THE ENCYCLOPEDIA OF
AMERICAN FACTS AND DATES

STAFF

Executive Editor	Raymond V. Hand, Jr.
Contributing Editors	Fon W. Boardman, Jr. David H. Scott
Managing Editor	Hayden Carruth
Copy Editor	Felice Levy
Indexer	Cynthia Crippen
Computer Keyboarder	Antje Munroe
Researchers	Sally Bunch Ellen Sackelman
Proofreaders	Barbara Bergeron Bernie Borok Rina Cascone Bitite Vinklers Brenda Woodward

THE ENCYCLOPEDIA OF
AMERICAN FACTS AND DATES

GORTON CARRUTH

NINTH EDITION

HarperCollins*Publishers*

FIRST EDITION

Library of Congress Catalog Card Number 92-54676
ISBN 0-06-270045-6

93 94 95 96 97 CC/RRD 10 9 8 7 6 5 4 3 2 1

To
Gisèle Carruth

Preface

From the milestones—Columbus's sightings, the Mayflower landing, the battle of Lexington, the admission of the states to the Union, the invention of the automobile, the first radio broadcast, the publication of *Uncle Tom's Cabin*, the launching of the first nuclear-powered submarine, the founding of the first baseball club, the relighting of the torch at the 100th anniversary of the Statue of Liberty, the placing into orbit of the Hubble Space Telescope—to the interesting and noteworthy—the development of the typewriter, the Lizzie Borden case, the first Army–Notre Dame football game, the Pulitzer Prize winners—to the small details—the favorite drink of colonial Americans, the first performance by Charlie Chaplin in the U.S., Hurricane Andrew, population figures throughout American History, the first recorded baptism on U.S. soil, the origins of street cleaning, epidemics, ship sinkings—*The Encyclopedia of American Facts & Dates* remains the best source of events from A.D. 986 to the present. And it is indeed an encyclopedia, not just a listing of dates. Entries are enriched with detail and overall coverage is exceptionally broad and colorful. Here you can find information ranging from explorations, treaties, battles, and politics to sports, theater, movies, crime, literature, philosophy, science, and religion.

This ninth edition has been completely revised and expanded. The yearly introductions that were so well received is earlier editions have been extended from 1931 back to the beginning of the book. The index, newly compiled and designed, is more detailed and useful. Since the first edition, *The Encyclopedia of American Facts & Dates* has been a standard reference book. It is now bigger and better.

The unique arrangement of *The Encyclopedia of American Facts & Dates*, which has proved useful and popular over the years, has been retained. It is the only encyclopedia of American history that is arranged in both concurrent and chronological order. You can read across time—learning about events that happened at the same time—as well as backward and forward in time.

As was done for the first and subsequent edition, new information in this edition was developed from original research and from many standard sources, but particular acknowledgement should be made to those single-volume American date and reference books that have been especially valuable: *The Reader's Encyclopedia* edited by William Rose Benét (HarperCollins); *Documents of American History* by Henry Steele Commager (Prentice-Hall); *The Columbia Encyclopedia* (Columbia University Press); *Information Please Almanac* (Houghton Mifflin); *Famous First Facts* by Joseph Nathan Kane (H. W. Wilson); *A Short Chronology of American History, 1492–1950* by Irving S. and Nell M. Kull (Greenwood); *The Encyclopedia of Sports* by Frank Menke (A. S. Barnes); *Encyclopedia of American History* edited by Richard B. Morris (HarperCollins); *The World Almanac* (Newspaper Enterprise Association). Acknowledgment should especially go to *The New York Times* for much of the recent detail. Thanks should go to the many readers who have made corrections and suggestions for improvement. Warm thanks must be extended to librarians across the country who have adopted *The Encyclopedia of American Facts & Dates* as a standard reference, but the staff of the Mount Pleasant Public Library in Pleasantville, N.Y., must be singled out for special thanks for their cheerful assistance given in every stage of our research.

GORTON CARRUTH

How to Use
The Encyclopedia of American Facts & Dates

The encyclopedia presents in one volume a vast number of the most interesting events from America's past arranged in both *concurrent* and *chronological* order. To make the encyclopedia even more useful, it has a detailed index for instant and easy consulting.

The subject matter is divided into four fields of interest arranged on every pair of facing pages in four vertical columns. **Each column continues on the following pair of facing pages.** The subjects listed at the tops of the columns are representative. Within the four columns you will find entries on the following topics:

I	II	III	IV
Colonization	Architecture	Agriculture	Crime
Disasters	Art	Business	Dress
Discovery, Exploration, Settlement	Ballet	Colleges and Universities	Expositions
	Books and Publishing		Fashions
Domestic Affairs	Censorship	Communications	Folklore
Foreign Affairs	Drama	Economics	Foods
Immigration	Jazz	Education	Furniture
Indian Affairs	Monuments	Finance	Games
Laws	Movies	Highways and Roads	Holidays
Military Affairs	Music		Manners
Politics and Government	Painting	Industry	Sayings
	Periodicals	Inventions	Social Issues
Slavery	Popular Entertainment	Labor	Sports
Statehood		Medicine	
Suffrage	Radio	Philosophy	
Tariffs	Sculpture	Religion	
Temperance	Songs	Scholarship	
Trade Agreements	Television	Science	
Treaties	Theater	Technology	
Vital Statistics		Transportation	
Wars and Battles			
Westward Expansion			
Women			

The text is in concurrent order. The four fields of interest are presented side by side in parallel columns. Thus, you can read across the page in order to learn what happened in all fields during the same time period.

The text is also in chronological order. Decade by decade, year by year, you can follow down the page the facts, dates, and events of American life by subject.

The index is your key not only to finding a specific event about which you want information but also to tracing a theme through American history. For example, if you want to learn about the major events in the history of America's westward expansion or in the development of baseball, turn to the index for a full listing of all the dates and events about those subjects. Please read "How to Use the Index" on page 859.

THE ENCYCLOPEDIA OF
AMERICAN FACTS AND DATES

986–1599

The first Europeans to see the North American continent were Norsemen, led by the navigator Bjarni Herjulfson, who, in 986, while seeking Eric the Red's settlement on the coast of Greenland, was blown off course and sighted an unidentified land mass. In 1000 Leif Ericson, a son of Eric the Red, explored the coast of North America and established a settlement he called Vinland. In the 1960s evidence of such a settlement was unearthed at L'Anse aux Meadows, Newfoundland. Between 1004 and 1008 Leif's brothers, Thorvald and Thorstein, carried out further exploration of the North American coast and may well have seen what is now New England. Thorfinn Karlsefni, a trader from Iceland, visited the coast of North America between 1010 and 1013. The last Norse voyage to the New World took place in 1014–1015 when, according to the Greenland Saga, Eric's daughter, Freydis, sailed with Thorfinn Karlsefni.

1492 Oct. 12   The expedition of **Christopher Columbus** sighted what was probably present-day Watling Island, in the Bahamas. That day they went ashore and claimed the island for the king and queen of Spain. Columbus explored the northeastern coast of Cuba and northern coast of Hispaniola, then set sail for Spain on Jan. 16, 1493. On his second expedition (1493–1496) he discovered Jamaica, and on his third (1498–1500) he made further discoveries, including the island of Trinidad. During his fourth and final expedition (1502–1504) Columbus discovered Martinique and explored the coasts of present-day Honduras, Nicaragua, Costa Rica, and Panama.

1513 Apr. 2   **Juan Ponce de León** discovered Florida, claiming it for the king of Spain.

1526 Summer   The **first European settlement** in what is now the U.S., San Miguel de Guadalupe, was established by Lucas Vazquez de Ayllón, who led some 500 or 600 settlers from Hispaniola to the coast of South Carolina. The site of the settlement was thought to have been just north of the mouth of the Peedee R. Many of the settlers died of fever. After Ayllón succumbed on Oct. 18, the approximately 150 surviving settlers returned to Hispaniola.

1539 May 30   **Fernando de Soto** landed in Florida and began the consolidation of Spain's dominion over the peninsula.

1541 May 8   The **first Europeans to reach the Mississippi R.** were members of the de Soto expedition. De Soto died the next year and was buried in the river.

1542   The **first Europeans to reach the Pacific coast** of what is now the U.S. were members of the expedition of Juan Rodriquez Cabrillo, who was sent on an exploratory voyage by Spanish administrators in Mexico. Cabrillo landed near what is now Ballast Point,

Almost as soon as the early explorers of America returned to Europe, they wrote accounts of their adventures. These accounts expressed great enthusiasm and, like later accounts, might be classed as promotional material. The first eyewitness report in English of what today is part of the U.S. was written in 1588 by Thomas Hariot, who took part in the Roanoke Island adventure sponsored by Sir Walter Raleigh. Hariot's account was entitled *A Brief and True Report of the New Found Land of Virginia.* It depicted America as a paradise where a little work would yield great prosperity. In the following year appeared *The Principal Navigations, Voyages, Traffics, and Discoveries of the English Nation* by Richard Hakluyt. Not an explorer himself but a collector of the reports of others, Hakluyt later enlarged his book and included the adventures of Sir Francis Drake, Sir Humphrey Gilbert, Sir Martin Frobisher, and others. In the early seventeenth century, further works were written by such explorers as John Smith and Samuel de Champlain. Mapmakers also went to work almost as soon as the New World was found, although their maps were very inexact by today's standards and reflected the prevailing belief or hope that America was but a minor obstacle in the way of ships seeking the riches of the Far East. One such map was prepared by Sebastian Cabot in 1544 and another by Gerardus Mercator in 1569.

1507   The term *America* was first used for the New World in Martin Waldseemüller's short geography book *Cosmographiae Introductio.* Wrote Waldseemüller, "But now that these parts have been more extensively examined, and another fourth part has been discovered by Americus Vespuccius . . . I do not see why anyone should by right object to name it America . . . after its discoverer, Americus, a man of sagacious mind, since both Europe and Asia took their names from women." Waldseemüller mistakenly attributed discovery of the New World to Amerigo Vespucci.

1519   A **portrait of Christopher Columbus** was completed by Sebastiano del Piombo, the Italian painter, 13 years after the explorer's death in 1506. Sebastiano, whose real name was Sebastiano Luciana, was but one of many artists who portrayed Columbus; however, none of the portraits were painted from life. Columbus had died in poverty, his achievements unrecognized. He went to his death still believing he

| Business and Industry; Science; Education; Philosophy and Religion   III | | IV   Sports; Social Issues and Crime; Folkways; Fashion; Holidays |

986–1599

When John Cabot discovered Newfoundland in 1497, he also discovered one of the world's great fishing areas. He enjoyed the codfish his crew found and he saw nets on shore, but not their Indian owners. England, however, was slow to develop this economic and trade resource. The French and Portuguese were the first to exploit it. They took fish home for trading purposes and also traded fish, which they cured on shore, with the Indians for furs. By 1577, according to Richard Hakluyt, there were 150 French fishing craft, 100 Spanish, and 50 Portuguese, but only 15 English vessels fishing in Newfoundland. English fishing, however, became dominant in the next century. Despite the competition of the European nations in other areas, this fertile fishing ground provided a peaceful international exchange.

1112 The **first bishop of America** was appointed. He was Eric Gnupsson, named by Pope Paschal II. His see included Greenland and Vinland.

1540 The **first recorded baptism** in what is now the U.S. was performed by priests accompanying the Fernando de Soto expedition. They baptized an Indian guide, Peter, in the waters of the Acmulgee R., near present-day Macon, Ga.

1550–1600 Discovery of **new agricultural products** during the Spanish explorations of the New World proved a great benefit to European economic development. Spanish expeditions brought back to the Old World such things as potatoes, tomatoes, quinine extracted from the bark of the cinchona tree, cocoa, tapioca from the cassava root, and tobacco. In return settlers brought to the Americas such things as barley, oats, rye, sugar cane, cattle, pigs, poultry, rabbits, and horses, which later found a natural home on the plains.

1564 Spring The **first successful Atlantic crossing** by a ship built in North America was accomplished by French Huguenots who had settled on Parris Island, S.C., but who had decided to return to France because their group was destitute. They built a pinnace, using bedding and shirts for sails. They actually arrived within sight of the French shoreline, half starved, where they were rescued by English sailors.

At the beginning of European colonization, there were some 600 tribes of North American Indians, speaking some 500 different dialects. They were chiefly hunters and gatherers, but some tribes had developed agriculture, and bartered or used wampum to exchange goods. There was a good deal of warfare between tribes and most Indians prided themselves on their courage in battle. But the Indians' chief weapon, the bow and arrow, was no match for European firearms, and against Old World diseases such as smallpox they had no defense. As soon as European settlement began in the early sixteenth century, the fragile structure of North American Indian society began to crumble.

1007 The **first white child** born in North America was Snorro, the son of Thorfinn and Gudrid Karlsefni, members of Leif Ericson's expedition to Vinland. Later Snorro became an important member of the Norse community in Iceland.

1540 The **horse was first introduced** on a large scale into what is now the U.S. by Francisco Coronado, the Spanish explorer, who traveled through Kansas with 260 horses, most escaping to the Midwest, Mexico, and Canada. These animals eventually mingled with large French Norman horses brought to Canada by French settlers, producing the wild horses later found in North America.

1564 The **earliest hunting pictures** in what is now the U.S. were in Jacques le Moyne's account of the René de Laudonnière expedition. Some drawings showed Indians stalking deer under a deerskin, capturing alligators by ramming long poles down their throats, and fishing from pirogues, tree trunks hollowed out to make crude boats.

1565 **Smoking** of tobacco was introduced to England by John Hawkins. Hawkins was primarily a slave trader, carrying Africans to the West Indies. Most of his dealings were with the Spanish in the West Indies, but during his second trip to the region (1564–1566) he visited the small French colony in Florida and learned to smoke tobacco from the colonists, who had

San Diego, Calif., then continued his explorations and discovered Santa Catalina Island, San Pedro Bay, the Santa Barbara Channel, and other West Coast landmarks.

1562 Apr. 30 The first French colonizers in what was to become the U.S., Huguenots led by Jean Ribaut, established Port Royal on Parris Island, off the coast of present-day South Carolina. In early 1564, when supplies failed to arrive from France, the colony was abandoned.

1565 Sept. 8 The first permanent white colony in what is now the U.S. was founded at St. Augustine, Fla., by the Spanish under Pedro Menéndez de Avilés, a naval officer.

1565 Sept. 20 Fort Caroline was destroyed by the Spanish under Menéndez, who massacred most of its inhabitants. He renamed it San Mateo and in the next two years built a string of forts to Tampa Bay while looking for a water passage across Florida.

1579 June 17 The expedition of **Sir Francis Drake** anchored in a harbor just north of present-day San Francisco Bay in California, during Drake's celebrated circumnavigation of the globe. Drake named the land Nova Albion and claimed it for England. The members of the expedition spent a month repairing their ship. Then on July 26 Drake sailed from California, continuing north and then west across the Pacific Ocean.

1585 Aug. The **Roanoke Island colony,** sponsored by Sir Walter Raleigh, was established on Roanoke Island, off the northeast coast of what is now North Carolina, under the leadership of Sir Richard Grenville and Sir Ralph Lane. The settlers fared badly and returned to England in June of 1586. In 1587 Raleigh sent out another group, under John White, consisting of 117 men, women, and children. White returned to England for supplies but was unable to get back to Roanoke until Aug. 17, 1590. He found all the colonists gone; the only clue to their fate was the word *Croatoan* carved on a tree. The meaning of this remains unexplained and no trace was ever found of the settlers.

had discovered part of Asia, and only years after his death did he attain fame. The various posthumous portraits of Columbus showed him lean-faced, fat-faced, blond or swarthy, clean-shaven or bearded, in many different styles of dress. Some 71 of these portraits were exhibited at the World's Columbian Exposition in 1893, and most of them did not in the least resemble contemporary descriptions of Columbus. Sebastiano's portrait is now in the Metropolitan Museum of Art in New York City.

1584 Richard Hakluyt wrote *A Discourse Concerning Western Planting,* at the request of Sir Walter Raleigh, for Queen Elizabeth I of England. This work urged that the queen promote English settlement in America and offered a complete plan for such a program. Hakluyt said such settlement would help promote religion, supply goods for England, employ men who would otherwise be idle, increase revenues, provide overseas bases for use in the event of war with Spain, and be useful in the search for a Northwest Passage to the Orient. Hakluyt wrote enthusiastically that "this Realm shall have by that meane Shippes of great burden and of great strengthe" for defense. Further, he wrote, colonial trade would "breed more skilfull, connynge and stowte pilotts and maryners than any other belonging to this land: For it is the long voyaiges ... that harden seamen and open unto them the secrets of navigation." The queen apparently read the *Discourse* but did not act on it. It was not published until almost three centuries later, when it was issued by the Maine Historical Society. As for Hakluyt, an ordained clergyman of the Church of England, he never saw America. Although he had intended to go to Jamestown, Va., in 1607 as rector, he was not physically able to make the trip. He died and was buried in Westminster Abbey in 1616.

1600–1609

From the beginning a chief purpose of voyages to the New World was to find a trade route to the Far East. When it became clear that there was a large land mass between Europe and the East, the search for a sea route became a search for the Northwest Passage, a way around the northern part of North America. Sir Martin Frobisher in 1576–1578 was the first European to search for such a route. John Davis made a similar attempt in 1585–1587. When Henry Hudson sailed up the Hudson

The key factor determining the design of the first colonial structures was the availability of building materials. In New England, the settlers tried to copy the architecture of their homelands, using wood, which was in abundance. In the South, brick soon displaced wood as the favorite building material. In the Southwest, the Spaniards adapted Indian materials and methods for their buildings. Such a structure, the oldest surviving non-Indian building in the U.S., was the governor's

Business and Industry; Science; Education; Philosophy and Religion III		IV Sports; Social Issues and Crime; Folkways; Fashion; Holidays

1565 The **first introduction of European livestock,** such as black cattle, horses, sheep, and swine, into America was made by the Spanish in Florida.

1565 Sept. 8 The **first Catholic parish** in what is now the U.S., the parish of St. Augustine, Fla., was founded by Fr. Don Martin Francisco Lopez de Mendozo Grajales, chaplain of the Spanish expeditionary forces.

1566 The **first Jesuit missionaries** in what was to become the U.S., three Jesuits sponsored by Pedro Menéndez de Avilés, arrived in Spanish Florida, followed by a second group two years later. The first missions were established at Guale, in present-day Georgia, and Orista and Santa Elena, in present-day South Carolina. The Jesuits were forced out of Florida by the Indians within a few years.

1579 The **first Protestant service** in the New World, and the first religious service in English held there, was conducted in California. Participants were members of the crew of Adm. Francis Drake's expedition. Having sailed around South America, the expedition put into a bay at the 38th parallel where, according to the ship's log, "the admiral ordered divine service to be performed at his tent."

1583 **Newfoundland** was officially claimed by Humphrey Gilbert, who took possession in the name of the English throne.

1587 The **first Indian convert** to Protestant Christianity was Manteo, who was baptized into the Church of England by members of Sir Walter Raleigh's expedition to Roanoke. Manteo was later named Lord of Roanoke by Raleigh.

learned from the Indians. Hawkins returned to England with a shipload of tobacco. He described the Indian use of the plant this way: "The Floridians when they travell have a kinde of herbe dried, who with a cane and an earthen cap in the end, with fire, and dried herbs put together, doe sucke thorow the cane the smoke thereof, which smoke satisfieth their hunger, and therwith they live foure or five days without meat or drinke, and this all the Frenchmen used for this purpose."

1577 **Shipboard provisions** for early explorers were characterized by the stock carried by Sir Martin Frobisher's second expedition to America to seek the Northwest Passage. The officers and crew, numbering about 150 on three ships, ate hardtack, flour, pickled beef and pork, dried peas and codfish, butter, cheese, oatmeal, rice, honey, and vinegar. The expedition also carried eight tuns of beer, which figured to about a gallon of beer for each crewman for six months.

1585 The first eyewitness picture of **American Indians at play,** a drawing by John White, showed Indians participating in lacrosse, archery, and foot racing, and pitching balls at a target on top of a high tree.

1587 Aug. 18 The **first English child** born in North America was Virginia Dare. Her parents were Ananias and Ellinor Dare, members of Sir Walter Raleigh's colony at Roanoke Island, in present-day North Carolina. Ellinor Dare was the daughter of Gov. John White, who had led a company of 150 householders to establish a colony on the island.

1600–1609

In the early days of the English colonies, trade was a one-way street. The colonists badly needed supplies from the homeland. The colony at Jamestown, Va., for example, was not self-sufficient for many years. On June 22, 1607, Capt. Christopher Newport left Jamestown with a cargo for England. Unfortunately, the cargo was fool's gold, but it was an indication of the economic motives of those who sponsored outposts in the New World. In Dec. 1608 Newport sailed with a more

Settlers as well as explorers were beginning to come to the English territories on the Atlantic coast. Unfortunately, some of the earliest pioneers, as at Jamestown, Va., were adventurers interested more in making a quick fortune from the alleged riches of the New World than in engaging in agriculture or forestry. In later years, though, a greater diversity of settlers arrived and brought with them a variety of skills. They ranged from wealthy Englishmen, who wanted to carve out large

| Exploration and Settlement; Wars; Government; Civil Rights; Statistics | I | | II | Publishing; Arts and Music; Popular Entertainment; Architecture; Theater |

R. in 1609 he hoped he had found the route, and in 1610 when he discovered Hudson Bay he was on a similar mission. In 1616 William Baffin discovered Baffin Bay, which many years later was to provide a key to the actual route, long after the Northwest Passage had lost any commercial appeal.

1602 May 15 The **first Englishman** to land in what is now New England was Capt. Bartholomew Gosnold, who anchored at what is now New Bedford, Mass. He had sailed on Mar. 26 from Falmouth, England, on the *Concord,* touched at the Maine coast, and explored the New England coastline. He named Cape Cod, Martha's Vineyard, and other landmarks.

1604 The **first northern French colony** was established by Pierre du Guast, Sieur de Monts, at Neutral Island in the St. Croix R. in southeastern Maine. His patent had been granted by the French king.

1606 **Colonial charters** were granted to the Virginia Company of London and the Virginia Company of Plymouth by the English Crown. The grants extended from Cape Fear, N.C., to the St. Croix R. on the border between what are now Maine and New Brunswick, Canada. The London Company was permitted to establish settlements in a tract between 34 and 41 degrees north latitude. The Plymouth Company was granted an equal tract between 38 and 45 degrees north latitude. The overlapping area was a neutral zone where both companies could establish settlements.

1607 May 13 The **first permanent English colony** in North America, Jamestown, Va., was founded by more than 100 colonists on the left bank of the "River of Powhatan" (James R.). Dispatched by the London Company, the colonists had sailed aboard the *Sarah Constant, Goodspeed,* and *Discovery.*

1607 Dec. Capt. **John Smith** and two companions were captured by Indians while in search of provisions. His companions were killed, but he was spared, Smith reported, by the intercession of Pocahontas, Chief Powhatan's daughter.

1609–10 This winter was the so-called **starving time** of the Jamestown colony. Many died and Deputy Gov. Sir Thomas Gates was about to take the colonists away when, on June 10, 1610, Thomas West De La Warr, newly appointed governor of Virginia, arrived. He encouraged the settlers to remain, sent for supplies, and threatened to punish colonists who did not work harder to raise food. As a result, conditions improved during the winter of 1610–1611.

palace in Santa Fe, N. Mex., built in 1609 by Don Pedro de Peralta. The building of forts, usually of logs, for defense against Indian attacks, became a necessity. The Jamestown colonists began such work less than a month after they landed in 1607. In August of that year, a Plymouth Company expedition to Maine erected a fort that encompassed other structures.

1606 Nov. 14 One of the **earliest theatrical performances** in North America, the French masque *Le Théâtre de Neptune en la Nouvelle-France* (Neptune's Theater in New France), took place at Port Royal, Acadia (Nova Scotia).

1608 What is considered the **first American book,** *A True Relation of Such Occurrences and Accidents of Noate as Hath Hapned in Virginia Since the First Planting of that Collony* by Capt. John Smith, was printed in London. The book strangely omitted the famous tale of Pocahontas. It was not until 1624, with the publication of his book *The Generall Historie of Virginia, New-England, and the Summer Isles,* that Smith included a reference to the famous romance.

1609 The last work of **Richard Hakluyt,** *Virginia Richly Valued,* was published. It was based upon a Portuguese work, *Relacam,* which was written by a voyager who claimed to have been with Fernando de Soto on the expedition through Florida, Georgia, Alabama, Arkansas, and Louisiana. One of three extant histories of this voyage, *Virginia Richly Valued* has been attributed to the original authorship of de Soto.

1609 *Good Speed to Virginia* by Robert Gray, the third work relating to Virginia, was published in London. A tract in the form of a sermon, it was intended to promote colonization. Gray's main argument for such emigration was that England was overpopulated. This work was followed in 1610 by *Newes from Virginia* by Richard Rich, an English soldier who had been in Virginia in June of that year, when the colony was very nearly abandoned. His work was a ballad based on his experiences, and it may have contributed to the dispatch of two more fleets to Virginia in 1611.

Business and Industry; Science; Education; Philosophy and Religion	III		IV	Sports; Social Issues and Crime; Folkways; Fashion; Holidays

practical cargo: pitch, tar, soap, ashes, and glass. There is evidence that sassafras was shipped from Cape Cod earlier, but this Jamestown cargo was the first instance of American manufactures being exported.

1603 A **monopoly of the fur trade,** granted for a ten-year period to Pierre du Guast, Sieur de Monts, by the king of France, reflected the importance the French placed on the trade. The English and Dutch were far behind in developing a fur trade with the Indians. Monts was associated with Pierre Chauvin, Sieur de Tonnetuit, a naval officer and trader; and with Samuel de Champlain, who in 1608 founded Quebec and the following year discovered the lake that now bears his name, in what is now New York State. They established trading posts in eastern Canada, working their way south to the Penobscot R. in what is now Maine. Monts' monopoly of the fur trade was rescinded in 1607, then restored for a year in 1608. He withdrew from the trade about 1612. Even with a monopoly, it was difficult to prevent others from engaging in fur trading. Eventually the English and Dutch became strong competitors in the fur trade.

1607 **Glassmaking** was practiced in the first English colony at Jamestown with techniques that differed little from those of ancient civilizations. In 1608 the first glass beads were made for trade with the Indians.

estates, to servants. Merchants saw the opportunity for trade as populations grew. Groups seeking religious freedom were also prominent, bringing with them a tradition of hard work and a willingness to start life anew.

1600 The **Indian population** of what was to become the U.S. was about 1,000,000 when European exploration began. Because the pattern of settlement here differed from that of the Spanish penetration of Central and South America, the change in customs of the Indians was, at first, comparatively slow. Pioneer groups of European colonists were small. They entered regions with sparser populations and more fluid cultures than the larger and more stable Indian communities of Central America, the Andes, and the Caribbean islands. Contact was sometimes mutually beneficial, but there was no fusion of European and Indian cultures as occurred in South America. In retrospect, the first decade of the seventeenth century was the twilight of aboriginal Indian life.

1607 A measure of **social position** among the male settlers of Jamestown, Va., the first permanent English settlement in America, was the fact that of some 105 men, 35 were considered gentlemen, persons whose means freed them from the need to work or engage actively in trade. The second expedition to Jamestown contained 33 gentlemen out of 120.

1608 John Smith had two Indians teach him how to raise **Indian corn.** Faced with starvation the colonists accepted this new grain, although opposition to it existed everywhere. In French Louisiana, the women, accustomed to fancier European fare, staged a petticoat rebellion against daily consumption of corn. The governor reported that the women " . . . inveigh bitterly against His Grace, the Bishop of Quebec, who, they say has enticed them away from home under the pretext of sending them to enjoy the milk and honey of the land of promise."

1609 In what was probably the **first marriage** in the American colonies, Anne Burrows and John Laydon were wed in Virginia.

1610–1619

The colonies, as soon as they were established, had to have leadership and a system of government. The proprietors of the companies that were granted colonizing rights appointed their own colonial governors. The Virginia Company, on Feb. 28, 1610, named Thomas West De La Warr, Lord Delaware, the first lord governor and captain general of the Virginia colony. On May 23, 1611, he was succeeded by Sir Thomas Dale, whose new law code amounted almost to martial law. Within a few years, however, the colonists had more voice in government, and the New England colonies, although theocratic, were not under comparably absolute rule.

The estimated European **population** in the colonies was 210.

1612   The **foundation of New York City** was laid when the Dutch sent two ships, *Tiger* and *Fortune*, to trade with the Indians on the Hudson R. Huts were built on Manhattan Island (approximately where 45 Broadway now stands) to house trade goods. One year later, a permanent trading post was established. The next year a fort was erected on the tip of the island.

1613   A small **French settlement**, established at Somes Sound, near Mount Desert on the Maine coast, was forced out by English settlers from Jamestown, Va., led by Samuel Argall.

1614   The **first important Dutch settlement** in the New World, preceding New Amsterdam, was Fort Nassau, a stockaded post at Castle Island, near present-day Albany, N.Y. Established by Dutch fur traders, it was abandoned in 1617 and a new fort was built on the shore of the Hudson R. Fort Orange, near Albany, was established in 1624 by the Walloons. The region was later dominated by the patroonship of Rensselaerswyck.

1619 July 30   The **first legislative assembly** in America, the House of Burgesses, convened at Old Church, Jamestown, Va. All legislation needed the approval of the London Company.

1619 Aug.   The **first slaves** arrived in Virginia when a Dutch ship carried 20 blacks to Jamestown, Va., for sale.

An important figure in early colonial literature was John Smith, the explorer and adventurer who wrote seven books about the New World. Among these were *A Map of Virginia* (1612), probably his best-known work; *A Description of New England* (1616); and *New England's Trials* (1620). These works contributed to further exploration and settlement and offer excellent views of early colonization. Smith's autobiography, *The True Travels, Adventures, and Observations of Captaine John Smith*, was published in 1630, the year before his death.

1610   An **early report of Virginia** was contained in *A True Reportory of the Wrack and Redemption of Sir Thomas Gates, Knight, upon and from the Islands of the Bermudas, his coming to Virginia and the Estate of that Colony then and after the Government of the Lord La Ware*, a firsthand account of New World settlement by William Strachey. First published in 1625, the manuscript has been offered as one of the sources that might have suggested *The Tempest* to William Shakespeare.

1612   An early **detailed study of Virginia** was provided in *A Map of Virginia* by Capt. John Smith. The book, describing Virginia's land, its commodities, people, government, and religion, was published in Oxford, England.

1613   *Purchas His Pilgrimes* by Samuel Purchas, published in England, took a skeptical view of New World settlements. Typical of his remarks is "For what haue they to oppose our Elephants, Rinocerotes, Camels, Horses, Kine, &c. Neither are the naturall fruits of America comparable to those of our World. Whence are their Spices, and best Fruits, but from hence, by transportation or transplantation? As for Arts, States, Literature, Diuine and Humane, multitudes of Cities, Lawes, and other Excellencies, our World enjoyeth still the priuiledge of the First-borne. America is a younger brother, and hath in these things almost no inheritance at all, till it bought somewhat herof of the Spaniards, with the price of her Freedome."

| Business and Industry; Science; Education; Philosophy and Religion III | | IV Sports; Social Issues and Crime; Folkways; Fashion; Holidays |

1610-1619

Early explorers were astonished to see Indians smoking tobacco, a plant unknown in Europe. Tobacco leaves were soon taken to Europe, where smoking became a rage. For a time it was believed that the fumes had miraculous curative powers. As a result of its popularity, tobacco became an economic asset in America, especially in Virginia, where a young planter, John Rolfe, planted the first successful crop in 1612. By 1619 tobacco was the leading export of Virginia, and it was later used as a basis for currency. Unfortunately, tobacco production came to require a large number of slaves, and the crop quickly depleted the soil.

1610 The **first doctor** in the English colonies, Lawrence Bohune, arrived in Virginia. In 1620 he was appointed surgeon general of the London Company in Virginia.

1611 The **first Presbyterian congregation** in America was established at Jamestown, Va., by the Rev. Alexander Whitaker, a volunteer from the Puritan community at Cambridge, England. He is best known as the clergyman who instructed Pocahontas in Christianity and baptized her.

1613 **Pocahontas,** daughter of Powhatan, head of a confederacy of Algonquian tribes in Virginia, was baptized, perhaps the first Indian convert in the colony. Taken hostage to compel the release of colonists held by her father's tribe, she came into contact with the Rev. Alexander Whitaker, was converted, baptized, and given the Christian name of Rebecca. On Apr. 14, 1614, she married the young planter John Rolfe. On a trip to England, her old friend, Capt. John Smith, introduced her to the royal court.

1614 The **first large-scale fishing expedition** in America, led by Capt. John Smith, sailed from Virginia in search of gold, copper, whales, and, finally, fish off the coast of Maine. The expedition caught 60,000 fish in one month.

1616 A **smallpox epidemic** among Indians relieved future New England colonies of the threat of major hostilites with the Indians. The tribes from the Penobscot R. in Maine to Narragansett Bay in Rhode Island were virtually destroyed.

Colonists from Europe brought with them their customs with regard to recreation. As early as May of 1611, the men of Jamestown, Va., played a game of bowls in the street, the first such event on record. At Christmas in 1625, a Virginian recorded that "the extreame winde, rayne, froste and snow caused us to keepe Christmas among the savages where we were never more merry, nor fed on more plenty of good Oysters, Fish, Flesh, Wilde fowl and good bread, nor never had better fires in England." In 1619, however, Virginia prohibited gaming at dice or cards. A few years later the Pilgrim and Puritan fathers of New England frowned on almost all frivolity.

1617 **Women** started to arrive in Virginia. Unlike the Puritans in the North, Virginia settlers came over "not as men, but more as soldiers sent out to occupy an enemy's country." The arrival of women insured the growth and development of permanent communities.

1618 In a move to **compel church attendance,** Gov. Samuel Argall of Virginia decreed that all who failed to attend church service would be imprisoned in the guardhouse, "lying neck and heels in the Corps of Gard ye night following and be a slave ye week following." Sunday dancing, fiddling, card playing, hunting, and fishing were also forbidden.

1619 **Laws restricting personal behavior** were enacted in Virginia. Penalties were provided for excesses in apparel unbefitting a person's station in life; gambling at dice or cards was prohibited; drinking was strictly regulated; Sabbath observance was required; and anyone found idle was to be bound over to perform compulsory work. According to court records, violations of these laws were strictly enforced.

1620–1629

In 1629 the Dutch West India Company introduced the patroon system to New Netherland. To encourage emigration, the company on June 7 proclaimed a Charter of Freedoms and Exemptions, by which large tracts of land were granted to those who could establish settlements of 50 persons within four years. In return, the landholder, or patroon, received what amounted to feudal rights and authority. By 1630 five such patroonships had been established, but only three were ever colonized: Pavonia, which included what is now Staten Island, N.Y.; Swaanendael on Delaware Bay; and Rensselaerswyck on the upper Hudson R. Of these, only Rensselaerswyck was successful.

The estimated colonial **population** was 2499.

1620 June 29   An early colonial **trade agreement** concluded between the English Crown and the Virginia Company provided that tobacco would not be grown in England. In return, England would receive one shilling per lb. duty on tobacco produced in Virginia.

1620 Nov. 21   The **Mayflower Compact,** the first social contract for a New England colony, was drafted and signed by 41 adult males in Provincetown Harbor, Mass. The Pilgrims did not settle there, but went on after a time to Plymouth.

1620 Dec. 26   The **Pilgrims reached Plymouth,** Mass., aboard the *Mayflower* after setting out from England on Sept. 16. The company consisted of 41 men and their families.

1621   A **peace treaty and defensive alliance** between the Wampanoag Indians and the Pilgrims was concluded at Strawberry Hill, Plymouth, Mass. Arranged by Squanto, an English-speaking Indian, it was one of the earliest recorded treaties between Europeans and Indians in North America. Squanto had been kidnaped and sold as a slave in Spain. He escaped to England, where he learned English, and lived in Newfoundland for a time before returning to Massachusetts in 1619.

1622 Mar. 22   The **first Indian massacre,** led by Powhatan's brother, almost wiped out the settlements outside Jamestown, Va., which was itself heavily fortified.

1622 Aug. 10   The province of **Maine** was granted to John Mason and Ferdinando Gorges. It included the land between the Merrimack and Kennebec rivers.

1623   The **first colonists** sent by the Dutch West India Company settled along the Hudson R.

1624 May   The Dutch colony of **New Netherland,** which at this time consisted of the Hudson River Valley north to Fort Orange, was established when Cornelis J. Mey reached what is now New York Bay with 30 families. Mey was the first governor of New Netherland.

One of the great stories of American literature concerns Myles Standish, military leader of Plymouth colony. According to tradition, in 1621 Standish, whose wife Rose had just died, asked John Alden, a young Pilgrim rising in importance, to court Priscilla Mullens on his behalf. When Alden did so, the maiden said to Alden, "Prithee, John, why do you not speak for yourself?" John did so, they were married, and Standish forgave Alden. This tale, although historically unfounded, was enshrined in American tradition by Henry Wadsworth Longfellow's poem "The Courtship of Miles Standish" (1858).

1620   Perhaps the **first music book** in America, Henry Ainsworth's *Psalm Book,* published in Amsterdam in 1612, was brought to the New World by the Plymouth Pilgrims. It brought together tunes from earlier English, French, and Swiss psalters, and was the best collection of its kind at the time.

1620   The **first public library** in the English colonies was established at a college planned for Henrico, Va. The library received bequests of books from English estates; but the college was never developed, and the collection of books was soon broken up.

1622   The journal of William Bradford and Edward Winslow, long known as *Mourt's Relation* and containing the first detailed and accurate account of the landing of the Pilgrims at Plymouth, was published. Printed anonymously in England as *A Relation or Journall of the Beginning and Proceedings of the English Plantation Setled at Plimoth in New England,* it included a preface bearing the signature G. Mourt, possibly that of George Morton, who served as an agent for the colony.

1622 Summer   The **first substantial building** in New England, a fort of hewn oak timbers, was built by the Plymouth settlers.

1624   *The Generall Historie of Virginia, New England, and the Summer Isles* by John Smith was published in England. The book consisted of accounts of his observations in the New World. Besides helping to found Virginia, he had mapped the coastal area of New England around Cape Cod in 1614. This exciting

| Business and Industry; Science; Education; Philosophy and Religion | III | | IV | Sports; Social Issues and Crime; Folkways; Fashion; Holidays |

1620–1629

A major factor in the establishment of the English colonies was the search for religious freedom. Much of the seventeenth century was a period of religious dissent in the British Isles against the established Church of England. The best known of the dissenters were the Pilgrims, who were Separatists, and the more numerous Puritans, who established the Massachusetts Bay Colony. Their church, the Congregational Church, became established in New England and was supported by taxes. Maryland was founded as a Roman Catholic sanctuary, and later the persecuted Quakers found a haven in Pennsylvania. Baptists, Presbyterians, and, later, Methodists added to the denominational mix of English colonists in America. Virginia was settled largely by Anglicans.

1620 A **Congregational Church** was founded in Plymouth, Mass., by 102 Pilgrim Separatists under William Brewster, William Bradford, and Edward Winslow, all of whom were part of the Scrooby-Leiden congregation in Holland. In England, Congregationalists were known as Independents. Ralph Smith, the first successful pastor of the church, arrived later.

1620 The **first American iron works** was planned by Virginia colonists at Falling Creek, 66 miles north of Jamestown. In 1622, before work could begin, 348 people of the settlement were massacred by Indians. Only a boy escaped.

1620 Dec. 21 The **first physician** for the Plymouth colony, Dr. Samuel Fuller, arrived on the *Mayflower*. As both doctor and administrator, he was one of the prominent members of the Pilgrim band.

1623 In order to promote **silk production** in America, the Virginia Legislature compelled all settlers to grow mulberry trees. Mulberry leaves were the food source for silkworms.

1623 Sept. 10 The **first cargo** shipped from Plymouth consisted of lumber and furs. It was dispatched to England aboard the *Anne*, a vessel of 140 tons, with William Pierce in command.

1624 The **first appointed minister** for the Pilgrim colony arrived at Plymouth. John Lyford, an Anglican minister, was sent by the London merchants who sponsored Plymouth colony. Charges of Anglican bias and conspiracy to establish a rival colony were leveled at Lyford by the Pilgrims. Lyford was tried, convicted, and expelled from the colony. He settled at Cape Anne, then Naumkeag (later Salem), then went to Virginia, where he died.

An important albeit lowly position in the colonial social structure, between free men and slaves, was that of the indentured servant. Indentured servants, in return for passage to America, agreed to work for a period of time, usually five years, in return for little more than their keep. Many came of their own free will, but the English government also sent over hundreds of hardened criminals on such terms. Often, after the servants' terms of service had expired, they were granted plots of land. Others became tenant farmers, as in Virginia, where by 1619 their farms extended for 20 miles along the James R.

1620 A **promotion scheme** launched by the Virginia Company of London, also known as the London Company, to exploit the New World included shipment of many English virgins to Virginia and their sale to colonists for 100 to 200 lbs. of tobacco each.

1621 Dec. The **earliest American harvest festival** was celebrated by the Pilgrims at Plymouth, Mass.

1621 Dec. 25 **Game playing** on Christmas Day by newcomers to Plymouth colony was halted by Gov. William Bradford. The governor, scandalized at the settlers' playing of such games as "pitching the barr" and "stoole-ball," confiscated the equipment needed to play the games.

1623 Plymouth colonists were ordered to **raise their own corn** by Gov. Bradford, after three very lean years. Besides the planting of corn, the colonists were taught by Indians how to grind and cook it. Many Indian names relating to corn have passed into English, including *hominy, pone, samp,* and *succotash.*

1623 **Seafood** was the main source of nutrition for women and children arriving in New England this year to join their Pilgrim husbands and fathers. The settlers were feasted with "a lobster or a piece of fish without bread or anything else but a cup of spring water." Many lobsters weighed 25 lbs. and were so abundant that the smallest child could catch them.

1623 **Social stratification** in Virginia was reflected in a law excepting "persons of quality" from penal whipping because they were not considered "fit to undergo corporal punishment."

1624 **Mandatory church attendance** on Sunday was required by an early Virginia law. The penalty for absence was 1 lb. of tobacco. The law also stipulated that each plantation have a house or room for worship.

1624 Dec. 21 The first Swedish colony in America was authorized by a charter granted to the South Company of Sweden. No colony was established until 1638, after organization of the New Sweden Company (1637).

1625 Spring The Dutch settlement of **New Amsterdam** was constructed at the tip of Manhattan, or Manhattes, Island. The settlement was under the direction of Willem Verhulst, who succeeded Cornelis Mey as governor of New Netherland. On May 4, 1626, Peter Minuit arrived with a new group of settlers and succeeded Verhulst, with the title director general of New Netherland.

1626 Manhattan Island was sold by the Indians for goods valued at 60 guilders, later calculated as the legendary sum of $24. The purchase was made by Peter Minuit.

1629 June 27 The first settlers of **Massachusetts Bay Colony** entered Salem Harbor. Led by John Winthrop, they were 900 strong, and arrived in five ships.

report, which included the first complete account of Smith's rescue by Pocahontas, was in part promotional literature designed to encourage immigration.

1625 The Rev. William Morrell's *Nova Anglia,* a Latin poem with English paraphrase, provided an early picture of New England. A typical stanza:

> Westward a thousand leagues, a spacious land
> Is made, unknown to them that it command
> Of fruitful mould, and no less fruitful main,
> Inrich with springs and prey, highland and
>   plain . . .

Morrell had lived in New England in 1623 and 1624 before returning to England, where his poem was published.

1630–1639

The first of the many wars between whites and Indians was fought in 1637 between the Pequots and New England settlers. The Pequots were a warlike tribe centered along the Thames R. in southeastern Connecticut. By 1630, under their chief, Sassacus, they had pushed west to the Connecticut R. There they had numerous quarrels with colonists, culminating in the murder by the Pequots of a trader, John Oldham, on July 20, 1636. On Aug. 24 Gov. John Endicott of Massachusetts Bay Colony organized a military force to punish the Indians, and on May 26, 1637, the first battle of the Pequot War took place when the New Englanders, under John Mason and John Underhill, attacked the Pequot stronghold near present-day New Haven, Conn. The Indian forts were burned and about 500 men, women, and children were killed. The survivors fled in small groups. One group, led by Sassacus, was caught near present-day Fairfield, Conn., on July 28, and nearly all were killed or captured. The captives were made slaves by the colonists or were sold in the West Indies. Sassacus and the few who escaped with him were put to death by Mohawk Indians. The few remaining Pequots were scattered among other southern New England tribes.

The estimated colonial **population** was 5700.

1630 The **Great Migration** into Massachusetts, which occurred between 1630 and 1640, brought some 16,000 settlers to the colony.

The history of American publishing dates from 1638, when the first printing press in the colonies arrived in Cambridge, Mass. It was the property of the Rev. Jose Glover, who died on the voyage from England. He had brought it with him under contract with Stephen Daye. In Cambridge, Glover's widow and Matthew Daye, Stephen's son, helped set up the press. In 1639 the press produced the first English document printed in America, "Oath of a Free-Man." This broadsheet read in part: "I doe solemnly bind myself in the sight of God, that when I shal be called to give my voyce touching any such matter of this State, in which Freemen are to deal, I will give my vote and suffrage as I shal judge in mine own conscience may best conduce and tend to the publike weal of the body, without respect of persons, or favour of any man." An almanac soon followed this broadsheet and in the course of the next decade more than 20 items were printed.

1630 *History of Plimmoth Plantation* by William Bradford, the first account of the settlement of Plymouth colony, was begun. Bradford was the second governor of Plymouth colony. His book took more than 20 years to complete and was first published in full in 1856. Devout, sincere, and learned, Bradford wrote feelingly of the *Mayflower* crossing and of the pioneer life of the early settlers. His authenticity earned him the title "father of American history."

Business and Industry; Science; Education; Philosophy and Religion III		Sports; Social Issues and Crime; Folkways; Fashion; Holidays IV

1628 The **Reformed Protestant Dutch Church** was established in New Amsterdam under the leadership of the Rev. Jonas Michaelius. Before this date Dutch settlers had held informal meetings of worship. The Rev. Michaelius also established the first school in New Netherland. The Reformed Church was the established church of the colony until the English conquest in 1664. Four churches in New York City—Fort Washington Collegiate Church, Middle Collegiate Church, Marble Collegiate Church, and West End Collegiate Church—now collectively known as the Collegiate Reformed Dutch Church, grew out of this early church.

1629 The **first successful pastor of Plymouth colony**, Ralph Smith, arrived. The year before, a Mr. Rogers had been sent from England, but he had proven, in the words of William Bradford, "crased in his braine" and was sent back to England the next year. Smith served as pastor until 1636, assisted for a time by Roger Williams.

1625 The **first child** born in New Amsterdam was in the family of Jan Joris Rapaelje, marking the beginning of family life in the Dutch settlement.

1627 **1500 kidnaped children** arrived in Virginia. They came from Europe and some became great successes. A six-year-old, kidnaped by a sailor and sold in America, married his master's daughter, inherited his fortune, and bought the sailor, by then a prisoner.

1628 May 1 The celebration of **May Day** at Mare Mount, Thomas Morton's settlement at what is now Quincy, Mass., was colorfully although bitterly described by Gov. Bradford: "They allso set up a May-Pole, drinking and dancing aboute it many days together, inviting the Indean women, for their consorts, dancing and frisking together, (like so many faries or furies rather) and worse practices. As they had anew revived and celebrated the feasts of the Roman Goddes Flora, or the beastly practiseses of the Madd Bacchinalians."

1630–1639

Education was an early concern of the colonists, in large part because it was believed necessary, especially in New England, that everyone be able to read the Bible. Also, many of the early settlers had some education—there were, in fact, about 130 university alumni in New England by 1640. The first schoolmaster was a Dutchman, Adam Roelantsen, who arrived in New Amsterdam in 1633 and set up the first school in America. It was an adjunct of the Dutch Reformed Church. That same year the first secondary school in America, the Boston Latin School, was established with a classical curriculum derived from English schools. By 1720 five public schools were maintained in Boston and were so well regarded that they enrolled students from as far away as the West Indies. Boston Latin School, the oldest public school in the U.S., is still in existence.

1630 Summer **Boston's first church** was founded. It had been formed under a covenant adopted by John Winthrop, Thomas Dudley, Isaac Johnson, and the pastor, John Wilson, in Charlestown before these men and their followers crossed the Charles R. and founded the settlement that became Boston. It was a Puritan but non-Separatist Congregational church.

1630 Nov. 9 The **first ferry route** was established by the Massachusetts Court of Assistants in Boston. Every approved ferry operator between Boston and Charlestown on the Charles R. could charge a penny for each passenger and the same amount for each 100 lbs. of cargo.

The tavern, a favorite European institution, began to thrive in America about this time. Drinking was looked on with tolerance in some circles, deplored and opposed in others. The first tavern in Boston was opened by Samuel Cole on Mar. 4, 1634. Taverns became important social institutions and at the time of the American Revolution were meeting places for patriotic groups. Nevertheless, they were frowned on by the authorities. In 1637 Gov. Willem Kieft of New Amsterdam lamented that one-quarter of all the buildings there were occupied by "grog-shops or houses where nothing is to be got but tobacco and beer." On Sept. 4, 1639, the General Court of Massachusetts enacted a law against drinking toasts, saying that, "The common custom of drinking to one another is a mere useless ceremony, and draweth on the abominable practice of drinking healths." It proved impossible to suppress such a time-honored custom, and the law was repealed in 1645.

1631 Feb. 22 The **first public thanksgiving**, a fast day, was celebrated in Massachusetts Bay Colony, though many private celebrations had been recorded before this.

1632 News of a **pirate raid** on Bristol, Maine, reached Gov. John Winthrop of Massachusetts Bay Colony. The raid was conducted by Dixy Bull and 15 other Englishmen. Bull was probably the first pirate to appear on the New England coast.

| Exploration and Settlement; Wars; Government; Civil Rights; Statistics **I** | | **II** Publishing; Arts and Music; Popular Entertainment; Architecture; Theater |

1630 Rensselaerswyck, the only successful Dutch patroonship, was founded by Kiliaen Van Rensselaer, a director of the Dutch West India Company. The patroonship, comprising present-day Albany and Rensselaer counties, extended 24 miles on both sides of the Hudson R., and its inhabitants numbered several thousand tenants. It was never seen by Van Rensselaer, who managed the entire enterprise from his home in Old Amsterdam.

1630 Sept. 30 The **first criminal executed** in the American colonies, John Billington, was hanged for murder. A member of the original Pilgrim band, he had waylaid and shot a man with whom he had quarreled.

1631 May 18 A restrictive suffrage act was passed by the Massachusetts General Court. The act limited privileges of citizenship to church members.

1632 June 20 A charter for the settlement of **Maryland** was granted to Cecilius Calvert, second Lord Baltimore. Under his proprietorship, the Roman Catholic settlement of St. Marys was established. Leonard Calvert, his brother, was the first governor of Maryland.

1635 Aug. 17 **Richard Mather** arrived in Boston. There he founded the so-called Mather dynasty, a sequence of New England ministers who often dominated the Puritan community by the power of their religious position and intellect.

1636 The **first pensions** in America were awarded to wounded soldiers by the Plymouth Pilgrims.

1636 June **Rhode Island** was founded by Roger Williams, who established Providence with a small group of colonists from Massachusetts Bay. It was the first English colony in America to grant complete religious tolerance.

1638 Mar. The **first Swedish settlers** in America landed at Fort Christiana, Del., after crossing in Dutch ships under Peter Minuit. They established the first Lutheran congregation in America, led by Rev. Reorus Rorkillus. In 1643 Swedish colonists from Delaware, under John Printz, settled at Upland, now Chester, Pa.

1639 In an early action for **woman suffrage,** Margaret Brent appeared before the Maryland Assembly and requested the right to vote, an unprecedented gesture for a woman of this time. Brent subsequently

1630 May 29 *The History of New England,* a chronicle of events from 1630 to 1649, was begun by John Winthrop, first governor of Massachusetts Bay Colony. The journal was the inspiration for many of Henry Wadsworth Longfellow's *New England Tragedies.* It was published in a two-volume edition in 1790. When an additional manuscript was found some time later, the whole work finally appeared as *The History of New England,* published in 1825–1826. Winthrop touched upon all major aspects of life. His work is a vast compendium of what the early colonists felt and thought and traces the evolution of their ideas and ideals. It remains an unparalleled primary source for the history of the period.

1634 The **first Roman Catholic** church built by English colonists was raised at St. Marys City, Md. Excavations have revealed its foundation, but nothing else is known about its appearance.

1636 The **oldest extant house** of the English-speaking colonies, the Adam Thoroughgood House, was built near Norfolk, Va. Its design typified that of the small, southern colonial brick farmhouse of the seventeenth century.

1637 The **oldest frame house** still standing in the U.S., the Fairbanks House, was built at Dedham, Mass.

1637 The *New English Canaan,* a book by Thomas Morton describing New England life and satirizing the Plymouth Pilgrims, was published in Amsterdam. Morton founded the colony at Mare Mount, where Maypole dances and other so-called debauched customs stirred the wrath of Puritan leaders. Morton was the square peg in the round hole of New England Puritanism. He spent his life traveling back and forth across the Atlantic, spending enough time in various colonies to outrage the local authorities and be shipped back to England and prison. Before he published his book, he was engaged by the English as an informer against the Massachusetts Bay Colony. The book served partly as revenge for the treatment he had received from the Puritans and partly as justification for his own activities. Nathaniel Hawthorne wrote about Morton in "The Maypole of Merry-Mount."

1638 Construction of **Old College** was begun at Harvard College in Cambridge, Mass. The most ambitious building of its time in the U.S., it housed the entire student body, library, lecture halls, etc.

Business and Industry; Science; Education; Philosophy and Religion	III		IV	Sports; Social Issues and Crime; Folkways; Fashion; Holidays

1631 Compulsory religious education in Virginia was enforced by requiring each churchwarden to take a monthly oath that he was not delinquent in catechizing the young. Ministers were ordered to "examine, catechise, and instruct the youth and ignorant persons" of the parish "in the ten commandments, the articles of the beliefe and in the Lord's prayer."

1631 Feb. 5 Roger Williams, the great early American dissenter and the founder of the American Baptist Church, arrived at Boston from England. He became pastor of the Separatist church at Plymouth in 1632.

1631 Nov. 3 The Rev. John Eliot, who became the first Protestant minister in America to dedicate himself to the religious conversion of Indians, arrived at Boston from England. Settling as a teacher at Roxbury, now part of Boston, he began preaching to the Indians in 1646 and came to be called the apostle of the Indians.

1633 Adam Roelantsen, the **first licensed schoolmaster in America,** took over the school of the Reformed Protestant Dutch Church established five years earlier by the Rev. Jonas Michaelius. The school remained in existence in New York City and today is the Collegiate School, affiliated with but independent of the Collegiate Reformed Dutch Church.

1634 Permission to build what may have been the **first bridge** in the English colonies was granted by the General Court at Boston. Israel Stoughton was authorized to construct a mill and bridge on the Naponsett R. at Dorchester, Mass.

1634 Mar. 25 The **Roman Catholic Church** gained a permanent foothold in America when the *Dove* and the *Ark* arrived in Maryland with colonists carefully selected by Cecilius Calvert, second Lord Baltimore, proprietor of Maryland and a Roman Catholic. The colony was led by Leonard Calvert, Lord Baltimore's brother.

1636 The **first church** in Hartford, Conn., was founded by religious refugees from England and Massachusetts. Led by Thomas Hooker, a Puritan clergyman, the group proclaimed its independence of all authority except that of God.

1636 Oct. 28 Harvard College was founded by an act of the General Court of Massachusetts that allowed £400 for the establishment of a school. Its entrance requirements were: "When any scholar is able to understand Tully or such like classical author extempore, and make and speak true Latin in verse and prose ... and decline perfectly the paradigms of nouns and verbs in the Greek tongue, let him then and not before, be capable of admission into the college." The Rev. Henry Dunster was Harvard's first president.

1637 Nov. 7 Anne Hutchinson was banished from Massachusetts Bay Colony. Charged with heresy for

1633 Price fixing was introduced in the town of Salem, Mass. The maximum price of a meal at an inn was sixpence. At the Ship Tavern, a famous hostelry in New England, board, lodging, and wine at dinner (beer on occasion) cost three shillings a day. Strong intoxicating liquors were forbidden, as well as games, dancing, and singing.

1634 A sumptuary law was passed by the Massachusetts General Court prohibiting the purchase of woolen, linen, or silk clothes with silver, gold, silk, or thread lace on them. Slashed clothing was limited to one slash in each sleeve and in the back.

1634 Mar. 25 Maryland Day, the state holiday, commemorates the landing of the first colonists on St. Clement's Island on this date.

1637 Taunton, Mass., was founded by a so-called ancient maid of 48. This characterization hints at the difficulties faced by **unmarried women** in early America. After the age of 25, unmarried women not only had to bear ridicule but often the penalties of law.

1638 Anne Walker was forcibly excluded from a Boston church for "intemperate drinking from one inn to another and for light and wanton behaviour." Public houses caused much disturbance.

1638 Dutch justice was prompt and harsh during the early days of Manhattan. Guysbert Van Regerslard was sentenced to throw himself from the sail-yard of a yacht three times and receive three lashes from each sailor for "drawing his knife upon a person."

1638 Dr. Hans Kiersted arrived in New Amsterdam. His Kiersted Ointment was used for more than 300 years, its formula a closely guarded family secret.

1639 New England laws governing the **clothing of men** reflected the gay attire of the day: men were censured for wearing "immoderate great breeches," broad shoulder-bands, capes, and double ruffles. Silk roses were worn as adornment on shoes.

initiated the woman suffrage movement in America.

1639   The **first American post office** was authorized in the Massachusetts Bay Colony. Richard Fairbanks, its postmaster, handled the mail in his home in Boston. He received one penny for each letter.

1639 Jan. 14   The **first constitution** in the colonies, the Fundamental Orders, composed by Roger Ludlow, was adopted by representatives from Hartford, Windsor, and Wethersfield in Connecticut. The resulting instrument, with some changes, remained in force until 1818.

1638   The **American log cabin,** originally a Finnish building, was introduced to the New World by the Swedish settlers of Delaware. Unlike other colonists, they brought over their own timber. The colonists also introduced the steam bath.

1638   The **first almanac** in the English colonies, *An Almanak for the Year of Our Lord, 1639, Calculated for New England* by William Pierce, was published at Cambridge, Mass., by Stephen Daye. Pierce, a shipmaster, used the almanac as a broadside to attract new settlers for the colonies and passengers for his ship.

1640–1649

The first federation of American colonies was formed on May 19, 1643, when representatives of Connecticut, Massachusetts Bay, New Haven, and Plymouth colonies met in Boston and organized the United Colonies of New England. The federation was to provide a "firm and perpetual league of friendship and amity, for offense and defense, mutual advice and succor upon all just occasions." John Winthrop of Massachusetts Bay Colony was the first president. Two commissioners from each colony administered the federation, which could not interfere in internal affairs but could resolve boundary disputes among themselves and with the Dutch, who were attempting to encroach on territory claimed by New Englanders. The federation was also intended to provide support against the Indians when necessary. Provision was made for the return of runaway indentured servants, and a fund for the conversion of Indians to Christianity was administered. In 1653 Massachusetts Bay Colony, with the largest population and therefore liable for more soldiers and money than the others, refused to join a proposed war against the Dutch. The federation gradually declined but revived in 1675 on the occasion of King Philip's War. It was dissolved in 1684.

The estimated colonial **population** was 27,947.

c1640   The **first woman barrister** in America was Margaret Brent, colonial attorney for Cecilius Calvert, Lord Proprietor of Maryland.

As mid-century approached, houses and commercial buildings in the colonies became larger, more imposing, and more like those of Europe than, for example, the first homes of Boston, which had been one-story structures covered with thatch and put up at random. By 1636 the Dutch West India Company had built in New Amsterdam five large stone structures for use as shops, although most houses there were built of wood. William Coddington, who founded Newport, R.I., in 1639, two years later built a large townhouse of the type that had a central chimney and two or four rooms on a floor, rather than the older pioneer style house of one room with the fireplace at one end. The City Tavern, the first inn built in New Amsterdam, in 1641, was a four-story stone house, an excellent example of the Dutch colonial style. In 1654 it became the Stadthuys, or Town-House. The first of the great Virginia mansions was erected in 1642 by Gov. William Berkeley about three miles north of Jamestown. Called Greenspring, it was L-shaped, with a brick main wing nearly 100 feet long.

1640   The **first book printed** in America, *The Whole Booke of Psalmes Faithfully Translated into English Metre,* was published in Cambridge, Mass. More commonly called the *Bay Psalm Book,* it contained new versions of all the psalms. Early editions had no music, but included explicit instructions on which tunes should be used for each psalm. Translations and tunes were crude, jog-trot ballads, easier to sing but much less interesting than older versions in Henry Ainsworth's or Thomas Sternhold and John Hopkins' psalters.

Business and Industry; Science; Education; Philosophy and Religion **III**	**IV** Sports; Social Issues and Crime; Folkways; Fashion; Holidays

preaching that faith alone was sufficient for salvation, a belief that contradicted Puritan orthodoxy, she was condemned by an ecclesiastical synod at Newtown, Mass., and fled to Rhode Island.

1638 The **first Baptist church** in America was established at Providence by Roger Williams, who became its first pastor but remained in the church for only a few months.

1639 May 20 The **first school maintained by community taxes** was established by the Council of Dorchester, Mass. Only certain property owners were taxed, and no general tax rates were established.

1639 June 6 A land grant of 500 acres at Pecoit, Mass., for a **gunpowder mill,** probably the first in America, was made to Edmund Rauson by the governors of the Massachusetts Bay Colony.

1639 A charge of **unfair trade** was brought against one Capt. Keane, a colonial shopkeeper, for taking more than sixpence in the shilling profit. Convicted and fined in court, he was severely censured by church authorities, some of whom favored having him excommunicated.

1639 A woman of Plymouth convicted of **adultery** was sentenced to "be whipt at a cart tayle" and to "weare a badge upon her left sleeue during her aboad" in the community. If found in public without the badge, she was to be "burned in the face with a hott iron." Generally the letters AD made up the badge.

1640–1649

It was many years before manufacturing was of much importance in the colonies compared with agriculture, forestry, and fishing, but by this period stirrings of the entrepreneurial spirit could be seen. In 1642 Joseph Jencks, a skilled English ironmaker, was induced to come to America to help develop the iron and brass works at Lynn, Mass. Jencks obtained a Massachusetts patent for a scythe-grinding machine in 1646, the first American patent for machinery. In 1643, what was probably the first American textile factory, a small woolen and fulling mill, was established at Rowley, Mass. The next year the first successful ironworks in what is now the U.S. was founded on the Saugus R. near Lynn, Mass. Its founders were called the Company of Undertakers of Ironworks. They were headed by John Winthrop, a colonial governor who in 1663 became the first resident of the American colonies to become a member of the Royal Society.

1640 Aug. 6 The first major allotment of **public land for education** was made by Newport, R.I. Income from the tract was to be used to educate poor children of the community.

1641 Oct. The **first patent** in the colonies was awarded to Samuel Winslow of Massachusetts for a process of manufacturing salt, the term of the patent to extend ten years.

1644 The **first ship** built in Boston was completed and named *Trial.* This marked the beginning of the great shipbuilding industry of New England.

1646 The first law in Virginia providing for **education of the poor** directed justices of the peace to bind out children of poor parents as apprentices in industrial or agricultural trades. No specific provision was made for book learning although many justices made such a stipulation in their apprentice contracts.

As towns grew and more houses were crowded together, the danger of fire led to development of the volunteer firefighting system. In Massachusetts, laws of 1638 and 1646 forbade smoking "out of dores." This move was inspired not so much by Puritan mores as because "fires have beene often occasioned by taking tobacco." Boston in 1649 required that between nine in the evening and half past four in the morning all fires be covered or put out. In 1648 in New Amsterdam, Gov. Peter Stuyvesant forbade construction of chimneys of "wood or plaister in any house," since defective chimneys caused most fires. He appointed four firemasters to inspect chimneys and to collect three guilders for any chimney found "neglected and foul." The fines were to be used to buy hooks, ladders, and leather buckets for a firefighting organization called The Prowlers, a group of eight men who patrolled the streets at night.

1640 The **high-backed settle** appeared in American households. Designed to rest in front of fireplaces, it was fitted with a high back and arms to ward off drafts, with seats extremely narrow and left unupholstered.

1643 The **first "cook's shop,"** or restaurant, was opened in Boston after Goody Armitage, William Hudson, Jr., and "William Knop's wife" received licenses. They were permitted to keep "the ordinary, but not to draw wine."

1644 The **first Thanksgiving Day** celebrated in New Amsterdam commemorated the safe return of Dutch

1640 **Boston Common** was reserved for the use of the municipality in order to maintain a natural retreat for city dwellers.

1641 Dec. The **Body of Liberties,** a legal code framed by the General Court of Massachusetts, contained strong hints of the growing spirit of colonial independence. Five years later, in 1646, the court had occasion to reply to criticism of its provisions: "Our allegiance binds us not to the laws of England any longer than while we live in England."

1643 The **cosmopolitan population** of New York City showed itself early. Although the city was administered by the Dutch until 1674, there were over 20 different nationalities and sects on Manhattan Island in 1643, speaking 18 languages.

1643 Development of the coastal towns of **Boston, Salem, Dorchester, and Charleston** in Massachusetts Bay colony dwarfed the Plymouth settlement. There were an estimated 20,000 inhabitants in the London Company's Bay Colony.

1643 Mar. **Roger Williams** left Providence for England to obtain a formal charter. In this way Rhode Island secured a legal position from which to fight against pressure from hostile New England colonies.

1644 Mar. 18 An **Indian uprising,** led by Opechancanough, threatened Jamestown, Va. The uprising was suppressed by the colonists, and the resulting treaty forced the Indians to cede additional territory and effected a peace that lasted until 1675.

1646 The **first American battle cruiser** was commissioned by the united colonies of New Haven and Hartford for patrolling Long Island Sound against incursions by the Dutch.

1647 May 29–31 The **Rhode Island General Assembly** convened at Portsmouth, drawing from the towns of Providence, Portsmouth, Newport, and Warwick. This body drafted a remarkably liberal constitution which, among other things, called for separation between church and state.

1641 *The Sincere Convert* by Thomas Shepard was published. The book presented Calvinistic theology in its most attractive form and gained such popularity that it went through 20 editions.

1643 The **first American word book,** *A Key into the Language of America, or an help to the language of the natives of that part of America called New England,* by Roger Williams, founder of Providence, R.I., was published in London. Williams compiled his Indian language dictionary aboard ship during a journey to Southampton, England.

1643 The **oldest tide mill,** a gristmill operated by the movement of the tides, was built at Hingham, Mass. It is one of the earliest examples of industrial architecture in the U.S.

1644 The **first great democratic note** struck in the colonies was Roger Williams' *The Bloudy Tenent of Persecution for Cause of Conscience,* which asserted that the basis of power lies in the people and "that such Governments as are by them erected and established, have no more power, nor for no longer time, than the civill power or people consenting and agreeing shall betrust them with." Considered a dangerous book, it was burned by the public hangman in London. Williams fortunately had not signed his name to it.

c1645 One of the **earliest American books for children,** *Spiritual Milk for Boston babes in either England. Drawn out of the breasts of both Testaments for their souls nourishment,* by John Cotton, was published in England.

1647 A severe **attack on toleration** was *The Simple Cobler of Aggawam in America* by Nathaniel Ward. Professing to be the reflections of a shoemaker, the book attacked women's fashions, men with long hair, etc., yet proved one of the most amusing works of the seventeenth century.

1647 The **earliest painting** of New York, by an unknown artist, also provided the first representation of a striped flag. The flag's four stripes symbolized the confederacy of four colonies: Plymouth, New Haven, Connecticut, and Massachusetts.

Business and Industry; Science;   **III**   **IV**   **Sports; Social Issues and Crime;**
Education; Philosophy and Religion   **Folkways; Fashion; Holidays**

1646 Sept. 1 The **Cambridge Synod** of Congregational Churches was convened by the General Court
of Massachusetts to draw up the *Cambridge Platform,*
the constitution of Congressional churches in the Massachusetts, Plymouth, New Haven, and Connecticut
colonies. The form of church agreed upon was partly
Congregational and partly Presbyterian.

1646 Oct. 28 The **first Protestant service** for Indians
in America was held by the Rev. John Eliot at Nonan-
tum, Mass.

1647 The **first important public education law** in
America was passed in Massachusetts, providing that
every community of 50 homeowners maintain free
elementary education and that communities of more
than 100 households provide secondary school education as well.

1647 May 26 **Roman Catholic priests** were forbidden
to enter territory under Puritan jurisdiction, according to a law passed in Massachusetts. Any person suspected who could not clear himself was to be banished. For a second offense death was the penalty.

1647 Nov. 11 The **first American compulsory school
law** was passed in Massachusetts. It provided for the
appointment of a teacher in every community of
more than 50 families and for the establishment of a
grammar school in every community of more than
100 families.

1648 The **first person executed for witchcraft** in America was Margaret Jones of Charlestown, Mass. Gov.
John Winthrop wrote "that she was found to have
such a malignant touch, as many persons, (men,
women and children), whom she stroked or touched
with any affection or displeasure, etc., were taken
with deafness . . . or other violent pains or sickness . . .
Her behaviour at the trial was very intemperate, lying
notoriously, and railing upon the jury and witnesses,
etc., and in the like distemper she died."

1648 Oct.18 The **first labor organization** in America
was authorized by the Massachusetts Bay Colony.
"The shoomakers of Boston" were permitted to meet
whenever they wanted to choose officers and clerks.

1649 Apr. 21 The **Toleration Act** was pushed through
the Maryland Assembly by Lord Baltimore, Roman
Catholic Proprietor of Maryland. Though the colony
was a haven for Roman Catholics, Lord Baltimore had
from the beginning encouraged Protestant immigration. As Protestant groups became more numerous,
religious disturbances became frequent and bitter.
The rise of Oliver Cromwell in England in 1642 intensified anti-Catholic feeling among the Puritans in
Maryland and other colonies. Increased pressure from
England for the suppression of Catholicism in the colonies led Baltimore to sponsor the Act of Toleration
as a means of averting a serious test of authority.

soldiers from the battle with Connecticut Indians
near Stamford.

1645 June An early mention of the **maypole** in New
Netherland appeared in the sentencing of one William Garritse who, because he sang a libelous song,
was tied to a maypole.

1646 A law limiting the **smoking of tobacco** was passed
by the General Court of Massachusetts. Settlers were
permitted to smoke only when on a journey of five
miles or more from any town. Unlike earlier laws governing smoking, this one was not based on moral
objections, but on danger of fire.

1647 An unusual blue law forbidding **social smoking**
was enacted in Connecticut. Tobacco could be used
once a day, at meals or elsewhere, "and then not in
company with any other." Tobacco could only be used
in one's own house. Behind this law lay the belief that
smoking in a group paved the way to dissipation.

1647 The first **rice planting** in the American colonies
was attempted by Sir William Berkeley, governor of
Virginia. The crop did not succeed.

1647 The first commercially successful **American
wines** were produced by a Capt. Brocas.

1647 **Tavern and innkeeping** provided a means of livelihood for many widows in colonial times. In Salem,
Mass., a Mrs. Clark was given a license to open a tavern on the condition that she "provide a fitt man that
is godlie to manage ye business."

1647 **Marriages by agreement** were declared illegal in
Rhode Island. Cases of common law marriage were
frequent in the colonies, especially among the Quakers. In one case a New England woman, after living
with her "husband" for 20 years, petitioned for separation and her property. The court stigmatized her as
a fornicator, fined both £20, and ordered them "not
to lead soe scandalose life."

1649–1660 Proper **sexual conduct** was rigidly
enforced by Puritan law, as reflected in 122 indictments for sexual offenses in sparsely settled Essex
County in northeastern Massachusetts between 1649
and 1660.

1650–1659

Of all the Indians the English colonists encountered in the colonies, none were more powerful or better organized than the Iroquois. The five tribes—Mohawk, Oneida, Onondaga, Cayuga, and Seneca—were concentrated in New York in that order between the Hudson R. and the Genesee R. to the west. Their league, possibly organized as early as 1570, numbered no more than 25,-000 persons by about 1650 but it dominated others in all directions. Their particular enemies were the Hurons to the north, who with their French allies dominated the fur trade. In 1649 the Iroquois won a resounding victory over the Hurons; in 1651 they nearly wiped out the Neutral Nation along the northern shore of Lake Erie; and in 1656 they defeated and dispersed the Eries. They continued to increase their power and became allies of the English after the Dutch lost New Netherland. As a result, the Iroquois were a serious problem for the patriot forces during the American Revolution.

The estimated colonial **population** was 51,700.

c1650   A **Maryland plantation** called "Aha, the Cow Pasture" was established. Other house and plantation names in seventeenth-century Maryland included Hard Bargain, Bachelor's Hope, Thrumcapped, Want Water, Dear Bought, Peddy Coat's Wish, and Parrott's Cage.

1652   Exportation of **African slaves** to New Netherland was approved by the Dutch government. In the colony strict laws prevented mistreatment of slaves. Whipping was forbidden unless the owner received permission from the authorities.

1652   **New Amsterdam was granted self-government** by the Dutch authorities in the Netherlands. Peter Stuyvesant, since his arrival in the town in 1647 as governor of New Netherland, had ruled as an autocrat. A board of advisers he appointed was dismissed by him in 1651 when they complained of his rule to the homeland. By Feb. 2, 1653, Stuyvesant had no choice but to proclaim New Amsterdam a self-governing municipality, but he reserved the right to enact laws and ordinances.

1652 May 31   **Maine** was part of the Massachusetts Bay colony, according to a ruling by the Massachusetts General Court. Despite an appeal to the English Parliament, Maine was unable to resist and so was annexed.

1652 June 10   The **first mint** in America was established in Boston in defiance of English colonial law, with John Hull as its first master. It issued the famous Pine Tree Shilling, designed by Hull, a silversmith.

1653   Settlement of **North Carolina** by Virginia colonists began. They migrated through the Nansemond Valley and settled north of Albemarle Sound between the Chowan R. and the sea. The move was endorsed

The Puritan settlers of New England were quick to defend their actions and their beliefs, and many felt that the substantial criticism of them being voiced in England during this time required answering. One of the stalwart defenders was Edward Johnson, who first emigrated to Boston in 1630. In 1653 he published in London *The Wonder-Working Providence of Sions Saviour in New England,* a history of Puritan settlement from 1628 to 1652. Johnson pictured the Puritan settlers as soldiers of Christ waging war against the wilderness and unbelievers.

1650   **Anne Bradstreet** became New England's first published poet when a volume of her verse, *The Tenth Muse Lately Sprung Up in America,* was published in London. Bradstreet was the wife of Simon Bradstreet, who later served as governor of Massachusetts colony from 1679 to 1686 and again from 1689 to 1692. The manuscript for her book had been taken to London by a brother-in-law who so admired her work that he arranged to have it published without her knowledge. Her poetry showed the influence of Edmund Spenser, Francis Quarles, Sir Philip Sydney, and others. The longer poems dealt with a variety of subjects, such as the four seasons and the four ages of man. Her shorter poems dealt with her New England experiences. Among the latter were "The Flesh and the Spirit," "On the Burning of Her House," "On My Son's Returning Out of England," and "The Author to Her Book." Cotton Mather and other eminent New England figures praised her poetry. A second edition of her poetry, *Several Poems,* was published posthumously in Boston in 1678.

1653   The beauty of the **Dutch gardens** in New Amsterdam was reported by an early traveler who cited "white and red roses, stock roses, cornelian roses, eglantine, jenoffelins, gillyflowers, different varieties of fine tulips, crown-imperials, white lilies, anemones, bare-dames, violets, marigolds, summersots, clove trees."

1653   The **first Indian book** was a *Catechism* translated into a dialect of the Algonquian language by John Eliot, missionary to the Indians. Eliot later translated the complete Bible into Algonquian, the first Bible printed (1661, 1663) in the colonies.

Business and Industry; Science; Education; Philosophy and Religion **III**		**IV** Sports; Social Issues and Crime; Folkways; Fashion; Holidays

1650–1659

Although many of the early settlers came to America to secure religious freedom, they were not always willing to extend this freedom to others. When the first Quakers, Mary Fisher and Ann Austin, arrived in Boston from Barbados on July 1, 1656, they were imprisoned and mistreated, then expelled by Massachusetts authorities. On Oct. 2 Connecticut enacted a law to fine and banish Quakers. Massachusetts legislation enacted on Oct. 14 decreed that 40-shilling fines be levied against anyone sheltering Quakers and prescribed various physical mutilations for those who returned to the colony after having been banished. The commissioners of the United Colonies of New England expressed their support for such legislation. The first five Quakers to land in New Amsterdam, on June 1, 1657, were imprisoned for eight days before they were allowed to leave for Rhode Island. On May 29, 1658, the Massachusetts General Court passed a law forbidding the holding of Quaker meetings. The first two Quakers hanged on Boston Common, on Oct. 27, 1659, for violating the law against returning to Massachusetts after they had been banished, were William Robinson and Marmaduke Stevenson. Except in Rhode Island, Quakers were persecuted in all the colonies in this period. It was not until the founding of Pennsylvania in 1682 that the Quakers had a haven in the New World.

1651 A famous case of **persecution of Baptists** in Massachusetts involved two Baptist ministers, John Clarke and Obediah Holmes, who were arrested during a service in a private home. Clarke was released against his wishes by a friend's payment of his fine, but Holmes was whipped in the streets of Boston.

1654 Jan Smede, an early Dutch **glassmaker** of New Amsterdam, was allotted ground upon which to set up his works. His firm prospered to such an extent that Glass-makers St., where it was located, was renamed Smede St. (later Smith St. and now William St.).

1654 A commission for the **first fire engine** in America was awarded by the Boston selectmen to Joseph Jencks, an ironmonger from Lynn, Mass. The machine, set on wheels, spurted water from a cistern filled by a bucket brigade.

1654 Probably the **first toll bridge** in what became the U.S. was authorized by the General Court of Massachusetts, which licensed Richard Thurley to build and maintain a toll bridge over the Newbury R. at Rowley. The court fixed the toll at two shillings for horses, cows, and oxen; one-half shilling for hogs, sheep, and goats. Humans crossed free.

Furniture manufacture in the colonies began about this time. Production was hampered for some time by a shortage of carpenters and cabinetmakers. Since the early houses were small, there was not a great deal of space for furniture, and a cramped effect was not unusual. Chests and cupboards provided storage space. An alcove bed was common. Sometimes the parlor, the best room in the house, also seved as the parents' bedroom. The so-called Turkish carpet was placed on table tops, not on the floor. The first known American cabinetmaker, an example of whose work is still extant, worked during this period. He was Nicholas Disbrowe, active in the Connecticut Valley. This area, then the frontier, became the site of a flourishing furniture industry.

c1650 The **settle table,** whose design demonstrated American ingenuity, was a dining table that could easily be changed into a settle, a high-backed wooden seat, by removal of two wooden pins. In 1844 the J.W. Mason Company of New York was established to make and sell these tables. They were in great demand.

1651 The sale of **toys and dolls** in stores in Boston and Salem reflected a relaxation of Puritan asceticism.

1652 A form of **miniature golf** appeared in New Netherland and became quite popular. A small ball was putted around a green by means of a crooked club.

1653 An interesting example of **New England snobbery** was demonstrated by the arrest of two women in Newbury, Mass., for adorning themselves with silk hoods and scarves. They were released when they presented proof that both their husbands had net worths of £200.

1656 A Capt. **Kemble** of Boston was made to sit for two hours in the stocks for his "lewd and unseemly behavior" in kissing his wife "publicquely" on Sunday. He had just returned from a three-year sea voyage.

1656 To ensure that **Sunday** would be a day of rest, the burgomasters of New Netherland passed a law forbidding drinking, sowing, mowing, building, sawing, smithing, bleaching, hunting, fishing, dancing, cardplaying, tick-tacking, bowling, jaunting in a boat or carriage, etc.

1656 A law governing the **baking of bread** was passed in New Amsterdam. Bakers had to bake coarse and white bread twice a week, both for Christians and Indians. The price of a coarse loaf of 8 lbs. was regulated at 14 stuyvers.

by the Virginia Assembly, which wanted a buffer settlement as protection for Virginia's southern frontier.

1655 New Netherland took **control of New Sweden,** the Swedish colony on the Delaware R., after years of pressure on the colony by Peter Stuyvesant. Much later, in 1683, the Swedes and Finns along the Delaware R. gladly became English citizens when William Penn founded Pennsylvania.

1655 Mar. 25 The **civil war** in Maryland between Catholics and Puritans was ended. The war had been sparked by repeal of the Toleration Act (1654), a move that denied Catholics protection under the law. The ensuing struggle was won by Puritans. In the subsequent struggle for control of the colony, the Calverts lost proprietary control of Maryland, then regained it once more (Nov. 30, 1657).

1656 Sept. 22 The **first all-woman jury** in the colonies was empaneled by the General Provincial Court in session at Patuxent, Md., to hear evidence against Judith Catchpole. The defendant, accused of murdering her child, claimed she had never even been pregnant. After hearing her evidence, the jury acquitted her.

1658 Aug. 12 The **first police force,** or *ratelwacht,* was formed in New Amsterdam. It consisted of ten watchmen who were paid 24 stuyvers (about 50 cents) a night, the money collected from the town's inhabitants each month. Any guard caught sleeping on duty was fined ten stuyvers. Guards were enjoined not to swear, fight, or drink.

1657 The **first church edifice in New Hampshire** colony, the Old North Church, was constructed in Portsmouth, N.H. It served its congregation until 1708. The church was located on a site offering maximum protection against Indian attacks.

1659 *The Christian Commonwealth* by John Eliot, outlining the Puritan notion of the relation of God and state, was published. The supremacy of the clergy in the seventeenth century was based on the belief that "there is undoubtedly a form of Civil Government, instituted by God himself in the holy Scriptures."

1659 An *Almanack* issued at Cambridge, Mass., contained probably the first description of Copernican astronomy in the colonies, "A brief Explication and proof of the Philolaick Systeme," by Sechariah Brigden. Young Harvard graduates often edited these New England almanacs, which consequently included verse of their editors and featured the latest popular scientific information.

1660–1669

Some seeds of the American Revolution were sown at this time by the Navigation Acts of the English Parliament, aimed at the rising power of the Dutch merchant fleet. A law passed in 1651 required that most products be shipped to England in English-owned vessels. The First Navigation Act, of 1660, listed colonial articles that could be supplied only to England. Other Navigation Acts followed in 1662, 1663, 1670, and 1673. The 1663 law required that all foreign goods be shipped to the colonies through English ports. Colonists benefited from the laws to the extent that they were given a monopoly on the shipment of some products to England and preferential tariff treatment in some instances. Colonial businessmen nevertheless resented the restrictions imposed upon them.

The estimated colonial **population** was 84,800.

1660 Dec. 1 The **First Navigation Act,** passed by the English Parliament to govern colonial trade, stated that all goods carried to and from England must be transported by British ships manned chiefly by British

Puritans resorted to poetry as well as prose to defend and extend their beliefs. The poetry was always stronger on the theological side than on the poetic. Most famous of such seventeenth-century poet-preachers was Michael Wigglesworth, a clergyman in Malden, Mass. In 1662 his volume *The Day of Doom,* accurately labeled in its subtitle *A Poetical Description of the Great and Last Judgement,* was published. Eighteen hundred copies were sold the first year. It was estimated that one of every twenty persons in New England and one in every forty-five in all the colonies bought a copy. Wigglesworth continued his poetic efforts with *Meat Out of the Eater* (1670), a long poem presenting the Christian view of suffering and the benefits to be derived from it.

1661 The **first Bible printed in America,** the New Testament translated by John Eliot into the Algonquian language and financed by the Corporation for Propagating the Gospel in New England, was published. Of this remarkable work, Cotton Mather wrote: "Behold,

Business and Industry; Science;
Education; Philosophy and Religion   **III**

IV   **Sports; Social Issues and Crime;**
Folkways; Fashion; Holidays

1654 July 8 The first Jew to settle in North America, Jacob Barsimson, arrived on Manhattan Island, first of 24 Jewish immigrants that year. In September three Jews fleeing the Spanish Inquisition in Brazil arrived in New Amsterdam, and more followed. Their right to stay was upheld by the Dutch West India Company against the wishes of Gov. Peter Stuyvesant. They founded Congregation Shearith Israel, with Saul Brown as first rabbi.

1655 **Illiteracy among women** was about 50%, as shown by an examination of legal documents that required signatures of women in Massachusetts. More than half were obliged to sign with a cross. In New Netherland the rate was 60% and in Virginia 75%.

1656 The **Copernican system,** the conception of the solar system that has the sun rather than Earth at its center, was formally accepted by Harvard College only 23 years after Galileo Galilei had been forced by the Roman Catholic Inquisition to repudiate it.

1658 Perhaps the **first hospital** in what is now the U.S. was set up in New Amsterdam by a Dr. Varravanger, surgeon of the Dutch West India Company. It consisted of a clean house with plenty of firewood and a fire, and was supervised by a matron.

1659 The **first classical elementary school** in New Amsterdam was established.

1657 The first reference to **golf** in America was a complaint issued by the sheriff of Fort Orange, now Albany, N.Y., against three men for playing kolven on Sunday. Kolven is believed to have been an early form of golf.

1657 **Horse racing** within the city limits of New Amsterdam was forbidden by Peter Stuyvesant, governor of New Netherland.

1658 A colonial writer took note of the **fortunes of women** in America: "They no sooner arrive than they are besieged with offers of matrimony, husbands being ready soon for those whom nature had apparently marked out and predestined for lives of single blessedness." Many servants, innocent country girls kidnaped in England and sent penniless to America, married well and attained distinction.

1659 Jan. The severity of **colonial punishments** was demonstrated by an ordinance passed in New Amsterdam: "No person shall strip the fences of posts or rails under penalty for the first offence of being whipped and branded, and for the second, of punishment with the cord until death ensues."

1659 Sept. 30 The first mention of **tennis** in America appeared in a proclamation issued by Gov. Peter Stuyvesant of New Netherland forbidding tennis playing, among other things, on certain days.

1660–1669

An early political document stressing religious toleration in America was *Fundamental Constitutions,* drawn up for the governance of the Carolinas in 1669. It was the work of the English philosopher John Locke, who prepared it for his friend Anthony Ashley Cooper, later first earl of Shaftesbury, one of the proprietors of Carolina. The document combined liberal principles and an aristocratic social system while stressing religious tolerance. Although it never became law, it exercised a profound influence on colonial religion, particularly in the Carolinas. *Fundamental Constitutions* provided that "Noe person whatever shall disturb, molest or persecute another for his speculative opinions in Religion or his way of worship." Official recognition and support could be granted only to the Church of England, but it was specified that any seven adherents of a religious faith could establish a church under any name they desired, with the provisos that they accept the existence of God and declare that the parishioners of the church would worship Him.

Seventeenth-century colonists enjoyed a variety of sports and games. Since horses were a part of everyday life, it was not surprising that, in 1664, horse racing became the first organized sport in the colonies. Before then the governor of Virginia and his friends had raced their horses on a short stretch of road after church services, thereby developing the fast "quarter horse." The Dutch in New Amsterdam enjoyed the cruel sport of "riding the goose" until it was banned in 1658. In Boston, in spite of the Puritan atmosphere, football was played on the streets. Gambling and card playing also were popular there until laws were passed to forbid them. At Newport, R.I., from 1640 to 1690, men amused themselves by bowling on the green.

c1660 **Pinkster Day,** the Dutch name for Pentecost, was celebrated with much rejoicing and riotous activity among the Dutch in New Netherland. The celebration was at its greatest among the African slaves of Fort Orange (Albany). Congo dances were staged, accompanied by tom-tom rhythms and African airs.

sailors. It further provided that certain articles, which included sugar, tobacco, cotton, wool, ginger, and dyestuffs, were to be exported to England only.

1662 May 3   A **legal charter for Connecticut** was secured through the efforts of Gov. John Winthrop, Jr. The charter united the colonies of New Haven and Connecticut, neither of which was protected by royal charter. New Haven, however, opposed merger with Connecticut.

1664   A **slavery act** in Maryland provided for lifelong servitude for black slaves. The law was designed to prevent slaves who had converted to Christianity from claiming freedom on the basis of English court decisions holding that infidel slaves must be freed once they had been baptized as Christians and had taken legal residence in the country. Similar acts were passed in Virginia, North Carolina, New York, South Carolina, and New Jersey. Such action was not taken in Georgia, Pennsylvania, or Delaware.

1664 Mar. 12   A **land grant** of territory between the Connecticut and Delaware rivers, including lands currently held by the Dutch, was made by King Charles II of England to his younger brother, James, Duke of York. On Apr. 2 James appointed Col. Richard Nicolls to head a force to conquer New Netherland.

1664 June 24   Proprietorship of **New Jersey,** land between the Hudson and Delaware rivers, was granted by James, Duke of York, to Lord John Berkeley and Sir George Carteret. The new grant was named New Jersey for Carteret, who had been governor of the Isle of Jersey.

1664 Sept. 7   Gov. **Peter Stuyvesant surrendered New Netherland** to an English naval force led by Col. Richard Nicolls. Not a shot was fired. Thus ended Dutch power in the New World. Dutch holdings were reorganized into the English colonies of New York and New Jersey. New Amsterdam was renamed New York, and Fort Orange was renamed Albany.

1665 Feb. 28   The **Duke's Laws,** sponsored by the English proprietor of New York, James, Duke of York, provided for official recognition of all Protestant sects within the colony. Specific mention was made of the Reformed Protestant Dutch Church, the only church recognized by name. This unusual toleration of the Dutch Church by English authorities contrasted sharply with the restrictive policies of the Dutch West India Company before its loss of the colony to the British in 1664. Up to 1664 the Reformed Protestant Dutch Church was the only legal church in the colony. Despite this restriction, a great many unauthorized religious groups established footholds in the Dutch colony. This religious diversity inherited by the English proprietor in 1664 made the policy of toleration a practical necessity.

ye Americans, the greatest honor that ever you were partakers of! This is the only Bible that ever was printed in all America from the very foundation of the world." Eliot's translation into Algonquian of the Old Testament was published in 1663.

1662   Strict **censorship** of printed material in Puritan New England was revealed in the appointment of two licensers to prevent distribution of certain books that might tend "to open the door of heresy."

1664   The **Richard Jackson House** was constructed in Portsmouth, N.H. Built in the traditional English style of the time, the dwelling is reputed to be the oldest building in the state. Richard Jackson was a shipbuilder.

1664   The **first mention of a musical instrument** in the colonies was made in the will of one Mr. Nathaniell Rogers of Rowley, Mass. The document mentioned a "treble vial" valued at ten shillings.

1664   The **first best-selling book of sermons** in America was *A Call to the Unconverted* by Richard Baxter. Baxter was a celebrated British Puritan preacher and author.

1664   The emergence of the **Renaissance style** in Dutch colonial houses at New Amsterdam was noted by contemporary observers. The Renaissance style was characterized by the adaptation of architectural elements from Roman antiquity. The Dutch influence continued to prevail after the colony became New York.

1665   *The Practice of Piety* by Lewis Bayly, bishop of Bangor, England, was a widely read book in colonial America. It was a book of prayer, meditation, and especially exhortations, written with Calvinistic fire.

1665 Aug. 27   The **first play performed in the North American colonies, Ye Bare and Ye Cubb** by Philip Alexander Bruce, was presented at Acomac, Va. Three local residents were fined for acting in this play. Most colonies had laws forbidding public performances. What is strange is that this incident occurred in Virginia, where no such legislation existed.

1666   *A Character of the Province of Maryland,* a rollicking account of **life in early Maryland** by George Alsop, was published. Full of raw humor, often coarse and obscene, the book was rich in such phrases as: "Herds of deer are as numerous in this province of Maryland as cuckolds can be in London, only their horns are not so well dressed and tipped with silver."

| Business and Industry; Science; Education; Philosophy and Religion | III | | IV | Sports; Social Issues and Crime; Folkways; Fashion; Holidays |

1660 The **first Indian church** in New England was founded by John Eliot at Natick, Mass., on the Charles R. He had established Natick as a native village for "praying Indians" in 1657.

1661 The **first annual meeting of American Quakers** was held in Rhode Island.

1661 Pressures for the **cultivation of silk** in Virginia were increased following coronation of King Charles II of England, who wore a robe woven of Virginia silk.

1661 Mar. 24 The **last Quaker executed** in Boston was William Leddra, who suffered the death penalty for returning from banishment.

1661 Sept. **Persecution of Quakers** in Massachusetts was halted by Gov. John Endicott on orders from Charles II, a personal friend of William Penn.

1662 Jan. The **first lime was produced in America** by a Mr. Hacklett of Providence, R.I.

1662 Mar. Adoption of the **Half-Way Covenant** by a general synod of Massachusetts churches led to a schism in New England Congregationalism. The covenant permitted parents who had been baptized in the church, but who no longer professed their faith, to have their children baptized. The Half-Way Covenant was symptomatic of the decline of power of the New England founders and the emergence of a more liberal second generation.

1666 Construction began of the **First Presbyterian Church** in Elizabeth, N.J., to serve the first English-speaking church group in the colony.

1666 The **first church in Breuckelen (Brooklyn)** was completed, a heavy, square building situated on what is now Fulton St. It continued to be used until 1810.

1660 The **first divorce case** in Delaware involved a Finnish couple. It was said that the "wife receives daily a severe drubbing and is expelled from the house like a dog." The husband was an adulterer, and the divorce was granted. New England at this time showed the most liberality in granting divorces. New Netherland and the rest of the Middle Atlantic colonies made divorce almost impossible except in cases of proved or confessed adultery.

1660 To promote **stable marriages,** a Connecticut law ordered all married men to live with their wives. Any man who was separated from his wife for more than three years was ordered out of the colony.

1660 A **sumptuary law** passed in Virginia forbade settlers from importing "silke stuffe in garments or in peeces except for whoods and scarfs, nor silver or gold lace, nor bone lace of silk or threads, nor ribbands wrought with gold or silver in them." But with the Restoration in England in 1660, periwigs came into fashion on both sides of the Atlantic. Authorities in New England made repeated efforts to prevent their use.

1660 May The celebration of **Christmas** was forbidden by a law of Massachusetts, with a fine of five shillings levied on violators.

1662 A Virginia edict on **baptism** decreed that any parents who failed to have their children baptized were to be fined 2000 lbs. of tobacco.

1662 The anniversary of the **beheading of Charles I,** Jan. 30, was declared by the Virginia General Assembly to be a day of fasting in the colony. Charles II had issued a similar edict in England upon his restoration in 1660.

1664 **Marriage** by a justice of the peace instead of a clergyman was made lawful in New York by the Duke's Laws, actually a continuation of a Dutch law of 1590. The law has never been altered.

1664 The **first organized sport** in America, horse racing, began when New York's first governor, Richard Nicolls, established the Newmarket Course at Hempstead Plains, Long Island, instituted rules of racing, and offered prizes to winners. His purpose was to improve the breed of horses in the colonies.

1665 Nov. 5 **Guy Fawkes Day** was celebrated in New York. A law ordered all ministers to preach a sermon on this date in commemoration of the discovery of the plot to blow up the English House of Lords in 1605.

1666 South Carolina publicized in England this **inducement to women:** "If any maid or single woman have a desire to go over, they will think themselves in the golden age, when men paid a dowry for their wives; for if they be but civil, and under fifty years of

1667   The Virginia legislature decreed that persons born in **slavery** did not become free once they were baptized in the Christian faith. The preamble to this law expressed the hope that slave owners would, by passage of this law, become more diligent in converting their slaves to Christianity.

1667 July 21   **New Netherland was ceded** to England by the Dutch by the Peace of Breda, which ended the Second Anglo-Dutch War (1664–1667).

1669   The first comprehensive **history of New England** was published in Boston, Mass.: *New England's Memoriall, or a Brief Relation of the Most Memorable and Remarkable Passages of the Providence of God, Manifested to the Planters of New England in America; With Special Reference to the First Colony Therefore, Called New Plymouth* by Nathaniel Morton, secretary of Plymouth colony.

1670–1679

While the English colonists were settling along the Atlantic coast and river valleys, the French, from their bases in Canada, were using the St. Lawrence R. and the Great Lakes to explore and claim western North America. At Sault Sainte Marie in 1671, Daumont de St. Lusson claimed the entire interior for France. In 1673 the explorer Louis Joliet and the missionary Jacques Marquette reached the upper Mississippi R. and traveled down it as far as Arkansas. Marquette established a mission at what is now Chicago on Dec. 4, 1674. Another expedition began in late 1678 under the leadership of Robert Cavelier, Sieur de La Salle, and Father Louis Hennepin. They passed Niagara Falls, and later Hennepin was the first European to write a description of it. The party explored the upper Mississippi River Valley. On Apr. 9, 1682, La Salle reached the mouth of the Mississippi, where he claimed control of the whole valley for France and named it Louisiana after King Louis XIV of France.

The estimated colonial **population** was 114,500.

1670   A **Virginia slavery act** decreed that slaves who had become Christians before their importation were not liable to lifelong servitude. This law reflected the moral concern felt in America over the enslavement of Christians.

1670   A law prohibiting the **importation of convicts** as indentured servants was passed by the Virginia legislature. This act was sustained for a time in the English Parliament but finally was repealed in 1717 by an act authorizing transportation of convicts to America.

1670 Apr.   **Charleston, S.C., was founded.** English colonists under Joseph West settled at Port Royal Sound, then moved northward to the Ashley R. at Albemarle Sound for fear of Spaniards. There they established Charles Town, later known as Old Charles Town. In 1680, this settlement was moved once again to the juncture of the Ashley and Cooper rivers, the present site of the city.

1671   The first of the great **Hudson Valley manors** was established at Fordham by the English colony of New

A colonial tradition in architecture was that a house should be designed and built to last, and to grow as the family that owned it grew. This was reflected in the history of the House of the Seven Gables in Salem, Mass. Originally known as the Turner House, its first two rooms were built in 1670. Successive additions greatly expanded the structure, and it eventually came to have eight gables. Nathaniel Hawthorne was thought to have modeled the house in his novel *The House of the Seven Gables* (1851) after this structure, which he had visited in his youth.

1670   An early painting attributed to **John Foster** was the portrait *John Davenport,* now at Yale University. A Harvard graduate who devoted his spare time to woodcuts, Foster painted his portrait in a stiff, flat manner. He became known later as one of the earliest primitives.

1670   *A Brief Description of New York* by Daniel Denton, the first printed account of New York City, was published. Designed to encourage immigrants to this growing community, the book described "the woods and fields so curiously bedecked with roses" and "divers sorts of singing birds, whose chirping notes salute the ear of travellers."

1670   The **first portrait engraving** in colonial America was a woodcut of Richard Mather, the Puritan leader and theological writer of Massachusetts.

Business and Industry; Science; Education; Philosophy and Religion III		IV Sports; Social Issues and Crime; Folkways; Fashion; Holidays

1668 May 27 The first Baptists sentenced to exile from Massachusetts were Thomas Gold, William Turner, and John Farnum.

1669 The first Sunday school of record was established at Plymouth, Mass.

age, some honest man or other, will purchase them for their wives."

1668 America's first sports trophy, a silver porringer, wrought by Pieter van Inburg, was presented to the winner of a horse race at the Newmarket Course at Hempstead Plains, Long Island.

1669 Horse racing was firmly established in New York when Gov. Francis Lovelace personally arranged a race for the silver crown at Newmarket Course at Hempstead Plains.

1670–1679

By 1675 more than 600 ships and 4000 New England men were engaged in fishing. From early times, fishing had been important to the colonies not just for food for the settlers but for commerce. When the Pilgrims sailed for America in 1620, they intended their colony to be in part a fishing settlement. In the 1630s the Puritans entered the field. The Rev. Hugh Peter organized fisheries at Marblehead, Mass., and discovered a market for dried codfish. Fishing for cod became so important in the Massachusetts Bay Colony that a wooden image of a cod was installed in the capitol in Boston. Salted fish was in demand in Catholic Europe and in the West Indies. New England fishermen divided their catch into three classes. The largest and fattest, the most difficult to cure, were consumed at home. Somewhat smaller fish were cured and exported to Europe. The smallest were sold, usually traded for molasses, in the West Indies as food for slaves.

1670 Aug. 22 An Indian church was founded on Martha's Vineyard by John Eliot and John Cotton of the Massachusetts Bay Colony. Hiacoomes and Tackanash, two educated Indians, were appointed pastor and teacher. Hiacoomes continued in his office for many years as a well-liked and faithful minister.

1671 The first Seventh Day Baptist Church was established at Newport, R.I., by Stephen Mumford. An English Sabbatarian Baptist, Mumford argued that the Sabbath should be observed on the last day of the week.

From the beginning, dress styles had varied from colony to colony, in large part because of national origin, class, or religion. New Englanders tended to be plain of dress, although not as austere as they were later depicted, while many Virginians copied the fashions of upper-class English men and women. By the later seventeenth century, colonial life had improved to where fashion became substantially more elegant and luxurious. This gave rise, particularly in New England, to sumptuary laws intended by colonial authorities to control excesses in dress, hairstyle, and the like.

1670–1690 Growth of the southern aristocracy became apparent early in Virginia, where practically every position in Henrico County was filled by a member of the Randolph family.

1670 The following game was available to hunters on Long Island, N.Y., a popular hunting area: "Deer, Bear, Wolves, Foxes, Racoon, Otters, Musquashes, and Skunks; Wild Fowl ... Turkies, Heath Hen, Quailes, Partridges, Pigeon, Cranes, Geese of several sorts, Brants, Ducks, Widges, Teal, and divers others."

1670 The coffee house appeared in America when a license was given by Boston authorities to a woman to sell coffee and chocolate.

1672 Indian mail carriers were hired by New York City officials to carry winter mail to Albany because of the extreme hardships involved. As late as 1730 a notice was posted that "whoever inclines to perform the foot-post to Albany this winter may make application to the Post-Master."

1673 Early horse racing in Virginia was strictly for aristocrats. James Bullock, a York County tailor, ran his mare against that of Mathew Slader for 200 lbs. of

York. Others followed: Fox Hall (Kingston), 1672; Rensselaerswyck, 1685; Livingston, 1686; Pelham, 1687; Philipsborough, 1693; Morrisania, 1697; Cortlandt, 1697; and Scarsdale, 1701.

1671 A new **slavery act** in Maryland extended the scope of the slavery law passed in 1664 by declaring that conversion or baptism of slaves before or after their importation did not entitle them to freedom. The act was passed on behalf of slave owners who hesitated to import slaves for fear of losing their investments through prior or subsequent conversion and, also, to encourage slave owners to convert their slaves to Christianity.

1672 May 15 The **first copyright law** in the American colonies was enacted by the Massachusetts General Court, which issued a copyright to John Usher, bookseller, to publish a new edition of *The General Laws and Liberties of the Massachusetts Colony.* Copyright protection was for seven years. The penalty for infringement was a fine three times the manufacturing cost.

1673 The **first native-born governor** of an American colony, Josiah Winslow of Plymouth, was elected governor of Plymouth colony. His term extended until his death in 1680. Winslow also succeeded Myles Standish as commander in chief of the Plymouth military defense.

1673 Aug. 8 The **surrender of New York** was demanded by a Dutch force of 23 ships and 1600 men anchored near Sandy Hook. They held possession of the colony until Feb. 9, 1674, when the English regained control.

1675–1676 Pressures on the **Indian population** of New England resulted in King Philip's War. The tribes most affected by early colonial expansion were the Wampanoags, originally from the Atlantic coast, now forced back to east of Narragansett Bay; the Narragansetts, whose territory between Narragansett Bay and the Thames R. was menaced by a land company that claimed it held a mortgage to the areas; the Mohegans, between the Connecticut and Thames rivers; the Podunks, directly to the north; and the Nipmucks, who ranged over the northern parts of the Thames and Pawtucket rivers. A coalition of these tribes, known as the Five Nations, was headed by King Philip, Indian name Metacomet, chief of the Wampanoags.

1675 June 24 **King Philip's War** (1675–1676) began with a massacre of colonists at Swansea, Plymouth, by a band of Indians. The war was started by King Philip after three of his people were executed by the English for murdering an Indian in English employ.

1675 Aug. 2 **Brookfield, Mass., was attacked** and destroyed by Indians. They were later forced to retreat under an assault led by Maj. Simon Willard.

1670 An early example of **colonial portraiture** was *Margaret Gibbs* by a "Freake Painter" of Boston. Adorned in lacery, the young subject attested to an aspect of Puritan life that was hardly religious. Though most painters of the period are unknown, the fact that Boston could claim from five to ten painters about this time reveals a lively interest in portraiture.

1672 Oct. 2 The **Castillo de San Marcos,** a fort at St. Augustine, Fla., and one of the most impressive structures of Spanish colonial style, was begun. The fort was completed in 1756. Nine previous forts of wood and earth construction had been built and demolished on its site.

1674 An early colonial **study of nature** reflecting true scientific discipline was an *Account of Two Voyages to New England* by John Josselyn. His book included geological and botanical observations.

1674 **Samuel Sewall** began his famous diary, which covered the years 1674 to 1729. Like Samuel Pepys, he loved to record commonplace events of his time. A judge at the Salem witchcraft trials in 1692, he later recanted his role in them.

1676 An example of **early American satire** was the ballad *A Looking-Glass for the Times; or, The former spirit of New England revived in this generation* by Peter Folger, grandfather of Benjamin Franklin. In strong, manly doggerel, he lashed into the Christians of New England for their behavior toward Quakers, Baptists, and others.

1677 A **classic historical book,** *Narrative of the Trouble with the Indians in New England* by William Hubbard, was published. The book reflected the colonials' hostility to red men, who were described as "treacherous villians," "children of the Devil," "the dross of mankind," and "dregs and lees of the earth."

Business and Industry; Science;   **III**   **IV**   Sports; Social Issues and Crime;
Education; Philosophy and Religion   Folkways; Fashion; Holidays

1673 Jan. 1 The first regular **mounted mail service** was inaugurated between New York and Boston. A postman rode without a change of horse from New York to Hartford, through woods and over streams, keeping a lookout for runaway servants and soldiers. The road was little more than a trail but it would soon become the Boston Post Road, the first important highway in the colonies. A post road was so called because men or horses were posted at intervals along the route. They would take packages or messages and carry them to the next post. In this way goods and information were relayed with relative speed. Nonetheless, it still took three weeks to get the mail from Boston to New York City.

1674 **Increase Mather** was appointed a fellow at Harvard College, beginning a distinguished career in education. Although he once refused the presidency of Harvard, Mather was named acting president in 1685. The following year he took charge, with the title of rector, and held that post until 1701. Mather promoted the study of scientific subjects while maintaining the college's Congregationalist ties. In 1675 his eldest son, Cotton Mather, was admitted to Harvard at the age of 12. He was the youngest person ever admitted to the school. Cotton Mather, the son and grandson of Puritan clergymen, even at this early age believed himself destined to follow in their footsteps and become the preeminent religious and political leader of Massachusetts. Perhaps it was young Mather's sense of destiny that led his fellow students to consider him something of a prig.

1675 Perhaps the **first business corporation** in America, a fishing corporation in New York, was established by a charter issued by the Duke of York. It was a joint-stock company with capital shares valued at £10, but the other aspects of the incorporation are not known.

tobacco. When he tried to collect, the court fined him 100 lbs. of tobacco, declaring "racing to be a sport for gentlemen only."

1673 The appearance of a **fencing school** in Boston indicated increased interest in recreation in Puritan life.

1674 A rule against **horse racing** on public thoroughfares in Plymouth colony stated that "whatsoever person ran a race with any horse in any street or common road should forfeit five shillings or sit in the stocks for one hour."

1675 **New York City**, which had always had a mixed population, began to take on a really cosmopolitan air. The combination of religious toleration and commercial activity encouraged an influx of Englishmen, Jews, Africans, Indians, Madagascan pirates, and French Huguenots.

1675 Laws upbraiding **current fashions** were enacted by the Massachusetts General Court. Indian attacks were blamed on the sins of the people, among which was "the manifest pride openly appearing amongst us in that long hair, like women's hair, is worn by some men, either their own or others' hair made into periwigs."

1675 In a case involving **sumptuary laws** in Connecticut, 38 women were brought before a magistrate for wearing clothes not befitting their social position. One young girl was accused of "wearing silk in a flaunting manner, in an offensive way and garb not only before but when she stood presented." This year 30 young men were arrested for wearing silk and sporting long hair.

1675 May 3 The **locking of church doors** during service was required by a Massachusetts law enacted because too many people were leaving before the long sermons were completed.

1676 A **caste law** passed in Connecticut provided that anyone adorned with silk ribbons, gold or silver lace, or any other luxurious fabric or metal was to be assessed for taxable property of £150 with the significant exception of "those whose quality and estate have been above the ordinary degree though now decayed."

| Exploration and Settlement; Wars; Government; Civil Rights; Statistics **I** | | **II** Publishing; Arts and Music; Popular Entertainment; Architecture; Theater |

1675 Sept. 1 Deerfield, Mass., was set aflame by attacking Indians.

1676 Feb. 10 Lancaster, Mass. was attacked by Indians led by King Philip. The settlement was destroyed by fire after all the men were killed and the women and children taken prisoners.

1676 Aug. 12 **King Philip's War** (1675–1676) ended when the Wampanoag leader was surprised and shot by an Indian in the service of Capt. Benjamin Church. The conflict had grown to include the Wampanoag, Nipmuck, Narragansett, Mohegan, and Podunk tribes and ended with their virtual destruction, opening southern New England to unimpeded colonial expansion.

1676 Sept. 19 Jamestown, Va., was burned in **Bacon's Rebellion,** an uprising led by Nathaniel Bacon. The rebellion was prompted by Virginia Gov. William Berkeley's repeated refusal to organize necessary defensive measures against marauding Indians. Among the buildings destroyed was the Episcopal Church in Jamestown, the first Protestant church in America. The ruins of the church tower are still standing on the site of the community.

1677 Aug. The first large group of **Quakers** from England to emigrate to America settled in West Jersey, founding the city of Burlington.

1678 The **first vessel** to penetrate Lake Ontario, the *Griffin,* carried a French expedition led by Robert Cavelier, Sieur de La Salle, from Fort Frontenac (later Kingston) to the present site of Fort Niagara.

1679 A **Boston fire,** the worst in the colonies in the seventeenth century, destroyed 150 houses in Boston. Thereafter, frame houses were abandoned by city ordinance, and all houses were constructed of "stone or bricke, & covered with slate or tyle."

1677 *Elegy on the Reverend Thomas Shepard* by Urian Oakes, one of the finest poems written in America during this era, was published. Increase Mather considered Oakes "one of the greatest lights that ever shone in this part of the world, or that is ever like to arise in this horizon."

1678 **Anne Bradstreet**'s first book of poems, published in London in 1650, was revised posthumously in Massachusetts, becoming the first collection of poetry by a woman published in the colonies. It was entitled *Several Poems Compiled with Great Variety of Wit and Learning.* Coming from a cultivated background in England, and thrust into the wilderness of the New World, Bradstreet revealed her leaning toward such poets as Philip Sidney, Edmund Spenser, and George Herbert and the feelings of a sensitive woman in contact with rude nature.

1679 A colonial **best seller,** *A Guide to Heaven* by Samuel Hardy, was published in Boston. A book of Puritan rules and practices of piety, it was less fiery than Bishop Lewis Bayly's *The Practice of Piety.*

1680–1689

The flight of King James II of England to France, and his succession on the English throne by William of Orange and his wife Mary on Feb. 13, 1689, marked the climax of the Glorious Revolution, by which the English Parliament asserted its authority over the king and ensured the succession of a Protestant to the throne. The abdication of James II, a Catholic and an autocratic ruler, had almost immediate repercussions in the colonies. In 1689 the unpopular governor of Virginia, Lord Howard, was removed; Gov. Edmund Andros surrendered in Boston; the counties of New York, Queens, and Westchester in New York ousted the royal government and set up their own rule; Rhode Island and Connecticut reestablished governments under their old charters;

A leading figure in colonial literature during this time was William Penn, one of the more unusual personalities among those who founded English colonies in America. The son of an English admiral, he became a Quaker in 1666, when he was 22. Two years later he was imprisoned for writing a religious tract. While in the Tower of London he composed another. Although a liberal in government and deeply religious, he was also politically adept at the royal court. During this period he founded Pennsylvania and wrote both in praise of the colony and in defense of his Quaker beliefs.

| Business and Industry; Science; Education; Philosophy and Religion   III | | Sports; Social Issues and Crime; Folkways; Fashion; Holidays   IV |

1676 Regulations on **shoe prices** were instituted in Massachusetts: "Five pence half penny a size for all pleyne and wooden heel'd shoes, and above seven pence half penny a size for well wrought 'French falls.' " Shoes with wooden heels were worn throughout the seventeenth century.

1677 The first charter guaranteeing **separation of church and state** in the American colonies was framed by William Penn at the Quaker colony of West Jersey.

1677 Puritan **hostility to Quakers** was reflected in a passage of Samuel Sewall's diary about the unruly gestures and appearance of a proselytizing Quaker woman bursting in on a Congregational meeting.

1676 An order regulating **church attendance** in Salem, Mass., required "all ye boyes of ye towne are appointed to sitt upon ye three paire of stairs in ye meeting-house, and Wm. Lord is appointed to look after ye boys upon ye pulpitt stairs." Little girls, on the contrary, sat with their mothers. Men and women generally sat on different sides of the hall.

1678 **Tobacco** consumption of the Dutch inhabitants of New York was substantial. An English chaplain reported that "the Dutch are obstinate and incessant smokers, whose diet . . . being sallets and brawn and very often picked buttermilk, require the use of that herb to keep their phlegm from coagulating and curdling."

1679 A suit for **nonpayment of dowry** was filed by James Willet against his father-in-law, Lt. Peter Hunt, for not paying the £100 dowry he had offered. Marriage was permeated by economics among fashionable Puritans. Fathers often haggled over their daughters' dowries.

1679 Sept. The first methodical **plan for naming streets** appeared in an order of the Town Meeting of Newport "to consider of making foure equall divisions of this Towne . . . (which) will be useful about ye naming of ye highways." Boston itself had no plan until later. It designated streets as "the street leading to the Neck" or "John Thwings land to the lane by Houghton's house."

1680–1689

By the late seventeenth century, the African slave trade was a large-scale business enterprise. Largely in the hands of the Dutch until the 1660s, it was continued by the English, with New Englanders especially active after the Royal Africa Trade Company lost its monopoly in 1696. In the trade, a ship sailed from New England with rum and other goods for the Slave Coast. The slaves were then carried, under the most miserable conditions, to the West Indies or to the colonial South, where they were exchanged for sugar, molasses, and tobacco for the North. During this period Virginia planters relied more on white indentured servants from Europe than on slaves from Africa. There were 6000 indentured servants in Virginia in 1681, compared with 2000 slaves. Some indentured servants came voluntarily, signing

A new element was added to colonial society when in France the Edict of Nantes was revoked in 1685 by King Louis XIV. The edict had protected the Huguenots, French Protestants, from persecution, and its revocation led to a wave of Huguenot emigration to the New World. Thrifty and industrious middle-class merchants and artisans, they settled in New York, Massachusetts, Rhode Island, Virginia, and South Carolina, and established such illustrious family names as Jay, Revere, DeLancey, Faneuil, Bowdoin, and Maury. In New York they founded and named New Rochelle in 1688. The Huguenots were especially important in South Carolina, where 500 of them took up 50,000 acres along the Santee R. They were prominent in Charleston life, and in

and a Protestant Association overthrew the old government in Maryland.

The estimated colonial **population** was 155,600.

1680 Sept. **New Hampshire** was separated from Massachusetts by royal commission.

1681 Mar. 4 What is now roughly the state of **Pennsylvania was granted to William Penn,** a member of the Society of Friends (Quakers) by King Charles II of England. The grant was apparently made to offset a debt of £16,000 the king owed to Penn's father, Sir William Penn.

1682 The **slavery law** of 1670, which had exempted from lifelong servitude all slaves who had been converted to Christianity before their importation, was repealed by the Virginia legislature. Repeal of the statute was dictated by the sharp decline in slave importation following its passage.

1682 A site for the city of **Philadelphia** was laid out by Thomas Holme, one of four commissioners who had been sent to Pennsylvania by William Penn to prepare settlers for the new government. Penn, who was in the colony at the time, helped in planning the city.

1682 The **first European settlement in Texas** was made by Spaniards at Yselta, on the site of present-day El Paso. The settlers were refugees from New Mexico who had been driven out after the Pueblo revolt of 1680. Several missions were established in this area but they did not flourish because the Comanche, Apache, and other Indian tribes were unfriendly.

1682 May 5 William Penn's *Frame of Government* was put into effect. An unusually liberal document, it provided for a governor, council, and assembly to be elected by freeholders. The council had legislative, judicial, and administrative powers. At first, the assembly could not initiate legislation, but this was altered in 1696.

1682 Aug. 13 The **first Welsh settlers** in America established a community near Philadelphia.

1682 Aug. 24 **Delaware** was awarded to William Penn by James, Duke of York, who had no legal title to the land. This made Penn's control over Delaware tenuous, particularly since it conflicted with other claims. The issue was finally resolved by the Charter of 1701, which gave Delaware autonomy.

1683 Oct. 6 The **first German settlers** in America, Mennonites from Krefeld, Germany, arrived at Philadelphia. They settled Germantown, near Philadelphia, at the bidding of William Penn. Their leader, Francis Daniel Pastorius, was considered by many the most learned man in America at the time.

1684 June 21 The **Massachusetts Bay Colony charter was revoked** by King Charles II of England, acting through the Court of Chancery. Massachusetts had violated its charter by discriminating against the Church of England, setting religious rather than

1680 The **first hipped, or Italian, roof** in the present-day U.S. was built on the Talbot County Court House in Maryland. The style later became popular in Georgian architecture of the Revolutionary era.

1681 An **early description of Pennsylvania** was provided in *Some Account of the Province of Pennsylvania* by William Penn. Like numerous other accounts of the colonies, this was intended to induce emigration from England by indicating ways in which one could earn a living in the New World.

1681 *The Pilgrim's Progress* by John Bunyan, one of the biggest best sellers in America (relative to population), was published in the colonies, only three years after its first English publication. The Library of Congress records more than 120 American editions, a far from complete list. Some editions sold for only ten cents.

1681 The **Old Ship Meeting House** was erected at Hingham, Mass., by the Puritans, who never referred to a house of worship as a church. This meeting house has been in continuous service since its completion, and it is the last remaining example of the four-square meeting house, a native American contribution to church construction. The meeting house was intentionally denied a cross or spire. Instead a functional tower held a bell and supported a practical weather vane.

1682 The **first printing press in Virginia,** established by William Nuthead, printed the Acts of the Virginia Assembly. This caused an uproar, and in 1683 King Charles II of England directed that no press be operated in Virginia.

| Business and Industry; Science; Education; Philosophy and Religion **III** | | **IV** Sports; Social Issues and Crime; Folkways; Fashion; Holidays |

papers for five or more years, at the end of which time they would receive some clothing and perhaps a parcel of land. They often then became tenant farmers. Criminals, vagrants, and debtors were sent involuntarily to the New World, usually for a term of service of seven years; they were known as "His Majesty's Seven Year Passengers." Others, children and adults, were victims of kidnaping. They were sold to shipmasters who in turn sold them into servitude in America. Many servants caused trouble in the colonies. As a result, the end of the seventeenth century saw a steady growth in the slave trade.

1680 A **catalog of Virginia plants** compiled by John Banister, the first organized study of American plants, was sent by Banister to the English naturalist John Ray. It was published in Ray's three-volume work *Historia Plantarum* (1686–1704). Banister had kept in touch with his fellow naturalists back in England, sending back specimens as well as descriptions of American insects.

1680 A major **scientific achievement** of colonial America was the calculation of the orbit of a comet of 1680 by Thomas Brattle, an early Boston mathematician. He sent word of his discovery to the royal astronomer at Greenwich, England, who checked Brattle's observation. Brattle's calculation supported Isaac Newton's theory of cometary orbits, and Newton acknowledged Brattle's work. Nonetheless, a curious mix-up by the Royal Society left Brattle's contribution to science unrewarded. In 1714, a year after he died, the society elected his brother, William, to membership. William Brattle declined the honor.

1681 July 11 An early attempt at **regulation of real estate transactions** was drafted by William Penn, who was attempting to organize the new colony of Pennsylvania. The following April Penn instructed Thomas Holme, the surveyor general of the colony, to map out the streets for what was to become the city of Philadelphia.

1684 The **first excise tax** on liquor in America was levied in Pennsylvania to pay the governor's expenses. Gov. William Penn refunded the revenues. Later

their cultivation of rice in the lowlands they did much to increase the use of slaves in the colony.

c1680 The **banister-back side chair** made its first appearance. It was a simple chair, deriving its name from a series of banisters, generally vase-shaped, set between the upper and lower rails of the back.

c1680 The **long straight coat** was introduced into New England. Manufactured without a collar, the coat was worn with a neck cloth fastened under the hair in back by a silver buckle. Later the coat appeared in flowered brocade with very large cuffs.

1681 The appearance of the **first dancing master** in Boston provoked an outburst from the authorities. He was cited as "a person of very insolent & ill fame that Raues & scoffes at Religion." He soon was driven out. Dancing was a constant source of complaint among the ministers. Shortly after ouster of the first dancing master, Increase Mather thundered forth his condemnation in the tract *An Arrow against Profane and Promiscuous Dancing, Drawn out of the Quiver of the Scriptures.*

1682 The **first Freemason** to settle in America, John Skene, arrived in Burlington, N.J. He belonged to the lodge in Aberdeen, Scotland, and came to the colonies through arrangements made by the Earl of Perth, chief proprietor of New Jersey and an outstanding Freemason.

1682 The **first marriage** in Pennsylvania was that of Priscilla Allen and Thomas Smith, who had met only once before, on the Isle of Wight.

c1685 The **Pennsylvania walnut stretcher table** made its appearance. Ranging in size from 30 in. in length to 8 ft., the table had sturdy legs framed by a skirt on top containing drawers. At the bottom the legs were braced by a stretcher all around.

1685 For **performing marriages in Boston**, a Huguenot minister was haled before a New England court. A growing tendency to make marriage an ecclesiastical function was strongly suppressed. Marriage was

property qualifications for suffrage, and establishing an illegal mint. The revocation had been prompted by Edward Randolph, who had been appointed surveyor of customs and collector in 1678. He sent two unfavorable reports to England in 1682, then returned to England the next year to help prosecute Massachusetts for its charter violations. Revocation of the charter led to dissolution of the New England Confederation.

1685 Jan. A **French expedition to Texas** led by Robert Cavelier, Sieur de La Salle, landed at Matagorda Bay and soon built a fort there. The settlers did not remain, but the excursion inspired the Spanish to build more missions in the region.

1687 The **Charter Oak incident** occurred as the result of the high-handed actions of Sir Edmund Andros, the English colonial governor. In 1685 King James II of England decided to consolidate the New England colonies into the Dominion of New England and named Andros governor. The dominion came to include New York and East and West Jersey. Andros dissolved colonial assemblies and infringed on other rights and customs. He also demanded that the colonial charters be turned over to him. According to legend, when he met with Connecticut officials in Hartford to demand their charter, the candles in the room were suddenly blown out and the royal charter, which had been granted Connecticut in 1662, disappeared. It was then hidden by Capt. Joseph Wadsworth in a hollow in a white oak tree, which became known as the Charter Oak. The tree was said to be 1000 years old and it stood until 1856.

1689 An **insurrection in New York** against its economic and aristocratic oligarchy was led by Jacob Leisler, a German merchant of New York City. Following the overthrow of the Catholic King James II of England (1688), Leisler, a Protestant, led a successful revolt. He forced Gov. Francis Nicholson to flee, proclaimed William and Mary the rightful sovereigns in England, and ruled as lieutenant governor. In 1691 he surrendered to Gov. Henry Sloughter, who had been appointed by William, and was executed for treason.

1689 England's **Glorious Revolution** had the effect in New England of ousting the unpopular Gov. Andros. On Apr. 18 an armed uprising in Boston forced Andros to surrender. A manifesto, written principally by Cotton Mather, listed the grievances of the colonists and justified the rebellion. Andros was returned to England to stand trial for misconduct.

1689 Aug. 1 A **Protestant rebellion in Maryland** was ended by peace treaty. The rebellion had begun when rumor convinced many that the colony was about to be taken over by Catholics. A Protestant Association was quickly formed by John Coode, who led a force to St. Marys to demand the resignation of

1682 A famous **account of Indian life,** *The Sovereignty & Goodness of God, Together With the Faithfulness of His Promises Displayed; Being a Narrative of the Captivity and Restoration of Mrs. Mary Rowlandson* by Mary Rowlandson, was published. It was the first example of an American literary genre, the Indian captivity narrative. It reflected the hostile attitude of colonists to the American Indian. The book went through more than 30 editions.

1682 The **Newport Parish Church,** the most complete and authentic of extant seventeenth- century Virginia churches, was built at Smithfield, Isle of Wight County. Also called the Old Brick Church, it is a remarkable example of Tudor Gothic (late medieval) architecture transferred to America.

1683 The **Parson Capen house,** a typical two-room colonial structure, was built at Topsfield, Mass. Careful restoration in 1913 made it the best image extant of seventeenth-century New England style.

1685 The **first successful printing press** outside New England was assembled by William Bradford in Philadelphia, Pa.

1687 *The Excellent Privilege of Liberty and Property* by William Penn was published in Philadelphia. It contained the text of the Magna Charta and other English statutes on freedom and property.

1687 **Francis Bacon's** *Essays,* one of the most widely read books in colonial times, was published in America, nearly a century after first publication in England in 1597. Bacon's *Essays* and John Bunyan's *The Pilgrim's Progress,* both widely read colonial books, are today considered classics.

Business and Industry; Science; Education; Philosophy and Religion	III		IV	Sports; Social Issues and Crime; Folkways; Fashion; Holidays

regretting his action, Penn was unable to secure the consent of his legislature for reimposition of the tax.

1686 The **importance of water transportation** to early colonial commerce was remarked on by a Frenchman traveling in Virginia, who noted: "None of the plantation houses, even the most remote, is more than 100 or 150 feet from a 'crik' and the people are thus enabled not only to pay visits in their canoes, but to do all their freight carrying by the same means." Until the coming of the railroads in the nineteenth century, most American commerce, particularly transportation of heavy goods, was conducted by water transportation.

1686 May 15 Bearing orders to found an **Anglican church** in Massachusetts, the Reverend Robert Ratcliffe arrived in Boston. Ratcliffe's visit represented the culmination of a campaign by King Charles II to establish the Church of England on the hostile soil of Congregationalism. Charles II had initiated his campaign as far back as 1664, and had been confronted with the unusual situation of demanding toleration in a British colony for the Church of England.

1687 Mar. 22 Seeking a site for the **first Anglican service** in Boston, Edmund Andros, royal governor of the Dominion of New England and an adherent of the Anglican Church, inspected three Puritan meeting houses in Boston. The South Meeting House was selected and the service was held there on Good Friday. A subsequent Anglican service was held on Easter Sunday from 11 A.M. to 2 P.M., to the great inconvenience of the Congregationalist parishioners who waited outside for the termination of the Anglican service. More satisfactory terms were later arranged for joint use of the South Meeting House by Anglican and Congregationalist parishes until the Anglicans were able to move into their projected church, King's Chapel, which was built the next year.

1689 The **first public school** in America with such practical subjects as science and inventions, the William Penn Charter School, was founded in Philadelphia. The school charged tuition only for students who could afford it.

regarded as a civil contract and the courts were determined to enforce this.

1685 **Caves** used for dwellings were ordered evacuated and filled in by the Governor's Council of Pennsylvania. Early settlers in Pennsylvania, New York, and Massachusetts lacked sawmills, even saws, as well as facilities for cutting and using stone. Many poor and rich lived in caves dug into the sides of hills.

1687 June 28 William Phipps, the first **knighted native American,** was dubbed by King James II of England in ceremonies at Windsor Castle. He was so honored for having found a treasure ship off the coast of Hispaniola. Later he returned to Massachusetts and became governor of the colony.

1688 According to Cotton Mather **supernatural happenings** this year made it a veritable *annus mirabilis:* In the summer a cabbage root was seen in Boston, out of which sprang three wonderful branches, "one of them exactly resembling a Cutlace, another of them, as exactly resembling a Rapier, and a third, extreamly like to a Club used by the Indians in their Barbarous Executions." In the winter "Red Snow" covered the ground. But extraordinary signs were not reserved for this year only. For example, on Oct. 1, 1689, a flaming sword blazed in the sky and threw into deathly fear thousands who observed it.

1689 June 30 An appeal for **garrison aid** typical of the period was sent to the governor and council of Massachusetts Bay. It asked for "twenty eight good brisk men that may be serviceable as a guard to us whilest we get in our harvest of hay & corn." Many early frontier settlements were not covered by a regular string of garrison forts set up for their protection, making it hard for settlers to do their work while fighting off drunken Indians and white renegades.

1689 Summer The legend of the naming of **Nix Mate's Island** in Massachusetts Bay originated this year. Captain Nix anchored his boat off the nameless island one night. Screams were heard by the inhabitants of Boston, and investigators found the captain murdered. His mate was accused, tried, and sentenced to hang. As a final statement the mate said that the island would wash away as proof of his innocence. By the beginning of the nineteenth century, a good

Lord Baltimore's representative. On Aug. 22 the association asked the English Crown to assume control of the colony. This was done in 1691.

1690–1699

King William's War (1689–1697) was the first of what came to be known in America as the French and Indian Wars. In fact, the French and Indian Wars were a series of colonial wars between Great Britain and France that lasted three-quarters of a century. Hostilities in King William's War began in 1690, when in the course of a few months Schenectady, N.Y., was burned by the French and Indians, and colonial English forces launched attacks on Port Royal (now Annapolis Royal), Nova Scotia, and on Quebec. Despite further raids by the French and Indians, the war ended in a stalemate. The Treaty of Ryswick, by which were ended the war and its European counterpart, the War of the Grand Alliance, restored all colonial possessions to their prewar status.

The estimated colonial **population** was 213,500.

1690 A **Spanish mission** was established near the Neches R. in Texas. Hostile Indians forced the missionaries to withdraw in 1693.

1690 In a move to provide **security for frontier settlements,** a committee of the General Court of Massachusetts recommended that the court decide exactly where the frontier was and maintain a garrison with 40 soldiers at each frontier town. Two hundred years later there was no frontier line in the U.S., and westward expansion, "the most important single process in American history," was over. By this time the word "frontier" had a special American meaning, denoting the edge of western settlement rather than a political boundary.

1690 Feb. 3 The **first paper money** was issued. It was used by Massachusetts to pay soldiers who had served the campaign in Quebec.

1690 Feb. 8 In **King William's War** (1689–1697) French and Indian forces from Montreal attacked and burned Schenectady, N.Y.

1690 Oct. 7 The city of **Quebec was attacked** by English forces in the first major military operation of King William's War. They were repulsed by the French under Louis de Buade, comte de Palluau et de Frontenac.

1691 A **charter** uniting the colonies of Plymouth and Massachusetts Bay provided "liberty of conscience to all Christians, except Papists."

1691 Albemarle was renamed **North Carolina** and put under the governorship of a deputy answerable to the Crown.

Printing and publishing, although hampered by government restrictions, had become more or less common in the larger cities by the end of the seventeenth century. John Foster had established Boston's first press in 1674, and by 1700 presses in Boston were producing more print than those in any English city except London. The first press in Philadelphia had been set up in 1685 by William Bradford, who that year issued an almanac, *Kalendarium Pennsilvaniense or America's Messenger.* Bradford, however, had trouble with the city council in 1693 and moved to New York City. In Philadelphia, Regnier Jansen established another press in 1698. In New York, Bradford began issuing almanacs in 1694, and in 1696 he published *Le Trésor des Consolations Divine et Humaine* [Treasury of Comforts Divine and Human]. Almanacs became popular in the eighteenth century. The most famous, *Poor Richard's Almanack,* was first issued by Benjamin Franklin in 1733.

Wadsworth Longfellow's *Tales of a Wayside Inn* (1886) was built in Sudbury, Mass. It was called the Red Horse Tavern, and was characterized by a raftered ceiling and a bar in the form of a cage. It was damaged by fire in 1955 but was restored.

1690 The *New England Primer,* a standard colonial elementary textbook, made its first appearance. It combined the teaching of the alphabet and Puritan theology in moral couplets, as "In Adam's fall/We sinned all."

1690 Sept. 25 The **first newspaper** in the colonies appeared in Boston. It was Benjamin Harris's *Publick Occurrences.* It expired four days later because Harris had presumed to publish without official permission.

1693 The earliest known example of the **jerkin-head roof** in America was on the Thomas Sessions house, built at Yorktown, Va. Also called a "clipped gable" or "a roof hipped above the wind-beams," it was a gable with its top corner flattened to form an additional, triangular, downswept surface.

1694 The **first brick meeting house** in Boston was constructed, replacing the old wooden house on Brattle Street.

portion of Nix Mate's Island had disappeared.

1690–1699

The history of New England's great religious leaders was magnified and epitomized in the prolific yet contradictory career of Cotton Mather, last and greatest of the Puritan divines. Pictured as a central figure in the Salem witch hunts because he helped bring on the witchcraft trials there in 1692, he later had second thoughts on witchcraft. He was smug and stern but was also a leader in the revolt against the autocratic rule of Gov. Edmund Andros in Massachusetts. Mather did much to promote education and was deeply interested in science. He wrote more than 440 works and collected a library of 4000 books. He was a man of his time in whom all traits good and bad were greatly magnified.

1690 An important theological treatise, *Vier Kleine Doch Ungemeine und Sehr Nützliche Tractätlein* [Four Short yet Uncommon and Very Useful Tracts] by Francis Daniel Pastorius, was printed in Germantown, now a section of Philadelphia. Pastorius, as agent for the Frankfort Land Company, had led a group of Mennonites from Krefeld, Germany, to found Germantown; he became one of its leading citizens. In 1688 he and several others had signed a religious protest against the keeping of slaves, the first such document in the English colonies.

1690 The **first paper mill** in America was set up by German settlers in Pennsylvania. The paper was handmade from linen rags pounded into pulp. The first American watermark was the word "company" formed in paper made by William Rittenhouse.

1690 The American **whaling industry** first began large-scale operations out of Nantucket, Mass.

1692 Authorization to **perform marriages** was given to clergymen by the Massachusetts Assembly, reversing a long-established policy. Connecticut followed in 1694.

1692 The **first divinity degree** conferred in the American colonies was given to Increase Mather, sixth president of Harvard College. Mather received a Doctor of Divinity degree from Harvard under a new charter just granted by William and Mary, the English sovereigns.

As towns and cities grew, the problem of street cleaning arose. Throwing rubbish of all kinds into the street was an old English custom. The tidy Dutch in New Amsterdam were the first to do something about the problem when they forbade in 1657 the throwing of "any rubbish, filth, oyster shells, dead animal or anything like it" into the street. Boston first took action in 1662 when Thomas Willsheer was hired as a scavenger to get rid of "all Carrion & matters of Offenciue natuer." Beginning in 1684 four scavengers were at work. Street cleaning was introduced in New York in 1695 when a Mr. Vanderspiegle was hired at £30 a year. By 1710 the city was employing public cartmen to remove trash placed before houses.

c1690 The **highboy** was created by adding short legs to the all-purpose chest. This innovative piece of furniture became very popular.

1690 Capt. **Paddock**, the legendary hero of "Old Yarmouth," Mass., came to Nantucket to instruct people "in the art of killing whales." His greatest adventure was against the monster Crook-Jaw, into whose mouth he wandered to pay a visit to the Devil and a sorceress.

1691 The Dutch custom of *aanspreecker,* or funeral inviter, was given official status by making the inviter a public officer in New York. A death was marked by the tolling of bells and the solemn march of the *aanspreecker* from the house of the deceased to the homes of relatives and friends, whom he informed of the death and whom he invited to the funeral. Etiquette forbade attendance at a funeral unless invited.

1691 The **ducking stool,** a form of punishment for scolds, was ordered built on the wharf in front of City Hall, New York. Although this form of punishment by plunging into water was not used frequently in New York City, it was common in the South.

1693 A book of tremendous influence on **child rearing** in the colonies, *Some Thoughts Concerning Education* by John Locke, was published in England. Based on letters written by Locke to a friend, Edward Clarke, on the raising of his son, the book emphasized the value of character and wisdom as well as learning, nutrition, sleep, exercise, play, and the opportunity for children to express their feelings.

1692 Provincial antagonism was somewhat abated when Connecticut sent soldiers to protect Massachusetts frontier towns along the Connecticut R. Frontier settlements were also learning to unite against their common enemies and reduce their hardships.

1692 The **first act of establishment** passed in the Maryland Assembly provided for official recognition of the Church of England in this royal colony. The act was rejected by the Board of Trade and Plantations in London. It represented the will of the Protestant majority in the assembly, but aroused the strong opposition of Roman Catholic and Quaker groups sympathetic to the Toleration Act of 1649.

1692 Apr. A patent to found a **post office** in the English colonies was issued to the Englishman Thomas Neale. It was first put into effect in Virginia. Andrew Hamilton, Neale's colonial deputy, later did much to organize widespread postal service.

1696 Slave trading in New England was begun on a large scale with the termination of the monopoly of the Royal African Trade Company.

1696 The **importation of slaves** by Quakers was forbidden at the yearly meeting of American Quakers, with expulsion from membership the penalty for violators.

1696 A **Board of Trade for the Plantations** was named by King William III of England. Its 15 members were given jurisdiction over trade and fisheries, care of the poor, all plantation affairs, appointments of colonial officials, and colonial legislation, which the board was empowered to review. The board's decisions were referred to the Privy Council.

1697 An epidemic of **smallpox** ravaged Charleston, S.C. After running its course for over a year, it diminished, only to be followed in Aug. 1699 by yellow fever, which killed 150 people in six days. Infections were generally brought from the West Indies.

1697 Fire wardens were probably the **first paid firemen** in America appointed for each ward in New York City. The wardens' main task was to enforce fire laws. Homeowners could be fined for dangerous chimneys as well as fires caused by negligence.

1697 Sept. 3 **King William's War** (1689–1697) was ended by the Treaty of Ryswick. From the standpoint of the American colonies, the war was completely pointless. Both French and English forces won a number of engagements and managed to occupy part of each other's territory. However, the treaty restored all possessions to their prewar status.

1694 The **Quaker Meeting House** in Flushing, N.Y., was built in simple rectangular form with a hipped roof. The oldest religious building on Long Island, it has been in continuous use.

1695 The cornerstone was laid for the first building at the **College of William and Mary in Virginia,** based on plans said to have been drawn in London by Christopher Wren. The building, an excellent example of early Georgian style in its purest, Virginian form, was completed in 1702.

1698 The **Old Swedes Church** in Wilmington, Del., said to be the oldest Protestant church in continuous use in America, was erected by Swedish Lutherans. It is now a Protestant Episcopal church.

1698 The **first book containing sheet music** published in America was *Psalms, Hymns, and Spiritual songs,* the ninth edition of *The Bay Psalm Book*. It had 12 tunes.

1698 May 29 **Trinity Church** of Wilmington, Del., was begun. It was completed at a cost to its parishioners of £800, a considerable sum for that time. The completed church of granite measured 60 ft. long, 30 ft. wide, and 20 ft. tall.

1699 A best seller, *God's Protecting Providence* by Jonathan Dickinson, a Quaker, was published. It told the story of a group of castaways in Florida, who, naked and starving, made their way to St. Augustine, being continually captured by but escaping from ferocious Indians. This was one of the best adventure stories of colonial days. It went through many editions in both the U.S. and Europe, where it was translated into Dutch and German.

1699 The first known **sliding-sash windows** in the Virginia colony were ordered from England for the capitol in Williamsburg. All windows previously had been leaded casements, usually very small, of a medieval type.

| Business and Industry; Science;
Education; Philosophy and Religion | III | | IV | Sports; Social Issues and Crime;
Folkways; Fashion; Holidays |

1692 Mar. The **Salem witch hunt** was unleashed when some children, called upon to explain their odd behavior, claimed that three old women had bewitched them. The women were tried, convicted, and condemned on the testimony of the children. Although Gov. William Phips halted the trials in Oct. 1692, by Jan. 1693 twenty persons condemned for witchcraft had been executed and two had died in prison.

1692 Oct. Reaction against the **Salem witch trials** was reflected in *The Wonders of the Invisible World* by Cotton Mather, a mystic defense of witchcraft.

1693 Feb. 8 A charter founding the **College of William and Mary in Virginia** was signed. A grant was given to James Blair to "furnish Virginia with a seminary of ministers, to educate the youth in piety, letters and good manners and to propagate Christianity among the Indians."

1695 An **epidemic** in the South destroyed 100,000 head of cattle. These quickly were replaced. By 1703 the colonial government ordered hunters to kill cattle that were unmarked and found straying. In Virginia they were hunted like game.

1697 *Four Boasting Disputers of This World Briefly Rebuked* by Francis Daniel Pastorius was published. It was a theological tract directed chiefly against George Keith, a Scottish-born preacher whose dissenting faction, known as Christian Quakers, had been denounced by William Penn.

1697 Official repentance for the **Salem witch trials** was highlighted by a day of prayer for forgiveness by the Massachusetts Court. Samuel Sewall, one of the Salem judges, publicly confessed his feeling of guilt from his pew in the South Church.

1697 Oct. A severe enactment against **blasphemers and atheists** was passed in Massachusetts. Anyone denying the divine nature of the Bible could be imprisoned for six months, confined to the pillory, whipped, bored through the tongue with a hot iron, or forced to sit on the gallows with a rope around his neck.

1693 The **Huguenots** of South Carolina, considered foreigners, were threatened with the loss of their estates upon death. Discrimination against the French was marked throughout the century in South Carolina, probably because of envy of their refinement, education, and superior economic ability.

1693 The earliest description of **buffalo** or **bison hunting** in America appeared in French traveler Fr. Louis Hennepin's account of Louisiana. Coming upon a large group of buffalo, the Indians would surround them with a circle of grass fire, leaving a few openings where they waited to ambush the escaping animals.

1693 **Philipsborough,** a manorial tract on the Hudson R. north of New York City, was awarded to Frederick Philipse.

1695 Overseers to administer **public relief** to the poor were appointed in New York City. They estimated the amount to be handed out as well as the poor tax. Paupers clothed by the city had to sew a badge on their garments "with this Mark N.Y. in blew or Red Cloath."

1695 Early **colonial prices** were illustrated by the fact that ninepence would buy a quarter of venison. Indians could exchange a stag for a jackknife. In Georgia, less heavily populated, a deer cost only sixpence as late as 1735.

1699 Spring Capt. **William Kidd,** the notorious pirate, paid a visit to an old friend in Narrangansett, R.I., and left some treasure. Thus began the myth of Capt. Kidd's buried treasure, which has sent thousands digging up beaches for trinkets and pieces of eight. Legend says that Kidd murdered a helper and buried him with the treasure chest as a means or warding off searchers.

1699 June A **card game** was suppressed by Judge Samuel Sewall of Boston. A few days later he found a pack of cards strewn over his lawn, as if to mock his efforts. Gambling was rampant in all the colonies despite numerous laws against it. Even lotteries came under ban in New England by an order promulgated in 1719.

I

II

1700–1704

Queen Anne's War (1702–1713), the second of the French and Indian Wars, began May 4, 1702. In Europe it was known as the War of the Spanish Succession. The Grand Alliance (England, the League of Augsburg, Denmark, Portugal, and the Netherlands) declared war on France and Spain to prevent union of the French and Spanish thrones following the death of King Charles II of Spain. In North America British and French colonial forces, with their Indian allies, raided and attempted to capture a number of border settlements. New England colonists successfully attacked the French settlements of Minas and Beaubassin in Nova Scotia in July 1704, while the French destroyed Deerfield, Mass., in February and took the English colony of Bonavista on Newfoundland in August. The most notable colonial success was the British capture of Port Royal, Nova Scotia, on Oct. 16, 1710, following unsuccessful assaults in 1704 and 1707; however, a British naval attack on Quebec in 1711 failed. In the South, Carolina forces captured the town of St. Augustine, Fla., in Sept. 1702, although the fort there held out. Another force wiped out all but one of fourteen missions in northwestern Florida in 1704.

c1700 The **population** of the colonies was sparsely scattered over the large area. Below the Delaware R. an isolated farm was the usual settlement, save for Charleston, which had about 250 families. Philadelphia had approximately 700 houses, New York about 5000 inhabitants, Newport less than 2000, and Boston, the largest city, about 7000. There were approximately 275,000 inhabitants in the colonies.

1701 The **Vestry Act,** providing for establishment of the Church of England in North Carolina, was passed by the Anglican majority in the colonial assembly over the violent opposition of dissenting groups, especially the Quakers and Presbyterians. Because of this spirited opposition and the dangerous possibilities it represented, the proprietors of the colony disallowed the act. This action reflected the religious diversity in North Carolina.

1701 The rising **status of women** in colonial America was indicated by the fact that six women were empaneled on an Albany, N.Y., jury engaged for special duty.

1701 July 24 A settlement at **Detroit** was established by Antoine de la Mothe Cadillac. The area of Michigan was early known to trappers, priests, and traders from French Canada. The Jesuits, led by Isaac Jogues, founded a mission at Sault Ste. Marie in 1641. There, in 1668, Jacques Marquette established the first permanent settlement in Michigan. When the French government lost interest in outposts in the West, Cadillac went to France with a proposal that would save the fur trade from the English. He was granted the land by the narrows of the river connecting Lake

Journalism was one of the trades that followed the colonists to America. The first successful newspaper in the English colonies appeared on Apr. 24, 1704. This was the Boston *News-Letter,* founded by John Campbell, the Boston postmaster. It published until 1776. Although its early circulation was only about 300, the paper was passed from person to person and was available in coffee houses and taverns. It carried advertising, including notices placed by dancing and music teachers. Other early newspapers were the Boston *Gazette* (1719), Philadelphia *American Mercury* (1719), *New England Courant* (Boston, 1721), New York *Gazette* (1725), Maryland *Gazette* (Annapolis, 1727), and *Pennsylvania Gazette* (Philadelphia, 1728).

1700 Perhaps the **first denunciation of slavery** in the colonies was *The Selling of Joseph* by Samuel Sewall, which put forth antislavery arguments. Typical of his time, Sewall relied mainly on biblical citations.

1700 The **first pipe organs** arrived in America. They were imported by the Episcopal Church of Port Royal, Pa., and the Gloria Dei (Swedish Lutheran) Church of Philadelphia, Pa.

1700 *A Token for Children,* a popular colonial book by James Janeway, was published. Its subtitle was *Being an exact Account of the Conversion, Holy and Exemplary Lives, and Joyful Deaths of Several Young Children.*

1702 *Magnalis Christi Americana; or the Ecclesiastical History of New England,* the *magnum opus* of Cotton Mather, was published. Mather wanted to bring people back to the early spirit of Puritanism at a time when feeling against the clergy ran high because of witch burnings.

1702 The first mention of the **stove** in the American house was in the diary of Judge Samuel Sewall of Boston under the date of Jan. 16. What kind of stove he meant is not known. Heat for warmth and cooking was still provided by fireplaces, and stoves did not become common for another 60 years.

| Business and Industry; Science; Education; Philosophy and Religion III | | Sports; Social Issues and Crime; Folkways; Fashion; Holidays IV |

1700–1704

The Church of England made great efforts in the eighteenth century to propagate its cause in the English colonies. The Society for the Propagation of the Gospel in Foreign Parts was granted a charter in 1701 by King William III of England. This charter was granted at the instigation of the Rev. Thomas Bray of London, who had been chosen in 1696 to establish the Anglican Church in Maryland. Bray recruited missionaries and sent out more than 30 parish libraries. Between 1702 and 1783 the society maintained 54 missionaries in South Carolina, 33 in North Carolina, 84 in New England, 47 in Pennsylvania, 58 in New York, 44 in New Jersey, 13 in Georgia, 5 in Maryland, and 2 in Virginia. In all, 202 central missions were maintained and the society spent £227,454 in this period. Although the Anglican Church made some gains as a result of this effort, the various other Protestant sects and denominations—Presbyterian, Congregationalist, Quaker, and Baptist—held their ground, as did the small Roman Catholic community. American Anglicans fought the establishment of an episcopate because the selection would be imposed from England. Southern laymen especially insisted on the right to choose their own clergymen. During the American Revolution the Patriot leadership was dominated by such southern Anglicans as George Washington and such northern Congregationalists as John Adams. The Loyalists for the most part were Anglicans.

1700 Fur traders from Carolina had by this time pushed west to the Mississippi R. Their advance had been aided by the fact that, unlike traders in the north, they did not have to contend with a mountain barrier. In the region just north of the Gulf of Mexico, they bought deer and buffalo skins in a trading system akin to the earlier French system in Canada. These skins were much valued in the Old World as a source of fine leather.

1700 June 17 Massachusetts enacted a law requiring **Roman Catholic priests** to leave the colony within three months. If any priest remained, he was to be considered an "incendiary and disturber of the public peace and safety and an enemy to the true Christian religion." If found guilty, he could be imprisoned for life or executed.

The Bowery, about three miles north of New York City, was a popular recreation center. The well-known traveler Sarah Kemble Knight visited the Bowery in 1704 and found that visitors did not "spare for any diversion the place offered, and sociable to a degree." John Clap, a tavern keeper there, offered "any Gentlemen Travellers that are strangers to the City . . . good Entertainment, for themselves and Horses." Knight reached the Bowery by sleigh and on one occasion noted that she met "50 or 60 sleys."

c1700 The American **slat-back chair** made its first appearance simultaneously in New England, Pennsylvania, and New York. In the nineteenth century Shakers produced quantities of this type of chair, popular for general home use. An early type used a rope seat. This design should not be confused with the splat-back chair, which showed the influence of Dutch craftsmanship and design and was a product of this period.

1701 The **naming of streets** was authorized by the Boston Town Meeting. Previously, only Newport and Philadelphia had officially assigned street names. At the end of seven years 109 names were submitted for ratification.

1702 To combat **delinquency** in Massachusetts Cotton Mather formed the Society for the Suppression of Disorders, a sort of vigilante committee to monitor swearing, blaspheming, and patronage of bawdy houses. Soon Mather had collected a list of young men who frequented disreputable establishments. The committee in turn warned each of the young men.

1703 Fall The use of **dogs** "to hunt Indians as they do bears" was urged by the Rev. Solomon Stoddard to the authorities of the Massachusetts Bay frontier town of Northampton. Indians were too fast on their feet for frontiersmen and "act like wolves and are to be dealt with as wolves."

1704 New York **women's fashions** were described by a contemporary traveler and diarist: "The English go very fasheonable in their dress. The Dutch, especially

Huron with Lake Erie. There he set up a large colony he called Fort Pontchartrain. The name Detroit comes from the French words for the narrows (*détroit*), where the fort was located.

1702 An **act of establishment** passed by the Maryland Assembly became law after two previous acts in 1692 and 1696 were rejected by the Board of Trade and Plantations in England. The act provided for official recognition of the Church of England. Its final passage was secured largely as a result of the efforts of Dr. Thomas Bray, the bishop of London's Commissary, who arrived in Maryland in 1700 to push its enactment and then returned to England to argue for final approval before the board. Taxes for support of ministers were levied on all free males over 16, all male servants over 16, and all male and female slaves over 16. Appointment of ministers was the prerogative of the royal governor of the colony. The most spirited opposition to the act of establishment came from Quaker and Catholic settlers.

1704 Feb. 29 **Deerfield,** a western outpost of Massachusetts, was attacked by a force of French and Indians, who massacred 50 men, women, and children and carried off over 100 more after burning the town to the ground. The raid was one of the bloodiest events of Queen Anne's War (1702–1713), the second of the French and Indian Wars.

1703 The **first professional actors** in America performed in Charleston, S.C., but no important theater developed in the colonies until at least a generation later because of the belief that theater bred immorality and disorder.

1704 The earliest known example of a **Dutch gambrel roof** in America was built on the Ackerman house in Hackensack, N.J. This roof type became common throughout New York and northern New Jersey in the eighteenth century.

1704 Oct. A classic travel book, *Private Journal*, was begun by Sarah Kemble Knight; she made entries until Mar. 1705. A schoolmistress (young Benjamin Franklin attended her school in Boston), she took a trip alone to New York and reported on her experiences. She also commented on the character and mores of the Yankee inhabitants she encountered. Her book was not published until 1825.

1705–1709

In the early nineteenth century the prevailing political and economic theory held that colonies existed for the benefit of the mother country and that the colonies should produce only raw materials, accepting in return manufactured goods from the homeland. An English law of 1705, for example, expanded the list of goods that the American colonies could export to English ports only. Among these were rice, molasses, and naval stores—pitch, rosin, tar, hemp, masts, yards, and bowsprits. At this time there was little organized political opposition to the rule of Crown and Parliament. As long as home nation and colonies prospered, the political situation remained manageable.

1705 The **Second Vestry Act,** providing for establishment of the Church of England in North Carolina, was passed by the Anglican majority in the assembly after the first act had been disallowed by colonial proprietors in 1701. The second act, like the first, caused violent controversy between Anglican interests and dissenting groups, mainly Quakers and Presbyterians. Violent civil disturbances stymied enforcement of the act and the matter was soon dropped.

1705 A Virginia **slavery act** decreed that all imported servants were to remain in lifelong servitude.

Accounts of persons who had been held captive by Indians provided popular reading matter in colonial times. One of the best examples of the genre, and a best seller in the early eighteenth century, was *The Redeemed Captive, Returning to Zion* (1707) by John Williams, Congregational minister of Deerfield, Mass. Williams and his family were captured by the Indians in 1704 during the raid on Deerfield in Queen Anne's War. His book, written at the urging of Cotton Mather, recounted the cruelties he witnessed and suffered during two years of captivity; it also detailed attempts by Jesuits to convert him to Catholicism. William's narrative and an earlier account, *The Sovereignty of God, Together with the Faithfulness of His Promises Displayed; Being a Narrative of the Captivity and Restauration of Mrs. Mary Rowlandson* (1682) by Mary Rowlandson, were models for a number of books about Indian captivity published during the eighteenth and early nineteenth century.

1705 *The History and Present State of Virginia* by Robert Beverley was published. This early account of Virginia was popular in England and France. A man of wealth, sprung from an ancient English family, Beverley, often motivated by what he felt was an

| Business and Industry; Science; Education; Philosophy and Religion **III** | | **IV** Sports; Social Issues and Crime; Folkways; Fashion; Holidays |

1701 Oct. 16 Yale was founded as Collegiate School in Killingworth, Conn., by Congregationalists dissatisfied with the growing liberalism at Harvard. The school was named after Elihu Yale, son of one of the founders of New Haven, who had gained great riches in India as governor for the East India Company. The school was moved in 1745 to New Haven, Conn., where it became Yale College. Yale became a university in 1887. Its first degrees were awarded in 1716.

1703 Mar. 28 Construction of the **oldest Episcopal church in New Jersey**, St. Mary's Church in Burlington, was begun. The first service was held on Aug. 22, before the church, in early Georgian style, was completed.

the middling sort, differ from our women, in their habitt go loose, were French muches which are like a Capp and a head band in one, leaving their ears bare, which are sett out with Jewells of a large size and many in number. And their fingers hoop't with Rings, some with large stones in them of many Coullers as were their pendants in their ears, which You should see very old women wear as well as Young."

1704 The **first underground sewer** in Boston was constructed by Francis Thrasher, at his own expense. The move led to municipal regulations governing disposal of refuse and garbage. By 1710 the selectmen of Boston were giving licenses to private citizens for digging up streets for sewer construction.

1704 Sept. 28 **Separation of couples** by a minister was legalized by a statute passed in Maryland. A minister could separate a man and woman if he disapproved of the woman. If the man did not obey, he was haled into court and, if convicted, fined or whipped until blood began to flow.

1705-1709

The various Protestant denominations were active in establishing themselves in the English colonies in the early eighteenth century. The first Anglican parish in Connecticut was established in 1706 at Stratford through the efforts of Caleb Heathcote. He was a wealthy merchant and public official who in 1701 had been granted the manor of Scarsdale in Westchester County, N.Y., the last manor to be granted in the colonies. In Mar. 1706 the first presbytery was established in Philadelphia, Pa., through the efforts of the Rev. Francis Makemie. Born in Ireland, Makemie first came to America in 1683 and began organizing Presbyterian churches. In 1707 he was arrested in New York, charged with preaching without a license. Although he was acquitted, he incurred heavy costs. About this time the Baptists in Philadelphia organized their first church, which had quarters in a brew house. In 1707 the first meeting of a Baptist association was held in Philadelphia, with five churches represented. Connecticut Congregational churches, meeting at Saybrook, Conn., adopted the Saybrook Platform in 1708, which moved toward a church system like that of the Presbyterians rather than the more democratic Massachusetts Congregationalists. In Charleston, S.C., both the Baptists

With the introduction of paper money in the colonies, counterfeiting was not long in appearing. In 1705 Thomas Odell of Boston counterfeited the £4 notes of Massachusetts and tried to pass them in Pennsylvania. He was arrested and sentenced in Boston to a fine of £300 and a year in prison. James Mar, a New York engraver, applied his skill to counterfeit bills. He was sentenced to be hanged, but was granted clemency by the governor, who could not refuse a tearful petition from "Most of the Gentlewomen of the City." In Philadelphia in 1720 Edward and Martha Hunt were implicated in counterfeiting and sentenced to death and life imprisonment respectively.

1705 **Intermarriage** between a white person and a black was declared illegal in Massachusetts. Any minister performing such a marriage was fined £50. This prohibition remained in force until 1843, when the law was repealed.

Excepted were those who had been Christians in their native country or who had been free in a Christian country. This law limited slavery to blacks and confined almost all imported blacks to slavery. An interesting exception was inserted for "Turks and Moors in amity with her majesty."

1706 An important American **customhouse** was built at Yorktown, Va. Yorktown had been appointed the port of entry for New York, Philadelphia, and other northern cities, though many merchants disregarded the law. Yorktown was the site of Virginia's "tea party" in 1774, when Richard Ambler, collector of revenue, led a boarding party to the *Virginia* and tossed its tea cargo overboard. The customhouse was restored in 1928.

1706 Jan. 17 **Benjamin Franklin** was born in Boston. His father, Josiah, a nonconformist, had fled England in 1682 and settled in New England, rearing 17 children.

1708 Aug. 30 **Haverhill**, Mass., was attacked and razed by the French and Indians.

1709 Sept. 3 The first major influx of **Swiss and German immigrants** came to the Carolinas. They had been encouraged by a grant of 13,500 acres by the proprietors to two sponsors representing German refugees from the Palatinate and Swiss emigrants from Berne.

English misconception of the colony, painted a robust picture of plantation life.

1706 Work was begun on the **Governor's Palace** at Williamsburg, Va., the finest residence of its time in the colonies. It was not formally completed until 1720. The Governor's Palace was occupied by royal governors until the Revolutionary War, and thereafter by the state governors, Patrick Henry and Thomas Jefferson, until the capital was moved to Richmond in 1780.

1706 The **first Latin grammar published in America**, the phenomenally popular *Accidence, A Short Introduction to the Latin Tongue* by Ezekiel Cheever, was published. The book went through 20 editions, the last appearing in 1785.

1706 *The Good Old Way* by Cotton Mather reflected the weakening of Puritan influence in America. In the book, Mather complained that people had lost their reverence for members of the clergy and did not support them as generously as before.

1708 A **popular satirical poem** by one Ebenezer Cook was *The Sot-Weed Factor; or, A Voyage to Maryland,—a satire in which is described the laws, government, courts, and constitution of the country, and also the buildings, feasts, frolics, entertainments, and drunken humors of the inhabitants in that part of America.* Little is known about the author.

1710–1714

Settlers from European lands other than the British Isles began to come to the English colonies in large numbers. On Sept. 3, 1700, the proprietors of Carolina granted a tract of 13,500 acres to agents representing Swiss and German Palatine emigrants. Besides wanting to better themselves economically, many of the emigrants sought religious freedom. New Bern, the second town in North Carolina, was settled in 1710 by some 650 Swiss and German colonists under the leadership of Baron Christopher de Graffenried and John Dawson. The same year 3000 Germans from the Palatinate settled near Livingston Manor, N.Y., intending to produce naval stores. They were brought to America by Robert Hunter, commissioned governor of New York and the Jerseys in 1709. The settlement was not successful and in 1713, under the leadership of Conrad Weiser, the settlers moved first to the Schoharie Valley and then to the Mohawk Valley. Eventually many of them moved to Berks and Bucks counties in Pennsylvania.

The estimated colonial **population** was 357,500.

Bookselling in the colonies began before the turn of the century and so was flourishing by this time. Around 1698 Regnier Jansen, a printer in Philadelphia, was selling books. By 1714 Andrew Bradford's Philadelphia store, the Bible and Crown, was filling orders from as far away as Barbados. In 1718 John Copson sold books along with other merchandise, a common practice. William Bradford, who set up in New York as a printer in 1694, also ran a bookshop, as did Thomas Adams, a stationer, after 1698. Boston, however, led the way in the book business, with about 30 stores there by 1711. In 1724 the Boston booksellers formed an association to fix prices and otherwise regulate the trade. Boston supplied books to all the other colonies, but its trade was especially brisk in New England.

1710 One of the most popular **books for farmers** in the American colonies was published in Boston, Mass.: *The Husband-Man's Guide, in Four Parts—Part first, containing many excellent rules for setting and planting. Part second, choice physical receipts for divers dangerous distempers in men, women, and children. Part third, the experienced farrier. Part fourth, containing rare receipts.* The author was Eleazar Phillips.

and the Quakers organized churches as early as 1699, but the largest religious groups there were the Huguenots and the Anglicans.

1706 What was perhaps the **first lithotomy** (surgical removal of stones from the bladder) in New England gave prominence to Zabdiel Boylston, the Boston surgeon who performed it. Following this, he performed many successful operations; in 1718 he removed a cancerous breast from a woman.

1709 The **first mining company charter** in America was granted by the Connecticut General Assembly to a copper mine at Simsbury, Conn. The mine produced 15 to 20% ore, which was exported to England. During the Revolutionary War, its diggings were used as a prison for Tories.

1709 The **first private home for mental illness** in America was established by the Quakers of Philadelphia, Pa. In 1751 it became a part of Pennsylvania Hospital.

1705 Methods of **hunting** in the South were described in Robert Beverley's *The History and Present State of Virginia:* Horses were taught to walk quietly at their master's side when stalking game to keep him out of sight; rabbits were hunted with fast mongrel dogs, which caught them or forced them into a hollow tree; raccoons and opossums, hunted on foot with small dogs by the light of the moon, were treed, and agile lads climbed trees after them and shook them down; wolves were trapped; turkeys were shot or trapped.

1706 A **closed season on deer hunting** was established on Long Island, where continual hunting had almost eliminated this popular game.

1708 A **closed season,** Apr. 1 to July 31, was established on turkeys, heath hens, partridges, and quail in Kings, Queens, and Suffolk counties in New York.

1710–1714

Deism, a rationalistic theology holding that the course of the universe demonstrates the existence of God, so no formal exercise of religion is necessary, made considerable headway in the colonies. Published in 1711, *Characteristicks of Men, Manners, Opinions, Times* by Anthony Ashley Cooper, third earl of Shaftesbury, had much influence in America. Shaftesbury postulated an innate moral sense that did not require religious incentives to reveal itself. Many of his admirers in America seized upon this idea as the basis of deistic thought. Deism was strongest in the large towns, especially in Philadelphia, where men such as Benjamin Franklin became believers. In New England even Cotton Mather, of the leading family of Puritan divines, flirted with the idea of "Nature and Nature's God" by 1715. The painter Robert Feke led a group in Newport, R.I., that read and discussed deistic works. Later in the century men as prominent as Thomas Jefferson were deists.

1710 **Trinity School** was established in New York City under the auspices of the Society for the Propagation of the Gospel. The founding of Trinity School represented a victory of private and parochial school

By 1710 the favorite nonalcoholic beverage of the colonists was probably chocolate. This drink resulted from the discovery of the cacao tree and its seed by Spanish explorers in Mexico. They took it to Europe, where it spread to England and then back to the North American colonies. Coffee was introduced into North America about 1668, and the first coffee house was opened in October 1676 in Boston by John Sparry. It soon became the place where businessmen gathered to exchange news. Tea was first brought to Europe by the Dutch East India Company in the early seventeenth century. It was carried by settlers to America almost as soon as colonization began. Coffee did not take first place over tea and chocolate until the time of the Boston Tea Party (1773), when it became a patriotic duty not to drink English tea because of the tax on it and the monopoly on its trade. However, the popularity of tea actually increased in the first half of the eighteenth century because of widespread smuggling, which provided a plentiful and inexpensive supply. Among alcoholic beverages, rum was a favorite in New England and beer in the middle colonies. Madeira took first place in wines followed by canary, claret, burgundy, port, brandy, and champagne.

| Exploration and Settlement; Wars; Government; Civil Rights; Statistics | I | | II | Publishing; Arts and Music; Popular Entertainment; Architecture; Theater |

1711 Sept. 22 The **Tuscarora Indian War** (1711–1713) began with a massacre of settlers on the Chowan and Roanoke rivers in northeastern North Carolina. The settlement at New Bern was abandoned. White encroachment, which included the enslaving of Indian children, led to the war.

1712 May 9 The **Territory of the Carolinas** was provided with two governors, one for the north and one for the south. Though theoretically a single province, the settlements were far apart, and so each section was accorded its own governor. From 1691 to 1712 a single governor usually resided in Charleston.

1713 Mar. 23 The **Tuscarora War** ended with the capture of the Indian stronghold at Fort Nohucke, S.C. The Indians fled northward and were admitted into the League of the Iroquois as a sixth nation.

1713 Apr. 11 **Queen Anne's War** (1702–1713) was ended by the Treaty of Utrecht, which brought the War of the Spanish Succession to a close in Europe. By the treaty France ceded the Hudson Bay territory, Newfoundland, and Nova Scotia to Great Britain. France also agreed to a British protectorate over the Iroquois Indians. France kept Cape Breton Island and the islands of the St. Lawrence.

1710–1717 Two famous pamphlets by **John Wise, The Churches Quarrel Espoused** (1710) and *Vindication of the Government of New England Churches* (1717), were published. Wise, pastor of Ipswich, Mass., led liberal Congregationalists against the forces seeking centralization of Massachusetts churches.

1711 The **first cruciform church** in America was begun in Bruton Parish, Williamsburg, Va.; the architect is unknown. Though the cruciform plan was usually a feature of Gothic architecture, the church was in all other details characteristic of early Georgian architecture.

1713 **King's Chapel,** the Anglican church in Boston, acquired an organ in a bequest from Thomas Brattle. Few organs were to be found in colonial churches, since Puritan practice prohibited instrumental music in religious services and most congregations of other denominations could not afford to import instruments from England.

1714 The **first play** to be printed in the colonies, *Androboros* by Robert Hunter of New York, was published. The play was a political satire. Hunter was the military and political head of New York and New Jersey. In his play he lampooned the senate and the lieutenant governor. It is doubtful that the farce was ever produced, though it is reputed to have made people laugh. The Huntington Library in California preserves a copy of *Androboros.*

1715–1719

Another of the many conflicts between whites and Indians that were to go on until the late nineteenth century occurred at this time. The Yamassee Indians, encouraged by the Spanish, massacred several hundred Carolina settlers in Apr. 1715. In Jan. 1716 the South Carolina settlers, aided by Cherokee Indians, defeated the Yamassee northwest of Port Royal, at the southern tip of what is now South Carolina. The conflict was a result of the desire of Carolina settlers moving into Yamassee territory to take up large areas of coastal land for raising cattle. This southward movement also brought the English colonists into areas claimed by the Spanish.

1715 The **Third Vestry Act** was passed by the Anglican majority in the North Carolina Assembly. The act, providing for official recognition and support of the Church of England, was accepted by the colonial proprietors, who had disallowed previous acts in 1701 and 1705. Passage of the act was due largely to the efforts of the Society for the Propagation of the Gospel, a missionary organization supported by the Church of England. Ministers were to be supported

When the colonists left England for new homes in America, they brought their music with them and in the eighteenth century were practicing and enjoying music in a variety of ways. In 1715 appeared the *Introduction to the Singing of Psalm-Tunes* by Rev. John Tufts. This was the first American instruction manual, and no copy of it is known to exist. In New York in 1720 gentlemen might gather at someone's home "to hear some good Musick, and to take a Tiff of fresh Lime Punch." The first public "Concert of Musick on Sundry Instruments" took place on Feb. 18, 1729, in Boston. The first piece of music criticism in America was perhaps an article in the *Philadelphia Mercury* in 1729. And in 1732 a school of "Vocal Musick" was opened at Newport, R.I., by a Mr. Beal, who had previously taught singing at Yale.

1716 The **first theater** in the colonies was built in Williamsburg, Va., by William Levingston.

1719 *Divine and Moral Songs for the Use of Children,* a juvenile best seller by Isaac Watts, was published. The book was popular for at least 150 years, with more than 240 editions being published in England and America.

| Business and Industry; Science; Education; Philosophy and Religion III | | IV Sports; Social Issues and Crime; Folkways; Fashion; Holidays |

adherents over supporters of free public schools.

1712 The **first sperm whale** captured by an American was taken by Christopher Hussey, of Nantucket, Mass. The event radically changed the character of the Nantucket whaling business. Whalers previously had plied close to shore, seeking right whales. Thereafter they hunted in deep waters on longer voyages. In 1715 Nantucket had a fleet of six sloops engaged in sperm whaling.

1713 The **first American schooner** was built by Capt. Andrew Robinson in Gloucester, Mass.

1714 **Iron furnaces** were established along the Rapidan R. by Gov. Alexander Spotswood of Virginia. He imported German settlers as labor.

1714 Support for **scientific observation** over dogma was demonstrated by the famous Puritan theologian Cotton Mather, who accepted the Copernican theory of the universe as against the Ptolemaic. His sermon of acceptance was unfavorably received by the eminent Puritan moralist Judge Samuel Sewall, who considered the subject too controversial.

c1710 In contrast to the sober dress of the Quakers, **colonial fashions** were often extravagant. High heels, stiff stays, and large curled wigs were worn by both men and women. Men's coat skirts were stiffened with buckram, and sleeve cuffs often reached the elbows. The invention of the hoop in England in 1711 governed dress styles in America for many years. Originally these hoops were flat, projecting only at the sides. Over them were worn layers of skirts, and a sacque, or overdress, was hung on top. Women's hairstyles were characterized by the "tower," or "commode." From the top of this tower "lappets," or lace pendants, hung down alongside the face.

1712 The **first fines for speeding** were levied against reckless carters in Philadelphia.

1714 May 12 The first record of a **wild animal on exhibition** in America was made in Samuel Sewall's diary of this date. Sewall reported the sale of "a large Dromedary seven foot high, and 12 foot long, taken from the Turks at the Siege of Vienna." There is some doubt whether the dromedary, a one-humped Arabian camel, actually appeared in America.

1715–1719

The growth of shipping and commercial trade was encouraged in 1717 when colonial merchants were allowed to send ships to the French West Indies. The chief item of this lucrative trade was molasses, from which New England distilleries produced rum, a profitable staple of colonial trade. The Treaty of Utrecht (1713) provided for trading concessions with the Spanish colonies. Commercial fishing was also booming and shipbuilding began to be important in the economy. An early shipbuilder was Capt. Andrew Robinson of Gloucester, Mass., who in 1713 built a schooner of his own design. From Charleston, S.C., much trade was carried on, not only with the West Indies but also with Dutch settlements in South America. In 1718 £150,000 worth of goods, mostly woolens from England, came into Charleston. New York, Newport, and Philadelphia were also growing as shipping and trading centers, but Boston was the leading commercial center of the colonies in the early eighteenth century.

1716 Probably the **first lighthouse** in the colonies was

Piracy, although declining, still existed on a fairly large scale and was not entirely frowned upon. This reflected the narrow difference between privateering, a wartime act in which a shipowner could legitimately attempt to capture merchant ships owned by his country's enemy, and piracy, which was much the same act in time of peace. Nevertheless, steps were taken to end piracy. The English Parliament in 1700 had ordered establishment of special courts in the colonies to try those accused of piracy. In 1718 Gov. Alexander Spotswood of Virginia offered a reward for capture of Blackbeard, the most notorious pirate of the time, whose real name was Edward Teach. He had been both a privateer and a pirate. Even though protected by the governor of North Carolina, who shared some of his booty, Blackbeard was caught and hanged. Also in 1718 another pirate, Stede Bonnet, was captured by an expedition from Carolina, and he too was hanged.

1719 Perhaps the **first street light** in America, a single lantern, was presented to the town of Boston by

Exploration and Settlement; Wars; Government; Civil Rights; Statistics I		Publishing; Arts and Music; Popular Entertainment; Architecture; Theater II

by a head tax not to exceed five shillings per person, to be assessed on both freemen and slaves over 16 years of age.

1718 New Orleans was founded by French settlers from Canada and France. The Canadians generally brought their wives and families with them. French officers, however, usually younger sons of nobility, refused to marry below their rank, inspiring the plea of one of the early governors to France: "Send me wives for my Canadians; they are running in the woods after Indian girls."

1719 The *Boston Gazette,* a nationalistic newspaper, was founded by William Brooker. In 1741 it was combined with the *New England Weekly Journal* and launched attacks on the stamp tax.

1719 Fraunces Tavern, the earliest residential building remaining in Manhattan, was built at Pearl and Broad streets in New York. Originally built as a residence for Stephen De Lancey, it was purchased for a tavern by Samuel Fraunces in 1762. It became famous for its Long Room, where George Washington delivered his Farewell Address to his officers in 1783.

1720–1724

In the eighteenth century northern New England was claimed both by the English and the French, and both established forts and settlements in the disputed area. The English in 1724 built Fort Dummer, named for William Dummer, lieutenant governor and acting governor of Massachusetts. It was near the site of present-day Brattleboro, Vt., named for William Brattle, who with Dummer had purchased the tract of land on which the fort stood. Brattleboro was the first permanent European settlement in Vermont. A French stronghold at this time was the Abnaki Indian village of Norridgewock on the Kennebec R. in Maine. The leader there was a French Jesuit missionary, Father Sébastien Rasle. Father Rasle escaped a British raid in 1721, leaving behind a dictionary of the Abnaki language he had been preparing. The raiders took it away, and it was not published until 1833. In 1724 the British again raided Norridgewock, captured it, and killed Father Rasle, gun in hand. These and similar events of the period became known as Dummer's or Lovewell's War (1721–1725). The Lovewell in question was John Lovewell, a Massachusetts Indian fighter who was killed in a skirmish with Pigwacket Indians at Fryeburg, Maine, on May 8, 1725.

c1720 A period of **French expansion and entrenchment** in the Mississippi Valley began. The French erected forts in 1720 and 1726 at the mouths of the Kaskaskia and Illinois rivers, and made peace with the Indians in the South. Fort Toulouse was erected among the Creeks on the Alabama R. In the North powerful Fort Louisbourg on Cape Breton Island, constructed in 1720, guarded the entrance to the St. Lawrence R. Farther south the French established fortifications at Crown Point on Lake Champlain in 1731. Fort Miami, constructed in 1704, protected the northern approach to the Mississippi Valley. Fort Ouiataon on the Wabash R. was built about 1719, and Fort Vincennes on the lower Wabash R. about 1724.

1720 The estimated colonial **population** was 474,388. City populations were: Boston, 12,000; Philadelphia,

Georgian architecture came into fashion in England and the English colonies at about this time. The style, named in honor of the three kings of England who reigned during the period, marked a return to classical forms. It was greatly influenced by the designs of the sixteenth-century Italian architect Andrea Palladio and the seventeenth-century English architect Inigo Jones. In Apr. 1723 the cornerstone was laid for Christ Church, known as Old North Church, in Boston. Designed by William Price, who had studied Christopher Wren's London churches, it was the first Georgian church in New England. Today it is the oldest church in Boston. From its steeple in 1775 were hung lanterns that started Paul Revere on his ride by horseback to Lexington and Concord to warn of the approach of British troops. In Philadelphia James Porteus designed a new Christ Church, completed in 1731 and the most ornate example of the Georgian style in America. A new state house for the Pennsylvania Assembly, completed in 1735, was the largest and most elaborately formal structure in the colonies. Perhaps the most distinguished private residence of the type was Westover, built about 1734 for William Byrd II, on the James R. in Virginia. Another practitioner of the Georgian style was the Newport, R.I., architect Peter Harrison, sometimes called the first American architect. Among his works were Newport's Touro Synagogue and the Redwood Library.

1720 **"The Reasonableness of Regular Singing, or Singing by Note,"** an essay by the Rev. Thomas Symmes of Bradford, Mass., was published. In it he stated that "singing by note" was studied at Harvard from the founding of the college (1636), proving that Puritans were not averse to secular music.

1721 A portrait of **Ann Pollard,** artist unknown, prefigured the development of twentieth-century expressionism. The subject, an innkeeper more than 100 years old, claimed she was the first to leave the boat when the Pilgrims landed in New England.

Business and Industry; Science; Education; Philosophy and Religion **III**		**IV** Sports; Social Issues and Crime; Folkways; Fashion; Holidays

put up by Massachusetts Colony on Little Brewster Island to guard Boston Harbor.

1716 The **first black slaves** in French Louisiana were delivered by two slave ships of the Company of the West.

1717 The **first professorship** in philosophy and mathematics in America was assumed by the Rev. Hugh Jones at the College of William and Mary in Virginia.

1719 **Potato cultivation** in the colonies began with the settlement of Londonderry, N.H., by Scottish-Irish immigrants.

Eliakim Hutchinson. Boston's selectmen ordered that the town be "well fixed with Lights on all or Stormy Nights."

1719 Mar. New Jersey enacted its most important **marriage statute.** It provided that no person under 21 years of age could be married without the consent of a parent or guardian. It was the result of many instances of young people being enticed into clandestine marriages.

1720–1724

A major step forward in preventive medicine was introduced to the colonies. The first smallpox inoculations in America were given on June 26, 1721, in Boston by Dr. Zabdiel Boylston. He had been urged to do so by Cotton Mather, the influential Puritan clergyman. Even though an epidemic was raging in Boston at the time, many persons objected fiercely on religious grounds. The homes of both Mather and Boylston were stoned by mobs. Dr. Boylston first inoculated his son, Thomas, and two black slaves. In all he inoculated 240 persons, of whom all but six survived. During the epidemic there were 5889 cases of smallpox in Boston, and 844 persons died. It is said that Dr. Boylston's slave, Onesimus, had previously told him of similar inoculations administered in Africa. Smallpox epidemics were a constant menace in colonial times. In Charleston, S.C., in 1698 an epidemic raged unchecked for about ten months. During another Boston epidemic, in 1702, it was ordered that bodies be buried without elaborate funerals so as to prevent the spread of infection. There were serious outbreaks in New York and Philadelphia in 1731–1732. In New York it was estimated that 6% of the population died of smallpox at the time.

1721 A **Jesuit college,** founded at Kaskaskia, in what is now Illinois, was one of the first institutions of higher learning in the Middle West. It had an especially distinguished library containing many volumes of eighteenth-century French philosophers.

1721 May 25 The **first marine and fire insurance company** in America was opened on High Street, Philadelphia, Pa., by John Copson.

1722 Jan. 24 Probably the **first professor of divinity** in the colonies was Edward Wigglesworth, who was named the first Thomas Hollis Professor of Divinity at Harvard College.

An increase in crime was noted in the colonies. The cause was attributed to the growth of cities, increasing wealth, and the changes brought on by the colonial wars, the first of which began in 1689. From then on, Boston, New York, Philadelphia, and Charleston, S.C., had night watches most of the time. By 1709, for example, Charleston had an armed watch of ten men who patrolled the town nightly. In New York in 1711 one John Riemer reported the theft of 25 gallons of cider, beer, and Madeira from his house. There was a great deal of theft in Boston in 1720, and it was blamed on the fact that there was much wealth there. Also at that time some people felt that Bostonians were "inclined to Riots and Tumults." Death was the usual penalty for theft, and in Philadelphia in Mar. 1720 William Smith and Hannah Travis, the latter known as Dancing Hannah, were convicted of theft and received death sentences. By 1723 the Boston police force consisted of 12 men who were instructed "to walke Silently and Slowly, now and then to Stand Still and Listen in order to make discovery. And no smoking to be on their walking rounds."

c1720 The **servants' staircase** was a striking interior feature of the new Georgian homes of wealthy Americans. It was said to have been introduced so that servants could carry full commodes from upper chambers without passing family or guests.

1720 The completed **Governor's Palace** in Williamsburg, Va., became the center of fashion and social life in Virginia.

Exploration and Settlement; Wars; Government; Civil Rights; Statistics I		II Publishing; Arts and Music; Popular Entertainment; Architecture; Theater

10,000; New York, 7000; Charleston, 3500; and Newport, 3800. All urban dwellers at this time were only 8% of the total population.

1720 Oct. The **Mississippi Bubble,** or Mississippi Scheme, devised by John Law to promote and finance French colonization in Louisiana ruined thousands of investors. The Duke of Orleans, regent of France, had encouraged Law, a Scottish financier and speculator, to start a bank. Under the name of the Western Company (also known as the Company of the West, *Compagnie D'Occident,* and the Mississippi Company), the bank gained control of trade on the Mississippi R. and issued paper money in excess of available security. The collapse of the bank ruined Law and caused great trouble in France. Although his financial scheme ended in failure, it did promote colonization in Louisiana. Law died in 1725.

1722 The **League of Six Nations,** an Iroquois confederation that included the Tuscarora tribe, concluded in Albany, N.Y., a treaty with Gov. Alexander Spotswood of Virginia. The Indians agreed not to cross the Potomac R. or Blue Ridge Mts. The Iroquois league always remained friendly to the English and hostile to the French, mainly because the latter often aided Indian tribes who were enemies of the Iroquois. Thus the League of Six Nations was an effective and necessary guard for the English colonies' western borders during this period of French expansion in the Mississippi R. Valley.

1722 June 4 Some 250 **German immigrants** landed at Mobile, Ala.

1723 **Benjamin Franklin,** discontent with the manner in which his brother treated him, left Boston and settled in Philadelphia, where he was to become famous.

1721 The **first American music book** with barred music notes, *The Grounds and Rules of Musick Explained, or, an Introduction to the Art of Singing by Note* by the Rev. Thomas Walter of Roxbury, Mass., was published.

1721 *Antiquities of the Jews* by Flavius Josephus was favorite reading for colonial settlers.

1721 The **first recorded public art commission** in America was given to Gustavius Hesselius by the Vestry of St. Barnabas's Church, Prince George's County, Md., for a painted altarpiece depicting the Last Supper.

1722 An **early account of western lands,** *Descriptions of La Louisiana; as also of the Great and Famous River, Meschacebe or Mississippi, the Five Navigable Lakes of Fresh Water etc . . .* by Daniel Coxe, was published.

1722 **The Alamo,** to become famous as the site of a great battle of the war for Texan independence in 1836, was constructed at about this time as a Franciscan mission.

1723 Perhaps the **first house with running water** in America was John Headly's in Newport, R.I. It was equipped in this year with a pipe "underground from the Spring."

1723 Aug.1–8 Probably the **first advertisement of an exhibition** in a colonial newspaper appeared in the *American Weekly Mercury,* describing the showing in Philadelphia of a "curious and exact Modell of the Czar of Muscovia's Country seat, near Moscow." The exhibition was apparently very successful.

1725–1729

The French and English began to compete for control of the area west of the Allegheny Mts., especially in the Ohio R. Valley. The French, who claimed the region and had done the most to explore it, were alarmed by the number of English colonists beginning to cross the mountains. In 1729 they sent Chaussegros de Léry to fortify the river down to the Miami R. in Ohio. Earlier, in 1724, the French had built Fort Vincennes on the lower Wabash R. The British government had done little to oppose the French, even though the English colonies claimed their land grants extended westward to include the Ohio Valley. King George I had been petitioned by the Lords of Trade in 1721 to "fortify the passes in the back of Virginia" to interrupt French communications, but nothing was done. Meanwhile, the French built another fort in 1726 on the Mississippi R.

Printing and publishing in the colonies began to thrive during this period, and one of the leading figures in the field was William Bradford. Born in England, he became in 1685 the first printer in Philadelphia. In 1690 he was one of the founders of the first paper mill in the colonies. In 1693 he moved to New York, where, in the course of 50 years, he issued some 400 items, including the first American *Book of Common Prayer* (1710); the first printed American play, *Androboros* (1714) by Gov. Robert Hunter of New York; and many almanacs and pamphlets. In 1725 he established the first newspaper in the colony, the *New York Gazette* (1725–1744). The paper was royalist in its politics, as Bradford was the official government printer. Andrew Bradford, William Bradford, and other Bradford descendants also became printers.

| Business and Industry; Science; Education; Philosophy and Religion | III | | IV | Sports; Social Issues and Crime; Folkways; Fashion; Holidays |

1722 Oct. 23 In a triumph for **Anglicanism in New England,** Timothy Cutler, Daniel Brown, and Samuel Johnson sailed for England to be ordained as Anglican ministers. The three men, leading Congregational ministers in Connecticut, had been affiliated with Yale College.

1723 The **first permanent school for Indians** in the colonies was established at Bafferton Hall, built at the College of William and Mary in Williamsburg, Va. The school was maintained by funds left for the purpose by Robert Boyle, the English scientist.

1723 The **first recorded commercial corporation** in America, a Connecticut trading company, was organized. Up to this time, land companies, universities, and philanthropic enterprises were the only forms of corporate enterprise. Colonial restrictions on the distribution of currency and restrictions from England on local trade and industry served to inhibit the formation of corporations in the modern sense.

1723 The **first Dunkard church** in America was formally organized at Germantown, Pa. A German Baptist sect, the members of it were known as Dunkards or Dunkers, from the German "dip," because of their method of baptism. The first congregation was organized in Germany in 1708. Persecuted, the Dunkards came to America under the leadership of Peter Becker and settled in Germantown in 1719. Six new converts were baptized in Wissahickon Creek the day the Germantown church was formed.

1724 The **first horticulturist** in America was Paul Dudley, who launched the science with his study of fruit trees in New England.

1721 In a move to increase the number of **women in Louisiana,** the French government sent 25 prostitutes, collected from a house of correction, to the colony. Officials sought to provide some means of getting Canadian settlers away from their Indian mistresses.

1721 May After a succession of **blue laws** limiting travel on Sunday, Connecticut passed a law providing that people could not go from their homes unless to attend worship or perform some indispensable task.

1722 Apr. 30 The game of **billiards** was mentioned in the *New England Courant,* which reported that a public house in Charlestown, Mass., had set up tables for customers who wished "to Recreate themselves with a Game of Billiards."

1723 Philadelphians opposing **racial intermarriage** petitioned the colonial assembly to do something "concerning the Intermarriages of Negroes and Whites." In Charleston, S.C., references were made to young men and their "black Loves." In 1735 a sea captain and a young southerner fought a duel over "the Favours of a certain sable Beauty."

1725–1729

Although few in number, Jewish immigrants were strong contributors to the religious life of America. The first permanent Hebrew congregation in the colonies was formed in 1729 in New York City; the next year the members constructed a synagogue on Mill St. that was described as a "solid, neat, stone Temple." The congregation later added the first school for Jewish children. Around this time Jewish communities were also developing in Charleston, S.C., Newport, R.I., and Philadelphia, Pa., and by the time of the American Revolution, there were between 2000 and 3000 Jews in the colonies, mostly merchants and traders. An act of Parliament in 1740 allowed Jews to be naturalized, and in the colonies they found more political and religious freedom than anywhere else in the world.

Voluntary associations formed for a variety of purposes became a feature of colonial life. One of the prime movers was Benjamin Franklin of Philadelphia, who in 1727 organized a group of artisans and tradesmen into the Leather Apron Club, later called the Junto. The club held meetings in taverns to discuss morals, politics, literature, and science, and to exchange books. The idea for a subscription library grew out of this last function, and on July 1, 1731, the Library Company was formed with 24 members. It imported its first books from England the next year. The club registered formal opposition to slavery and what it considered other inhumane practices. Out of the Junto grew the American Philosophical Society, founded in 1743.

1725 Queen Anne style furniture, characterized by double curves, broken pediments, and curved legs in

at the mouth of the Illinois R., and, to protect their routes to the Ohio country from Quebec, had that same year erected Fort Niagara on the Niagara R. at its junction with Lake Ontario.

1725 The **slave population** in the American colonies reached 75,000.

1725–1729 In a crackdown on the **black market fur trade,** a number of Albany merchants were tried and sentenced. English colonists were forbidden by law to traffic in furs trapped by Indians living in French territory. A similar ban restricted commerce between the French colonists and the Indians living in English territory. By 1725 a two-way illegal trade was flourishing. The law began to be enforced and several English traders were prosecuted and punished.

1726 A **riot in Philadelphia** by the city's poorer residents broke out in the heart of town. The rioters tore down the pillory and stocks and set them on fire before the governor of Pennsylvania put down the uprising. Similar outbursts continued to crop up in the city: in 1729 crowds broke into the mayor's gardens and destroyed his plants; in 1738 a riot ensued when the administration limited fishing on the Schuylkill R.

1729 **Royal control in South Carolina** was reestablished. The colonists of South Carolina, chafing under proprietary rule, had rebelled and petitioned for a royal government. Their grievances were of long standing. They resented the failure of the proprietors to give them adequate protection against the Yamassee Indians, who had been goaded by the Spanish to wage war against them from 1715 to 1728. In 1719, when the proprietors vetoed the more liberal election laws of the assembly, the colonists rebelled and appointed a governor who would be responsible only to the king. The proprietors were finally forced to relinquish their rights, and Parliament instituted a royal government for the colony.

1729 June The **Carolina grant was purchased** by the English Crown from its proprietors for £17,500. Carolina was divided into two royal provinces, North Carolina and South Carolina, in 1730. Even after independence there were disputes as to the exact boundary between the two states. These were not resolved until 1815.

1725 The *Astronomical Diary and Almanack* by Nathaniel Ames, a Massachusetts physician, was published. Extremely popular, it may have been used by Benjamin Franklin in preparing his own almanac. Typical of its entries were:

> Dec 7–10 Ladies take heed,
> Lay down your fans,
> And handle well
> Your warming pans.
> Dec 15–18 This cold, uncomfortable weather
> Makes Jack and Gill lie close together.

1725 The **Union Oyster House,** a famed Boston restaurant, was built as a private residence. It became a public eating place in 1826.

1726 The **largest book** printed in America up to this time, a folio volume entitled *Compleat Body of Divinity* by the Rev. Samuel Willard, president of Harvard University, was published.

1728 *The Mouse-Trap, or the Battle of the Cambrians and the Mice* by Richard Lewis, an important poetical work from Maryland, was printed by William Parks in Annapolis, Md. The poem was a translation of Edward Holdsworth's Latin poem *Muscipula,* a lampoon on the Welsh.

1729 The **Old South Meeting House** was built in Boston by Joshua Blanchard, a master mason who later built Faneuil Hall in Boston. The meeting house has been a museum since 1876.

1729 The **first serial** in an American newspaper, Daniel Defoe's *Religious Courtship,* appeared in the *Pennsylvania Gazette.*

1729 The **first arithmetic textbook** by an American, *Arithmetick Vulgar and Decimal: with the Application Thereof to a Variety of Cases in Trade and Commerce* by Isaac Greenwood, was published in Boston, Mass.

1729 Oct. The *Pennsylvania Gazette* was bought by Benjamin Franklin. Under the title *Universal Instructor in All Arts and Sciences and Pennsylvania Gazette,* it was founded by Samuel Keimer in 1728. At that time it had a subscription list of 90. Under Franklin it became in time the leading newspaper between New York and Charleston. He managed the *Gazette* until 1766, and it was continued until 1815 by David Hall, Franklin's partner from 1748, and by Hall's descendants. The claim of the popular magazine *The Saturday Evening Post* that it was a continuation of the Gazette *is a* myth. The *Post* was founded in 1821, six years after the *Gazette* had expired, by men with no connection with the *Gazette.*

| Business and Industry; Science; Education; Philosophy and Religion   III | | IV   Sports; Social Issues and Crime; Folkways; Fashion; Holidays |

1725 The first separate church of **colored Baptists** was established at Williamsburg, Va.

1725 The **U.S. Reformed Church** was established by John Philip Boehm at Falkner Swamp, Pa.

1726 The **first college** established in the middle colonies was the Log College in Bucks County, Pa.

1727 **Jonathan Edwards,** the leading religious figure of the eighteenth century in America, succeeded his grandfather in the pulpit of Northampton Church, the most prominent church in New England outside of Boston.

1728 **Benjamin Franklin** demonstrated his belief in reason as the basis of religious faith with the writing of his prayer manual entitled *Articles of Belief and Acts of Religion.* Franklin subordinated formal religious doctrines to common sense and logic.

1729 The **third Anglican parish** in Boston was established in Trinity Church. The new parish reflected the rapid expansion of Anglicanism in New England.

1729 **Presbyterian churches** adopted as their doctrinal standard the Westminster Confession of Faith and Catechisms.

1729 Mar. 15 The **first Catholic nun** to be professed in the colonies was Sister St. Stanislaus Hachard, who celebrated the Ceremony of Profession at the Ursuline Convent in New Orleans, La.

furniture of walnut, became fashionable in the colonies five years after its greatest popularity passed in England and some 11 years after the death of Queen Anne of England. This period marked the first appearance of the cabriole, or curved, style for table and chair legs; and the first appearance of the American Windsor chair, in Philadelphia. Windsor chairs were generally painted green, brown, or red, but rarely white.

1728 **Boston Common** was enclosed in order to preserve its grass from carts and horses. Soon it became the custom after tea for gentlemen and ladies to stroll about the green before going to their homes.

1728 The *New England Weekly* estimated that the living expenses of a middle-class tradesman, having no more than eight in his family, were about £265. 18s. 9d. per year. Most families employed a maid-of-all-work at a cost of £10 a year.

1728 The arrival in Louisiana of **casket girls,** so called because they received a dress in a casket as a gift for their immigration, introduced a new element into Louisiana society. Since these girls were not inmates of penal institutions, as were many of their predecessors, it became and has remained an honor to be descended from a casket girl.

1728 **Importation of rum** in the colonies for this year amounted to 2,124,500 gal., or £25,000 of liquor. Drinking was extremely heavy. This printed doggerel gave one reason why people did not drink:

> There's but one Reason I can Think
> Why People ever cease to drink,
> Sobriety the Cause is not,
> Nor Fear of being deam'd a Sot,
> But if Liquor can't be got.

1729 **Discrimination** in Rhode Island forced ship captains to post £50 for each immigrant coming from any place other than England, Ireland, Jersey, or Guernsey.

1729 Mar. 1 **St. David's Day,** in honor of the patron saint of Wales, was formally celebrated by Welsh inhabitants of Philadelphia, who formed the Society of Ancient Britons, gathering in Queen's Head Tavern. From there, members of the Society marched through the streets, wearing leeks in their hats, to Christ Church, where a Rev. Dr. Weyman delivered a sermon in Cymric, after which the celebrants repaired to a tavern for further ceremonies.

1729 Apr. 23 The first celebration of **St. George's Day** in America was held in Tun Tavern by St. George's Society of Philadelphia, a group of Philadelphians of English extraction.

1730–1734

Georgia, the last of the 13 original colonies to be founded, came into being under somewhat different circumstances than the others. On June 9, 1732, a royal charter was granted by King George II of England to James Edward Oglethorpe, an English general and philanthropist. Originally this region had been part of the grant of the Carolinas; it also was claimed by Spain. One of the purposes of founding Georgia, therefore, was to protect the other southern colonies from Spanish intrusion. Oglethorpe saw the colony as a refuge for English debtors. The first colonists, led by Oglethorpe, arrived on Feb. 12, 1733, and founded Savannah, the first settlement in Georgia. Forts were built and the friendship of the Creek Indians was secured. Slavery was originally prohibited, but members of Georgia's ruling class felt this would hinder them economically. In 1752 the colony was turned over to the Crown and thereafter became profitable, but by then it had already achieved its major objective, the blocking of Spanish northern expansion.

The estimated colonial **population** was 654,950.

1730 The **most populous area** of colonial America was New England, with 275,000 Europeans. By 1760 this number rose to 425,000, and at the close of the Revolution to 800,000.

1730 Baltimore, Md., was settled. Two previous efforts had been made to found a city named after the Lords Baltimore, but the site of the first is in question and only one house and some ruins remain of the second. Baltimore was important as a seaport for the rich grain and tobacco lands around the head of the Chesapeake Bay. The land for Baltimore had been bought by the Maryland legislature in 1729.

1732 Jan. The **concession in Louisiana** was surrendered to the French Crown by the Western Company of John Law. Antoine Crozat, a French trader, had held the concession from 1712. He made the grant in 1717 to John Law, a Scottish financier and speculator. The Western Company (also called the Company of the West, *Compagnie D'Occident,* and the Mississippi

Growth of American music was stimulated in colonial times by immigrant European musicians, many of whom were talented and creative composers as well as accomplished performers. Often the musicians were obliged to travel from place to place seeking work as church organists, teachers, or the like. Such a musician was Carl Theodorus Pachelbel, an organist and composer and son of Johann Pachelbel, who had been a noted influence on his younger contemporary Johann Sebastian Bach. Carl Theodorus Pachelbel emigrated from Germany to Boston in 1733. There he taught children to play the harpsichord and the spinet. He soon moved on to Newport, R.I., where he became organist at Trinity Church. In Jan. 1736 he gave a concert of vocal and instrumental music at Todd's Tavern in New York City, "the Harpsichord Part Perform'd by himself. The Songs, Violins, and German Flute by private hands." Enough people paid four shillings apiece to attend to allow another performance to be given in March. Later Pachelbel moved to Charleston, S.C., where he died on Sept. 14, 1750.

1730 An **early collection of hymns,** *Göttliche Liebes und Lobes Gethöne* (also known as the *Ephrata Hymnbook*) compiled by Conrad Beissel, was printed in Philadelphia, Pa., by Benjamin Franklin.

1730 Probably the **first algebra book** printed in America was *Arithmetica ot Cyffer-Konst Volgens de Muten Maten en Gewigten, te Niew-York, gebruykelyk als mede een kort ontwerp van de Algebra* by Peter Venema. It was published by John Peter Zenger in New York City.

1730 The **Old State House** in Philadelphia, known as Independence Hall, was designed by Andrew Hamilton. Completed in 1753 and rebuilt in 1828, it is an excellent example of Georgian public architectural style.

1730 "**Father Abbey's Will**" by John Seccomb, a New England minister, was an extremely popular piece of humorous verse that caught the fancy of the English public when printed in the *Gentleman's Magazine.* In the poem, Father Abbey, dying, bequeathed in part the following to his widow:

> A greasy hat,
> My old ram cat,
> A yard and half of linen,
> A woolen fleece
> A pot of grease
> In order for your spinning.

1732 The **first guidebook** in America, *Vade Mecum for America; or, A Companion for Traders and Travellers* by Daniel Henchman and T. Hancock, was printed. It

| Business and Industry; Science; Education; Philosophy and Religion III | | IV Sports; Social Issues and Crime; Folkways; Fashion; Holidays |

1730–1734

The prominent part religion played in the settlement and development of the English colonies was emphasized by the revival movement known as the Great Awakening, which began in New England in 1734, triggered by the preaching at a revival in Northampton, Mass., of Jonathan Edwards, the theologian and philosopher. Edwards emphasized man's sinful nature and the torments of eternal damnation. His fame spread widely and he received many invitations to preach. His influence was strong among young people. Many converts were made, amid public scenes of great emotion. In the middle colonies, William Tennent, a Presbyterian clergyman, led the movement. The Great Awakening reached all the colonies with the 1739–1741 visit to America of George Whitefield, the Methodist evangelist who preached from New England to Georgia. In the South Samuel Davies carried the message to the Presbyterians of Virginia. The movement reached the Baptists of North Carolina in the 1760s, but by that time it had already died out in New England. The Great Awakening resulted in bitter doctrinal disputes in New England between two groups known as the New Lights and the Old Lights. The latter opposed revivalism as extravagant and impermanent. The Old Lights were led by Charles Chauncy, a Boston clergyman who became the leader of the theological liberals. His beliefs developed into Universalism, or Unitarianism. The theology of the New Lights was more conservative and developed into a somewhat modified Calvinism.

1730 The **first stoneware furnace,** or kiln, was established in New York City. New York eventually became a center of pottery manufacture, evidenced by the designation "Potter's Hill" on an early map of the city.

1730 Wallpaper, "Stampt Paper in Rolls for to paper Rooms," was sold to wealthy merchants of the colonies.

1730 The **first practical navigating quadrant,** Hadley's Mariner's Quadrant, was invented by Thomas Godfrey.

1731 The **Library Company of Philadelphia,** the first circulating library in the New World, was founded by Benjamin Franklin. The extent to which libraries were to grow and flourish in the U.S. is indicated by the fact that by 1984 there were 8796 public libraries, with an additional 6260 branches, in the U.S.

By 1730 summer resorts were being patronized by the well-to-do. A Dr. Thomas Bond encouraged his patients to picnic and take the waters at Spring Garden on the outskirts of Philadelphia. Near Bristol, Pa., was the so-called Bath spring, which also became a popular summer resort. The most popular and fashionable resort was Newport, R.I., whose climate attracted patrons from the Carolinas and the West Indies who came ostensibly for reasons of health. Newport's offerings included excursions to New Shoreham and Prudence Island. There were races on the beach by Narragansett pacers, and the winners were awarded silver tankards. Tea parties, dances, and lavish dinners added to the atmosphere of pleasure and sophistication. Newport's popularity contributed to its growth as a cultural and trade center as well. In 1730 a Philosophical Society was established, out of which the Redwood Library was formed 20 years later. Within a few years Newport became an important port in the "triangular trade," whereby rum was traded for slaves in Africa and the slaves were exchanged for sugar and molasses in the West Indies.

c1730 A great craze for **white stockings** for men and women set in, replacing varicolored hose of the seventeenth century. The stockings were made of thread, silk, cotton, or worsted, and were supported by ornate garters. Often the name of the wearer was woven into the garter with a "posy." White hose were worn until the end of the century.

1730 In order to improve **fox hunting** in the colonies, a Mr. Smith of Maryland imported a number of English red foxes and set them loose along banks of the Chesapeake.

1730 Daniel Coxe became the **first appointed grand master of Masons** in America when he was designated "Provincial Grand Master of the Provinces of New York, New Jersey, and Pennsylvania."

1732 In order to establish a **bowling green** in New York City, "A piece of land at the lower end of Broadway fronting to the fort" was leased to three well-known New Yorkers, John Chambers, Peter Bayard, and Peter Jay.

1732 The **oldest sporting organization** and first fishing club in North America was formed as the Schuylkill

Company) was pledged to develop Louisiana and had been given exclusive right to trade on the Mississippi R.

1732 Feb. 22 George Washington was born at Bridges Creek, Va.

1733 An **epidemic of influenza,** the first outbreak in North America, swept New York City and Philadelphia.

1733 May 17 The **Molasses Act** was passed, placing high duties on rum and molasses imported from the French and Spanish West Indies. Admission of American merchants into the rum trade of the French West Indies (1713) caused a boom in sugar on those islands. Planters on the English islands lost out as New England ships put into French and Dutch ports to load up with cheap sugar. The English planters petitioned Parliament and forced passage of the Molasses Act, which levied prohibitive duties on sugar and molasses brought to the colonies from other than British possessions.

1733 July Forty **Jews,** admitted to Georgia colony by its proprietors, settled in Savannah.

provided information on all roads and taverns from Maine to Virginia, and also included a directory of the streets of Boston.

1732 The **second theater building** in the colonies, the New Theater, Nassau Street, New York City, was opened. On Dec. 6 it staged *The Recruiting Officer* by George Farquhar. It also produced this season *The Beaux' Stratagem* by George Farquhar, *The Busybody* by Susannah Centlivre, and *Cato* by Joseph Addison.

1732 The **Adams mansion** in Quincy, Mass., the Georgian residence of the famous Adams family throughout the eighteenth and nineteenth centuries, was built. It was enlarged several times and shows successive changes in architectural style.

1732 May The *Philadelphische Zeitung* [Philadelphia Newspaper], the first foreign-language newspaper in the English colonies, was founded by Benjamin Franklin in Philadelphia, Pa.

1732 Dec. 19 *Poor Richard's Almanack* was first published by Benjamin Franklin at Philadelphia, Pa. In continuous publication for 25 years, Franklin's *Almanack* sold on average more than 10,000 copies yearly and thus was one of the most popular writings of colonial America.

1734 Oct. In a landmark case involving **freedom of the press,** John Peter Zenger, founder and publisher of the New York *Weekly Journal,* was arrested for libel. Zenger had founded the *Weekly Journal* on Nov. 5, 1733, and had used its pages to oppose the administration and policies of Gov. William Cosby of New York. In 1735 he was acquitted after a defense by Andrew Hamilton that was later cited in many cases involving freedom of the press. The Sons of Liberty, an organization founded to aid Zenger's defense, later became the Tammany Society of New York. The *Weekly Journal* was published until 1751.

1735-1739

The War of Jenkins' Ear (1739-1742), which began in Europe on Oct. 19, 1739, and a year later merged into the War of the Austrian Succession, had its repercussions in the southern colonies. England went to war with Spain over the mistreatment of English seamen whom the Spaniards accused of smuggling. The war took its name from Robert Jenkins, captain of the ship *Rebecca,* who claimed Spanish coast guards had cut off his ear in 1731. He exhibited the ear in the House of Commons and so aroused public opinion that the government of the British Prime Minister Robert Walpole reluctantly declared war on Oct. 23, 1739. Basically, the war was one of commercial rivalry between England and Spain. By the Treaty of Utrecht (1713), which ended Queen

Many colonists were deeply concerned with religion, and hymn singing was of major importance. This led to the publication of hymnals. When John Wesley, the founder of Methodism, visited America in 1737 he had published at Charleston, S.C., *A Collection of Psalms and Hymns.* Some of the selections were adaptations from the German Moravian *Gesangbuch.* Wesley had met Gov. James Edward Oglethorpe of Georgia in 1735, when Oglethorpe was in England. Oglethorpe invited Wesley and his brother Charles, then students at Oxford and members of an Oxford group known variously as the Holy Club, Bible Moths, and Methodists, to come to Georgia. They arrived in Georgia Feb. 5, 1736. Notwithstanding Oglethorpe's invitation, the visit was marked

Business and Industry; Science; **III**
Education; Philosophy and Religion

IV **Sports; Social Issues and Crime;**
Folkways; Fashion; Holidays

1731 The **first efficient fire engine** in America, invented in England, arrived in Philadelphia and became part of the Union Fire Company of Philadelphia, headed by Benjamin Franklin.

1732 An early indication of **Quaker humanitarianism** in America was the founding of a public almshouse in Philadelphia supported by public funds.

1732 The **first stage coach line** was established between Burlington and Amboy, N.J. Connections could be made from Amboy to New York City and from Burlington to Philadelphia by boat.

1732 Feb. 26 The **only Roman Catholic Church** built and maintained in the colonies until the Revolutionary War held its first mass in Philadelphia.

c1733 **Pennsylvania Dutch kilns** produced perhaps the finest pottery in America. The earliest specimen dates from this period—a barber basin inscribed "Putz und Balwir mich heibsh und fein das ich gefal der liebste mein [Clean and shave me nicely and fine so that I'll please my loved one]." Later Pennsylvania Dutch sgraffito, pottery in which a design is etched through the surface coating to show the layer beneath, and slipware bore short verses like the following:

> In the dish on the table
> Merry he who yet is single
> Sad is he who is engaged.
> If loving were unhealthy
> Surely the doctor would avoid it
> And if it would hurt the wivet
> Surely they would not allow it.

Fishing Company in Philadelphia. It is now known as the Fish House Club, its membership limited to 30, its function limited to annual meetings at the Andalusia, Pa., headquarters.

1733 New York gentry began to form **social clubs,** one of the earliest being the Political Club, which met this year at Todd's Tavern. It was followed by the Hum Drum Club, the Hungarian Club, and the New Club, Lodge, or Society of Free Masons (1738).

1734 **Benjamin Franklin** contributed what was to become a famous epigram on marriage to his *Poor Richard's Almanack* when he observed that "where there's marriage without love, there will be love without marriage."

1734 The **first jockey club** in the world was formed as the South Carolina Jockey Club. It was disbanded in 1900.

1734 Mar. A commercial notice in Boston said that a shipment of **Nassau silk** "of the Colour provided for the royal wedding" had been shipped from England "early, that . . . Ladys may have them as soon as some of ours." The royal wedding was that of Princess Anne, the eldest daughter of King George II of England, who was married to the Prince of Orange on Mar. 14, 1734. Boston provided a good market for the merchants of London, since the latest fashions were in great demand by the wealthy.

1735–1739

Science and scientists were flourishing in the colonies. The first chair in mathematics and natural philosophy was endowed at Harvard in 1727, and its first incumbent was Isaac Greenwood, who gave a course in fluxions (calculus). He retired in 1737, his lectures having done much to stimulate interest in science. Greenwood was succeeded by John Winthrop IV, who is sometimes called the father of seismology because of his studies of earthquakes. In 1746 he gave the first laboratory demonstration of magnetism and electricity. In 1766 Winthrop was elected a fellow of the Royal Society and in 1773 Harvard conferred on him an L.L.D. degree, the first ever awarded in America. The Rev. Jared Eliot of Connecticut, the first American experimenter in

Because of the religious atmosphere and growing colonial affluence, funerals became more elaborate and expensive. It was customary to give away mourning rings or gloves at funerals. At the funeral of Gov. Jonathan Belcher of Massachusetts in 1741, his widow gave away 1000 pairs of gloves. Clergymen and doctors accumulated hundreds of such items over their careers. In 1721 the General Court of Massachusetts passed laws against "extraordinary expenditures for funerals" to protect those who could not afford "gloves, scarfs and scutcheons," but when Andrew Faneuil was buried in 1738 more than 1100 persons accompanied his funeral cortege, which was described as "generous and expensive." Newport, R.I., also witnessed elaborate funerals,

Anne's War, Britain was to be allowed to participate in slave traffic with the Spanish colonies. A special Spanish fleet, however, interfered with this activity and the Spanish also objected to the English logwooders operating on the coast of Honduras. The other cause of the war was the continued dispute over the boundary of Spanish Florida in relation to Georgia. As soon as war was declared, Gov. James Edward Oglethorpe called on the citizens of Georgia and South Carolina to join in an invasion of Florida. The Spanish retaliated by attempting to invade those colonies by sea.

1735 **Augusta** was established when James Oglethorpe, proprietor of the colony of Georgia, fortified and renamed a trading post on the Savannah R. The post had been established in 1717. Augusta was so named in honor of the mother of King George III of England. Also this year, Oglethorpe established Fort Okfuskee on the Talapoosa R. By 1739 he had completed military fortifications on Amelia, Cumberland, St. Andrew's, and St. Simon's islands as a line of defense against possible Spanish encroachment. He also had reached peace agreements with the Creeks and other Indian tribes in the region.

1735 Oct. 30 **John Adams,** second president of the United States, was born in Braintree, Mass.

1737 Friendly relations between the **Delaware Indians** and the Pennsylvania proprietors deteriorated when Thomas Penn, son of William Penn and manager of the proprietorship, hired expert walkers to pace off land deeded to his father by the tribe. By the terms of the deed, the grant was to include all the land a man could walk across in a day and a half. Penn's experts walked 66½ miles.

1738 **Lewis Morris** was named the first governor of New Jersey colony. Since 1702 New York and New Jersey had shared the same governor, although New Jersey had become autonomous for all practical purposes. Morris, who had been born in New York to a wealthy and prominent family, served as governor of New Jersey until his death in 1746.

1739 Three **slave uprisings** broke out in South Carolina this year. The incidents have been attributed to the preaching of the Spanish missionaries who allegedly created in the slaves a false expectation of deliverance. On Sept. 9 a band of slaves from Charleston set out for St. Augustine, Fla., and freedom, slaying all Europeans they met on the way. They were themselves surrounded and massacred. Twenty-one

by difficulties. In Savannah John was charged with inserting into the Anglican church service unauthorized psalms and hymns. Charles Wesley is said to have produced about 5000 hymns in his lifetime, many of which became popular in America, including "Hark! The Herald Angels Sing." Another prolific and popular hymn writer was Isaac Watts, an English clergyman. The first American edition of his *Hymns and Spiritual Songs,* which appeared in England in 1707, was published in America in 1739, although his hymns had been sung there before that. Watts wrote "O God, Our Help in Ages Past," among several hundred hymns that reflected a stern Calvinism with touches of sympathy and tenderness.

1735 Feb. 8 The **first opera** produced in the colonies was performed at the Courtroom, in Charleston, S.C. It was *Flora; or The Hob in the Well* by Colley Cibber.

1735 Feb. 12 The **third theater** in the colonies, the Dock Street Theater in Charleston, S.C., opened with a performance of *The Recruiting Officer* by George Farquhar. On Feb. 23 it staged *The Orphan* by Thomas Otway. Performances were given until May 1737. Box seats were 30 shillings; pit, 20 shillings; gallery, 15 shillings.

c1737 The **oldest extant house** in the U.S. Midwest was built by an unknown French colonist at Cahokia, Ill. The house later became the Cahokia County Courthouse. The structure was of poteaux-sur-sole style construction, characterized by upright posts driven into the earth and chinked with clay, with a double-pitched, hipped roof, and a surrounding balcony.

1737 *A Faithful Narrative of the Surprising Work of God* by Jonathan Edwards, the clergyman who launched the Great Awakening with his sermons in Northampton, Mass., was published. The book described and defended the religious revival. Edwards considered it of vital importance although he deplored some of the hysteria it engendered.

1739 *An Historical Discourse,* a notable sketch of the history of Rhode Island by John Callender, minister of the Baptist Church in Newport, was published. The book traced the series of acts of intolerance and

Business and Industry; Science;   **III**   **IV**   **Sports; Social Issues and Crime;**
Education; Philosophy and Religion   **Folkways; Fashion; Holidays**

physiological botany, was interested in making agriculture more scientific and worked on the fructification of maize before 1739. He also developed a process for smelting iron from black magnetic sand. Ezra Stiles, a theologian as well as a scientist, calculated the true position of the sun and moon, using the work of Sir Isaac Newton. As president of Yale from 1778 to 1795, he liberalized the curriculum, bringing in the thought of the enlightenment of the eighteenth century.

1735 The **first Moravian community** in America was established at Savannah, Ga., under the leadership of Rev. Augustus Gootlieb Spangenberg. A Moravian evangelist had been in Pennsylvania the year before.

1735 Probably the **first fire insurance company** in the colonies, The Friendly Society for the Mutual Insurance of Houses Against Fire, was established in Charleston, S.C. The company was ruined in the great fire of Nov. 18, 1740, which consumed half of Charleston.

1735 The growth of **Massachusetts trade** was reflected in the fact that Boston and Salem between them had some 25,000 tons of shipping.

1735 The first published account of **lead poisoning** as a result of drinking rum distilled with lead pipes was written by Thomas Cadwallader.

1736 The **first adequate clinical diagnosis of scarlet fever** was published by Dr. William Douglass of Boston. It was a significant contribution to the science of medicine.

1736 Feb. 5 The history of **Methodism** in America began with the arrival in Georgia of John Wesley, at the invitation of Gov. James Edward Oglethorpe. When Wesley came to America his career had not yet reached the spectacular proportions later brought on by his achievements as a public preacher. Six years earlier the name Methodists had been applied to his group of religious ascetics, but Methodism as a religious movement was still in the future. His stay in America was notable for his romance with Sophia Hopkey, who wooed but did not win him. When Sophia married another, Wesley barred her from his congregation and her new husband retaliated with the threat of a lawsuit. Wesley then decided to return to England.

1739 **Caspar Wistar,** the glass designer and manufacturer, set up his glassworks at Allowaystown, N.J., on tracts of land ideal for production of window and bottle glass. The factory went into operation July 30, 1740, and was staffed by Belgian glassblowers specially drafted from Europe. Wistar's enterprise was responsible for the most distinctive type of early American glass, South Jersey glass, known for its wide, bulbous forms, often with superimposed winding thicknesses on the bottom. Wistar's glassworks was one of the first successful co-ops in America.

that of Rosewell Lavine in 1716 costing £55. One livery stable in Boston kept black horses for hire for funerals, while a "Mr. C.H." offered to supply engraved sets of ready-to-use obituaries, "With Void Spaces for the Name, Age, Distinction, and Profession, or such Particular and Eminent Qualities as do not properly fall under the Notice of General Description."

c1735 The **status of women** changed with the increase of wealth in the colonies. More women left their husbands when they found living together incompatible; newspaper items told of runaway wives and elopements.

1735 **Public balls** came into vogue in colonial New York. In 1736 the birthday of the Prince of Wales was celebrated in a magnificent ball at the Black Horse Tavern.

1735 Jan. The often tense **relations between Europeans and blacks** in New York was demonstrated when John van Zandt, a Dutch burgher of New York, horsewhipped his slave to death for having been picked up at night by a watch. The coroner's jury judged the "Correction given by the Master was not the Cause of his Death, but it was by the Visitation of God." One reason for such tension was that the slave population was about one-fifth that of the entire colony. Blacks were lynched and burned for theft, rape, etc.

1736 A **shortage of marriageable women** in the colonies led 60 maidens from the Bahamas to sail to Charleston, S.C., where they advertised in the local press for husbands.

1737 Mar. 9 A **movement for social reform** in Boston got out of hand when a mob smashed up a bawdy house in the city "for harbouring lewd and dissoulute Persons." Prostitutes roamed the waterfront of Boston. One woman, who entertained "Lawyers, Officers, Journeymen, Gentlemen, Merchants, Apprentices," had to be cautioned not to display her behavior "at the Window on the Lord's Day" for fear of the minister.

1737 Mar. 17 The first celebration of **St. Patrick's Day** outside the confines of the Roman Catholic Church was held in Boston by the Charitable Irish Society, which had been founded that year. The Friendly Sons of St. Patrick in New York City followed suit in 1784. An oddity of the New York society was its joint sponsorship by Irish Roman Catholics and Presbyterians, with the first president of the organization being a Presbyterian.

1738 A Masonic warrant for the **first Masonic lodge** was issued by the Grand Lodge of Massachusetts to Abraham Savage. A similar authority was granted to Richard Gridley in 1756 for a military expedition

| **Exploration and Settlement; Wars; Government; Civil Rights; Statistics**   I | | II   **Publishing; Arts and Music; Popular Entertainment; Architecture; Theater** |

Europeans and 44 blacks perished. At Stone River a slave named Cato led another insurrection. The third uprising was in St. John's Parish in Berkeley County.

bigotry in the Massachusetts Bay Colony that led to the emigration to and formation of Rhode Island.

1740–1744

King George's War (1744–1748), the third of the French and Indian wars, was known as the War of the Austrian Succession in Europe, where it began in 1740. The war included most of the European nations in a complicated series of alliances. It began after the death of Charles VI, the Holy Roman Emperor and ruler of the Hapsburg lands. The Archduchess Maria Theresa succeeded her father but there were counterclaimants. Fighting began when King Frederick II of Prussia invaded Austrian-held Silesia. In America and elsewhere in the world, France and England fought for colonial power and possessions. The French unsuccessfully attacked Port Royal, Nova Scotia, in 1744, the year in which fighting broke out in America.

The estimated colonial **population** was 889,000.

1740 A powerful **political attack** on Gov. James Edward Oglethorpe and his administration of the new colony of Georgia was published in *A True and Historical Narrative of the Colony of Georgia* by Patrick Tailfer, Hugh Anderson, and David Douglass, three colonists who had fled to Charleston, S.C. The account read in part: "Thus, while the nation at home was amused with the fame of the happiness and flourishing of the colony, ... the poor miserable settlers and inhabitants were exposed to as arbitrary a government as Turkey or Muscovy ever felt."

1740 Jan. The **War of Jenkins' Ear** (1739–1742) continued with an invasion of Florida led by Gov. Oglethorpe of Georgia. He was protected on the west from the French by friendly Indians. He captured forts San Francisco de Pupo and Picolata on the San Juan R. From May to July he besieged St. Augustine, but broke off the attack when his rear guard was threatened by the Spanish.

1741 A group of **German Moravians** moved from Georgia, where their colony had been unsuccessful, to Pennsylvania. They joined others of their faith in the establishment of Bethlehem on the Lehigh R. Count Nikolaus Ludwig Zinzendorf, their leader, arrived from Europe this year, bringing with him a band of

Before the American Revolution, about 15 magazines began publication in the colonies, but they had an average life of only ten months. The first of these, published by Andrew Bradford, was the *American Magazine; or, A Monthly View of the Political State of the British Colonies*. Bradford's magazine began in Philadelphia in Jan. 1741 but published only three monthly issues. Bradford by three days had beaten Benjamin Franklin, who started his *General Magazine and Historical Chronicle* also in Philadelphia and also in January. Franklin's magazine lasted for six issues. In Boston in 1743, Gamaliel Rogers and John Fowle began the *Boston Weekly Museum*, which died that same year. More successful was the *American Magazine and Historical Chronicle*, which began publication in Boston in 1743. It was edited by Jeremy Gridley and published for more than three years. Gridley was a lawyer, and while the magazine was devoted largely to politics, he also wrote about literary and cultural subjects.

1741 The **first symphony orchestra** in America was organized by Moravian settlers in Bethlehem, Pa. By 1748 it had 14 pieces: two first violins, two second violins, two violas, one cello, one double bass, two flutes, two trumpets, and two French horns.

1741 Aug. Probably the **first organ** built in the colonies, the organ for Trinity Church in New York City, was completed by Philadelphian Johann Gottlob Klemm. Klemm took more than two years to construct the instrument.

1742 Jonathan Edwards's *Some Thoughts concerning the Present Revival of Religion in New England*, a work reflecting the revivalism in colonial times, was published.

1742 The **Carpenters' Company** was established by the master carpenters of Philadelphia, who sought to establish an architectural library and teach themselves the elements of design and craftsmanship. In 1770 they built Carpenters' Hall, which became the meeting place of the first Continental Congress in 1775.

1742 Sept. 24 **Faneuil Hall** in Boston was opened to the public. A Georgian structure designed by the painter John Smibert, it was enlarged in 1805 according to plans by Charles Bulfinch that retained the original Georgian style. The famous weather vane on

| Business and Industry; Science; Education; Philosophy and Religion   III | | Sports; Social Issues and Crime; Folkways; Fashion; Holidays   IV |

1739 Aug. George Whitefield, a celebrated English preacher and associate of John Wesley, arrived at Lewes, Del., to begin an evangelistic tour that was to help promote Methodism in America.

against Crown Point, N.Y., during the French and Indian War (1754–1763).

1739 Benjamin Franklin coined the famous epigram on self-adulation in *Poor Richard's Almanack:* "He that falls in love with himself will have no rivals."

1740-1744

The first American scientific association, the American Philosophical Society, was founded in Philadelphia in 1743 as an outgrowth of the Junto, a club Benjamin Franklin and a group of friends had begun in 1727. The society was formed "for the promotion of useful knowledge among the British planters in America." Its first president was a lawyer named Thomas Hopkinson, and Franklin was the first secretary. In 1769 it merged with the American Society for Promoting Useful Knowledge, and Franklin was elected the first president of the combined organization. He held the post until his death in 1790. He was succeeded by David Rittenhouse, an astronomer and instrument maker, who was succeeded by Thomas Jefferson. In 1769 the society began publication of its *Transactions.* The original inspiration for the society was the Royal Society of England. The society continues to exist with a membership of distinguished persons in intellectual and scientific fields. It has a large library especially rich in materials dealing with the American Revolution and the history of science in America.

1740 Jonathan Edwards began to write his "Personal Narrative" about this time. An account of Edwards's personal conversion, it was first published in *The Life and Character of the Late Reverend, Learned and Pious Mr. Jonathan Edwards* by Samuel Hopkins, which was printed in Boston in 1765.

1740 The first brewery in Georgia was erected by Gov. James Edward Oglethorpe, supplying ample quantities of beer for his colonial troops.

The growth of the fishing industry in New England was reflected in the existence of some 1000 fishing ships.

1741 The Great Awakening, a religious revival movement in New England, reached an oratorical peak with the famous sermon delivered by Jonathan Edwards at Endfield, Mass. Entitled "Sinners in the Hands of an Angry God," Edwards's sermon proclaimed man's "abominable" sinfulness in the eyes of God.

1741 The first true porcelain manufactured in the colonies was produced by Andrew Duché, a craftsman of Huguenot descent who had founded a pottery in

The growing problem of crime and racism in the increasingly populous cities, and a decline in social and economic stability, was reflected in the so-called Negro Conspiracy of 1741 in New York City. A number of robberies in February were attributed to the customers of John Hughson's dram shop, which was frequented by blacks. Hughson had a bad reputation and it was suspected that he was a fence for stolen goods. In March Fort George burned and the fire was thought to have some connection with the robberies. Many people panicked for fear of crimes by blacks, and their fears were fed by sensational tales of a conspiracy, described by one Mary Burton, a European servant. Hundreds of people fled to the Bowery and Harlem, and then outside the city proper, for fear of a black uprising. The militia was called out and many blacks were jailed and given summary judicial treatment. Two slaves, Quack and Cuffee, were burned at the stake, and Hughson and his wife were hanged. Before the frenzy subsided, 13 blacks had been burned alive, eight hanged, and 71 transported out of the colony. The claim of a conspiracy had no basis. Even Daniel Horsemanden, the prosecutor, admitted later that there had been no plot.

1740 Mineral springs in the mountains of Virginia were found to have medicinal qualities, inducing many plantation owners to travel there with their families to bathe and vacation. George Washington in 1769 spent a season there with his wife and stepdaughter.

1740 Mar. 25 Construction of Bethesda Orphanage in Savannah, Ga., began under the auspices of the English evangelist George Whitefield. Georgia authorities had granted Whitefield 500 acres of land for the orphanage, and he had raised some £2530 to finance it. Whitefield visited America seven times between 1738 and 1770, preaching from New England to Georgia, and maintaining an active interest in management of the orphanage until his death in New Hampshire on Sept. 30, 1770. The main building of the orphanage, which was sometimes called Bethesda College, burned in June 1773 and was never rebuilt.

1741 The legend of Tom Cook, the Leveler, may be said to have commenced this year. The lad was sick unto death and his mother prayed, "Only spare his

new immigrants. Zinzendorf returned to Europe in 1743.

1742 June 9 In the **Battle of Bloody Marsh** on St. Simons Island, one of the Sea Islands off the southeast coast of Georgia, the Spanish attacked Fort Frederica, which had been constructed by Gov. Oglethorpe in 1736 to protect the colony. The Spanish were repulsed in a bloody battle that was a decisive engagement of the War of Jenkins' Ear.

1743 John Woolman began preaching the evils of slavery to Quaker meetings throughout the colonies.

1743 Apr. 13 **Thomas Jefferson**, third president of the United States, was born in Shadwell, Va.

1744 An **Indian treaty** signed with the Iroquois League at Lancaster, Pa., ceded to England the territory of the Ohio R. Valley north of the Ohio R.

its cupola is a giant grasshopper of beaten copper.

1744 *A Collection of Poems by Several Hands,* hailed as proof of poetic excellence in the American colonies, was published. The volume contained poems by various authors that echoed the poetry of Alexander Pope.

1744 The best-selling novel *Pamela* by the English novelist Samuel Richardson was first published in America. This and Richardson's subsequent novels, *Clarissa* (1747–1748) and *Sir Charles Grandison* (1753), were the first examples of the so-called sentimental novels popular in America from the mid-eighteenth to mid-nineteenth century.

1744 A **Collegium Musicum** for the performance of the chamber music and symphonies of Johann Sebastian Bach, Joseph Haydn, Johann Stamitz, and other European composers was established at Bethlehem, Pa., by the Moravians, the most musical of the dissenting religious sects in America. It was the first such organization in the colonies.

1745–1749

The Treaty of Aix-la-Chapelle was signed on Oct. 18, 1748, ending the War of the Austrian Succession, known in America as King George's War (1744–1748). For the most part it restored the status quo in the New World, returning Fort Louisbourg, on Cape Breton Island in Canada, to France. The New Englanders, whose forces had fought brilliantly to capture heavily defended Louisbourg, were outraged. As a result, the English Crown agreed to bear the cost of the expedition. Great Britain's privilege of transporting slaves to Spanish America was renewed, but the treaty turned out to be merely a truce before the last and greatest of the French and Indian Wars.

1745 In **King George's War** (1744–1748), French and Indian forces began the year with raids on English fortifications in Maine.

1745 June 16 **Fort Louisbourg**, a powerful French stronghold on Cape Breton Island in Nova Scotia, was captured by New Englanders under William Pepperell and an English fleet under Sir Peter Warren.

1745 Nov. 28–29 Saratoga, N.Y., was attacked and burned by French and Indian forces after the English had succeeded in persuading the Iroquois league to enter the war against the French.

1747 Some of the **first flags** created in the American colonies were those designed by Benjamin Franklin.

In the mid-eighteenth century portrait painting flourished. The best colonial painter of this period was Robert Feke. He probably studied in Europe at one time, but he developed a personal style of painting. Feke practiced in New York City, Philadelphia, Newport, and Boston, painting excellent portraits of leading citizens. Perhaps his best, in terms of characterization, was a portrait of the Rev. Thomas Hiscox done in 1745. Feke's portraits were noted for their charm and for the elegance of the costumes worn by his subjects. Examples of his work include a portrait of Mrs. Barlow Trecothick done in Boston; and *Unknown Lady,* now in the Brooklyn Museum, noted for its almost cubist depiction of the subject's bell-shaped skirt and funnel-shaped torso. Feke's work was influenced by John Smibert, the first painter of skill in New England. Feke disappeared at sea in 1750.

1745 Selections from the writings of Charles de Secondat, Baron de la Brède et de **Montesquieu**, were first published in American periodicals. The selections were from *Lettres Persanes (Persian Letters,* 1721). These were followed several years later by excerpts from *L'Esprit des Lois (Spirit of the Laws,* 1748) in the Boston *Gazette.* This book had a profound effect on the evolution of American political theory and the formulation, some 40 years later, of the U.S. Constitution.

1745 Summer The **first carillon** in America, an eight-bell instrument, was placed in Christ Church belfry, in Boston, Mass. It was paid for by public subscription

Business and Industry; Science; Education; Philosophy and Religion III		IV Sports; Social Issues and Crime; Folkways; Fashion; Holidays

Savannah, Ga., in 1730. Lack of financial backing hampered pottery manufacture, but Duché prospered by exporting his clay to England. In 1764 the *Bristol Journal* acknowledged that the first porcelain made in an English-speaking country came from North America.

1742   The **Moravian Seminary for Women** was founded at Bethlehem, Pa. Men were first admitted in 1746, and in 1807 a full college curriculum was adopted. The institution is now known as Moravian College.

1742   The so-called **Franklin stove,** a variation on an open firebox of German design, was invented by Benjamin Franklin.

1744   The **first brewery in Baltimore** was established on the southwest corner of Baltimore and Hanover streets by Leonard and Daniel Barnetz of York, Pa.

life, and I care not what he becomes." He became a semilegendary evildoer, a sort of Robin Hood, whose name came up in scores of New England villages. Legend has it that he sold his soul to the Devil, but managed to rob even Satan of his due.

1741   The prevalence of **alcohol abuse** in the colonies was demonstrated in the death of a child about five years old after consuming a great quantity of rum. Drunkenness was the most prevalent vice of colonial settlers. Each colony had stringent laws meant to suppress excess drinking. Boston even went so far as to post the names of drunkards. A contemporary quatrain sounded this note:

> This town would quickly be reclaimed,
> If drams no more had vent,
> And all the sorts that could be named,
> To *Strombolo* were sent.

1745-1749

Seven colleges—Harvard, the College of William and Mary, Yale, Princeton, Columbia, Brown, and Rutgers—were established before the Revolution. Typical of them was Princeton, chartered Oct. 22, 1746, as the College of New Jersey and opened in 1747 in Elizabethtown, N.J. Its first president was Jonathan Dickinson, who taught the first classes in his home. He was a leading preacher of the Great Awakening and founded the college to train leaders for the revival movement. Its first degrees were conferred in 1748. In 1756 the college moved to Princeton, N.J., where its name was changed. In the years following its founding, Princeton became a stronghold of conservative doctrine in the bitter theological conflicts within the Presbyterian Church. Princeton's second president was Aaron Burr, whose son, also named Aaron Burr, was to kill Alexander Hamilton in a duel. During the Revolution both sides occupied the school buildings, which were heavily damaged. As time passed, the original purpose of training clergymen disappeared and the university devoted itself to higher education.

1745   The growth of **literacy** in early America was spurred by the founding of 22 newspapers between 1713 and 1745.

1745-1763   An **early Texas history** was compiled by Franciscan fathers, who wrote books on the techniques of missionaries and on the language and character of the Texas Indians.

Coffee houses began to gain popularity about this time, as the populations of cities grew. New York had two coffee houses in 1744. A coffee house was opened in Charleston, S.C., by William Monat in 1743, but lost business to Charles Shepheard, whose British Coffee House grew in popularity after its owner became deputy postmaster. Three coffee houses were available to Philadelphians before 1750, two of them named the Widow Robert's and the Widow Jones's. The former was the most popular, providing newspapers and magazines, tea, coffee, and chocolate, and the "constant Attendance" of the proprietor until the Widow Roberts died in 1754. Boston had the Crown and the North End. Jacob Hassey, described as "a comicall old whimsical fellow," kept a coffee house at Newport, R.I. Prior to the opening of coffee houses, taverns fulfilled some of the same purposes, but many taverns became notorious for their patrons' heavy drinking and lawlessness. As a result, coffee houses became centers where businessmen met and where notices of ship sailings, sales, and other matters were posted.

c1745   **Whist** became very popular in the colonies, having been brought over from England, where it was the rage. The game afforded men the opportunity to keep company with women. Ladies often played for money, as evidenced in accounts of Thomas Jefferson and George Washington concerning their wives' expenses.

They were to be employed by military units opposing attacks by the French.

1748   Drapers Meadows was founded on Virginia's frontier. It was the first English settlement west of the Allegheny Divide.

1749 May 19   The **Ohio Company** was chartered by King George II of England. Organized by Virginians and Englishmen, it had a grant of 500,000 acres on the upper Ohio R. During this year Jean Baptiste Le Moyne, Sieur de Bienville, led a French expedition into the Ohio Valley to establish the French claim. He deposited inscribed lead plates at the mouth of each important river.

1749 Oct. 26   Slavery in Georgia was officially sanctioned by the colony's proprietors. The importation of rum was also permitted. This action repealed a parliamentary act of 1735 that prohibited both rum and slavery. Thus ended the timidity of Parliament about the presence of slaves in the colonies who might have allied themselves with the Spanish in time of crisis. The act of 1735 had already been repudiated by the colonists, especially in Georgia, where the necessity for field and house hands had encouraged the settlers to flout the prohibition. In England, too, shippers and traders were besieging Parliament to lift the ban. Finally, in 1749, the trustees of Georgia requested a change in policy. Parliament yielded. The legal introduction and extension of slavery into the colonies in this year marked the beginning of the plantation system in the South.

in Boston and London. Its bells were cast in Gloucester, England.

1745 Sept. 4   At a **Moravian concert** in Bethlehem, Pa., the hymn "In Dulce Jubilo" was sung in 13 languages simultaneously: Bohemian, Dutch, English, French, German, Greek, Irish, Latin, Mohawk, Mohican, Swedish, Welsh, and Wendish. A Dane, a Pole, and a Hungarian were also present but did not join in.

1747   Alexander Pope's *Essay on Man*, probably the most popular poem in the eighteenth century, was published in America. First published in England in 1733, it was reprinted all over the American colonies. A reflection of its popularity is the fact that, nearly two centuries after its first publication, it sold 50,000 copies in the Little Blue Books edition of 1920.

1747   *Turtel Taube* [Turtle Dove], the first book of original hymns published in America, was issued in Ephrata, Pa. The hymns were written in German by J. Conrad Beissel and his followers. Beissel had come to America from Germany in 1720, and in 1732 established and administered a monastic society at Ephrata. Beissel's foreword to *Turtel Taube* was the first writing in America on the subject of hymns.

1748   *An Essay on Field Husbandry* by Jared Eliot, a New England preacher, physician, and farmer, was published. It was one of the earliest attempts to adapt scientific method to agriculture.

1749   King's Chapel, the first building in Boston to be built from Quincy granite, was erected from designs by Peter Harrison of Newport, R.I. It superseded the first King's Chapel, built in 1688.

1749 Aug. 22   Colonial **opposition to acting** was demonstrated when an early troupe of English actors, Murray and Kean's, performed Joseph Addison's *Cato* (1713) in a Philadelphia warehouse. Protests by the city council forced them to leave for New York.

1750–1754

The first attempt to unite the English colonies was made at the Albany Congress, which was called in Albany, N.Y., in 1754 to negotiate a treaty with the Iroquois Indians in the event of further war with the French. Represented at the Albany Congress were the four New England colonies and New York, Pennsylvania, and Maryland. Benjamin Franklin took the occasion to present his "Plan of the Union" of the colonies, which the delegates approved on July 19, 1754. The plan included amendments proposed by Thomas Hutchinson of Massachusetts and would have united all the American English colonies, except Georgia and Nova Scotia, under a president general who would be named by the British government and paid by it. The various colonial assemblies would elect a grand council that would have

The fortunes of American theater rose considerably when Lewis Hallam brought his theatrical troupe to America in 1752. The company's first performance was *The Merchant of Venice* in Williamsburg, Va. Moving to New York City in 1753, Hallam built a new theater on Nassau St. that was well patronized by upper-class New Yorkers. In April the company moved on to Philadelphia, where it gave 30 performances at Plumstead's Theater, which had been renovated for them. The performance of *The Fair Penitent* was received "with universal applause." After touring the South, Hallam went to Jamaica in the West Indies, where he died in 1756. The company was said to have had a repertoire of over 40 plays. Hallam's widow married David Douglass. With him she formed the American Company, which came to

Business and Industry; Science; Education; Philosophy and Religion III		IV Sports; Social Issues and Crime; Folkways; Fashion; Holidays

1746 The first university lectures on **electricity** in America were given by John Winthrop IV at Harvard.

1746 Father Sébastien Louis Meurin arrived in the Illinois Country, the last Jesuit missionary sent there before France lost the region to England in 1763. During his career in America, Father Meurin studied Indian languages and compiled a dictionary of various dialects. On June 24, 1770, he blessed the first log cabin church in the new village of St. Louis, Mo.

1747 Jonathan Mayhew, the first New England minister to challenge openly the traditional doctrine of the Trinity, assumed the pulpit at the West Church in Boston.

1747 The **New York Bar Association**, the first legal society in America, was organized by lawyers of New York City to defend themselves against attacks by Lt. Gov. Cadwallader Colden. In 1765 the group spearheaded colonial resistance to the Stamp Act.

1749 The importance of **Boston** as a colonial seaport was reflected in the fact that no fewer than 489 ships used the harbor as home port during the year.

1749 Nov. 13 The **University of Pennsylvania** originated as an academy established by 24 citizens of Philadelphia, Pa. They had been inspired by a pamphlet on education written by Benjamin Franklin, and Franklin was the first president of the school's trustees. In 1753 the proprietors of Pennsylvania gave $15,000 to the academy, and in 1755 it became the College, Academy, and Charitable School of Philadelphia, from which grew the University of Pennsylvania.

1747 **Benjamin Franklin** coined the oft-quoted proverb of prudence in *Poor Richard's Almanack:* "A Slip of the Foot you may soon recover, But a Slip of the Tongue you may never get over."

1749 The **consumption of cider** in New York rivaled that of beer. A Swedish visitor to the colonies noted the abundance of apple orchards and number of cider presses in New York. In winter cider was used extensively; in summer it was mixed with water, sweetened, and spiced with nutmeg.

1749 Philadelphia **social life** was enhanced by establishment of a Dancing Assembly. Positions in the dance were determined by lot, and a gentleman and his partner were engaged for an entire evening. On the day following a dance a gentleman usually had tea with his partner in order to develop his acquaintanceship.

1749 The **eating habits** of the Dutch in New York were carefully recorded by a foreign traveler: "Their Breakfast is tea, commonly without milk. . . . They never put sugar into the cup but put a small bit of it into their mouths while they drink. Along with tea they eat bread and butter with slices of hung beef. . . . They breakfast generally about seven. Their dinner is buttermilk and bread. . . . They sometimes make use of buttermilk instead of fresh milk to boil a thin kind of porridge with, which tastes very sour but not disagreeable in hot weather. To each dinner they have a great salad prepared with abundance of vinegar and little or no oil [probably koolslaa—modern coleslaw]. Their supper is generally bread and butter, or milk and bread."

1750–1754

Medical care in the colonies was somewhat primitive and unorganized in the early eighteenth century. During this period both the quality and availability of medical treatment improved as medical education increased and general hospitals made their first appearance. In 1734 William Bull of South Carolina received a medical degree in Europe, the first of 40 or so colonial physicians to be educated abroad. Forerunners of hospitals were the pesthouses, such as those established in Boston (1717), Philadelphia (1742), Charleston, S.C. (before 1752), and New York City (1757). The first general hospital was organized in Philadelphia by Dr. Thomas Bond; it opened its doors Feb. 6, 1752, as the Pennsylvania Hospital. Admission was on a paying or charity basis for persons who were mentally or physically ill, except

By the mid-eighteenth century social customs and forms of entertainment were somewhat relaxed compared with earlier periods. At the same time, many forms of entertainment and recreation were those to be expected of small towns and farming areas—hunting, fishing, folk dancing, and corn husking bees, for example. One observer noted that at one of the husking bees the "neighboring Swains . . . cannot carry in the husks without a Rhum bottle." There was widespread observance of the custom that any young man who found a red ear of corn could kiss any girl he chose. It was recorded that one young woman, Sarah Tuttle, charged with having enjoyed the occasion too much, was brought before a magistrate who denounced her as a "Bould Virgin."

| Exploration and Settlement; Wars; Government; Civil Rights; Statistics | **I** | | **II** | Publishing; Arts and Music; Popular Entertainment; Architecture; Theater |

legislative power, subject to the president general and the English Crown. However, the plan was rejected by the colonies and by the Crown. England proposed a looser union with a commander in chief and a commissioner for Indian affairs, but nothing came of the idea.

The estimated colonial **population** was 1,207,000.

1750 **Christopher Gist** was sent by the Ohio Company to explore the large tract of land on the upper Ohio R. that it had obtained by royal charter the year before. Gist was a neighbor of Daniel Boone and, by this commission, beat Boone in becoming the first European to survey northeastern Kentucky. Gist studied the lands of the Ohio R. and their inhabitants with such care that to this day the charts he made of the region and his observations of the customs of the Indians are esteemed as "models in mathematical exactness and precision in drawing."

1751 Mar. 16 **James Madison,** the fourth president of the United States, was born in Port Conway, Va.

1753 In a search for the **Northwest Passage,** the *Argo,* a schooner commanded by Capt. Charles Swaine, set out from Philadelphia, Pa. The expedition had been fitted out chiefly through the efforts of Benjamin Franklin. The expedition explored Hudson's Straits and returned the same year.

1753 Oct. 31 **George Washington** was sent by Gov. Robert Dinwiddie of Virginia to demand French withdrawal from the Ohio territory. Dinwiddie had been impressed by Washington's achievement as surveyor and fieldsman, and picked him for the commission although he was only 21. As adjutant general of the Northern Division, Washington set out from Williamsburg, Va. With Christopher Gist as his guide, he made observations of French fortifications and estimations about needed English fortifications. During the expedition he kept a journal, which Dinwiddie later obtained and had printed. It indicted French intentions for the territory and attributed to a French officer the indiscreet admission that " . . . it was their absolute Design to take possession of the Ohio, and by G— they would do it."

1754 Continuing his **campaign against slavery,** John Woolman wrote his essay *Some Considerations on the Keeping of Negroes.* Woolman, a Quaker, relentlessly tried to persuade Quaker slave owners to give up their slaves. His was the strongest voice against slavery during this period.

1754 Apr. 17 The **French continued to advance** on the Ohio River Valley with the occupation of the

New York in 1759. The opening bill at Cruger's Wharf was *Jane Shore,* which played to "great applause, to a most crowded audience." Hallam's son, Lewis, Jr., was a member of this troupe and a noted performer of comedy. In 1767 he appeared in Thomas Godfrey's *Prince of Parthia,* the first American drama to be produced professionally.

1750 Probably the **first use of imitation materials** in an American building was in construction of the Redwood Library of Newport, R.I. A temple-form structure in late Georgian style, it was finished with pine plank siding worked to imitate stone.

1750 **Parlange,** one of the finest plantation houses of the bayou country in Louisiana and a classic example of French colonial architecture, was built at New Roads, Pointe Coupée Parish, La., by Marquis Vincent de Ternant, whose descendants still own it.

1750 Mar. 5 The **Murray-Kean Company of Comedians** of London began presenting theatrical performances in New York in a building on Nassau St. owned by a Rip Van Dam. They offered such English favorites as *The Beggar's Opera* and *The Recruiting Officer* to full houses, leading one James Parker to remark that "the Taste of this Place is not so much vitiated" as many thought. The company, headed by Thomas Kean and Walter Murray, first performed in Philadelphia but had not found receptive audiences.

1751 *Observations Concerning the Increase of Mankind* by Benjamin Franklin was published. A significant volume on economic theory, it advanced the idea that the wages of workers in America must be high because of the abundance of free land. This year also saw publication in London of Franklin's famous *Experiments and Observations in Electricity, Made at Philadelphia in America.*

1751 Apr. 2 **John Smibert,** perhaps the earliest American artist of merit, died. Born in 1688, he studied in England and Italy. Coming to America with Bishop George Berkeley, he finally settled in Boston where he achieved fame and wealth as a portrait painter. In 1730 in Boston he presented what was probably the first art show in America, exhibiting his own copies of works by old masters. Smibert's most famous work was the *Family of Bishop Berkeley,* now in the Dining Hall of Yale University.

1751 Dec. **Peter Pelham,** an early engraver and the stepfather of the celebrated American painter John Singleton Copley, died. During his life he engraved many portraits of New England ministers, that of Cotton Mather being one of his best known.

for incurables and those having infectious diseases.

1750 The **first essay on human dissection** was written by doctors John Bard and Peter Middleton of New York City. The dissection was performed on the body of Hermannus Carrol, an executed murderer.

1750 The **Great Awakening,** the New England religious revival sparked by Jonathan Edwards, came to an end when Edwards was compelled to resign from his pulpit at Northampton, Mass., by liberal members of his congregation. The liberals opposed his emphasis on the sinful nature of mankind.

1750 The **flatboat** was invented by Jacob Yoder of Pennsylvania. It was a boon to colonial inland navigation.

1750 Probably the first free **manual training classes** in America were established by the Rev. Thomas Bacon in Maryland. Enrollment was open to all without distinction as to sex or racial origin.

1751 The **first sugar cane** grown in America was introduced into Louisiana by Catholic missionaries from San Domingo on the island of Hispaniola. It was used to make taffia, a kind of rum.

1752 Jan. 31 The **first American-born nun** in the Roman Catholic Church was Sister St. Martha Turpin, who celebrated the Ceremony for the Profession at the Ursuline Convent, in New Orleans, La.

1752 June **Benjamin Franklin** conducted his celebrated experiment with kite and key to prove lightning a manifestation of electricity. A kite with a projecting wire was flown during a thunderstorm, and an electrical charge was conducted to the key through light twine. The experiment was conducted in a pasture near what is now the corner of Fourth and Vine streets in Philadelphia, Pa.

1753 **Benjamin Franklin** received the Copley Medal of the Royal Society of London in recognition of his research in electricity. The award was voted unanimously by the Royal Society. Franklin's reputation as a scientist had grown rapidly in Europe after publication there of his works on electricity.

1753 The **practice of medicine** in New York City was regulated for the first time. An ordinance required that "all the physicians and surgeons and apothecaries in the province are to be licensed. ... " The law was not strictly enforced until 1760, when the New York General Assembly provided a system of examination and licensing for those who intended to practice medicine or surgery within the province. Illegal practice was punishable by a fine of £5.

1753 The **first steam engine** in the colonies was brought to North Arlington, N.J., by John Schuyler to pump water from his copper mine. The machine came from England and was assembled in America by Joshua Hornblower.

1750 A big **horse race** on the Newmarket Course on Hempstead Plains, Long Island, brought heavy business to the Brooklyn ferry, which carried more than 70 chairs and chaises and more than 1000 horses in one day.

1750 Col. Tasker of Belair, Md., imported **Selima,** daughter of Godolphin Arabian, one of the original thoroughbred horses. Selima became dam of several good American racers.

1752 Col. Tasker's **Selima** defeated Col. Bird's Tyrall in a horse race in Maryland. Col. Tasker was so successful with the offspring of Selima that Maryland-bred horses were barred from Virginia Jockey Club purses for several years. The colonel then sent his horses to Virginia to foal and soon was winning again.

1752 The inscription for the **Liberty Bell,** the biblical sentence "Proclaim liberty throughout all the land unto all the inhabitants thereof," was chosen by the Pennsylvania Provincial Assembly. The bell was cast in England and delivered to the colony in this year. While being tested in Philadelphia, it suffered its first crack.

1752 May 11 "Hand-in-hand," the celebrated motto of the early colonial fire insurance company, the Philadelphia Contributorship for the Insurance of Homes, dates from the adoption of the company's famous seal at the first meeting of the board of directors. The company's 12 directors had been chosen Apr. 13, but it was not until the following month that they met.

1753 May 10 In a tribute to the **beauty of Carolinian women,** the Society for the Regulation of Manners decreed that after this day "no Lady do presume to walk the Streets in a Mask, unless either the Sun or Wind is in her Face; such as are very ugly or have sore Eyes always excepted."

1754 An important influence on **American furniture design,** *The Gentleman and Cabinetmaker's Director* by Thomas Chippendale, was first published in England. The book stressed elaborate rococo designs with formal adaptations of French, Gothic, and Oriental styles.

1754 Wearing of the **banyan,** a nightgown made of silk and damask that was worn as a dressing gown, was forbidden to students at Harvard College.

1754 Curious **Valentine customs** were recorded by a colonial girl: "Last Friday was St. Valentine's Day, and the night before I got five bay leaves and pinned four on the corners of my pillow and the fifth to the middle; and then if I dreamt of my sweetheart, Betty said

junction of the Allegheny and Monongahela rivers on the site of present-day Pittsburgh, Pa. There they built Fort Duquesne. The move anticipated similar intentions by an English force led by George Washington and dispatched by Gov. Dinwiddie.

1754 May 28 The **first skirmish of the French and Indian War** (1754–1763), the last and most significant of the French and Indian Wars, occurred when a small force under George Washington engaged and defeated a reconnaissance party of French and Indians near Fort Duquesne. Unable to proceed against the superior French forces in the fort, Washington erected Fort Necessity at nearby Great Meadows.

1754 July 4 George Washington surrendered **Fort Necessity** when attacked by a large French contingent from Fort Duquesne. This defeat left the French in possession of the Ohio River Valley.

1752 The **Georg Muller House,** the best surviving example of Pennsylvania Dutch architecture, was built at Milbach, Pa. Its layout was based on designs common in the Rhine Valley.

1753 *A General Idea of the College of Miriana* by William Smith was published. An early tract in the form of a romance, it outlined plans for an ideal college in America. The book influenced Benjamin Franklin in his plans for establishing a college in Philadelphia.

1754 What was perhaps the **first American political cartoon** was published by Benjamin Franklin in his *Pennsylvania Gazette.* The cartoon showed a snake cut into eight parts, the head representing New England and the other seven parts representing the remaining colonies. The caption was "Join or Die." The cartoon was prompted by rumors of an impending war with the French.

1755–1759

The Seven Years' War (1756–1763), the European counterpart to the French and Indian War (1754–1763), began officially between France and England on May 15, 1756, when the latter made a formal declaration of war. Actually, fighting had been going on in America for two years. The war involved all the major European powers and was worldwide in scope, but to the colonists it was a struggle against the French for control of North America. The war did not go well for England until the elder William Pitt came to power in 1756. He concentrated on fighting the French and sent badly needed troop reinforcements to North America.

1755 July 9 In the **French and Indian War** (1754–1763), British Gen. Edward Braddock was mortally wounded when he and his force of British troops and colonial militia were caught in a French and Indian ambush. Braddock had just crossed the Monongahela R. on his way to attack Fort Duquesne, on the site of what is now Pittsburgh, Pa. Braddock died July 13, and George Washington assumed command of the retreating army.

1755 Nov. 27 Land for the **first Jewish settlement** in America was purchased by Joseph Salvador, who bought 100,000 acres near Fort Ninety-Six, S.C.

1755 Nov. 30 The **first refugees** from the French and Indian War, some 900 Acadian French deported by British authorities from Nova Scotia, arrived in Maryland. Years later Henry Wadsworth Longfellow used this exile as the background for his poem *Evangeline* (1847).

Colonial America was developing its own intellectual class, whose members were noted for their wide-ranging interests and varied talents. None of them was more versatile than Francis Hopkinson, a musician and poet, accomplished harpsichordist, and leader of musical pursuits in Philadelphia. In 1759 Hopkinson wrote what was probably the first secular song written by a native American, "My Days Have Been So Wonderous Free." The song, based on the poem by Thomas Parnell, was not published until the twentieth century. Hopkinson went on to become a signer of the Declaration of Independence, wrote the celebrated Revolutionary poem "The Battle of the Kegs" (1778), and, as a member of the Continental Navy Board (1776–1778), may have designed the American flag. His book *Seven songs, for the Harpsichord or Forte-Piano* (1788) was the first book of music published by an American composer.

1755 According to legend, the words of the song "**Yankee Doodle**" were written by Dr. Richard Shuckburg, a British army surgeon, as a satire on the ragged American troops. More likely the song was of folk origin among the British soldiers. Adopted as a favorite marching tune by American troops, "Yankee Doodle" quickly lost its satirical aspect. In 1781, during the American Revolution, the song was played at the British surrender at Yorktown, Va.

1755 A prophetic reference to the destiny of **George Washington** was made in a sermon preached in

Business and Industry; Science; Education; Philosophy and Religion III		IV Sports; Social Issues and Crime; Folkways; Fashion; Holidays

1754 The **first clock made entirely in America** was constructed by Benjamin Banneker, a 30–year-old black who had never seen a clock before. It continued to run accurately, striking all hours regularly, for 20 years.

1754 Oct. 31 **King's College** was chartered in New York City. Its first degrees were awarded in 1758. Sponsored by Episcopalian groups, King's College was incorporated as Columbia College, the dominant institution in the state of New York in an act passed in 1784. Bitter conflict between advocates of free public education and backers of Columbia College led to the separation of the college from the University of the State of New York by an act of the state legislature in 1787. The University of the State of New York, a university in name only, then concerned itself with primary and secondary school education while Columbia College remained the only institution of higher learning in the state. Columbia College became a university in 1912.

we should be married before the year was out. But to make it more sure I boiled an egg hard and took out the yolk and filled it with salt; and when I went to bed ate it shell and all, without speaking or drinking after it. We also wrote our lovers' names on bits of paper, and rolled them up in clay and put them into water; and the first that rose up was to be our Valentine. Would you think it? Mr. Blossom was my man. I lay abed and shut my eyes all the morning, till he came to our house, for I would not have seen another man before him for all the world." It was about this time, in the middle of the century, that the history of American valentines began. A certain simplicity was apparent in the style of the sketches and verses of early valentines, though they often displayed some talent. So-called valentine writers, guides to the composition of valentines containing sample verses, were imported from England from 1723 on, and many senders were willing merely to copy their verses from these.

1755-1759

The opening in 1756 of a through stage route linking Philadelphia and New York City marked another step forward in the development of colonial transportation. As the first colonial settlements grew into towns and then into cities, the need for roads and reliable means of transportation also grew. By 1717 there was a continuous road along the East Coast connecting all the colonies. Other roads went into the interior, but many were rough. The first stage line between Boston and Newport, R.I., began to operate in 1736. Beginning in 1744, part of the heavily traveled route between New York and Philadelphia was served by twice-weekly stages between New Brunswick and Trenton, N.J. Perhaps the most heavily traveled road was the Great Philadelphia Wagon Road, which ran west to Lancaster and then to York. The 1756 Philadelphia–New York stage used Jersey Wagons, wagons without spring suspensions, which operated in relays. Faster passenger service was offered in 1766 by the Flying Machine, a box wagon that ran from Camden, N.J., to what is now Jersey City, N.J. The 90–mile trip took two days and passengers had to use a ferry at each end.

As soon as streets were laid out in colonial cities, citizens and city councils alike pointed to the necessity and desirability of paving them. Paving not only made streets drier and smoother, but also contributed to public health by providing drainage. After 1700, Boston, New York City, and Newport, R.I., began to pave streets. Later, between 1743 and 1760, paving became more common and colonial streets were probably in better shape than those in England. In 1757 over 16,000 yards of roadway on Boston Neck were paved at a cost of £3000. A lottery in Newport in 1752 provided funds for paving more streets. Philadelphia also used a lottery to pay the cost of paving.

1755 A **scene of rural frolic** was described by Jacob Bailey, a Kingston, N.H., schoolteacher, in a poem:

> The chairs in wild disorder
> flew quite around the room,
> Some threatened with firebrands,
> some brandished a broom,
> While others,
> resolved to increase the uproar,
> Lay tussling the girls
> in wide heaps on the floor.

1755 June 16 The **first nonsectarian college** in America, the University of Pennsylvania, was chartered as the College, Academy, and Charitable School in Philadelphia through the efforts of Benjamin Franklin. Its first degrees were awarded in 1757.

1756 Aug. 14 **Fort Oswego** in north central New York was captured by the French under Gen. Joseph de Montcalm de Saint-Véran. Gen. Montcalm rendered the fort useless for military purposes and returned to Montreal.

1757 Aug. 9 **Fort William Henry,** at the southern tip of Lake George in northeastern New York, capitulated to the French commanded by Gen. Montcalm. Many of the British soldiers in the garrison were killed by the Indian allies of the French on the next day.

1758 Apr. 28 **James Monroe,** the fifth president of the United States, was born in Monroe's Creek, Va.

1758 July 8 A British and colonial assault on **Ticonderoga,** at the northern end of Lake George in New York, was beaten back by the French under Gen. Montcalm. Nearly 2000 of the attacking force of 17,-000 were killed or wounded.

1758 July 26 The French at the **fortress of Louisbourg,** Nova Scotia, surrendered to the British under Adm. Edward Boscawen and Gen. Jeffrey Amherst after a 48–day siege. Almost 6000 prisoners were captured and the fortress was razed.

1758 Aug. The **first Indian reservation** in North America was established by the New Jersey colonial assembly. The reservation was founded on a 3000–acre tract called Edge Pillock in Burlington County, on the site of the present village of Indian Mills. About 100 Indians, chiefly Unamis, settled on the reservation and attempted to set up a self-sustaining community.

1758 Aug. 27 **Fort Frontenac,** located on the site of what is now Kingston, Ontario, was captured by British forces under Col. John Bradstreet.

1758 Oct. The **Treaty of Easton** was negotiated between the colony of Pennsylvania and the Indian tribes in the western part of the colony. By its terms Pennsylvania promised not to found any settlements west of the Allegheny Mts. However, the French abandonment of Fort Duquesne in November resulted in a rush of settlers. The treaty took its name from the town of Easton, Pa., where several treaty conferences were held with the Indians.

1758 Nov. 25 British forces drove the French from **Fort Duquesne,** which the British renamed Pittsburgh.

1759 July 26 **Ticonderoga was abandoned** by the French as Gen. Amherst threatened a siege. The French commander, the Chevalier de Bourlamaque, withdrew to Crown Point, N.Y.

Virginia by a popular minister, Samuel Davis. At about the time of Gen. Edward Braddock's defeat and death, he said: "I may point out to the public that heroic youth, Colonel Washington, whom I cannot but hope Providence has hitherto preserved in so signal a manner, for some important service to his country."

1756 The *New Hampshire Gazette,* the oldest continuing newspaper in America, began publication in Portsmouth under the editorship of Daniel Fowles.

1757 **Mount Vernon,** a cottage of one and one-half stories acquired by George Washington, was remodeled for the first time. It was enlarged and remodeled at least three more times in the next 30 years, probably in accordance with Washington's own designs. The result was a structure not as well designed as other Virginia mansions but, aside from its historical associations, interesting for its record of architectural growth.

1757 Oct. *The American Magazine,* probably the most admired of early literary magazines, began publication. It ran until Oct. 1758. Conducted "by a society of gentlemen," this Philadelphia publication printed choice articles on philosophy and science, as well as a sprinkling of belles-lettres.

1758 **Mount Airy,** one of the best examples of late Georgian architecture in Virginia, was built near Richmond. Designed by John Ariss, the most important architect in Virginia at the time, it was more massive and more highly decorated than earlier Georgian homes.

1759 May 31 **Opposition to theater** by religious groups, especially Baptists, was reflected in passage of a Pennsylvania law forbidding performance of plays, under penalty of a £500 fine.

1759 Dec. 13 The **first music store** in America was opened by Michael Hillegas in Philadelphia.

Business and Industry; Science;   **Sports; Social Issues and Crime;**
III   **IV**
Education; Philosophy and Religion   **Folkways; Fashion; Holidays**

1755 June 28 The first English-made vessel on Lake Ontario, a schooner with a 40–ft. keel, equipped with 14 oars and 12 swivel guns, was launched from its berth.

1756 The rise of **rationalistic thinking** in American religion was reflected in the republication of *The Humble Inquiry into the Scripture Account of Jesus Christ* by Thomas Emlyn, the first self-styled Unitarian minister in Great Britain.

1758 **Salaries for clergymen** and some public officials in Virginia were authorized by the so-called Two Penny Act, which was passed by the Virginia Assembly. Clergy and some public officials, by provisions of the act, were to receive regular salaries rather than proportionate shares of the tobacco crop. Due to the small size of the tobacco crop, this act cut into the real income of the designated parties by keeping them from selling tobacco in a demand market. It was, consequently, extremely unpopular. One affected clergyman was the Rev. James Maury, with whom Thomas Jefferson, then 14, began that year to study. Maury had set up a log cabin on his place, where he added to his income by teaching school. Jefferson boarded with the family, was one in a class of five, and paid tuition of £20 a year.

1758 A **school for blacks** was established in Philadelphia under the auspices of the "Associates of Dr. Bray." The organization, founded by the Rev. Thomas Bray of Maryland in 1723, was an Anglican missionary group closely linked to the Society for the Propagation of the Gospel in Foreign Parts.

1759 The **first recorded life insurance company** in America, the Presbyterian Ministers Fund, was established by Thomas and Richard Penn of Philadelphia, Pa.

1756 July 26 **Bosom bottles** were advertised in the *Boston Evening Post*. They were small, beribboned glasses worn on stiff dresses of the period, filled with water, and containing flowers that served much the same function as corsages do today.

1757 **American Childers,** Lewis Morris's famous horse, won a race around Beaver Pond in Jamaica, Long Island.

1757 **Street lights** appeared in Philadelphia on a small scale. Whale oil lamps, specially designed by Benjamin Franklin, were installed on a few streets. The year before, Franklin had introduced a bill to the Pennsylvania Assembly for street illumination.

1758 **Benjamin Franklin** circulated this famous parable on thrift in *Poor Richard's Almanack:*

A little neglect may breed mischief:
For the want of a nail the shoe was lost,
For the want of a shoe the horse was lost,
For the want of a horse the rider was lost,
For the want of a rider the battle was lost,
For the want of a battle the kingdom was lost—
And all for the want of a horseshoe nail.

This year he also composed: "Early to bed and early to rise/Makes a man, healthy, wealthy and wise."

1758 July The celebrated legend of the **Windham Frogs** began in Windham, Conn. Inhabitants of the town were awakened by a tremendous roaring and clashing that drove them in nightdress from their homes and they remained outside until dawn waiting for judgment day. In the morning they discovered that two armies of bullfrogs had fought for possession of a pond. According to the story, each army had repeatedly called out the names of Col. Dyer and Col. Elderkin, both well-known lawyers. The town's inhabitants swore they heard these names amid the roaring and hubbub.

1760–1764

The Treaty of Paris, signed by Great Britain, France, and Spain on Feb. 10, 1763, ended the Seven Years' War and its American counterpart, the French and Indian War (1754–1763). By terms of the treaty, France ceded Canada and all its territory east of the Mississippi R. to England, and Spain yielded Florida to England. France retained the islands of St. Pierre and Miquelon in the Gulf of St. Lawrence. Worldwide, France was humbled and the treaty marked the start of the colonial and maritime supremacy of Great Britain. Britain's success was costly, however, and Parliament's attempt to cover its debts, and to pay for a continuing military presence in America, by direct taxation of the colonists soon caused strained relations between mother country and colonies.

The estimated colonial **population** was 1,610,000.

1760 Aug. 7 In the **French and Indian War** (1754–1763), Fort Loudon, Tenn., capitulated to the Cherokee Indians. Capt. Demere surrendered under condition that his troops be allowed to retreat unimpeded. On Aug. 10 the garrison was massacred by Indians while retreating to Fort Prince George in South Carolina.

1760 Nov. 29 **Detroit was surrendered** to Maj. Robert Rogers by the French Commander Belêtre.

1761 Feb. 24 Strong **colonial opposition to English rule** was inaugurated by James Otis in his controversial political speech against writs of assistance before the Supreme Court of Massachusetts. Later (1764) he published his famous pamphlet, *The Rights of the British Colonies Asserted and Proved*, in which he stated that power ultimately derives from the people.

1761 Dec. 2 In an effort to control **colonial encroachment on Indian territories**, governors of the frontier colonies were instructed to gain royal approval for any land grants that might include Indian lands.

1763 The beginning of a **free black tradition** in New England was reflected in the fact that of a Massachusetts population of 235,810, there were 5214 blacks. Most worked at menial jobs in shipyards and homes.

1763 An unusually strong presentation of the Loyalist point of view was put forth in sermons by **Jonathan Boucher**, Anglican clergyman of Virginia. Because of his royalist views, Boucher fled to England in 1775. Thirteen of his American sermons were published in 1797 under the title *A View of the Causes and Consequences of the American Revolution*. Boucher believed monarchical government was a divine instrument functioning under God's sanction.

1763 May 7 **Pontiac's Rebellion**, named for the Ottawa Indian chief who led the uprising, began when Pontiac led an attack on the fort at Detroit. The raid failed and the Indians began a siege. News of the

The growth of the colonies brought with it a strong interest in cultural activities. In the mid-eighteenth century musical concerts were flourishing in the colonial centers, and musical societies, music dealers, and instrument makers all benefited. As in other matters, Boston, New York City, Philadelphia, and Charleston, S.C., led the way, with Charleston seeming to have a special affinity for music. The first music society in America, the St. Cecilia Society, was founded there in 1762. In Europe, Charleston was considered the chief cultural center of the colonies, and many artists, actors, and musicians chose to settle there when they emigrated to America. Other cities could boast of cultural achievements as well. In Boston a group of gentlemen sponsored a concert in Faneuil Hall as early as 1744, and in 1754 the first concert hall in Boston was opened by Gilbert Deblois. Philadelphia boasted four organ makers who produced spinets and virginals as well as organs.

c1760 **John Copley** completed portraits of *Colonel Epes Sargent* and *Mrs. Thomas Boylston*, both of which showed the painstaking care he took in realistic portraiture. Colonial sitters posed for hours on end for many days. In contrast, Sir Joshua Reynolds wrote of his craft in England: "A portrait requires in general three sittings, about an hour and a half each, but if the sitter chooses it the face could be begun and finished the same day. When the face is finished the rest is done without troubling the sitter."

1761 An **early American hymn book**, *Urania, or a Choice Collection of Psalm-Tunes, Anthems, and Hymns* written and compiled by James Lyon, was published in Philadelphia. Lyon, a Presbyterian minister, was one of the earliest American writers of psalms and hymns. His volume replaced older psalm books and ushered in a new period in church music.

1761 The **glassychord**, a musical instrument later known as the armonica, was invented by Benjamin Franklin. It was based on musical glasses, which had been introduced in Europe 20 years before. Instead of filling glasses with water, Franklin made them of different sizes and balanced them on spindles that were rotated by foot action, like a spinning wheel. The performer could reach a wide range of notes and play rapid passages. The instrument achieved considerable popularity, and armonica concerts were given in London and Paris as well as in the colonies.

1760–1764

The most useful contribution to transportation produced in the colonies was the Conestoga Wagon. Although it existed in primitive form by about 1725, it came into its own after 1760, by which time craftsmen of Lancaster, Pa., living along the Conestoga Creek, had converted the wagon into an enormous conveyance using six horses and carrying up to eight tons of goods. The bottom was curved to help keep the load in place whether going uphill or down. The top was a huge white cover, first made of homespun hempen and later of canvas. It rose out and up at each end, giving a poke bonnet effect. The driver rode on the left wheelhorse or on a lazyboard that could be pulled out from the side of the wagon. By so doing, he could see oncoming traffic. This arrangement is thought to be the origin of the custom of driving on the right-hand side of the road. The Conestoga Wagon was vital to the settlement of the Allegheny region. Thousands of these wagons carried farm produce to the cities and hauled to the west the goods needed by pioneer settlers. The prairie schooner, which made up the wagon trains that later took settlers to Mississippi regions, was a light version of the Conestoga Wagon.

c1760   The **first bifocal lenses** were invented by Benjamin Franklin. Twenty years later Franklin wrote to a friend that he had become tired of carrying two pairs of spectacles and had ordered a pair made with two kinds of lenses cut in the same circle of glass.

1761   John Winthrop led a **scientific expedition** to Newfoundland to observe the transit of Venus across the sun. Harvard College sponsored the expedition for the specific purpose of gathering data on the parallax of the sun. The years of the transits were 1761 and 1769. Winthrop wrote of this expedition in a *Relation of a Voyage from Boston to Newfoundland for the Observation of the Transit of Venus.*

1761   One of the earliest known **American cookbooks,** *The Complete Housewife; or, Accomplished Gentlewoman's Companion; Being a Collection of Several Hundred of the most Approved Receipts in Cookery, Pastry, etc.,* by (Mrs.) E. Smith, was published in New York City.

1763   A pioneer attempt at **steam navigation** was made by Henry Williams. Inspired by the work of James Watt in England, Williams built the first steam-powered boat and tested it on the Conestoga Creek in Lancaster, Pa. Although the tests were a failure,

Student life at colonial colleges was reflected in the experience of Thomas Jefferson, who entered the College of William and Mary at Williamsburg, Va., on Mar. 25, 1760, when not quite 17. About this time the students complained about the food. The faculty told the housekeeper, Isabella Cocke, that both salt and fresh meat must be served at dinner, puddings and pies provided on Sunday and two weekdays, and supper must be the same at all tables, even if made up of scraps. Jefferson described the buildings as "rude, mis-shapen piles, which, but that they have roofs, would be taken for brick-kilns." The College of William and Mary was the second oldest college in the colonies, opened in 1694, and its main building was already 60 years old.

1761 June 10   The influence of **Puritan morality** on colonial society was demonstrated in the production of a play presented at Newport, R.I., by the Douglass Company: *Moral Dialogues in 5 parts, Depicting the Evil Effects of Jealousy and other Bad Passions, and Proving that Happines can only Spring from the Pursuit of Virtue.* The play was actually Shakespeare's *Othello.* The advertisement for the performance read: " . . . Commencement at 7, conclusion at half past 10, in order that every spectator may go home at a sober hour and reflect upon what he has seen before he retires to rest." This description failed to disarm Puritan critics of theater. After a few performances by the company in Newport and Providence, the Rhode Island Assembly enacted legislation barring theatrical performances in the colony, with a penalty of £100 for each actor.

1762 May 3   A commentary on the quality of **colonial theater** was made in the playbill of the Douglass Company: "A Pistole reward will be given to whoever can discover the person who was so very rude as to throw eggs from the gallery upon the stage last Monday, by which the cloaths of some ladies and gentlemen were spoiled and the performance in some measure interrupted. . . . "

attack sparked similar raids throughout the region until all but three forts—Detroit, Pitt, and Niagara—had fallen. British forces rushed to their relief. With no French aid materializing, Pontiac in October secured a truce and withdrew to the west. A final peace agreement in 1766 marked the end of the rebellion.

1763 June 2 A surprise **Indian attack** on Fort Michilimackinak at what is now Mackinaw City, Mich., led to the razing of the fort and slaughter of its occupants. The Indians had disguised their intentions by staging a game of lacrosse between two enormous teams outside the fort. After the British troops manning the fort gathered to watch the game, the Indians seized concealed weapons and began the massacre. Those who were not killed were taken as slaves.

1763 Aug. 5 At the **Battle of Bushy Run** the Indians were decisively defeated by the British under Col. Henry Bouquet, who then proceeded to the relief of Fort Pitt.

1763 A collection of **hymns in the Delaware Indian language** was published by the Moravians of Pennsylvania.

1764 *A Collection of the Best Psalm Tunes* by Josiah Flagg was published. The book recorded significant development in the use of harmony in hymns and psalms.

1764 The *Connecticut Courant* began publishing as a weekly newspaper in Hartford, Conn. Renamed the *Hartford Daily Courant,* it became a daily in 1837, changing to its present name, the *Hartford Courant,* in 1887. It became the oldest continuously published newspaper in the U.S. The *Courant* was a patriotic journal during the Revolution and after independence supported the Federalist Party.

1765–1769

The Stamp Act, passed by Parliament on Mar. 22, 1765, raised the subject that was to be a major cause of the American Revolution, taxation without representation. The act levied a tax on all newspapers, legal documents, pamphlets, almanacs, playing cards, and dice by requiring that they bear a stamp. The receipts from the tax were to be used to pay for defense of the colonies. The tax was to take effect on Nov. 1, but even before then American opposition was intense. Merchants refused to buy English goods, stamp agents were threatened with harm if they did not resign, and in some places the official stamps were destroyed. As a result the tax was repealed on Mar. 18, 1766, but not before delegates from nine of the thirteen colonies attended the Stamp Act Congress in Oct. 1765. The congress issued a series of resolutions stating the reasons for colonial opposition to the tax. The same day the tax was repealed, Parliament passed the Declaratory Act, asserting that the British government had the right to make any laws it wished concerning the American colonies.

1765 The **Establishment Act** was passed by the Anglican majority in the North Carolina Assembly. The act supplemented the Vestry Act of 1715 by fixing the salary of ministers at a little over £133 a year and placing control of ministerial appointments in the hands of the governor. This law was the first of its type in North Carolina to receive approval of the British authorities. The power of appointment granted to the governor antagonized local parishes, causing resistance to ministers appointed by the governor and a general

The American school of painting, still in its infancy during this period, was diminished by the death in 1765 of Joseph Badger, whose use of realism in portraiture was a significant move away from traditional European techniques. Badger's works owed nothing to the more refined and technically superior British school of portraiture. Badger was a glazier and house painter who became Boston's favorite artist. His work had charm, but a stiff, archaic style. His best work portrayed children, such as Jeremiah Belknap. He also did portraits of Revolutionary era notables such as Jonathan Edwards and John Adams. Many thought his plain style was more suited to the young, raw, and vigorous colonials than to studied portraits of English nobles. His work reflected the general tendency in all the colonial arts during this period to establish independent styles and techniques.

1765 Probably the **first college arts and letters society** in the U.S., the Well Meaning Society, was founded by William Paterson, a Princeton College student. The organization later became the Cliosophic Society.

1765 **John Singleton Copley** completed a portrait of *John Hancock.* The painting revealed a simple, unsophisticated style and native talent. Although Copley departed from his style upon settling in London about 1775, his impact upon young American artists was great. Their unpretentious portraits formed a characteristic school. This year he also completed his

| Business and Industry; Science; Education; Philosophy and Religion   III | IV   Sports; Social Issues and Crime; Folkways; Fashion; Holidays |

they helped encourage Robert Fulton and his experiments.

1763   A turning from strict **Calvinism** to a more liberal concept of God's nature was shown in two sermons by Jonathan Mayhes, published as *On the Nature, Extent, and Perfection of the Divine Goodness.* Mayhew turned away from the conception of God wielding arbitrary power and characterized by a spirit of anger.

1763   **French Jesuit missionaries were expelled** from the Appalachian area by the British. The move deprived French settlers in the region of effective leadership.

1764   **Spinning and carding machinery** was invented by James Davenport of Pennsylvania. On Feb. 14 a patent was granted and Davenport founded the Globe Mills in Philadelphia.

1763 Oct. Vermont was named. Standing on a high tor, the Rev. Dr. Richard Peters pronounced: "We have here met on the rock Etam, standing on Mount Pisagh . . . to dedicate and consecrate this extensive wilderness to *God manifested in human flesh,* and to give it a new name, worthy of the Athenians and ancient Spartans; which new name is Verd-mont, in token that her mountains and hills shall be ever green, and shall never die."

1764   The **first Dutch Reformed minister to preach in English,** the Rev. Dr. Archibald Laidlie, arrived in Manhattan and soon tried to have dancing banned in the colony. He was unsuccessful; the Dutch continued most of their festivals and frequent supper dances.

1765–1769

The last of the large Protestant denominations to establish itself in America was the Methodist Church. In England it did not formally separate from the Church of England until late in the century. In 1766 Philip Embury, originally from Ireland, formed the John Street church in New York City and preached there. About the same time Robert Strawbridge started a congregation in Maryland, and in Virginia the Rev. Devereux Jarratt, an Anglican, acted as chaplain to the Methodists. Francis Asbury came from England in 1771 and made many converts to Methodism. The first annual Methodist conference in America was held in 1773. In 1784, with authority from John Wesley, the founder of Methodism, Thomas Coke formally organized the Methodist Episcopal Church in America.

1765   The **first chocolate** manufactured in North America was produced at Dorchester Lower Mills on the Neponset R. in Massachusetts by John Harmon. In 1780 the plant came into the possession of Dr. James Baker, who had sponsored Harmon. From Baker's business evolved the world-famous Walter Baker & Co., Ltd., chocolate manufacturers.

1765   **Latin schools** were maintained in at least 48 of 140 Massachusetts communities with a population in excess of 100 families.

1765 May 3   The **first medical school** in the colonies, the medical department of the College of Philadelphia, was organized by Drs. John Morgan and William

This period, following the last of the French and Indian Wars, saw the opening of vast new tracts for westward expansion and the rise of the western frontiersman as an American folk hero. The most celebrated folk hero was Daniel Boone who, after hunting and exploring his way through the Cumberland Gap, saw Kentucky for the first time on June 7, 1769. Boone spent two years exploring the region, then in 1773 made an unsuccessful attempt to settle Kentucky. In 1775, with a company of 30 men, he blazed the Wilderness Road and founded Boonesborough, Ky. The next year he joined the Patriot cause in the American Revolution as a captain in the Virginia militia. In 1778 he was captured by the Shawnee Indians but managed to escape and alert Boonesborough to an impending Indian raid. Boone's land titles in Kentucky were overturned in the courts on technicalities, and he eventually moved to Missouri, where he continued his pioneer existence until his death in 1820. Boone's adventures became widely known after publication in 1784 of *Discovery, Settlement, and Present State of Kentucky* by John Filson, which contained material purporting to be autobiographical.

1765   The term **Sons of Liberty** was first used in the English Parliament by Col. Isaac Barré, one of the few English opponents of the Stamp Act. Later that year, groups formed in Boston and elsewhere in the colonies were called The Sons of Liberty and in some places Liberty Boys.

| Exploration and Settlement; Wars; Government; Civil Rights; Statistics | I | | II | Publishing; Arts and Music; Popular Entertainment; Architecture; Theater |

diminution in prestige of the Church of England in North Carolina.

1765 Mar. 24 The **Quartering Act,** passed the previous year by Parliament, went into effect in the American colonies. It required the colonies to provide housing for British troops stationed in the colonies and to keep them supplied with food and other necessities. The act further enraged the colonists, already provoked by the Stamp Act and other measures considered repressive.

1765 May 29 **Patrick Henry** attacked the Stamp Act in the Virginia House of Burgesses, declaring that only colonial legislatures could impose taxes on their respective colonies. Shouts of "Treason!" interrupted Henry's speech, to which he replied: "If this be treason, make the most of it."

1765 Oct. 7–25 The **Stamp Act Congress** met at City Hall, New York City, in answer to a circular from the Massachusetts House of Representatives. Twenty-eight delegates from nine colonies attended to organize a united resistance to the Stamp Act. On Oct. 19 the congress adopted the Declaration of Rights and Grievances, a series of resolutions protesting taxes imposed by the act, and resolved not to import any goods that required payment of duty. This led to the Petition of London Merchants in 1766, which urged repeal of the act and stressed the injury to English trade caused by the colonial policy of nonimportation.

1765 Nov. 1 A **Stamp Act riot** in New York City coincided with preparations for celebration of Guy Fawkes Day. Colonists executed and buried "Liberty" and then proceeded to break windows, burn an effigy of the governor, mock soldiers, and loot homes of officials. The riot was gradually quelled by fearful citizens.

1766 Mar. 17 The **Stamp Act was repealed** by Parliament. The repeal was approved the next day by King George III and became effective on May 1.

1766 Mar. 18 Parliament passed the **Declaratory Act** stating that Parliament had the power to pass laws binding the colonies.

1767 Mar. 15 **Andrew Jackson,** seventh president of the United States, was born at Cureton's Pond, N.C.

1767 June 29 The **Townshend Revenue Act** was passed by Parliament. It required that colonists pay an import duty on tea, glass, painter's colors, oil, lead, and paper. The £40,000 that the act was expected to yield was to pay salaries of royal governors and judges in the colonies. In Feb. 1768 the Massachusetts House of Representatives sent a letter to other colonial legislatures calling upon them to join with it in action against the duties. The British ordered the letter repudiated and threatened to dissolve any assembly in sympathy with Massachusetts. In Virginia the burgesses responded with a declaration that they had the

Portrait of Lady Wentworth. His portrait of *John Amory* was finished in 1768.

1766 **St. Paul's Chapel,** the oldest church surviving in Manhattan, was built as a subsidiary to Trinity Church.

1766 *Ponteach, or the Savages of America* by Robert Rogers, the first play about American Indians, was published in London.

1766 Oct. The **first permanent theater** in the colonies, the Southwark Theater, was erected on South St. in Philadelphia by David Douglass, owner and manager of the American Company of Comedians. Douglass also built New York City's first permanent theater, the John Street Theater, in 1767.

1767 *Plain Tunes* by Andrew Law, a collection of compositions, was published. The son of the governor of Connecticut, Law cultivated music assiduously and was a "better music booster" of his day. He introduced a system of musical notation that used no staff lines and employed notes of various shapes to signify pitch.

1767 Probably the **first libretto published in the English colonies** was *The Disappointment: or The Force of Credulity,* a light opera by Andrew Barton. It was printed in New York City.

1767 Apr. 24 Probably the **first professionally performed American play,** *The Prince of Parthia* by Thomas Godfrey, opened at the Southwark Theater in Philadelphia.

1768 A commemorative bowl molded in silver by **Paul Revere** was presented to each of 92 legislators in the Massachusetts House of Representatives who resisted royal authority by protesting to King George III about restrictive trade measures.

1768 July 18 Probably the **first American patriotic song,** "The Liberty Song," appeared in the *Boston Gazette.*

Business and Industry; Science; Education; Philosophy and Religion **III**		**IV** Sports; Social Issues and Crime; Folkways; Fashion; Holidays

Shippen, Jr. The school later became the University of Pennsylvania School of Medicine.

1766 A **stagecoach** operating between New York City and Philadelphia advertised itself as a "flying-machine, a good stage-wagon set on springs." Trips took two days in good weather.

1766 Nov. 10 **Rutgers University** was first chartered as Queen's College in New Brunswick, N.J. Established under Dutch Reformed auspices, Queen's College was renamed Rutgers College in 1825 and Rutgers University in 1924. Its first degrees were awarded in 1774.

1767 The **first planetarium** in America was built by David Rittenhouse of Philadelphia. Rittenhouse, a noted clockmaker, plotted the orbits of Venus and Mercury in 1769.

1768 The **first cottonseed oil** made in America was presented to the American Philosophical Society by one Dr. Otto of Bethlehem, Pa. He submitted samples and said he had obtained nine pints of oil from a bushel and a half of seed.

1768 The **first botany professor** in the colonies was Adam Kuhn, who gave his first course at the College of Philadelphia in 1768.

1768 Apr. 5 John Cruger was elected the first president of the **New York Chamber of Commerce** at the founding meeting held in New York City. The organization was probably the first of its kind in America.

1768 Oct. 30 The **first Methodist Church** in America was dedicated. It was the Wesley Chapel on John St. in New York City. The church was rebuilt in 1817 and again in 1840.

1769 A famous American **glassmaking plant** opened at Manheim, Pa., by Henry William Stiegel, whose name became identified with a type of American glassware that reflected a German tradition.

1769 **Porcelain** was advertised for sale by Gousse Bonnin and George Morris of Philadelphia, probably the first commercial manufacturers of this product in the colonies. They produced an elaborate, pierced fruit dish, the decoration and design of which closely resemble Worcester porcelain. Bonnin and Morris apparently ceased production by 1779.

1769 The ties between **American Lutherans** and their German brethren were strengthened by the arrival in

1765 A typical **colonial curriculum** for wealthy young southerners was described by William Kean, director of Queen Anne Country School in Virginia. He instructed "in Latin, Greek, Hebrew, the Grecian and Roman Histories and Antiquities . . . reading, writing, arithmetic-vulgar, decimal, and duodecimal-geometry, planometry, trigonometry, surveying, gauging, Italian bookkeeping, navigation and the proportions of the horizontal dials."

1765 The **marriage custom** outside of New England by this time was to obtain a license by special permission of a magistrate. In New England, custom still called for posting of the marriage banns.

1765 **Education for women** in colonial America emphasized practical learning, as illustrated by the advertisement of a Philadelphia teacher who promised to teach young ladies to spell and print with propriety. He advised them not to be discouraged in their pursuit of knowledge by their age or fear of not obtaining a husband, since he had given "the finishing stroke" to several New York ladies who married shortly afterward.

1765–1775 **Horse racing** in Maryland entered its greatest period of fashion and popularity under Gov. Robert Eden. The racecourse at Annapolis, Md., was one of the best in the colonies.

1766 The **Gloucester Fox Hunting Club**, the first regularly organized fox-hunting group in America, was founded in Philadelphia. Most of its hunting was done across the Delaware R. in Gloucester County, N.J.

1766 Some **popular games** in New York City were suggested by James Rivington's advertisement that he imported "battledores, shuttlecocks, cricket balls, pellets, racquets for tennis and fives, and backgammon tables."

1767 Dec. 21 An incredible **hunting story**, and one of the earliest examples of the American tall tale, appeared in the Boston *Evening-Post.* It told of Josiah Prescott of Deerfield, Mass., who spied a moose 100 yards away and shot it dead. Immediately two more appeared and his aim was perfect; then another suffered the same fate. "One of the old ones was ten feet high and ten feet long; the other eight feet high and ten feet long. . . . After this extraordinary exploit was over, he was joined by a partner, who being at a little distance, heard the guns, came up to his assistance; and in going home he got help to dress the Mooses: A wild Cat they also killed on their return. This is a fact."

1768 According to New England legend, an **army of caterpillars** invaded both sides of the Connecticut R. this year—three miles front and two in depth—and in

exclusive right of taxation in the colony. While protesting loyalty to the king, they entered into an agreement not to import goods on which Parliament raised revenues and, after a certain date, to stop buying a long list of embargoed items.

1767 July 11 **John Quincy Adams,** the sixth president of the United States, was born in Braintree, Mass.

1768 Oct. 1 **British troops landed in Boston.** British warships had arrived from Halifax in Boston harbor on Sept. 28. Two regiments of troops came ashore and took up quarters in the city.

1769 The **first California mission,** San Diego de Alcala, was established by Father Junipero Serra, a Franciscan friar. Within 15 years he established eight others along the Camino Real (King's Highway), the northernmost at San Francisco Bay. These were the first permanent settlements in California.

1769 **Whitehall,** an impressive late Georgian mansion, was built in Anne Arundel County, Md. It was equipped with the only known interior water closet in colonial America.

1769 The first known American sculptor, Mrs. **Patricia Lovell Wright** of Bordentown, N.J., left America for London. Earlier she did the bust of *Thomas Penn* now housed in Independence Hall, Philadelphia.

1769 Sept. 18 Possibly the **first spinet** made in America was constructed by John Harris of Boston. Some have said that Gustavus Hesselius had made spinets as early as 1743 in Philadelphia.

1770–1774

The first clashes of the coming revolution occurred during this period, among them the Boston Massacre in 1770 and the Boston Tea Party in 1773. This period also saw the rise of organized political resistance to parliamentary and royal excesses in the form of the first Continental Congress, which met from Sept. 5 to Oct. 26, 1774, in Philadelphia. There were 55 delegates representing all the colonies except Georgia. Peyton Randolph of Virginia was elected president and Charles Thompson of Pennsylvania secretary. The most important action, taken on Oct. 20, was the formation of the Continental Association, which forbade the importation and use of English products and proposed that colonial exports be prohibited. The delegates also adopted a number of resolutions opposing the Intolerable Acts, the Quebec Act, the maintenance of British troops in towns in peacetime, and the dissolution of colonial assemblies. The rights of the colonists, including rights to "life, liberty, and property," were also expressed. The congress voted to assemble again on May 10, 1775.

The estimated colonial **population** was 2,205,000.

1770 Mar. 5 In what came to be called the **Boston Massacre,** five colonists were killed when British troops fired on a mob of men and boys who had been taunting them and throwing stones. Capt. Thomas Preston, commander of the British contingent, and six of his men were charged with murder. They were defended in court by John Adams and Josiah Quincy. All were acquitted but two soldiers who were found guilty of manslaughter.

1770 Apr. 12 The **Townshend Acts** were repealed through the efforts of Lord Frederick North. Realizing that the colonies were being pushed too far,

The rising prestige of American artists in the world was reflected in the career of John Singleton Copley, who was at the peak of his powers at this time, and was soon to become one of America's earliest expatriate artists. A Bostonian and a successful portrait painter by the time he was 20, Copley moved to England about 1775 and remained there for the rest of his life. In England he enjoyed great popularity, and completed a number of his best historical paintings, such as *The Death of Lord Chatham* (c1780), which won him election to the Royal Academy, and the *Siege of Gibraltar* (1790). He also painted portraits of the royal family and the famous *Family Picture* of his wife and children. Nevertheless, Copley's reputation rests primarily on the portraits he painted in America, including those of many of the leading citizens of New England.

1770 *The New England Psalm singer, or American Chorister* by William Billings of Boston, containing psalms, anthems, and canons, was published. Billings, the most popular composer among native-born Americans of the second half of the eighteenth century, produced several collections, including: *The Singing Master's Assistant* (1778); *Music in Miniature* (1779); and *The Suffolk Harmony* (1786). Among his most famous hymn tunes were "Majesty," "Chester," and "The Bird."

| Business and Industry; Science;
Education; Philosophy and Religion III | | IV Sports; Social Issues and Crime;
Folkways; Fashion; Holidays |

Pennsylvania of Justus Henry Christian Helmuth, a distinguished theologian. He wrote a number of devotional and theological tracts that kept Lutherans in the colonies in touch with Lutheran scholarship in Europe.

1769 The continued dominance of **religious tradition** over America's scientific community was reflected in a conclusion accepted at Harvard that reptiles in America were descendants of Noah's creatures.

1769 **Anthracite coal** was used in a forge for the first time in Wilkes-Barre, Pa. It had been discovered as early as 1762 by Connecticut pioneers in Pennsylvania. It was little used until the beginning of the nineteenth century.

spite of efforts of 1000 frantic men, devoured everything for 100 miles. Then they marched into the river and drowned, poisoning the waters. Only the arrival of millions of pigeons, which were hunted for food, kept settlers in Vermont from starvation.

1769 Nov. 30 The employment of **amateur musicians in professional orchestras** of the day was reflected in the following advertisement, which appeared in the *Pennsylvania Gazette* of Philadelphia: "The Orchestra, on Opera Nights, will be assisted by some musical Persons, who as they have no View but to contribute to the Entertainment of the Public, certainly claim a Protection from any Manner of Insult." It was a widespread custom in the eighteenth century to fill out inadequately staffed professional orchestras with gentleman amateurs, wealthy performers who donated their services out of love for music.

1770–1774

The curious history of the American Shaker movement began during this period. The Shakers, officially the United Society of Believers in Christ's Second Coming, had been established in England for a number of years when Ann Lee, known as Mother Ann, arrived in New York State on Aug. 6, 1774, following a vision that told her to travel to America. In 1776 she and eight followers—six men and two women—settled at Watervliet, near Albany. Members of the movement became known as Shakers because of the trembling movements their bodies made when they were in a state of religious fervor. Mother Ann's tour of New England in 1781 aroused animosity because her followers claimed she embodied the second coming of Christ. The Shaker faith centered upon public confession of sins and preparation for the second coming, and Mother Ann added strictures against sexual intercourse and marriage (which ultimately doomed the sect), war, the bearing of arms, and oath-taking. After her death in 1785, her followers composed a life story that made much of the persecutions she encountered in England and America and the supposedly miraculous manner of her deliverance from them. By 1825, eighteen Shaker communities had been founded in eight states, as far west as Indiana, but by 1860 the movement had begun to decline. Today the movement is known especially for its furniture and handcrafts, which were famous for their simplicity and high quality of workmanship.

1770 The **first chemistry textbook**, *A Syllabus of a Course of Lectures on Chemistry* by Benjamin Rush,

The first large-scale street lighting projects began during this period, although street lighting had begun in the major colonial cities in the 1750s. Philadelphia had installed some 320 oil lamps by 1767, and in Charleston, S.C., in 1762 one Joseph Wilson contributed £300 for street lamps and three months of maintenance. The need for street lighting as an aid to citizens engaged in evening commerce or cultural activities and also as a deterrent to steadily rising urban crime, had been growing throughout the mid-eighteenth century. In 1770 Charleston began a program of street lighting at public expense, and in 1771 Philadelphia purchased a large number of new lamps. It also levied a £20 fine for breaking a lamp. Boston street lighting came comparatively late, but on Mar. 2, 1774, its streets were illuminated by 310 lamps, tended by one Edward Smith with the assistance of seven lamplighters. The lamps were kept lighted in the evenings from Oct. 1 to May 1.

c1770 The **tower hairstyle**, which first came into vogue in 1710, made a reappearance on the colonial fashion scene, this time in a highly exaggerated form. After being frizzled, hair was piled up high over pads until there was a mountain of curls. It was then greased with pomatum, powdered, and finally decked with all kinds of paraphernalia—beads, jewels, ribbons, lace, feathers, and flowers. From the tower thick false curls dangled alongside the cheeks. Sometimes an ostrich feather a yard high flew above the tower. Hairdressing took hours and hairdressers were in great demand.

Parliament was persuaded to withdraw all Townshend duties except that on tea. The colonies responded by lifting their embargo on goods shipped from England, thus improving relations between England and America. The tax on tea remained, as did the colonial embargo on tea.

1772 The **Watauga Association,** formed to govern an area outside the normal jurisdiction of any colony, became the first independent local government in North America. The land was originally ceded by the Six Nations to the British in what is now Tennessee. Not knowing what else to do with it, the British turned the area over to an elected committee of five, who ruled according to the Articles of the Watauga Association.

1773 Feb. 9 **William Henry Harrison,** the ninth president of the United States, was born at Berkeley, Va.

1773 Apr. 27 The **Tea Act** was passed by Parliament. The act was designed to save the East Indian Company from bankruptcy by remitting all British duties on tea while retaining the tax on tea exported to America. This enabled the company to cut its price and undersell colonial competition. The company's resulting monopoly all but destroyed American tea merchants.

1773 Dec. 16 In the celebrated **Boston Tea Party,** a group of men dressed as Indians boarded three British ships in Boston harbor and threw their cargoes of tea, 342 chests worth £18,000, into the water. The action was the climax of growing colonial opposition to the Tea Act.

1774 Mar. 31 The first of the **Intolerable Acts,** also known as the Coercive Acts, was passed by Parliament. The Coercive Acts were punitive measures against Massachusetts for the Boston Tea Party. This act closed the port of Boston until payment was made for the destroyed tea. The three subsequent acts were the Massachusetts Government Act (May 20), which forbade public meetings unless sanctioned by the governor; the Administration of Justice Act (May 20), under which any British officials accused of capital offenses were to be transferred from Massachusetts to England or to another colony for trial; and the Quartering Act (June 2), which required Massachusetts residents to house and feed British troops.

1774 May 17 The first call for an **intercolonial congress** was issued by Rhode Island. The appeal was echoed almost immediately by Philadelphia and New York, and led to the First Continental Congress.

1774 June 2 The old **Quartering Act** was extended. It required that colonial homes be made available to soldiers wherever existing quarters were inadequate, and applied to all the colonies.

1774 June 22 The **Quebec Act** was passed by Parliament. It established a permanent government

1770 The first house at **Monticello** was built by Thomas Jefferson from his own designs. Its plan showed his great interest in pure classicism and in the temple forms of Greek and Roman architecture, especially as evidenced by large porticoes. Monticello later was completely rebuilt and enlarged, but still in keeping with classical forms. Plans for Monticello absorbed Jefferson's attention from his early manhood. Its foundations were dug in 1769, the year of his first election to the House of Burgesses. Monticello stands to this day.

1771 **Benjamin Franklin** began writing his *Autobiography,* which he took up again in 1784, and again in 1788–1789. The work, never completed, carried the story of his life up to 1759 and was originally designed to inform his son, William, then governor of New Jersey, of his background. Franklin included a wealth of remarks on religion, literary life, and utilitarian philosophy, as well as a colorful account of his experiences in Philadelphia, Boston, and London.

1772 **Charles Willson Peale,** a versatile artist from Maryland, completed the first life-size portrait of George Wahington. The first of many Peale renderings of Washington, the portrait depicted him at the age of 40 as a colonel, in the uniform he wore during the French and Indian War.

1774 The influence of **politics in American drama** was reflected in an anonymous play attributed to a southerner, *A Dialogue Between a Southern Delegate and His Spouse on His Return from the Grand Continental Congress.* The play, expressing the Tory viewpoint on the political situation of the time, was a sharp satire on the workings of congress. Other Tory dramas were *The Americans Roused* (1775) by Jonathan Sewall; *The Blockade* by Gen. John Burgoyne, which was performed in Boston in 1775 but not published; and the anonymous *Battle of Brooklyn* (1776). Burgoyne's opus prompted the fiercely patriotic, albeit anonymous, farce *The Blockheads* (1776).

1774 The novel *Die Leiden des Jungen Werthers* [The Sorrows of Young Werther] by Johann Wolfgang von Goethe attained a phenomenal popularity in the colonies. Based on Goethe's unrequited love for Charlotte

was published in Philadelphia, Pa. Rush, who taught at the College of Philadelphia, held the first chemistry professorship in America.

1770 The **College of Charleston** was established. A charter was granted in 1785 and classes began in 1790. In 1837 it became the first municipal college in the U.S.

1770 The **first mental hospital** in the colonies, the Public Hospital for Persons of Insane and Disordered Minds, was opened at Williamsburg, Va. It later became the Eastern Lunatic Asylum, and still later the Eastern State Hospital.

1772 The **first foundry for casting type** in America was completed. It could not produce enough type to fill the needs of colonial newspapers. Consequently, when the Revolution broke out, the colonies were cut off from imported type from England and journalism in America was seriously disrupted.

1773 The **first commercial roster** by Robert Aitken of Philadelphia, Pa., was published. It was *Aitken's General Register and the Gentleman's and Tradesman's Complete Annual Account Book, and Calendar, for the Pocket or Desk, for the year of our Lord, 1773.*

1773 Oliver Evans had his first successes in his experiments in **steam propulsion.** The inventor of a cylinder flue boiler for high-pressure steam engines, Evans demonstrated the first practical steam-powered vehicle in Philadelphia in 1804.

1773 John Winthrop, the astronomer and mathematician, received the first honorary LL.D degree granted by Harvard College.

1771 The **umbrella** as protection against the sun was introduced in Philadelphia amid a storm of ridicule. Newspapers considered it effeminate. Doctors, however, recommended it as a means of avoiding vertigo, epilepsy, sore eyes, fevers, etc.

1771 Mar. 15 An unusual **marriage** was recorded in the *Virginia Gazette:* "Yesterday was married, in Henrico, Mr. William Carter, aged 23, to Mrs. Sarah Ellyson, Relict of Mr. Gerard Ellyson, deceased, aged 85, a sprightly old Tit, with three Thousand Pounds Fortune." Publication of the bride's wealth was common throughout the colonies. As for marrying late, many widows survived three or four husbands.

1772 Nearly 100 **private carriages** were owned in Philadelphia, indicating the city's reputation as a center of high society.

1773 In a comment on **women's fashions,** a Virginia diarist sadly noted the arrival of a batch of women's stays (corsets): "[They] are produced upwards so high that we can have scarce any view at all of the Ladies' Snowy Bosoms; and on the contrary, they are extended downwards so low that whenever ladies who wear them, either young or old, have occasion to walk, the motion necessary for Walking, must, I think, cause a disagreeable Friction of some part of the body against the lower edge of the Stays which is hard and unyielding." Stays were worn by old and young alike. Even ten-year-old girls were forced to girdle their bodies.

1773 **Thomas Burling,** an eminent cabinetmaker of the colonial period, began his career as a craftsman in New York City.

1773 **Student listings by social position** in the Harvard College catalog were discontinued after this year.

1773 Mar. The rioting and wild festivities that marked **New Year's Day** in New York were somewhat curbed by the colonial legislature, which outlawed the discharge of firearms and explosives. New Year's Day had been the most important holiday in the colony during Dutch rule, when it was the traditional day to visit and exchange gifts. When the English took over the colony in 1664, they adopted Dutch customs completely and added a turkey shoot to the day's festivities.

in Quebec and extended its boundaries south to the Ohio R. to include land contested by several American colonies. For this, it was considered by the colonists to be one of the Intolerable Acts.

1774 Sept. 17 The **Suffolk Resolves** were approved by the First Continental Congress. Originally passed by a Suffolk County, Mass., convention, the resolves called for organized opposition to the Intolerable Acts and sanctions against British authority until repeal.

1774 Nov. 17 The **Philadelphia Troop of Light Horse,** one of the earliest revolutionary military groups established in the colonies, was founded by 26 patriots of Philadelphia after the meeting of the First General Continental Congress. The troop later became The First Troop Philadelphia City Cavalry.

1774 Dec. 14 The **first military encounter of the American Revolution** occurred. On the report (the news was carried by Paul Revere) that the British intended to station a garrison at Portsmouth, N.H., Maj. John Sullivan led a band of militia to Fort William and Mary, broke into its arsenal, and carried off a store of arms and ammunition. Neither side suffered casualties.

Buff, the novel made the author famous but inspired many of its readers to morbid speculation and emotion. This in turn occasioned numerous warnings in books and periodicals against the effects of what came to be called Wertherism. In one novel of the time, the hero died holding a copy of Goethe's novel in his hands.

1774 Jan. The *Royal American Magazine,* the first American magazine to make frequent use of illustrations, began publication.

1774 Oct. 20 American theater was suspended after an order of the Continental Congress that the colonies "discountenance and discourage all horse racing and all kinds of gaming, cock fighting, exhibitions of shows, plays and other expensive diversions and entertainments."

1775–1779

This period saw the beginning of the American Revolution (1775–1783). Of the numerous events that occurred, none was more momentous than the drafting and adoption of the Declaration of Independence at the Second Continental Congress, which convened in Philadelphia in May 1775. On June 6, 1776, Richard Henry Lee of Virginia introduced a resolution that "these united colonies are, and of right ought to be, free and independent states." On June 11 John Adams, Benjamin Franklin, Thomas Jefferson, Robert R. Livingston, and Roger Sherman were appointed to draft a declaration. Jefferson prepared the first draft; then improvements by Adams and Franklin were incorporated. Lee's resolution of independence was adopted on July 2 by a vote of 12 to 0, New York abstaining. The actual Declaration was approved July 4, after the congress made some further changes. It was not until Aug. 2, however, that a formal parchment copy was ready for signing. Eventually 61 patriots affixed their signatures. The importance of the document lay in its declaration that each person has certain unalienable rights, and that governments derive their powers from the consent of the governed. In an age of kings who were thought to rule by divine right, this was truly a revolutionary philosophy. The Declaration of Independence, combined with the ultimate success of the American Revolution, was destined to usher in a new political age.

The American Revolution provided fresh material for the new nation's poets. Philip Freneau, who was later to earn the title "poet of the American Revolution," wrote a number of satirical poems, among them "General Gage's Soliloquy" (1775) and "General Gage's Confession" (1775), before leaving America in 1776 for the Caribbean. Returning in 1778, he was captured by the British and released. He then turned his poetic talents to the revolutionary cause. Francis Hopkinson, in his ballad "The Battle of the Kegs" (1778), satirized the British reaction during an actual incident, a mine attack launched by David Bushnell on the British fleet in Philadelphia in Jan. 1778. The poem enraged the British and delighted the Patriots, and was the most popular poem of its day. Later poets found the American Revolution a rich source of material. Henry Wadsworth Longfellow immortalized Paul Revere's 1775 ride to alert the Minutemen at Lexington and Concord in his classic American poem "Paul Revere's Ride" (1861).

| Business and Industry; Science; Education; Philosophy and Religion **III** | | **IV** Sports; Social Issues and Crime; Folkways; Fashion; Holidays |

1773 Jan. 12 The **first museum** officially established in the American colonies was founded at Charleston, S.C. In 1915 it was incorporated as the Charleston Museum.

1773 Feb. 27 **Christ Church** in Alexandria, Va., was completed after six years of construction and a total cost of approximately $4070. George Washington purchased a pew for himself and his family at a cost of about $100. He also donated a handsome brass chandelier to the church.

1773 July 14 The first annual **conference of American Methodists** convened at St. George's Church, Philadelphia, Pa.

1774 **Bull baiting** was scheduled for every Thursday afternoon at 3 P.M. on Tower Hill in New York City, according to an advertisement.

1774 The Continental Congress proposed a **ban on frivolous activities** by colonials, including horse racing, cockfighting, gambling, and theatrical exhibitions as an austerity measure during the political crisis with England. Opposition to these diversions persisted well after the end of the American Revolution.

1774 The **first hunting scene** engraved and published in the colonies appeared at the head of "The Hill Tops, A New Hunting Song," in the *Royal American Magazine* in Boston. The scene depicted the death of a stag.

1774 May The rigidity of the **social code in Virginia** was reflected in the publication of a code of etiquette at the colonial assembly in Williamsburg. The code regulated the social behavior of the community, strictly following British customs.

1775–1779

Despite the outbreak of war, new religious groups continued to find the colonies an excellent place in which to grow. Among them was the Universalist Church of America, founded by John Murray, a convert from Methodism who came to America from England in 1770. He traveled and preached for four years in New Jersey, New York, and New England before settling in Gloucester, Mass. In 1775 George Washington named him chaplain to the Rhode Island troops. In 1779 Murray became pastor of the Gloucester First Church, the first Universalist church in the U.S. The Universalist movement spread and in 1790 a convention was held in Philadelphia that drew up a profession of faith and a congregational organization. Murray's Universalism was basically Calvinistic. Later, under Hosea Ballou, pastor for may years of the Second Universalist Society in Boston, the Calvinist strains of Universalism began to diminish.

The somewhat obscure and uncertain history of the American flag began during this period. In Oct. 1775, when Congress created the first naval force, it also set down rules for creation of a flag. The result, variously called Congress Colors, the Grand Union Flag, or the First Navy Ensign, was a flag of 13 alternating red and white stripes, with a field of blue bearing the crosses of St. George and St. Andrew. This flag is believed to be the one raised by Lt. John Paul Jones aboard Commodore Esek Hopkins's flagship *Alfred* on the Delaware R. at Philadelphia on Dec. 3, 1775. The first land raising of the Grand Union Flag occurred at Prospect Hill in Somerville, Mass., on Jan. 1, 1776, during the American siege of Boston. On June 14, 1777, Congress adopted what became known as the Stars and Stripes, a flag of 13 red and white stripes with a blue field bearing 13 stars, one for each state. The tradition that Betsy Ross designed the flag has been almost completely discredited. It has been suggested that Francis Hopkinson, a member of the Continental Navy Board from 1776 to 1778, was the father of the Stars and Stripes.

1775 Jan. 11 Francis Salvador, the first Jew to hold elective post in the New World, became a member of the South Carolina Provincial Congress. On July 31, 1776, he was killed in a skirmish, thus becoming the first Jew to die for American independence.

1775 Mar. 23 Patrick Henry, addressing the second Virginia convention in Richmond, Va., delivered his immortal speech against arbitrary British rule, closing with "Give me liberty or give me death."

1775 Apr. 14 The first abolition society in America, The Society for the Relief of Free Negroes Unlawfully Held in Bondage, was organized at Philadelphia, Pa., by Benjamin Franklin and Benjamin Rush.

1775 Apr. 19 The opening volleys of the American Revolution were exchanged at the Battle of Lexington in Massachusetts. Capt. John Parker, commanding some 70 Minutemen, engaged a British column marching on Concord, Mass., to seize military stores there. The brief fight at Lexington left eight Minutemen dead and ten wounded. The British then marched to Concord, destroyed some colonial supplies, and fought another engagement before beginning a long and costly retreat under colonial fire back to Boston. By day's end, the British had suffered about 273 casualties, the Americans 93.

1775 May 10 Fort Ticonderoga, N.Y., was taken by American forces under the command of Col. Ethan Allen.

1775 May 10 The Second Continental Congress convened in Philadelphia, Pa.

1775 May 16 A Massachusetts draft constitution, the first constitution in America to be tested by popular vote, was completed by the Provincial Congress of Massachusetts, but it was subsequently rejected. An acceptable constitution was finally ratified on June 7, 1778.

1775 May 20 The Mecklenburg Declaration of Independence was supposedly proclaimed at Charlotte, N.C., by the citizens of Mecklenburg County. The declaration, although it bears the North Carolina seal and flag, is generally considered spurious. The Mecklenburg citizens on May 31 did adopt strong anti-British resolutions, the Mecklenburg Resolves, which declared all royal officials suspended from office. This implied independence but did not actually declare it.

1775 May 25 British reinforcements arrived at Boston. They were under the command of Gen. Sir William Howe, Gen. Sir Henry Clinton, and Gen. John Burgoyne.

1775 June 15 The Second Continental Congress chose George Washington commander in chief of the Continental Army. He declined to accept pay for his services, but in 1783, after eight years of war, submitted records of his expenses totaling £24,700.

c1775 The movement toward realism in portraiture was reflected in *Roger Sherman* by Ralph Earl. The subject, a self-made man who was a delegate from Connecticut to the Continental Congress and a signer of the Declaration of Independence, was depicted sitting in a hard wooden chair, stiff and ungainly, the epitome of Puritan vigor and intransigence.

1775 The first two cantos of *M'Fingal* by John Trumbull, a satire on American Tories in the Revolution, were published. Trumbull labored seven more years on the poem, which was published complete in 1782. Although extremely popular, the work was derivative, borrowing from such works as *Hudibras* (1663–1678) by Samuel Butler and *The Ghost* (1763) by Charles Churchill.

1775 Perhaps the first note of romanticism in painting by an American was struck by John Singleton Copley, then in London, in his painting *Brook Watson and the Shark*. The painting depicted a naked boy being attacked by a shark while his companions in a skiff attempt to save him. Unlike other eighteenth-century masters, Copley did not try to point out a moral or load the painting with intellectual content.

| Business and Industry; Science; Education; Philosophy and Religion III | | IV Sports; Social Issues and Crime; Folkways; Fashion; Holidays |

1775 Feb. 22 The first joint stock manufacturing **company** in America, the American Manufactory of Woolens, Linens, and Cottons, was established to promote the production and distribution of textile products. Shares sold on a subscription basis at £10 apiece.

1775 Colonial workmanship was reflected in the response by seamstresses throughout the colonies to an appeal by the Continental Congress for 13,000 winter coats for the Continental Army. The quality of the coats was generally so high that many troops chose to accept coats rather than their bounty. The names of these troops and the makers of their coats are still listed in many New England communities on what is called a Coat Roll.

1775 Mar. 10 Daniel Boone began blazing the **Wilderness Road,** from Fort Chiswell in the Shenandoah Valley of Virginia, southwest then west through the Cumberland Gap into Kentucky and to the Ohio R., where Boone established a fort and terminal station he named Boonesborough. Although the Wilderness Road was for many years the main route for western traffic, it was not improved for wagon traffic until 1795.

1775 James Adair wrote a description of a **lacrosse** game played by Cherokee Indians in Florida. They used a deerskin ball stuffed hard with deer's hair and bats two feet long with deerskin thongs. The game usually was played for high stakes between two large groups, equal in number, and the ball was kept in the air for long periods of time. The Indians were evidently very good at the game.

1775 June 16 Defense works on **Breed's Hill** overlooking Boston were built under the direction of Col. Richard Gridley, the first chief engineer of the Continental Army.

1775 June 17 The Battle of **Bunker Hill** was actually fought on Breed's Hill. British forces under Gen. Howe assaulted the Continental positions three times before the Americans, under Col. William Prescott, ran out of gunpowder and were forced to retreat. The British then occupied Bunker Hill after another skirmish.

1775 June 22 The Second Continental Congress resolved to issue **paper currency** of a "sum not exceeding 2,000,000 Spanish milled dollars." It was decided that the represented colonies (Georgia was absent) should pledge themselves to redeem the bills.

1775 July 3 Gen. **George Washington** assumed command of the troops at Cambridge, Mass., that were laying siege to Boston.

1775 July 26 A **postal system** was established by the Second Continental Congress. Benjamin Franklin was chosen postmaster general.

1775 Sept. 25 Col. **Ethan Allen** was captured while attacking Montreal. He was taken to England and held prisoner until the end of the war.

1775 Oct. 13 A naval **force was established** by the Continental Congress when it authorized construction of two warships, increasing the number to four on Oct. 30. The Continental Navy was formally established on Nov. 28 and rules for its regulation approved.

1775 Nov. 10 Two battalions of **Continental Marines** were organized by the Continental Congress as a component of its naval force. The U.S. Marine Corps was not formally established until July 11, 1789.

1775 Nov. 29 A **Committee of Secret Correspondence** was formed by the Continental Congress, which resolved that a committee of five be appointed to correspond with "our friends" in England, Ireland, and France. Its members were Thomas Johnson, Benjamin Harrison, Benjamin Franklin, John Jay, and John Dickinson.

1775 Nov. 29 In an important **naval victory,** the American cruiser *Lee* captured the British brig *Nancy*, which was laden with guns and ammunition destined for Quebec. *Nancy* was renamed *Congress* and played a key role in forcing the British evacuation of Boston in Mar. 1776.

1775 Dec. 22 Esek Hopkins was appointed the **first commander in chief of the Continental Navy.** His rank was to correspond with Gen. Washington's. His first fleet consisted of the *Alfred, Columbus, Andrea Doria,* and *Cabot,* to which four more converted merchant ships were soon added. On Jan. 2, 1777, Hopkins was formally dismissed because he failed to

1775 *The Group,* a satirical play by Mrs. Mercy Otis Warren, was published but, owing to the outbreak of the American Revolution, apparently never produced. The play satirized Gov. Thomas Hutchinson of Massachusetts and other colonial figures, as did her earlier satire, *The Adulateur* (1773).

1775 The **first pianoforte** made in America was produced by John Behrent in Philadelphia.

1776 *The Fall of British Tyranny, or American Liberty Triumphant* by John Leacock of Philadelphia, a political satire dealing with the conditions that brought about the American Revolution, was published.

| Business and Industry; Science; Education; Philosophy and Religion | III | | IV | Sports; Social Issues and Crime; Folkways; Fashion; Holidays |

1775 July 25 Dr. Benjamin Church became the **first surgeon general of the Continental Army.** On Oct. 4, 1775, with Gen. George Washington presiding, Church was court-martialed for having held "criminal correspondence with the enemy." He was sentenced to life imprisonment, but because of ill-health he was permitted to live in Massachusetts providing he did not leave the colony. It is said that he later sailed for London, but the ship was apparently lost at sea, and Church was never heard from again.

1775 June 17 The memorable words **"Don't fire until you see the whites of their eyes"** were uttered, according to tradition, by Col. William Prescott at the Battle of Bunker Hill. The injunction, by no means completely original, was also ascribed to Gen. Israel Putnam.

1775 Sept. 15 An early but unofficial **American flag** was raised over Fort Johnson on James Island in the harbor of Charleston, S.C. Three companies of Americans led by Lt. Col. Isaac Motte took possession of the fort from the British and ran down the Union Jack. It was replaced by the ensign designed by Col. William Moultrie: a dark blue ground with a white crescent in the upper left corner and the word "Liberty" in white letters across the flag.

1776 July 3 A wartime incentive to promote **warship construction** on Lake Champlain was provided by the Cintinental Congress in a measure authorizing the Marine Committee to hire skilled shipworkers from seaports on the Atlantic coast at a wage of $37⅔ a month and a half pint of rum a day.

follow orders from the Continental Congress.

1776 Jan. 1 **Norfolk, Va., was burned** by the British after American forces defeated a Loyalist contingent (Dec. 11, 1775) led by Gov. John Murray Dunmore of Virginia.

1776 Mar. Charleston, S.C., set up an **independent government** under a temporary local constitution that was to be in effect until an agreement with England could be reached. John Rutledge was chosen president. This government, said to be the first independent government within the recognized borders of the colonies, successfully defended Charleston against the British army and fleet on June 28, 1776, thus freeing the South from attack for nearly three years.

1776 Mar. 17 The **British evacuated Boston** after American forces seized and fortified Dorchester Heights on Mar. 4. Gen. Howe sailed for Halifax, Nova Scotia, to await reinforcements.

1776 Apr. 12 North Carolina became the **first colony to propose independence** formally when the North Carolina Provincial Congress instructed its delegates to the Continental Congress to vote for independence.

1776 June 27 The **first American soldier executed** by order of a military court, Thomas Hickey, was hanged near Bowery Lane in New York City. Hickey had been condemned as a traitor for conspiring to deliver Gen. Washington to the British.

1776 July 2 The first colonial statute granting **women's suffrage** was passed by New Jersey. It remained in force until 1807, when it was reversed.

1776 July 8 The **first public reading of the Declaration of Independence** was given by John Nixon to an assembly of Philadelphians. He had been chosen for this distinction by the sheriff of Philadelphia. The next day the Declaration was read before George Washington's troops in New York City.

1776 Aug. 2 The **Declaration of Independence was signed** by the members of the Continental Congress. Though it had been approved on July 4, the draft document had been signed only by John Hancock and Charles Thomson, the president and secretary. The names of the signers were withheld from the public for more than six months because, if independence were not achieved, their treasonable act might result in their deaths.

1776 Aug. 27 In the Battle of **Long Island, N.Y.,** American forces commanded by Gen. Israel Putnam and Gen. John Sullivan were defeated by the British under Gen. Sir William Howe and Gen. Sir Henry Clinton. Howe took Gen. Sullivan prisoner. On Aug. 30 the Americans evacuated Long Island and crossed to Manhattan.

1776 Sept. Benjamin Franklin was chosen by the Continental Congress to represent the U.S. in

1776 Jan. 8 During a production in Boston of *The Blockade* by Gen. John Burgoyne, a sergeant of the British army jumped on stage and announced "The Yankees are attacking our work on Bunker's Hill."

1776 Jan. 10 *Common Sense* by Thomas Paine was published. The pamphlet, which contained the first demand for complete independence for the American colonies, sold 100,000 copies in less than three months. No other book in the U.S. has had such a quick or large sale relative to population. The pamphlet was highly influential in swinging the tide of popular opinion toward a clean break with the mother country.

1776 July 6 The **Declaration of Independence was published** for the first time in the *Pennsylvania Evening Post* under the title "A Declaration by the Representatives of the United States of America, in General Congress assembled." The *Post* was sold for "only two coppers" and was published every Tuesday, Thursday, and Saturday evening. A four-page paper, it devoted its entire front page and the first column of its second page to the Declaration.

Business and Industry; Science; Education; Philosophy and Religion		Sports; Social Issues and Crime; Folkways; Fashion; Holidays
III		**IV**

1776 Dec. 5 The **Phi Beta Kappa** fraternity was founded at the College of William and Mary as a social fraternity of five students. It was the first social fraternity at an American college. In 1831 Phi Beta Kappa became an honorary fraternity for students of academic distinction.

1775 Dec. 3 Raising of the **first official American flag** took place aboard the *Alfred,* the flagship of Commodore Esek Hopkins, on the Delaware R. Because the Navy was governed by Congress the flag was called Congress Colors, and was later variously known as the Grand Union Flag and First Navy Ensign. This standard remained the colonial flag until superseded by the Stars and Stripes on June 14, 1777.

1776 The **first cocktail** was said to have been made by Betsy Flanagan, a barmaid at Halls Corners, Elmsford, N.Y. The back of the bar was decorated with tail feathers. According to tradition, when an already inebriated customer called for a glass of "those cocktails," she made him a mixed drink and put a feather in it.

1777 A new process for manufacturing **nails** from cold iron was invented by Jeremiah Wilkinson of Cumberland, R.I.

negotiations with France for a treaty of commerce.

1776 Sept. 6   The first **submarine attack,** by David Bushnell's submersible craft *Turtle,* was initiated unsuccessfully against Adm. Richard Howe's flagship *Eagle* in New York Bay off Manhattan Island. A second attempt to sink British shipping later in September also failed.

1776 Sept. 9   The Continental Congress resolved that the words "**United States**" were to replace the words "United Colonies."

1776 Sept. 15   The **Continental Army evacuated New York City,** which was then occupied by the British under Howe.

1776 Sept. 21   A **New York City fire** destroyed most of the older part of the city, including many of the best Dutch colonial structures in America.

1776 Sept. 22   Capt. **Nathan Hale** of Connecticut was executed by the British in New York City for spying. Before he was hanged he said, "I only regret that I have but one life to lose for my country."

1776 Nov. 16   **Fort Washington** on Manhattan Island fell to the British, who took about 2000 prisoners.

1776 Dec. 19   The first number of *The Crisis* by Thomas Paine, a series of pamphlets written to bolster the morale of the Continental Army, was issued. It was immortalized by its famous first sentence, "These are the times that try men's souls."

1776 Dec. 26   In the Battle of **Trenton,** N.J., Gen. Washington captured nearly 1000 mercenary Hessian troops in an early morning surprise raid.

1777 Jan. 3   The Battle of **Princeton,** N.J., was fought and won by the Continental Army. Gen. Washington again attacked in the early morning, as he had at Trenton the previous week.

1777 July   The **Vermont state constitution,** drafted this month, made Vermont the first state to abolish slavery and adopt universal male suffrage without regard to property. It was followed to a lesser degree by other New England states, which with Vermont were destined to become strongholds of abolitionism in the 1850s. Vermont had declared itself an independent state on Jan. 16, 1777.

1777 July 6   **Fort Ticonderoga,** N.Y., was abandoned by Patriot forces under Gen. Arthur St. Clair to a superior British force commanded by Gen. Burgoyne. St. Clair, with approximately 3000 troops, joined Gen. Philip Schuyler at Fort Edward, N.Y.

1777 Aug. 16   Americans under Gen. John Stark defeated the British at **Bennington,** Vt., killing about 200 and capturing 600. The British detachment commanded by Lt. Col. Friedrich Baum had been sent by Gen. Burgoyne in search of provisions.

1777 Sept. 11   In the Battle of **Brandywine,** Pa., the Continental Army under Gen. Washington was defeated by British forces under Gen. Howe, who

1777   *Night Thoughts* by the Rev. Edward Young, a best-selling book of poems, was published. A great success in Europe as well as America, the book remained popular well into the nineteenth century.

1777   **California's oldest building,** the chapel of San Juan Capistrano mission, was completed. The mission had been established the year before.

1777   The first American edition of the **Bible** in English was published. It consisted of the New Testament alone. The first complete Bible in English published in America appeared in 1782.

| Business and Industry; Science; Education; Philosophy and Religion III | | IV Sports; Social Issues and Crime; Folkways; Fashion; Holidays |

1777 In Virginia an advertisement for **weaver apprentices** was placed by the Manufacturing Society of Williamsburg, offering employment for young blacks, boys to be aged 15 to 20 and girls 12 to 15. All apprentices, however, were to be retained as slaves.

1776 The first community in America to adopt the name **Washington** in honor of the commander of the Continental Army was a town in eastern North Carolina at the head of the Pamlico R. estuary.

1776 July 13 Opposition to the use of **titles of rank** by persons in America was spearheaded by the *Pennsylvania Evening Post.*

1778 Probably the **first pharmacopoeia** published in the U.S., *Pharmacopoeia Simpliciorum & Efficaciorum* by William Brown, chief physician of government hospitals, was issued in Philadelphia, Pa.

1776 Nov. 16 The **first salute to a U.S. flag** (Grand Union Ensign) was a volley of 11 guns fired by Fort Orange on St. Eustatius, Dutch West Indies. The salute was in response to a volley fired from the *Andrea Doria* commanded by Capt. Isaiah Robinson.

continued to advance on Philadelphia.

1777 Sept. 14 Gen. **Burgoyne crossed the Hudson** R. over a bridge of boats and encamped at Saratoga, N.Y.

1777 Sept. 19 In the first Battle of **Bemis Heights,** also known as the Battle of Freeman's Farm, the British under Gen. Burgoyne gained some ground from the Americans under Gen. Horatio Gates but lost 500 men. Almost 300 Americans were killed.

1777 Sept. 19 The **Continental Congress fled Philadelphia,** which was threatened by British forces.

1777 Sept. 25–Dec. 23 The **Conway Cabal,** an alleged plot to remove George Washington as commander of the Continental Army, followed Washington's defeats at Brandywine and Germantown and Gen. Horatio Gates's victory at Saratoga. The plotters wished to put Gates in Washington's place. Gen. Thomas Conway, whose promotion had been opposed by Washington, wrote an indiscreet letter to Gates. Its contents, in distorted form, were then reported to Washington. When details of the plot leaked out, public opinion was overwhelmingly on Washington's side. Actually, Conway seems to have been more the victim of the plotters than the guilty party. He resigned from the army in 1778.

1777 Sept. 26 Philadelphia was occupied by British forces under Gen. Howe.

1777 Oct. 4 At **Germantown,** near Philadelphia, Gen. Washington attacked the British but was repulsed by Gen. Howe. The Americans lost about 600 men in this battle.

1777 Oct. 7 In the second Battle of **Bemis Heights,** near Saratoga, N.Y., the Americans routed a force of some 1500 British. Benedict Arnold was wounded while attempting to force an entrance into the Hessian camp, and British Gen. Simon Fraser was killed.

1777 Oct. 8 Gen. Burgoyne retreated to **Saratoga.**

1777 Oct. 17 At **Saratoga** Gen. Burgoyne, surrounded by a superior force, capitulated to Gen. Horatio Gates, surrendering 5642 British and German troops.

1777 Nov. San José, the first secular community in California, was established on the Guadalupe R. Called a *pueblo,* it had 66 inhabitants whose dissolute lives scandalized the *padres* at nearby Mission Santa Clara. The priests built a road lined by shady willows from the mission to San José to encourage church attendance, but the colonists stayed away.

1777 Nov. 15 The **Articles of Confederation** were adopted by the Continental Congress at York, Pa. They were ratified in 1781.

1777 Dec. 17 Gen. Washington retired with his troops to **Valley Forge,** Pa., for the winter.

1778 Jan. 5 In a **mine attack** against British shipping in the Delaware R. at Philadelphia, four persons were killed aboard a barge after one of the floating mines

1777 *The Seasons* (1726–1730), a collection of four poems in blank verse by the Scottish poet James Thomson, received its first American publication.

1777 The **Lefferts Homestead,** a fine example of late colonial Dutch-style architecture, was built in Brooklyn, N.Y., by Lt. Peter Lefferts. The house featured a low gambrel roof that curved out to form a wide overhang supported by slender columns. Its front door was richly paneled and featured paned-glass side lights and top light. The house, since moved from its original site, is open to visitors.

1779 *The Motley Assembly,* a play attributed to Mrs. Mercy Otis Warren, was a rollicking satire on Bostonians who avoided support of the Revolution for fear they might lose their elevated social status. Some characters in the play were Esq. Runt, "a short fat old fellow: fond of gallanting the ladies"; Mrs. Flourish, Mrs. Taxall, and Mrs. Bubble—all women who preferred British scarlet to Yankee blue.

| Business and Industry; Science; Education; Philosophy and Religion **III** | **IV** Sports; Social Issues and Crime; Folkways; Fashion; Holidays |

1778 A proposal for federal subsidy of **steamboat building** in America was made by Thomas Paine, who recommended the ship design of Jonathan Hulls. In 1736 Hulls had patented in England a ship that would surmount both "wind and tide."

1777 June 14 Congress authorized the **Stars and Stripes,** a flag consisting of 13 stripes alternating red and white, and 13 white stars on a field of blue "representing the new constellation." June 14 has since been observed as Flag Day, although the resolution did not go into effect until Sept. 3, 1777.

1778 Feb. 14 The **first salute to the Stars and Stripes** was fired by the French ship *Admiral La-Motte Picquet* in answer to a 13-gun salute by the *Ranger,* commanded by John Paul Jones. The French volley was, in effect, acknowledgment of American independence.

1779 The **College of William and Mary,** under the direction of Thomas Jefferson, became a university by discontinuing its grammar and divinity schools and creating schools of medicine, law, and modern languages. An elective system was adopted at the same time.

1779 **Sprint races,** a popular diversion of the lower and middle classes around Charlottesville, Va., were

was hauled aboard. The mines had been set afloat upriver by David Bushnell in late Dec. 1777. The attack put British troops and Philadelphians alike into a complete panic.

1778 Feb. 6 A **Treaty of Alliance with France** was signed. It was in part commercial and in part political and military. France recognized U.S. independence, which was for the Americans the goal of the treaty. It was the first and only treaty of alliance made by the U.S. until the North Atlantic Treaty Organization pact of 1949.

1778 May 4 The **Treaty of Alliance with France** was ratified by the Continental Congress.

1778 June The **Secret Service** was organized as Headquarters Secret Service, the first such organization in the U.S. It was directed by Aaron Burr.

1778 June 18 The **British evacuated Philadelphia,** fearing blockade by French ships.

1778 June 28 In the Battle of **Monmouth,** N.J., American forces under Gen. Washington defeated the British under Gen. Clinton after initial reversals.

1778 July The **first foreign diplomat** accredited to the U.S., Conrad Alexandre Gerard, arrived in America. He had been appointed by King Louis XVI of France.

1778 July 3–4 The **Wyoming Valley massacre** was conducted by Tory and Indian forces led by Sir John Butler against the inhabitants of the Wyoming Valley in Pennsylvania. Some 200 were scalped and many others were burned alive when the fort at Kingston was set aflame.

1778 Aug. 30 **American forces withdrew from Rhode Island** after an unsuccessful attempt, led by Gen. John Sullivan, to recapture Newport (Aug. 29) from the British.

1778 Dec. 29 **Savannah, Ga., was occupied** by British forces under Col. Archibald Campbell.

1779 Mar. 3 The British were victorious at **Briar Creek,** Ga., where more than 300 Americans under Gen. John Ashe were lost.

1779 July 15 The fort at **Stony Point,** N.Y., was seized by American forces under Gen. Anthony Wayne. More than 600 British were killed or taken prisoner.

1779 July 26 The **first decoration to a foreign national** was awarded by Congress to Lt. Col. François Louis Teisseidre de Fleury. He was presented with a silver medallion for his part in the attack on the fort at Stony Point, N.Y., where he commanded part of the American attack forces himself and captured the British flag.

1779 Sept. 3–Oct. 28 An unsuccessful **siege of Savannah,** Ga., which had been captured by the British in late 1778, was conducted by a French fleet under Adm. d'Estaing supported by American forces on land. On Oct. 9 Count Casimir Pulaski, a Polish officer

1779 Jan. 9 A **theater notice** advertising the opening night of the season at the John Street Theater in British-occupied New York City stated that all parts would by played "by young ladies and grown gentlewomen who never appeared on any stage before."

1779 A broad democratic program for **public education** in Virginia was proposed by Thomas Jefferson. The plan provided for universal elementary education in schools supported by local districts, with boys of proven ability being provided with further education in academies and colleges. Scholarships would go to those gifted students who could not afford to pay for higher education.

quarter-mile races between two horses of great speed. This was also called quarter-racing, according to Thomas Anbury, a British officer who distinguished between sprints and the two-, three-, and four-mile races held every spring and fall in the big towns of Richmond and Williamsburg. The latter races compared favorably with the big purse races held in England.

in American service, was mortally wounded in a disastrous assault on the city.

1779 Sept. 23 John Paul Jones, commanding the *Bonhomme Richard*, defeated and captured the *Serapis*, a British man-of-war commanded by Capt. Richard Pearson. It was during this engagement that Jones, when asked if he had struck his colors (surrendered), replied "I have not yet begun to fight." After three hours of brutal fighting, Pearson surrendered to Jones. The Americans transferred to the *Serapis* from their own ship, which sank a day later.

1780–1784

By 1780 the Continental Army had suffered its worst privations, its greatest defeats, and its darkest hours. It would continue to lose battles but, by this time turned into a well-trained fighting force by European officers and aided by allied French forces, it endured and marched to ultimate victory at Yorktown, Va., in Aug. 1781. The military phase of the conflict ended at Yorktown, but the diplomatic struggle continued. Preliminary articles of peace were secured on Nov. 30, 1782, after long and difficult negotiations. The Treaty of Paris, by which the war was officially ended and independence formally acknowledged by Great Britain, was not signed until Sept. 3, 1783.

1780 The estimated colonial **population** was 2,781,-000.

1780 Mar. 1 Pennsylvania became the **first state to abolish slavery** (Vermont had not yet joined the Union). The law provided that no child born after the date of its passage would be a slave.

1780 Aug. 16 In the Battle of **Camden,** S.C., American forces uder Gen. Horatio Gates were defeated by the British under Gen. Charles Cornwallis. Baron Johann de Kalb, a Prussian officer who was commissioned a general in the Continental Army, was mortally wounded in the battle.

1780 Oct. 2 Maj. **John André,** adjutant general to British Gen. Sir Henry Clinton, was hanged as a spy at Tappan, N.Y. André had been apprehended on Sept. 23 by three militiamen as he returned from a secret meeting with Gen. Benedict Arnold, who, as commander of West Point, had agreed to surrender the key American fort on the Hudson R. to the British. The plot uncovered, Arnold fled to safety in New York City.

1780 Oct. 7 British and Tory forces were defeated at **King's Mountain,** S.C., by Americans under Col. William Campbell, Col. Isaac Shelby, and Col. Benjamin Cleveland. The British commander, Maj. Patrick Ferguson, and 150 others were killed. Nearly 800 prisoners were taken.

During the American Revolution and the early uncertain days of independence, American intellectual life continued its steady development. The American Academy of Arts and Sciences, the second oldest learned society in the U.S., was founded in Boston on May 4, 1780. The academy, like others of the period, was largely local but kept in touch with other groups. It joined, for example, in an unsuccessful attempt to have the duty on foreign books repealed. The academy began publishing *Memoirs* in 1785 and *Proceedings* in 1846. The moving spirit in starting the academy was James Bowdoin, a leading political figure in Massachusetts who, like many other public figures of the time, was interested in arts and sciences. He was the academy's first president. Bowdoin College in Maine was named for him.

1782 The **first complete English Bible** printed in the U.S. was published in Philadelphia by Robert Aitken. British copyright laws prevented earlier printing of the English Bible, so the publication had to be held off until the colonies were virtually independent.

1782 The fortunes of **Gilbert Stuart** skyrocketed with the reception in London of his painting *The Skater.* It was originally intended as a portrait, but the idea of portraying his subject as a skater struck him when the sitter suggested they leave his cold studio and go skating in St. James's Park in London. The unconventionality of the composition and Stuart's masterful handling won him hundreds of commissions for portraits.

1782 Less than half as much **printed matter** was published in the U.S. as was published in 1775 at the beginning of the American Revolution.

1782 *M'Fingal* by John Trumbull was published in its complete form. The first two of its four sections had been published in 1775. A lively debate on revolutionary matters, it was for a time considered one of the greatest of the American poems.

Business and Industry; Science;
Education; Philosophy and Religion   **III**

IV   **Sports; Social Issues and Crime;**
Folkways; Fashion; Holidays

1780–1784

By the late eighteenth century medical scientists in Europe and America were questioning older practices and theories. In the U.S. Benjamin Rush was the foremost medical scientist of his time, and he typified the new attitude. He was the author of the earliest important work on mental disorders, *Medical Inquiries and Observations upon the Diseases of the Mind* (1812). Another of Rush's studies, *An Inquiry into the Effects of Spiritous Liquors on the Human Body and Mind* (1784), provided scientific support for the temperance movement. Rush, a signer of the Declaration of Independence, became the first professor of chemistry in America in 1769, at the College of Philadelphia and, at the University of Pennsylvania after 1792 he developed the best medical school in the U.S. Unfortunately, in spite of his pioneering investigations of the relationship of bodily and mental illnesses, Rush also remained a strong advocate of bloodletting and purging and so delayed discontinuance of these practices.

1780 The establishment of **scientific associations** was encouraged by a clause in the Massachusetts constitution.

1780 The **first town clock** in the U.S. was built and installed in the Old Dutch Church in New York City by Col. Benjamin Hanks of Litchfield, Conn. Hanks had already cast the first brass cannon and the first bells in America.

1781 Dec. 31 The **Bank of North America** was established by Congress. Under the Articles of Confederation, Congress could not tax, so the Bank of North America was founded with a capitalization of $400,-000 to supply the federal government with money.

1782 The opening of **Harvard Medical School** signaled a movement in America to end dependence on

American cabinetmakers and furniture designers were becoming the equal of any in artistic ability. Chief among them were William Savery, John Goddard, Jonathan Gostelow, and, beginning in the 1790s, Duncan Phyfe. Savery is believed to have lived in Philadelphia from about 1740 and was noted for his original interpretation of eighteenth-century English designs, especially the Queen Anne style. John Goddard was a member of a Newport, R.I., Quaker family of cabinetmakers. His pieces, especially his secretaries, were known for their stateliness. Goddard developed a characteristic block front design that divided the front of his pieces into three equal sections. Examples of Goddard's work are quite scarce. Gostelow worked in Philadelphia and showed originality at a time when many Americans were following English designs. His work had graceful but substantial lines rather than elaboration or ornamentation. In 1788 Gostelow was elected chairman of the Gentlemen Cabinet and Chair Makers of Philadelphia, and in 1789 he made and presented an elaborate font to Christ Church. Phyfe emigrated from Scotland and about 1792 set up shop in New York. He was noted for his use of mahogany and held to high standards of workmanship. His early designs boasted excellent proportions and graceful curves. Later he adopted the Empire style. His final designs were heavily ornamented. He was so much copied that a Duncan Phyfe style came into being.

1780 Nov. Three days of **horse racing** on Hempstead Plains, Long Island, included a Gentleman's Purse, a Ladies' Subscription, and a race run by women riders. Gentlemen who were fond of fox hunting met daily at dawn at Loosely's King's Head Tavern.

1781 The **splendor of Annapolis**, Md., was described in an account by an eighteenth-century French traveler, who noted the city's fine women, elegant horses,

1781 Jan. 17 In the Battle of **Cowpens**, S.C., American forces under Gen. Daniel Morgan inflicted severe losses on a British force led by Col. Banastre Tarleton.

1781 Mar. 1 The **Articles of Confederation** were ratified by Maryland, the last state to do so.

1781 Mar. 15 In the Battle of **Guilford Court House**, N.C., Gen. Cornwallis defeated an American force led by Gen. Nathanael Greene, but heavy losses were suffered by both the British and Americans.

1781 Aug. 1 Yorktown, Va., was occupied by the British under Gen. Cornwallis, who sought supplies and reinforcements from Gen. Clinton in New York City.

1781 Sept. 5 A naval engagement on Chesapeake Bay was fought between a French fleet under Adm. de Grasse, which had Cornwallis bottled up at Yorktown, and a British relief fleet under Adm. Thomas Graves. De Grasse drove the British back to New York City, precluding aid to Cornwallis.

1781 Sept. 8 New London, Conn., was looted and partially burned by British troops under Gen. Benedict Arnold, who had joined the British. He also captured Fort Griswold at Groton across the Thames R. from New London. Arnold treated American soldiers with unnecessary brutality.

1781 Sept. 9 At Eutaw Springs, S.C., the American forces under Gen. Nathanael Greene were forced to withdraw after an assault upon the British under Col. Alexander Stewart.

1781 Oct. 9 At Yorktown, Va., American and French forces began shelling Gen. Cornwallis's encircled army.

1781 Oct. 19 Gen. **Cornwallis surrendered at Yorktown.** The capitulation, which yielded about 8000 British prisoners, virtually brought the war to an end.

1782 An **emancipation law** was enacted by the Virginia legislature under urging by Thomas Jefferson. The bill made it lawful for any man "by last will and testament or other instrument in writing sealed and witnessed, to emancipate and set free his slaves."

1782 The **Great Seal of the United States** was adopted. It was first used on Sept. 16, 1782, on a document granting Gen. Washington authority to consult with the British about prisoner exchanges. On Sept. 15, 1789, Congress declared that the Great Seal was to be the official seal of the U.S. and that it was to be kept in custody of the secretary of state. Since then six dies of the seal have been officially cut and used.

1782 Aug. 7 The **Badge of Military Merit**, popularly known as the Purple Heart, was instituted by Gen. Washington. Only three men of the Continental Army are known to have received the award. It came into disuse after the American Revolution, but was revived in Feb. 1932.

1782 *Letters from an American Farmer* by J. Hector St. John de Crèvecoeur, an extremely popular book on early American life around the time of the American Revolution, was published. The author, whose real name was Michel Guillaume Jean de Crèvecoeur, was a Frenchman who settled in New York, where he collected his famous impressions of the New World. The *Letters* reflected the "noble savage" views of the eighteenth century. The book was reprinted five times in English and appeared in three French editions and two German translations. Crèvecoeur traveled extensively in America, became a naturalized citizen, and was an experienced woodsman and farmer. *Letters from an American Farmer* contains 12 letters reflecting in warm and vivid detail his knowledge of farm life, animals, and the geography of the colonies. He believed in the simple life espoused by Jean Jacques Rousseau and popularized the idea of the Physiocrats that the goodness of man was traced from his connection with the soil. Crèvecoeur in his writings idealized the new man who was to come from the American experiment.

1782 Dec. 5 The **first depiction of the U.S. flag in England** was the work of John Singleton Copley, who painted the Stars and Stripes flying over a ship in the background of his portrait of Elkanah Watson, a well-known sponsor of agricultural fairs in the U.S. Copley did this after hearing the speech in which King George III of England formally acknowledged the independence of the U.S. Watson was on hand when Copley painted the flag.

1783 *The American Speller* by Noah Webster was published. It was the first part of Webster's *A Grammatical Institute of the English Language*, which included a grammar (1784) and a reader (1785). As a separate work, Webster's *Speller* supplanted for a time the *New England Primer* as the principal text for the early grades of public school. It included stories, aphorisms, and maxims on ethical behavior.

1783 May 30 The **first daily newspaper** in the U.S., the *Pennsylvania Evening Post* published by Benjamin Towne, began publication in Philadelphia, Pa.

1784 The English portrait painter **Robert Edge Pine** arrived in the U.S., bringing with him one of the earliest casts of the Venus de Medici statue. Its nudity so shocked Philadelphians that it was kept in a case and only shown privately. Later Joseph Hopkinson, second president of the Pennsylvania Academy, said, "The manners of our country, at that time, would not tolerate the public exhibition of such a figure." Pine became noted for his portraits of such contemporary

Europe for the professional training of American physicians.

1782 The growth of **rationalism** in America was reflected in the fact that Princeton College could claim only two church members in its student body.

1782 Apr. **Washington College** was chartered in Chestertown, Md. Established under Episcopalian auspices, Washington College awarded its first degrees in 1783.

1782 Oct. **Liberty Hall Academy** was chartered in Lexington, Va. The school had developed from Augusta Academy, which had been founded in 1749 about 15 miles southwest of what is now Staunton, Va. Liberty Hall, established under Presbyterian auspices, became Washington Academy in 1789, Washington College in 1813, and Washington and Lee University in 1871.

1783 The **first Protestant Episcopal bishop** in America, Dr. Samuel Seabury, was elected by ten of his fellow ministers at Woodbury, Conn.

1784 A major **depression** crippled the U.S. economy, prompting the states to institute separate measures to aid recovery. The hardships suffered during this depression, which did not end until 1788, led to Shays' Rebellion in 1787.

1784 A lucrative new **trade route** was opened to American merchantmen when the *Empress of China* sailed from Sandy Hook, N.J., around Cape Horn with a cargo of ginseng root for which the Chinese were willing to pay enormous prices. The voyage lasted a year and was very profitable. The trade route enabled American commerce to recover from the crippling British blockade during the American Revolution. By 1789, 18 American merchantmen were plying their way to the harbor of Canton. Salem, Mass., had become the main American port for the China trade.

1784 Probably the **first seed business** in the U.S. was founded by David Landreth of Philadelphia, Pa. The Price family of Flushing, Long Island, preceded him as nurserymen.

1784 Nov. St. John's College was chartered in Annapolis, Md., under Episcopalian auspices. Its first degrees were awarded in 1793. Saint John's, under the name of King William's School, dated back originally to 1696. Gov. William Paca of Maryland, who

coaches, and sumptuous dinners and balls. He also noted that "A French hair dresser is a man of importance among them, and it is said, a certain dame here hires one of that craft at a thousand crowns a year salary."

1782 A state **liquor excise** was opposed by a Worcester, Mass., town meeting on the grounds that the tax was "contrary to the genius of a free people." Liquor was, said the meeting, "absolutely necessary" for the morale of farm workers.

1782 Use of the **scarlet letter,** a letter "A" branded on the skin, or a cloth letter "A" sewn on a garment, to identify adulterers was discontinued in New England.

1782 A major influence on **American hairstyles** in its day, *Plocacosmos or the Whole Art of Hair Dressing,* was published. It was a practical book with many rules for all classes of persons and interspersed with homilies.

1783 The term *Know Ye Men* came into use in Rhode Island to denote advocates of a paper money policy. They were so called because one of their pamphlets on the subject began with the words "Know ye men."

1783 **Enrollment at Yale** reached 270 students, the greatest number at any U.S. college.

1783 The **pace of public transportation** in the U.S. was painfully slow. It took Thomas Jefferson five days to travel from Philadelphia to Baltimore.

1783 By this time some **100,000 Loyalists had fled the U.S.** Also known as Tories, they had suffered various penalties for their loyalty to the Crown, including confiscation of property, removal from public office, and punitive taxation. Probably no more than 10% of the colonials were Tories, who were generally well-to-do, engaged in commerce or the professions, or public officials. Many fled to Canada, some to England. Some returned after the war. Many, however, had remained behind. After the conflict many were able to recover at least some of their confiscated property.

1783 May 13 The **Society of Cincinnati** was founded by veteran officers of the American Revolution. Its

1782 Dec. 5   Martin Van Buren, the eighth president of the United States, was born in Kinderhook, N.Y. He was the first president to be a U.S. citizen at birth. All previous presidents had been born during colonial times.

1783   Slavery was made illegal in Massachusetts by a judicial interpretation of the state constitution of 1780, in which text stating that all men were "born free and equal" was construed as legal nullification of slavery. This year also saw the slave trade outlawed in Maryland.

1783 Sept. 3   The Treaty of Paris was signed by representatives of the U. S. and Great Britain, thus ending the American Revolution. American independence was recognized by the British and the boundaries of the new republic agreed upon: the Great Lakes and Florida to the north and south, and the Mississippi R. to the west. Benjamin Franklin, John Jay, and John Adams were the American agents during the peace negotiations in Paris.

1783 Dec. 24   Gen. Washington resigned his commission as commander in chief of the Continental Army.

1784   Slavery was abolished in Connecticut and Rhode Island.

1784 Nov. 24   Zachary Taylor, 12th president of the United States, was born in Orange Court House, Va.

leaders as Gen. Horatio Gates, Charles Carroll, Baron von Steuben, and George Washington.

1784   Joel Barlow, the poet of Connecticut, was appointed to "Americanize" the hymns of Dr. Isaac Watts, the most popular religious music of the eighteenth century. Barlow's versions were criticized by some for being too far from Watts's originals.

1784   San Xavier del Bac, the single surviving church of the Franciscan missions in Arizona and the most ambitious of all Spanish colonial churches, was begun at Tucson. It was completed in 1797. The church marked the height of Spanish-Mexican baroque style in America.

1784 Apr. 1   Theater performances were revived in Philadelphia with the reopening of the Southwark Theater under the direction of Lewis Hallam, Jr. He delivered a *Monody to the Memory of the Chiefs who have fallen in the Cause of American Liberty.*

1784 May   *Gentlemen and Ladies' Town and Country Magazine,* the first magazine directed at women, began publication in Boston. The magazine included fiction and advice to young ladies but lasted through only eight numbers.

1785–1789

In the nation's early years, it became clear that the Articles of Confederation, which had gone into effect in 1781, were inadequate for the effective government of the United States. On May 25, 1787, the Constitutional Convention convened in Philadelphia. Eventually, all the newly independent states except Rhode Island sent delegates to the session that at first was expected merely to amend the Articles of Confederation. As it turned out, the delegates wrote a new charter, the Constitution of the U.S. Many problems were solved after long debate, such as the question of fair representation for large and small states. This issue resulted in a compromise whereby in the Senate all states would be equally represented but in the House of Representatives representation would be based on population. George Washington was president of the convention and other leading delegates included Benjamin Franklin, James Madison, Gouverneur Morris, Roger Sherman, and Edmund Randolph. Final agreement was reached on Sept. 17 and the document was submitted to the states for ratification. This process reached a conclusion on June 21, 1788, by which time nine states had ratified, the number necessary to put the Constitution into effect. The debate had been long and aroused great passion along with much

The leading publishing event of the period was the serial publication, beginning Oct. 27, 1787, of *The Federalist,* probably the greatest American work on political theory. This series of essays, an outgrowth of the debate over adoption of the Constitution, began with the intent of persuading New York State and others to ratify the new document. The last essay was published on Apr. 4, 1788. The series of 85 essays was initiated by Alexander Hamilton of New York, who wrote at least 51 of the papers. James Madison of Virginia wrote 14 and John Jay of New York wrote five. The authorship of the other 15 is debatable as between Hamilton and Madison. The essays were widely read as they appeared in newspapers, but actually had little effect on the debate over ratification. They did, however, make clear the basic problems of republican government and defended federalism as a means of creating a strong state while perserving individuals from tyranny. The essays appeared in book form in two volumes published between March and May of 1788.

1785   John Singleton Copley, at the crest of phenomenal international fame, was commissioned to paint *Children of George III.*

| Business and Industry; Science; Education; Philosophy and Religion III | | IV Sports; Social Issues and Crime; Folkways; Fashion; Holidays |

had laid the cornerstone at Washington College the year before, was joined by Samuel Chase, Charles Carroll, and Thomas Stone on the Board of Visitors and Governors.

1784 Nov. 18 Samuel Seabury, the first American Protestant Episcopal bishop, was consecrated by the Scottish bishops in Aberdeen and Moray in contravention of the wishes of the Archbishop of Canterbury.

1784 Dec. 24 The **Methodist Church** was organized in America at a conference in Baltimore, Md., even though in England the Methodists did not formally separate from the Church of England until 1791. John Wesley, the founder of Methodism, had sent the Rev. Thomas Coke to America this year as superintendent of the Methodist societies. Francis Asbury was to be associate superintendent. Asbury, however, dominated the conference, was elected superintendent, and then assumed the title of bishop. Although in ill health all his life, Asbury traveled on horseback more than 5000 miles a year to supervise and expand the Methodist Church.

membership was restricted to the eldest male descendants of Revolutionary soldiers. George Washington was its first president-general and Gen. Alexander Hamilton its second.

1784 The **Society of the Friendly Sons of St. Patrick** was organized in New York by Irish veterans of the American Revolution. A century later the society acquired new vigor from U.S. sympathies with the cause of Irish independence.

1784 Nocturnal deer hunting in the Carolinas was made a misdemeanor because of the accidental slaughter of many domestic cows and horses.

1784 A relaxation of American **resentment toward Tories** was reflected in a vote by a New Haven town meeting approving the return to business and to the general life of the community of those whose sympathies were with the Crown during the American Revolution.

1785–1789

Unitarianism took root in the U.S. during this period. Although the foundations of Unitarianism—the belief that God exists in only one being rather than in the trinity of Father, Son, and Holy Spirit—originated in the sixteenth century, it was 1785 before the doctrine came to the U.S. The Unitarian movement in America originated from a change in the Episcopalian liturgy at King's Chapel in Boston. The clergyman responsible was James Freeman, a Harvard graduate. In 1796 Joseph Priestley, the English scientist, established a Unitarian church in Philadelphia. Separate congregations gradually formed themselves into a denomination, adopting the name Unitarian about 1815. Unitarianism grew out of the liberal wing of Congregationalism and was strongest in New England.

1785 The **first dispensary** in America, the Philadelphia Dispensary, was established by Dr. Benjamin Rush.

1785 The **importance of education** to achievement was stressed in a speech by Gov. James Bowdoin before an assembly of the American Academy of Arts and Sciences. Bowdoin, addressing the subject of race and intelligence, stated that the apparently inferior accomplishments of free blacks were due not to any racial inferiority but to the lack of educational

The widely practiced custom of bundling, prevalent in colonial days in New England and Pennsylvania especially, was dying out. The cold of northern winters, which had been a major contributor to the custom's popularity, was now alleviated by better heating and sturdier houses. To bundle, engaged or courting couples got into bed together, but with most or all of their clothes on. The couple was sometimes separated by a board and some girls tied their ankles together. Although bundling implied no improper relationship, it became the target of reformers and was abandoned by the early nineteenth century, although there were reports of bundling in the backwoods of western Pennsylvania in the 1840s.

c1785 The style of **men's clothing** during this period was reflected in a description by a printer of Boston: "He wore a pea-green coat, white vest, nankeen small clothes, white silk stockings, and pumps fastened with silver buckles which covered at least half the foot from instep to toe. His small clothes were tied at the knees with ribbon of the same colour in double bows, the ends reaching down to the ancles. His hair in front was loaded with pomatum, frizzled or craped and

Exploration and Settlement; Wars; Government; Civil Rights; Statistics **I**

II **Publishing; Arts and Music; Popular Entertainment; Architecture; Theater**

1785   Slavery was made illegal in New York.

1785 Feb. 24   Congress appointed **John Adams** minister to England.

1785 Mar. 10   Congress appointed **Thomas Jefferson** minister to France.

1785 May 20   A **land ordinance** passed by the Continental Congress provided the first federal land grant for schools. The act authorized the surveying of townships in the Western Reserve, a tract in Ohio. Each township was to be divided into 36 lots, one of which was to be set aside for support of public schools.

1785 July 6   A new **coinage system,** based on the Spanish milled dollar, was proposed in Congress by Thomas Jefferson. He proposed a gold piece with a value of ten dollars, a dollar in silver, a tenth of a dollar in silver, and a hundredth of a dollar in copper. This proposal was adopted by Congress, and on Aug. 8, 1786, a full plan of coinage was enacted.

1786   Slavery was outlawed in New Jersey.

1786   The **first consul** appointed in the U.S. foreign service, Maj. Samuel Shaw of Massachusetts, was named U.S. consul to China. Shaw established himself in Canton, China, and was reappointed in 1790.

1787 Jan. 25   **Shays' Rebellion,** a farmers' uprising named for its leader Daniel Shays, reached its climax when Shays led 1100 men in an attempt to seize the arsenal in Springfield, Mass. State militia commanded by Gen. William Shepherd routed the insurgents. The uprising had been caused by the harsh economic conditions faced by Massachusetts farmers, who sought reforms and the issuance of paper money.

1787 July 13   The **Northwest Ordinance,** enacted by Congress under the Articles of Confederation, established the Northwest Territory, the region bounded by the Great Lakes on the north, the Ohio R. on the south, and the Mississippi R. on the west. The ordinance established a government for the territory, provided that it could form no fewer than three nor more than five states, set up the procedure by which statehood was to be achieved, and barred slavery in the territory.

1787 Dec. 7   **Delaware** became the first state to ratify the Constitution.

1787 Dec. 12   **Pennsylvania** ratified the Constitution and became the second state of the Union.

1787 Dec. 18   **New Jersey** ratified the Constitution and became the third state of the Union.

1788 Jan. 2   **Georgia** ratified the Constitution and became the fourth state of the Union.

1788 Jan. 9   **Connecticut** ratified the Constitution and became the fifth state of the Union.

1788 Feb. 6   **Massachusetts** ratified the Constitution and became the sixth state of the Union.

1785   The **Rocky Hill Meeting House,** the finest example of a late colonial meeting house in Massachusetts, was built at Amesbury. Its parsonage was constructed in the Georgian style.

1786   The **first extended theatrical engagements** in America were seen this year. Lewis Hallam, Jr.'s, American Company, performing in New York City, gave seven performances of Richard Brinsley Sheridan's *The School for Scandal* (1777) and 18 of John O'Keefe's *The Poor Soldier.* This year also saw the first U.S. performance of *Hamlet,* in New York City at the John Street Theater by Hallam's company with the Irish actor John Henry.

1786   *The Worcester Collection of Sacred Harmony,* which became one of the most popular hymn books of the time, first appeared at Worcester, Mass.

1786 May   The **first musical periodical** in America, *American Musical Magazine,* began publication. A collection of tunes and hymns, it was published and edited by Daniel Read in New Haven, Conn.

1786 Sept.   *Columbian Magazine,* one of the most important periodicals of early American times, began publication. In 1790 its name was changed to *Universal Asylum and Columbian Magazine.* It ceased publication in Dec. 1792.

1787   One of the earliest **collections of secular music** published in the U.S., *A Select Collection of the Most Favorite Scot Tunes* compiled by Alexander Reinagle, was published in New Haven, Conn.

1787   **Erasmus Hall High School,** an excellent example of early Georgian architecture, was erected in Brooklyn, N.Y. Originally a private academy with 26 students, it was the first secondary school to be chartered by the regents of the University of the State of New York.

1787 Jan.   *American Museum,* perhaps the most important American magazine of the eighteenth century, began publication. Its contents were especially rich in early American material. It ceased publication in Dec. 1792.

1787 Apr. 16   *The Contrast* by Royall Tyler, the first American comedy to be performed on a regular stage by a company of professional actors, opened at the John Street Theater in New York City. It became an immediate success. The first stage Yankee in American history appeared as the hero in this prodemocratic play, which ridiculed aristocratic values while extolling the rustic virtues of the hero.

| Business and Industry; Science; Education; Philosophy and Religion   III | IV   Sports; Social Issues and Crime; Folkways; Fashion; Holidays |

opportunities afforded them.

1785 Regular stage routes linking New York City, Boston, Albany, and Philadelphia were initiated. The trip from Boston to New York took six days with coaches traveling from 3 A.M. until 10 P.M.

1785 The first American turnpike, known as the Little River Turnpike, was authorized by the state of Virginia.

1785 The charter of the Bank of North America was revoked by the Pennsylvania legislature. The bank's enemies charged it with causing the economic depression that had begun in 1784. When things did not get better, supporters of the bank claimed that trade was bad because the bank's charter had been lost. In 1787 Democratic-Republicans won control of the state legislature and rechartered the bank. It was the first bank owned and operated by and for merchants. It acquired capital and influence so quickly that it became a center of political rivalry and ambition.

1785 An early trade association, the Association of the Tradesmen and Manufacturers of the Town of Boston, was formed by representatives of 26 trades who convened in Boston. The association grew out of the demands of manufacturers, mostly small artisans engaged in shop and home production, for legislative protection against foreign competition.

1785 Jan. 27 The University of Georgia was chartered in Athens, Ga., as a state university with no denominational ties. The oldest state university in America, it awarded its first degrees in 1804.

1785 Oct. 1 The first city directory in the U.S., *MacPherson's Directory for the City and Suburbs of Philadelphia*, printed by Francis Bailey, was published.

1786 The first steamboat in America, built by John Fitch, sailed on the Delaware R. On Aug. 22, 1787, Fitch ran his second and improved boat on the Delaware R. It used a system of upright paddles at the sides of the boat and attained a speed of 3 mph.

1786 The first recorded strike in the U.S. was called by the printers of Philadelphia, Pa. They were successful in obtaining a wage of $6 a week.

1786 Aug. 7 An early federal Indian act was passed by Congress, establishing two departments, or reservations: a northern department, north of the Ohio R.; and a southern department, south of the Ohio R. Department directors for each were authorized to grant licenses for trading or settling within their department.

powdered. Behind, his natural hair was augmented by the addition of a large queue called vulgarly a false tail, which, enrolled in some yards of black ribbon, hung half-way down his back."

1785 The phrase *facing the music* entered into popular talk from theater jargon. It originally characterized the difficulty an actor faced when stepping before the footlights.

1785 Canton ware became very popular in America. It was imported from potteries located near Canton and Ch'ing-te-chen, China.

1785 George Washington retired from active hunting, giving away his valuable kennel of hounds, which he had renewed after the American Revolution. Washington enjoyed riding to hounds, and between 1783 and 1785 went on three hunts a week during the season.

1785 Primogeniture, or the preserving of a large estate by conveying it intact to the oldest son in a family, was abolished in the Virginia legislature largely through the efforts of Thomas Jefferson.

1786 Aug. 17 David Crockett, legendary frontiersman, congressman, and one of the defenders of the Alamo, was born in Hawkins County, Tenn.

1787 The abundance of commodities that had become available to Americans was saluted by August Tench Coxe in a speech before an assembly in Philadelphia: " . . . we now make ourselves . . . meal of all kinds, ships and boats, malt liquors, distilled spirits, potash, gun-powder, cordage, loaf-sugar, paste-boards, cards and paper of every kind, books in various languages, snuff, tobacco, starch, cannon, muskets, anchors, nails, and very many other articles of iron, bricks, tiles, potters ware, millstones, and other stone work, cabinet work, trunks and windsor chairs, carriages and harness of all kinds, cornfans, ploughs and many other implements of husbandry, saddlery and whips, shoes and boots, leather of various kinds, hosiery, hats and gloves, wearing apparel, coarse linens and woolens, and some cotton goods, linseed and fish oil, wares of gold, silver, tin, pewter, lead, brass and copper, clocks and watches, wool and cotton cards, printing types, glass and stoneware, candles, soap and several other

| Exploration and Settlement; Wars; Government; Civil Rights; Statistics | I | | II | Publishing; Arts and Music; Popular Entertainment; Architecture; Theater |

1788 Mar. 21 A tremendous **New Orleans fire** destroyed some 800 buildings and virtually wiped out the city's old French and Spanish style of architecture. A second fire in 1794 completed the process.

1788 Apr. 28 **Maryland** ratified the Constitution and became the seventh state of the Union.

1788 May 23 **South Carolina** ratified the Constitution and became the eighth state of the Union.

1788 June 21 **New Hampshire** ratified the Constitution and became the ninth state of the Union. With this ratification the Constitution became effective, though not declared in effect until Mar. 4, 1789.

1788 June 25 **Virginia** ratified the Constitution and became the tenth state of the Union.

1788 July 26 **New York** ratified the Constitution and became the 11th state of the Union. For a time North Carolina and Rhode Island refused to ratify, but the introduction of a bill of rights and the threat of economic sanctions eventually induced them to join.

1789 The **Federalist Party** was formed by those who had supported ratification of the Constitution. Considered pro-English, they enjoyed considerable success until 1800, when Thomas Jefferson, a Democratic-Republican, defeated John Adams for the presidency. Eventually the party lost its supporters and ceased to exist about 1820. Alexander Hamilton was one of the party's founders and foremost leaders.

1789 The **first organized temperance group** in America was formed by 200 farmers in Litchfield County, Conn. They pledged not to partake of alcoholic beverages during the farming season.

1789 Mar. 4 The **first session of the U.S. Congress** convened, but only 9 of 22 senators and 13 of 59 representatives appeared. The House had its first quorum on Apr. 1, the Senate on Apr. 5. On Apr. 6 the first Congress was formally organized. By its end in 1791 the first Congress consisted of 26 senators of whom 17 supported the Washington administration and 9 were generally in opposition. In the House the division was 38 and 26.

1789 Apr. 30 **George Washington,** Federalist of Virginia, was inaugurated president of the United States.

1789 June 1 The **first legislation** enacted by Congress was signed into law by Pres. Washington. It was an act to legalize certain oaths.

1789 July 27 The U.S. **State Department** was established by Congress. Thomas Jefferson became the first secretary of state in Feb. 1790.

1789 Aug. 7 The U.S. **War Department** was established. Pres. Washington selected Henry Knox to be the first secretary of war. At this time the regular army numbered 840 men who supervised public lands and guarded the Indian frontier.

1788 A volume of **Miscellaneous Works** by Philip Freneau was published. This book, combined with Freneau's collected *Poems* (1786), marked Freneau's emergence as a major American poet. Some memorable poems appeared in these volumes, for example, "To the Hurricane" and "The Indian Burying Ground." "The Wild Honey Suckle" was considered Freneau's finest poem.

1788 The first American edition of **The Royal Standard English Dictionary** by William Perry, a well-known English dictionary, was published at Worcester, Mass.

1789 **Noah Webster**'s *Dissertations on the English Language,* a scholarly work that reflected the spirit of American nationalism inspired by the Revolution, was published. In this work, Webster sought to set up a characteristically American language, republican in nature as opposed to the language of royalist England. The *Dissertations* grew out of a series of lectures Webster had given in Baltimore four years earlier. They called for a radical revision of native speech, but Webster failed to realize these early ambitions for the language. Webster never outgrew his nationalism, and the line he forged between language and loyalty has left an inheritance of memorable maxims: "a *national language* is a bond of *national union*"; "as independent in *literature* as she is in *politics*—as famous for *arts* as for *arms*."

1789 What has been called the **first American novel,** *The Power of Sympathy; or The Triumph of Nature* by William Hill Brown, was published. The book was written "to expose the dangerous Consequences of Seduction and to set forth the advantages of female Education."

1789 The **Virginia Capitol** was built at Richmond from plans by Thomas Jefferson. It was generally considered the first building of the Classic Revival style in the U.S.

1789 The **Methodist Book Concern** was established in New York City by the Methodist Church to publish religious material and further Christian education. It became part of the United Methodist Publishing House, whose Abingdon Press is the oldest book publishing house in continuous operation in the U.S.

1789 Jan. The first issue of **Arminian Magazine,** the first American sectarian magazine, was published. Edited by Bishop Thomas Coke and Bishop Francis

Business and Industry; Science; Education; Philosophy and Religion III		IV Sports; Social Issues and Crime; Folkways; Fashion; Holidays

1786 Oct. 20 Probably the **first astronomical field expedition** in America was organized by Prof. Samuel Williams of Harvard College, who led a party of students to observe a total eclipse of the sun at Penobscot Bay in Maine.

1787 A growing American belief in **women's education** was reflected in the publication of *Thoughts on Female Education* by Dr. Benjamin Rush. The book supported the argument that to have educated children there must be educated mothers.

1787 **William Samuel Johnson,** the first noncleric appointed president of any English or American college, became president of Columbia College, serving until 1800. He was the son of Samuel Johnson, the first president (1753–1763) of the school, then called King's College.

1787 The **first cotton factory** in New England was established at Beverly, Mass., under the management of John Cabot and Joshua Fisher.

1787 In a move to promote **manufacturing,** the Pennsylvania Society for the Encouragement of Manufactures and Useful Acts was organized. It supported a protective tariff, inventions, and research. Its Committee on Manufactures, chosen by subscribers to a manufacturing fund, agreed to promote cotton manufacturing and ordered two English carding and spinning machines. By the end of 1788, its factory put out 10,000 yards of cotton and linen. New York City, Boston, and Baltimore established similar societies in the same year, and were soon followed by other cities.

1787 Mar. 10 **Franklin College** was chartered in Lancaster, Pa., under German Reformed auspices. In 1850 the college merged with Marshall College, which had been chartered in 1836 at Mercersburg, Pa., to form Franklin and Marshall College. The two branches of the school were merged at Lancaster in 1853.

1787 Dec. **Cokesbury College,** the first Methodist college in the U.S., opened. The college was named for Thomas Coke and Francis Asbury, the first two Methodist bishops in the U.S. Located first at Abingdon, Md., the college moved later to Baltimore.

1787 Dec. 3 The **first steam-powered boat** was demonstrated on the Potomac R. by its inventor, James Rumsey. The boat was propelled by a stream of water forced astern by a steam-powered pump. Rumsey was awarded a patent in 1791 but died a year later.

1789 The first known **road maps** published in the U.S. were contained in *A Survey of the Roads of the United States of America,* compiled by Christopher Colles and published in New York City.

valuable articles, with which the memory cannot supply at once."

1788 A new era in **furniture design** in America was initiated with the publication in England of George Hepplewhite's *Cabinetmaker, and Upholsterer's Guide.* The trend was away from the rococo designs of Thomas Chippendale toward subtler, more graceful lines. The book was known to most furniture manufacturers in America.

1788 May A celebrated gray stallion, **Messenger,** believed to be the original sire of a fine breed of trotting horses, arrived from England. His line was so successful that upon his death he was buried with military honors on Jan. 8, 1808.

1789 The beginning of a **social courtesy** that was soon to spread elsewhere was seen in the following announcement at a performance in the Park Theater, New York City: "The offensive practice to Ladies, and dangerous to the House, of smoking segars during the performance, it is hoped, every gentlemen will consent to an absolute prohibition of."

1789 The frequent appearance of **George Washington** in his box at the John Street Theater in New York City during the year lent respectability to the theater but also evoked disapproval in certain prominent citizens.

1789 Apr. 23 The **style of address** for the president of the U.S. was a topic of serious discussion. A committee was formed in Congress to devise a suitably lofty style. Sen. Ralph Izard proposed the term "Excellency" while Sen. Richard Henry Lee considered "Highness" appropriate.

1789 May 7 The **first inaugural ball,** to honor Pres. Washington, was held at the Assembly Rooms, New York City.

1789 May 12 The **Society of Tammany** held its first meeting in New York. Its name was derived from an ancient and wise chief of the Delaware Indians, Tammany, and the society was essentially anti-Federalist in character. Its chief founder and first grand sachem was William Mooney.

Exploration and Settlement; Wars; Government; Civil Rights; Statistics	**I**		**II**	Publishing; Arts and Music; Popular Entertainment; Architecture; Theater

1789 Sept. 2 The U.S. **Treasury Department** was established by Congress. Alexander Hamilton became the first secretary of the treasury.

1789 Sept. 26 Congress confirmed John Jay's appointment as the **first chief justice of the U.S. Supreme Court.** He was appointed by Pres. Washington and served for six years.

1789 Sept. 26 Samuel Osgood was appointed the **first postmaster general** of the U.S. by Pres. Washington. Osgood resigned in Aug. 1791 because of the government's removal from New York City to Philadelphia.

1789 Sept. 26 Edmund J. Randolph was appointed **attorney general** of the U.S. by Pres. Washington. In 1794 he succeeded Thomas Jefferson as secretary of state.

1789 Nov. 21 **North Carolina** ratified the Constitution and became the 12th state of the Union.

Asbury of Philadelphia, the magazine was published for two years.

1789 Jan. The **first juvenile magazine** in the U.S., *Children's Magazine,* began publication in Hartford, Conn. It issued only three numbers.

1789 Mar. 2 A law prohibiting theatrical performances was repealed in Pennsylvania. A more permissive attitude toward theater was seen in all the states.

1789 Apr. 11 The *Gazette of the United States,* a celebrated weekly newspaper established to support the Federalist cause, began publication in New York City. It was backed financially by Alexander Hamilton and edited by John Fenno.

1790–1794

Probably the most important political event of this period was adoption of the Bill of Rights, the first ten amendments to the U.S. Constitution. Some had opposed adoption of the Constitution because of its lack of guarantees of such rights as freedom of worship, freedom of speech, freedom of the press, and freedom of assembly. Supporters of the Constitution had promised that if ratified, it would be amended in these respects. Accordingly, on Sept. 25, 1789, Congress voted to submit the amendments to the states. They became part of the Constitution on Dec. 15, 1791, when Virginia ratified them, thereby completing the required number of state ratifications for passage into law.

1790 Mar. A sizable **French colony** was founded at Gallipolis, Ohio, by immigrants who had come to America in response to the glowing claims of the Scioto Company. Named for a river in Ohio, the Scioto Company was organized in 1787 to purchase holdings beside the Ohio and Scioto rivers. It proved a disastrous undertaking and is considered one of the great American swindles. Of 218 French immigrants, about 150 bought land and settled at Gallipolis, the rest at Marietta where a subsidiary of the Scioto Company had another claim. The settlers were in for a miserable time. They were left stranded without supplies and there were legal doubts as to the validity of their holdings. The company itself went bankrupt and was finally charged with fraud. Through the Scioto Company Joel Barlow, the "first American Milton" and a member of the group of writers known as the Hartford Wits, left for Europe to huckster lands to the unsuspecting French. For the most part he was a failure. His enterprise, *La Compagnie du Scioto,* expired

Scientists traveled widely in the U.S. because there was much to study that was new and because there were unique flora and fauna. Invariably, such men wrote about their journeys. While these men wrote as scientists, their writings can also be categorized as travel books. The travelers gloried in the beauty and magnitude of American scenery and often were imbued with the spirit of the Romantic movement. Such a naturalist-author was William Bartram, son of John Bartram, who had earlier recorded his trips to Lake Ontario and Florida. William wrote *Travels Through North and South Carolina, Georgia, East and West Florida, the Cherokee Country, the Extensive Territories of the Muscogulges, or Creek Confederacy, and the Country of the Chactaws* (1791). In the book Bartram revealed a vision of "natural man." His enthusiastic descriptions of scenery influenced such writers as William Wordsworth and Samuel Taylor Coleridge, the latter terming the book one of "high merit."

c1790 Alexander Reinagle composed four sonatas for the pianoforte, the **first piano pieces composed in America.** Reinagle came to the U.S. from England in 1786. After giving concerts in New York City he went to Philadelphia, where he had a successful career as a composer and opera producer. He wrote incidental music for plays and the complete scores for *The Sicilian* (1795) and *The Volunteers* (1795). Most of his works were destroyed in a fire in 1820 but the pianoforte pieces were found among his daughter's effects.

1790 Printing began on *Dobson's Encyclopaedia,* a magnificent American edition in 18 volumes of the *Encyclopaedia Britannica.* Special types were

Business and Industry; Science;
Education; Philosophy and Religion   III   IV   **Sports; Social Issues and Crime;**
Folkways; Fashion; Holidays

1789 Jan. 23 Georgetown College, the first Catholic college in the U.S., was founded by Father John Carroll at Georgetown, now in the District of Columbia. In 1805 the college came under the direction of the Society of Jesus.

1789 Apr. 23 Probably the **first Catholic newspaper** in the U.S., the *Courrier de Boston*, began publication. It published until Oct. 15.

1789 July 4 The **first tariff bill** enacted by Congress set up protective duties on more than 30 different commodities.

1789 Dec. 11 The **University of North Carolina** was chartered in Chapel Hill, N.C., as a state university. Its first degrees were awarded in 1798.

1789 Oct. 7 A **satanic visitation** was reported by the *Hampshire Gazette.* A Connecticut man, imprisoned for theft, told his guards that he was awaiting the devil, with whom he had made a pact. While talking he spread gunpowder over the floor. " . . . When the time arrived . . . that the Devil was to call him—he by some means conveyed fire to the powder, by which means the room appeared to be in flames, and while the guards were in the greatest consternation and surprise—*The Devil carried off the Prisoner!"*

1789 Nov. 26 Thanksgiving Day was celebrated for the first time as a national holiday. Pres. Washington, at the request of Congress, had proclaimed it a day of thanksgiving for the Constitution. Anti-Federalists protested that his proclamation violated states' rights.

1790–1794

Although the U.S. was primarily an agricultural nation, some manufacturing had begun. There were those who thought that with independence the new nation should encourage manufacturing as a way of avoiding dependence on other nations. Chief among these persons was Alexander Hamilton, first secretary of the treasury, who submitted his *Report on the Subject of Manufactures* in 1791. The report favored tariffs and government bounties and said such policies would create employment, attract immigrants, and stimulate investment. Hamilton, however, received little support. Merchant and shipping interests had more to gain from free trade, and the expanding cotton regions of the South did not want tariffs that would increase their costs.

1790 The **oldest lighthouse** still in operation, the Portland Head Lighthouse at Portland, Maine, was ordered built by Pres. George Washington.

1790 The wide use of the **Wilderness Road** by early American pioneers was reflected in the fact that of Kentucky's 75,000 people, more than 90% had traversed the road on their way to the new territory.

1790 The **first cotton mill** in the U.S. was erected by Samuel Slater at Pawtucket, R.I. Slater had been an apprentice of Sir Richard Arkwright in England.

1790 The **first Catholic Bible** in America was printed in Philadelphia by Mathew Carey, the first major U.S. publisher of Catholic works.

During and after the American Revolution patriotic societies sprang up in several cities. Among them were the Tammany societies founded in New York City, Philadelphia, and other cities. The societies were named for the Delaware Indian chief Tammany, who was said to have welcomed William Penn to Pennsylvania. The Tammany Society, or Columbian Order of New York City, was formed in 1786 and incorporated in 1789. The first Columbus Day was celebrated on Oct. 12, 1792, under the auspices of this society. The New York Tammany was the only such society to have a long life, and it became the most powerful political organization in the city in the nineteenth century. Its headquarters, Tammany Hall, became a symbol of graft, corruption, and machine politics in the 1860s and 1870s. The organization maintained substantial political influence well into the twentieth century.

c1790 Followers of **horse racing** began to take an interest in the breeding of horses. Belair, Gimcrack, and Calypso, the offspring of Medley, an earlier champion, won repeatedly at races.

1790 New York City, the state's capital, had a population of 30,000 and five markets. Gov. George Clinton moved into Government House to save the $750 per year rent he was paying for his own house.

1790 The **ascendancy of commerce** in American life

in 1789. Left adrift in Europe, Barlow immersed himself in the revolutionary ferment, established himself on intimate terms with leading European intellectuals, and entered upon a colorful career with the American state department. He died in 1812 while minister to France.

1790 Mar. 1 The first U.S. Census was authorized by Congress. It was completed on Aug. 1. The population was placed at 3,929,625, including 697,624 slaves and 59,557 free blacks. The most populous state was Virginia, with 747,610 people, and the largest city was Philadelphia, with a population of 42,444. The center of U.S. population was about equally divided between New England and the Middle Atlantic States, and the South. Massachusetts was the only state to report no slaves.

1790 Mar. 26 A federal naturalization act was passed. It provided uniform rules for naturalization after two years of residence.

1790 Mar. 29 John Tyler, tenth president of the United States, was born in Greenway, Va.

1790 Apr. 10 The first patent law was passed. It provided for a three-man board with the power to grant patents. Its board members included the secretaries of state and war, and the attorney general. The board's first incumbents were Thomas Jefferson, Henry Knox, and Edmund Randolph.

1790 Apr. 10 The first circumnavigation of the globe by an American vessel was accomplished when Capt. Robert Gray docked the *Columbia* in Boston harbor. On a voyage for a group of Boston merchants, Gray had sailed from Boston in Sept. 1787 with a cargo of goods to be traded for furs with Indians of the Pacific Northwest. Gray then carried a valuable cargo of sea otter skins to Canton, China, and sailed on around the world, a voyage of almost 42,000 miles. His trip opened up trade between New England and the Pacific Northwest, which brought great wealth to New England merchants. The trip also helped establish U.S. claims to the Oregon Territory. On May 11, 1792, during a second voyage, Gray became the first white man to enter the Columbia R.

1790 Apr. 17 Benjamin Franklin died in Philadelphia at 84. Lord Jeffrey, editor of the *Edinburgh Review,* wrote of him: "In one point of view the name of Franklin must be considered as standing higher than any of the others which illustrated the Eighteenth Century. Distinguished as a statesman he was equally great as a philosopher, thus united in himself a rare degree of excellence in both these pursuits, to excel in either of which is deemed the highest praise." Franklin's funeral and burial in Christ Church Yard drew 20,000 spectators, the largest gathering in the U.S. to that time.

prepared for the task, and a great number of engravings of fine workmanship were made on Pennsylvania paper. Printing required seven years, the cost of the venture being covered by subscription. When completed, the encyclopedia was hailed as the greatest achievement of the press in America up to that time.

1790 *The Contrast,* a play by Royall Tyler, was published. The first American comedy to be produced and performed in public, it satirized Americans who continued to ape British customs.

1791 *The Cabinet-maker and Upholsterer's Drawing Book* by Thomas Sheraton was published in England. The book was widely read by American furniture makers. Sheraton's delicate designs followed the tradition of George Hepplewhite.

1791 The first New Orleans opera house, the Théâtre de St. Pierre, opened. From this beginning the city became the opera center of the U.S. until the Civil War.

1791 *The Prompter* by Noah Webster, a popular essay dealing with political and educational matters, was published. Written in simple workaday prose, the essay went through seven editions before 1800.

1791 Mar. The first part of *The Rights of Man* by Thomas Paine was published in England. An incendiary document, it attacked monarchy, supported the French Revolution, and argued forcibly in favor of democracy, republican government, and personal freedom and rights. The British government considered the work seditious and charged Paine with treason. He fled to France in 1792, was tried in absentia, and was banished from Great Britain.

1791 Mar. The first printed orchestral score in America, "The Death Song of an Indian Chief," was published in Boston in the March issue of *The Massachusetts Magazine.*

1792 The cornerstone of the Capitol was laid in Washington, D.C. The building was completed about 1830, though it was in use before then. It was designed by William Thornton following lines of English country mansions in the Palladian mode.

1792 Work on the White House in Washington, D.C., was begun, following plans by James Hoban. The building was a sumptuous example of post-colonial architecture, modeled after the palace of the Duke of Leinster in Ireland. Burned by the British in 1814, it was rebuilt in 1818 and restored in 1951.

1792 The organist, composer, and teacher Raynor Taylor arrived in America, having come from England at the suggestion of his former pupil Alexander Reinagle. Taylor taught and performed in Baltimore and Annapolis, Md., before settling in Philadelphia.

| Business and Industry; Science; Education; Philosophy and Religion **III** | | **IV** Sports; Social Issues and Crime; Folkways; Fashion; Holidays |

1790 **Trinity Church** in New York City, which was burned during the American Revolution, was rebuilt and rededicated by Bishop Samuel Provoost of the Episcopal Church. Pres. Washington attended the ceremony. From then on, the president had a special pew reserved for him, distinctively ornamented and covered by a baldachin, or canopy.

1790 Delegates to the **Universalist convention** in Philadelphia, under the leadership of Rev. Elhanan Winchester and Dr. Benjamin Rush, took a position against the dogma of the Holy Trinity. The meeting declared that Jesus was the human intermediary between man and God rather than the son of God.

1790 July 31 The **U.S. Patent Office** was opened. It has been said that a dozen men from Connecticut were waiting at the door, a colorful way of noting that traditionally more inventors from Connecticut have registered patents than from any other state. However, the first U.S. patent was issued to Samuel Hopkins of Vermont for a new method of making pearlash and potash.

1790 Aug. 4 Interest-bearing **government bonds** were authorized by Congress. The 6% bonds were sold to pay off the federal debt.

1790 Aug. 15 The **first Roman Catholic bishop** in the U.S., Father John Carroll, was consecrated at Lulworth Castle, England. He was selected by Pope Pius VI, who also chose Baltimore as the first episcopal see in America. Bishop Carroll held his first synod on Nov. 7, 1791.

1790 Dec. 21 The **cotton mill** of Almy, Brown, and Slater began operation in Pawtucket, R.I., using British industrial methods. Samuel Slater had come to America with a thorough understanding of the new machinery invented in Britain by Richard Arkwright, Samuel Crompton, and James Hargreaves. His factory was manned by children between four and ten years of age. Slater was the first American industrialist to break down the production process into simple parts, enabling child labor to outproduce skilled artisans.

1791 The **Massachusetts Historical Society,** the first historical association in the U.S., was founded by Jeremy Belknap, a Boston clergyman and historian. The society was organized to collect important historical documents.

1791 The **carpet industry** in Philadelphia began with the manufacture of Turkish and Axminster carpets by William Peter Sprague.

was symbolized in Philadelphia when High St. was renamed Market St.

1790 The phrase *not worth a continental* expressed a common attitude toward the continental currency issued by Congress at the end of the American Revolution. Paper money valued at $200,000,000 shrank rapidly in purchasing power until it took $40 in paper to buy one silver dollar.

1790 Major changes in **prison conditions** in Pennsylvania were effected through the relentless activity of the Society for Alleviating the Miseries of the Public Prisons, led by such Pennsylvanians as Tench Coxe, William Howard, and Benjamin Rush. Among the improvements were greater privacy, adequate clothing, religious instruction, separation of different types of criminals, and protection of the rights of prisoners from avaricious keepers.

1790 The **Pennsylvania system** of prison management, based on the concept of absolute solitary confinement, was introduced at the Walnut St. Prison in Philadelphia. It was supposed to promote moral regeneration by means of enforced meditation. The philosophy of the Pennsylvania system was opposed to that of the later Auburn system, which was initiated by the state penitentiary at Auburn, N.Y., in 1816, and which permitted congregation of prisoners during the day. At night, however, Auburn prisoners slept in separate cells. In general, the Auburn system came to prevail in the U.S.

1790 **High heels** went out of fashion in America and were replaced by sandal-like footwear, with low quarters and bows and ribbons instead of buckles.

1790 June 30–July 7 An **exhibition of two Arabian camels** was advertised in the *Connecticut Journal,* which described the creatures as "the greatest natural Curiosity ever exhibited to the Public on this Continent." It is not certain, however, that these were the first camels ever exhibited in America. Samuel Sewall reported the appearance of a dromedary, or Arabian camel, in 1714.

1790 July 14 Americans celebrated **Bastille Day** on the first anniversary of the storming of the Bastille as an expression of their revolutionary sentiments. The

1790 May 29 Rhode Island ratified the Constitution and became the 13th state of the Union.

1790 May 31 The **first U.S. copyright act** was signed by Pres. George Washington. The new law protected plays, maps, and books. The term of protection was for 14 years, with the right of renewal for another 14 years. The work's title page had to be deposited in the clerk's office of the local U.S. district court. Passage of the law was credited largely to the efforts of Noah Webster. Until the eighteenth century copyright had remained, on the whole, a matter of common law, and protection ebbed and flowed with the tides of political fortune. But in 1710 Parliament passed the Statute of Anne, which provided protection for up to 28 years. It became standard in the colonies as well as in England. After the American Revolution, however, the various states were lax about establishing copyright prerogatives. When Webster was ready to publish his *American Spelling Book,* he soon discovered that he would have no say in the disposition of his work. He began a tour of the states to campaign for new legislation. His campaign for a uniform copyright law coincided with the Federalists' desire for a strong central government, and the measure was passed.

1791 Mar. 3 The **first internal revenue law** was passed by Congress. Fourteen revenue districts were created and a tax of 20 to 30 cents a gallon put on distilled spirits. The legislatures of North Carolina, Virginia, and Maryland passed resolutions of disapproval shortly thereafter.

1791 Mar. 4 Vermont joined the Union, becoming the 14th state. It had ratified the Constitution in January.

1791 Apr. 23 James Buchanan, the 15th president of the United States, was born in Cove Gap, Pa.

1791–1793 The **second Congress** had 30 senators of whom 17, now known as Federalists, supported the administration and 13, becoming known in 1792 as Democratic-Republicans, were in opposition. In the House the count was 37 Federalists and 33 Democratic-Republicans.

1792 The **Democratic-Republican party was formally organized.** It was sometimes called simply the Republican party and was anti-Federalist. It became the Democratic party in 1828. The Democratic-Republicans were liberal, looked with favor on the French Revolution, and had as their leader Thomas Jefferson. The party enjoyed the support of the majority until the 1824 presidential election. The Federalists were conservative, supported by the business interests, and friendly to England.

1792 Jan. 12 Thomas Pinckney was appointed the first **U.S. minister to England** by Pres. Washington. Pinckney, governor of South Carolina, was instructed to express "that spirit of sincere friendship, which we

There he was a church organist, composer, and a colleague of Reinagle, and in 1820 one of the founders of the Musical Fund Society.

1792 The first two parts of *Modern Chivalry* by Hugh Henry Brackenridge were published. This novel was a rollicking satire on the manners of the author's American contemporaries, and showed the influence of Miguel de Cervantes. More parts of the novel were published in 1793 and 1797, and all were collected in 1805. A new edition with additional material appeared in 1815.

1792 Benjamin West was appointed president of the Royal Academy of London. West, an American-born artist, settled in England in 1763 and remained there until his death in 1820. He was the foremost portrait painter of his day.

1792 Apr. 24 *The Yorker's Stratagem, or Banana's Wedding* by J. Robinson, an early American farce, opened. In the play a New Yorker disguises himself as a bumpkin and under the name of Banana woos and wins a West Indian heiress. The play introduced black characters, but not American, for the first time on stage.

1792 Oct. 12 The first **memorial to Christopher Columbus** in America was dedicated at Baltimore, Md. Built of English brick and coated with cement, it was put up at North Ave. and Bond St.

1792 Dec. 5 Boston's first theater was closed and its manager, Joseph Harper, was arrested by the sheriff. Called The New Exhibition Room in an attempt to circumvent Boston's ban against theaters, it had been built the same year.

1793 *American Poems, Selected and Original,* an anthology of poems selected by Elihu Hubbard Smith, was published at Litchfield, Conn. The anthology was devoted largely to the group of writers who became known as the Hartford Wits or Connecticut Wits, including John Trumbull, Joel Barlow, Timothy Dwight, and Lemuel Hopkins, all of whom were friends of Smith.

1793 New York City's first daily newspaper and the second daily in the country, the *American Minerva,* was founded by Noah Webster. He edited the paper for ten years, during which time it was strongly Federalist and anti-French. In 1797 the name was changed to the *Commercial Advertiser.* In 1905 the *Advertiser* in turn was combined with the New York *Globe,* which in turn was absorbed by the New York *Sun* in 1923.

1793 An essay by John Woolman was published under the title "A Word of Remembrance and Caution to the Rich." Woolman, a Quaker tailor of New Jersey

1791 Nov. 3   The **University of Vermont** was chartered in Burlington. Its first degrees were awarded in 1804.

1791 Dec. 12   The **Bank of the U.S.** opened its main branch in Philadelphia and additional branches in the main urban centers of America. The bank served the federal government as its fiscal representative.

1792   The **Russian Orthodox Church** initiated a missionary program in Alaska, then owned by Russia. The resident bishop in Sitka coordinated missionary work.

1792   The **Chemical Society of Philadelphia,** one of the earliest scientific societies in America, was organized by James Woodhouse.

1792   The first important **wooden truss bridge,** invented to suit American needs, was completed by Col. Ewel Hale at Bellows Falls, Vt. Wood was plentiful in the area but rafts and barges would have been impeded by a bridge built on piles or with rows of arches. Hale's bridge consisted of two spans of 175 ft. each resting on an island.

1792 May 17   The **New York Stock Exchange** was organized at the Merchants Coffee House, New York City.

1793   A famous **American geography,** the *American Universal Geography; or, a View of the Present State of All the Empires, Kingdoms, States and Republics in the Known World, and of the United States of America in Particular,* was published. It was illustrated with maps by Jedidiah Morse of Boston. Morse was a famous geographer, and in 1797 he finished what was probably the first American gazetteer, *The American Gazetteer, exhibiting, in Alphabetical Order, a much more full and accurate Account, than has been given, of the States, Provinces, counties, Cities, Towns . . . on the American Continent, also of the West-Indies Islands, etc.* This gazetteer went through many editions.

1793 Feb. 22   **Williams College** was chartered in Williamstown, Mass. Its entrance requirements reflected a vogue for learning French, a result of close ties between France and the U.S. formed during the American Revolution. French was accepted as a substitute prerequisite for classical languages.

1793 May 25   The first **Roman Catholic priest ordained** in the U.S., Father Stephen Theodore Badin, was ordained in Baltimore, Md. He was a refugee from the French Revolution. After his ordination he served in Kentucky where he dedicated the first

main public ceremony of the event was held in Philadelphia. After a few years, Bastille Day was not celebrated in any formal manner except by French societies and those interested in France and its language. On July 14, 1918, a special observance of Bastille Day in America was arranged by a committee organized by William Howard Taft.

1790 Dec. 6   **Philadelphia** became the nation's capital when Congress opened its legislative session there. On July 10, 1790, the House of Representatives had approved, by a vote of 32 to 29, the move from New York City to Philadelphia as part of a deal to establish a permanent capital. Congress had authorized George Washington to select a site for a new capital on the Potomac R. Philadelphia remained the nation's capital until 1800, when Washington, D.C., became the permanent seat of government. In 1799 Philadelphia had ceased to be the capital of Pennsylvania when the state government moved to Lancaster.

1791 Jan. 1   The custom of a **presidential reception on New Year's Day** was initiated by Pres. George Washington. The custom was continued by the first Democratic president, Thomas Jefferson, and remained in practice until Jan. 1, 1934, when it was suspended by Pres. Franklin D. Roosevelt who, because of his paralysis, found it too difficult to stand in a receiving line.

1792   The first edition of *The Farmer's Almanac* was published. Edited by Robert Bailey Thomas, a native of Grafton, Mass., it contained much information about New England life and manners along with valuable data on weather and other practical matters. Its homespun flavor and its depiction of New England ways captivated readers and turned the almanac into an American institution. Thomas, until his death in 1746, edited *The Farmer's Almanac,* later retitled *The Old Farmer's Almanac* to differentiate it from its numerous imitators.

1792 June 1   **Statehood Day** in Kentucky was instituted to commemorate admission of the Blue Grass State to the Union on this date.

1792 Oct. 12   The first celebration of **Columbus Day** in America was held in New York City under the auspices of the Society of St. Tammany. St. Tammany had been chosen as the patron saint in a spirit of ridicule since he had been an Indian savant. The ridicule was

bear to the English nation" and also to seek the liberation of American commerce from British restrictions.

1792 Apr. 2 Congress passed the **Coinage Act,** establishing the first U.S. Mint, to be constructed in Philadelphia, Pa. The act provided for a decimal system of coinage and a standard of bimetallism, with silver and gold as legal tender at a ratio of 15 to 1 by weight. David Rittenhouse, the astronomer and instrument maker who had succeeded Benjamin Franklin as president of the American Philosophical Society in 1791, was named first director of the mint.

1792 May 8 A **national conscription act** was passed by Congress, requiring "each and every free able-bodied white male citizen of the republic" to serve in the U.S. militia.

1792 June 1 **Kentucky** became the 15th state. It previously had been part of Virginia territory.

1792 Dec. 5 **George Washington was reelected** president of the United States. John Adams was elected vice president. The electoral vote was Washington, 132; Adams, Federalist of Massachusetts, 77; George Clinton, anti-Federalist of New York, 50.

1793–1795 The **third Congress** consisted of 30 senators of whom 17 were Federalists and 13 Democratic-Republicans. In the House the count was 57 Democratic-Republicans and 48 Federalists.

1793 Mar. 4 **Pres. Washington was inaugurated** for his second term.

1793 Apr. 22 A **proclamation of neutrality** was issued by Pres. Washington. It warned Americans to avoid aiding either side in the war between Great Britain and France.

1794 Feb. 28 **Sen. Abraham Alfonse Albert Gallatin** of Pennsylvania, later secretary of the treasury, was barred from the Senate after a dispute concerning his election. His seat was declared void because he had not fulfilled the nine-year residence requirement for election to the Senate. Gallatin had incurred the enmity of Alexander Hamilton and the Federalists when he introduced a motion demanding that the administration present a record of its finances.

1794 Apr. 22 **Capital punishment** was eliminated in Pennsylvania, except as a penalty for murder in the first degree.

1794 July-Nov. The **Whiskey Rebellion** broke out in western Pennsylvania among farmers opposed to a federal excise tax on liquor passed in 1791. On Aug. 7 Pres. Washington issued a proclamation ordering the insurgents to go home and calling out a militia force of several thousand from four states. He issued another proclamation on Sept. 24 and ordered the militia to suppress the uprising. For a time Washington led this force in person. By mid-November the trouble was over. Two men were convicted of treason but Washington pardoned them.

who died in 1772, had written the essay, one of the best examples of the humanitarian spirit of the eighteenth century, in 1763. It advocated vast social reforms, including the abolition of slavery. The tract was reprinted by the Fabians in 1898, who referred to Woolman as "the voice in the wilderness, the John the Baptist of the Gospel of Socialism."

1793 *Letters from an American Farmer* by J. Hector St. John de Crèvecoeur (Michel Guillaume Jean de Crèvecoeur) had its first American publication in Philadelphia. It had been issued in London in 1782.

1793 **Philip Freneau** endorsed the French Revolution in his poem *On the Anniversary of the Storming of the Bastille.* Freneau continued to espouse the cause of the French Revolution even after the support of his contemporaries began to cool.

c1794 **John L. Berkenhead,** a blind pianist from London, became the most popular musician in Boston for his realistic renditions of *The Demolition of the Bastille,* one of the pieces of descriptive music that were popular toward the close of the eighteenth century.

1794 The **Boston Theater** was opened under the management of Charles Stuart Powell after repeal of the law of 1750 prohibiting plays in Boston.

1794 The first phase of the **Classic Revival** period in architecture gained momentum when Charles Bullfinch began construction of attached houses on Tontine Crescent, Franklin Place, Boston. The houses were done in what came to be known as the Federal style.

1794 The continuing **Dutch influence** in New York City publishing was reflected in the issuance of some 50 books in the Dutch language between 1708 and 1794.

1794 *The Harmony of Maine,* a collection of songs by Supply Belcher, was published in Boston. Belcher, known as "the Handel of Maine," was a politician, schoolteacher, and tavernkeeper on the northern frontier, as well as a composer of simple hymns and fugues that were very popular among rural audiences.

1794 *Charlotte Temple,* a sentimental romance by Susanna Rowson, was published in America. The highly successful novel, concerning the seduction of a girl by an army officer and her tragic fate in America, was first published in England in 1791, but it did not achieve its enormous popularity until it was published in Philadelphia this year.

1794 The first part of *The Age of Reason* by Thomas Paine was published in Paris. This deistic work was written with frequently faulty logic but unmistakable fervor and conviction. The book had a profound effect and was especially popular with common people, who

Catholic chapel in Lexington in 1800.

1793 Oct. 28 Eli Whitney of Mulberry Grove, Ga., filed an application for a patent on the cotton gin. The patent was granted on Mar. 14, 1794. Cotton production mounted spectacularly after Whitney's invention, rising from 138,000 lbs. exported in 1800. Whitney, however, received very little in return for his invention. His machine's operating principle was stolen or duplicated by others in spite of his patent, and powerful interests opposed his fight for royalties. In 1812 Congress refused to renew his patent.

1794 Charles Willson Peale, a major force in American mass education, opened his museum in Philadelphia, which began disseminating historical and scientific knowledge to the public. The museum featured displays of wampum, tomahawks, scalps, and other antiquities against realistically painted backgrounds.

1794 An early American union, the Federal Society of Journeymen Cordwainers, was organized in Philadelphia. It called a strike this year and succeeded in raising the rates of its members.

1794 The first independent Methodist Church for blacks was established in Philadelphia by Richard Allen, a former slave. In 1816 Allen became the first bishop of the African Methodist Episcopal Church when 16 black congregations united to form the new denomination.

1794 The first major turnpike in America was completed between Philadelphia and Lancaster, Pa. The large profits that could be realized by sponsoring such a company led to the construction of many such roads throughout America, often in areas where they were not necessary. Lancaster Turnpike, 62 mi. long, was the first macadam road in the U.S.

1794 One of the earliest American canals was built to circumnavigate South Hadley's falls on the Connecticut R. in Massachusetts. Its lift operated by means of inclined planes and cables powered by the current. At about the same time construction of the Middlesex Canal from Boston to the Merrimack R. was begun. Its first section opened in 1804. The Middlesex Canal was 27 miles long, and it cost about $3.50 for a standard barge to go its length. The sizes of the barges were fixed by regulations. The barges were pulled by horses.

1794 June 24 Bowdoin College was chartered in Brunswick, Maine, under Congregational auspices. Its first degrees were awarded in 1806.

directed at such societies as those of St. George, St. Andrew, and St. David.

1793 Anthelme Brillat-Savarin, a French émigré, arrived in New York City. Savarin supported himself by giving French lessons and playing in a theater orchestra. He ate in Little's Tavern and soon began to apply his gustatory art and continental tact to counteracting the English influence in American cooking.

1793 Horse racing in public thoroughfares in Lexington, Ky., was outlawed by the town's trustees. Such races had been frightening pedestrians.

1793 The method of house numbering in Philadelphia, Pa., with even numbers on one side of the street and odd numbers on the other, so intrigued Médéric Louis élie Moreau de Saint-Méry, a refugee from the Reign of Terror in France, that upon his return to Europe he introduced the practice in various European cities.

1793 Ricketts' Circus, John Bill Ricketts, proprietor, gave performances in Philadelphia, Pa. The performance of Apr. 22 was seen by Gen. George Washington. Ricketts later moved his circus to New York City, where he exhibited at Greenwich Theatre near the Battery in 1795.

1794 A widely read indictment of women's inferior social status, A Vindication of the Rights of Women (1792) by the English author Mary Wollstonecraft, had a great influence in American intellectual circles.

1794 Powdering of men's hair went out of fashion after more than 100 years. However, men's hair was still worn in a queue tied with a black ribbon.

1794 Penal reform undertaken in Pennsylvania resulted in the decrease in the number of crimes for which capital punishment was decreed.

1794 A barber-hairdresser, specializing in men's wigs, hired out in Philadelphia for 22 shillings a month.

1794 American sympathy for the French Revolution was demonstrated by Philadelphians who saluted one

| Exploration and Settlement; Wars; Government; Civil Rights; Statistics I | Publishing; Arts and Music; Popular Entertainment; Architecture; Theater II |

1794 Aug. 20 A major **Indian defeat** in the Northwest Territory occurred when Gen. Anthony Wayne routed 2000 Indians, killing and wounding many, on the Miami R. in Ohio. The victory virtually ended a war that had started in 1790, and secured the region for settlement.

1794 Nov. 19 The **Jay Treaty** was concluded between Great Britain and the U.S. It was widely denounced in America because it continued to allow the British the right to search U.S. ships and impress American seamen on the grounds that they were actually of British birth and citizenship.

resented religious as well as political tyranny. On Dec. 27, 1793, after completing the first part of the book, Paine was thrown into prison for his opposition to the Reign of Terror then raging in revolutionary France. He completed the rest of his book under the shadow of the guillotine, and it was published on his release in 1795.

1794 Feb. 17 The **New Theatre** on Chestnut St. in Philadelphia opened with a performance of Samuel Arnold's opera *The Castle of Andalusia.* The theater's opening had been long delayed by a yellow fever epidemic that swept through Philadelphia in 1793.

1795–1799

What came to be known as the XYZ Affair marked a new low in Franco-American relations at the end of the eighteenth century. A three-man commission, consisting of Elbridge Gerry, John Marshall, and Charles Cotesworth Pinckney, was sent to France in 1797 by Pres. John Adams to negotiate a treaty of commerce and amity. The French foreign minister, Charles Maurice de Talleyrand, refused to deal with them directly and instead on Oct. 18 sent three agents who later were designated X, Y, and Z in the reports of the American delegation. The French agents suggested that the U.S. make a loan to France and also offer a bribe of about $250,000 to Talleyrand. The Americans refused, with Pinckney replying, "No, no, not a sixpence." On Apr. 3, 1798, Pres. Adams submitted the XYZ correspondence to Congress, and the disclosure aroused great resentment in the U.S. against France.

1795 The **Yazoo land fraud,** one of the earliest and most spectacular incidents of fraud in American history, rocked Georgia. The Yazoo lands were located in what is now Mississippi and Alabama, and were owned by Georgia. The Georgia legislature granted 35,000,000 acres of this land for settlement to four companies at a price of $500,000. It then was discovered that every legislator but one had an interest in the grants when the measure was passed. Although the contract was repealed by a new legislature elected in 1796 and led by James Jackson, who had left the U.S. Senate to run for the state legislature and reclaim the lands, the original grants could not be overturned in the courts. A unanimous Supreme Court decision delivered by Chief Justice John Marshall in the case of *Fletcher v. Peck* (1810) upheld the grant and declared that the Georgia legislature had acted unconstitutionally in nullifying the contract. That year, the U.S. Congress passed a bill appropriating up to $8,000,000 to settle the original Yazoo claims, which Georgia had refused to honor.

After American independence was won, more and more periodicals began to be published, with over 70 appearing before 1800. Most of them did not last long. Among the periodicals were *Columbian Magazine* (1786–1792), *Massachusetts Magazine* (1786–1796), *New York Magazine* (1790–1797), and *Monthly Magazine and American Review.* The last one was established in New York in April of 1799 by Charles Brockden Brown, the nation's first professional novelist. In 1801 it became a quarterly under the title *American Review and Literary Journal*; it published until the end of 1802. Brown also edited the *Literary Magazine and American Register* from its founding in Philadelphia in 1803 until 1807, when it too failed. Most magazines of the time carried a mix of educational, literary, and scientific material.

1795 An *English Grammar* by Lindley Murray, a Pennsylvania native of Scottish descent who immigrated to England, was published. The best known of Murray's works, this book was accepted for four generations as the standard authority on English grammar. Murray also compiled a popular *English Reader* (1779).

1795 The **Massachusetts State House,** one of the best post-Revolutionary public buildings, was built in Boston from designs by Charles Bulfinch.

1795 May 22 The **first American-born black character** in American theater was Sambo in *The Triumphs of Love, or Happy Reconciliation* by John Murdock. The play also included the first Quaker characters.

1796 **Joseph Jefferson,** the English actor, made his first New York City appearance with the American Company. He was the first of a long line of celebrated actors of the nineteenth century.

1796 **Gilbert Stuart** completed his portrait *George Washington,* probably the most famous portrait of the

| Business and Industry; Science; Education; Philosophy and Religion III | | IV Sports; Social Issues and Crime; Folkways; Fashion; Holidays |

1794 Sept. 10 The **University of Tennessee** was first chartered as Blount College in Knoxville, Tenn. Established under Presbyterian auspices, Blount College conferred its first degrees in 1806, the same year it became a state university through a federal grant providing for two state universities, one in the eastern part of the state and the other in the western part. Blount College was chosen as the eastern member and, in 1807, was renamed East Tennessee College. It became East Tennessee University in 1840 and the University of Tennessee in 1879.

another as *citizen*, the form of address adopted by the French. More evidence of American support for the French was displayed on Nov. 21 at The Sign of the Black Bear in Philadelphia, which advertised a performance of the guillotining of Louis XVI, who had been executed in 1793. The climax was described as the point at which "the head falls in a basket, and the lips, which are first red, turn blue." Supporters of Thomas Jefferson and his party flocked to applaud this revolutionary reenactment "performed to the life by an invisible machine without any perceivable assistance."

1795–1799

Both in the U.S. and abroad, the day of the general scientists, who took many fields of inquiry as their province, was coming to an end. Professional, or at least more specialized, scientists were taking over. An outstanding example of the generalists who had contributed so much to eighteenth-century progress was Samuel Latham Mitchill. His accomplishments and interests revealed the scope of his life's work. Mitchill established the first medical journal, *Medical Repository,* in 1797; was professor of natural history at Columbia College from 1798 to 1801; published the first good description of the geology of eastern New York State in 1798; was professor of the College of Physicians and Surgeons in New York City from 1807 to 1826; and served in the New York State Assembly and the House of Representatives and the U.S. Senate. In addition, he introduced into American science the chemical nomenclature of Antoine Lavoisier, founder of modern chemistry, and by 1814 was the foremost zoologist as a result of his work on the fish of New York.

1795 The **first Kentucky library** was founded at Lexington. It reflected the city's cultural ascendancy in the early frontier region.

1795 An early influence in the development of American **Utopianism** was Constantin François de Chasseboeuf, Comte de Volney. He visited the U.S., where his work *The Ruins; or, A Survey of the Revolution of Empires* (1791) had been favorably received and translated by Thomas Jefferson and Joel Barlow. *The Ruins* was a study of the philosophy of history, and the cultivated deism of the author greatly appealed to American intellectuals. Unfortunately, Volney's arrival was followed closely by the crisis with France.

Americans—at least those who could afford to—dined well and heartily on holiday occasions, as the menus of some presidential Christmas dinners indicated. A Christmas menu from Mount Vernon showed that George and Martha Washington served 34 different dishes and wines on one holiday, beginning with onion soup and ending with port and Madeira. Five different meat dishes were available. In the White House John and Abigail Adams called one of their holiday repasts "A Most Sinful Feast." Among the 29 dishes was "Skillet Cranberries for a Slack Oven."

1796–1799 **Louis Philippe,** who in 1830 would be proclaimed "king of the French" by the deposed King Charles X of France, was living in a one-room flat over a bar in Philadelphia, Pa. He managed, however, to travel in the best circles. He met one of the two daughters of William Bingham, a banker and U.S. senator from Pennsylvania, and husband of Washington's most colorful and celebrated hostess, Anne Willing Bingham. Bingham had founded the Bank of North America as well as the city of Binghamton, N.Y. Louis Philippe proposed marriage to the younger Miss Bingham, but the senator refused permission on the ground that she was not good enough for Louis if Louis were to become king, and too good for him if he were not. Louis Philippe left Philadelphia in 1800 and in 1830 became "citizen king" of France. As for Bingham's daughters, one married the Comte de Tilly and the other married Alexander Baring, Baron Ashburton, an English financier and banker.

1796 A social trend away from **capital punishment** was reflected in reforms in the criminal code of Virginia, which reduced the number of crimes for which capital punishment was decreed.

Exploration and Settlement; Wars; Government; Civil Rights; Statistics	Publishing; Arts and Music; Popular Entertainment; Architecture; Theater

I   **II**

1795 An **Indian factory system** was established by the federal government to assist Indians in their dealing with white traders. Under the supervision of the factors, agents who supplied money on the basis of outstanding business accounts, the system was designed to get fair prices for the products of Indians.

1795–1797 The **fourth Congress** consisted of 32 senators of whom 19 were Federalists and 13 Democratic-Republicans. In the House 54 were Federalists and 52 Democratic-Republicans.

1795 Jan. 29 The **Naturalization Act** was passed. It required a residence period of five years and renunciation of allegiances and titles of nobility as prerequisites to citizenship.

1795 Nov. 2 James K. Polk, 11th president of the United States, was born in Pineville, N.C.

1796 May 19 A **game protection law** was passed by Congress to restrict encroachment by whites on Indian hunting grounds. The act provided fines or imprisonment as penalties for hunting game in Indian territory.

1796 June 1 Tennessee became the 16th state of the Union.

1796 Sept. 17 What has come to be known as **Washington's Farewell Address** was delivered by Pres. Washington before Congress. One of the outstanding American political documents, the address warned against America's involvement in foreign disputes and thus paved the way for the isolationist policy of the nineteenth century.

1796 Dec. John Adams was elected president of the United States. Adams was the last Federalist candidate to gain the presidency. The electoral vote was Adams, 71; Thomas Jefferson, Democratic-Republican of Virginia, 68; Aaron Burr, Democratic-Republican of New York, 30; and Thomas Pinckney, Federalist of South Carolina, 59. Jefferson, the candidate with the second highest electoral vote, became vice president.

1797–1799 In the **fifth Congress** 20 senators were Federalists and 12 Democratic-Republicans; in the House the division was 58 and 48.

1797 Mar. 4 John Adams was inaugurated president of the United States. The second president, he served one term.

1797 May 15 The **first special session of Congress** was called by Pres. Adams to debate a crisis in French-American relations. The American envoy to France, Charles Cotesworth Pinckney, had left France after being insulted by the French foreign minister. The situation deteriorated rapidly and caused growing concern in the U.S.

1798 A severe **yellow fever epidemic** in New York

first president. It also came to be known as the Athenaeum head. Stuart made numerous tries before this successful result. Nothing but the head of Washington can be seen, his character being derived from his facial features alone. This likeness is the accepted one and has become familiar to millions. The portrait was placed in the Boston Athenaeum, and later on permanent loan to the Boston Museum of Fine Arts.

1796 *The Hasty Pudding* by Joel Barlow was published. Barlow wrote the poem, a mock epic singing the virtues of the American dish, cornmeal mush, in France in 1793. It became his most popular work.

1796 The first complete American edition of **William Shakespeare's** *Plays* was published.

1796 The **Harrison Gray Otis House** was built in Boston. Its design reflected the influence of the so-called Adam style popular in England, named after Robert and James Adam, Scottish architects. The Otis House later became headquarters of The Society for the Preservation of New England Antiquities.

1796 An early American opera, *The Archers, or the Mountaineers of Switzerland,* was staged in New York City. An adaptation of Friedrich von Schiller's *William Tell,* it was composed by William Dunlap and Benjamin Carr.

1797 Thomas Paine's *Agrarian Justice* was published while the author was living in France. It put forward a belief in a rational basis for the perfectability of social institutions. This tenet was shared by Paine with other leaders of the eighteenth-century Enlightenment. The full title of Paine's work was *Agrarian Justice opposed to Agrarian Law and to Agrarian Monopoly; being a Plan for ameliorating the Condition of Man by creating in every Nation a National Fund, etc.*

1797 Construction of the main church began at the mission **San Juan Capistrano,** the most ambitious of colonial buildings in California. Designed by Isidoro Aguilar, a stonemason from Mexico, it had a 120-ft. bell tower and many carved ornaments. It was completed in 1806 but was destroyed in an earthquake on Dec. 8, 1812. The ruins are still a favorite tourist attraction.

1797 Feb. 17 The play *Bunker Hill* by John Daly Burk provided a dramatic spectacle in its last act, in which a realistic reenactment of the assault was staged. The play was often revived in Fourth of July celebrations.

1798 The poem "Hail, Columbia" by **Joseph Hopkinson** was published. It stirred Americans' patriotic fervor at a time when war with France appeared imminent.

Business and Industry; Science; Education; Philosophy and Religion III		IV Sports; Social Issues and Crime; Folkways; Fashion; Holidays

He was charged with spying and forced to leave for home the next year.

1795 Feb. 25 **Union College** was chartered at Schenectady, N.Y., under Presbyterian auspices. Its first degrees were awarded in 1800.

1796 The first experiments with **gas illumination** were conducted in Philadelphia, Pa.

1796 The first important **suspension bridge** in the U.S. was built between Uniontown and Greensborough, Pa., over Jacob's Creek. The bridge, no longer standing, was based on a principle of suspension developed mainly by James Finley of Fayette County, Pa.

1796–1797 **John Fitch** made a final effort to raise financial backing for his steamboat experiments. In New York City, on Collect Pond, where the Tombs stood on Centre Street, he sailed a steamboat driven by a screw propeller. No one was interested. Fitch committed suicide in Bardstown, Ky., on July 2, 1798.

1797 The first instruction booklet in **experimental chemistry** in America was published by Dr. James Woodhouse in Philadelphia, Pa.

1797 The **first glassworks** in what was then the American midwest was established in Pittsburgh, Pa., by the firm of O'Hara and Craig.

1797 The first U.S. **clock patent** was awarded to Eli Terry for his newly devised method of employing wooden works in his clocks. Terry's clocks were sold rather cheaply—$18 to $70—and sales were brisk. Terry became the first manufacturer to use water power to cut parts.

1797 June 26 The first U.S. **plow patent** was issued to Charles Newbold of New Jersey. After expending his entire fortune in developing a practical plow of cast iron, Newbold was unable to sell it to farmers because of their fear of harmful effects of iron on soil. Thomas Jefferson had made the first studies of plows in America and designed a moldboard plow according to the distinctive requirements of American soil, but he never applied for a patent.

1796 The popularity of **billiards** in the South was noted by Francis Baily, the English astronomer, who began a two-year, 2000-mile tour of the U.S. this year. Baily observed that there were a dozen billiard tables in Norfolk, Va., alone. His narrative, *Journal of a Tour in Unsettled Parts of North America in 1796 and 1797,* was published in 1856.

1796 **Travel** between the cities of America frequently presented challenges and dangers to tradesmen and vacationers. Harried travelers on the Philadelphia-Baltimore roads complained of chasms six to ten feet deep along the way. They were lucky when their vehicles did not overturn. It sometimes took a stagecoach five days to make a trip.

1797 **Equality** of men and women in the spheres of culture, economics, politics, and society was propounded by Charles Brockden Brown in *Alcuin,* a novel holding that men and women had more in common than in dispute.

1797 A new **water supply** for Philadelphia, Pa., drawing from the Schuylkill R., went into operation. There were three underground tunnels for distributing water in the city, and these were supplied from a tower in the center of the city. This was the first attempt in the U.S. to construct a centralized water distribution system.

1798 The **breeding of horses** in the U.S. began in earnest. This year Diomed, the great English champion that had won the Epsom Derby in 1780, was brought to the U.S. by Col. John Hoomes of Virginia. Diomed sired many famous American horses, including Eclipse and Lexington.

1798 The **first model train** was said to have been built by John Fitch, who turned to the construction of miniature steam-powered vehicles after his dismal failure as a steamboat salesman. The model he built has been described as the first free-moving railway steam engine in miniature.

1798 June 18 "Millions for defense, but not one cent for tribute" entered American political history at a banquet at O'Eller's Tavern in Philadelphia, Pa., in honor of John Marshall, one of the three presidential

City caused 2086 deaths out of a total population of 50,000.

1798 Daniel Boone received a grant of 850 acres of land from the Spanish government in the Femme Osage district of Louisiana Territory.

1798 The **first secretary of the Navy** was appointed by Pres. Adams. He was Benjamin Stoddert, and he found himself with a weak navy in a time of trouble with France. Within two years he acquired 50 ships and planned a marine corps, naval hospital, and dock yards.

1798 Jan. 8 The **Eleventh Amendment** to the Constitution was adopted. It stipulated that federal courts shall not have jurisdiction over litigation between individuals from one state against individuals from another state.

1798 June 18 The first of four acts known collectively as the **Alien and Sedition Acts,** amending the Naturalization Act of 1795, was adopted. The act required of prospective citizens a residence period of 14 years and a declaration of intention for five years.

1798 June 25 The **Alien Act,** second of the Alien and Sedition Acts, was passed, granting the president power for two years to deport any alien he deemed dangerous to the country's safety.

1798 July 6 The **Alien Enemies Act,** third of the Alien and Sedition Acts, was passed. It provided for the apprehension and deportation of male aliens who were subjects or citizens of a hostile country.

1798 July 7 The first case of outright **abrogation of a treaty** by the U.S. occurred when Congress pronounced the U.S. "freed and exonerated from the stipulations" of the treaties of 1778 with France.

1798 July 14 The **Sedition Act,** fourth and last of the Alien and Sedition Acts, was passed. It provided for arrest and imprisonment of any person who attempted to impede the lawful processes of government, foment insurrection, or write, publish, or utter any false or malicious statement about the president, Congress, or government of the U.S. The Alien and Sedition Acts reflected the panic of the Federalist Party in the face of the XYZ Affair, the general conflict with France, and the growing strength of the Democratic-Republican Party. Intended to curb domestic opposition, the acts caused confusion and injustice and brought the Federalist Party ultimately into contempt, political defeat, and dissolution.

1799 Dec. 14 George Washington died at 67. He was buried on his estate in Mount Vernon, Va.

1798 The novel *Wieland* by Charles Brockden Brown, considered America's first professional writer, was published. This Gothic romance reflected the influence of European literature yet dealt with American subjects and locales. It was followed by *Arthur Mervyn, Ormond,* and *Edgar Huntly,* three novels published in 1799. Brown incorporated into his novels such elements as superstition, ventriloquism, diabolical heroes, sleepwalking, and Indian massacres.

1798 Apr. *Female Patriotism, or the Death of Joan d'Arc,* a remarkable dramatic tour-de-force by John Daly Burk, was produced at the Park Theater in New York City. Burk was able to instill Elizabethan vigor in his lines. The spirit of liberty suffuses the entire play.

1798 Dec. 10 The play *The Stranger* by William Dunlap, an adaptation of *Menschenhass und Reue* by the German writer August Friedrich Ferdinand von Kotzebue, opened in New York City. Its success reflected a great vogue for adaptations of Kotzebue's works, among which were *Lovers' Vows* (1799), *Count Benyowski* (1799), *False Shame* (1799), *Force of Calumny* (1800), *Count of Burgundy* (1800), and *Virgin of the Sun* (1800).

1799 The *Baltimore American,* the first newspaper outside Washington, D.C., to give verbatim reports of Congressional debates, began publication. The paper published for 130 years.

1799 Gracie Mansion in New York City, one of the few remaining examples of the country mansions that were built in upper Manhattan during the eighteenth century, was constructed in what is now Carl Schurz Park. It was acquired as the official residence for mayors of New York City in 1942.

1799 St. Mark's in-the-Bouwerie, an example of New York City's best small church architecture, was built on the site of the former farm of Gov. Peter Stuyvesant.

1799 The **Bank of Pennsylvania** in Philadelphia was built from plans by Benjamin H. Latrobe, one of the leaders of the Greek Revival movement in America. In this building he used an Ionic hexastyle portico that presaged the introduction of heavy, monumental public buildings.

1798 The first professional **nursing instruction** in the U.S. was given by Dr. Valentine Seaman, who lectured on anatomy, physiology, obstetrics, and pediatrics. Seaman later published an outline of these lectures, probably the first attempt in the U.S. at publishing a nursing text.

1798 The revolutionary concept of manufacturing **interchangeable parts** was incorporated by Eli Whitney in production of firearms for the U.S. government.

1798 The first American **ship built on Lake Ontario,** the 30-ton vessel *Jemima,* was constructed just outside of Rochester, N.Y.

1798 June An example of active **religious pacifism** was seen in the expedition of George Logan. Worried about the imminence of war with France, Logan sailed on a peace ship to do what he could as a private citizen to prevent the outbreak of hostilities. Logan, an erstwhile doctor, was an active Pennsylvania politician, friend of Thomas Jefferson, and a lifelong Quaker. His mission to France was an expression of his religious pacifism. He was further influenced by the sympathy of the Democratic-Republican Party, of which he had become a member, for France. Despite personal threats from Federalists, he equipped himself for the mission and set sail. With assistance from the Marquis de Lafayette, himself in exile in Germany, he got into France and presented his pleas to the French minister after U.S. relations with France had been severed and the last representative had left. Logan was credited with having influenced the course of peace, but he was strongly censured at home for his action, which brought about passage of the so-called Logan Act (1798). The legislation prohibited private citizens from engaging in diplomatic exchanges unless expressly authorized to do so.

1798 Dec. 14 A patent for a **screw threading machine** was awarded to David Wilkinson of Rhode Island. In Aug. 1848, Congress awarded Wilkinson $10,000 for his invention.

envoys to French Foreign Minister Charles Maurice de Talleyrand-Périgord. Honored by the Federalists for refusing a bribe by one of Talleyrand's agents, Marshall listened to 16 toasts in honor of his part in the XYZ Affair. The 13th toast, proposed by Rep. Robert Goodloe Harper, Federalist of South Carolina, contained the well-known phrase. Although the statement was correctly attributed to Harper in Philadelphia's *American Daily Advertiser* on June 20, the expression came to be identified with Charles Cotesworth Pinckney, another of the American envoys to whom the bribe request had been directed. Pinckney, shortly before his death, denied ever having made the statement, but because the expression seemed more apt as a diplomatic reply than as a toast, the legend persisted that Pinckney had spoken these words to the French agent.

1799 The first recorded use of the word *scab* in labor-management conflicts occurred during a shoemakers' strike in Philadelphia, Pa. The term applied to workers hired at establishments during a strike. At the same time the term *paid walking delegate* was born. It was the duty of the paid walking delegate to inspect struck establishments for the presence of scabs and to take necessary measures.

1799 **Academic precocity,** frequent throughout early American history, was illustrated by the graduation this year of a boy of 14 from Rhode Island College. Infants of three years of age were sometimes taught to read Latin as soon as English. Timothy Dwight was able to read the Bible at the age of four.

1799 Dec. 26 "First in war, first in peace, first in the **hearts of his countrymen,**" forever associated with George Washington, was first said as part of Henry Lee's funeral oration before Congress, after Washington's death on Dec. 14. Lee, known as "Light Horse Harry" Lee, had served under Washington in the Revolution and become his close friend. He was the father of Robert E. Lee. On the same day as Lee's eulogy, the House of Representatives passed a resolution incorporating Lee's words almost verbatim: "First in war, first in peace, first in the hearts of his fellow citizens."

1800 *PRES.* JOHN ADAMS

120

Exploration and Settlement; Wars;
Government; Civil Rights; Statistics

I

II

Publishing; Arts and Music; Popular
Entertainment; Architecture; Theater

1800

This year's contest for the presidency revealed a sharp political division between the Federalist Party and the Republican, or Democratic-Republican, Party (forerunner of the Democratic Party). The Federalists, advocates of a strong central government and representing the well-to-do business class, chose as their candidate Pres. John Adams. The Republicans, the party of limited government and the agricultural interests, selected Thomas Jefferson of Virginia. The Constitution provided for each elector in the electoral college to vote for two candidates. The candidate with the most votes would become president and the one with the second highest total, vice president. The Republican electors cast 73 votes for Jefferson and the same number for Aaron Burr, the Republican candidate for vice president. The Federalist electors cast 65 votes for Adams; 64 for Charles Cotesworth Pinckney, their candidate for the vice presidency; and one for John Jay. The tie between Burr and Jefferson for the presidency meant the election would have to be decided in early 1801 by the House of Representatives. The problems caused by this election contributed to the passage, and ratification in 1804, of the Twelfth Amendment to the Constitution.

The second U.S. **Census** recorded a population of 5,308,483, including 896,849 slaves. The total number represented a ten-year increase of 1,379,269; the number of slaves increased by 199,168. The center of U.S. population was 18 miles southwest of Baltimore, a westward shift from 1790 reflecting the expansion of the frontier.

African resettlement of black slaves in Virginia was proposed for the first time by the Virginia Assembly. The nonbinding resolution and its successors reflected antislavery attitudes in the South in the early years of the nineteenth century, even among influential slaveholders. In 1802, 1805, and 1816 similar resolutions were passed by the Virginia Assembly.

1800–1801 In **congressional elections** the Republicans gained six Senate seats to take an 18–13 majority over the Federalists. In the House they gained 27 seats to take a 69–36 majority.

Jan. 7 Millard Fillmore, 13th president of the United States, was born in Locke, now Summerhill, in northwestern New York.

May 7 The **Northwest Territory was divided** by a law enacted by Congress into two territories, Ohio and Indiana, the latter out of the western portion, including Illinois, Wisconsin, Indiana, and parts of Michigan and Minnesota. The provisions of the Treaty of Paris (1783), which ended the Revolutionary War, had defined the borders of the U.S. Among other concessions, Great Britain agreed to a line through the Great Lakes that placed in U.S. control the territory called

Almost as soon as George Washington died in 1799, writers began to depict him as a hero of almost mythical proportions. Chief contributor to this legend was Mason Locke Weems, an Episcopal clergyman usually referred to as Parson Weems, who is supposed to have had Washington as a parishioner in Virginia. In 1800 the first edition of his best-known work appeared, *The Life and Memorable Actions of George Washington.* There were nine editions of the book by 1809. It was in the fifth edition, issued in 1806, that Weems first included the story of Washington and the cherry tree. In all, the biography went through 86 printings between 1800 and 1927. Weems's practice was to fictionalize biographies to increase their sales. For more than 30 years he was primarily a book peddler, selling his own books as well as those of other authors. He worked for Mathew Carey, the leading publisher and bookseller of Philadelphia. Weems wrote biographies of Francis Marion, Benjamin Franklin, and William Penn. He also composed moral tracts such as *The Drunkard's Looking Glass* (1812) and *Hymen's Recruiting Sergeant* (c1799).

Ralph Earl, who earned his living as an itinerant artist, was probably the first American painter to show genuine feeling for nature. He completed *Looking East from Leicester Hills* in 1800. The painting depicted a broad landscape viewed through an open window. It was commissioned by a landowner who probably desired to immortalize his holdings.

Hymns and Odes Composed on the Death of General George Washington, a volume collecting some of the countless poems occasioned by the death of George Washington in 1799, was published. Among the contributors to the book were Thomas Paine, Charles Brockden Brown, and Richard Alsop.

Isaiah Thomas, printer and publisher of Worcester, Mass., issued the first Greek New Testament printed in the U.S. Thomas was the leading U.S. book publisher from the end of the Revolutionary War to the end of the century, issuing 400 titles, well designed and manufactured. His biweekly newspaper, *Massachusetts Spy,* which he started in 1770, was published until 1904.

| Business and Industry; Science; Education; Philosophy and Religion **III** | | **IV** Sports; Social Issues and Crime; Folkways; Fashion; Holidays |

1800

The need to improve transportation facilities sparked a boom in canal building in the early nineteenth century. In South Carolina the Santee Canal, the first true canal in the U.S., was constructed between 1792 and 1800 to connect the Santee and Cooper rivers. This canal was 22 miles long, with ten locks that raised and lowered boats 103 feet. Its construction was directed by Christian Senf, a Swedish engineer imported for the job. He employed 110 men and women, mostly black slaves, to do the hard work. The canal cost $1,000,000 but ultimately failed because of inadequate supply of water. In New York State the Western Inland Lock Navigation Company had started a canal at the same time. This was only one mile long, with five locks. It was constructed to make navigation possible around the rapids of the Little Falls Gorge, on the Mohawk R.

The **Library of Congress** was established by the federal government. Housed at first in the Capitol, it was moved in 1897 to its own building, the largest and most costly library building in the world.

A **famous strike** in early U.S. history was the sailors' strike in New York City. Sailors demanded a raise in wages from $10 to $14 per month. They actively agitated throughout the city, urging other seamen to join the demonstrations. The strike was broken with the arrest of its leader for disturbing the peace and inciting to riot.

The first shoemaker in America to make **shoes designed specifically for the right and left feet** was William Young of Philadelphia.

The **Church of the United Brethren in Christ** was organized. Philip William Otterbein and Martin Boehm were elected bishops. The movement to form the church had originated among Mennonites in Lancaster County, Pa., in 1766 and spread among the German settlers of Pennsylvania, Maryland, and Virginia through the evangelistic labors of Otterbein and Boehm.

The **first cowpox vaccination** in the U.S. was performed by Dr. Benjamin Waterhouse in Philadelphia.

1800–1819 Renewed interest in **German culture** in America was spurred by the Rev. William Bentley of Salem, whose *Impartial Register,* released

The remarkable career of Johnny Appleseed began about 1800. Born John Chapman in Massachusetts about 1775, he moved to Pennsylvania, where he sold or gave away saplings and apple seeds to settlers moving west. Chapman then moved on to Ohio, sowing and giving away apple seeds en route. For more than 40 years he traveled throughout Ohio, Indiana, and western Pennsylvania. He pruned trees he had previously planted and helped pioneers care for the orchards grown from his seeds. His work bore fruit, literally, over an area of perhaps 100,000 sq. mi. Chapman was ragged in dress and eccentric in his ways. He was also an itinerant preacher, expounding his faith in the Church of the New Jerusalem, the religious organization that grew out of the teachings of Emanuel Swedenborg, the Swedish mystic whose teachings had been introduced to the U.S. in 1784 and whose empathy with the natural world apparently appealed to Chapman. During the War of 1812 Chapman traveled 30 miles to bring troops to Mansfield, Ohio, to forestall a raid by Indian allies of the British. Chapman also introduced and encouraged the raising of many useful medicinal herbs. He died near Fort Wayne, Ind., in 1847.

Four-tined forks came into common use in American homes at about this time. Two- and three-tined forks had been customary.

The **Sheraton and Directoire styles** in furniture, both reflecting a continued classical influence and a return to simpler design, appealed strongly to public taste. The New York City workshop of Duncan Phyfe turned out many superb examples.

The well-known cabinetmaker **Michael Allison** began producing cabinets of distinctive craftsmanship in New York City.

The method of **payment of American actors** was reflected in the hiring of Mrs. Merry as "star" for the American Company, performing in New York City. Her salary was $100 a week plus a "benefit." This benefit was usually the third performance of the play, the actor receiving a share of the proceeds.

Gouging, a popular frontier sport, reached its peak of popularity in the Ohio R. Valley. The ultimate goal was

| Exploration and Settlement; Wars; Government; Civil Rights; Statistics | I | | II | Publishing; Arts and Music; Popular Entertainment; Architecture; Theater |

the Old Northwest, between the Ohio and Mississippi rivers. States that had previously laid claim to parts of the region had ceded their territories in anticipation of the Northwest Ordinance of 1787.

June The new city of **Washington** in the District of Columbia became the U.S. capital, succeeding Philadelphia. This occurred when government departments began to move into their new buildings on land ceded to the federal government by Maryland and Virginia. The radial design of the city was created by the French architect Pierre Charles L'Enfant. Construction began in 1791 but was delayed following L'Enfant's dismissal in 1792. The first Congress to sit in Washington convened on Nov. 17, 1800. The first president to live in the Executive Mansion, John Adams, moved in, also in November. The first president to be inaugurated there, Thomas Jefferson, was sworn into office March 4, 1801. The U.S. was probably the first modern nation to design a city exclusively as a capital.

Oct. 1 The territory of **Louisiana**, the entire region of the Missouri-Mississippi river valleys, was ceded by Spain to France in the secret treaty of San Ildefonso, in effect giving back territory awarded Spain by France in the Treaty of Fontainebleau in 1762. This territory was acquired by the U.S. in 1803 through the Louisiana Purchase.

The first issue of ***Musical Journal,*** a weekly published and edited by Benjamin Carr, appeared in Philadelphia. Carr announced he would publish "a regular supply of new music from Europe" and would draw on "the assistance of Men of Genius in this Country."

The number of **libraries** in the U.S. was about 50, with holdings of some 80,000 volumes. Most of these libraries required membership or payment of a fee for access to their books. By 1825, however, the nation's four largest cities could claim a total of 50 libraries, including some 1,500,000 volumes. Between 1800 and 1830 about 50,-000 pamphlets, books, and magazine titles were issued in the U.S. Most of the books sold no more than 1000 copies, a respectable number considering the population of the country.

July 9 The **first summer theater** in New York opened at Mount Vernon Gardens at Broadway and Leonard St. Performances began at 9 P.M., tickets selling at four and five shillings.

1801

As a result of the tie vote between Thomas Jefferson and Aaron Burr in the electoral college in the 1800 presidential election, the process of presidential selection went to the House of Representatives, where each state would have one vote. Burr publicly professed support for Jefferson, his fellow Republican, but did nothing to take himself out of the race, even though the Republicans intended that Burr become vice president. Many Federalists favored Burr for president, but Alexander Hamilton, the leading Federalist, detested Burr and worked behind the scenes on Jefferson's behalf, despite his disagreement with Jefferson's policies. Beginning Feb. 11, the House took 35 ballots without breaking the deadlock. On the 36th ballot, on Feb. 17, barely two weeks before a new president was to be inaugurated, Jefferson received a majority vote when certain Federalists gave up their support of Burr. Burr was elected vice president.

Jan. 20 **John Marshall** was appointed chief justice of the U.S. Supreme Court. He became one of the greatest judges in U.S. history, establishing the Supreme Court as final authority in determining state and federal powers.

With the new century and the establishment of political parties came newspapers and journals that strongly supported one side or another. Among the leading editors of such publications was Joseph Dennie, who first edited the *Farmer's Weekly Museum* in Walpole, N.H. The publication became influential because of the "Lay Preacher" essays Dennie wrote for it. Later, in Philadelphia, he edited *The Port Folio* from 1801 to 1809. An avid Federalist, Dennie made such strong verbal attacks on Thomas Jefferson that he was tried in 1805 for seditious libel but was acquitted. He did, however, publish literary articles of quality, including works of Thomas Moore, Leigh Hunt, and Thomas Campbell. Dennie was a founder of the Tuesday Club of Philadelphia, which supported both the magazine and the Federalist cause.

City Hall at Charleston, S.C., one of the best examples of post-colonial, "studied" architecture, was built from plans by Joseph Manigault.

The **New York** *Evening Post,* a newspaper that enlisted some of the foremost editorial writers of the nineteenth century, was established. Under the editorship of William Cullen Bryant from 1826–1878, it was Free-soil and supported Abraham Lincoln. In the 1880s

| Business and Industry; Science; Education; Philosophy and Religion   **III** | | **IV**   Sports; Social Issues and Crime; Folkways; Fashion; Holidays |

periodically over two decades, reported on cultural, intellectual, and scientific advances in Germany.

July The **first recorded Methodist camp meeting** was held in Logan County, Ky., near the Gaspar R. Church.

Sept. **Cayuga Bridge,** an engineering marvel of its time, was completed. It crossed the northern end of Cayuga Lake and the Montezuma Swamp in west central New York. The bridge, one and one-eighth of a mile long, was built of wood and was wide enough for wagons to pass abreast. Stages of the Genesee Turnpike used it, as did American troops in the War of 1812 on their way to the Niagara frontier. The bridge cost $150,000. It was financed by a loan from the Manhattan Company of New York City, which was founded in 1799 by Aaron Burr. Ostensibly established as a water supply company, the Manhattan Company had a charter broad enough so that it could function as a bank.

Nov. 1 **Middlebury College** was chartered in Middlebury, Vt. Its first degrees were awarded in 1802.

to gouge out an opponent's eye with the thumbnail. Thumbnails were grown long for this purpose. This style of fighting was imported from England into the South and spread westward.

Apr. 3 **Martha Washington** was granted the franking privilege. A special act of Congress allowed her to receive and send mail free of charge. Mrs. Washington lived to enjoy her privilege only two years. Franking, extended to veterans of the Revolutionary War, became so widespread that a complete revision of the practice soon became necessary.

Sept. 23 **Thomas Jefferson** penned one of his best known quotes in a letter to his friend Benjamin Rush. He summed up his strong views on freedom of speech, the press, and religion in the comment, "I have sworn upon the altar of God, eternal hostility against every form of tyranny over the mind of man." This, he continued, was all his opponents had to fear from him. Rush, a physician and scientist and a signer of the Declaration of Independence, was treasurer of the U.S. Mint in Philadelphia.

1801

A religious revival began to sweep the West in this period. It started with the preaching of James McGready, a Presbyterian minister who began preaching in Logan County, Ky., in 1797. Encampments at which he preached formed the beginnings of the camp meeting, a gathering that for many typified evangelical Protestantism on the frontier. Such meetings generally featured hell-fire sermons preached at congregations gathered in open fields or groves of trees.

The **Plan of Union** was adopted by Congregationalists and Presbyterians to combine their resources in bringing religion to frontier settlements. This proved to be one of the most fruitful cooperative ventures in American church history. The expansion of the frontier westward had placed serious organizational burdens on both denominations. Settlements were scattered and poorly serviced. To make the most of available resources, the Plan of Union permitted Congregationalist and Presbyterian ministers to serve in one another's churches.

The **American Company of Booksellers** was organized in New York City. It was promoted especially by the Philadelphia publisher Mathew Carey. This

Pioneer farmers in the backwoods had no opportunity to go to concerts or plays, but they created their own recreation, geared to their circumstances and their way of life. They met their neighbors at log-rollings, barbecues, and religious camp meetings. Some of them drank too much of the raw whiskey produced on the frontier, or gambled on horses or at cards. Since good marksmanship was a necessity, competition arose out of men's pride in their skill. There were competitive squirrel hunts and shooting at targets for such prizes as a turkey or a barrel of whiskey. Dances such as Virginia reels and country jigs were popular; they gave the women some much-needed social life.

Cold water crackers first began to appear in New England. Josiah Bent of Milton, Mass., constructed a Dutch oven in his home; the first crackers were probably made in it. They were made with wheat flour and cold water, then cooked in a wood-fired brick oven. He peddled the crackers himself. They soon became widespread in New England, and eventually gained international recognition. Their popularity probably was aided by the belief that crackers helped the digestion. Bent's Cold Water Crackers are still produced.

Exploration and Settlement; Wars; Government; Civil Rights; Statistics		Publishing; Arts and Music; Popular Entertainment; Architecture; Theater

I Exploration and Settlement; Wars; Government; Civil Rights; Statistics

II Publishing; Arts and Music; Popular Entertainment; Architecture; Theater

Mar. 4 Thomas Jefferson, third president of the United States, became the first president to be inaugurated in Washington, D.C. He held the office for eight years, and was the first of the Republican (later Democratic) Party elected to the presidency.

May 14 Yusuf Karamanli, pasha of Tripoli, opened the **Tripolitan War** (1801–1805) by the symbolic act of ordering his soldiers to cut down the flagpole at the U.S. consulate. The action followed U.S. refusal to satisfy Tripolitan demands for more tribute to guarantee protection from piracy against American ships.

Carl Schurz and Edwin Lawrence Godkin steered the paper in its attack on local corruption. After passing through many hands, it became the New York *Post* in Mar. 1934.

Feb. 11 *Abaellino, the Great Bandit,* a play by William Dunlap, opened. Adapted from *Aböllino* (novel, 1794; play, 1795) by the German writer Johann Heinrich Daniel Zschokke, it ran in American theaters for 25 years and was translated into many languages for production abroad.

1802

In April the U.S. learned that Napoleon I of France in 1800 had secured through a secret agreement the return of the Louisiana territory from Spain. This was alarming news because the mouth of the Mississippi R. was now in the hands of an aggressive power, and Americans west of the Allegheny Mts. depended on free passage and use of the port of New Orleans to transfer their products to oceangoing ships. Pres. Thomas Jefferson ordered Robert R. Livingston, U.S. minister to France, to buy land on the lower Mississippi for use as a port, or to secure a guarantee of free navigation. In October Spanish officials, still in New Orleans, refused to allow Americans to use the port. This serious disruption of American commerce led Jefferson in the next year to begin negotiations for purchase of Louisiana.

1802–1803 In **congressional elections** the Republicans gained seven Senate seats for a 25–9 majority over the Federalists. In the House they gained 33 seats to the Federalists' gain of three, for a 102–39 majority.

Jan. 29 The first librarian of the **Library of Congress** was John Beckley of Virginia, previously clerk of the House of Representatives. The library had its beginnings as a parliamentary library.

Feb. 6 To protect U.S. ships against **Tripolitan pirates,** Congress empowered the president to arm U.S. vessels. Congress did not declare war, implying instead that the U.S. might use force at sea but not against Tripolitan ports. A squadron under Commodore Richard Dale blockaded Tripoli later in the year.

Mar. 16 The **U.S. Military Academy** at West Point, N.Y., was established by Congress. The academy opened officially on July 4.

Apr. 30 Pres. Jefferson signed the **Enabling Act,** establishing procedures under which a territory organized by the provisions of the Ordinance of 1787 could become a state. The law authorized the people of Ohio Territory to hold a convention and frame a constitution. Subsequently, in 1803, Ohio became the

In the nineteenth century almost all American artists studied abroad and many of them became expatriates, chiefly in England and Italy. The first of these was Benjamin West, one of the best historical painters. West settled in London in 1763, becoming prominent as historical painter to King George III and president of the Royal Academy. He trained or advised a number of younger American painters. Among his paintings were *Saul and the Witch of Endor* and *The Death of Wolfe.* His paintings treating American subjects included *William Penn's Treaty with the Indians* (1772) and *Franklin Drawing Electricity from the Sky* (c1805). He completed an enormous canvas of *Christ Healing the Sick* in 1816, intended as a gift for the Pennsylvania Hospital in Philadelphia. It created such a sensation in London that he was offered 3000 guineas for it, so he painted a duplicate to send to America. The picture was so large that a special gallery had to be built to house it.

The **American Academy of Arts** was established in New York City. Shares of stock in the organization were sold as if the academy were a business corporation, reflecting the domination of the upper class in American culture.

The **Greek Revival, or Classical, style** of architecture became popular in the U.S. around the turn of the nineteenth century. Construction of one of the most outstanding examples of this style, Arlington House, also called the Custis-Lee mansion, was begun this year in Arlington, Va., across the Potomac R. from Washington, D.C. Built for George Washington Parke Custis, grandson of Martha Washington, it later became the home of Robert E. Lee. During the Civil War it was confiscated and its grounds turned into a military cemetery, from which Arlington National Cemetery was formed. It is now known as Arlington House National Memorial.

Apr. The **Library of Congress** issued the first known catalog of books in the U.S., entitled *Catalogue of*

| Business and Industry; Science; Education; Philosophy and Religion **III** | | Sports; Social Issues and Crime; Folkways; Fashion; Holidays **IV** |

organization sponsored five book fairs between 1802 and 1806.

South Carolina College was chartered in Columbia, S.C. It opened for instruction in 1805 and awarded its first degrees in 1806. It was renamed the University of South Carolina in 1865.

Oct. 19 The **first Philadelphia aqueduct** was opened, providing a new supply of fresh water for the growing city.

Mar. 4 The expression *entangling alliances* was coined by Thomas Jefferson and used in his first inaugural address: "Peace, commerce, and honest friendship with all nations—entangling alliances with none." These words have been commonly attributed to George Washington; although Washington supported the idea expressed, there is no record of his having used this phraseology.

1802

American scientists, often self-taught, showed a bent for practical matters rather than research in theoretical problems. A good example was Nathaniel Bowditch. After having learned algebra at age 14, Bowditch made five sea voyages between 1795 and 1803, during which he perfected his knowledge of mathematics and navigation. As a result he corrected some 8000 errors in J. Hamilton Moore's *The Practical Navigator*, a standard work. Bowditch devised a practical method of computing longitude with a sextant, by measuring the angular distances between certain fixed stars and the moon. A new edition of Moore's work appeared under Bowditch's name in 1802 as *The New Practical American Navigator*. Nine more editions appeared in his lifetime, and in 1867 the rights were acquired by the U.S. Hydrographic Office, which has published it since. Bowditch also found time to translate four volumes of Pierre Simon, Marquis de Laplace's *Mécanique Celeste*, and to be president of the Essex Fire and Marine Insurance Co.

Sheep breeding in the U.S. received a powerful impetus when 100 Merino sheep were brought back from Spain by Col. David Humphreys at the end of his tour of duty there as U.S. minister. This first introduction into the U.S. of the fine wool of the Merino breed led to vastly improved domestic sheep. In less than a decade over a score of woolen mills were operating in the U.S., chiefly in New England.

The **first brass mill**, built by Abel Porter & Co. and operated by horsepower, began operation in Waterbury, Conn., which became the leading brass manufacturing center in America.

Jan. 9 Ohio University in Athens, Ohio, received its original charter as American Western University. In 1804 the name Ohio University was adopted. Its first degrees were awarded in 1815.

Jan. 15 **Washington and Jefferson College,** now located in Washington, Pa., had its beginnings when Jefferson Academy in Canonsburg, Pa., was chartered as Jefferson College. In 1806 Washington Academy in nearby Washington, Pa., was chartered as Washington

By the early nineteenth century the division between North and South on the question of slavery was becoming clear-cut. By 1802 all states north of the Mason-Dixon line, except for New Jersey, had passed antislavery laws or measures for gradual emancipation. In Congress a bill to make the Fugitive Slave Law of 1793 more stringent was defeated by a narrow margin. In the South there was fear of slave insurrections, which were reported in six North Carolina counties and nine Virginia counties in 1802.

The **banjo clock** first appeared in American homes. Designed by Simon Willard, the famous clockmaker of Roxbury, Mass., the banjo clock was constructed to hang on a wall, against which it was supported by a small gilt bracket.

The **first hotel** in the U.S., the Union Hotel in Saratoga Springs, N.Y., was built by Gideon Putnam. What distinguished the Union as a hotel was its emphasis on lodging and services rather than food and drink.

Public horse racing was forbidden by a New York State law. Racing was conducted by several private organizations, so-called jockey clubs.

Expectation, a powerful horse owned by Colonel Tayloe, won a sweepstakes race at Richmond, Va., doing two miles in 3:47. After the race, Expectation was sold to Colonel Alston for $4000.

17th state of the Union and the first created out of the Northwest Territory. This precedent was later followed by other parts of the territory.

Books, Maps, and Charts, Belonging to the Library of the Two Houses of Congress.

1803

A landmark decision was handed down by the Supreme Court this year in the case of *Marbury* v. *Madison*. In Mar. 1801, in the last hours of John Adams's presidency, William Marbury was awarded a commission as justice of the peace of the District of Columbia. The new president, Thomas Jefferson, instructed his secretary of state, James Madison, not to deliver the commission. Marbury and three other men in the same situation sued Madison. The Court's decision, written by Chief Justice John Marshall and issued on Feb. 24, held that the law under which the suit was brought was null and void because it contravened the Constitution. This was the first decision of the Supreme Court to declare an act of Congress unconstitutional, thereby establishing the doctrine of judicial review and expanding the power of the judiciary.

Jan. 11 Pres. Thomas Jefferson appointed **James Monroe** minister plenipotentiary and envoy extraordinary to France and Spain, instructing him to purchase New Orleans and East and West Florida. The U.S. minister in Paris, Robert R. Livingston, was surprised when Napoleon offered to sell the entire Louisiana territory.

Feb. 19 **Ohio** became the 17th state. Although slavery had been outlawed in the Northwest Territory by the Northwest Ordinance in 1787, Ohio was the first state in which slavery was forbidden by law from the beginning of statehood. Vermont had outlawed slavery with the adoption of its constitution in July 1777, some six months after its declaration of independence as a republic.

Apr. 30 The **Louisiana Purchase,** the first territorial acquisition made by the U.S., added to the country some 828,000 sq. mi. of land between the Mississippi R. and the Rocky Mts. It was bought from France for 80,000,000 francs (about $15,000,000). The price included 20,000,000 francs for assumption by the U.S. of claims against France by U.S. citizens. The Louisiana Purchase increased U.S. national territory about 140%. The territory later formed Missouri, Nebraska, Iowa, Arkansas, North and South Dakota, most of Louisiana, Kansas, Minnesota, Montana, Wyoming, and parts of Colorado and Oklahoma.

May 23 In the **Tripolitan War** (1801–1805), Commodore Edward Preble was commissioned as commander of a U.S. Navy squadron to be sent against Tripoli.

A versatile American of the early national period was William Wirt of Virginia. A lawyer, politician, and essayist, he served as U.S. attorney general for 12 years. His most popular literary work was *Letters of a British Spy,* purporting to be written by a member of the British Parliament during a visit to the southern U.S. Wirt's essays, attempting to mimic the style of Joseph Addison, first appeared anonymously in a Richmond, Va., newspaper. They followed the example of eighteenth-century commentators who posed as foreign observers of the customs of a strange society. Published in book form in 1803, the essays became very popular and went through 12 editions. The essays dealt with southern customs, education, politics, and history. In 1817 Wirt published *Life and Character of Patrick Henry,* the first book to appear under his own name. In it he recreated many of Henry's speeches.

Thomas G. Fessenden employed social and political satire in *A Terrible Tractoration,* which ridiculed medical quackery, vivisection, animal crossbreeding, and the scientific theories of such French and English naturalists as Comte Georges Louis Leclerc de Buffon and Erasmus Darwin. His *Democracy Unveiled* (1805) attacked Thomas Jefferson, and his *Pills, Poetical and Philosophical* (1809) again satirized the medical profession.

New York City Hall, one of the country's best examples of Georgian architecture, was erected from plans made by the city's supervising architect, John McComb.

Feb. 4 **William Dunlap,** often called America's first professional playwright, adapted the French melodrama *La Voix de Nature* by L.C. Caigniez, and produced it in New York City. Melodrama, newly developed abroad, notably in France, involved virtuous and villainous stock characters, with the virtuous always triumphant. *The Voice of Nature* was the first melodrama to reach the American stage.

| Business and Industry; Science; Education; Philosophy and Religion | III | | IV | Sports; Social Issues and Crime; Folkways; Fashion; Holidays |

College. The two were united in 1865.

Nov. 18 The **first sheet copper** produced in the U.S. was manufactured in Boston, Mass.

1803

Among the religious groups that attempted to fund utopias in the U.S. were the Rappites, so-called after their leader George Rapp, who emigrated from Germany in 1803. In 1805 he and his followers founded Harmony, Pa., where they developed a prosperous industrial and agricultural community. In 1814 and 1815 they moved to Indiana and founded another Harmony. There they also prospered but in 1825 sold their property to Robert Owen, the English manufacturer and social reformer. Moving back to Pennsylvania, the Rappites established Economy (now Ambridge), northwest of Pittsburgh. The Harmony Society was an austere group who practiced celibacy. The group weakened after Rapp's death and faded as its members grew old. It ceased to exist in 1906.

The **first tax-supported public library** was founded in Salisbury, Conn. It was launched by a gift from Caleb Bingham, a Boston publisher, and was continued by grants of town moneys.

Jacob Albright of Lebanon County, Pa., was ordained an elder in a religious group that came to be known as the Albrights. A layman of Lutheran upbringing and Methodist ideas, Albright had begun to preach in 1796 and had attracted a personal following among the German-speaking people of Lebanon County. In 1807 this group held its first annual conference, elected Albright bishop, and adopted articles of faith. In 1816, after Albright's death, it took the name Evangelical Association.

Apr. John James Audubon became the first American to band birds for scientific purposes by tagging a number of phoebes.

May The future of **steam engines** was addressed by U.S. architect Benjamin Henry Latrobe in a less than enthusiastic report to the American Philosophical Society. Latrobe's report was in response to a request from the Philosophical Society of Rotterdam concerning U.S. engineering developments. Latrobe, Pres. Jefferson's surveyor of public buildings and an architect of distinction, lacked insight into the future of science. In 1807 Robert Fulton's steam-driven vessel, *Clermont,* launched on the Hudson R., was operating successfully.

Sept. 29 The first **Roman Catholic Church** built in Boston was formally dedicated.

The British Passenger Act of 1803 appeared to be a humanitarian measure, but its practical effect was to cut down dramatically on the number of immigrants coming to the U.S. Ships from Londonderry and Belfast, Ireland, had been carrying 400 to 500 emigrants on each voyage, but the new law required that 43 sq. ft. of space be allowed for each passenger, so they soon could transport only a few score. As a result, fares increased so after 1803 only about 1000 emigrants a year left Ireland for the U.S. Between 1810 and 1812 these ships were preyed upon by British naval vessels, which impressed hundreds of young men into service. The falling off of immigration to the U.S. during the early years of independence gave more time for earlier settlers to become assimilated before the next influx.

The personal nature of **medical practice** in early America was demonstrated by a doctor who, in setting up his practice, advertised that he would be glad to wait upon the public but that his first concern was for "his friends in particular."

The racehorse **Peacemaking,** by running two miles in 3:54, set a record that was to stand for 30 years.

John Randolph of Roanoke, an aristocratic Virginia congressman, set tongues wagging in Philadelphia with an announcement that he had fathered an illegitimate child.

A **subscription** to the Philadelphia periodical *Port Folio* cost $5.00 a year. It was suggested that the price would be negligible if readers organized themselves into reading clubs and shared each issue.

| Exploration and Settlement; Wars; Government; Civil Rights; Statistics | I | | II | Publishing; Arts and Music; Popular Entertainment; Architecture; Theater |

1804

Pres. Thomas Jefferson's scientific curiosity, and his concern for the economic and political security of the western U.S., were reflected in his sponsorship of the Lewis and Clark Expedition of 1804–1806. The expedition was headed by Merriwether Lewis, Jefferson's private secretary, and William Clark, an Army officer. The expedition was to explore the Northwest from the Mississippi R. to the Pacific Ocean, find the best travel route, and establish U.S. claims to the Oregon Territory. The expedition, including about 30 persons, left St. Louis, Mo., on May 14, 1804, and traveled up the Missouri R., spending the winter in North Dakota. In July 1805, the group found the headwaters of the Missouri and learned there was no easy route to the Pacific. They were also the first Americans to cross the Continental Divide. Traveling down the Columbia R., the expedition reached the Pacific on Nov. 8, 1805, and wintered there. On Sept. 23, 1806, the expedition arrived back at St. Louis, bringing with it great quantities of information on vegetation, animals, Indians, and the geography of the region. As Theodore Roosevelt wrote later, the expedition "opened the door into the heart of the Far West."

1804–1805 In **congressional elections** the Republicans gained two Senate seats for a 27–7 majority over the Federalists. In the House they gained 14 seats for a 116–25 majority.

Feb. 16 Lt. **Stephen Decatur,** commanding the *Intrepid,* burned the captured U.S. frigate *Philadelphia* while it was docked in Tripoli harbor. The American ship had been captured by Tripolitan gunboats in the previous October when it ran onto a reef.

Mar. 26 The **Louisiana Territory Act** was passed by Congress. It divided the Louisiana Purchase into the Territory of Orleans (present-day Louisiana west of the Mississippi R.) in the south, and the District of Louisiana (renamed the Territory of Louisiana in 1805) in the north.

July 11 **Alexander Hamilton was fatally wounded** in a pistol duel with Aaron Burr. Hamilton had fought Burr's run for the presidency in 1800, and for the governorship of New York in 1804, when Hamilton and others suspected that Burr intended to attach New York to the disgruntled New England states in a plan to disunite from the Union and form a northern confederacy. Burr challenged Hamilton, who deliberately misfired before Burr fired with intent to kill.

Sept. 25 The **Twelfth Amendment** to the U.S. Constitution was ratified, providing in part that voters shall "name in their ballots the person voted for as President and in distinct ballots the person voted for as vice president." In the election of this year, electors for the first time voted separately for president and vice

Like other American artists before and after them, Washington Allston and John Vanderlyn found Europe more congenial for exercising their talents than the U.S. Beginning in 1801, Allston studied in England under Benjamin West, then spent four years in Rome. The period from 1810 to 1818, spent in England, was Allston's most productive. He was an early and important artist of the Romantic school, as exemplified in such works as *The Deluge* (1804) and *The Rising of a Thunderstorm at Sea* (1804). His work lost its vitality when he returned to the U.S. and was marked by such failures as *Belshazzar's Feast,* over which he labored for 26 years. John Vanderlyn was the first American painter to study in Paris instead of London or Rome. He spent the years from 1796 to 1815 in the French capital and in Rome. His early work featured nudes painted so realistically that they shocked viewers. Vanderlyn was primarily a historical painter, and such works as *Marius Amid the Ruins at Carthage* won him a high reputation but did not sell. He also did excellent portraits but worked so slowly that few people had the patience to pose for him.

The Hermitage, now a national shrine, was begun by Andrew Jackson and his wife as a three-room cabin in the Tennessee wilderness north of Nashville.

St. Stephen's Catholic Church was built, the only extant church in Boston designed by Charles Bulfinch. It is sometimes called the New North Church.

One of the earliest **book catalogs** issued in the U.S. made its appearance. Entitled *The Catalogue of All the Books Printed in the United States,* the publication was a joint effort of Boston booksellers.

The first volume of *Life of George Washington* by John Marshall was published. The fifth and final volume appeared in 1807. Although the work reflected

| Business and Industry; Science; Education; Philosophy and Religion   **III** | | **IV**   Sports; Social Issues and Crime; Folkways; Fashion; Holidays |

1804

Even as late as the eighteenth century, religious and political persecution was spurring men of above ordinary talent to immigrate to the U.S. Such a man was Joseph Priestley, theologian and scientist. His greatest scientific achievement was the discovery of oxygen, although he did not realize the importance of his work. His strongly expressed Unitarian views and his support of the French Revolution made him many enemies. A mob wrecked his house and destroyed his scientific apparatus in 1791, prompting him to leave England for the U.S. in 1794. Among his friends and correspondents was Thomas Jefferson. Priestley settled at Northumberland, Pa., and spent the last years of his life writing and continuing his scientific studies. He died at Northumberland on Feb. 6, 1804.

The New-York Historical Society, founded mainly through the efforts of businessman John Pintard, began making contributions to scholarship and establishing enduring historical records. Pintard had lost his money through a bad investment, but he was able to reestablish himself and concentrate on what was to become his vocation: promoting cultural institutions. He is credited with having encouraged the start of the Massachusetts Historical Society and similar groups. Pintard also helped establish the General Theological Seminary and the American Bible Society in New York City, and he installed an improved method for keeping the vital statistics of New York City.

What was perhaps the **first automobile** was built by Oliver Evans, an American inventor, who was commissioned by the Philadelphia Board of Health to build a steam engine for dredging the Schuylkill R. and cleaning the city docks. His five-hp engine propelled a scow 12 ft. wide and 30 ft. long. The scow weighed 15½ tons and was driven 1½ miles from its construction shed, down Center St., much to the amusement of Philadelphians. Evans offered to bet an onlooker $3000 that he could build a steam-driven vehicle that would go faster than any horse in the world. The scow's drive belt was shifted from its rollers to paddlewheels and it went steaming down the river against the wind, leaving all sailboats behind. Despite this demonstration, the public was not much impressed with the principle of steam locomotion.

One result of Napoleon's establishment of the French Empire in Europe in 1804 was the development of the Empire style in furniture and house furnishings. The style was not long in reaching the U.S. and dominated until after Napoleon's fall in 1815. By contrast with late eighteenth-century styles, which favored the classical manner of straight lines and minimal carving, Empire furniture was heavier and more massive. There were combinations of marble and brass, and ormolu and wood. Animal forms, such as claw feet and eagle heads, were used together with elaborate decorative carvings. Heavy textiles were used in upholstery. Larger and more imposing interiors were needed to set off the monumental furniture so couches were modeled after Roman beds and bookcases with facades like temples appeared. Although most American pieces were not as lush as the French originals, the furniture suggested wealth and power in the Napoleonic manner but did not provide a relaxed setting for social life.

The **Coonskin Library** was founded in Marietta, Ohio. This unique institution came into being when settlers along the Ohio R. bartered coonskins for books from Boston merchants.

The **first agricultural fair** was held in Washington, D.C. There existed before this time various societies that promoted agriculture, commerce, and the arts. These groups distributed literature, with some bulletins devoted exclusively to agriculture.

The first recorded shipment of **bananas** to the U.S. arrived on the schooner *Reynard,* apparently from Cuba. Commercial organization of the banana trade did not begin until 1885, when the Boston Fruit Company was formed, as large-scale importation required refrigeration and ships especially designed for shipping the fruit.

Feb. 1   Thomas Jefferson's vision of an **agrarian society** rising in the U.S. was reflected in a letter to the French economist Jean Baptiste Say, who had sent Jefferson two volumes on political economy. Jefferson noted that in Europe "the quantity of food is fixed, or

president. Previously the candidate having the second largest number of votes in the electoral college became vice president.

Dec. 5 Thomas Jefferson was reelected president of the United States. George Clinton, first governor of New York and like Jefferson a Democratic-Republican, was elected vice president. The electoral vote was Jefferson, 162; Charles C. Pinckney, Federalist of South Carolina, 14. This was the first election with separate ballots for president and vice president.

Marshall's Federalist bias and lacked literary style, it was considered the most impressive and authoritative biography of the first president to appear in the 50 years following Washington's death. Shorter biographies of Washington were written by Aaron Bancroft (1807) and David Ramsay (1807).

1805

U.S. merchant shipping, as it grew in volume, was increasingly preyed upon by pirates of the states of the Barbary Coast of North Africa, who had attacked the shipping of European nations for many years. These states were Tripolitania, Tunisia, Algeria, and Morocco. The Tripolitan War (1801–1805), the first of a number of conflicts, began when the American government refused to pay tribute to the rulers of these states in return for a guarantee of protection. After sporadic fighting, John Rodgers, a naval officer, negotiated a peace treaty, which was signed June 4, 1805. Tripoli renounced all rights to collect tribute or halt U.S. shipping. The U.S. agreed to pay $60,000 to ransom the crew of the warship *Philadelphia*, which had been captured after having drifted aground. The treaty was the most favorable any nation had negotiated with the pirate states, but it did not put an end to piracy. Another decade was to pass before the threat was entirely ended.

Mar. 4 Pres. **Thomas Jefferson was inaugurated** for his second term. George Clinton succeeded Aaron Burr as vice president.

Apr. 27 In the **Tripolitan War,** the U.S. achieved its major victory when William Eaton, a special U.S. naval agent, led a small force of Marines and Arab mercenaries in capturing the Tripolitan port city of Derna. Eaton's force, a squad of U.S. Marines under Lt. Preston N. O'Bannon and about 100 Arab mercenaries, had marched 500 miles from Egypt to Derna and were assisted by a coordinated bombardment of Derna by U.S. naval vessels. Eaton's ultimate mission, approved by Pres. Thomas Jefferson, was to replace the ruling pasha of Tripoli with the rightful ruler. However, the coming of peace in early June aborted the plan. The phrase "to the shores of Tripoli" in the

In the early years of independence the U.S. was still dependent on Europe, especially England, for architects and architectural styles. Benjamin Henry Latrobe, who came to the U.S. from England in 1796, is considered the first professional architect in the U.S. Pres. Thomas Jefferson appointed him surveyor of public buildings in 1803. Latrobe introduced classical Greek designs and styles, which contributed greatly to the Classical revival. His 1799 design for the Bank of Pennsylvania in Philadelphia was modeled after a Greek Ionic temple. Latrobe also designed the Roman Catholic Cathedral in Baltimore. Built between 1805 and 1815, it was the first cathedral in the U.S. and represented the best monumental architecture of the period. In 1800 Latrobe designed Sedgeley, a residence near Philadelphia, said to be the first executed example of the Gothic revival in the U.S. After the British burned the Capitol in Washington, D.C., in 1814, Latrobe took charge of its rebuilding.

The **Pennsylvania Academy of Fine Arts** was founded by Charles Willson Peale. It is the oldest extant art institution in the U.S. The New York Academy was founded in 1801 but survived only four years.

Mrs. **Mercy Otis Warren,** sister of James Otis and wife of James Warren, both prominent Massachusetts politicians, provided a lively contemporary account of the American Revolution in her three-volume *Rise, Progress, and Termination of the American Revolution.* Her acquaintance and correspondence with many of the Revolutionary leaders enabled her to focus on individual participants in the war. Her sketches of these figures provided later writers with a mine of anecdotes.

Matthew Pratt, an early student of Benjamin West, died in Philadelphia. During his early life he displayed great skill in painting wooden signboards, which were still to be seen after the Civil War. Pratt studied with West in London for two and a half years, immortalizing his stay there in his painting *The American School,* which shows West instructing four pupils.

Gore Place, perhaps the finest New England example

Business and Industry; Science; Education; Philosophy and Religion **III**		**IV** Sports; Social Issues and Crime; Folkways; Fashion; Holidays

Two patents for **galluses,** or suspenders, were granted.

increasing in a slow and only arithmetical ratio. . . . Here the immense extent of uncultivated and fertile lands enables every one who will labor to marry young, and to raise a family of any size. Our food, then, may increase geometrically with our laborers, and our births, however multiplied, become effective."

1805

A book of theological thought published this year marked a change in the course of belief within the Universalist Church. The book was *A Treatise on the Atonement* by Hosea Ballou, who for about 34 years was pastor of the Second Universalist Society in Boston. After about 1796 Ballou was the most influential voice in the denomination and turned it away from its Calvinistic tendencies. Ballou emphasized "Christ's subordination to the Father," giving Universalism a position much the same as that of Unitarianism. His basic viewpoint was that of anti-Trinitarianism, with God the universal father and Jesus Christ, His son, the spiritual authority and leader in uniting man with God. Ballou affirmed the freedom of man's will, with the sacrifice of Christ an example of the perfection man can attain by turning away from sin. The Winchester Profession, stating the doctrinal position of the church, had been adopted in 1803.

Not all commentators praised the morals and manners of the young U.S. Among those who emphasized the excesses of a raw democracy was Scottish-born Hugh Henry Brackenridge, author and jurist. The influence of satirists such as Miguel de Cervantes and Jonathan Swift was evident in his novel, *Modern Chivalry*, published between 1792 and 1815 in four volumes, a revision, and a final edition. In it he wrote: "In the American republic, we retain yet a great deal of the spirit of monarchy. . . . The first lesson I would give to a son of mine would be to have nothing to do with public business, but as a duty to his country. . . . beware of flatterers, whose object is not to serve them, but themselves. The demagogue in a democracy, and the courtier in a monarchy, are identical."

The first important **shipment of ice** from New England was made by Frederick Tudor, an inventive Boston businessman, who loaded the brig *Favorite* with ice and sent the cargo to Martinique. Tudor lost $4500 on the transaction, but a later shipment, aboard the vessel *Trident,* was more successful. It took another 15 years for the ice-exporting industry to show its potential. New techniques for cutting, storing, and shipping ice provided the groundwork for profitable shipments to Havana, New Orleans and, by 1833, to India.

Sacajawea, a Shoshone Indian woman, gained a place in American folklore by her activities this year. The wife of the Lewis and Clark expedition's official interpreter, Toussaint Charbonneau, she joined the expedition in what is now South Dakota, and accompanied the party to the Pacific and part of the way back east. Her presence with the explorers helped convince the Indians they met en route that the newcomers were not members of a war party. Her knowledge of edible wild plants was a great help to the expedition. In February she gave birth to a baby boy. The midwife was Meriwether Lewis.

Mar. 4 An **idyllic description of the American taxpayer** was presented by Pres. Thomas Jefferson in his second inaugural address. After noting that "internal taxes" had been discontinued, Jefferson reported: "The remaining revenue on the consumption of foreign articles is paid cheerfully by those who can afford

A **labor dispute** was taken into court for the first time by a struck employer. The result was conviction of leaders of the Philadelphia Society of Cordwainers, workers

official song of the U.S. Marine Corps refers to the Derna campaign, which was the first engagement of U.S. land forces in North Africa. The campaign marked the first time that the U.S. flag was raised over an Old World fort.

of late Georgian or Federal architecture in private residences, was built at Waltham, Mass.

Feb. 22 The **Park Theatre** in New York City was forced to close because of the bankruptcy of its producer, William Dunlap, the dominant force in the American stage during this period. Dunlap's operation had been hampered by displays of temperament among his actors and actresses and by frequent outbreaks of yellow fever.

1806

One of the most puzzling incidents of the early nineteenth century involved Aaron Burr, the brilliant but erratic political figure. Shortly after he fatally wounded Alexander Hamilton in a duel in 1804, Burr journeyed to New Orleans and entered into a conspiracy with U.S. Gen. James Wilkinson, although it is not clear what they conspired about. Wilkinson was actually in the pay of Spain at the time. Speculation was that Burr intended either to establish an independent nation in the Southwest or to seize territory for the same purpose in Spanish America. Burr secured financing from Harman Blennerhassett, of Blennerhassett Island in the Ohio R. near present-day Parkersburg, W. Va. He set out from there in the fall of 1806 with about 60 well-armed men and headed downstream. The expedition aroused suspicion and Wilkinson, seeking to save his own skin, turned against Burr. He spread stories of Burr's intentions and sent dispatches to the government in Washington accusing Burr of treason. Burr was arrested and charged with treason, but he was acquitted in 1807.

1806–1807 In **congressional elections** the Republicans gained one Senate seat for a 28–6 majority over the Federalists. In the House they gained two seats for a 118–24 majority.

Apr. 18 The **importation of many British products** was prohibited by an act of Congress in protest against the seizure of American ships and the impressment of American sailors by the British.

May 16 A **blockade** of the European coast from Brest to the Elbe R. was declared by Great Britain in an attempt to weaken Napoleon's military power. On Nov. 21 Napoleon responded with the Berlin Decree, which declared the British Isles under blockade. Both actions in time affected U.S. trade and foreign relations.

July 15 **Zebulon Pike** began his exploration of what is now the southwestern U.S. He traveled up the Missouri R., through Kansas and southern Nebraska to New Mexico, through the Rio Grande Valley and on to Mexico City. On Nov. 15 Pike first saw the famous mountain named for him, Pike's Peak, in what is now Colorado.

More and larger book publishing firms began to emerge as the nation grew. The most important publisher before the turn of the century was Isaiah Thomas of Worcester, Mass., whose firm published everything from magazines to reference books to almanacs. Thomas wrote a valuable *History of Printing in America* (1810). Another publisher was Matthew Carey of Philadelphia, who also labored for a protective tariff system. His son, Henry Charles Carey, became the head of Carey, Lea, and Carey, whose authors included Washington Irving. Henry Carey, like his father, was deeply interested in economics and the protective tariff.

The **Old West Church** at 131 Cambridge St., Boston, Mass., was built. It was designed by Asher Benjamin, who planned houses and churches in many New England towns. Built in the Federal style, the church had two stories of brick construction, with a stepped gable roof, decorative interior galleries, and a rotunda. The restored building is now privately owned.

Noah Webster's *Compendious Dictionary of the English Language* represented a retreat from Webster's earlier attempts to Americanize the English language. Although many supporters of a purely American language continued to agitate for linguistic change, Webster's dictionary compromised with the British mother tongue, and its standards became the accepted practice in the U.S. The dictionary was the culmination of a series of works by Webster, beginning in 1783 with *The Grammatical Institute of the English Language* and including readers, spellers, and grammars with enormous circulation in America.

Exhumation of the **first complete skeleton of an American mastodon** was depicted in a painting by Charles Willson Peale, a Philadelphia artist and naturalist. In 1801 Peale had heard of the discovery of the bones on a farm in upstate New York. He organized the first scientific expedition in the history of the U.S. to supervise the digging. Peale brought the bones to Philadelphia, assembled them, and exhibited them in his museum.

Nov. 15 The **first college magazine** appeared, the Yale University *Literary Cabinet.*

in cordovan leather, for criminal conspiracy for the purpose of increasing their wages. The conviction was secured under English common-law doctrine.

to add foreign luxuries to domestic comforts, being collected on our seaboards and frontiers only, and incorporated with the transactions of our mercantile citizens. . . . "

1806

Many trails long used by the Indians became roads for pioneer settlers. Such a trail was the Natchez Trace, which ran from present-day Nashville, Tenn., southwest to Natchez, Miss. By 1806 it was much used by traders, causing Congress to pass legislation for construction of a better road over its route. In the War of 1812 Andrew Jackson marched troops on the Natchez Trace as he moved on New Orleans to oppose the British.

The **first industry-wide strike** in the U.S. resulted when 200 journeymen shoemakers in New York City, suspecting that struck employers were having their work done in other establishments, obtained a nationwide strike order from the Journeyman Cordwainers' Society of Baltimore. Leaders of the strike were indicted for criminal conspiracy in their attempt to secure higher wages.

The **Lancaster system,** an English system of education named after its originator, Joseph Lancaster, was introduced in the U.S. in a New York City school. The system provided for use of pupil-teachers who, having once learned their lessons from other pupil-teachers or from master teachers, would pass on their knowledge to other pupils. Lancaster emigrated to America in 1818 to supervise implementation of his ideas. The system was economical and very popular among wealthy citizens, who preferred such schools to more costly public schools.

The **popularization of scientific knowledge** was successfully attempted in *The Wonders of Nature and Art* by Smith and Mease. The net effect of a book of this nature was to break the monopoly of knowledge held largely by the well-to-do classes in the U.S.

Dueling was dying out but had not yet disappeared. One of its most active practitioners was a future president of the U.S., Andrew Jackson. In 1803 he became embroiled in a dispute with Gov. John Sevier of Tennessee, who was said to have insulted Jackson's wife. A duel was arranged, but the confrontation was averted because of confusion at the scene. In 1806 a duel resulted from a bet on a horse race and yet another insult to Jackson's wife, this time by a lawyer, Charles Dickinson. When Jackson and Dickinson met on May 30, both men fired and Jackson suffered a broken rib. His shot felled Dickinson, who bled to death.

Street lighting by gas was introduced in the U.S. by David Melville, who constructed the lamps on Pelham St., Newport, R.I. There were legal complications, and the project was a failure for Melville.

The first picture of a soccer-type **football game** in America showed president Timothy Dwight watching Yale students kicking a ball. According to Yale tradition, the game of football had been played there for 45 years. The modern American game of football, however, did not begin to develop until about 1869.

Some **expressions** that Noah Webster included in his *Compendious Dictionary* were *lengthy, sot, spry, gunning, belittle,* and *caucus.* These Americanisms were denounced as so-called wigwam words, and the dictionary was criticized for containing vulgar New Englandisms.

June 5 A new **trotting record** was established at Harlem, N.Y., when the horse Yankee trotted a mile in 2:59, becoming the first trotter to break the three-minute mile.

1807

An early incident presaging the War of 1812 was the *Chesapeake-Leopard* affair of June 22, 1807. The U.S. warship *Chesapeake* was stopped by the British frigate *Leopard* off Norfolk, Va. The British commander insisted that the Chesapeake had four British deserters on board. When James Barron, commanding the *Chesapeake*, refused to surrender the men, the British ship opened fire, killing three Americans and wounding 18. The four alleged deserters were forcibly removed. In spite of Pres. Thomas Jefferson's protest, the British government on Oct. 17 announced it would continue its policy of impressing seamen on American ships who were thought to be British. As for Barron, he was court-martialed and suspended from active duty for five years, during which time he served in the French navy. In 1820 Barron killed Stephen Decatur in a duel sparked by Decatur's opposition to Barron's reinstatement.

The nation's new sense of political independence was reflected in the lives and works of its writers, who felt that American letters should also be independent of the Old World. Leaders in this movement were the Connecticut Wits, also known as the Hartford Wits because they were centered in that Connecticut city. This informal group began as one devoted to modernizing the Yale College curriculum. The members soon, however, entered the political arena. They shared the views of the conservative Federalists and collaborated on satirical verse attacking the liberal position. Among the group's members were Joel Barlow, John Trumbull, Timothy Dwight, Theodore Dwight, and Lemuel Hopkins. The group's political and literary importance was greatest in the late 1700s but continued to be an influence into the early 1800s.

Mar. 2 The **African slave trade** was prohibited after Jan. 1, 1808, by an act of Congress, which outlawed importation of slaves into any place within the jurisdiction of the U.S.

The **American college student** was satirized for the first time in the character of Dick Dashaway in a comedy by A. B. Lindsley, *Love and Friendship,* or *Yankee Notions,* performed in New York City. Dick, a fop, was contrasted with Yankee characters.

Sept. 1 **Aaron Burr** was acquitted of treason by a circuit court in Richmond, Va., on the grounds that he was not present when an overt act was committed. Pres. Thomas Jefferson, having been warned of Burr's activities with respect to annexation of Spanish territory, had issued a warning on Nov. 27, 1806, to all citizens forbidding any expedition against Spanish territory. Burr had been arrested in Alabama on Feb. 19 and indicted on June 24 on charges of treason.

Jan. 24 The first number of *Salmagundi,* a series of whimsical, mildly satirical, and very popular essays written by William and Washington Irving and James Kirke Paulding, was published. Following the informal style of London essayists of the previous century, these pieces afforded delightful glimpses of New York's social, cultural, and political life in the early 1800s. They also marked the beginning of what came to be called the Knickerbocker movement in American literature. Many imitations followed at once. Paulding and the Irvings were men of affluent background and similar literary taste. At this point in their lives they were little concerned with the major issues of the day. *Salmagundi,* therefore, remains charming embroidery rather than basic fabric in the development of American literature. But the essays are a lasting memorial to the old days of New York City and its Hudson R. Valley suburbs, and they established the tradition of metropolitan wit that continues unbroken to our day.

Dec. 22 The **Embargo Act** was signed by Pres. Jefferson. Britain and France had refused to recognize U.S. neutral rights and had hampered its shipping. The act was a retaliatory measure based on Jefferson's idea of commercial exclusion; U.S. exports to Britain and France were prohibited. This attempt to force France and England to remove restrictions on U.S. trade was considered by many a "cure that killed," since it seriously crippled American commerce.

1807

In the late eighteenth and early nineteenth centuries, American physicians and surgeons made significant contributions to medical science. Samuel Bard wrote a manual on midwifery and a forward-looking report on medical education. Nathan Smith helped found Yale's medical school and wrote a treatise on typhus fever. Philip Syng Physick performed many operations for cataracts and improved methods for treating fractures. Ephraim McDowell, who practiced in Kentucky, performed the first ovariotomy on record in 1808.

Most Americans had plenty to eat, but few enjoyed a balanced diet. Farmers grew their own food and shot wild game. In the cities the lack of refrigeration and even of canning until about 1820 meant that much salt pork and other preserved items were staples. Fresh fruits and vegetables were not available for much of the year. Foreign visitors were impressed by the amount of greasy food consumed by Americans and the speed at which it was eaten. A visiting French count reported that he was nearly made ill by a breakfast that included fish, steak, ham, sausage, salt beef, and hot breads. "The whole day passes in heaping indigestions on one another," he complained.

The **Boston Athenaeum,** a major institution fostering scholarship in the U.S., was founded out of the old Anthology Society. It combined the functions of an exclusive subscription library limited to the commercial, professional, and academic citizens of Boston; a social meeting place for these groups; a superior reference library; and a museum of natural history.

The general **social and intellectual lull** that pervaded New England in the early nineteenth century was epitomized by publication of *Life of Washington,* by Aaron Bancroft, a work of some scholarship but little inspiration. Years later Ralph Waldo Emerson would describe the period between 1790 and 1820 as a time when "there was not a book, a speech, or a conversation, or a thought" in Massachusetts. This intellectual lethargy was but an indicator of the social stability that seemed to contradict New England's growing trade, industry, and population. Fortunately, a new generation of writers was being born, including Henry Wadsworth Longfellow, on Feb. 27 of this year, and John Greenleaf Whittier, on Dec. 17.

Aug. 11 Robert Fulton's steamboat *Clermont* made its first run to Albany from New York in 32 hours, traveling at about 5 mph. The initial trial of the *Clermont* had taken place the previous spring when it crossed the Hudson R. from New York to New Jersey. Also in 1807 Pres. Jefferson corresponded with Fulton about the torpedoes Fulton was proposing as the chief defense of harbors. But Jefferson could not see gambling the safety of the nation on the success of a single weapon. Fulton had also proposed the development of submarines. Jefferson noted how effective torpedoes launched from submarines would be, and encouraged Fulton in his research and experiments.

Feb. 27 Henry Wadsworth Longfellow, one of America's most popular and revered poets, was born in Portland, Me. His birthday came to be celebrated for many years in public schools throughout the nation. One of the earliest records of such a celebration appeared in the biennial report of the superintendent of schools in West Virginia in 1905. The Historical Society of Cambridge, Mass., celebrated the centenary of Longfellow's birth in 1907 with addresses by William Dean Howells, Charles W. Eliot, Charles Eliot Norton, and Thomas Wentworth Higginson.

Exploration and Settlement; Wars;   Publishing; Arts and Music; Popular
Government; Civil Rights; Statistics   Entertainment; Architecture; Theater

I   II

1808

The war between Great Britain and Napoleonic France in the early nineteenth century caused great damage to America's economy and led to government action to solve the problem. On Dec. 22, 1807, an Embargo Act became law. In effect the act banned all trade with foreign countries in an attempt to show England and France, who were trying to keep U.S. ships from reaching each other's ports, the importance of U.S. products and markets. Another Embargo Act was passed on Jan. 9, 1808, and still a third on Mar. 12. None of the acts had the desired effect. Trade to and from Canada was difficult to stop, and neither Britain nor France suffered. The chief result was damage to shipping and commercial interests of the North, especially New England.

1808–1809 In congressional elections the Republicans maintained their 28–6 Senate majority over the Federalists. In the House they lost 24 seats but kept a majority, 94–48.

Apr. 17 French seizure of American shipping was authorized by Napoleon. His Bayonne Decree ordered seizure of all U.S. vessels entering French and Italian ports and all ports of the Hanseatic League. The U.S. was helpless before this legalized piracy. The French took the position that all American shipping in those waters was really British and operating under false registration. In addition, the French contended that any actual U.S. shipping was prohibited by the U.S. Embargo Act and should be confiscated as a favor to the U.S. government. Through his Bayonne Decree, Napoleon increased his nation's wealth by some $10,000,000 worth of U.S. ships and cargo.

Dec. 7 James Madison was elected president of the United States. George Clinton, Republican of New York, was elected vice president. The electoral vote was Madison, Democratic-Republican of Virginia, 122; Charles Cotesworth Pinckney, Federalist of South Carolina, 47; George Clinton, 6. In the vice presidential race the electoral vote was Clinton, 113; Rufus King, Federalist of New York, 47.

Dec. 29 Andrew Johnson, 17th president of the United States, was born in Raleigh, N.C.

Pocahontas (real name, Matoaka), daughter of the Indian chief Powhatan, became a favorite subject of American writers as a result of John Smith's tale of her intercession to save his life. The first book to treat Pocahontas as a literary figure was a novel, *The First Settlers of Virginia* (1805) by John Davis. The first play to use an American Indian as its subject was *The Indian Princess; or, La Belle Sauvage* by James N. Barker; it was first staged in Philadelphia on Apr. 6, 1808. The play was interspersed with songs and told the story of Pocahontas in a romantic vein. Another play, *Pocahontas* appeared in 1830; it was the work of George Washington Parke Custis, grandson of Martha Washington. Another drama with the same title, by Robert Dale Owen, the social reformer, appeared in 1837. Seba Smith, the humorist and journalist, wrote a verse romance, *Powhatan* (1841).

The New York Academy of Fine Arts was founded, helping New York City's rise as an American art center. Robert R. Livingston, U.S. ambassador to France, was its first president. The academy's European orientation made it popular with New York upper classes.

The *Théâtre d'Orleans* was built at a cost of $100,000, establishing New Orleans as America's operatic capital.

Poems on Various Occasions by George Gordon, Lord Byron, was published in America. Byron's poetry sold slowly at first. His death in 1824 in the cause of Greek independence made him a hero in the U.S., and eventually his works sold hundreds of thousands of copies.

1808

One of America's first and most successful entrepreneurs was German-born John Jacob Astor, who came to the U.S. in 1784. On Apr. 6, 1808, he received a charter for the American Fur Company, planning to compete in the far Northwest with the long established Canadian firms. In 1811 a subsidiary company established Fort Astoria (now Astoria, Oreg.) on the Columbia R. estuary, the first permanent U.S. settlement on the Pacific coast. By the 1820s Astor held a virtual monopoly on fur trading in the U.S. West. Manuel Lisa, William Clark, Pierre Chouteau, and others operating out of St. Louis, Mo., formed the Missouri Fur Company on July 16, 1808, to compete but in 1821 Astor formed an alliance with them. Astor retired in 1834 and at his death on Mar. 29, 1848, was the wealthiest man in the U.S.

Horses and horse racing continued to fascinate a large part of the population. The thoroughbred stallion Diomed was imported from England in 1798 and put out to stud. Diomed sired Sir Archie, sold to Gen. William R. Davie, a veteran of the American Revolution, for the unheard of sum of $5000. There was widespread mourning when Diomed died in 1808 in Virginia. The most important horse of the period was Justin Morgan, foaled in 1792 and the sire of the breed that became known by his name. The horse was named for its owner, a schoolteacher who brought him to Vermont, where there still is a Morgan horse farm near Middlebury. The Morgan horse is small, has great endurance, and can do almost anything but hunt or run well in long races.

What was probably the **first legal journal** in the U.S., the *American Law Journal,* was founded in Baltimore, Md., by John Elihu Hall, professor of rhetoric at the University of Maryland. It published until 1817.

The first volume of ***American Ornithology*** by Alexander Wilson, a major contribution to American scientific scholarship, was published. Wilson's study ran to nine volumes and was completed in 1814. A pioneer work, it also appealed to laymen because of its attractive illustrations and frequent analogies to human nature.

The **first recorded duel between two congressmen** was fought on what became a famous dueling ground at Bladensburg, Md. The duel was between George W. Campbell, a Jeffersonian Republican of Tennessee, and Barent Gardenier, Federalist of New York. Gardenier had attacked Campbell on the floor of Congress, charging that the House was controlled by French influence. Gardenier was seriously wounded but he recovered.

Feb. 11 **Anthracite coal** was burned for the first time in an open-grate experiment conducted by Judge Jesse Fell in his home at Wilkes-Barre, Pa. Anthracite was too hot a fuel for most domestic stoves of the period and was considered generally useless except for small manufacturing and forging operations.

Oct. 30 **Benjamin Ireson,** skipper of the schooner *Betty,* brought his vessel into Marblehead, Mass., where he was accused unjustly of sailing away from another skipper's sinking ship because he feared losing his own vessel. The women of Marblehead tarred and feathered him and ran him out of town in a cart. This story was related years later by John Greenleaf Whittier in his ballad "Skipper Ireson's Ride" (1857).

Dec. 12 The **first Bible Society** in the U.S. was formed in Philadelphia. Its first president was the Rev. William White.

| Exploration and Settlement; Wars; Government; Civil Rights; Statistics | I | | II | Publishing; Arts and Music; Popular Entertainment; Architecture; Theater |

1809

Great Britain's attempts to restrict U.S. shipping during Britain's war with France continued to cause dissension in the U.S. The ineffective Embargo Act of 1807 was repealed on Mar. 1, 1809, largely through the efforts of Sen. Timothy Pickering of Massachusetts. Pickering was an ardent Federalist who typified the bitter opposition of New England to the law that had almost destroyed its shipping. The Non-Intercourse Act was passed the same day, permitting trade with all nations except England and France. Trade with the belligerents would be resumed when they agreed to respect the rights of the U.S. On Apr. 19 Pres. James Madison issued a proclamation allowing trade with England; the British minister to the U.S. had stated that British orders against U.S. shipping would be withdrawn on June 10. Unfortunately, the minister did not have the authority to make this promise, and on Aug. 9 Pres. Madison reinstated the Non-Intercourse Act.

Feb. 12 **Abraham Lincoln,** 16th president of the United States, was born in Hodgenville, Ky.

Mar. 1 The **Embargo Act** was repealed because it was considered detrimental to U.S. economic interests.

Mar. 1 The **Non-Intercourse Act** was signed by Pres. Thomas Jefferson in retaliation for English and French interference with American commerce. The act closed ports of the U.S. to France and England and outlawed their imports. It was repealed when the loss in customs revenue became excessive.

Mar. 4 **James Madison** was inaugurated **president** of the United States. The fourth president, he served two terms.

Mar. 4 **Thomas Jefferson** retired to private life at Monticello, near Charlottesville, Va. Impoverished after 44 years of nearly continuous public service, Jefferson returned to his studies of science, philosophy, and architecture. He became the key figure in the establishment of the University of Virginia in 1819.

The Wyoming Valley Massacre of 1778, a relatively minor event in the course of the American Revolution, was remembered because of a later poem about it. On July 3, 1778, a force of Loyalists and Indians commanded by John Butler of Connecticut attacked a settlement in the Wyoming Valley of northeastern Pennsylvania. The Americans were promised safe conduct, but when they surrendered on July 4, the Indians killed the settlers and looted and burned their homes. In 1809 Thomas Campbell, a Scottish poet, wrote *Gertrude of Wyoming,* a long narrative poem that described horrible events that had never occurred. It also told the sad story of two fictional lovers whose future happiness was doomed by the massacre. The poem was one of the earliest works by a European writer based on an American historical incident.

A History of New York by Washington Irving, the first American humorous masterpiece, was published. It was also the first American work to impress European critics and readers. Written under the pseudonym Diedrich Knickerbocker, a comic scholar "a little queer in his ways," Irving's book was a tongue-in-cheek history of Dutch New Amsterdam. It became a best seller. Although it has been said that the descendants of the original Dutch settlers were put out by the treatment Irving gave their ancestors, the Dutch patroons were but one target among many. Irving had as good a time with Thomas Jefferson, Republicans, Yankees, Swedes, European literature, and historians who wrote the sort of books that did please the descendants of the Dutch. He also possessed the redeeming quality of being able to laugh at himself.

Charles Willson Peale completed his painting *Family Group,* which brought to American art the influences of scientific study: careful observation and objective rendering of the subject. A Philadelphian, Peale had been intensely interested in science for many years and, in 1794, had established America's first privately run museum of natural history.

| Business and Industry; Science; Education; Philosophy and Religion   III | | IV   Sports; Social Issues and Crime; Folkways; Fashion; Holidays |

1809

Among those who contributed to the growing knowledge about the U.S. and to the achievements of American scientists was William Maclure, a well-to-do Scottish merchant who became a U.S. citizen in 1796. His *Observations on the Geology of the United States* (1809) included the first geological map of the U.S. In preparing a revised edition (1817), Maclure crossed the Allegheny Mts. dozens of times. He also introduced to the U.S. the educational theories of Johann Heinrich Pestalozzi, the Swiss educational reformer. Pestalozzi emphasized individual development and the study of nature.

The **first screw-cutting machine** in the U.S. was designed and produced by Abel Stowel in Massachusetts.

The **first successful sea voyage by steamboat** was made by John Stevens's *Phoenix*, which sailed from New York City to Philadelphia. Stevens had designed a screw propeller in 1802. He was one of America's most important early inventors and was influential in the establishment of the first federal patent laws.

Among the **quack medicines** offered to Americans was a concoction known as "Hamilton's Essense and Extract of Mustard: for rheumatism, gout, Palsy, Swelling, Numbness, etc."

The **Boston Crown Glass Company** was incorporated. The company had been in business since 1792, when it made the first successful window glass in the U.S. Its glass was said to be superior to any imported product. The charter of incorporation suspended company taxes and freed employees from military service.

Feb. 17   **Miami University** in Oxford, Ohio, was chartered as a state university. Its first degrees were conferred in 1826.

Feb. 25   Thomas Jefferson, seeking to qualify his earlier comments on **racial inequality,** wrote to Henri Grégoire, the French Roman Catholic priest and political dissident, thanking him for sending a copy of *Literature of Negroes.* Grégoire had wanted to refute the contention of Jefferson, expressed in *Notes on Virginia,* that blacks were mentally and physically inferior to whites. He presented evidence that Jefferson's opinions were based on limited acquaintance with blacks. Jefferson acknowledged that his conclusions had been tentative and drawn solely from what he had observed in Virginia. He recognized the social value of Grégoire's work.

One of the most impressive American Indian leaders was Tecumseh, chief of the Shawnees. Alarmed by the steady westward movement of settlers, Tecumseh on July 2, 1809, began a campaign to unite in a defensive confederacy the Indian tribes of the Old Northwest, the South, and the eastern Mississippi R. Valley. Americans had by treaty already acquired 30,000,000 acres of land in the region. Tecumseh was aided by his brother, Tenskwatawa, called the Shawnee Prophet. In spite of Tecumseh's efforts, on Sept. 30 William Henry Harrison, governor of the Indiana Territory, signed a treaty at Fort Wayne by which the Indian tribes ceded three more tracts of land along the Wabash R. Tecumseh's continuing efforts to halt further encroachment on Indian lands alarmed the settlers, who urged military action against him. The dream of an Indian confederacy died for good with the battle of Tippecanoe in Nov. 1811.

Two upper-class families of New York and Virginia merged with the wedding of Gouverneur Morris and Anne Cary Randolph. Among the wealthy families of New York, only the Morrises were not engaged in trade.

May 31   A theatrical **benefit performance** at the New Theater for an actor called Master Payne was advertised in the New York *Post.* The play was to be Shakespeare's *Hamlet,* with Payne in the title role. The drama would be followed by a "musical afterpiece" called "Agreeable Surprise." The doors would open at a quarter past six o'clock, with the curtain rising at a quarter past seven.

Oct. 31   A **missing persons advertisement** was placed by one George Hicks of Brooklyn in the New York *Post.* Hicks offered a $25 reward for the return of a "Negro woman named Charity and her female child . . . 25 years of age, five feet high, of a yellowish complexion . . . has lost the use of one of her fingers, occasioned by a fellon . . . took with her several suits of clothes."

Nov. 1   An exhibit opened in New York City featuring a **Grand Panorama,** a view of the city and its surrounding countryside "as seen from an eminence in the neighborhood of the Park." Admission was 50 cents, and children paid half price. A $2.00 lifetime ticket was also available.

1810

The western and northern boundaries of the area known as West Florida were long in dispute between the U.S. and Spain, England, or France—all three controlled it at various times. The U.S. claimed some of the area as part of the Louisiana Purchase of 1803. In dispute was the land between the Mississippi R. on the west and the Perdido R. on the east. In 1810 American settlers in the region rebelled against Spanish control. On Sept. 26 they captured the fort at Baton Rouge and proclaimed a republic. On Oct. 27 Pres. James Madison proclaimed U.S. annexation of West Florida and declared it part of Orleans Territory.

The third U.S. **Census** recorded a population of 7,239,881, an increase of 1,931,398 over 1800. Black population rose by 481,361 to 1,378,110. Of this total, 186,746 were free citizens, a group omitted in the 1800 census. The center of population moved to a point 40 mi. northwest of Washington, D.C.

Elbridge Gerry, later to serve as vice president of the United States under James Madison, was elected governor of Massachusetts. In his second term as governor, the state legislature passed measures to redistrict the state for the election of state senators. The legislators intended to ensure a Democratic-Republican (present-day Democratic Party) majority. The stratagem, approved by former Pres. Thomas Jefferson, came to be known as *gerrymandering.*

1810–1811 In **congressional elections** the Republicans gained two Senate seats for a 30–6 majority over the Federalists. In the House they gained 14 seats for a 108–36 majority.

Mar. 23 Napoleon signed his **Rambouillet Decree,** ordering seizure and confiscation of all American shipping in any French port.

May 1 **Macon's Bill No. Two** was passed by Congress. It was a substitute measure designed to replace the Non-Intercourse Act, which was to expire later that year. Introduced by Rep. Nathaniel Macon, Republican of North Carolina, it authorized the president to restore trade with England and France despite their antagonistic commercial policies. The bill also provided that if either England or France repealed its offensive policies before Mar. 3, 1811, the president was empowered to terminate all trade with the other.

Aug. 5 **Napoleon** instructed the French foreign minister, Jean Baptiste Nompère Champagny, to advise the U.S. government that France would revoke the

Interest and support for musical enterprises continued to grow. The first regular orchestra in the U.S. was formed about this time in Boston by Gottlieb Graupner, a German-born musician who came to the U.S. in 1795. For nearly 25 years Graupner played a leading role in the musical life of Boston, especially as the founder of the Handel and Haydn Society. The semiprofessional Philharmonic Orchestra he founded played a significant role in the development of Boston's cultural life. The orchestra gave its last performance on Nov. 24, 1824, at the Pantheon, on Boylston Square.

The **Park Street Church** was built in Boston by Peter Banner, with capitals on its tower carved by Solomon Willard.

The Society of Artists of the United States was organized. Painters revealed their contempt for the American milieu by remarking that American art began when Benjamin West sailed for Europe.

Inchiquin, The Jesuit's Letters by Charles Ingersoll, a Philadelphia lawyer and writer, was published. The book was a collection of essays purportedly written by a Jesuit traveling in the U.S. In the essays the self-conscious nation found a voice in defense against European charges of cultural barbarism. Ingersoll's book, attacked in England, was stoutly defended by Timothy Dwight and James Kirke Paulding.

The tremendous popularity in the U.S. of *Scottish Chiefs* by **Jane Porter** anticipated the success of the novels of her friend Sir Walter Scott. Porter and Scott wrote in reaction to the novels of sensibility and high life, and to the Gothic novels characteristic of the late eighteenth century. *Scottish Chiefs,* a romantic adventure story, was still popular a century after it first appeared.

A **theater season** was launched in Lexington, Ky., the first time west of the Appalachians. From then on, road companies mostly offering contemporary melodramas and farces brought stage presentations to the smaller cities of the U.S. until the high costs of production and travel in the mid-twentieth century made the business unprofitable.

| Business and Industry; Science; Education; Philosophy and Religion III | | Sports; Social Issues and Crime; Folkways; Fashion; Holidays IV |

1810

Because of the vast expanse of the U.S., the development of new means of transportation was inevitable. Cornelius Vanderbilt was one of the first of the new developers. He began his career in 1810, operating a small boat as a ferry between Staten Island and Manhattan, New York. By age 40 he was worth a small fortune as a result of his major share in shipping interests around New York harbor and on the Hudson R. During the gold rush of the mid-nineteenth century, he operated a shipping line to the West Coast by way of Nicaragua, where he put together a combined land and water route across Central America. Turning his attention to railroads after the Civil War, Vanderbilt built or secured control of the lines that became the New York Central Railroad between New York and Chicago. Some of his methods, like those of his competitors, were ethically questionable, but at his death in 1877 Vanderbilt was said to be worth $100,000,000.

The **Newburyport Bridge** over the Merrimack R. in Massachusetts, the most famous suspension bridge in nineteenth-century America, was erected by John Templeman, holder of several patents on suspension bridge improvements. The bridge had a span of 224 ft. In 1909 it was rebuilt, with its original structure carefully preserved.

The **American Board of Commissioners for Foreign Missions** was formed. Created by Congregationalists, it became interdenominational in 1812 and remained so for nearly four decades. It was the first missionary society in the U.S. In 1812 it sent famed missionary Adoniram Judson to India, but his great work was done in Burma.

Growth of higher education in the U.S. was reflected in the establishment of seven new colleges during the decade beginning in 1810. The new schools brought to 37 the number of institutions of higher learning in the nation.

Thomas and Alexander Campbell, father and son and both Presbyterian ministers in Washington County, Pa., opposed the Calvinistic doctrines and restrictions on communion in their denomination. They organized the Brush Run (Pa.) Church, with Alexander as its pastor. The church formed a connection with an association of Baptist churches, but after a decade disagreements between the two groups began to arise because of the liberal views of the Campbellites.

July The **first agricultural magazine** in the U.S., the *Agricultural Museum,* began publication in Georgetown, D.C. The magazine published until May 1812.

July 12 The **Journeymen Cordwainers** trial began in New York City. Members of this trade union were accused of conspiring to raise their wages by calling a strike. They were found guilty and fined $1.00 each

Although cricket had a long headstart over baseball, it quickly lost out in popularity once baseball was introduced later in the century. A form of cricket was played in Virginia as early as 1709, and a match was played in New York City in 1751. Boston's first cricket club was organized in 1809, and the sport spread west with English settlers. There were reports of cricket being played in Kentucky in 1818 and in Illinois a year later. Chicago in 1840 had three teams. But Philadelphia was the center of cricket in the U.S., and its factory workers of English origin played weekly matches.

The **Connecticut Moral Society** was organized to combat "Sabbath-breakers, rum-selling, tippling folk, infidels and ruff-scruff" among the Protestant clergy. Among the charter members was the Rev. Lyman Beecher, father of Harriet Beecher Stowe and Henry Ward Beecher.

A **lottery** was held at Union College, Schenectady, N.Y. The holder of winning ticket could draw up to $100,000.

Contemporary remedies. For asthma take ½ oz. senna, ½ oz. flour of sulphur, 2 drams ginger, ½ dram pounded saffron, and mix up 4 oz. honey. For consumption take yolks of 2 new-laid eggs and beat in three tablespoons rosewater, then mix well in ½ pt. (English) of milk fresh from the cow and sweeten with syrup of capillaire and a little nutmeg grated over. Take this mixture early every morning.

A **popular lyric** of the day:

> Swans sing before they die . . .
> 'Twere no bad thing,
> Should certain persons die
> Before they sing.

Oct. 1 The **Berkshire Cattle Show** in Pittsfield, Mass., was the forerunner of what was to become one of America's most popular institutions, the county fair. In 1807 Elkanah Watson, a pioneer in scientific agriculture, had exhibited two Merino sheep in the center of Pittsfield. He then organized the 1810 cattle show, which led to formation of the Berkshire Agricultural Society. The society promoted crop rotation and the use of fertilizer, and sponsored the first county fair in the U.S.

Exploration and Settlement; Wars; Government; Civil Rights; Statistics I		II Publishing; Arts and Music; Popular Entertainment; Architecture; Theater

Berlin and Milan decrees insofar as they applied to the confiscation of U.S. vessels if Pres. Madison would enforce non-intercourse with Great Britain. Madison, unaware of Napoleon's intended deceit, waited to see whether Great Britain would likewise revoke its blockade edicts. He invoked non-intercourse with Great Britain in Feb. 1811.

George Frederick Cooke, a popular British actor, played at the Park Theatre in New York City to large and enthusiastic audiences. His popularity declined in the following year, when his drinking made him unreliable. He toured the U.S. with William Dunlap as his manager until an early death in 1812.

1811

Two incidents involving warships were portents of the coming war between the U.S. and Great Britain. On May 1, off Sandy Hook, N.Y., the 38-gun British frigate *Guerrière* stopped the American brig *Spitfire* and seized an American-born seaman. On May 6 the 44-gun American frigate *President* was ordered to the area to protect U.S. shipping; en route it came upon a ship thought to be the *Guerrière.* Actually it was a British 20-gun corvette, *Little Belt.* The *President* attacked the *Little Belt* on May 16, disabling it, killing nine, and wounding 23 of the crew. The U.S. government told the British minister in Washington on Nov. 1 that it would reach an agreement about the incident if Great Britain would rescind orders that restricted American commercial shipping. The British refused to negotiate.

Feb. 11 **Trade with Britain** was prohibited by Pres. Madison, the third time in four years that such action was taken. Madison hoped to effect repeal of the Orders in Council by which Britain placed restrictions on neutral commerce.

Apr. 12 Colonists sent by **John Jacob Astor** on the *Tonquin* to operate a Pacific coast fur-trading center of the newly formed Pacific Fur Company arrived at the mouth of the Columbia R. via Cape Horn. Under the leadership of a Capt. Thorn, they disembarked at Cape Disappointment, Wash., but soon moved a few miles upstream and founded Astoria in what is now Oregon. This was the first permanent American colony in the Pacific Northwest.

Nov. 7 **William Henry Harrison,** commander of 800 U.S. soldiers fighting marauding Indians organized by Tecumseh, beat off a surprise attack led by Tecumseh's brother Tenskwatawa, called the Prophet, at Tippecanoe R. in northcentral Indiana. The toll of U.S. soldiers was 61 dead, 127 wounded. Subsequently, Harrison's troops destroyed the Indian confederacy. Tecumseh and many of his followers crossed over into Canada and joined British forces in the War of 1812.

Dec. 16 **One of the greatest earthquakes in history** occurred. It was centered on New Madrid, Mo., and it changed the topography of a 30,000-sq.-mi. area. Tremors were felt over a region ten times as great. The quake raised and lowered parts of the Mississippi

An unusual case of plagiarism involved one of the most popular American novels of the early nineteenth century. Isaac Mitchell, a newspaper editor, serialized in 1811 in his Poughkeepsie, N.Y., *Political Barometer,* a novel he had written, *The Asylum; or, Alonzo and Melissa.* In the same year there appeared *Alonzo and Melissa; or, The Unfeeling Father,* signed by Daniel Jackson, a teacher at the Plattsburgh, N.Y., Academy. Mitchell died before he could sue for damages, but authorship later was restored to him. The novel, a Gothic romance, featured ghosts, separated lovers, haunted castles, and a happy ending for the young couple. It sold well for some 40 years.

William and Ellen by Eaglesfield Smith, the first noteworthy imitation of the romanticism of Sir Walter Scott, was published. Scott's influence on American writers was reflected in numerous books of the period, notably *Crystalina* (1812) by John Milton Harney, which dealt with the Scottish Highlands; *The Fall of Palmyra* (1816) by H.H. Wright; and *Bride of Vaumond* (1817) by Robert Charles Sands.

Efforts to promote **cultural ties with Latin America** were recorded in a congressional report by Rep. Samuel Latham Mitchill of New York. Dr. Mitchill, a physician, was also a recognized authority on Spanish and Portuguese literature in Latin America.

James Fenimore Cooper left the U.S. Navy to marry Susan De Lancey and settle down in Mamaroneck, N.Y., as a gentleman farmer. Cooper did not begin his career in letters for another nine years. In 1814 Cooper moved to Cooperstown, N.Y., then to Scarsdale, N.Y., in 1817. There, it is said, he claimed he could write a better book

| Business and Industry; Science; Education; Philosophy and Religion | III | | IV | Sports; Social Issues and Crime; Folkways; Fashion; Holidays |

plus costs because "Even to do a thing which is lawful in itself, by conspiracy, is unlawful." This decision followed the precedent established in the 1806 trial of bootmakers in Philadelphia. In 1842 the Supreme Court of Massachusetts reversed the trend by stating that the legal definition of *conspiracy* excluded union actions.

Dec. 10   The first unofficial **heavyweight champion** of the U.S., Tom Molineaux, a freed slave from Virginia, was beaten in the 40th round by Tom Cribb, the English champion, in a boxing match at Copthall Common, London.

1811

The first large-scale highway construction project of the federal government began this year. The project was the National Road, the first part of which was known as the Cumberland Road because it connected Cumberland, Md., already linked to Baltimore, with Wheeling, in present-day West Virginia. The Cumberland Road was completed in 1818. Originally the National Road was to run to the Mississippi R., but after it reached Vandalia, Ill., in 1830 construction stopped. Until it lost its importance, first to canals and then to railroads, the National Road was the main route west for settlers and a vital commercial artery for farm products moving to eastern cities.

The **first steamboat** to sail down the Mississippi R. was owned by a Mr. & Mrs. Roosevelt. After several interruptions, including an earthquake at New Madrid, Mo., and the birth of a baby to Mrs. Roosevelt, the boat reached New Orleans on Jan. 12, 1812, where it caused a sensation. The boat then commenced regular runs between New Orleans and Natchez, charging $18 for the downstream trip and $25 for the upstream trip.

The opening of the **American Museum** in New York City reflected popular interest in science and art. On display were stuffed and live animals, paintings, etc. Lectures were given to the public. In 1841 P.T. Barnum purchased the museum's contents and used them in his own museum.

The first edition of *Singsters Repository of ballads collected from New Yorkers* was published by Nathaniel Dearborn. It sold for 25 cents a copy.

An **important road** in the development of Illinois was chartered. Called the Kaskaskia and Cahokia Road, it ran from Kaskaskia, a town on the Mississippi R., about 75 mi. north to Cahokia, opposite St. Louis, Mo.

The **first steamboat ferry** in the U.S. began operating from Hoboken, N.J., to New York City. Named *Juliana,* it was designed and built by engineer-inventor John Stevens. However, Robert Fulton and Robert R. Livingston, Fulton's partner, had a monopoly on steamboat

Even as the nation grew in size, its social fabric was being enriched by the introduction of new national groups. In 1811 Russians were exploring and claiming areas of the Far West that eventually became U.S. territory. On Feb. 2 Russians landed at Bodega Bay, north of San Francisco, and established Fort Ross, a fur-trading post. Russians had been the first Europeans to reach Alaska, in 1741, under the leadership of Vitus Bering, a Dane in Russian employ. They established the first settlement in Alaska in 1784 on Kodiak Island, and further strengthened their claim to the region with the founding of the Russian-American Company in 1799.

The first noteworthy **rowing race** in the U.S. was between two four-oared barges. *Knickerbocker* of New York City defeated *Invincible* of Long Island for a wager in a well-publicized race that attracted thousands of spectators. The boats started at Harsimus, N.J., and finished at New York City's Battery.

Instruction in **painting on velvet** was offered by a Mrs. and Miss Andrews at their apartments at 65 Maiden Lane, New York City.

Jan.   A **slave insurrection** took place in Louisiana when some 400 slaves rose up, killed the son of a plantation owner, and marched on New Orleans. Armed soldiers and planters put down the uprising, and some 75 of the slaves were killed. The uprising was an indication of the frail foundation on which the southern economy and social fabric were based. Fear of further bloody uprisings was to play an important role in the nation's political and social history leading up to the Civil War.

Dec. 12   J. Delacroix's **Vauxhall** opened for the winter season in New York City. Advertisements announced

Valley region by as much as 15 ft. It changed the course of the Mississippi R., causing it to flow backward and thereby create Reelfoot Lake in northwestern Tennessee. Aftershocks were felt for weeks, but because of the small population of the area and the small number of buildings, damage was relatively light.

than the novel he was then reading, and his wife challenged him to do so. Thus began the career of one of the most popular novelists in American literary history.

1812

The War of 1812 began on June 18, when Pres. James Madison officially proclaimed the U.S. to be at war with Great Britain. Congress had voted for war on June 4 and June 8. The war, which caused great harm to the U.S. economy, came after a long period of troubled relations between the two countries, caused mainly by Britain's conflict with Napoleonic France. The British seized American ships, impressed seamen from them, some of whom were U.S. citizens, and attempted to keep U.S. ships from reaching French ports. The war was also the result of the influence of the so-called War Hawks in Congress, Henry Clay and other westerners who wanted to acquire more land by conquering Canada. Ironically, on June 23 Great Britain, not yet aware of the declaration of war, suspended the orders that had hampered U.S. shipping.

1812–1813 In **congressional elections** the Republicans lost three Senate seats but still led the Federalists 27–9. In the House the Federalists gained 32 seats to the Republicans' four, but the latter maintained a majority, 112–68.

Feb. 15 **William Hunt** arrived in Astoria, Oreg. He had started from St. Louis to establish a route and a fur-trading post on the Columbia R. for John Jacob Astor. Hunt crossed much unexplored territory, and the last part of his route was almost identical with the later Oregon Trail.

Mar. 3 The first **foreign aid act** ever passed by Congress authorized $50,000 for the relief of Venezuelan victims of a severe earthquake. Congressional opposition to the act was based on the question of whether such an act was permitted under the legislative provisions of the Constitution. James Monroe reportedly observed in 1820 that Congress had no express authority, but rather an implied power, from the Constitution for such an act.

Mar. 14 The **first U.S. war bonds,** valued at $11,000,-000, were authorized by Congress. This was the first of six war loans floated to finance the War of 1812.

Apr. 30 **Louisiana** was admitted to the Union, the 18th state. Formerly known as Orleans Territory, it was made up mainly of land from the Louisiana Purchase of 1803, but also included the part of West Florida annexed in 1810 west of the Pearl R.

Thomas Sully was an Anglo-American who became the leading portrait painter of his day. Born in England, Sully came to the U.S. as a child and later lived and worked in both countries. He was influenced by Benjamin West and Sir Thomas Lawrence, and his portraits were in the Romantic style, urbane and elegant. They included likenesses of Queen Victoria, Fanny Kemble, Andrew Jackson, and Samuel Coates. The Coates portrait shows the subject standing by his desk, quill pen in hand, a cosmopolitan gentleman. Sully also did historical paintings, his best known being *Washington's Passage of the Delaware.* He produced some 2000 portraits in all as well as miniatures.

The Diverting History of John Bull and Brother Jonathan by James Kirke Paulding, written under the pseudonym Hector Bull-Us, was published. The first comic history of the U.S., the book was an attack on British attitudes and policies.

John Vanderlyn exhibited his nude painting *Ariadne.* It shocked Americans but was favorably received in Paris. He was the first American painter to study in Paris instead of London or Rome. In 1808 Vanderlyn had received the praise of Napoleon for his *Marius.*

The Classic Revival style of architecture was exemplified by the **Monumental Church** of Richmond, Va., built in 1812 in an octagonal design with a columned portico. The Classic Revival was characterized by the adaptation of architectural models of Greece and Rome. The grandiosity of the Classic Revival also gave concrete expression to Revolutionary patriotic sentiments. The style reached its peak in Thomas Jefferson's plan for a native architecture. Jefferson was deeply impressed by the work of the sixteenth-century Italian master Andrea Palladio, and the ancient Roman models Palladio had imitated came to represent for him an approach to perfection. The first phase of the Classic Revival (1789–

Business and Industry; Science; Education; Philosophy and Religion III		IV Sports; Social Issues and Crime; Folkways; Fashion; Holidays

operations in New York State. They threatened lawsuits and Stevens abandoned his project.

John Jacob Astor's increasing monopoly on fur trading in the U.S. was marked by the formation of the South West Company, controlled by Astor through a two-thirds interest.

that there was a large saloon for more than 200 people; a tea room for 100; card rooms and dressing rooms; choicest liquors. It was to be an establishment "for the accommodation of genteel company" and would be open on fair days only.

1812

American religious groups, which in colonial days had been the object of missionary efforts from England and other countries, in the early nineteenth century began to proselytize abroad. The American Board of Commissioners for Foreign Missions was formed in 1810. The Baptists established a group to support missions in 1814, the Methodists in 1819, the Episcopalians in 1820, and the Presbyterians in 1837, although work by the Presbyterians had begun much earlier. Adoniram Judson, a leader of the missionary movement that had spawned the American Board, went to India in 1812. In 1813 he traveled to Burma, where he remained for 30 years and where he translated the Bible into Burmese. By 1848 there were 283 American missionaries in the Orient.

Dr. **Benjamin Rush**, Philadelphia physician and reformer, published the first American treatise on mental disorders. It was entitled *Medical Inquiries and Observations upon the Diseases of the Mind.*

The formation of **banking institutions** was greatly stimulated by the War of 1812. Between 1812 and 1815, a total of 120 new banks received charters.

Life insurance as the primary interest of an American insurance company was first seen in the Pennsylvania Company for Insurance on Lives and Granting Annuities, incorporated in Philadelphia. It was the first company to use actuarial tables.

The **first lead pencils** produced in the U.S. were manufactured by William Monroe, a cabinetmaker of Concord, Mass. The pencils used domestic graphite.

The **Academy of Natural Sciences of Philadelphia** was founded, dedicated to the advancement of the natural sciences. It was immediately popular and generously

The first use of *Uncle Sam* to personify the federal government occurred during the War of 1812. It seems to have been used derisively at first by those opposed to the war and stemmed probably from the "U.S." stamped on uniforms and government wagons. Some attribute the origin of the term to Samuel Wilson of Troy, N.Y. His nickname was Uncle Sam and he was an inspector of Army supplies. The "U.S." stamped on supplies was referred to by workmen as Uncle Sam. The first recorded use of the term in print was in the Troy *Post* of Sept. 3, 1813, and the first appearance in a book was in *Adventures of Uncle Sam* (1816) by an author who used the name Frederick Augustus Fidfaddy, Esq.

The term *Coodies* was applied derisively to the faction of the Federalist Party that urged support for the War of 1812, a position highly unpopular with the majority of the party. The term derived from the series of prowar articles written by Gulian Crommelin Verplanck under the pen name *Abimeleck Coody.* Verplanck was a distinguished editor, author, and Shakespearean scholar. The epithet *King Coody* was applied to Rep. Roger Brooke Taney of Maryland, later chief justice of the U.S. Supreme Court.

A report on the U.S. hinterland by Samuel J. Mills, a missionary sponsored by the Connecticut and Massachusetts Missionary Societies, confirmed the suspicions of easterners about their backwoods compatriots. Mills, describing the first of two celebrated tours of the U.S. frontier, spoke of "the nakedness of the land" and "the heartrending report reached the ears of the Church. . . . South of New Connecticut, few Bibles or religious tracts have been received for distribution among the inhabitants. The Sabbath is greatly profaned and but few good people can be found in any one place . . . within 30 miles of the falls of the Ohio. . . . We found the inhabitants in a very destitute state; very ignorant of the doctrines of the Gospel; and in many instances without Bibles, or any other religious books. The Methodist preachers pass through this country, in their circuits, occasionally. There are a number of good people in the Territory,

May 14 Annexation by a congressional act added the **West Florida territory** to the territory of Mississippi and to the nation.

Aug. 15 A **massacre at Fort Dearborn,** on the site of what is now Chicago, took place when American soldiers, traders, and their families evacuated the fort. Indians attacked the fleeing Americans along a trail that later became Indiana Ave. Only two women and one trader survived. After the massacre the fort was razed. British-supported Indians controlled the area for several years after.

Aug. 16 Brig. Gen. **William Hull surrendered Detroit** to British forces under Gen. Isaac Brock, making no attempt to defend the city though the attacking force was smaller than his own. Hull was court-martialed two years later for yielding without resistance.

Aug. 19 The U.S. frigate *Old Ironsides* (*Constitution*) defeated the British ship *Guerrière* off Nova Scotia. The *Constitution* was commanded by Commodore Isaac Hull.

Oct. 9 In a **naval engagement on Lake Erie,** American forces under the command of Lt. Jesse Duncan Elliott captured two British brigs, *Detroit* and *Caledonia.* Elliott was later forced to set fire to the *Detroit.*

Oct. 13 Gen. **Stephen Van Rensselaer** was defeated in the battle of Queenstown Heights, Canada, on the Niagara frontier by the British and Indians. About 1000 U.S. troops were killed or wounded. British Gen. Isaac Brock, captor of Detroit, was killed during the engagement.

Dec. 2 **James Madison was reelected president** of the United States, defeating De Witt Clinton of New York, who had been endorsed by the Federalists and by Democratic-Republicans opposed to the war. Elbridge Gerry, Democratic-Republican of Massachusetts, was elected vice president. The presidential electoral vote was Madison, 128; Clinton, 89. The vice presidential electoral vote was Gerry, 131; Charles Jared Ingersoll, Federalist of Pennsylvania, 86.

Dec. 29 The U.S. frigate *Constitution* destroyed the British frigate *Java* in a fight off the coast of Brazil. *Old Ironsides* was under the command of Commodore William Bainbridge.

1820) was a Roman revival, characterized by simple lines, sparse decoration, and superb discipline. The Greek revival (1820–1860) introduced greater structural variety and a liberal use of Greek columns, mantletrees, and doors.

Travels in the United States by John Melish was published. Melish, a Scotsman who settled in the U.S. in 1809, described journeys he had made around the country in an attempt to encourage emigration from Europe. Melish drew his own maps for this book. It was followed in 1813 by *A Military and Topographical Atlas of the United States,* and in 1819 by *Information and Advice to Emigrants to the United States.*

New York City Hall, at Broadway and Park Row, was completed. Designed by Joseph F. Mangin, a French architect who worked on the layout of the Place de la Concorde in Paris, the building is still used for the office of the mayor of New York City. Mangin was an exponent of a new style, called Rationalism, which emphasized the use of simple but massive geometrical shapes in building design. Other French architects of this school included Joseph Jacques Ramée, who lived in the U.S. from 1811 to 1816 and designed the campus of Union College in Schenectady, N.Y.; and Maximilian Godefroy, who in 1817–1818 designed the First Unitarian Church in Baltimore, Md.

Apr. 13 *Marmion* by James N. Barker, a highly successful dramatization of the poem by Sir Walter Scott, opened in New York City. With the U.S. at war with Great Britain, the anti-English sentiments expressed by Scott's characters held great appeal for New York audiences. Yet the producer listed the play as written by an Englishman, Thomas Morton, to cater to the esteem Americans placed on British culture.

1813

An Indian uprising in the South brought on the Creek Indian War (1813–1814). Creeks who lived mainly in Alabama and Georgia were alarmed by encroachments on their lands and were convinced by Tecumseh, the Shawnee chief, to unite with many other tribes against the settlers. The leader of the Creeks was William Weatherford, also known as Red Eagle. On Aug. 30, 1813, he

The most successful woman author of the late eighteenth and early nineteenth centuries was Susanna Rowson, who had come to America from England in 1793. In England she had published in 1791 the sentimental and didactic novel *Charlotte Temple: A Tale of Truth.* It was issued in America in 1794, described as "designed ... for the perusal of the young and

Business and Industry; Science; **III**   **IV** **Sports; Social Issues and Crime;**
Education; Philosophy and Religion   **Folkways; Fashion; Holidays**

supported. Within two years the original membership of seven doubled, 33 correspondents were making contributions, and a program of lectures on plants and insects was scheduled. The public was admitted in 1828, two years after the museum had been expanded by the addition of another building. Among today's more than 140,-000 volumes, those presented by the original donors maintain a place of honor.

May 26 **Hamilton College** was chartered in Clinton, N.Y., under Presbyterian auspices. Its first degrees were conferred in 1814.

June 30 Congress authorized **Treasury notes** in an issue not to exceed $5,000,000. This was the first of five war issues.

July 23 **William Ellery Channing,** an apostle of modern pacifism, weighed the negativism of New England toward the War of 1812 in a sermon that cautioned loyalty toward the just acts of a good government. "It is the time," he said, "to be firm without passion." Channing denounced attempts to stifle opposition and criticism in the name of patriotism. "The sum of my remarks is this. It is your duty to hold fast and to assert with firmness those truths and principles on which the welfare of your country seems to depend, but do this with calmness, with a love of peace, without ill will and revenge."

Dec. 29 The **University of Maryland** was chartered as the state university in Baltimore, Md. It was organized around the College of Medicine of Maryland, founded in 1807. In 1920 Maryland State College formally merged with it.

who are anxious to have Presbyterian ministers amongst them. They likewise wish to be remembered by Bible and Religious Tract Societies. . . . At New Orleans . . . the greater part of the inhabitants are French Catholics, ignorant of almost every thing except what relates to the increase of their property; destitute to schools, Bibles and religious instruction. In attempting to learn the religious state of the people, we were frequently told, that they had no Bibles, and that the priests did not allow of their distribution among them."

Gerrymandering entered the national vocabulary as a term indicating political abuse. The Massachusetts legislature had passed a bill that would facilitate the rigging of contests for senatorial offices by a systematic reapportionment of the electoral districts within the state. In 1812 the senatorial districts corresponded to the areas of the counties. When the Republicans gained control of the legislature, they cited a provision of the state constitution that invested the legislature with the power of determining electoral districts. Elbridge Gerry, the governor, signed the bill into a law. The districts followed no regular lines. One district resembled a salamander or, in the words of a Federalist, a *Gerrymander.*

The **American Antiquarian Society** was founded and endowed in Worcester, Mass., by Isaiah Thomas, the foremost U.S. printer and publisher of the day. Thomas also served as the society's first president. The society's vast collection includes hundreds of thousands of manuscripts dealing with early American history, a collection of American newspapers published before 1820, and numerous state, county, and local histories. Its publication, *Proceedings,* was first issued in 1843.

Aug. 19 **Lucy Brewer,** under the name Nicolas Baker, served as a member of the crew of the *Constitution* in the naval battle with the British *Guerrière.* She spent three years aboard the *Constitution* and successfully disguised her sex during the entire time.

1813

In 1813 Jethro Wood, a farmer in New York State, invented a cast-iron plow that he patented the following year. This was the 19th patent for a plow issued in the U.S. Charles Newbold had patented the first cast-iron plow in 1797. In 1819 Wood patented an improved plow that had replaceable iron parts and a curved plate, the moldboard. The modern moldboard derives from

The gambling game of craps, derived from the English and French game of hazard, began to be played in the U.S. at about this time. At least as early as the sixteenth century, the throw of 1-1 with dice was called crabs, and the word *craps* stems from this term. According to one legend, blacks around New Orleans, La., began playing hazard about 1800, when the game was

led an attack on Fort Mims, a temporary stockade near the confluence of the Tombigbee and Alabama rivers. Although Weatherford attempted to restrain his warriors, they massacred some 500 whites. The U.S. retaliated on Nov. 3 when Gen. John Coffee attacked and destroyed the Indian village Talladega, in Alabama, killing more than 500 warriors. In Jan. 1814, however, Tennessee militiamen were defeated in three minor engagements. The war did not end until the Battle of Horsehoe Bend in Mar. 1814.

Feb. 24 In the **War of 1812** (1812–1814), Capt. James Lawrence, commanding the U.S. frigate *Hornet,* captured the British ship *Peacock.*

Mar. 4 Pres. **James Madison was inaugurated** for his second term. Elbridge Gerry succeeded George Clinton as vice president. Clinton had died in office in 1812.

Apr. 27 British forces surrendered **York, Canada,** now Toronto, to Americans commanded by Brig. Gen. Zebulon M. Pike, who was killed in the battle.

June 1 Capt. **James Lawrence** cried "Don't give up the ship" to his crew as he lay mortally wounded aboard the *Chesapeake,* which was subsequently defeated and captured by the British frigate *Shannon* in an engagement off the Massachusetts coast.

Aug. 14 A **British naval victory** off the coast of England was scored by the *Pelican* when it captured the American ship *Argus,* which had previously captured 27 British merchant vessels.

Sept. 10 The **Battle of Lake Erie** was a significant American naval victory. An improvised American fleet commanded by Oliver Hazard Perry decisively defeated the British after a bloody engagement. During the battle Perry's flagship *Lawrence* was crippled and he had to continue the fight from another ship. He returned to the *Lawrence* to accept the British surrender, then sent to Gen. William Henry Harrison, commander in the west, the victory dispatch containing the words "We have met the enemy, and they are ours." The Americans gained control of Lake Erie, and the British were obliged to withdraw from Detroit, further strengthening the U.S. position in the Great Lakes.

Oct. 5 Gen. Harrison defeated the British under Gen. Henry A. Proctor at the **Battle of the Thames,** Ontario, Canada. Tecumseh, Shawnee Indian chief and ally of the British, was killed during the engagement. His death broke the Indian confederacy.

thoughtful of the fair sex." By 1933 it had gone through 161 editions in the U.S. Mrs. Rowson was also an actress and author of comedies and comic operas. Although she left the stage in 1797 and opened a girls' boarding school near Boston, Mrs. Rowson continued to write, her work including the novel *Sarah; or, The Exemplary Wife* (1813).

The *Boston Daily Advertiser,* a strong supporter of the Whig Party, was started under the editorship of Nathan Hale. In 1917 it was purchased by William Randolph Hearst and combined with the *Boston Record.*

The Sylphs of the Season, the first book of poems by the American poet and painter Washington Allston, was published. Also in 1813 Allston, then living in England, completed his first important painting, *Dead Men Revived by Touching the Bones of the Prophet Elisha.* His poetry was praised by Samuel Taylor Coleridge, Robert Southey, Wilkie Collins, and others. His painting won an award and praise from William Wordsworth. Allston introduced the Romantic style to U.S. painting on his return to the U.S. in 1818.

A unique **choir book** for use in Catholic missions among the Indians of the Southwest was compiled by Padre Narciso Durán, choirmaster at San José Mission in California. Members of the choirs adapted religious music to their growing folk tradition.

The Lay of the Scottish Fiddle by James Kirke Paulding was published. Paulding's work was a verse parody of the romantic heroic poetry of Sir Walter Scott. In 1818 Paulding would publish another long poem, *The Backwoodsman,* offering a hero quite different from Scott's heroes. But Paulding's satire and his preference for American qualities could do nothing to halt the popularity of the romantic period in Anglo-Saxon literature.

Sept. 4 The **first religious weekly** in America, *Religious Remembrancer,* founded in Philadelphia by John W. Scott, began publication. Through successive mergers the magazine grew, and eventually became the *Christian Observer.*

Wood's moldboard. Wood's design remains little changed today, but John Deere's substitution of steel for cast iron two decades later proved more effective in turning the heavy, sticky soil of the prairies.

William Ellery Channing, influential Congregationalist Unitarian minister of Boston, helped found the *Christian Disciple*, a liberal Protestant magazine. Channing hoped to challenge the more conservative *The Panoplist*, a newspaper published by the Rev. Jedidiah Morse, father of Samuel F. B. Morse. The conflict between the two publications mirrored the conflict between liberal and conservative Protestantism that has continued in America to this day. Channing resisted any attempt to define his ideas within the logical limits of a creed. Nor did he particularly relish the notoriety his ideas gained for him. Six years passed before he was to define his position as a Unitarian. In the meantime the ferment continued in the religious life of New England. In 1815 there was a flurry of excitement about a heresy within the Congregational churches of Boston. This resulted in the Congregationalists being labeled Unitarian by orthodox Trinitarians. The liberals proposed that Christ was not of the same nature as God but was sent as a moral teacher rather than a divine mediator. It was not until 1819 that Channing publicly identified himself with this position.

Feb. 26   Robert R. Livingston, one of the leading figures in the development of steam transportation, died. Livingston had financed Robert Fulton's first successful steamboat, the *Clermont*, which had sailed up the Hudson R. in 1807. As a result of Fulton's early support, Livingston had secured a monopoly on steamboat shipping in New York waters. Livingston was a man of many achievements. He had been a member of the committee that drafted the Declaration of Independence in 1776. As the first chancellor of the State of New York, he had administered the presidential oath of office to George Washington in 1789, and in 1801, as U.S. minister to France, conducted the negotiations that led to the Louisiana Purchase.

already sometimes called crabs or craps. Rules were so modified that craps became a separate game. Another explanation is that a rich playboy of New Orleans, Bernard Xavier Philippe de Marigny de Mandeville, introduced craps to America. He is said to have lost most of his money shooting craps. In any event, New Orleans seems to have been the starting point for the game of craps.

The celebrated "witch" **Moll Pitcher** died in Lynn, Mass. Her fame had spread throughout the region. Hundreds went to her for prophecy, love potions, and knowledge of lost things. She is reputed to have presided at conventions of witches at Lynn. Every time she visited a community, she entered its folklore. Years later she became the subject of the long poem *Moll Pitcher* (1832) by John Greenleaf Whittier.

Aug. 9   The first blackout in U.S. history occurred at St. Michaels, Md. Upon the report that British naval vessels were entering the St. Michaels R., and that an attack on the shipbuilding town was planned for that night, women, children, and old folk were evacuated inland. The commanding officer of the county militia then ordered lanterns placed in the tops of the tallest trees of St. Michaels and atop the masts of vessels in the harbor; all other lights were extinguished. In the misty darkness the British gunships directed their fire too high and overshot the town before sailing away to rejoin their fleet.

1814

The Treaty of Ghent, ending the War of 1812, was signed on Dec. 24 by representatives of the U.S. and Great Britain. The Senate ratified the treaty in Feb. 1815. The American negotiators were John Quincy Adams, James A. Bayard, Henry Clay, Jonathan Russell, and Albert Gallatin. By terms of the treaty, all conquered territory was to be returned by both sides, and a commission was to settle the boundary between the U.S. and Canada from the St. Croix R. west to Lake of the Woods. The British did not achieve their aim to set up an Indian buffer state in the Northwest. The emotional issues that helped cause the war—impressment of American seamen and the rights of neutral commerce—were not mentioned.

1814–1815 In **congressional elections** the Republicans lost two Senate seats but led the Federalists 25–11. In the House they gained five seats for a 117–65 majority.

Mar. 29 The **Creek War** (1813–1814) ended as Gen. Andrew Jackson defeated the Creeks under Chief Weatherford at the decisive battle of Horseshoe Bend, Ala., where nearly 900 of 1000 Indians were killed. The Creeks had fought with British troops against the Americans in the War of 1812.

Aug. 24 **Washington, D.C., was captured** by British troops under Gen. Robert Ross. The Capitol, White House, and other government buildings were set afire in retaliation for the earlier burning of Canadian government buildings in York, Toronto, by U.S. troops.

Sept. 11 At the **Battle of Lake Champlain** a newly built U.S. fleet under Master-Commandant Thomas Macdonough annihilated a British squadron. This forced British Gen. Sir George Prevost and his army to abandon their siege of the U.S. fort at Plattsburgh and to retreat to Canada on foot.

Dec. 15–Jan. 4, 1815 The **Hartford Convention,** held in secret, adopted a strong states' rights position while the nation was at war. All the delegates were from the five New England states. The war was unpopular in those states because they bore a heavy share of the expenses yet were given virtually no military or naval protection. The delegates were largely Federalists. Many grievances were aired and secession was discussed but rejected. The final proposals were for amendments to the Constitution that would protect sectional interests; the proposals in practice would have threatened the existence of the nation. News of the Treaty of Ghent and the Treaty of the Battle of New Orleans put an end to the convention's proposals and marked the end of the Federalist Party's influence in American affairs.

The words to "The Star Spangled Banner" were written during the War of 1812 by Francis Scott Key, a lawyer, on the night of Sept. 13–14, 1814, during the unsuccessful bombardment of an American fort by British warships. Key was on his way to the British fleet to try to secure release of an American citizen held by the British. He was detained by the British during their attempt to capture Fort McHenry, near Baltimore. Key was inspired by the sight of the American flag still flying and wrote the words that were set to the music of "Anacreon in Heaven," anthem of the Anacreontic Societies of England, which were clubs of amateur musicians. Key's song was first printed as a handbill; on Sept. 20 it appeared in the Baltimore *Patriot*. Although long considered the national anthem of the U.S., "The Star Spangled Banner" did not officially gain that status until 1931.

A report on the **Lewis and Clark Expedition** (1803–1806), based on the papers of Meriwether Lewis and made available by William Clark, was published by editors Nicholas Biddle and Paul Allen. The report, *History of the Expedition under the Command of Captains Lewis and Clark,* carried a preface by Thomas Jefferson in which the career of Lewis was related in succinct but memorable detail. In 1806 Jefferson himself had given advance notice of the findings of the expedition in his *Message from the President of the United States, Communicating Discoveries Made by Captains Lewis and Clark.* Lewis had intended to arrange publication of the material himself. But immediately after the expedition and retirement from the Army, Jefferson appointed Lewis governor of the Louisiana Territory. Lewis was so busy with the affairs of his office that he found no time to finish his revision before his mysterious death in an inn in Tennessee in 1809. Clark contributed to this edition of the journals, but final discretion was left to his editors. The complete papers remained unpublished until 1903.

The romantic novel *Waverley* by Sir Walter Scott was issued in America and became enormously popular. This novel, and the five additional Waverley novels published in the following four years, sold some 5,000,000 copies by 1824 and marked the firm establishment of romanticism in American literature.

The **first American-born sculptor of note,** William Rush, carved a full-length statue in wood of George Washington. Rush had made his name as a sculptor of wooden figureheads for boats.

1814

Important improvements in education in the early nineteenth century, especially education of women, were the result of the efforts of Emma Willard. In 1807, when only 20, she took charge of the Female Academy at Middlebury, Vt. She opened a school of her own in 1814. There she taught subjects not otherwise available to women. An appeal to the New York State legislature in 1818 to support her plan for improving the education of women induced Gov. De Witt Clinton to invite Mrs. Willard to move to New York. She accepted, and opened a school at Waterford in 1819. In 1821 she moved to Troy and established the Troy Female Academy. Mrs. Willard wrote textbooks and a volume of poems (1831), which included the popular "Rocked in the Cradle of the Deep."

The **first large library network** west of the Alleghenies was established from several circulating libraries in Pittsburgh. The network formed the Pittsburgh permanent library.

Francis Cabot Lowell built the first U.S. plant designed to manufacture cloth from raw cotton by power machinery. A Boston importer, Lowell had observed power machinery in British textile plants and had violated British laws by smuggling secretly drawn sketches of that machinery out of the country. With the financial backing of his brother-in-law, Patrick Tracy Jackson, and the mechanical skill of machinist Paul Moody, Lowell secured a charter for the Boston Manufacturing Company, with a capitalization of $300,000. The machinery used in the Waltham factory and all subsequent equipment of the company came to be known as Lowell-Moody machinery and soon was quite different from the English models upon which they had been based. The city of Lowell, Mass., was named after Lowell.

Admiration for **German culture,** especially German romanticism and philosophy, was boosted by publication of a translation of *De l'Allemagne* by Anne Louise Germaine, Mme. de Staël. The immediate interest in this work foreshadowed the dominant position German thinking was to assume in the intellectual life of nineteenth-century America.

Oct. 29 The **first steam-powered warship,** *Demologos,* was launched in New York harbor. Designed and constructed by Robert Fulton, the ship was later officially christened *Fulton the First.*

A ubiquitous institution of the period was the country store. Most communities were too small to support a variety of retail stores, each specializing in a particular line of goods. The result was the country store, carrying virtually everything—food, clothing, farm equipment, housewares, and more. The Great Western Store, opened by Jedediah Barber at Homer, N.Y., in the central part of the state in 1813, was typical. Starting in one medium-sized room, Barber expanded his establishment to three stories, attic, and cellar. Like other storekeepers of the time, Barber did much of his business in barter, with customers exchanging products they had made or grown for store goods. Storekeepers often became leading citizens of their communities, sometimes adding real estate and banking to their business enterprises.

The **cost of education at Harvard** was about $300 a year. John Thornton Kirkland became president in 1810 and continued the innovations that had established the liberal bent of the college. He made it possible for poor students to meet fees by offering a number of jobs in which they could earn some money. He also supervised grants and scholarships, as well as an annual subsidy of $2500 that Massachusetts donated to encourage gifted but needy students. In Kirkland's time Harvard had the reputation of being a poor man's school, because he did so much to make it easy for indigent students to attend. Yet the tradition of gentility was already apparent, since the aim of the college was to create the same kind of gentlemen who were described in prospectuses of Cambridge and Oxford. Students attended classes five days a week from 6 A.M. to 4 P.M., with an hour free between the morning and afternoon sessions. Campus social life was encouraged by Kirkland. He contributed to the beginnings of some of the most famous clubs, including Hasty Pudding, Porcellian, Hermetic Society, and Speaking Club. There were extracurricular pleasures in parties and dances, and the college was just far enough from Boston to provide the attractions of both city and country life.

1815

The greatest battle of the War of 1812 and its finest American victory came on Jan. 8, 1815, two weeks after the war had been ended officially by the Treaty of Ghent. The Battle of New Orleans was fought on the British side by 7500 veterans under the command of Gen. Sir Edward Pakenham. The U.S. force, under the command of Gen. Andrew Jackson, comprised about 4500 troops, many of them expert marksmen from Kentucky and Tennessee armed with exceedingly accurate long rifles. The U.S. troops were strongly entrenched when on the morning of Jan. 8 the British, in close ranks, made two assaults on their lines. In half an hour the British were driven back, Pakenham was killed, and 2036 of his men were killed or wounded. U.S. forces suffered 8 killed and 13 wounded. Although the battle had no bearing on the outcome of the war, it was a stimulus to U.S. pride, which had suffered from several embarrassing defeats during the conflict. The battle made a military hero of Gen. Jackson, whose political career was advanced.

Feb. 11 News of the **Treaty of Ghent** reached New York City.

Mar. 3 **War against Algeria** was declared by Congress. The dey of Algiers had molested U.S. ships and insisted on payment of tribute.

June 17 Commodore **Stephen Decatur** captured the Algerian frigate *Mashouda*. Hammida, the renowned Algerian admiral, was killed during this engagement.

June 30 The **war against Algeria** and the Barbary Coast pirates ended when a peace treaty was signed with the dey of Algiers. It was followed by similar treaties with Tunis on July 26 and Tripoli on Aug. 5. The treaties, exacted by Commodore Stephen Decatur, required the pirates to cease their hostile acts, free all American prisoners, and compensate the U.S. for vessels seized.

Dec. 5 Pres. James Madison, in a **message to Congress**, asked for improvements in the armed forces, creation of a national currency, construction of roads and canals, and establishment of a national university. This was a major divergence from the policy of Thomas Jefferson, Madison's predecessor, who had urged careful protection of the rights and powers of the states.

America's first professional journalist, Philip Freneau, was also the "poet of the American Revolution." In 1775, at the beginning of the war, he wrote eight satirical poems, such as "General Gage's Confession." During the war he was captured by the British on a voyage from the West Indies and in 1781 wrote of the brutal treatment he had received in "The British Prison Ship." Freneau's anti-British sentiments were also expressed during the War of 1812 in such poems as "On British Commercial Depredations." Freneau edited various newspapers, such as the *National Gazette* in Philadelphia from 1791 to 1793. As an editor he was a vigorous Jeffersonian, often involved in editorial quarrels. Beyond his political and patriotic activities, Freneau was the earliest American lyrical poet of importance, writing such poems as "The Wild Honeysuckle" and "Eutaw Springs." An edition of his *Collected Poems* was published in 1815.

The *Life of Doctor Benjamin Franklin* by Mason Locke Weems, based largely on Franklin's *Autobiography*, was published in the U.S. The first version of the life was issued in Paris in 1791 as *Memoires de la Vie Privée*. This edition was retranslated into English and published in London in 1793. Another version, heavily edited by Franklin's grandson, William Temple Franklin, appeared in London in 1817. It was not until 1868 that a complete *Autobiography* was published in the U.S. It was edited by John Bigelow, author and diplomat, who had discovered the original manuscript in Paris.

The *North American Review,* for a century the most influential review in the U.S., was founded by William Tudor, Edward T. Channing, and Richard Henry Dana, Sr. It soon became a major influence among educated readers. The review published articles by leading American writers, who wrote in professional and scholarly fashion.

July 4 The cornerstone for the **first monument to George Washington** was laid in Baltimore, Md. The monument was designed by Robert Mills, a leader in the Greek Revival movement in U.S. architecture.

| Business and Industry; Science; Education; Philosophy and Religion   III | | IV   Sports; Social Issues and Crime; Folkways; Fashion; Holidays |

1815

One of the most important economic activities in the U.S. from the late eighteenth century to the middle of the nineteenth century was whaling. In 1791 American whalers for the first time rounded Cape Horn to hunt whales in the South Pacific. New Bedford, Mass., became the greatest whaling port in the world. Although set back by the War of 1812, whalers prospered more than ever after the virtual disappearance of British whaling ships. U.S. ships sailed throughout the Pacific Ocean, often on hunts of three years or more. Shortly before the Civil War, the whaling industry declined because the demand for sperm oil lessened with the coming of the petroleum industry. In addition, the number of whales had been reduced by overhunting.

The **Library of Congress** acquired Thomas Jefferson's collection of rare and significant books. This acquisition helped replace volumes lost in the fire set by the British in the War of 1812.

The rise of the U.S. **whaling industry** made greater amounts of whale oil and tallow available for illuminating U.S. homes.

The **Conestoga wagon** proved to be the most efficient mode of transportation for long treks from the East into the prairie regions. The "prairie schooner" was often bedecked with lively colors, its team of four-to-six horses festooned with bells. It carried a load of several tons and sometimes was built to a length of 60 ft.

Georgetown College, founded in Washington in 1789 by John Carroll and the first college in the U.S. established under Catholic auspices, was chartered by Congress as a university and empowered to grant degrees. In 1805 the operation of the college had been transferred to the Society of Jesus.

Allegheny College was founded at Meadville, Pa., and began instruction in the following year. It was chartered on Mar. 24, 1817.

With the end of the Napoleonic wars in Europe, immigration to the U.S. increased to new levels. Between 1815 and 1860, 5,000,000 persons came to the U.S. Over half of the immigrants came from the British Isles, mostly from Ireland. The next largest contingent arrived from Germany, 1,500,000, not counting German-speaking French citizens from Alsace and Lorraine. More than half the German immigrants settled in the upper Mississippi and Ohio river valleys.

Ohio glassware was a superior type of glassware manufactured from 1815 to 1850. The designation *Ohio* was generally applied both to the blown and molded glass produced in the Ohio R. Valley region. Three of the leading manufacturers of this glassware were located in Mantua, Kent, and Zanesville, all cities of Ohio. The designation *Ohio* was also used to identify glass factories in the neighboring regions of West Virginia and western Pennsylvania.

The **Boston Society for the Moral and Religious Instruction of the Poor** was established. It promoted Sunday school education in the city.

Jean Lafitte, the pirate, became an American folk hero because of his actions at the Battle of New Orleans. Since 1810 Lafitte had been operating off the Baratarian coast, south of New Orleans, as a privateer, preying on Spanish commerce for several Latin American nations. In Sept. 1814, a few days after a U.S. naval force raided his base at Barataria, Lafitte was offered a commission by the Royal Navy. Instead of accepting, Lafitte offered to help Andrew Jackson in return for a U.S. pardon for his piratical offenses. Lafitte and his men acquitted themselves admirably in the Battle of New Orleans, but in 1817 he moved his crew to the site of present-day Galveston, Tex., where they resumed a life of piracy.

1816

The presidential election of 1816 resulted in continuation of the so-called Virginia dynasty of presidents that had begun with Thomas Jefferson's election in 1800. The Democratic-Republican candidate was James Monroe of Virginia, who had been wounded in the American Revolution, and had served as diplomat, senator, and secretary of state. The Federalists by now scarcely existed as a national political party. They nominated Rufus King, who had been a delegate to the Constitutional Convention and one of New York's first senators. He carried only Massachusetts, Connecticut, and Delaware. The election was yet one more indication of the moribund condition of the Federalist Party. From this election on, it became ever weaker and ceased to exist in the 1820s.

1816–1817 In **congressional elections** the Republicans gained nine Senate seats for a 34–10 majority over the Federalists. In the House they gained 24 seats for a 141–42 majority.

Jan. 1 The **public debt** stood at $127,335,000, exceeding $100,000,000 for the first time. It amounted to about $15 per person.

Mar. 20 The power of the **Supreme Court** was further consolidated in the case of *Martin v. Hunter's Lessee*, which gave the Court jurisdiction over Virginia's state court.

Mar. 20 The draft of a **tariff bill** kept virtually the same tariff on imports that had been added earlier to raise money for the War of 1812. The measure was continued for protection of domestic manufacturers and eventual lessening dependence on foreign goods.

Dec. 4 **James Monroe was elected president** of the United States. Daniel D. Tompkins was elected vice president. Monroe, secretary of state under Pres. James Madison, gained the presidency in a landslide victory over his Federalist opponent, Rufus King of New York. The presidential electoral vote was Madison, 183; King, 34; and four abstentions.

Dec. 11 **Indiana** was admitted into the Union as the 19th state. Five years earlier, at the Tippecanoe R., it had been the scene of a decisive encounter between the confederated Indians under Tecumseh and U.S. forces under Gen. William Henry Harrison. After that encounter the Indians had made one last major raid, in 1812, then chose to sell out to the settlers and move beyond the Mississippi R. In June 1816 a constitution for the new state was drafted in the Indiana state capital at Corydon. In 1825 the state capital was moved to Indianapolis.

It was believed in some quarters and hoped in others that one result of securing independence from England would be development of an American language. Differences in spelling and vocabulary increased, but the American language has never achieved true independence from the mother tongue.

Champions of Freedom, a moral, romantic, historical novel by Samuel Woodworth, was published. Set against the events of the War of 1812, its plot involved the spirit of George Washington guiding the destinies of such heroes as Stephen Decatur, W. H. Harrison, Andrew Jackson, and the pirate Jean Laffite.

A great improvement in the **hand-press** was completed by George Clymer, a Philadelphia inventor who had been working on improving the printing press for 16 years. The invention improved the press originally devised by the Earl of Stanhope and was the first real American invention in the printing field. The $400 price of the press was high for American printers, so Clymer in 1817 took his invention to England, where his press was widely used for many years.

Airs of Palestine by John Pierpont, a popular long poem, was published and quickly went through three editions. With the correctness of a disciple of Alexander Pope, Pierpont traced the influence of music on Jewish history and paid tribute to François René de Chateaubriand, whom he called "the poetic pilgrim of the West."

Aug. "The Culprit Fay," a poem of more than 600 lines, was written in three days by Joseph Rodman Drake. Drake died of tuberculosis in 1820, and his poem was not published until 1835, in the volume *The Culprit Fay and Other Poems*. On his deathbed Drake had ordered his wife to destroy the manuscripts of what he described as his "trifles in rhyme." Fortunately, she did not do so. "The Culprit Fay," set against the background of the Hudson R. Valley, is considered an important milestone in the development of American literature.

1816

Black religious groups began to break away from largely white Protestant denominations to form their own churches. In 1796 black members of the Methodist Episcopal Church in New York City formed the African Methodist Episcopal Zion Church, which in 1821 was organized as a national group. The African Methodist Episcopal Church was founded in 1816 by Richard Allen, a clergyman who had been born a slave. He was pastor of a group that broke away from the Methodist Church in Philadelphia. On Apr. 11 he became the first bishop of the new denomination.

A *Vocabulary of Words and Phrases Peculiar to the United States* by John Pickering, the first formal study of American speech, was published. It was a dictionary of some 500 distinctly American words and phrases, and reflected the rising cultural differences between America and England. Although changes in vocabulary and spelling have been extensive and continue to accumulate, the American language has not yet achieved the independence from the mother tongue that some of its partisans expected.

The **American Bible Society** was founded in New York City. The purpose of the organization was to increase circulation of the Bible. Through the society translations of the Bible in over 1000 tongues have been printed and distributed around the world. The society emphasizes distribution of the Bible to the poor. It was incorporated in 1841 and in cooperation with the British and Foreign Bible Society has developed into an organization of worldwide influence with a large membership and many auxiliaries.

Feb. 6 Probably the **first railroad charter** granted in the U.S. was that of the New Jersey legislature to Col. John Stevens for a railroad between the Delaware and Raritan rivers. The project was never developed.

Apr. 10 The **second national bank** was chartered by Congress for a period of 20 years. It began with capital of $35,000,000, of which $28,000,000 was to be sold in shares of $100 each to private stockholders and $7,000,000 subscribed by the federal government.

June Baltimore, Md., became the first city in the U.S. to launch a **gas company.** The Gas Light Company of Baltimore was organized to provide coal gas for lighting the city's streets.

Dec. 13 The **first savings bank** in the U.S. was organized in Boston as The Provident Institution for Savings.

Transportation of blacks from the U.S. to Africa was often proposed as a partial solution for the slavery question. The first important step along these lines was taken at a meeting in Washington, D.C., in Dec. 1816 and Jan. 1817, when the American Colonization Society was formed. The principal founder was Robert Finley, a clergyman. Freeing many black slaves created a new problem: freedmen did not enjoy equal status with whites. In 1821 land was secured in Africa that later became the independent nation of Liberia, but by 1860 only about 11,000 blacks had been transported there. Abolitionists opposed resettlement, claiming it merely made slavery stronger in the South by removing free blacks. At the same time, many blacks born in the U.S. showed little enthusiasm for resettlement in Africa.

A new **mile record** in horse racing was set by Timoleon. The time was 1:47.

Freak summer weather in New England brought ten inches of snow on June 6. July and August were no better, with half an inch of ice spread over Vermont and New Hampshire. This year was entered into records as "the year in which there was no summer."

"Our country, right or wrong" was included in a toast offered by Stephen Decatur at a Virginia dinner commemorating his success against the pirates of the Barbary Coast. Called on to propose a toast he said: "Our Country! In her intercourse with foreign governments may she always be in the right; but our country, right or wrong."

The **first recorded boxing champion** in America was Jacob Hyer. In a grudge match billed as a "pugilistic encounter," Hyer beat Tom Beasley in a bare-knuckles contest under London Prize Ring Rules. Hyer then designated himself "America's first champion" and retired. The record books have accepted his self-designation.

The **Peace Society of Massachusetts** was established as a result of an antiwar sermon by the Rev. William Ellery Channing. Channing was not a total pacifist, however, since he conceded the necessity of waging war in self-defense or in defense of a moral principle.

June 22 The **Grand Encampment of Knights Templar** was started in New York City. De Witt Clinton was elected grand master.

| Exploration and Settlement; Wars; Government; Civil Rights; Statistics | I | | II | Publishing; Arts and Music; Popular Entertainment; Architecture; Theater |

1817

The first step in a process of mutual disarmament along the U.S.-Canadian border was taken this year in the Rush-Bagot Convention, signed on Apr. 28–29. The agreement was contained in an exchange of notes in Washington, D.C., between Richard Rush, acting secretary of state, and Charles Bagot, the British minister to the U.S. By its terms, each nation would have no more than four warships on the Great Lakes and Lake Champlain, and none would exceed 100 tons. The Senate unanimously approved the agreement on Apr. 16, 1818. The agreement set a precedent for solving Anglo-American disagreements by negotiation, although it was not until the Treaty of Washington of 1871 that complete mutual disarmament obtained along the U.S.-Canadian border.

Jan. 7 The second **Bank of the United States** opened in Philadelphia, Pa.

Mar. 3 The **Mississippi Territory** was divided into the Territory of Alabama and the state of Mississippi, about to be admitted into the Union.

Mar. 3 The so-called **Bonus Bill** was vetoed by Pres. James Madison on his last day in office. On Dec. 23, 1816, Rep. John C. Calhoun of South Carolina had introduced a bill to create a permanent fund for internal improvements (roads and canals). The bill set aside the $1,500,000 the Bank of the U.S. had paid the federal government for its charter and all future dividends the bank might pay the government on stock it held. Pres. Madison favored internal improvements but vetoed the bill because he believed a constitutional amendment was necessary to legalize them.

Mar. 4 **James Monroe was inaugurated president** of the United States. The fifth president, Monroe served two terms, a period characterized by an editorial writer on the Boston *Columbian Centinel* in June 1817 as "the era of good feeling."

Nov. 20 The **First Seminole War** (1817–1818) began when settlers attacked Florida Indians and the Indians retaliated by raiding isolated Georgia homesteads. Americans believed Spain had incited the Seminoles against the white settlers.

Dec. 10 **Mississippi** was admitted into the Union, the 20th state.

More than any other painter, John Trumbull provided future generations with a record of the Revolutionary era. After studying under Benjamin West in London, he began copying his teacher's grand style in historical paintings. An early and moving example was *The Death of General Montgomery at Quebec.* In 1816 Trumbull secured a commission from Congress to decorate the Capitol, and the best known result was *Signing of the Declaration of Independence* (1818). Others were *Surrender of Burgoyne at Saratoga, Surrender of Cornwallis at Yorktown,* and *Resignation of Washington.* In 1831 he founded Trumbull Gallery at Yale and placed much of his work in it.

Widespread literacy among Americans was noted by William Cobbett, an English journalist-reformer traveling widely in the U.S. Cobbett stated that American farmers read much more than the peasants of Europe.

Lalla Rookh, by the Irish poet Thomas Moore, became a best seller on its publication in the U.S. A long narrative poem of Oriental setting, for decades it rivaled the popularity of the heroic poems of Sir Walter Scott and Lord Byron.

Aug. 29 *Philanthropist,* an abolitionist newspaper, began publication in Mt. Pleasant, Ohio. Its founder and editor was Charles Osborn, one of the first, if not the first, to advocate immediate emancipation of all slaves. The paper, an eight-page weekly, ceased publication on Oct. 8, 1818.

Sept. The poem "Thanatopsis" by William Cullen Bryant won for American poetry its first attention and respect from British critics. Printed in the *North American Review,* the poem's appearance was "much as if a classic temple had been exorcised from the wilderness by the strains of a new Amphion." Its quiet reflections on death and nature created an entire school of American poets.

1817

The distribution by religious groups of Christian literature not only spread religion but also contributed significantly to education. The Connecticut Tract Society was formed in 1807. In 1814 it joined with half a dozen similar groups to form a national organization, the American Tract Society. After 1817 the society supplied much religious literature, which was distributed widely by circuit riders. In many homes these were the only books, and from them children learned to read and spell. Peter Cartwright, a Methodist circuit rider for nearly 50 years, wondered whether he "had done the most good by preaching or by distributing religious books." He felt "it was part and parcel of a Methodist preacher's most sacred duty to circulate good books." Cartwright sometimes handed out $1,000 worth of books a year, a large amount at that time.

The first free **public school for the deaf** was founded in Hartford, Conn., by Thomas Hopkins Gallaudet. The school is now the American School for the Deaf.

The **first insane asylum** in the U.S. was established at Frankford, Pa.

Machine-made **paper** was manufactured by Thomas Gilpin near Wilmington, Del. For the first time in the U.S., custom-made paper was available.

Rolled iron was produced in Pennsylvania at the Plumstock Rolling Mill, financed by Isaac Mason.

July 4 Construction of the **Erie Canal** was begun under Gov. De Witt Clinton of New York, elected in spring of 1817. The canal was to affect the development of New York, both city and state, bringing Great Lakes trade to the Atlantic Ocean.

Fashions in clothing changed considerably in the early nineteenth century. Under the influence of the romantic movement and the French Revolution, women's fashions became simpler. Light dresses, low-cut and sleeveless, replaced the elaborate billowing gowns of the old aristocracy. Hair was cut shorter, not piled high. About 1815 fashion began moving back to the era of stiff corsets, leg-of-mutton sleeves, and full skirts that developed into the hoop skirt. Men's fashions also changed. Knee-length pantaloons, with buckles, silk stockings, and low-cut shoes, as well as the wig, were on their way out by 1800. Pres. James Monroe was the last chief executive to dress this way, and an 1823 painting of him and his cabinet shows Monroe the only person so clothed. Long trousers came in, reflecting the French Revolution, whose supporters came from the middle and lower classes and dressed this way to contrast with the nobility. The style seemed appropriate for democratic America.

Cup plates became the rage at about this time. They were miniature plates with a center cavity about the diameter of a cup bottom used as a dainty but practical perch for cups while a drinker sipped from his saucer. Cup plates were decorated with lavish attention to detail, came in a great variety of patterns, and fairly chronicled the taste of the period. They were introduced first as chinaware. The development of the glass industry, especially of the glass press, made them even more plentiful and, considering their use, necessary. Cup plates lasted as long as it was considered polite to drink from a saucer but went out of vogue before the Civil War.

The **linguistic conservatism** of southern planters was commented on by James Kirke Paulding in his book *Letters from the South.* Paulding wrote that he was astonished that these planters opposed modernization even by English writers, preferring the eighteenth-century prose styles of John Milton, Isaac Newton, John Locke, and Joseph Addison to the nineteenth-century innovations of such writers as Lord Byron.

| Exploration and Settlement; Wars; Government; Civil Rights; Statistics | I | | II | Publishing; Arts and Music; Popular Entertainment; Architecture; Theater |

1818

The First Seminole War (1817–1818) began in earnest this year with a U.S. invasion of East Florida to punish hostile Seminole Indians, whose territory had become a refuge for runaway slaves. American troops on July 27, 1816, had destroyed the Seminole stronghold of Fort Apalachicola, on the river of that name. On Dec. 27, 1817, Gen. Andrew Jackson took command, with orders to pursue the Indians across the Florida boundary. Jackson marched his troops into Florida and captured St. Marks on Apr. 7, 1818, and Pensacola on May 24. In the course of his campaign, Jackson seized two British traders, Alexander Arbuthnot and Robert Ambrister. He accused them of aiding the enemy and had the former hanged and the latter shot. There was a great outcry in England and considerable criticism in Washington. Nevertheless, popular opinion approved the campaign, which brought East Florida under American control and resulted in its cession to the U.S. by Spain in 1819.

Laws extending **suffrage** were adopted in Connecticut this year, in Massachusetts in 1820, and in New York in 1821. Such laws reduced or did away with property qualifications for voting. The new western states came into the Union with few if any restrictions on male suffrage, putting pressure on the older states. By 1824 virtually all white males could vote in presidential elections except in Rhode Island, Virginia, and Louisiana.

1818–1819 In **congressional elections** the Republicans gained one Senate seat for a 35–7 majority over the Federalists. In the House they gained 15 seats for a 156–27 majority.

Oct. 20 A **diplomatic convention** signed between Britain and the U.S. gave fishing rights to American seamen off parts of Newfoundland and the coast of Labrador. The U.S. renounced such activity within three miles of any other British territory. The boundary between Canada and the U.S. between Lake of the Woods and the crest of the Rocky Mts. was fixed at the 49th parallel. No boundary was decided upon farther west, and Oregon was declared open territory for ten years.

Dec. 3 **Illinois** was admitted into the Union, the 21st state.

An unusual example of an American playwright of the early years of independence who won acclaim, although not riches, on both sides of the Atlantic was John Howard Payne (1791–1852). Showing a precocious interest in the drama, he published the *Thespian Mirror* in New York City when he was only 14. It so impressed the literary and theater world that he was encouraged to write. He proceeded to write a melodrama, *Julia; or, The Wanderer* in 1806. His early fame waned, and it was not until 1818, in England, that he regained recognition. Success stemmed from the production by Edmund Kean, the noted British actor, of Payne's *Brutus; or, The Fall of Tarquin*, which opened on Dec. 3. This romantic tragedy, in blank verse, was equally successful in New York in 1819. It was performed for many years. By 1832, after other successes and writing the poem "Home, Sweet Home," which was put to music, Payne was honored but died in debt while working on further literary and dramatic works.

Pirating of English novels became a highly competitive sport among U.S. publishers with the appearance here of Sir Walter Scott's tremendous success, *Rob Roy.* In the absence of copyright protection in the U.S. for foreign works, representatives of U.S. publishers sent clandestinely obtained proofs here by fastest boat, and printers worked around the clock to get the books to market.

The **first lithograph** produced in the U.S. was prepared by Bass Otis, a portrait painter and mezzotint engraver. The lithograph was a portrait of the Rev. Abner Kneeland, a Universalist clergyman and editor of religious magazines. It appeared as frontispiece for a volume of Kneeland's sermons. Some experts claim the portrait was technically not a lithograph because Bass etched it in stone, thus making it an intaglio instead of a surface process.

Jan. 1 The **White House,** as the restored Executive Mansion in Washington, D.C., was now called because of its gleaming new coat of white paint, was opened for a general reception. Burned out by the British in 1814, the building was ready for occupancy in the fall of 1817, but lacked proper furnishings.

| Business and Industry; Science; Education; Philosophy and Religion **III** | | **IV** Sports; Social Issues and Crime; Folkways; Fashion; Holidays |

1818

Americans in the early nineteenth century continued to show interest in science. One of the foremost scientists was Benjamin Silliman, who in 1802 became the first professor of chemistry and natural history at Yale. In 1813 he began an illustrated lecture course in geology and mineralogy and in 1818 was one of the founders of the Yale Medical School. Also in 1818 he became one of the founders of the *American Journal of Science and Arts,* the first important scientific journal in the U.S., which he edited for nearly 28 years.

The **West Point Foundry** was established at Cold Spring, N.Y., across the Hudson R. from the U.S. Military Academy. Beginning as a small forge, the foundry became the Union's main source of artillery and projectiles, producing in the course of the Civil War over 3000 heavy cannon and 1,600,000 shells. Gouverneur Kemble, a leading American ironmaster and operator of the foundry, was largely responsible for the quality of ordnance produced at the foundry.

The **tin can** was introduced to the U.S. by Peter Durand, an Englishman, who hit on the idea of sealing hot perishable foods in suitable containers and took out a patent on the process in 1810. He put tin at the top of a list of recommended materials for containers. Glass had already been used for similar purpose in France by François Appert, author of *Art of Preserving Animal and Vegetable Substances for Many Years,* published in 1810.

Jan. Transatlantic ship crossings on a regular monthly basis were initiated between U.S. and British ports when the *James Monroe* sailed from New York City and the *Courier* from Liverpool, England. Four ships formed the Black Ball Line.

Sept. 20 Patent leather was manufactured in the U.S. for the first time by Seth Boyden in Newark, N.J. Boyden had developed a lacquer for treating leather in the fashion of European decorative leather. One of the great early American inventors, Boyden later sold the factory and turned to production of malleable iron, locomotives, steam engines, and other items.

Bowling had been introduced to America by the Dutch in the seventeenth century, when the game became a ten-pin rather than nine-pin game. There is an 1803 picture of ten-pin bowling in progress in Suffolk County, N.Y. By mid-nineteenth century there was a boom in the building of indoor alleys. Gambling began to invade the sport, and in 1841 bowling was banned in Connecticut for this reason. Still it remained a regular amusement at the fashionable Saratoga, N.Y., spa. In literature, the game of ninepins plays an important part in Washington Irving's "Rip Van Winkle," probably his most popular story, issued serially in *The Sketch Book* (1819–1820).

Thin muslin dresses, low-cut and fitted, came into vogue. Concern was expressed for women who went out attired in these dresses. Was the fashion in the best interests of the ladies' health? Were the ladies in physical danger from fire? Most important, did such dresses reflect on the virtue of the wearer?

Vocal recitals were highly popular entertainment. Among the successful vocalists was a Mr. Philips, who offered at the New York Theater "Behold in his soft expressive face," "Robin Adair," and "Lilla come down to me" among other selections.

The City Hotel in New York featured the exhibition of a female albino, referred to as the Albiness, until Feb. 5.

Apr. 4 A **U.S. flag with 13 stripes** was settled on by Congress. On admission of each new state to the Union, another star would be added to the flag, the number and pattern of stripes remaining the same.

1819

The Supreme Court, under the leadership of Chief Justice John Marshall, continued to set precedents increasing the power of the judiciary and the national government. In the case of *McCullock v. Maryland* in 1819, Marshall found an opportunity to assert the power of the federal government over the states. Maryland had levied a tax on a branch of the Bank of the United States. Marshall argued that if the government had the right to coin money, which the Constitution gave it, it had the implied right to establish a bank. Thus, the government was supreme in that sphere and a state could not tax an instrument of the central government. This argument is generally agreed to be Marshall's most brilliant opinion on constitutional law, but it was not universally accepted at the time.

A financial panic struck the U.S. in 1819. State banks closed and much western property was turned over to the Bank of the United States. Immigration slowed to a trickle for almost a decade.

Feb. 13   The first major division over **slavery** followed introduction of an amendment by Rep. James Tallmadge of New York to the bill creating statehood for Missouri. States were evenly divided between slave and free. Missouri's status appeared crucial to both North and South. The amendment proposed that all children born in Missouri be free at age 25, and that further introduction of slavery be prohibited. The right of Congress to impose restrictions on new states that the Constitution did not impose on the original commonwealths was questioned. The Tallmadge amendment was ultimately dropped.

Feb. 22   The **Florida Purchase Treaty** was signed by Spain and the U.S. In a triumph of diplomacy by Sec. of State John Quincy Adams, Spain ceded the remainder of its old province of Florida at no cost beyond that of U.S. assumption of up to $5,000,000 of the claims of U.S. citizens against Spain. Adams also obtained for the U.S. a transcontinental southern boundary that legitimized U.S. interests on the northern side of the line to the Pacific.

Mar. 2   The **first immigration law** enacted by Congress established rules and procedures for passenger ships bringing immigrants to the U.S. The most important procedure was the numerical registry of immigration, which made it possible to compile accurate statistics on immigration in later years.

Dec. 14   **Alabama** was admitted into the Union, the 22nd state.

One of the earliest satirical writers on public affairs in the U.S. was Joseph Rodman Drake, a poet of New York. A series of satirical poems called "The Croaker Papers" appeared anonymously in the New York *Evening Post* and *National Advertiser* this year. Of the 35 poems, Drake wrote 14 and collaborated on eight with his friend Fitz-Greene Halleck. Drake also wrote "The Culprit Fay," a serious poem, and "The American Flag," a patriotic poem that was declaimed on many occasions for years after. Drake died of consumption on Sept. 21, 1820, at 25. Halleck's poem "On the Death of Joseph Rodman Drake" is considered one of the finest elegies in American literature.

The building designed by **Benjamin Latrobe** for the Second Bank of the U.S. in Philadelphia was completed. Latrobe, a skilled engineer, was a prominent and influential leader of the Greek Revival movement. In his building for the Second Bank he introduced a Doric portico similar to the one used in the Parthenon. Porticoes were widely employed by Latrobe in his public buildings and by architects of homes for clients who favored the Greek Revival style.

Washington Allston captured the romantic feeling for nature admirably in his *Moonlit Landscape,* a canvas flooded with mystery. His friend Samuel Taylor Coleridge said of him that he alone was able to capture true aspects of nature, "not the dead shapes, the outward letter, but the life of nature revealing itself in the phenomenon."

Washington Irving's *Sketch Book* became an immediate best seller and still ranks among the most popular American books of all time. With this book Irving established himself as a beloved literary genius.

St. Paul's Episcopal Church in Augusta, Ga., an excellent example of southern Greek Revival architecure, was built from plans by an architect unknown to history.

1819

In the Dartmouth College case the Supreme Court, under Chief Justice John Marshall, continued to uphold the power of the federal government. In 1816 New Hampshire, without the consent of Dartmouth College, amended the college charter, which in legal terms was a contract. The college brought suit, with Daniel Webster as counsel. Marshall wrote the court's opinion, holding that New Hampshire acted unconstitutionally, violating the Constitution's prohibition against any state passing laws "impairing the Obligation of Contracts." The decision became a major instrument for protection of property rights against state abridgment.

Norwich University, the first private military college in the U.S., opened in Northfield, Vt. Specializing in technical training, it marked a significant advance in American higher education.

Ebenezer Brown, the first missionary sent out by the Methodist Church in the U.S., was dispatched by Bishop George to preach to the French-speaking inhabitants of Louisiana. The mission failed and Brown turned to a pastoral ministry. In 1829 at Troy, N.Y., he conceived the idea of a detachable collar for shirts and began making them with part-time female labor; this later became a full-scale business. These were the first such collars made in the U.S.

What was probably the **first food canning business** was begun in New York City when Ezra Daggett and Thomas Kensett started canning fish as a commercial enterprise. In 1825 Kensett obtained a patent, the first, for tin-plated cans. In Boston William Underwood opened a successful canning plant in 1820.

William Ellery Channing delivered his famous sermon, "Unitarian Christianity," in Baltimore. In it he outlined the Unitarian view and provided liberals with a platform. The sermon heightened tensions among Protestant factions and led to formation of the American Unitarian Association.

The **University of Virginia** at Charlottesville was founded under sponsorship of former President Thomas Jefferson and chartered by the state. Instruction at the post-secondary level was first given in 1825, and the first degrees were granted in 1828.

Apr. 2 The **first successful agricultural journal** in the U.S., *American Farmer,* was founded in Baltimore, Md., by John Stuart Skinner. It became widely popular and continued publishing until 1897.

May 26 The **first American steamboat** to cross the Atlantic left Savannah, Ga., bound for Liverpool. It made the crossing in 25 days, all but seven on steam.

The eastern U.S. was slowly becoming urbanized, but the frontier, moving ever westward, was still the place for the vigorous outdoor activities associated with newly settled rural areas. Marksmanship was highly prized and involved such sports as squirrel shooting by four-man teams. On one occasion, a team shot 152 squirrels by nightfall and the other, 141. A brutal sport was the rough-and-tumble fight. There were no rules and the two contestants were free to bite off ears or gouge out eyes until a fighter gave up or was knocked unconscious.

The **New York Picture Gallery** was opened for display and sale of art. It advertised showings of old and modern pictures, sculptures, and bronzes.

A **six-cent reward** was offered for return of a lost, strayed, or stolen 19-year-old apprentice blacksmith in the New York *Evening Post.*

Feb. G. Geib advertised his **Patent Analytical Grammatical system** of teaching the composition and practice of music. Lessons were $30 a quarter. The money would be refunded if the pupil was not satisfied. Geib bonded himself for $1000 against failures.

Feb. 5 **Double-feature theatrical performances** offered theater buffs such plays as *Rob Roy McGregor* or *Auld Lang Syne,* followed after an intermission by *Dr. Last's Examination* or the comic ballet *Little Red Riding Hood.*

Apr. 26 The **Independent Order of Odd Fellows** made its first appearance in the U.S. with the organization of Washington Lodge No. 1 in Baltimore, Md., by Thomas Wildey, who had arrived from England in 1818. On Feb. 1, 1820, the new lodge was chartered by Duke of York Lodge, Preston, England.

June 1 A noted European **tightrope performer,** Mme. Adolphe, made her American debut at the Anthony Street Theater, New York City.

1820

The first serious clash between slavery and antislavery interests, in 1819 and 1820, strained relations between the North and the South and hinted at worse trouble to come. At the end of 1818 the Union consisted of 11 free and 11 slave states. The North, however, was rapidly outdistancing the South in population and held a growing numerical advantage in the House of Representatives. Southern leaders felt strongly, therefore, that the number of free and slave states should remain balanced so that the South would be equal to the North in the Senate. Ready for statehood were Maine, certain to be a free state, and Missouri, part of the Louisiana Purchase and likely to be a slave state. After much political maneuvering, Congress passed on Mar. 3, 1820, a bill that became known as the Missouri Compromise. By its terms Maine was to be admitted as a free state and Missouri as a slave state, but slavery was to be forever prohibited in the rest of the Louisiana Purchase north of the line of latitude 36° 30', which was the southern boundary of Missouri.

The fourth U.S. **Census** recorded a population of 9,638,453. The center of population was placed 16 miles east of Moorefield, W.Va.

Big-time **machine politics** was introduced to the U.S. by a group of New York Democrats known as the Albany Regency. Martin Van Buren was among the leaders of the group, which controlled New York politics for two decades.

Capt. **Nathaniel Brown Palmer** and a crew of six sighted the Antarctic Peninsula, later called Palmerland. This was believed to have been the first discovery of Antarctica. Palmer commanded the sloop *Hero*, out of Stonington, Conn.

1820–1821   In **congressional elections** the Republicans gained nine Senate seats for a 44–4 majority over the Federalists. In the House they gained two seats for a 158–25 majority.

Feb. 6   The first organized **immigration of blacks** to Africa from the U.S. began with a group of 86 sailing from New York City to Sierra Leone.

Mar. 15   **Maine** was admitted into the Union, the 23rd state.

June 6   The expedition of Maj. **Stephen Long** set out from Pittsburgh to explore the region south of the Missouri R. and the Rocky Mts. The only important geographical discovery of the expedition was the course of the Canadian R., later an important part of the route to New Mexico.

Dec. 6   **James Monroe was reelected president** of the United States. Daniel D. Tompkins was reelected vice president. The electoral vote was Monroe, 231; John Quincy Adams, a Federalist and Monroe's secretary of state, 1.

The Knickerbocker Group was a school of writers with similar literary tastes who were associated with New York City. The name was a tribute to Washington Irving's *Knickerbocker's History of New York* (1809); those who followed Irving tried to carry on his spirit and style. Among the Knickerbockers were William Cullen Bryant, James Kirke Paulding, Joseph Rodman Drake, Lydia Maria Child, and Fitz-Greene Halleck. In 1819 Halleck's long poem *Fanny* was published. In it, in imitation of the style of Lord Byron, he satirized in rollicking fashion life in New York—finance, society, women, etc. Halleck also found time to be personal secretary to the entrepreneur John Jacob Astor.

A great **literary theme** of the 1820s was the romantic treatment of the Indian. Works in this vein included *Frontier Maid, or the Fall of Wyoming* (1819); *Yamoyden* (1820) by Eastburn and Sands; *Logan, an Indian Tale* (1821) by Samuel Webber; *The Land of Powhatten* (1821) by a Virginian; and *Ontwa, Son of the Forest* (1822) by Henry Whiting.

The **Grove Street houses** built in Greenwich Village, New York City, were good examples of the nineteenth-century New York style, before the emergence of the Greek Revival.

A book by **Anton Philip Heinrich** calling for nationalistic music, *Dawning of Music in Kentucky, or the Pleasures of Harmony in the Solitudes of Nature,* was published. Heinrich had emigrated from Hamburg, Germany, two years earlier. Among his compositions were: *The Columbiad; Grand American National Chivalrous Symphony; Jubilee;* and *Yankee Doodiad.*

Ivanhoe by **Sir Walter Scott,** published in 1820, sold over 2,500,000 copies. Scott and, some years later, Charles Dickens were the two most republished authors in the U.S.

Jan.   This was the year that **Sydney Smith,** an English clergyman, writer, and wit, taunted American culture with his widely quoted query: "In the four quarters of the globe, who reads an American book? or goes to an American play? or looks at an American picture or statue?"

Nov. 27   **Edwin Forrest,** a celebrated actor of the nineteenth-century American stage, made his debut at the Walnut Street Theater, Philadelphia, as young Norval in John Home's *Douglas.* Not quite 15, Forrest did not overwhelm his audience or the critics with his ability. Nonetheless, he later became America's foremost stage idol.

| Business and Industry; Science; Education; Philosophy and Religion | III | | IV | Sports; Social Issues and Crime; Folkways; Fashion; Holidays |

1820

Americans were beginning to take an interest in the history and culture of the Indians. The foremost pioneer in this field was Henry Rowe Schoolcraft, a self-taught ethnologist and geologist. This year Schoolcraft accompanied an expedition to the upper Mississippi R. and Lake Superior region, and two years later he was appointed Indian agent for the tribes in that area. This enabled Schoolcraft to carry on his research into Indian history and culture and resulted in voluminous writings. These included a six-volume history published between 1851 and 1857. Schoolcraft married the daughter of an Ojibwa woman and a fur trader. Henry Wadsworth Longfellow used Schoolcraft's writings as source material for his narrative poem *The Song of Hiawatha* (1855).

Libraries as institutional sources of reading material for the eager American middle class were boosted by the establishment in New York City of the Mercantile Library Association and the Apprentices Library Association. They were followed shortly by similar libraries in Boston and Philadelphia.

Major **Stephen Long,** Army officer, explorer, and engineer, completed an expedition, which had been suggested by Sec. of War John C. Calhoun, into the region of the Platte and Arkansas rivers and their headwaters. In addition to being the first person to sight Mt. Long, northwest of Denver, he came upon and reported on 60 rare or previously unknown animals, hundreds of new insects, and many previously unknown plants.

The **first state-supported libraries** in the U.S. were established in New York and New Hampshire. This marked a major advance in public readership and scholarly endeavors.

The **number of college graduates** in the U.S. was estimated by James Fenimore Cooper to be 8000, in a population of 10,000,000.

The evolution of **interchangeable machine parts** was stepped up by Thomas Blanchard's invention of a special lathe to finish off wooden stocks of firearms. Stocks could be cut out in rapid order and used with standardized metal parts of guns. Success with his lathe encouraged Blanchard to apply his invention to more general industrial uses.

Elihu Embree began publication of *Emancipator* at Jonesboro, Tenn. In 1819 he started his crusade against slavery with a weekly paper, *Manumission Intelligencer.* Forced to convert to a monthly, Embree renamed his publication *Emancipator.* It was a popular and powerful organ of agitation, denouncing slaveholding as evil. Embree, a convert to Quakerism, was strongly influenced by the Quaker argument that all men are entitled to exercise the freedom given them by God. He died before the end of the year, and his monthly with him.

The frontier attracted rugged types who liked to boast of their toughness, since the West was a region where physical strength was often a necessity. The phrase *half horse, half alligator,* first recorded in 1809 by Washington Irving, was an appellation such persons liked to use in referring to themselves. Mark Twain later wrote of a rough-and-tumble fighter who introduced himself in this way: "the original iron-jawed, brass-mounted, copper-bellied corpse-maker from the wilds of Arkansaw," concluding with "cast your eye on me, gentlemen, and lay low and hold your breath, for I'm 'bout to turn myself loose."

During this decade the **first soccerlike games** appeared in American colleges. A large round ball was kicked toward a goal. The game served as a form of hazing, especially at Yale and Harvard. Sophomores and freshmen were supposed to kick the ball, but sophomores generally kicked freshmen instead. The games were banned during the 1830s because of the large number of injuries sustained by students.

A notable **chair factory** was started by Lambert Hitchcock at Hitchcockville (now Riverton), Conn. This factory produced chair parts, which were sent to South Carolina for assembly. The Hitchcock chair thus became popular in the South. In 1823 the chair was manufactured completely in Hitchcockville.

Popular attitudes and actions, John C. Calhoun reported to John Quincy Adams early this year, deserve careful attention. The panic of 1819 had wrought great changes in people's economic status. A period of wild speculation had ended with wholesale foreclosures by banks, and much property in the South and West reverted to the national bank. There were, said Calhoun, "enormous multitudes in deep distress" who were disenchanted with government, alert to the main chance and "looking out anywhere for a leader." This proved to be a shrewd political insight into the factors ushering in the age of Jackson.

Apr. 12 The term *doughface* was popularized by Rep. John Randolph of Roanoke, Va., according to a report in the *New Brunswick Times.* The term was applied to northern congressmen who voted with southern slaveholding interests. John Quincy Adams continued to use the term in this way until 1843.

1821

As part of the westward movement, American traders probed the Southwest, which put them in contact with Spanish regions. Traffic over what was to become the Santa Fe Trail began on Sept. 1, 1821, when William Becknell led a party from Independence, Mo., headed for Santa Fe, N.Mex. Spanish authorities had forbidden trading with Americans, but such trade was welcome after Mexico won its independence in Nov. 1821. The trip of about 780 miles was made yearly by caravans comprising as many as 100 wagons, the trip taking 40 to 60 days. The caravans carried textiles and hardware to Santa Fe, where the traders usually remained for four or five weeks before returning to Missouri.

Music was made more available to amateurs and students by the publication of songbooks and by the introduction into schools of music education. A pioneer in this field was Lowell Mason, a banker and church organist in Savannah, Ga. In 1821 he helped compile the *Boston Handel and Haydn Society's Collection of Church Music.* Its success was one reason why Mason gave up banking and turned to music, becoming the musical director of three Boston churches. He was a founder of the Boston Academy of Music in 1832. Mason also found time to compose 1210 hymns, including "Nearer, My God, to Thee."

Mar. 5   Pres. **James Monroe was inaugurated** for a second term. As Mar. 4 fell on a Sunday, Monroe moved the ceremony to the following Monday. This was the first time that inauguration ceremonies were moved ahead because the designated day fell on a Sunday.

Kenilworth by Sir Walter Scott was published. Scott's colorful novels were read eagerly by Americans as quickly as publishers could turn out American editions from pages shipped from England.

Aug. 10   **Missouri** was admitted into the Union, the 24th state.

The Spy by James Fenimore Cooper, a romance of the American Revolution, was published and quickly went through three printings in its first year.

Sept.   A treaty was concluded by which the **Seminole Indians** agreed to retire to the center of the Florida peninsula, an almost uninhabitable territory. They were to move west 20 years from the date of the treaty, and the U.S. was to pay them annuities and assure them of protection and care.

The sole sculpture of an American by **Antonio Canova,** the Italian master, a statue of George Washington, was erected in Raleigh, the capital of North Carolina—an unlikely location for what was probably the finest piece of sculpture then in the U.S. It was later destroyed by fire.

Dec.   The **first American settlement in Texas,** San Felipe de Austin, was established by Stephen Austin.

The Genius of Universal Emancipation, an antislavery publication, was first issued in Ohio by Benjamin Lundy, who articulated the widespread hope of resettling blacks in Africa.

1821

The need for more and better roads to transport people and goods also meant that more and better bridges were needed. Ithiel Town, an architect, contributed to the cause by patenting in 1820 a form of truss bridge with a diamond pattern of closely spaced diagonals. This was simple to construct and required no special materials. In 1821 he wrote an article that considered the problem of rigid iron bridges. It was to take 15 years before such structures were built in the U.S.

Emma Willard, with the founding of her Troy Female Seminary in Troy, N.Y., initiated higher education for women. Her curriculum, including science, was considered rigorous, offering virtually collegiate education for which Mrs. Willard devised new teaching methods. The seminary became a model for European and American education institutions for women and trained hundreds of women for the teaching profession.

The **first natural gas well** in the U.S. drilled intentionally began production in Fredonia, N.Y., near Buffalo.

Feb. 6 **George Washington University,** first chartered as Columbian College, was established in Washington, D.C., under Baptist auspices. The college awarded its first degrees in 1824. Columbian College was renamed Columbian University in 1873 and George Washington University in 1904.

May **English Classical School,** later renamed English High School, opened in Boston, Mass. This was the first free, publicly supported high school anywhere. In addition, the term *high school* was used for the first time.

May 31 The **first Catholic cathedral** in the U.S., the Cathedral of the Assumption of the Blessed Virgin Mary, Baltimore, Md., was dedicated by Archbishop Maréchal. The cornerstone had been laid in 1806.

The most serious attempt to find a home outside the U.S. for freed black slaves was the establishment in 1821 of the colony of Liberia in western Africa. With government and private funds, the American Colonization Society purchased the area from local tribal chiefs. Settlement began in 1822, when the first of about 15,000 persons arrived in Liberia. The colony had many difficulties, and its survival in the early years was due mainly to the efforts of Jehudi Ashmun, who was sent there by the society and who built up the colony in spite of epidemics and native attacks. The colony was declared independent in 1847. Immigration of American blacks ended for the most part after the Civil War.

During the next decade and a half **coffee** came into general use in America. But temperance movements directed heavy campaigns against it, and in some quarters it was considered an aphrodisiac.

Laws against **public horse racing** were relaxed in New York, permitting tracks to open in Queens County. This led to the building of the Union Course on Long Island.

Dr. **Charles Caldwell,** trained in medicine by the great Benjamin Rush, and a faculty member in medicine at Transylvania College, Lexington, Ky., traveled to Europe with $10,000 contributed by the state of Kentucky to buy a library for the college. The books he brought back formed the first collection west of the Alleghenies. He also brought back an enthusiasm for phrenology, gained from meetings in Vienna with its founder, J.H. Spurzheim. Caldwell's publicizing of phrenology earned him the sobriquet "American Spurzheim," overshadowing his contribution to medical science in the Midwest.

1822

Fear of slave insurrections was common in the South in the early nineteenth century. While there were few actual instances of trouble, a serious uprising took place in Charleston, S.C., this year. It was led by a free black, Denmark Vesey, who had purchased his freedom in 1800. Over the years Vesey had organized a plot to seize control of Charleston, but word leaked out in June. Militia and federal troops were called out, many slaves were arrested, and Vesey and 34 others were executed. Some estimates put the number of slaves involved as high as 9000.

1822–1823   In **congressional elections** the Republicans kept their 44–4 Senate majority over the Federalists. In the House they gained 29 seats to the Federalists' gain of one, for a 187–26 majority.

Mar. 8   **Recognition of several Latin American republics** was urged by Pres. James Monroe in a message to Congress. The states were La Plata (Argentina), Brazil, Chile, Peru, Colombia, Mexico, and the Federation of Central American States. A Congressional Act of May 4 provided for diplomatic recognition of these nations.

Apr. 27   **Ulysses S. Grant,** 18th president of the United States, was born in Point Pleasant, Ohio.

May 4   **A transportation bill** appropriating money for repair of the Cumberland Road and authorizing toll charges was vetoed by Pres. Monroe, who asserted that the federal government did not have the right to operate and hold jurisdiction over a public road. The bill did not pass over his veto.

Oct. 4   **Rutherford B. Hayes,** 19th president of the United States, was born in Delaware, Ohio.

Men with a variety of talents aided progress in literature, religion, and education in the first quarter of the nineteenth century. One of these was Timothy Dwight of New England, a leader of the Connecticut Wits, clergyman, and educator. His long poem *Greenfield Hill* (1794) was an attempt to convince Europeans that America provided suitable material for poetry. His *Travels in New England and New York* (four volumes, 1821–1822) is an indispensable source for the life of the period. An orthodox Congregational minister, Dwight was sometimes called the "Protestant pope of New England." He was president of Yale from 1795 to 1817 and did much to modernize its curriculum.

The Pilot by James Fenimore Cooper was published and became a best seller. Cooper's fourth novel, and the first with a maritime setting and theme, was a product of Cooper's determination to outdo Sir Walter Scott in the production of a sea novel. The unnamed hero, known only as the Pilot, represents John Paul Jones, the foremost U.S. naval figure of the time. The novel's action takes place during the American Revolution. Cooper's novel was long popular.

Washington Irving continued his literary quest among the treasures of antiquity with his *Bracebridge Hall.* Like his *Sketch Book,* it comprised sketches, stories, and essays, many of which romanticized the English countryside. "The Stout Gentleman" was considered one of the best stories in the collection.

1822

Agitation by manufacturing interests for a protective tariff system, which had begun with Alexander Hamilton in the late eighteenth century, continued as industry grew. The chief proponent was Mathew Carey of Philadelphia. One of the most important publishers and booksellers of his day, Carey was also a self-taught economist who wrote and spoke in favor of what was beginning to be called the American system: tariffs and internal improvements at the federal government's expense. Carey's *Essays on Political Economy* was published in 1822. His frequent addresses before the Philadelphia Society for the Promotion of National Industry reflected the rise of protectionist sentiment.

Exploration of the western U.S. was aided by fur trappers and those who organized the fur trade. One such man was William Henry Ashley, whose 1822 expedition built a post at the confluence of the Yellowstone and Missouri rivers. Ashley's innovation in the fur trade was to initiate an annual rendezvous at which time the trappers gathered to sell their furs and purchase supplies. The trappers, who had had no taste of civilization for a year, sometimes spent on drinking and gambling everything they had earned for the year's work.

The primitive U.S. form of **football** was prohibited at Yale College by Pres. Timothy Dwight, who ordered any violations to be reported and violators to be penalized by a fine not to exceed half a dollar.

John Jacob Astor moved a step closer to his monopoly of the fur trade in the Northwest when Congress abandoned its program of operating Indian factories, or fur-trading posts. Following this development, Astor bought out the few rival companies and established total control in the fur market.

"**The Hunters of Kentucky**" was performed by the comedian Noah Ludlow before an enthusiastic audience in New Orleans consisting mostly of river boatmen. The song turned the already celebrated Battle of New Orleans into a Jacksonian legend. Its fifth stanza goes:

> But Jackson, he was wide awake,
> And wasn't scared at trifles;
> For well he knew what aim to take,
> With our Kentucky rifles;
> So he led us down to Cypress swamp,
> The ground was low and mucky;
> There stood John Bull, in martial pomp,
> And here was old Kentucky.
> Oh! Kentucky, the hunters of Kentucky,
> The hunters of Kentucky.

Apr. 10 The future **Hobart College** was founded as Geneva College at Geneva, N.Y. It adopted the name Hobart in 1860. Geneva offered the first nonclassical course in the U.S.; called "English Course," it offered to equip "the Agriculturist, the Merchant, and the Mechanic" with a "practical knowledge of what genius and experience have discovered."

1823

Many Americans, especially in the South, were beginning to cast eyes at Texas as an area for agricultural expansion. Long part of the Spanish Empire, Texas had become part of the independent nation of Mexico in 1821. Spain had made a grant of land and in 1820 given Moses Austin permission to bring in 300 settlers. The Mexican government having confirmed the grant, Moses's son Stephen took up the work of his late father and brought in settlers in Dec. 1821. Mexico further encouraged American settlement in 1823 with an offer of cheap land. More Americans came, and half a dozen settlements had been established within a decade.

The portrayal of blacks on the stage posed problems in a nation in which most blacks were slaves. The first acting group of blacks, the African Company, began giving performances in New York City in 1821. Both Shakespearean drama and lighter plays were produced. In 1823 Edwin Forrest, who was to become a national idol and one of the great tragedians of the century, appeared in blackface as Ruban in a farce by Sol Smith, *Tailor in Distress.* No white actress would black her face, so a black woman was engaged to play opposite Forrest.

The **Hudson River school,** an unorganized group of American painters who rebelled against the classical tradition and adopted the romantic attitude of European artists toward nature, began to attract attention. The grandeur of the scenery in the Hudson River Valley was frequently treated in a lush, highly romantic manner. Thomas Cole, Asher B. Durand, and Thomas Dought were among the school's forerunners.

Dec. 2 What came to be called the **Monroe Doctrine** was enunciated by Pres. James Monroe. His annual message to Congress expounded a foreign policy based on two principles. First, any attempt by Europeans to colonize the Americas or interfere in the internal affairs of the Western Hemisphere would be viewed with displeasure by the U.S. Secondly, the U.S. would remain aloof from European quarrels. In essence, this was the foreign policy advocated by John Quincy Adams, Monroe's secretary of state.

May 8 "Home Sweet Home" by John Howard Payne, the most popular song yet written by an American, was sung for the first time at Covent Garden in London. It was an aria sung by the homesick heroine in a play by Payne with music composed by Sir Henry Bishop.

1823

The banking system of the U.S. centered on the second Bank of the United States, chartered in 1816 by the federal government. Its headquarters was in Philadelphia and it had 25 branches around the land. It prospered under the presidency of Langdon Cheves, a legislator from South Carolina who assumed the post in 1819, and even more under Nicholas Biddle, who took over in 1823. Biddle was a financier, editor, and diplomat. State-chartered banks were growing in numbers. The leading private banker was Stephen Girard, a French-born financier who had helped the government finance the War of 1812.

In an era when entertainment in the home had to be supplied by family and guests, music with humorous or sentimental words that could be sung to well-known melodies, was popular. Among such songs were "Believe Me if All Those Endearing Young Charms" (1808); "'Tis the Last Rose of Summer" (1813); "The Minstrel's Return from the War" (1827); and "Zip Coon" (c1834), later known as "Turkey in the Straw."

Hydrofluoric acid was prepared for the first time in the U.S. by Benjamin Silliman, professor of chemistry at Yale.

Charles J. Ingersoll offered a major defense of American culture against the criticism of British intellectuals in an address before the American Philosophical Society. In his *Discourse Concerning the Influence of America on the Mind,* he accepted the challenge of British critics by comparing American culture with European, suggesting that the average intellect in America far surpassed the corresponding intellect in Europe. He suggested that America's great contribution to world civilization had been self-government.

May The **first major horse race** in the U.S. was between American Eclipse from the North and the challenger Sir Henry from the South for a purse of $20,000. About 100,000 spectators jammed the Union Course on Long Island to see American Eclipse take two out of three heats, doing the four-miles in 7:49 and 8:24. Victory of the northern horse spread gloom in the South.

1824

Russia and the U.S. settled a territorial dispute involving regions in the far Northwest. On Sept. 4, 1821, Czar Alexander I asserted a claim on all of the Pacific coast north of the 51st parallel, bisecting the Oregon Territory claimed jointly by the U.S. and Great Britain. On July 17, 1823, Secretary of State John Quincy Adams notified Russia that this claim was unacceptable under the principles set forth by Pres. James Monroe the following December. On Apr. 17, 1824, Russia and the U.S. signed a treaty by which Russia agreed to 54°40' as the southern limit of its claim. The treaty also removed a ban Russia had tried to impose on commercial fishing off the coast of the land it claimed.

A **gateway through the Rocky Mts.** was found by a party led by Jedediah Strong Smith, a fur trader and explorer. This was at South Pass, providing access to the Green River Valley.

1824–1825 In **congressional elections** the traditional parties broke down. The Federalist party disappeared as a national force and the Republican party split into Administration supporters, who backed John Quincy Adams, and Jacksonians, who supported Andrew Jackson. In the Senate the Administration faction led the Jacksonians 26–20. In the House they took a 105–97 majority.

Mar. 2 Federal control of **interstate commerce** was established by the *Gibbons v. Ogden* steamboat case, argued before the Supreme Court.

Aug. The **first nominating convention** was held at Utica, N.Y. For the first time, electors of nominees for office were chosen by popular vote. Nominations for president and for state offices had previously been made in caucus, but this method was replaced by the convention. The Utica convention nominated candidates for the offices of governor and lieutenant governor of New York.

Dec. 1 In the **1824 presidential election** no candidate received an electoral majority. John Quincy Adams of Massachusetts received 84 votes; Andrew Jackson of Tennessee, 99; Secretary of State William H. Crawford, who had suffered a stroke and was effectively out of the running, 41; Henry Clay, 37. John C. Calhoun of South Carolina was elected vice president. On Feb. 9, 1825, John Quincy Adams was chosen as president by the House of Representatives.

Of the many accounts of Indian captivity, none was more popular than *A Narrative of the Life of Mrs. Mary Jemison* by James E. Seaver, published in 1824. Mary Jemison was captured by a French and Indian war party in western Pennsylvania in 1758, when she was 15. She was married twice, once to a Delaware and once to a Seneca, and had eight children. Becoming known as the "White Woman of the Genesee," Mrs. Jemison refused to leave the Senecas. In 1817 New York State confirmed her possession of a tract of land on the Genesee R. that had first been given to her in 1797.

The Gothic tale as developed by German romanticists found American expression in **Washington Irving**'s collection of tales and sketches, *Tales of a Traveler.* Noteworthy among Irving's Gothic stories were "Adventure of the German Student" and "The Devil and Tom Walker."

The **Meeting House** at Deerfield, Mass., was built from plans by Isaac Damon, the most popular country architect of New England in the early nineteenth century. The building is considered a very good example of his somewhat monumental style.

May 12 *Superstition* by James N. Barker, a tragedy based on Indian warfare and the witch trials of early New England history, opened a successful run at the Chestnut Theater in Philadelphia. Barker was a pioneer dramatist in the use of American materials and themes.

May 27 Perhaps the best comedy from the pen of **John Howard Payne, Charles the Second, or the Merry Monarch,** opened in New York City. It was adapted from a French play, as was his *Richelieu* (1826). Payne in this productive period also wrote *'Twas I* (1825) and *The Lancers* (1826).

| Business and Industry; Science; Education; Philosophy and Religion III | | IV Sports; Social Issues and Crime; Folkways; Fashion; Holidays |

1824

A new institution with religious and secular functions was the Sunday school. Originating in England, Sunday schools were first established to educate children who worked in mines and factories. Under church sponsorship, the schools soon came to offer religious instruction. The Methodist leader, Francis Asbury, established the first Sunday school in the U.S. in 1786 in Hanover County, Va. On May 25, 1824, representatives of a number of denominations from several states founded the American Sunday School Union to coordinate activities of these schools. Publication of *Sunday School Magazine* began in 1824, and over the years an enormous amount of literature was issued to serve the widespread institution.

The first recorded **strike involving female employees** in the U.S. occurred in Pawtucket, R.I. Male and female weavers struck against a proposed decrease in wages and an increase in hours. Prior to this time, organized labor had met with little success in or out of court in improving working conditions. By 1820, however, textile mill workers had been organized into a union numbering some 100,000. This growth in union strength was one of the factors that contributed to the strike in Pawtucket.

Jan. 24 **Kenyon College** was chartered in Gambier, Ohio, as the Theological Seminary of the Protestant Episcopal Church. Its first degrees were awarded in 1829. The present name was adopted in 1891.

Oct. 3 **Rensselaer Polytechnic Institute** at Troy, N.Y., was established as the Rennselaer School. It was the first private technical school in the U.S. and awarded the first U.S. engineering degrees in 1835.

Memories of the American Revolution were revived when the Marquis de Lafayette, who had come from France in 1777 to fight on the Patriot side, arrived in the U.S. on Aug. 14, 1824. He was 67 years old when he returned. In October of 1824, Gen. Lafayette met Pres. James Monroe, the last U.S. president to have fought in the Revolution. On his tour of the U.S., which lasted until Sept. 1825, Lafayette was welcomed with enthusiasm, his natural charm and easy self-confidence winning over men and women alike.

A **boat race** in New York harbor for a purse of $1000 attracted an estimated crowd of 50,000. The crew of the victorious craft, *Whitehall*, became civic heroes and received a tumultuous ovation on their appearance at the Park Theater in New York City.

Frances Wright, a well-known reformer and lecturer of the period, arrived from Scotland. She traveled throughout the country, advocating free thought, birth control, public education, abolition, and women's rights.

The **first written American Indian language**, Cherokee, was finished by Sequoyah, the son of a white trader and a Cherokee Indian woman. Sequoyah, who also used the name George Guess, devised a syllabary of 85 characters to represent the spoken sounds of the Cherokee language. He demonstrated the alphabet's utility in a dramatic way. He had his young daughter transcribe speeches at a tribal council in his absence. Then he entered the council chamber and read the speeches aloud from his daughter's transcription. In the years following, Sequoyah taught thousands of Cherokee Indians to read and write. He also translated parts of the Bible into the new language, and in 1828 began publication of a weekly newspaper.

Aug. 2 **Emancipation Day** in Illinois commemorated this date, when slavery was abolished in the state. Even after Pres. Abraham Lincoln issued his Emancipation Proclamation on Jan. 1, 1863, blacks in Illinois celebrated their freedom every Aug. 2.

1825

The first secular Utopian society in the U.S. was established on Jan. 3 by Robert Owen, a social reformer who had made a fortune as a cotton manufacturer in Great Britain. He took over Harmony, Ind., from the followers of George Rapp and set up New Harmony, a community that was to have complete equality of property and opportunity. About 1000 settlers were attracted to the 20,000 acres of New Harmony, including educators, scientists, and writers. However, dissension arose and there was lack of direction among those who were supposed to cooperate. Owen left in 1827. In 1828 the community ceased to exist as a Utopian enterprise.

The **Albany Regency,** led by Martin Van Buren, was in high gear in Albany, N.Y., the capital. The name Regency was applied to the men who managed the state Democratic machine for Van Buren after he went to the U.S. Senate in 1821. Associates in the so-called Regency were William L. Marcy, Silas Wright, John A. Dix, all past or future governors, and Azariah C. Flagg, Benjamin F. Butler, Edwin Crosswell, and Michael Hoffman. This group exercised great influence on state and national politics for about 20 years before splitting into factions.

Feb. 9 John Quincy Adams was elected president of the United States by the House of Representatives, into which the election had been thrown by the failure of any of the four candidates to win a majority in the electoral college. In the four-way race of Adams, Andrew Jackson, Henry Clay, and William Crawford, Jackson had received more electoral votes than Adams, but no majority. Clay assisted the Adams cause in the House.

Feb. 12 The **Creek Indian treaty was signed.** Tribal leaders agreed to turn over all their lands in Georgia to the government and promised to migrate west by Sept. 1, 1826. The treaty was rejected by most Creeks.

Mar. 4 John Quincy Adams was inaugurated president of the United States. The sixth president, he served one term.

Mar. 7 The **first minister to Mexico,** Joel R. Poinsett, was named. His appointment was approved by the Senate on the following day. On his return to the U.S. in 1828, he introduced a Mexican shrub of the spurge family that now is named after him, poinsettia.

Mar. 24 **American colonization of Texas** was authorized by a law passed by the new Mexican state of Texas-Coahuila. In 1823, Stephen Austin had been given authorization by law and decree to bring settlers into the region, but in 1824 a new republic was established in Mexico and a new constitution enacted. A Mexican federal law on colonization was passed that year, but it allowed each state to set conditions for colonization not expressed in the federal law.

Henry Wadsworth Longfellow, one of the first American poets destined to be read and honored in the U.S. and Europe, began to see his poems appear in print. His first poem to be published was "The Battle of Lovell's Pond," on Nov. 17, 1820, in the Portland, Maine, *Gazette.* In 1825, the year he was graduated from Bowdoin College, a number of Longfellow's early poems were published in the *United States Literary Gazette.* They included "Autumnal Nightfall," "Woods in Winter," "The Angler's Song," and "Hymn of the Moravian Nuns." Longfellow soon left for Europe to prepare for a teaching position at Bowdoin, to which he returned in 1829.

The **Yankee** as a stock stage figure reached an early peak in its development, in the character of Jonathan Ploughboy in Samuel Woodworth's *The Forest Rose,* which opened in 1825. James E. Hackett played the part and made the Yankee famous. Under various titles— Uncle Ben, Solomon Swap, Industrious Doolittle, Jonathan Doubikins—the Yankee type became a stock role for comedians.

Readers published by **John Pierpont** came into use this year, especially in the public schools of New England. John Pierpont was the grandfather of John Pierpont Morgan, the celebrated industrialist and financier of the late nineteenth century.

June 17 Word of the oratorical brilliance of **Daniel Webster** spread after his celebrated "Bunker Hill Oration" at the laying of the cornerstone for the Bunker Hill Monument in Boston. His other early speeches included "The Dartmouth College Case" (1818) and "The Landing of the Pilgrims" (1820), matched perhaps only by Webster's "Reply to Hayne" in the U.S. Senate in 1830.

Nov. 8 The New York Drawing Association, renamed the **National Academy of Design** in 1828, was organized in New York City by young artists dissatisfied with the operation of the American Academy of Fine Arts. Samuel F. B. Morse, one of the founders of the association, was chosen as its first president.

Nov. 29 **Opera** in the grand romantic Italian style of the age was introduced to New York at the Park Theater with the performance of *Il Barbiere di Siviglia.* The company was led by the famous tenor Signor Garcia, and its cast included Signorina Maria Garcia, who later became widely known as Mme. Malibran.

| Business and Industry; Science; Education; Philosophy and Religion | III | | IV | Sports; Social Issues and Crime; Folkways; Fashion; Holidays |

1825

The era of canal building was gathering momentum. On Oct. 26, 1825, the most important and successful of all American canals, the Erie, was officially opened. The Erie Canal stretched for more than 350 miles between Lake Erie and the Hudson R. at Albany and thus connected the Great Lakes with the Atlantic Ocean at New York City by way of the Hudson R. The father of the Erie Canal was Gov. De Witt Clinton of New York, whose enthusiasm had gotten the project under way. Construction had begun on July 4, 1817, and on Oct. 22, 1819, the first boat to travel on the canal went from Rome to Utica. The canal cost $7,000,000, which was returned many times over by the traffic it attracted. The Erie Canal became the most important passenger and freight route from the East to the Midwest and made New York the Empire State.

A **strike** was called in Boston by 600 carpenters.

Mechanical pressing of glass, the first technical innovation in glassmaking since ancient times, was introduced into American factories. The change enabled production of intricately designed glassware. Famous glassworks established this year by Deming Jarves at Sandwich, Mass., were noted for their large-scale production of pressed glass.

The manufacture of **telescopes,** reflecting and achromatic, was begun about this time by Amasa Holcomb of Southwick, Mass. These were probably the first telescopes made in the U.S.

Homeopathy was introduced in the U.S. from Germany by Dr. Hans Burch Gram. Homeopathy was the creation of Samuel Hahnemann, a German physician, who was forbidden by law in 1820 to practice his treatments but was protected and encouraged to continue research by Duke Ferdinand of Anhalt-Cöthen. According to the homeopathic formula, a person suffering from a particular disease can be cured by a medicine that produces symptoms of the same disease in a healthy person. It was a radical departure from established theory, and persecution of Hahnemann drove him from place to place, indirectly ensuring rapid propagation of his ideas.

Feb. 21 **Amherst College** was chartered by Massachusetts in Amherst. However, classes had begun on Sept. 19, 1821, under the Rev. Zephaniah Swift Moore, at that time president of Williams College. Moore became Amherst's first president, bringing 15 Williams students with him to Amherst.

Controversy over women's place in society was stimulated by Frances Wright, who had moved from England to the U.S. in 1824. An earlier visit (1818–1820) had resulted in her volume *Views of Society and Manners in America* (1821), which praised the country enthusiastically. Now, however, she was lecturing from public platforms, addressing workmen's groups and openly discussing such forbidden subjects as equal rights, birth control, and abolition. One newspaper editor denounced her as a "bold blasphemer and voluptuous preacher of licentiousness."

Guidebooks for American travel became available. Stagecoach travelers for the first time had a guide to the whole country in *The American Traveller* by Daniel Hewett. In addition, the first newspaper in America especially devoted to coach interests, entitled *American Traveller,* appeared in Boston, and a popular travel booklet, "The Fashionable Tour," was published.

The **New York Trotting Club** was organized. It constructed a race course on Long Island, the first especially devoted to trotting.

The **first gymnasium** in the U.S. was established at Northampton, Mass., by Charles Beck, a disciple of Friedrich Jahn, founder of the first *turnplatz* in Germany. Widespread interest in German gymnastics was also stimulated by Charles Follen, a refugee student leader from Germany, who introduced the sport in Boston. Follen later taught at Harvard.

Glassware in cheap, standardized sets appeared for the first time on store counters in the U.S. The sets marked the transition from blown to pressed glass. The mechanical press introduced a new method of stamping out molds in glassmaking factories, bringing quicker, less expensive, more uniform products. Housewives eagerly bought the new pieces to fill their cabinets with ornamental glass. At first, glassware made on presses was heavy, though its thickness was balanced by patterns worked in tiny raised dots to give an appearance of delicacy. In 1825 the opening of the famous Jarves works at Sandwich, Mass., gave additional impetus to the flood of new ware. These Sandwich pieces, named for their place of origin, were associated with pressed glass in particular and soon became collectors' items. The Sandwich factory operated until 1888.

1826

Trappers, explorers, adventurers, and scientists were beginning to unlock the secrets of the immense expanse of the American West, much of it still unknown to settlers. One of the most daring yet practical of these men was Jedediah Strong Smith. Already a veteran of various expeditions, Smith set out on Aug. 22, 1826, with a small band of men from Great Salt Lake, Utah. They crossed the Colorado R. and the Mojave Desert before arriving at the San Gabriel Mission on Nov. 27. On leaving California, Smith and two of his men became the first men other than Indians to cross the Sierra Nevada and the Great Salt Desert from west to east. In 1831, while traveling along the Santa Fe Trail, Smith was killed by Comanches. Smith's most important contributions were his mapping and establishment of trails in the areas he explored.

Free Mason **William Morgan** of Batavia, N.Y., was kidnaped and presumably killed because he allegedly revealed Masonic secrets. Morgan's supporters subsequently founded the Anti-Masonic Party.

The federal **Fugitive Slave Act of 1793** was largely nullified by a Pennsylvania law making kidnaping a crime. The Pennsylvania statute was to be declared unconstitutional by the Supreme Court in 1842 in the case of *Priss v. Pennsylvania.* The decision stated that states could not be obliged to enforce fugitive slave laws through state officers. This led to a series of laws directed at personal liberty in Northern states, giving fugitives jury trials and forbidding states from extraditing them.

1826–1827 In **congressional elections** the Jacksonians gained eight Senate seats for a 28–20 majority over the Administration faction. In the House they gained 22 seats for a 119–94 majority.

Jan. 24 The Creek Indians signed the **Treaty of Washington** with the federal government. It nullified a previous treaty and ceded less territory to the government. It also granted the Indians the right to stay on their lands until Jan. 1, 1827.

June The **Panama Conference** of Latin American states called by Simon Bolivar, to which the U.S. was invited, provided a test of the administration of Pres. Adams. He had forwarded to the Senate for confirmation the names of two delegates. A coalition led by John C. Calhoun and Martin Van Buren opposed U.S. attendance, chiefly on the ground that it broke the tradition of U.S. independence and neutrality. Several southern senators objected because some participating nations were controlled by blacks. The Senate ultimately confirmed the appointments, but neither delegate reached the conference before it adjourned; one died en route and the other got only as far as Mexico.

American actors were competing with their British counterparts, who long had dominated the stage. The most notable rivalry was between the American Edwin Forrest and William Charles Macready of Great Britain. Forrest became a great tragedian, first playing Othello in 1826. He was very popular but some thought he displayed his powerful voice too often. Macready made his first visit to the U.S. in 1826, making his debut Oct. 2 at the Park Theater in New York in the play *Virginius* by James Sheridan Knowles. He, too, was a great tragedian. Forrest played Macbeth in England in 1845 but met with hostility from those who preferred Macready. Their rivalry was to have fatal consequences in 1849.

James Fenimore Cooper's *The Last of the Mohicans* began its phenomenal publishing record. The most popular of Cooper's novels, selling over 2,000,000 copies, it was also a best seller across the Atlantic. The Leatherstocking Tales, of which *The Last of the Mohicans* is the second novel of five, are still popular in the U.S. and Europe, especially France.

William Cullen Bryant, already recognized as an accomplished poet, became assistant editor of the New York *Evening Post.* In 1829 he became editor of the paper, remaining at that post and wielding enormous literary and political influence until his death in 1878.

The great vogue of **annuals** began. An annual was a publication bound in beautiful leather and exquisitely printed, used mostly as a gift for ladies. Schools of poetasters contributed to these publications.

Melodies, Duets, Songs, and Ballads by Samuel Woodworth was published. It included his classic poem "The Bucket," which was set to music and gained enormous popularity as "The Old Oaken Bucket." Woodworth's poem was first published in 1817 and first collected in the following year.

Quincy Market, an area adjacent to Faneuil Hall in Boston, was laid out by Alexander Parris. In his facades Parris used individual granite slabs rather than blocks and mortar to form piers and lintels.

Manuel del Pópolo Vincente García, a celebrated European tenor, for his New York season of Italian opera (1825–1826) rented the Park Theater for two nights a week and set admission prices at $2.00 for box seats, and $1.00 for the pit. Garcia aspired to build a permanent New York company for Italian opera.

Oct. 23 The **Bowery Theater** opened. Boasting the largest stage in New York City at the time, it was built

1826

Legal scholarship flourished in the U.S. as the American legal system began to separate from British tradition and establish its own foundations and precedents. America's first great legal scholar was James Kent, who in 1794 became the first professor of law at Columbia and later became chief justice of New York State courts. Kent modified English chancery practice to conform to American institutions and virtually created equity jurisdiction in the U.S. Out of his opinions and lectures came his *Commentaries on American Law* (4 volumes, 1826–1830). The section on constitutional law was Federalist in approach. The *Commentaries* were an immediate success. Kent updated them five times and they have been revised many times since. Kent's influence on the legal profession and the teaching of law in the U.S. was second only to that of John Marshall. Kent's classic work has been compared with that of William Blackstone, the English jurist who wrote a similar four-volume work (1765–1769).

The **first railway steam locomotive** in America was run on a small circular track in Hoboken, N.J., by its builders, Col. John Stevens and his sons Robert and Edwin.

The **American Home Missionary Society** was established by the Congregational Church. This organization was especially active in the South, before and during the Civil War, on behalf of blacks.

Feb. 7 **Western Reserve University** was first chartered as Western Reserve College in Hudson, Ohio. It was established under the joint auspices of the Presbyterian and Congregational denominations during a period when these two churches were cooperating in the Midwest. The college awarded its first degrees in 1830. Western Reserve College moved to Cleveland in 1882 and became Western Reserve University in 1884 and, much later, Case-Western Reserve.

Mar. 9 **Lafayette College,** founded by the people of Easton, Pa., and named for the French hero of the American Revolution, was chartered. It granted its first degrees in 1830. Lafayette became affiliated with the Presbyterian denomination in 1832.

Apr. 1 The design for an **internal combustion engine,** submitted by Samuel Morey of Orford, N.H., was

Combining entertainment with education, the lyceum movement became a familiar part of American life. A lyceum was an organization that provided a platform for speakers on a great variety of subjects. The first lyceum was organized in 1826 in Millbury, Mass., by Josiah Holbrook, a teacher whose Agricultural Seminary had failed in 1825. Within two years he helped establish more than 100 lyceums. The National American Lyceum was formed in 1831, and by 1834 some 3000 lyceums were in operation, offering information on the arts, science, history, and public affairs. Many so-called reformers took advantage of this platform to promote their notions, but leading figures of the day, such as Daniel Webster and Ralph Waldo Emerson, also were happy to appear on lyceum platforms.

Physical education, more specifically the new art of gymnastics, was introduced into U.S. colleges by Charles Follen, an instructor in German literature at Harvard College. Follen was a devotee of the system taught in Germany by Friedrich Ludwig Jahn. He was also a preacher, and in 1836 wrote a perceptive article for *Quarterly Antislavery Magazine* on various forms of oppression in the U.S.

Jan. 17 One of the earliest **celebrations of Benjamin Franklin's birth** was arranged by the Franklin Typographical Society of Boston, a group organized to assist needy printers. It honored the 120th anniversary of Franklin's birth.

Feb. 13 The **first national temperance organization,** The American Temperance Society, was founded. *The National Philanthropist,* the first journal devoted entirely to temperance, was also founded this year by the Rev. William Collier, a Baptist missionary.

June 30 "**Independence now and Independence forever!**" was penned by John Adams in response to a request for a toast to be offered in his name on July Fourth. The entire toast by Adams read: "It is my living sentiment, and by the blessing of God it shall be my dying sentiment—Independence now and Independence forever!"

Aug. 2 The sentence "**Sink or swim, live or die, survive or perish, I give my hand and my heart to this vote**" was attributed to John Adams by Daniel Webster in a speech eulogizing the former president. Whether Adams said these words during the debate over adoption of the Declaration of Independence is dubious,

July 4 Thomas Jefferson and John Adams **died** on this, the 50th anniversary of the Declaration of Independence, which both men had helped to frame.

for popular musical and minstrel shows. It continued as a melodrama and vaudeville theater for over a century.

1827

Oregon Country, the region north of the California border and extending to Alaska, was still claimed by both the U.S. and Great Britain. On Aug. 6, 1827, the two nations signed a treaty extending an 1818 agreement to continue joint occupation of the territory. American and British fur-trading companies were in competition in the region, with the English Hudson's Bay Company having the better of it. At the same time, Americans were exploring the area, and in 1829 Hall J. Kelley of Boston founded the American Society for Encouraging the Settlement of the Oregon Territory.

Fort Leavenworth was built by Col. Henry H. Leavenworth on the Missouri R., about 25 miles northwest of present-day Kansas City. It was constructed as a strongpoint for military units patrolling the Santa Fe trade route. Leavenworth became a permanent settlement when the Santa Fe Trail was increasingly used by traders who needed a safe starting point. From 1825 to 1854 a town gradually formed around the fort. The town was finally defined and established by a group of Missouri squatters in 1855 as the first incorporated city of Kansas.

Feb. 2 The Supreme Court of the U.S. gave the president final authority to call out the **militia**. The decision was handed down in the case of *Martin v. Mott.*

Feb. 28 The **Woolens Bill** stalled in the Senate. The bill, which increased tariffs on raw and manufactured wool, had been passed by the House but was tabled in the Senate by the tie-breaking vote of Vice Pres. John C. Calhoun. Rejection of the bill stimulated the high-tariff forces in the manufacturing centers of the North; at the same time, the South opposed the tariffs because they disturbed world markets on which its agricultural economy depended. The western states were undecided. The tariff issue led to sectional differences in the U.S. and was one reason for increasing dissension between the North and South.

Nov. 15 The **Creeks** ceded their remaining territory in the Southeast to the U.S. The area included all their lands in Georgia.

The birds of North America, abundant and colorful, attracted scientists and nature lovers alike. It remained for an artist and ornithologist, John James Audubon, to give them recognition by painting some 500 of the birds in all their splendor. Later paintings may be more scientific, but none has ever matched Audubon's in popular appeal. *The Birds of America* was published in elephant folio size in parts between 1827 and 1838 in London. An accompanying text, *Ornithological Biography,* was issued in five volumes between 1831 and 1839. In the text Audubon had the help of William MacGillivray, who supplied scientific information. Earlier, in the course of observing birds, Audubon had made the first American bird-banding experiments.

The first book of poems by **Edgar Allan Poe,** *Tamerlane and Other Poems,* was printed in Boston. Little attention was paid the slim volume. In 1829 a second volume, *Al Aaraaf, Tamerlane and Minor Poems,* also went unnoticed.

The ***American Quarterly Review,*** a scholarly and literary journal, was founded in Philadelphia by Robert Walsh. Contributions included articles on travel, biography, law, political economy, and hieroglyphics. Such writers as George Ticknor, George Bancroft, and James Kirke Paulding wrote for it.

The Prairie by James Fenimore Cooper was published and became a best seller. Cooper's novels owed some of their success to their stories of adventure laid in primitive areas, to readers' growing pride in America, and to popular reaction against novels of sensibility.

Feb. 7 **Ballet** was introduced to the U.S. by Mme. Francisquy Hutin, famed French danseuse, with *The Deserter,* staged at the Bowery Theater, New York City. Mme. Hutin's light and scanty attire so shocked the public that every woman in the lower tier of boxes immediately left the theater.

Dec. Mrs. **Frances Trollope** arrived in the U.S. on a visit from England. She later wrote *Domestic Manners of the Americans* (1832), one of the first of many books by English authors who criticized American intellectual life, tastes, and customs.

granted a patent, one of the first for such an engine. His design was for a two-cylinder engine.

but Adams is known to have used much the same language in 1774 in discussing independence.

1827

As the U.S. economy began to shift from agriculture to manufacturing, causing a relative decline in commerce and shipping, economists who favored manufacturing began finding arguments for protecting and encouraging it. Among these was a German-born economist, Friedrich List, who emigrated to the U.S. in 1820 and returned to Germany in 1832. List wrote *Outlines of American Political Economy* (1827), arguing that a nation's true wealth stemmed from its productive industrial forces rather than from commercial transactions. Such a view was especially popular in New England, where the shift to light and heavy manufacturing was most pronounced. Thus, New England favored high tariffs on imported goods to protect the young American industries.

The **first state high school law** was passed. It was enacted by Massachusetts and called for a tax-supported high school in every community of 500 families or more. An additional clause made the study of U.S. history mandatory.

Arthur Tappan founded *Journal of Commerce* in New York City. The first number announced that the newspaper would be free of "immoral advertisements" and be "regardful of the Sabbath."

Encyclopedia Americana was begun by the German refugee political philosopher, Francis Lieber. Organized along Germanic principles of research and scholarship, the 13-volume work began to appear in 1829. It made a significant contribution to American culture.

May   Josiah **Warren** of Cincinnati, Ohio, founder of philosophical anarchism in the U.S., opened his "equity" store to prove his theory of "labor for labor." Warren sold goods almost at cost, and the store closed in two years. Warren was something of an inventor, having devised a speed press which, after he had failed to patent it, was incorporated into the famous Roe presses. His ingenuity was again displayed in his construction of a press and his making of type for his publication *The Peaceful Revolutionist*, a periodical that lasted less than a year. Though a thoroughgoing individualist and disbeliever in all government, in the 1850s he established Modern Times, a town on Long Island. Modern Times was a center for philosophical anarchists and for eccentrics.

During the first half of the nineteenth century, the American diet and eating habits amazed English visitors. Frances Trollope noted: "They eat with the greatest possible rapidity and in total silence." Harriet Martineau reported a breakfast that consisted of "cornbread, buns, buckwheat cakes, broiled chicken, bacon, eggs, rich hominy, fish, fresh and pickled, and beef-steak." And Charles Dickens was repelled by "those dyspeptic ladies and gentlemen who eat unheard-of quantities of hot corn bread (almost as good for the digestion as a kneaded pincushion), for breakfast and supper."

The **first Mardi Gras** celebration in New Orleans was initiated by French-American students who, returning home on holiday, organized a procession of street maskers on Shrove Tuesday.

The *American Shooter's Manual* was published in Philadelphia. It treated the new sport of shooting birds on the wing, offering much practical advice.

Theaters in New York City were plagued with fires, inadequate houses, and crowded bookings. The Bowery Theater, showplace of the previous season, was destroyed by fire. It was later rebuilt. The Chatham played out the season, then closed for alterations. The Park Theater was running Signor Garcia's Grand Opera Company two nights weekly, forcing the Park Company to barnstorm at the Broadway Circus on those nights. But shows did go on. The Lafayette Theater was rebuilt and hailed as the biggest and best in the nation. One improvement introduced was overhead manipulation of stage lighting and machinery.

July 23   The **first swimming school** in the U.S. opened in Boston, Mass. Swimming was taught by placing a belt "around the bodies, under the arms, attached to a rope and pole, by which the head and body are kept in the proper position in the water, while the pupil is learning the use of his limbs." The school was attended by many notables, including John James Audubon and John Quincy Adams. Adams is reputed to have done some diving from the 6-foot board when he was 61 years old.

1828

Growing discord between North and South over the tariff came to the fore this year when, on May 19, Pres. John Quincy Adams signed into law what became known as the Tariff of Abominations. Political maneuvering between supporters of Pres. Adams and those of Andrew Jackson caused much bitterness. The Jacksonians had hoped to discredit Adams by making the bill so objectionable that it would be defeated. Southerners, led by Vice Pres. John C. Calhoun, felt the law discriminated against the agricultural South, which relied on imports from abroad, and favored the North and West. With strong New England support, the bill passed both houses of Congress.

The **Democratic Party** was formed. Essentially it was an extension of the Democratic-Republican (Jeffersonian) Party (formed May 13, 1792), and was backed by southern agrarians and northern urban workers. It advocated Jeffersonian principles of personal liberty and attacked special privilege. Andrew Jackson became the new party's first nominee for president.

The **National Republican Party** was formed during Pres. John Quincy Adams's term of office (1824–1828). Ill feeling between Adams and Jackson was polarizing U.S. politics. The National Republican Party of Adams advocated a nationalistic program including a national bank, protective tariffs, federally sponsored internal improvements, and a conservative land-sale policy. This package, called the American System, was put together by Henry Clay, an ally of Adams, to appeal to the North and West. After loss of the election to Jackson, the coalition of National Republicans, Whigs, and splinter groups fell apart, and the Whig Party emerged as the party of opposition to the Jacksonian Democrats.

1828–1829   In **congressional elections** the Democrats gained a 26–22 Senate majority over the National Republicans. In the House they took a 139–74 majority.

Dec. 3   **Andrew Jackson was elected seventh president** of the United States. Jackson, a senator from Tennessee until his nomination, received 647,231 popular votes and 178 electoral votes against 509,097 popular votes and 83 electoral votes for John Quincy Adams, candidate of the National Republican Party. John C. Calhoun was reelected vice president, receiving 171 electoral votes. The election was swung by Martin Van Buren of New York on the understanding that he would continue to exercise power in the state through the spoils system.

Dec. 19   The **Tariff of Abominations** was declared by the South Carolina legislature to be oppressive, unjust, and unconstitutional. The motion was supported by the legislatures of Georgia, Mississippi, and Virginia. These resolutions caused publication of

Women were beginning to enter journalism, and the most prominent woman journalist was Sarah Josepha Hale. In 1828 in Boston she became editor of a new journal, *Ladies' Magazine.* She moved to Philadelphia in 1837, becoming editor of *Godey's Lady's Book* and holding that post for 40 years. In 1846 Mrs. Hale began using the pages of the magazine to agitate for a national Thanksgiving Day, and by 1858 all but six states celebrated thanksgiving on the last Thursday in November. Mrs. Hale had great influence on fashions and manners and regularly urged higher education for women. Her volume *Poems for Our Children* (1830) contained "Mary Had a Little Lamb."

Fanshawe, the anonymous first novel of **Nathaniel Hawthorne,** was published. The setting of the short novel resembled Bowdoin College in Maine, from which Hawthorne was graduated in 1825.

The monumental *American Dictionary of the English Language* by Noah Webster was published, a labor of more than 20 years. Webster spent much time in England gathering material for his work and completed it while living in Cambridge, England.

Washington Irving, now a diplomatic attaché in Spain, turned from Knickerbocker settings to Spanish history in his *History of the Life and Voyages of Christopher Columbus* (1828) and *Conquest of Granada* (1829). Irving's international point of view earned him the title "ambassador-at-large from the New World to the Old."

The **First Church** (Unitarian) at Quincy, Mass., was built by Alexander Parris from local granite. It has been called the Stone Temple.

The story of **Rip Van Winkle,** Washington Irving's delightful character, was given its first theatrical expression in Albany, N.Y., in a play by a playwright unknown. On Oct. 30, 1829, another version by John Kerr was successful in Philadelphia. The most famous of all versions was the adaptation by Dion Boucicault performed by Joseph Jefferson, a prominent American actor for decades.

Feb. 21   The **first newspaper for Indians** in the U.S. followed the arrival on this date of a printing press at the headquarters of the Cherokee Council in Echota, Ga. There the Cherokee Indian leader Sequoyah created a written Cherokee language based on letter symbols.

| Business and Industry; Science; Education; Philosophy and Religion | III | | IV | Sports; Social Issues and Crime; Folkways; Fashion; Holidays |

1828

For practical purposes, the age of the railroad in the U.S. began on July 4, 1828, when ground-breaking ceremonies for the Baltimore and Ohio Railroad, led by Charles Carroll, the last surviving signer of the Declaration of Independence, were held in Baltimore, Md. The first section of the B&O, as it came to be known, opened in May 1830 between Baltimore and Ellicott's Mills, Md. The first source of power was the horse, but on August 30 the line was converted to steampower. The B&O kept laying rails westward and reached St. Louis, Mo., in 1857.

The total value of **gold** mined in the U.S. up to 1828 amounted to $110,000. It was derived from small deposits in North Carolina.

New England's economic transition from a commercial to an industrial economy was reflected in a shift by Sen. Daniel Webster of Massachusetts to advocacy of protective tariffs. Webster was supported by the arguments of Willard Phillips, Boston businessman, lawyer, and editor. Phillips's *A Manual of Political Economy,* published this year, skillfully identified the needs of New England industrialists with the economic welfare of the entire nation.

Chinaware began to be produced in significant amounts at the factory of the American Pottery Manufacturing Company in Jersey City. Up to this time, china almost entirely had been imported, from France, Germany, England, and China.

A strike of factory workers, the first recorded, occurred in a textile plant in Paterson, N.J. The strike was doubly significant because it led to the first recorded summoning of the militia to end labor violence. The workers' agitation for a ten-hour day ended in failure.

Jan. 24 **Indiana University** was chartered in Bloomington, Ind., by the state's general assembly as Indiana College. Indiana College, a state-supported institution, granted its first degrees in 1830 and was given its present name in 1838. The basis of Indiana College was the founding of a state seminary in Jan. 20, 1820, by the general assembly.

Dec. 30 **Hanover College** was chartered by the general assembly of Indiana. It had been founded by

Performances by white entertainers in blackface, destined to develop into the popular minstrel shows of the 1840s and 1850s, probably got their start in 1828. In that year Thomas Dartmouth Rice gave a solo performance in blackface, dancing and singing "Jim Crow." Rice is said to have taken the tune from an elderly black who worked near the Louisville Theater, in Louisville, Ky. When Rice went to England in 1836, "Jim Crow" became an international hit song and the term Jim Crow became a synonym for blacks. Rice became known as "the father of American minstrelsy."

The **American Peace Society** was established by William Ladd, who edited its periodical and was its chief publicist. The society maintained close relations with similar organizations in Europe and repeatedly petitioned Congress and state legislatures to set apart an annual day for peace prayers.

The phrase *Tariff of Abominations* was used to characterize the high protective tariffs pushed through Congress by the efforts of Henry Clay.

America's **first archery club** was formed by a group of famous artists. The United Bowmen of Philadelphia was formally organized by Franklin Peale, Titian Ramsey Peale, Samuel P. Griffith, Jr., Thomas Sully, and others. The initiation fee was $5.00 and dues 50 cents a month. Members wore Lincoln green frock coats with gold trim and broad straw hats decorated with three black ostrich plumes. It held annual tournaments and awarded silver trophies until it disbanded in 1859. It was the forerunner of the National Archery Association, founded in 1879. The National Field Archery Association was founded in 1939.

New York City's growth and transformation were noted by James Fenimore Cooper, who observed that fewer than 500 buildings were still standing that antedated 1783.

| Exploration and Settlement; Wars; Government; Civil Rights; Statistics | I | | II | Publishing; Arts and Music; Popular Entertainment; Architecture; Theater |

South Carolina Exposition and Protest by John C. Calhoun. Calhoun rejected nationalism and identified himself with the economic and political interests of the southern states.

The Cherokee Phoenix, written and printed in this language, was edited by Elias Boudinot, a Cherokee. The sequoia tree is named after Sequoyah.

1829

Inauguration of Andrew Jackson as seventh president was a turning point in the history of the executive office. Jackson was a self-made man, in contrast with his six predecessors, four of them upper-class Virginians and two affluent New Englanders. Jackson was also the first president nominated by the Democratic Party, which had evolved from the old Jeffersonian Democratic-Republican Party. The events of his inauguration symbolized the new Jacksonian era. After the ceremony thousands of his followers accompanied him back to the White House where, uninvited, they took over the reception, standing on chairs and crowding so that people were trampled and china and glassware broken. Tubs of punch were set out on the White House lawn to lure some of the crowd before a disaster occurred. The new president himself had to be eased out a rear door for protection against his surging admirers. Jacksonians felt that the true democracy of America had triumphed.

The **spoils system,** by which victorious political candidates reward supporters with government positions, was introduced into national politics by Pres. Andrew Jackson. Contrary to popular belief, he did not make wholesale political appointments and removals. During his first year in office, only about 9% of federal officeholders were replaced.

Pres. Jackson formed a **kitchen cabinet,** a small group of unofficial political advisers to whom Jackson's opponents gave its scornful name. Its influence was highest from 1829 to 1831.

The **American Society for Encouraging the Settlement of Oregon** was organized by Hall Jackson Kelley in Boston, Mass.

Mar. 4   Andrew Jackson was inaugurated president of the United States. The seventh president, Jackson was the first successful candidate of the Democratic Party and served two terms.

Aug. 25   An offer to purchase **Texas** from Mexico was made by Pres. Andrew Jackson. The offer was refused.

Sculptors were never as numerous as painters in nineteenth-century America, but the making of statues was becoming a profession. Horatio Greenough was America's first professional sculptor. He is best known for his colossal statue of George Washington, but he did other notable work, such as *The Rescue* (1846) for the Capitol in Washington, D.C., depicting a settler saving his wife and children from attacking Indians. He also created *The Chanting Cherubs* (1829) for the novelist James Fenimore Cooper, but the nude cherubs shocked public taste. Greenough is remembered as well for his writings on architecture, in which he advocated that form follow function.

Scrimshaw, the art of making pictures on or carving the teeth or jaw of a sperm whale, flourished during this period. Busks for corsets, chessmen, vases, cutlery, etc. were carved as were historical scenes. The hobby filled long, lonely hours on whaling cruises.

Lectures on American Literature by Samuel Knapp, the first history of American literature, was published. Knapp's work was more comprehensive than earlier studies, but he could not find enough material of substance and was not sufficiently versed in the subject.

Mar. 26   **Richard Penn Smith** exemplified the growing tendency of American dramatists to write melodrama. His *Disowned, or the Prodigals,* adapted from the French, had all the trappings: the villain Malfort out to win the virgin Pauline and her fortune; Gustavus, the hero, who loves a widow, Amelia, instead of Pauline; Bertrand, the villain's accomplice, who mistakenly stabs his sister Amelia, etc.

Sept. 14   **Peters the Antipodean** performed spectacular feats in a program offered at the Bowery Theater in New York City. Peters walked on the ceiling with his head down and lifted from the stage 16 men and 10 coach wheels. It is not known how he performed these feats.

Business and Industry; Science; Education; Philosophy and Religion	III		IV	Sports; Social Issues and Crime; Folkways; Fashion; Holidays

the Rev. John Finley Crowe under Presbyterian auspices in 1827 as a seminary to train ministers in the "wilderness." Hanover's first degrees were awarded in 1834.

Boots with side lacing and decorative fringes at the top came into vogue for women.

1829

A landmark in American education and publishing was the work of a German-born political philosopher, Francis Lieber, who came to the U.S. in 1827. Between 1829 and 1833 he edited the 13-volume *Encyclopedia Americana,* the first such reference work published in the U.S. Important to the work was the fact that Lieber persuaded specialists in various fields to write for the general public. As a professor at the University of South Carolina (1835–1836), he wrote the first works in political science by an American scholar not in public life. Among his other activities was popularization of physical education, which he saw as contributing to the well-being of a cultivated mind. During the Civil War he wrote *Instructions for the Government of Armies of the United States in the Field* (1863).

Americans have always liked tales of men of outsized stature and achievement, and Mike Fink was an early favorite. Born at Fort Pitt, Pa., before the American Revolution, Fink was an Indian scout but most of his fame came from his exploits as a keel-boatman on the Ohio and Mississippi rivers. The first account of his adventures appeared in print in 1829 in *The Western Souvenir,* in an article by Morgan Neville. The account told of Fink's marksmanship, physical prowess, and tall tales. There are about 11 versions of his death, but he probably was shot dead somewhere near the mouth of the Yellowstone R. while trapping and exploring up the Missouri R. in 1822. Bernard DeVoto described this legendary figure as one in which "Casanova, together with Paul Bunyan, merges with Thor."

Mar. 2 The **first school for the blind in the U.S.,** the New England Asylum for the Blind, was incorporated in Boston, Mass. It was founded by Dr. John Dix Fisher, and in Aug. 1832 it opened under the direction of Dr. Samuel Gridley Howe. In 1839 it was renamed Perkins Institution and Massachusetts Asylum (now School) for the Blind. It now is located in Watertown, Mass.

The **first fancy dress ball** of record in New York City society was held at the house of a Mme. Brugière at Bowling Green in lower Manhattan.

July 23 The **first typewriter patent** of any consequence was issued by the Patent Office to William Austin Burt of Detroit, who called his crude machine a typographer. In a few years it was surpassed by a machine with the first movable keyboard.

Oct. 16 The **Tremont Hotel** in Boston, the first luxurious hotel in the New World, opened with a dollar-a-plate dinner attended by such notables as Daniel Webster and Edward Everett. The 170-room hotel offered many first-time-ever luxuries and conveniences: private bedrooms with door locks, soap and a pitcher of water in each room, indoor toilets (eight water closets), menus in the dining room, room clerks, and bellboys, called rotunda men. Architects of luxury hotels in the next few decades generally used the Tremont as their model.

Oct. 17 The **Chesapeake and Delaware Canal** was formally opened. Linking the Delaware R. and Chesapeake Bay, the canal was 14 miles long and cost some $2,250,000, which was shared by the U.S. government, Delaware, Maryland, and Pennsylvania, and various private citizens.

Nov. 13 **Sam Patch,** a high diver, died in a 125-foot dive into the Genesee Falls. His body was found months later at the river's mouth. Patch had earlier made a dive of 80 to 90 feet from the Passaic River's Chasm Bridge, a Niagara Falls jump from Goat Island, and many leaps and dives from cliffs, masts, and other bridges.

1830

The constitutionality of internal improvements (roads and canals) carried out by the federal government continued to be debated and to cause political divisions. On May 27, 1830, Pres. Andrew Jackson vetoed the Maysville Road bill, which would have provided government financial support for a 60-mile road construction project entirely in Kentucky. On May 31 Jackson approved a bill to provide funds for the Cumberland Road because it involved more than one state. Jackson believed in internal improvements in principle but felt a consititutional amendment was necessary. His stand helped him politically. The South's belief in states' rights was supported by his veto, which was also aimed at Henry Clay and the National Republicans.

The U.S. **Census** recorded a population of 12,866,020. The center of population was placed 19 miles west-southwest of Moorefield, W.Va.

The **Indian Removal Act,** under which Indians east of the Mississippi R. were to be resettled in the Oklahoma Territory, was enacted by Congress.

1830–1831 In **congressional elections** the Democrats and National Republicans each lost a Senate seat to minor parties, but the Democrats held a majority of 25–21. In the House they gained two seats for a 141–58 majority, with 14 seats going to minor parties.

Jan. 19–27 The **Webster-Hayne debates** took place. They began when Sen. Samuel A. Foot of Connecticut offered a resolution to restrain sale of public lands in the West. Sen. Thomas Hart Benton of Missouri replied by declaring that eastern interests were trying to check the prosperity of the West. He was supported by Sen. Robert Y. Hayne of South Carolina, who defended states' rights. Hayne stated that "the very life of our system is the independence of the states, and that there is no evil more to be deprecated than the consolidation of this government." Sen. Daniel Webster of Massachusetts replied by criticizing the tendency of some senators "to habitually speak of the union in terms of indifference, or even of disparagement." The debate evolved into a discussion of the powers of the Constitution and the nature of the Union. In his speech of Jan. 26–27, Webster declared that the states were sovereign only in that area where their power is not qualified by the Constitution, and that the Constitution and the government were sovereign over the people.

Apr. 6 Further **colonization of Texas** by U.S. citizens was forbidden by Mexico, which also prohibited importation of slaves.

Apr. 10–July 16 Jedediah Strong Smith and William Sublette led a covered wagon train from the Missouri R. to the Rockies to the annual rendezvous of Mountain Men on the Wind R. in Wyoming. This year Smith

Inspired by the Romantic movement while studying in Europe, a group of American painters, beginning about 1825 and lasting for half a century, formed what came to be called the Hudson River school. They took interest in the natural beauty of the U.S. and concentrated on painting the Hudson River Valley, Catskill Mts., White Mts., and Niagara Falls. Best known of the school were Thomas Doughty, Asher B. Durand, Thomas Cole, John Frederick Kensett, and George Innes.

William Prior was one of many traveling portrait painters who flourished in the early 1830s. He traveled extensively along the Atlantic coast painting portraits in naive American style, which ranged from flat, shadowless linear representations with high foreheads and wide-open eyes to more lifelike techniques, depending on the price sitters could pay. Today Prior's less expensive works, considered more primitive, are more highly thought of.

Primitivism was characteristic of the many anonymous folk paintings of this period. *The Quilting Party* (c1840), *Portrait of a Woman* (c1830), *The Buffalo Hunter* (c1830), and *Meditation by the Sea* (c1860) all reveal crudeness of color and flatness of surface that derive from early colonial painting.

The Shoshone Valley, the last novel of Timothy Flint, a Massachusetts preacher, missionary, and journalist, was published. Always a romantic, Flint wrote in this work of a New England mariner who married a Chinese woman. They turned their backs on humdrum civilization to live among the Indians. Flint's plots were melodramatic and improbable, at times even banal, and his characters were clichés. But his depictions of frontier settings, pioneer ways, and scenery were realistic and informative.

Plays about Indians flooded the American stage in the decades before the Civil War. Among the more successful were the anonymous *Indian Wife* (1830), *Pontiac, or the Siege of Detroit* by General Alexander Macomb, and *Metamora, or The Last of the Wampanoags* by John A. Stone. Approximately 50 plays about Indians appeared between 1825 and 1860.

Approximately 8200 **makers of fancy chairs** in America supplied a population of 12,700,000. Chairs made in

1830

The Church of Jesus Christ of Latter-Day Saints, known as the Mormon Church, was founded on Apr. 6, 1830, by Joseph Smith at Fayette, N.Y., with 30 members. Smith in 1827 said he had unearthed golden tablets near Palmyra, N.Y., the writing on which he translated and published in 1829 as *Book of Mormon.* These writings of the prophet Mormon were an early history of America from about 600 B.C. to about A.D. 420, showing that colonization of America had been carried out by a lost tribe of Israel. Mormon also revealed God's special message for America. This made Mormonism a distinctly American religion at a time when nationalistic feeling was strong. Smith set up the headquarters of his church in Kirtland, Ohio, in 1831.

Canal mileage in America totaled 1277 as against 73 miles of railroads. By 1840 there were 3326 miles of canals and 2818 miles of railroads. By 1850 there were 3698 miles of canals and 9021 miles of railroads. In 1830 New York was first in canals, with 546 miles, while Pennsylvania had virtually all railroads, 70 out of 73 miles. In 1840 Pennsylvania seized first place with 954 miles of canals, keeping its lead in rail mileage with 576 miles. In 1850 Pennsylvania retained its lead in canal mileage with 954 miles, yielding rail leadership to New York with its 1361 miles.

The **largest library west of the Alleghenies** was that at Transylvania University, acquired in 1821, and possessing 2000 volumes.

Robert L. Stevens invented the **T-rail,** a major innovation in the development of the railroad. Stevens, a Promethean figure in American engineering, made significant contributions to steamship and weapon development as well as to railroad engineering. He established the Hoboken ferry line between New York City and New Jersey, the first scheduled steamship ferry system in the world. Through his family holdings he became president of the Camden and Amboy Railroad. It was this interest in railroad operations that stimulated his design of the T-rail. So-called because a vertical cross-section of Stevens's rail resembles the letter "T," the T-rail became standard on all American track. Stevens completed the task of joining the rail sections by also inventing the iron tongue, a plate that fastens rail end to rail end; the hook-headed spike, a special spike used to fasten rail to ties; and accessory bolts and nuts to fasten sections of rail together.

Fads and reforms in diet attracted reformers and dieters alike. The most successful experimenter was Sylvester Graham, a clergyman and temperance lecturer of the period who believed proper diet would prevent alcoholism. He developed Graham bread, or Graham crackers, the name still linked to his product. Made of coarsely ground whole wheat flour, Graham's bread preserved vitamins, although nothing was known about vitamins at the time. His name also became attached to health clubs and boardinghouses. Graham advocated bathing at least three times a week, daily exercise, open bedroom windows in winter, and cheerful dispositions at meals. The well-known newspaper editor Horace Greeley at one time lived on a diet of beans, potatoes, boiled rice, milk, and Graham bread. In 1850 the American Vegetarian Society was founded.

John Nepomuk Maelzel arrived from a successful tour of Europe with an exhibition of his generally impractical inventions, including a universal orchestral instrument called a panharmonicum, an automatic trumpeter, speaking dolls, tiny birds that flew out of little boxes, an act called the Conflagration of Moscow, and a mechanical chess player. Although Edgar Allan Poe and others exposed the mechanical chess player as a hoax, Maelzel's exhibitions attracted large crowds in the U.S. for many years.

Town ball, based on the English game of rounders, became popular in New England. There were several teams in Boston.

A **thousand-mile walk** taking 18 days was completed by Joshua Newsam of Philadelphia, Pa.

Jan. 27 "Liberty and Union, now and forever, one and inseparable!" was included in a speech delivered by Sen. Daniel Webster of Massachusetts in debate with Sen. Robert Y. Hayne of South Carolina. Webster held that the Union was stronger than the separate states, and that its acts could not be nullified by them.

and his associates sold their interests in their trading enterprise, which was reorganized as the Rocky Mountain Fur Company.

May 28   The **Indian Removal Act** was signed by Pres. Andrew Jackson. It called for resettlement of all Indians east of the Mississippi R. to lands west of it. The sum of $500,000 was appropriated by Congress to compensate Indians and pay the costs of resettlement.

July 15   The **Sauk and Fox Indians** concluded a treaty with the U.S. government in which they ceded to the U.S. portions of their lands lying in southern Wisconsin and northern Illinois. Most of them resettled in Iowa.

Sept.   The **Anti-Masonic Party,** the first major third party in the history of U.S. politics, held its first national convention in Philadelphia. Its candidate was William Wirt of Maryland. It would draw votes from Henry Clay in the 1832 elections and win several House seats in New England.

Oct. 5   **Chester A. Arthur,** the 21st president of the United States, was born in Fairfield, Vt.

the Adam, Sheraton, Directoire, and Empire styles were in great demand.

William Ellery Channing delivered his "Remarks on American Literature," one of the more significant addresses on the dependence of U.S. writers on European models.

Washington Square North, on the northern edge of expanding New York City, was given a row of private houses with uniform facades by the architect Martin Thompson. The houses were excellent examples of the Greek Revival style.

Sept. 16   **Oliver Wendell Holmes** wrote the poem "Old Ironsides" for the Boston *Daily Advertiser.* Stirred by the notice that the frigate *Constitution* was to be dismantled, he composed his impassioned poem, which became so popular that the order for destruction of the ship was rescinded.

1831

A bloody slave insurrection, long feared by many southerners, began on Aug. 21 in Southampton County, Va. It was led by Nat Turner, a black who believed he had been chosen to lead his people out of slavery. With about 70 followers, Turner first killed his master, Joseph Travis, and his family. Within 24 hours, 60 or 70 whites had been murdered. Militia and federal troops who were called out killed about 100 blacks. Turner was captured on Oct. 30 and, after confessing to the uprising, was hanged on Nov. 11. The shaken South retaliated by passing more stringent laws relating to slaves. Southerners blamed abolitionists for inciting the slaves.

Rising tension in the U.S. over **slavery** was seen in a resolution of the Georgia Senate that offered a $5000 reward for apprehension and conviction in a Georgia court of William Lloyd Garrison, editor and publisher of *The Liberator.*

Mar. 4   **John Quincy Adams** returned to Congress, the first former president to do so. He represented the Plymouth, Mass., district in the House of Representatives for eight terms.

June 27   **Black Hawk,** leader of the Sauk Indians, and Gen. Edmund P. Gaines, commanding U.S. troops, reached an agreement under which the Sauks would move out of the Rock R. area of Illinois and across the Mississippi R. into Iowa. Once there, the Sauks nearly

The early nineteenth century was a period of strong patriotic feeling on the part of Americans. Independence had been confirmed by the War of 1812, and the growing population was spreading over a vast continent. One result of this fervor was the writing of patriotic verse and song. The most notable song, after "The Star Spangled Banner," was "America," which was first sung in public on July 4, 1831, at a service in the Park Street Church, Boston. The words had been written by the Rev. Samuel Francis Smith, a Baptist clergyman, earlier in the year. The words of this American hymn were sung to the tune of "God Save the King," and it is said that Smith did not know it was the British anthem.

Gramercy Park, one of the few private parks in the U.S., was formed in New York City to attract wealthy residents and establish an exclusive neighborhood.

Jan. 1   The first issue of *The Liberator,* edited and published by William Lloyd Garrison in Boston, was issued. Probably the leading abolitionist journal, *The Liberator* was published until 1865.

June 21   The famed **statue of George Washington** by the Italian sculptor Antonio Canova was destroyed in a great fire in the state house at Raleigh, N.C. The loss was felt throughout the states, and Congress was spurred to commission a statue of the first president.

Sept. 26   *The Gladiator* by Robert Montgomery Bird represented a high-water mark in romantic tragedy. With Edwin Forrest in the hero's role, the play had tremendous success in New York City. It dealt with

Business and Industry; Science;
Education; Philosophy and Religion   **III**

IV   **Sports; Social Issues and Crime;**
Folkways; Fashion; Holidays

Alexander Campbell and his followers, often called Campbellites, formed the Disciples of Christ. The denomination rejected all creeds and confessions and urged restoration of New Testament beliefs, practices, and polity. Undivided on the issue of slavery, the Disciples grew rapidly in number and influence throughout the last half of the nineteenth century.

The **American Institute of Instruction,** oldest educational association in the U.S., was founded at Boston, Mass. Francis Wayland, president of Brown University, was chosen its first president. Its purpose was the "diffusion of useful knowledge in regard to education."

Dec.   The first American book on **birth control,** *Moral Physiology* by Robert Dale Owen, was published. About 25,000 copies were sold in authorized and pirated editions, despite the refusal of reputable newspapers and magazines to carry advertisements for it.

Feb. 11   The continued appeal of **cock fighting** was indicated by a great series of fights held in Harrisburg, Pa., in which $100 was put up for each fight.

Sept. 18   A celebrated **race between horse and steam** was won by the horse over the Tom Thumb, the first locomotive built in America. During the race the locomotive pulled 40 passengers over a nine-mile course from Riley's Tavern to Baltimore, Md. Mechanical failure, ever the plague of railroads, caused Tom Thumb's poor showing. The engine sprang a leak in the boiler and failed to finish the course.

1831

American inventors, less hampered by tradition than their European counterparts, and faced with a labor shortage and an almost limitless expanse of arable land, were early encouraged to invent labor-saving devices for farmers. Chief among the inventors was Cyrus H. McCormick, who demonstrated his reaper in 1831 and patented it in 1834. A similar machine was invented independently by Obed Hussey, who first announced his invention in 1834. McCormick in 1847 built a factory in Chicago to produce his own reaper and by 1850 had established a nationwide business. In 1851 he introduced the reaper in England and later on the Continent. During the Civil War McCormick's reaper helped make it possible to feed Union armies.

Joseph Henry devised the **electric bell.** In demonstrating that it was possible to magnetize iron at a distance, Henry made use of a magnet that vibrated the armature of an intensity battery, causing a bell at the other end of a mile of insulated copper wire to strike. The electric bell was among the first items of electrical equipment to be used in the home.

Chloroform, called chloric ether, was synthesized by Dr. James Guthrie in his laboratory at Sacketts Harbor, N.Y. The anesthetic properties of chloroform were discovered in 1847 by a Scottish surgeon, Sir James Young Simpson.

Apr.   Timothy Bailey of Cohoes, N.Y., perfected a **powered knitting machine,** used the following year in

In the first half of the nineteenth century the diet and health of Americans were improved by the introduction of canning and refrigeration. Canned foods began to be produced commercially in 1820 by William Underwood in Boston and Thomas Kensett in New York. Canning became more efficient after introduction of the tin can, first patented in the U.S. in 1825. By the 1840s canning was being done on a large scale. By this time, too, improvements in the cutting and storing of ice made ice cheaper, so refrigeration came into common use.

Jan. 1   The passionate abolitionist sentiment "**I will not retreat a single inch, and I will be heard**" concluded the lead article by William Lloyd Garrison in the first issue of his abolitionist weekly, *The Liberator.* "I will be as harsh as truth and as uncompromising as justice, on this subject [slavery]. I do not want to think or write with moderation. No! No!" His uncompromising stand caused immeasurable trouble for Garrison and his followers. He was maligned, threatened, and beaten in Boston. *The Liberator,* understaffed and operating on a shoestring budget, overcame almost insurmountable obstacles in getting to press. Garrison's experiences from the time he began his antislavery crusade in Boston in 1829 would have defeated a less inspired person. In 1830 Garrison was convicted of libel and imprisoned.

Apr. 25   The **frontiersman,** one of the hardy comedic figures in American literature, first appeared in James Kirke Paulding's play *The Lion of the West* at the Park

starved and in the srping of 1832 returned to their old corn fields in Illinois.

July 4   Former Pres. **James Monroe** died at 73. He was buried at Richmond, Va.

Sept. 26   The **Anti-Masonic Party** convened in Baltimore, Md., and nominated for president William Wirt, attorney general in the cabinets of James Monroe and John Quincy Adams. In the 1832 election Wirt received seven electoral votes and drew support from Henry Clay.

Nov. 19   **James A. Garfield,** 20th president of the United States, was born in Orange Township near Cleveland, Ohio.

Dec. 12   The **first nominating convention** of a major party was held by the National Republican Party. It nominated Henry Clay for President.

the revolt of the gladiator Spartacus. Abolitionist sentiment and hatred of tyranny dominated the piece.

Oct. 13   **Riots** occurred at the Park Theater in New York City when Joshua R. Anderson, an English actor who had strongly criticized America, made his appearance on stage.

Dec. 26   **Stephen Girard** died. One of the wealthiest men in the U.S., he left his fortune to Philadelphia, Pa., for the founding of Girard College, an elementary and secondary school for "poor, male white orphans." The will was contested and the college was not built for several years. When the college building was completed, it was the most complete example of Greek Revival style in the U.S. Unfortunately, its vaulted rooms, lack of windows, and complete peripheral colonnade of Corinthian columns were inappropriate for a school. The failure of the building helped end the Greek Revival in the U.S.

1832

The issue of states' rights had come to the fore as a result of the tariff bill of 1828, known to its enemies in the South as the Tariff of Abominations. This year, for the first time, a state threatened both nullification and secession. On Nov. 24, 1832, a South Carolina convention passed an ordinance declaring null and void both the 1828 tariff and one enacted in 1832, reducing somewhat the tariff duties to which the South objected. The ordinance stated further that the state would secede if the federal government used force. Pres. Andrew Jackson reacted strongly to this declaration on Dec. 10 with a proclamation to South Carolina asserting supremacy of federal law and calling nullification an act of rebellion.

The **first epidemic of Asiatic cholera** struck the U.S., spreading from Canada south to the U.S. and down the Mississippi R. It appeared on June 28 in New York City and soon spread to other large cities throughout the Northeast. New York City alone reported 2251 deaths. In the Mohawk Valley thousands died from it. During a 12-day period beginning Oct. 25, more than 6000 perished in New Orleans. Some corpses were weighted with bricks and stones and thrown into a river; others were heaped in long trenches and covered. The epidemic subsided by 1838 but reappeared during the next decade, when the disease swept the Indian nations of the Great Plains, drastically reducing their populations and their ability to resist the advance of settlers.

1832–1833   In **congressional elections** the Democrats and National Republicans fell into a 20–20 Senate tie, with eight seats held by minor parties. In the House

As in the past, many of the most popular figures on the American stage during this period were English actors and actresses, some of whom remained in the U.S. and made careers there. The most popular of them all was Fanny Kemble, who made her debut with her father Charles at the Park Theater, New York City, in 1832. Two years later Miss Kemble married Pierce Butler, whose family owned a large plantation in Georgia. The marriage was a failure, largely because she could not stand life on a slave-operated estate. She wrote *Journal of a Residence on a Georgia Plantation in 1838–39,* which was published in 1863. She hoped it would turn British opinion against the South.

The **Old Merchant's House** was built in New York City, a fine example of urban architecture of its time. Today it is a museum with all its original furnishings preserved.

Indians hired as extras for a performance of Richard Brinsley Sheridan's play *Pizarro* (1799) in Columbus, Ga., gave the audience an unexpected thrill. Paid 50 cents and a glass of whiskey each, the Creeks made their stage entrance the occasion for a genuine war dance, culminating in the scalping, or wig removal, of King Atalibe, the demolition of the sets, and the frightened exit of the female extras who played the roles of virgin maidens.

The song **"Clare de Kitchen"** was copyrighted by George Willig, Jr., a Baltimore music publisher. It was made popular by Thomas Dartmouth "Jim Crow" Rice, a noted minstrel singer, who used several versions. It was a nonsense song about animals, chiefly a blind horse.

a factory operated by Bailey and Egbert Egberts.

Apr. 18 Today's **New York University** was chartered as the University of the City of New York. The university issued its first degrees in 1833. Its name was changed to New York University in 1896.

May 26 **Wesleyan University** was chartered in Middletown, Conn. It is the oldest institution of higher education founded in the U.S. by Methodists. Its first degrees were granted in 1833.

Aug. The **Adventist movement** in American Protestantism was born when William Miller, a Baptist, began public preaching. His theme was the imminence of Christ's return to earth, based on his interpretation of passages from Daniel and Revelation. Miller predicted that the "cleansing by fire" would begin at some point between March 21, 1843, and March 21, 1844.

Theater in New York City. Col. Nimrod Wildfire, a character in the play, was described as "a raw Kentuckian recently elected to Congress." Although the playwright denied he was satirizing Davy Crockett, then approaching the end of his second term in Congress, suspicion persisted. The colonel was a Kentucky character who visited the Northeast and outsmarted city folk. The play has not survived except for a speech from it that appeared in several periodicals.

Aug. 10 The term *Old Glory,* denoting the U.S. flag, was first used by William Driver, of Salem, Mass., captain of the *Charles Daggett.* Presented with a large American flag, Driver raised it to the masthead and proclaimed: "I name thee Old Glory." By the end of the 1850s, the term was in widespread use.

Dec. 10 A popular weekly **racing sheet**, *Spirit of the Times,* founded by William Trotter Porter, began publication. Its stated purpose was to raise the reputation of horse racing and other sports.

1832

The need for faster ships to connect the East and West coasts of the U.S. by way of Cape Horn, and to carry on the lucrative trade with China, resulted in the development of the clipper ship, the fastest merchant sailing vessel ever built. The clippers were characterized by great length in proportion to beam and an enormous area of sail. The first true clipper, the *Ann McKim,* was built in Baltimore in 1832. Donald McKay of Boston became the foremost builder, completing such famous clippers as *Flying Cloud* and *Lightning.* In 1854 *Flying Cloud* set a record for the Boston to San Francisco route of 89 days, 8 hours. The clipper as a type ruled the seas until the development of steam-powered vessels.

The so-called science of **phrenology** was introduced to America in Boston by Johann Kaspar Spurzheim of Vienna, a disciple of the founder of phrenology, Dr. Franz Joseph Gall of Vienna and Paris. Phrenology was based on the premise that a person's moral character and intellectual capacity could be determined by studying the shape and protuberances of the skull. Many distinguished Americans, like John Quincy Adams, questioned the claims of this science; but others, like Daniel Webster and Andrew Jackson, endorsed phrenology, perhaps because phrenologists had given flattering analyses of the craniums of these distinguished men.

The **Ohio and Erie Canal** connected Cleveland to the Ohio R. at Portsmouth. Construction of the canal took seven years, with malaria and a shortage of funds

A unique link with the birth of the nation was broken this year when Charles Carroll, the last surviving signer of the Declaration of Independence, died on Nov. 14, at 95. He had inherited a large estate from his father near Frederick, Md., known as Carrollton Manor. Carroll was one of a delegation that tried unsuccessfully in 1776 to get support from Canada for the Revolutionary cause. Later he was a U.S. senator from Maryland (1789–1792). Said to be the wealthiest man in America in his time, Carroll was a pioneer in promoting transportation projects and was chairman in 1828, of the first board of directors of the Baltimore and Ohio Railroad.

Oranges and lemons entered the American diet with the arrival of the first large shipment, direct from Sicily. Previously they had been a delicacy for the rich. Oranges and lemons have both been traced to Asia. It was not until the conquests and migrations of the Arabs that the fruit became of major agricultural consequence. The Arabs planted lemon trees in Spain during their occupation. Christopher Columbus was credited with planting the first orange tree in the New World. Trees were distributed by the Spaniards throughout the regions they explored and settled. Neither the orange nor the lemon became of commercial importance in the U.S. until years later.

The Young Man's Guide, a moralistic book of manners for personal and domestic situations by William A. Alcott, was published and became widely read. The author was an educator.

the Democrats had a 147–53 majority over the Anti-Masonic Party, with 60 seats held by minor parties.

Apr. 6 The **Black Hawk War** began soon after the Sauk Indians, led by Black Hawk, faring poorly in Iowa where the government had moved them, recrossed the Mississippi R. and moved back to their former corn fields to plant a new crop. As tensions mounted, panicky settlers killed two Indians seeking a parley and bearing a white flag. Black Hawk, enraged, began killing white settlers.

May 9 The **Treaty of Payne's Landing** was concluded with some Seminole chiefs in Florida who accepted resettlement in lands allotted to their related nation, the Creek, west of the Mississippi R. But other chiefs and their followers demurred and remained on their Florida lands. White settlers stepped up their campaign of harassment and insisted that the U.S. government force the Seminoles to obey the provisions of the treaty. Continued resistance to resettlement led to the Second Seminole War (1835–1842).

May 21 The **Democratic Party,** formerly known as "Republican Delegates from the Several States" and called both Republican and Democratic-Republican, formally adopted its present name at its convention in Baltimore, Md. The convention nominated Pres. Andrew Jackson for a second term and nominated Martin Van Buren of New York for vice president.

July 10 The congressional bill to renew the charter of the **Bank of the U.S.** was vetoed by Pres. Jackson. Jackson charged that the bank was a monopoly and saw the danger of its being principally controlled by foreigners, who owned about $8,000,000 of the bank's stock.

Aug. 2 Sauk followers of **Black Hawk** were massacred at the mouth of the Bad Axe R. in Wisconsin by Illinois militia led by Gen. Henry Atkinson. Old men, women, and children were all killed without regard for pleas of mercy or white flags.

Aug. 27 **Black Hawk,** deserted by his Winnebago allies, surrendered, thus ending the Black Hawk War.

Dec. 5 **Andrew Jackson was reelected president** of the United States by 687,502 popular votes and 219 electoral votes, against 530,189 popular votes and 49 electoral votes for Henry Clay. Martin Van Buren was elected vice president.

Swiss Family Robinson, the classic novel for children by Johann Rudolph Wyss, was published for the first time in the U.S., nearly 20 years after its appearance abroad. It has sold well over 1,000,000 copies in the U.S. since.

The popular versifier **Hannah F. Gould** published an edition of her *Poems.* Generally short, her verses had little poetic quality, but were sincere and good-humored, dealing with the commonplaces of domestic life, nature, and patriotic and religious themes. *Poems* was well adapted to the gift book vogue of the times. Over two decades, *Poems* and its successors were reprinted several times.

The collected *Poems* of **William Cullen Bryant** were published and hailed by the *North American Review* as "the best volume of American verse that has appeared." Among the 89 poems were such favorites as "O Fairest of the Rural Maids," "The Death of the Flowers," "June," "A Forest Hymn," "Hymn to Death," "A Meditation on Rhode Island," and "To a Fringed Gentian."

Literary Remains, the posthumous work of John Gardiner Brainard, the Connecticut poet, editor, and folklorist, was published. John Greenleaf Whittier, who admired Brainard's work, edited the volume and supplied a biographical sketch of Brainard, who died in 1828.

The Heidenmauer by James Fenimore Cooper, a romantic novel set in sixteenth-century Bavaria, was published. In the period 1826–1833, while living and traveling in Europe, Cooper wrote three novels with European settings and five nonfiction books, a remarkable rate of production. Even in his European novels Cooper could not mute his lifelong contention that democracy, the American frontier, and the American character were better than European aristocracy and the lingering remains of feudalism. *The Heidenmauer* was moderately successful because Cooper could tell a story. Not until his return to the U.S. did Cooper turn again to the American frontier settings he knew so well.

June 17 **Joseph Stevens Jones,** author of scores of farces and melodramas, began to exploit the shrewd Yankee type. *The Liberty Tree,* produced this year, contains Bill Ball; his *Green Mountain Boy* (1833), a character named Jedediah Homebred; *People's Lawyer* (1839), the well-known Solon Shingle; *Silver Spoon* (1852), the Honorable Jefferson S. Batkins. Actor George Handel Hill excelled in these parts.

| Business and Industry; Science; Education; Philosophy and Religion III | Sports; Social Issues and Crime; Folkways; Fashion; Holidays IV |

crippling the year-round labor of some 2000 workers. The canal, opened in 1833, gave Ohio farmers an outlet to the Mississippi R. and to the markets of the South.

A machine to make **pins** in one operation was invented by John Ireland Howe of Salem, N.Y. A similar machine had been in use in England since 1824. In 1833 Howe improved it and obtained foreign patents. In 1835 he founded Howe Manufacturing Company, and soon had five machines in operation.

Feb. 2 **Denison University** in Granville, Ohio, was chartered as Granville Literary and Theological Institution. Established under Baptist auspices, the institution awarded its first degrees in 1840. It became Granville College in 1845 and Denison University in 1856.

Feb. 6 A **transcontinental railroad** was suggested in print for the first time in the *Emigrant*, a weekly newspaper published in Ann Arbor, Mich.

Apr. 7 **Gettysburg College** in Gettysburg, Pa., received its charter as Pennsylvania College. Founded under Lutheran auspices, the college awarded its first degrees in 1834. Pennsylvania College became Gettysburg College in 1921. It was the first Lutheran-sponsored institution of higher learning in the U.S.

Nov. 26 The **first streetcar in the world** was put into operation by the New York & Harlem Railroad in New York City. Built by John Stephenson, it was named *John Mason* and was a horse-drawn car that ran on lower Fourth Ave.

Dec. 28 **St. Louis University** was chartered in St. Louis, Mo., under Catholic auspices. It had been founded in 1818. It was the first Catholic university west of the Alleghenies.

The **first sports editor** in the U.S. was William Trotter Porter. He was given that position and title after he sold his newspaper, *The Spirit of the Times*, to *The Traveller*.

Calisthenics was prescribed for urban women in *Atkinson's Casket*. The suggestion reflected a growing fear of the physical deterioration of city dwellers. Illustrated exercises stressed muscular development of the arms and shoulders, but above all, the back.

Jan. 21 "To the victors belong the spoils" was an expression originated by Sen. William Learned Marcy of New York. He used the expression in a speech defending the system of party patronage, initiated under the Democrats, against the attack of Henry Clay. The entire sentence read, "They see nothing wrong in this rule, that to the victor belong the spoils of the enemy."

Apr. 1 **Robert the Hermit,** of Massachusetts, one of the most colorful and famous hermits in American history, died in his hermitage at Seekonk, Mass. Robert was a bonded slave, born of an African mother and probably an Anglo-Saxon father, in Princeton, N.J. He obtained his freedom, was swindled out of it and shipped to a foreign slave market, escaped to America, was parted from his first wife by force, rejected by his second wife after a long voyage at sea, and otherwise buffeted about before withdrawing from the society of men.

July 9 The **National Fast Day** that Sen. Henry Clay of Kentucky proposed in a resolution was defeated after a bitter debate. Clay wanted the day proclaimed by Congress and the president so the nation might officially pray for relief from a cholera epidemic. The opposing Democrats held that "prayer and humiliation" should be "prompted by the devotion of the heart, and not the bidding of the state." Pres. Jackson had already declined on the principle of separation of church and state, following Thomas Jefferson's example. However, other presidents both before and after Jackson have proclaimed days of thanksgiving and prayer.

1833

That the abolition movement was gaining strength was demonstrated this year when the first national abolitionist organization, the American Anti-Slavery Society, was formed in Philadelphia on Dec. 4. Its first president was Arthur Tappan, who like his brother Lewis was a wealthy New York City businessman. Both were active in the antislavery cause for many years. Also prominent in the movement was William Lloyd Garrison, the fiery editor of *The Liberator,* who with his followers seized control of the society in 1840 because he did not think it was radical enough. The society saw slavery as a moral evil and called for immediate abolition. In 1835 it began a propaganda campaign that flooded the slave states with abolitionist literature.

Mar. 2 In the continuing **controversy over nullification,** Pres. Andrew Jackson signed two bills. The first was Henry Clay's compromise Tariff of 1833, which was intended to ease the trouble between the federal government and South Carolina. The second was called the Force Act; it authorized the president to enforce collection of tariffs by use of the Army and Navy if necessary.

Mar. 4 Pres. Andrew Jackson was inaugurated for his second term. Martin Van Buren of New York succeeded John C. Calhoun as vice president.

Mar. 15 The South Carolina **Ordinance of Nullification** was revoked by a state convention. However, on Mar. 18 the convention passed an ordinance nullifying the Force Act.

Mar. 20 The U.S. signed a **commercial treaty** with Siam at Bangkok.

Aug. 20 **Benjamin Harrison,** 23rd president of the United States, was born in North Bend, Ohio.

Sept. 21 The U.S. signed a **commercial treaty** with the Sultan of Muscat (Oman).

Sept. 23 William J. Duane, secretary of the treasury, was removed from office by Pres. Jackson because he refused to withdraw government deposits from the Bank of the U.S. and place them in state banks. Roger B. Taney was appointed by Pres. Jackson to succeed Duane.

The day of newspaper sensationalism dawned with the establishment of the New York *Sun* on Sept. 3. Founded by 23-year-old Benjamin H. Day, its first issue consisted of four pages, which Day wrote and set in type himself. The paper sold for one penny while all other New York papers sold for 6 cents. Day was the first publisher in the city to use newsboys and by 1835 he claimed that the 19,360 circulation of the *Sun* was the largest in the world.

A commission for a **statue of George Washington,** a monumental figure in marble to be placed in the Capitol in Washington, D.C., was awarded to Horatio Greenough. Influenced by classical forms, Greenough delivered a decade later a huge sculpture depicting Washington half-nude and resembling a Greek god. It was too heavy for its planned site under the dome and had to be placed in an outside location for which it was ill-suited. The public scorned it. Later it was removed to the Smithsonian Institution.

Edgar Allan Poe's story "MS Found in a Bottle" won a prize of $50 in a competition sponsored by the *Baltimore Saturday Visiter.* More important, the award brought Poe in contact with John Pendleton Kennedy, an established literary figure who helped him find work on the *Southern Literary Messenger.*

A **bowdlerized version of the Bible** was completed by Noah Webster, who deleted many verses altogether and substituted *breast* for *teat, in embryo* for *in the belly, smell* for *stink, to nurse* or *to nourish* for *to give suck,* and so on.

Nathaniel Currier moved his lithography business from Philadelphia, Pa., to New York City, going into business with J. H. Bufford. In 1850 Currier went into business with James Merritt Ives, and by 1857 all of the prints issued by the company bore the Currier & Ives imprint. The lithographs, inexpensive and enormously popular, gave an eloquent pictorial account of sights and events of nineteenth-century America.

One of the earliest **blackface minstrel songs,** "Sambo's Address to He' Bred'rin" or "Ching a Ring Chaw," was published in Boston. Its lyrics urged blacks to immigrate to "Hetee" (Haiti), where they would be free and wealthy.

The **Boston Academy of Music** was founded by Lowell Mason to instruct children and music teachers.

Jan. 17 **William Rush,** the first native American sculptor, died at 76. Working in wood and clay, Rush in his work reflected the neoclassical influence. His work included busts of many notables, American and European; carved wooden female figureheads for ships; the personifications of Tragedy and Comedy seen at the Actor's Home outside Philadelphia; and

| Business and Industry; Science; Education; Philosophy and Religion | III | | IV | Sports; Social Issues and Crime; Folkways; Fashion; Holidays |

1833

An invention that contributed as much to the history and folklore of the American West as it did to the firearms industry was the Colt revolver, invented by Samuel Colt in 1833 and patented on Feb. 25, 1836. Colt began producing the weapon at the Patent Arms Company in Paterson, N.J. As the first firearm that could be used effectively by a man on horseback, this six-shooter soon became associated with the frontier and the Great Plains. In time the name Colt became almost synonymous with the term revolver. Colt's business failed, but it was revived by an order from the government for 100 revolvers in 1847 for use in the Mexican War. Colt established a new company and plant in Hartford, Conn.

Disestablishment of its church came finally to Massachusetts, the last state to do so. From this date on, the legal separation of church and state has been complete in the U.S.

Paternalism in industry made its first appearance at Kensington Glass Works in Philadelphia, Pa. The company was founded by Thomas W. Dyott, who had already built up the first large patent medicine business in the U.S. Dyott employed 450 persons, including 100 apprentices, on a 12-month basis, each working 11 hours a day. In the company housing (Dyottville) no liquor was allowed, children had to be in bed by 8:30 P.M., and gates were closed for adults at 9:30 P.M. Dyott provided medical assistance and a sick room, baths on schedule, a library, recreation, and a singing school. The rising bell came at daybreak. At scheduled intermissions, crackers were served. The scheme collapsed when Dyott's bank failed in 1836.

A **tax-supported public library** was established in Peterborough, N.H., under the leadership of the Rev. Abiel Abbot. The library charged a small membership fee. It is considered the oldest public library in the U.S. except for the Library of Congress, established in 1800 by an act of Congress.

Haverford College, the **first Quaker college** in the U.S., was founded in Haverford, Pa. It was chartered as the Haverford School Association in 1856, the year its first degrees were awarded. In 1875 the school adopted the name Haverford College.

The new **Oberlin Collegiate Institute**, Oberlin, Ohio, opened its doors to both sexes, the first college to do so. In 1835 it admitted students "without respect to color." In 1837 it awarded its first degrees. The school changed its name to Oberlin College in 1850.

The frontier and the westward movement produced a number of semilegendary folk heroes. None of these figures has ever surpassed Davy Crockett in popularity or scope and number of alleged exploits. Crockett began as a frontiersman and Indian fighter, but by 1833 he was serving his third term as a congressman from Tennessee. As a legislator, he made the most of his backwoods humor, style of dress, racy language, and naive but often shrewd comments on public affairs. More sophisticated politicians used Crockett, who opposed Pres. Andrew Jackson's policies, to lure Democratic backwoodsmen to the Whig Party. One of their ploys was to prepare books and attribute them to Crockett, who may have had a hand in some of them. *Sketches and Eccentricities of Col. David Crockett* appeared in 1833. He died in 1836 as one of the defenders of the Alamo in San Antonio, Tex. That year there appeared posthumously *Col. Crockett's Exploits and Adventures in Texas.*

Henry Perrine, a physician, U.S. consul in Mexico, and botanical collector, brought the avocado tree from Mexico to his experimental nursery in southern Florida. The avocado may have been introduced earlier by Spaniards. However, Perrine brought back over 200 tropical species, many useful, including the sisal, valuable for its fibers.

A rudimentary form of **baseball** was played in Philadelphia, Pa., by the Olympic Ball Club. Home plate was situated between two bases. As in cricket, a ball hit behind the batter was considered a hit, and runners struck by the ball were out.

The American appetite for **liquor** was evidenced by the founding in Washington, D.C., of the Congressional Temperance Society. The nation's legislators hoped to discourage "the use of ardent spirit and the traffic in it, by example and by kind moral influence." The society declined shortly after its founding but in 1842 was suddenly revived by John H. W. Hawkins, a temperance lecturer who, in his first ten years of crusading activity, traveled more than 100,000 miles and spoke on at least 2500 separate occasions.

The **Opera House** opened at Leonard and Church streets in New York City was something entirely new to Americans. There was a second balcony of boxes that ran around the back of the house, painted white with decorations in gold, red, and blue. The upholstery of the divans and orchestra seats was in blue, and the floors were carpeted from wall to wall. It was a fitting abode for the Muses, who peered from pastel bowers in the

Oct. 1 Government deposits of public funds were withdrawn from the **Bank of the U.S.** in accordance with an executive order. The funds were redeposited in a number of state banks, known as "pet banks."

Dec. 26 Sen. **Henry Clay** introduced two censure resolutions in the Senate on the question of withdrawing deposits from the Bank of the U.S. Both were directed at Pres. Jackson.

also the *Spirit of the Schuylkill*, in Fairmount Park in Philadelphia.

Nov. 16 The newly constructed **Italian Opera House** opened at Leonard and Church streets in New York City. It was partly sponsored by various leaders of New York society who subscribed to season boxes at prices up to $6000. Admission prices to the first performance, a Rossini opera, were $1.50 for box, $2.00 for sofa seats, $1.00 for the pit, and 75 cents for the gallery.

1834

A new national political party coalesced this year out of several groups whose common cause was opposition to Pres. Andrew Jackson and his policies. In 1834 this coalition formally adopted the name Whig, after the English political party that opposed excessive royal prerogatives. Its leaders were Henry Clay of Kentucky, John C. Calhoun of South Carolina, and Daniel Webster of Massachusetts. The party brought together those who favored the so-called American system of protective tariffs combined with internal improvements, states' rights groups, those opposed to Jackson's Bank of the United States policy, southern planters, and northern industrialists. In 1836 the party absorbed the remnants of the Anti-Masonic Party. Although in general it represented the conservative political view, the party lacked leadership and disappeared after it failed dismally in the 1852 presidential election.

British immigration to the U.S. was spurred dramatically by a tightening by Parliament of the Poor Laws, which almost equated unemployment of the able-bodied with moral failure. For the next century, whenever employment conditions were bad in Europe and bright in the U.S., immigration to the U.S. jumped sharply.

1834–1835 In congressional elections the Democrats took a 27–25 Senate majority over the Whigs. In the House they lost two seats but held a majority of 145–98 over the Whigs.

Mar. 28 Senate resolutions of censure against Pres. Jackson, introduced by Sen. Henry Clay of Kentucky, were adopted. The censure was for Jackson's removal of public deposits from the Bank of the U.S.

Apr. 15 The Senate censure resolutions were formally protested by Pres. Jackson. He succeeded in having them removed from the Senate journal in the following year.

June 15 Fort Hall, Idaho's first settlement, was founded by Nathaniel Jarvis Wyeth, a trader and explorer, as a fur-trading center. Located on the Snake R. in southeast Idaho, Fort Hall became a well-known station on the Oregon Trail.

American historians of the middle years of the nineteenth century were not as objective in their treatment of the nation's history as most of those who came later. The last great subjective historian was George Bancroft, whose ten-volume *History of the United States* appeared between 1834 and 1874. Bancroft was professionally trained as a historian, but he was nationalistic and rhetorical, using the story of the U.S. to express commonly held beliefs in democracy, manifest destiny, and the virtues of Anglo-American Protestantism. Bancroft also held public office and as secretary of the navy in 1845–1846 he established the U.S. Naval Academy at Annapolis, Md.

The song **"Zip Coon"** was performed in New York City by Bob Farrell. It would soon become known as "Turkey in the Straw" and gain popularity in minstrel shows. It originated as a folk song about 1815 in the frontier states of the Southwest.

A *History of the Rise and Progress of the Arts of Design in the U.S.* by William Dunlap, the dramatist and theatrical entrepreneur, was published. This work is the source for most of the information concerning early American painters. Dunlap helped to found the National Academy of Design.

The **Merchant's Exchange** was built in Philadelphia, Pa., from plans by William Strickland. It was a good example of Greek Revival style at its most ornate.

The Last Days of Pompeii, a historical novel by Edward Bulwer-Lytton, was published. It was an instant and long-lasting success.

Feb. 5 Newark College was chartered in Newark, Del. Established under Presbyterian auspices, it was merged with Newark Academy, a preparatory school founded in New London, Pa., in 1743 and moved to Newark in 1765. Newark College opened on May 8, 1834, and conferred its first degrees in 1836. It became Delaware College in 1843 and the University of Delaware on Mar. 28, 1921.

domed ceiling. Attraction of women to the theater was the purpose behind the sumptuous decor of the Opera House. Gentility even surrounded the purchase of tickets—there was no charge for ordering seats in advance. But beauty and thrift in this case were small compensation for the main drawback of the Opera House: Unattended ladies could not come because the neighborhood had a bad reputation.

1834

Growing interest in science brought with it advocates and followers of pseudo-sciences. One was phrenology, which began in Germany and was now being popularized in the U.S. by Orson Fowler. Phrenology claimed that from the shape of the human skull one could determine character traits and mental abilities. Furthermore, phrenology taught that man could alter his personality and develop the brain by training. The lectures and writings of Fowler, self-appointed professor of phrenology, became very popular, and even so eminent a person as Horace Mann, the educator, said it helped him in his work.

From about 1825 to the outbreak of the Civil War in 1861, there was a strong atmosphere of reform in the U.S. Most noticeable was the antislavery movement, but it was only one of many causes for which people organized, labored, and contributed money. Dedicated people worked for women's rights, prison reform, educational reform, religious liberalism, social welfare, and other causes. One group called itself the Society to Improve the Condition of the Sailors. This urge to reform had several sources: the religious revival that began in the 1820s; the rational spirit of the Enlightenment with its idea of the possibility of progress, and the spirit of romanticism, which was related to the older notion that the New World was a second Eden where people could start over.

Albert Brisbane returned to the U.S. hoping to establish a Utopian community along the lines projected in Charles Fourier's *Traité de l'Association Domestique-Agricole*. Brisbane was sympathetic to the Fourierian plan to dignify the labor class by making their work attractive. He later organized a society and publicized the theories of Fourier in addresses and articles, many of which were bought by Horace Greeley for the New York *Tribune.*

The **Park Theater** in New York City, in keeping with the trend toward heightened elegance in theatrical decor, was completely renovated for the coming season. William Shakespeare was the decided theme. All details complemented the portrait of Shakespeare that graced the center of the proscenium. On the fronts of boxes were reproductions of scenes from his plays, as well as replicas of buildings that he immortalized, including his home, the Globe, the Falcon Inn, and Charlecot Hall. The old mirrors which had stood on either side of the stage were replaced with figures of Tragedy and Comedy. The theater gleamed with gold and crimson on a cream-colored ground.

A true prototype of the modern **electric motor** was constructed by Thomas Davenport, a Vermont blacksmith. Davenport recognized the versatility of Joseph Henry's electromagnet and saw that it could be adapted for use in an electric power machine. He connected four electromagnets to a battery and set them up on a wheel that rotated rapidly when current was turned on. This is the basic design of the standard electric motor of today. Davenport received a patent in 1837, but could not create a market for his device before his death in 1851.

The legend of **Davy Crockett** was augmented by publication of his supposed autobiography, *A Narrative of the Life of David Crockett.* He was featured as a great bear hunter and congressman. Interspersed were tall tales. Anti-Jacksonians, of whom Crockett was one, expected to profit politically from promotion of Crockett's image. Political opponents meanwhile characterized him as "fresh from the backwoods, half-horse, half-alligator, a little touched with the snapping-turtle."

| Exploration and Settlement; Wars; Government; Civil Rights; Statistics | I | | II | Publishing; Arts and Music; Popular Entertainment; Architecture; Theater |

June 24 Roger Brooke Taney, serving as secretary of the treasury on a recess appointment from Pres. Jackson, was rejected by the Senate when his name was sent up for confirmation. Again in 1835 Taney was rejected when nominated to be an associate justice of the Supreme Court, but in 1836 he was nominated and confirmed as chief justice.

June 28 The **Second Coinage Act** established the historic 16 to 1 ratio between silver and gold. The previous 15 to 1 ratio had undervalued gold coins, which were being hoarded. The new relationship was achieved by a small reduction of the fine gold content of the gold pieces.

June 30 The **Department of Indian Affairs** was established by an act of Congress.

Oct. **Proslavery rioting** erupted in Philadelphia, Pa., destroying about 40 homes in the black community.

Oct. 28 The **Seminole Indians** were ordered to evacuate Florida and move west of the Mississippi R. The government acted under a treaty signed May 9, 1832.

Nicholas Biddle, Philadelphia financier and perhaps the first native-born American to study Greek civilization on its home grounds, built his country seat at Andalusia, in Bucks County, Pa. A full row of Doric columns supported the roof all around—one of few such residences in the U.S. Biddle retired to it in 1839.

July 10 James McNeill Whistler, painter and etcher, was born in Lowell, Mass. Later in life, when his birthplace was brought up in conversation, he remarked, "I shall be born when and where I want, and I do not choose to be born in Lowell." All his adult life was lived abroad.

1835

The federal government was committed to a policy of removing all eastern Indians to reservations west of the Mississippi R. To that end a treaty had been signed in 1832 with the Seminole Indians of Florida. When the time came in 1835 to begin the move, many Seminoles refused to go. Resistance was led by the Indian chief Osceola, whose father was not an Indian. In November the Second Seminole War (1835–1842) erupted. Federal troops were sent to Florida but had little success against the Indians, whose raiding parties struck quickly and then vanished. Osceola was taken prisoner in 1837 while negotiating under a flag of truce; he died in prison on Jan. 30, 1838. The American forces did not overcome Seminole resistance until 1842. The cost to the U.S. was 1500 dead and $20,000,000.

Theodore Dwight Weld, having redirected his zeal from the temperance movement to the antislavery movement, was now selecting and training agents for the American Anti-Slavery Society. Within a year his group, known as The Seventy, would be spreading the abolitionist gospel throughout the rural areas of the North and the border states. His strategy would win thousands of converts and create a groundswell of public opinion against slavery.

Jan. Daniel Webster of Massachusetts was nominated for president by the Whigs of the Massachusetts legislature. With other Whig candidates in the field and the Anti-Jacksonians divided, Webster won only his home state.

Compared with that of Europe, the history of the U.S. did not go back very far, but already it was being recorded professionally. Scholars began to edit papers and documents of the first heroes of the nation. Among these historians was Jared Sparks who, at Harvard in 1839, became the first professor of American history in the U.S. Sparks did much to find and publish previously unprinted manuscripts, but he bowdlerized them to enhance the reputations of his subjects. His largest work was *The Writings of George Washington* (12 volumes, 1834–1837). The initial volume was a biography of the first president.

Slavery, an influential tract of the abolitionist cause by William Ellery Channing, was published.

The *Collected Works* of **James Kirke Paulding** was published, a literary event of the year. In the collection were his two novels written during the decade, *The Dutchman's Fireside* (1831), about eighteenth-century Albany, and *Westward Ho!* (1832), a popular romance. Though Paulding lived until 1860, he wrote little after 1835.

The Linwoods by Catherine Maria Sedgwick was published. It was a novel about social life in New York City toward the end of the American Revolution. An extravagant romantic and the most popular woman author of the period, Sedgwick used the natural beauties

Cyrus McCormick patented an early model of his famous reaper. Although 20 patents for reapers in the U.S. preceded his, McCormick's persistent experimentation and technical improvements soon made his product preeminent in its field. He did not put his reaper on the market until certain defects had been eliminated. He sold his first two reapers in 1841; produced 4000 in 1856; and 23,000 in 1857. McCormick's reapers revolutionized American agriculture.

Wabash College in Crawfordsville, Ind., founded in 1832 under Presbyterian auspices, received its charter as Wabash Manual Labor College. It awarded its first degrees in 1838 and adopted its present name in 1851.

Americans began to eat **tomatoes** at about this time, but not until 1900 would they become popular. Despite the fact that tomatoes had been introduced into Europe from Mexico as ornamental plants c1550, and were soon afterward eaten in Italy, they were popularly regarded in the U.S. as poisonous and in France as an aphrodisiac.

In **horse racing,** hurdles were introduced in a race at Washington, D.C., perhaps for the first time in the U.S. Six fences were placed at intervals over the one-mile course. The winner was awarded a plate valued at £100.

The **Philadelphia Club,** oldest club for gentlemen in the U.S. and at first called the Adelphi Club, was formed in Philadelphia, Pa.

Rules for a game called **baseball** appeared in *The Book of Sports* by Robin Carver. However, the rules were for a game known to Englishmen as rounders and were copied from an English book. Rounders bore little resemblance to American baseball.

1835

Almost since its discovery, America had been popular with European intellectuals, who visited here because of its novelty. Now the U.S. began to attract visitors who wanted to study the world's preeminent experiment in democracy. Perhaps the most thoughtful of these visitors was Alexis de Tocqueville, a French liberal who visited the U.S. in 1831–1832. In 1835 his classic volume *De la Démocratie en Amérique* was published in Belgium. It was issued in the U.S. in an English-language edition, *Democracy in America,* in 1838. Tocqueville had been favorably impressed with the U.S. and its attempt to have both liberty and equality. His book, objective for the most part, was the earliest important analysis of the American system of government.

A **wheat crop failure** in western farming areas caused a severe economic crisis in that region, with attendant strain on banking and loan facilities.

A model **telegraph** was constructed by Samuel F. B. Morse and demonstrated for a few friends. Morse's model was severely limited and inefficient because he was unfamiliar with advances made in electromagnetism by his contemporaries. It had about the same applicability as a telephone with a range of 40 feet. In the next two years he applied the results of more recent research, improved his equipment, and extended the

Although the nation was still basically one of farms and small towns, a trend toward urbanization was becoming apparent. Between 1820 and 1850 the combined population of New York City, Philadelphia, Baltimore, and Boston nearly tripled. In 1830 farmers outnumbered city dwellers by about 10.5 to 1; by 1840 the ratio was only 5.5 to 1. The population of towns of 8000 or more nearly doubled between 1830 and 1850. Urbanization brought with it such problems as slums, poor sanitation, and crime. In 1835 *The People's Magazine* blamed the growth of cities for a new type of young man, characterized as unhealthy, badly postured, pale, and nervous.

Social welfare in the U.S. took a step forward with the formation in Boston of the Association of Delegates from the Benevolent Societies of Boston. Conditions in that city were reported on. Joseph Tuckerman, a clergyman, pioneered in the formation of this association. He also organized during this year the Society for the Prevention of Pauperism. He saw low wages and the uncertainties of seasonal work, among other economic factors, as obstacles to reducing pauperism.

The temperance stories of **Lucius Manlius Sargent** began to appear. Sargent became the most popular writer on this subject. No other temperance stories were as widely circulated or often reprinted in the next 25

Jan. Sen. **Hugh L. White** of Tennessee was nominated for president by independent anti-Jacksonian Democrats in the legislatures of Tennessee and Alabama. John Tyler was his running mate. White won the electoral votes of Tennessee and Alabama in the 1836 election.

Jan. 30 Pres. **Andrew Jackson** was attacked in the first attempt on the life of a U.S. president. Richard Lawrence fired twice while Jackson was attending the funeral of Rep. Warren Ransom Davis of South Carolina, but both shots misfired. Lawrence was later declared insane.

May 20 The **Democratic National Convention** nominated **Martin Van Buren** of New York for the presidency. Richard M. Johnson of Kentucky was nominated for the vice presidency.

July 8 The **Liberty Bell** cracked while it tolled the death of Chief Justice John Marshall, who died on July 6.

Oct. 21 **William Lloyd Garrison,** the noted abolitionist, was rescued from a Boston mob of some 2000 people. He was lodged for safety in the Leverett Street Jail. The mob was angered by his preaching that "all men are created equal. . . . "

Nov. 24 The **Texas Rangers,** a mounted police force, was authorized by the Texas Provincial Government.

Dec. In the **Treaty of New Echota** a faction of the Cherokee Indians in Georgia ceded all Cherokee lands to the U.S. for $5,600,000 and free transportation to the Indian Territory (Oklahoma). The majority of the Cherokees opposed the treaty but were powerless. Forced removal along the Trail of Tears began in 1838.

Dec. 16 The **Anti-Masonic Party** nominated **William Henry Harrison** of Ohio for the presidency and Francis Granger of New York for the vice presidency.

of the Northeast, local customs, and simple American home life as backdrops. She was a pioneer of the American domestic novel.

A *History of the Condition of Women in Various Ages and Nations* by Lydia Maria Child was published. Reflecting the growing interest in feminism in the U.S., the work went through 20 editions in seven years.

Augustus B. Longstreet, Georgia essayist and humorist, drew realistic word pictures of life in Georgia in *Georgia Scenes.* His sketches, first published in newspapers, drew on the distinctive characters, customs, manners, idioms, wit, and pastimes of southern life. Longstreet's success showed U.S. writers that, wherever they were, material lay all around them.

The **New York** *Herald,* a penny daily, was begun by James Gordon Bennett. It soon became pro-Tammany and proslavery. In 1869 it astounded everyone by sending Stanley to Africa to find Livingstone. In 1924 it was merged with the New York *Tribune* to form the *Herald Tribune.*

Washington Irving bought and remodeled a Dutch farmhouse near Tarrytown, N.Y., creating one of the first Gothic Revival buildings in the U.S. Called Sunnyside, it has become one of the most popular literary sites in America.

St. Philip's Church, Charleston, S.C., known as "the Westminster Abbey of South Carolina" because of the number of distinguished men buried in its cemetery, was built in the ornate tradition of the Greek Revival.

1836

The presidential election campaign of 1836 pitted Democratic Vice Pres. Martin Van Buren against a field of three Whig candidates. They were William Henry Harrison, who also ran on the Anti-Masonic ticket; Daniel Webster, representing the North; and Hugh L. White, whose support came from the South and Southwest. The Whig Party hoped the vote would be split enough to throw the election into the House of Representatives, where they had a chance of prevailing. Issues played little part in the campaign. Those who approved of Pres. Andrew Jackson's policies of the past eight years were for Van Buren; those who were anti-Jackson backed a Whig candidate.

A **feminist's petition** to the New York State legislature requesting that it grant married women the right to

This year proved a turning point in American intellectual life. Ralph Waldo Emerson's first book, *Nature,* in which he stated his fundamental philosophy, was published anonymously. Emerson had visited Europe in 1832 and 1833, where he met Thomas Carlyle, William Wordsworth, and Samuel Taylor Coleridge. Through them he was introduced to transcendental thought, derived from Immanuel Kant and German idealism. In *Nature* he set forth the principles of American Transcendentalism, which was to become the most influential school of philosophy of the nineteenth century. Transcendentalism also owed much to the Romantic movement. Emerson expressed a deeply felt love for the natural world in *Nature* and went on to combine

| Business and Industry; Science; Education; Philosophy and Religion **III** | | **IV** Sports; Social Issues and Crime; Folkways; Fashion; Holidays |

range of his system to ten miles. He received a patent in 1840.

Gas lighting for hotel guest rooms and upstairs halls was provided for the first time in the American House in Boston, opened by Lewis Rice.

The **Bowie knife,** according to popular legend, was invented by Col. James Bowie, who died in 1836 at the Alamo in San Antonio, Tex.

Feb. 14   Marietta College in Marietta, Ohio, was chartered under Congregational auspices. Its first degrees were awarded in 1838.

Nov. 23   A machine to manufacture **horseshoes** was patented by Henry Burden of Troy, N.Y., a Scottish immigrant. The machine could produce 60 horseshoes a minute. In the Civil War most of the shoes for Union cavalry came from Burden's plant in Troy.

Dec. 21   Oglethorpe University, originally chartered as Oglethorpe College in Milledgeville, Ga., was founded under Presbyterian auspices. The college awarded its first degrees in 1839. It was moved from Milledgeville to Atlanta, Ga., in 1913, when it became Oglethorpe University.

years. Sargent was a Boston lawyer and antiquary of independent means. He wrote verse in Latin and translated Virgil while maintaining his steady stream of temperance tracts, which were collected in *The Temperance Tales* (6 vols., 1863–1864). An opponent of abolition, he also wrote *The Ballad of the Abolition Blunderbuss* (1861), an attack on Ralph Waldo Emerson and other leaders of the antislavery movement.

A well publicized **ten-mile foot race** at Union Course, L.I., was watched by nearly 30,000 spectators. The offer of $1000 to any man who could run ten miles in less than an hour drew nine contestants. Henry Stannard of Killingsworth, Conn., won. He covered the first mile in 5:36, the last mile in 5:54, and the entire course in 59:44. At the conclusion of the race, amid great jubilation, Stannard leaped on a horse and triumphantly retraced his winning course.

Speaking on **alcohol abuse,** the Rev. Charles Giles, a temperance advocate, declared that 56,000 people in the U.S. were destroyed annually by drink and that "500,000 drunkards are now living in our blessed America, all moving onward to the dreadful verge. What a scene of immolation."

Halley's Comet passed by Earth on its cycle of approximately 76 years. Also this year, Samuel Langhorne Clemens, who would achieve international fame as Mark Twain, was born on Nov. 30. By coincidence, Twain died on Apr. 21, 1910, during the comet's next journey past Earth.

1836

Politics, religion, and education all shaped American thought and action. In the field of education, nothing was more influential than the *Eclectic Readers,* compiled by William Holmes McGuffey, a clergyman and teacher. His first and second readers appeared in 1836, the third and fourth in 1837, the fifth in 1844, and the sixth in 1857. They became almost universally used in the public schools of America and were often revised. After nearly two generations of use, they had sold 122,-000,000 copies. The readers taught literary and moral lessons, and included selected writings of the best English-language authors.

In the 1830s circuses developed into tent shows when acrobatic troupes merged with menageries and equestrian shows. By this time, 30 shows were traveling around the country and one, the Zoological Institute, boasted 47 carriages and wagons, over 100 horses, 14 musicians, and 60 performers. An integral part of the entertainment was a parade heralding the arrival of the circus in a town. Floating theaters in the form of showboats on the Mississippi and Ohio rivers in particular added to the entertainment. The first showboat was built in Pittsburgh, Pa., in 1831.

The political slogan *Tippecanoe and Tyler too* caught the public fancy during this year's presidential campaign. Troops under William Henry Harrison, the Whig

1836 *PRES.* ANDREW JACKSON   198

| Exploration and Settlement; Wars; Government; Civil Rights; Statistics | I | | II | Publishing; Arts and Music; Popular Entertainment; Architecture; Theater |

hold property in their own names was circulated by Ernestine L. Rose. Her petition held five signatures.

1836–1837 In **congressional elections** the Democrats gained four Senate seats for a 30–18 majority over the Whigs, with four seats going to minor parties. In the House they lost 37 seats for a nominal majority of 108–107, with 24 seats going to minor parties.

Mar. 2 **Texas** declared itself an independent republic. Two weeks later it wrote a constitution and organized a government. The new republic sent commissioners George Childress and Robert Hamilton to Washington, D.C., where their authority was not accepted because the U.S. was unwilling to recognize the Republic of Texas.

Mar. 6 **The Alamo,** a fortified mission at San Antonio, Tex., where fewer than 200 Texans were garrisoned, was captured by the Mexican leader Gen. Antonio López de Santa Anna, who had led 3000 troops across the Rio Grande. Every Texan except a mother, a child, and a servant was killed.

Apr. 21 At the **Battle of San Jacinto,** the Texas army under Gen. Sam Houston defeated the Mexican army under Santa Anna. This battle ended the war, and Texas earned its independence from Mexico.

May 25 **Gag rules** were for the first time adopted by the House of Representatives in connection with resolutions on slavery and the right to petition. Congress had been inundated by abolitionists' petitions, especially in an effort to end slavery in the District of Columbia, which the House governed. The House voted to table all such petitions without discussion or action for the rest of the session.

June 15 **Arkansas** was admitted into the Union, the 25th state.

June 28 **James Madison** died at the age of 85. He was buried in a family plot near his estate in Montpelier, Va.

July 2 The **Post Office Department** was directed by Congress to accept newspapers and pamphlets for delivery. The act also ordered that any postmaster intentionally keeping mail from an addressee be fined and imprisoned and lose all rights to serve again. Occasional refusal to deliver abolitionist literature lay behind the act.

July 11 The so-called **species circular** was issued by the Treasury on Pres. Andrew Jackson's orders. It stated that nothing but gold or silver would be received in payment for public lands. Opponents of the president later charged that the circular helped cause the financial panic of 1837.

Sept. 1 The northern part of **Oregon Territory** was given its first American settlement near what today is Walla Walla, Wash., by two missionaries, Dr. Marcus Whitman and H. H. Spalding, their wives, and a friend.

this with a belief in the spiritual nature of reality and the importance of self-reliance.

The shift in focus of **American painters** from classical imitations of the eighteenth century to the study of American landscape is best marked in the work of Thomas Cole. In his *Oxbow of the Connecticut,* painted this year, nature is depicted in its wildness: a storm brews in the background, bending the trees lining the river. Cole made landscape painting a worthy and attractive field.

Shobal Vail Clevenger, formerly an apprentice stone-cutter in the shop of David Guion of Cincinnati, Ohio, emerged at this time as an exceptional sculptor in marble and stone. His many busts of notables were marked by careful workmanship and precision of representation.

Building of the **Washington Monument** in Washington, D.C., was begun from plans by Robert Mills. The monument was outstanding for its freedom from ornamentation in a period when taste ran toward the decorative.

The **Hodges-Field House,** one of the best examples of Greek Revival architecture in the U.S., was built in North Andover, Mass.

James Kirke Paulding, a prolific story writer and interpreter of the New York Dutch, collected a series of his tales dealing with Nieuw Amsterdam in *The Book of Saint Nicholas.* Favorites such as "Cobus Yerks" and "Claas Schlaschenschlinger" were included.

A collection of early *Poems* by **Oliver Wendell Holmes** was published. The collection revealed a jocose spirit that pointed back to the light verse of the eighteenth century. Poems such as the "Ballad of the Oysterman" and "My Aunt" reflect this touch, while pathos is seen in the ever popular "The Last Leaf."

The Abolitionist by William Ellery Channing, the influential Unitarian minister, was published. The work was a powerful statement of his position on the moral implications of slavery.

The celebrated actor **James E. Murdoch** made his New York debut at the Richmond Hill Theater. He was already well known as a star on the road.

James N. Barker produced his play *Court of Love* at the Arch Street Theatre in Philadelphia. Written in 1817 under the title *How to Try a Lover,* but never before played, *Court of Love* was received enthusiastically. Like many of Barker's plays, it was an adaptation of a French work. Barker later said that it was the only one of his many plays that satisfied him.

| Business and Industry; Science; Education; Philosophy and Religion   III | | IV   Sports; Social Issues and Crime; Folkways; Fashion; Holidays |

The **Transcendental Club,** with Ralph Waldo Emerson, A. Bronson Alcott, George Ripley, Henry Hedges, Orestes Brownson, Theodore Parker, Margaret Fuller, William Ellery Channing, Nathaniel Hawthorne, Elizabeth Peabody, Henry David Thoreau, James Freeman Clark, and others as participants, began as a casual discussion group. The group convened frequently, but the note of informality was never lost. The club had no officers, office, or schedule, and membership waxed and waned. One outcome of the Transcendental Club was the beginning, in 1840, of the Transcendental organ, *The Dial.*

Constantine Hering, an immigrant German physician, established the North American Academy of the Homeopathic Healing Art at Allentown, Pa., under a charter granted in 1836. This was the first school of homeopathic therapeutics anywhere. Hering became the outstanding figure in homeopathy in the U.S.

Jan. 9 **Spring Hill College** was chartered in Spring Hill, Ala., under Roman Catholic auspices. The first Roman Catholic college in the deep South, Spring Hill issued its first degree in 1837. It had been founded in 1830.

Jan. 30 **Franklin College** received its charter as Indiana Baptist Manual Labor Institute in Franklin, Ind. It was renamed Franklin College in 1843.

Mar. 23 The **U.S. Mint** produced its first coins made by a press operated by steam power. The press was designed by Franklin Beale.

May 27 **Jay Gould,** who was to become one of the most hated of America's so-called robber barons, was born on his family's farm in Roxbury, N.Y. Christened Jason Gould, he left school at 14, clerked in a store, studied surveying, took a job as a surveyor's assistant at $20 a month, and in 1856 completed a history of Delaware County. By the time he was 21 he had amassed $5000. He bought an interest in a tannery in

candidate, had engaged the Indians at Tippecanoe and beaten them off with heavy losses. Harrison thus became identified with the place. John Tyler, a former Democratic senator from Virginia, was his running mate.

Remember the Alamo was the stirring battle cry of Texans at San Jacinto, where the army of Gen. Antonio López de Santa Anna was routed and revenge taken for the massacre of the previous year. The Alamo, a fort in San Antonio, had been besieged for ten days. After being taken, its defenders were slaughtered. Among the dead were Davy Crockett and James Bowie.

In **horse racing,** the South made up for its loss to the North in 1823 in a return race at the Union Course on Long Island. The southern horse, John Bascombe, defeated Post Boy, taking both heats of a four-mile race. Its times: 7:49 and 7:51½.

The **Union Club,** a gathering place "for gentlemen," was founded in New York City.

William A. Alcott, educational reformer and an arbiter of manners in the U.S., had two of his works published: *The Young Woman's Guide* and *The Young Mother.* He upheld traditional moral standards in both. *The Young Wife* (1837) and *The Young Husband* (1838) extended the scope of his approach to manners of the marriage relationship.

A pledge of **total abstinence** became the official policy of most Protestant ministries, but even before official pressure was exerted, over 300,000 ministers took the pledge.

So-called **cold water societies** were introduced by the Rev. Thomas P. Hunt, who enlisted children, mainly through Sunday schools, in a temperance crusade. Each child was issued a pledge card and sent out to gather signatures of those who agreed to abstain from drink.

Mar. 2 **Texas Independence Day,** a legal holiday in Texas, commemorates drafting and signing of a declaration of independence from Mexico on this date.

Apr. 21 **San Jacinto Day,** a holiday in Texas, commemorates the Battle of San Jacinto.

May 31 The **Astor Hotel** opened in New York City. Built by John Jacob Astor on a plot facing City Hall Park, it was the most impressive hotel in the U.S. and the most fashionable meeting place in New York City.

Oct. 22 **Sam Houston** was sworn in as the first president of the Republic of Texas. He later became a U.S. senator from Texas.

Dec. 7 **Martin Van Buren was elected president** of the United States. The electoral vote was Van Buren, 170; William Henry Harrison, Anti-Masonic candidate, 73; Sen. Hugh L. White of Tennessee, anti-Jacksonian Democrat, 26; Daniel Webster, Massachusetts Whig candidate, 14; and Willie P. Mangum of North Carolina, 11. The popular vote was Van Buren, 761,549; Harrison, 549,567; White, 145,396; Webster, 41,287. None of the four vice presidential candidates received a majority of the electoral votes. The Senate, for the first and only time, had to choose, naming Richard M. Johnson of Kentucky to the office.

American drama was marked by the adaptation of foreign plays. Richard Penn Smith's work was typical. His *The Daughter*, produced in Philadelphia in 1836, was a literal adaptation of a French play; *Actress of Padua* was based on Victor Hugo's *Angelo, Tyran de Padoue;* and *The Bombardement of Algiers* (1829) on a French play by Frédéric du Petit-Méré.

Jan. The first number of *Philanthropist,* one of the most radical antislavery journals in the U.S., was issued by James G. Birney in New Richmond, Ohio, near Cincinnati. Birney left the paper in 1837 when he moved to New York to agitate for abolition. He ran for the presidency on the Liberty Party ticket in 1840 and 1844.

1837

A severe financial panic struck the U.S. in 1837. It was triggered on May 10, when New York banks stopped making payments in specie, but the causes were more deep-seated. Pres. Andrew Jackson's administration had created too much credit. The result was inflation and speculation in western lands. The Specie Circular drained gold and silver to the West. During the year 618 banks failed. A depression followed, bringing widespread unemployment. The panic did not end until 1843.

The **American Peace Society** formally condemned all war.

Jan. 1 The **Distribution Bill** took effect. It was a measure designed to relieve the government of the surplus money collected in the recent period of financial boom. The federal books were to be balanced, a working capital of $5,000,000 set aside, and the rest of the funds distributed to the states in four installments. But when the effects of the financial panic of 1837 hit the nation, the fourth installment was not made.

Jan. 26 **Michigan** was admitted into the Union as the 26th state.

Feb. A New York State law requiring **reports on immigrants,** to be filed by ships' captains as the immigrants landed, was upheld by the U.S. Supreme Court in the case of *New York v. Miln.*

Feb. 6 A **slavery resolution** passed in the House of Representatives asserted that slaves did not have the right of petition given to the people of the U.S. by the Constitution.

While authors such as Nathaniel Hawthorne and Ralph Waldo Emerson were writing novels and essays that are still read and honored, other authors were publishing books of less than permanent quality. A good example of popular taste in historical fiction was a trilogy by William Ware, a Unitarian clergyman. The first part of the trilogy, *Zenobia,* appeared in 1837; the second, *Aurelian,* in 1838; and the final volume, *Julian,* in 1841. These epistolary novels dealt with the political and social struggles of Christians against the Roman Empire.

William Hickling Prescott brought his *History of the Reign of Ferdinand and Isabella* to a conclusion. The work was published in three volumes in 1838 and brought him immediate honor. It was distinctive in its capture of the pageantry of the times. Above all, Prescott's prose was wonderfully readable and has been translated into many languages.

The English visitor **Harriet Martineau** wrote a favorable account of her impressions of the U.S. and its institutions in the book *Society in America,* which became very popular in England and France. Even she, however, remarked that "If the American nation be judged by its literature, it may be pronounced to have no mind at all."

Nick of the Woods by Robert Montgomery Bird, a popular melodramatic novel of backwoods Kentucky, was published. Bird saw the Indian as a vicious, dirty, unforgiving, unforgetting "varmint" deserving extermination. The book has gone through more than 25 printings in the U.S.

| Business and Industry; Science; Education; Philosophy and Religion **III** | | Sports; Social Issues and Crime; Folkways; Fashion; Holidays **IV** |

Pennsylvania and began a career in business and finance that would bring him vast wealth and many enemies.

Dec. 10 **Emory University** received its charter as Emory College in Oxford, Ga. Established under Methodist auspices, Emory College granted its first degrees in 1841. It became Emory University in 1915 and moved to Atlanta, Ga., in 1919.

July 4 The **first white women to cross the Rockies** into the Oregon Territory were Narcissa Prentiss Whitman and Eliza Hart Spalding, wives of missionaries in the party organized by the American Board of Commissioners for Foreign Missions. Success of this expedition greatly stimulated immigration to the Northwest territories.

Nov. 12 The telling phrase *the almighty dollar* was coined by Washington Irving in his story "The Creole Village," which appeared in *The Knickerbocker Magazine* on this date. The full phrase was "The Almighty Dollar, that great object of universal devotion throughout the land."

1837

The U.S. was beginning to develop its own economists. These new economists approached their subject from the point of view of American optimism, in contrast to the pessimism of English economists. Chief among the Americans was Henry C. Carey of Philadelphia, who had gained substantial business experience by running efficiently the large bookstore he inherited from his father. In general, Carey believed in laissez-faire capitalism but favored a protective tariff for American industries. In his three-volume work *Principles of Political Economy* (1837–1840), his economic nationalism was apparent.

John Deere produced his first plow incorporating a steel blade at his blacksmith shop in Grand Detour, Ill. While visiting a sawmill he noticed a smooth-surfaced saw blade and thought that, shaped into a plow blade, it might easily cut furrows in the moist and sticky midwestern soil without clogging. His experiments proved successful and he soon moved to Moline, Ill., where he began to manufacture steel plows. Deere plows, known as singing plows, contributed greatly to the expansion of farming in the Midwest and West.

A report on *Elementary Instruction in Europe* by Calvin Stowe was published. The report was prepared for the Ohio legislature. Stowe, husband of Harriet Beecher Stowe, visited schools in England, Germany, and France and returned with his report, which he delivered to the legislature. The report became the basis for the free common school system of Ohio.

The expansion of **credit facilities** in the U.S. between 1834 and 1837 was facilitated by charters for 194 new banks.

William W. Gerard, a Philadelphia physician, made a significant contribution to American medicine with his

Americans liked showmanship, natural wonders, freaks, and all kinds of believe-it-or-not items. One man in the mid-nineteenth century gave them all this and more. He was Phineas T. Barnum, who began his career this year by exhibiting an old black woman, Joyce Heth. He claimed she was 161 years old and had been George Washington's nurse. She was actually about 80. A crowd of some 10,000 flocked to see her at Niblo's Garden in New York City. In 1842 Barnum opened his American Museum in New York City. There at various times he was to exhibit the original Siamese twins, Chang and Eng, and the Fiji Mermaid, half monkey and half fish. The most popular attraction, though, was Tom Thumb, a dwarf who stood only 40 inches tall. Exhibited in the U.S. and abroad, Thumb was seen by 20,000,000 people.

American **tastes in popular literature** were reflected by the vogue for temperance stories, which began to appear frequently in American magazines. The plots of these stories generally emphasized the evils of drink on the part of sinning husbands, who often died in sorrow. Sentimental stories of this stripe began to replace didactic pieces on temperance such as Lyman Beecher's *Six Sermons*. Temperance annuals and gift books soon became common items in American bookshops.

A Manual of Politeness for Both Sexes published this year gave advice on the disposition of ladies' knees: "To cross them one over the other, and to embrace them with the hands joined, is deemed vulgar."

Mar. 3 **Supreme Court membership** was increased from seven to nine by an act of Congress.

Mar. 3 The **Republic of Texas** was recognized by Pres. Andrew Jackson and approved by Congress.

Mar. 4 **Martin Van Buren was inaugurated president** of the United States. The eighth president, he was the first to be born after the signing of the Declaration of Independence. Conscious of this fact, Van Buren deferentially mentioned it in his inaugural: "Unlike all who have preceded me, the Revolution that gave us existence as one people was achieved at the period of my birth; and whilst I contemplate with gratified reverence that memorable event, I feel that I belong to a later age and that I may not expect my countrymen to weigh my actions with the same kind and partial hand."

Mar. 18 **Grover Cleveland**, 22nd and 24th president of the United States, was born in Caldwell, N.J.

Nov. 7 **Elijah P. Lovejoy was killed** by proslavery rioters at Alton, Ill. His antislavery printing press had previously been smashed several times but was replaced by the Ohio Anti-Slavery Society. Lovejoy became known as the martyr abolitionist.

Dec. 8 **Wendell Phillips** delivered his first abolition speech in Faneuil Hall, Boston, Mass. It was a passionate response to the murder of Elijah P. Lovejoy.

Dec. 29 The *Caroline* **Affair** (1837–1842) began when, on the U.S. shore of the Niagara R. near Buffalo, Canadian authorities seized and burned the American vessel *Caroline*. The ship was leased to run supplies to Navy Island for support of Canadian revolutionaries led by William Lyon MacKenzie. In the fracas an American was killed by a Canadian militiaman. Ultimately the Canadian was acquitted.

Twice-Told Tales by Nathaniel Hawthorne, the author's second book and first collection of tales, was published. Digging deep into chronicles and histories of colonial New England and adding symbolic overtones, Hawthorne achieved some of the finest moral allegory ever written.

The first book of **Charles Dickens** published in America, *The Pickwick Papers*, inaugurated an unmatched popularity for its author.

Thomas Cole produced a masterpiece of the Hudson River school of landscape artists, *In the Catskills*. A resident of the region, Cole as usual romanticized the rural setting. In a clearing surrounded by trees, two figures rest by a winding stream that loses itself in the foliage of the background. In the rear the mountains rise gently.

There were eight **New York City theaters** in operating condition at the beginning of the season: the Bowery, Broadway, Franklin, National, Niblo's, Olympic, Park, and Vauxhall Gardens. For concerts there were Castle Garden and the Richmond Hill Circus.

Mar. 20 *The Prophet of St. Paul's,* a romantic comedy by David Paul Brown, opened in Philadelphia and closed after three performances. Its romantic theme reappeared in later books and plays, notably the celebrated historical novel *When Knighthood Was in Flower* (1898) by Charles Major.

Aug. 31 **Ralph Waldo Emerson** delivered his celebrated *American Scholar* address before the Phi Beta Kappa Society at Harvard. Oliver Wendell Holmes called it "our intellectual Declaration of Independence." Although many previous writers and speakers had dealt with the same theme, Emerson raised the subject to the level of philosophy.

1838

The Underground Railroad was a loosely organized apparatus operated by northern abolitionists to bring slaves from the South and set them free. More than 3000 persons were involved in the effort. The name apparently was first used in 1831. The best known leaders were Levi Coffin, who is said to have assisted 3000 slaves, and Harriet Tubman, an escaped slave. Slaves were passed along from one safe station to another until they reached a free state. Some went on to Canada. By the time of the Civil War, the Underground Railroad

Although the North seemed to supply most of the nation's authors, the South was not without its contributors to the literary world. A worthy example was John Pendleton Kennedy, a lawyer and politician as well as author. His *Swallow Barn* (1832) was a series of sketches about Virginia, written in the manner of Washington Irving. Kennedy wrote two novels, *Horse-Shoe Robinson* (1832) and *Rob of the Bowl* (1838). Although its subject matter was melodramatic, the latter novel was a realistic tale of Maryland in 1681. It concerned an

| Business and Industry; Science; Education; Philosophy and Religion | III | | IV | Sports; Social Issues and Crime; Folkways; Fashion; Holidays |

clinical tests of typhus and typhoid fever. Through the tests he succeeded in differentiating the two dread diseases.

Mar. 18 The **University of Michigan** was chartered in Ann Arbor as a state university. It had been preceded by the founding of another University of Michigan in 1817, but that institution never taught a course on a collegiate level. This second university opened its doors in 1841 and conferred its first degrees in 1845.

Apr. 20 A **state board of education,** probably the first in the U.S., was created by the Massachusetts senate to supervise the public school system. Horace Mann, then president of the state senate, served as secretary of the board until 1848.

Sept. **Samuel F. B. Morse** filed for a patent on his telegraph. It was not granted until 1844.

Nov. 8 **Mt. Holyoke Seminary** opened for classes. The first college in the U.S. intended specifically for women, it had been founded in 1836 by Mary Lyon. It accommodated 80 students; in the next year 400 were turned away for lack of room. Mt. Holyoke established higher standards for admission than had previously been demanded of women. A girl had to be 16, and entrance examinations were required. The course of instruction ran three rather than two years, and it included rudimentary training in home economics; the students cooked and cleaned and spent Monday, their day for recreation, polishing up the school. Diplomas were granted to seniors who successfully passed the final year of chemistry, astronomy, geology, rhetoric, logic, moral philosophy, natural theology, and ecclesiastical history. The initial enrollment was 116, of whom three were graduated at the first commencement, Aug. 23, 1838.

Dec. 29 A portable **combined thresher and fanning mill** earned a patent for the inventors, Hiram Avery and John Avery Pitts of Winthrop, Me. Eventually Hiram moved to Chicago where he manufactured Chicago-Pitts brand threshers, which were widely used throughout the grain belt for more than half a century.

About this time **Amos Lawrence** became a well-known model of the virtuous merchant by his practicing of moral hygiene. Lawrence gave up tea and coffee in 1832, fish, meat, and gravies in 1835, and butter in 1836. Lawrence conducted regular family prayers, conscientiously observed the Sabbath, and contributed to many worthy charities. In the midst of his piety, Lawrence prospered as a landlord and businessman to such an extent that his example was cited as evidence of the rewards of good living. Lawrence died on Dec. 31, 1852. His sons collected his papers, published as *Extracts from the Diary and Correspondence of the Late Amos Lawrence* (1855).

The **American Moral Reform Society** held its first convention in Philadelphia. It adopted a resolution pledging "to practice and sustain the principles of Moral Reform in the United States, especially Education, Temperance, Economy, and Universal Liberty." The convention also praised George Thompson, an English abolitionist, and Benjamin Lundy, a Quaker leader in the antislavery movement. Resolutions were adopted against the custom of donning mourning clothes for the dead and against the pomp and ceremony of funerals on the grounds that this fashion imposed an unfair burden on the poor.

Mustaches, Nathaniel Hawthorne reported, had been adopted among young officers at the Charlestown, Mass., Navy Yard—a fashion imported from England.

Horseback riding for women was characterized in Donald Walker's *Exercises for Ladies.* Walker held that horseback riding tended to consolidate unnaturally the bones of the lower part of the body, causing difficulties in the performance of unspecified future womanly duties.

1838

The **Mormon Church** was going through a difficult period. On Jan. 12, 1838, Joseph Smith, the founder, and his followers left Kirtland, Ohio, partly as a result of the panic of 1837. They moved to Independence, Mo., where they met with hostility, partly because of their beliefs and partly because of their communal economic organization and efficiency. Moving back east in 1839, the Mormons founded Nauvoo, Ill. By 1844 Nauvoo had a population of 15,000 and was the most prosperous city in Illinois. Again, however, the Mormons were

Comparatively brief as American history was, Americans were exceedingly proud of it and were beginning to give a mythological flavor to the Revolutionary War period and its heroes. Foremost among these, of course, was George Washington. In 1832, on the 100th anniversary of Washington's birth, Daniel Webster had declaimed: "His age and his country are equally full of wonders; and of both he is the chief." An attempt in Congress at this time to have the remains of the first president removed from their Mount Vernon, Va., tomb

may have assisted as many as 50,000 slaves to escape bondage, although after the passage of the Fugitive Slave Law of 1850 the number decreased to 500 to 1000 a year.

1838–1839 In congressional elections the Democrats lost two Senate seats but still led the Whigs 28–22. In the House the Democrats picked up 16 seats and the Whigs gained 11, for a Democratic majority of 124–118.

Jan. 5 A neutrality proclamation was issued by Pres. Martin Van Buren, forbidding Americans to take sides in the Canadian insurrection. This was a continuation of the *Caroline* affair. On Jan. 13, Canadian rebels, who had been operating from Navy Island against Canada, surrendered to the U.S. Public opinion in the U.S. at this time was anti-British, and there were numerous border violations. Pres. Van Buren issued a second neutrality proclamation on Nov. 21; he ordered swift punishment of Americans who violated its provisions.

Jan. 26 The first prohibition law in the U.S. was passed in Tennessee, making it a misdemeanor to sell alcoholic beverages in taverns and stores. Later in the year a political storm erupted in Massachusetts over a law prohibiting the sale of alcoholic beverages in amounts of less than 15 gallons, except for "medicinal or mechanical purposes."

Apr. 25 The steamer *Moselle* exploded on the Ohio R. near Cincinnati, Ohio, killing 100 persons.

May 18 Charles Wickes was placed by Congress in command of a naval exploring and surveying expedition of the South Seas. On Aug. 18 his fleet of six ships left Hampton Roads, Va., to explore hundreds of islands of the Pacific; a large sector of Antarctica, later named Wickes Land; and the American Northwest coastline. The expedition returned in July 1842. Wickes's five-volume report was published in 1844.

June 12 A new Iowa Territory, including the two Dakotas and much of Minnesota in addition to Iowa, was formed with its separation from Wisconsin Territory.

June 14 The steamer *Pulaski* exploded off the coast of North Carolina, killing 140 persons.

Oct. 12 The Republic of Texas withdrew its annexation request.

Dec. Cherokee Indians remaining in Georgia and southeastern Tennessee, 14,000 in all, were forcibly removed from their lands by 7000 U.S. soldiers and herded into Oklahoma. The phrase *Trail of Tears* refers to this final tragic act in the enforcement of the fraudulent treaty of New Echota in 1835. Four thousand Cherokees died en route; perhaps 1000 escaped. In the end 7,000,000 acres of Cherokee land had been seized by whites.

attempt by Protestants to overthrow Lord Baltimore, a Catholic.

John Greenleaf Whittier joined the list of authors of books supporting abolition with the publication of his *Ballads and Anti-Slavery Poems.* Noteworthy among the pieces were "To William Lloyd Garrison," "The Hunters of Men," "The Slave Ships," "Stanzas for the Time," "Toussaint L'Ouverture," "Hymn," the extremely popular "Stanzas," and "The Moral Warfare."

James Fenimore Cooper, upon his return from Europe, turned to social criticism in *The American Democrat,* a nonfiction work published in 1838. Though believing in equality of rights, Cooper could not accept equality of conditions. The dangers of democracy from an aristocratic social point of view were cogently presented.

Thomas Cole, a popular painter of romantic landscapes, wrote in his diary: "I am out of place . . . ; there are few persons of real taste; and no opportunity for the true artist to develop his powers. The tide of utility sets against the fine arts." This attitude was common among American artists for several generations. Most known American artists resided in Europe. An indication of their reception in London was shown in the following newspaper comment, referring to the Pall Mall Exhibit, in which many Americans were represented: "The cognoscenti first stared, then wondered, and finally admired."

Lowell Mason finally persuaded the Boston School Committee to authorize its public schools to include music instruction. Mason, who had conducted music classes in the Boston schools without pay during 1837–1838, was appointed the first superintendent of music in a U.S. public school system.

Ole Rynning, a Norwegian farmer and immigrant leader, wrote a book published in Norway and called *A True Account of America for the Information and Help of Peasant and Commoner.* The book started a flow of Scandinavian immigration to the U.S. Early in 1837, Rynning, certain that prospects in the U.S. were brighter for land-poor Norwegian farmers, had persuaded 80 others to emigrate with him. Rynning chose Illinois as the place for their settlement. By Feb. 1838, Rynning had finished his book, which a friend carried

distrusted for their religious beliefs and disliked for their economic competition.

Manila paper was created by John and Lyman Hollingsworth, brothers of South Braintree, Mass., from hemp rope, sails, canvas, etc. Their experiments were stimulated by the panic of 1837, which left them with no money and no stock for their paper business. A patent was issued to them in 1843.

Standardized brass clock works were first introduced by Chauncey Jerome of Bristol, Conn. His one-day brass clock sold for $2.00, compared with $40 for a wooden clock. Jerome soon was manufacturing 600 clocks a day.

Turnpikes in Pennsylvania now totaled 2500 miles. Their cost was $37,000,000.

Railroads were declared legal carriers of U.S. mails by Congress. The use of the stage, which had previously conveyed the mails, declined after 1838 when a presidential message went by rail from Philadelphia to New York City one hour faster than the stage could carry it. However, mail stages remained in use for many years in areas between rail lines.

Apr. 23 The **first transatlantic steamship service** began with the arrival in New York harbor of the steamer *Great Western* after less than 16 days at sea. The previous day the *Sirius* had arrived from England. Both ships were British steam-sail packets. For the next generation Great Britain led the world in transatlantic steamer service. Scheduled service was not established until 1840.

Dec. 26 **Wake Forest College** was chartered in Wake Forest, N.C. It had been founded under Baptist auspices in 1834. It granted its first degrees in 1839.

Dec. 28 **Greensboro College** was first chartered as Greensborough Female College in Greensborough, N.C. Sponsored by Methodist groups, Greensborough Female College awarded its first degrees in 1913

and reburied in the capital city caused bitter debate. Southerners refused to have such a precious possession moved even a few miles north.

The term **Trail of Tears** referred to the route taken by the Cherokee Indians on their removal from Georgia to new lands in Oklahoma. The Indians were forced into prison camps by troops under Gen. Winfield Scott. The first migration began in October. Conservative estimates placed the Indian death toll at 10% of the population. The removal had been legalized by the Treaty of New Echota in 1835.

The expression **Here she goes; there she goes!** achieved great popularity through an advertising stunt. In front of the Bradshaw Hotel in Harlem a man sat and in unison with a large pendulum clock repeated the sentence over and over. Crowds collected, and soon Bradshaw's became a popular gathering place. A play, *The Old Clock; or, Here She Goes—There She Goes,* was produced at the Franklin Theater this year.

Quack remedies dominated the advertising space of the New York *Herald* and the Boston *Transcript.* On one day the *Herald* printed 130 inches of advertising, of which 54 were devoted to doctors and their nostrums. Advertising figures for the *Transcript* were 224 and 134 inches respectively.

The celebrated English exponent of **phrenology,** George Combe, came to the U.S., beginning a two-year lecture tour. Combe succeeded in making phrenology fashionable through his lectures and textbooks.

A comment on the **dangers of drink** was made by Eliphalet Nott, president of Union College in Schenectady, N.Y., who declared to his students that such a large number of drunkards had died from internal fires caused by alcoholic fumes "that I presume no person of information will be found to call the reality of their existence [internal fires] into question."

Jan. **U.S. newspapers** were given a modern-sounding criticism in the *American Monthly Review:* "The newspaper now is a lame thing, and quite uniform from New York to Maine, Arkansas and Mississippi."

Mar. 3 **Dinner conversation** was the subject of advice in the New York *Mirror,* which recommended to male readers: "When you are seated next a lady, you should be only polite during the first course; you may be gallant in the second; but you must not be tender till the dessert."

Dec. 15 A **wise saying** of Benjamin Franklin's *Poor Richard's Almanack* was echoed, with considerable loss of brevity, in the New York *Mirror:* "Keep your

Dec. 11 The so-called **Atherton Gag** was adopted by the House of Representatives. Named for a New Hampshire representative, Charles G. Atherton, this was the 1838 version of the 1836 gag rule that tabled automatically any petition to discuss slavery in the House.

back to Norway and which became known as the "America Book." It described all aspects of American life. Rynning died of malaria in late 1838.

1839

An unusual incident involving a mutiny on a slave ship added to the tension between North and South. A Spanish ship, the *Amistad,* sailed from Havana, Cuba, in June 1839 with 54 black slaves aboard. An uprising by the slaves on July 1, in which two men were killed, gave them control of the ship and they attempted to sail to Africa. However, the vessel was captured by a U.S. Navy ship off Long Island. Slave interests, led by Sec. of State John Forsyth, attempted to turn the slaves over to Spain. Abolitionists brought suit to prevent this, and the case reached the Supreme Court, which in Mar. 9, 1841, found that the slaves had been illegally kidnaped and set them free. Former Pres. John Quincy Adams defended the blacks.

Theodore Dwight Weld, Massachusetts abolitionist, issued *American Slavery as It Is,* a report on the evils of slavery culled from southern newspapers and the eyewitness testimony of former slaves and Southern abolitionists. In this important work he was assisted by Angelina Grimké, daughter of a South Carolina slaveholder, whom he married in 1839. Weld is credited with gaining important converts to the abolitionist cause. Harriet Beecher Stowe credited Weld's book with inspiring her *Uncle Tom's Cabin.*

In Albany County, N.Y., the **Antirent War,** also known as the Helderberg War after the mountain group in the area, broke out when tenant farmers resisted the attempts of the descendants of Stephen Van Rensselaer to collect back rent. Sporadic conflicts continued until 1846, when Gov. Silas Wright moved to solve the crisis through legislation. The result was the New York State constitution of 1846, which outlawed the practice of perpetual leases on the old Dutch patroonships, and provided for a just settlement of the conflict.

Feb. 12 The **Aroostock War** began with the seizure of Rufus McIntire, a U.S. land agent sent to the Aroostock region between New Brunswick, Canada, and Maine, to expel Canadian lumberjacks who had entered the disputed area. The boundary question had been an Anglo-American issue since 1783 and had never been satisfactorily settled. After McIntire's arrest, Maine and New Brunswick called out their militias, and the Nova Scotia legislature appropriated war funds. Congress authorized a conscription of 50,-000 men and voted $10,000,000 toward the

In architecture the Gothic Revival, beginning in the late 1830s, competed with the earlier Classic Revival. Copying the tall towers and pointed arches of the Middle Ages, the Gothic style was used primarily for churches, schools, and libraries, but was adapted to country houses also. The first important architect of the Gothic Revival was Richard Upjohn, who in 1839 was given the task of rebuilding Trinity Church in New York City. His design was soon copied by other churches. James Renwick was also a leading architect of the style. He planned beautiful Grace Church in New York City (1843–1846), and was then chosen in 1853 to be the architect for St. Patrick's Cathedral, also in New York City. This was the most ambitious structure of the Gothic Revival. In the field of country houses and landscape gardening, Andrew Jackson Downing was the leading figure. His book, *Treatise on the Theory and Practice of Landscape Gardening Adapted to North America,* appeared in 1841. It at once became the standard work in its field, going through ten editions.

The formation of the **American Art Union** in New York City stimulated popular appreciation of classics in the fine arts. The union's activities were financed by subscription, and paintings purchased by excess funds were raffled off to subscribers on Christmas night. This practice violated New York State's antilottery laws and led to dissolution of the organization.

An Englishman, **Alexander Forbes,** wrote *California,* the first book in English about the territory. A businessman, Forbes stopped off at Yerba Buena (San Francisco) on a voyage to the Pacific and saw the possibilities of the new land. He urged the British government to take over the territory before Russian or American settlers pushed into it. To make the territory more accessible, he suggested cutting a canal across the Isthmus of Panama.

Voices of the Night, the first collection of poems by Henry Wadsworth Longfellow, was published. This year also saw the publication of *Hyperion,* a prose romance. Longfellow did not gain fame as a poet until the publication of *Evangeline* in 1847.

Business and Industry; Science; Education; Philosophy and Religion III		IV Sports; Social Issues and Crime; Folkways; Fashion; Holidays

when it became Greensboro College for Women. It became coeducational and was renamed Greensboro College in 1920.

head cool by temperance, your feet warm by exercise, rise early and go soon to bed; and if you are inclined to get fleshy, keep your eyes open and your mouth shut."

1839

Increased attention was now being paid to education: in requiring school attendance, in providing free public schools, and in teacher education. The leader in the field was Horace Mann of Massachusetts. It was through his efforts that in 1839 the first state-supported school to educate teachers was established in the U.S., in Massachusetts. As secretary of the state board of education there, Mann instituted longer school terms, insisted on better schoolhouses, and secured higher pay for teachers. His successful upgrading of education influenced states throughout the nation.

The **first photographic equipment** in the U.S. was brought from Paris by Samuel F. B. Morse, painter and inventor. Morse had learned the process from Louis Daguerre, and he made the first daguerreotype portraits in America.

Vulcanized rubber was first made by Charles Goodyear, after many failed experiments. This was the first successful attempt to make rubber nonsticky and solid at high temperatures. Rubber had interested inventors for years but none had succeeded in creating a product that did not melt easily when subjected to heat. Goodyear made his first tests with rubber while in jail for debt in 1834. His ultimate success was the result of an accident—he dropped a mixture of sulfur and rubber on top of a hot stove, thereby discovering a process he called vulcanization. Goodyear secured patents for his process and made arrangements for royalties, but he became entangled in lawsuits. At the time of his death in 1860, he was $200,000 in debt.

The importance of **wheat** as a cash crop was increasing steadily. In 1839 production amounted to 84,823,-000 bushels. Ten years later the number had climbed to 100,485,000 bushels. By the 1840s large areas of Iowa and Nebraska were being used to grow wheat. Canals and railroads were used to transport the bulky crop, and by 1840 there were 4354 grist mills in the U.S. to grind the wheat into flour. Large mills were located in Baltimore, Buffalo, and Rochester.

Even though a commission reported in 1908 that Gen. Abner Doubleday, veteran of the Mexican and Civil wars, had invented baseball in 1839 at Cooperstown, N.Y., hardly anyone credits this story any more. Too many other similar games, such as rounders, played mostly by children, antedated 1839. In addition, the game lacked many phases of its development until later in the century, when it became the American national sport. The first organized baseball team of which much is known was the Knickerbocker Base Ball Club in New York, organized in 1842. Three years later the club found a permanent home at the Elysian Fields in Hoboken, N.J., and adopted a set of rules.

The **first woman horse thief** of record in the U.S., Josephine Amelia Perkins achieved notoriety by a confession that was published with the following description of herself: "A young woman, who, in early life was deservedly esteemed for her exemplary behavior, yet for three years last past (friendless and unprotected) has been unhappily addicted to a criminal propensity, more singular and surprising in its nature (for one of her sex) than can be found on record; in the commission of which, she has been four times detected, twice pardoned on account of her sex, once for reasons of supposed insanity, and the fourth and last time, convicted and sentenced to two years imprisonment in Madison County jail, Kentucky. Annexed is a well-written Address to Parents and Children." Miss Perkins was born in Devonshire, England, in 1818. She stole her first horse from her father to make an elopement journey of 117 miles. Through a series of misadventures, she landed in America without any money and with only the clothes on her back. Her career in horse stealing soon began.

The **sale of alcoholic beverages** in amounts of less than a gallon was prohibited in Mississippi.

prosecution of this action. Calmer voices prevailed: Gen. Winfield Scott arranged a truce, and both parties agreed to refer the dispute to a boundary commission. The issue was settled in 1842 by the Webster-Ashburton Treaty.

Nov. 13 The **Liberty Party,** an antislavery party, held its first national convention at Warsaw, N.Y. It nominated James G. Birney of New York for president. Birney, a former Kentuckian and slaveholder, wielded strong political influence in western New York and the Ohio R. Valley. Francis J. Lemoyne was nominated for vice president.

Dec. 4–7 The **Whig National Convention nominated William Henry Harrison** for the presidency. John Tyler of Virginia was nominated for the vice presidency.

The Green Mountain Boys by Daniel Pierce Thompson, a novel blending romance, adventure, and history and set during the early days of Vermont, was published. Less imaginative than James Fenimore Cooper, Thompson was able nonetheless to win, through his narrative ability, a huge readership. By 1860 *The Green Mountain Boys* had gone through 50 printings.

Plans for a new **Trinity Church** at Wall St. and Broadway were submitted by architect Richard Upjohn, who was soon commissioned for the project. Founded in 1697, Trinity Church had received valuable land endowments from Queen Anne in 1705; these endowments ultimately made it the wealthiest church in New York City. The new church building, the first in the U.S. in a relatively pure Gothic style, was the third on the site. It was completed in 1846.

1840

The presidential election campaign of 1840 was something new in American life, engaging as it did in the use of slogans, parades, campaign hats, and mud-slinging. The Democrats renominated Pres. Martin Van Buren, but could not agree on a vice presidential candidate. The Whigs nominated William Henry Harrison of Ohio and, for vice president, John Tyler of Virginia. The Democrats ran on a platform that emphasized strict construction of the Constitution. They opposed congressional interference with slavery, a national bank, and internal improvements paid for by the federal government. The Whigs, on the other hand, based their campaign on personalities. They pictured Van Buren as luxury-loving and aristocratic. Most of all, they made use of a remark of a Democratic newspaper, the Baltimore *Republican,* "that upon condition of his receiving a pension of $2000 and a barrel of cider, Gen. Harrison would no doubt consent to withdraw his pretensions, and spend his days in a log cabin on the banks of the Ohio." The Whigs used this statement to run a "Log Cabin and Hard Cider" campaign. They presented the hero of the Battle of Tippecanoe as a simple man of the people, although he came from an aristocratic Virginia family. The Whig campaign song was "Tippecanoe and Tyler Too," with a refrain, "Van, Van is a used up man." Their placards portrayed Harrison at the door of a log cabin, welcoming visitors to his humble home.

The U.S. **Census** recorded a population of 17,069,453. The center of population was placed 16 miles south of Clarksburg, W.Va.

Approximately 40,000 **Indians** from the Five Civilized Nations of the East, the Cherokee, Creek, Seminole, Choctaw, and Chickasaw, were resettled in Indian Territory by this time. Most of the tribes were organized

Magazines with high standards and espousing particular points of view were established in this period. The most notable was *The Dial,* first published in July 1840 and lasting only until April 1844. It was the voice of the transcendentalists and was edited by Margaret Fuller. It published articles by Ralph Waldo Emerson, Henry David Thoreau, Theodore Parker, and others. *The Living Age* was founded in 1844 by Eliakim Littel and edited by him until his death in 1870. It was a general magazine of fiction, poetry, and comment. *Brownson's Quarterly Review* was also first published in 1844, by Orestes Brownson; it reflected Brownson's conversion to Catholicism. *The Southern Literary Messenger* was founded in Richmond, Va., in 1834, while the year before James Hall had brought out the *Illinois Monthly Magazine,* the first literary magazine west of the Ohio R.

Panorama-type painting, a forerunner of a sort of twentieth-century documentary film, flourished during this period. Canvases were rolled on one or two drums, and unfolded yard by yard to the spectator, often taking an hour and a half for the presentation. A famous panoramic painter was John Banvard. His Mississippi R. scenic series was advertised as three miles long; it depicted 1200 miles of scenery.

Two Years Before the Mast by Richard Henry Dana, Jr., an American classic dealing with the nineteenth-century maritime industry, was published. The book drew on the author's experience as a sailor to the West Coast and back (1834–1836). A sensitive man, Dana was revolted by the cruelty, especially the flogging, aboard ship, and later was instrumental in having the practice outlawed. His realistic approach to writing about life at

| Business and Industry; Science; Education; Philosophy and Religion | III | | IV | Sports; Social Issues and Crime; Folkways; Fashion; Holidays |

Jan. 7 The **first silver-mining company** in the U.S., the Washington Mining Company, was chartered in North Carolina to work the newly discovered Silver Hill Mine near Lexington, N.C. The company began mining operations in 1842.

Feb. 11 The **University of Missouri** in Columbia, Mo., was originally chartered as the University of the State of Missouri. State-supported, the university issued its first degrees in 1843. The name was changed to University of Missouri in 1913.

The **Olympic Theater** in New York City was reopened by William Mitchell as a cut-rate house that specialized in the production of burlettas and musical novelties. The price of boxes was 50 cents, and seats went for 25 cents. This liberal policy pleased particularly the men of the city, who made the Olympic a "fashionable resort" and "honored it with their constant patronage for the next ten years."

1840

Dentistry was about to become a separate profession and the U.S. took the lead. The first dental school in the world, the Baltimore College of Dental Surgery, was founded this year in Baltimore, Md. It later became part of the University of Maryland. Chapin Aaron Harris, a pioneer in the field, was the founder. The previous year he had established the *American Journal of Dental Science* and in 1840 helped organize the American Society of Dental Surgeons.

Railroads in the U.S. now ran over 2818 miles of track.

An early **astronomical observatory** in America was constructed at Harvard by William Cranch Bond. For a decade his observatory had been his home in Dorchester.

The first normal **transatlantic steamer service** was inaugurated by the British and North American Royal Mail Steam Packet Company (now the Cunard Steamship Company).

Railroad investment continued in the 1840s, and complicated financial schemes were adopted to serve their rapid expansion. Soon, financiers found ways of milking railroad funds, although not on a scale comparable with the financial manipulations that occurred after the Civil War.

Dr. **Willard Parker** opened the first clinic in an American college at the College of Physicians and Surgeons, New York City. Later, in 1850, Parker performed the first cystotomy in the U.S.

An indication of the social issues confronting Americans during this period was the burgeoning of societies and associations formed to improve health, labor conditions, moral values, education, and other social conditions. The Washington Temperance Society, formed this year by a small group, held a series of meetings in which alcoholics discussed their problems with one another. Within three years the society claimed that 500,000 intemperate drinkers and 100,000 confirmed alcoholics had reformed under its auspices. As early as 1834 the North Carolina Temperance Society had 50 branches with 4700 members. A temperance novel, *My Mother's Gold Ring*, by Lucius Manlius Sargent, was published in 1833 and sold 113,000 copies. What had begun as a movement for temperance in drinking alcoholic beverages turned into a moral crusade for total abstinence, led primarily by Protestant clergymen. Many employers backed the drive on the grounds that nondrinking workers would be more efficient. Among laymen, Neal Dow of Maine was the foremost champion of temperance. He made his first temperance speech when he was 24 and in 1838 was instrumental in the founding of the Maine Temperance Union.

The expression *O.K.* came into popular use this year. The first recorded use of the term was in the Boston *Morning Post* of Mar. 23, 1839, as the initials of the jocularly misspelled phrase *oll korrect*. It came into use in Boston and New York City, then in the presidential election of 1840 was used also to mean *Old Kinderhook*, a reference to Martin Van Buren, whose birthplace and home were in Kinderhook, N.Y.

into self-governing republics, patterned after the U.S. government, with written constitutions and laws.

Capt. **Gabriel J. Rains,** serving in the campaign against the Seminole Indians, began to experiment with the first land mines. Their first significant use by Rains, then an officer of the Confederate Army, was in 1862 at Yorktown and Williamsburg, Va.

1840–1841 In **congressional elections** the Whigs gained six Senate seats for a 28–22 majority over the Democrats, with two seats held by minor parties. In the House the Whigs gained 15 seats for a 133–102 majority, with six seats going to minor parties.

Jan. 8 A **gag rule** was again adopted in Congress by a House resolution. It stated that no petition or resolution concerning the abolition of slavery "shall be received by this House, or entertained in any way whatever."

Jan. 13 A **ship fire** caused the death of 140 persons when the steamboat *Lexington* caught fire near Eaton's Neck, N.Y.

Jan. 19 The **U.S. expedition** to the South Seas led by Capt. Charles Wilkes laid claim to a portion of the continent of Antarctica for the U.S.

May 5 The **Democratic National Convention** nominated **Pres. Martin Van Buren** for a second term. The convention was unable to agree on a vice presidential candidate.

Dec. 2 **William Henry Harrison was elected president** of the United States. John Tyler of Virginia was elected vice president in a Whig landslide. The electoral vote was Harrison, 234; Martin Van Buren, incumbent Democrat, 60. The popular vote was Harrison, 1,275,017; Van Buren, 1,128,702; James G. Birney, Liberty Party candidate, 7059.

sea set the standard for later writers.

James Fenimore Cooper returned to the American frontier and the Leather Stocking series in his novel *The Pathfinder,* a tale set during the French and Indian War. Most of the action in the novel was set near Fort Oswego on Lake Ontario.

This year marked the high point in the career of **Nathaniel Parker Willis,** co-editor of the New York *Mirror,* sometime poet and dramatist, and widely traveled author of sketches and worldly essays and letters for American journals. Two of his romantic tragedies had been recent successes, *Bianca Viscati* (1837) and *Tortessa the Usurer* (1839). This year he published *Loiterings of Travel* and *American Scenery,* both collections of pieces previously published in magazines. He also employed Edgar Allan Poe as literary critic of the New York *Mirror.* In contrast to his friend Poe, Willis was the best-paid magazine writer of the period. At one time he was receiving $100 a month from four magazines for his stories and sketches. Nevertheless, he left little mark on American literature.

Tales of the Grotesque and Arabesque, the first collection of short stories by Edgar Allan Poe, was published in Philadelphia in Dec. 1839 but bore the date 1840 on its title page. The two-volume collection included such classic tales of the macabre as "MS. Found in a Bottle," "The Fall of the House of Usher," and "William Wilson." Although Poe was gaining a substantial literary reputation, he failed to find a wide readership or any financial security from his writing. He spent his entire career in virtual penury.

1841

For the first time a vice president succeeded to the presidency because of the death of an incumbent. William Henry Harrison, 68, who caught cold at his inauguration on Mar. 4, died of pneumonia on Apr. 4. Harrison was succeeded by Vice Pres. John Tyler who, although he had run on the Whig ticket, was not a Whig at heart. He had previously supported the Democrat, Pres. Andrew Jackson, in 1828 and 1832, and had major political disagreements with the northern, conservative wing of the Whig Party. His administration was characterized by bickering and frustration, as Henry Clay and Daniel Webster tried to control Tyler and shape the Whig Party to their own interests.

Mar. 4 **William Henry Harrison was inaugurated president** of the United States. John Tyler was inaugurated vice president. Harrison, the ninth president and the

A new literary genre, the detective story, was created in the U.S. this year. It was introduced by Edgar Allan Poe with "The Murders in the Rue Morgue." The story appeared in the April issue of *Graham's Lady's and Gentleman's Magazine,* of which Poe was editor. Poe followed this with "The Mystery of Marie Rogêt" in 1842–1843 and "The Purloined Letter" in 1845. The forerunner of the modern fictional detective appeared in these stories in the person of C. Auguste Dupin, an amateur who demonstrated his ability to find and analyze clues that baffled the police. Thus Poe introduced the puzzling crime, the eccentric detective, his loyal but unperceptive companion, the dull-witted policeman, the surprise solution, and the rational explanation. These works of Poe were popular, but it was later in the century that detective stories by foreign authors such as

Business and Industry; Science; Education; Philosophy and Religion III	IV Sports; Social Issues and Crime; Folkways; Fashion; Holidays

Photography of the moon was accomplished for the first time by John William Draper, a physicist and astronomer at New York University. Draper's photograph of the moon was not impressive by later standards, but it foreshadowed America's pioneering role in astronomical photography. Draper also had the distinction of being the first photographer to capture an image showing a human subject with eyes open.

The **American Society of Dental Surgeons,** the first national association of dentists, was founded in New York City. Dr. Horace A. Hayden was prominent among the founders and among U.S. dentists who established dentistry as a profession.

The Beacon, a leading antireligious magazine, began publication in New York City. It linked the rights of labor to the repudiation of all religious doctrines. It was a typical effort of the times in seeking to popularize such challenges to organized religion as deism and agnosticism, while appealing at the same time for greater social justice.

Mar. 2 **Bethany College** was chartered in Bethany, W.Va., under the auspices of the Disciples of Christ. Its first degrees were granted in 1844.

Mar. 4 The **University of Richmond** was first chartered in Richmond, Va., as Richmond College. Founded by Baptist groups in 1830, the college issued its first degrees in 1849 and became a university in 1920.

Mar. 31 A **ten-hour workday** was established by executive order for all federal employees engaged on public works. It had long been a goal of U.S. labor.

Growing poverty in New York City led to the organization of more than 30 relief agencies in the city.

The **World's Anti-Slavery Convention** in London refused to admit several women delegates who had been sent to the convention by American antislavery societies. Mrs. Lucretia Mott, one of the rejected delegates, became a leading champion of women's rights in America.

Hydrotherapy was introduced into America at this time. It was a health fad fashioned after the popular water cures of Vincent Priessnitz in Europe. By the 1850s there were some 27 hydropathic sanitariums in America. Establishments like the one at Saratoga Springs, N.Y., became gathering points for members of high society.

The **first international cricket match** in which a U.S. team participated took place in Toronto, Canada, where an underrated New York club beat the Toronto club by the margin of one run. Stakes for the match were $500 a side.

1841

Nativism, chiefly an anti-Catholic movement, increased as the number of Catholic immigrants grew. By 1841 it began to involve education. At this time there were about 200 parochial schools in the country. In New York, on Oct. 29, Bishop John Joseph Hughes urged state support for such schools and encouraged Catholics to use their votes to achieve this purpose. His efforts led to the establishment of an independent Catholic school system, and aroused anger and fear among many American Protestants. Agitation over government support for parochial schools contributed to the founding of the Native American Party, which consisted of Protestants who saw a conspiracy on the part of the growing Catholic population and especially its clergy. Riots resulted, including an attack on Bishop Hughes's home in 1842.

Foreign visitors continued to arrive in the U.S., look about them, return home, and publish their impressions. Perhaps the most indefatigable of all, both as to miles traveled and words written, was James Buckingham, a British lecturer and a member of Parliament. He made a four-year tour of the U.S., from 1837 to 1840. In 1841 appeared his *America: Historical, Statistical, and Descriptive,* in two volumes. In the following year he published four more volumes, two devoted to the eastern and western states and two to the slave states. His encyclopedic approach yielded a more or less impartial guide. In one observation he found upstate New York frugal and staid, but New York City speculative and extravagant.

first Whig president, refused to wear a jacket during the inauguration. He caught pneumonia and died on Apr. 4. John Tyler was sworn in as the tenth president of the United States. Harrison was buried at North Bend, Ohio. Tyler was the first person to succeed to the presidency because of the death of a president.

May The **first covered wagon train to California** departed from Sapling Grove in northeastern Kansas. At the end of October the wagon train reached the Stanislaus R. The expedition followed it into central California and reached present-day Sonora in early November.

June 12 A bill to establish a **Fiscal Bank of the U.S.** was introduced in the Senate. Approved by the Senate (July 28) and the House (Aug. 6), it was vetoed by Pres. Tyler on the grounds that it did not specify that state approval for branch banks would be required for the banks to be established. A second act, which also omitted this stipulation, was also vetoed by Tyler. The Whig leadership was enraged by Tyler's veto. They believed Tyler had agreed to sign the bill and that he had reneged on a promise.

Aug. 9 A **steamboat fire** took 175 lives when the *Erie* burned on Lake Erie.

Aug. 19 A **federal bankruptcy law** was enacted by Congress as a result of the panic of 1837. The law was repealed in 1843 when state insolvency laws came into force. Other federal laws were enacted in 1874 and 1898, after periods of economic disaster.

Sept. 11 Pres. **Tyler's entire Cabinet resigned,** with the exception of Sec. of State Daniel Webster, because of Tyler's bank bill veto.

Oct. 27 What came to be called the *Creole incident* began when the U.S. brig *Creole* sailed from Hampton Roads, Va. At sea its cargo of slaves mutinied and took over the vessel, then made for the Bahamas, where the mutineers were arrested and the crew allowed to go free. Sec. of State Daniel Webster, arguing that the slaves were on an American vessel and therefore subject to U.S. law, led the attempt to recover the slaves. Rep. Joshua Giddings, Whig of Ohio, introduced a series of resolutions (Mar. 21–22, 1842) against federal sanction of slavery, and particularly against the coastal slave trade, and was censured (Mar. 23, 1842). He resigned from Congress but was returned the next month by his constituents in a special election.

Wilkie Collins and Arthur Conan Doyle brought wide readership of the genre. Nevertheless, Poe brought this distinct form of fiction to a level matched by only a few later writers.

Essays (first series) by Ralph Waldo Emerson appeared. His second series of *Essays* was published in 1844. Initially both books had only a small sale, but with the advent of the "cheap libraries" of the 1870s and 1890s the *Essays* reached best-seller status. Transcendentalism found its best expression in these essays.

The Deerslayer by James Fenimore Cooper, the last of the frontier novels known as the Leather-Stocking Tales, was published. Leatherstocking, also called Natty Bumppo and Hawkeye, was shown in his youth, skillful in the hunt, resourceful, tough, and sinewy. Above all he was virtuous, sincere, and unspoiled by civilization. When asked about his church, he replied: "I am in church now; I eat in church, drink in church, sleep in church. The 'arth is the temple of the Lord. . . . "

The Big Bear of Arkansas by Thomas Bangs Thorpe was published. A tall tale of Arkansas, noted for its broad exaggeration and studied blend of colorful characters and impossible experiences, it brought its author great popularity.

Henry Wadsworth Longfellow gained wide readership with the publication of his *Ballads and Other Poems,* in which he displayed a spirited narrative technique. Poems such as "The Skeleton in Armor" and "The Wreck of the Hesperus" have become part of the American folk heritage. In seven years the Longfellow collection went through ten printings.

Andrew Jackson Downing published his *Treatise on the Theory and Practice of Landscape Gardening.* Downing was the first great American landscape gardener and horticulturist.

Hibernian Hall, Charleston, S.C., was built in 1841, the heyday of Greek Revival. Its hexastyle Ionic portico was one of the best in the U.S.

Apr. 10 The **New York** *Tribune,* edited and published by Horace Greeley, began publication. A prominent figure in the Whig Party, Greeley skillfully built the paper into a Whig, and later a Republican, publication of great influence. In September he merged his earlier periodicals, *The New Yorker* and *The Log Cabin,* into the *Weekly Tribune.*

1842

A turning point in U.S.-British relations came with the signing on Aug. 9, 1842, of the Webster-Ashburton Treaty, which settled several matters between the two nations. The treaty took its name from Sec. of State

Growing interest in classical music was indicated by the number of musical organizations founded in the mid-nineteenth century. Foremost among them was the New York Philharmonic Society, established on Apr. 2,

| Business and Industry; Science; Education; Philosophy and Religion   III | | Sports; Social Issues and Crime; Folkways; Fashion; Holidays   IV |

The **earliest commercial use for oil** in the U.S. was found by Samuel M. Kier. When seepage oil began this year to flow from his father's salt wells at Tarentum, Pa., he decided to peddle it bottled as a cure for most ills. His first sales medium was the "medicine road show," but soon he was distributing oil through druggists as Kier's Rock Oil. Later, Kier refined his oil for purposes of illumination, and so is regarded as the pioneer oil refiner in the U.S.

A famous sermon by the Rev. **Theodore Parker,** "The Transient and Permanent in Christianity," caused a sensation at the South Boston Unitarian Church, where it was delivered at an ordination ceremony. It led ultimately to Parker's virtual ostracism, even by fellow Unitarians, and to denunciation in the press by the orthodox. Parker held that the ritualistic elements of Christianity were transient expressions of particular churches in particular periods in history. The permanent quality of Christianity derived, as Parker put it, from the rational truth of the teachings of Jesus rather than from His personal authority. Parker recommended that contemporary Christians imitate Jesus's way of worshipping God directly, with no mediator.

The **Brook Farm Association** was created by members of the Transcendental Club to apply their theories in an experimental cooperative community on a farm nine miles from Boston. A stock company was formed, with George Ripley as its prime organizer and first manager. On April 1 he and his wife and some 20 others began seeking a life balanced between manual labor and intellectual pursuits. Emerson was a party to discussions but never committed himself. Hawthorne and two other transcendentalists lived at Brook Farm for a period. The experiment ended after a serious fire in 1847, with the problems of combining plain living and high ideals unresolved.

The nickname **"Old Fuss and Feathers"** was coined by soldiers to characterize the vain and pompous Gen. Winfield Scott. A stickler for Army dress and etiquette, he used to parade before his troops in a feathered hat.

The unofficial **boxing championship** was claimed by Tom Hyer, son of the previous claimant, Jacob Hyer. Young Tom was challenged by John McCluster. Hyer, who weighed 205 pounds, defeated McCluster in short order.

Dorothea Dix began a long, energetic campaign to eliminate mistreatment of the insane. She embarked on a two-year investigation of conditions in Massachusetts almshouses and houses of correction, where the insane often were kept in cages, cellars, stalls, or pens. By 1854 she had influenced the legislatures of 11 states to remove the insane from such places and put them under medical care. A law sponsored by Miss Dix authorizing a $12,000,000 appropriation for maintenance of insane asylums was passed by Congress in 1854 but vetoed by Pres. Franklin Pierce.

The **social responsibility of newspapers** was a concern of Horace Greeley as he launched his New York *Tribune* this year. Greeley promised to exclude from his pages "the unmoral and degrading Police Reports, Advertisements, and other matters which have been allowed to disgrace the columns of our leading Penny Papers," and to exert every effort to render the *Tribune* "worthy of the beauty approved of the virtuous and refined, and a welcome visitant to the family fireside."

The current vogue in **ladies' dresses,** *Godey's Lady's Book* commented, was for tight sleeves. Further, it predicted that the style would last and "again exhibit the beautiful contour of a lady's arm." Yet bare limbs were not proper. Ladies who attended summer resorts were warned against "brocade breakfast dresses" with sleeves and necklines so short that they caused brothers to blush "through the tediousness of three courses and dessert."

New York society was characterized by James Buckingham in his *America: Historical, Statistical, and Descriptive,* as follows: upstate, frugal and staid; New York City, speculative, extravagant, and loaded with *nouveaux riches.*

1842

Of the nineteenth-century advances in medical science, none was more welcome to patients than the development of anesthetics. The properties of chloroform had been discovered in 1831, but it was not used

At this time horse racing was the most popular spectator sport. It was also popular with those who liked to wager on sporting events. The Union Course, on Long Island, N.Y., held a series of intersectional races that

Daniel Webster and Lord Ashburton, the British envoy in Washington. It adjusted the Maine-New Brunswick boundary, which had been the cause of the Aroostock War of 1838–1839. The U.S. received most of the territory in dispute as well as navigational rights on the St. John R. The treaty also settled the question of the U.S.-Canada boundary between Lake Superior and Lake of the Woods. As a result, the U.S. gained territory that included the rich Mesabi iron deposits discovered later. The two nations also agreed to cooperate in suppressing the slave trade. In a separate action Ashburton apologized for the *Caroline* affair, which involved the seizure in 1837 of that American-owned small steamer on the Niagara R.

The **first expedition of John Frémont** began this year. Frémont was placed at the head of a party sent to explore the route to Oregon beyond the Mississippi R. as far as the South Pass of the Continental Divide in Wyoming. Frémont had previously traced the headwaters of the Des Moines R. in 1841.

Dorr's Rebellion, named for its leader, Thomas W. Dorr, was directed against the government of Rhode Island, which was still operating under the charter of 1663. The legislature had failed to liberalize the constitution by extending voting rights, enacting a bill of rights, or reapportioning the legislature. The Dorrites held an extralegal convention, drafted a new constitution and submitted it to the electorate, whose numbers had been enlarged by the new Dorrite provisions. Simultaneously, on Apr. 18, with Gov. Samuel W. King legally still in power, Dorr was named governor in a so-called election. King imposed martial law. On May 18 Dorr and a contingent of followers unsuccessfully attempted to seize a state armory. In 1843 Dorr was sentenced to life imprisonment, but was fully pardoned after serving one year. Reforms in the state constitution were quickly adopted.

1842–1843 In **congressional elections** the Democrats gained three Senate seats but the Whigs kept a majority, 28–25, with one seat going to a minor party. In the House the Democrats picked up 40 seats for a 142–79 lead, with one seat going to a minor party.

June 25 A **congressional reapportionment act** was passed. It provided that all congressmen were to be elected by districts equal in number to each state's quota of representatives.

1842. The orchestra was led by a German-trained musician from Connecticut, Ureli Corelli Hill. It gave its first performance on Dec. 7. Only Hill and the librarian received salaries, while the 60-odd orchestra members, mostly Germans, shared in the modest ticket receipts. The Chicago Philharmonic Society was formed in 1850 but lasted only four years. The first important chamber music group was the Mendelssohn Quintette Club of Boston, founded in 1849.

Charles Dickens and his wife arrived in January for a five-month tour. He was lionized in Boston and New York, then journeyed to Philadelphia, Washington, Pittsburgh, and down the Ohio R. The last half of his visit was marked by attacks in the press sparked by the popular author's continual outspokenness over the issue of copyright laws in the U.S. and the pirating practices of the eastern press. Back home, Dickens wrote *American Notes*, a largely descriptive account but with criticisms of the American penal system, slavery, and the lack of U.S. copyright protection for foreign authors.

James Fenimore Cooper returned to the sea for the setting of several new historical and romantic novels. This year two appeared, *The Two Admirals* and *The Wing-and-Wing*. These were followed by *Afloat and Ashore* and its sequel, *Miles Wallingford* (1844), *The Crater* (1847), *Jack Tier* (1848), and *Sea Lions* (1849). Cooper produced six additional books in this eight-year period.

Poems by **Alfred Tennyson** marked his first appearance in American bookstores. Eventually the volume sold over 1,500,000 copies.

Rufus Wilmot Griswold published a popular anthology entitled *The Poets and Poetry of America*, accompanied by critical remarks that show Griswold to be a better compiler and editor than literary critic.

Cheap publishing made its first appearance in the U.S. Because of low postal rates for newspapers and improvements in printing, novels were published in a newspaper format and sold for as little as 6¼ cents. This forced regular publishers to produce cheap paperbacks. The newspaper extras lasted only four or five years, having been killed off by the handier paperbacks.

Feb. 14 The **Boz Ball,** at the Park Theater in New York City, was one of the highlights of the U.S. tour of Charles Dickens. Named for his early pseudonym "Boz," it was a select affair, with the pedigree of every guest rigorously checked by a committee beforehand. The tickets to the ball sold for $10 each, preliminary insurance that the unwanted would not attend. The affair was a sellout. Between dances the record crowd was entertained and edified with representations of scenes from the works of Dickens. After the ball the decorations were left up, for the management realized that other audiences might like to see Dickens. Two additional balls were arranged at somewhat less

as an anesthetic until 1847 in Great Britain. In the meantime, on Mar. 30, 1842, Dr. Crawford W. Long of Jefferson, Ga., used ethyl ether while removing a tumor from the neck of a patient. For several years thereafter he continued to use ether. He even administered it to his wife during childbirth. Long, however, did not make his work public until 1849, after others had demonstrated the value of anesthetics. Dr. William T. G. Morton demonstrated the beneficial effects of ether in Boston on Oct. 16, 1846, before members of the medical profession.

Samuel Colt, inventor of the famous Colt .45 revolver, began a series of experiments to develop a submarine battery for detonating underwater mines.

The **legality of labor unions** was established by the Massachusetts Supreme Court in the case of *Commonwealth v. Hunt.* This included the right of workers to strike in order to obtain a closed shop, higher wages, shorter working hours, and better working conditions. It was held further that individual members of unions could not be indicted collectively for the illegal actions of other union members. This decision was significant in its reversal of traditional judicial hostility to labor organizations.

Mar. 3 **Child labor legislation** was advanced when Gov. John Davis of Massachusetts signed a law to regulate the workday of children under 12 years of age. Such children were limited to a ten-hour day. But the law applied only to "manufacturing establishments" and was not easily enforceable. Similar laws were passed in other states, particularly in New England and the Middle Atlantic states, but it was not until after the Civil War that enforcement of minimum age and maximum hour provisions began to affect child employment practices.

Mar. 7 **Ohio Wesleyan University** was chartered in Delaware, Ohio. Founded under Methodist auspices, the university granted its first degrees in 1846.

Apr. 12 The **first mutual life insurance company** in the U.S., the Mutual Life Insurance Company of New York, was granted a charter. This charter is often called the Magna Charta of American insurance.

drew large crowds. On May 20, 1842, the entry from the South, Fashion, and the entry from the North, Boston, raced for a purse of $20,000. Although Boston was the outstanding horse of the period, it lost to Fashion, which ran the four-mile course in a record 7:32. In 1845 Fashion raced Peytona, from Alabama, on the same course; the latter won. This time it was estimated that 50,000 people tried to reach the track, tying up traffic to the extent that some fans never arrived.

The **Sons of Temperance** was founded at Teetotalers' Hall in New York City with these objectives: to protect its members from intemperance, elevate their characters, and provide mutual aid in case of sickness. The Sons of Temperance, financed by dues and initiation fees, practiced many of the secret rituals of Masonic organizations. This secrecy drew fire from John Marsh of the American Temperance Union, who objected to the exclusion of nonmembers at Sons of Temperance meetings.

Annual mortality rates, as published in *Godey's Lady's Book,* were broken down by cities. In Boston the rate was one death for each 45 residents; in Philadelphia, one in 42.3; and in New York City, one in 37.83.

In **women's fashions,** the pelerine, a type of cape or mantle, was very popular, as were watered silk and velvet cardinals (short cloaks) and scarves. However, it was not considered good taste to wear a cardinal with a dress of the same color.

Edwin P. Christy organized the Christy Minstrels. However, it was another four years before the troupe appeared at Mechanics Society Hall on Apr. 27, 1846. The American audiences who applauded the minstrels wanted entertainment, especially burlesque. The trend was clear to William Mitchell, the English impresario, who had reopened the Olympic Theater in 1839. He created a loud, mocking, and completely American comedy.

Aug. 30 A new **Tariff Act** was passed by Congress. It restored the generally high protective level of 1832.

expensive admission fees; the crowds continued to come.

1843

The U.S. was concerned over the interest shown in the Hawaiian Islands by France and Great Britain. In 1842 the U.S. recognized the islands' independence and Pres. John Tyler said the U.S. would be "dissatisfied" if any nation took possession of them. To affirm its interest, the U.S. signed a trade treaty with Hawaii in 1843 and sent a diplomatic agent, George Brown, to represent American interests. Earlier in the year the commander of a British frigate had made an abortive attempt to obtain cession to Great Britain from King Kamehameha III.

Jan. 29 **William McKinley,** 25th president of the United States, was born in Niles, Ohio.

May 2 **Oregon** settlers determined to form a local government at a meeting at Champoeg. They prepared a constitution modeled on that of Iowa.

May 22 Over 1000 settlers left Independence, Mo., on their way to **Oregon.** Using wagons all the way, they arrived in October.

May 29 The second and most fruitful **Frémont expedition,** under John C. Frémont, left Kansas City. The journey yielded an accurate survey of the emigrant route to Oregon. The return journey allowed members of the expedition to correct many misconceptions about the geography of California. Frémont discovered the nature of the Great Basin, and probably first used that term to describe the independent system of lakes and rivers divided from the ocean by the mountains. Frémont made a great contribution to geographical knowledge. He arrived back in St. Louis on Aug. 7, 1844.

June The **American Republican Party** was formed at New York City largely through the efforts of the Native American Association, an anti-Catholic, anti-immigrant organization. In 1845, this party evolved into the Native American Party, which called for sweeping changes in immigration laws. Having no position on the Mexican War, it failed. Revived in 1853, it collapsed again in division over the slavery issue.

Aug. 31 The abolitionist **Liberty Party nominated** James G. Birney of Kentucky for the presidency and Thomas Morris of Ohio for the vice presidency.

American humor continued to favor the regional, folksy approach of the naive but shrewd storyteller. Two such storytellers were Seba Smith and William Tappan Thompson. The latter was the editor of the Savannah, Ga., *Morning News.* His humorous accounts of Georgia characters, which had first appeared in his paper, were collected in 1843 in *Major Jones's Courtship.* The sketches were written as letters to the editor, and the supposed author, Major Jones, appeared to be a semiliterate Georgia planter. The pieces were filled with descriptions of everyday events, weddings, military service, and the like, all in dialect. Thompson's book went through 20 printings. He published four more books in a similar vein. Seba Smith founded the Portland, Me., *Courier* and published in it letters from the fictional "Major Jack Downing," a Down East Yankee whose forte was political commentary. Smith, through his alter ego, was thus the first of a line of homespun political philosophers to delight American readers. Smith collected Downing's writings in book form first in 1833.

The Conquest of Mexico, an American historical and literary classic by William Hickling Prescott, was published. It was a monumental work for which he had to import a small reference library. Concerned always with style, Prescott had a passion for fact, making his work authoritative as well as compelling. In 1847 he added *The Conquest of Peru* to his history of Spanish America. Both books have sold hundreds of thousands of copies.

The first **minstrel troupe** in New York City was formed by Daniel Decatur "Dan" Emmett, who later wrote the song "Dixie." His quartet of blackface singers and musicians played in several Bowery theaters and established many of the basic routines followed by later minstrel shows.

John Greenleaf Whittier continued his verse descriptions of New England in his *Lays of My Home,* containing such distinctive pieces as "The Merrimack," "Cassandra Southwick," "The Funeral Tree of the Sokokis," "Extract from 'A New England Legend,'" and "St. John."

The **Virginia Minstrels** made their New York City debut at the Bowery Amphitheater. Composed of Daniel Decatur Emmett, Billy Whitlock, Frank Brower, and Dick Pelham, the Virginia Minstrels became the first blackface entertainers to achieve widespread popularity.

1843

The era of nineteenth-century Utopian communities came to a climax with the establishment this year of the North American Phalanx at Red Bank, N.J. Its founder was Albert Brisbane, a disciple of the social philosophy of Charles Fourier of France, who proposed organizing people into economic units called phalanxes. About 1200 formed the Red Bank group, which built a three-story phalanstery and a gristmill. The land was fertile and the group's members, mostly people of culture and refinement, developed a successful truck gardening operation. The members ate their meals together but each family had separate quarters. After the mill burned down in 1854, the association was dissolved, having enjoyed a longer life until then than any other community of its type.

A primitive **typewriter,** more properly a hand-printing machine, was invented by Charles Thurber of Worcester, Mass. It had a movable carriage and a way of turning the paper, but was extremely slow. The first efficient typewriter appeared in 1867.

American medical science gained international stature with the publication of "The Contagiousness of Puerperal Fever" by Dr. Oliver Wendell Holmes in *The New England Quarterly Journal of Medicine.*

Benjamin T. Babbitt, an ingenious Yankee chemist, inventor, and soapmaker, introduced soap powder at about this time. His patented devices made soapmaking a leader in industrial efficiency. "Babbitt's Best Soap," advertised by distributing free samples, was known throughout the U.S.

The **Harvard Astronomical Observatory** acquired by private subscription was the largest telescope available. In March a comet had appeared in daytime and aroused such interest that a subscription for fitting out the observatory with the latest astronomical equipment had been proposed. The purchase of the telescope indicated that lectures and public addresses by scientists were having the intended effect: establishing American astronomy. Harvard Observatory was begun through the initiative of William Cranch Bond, who had made observations for some years at his home and then moved to Dana House in 1839. A main branch of the Harvard Observatory is still maintained at Cambridge, Mass.

Dec. 30 **Cumberland University** was chartered in Lebanon, Tenn., under Presbyterian auspices. It had been founded in 1842. Its first degrees were awarded this year.

Rowing and sailing were popular sports. They were mainly enjoyed by the well-to-do and hence had high social status. Rowing was introduced at Harvard this year by a student, William Weeks, who bought and out-fitted a shell. Yale took up the sport the next year. On Aug. 3, 1852, the Harvard crew defeated the Yale crew on Lake Winnepesaukee, N.H., in the first intercollegiate sports event of any kind. In the 1830s and 1840s in New York City, the Castle Garden Amateur Boat Club Association was restricted to "young men of the highest respectability, who were determined to combine with pleasure the utmost propriety of conduct."

The term *millionaire,* first cited in England in the 1820s, was popularized in the U.S. by newspaper reports of the death of Pierre Lorillard, a banker, landlord, and tobacconist. His fortune of some $1,000,000 was notable at this time, but within five years such personal wealth became more common.

The **Association for Improving the Condition of the Poor of New York City** was founded after an investigating committee reported that relief societies in the city were derelict in their duty because of their failure to learn the "wants, capacities, and susceptibilities" of the poor by visiting their homes. The Association for Improving the Condition of the Poor of New York City was a comprehensive organization that integrated the programs of myriad private agencies. It was later copied elsewhere, notably in Brooklyn, Baltimore, Boston, and Chicago.

Jan. **Dorothea Dix** published her *Memorial to the Legislature of Massachusetts,* which contained a scathing indictment of the treatment of the insane based on her firsthand investigations.

July 12 **Joseph Smith,** leader of the Mormon Church, announced that a divine revelation had sanctioned the practice of polygamy. This announcement caused bitter feeling both within Mormon ranks and between Mormons and non-Mormons around Nauvoo, Ill., where Smith's followers were settled at this time.

1844

The presidential election campaign of 1844 saw some unusual happenings in American politics. Pres. John Tyler wanted a term in his own right, and a Democratic faction nominated him in 1844. It was clear, however, that he stood no chance, and he withdrew on Aug. 20, becoming the first president who did not stand for a second term. At the Democratic National Convention, former Pres. Martin Van Buren tried to secure the nomination but could not muster enough support, largely because of his opposition to the annexation of Texas. The Democrats nominated the first so-called dark horse in U.S. history, James K. Polk of Tennessee. The Whigs unanimously nominated Henry Clay of Kentucky for the presidency. There was a third party this year, the Liberty Party, which in 1843 had nominated James G. Birney of Kentucky on an antislavery platform. The Democratic platform was nationalistic, calling for annexation of Texas and control of the entire Oregon Territory, then shared with England. The Whig platform was more general, making no reference to Texas or to the question of a national bank.

A series of **riots broke out in Philadelphia** between Catholics and non-Catholics. Before order could be restored, 24 persons were dead, two Catholic churches burned, and extensive damage done to other Catholic property.

1844–1845 In **congressional elections** the Democrats gained six seats for a 31–25 majority over the Whigs. In the House the Democrats gained one seat for a 143–77 majority, with six seats going to minor parties.

Apr. 12 The **Texas Annexation Treaty** was signed by the U.S. and the Republic of Texas. It provided for the admission of Texas as a territory.

Apr. 27 **Opposition to annexation of Texas** without the consent of Mexico was expressed by former Pres. Martin Van Buren and Henry Clay of Kentucky. Both had presidential ambitions and wanted to eliminate Texas as an election issue.

May 1 The **Whig National Convention nominated Henry Clay** of Kentucky for the presidency. Theodore Frelinghuysen of New Jersey was nominated for the vice presidency.

May 27 **John Tyler was nominated for president** by Tyler Democrats at their convention in Baltimore, Md. Tyler withdrew from the race on Aug. 20.

May 27–29 The **Democratic National Convention nominated James K. Polk** of Tennessee for the presidency on the ninth ballot. Polk won the nomination after all other candidates withdrew. Former Pres. Martin Van Buren was unable to secure the nomination largely because of his opposition to the annexation of Texas. George M. Dallas of Pennsylvania was nominated for the vice presidency. This was the first

Fictional tales of the violence, real or imagined, of the western frontier were popular. One of the most successful authors of such works was Charles W. Webber, who served in the Texas Rangers, studied at Princeton Divinity School, and died on an expedition to Nicaragua. Among his novels were *Jack Long; or, The Shot in the Eye* (1844) and *Old Hicks* (1848). Emerson Bennett wrote 50 novels of adventure and intrigue, most of them with western settings. *Prairie Flower* and *Leni-Leoti*, both published in 1849, sold about 100,000 copies each.

The **American Revolution** as a setting for drama was popular during this period, including the representation of George Washington, Benjamin Franklin, Ethan Allen, and Nathan Hale. A marked success was achieved this year by Nathaniel Harrington Bannister with the performance of his play *Putnam, the Iron Son of '76* (1857); and by J. G. Burnett with the play *Blanche of Brandywine* (1858).

The song **"Lubly Fan"** was copyrighted by Cool White. The song was later used by the Christy Minstrels as "Bowery Gals," and after that by the Ethiopian Serenaders as "Buffalo Gals," in which form it entered folklore.

Stephen Foster's first published song, "Open Thy Lattice, Love," was published by George Willig of Philadelphia. Based on a poem by George Pope Morris, it was a sentimental and genteel ballad.

The Three Musketeers by Alexandre Dumas was published by several houses in cheap and library editions. Instantly popular, it eventually sold more than 1,000,000 copies; it still sells well. Dumas' *The Count of Monte Cristo* (1845) also achieved instant and continuing popularity among American readers.

A Christmas Carol by Charles Dickens was published in the U.S. It had low sales in the beginning, but eventually topped all Dickens's titles, selling over 2,000,000 copies in the U.S.

The **home of James F. D. Lanier** was built in Madison, Ind., at a cost of $40,000—an extraordinary sum at the

1844

American inventors tended to concentrate on the development of practical and marketable devices. Such a man was Charles Goodyear, who on June 15, 1844, received a patent for vulcanizing rubber. In 1839 Goodyear, while trying to find a way of making rubber useful at high temperatures, accidentally dropped some rubber that had been mixed with sulfur on a hot stove, and the vulcanization process was discovered. Poor and in debt, Goodyear sold his patent for far less than it was worth. He died in poverty.

The **Alphadelphia Phalanx,** another of Albert Brisbane's cooperative, socialized communities, was established on some 3000 acres in Kalamazoo County, Mich., with a membership of almost 500. Internal dissension caused its dissolution within three years.

The first name of the **American Psychiatric Association** was the Association of Medical Superintendents of American Institutions for the Insane. It was established in 1844.

Jan. 15   The **University of Notre Dame** was chartered in South Bend, Ind., under Roman Catholic auspices. It had been founded in 1842 by Rev. Edward Frederick Sorin and six other brothers of the Congregation of the Holy Cross. Its first degrees were awarded in 1849.

Feb. 23   The **University of Mississippi** was chartered as a state university in Oxford, Miss. It opened on Nov. 6, 1848, and its first degrees were awarded in 1851.

Mar. 21   The Adventist **William Miller** had predicted the second coming of Christ on this date. When nothing happened, Miller revised the date to Oct. 22. Again nothing happened. Many Adventists returned to more conservative folds, but some remained and formed new Adventist organizations.

May 24   The **first telegraph message,** "What hath God wrought," was sent from the U.S. Supreme Court room in Washington, D.C., to Alfred Vail in Baltimore, Md., by Samuel F. B. Morse, the inventor of the

Foot racing was a popular sport, largely because it offered a fine opportunity for betting. The runners of the time were professionals and were called pedestrians. In 1835 in New York City a $1000 purse was offered to anyone who could run a ten-mile course in less than an hour. An enormous and unruly crowd turned out to see one of the nine starters finish in just under an hour. In 1844 at Hoboken, N.J., a similar race was run in which John Gildersleeve of New York triumphed out over several British entrants. Gildersleeve finished in 57:01.5 and won $1000. A crowd estimated at 25,000 watched the race and was again unruly.

The catchy phrase *Fifty-four Forty or Fight* was adopted as a campaign slogan by forces supporting James K. Polk, the expansionist Democrat, for the presidency. It applied to the Oregon controversy between Great Britain and the U.S. Many Americans felt that the country should press U.S. claims to the 54°40'th parallel. Settlement was finally made on the 49th parallel, with everything north becoming part of Canada and everything south part of the U.S. Northwest.

The **first private bath** in an American hotel was introduced at the New York Hotel. The first bridal suite in an American hotel was introduced at the Irving House in New York City.

Moses Yale Beach, owner of the New York *Sun,* published the first practical guidebook of credit standings and marriage possibilities, *The Wealth and Biography of the Wealthy Citizens of New York.* The booklet, priced at 25 cents, ran through ten somewhat revised editions by 1846; it was revised twice more in the next ten years. The 1846 edition had approximately 850 names in its select list out of a total New York City population of 400,000.

The **first female mannequin** ever exhibited in America was employed by Paulina Wright in her public lectures on the physiology of women before female audiences.

The **New York Prison Association** was established "to take into consideration the destitute condition of

convention at which a dark horse candidate won, and also the first to be reported by telegraph.

June 8 The **Texas Annexation Treaty** failed to win the necessary two-thirds vote for passage in the Senate.

July 1–27 Henry Clay, in the so-called **Alabama letters**, stated that he had no objection to the annexation of Texas if it could be done "without dishonor, without war." Clay's ambivalence on Texas probably lost him the presidency.

July 3 A **commercial treaty with China** was negotiated by Caleb Cushing, Pres. Tyler's commissioner, and a representative of the emperor. The treaty opened five ports to American merchants and provided that U.S. citizens living in China would be subject to U.S. laws and officials only. The Senate ratified the treaty on Jan. 16, 1845.

Dec. 3 A **gag rule** affecting slavery petitions was finally lifted by the House under a resolution offered by John Quincy Adams. The vote was 108–80.

Dec. 4 **James K. Polk was elected president** of the United States by a popular vote of 1,337,243 against 1,299,068 for Henry Clay, the Whig candidate, and 62,300 for James B. Birney, the Liberty candidate. Birney's strong showing in New York cost Clay the state's electoral votes and the election. The electoral vote was Polk, 170; Clay, 105.

time. It was in the full Greek Revival style, with tetrastyle Doric colonnade.

The second series of *Essays* by Ralph Waldo Emerson was published. Among the essays included were "Experience," "Gifts," "New England Reformers," "The Poet," "Character," "Politics," "Nature," and "Manners." It proved more popular than Emerson's first series of *Essays* (1841), but it has not enjoyed equal literary reputation.

The Dial suspended publication. Founded in 1840, the publication was never popular and its 16 issues did not, from circulation reports, indicate that it ever would be. Yet it was of crucial importance in the history of New England transcendentalism and has had an influence on American life and letters that is belied by its short life. *The Dial* remains a primary source for an understanding of the views of the transcendentalists. As first editor, Margaret Fuller drew on an outstanding list of contributors, among them Ralph Waldo Emerson and Henry David Thoreau.

1845

The annexation of Texas finally became a reality after long political bickering. Antislavery forces were opposed to annexation because Texas was certain to become a slave state. Others wanted to act lest Great Britain or France develop a relationship with the Republic of Texas, whose independence Mexico refused to recognize. In Apr. 1844 Pres. John Tyler submitted to the Senate a treaty of annexation, but the Senate rejected it in June. In December Tyler offered a joint resolution to cover annexation. This required only a majority vote by both houses of Congress instead of the two-thirds vote needed to ratify a treaty. Action on the resolution was completed on Feb. 28, 1845, when the House accepted it in revised form. On June 23 the congress of Texas accepted annexation.

Jan. 23 A **uniform election day for presidential elections** was established by an act of Congress. States had previously set their own election days. The act named the first Tuesday after the first Monday in November as Election Day. The first national election fell on Nov. 4.

Mar. 3 **Florida** was admitted to the Union, becoming the 27th state.

Writings about the western frontier now included works by authors who saw the process of pioneering in realistic terms. One such author was Caroline Kirkland, an early settler of Pinckney, Mich. Her first book was *A New Home—Who'll Follow?* (1839). In it she described many aspects of frontier life, from log houses to land booms, as well as social life, politics, and teaching methods, etc. Later Mrs. Kirkland wrote *Forest Life* (1842) and *Western Clearings* (1845), which were more sentimental and self-conscious than her first and more humorous book had been.

Woman in the Nineteenth Century, a strongly feminist book by Margaret Fuller, was published. The author, a remarkably modern-thinking woman, was a friend and intellectual equal of Ralph Waldo Emerson, William Henry Channing, and other members of the transcendental school. Her life was cut short in a shipwreck in 1850.

Mar. 24 *Fashion,* a play by Anna Cora Mowatt, brought the comedy of social satire into vogue. *Fashion* was the story of a *nouveau riche* family and the social aspirations of the wife. The introduction of foreign characters heightened the contrasts between Americans and Europeans. This latter element influenced many plays: *Nature's Nobleman* (1851) by

Business and Industry; Science; Education; Philosophy and Religion III	IV Sports; Social Issues and Crime; Folkways; Fashion; Holidays

telegraph. The federal government appropriated the money for the line.

May 25 A patent for an early **gas engine** was awarded to Stuart Perry of Newport, N.Y. Perry was issued a second patent for an improved engine on Oct. 7, 1846.

June 27 The founder of Mormonism, **Joseph Smith,** and his brother, Hiram Smith, were murdered by a mob in Carthage, Ill.

Sept. 19 The **Marquette iron range** in the Upper Peninsula of Michigan near Lake Superior was discovered accidentally by a group of government surveyors headed by William A. Burt. Burt observed that his compass was deviating 87 degrees from normal. Upon investigating the soil, he found evidence of large deposits of iron ore.

discharged convicts." A department for women, "The Home," was opened in 1845 to provide for the practical education of released female convicts.

The celebrated **balloon hoax** was perpetrated by Edgar Allan Poe with Moses Yale Beach, owner of the New York *Sun,* as co-conspirator. The *Sun* reported at length on a balloon crossing of the Atlantic that allegedly brought passengers from Europe to America. The hoax was accepted by readers at face value.

June 26 Pres. **John Tyler was married** to Miss Julia Gardiner at the Church of the Ascension in New York City. Tyler was the first president to marry during his term of office.

July 29 The **New York Yacht Club** was founded on board the schooner *Gimcrack* docked off the Battery. John C. Stevens was elected its commodore. It is the oldest surviving yacht club in the U.S.

1845

There were as yet few leaders or writers who took up labor's cause, and those who did generally cloaked their efforts under the broad heading of social reform. There were also few attempts to form labor unions. Unusual for his time was George Henry Evans, who had retired in 1836. He emerged again in 1844, reestablishing his former paper, the *Workingman's Advocate.* In 1845 he formed the National Reform Association. At the heart of Evans's reform was his proposal to have the government give every workingman a free homestead of 160 acres. His strategy was to get candidates for public office to support this idea if they wanted the votes of labor.

The **first written examination** in American elementary schools was initiated in Boston.

The **Industrial Congress of the United States,** one of the earliest labor organizations in America, was organized in New York City. The congress organized local congresses throughout the country. By 1856, however, the organization had weakened through internal confusion and was invaded by Tammany political forces.

The exuberant, nationalistic, even jingoistic, spirit of the times was perfectly exemplified in the phrase *manifest destiny,* which first appeared this year in connection with the annexation of Texas. In the July issue of the *United States Magazine and Democratic Review,* John L. O'Sullivan, its editor, wrote of "our manifest destiny to overspread the continent allotted by Providence for the free development of our yearly multiplying millions." The phrase soon gained wide usage in connection with the dispute over the Oregon Territory, even by those who wanted to annex Cuba.

The **Temple of Honor** was established in New York City as a combination temperance society and Protestant fraternal order. William L. Stacey, who became most worthy templar of the national temple in 1849, described the temple as "all that is excellent in older associations with additional advantages." Temple members practiced "unceasing and universal abstinence." No one was admitted to membership who did not acknowledge the existence of God. Embellished with passwords and colorful ceremonial costumes, the Temple of Honor flourished most in the plantation regions of the South.

Mar. 4 James K. Polk was inaugurated president of the United States. A Democrat, he served one term. George M. Dallas was sworn in as vice president.

Mar. 28 Mexico broke off diplomatic relations with the U.S.

Spring John C. Frémont left on his third expedition, this time directly to California, with 60 armed men. Ostensibly their mission was to survey the central Rockies and the Great Salt Lake region. However, war with Mexico was in the air. In 1846 Frémont supported and may have instigated the Bear Flag Revolt, in which American settlers in the San Francisco Bay area seized the town of Sonoma. The settlers raised a flag with the figure of a bear on it and proclaimed the Republic of California.

June 8 Andrew Jackson, seventh president of the United States, died at 78. He was the first president to belong truly to the common people. Much of his popularity originated from his ability as an Army general. He was buried at his country home, The Hermitage, north of Nashville, Tenn.

June 15 U.S. protection of Texas was assured if it agreed to annexation. Tangible evidence was given to the Texans when Gen. Zachary Taylor was ordered to defend a line "on or near the Rio Grande."

Dec. 29 Texas was admitted to the Union, the 28th state.

Harry Watkins set an English earl in America; *The Golden Calf* (1857) by Mrs. Sidney Frances Bateman contrasted the English, French, and Americans and satirized snobbery and the craze for money; *Americans in Paris* (1858) by William Henry Hurlbert dealt with American couples in France.

June *Tales* by Edgar A. Poe was published in New York City by Wiley & Putnam, which also issued Poe's *The Raven and Other Poems* in October. The former contained 12 stories, including "The Gold-Bug," "The Fall of the House of Usher," "A Descent into the Maelstrom," and "The Murders in the Rue Morgue." The latter included all of Poe's best poems to date. Despite growing recognition and the publication of these volumes, his eighth and ninth books, Poe was in such dire need of money that his magazine, *Broadway Journal*, failed in December, ending a remarkably productive two years.

June 4 The first American grand opera, *Leonora*, composed by William Henry Fry, was presented at the author's expense at the Chestnut Street Theater in Philadelphia. It ran for 12 nights. It was given several performances at the New York Academy of Music and was revived briefly in 1856. Fry was the first native American to have his opera performed publicly.

1846

With the annexation of Texas in early 1845, war with Mexico became all but inevitable. Pres. James K. Polk hoped to settle matters peacefully but was determined to have his way by war if necessary. In Nov. 1845 he sent John Slidell to Mexico with an offer of $5,000,000 for the purchase of New Mexico and $25,000,000 for California. The offer was refused. On May 9, 1846, word reached Washington, D.C., that American troops had been attacked by Mexican forces on Apr. 24. Polk asked Congress for, and was granted, a declaration of war. Congress authorized the president to call for 50,000 volunteers and appropriated $10,000,000. Congress and the nation, however, were far from united on the idea of waging war. Southerners favored war as likely to extend slave territory, while northerners opposed the war for the same reason.

1846–1847 In congressional elections the Democrats increased their Senate majority to 36–21, with one seat going to a minor party. In the House the Whigs gained 38 seats to take a 115–108 majority, with four seats going to minor parties.

Jan. Pres. James K. Polk ordered U.S. troops into the region in southern Texas disputed with Mexico,

The talented author whose career becomes disjointed and whose works lapse into obscurity, only to be revived and hailed by a later generation, is not unique in literary history. No one fitted this situation better than Herman Melville, in 1846 deemed one of America's most promising new writers. In his lifetime Melville worked as a bank clerk, farmer, teacher, and sailor; he spent 19 of his later years working as customs inspector in New York City. His career seemed more than ensured when his first novel, *Typee,* was published in 1846. This romance of the South Seas, based on his own experiences, was followed by several more well received novels. His greatest work, *Moby-Dick* (1851), was misunderstood by readers and critics alike, and Melville began a long, heartbreaking slide into literary oblivion. His greatness was not fully appreciated until well into the twentieth century.

Napoleon and His Marshals by Joel T. Headley, associate editor of the New York *Tribune,* was

| Business and Industry; Science; Education; Philosophy and Religion | III | | IV | Sports; Social Issues and Crime; Folkways; Fashion; Holidays |

Dr. **William Keil** founded the communal settlement of Bethel in Shelby County, Mo. He led 500 German immigrants with Anabaptist backgrounds and Utopian ideas into this haven. There he established his Church of the Living God, a successful enterprise. Keil held autocratic power. His subjects seldom received any money for their efforts, but all their needs were satisfied—food, clothing, shelter, education for their children, and other benefits.

Feb. 1 **Baylor University** was chartered by the Republic of Texas in Independence, Tex., under Baptist auspices. Its first degrees were awarded in 1855. Baylor moved to Waco, Tex., in 1886 when it merged with Waco University.

Oct. 10 **The U.S. Naval Academy** opened at Annapolis, Md. It combined at one site a group of schools previously located in the port cities of New York, Boston, Philadelphia, and Norfolk. Its first graduation exercises were held on June 10, 1854.

The popularity of **lectures** among American audiences was reflected in the career of John Bartholomew Gough, an English-born reformed alcoholic who made a handsome living giving lectures on his victory over drink. Every lecture ended with the taking of pledges of abstinence. At his peak Gough was paid $175 per lecture, many times the fee of the average temperance speaker. Before his death Gough estimated he had given 9600 temperance lectures to 9,000,000 people. In 1843 he traveled 6840 miles to make 383 addresses.

Baseball took a giant step toward the modern game when Alexander J. Cartwright, a New York City fireman, drew up a set of rules and organized the first baseball club, The Knickerbockers. Other clubs were formed and adopted Cartwright's rules. Cartwright fixed four as the number of bases, not two, three, or five; set them 90 feet apart; stood the batter in a box at home plate, not at some distance from it; made the bases flat; and ruled out "plugging" a baserunner with a thrown ball to put him out.

1846

One of the most important events in the scientific world at this time was the establishment by Congress this year of the Smithsonian Institution in Washington, D.C. In 1829 James Smithson, an illegitimate son of the Duke of Northumberland, left about $550,000 in his will to establish such an institution. Congress, however, did not resolve exactly how to use the money for 17 years, finally determining that it should be "for the increase and diffusion of knowledge among men." The Smithsonian over the years has grown into a complex of museums and other facilities serving professionals and nonprofessionals alike. It supports many scientific endeavors.

The **Eastern Exchange Hotel,** the first public building heated by steam, opened in Boston.

Erastus Brigham Bigelow built the first gingham factory in the U.S. at Clinton, Mass. He developed power looms to make tapestries and carpets and made Clinton the center for his specialized textile mills.

The lecture circuit was popular with Americans, who found lyceum speakers entertaining and sometimes inspiring. The lecture hall became a center for promotion of social movements, including the rising agitation for prohibition laws. At this time there emerged a new voice for temperance, John Bartholomew Gough, an Englishman and reformed alcoholic. He lectured for 40 years, and thousands of people signed the teetotaler's pledge after hearing his story of the evils of drink. Gough advocated that a prohibition amendment be added to the Constitution.

Tall stories of the frontier were in many cases first told in *Mince Pie for the Million,* author unknown. Included were "Skinning a Bear," "The Death Hug," and "A Sensible Varmint," the last involving the ubiquitous Davy Crockett. The stories were written in frontier dialect with colorful misspellings. They generally involved animals, particularly bears and game animals, such as the raccoon (spelled *rakkoon* in "A Sensible Varmint").

between the roughly parallel Nueces and Rio Grande rivers. The commanding general was Zachary Taylor.

Feb. 10 The **Mormon migration** westward from Nauvoo, Ill., began. It was organized and led by Brigham Young after the murder of Joseph Smith, founder of Mormonism.

Apr. 27 The **Oregon question** was pushed toward resolution by the recommendation of Congress to the president that he give notice to Great Britain of the intent of the U.S. to terminate the agreement of 1818 providing for joint occupation of disputed Northwest territory.

May 4 **Capital punishment** was abolished for the first time in the U.S. by the Michigan legislature, effective Jan. 1, 1847. Treason against the state remained a capital crime.

May 8 The **Battle of Palo Alto,** the first important engagement of the Mexican War, was fought, with the Mexicans on the losing side.

May 9 In the **Battle of Resaca de la Palma,** U.S. forces under Gen. Taylor forced the Mexican army back across the Rio Grande.

May 13 A **declaration of war** against Mexico was passed several days after hostilities commenced. War measures were passed over Whig opposition, which increased as the war progressed.

May 18 **U.S. forces crossed the Rio Grande,** led by Gen. Zachary Taylor. The Americans occupied Matamoros.

June 14 The **Bear Flag Revolt** began with the proclamation by a group of California settlers of the Republic of California. The name came from their standard, which included the name of the republic, a grizzly bear, and a star on a field of white. On Aug. 17 Robert F. Stockton, a naval officer commanding U.S. forces on the Pacific coast, issued a proclamation declaring the annexation of California by the U.S., and establishing himself as governor.

June 15 The **Oregon Treaty** with Great Britain was signed. It established the 49th parallel as the boundary between the U.S. and the British Northwest territory. Idaho, Oregon, Washington, and part of Montana became undisputed U.S. territory. This was a compromise from the campaign slogan of Polk in 1844: "Fifty-four Forty or Fight." Canada was granted navigation rights to part of the Columbia R. south of the 49th parallel.

Aug. The **Wilmot Proviso** was formulated by Rep. David Wilmot of Pennsylvania and tacked on to the bill in which Pres. Polk asked for $2,000,000 to buy additional territory from Mexico. The intent was to prohibit slavery in any territory acquired from Mexico. It passed the House, but lost in the Senate. Resurrected in 1847, the proviso again passed in the House but lost in the Senate, with John Calhoun leading the

published. The book went through 50 printings in 15 years.

Margaret Fuller published her critical essays as *Papers on Literature and Art.* Up to and even past her time, Fuller was the most formidable American female intellectual. She was known in her own time for her support of the rights of women, her intellect, her knowledge of German, and her understanding of philosophy. From 1840–1842 she edited *The Dial,* and she was considered the best American critic up to 1850, but her writings had a limited and select audience. Hawthorne used her in conceiving his character Zenobia in *The Blithedale Romance.*

Industrial architecture of the second quarter of the nineteenth century found commendable expression in the two original units of the mills of the Essex Company, built of granite at Lawrence, Mass.

Grace Church, designed by James Renwick, was constructed at Broadway and 10th St., New York City. It was an important early example of Gothic Revival architecture in the U.S.

The literary art of **Nathaniel Hawthorne** was again seen in a collection of short stories, *Mosses from an Old Manse.* As in an earlier collection, *Twice-told Tales, Second Series* (1842), all the puritanical themes for which he was known were touched upon: isolation, secret guilt, spiritual arrogance, and the search for perfection.

Feb. 9 **Southern mountain folk** as types were introduced on the stage for the first time in *The Hoosier at the Circus* by a playwright named Carrol.

Business and Industry; Science; III
Education; Philosophy and Religion

IV **Sports; Social Issues and Crime;**
Folkways; Fashion; Holidays

The **first rotary printing press** was devised and produced by Richard M. Hoe. It was capable of turning out 8000 newspapers an hour. The press was first installed in 1847 by Philadelphia's *Public Ledger.*

Jan. The *Commercial Review of the South and Southwest* began publication in New Orleans. Edited by James De Bow, a statistician, the periodical gave an outstanding picture of the social and economic life of the antebellum South. Known as *De Bow's Review,* the publication enjoyed the largest number of subscribers of any southern magazine until 1880.

Feb. 5 **Bucknell University** was chartered in Lewisburg, Pa., as the University of Lewisburg. Established under Baptist auspices, the university issued its first degrees in 1851. The University of Lewisburg became Bucknell University in 1886.

Mar. 26 **Colgate University** was chartered in Hamilton, N.Y., as Madison University. It was renamed Colgate in 1890 in recognition of its benefactor, William Colgate, a soap manufacturer. It had been founded Mar. 5, 1819, under Baptist auspices.

Apr. 10 **Fordham University** was chartered in the Bronx, New York City, as St. John's College. Established in 1841 under Catholic auspices, the college granted its first degrees in 1846. It became Fordham University in 1907.

Apr. 13 The **Pennsylvania Railroad,** one of the most famous rail systems in history, was chartered.

June 17 **Grinnell College** was chartered in Davenport, Iowa, as Iowa College under Congregational and Presbyterian auspices. Its first degrees were awarded in 1854. The college was moved to Grinnell, Iowa, in 1859 and renamed Grinnell College in 1909.

Sept. 10 The **first sewing machine** in the U.S. with an eye-pointed needle was patented by Elias Howe, called the father of the modern sewing machine.

The **exodus of the Mormons** from Nauvoo, Ill., after open hostilities with their Illinois neighbors came on the heels of a hard winter of preparation. The Mormons had turned their homes into workshops and equipped 12,-000 wagons to carry their families and belongings. Beginning in February, small groups began to leave Nauvoo. They crossed the Mississippi R. by flatboat. Later in the month the river froze and some groups were able to cross on the ice. By the end of the month, 2000 men, women, and children were in Iowa and ready to move on. The sprawling caravan was broken into companies of 50 wagons. The leading parties advanced slowly, setting up resting spots along the route where tired people and cattle could recover from the ravages of ice, snow, and rain. By the middle of May 16,000 Mormons had crossed the Mississippi. The stragglers left Nauvoo by September. Through the fall and following winter, from fear of winter and Indians on the plain ahead, the main body of the wagon train was bogged down in the bottomlands of the Missouri R., near Council Bluffs, Iowa.

The **panorama,** a moving picture mounted on rollers in such a way that a viewer saw only a portion of it, was a popular attraction during this period. This year John Barnard exhibited one of the best known panoramas, a scenic masterpiece designed to give the viewer the sensation of traveling along the Mississippi R. This work was said to be 10 feet high and 3 miles long. However, the longest panoramas were probably no longer than 4000 feet. Some panoramas were mounted on the walls of circular buildings. Among the most popular subjects for these visual displays were the burning of Moscow and the life of Napoleon Bonaparte.

The great **Irish potato famine,** which had begun in 1845, prompted a wave of Irish immigration to the U.S. A blight had destroyed the Irish potato crop, and British trade policies had contributed to what became one of the great disasters of world history. The population of Ireland dropped from about 8,500,000 to 6,550,000, partly from starvation but also from the departure of an estimated 1,600,000 Irish to the U.S. Some famine relief was sent by groups in the U.S. to Ireland, but not enough to ease the suffering appreciably. The immigrants who arrived in the U.S. were not particularly welcome. Most ended up in the big cities, where they worked as cheap domestic and menial laborers.

Orson Squire Fowler, a noted phrenologist and publisher, issued *Matrimony; or, Phrenology and Physiology applied to the Selection of Congenial Companions for Life.* This book sold well and was noted for its motto

opposition. The debate brought into focus the sectional differences over slavery and contributed to the formation of the Republican Party.

Sept. 25 **Monterrey, Mexico,** was captured by U.S. forces under Gen. Zachary Taylor after a four-day engagement that made "Old Rough and Ready" Taylor, a Whig, into a national hero. His relations with Pres. Polk, a Democrat, cooled subsequently.

Dec. 28 **Iowa** was admitted into the Union, becoming the 29th state.

Apr. 27 The **Christy Minstrels** of Albert Christy opened at Palmo's Opera House in New York City. They were acknowledged to have brought minstrelsy to its peak as an entertainment form.

1847

One of the most horrifying incidents in the history of the westward movement occurred in early 1847 in the Sierra Nevada range of California. The previous December a pioneer group of 87 persons, headed by two brothers, Jacob and George Donner, had attempted to take a shortcut through the Wasatch Mountains, only to find themselves trapped by snow when they reached the Sierra Nevada. A party of eight men, five women, and two Indian guides set out for help. While they were gone, the rest of the party realized that no one would survive unless they practiced cannibalism on those who died. When relief reached the stranded party on Feb. 19, there were only 45 survivors.

Feb. 22–23 At the **Battle of Buena Vista,** U.S. forces under Gen. Zachary Taylor defeated the Mexicans under Gen. Antonio López de Santa Anna.

Mar. 9 U.S. forces under Gen. Winfield Scott landed near **Vera Cruz,** Mexico. Some 10,000 troops landed just south of the city, site of the most powerful fortress in the Western Hemisphere, in what was the first large-scale amphibious operation in U.S. history. Scott began a siege of Vera Cruz on Mar. 22. The fortress fell on Mar. 27 and was occupied two days later. On Apr. 8 Scott moved toward Mexico City.

Apr. 15 To negotiate **peace with Mexico,** Pres. James K. Polk appointed as his special agent Nicholas P. Trist, a State Department veteran.

Apr. 18 At Cerro Gordo Gen. Winfield Scott, marching on Mexico City, met and defeated a Mexican force of about 13,000.

June 6 **Peace negotiations** with Mexico were initiated through the British minister, Charles Bankhead.

July 24 **Mormon emigrants** arrived in Utah, settling what later was to become Salt Lake City. The party consisted of 143 men, 3 women, and 2 children.

The death in New York City on Nov. 2 of Nathaniel Bannister, a prolific southern playwright who ended his days in poverty, was a reminder of the period's love of historical and melodramatic plays. Bannister's work also reflected the vogue for foreign settings, as in *Gaulantus* (1837), *England's Iron Days* (1837), and *Gentleman of Lyons* (1838). His most popular play, *Putnam*, however, which had been produced at the Bowery Theater in New York City in 1844, had a Revolutionary War setting.

The **first life-sized bronze statue** to be cast in the U.S. was made by Robert Ball Hughes. It was a likeness of mathematician Nathaniel Bowditch and was placed on his grave at Mt. Auburn Cemetery, Cambridge, Mass. In 1886 the original casting was replaced by one made in Paris by Gruet Jeune. A plaster cast is in the Boston Athenaeum.

Herman Melville continued his fictional treatment of life in the South Seas with *Omoo,* a tale set in Tahiti.

An idyllic tale in verse, *Evangeline* by Henry Wadsworth Longfellow, was published. Based on an account told to the poet by Nathaniel Hawthorne, the narrative concerns the fate of two lovers in French Acadie (Nova Scotia) who are separated when the French are expelled from Nova Scotia. It is a tale of virginal love that maintains itself through disappointments and frustrations.

The **Unitarian Church of Lexington,** Mass., a good example of mid-nineteenth-century ornate style, was built by Isaac Melvin.

| **Business and Industry; Science;**
Education; Philosophy and Religion   III | | IV   **Sports; Social Issues and Crime;**
Folkways; Fashion; Holidays |

Oct. 16 Anesthesia was given its first public demonstration before doctors by William T. G. Morton, a Boston dentist. Morton administered sulfuric ether during an operation performed by John Collins Warren at the Massachusetts General Hospital. A neck tumor was removed. Earlier, on Sept. 30, Morton had painlessly removed an ulcerated tooth from a patient anesthetized by ether.

on the title page: "Natural waists or no wives."

June 19 The first recorded baseball game in history resembling the modern sport was played at Elysian Field, Hoboken, N.J., between the New York Club and the Knickerbockers. The New York Club won 23–1. Davis, their pitcher, was fined six cents for swearing at the umpire. Alexander J. Cartwright, founder of the Knickerbockers, had written the rules under which the game was played.

1847

Liberal Protestant clergymen were stirring controversy by their espousal of a less harsh view of humanity than that offered by Calvinism. The early intellectual leader of this group was Horace Bushnell, a Congregational clergyman who emphasized the divine in humanity and in nature. His views were expressed in *Christian Nurture* (1847) and *God in Christ* (1849). *Nature and the Supernatural* (1858) attacked transcendentalism. Bushnell was accused of heresy for his views on the Trinity but was never brought to trial.

Lawrence College was chartered in Appleton, Wis. The second oldest coeducational college in the U.S., it received its initial financial backing from Amos Adams Lawrence, a Massachusetts textile manufacturer and philanthropist.

Jan. 18 Taylor University was chartered in Fort Wayne, Ind., as Fort Wayne Female College. Established under Methodist auspices in 1846, the college became Fort Wayne Methodist Episcopal College between 1852 and 1855. It moved to Upland, Ind., in 1893, when it was renamed Taylor University after the Methodist bishop William Taylor.

Feb. 16 The University of Louisiana was established as a state institution in New Orleans and took over the Medical College of Louisiana, founded in 1834. In 1884 the state legislature transferred the University of Louisiana to the administrators of the Tulane Education Fund for operation as a privately endowed institution, changing its name to Tulane University.

Feb. 25 The State University of Iowa was chartered in Iowa City by the new state's first General Assembly. The first degrees were granted in 1858. It was renamed the University of Iowa in 1964.

Apr. 16 The first telegraph company, the Magnetic Telegraph Company, was given the experimental Baltimore to Washington, D.C., line. The company had been formed by Samuel F. B. Morse and his associates. Morse had been unsuccessful in his efforts to interest the federal government in the new technology.

Light entertainment in the 1840s consisted of burlesque and *tableaux vivants*. Burlesque usually took the form of musical satire. Even William Shakespeare was burlesqued, as in *Much Ado about the Merchant of Venice*. Most daring were *tableaux vivants* in which scantily clad men and women posed in such classical scenes as "Venus Rising from the Sea" and "Psyche Going to the Bath."

The new **Astor Place Opera House** typified the union of high society and grand opera in New York City. Its construction was subsidized by wealthy subscribers. Typical of its ostentatious decor was a huge chandelier that blocked the view of the stage from the 50-cent balcony seats.

The **legal status of women** was slightly improved in Vermont by passage of a state law that guaranteed to the wife full ownership of real estate held by her at the time of her marriage or gained by gift or bequest afterward. The husband's consent was still necessary, however, if the wife wished to transfer ownership of the property.

Tailors were the target of George V. Callendines, author of *The Geometrical Regulator, or Circular Transfer; being a Scientific Guide for Draughting, Balancing and Cutting Pantaloons*. Not one in 20 tailors, Callendines wrathfully declared, knew how to fold a new pair of pantaloons correctly.

Flogging boys and girls as an educational practice was attacked by Lyman Cobb in *The Evil Tendencies of Corporal Punishment as a Means of Moral Discipline in Families and Schools*. Cobb listed some 60 arguments against the practice. An advanced educator, Cobb even announced that he did not want his pupils to suffer over tedious reading. His views were widely held by those opposing the old-fashioned "school of the rod."

A popular **etiquette manual** of this period was *True Politeness; a Hand-book of Etiquette for Ladies*. It

| Exploration and Settlement; Wars; Government; Civil Rights; Statistics | I | | II | Publishing; Arts and Music; Popular Entertainment; Architecture; Theater |

Aug. 20 At **Churubusco** Gen. Winfield Scott defeated a Mexican army of 20,000.

Sept. The **Native American Party** convention at Philadelphia, Pa., nominated Gen. Zachary Taylor for president and Henry A. S. Dearborn of Massachusetts for vice president.

Sept. 8 At the **Battle of Molino del Rey** U.S. forces under Gen. Winfield Scott defeated an estimated 12,-000 Mexicans.

Sept. 13 The fortified hill of **Chapultepec**, the last obstacle before Mexico City, was taken by U.S. forces under Gen. Winfield Scott.

Sept. 14 Gen. **Winfield Scott entered Mexico City.** A battalion of U.S. Marines made its presence felt at the "halls of Montezuma."

Nov. The **Liberty Party nominated John P. Hale** for president and Leicester King for vice president at their convention in New York City. Before the election in 1848, the Liberty Party merged with the Free Soil Party, whose nominee was Martin Van Buren. Hale withdrew.

Nov. 19 A **steamboat collision** on the Ohio R. of the *Talisman* and the *Tempest* killed 100 persons.

Nov. 22 A **ship fire** aboard the *Phoenix* on Lake Michigan killed 200 Dutch immigrants.

The **Plymouth Church of the Pilgrims,** an example of the late meeting house style, was built in Brooklyn, N.Y. It was noted chiefly as the church of the Rev. Henry Ward Beecher and as a center of abolitionist activity before the Civil War.

Jan. 30 **Edgar Allan Poe** began a dark year with the death of his sickly wife, Virginia. Except for "Ulalume," a haunting poem on death written in an effort to console himself, Poe wasted most of the year on fruitless quarrels and plagiarism suits against editors and other authors. His physical condition worsened.

Sept. 11 "Susanna," by Stephen Foster, was performed for the first time at a concert in the Eagle Saloon, Pittsburgh, Pa. It became Foster's first widespread success, being taken up by minstrel troupes and carried to the West Coast by the forty-niners.

1848

The Treaty of Guadalupe Hidalgo, signed by the U.S. and Mexico on Feb. 2, 1848, formally ended the Mexican War (1846–1848). By its terms Mexico recognized Texas as part of the U.S. and ceded to the U.S. over 500,-000 square miles of territory, including all of the future states of California, Nevada, and Utah, almost all of New Mexico and Arizona, and parts of Colorado and Wyoming. In return the U.S. agreed to pay Mexico $15,000,-000 and to assume the claims of U.S. citizens against Mexico, amounting to $3,250,000. The U.S. became an enormous continental republic, but the acquisition of the new territory aggravated the dispute between slavery and antislavery forces. The war resulted in 1721 dead and 4102 wounded. In addition, some 11,155 Americans died of disease as a result of the war. The total cost of the war was estimated at $97,500,000.

The **first Chinese immigrants,** three men, reached San Francisco on the *Eagle.* During the next two years several Chinese laborers who had escaped from Peru reached the West Coast, and immigration direct from

New developments in cast-iron production combined during this period with innovative architectural concepts to produce a new kind of structure, both as to materials and design. Pioneer architect James Bogardus built in 1848 and 1849 the first cast-iron building, a five-story structure located in New York City at Centre and Duane streets. It consisted of cast iron instead of masonry, except that the floor beams may have been timber. The facade consisted of cast-iron columns similar to the stone columns of the Classical style, interspersed with windows. The style remained popular for the rest of the century. Foundries such as Badger's Iron Works in New York City began to turn out prefabricated parts for columns and capitals.

Membership in the **American Art Union** had grown to the point where the annual lottery distributed more than 450 paintings, for which the artists received $40,-907.

Edgar Allan Poe published his memorable lyric poem "The Bells" and an unmemorable prose work called

| Business and Industry; Science; Education; Philosophy and Religion | III | | IV | Sports; Social Issues and Crime; Folkways; Fashion; Holidays |

May 1 The **Smithsonian Institution** was formally dedicated in Washington, D.C. Joseph Henry, a Princeton physicist, was named its first secretary.

May 7 The **American Medical Association** was organized in Philadelphia, Pa. In the previous year representatives of all national medical societies and schools held a national medical convention in New York City. They decided to hold a second convention in the following year. The A.M.A. grew out of the discussions and decisions of the Philadelphia convention.

July 1 The **first official U.S. postage stamps** were issued by the Post Office Department in five-cent and ten-cent denominations. This action had been authorized by Congress on Mar. 3. The new stamps were also the first adhesive postage stamps in the U.S.

July 24 **Brigham Young,** with a party of 143, reached the valley of Great Salt Lake. The flight of Joseph Smith from Missouri to Illinois had ended with a quarrel among the factions of the Mormon Church, the imprisonment of Smith by order of the Illinois governor, and his assassination by a mob that stormed the jail at Carthage and shot him and his brother to death. Brigham Young had been chosen to succeed Smith as leader of the Mormons. Hostility toward the Mormons continued and violence increased. Young was compelled to lead the Mormons' western trek, which was one of the great migrations of the American West. When Salt Lake City was established, Young returned to lead the rest of the eastern Mormons from Council Bluffs, Iowa, to their permanent home in Utah.

warned against the use of double entendres by women, "especially when perpetrated in the presence of men." The manual continued, "It is, in general, bad taste for ladies to kiss each other in the presence of gentlemen with whom they are but slightly acquainted." Ladies were warned also, "Never sing more than one or two songs consecutively" and "Be very cautious of giving a gentleman a letter of introduction to a lady,—it may be the means of settling the weal or woe of the persons for life."

July 26 A miniature electric train on which children could ride was built by Moses Gerrish Farmer in Dover, N.H. There were two cars, one for the motor and batteries, the other for passengers. Farmer exhibited it in town halls and on lawns and fairgrounds, charging children a penny a ride. In 1850 he devised for Boston the first electric fire alarm system in the U.S.

Oct. Maria Mitchell, a Nantucket, Mass., librarian and astronomical observer, discovered a new comet. For this she received a gold medal from the astronomy-minded King of Denmark and election into the American Academy of Arts and Sciences, the first woman so honored. When Vassar College opened in 1865 she was named to the staff as the first woman professor of astronomy in the U.S.

1848

The only successful industrial Utopian community was established in 1848 in Oneida, N.Y. It was founded by John Humphrey Noyes and his followers. In 1839 Noyes had established a so-called Perfectionist community at Putney, Vt. His system of polygamous marriage so outraged his neighbors that the group was forced to flee. They moved to Oneida where they established the Oneida Community. There the group held all property in common and children were raised in a communal nursery. The community prospered, at first by manufacturing a trap for small animals and later by producing silverware. In 1879, however, opposition again arose to the community's style of living and Noyes went to Canada, where he remained for the rest of his life. In 1881 the group, having abandoned Noyes's theories, was reorganized as a business corporation.

The **Associated Press** (AP) was organized by a group of New York City journalists. The AP was a result of the impatience of Moses Beach, publisher of the New York *Sun,* with established news lines. He experimented with

The first significant sign that women were becoming an organized force in American society was seen in 1848. A group of women called a convention to be held in Seneca Falls, N.Y., on July 19. There they formulated a "Declaration of Sentiments," which cleverly paraphrased the Declaration of Independence, addressing "man" rather than King George III of England. The document called for women's "immediate admission to all the rights and privileges which belong to them as citizens of the United States." The organizers of the convention were Lucretia Mott and Elizabeth Cady Stanton; they led the movement for many years. Mrs. Mott was one of the earliest women lecturers for temperance, the rights of labor, and abolition. Mrs. Stanton was particularly interested in securing the right to vote. When she married Henry B. Stanton in 1840, she refused to have the word "obey" used in the ceremony.

China increased. By 1852 the number of Chinese in the U.S. was estimated at 18,000.

1848–1849 In **congressional elections** the Democrats lost one Senate seat for a 35–25 majority over the Whigs, with one seat held by a minor party. In the House they gained four seats for a 112–109 majority, with nine seats held by minor parties.

Jan. 24 **Gold was discovered** at John A. Sutter's mill on the American R. near Sacramento, Calif., by one of his employees. The discovery resulted in the great gold rush of 1849.

Feb. 23 **John Quincy Adams,** sixth president of the United States, died at 80. He was buried at Quincy, Mass.

May 22–26 The **Democratic National Convention** nominated **Lewis Cass** of Michigan for the presidency and William O. Butler of Kentucky for the vice presidency.

May 29 **Wisconsin** was admitted to the Union, becoming the 30th state.

June 3 The **Treaty of New Granada** between the U.S. and the Republic of New Granada (now Colombia) was approved by the U.S. Senate. It provided a U.S. right of way across the Isthmus of Panama in return for a guarantee of neutrality for the area.

June 7–9 The **Whig National Convention nominated Gen. Zachary Taylor** of Louisiana for the presidency and Millard Fillmore of New York for the vice presidency.

June 22 The **Barnburners,** the progressive faction of the Democratic Party, withdrew from the national convention in Baltimore, Md., and met at Utica, N.Y. They nominated Martin Van Buren of New York for the presidency and Henry Dodge of Wisconsin for the vice presidency.

July 19–20 A **women's convention at Seneca Falls,** N.Y., called by Lucretia Mott and Elizabeth Cady Stanton, discussed women's rights. Susan B. Anthony joined the convention, where such subjects as voting, property rights, and divorce were debated. Similar conventions were held annually until the Civil War.

Aug. 9 The **Free Soil Party nominated Martin Van Buren** of New York for the presidency and Charles Francis Adams of Massachusetts for the vice presidency. The party urged prohibition of slavery in the new territory added to the Union after the Mexican War.

Aug. 24 A **ship fire** aboard the *Ocean Monarch* off Caernarvonshire, North Wales, killed 200 Americans.

Nov. 7 **Zachary Taylor was elected president** of the United States. Millard Fillmore was elected vice president. The electoral vote was Taylor, 163, Lewis Cass, Democratic candidate, 127. The popular vote was Taylor, 1,360,101; Cass, 1,220,544; Martin Van Buren, Free-Soil and Barnburners candidate, 291,263.

Eureka, which was based on a lecture he had given. In *Eureka* Poe put forward an ingenious theory of the evolution of the universe, while displaying frequent misunderstandings of science. This year Poe displayed erratic behavior, notably his courting of three widows, an attempt at suicide, recurring problems with alcohol, and swiftly deteriorating health.

The *Temperance Tales* of Lucius Manlius Sargent, in two volumes, proved a popular success. The 21 stories had previously appeared in temperance journals and been given wide circulation by religious organizations. The tone of the tales may be judged from titles such as "My Mother's Gold Ring" and "Groggy Harbor."

James Russell Lowell had a banner year with the publication of three major poetic works. *The Biglow Papers* (first series) consisted of nine poems that humorously voiced opposition to the war with Mexico and the annexation of Texas. The Yankee dialect of Ezekiel and Hosea Biglow immediately caught popular fancy. *A Fable for Critics,* in the tradition of Pope's *Dunciad* and Byron's *Vision of Judgment,* dealt with contemporary writers and critics. Lowell also published *Poems: Second Series* and *The Vision of Sir Launfal.*

Wuthering Heights by Emily Brontë was published in the U.S. Not very popular at first, it eventually sold about 1,000,000 copies. Emily Brontë died of tuberculosis in Dec. 1848.

A Home for All, or the Octagon Mode of Building by Orson Squire Fowler, a former theological student and popular phrenologist and publisher, was issued. The book, coupled with Fowler's efforts to promote the Octagon style of architecture, led to a vogue for octagonal houses in the mid-nineteenth century. A number of the best have survived and been restored.

Jane Eyre by the English novelist Charlotte Brontë became immediately popular following publication in the U.S. An emotional story of the love between a governess and her married master, it proved to be sensational literary material.

Hans Christian Andersen was given his first U.S. publication with *Shoes of Fortune and Other Tales.* The stories ultimately were included in his classic *Fairy Tales.*

Gothic Revival architectural detail was precisely exemplified in the First Congregational Church at Haverhill, Mass. The designer was Richard Bond.

A Glance at New York by Benjamin A. Bacon, starring the mimic Joseph Chanfrau, started a vogue for plays dealing with the life of cities. *New York* had a cast of characters different from what had been seen before: assorted scoundrels, firemen, show girls, etc. The "hero," Mose, was a likable ruffian. Chanfrau took the play on the road across America.

| Business and Industry; Science; Education; Philosophy and Religion   III | IV   Sports; Social Issues and Crime; Folkways; Fashion; Holidays |

ways of getting the news faster, including use of carrier pigeons. Reports from the Mexican War came in so slowly that Beach finally set up his own express service. The arrangement was successful enough to convince other New York publishers to carry the expense of a private news-gathering service, which became the Associated Press.

A **power loom** to weave Brussels, Wilton, velvet, and tapestry carpets was invented by Erastus B. Bigelow.

Jan. 3   **Girard College** in Philadelphia, Pa., opened its doors. Founded by Stephen Girard, it consisted of a free home, secondary school, and junior college for fatherless white boys. In 1968 the school accepted blacks for the first time.

Mar. 10   **Villanova University** was chartered in Villanova, Pa. It had been founded by the Order of St. Augustine (the Augustinian Fathers) in 1842. Its original name was Augustinian College of Villanova.

June 27   **Air conditioning** for a theater was offered by the Broadway Theater in New York City, perhaps for the first time. The theater issued this notice in its bill: "The public is respectfully informed that an Extensive Apparatus for the Perfect Ventilation of the Entire Building is now in operation. The Steam Power by which it is impelled, being capable of conveying to the Audience part along, 3000 Feet of Cool Air per minute, thus rendering the Establishment during the hottest and most crowded nights in all respects comfortable. The machinery patented by Mr. J. E. Coffee."

July 26   The **University of Wisconsin** was chartered in Madison, Wis., as a state university. Its first degrees were granted in 1854.

Sept.   The **American Association for the Advancement of Science** was founded. The charter of the association expressed a determination to "advance science in the New World" in every possible way. The association developed as a joint endeavor of American and Canadian scientists.

Nov. 1   The **first medical school for women** opened with an enrollment of twelve. It was founded and further developed by Samuel Gregory, a pioneer in medical education for women. Known as the Boston Female Medical School, it was merged in 1874 with the Boston University School of Medicine to form one of the first coed medical schools in the world.

Baseball rules were altered to provide that a runner was out at first base if the ball was held by a fielder on the bag before the runner could reach it.

New York State granted **property rights for women** equal to those of men. This was a significant improvement in women's legal status, but New York's example was not copied elsewhere. Similar women's property rights laws had been passed in Mississippi (1839) and Maine (1844).

John B. Curtis of Bangor, Maine, manufactured the first chewing gum commercially sold in the U.S. Curtis later traveled as a drummer throughout western territories and is reputed to be the first commercial traveler for an eastern firm in the West.

Jan. 24   **Discovery of gold** on the estate of John Sutter made California and broke Sutter. From the day he settled in Nueva Helvetia, at the junction of the American and Sacramento rivers, Sutter prospered. Then gold was found by James W. Marshall, who was building a sawmill for Sutter. The workers on the estate left to look for gold. Every kind of adventurer squatted on Sutter's land. In four years he was ruined. For the rest of his life, Sutter petitioned the state and the federal government for aid. He died on June 18, 1880, at age 77, while the bill he sought was being argued in the House of Representatives. The boom provided a wealth of material for writers. Mark Twain, Joaquin Miller, Bret Harte, Ambrose Bierce, George Horatio Derby, Charles Warren Stoddard, and Edward Rowland Sill were all in the ranks of those who found inspiration in the volatile new atmosphere. There were few voices in the whole country to caution against the excesses of the gold rush. However, the Mormon Church in Salt Lake City, having heard reports of gold in California, cautioned its children to hoard up other riches: "The true use of gold is for paving streets. . . . When the Saints shall have preached the gospel . . . and built up cities enough, the Lord will open up the way for a supply of gold to the perfect satisfaction of his children. . . . Let them not be over-anxious, for the treasures of the earth are in the Lord's storehouses."

1849

News of the discovery of gold in California in Jan. 1848 was slow in reaching the East. Word of it first appeared in the New York *Herald* on Aug. 19, but no great excitement was created until Pres. James K. Polk expressed enthusiasm about it in his message to Congress on Dec. 5. The rush began by land across the continent and by sea and land via the Isthmus of Panama. The first shipload of prospectors arrived in San Francisco via Cape Horn on Feb. 28. About 80,000 people made their way to California in 1849—55,000 overland and 25,000 by sea. About 5000 who started out overland never made it because Asiatic cholera swept their ranks. By the end of 1849, gold worth $10,000,000 had been mined.

Mar. 3 The **U.S. Department of the Interior** was created by Congress as an administrative catchall for the General Land Office, the Bureau of Indian Affairs, the Pension Office, the Patent Office, and the Bureau of the Census. Its prime purpose for many decades seemed to be to locate resources in the West for exploitation by white settlers. Not until the end of the century would the department regard the protection of natural resources as a part of its responsibility.

Mar. 3 **Minnesota Territory** was established by Congress. Slavery within the territory was prohibited.

Mar. 5 **Zachary Taylor was inaugurated as 12th president** of the United States. Millard Fillmore was inaugurated as vice president. Taylor, the second and last Whig president, died after 16 months in office.

Mar. 10 The **Missouri legislature** took the position that "the right to prohibit slavery in any territory belongs exclusively to the people thereof."

May 17 A fire in **St. Louis,** Mo., destroyed 400 buildings and 27 freight and passenger steamships. A serious cholera epidemic ensued.

Sept. 1 A **California convention** called by the territorial governor, Gen. Bennett Riley, met in Monterey. The convention created a state government without waiting for congressional action. On Oct. 20 the delegates adopted a constitution. On Nov. 13 the constitution was ratified by California voters, and a governor and legislative representatives were chosen. Slavery was prohibited.

Civil disobedience, which had been practiced by many patriots before the Revolution and was to be used as a means of protest again late in the twentieth century, in 1849 found its most eloquent spokesman in Henry David Thoreau. A transcendentalist and observer of nature and of man, he opposed the Mexican War. In protest, Thoreau refused to pay his poll tax. He was jailed just overnight because, to his distress, a friend paid the tax for him. As a result of the experience, Thoreau wrote the essay "Civil Disobedience," in which he stated: "There will never be a really free and enlightened State until the State comes to recognize the individual as a higher and independent power, from which all its own power and authority are derived. . . . "

A second edition of *Poems* by John Greenleaf Whittier was published. An enlarged and updated edition of the poet's 1838 volume, it collected Whittier's poems from 1831 to date. Whittier did not become popular with readers until after the Civil War.

In Philadelphia, Pa., a shop specializing in **cameo portraiture** was opened by a Mr. Peabody, one of the last practitioners of the art. Cameo portraiture would soon be superseded by daguerreotype photography.

May 10 The **Astor Place riot,** a notorious theater riot, erupted outside the Astor Place Opera House in New York City, where the celebrated British actor William Charles Macready was performing. Angry crowds reacted against dress requirements for admission to the theater and against Macready's scornful public utterances on the vulgarity of American life. Macready's rival, the American actor Edwin Forrest, who had asserted the cause of the masses both in his stage roles and in his public statements, fueled the indignation of common citizens. On May 8 Macready's performance of *Macbeth* was stopped by Forrest's followers. Two days later, a mob led by E. Z. C. Judson, later to gain fame as Ned Buntline, used clubs, paving stones, and brickbats to shatter the windows of the theater during Macready's performance. Troops were summoned and when order could not be restored by their presence, they were ordered to fire, killing 22 and wounding 56.

| Business and Industry; Science; Education; Philosophy and Religion **III** | | IV Sports; Social Issues and Crime; Folkways; Fashion; Holidays |

1849

Spiritualism began to attract believers, who held that the human personality continues to exist after death and can communicate through a medium with the living. In 1848 two adolescent sisters of Wayne County, N.Y., claimed they heard rappings on floors and walls and that these spelled out messages from the spirit world. Margaret Fox was the central figure in this new cult, along with her sister Katherine. Margaret later admitted it was all a fraud and that the sounds were made by cracking toe knuckles. Nevertheless, there were many believers. In the next decade séances became common and there were at least six spiritualist publications.

The **American Horologe Company,** later (1854) the Waltham Watch Company, was established at Roxbury, Mass. It was the first successful U.S. watch business.

A **safety pin** was patented by Walter Hunt of New York City.

Elizabeth Blackwell became the first woman in the U.S. to receive a medical degree and the first female doctor of medicine of modern times. After some hospital experience in Paris and London, she and her sister in 1853 founded the New York Infirmary and College for Women, the first hospital run entirely by women.

Feb. 13 Otterbein College, founded in 1847, was chartered in Westerville, Ohio, as Otterbein University under United Brethren auspices. Its first degrees were granted in 1857. It became Otterbein College in 1917.

Feb. 27 William Jewell College was chartered in Liberty, Mo., under Baptist auspices. Its first degrees were granted in 1855.

Nov. 22 Austin College was chartered in Huntsville, Tex., under Presbyterian auspices. Its first degrees were issued in 1850. The college moved to Sherman, Tex., in 1876.

Prize fighting was illegal but popular. Condemned for its brutality by many, the sport had many ardent followers. When Tom Hyer, the unofficial American champion, fought Yankee Sullivan this year, the participants and spectators were chased by militia and had to flee Peel Island, Md., the site of the match, to woods on the Western Shore. A few years later, when John C. Morrissey claimed the title vacated by Hyer, the site again had to be changed at the last minute. Bare fist boxing was brutal and there were few rules. In one bout that lasted three hours, one fighter, after being knocked down 81 times, dropped dead. A history of boxing in America was published this year. It was *The American Fistiana;* the book recorded the most important bouts of the previous four decades.

The Great Chinese Museum opened on Broadway between Spring and Prince streets, New York City. It was the only museum of its kind in the country. All of the typical features of Chinese life were displayed, including a large number of life-size wax figures representing all classes; a collection of hundreds of Chinese paintings, house furnishings, models of pagodas, temples, and bridges; and specimens of Chinese manufacture.

Jan. Amelia Bloomer, the temperance and woman's suffrage advocate, began publication of *Lily.* The first issue printed 200 copies, but by 1853 Bloomer was issuing 4000 copies twice monthly. The articles dealt with contemporary education, marriage laws, woman's suffrage, etc. Bloomer began to have a major influence on American society.

Feb. 7 Tom Hyer, unofficial American heavyweight bare knuckle boxing champion, met Yankee Sullivan, an Englishman who was touring the country, and knocked him out. This was Hyer's last fight, for no one else challenged him.

| Exploration and Settlement; Wars; Government; Civil Rights; Statistics **I** | | **II** Publishing; Arts and Music; Popular Entertainment; Architecture; Theater |

1850

The territory acquired from Mexico in the Mexican War, particularly California, caused the reopening of the question of free or slave status for new states. After acrimonious debate, Congress passed five bills on the subject between Sept. 9 and Sept. 20. As signed by Pres. Millard Fillmore, they constituted what became known as the Compromise of 1850 and once more postponed a showdown on slavery. The compromise was the result of eight resolutions that had been introduced in the Senate on Jan. 29 by Henry Clay of Kentucky. The five final bills dealt with all the pressing questions, and for the most part reaction was favorable, but extremists in the North and South were displeased.

The seventh U.S. **Census** fixed the population of the 31 states of the Union at 23,191,876. The center of population was located 23 miles southeast of Parkersburg, W.Va.

The **number of immigrants** entering America in 1850 totaled 369,980. The figures reflected the Irish famine of the late 1840s, and social and political unrest in northwest Europe.

1850–1851 In **congressional elections** the Whigs lost one Senate seat, resulting in a Democratic majority of 35–24 with three seats going to minor parties. In the House the Democrats gained 28 seats for a 140–88 majority with five seats going to minor parties.

Mar. 7 **Daniel Webster** supported Sen. Henry Clay's compromise in a famous speech to the Senate in which he espoused the provisions of the Fugitive Slave Bill. John Greenleaf Whittier had Webster in mind when he wrote in his poem "Ichabod":

> All else is gone; from those great eyes
> The soul has fled;
> When faith is lost, when honor dies
> The man is dead.

Apr. 19 The **Clayton-Bulwer Treaty** was signed. The U.S. and Great Britain agreed to the neutrality of a canal to be built across Central America. Both governments were to act as joint protectors of the territory, and neither was to establish any military post on, or assume control over, any part of Central America.

May 4 A **fire** struck the burgeoning town of San Francisco, an odd collection of wood houses, tents, and shacks. Fires struck again on June 14 and Sept. 17.

May 22 Sir **John Franklin,** an English explorer who was lost in the Arctic in 1845 in an attempt to find the Northwest Passage, was the object of an American rescue expedition. Henry Grinnell, the New York merchant and philanthropist, bore the expense of fitting out two vessels, the *Advance* and the *Rescue,* which sailed under command of Lt. Edwin Jesse De Haven.

The extremes to which the public would go in its adulation of popular entertainers, especially when urged on by clever promotion, was nowhere better shown than in connection with the American tour of Jenny Lind, called the "Swedish Nightingale." Miss Lind was brought to the U.S. in 1850 by master showman and promoter Phineas T. Barnum. On her arrival 30,000 people surrounded her New York City hotel, hoping to see the coloratura soprano. Tickets for her Sept. 11 debut at Castle Garden Theater were auctioned at $225. Boston topped that with a $625 bid when she sang there. Miss Lind gave 95 concerts around the country from 1850 to 1852, for which she received $17,675. Barnum made a fortune.

Louis Moreau Gottschalk, American pianist and composer, toured the French provinces, Switzerland, and Savoy and was widely acclaimed.

Harper's Monthly Magazine began its notable career in New York City. It promised "to place within the reach of the great mass of American people the unbounded treasures of the periodical literature." Most of the contributions were serializations of the novels of Charles Dickens, William Makepeace Thackeray, Anthony Trollope, and George Eliot. In most cases *Harper's* paid its authors more than the English publishers did.

The Scarlet Letter, a classic American novel by Nathaniel Hawthorne, was a best seller from the beginning. Four thousand copies were sold in the first ten days; the second printing immediately sold out. Its daring subject matter accounted in part for its immediate success.

White-Jacket by Herman Melville was published. In this partly autobiographical novel, Melville, who had spent 15 months on a U.S. man-of-war (1843–1844), gave his readers a striking set of characters and a realistic picture of the daily and often frightening activities in the Navy at mid-century.

Representative Men by Ralph Waldo Emerson was published. It was a collection of lectures he had given on Plato, Swedenborg, Montaigne, Napoleon, Goethe and others. Emerson set forth his view of the roles played by great men. He believed that man was not the victim of his environment but had creative powers within him to change things and live his own life.

William Sidney Mount was at his peak as a painter of the life and landscapes of his hometown, Setauket, and of Suffolk County on eastern Long Island, N.Y. *Dancing on the Barn Floor, Raffling for the Goose,* and *Bargain-*

1850

The textile industry was the first U.S. manufacturing group to develop on a sizable scale. More than two-thirds of all cotton manufacturing was carried out in New England, where by 1850 there were 564 plants, capitalized at more than $58,000,000 and employing 61,893 operators. The South, by contrast, had only 166 plants, capitalized at $7,250,000 and employing 10,043 workers. The New England textile industry employed many female workers, most of them young girls.

A **cholera epidemic** swept through the Middle West after passing through the South the previous year. From New Orleans it fanned through the U.S. and was checked in successive advances only by cold weather.

Aaron Lufkin Dennison, pioneer U.S. watchmaker, established a factory to manufacture the first commercial eight-day watch. The mainspring was too long, however, and the model was abandoned in favor of a 36-hour watch.

The **first agricultural binder** for tying grain was invented by John E. Heath.

James N. Richmond, glassmaker of Cheshire, Mass., built a glass house that attracted visitors from many areas. Later Richmond became the first manufacturer of plate glass in the U.S.

Newspaper distribution in the U.S. reflected increased accessibility. For each person in the U.S. the annual distribution figure was 22, as compared with 8 in 1828.

Fares for **immigrants** to the U.S. dropped as low as $10, but living conditions in the steerages of ocean vessels remained atrocious until late in the century.

A **park** in New York City large enough to provide a healthy atmosphere for all the citizens was first proposed. Here began the concept of a central park.

Aid to Roman Catholic churches and missions in the U.S. by the Lyon Propaganda, a French missionary group organized in 1822 to help American Catholics, amounted to 9,000,000 francs.

The **house sparrow,** also known as the English sparrow, was imported from England by Nicholas Pike. The first flock of eight pairs died. In 1851 a new flock of sparrows was imported and released at Brooklyn, N.Y. They flourished and soon spread across the country.

Some advocates of women's rights attracted attention by means of odd dress. Amelia Bloomer, who edited *Lily,* a women's rights and temperance magazine, began wearing in public a skirt over full trousers, much like Turkish trousers. As a result, the fashion became known as the *bloomer costume,* although it had been designed in the mid-1840s by Elizabeth Smith Miller. With the pantaloon, called *bloomers,* Mrs. Bloomer wore an ordinary vest over her blouse. Because the outfit evoked derision, she abandoned it, but not before bloomers gathered higher on the leg were found suitable for women's gymnastics.

Madame Restell, a notorious practitioner of **abortion** in New York City, advertised herself as a "woman's physician." Thus she unwittingly discouraged women who heard of her from considering medicine as a profession.

The phrase *sold down the river* entered the American idiom. Slaves on the older plantations, where their treatment was relatively good, contrasted their situation with that of slaves on the Mississippi and in the deep South. To be sold down the river meant to be cut off from family and home—a dreadful fate. The term was later used to characterize any summary action that did not consider the feelings of those affected.

Female clerks were employed for the first time in the U.S. by Philadelphia storekeepers.

The memorable quote **"I would rather be right than be president"** was uttered by Henry Clay in the Senate during his impassioned plea for the compromises proposed by him to settle the dispute between slave and free factions. Bitter because of his failure to achieve the presidency, he threw off his famous remark when taunted by his colleagues.

A reflection of the rise of a new class, **the homeless,** was seen in the 18,456 persons sheltered in 8141 cellars in New York City. By 1856 tenements had been built to house some of these unfortunates.

The **Turnverein,** or Turners, gymnastic societies made up of German immigrants, combined as a single organization in Cincinnati, Ohio. The Turnverein was started in Germany by Friedrich Jahn to foster physical and mental development in German youth. In 1848, a time of social unrest in Germany, it came under suspicion and

Though Grinnell Land was discovered, the expedition was unsuccessful in its main purpose.

June 17   A steamship fire aboard the *Griffith* on Lake Erie killed 300 persons.

July 1   Overland mail delivery west of the Missouri R. was organized for the first time on a monthly basis from Independence, Mo., to Salt Lake City, Utah.

July 8   The overland gold rush to California through Fort Laramie, Wyo., involved 42,300 emigrants and 9720 wagons between Jan. 1 and July 8. Over 90% of the population of California was male. Nine years later men still outnumbered women six to one.

July 9   Pres. Zachary Taylor died of cholera at the age of 55. Vice Pres. Millard Fillmore was sworn in as the 13th president of the United States on July 10.

Sept. 9   California was admitted to the Union as a free state, giving free states a majority in the Senate. This was one of the bargains of the Compromise of 1850 and a concession to the North. California was the 31st state admitted to the Union.

Sept. 9   The Texas and New Mexico Act was passed by Congress. The act established the Texas boundaries, authorized payment to Texas of $10,000,000 for relinquishing its claims to territories beyond the new state lines, and established the boundaries of New Mexico Territory. As a concession to the South, New Mexico would be a free or a slave state according to its constitution upon admission to the Union. This option was part of the Compromise of 1850.

Sept. 9   The Utah Act established the territorial boundaries of Utah. It was to be a free or slave state according to the constitution it adopted on admission to the Union. Part of the Compromise of 1850, this option was a concession to the South.

Sept. 18   The Fugitive Slave Bill was passed by Congress. Known as the second Fugitive Slave Law (a first, enacted on Feb. 1, 1793, was largely circumvented in the North), this legislation required return of escaped slaves to their owners. Fugitives were not permitted a jury trial and could not testify in their own behalf. The commissioners earned $10 if their decision favored the claimant but only $5 if it favored the fugitive. This law was part of the Compromise of 1850 and a concession to the South.

Sept. 20   Slave trade was abolished in the District of Columbia. This was a concession to the North in the Compromise of 1850.

Sept. 28   Brigham Young, Mormon leader, was named first governor of the territory of Utah by Pres. Fillmore.

Sept. 28   Flogging was outlawed in the Navy and Merchant Marine.

Oct. 23–24   The first national women's rights convention, held in Worcester, Mass., was attended by delegates from nine states. The first women's convention

ing for a Horse were among his many paintings. Mount was also a fine portrait artist.

Washington Crossing the Delaware was painted in Düsseldorf, Germany, by Emanuel Leutze, an American historical and portrait painter residing abroad. Gen. Washington stands in a theatrical, unseamanlike pose in the boat; the Delaware R. is really the Rhine R. as seen from the artist's window. But in this and other U.S. historical subjects, such as *Westward the Course of Empire*, the gigantic mural on the wall of the west staircase of the House of Representatives, Leutze communicated the fortitude and courage of American national heroes and contributed significantly, if not realistically, to people's conceptions of American history.

George Washington Lafayette Fox, the celebrated clown and pantomimist, made his New York City debut. Fox achieved his greatest fame in *Humpty Dumpty* (1868), which he performed 1268 times in New York. His travesty of *Hamlet* delighted audiences, as well as the great tragedian Edwin Booth.

Far western newspaper publishing saw the first issues of the *Weekly Oregonian* in Portland, Ore., and of the *Deseret News* in Salt Lake City, Utah. The latter was a publication of the Mormon Church.

Mar. 18   *The Oath of Office* by Charles James Cannon, a romantic tragedy set in the fifteenth century, was given its first performance.

July 22   *New York Fireman and Bond Street Heiress* by S.D. Johnson opened. The play exemplified the type of drama that contrasted the lives of rich and poor, a theme coming into vogue. A Philadelphia play of this year was entitled *Democracy and Aristocracy.*

Aug. 19   William Davidge, the celebrated English comedian, made his American debut at the Broadway Theater, New York City, as Sir Peter Teazle in Sheridan's *The School for Scandal.* Davidge became noted for Shakespearean low-comedy roles, such as Dogberry, Touchstone, and Holofernes. He later played Dick Deadeye in *H. M. S. Pinafore* by Gilbert and Sullivan.

Sept. 27   The great American actor Edwin Booth made his New York City debut at age 16 as Wilford in the play *The Iron Chest* at the National Theater. His acting debut had been at the Boston Museum on Sept. 10, 1849, when he played the role of Tressel in Colley Cibber's version of *Richard III.* His first major role also came at the National Theater, when he took over the role of Richard III in 1851 after his father, Junius Brutus Booth, became ill.

Dec. 3   A new theater, Brougham's Lyceum (later Wallack's Theater), opened in New York City. Private

| Business and Industry; Science; Education; Philosophy and Religion **III** | **IV** Sports; Social Issues and Crime; Folkways; Fashion; Holidays |

An **anti-Catholic organization** called The Supreme Order of the Star-Spangled Banner was secretly formed. This organization soon helped to create the Know-Nothing Party. The order agitated against rising immigration of Irish and German Catholics and activities of foreign Catholic missionary groups in the U.S.

A large **federal land grant for railroad construction** was made for the first time. It provided a right of way on land in Illinois, Mississippi, and Alabama for a railroad from Chicago to Mobile.

A new **speed record for sailing ships,** 13 days from Boston Light to the Equator, was set by the *Stag Hound,* a clipper designed by Donald McKay, premier U.S. shipbuilder.

Jan. 2 The first U.S. **commercial treaty with El Salvador** was ratified.

Mar. 4 Ailing Sen. **John C. Calhoun** of South Carolina had his final speech read to the Senate by a colleague as he sat by. It was his final attack on Sen. Henry Clay's compromise resolutions. Calhoun claimed they failed to provide guarantees that met the concerns of the South. Calhoun died on Mar. 31.

Mar. 11 The **Woman's Medical College of Pennsylvania,** the first medical school entirely for women, was incorporated. Classes began Oct. 12.

Apr. 27 A **regular transatlantic schedule** between Great Britain and the U.S. was inaugurated by the Collins Line, subsidized by carrying U.S. mail. Four new ships designed by naval architect John Willis Griffiths were the best and fastest afloat. Misfortune struck the *Arctic,* however, when it collided with a French vessel off Cape Race, Newfoundland, and sank on Sept. 27. In January of 1856 the *Pacific* was to leave Liverpool for the U.S. and never be heard from again, presumably victim of a collision with an iceberg.

June 1 Native-born U.S. **military personnel** figures were as follows: Army, of 10,540 officers and men, one-third; Navy, of 7500 men, nine-elevenths. Of the combined 18,000 men, 6638 were at sea.

July 8 The **Mormon colony** on Beaver Island in Lake Michigan near the Straits of Mackinac crowned as its king James Jesse Strang, who founded the colony in 1847. In 1856 Strang was assassinated by disaffected followers. An expedition of mainlanders then broke up the colony, and some 2500 Mormons left Michigan.

was disbanded, but later reinstated. German immigrants brought the institution to America, where it was soon functioning as a physical, social, and cultural center.

The most prevalent **American habits,** according to English travelers, were bragging, tobacco chewing, and spitting. American industry and hospitality were also mentioned frequently in the many accounts of the U.S. offered by English visitors, some of whom stayed on.

Tammany Hall, under the leadership of Fernando Wood, was becoming the dominant influence among the many immigrants flooding into New York City. Its charitable services helped win support for developing the political machine.

The **federal policy toward Indians** at this time was summed up in the dictum that it was "cheaper to feed the Indians for a year than fight them for a day."

Approximately 40 **communal settlements,** largely derived from the social reconstruction plans propounded by Charles Fourier and Arthur Brisbane, were founded in the U.S. between 1840 and 1850.

Spring fashions emphasized a "decided tendency to depart from simplicity in dress and adopt ornamental elegance of the middle ages." Bonnets, mantles, and dresses were trimmed with puffings of net, lace, and flowers.

Apr. A **drinking contest** between two bar habitués in Auburn, N.Y., it was reported by Amelia Bloomer in her magazine *Lily,* had tragic consequences. Each contestant downed three pints of Irish whiskey, after which the defending champion sank to the floor and died. Mrs. Bloomer ended her denunciation of this exhibition with a sympathetic thought for the dead man's mother and sister, "for we know they mourn as those who have no hope."

July Some 500 **deserted ships** were counted in the San Francisco Bay area. Sailors had left them to find their fortunes in California's newly discovered gold fields.

July 25 **Gold in Oregon** was discovered on the Rogue R., providing new prospecting territory for the forty-niners of California's gold rush.

Exploration and Settlement; Wars; Government; Civil Rights; Statistics	I		II	Publishing; Arts and Music; Popular Entertainment; Architecture; Theater

in history had been held in Seneca Falls, N.Y., in 1848.

boxes were $5, orchestra stalls $1, dress circle and parquet 50 cents, and family circle 25 cents.

1851

The new, harsher Fugitive Slave Law of 1850 aroused immediate anger in the North. In turn, landowners and legislators in the South became upset because northern states refused to help enforce the act. The law provided for federal commissioners who could order warrants for arrest of fugitive slaves; it also provided heavy penalties for interfering with enforcement. Anyone aiding a fugitive slave could be fined and jailed. In reaction, a number of free states enacted "personal liberty laws," intended to make it difficult for a slave owner to repossess his property. The actual number of runaway slaves was small, estimated in 1850 at about 1000 out of 3,000,-000 slaves. Most of the runaways were ultimately captured.

Feb. 15 Shadrach, a **fugitive slave,** was rescued from forcible return to his master by a mob in Boston. Attempts to put the Fugitive Slave Act of 1850 into effect caused much bitterness in the North and increased abolitionist sentiment. Many states (Vermont, 1850; Connecticut, 1854; Rhode Island, 1854; Massachusetts, 1855; Michigan, 1855; Maine, 1855 and 1857; Kansas, 1858; and Wisconsin, 1858) passed personal liberty laws, in large part designed to circumvent the federal fugitive slave law. These state laws aroused much controversy and contributed greatly to the split between North and South that led to the Civil War. South Carolina later cited these laws as one of the grievances justifying its secession from the Union. Other outstanding rescues or attempted rescues included that of James Hamlet in New York City (1850), Thomas Simms in Boston (1851), "Jerry" M'Henry in Syracuse, N.Y. (1851), and Anthony Burns in Boston (1854).

Mar. 3 **Coinage of three-cent pieces** was authorized by Congress. At the same time cheaper postage rates were set by Congress. A half ounce could be sent up to 3000 miles for three cents.

May 3 A San Francisco **fire** destroyed 2500 buildings, causing damage estimated at $12,000,000.

June 2 A **prohibition law,** passed by the Maine legislature, forbade the manufacture and sale of alcoholic beverages throughout the state.

Aug. 24 The **López expedition,** unauthorized by the federal government and formed for the purpose of taking Cuba by force, dissolved with the death of Gen. Narciso López and dispersal of his men by Spanish troops at Havana. López was a leader of Spanish refugees agitating for liberation of Cuba which, they

Americans in several fields were beginning to acquire reputations in Europe. In sculpture, the first was Hiram Powers, who had gone to Italy to study classical art in 1837. There in 1843 he produced his marble *Greek Slave* which, when exhibited in London in 1851 at the Crystal Palace, became the most celebrated statue of its time. The nude, a Greek maiden in chains, symbolized Greece's subjection to Turkey. The statue's nudity shocked many, but critics, including many clergymen, ultimately recognized the sculptor's moral purpose and the symbolism of the stark nudity. Several copies of the statue were made. Powers became wealthy and famous as a result of the busts he sculpted, but his fame did not last. Marble busts went out of fashion after his death.

The New York Daily Times was begun as a Whig paper under the editorship of Henry Jarvis Raymond. Its name was changed to *The New York Times* in 1857. During the Civil War it strongly supported Lincoln and his policies, while after the war it fought the Tweed Ring and Tammany in New York City. In 1896 it was purchased by Adolph S. Ochs. In 1935 control passed to Ochs's son-in-law, Arthur Hays Sulzberger.

The House of the Seven Gables by Nathaniel Hawthorne was published. The story centered on a curse laid on a house in Salem at the time of the witch trials (1792).

Moby-Dick, Herman Melville's powerful novel of the sea, was published and little understood. Ostensibly the story of a whaling captain's obsessive search for a white whale, it deals with man's conflict with evil in the universe. Not until 70 years later was the novel widely accepted as a masterpiece.

Francis Parkman began his multivolume account of the colonial French in America and their struggles with the British. The first volume was *The Conspiracy of Pontiac,* which ultimately proved to be the last of the series chronologically. Parkman combined a historian's temperament for painstaking scholarship with a love for the wilderness and respect for the Indians.

Stephen Foster composed "Old Folks at Home." Noting the prejudice against "Ethiopian songs" and wanting to preserve his name for more genteel compositions, Foster sold the first performance rights to Edwin P. Christy, the famous minstrel, and allowed Christy's name to appear on the published music as composer.

The American composer and pianist **Louis Moreau Gottschalk** toured Spain. Compositions that were

Aug. 21 A new transatlantic speed record was set by the Collins Line's steamer *Pacific*, which made the crossing in ten days, four and a half hours.

1851

The Young Men's Christian Association, founded in England in 1844, came to North America in 1851 with the organization of chapters in Boston, Mass., and Montreal, Canada. Other U.S. cities soon formed similar groups. The first convention of the North American association was held in Buffalo, N.Y., in 1854. In 1858 chapters for students were formed at the universities of Michigan and Virginia. The organization emphasized the improvement of the spiritual and moral well-being of young men. It also sponsored social and athletic activities.

The **first electric fire alarm** in America was installed in Boston by Dr. William P. Channing and Moses Gerrish Farmer.

Jan. 28 Northwestern University was chartered in Evanston, Ill., under Methodist auspices as North Western University. The words North and Western were combined in 1867.

Jan. 29 Ripon College was chartered in Ripon, Wis., as Brockway College under the joint auspices of Congregational and Presbyterian groups. The name was changed to Ripon College in 1864. Its first degrees were awarded in 1867.

Feb. 13 The **University of Minnesota** was established by an act of the new territorial legislature, but it did not begin instruction until 1869. Its first degrees were granted in 1873. It is now one of the largest of American universities.

Feb. 13 Heidelberg College, founded in 1850, was chartered in Tiffin, Ohio, under German Reformed auspices. Its first degrees were awarded in 1854. The college was a university between 1890 and 1926.

Feb. 18 Westminster College was chartered in Fulton, Mo., under Presbyterian auspices as Fulton College. Its name was changed to Westminster College in 1853. It issued its first degrees in 1855.

May 6 The first U.S. patent for an **ice-making machine** was awarded to John Gorrie. He died in 1855 after exhausting and futile efforts to raise capital for manufacture of his machine.

May 15 The **longest railroad line** in the world up to this time, the Erie Railroad, opened with a 483-mile route between Piermont, N.Y., on the west side of the Hudson R. and Dunkirk, N.Y., on Lake Erie.

The first important U.S. victory in international sports came on Aug. 22, 1851, when the 170-ton schooner-rigged yacht *America* defeated 14 British vessels in a race around the Isle of Wight for the Hundred Guinea Cup. *America* was built for $30,000 by a syndicate headed by Commodore John C. Stevens, a wealthy Hoboken, N.J., financier and yachtsman who also served as captain. The trophy won became known as the *America's Cup* and has been in competition ever since. The cup was successfully defended by U.S. boats until 1984, when Australia became the first foreign country to win the event.

The **Asylum for Friendless Boys** was founded in New York City. The asylum was reorganized in 1853 into a semimunicipal institution, the Juvenile Asylum, to which courts were empowered to commit not only young vagrants but also children who had been neglected, abused, or exploited by their parents. This civic statute constituted the first legal challenge to the supremacy of the family head in determining a child's welfare.

Horace Greeley won an essay contest in Palmer's *Business Men's Almanac* for 1851 with an article entitled "The Philosophy of Advertising." Greeley contended that the days of large unit-sale profits were all but gone. "The general diffusion of intelligence and the improvement of the facilities for direct exchanges between producer and consumer render extensive and regular trade on the basis of small sales and large profits impossible."

Wendell Phillips, a Boston lawyer, reformer, and orator, made a famous, if pessimistic, observation on human improvement while addressing a rally for women's rights. Said Phillips, "Every step of progress the world has made has been from scaffold to scaffold and from stake to stake."

claimed, was on the verge of revolution against Spanish rule. López attracted a group of Americans in New Orleans who thought Cuba could be annexed to the U.S. and thus become ripe for speculation. They issued bonds against the success of the López mission and organized a band of recruits who were enticed by promises of plunder. The *Pampero,* with a vest-pocket army of 500, many mere boys, sailed from New Orleans on Aug. 3. Both Pres. Zachary Taylor and Pres. Millard Fillmore had forbidden the expedition and pledged the security of Spanish property. The illegal voyage, with no support, ended in disaster. Col. William Crittenden of Kentucky and his company of volunteers were caught and shot. López was publicly executed in Havana. One hundred and sixty-two prisoners, at least half of them Americans, were sent to Spain. When news of the rout reached New Orleans, a mob attacked the Spanish consulate there, tore the Spanish flag to shreds, and mutilated the portrait of the Spanish queen. Congress was forced to pay a $25,000 indemnity for the damage done in New Orleans before the Americans were released by Spain.

Dec. 24   **A fire at the Library of Congress** in Washington, D.C., destroyed two-thirds of its collection.

written or first conceived by Gottschalk during this tour included *Midnight in Seville, Manchega,* and *The Siege of Saragossa.* On his return to the U.S. in 1853, Gottschalk achieved unmatched popularity as a concert performer.

Andrew Jackson Downing was commissioned at an annual salary of $2500 to landscape the public gardens near the Capitol and the White House in Washington, D.C.

Karl Marx, a German exile living in London since 1848, made his first appearance in print in the columns of the New York *Tribune* in a series called "Revolution and Counter-Revolution." Marx had met Charles A. Dana, managing editor of the *Tribune,* in Cologne, Germany, in 1848.

July 4   **Enlargement of the Capitol** in Washington, D.C., was begun with the laying of a cornerstone for an extension. Chief architect of the new wings and of most interior details was Thomas W. Walter, who included a final touch of Greek Revival influence, which had by then run its course. Walter also designed other federal buildings and enlargements in this period.

1852

Disagreement over the Compromise of 1850 was not the only matter dividing the nation. The North was becoming more industrial, but the South remained tied to its slave-operated agricultural system. There were now 16 free and 15 slave states, causing the South to be outnumbered in the Senate as well as in the House, where the North had 144 seats to 90 for slave states. With improvement of transportation, the East and West were becoming more closely integrated by mutual economic interests. The West's interests were reflected particularly in the demand for laws to make it easier to acquire public land. Thus a prosperous and growing nation approached another presidential election with some disunity.

1852–1853   In **congressional elections** the Democrats gained three Senate seats for a 38–22 majority over the Whigs, with two seats going to minor parties. In the House they gained 19 seats for a 159–71 majority, with four seats going to minor parties.

June 1–6   The **Democratic National Convention nominated Franklin Pierce** of New Hampshire for the presidency and William R. King of Alabama for the vice presidency. The convention adopted a platform

The most important book of the 1850s, not for literary quality but for impact on the growing controversy over slavery, was *Uncle Tom's Cabin, or Life Among the Lowly* by Harriet Beecher Stowe. Her book appeared in 1852 and within a year 300,000 copies had been sold. For the first time blacks were treated as individuals, not stereotypes. The South denounced the book but in the North it was taken to be a true picture of the horrors of slavery. The novel may have hastened the final break between North and South. George L. Aiken, actor and playwright, dramatized *Uncle Tom's Cabin* and performed in it. It was first performed at Troy, N.Y., on Sept. 27, 1852, where it ran for 100 nights.

A Western paper, the ***Missouri Democrat,*** was established. It strongly urged emancipation.

The ***Cleveland Leader*** was established by Joseph Medill. In 1855 Medill bought an interest in the Chicago *Tribune.* After the Whig defeat in the 1852 election he became active in forming the Republican Party, which he may have named.

July 10 The **College of the Pacific** was chartered in Santa Clara, Calif., as California Wesleyan College. Established under Methodist auspices, it was renamed the University of the Pacific in 1852. It granted its first degrees in 1858, was transferred to San Jose, Calif., in 1871, integrated with Napa College of Napa, Calif., in 1896, and became the College of the Pacific in 1911. It was moved to Stockton, Calif., in 1924.

Aug. 12 A patent for a **practical sewing machine** was granted to Isaac Merrit Singer, who quickly organized I. M. Singer & Company. The unique feature of Singer's machine was its continuous stitching action. Elias Howe, whose machine was then the most popular, initiated a royalty suit against Singer for producing a machine similar to Howe's. Singer lost and was forced to make a settlement of $15,000; his machine in the meantime had achieved a leading position. It was improved in the next decade by additional patented devices.

Dec. 16 The first patent for a **process of shaping brass into bowls** was issued to Hiram Hayden of Waterbury, Conn. Dishes of brass, fastened to spinning dies, were pressed to the shape of the die.

"**Go West, young man, go West**" originated as the title of an editorial by John B. L. Soule, editor of the Terre Haute *Express*. Horace Greeley, editor of the New York *Tribune* who had been deeply impressed with the West on his travels, reprinted the piece with full credit to Soule. Later, in a letter to a friend, Greeley repeated the advice, adding "and grow up with the country." The quote has since been attributed to Greeley because of his prominence in national affairs.

A sculling match that excited much popular interest in New York City took place around Bedloe's Island. The contestants were William Decker and James Lee. A crowd, betting heavily, gathered at the Battery and saw Decker win by 300 yds.

June 3 The **first baseball uniforms** were worn by the New York Knickerbockers. The outfits consisted of straw hats, white shirts, and blue full-length trousers.

1852

The trend toward taller and taller buildings could only continue if two conditions were satisfied. Iron and steel to support such structures had to be readily available, and a practical way to get up and down had to be devised. Elisha Graves Otis, a Vermont-born inventor, solved the latter problem in 1852 when, while supervising construction of an industrial plant in Yonkers, N.Y., he developed a device to keep hoisting machinery from falling even if the lift chain or rope broke. From this start he developed a safe passenger elevator. The first of its kind was installed in E. V. Haughwout's store at 488 Broadway, New York City, on Mar. 23, 1857.

A steam fire engine that was effective was invented by locomotive engineer Alexander Bonner Latta and sold to Cincinnati, Ohio, the first city to adopt use of steam in its fire-fighting apparatus. Its chief feature was a boiler made of two square chambers, the inner one a firebox, the outer a space for water and steam. The machine could shoot as many as six jets.

A school attendance law was enacted by Massachusetts. It required all children between the ages of 8 and 14 to attend school at least 12 weeks a year, 6 of them to be consecutive.

About this time a Norwegian musician with a love for America and independence initiated a grandiose settlement scheme in western Pennsylvania. Ole Broneman Bull of Norway was a violinist who toured Europe and the U.S. giving concerts to raise money for his project. In 1852 he bought 125,000 acres, which he called Oleana and which was to be a colony for his countrymen, "consecrated to freedom, baptized in independence, and protected by the mighty flag of the Union." The plan failed and Bull lost a great deal of money.

Godey's Lady's Book began featuring paragraphs with the heading "Employment of Women." The items told of the most recent entries of women into the world of business and industry. *Godey's* itself was staffed largely by women in both editorial and press rooms.

The trend toward **women teachers** in public schools was reflected in the following figures. In Boston, 6000 of 8000 teachers were women; in Brooklyn, 103 of 120 teachers were women; and in Philadelphia, 699 of 781 teachers were women.

Matrimonial agencies were becoming popular. The Caroline Fry Marriage Association advertised in the New York *Tribune:* "CHEAP WIVES for poor and deserving young men . . . particular attention paid to the proper matching of temperaments."

that favored the Compromise of 1850 as a solution to the slavery question.

June 16–21 The **Whig National Convention** nominated Gen. Winfield Scott of New Jersey for the presidency and William A. Graham of North Carolina for the vice presidency. The candidates were committed to strict enforcement of the Compromise of 1850.

Aug. 11 The **Free-Soil National Convention** nominated John P. Hale of New Hampshire for the presidency and George W. Julian of Indiana for the vice presidency.

Nov. 2 **Franklin Pierce was elected president** of the United States. William R. King was elected vice president. The electoral vote was Pierce, 254; Winfield Scott, Whig candidate, 42. The popular vote was Pierce, 1,601,474; Scott, 1,386,578; John P. Hale, Free-Soil candidate, 156,149.

Stephen Foster composed "Massa's in de Cold Ground" and in 1853 "My Old Kentucky Home." In the latter, he dropped black dialect for standard English, thus ensuring widespread popularity for the song.

A noted portraitist of the period was **Isaac Augustus Wetherby,** who traveled west making a living where he could with his pen and brush. He lithographed caricatures of members of the Democratic Party and sold them at seven cents apiece. In Iowa in 1856 he offered to paint at a price for both political parties. He experimented in early daguerreotypes, drew heads for itinerant phrenologists and patent medicine retailers, illustrated temperance books, and painted portraits of subjects live and dead.

Sept. 6 **A celebration of drama,** commemorating its supposed introduction to America in 1752 with the arrival of Lewis Hallam's theatrical company in Williamsburg, Va., was held at Castle Garden in New York City. Prominent American players performed in *The Merchant of Venice* and David Garrick's *Lethe.*

1853

The U.S. became the first western nation to establish relations with Japan since the country was closed to foreigners in 1683. On July 8, 1853, Commodore Matthew Calbraith Perry sailed into Yedo (now Tokyo) Bay with a squadron of four vessels. For a time Japanese officials would have nothing to do with Perry, but on July 14 he was able to deliver the documents he carried from Pres. Millard Fillmore to two royal princes at the village of Kurihama. Perry then sailed away to give the Japanese time to consider the idea of external relations. He returned to Yedo the following March and on Mar. 31, 1854, signed a treaty that opened Japan to trade with the West.

Yellow fever took the lives of over 5000 persons in New Orleans, La., from 1853 to 1855. A few cases were reported in the spring, but epidemic proportions were not reached until mid-summer. Two hundred deaths were recorded in the week ending July 16. Vicksburg, Miss., lost one-sixth of its population in the epidemic.

The **Native American, or Know-Nothing, Party** was formed. Its adherents viewed with alarm the steadily growing number of immigrants. The party hoped to exclude anyone not native-born from holding federal, state, or municipal office, and urged the repeal of naturalization laws. "Know Nothing" became the party's unofficial name because its followers' typical response to

The distinctive culture and humor of the old Southwest, along the Gulf of Mexico, were colorfully recorded by Joseph Glover Baldwin in *The Flush Times of Alabama and Mississippi,* which was published this year. The 26 sketches included a mixture of comic anecdotes and biographies of notable lawyers and judges of the 1830s and 1840s. The book was both realistic and satirical and typified the humorous exaggeration of the time as practiced by the region's best orators, gamblers, and tellers of tall tales.

Fern Leaves from Fanny's Portfolio by Fanny Fern (Sara Payson Willis) was published. A collection of sentimental verse, a genre extremely popular at this time, it sold more than 70,000 copies in its first year. The 1850s were noted for the number of women writers who consistently sold more books than such literary lights as Ralph Waldo Emerson, Nathaniel Hawthorne, Herman Melville, and Walt Whitman.

The **Crystal Palace** was built in New York City to house the 1853 exhibition. Constructed of cast iron and glass, it had the largest dome yet erected in the U.S. It was hailed for integrating engineering and decoration in a new national architectural style.

The publishing firm of **Harper & Brothers** in New York City was swept by a fire that destroyed the firm's building, plates, and inventory. The loss was estimated

| Business and Industry; Science; Education; Philosophy and Religion **III** | | **IV** Sports; Social Issues and Crime; Folkways; Fashion; Holidays |

Jan. 15 The **first Jewish hospital** in the U.S. was incorporated by Sampson Simson and eight associates in New York City. Called Jews' Hospital, it later became Mt. Sinai Hospital.

May 9 The **first U.S. Roman Catholic Church Council** was held at the Cathedral in Baltimore, Md.

Nov. 5 The **American Society of Civil Engineers** was established in New York City. First called the American Society of Engineers and Architects, it did not hold its first annual meeting until 1869, when membership was 160.

Nov. 21 **Duke University,** founded in 1838 as Union Institute, was chartered in Randolph County, N.C., as Normal College. Established under Methodist auspices, it awarded its first degrees in 1853 and was renamed Trinity College in 1859. It moved to Durham, N.C., in 1892. In 1924 it became Duke University after becoming the major beneficiary of the Duke Foundation.

The word *lingerie* came into general circulation, replacing such euphemisms as *white work, white sewing,* and *the under wardrobe.*

Jan. 28 The famous sentence "**Eternal vigilance is the price of Liberty**" was uttered by abolitionist Wendell Phillips in an address before the Massachusetts Anti-Slavery Society. Phillips' words are thought to have been based on the statement "The condition upon which God hath given liberty to man is eternal vigilance . . . ," made in a speech by the Irish politician John Philpot Curran on July 10, 1790.

Apr. 6 The word *telegram* was first used in the Albany *Evening Journal.* It read in part: "A friend desires us to give notice that he will ask leave . . . to introduce a new word. . . . It is 'telegram,' instead of 'telegraphic dispatch' or 'telegraphic communication.'" The British refused to accept this piece of Yankee slang until 1857, when the London *Times* used the word in a heading over an official British dispatch.

Aug. 3 The **first intercollegiate rowing race** was conducted by Harvard and Yale, whose crews rowed a two-mile course on Lake Winnepesaukee, N.H. Harvard won by four lengths.

1853

The iron rails of the railroads were weaving a network of lines around the nation at an ever greater rate. In 1850 there were about 9000 miles of track, by 1860 more than 30,000. The Pennsylvania Railroad connected Philadelphia and Pittsburgh in 1852. The New York Central came into being in 1853, combining seven short lines between Albany and Buffalo, N.Y., into one. On Jan. 12, 1853, the Baltimore & Ohio Railroad began rail service to Wheeling, W.Va., from Baltimore. Rail service between New York and Chicago was available, although not in one continuous line. In 1856 the Illinois Central became the longest railroad in the world, with 700 miles of main line track. The Illinois Central was also the first railroad to which the federal government granted large tracts of public land as a subsidy; it was given 3,736,000 acres.

The **first terra cotta** in the U.S. was produced by James Renwick, professor of natural philosophy and experimental chemistry at Columbia University in New York City. Renwick, the father of the architect of the same name, proposed its use as paving material.

Improvement of the **sluicing process** by E. E. Matteson proved beneficial in California gold fields and later in the Klondike.

The **College of the City of New York,** founded in 1847 as the Free Academy, was incorporated this year.

Popular entertainment was taking new forms, and larger theaters were built to serve growing audiences. The Hippodrome, in New York City, which opened in 1853, could seat 4600 people. It offered chariot races as well as acrobats and clowns. Other entertainment included Swiss bell ringers and a steam calliope drawn by 40 horses.

The wearing of **knee breeches or medals,** Sec. of State William L. Marcy warned all members of the diplomatic service, would not be accepted under any circumstances.

The **Mount Vernon Ladies' Association** was organized by Anne Pamela Cunningham for the purpose of purchasing George Washington's plantation home. Edward Everett donated to it all fees from his Lyceum lecture on the moral qualities of Washington. This came to more than one-third of the necessary $200,000. The Mount Vernon Ball at the Boston Theater in 1859, sponsored by Mrs. Harrison Gray Otis, provided the final $10,000.

"**Woman,**" Dinah Taylor wrote in an 1853 issue of Amelia Bloomer's feminist magazine *Lily,* "is the great and grand Archimedian lever, whose fulcrum is

questions regarding policy was, "I don't know." The reply was not from ignorance but secrecy.

Feb. 21 The **silver content of all coins** except the silver dollar was reduced. The Coinage Act was passed to keep smaller coins in circulation. It also provided for the minting of $3.00 gold pieces.

Mar. 2 The **Territory of Washington** was formed after separation from the Oregon Territory.

Mar. 3 A **transcontinental railroad survey** was authorized by Congress. $150,000 was appropriated to find the most practical railroad route across the country. The survey was to be conducted by the War Department.

Mar. 4 **Franklin Pierce was inaugurated president** of the United States. The 14th president and a Democrat, he was not renominated by his party in 1856.

May 31 A **second Arctic expedition** to find the missing British explorer Sir John Franklin left New York harbor aboard the cutter *Advance.* The expedition was financed by Henry Grinnell, who had also financed the first expedition in 1850. Elisha Kent Kane was the commanding officer. The ship was caught in freezing weather and remained icebound in Kane Basin for 21 months. The entire party abandoned ship on May 25, 1855, and made a heroic trek to Upernivik, Greenland, in 83 days. There, Kane and his party were rescued by a relief expedition.

Dec. 24 The steamship *San Francisco* sank at sea on its way to California. Some 240 of its 700 passengers were lost at sea.

Dec. 30 The **Gadsden Purchase,** negotiated by James Gadsden, U.S. minister to Mexico, was signed. By its terms the U.S. acquired 29,644 sq. mi. of territory, comprising the southernmost portions of present-day Arizona and New Mexico, for $15,000,000 (later reduced to $10,000,000). The purchase established the final boundaries of the contiguous United States. The treaty, amended with consent of the Mexican government, was ratified on June 30, 1854. The territory had been sought for a route for the Southern Pacific Railroad.

at $1,500,000, the costliest fire in the U.S. to date for a company.

The Bryan Gallery of Christian Art was opened in a loft on Broadway, New York City, by Thomas Jefferson Bryan, a wealthy art collector who tried to stimulate public taste. The collection included works by Albrecht Dürer, Hubert van Eyck, Andrea Mantegna, and others. Bryan charged 25 cents for admission. In an introduction to the gallery's catalog Richard Grant White described the popular art of the day: "Floras and Doras, with big eyes and little mouths, big arms and little hands, big busts and little waists, big bustles and little feet ... portraits of homely old women flattered, in Books of Beauty, into a conventional prettiness and unnatural youth, far more repulsive than their own actual comeliness: such are the works of art which 'sell.'"

Jan. 8 The **first equestrian bronze casting** made in the U.S., that of Gen. Andrew Jackson, was dedicated in New Orleans on the 38th anniversary of Jackson's greatest military triumph. The artist was the resourceful Clark Mills, who solved the problem of balancing the largest bronze casting yet attempted with the horse standing on his rear legs and the general raising his cap. Congress had appropriated $12,000 in advance and liked the sculpture so much it appropriated another $20,000 on its completion. Congress later commissioned Mills to do an equestrian statue of George Washington, for which it paid him $50,000.

Feb. The women's suffrage magazine *Una,* published by Paulina Wright Davis and edited by Caroline H. Dall, issued its first number in Washington, D.C.

Feb. 11 **Louis Moreau Gottschalk** made his formal debut at Niblo's Garden, New York City. Only 24 years old, Gottschalk was widely acclaimed as a pianist and composer. He was offered a long-term contract by P. T. Barnum, which he refused. Instead he embarked on a concert career under the management of Max Strakosch.

Aug. 15 **Attitudes toward blacks** in New York City were reflected in the notice issued by Purdy's Theater during its successful run of *Uncle Tom's Cabin:* Respectable colored people would be accommodated in a comfortable parquet, set off from the rest of the house; a special entrance would be provided, and admission would be 25 cents.

| Business and Industry; Science; Education; Philosophy and Religion **III** | | **IV** Sports; Social Issues and Crime; Folkways; Fashion; Holidays |

Jan. 12 Willamette University was chartered in Salem, Ore., under Methodist auspices. Its first degrees were awarded in 1859. It had been founded in 1842.

Feb. 12 Illinois Wesleyan University was chartered in Bloomington, Ill., under Methodist auspices. Its first degrees were awarded in 1853. It had been founded in 1850.

Feb. 22 Washington University was chartered in St. Louis, Mo., as Eliot Seminary. Established under Unitarian auspices, the seminary became Washington University in 1857. It awarded its first degrees in 1862.

Mar. 31 Louisiana State University was chartered in Alexandria, La., as the Louisiana State Seminary of Learning and Military Academy. State-supported, the seminary awarded its first degrees in 1869. It moved to Baton Rouge, La., in 1870, when it was renamed Louisiana State University.

Apr. 1 Ohio Wesleyan Female College was chartered in Delaware, Ohio. It was combined with Ohio Wesleyan University in 1877.

Apr. 13 Loyola College was chartered in Baltimore, Md., under Catholic auspices. Its first degrees were awarded in 1853. It had been founded in 1852.

May Gail Borden applied for a patent on his process for making evaporated milk in a vacuum. The Patent Office doubted its patentability until Borden reargued his application, after which the patent was issued, on Aug. 19, 1856. Production began in 1858. Originally conceived as a boon for immigrant and tenement-dwelling children who needed a source of safe, nutritious milk, evaporated milk skyrocketed in sales during the Civil War because of Army purchases.

June 3 Central College was chartered in Pella, Iowa, under Baptist auspices. Its first degrees were awarded in 1861. The university passed from Baptist to Dutch Reformed control in 1916.

Sept. Antioch College, which welcomed both male and female students, began operation. The first president of this nonsectarian school was Horace Mann.

Sept. 15 The **first national librarians' convention** was held at the newly incorporated College of the City of New York. Presiding was Charles Jewett, librarian of the Smithsonian Institution.

childhood, whose weight is the world, whose length is all time, whose sweep is vast and endless eternity."

The **Crystal Palace Exhibition of the Industry of All Nations** was held in New York City to demonstrate American inventions and industrial progress. Called a world's fair, it was inspired by the London Exhibition of 1851. The building that housed the exhibition was impressive enough to be referred to as Aladdin's palace.

Waitresses, now beginning to appear, were commented on by Amelia Bloomer, American feminist: "Stopping over night at the Delavan House in Albany, we were very agreeably surprised on entering the dining-room for supper to see about a dozen young women in attendance on the tables. This was something new. When we visited the house last winter the waiters were all men, as is usual in such places. Now not a man was to be seen in that capacity; but in place of their heavy tread, and awkward motions, was woman's light footfall and easy, graceful movements. In a conversation with the proprietor we learned that the change was made in May . . . entirely satisfactory . . . the only objectors being a few women . . . preferring black men."

The celebrated New York–Brooklyn **baseball rivalry** began when an all–New York team defeated an all-Brooklyn team in a best-of-three series, two games to one.

The **first newspaper story on baseball** was published in the New York *Mercury.* The report was by Sen. William Cauldwell, the newspaper's owner and editor.

Oct. 12 The **heavyweight boxing championship** was decided on a technicality. John C. Morrissey, claiming the title vacated by Tom Hyer, was losing to challenger Yankee Sullivan. But between rounds Sullivan left the ring to slug a few Morrissey supporters who had heckled him. He failed to get back into the ring to answer the bell for the next round, and the referee awarded the decision to Morrissey.

Exploration and Settlement; Wars; Government; Civil Rights; Statistics I		II Publishing; Arts and Music; Popular Entertainment; Architecture; Theater

1854

The signing of the Kansas-Nebraska Act on May 30 by Pres. Franklin Pierce brought civil war a step nearer. The bill, sponsored by Sen. Stephen A. Douglas, Democrat of Illinois, created two new territories and provided what Douglas called "popular sovereignty," also called "squatter sovereignty." This meant that those who settled in each territory would have the right to decide whether the territory, when admitted as a state, would be free or slave. In the North some people were infuriated because the law had the effect of repealing the Missouri Compromise of 1820, which said that there would never be slavery north of the southern boundary of Missouri, except for Missouri itself. Douglas was harmed politically by his sponsorship of the bill.

1854–1855 In **congressional elections** the fledgling Republican party gained 15 Senate seats but trailed the Democrats 40–15, with five seats held by minor parties. In the House the Republicans took a 108–83 majority, with 43 seats held by minor parties.

Mar. 31 The **Treaty of Kanagawa** was signed by Commodore Matthew C. Perry with Japan. The U.S. was permitted a consulate, and American ships were permitted to enter certain Japanese ports for limited trade.

Apr. 26 The **Massachusetts Emigrant Aid Society** was founded by Eli Thayer to encourage immigration to Kansas by opponents of slavery. It was renamed New England Emigrant Aid Society on Feb. 21, 1855. Lawrence, Kans., was settled this year by emigrants from the Northeast sent by the society. The town was named for Amos Adams Lawrence, supporter of the new community.

June 5 The **Canadian Reciprocity Treaty** opened the U.S. market to Canadian agricultural products, timber, and fish. In return American fishermen received new rights in Canadian waters and freedom of operation on the Great Lakes and the St. Lawrence R.

July 6 The **Republican Party was formed** in Jackson, Mich., and nominated the first Republican state ticket for the November elections. A preliminary meeting had been held at Ripon, Wis., on Feb. 28 by 50 disaffected Whigs, Free-Soilers, and northern Democrats, and the name "Republican" proposed. The Jackson meeting also attracted individuals from other splinter groups. The common bond was antislavery, more specifically anger over the Kansas-Nebraska Act.

Oct. 18 The **Ostend Manifesto,** written chiefly by Pierre Soulé, U.S. minister to Spain, after consultation with two other U.S. ministers to European capitals, was forwarded from Ostend city to Sec. of State William L. Marcy, who had requested their recommendation. The manifesto assumed that the U.S. intended to acquire Cuba from Spain. It recommended offering

Opera was thriving, as witnessed by a new and opulent opera house, the Academy of Music, which opened this year on 14th St. at Irving Place in New York City. It replaced the Astor Place Opera House, built in 1847. The new structure, which cost $335,000, opened on Oct. 2 with a performance of Vincenzo Bellini's *Norma.* The cast included two well-known artists of the day, Giulia Grisi and Giuseppe Mario, and was conducted by Luigi Arditi.

The **first newspaper in Nebraska Territory,** the *Nebraska Palladium,* was started in neighboring Iowa.

Walden, an American classic and the most famous work of Henry David Thoreau, was published. It was a series of 18 essays based on the two years Thoreau spent close to nature. The book stresses simplicity and holds that happiness is not to be had by pursuit of wealth. Descriptions of plants, birds, and animals are interspersed with reflections on life.

Novelist **Mary Jane Holmes** began her highly successful publishing career with *Tempest and Sunshine; or, Life in Kentucky.* By 1905 Mrs. Holmes had written 39 novels, many appearing originally in paperback, and had sold over 2,000,000 copies. In the decade or two after the Civil War, she was probably the most popular U.S. novelist. Her hallmark was highly sensitive heroines and noble heroes going through a series of stereotyped situations supported by a simplistic moral code.

The melodramatic *Ten Nights in a Barroom and What I Saw There* by Timothy S. Arthur was published. *Ten Nights* was second in sales to Harriet Beecher Stowe's *Uncle Tom's Cabin.* This favorite of the temperance forces was dramatized successfully by W. W. Pratt in 1858.

Intended as a reply to *Uncle Tom's Cabin, The Hireling and the Slave* by William Grayson was a long, didactic poem in couplets. It contrasted the wretched life of the wage slaves of the North with the ideal life of slaves on southern plantations.

New American plays, mostly comedies and burlesques, marked the beginning of the end for classical drama in the U.S. Adaptations of French comedies appealed to new and wider audiences and were relatively easy for such talented playwrights as Dion Boucicault, John Brougham, and Fitz-James O'Brien, all Irish-born. In the absence of any international copyright convention, adaptations were profitable to authors and producers alike. Livening the scene further was the American debut of the English actress Agnes Robertson on Oct. 22 in *The Young Actress,* a major play by the prolific Boucicault. She was an immediate hit in New York City and later delighted Bostonians for nine weeks.

Business and Industry; Science; Education; Philosophy and Religion III		IV Sports; Social Issues and Crime; Folkways; Fashion; Holidays

1854

The era of public libraries was beginning, and this year it received an important impetus with the opening of the Astor Library in New York City. The library was made possible by a bequest of $400,000 from John Jacob Astor, the wealthiest man in the U.S. at his death in 1848. The library was chartered in 1849 and opened its own building on Lafayette Place as a reference library in 1854. Astor had little formal education but maintained a lifelong interest in literature and science. Fitz-Greene Halleck and Washington Irving, two of America's leading authors, are said to have been instrumental in persuading Astor to make the bequest.

The **paper collar** was invented by Walter Hunt, who had patented the safety pin in 1849.

The **Boston Public Library** was opened to the public. The library had been founded two years earlier. The library is credited with having inaugurated the practice of having popular books kept in large enough supply to fill the demands of many readers while keeping a regular complement of books of more limited circulation. This policy permitted development of the libraries of manuscripts and rare books for which Boston Public Library is famous. The original building was replaced in 1895 with a new structure designed by Charles McKim. It is a masterpiece of the new Italian Renaissance style.

Pennsylvania State College, University Park, Pa., was chartered by the Pennsylvania legislature as Farmers High School of Pennsylvania, the first such state school. It opened in 1859 and became the state's agricultural college in 1862. The name was changed to Pennsylvania State College in 1874.

Jan. 13 **Pacific University** was chartered in Forest Grove, Ore., as Tualatin Academy and Pacific University. It had been founded in 1849 under the joint auspices of Presbyterian and Congregational groups. The university awarded its first degrees in 1863 and became Pacific University in 1922.

Feb. **Cornell College** was chartered in Mt. Vernon, Iowa, as the Iowa Conference Seminary, under Methodist auspices. It had been founded the previous year. The seminary became Cornell College in 1855 and granted its first degrees in 1858.

May 6 **Transatlantic cable communication** became possible when a company headed by Cyrus W. Field was granted a charter and a 50-year monopoly. Not until 1866 was a permanently successful cable laid.

Dec. 30 The Pennsylvania Rock Oil Co., the **first U.S. oil corporation,** was formed in New Haven, Conn., by George H. Bissell and Jonathan J. Eveleth, New York

Paris set the style in women's dress and the Empress Eugenie of France set the Paris style. This was the dawn of the era of the hoop skirt, which ballooned out from a woman's waist. Around 1870 the bustle, a horsehair pad or wire cage worn in back under a woman's skirt, became the fashion. With it went very long, elaborate dresses with puffed upper sleeves. For men, the long cutaway coat of the 1850s went out of fashion, but black suits and white shirts were still in style.

The words *popular sovereignty* were introduced in the slavery issue by Sen. Stephen A. Douglas during debate on his bill to organize the territory of Nebraska into two separate territories. He advanced the principle that each territory had the right to accept or outlaw slavery within its borders. "Popular sovereignty," originated by Lewis Cass, was called "squatter sovereignty" by opponents of slavery.

The phrase *Beecher's Bibles* was introduced to characterize the Sharps rifles shipped to the settlers of Kansas after passage of the Kansas-Nebraska Act. Determined to keep the territory free, northerners rushed in thousands of rifles, which the Rev. Henry Ward Beecher had stated would be more convincing to proslavery forces than any biblical argument against slavery.

William Stuart of Connecticut became one of the best-known counterfeiters in American history with the publication of his *Life,* a vivid account of crime that has become a collector's item.

A **comment on American life,** emphasizing the evils of drink, was offered in the successful tear-jerker *Little Katy; or, The Hot Corn Girl.* The play opened on a happy home. The husband began to drink and gamble. To recoup his losses he committed forgery and was apprehended. His wife began to drink while toiling at her sewing, the rum destroying her maternal feelings. Little Katy was driven into the street to sell hot corn, finally dying of pneumonia.

The trotting horse **Flora Temple** broke all records by running the mile at Kalamazoo, Mich., in 2:19½—the first time a horse had run a mile faster than 2:20. The news, flashed immediately throughout the nation by telegraph, made Flora Temple a national celebrity.

The **Children's Aid Society** in New York City opened a lodging house for boys and integrated it with an industrial school, and with boys meetings, which stressed religious education.

Baseball rules stipulated the exact weight and size of the baseball for the first time. The ball had to weigh

| Exploration and Settlement; Wars; Government; Civil Rights; Statistics | I | | II | Publishing; Arts and Music; Popular Entertainment; Architecture; Theater |

Spain $130,000,000 for Cuba, and if the offer was rejected, taking the island by force. In the face of rising opposition to such an acquisition, Sec. Marcy rejected the recommendation on Nov. 13.

Nov. 13   A shipwreck off the New Jersey coast of the emigrant ship *New Era*, en route to New York City from Bremen, Germany, killed nearly 300 persons.

The **first fireproof building** in the U.S. was constructed for Harper & Brothers for its publishing headquarters in New York City. It was built with wrought-iron beams set in masonry walls.

Sept. 15   The **first newspaper in Kansas**, the *Kansas Weekly Herald*, began publication at Leavenworth.

1855

This period showed a great increase in immigration to America from Europe, both for economic and political reasons. The growth was reflected in the fact that this year the New York State Immigration Commission leased Castle Garden, at the tip of Manhattan Island, as a reception center. During the 1850s a total of 2,314,000 people arrived in the U.S. Almost all came from Germany, Ireland, England, Scotland, and Wales. Immigrants for the most part settled in the northeastern part of the country. The Irish tended to remain in the large cities, but many Germans moved west to farmland.

William Walker landed a company of filibusters, military adventurers, in Nicaragua, overthrew the government, and set himself up as ruler. Walker, a sometime lawyer, doctor, and newspaper editor, had seized Lower California in 1853 and made himself president. When his regime collapsed, he was tried and acquitted by a San Francisco court for breaking neutrality laws. He went to Nicaragua at the request of a revolutionary party and became the leader of the rebellion. By 1856 he was again a president, and his regime was recognized by the U.S. He was forced out of power by British and French interests and by the maneuvers of Cornelius Vanderbilt, who resented Walker's interference in Nicaraguan administration of the Accessory Transit Company. Walker was executed in 1860 by a Honduran court when his attempt to return to Nicaragua was foiled by the British.

Omaha, which had begun its first boom only a year earlier, when the Indians left the region, became the site of Nebraska's first territorial legislature. A ferry company's building was used for the assembly.

Feb. 10   U.S. **citizenship laws** were amended to provide that all children born abroad of U.S. parents be granted U.S. citizenship.

Feb. 24   An act creating the **first U.S. Court of Claims** was signed by Pres. Franklin Pierce. Previously citizens could present claims against the federal government only by petitioning Congress.

Mar. 30   **Kansas's first territorial election** chose legislators amid armed violence. Some 5000 so-called Border Ruffians invaded territory from western Missouri

American composers were still few in number. Two who became pioneer composers of opera in the U.S. were William H. Fry and George F. Bristow. Fry wrote the first American opera, *Leonora*, in 1845, but it was not successful. Bristow's *Rip Van Winkle*, the second American opera, opened at Niblo's Garden in New York City on Sept. 27, 1855, and ran for four weeks. Richard Storrs, contemporary critic, announced, "A new American opera has succeeded in New York!" Fry and Bristow tried to encourage compositions by American composers.

Israel Potter: His Fifty Years of Exile by Herman Melville was published. This historical romance was based on an earlier account of an American Revolutionary soldier who was captured by the British and taken to England, where he escaped and joined an underground group of rebel agents. Later Potter meets Ben Franklin, John Paul Jones, and Ethan Allen, and participates in the great naval battle between the *Bonhomme Richard* and the *Serapis,* which Melville vividly recreates.

Familiar Quotations, the now famous compilation by John Bartlett, a Cambridge, Mass., bookstore owner, was published. The book *Quotations* has often been revised, the 15th edition having appeared in 1980.

The *Daily News,* the powerful organ of Tammany Hall in New York City, was established. Strongly opposed to the Civil War, it led all U.S. newspapers in circulation until 1901, the year of its demise.

Leaves of Grass by Walt Whitman, one of the most famous books of poetry of all time, was published at the author's expense. The first edition, containing only 12 poems, fared badly in the marketplace, but it did receive helpful praise from Ralph Waldo Emerson, ending with "I greet you at the beginning of a great career." A second edition, with 33 poems added, appeared in 1856; in 1860 a third, greatly enlarged and rearranged edition appeared. After the Civil War, revised and enlarged editions were published periodically; the final, ninth edition, under the author's direction, is dated 1892. In the 1940s a book club distributed 250,000

| **Business and Industry; Science; Education; Philosophy and Religion** III | | IV **Sports; Social Issues and Crime; Folkways; Fashion; Holidays** |

City law partners. Samples of surface oil found in Cherrytree Township, Venango County, Pa., had been analyzed by Prof. Benjamin Silliman of Yale, who found eight commercially feasible uses for the oil. Bissell and Eveleth then leased 200 acres and went into business with $500,000 in capital. The oil was obtained by digging wells and trenching.

between 5½ and 6 oz. and have a diameter of between 2¾ and 3½ in.

Growing interest in **baseball** in New York City was evidenced by the establishment of many clubs, including: the Eagle and the Empire of New York City and the Excelsior of Brooklyn. By 1855 Morrisania had the Union Club and Brooklyn had added the Atlantic and the Eckford.

1855

Bridge building continued, and structures were getting longer and stronger. The most expert designer and builder of bridges was John Augustus Roebling. Roebling came to the U.S. from his native Germany in 1831 and became a citizen in 1837. He was a pioneer in suspension bridge construction, completing the Allegheny Suspension Bridge at Pittsburgh in 1845 and the Niagara Suspension Bridge in 1855. In the latter bridge Roebling made the first full-scale use of a wire cable of his own design; the cable was made up of parallel wires that were wire-bound. Previous cables had consisted of twisted wire. Roebling first developed this wire cable, or wire rope, in 1841.

The *American Journal of Education,* the first national publication of the teaching profession in the U.S., was published by Henry Barnard. In 1867 Barnard became the first U.S. commissioner of education.

The **first lighthouse** on the Pacific coast was built on Point Loma, San Diego, Calif.

The **Panama Railroad,** owned and built by a U.S. company, was completed across the Isthmus of Panama.

Jan. 25 **Iowa Wesleyan College** was chartered in Mt. Pleasant, Iowa, as Iowa Wesleyan University. Founded under Methodist auspices in 1842, it awarded its first degrees in 1856. It became a college in 1912.

Feb. 6 **Eureka College** was chartered in Eureka, Ill., under the auspices of the Disciples of Christ. Its first degrees were granted in 1860.

Feb. 10 **Kalamazoo College** was chartered in Kalamazoo, Mich., under Baptist auspices. It presented its

Few blacks achieved any prominence or became well-known to the general public in the age of slavery. An exception was Frederick Douglass. Born a slave in Maryland, he escaped and made his way to Massachusetts in 1838. A speech delivered by Douglass at an antislavery meeting so impressed his hearers that the American Anti-Slavery Society engaged him as one of its lecturers. In 1847 Douglass founded an abolitionist newspaper, the *North Star.* During the Civil War he persuaded Pres. Abraham Lincoln to use blacks as soldiers. In 1889 he became U.S. ambassador to Haiti.

Mrs. **Sarah Josepha Hale** launched a campaign in the columns of *Godey's* against the use of the word "female" in reference to women in public life. Elimination of the term became one of the objectives of feminism in America.

The phrase *cotton is king* came into prominence. It was taken from the title of a book, *Cotton is King, or the Economical Relations of Slavery,* by David Christy, which was published this year. At this time export of cotton amounted to one-half of all U.S. exports. Its value was more than $100,000,000 annually.

The vogue for **horseback riding** among American ladies was now widespread. In Boston and New York City numerous riding academies were set up to help women adjust to side saddle riding. A newspaper editorial commented: "A lot of cynical old fogies . . . have recently been startled . . . by the rushing, galloping, slashing, and dashing exploits of the lady equestrians at the agricultural fairs. This jocund spectacle like everything else that is new . . . does not suit the still veins of these respectable old goats. . . . But still the ladies go on riding. . . . "

The **American penchant for travel** was evident for many years, but it became increasingly so at midcentury. By 1855 the eastern railroad system was already beginning to function. It was possible to make a trip between most of the large cities, but schedules

and forced the election of a proslavery legislature. The number of votes cast far exceeded the number of eligible voters. To prevent widespread bloodshed, Andrew H. Reeder, appointed territorial governor by Pres. Pierce, reluctantly allowed the fraudulent election to stand.

June 5 The **American Party** was chosen as the new name for the Native American Party, commonly called the Know-Nothing Party, during its national meeting at Philadelphia. Control had been won by southern and proslavery forces, resulting in the disaffection of northern members, most of whom turned to the Republicans. The party virtually ceased to exist after the 1856 presidential election.

Sept. 5 **Antislavery settlers in Kansas,** at a convention held in Big Springs, repudiated the fraudulently elected territorial legislature. Arms were sent to the settlers from northern states and an army was formed, called the Free State forces. The abolitionist firebrand, John Brown, arrived in Kansas and became a leader of these forces.

Oct. 23 The **Topeka Constitution** drawn up by Kansas Free State forces set up a governor and a legislature. Kansas now had two governments. The Topeka Constitution outlawed slavery.

Nov. 26 The **Wakarusa War** threatened Lawrence, Kans., when some 1500 Border Ruffians, camped on the Wakarusa R., advanced on the town. They withdrew when they found the town was heavily defended by Free State forces. They returned in 1856.

copies to its members. *Leaves of Grass* today is in many reprint series.

The Song of Hiawatha by Henry Wadsworth Longfellow was published. The poem was a broad collection of Indian legends tied together by a fictional character. Its publication marked the peak of Longfellow's fame. Using the meter of the Finnish epic *Kalevala*, Longfellow obtained musical effects by his repeated use of euphonious names for Indian persons and places. The poem epitomized the glorification of the American literary concept of the noble savage.

***The Age of Fable*,** the classic work popularly known as Bullfinch's Mythology, was published. Thomas Bullfinch, a Boston businessman and son of a celebrated architect, assembled the great myths from Greek, Roman, Scandinavian, Celtic, and Oriental mythology and retold them for a wide readership.

The plates and rights of **Noah Webster's** *A Grammatical Institute of the English Language*, called by many generations of schoolchildren the Blue-back Speller, were acquired by D. Appleton & Company, New York City publishers. Originally published in 1783, the book was reissued as the *Spelling Book.* It sold 1,000,000 or more copies a year for 40 years after Appleton became its publisher.

Oct. 9 A patent for a **steam calliope** was awarded to Joshua C. Stoddard of Worcester, Mass. Stoddard later extended his scope to the invention of farm implements, including a horse-drawn hay rake and a fruit parer.

1856

The presidential election campaign of 1856 saw two new parties fielding candidates for the presidency. One was the American Party, the Know-Nothings, which had reached its peak in 1854 and was disintegrating over the slavery issue. The other was the Republican Party, whose strength lay in the North and West and among antislavery forces. The main issue of the campaign was the fight between slavery and antislavery forces for control of Kansas Territory. Although the Democrats won the presidency, the combined popular vote for the American, Republican, and Whig candidates was more than that for the Democratic winner, James Buchanan.

1856–1857 In **congressional elections** the Democrats lost four Senate seats but kept a majority, 36–20, over the Republicans, with eight seats going to minor parties. In the House the Democrats took a 118–92 majority, with 26 seats going to minor parties.

Feb. 22 The **Republican Party** held its first national meeting at Pittsburgh, Pa. Delegates met to plan a

Until this time American historians had mostly confined their writings to American and related British subjects. John Lothrop Motley went further afield and devoted his life's work to a study of the Netherlands. *The Rise of the Dutch Republic* appeared in 1856 in three volumes; it was followed by six more volumes in later years. Motley, writing with great enthusiasm for his subject, attempted to show how Protestantism in northern Europe had brought freedom there. Warmly partisan toward William of Orange, he created a dramatic narrative of the Dutch struggle against Spanish oppression. He drew analogies with the struggles of the U.S. and George Washington. The work sold over 30,000 copies in England and the U.S. in its first year.

"**The Barefoot Boy**" by John Greenleaf Whittier, one of America's most endearing poems, was included in his *The Panorama and Other Poems,* published this year. Turning here from his concerns about slavery, Whittier

Business and Industry; Science; Education; Philosophy and Religion	III	IV	Sports; Social Issues and Crime; Folkways; Fashion; Holidays

first degrees in 1855. It had been established in 1833 as a literary institute.

Apr. 28 The **University of Santa Clara** was chartered in Santa Clara, Calif., under Catholic auspices. Its first degrees were awarded in 1857. It had been founded Mar. 19, 1851, as Santa Clara College, its name until 1912.

Apr. 30 The **College of California** was chartered in Oakland, Calif., under control of Congregational and Presbyterian denominations. Its first degrees were awarded in 1864. It was the first institution in California to offer courses on the model and scale of the leading colleges of the East.

Sept. 17 The **Boston Public Library,** the first public library in Massachusetts supported by taxation, was dedicated. George Ticknor was a major benefactor and Edward Everett a vigorous promoter. A public library at Wayland, Mass., had been founded in 1850 by an endowment from Francis Wayland, president of Brown University.

Oct. 17 The **first conference of rabbis** in the U.S. met at Medical College in Cleveland, Ohio. The Reform rabbi, Isidor Kalisch, a German immigrant, was a chairman of the convention.

and services were hardly efficient or oriented to passenger convenience. There was, for example, only a single train each day out of Washington, D.C., that connected with other trains on the way to Boston. The run included changes and stopovers in Baltimore, Philadelphia, and New York City, which varied in length from half an hour in Baltimore to nine hours in New York. The total traveling time of the run was 35½ hours. The trip from Washington to Boston cost $11.60.

The practice of **selective law enforcement** was exemplified this year in instructions issued to New York City police by Mayor Fernando Wood concerning prohibition. A statewide prohibition law had gone into effect on July 4. Mayor Wood's instructions read in part: "Whether liquors exhibited in your presence . . . are intoxicating liquors . . . you must judge with great circumspection, and be careful to avoid seizing any thus exempt. An error in this regard may lay you liable to severe personal responsibility. . . . Keeping liquor with intent to sell or give away, is not an offense fully within the scope of the eye. . . . You can not see the violation . . . for an intent can not be seen. . . . These violations . . . do not . . . compel you to arrest or seize without complaints." This situation of selective law enforcement was disposed of by the judiciary when it declared the New York State statute unconstitutional in Mar. 1856. Twelve states and two territories had prohibition by the end of 1855, but drinking was an established American habit. Even the cop on the beat liked his beer.

1856

Along with the growing railroad system, the telegraph was vital to the transportation and communication network that was uniting the nation from coast to coast. Ezra Cornell, a financier who had supported the experiments of Samuel F. B. Morse that led to the invention of the telegraph, set out in 1855 to organize a national telegraph system. Given the name Western Union Telegraph Company on Apr. 1, 1856, Cornell's company by 1866 became a national system controlling some 75,000 miles of telegraph lines. The telegraph was essential to the railroads because it was the only way a message could be sent ahead of trains to give operational orders.

The **first kindergarten** in the U.S. was opened in Watertown, Wis., under the guidance of Mrs. Carl Schurz, wife of the prominent German refugee and leading Republican figure in the Lincoln-Hayes administration. It was a German-language school. Mrs. Schurz was an ardent disciple of Friedrich Froebel, the

Gambling continued to be a favorite pastime of Americans. It was estimated that in the 1850s there were 2000 professional gamblers working the riverboats. Faro, monte, and chuck-a-luck were the favorite games. There was also three-card monte to help innocents lose their money even faster. The gamblers were easily recognized by their elegant, if gaudy, clothing, which featured a broadcloth coat and a ruffled white shirt.

By 1856 **baseball** was already considered a national pastime, as evidenced by the following passage from the sporting paper *Spirit of the Times:* "With the fall of the leaf and the diminution of the daylight, many of the out-of-door sports and pastimes come to a close for the season. The manly and exhilarating pastimes of Base Ball, Cricket, Foot Ball, and Racket are not playable. . . . We feel a degree of old Knickerbocker pride at the continued prevalence of Base Ball as the National game in the region of the Manhattanese."

national presidential nominating convention to be held in June.

Feb. 22 The **national convention of the American, or Know-Nothing, Party** met at Philadelphia and nominated former Pres. Millard Fillmore for president and Andrew J. Donelson of Tennessee for vice president.

May 21 **Lawrence, Kans.,** a station on the underground railroad, was sacked by Border Ruffians and proslavery supporters. Loss of life was not great, but the act inflamed northern sentiment. In retaliation John Brown, with four sons and three companions, massacred five proslavery Kansans along the Pottawatomie Creek on May 24.

May 22 Sen. **Charles Sumner** of Massachusetts was severely beaten by cane-wielding Preston S. Brooks, a member of the House from South Carolina. Two days before, during the Senate debate on the admission of Kansas, Sumner referred to Sen. Andrew P. Butler of South Carolina, a proslavery opponent of admission, in these terms: "The Senator touches nothing which he does not disfigure with error, sometimes of principle, sometimes of fact. He shows an incapacity for accuracy, whether in stating the Constitution, or in stating the law, whether in details of statistics or the diversions of scholarship." Sumner also delivered derogatory comments about South Carolina. Rep. Brooks, Sen. Butler's nephew, feeling personally affronted, caned Sumner while he was seated at his Senate desk. Brooks was arrested and fined $500, which he later paid. Expulsion proceedings in the House failed, but Rep. Brooks resigned. However, he was reelected to Congress by his district in the next election. He later challenged a northern congressman to a duel, which never took place. Sen. Sumner was so severely injured by the caning that his recovery took three years.

June 2 An antislavery section of the **Know-Nothing Party** met in New York City and nominated John C. Frémont of California for president and W. F. Johnston of Pennsylvania for vice president.

June 2–5 The **Democratic National Convention** nominated James Buchanan of Pennsylvania for president and John C. Breckinridge of Kentucky for vice president.

June 17–19 The **Republican National Convention** nominated John C. Frémont of California for president and William L. Dayton of New Jersey for vice president.

July 17 A railroad disaster cost the lives of 66 children on a Sunday-school outing outside Philadelphia, Pa.

Aug. 1 **Bleeding Kansas,** as the territory was known at this time, was without any settled government. Raids between the two factions continued, with an estimated 200 killed and $2,000,000 in property lost between Nov. 1855 and Dec. 1856. The House

called up memories of his own boyhood and created a small masterpiece of local color.

John Halifax, Gentleman, by Dinah Maria Mulock Craik, was published. Its popularity was long lasting, and it is still being reissued.

Dred, A Tale of the Great Dismal Swamp by Harriet Beecher Stowe was published. *Dred* was popular both in the U.S. and in Europe, but did not rival *Uncle Tom's Cabin. Dred* attempted to emphasize the economic as well as the moral evils of slavery, especially its demoralizing effect on whites.

The vogue for **romantic and emotional paintings** was reflected in the works of Thomas P. Rossiter, who had returned to New York after an extended stay in Paris. The titles of his paintings reflect the demands of the day: *The Last Hours of Tasso; The Parting between Ruth, Orpah, and Naomi; The Return of the Dove to the Ark; Morn, Noon, and Evening in Eden.* In 1857 Rossiter began his well-known *Washington and Lafayette at Mount Vernon, 1776,* now in the Metropolitan Museum, New York City.

A **pantomime** called *Planche or Lively Fairies* opened in New York City. *Planche* was a London original. Several thousand dollars had been spent importing the London sets and readying the lavish, multi-act show for its New York City premiere.

George William Curtis published *Prue and I* (1856–1857), a collection of satirical essays about life in New York City in the vein of *Salmagundi* by Washington Irving. Curtis, a well-established editor, also delivered this year a famous address against slavery, "The Duty of the American Scholar to Politics and the Times."

Of **American painting,** John Ruskin, famous English art critic, had this to say: "I have just been seeing a number of landscapes by an American painter of some repute; and the ugliness of them is Wonderful. I see that they are true studies and that the ugliness of the country must be unfathomable." But Ruskin was hardly more complimentary toward British art and architecture.

English Traits by Ralph Waldo Emerson was published. Emerson had been lecturing on the English since his second visit to England in 1847. He had come to admire Englishmen during his first visit in 1833, when he first met Samuel Taylor Coleridge, William Wordsworth, Walter Savage Landor, and Thomas Carlyle. Emerson's style was relaxed and his comments were keen and amusing. In 1847 England was, he found, the "best of all actual nations," though it was "no ideal framework."

| Business and Industry; Science; Education; Philosophy and Religion III | IV Sports; Social Issues and Crime; Folkways; Fashion; Holidays |

progressive educator in Thuringia whose theories, including those on the kindergarten, had great influence on American education.

The **first railroad in California** was built from Sacramento to Folsom.

Caloric engines were invented and developed by John Ericsson in this period. Ericsson called the engines caloric because they were propelled by hot air. Too large for locomotive use, they nevertheless were sold for stationary industrial service. Ericsson attempted unsuccessfully to adapt the caloric engine to power ships. He found greater success when he later designed and constructed the steam-powered ironclad *Monitor.*

The **Illinois Central Railroad** completed its line from Galena and Chicago in the north to Cairo in the south, the longest in the U.S. at this time. The effect was to open the entire southern part of the state to farming and mining. Lake Michigan was now linked with the Mississippi and Ohio rivers. Sen. Stephen A. Douglas of Illinois had persuaded Congress to grant some 4000 sq. mi. of land for use as a railroad right-of-way. The Illinois legislature had granted articles of incorporation to the new railroad company. Investment money poured into Illinois.

Arguing that America was the **Promised Land** of the Bible, Dr. Joseph F. Berg, pastor of the Second Dutch Reformed Church of Philadelphia, published *The Stone and the Image, or The American Republic, the Base and Ruin of Despotism.*

A patent for a **milk-condensing process** was awarded to Gail Borden. Manufacture began in 1858. In 1851 Borden had won the Great Council Medal at the London Exposition for his development of a one-pound meat biscuit containing the nutritional qualities of five pounds of meat and ten ounces of flour. Borden was the first American food producer to win such an honor.

Jan. 8 **Borax** was found for the first time in the southern U.S. by Dr. John A. Veatch at a spring in California.

Mar. 26 The **first street trains** in New England began running between Boston and Cambridge. They were drawn by steam engines.

Apr. 3 **St. Lawrence University** was chartered in Canton, N.Y., under Universalist auspices. Its first degrees were awarded in 1863.

Apr. 21 The **first railroad bridge over the Mississippi R.** opened with the first crossing of a locomotive. The

Children's Day was given its first recorded observance in the Universalist Church of the Redeemer in Chelsea, Mass., when the Rev. Dr. Charles H. Leonard conducted a special service for the children of the parish. Since that time it has been the custom in American Protestant churches to observe Children's Day on the second Sunday in June each year.

An **advertisement** in *The New York Daily Times* read as follows: "Two well-educated young men would like to make acquaintance of two young ladies, with a view to matrimony. They must be well-educated, of loving temperament, and above all religiously disposed." The young men, a lawyer and a theologian, declared that they were each financially able to support a wife and gave their forwarding address as: Columbians, Box #272, Union-Square Post Office, New York City.

Freeman Hunt wrote *Wealth and Worth.* Hunt, an experienced editor of commercial magazines, was a leading defender of the American business ethos against the champions of the arts and sciences. He argued that commerce had taken such a commanding position in the modern world that the concept of culture had to be broadened to include business. He predicted that the study of business would soon be developed and pursued not merely as a technique but as a culture on a par with medicine and law.

A popular and authoritative **home health book,** *The Home Book of Life and Health* by William Andrus Alcott, was published. Alcott, a pioneer in physical education, wrote more than 100 books, including *Forty Years in the Wilderness of Pills and Powders,* which was published in 1859, the year of his death.

The *house divided* theme, developed later by Abraham Lincoln, had its source this year in an editorial by George Fitzhugh in the Richmond (Va.) *Examiner.* Fitzhugh declared that the slave system of the South and the free labor market of the North were antagonistic and would eventually come into conflict with each other. This perception was echoed by Lincoln in his great speech of June 16, 1858, in which he declared: " ' A house divided against itself cannot stand.' I believe this government cannot endure permanently half slave and half free."

refused to seat either proslavery or Free State territorial delegates from Kansas.

Aug. 10 A hurricane took the lives of 400 people at a ball on Last Island, La. Winds drove waves over the gulf resort, inundating the island.

Sept. 17 The Whig National Convention nominated Millard Fillmore for the presidency and Andrew J. Donelson for the vice presidency. Fillmore and Donelson were also the candidates of the Know-Nothing Party.

Nov. 4 James Buchanan was elected president of the United States. John C. Breckinridge was elected vice president. The electoral vote was Buchanan, 174; John C. Frémont, Republican, 114. The popular vote was Buchanan, 1,838,169; Frémont, 1,335,264; Millard Fillmore, Whig and American (Know-Nothing) Party candidate, 874,534. The election marked the end of the Whig Party as a national force.

Dec. 28 Woodrow Wilson, 28th president of the United States, was born at Staunton, Va.

Lena Rivers by Mary Jane Holmes was published. This sentimental novel sold about 1,000,000 copies. Holmes, author of 38 similar novels, provided reading for the taste of the masses.

Mar. 1 George F. Bristow's *Second Symphony in D Minor* was performed by the New York Philharmonic Society. This was one of the few orchestral works by a native-born composer that it presented during the mid-nineteenth century.

July 4 An early equestrian statue, the masterpiece of Henry Kirke Brown, was his *George Washington*, unveiled at Union Square, New York City. The funding was provided by $500 subscriptions from art patrons and merchants.

Aug. 18 A copyright law was passed by Congress, giving the author of a play "along with the sole right to print and publish the said composition, the sole right also to act, perform, or represent the same."

1857

A Supreme Court decision handed down on Mar. 6 in the case of *Dred Scott v. Sandford* was a setback for antislavery forces and further aggravated the growing ill feeling between North and South. Dred Scott was a slave whose owner had taken him from Missouri to Illinois, a free state, in 1834. Scott later returned to Missouri and in 1846 sued for his liberty on the grounds that his stay in free territory ended his slavery. The Court ruled, however, that Scott could not sue because slaves were not citizens. Going beyond the specific case, the Court also said that Congress had no power to prohibit slavery in territories and therefore the Missouri Compromise of 1820, already repealed by the Kansas-Nebraska Act, was unconstitutional.

Jan. 15 The State Disunion Convention, favoring peaceful separation of North and South, met at Worcester, Mass. The most fiery speech was delivered by William Lloyd Garrison, who declared, "No union with slaveholders."

Feb. 21 Foreign coins were declared no longer legal tender by an act of Congress.

Mar. 3 Import duties were lowered to about 20% by the Tariff Act, and the free list was enlarged.

Mar. 4 James Buchanan was inaugurated president of the United States, the 15th president. A Democrat, he served one term.

May 1 A literacy test as a requirement for voting was adopted as an amendment to the Massachusetts state constitution.

Books and articles attacking and defending slavery began to appear in increasing numbers. This year *Cannibals All! or, Slaves Without Masters* by George Fitzhugh, a lawyer and editor of the Richmond, Va., *Examiner,* challenged the idea that freedom was inherently better than slavery. Fitzhugh compared the northern wage system unfavorably with the slave system, arguing that factory workers were "slaves without masters" who had no guarantee of care in illness or old age. Another southerner, Hinton Rowan Helper of North Carolina, also published a book in 1857, *The Impending Crisis of the South,* which was at the same time antislavery and antiblack. He argued that slavery retarded the South and that white farmers who had no slaves suffered from competition with large plantations operated by slaves. Helper's book enraged the South. In 1860 the Republicans distributed 100,000 copies in a condensed version to aid Abraham Lincoln's presidential campaign.

The *Atlantic Monthly* was founded in Boston under the editorship of James Russell Lowell. All the famous New England writers soon contributed to it. In its first issue Oliver Wendell Holmes initiated a series of personal essays under the title "The Autocrat of the Breakfast Table."

Russell's Magazine was founded in Charlestown, S.C., with Paul Hamilton Hayne as editor. A literary journal, it achieved distinction during its three years of life presenting studies of southern life and literature, but also considering science, poetry, travel, and literary criticism. Among its supporters and contributors were

Business and Industry; Science; Education; Philosophy and Religion **III**		**IV** Sports; Social Issues and Crime; Folkways; Fashion; Holidays

bridge ran between Rock Island, Ill., and Davenport, Iowa.

Oct. 7 The **first practical folding machine** to fold book and newspaper sheets was patented by Cyrus Chambers, Jr., a Pennsylvania inventor. Installed in the printing house of Jasper Harding & Son, Philadelphia, Pa., it proved defective for use in handling lightweight Bible sheets but was practical, rapid, and economical in folding almanacs. Chambers, a prolific inventor, built a gold and silver steam engine weighing less than half an ounce; constructed of 150 parts with screws invisible to the naked eye, it was pronounced a marvel of the age.

Dec. 20 **Newberry College** was chartered in Newberry, S.C., under Lutheran auspices. Its first degrees were granted in 1869. The college was moved to Walhalla, S.C., in 1868 but returned to Newberry in 1877.

Lola Montez, an entertainer noted more for her charm and flamboyance than for her dancing skill, returned to the U.S. after a tour of Australia. Montez, born Marie Dolores Eliza Rosanna Gilbert, claimed Spanish descent but actually had been born in Limerick, Ireland. One of the most colorful characters of the midnineteenth century, she had had affairs with Franz Liszt and the elder Alexander Dumas, and had been the mistress of King Louis I of Bavaria before coming to the U.S. in 1851. She married a San Francisco newspaperman and in 1852 took to the stage in a production entitled *Lola Montez in Bavaria.* One of her protégées was Lotta Crabtree, whom she taught to dance when Crabtree was only six. Crabtree was a favorite child performer in California mining camps. Montez also lectured on beauty and fashion and was the author of *The Art of Beauty* (1858). She died in Astoria, N.Y., on Jan. 17, 1861.

1857

Awarding on June 23 of a patent for a process for the economical production of steel marked an important advance in a basic industry. The patent was awarded to William Kelly, whose process involved the oxidation of impurities in iron by blowing air through molten iron. He had first developed the process in 1851. Independently, Henry Bessemer had perfected the technique in England in 1856. Their rival claims were settled in 1866. The first Bessemer converter was built at Troy, N.Y., in 1864. Kelly's process was used in a converter at Wyandotte, Mich., the same year. Steel at once began to replace iron for railroad tracks, with 259,699 tons of steel rail produced in 1875.

A machine for **postmarking and stamp-canceling** was granted a patent for the first time.

Mar. 3 A **U.S. subsidy of overseas cable** was voted by Congress, paying the company formed by Cyrus W. Field $70,000. The project was also supported by England and private resources on both sides of the Atlantic. The laying of cable from Ireland to Newfoundland began this year, but the cable broke some several hundred miles out from Valentia, Ireland. It was decided to use two ships, beginning from the midpoint between Newfoundland and Ireland and traveling in opposite directions. After three more failures, a copper wire 1950 miles long was laid between Trinity Bay and Valentia, the ships both arriving at their destinations on Aug. 5, 1858. Queen Victoria of England

One of the first large and well-planned city parks, and one that set an example, began to be laid out this year. It was Central Park in Manhattan, New York City, comprising 840 acres acquired in 1856. Frederick Law Olmsted and Calvert Vaux won a competition for designing it in 1857; Olmsted was appointed the park's chief architect in 1858. He and Vaux laid out a park that embodied the naturalistic and romantic ideas of the time. Olmsted spent most of his life designing parks and park systems in such cities as Brooklyn, Chicago, Buffalo, and Boston.

Charity balls were originated in New York City. The balls enabled society to dispense with its charitable obligations while displaying its wealth. The first annual charity ball was given at the Academy of Music.

Variety performances at eating places were growing in popularity. The admission fee at many places was 12 cents.

The **first baseball association** was formed. Some 25 amateur baseball clubs agreed to meet in 1858 and establish themselves as the National Association of Baseball Players. Within two years the association had doubled in size.

A new **baseball rule** fixed the length of a game at nine innings and provided that an interrupted game would be regarded as completed after five innings.

Sept. 11 The **Mountain Meadows Massacre** resulted in the death of 120 emigrants headed for California. They were killed in Utah by Indians incited by the Mormon fanatic John D. Lee. Lee's justification was that he was retaliating against Pres. Buchanan's order removing Brigham Young as governor of Utah.

Sept. 15 **William Howard Taft,** 27th president, was born in Cincinnati, Ohio.

Oct. 5 **Kansas** elected a free-state legislature under Gov. Robert J. Walker. The elections were held under supervision, and thousands of fraudulent proslavery votes were rejected.

Oct. 19 The **Lecompton Constitutional Convention** met in Lecompton, territorial capital of Kansas, to prepare a constitution for popular approval. The proposed constitutional referendum was rigged by proslavery elements so that slavery could not be eliminated from the territory even by a negative majority vote. Free-staters consequently refused to vote, and the constitution, permitting slavery, won approval on Dec. 21. The Free-State Party, however, succeeded in convening an extra-legal state legislature, which set another election, this time permitting an unequivocal vote. On Jan. 4, 1858, the constitution lost by an overwhelming vote. Three years before, Stephen Douglas had converted a simple bill for the government of Kansas and Nebraska into the subtle Kansas-Nebraska Bill. With the support of Pres. Franklin Pierce and the southern leaders, Douglas effectively repealed the Missouri Compromise by giving the decision about slavery to the people of Kansas.

William Gilmore Simms, Henry Timrod, and Basil Gildersleeve.

Harper's Weekly was founded under the editorship of George William Curtis.

The famed **Boston Custom House,** the finest granite commercial edifice in the downtown area, was built in the severe style of an earlier period.

The **Studio Building,** New York City's first structure designed for artists' studios, was built by Richard Morris Hunt. Hunt was also influential in the founding this year of the American Institute of Architects.

Oct. 10 **Thomas Crawford,** one of the most productive and original of early American sculptors, died in London at 44. Most of his life was spent in Rome where he had gone to study with Albert Bertel Thorvaldsen. Among his noteworthy works were the bronze doors of the Senate portico, sculptural studies of James Otis and Beethoven, the Washington Monument in Richmond, Va., and the Armed Liberty, crowning the Capitol dome in Washington, D.C.

Dec. 8 *The Poor of New York* by Dion Boucicault, the Irish actor-playwright, opened in New York City during the panic of 1857, an event that was incorporated into the play. Boucicault wrote or adapted over 100 plays, among them *London Assurance,* produced in London Mar. 4, 1841, before he emigrated to the U.S.; *The Octoroon* (1859), dealing with the love of a white man for a black girl; and *Rip Van Winkle* (1865), in which the famous actor Joseph Jefferson played with so much success. Boucicault is credited with inaugurating the "road system." The revision of the copyright law that guaranteed a dramatist the sole right to "act, perform, or represent" his play was the result of his efforts.

1858

A landmark series of political debates took place this year between Aug. 21 and Oct. 15, when Sen. Stephen A. Douglas of Illinois and Abraham Lincoln, little known Republican of Illinois, held a series of seven debates in towns across Illinois, competing for a seat in the Senate. Their points of view showed clearly the growing gap between North and South. Lincoln opposed slavery. The nation, he said, would have to decide on the issue—either the whole country should accept slavery or eliminate it. Douglas did not defend slavery, but he did uphold the right of the people in a given territory to decide the issue for themselves. The Democratic majority in the Illinois legislature elected Douglas to the Senate seat, but Lincoln's efforts brought him into the national spotlight.

1858–1859 In **congressional elections** the Republican Party made a strong showing. In the Senate the

Changing critical standards in historiography were exemplified in the work of John Gorham Palfrey, a Unitarian clergyman of Boston and a former editor of the *North American Review.* He was the author of *History of New England,* which appeared in five volumes between 1858 and 1890. At the time the work was considered impartial and was praised for bringing colonial and English events together in its chronology. Later critics, however, considered the volumes biased in favor of New England, especially Massachusetts, and the clergy.

Sales of Lowell Mason's *Carmina Sacra,* published in 1841, now exceeded 500,000 copies, making it the most popular book of music in the U.S. Mason had been editor of the famous Boston *Handel and Haydn Society*

sent the first message on Aug. 16, 1858, to Pres. Buchanan. The feat was considered a glorious achievement until the cable broke two weeks later, perhaps from faulty insulation. After financial reverses and the interruption of the Civil War, Field succeeded in laying the cable in 1866, using the largest steamship of the time, *Great Eastern.*

May   Channing Home, a hospital for poverty-stricken women, opened in Boston, Mass., under the guidance of Harriet Ryan Albee. It became one of the best-known charity hospitals in the U.S. and one of the first to accept tubercular patients. The home and Mrs. Albee were subjects of poems by Oliver Wendell Holmes, James Russell Lowell, and Ralph Waldo Emerson.

June 2   A sewing machine patent was issued to James Ethan Allen Gibbs of Mill Point, Va., a farmer. Gibbs had perfected his twisted-loop, rotary hook machine, toward which his previously patented sewing machine devices had been leading. In 1858 he entered into partnership with James Willcox of Philadelphia to market the sewing machine. For decades thereafter, Gibbs continued to devise improvements.

Aug. 24   A financial panic was precipitated by the failure of the New York City branch of the Ohio Life Insurance Company. Some 4932 businesses failed this year. By 1859 another 8000 had failed. The bankruptcies were primarily the result of overspeculation in railway securities and real estate.

The **New Orleans Mardi Gras** for the first time offered a pageant of decorative floats organized and paid for by societies called Krewes. The first society, Comus, began functioning this year as a patron and promoter of the festivities.

The **America's Cup,** won in England by the U.S. schooner-yacht *America,* was presented to the New York Yacht Club by members who owned *America:* J. C. Stevens, Edwin A. Stevens, Hamilton Wilkes, J. Beekman Finley, and George L. Schuyler. The gift stipulated that the cup be used perpetually as a trophy in international challenge yacht races.

The **first U.S. horse to race in Europe,** Prioress, owned by Richard Ten Broeck, won the English Cesarewitch Handicap. The race ended in a dead heat; Prioress won a runoff against El Hakim and Queen Bess at the end of the day's program. The time for the two-mile 468-yard course was 4:15.

Oct. 6   The American Chess Association was organized at the first American Chess Congress, held in New York City. There Paul C. Morphy, a 20-year-old chess wizard from New Orleans, La., won the American championship. Morphy toured Europe in 1858 and 1859, defeating all the masters who would meet him. Although he played only sporadically thereafter, he was recognized as the first American international chess master.

1858

Japan was further opened to American commerce in 1858, following Commodore Matthew C. Perry's original treaty of 1854. In 1855 the U.S. sent Townsend Harris, a New York merchant, to Japan as its first diplomatic representative. Harris came to exercise considerable influence with the Japanese government because of his sound advice. He signed agreements on June 18, 1857, and July 29, 1858, that opened more ports to U.S. commerce and gave Americans residence rights.

Cooper Union, a New York adult educational institution for the working class named for the industrialist-philanthropist Peter Cooper, opened. It offered free technical and art courses, public lectures, and the city's first public library.

Steel pens were successfully produced for the first

Another gold rush captured the nation's attention when gold was discovered in Colorado in the Pike's Peak area in 1857 and at Cherry Creek, Denver, in 1858. About 100,000 gold seekers headed west, but about half never made it to the gold regions. Within two years Denver was enough of a city to have a theater, circulating library, and debating club. The town of El Dorado, near present-day Colorado Springs, was founded by miners as Fountain Creek in 1859. The rallying cry of the fortune hunters in this period was "Pike's Peak or bust."

Birth control came to the fore with H. C. Wright's popular *The Unwelcomed Child; or the Crime of an Undesigned and Undesired Maternity.* It indicated a growing frankness about sexual matters in American society.

Democrats took a majority of 38–26 over the Republicans, with two seats held by minor parties. In the House the Republicans took a 113–101 majority over the Democrats, with 23 seats going to minor parties. Abraham Lincoln, Republican candidate for senator from Illinois, was defeated by his Democratic rival Stephen A. Douglas.

Mar. 23 The Senate voted to accept Kansas into the Union under the **Lecompton Constitution** after the constitution had been rejected by Kansas. The House, however, voted to resubmit the constitution to a popular vote.

May 4 Congress passed the **English bill,** named for Rep. William H. English of Indiana, devised as a compromise between the House and Senate bills on the admission of Kansas. In effect the English bill resubmitted to the voters of Kansas the Lecompton Constitution with an attached incentive of public land if they ratified it.

May 11 **Minnesota was admitted as a state,** the 32nd to join the Union.

June 13 A steamship explosion aboard the *Pennsylvania* on the Mississippi R. near Memphis, Tenn., killed 160 persons.

Aug. 2 The **Lecompton Constitution** was submitted by the federal government to the people of Kansas for popular vote for the third time. It was rejected and the territory became nonslaveholding. Kansas did not enter the Union until 1861.

Oct. 27 **Theodore Roosevelt,** 26th president of the United States, was born in New York City.

Collection of Church Music, published in 1821, which also enjoyed remarkable success.

St. Patrick's Cathedral, New York City, was begun; it was completed in 1879. A late example of Gothic Revival in U.S. architecture, it was designed by James Renwick.

The Autocrat of the Breakfast Table by Oliver Wendell Holmes was published. The title had been used by Holmes in 1831–1832 for two contributions to *New England Magazine.* Holmes's intellect, wit, and humanity found a perfect medium of expression in the imagined conversations at a Boston boardinghouse on subjects that intrigued him: trees, books, sports, poetry, painting, the human mind, etc. All was grist for the "autocrat." Later Holmes would employ the same method in *Professor at the Breakfast Table* (1860), *The Poet at the Breakfast Table* (1872), and *Over the Teacups* (1891).

"The Courtship of Miles Standish" by Henry Wadsworth Longfellow, a verse account of a bit of Puritan history of the domestic kind, was published. Miles Standish, John Alden, and Priscilla became living traditions to millions through this work. In London 10,000 copies were sold on the day of its appearance. Longfellow's popularity among his contemporaries is revealed by the fact that over 300,000 of his books had been sold by 1857.

1859

A court case stemming from opposition to the Fugitive Slave Law of 1850 found a northern free state arguing for states' rights, usually the preserve of the South. In 1854 the Wisconsin Supreme Court freed Sherman M. Booth, an abolitionist editor who had been convicted in federal court of violating the Fugitive Slave Law, on the grounds that the law was unconstitutional. In *Abelman v. Booth* (Abelman was a U.S. marshall), the Supreme Court on Mar. 7, 1859, denied the right of a state to interfere in a federal case, and upheld the constitutionality of the law. The Wisconsin legislature then adopted a resolution defending state sovereignty.

The **Comstock Lode,** the richest known U.S. silver deposit, was discovered in western Nevada. It was the first major U.S. silver strike.

Most of the opera singers heard in America were European-born and trained, and it was rare for an American-trained singer to reach the top ranks in Europe. The first to accomplish this was Adelina Patti, a coloratura soprano born of Italian parents in Madrid, Spain. She made her operatic debut in New York City on Nov. 24, 1859, in the title role of *Lucia di Lammermoor.* For years after that she sang in such cities as London, Paris, and Milan, returning to the U.S. in 1881. Patti was the most popular and highest paid singer of her time. It became a custom for audiences to demand that she sing "Home, Sweet Home" as one of her encores.

The Hidden Hand by Mrs. E. D. E. N. Southworth, the popular novelist, was published and soon became a best seller. Mrs. Southworth wrote some 60 popular novels, mostly set in the South. *The Hidden Hand* sold nearly 2,000,000 copies.

Business and Industry; Science;
Education; Philosophy and Religion **III**

IV **Sports; Social Issues and Crime;**
Folkways; Fashion; Holidays

time by Richard Esterbrook in Philadelphia, Pa., and later in Camden, N.J.

Philadelphia's first horsecar went into operation. As in New York City, where regular passenger runs began in 1852, the horsecar soon replaced the older omnibus. The horsecar effected a minor revolution in city planning, for the tracks it ran on were permanent and inflexible. Boston adopted a horsecar line in 1852, Chicago in 1859.

A **religious revival,** often characterized as a prayer meeting revival, began in New York City and Philadelphia and swept across the country. The revival has been associated with the financial panic of 1857, but the religious history of nineteenth-century America was noted for its emotionalism. In addition, the campmeeting, so characteristic of outdoor evangelism, had been established as early as 1830. The revival of 1858 was marked by daily prayer meetings in every major city, and conversions to the various churches reached unprecedented numbers. The revivalist spirit soon caught on in the British Isles.

Jan. 6 The **University of the South** was founded and chartered in Sewanee, Tenn., under Episcopalian auspices. Its first degrees were granted in 1873.

Aug. 16 The **first cable message** was sent across the Atlantic Ocean from Queen Victoria of England to Pres. James Buchanan.

Oct. 9 The stage inaugurating the **first overland mail service** connecting the West and East coasts reached St. Louis from San Francisco after a trip of 23 days, 4 hrs. At St. Louis the mail was transferred to a train for the remainder of the journey to the East.

The first meeting of the **National Association of Baseball Players** was held. The association adopted, with a few changes, rules created by the New York Knickerbocker baseball club, including standardized measurements for the ball and bat and for the distance between bases. Many of these rules are still in force today.

Apr. 12 The **first U.S. billiard championship** was held at Fireman's Hall, Detroit, Mich. Michael J. Phelan defeated John Seereiter in a match lasting nine and a half hours. It was witnessed by a "genteel" audience that included a few ladies.

June 16 **"A house divided against itself cannot stand"** was included by Abraham Lincoln in his speech of acceptance of the Republican nomination for the U.S. Senate. "I believe," he went on, "this government cannot endure permanently half slave and half free."

July 20 The **first admission charge to a baseball game** (50 cents) was levied for the contest between Brooklyn and the New York All Stars at Fashion Race Course in Long Island. About 1500 spectators saw New York defeat Brooklyn 22–18.

Oct. 25 The phrase *an irrepressible conflict,* used in relation to the slavery issue, was first heard from William Henry Seward in a speech delivered in Rochester, N.Y.

1859

A turning point in the economic history of the U.S. came this year when on Aug. 27 the first producing oil well began to flow at the rate of 20 barrels a day. The well had been drilled to a depth of 60 feet by Edwin L. Drake, near Titusville, Pa. An oil rush, reminiscent of the California gold rush, began almost at once. Boom towns grew up overnight and within three years of Drake's discovery 128,000,000 gallons had been produced. Oil became an important export product and kerosene displaced whale oil and candles as a source of illumination.

Even though prizefighting was still bare-knuckled and brutal, it fascinated people of all classes. This was shown by the interest aroused when John C. Heenan sailed for England in 1859 to meet the British champion, Tom Sayers. Heenan had justly claimed the American heavyweight title on the retirement of John C. Morrissey. On Oct. 20, 1858, Morrissey had been awarded a decision over Heenan on a technicality. When Heenan and Sayers met on Apr. 17, 1860, they fought for 42 rounds in a bout that lasted 2 hrs. and 20 min. Heenan battered Sayers but the police broke up the illegal match. The crowd invaded the ring, and the bout was declared a draw. Even so, *The Spirit of the Times,* in an extra edition of 100,000 copies, hailed Heenan as the world champion.

The **Massachusetts Institute of Technology** was established at Cambridge, Mass. Its first classes met in 1865.

Mount Vernon, George Washington's estate on the Potomac R. in Virginia, was dedicated as a national monument.

Exploration and Settlement; Wars; Government; Civil Rights; Statistics	I		II	Publishing; Arts and Music; Popular Entertainment; Architecture; Theater

Feb. 14   **Oregon** was admitted to the Union, the 33rd state.

May 12   Reopening of the **African slave trade** was urged by the Vicksburg Commercial Convention. An act passed in 1820 forbade further importation of slaves from Africa. The Vicksburg convention took the position that all laws, state and federal, restricting slave trade should be repealed.

July 5   The **Kansas constitutional convention** convened at Wyandotte, Kans. The chief issue was whether the state should be free or slave. On Oct. 4 an antislavery constitution was ratified by a vote of 10, 421 to 5530.

Oct. 16   The federal arsenal at **Harpers Ferry** (now in W.Va.) was seized by John Brown and 21 followers. Brown wanted to establish an abolitionist republic in the Appalachians and to fight slavery with fugitive slaves and abolitionist whites. On Dec. 2 he was hanged at Charles Town, Va., for murder, conspiracy, and treason against Virginia. In the South he was thought of as a murderer and traitor who deserved the gallows, but in the North his gibbet was described as "the cross of a martyr." In Concord, Mass., Henry David Thoreau wrote of Brown: "When a government puts forth its strength . . . to kill the liberators of the slave, what a merely brute . . . force it is seen to be." Lincoln was philosophical and brooded over the fates of historical zealots who had taken it upon themselves to end oppression. Longfellow sounded a prophetic note: "This will be a great day in our history, the date of a new revolution. . . . As I write, they are leading old John Brown to execution. . . . This is sowing the wind to reap the whirlwind, which will soon come."

"**Dixie**," first known as "I Wish I Was in Dixie's Land," was composed by Dan Emmett as a "walk-around" for Bryant's Minstrels. The song was later claimed by both sides during the Civil War, but eventually became associated almost completely with the Confederacy. Emmett was a northerner from Ohio.

South Dakota's first newspaper, *The Democrat,* was published at Sioux Falls. Later it was called the *Northwestern Independent.* At this time there were few settlers in the Sioux Valley, and in 1862 homes were abandoned after an uprising by Sioux Indians in Minnesota.

Two pieces of sculpture by **William Randolph Barbee,** *Coquette* and *The Fisher Girl,* stirred excitement when exhibited in a New York City salon. One critic wrote of *The Fisher Girl,* "We unhesitatingly pronounce the carving of that fishing-net one of the most perfect triumphs of the chisel that we have ever beheld. . . . "

"**Out of the Cradle Endlessly Rocking**," one of Walt Whitman's greatest poems, was written.

The Minister's Wooing by Harriet Beecher Stowe, a romantic novel set in Puritan New England, was published.

Jan. 28   **William Hickling Prescott** died at 62, while working on the fourth and final volume of *History of the Reign of Philip the Second, King of Spain.* His Spanish histories have stood the test of time.

Mar. 26   **George F. Bristow's** *Third Symphony in F Sharp* was performed by the New York Philharmonic Society Orchestra. Bristow was the most noted American composer of the mid-nineteenth century.

Apr. 23   The **first newspaper in Colorado**, the *Rocky Mountain News,* began publication in Auraria, now part of Denver.

Sept. 5   Probably the **first novel by a black** to appear in the U.S., *Our Nig; or Sketches from the Life of a Free Black* by Harriet E. Wilson, was issued in Boston. It had been privately printed for the author, about whom little is known, by the Boston printing firm of George C. Rand and Avery. Autobiographical in nature, the novel was intended by Mrs. Wilson to raise funds to care for her son, who died in 1860. Despite its significance, the novel remained virtually unrecognized until its rediscovery and republication in 1983.

1860

Even before the presidential election campaign of 1860 began, it was clear that slavery would be the only issue. The first result of this situation was a complete split in the Democratic Party between its northern and southern supporters. The Republican Party, drawing its strength from the North and West, was united in its antislavery stand and represented the largest part of the nation. There was also an attempt at a coalition of

Poets of the period often devoted their talents to the controversy over slavery and the events of the Civil War. The leading voice of the South was Henry Timrod of South Carolina, who was to become known as the poet laureate of the Confederacy. Timrod's collection of *Poems* was published this year, but it was not until 1873 that his poetry dealing with the war appeared. Most notable was "Ode Sung at the Occasion of Decorating

The **first medical college on the Pacific coast** was founded by Dr. Elias Samuel Cooper. It began as the medical department of the University of the Pacific in San Francisco. After a period of discontinuance it was reorganized (1880) as Cooper Medical College. It was taken over by Stanford University in 1908.

The **first hotel passenger elevator** in the U.S. was installed in the Fifth Avenue Hotel, New York City. Many patrons continued to climb the stairs.

A **device to bind sheaves of grain** as they were cut by the reaper was invented by a youthful Wisconsin farmhand, John Francis Appleby. The Appleby Knotter was adapted for use on the Marsh harvester in 1875.

July   **Electric home lighting** was given its first successful demonstration by Prof. Moses G. Farmer in the parlor of his home at Salem, Mass. Current, supplied by a voltaic battery, was conducted to two lamps on a mantelpiece. Strips of platinum provided the illuminating medium. This device produced the best artificial light then known but was much more expensive than gaslight.

Sept. 1   George M. Pullman's **first sleeping car** made its first run. It was a converted coach. In 1863 he built the *Pioneer,* the first modern sleeping coach with a folding upper berth and extensible seat cushions to form a lower berth. In 1868 he introduced a dining car, in 1875 a chair car.

George W. Henry of Oneida, N.Y., known to his contemporaries as Henry the Holy Shouter, published his "Shouting: Genuine and Spurious in all Ages of the Church . . . Giving a History of the Outward Demonstrations of the Spirit, such as Laughing, Screaming, Shouting, Leaping, Jerking and Falling under the Power." Mr. Henry advocated a violent form of revivalism and cited Church fathers who leaped and sang with joy over their conversion to God.

The **first national billiards champion** was Michael Phelan of New York. He defeated John Seereiter of Detroit, Mich., in a 2000-point match for a $15,000 stake. The game played was four-ball carom on a six-pocket table.

June 30   Niagara Falls was crossed by a **tightrope walker,** Charles Blondin. In five minutes the sensational Frenchman, watched by 25,000 spectators, passed across a cable 1100 feet long and 160 feet above the seething water. In later performances Blondin made the same crossing blindfolded, pushing a wheelbarrow (July 4); carrying a man on his back (Aug. 19); and walking on stilts (Sept. 14, 1860). At age 72, in 1888, Blondin was still thrilling crowds in the U.S. and abroad with his high-wire skills.

July 1   In the **first intercollegiate baseball game** in history, Amherst defeated Williams, 66–32.

July 26   In the **first intercollegiate regatta,** Harvard defeated Yale and Brown at Lake Quinsigamond, Worcester, Mass. The race was in six-oared shells, at three miles. A similar regatta planned for the previous year was cancelled when the Yale stroke, George E. Dunham, drowned.

Oct. 3   An **international cricket match** took place in Hoboken, N.J., between an All-England 11 and an All-U.S. 22 from Philadelphia and New York City. The English team was victorious by 64 runs and an inning, after a match that lasted three days.

1860

Education of children at a very early age was a European innovation that now came to America. The first English-language kindergarten in the U.S. was opened in Boston this year by Elizabeth Palmer Peabody, a member of the New England intellectual elite. (A German-language kindergarten had been established in Watertown, Wis., in 1856.) Miss Peabody was interested in social reform and education and had been associated

The game of croquet was introduced to America from England. It was soon popular but did not reach the height of its popularity until after the Civil War. Croquet was the first outdoor athletic activity in which women participated. Even more important, it could be played by men and women together. Consequently, it became as much a social as an athletic activity and afforded fine opportunity for courting. In the 1870s the

factions to hold the Union together at any cost. There were now 33 states, 18 of them free and 15 slave. This situation, combined with the split in the Democratic Party, made a Republican victory inevitable. Abraham Lincoln carried all the free states, except for a split in New Jersey. He won a clear majority in the electoral college but not in the popular vote.

The U.S. **Census** recorded a population of 31,443,321. The center of population was located 20 miles southeast of Chillicothe, Ohio. There were 448,070 free blacks and 3,953,760 slaves in the country.

1860–1861 In **congressional elections** the Republicans took control of both houses of Congress. As southern states seceded, the 37th Congress had the following representation: Senate, 31 Republicans, 10 Democrats, 8 other parties; House, 105 Republicans, 43 Democrats, 30 others.

Feb. 27 **Abraham Lincoln** delivered his memorable address at Cooper Union, New York City. He set forth the issues on which the new Republican Party would appeal to voters and his no-compromise position on slavery. This projected Lincoln into the lead for the Republican presidential nomination.

Mar. 9 The staff of the **first Japanese embassy to a foreign power,** led by Niimi Masaoki, reached San Francisco aboard the *Powhatan*. The staff reached Washington, D.C., on Apr. 25 and remained in the U.S. for six weeks.

Apr. 23 The **national convention of the Democratic Party** met at Charleston, S.C. On Apr. 30 delegates from the South walked out over platform disputes. The remainder, led by Stephen A. Douglas, supported constitutional decisions and congressional noninterference on the issue of slavery in the territories. The convention adjourned on May 3 without making any nominations.

May 9 The national convention of the **Constitutional Union Party** nominated John Bell of Tennessee for the presidency and Edward Everett of Massachusetts for the vice presidency. The party was composed of remnants of the Whig and American parties.

May 16–18 The **Republican National Convention** nominated **Abraham Lincoln** of Illinois for the presidency and Hannibal Hamlin of Maine for the vice presidency.

June 18–23 Reconvening in Baltimore, Md., the **Democratic Party** nominated **Stephen A. Douglas** of Illinois for the presidency and Herschel V. Johnson of Georgia for the vice presidency.

June 28 The **southern Democrats** nominated **John C. Breckinridge** of Kentucky for the presidency and Joseph Lane of Oregon for the vice presidency. Their platform supported slavery in the territories.

the Graves of the Confederate Dead," written in 1867, the year of his early death.

Dime novels made their first appearance under the aegis of the publisher Erastus Beadle. The first dime novel was *Malaeska; The Indian Wife of the White Hunter* by Mrs. Anna Sophia Stephens; it sold more than 300,000 copies in its first year. Another dime novel, *Seth Jones; or, the Captives of the Frontier* by Edward S. Ellis, also published this year, sold some 450,000 copies in less than a year. By 1865 Beadle's dime novel series had sold over 4,000,000 copies. The novels featured such larger-than-life characters as Deadwood Dick, Calamity Jane, and Kit Carson. Published in orange jackets, the books were read extensively by soldiers in camp. In 1870 a second series, Beadle's Pocket Novels, was begun. Literary fare in these novels consisted of tales of the West, Indians, hunters, pioneers, and the gunmen. In general, the morality of the books was unobjectionable if simplistic, for the villain and the hero were obvious from the opening pages, and evil was always punished.

Mrs. **Miriam Coles Harris** published anonymously her all-time best seller, *Rutledge,* a novel of the perilous love of a young woman for a middle-aged man. Mrs. Harris published 130 other novels of the same type. They were marked by stilted actions and conversations, artificial and melodramatic plots, and moralistic intrusions by the author. Still, her readers craved more of the same.

The Marble Faun, Nathaniel Hawthorne's last completed novel, was published. Even in this romantic novel with its Italian setting, Hawthorne burdened his characters with heavy moral conflicts. His descriptions of the Eternal City in which his tragic romance is played out attest to the keenness of his observations. Even today *The Marble Faun* has interest as a travel guide.

"Old Black Joe," the last of Stephen Foster's "plantation songs," was published. Foster, suffering from alcoholism and financial problems, moved to New York City and began to write sentimental potboilers—as many as 46 songs in one year. He died in Bellevue Hospital, New York City, on Jan. 13, 1864.

Harriet G. Hosmer, the most famous woman sculptor of her day, achieved financial success with her marble statue *Puck,* a bat-winged elf astride a mushroom. The Prince of Wales (the future Edward VII) bought a copy, and the demand for replicas kept her studio and 20 Italian stonecutters busy. Previously known for her classical sculptures, Hosmer created several more popular works, including *Siren Fountain, Sleeping Faun,* and *Waking Faun.*

with A. Bronson Alcott and his experimental Temple School. In her kindergarten she followed the precepts of Friedrich Froebel, the German educator and founder of the kindergarten system. Miss Peabody was a member of the Transcendental Club, and her home was the setting of the notable conversation classes of Margaret Fuller, another of the transcendentalists.

A **U.S. Department of Education survey** showed a total of 321 high schools in the country; more than half were in Massachusetts, New York, and Ohio.

The masterwork of **Charles Darwin,** *On the Origin of Species by Means of Natural Selection* (1859), was published in the U.S. on the eve of the Civil War, when the press was preoccupied with politics. Louis Agassiz of Harvard, the brilliant Swiss-American naturalist, rejected Darwin's contentions, holding that all species were immutable from the time of creation. Agassiz's position was challenged by his Harvard colleague, the botanist Asa Gray, who defended Darwinism as an enrichment of the concept of divine creation.

The **first professor of the diseases of children** in the U.S., Dr. Abraham Jacobi, was appointed by New York Medical College. Dr. Jacobi at once created the first free clinic for children's diseases. In 1862 he issued the first report on the subject, based on the clinic's findings.

The **first widely accepted repeating rifle** was produced by Oliver F. Winchester and his New Haven Arms Company. Over the next decade this rifle was adopted by many state militia regiments and by settlers in the far West. Winchester continued to improve his rifle and to absorb other manufacturers until the Winchester name became preeminent.

Feb. 15 **Wheaton College** was chartered in Wheaton, Ill., as the Illinois Institute. Established under Methodist auspices, the institute awarded its first degrees in 1860. It passed under Congregational control in 1861 when it became Wheaton College. Today it is not affiliated with any denomination.

Feb. 22 The **most significant strike of the period** began in Lynn, Mass. Shoemakers there struck for higher wages and union recognition. The strike, which followed the introduction of new machinery in the shoe industry, soon spread to include 25 towns and 20,000 shoemakers. The workers protested because youngsters were being brought in to work the new machines, cutting the salary of skilled men to $3.00 a week. The Mechanics' Association, formed in 1859 at Lynn, organized the strike. On Apr. 10 the manufacturers agreed to a 10% wage increase. Some 1000 workers went back to their jobs. The effort to win general union recognition was largely frustrated.

Mar. 20 **St. Stephen's College** was chartered in Annandale, N.Y., under Episcopalian auspices. Its first degrees were granted in 1861. It was rechartered in

vogue for croquet was so great that sets with candle sockets for night playing were introduced.

Olympia Brown, a graduate of Antioch College, was admitted to the Theological School of St. Lawrence University. She became the first woman in the U.S. to be permitted to study theology along with men, and later (1863) the first woman to be ordained in the ministry of a properly constituted ecclesiastical body.

Prices for shaves, haircuts, and curling were raised at Tony Delight's in Chicago, one of the famous tonsorial enterprises in America. Shaves went up from 5 cents to 6 cents, haircuts from 10 cents to 12 cents, and curling from 15 or 20 cents to 25 cents. Shampoos were priced at 25 cents.

Intercollegiate rowing contests became institutionalized. This year's regatta saw Harvard, Yale, and Brown competing. Harvard won.

The term *seventh-inning stretch* became common at baseball games. It referred to the custom of spectators standing up and stretching just before the home team came to bat in the seventh inning. The custom served two functions, one practical and one superstitious. Spectators relieved cramped muscles and brought good luck to their team as well, since the number seven was seen as lucky.

The **popular attitude toward strikes** was reflected in the reaction of the U.S. press this year to the Massachusetts shoemakers' strike, which was looked upon as a virtual revolution. "Rebellion among the workers in New England" and "Revolution at the North" were among the warnings that greeted newspaper readers over their morning coffee. Some of the newspapers were shocked by the part played by women workers in the strike and bewailed the effects of the feminist movement. Churches generally supported the strikers, while the New England manufacturers threatened the German and Irish immigrants, who formed the bulk of the strikers, with legislative retaliation that would take away their voting privileges.

Baseball came to San Francisco in an organized game for the first time.

Sept. 7–8 A **collision** of the steamship *Lady Elgin* with the schooner *Augusta* on Lake Michigan killed nearly 400 persons. Edward Spencer, a student at Northwestern University, entered the icy waters 16 times to recover 17 victims of the collision. A bronze tablet on the university campus memorialized his heroism.

Nov. 6 **Abraham Lincoln was elected president** of the United States in a Republican victory over the divided Democrats. Hannibal Hamlin was elected vice president. The electoral vote was Lincoln, 180; John C. Breckinridge, southern Democrat, 72; John Bell, Constitutional Union candidate, 39; Stephen A. Douglas, Democrat, 12. The popular vote was Lincoln, 1,866,252; Douglas, 1,375,157; Breckinridge, 849,781; Bell, 589,581.

Dec. 18 The **Crittenden Compromise**, a last minute attempt to persuade the southern states to remain in the Union, was proposed by Sen. John J. Crittenden of Kentucky. Crittenden proposed constitutional amendments extending the Missouri Compromise line across the country and allowing slavery south of the line. President-elect Lincoln opposed the plan.

Dec. 20 **South Carolina seceded from the Union,** the first state to do so. Its action was taken as a consequence of Lincoln's election.

Dec. 22 **South Carolina** appointed three commissioners to arrange with Pres. James Buchanan and Congress for delivery of public lands to the state. On Dec. 27, after Fort Moultrie had been abandoned as indefensible by Maj. Robert Anderson, the state seized it and Castle Pinckney. On Dec. 30 South Carolina troops seized the U.S. arsenal at Charleston.

The Conduct of Life by Ralph Waldo Emerson was published. For several years Emerson had lectured on the subject popularly and effectively. At the peak of his powers, he was now clearly an astute social commentator as well as moral philosopher. Among the book's topics were the discoveries of science, evolution, uses of wealth, importance of culture, faith, art, and a reevaluation of the position of the transcendentalists.

Home Ballads, Poems and Lyrics by John Greenleaf Whittier was published.

Avolio, A Legend of the Island of Cos by Paul Hamilton Hayne was published. Hayne, a Charleston, S.C., lawyer, editor, critic, and poet, later made a more lasting impression with his sonnets and lyrics about post-Civil War South Carolina.

The **golden day of American art,** an expression once applied to the era prior to the Civil War, had validity only with regard to literature. There was little painting of note, and sculpture fared even worse. The Hudson River school, which specialized in landscape painting, was the notable exception to the general mediocrity of painting.

Mar. 29 **Dion Boucicault** turned to an Irish setting and characters in the first of his smash comedy-drama hits, *The Colleen Bawn.* Other Boucicault plays based on Ireland are *Arrah-na-Pogue* (1864), *The O'Dowd* (1873), *The Shaughraun* (1874), and *Cuishla Machree* (1888).

1861

The Civil War (1861–1865) began in the early morning hours of Apr. 12 when Confederate forces at Charleston, S.C., opened fire on the federal garrison at Fort Sumter in Charleston harbor. The action was the culmination of months of effort by Confederate officials to force federal troops out of Charleston harbor. They had been successful elsewhere in occupying federal arsenals and forts and in removing federal garrisons. Pres. Abraham Lincoln tried to deal firmly with South Carolina authorities without provoking violence, but the attempt failed. When the federal garrison at Fort Sumter surrendered on Apr. 13, the citizens of Charleston were filled with joy. Little did they realize that they had witnessed the beginning of four years of vicious warfare.

Jan. 9 *Star of the West,* an unarmed federal supply ship, was fired on by the South Carolina state battery

East Lynne, a phenomenally successful novel and dramatization by Mrs. Henry Wood, an English author, was published in the U.S. this year. The tearjerker sold at least 1,000,000 copies, but its greatest success came as a stage play. The drama packed theaters for most of the rest of the century. *East Lynne* later became a synonym for the crudest of melodramas.

Business and Industry; Science; Education; Philosophy and Religion III

IV Sports; Social Issues and Crime; Folkways; Fashion; Holidays

1935 as Bard College and became coeducational in 1944.

Apr. 3   The first relay of the **Pony Express** mail service left St. Joseph, Mo., and arrived in Sacramento, Calif., on Apr. 13. The cost of mailing a letter was at first $5.00 a half-ounce, later reduced to $1.00. The Pony Express was discontinued in Oct. 1861, when the transcontinental telegraph began service.

Apr. 14   **Idaho's first permanent settlement** was established by Mormons and called Franklin. All previous settlements had been abandoned in the face of Indian hostility.

May 10   The **Morrill Tariff Bill** was passed by the House of Representatives, opening the era of protectionism. The tariff became law in Mar. 1861. It became the regulator of imports and was superseded only by the McKinley Bill, passed by the 51st Congress in 1890.

May 28   The **American Peace Society**, founded in 1828 by William Ladd, met without a quorum. The society was dedicated to arbitration and peace and would not countenance even a defensive war. The waning of its popularity before the Civil War reflected the shift in popular sentiment regarding the approaching conflict. In Jan. 1861 the society sent a plea to 500 newspapers, advising a more temperate presentation of the issues that were leading the country toward war.

June 23   The **Government Printing Office** was established by an act of Congress. Later the government bought an existing commercial press in Washington, D.C. Today, the Government Printing Office is the largest printing establishment in the world, with the plant valued at over $20,000,000.

The **first intercollegiate billiards match** in the U.S. was held between Harvard and Yale.

A **$5.00 chemistry set,** the Youth's Chemical Cabinet, was advertised in *The New York Times* as being "perfectly safe in the hands of youth." The set included directions for experiments, none of which called for strong acids or other "deleterious or dangerous articles."

Mink muffs were advertised in *The New York Times.* They were on sale for $10, reduced from their regular price of $14.

An **Exhibition of the Great Paintings** was announced in *The New York Times.* The chefs-d'oeuvre on display were Thomas B. Thomp's *Niagara As It Is!;* the "last and greatest" of William Page, *Moses on Mount Horeb;* and Thomas Rossiter's "three great paintings," *Miriam, Noah,* and *Jeremiah.* An exhibition of famous sculptures was also promised; it included *The Dead Pearl Diver, The Fisher Girl,* and *Flora.*

Oct. 4   The **Prince of Wales,** bored by a reception at the White House, slipped off with Harriet Lane, the niece of Pres. James Buchanan, to the gym of Mrs. Smith's Institute for Young Ladies. There the prince and his partner played tenpins.

1861

An important step in the development of the nation's communication system came on Oct. 24, 1861, when Pres. Abraham Lincoln in Washington, D.C., received the first transcontinental telegraph message, from Sacramento, Calif. The lines of the Overland and the Pacific telegraph companies had been linked at Fort Bridger, Utah. A side effect of the completion of the transcontinental line was the almost immediate demise of the far more romantic Pony Express, which had begun operating in Apr. 1860 between St. Joseph, Mo., and Sacramento.

A change in American society's attitude toward light entertainment came in 1861 when Antonio "Tony" Pastor, a singer and dancer, opened his first theater at 444 Broadway in New York City. The variety theater had had a reputation for vulgarity, but Pastor's performers and acts were suitable for the whole family. He attracted women patrons by offering door prizes such as kitchenware and dress patterns. Pastor eventually became known as the father of American vaudeville. He introduced performers who were to become famous, such as Lillian Russell (born this year). His style of entertainment was soon copied in other cities.

at Charleston harbor; the command to fire was given by Francis Wilkinson Pickens, governor of the state. The ship had been sent under orders from Pres. James Buchanan to supply and reinforce the federal garrison at Fort Sumter in Charleston harbor.

Jan. 9 **Mississippi** became the second state to secede from the Union.

Jan. 10 A **Florida convention** voted for secession from the Union. "United States" was changed to "Confederate States" in their constitution.

Jan. 11 **Alabama seceded** from the Union.

Jan. 19 **Georgia seceded** from the Union.

Jan. 26 **Louisiana seceded** from the Union.

Jan. 29 **Kansas was admitted to the Union,** the 34th state. It entered as a free state.

Feb. 4 The **Confederate States of America was formed** at Montgomery, Ala. Jefferson Davis of Mississippi was elected president, Alexander H. Stephens of Georgia vice president. Both were chosen on Feb. 9.

Feb. 9 The **Confederate Provisional Congress** asserted that all laws under the U.S. Constitution that were not inconsistent with the constitution of the Confederate states would be recognized.

Feb. 13 The action that led to the awarding of the **first U.S. Medal of Honor** took place at Apache Pass, Ariz., where Col. Bernard John Dowling Irwin led his troops to victory over hostile Chiricahua Apache Indians. The medal was not given to Irwin until Jan. 24, 1894.

Feb. 18 **Jefferson Davis was inaugurated** president of the Confederacy. The Confederate capital was established in Montgomery, Ala., where Davis lived at 626 Washington St., in a building known as the White House of the Confederacy. The capital was later moved to Richmond, Va.

Feb. 23 **Texas seceded** from the Union, following a state convention's recommendation of Feb. 1. It was the seventh state to secede.

Mar. 2 A congressional act establishing the **territories of Nevada and Dakota** was signed by Pres. James Buchanan. Nevada Territory was formed from Utah Territory, Dakota Territory from Nebraska Territory.

Mar. 4 An official **Confederate flag,** "Stars and Bars," was adopted by a Confederate convention at Montgomery, Ala. The flag had seven stars and three stripes, and was raised over the Confederate capitol at Montgomery. Later, after the similarity between Union and Confederate flags created confusion at the Battle of Bull Run, the Confederate army adopted a battle flag consisting of a red field and the blue cross of St. Andrew, with 13 stars.

Mar. 4 **Abraham Lincoln was inaugurated president** of the United States. A Republican, he was elected to two terms but was assassinated early in his second term. Hannibal Hamlin was inaugurated vice president.

Several **theaters closed** because of the Civil War, notably Niblo's Garden and the Bowery in New York City, the Boston Theater, and some in Philadelphia and Richmond.

"All Quiet Along the Potomac Tonight" appeared as one of the hit tunes of the Civil War. It was composed by John Hill Hewitt, a northern journalist and musician living in Richmond.

Impressionism in American painting was represented in George Inness's *Delaware Water Gap* and in his writing: "The purpose of the painter is simply to reproduce in other minds the impression which a scene has made upon him. A work of art does not appeal to the intellect. It does not appeal to the moral sense. Its aim is not to instruct, not to edify, but to awaken an emotion."

Business and Industry; Science; Education; Philosophy and Religion III	IV Sports; Social Issues and Crime; Folkways; Fashion; Holidays

The **first Ph.D. degree** in the U.S. was conferred by Yale University.

Edward P. Weston's walking feats this year included a foot journey from Boston to Washington, D.C., 478 miles in 208 hrs. The Union Army studied this feat to determine how far troops could be made to travel on forced marches.

The **University of Boulder** was chartered at Boulder, Colo. It was reorganized in 1876 as the University of Colorado.

The **Seneca Indian foot racer Deerfoot** was a sensation in England this year. Running in breechcloth and moccasins, Deerfoot outran every available British runner. The largest crowds ever to attend a meet, which included the royal family, flocked to see him run.

The **University of Washington** began its existence as the Territorial University of Washington with a congressional award to the territorial legislature of two townships in what is now downtown Seattle. The present name was adopted in 1889. In 1895 the university moved to its present site outside Seattle.

Jan. 18   **Vassar Female College,** since 1867 called Vassar College, was founded and endowed by Matthew Vassar, a Poughkeepsie brewer and philanthropist who insisted its curriculum be comparable to that of men's colleges. It became coeducational in 1968.

The **first baseball trophy** was offered by a newspaper, the New York *Clipper.*

Mar. 9 A **coinage bill** was enacted by the Confederate congress. It authorized issuance of treasury notes in denominations up to $1,000,000 and not less than $50.

Mar. 11 The **Confederate constitution** was adopted unanimously by the Confederate congress in session at Montgomery, Ala. It declared the sovereignty of states and forbade passage of any law prohibiting slavery.

Apr. 6 In a **message to South Carolina Gov. Francis W. Pickens,** Pres. Lincoln stated that a relief expedition was on its way to Fort Sumter with the sole purpose of supplying its garrison with provisions.

Apr. 11 At **Fort Sumter,** surrender of the federal garrison was demanded by South Carolina authorities. Maj. Robert Anderson refused to surrender, but added that he would soon be forced to do so if supplies were not forthcoming.

Apr. 12 The **Civil War began** at 4:30 A.M. when Confederate shore batteries under command of Gen. P. G. T. Beauregard opened fire on Fort Sumter. The federal garrison, out of supplies, surrendered on Apr. 13 and evacuated the fort the following day.

Apr. 15 **Volunteer troops (militia)** were called for by Pres. Lincoln, who declared the existence of an "insurrection." This first call was for 75,000 men for three months' service.

Apr. 17 A **Virginia convention voted for secession** from the Union as a result of Lincoln's call for troops. The proposal was put before the people of Virginia on May 23 and passed. Virginia was the eighth state to secede.

Apr. 19 The **first casualties of the Civil War** occurred when troops of the Sixth Massachusetts Regiment, en route to Washington, D.C., were stoned by mobs in Baltimore, Md.; four soldiers were killed.

Apr. 19 A **blockade** of Confederate ports was ordered by Pres. Lincoln. The blockade would ultimately weaken the Confederacy by disrupting the importation of war supplies.

Apr. 19–20 **Norfolk Navy Yard** was destroyed and evacuated by Union forces. Among the ships scuttled was the steam frigate *Merrimack,* which was burned to the waterline.

May 6 **Arkansas seceded** from the Union, the ninth state to join the Confederacy.

May 20 **North Carolina seceded** from the Union.

May 21 **Richmond,** Va., was made capital of the Confederate States of America. Virginia at this time was the most populous of the southern states.

June 8 **Tennessee seceded** from the Union.

July 21 At the first Battle of **Bull Run,** near Manassas, Va., Union forces under Gen. Irvin McDowell were defeated by the Confederates. McDowell delayed the attack for two days, allowing Confederate Gen.

The Cloister and the Hearth by the English novelist Charles Reade was published in the U.S. Some early critics regarded it as the best of all historical novels. The setting was fifteenth-century Europe; the central character, the father of Erasmus.

Landscape artist **Frederick Bierstadt** finished the first of his many vast canvases of western scenes, *Laramie Peak.* For the next 25 years he would produce many huge, realistic, impressive, but charmless paintings. His *Discovery of the Hudson River* and *Settlement of California* are in the Capitol at Washington, D.C.

Elsie Venner, a novel by Oliver Wendell Holmes, was published. Like his poem "The Deacon's Masterpiece," *Elsie Venner* was critical of Calvinism. Holmes used his novel to support the determinism that dominated the intellectual life of his day.

Apr. 20 **Thaddeus Sobieski Coulincourt Lowe,** inventor and balloonist, made a record balloon voyage from Cincinnati, Ohio, to near the coast of South Carolina—900 miles in 9 hrs.—to demonstrate the value of balloons for observation by the military. He was briefly held as a Union spy. On Oct. 1 Pres. Lincoln made him chief of the Army's aeronautic section.

Mar. 4 In Abraham Lincoln's **first inaugural address** the new president began with a sentiment that has become an integral part of the literature and history of America: "This country, with its institutions, belongs to the people who inhabit it. Whenever they shall have grown weary of the existing government, they can exercise their constitutional right of amending it, or their revolutionary right to dismember or overthrow it." He concluded: "We are not enemies, but friends. We must not be enemies. . . . The mystic chords of memory . . . will yet swell the chorus of the Union, when again touched, as they surely will be, by the better angels of our nature."

Aug. 5 Congress adopted an **income tax law** as a war finance measure. Income was defined broadly as "derived from any source whatever." The rates were 3% on incomes from $600 to $10,000 and 5% for incomes above $10,000.

June 10 **Dorothea Dix,** famous penal and hospital reformer, was appointed superintendent of women nurses, serving as head of hospital nursing for the Union Army.

Oct. 4 **Construction of the** *Monitor* was authorized by the U.S. Navy. This steam-powered, propeller-driven, armored, and rotary-turreted warship was designed

Aug. A **summer camp** for boys, perhaps the first in the country, was founded at Welch's Point, Milford,

Beauregard to call on reinforcements from the Shenandoah Valley. Their arrival late in the day gave the Confederates a numerical advantage. It was in this battle that Confederate Gen. Thomas J. Jackson was nicknamed "Stonewall" for his firm stand at a crucial moment.

July 25 **Volunteers were sanctioned** by Congress for use in putting down the insurrection in the South. A bonus of $100 was paid to those who volunteered for at least two years.

Aug. 10 The Battle of **Wilson's Creek** in Missouri was won by the Confederacy under Generals Sterling Price and Ben McCulloch. Gen. Nathaniel Lyon, who commanded the outnumbered Union forces, was killed during the battle.

Sept. 13 The **first naval engagement** of the Civil War took place at Pensacola, Fla. Lt. John Henry Russell sailed the frigate *Colorado* past shore batteries at night and, as day broke, with a force of 100 sailors and Marines, went for the southern privateer *Judah* in the shipyard. After hand-to-hand fighting, the contingent burned the vessel to the waterline and left with few losses. Pres. Lincoln thanked Russell personally, and the Navy Department honored him.

Oct. 21 Union troops were ambushed at **Ball's Bluff,** Leesburg, Va. Some 1900 Union soldiers were killed.

Oct. 31 Gen. **Winfield Scott,** the greatest U.S. military figure since the War of 1812, retired as commander in chief of Army forces at age 75.

Nov. 1 Pres. Lincoln named Gen. **George B. McClellan** to succeed Gen. Scott as Army commander in chief.

Nov. 7 **Union forces captured Port Royal Island** on the South Carolina coast. A Navy fleet under Samuel F. Du Pont bombarded the protecting forts, Beauregard and Walker, which were then overrun by Army troops under Lt. Col. Thomas W. Sherman. The victory was important to the North, for it now had a base on the flank of the South. From this base its South Atlantic Blockading Squadron under Du Pont proceeded to capture or render inoperative nearly all the South's Atlantic ports below North Carolina.

Aug. 15 **Civil War events became theatrical material.** Charles Gayler's *Bull Run* was presented in New York City less than a month after the battle itself. Other plays dealing with the war were *Capture of Fort Donelson* (1862) by Henry Seymour; *How to Avoid Drafting* (1862), anonymous; *A Supper in Dixie* (1865) by William C. Reynolds; *The Guerrillas* (1862) by James D. McCabe, Jr.; and *Grant's Campaign* (1865) by John Poole.

1862

An important milestone in settling the West was the signing of the Homestead Act on May 20 by Pres. Abraham Lincoln. This law gave 160 acres of public land to any person who was head of a household and 21 years of age or older, provided that the person settled on the land for five years and then paid a nominal fee. If settlers wished to acquire title earlier, they could do so after six months by paying $1.25 an acre. The law was a boon to the approximately 2,000,000 people who

Typical of the style of humor favored by Americans of the period was that of Charles Farrar Browne, who wrote under the name of Artemus Ward. His writings began as newspaper columns in 1857, and in 1861 some of them were collected in *Artemus Ward, His Book.* Browne's column recounted the fictional adventures of Ward, a traveling carnival man. Ward's humor was based on naive sounding but shrewd comments on current events, with a great many misspellings that were

and made by John Ericsson. It was launched at Greenpoint, Long Island, on Jan. 30, 1862, less than 100 days after its keel was laid. Naval warfare was changed irrevocably by its design.

Conn., by Frederick William Gunn, founder and head of the Gunnery School at Washington, Conn.

Dec. 24 Waco University was chartered in Waco, Tex., under Baptist auspices. In 1886 another Baptist college, Baylor (chartered in 1845), was moved to Waco from Independence, Tex., and consolidated with Waco University under the Baylor name.

1862

What eventually proved to be a cornerstone of higher education, especially in its practical aspects, was the Morrill Act, signed July 2 by Pres. Abraham Lincoln. The law took its name from Rep. Justin Smith Morrill, Republican of Vermont, who had first introduced the bill in 1857. The law granted to each loyal state 30,000 acres of land for each senator and representative serving in Congress. The schools to be established on the land were to emphasize agriculture, home economics,

Strong emotions aroused by the war were reflected in the use of such epithets as *Copperhead.* The term was applied to northern Democrats who opposed the war and the Republican administration. The Copperheads were particularly strong in Ohio, Indiana, and Illinois. The name came from the Copperheads' custom of cutting the head of the goddess of liberty from copper pennies to wear in lapels; it also referred to the venomous snake. Some Republicans used the term to condemn the

ultimately found new homes under it, but it was not the major contributor to the overall settlement of the West. Far greater acreage was available from other sources, particularly the railroads, which received enormous grants of good land as subsidies.

1862–1863 In **congressional elections,** the Republicans kept control of both houses of Congress with a 39–12 majority in the Senate and 103–80 majority in the House.

Feb. 8 **Union forces captured Roanoke Island,** N.C. Gen. Henry A. Wise and his Confederate garrison of 2675 men were taken prisoner.

Mar. 6–7 The Battle of **Pea Ridge,** Ark., was fought. A Confederate army of 16,000 under Gen. Earl Van Dorn attacked a Union army of 10,500 under Brig. Gen. Samuel Ryan Curtis, whose last reserves prevented a Union disaster on the second day. Among the heavy losses on both sides were two Confederate generals, Benjamin McCulloch and James McQueen McIntosh.

Mar. 8 The **Confederate ironclad** *Virginia* destroyed two Union frigates at Hampton Roads, Va., sinking the *Cumberland* and setting the *Congress* on fire. The *Virginia* had been built from the raised hull of the Union ship *Merrimack,* which had been burned to the waterline when Union forces evacuated Norfolk Navy Yard in Apr. 1861.

Mar. 9 In the **first battle between ironclad warships,** the Confederate ship *Virginia* and Union ironclad *Monitor* fought to a draw at Hampton Roads, Va., whereupon the *Virginia* retired, leaving the Union blockade intact. The crew of the *Monitor,* following naval regulations, had been using only half charges in its two 12-inch guns.

Apr. 6–7 The Battle of **Shiloh** was fought near Pittsburg Landing, Tenn. The Union army of Tennessee was commanded by Gen. Ulysses S. Grant, the Confederate army of Mississippi by Gen. Albert S. Johnston. Over 100,000 men were engaged, the largest number yet in the Western Hemisphere. Johnston was close to a brilliant victory on the first day, but it cost him his life. Grant, with timely reinforcements on the second day, turned the tide against Gen. P. G. T. Beauregard. Losses were severe on both sides, sobering Washington and Richmond and the public perception of the struggle.

May 1 Capt. David G. Farragut and Union forces took **possession of New Orleans** after running past Forts Jackson and St. Philip on the Mississippi R. at night and then defeating a small Confederate flotilla. Farragut was promoted to rear admiral in July.

May 11 The Confederate ironclad *Virginia* was destroyed by its crew on the evacuation of Norfolk, Va.

considered amusing. Ward was an early influence on another writer, Samuel Langhorne Clemens, who began writing for the Virginia City, Nev., *Territorial Enterprise* this year. Clemens adopted the pseudonym Mark Twain in 1863.

The **first newspaper published in Idaho** was the *Golden Age* of Lewiston.

An early romantic **western novel** set in the Rockies, *John Brent* by Theodore Winthrop, was published. The author, a Connecticut gentleman of leisure, had been killed in a Civil War skirmish in June 1861. That year saw the posthumous publication of Winthrop's novel *Cecil Dreeme,* about a young woman masquerading as a male artist in Washington Square, New York City. Another novel, *Edwin Brothertoft* (1862), and two travel books followed *John Brent.* Winthrop's popularity lasted for a generation.

Business and Industry; Science; Education; Philosophy and Religion **III**	**IV** Sports; Social Issues and Crime; Folkways; Fashion; Holidays

engineering, and mechanical arts. These land-grant colleges still exist in most states.

John D. Rockefeller, 23 years old, invested in an oil refining business $4000 he had accumulated through a partnership in a produce commission house, Clark & Rockefeller. Five years later he was the major owner of Rockefeller, Andrews, and Flagler, the progenitor of Standard Oil Company of Ohio, incorporated in 1870.

The **first public clinic for throat diseases** was opened at the Medical College of New York by Dr. Louis Elsberg. The previous year he had given the first course in the U.S. on laryngology. In 1865 the American Medical Association awarded him its gold medal for his essay "Laryngoscopal Surgery."

Aerial reconnaissance for Union forces was carried out by American balloonist Thaddeus Lowe, who photographed Confederate ground emplacements around Richmond, Va., at an altitude of 1000 ft. This was the earliest use of cameras to provide panoramic shots of military positions.

entire Democratic party as disloyal to the Union. The term probably first appeared in print in the Cincinnati *Gazette* on July 30, 1862.

The popularity of **trotting races** was not diminished by the war. A new track was established in New York City at 144 St. between 7th and 8th Aves.

The **first enclosed baseball field** opened at Union Grounds, Brooklyn, N.Y.

May 31–June 1 At the twin battles of **Seven Pines and Fair Oaks,** Confederate forces under Gen. Joseph E. Johnston stalled the Union advance toward Richmond, Va., in Gen. George B. McClellan's Peninsular Campaign. Johnston was wounded at Fair Oaks and succeeded by Gen. Robert E. Lee.

June 1 Gen. **Robert E. Lee** was appointed commander of the Confederate Army of Northern Virginia.

July The **first black troops** were organized by Maj. Gen. David Hunter in the Union's First Carolina Regiment. Many of the soldiers were former slaves.

July 1 The **public debt** rose to $524,176,412.13, exceeding $500,000,000 for the first time. One year before it had been only $90,000,000; one year later it exceeded $1,000,000,000.

July 1 Congress enacted **antipolygamy legislation,** the Morrill Act, "to punish and prevent the practice of polygamy in the territories." Directed against the Mormons, the law proved defective and unenforceable. The Edmunds Act of 1882 and Edmunds-Taylor Act of 1887 were more effective.

July 1 The **Seven Days Campaign** ended with the indecisive Battle of Malvern Hill (Va.). Gen. Lee had started the campaign with an attack on McClellan's Union army at Mechanicsville, Va., on June 26. The Confederates gradually pushed the timid McClellan back to the safety of his base on the James River. McClellan's Peninsular Campaign had failed and his army was withdrawn. Casualties for the week stood at Union, 15,849; Confederate, 20,141.

July 11 Maj. Gen. **Henry W. Halleck** was named commander in chief of the Union armies by Pres. Lincoln.

July 12 Congress authorized the **Medal of Honor** for noncommissioned Army officers and privates who exhibited supreme gallantry in action. This highest U.S. military decoration had been authorized for men of the Navy in 1861. In 1863 the award was extended to include commissioned officers.

July 22 An intention to issue an **Emancipation Proclamation** was announced by Pres. Lincoln to his Cabinet as a strictly military effort to cripple Confederate manpower. He was persuaded to wait for a more favorable military situation to avoid the appearance of desperation.

July 24 **Martin Van Buren,** eighth president of the United States, died at 79. He was buried in his hometown, Kinderhook, N.Y.

Aug. 9 In the Battle of **Cedar Mountain,** Va., near the Rappahannock R. northwest of Richmond, Confederate troops under Gen. Stonewall Jackson, planning a move northward in advance of Gen. Lee's larger forces, defeated two brigades of Union forces led by Gen. John Pope and Gen. N. P. Banks. Badly outnum-

A best seller for 1862 was *Parson Brownlow's Book,* published as *The Rise, Progress, and Decline of Secession,* by William G. Brownlow. An influential preacher-editor in Knoxville, Tenn., Brownlow championed the federal government in a region devoted to secession. After imprisonment in 1861, Brownlow was released in the North on Mar. 3, 1862. The North loved his denunciation of the South; over 100,000 copies of the book were sold within six months.

Apr. **Variety programs** and waitresses serving liquor in resorts and restaurants were banned by a law passed by the state legislature of New York

Apr. 6 **Fitz-James O'Brien,** author of such stories as "What Was It?" and "The Diamond Lens," died of a wound received in combat.

| Business and Industry; Science;
Education; Philosophy and Religion | III | | IV | Sports; Social Issues and Crime;
Folkways; Fashion; Holidays |

The **University of Maine** was established as a land-grant institution at Orono under the name State College of Agriculture and the Mechanic Arts. Its first college-level instruction began in 1868. The present name dates from 1897.

The **largest retail store** in the world was that built for Alexander T. Stewart on the block bounded by Broadway, Fourth Ave., and 9th and 10th Sts., in New York City. Eight stories high and built of steel and stone, it cost nearly $3,000,000. Stewart's employed 2000 persons. In 1896 the company and building were bought by John Wanamaker of Philadelphia. The landmark building, designed by John Kellum, burned in 1956.

Congress established the **Department of Agriculture** "to acquire and diffuse useful information." In its first years its annual budget was about $50,000. Previously agriculture had been handled by the Patent Office, since many patents pertained to farm machinery.

July 16 "**We Are Coming, Father Abraham, Three Hundred Thousand More,**" a popular Civil War slogan, appeared in the poem by James Sloan Gibbons published in the New York *Evening Post.* Pres. Abraham Lincoln had urged Congress to raise an army of 500,000. The poem was written to aid the call for volunteers. It was set to music by Luther O. Emerson and Stephen Foster.

July 1 A **transcontinental railroad** became a certainty when Pres. Abraham Lincoln signed a bill incorporating the Union Pacific Company. The company was subsidized with federal funds to enable it to construct a line from Nebraska to Utah, where it would meet the Central Pacific.

Dec. 29 **Walt Whitman** wrote from Washington, D.C., to tell his mother about his brother George, whom he had visited in camp. He had a hard time locating his

bered, the Union army suffered 2381 killed or wounded; the Confederates, 1276.

Aug. 18 A **Sioux uprising** led by Chief Little Crow began. The cause was tardy payment of the cash annuity promised by the government under Indian land treaties. For five weeks the Sioux pillaged and burned settlements in Minnesota and massacred about 1000 people. On Sept. 23 the Sioux were badly defeated by Col. Henry H. Sibley at Wood Lake.

Aug. 29–30 At the second Battle of **Bull Run,** the maneuvers of Gen. Stonewall Jackson and his teamwork with Gen. Lee were too much for the 45,000 Union troops under Gen. John Pope, who broke and retreated to Washington, D.C. Union losses were 1724 killed, 8372 wounded, 5958 missing. Confederate losses stood at 1481 killed, 7627 wounded, 89 missing.

Sept. 15 The Union arsenal at **Harpers Ferry,** W.Va., was captured by Gen. Stonewall Jackson. A tremendous quantity of materiel was seized, and 12,500 men were captured. Harpers Ferry was abandoned and the captured troops set free by the Confederates on Sept. 20 and reoccupied by the North on the 22nd.

Sept. 17 At the Battle of **Antietam** Creek near Sharpsburg in western Maryland, Gen. Lee's first invasion of the North was halted by Union troops under Gen. McClellan. This was the bloodiest one-day battle of the Civil War. Each side lost over 2000 killed and 9000 wounded.

Sept. 22 A preliminary **Emancipation Proclamation** was issued by Pres. Lincoln. It was announced that on Jan. 1, 1863, slaves within all areas still in rebellion would be declared free forever.

Nov. 5 Gen. **Ambrose E. Burnside** was named by Pres. Lincoln to replace Gen. McClellan as commander of the Army of the Potomac.

Dec. 13 The Battle of **Fredericksburg,** Va., was a grave defeat for the North under Gen. Burnside. Gen. Lee's men killed or wounded 12,653 Union soldiers. Confederate casualties were 5300.

Dec. 31 The Union ironclad *Monitor* sank in a gale off Cape Hatteras, N.C.

Dec. 8 The opening of *Leah the Forsaken* by Augustin Daly, an adaptation of a German play by S. H. von Mosenthal, marked the beginning of Daly's brilliant career. Daly was responsible for scores of adaptations from the French, German, and English. He assembled a company of players that at various times included Ada Rehan, Otis Skinner, John Drew, Maurice Barrymore, and Joseph Jefferson.

1863

On Jan. 1, 1863, Pres. Abraham Lincoln issued his Emancipation Proclamation, which in spite of its title neither freed all the slaves nor satisfied the abolitionists. The proclamation applied only to slaves in territory under control of the Confederacy. It did not apply to areas occupied by Union forces or to the four slave states that had not seceded (Delaware, Kentucky, Maryland, and Missouri). In effect, it freed the slaves where Lincoln could not enforce the proclamation, and left slavery intact where the slaves could have been freed.

The Civil War continued to influence American literature. This year marked the appearance of a short novel that was destined to become a classic. *The Man Without a Country* by Edward Everett Hale, clergyman and author, first appeared anonymously in *Atlantic Monthly* in December. The story was inspired by a remark that had been made by Clement L. Vallandigham, leader of the northern antiwar Copperheads, in which he implied he did not care to live in a country that had Abraham Lincoln as president. In the story, Philip Nolan, charged

Aug. 28 The **Bureau of Engraving and Printing** was created to design and print financial papers for the federal government. It began with five employees.

Nov. 4 The **Gatling gun,** designed by Richard Jordan Gatling, was given a patent. Its chief feature, six barrels revolving around a central axis, permitted high rates of fire. It was not employed by Union forces until the siege of Petersburg, Va., in 1864–1865.

brother's outfit, and his pocket had been picked while he was changing trains in Philadelphia. But he found George safe and promoted to captain of the 51st New York Volunteers, at Falmont, Va., near Fredericksburg. George Whitman was sharing a tent with a Capt. Francis, and Walt lived with them: "There were five of us altogether, to eat, sleep, write, etc., in a space twelve feet square. George is about building a place, half hut and half tent, for himself. Every captain has a tent, in which he lives, transacts company business . . . has a cook (or a man of all work) and in the same tent mess and sleep his lieutenants, and perhaps the first sergeant. They have a kind of fireplace—and the cook's fire is outside on the open ground. . . . "

1863

The Civil War increased the pace at which labor unions were organized. The war raised economic and social questions concerning free versus slave labor. At the same time, the increase in the cost of living caused by the war brought agitation for higher wages. As a result, at least ten national unions were organized between 1863 and 1866. Among them was the first of the railroad brotherhoods, the Brotherhood of Locomotive Engineers, formed this year as the Brotherhood of the Footboard. Conductors organized in 1868, trainmen

A new sport became available to Americans this year with the introduction of roller skating by James L. Plimpton. Plimpton invented the four-wheel skate, which worked on rubber pads, thus permitting skaters to change direction by shifting their weight to one side or the other without lifting the wheels of the skate off the ground. Roller skating became fashionable in New York City and soon spread to other cities. In Newport, R.I., the Roller Skating Association leased the Atlantic House and turned its dining hall and plaza into a skating

| Exploration and Settlement; Wars; Government; Civil Rights; Statistics **I** | | **II** Publishing; Arts and Music; Popular Entertainment; Architecture; Theater |

Lincoln had no intention of driving the loyal slave states into the Confederate camp. The proclamation enraged many southerners, who saw it as an attempt to spark a slave insurrection.

Henry Ward Beecher, the celebrated pastor of the Plymouth (Congregational) Church in Brooklyn, N.Y., journeyed to England on a lecture tour during which he defended the Union position before English audiences sympathetic to the South.

Free delivery of mail in cities was initiated by Congress. Rural free delivery (RFD) did not begin until 1896.

Feb. 24 The **Territory of Arizona** was formed from the Territory of New Mexico. Its first capital was established at Fort Whipple in 1864.

Feb. 25 Congress passed the **National Banking Act,** designed by Salmon P. Chase, providing for a system of national banks. To supervise the system Congress created the post of Comptroller of the Currency. Hugh McCulloch was appointed to the position on May 9.

Mar. 3 The **Territory of Idaho** was carved from four existing territories: Washington, Utah, Dakota, and Nebraska. It included the later states of Montana and Wyoming.

Mar. 3 A **conscription act,** first in the nation's history, was passed by Congress. It called for registration of all male citizens between 20 and 45 years of age and aliens in the same age bracket who had declared their intention of becoming citizens. Conscripts could be exempted from military service by payment of $300 or by providing a substitute.

May 1–4 At the Battle of **Chancellorsville,** 50 miles southwest of Washington, D.C., Gen. Robert E. Lee won his greatest victory over huge Union forces under Gen. Joseph Hooker. In the North, 17,275 were killed or wounded; in the South, 12,821. Gen. Stonewall Jackson, one of the wounded, died a few days later.

May 2 Gen. **Stonewall Jackson,** leading a large part of Gen. Lee's army, delivered a devastating blow on Gen. Hooker's right flank. Reconnoitering with his staff at day's end, Jackson and his group were mistaken for Union soldiers and fired on by their own forces. Jackson's shattered left arm had to be amputated. While he was hospitalized pneumonia set in; his death came on May 10.

June 20 **West Virginia** was admitted to the Union, the 35th state.

July 1–3 At the Battle of **Gettysburg,** Gen. Lee made a desperate bid to smash through Union forces and approach Washington, D.C., from the west. Gen. George G. Meade met him accidentally at Gettysburg, Pa. Lee's assaults on federal positions brought heavy losses to both sides. On July 3, when the famous

with treason, declares that he never wants to hear of the U.S. again. He is sentenced to spend the rest of his life at sea, with all news of the U.S. withheld from him.

James Abbott McNeill Whistler, expatriate U.S. painter-etcher-engraver, displayed *The White Girl* in the Salon des Refusées in Paris, causing a furor in the art world. Whistler opposed the English fashion for storytelling in art, holding that art had no mission to fill, but was self-justified. His most famous painting, called originally *Arrangement in Grey and Black,* but soon known as *Whistler's Mother,* was probably done in 1865.

The most influential **labor paper** of the Civil War period, *Fincher's Trades' Review,* was established in Philadelphia, Pa.

The **first newspaper in Wyoming** was the *Daily Telegram,* published at Fort Bridges.

The first part of *Tales of a Wayside Inn,* stories in verse by Henry Wadsworth Longfellow, was published, demonstrating Longfellow's narrative skill. Using the convention of Chaucer and Boccaccio, he and six congenial acquaintances gather at an inn in Sudbury, Mass., and tell tales, including such favorites as "Paul Revere's

in 1873, and firemen in 1883.

The **University of Massachusetts,** at Amherst, Mass., was founded as Massachusetts Agricultural College. Its first classes met in 1867. Its name was changed to Massachusetts State College in 1931; the present name was adopted in 1947.

The **Travelers Insurance Company,** offering the first travelers' accident insurance in the U.S., was founded. The first premium received was two cents for insuring a Hartford banker while walking from the post office to his home. The founder was James G. Batterson.

Butterick paper clothes patterns began when Ebenezer Butterick, a tailor and shirtmaker of Sterling, Mass., received a patent. The first patterns were cut from stiff paper and limited to children's wear, but were immediately successful. By 1864 Butterick had an office at 192 Broadway, New York City, and was making his patterns of tissue paper. In 1871 he sold 6,000,000 patterns.

Jan.   **Confederate churches** behind federal lines were given protection against interference by the military in their internal affairs in an order from Pres. Lincoln. The policy was stated in a letter to the commanding general of the Union forces at St. Louis, Mo.

Mar. 2   Congress authorized a **railway gauge** of 4 ft. 8½ in. for the track width of the Union Pacific Railroad. This act rejected Pres. Lincoln's recommendation of 5 ft. The gauge set by Congress has become the generally accepted measure on most of the world's railways.

rink. In Chicago, the Casino could accommodate 3000 spectators and 1000 skaters. In San Francisco, a rink advertised 5000 pairs of skates available for rent.

Adah Isaacs Menken, a lovely and much talked about actress, scored a spectacular triumph in Virginia City, Nev., with her performance in *Mazeppa, or The Wild Horse.* At the climax of the show she was strapped to the back of a wild horse and, in a flimsy gauze garment, driven up a mountain trail. The audiences of miners stood on their chairs and cheered wildly. Virginia City was so impressed that it named a new mining district the Menken and established a Menken Shaft and Tunnel Company.

A new **baseball rule** provided that both balls and strikes were to be called.

The first attempt at **base-stealing** in baseball history was made by Eddie Cuthbert of Philadelphia, Pa., when his team, the Keystones, played against the Brooklyn Atlantics.

The English sport of **racquets** was greatly encouraged by the construction of excellent courts on West 13th St., New York City, and the engagement of Frederick Foulkes of England as a professional player. In 1867 an international match with England was staged, in which William Gray, the British champion, beat the American entry.

Life on the battlefront was vividly described by Walt Whitman in a letter to Nat and Fred Gray: "I . . . have

charge of Gen. George E. Pickett's division failed, with one unit leaving 3393 out of 4800 men dead or wounded on the field, the battle was lost to the South. On July 4 both sides were exhausted. On July 5 Lee's army retreated across the Potomac R., never to return to northern territory. The South suffered 30,000 killed, wounded, or missing; the North, 23,000.

July 4 At the Battle of **Vicksburg** a Confederate army under Gen. John C. Pemberton surrendered to Gen. Ulysses S. Grant after a campaign that had begun on Mar. 29. The South lost 8000 killed and wounded; and more than 29,000 surrendered. Union casualties were 8910. This loss of manpower and control of the Mississippi R., atop the loss at Gettysburg, doomed the Confederacy.

July 8 At the Battle of **Port Hudson,** Miss., Confederate Maj. Gen. Franklin Gardner surrendered his garrison of 5500 men to Gen. Nathaniel P. Banks after a siege of six weeks.

July 13–16 **Antidraft riots** broke out in New York City, and nearly 1000 persons were killed or wounded before federal troops restored order.

Sept. 19–20 At the Battle of **Chickamauga,** Tenn., Union forces under Gen. William S. Rosecrans were defeated by troops under Gen. Braxton Bragg. Both sides, evenly matched, saw over a quarter of their men killed or wounded. Union forces retreated to Chattanooga, Tenn.

Nov. 23–25 At the Battle of **Chattanooga,** Tenn., Union reinforcements under Gen. Grant systematically captured Confederate positions around the city. The siege was broken and Confederate forces under Gen. Bragg fled to Dalton, Ga. Tennessee was no longer a battleground.

Dec. 8 Pres. Lincoln issued a **proclamation of amnesty and reconstruction,** offering full pardon to all southerners who voluntarily took a "prescribed oath."

Ride," "The Saga of King Olaf," "The Legend of Rabbi Ben Levi," and "The Birds of Killingworth."

June 1 Respect for **freedom of the press** was strikingly exemplified by Pres. Lincoln's revocation of an order given three days earlier by Gen. Ambrose E. Burnside suppressing the *Chicago Times* because of its violently anti-Lincoln and pro-southern opinions.

Nov. 19 The **Gettysburg Address** was delivered on the bloodstained battlefield at Gettysburg, Pa., by Pres. Abraham Lincoln, at ceremonies dedicating a national cemetery. The three brief paragraphs are marked by orderly thought, lucid expression, and a noble sense of the tragedy of the conflict.

1864

A presidential election while the Civil War was being fought posed special problems. In the North there was considerable dissatisfaction with the progress being made in defeating the Confederacy, so Pres. Abraham Lincoln did not think his chances of reelection were good. The Democrats were split between those who supported the war and those who wanted peace at almost any price. The Democratic nominee was Gen. George B. McClellan, commander of the Union Army, who had let several opportunities for victory slip away. The Democratic platform called for peace through reunification of the states but did not say how this was to be done. Fortunately for Lincoln and the Republicans, several important military victories were won in

The Civil War created a large demand for statues of leading figures in the conflict. A sculptor who provided many such works was John Quincy Adams Ward. In 1861 Ward set up his studio in New York City. This year he completed what was perhaps his finest work, *Indian Hunter,* for New York City's Central Park. He completed this after a long trip among Indians in the West and Northwest. Ward later did other statues for Central Park and for several cities, including statues of Gen. William T. Sherman and Gen. George H. Thomas, as well as *Private of the Seventh Regiment.*

| Business and Industry; Science; Education; Philosophy and Religion III | | IV Sports; Social Issues and Crime; Folkways; Fashion; Holidays |

Mar. 3 The **National Academy of Sciences** was founded in Washington, D.C., as a private nonprofit organization to promote science and investigate scientific problems for the government. Today it has about 1250 members.

Apr. 14 A **continuous-roll printing press** was patented by William Bullock, who put a press of this type into operation in his Pittsburgh, Pa., printing plant. He turned to manufacture of the press as soon as the Civil War ended. This was the first printing press capable of printing on both sides of a sheet.

May 1 The **New York Hospital for Ruptured and Crippled Children** opened in New York City, the first orthopedic hospital in the U.S. In 1940 the institution was renamed the Hospital for Special Surgery.

Dec. 1 The **stereoscope** continued to be improved by U.S. inventors during the Civil War. Samuel D. Goodale of Cincinnati, Ohio, secured a patent for a stereoscopic apparatus to show scenes in motion. Operated by hand, it was the forerunner of peep-show devices.

seen warlife, the real article—folded myself in a blanket, lying down in the mud with composure—relished salt pork and hard tack—have been on the battlefield among the wounded, the faint and the bleeding . . . have gone over with a flag of truce the next day to help direct the burial of the dead. . . . " Whitman also visited army hospitals: "These Hospitals, so different from all others—these thousands, and tens and twenty of thousands of American young men, badly wounded, all sorts of wounds, operated on, pallid with diarrhoea, languishing, dying with fever, pneumonia, etc."

May 5 The **U.S. heavyweight boxing championship** was won by Joe Coburn, who knocked out Mike McCoole in the 63rd round at Charleston, Md. In 1865 Coburn retired and McCoole claimed the title.

Oct. 3 **Thanksgiving Day** was proclaimed a national holiday by Pres. Lincoln, to be observed on the last Thursday in November. In 1939 Pres. Franklin D. Roosevelt moved Thanksgiving Day one week back to stimulate Christmas shopping. In 1941 Congress adopted a joint resolution confirming the fourth Thursday, not the last Thursday, as Thanksgiving Day.

1864

Efforts to educate the deaf, almost entirely the work of the Gallaudet family during the nineteenth century, were rewarded in 1864 when Congress authorized the granting of degrees by the new college division of the Columbia Institution for the Deaf, Dumb, and Blind, in Washington, D.C. The school was renamed Gallaudet College in 1894. Early in the century Thomas Hopkins Gallaudet had pioneered in the field. His eldest son, Thomas Gallaudet, was a clergyman who devoted almost all his time to missionary work among the deaf; he founded St. Ann's Church for Deaf-Mutes in New York City. The youngest son, Edward Miner Gallaudet, had opened the Washington school about 1857. It

In the early days of baseball there was a rule against paying players. However, by 1864 the rule had been stretched or broken a number of times. At least as early as 1860 the Brooklyn Excelsiors reputedly paid Jim Creighton (under the table, of course), although Albert J. "Al" Reach is often cited as the first professional baseball player. He accepted money in 1864 to leave the Brooklyn Eckfords for the Philadelphia Athletics. Reach later became a prominent manufacturer of sporting goods.

| Exploration and Settlement; Wars; Government; Civil Rights; Statistics | I | | II | Publishing; Arts and Music; Popular Entertainment; Architecture; Theater |

time to influence the outcome.

1864–1865 In **congressional elections** the Republicans increased their majorities to 42–10 in the Senate and 149–42 in the House.

Feb. 7 A **Union expedition to Florida** to return the state to Union allegiance entered Jacksonville under command of Gen. Truman Seymour.

Feb. 20 At the Battle of **Olustee**, Fla., near Jacksonville, Union forces under Gen. Seymour were badly defeated by Confederate troops under Gen. Joseph Finegan. The Union lost some 2000 killed or wounded. The effort to set up a loyal state government was severely hampered in what was the largest land engagement in Florida.

Mar. 10 Gen. **Ulysses S. Grant** was made general in chief by Pres. Lincoln, replacing Gen. Henry W. Halleck.

Apr. 12 The **Fort Pillow massacre** followed capture of the Union-held fort on the Mississippi R. in Tennessee by the Confederate cavalry officer Maj. Gen. Nathan B. Forrest. Northern accounts, supported later by a federal investigation, held that the black Union troops were massacred in cold blood after the fort's surrender. Southern accounts denied the charge.

Apr. 17 The **exchange of prisoners of war** was discontinued by Gen. Grant. He stated that the practice served to prolong the conflict.

Apr. 20 **Rations** of Confederate captives were reduced by the War Department in retaliation for mistreatment of Union prisoners.

May 5–6 The Battle of the **Wilderness** ended indecisively as the armies of Robert E. Lee and Ulysses S. Grant wrought mutual destruction near Chancellorsville, Va. Because of thick forest growth, most of the fighting was done at close hand. Despite heavy Union losses, Grant's progress southward was only briefly halted.

May 7–20 In the **Spotsylvania campaign,** Gen. Grant continued hammering at Lee's waning forces.

May 11 **James Ewell Brown "Jeb" Stuart,** Confederate general and cavalry leader, was mortally wounded at Yellow Tavern, Va., where an inadequate Confederate force was attempting to block Gen. Philip H. Sheridan. Sheridan, with Gen. Grant's approval, was making his first independent cavalry action.

May 12 The heaviest action of the Battle of **Spotsylvania** began at dawn, when Gen. Winfield Scott Hancock, with 20,000 men, attacked a Confederate salient. Creating a gap, Hancock's men captured some 4000 men and 20 guns.

May 26 The **Territory of Montana** was formed by Congress from the Territory of Idaho.

June 3 At the Battle of **Cold Harbor,** Gen. Lee won his last victory over Union forces, numbering 108,000 against his 59,000. On this day federal troops lost 7000

Three books of **wartime poems** were published: *Thirty Poems* by William Cullen Bryant, *Poems of the War* by George Henry Boker, and *In War Time* by John Greenleaf Whittier.

North Dakota's first newspaper, *Frontier Scout,* was started at Fort Union.

The **first newspaper in Montana Territory,** the *Montana Post,* began publication.

The adaptation by **Augustin Daly** of *Le Papillon,* by the French playwright Victorien Sardou, initiated other Daly adaptations of plays written by the prolific French-

Business and Industry; Science; Education; Philosophy and Religion	III		IV	Sports; Social Issues and Crime; Folkways; Fashion; Holidays

remains the only liberal arts college in the world for the deaf.

The motto "**In God We Trust**" appeared on a coin for the first time, on the 1864 two-cent piece.

The **University of Kansas** was established at Lawrence, Kans. Its first classes met in 1866.

A **new political expression** was coined by Pres. Lincoln in his campaign of 1864 when he observed, " . . . it was not best to swap horses while crossing the stream, and . . . I am not so poor a horse that they might not make a botch of it in trying to swap."

The **first successful U.S. advertising agency** was started by George Presbury Rowell. Its first job was to prepare a theatrical program for the holiday season in Boston. Rowell later published an important newspaper directory. The first modern-style agency was N. W. Ayer & Son, established in Philadelphia, Pa., in 1869.

The **Saratoga, N.Y., race track** was built by John Morrissey, former boxing champion, and the first organized meets in the U.S. were held there. Morrissey named the first stakes race The Travers after a local family. Still run today, it is the oldest stakes race in the U.S.

Tremont Temple, in Boston, organized the first Baptist social union in the U.S., a pioneer lay organization. Similar church lay organizations followed in other churches, reflecting the growing influence of businessmen and professionals in church affairs.

The **first American croquet club** was founded, the Park Place Croquet Club of Brooklyn, N.Y.

men against 1500 for the Confederate troops. In an eight-minute period more men fell in an assault on entrenched Confederate troops than in any other like period of time. Between May 7 and June 3, federal losses were 50,000 men, Confederate 32,000. The North could replace its losses fully, but the South could not.

June 7 The **Republican National Convention** nominated **Pres. Lincoln** for a second term. Andrew Johnson of Tennessee was nominated for the vice presidency.

June 14 The **James River Bridge,** the longest (2100 ft.) pontoon bridge ever used in war, was constructed in eight hours by 450 Union engineers. Extending from Windmill Point to Fort Powhatan in Virginia, the structure enabled Grant's forces to cross the James R. and to move on Petersburg, a vital communications center south of Richmond.

June 15–18 At the Battle of **Petersburg,** Va., Union forces were unable to take the strategic city in the face of brilliant strategy by Gen. Lee. Gen. Grant began a siege that continued until Apr. 1865.

June 19 The Confederate cruiser *Alabama* was sunk by the U.S.S. *Kearsarge* off Cherbourg, France, while trying to escape into the Atlantic. Fifteen thousand Frenchmen watched the battle from shoreline cliffs. In two years of roaming the Atlantic, the *Alabama* had destroyed or captured 69 vessels.

July 5 **Horace Greeley,** eager for Pres. Lincoln to open peace negotiations, advised him that Confederate emissaries from Jefferson Davis were in Canada. Lincoln authorized Greeley to open negotiations with the men at Niagara Falls, N.Y. The negotiators were found to be without proper authority, and the peace attempt failed.

July 11 Gen. **Jubal A. Early,** commanding Confederate troops attempting to draw Union forces away from Richmond, broke through inadequate Union forces southeast of Frederick, Md., and entered the District of Columbia. Noting that hastily ordered federal reserves were arriving in significant numbers, Early withdrew the next night. He continued to harass Union forces from the Shenandoah Valley until the Battle of Cedar Creek in October.

Aug. 5–23 At the Battle of **Mobile Bay,** Ala., David G. Farragut commanded a fleet of fourteen wooden ships and four ironclads. Running through a minefield and past Confederate forts Gaines, Morgan, and Powell, Farragut's fleet defeated a Confederate flotilla, including the Confederate ironclad *Tennessee,* and took one of the South's last major ports. The city of Mobile was taken in 1865.

Aug. 29 The **Democratic National Convention** nominated **Gen. George B. McClellan** for the presidency and George H. Pendleton of Ohio for the vice

man: *King Carrot* (1872), *Folline* (1874), *Odette* (1882), and *The Golden Widow* (1889).

Japanese influence on U.S. art began to appear, stemming from the opening of Japan to foreign trade in 1854. James Whistler's *La Princesse du Pays de la Porcelaine* clearly reflects an acquaintance with the art of the Japanese print.

An **outstanding equestrian statue** is *Washington,* in the Boston Public Gardens, by Thomas Ball of Boston. Since there were no funds for the casting, Ball kept the statue until July 3, 1869, when it was finally unveiled.

| Business and Industry; Science; Education; Philosophy and Religion | III | | IV | Sports; Social Issues and Crime; Folkways; Fashion; Holidays |

An **underground transit system** for New York City was planned by Hugh B. Wilson, to be the first in the U.S. Wilson established a company, capitalized at $5,000,-000, to advance the project, but his request for a franchise was rejected by the N.Y. State legislature. London had opened a subway in 1863.

The **first curve ball** by a baseball pitcher was thrown by William A. "Candy" Cummings of the Brooklyn Stars. He was pitching against the Brooklyn Atlantics. Skeptics thought it was an optical illusion.

A **salmon cannery,** probably the first in the U.S., was built by William, John, and George Hume, and Andrew S. Hapgood next to the Sacramento R., in Washington, Calif. It failed, but they built another one the next year at Eagle Fish, Wash. It became a success and led to the proliferation of salmon canneries in the Northwest.

Feb. 19 The **Knights of Pythias** had their start in Washington, D.C. Justus H. Rathbone and 12 other charter members organized in Temperance Hall, now Washington Lodge No. 1. Over 3000 subordinate lodges of this fraternal and benevolent organization exist today.

The **formation of unions** was spurred by rising living costs. In the next ten years 26 would be created. They would have 300,000 members by 1872.

May 11 "I propose to fight it out on this line if it takes all summer" was said by Gen. Ulysses S. Grant during the Spotsylvania campaign, reflecting the Union general's determination to take Richmond, Va., and win the war, despite the heavy losses he would suffer.

Feb. 17 The **first successful submarine attack** was made by the Confederate vessel *Hunley*, which sank the federal sloop *Housatonic* while it was blockading Charleston, S.C. In 1863 the Confederate submarine

May 16 Platt Rogers Spencer, creator of Spencerian penmanship, died at 63. As a young teacher he had

Exploration and Settlement; Wars; Government; Civil Rights; Statistics	I		II	Publishing; Arts and Music; Popular Entertainment; Architecture; Theater

presidency. The party platform attacked Pres. Lincoln's prosecution of the war, calling his program a failure.

Sept. 1 Atlanta, Ga., was evacuated by Confederate forces under Gen. John B. Hood. The next day the city was occupied by Union forces under Gen. William Tecumseh Sherman.

Oct. 19 A Confederate **raid on St. Albans,** Vt., led by Lt. Bennett H. Young, netted the raiders some $208,-000 from the town's three banks. The raiders attempted unsuccessfully to burn the town, then rode off to the Canadian border, where they were arrested. They were subsequently released.

Oct. 19 At the Battle of **Cedar Creek,** Va., the last in the Shenandoah Valley, Gen. Early's Confederates missed an opportunity for a significant victory by failure to follow up an advantage. Regrouped, and with Gen. Philip H. Sheridan arriving back from Washington, Union forces counterattacked in the afternoon and forced the Confederates to withdraw. The poem "Sheridan's Ride" by Thomas Buchanan Read dramatized the general's return to the field.

Oct. 31 **Nevada was admitted** to the Union, the 36th state.

Nov. 8 **Abraham Lincoln was reelected president** of the United States. Andrew Johnson of Tennessee was elected vice president. The electoral vote was Lincoln, 212; Gen. George B. McClellan, Democratic candidate, 21. The popular vote was Lincoln, 2,216,-067; McClellan, 1,808,725.

Nov. 16 **Gen. Sherman's march to the sea** with 62,000 men began. Leaving Atlanta, Ga., in flames and sweeping across a 60-mile front with little serious opposition, his army destroyed everything useful to the Confederates and ravaged the countryside. The South was cut in two. Gen. William J. Hardee and his remaining Confederate forces evacuated Savannah, Ga., on Dec. 21. Sherman occupied the city that day.

Nov. 25 A Confederate **attempt to burn New York City** ended in failure. Twelve fires were set by arsonists at hotels, theaters, and docks, but all were put out quickly and no one was hurt. Among the targets were Barnum's Museum, the Astor House, and the Hudson River dock.

Dec. **Salmon P. Chase was appointed chief justice** of the Supreme Court. His most significant achievements came when he held the office of secretary of the treasury under Lincoln. He was partly responsible for saving the country from financial ruin with the Legal Tender Act, which he sponsored in 1862. The act allowed 150,000,000 greenbacks to be issued. The phrase "In God We Trust" was put on national coins by order of Chase.

Bayard Taylor, traveler, journalist, poet, and novelist, published *John Godfrey's Fortunes,* a realistic novel of the contemporary New York literary scene with autobiographical elements. One of four fiction works he produced in the 1860s, it was popular then but little read now.

The Nasby Papers by Petroleum Vesuvius Nasby, pseudonym of the Ohio journalist David Ross Locke, was published. It was a collection of Locke's satiric "letters" to a newspaper by Nasby, an illiterate country preacher supposedly supporting the South but in effect caricaturing its positions. Pres. Abraham Lincoln enjoyed the Nasby letters, often reading them to his Cabinet and visitors.

Business and Industry; Science; Education; Philosophy and Religion	III		IV	Sports; Social Issues and Crime; Folkways; Fashion; Holidays

David had damaged the federal ship *Ironsides.* Both the *Hunley* and the *David* were lost in these engagements.

June 30 A new **Internal Revenue Act** was passed by Congress. It increased taxes on many items, including tobacco, and introduced a second income tax. The tax rate was 5% on incomes between $600 and $10,000 and 10% on incomes over $10,000.

July 4 **Immigration to the U.S.** was spurred by passage of a federal contract labor act, which guaranteed 12-month wage contracts for immigrant workers.

helped found boys' schools in New York and New England where expert penmanship was taught as a way to achieve success.

Aug. 5 Adm. David G. Farragut exclaimed, "**Damn the torpedoes! Full speed ahead**" when the lead ship of his flotilla, the *Tecumseh,* struck a mine, then called a torpedo, and sank at the entrance to Mobile Bay. The federal fleet ran the minefield and the forts at the entrance and captured the small Confederate flotilla in the harbor.

1865

The Civil War was scarcely over before Pres. Abraham Lincoln was assassinated, the first president to be killed. The assassin struck as Lincoln watched a comedy, *Our American Cousin,* at Ford's Theater in Washington, D.C., on the evening of Apr. 14. He died at 7:22 A.M. the next day. The assassin, John Wilkes Booth, an actor and Confederate sympathizer, escaped from Washington but broke his leg jumping from the president's box to the stage. He was cornered in a barn near Bowling Green, Va., on Apr. 26 and shot to death. Of the nine persons charged with the conspiracy, four were hanged and four were jailed. Dr. Samuel A. Mudd, the physician who, not recognizing Booth, set his broken leg, was sentenced to life imprisonment but was pardoned in 1869.

Jan. 15 **Fort Fisher,** N.C., fell to Union forces under a joint sea and land assault. Some 2000 soldiers were captured, including Maj. Gen. William H.C. Whiting, mortally wounded. This engagement gave the federals control of Cape Fear R. Wilmington, the last Confederate port, was now closed.

Feb. 3 At the **Hampton Roads Peace Conference,** Pres. Abraham Lincoln met with Confederate peace commissioners aboard the *River Queen* in Hampton Roads, Va. Negotiations were deadlocked because the Confederates insisted on southern autonomy.

Feb. 6 Gen. **Robert E. Lee** was given overall command of the Confederate armies by the Confederate congress at Richmond. Previously, Pres. Jefferson Davis had commanded all armies himself.

Feb. 17 **Columbia,** S.C., was set afire while being entered by federal troops under Gen. William Tecumseh Sherman. Bales of cotton were put to the torch, perhaps by Confederates to prevent their falling into federal hands. Strong winds scattered the burning cotton across most of the city.

Mar. 2 **Gen. Lee asked Gen. Grant for a conference** to iron out differences between North and South. Pres. Lincoln rejected the proposal, demanding the surrender of the Confederates before such negotiations could take place.

Mar. 3 The **Freedmen's Bureau was created by Congress** to help the destitute but free blacks of the South. In 1866 Congress greatly extended the bureau's power, over Pres. Andrew Johnson's veto. The first bureau commissioner was Union Gen. Oliver O. Howard, who later founded Howard University in Washington, D.C.

Mar. 4 Pres. **Lincoln was inaugurated** for his second term. Sen. Andrew Johnson, Republican of Tennessee, succeeded Hannibal Hamlin as vice president.

Mar. 13 **Slaves were subject to military duty** in the Confederate Army by a bill signed by Pres. Jefferson Davis.

The end of the Civil War was marked by an outpouring of war-related writings: poetry commemorating the dead, accounts of wartime experiences, and reflections on its causes and consequences. One of the first and best of the war poems was James Russell Lowell's "Ode Recited at the Commemoration to the Living and Dead Soldiers of Harvard University," read on July 21, 1865. It was first privately printed and did not attract much attention until it appeared in the Sept. 1865 *Atlantic Monthly.* Lowell, who had lost three nephews in the war, portrayed Abraham Lincoln as the symbol of the courageous warrior. During the war Lowell had written two series of verses, *The Biglow Papers,* for the *Atlantic.* These were published in book form in 1867. They strongly supported the Union and criticized England for its unfriendly attitude toward the North.

The popular children's story ***Hans Brinker; or The Silver Skates*** by Mary Mapes Dodge, begun as a serial, quickly became a best seller.

Josh Billings, His Sayings by Henry Wheeler Shaw, rural apostle of horse sense, was published with the assistance of Charles Farrar Browne (Artemus Ward). Shaw's aphorisms, in the semiliterate vernacular, delighted the public and earned him the title of "Aesop and Ben Franklin condensed and abridged." Typical of his aphorisms is the following: "The muel iz haf hoss and haf Jackass, and then kums tu a full stop, natur diskovering her mistake."

Petroleum Vesuvius Nasby (David Ross Locke) offered another collection of his humorous political commentaries, *Divers Opinions of Yours Trooly.* Again Locke cast Nasby as a stupid, semiliterate, hypocritical, corrupt Copperhead preacher—a straw man used to convey Locke's political views. Locke soon became famous and rich as a lecturer and writer.

Walt Whitman's ***Drum-Taps*** drew on the poet's experience as a nurse in Washington, D.C., during the Civil War. Later incorporated into Whitman's everexpanding *Leaves of Grass,* this volume included such favorites as "Pioneers! O Pioneers!" and "Beat! Beat! Drums." A supplement published after Lincoln's death contained "O Captain! My Captain!" and "When Lilacs Last in the Dooryard Bloom'd."

Francis Parkman's ***Pioneers of France in the New World*** continued the historian's magnificent account of the conflict between nations for domination in the New World. It was ultimately completed in seven volumes.

| Business and Industry; Science; Education; Philosophy and Religion III | IV Sports; Social Issues and Crime; Folkways; Fashion; Holidays |

1865

Women were slowly being accepted in the professions and the sciences. Among them was Maria Mitchell, an astronomer. She discovered a comet in 1847. In 1865 she became the first woman professor of astronomy in the U.S., being appointed to a chair at Vassar College. Mitchell was noted especially for her studies of satellites, nebulas, and sunspots. She was the first woman to be elected to the American Academy of Arts and Sciences. Her reputation in the U.S. and abroad was a significant reflection of the rising reputation of Vassar.

The **first department of fine arts** in a U.S. college was opened at Yale University. Under the direction of Prof. John F. Weir, the Yale School of Fine Arts began with four students.

Purdue University, West Lafayette, Ind., was chartered as Indiana Agricultural College. Its present name was adopted in 1869. Its first classes met in 1874.

Cornell University was founded at Ithaca, N.Y., by Ezra Cornell and Andrew Dickson White. Cornell secured the site and endowed $500,000 for the school. White became its first president. The first classes were held in 1868.

The **University of Kentucky,** Lexington, Ky., was established as the Agricultural and Mechanical College of Kentucky University. Its first classes were held in 1865. After name changes in 1878 and 1908, the present name was adopted in 1916.

The **number of dollars in circulation** in the U.S. rose to 1,081,540,514, more than double the number in 1860, as the federal government inflated the currency to pay for the Civil War.

Natural gas was sold for the first time in the U.S. by the Fredonia Gas Light and Water Works Company, Fredonia, N.Y. Small natural gas wells had been brought in at Fredonia in 1821, and the gas had been piped to

Beards were fashionable at this time. Scarcely a picture exists of a Civil War general on either side who did not sport one. All presidents from Ulysses S. Grant (elected in 1868) to Chester A. Arthur had beards. Pres. Grover Cleveland (elected in 1884) broke the custom, although he had a large, drooping mustache. Men's clothing continued to be plain and conservative. Collars, cravats, and waistcoats were worn regardless of the weather, although some men were beginning to wear white linen or seersucker suits in summer.

Clara Barton was placed in charge of a government-sponsored search for missing soldiers of the Civil War. During the war, as a personal enterprise, she had obtained and distributed hospital supplies for Union troops. Her distribution agency often delivered supplies right at the front.

Interest in **baseball** had a tremendous surge after the Civil War. This year saw 91 clubs included in the National Association of Base Ball Players. In 1866 Arthur P. Gorman was named president of the organization. A year later 237 teams were represented.

John Wesley Hyatt received a patent for a composition billiard ball and was awarded a $10,000 prize by a billiard ball manufacturer who up to this time had to use expensive ivory. Hyatt, one of the most prolific inventors of his time, later discovered the process for the production of celluloid, thus creating a revolution in American industry. His other inventions included a type of roller bearing still in use, a water filter, and a sugar cane mill.

The popular **Stetson hat** had its origin this year when John Batterson Stetson opened a one-man hat factory in Philadelphia, Pa. Stetson, the son of a hatmaker, had previously attempted to establish himself in the business, but ill health had forced him to travel to Illinois, Missouri, and Colorado. During his travels he had noticed the style of hat favored by westerners and, after a slow start in Philadelphia, he began to design new hats based on the western styles. His business began to expand rapidly. By 1906 he employed 3500 workers and was selling 2,000,000 hats a year. The Stetson hat had a broad brim and its crown was tall enough to sport ten ornamental braids, known as galloons. It was the mispronunciation of the word *galloon* that gave the world the term *ten-gallon hat.*

Mar. 25 At the Union siege of **Petersburg**, Va., Gen. Lee made a desperate attempt to break through the Union line at its weakest point, Ft. Stedman, east of the city. Despite initial success the Confederates were beaten back. Losses on both sides were heavy.

Apr. 1 At the Battle of **Five Forks,** a strategic crossroads outside Petersburg, Gen. Philip H. Sheridan routed Confederates under Gen. George E. Pickett. Some 5000 Confederate prisoners were taken.

Apr. 2 The **evacuation of Richmond** was urged by Gen. Lee, who informed Confederate Pres. Davis that he himself must withdraw from Petersburg, Va. Davis left the city that night with his cabinet, retreating to Danville. The now small Confederate army began evacuation of Petersburg.

Apr. 3 **Union forces occupied Petersburg,** Va., one day after the Confederate evacuation. Lee's forces moved south but were blocked by Union units.

Apr. 9 At **Appomattox** Court House, Va., Gen. Lee surrendered to Gen. Grant. The Civil War was virtually ended.

Apr. 14 Pres. **Lincoln was shot** by John Wilkes Booth at Ford's Theater in Washington, D.C. He died the following morning.

Apr. 15 Vice Pres. **Andrew Johnson was sworn in** as 17th president of the United States. He completed Lincoln's term.

Apr. 26 Gen. **Joseph E. Johnston surrendered** the Confederate Army of Tennessee to Gen. Sherman near Durham Station, N.C.

Apr. 26 **John Wilkes Booth** was hunted down by military police in a barn near Fort Royal, Va. The barn was set afire, and Booth was mortally wounded, possibly by his own hand.

Apr. 27 The **worst ship disaster in U.S. history** took the lives of 1700 persons when the steamer *Sultana* exploded on the Mississippi R. Of 2300 persons on board, 2134 were Union soldiers returning from Confederate prison camps.

May 10 **Jefferson Davis was captured** at Irwinville, Ga., by a contingent of Gen. James H. Wilson's cavalry, led by Lt. Col. Benjamin Pritchard.

May 29 Pres. Johnson issued a **proclamation of amnesty,** specifying classes of persons who must make application for pardon. A second proclamation looked toward establishment of a loyal government in North Carolina, with the state to determine the voting rules.

Aug. 14 **Mississippi overturned its secession ordinance** of 1861 at a state convention that also abolished slavery in the state.

Nov. 9 **North Carolina overturned its secession ordinance,** prohibited slavery, and elected representatives to the U.S. Congress. The state was readmitted to the Union in 1868.

The **San Francisco *Examiner,*** soon to become the leading Democratic newspaper in the far West, was started by William Moss. William Randolph Hearst purchased the paper in 1880 and relied heavily on sensationalism in his treatment of the news.

The **San Francisco *Chronicle*** was founded as the *Daily Dramatic Chronicle* by Michael Harry DeYoung, age 16, and his brother Charles, age 18. At first only a bulletin of entertainment events, it carried advertisements and was distributed free. However, it soon expanded into a publication with news and feature articles. Mark Twain and Bret Harte were early contributors. The *Chronicle* later (1872) became a champion of reform in city and state governments.

Landscape painter **George Inness** completed one of his loveliest pictures, *Peace and Plenty.* His grandly conceived and executed landscapes were in the manner of the seventeenth-century French painter Nicolas Poussin, and of the French romantic landscape painters of the 1830s, such as Pierre Rousseau. Not for another decade, however, would canvases by Inness command high prices.

Winslow Homer's *Prisoners from the Front* presented a series of paintings depicting the plight of men at the front during the Civil War. Homer, now 25, had been engaged by *Harper's Weekly* as a special correspondent and artist.

Actor-producer-playwright **David Belasco** began his career with a romantic play, *Jim Black, or the Regulator's Revenge.* He wrote it at age 12.

The Nation, a weekly magazine focusing on current affairs, was founded by James Miller McKim. The first editor was Edwin Lawrence Godkin (1865–1881), and the second was Wendell Phillips Garrison (1881–1906). *The Nation* quickly established itself as a leading liberal voice in politics, literature, and art. Its nineteenth-century crusades were directed toward revision of the tariff and civil service, and against political corruption.

French influence on American architecture was demonstrated in the first buildings for Vassar College, designed by James Renwick. The age that succeeded the romantic era adopted variety but no definite style of its own. Novelty was enjoyed for its own sake. In the maze of forms that characterized the Civil War period, the French touch could be felt even where it was not immediately seen. Imitation was usually frank and sometimes blatant. Washington, Boston, Philadelphia, and Detroit all modeled public buildings on the style then current in France. Renwick followed the fashion of his times and

the Fredonia Hotel, where it was used for lighting and cooking.

Free delivery of mail was provided in all cities with populations of 50,000 or more.

Louis Agassiz began a 19-month expedition with his wife and six assistants to study the natural history of Brazil and add to his collection of specimens. Agassiz, who had become a naturalized American citizen, began his career at the University of Munich where, at 21, he published *The Fishes of Brazil* (1829), the most important work yet published in ichthyology. The study was based on a collection brought back to Germany by an expedition to Brazil in 1821. Agassiz always cherished the ambition to see the natural life of Brazil firsthand. The trip was financed primarily by Nathaniel Thayer of Boston, but other people, organizations, and government officials in the U.S. and Brazil also lent support. *A Journey to Brazil,* by Mrs. Agassiz, published in 1868, recounted the day-to-day experiences of the expedition.

The opening of the **Union stockyards** in Chicago, Ill., led within the decade to the phenomenal growth of Chicago as the world's greatest meat-producing and meat-packing center. Cincinnati, Ohio, had been at the top of the meat industry for over 20 years. Chicago was just emerging as a rival when the Union stockyards combined the various yards of the city into a common, efficient center. Production was stepped up to the point where the output of Cincinnati was soon surpassed. Consolidation of companies within the industry also accelerated the pace of production. Chicago, as a railroad center, was in the direct line of livestock shipments from western ranches. It also had immediate access to all the principal railroad lines of the country.

Benjamin Altman opened up his first dry-goods store, on Third Ave. near Tenth St. in New York City. Altman had worked in a number of such stores in New York and New Jersey, and his experience helped turn this venture into a great success. In 1870 he moved the business to Sixth Ave. and concentrated on turning it into a first-rate department store. In 1906 the firm moved to Fifth Ave. and 34th St. B. Altman & Co. was such an enormous success that Altman was able to become a noted philanthropist and patron of the arts. He died on Oct.

Mar. 4 Pres. **Lincoln's second inaugural address** brought tears to the eyes of many in the audience. It was a silent audience, befitting an occasion made even more solemn by Lincoln's words. The war was not over, but there was room for hope, if not certainty. Lincoln began by saying that the occasion did not call for an extended address, such as the one delivered at his first inaugural. The audience was as familiar as he with the progress of the war. Lincoln asked his listeners to relive with him the forebodings of four years before, when both sides were rushing toward war, though "neither party expected the magnitude or duration which it has already attained. Neither anticipated that the cause of the conflict might cease before the conflict itself should cease. Each looked for an easier triumph and a result less fundamental and astonishing. Both read the same Bible and pray to the same God. Each invokes His aid against the other. It may seem strange that any man should dare to ask a just God's assistance in wringing bread from the sweat of other men's faces; but let us judge not, that we be not judged." He expressed the common hope that the war would soon end, and bade his hearers to continue what they had begun: "With malice toward none, with charity for all, with firmness in the right, as God gives us to see the right, let us strive on to finish the work we are in, to bind up the nation's wounds, to care for him who shall have borne the battle, and for his widow and orphans; to do all which may achieve and cherish a just and lasting peace among ourselves and with all nations." The address was not followed by any demonstration, either public or personal, to indicate to Lincoln whether it had been effective. He felt himself that it was among the best he had ever delivered, and he expressed this sentiment in a letter to Thurlow Weed, thanking Weed for a few words of congratulation.

Apr. 26 **Confederate Memorial Day,** a legal holiday in Mississippi, was born of the visit of Mrs. Sue Landon Vaughn, a descendant of Pres. John Adams, and other ladies to the military cemetery in Vicksburg, Miss.

May 5 The **first railroad train robbery** took place at dawn at North Bend, Ohio, when an Ohio & Mississippi Railroad train was derailed by a gang. Male passengers were robbed and the express car looted.

| Exploration and Settlement; Wars; Government; Civil Rights; Statistics | I | | II | Publishing; Arts and Music; Popular Entertainment; Architecture; Theater |

Dec. 2 Adoption of the **Thirteenth Amendment,** prohibiting slavery, became a certainty when Alabama became the 27th state to ratify it, raising state ratifications to the necessary two-thirds. The declaration of ratification was issued on Dec. 18.

Dec. 4 A **Joint Committee on Reconstruction** was established under the guidance of Rep. Thaddeus Stevens of Pennsylvania, who became its chairman. Stevens led the radical Republicans, who were opposed to Pres. Johnson's attempts to follow Pres. Lincoln's plans for reconciliation with the South. Stevens, Sen. Charles Sumner of Massachusetts, and others were determined to reduce the South to territorial status unless it permitted black suffrage and accepted other pro-Republican conditions.

wove French themes into the buildings that he designed.

Apr. 15 All **New York City theaters were closed** until Apr. 26 because of the death of Abraham Lincoln.

Nov. 18 **Mark Twain** (Samuel Langhorne Clemens) was catapulted to fame when his version of a California tall tale, "Jim Smiley and His Jumping Frog," was printed in the New York *Saturday Press.* It was quickly reprinted by major newspapers across the country. It is now known under the title "The Celebrated Jumping Frog of Calaveras County."

1866

Reconstruction, the process of dealing with the former Confederate states and the millions of freed black slaves, was to occupy the government and the nation for the next decade. Pres. Andrew Johnson proposed fairly lenient treatment of the secessionists but showed no interest in securing civil rights for blacks. Opposing him was a group of radical Republicans who wanted the South severely punished. The congressional election in the fall gave the radicals an overwhelming victory that paved the way for harsh treatment of the South.

A **cholera** epidemic decimated many U.S. cities. About 200 a day died in St. Louis, Mo., during the height of the epidemic.

1866–1867 In **congressional elections** the Republicans held a Senate majority of 42–11, the Democrats gaining one seat. In the House the Republican majority was 143–49.

Feb. 19 The **New Freedmen's Bureau bill** was passed by Congress. The law authorized military trials for those accused of depriving newly freed blacks of their civil rights. Pres. Andrew Johnson vetoed the bill on the grounds that it violated the Fifth Amendment, and that the legislation affected 11 southern states not represented in Congress. The veto served to widen the rift between Congress and the president. Legislators retaliated by overriding the veto on July 16.

Apr. 2 The **state of insurrection** was declared over by presidential proclamation in Georgia, South Carolina, Virginia, North Carolina, Tennessee, Alabama, Mississippi, Louisiana, Arkansas, and Florida. On Aug. 2 the president announced that the insurrection was at an end in Texas, and that civil authority existed in the U.S.

Southern writers of the war and postwar period tended to idealize both the recent and the colonial past, perhaps to compensate for loss of the struggle for secession. One such writer was John Esten Cooke, a Virginian who had served as a captain in the Confederate army. This year Cooke began a series of wartime romances with the publication of *Surry of Eagle's Nest.* The series continued with *Hilt to Hilt* (1869), *Mohun* (1869), and *Hammer and Rapier* (1871). Cooke's writing showed sentimentality, but he achieved his aim: to entertain. Cooke also wrote *Life of Stonewall Jackson* (1863) and *Life of General Robert E. Lee* (1871).

Among the **books published** this year was *Snow-Bound,* the most famous poem by John Greenleaf Whittier. Drawing on his memories of youth and home life in rural New England, Whittier painted an inviting picture of a homestead buried in snow. The poem described the blazing hearth, the family members, the sparkling snowbanks, the schoolmaster, etc. Other books published this year included *Surry of Eagle's Nest* by John Esten Cooke, which harked back to the chivalry of antebellum Virginia and evoked vivid pictures of southern leaders and Civil War battles; and *Venetian Life* by William Dean Howells, who served as U.S. consul to Venice throughout the Civil War and described his impressions of the city, its life and literature.

Alice's Adventures in Wonderland by Lewis Carroll was first published in America. An estimated 2,000,000 copies or more have been sold in the U.S. The original manuscript was sold in 1928 for $75,250.

The first course in **architecture** at an American

7, 1913, the same year the business was incorporated. At his death his estate was valued at about $35,000,000, including a $20,000,000 art collection that was given to the Metropolitan Museum of Art. The store closed in 1991.

May 2 The **first fire department** with paid firemen was established in New York City by an act of the state legislature.

June 19 **Emancipation Day** was established in Texas by the proclamation of Gen. Robert S. Granger, commander of the Texas military district, who officially notified the former slaves that they were free. Emancipation Day was celebrated on various dates by a number of states. Most chose Jan. 1, the date the Emancipation Proclamation went into effect in 1863.

Dec. 24 The **Ku Klux Klan** had its beginning in the law office of Thomas M. Jones in Pulaski, Tenn. The name evolved from Greek *kyklos* (circle), suggested by John B. Kennedy. It was broken up into the more euphonious Ku Klux by James R. Crowe, who added Klan as a reflection of the predominantly Scotch-Irish population of the area.

1866

The steadily growing movement to promote animal welfare scored a major victory this year with the founding on Apr. 10 of the American Society for the Prevention of Cruelty to Animals. It was patterned after the Royal Society for the Prevention of Cruelty to Animals in England, which had been founded in 1824. The founder and first president of the ASPCA was the philanthropist Henry Bergh. Its purpose was to shelter homeless animals, help enforce game laws, and guide farmers in caring for livestock.

The **University of New Hampshire,** Durham, N.H., was founded as New Hampshire College of Agriculture and Mechanic Arts at Hanover, N.H. Its first classes were held in 1868. The school moved to its present site in 1893 and adopted its present name in 1923.

Apr. 1 **Western Union,** with capital of about $40,000,-000, absorbed the U.S. Telegraph Company, with $6,-000,000 worth of shares. This was on the tenth anniversary of the day that Western Union was named. The absorption of U.S. Telegraph made Western Union the first complete monopoly serving all parts of the country with uniform rates.

July 27 Final laying of the **Atlantic cable** between Great Britain and the U.S. was completed when the steamship *Great Eastern* reached the U.S. The final cable-laying voyage of the *Great Eastern* took two weeks, July 13 to July 27. The previous year the steamship had attempted to complete the laying of the cable, only to have it break in mid-ocean. Success came after 12 years of effort. Cyrus Field chartered his company on May 6, 1854, with Peter Cooper, Moses Taylor, Marshall Roberts, and Chandler White on the board of directors. Six hundred men worked on

A lighter and more daring form of entertainment heralded the coming of what was to be known as burlesque. The first long-running musical show on Broadway, combining melodrama and ballet in a lavish production, was *The Black Crook,* which opened on Sept. 12 at Niblo's Garden and ran for 474 performances. Some considered it immoral because of its 50 lightly-clad dancing girls. Even more daring was *British Blondes,* imported from England two years later. It played around the country for 20 years.

The first **Young Women's Christian Association** in the U.S. opened in Boston, Mass. The organization had its beginnings in England.

The expression "**Forty acres and a mule**" gained currency during the Reconstruction period. Many freed blacks had their hopes built up by the promise that Congress would divide southern estates and distribute acreage to each freed slave. The expression came to characterize vain expectations foisted on blacks by Reconstructionists.

The unofficial U.S. **baseball championship** game was played by the Brooklyn, N.Y., Atlantics and the Philadelphia, Pa., Athletics. An enthusiastic crowd smashed its way to the field, causing the game to be halted and finally moved to Long Island. Brooklyn defeated the Athletics 27–10.

The first deliberate **bunt** in baseball was laid down by Dickey Pierce of the Brooklyn Atlantics.

The **first transoceanic yacht race** was won by James Gordon Bennett's 107-ft. schooner *Henrietta.* The *Henrietta* engaged two other schooners in a race from Sandy Hook, N.J., to the Isle of Wight. The winning time was 13 days, 21 hrs., 45 min.

The number of **public balls** held in New York City in 1866 was estimated at 600 "more or less." The cost of

Apr. 9 A **Civil Rights Act** was passed over Pres. Johnson's veto. It granted citizenship to all persons born in the U.S., except Indians. It declared that all citizens had the same civil rights and provided for the punishment of persons who prevented free exercise of these rights. The Fourteenth Amendment was proposed when the constitutionality of the first section of this act was questioned.

May 16 Issuance of the **nickel,** a new five-cent coin, was authorized by Congress. It was minted of copper and nickel with not more than 25% nickel.

July 4 A **fire** in Portland, Maine, destroyed 1500 buildings. Property loss was estimated at $10,000,000.

Oct. 3 The steamer *Evening Star* foundered at sea on its way from New York City to New Orleans. Two hundred fifty lives were lost.

college opened at Massachusetts Institute of Technology.

A commission for a **statue of Abraham Lincoln** was given to a New Hampshire sculptor. The price of the monument was $200,000, surpassing the cost of all other monuments built to date in the U.S. The completed work was unveiled in 1874 at Springfield, Ill., and used as a tomb for the assassinated president.

Dec. 29 An interesting performance of *Othello* was given at the Winter Garden, New York City. Bogumil Dawison, a Polish actor, played the part of Othello in German; Edwin Booth played Iago in English; and Madame Methua-Scheller played Desdemona alternately in English and German.

1867

Purchase of Alaska, 586,400 sq. mi. of almost unknown land in the far northwest of North America, added an unusual chapter to the story of the expansion of the U.S. On Mar. 30, 1867, Sec. of State William Henry Seward concluded negotiations with Russia whereby the U.S. agreed to pay $7,200,000, about two cents an acre, for the territory. The Senate ratified the purchase on Apr. 9, and ownership was transferred on Oct. 18. Alaska was known to be rich in furs and fish, but otherwise it seemed useless. It was many years before the natural riches of Alaska were appreciated and Americans began to settle it as a new frontier.

The **first tenement-house law** in America was enacted in New York City. Despite supplementary laws enacted in 1879, 1887, and 1895, housing conditions became worse instead of better because of inadequate enforcement of the laws and increasing population.

An important event in what became known as the **Crédit Mobilier** scandal occurred when Rep. Oakes Ames, Republican of Massachusetts, bought off Col. H. K. McComb and at the same time revealed to him the names of the politicians behind the Crédit Mobilier of America. In 1872 McComb turned these names over to the New York *Sun.* Their publication and the resulting congressional investigation uncovered the most flagrant political scandal of the period. Ames, a director of the Union Pacific Railroad, was also a member of the House committee that authorized the railroad to issue bonds the government stood pledged to redeem. Railroad construction began but soon stopped for lack of funds. A second company, the Crédit Mobilier, was formed to continue the construction; in payment it received the stocks and bonds of the railroad. While the railroad

In keeping with the spirit of the times were the novels of Horatio Alger, Jr. The mid-nineteenth century was an age when many proclaimed the virtues of the self-made man. Alger's books gave the formula for success. His first of the Ragged Dick series appeared in 1867. Like all those to come, it preached hard work and resistance to temptation as the road to wealth and renown. In most of the books, though, the young hero first gets a break by catching the eye of a well-to-do patron, perhaps by rescuing his pretty daughter from a runaway horse. Alger followed with the Luck and Pluck series (1869) and Tattered Tom tales (1871). These stories found a ready market in the steady wave of boys moving from farms or small towns to the cities to seek work. More than 20,000,000 copies of Alger's novels were sold.

Among the **books published** this year was *Tiger-Lilies,* the only novel by poet-musician Sidney Lanier. A war novel drawing on Lanier's experiences in the Civil War, the book contained a realistic depiction of the soldier's life but rambled on about art, romanticism, and music. Other books published this year included *Miss Ravenel's Conversion from Secession to Loyalty* by John William De Forest, a realistic novel based on the author's military experiences, once rated the best Civil War novel; *St. Elmo* by Augusta Jane Evans, a best-selling novel that included such elements as a long love affair, an attack on the rich, and the success of a poor girl, which sold about 1,000,000 copies and inspired people to name towns, streets, and babies after it; *Sut Lovingood Yarns* by George W. Harris, a humorous collection of tales about Sut Lovingood, "a nat'ral born durn'd fool" and prankish roughneck who took advantage of the foibles

the first line, which had to be cut at sea because of a gale. Seven more efforts were needed before the cable was completed. A cable laid in 1858 was able to carry a message, but was probably badly insulated, and went out after three weeks of operation.

Aug. 20 The **first National Labor Congress** met at Baltimore, Md., and met annually in different cities for several years.

Aug. 29 The famous **Mt. Washington Cog Railroad,** at Mt. Washington, N.H., was opened for public viewing. The invention of Sylvester Marsh of New Hampshire, the railroad was the first mountain-climbing railroad in the world and remained the steepest. Work on it was finished in 1869.

the balls was estimated at $7,000,000, and the average cost of a gown was computed to be $1000, not including jewelry.

Feb. 12 The first formal observance of **Lincoln's birthday** was held in the Capitol of the U.S. with most of the high government officials, including Pres. Andrew Johnson, in attendance.

Sept. 15 A report on **annual income** in *Scientific American* stated that there were "more men in New York today whose annual incomes reach $100,000 than there were twenty-five years ago of those whose entire possessions amounted to as much."

Nov. 20 The **first national encampment** of the Grand Army of the Republic, comprising Union veterans of the Civil War, was held at Indianapolis, Ind.

1867

The first organization of American farmers was founded in 1867 when Oliver H. Kelley, a Minnesota farmer and an employee of the Bureau of Agriculture in Washington, D.C., established the National Grange of the Patrons of Husbandry. The Grange movement had a slow start, but it greatly expanded as a result of the panic of 1873 and reached a membership peak of 858,000 in 1875. The Grange began as a social and educational organization but soon became involved in politics. Its main targets were the railroads and the owners of grain storage elevators who, the Grange claimed, charged exorbitant prices for their services. As a result of pressure from the Grange, some midwestern states passed laws to limit such rates.

When the quarrels of insiders in the **Crédit Mobilier** scandal began to boil over, Rep. Oakes Ames, Republican of Massachusetts, took out 343 shares of stock and palmed them off "where they will do the most good." He had politicians in high places in mind for his plums. When the scandal broke, his turn of phrase quickly became popular.

The **eight-hour day,** a main goal of labor unions, was enacted in Illinois, New York, and Missouri, but it was not enforced.

Howard Theological Seminary, later Howard University, was chartered in Washington, D.C., and named after Gen. Oliver O. Howard, its first president. It was the first predominantly black college to offer comprehensive university facilities.

West Virginia University was established at Morgantown, W.Va., as the Agricultural College of West Virginia. The first classes were held in 1868, the year its present name was adopted.

Life in the mining towns of the far West was boisterous and extravagant. The height of fun and games was achieved in Virginia City, Nev., site of the fabulous Comstock Lode, in the period from 1860 to 1880. The town had more than 100 saloons, five legitimate theaters, six variety houses, and other establishments such as dance halls. The single most popular performer was Adah Isaacs Menken, known for performing while clad only in a flimsy gown.

The phrase *Seward's folly* was coined to characterize the purchase of Alaska from Russia. The purchase was negotiated by Sec. of State William Henry Seward. Alaska was also ridiculed as *Seward's icebox.*

"Now is the time for all good men to come to the aid of the party," a slogan created by Charles Weller, a court reporter, was used to test the efficiency of the first practical typewriter, invented by his friend, Christopher Sholes.

Harper's New Monthly Magazine published an account by George Ward Nichols of a visit to the city of Springfield, Mo., where he met and interviewed **"Wild Bill" Hickok.** Nichols swore that he recorded only what William Hitchcock (as Nichols called him) told him, that the facts were confirmed by witnesses, and that he himself did not doubt their truth. The article fitted nicely into the literature of the tall tale, which had been growing ever taller and more popular since the century

company went to ruin, the profits of the Crédit Mobilier mounted. During the presidential campaign of 1872, McComb revealed the setup to the public. The House made its sensational report on Feb. 18, 1873.

Jan. 8 **Suffrage** was given to blacks in Washington, D.C., by a bill passed over Pres. Andrew Johnson's veto.

Feb. 25 A survey for a **canal** at Darien, Panama, to connect the Atlantic and Pacific oceans was provided for by a resolution adopted by Congress.

Mar. 1 **Nebraska** was admitted as a state, the 37th to join the Union.

Mar. 2 The **first Reconstruction Act** was passed by Congress over Pres. Johnson's veto. The bill imposed martial law on the southern states, which were split into five districts, and provided for the restoration of civil government as soon as the states were restored into the Union and passed the Fourteenth Amendment.

Mar. 2 The **Tenure of Office Act** was passed. In substance, it denied power to the president to remove officials who had been appointed by and with the consent of the Senate. This act was ruled unconstitutional by the Court of Claims in 1926 in the case of *Myers v. U.S.*

Mar. 5 **Voting rights of blacks** were challenged at Alexandria, Va., when the votes of some 1000 blacks were rejected. The black voters had attempted to exercise suffrage granted under the Reconstruction Act.

Mar. 23 The **second Reconstruction Act** was passed over Pres. Johnson's veto. It provided for the registration of all qualified voters, who were subsequently to decide on readmittance to the Union.

July 19 The **third Reconstruction Act** was passed over Pres. Johnson's veto. The bill was essentially a restatement of the two previous acts except for the added provision that the Fifteenth Amendment must be ratified before the southern states could be admitted to the Union.

of mankind; *The Lost Galleon and Other Tales,* a first volume of poems by Bret Harte; and *Katherine,* a narrative poem by Timothy Titcomb, the nom de plume of Josiah Gilbert Holland. The poem sold 30,000 copies in the first three months of publication.

Three **sculptures** of Civil War scenes were presented at the Paris Exposition by John Rogers, a popular American sculptor noted for his group statuary. The three groups in bronze were *One More Shot, Taking the Oath,* and *Wounded Scout.* Earlier his realism was reflected in *Checkers up at the Farm* and *Football Game.*

The **American Water Color Society** was founded as the American Society of Painters in Water Color by Samuel Colman and John D. Smillie, two young painters. Colman was the society's first president.

James Redpath established a **central booking office** for lecture circuits and introduced order into the helter-skelter system of hiring speakers. He made it possible for local committees to fill their engagements through the national agency he set up.

Aug. 12 *Under the Gaslight* by Augustin Daly opened in New York City. The melodrama, which was performed in New York and London for many years, had all the trappings: a villain who bound the hero to the railroad tracks, a pure heroine harried by a blackmailer, a wounded soldier, etc.

Dec. 2 **Charles Dickens** gave his first reading in a theater in New York City. This was his second visit to the U.S. Before the box office opened, people were standing in two lines, almost a mile long, waiting for tickets. Scalpers were asking $20 for a ticket. Thirty-one different editions of Dickens's collected works were published in 1867.

1868

For the first time in the nation's history a president was impeached. Pres. Andrew Johnson was accused by Congress of having violated the Tenure of Office Act of 1867, which forbade the president to discharge any federal officeholder appointed "by and with the consent of

The literary genre known as juvenile or children's literature received new vitality this year with publication of *Little Women* by Louisa May Alcott, daughter of A. Bronson Alcott. Up to this time, many of the books intended for children moralized to the extent that they

Business and Industry; Science; Education; Philosophy and Religion III		IV Sports; Social Issues and Crime; Folkways; Fashion; Holidays

The **Johns Hopkins University** was chartered at Baltimore, Md. Its first classes met in 1876.

The **University of Illinois,** at Urbana, Ill., was founded as Illinois Industrial University. The university's first classes met in 1868. Its present name was adopted in 1885.

James Cruikshank's ***Primary Geography,*** the chief school geography during the last three decades of the nineteenth century, was published. Of the U.S. it said: "There are now more than 30,000,000 of people and the United States are the freest, most enlightened, and powerful government on earth."

Cigarettes began to appear in America. Cigarette production had formerly been confined to Europe. Production in America did not provide a major source of revenue until the 1880s.

The **first successful typewriter** was constructed by Christopher Latham Sholes, who also first used the word *typewriter.* Patents for the invention were awarded jointly to Sholes, Samuel W. Soulé, and Carlos Glidden in the following year.

Abilene, Kans., became a leading cattle terminal through the foresight of J. G. McCoy, a Chicago cattle dealer who built a cattle yard in the town. He had selected Abilene as the closest point to the intersection of the Texas cattle trail and the railroad. The most celebrated trail from Texas to Abilene was established by a cattle driver named Jesse Chisholm. His Chisholm Trail became part of the folklore of the West.

George Pullman incorporated the Pullman Palace Car Company. Within two years, he was operating 48 cars on three different railroads with an investment in rolling stock of $1,000,000.

The **first elevated railroad** in America began operation in New York City. Built by the West Side Elevated Railroad Company, its single track ran from Battery Place through Greenwich St. and 9th Ave. to 30th St.

Mar. 7 The **Order of the Knights of St. Crispin** was founded to halt rising unemployment in the U.S. shoe industry. The order's main objective was protection of seniority rights against the cheaper competition of beginners.

Oct. 25 The **first rabbinical college** in the U.S., Maimonides College, opened in Philadelphia, Pa. It closed in 1873 for lack of support. A second Maimonides College opened in New York City in 1927.

began. The author painted vivid portraits of Springfield and James Butler Hickok. Springfield was, he found, "not a burgh of extensive dimensions," though it was the local crossroads. The people, "strange, half-civilized," came to Springfield to market. "Men and women dressed in queer costumes; men with coats and trousers made of skin" so thick with dirt and grease as to defy identity of the animals that grew them. Homespun was common. The men were, said Nichols, so lazy that their highest ambition seemed to be to let their hair and beards grow. They lolled in front of the shops lining either side of the main street, or even lay on the wooden sidewalks. There were some still wearing Army blue— the liveliest men of the lot. Everyone wore a pistol. Hickok was 6'1" tall in moccasins. He wore a deerskin shirt, which hung "jauntily" over his shoulders, revealing a "remarkable" breadth and depth of chest. Around his "small round waist" were two Colt revolvers on a belt. His toes turned inward when he walked. On his head was a large sombrero. He had thin, sensitive lips, not-too-square jaw, and slightly prominent cheekbones.

A long-distance **walking record** was set by Edward P. Weston, who did the distance from Portland, Maine, to Chicago in 26 days, and won for his efforts $10,000.

Jan. 23 The **East R. was frozen over** after a series of heavy snowstorms. Thousands crossed the river on foot.

June 19 The **first annual Belmont Stakes** was won by Ruthless, with a time of 3:05. The jockey was J. Gilpatrick. The race was held at Jerome Park, N.Y., from 1867 to 1889; at Morris Park, N.Y., from 1890 to 1905; and at Belmont Park, N.Y., from 1906 to the present. In the beginning the distance was 1⅝ miles, but it has been changed from time to time. The Belmont Stakes is the oldest of the American Triple Crown races.

1868

As important as rail transportation had become, it still remained potentially dangerous for both passengers and freight. This year George Westinghouse solved a major problem with the invention of the air brake. This allowed equal and simultaneous braking, through one

Ice skating, which had begun a rise in popularity around the 1850s, had become a major winter pastime. Steel skates had first been made in the 1850s. They had straps and clamps to fasten them to shoes. In the 1860s Jackson Haines, an American, invented figure skating.

the Senate." Johnson tested the act by removing Sec. of War Edwin M. Stanton on Feb. 21. The impeachment was brought largely because the radical Republicans bitterly opposed Johnson's plans for Reconstruction. Johnson's firing of Stanton gave them the opportunity they had been seeking. On Feb. 24 the House of Representatives voted to impeach. The trial, conducted by the Senate, began on Mar. 13. On May 16 and again on May 26 the Senate voted on the charges brought against Pres. Johnson. Both times the vote was 35 for conviction and 19 for acquittal. Because a two-thirds vote was needed to convict, Johnson was judged not guilty. The radicals then dropped the matter.

Organization of the **New England Woman's Club** was completed by Carolina Severance. Julia Ward Howe, a founder of the club, served as president for 18 years beginning in 1871. The organization's objective was to promote the efforts of women to gain their rights.

Susan B. Anthony founded the suffragette newspaper *The Revolution.* It adopted the motto "The true Republic—men, their rights and nothing more; women, their rights and nothing less."

The **Ku Klux Klan** formulated its revised constitution, which declared that the organization was to be guided by chivalry, humanity, mercy, and patriotism. The southern states were to be its empire, with the grand wizard as supreme leader and its body of officers designated as "ghouls." In reality, the order was formed to intimidate blacks and carpetbaggers and to regain white supremacy in the South.

1868–1869 In **congressional elections** the Republicans kept majorities in both houses: 56–11 in the Senate and 149–63 in the House.

Mar. 11 The **fourth Reconstruction Act** was passed. Under its provisions a majority of the votes actually cast would decide the adoption or rejection of a state constitution (the second Reconstruction Act required a majority of the registered voters). The measure was taken to counter the intimidation of black voters by the Ku Klux Klan and disenfranchised whites.

May 20–21 The **Republican National Convention** nominated Gen. Ulysses S. Grant for the presidency and Schuyler Colfax of Indiana for the vice presidency. At the same meeting, the convention adopted the name National Republican Party.

June 25 Congress passed a law providing an **eight-hour day** for laborers and workmen employed by the government. The concept of the eight-hour day was still something of a novelty, although ineffectual eight-hour laws had already been passed in a few states.

June 25 **Congressional representation** was granted to North Carolina, South Carolina, Louisiana, Georgia, Alabama, and Florida by an omnibus bill passed over Pres. Johnson's veto.

did not entertain their readers. Miss Alcott's book, based on her own family experiences, was more realistic and less sentimental than most. The book became the most popular girls' story in American literature and has sold more than 2,000,000 copies. It earned its author about $200,000 by the time she died. Miss Alcott also wrote *Little Men* (1871), *Jo's Boys* (1886), and other books. Her writings brought financial security to her family, the head of which was well-intentioned but improvident. Miss Alcott greatly influenced the trend of juvenile literature by avoiding didacticism and by using characters drawn from life.

Among the **books published** this year was *The New England Tragedies,* part III of *Christus—A Mystery* by Henry Wadsworth Longfellow. The writing of *Christus* occupied Longfellow for more than 20 years. In 1851 he finished *The Golden Legend,* which was based on the typical miracle tales of medieval literature, with a prince as hero who is, like Faust, under the power of Lucifer. *The Golden Legend* became part II of *Christus.* Part I, *The Divine Tragedy,* was published in 1871. It was a dramatization of the Gospel story, which included a miracle play, *The Nativity. The New England Tragedies* was based on incidents in American colonial history that the author turned into two five-act plays, *John Endicott* and *Giles Gorey of the Salem Farms.* In spite of his efforts, *Christus* was not a literary success and was too complicated and lifeless to win popular favor. All three parts were published together in 1872. Also published in 1868 were *Men of Our Times* and *The Chimney Corner* by Harriet Beecher Stowe; and *The Golden Wedding: A Masque* by Bayard Taylor.

The first issue of ***The World Almanac*** was published by the New York *World.* It was published annually until 1876, then was revived in 1886 by Joseph Pulitzer. It has been published annually ever since.

The Moonstone by Wilkie Collins, a mystery classic, was published serially in *Harper's Weekly.* Some think it the finest mystery story ever written.

Hiram Powers completed his celebrated sculpture *Clytie.* Powers, who had settled in Florence, Italy, in 1837, was then enjoying great popularity, largely on the strength of such works as his statue of *Daniel Webster* (1859) in front of the Boston State House, as well as works in marble of other famous Americans, including John C. Calhoun, Andrew Jackson, and George Washington.

Charles A. Dana, who had served as managing editor of the New York *Tribune* under Horace Greeley, became editor of the New York *Sun.*

| Business and Industry; Science; Education; Philosophy and Religion   III | IV   Sports; Social Issues and Crime; Folkways; Fashion; Holidays |

control, of each car in a train, and also provided for automatic braking if cars should accidentally uncouple or brake lines become disabled. Westinghouse's system was first put to use on a train this year. It made possible the safe braking of both long trains and high-speed trains, paving the way for a revolution in rail travel.

The **University of Minnesota,** at Minneapolis, was chartered. Its first classes met in 1869.

The **open-hearth process** in the American steel industry was introduced from England by Abram S. Hewitt in Trenton, N.J. The process expanded steel production by making more ore available through the extraction of sulfur and phosphorus.

A **pork-packing plant** was added by Philip and Herman Armour to the original Chicago Grain Commission of H. O. Armour and Company. It became Armour and Company in 1870.

A $2,000,000 endowment for establishment of a **free public reference library** in Chicago was left by Walter Loomis Miller. Miller, a merchant banker, had founded the Young Men's Library Association in 1841, which became the nucleus of the Chicago public library system. Miller was president of the Historical Society in 1863. The money he provided for Chicago's Newberry Library was drawn from undeveloped real estate. It represented half of his estate. The Newberry Library has, through its collection, become world famous; it concentrates on history, music, literature, and philology.

The rise of **railroad brotherhoods** continued with the formation of a union of railway conductors.

Opposition to **labor** led the National Labor Union to concentrate on political organization.

The **first office building** to have an elevator installed in it was the Equitable Life Assurance Society building, built in New York City.

Jan. 16 A patent for a **refrigerator car** was granted to William Davis, a fish dealer in Detroit, Mich. Davis, wanting to increase his area of sales, had worked for many years to develop his "ice box on wheels." He used his new invention for the transportation of fish and fruit. He also designed the first railroad refrigerated car, which was built in 1869.

By 1868 ice skating was so widespread that a skating congress was held in Pittsburgh to set regulations and encourage the sport. In a single winter some 200,000 skaters used the lakes in New York City's Central Park. In Boston daily excursion trains carried a thousand or more skaters to Jamaica Pond. One reason for the sport's popularity was that both sexes could participate, making skating a social as well as athletic occasion.

The new sport of **velocipeding** (cycling) attained great vogue in America three years after it had been perfected in Paris. Schools for all ages and both sexes were set up throughout the large cities. Newspapers reported on the vogue. The fact that women could participate added greatly to its rapid spread.

The **Benevolent Protective Order of Elks** was formed in New York City.

A newspaper campaign against **customs regulations** requiring all passengers on arriving boats to stay on board until all baggage had been removed to the docks was launched by *The New York Times.* The homecoming of passengers was also inconvenienced because guests were not permitted to go on board to greet friends. Delays were compounded because none of the baggage was sorted until the whole lot had been taken off a ship.

Sunday sermons of Henry Ward Beecher, pastor of the Plymouth Congregational Church in Brooklyn, N.Y., were so popular that they reappeared in print in the papers on Tuesday mornings and sold for as much as five cents.

Hazing of underclassmen was condemned by a resolution passed by seniors at Amherst College in Amherst, Mass.

May 30 **Decoration Day** was celebrated nationally for the first time. The day was chosen by John A. Logan, national commander of the Grand Army of the Republic, for decoration of Civil War graves. Previously, local communities had held decoration days at various times.

July 4–9 The **Democratic National Convention** nominated Horatio Seymour of New York for the presidency and Francis P. Blair, Jr., of Missouri for the vice presidency.

July 28 The **Fourteenth Amendment,** which granted citizenship to all those born or naturalized in the U.S., notably slaves freed by the Civil War, was adopted. It also validated debts incurred during the Civil War but denied federal or state responsibility for any debts incurred in aid of conspiracy or insurrection against the U.S.

Nov. 3 **Ulysses S. Grant was elected president** of the United States, defeating Horatio Seymour. Schuyler Colfax was elected vice president. Grant's popular majority was a scant 306,000 out of 5,715,000 votes, although his margin in the electoral college count was 214 to 80. The black vote, which totaled over 700,000, decided the election for Grant.

Dec. 3 The **treason trial** of Jefferson Davis, president of the Confederacy, began in Richmond, Va., before Circuit Court Judges Salmon P. Chase and John C. Underwood. The charge was dropped on Feb. 15, 1869, after Pres. Johnson's proclamation of general amnesty.

Dec. 25 Unqualified **amnesty** was granted by presidential proclamation to all who participated in the "insurrection or rebellion" against the U.S.

The *Atlanta Constitution,* destined to become one of the largest daily newspapers of the East, was started by W. A. Hemphill.

The *Louisville Courier-Journal,* a newspaper that maintained the liberal Republican point of view, was established in Louisville, Ky. It was to support Horace Greeley for president and, much later, establishment of the League of Nations.

July *The Overland Monthly,* founded in San Francisco, Calif., by Anton Roman, a publisher and bookseller, issued its first number. The new magazine's chief editor was Bret Harte, who was then secretary to the director of the San Francisco Mint and had previously written for the *Golden Era* and the *Californian.* The second issue contained Harte's story "The Luck of Roaring Camp," which met with immediate and phenomenal success and made Harte's reputation as a writer. Later issues contained "The Outcasts of Poker Flat" and "Plain Language from Truthful James." In 1870 Harte resigned from the magazine and moved east to capitalize on his celebrity. The magazine continued until 1875, when it was suspended. Revived in 1883, it continued until 1935, carrying works by Joaquin Miller, Jack London, Willa Cather, and many others.

1869

This year, Ulysses S. Grant was inaugurated 18th president of the United States. After a checkered career in and out of the Army, Grant began to rise in public esteem through his military exploits in the Civil War. Until 1862 it had seemed as though no Union commander was competent to win the war. By war's end Grant had become, after Abraham Lincoln, the leading figure in the Union war effort. Although Grant had had nothing to do with politics, the Republicans in 1868 were glad to nominate him, a certain winner, for the presidency. As it turned out, while Grant was honest and well-intentioned, he had almost none of the abilities required in a president and was fated to be the victim of dishonest friends and associates.

Arabella Mansfield was admitted to the Iowa bar as the **first woman lawyer** in the U.S. and the first woman lawyer in America since Mistress Margaret Brent, attorney for Cecilius Calvert, lord proprietor of Maryland in the 1640s.

A major contribution to **knowledge of the West** was made by John Wesley Powell, a one-armed casualty of the Civil War, and the first non-Indian to navigate the stretch of the Colorado R. that runs through the Grand

Musical performances were becoming widely available, although many of those providing music for American audiences were born abroad. One of the most able and energetic among them was Theodore Thomas, who came from Germany in 1845 and organized his own orchestra in 1862. Every year from 1869 to 1878 he toured the U.S. with the orchestra, introducing to Americans major works by Franz Liszt, Richard Wagner, Johannes Brahms, and others.

Among **books published** this year was *Innocents Abroad* by Mark Twain, a collection of articles written by Twain during a tour of Europe and the Near East. The extremely popular and humorous book poked fun at Old World institutions and distorted historical facts. Also published this year was *Oldtown Folks* by Harriet Beecher Stowe. The series of sketches, which demonstrated admirable use of local color, was based on Mrs. Stowe's memories of Litchfield, Conn., and those of her husband. Her description of New England life contrib-

Business and Industry; Science; Education; Philosophy and Religion III	IV Sports; Social Issues and Crime; Folkways; Fashion; Holidays

Mar. 23 The **University of California** was chartered in Berkeley, Calif., by merger with the College of California under provisions of the Morrill Land-Grant College Act of 1866. The trustees of the College of California, which was the first California institution to adopt the educational standards of the leading colleges of the East, turned over the rights and sites of the college of the state, giving the University of California the campus at Berkeley. The first classes there met in 1873.

June 23 Two patents for the **typewriter** were granted to Christopher Sholes, Samuel Soulé, and Carlos Glidden. For five years afterward, Sholes worked to complete his machine but did not succeed. In 1871 he received an additional patent for improvements he had made to his original invention. Two years later he sold his rights to the Remington Arms Company for $12,000. Remington mechanics quickly converted Sholes's crude machine into a marketable product. The Remington Company had an improved model by 1873. Sholes carried on with ideas for improvements and took out another patent in 1875, but finally turned all of his work over to Remington, which marketed the machine as the Remington typewriter.

June 10 The second annual **Belmont Stakes** was won by General Duke, with a time of 3:02. The jockey was R. Swim.

Oct. 1 The **Rochester Agricultural Fair** in upstate New York brought 50,000 visitors to the city. Some 40,000 attended the fair on Oct. 1, for a record $11,000 in gate receipts.

Oct. 1 A tremendous demand for **advertising space** led *The New York Times* to apologize to readers for increasing the number of its pages from a convenient eight to a cumbersome twelve. The newspaper explained that it was compelled from time to time to introduce the additional pages.

Nov. 11 The first indoor **amateur track and field meet** was held by the New York Athletic Club. The club, which had been organized Sept. 8, later held outdoor meets, established rules for the conduct of meets, and built the first cinder track. It continues to this day to promote track and field and other sports.

1869

Higher education was undergoing changes in the U.S., particularly at Harvard College in Cambridge, Mass., where Charles W. Eliot was inaugurated president on Mar. 10. Eliot was the first non-clergyman to hold the post and was an administrator rather than a teacher. He changed Harvard from a small undergraduate college into a modern university. Eliot introduced the elective system, organized graduate schools, insisted on written exams, and relaxed student discipline. He greatly influenced higher education throughout the country.

The **University of Nebraska** was chartered at Lincoln, Nebr. Its first classes were held in 1871.

The **first state board of health** in the U.S. was established in Massachusetts.

Thomas Edison's electric voting machine proved an operational success but a commercial failure. The invention was first used in an election in 1892.

Henry J. Heinz and L. C. Noble established a food-packing company at Sharpsburg, Pa. Its first product was grated horseradish. Heinz eventually had widespread commercial success.

Although boxing would not become a major American sport until the 1880s, when John L. Sullivan popularized it, an important bare knuckle boxing match was fought this year between Tom Allen, an English boxer who had moved to the U.S., and Mike McCoole, an American who claimed the U.S. title. Allen challenged McCoole and the two squared off in St. Louis on June 15. McCoole won the fight on a ninth-round foul and claimed the American championship. The following year Allen lost a bid for the international bare knuckle championship. Allen and McCoole met again in 1873 for a bout near St. Louis. Allen beat McCoole, this time in seven rounds. McCoole quit the ring. Allen claimed the world championship but was whipped soundly in 1876 by the English fighter Joe Goss in a 27-round bout in Kentucky.

The term *battery* was first employed in baseball parlance to denote a pitcher and catcher. The term derived from telegraphy, where the combination of a transmitter and receiver formed a battery.

Canyon, replete with 1000 miles of torrents and dangerous rapids. Powell later became director of the U.S. Geological Survey.

Feb. 6 The first caricature of **Uncle Sam** with chin whiskers appeared in *Harper's Weekly*. The figure had been used without whiskers by cartoonists for several years and had evolved from the Revolutionary caricature of Brother Jonathan. After 1869 Uncle Sam became a stock device of political cartoonists.

Mar. 4 **Ulysses S. Grant was inaugurated president** of the United States. The 18th president, Grant served two terms.

Apr. 10 The **Fifteenth Amendment** was ratified by Georgia, Mississippi, Texas, and Virginia, and these states were then readmitted into the Union. This amendment states that suffrage shall not be denied or abridged because of race, color, or previous condition of servitude.

May 15 The **National Woman Suffrage Association** was formed. Elizabeth Cady Stanton was chosen as first president and held the post until 1890. The other chief founder of the association was Susan B. Anthony.

Sept. 1 The **Prohibition Party** was organized during the National Prohibition Convention in Chicago. The convention was called by the National Temperance Convention in Cleveland.

Sept. 6 In a **coal mine disaster** in Avondale, Pa., 108 miners were killed by suffocation.

Oct. 8 **Franklin Pierce,** 14th president of the United States, died at 64. He was buried at Concord, N.H.

Oct. 27 A **steamboat fire** killed 200 when the steamer *Stonewall* caught fire on the Ohio R. near Cairo, Ill.

Dec. 10 The **first women's suffrage** in the U.S. was granted by Wyoming Territory.

uted to the later success of Sarah Orne Jewett and Mary Wilkins Freeman.

St. Anne's Church, designed by Renwick and Sands, was built in Brooklyn, N.Y. The church is considered an example of the worst of the Italian Gothic Revival style in the U.S.

The **plight of the dramatist,** who could not publish plays unless given permission by the producer, was reflected in the reply of actor-producer Edwin Forrest to the son of Robert Montgomery Bird, who asked for permission to publish his father's plays. Forrest wrote: "The heirs of the late Dr. R. M. Bird have neither right, title, nor any legal interest whatever in the plays written by him for me. . . . These plays are my exclusive property, by right of purchase, and for many years by the law of copyright."

West Wind, a statue by Thomas Gould, created a sensation in America. The work, the figure of a young girl surrounded by drapery, was thought to be a reproduction of a statue by the Italian sculptor Antonio Canova. Gould was commissioned to make seven replicas of the work.

1870

A short chapter in the history of American expansion ended this year in a personal defeat for Pres. Ulysses S. Grant. A group of land speculators interested Pres. Grant in a scheme to annex the Dominican Republic, which had gained independence from Spain in 1865. Ignoring the State Department and normal diplomatic procedure, Grant sent his private secretary, Orville E. Babcock, to negotiate a treaty of annexation. This treaty was submitted to the Senate on Jan. 10, and although Grant did his best to force its acceptance, the Senate rejected it on June 30.

The ninth U.S. **Census** recorded a population of 39,-818,449. America's center of population was located 48 miles east by north of Cincinnati, Ohio.

Woman's Journal, the official organ of the National Woman Suffrage Association, was founded by Lucy

John La Farge, a talented author and artist, was a pioneer in the art of stained glass. His celebrated work *Battle Window,* in Memorial Hall at Harvard University, was installed in 1870. In 1876 he did the mural decorations for Trinity Church in Boston. La Farge also executed stained glass windows for churches in Buffalo, N.Y., and Worcester, Mass., and for the chapel of Columbia University in New York City. What is referred to as American glass is an outgrowth of his experimentation.

Among the **books published** this year was *The Story of a Bad Boy,* a favorite boys' book by Thomas Bailey Aldrich. Semiautobiographical, the book provided a fresh account of boyhood, eschewing the moralizing that characterized most juvenile fiction. Other books

Business and Industry; Science; Education; Philosophy and Religion **III**		**IV** Sports; Social Issues and Crime; Folkways; Fashion; Holidays

The **first summer university course** was offered by Dean Nathaniel S. Shaler of Harvard University. It consisted of lectures in geology and was taken for recreation rather than for credit. The first formal summer course in education for public school teachers consisted of a six-week series of lectures held at Martha's Vineyard, Mass., in 1878.

The **Noble Order of the Knights of Labor** was established in Philadelphia, Pa. Its nine original members, all garment-cutters, were headed by Uriah S. Stephens. This secret order was formally organized in 1871.

Jan. 23   The **first state bureau of labor** in the U.S. was organized in Massachusetts.

Feb. 15   The **University of Nebraska** obtained its charter. It opened in 1871.

May 10   The **first transcontinental railroad** in the U.S. was completed at Promontory Point, Utah, with the linkup of the Central Pacific Railroad from the west and the Union Pacific Railroad from the east.

June 8   The first U.S. patent for a suction **vacuum cleaner** was awarded to Ives W. McGaffey of Chicago, Ill.

Sept. 24   **Black Friday,** a day of financial panic on Wall Street caused by the manipulation of Jay Gould and James Fisk, ruined thousands of gold speculators. In an attempt to corner the gold market, Gould and Fisk tried to keep Pres. Grant from selling government gold, and assured the public that they had been successful. However, Grant ordered the sale of $4,000,000 in gold, forcing the price down.

Dec. 6   The **first national black labor group** in America, the Colored National Labor Convention, met in Washington, D.C.

The **first ice yacht club** in the U.S., the Poughkeepsie, N.Y., Ice Yacht Club, was formed. It was followed by the New Hamburgh and Hudson River ice yacht clubs.

Jan.   The sentence **"The only good Indian is a dead Indian"** was credited to Gen. Philip H. Sheridan, one of the Union's great cavalry officers during the Civil War. Sheridan is said to have made the statement in reply to Comanche Chief Toch-a-way's remark, "Me good Indian," when they met at Fort Cobb, Mo.

Mar. 15   The **first professional baseball team** was the Cincinnati Red Stockings. The team announced regular payments to players and began a successful eight-month tour of the East and Middle West.

June 5   The third annual **Belmont Stakes** was won by Fenian, with a time of 3:04¼. The jockey was C. Miller.

Nov. 6   The **first intercollegiate football game** was played at New Brunswick, N.J. Rutgers beat Princeton 6–4 in a game more like soccer than football. There were 25 men on each team, and no running with the ball was allowed.

1870

Formation of the Standard Oil Company this year marked the start of what was to become the biggest influence by far in the growing oil industry, and the first industrial combination to exercise a virtual monopoly. The moving spirit in the company was John D. Rockefeller, who had begun his career as a bookkeeper in Cleveland, Ohio, center of the oil refining industry at this time. Rockefeller and his partners, including his brother William, started with two refineries in Cleveland and a sales agency in New York City. From this modest beginning, Rockefeller set out to control not only the refining of oil but also its transportation from the oil fields and marketing of the finished product.

The first comprehensive **graduate program of studies** was initiated at Yale and Harvard.

The sporting year was marked by an important event in international yachting. For the first time since the U.S. won the America's Cup from England in 1851, a British yacht issued a challenge to win it back. Accordingly, on Aug. 8 in New York Bay, the *Cambria* sailed against 23 American boats of the New York Yacht Club. The winner was *Magic,* owned by Franklin Osgood. *Cambria* came in tenth. The bay was dotted with ships of all descriptions, and an estimated 100,000 people lined the shores to see the spectacle.

The craze for **roller skating** spread throughout the U.S. as it did throughout the world. By 1863 four rollers had been added to "parlor skates" and a young skater, William H. Fuller, developed the art of figure skating, which he displayed on a tour around the world.

Stone, who guided its policies until her death in 1893.

1870–1871 In **congressional elections** the Democrats gained six seats in the Senate, but the Republicans still enjoyed a 52–17 majority, with five seats going to minor parties. In the House the Republicans lost 31 seats but still led 134–104, with five seats going to minor parties.

Jan. 15 The first political cartoon to use the **donkey** as a symbol for the Democratic Party appeared in *Harper's Weekly.* The cartoon, by Thomas Nast, was called "A Live Jackass Kicking a Dead Lion."

Jan. 26 **Virginia was granted representation** in the U.S. Congress on condition that the members of the Virginia legislature take an oath never to amend their constitution to deny blacks the right to vote, hold office, or gain an education.

Feb. 23 **Mississippi was granted representation** in the U.S. Congress. The provisions were the same as those contained in the bill admitting Virginia, except that the representatives were permitted an affirmation instead of an oath.

Feb. 25 The **first black in Congress,** Sen. Hiram R. Revels, Republican of Mississippi, took his seat. The first black member of the House was Joseph H. Rainey, Republican of South Carolina, who also entered Congress this year.

Mar. 30 **Texas was granted representation** in the U.S. Congress. The provisions were the same as those contained in the bill admitting Mississippi.

Mar. 30 The **Fifteenth Amendment was adopted.** It stipulated that no state shall deprive any citizen of the right to vote because of race, color, or previous condition of servitude.

Apr. 27 A **building collapse** in Richmond, Va., killed 61 persons and injured 12. The floor of the Supreme Court room caved in.

June 22 Congress passed an act to create the **Department of Justice** under direction of the attorney general. The department today supervises all government police, the FBI, and the Bureau of Prisons.

July 15 **Georgia was granted representation** in the U.S. Congress.

Oct. 12 Gen. **Robert E. Lee** died at Lexington, Va., at 63. A graduate of West Point and a brilliant military strategist, he offered his services to the Confederacy at the outbreak of the Civil War and rose to become commander in chief of the Confederate army.

published this year included the *Rubáiyát* of Omar Khayyám, translated by Edward Fitzgerald, and *The Luck of Roaring Camp and Other Sketches* by Bret Harte, which catapulted the author to international fame.

A great impetus was given to **vaudeville** in New York City by the team of Edward Harrigan and Tom Hart. Portraying a male and female combination, they satirized baseball, politics, the armed forces, blacks, Germans, Italians, and many aspects of city life.

Scribner's Monthly, the leading periodical of the 1870s, was founded. Unlike other literary magazines, it gave preference to American writers, including Edward Eggleston, Joaquin Miller, Bret Harte, and Frank Stockton.

Corcoran Art Gallery, in Washington, D.C., was incorporated by an act of Congress. William C. Corcoran, a financier, had given $300,000 to build the gallery, which was completed in 1859. During the Civil War it had been used for military purposes. Corcoran also gave $1,000,000 to acquire a collection, as well as 79 paintings from his own collection.

The **mecca for American painters** was no longer London, Rome, or Düsseldorf, but Paris. Painters such as William Morris Hunt, John La Farge, and James Abbott McNeill Whistler were influenced by the prominent French schools.

Saratoga, a play by Bronson Howard, was produced on the New York stage. Howard was the only U.S. dramatist of the nineteenth century who was able to earn his living by writing for the stage.

Feb. 14 **Frontier drama** burst on the stage with the popular *Kit the Arkansas Traveler* by Thomas Blades DeWalden. It was followed by *Horizon* (1871) by Augustin Daly, *Davy Crockett* (1872) by Frank Murdock, *The Gilded Age* (1874) by Mark Twain and Charles Dudley Warner, *The Two Men from Sandy Bar* (1876) by Bret Harte, and *The Danites in the Sierras* (1877) by Joaquin Miller.

The **Great Atlantic and Pacific Tea Company** was organized "for the purpose of importing and distributing pure and reliable teas and coffees and subjecting the purchaser to but one profit from the foreign factor." The company grew into the largest single chain of grocery stores in the U.S. in terms of volume of business. The company's early advertising stressed that the chain could provide bargains by eliminating middlemen from grocery sales.

Stevens Institute of Technology was established at Hoboken, N.J. Its first classes were held in 1871.

Syracuse University was established at Syracuse, N.Y. Its first classes met in 1871.

Wellesley College was founded as Wellesley Female Seminary. Its first classes began in 1875.

Ohio State University at Columbus, Ohio, was chartered as Ohio Agricultural and Mechanical College. Its first classes met in 1873. Its present name was adopted in 1877.

Loyola University, Chicago, Ill., was chartered as St. Ignatius College. The change to its present name was made in the same year. The first classes met in 1869, the year before official chartering.

The **refrigerated railroad car** emerged in the 1870s as an important factor in the development of certain industries. Pioneer development of the refrigerated car is credited to Gustavus Franklin Swift, who in the 1870s began to ship dressed beef from Chicago to the East, the first time this was done successfully. He employed a railroad car in which fresh air was forced over ice and then circulated through the storage compartments. George Henry Hammond also pioneered at about this time in the use of refrigerated cars, shipping meat from Omaha, Nebr., and from Hammond, Ind.

The **growth of unions** in America was reflected in a total membership of 300,000.

Jan. 2 Construction of the **Brooklyn Bridge** began. It was to span the East R. from Park Row, Manhattan, to Sands and Washington streets in Brooklyn.

Feb. 9 The **U.S. Weather Bureau** was established by Congress. Originally part of the Signal Corps, it became part of the Department of Agriculture on July 1, 1891. On June 30, 1940, it was transferred to the Commerce Department.

July 12 A U.S. patent for a process by which **celluloid** is produced was awarded to John W. Hyatt, Jr., and Isaiah S. Hyatt of Albany, N.Y. The discovery of celluloid was a significant advance in the science of photography, as later developed by George Eastman.

Dec. 16 The **Colored Methodist Episcopal Church** of America was established at Jackson, Tenn., by Bishop Robert Paine.

Walking became one of the most popular spectator sports. Gilmore's Gardens in New York City would usually sell out when famous heel-and-toers raced there. About 1900, bicycle riders replaced walkers in popularity.

Two **popular sports** were cricket and baseball. Cricket was generally favored in the press because of its gentility.

Pimlico racetrack was built in Baltimore, Md., by a group of racing enthusiasts who were encouraged by the success of the course at Saratoga Springs, N.Y., in 1864.

The **first boardwalk** in America was completed at Atlantic City, N.J.

Early **football matches** were played by Columbia, Princeton, and Rutgers. Technically, the game played was soccer.

Yale and Harvard met in a **crew race** on a circular course at Worcester, Mass. Yale came in first but was disqualified for having run into the Harvard team.

May 10 The **world heavyweight boxing championship** was won by Jem Mace of England, who had claimed the title after retirement of Tom King, also an Englishman. To defend the claim, Mace defeated Tom Allen, another claimant, in a ten-round bout near Kennersville, La.

June 4 The fourth annual **Belmont Stakes** was won by Kingfisher, with a time of 2:59½. The jockey was W. Dick.

Aug. 16 Fred Goldsmith demonstrated that the **curve ball** was not an optical illusion. Before a large crowd at the Capitoline Grounds, Brooklyn, N.Y., Goldsmith set up three poles in a straight line and hurled a ball that went to the right of the first pole, to the left of the second, and to the right of the third.

1871

One of the great disasters in American history occurred between Oct. 8 and Oct. 11, when Chicago was burned nearly to the ground. According to legend, the fire began when a cow belonging to a Mrs. O'Leary kicked over a lantern. In fact, the fire started in the barn of a laborer named Patrick O'Leary, who lived on DeKoven Street on the West Side. Before the fire was out, about 17,500 buildings had been destroyed over an area of 2124 acres, with damage estimated at about $200,000,000. Some 250 people were killed and about 98,500 left homeless. It was a tribute to the spirit of the city and the times that rebuilding began at once and recovery took a surprisingly short time. Lost to fire was the original draft of Pres. Abraham Lincoln's Emancipation Proclamation, destroyed when the Chicago Historical Society building burned.

Feb. 21 The **District of Columbia** was provided with a territorial government. Several systems of government were tried, and the one in present use was adopted in 1878.

Feb. 28 A **federal election law** was passed, providing for federal supervision of elections in any city having more than 20,000 inhabitants. The measure was taken primarily to protect black voters in the South.

Mar. 3 The **Indian Appropriation Act** was passed. It made all Indians national wards and nullified all Indian treaties.

Mar. 4 Pres. Ulysses S. Grant established the **first civil service commission,** headed by George William Curtis of New York City. The unwillingness of Congress to make additional appropriations rendered the commission ineffective.

May 8 The **Treaty of Washington** was signed between the U.S. and Great Britain at Washington, D.C. It provided for arbitration for the *Alabama* claims by an international tribunal to meet at Geneva. These claims were for damages to U.S. shipping during the Civil War by the raider *Alabama* and other Confederate vessels built or armed by the British. The treaty also renewed Canadian-American fishing arrangements in the North Atlantic.

July 12 A **riot** between Irish Catholics and Irish Protestants in New York City left 52 persons dead and many more wounded.

Sept. 4 A citizen commission to investigate **Tammany Hall** was formed when 70 citizens were appointed at a mass meeting at Cooper Institute, New York City. The group investigated corruption by the political machine led by William Marcy "Boss" Tweed. By the

America had never lacked for nature writers and in the later nineteenth century the best was John Burroughs, who followed in the footsteps of Ralph Waldo Emerson and Henry David Thoreau. His first work, *Wake-Robin,* was published this year. The book was poetic in manner, as was *Birds and Poets* (1877). *Wake-Robin* was an invitation to ornithology and imparted the author's enthusiasm for bird watching. Burroughs' later writings paid more attention to scientific observation, although in his final years he believed that the salvation of society depended more on teachers, prophets, poets, and mystics than on science.

Among **books published** this year was the best seller *The Hoosier Schoolmaster* by Edward Eggleston. A classic of regional literature, Eggleston's novel sold some 500,000 copies, a circulation never reached by Eggleston's *The Circuit Rider* (1874) or *Roxy* (1878), considered better novels. Also published this year were *Their Wedding Journey,* the first novel of William Dean Howells, a combination of travelogue and novel of manners tracing the honeymoon journey of the Marches (who appear in later novels) to Niagara, Montreal, and Quebec; and *Passage to India,* a collection of poems by Walt Whitman that reflected a broadening of the poet's scope and subject matter. In the 72 poems, Whitman's artistic powers embraced peoples of all lands.

Probably the **best-known painting** by an American, popularly known as *Whistler's Mother,* was exhibited by James McNeill Whistler at the Pennsylvania Academy of Fine Arts. It was entitled *Arrangement in Grey and Black.* Whistler remarked relative to the title that no one would have an interest in the identity of the sitter. Actually millions since have identified the canvas with their feelings for their own mothers.

Lenox Library in New York City was built from plans by Richard Morris Hunt, who was one of the first Americans to study at the Ecole des Beaux-Arts in Paris and was influential in introducing French architecture to the U.S.

A patent for the **first hollow tile design** was issued to Balthaser Kreischer, a New York manufacturer. Hollow tile, light and fireproof, came into extensive use for industrial buildings.

1871

As communication and transportation improved, and as the U.S. came to be more concerned with events on other continents, an interest in religions other than Christianity was aroused. The outstanding scholar in this field was James Freeman Clarke, a Unitarian clergyman and liberal reformer. His *Ten Great Religions* (2 volumes, 1871–1883) was an important work in comparative religion. It went through 21 editions by 1886.

A greater emphasis on **science in education** was reflected in the publication of an official Yale pamphlet entitled *The Needs of the University.* Without renouncing the virtues of classical education, the authorities at Yale admitted the utility of laboratory courses in the sciences.

The **first undergraduate daily newspaper** in U.S. was the *Daily Illinois,* published at the University of Illinois.

Smith College was chartered at Northampton, Mass. Its first classes met in 1875.

Two devices making the **cable car** possible, an underground continuous moving cable and a mechanical gripper for the underside of streetcars, were invented by Andrew Smith Hallidie. His inventions prepared the way for introduction of the cable car in San Francisco and other cities by 1873.

Mar. 27 The **University of Arkansas** was founded as Arkansas Industrial University at Fayetteville, Ark. Its first classes met in 1872.

May 1 The **Legal Tender Act** was declared constitutional by a Supreme Court decision in the case of *Knox v. Lee.* Passed in 1862, when national credit was ebbing, the Legal Tender Act had authorized issuance of $450,000,000 in treasury notes, making them legal tender for all private debts and public dues except import duties and interest on public debt. A second act was passed in 1863. The Supreme Court, reduced to seven members, declared the Legal Tender Acts unconstitutional on Feb. 7, 1870, in the case of *Hepburn v. Griswold,* on the grounds that they exceeded any delegated or implied powers of Congress, violated the spirit of the Constitution, and deprived creditors of property without due process of law. Pres. Ulysses S. Grant made nominations to the empty Supreme Court posts on the same day the decision was handed down; four days later the Supreme Court voted to reargue the issues. The decision of May

An American type still popular in song, story, and movies is the cowboy of the western cattle country. He flourished from the late 1860s to the late 1880s, when cattle were driven long distances to market. The cowboy's heyday was brief; it was ended by the spread of railroad lines and by the fencing in of ranges and farms. The cowboy's life was not glamorous. It meant hard work, danger, and low pay. After a drive he would frequently spend all his pay in the saloons of such cow towns as Abilene, Kans. Between 1867 and 1871 cowboys drove 1,460,000 cattle into Abilene, the first of the famous western railheads.

The **National Rifle Association** was formed in response to the revived interest in rifle shooting produced by the Civil War. Shooting at a target replaced shooting for a game prize.

Henry James made a trip to **Niagara Falls,** sailing down from Toronto across Lake Ontario. He recorded his impressions in an early travel essay. Much of what he experienced is still echoed by visitors to the falls: "There is every appearance that the spectacle you have come so far to see is to be choked in the horribly vulgar shops and booths and catchpenny artifices which have pushed and elbowed to within the very spray of the Falls, and ply their importunities in shrill competition with its thunder. You see a multitude of hotels and taverns and stores, glaring with white paint, bedizened with placards and advertisements, and decorated by groups of those gentlemen who flourish most rankly on the soil of New York and in the vicinage of hotels; who carry their hands in their pockets, wear their hats always and every way, and, although of a stationary habit, yet spurn the earth with their heels. A side glimpse of the Falls, however, calls out your philosophy; you reflect that this may be regarded as one of those sordid foregrounds which Turner liked to use, and which may be effective as a foil; you hurry to where the roar grows louder, and, I was going to say, you escape from the village. In fact, however, you don't escape from it; it is constantly at your elbow, just to the right or left of the line of contemplation. It would be paying Niagara a poor compliment to say that, practically she does not hurl away this chaffering by-play from her edge; but as you value the integrity of your impression, you are bound to affirm that it suffers appreciable abatement from such sources. You wonder, as you stroll about, whether it is altogether an unrighteous dream that with the slow progress of taste and the possible or impossible growth of some larger comprehension of beauty and fitness, the public conscience may not tend to confer upon such sovereign places of nature something of the inviolability and privacy which we are slow to bestow, indeed, upon fame, but which we do not grudge at least to art."

Exploration and Settlement; Wars; Government; Civil Rights; Statistics	I		II	Publishing; Arts and Music; Popular Entertainment; Architecture; Theater

end of the year he had been twice arrested and released on bail.

Oct. 8 Fire destroyed the community of Peshtigo, Wis., leaving some 600 dead. About 50 persons seeking refuge in a brick building were consumed by the intense flames.

The first **Grand Central Station** opened in New York City, with tracks running into a huge vault of open, webbed wrought iron. The building was demolished later to make way for the present terminal.

1872

The presidential election campaign of 1872 was a strange one. As a result of the scandals in Pres. Ulysses S. Grant's administration, and because Grant sided with the radical Republicans in Reconstruction policies, many Republicans, liberals, and reformers split off to nominate their own candidate, Horace Greeley, editor of the New York *Tribune.* Greeley had been a leading figure in the antislavery movement and a key figure in the election of Abraham Lincoln. He was a champion of universal suffrage and other radical causes. He was also viewed by many as a champion of fads, a visionary. Even though the Democrats also nominated Greeley, Grant won the election handily. Greeley died less than a month after the election.

The **Crédit Mobilier scandal** came to a head when the New York *Sun* published the names of congressmen who had received shares of Union Pacific stock virtually free from Rep. Oakes Ames of Massachusetts. A congressional investigation was begun in late 1872. Its report in 1873 prompted little more than the censure of Ames and Rep. James Brooks of Massachusetts.

Susan B. Anthony tested the Fourteenth Amendment by leading a group of women to cast ballots in the presidential election. She was arrested, found guilty, and fined $100. She refused to pay the fine and never did. Her reward came 14 years after her death when in 1920 the Nineteenth Amendment, guaranteeing women's suffrage, was adopted.

The **National Labor Reform Party,** a new American political party formed out of the National Labor Union, prepared for the presidential election with the nomination of Judge David Davis of Illinois at its convention in Columbus, Ohio. His subsequent withdrawal from the race dealt a death blow to both the party and the labor federation that had spawned it.

1872–1873 In **congressional elections** the Republicans lost two Senate seats, for a 49–19 majority, with five seats held by minor parties. In the House, which had gained 50 seats since 1870, the Republicans made spectacular gains, leading 194–92, with 14 seats going to minor parties.

Feb. 22 The **Prohibition Party** held its first national nominating convention in Columbus, Ohio. James

Of the scores of magazines first published this year, two were especially notable. The first was *Publishers' Weekly,* originally issued with the title *The Publishers' and Stationers' Weekly Trade Circular.* Founded in New York City by Frederick Leypoldt, the first issue was dated Jan. 18, 1872. The second magazine of note was *Popular Science Monthly,* published by D. Appleton & Company and edited by Edward L. Youmans. Its first issue, which appeared in May 1872, carried the first part of *The Study of Sociology* by the British philosopher Herbert Spencer, and the first part of *Natural History of Man* by the French anthropologist Armand de Quatrefages. The magazine scored an immediate success, reflecting the growing American interest in science.

Among **books published** this year was *Roughing It* by Mark Twain, a "record of several years of variegated vagabondizing" in the West. A boisterous and exciting book, it described the rough-and-tumble life of the Nevada miners, stagecoach days on the Overland Trail, Western tall tales, hilarious optimism, and desperadoes and pioneers. Twain also included chapters on his stay in Hawaii. Other books published this year included *The Poet of the Breakfast Table* by Oliver Wendell Holmes; and *Barriers Burned Away* by Edward Payson Roe, a best-selling novel based on the Chicago fire of 1871.

The *North American Review* declared that the true fiction writer must idealize what he finds. In the end, the *Review* judged, **idealist fiction** would be the true realistic fiction, since truth was not to be found in facts alone. The American writer, in particular, said the *Review,* must look beyond his native land, which had neither depth nor antiquity, to the uncharted fields of the imagination.

Business and Industry; Science; Education; Philosophy and Religion **III**		**IV** Sports; Social Issues and Crime; Folkways; Fashion; Holidays

1, 1871, found the power to issue legal tender implied in the power to coin money and wage war. It also declared that the Constitution forbade the states, but not Congress, from impairing contracts. Whether Pres. Grant actually packed the Court is still argued among historians.

Mar. 17   The **first professional baseball asssociation**, the National Association of Professional Baseball Players, was organized. It replaced the amateur National Association.

June 10   The fifth annual **Belmont Stakes** was won by the horse Harry Bassett, with a time of 2:56. The jockey was W. Miller.

1872

A new era in retail merchandising began in 1872 with the establishment of Montgomery Ward & Company in Chicago. Its founder was Aaron Montgomery Ward, a clerk and traveling salesman who thought he could sell goods directly to people in rural areas by mail. He began with a one-sheet leaflet that offered bargains to Granges. Ward's business expanded and was copied by others.

The **Russian Orthodox Church** transferred its Episcopal see from Sitka, Alaska, to San Francisco, Calif. Purchase of Alaska by the U.S. ended the official influence of the Russian Orthodox Church in Alaska.

The **Jehovah's Witnesses** was organized by Charles Taze Russell, a lay member of the Presbyterian Church. First called Russellites, International Bible Students, and Millennial Darwinists, Russell's fundamental followers officially became Jehovah's Witnesses in 1931. In 1939 the sect was incorporated in New York as the Watch Tower Bible and Tract Society.

Early experiments in **photographing moving objects** were conducted by Eadweard Muybridge, an English photographer, in a project sponsored by the U.S. government. Later he photographed a running horse by tripping a series of cameras synchronized by electric circuits with 12 clocks. In 1881 he invented the zoopraxiscope, a forerunner of the moving picture, for the projection of animal pictures on a screen.

The **University of Oregon** at Eugene and Portland, Ore., was established. Its first classes were held in 1876.

A contract calling for **secret rebates** and drawbacks was signed between the Pennsylvania Railroad and the South Improvement Company, a Rockefeller interest. This agreement later became the most celebrated example of pernicious business practice among large corporations.

The **first mercantile corporation** in the U.S. was formed, the Simmons Hardware Company, controlled by Edward Campbell Simmons of St. Louis, Mo.

The nation was in its Gilded Age, and those who were reaping fortunes from enterprises honest or dishonest were eager to display their new wealth. Society in New York City came to be based almost entirely on wealth. A self-appointed leader of this glittering society was Ward McAllister, who had married a millionaire's daughter. In 1872 he chose a group of men from prominent New York families who were to lead society as "patriarchs." McAllister also groomed Mrs. William Astor to become the grande dame of New York high society.

The earliest recorded use of the word *mugwump* occurred this year in the Indianapolis *Sentinel.* On Mar. 23, 1884, the New York *Sun* began to use the word to describe Republicans who were against James G. Blaine, Republican candidate for the presidency. In a series of editorials, the word became widely known. It was roughly equivalent to the later political classification *egghead.*

Yellowstone National Park Reserve was established for the enjoyment of the public. It was designated the first Federal Forest Reserve by Congress in 1891. John Colter, a member of the Lewis and Clark expedition, is credited with reaching the region in 1806. His report on his adventures and the things he saw set the pattern for the fantastic stories about Yellowstone that were to circulate for years to come. The government finally sent exploratory parties to the area in 1859 and 1870. The reports on these expeditions were widely read and became the grounds for the act of Congress that established Yellowstone as a public park. Yellowstone is the oldest and biggest of the national parks. The area was originally marked off as 3348 sq. mi. In subsequent years, the boundaries of Yellowstone were substantially increased, and the Shoshone National Forest, a timber and land reserve, was added.

A new **baseball rule** permitted the pitcher to snap his delivery of the ball. However, the pitcher was still restricted to an underhand, below-the-waist motion. Present-day regulations for the size of the ball also were

Black of Pennsylvania was nominated for the presidency and the Rev. John Russell of Michigan for the vice presidency.

May 1 The first national convention of the **Liberal Republican Party nominated Horace Greeley** for the presidency and Gov. Benjamin Gratz Brown of Missouri for the vice presidency. The same slate was nominated by the Democratic convention on July 9.

May 23 The **Workingmen's National Convention** nominated Pres. Grant as its presidential candidate, and named Sen. Henry Wilson of Massachusetts as its vice presidential candidate.

June 5–6 The **Republican National Convention** nominated Pres. Grant for reelection. Sen. Henry Wilson of Massachusetts was nominated for the vice presidency. This was the first major party convention in which black delegates participated. Speeches were delivered from the rostrum by three black delegates, William E. Gray of Arkansas, B. B. Elliott of South Carolina, and John Roy Lynch of Mississippi.

July 9 The **Democratic National Convention** nominated **Horace Greeley,** editor of the New York *Tribune,* for the presidency and Gov. Benjamin Gratz Brown of Missouri for the vice presidency.

Nov. 5 Ulysses S. Grant was reelected president of the United States, defeating Horace Greeley by an electoral vote of 286 to 66. Pres. Grant received a popular vote of 3,597,132 against 2,384,124 for Greeley.

Nov. 9 A fire started in Boston, Mass., and raged for three days, destroying some 65 acres of the city. The fire killed 13 persons and destroyed $75,000,000 in property.

William H. Rinehart completed what was considered his greatest sculpture, the marble nude *Clytie,* now on exhibit in the Peabody Institute of Baltimore. Its naturalism was in direct opposition to neoclassical representations of the nude.

The **First Baptist Church,** originally the New Brattle Square Church, was built in Boston by Henry Hobson Richardson. The church was one of his first truly distinguished works.

Work was begun on the **Old Art Museum** in Boston, a huge example of Victorian Gothic style in U.S. architecture. In this building the first domestic terra cotta was used. The museum hewed closely to the aesthetic principles of John Ruskin. The period after the Civil War was deeply influenced by the theories of Ruskin, who defended medieval architecture against the supposedly immoral forms of the Renaissance. He was so successful in his campaign that Victorian Gothic is also known as Ruskinian Gothic.

1873

After a period of unprecedented prosperity, fueled originally by the economic demands of the Civil War, the nation plunged into a depression. The panic of 1873 was triggered by the failure on Sept. 18 of the leading brokerage firm, Jay Cooke & Company, which had been financing construction of the Northern Pacific Railroad. The actual causes lay deeper: overspeculation in land and securities, issuance of too much paper money, and increasing inflation. Over 5000 businesses failed this year and another 5000 or so failed before recovery was complete about six years later.

The **Farmer's Alliance,** which soon became a national farmers' welfare organization, began with small local meetings. It grew into a statewide group in Texas in 1876, and a nationwide alliance in 1887, when all state groups formed by that date joined in a cooperative union. The program of the alliance soon concentrated

The founding of *St. Nicholas* magazine and the appointment of Mary Mapes Dodge as its editor marked 1873 as a notable year for children's literature. Mrs. Dodge edited the magazine and contributed to it until her death in 1905. In the process she had more influence on literature for young people than any other contemporary person or publication. Among the many contributors to *St. Nicholas* were Louisa May Alcott, Rudyard Kipling, Howard Pyle, Robert Louis Stevenson, Frank Stockton, and Mark Twain.

Among **books published** this year was the classic science fiction adventure story *Twenty Thousand Leagues Under the Sea* by Jules Verne, a French writer. Another Verne novel, *Around the World in Eighty Days,* topped the 1,000,000 mark in sales. Other books published this

The **Burbank potato** had its origin this year when Luther Burbank found an Early Rose potato plant that had produced a seed ball, a rare event for that type of potato. Burbank had bought a 17-acre plot in Lunenburg, Mass., in 1871 and had taken up market gardening as a livelihood. He collected the seeds and planted them the following year. Of the 23 seeds, only two produced plants worth investigating. In 1874 Burbank grew both varieties, then picked the more promising one. In Oct. 1875 Burbank sold this potato variety to James J.H. Gregory of Marblehead, Mass., for $150 and moved to California to continue his horticultural research. Gregory named the new variety the Burbank and made a fortune.

Nov. 1 The **failure of the velocipede, or bicycle,** as a mode of transportation was reflected in an editorial in *The New York Times.* New York City was then in the throes of an epidemic of equine distemper. The *Times* reported that "the utter failure of the velocipede as a substitute for the saddle-horse is just now emphasized by the fact that, in the present dearth of horses, no one has alluded to the velocipede as a possible solution of the problem how the business man is to reach his office, in case the cars and stages should cease running." The *Times* noted that the failure of the velocipede to gain popularity was the result of "the tyranny of the small boy," a "shameless and exasperating mouthpiece of crude and unreasoning public opinion" who jeered and insulted cyclists right off the streets.

set this year: not less than five nor more than five and one-quarter ounces, and not less than nine nor more than nine and one-quarter inches in circumference.

Apr. 10 **Arbor Day,** a festival of tree planting, was inaugurated in the state of Nebraska through the efforts of Julius Sterling Morton, later secretary of agriculture. In 1885, Apr. 22 was officially designated as Arbor Day by the Nebraska legislature. Other states followed suit: Michigan and Minnesota (1876), and New York (1888). Ontario, Canada, inaugurated Arbor Day in 1887.

June 1 The sixth annual **Belmont Stakes** was won by the horse Joe Daniels, with a time of 2:58¼. The jockey was James Rowe.

Nov. 7 The brigantine *Mary Celeste,* commanded by Capt. Benjamin S. Briggs, sailed from New York harbor bound for Genoa, Italy, carrying some 1700 barrels of alcohol. On Dec. 4 the British brigantine *Dei Gratia* found the *Mary Celeste* between the Azores and Portugal, her sails slightly damaged, several feet of water in her hold, and completely abandoned. The cargo was intact, the ship was in good order, and there was plenty of food and water aboard, but the lifeboat was gone. The mystery of the disappearance of Capt. Briggs, his wife and daughter, and the eight crewmen aboard has never been solved, and the story of the *Mary Celeste*'s voyage has become a classic of sea lore.

1873

The first important railroad tunnel in the U.S., and the longest until 1927, was completed on Nov. 27. This was the Hoosac Tunnel, through the Hoosac Range in northwestern Massachusetts. Work on the tunnel had begun in 1851. The new explosive nitroglycerin had its first practical use in the U.S. in construction of the tunnel. So did the compressed air drill, which earlier had been used in the Mont Cenis Tunnel in the Swiss Alps, the only tunnel in the world longer than the Hoosac at that time. The Hoosac Tunnel was 4.75 miles long. It was traveled by trains of the Boston and Maine Railroad from New England to New York City. It was 20 feet high and 24 feet wide, and required 20,000,000 bricks for archwork support. It cost $20,000,000 to build and took the lives of nearly 200 workmen.

By 1873 the American bison, also called the buffalo, was almost extinct, even though at the start of the nineteenth century estimates placed the North American bison population as high as 60,000,000. Bison were essential to the way of life of the Indians of the Great Plains, who depended on them for food, clothing, and shelter. The symbiotic relationship of the Indians and the bison threatened neither group. However, with the coming of the railroad, professional buffalo hunters, and the settlement of the West, the situation changed. Bison were slaughtered far beyond any need for food or hides. Although in 1865 about 10,000,000 bison still roamed the plains, by 1890 only 1000 or so were left.

Memorial Day became a legal holiday in New York, the first state to recognize it. Rhode Island followed suit in 1874; Vermont in 1876; New Hampshire in 1877; and Wisconsin in 1879.

on free silver, greenbacks, national railroads, curtailment of speculation, and decentralized banking, emphasizing the common grievances of the straitened farmers. When the alliance joined with the Knights of Labor in 1889, these issues were discussed on a broader basis and became the major radical demands of the last decade of the century.

Feb. 12 A routine **coinage act** of Congress omitted all silver currency because silver was so scarce it brought more as bullion than as dollars. Three years later, when Nevada mines were producing unprecedented quantities of silver, mine owners demanded that the government buy their product for coinage. At that time the coinage act became known as the Crime of '73.

Mar. 3 An act prohibiting the **mailing of obscene literature** was passed by Congress. The bill was promoted by Anthony Comstock, secretary of the Society for the Suppression of Vice. Comstock, formerly a dry-goods store clerk, joined the YMCA and began to agitate for a New York vice society. He drew his inspiration from a London society that for 75 years had been engaged in ferreting out and bringing to trial moral offenders.

Mar. 4 Pres. Ulysses S. Grant **was inaugurated** for his second term. Henry Wilson was sworn in as vice president.

Sept. 20 The **New York Stock Exchange closed.** The same day the secretary of the treasury reissued $26,-000,000 in legal tender. Ten days later the exchange reopened.

Nov. 19 **William Marcy "Boss" Tweed** was convicted on 204 charges of fraud. He was sentenced to 12 years in prison and fined $12,550.

year included *Marjorie Daw* by Thomas Bailey Aldrich, a collection whose title story achieved both critical and popular success; *The Mystery of Metropolisville* by Edward Eggleston, a novel that included a preface by the author declaring that he considered the novel a proper vehicle for contributing to the history of civilization in America; and *Mrs. Skaggs's Husbands and Other Stories* by Bret Harte, which included some of the author's best writing of this period, notably the story "The Head of Sandy Bar."

Interest in romantic **landscapes** reached a peak with *Home of the Heron* by George Inness. He believed, along with the French school of Jean Baptiste Camille Corot, that greatness lies in the area of the emotions. The effect of Inness on younger painters was great. The sentimentalism evident in their paintings persisted well into the twentieth century.

An early painting by **Thomas Eakins,** probably the most influential painter America has produced, was *Turning Stake Boat,* depicting a number of sculls on a flat surface of water. Eakins confessed to using trigonometric tables to fashion perspective, and to studying refraction to get the exact shimmer on the water. His attitude, like that of Renaissance painters, was often scientific rather than aesthetic.

Sidney Lanier composed "Field-larks and Blackbirds," "Swamp Robin," and "Danse des Moucherons"—all compositions for the flute.

1874

Growing out of the hardships caused by the panic of 1873, a convention in Indianapolis, Ind., formed the Greenback Party on Nov. 25, 1876. Its supporters were mostly farmers from the West and the South who wanted to inflate the currency so as to relieve themselves of the burden of debt they had incurred in times of high prices. Originally, the Greenback Party hoped to gain control of the Democratic Party, but it could not do so. It fielded its own candidates until 1884, when the party did so badly that it disbanded. In 1878, with the

The American theater prospered in the late nineteenth century and became completely professional, counting among its ranks numerous stars and a number of energetic and able producers. Among comediennes no one was better or more successful than Ada Rehan, who first appeared on the stage in 1863 at the age of 13. She was for many years the leading lady of Augustin Daly's company, popular both in America and England. Her most famous part was Katherine in *The Taming of the Shrew.*

Business and Industry; Science; Education; Philosophy and Religion III	IV Sports; Social Issues and Crime; Folkways; Fashion; Holidays

The **Union of American Hebrew Congregations,** the first national grouping of Jewish congregations, was organized. Two years later this group founded Hebrew Union College in Cincinnati, Ohio, the oldest rabbinical seminary in the U.S. A conference in Cleveland in 1855 had resulted in a breach between the eastern and the western rabbis; their division was not bridged until 1879. The Union of American Hebrew Congregations, therefore, consisted of congregations from the South and the West only.

The rise of **railroad brotherhoods** continued with the organization of railroad firemen.

Epidemics of yellow fever, cholera, and smallpox swept through many southern cities.

The **cable car,** invented by Andrew S. Hallidie, was first used in San Francisco, Calif.

The first major **nursing education institution** was founded at Bellevue Hospital, New York City. It based its teaching on the theories of Florence Nightingale.

Free mail delivery was provided in all cities with a population of at least 20,000.

May 1   The **first penny postcards** in the U.S. were issued.

Oct. 27   A patent for an improvement in **barbed wire** was issued to Joseph F. Glidden of Illinois. His innovation became widely popular and is the basis for the manufacture of barbed wire today.

Bookmakers first appeared at U.S. racetracks. The first few were English but Americans soon learned the skill. The days of informal wagering between owners or spectators were over.

The **Fair Grounds racecourse** was opened in New Orleans, La. It was to operate on a system of prolonged meetings patterned after John Morrissey's races begun in Saratoga Springs in 1864.

Riflemen were the top sports idols during the 1870s. More than 100,000 people attended one national rifle shooting tournament held at Creedmoor, Long Island, N.Y., in 1873. Oarsmen were the second favorite sports figures. As many as 60,000 men, women, and children lined the banks of the Harlem R. in New York City to watch and wager on the sculling contests held there.

May 27   The first annual **Preakness Stakes** was won by Survivor, with a time of 2:43. The jockey was G. Barbee. The race was run at Pimlico, Md. The Preakness Stakes is one of the three classic races in American racing. It is grouped with the Kentucky Derby and the Belmont Stakes in importance. A horse that has won all three has earned the Triple Crown of American racing. The Preakness Stakes has been run over varying distances.

June 7   The seventh annual **Belmont Stakes** was won by Springbok, with a time of 3:01¾. The jockey was James Rowe.

Aug. 18   **Mt. Whitney,** the second highest mountain in the U.S., was scaled by an American team for the first time. The climbers were John Lucas, Charles D. Begole, and A. H. Johnson.

Sept. 23   The **world heavyweight boxing championship** was won by Tom Allen of England, who fought Mike McCoole near St. Louis, Mo.

Oct. 19   The first code of **football rules** was drafted by representatives from Yale, Princeton, Columbia, and Rutgers universities; they met in a Fifth Ave. hotel in New York City. The rules chosen were more like soccer than modern football and were abandoned in a few years in favor of the "Boston game" played at Harvard.

1874

An invention that revolutionized life on the Great Plains had its first practical use in 1874. The invention was barbed wire, the work of Joseph F. Glidden of Illinois. Until 1874, considering the lack of timber on the Great Plains, there had been no economical way to fence the land. Cattle roamed where they would. Now the range was fenced in. Cowboys had to become ranchers and farmers had to protect their crops from marauding cattle. At first there were battles between ranchers and farmers, but eventually barbed wire won. In 1874

A new sport, lawn tennis, appeared in the U.S. this year. Invented in England, the game came to the U.S. by way of Bermuda, where a New Yorker, Mary Ewing Outerbridge, was introduced to the game. She returned home with a net, balls, and rackets, and had the first lawn tennis court in the U.S. laid out on Staten Island. Another court soon was laid out in Nahant, Mass., and the game spread around the country. Tennis was such a genteel game that women could play despite their long skirts, since they were not expected to run about.

assistance of labor organizations, the Greenback-Labor Party elected 14 representatives to Congress. At the 1874 convention the party nominated Peter Cooper, New York industrialist and philanthropist, as its candidate for the presidency in 1876.

The **Woman's Christian Temperance Union**, called the WCTU, was established at Cleveland, Ohio. It stemmed from the women's crusade against liquor traffic in midwestern states. Mrs. Annie Wittenmyer was elected first president.

1874–1875 In **congressional elections** the Democrats picked up ten seats in the Senate but still lagged behind the Republicans 45–29, with two seats going to minor parties. In the House the Democrats took a 169–109 majority, with 14 seats going to minor parties.

May 16 The Ashfield Reservoir **dam collapsed** above Williamsburg, Mass., inundating Mill R. Valley. More than 100 persons were killed. Property loss was in the millions of dollars.

June 20 Territorial government in the **District of Columbia** was abolished and replaced by a commission.

Nov. 7 The first cartoon featuring an **elephant** to symbolize the Republican Party appeared in *Harper's Weekly*. Entitled "Third Term Panic," the cartoon by Thomas Nast showed Republican concern that Pres. Grant would be elected for a third term on the Democratic ticket.

Dec. 7 About **70 blacks were killed** when they attacked the courthouse at Vicksburg, Miss. The blacks rioted over the intimidation and ejection of a carpetbag sheriff by the whites of Vicksburg.

Among **books published** this year was *The Gilded Age* by Mark Twain and Charles Dudley Warner, a novel that epitomized the corruption of post–Civil War America. In the character of Colonel Sellers the authors represented "the grandfather of all American boosters ... with his dreams of an immediate future gilding a present of poverty-stricken, whiskey-soaked, rough-and-tumble frontier." Other books published this year included the first American edition of *Lorna Doone* by Richard Doddridge Blackmore; *The Circuit Rider,* a major novel by Edward Eggleston, with a pioneer preacher as its main character whose pulpit was the saddle of his horse and whose flock was the citizenry of communities without churches; *The Hanging of the Crane,* an ambitious long poem by Henry Wadsworth Longfellow, not generally classed among his best works; and *The Old Regime in Canada* by Francis Parkman, a volume in his cycle of histories about the struggles of the English and the French for dominion over North America.

Erection of **Soldiers' and Sailors' Monument** on Boston Common marked the beginning of a distinctive type of American public sculpture. The monument, by Martin Milmore, typified a style characterized by a heavy base crowned by an allegorical figure such as Liberty or Victory, with statues of men beneath.

Pneumatic foundation caissons in bridge construction were first used on the Eads Bridge over the Mississippi R. at St. Louis, Mo.

1875

One of the worst scandals of the administration of Pres. Ulysses S. Grant surfaced this year with revelations involving what was called the Whiskey Ring. A group of distillers, chiefly in St. Louis, Mo., and corrupt Treasury Department officials had conspired to defraud the government of millions of dollars in taxes on liquor. Two hundred thirty-eight persons were indicted on May 10. Later in the year Grant's private secretary, Orville E. Babcock, was also indicted. Grant intervened to make sure Babcock was not convicted. Babcock retired shortly after his acquittal.

Jan. 14 The **Specie Resumption Act** was passed, providing for redemption of fractional currency for specie beginning on Jan. 1, 1879. Circulating greenbacks were to be reduced to $300,000,000.

Jan. 30 The **Hawaiian Reciprocity Treaty** was signed.

The growing place of music in cultural life was indicated by the appointment in 1875 of John Knowles Paine to a professorship of music at Harvard, the first such post at any American university. Paine was a composer and organist, but his importance in American music lay in his educational efforts. Many of his pupils became notable composers.

Among **books published** this year was *A Passionate Pilgrim and Other Tales* by Henry James. This early collection showed the author's insight and psychological realism in such tales as "The Madonna of the Future" and "Madame de Mauves." An international theme runs through most of the stories. Other books published this year included *Honest John Vane* by John William De Forest, a novel dealing with the economic and political corruption of the period, with particular reference to the Crédit Mobilier scandal; *Sevenoaks* by Josiah Gilbert

only 10,000 lbs. of it were produced, but in 1880 the output was 80,500,000 lbs.

The **Chautauqua movement** was founded by Lewis Miller, an Ohio industrialist, and John H. Vincent, a Methodist clergyman, as an annual summer meeting for the training of Sunday school teachers. The movement derived its name from the site of its meetings on the shores of Lake Chautauqua, N.Y. The meetings gradually expanded their educational scope and the size of the student body.

Osteopathy, a new medical discipline, was developed by Dr. Andrew T. Still of Baldwin, Kans.

The **first steel arch bridge** to span the Mississippi R., built by James Eads, opened at St. Louis, Mo. Construction was in process for seven years. Immediately afterward, Eads began work on the South Pass of the Mississippi delta, to clear the river of mud and improve navigability. He built jetties of willow mattress, which turned the current so that it cut through and washed out the bars of silt blocking the mouth of the river and made the port of New Orleans deep enough for ocean vessels.

The **third rail,** which revolutionized municipal rail transportation by providing convenient distribution of electric power, was invented by Stephen Field of New York City.

Mar. 22   The first **Young Men's Hebrew Association** in the U.S. was organized in New York City. Its first president was Lewis May.

The **first public zoo** in the U.S., the Philadelphia Zoological Gardens of Philadelphia, Pa., was opened.

The **potato bug,** also known as the Colorado beetle, was discovered in the Rocky Mts. in 1824. By 1874 it reached the states along the Atlantic coast. The female beetle lays batches of 500–1000 orange eggs in clusters on the back of leaves where the larva have a ready supply of food. Indigenous to the U.S., the potato bug does great damage to potato crops when uncontrolled.

May 26   The second annual **Preakness Stakes** was won by Culpepper, with a time of 2:56½. The jockey was W. Donohue.

June 13   The eighth annual **Belmont Stakes** was won by Saxon, with a time of 2:39½. The jockey was G. Barbee. From this year to 1889 the distance run was one and one-half miles.

Aug. 21   **Henry Ward Beecher** was sued for $100,000 by Theodore Tilton, accusing the famous preacher of committing adultery with Tilton's wife. The trial attracted national publicity and controversy, especially since the jury handed down a split decision, 9–3, in favor of Beecher. A special investigating committee made up of members of his congregation, the Plymouth Congregational Church, Brooklyn, N.Y., had previously exonerated Beecher after interviewing 36 people, including Tilton.

1875

Dwight L. Moody, a new, forceful personality in evangelical Christianity, began his life's work this year with revival meetings in the East. Moody was to play a major role in the religious life of the country to the end of the nineteenth century. He preached a simple biblical message, concentrating on the salvation of individual souls at a time when many clergymen were turning to social reform. Moody founded the Northfield School for Girls (1879) and the Mt. Hermon School for Boys (1881) in his native town of Northfield, Mass., and the Moody Institute (1889) in Chicago.

Hebrew Union College, one of the oldest rabbinical seminaries in the U.S., was founded in Cincinnati, Ohio. Its first president was Isaac Mayer Wise. The college opened with an enrollment of nine students.

Luther Burbank set up a plant nursery in Santa Rosa,

The traveling circus was evolving into "the greatest show on earth," aided by that master of showmanship, Phineas T. Barnum, who had organized such a show in 1871. His tent covered the largest area of any in the world and he introduced the three-ring circus. In 1881 Barnum merged his circus with that of James A. Bailey to form an even bigger enterprise. Barnum's greatest single coup came in 1882 when he purchased Jumbo, the world's largest elephant, from the Royal Zoological Gardens of London.

Football uniforms were first worn at a match between Harvard and Tufts.

The **baseball glove** was introduced by Charles G. Waite, first baseman for a Boston team. The glove was unpadded.

May 17   The **first Kentucky Derby** was run at Churchill Downs, Ky. The winner was Aristides, with a time of 2:37¼. The jockey was Oliver Lewis.

It provided that no Hawaiian territory be turned over to any third power.

Mar. 1 A **Civil Rights Act** was passed guaranteeing blacks equal rights in public places. The law also prohibited exclusion of blacks from jury duty.

May 7 In a **steamship disaster,** some 200 persons were killed when the steamer *Schiller,* en route from New York City to Hamburg, ran aground on the Scilly Isles, off the southwest coast of England.

May 27 A **fire** destroyed the French Catholic Church in South Holyoke, Mass., killing 120 persons.

Nov. 4 **Two hundred thirty-six persons drowned** off Cape Flattery, Wash., when the steamer *Pacific* sank after a collision.

Dec. 4 **William Marcy "Boss" Tweed** escaped from prison at Ludlow St., New York City, and fled to Cuba.

Dec. 15 A resolution against **presidential third terms** was overwhelmingly approved by the House of Representatives. It was directed against Pres. Ulysses S. Grant's third-term ambitions, although he had reluctantly disclaimed any intention of running in a statement made on May 29.

Holland, a novel about a powerful and corrupt New England businessman; *A Foregone Conclusion* by William Dean Howells, a novel set in Venice; and *From Jest to Earnest,* a novel by Edward Payson Roe.

A vogue for small plaster statuary groups from casts by **John Rogers** reached its height. Most of his groups were narrative in intent, depicting such scenes as *The Checker Players,* and *The Slave Market.* Rogers cast and sold the reproductions himself, selling more than 100,000 altogether.

A **masterpiece of realism** in the style of Jean Léon Gérôme and Léon Joseph Florentin Bonnat was Thomas Eakins' *Gross Clinic.* The objectivity with which Eakins approached the subject corresponded to the scientific objectivity of the doctor who is the subject.

Dec. 25 The **Chicago *Daily News*** was founded by Melville E. Stone, William Dougherty, and Percy Meggy with a trial issue. Daily publication began in Jan. 1876. In a few months it was purchased by Victor F. Lawson, who hired Stone as editor and later made him a partner.

1876

For the first time since the Civil War, the Democratic Party was optimistic about its chances of winning a presidential election. The Grant administration was riddled with scandals, and the depression that had begun in 1873 had not completely disappeared. The Republicans were in disarray. Pres. Ulysses S. Grant would have liked a third term, but had strong opposition within the party. Rep. James G. Blaine, Republican of Maine, was favored by one faction but he too was touched by scandal. He lost the nomination but in July took a seat in the Senate. In the campaign the Democrats blamed the Republicans for the nation's ills, while the Republicans "waved the bloody shirt," still taking credit for having saved the Union during the Civil War. Neither party discussed the long-standing argument between so-called hard money businessmen and soft money proponents, mostly farmers.

Southern congressmen, in an almost solid bloc, won enough northern support to enact **repeal of the Southern Homestead Act** of 1866, which had been designed to prevent domination of public lands in the South by speculators, monopolists, and former Confederates. The act had preserved 47,500,000 acres of the public lands in Alabama, Arkansas, Florida, Louisiana, and Mississippi exclusively for homesteaders by ruling out cash purchases and rights of preemption. The act, applying

An unusual book published this year was not intended for personal reading but to help organizations of all kinds conduct their meetings with standard rules. The book was *Pocket Manual of Rules of Order for Deliberative Assemblies;* the author was Henry M. Robert, an Army engineer. The small volume was at once popular, as many groups recognized it as a means of ensuring order and fairness in business meetings. It was revised in 1915 and 1943 and has continued to be the standard work, known to millions as *Robert's Rules of Order.*

Among **books published** this year was *Clarel: A Poem and Pilgrimage in the Holy Land* by Herman Melville. Published in two volumes, the work was based on Melville's trip to the Holy Land in 1857. Its publication did nothing to enhance the reputation of the author, then working as a customs inspector in New York City. Other books published this year included *Helen's Babies* by John Habberton, a humorous novel that was enormously popular; *Roderick Hudson,* a novel by Henry James; *Among My Books: Second Series* by James Russell Lowell; *The One Fair Woman,* a novel by Joaquin Miller, the "poet of the Sierras"; *The Adventures of Tom Sawyer* by Mark Twain, an American classic that became his most popular book but was barred from libraries in Brooklyn,

Business and Industry; Science; Education; Philosophy and Religion III	IV Sports; Social Issues and Crime; Folkways; Fashion; Holidays

Calif., in which he developed new strains of berries, fruits, vegetables, grains, and grasses.

Henry Bergh became the first president of the new **Society for the Prevention of Cruelty to Children.** In 1866 Bergh had incorporated the Society for the Prevention of Cruelty to Animals after a long and lonely crusade. The Society for the Prevention of Cruelty to Children was organized with the help of Elbridge T. Gerry, and quickly became the more prominent society, though Bergh remained more intimately asssociated with efforts to eliminate cruelty to animals.

The **Christian Science** movement received a powerful impetus with publication of *Science and Health* by Mary Baker Eddy.

Mar. 15 The **first American cardinal,** Archbishop John McCloskey of New York City, was invested at St. Patrick's Cathedral.

Nov. 17 The **Theosophical Society of America** was founded in New York City by Mme. Helena Petrovna Blavatsky. The society was formed to unite humanity in universal brotherhood without distinctions as to race or creed; encourage the study of Eastern cultures; and to investigate unexplained laws of nature and the psychical powers latent in people.

May 28 The third annual **Preakness Stakes** was won by Tom Ochiltree, with a time of 2:43½. The jockey was L. Hughes.

June 12 The ninth annual **Belmont Stakes** was won by Calvin, with a time of 2:42¼. The jockey was Robert Swim.

Nov. 23 A **National Railroad Convention** was held at St. Louis, Mo., for two days beginning Nov. 23. The citizens of St. Louis were the formal sponsors of the convention and issued invitations after a mass meeting that also drew up an entertainment program. Over 800 delegates, representing 31 states and territories, attended. It was claimed to be the largest formal delegation ever convened in the West. The assembly hall was decorated with banners that read "Westward the Star of Empire Takes Its Way," "Twenty Millions of People seek an acceptable Route to the Pacific," "There is the East—There is India," and "The Grange Railway—The Texas Pacific." Jefferson Davis, chairman of the Mississippi delegation, declined a seat on the dais after protesting that, if all the commanding generals from either side of the war were to sit in the place of honor, there would not be enough room.

1876

Before the twentieth century most American scientists worked with practical objectives in mind. One of the few who devoted himself to what may be called pure research was Josiah Willard Gibbs, at Yale University. His work later had practical applications in industry. Gibbs's most important contribution was his theory of thermodynamics, the basis for modern physical chemistry and chemical engineering. His most important publication was "On the Equilibrium of Heterogeneous Substances," which appeared this year in *Transactions of the Connecticut Academy of Arts and Sciences.* The second half of this classic paper was published in 1878. Gibbs also contributed to statistical mechanics, vector analysis, crystallography, and electromagnetic theory.

Formation of the **American Chemical Society** reflected the growing specialization of American science scholarship. The society was incorporated in 1877, reorganized in 1891 to permit national participation, and finally incorporated under a federal charter in 1937. The purpose of the society was to encourage the broad and liberal advancement of all branches of chemistry, promote research, raise the standards of practice and ethics among chemists, add to and disseminate chemical

The nation celebrated its 100th birthday with a world's fair, the Centennial Exposition, held appropriately in Philadelphia, where the Declaration of Independence was written and proclaimed in 1776. The exposition covered 450 acres. Each state had its own building and 50 foreign nations sent exhibits. Between May and November, almost 10,000,000 people visited the fairgrounds. The most popular attraction proved to be Machinery Hall, with its vast displays of inventions heralding the latest technology.

Polo was brought to the U.S. by James Gordon Bennett, publisher of the New York *Herald.* The sport was launched at Dickel's Riding Academy, New York City.

The **first fraternity house** in the U.S. was opened at Williams College, Williamstown, Mass. It was occupied by a chapter of Kappa Alpha Society.

The **catcher's mask** used in baseball was invented by Fred W. Thayer of Harvard University.

In track, the **100-yard race** was run for the first time in ten seconds, by Horace H. Lee of Pennsylvania.

The **tenderloin section of New York City** (24th to 40th streets between 5th and 7th avenues) was so named by Police Captain A. S. Williams, who is reported to have said, on being transferred to the West 30th St. precinct: "I've been having chuck steak ever since I've been on

Exploration and Settlement; Wars; Government; Civil Rights; Statistics   **I**

II   **Publishing; Arts and Music; Popular Entertainment; Architecture; Theater**

to public lands of the South alone, aimed to ensure that freedmen would get their promised 40 acres and a mule. When the southerners returned to the Senate and the House, they joined in an effort to force repeal of the Southern Homestead Act, but the opposition held firm for ten years. Repeal of the act opened the way for speculators to snatch up rich southern timberland. Most of the dealers were from the North. They did not use the lands to contribute to the general development of the South but held on to them and kept the South from competing with northern industry and agriculture.

1876–1877   In **congressional elections** the Republicans lost ground in the Senate but held a 39–36 majority, with one seat going to a minor party. In the House the Democrats held a 153–140 majority.

May 17   The **Prohibition Party** held its second national convention in Cleveland, Ohio. Green Clay Smith of Kentucky was nominated for president and Gideon T. Stewart of Ohio for vice president.

May 18   The **Greenback Party** held its first national convention at Indianapolis, Ind. The convention named Peter Cooper of New York for president and Samuel F. Perry of Ohio for vice president.

June 14–16   The **Republican National Convention** nominated **Rutherford B. Hayes** of Ohio for president. His running mate was William A. Wheeler of New York.

June 25   At the Battle of **Little Big Horn** in Montana, Gen. George A. Custer and all of the 265 men of the Seventh Cavalry were slaughtered by Sitting Bull's Sioux Indians.

June 27–29   The **Democratic National Convention** nominated **Samuel J. Tilden** of New York for president and Thomas A. Hendricks of Indiana for vice president.

July 25   Free and unlimited **coinage of silver** was proposed in a bill introduced in the House by Richard P. Bland of Missouri.

Aug. 1   **Colorado was admitted to the Union**, the 38th state.

Nov. 7   The **presidential election** gave Samuel J. Tilden, the Democratic candidate, a popular vote plurality of 250,000, but Republicans refused to concede on the grounds that returns from Florida, Louisiana, South Carolina, and Oregon were in dispute. Hayes needed the electoral votes of those states to win. On Dec. 6 two different sets of electoral returns were reported from the four states. The electoral vote ultimately was to be determined by a special 15-member electoral commission.

Nov. 23   William Marcy "Boss" Tweed, after his capture in Spain, was delivered to authorities in New York City to serve his prison sentence.

Dec. 5   New York City's worst **theater fire** occurred at

N.Y., Denver, Colo., and elsewhere as being unfit for young readers; and *My Winter on the Nile* by Charles Dudley Warner, a book of travel sketches based on the author's 1875 trip to Africa and the Middle East.

Sidney Lanier composed an ode, "Psalm of the West," which commemorated the 100 years of American history since the American Revolution.

William Cullen Bryant composed two of his most memorable poems, "A Lifetime" and "The Flood of Years."

James Russell Lowell wrote "An Ode for the Fourth of July, 1876."

Emma Lazarus wrote "The Spagnoletto," a verse tragedy set in Italy in the age of the Baroque.

Joel Chandler Harris began a 31-year association with the *Atlanta Constitution*. His first Uncle Remus story appeared there in 1879.

The painter **John La Farge** was given the first major assignment for mural decoration in a U.S. church by the architect of Trinity Church, Boston, H. H. Richardson. The Romanesque church provided La Farge with ample space to display his talents.

Winslow Homer produced a lively painting evoking the sea and the exhilaration of sailing before the wind in his *Breezing Up*. It foreshadowed his later concentration on sea subjects.

The gigantic **statue of *Daniel Webster*** now standing in Central Park, the work of Thomas Ball, was unveiled. Fourteen feet in height, the statue was cast in Munich. Popularity of the work brought Ball orders for statues of Josiah Quincy and Charles Sumner.

An excellent piece of **public statuary** was the bronze *Chancellor Robert R. Livingston* in the National Hall of Statuary in the U.S. Capitol, by Erastus D. Palmer of Albany. Exhibited at the Centennial Exposition at Philadelphia, it received a medal of the first class.

The **nature of sculpture** changed in America after the Centennial Exposition of 1876 in Philadelphia. American sculptors were able to study works of Europeans

| Business and Industry; Science; Education; Philosophy and Religion | III | | IV | Sports; Social Issues and Crime; Folkways; Fashion; Holidays |

knowledge, and promote scientific interests for the betterment of public welfare and education.

The **first photograph of the solar spectrum** was taken by John William Draper, a physicist and astronomer at New York University. Draper was credited in 1840 with the first photograph of the moon.

A **mimeograph** device was invented by Thomas A. Edison in his laboratory at Menlo Park, N.J. The machine employed a stencil for making impressions. The impressions were inserted into a set frame and ink was applied. It was probably the first practical duplicating machine.

The **New York Society for Ethical Culture** was established by Dr. Felix Adler. In the same year Adler founded the first free kindergarten in New York City in connection with his Ethical Culture School.

Central Park was completed along the design of its planners, Frederick Law Olmsted and Calvert Vaux, as a growing part of New York City. It was to be expanded as the city expanded.

The *Harvard Lampoon,* the first undergraduate humor magazine in the U.S., was started at Harvard University.

The world's longest **cantilever bridge** (1200 feet) was designed and constructed by Charles S. Smith for the Cincinnati Southern Railway. The bridge crossed a canyon 275 feet deep. A professional and financial risk for Smith, the bridge had no precedent anywhere and was a technical achievement of the first magnitude.

The **Dewey Decimal System** of classification of library books was originated by Melvil Dewey. The Dewey system permits subdivision and expansion of file entries without the necessity of rearrangement. Dewey divided knowledge into nine classes and assigned a number to each: (1) philosophy, (2) religion, (3) sociology, (4) philology, (5) natural science, (6) useful arts, (7) fine arts, (8) literature, and (9) history. These nine classes were broken down into nine subdivisions, numbered one to nine, and each subdivision was further separated into nine sections. The Dewey Decimal System was intended for use by the American Library Association, established in the same year with Dewey as one of the original founders.

Charles Sanders Peirce, Harvard logician-philosopher, was the inventor of pragmatism, the most typical of American philosophies. He formulated his famous original pragmatist maxim: "Consider what effects, that might conceivably have practical bearings, we conceive the object of our conception to have. Then, our conception of these effects is the whole of our conception of the object."

the force, and now I'm going to have a bit of tender-loin." The expression was taken up by the press and soon was applied to the vice-laden sections of any city.

The **Intercollegiate Association of Amateur Athletes of America** (ICAAAA) was founded at Saratoga, N.Y., by delegates from 14 U.S. colleges participating in crew and track events held July 20–21. The organization was the earliest significant intercollegiate sports association in the U.S. Amherst, Bowdoin, Brown, CCNY, Columbia, Cornell, Dartmouth, Harvard, Princeton, Trinity, Union, Wesleyan, Williams, and Yale were original members.

Jan. 1 The **Philadelphia Mummers' parade** was organized in its present form in celebration of the American centennial. The parade was sponsored mainly by the Silver Crown New Year's Association. The Mummers' parade dates back to early colonial times. It combines the boisterous Swedish custom of celebrating the New Year with the English tradition of the Mummers' play, in which St. George slays the dragon. The city of Philadelphia did not officially recognize the parade until 1901, when 42 fraternal organizations received permits to stage a parade for which prizes would be awarded for costumes, music, and comic antics.

Feb. 2 **Professional baseball** became entrenched in the U.S. with the formation of the National League, consisting of teams in Philadelphia, Hartford, Boston, Chicago, Cincinnati, Louisville, St. Louis, and New York. The first president of the league was Morgan G. Bulkley. Chicago won the pennant with a season's record of 52 wins and 14 losses.

Apr. 2 In the **first official National League baseball game,** Boston beat Philadelphia 6–5, with Jim O'Rourke getting the first hit.

May 15 The second annual **Kentucky Derby** was won by Vagrant, with a time of 2:38¼. The jockey was Robert Swim.

May 23 The **first no-hitter** in National League history was pitched by Joe Borden of Boston. Borden lost his effectiveness soon after and ended the season as the club's groundskeeper.

May 25 The fourth annual **Preakness Stakes** was won by Shirley, with a time of 2:44¾. The jockey was G. Barbee.

June 10 The tenth annual **Belmont Stakes** was won by Algerine, with a time of 2:40½. The jockey was W. Donohue.

Aug. 11–12 The **America's Cup** was successfully defended by the yacht *Madeleine,* which won two straight races from the Canadian challenger *Countess of Dufferin.*

1876 – 1877 *PRES.* ULYSSES S. GRANT, RUTHERFORD B. HAYES   320

| Exploration and Settlement; Wars; Government; Civil Rights; Statistics | I | | II | Publishing; Arts and Music; Popular Entertainment; Architecture; Theater |

the Brooklyn Theater, when 289 of 1200 in the audience were killed.

Dec. 12 A **prohibition amendment** to the Constitution was introduced for the first time. It was proposed before the House in a bill by Henry W. Blair of New Hampshire.

Dec. 29 A **railroad accident killed 84** when the *Pacific Express* plunged into a gorge at Ashtabula, Ohio. The accident occurred when the bridge spanning the gorge cracked in the center as the passenger train passed over it.

who had turned away from neoclassical style. Among the artists exhibited were Cordier, Cain, Dalou, De Groot, Rodin, and Vincotte.

Feb. 28 A **monument** of excellence is the statue of *Ethan Allen,* Revolutionary hero, by Larkin G. Mead, today standing in the National Hall of Statuary in the Capitol. Mead depicted Col. Allen demanding surrender of Fort Ticonderoga.

1877

The nation had never before faced a dispute over the results of a presidential election but it did this year. A candidate needed 185 electoral votes to win and Samuel J. Tilden, the Democratic candidate, clearly had 184. In dispute were the 19 electoral votes of three states still under carpetbag rule—Florida, Louisiana, and South Carolina—plus one vote in Oregon. In Congress both parties agreed on Jan. 29 to establish an electoral commission to decide the issue. The commission, with five members from each house of Congress and five members from the Supreme Court, was made up of eight Republicans and seven Democrats. All the commission's decisions were to fall along party lines. On Mar. 2 Congress accepted the commission's decision, which awarded all the disputed votes to the Republican candidate, Rutherford B. Hayes, who thus received 185 electoral votes to Tilden's 184. The Republicans were accused of offering southern Democrats economic favors for their region if they supported Hayes's claim. In any event, the new president showed a conciliatory attitude toward the South: the last federal troops were withdrawn and there was no further effort to protect the rights of blacks. Reconstruction was over.

Anti-Chinese riots broke out in California. They were incited by the Workingmen's Party, formed by Denis Kearney to protest the use of cheap Chinese labor.

Jan. 2 **Carpetbag government** ended in Florida when George F. Drew, Democrat, was inaugurated as governor.

Mar. 5 **Rutherford B. Hayes was inaugurated president** of the United States. He had been sworn in on Saturday, Mar. 3, and the inauguration was held a day late because Mar. 4 fell on a Sunday. A Republican, Hayes served one term.

Apr. 10 **Carpetbag government** ended in South Carolina when federal troops evacuated Columbia.

Apr. 24 **Carpetbag rule** ended in Louisiana, the last southern state to regain control of its internal government. Withdrawal of federal troops here and in South

Two actors destined to appear together many times and to be among the most popular and successful of their era made their debuts this year on opposite coasts. In Philadelphia, Otis Skinner appeared at the Museum Theater, and in San Francisco the Polish actress Helena Modjeska played the lead role in *Adrienne Lecouvreur.* The two would ultimately tour the U.S. together. Skinner became best known for his role in *Kismet* (1911). Madame Modjeska in 1883 played the role of Nora in *A Doll's House* in Louisville, Ky., the first American production of a play by Henrik Ibsen.

Among **books published** this year was *Deephaven* by Sarah Orne Jewett, one of America's finest novelists in the use of local color. The author's first major work, *Deephaven* contained sketches of a New England town that resembled her own South Berwick, Maine. Other books published this year included *Birds and Poets* by John Burroughs, marking the author as a worthy successor to Henry David Thoreau; *The American* by Henry James, continuing the author's exploration of contrasts and conflicts of American life in Europe; and *Poems* by Sidney Lanier, a volume which would be enlarged and reissued in 1884.

American provincialism, particularly puritanical objections to the nude, was highlighted in a painting by Thomas Eakins, *William Rush Carving the Allegorical Figure of the Schuylkill River.* In addition to the artist and a nude figure, a chaperone is shown seated with her knitting. Eakins' insistence on his students drawing from the nude caused a demand for his resignation from the Pennsylvania Academy of the Fine Arts. In support of Eakins, Walt Whitman said, "Eakins is not a painter; he is a force."

A **libel suit** by James Abbott McNeill Whistler against the English critic John Ruskin grew out of the exhibition of Whistler's *The Falling Rocket.* Writing of Whistler, Ruskin remarked, "His ill-educated conceit so nearly approached imposture. I have seen and heard much Cockney impudence before now, but never expected to

| Business and Industry; Science; Education; Philosophy and Religion | III | | IV | Sports; Social Issues and Crime; Folkways; Fashion; Holidays |

Mar. 7 The first U.S. patent for the **telephone** was awarded to Alexander Graham Bell.

Oct. 6 The **American Library Association was established** in Philadelphia by a group of leading public and university librarians for the purpose of supplying "the best reading for the largest number at the least expense." Melvil Dewey, librarian at Columbia and originator of the Dewey Decimal System, F. W. Poole of the Chicago Public Library, and Charles Cutter of the Boston Athenaeum were prominent founders of the association.

Sept. 7 The **world heavyweight bare knuckle boxing championship** was won by Joe Goss of England, who beat Tom Allen in a 27-round bout at Covington, Ky.

Nov. 23 **Rules for football** were discussed at the invitation of Princeton, by delegates from Yale, Harvard, Rutgers, Columbia, and Princeton meeting at Massasoit House, Springfield, Mass. Princeton had recently adopted Harvard's rules, which in turn were chiefly based on the rules of the British Rugby Union, and these were adopted by all colleges represented at the meeting. The Intercollegiate Football Association grew out of the meeting.

1877

Strikes on a national scale, accompanied by violence, occurred this year for the first time in American history. The labor trouble began on July 17 when Baltimore & Ohio Railroad workers struck. The line had cut wages 10% even though it was paying large dividends to its stockholders. Violence broke out first in Martinsburg, W.Va., where federal troops were used to restore order. On July 20 nine strikers were killed in Baltimore when state militia fired on a crowd. On July 21 strikers in Pittsburgh rioted, destroying some 2000 freight cars. Police aided by cavalry troops attacked a gathering in Chicago on July 26, causing more bloodshed. The strikes spread to other railroads and to many other industries. In the end, most rail workers gained little or nothing, but coal miners won a 10% wage increase. Although the strikes were not especially successful, they did bring more unity to labor and generally promoted the growth of labor unions, which had suffered during the recent depression.

Labor union influence was in decline as the number of national unions dwindled from 30 to 9 and membership dropped from 300,000 to 50,000.

Root beer came on the market, produced and distributed by Charles Elmer Hires. The popularity of his product led to a worldwide business.

The detection of two **satellites of Mars** by Asaph Hall made a major contribution to astronomy. This discovery, made at the Naval Observatory in Washington, D.C., was ranked as the most significant since the discovery of Neptune in 1846.

The first interconnection of lines by a **telephone switchboard** was made in Boston. A crude system of metal blocks and plugs at a burglar alarm office permitted connection of lines from several outside stations. The first regular exchange went into operation following year in New Haven.

Flag Day was observed for the first time this year, on June 14, to mark the centennial of the adoption of the stars and stripes design by the Continental Congress. It is not a legal holiday, but is observed by presidential proclamation. The question of who designed the flag has never been resolved. Possibly it was Francis Hopkinson, who was chairman of the Navy board of the Congress, where the design originated.

The first annual **Westminster Kennel Club dog show** was held at Gilmore's Garden in New York City; it was sponsored by the Westminster Kennel Club. Setters of English, Irish, and Gordon types, pointers, spaniels, mastiffs, St. Bernards, terriers, and poodles were well represented.

A new **baseball rule** exempted the batter from a time at bat if he was walked. This rule affected the determination of a batter's average rather than actual play. Another new rule stipulated that a substitute player could replace a starting player only before the fourth inning. The National League pennant winner was Boston, with a record of 31 wins, 17 losses.

May 22 The third annual **Kentucky Derby** was won by Baden Baden, with a time of 2:38. The jockey was William Walker.

Carolina was a part of the bargain between Republicans and southern Democrats for quiet acceptance of the decision of the electoral commission.

June–Oct. **Nez Percé Indians** went to war with the U.S. in Idaho. The war ended when federal troops captured Chief Joseph and evacuated the Indians to a reservation.

June 15 The **first black was graduated** from the U.S. Military Academy at West Point, Henry O. Flipper.

Nov. 23 The perennial **fishing rights problem** along the eastern coastline of North America was settled by a commission created by the Treaty of Washington (1871). Reciprocity between Canada and the U.S. was agreed on, and Canada was awarded $5,500,000 because of its greater concessions.

hear a coxcomb ask two hundred guineas for flinging a pot of paint in the public's face." Whistler sued for libel and was awarded one farthing.

The **cakewalk** became a popular feature of minstrel shows following the success of a number called "Walking for Dat Cake" by the New York musical comedy team of Harrigan and Hart. The cakewalk now was an imitation of antebellum plantation cakewalks, set to syncopated tunes taken from black sources and later developed into ragtime.

June 1 The **Society of American Artists** was founded by Augustus Saint-Gaudens, Wyatt Eaton, Walter Shirlaw, and Miss Helena De Kay. The new society was formed to exhibit the works of artists who were being held back by the Academy of Design.

1878

Epidemics struck the nation fairly often during this period, when causes and cures were not known. Especially rampant this year was yellow fever, which swept through the South. New Orleans was hardest hit, and as people fled the disease there they spread it elsewhere. Louisiana, Alabama, Mississippi, and Tennessee were most affected, but the epidemic reached as far north as Cincinnati, Ohio. There were 24,000 cases in New Orleans and 4000 fatalities. The national toll was 14,000. Cigars and whiskey were recommended by some as remedies. In Memphis, Anna "Madame Annie" Cook, who operated the Mansion House brothel, discharged her prostitutes to provide hospital quarters. She died in September of yellow fever contracted while caring for patients. The epidemic broke out again in 1879.

1878–1879 In **congressional elections** the Democrats gained control of both houses of Congress for the first time since 1858. The Democratic majorities were 42–33 in the Senate, with one seat going to a minor party; 149–130 in the House, with 14 minor party seats.

Jan. 14 The **Supreme Court** declared unconstitutional any state law requiring a railroad to provide equal accommodations for all passengers regardless of race or color.

Jan. 17 A **commercial treaty** with Samoa was signed. The harbor at Pago Pago was reserved for a coaling station for U.S. naval vessels.

Feb. 22 The **Greenback-Labor Party** was formed at a convention held in Toledo, Ohio. Ohio workers had founded the National Party in 1877, while workers in other states had already joined the Greenback Party. The new party was a fusion of both elements. At its first nominating convention, held June 9–10, 1880, in Chicago, Ill., the party chose Gen. James B. Weaver

This was a landmark year for newspaper publishing in the U.S., although it was not perceived as such at the time. On Dec. 9 Joseph Pulitzer, who had been involved in politics and publishing for a number of years, bought the St. Louis *Dispatch*, a bankrupt evening newspaper, for $2500. Pulitzer calculated that after the purchase he had enough operating capital to keep going for 17 weeks. Almost immediately he merged his paper with John A. Dillon's St. Louis *Post,* and within a year the new paper, the St. Louis *Post-Dispatch,* had doubled in circulation and was making money. From this point Pulitzer turned his interest away from politics and toward journalism. His influence would eventually change the newspaper business around the world.

Among **books published** this year was *The Leavenworth Case* by Anna Katharine Green, the first in a score or more of best-selling mystery novels. Other books published this year included *Roxy* by Edward Eggleston, a novel set in nineteenth-century Indiana; *The Europeans* by Henry James, which reversed the usual plot in the author's novels by introducing European characters into an American setting; *Through the Dark Continent* by Henry M. Stanley, the explorer; and *History of American Literature, 1607–1765* by Moses Coit Tyler, a pioneering study of early American literature.

Fire hazards in U.S. theaters were found by a survey to cause one theater in every four to burn down within four years of erection. The average life of theater buildings was 12 years. Gas lighting, inflammable scenery, and too few exits combined to make theater-going risky.

The first successful **Sunday edition** of a daily newspaper was published by the *Philadelphia Times.*

| Business and Industry; Science; Education; Philosophy and Religion III | IV Sports; Social Issues and Crime; Folkways; Fashion; Holidays |

Oct.   The **American Humane Association** was formed at Cleveland, Ohio, by representatives of various societies for the prevention of cruelty to animals. Delegates were particularly concerned about the conditions under which livestock were transported to slaughterhouses and called on cattlemen and railroad companies to develop a cattle car that would provide facilities for water and food.

Dec. 6   Thomas A. Edison completed his **phonograph.** He filed for a patent for the device on Dec. 15. The first full description of the phonograph appeared in *Scientific American* (Dec. 22), at whose New York offices Edison demonstrated its operation.

May 24   The fifth annual **Preakness Stakes** was won by Cloverbrook, with a time of 2:45½. The jockey was C. Holloway.

June 9   The 11th annual **Belmont Stakes** was won by Cloverbrook, with a time of 2:46. The jockey was C. Holloway.

1878

Law had been a widely practiced profession in the U.S. from the start. It was taught as early as 1779 by George Wythe in Virginia, and in 1784 by Tapping Reeve in Connecticut. There was not, however, a national organization for the legal profession until Aug. 21, 1878, when the American Bar Association was formed at Saratoga, N.Y., at a meeting called by the Connecticut Bar Association. James O. Broadhead was chosen the first president.

The **conflict between fundamentalism and science** had an early manifestation at Methodist-sponsored Vanderbilt University in Nashville, Tenn., where geologist Alexander Winchell was dismissed for his scientific contradictions of biblical chronology.

Albert A. Michelson published his first paper in the *American Journal of Science,* which he called "On a Method of Measuring the Velocity of Light." It was devoted to a method of determining the velocity of light, a project that occupied him for the rest of his life and made him the international authority on all questions relating to the subject. Michelson was equally concerned with experiments on the interference of light, helped clear the way for the discoveries of Albert Einstein, and, with Edward Morley, established the basic equipment and theory in spectroscopy.

A monograph by **John Wesley Powell, Report on the Lands of the Arid Region of the U.S.,** was published. In 1869, with a party of 11 men, Powell successfully navigated the gorges of the Green and Colorado rivers. In 1875 he published *Explorations of the Colorado River of the West,* in which he pointed out that the Uinta canyons were caused by rivers cutting through rock that was being gradually elevated.

Jan. 1   The **Knights of Labor** was established as a national organization at its first general assembly.

The bicycle first attracted attention when exhibited at Philadelphia's Centennial Exposition in 1876. It was first manufactured in the U.S. in 1878. These bicycles had front wheels about five feet in diameter, but the rear wheels were no more than a third this size. Such a machine was difficult and dangerous to ride. Nevertheless, bicycling became a fad. It became a popular sport after the safety bike, basically like the modern bicycle, was introduced in 1887. By 1882 there were about 20,-000 cyclists in the country; the League of American Wheelmen was formed in 1880. Cycling clubs held parades and competitive meets. Women could not ride the high-wheeled bikes but the tricycle was available to them.

Interest in **etiquette,** alongside the rising social aspirations of many Americans, was manifested in the publication *The Social Etiquette of New York.* In the next decade other books that had good sales were *P.G. or Perfect Gentleman* and *Success in Society.*

Wild West shows had their beginnings in exhibitions such as that given by Dr. W. F. Carver, who came to New York from California to show his art of shooting from the back of a racing horse.

The **National League baseball pennant** winner was Boston, with a season record of 41 wins and 19 defeats.

May 21   The fourth annual **Kentucky Derby** was won by Day Star, with a time of 2:37¼. The jockey was Jimmie Carter.

May 27   The sixth annual **Preakness Stakes** was won by Duke of Magenta, with a time of 2:41¾. The jockey was C. Holloway.

June 8   The 12th annual **Belmont Stakes** was won by

| Exploration and Settlement; Wars; Government; Civil Rights; Statistics | I | | II | Publishing; Arts and Music; Popular Entertainment; Architecture; Theater |

of Iowa and B. J. Chambers of Texas for the presidency and vice presidency respectively.

June 11 The **District of Columbia** was given a new government by Congress. The three commissioners, two residents and one U.S. Army engineer, were empowered to recommend governing legislation to Congress. Residents would have no direct voice in either local or national government. The president made appointments to the commission on June 23.

Dec. 17 **Greenbacks** reached par value on the Wall Street exchange for the first time since 1862.

Edward Kemeys, foremost among American sculptors of animals, exhibited his group *Bison and Wolves* at the Paris Salon. Returning to New York City he later produced, among others, the *Still Hunt* of Central Park, New York, and the *Wolves* of Fairmount Park, Philadelphia.

"The Marshes of Glynn," one of Sidney Lanier's finest poems, appeared anonymously in *Masque of Poets*, an anthology.

1879

Opposition to Chinese immigration, growing stronger in California in particular, came to a head with passage by Congress of a bill to restrict such immigration. Pres. Rutherford B. Hayes vetoed the bill on May 11 on the grounds that it violated the Burlingame Treaty of 1868, which established free immigration between the two countries. On May 7 California adopted a new constitution that forbade employment of Chinese laborers. Between 1850 and 1882 about 300,000 Chinese came to the U.S., almost all remaining on the Pacific coast. Chinese laborers had first been brought in large numbers in the 1860s to work on construction of the transcontinental railroad. The feeling against them at this time was economic rather than racial, since they worked for less than American workers.

Jan. 1 **Specie payment** was resumed by the U.S. government for the first time since it was suspended in 1861. Lack of specie payment had kept the currency in an unsettled state, partly contributing to the panic of 1873. Its approaching resumption caused much apprehension that the government could not provide enough coin to meet the expected demand. Mints had been kept open after hours to produce additional coinage, and there was surprise when little currency was presented by the public for redemption. This showed the extent to which public confidence in government fiscal policies had been restored since the Civil War. Payment of specie has been maintained ever since.

Feb. 15 **Women attorneys** won the right to argue cases before the U.S. Supreme Court by an act of Congress.

The history of one of the world's great entertainment palaces began this year when Madison Square Garden opened to the public in New York City. The first Garden was not elaborate, just a converted railroad structure at 26th St. In 1890 it was replaced by an elegant structure designed by the firm of McKim, Mead, and White; it featured a tower modeled after the Giralda in Seville, Spain. The second Garden was designed not for the average sports fan but for the wealthy and cultured citizens of New York and such events as the annual horse show of the Equestrian Society. This building was torn down and in 1925 replaced by a third Garden, on Eighth Ave. and 50th St. It was in turn replaced by the fourth and present Madison Square Garden, 31st to 33rd streets between Seventh and Eighth avenues.

Among **books published** this year was *Daisy Miller* by Henry James. It became the most popular of the author's early novels, perhaps because of an endearing young American heroine pitted against the complexities of Continental society. Other books published this year included *Old Creole Days* by George Washington Cable, the author's first collection of short stories, many of which first had appeared in *Scribner's Monthly*; *Progress and Poverty* by Henry George, a landmark work in economics concentrating on land and its value and advocating a "single tax" on land to replace all other forms of taxation; *A Lady of Aroostook* by William Dean Howells, the author's fourth novel; and *Rudder Grange* by Frank R. Stockton, a whimsically humorous novel that was so popular it inspired a sequel, *The Rudder Grangers Abroad* (1891).

The New England sculptor **Daniel Chester French** finished his bust of *Ralph Waldo Emerson* modeled from life. The face combines strength and vigor in general form with delicacy and sensitiveness in details. Other busts by French are *John Harvard* (1882), *General Cass* (1888), and *Thomas Starr King* (1890).

| Business and Industry; Science; Education; Philosophy and Religion   III | | IV   Sports; Social Issues and Crime; Folkways; Fashion; Holidays |

This was the first labor union to attempt to organize all workers into a single union. Its growth was rapid after the election in 1879 of Terence Vincent Powderly as its grand master workman.

Jan. 28 The first commercial **telephone exchange** opened at New Haven, Conn. It provided eight lines and served 21 telephones.

Oct. 15 The **first electric light company** was formed. It was the Edison Electric Light Company, located at 65 Fifth Ave., New York City.

Duke of Magenta, with a time of 2:43½. The jockey was L. Hughes.

Oct. 27 A celebrated **robbery** of $3,000,000 from the Manhattan Savings Institution in New York City was credited to a gang leader called George L. "Western" Leslie. Although two of his accomplices were convicted of the robbery, Leslie was not brought to trial because of lack of evidence. New York's chief of police attributed four-fifths of the bank holdups in the U.S. to Leslie, whose career was terminated by his murder in 1884.

1879

A venture in retailing that began in 1879 set the stage for development of nationwide chains of stores in various merchandising fields. This year, Frank W. Woolworth, having had a five-cent store fail in Utica, N.Y., opened a five-and-ten-cent store in Lancaster, Pa. It was a success and by the 1890s Woolworth operated 28 stores. By 1911 the F. W. Woolworth Company owned over 1000 such outlets. Chain stores aroused the antagonism of local merchants, but the public approved, as their steadily increasing patronage showed.

The first public **electrical street lighting** system in the U.S. was installed in Cleveland, Ohio, by Charles F. Brush. Wabash, Ind., was the first city to be completely lighted by electricity (Mar. 31, 1880). Brush used arc lights for illumination rather than incandescent lamps.

The **first intercity telephone** system was established between Boston and Lowell, Mass.

Carlisle Indian School was founded by Richard Henry Pratt at Carlisle, Pa., in unused Army barracks there. The first students, 82 Sioux, arrived on Oct. 6. At first offering only grammar school classwork, it later provided high school and teacher training curricula, with emphasis on English. The school was formally authorized by Congress in 1882. Pratt retired in 1904. Once famed for its football team, especially in the era of Jim Thorpe (1911–1912), the school declined and was abandoned in 1918.

Radcliffe College, Cambridge, Mass., was established as an adjunct to Harvard University. It was incorporated as The Society for the Collegiate Instruction of Women in 1882 and chartered under its present name in 1894. In the early 1970s Harvard and Radcliffe merged their admissions and administrative offices and provided equal access to facilities to men and women.

The **Church of Christ, Scientist** was organized by Mary Baker Eddy, founder of Christian Science. Mrs. Eddy, who resided in Lynn, Mass., was the author of *Science and Health with Key to the Scriptures,* published in 1875.

Two popular forms of recreation during this period were fox hunting and coaching. Clubs of wealthy persons on Long Island, in the suburbs of Philadelphia, and in New England, Virginia, and Maryland took up fox hunting in the English style. One newspaper described the last hunt of the season at Newport, R.I., this way: "All Newport mustered at the meet, the road to Southwick's Grove being literally chock-full of vehicles of every sort, shape, size, and description." Coaching was also imported from England and such resorts as Tuxedo, N.Y., and Lenox, Mass., found roads jammed with expensive dog-carts, buckboards, landaus, and phaetons. In New York City there was an annual coaching parade during which such rigs as four-in-hands and tally-hos coursed down Fifth Ave. The elite of society rode atop these magnificent vehicles, the men in striped waistcoats and silk top hats, the ladies with parasols held over enormous picture hats.

A new **baseball rule** allowed a batter to reach first base after receiving nine balls. The requirements for a walk to first base were reduced to eight balls in 1880, seven in 1881, six in 1884, raised to seven again in 1885, reduced to five in 1887, and four in 1889. This last requirement for a base on balls has persisted until the present time.

May 20 The fifth annual **Kentucky Derby** was won by Lord Murphy, with a time of 2:37. The jockey was Charlie Shauer.

May 24 The seventh annual **Preakness Stakes** was won by Harold, with a time of 2:40½. The jockey was L. Hughes.

June 5 The 13th annual **Belmont Stakes** was won by Spendthrift, with a time of 2:48¾. The jockey was Evans.

June 24 The first crew race for the **Childs Cup** was won by the University of Pennsylvania. The perpetual trophy was presented by George W. Childs of Phila-

Mar. 3 The **U.S. Geological Survey** was created within the Department of the Interior. It brought into one office four independent but government-subsidized surveys. Appointed director was the geologist and mining engineer Clarence King, who was experienced in survey work and a stickler for high professional standards.

Jan. 13 The second of the popular **Mulligan Guard plays**, *The Mulligan Guard Ball*, opened in New York City. This and its predecessor, *The Mulligan Guard Picnic* (1878), and its several successors, were farcical comedies containing music-hall lyrics satirizing burgeoning postwar military organizations. They featured Edward Harrigan playing a stereotyped Irishman and his partner, Tony Hart, as a German.

June 16 **Gilbert and Sullivan** were introduced to New York City with the U.S. opening of *H.M.S. Pinafore* at the Bowery Theater.

1880

The field for the presidential nominations of 1880 was wide open, Pres. Rutherford B. Hayes having announced he would not seek a second term. For the first time since the Civil War, the Republicans could not claim they alone saved the Union: the Democratic nominee, Gen. Winfield Scott Hancock, had fought in both the Mexican and Civil wars. The tariff was the only major issue and Hancock was inept at discussing it. The candidates for the most part stayed home, and for the first time interested supporters came in large numbers to visit them at their homes. James A. Garfield especially received gifts and poems composed for the occasion, watching silently as supporters trampled his flowers and shrubs.

The U.S. **Census** recorded a population of 50,155,783. The center of population was located at eight miles west by south of Cincinnati, Ohio (in western Kentucky). New York became the first state with a population above 5,000,000.

Mar. 1 **Excluding blacks from jury duty** was held unconstitutional by the Supreme Court. The decision was based on section five of the Fourteenth Amendment. It advised jury commissioners that they were forbidden to carry out their offices in such a way as to discriminate on racial grounds in the selection of jurors.

Apr. The **National Farmers' Alliance** was organized in Chicago, Ill. It was the forerunner of the Peoples' Party. The alliance was formed because the Grange had put itself in jeopardy through its political activity. The intention of the alliance was to unite farmers against discriminatory legislation. It was an open union without a central organization and, as a result, offered little on which to establish a national union, except such common bonds as the transportation problem.

The riches accumulated by the new millionaires of the Gilded Age provided them with the opportunity to become art collectors. This was also the period when public art museums began to appear, led by the Metropolitan Museum of Art in New York City. Formed in 1870, it opened its doors ten years later on its present site in Central Park, facing Fifth Ave. It was destined to become the most comprehensive art museum in the U.S. and one of the great museums of the world. Its early sponsors were from families of wealth and social position who tended to look down on the new rich. However, the latter were not ignored for long; their financial support was vital to the growth of such institutions as the Metropolitan. The new rich, in turn, were eager to secure the favorable publicity that came through substantial gifts to the arts.

Among **books published** this year was *Ben-Hur* by Lew Wallace, a highly successful historical romance about early Christians in the Roman Empire. It has not been out of print since and has twice been made into Hollywood movie extravaganzas. Other books published this year included *Democracy* by Henry Adams, a novel set in Washington, D.C.; *Ultima Thule* by Henry Wadsworth Longfellow, the venerable poet's next to last collection; *Bricks Without Straw* by Albion W. Tourgee, a novel of life in postwar North Carolina; and *A Tramp Abroad* by Mark Twain, another delightful travel narrative, based on a walking tour of Germany, Switzerland, and Italy.

Harriet Lothrop, writing under the name **Margaret Sidney,** saw the serial publication of her work *Five Little Peppers and How They Grew* in the periodical *Wide Awake.* Published in book form in 1881, it became a chil-

| Business and Industry; Science; Education; Philosophy and Religion | III | | IV | Sports; Social Issues and Crime; Folkways; Fashion; Holidays |

May 8 George B. Selden, inventor and patent attorney of Rochester, N.Y., filed the first patent application for a gasoline-driven automobile. His vehicle had a two-cycle engine, running gear, driving wheels, propeller shaft and clutch, and carriage body. Because of Selden's changes and his delays in answering Patent Office objections, the patent for his horseless carriage was not issued until Nov. 5, 1895.

Oct. 21 The first practical **incandescent electric lamp** was perfected by Thomas A. Edison in his laboratories at Menlo Park, N.J. He found that a carbonized filament of cotton would last for about 40 hrs.

delphia, Pa., for competition among Columbia, Pennsylvania, and Princeton universities. Cornell and Navy occasionally participate by invitation, but if they win, they may not claim the prize. The Childs Cup is the oldest trophy in sprint racing; it was contested by four-oared crews until 1887; by eight-oared crews since 1889. (There was no competition in 1888.)

Fall Providence won the **National League baseball pennant** with a season record of 55 victories, 23 defeats.

1880

The Salvation Army, one of the most energetic and successful evangelical and philanthropic organizations in the world, made its debut in the U.S. this year. The Salvation Army had been founded in England in 1865 by William Booth and his wife Catherine. In 1880 Commissioner George Railton and seven women members arrived in the U.S. to found a branch in Pennsylvania. In 1904 Evangeline Booth, daughter of the founder, took charge of the U.S. branch. From its early days the street bands of the Army have been familiar and popular. The organization has from the beginning treated its women workers the same as its men.

The **American Society of Mechanical Engineers** was formed, reflecting the rising specialization of American scholarship in science.

Illiteracy in America was estimated at 17% of the population, a decrease of 3% over the previous decade.

The **U.S. railroads** had increased to a total of 93,671 miles of track, covering broadly all the settled parts of the country.

A charter for **Bryn Mawr College** for women at Bryn Mawr, Pa., was obtained by a group of men and women belonging to the Society of Friends. After careful planning, the first students were admitted in 1885. The strongly feminist Martha Carey Thomas, holding a Ph.D. from the University of Zurich, was appointed professor of English and also dean, the first woman college faculty member in the U.S. to be so designated. Thomas later organized at Bryn Mawr the first graduate program at a women's college.

The **diversification of crops** in the U.S. was reflected in the large-scale cultivation of corn, wheat, potatoes, and hay on southern farms during the 1880s. Conversely, there was a movement away from reliance on one or two basic crops, such as cotton and tobacco. New markets were opened for wine grapes from North Carolina, watermelons from Georgia, peanuts and apples

Wrestling was more popular than boxing as an American combat sport, especially on the frontier and in mining towns, until well into the nineteenth century. Abraham Lincoln in his younger days had been a skilled wrestler. In 1880 the leading wrestler in the U.S. was William Muldoon, who won the heavyweight title this year. Muldoon wrestled in the U.S. and in England and toured America with John L. Sullivan, the boxing champion. Muldoon once had an eight-hour match with Clarence Whistler; the bout ended in a draw. Muldoon also organized the Police Athletic Association and invented the medicine ball.

The **participation of women in sports** increased sharply during this decade. Besides tennis, archery, and croquet, they engaged in riding, cycling, swimming, boat racing, fencing, and skating. Woodcuts of the period even show women bowling.

The **gold brick swindle** was brought to New York City by Reed Waddell, who was originally from Springfield, Ill. It is estimated that Waddell amassed more than $250,000 in ten years through the sale of gilded lead bricks and counterfeit currency.

The **Edwards heirs fraud** was initiated by Dr. Herbert H. Edwards of Cleveland, Ohio, who claimed he was a descendant of Robert Edwards, the alleged owner of 65 acres of valuable property on Manhattan Island in 1770. This property included the site of the Woolworth Building. Dr. Edwards founded the International Edwards Heirs Association to litigate for return of the property to its rightful owners. Applicants for the inheritance were subject to an enrollment fee of $26. A pretended genealogical investigation of each applicant was conducted by Milo Pressel, a carpenter. By the time the U.S. Post Office Department exposed the hoax, $10,000 had been deposited in the name of the association.

The **world heavyweight bare knuckle boxing championship** was won by Paddy Ryan this year. Ryan beat the

June 2–8 The **Republican National Convention** nominated James A. Garfield of Ohio for the presidency. Chester A. Arthur of New York was named as his running mate. During the convention's meetings Sen. Blanche Kelso Bruce of Mississippi was made temporary chairman of the convention, becoming the first black to preside over a major party convention.

June 9 The **National Convention of the Greenback-Labor Party** nominated James B. Weaver of Iowa and B. J. Chambers of Texas for the presidency and vice presidency respectively. The convention was held in Chicago, Ill.

June 17 The **Prohibition Party National Convention** nominated Neal Dow of Maine for the presidency and Dr. Henry A. Thompson, president of Otterbein University in Ohio, for the vice presidency.

June 22–24 The **Democratic National Convention** nominated Winfield S. Hancock of Pennsylvania for the presidency and William H. English of Indiana for the vice presidency.

Nov. 2 **James A. Garfield was elected president** of the United States. Chester A. Arthur was elected vice president. The electoral vote was Garfield, 214; Winfield S. Hancock, Democratic candidate, 155. The popular vote was Garfield, 4,449,053; Hancock, 4,442,035; James B. Weaver, Greenback-Labor candidate, 308,578; Neal Dow, Prohibition candidate, 10,305. In congressional elections the Republicans fell into a 37–37 tie with the Democrats in the Senate, with one seat going to a minor party. In the House the Republicans took a 147–135 majority, with 11 seats going to minor parties.

Nov. 17 The **Chinese Exclusion Treaty** was signed with China at Peking. It gave the U.S. the right to "regulate, limit, or suspend" but not to exclude completely the entry of Chinese nationals.

dren's classic, with more than 2,000,000 copies sold in 50 years.

Bellaman House, the first of architect Henry Hobson Richardson's influential shingled houses, was built in Cohasset, Mass.

The *Second Symphony* of **John Knowles Paine** was given its first performance in Boston, where audiences went wild with enthusiasm. Paine, professor of music at Harvard University, wrote themes imitative of the popular German motifs of the time.

Glorification of the American girl found expression in paintings of Paris-trained young artists, who were nevertheless forced to avoid the nude because of prevailing prejudices. In the works of Abbott Thayer and Thomas Dewing, young girls are presented as angels, fairies, virgins, etc., as in *Spirit of the Water Lily*.

Steele MacKaye brought his **domestic melodrama Hazel Kirke** to a New York City stage. The audience was provided with an elopement by Hazel and a disguised English lord, in addition to Hazel's angry father, an antagonistic mother-in-law, Hazel's attempt to commit suicide by drowning, her rescue by her husband, and forgiveness and domestic bliss at the final curtain.

Nov. 8 **Sarah Bernhardt,** the celebrated French actress, made her American debut at Booth's Theater in New York City. During the season she performed in Alexandre Dumas' *La Dame aux Camélias* and three other plays that displayed her dramatic strengths.

1881

For the third time in U.S. history, a vice president succeeded to the highest office after death of the incumbent. Chester A. Arthur of New York came to the presidency on the death of Pres. James A. Garfield. Arthur had a poor reputation, a result of his association with Sen. Roscoe Conkling of New York, who had made the most of the spoils system. Arthur was also considered too fond of high living. Nevertheless, his administration brought no scandal to the office and, to the surprise of many, supported badly needed civil service reform. Arthur also supported the rebuilding of the U.S. Navy, which had languished since the Civil War.

Literary magazines and their editors exercised great influence in this era. Among the best was Richard Watson Gilder, who this year became editor of *The Century Illustrated Monthly*, the successor to the celebrated literary journal *Scribner's Monthly*. He continued as editor until his death in 1909. In its first years *The Century* specialized in the memoirs of Civil War generals. The magazine published the works of such leading authors as William Dean Howells, Josh Billings, F. Marion Crawford, and Joel Chandler Harris. Gilder also wrote 16 volumes of poetry. His sister, Jeannette, assisted him at editing and wrote for newspapers what was probably the first American literary gossip column.

| Business and Industry; Science; Education; Philosophy and Religion | III | | IV | Sports; Social Issues and Crime; Folkways; Fashion; Holidays |

from Virginia, and subtropical fruits from Florida, notably oranges, lemons, and pineapples.

The **first major gold strike in Alaska** led to rapid development of the Alaskan village of Juneau.

Major improvements were made in **plumbing facilities** for the home during this decade, largely through the pressures of city and state inspection codes.

At about this time the **first municipal electric lighting plant** was established in New Britain, Conn., by Charles Leonard Newcomb.

A **successful roll film** for cameras was patented by George Eastman of Rochester, N.Y. In 1885 he placed on the market his first commercial film, cut into strips and sealed in a box camera that was returned to the factory for removal and developing. The introduction of daylight loading film came in 1891, and the first pocket Kodak in 1895.

A **safety razor** was devised by Kampfe Bros. of New York City.

House paint was manufactured for the first time from standard formulas. The Sherwin-Williams Company of Cleveland, Ohio, began producing an all-purpose paint for wood from an unvarying formula. This production method was later applied to stains, varnish stains, varnishes, and enamels.

Jan. 27 A patent for an **incandescent lamp** was received by Thomas A. Edison. The filament was made with a carbonized cotton thread. The first public demonstrations of the lamp had been held on Dec. 31, 1879, at Edison's laboratories at Menlo Park, N.J. The first commercial installation of these lamps was made in the steamship *Columbia* of the Oregon Railroad and Navigation Company.

Oct. 4 The **University of Southern California** was founded at Los Angeles, Calif. The first classes met this year.

defender, Joe Goss of England, in an 87-round bout near Colliers Station, W.Va.

Orange Blossom, a pseudonym for Joseph M. Mulholland of Washington, Pa., became famous as the byline for implausible stories printed as serious news items. Mulholland's most spectacular hoax was his account of a flaming meteor that supposedly landed in western Pennsylvania, setting fire to a huge area. In later years his stories came to be printed as short works of the imagination, not to be taken literally.

The term *hot corner* became baseball parlance for third base. The term was coined by Ren Mulford, a writer of this period who watched a game in which the Cincinnati third baseman Hick Carpenter was bombarded by several balls hit sharply in his direction.

A new **baseball rule** stipulated that a baserunner was out if he was hit by a batted ball.

Mar. 12 A *dead line* at Fulton St. in New York City, south of which any known criminal would be arrested on sight, was established by Inspector Thomas Byrnes of the New York City police. Byrnes was attempting to stem a wave of bank robberies.

May 18 The sixth annual **Kentucky Derby** was won by Fonso, with a time of 2:37½. The jockey was George Lewis.

May 28 The eighth annual **Preakness Stakes** was won by Grenada, with a time of 2:40½. The jockey was L. Hughes.

June 5 "He will hew to the line of right, let the chips fall where they may" was declaimed by Sen. Roscoe Conkling of New York in nominating Ulysses S. Grant for a third presidential term. Grant failed in his bid, losing to James A. Garfield.

June 14 The 14th annual **Belmont Stakes** was won by Grenada, with a time of 2:47. The jockey was L. Hughes.

Fall The **National League championship** was won by Chicago with a season record of 67 wins and 17 losses.

1881

Founding of an American branch of the Red Cross on May 21, 1881, inspired by the establishment of the International Red Cross in Europe in 1863, was largely the work of one woman, Clara Barton. Miss Barton, a teacher, volunteered to nurse wounded Union soldiers during the Civil War; in 1864 she was put in charge of all hospitals of the Union Army of the James. She became known to the soldiers as "the angel of the battlefield." At the request of Pres. Abraham Lincoln, she headed a search for missing Union soldiers after the war. The American National Red Cross received a federal charter in 1900 and is the only organization with such a charter. Miss Barton headed the Red Cross until 1904.

There were many organizations for Americans to join at this time. Some were patriotic, some religious, some social. Others, such as volunteer fire companies, combined civic service with sociability. Some carried extravagant names, such as the Ancient Arabic Order of Nobles of the Mystic Shrine, or Daughters of Isis. Some went in for gaudy uniforms and much ceremony and ritual. Patriotic groups were especially popular in the late nineteenth century. The Sons of the American Revolution, the Daughters of the American Revolution, and the Colonial Dames of America were all founded between 1875 and 1894. Largest of all was the Grand Army of the Republic, made up of veterans of the Union

Exploration and Settlement; Wars; Government; Civil Rights; Statistics	**I**	**II**	Publishing; Arts and Music; Popular Entertainment; Architecture; Theater

Jan. 24 The federal income tax law of 1862 was declared constitutional by the Supreme Court in the case of *Springer v. United States.* Counsel for Springer argued that the tax was a direct tax, forbidden by Article 1, sections 2 and 9 of the Constitution. The Supreme Court ruled that there were only two kinds of direct tax—real property tax and poll tax—and the income tax was neither of these.

Mar. 4 James A. Garfield was inaugurated president of the United States. The 20th president and a Republican, he served only 6 months and 15 days.

July 2 Pres. **Garfield was shot** in a Washington, D.C., railroad station by Charles J. Guiteau, a disgruntled and perhaps insane office seeker. Garfield survived for 80 days after he was shot, being treated in Washington and Elberon, N.J., where the Garfield family was summering at the seashore. The doctors' reports provided no guidance on the president's ability to fulfill his duties. Vice Pres. Chester A. Arthur served as acting president. Garfield died Sept. 19, 1881, without ever leaving his bed. He was buried in Cleveland, Ohio. Guiteau was hanged in Washington on June 30, 1882.

Sept. 20 Chester A. Arthur was inaugurated president of the United States, succeeding to the presidency on the death of Pres. Garfield. The 21st president and a Republican, he served three years and five months.

Nov. 14 The **trial of Charles J. Guiteau,** who assassinated Pres. Garfield, began in Washington, D.C. From the beginning, Guiteau's behavior was remarkable. When his attorney sought a delay in the trial, Guiteau stated he wanted the trial to begin and that he wanted to represent himself. He released for publication an address that virtually admitted his action and called on those who benefited from Garfield's death to aid his case financially. Guiteau was convicted on Jan. 25, 1882, and was executed in Washington on June 30, 1882.

Nov. 29 U.S. interest in **Pan-American cooperation** was briefly aroused when Sec. of State James G. Blaine invited Latin American states to Washington for a congress to be held in 1882. But Blaine left Pres. Arthur's Cabinet on Dec. 19. His successor, Frederick T. Frelinghuysen, revoked the invitation and the meeting was canceled.

Among **books published** this year was *A Century of Dishonor* by Helen Hunt Jackson. Previously a writer of popular but minor fiction, poems, and prose sketches, and now living in the West, Mrs. Jackson provided an eye-opening account of the U.S. government's ruthless treatment of Indians. Among other books of this year were *Uncle Remus: His Songs and His Sayings* by Joel Chandler Harris, full of authentic black folklore in dialect; *Dr. Breen's Practice,* a novel about a society woman as a physician by William Dean Howells; and two novels by Henry James, *Portrait of a Lady,* the masterpiece of his early novels, and *Washington Square,* a story unusual for James about Americans in their home environment.

Henry Hobson Richardson, architect of Trinity Church, Boston (1877), displayed his functional approach to public buildings in his design of suburban railroad stations for the Boston & Albany Railroad in the Boston area. The station at Auburndale, Mass., is regarded by many as his best in this field.

America's most talented woman painter, **Mary Cassatt,** an expatriate, for the third year in a row exhibited her work in Paris beside the works of other Impressionists. Cassatt, owing much to Edgar Degas and Gustave Courbet, abhorred conventional art and espoused naturalism. Her renderings of mothers and children in intimate scenes, her etchings and color prints soon won her an international reputation.

The **Newport Casino** at Newport, R.I., was built from designs by Stanford White. At the time he was inclined toward informal but enormous shingle buildings suitable for life in the great resorts. Included in the casino complex was a theater for a summer stock company.

The portrait artistry of **Eastman Johnson** was exemplified in his *Two Men,* a representation of Samuel Rowse and Robert W. Rutherford in conversation. Trained in Düsseldorf, Eastman was never at a loss for commissions after 1859.

John Singer Sargent in his *Vernon Lee* and *Portrait of a Lady* foreshadowed the brilliant success of *Madame X* (1884) and the stream of portraits of the great and near great that followed. His work was marked by an air of aloof elegance, seemingly spontaneous poses, and technically brilliant use of light colors to reveal shapes.

June 1 **William Gillette,** better known as an actor, made his debut as a playwright with *The Professor* and, later in the year, *Esmeralda,* the latter written with Frances Hodgson Burnett. The Gillette plays were melodramas, but were given detailed, realistic settings. Their leading roles were played by Gillette without the flamboyance of nineteenth-century matinee idols.

| Business and Industry; Science; Education; Philosophy and Religion **III** | | **IV** Sports; Social Issues and Crime; Folkways; Fashion; Holidays |

The **first summer camp** in the U.S. for city children was established at Squam Lake, N.H. Its success encouraged the founding of similar camps in New England, New York, Pennsylvania, and other states.

The **first central electric power plant** in the world was constructed on Pearl St., New York City, under the direction of Thomas Edison. Operations began with one generator. Edison had solved the problem of designing a system for the efficient distribution of power from a central generating system.

The **Wharton School of Finance and Economy,** the first of its kind in the U.S., was founded within the University of Pennsylvania. It was named for Joseph Wharton, manufacturer of metal alloys and philanthropist, who gave $100,000 for the project, later increased to $500,000.

The **University of Connecticut** was established as the Storrs Agricultural School at Storrs, Conn. The name was changed to Storrs Agricultural College in 1893, to Connecticut Agricultural College in 1899, to Connecticut State College in 1933, and to its present name in 1939.

The **loganberry** was developed by Judge James J. Logan of Santa Cruz, Calif. He attempted to cross the Texas Early blackberry and the wild California blackberry, but placed a row of Red Antwerp raspberries alongside the wild berries. He succeeded in crossing the blackberries, producing a variety he called Mammoth. Also produced was one plant closer in nature to a raspberry than a blackberry and with its own distinctive flavor. From this one plant, propagated by cuttings at the University of California, Berkeley, came loganberries.

By 1881 all the major **elevated railroads in Manhattan** were completed. The first el in New York City had been finished in 1869. During the following decade, the progress of the elevated was at a standstill. It has been said that it took New Yorkers at least that long to get used to the shock of the original el. But the men who were to lay the iron arteries up and across Manhattan Island, led by Cyrus W. Field, had mapped out the island and, in 1878, went to work. The vacant lots through which the els often ran, and the vast outlying areas they penetrated, would shortly be developed through the magic of mass transportation. The trains were powered by steam locomotives.

July 4 The doors were opened to **Tuskegee Institute,** established by the Alabama legislature in February. Booker T. Washington was its president. Until 1937 it was known as Tuskegee Normal and Industrial Institute.

Army, which reached a peak membership of 400,000 in 1890.

A new **baseball rule** increased the distance of the pitcher's slab from home plate from 45 ft. to 50 ft. Another new rule provided that a pitcher be fined for hitting a batter deliberately with a pitched ball. This rule was abolished in 1882.

The **United States Lawn Tennis Association** was born at a meeting of leaders of eastern clubs, at which tennis was traditionally played. A pattern of play was set and adopted all over the world. The national championship was held at Newport, R.I., starting on Aug. 31. Richard D. Sears won the first men's singles crown.

Coney Island, which had been a deserted sandbank four years earlier, had by this time become famous as a place for sun and recreation. Manhattan, Rockaway, and Brighton beaches were all considered to be under the umbrella term Coney Island, but it was Cable Beach, with its boardwalk, that was to become the nucleus of Coney Island. The Boardwalk, built on sturdy steel girders, ran three-fourths of a mile out over the water and included a hotel shipped piece by piece from the 1876 Centennial Exposition in Philadelphia. Coney Island also boasted museums, sideshows, orchestras, rides, and sandy beaches.

The home of **William Kissam Vanderbilt,** at the corner of Fifth Ave. and 52nd St., was completed at a cost of $3,000,000. It marked the beginning of the great and often monumental edifices erected by American millionaires in imitation of the chateaus and palaces of Europe.

May 17 The seventh annual **Kentucky Derby** was won by Hindoo, with a time of 2:40. The jockey was Jimmy McLaughlin.

May 27 The ninth annual **Preakness Stakes** was won by Saunterer, with a time of 2:40½. The jockey was T. Costello.

June 7 The 15th annual **Belmont Stakes** was won by Saunterer, with a time of 2:47. The jockey was T. Costello.

Fall Chicago won the **National League baseball pennant** with a season's record of 56 victories, 28 defeats.

Nov. 9–10 The **America's Cup** was successfully defended by the yacht *Mischief,* which won two straight races from the Canadian challenger *Atlanta.*

1882

The first federal law restricting immigration was passed by Congress on Aug. 3. It set a head tax of 50 cents on each immigrant and excluded convicts, the insane, and persons likely to become public charges. The law was the result of agitation by states controlling the main ports of entry. They had attempted to regulate immigration with state laws and to set a tax in order to support needy newcomers. The Supreme Court declared such laws unconstitutional in 1876 on the grounds that they attempted to regulate foreign commerce, a right reserved to Congress. In the decade from 1881 to 1890, over 5,000,000 immigrants arrived in the U.S.

The **first U.S. naval attaché**, Lt. Commander French Ensor Chadwick, was named to the U.S. embassy in London. Chadwick, an experienced investigator of foreign naval systems, served in London until 1889.

Mar. **Floods** along the Mississippi R. left some 85,000 persons homeless.

Mar. 16 The **Geneva Convention** of 1864 for the care of wounded war personnel, accepted by most European nations, was ratified by the U.S. Senate. Clara Barton, founder of the American branch of the Red Cross in 1881, did much to promote public sentiment in favor of ratification.

Mar. 22 The **Edmunds Act** was adopted by the U.S. Congress to suppress polygamy in the territories, especially in Mormon Utah.

Mar. 31 A **pension for widows of presidents** was voted by Congress. Mrs. Polk, Mrs. Tyler, and Mrs. Garfield were each voted $5000 a year. This initiated the custom of voting pensions to widows of presidents.

May 6 The first **Exclusion Act** barred further Chinese immigration for ten years. The act was regularly renewed by Congress and was still on the books in 1920.

English actors and actresses continued to be popular in the U.S., although in some cases not entirely for their abilities on stage. Such a figure was Lillie Langtry, who married into London society and became the first society woman to go on the stage. Having made her debut in London in Dec. 1881, she made her first visit to the U.S. this year. On Nov. 6 she appeared as Rosalind in Shakespeare's *As You Like It* at the Fifth Avenue Theatre in New York City. Although not a great actress, Langtry was welcomed wherever she appeared in the U.S., as much for her beauty and her scandalous reputation as for her acting.

Among **books published** this year was the realistic novel by William Dean Howells, *A Modern Instance*. In it Howells traced the history of a marriage that led to divorce and the disintegration of character. Other books published included *John Randolph* by Henry Adams, a biography that reflected the author's sustained interest in the Founding Fathers of the U.S.; *Mr. Isaacs*, the first of many romantic novels by Francis Marion Crawford, based on the adventures of a gem dealer the author had met in India; *L'Abbé Constantin*, by a French dramatist and novelist, Ludovic Halévy, which delighted American readers in translation with its likable village priest and his problems, including two American women who had acquired a home in his idyllic parish; *The Prince and the Pauper* by Mark Twain, set in the reign of England's King Edward VI; and *Anne* by Constance Fenimore Woolson, the first of her five novels dealing realistically with life in northern Michigan.

"**The Lady or the Tiger?**" by Frank R. Stockton was published in *Century Magazine*. Sensationally popular at the time, this short story has since appeared in nearly every American anthology of fiction.

A bust of **Henry Wadsworth Longfellow**, the first American to make a living from poetry, was placed in poet's corner in Westminster Abbey in London. He was the first American to be so honored.

| Business and Industry; Science; Education; Philosophy and Religion | III | | IV | Sports; Social Issues and Crime; Folkways; Fashion; Holidays |

1882

A development in 1882 in the way large businesses were organized had economic repercussions for many years. John D. Rockefeller of the Standard Oil Company sought a means of legally controlling under one management companies owned in several states. A lawyer, Samuel C. T. Dodd, hit on the idea of the trust. Stockholders set up a board of trustees to whom were turned over the stocks of about 40 companies. The stockholders received trust certificates, which gave the trustees, Rockefeller and his close associates, the right to operate the companies as they saw fit. The Standard Oil trust, organized on Jan. 2, 1882, was capitalized at $70,000,-000. Rockefeller himself owned about a third of all the trust certificates. The trust idea was soon copied in such fields as sugar and tobacco processing. The result was monopolistic control of a number of industries, leading eventually to political action to restore competition.

Prof. **Granville Stanley Hall** of The Johns Hopkins University, Baltimore, Md., was appointed to a special lectureship in psychology and given $1000 to establish a psychological laboratory. William James at Harvard University had previously organized a laboratory for work in "psycho-physics," but Johns Hopkins soon took over leadership.

The **University of South Dakota,** chartered in 1862 as the University of Dakota (territory), a name retained until 1891, opened its doors at Vermillion, S.D.

Founding of the **American School of Classical Studies** at Athens, Greece, encouraged study of the classics by Americans. The success of this enterprise led to establishment of a similar institution in Rome, Italy, in 1885.

An **electric flatiron** was patented by a New Yorker, Henry W. Seely.

Formation of the **American Forestry Association** reflected the growing specialization of American scientific scholarship and alarm over condition of forestlands.

An **electric fan** was developed by Schuyler Skaats Wheeler, a New York City engineer and inventor.

The nation's **first hydroelectric plant** was built at Appleton, Wis., where the first electric streetcar went into service in 1886.

Americans have a tendency to make folk heroes of outlaws; one of the first of these heroes was Jesse James. Born on Sept. 5, 1847, in Missouri, Jesse Woodson James fought for the Confederacy in Quantrill's Raiders. In 1866 he and his brother, Frank, became leaders of a Midwest gang that first held up banks, then turned to train robbery. A reward offered by the governor of Missouri tempted a member of the gang, Robert Ford, to shoot and kill Jesse on Apr. 3, 1882. After Jesse's death Frank James surrendered, was acquitted of the charges against him, and lived out his life on a Missouri farm. Much has been written about the James gang, including a song, "The Ballad of Jesse James."

A **new baseball league,** the American Association, was formed. It flourished for several years, formed a working agreement with the established National League in 1886, then suffered a poor season in 1891 and disbanded.

The **National Croquet Association** was formed to revise and standardize the rules of the game.

The phrase **"the public be damned"** was offered by William H. Vanderbilt in answer to a question by Clarence Dresser, a reporter for the Chicago *Daily News.* When asked whether Vanderbilt, owner of the New York Central Railroad, was running the railroad for the public or the stockholders, Vanderbilt tossed off his remark, which was to become a symbol of the arrogance of the railroad barons.

The **first malted milk** was produced by William Horlick of Racine, Wis. He added milk to a mixture of extract of wheat and malted barley; the resulting mixture was then evaporated to a powder. Horlick began to manufacture his product commercially in 1883. He used the name "malted milk" for the first time in 1886. Originally, malted milk was primarily a supplemental food for infants and invalids.

The **U.S. Intercollegiate Lacrosse Association** was founded. The original members were Harvard, Princeton, and Columbia; Yale and New York University were admitted in the following year.

The **U.S. Lawn Tennis Association singles championship** was won by Richard D. Sears.

Feb. 7 The **world heavyweight bare knuckle boxing championship** was won by John L. Sullivan, who defeated Paddy Ryan in a nine-round bout in Mississippi City, Miss. This year Sullivan toured the country, giving boxing exhibitions under Marquis of Queensberry rules, and offering $500 to any person who could last four rounds with him. His efforts gave boxing new respectability and wider popularity.

May 16 The eighth annual **Kentucky Derby** was won by Apollo, with a time of 2:40½. The jockey was Babe Hurd.

May 22 The **independence of Korea,** uncertain as it was in the face of Chinese, Russian, and Japanese manipulations, was recognized by the U.S. government and a commercial treaty was signed.

Aug. 2 A **River and Harbors Bill,** authorizing expenditure of over $18,000,000 for public works, was passed by Congress, overriding a veto by Pres. Chester A. Arthur.

Nov. 7 In **congressional elections** the Democrats gained 50 seats in the House to take a 197–118 majority, with ten seats going to minor parties. In the Senate the Republicans gained one seat to take a 38–36 majority over the Democrats, with two seats going to minor parties.

The popular **Lovell's Library** made its first appearance. John W. Lovell was the leading publisher of cheap "regular" sized books, selling at 10 to 20 cents each. For a time there was a new title every day, bearing a date like a newspaper. Lovell eventually issued Lovell's Popular Library, clothbound at 50 cents, and Lovell's Standard Library, at $1.00 a copy.

The **New York** *Morning Journal,* a newspaper characterized by sensationalism, was begun by Albert Pulitzer. Sold to William Randolph Hearst in 1895, it was renamed the New York *Journal* and supported William Jennings Bryan and the free silver movement. Edited by Arthur Brisbane, it clamored for war with Spain and the independence of Cuba.

1883

Shocked by the suggestion that the assassination of Pres. James A. Garfield in 1881 by a disappointed office seeker was an indirect result of the spoils system, Congress on Jan. 16 passed the Pendleton Act, which was signed into law by Pres. Chester A. Arthur. The law established a three-man Civil Service Commission and specified rules for filling federal government positions by a merit system, including competitive examinations. At the start, only about 14,000 of 100,000 positions were covered by the act, but by 1900 about 106,000 of 250,-000 were covered. The worst evils of political patronage were ended, but the question of whether the act improved the efficiency of government, as reformers declared it would, remained unanswered.

The **Southern Immigration Association** was formed. The organization promoted European immigration to the South. At the same time the Northern Pacific Railroad dispatched agents to Europe and England to encourage immigration to the Northwest.

Jan. 10 **Fire** consumed the Newhall House in Milwaukee, Wis., causing the death of 71 persons. This was the worst hotel fire in U.S. history until Dec. 7, 1946, when the Winecoff Hotel fire in Atlanta, Ga., caused 121 deaths.

Mar. 3 U.S. **postage** was reduced to two cents per half ounce by an act of Congress. On the same day the so-called Mongrel Tariff Act was passed by Congress.

A marvel of design and engineering that captured the imagination of the public was officially opened on May 24. This was the Brooklyn Bridge, spanning the East R. between Brooklyn and New York City. John A. Roebling, a pioneer in suspension bridge design, planned the bridge. Shortly after work began in 1869, Roebling was injured when a barge crushed his foot against a pier. Tetanus set in and he died on July 22, 1869. His son, Washington A. Roebling, took over. In 1872 he too was felled, by nitrogen narcosis, or the bends, the result of too much time spent in the underground caissons built to sink the massive foundations of the bridge towers. From 1872 on, he directed construction from an apartment overlooking the bridge site. The bridge has a span of 1595 feet. The striking towers at either end are 272 feet high, with foundations 78 feet below water level. A great civic celebration, attended by Pres. Chester A. Arthur and Gov. Grover Cleveland, marked opening day.

Among **books published** this year was the semiautobiographical *Life on the Mississippi* by Mark Twain. Although soon recognized as a classic account of the difficult art of piloting steamboats on the Mississippi R., and written with the verve of Twain at his peak, the book was not a best seller until it was issued in a paperback edition in the 1940s. Other books published included *The Story of a Country Town* by Edgar Watson Howe, published privately after rejection by many commercial publishers. It was a frequently republished pioneering work of naturalistic fiction set in a midwestern

| Business and Industry; Science; Education; Philosophy and Religion   III | | IV   Sports; Social Issues and Crime; Folkways; Fashion; Holidays |

Feb. 2 The **Knights of Columbus,** the first fraternal benefit society of Catholic men, was founded in New Haven, Conn., by the Rev. Michael Joseph McGivney. The society was chartered on March 29, 1882.

Apr. 28 The **John F. Slater Fund** for education of emancipated blacks was incorporated in New York. It was funded by a gift of $1,000,000 from textile manufacturer John Fox Slater. This was the first major philanthropy in this field. In 1937 the fund merged with similar foundations to form the Southern Education Foundation.

Dec. 11 **Incandescent stage lighting** was first used in the U.S. at the Bijou Theater in Boston at a performance of *Iolanthe,* by Gilbert and Sullivan. Some 650 incandescent bulbs were used. In London the Savoy Theater first employed incandescent bulbs in 1881.

May 27 The tenth annual **Preakness Stakes** was won by Vanguard, with a time of 2:44½. The jockey was T. Costello.

June 8 The 16th annual **Belmont Stakes** was won by Forester, with a time of 2:43. The jockey was Jimmy McLaughlin.

June 24 The only major league **baseball umpire expelled for dishonesty,** Richard Higham, left the National League.

Fall The **National League baseball championship** was won by Chicago, with a record of 55 wins and 29 losses. Chicago split a two-game interleague playoff with Cincinnati, of the American Association. It was the first such series, the forerunner of the World Series.

Sept. 5 The **first Labor Day parade,** sponsored by the Knights of Labor, was held in New York City.

Sept. 25 The **first major league double header** was played between the Providence and Worcester teams.

1883

Two American scholars were the leading sociologists of the time, but differed completely on the meaning of the theory of evolution, which was much discussed by intellectuals. They were Lester Frank Ward and William Graham Sumner. Ward, whose *Dynamic Sociology* was published this year, believed that the human mind, when properly used, could take an active part in the process of human evolution. He did not believe that evolution is an inevitable and uncontrollable process. Ward further developed his ideas in *Psychic Factors in Civilization* (1893) and *Pure Sociology* (1903). Sumner, on the other hand, believed that the fittest survived and deserved to survive, and that the fittest were those who lived by hard work and individualism. His views were expressed in *What Social Classes Owe to Each Other* (1883).

Experiments leading to development of the **fountain pen** were begun by Lewis E. Waterman. The first to apply the principle of capillary action, Waterman obtained patents and produced a practical pen in 1884, thus founding the Ideal Pen Company in New York City. By 1887 his business had expanded vastly and a new L. E. Waterman Company was incorporated.

The **Modern Language Association** was founded at Baltimore, Md., for the advancement of literary and linguistic studies. Membership was open to all teachers of

The far West fascinated Americans in the late nineteenth century, as it has continued to do ever since. A taste of that region was brought east and to Europe with some authenticity by William Frederick "Buffalo Bill" Cody. A Pony Express rider, buffalo hunter, and Army scout, he organized "Buffalo Bill's Wild West Show" in 1883. The show may have given its first performance at North Platte, Neb., on July 4. Buffalo Bill toured with the show for years, both in the U.S. and abroad. It was a smash hit in England. Queen Victoria enjoyed watching stage coaches being held up and Indian attacks repulsed, all to the accompaniment of heavy gunfire.

This year the **first national college football championship** was won by Yale, with a record of eight wins, no losses, no ties. The yearly ranking of the top college football teams was begun by the Citizens Savings Athletic Foundation. In 1936 the Associated Press inaugurated an annual poll of its sportswriters to select the champion team of the year. In 1950 United Press International began its own poll of college coaches.

G. M. Hendrie of Springfield, Mass., won the first recorded bicycle race; it was called a race for the championship although only two riders participated. Hendrie later became a successful automobile and motorcycle builder.

The **U.S. lawn tennis men's singles championship** was won by Richard D. Sears.

The original intent of the act had been to reduce the annual Treasury surpluses, which encouraged reckless government spending. Excise taxes were removed from everything but liquor and tobacco, but an unsystematic increase in protective tariffs was declared in spite of recommendations to the contrary by a special tariff committee. Treasury surpluses continued.

Mar. 3 Rebuilding of the United States Navy began with appropriation by Congress of funds for the first steel vessels, three cruisers and a dispatch boat. Sec. of the Navy William H. Hunt was the first of four successive secretaries to build, with congressional approval, the new Navy.

Oct. 15 The **Civil Rights Act of 1875,** which forbade racial discrimination or separation in public accommodations, was vitiated by a narrow Supreme Court decision. The Court held that only state-imposed discrimination was forbidden, not that by individuals or corporations.

Nov. 18 A system of **standard time** was adopted by the railroads of the U.S. and Canada to eliminate problems in printed schedules caused by the unsystematic setting of local times. In 1884, at an international conference in Washington, D.C., a worldwide system of standard time was adopted. The prime meridian was assigned to the meridian passing through the British Royal Observatory at Greenwich, England.

community. *The Old Swimmin' Hole and 'Leven More Poems* by James Whitcomb Riley contained some of Riley's most famous verse depicting rustic life in Indiana. It was written in Hoosier dialect and reached a wide audience.

The **highest masonry building** in the U.S., the Monadnock Building, was erected in Chicago. All 16 stories rest entirely on masonry walls, which are five feet thick at the base.

Life, a satirical magazine that included serious criticism of books and the theater, was founded by two young Harvard graduates, John Ames Mitchell and Edward Sandford Martin. It became the outstanding humor magazine, focusing on topics of current interest.

The *Ladies' Home Journal* was established by Cyrus H. K. Curtis. It became the model for later entrants into the field of women's magazines. Edward W. Bok took over the editorship in 1889 and solidified the magazine's reputation for outstanding feature articles, well-selected fiction, and reliable advertisements.

In Boston **Benjamin Franklin Keith** opened the first of the 400 theaters bearing his name at his death in 1914. Keith introduced the first continuous shows in the U.S. and gradually built a vaudeville circuit that offered much of the best American entertainment at popular prices across the country.

May 9 The New York *World* was purchased by Joseph Pulitzer from Jay Gould. For a decade it was staunchly Democratic. In the 1890s Pulitzer began a circulation war with William Randolph Hearst, owner of the New York *Morning Journal.* The *World* crusaded for reform of city government and for war with Spain.

1884

The presidential election campaign of 1884 was fought mainly with attacks on the reputations of the rival candidates. The Republican candidate, James G. Blaine, on the basis of letters he had written, was accused of having profited from the Crédit Mobilier scandal involving the building of the Union Pacific Railroad. His opponents sang: "Blaine, Blaine, James G. Blaine, the continental liar from the state of Maine." The Democratic candidate, Grover Cleveland, was accused of having fathered an illegitimate child, which in his forthright manner he admitted. The turning point of the election was a remark made on Oct. 9 by the Rev. Samuel D. Burchard in New York, in the presence of Blaine, that the Democrats were the party of "Rum, Romanism, and Rebellion." Blaine did not disavow the remark, and the Irish-American Roman Catholics of New York were outraged. Cleveland carried the state by 1149 votes and thereby won the presidency.

Although newspaper chains had not yet come into existence, there was a market for news and feature material gathered by a news organization and made available for a fee to newspapers all over the country. The first such syndicate was founded on Nov. 8 by Samuel Sidney McClure, who had come to America from Ireland as a boy. In 1893 he founded *McClure's Magazine,* which became a great success under his editorship. The magazine was especially noted for the articles it published in the early twentieth century by such leading muckrakers as Ida Tarbell and Lincoln Steffens.

Among **books published** this year was *Huckleberry Finn* by Mark Twain. A world classic, this picaresque novel of Huck's adventures with his black friend Jim

Business and Industry; Science; Education; Philosophy and Religion III		IV Sports; Social Issues and Crime; Folkways; Fashion; Holidays

English and modern foreign languages in higher education.

The earliest recorded U.S. **heavier-than-air glider flight** was made by John J. Montgomery. He launched his glider from a 300-foot hill near Otay, Calif., and covered a distance of 600 feet.

Feb. 23 The **University of North Dakota** was chartered at Grand Forks. It had been authorized by the Dakota Territory legislature six years before North Dakota became a state. Instruction began in 1884.

Feb. 27 The first practical **cigar-rolling machine** was patented by Oscar Hammerstein. Hammerstein was also a composer, opera impresario, inventor of nearly 100 devices, and founder of the *United States Tobacco Journal.* Oscar Hammerstein II, the librettist, was his grandson.

Mar. 24 The **first telephone service** between New York and Chicago was initiated.

Sept. 15 Instruction began at the **University of Texas** at Austin. The university had been authorized by the state legislature in 1876.

Sept. 21 The first direct **telegraph service to Brazil** from the U.S. was established.

May 23 The ninth annual **Kentucky Derby** was won by Leonatus, with a time of 2:43. The jockey was Billy Donohue.

May 26 The 11th annual **Preakness Stakes** was won by Jacobus, with a time of 2:42½. The jockey was G. Barbee.

June 2 The **first baseball game played under electric lights** took place in Fort Wayne, Ind. Fort Wayne beat Quincy 19–11 in seven innings.

June 9 The 17th annual **Belmont Stakes** was won by George Kinney, with a time of 2:47½. The jockey was Jimmy McLaughlin.

June 16 The **first Ladies' Day baseball game** was staged by the New York Giants. On Ladies' Day, both escorted and unescorted ladies were admitted to the park free.

Fall Boston won the **National League baseball championship** with a season's record of 63 victories, 35 defeats.

Oct. 22 The **first annual New York Horse Show** opened at Gilmore's Gardens, New York City. It was organized by the National Horse Show Association of America. Represented were 165 exhibitors and 299 horses; many workhorses, including fire-engine horses, police mounts, and draught horses, were shown. The show was immediately popular and became an annual event. After 1913 the character of the show altered; working breeds were no longer allowed, and entries were limited to show horses, gaited horses, and the like.

1884

The formation of national and local learned societies accelerated. At least 79 were organized in the 1870s and 121 in the 1880s. The American Historical Association, founded at Saratoga, N.Y., in 1884, was among the most important of these societies; it began publishing the *American Historical Review* in 1895. There were also more specialized groups, such as the American Society for Church History (1897) and the American Irish Historical Association (1897).

Memorial Hospital for the Treatment of Cancer was founded in New York City. It was one of the first hospitals in the U.S. devoted exclusively to cancer treatment and research.

One method of showing off newly acquired wealth in the Gilded Age was to build an elaborate and costly mansion. This went on chiefly in New York City, Chicago, and San Francisco, and at such summer resorts as Newport, R.I. At Fifth Ave. and 91st St. in New York City, Andrew Carnegie, the steel magnate, erected a mansion with gold plumbing fixtures. In Chicago the Potter Palmers, society leaders, constructed a castlelike home with a tower 80 feet high. On Nob Hill in San Francisco, James C. Flood, whose wealth came from mining, built a 42-room house that was surrounded by a block-long bronze fence. It took the full-time services of a man to keep it polished.

The derisive term *mugwump* had wide currency during this election year. It was applied to those Republicans, reformist or liberal, who bolted the party to vote for the Democratic nominee, Grover Cleveland. The

The **National Equal Rights Party** was formed by a group of suffragists who nominated Mrs. Belva A. Lockwood of Washington, D.C., for president. Mrs. Lockwood, a lawyer and the first woman admitted to practice before the Supreme Court, was renominated in 1888. She was the first woman candidate for the presidency.

Feb. 9 A **tornado** that swept across the southern states killed 700 persons.

May 14 The **Anti-Monopoly Party of the United States** was founded at a convention in Chicago. Former Gen. Benjamin F. Butler of Massachusetts was nominated for the presidency. Butler, an active politician, had been first a Democrat but was now a radical Republican. The Anti-Monopoly Party platform called for many liberal measures, including a graduated income tax and repeal of all tariffs.

May 28 The **Greenback Party National Convention** nominated Benjamin F. Butler of Massachusetts for the presidency and Alanson M. West of Mississippi for the vice presidency.

June 3–6 The **Republican National Convention** nominated James G. Blaine of Maine for the presidency on the first ballot. Gen. John A. Logan of Illinois was nominated for the vice presidency.

June 6 **Mugwumps,** the independent Republicans, walked out of the national convention in Chicago, Ill., when the party nominated James G. Blaine. They felt he would not support civil service reform. On June 16 they held a convention of their own in New York City, pledging support to the Democratic Party if a liberal candidate were named.

June 27 The **U.S. Bureau of Labor** was created within the Dept. of the Interior. An independent Dept. of Labor was not authorized until 1913.

July 8–11 The **Democratic National Convention** nominated Gov. Grover Cleveland of New York for the presidency and Thomas A. Hendricks of Indiana for the vice presidency.

July 23 The **Prohibition Party National Convention** nominated John P. St. John of Kansas for the presidency and William Daniel of Maryland for the vice presidency.

July 30 The **Labor Party National Convention** met in Chicago, Ill. It supported the slate named by the Democratic Party earlier in the month.

Aug. 5 The cornerstone of the pedestal of the **Statue of Liberty** was laid at Bedloe's Island (now Liberty Island) in New York harbor. The pedestal, which holds the statue by the French sculptor Frédéric Auguste Bartholdi, is 151 feet high.

Nov. 4 **Grover Cleveland was elected president** of the United States. Thomas A. Hendricks was elected vice president. The electoral vote was Cleveland, 219; James G. Blaine, Republican of Maine, 182. The

drew on the author's experiences on the Mississippi R. The river also served as a backdrop for a variety of rivermen, actors, and rascals, authentic vernacular speech, tall tales, and folklore. Also published this year were *A Roman Singer* and *To Leeward,* novels with an Italian setting by Francis Marion Crawford; *Excursions of an Evolutionist* and *The Destiny of Man in the Light of His Origin* by John Fiske, the best-known defender of Darwinism in the U.S.; the romantic novel *Ramona* by Helen Hunt Jackson, which reached millions of readers with its impassioned plea for justice for American Indians; *A Country Doctor,* another minor but solid novel by Sarah Orne Jewett; *In the Tennessee Mountains* by Mary Noailles Murfree, using the pseudonym Charles Egbert Craddock, the first collection of short stories with realistic settings and genuine Cumberland Mts. dialect; and *Montcalm and Wolfe,* the sixth and next-to-last of Francis Parkman's volumes in his mammoth history of French and English relations in North America.

Winslow Homer moved into a cottage studio at Prout's Neck, Scarborough, Maine, where he lived for the rest of his life except for winter trips to the tropics. He became a marine painter, producing such works as *The Life Line, The Fog Warning, Banks Fishermen, Eight Bells,* and *Coast in Winter.*

Steel skeleton construction was used for the first time by architect William L. Jenney in a ten-story Chicago office building for the Home Insurance Company of New York. Each story was carried independently on the structural framework. This marked the beginning of the age of the skyscraper.

John Singer Sargent, the brilliant American painter living abroad, exhibited *Mme. Gautreau,* his portrait of a lady in a decolleté black dress. The painting caused a sensation. Critics accustomed to stodgy, rather unrealistic portraits charged Sargent with eroticism and provocativeness. Sargent withdrew the portrait to his studio, where as *Madame X* it remained until 1915. It was one of his masterpieces.

| Business and Industry; Science; Education; Philosophy and Religion III | | IV Sports; Social Issues and Crime; Folkways; Fashion; Holidays |

The **American Institute of Electrical Engineers** was founded. It became the parent organization of all trade associations in the American electrical industry. In 1963 it merged with the Institute of Radio Engineers to form the Institute of Electrical and Electronic Engineers.

Telephone service in New York City was expanding so rapidly and the number of poles on city streets was becoming so numerous that the city ordered the placement of all wires underground. This year also saw the installation of the first long-distance line between Boston and New York City.

The **Maxim machine gun,** invented by Hiram Percy Maxim, was put into production by the Maxim Gun Company. This single-barrel weapon was capable of firing 660 rounds a minute. It was used by every major power in World War I.

The **Linotype** automatic typesetting machine, which could form an entire line of type as one piece of metal, was patented by Ottmar Mergenthaler. Mergenthaler received patents for improvements in 1885. The first Linotype machines were put into operation by the New York *Tribune* on July 3, 1886. Mergenthaler's typesetter revolutionized the publishing industry.

Tulane University was established by the Louisiana legislature, which transferred the University of Louisiana to the administrators of the Tulane Education Fund. The fund had been founded by Paul Tulane, a New Orleans merchant, in 1882.

Mar. 12 The **Mississippi Industrial Institute and College,** the first state-supported women's college, was chartered at Columbus, Miss. It is now Mississippi University for Women.

May 29 The **Bureau of Animal Industry** was authorized by Congress as a section of the U.S. Dept. of Agriculture. It had been organized by Dr. Daniel Elmer Salmon the previous year; he became head of the bureau and held the post until 1905.

June **James Buchanan Eads,** noted American hydraulic and bridge engineer, received the Albert Medal from the British Society for the Encouragement of Art, Manufacture, and Commerce, the first American so honored. Eads was known for many projects. In

word derives from an Algonquian word meaning "big chief." Its first prominent use was by Charles Dana, editor of the New York *Sun,* with the implication that Republican bolters thought themselves above party affiliations. The term is now applied to bolters of any party.

A celebrated **presidential campaign slogan** aimed at Grover Cleveland was, "Ma, Ma, where's my Pa?"— a reference to Cleveland's admission that he fathered a child out of wedlock. To this query the Democrats would reply, "Gone to the White House, ha, ha, ha."

The Knights of Labor, at their convention, designated that **Labor Day** be celebrated annually on the first Monday in September. Previously, the holiday had been celebrated sporadically. In 1887 several states established the first Monday in September as Labor Day; others followed suit shortly. Not until 1894 did Congress declare Labor Day a legal holiday for federal employees.

This year's **national college football championship** was awarded to Yale, with a record of eight wins, no losses, one tie.

A new **baseball regulation** removed all restrictions on the manner in which a pitcher might throw the ball. By another rule of this year, a pitcher might take only one step before delivering his pitch.

The **first black major league baseball player** was Moses Fleetwood Walker, who played for Toledo in the American Association.

Greyhound racing was introduced in Philadelphia, Pa.

The **U.S. Lawn Tennis Association men's singles championship** was won for the fourth year in a row by Richard D. Sears.

May 16 The tenth annual **Kentucky Derby** was won by Buchanan, with a time of 2:40¼. The jockey was Isaac Murphy, one of the greatest of all time.

May 23 The 12th annual **Preakness Stakes** was won by Knight of Ellerslie, with a time of 2:39½. The jockey was S. Fisher.

June 4 The 18th annual **Belmont Stakes** was won by Panique, with a time of 2:42. The jockey was Jimmy McLaughlin.

June 5 Gen. **William Tecumseh Sherman,** a hero of the Civil War, declined the offer of the Republican presidential nomination with these words to the Republican convention: "I will not accept if nomi-

popular vote was Cleveland, 4,911,017; Blaine, 4,848,-334; Benjamin F. Butler, Greenback Party candidate, 175,370; John P. St. John, Prohibition candidate, 150,-369. In congressional elections the Republicans gained five seats in the Senate to gain a 43–34 majority. In the House the Republicans gained 22 seats but the Democrats held a 183–140 majority. Robert M. La Follette, Republican of Wisconsin, was elected to his first term in the House of Representatives.

Elihu Vedder drew over 50 illustrations for *The Rubáiyát of Omar Khayyám,* one of the finest accompaniments to a poetic text in literary history. Vedder, then living abroad, was ideally suited to the task, which called for supplementing the poet's ideas and reflecting accurately the philosophy of the text.

1885

Under pressure from the Knights of Labor and other workers' groups, Congress on Feb. 26 passed the Contract Labor Law, or Foran Act, to further restrict immigration. The Knights had charged that American employers were signing up foreign workers with the promise of paying their passage to the U.S. and then were bringing them in for use as strikebreakers. Actually, most strikebreakers were hired from private labor agencies in large cities. The new law, virtually outlawing alien contract labor, did not, however, apply to skilled laborers needed by new industries or to certain other groups, such as actors and servants.

Feb. 25 **Fencing of public lands** in the West was prohibited by an act of Congress. On Aug. 17 Pres. Grover Cleveland reinforced the act with orders to remove all illegal enclosures. Five years before, Carl Schurz, secretary of the treasury, had conducted an investigation into public land abuses. Since then, pressure mounted steadily to prevent railroad and cattle interests from exploiting the weak postwar management of western lands. By fencing in all water sources, special interests were concentrating great holdings. They reacted to the strictures of 1885 by forcing William A. J. Sparks, in 1887, from his presidential appointment as land commissioner. Agitation for reform persisted and eventually won out.

Mar. 3 **Special delivery service** was inaugurated by the U.S. Post Office Dept.

Mar. 4 **Grover Cleveland was inaugurated president** of the United States. The 22nd president and a Democrat, he served two terms but not consecutively.

July 1 **Postal rates** were lowered to two cents an ounce by an act of Congress. Second-class postage was reduced to one cent a pound. A persistent deficit in the Post Office Dept. resulted.

July 23 **Ulysses S. Grant died** at 63 and was buried in a mausoleum on Riverside Drive, New York City,

Ragtime, the earliest form of jazz, began its rise to popularity with the arrival this year in St. Louis, Mo., of Scott Joplin. Joplin was born in Texarkana, Tex., in 1868, the son of a former slave. A self-taught musician, he was only 17 when he arrived in St. Louis. He began playing the piano in honky-tonks along Chestnut and Market streets. In ragtime the melody is syncopated on the piano with the right hand while the left keeps a regular beat in march style. In the late 1890s Joplin turned to composing. Among his best known works are "Maple Leaf Rag" and "The Entertainer," the latter supplying the background music for the 1973 movie *The Sting.* Joplin also composed a ragtime opera, *Treemonisha.*

Among **books published** this year, *The Rise of Silas Lapham* by William Dean Howells showed Howells at the peak of his form in depicting a self-made man and his family transplanted into Boston society. Also published were Ulysses S. Grant's unassuming *Personal Memoirs* in two volumes, a work that became a best seller and saved his heirs from penury; and the first major work by the Harvard philosopher and teacher Josiah Royce, *The Spirit of Modern Philosophy.*

The **Marshall Field Building,** designed by Henry Hobson Richardson, was completed, marking the beginning of a new era in commercial architecture. One of the Boston architect's masterpieces, it reflected Richardson's grasp of the realities of commercial problems and his talent for achieving, despite functional requirements, a logical, even exuberant, effect. His influence on Louis Sullivan and later Chicago architects is clear.

Asbestos curtains as protection against fire came into use in theaters in large U.S. cities. Theater managers were proud of the innovation and had artists paint "Fireproof Asbestos Curtain" on the curtain in fancy lettering. Sometimes they ran the curtain up and down a half-dozen times before each performance.

One of the many trompe l'oeil paintings of **William Michael Harnett** found its way into a barroom. His *After the Hunt* was purchased by a New York City saloonkeeper after fascinating crowds in Paris. The painting shows dead game and the hunter's paraphernalia hanging from a wooden door. The objects were painted with

1861 he built the first ironclad warship. In 1874 he built an arched steel bridge across the Mississippi at St. Louis, and in 1879 he deepened the South Pass at the mouth of the river by building a series of jetties so arranged that the river's flow would deposit its sediments where engineers desired. The Albert Medal was awarded to him for "services rendered to the science of engineering."

nated and will not serve if elected." Sherman was without political experience or inclination.

Fall The **National League baseball championship** was won by Providence, with a record of 84 wins and 28 losses. Providence went on to defeat the New York Metropolitans, of the American Association, in a three-game series at the Polo Grounds in New York City.

1885

One of the most dreaded diseases of the time was tuberculosis, for which there was no specific remedy. Edward Livingston Trudeau, a New York physician, contracted the disease while taking care of his tubercular brother and went to live in the Adirondack Mts. in New York State. There, spending much time in the open air, he regained his health. He believed the cold dry air of the mountains and his way of life, which included much rest, were the cause of his cure. As a result, he opened the Adirondack Cottage Sanatorium in 1885 at Saranac Lake, N.Y. This first institution of its kind in the U.S. was initially a one-room cottage with simple furnishings and facilities. The sanatorium functioned until 1954, when it closed for lack of patients, modern methods of diagnosis and treatment having by then reduced deaths from tuberculosis in the U.S. by 95%.

The **American Economic Association** (AEA) was founded at Saratoga Springs, N.Y. It was formed principally by young German-trained economists in revolt against determinist economics. The members of the AEA, 186 at the start, were philosophical moderates. They were impressed by the scientific climate of the latter part of the century and declared that laissez-faire principles of the previous generation were "unsafe in politics and unsound in morals." They argued that the state must contribute "positive aid" as "an indispensable condition of human progress," but their program was a middle course between laissez-faire and the German political philosophy and tolerated a wide spectrum of political opinion. Among its early members were Henry C. Adams, John B. Clark, Richard R. Fly, Woodrow Wilson, Carrol Wright, and Andrew Carnegie.

Furnaces for **garbage disposal** began to be introduced in many cities, particularly in the landlocked Middle West, as a health measure. It had been discovered that swine fed with garbage from the cities contracted trichinosis, which could be transmitted to consumers of the infected meat.

The life and writings of **Josiah Strong**, Protestant minister and reformer, marked the beginning of the so-

A world's fair in the U.S., the New Orleans Exposition, attracted international attention when it opened on Jan. 24, 1885. It was the largest yet held in the U.S., being a third again larger than the Centennial Exposition in Philadelphia in 1876. Many nations, including England, France, China, Japan, Austria, and all the nations of South America, had exhibits. The U.S. was represented by exhibits from each department of the federal government and from the Smithsonian Institution, which had a display of "almost every survival of prehistoric times." Americans took special pride in what one observer termed "the unrivaled collection of American products and resources."

The **fashion in clothing** was described thus in *Harper's Bazaar:* " 'Moyen âge' is the term used to describe the new fashion in the spring of 1885. Scarfs, handkerchiefs, wide ribbons and fabrics are emblazoned to imitate medieval banners. Vieux rouge (old red) is showing two tones while the new blue is called vieille blouse usée, the color of workmen's shirts. Much beige and cream color and bright gold is being shown. Flowers and scarfs are replacing feathers on hats. Combinations of two materials with long drapery and plain lawn skirts are being used in both suits and dresses."

The **U.S. Lawn Tennis Association championship** was won for the fifth successive year by Richard D. Sears.

This year's **national college football championship** was won by Princeton, with a record of nine wins, no losses, no ties.

Jan. 17 **Benjamin Franklin's birthday** was celebrated for the first time by the Old Time Printers Association of Chicago. Regarded as one of the founding fathers of American printing, Franklin has been honored by printing associations in many of the major American cities.

May 14 The 11th annual **Kentucky Derby** was won by Joe Cotton, with a time of 2:37¼. The jockey was Erskine Henderson.

overlooking the Hudson R. The funeral of Gen. Grant was designated a day of national mourning. The body was taken to New York City on a special train shrouded in black curtains. The former president lay in state at City Hall, where citizens who wished to pay their last respects gathered in a line a mile long. Day and night for two days the mourners filed past. The funeral procession to the tomb was enormous and people packed the sidewalks and rooftops along its route.

Nov. 25 Vice Pres. **Thomas A. Hendricks died** in Indianapolis, Ind., at 66. He was buried in Crown Hill cemetery in Indianapolis.

Dec. Suspension of **compulsory coinage of silver dollars** was recommended by Pres. Cleveland in his message to Congress. The Bland-Allison Act of 1878 had required the Treasury to issue between 2,000,000 and 4,000,000 silver dollars each month. Pres. Cleveland saw inflationary dangers in bimetallism.

such realism that many a tippler reached for the painted jug.

The sculptor **John Donoghue** modeled his best-known work, a delightful *Young Sophocles.* Donoghue is best remembered for his classical statuary, for example, *Hunting Nymph, Kypris, Hannibal,* and *St. Paul,* rather than for his busts of contemporaries. Donoghue committed suicide in 1903, his youthful promise unfulfilled.

Douglas Tilden, a gifted West Coast sculptor, created his first work on an athletic theme, *Tired Wrestler.* Among his later works in this vein were *Baseball Player, Young Acrobat,* and *Football Players.*

Feb. 21 The **Washington Monument** was dedicated in the nation's capital, 37 years after the cornerstone was laid, four and a half years after construction began. Total cost was a bit less than $1,200,000. The monument is 555 feet 5 and one-eighth inches high. Ascent and descent can be made by elevator or by negotiating 898 steps. The monument was opened to the public on Oct. 9, 1888.

1886

The nation was stirred by an incident on May 4 in Chicago's Haymarket Square. A labor rally there, which included speeches by anarchists, was breaking up when a large force of police arrived. A bomb exploded among them, killing seven officers and wounding about 60. The anarchists were blamed and the police arrested eight leaders of what came to be known as the Haymarket Riot. Their trial began on June 19. Although no evidence was ever presented to identify any of the accused as the bomb thrower, all eight were convicted on Aug. 20. Seven were sentenced to death, one to jail. Of the condemned, four were hanged on Nov. 11, one committed suicide in jail, and two had their sentences changed to life imprisonment. Seven years later, on June 26, 1893, Gov. John Peter Altgeld of Illinois pardoned the three still in jail. For this act he was denounced by some as little better than an anarchist himself.

Jan. 19 A **Presidential Succession Act** was passed by Congress. It provided that in the event of removal, death, resignation, or inability of the president and vice president, the heads of the executive departments, in the order of the creation of their offices, would succeed to the presidency. A new order of succession was adopted in 1947, and it was superseded by the Twenty-fifth Amendment to the Constitution in 1967.

May 10 An **alien,** the Supreme Court declared, is a person in the eyes of the law. The Court ruled thus in the case of *Yick Wo v. Hopkins,* declaring that municipal ordinances discriminating against Chinese

Not surprisingly, the Civil War became the source of material for playwrights. The first important drama using this subject opened in Brooklyn, N.Y., on Feb. 22. It was *Held by the Enemy* by William Gillette, the actor and dramatist. Its plot concerned two soldiers in love with the same woman in an occupied southern city. In 1895 Gillette again used a Civil War setting, this time in a spy episode in *Secret Service.* Gillette's most popular play, however, was *Sherlock Holmes* (1899), in which Gillette was to act the title role until a few years before his death in 1937.

Among **books published** this year was an immensely popular story for children, *Little Lord Fauntleroy* by Frances Hodgson Burnett. The little gentleman-hero has long since lost any appeal for youngsters, but the illustrations by Reginald Bathurst Birch set a durable fashion for children's clothing, and 40 years later Mary Pickford played Fauntleroy in one of her box office successes. Also published were *The Midge* by Henry Cuyler Bunner, a graceful novelette by the poet-editor of *Puck; Indian Summer,* a romantic novel set in Florence, *Tuscan Cities,* a travel book, and *The Garroters,* a farcical play, all by William Dean Howells; *Princess Casamassima,* a novel by Henry James in which he uncovered the social ferment underlying the surface placidity of upper-class life in London; and *Hugh Wynne* by Silas Weir Mitchell, a noted Philadelphia physician and neurologist, partly a historical romance, partly a novel of

called social gospel in the U.S. His *Our Country*, published this year for the Congregational Home Missionary Society, aroused the social and spiritual idealism latent within Protestantism. The book exposed the dangers of accumulated wealth and the concentration of capitalism, and challenged the church to concern itself with social problems. This book and *The New Era* (1893) made Strong a national figure in religious and intellectual circles. His work was translated into several European languages, Chinese, and Japanese.

Stanford University was founded at Palo Alto, Calif., by Leland and Jane Stanford. Officially named Leland Stanford Junior University after their only child, Stanford today operates branch campuses in England, France, Germany, Austria, and Italy.

The **University of Arizona** was established at Tucson by the Arizona territorial legislature. It opened in 1891. Also established in 1885 was Arizona Territorial Normal School, since 1958 named Arizona State University.

May 22 The 13th annual **Preakness Stakes** was won by Tecumseh, with a time of 2:49. The jockey was Jimmy McLaughlin.

June 6 The 19th annual **Belmont Stakes** was won by Tyrant, with a time of 2:43. The jockey was P. Duffy.

Fall The **National League baseball championship** was won by Chicago, with a record of 87 wins and 25 losses. The third interleague playoff series (seven games), with St. Louis of the American Association, ended in a 3–3 split, with one game a draw.

Sept. 14–16 The **America's Cup** was successfully defended by the U.S. yacht *Puritan*, which won two straight races from the British challenger *Genesta*.

Dec. 20 A **weightlifting feat** of incredible proportions was accomplished by William B. Curtis, who was reported to have lifted 3239 lbs. "with harness."

1886

A significant step in the growth of the labor movement was taken on Dec. 8 in Columbus, Ohio, when the American Federation of Labor (AFL) was organized by about 25 labor groups representing 150,000 members. The new union grew out of the Federation of Organized Trades and Labor Unions, formed in 1881. The first president of the AFL was Samuel Gompers, president of the Cigarmakers Union, who held the office except for one year until his death in 1924. The AFL was craft-oriented and favored skilled labor. Under Gompers' leadership, it had nothing to do with politics or socialistic programs, but put its efforts into securing higher wages, shorter working hours, and better working conditions. By 1890 the AFL had 225,000 members; by 1900 its membership was 550,000.

A cheap process for extracting **aluminum** from its ore was invented by Charles Martin Hall. His electrolytic method caused the price of aluminum to drop from $5.00 a lb. in 1888 to 18 cents in 1914.

The **Andover Controversy** typified the bitter conflict between liberal and orthodox religious forces in the U.S. at this time. The controversy erupted at Andover Theological Seminary, a Congregational institution in Massachusetts, with the trial of five professors charged with theological liberalism and the finding by the board of visitors that one of the five was guilty of the charge. The

What a person will do to achieve instant notoriety was demonstrated on July 23 when Steve Brodie, a bookmaker, allegedly jumped off the Brooklyn Bridge into the East R., a drop of about 140 feet. Some said that a dummy was dropped while Brodie hid under a pier, waiting to appear at the proper moment. In any event, Brodie opened a profitable saloon on the strength of the feat. Brodie later took to the stage and repeated his act by jumping from a "bridge" in the melodrama *Mad Money*, first performed at Niblo's Garden in New York City on Feb. 22, 1891.

This year's **national college football championship** was won by Yale, with a record of nine wins, no losses, and one tie.

The **first international polo match** was held between England and the U.S. at Newport, R.I.; it was a gala occasion. Both teams were colorfully dressed in satin and full-length leather boots. The grounds were lined with members of the social set of New England and New York. The visiting team, more practiced, swept the match 10–4 and 14–2.

The **U.S. Lawn Tennis Association men's singles championship** was won for the sixth year in a row by Richard D. Sears.

Jan. 1 The **first Tournament of Roses** was held in Pasadena, Calif., staged by the Valley Hunt Club, which had been founded by Charles Frederick Holder, a distinguished naturalist. Mr. Holder suggested that the members of the Valley Hunt Club decorate their carriages with the natural flowers of California on New

laundries violated the Fourteenth Amendment.

June 30 Congress approved legislation recognizing the **Division of Forestry,** which had been established in 1881 in the Dept. of Agriculture. Dr. Bernhard E. Fernow, a professional forester, was put in charge. The division was the outgrowth of an agency established in 1876 to study American forests and their future supply of timber.

Sept. 4 Geronimo, the inveterate Apache raider along the Mexican border, surrendered to Gen. Nelson A. Miles in Arizona. All the Chiricahua Apaches were then resettled in Florida as war prisoners. They were relocated to Fort Sill, Okla., in 1894.

Sept. 16 The national convention of the **Anti-Saloon Republicans** was held in Chicago, Ill.

Oct. 12 A **flood** along the Texas Gulf Coast took 250 lives. The gulf waters were whipped onto the mainland by gale winds.

Oct. 28 The **Statue of Liberty** was unveiled and dedicated by Pres. Grover Cleveland in a ceremony on Bedloe's Island. The 225-ton, 152-ft. tall copper statue was presented to the U.S. by France in commemoration of 100 years of American independence.

Nov. 2 In **congressional elections** the Republicans lost four seats in the Senate but held a 39–37 majority over the Democrats. In the House the Democrats lost 14 seats but held a 169–152 majority, with four seats going to minor parties.

psychology, first appearing as a serial in *Century Magazine.*

Cosmopolitan magazine was founded in Rochester, N.Y. It moved to New York City in 1887 and attained a large circulation as a result of the widespread popularity of its stories and articles.

James Abbott McNeill Whistler was elected president of the Royal Society of British Artists. Later, failing to achieve reelection and with many of his followers resigning, he said, "The artists have come out and the British have remained."

Jan. 4 One of the first **comic operas** to be written by an American composer, *The Little Tycoon* by Willard Spenser, was produced in Philadelphia.

Aug. 19 Augustin Daly led the first invasion of the European continent by an English-speaking dramatic company in 300 years. The reception in Berlin and Paris was not enthusiastic.

1887

Growing agitation by farmers and others over the abuses of railroads in setting rates and in other matters resulted in the establishment of the first regulatory commission in U.S. history. This was the Interstate Commerce Commission, set up by the Interstate Commerce Act of 1887, which became law on Feb. 4. The law stated that interstate railroads must charge reasonable, not discriminatory, rates, and prohibited them from engaging in pooling operations. Drawbacks and rebates, both forms of rate reduction for preferred customers, were outlawed, and charging more for a short haul than a long haul was forbidden. In part, the law was an outgrowth of the Wabash case of 1886, in which the Supreme Court ruled that a state could not regulate an interstate railway that went through its territory. The railroads soon found ways to evade the act, and the Supreme Court reversed decisions of the commission.

Free delivery of mail was provided in all communities with a population of 10,000 or more.

Jan. 20 Pearl Harbor, on the island of Oahu, was leased by the U.S. from Hawaii for a naval station.

The variety of American stage offerings in the late nineteenth century could be seen in a listing of plays that opened in New York City in 1887. Rapidly becoming a favorite was the young Edward Hugh Sothern, who played in a popular comedy, *The Highest Bidder,* which opened at the Lyceum Theater on May 3. *The Still Alarm,* which opened at the 14th Street Theater on Aug. 30, featured Harry Lacey playing a fireman. *A Hole in the Ground,* with William Mack, opened at the same theater on Sept. 12. David Belasco and Henry C. De Mille scored a resounding success with their first collaboration, *The Wife,* which opened at the Lyceum Theater on Nov. 1. That same night Ada Rehan, already popular, starred in *The Railroad of Love* at Daly's Theater, with Mrs. George H. Gilbert and John Drew in the cast. This year Rehan also gave her New York debut performance as Kate in Shakespeare's *The Taming of the Shrew.*

| Business and Industry; Science; Education; Philosophy and Religion | III | | IV | Sports; Social Issues and Crime; Folkways; Fashion; Holidays |

celebrated trial had been preceded by several years of acrimonious disputes within the seminary.

The **first settlement house** in the U.S., the Neighborhood Guild in New York City, was established by Dr. Stanton Coit. Settlement houses provided many social services for the poorer inhabitants of the cities.

The **Whiskey Trust** was formed on the model of the Standard Oil Trust. It included 80 distilleries, of which all but 12 were closed down; profits were distributed pro rata.

Labor unrest marked the entire year. Especially notable was the massive strike of railroad workers (Mar.–May) on the Gould system in the Middle West, promoted by the Knights of Labor. The strike failed but it helped publicize the eight-hour day, a goal of the Knights of Labor. The Haymarket Riot in Chicago and Pres. Grover Cleveland's message to Congress stood as further evidence of labor unrest.

Mar. 4 The **University of Wyoming** was chartered at Laramie, Wyo.

May 10 The Supreme Court held **corporations** to be persons covered by the Fourteenth Amendment, especially in its so-called due process clause.

carriages with the natural flowers of California on New Year's Day and that after a parade of these carriages a program of athletic events be devised to round out the day. Holder's floral motif has remained a feature of the tournament to this day.

May 14 The 12th annual **Kentucky Derby** was won by Ben Ali, with a time of 2:36½. The jockey was Paul Duffy.

May 21 The 14th annual **Preakness Stakes** was won by The Bard, with a time of 2:45. The jockey was S. Fisher.

June 5 The 20th annual **Belmont Stakes** was won by Inspector, with a time of 2:41. The jockey was Jimmy McLaughlin.

Fall The **National League baseball championship** was won by Chicago, with a record of 90 wins, 34 losses. The interleague playoff was won by St. Louis of the American Association, beating Chicago four games to two.

Sept. 9–11 The **America's Cup** was successfully defended by the U.S. yacht *Mayflower,* which won two straight races from the British challenger *Galatea.*

Oct. The **tuxedo** made its first recorded appearance at the annual Autumn Ball of the Tuxedo Club, Tuxedo, N.Y. Griswold Lorillard wore a tailless dress coat, thereafter called a tuxedo. The Tuxedo Club, a sporting and social club, had been founded the previous year by Pierre Lorillard.

1887

Copying the lead of the Standard Oil trust in 1882, other industries rushed to establish trusts to secure monopolies and eliminate competition. In the decade beginning in 1887, 86 combinations of companies were made. Another 149 combinations were formed by 1900. This year saw formation of the Sugar Trust (American Sugar Refineries Company), the Whiskey Trust (Distillers' and Cattle Feeders' Trust), the Lead Trust, and the Cotton-Oil Trust, as well as monopolies in the wallpaper, shoelace, and oatmeal industries. When trusts were formed, some plants in the industry were closed to restrict supplies and raise prices, thus putting people out of work. In the case of the Sugar Trust, 11 out of 18 refineries were immediately shut down.

Congress enacted the **Edmunds-Tucker Act,** which dissolved the Mormon Church as a corporation. The effect was to limit Mormon power in Utah. In 1890 polygamy was renounced by the Mormon president, Wilford Woodruff.

Trade, manufacturing, transportation, and technology were greatly increasing the nation's wealth, yet there seemed to be a growing gap between the poorest and the richest Americans. For the poor, clothing tended to be drab and dark, as did furniture. Men went to work in overalls. Among women of all levels, clothing was mainly heavy and dark, except for the young and those in society who could spend freely. Gentlemen in society wore full dress suits to social affairs. The growing middle class enjoyed the good things of life to an increasing extent, living in comfortable homes. The average middle-class home was crowded with weighty furniture, thick draperies, and innumerable knickknacks.

This year's **national college football championship** was won by Yale, with a record of nine wins, no losses, no ties.

The **first true golf club** in the U.S. was probably the Foxbury Golf Club, founded in Foxbury, Pa., as a result of John Mickle Fox's trip to Scotland, where he learned the game. The club is still in existence. There were golf clubs calling themselves such in Savannah, Ga., and

Feb. 8   Congress passed the **Dawes Severalty Act.** On the surface, it attempted to replace the Indian reservation system by parceling out tracts of land (40, 80, or 160 acres) to individual Indians on the supposition that this would provide them with greater incentives to succeed. In practice it became a mechanism that enabled whites to acquire these allotments by purchase or in repayment of loans. By 1934, when the law was overturned, Indian lands had dwindled from 138,000,000 acres to 48,000,000.

Mar. 2   Pres. Grover Cleveland signed the **Hatch Act,** which called for establishment of an agricultural research and experiment station in each state with a land-grant college. The act also authorized annual appropriations to each state on the establishment of such a station.

Mar. 3   The **American Protective Association** was founded as a secret society in Clinton, Iowa. This anti-Catholic organization grew in number and power by appealing to fears of increasing Catholic influence in schools and public institutions. By 1900 the association became moribund.

Aug. 10   **A train wreck** at Chatsworth, Ill., killed about 100 people. A burning bridge hidden by a knoll crumbled when the train passed over it. Eight hundred passengers from Illinois, Iowa, and Wisconsin were making an excursion to Niagara Falls. In commemoration the ballad "The Bridge Was Burned at Chatsworth" was written.

Among **books published** this year was Sir Henry Rider Haggard's *She.* A romantic melodrama with an African setting, *She* was a best seller, like its predecessor *King Solomon's Mines* (1885). *She* also started a fad for pronouns as book titles: *He, It, Me,* etc. Also published this year was *Saracinesca,* a romantic novel of love in Italian society by F. M. Crawford; *Culture's Garland,* the first collection of Eugene Field's contributions to the Chicago *Morning News,* and two of his best loved poems, "Little Boy Blue" and "Dutch Lullaby" ("Wynken, Blynken, and Nod"); *A Humble Romance,* a book of short stories about restrictive village life in Massachusetts, by Mary E. Wilkins Freeman; *The Aspern Papers,* a novelette by Henry James; and *In Old Virginia* by Thomas Nelson Page, a native Virginian who recaptured gracefully if sentimentally the romantic aspects of the old South in stories and sketches.

Augustus Saint-Gaudens completed his famous standing statue of Abraham Lincoln for Lincoln Park, Chicago. Lincoln, with slightly bowed head, stands before a chair from which he has seemingly just risen.

1888

The main issue in the presidential election campaign of 1888 was whether the tariff should be reduced; Democrats said yes, Republicans no. Pres. Grover Cleveland, the Democratic candidate, did not campaign, feeling it was beneath the dignity of the office of president. Benjamin Harrison, the Republican candidate, brought the front porch campaign to its peak. Republican groups were told when to visit Harrison's home, and the candidate was well prepared for each, including the Republican White Hat Club of Ohio. In all, he addressed about 300,000 people without leaving home. Late in the campaign, on Oct. 26, the British minister to the U.S. was tricked into writing a letter saying it would be best for England if Cleveland were reelected. Sensing there was still some latent dislike of the mother country, the Republicans turned this against Cleveland even though he had sent the hapless diplomat home.

The **secret ballot** was first used in the U.S. in local elections in Louisville, Ky. Adopted in Australia as early as 1858, the secret ballot came to be referred to in America as "kangaroo voting." Henry George, proponent of

A new generation of musicians was emerging; they were to dominate American music until the time of World War I. These composers, whose works and writings reflected particularly the influence of Johannes Brahms, became known as the New England Academicians or Boston Classicists. Among them was Arthur William Foote, the only important American composer of the period educated entirely in the U.S. His choral work *The Wreck of the Hesperus* was enthusiastically received in Boston this year. He composed an overture, *In the Mountains,* in 1887 and *Suite for Strings* in 1889.

Among **books published** this year was *Looking Backward, 2000–1887,* a Utopian fantasy by Edward Bellamy, a little-known journalist and novelist. Bellamy hit on the right medium for expressing his concern with social problems in an industrialized society. The book sold 1,000,000 copies in a few years, and Bellamy clubs devoted to the nationalization of industry and redistribution of wealth sprang up everywhere. Also published this year were *The American Commonwealth,* a classic

| Business and Industry; Science; Education; Philosophy and Religion | III | | IV | Sports; Social Issues and Crime; Folkways; Fashion; Holidays |

The **Marine Biological Laboratory** was founded at Woods Hole, Mass. The prime mover was zoologist Stephen F. Baird, U.S. commissioner of fish and fisheries since 1871.

What became the first successful **electric trolley** system was contracted for by Frank J. Sprague for the city of Richmond, Va. It began operating in 1888.

Clark University, conceived by philanthropist James Gilman Clark as a graduate school that would provide higher education at a cost below that of other New England universities, was established at Worcester, Mass. Its first classes were held in 1889.

The interest of **Theodore Roosevelt** in the protection of big game and wildlife became manifest in his appeal for the formation of the Boone and Crockett Club, named for two of his heroes. Since 1883, Roosevelt had been buying Dakota ranchlands. He gave up these investments in 1887, but contact with the open spaces had stimulated his interest in nature. In 1888 he set down his western experiences in the book *Ranch Life and the Hunting Trail.*

Apr. 19   Catholic University in Washington, D.C., was chartered by Congress. It opened in 1889, the only university owned by the Roman Catholic hierarchy in the U.S.

Charleston, S.C., as far back as 1795 and 1796, but there is no record that their members ever played golf.

The **U.S. Lawn Tennis Association men's singles championship** was won for the seventh time in a row by Richard D. Sears. This year the first women's singles championship was held at the Philadelphia Cricket Club. Ellen Hansell was the winner.

Mar. 2   The **American Trotting Association** was organized at Detroit, Mich.

May 11   The 13th annual **Kentucky Derby** was won by Montrose, with a time of 2:39¼. The jockey was Isaac Lewis.

May 13   The 15th annual **Preakness Stakes** was won by Dunbine, with a time of 2:39½. The jockey was Billy Donohue.

May 26   **Racetrack betting** became legal for the first time in New York State.

June 9   The 21st annual **Belmont Stakes** was won by Hanover, with a time of 2:43½. The jockey was Jimmy McLaughlin.

Fall   The **National League baseball championship** was won by Detroit, with a record of 79 wins, 45 losses. This year's interleague playoff was notable for its 15-game road trip. Detroit bested St. Louis of the American Association ten games to five.

Sept. 5   **Labor Day** was first observed as a legal holiday in New York State.

Sept. 17–30   The **America's Cup** was successfully defended by the U.S. yacht *Volunteer,* which won two straight races from the British challenger *Thistle.*

1888

Scientists and inventors were beginning to put electricity to practical use. Among the leaders in this field was Nikola Tesla, who was born in Austria-Hungary in 1857 and came to the U.S. in 1884. In 1888 he invented the alternating current motor, one of his most important contributions. Other inventions included an arc lighting system (1886), an alternating current transmission system (1888), and high-frequency current generators (1890). Tesla also worked on a system for transmitting power without wires. In his later years he was occupied with telephony and telegraphy.

Continuing **specialization in American scholarship** was reflected in the founding this year of the Geological Society of America, the American Folklore Society, the American Mathematical Society, and the National Statistical Association.

Although it was not the first golf club established in the U.S., St. Andrews Club in Yonkers, N.Y., founded this year, clearly marked the point at which the game became firmly rooted in the U.S. Clubs were soon set up in Boston, New York, and Philadelphia. By 1892 the game was moving westward, soon reaching the Pacific coast. In 1893 a course for women only was opened in Morristown, N.J., and by 1894 there were 100 courses in the country. At this time golf was a game for the well-to-do, and the players, who wore rather odd costumes, including scarlet coats, were often objects of ridicule.

This year's **national college football championship** was won by Yale, with a record of 13 wins, no losses, no ties.

The political slogan **"As Maine goes, so goes the nation"** was adopted by the Republican Party after the election of Benjamin Harrison. State elections in Maine for decades to come were held weeks before national

the single land tax, was among the earliest American public figures urging adoption of the secret ballot. In 1950 South Carolina became the last state to adopt the secret ballot.

Feb. 19 A **cyclone** virtually destroyed Mount Vernon, Ill., killing 35 persons.

Mar. 12 A 36-hour **blizzard**, which struck the region around New York City, cost 400 lives and destroyed millions of dollars of property. The city was virtually isolated from the world when the heavy snows halted transportation and disrupted communications. Messages to Boston had to be relayed via England.

May 31 The **Prohibition Party National Convention** nominated Clinton B. Fisk of New Jersey for the presidency and John A. Brooks of Missouri for the vice presidency.

June 4 **Electrocution** replaced hanging as the method of execution in New York State. Gov. David B. Bill signed a bill authorizing electrocution effective Jan. 1, 1889.

June 5 The **Democratic National Convention** nominated **Pres. Grover Cleveland** for a second term. Allen G. Thurman of Ohio was nominated for the vice presidency.

June 25 The **Republican National Convention** nominated **Benjamin Harrison** of Indiana for the presidency and Levi P. Morton of New York for the vice presidency.

July 29 A **yellow fever epidemic** broke out in Jacksonville, Fla., and persisted until Dec. 7. Over 4500 cases were reported, and more than 400 persons died. Similar epidemics struck throughout the South during this period.

Nov. 6 **Benjamin Harrison was elected president** of the United States. Levi P. Morton was elected vice president. The electoral vote was Harrison, 233; Pres. Grover Cleveland, the Democratic candidate, 168. The popular vote was Harrison, 5,444,337; Cleveland, 5,540,050; Clinton B. Fisk, Prohibition candidate, 250,125; Alson J. Streeter, Union Labor candidate, 146,897; Robert H. Cowdrey, United Labor candidate, 2808. In congressional elections the Republicans kept their 39–37 majority in the Senate and gained 14 seats in the House to take a 166–159 majority.

Dec. 24 **Mississippi steamboat fires** killed 55 persons over the holiday. The steamer *Kate Adams* burned on this day, killing 25, and the steamer *John H. Hanna* burned Dec. 26, killing 30.

that ranks with Alexis de Tocqueville's *Democracy in America* as a sympathetic but penetrating analysis, by James Bryce, British historian, frequent visitor to the U.S., and later ambassador to the U.S. (1907–1913); *Acres of Diamonds* by Russell Conwell, an inspirational classic first delivered as a lecture in 1861 but polished through use on the Chautauqua circuit (over 6000 times); *The Critical Period of American History, 1783–1789* by John Fiske, who was now turning from evolution to history; *The History of the Inquisition in the Middle Ages* by Henry C. Lea, probably the best historical work to date by an American historian in a field other than U.S. history; *Political Essays*, the last published work of James Russell Lowell; and the first volumes in *The Library of American Literature*, edited by the poet, stockbroker, and critic Edmund Clarence Stedman.

Olin Levi Warner and John T. Boyle, working independently, used American Indian subjects for their art works and in Warner's case made an ethnologically valuable contribution. Warner at about this time, following a long trip through the West, was producing reliefs depicting Indian heads. Use of Indian themes in sculpture was characteristic of Boyle's work. In *The Stone Age*, modeled this year, an Indian woman was shown defending her children against a powerful eagle.

John La Farge, unrivaled U.S. church muralist, painted the *Ascension*, his vast mural in the academic tradition in the chancel of the Church of the Ascension, New York City.

. A new main building for the **Boston Public Library** was begun from designs by Charles Follen McKim, a member of McKim, Mead, and White, the great architectural firm of the nineteenth century. Standing near other architectural gems on Copley Square, this striking building in the Italian Renaissance style was enriched by decorative ideas from Stanford White and Augustus Saint-Gaudens. John Singer Sargent, Edwin A. Abbey, and the French painter Pierre Puvis de Chavannes were engaged to provide murals.

Edward MacDowell returned permanently to the U.S. after having studied for 12 years in France and Germany. He became the first American composer to be as highly regarded as his European contemporaries.

May "Casey at the Bat," by Ernest Thayer, was given its first public recitation by the popular actor DeWolf Hopper, at Wallack's Theater, New York City.

Business and Industry; Science; **III**		**IV** **Sports; Social Issues and Crime;**
Education; Philosophy and Religion		**Folkways; Fashion; Holidays**

Business combinations were being formed in every direction. By this year the following industries were organized in some form of combination: oil, whiskey, sugar, glass, copper, rubber, coal, beef, reaping and moving machinery, gas, lead, threshing machines, ploughs, steel rails, steel and iron beams, wrought-iron pipe, iron nuts, stoves, school slates, castor oil, and linseed oil.

The **Lick Observatory** was completed on Mt. Hamilton, east of San Jose, Calif., and turned over to the regents of the University of California. Funded by a bequest of $700,000 by San Francisco financier James Lick, the observatory housed the most powerful telescope yet devised.

George Eastman introduced the **Kodak,** a square box camera using roll film. Kodak camera No. 1 was at first marketed already loaded; the photographer mailed the Kodak to the factory, which returned prints and the reloaded camera. Photography became a practical hobby overnight, and sales skyrocketed.

Chinese laborers who left the U.S. were prohibited from returning by an act of Congress. The law cancelled provisions in the act of 1882 that permitted Chinese to return to the U.S. under certain conditions.

June 13 A **Department of Labor** without Cabinet status was established by an act of Congress. In 1903 it was reduced to the status of a bureau in the Dept. of Commerce and Labor. On Mar. 4, 1913, Congress created a Department of Labor headed by a Cabinet member.

July 27 The **first electric automobile,** designed by Philip W. Pratt, was demonstrated in Boston. It was a tricycle driven by storage batteries, and was built by the Fred W. Kimball Company of Boston.

Oct. 1 The beginnings of **federal labor arbitration** were marked by congressional authorization of a commission to mediate disputes between interstate railroads and their workers.

elections, so they were used as gauges for predicting the results in the national balloting. Maine remained staunchly Republican until the era of Franklin D. Roosevelt.

The **major league pitching record** for most consecutive games won in a season was set by Tim Keefe of New York. He won 19 straight games.

The **U.S. Lawn Tennis Association singles championships** were won by Bertha L. Townsend in the women's division and by Henry W. Slocum in the men's division.

Jan. 21 The **Amateur Athletic Union** of the U.S. (AAU) was formed, winning control over amateur athletics from unscrupulous promoters. The AAU's ideal was to preserve "sport for sport's sake." It came to supervise and conduct programs and competitions in about 20 sports and to represent the U.S. in international amateur sports federations. Its influence has been reduced since World War II by the takeover of collegiate sports by the National Collegiate Athletic Association (NCAA) and by the increasing professionalization of many sports.

May 11 The 16th annual **Preakness Stakes** was won by Refund, with a time of 2:49. The jockey was F. Littlefield.

May 14 The 14th annual **Kentucky Derby** was won by MacBeth, with a time of 2:38¼. The jockey was George Covington.

June 9 The 22nd annual **Belmont Stakes** was won by Sir Dixon, with a time of 2:40¼. The jockey was Jimmy McLaughlin, who picked up his sixth Belmont Stakes win. McLaughlin was the only jockey in Belmont history to twice win the race three times in a row (1882–1884, 1886–1888).

Fall The **National League baseball championship** was won by New York, with a record of 84 wins, 47 losses. The annual interleague playoff was won by New York, defeating St. Louis of the American Association six games to four.

| Exploration and Settlement; Wars; Government; Civil Rights; Statistics | I | | II | Publishing; Arts and Music; Popular Entertainment; Architecture; Theater |

1889

A controversy involving the U.S., Great Britain, and Germany over the Samoan Islands in the Pacific Ocean threatened to break out into armed conflict. In 1889 warships of the three nations converged in the region, reflecting the three powers' interest in the civil war being fought on the islands. A showdown among the naval vessels in the harbor of Apia was averted only when a fierce storm destroyed all the warships except one English vessel. On Apr. 29 a conference opened in Berlin and on June 14 the three nations agreed on a treaty that provided for a three-power protectorate to guarantee Samoan independence.

Holding companies were permitted by amendment to New Jersey's laws of incorporation. The companies were later used to circumvent provisions of the Sherman Antitrust Act. As a result New Jersey became the home of most of the early giant corporations. Delaware followed suit a few years later.

Jan. 28 A **transit workers strike** tied up virtually all of New York City's surface transportation. The strike ended a few days later when the workers realized their efforts were futile.

Feb. 11 The **Department of Agriculture** was raised to Cabinet status by Congress. Pres. Grover Cleveland appointed Norman J. Colman as its first secretary. He served less than three weeks before being replaced by Jeremiah M. Rusk, appointed by incoming Pres. Benjamin Harrison.

Mar. 2 The **first antitrust law** was passed by the Kansas legislature. North Carolina, Tennessee, and Michigan followed the same year; South Dakota, Kentucky, and Mississippi the next year; and eight more states in 1891. These state laws were ineffective, for no state could prohibit a corporation duly chartered elsewhere from doing business within its borders.

Mar. 4 **Benjamin Harrison was inaugurated president** of the United States, the 23rd. A Republican, he served one term.

Apr. 22 At noon the great **Oklahoma land rush** began. The federal government, pressured by cattlemen, opened for settlement 1,900,000 acres in central Oklahoma bought from the Creek and Seminole tribes. Thousands of settlers raced in after a pistol shot signaled the opening. Many Oklahomans had already

A new approach to women's magazines was introduced this year by Edward W. Bok, who took over editorship of the *Ladies' Home Journal.* Hitherto such periodicals had offered only light entertainment and household hints. By publishing serious articles on civic affairs, waging crusades against social ills, and printing the writings of leading authors such as Mark Twain and Rudyard Kipling, Bok demonstrated that women's interests were wider than had been assumed. By the time Bok retired in 1919, the *Journal's* circulation had increased from 440,000 to 2,000,000.

Among **books published** this year was *A Connecticut Yankee in King Arthur's Court* by Mark Twain, in which the author further explored the ironies of human nature and existence by setting a Yankee industrialist in the not-so-romantic days of chivalry. Also published were the first two volumes of *The History of the United States* by Henry Adams, for many years the best account of the administration of Thomas Jefferson; *Sant' Ilario,* one of Francis Marion Crawford's better romantic novels of life in Italian society, part of his trilogy begun in *Saracinesca* and concluded in *Dr. Orsino* (1892); *A Little Book of Western Verse* by Eugene Field, which brought the Chicago columnist-poet a wider following; *Chita: A Memory of Last Island* by Lafcadio Hearn, the first novel by an atypical American author on an atypical theme, the destruction of an island and the hazards faced by a lost child; *Annie Kilburn* by William Dean Howells, a novel in which Howells took up the cause of labor; and the first two volumes of *The Winning of the West* by Theodore Roosevelt.

Edward MacDowell performed his *Second Piano Concerto* in New York City, his first great success after his return to the U.S. from Germany. The concert was held at Chickering Hall.

The Charity Ball, another popular play written by David Belasco and Henry De Mille, opened at the Lyceum in New York City.

Feb. 2 The first number of *Munsey's Weekly* was issued by Frank A. Munsey. Munsey had burst on the New York publishing scene in 1882 as editor of *The Golden Argosy* (later *Argosy* magazine). He filled the pages of his new magazine with moralistic action stories, including tales by Horatio Alger, Jr., and other

1889

Liberal thinkers within American Protestantism reacted to the problems caused by rapid industrialization with a movement that came to be known as the Social Gospel, or Christian Socialism. These leaders believed that Christian churches should do more than strive for personal salvation. They worked to abolish child labor, secure better working conditions for women, and gain a living wage for all workers. They believed that the growing concentration of wealth was inimical to the teachings of Christ. The early leader of the Social Gospel movement was the Rev. Washington Gladden, who wrote *Burning Questions* (1890). Somewhat later, the Rev. Walter Rauschenbusch became an important figure. Among economists, Richard T. Ely took a forceful part. Others active in the Society of Christian Socialists, which held a meeting in Boston this year, were Josiah Strong, David Jayne Hill, and E. Benjamin Andrews.

Hull House, a settlement house that would become famous, was established in a slum neighborhood in Chicago by Jane Addams. Like other settlement houses of this period, Hull House was patterned after Toynbee Hall in London.

Barnard College for women in New York City was established as part of Columbia University. Its first classes met this year.

The **first scholar to record Indian speech** and music with a phonograph was J. Walker Fewkes, who had been commissioned by Mary Hemenway to study Indian folklore along the Passamaquoddy R. in Maine. Fewkes later became the outstanding ethnologist of the American Indians of the Southwest.

The **University of New Mexico** was chartered at Albuquerque, N.M. Students were admitted in 1892.

The **first Bessemer Steel I beam** in the U.S. was produced by Jones & Laughlin of Pittsburgh, Pa. I beams made possible rapid construction of steel-skeleton skyscrapers.

The **first movie film** was developed by Thomas A. Edison on a base devised by George Eastman.

The **Singer Manufacturing Company** of Elizabethport, N.J., produced and marketed the first electric sewing machine known in the U.S.

As methods of transportation improved, there was a temptation to see how far one could go in the shortest time. Nellie Bly (Elizabeth Cochrane Seaman), a reporter for Joseph Pulitzer's New York *World,* set out on Nov. 14 to better the record of 80 days around the world set by Jules Verne's fictional hero Phileas Fogg. Using trains, boats, bullock carts, and her own energy, Nellie made it back to New York City on Jan. 25, 1890, with a time of 72 days, 6 hrs., 10 min., 58 sec. She was much acclaimed, especially by the *World.* She recounted her trip in *Nellie Bly's Book: Around the World in Seventy-Two Days* (1890). The year it was published, someone named George Train went around the world in 67 days, 12 hrs., 3 min., but no one paid him much attention. This was not Nellie Bly's first headline-grabbing exploit. Earlier she had had herself committed to a facility for the mentally ill on Blackwell's Island, New York City, and in 1887 recounted her adventures in *Ten Days in a Mad House.*

The **General Federation of Women's Clubs** was founded, uniting the many influential clubs that flourished throughout the U.S. The relatively easy access of American women to higher education gave them community interests that found an outlet in women's clubs, which often held considerable political and social power.

The so-called **safety bicycle** was manufactured for the first time on a large scale. It was generally the same as bicycles today, having two wheels of equal size with the saddle above and between them. It replaced the dangerous high-wheelers that had one very large and one small wheel. Cycling became a popular method of transportation for workers, causing severe traffic and parking problems.

The term *Texas leaguer* became baseball parlance for a weak hit just over the heads of the infield but short of the outfield players. The term may first have been used to describe the short hits of Arthur Sunday, a player from Texas. Another version has it that the term was coined in Syracuse, N.Y., in 1886 by a pitcher who lost a game on such hits by several former Houston players on the Toledo team.

The **Sons of the American Revolution** was organized in New York City this year, centennial of the U.S. Constitution. The society was formed to keep alive the patriotic spirit of those who fought in the American Revolution, but its membership was restricted to male descendants of Revolutionary veterans.

Walter Camp listed in *Collier's Weekly* the first **All-American football team,** selecting 11 college football players as best in the nation at their positions. The selection was made by Caspar Whitney, who chose the All-American teams through 1896. The selections appeared

made illegal entry to stake claims to the best land. In fact, by 10 A.M. of the opening day, Guthrie, the designated central city for the new territory, had swelled with settlers seeking plots in the new territorial capital.

May 31 The disastrous **Johnstown flood** killed 2295 persons when the dam above Johnstown, Pa., broke after heavy rains had swelled the Conemaugh R. The flood destroyed four valley towns before drowning Johnstown in 30 feet of water. Every Johnstown survivor lost a relative or friend in this calamity.

June 10 The **United Confederate Veterans** was organized at New Orleans, La., for the purpose of uniting all Confederate veteran organizations. John B. Gordon, governor of Georgia, was elected the first general of the association.

Oct. 2 The **International Conference of American States** began in Washington, D.C. Chairman of this first Pan-American conference was James G. Blaine, secretary of state, who almost alone among U.S. statesmen had long been concerned with Latin American relations. Several trade and customs treaties were signed by Pres. Harrison.

Nov. 2 **North and South Dakota** were admitted into the Union, the 39th and 40th states.

Nov. 8 **Montana** was admitted into the Union, the 41st state.

Nov. 11 **Washington** was admitted into the Union, the 42nd state.

practitioners of the rags-to-riches school of literature. In 1891 the magazine was retitled *Munsey's Magazine* and made a monthly. After several years, it became an enormous success, largely because of Munsey's program of direct-mail and newspaper advertising. By the end of the century, it was one of the most successful monthlies in the U.S. It continued until 1929, when it was merged with an already merged publication, the *Argosy All-Story Weekly.*

July 8 The *Wall Street Journal* began publication when the Wall Street firm of Dow Jones & Co., which had been established in 1882 by Charles H. Dow and Edward T. Jones, converted an afternoon newsletter for its customers into a full-fledged afternoon daily. At first, the four-page paper was published from the firm's offices at 15 Wall Street. Over the years the paper has grown to become one of the world's biggest daily newspapers, with ten printing plants across the U.S. receiving copy by satellite transmission. It has a circulation of about 1,500,000.

July 12 Recognition of **American music** by Europeans was bestowed by the Paris Exposition. A concert of American works conducted by Frank Van der Stucken offered pieces by Edward MacDowell, Dudley Buck, George W. Chadwick, Arthur Foote, Henry Holden Huss, Margaret Ruthven Lang, John K. Paine, and Van der Stucken.

Sept. 9 *Shenandoah* by Bronson Howard was produced by Charles Frohman at the Star Theatre in New York City. The play, like many of Howard's best works, dealt with the Civil War.

1890

Mounting pressure for federal restraint of monopolistic industrial trusts resulted in the passage on July 2 of the Sherman Antitrust Act, named for Sen. John Sherman, Republican of Ohio. The law stated: "Every contract, combination in the form of trust or otherwise, or conspiracy, in restraint of trade or commerce among the several States, or with foreign nations, is hereby declared illegal." In practice, the lack of definition of such words as trust weakened the law. Also, it was not clear whether the law applied to labor unions. The act did not accomplish as much as its advocates hoped because of the way federal courts interpreted it and

Toward the end of the nineteenth century, light and comic operas became popular. The two leading composers were Victor Herbert and Reginald De Koven. The latter wrote 19 comic operas, of which the most popular by far was *Robin Hood*, first produced in Chicago this year on June 9. It contained his two most popular songs, "Brown October Ale" and "Oh, Promise Me." De Koven also wrote two grand operas, *Canterbury Pilgrims* (1917) and *Rip Van Winkle* (1920).

The **Tower Building,** probably the first steel-skeleton building in New York City, was built at 50 Broadway. In his plans, Bradford Gilbert specified a building of 11 stories, 129 ft. high and 21 ft. 6 in. wide. The Tower Building was the first in the world in which the total weight of walls and floors was carried through girders and columns to the foundation. The New York City Building Department altered the building code to permit the novel construction.

Jan. 30 The **University of Idaho** was chartered at Moscow, Idaho. First instruction was given in 1892.

June The **first systematic theory of philanthropy** in the U.S. appeared in the *North American Review* in an article by Andrew Carnegie entitled "Wealth." Carnegie combined a defense of the free enterprise system as a manifestation of natural law with an exhortation to businessmen to donate their wealth to worthy causes to adjust the inequities of capitalism.

Oct. 7 **Seth Low,** a merchant and public official, was chosen president of Columbia College. His 12-year tenure was marked by transformation of the small college into a large university. In 1901, campaigning as a reformer, Low became mayor of New York City.

Nov. 11 The **first Congress of the Roman Catholic laity** of the U.S. assembled at Baltimore, Md.

Dec. 14 The **American Academy of Political and Social Science** was founded in Philadelphia. This year also saw formation of the American Physical Association and the American Dialect Society. These organizations reflected the trend toward greater specialization in American scholarship.

in articles in *Collier's* annually until Camp's death in 1925, when Grantland Rice took over the task. Today selections are made by various polls of sportswriters and coaches.

The **U.S. Lawn Tennis Association singles championships** were won by Bertha L. Townsend in the women's division and Henry W. Slocum in the men's division.

This year's **national college football championship** was won by Princeton, with a record of ten wins, no losses, no ties.

Jan. 24 A **$500,000 robbery** of the Connecticut Mutual Life Insurance Company by Joseph A. Moore, an Indianapolis agent, was announced.

May 9 The 15th annual **Kentucky Derby** was won by Spokane, with a time of 2:34½, a new Derby record. The jockey was Thomas Kiley.

May 10 The 17th annual **Preakness Stakes** was won by Buddhist, with a time of 2:17½. The jockey was H. Anderson.

June 5 **James J. Corbett,** a bank teller turned amateur boxer, defeated the well-known pro boxer Joe Choynski in 27 bloody rounds. Corbett finished the struggle with a left hook, a punch he was said to have conceived after suffering two broken knuckles.

June 13 The 23rd annual **Belmont Stakes** was won by Eric, with a time of 2:47. The jockey was W. Hayward.

July 8 **Bare knuckle boxing** had its last and most memorable bout when John L. Sullivan knocked out Jake Kilrain in the 75th round for the U.S. heavyweight championship at Richburg, Miss. Sullivan then claimed the world's championship, for Kilrain had fought a draw with the champion of England, Jem Smith. After this bout boxing with gloves under Marquis of Queensberry rules was introduced.

Fall The **National League baseball championship** was won by New York, with a record of 83 wins, 43 losses. New York also won the annual interleague playoff, defeating Brooklyn of the American Association six games to three.

1890

As the century neared its end, the U.S. developed a school of philosophy of its own—pragmatism. The term had been used in a magazine article as early as 1878 by Charles Sanders Peirce. Pragmatism taught that truth was to be found not in theoretical speculation, but in the practical outcome of ideas. It judged ideas and actions by their consequences, if any. This truly American philosophy was developed by William James, who became the most influential thinker of his time. He earned an international reputation and brought the concept of pragmatism to a wide audience. James's *Principles of Psychology,* published this year, became a classic. The

The existence of urban slums was well known by many, but it was not until the publication this year of *How the Other Half Lives* by Jacob A. Riis, a Danish-born New York City journalist, that the reality of the miserable lives led by thousands in the slums was brought home to the general public. The book triggered efforts to alleviate these conditions by improving labor conditions and instituting building codes. In his book Riis cited facts and figures and told of his experiences in the slums. Battling alone at first, Riis gained many supporters and found a powerful ally in Theodore Roose-

because, for the first ten years at least, no vigorous attempt was made to enforce it.

The **Census** recorded a population of 62,947,714. The center of population was placed at 20 mi. east of Columbus, Ind.

The **melting pot** character of New York City was reflected in statistics revealing that there were half as many Italian New Yorkers as Neapolitans in Italy, as many German New Yorkers as Germans in Hamburg, twice as many Irish New Yorkers as Dubliners, and two and one-half times as many Jews as were living in Warsaw.

Feb. 4 The Senate ratified the **Samoan treaty** with Germany and Great Britain. This treaty placed the Samoan Islands under the joint control of the three powers, and thus made more secure the fueling station at Pago Pago for the growing U.S. Pacific fleet.

Feb. 10 Some 11,000,000 acres of **Sioux Indian territory,** ceded to the U.S. in 1889, were opened for general settlement.

Feb. 24 The **World's Columbian Exposition** of 1893 was designated to be held in Chicago by the House of Representatives. The fair was to commemorate the 400th anniversary of the discovery of America.

Apr. 14 The **Pan-American Union** was created by a resolution of the Pan-American conference held in Washington, D.C., between Oct. 2, 1889, and Apr. 21, 1890.

May 2 The **Oklahoma Territory,** the last territory in the contiguous United States, was created by an act of Congress. It was established by redefining Indian territory and creating an area for settlers within Indian lands.

May 24 **George Francis Train** completed a trip around the world. The journey took 67 days, 13 hrs., 3 min., 3 sec. This time bettered Nellie Bly's record.

July 3 **Idaho** was admitted to the Union, the 43rd state.

July 10 **Wyoming** was admitted to the Union, the 44th state. As a territory it had given women the vote in 1869. It was the first territory and the first state to do so.

July 13 A **tornado** caused the death of nearly 100 persons by drowning when it swept over Lake Pepin, Minn.

July 14 Congress passed the **Sherman Act,** requiring the federal government to purchase 4,500,000 oz. of silver a month and issue paper notes against it. The act, a compromise with the free silver interests in the West, was repealed in 1893.

Sept. 3 A **single tax platform** was adopted by the Single Tax National League of the U.S. at a conference in Cooper Union, New York City. The originator of the idea, Henry George, acted as chairman.

Among **books published** this year was *Poems,* a selection of poems among many by Emily Dickinson that were found after her death by her sister. It received mixed reviews because her poetry, often unrhymed and subtle, struck an unfamiliar note. Her place in U.S. poetry gradually became secure, and her popularity and reputation skyrocketed after World War II. Also published this year were *A Hazard of New Fortunes,* a long, complex novel by William Dean Howells, in which a cast of 15 major characters and many minor figures scramble for success in New York City; *The Influence of Sea Power upon History,* by Navy Capt. Alfred Thayer Mahan, a classic analysis of sea power; *Abraham Lincoln: A History* in ten volumes by John Nicolay and John M. Hay, wartime secretaries to the president, which became a standard biography; and *Black Beauty,* by Anna Sewell, an English book for children issued in the U.S. under the aegis of the American Humane Society.

U.S. acceptance of the **International Copyright** agreement came too late to protect Rudyard Kipling against pirating by U.S. publishers of his early books. This year he became popular in England with the publication of *Barrack-Room Ballads* and *Plain Tales from the Hills.* These and other early Kipling works were rushed into print in the U.S. before the act could become effective in 1891.

Censorship by the U.S. Post Office Dept. touched off a controversy when *The Kreutzer Sonata* by Leo Tolstoy was banned from the mails. Theodore Roosevelt called Tolstoy a "sexual and moral pervert."

Louis H. Sullivan's Wainwright Building was erected in St. Louis. The Chicago architect has been called the father of modern architecture and the inventor of the skyscraper. The Wainwright Building was one of his best works. Also this year, Sullivan's Chicago Auditorium was completed. It was for many years the greatest structure of its type anywhere.

Charles Buddy Bolden formed his own band in New Orleans. A cornetist, Bolden was one of the pioneers of instrumental jazz. Most of the early jazz musicians of New Orleans played in his band at one time or another.

Feb. The fictional character **Sherlock Holmes,** created by Arthur Conan Doyle, made his official debut in the U.S. when *Lippincott's Monthly Magazine* published

| Business and Industry; Science; Education; Philosophy and Religion III | IV Sports; Social Issues and Crime; Folkways; Fashion; Holidays |

book was thoroughly empirical and made a laboratory science of psychology.

The growth of **child labor** in the South was reflected in the fact that some 23,000 children were now employed in the factories of the 13 southern states. Adoption by industry of the traditional agricultural family system of employment was mainly responsible for the high number of children employed.

Illiteracy in America was estimated at 13.3% of the population, a decrease of 3.7% in a decade.

The first U.S. patent for a **pneumatic hammer** was awarded to Charles B. King. His hammer was exhibited at the Columbian Exposition of 1893.

John W. Burgess's *Political Science and Comparative Constitutional Law* charted a new course in American political science by rejecting passive notions of natural rights in favor of historic and legal analysis of the potentialities of social and political institutions. W. W. Willoughby's *An Examination of the Nature of the State* expresses the same spirit in its analysis of government.

The establishment of **Sequoia and Yosemite national parks** by the federal government assisted the cause of conservation in the U.S. by protecting native species of animal and plant life from hunters and timber interests.

The **cyanide process of extracting gold** from low-grade ore was introduced at about this time. Annual production of gold in the U.S. more than doubled within eight years, undermining arguments for free coinage of silver.

The value of **silver** produced in the U.S. for the year rose to $57,242,100, more than five times the value of silver produced in 1865. The rapid inflation of silver, as opposed to the deflation of gold, in the post–Civil War period led to political currency issues, the rise of William Jennings Bryan, and the formation of such interest groups as Greenbackers, populists, and Silverites.

Formation of the **American Tobacco Company**, after a price war among cigarette companies, created a monopoly organized by James Buchanan Duke. Duke later created similar monopolies for plug tobacco and snuff. Ultimately he established the Duke Endowment, principally for the benefit of Trinity College in Durham, N.C., in 1924 renamed Duke University.

Jan. 23 The **fastest railroad time** for an American train was claimed for the Atchison, Topeka & Santa Fe Railroad, which carried reporter Nellie Bly from La Junta, Colo., to Chicago at an average speed of 78.1 mph.

velt. He also made enemies of landlords and politicians who were profiting from the slums.

The observation "**Everybody talks about the weather, but nobody does anything about it**" was written by the editor Charles Dudley Warner in the Hartford *Courant.* The remark has been wrongly attributed to his Hartford friend Mark Twain.

Smoking by men at social functions became more acceptable during this decade, but the social taboo against women smoking in the company of men remained strong.

The **two-step** came into vogue. This lively dance step probably owed much to John Philip Sousa's fast "Washington Post March." In any case, the two-step replaced several older dances, such as the galop, quadrille, lancers, reel, polka, and Portland fancy.

The term *Baltimore chop* entered baseball parlance to mean a batted ball that bounced so high in the infield that the hitter could reach first base before the ball could be fielded and thrown. The Baltimore team, especially players John McGraw and Willie Keeler, were especially adept at this method of getting on base.

This year's **national college football championship** was won by Harvard, with a record of 11 wins, no losses, no ties.

The **U.S. Lawn Tennis Association singles championships** were won by Ellen C. Roosevelt in the women's division and Oliver S. Campbell in the men's division.

May 14 The 16th annual **Kentucky Derby** was won by Riley, with a time of 2:45. The jockey was Isaac Murphy.

June 10 The 18th annual **Preakness Stakes** was won by Montague, with a time of 2:36¾. The jockey was W. Martin.

June 10 The 24th annual **Belmont Stakes** was won by Burlington, with a time of 2:07¾. The jockey was S. Barnes.

Aug. 6 The **first electrocution** took place at Auburn Prison, Auburn, N.Y. The executed prisoner was

| Exploration and Settlement; Wars; Government; Civil Rights; Statistics I | II Publishing; Arts and Music; Popular Entertainment; Architecture; Theater |

Oct. 1 Congress passed the **McKinley Tariff Act,** which raised tariffs to the highest level yet known in the U.S. Among other items it taxed opium at $10 a lb. if manufactured for smoking.

Oct. 1 The **Weather Bureau** was created in the Dept. of Agriculture by an act of Congress. Weather information had previously come from the Army Signal Corps.

Nov. 1 The first state to restrict **black suffrage** was Mississippi, which adopted a new constitution that effectively disenfranchised most of the black population by requiring the ability to read and understand the U.S. Constitution.

Nov. 4 In **congressional elections** the Republicans gained eight seats in the Senate to lead the Democrats 47–39, with two seats going to minor parties. In the House a Democratic landslide gave Democrats a 235–88 majority, with nine seats going to minor parties.

Dec. 15 **Sitting Bull,** chief of the Sioux Indians, was killed in a skirmish with U.S. soldiers along the Grand R. in South Dakota.

Doyle's story "The Sign of the Four." Pirated editions of Doyle's story *A Study in Scarlet* (1887) had created a great demand for more Holmes stories. On Mar. 1, J. B. Lippincott Company published the authorized edition of *A Study in Scarlet.*

May 19 The American playwright **Clyde Fitch** began his career with a huge success, *Beau Brummell,* a romantic vehicle for matinee idol Richard Mansfield. Later Fitch would create dramas depending more on character development, thus breaking ground for twentieth-century dramatists.

May 30 The cornerstone of the **Washington Memorial Arch,** in marble, was laid. The arch was originally built of wood. This masterpiece by architect Stanford White stands at the foot of Fifth Ave. in New York City.

1891

The tide of immigration continued to flow strongly. To help deal with it, the position of superintendent of immigration was created on Mar. 3. In this one year, 560,319 immigrants arrived at American ports, and during the 1890s the total was 3,687,000. Until the 1880s, most of the immigrants had come from western and northern Europe. However, in the 1880s such immigration decreased and the numbers arriving from southern and eastern Europe and the Middle East swelled greatly. These new immigrants were less equipped to fit into American life, and almost all had to start at the bottom of the economic ladder.

Mar. 3 U.S. **Circuit Courts of Appeal** were created by an act of Congress. This relieved the Supreme Court of some of its appellate jurisdiction.

Mar. 4 Congress passed the **International Copyright Act,** which gave British, French, Belgian, and Swiss authors copyright protection in the U.S. American publishers had previously pirated works by foreign authors, depriving them of their royalties and injuring American authors, whose books had to be priced higher than those of foreign authors because of the inclusion of royalties in the price. Copyright protec-

One of the greatest careers of the American stage, extending over more than 40 years, came to an end on Apr. 4 at the Brooklyn, N.Y., Academy of Music when Edwin Booth appeared for the last time in *Hamlet.* Booth had always been popular and his restrained style of acting departed from the more emotional style of many others, but his career had been checkered, marked by bankruptcy and then by scandal when his brother, John Wilkes Booth, assassinated Pres. Abraham Lincoln. Among Booth's most notable achievements were the 100-night run of *Hamlet* in 1864 in New York City; the building of Booth's Theater in New York in 1869, where Booth presented the works of William Shakespeare; and the bequest of his New York home to the Players' Club, which he founded in 1888 and served as first president.

Among **books published** this year was *Tales of Soldiers and Civilians* by the San Francisco journalist Ambrose Bierce, a writer fascinated by the supernatural, the mysterious, the terrifying, and the intensely emotional. His *Tales,* based on his Civil War experiences, was later reissued under the title *In the Midst of Life.* It included the oft-anthologized "An Occurrence at Owl Creek Bridge" and "A Horseman in the Sky" and established his reputation in the East. Other books published were *Poems, Second Edition,* by Emily Dickinson; *The American Revolution* by the skillful popularizer of U.S. history, John Fiske; *A New England Nun and Other*

Mar. 10   The **Blair Education Bill,** introduced by Sen. Henry W. Blair of New Hampshire, died in the House. It would have provided for the funding of public schools from a $120,000,000 appropriation to be distributed among the states on the basis of the prevalence of illiteracy.

May 1   The **Bank of America** at Philadelphia, Pa., failed, causing the failure of several other banks and of the American Life Insurance Company of Philadelphia.

Aug. 8   A **strike** on the New York Central and Hudson River Railroad was called by the Knights of Labor. It lasted until Sept. 17.

Oct. 6   The sanctioning of **polygamy** was discontinued by the Mormon Church. Thereafter most cases in conflict with federal law concerned men who had married polygamously before 1890.

William Kemmler of Buffalo, who had been convicted of the hatchet murder of Matilde "Tillie" Ziegler, his common-law wife, on Mar. 28, 1889. The execution was botched. George Westinghouse, Jr., reported: "It has been a brutal affair. They could have done better with an axe."

Fall   The **National League baseball championship** was won by Brooklyn, with a record of 86 wins, 43 losses. The annual interleague playoff, with the American Association's Louisville team, ended in a tie, each team winning three games and one game ending in a tie.

Nov. 29   The **first Army-Navy football game** was played at West Point, N.Y. The score was Navy 24, Army 0. The contest became an annual event between the two service academies (except for 1909, 1917–1918, and 1928–1929).

1891

As the nation grew, it became increasingly industrialized. Industrial and agricultural production was rising, and imports and exports rose steadily as well. Agricultural products still represented the largest part of exports, but in the 1890s they declined from 74.5% of the total to 61% by 1900. During the decade, manufactured goods' share of exports rose from 17.87% to 31.65%. The value of imports increased from $789,310,404 in 1890 to $849,941,184 in 1900.

Henry O. Havemeyer created the **American Sugar Refining Company** under a New Jersey charter, after having his Sugar Refineries Company in New York broken up by the state's antitrust laws. Thus reorganized and without legal impediment, American Sugar went on to control half the sugar consumed in the U.S. by the time of Havemeyer's death in 1907.

The **University of Chicago** was created by funds from John D. Rockefeller, Sr., ultimately amounting to $35,000,000. It was built atop a Baptist institution. Further land was donated by Marshall Field. Chartered this year, it opened on Oct. 1, 1892. Its first president was the biblical scholar and educator William Rainey Harper, who promised complete academic freedom for his topnotch faculty.

California Institute of Technology (Caltech) was founded this year as Throop Polytechnic Institute in Pasadena, Calif. Its first classes met this year.

Photography of the sun was made possible for the first time by invention of the spectroheliograph by George

A unique event in sports history occurred this year when James Naismith, a physical education instructor at what is now Springfield College, Springfield, Mass., invented the game of basketball. No other sport is known to owe its origin to one person. Basketball is the only popular American game that does not have English origins. Naismith was seeking to create a game that could be played indoors in winter and allow fast action and competition but not be as rough as football, which was gaining a reputation for violence. The first basketball game employed a soccer ball and two peach baskets. The rules Naismith devised have not been changed basically in over 100 years.

A new **baseball rule** permitted player substitution at any time during a game, removing a restriction imposed in 1877 that allowed a substitute to enter the game only before the fourth inning.

Construction of **federal penitentiaries** was authorized by Congress at Ft. Leavenworth, Kans., Atlanta, Ga., and McNeil's Island, Puget Sound, Wash. These were the first nonmilitary prisons built by the federal government.

tion was later extended to include most other countries of the world.

Mar. 14 The **lynching** of 11 Sicilian immigrants who had been indicted for the murder of the Irish chief of police of New Orleans caused an international crisis, the recall of the Italian minister, and an indemnification by the federal government. A mob of New Orleans citizens was incensed by the acquittal of three of the suspects. The incident served to restrain subsequent official encouragement of immigration.

May 19 The **People's, or Populist, Party** was launched in Cincinnati, Ohio. Farmers in the West and South were in desperate economic plight, and backers of the new party, thinking eastern bankers were hoarding gold, advocated free coinage of silver. High railroad rates also were hurting farmers, so they advocated government ownership of railroads. Free silverites captured the Democratic Party in 1896, but lost the election by 600,000 votes.

Sept. 22 Nine hundred thousand acres of **Indian land** in Oklahoma were opened for general settlement by a presidential proclamation. The land had been ceded to the U.S. by Sauk, Fox, and Potawatomi Indians.

Oct. 16 A mob in **Valparaiso,** Chile, attacked American sailors from the cruiser U.S.S. *Baltimore.* Two were killed, several wounded. War became imminent because of Chile's delay in making settlements. Chile finally paid a total of $75,000 to the injured and the heirs of the dead.

Stories by Mary Wilkins Freeman, offering expert portrayals of Massachusetts farm folk undergoing deformation of character or spirit in an era that was leaving them behind; *Main-Traveled Roads,* stark short stories and sketches against a background of dreary midwestern farm life, by Hamlin Garland; *Colonel Carter of Cartersville,* a novelette about a gentleman of the old South down on his luck, which made Francis Hopkinson Smith a popular author; and a final collection of poems and prose by the aging Walt Whitman, *Goodbye, My Fancy.*

Augustus Saint-Gaudens completed his monumental memorial to Mrs. Henry Adams in Rock Creek Cemetery, Washington, D.C. The hooded figure, variously called *Grief* or *Death* or *Peace of God,* is perhaps the most moving and enigmatic sculpted figure done by an American.

The **Masonic Temple** in Chicago, one of the earliest modern buildings, was built from designs by Daniel H. Burnham and John W. Root, disciples of the Romanesque Revival of Henry Hobson Richardson. It was 20 stories high and the tallest building in the U.S.

George M. Cohan made his first stage appearance, at the age of 13, with his family in *Peck's Bad Boy.*

May 5 **Carnegie Hall** at Seventh Ave. and 57th St., New York City, opened with an all-Tchaikovsky program conducted by the composer himself. Funded principally by Andrew Carnegie, designed by William B. Tuthill, and originally called the Music Hall, the building was for many years the home of the New York Philharmonic.

Nov. 9 The **longest consecutive theatrical run** to date was begun with the opening of *A Trip to Chinatown,* a farce about San Francisco by Charles H. Hoyt. It ran 650 performances, closing on Aug. 17, 1893, and held the record until 1918. Hoyt had already satirized spiritualism, the plumbing industry, railroad operations, and politics.

1892

As the 1892 presidential election approached, there was dissatisfaction among voters with both the Democratic and the Republican parties. Many thought the tariff rates too high, the farmers complained of low prices for their products, and there was a feeling that the government favored bankers and industrialists at the expense of the common man. The only party to show much concern about these issues, the People's Party, usually referred to as the Populists, was organized this year. The Populists campaigned vigorously for such proposals as public ownership of the railroads, an eight-hour

The cornerstone for what was intended to be the largest church in America, the Protestant Episcopal Cathedral of St. John the Divine, was laid on St. John's Day, Dec. 27. It was located on 11.5 acres of land in upper Manhattan, New York City. In a competition, the architectural firm of George Lewis Heins and Christopher Grant La Farge had won the award with plans for a structure in the Romanesque style. It was to be 601 ft. long, 146 ft. wide at the nave, and 320 ft. wide at the transept. Construction proceeded in fits and starts because of the great amount of money needed. In 1911

| Business and Industry; Science; Education; Philosophy and Religion   **III** | **IV**   Sports; Social Issues and Crime; Folkways; Fashion; Holidays |

E. Hale while a student at M.I.T. Hale later became professor of astrophysics at the newly opened University of Chicago and director of the Mt. Wilson observatory.

The new **biblical criticism** was spread in the U.S. in large part by Orello Cone through his book *Gospel Criticism and Historical Christianity,* published this year. A scholar in New Testament studies, Cone set forth the principles and methods of the new discipline, well advanced in Germany but lagging in the U.S. He followed up in 1893 with *The Gospel and Its Earliest Interpreters.* Cone at the time was president of Buchtel College, now the University of Akron, Ohio.

Washington Gladden, Congregational minister in Columbus, Ohio, emerged as a popular interpreter of the new biblical criticism and a mediator between its proponents and holders of more orthodox views. In *Who Wrote the Bible?* Gladden set about to uncover the hitherto neglected riches of the Bible, literary, spiritual, and ethical, and to rekindle popular interest in it. The book became a text for YMCA instruction and adult Bible classes of several Protestant denominations.

May 19 A charter was granted to **Rice Institute,** founded by William Marsh Rice, in Houston, Tex. No instruction, however, was given until 1912. In 1960 the name was changed to Rice University.

Aug. 24 A patent for a motion picture camera, the first in its field in the U.S., was filed by Thomas A. Edison.

Oct. 16 The **first correspondence school** in the U.S. was opened by Thomas Jefferson Foster, editor of the Shenandoah *Herald.* Now known as the International Correspondence School, Scranton, Pa., it was begun to teach mining methods to workers to increase safety in coal mines.

Dec. 29 An early patent for **wireless telegraphy** was issued to Thomas Edison for a "means of transmitting signals electrically . . . without the use of wires." The patent was the result of experiments conducted in 1885. On Nov. 15, 1883, Edison had received a patent for his two-element vacuum lamp, the forerunner of the vacuum tube rectifier.

The year's **national college football championship** was won by Yale, with a record of 13 wins, no losses, no ties.

The **U.S. Lawn Tennis Association singles championships** were won by Mabel E. Cahill in the women's division and Oliver S. Campbell in the men's division.

This year the **Preakness Stakes** was not run. The annual event resumed with the 19th running in 1894.

May 13 The 17th annual **Kentucky Derby** was won by Kingman, with a time of 2:52¼. The jockey was Isaac Murphy, who scored his second straight Derby win.

June 10 The 25th annual **Belmont Stakes** was won by Foxford, with a time of 2:08¾. The jockey was Edward "Snapper" Garrison.

Fall The **National League baseball championship** was won by Boston, with a record of 87 wins, 51 losses. This year the rival American Association disbanded after a disappointing season. No interleague playoff was held.

Oct. 18 The **first International six-day bicycle race** in the U.S. was run in Madison Square Garden, New York City. Riders used high-wheelers and worked alone, pumping until exhausted, then resting and starting again for 142 hours. The first winner was "Plugger Bill" Martin. The record under one-man rules was established in 1898 by Charlie Miller at Madison Square Garden, who rode 2093.4 miles. Most of his competitors ended up in hospitals, suffering from exhaustion.

1892

The growing conflict between capital and labor resulted this year in violent conflict in the Homestead Strike. On July 1, when a contract between the Amalgamated Association of Iron and Steel Workers and the Carnegie Steel Company expired, the company cut wages and refused to recognize the union. The workers struck on June 26. On July 6 the company brought in 300 Pinkerton guards to protect the Homestead plant, near Pittsburgh, Pa. A pitched battle resulted. The Pinkertons were turned away with three dead and many wounded; ten strikers were killed. The company hired

One of the most intriguing murder cases in U.S. history began on Aug. 4 when Andrew J. Borden and his second wife, Abby, were murdered with blows from an ax in their Fall River, Mass., home. Mr. Borden's 32-year-old unmarried daughter, Lisbeth A. Borden, was accused of the crime, although she denied it. Miss Borden did not testify at her trial. She was acquitted and the case was never solved, although it gave the world a still well-known jingle:

day for labor, and a currency system controlled by the federal government, not the banks. In the election, the Populists became the first third party since 1860 to win electoral college votes, carrying Kansas, Colorado, Idaho, and Nevada.

Jan. 1 **Ellis Island** in upper New York Bay became the receiving station for immigrants. On Nov. 12, 1954, it was closed after 62 years and the processing of 20 million immigrants. It is now part of the Statue of Liberty National Monument.

Feb. 29 U.S. prohibition of the **hunting of fur seals** in the Bering Sea was submitted to international arbitration. The U.S. had earlier seized Canadian vessels, claiming that the Bering Sea was a closed sea under control of surrounding U.S. territories. On Aug. 15, 1893, the tribunal declared against the U.S. In 1898 Congress appropriated $473,151 to pay damages to the owners of the Canadian vessels.

Apr. 12 A **$25,000 indemnity** was paid by the U.S. government to families of the Italian subjects lynched at New Orleans in 1891.

May 5 **Chinese immigration** was further restricted by congressional legislation providing registration of Chinese laborers and deportation regulations for those not specifically authorized to remain. Called the Geary Chinese Exclusion Act, it extended existing exclusion laws another ten years.

June 7–11 The **Republican National Convention** nominated Pres. Benjamin Harrison for reelection and Whitelaw Reid of New York for the vice presidency.

June 21–23 The **Democratic National Convention** nominated Grover Cleveland of New York for the presidency and Adlai Ewing Stevenson of Illinois for the vice presidency.

June 29–July 1 The **Prohibition National Convention** nominated John Bidwell of California for the presidency and James B. Cranfill of Texas for the vice presidency.

July 4–5 The **People's (Populist) Party National Convention** nominated James B. Weaver of Iowa for the

the trustees decided to change the partly built cathedral to the Gothic style, which would make it the largest Gothic cathedral in the world. Plans originally submitted by the architect Ralph Adams Cram were adopted. Today the cathedral is still incomplete, although work is once more in progress.

Among **books published** this year was the final edition of *Leaves of Grass* by Walt Whitman. Also published were *The West from a Car Window* by Richard Harding Davis, editor of *Harper's Weekly*, which collected reports on his extensive travels in the U.S.; *The Adventures of Sherlock Holmes*, the first collection of the short stories by Arthur Conan Doyle about literature's most famous detective; *The Quality of Mercy*, a novel by William Dean Howells in which he again probes the relationship between the economic order and the crimes of individuals; *Barrack-Room Ballads* by Rudyard Kipling, demonstrating the English poet's heroic view of his nation's imperialism; *The Old South* by Thomas Nelson Page, offering vivid if sentimental essays and sketches about plantation life; *Green Fields and Running Brooks*, another collection of Hoosier poems by James Whitcomb Riley; and *The History of David Grieve* by Mrs. Humphry Ward, a novel promoting the social application of Christianity.

"**Daisy Bell**," the "bicycle built for two song," rode to popularity along with the new American pastime of cycling.

Jack "Papa" Laine formed the Reliance Brass Band in New Orleans. A white musician, Laine was one of the first to imitate black styles of hot music. His later organization, Jack Laine's Ragtime Band, was probably the first white Dixieland jazz band.

The **American Fine Arts Society** was formed by combining the Society of American Artists, the Art Students' League, and the Architectural League. The new group was housed on 57th St., New York City, and aided financially by George W. Vanderbilt, owner of the magnificent estate Biltmore, near Asheville, N.C.

Antonín Dvořák, the Bohemian composer, came to New York City in response to an invitation to direct the National Conservatory of Music. Dvořák was particularly interested in national movements in music, especially those allied to interest in folklore, independence, and romanticism. He arrived in Hoboken, N.J., on Sept. 27, 1892, with his family. From there he traveled to New York City, taking rooms near the National Conservatory. The composer's first public appearance was on Oct. 21, when in a series of performances at Carnegie

strikebreakers and at its request the governor of Pennsylvania, Robert E. Pattison, sent in the state militia on July 12. The militia protected the strikebreakers hired by Carnegie. The strike ended on Nov. 20 with the workers admitting defeat. The union was destroyed and many of the men never got their jobs back.

The **General Electric Company** was formed by a merger of the Edison General Electric Company with its biggest rival, the Thomson-Houston Electric Company.

Labor unrest, reflected in many strikes and much violence, characterized the year, especially in Pennsylvania, Tennessee, Wyoming, and Idaho. Unrest in Tennessee was the result of the use of convict labor. Pres. Harrison issued orders against strikers, especially in the West, and federal troops were used to enforce court injunctions.

Bacteriology came of age in the U.S. with the publication of *A Manual of Bacteriology,* the first comprehensive book on the subject. It was written by Lt. Col. George Miller Sternberg, who specialized in the cause and prevention of infectious disease.

The **fundamentalist-modernist controversy** was heated up by the heresy trial of Charles A. Briggs, professor of the Old Testament at Union Theological Seminary, New York City. Prof. Briggs, on his elevation to a distinguished chair at the seminary, delivered a paper taking a liberal approach on the authority of the Bible. Many orthodox Presbyterian ministers, sensing a threat in Briggs's modernist biblical views, persuaded the General Assembly of the Presbyterian Church, which held veto power over the seminary's appointments, to exercise its veto. The New York Presbytery then tried Briggs for heresy; he was acquitted. The prosecution appealed the decision to the assembly, which condemned Briggs and suspended him from the ministry. The case aroused partisan feelings among Presbyterian ministers across the country, and several defenders of Briggs were suspended, notably Prof. H. P. Smith of Lane Theological Seminary in Cincinnati, Ohio. At the end, the seminary broke off its Presbyterian relationship, became nondenominational, and kept its distinguished scholar.

The **First Church of Christ, Scientist** was founded in Boston, Mass., by Mary Baker Eddy and a small group of followers.

The **boll weevil,** a beetle of Mexican or Central American origin, was first seen in Texas; from there the pest spread widely, causing severe damage to U.S. cotton crops.

Formation of the **American Psychological Association** reflected the improved status of psychology as an independent discipline.

The **University of Chicago** integrated the summer session with the academic year. This policy was initiated by Pres. William Rainey Harper, one-time supervisor of the

Lizzie Borden took an ax,
Gave her mother 40 whacks.
When she saw what she had done,
She gave her father 41.

Lizzie Borden spent the rest of her life as a virtual recluse and died in her Fall River home on June 1, 1927, at 68.

The phrase *the 400* with reference to society's elite achieved an almost instant place in American idiom after it was used by New York City's social arbiter, Ward McAllister. Asked to shorten a long list of persons to be invited to a ball in the Astor ballroom, which would hold only 400, McAllister commented that there were "only 400 persons in New York society." Social commentators and society gossips quickly gave the remark wide circulation. Those with social pretensions who were left off the list were outraged.

The expression *Diamond Horseshoe* came into prominence to describe the U-shaped row of 35 newly constructed parterre boxes in the Metropolitan Opera House in New York City. The price of a box was $60,000.

George W. G. Ferris designed the **Ferris wheel.** He built the first one in 1893 for the Columbia Exposition. Forty passengers could be carried 250 feet high in its 36 cars.

This year's **national college football championship** was won by Yale, with a record of 13 wins, no losses, no ties.

The **U.S. Lawn Tennis Association singles championships** were won by Mable Cahill in the women's division and Oliver S. Campbell in the men's division.

Mar. 18 **Jockeys** were prohibited from using anything but a whip and a spur on a horse during a race. The ruling was prompted by discovery that jockey Cook used an electric spur while riding Gyda at Guttenburg, N.J. Cook was ruled off the track.

May 11 The 18th annual **Kentucky Derby** was won by Azra, with a time of 2:41½. The jockey was Alonzo Clayton.

June 3 **Jefferson Davis's birthday** was for the first time observed as an official holiday in Florida. The date has since been made a legal holiday in Alabama, Georgia, Louisiana, Mississippi, South Carolina, Tennessee, and Texas. It is a memorial day in Arkansas. Jefferson Davis was born in 1808.

June 9 The 26th annual **Belmont Stakes** was won by Patron, with a time of 2:47. The jockey was W. Hayward.

presidency and James G. Field of Virginia for the vice presidency.

Aug. 28 The **Socialist Labor Party** nominated Simon Wing of Massachusetts for the presidency and Charles H. Matchett of New York for the vice presidency.

Oct. 15 The **Crow Indian reservation** in Montana was opened to settlers by presidential proclamation. The territory covered 1,800,000 acres.

Oct. 28 A great fire in Milwaukee, Wis., destroyed $5,-000,000 worth of property over 26 acres.

Nov. 8 Grover Cleveland was elected president of the United States. Adlai E. Stevenson was elected vice president. The electoral vote was Cleveland, 277; Pres. Benjamin Harrison, Republican incumbent, 145; James B. Weaver, Populist candidate, 22. The popular vote was Cleveland, 5,554,414; Harrison, 5,190,802; Weaver, 1,027,329; John Bidwell, Prohibition candidate, 271,058; Simon Wing, Socialist Labor candidate, 21,164. In congressional elections the Democrats gained five seats in the Senate for a 44–38 majority, with three seats going to minor parties. In the House the Democrats lost ground but kept a 218–127 majority, with 11 seats going to minor parties.

Music Hall he conducted the first performance of *Te Deum,* which he had written for the occasion. The world premiere of his ninth symphony, *From the New World,* was performed in New York City in 1893. Dvořák traveled to Europe in May 1894 and returned to New York in November. He left the U.S. for the last time on Apr. 16, 1895.

"**After the Ball Is Over,**" a perennial favorite song in the U.S., was composed by Charles K. Harris, one of the most successful songwriters of the 1890s and early 1900s. "After the Ball" became a tremendous hit during the Columbian Exposition of 1893 in Chicago.

The first home designed by **Frank Lloyd Wright,** it is widely believed, was Charnley House, built in Chicago. Wright made the plans while still working for the firm of Adler & Sullivan.

Aug. 27 The **Metropolitan Opera House** in New York City was almost totally destroyed by fire. The fire started in the morning and in less than an hour destroyed the auditorium and stage, causing upward of $100,000 in damage. Other portions of the building, occupying the block between Broadway and Seventh avenues from 39th to 40th streets, sustained little damage. The opera house itself, which had opened on Oct. 22, 1883, was gutted.

1893

A bitter political battle was fought over repeal of the Sherman Silver Purchase Act of 1890, which required that the U.S. treasury buy at market value 4,500,000 ounces of silver a month. When, by Apr. 15, 1893, the gold reserve in the treasury fell below the $100,000,000 level because silver had been overvalued in relation to gold, Pres. Grover Cleveland and others blamed the Sherman Act for creating too much money. Cleveland called a special session of Congress for Aug. 7, but it was Oct. 30 before both houses of Congress, after much debate, voted repeal. Cleveland was thus able to keep the U.S. on the gold standard, but he alienated members of the Democratic Party who wanted easy credit.

Jan. 17 A revolution in Hawaii deposed Queen Liliuokalani with at least the foreknowledge of the U.S. minister to Hawaii, John L. Stevens. A provisional government headed by Sanford B. Dole was protected by 300 U.S. Marines from the cruiser *Boston.* The provisional government requested the U.S. to

American playwrights were relying more and more on domestic themes, characters, and settings for their plays, and were writing more realistic, if still melodramatic, plays. One such author, and also a leading actor, was James A. Herne, whose play *Shore Acres,* depicting life in New England, became a hit in 1893. The play deals with tensions in a family in a quietly realistic way. The play ran for 113 performances in Boston, beginning in Feb. 1893, and then became a success in New York City, opening on Dec. 25 at Daly's Theater.

Among **books published** this year was *Maggie: A Girl of the Streets,* by a 21-year-old newspaper reporter, Stephen Crane. Unable to find a publisher for a realistic novel about a prostitute, Crane published privately; no one paid attention to it until the success of his *Red Badge of Courage* in 1895. The significance of *Maggie* became clearer as grimly naturalistic portrayals of the seedy side of American life became increasingly the material of American writers. Also published this year were *Can*

| Business and Industry; Science; Education; Philosophy and Religion III | | Sports; Social Issues and Crime; Folkways; Fashion; Holidays IV |

summer meeting of the Chautauqua movement. Harper also created the first successful correspondence school courses.

The **first college of osteopathy** in the U.S. was established at Kirksville, Mo.

Nikola Tesla developed the first motor that could effectively utilize alternating current for power.

Astronomer **Edward Emerson Barnard** detected the fifth satellite of Jupiter from the Lick Observatory in California. During his career Barnard also developed the science of celestial photography, identified 16 comets, and had a star named for him.

Sept. The **first successful gas-powered automobile** made in the U.S. was built by Charles and Frank Duryea, bicycle designers and toolmakers, at Chicopee, Mass. Afraid of ridicule if they tested the vehicle publicly, the builders tested it indoors. A more powerful model was given a successful trial run at Springfield, Mass., in 1893.

Sept. An **electric automobile** made by William Morrison of Des Moines, Iowa, appeared in the streets of Chicago. The owner called on police to help him make his way through crowds of curious spectators.

Oct. 3 The **University of Idaho** was opened to students. It had been chartered Jan. 30, 1889, by the territorial legislature, and was thus 18 months older than the state itself.

Dec. 19 The **University of Oklahoma** was opened at Norman, Okla.

Fall Boston won the **National League baseball championship** with a record of 102 wins, 48 losses.

Sept. 7 James J. Corbett won the **world heavyweight boxing championship** by knocking out John L. Sullivan in the 21st round. The bout, held at New Orleans, La., has been considered the first heavyweight title bout fought with gloves under Marquis of Queensberry rules, including three-minute rounds.

Oct. 5 The notorious **Dalton gang** of robbers was virtually wiped out at Coffeyville, Kans., while attempting to rob a bank.

Oct. 20–23 The **World's Columbian Exposition** was opened with magnificent dedication ceremonies at Chicago. Vice Pres. Levi Morton gave the opening address. John Philip Sousa, who resigned from the Marine Corps this year to organize his own band, conducted. The exhibition was the result of public demand for fitting commemoration of the discovery of America. On Apr. 25, 1890, Congress had passed an act that authorized an "exhibition of the arts, industries, manufactures, and products of the soil, mine and sea." Pres. Benjamin Harrison had recommended that a sum of "not less than $10 millions" be allotted to the fair. Total expenditures have been estimated as over $22,000,000. The fair was set out on an area of 644 acres, with the exposition itself covering 150 acres. There were 50 acres of concessions and 55 acres of state, transportation, electric, arts, and liberal arts buildings. It officially opened May 1, 1893.

1893

A worldwide financial panic and economic depression began in the spring of 1893. Sensing weakness in the American economy, foreign investors began withdrawing their capital. Railroads began to go into bankruptcy, the steel industry declined, and the banking system was strained to the limit. On May 5 and June 27 stocks fell sharply on the New York Stock Exchange. On June 26 the value of the U.S. silver dollar had fallen from 67 cents to less than 60 cents in gold. A panic in New York City was averted on June 29 by a loan of $6,000,000 by clearinghouse banks. Pres. Cleveland directed the treasury to sell government bonds to New York City banks for gold; four issues of such bonds totaled $293,000,000. Nevertheless, by December about 600 banks had failed and by June 1894 no fewer than 194 railroads had gone bankrupt. Unemployment climbed, and by the winter of 1893–1894 there were about 2,500,000 persons out of work. Democrats blamed the high tariff and excess government spending by Republicans. Gold standard advocates blamed the depression on agitation for more and

The World's Columbian Exposition, on the shores of Lake Michigan in Chicago, was officially opened to the public on May 1 to mark the 400th anniversary of the discovery of America by Christopher Columbus. The exposition had been authorized by Congress in 1890 and formally dedicated on Oct. 12, 1892. The exposition's 150 buildings of Greek, Romanesque, and Renaissance styles of architecture became known as the White City; the buildings exhibited the talents of the foremost American architects and sculptors. Seven thousand workmen were employed in construction of the exposition. Popularly known as the Chicago World's Fair, the exposition covered 600 acres, brought exhibits from 72 countries, and by the time it closed on Oct. 30 attracted more than 27,000,000 visitors. The architecture and the landscaping had a powerful effect on the nation and was largely responsible for the so-called City Beautiful movement, which sought to make American cities more attractive and livable through the planning of buildings and parks.

annex the islands. The queen later protested her ouster to Pres. Grover Cleveland.

Feb. 1 The **provisional government of Hawaii** was recognized by the U.S. minister to Hawaii, John L. Stevens, who ordered the raising of the American flag and declared the islands a protectorate.

Feb. 15 A **Hawaiian annexation treaty** was submitted to the Senate. It had already been signed by the provisional government of Hawaii. On Mar. 9 Pres. Grover Cleveland, beginning to doubt the propriety of Minister Stevens's actions in Hawaii, withdrew the treaty from the Senate and commissioned James Henderson Blount to investigate and report.

Mar. 1 The **Diplomatic Appropriation Act** was passed by Congress; it authorized creation of the rank of ambassador. The act also stipulated that U.S. ministers hold a rank similar to that of the ministers from the countries to which they are assigned. By 1920, 15 legations had been raised to ambassadorial rank.

Mar. 4 **Grover Cleveland was inaugurated president** of the United States, the only president to serve two nonconsecutive terms. A Democrat, he was the 22nd and 24th president. Adlai E. Stevenson was sworn in as vice president.

Apr. 3 The **first U.S. ambassador to the Court of St. James** was named: Thomas Francis Bayard, secretary of state in Pres. Cleveland's first administration. Up to this time the highest U.S. diplomatic title had been minister.

Apr. 13 The **Hawaiian protectorate** was ended by Commissioner James H. Blount, who ordered U.S. troops back to their ship.

May 15 The Geary **Chinese Exclusion Act** of 1892 was declared unconstitutional by the Supreme Court. The act was enforced for the first time on Aug. 10, when Chinese immigrants were deported from San Francisco for nonregistration.

July 17 Commissioner James H. Blount's **report on the Hawaiian revolution,** delivered to Sec. of State Walter Q. Gresham, accused Minister Stevens of active participation in all phases of the Hawaiian uprising. Stevens's supporters countercharged Blount with compiling a lopsided report based on a small sampling of Hawaiian opinion and of failing to question Stevens himself. Not until 1898 was Hawaii annexed as a territory.

Aug. 13 A fire in Minneapolis, Minn., left 1500 persons homeless and destroyed about $2,000,000 in property.

Aug. 24 A devastating **cyclone** ripped through Savannah, Ga., and Charleston, S.C., killing some 1000 persons and causing terrible damage.

Sept. 7 The surveillance of **illegal immigration** into the U.S. was for the first time made the subject of an agreement between the U.S. and Canada. The major

Such Things Be? by Ambrose Bierce, hair-raising tales of the supernatural; *The Cliff Dwellers*, a novel about the relationships of people working in a Chicago skyscraper, by Henry Blake Fuller; *Nights with Uncle Remus*, another of the popular collections of tales by Joel Chandler Harris; *The World of Chance* by William Dean Howells, expressing a stark view of life and society; *The Heavenly Twins* by Sarah Grand (pen name of Mrs. Frances Elizabeth M'Fall, an English women's rights activist), a best seller treating hitherto taboo subjects fictionally; and *The Strange Case of Dr. Jekyll and Mr. Hyde* by Robert Louis Stevenson, six years after its appearance in England.

The world premiere of **Antonín Dvořák's** *New World Symphony* was given in New York City. Dvořák, who had been in the U.S. only a year, produced the most American composition of the nineteenth century. Though no theme of the symphony is specifically drawn from folk music, many are close to the spirit of plantation songs and Indian melodies.

Frederick W. MacMonnies executed the sculptural jewel of the Columbian Exposition: the great fountain of the Court of Honor, a group of 27 large, animated figures surrounding a great white ship. On the recommendation of Augustus Saint-Gaudens, his mentor, MacMonnies had been given $50,000 to carry out his concept. The Columbian fountain won him fame almost overnight.

Daniel Chester French contributed two sculpted highlights of the Columbian Exposition: his relief *The Angel of Death Staying the Sculptor's Hand* and his 75-foot-high *Republic*, symbolizing the U.S.

Two classical **sopranos**, Nellie Melba, a coloratura soprano from Australia, and Emma Calve, an exciting French soprano, made their U.S. debuts at the Metropolitan Opera. One effect of the Columbian Exposition was to widen interest in classical music and opera outside a few eastern cities, and to make musical tours attractive to performers. So popular was Melba that she had a form of toast and a peach dessert named after her.

The 17-story **Manhattan Life Insurance Building,** the first building in New York City to rise above Trinity Church's steeple, was erected.

The first completely independent architectural commission of **Frank Lloyd Wright,** the Winslow residence in Chicago, was built this year.

Louis H. Sullivan saw the construction at the Columbian Exposition in Chicago of one of his most impressive

cheaper money. The populists blamed everything on the gold standard and a shortage of currency. The economy gradually improved, but it was 1897 before it could be said that good times had returned.

Frederick Jackson Turner made his famous contribution to American historiography with "The Significance of the Frontier in American History," an address delivered before the American Historical Association. Turner argued that the ever-expanding frontier of the U.S. provided the key to understanding the differences between Europeans and Americans.

Leo H. Baekeland perfected the process by which Velox paper was produced. Although not immediately successful, Baekeland received $1,000,000 for his patent from Eastman Kodak Company in 1899. With this money, Baekeland constructed the private laboratory in which he made his monumental discoveries in plastics, including Bakelite.

A **zipper,** or slide fastener, was patented by Whitcomb L. Judson. It consisted of a series of hooks and eyes that fastened with a slider. An improved zipper with the meshed tooth type of slide familiar today was patented in 1913 by Gideon Sundbach.

The **Mormon Temple** was dedicated at Salt Lake City, Utah. The site of the temple was selected by Brigham Young six years before work began in 1853. The massive temple of white granite, which looks from a distance to be of marble, cost between $6,000,000 and $12,000,000. It was lavishly appointed, with sky-blue ceiling and marble tiled and seasoned oak floors.

Lillian D. Wald, a social worker, founded the Livingston Street Settlement in New York City, a nursing center in the slums of the Lower East Side. In 1895 Jacob Schiff, a banker and philanthropist, with others, provided funds for larger quarters on Henry St. Known first as Nurses' Settlement, the establishment soon became the justly famous Henry Street Settlement.

Feb. 1 Construction of a pioneer film studio, called the **Black Maria** because of its resemblance to police paddy wagons, was completed at the Edison laboratories in West Orange, N.J. The structure was covered with tarpaper and pivoted to turn with the sun.

Feb. 17 The **University of Montana,** in Missoula, was chartered by the Montana state legislature. Its first classes were held in 1895.

Aug. 1 The **National Bimetallic League** was formed by Populists and Republicans meeting in Chicago. The convention was attended by 810 delegates from 42 states. The convention demanded free coinage of silver at 15½ or 16 to 1 in return for repeal of the Sherman Silver Purchase Act. The delegates sought

Ice hockey was introduced from Canada to the U.S. Games were played at Yale and Johns Hopkins universities. Canadian hockey dates at least from 1855, when teams from the military played games in Ontario. In 1875 students at McGill University in Montreal formulated rules for the game. A flat puck replaced the previously used rubber ball.

The **rise of bicycling** as a means of transportation and recreation in the U.S. was indicated by the increase of bicycles in use from some 20,000 in 1882 to over 1,000,-000 in 1893.

The term *coochee-coochee* was given to a dance by Little Egypt (Catherine Devine), on the Midway at the Chicago Columbian Exposition. It was said that Little Egypt sometimes performed the dance in the nude. Later the term for such a solo performance became *hootchy-kootchy* and finally *the cooch.* This early belly dance made Little Egypt instantly famous and ultimately wealthy.

This year's **national college football championship** was won by Princeton, with a record of 11 wins, no losses, no ties.

The **U.S. Lawn Tennis Association singles championships** were won by Aline Terry in the women's division and Robert D. Wrenn in the men's division.

The **first national fly casting tournament** was held at the World's Columbian Exposition by the newly formed Chicago Fly Casting Club. Accuracy fly, delicacy fly, long-distance bait, and long-distance fly events were held at distances of 75, 80, and 85 feet. The club held national tournaments in 1897, 1903, and 1905. In 1906 a permanent organization, the National Association of Scientific Angling Clubs, was formed in Racine, Wis.; it held a national tournament in 1907. This organization, still strictly amateur, is now the National Association of Angling and Casting Clubs, the governing body of fly casting.

The **Anti-Saloon League** was organized at Oberlin, Ohio, by representatives of temperance societies and evangelical organizations. The league's goal was the prohibition of the manufacture and sale of liquor in Ohio.

A new **baseball rule** established the distance between the pitching slab and home plate at 60 ft. 6 in. This distance has remained unchanged to the present time.

May 10 The 19th annual **Kentucky Derby** was won by Lookout, with a time of 2:39¼. The jockey was Eddie Kunze.

June 10 The 27th **Belmont Stakes** was won by Comanche, with a time of 1:53¼. The jockey was W. Simms.

June 14 **Flag Day** was first officially observed by the city of Philadelphia by order of the mayor, who ordered that the flag be displayed over every public

target was Canadian Pacific coast ports.

Sept. 16 The **Cherokee Strip,** between Kansas and Oklahoma, was opened for land rush settlement. More than 100,000 persons rushed into an area of 6,000,000 acres that had been purchased from the Cherokee Indians in 1891.

Oct. 2 A cyclone raged along the Gulf Coast of Louisiana, killing some 2000 persons.

Nov. 7 Women's suffrage was adopted in Colorado.

projects in the modern style, the Transportation Building.

Oct. 23 *In Old Kentucky* by Charles T. Dazey opened in New York City, a melodrama so popular that it ran for 27 consecutive seasons either in New York City or on the road. The play makes use of fights, murder, horse racing, and conflict between mountaineers and plainsmen.

1894

A new form of protest over economic conditions appeared this year when Coxey's Army, a band of unemployed workers, began a march on Washington, D.C. Jacob S. Coxey was an Ohio businessman and social reformer who gathered together some hundred unemployed followers. Headed by a six-piece band, the group set out for the capital on Mar. 25 from Massilon, Ohio. Coxey expected to gather a large throng on the way to call attention to the plight of the unemployed and to demand government action, such as a large-scale road building program. The men were well received along the way but on Apr. 30, when they arrived in Washington, the army numbered only about 400 men. The next day Coxey and two others were arrested for trespassing on the Capitol lawn when they tried to present petitions to Congress. The army disbanded. Similar armies set out from other starting points, even from the West Coast, but of these, only 17 out of some 1200 persons reached Washington.

Jan. 8 A fire at the site of the Chicago World's Columbian Exposition destroyed virtually all the buildings, with property damages estimated at $2,000,000.

Jan. 17 The U.S. treasury offered a **bond issue** of $50,-000,000 to replenish its gold reserve. This issue proved insufficient, so the treasury offered a second bond issue of $50,000,000 on Nov. 13.

Jan. 30 Suspected **corruption** in the New York City police department prompted the New York State Senate to authorize an investigation.

Feb. 13 A **cave-in** at the Gaylord mine at Plymouth, Pa., killed 13 miners.

Mar. 17 A **Chinese Exclusion Treaty,** by which China agreed to exclusion of Chinese laborers from the U.S., was signed. The Senate ratified the treaty on Aug. 13.

Mar. 30 The **Bland Bill,** authorizing coinage of silver bullion, was vetoed by Pres. Grover Cleveland.

Few American women became professional painters at this time, but one who did so was Mary Cassatt, who spent most of her life in France. There she took part in the impressionist movement and became a friend of Edgar Degas and Edouard Manet. She was the only American invited by the impressionists to exhibit with them. Motherhood was one of her favorite subjects; she did several versions of *Mother and Child.* In 1893 she painted a mural, *Modern Women,* for the women's building at the Chicago World's Fair. In 1894 her painting *La Toilette* was exhibited in Paris.

Among **books published** this year was *Coin's Financial School* by William Hope Harvey, a free silver advocate. The book, on economics, was of little merit but sold 300,000 copies within a year. Also published this year were *A Kentucky Cardinal* by James Lane Allen, a novel about an amiable, nature-loving recluse in love with a girl of quite different interests; *Songs From Vagabondia* by Bliss Carman and Richard Hovey, the first of three refreshing poetic collaborations; *Glimpses of Japan* by Lafcadio Hearn, the best study to date of Japanese culture; *The Prisoner of Zenda* by Anthony Hope, a historical romance that became a classic; *A Traveler from Altruria* by William Dean Howells, a Utopian novel; *The Jungle Book* by Rudyard Kipling, a children's classic; *Wealth Against Commonwealth,* a study of the Standard Oil Company by Henry Demarest Lloyd, one of the first of the muckraking journalists; *Beautiful Joe* by Margaret Marshall Saunders, a dog story that eventually sold some 1,000,000 copies; and *The Tragedy of Pudd'nhead Wilson,* a generally underestimated novel by Mark Twain.

George Grey Barnard, in his first public show at the Paris Salon, achieved an immediate success with his huge marble sculpture *Struggle of the Two Natures in Man.* The work was suggested by a line of Victor Hugo: *Je sens deux hommes en moi* [I sense two men within me]. It depicts two figures grappling, one standing over

banking reforms and repeal of the tax on national bank circulation.

Dec. 24   **Henry Ford** completed construction of his first successful gasoline engine. His first motor car was assembled in 1896. It made a successful run on June 4 powered by a two-cylinder, four-cycle gasoline motor.

building in the city. The mayor's order was pursuant to a resolution of the Colonial Dames of the State, whose president, Mrs. Elizabeth Duane Gillespie, was directly descended from Benjamin Franklin.

Fall   The **National League baseball championship** was won by Boston, with a record of 86 wins, 44 losses.

Oct. 7–13   The **America's Cup** was successfully defended by the U.S. yacht *Vigilant*, which won three straight races from the British challenger *Valkyrie*.

1894

The Gilded Age might well have been called the Age of the Railroad. Railroad building and operation was the single largest economic enterprise by far. On the New York Stock Exchange in 1898, 60% of the stocks listed were those of railroads. The pace of track-laying was never surpassed: in 1880 the mileage was 93,261; in 1890, 167,191; in 1900, 198,964. By 1900 the railroads employed 1,018,000 persons and were valued at a little more than $10,000,000,000. One reason for the affluence of the lines was the generous way in which states and the federal government gave them public land as subsidies for building: nearly 50,000,000 acres from the states and about 130,000,000 acres from federal grants, most of it west of the Mississippi R.

Dr. **Edward Livingston Trudeau**, with the financial support of philanthropist George C. Cooper, opened his enlarged Adirondack Cottage Sanatorium for the treatment of tuberculosis; it was later renamed Trudeau Sanatorium. Himself a sufferer from tuberculosis, Dr. Trudeau founded the sanatorium a decade earlier, financing it from his own practice and solicitations. In his new laboratory Dr. Trudeau conducted the first large-scale experiments on the disease in the U.S.

The **American Federation of Labor** (AFL), under the leadership of Samuel Gompers, voted against adopting socialist reform programs. Gompers believed that U.S. labor should work with capitalism, not against it, and that the AFL's proper concerns were shorter hours, higher wages, and better working conditions. Gompers' victory set U.S. labor on a nonideological course quite different from that of labor in European countries.

The **Southern Railroad Company** was organized by J. P. Morgan. The first well-run railroad in the South, it connected major southern cities with the industrial Northeast, and the Gulf of Mexico with Ohio R. traffic. Morgan had earlier reorganized the Philadelphia & Ohio railroads. His businesslike approach to running railroads brought an end to the swashbuckling, manipulative methods used by Jay Gould, Jay Cooke, and other early railroad barons.

Apr. 20   A strike by **136,000 coal miners** for higher wages began at Columbus, Ohio. This year, like the

Golf was becoming popular in the U.S. but was still largely pursued by the well-to-do at private country clubs. The United States Golf Association (USGA) was formed on Dec. 22 at a meeting of five golf clubs from Long Island, N.Y., Mount Hope, N.Y., Brookline, Mass., Newport, R.I., and Chicago. The association was to standardize rules, conduct national championship tournaments, and stimulate interest in the game. The USGA held its first amateur and open golf tournaments in 1895 at Newport. The new association did much to organize golf and establish consistent rules and guidelines, but it took another 20 years for golf to catch on with the American public.

A new **baseball rule** stipulated that a wooden slab, called the rubber, 12 in. by 4 in., be sunk into the pitcher's mound 60 ft. 6 in. from the front edge of home plate, and that a pitcher be required to place both feet on it at the start of his delivery. Other new rules stipulated that a foul bunt with two strikes on the batter be called strike three, and that a player who sacrificed was not to be charged with a time at bat.

The **highest batting average** for a season ever compiled by a major league baseball player was Hugh Duffy's .438. He was a member of the Boston Nationals.

This year's **national college football championship** was won by Yale, with a record of 16 wins, no losses, no ties.

The **U.S. Lawn Tennis Association singles championships** were won by Helen Hellwig in the women's division and Robert D. Wrenn in the men's division.

Apr. 5 A **riot** of striking miners at Connellsville, Pa., left 11 miners dead.

Apr. 24 A **mine disaster** at Franklin, Wash., killed 37 miners.

June 21 The **Democratic Silver Convention** was held in Omaha, Neb.; 1000 delegates attended. William Jennings Bryan led the convention to the adoption of a free-coinage plank on a silver-to-gold ratio of 16 to 1.

Aug. 1 A **fire** in Chicago, Ill., destroyed $3,000,000 worth of property.

Aug. 8 The **Hawaiian Republic** was officially recognized by the U.S. government. On May 31 the U.S. had recognized that Hawaii should have its own government and that interference from any foreign power would be considered unfriendly to the U.S. On July 4 the Republic of Hawaii had been proclaimed and a progressive constitution adopted.

Aug. 18 The **Bureau of Immigration** was created by Congress.

Aug. 27 The **first graduated income tax law** was passed by a predominantly Democratic Congress after acrimonious debate. It was denounced by Sen. John Sherman (Ohio) as "socialism, communism, devilism." The law was declared unconstitutional in the next year by the Supreme Court. It was part of the Wilson-Gorman Tariff Act, which became law without the signature of Pres. Cleveland.

Sept. 1 A **fire** killed 500 persons in Hinckley, Minn., and 18 neighboring towns. Flames were swept along by a cyclone. Some 500 persons fled the burning Hinckley station in a train.

Nov. 6 In **congressional elections** the Republicans regained control of both houses of Congress, taking a 43–39 majority in the Senate, with six seats going to minor parties, and taking a 244–105 majority in the House, with seven seats going to minor parties. William Jennings Bryan of Nebraska, defeated in his bid for a Senate seat, became editor in chief of the Omaha *World-Herald*. He became an enormously popular speaker on the national lecture circuit.

Dec. 14 Evidence of **corruption** in the New York City police department was highlighted by the admission by Capt. Timothy J. Creeden to a state Senate investigating committee that he had paid $15,000 for his captaincy.

the prostrate form of the other. It is now in the Metropolitan Museum in New York City.

Victor Herbert, leader of the celebrated 22nd New York Regiment Band, composed and produced the first of his many successful operettas, *Prince Ananias.*

"The Sidewalks of New York" was written and composed by Charles Lawler, a buck-and-wing dancer in out-of-the-way music halls. The song was popular in the 1890s, but it became even more popular when Gov. Alfred E. Smith used it in his campaign for the Democratic presidential nomination in 1924.

Rudyard Kipling, then living in Brattleboro, Vt., saw the publication of one of his most enduring works, *The Jungle Book.* Kipling had come to live in Vermont in Feb. 1892, shortly after marrying Caroline Balestier, whose family lived in Brattleboro. The Kiplings lived in Vermont for four years, during which time Kipling's literary reputation was on the rise. During these years Kipling worked on *Captains Courageous* (1897) and saw the publication of a second *Jungle Book* (1895). Kipling loved Vermont, but after a series of unfortunate events the Kiplings left their Brattleboro home in 1896.

Mar. **William Sydney Porter,** who would later adopt the pen name O. Henry, made his first important literary foray when he bought the Austin, Tex., printing office used by William Cowper Brann in 1891 to publish his first issues of the *Iconoclast.* Porter published two issues using the title *Iconoclast,* then renamed his weekly *The Rolling Stone* as of its Apr. 28 issue. Porter supplied virtually all the copy, and in December he quit his job as a teller at the First National Bank in Austin to concentrate on his editorial duties. Neither paper nor author fared well. The last number of *The Rolling Stone* was dated Apr. 27, 1895, and not long after Porter was indicted for embezzling funds from the bank.

July 26 The opening in Chicago of *New Blood* by Augustus Thomas demonstrated the playwright's ability to craft characteristically American subjects and contemporary events into powerful drama. The play opened during the bitter Pullman strike and dealt with conflict between labor and capital. Also this year Thomas's *The Capitol,* set in Washington, D.C., offered a dramatic mix of congressional lobbying, coal strikes, railroad pools, religion, and government.

| Business and Industry; Science; Education; Philosophy and Religion III | | IV Sports; Social Issues and Crime; Folkways; Fashion; Holidays |

previous one, would be marked by widespread labor unrest.

May 11 The bitter **Pullman strike** began at the Pullman railroad car plant in south Chicago. The depression had induced the company to cut wages sharply without reducing the rents of the workers in company-owned housing. Considerable violence, pillaging, and burning of railroad cars ensued; mobs of non-workers joined in.

June 26 A **general railway strike** followed the boycotting of the servicing of Pullman cars by the American Railway Union (ARU), an industrial union headed by Eugene V. Debs. Earlier this year Debs had led a successful strike against the Great Northern Railway. The ARU boycott tied up railroads across the nation.

July 2 An **injunction** was granted to the U.S. government in a federal court in Illinois forbidding the officers of the American Railway Union from interfering with interstate commerce and obstructing the mails. This marked the introduction of court injunctions as a counterblow to labor's chief weapons, the strike and the boycott.

July 3 **Federal troops were ordered to Chicago** by Pres. Grover Cleveland to enforce the injunction against the American Railway Union. Gov. John P. Altgeld of Illinois protested on constitutional grounds. He contended that the disorders were local and did not call for massive federal military intervention.

July 6 **Violence in the railway strike** continued. Two men were killed and several injured when U.S. deputy marshals fired on strikers at Kensington, near Chicago.

July 10 **Eugene V. Debs,** head of the American Railway Union, was cited for contempt when he failed to obey the court injunction handed down on July 2.

July 20 **Federal troops** were withdrawn from Chicago.

Aug. 3 The **Pullman strike** was declared over by the American Railway Union. Labor had been dealt a blow by being brought under the Sherman Antitrust Act and by the introduction of the court injunction as a weapon against it. The ARU specifically had been crushed. No further attempt to create an industrial union was made until the Depression of the 1930s. Only the AFL and the railroad brotherhoods survived. The AFL had 1,675,000 members by 1904.

Sept. 4 A **garment workers' strike** was launched by some 12,000 tailors in New York City. They were protesting sweatshop conditions and the piecework system of payment.

Dec. 14 **Eugene V. Debs** was found guilty of criminal contempt for violating the injunction issued on July 2. He was sentenced to six months in jail. Clarence Darrow came into national prominence as legal counsel for Debs. The entire proceedings, beginning with the

Feb. The **Jockey Club** was incorporated as a result of a meeting of trainers and owners in the previous year. The club's purpose was to "encourage the development of the Thoroughbred horse" and "establish racing on such a footing that it may command the interest as well as the confidence and favorable opinion of the public."

May 15 The 20th annual **Kentucky Derby** was won by Chant, with a time of 2:41. The jockey was Frank Goodale.

May 17 The **Preakness Stakes** was resumed after a lapse of three years, with the 19th running, under the auspices of the Brooklyn Jockey Club at its Gravesend course. The winner was Assignee, with a time of 1:49¼. The jockey was Fred Taral. The Preakness was run in Brooklyn through 1908. In 1909 it returned to Pimlico Race Course in Maryland.

June 16 The **squeeze play** was first employed in baseball by George Case and Dutch Carter, players on the Yale team, in a game against Princeton. The squeeze play is a batting maneuver in which, with a runner at third base and with less than two out, the batter bunts the ball slowly to the infield, enabling the runner on third to come home safely. It was introduced in the major leagues in 1904 by Clark Griffith, manager of the New York Highlanders in the American League. Two types of squeeze play are now in use. One is called the delayed squeeze; in it the runner on third base does not run until the ball has been bunted. The other, more dramatic, type is called the suicide squeeze, in which the runner on third base breaks toward home plate as the pitcher begins his delivery.

June 19 The 28th annual **Belmont Stakes** was won by Henry of Navarre, with a time of 1:56½. The jockey was W. Simms.

June 28 **Labor Day** was made a legal holiday by a congressional resolution.

Fall The **National League baseball championship** was won by Baltimore, with a record of 89 wins, 39 losses.

Dec. 29 A fire during a Christmas festival at Silver Lake, Oreg., killed 40 persons.

1895

A boundary dispute between Great Britain and Venezuela drew England and the U.S. to the verge of war this year. The boundary between Venezuela and British Guiana had been in dispute for 80 years. Tension grew when gold was discovered and Venezuelan troops entered the disputed area. Great Britain refused to submit the quarrel to arbitration, which caused a belligerent reaction by Pres. Grover Cleveland's administration. Sec. of State Richard Olney, on July 20, as much as told Great Britain that the U.S. ruled the Western Hemisphere. This statement irritated Latin Americans and Canadians as well as the British. On Nov. 26 the British prime minister, Robert A. T. Gascoyne-Cecil, Lord Salisbury, replied that the dispute did not concern the U.S., but the U.S. would not yield, citing the Monroe Doctrine. On Dec. 21 Pres. Cleveland asked Congress to establish a commission to settle the dispute and Congress did so. Great Britain, faced with pressing problems elsewhere in the world, wanted no more trouble and on Feb. 27, 1897, agreed to arbitration. On Oct. 3, 1899, a boundary was agreed on which largely upheld England's claim. In the aftermath, many Americans were appalled at how close to war the two English-speaking nations had come, especially since Great Britain was far stronger militarily than the U.S.

Feb. 8 A **federal gold purchase** of $62,000,000 was made by the Treasury Dept. from the banking houses of J. P. Morgan & Company and August Belmont & Company. Gold reserves had fallen to $41,000,000. Revival of business activity in 1896 eased the seriousness of further falls, but gold hoarding did not cease until after the presidential election of 1896, when supporters of the gold standard triumphed over those supporting bimetallism.

Feb. 24 The **revolt of Cuba against Spain** broke out. On June 12 Pres. Cleveland called on U.S. citizens to avoid giving aid to the insurgents. A partial cause of the rebellion was the panic of 1893, which caused a severe depression in the Cuban sugar industry. Repressive measures taken by the Spanish aroused American sympathy, which was inflamed to a war pitch by the yellow journalism of William Randolph Hearst's New York *Journal* and Joseph Pulitzer's New York *World.*

Mar. 5 The **free coinage of silver** at a ratio of 16 to 1 was asked for by a minority of House Democrats. The

The influence of William Morris, the English poet, craftsman, social reformer, and above all a devotee of the Middle Ages, was reflected in the career of the writer and editor Elbert Hubbard. Born in Illinois in 1856, Hubbard abandoned a career in business and turned to writing. This year he established the Roycroft Press at East Aurora, N.Y., and attempted with little success to imitate Morris's Kelmscott Press. He began publishing the monthly magazine *The Philistine*, noted for its inspirational writings and platitudes, contributed mainly by Hubbard. He started another magazine, *The Fra*, in 1908, the title coming from the sobriquet Hubbard had bestowed on himself. Hubbard was best remembered for the essay "A Message to Garcia" (1899), an enormously successful inspirational piece based on an incident in the Spanish-American War. It so appealed to employers that they distributed copies freely to their employees. By 1940 the total circulation of the article was estimated at 40,000,000.

Among **books published** this year was *The Red Badge of Courage*, a realistic Civil War novel by Stephen Crane. It was a remarkable performance: the author was 23 and without any war experience. The novel put American fiction on a firm path toward naturalism. Also published this year were *A House Boat on the Styx* by John Kendrick Bangs, a novel in a humorous vein drawing together various historical figures; *With the Procession* by Henry Blake Fuller, a novel of social strivings in Chicago; *Rose of Dutcher's Coolly*, a novel by Hamlin Garland about a girl's revolt against the bleak life on a Dakota farm; a second *Jungle Book* by Rudyard Kipling; *Amos Judd* by John Mitchell, founder of the original *Life* magazine, a novel about a young Indian rajah brought to the U.S. to save his life; and *The Jucklins* by Opie Read, a best-selling novel by the former editor of *The Arkansas Traveler.*

"You've Been a Good Old Wagon but You've Done Broke Down," a song by Ben R. Harney, was published in Louisville, Ky. Although it was not called a rag, it contained authentic ragtime features. The tune later became a standard number in New Orleans jazz repertoires.

"The Purple Cow," an early humorous quatrain by Gelett Burgess, appeared in the first number of *The Lark*, an amateur magazine of humor and light comment. The four lines probably became as widely memorized and quoted as any piece of U.S. verse.

George W. Chadwick, an organist and composer, began publishing his *Symphonic Sketches* (1895–1904).

Business and Industry; Science; Education; Philosophy and Religion	III		IV	Sports; Social Issues and Crime; Folkways; Fashion; Holidays

use of a blanket injunction, caused concern among many Americans.

1895

Advances in science and technology in the late nineteenth century included great progress in the field of astronomy, particularly in the construction of observatories. As early as 1874–1875, the Lick Observatory on Mt. Hamilton, Calif., was established through gifts from James Lick. The Lowell Observatory was founded in Flagstaff, Ariz., in 1894 by the astronomer Percival Lowell, who caught popular attention with his belief that intelligent life might exist on Mars. The Yerkes Observatory, on the shores of Lake Geneva, Wis., was founded in 1892 with money from Charles T. Yerkes, the financier and urban transportation system magnate. The Yerkes Observatory's 40-inch refracting telescope, then the largest of its type in the world, was completed in 1897.

Power generators capable of the efficient production of hydroelectric power were constructed and put into operation at Niagara Falls, N.Y., by the Westinghouse Electric Company. George Westinghouse, inventor and manufacturer, made invaluable contributions to U.S. industry and commerce. Among his inventions were the air brake for railroad trains and an automatic signaling system for railroad yards and grade crossings.

Jan. 22 The first meeting of the **National Association of Manufacturers** was held in Cincinnati, Ohio. It was attended by representatives of several hundred manufacturing firms.

May 20 Clauses pertaining to **income tax** in the 1894 Tariff Act were declared null and void by the Supreme Court.

May 27 The Supreme Court ruled that **interference with interstate commerce** may legally be prevented by federal injunction.

June 11 The first U.S. patent for a **gasoline-driven automobile** by a U.S. inventor was issued to Charles E. Duryea. On June 26 of the previous year, the Patent Office had granted a patent for a motor car developed in Germany by Karl Benz.

Nov. 2 The **first contest between self-propelled vehicles** in the U.S. was held in Chicago, Ill. A Benz motor wagon, imported and improved by Oscar Bernhard Mueller, was the only car to finish the race.

The work of Charles Dana Gibson began to have a major influence on Americans' perceptions of themselves. Gibson's idealized depiction of the perfect American woman, who came to be known as the Gibson Girl, soon swept the country. She was slim, small-waisted, and had a pompadour hairstyle. She also had a cool, aloof beauty. The young man she was depicted with was created by Gibson somewhat in his own image. This ideal male was clean-shaven and had much to do with the disappearance of the hitherto popular mustache. He also had a strong jaw and broad shoulders, thus not needing padding in his jackets. Gibson's pair were frequently depicted in settings that made sharp and amusing comments on the social scene. Gibson's work appeared in many magazines and books, notably the works of Richard Harding Davis.

Women's skirts were shortened for bicycling wear. They were shortened an inch or two from the ankle, and the hems were weighted with lead.

This year's **national college football championship** was won by Pennsylvania, with a record of 14 wins, no losses, no ties.

The **U.S. Lawn Tennis Association singles championships** were won by Juliette P. Atkinson in the women's division and Fred H. Hovey in the men's division.

May 6 The 21st annual **Kentucky Derby** was won by Halma, with a time of 2:37½. The jockey was James "Soup" Perkins.

May 25 The 20th annual **Preakness Stakes** was won by Belmar, with a time of 1:50½. The jockey was Fred Taral.

Aug. 31 The **first professional football game** was played in Latrobe, Pa., when Latrobe's team of profit-sharing players met the Jeannette, Pa., team. Latrobe hired a substitute quarterback, John Brallier, for $10 in expense money, making him the game's first professional player.

Fall The **National League baseball championship** was won by Baltimore, with a record of 87 wins, 43 losses.

Sept. 7–12 The **America's Cup** was successfully defended by the U.S. yacht *Defender*, which won three straight races from the British challenger *Valkyrie II.*

1895 – 1896   *PRES.* GROVER CLEVELAND

372

Exploration and Settlement; Wars;   I

Government; Civil Rights; Statistics

II   Publishing; Arts and Music; Popular

Entertainment; Architecture; Theater

appeal was framed by Representatives Richard P. Bland of Missouri and William Jennings Bryan of Nebraska. This year saw several free-silver conventions in the South and West; the most notable was held in Salt Lake City on May 15 with delegates from 17 states and territories.

Mar. 18 **Emigration of U.S. blacks** to Liberia, which had begun in 1822 with the establishment of Monrovia by free black settlers, continued with the departure of 200 settlers from Savannah, Ga.

Sept. 27 The so-called **Irish National Convention** was held at Chicago, where physical force was discussed as a means of achieving freedom for Ireland from Great Britain.

Nov. 5 **Women's suffrage** was provided for in the constitution of Utah. The constitution came into effect Jan. 4, 1896, the day Utah entered the Union. It was the second state to give women the vote.

Nov. 6 A **boiler explosion** in the building of the *Evening Journal* at Detroit, Mich., killed 40 persons.

Though a member of the so-called Boston Classicists, Chadwick took a livelier view of contemporary America than did most other composers. His *Sketches* include "A Vagrom Ballad," which is based on hobo themes. The versatile Chadwick composed operas, choral compositions, orchestral pieces, chamber music, piano pieces, and songs.

An early **steel frame skyscraper,** the 16-story Reliance Building in Chicago, was completed by the firm of Burnham and Root. The first floor, designed by John W. Root, was completed in 1891. The remaining floors were designed by Charles B. Atwood, who joined the firm after Root's death in 1891. Daniel H. Burnham continued to pioneer steel frame architecture, notably in the Flatiron Building in New York City (1902).

June 1 **William Allen White** bought the Emporia, Kans., *Gazette* and began a brilliant career as journalist and political commentator. White's staunch Republican views soon brought him into conflict with many fellow Kansans, who were populist in outlook.

July 4 **"America the Beautiful"** by Katherine Lee Bates, a Wellesley College professor, was published in the *Congregationalist,* a church publication. The poem was revised in 1904 and put in final form in 1911.

1896

The presidential election of 1896 was decided after one of the hardest fought campaigns in U.S. history. The division between the Republicans and the Democrats was clear. Republicans were for hard money, a high tariff to protect American industry, and other conservative policies. The Democrats were now in the hands of the populists. The free coinage of silver was their primary campaign issue. This appealed to the farmers and miners of the South and West. The Republicans waged a front-porch campaign for William McKinley, spending about $7,000,000, mostly on mailings that reached 5,000,000 families a week. The Democrats, with only about $300,000 to spend, sent their candidate, William Jennings Bryan, on an 18,000-mile campaign trip, during which he made 600 speeches. But Bryan could not attract the votes of the urban workers, despite his personal attractiveness and oratorical power.

Jan. 4 Utah was admitted into the Union, the 45th state.

May 18 The so-called **Jim Crow Car Law** of Louisiana was declared constitutional by the Supreme Court in *Plessy v. Ferguson,* which advanced the separate but equal doctrine. The court held that segregation was legal if equal facilities were offered to both races. The U.S. Supreme Court reversed this doctrine in civil

A new form of American humor, art, and journalism came into being this year with the appearance of "The Yellow Kid," by Richard F. Outcault, in the New York *World.* It was soon to become the comic strip. A single-panel drawing, which appeared each week, showed the adventures of a boy in a long, yellow, sacklike garment; Outcault soon began to add words. This marked the first time a cartoon caption had appeared inside the frame of a picture. Circulation of the *World* boomed. In 1897 Rudolph Dirks introduced "The Katzenjammer Kids" and was the first to make use of a sequence of panels to tell a story. Another pioneer was Frederick Burr Opper with "Happy Hooligan" (1899). The first comic strip to appear six days a week made its appearance in 1907 in the San Francisco *Chronicle.* It was Harry C. "Bud" Fisher's "A. Mutt," a forerunner of "Mutt and Jeff."

Among **books published** this year was the immensely popular *Quo Vadis?* by the Polish novelist Henryk Sienkiewicz. This vivid, powerful tale of Roman life under Nero and of early Christians has been dramatized, filmed, and translated into all major languages. Also published were *Joan of Arc,* the last major work of Mark Twain, presenting a somewhat idealized Joan set against the malign forces arrayed against her; *Poems, Third Series* by Emily Dickinson, bringing to light more of the

Nov. 5 What came to be known as the **Selden patent,** originally applied for in 1879, was issued to George B. Selden for his gasoline-driven automobile. Alleged infringements on the patent brought about the most celebrated litigation in the history of the auto industry. In 1899 Selden assigned an exclusive license for his motor car to the Electric Vehicle Company. Suits initiated by this company led in 1903 to the formation of the Association of Licensed Automobile Manufacturers (ALAM); ALAM began to collect royalties from the industry for the Selden patent. Henry Ford and a few other automobile manufacturers not affiliated with the ALAM refused to pay the royalties, and suit was brought against the Ford company and one other firm in New York in 1903. The court upheld the validity of Selden's patent on Sept. 15, 1909. Ford appealed and the New York Court of Appeals on Jan. 9, 1911, again ruled in favor of the Selden patent. But it was a Pyrrhic victory for Selden and the Electric Vehicle Company: the patent was held to be restricted to the particular construction it described, and every important auto manufacturer used a motor significantly different from that described in Selden's patent.

Sept. 9 The **American Bowling Congress** (A.B.C.) was formed in Beethoven Hall, New York City, to revive waning interest in a once popular sport. Bowling alleys and matches had been taken over by gamblers and ruffians. Teams of businessmen or workers were often physically beaten in revenge after they had won their matches. The A.B.C. became the ruling body of bowling. It standardized rules and equipment and planned national tournaments. The modern ten-pin game became standard.

Oct. 4 The **first U.S. Open golf tournament,** held at Newport Golf Club in Newport, R.I., under the auspices of the U.S. Golf Association, was won by Horace Rawlins. Rawlins, 19, had come from England earlier in the year to work at the Newport club.

Nov. 2 The 29th annual **Belmont Stakes** was won by Belmar, with a time of 2:11½. The jockey was Fred Taral.

Nov. 28 The **first gasoline-powered automobile race** in the U.S., the Chicago to Evanston Thanksgiving Day Race, was won by the brothers Charles E. and J. Frank Duryea.

1896

Pulpit-thumping Christian evangelism was thriving as the twentieth century neared. In these years the most popular practitioner was William Ashley "Billy" Sunday. A professional baseball player from 1883 to 1900, Sunday had also worked for the YMCA in Chicago from 1891 until he turned evangelist in 1896. On Apr. 15, 1903, he was ordained a Presbyterian minister. Sunday was agile on the platform and colloquial in his speech. He preached the kind of Bible fundamentalism that many wanted to hear and promoted prohibition. It is said that by the time of his death in 1935 he had preached to more people than any other Christian.

Newspapers, in search of greater circulation and more advertising, were becoming less political and more concerned with everyday interests of average people. They began to publish material to entertain as well as inform the reader. Among the innovations was the advice to the lovelorn column, which made its debut in 1896 in the New Orleans *Picayune.* Its author was Elizabeth Meriwether Gilmer, who used the pen name Dorothy Dix. Her column was later syndicated, and collections of her advice on various topics appeared in book form into the 1930s.

Establishment of the **New York Aquarium** provided both a diversion for the public and an invaluable research source for American ichthyologists.

This year's **national college football championship** was won by Princeton, with a record of ten wins, no losses, one tie.

Seven-eighths of the **wealth of the U.S.** was controlled by one-eighth of the people.

The **U.S. Lawn Tennis Association singles championships** were won by Elizabeth H. Moore in the women's division and Robert D. Wrenn in the men's division.

Oliver Wendell Holmes, sitting on the Supreme Court of Massachusetts, dissented in a decision denying

rights decisions on May 17, 1954; May 31, 1955; and Nov. 7, 1955. Chief Justice Earl Warren said in the first of these decisions that the separate but equal doctrine had no place in the field of public education, and maintained that separate facilities were inherently unequal.

May 27 A **tornado** caused 400 deaths in St. Louis, Mo., and East St. Louis, Ill. Over 120 people were injured and more than 5000 left homeless as the twister, which was preceded by rain and winds up to 120 mph, swept through the cities.

May 27–28 The **Prohibition Party National Convention** nominated Joshua Levering of Maryland for the presidency and Hale Johnson of Illinois for the vice presidency.

June 18 The **Republican National Convention** nominated William McKinley of Ohio for the presidency and Garret A. Hobart of New Jersey for the vice presidency.

July 4–9 The **Socialist Labor Party National Convention** nominated Charles H. Matchett of New York for the presidency and Matthew Maguire of New Jersey for the vice presidency.

July 11 The **Democratic National Convention** nominated William Jennings Bryan of Nebraska, a dark horse, for the presidency. Bryan's famous "cross of gold" speech united the silverite wing of the party and took the convention by storm. The platform advocated "free and unlimited coinage of both silver and gold at the present legal ratio of sixteen to one." Arthur Sewall of Maine was nominated for the vice presidency.

July 22–24 The **National Silver Republican Convention** nominated William Jennings Bryan, the Democratic candidate, for the presidency and Arthur Sewall for the vice presidency. These western Republicans, under the leadership of Sen. Henry M. Teller of Colorado, had bolted the Republican Party when it adopted a gold plank.

July 25 The **People's Party National Convention** nominated William Jennings Bryan for the presidency and Thomas E. Watson of Georgia for the vice presidency.

Sept. 2–3 The **National Democratic Party (Sound Money Democrats)** nominated John M. Palmer of Illinois for the presidency and Simon P. Buckner of Kentucky for the vice presidency.

Oct. 1 **Rural free postal delivery** was established.

Nov. 3 **William McKinley was elected president** of the United States. Garret A. Hobart was elected vice president. The electoral vote was McKinley, 271: William Jennings Bryan, Democratic candidate, 176. The popular vote was McKinley, 7,104,779; Bryan, 6,502,925; John M. Palmer, National Democratic candidate, 133, 148; Joshua Levering, Prohibition candidate, 132,007;

hundreds of her poems found by Lavinia Dickinson, Emily's sister; *The Damnation of Theron Ware* by Harold Frederic, a realistic novel about a hypocritical small-town Methodist minister; *The Country of the Pointed Firs*, the masterpiece of the mistress of the local-color novel, Sarah Orne Jewett; *The Seats of the Mighty*, a historical novel by Sir Gilbert Parker about the capture of Quebec; the first story about the fabulous fictional character Frank Merriwell, the creation of Gilbert Patten under the pseudonym Burt L. Standish; *The Torrent and the Night Before*, poems by Edwin Arlington Robinson, noteworthy only because it was the first publication of this important American poet; the fourth and final volume of *The Winning of the West* by Theodore Roosevelt; *The Sense of Beauty* by George Santayana, his first major philosophical work and a classic study of aesthetics; *In His Steps* by Charles M. Sheldon, an all-time best seller about a Kansas minister following the example of Jesus, translated into 25 or more languages; and another religious classic, *The Story of the Other Wise Man* by Henry Van Dyke, still in print.

Edward A. MacDowell was appointed head of the new Music Department at Columbia University. He labored to raise the status of the musical arts in American universities. After his death, the MacDowell Colony at Peterborough, N.H., was founded by MacDowell's wife as a summer residence for composers, writers, and artists. MacDowell stimulated interest in American music through his use of Indian and black melodies in orchestral composition.

Mr. Dooley, the fictional Irish saloonkeeper-philosopher created by Chicago newspaperman Finley Peter Dunne, gained a nationwide following for his observations on the political and social scene. Dunne first introduced Mr. Dooley in 1893.

The song **"There'll Be a Hot Time in the Old Town To-Night"** was an adaptation of an old song written by Theodore A. Metz, with words by Joseph Hayden. Two years later, during the Spanish-American War, it was adopted by Roosevelt's Rough Riders. It was revived by U.S. troops during World War I.

Apr. 23 The **first moving pictures** on a public screen were shown at Koster and Bial's Music Hall in New York City. The program included films of two blonde girls performing the umbrella dance, a view of the surf breaking on a beach, a comic boxing exhibition, a bit of comic allegory entitled "The Monroe Doctrine," and a performance of the skirt dance. *The New York Times* review the following day described the exhibition as "all wonderfully real and singularly exhilarating."

Aug. 15 **William Allen White,** editor of the Emporia *Gazette,* published his editorial "What's the Matter

Business and Industry; Science; **III**	**IV** **Sports; Social Issues and Crime;**
Education; Philosophy and Religion	**Folkways; Fashion; Holidays**

workers the right to picket. Holmes wrote at the time that his dissent probably would shut him off from all chances of further advancement as a judge.

Auto production by the Duryea brothers rose to ten cars for the year. Charles E. and J. Frank Duryea were the outstanding figures in the early U.S. automotive industry. They easily won most of the road races in 1894, 1895, and 1896 with their cars.

Book matches became popular in the U.S. for the first time. They had been invented in 1892 by Joshua Pusey, an attorney; in 1895 the Diamond Match Company bought his patent. Initially the matchbooks were unpopular, but this year a brewery ordered 10,000,000 books for advertising and made the matchbook industry secure.

A **model airplane,** pilotless and steam-powered, designed by Samuel P. Langley, flew for a minute and a half, traveling half a mile over the Potomac R. The model weighed 26 lbs. and had a 14-ft. wingspan.

Jan. 29 X-ray treatment for breast cancer was first performed by Emil H. Grube.

June 4 Assembly of the **first Ford automobile** was completed at 2 A.M. in a brick workshed in Detroit, Mich., by Henry Ford and his associates. The road test of the car was delayed an hour or so because genius had overlooked one detail: the car was wider than the shed door. The men had to use an ax to knock bricks out of the framework.

Aug. 12 Gold was discovered on the Klondike R. about three miles from Dawson in the Yukon Territory of northwest Canada. This sparked the second great gold rush in U.S. history, the Klondike stampede of 1897–1898. News of the strike reached the U.S. in June of 1897, and within a month thousands were on their way by a variety of difficult routes. In 1898 there were about 25,000 people in the Klondike area. Total gold production there from 1885 to 1929 exceeded $175,000,000.

Sept. Rose Hawthorne Lathrop, daughter of Nathaniel Hawthorne, founded a free home for destitute cancer victims in New York City. She and her husband,

Apr. 6 The **first modern Olympic Games** began in Athens, Greece. The games were dominated by a small team of Americans who arrived just as athletes for the first events were being called. The U.S. team, out of condition from the long ocean trip, with no time to limber up, won nine of the 12 events. James B. Connolly, who won the first event—the hop, step, and jump—was the first Olympic champion to be crowned in 15 centuries. Revival of the games was brought about by the efforts of a young French baron, Pierre de Coubertin of Paris. His plan to hold international contests every four years has been carried out for the most part.

May 6 The 22nd annual **Kentucky Derby** was won by Ben Brush, with a time of 2:07¾. The jockey was Willie Simms. This year the course distance was set at a mile and a quarter.

June 2 The 30th annual **Belmont Stakes** was won by Hastings, with a time of 2:24½. The jockey was Henry Griffin. From this year to 1925 (1904–1905 excepted) the distance was one and three-eighths miles.

June 6 The 21st annual **Preakness Stakes** was won by Margrave, with a time of 1:51. The jockey was Henry Griffin.

July 7 The sentence **"You shall not crucify mankind upon a cross of gold"** marked William Jennings Bryan's stirring speech at the Democratic National Convention. The reference was to the insistence by the gold faction, which opposed free coinage of silver, on gold alone as the basis for U.S. currency.

July 18 The **U.S. Open golf tournament** was won by James Foulis.

Fall The **National League baseball championship** was won by Baltimore, with a record of 90 wins, 39 losses.

Nov. The **first U.S. ice hockey league,** the Amateur Hockey League, was organized in New York City. The

Charles H. Matchett, Socialist Labor candidate, 38, 274. In congressional elections the Republicans gained four seats in the Senate to lead 47–34, seven seats going to minor parties. In the House the Republicans lost 40 seats but still held a 204–113 majority, 40 seats going to minor parties.

with Kansas?" after being confronted by a group of irate local citizens two days earlier. This attack on populism was reprinted in every important paper in the U.S. and was used as campaign literature by the Republican candidate William McKinley. It made the reputation of its author overnight.

1897

The tariff continued to be a controversial issue, but after the presidential election of 1896 the Republican Party was free to have its way. Pres. William McKinley called a special session of Congress, and on July 7 the lawmakers passed the Dingley Tariff Bill, named for its sponsor, Rep. Nelson Dingley, Republican of Maine. This law, which remained in effect until 1909, put tariffs at the highest level ever, raising them an average of 57%. It reimposed the duty on woolen goods and set the rate at 91%. The new tariff rates were much higher than was necessary because many American industries no longer needed protection against foreign goods.

Jan. 12 The **National Monetary Conference** met at Indianapolis, Ind., and endorsed the existing gold standard. A commission appointed later in the year offered Congress a plan for the monetary system. With the free silver issue finally settled, the U.S. entered a decade of prosperity.

Feb. 2 **Fire** destroyed the Pennsylvania State Capitol at Harrisburg.

Mar. 2 An **immigration bill** that required a literacy test was vetoed by Pres. Grover Cleveland. He called it a "radical departure from our national policy."

Mar. 4 **William McKinley was inaugurated president** of the United States, the 25th. A Republican, he was elected to two terms but was assassinated before completing his second term.

May 5 An **enlarged New York City** was provided for by a new charter signed by the governor of the state; it went into effect Jan. 1, 1898. Total area was now 326 sq. mi.; total population, 3,400,000.

May 24 For relief of **Americans in Cuba,** Congress appropriated $50,000. Concessions made later this year by the liberal Sagasta ministry in Spain, which included the recall of the governor general, Valeriano Weyler y Nicolau, and the release of imprisoned Americans, satisfied neither side in the rebellion.

July 14 **Klondike gold,** $750,000 in a first shipment, arrived in San Francisco. Another shipment of $800,-000 arrived in Seattle on July 17.

Popular songs were being turned out by the hundreds. Many of them had a nostalgic air and expressed a yearning for rural life. Quite a few were humorous and, of course, many were about love. Among the most successful composers of the period was Paul Dresser, real name Dreiser, whose brother Theodore was to become one of America's greatest novelists. Dresser is remembered for "On the Banks of the Wabash, Far Away" (1897), on which his brother helped with the lyrics, and "My Gal Sal" (1905). Another popular songwriter of the day was Harry Von Tilzer, who is said to have composed more than 3000 songs, including "Wait Till the Sun Shines, Nelly" (1906).

Among **books published** this year was *Soldiers of Fortune* by Richard Harding Davis, a novel that became a best seller. Davis was a newspaperman, war correspondent, and author. His work found a large audience from the early 1890s to his death in 1916; however, his novels and many stories did not stand the test of time and, except for a few, are largely forgotten. Other books published this year included *The Spoils of Poynton* and *What Maisie Knew* by Henry James; *Captains Courageous* by Rudyard Kipling, a novel of the sea that became a classic; *Hugh Wynne, Free Quaker* by S. Weir Mitchell, a novel of the American Revolution considered by some to be Mitchell's masterpiece; *The Children of the Night* by Edwin Arlington Robinson, the author's second collection of poems, which included "Richard Cory" and other well-known poems; and *The Literary History of the American Revolution* by Moses Coit Taylor.

Work was begun on the **New York Public Library** on Fifth Ave. Among U.S. public buildings it was perhaps the finest example of a building embodying the principles of design taught at the Ecole des Beaux Arts in Paris. The architects were John Merven Carrère and Thomas Hastings. The building was completed in 1911.

Jan. 30 The 17-story **Astoria Hotel** in New York City, designed by Henry Janeway Hardenbergh, was opened to the public. The lavishly furnished hotel was connected to the ten-story Waldorf Hotel, which had also been designed by Hardenbergh and had opened on Mar. 14, 1893.

| Business and Industry; Science; Education; Philosophy and Religion III | | IV Sports; Social Issues and Crime; Folkways; Fashion; Holidays |

George Parsons Lathrop, converted to Catholicism, and she later joined a Dominican community of nuns at Sherman Park, N.Y. In 1901, as Mother Mary Alphonsa, she founded and directed the Rosary Hill Home, a charitable organization at Hawthorne, N.Y.

first league game was played a month later. The Canadian sport spread through the U.S. wherever natural ice was available in winter.

1897

As the population of cities grew and their geographical boundaries expanded, transportation of large numbers of people became a serious problem. Elevated railroads had already been built, but they were noisy and dirty. Municipalities now turned to underground railways, or subways, as a solution. An experimental underground railway had been built in New York City more than 30 years before, yet New York City officials were still working out plans to finance subway construction. The first practical and successful subway line in the U.S. was the Tremont St. subway in Boston, which opened in 1897 and was completed the next year. It ran for only 1.8 miles and the cars were ordinary trolley cars. Later the Boston subway was extended to 22 miles.

The **Yerkes Observatory,** built for the University of Chicago at Lake Geneva, Wis., by traction magnate Charles Tyson Yerkes, was dedicated and opened. The observatory soon became preeminent in photographic studies of the Milky Way and in spectroscopy.

At Kansas Agricultural College the entire **faculty was dismissed** on the grounds that it did not support the political doctrines of populism.

Formation of the **American Osteopathic Association** reflected the growing significance of osteopathy in the U.S.

Feb. 17 The **National Congress of Mothers** was organized in Washington, D.C., by Mrs. Theodore W. Birney. In 1898 it became the National Congress of Mothers and Parent-Teacher Associations, and in 1924 the National Congress of Parents and Teachers.

July 2 A **coal miners' strike** shut down mines in Pennsylvania, Ohio, and West Virginia and put 75,000 men out of work. On Sept. 10 more than 20 miners were killed at Hazelton and Latimer, Pa., when deputy sheriffs opened fire on them. One day later the strike was settled. The miners won an eight-hour work day, semimonthly pay, abolition of company stores, and biennial conferences.

Conspicuous consumption in the Gilded Age exceeded anything ever seen before in the U.S. The most lavish party of all was that given in 1897 by the Bradley Martins of New York City. The ballroom of the Waldorf-Astoria Hotel was turned into a replica of the Palace of Versailles. Mrs. Martin attended dressed as Mary Queen of Scots, wearing a necklace that had once belonged to Marie Antoinette. The ball was held just as the nation was emerging from its worst depression ever, and thus produced a wave of criticism in the press. So much disapproval descended on the Martins that they fled to England and stayed there.

The **first Frontier Day** was conceived and celebrated by citizens of Cheyenne, Wyo., at the town's fair grounds. The celebration has since become a five-day Wild West Show, held annually at Frontier Park.

This year's **national college football championship** was won by Pennsylvania, with a record of 15 wins, no losses, no ties.

The **U.S. Lawn Tennis Association singles championships** were won by Juliette P. Atkinson in the women's division and Robert D. Wrenn in the men's division.

Mar. 17 The **world heavyweight boxing championship** was won by Bob Fitzsimmons, who defeated James J. "Gentleman Jim" Corbett in a 14-round bout at Carson City, Nev. This was the first boxing match photographed by a motion picture camera.

Apr. 19 The **first Boston Marathon** was won by John J. McDermott of New York City, with a time of 2 hrs., 55 min., 10 sec.

May 4 The 23rd annual **Kentucky Derby** was won by Typhoon II, with a time of 2:12½. The jockey was F. "Buttons" Garner.

May 29 The 31st annual **Belmont Stakes** was won by Scottish Chieftain, with a time of 2:32¼. The jockey was J. Scherrer.

June 8 The 22nd annual **Preakness Stakes** was won by Paul Kauvar, with a time of 1:51¼. The jockey was T. Thorpe.

Fall The **National League baseball championship** was won by Boston, with a record of 93 wins, 39 losses.

Sept. 17 The **U.S. Open golf tournament** was won by Joe Lloyd of England.

1898 *PRES.* WILLIAM MCKINLEY   378

Exploration and Settlement; Wars;   Publishing; Arts and Music; Popular
Government; Civil Rights; Statistics   **I**   **II**   Entertainment; Architecture; Theater

1898

Victory in the Spanish-American War made the U.S. a nation with global interests. In one brief clash of arms the U.S. acquired Guam, Puerto Rico, and the Philippine Islands from Spain. In addition, Cuba was granted independence, with Spain assuming its national debt. Many Americans were appalled by the new U.S. foreign policy, which they equated with imperialism. Andrew Carnegie, the steel magnate and philanthropist, offered to buy the Philippines for $20,000,000 and give the country its freedom. Many other Americans, however, talked of manifest destiny and the duty of the U.S. to spread its form of civilization far and wide.

Jan. 25 The U.S. battleship *Maine* arrived at Havana, Cuba, on a friendly visit. The real purpose of the *Maine* was to protect American life and property.

Feb. 9 The **de Lôme letter,** written by the Spanish minister to the U.S., Enrique de Lôme, was published in William Randolph Hearst's New York *Journal.* This private letter was stolen by Cuban revolutionists from the mails in Havana. It characterized Pres. William McKinley as weak and questioned his political integrity. De Lôme immediately resigned.

Feb. 15 The U.S. **battleship Maine** exploded in Havana harbor; two officers and 258 crew members were killed. U.S. sympathies were already strongly with Cuba in its revolt against Spanish tyranny, and the *Maine* disaster made U.S. intervention inevitable. The cause of the explosion and the people responsible for it were never determined.

Apr. 11 Congressional **authorization to use armed force** to end the civil war in Cuba was requested by Pres. McKinley. In Spain Prime Minister Práxedes Mateo Sagasta made a last-minute attempt to avoid war by offering Cubans limited autonomy.

Apr. 19 Congress adopted a **joint resolution on Cuba,** which stated that the U.S. had no plans for Cuban annexation, demanded Spain's withdrawal, and authorized the president to use military force. Spain immediately severed diplomatic relations.

Apr. 20 An **ultimatum to Spain** was cabled to U.S. minister Stewart L. Woodford after Pres. McKinley had signed the Cuban resolution. The cable was intended for delivery to the Spanish government, but Woodford's credentials were returned to him on Apr. 21, before he could deliver his message.

Apr. 22 A **blockade of Cuban ports** was ordered by Pres. McKinley. Rear Adm. William T. Sampson sailed from Key West, Fla., with a sizable fleet.

Apr. 22 The Spanish ship *Buena Ventura* was captured by the U.S. gunboat *Nashville,* the first prize of the Spanish-American War.

Apr. 22 The **Volunteer Army Act** was passed by Congress. It authorized organization of the First

Sentimentality seemed to hold sway in the field of song, resulting in the composition of some musical pieces that were at least as popular for their words as for their music. An outstanding example, "The Rosary" by Ethelbert Nevin with lyrics by Robert Cameron Rogers, was published this year. It was the most popular song in the U.S. for a quarter of a century. Nevin was a pianist and composer who wrote other similar music, such as "Narcissus" (1891), and who set to music such poems as Eugene Field's "Little Boy Blue."

Among **books published** this year was *David Harum* by Edward Noyes Westcott, a Syracuse lawyer. The novel had been rejected by six publishers before being accepted by D. Appleton & Company. It was published shortly after Westcott's death from tuberculosis on Mar. 31. The story, centering on a shrewd, humorous, and lovable small-town banker, sold 400,000 copies by Feb. 1, 1901, and 1,000,000 in 35 years. It was dramatized in 1900 and twice made into a movie, the second time with Will Rogers in the title role. Other books published this year included *The Open Boat and Other Stories* by Stephen Crane; *Mr. Dooley in Peace and War* by Peter Finley Dunne; *The Turn of the Screw* by Henry James, a masterpiece of horror by a master of English prose; *Prisoners of Hope* by Mary Johnston, a novel of colonial Virginia; *When Knighthood Was in Flower* by Charles Major, a historical romance that became a best seller; *The Adventures of Francois* by S. Weir Mitchell, a picaresque novel of the French Revolution; and *Songs from the Ghetto* by Morris Rosenfeld, an immigrant from Russian Poland, translation by Leo Wiener.

Business and Industry; Science; Education; Philosophy and Religion III		IV Sports; Social Issues and Crime; Folkways; Fashion; Holidays

1898

As the end of the century neared, American industry was becoming the most productive in the world. Steel production had passed that of Great Britain in 1865; by 1900 it was 10,000,000 tons a year, and the U.S. was turning out more than Great Britain and Germany combined. Cotton textile mills were built in the South as well as the North, and by 1900 the two regions were using 3,500,000 bales of cotton a year. Meat packing was becoming an assembly line process, and large firms in the Midwest were leading the way. The Niagara Falls power plant had ushered in the era of hydroelectric power in 1894, and steam turbines and electric motors were beginning to change the face of American industry.

A great deal of entertainment for the general public was being provided by amusement parks, usually located on the outskirts of cities and often built by traction companies to create traffic for their trolley car lines. Whole families could enjoy parks such as Palisades Amusement Park in New Jersey, just across the Hudson R. from New York City, which opened in 1897. Among the many attractions at these parks were roller coasters, merry-go-rounds, shoot the chutes, dance halls, bathing beaches, and, of course, food and drink.

The impassioned slogan "**Remember the Maine**" became the war cry of Americans urging war with Spain. The battleship *Maine* had been destroyed by an explosion while docked at Havana. The American public was led to believe that it had been blown up by agents of Spain. This feeling supported American resentment against Spanish oppression of Cuban nationalism.

The **Biltmore Forest School** was opened by Dr. Carl A. Schenck in Biltmore, N.C. The school offered a one-year course in forestry plus a six-month course of field training. The school, which closed in 1914, was the first forestry school in the U.S.

This year's **national college football championship** was won by Harvard, with a record of 11 wins, no losses, no ties.

Volunteer Cavalry, or the Rough Riders, under command of Col. Leonard Wood and Lt. Col. Theodore Roosevelt.

Apr. 23 Pres. McKinley issued a **call for 125,000 volunteers** to fight in the war with Spain.

Apr. 24 The **Spanish-American War** officially began when Spain declared war on the U.S. The following day Congress passed a declaration of war, effective Apr. 21.

May 1 At the Battle of **Manila Bay,** the six-ship Asiatic squadron of Commodore George Dewey decisively defeated a larger but outgunned and underprepared Spanish fleet. The U.S. flotilla emerged virtually unscathed, with only eight wounded. The Spanish fleet was destroyed, with heavy casualties. The action cleared the way for U.S. occupation of Manila in August.

May 25 A new **call for volunteers,** 75,000 strong, was issued by Pres. McKinley.

May 25 The **first troop expedition to Manila** set sail from San Francisco with some 2500 men.

May 28 **Native citizenship,** the Supreme Court declared, is without respect to race or color; a child born of Chinese parents in this country is a U.S. citizen and cannot be deported under the Chinese Exclusion Act.

June 10 The **War Revenue Act** was passed by Congress and signed by the president on June 13. The bill authorized the government to make a loan of up to $400,000,000 and place a tax on liquor, tobacco, flour, and other items. Actually, the government sold only $200,000,000 of 3% bonds.

June 11 About 600 **U.S. Marines landed at Guantánamo,** Cuba. They engaged Spanish forces the next day.

June 12–14 **U.S. forces embarked from Key West,** Fla. Some 17,000 troops under Gen. William R. Shafter sailed to undertake capture of Santiago de Cuba, the chief Spanish naval base in Cuba.

June 15 **Annexation of Hawaii** was approved in a joint resolution adopted by the House of Representatives, and by the Senate on June 17. It was signed by Pres. McKinley on July 7.

June 21 **Guam,** one of the Mariana Islands in the western Pacific, surrendered to Capt. Henry Glass on the U.S.S. *Charleston.* The Spanish commander on the island obviously had not heard of the outbreak of the war, for on the previous day when Capt. Glass fired on the island a message was sent to the *Charleston* with an apology for not having returned the salute—there was no ammunition on the island.

June 24 At the Battle of **Las Guasimas,** U.S. troops won the first major land battle of the war with Spain. The division of cavalry volunteers led by the aggressive Maj. Gen. Joseph Wheeler, with Col. Leonard

The **National Institute of Arts and Letters** was established by the American Social Science Association "for the furtherance of literature and the fine arts in the United States."

The **Watch and Ward Society** of Boston brought an unsuccessful court action against booksellers handling Gabrielle D'Annunzio's novel *Il Trionfo della Morte* (1894), published in the U.S. as *The Triumph of Death.*

The **Bayard Building** (later renamed Condict Building), designed by Chicago architects Dankmar Adler and Louis H. Sullivan, was built in New York City. Its low-relief work in terra cotta was much favored by Louis Sullivan.

Business and Industry; Science; Education; Philosophy and Religion III		IV Sports; Social Issues and Crime; Folkways; Fashion; Holidays

Nome, Alaska, was founded as the result of a gold strike on the Seward Peninsula, for which it was the port. Nome was named for a misspelling of a nearby cape on a map. The cape was referred to as "no name."

The need for a **canal across Panama** was made clear by the 67 days (Mar. 19 to May 24) it took for the U.S. battleship *Oregon*, needed in the Gulf of Mexico during the Spanish-American War, to steam from San Francisco, Calif., to Key West, Fla.

June 1 The **Erdman Arbitration Act,** sponsored by Rep. Jacob Erdman, Democrat of Pennsylvania, was passed. It authorized governmental mediation between interstate carriers and their employees. It forbade interstate carriers to discriminate against or

The **U.S. Lawn Tennis Association** singles championships were won by Juliette P. Atkinson in the women's division and Malcolm D. Whitman in the men's division.

Apr. 19 The second **Boston Marathon** was won by Ronald J. McDonald of Cambridge, Mass., with a time of 2 hrs., 42 min.

May 4 The 24th annual **Kentucky Derby** was won by Plaudit, with a time of 2:09. The jockey was Willie Simms.

May 26 The 32nd annual **Belmont Stakes** was won by Bowling Brook, with a time of 2:32. The jockey was F. Littlefield.

Wood now a regimental commander and Col. Theodore Roosevelt leading the Rough Riders, performed well.

July 1–2 **El Caney and San Juan Heights,** Spanish outposts to Santiago de Cuba, were stormed and taken over stubborn resistance by U.S. troops. There were heavy casualties on both sides. The Rough Riders participated in the attack.

July 3 The **Spanish fleet at Cuba,** under Adm. Pascual Cervera y Topete, was destroyed by U.S. ships in an attempt to break out of Santiago. The Spanish lost 323 dead, 151 wounded. The U.S. lost one man. The war was virtually over.

July 8 **Isla Grande,** in Subic Bay near Manila, was occupied by forces under Adm. George Dewey. The German gunboat *Irene,* which had attempted to hamper American operations, was forced to withdraw.

July 17 **Santiago de Cuba** was surrendered along with 24,000 Spanish troops by Gen. José Toral to U.S. Gen. William R. Shafter.

July 25 **Puerto Rico** was invaded by U.S. forces led by Maj. Gen. Nelson D. Miles. The landing was made at Guanica, on the southern coast. Resistance was minimal.

July 28 **Ponce,** Puerto Rico's second largest city, surrendered to Gen. Miles.

July 31 A **Spanish assault at Malate,** near Manila, was repulsed by U.S. forces under Gen. Francis V. Greene. U.S. casualties were 10 dead, 33 wounded.

Aug. 1 **Casualties from disease** were exceedingly high during the conflict in Cuba. At this time there were some 4200 sick U.S. personnel in Cuba, most suffering from yellow fever or typhoid. Fewer than 400 troops were killed in battle or died of wounds in Cuba. Fully 90% of U.S. casualties were caused by disease.

Aug. 7 The **Rough Riders left Cuba,** along with other units, for Montauk Point, Long Island, to escape epidemics in Cuba.

Aug. 9 At **Coamo,** Puerto Rico, U.S. forces under Brig. Gen. Oswald H. Ernst defeated a Spanish force.

Aug. 12 **Hostilities between Spain and the U.S. were halted** by a protocol in which Spain agreed to give Cuba its independence and to cede Puerto Rico and Guam to the U.S. Spain agreed to negotiate the status of the Philippines in a postwar conference.

Sept. 9 **U.S. peace commissioners** were appointed, headed by Sec. of State William R. Day. They sailed for Paris, France, on Sept. 17.

Nov. 8 In **congressional elections** the Republicans continued to gain strength in the Senate and lose strength in the House, taking a 53–26 lead in the Senate, with eight seats going to minor parties, and holding a majority of 185–163 in the House, with nine seats held by minor parties. In New York State, Theodore Roosevelt was elected governor on the

Nov. 7 Mme. **Ernestine Schumann-Heink** made her first U.S. appearance in *Lohengrin* at Chicago. Her New York City debut was at the Metropolitan Opera House in the same opera on Jan. 9, 1899.

Business and Industry; Science; Education; Philosophy and Religion III		IV Sports; Social Issues and Crime; Folkways; Fashion; Holidays

blacklist union laborers. But on Jan. 27, 1908, the Supreme Court held the provision against discrimination unconstitutional according to the Fifth Amendment. On July 15, 1914, Congress replaced the Erdman Act by the Newlands Act, which set up a mediation board.

June 11 The 23rd annual **Preakness Stakes** was won by Sly Fox, with a time of 1:49¾. The jockey was Willie Simms.

June 18 The **U.S. Open** golf tournament was won by Fred Herd.

Oct. 12 A strikers' riot at Virden, Ill., resulted in 13 persons killed and 25 wounded. The strike broke out when employers attempted to replace striking members of the United Mine Workers with nonunion, black miners.

Fall The **National League baseball championship** was won by Boston, with a record of 102 wins, 47 losses.

1898 – 1899 *PRES.* WILLIAM MCKINLEY

384

Exploration and Settlement; Wars; I
Government; Civil Rights; Statistics

II Publishing; Arts and Music; Popular
Entertainment; Architecture; Theater

Republican ticket. The Republicans had chosen him partly because of his war service and partly to overcome the taint of corruption left by the previous administration.

Dec. 10 The **treaty ending the Spanish-American War** was signed in Paris.

1899

The first international discussion of the problems of armaments and warfare was held from May 18 to July 29 at The Hague, the Netherlands. Delegates from the U.S. and 25 other nations met at the invitation of Czar Nicholas II of Russia. The conference considered disarmament, limitations on methods of warfare, and establishment of a forum for arbitrating international disputes. Nothing was accomplished in disarmament and little in issues concerning warfare, except for conventions having to do with neutral shipping and the protection of noncombatants. The conference did establish the Permanent Court of International Arbitration, although arbitration was not compulsory and the U.S. specified reservations with regard to disputes that involved application of the Monroe Doctrine.

Feb. 4 Philippine guerrillas under **Emilio Aguinaldo** fired on American forces at Manila, starting skirmishes lasting several days. Before the insurgents were driven out and scattered, 57 Americans were killed and 215 wounded. Some 500 Filipinos were killed, 1000 wounded, and 500 made prisoners. This was the beginning of a rebellion against U.S. rule that lasted until Mar. 23, 1901, when Aguinaldo was captured by Gen. Frederick Funston at Palawan, Luzon.

Feb. 10 The **peace treaty** with Spain was signed by Pres. William McKinley. It had been ratified by Congress on Jan. 9. By its terms the U.S. acquired Puerto Rico and Guam, and Spain relinquished its claim to Cuba. The U.S. paid Spain $20,000,000 for specific Spanish holdings in the Philippines, but many interpreted the payment as purchase of the Philippines from Spain.

Mar. 30 Gen. Arthur MacArthur occupied **Malolos,** Luzon, Philippine Islands, forcing Gen. Aguinaldo to withdraw to Tarlac.

Apr. 27 A **tornado** that swept across northern Missouri killed more than 40 persons and injured at least 100 more.

The last few years of the nineteenth century saw publication of a number of popular songs that were to endure. Among them were "A Bird in a Gilded Cage" (1899) by Harry Von Tilzer, "My Wild Irish Rose" (1899) by Chauncey Olcott, and "The Stars and Stripes Forever" (1897) by John Philip Sousa. The first named was not widely popular at first, but in later years it came to be identified closely with the 1890s. For every song that found a permanent place in U.S. musical history, there were many that did not make it to the new century, such as "Gold Will Buy Most Anything but a True Girl's Heart" (1898), and "She Was Happy Till She Met You" (1899), both by Monroe H. Rosenfeld.

Among **books published** this year was *The Theory of the Leisure Class* by Thorstein Veblen, professor of political economy at the University of Chicago. Though little read except among students of economics, this outspoken assault on the moneyed class made Veblen famous in his field. Also published this year were *Fables in Slang* by George Ade, who eventually found in the follies and foibles of his fellow Americans enough material for 12 books; *Richard Carvel* by Winston Churchill, a Revolutionary War romance, the first important novel by a writer capable of probing beneath historical events to underlying forces and ideals; *The School and Society* by John Dewey, a work that revolutionized American educational theory and practice; *Janice Meredith* by Paul Leicester Ford, a historical novel widely read, perhaps because the heroine and members of her family were involved in many of the major events of the Revolutionary War; *The Man with the Hoe and Other Poems* by Edwin Markham; *McTeague,* by Frank Norris, a novel about unromantic lower-class people in San Francisco, written in a naturalistic manner; and *The Gentleman from Indiana* by Booth Tarkington, his first novel, about a crusading country editor.

Scott Joplin was heard playing piano at the Maple Leaf Club in Sedalia, Mo., by John Stillwell Stark, a music publisher. Stark persuaded Joplin to write down one of his tunes, and it was published under the title "Maple Leaf Rag." The tune was an immediate success and introduced the vogue for ragtime among white musicians and listeners throughout the U.S.

William Gillette wrote and played in *Sherlock Holmes,* based on the stories of Arthur Conan Doyle.

| Business and Industry; Science; Education; Philosophy and Religion | III | | IV | Sports; Social Issues and Crime; Folkways; Fashion; Holidays |

1899

Propagation of the Christian faith was not left to the clergy or the churches, especially among evangelical Protestants. One group that came to play a unique role in this endeavor was the Christian Commercial Men's Association of America, formed by a group of traveling salesmen meeting in Boscobel, Wis., on July 1. The organization became better known as the Gideons International, and best known for its chief work, placing Bibles in hotel rooms. The first Gideon Bible was placed in the Superior Hotel, Iron Mountain, Mont., in Nov. 1908.

Motorized mail collection was given a trial run by postal authorities in Cleveland, Ohio. Using a Winton truck, the Post Office completed a route of 126 stops along 22 miles of streets in 2 hrs., 27 min., less than half the time required by a horse-drawn wagon. Despite the test results, the Post Office did not create a motor vehicle division for 15 years.

Feb. 14 Congress authorized **voting machines** for federal elections if desired by the individual states.

Mar. An **Isthmian Canal Commission** was created by Congress to study plans for building an interocean canal in Central America.

Apr. 29 **Strike violence** erupted at Wardner, Idaho, after miners demanded (on Apr. 24) $3.50 a day for underground miners and a closed shop. Employers refused to grant the closed shop. The miners blew up mills and destroyed mining property estimated at $250,000.

More attention was being paid to providing parks and playgrounds in America's cities. By this time Manhattan Island, the heart of New York City, had 1140 acres of parks, but most of it was accounted for by Central Park; there was little parkland in crowded areas. An exception was Mulberry Park, opened in 1896, which consisted of only three acres but offered a little green space in one of the worst slum areas. Kansas City, Mo., in 1893 began planning a system of 16 miles of boulevards to connect 2000 acres of parkland. Boston began to organize a park system in the 1890s. By 1898 some 14 cities in the East had children's playgrounds, many of them in schoolyards.

A new **baseball rule** required a pitcher to complete a throw to first base if he had motioned in that direction to drive a base runner back to the bag.

This year's **national college football championship** was won by Harvard, with a record of ten wins, no losses, one tie.

The **U.S. Lawn Tennis Association singles championships** were won by Marion Jones in the women's division and Malcolm D. Whitman in the men's division.

Apr. 19 The third **Boston Marathon** was won by Lawrence J. Brignolla of Cambridge, Mass., with a time of 2 hrs., 54 min., 38 sec.

May 4 The 25th annual **Kentucky Derby** was won by Manuel, with a time of 2:12. The jockey was Fred Taral. This year only three horses were in the race.

May 25 The 33rd annual **Belmont Stakes** was won by Jean Bereaud, with a time of 2:23. The jockey was R. Clawson.

May 30 The 24th annual **Preakness Stakes** was won by Half Time, with a time of 1:47. The jockey was R. Clawson.

Apr. 28 Terms of armistice were proposed by a Filipino peace commission to Maj. Gen. Elwell Stephens Otis, who rejected the terms and demanded unconditional surrender.

June 12 A tornado that ripped through Minnesota and Wisconsin killed some 250 persons at New Richmond, Wis.

Nov. 24 U.S. control of central Luzon in the Philippines was reported to Washington, D.C., by Maj. Gen. Elwell S. Otis. The president of the Filipino Congress, the Filipino secretary of state, and the treasurer had been taken prisoner. Only small bands of insurgents continued to fight.

Dec. 2 The Samoan Partition Treaty was signed at Washington, D.C., with Germany and England. It partitioned the Samoan Islands between the U.S. and Germany, with the U.S. receiving Tutuila with Pago Pago, its harbor.

Gillette came to be identified with Doyle's famous sleuth, and this play was Gillette's most successful vehicle. He continued to perform the lead in revivals into the early 1930s.

Jan. 15 "The Man with the Hoe," a poem by Edwin Markham, a California schoolteacher, was published in the San Francisco *Examiner.* The poem was a social protest; it pictured a farmer brutalized by forces he could not control or understand. Within a week it had been reprinted by newspapers across the country. Antitrust forces called it "the cry of the Zeitgeist [cultural climate of the era]." It was the most popular poem in the U.S. by far.

Feb. 22 Elbert Hubbard wrote "A Message to Garcia," an inspirational piece for the March issue of the *Philistine.* It recounted the somewhat inaccurate story of one Capt. Andrew Rowan who, during the Spanish-American War, was supposedly handed a message by Pres. William McKinley to deliver to the Cuban leader Gen. Calixto García Iñiquez. Rowan did so without delay in the face of great difficulty, Hubbard wrote, and was the real hero of the war.

1900

Bitter antagonism against all foreigners in China broke into open warfare this year when a nationalist group, the Boxers, occupied Peking on June 20 and besieged members of the diplomatic corps, their families, and others in the British legation. The Boxers wanted to rid China of all foreigners. After a siege of nearly two months, troops from the U.S., Great Britain, France, Russia, Germany, and Japan reached Peking on Aug. 14 and put down the Boxer Rebellion. Under pressure from the U.S., the other powers agreed not to partition China further. On Sept. 7, 1901, China and eleven other nations signed the Boxer Protocol, by which China agreed to pay $333,000,000 in indemnity. The U.S. received $24,500,000, but in 1908 this amount was reduced and the money was used to educate Chinese students in the U.S.

The **temperance movement** turned less than temperate this year when Carry Nation led a group of anti-liquor agitators through Kansas. The agitators vandalized saloons and other establishments that sold liquor.

The **Census** recorded a population of 75,994,575. The center of population was placed at six miles southeast of Columbus, Ind.

Mar. 6–9 The **Social Democratic Party nominated Eugene V. Debs** of Indiana for the presidency and Job Harriman of California for the vice presidency.

Mar. 14 The currency act, which established a **gold standard** for all U.S. currency, was passed by Congress. The act was made possible by increased gold

The U.S. had produced painters of talent and accomplishment in the fields of portraiture, historical painting, and landscape studies. No American painter of standing, however, fell into quite the same class in this period as did Albert Pinkham Ryder. Mostly self-taught, Ryder many times used as his subject the sea or moonlight. His work evokes a feeling of loneliness and mysterious force of nature. Of some 160 paintings, perhaps his best known is *Toilers of the Sea* (1900), which includes a dark sail and a wan moon giving off an aura of ghostliness. Ryder also did paintings with such titles as *Death on a Pale Horse* and *Temple of the Mind.*

Among **books published** this year was *Sister Carrie,* a first novel by Theodore Dreiser. An unflinchingly naturalistic novel, it examined in economic and moral terms the rise of a young woman from rural obscurity to success on the New York stage. Steeped in tragedy, the story was published only after Dreiser made extensive cuts. The book was issued, then recalled, by the publisher. The book's failure sent Dreiser into a deep depression. Reissued in 1912, the book was eventually recognized as an American classic. In 1981 it was republished with Dreiser's deleted text restored. Other books published this year included *Eben Holden, A Tale of the North Country* by Irving Bacheller, which sold 300,000 copies within six months; *The Wonderful Wizard of Oz* by L. Frank Baum; *Whilomville Stories* by Stephen Crane, a posthumous collection; *Literary Friends and*

| Business and Industry; Science; Education; Philosophy and Religion | III | | IV | Sports; Social Issues and Crime; Folkways; Fashion; Holidays |

Oct. 14 "The ordinary **horseless carriage**," the *Literary Digest* pronounced, "is at present a luxury for the wealthy; and altho its price will probably fall in the future, it will never, of course, come into as common use as the bicycle."

Dec. 22 **Dwight L. Moody** died at 62. The most widely known and effective evangelist of the last quarter of the century, Moody also founded the Northfield (Mass.) school for boys and girls (now Northfield–Mt. Hermon) and the Moody Bible Institute in Chicago. With his organist, Ira D. Sankey, Moody wrote many popular hymns, including "The Ninety-and-Nine," "Hiding in Thee," and "Where is My Wand'ring Boy?"

Summer Pres. William McKinley became the **first president to ride in an automobile** when he took a ride in a Stanley Steamer at his home in Canton, Ohio.

June 9 The **world heavyweight boxing championship** was won by James J. Jeffries, who knocked out Bob Fitzsimmons in the 11th round of a bout at Coney Island, N.Y.

Fall The **National League baseball championship** was won by Brooklyn, with a record of 88 wins, 42 losses.

Sept. 15 The **U.S. Open golf tournament** was won by Willie Smith.

Oct. 16–20 The **America's Cup** was successfully defended by the U.S. yacht *Columbia*, which won three straight races from the British challenger *Shamrock I.*

1900

The new century brought with it the automobile as a practical means of transportation. In 1900 there were only 8000 autos registered in the entire country and only about ten miles of paved roads for them to travel on. Only 4000 autos were produced in 1900, but ten years later 187,000 rolled out of the factories. The appearance of cars was changing, too. New autos looked less like horseless carriages and more like powered vehicles. The Automobile Club of America held its first meeting on Oct. 16, 1900; it sponsored the first automobile show, in Madison Square Garden, New York City, from Nov. 3–10. Nevertheless, the auto was viewed with displeasure by some. One editor wrote, "It is well named the devil-wagon." At the turn of the century there were still about 18,000,000 horses and mules providing transportation and power, and 10,000,000 bicycles for pleasure and work.

Rural free delivery served 185,000 customers. By 1924 this number would rise to 6,500,000.

A survey of **Protestant religious sects** in the U.S. at the end of the nineteenth century showed reformed and evangelical denominations in the vast majority: 6,000,-000 Methodists; 5,000,000 Baptists; 1,500,000 Lutherans; 1,500,000 Presbyterians; 350,000 Mormons; and 80,000 Christian Scientists.

Illiteracy in the U.S. reached a new low of 10.7% of

The growth of tennis around the world received a tremendous impetus in 1900 when Dwight F. Davis, a player of championship caliber, offered a cup for international contests between male players of the U.S. and Great Britain. The first five-match event was played in Boston, Mass. The U.S. won three matches, one match was not finished, and the last match was not played. The annual competition was soon opened to teams of other nations. Within a few years Australia and France presented teams that gave the U.S. and Britain strong competition.

This year's **national college football championship** was won by Yale, with a record of 12 wins, no losses, no ties.

Only 12,572 dozen pairs of **silk stockings** were sold in the U.S. this year, a ratio of one pair for every 2000 Americans. By comparison, 18,088,841 pairs were sold in 1921, one pair for every six persons.

A new **baseball rule** introduced the five-sided home plate, which is still used.

production in South Africa and the Klondike fields. It put an end to the free silver controversy, although William Jennings Bryan and other advocates of the free coinage of silver continued to agitate for ten years more.

Apr. 30 An act establishing the **Territory of Hawaii** was passed by Congress. It went into effect on June 14. On that date Pres. McKinley appointed Sanford B. Dole the first governor of Hawaii. Dole had been born in Honolulu of American missionary parents.

May 1 A **mine explosion** at Scofield, Utah, killed more than 200 persons.

May 10 The so-called **middle-of-the-road Populists** nominated Wharton Barker of Pennsylvania for the presidency and Ignatius Donnelly of Minnesota for the vice presidency.

June 19–21 The **Republican National Convention nominated Pres. McKinley** for reelection. Gov. Theodore Roosevelt of New York was nominated for the vice presidency, but he felt he was being sidetracked from the center of political activity. Roosevelt nonetheless conducted one of the most vigorous campaigns on record, visiting 24 states, traveling 21,000 miles, and delivering some 700 speeches. McKinley conducted a front-porch campaign, never stirring from his home.

June 21 **Amnesty** was granted to the Filipino insurgents by a proclamation issued by Gen. Arthur MacArthur, military governor of the Philippines.

June 27–28 The **Prohibition Party** nominated John G. Woolley of Illinois for the presidency and Henry B. Metcalf of Rhode Island for the vice presidency.

June 30 A **pier and steamship fire** at Hoboken, N.J., killed 326 persons. Total damage was $10,000,000.

July 5 The **Democratic National Convention nominated William Jennings Bryan** of Nebraska for the presidency and Adlai E. Stevenson of Illinois for the vice presidency.

Sept. 8 A **hurricane** killed 6000 persons at Galveston, Tex. Winds up to 120 mph drove Gulf waters over land. Afterward looters were found with ringed fingers they had cut off the hands of the dead. Property damage amounted to $20,000,000.

Sept. 18 The **first direct primary** in the U.S. was tried in Hennepin County (including Minneapolis), Minn. It aroused considerable interest throughout the country. The first state to adopt the primary system was Wisconsin in 1903.

Nov. 6 **William McKinley was reelected president** of the United States. Gov. Theodore Roosevelt, Republican of New York, was elected vice president. The electoral vote was McKinley, 292; William Jennings Bryan of Nebraska, candidate on the Democratic and Populist tickets, 155. The popular vote was McKinley, 7,219,530; Bryan, 6,358,071; John G. Woolley of

Acquaintances by William Dean Howells, a collection of the author's essays; *To Have and to Hold* by Mary Johnston, the author's best-known romance; *The Son of the Wolf* by Jack London, a first collection of stories; and *Alice of Old Vincennes* by Maurice Thompson, a historical novel set in Indiana in the late eighteenth century.

An American sculptor noted at the 1900 Paris Exposition was **Hermon Atkins MacNeil,** whose figure of American Indian life won him a silver medal. Other of his Indian pieces include *The Moqui Runner, A Primitive Chant,* and *The Sun Vow.* Returning to the U.S., MacNeil produced the statue *President McKinley* for the McKinley Memorial in Columbus, Ohio, and a relief of George Washington for the Washington Arch on Washington Square, New York City.

The **most popular song** of the year was "Good-Bye, Dolly Gray," a wartime song about a soldier departing for the Philippines. This and "In the Good Old Summer Time" (1902) were among the best-known songs of the first decade of the twentieth century.

The White Rats, a union of actors, was patterned after the similarly named actors' organization in London. The union was established to counter a recently formed association of vaudeville managers, whose main function was to keep actors' wages down by means of a so-called gentleman's agreement. As a result of the surprise appearance of The White Rats, many vaudeville theaters shut down. Others retaliated by exhibiting motion pictures as the sole attraction. Thus, indirectly, The White Rats had a great influence on the development of motion pictures as a mass medium.

Spectacular **motion picture reportage** of disasters in Bayonne, N.J., and Galveston, Tex., was recorded in two on-the-spot films entitled *Destruction of the Standard Oil Company Plant at Bayonne* and *The Galveston Cyclone.*

Mar. The first issue of *The Smart Set,* a literary monthly, was published by William D'Alton Mann. Contributors in its early years included Mary Austin, Ambrose Bierce, Theodore Dreiser, O. Henry, and Jack London. In Nov. 1908 H. L. Mencken began contributing a monthly column to the magazine, which was to hit its peak under the co-editorship of Mencken and George Jean Nathan from 1914 to 1923. During that period, *The Smart Set* published the early works of F. Scott Fitzgerald, Eugene O'Neill, and others. In 1923 Mencken and Nathan left to start up the *American Mercury. The Smart Set,* which would never again attain such literary heights, continued until 1930.

Oct. 15 **Symphony Hall** in Boston, designed by the New York firm of McKim, Mead, and White, was opened to the public with a special concert that

| Business and Industry; Science; Education; Philosophy and Religion | III | | IV | Sports; Social Issues and Crime; Folkways; Fashion; Holidays |

the population, a decline of 2.6% from 1890 and a decline of 9.3% from 1870.

The **International Ladies' Garment Workers Union** was established at a time when the average work week in the trade was 70 hours. Jacob A. Riis reported that women sewing at home for the clothing industry were earning 30 cents a day at best.

Telephone service in the U.S. had grown to 1,335,911 telephones in use.

Annual **cigarette production** in the U.S. reached the 4,000,000,000 mark. Cigars, pipes, and chewing tobacco were much more popular than cigarettes, which were considered effete.

Wilbur and Orville Wright built their first full-scale glider after several years of reading and experimenting with models. The glider incorporated their idea of the warped wing, the predecessor of the aileron, the first successful device for lateral control of a flying airship. The glider was flown as a kite at Kitty Hawk, N.C., in September.

The first quantity-production **automobile factory** was established by the Olds Company in Detroit, Mich., with a capitalization of $350,000. Workers assembled one model at a time from parts bought in quantity from other manufacturers. Olds produced 400 cars in the first year, 1600 in the second, and 4000 in the third. The company paid 105% in cash dividends in the first two years, marking this venture as the real beginning of the automotive industry.

The **largest railroad** of its time, the New York Central, controlled 10,000 miles of track through five terminals in New York, Cincinnati, Boston, Chicago, and St. Louis. Spectacular railroad growth in the preceding four decades was reflected in the following figures: average freight weight went up from 15,000 tons to 100,000 tons; running time between New York City and Chicago went down from 50 hrs. to 24; and cost per ton of freight was cut from $2.00 to 73 cents.

Mar. 5 The **Hall of Fame** was founded in New York City for the purpose of commemorating great Americans. It still exists today. New members are voted on every five years by a committee of 100 men and women from all the states. To be elected a nominee must have been dead at least 25 years, have been a citizen of the United States, and have the approval of three-fifths of the committee. Any citizen may make a nomination. A bust of a person elected is placed in the open air colonnade at the former campus in The Bronx of New York University.

The **U.S. Lawn Tennis Association** singles championships were won by Myrtle McAteer in the women's division and Malcolm D. Whitman in the men's division.

Photography as a pastime received a tremendous boost when the Eastman Kodak Company introduced the Brownie Box Camera. The camera cost only $1.00 and a six-shot roll of film cost 10 to 15 cents, depending on the type of film the photographer chose. At these prices, virtually everyone who wanted to take pictures could afford to do so. The result was that photography made a grand leap out of the studio and into the real world. Brownie cameras were manufactured until the mid-1960s, when they were superseded by the equally popular Instamatic cameras.

Jan. 29 The **American League** was formed in Chicago, Ill. The new baseball league demanded recognition as a major league, but was refused by the National League until 1903 when the National, American, and minor leagues joined forces and set up a ruling body known as the National Commission.

Apr. 15 An early **automobile race** held at Springfield, Long Island, N.Y., was won by A. L. Riker in an electric car. He covered 50 miles in 2 hrs., 3 min.

Apr. 19 The fourth **Boston Marathon** was won by James J. Caffrey of Hamilton, Ontario, Canada, with a time of 2 hrs., 39 min., 44 sec.

Apr. 30 At 3:52 A.M. railroad engineer John Luther "Casey" Jones died at the throttle slowing down the *Cannon Ball* express train from Memphis, Tenn., to Canton, Miss., as it slammed into the rear of a stopped train. Although Jones was speeding to make up lost time, his final action saved his passengers' lives and he became a folk hero.

May 3 The 26th annual **Kentucky Derby** was won by Lieutenant Gibson, with a time of 2:06¼. The jockey was Jimmy Boland.

May 20–Oct. 28 At the **Olympic Games** in Paris, France, the U.S. finished with 20 gold medals. France was first with 29 gold medals.

Illinois, Prohibition candidate, 209,166; Eugene V. Debs of Indiana, Social Democratic candidate, 94,768; and Wharton Barker of Pennsylvania, middle-of-the-road Populist, 50,232. In congressional elections both major parties gained Senate seats from the minor parties, the Republicans taking a 55–31 majority, with four seats held by minor parties. In the House the Republicans led 197–151, with nine seats held by minor parties.

Dec. 29 The State Dept. announced that negotiations for purchase of the **Virgin Islands,** or the Danish West Indies, had been completed. Only an appropriation from Congress was needed to bring about the transfer. This did not occur until 1917.

included a chorale by J. S. Bach and Beethoven's *Solemn Mass in D.* Owen Wister, the novelist, read a poem entitled "The Bird of Passage, an Ode to Instrumental Music." Acoustics in the hall, which had cost about $750,000 to complete, were judged adequate; its furnishings were considered excellent. The building was designed exclusively for use as a music hall. No opera or theatrical performances could be presented. During the intermission, the elite of New York and Boston society mingled in the building's spacious corridors in what *The New York Times* called a "dress parade, quite equal in appearance to that which is seen on ordinary nights in the lower corridors of the Metropolitan Opera House."

1901

For the third time in the nation's history a president was assassinated. On Sept. 6 Pres. William McKinley visited the Pan-American Exposition in Buffalo, N.Y. While greeting visitors he was shot twice in the abdomen by a young anarchist, Leon Czolgosz, who was carrying a concealed pistol in a handkerchief. For a few days McKinley seemed to be recovering, but he took a turn for the worse and died on Sept. 14 at 2:15 A.M. McKinley, 58, was succeeded by Vice Pres. Theodore Roosevelt, who became the 26th president of the United States. Roosevelt took the presidential oath in the same house in Buffalo where the body of McKinley awaited transportation to Canton, Ohio, for burial. Roosevelt was not quite 43 years old and so was the youngest person to hold the office of president. Conservative Republicans, who had been happy with McKinley, were appalled. As governor of New York, Roosevelt had shown liberal tendencies. He had gained the vice presidential nomination in 1900 partly because Republican leaders sought to keep him in a harmless post.

The **Socialist Party** was organized by the merger of the Social Democratic Party under Eugene V. Debs with the reformist section of the Socialist Labor Party under Morris Hillquit.

Feb. 2 The **U.S. Army Dental Corps** was created by Congress.

Feb. 2 The **Army Nurse Corps** was organized as a branch of the U.S. Army.

Mar. 2 The **Platt Amendment,** sponsored by Sen. Orville H. Platt of Connecticut, was adopted by Congress as an amendment to the Army Appropriation Act of 1901. It consisted of a series of provisions that the Cubans had to append to their new constitution before the U.S. would withdraw its troops. In effect,

For a number of years journalists had been documenting the corruption of the railroads and trusts. This year Frank Norris turned his skills as a novelist to a campaign against the excesses of big business. Concerned about the social and economic evils he saw, Norris planned a trilogy of novels, his *Epic of the Wheat.* The first volume, *The Octopus,* was published in 1901. It dealt with the struggle of farmers in the San Joaquin Valley of California against the power of the Southern Pacific Railroad. In *The Pit* (1903) Norris told the story of speculation on the Chicago wheat exchange and the damage it brought to individuals and society. Norris died on Oct. 25, 1902, at 32. *The Wolf,* which was to have concluded the trilogy, was never written. Norris viewed social and economic factors and nature itself as the determining elements in molding human lives.

Among **books published** this year were *D'ri and I* by Irving Bacheller, a novel set during the War of 1812; *Cardigan* by Robert W. Chambers, a novel of the American Revolution; *Graustark* by George Barr McCutcheon, a best-selling romance about a mythical Balkan kingdom; *Mrs. Wiggs of the Cabbage Patch* by Alice Hegan Rice; and *Springtime and Harvest* by Upton Sinclair, the author's first novel, which later was retitled *King Midas.*

The paintings of **Maurice Prendergast** were characterized by a combination of impressionism and a Venetian love of pageantry. Returning from Paris, where he was the first important U.S. painter to recognize the genius of Paul Cézanne, he painted many beach scenes.

| Business and Industry; Science;
Education; Philosophy and Religion **III** | | **IV** Sports; Social Issues and Crime;
Folkways; Fashion; Holidays |

Mar. 24 The **Carnegie Steel Company,** organized in 1899, was incorporated in New Jersey with a capitalization of $160,000,000, making it one of the largest corporations in the U.S.

Apr. Dividend payments of the **Standard Oil Company** for the first quarter of 1900 amounted to $20,000,000, the largest quarterly dividend declared by a corporation to date.

Sept. 17 A **coal miners' strike** by 112,000 miners sent the price of anthracite in New York City from $1.00 to $6.50 per ton. The strike ended Oct. 25 with a settlement favorable to the workers.

Nov. 15 The **Carnegie Institute of Technology,** popularly known as Carnegie Tech, was established by Andrew Carnegie in Pittsburgh, Pa.

May 24 The 34th annual **Belmont Stakes** was won by Ildrim, with a time of 2:21½. The jockey was Nash Turner.

May 29 The 25th annual **Preakness Stakes** was won by Hindus, with a time of 1:48²⁄₅. The jockey was H. Spencer.

Fall The **National League baseball championship** was won by Brooklyn, with a record of 82 wins, 54 defeats.

Oct. 5 The **U.S. Open golf tournament** was won by Harry Vardon of England.

1901

·The extent to which the economy of the country had grown was made clear when the first billion-dollar corporation was formed this year. The United States Steel Corporation, formally organized on Mar. 3, was capitalized at $1,402,846,000. The actual value of the tangible property of the corporation was estimated at $682,000,000, indicating that a good deal of the capitalization was for good will. The enterprise netted the organizers, including the financier J. Pierpont Morgan, large sums. The corporation was formed primarily from the Carnegie Steel Company, but it brought in other mills as well. The new firm manufactured 60% of all iron and steel produced in the U.S. Andrew Carnegie received 5% bonds with a par value of $225,639,000 for his company and spent the next 20 years distributing his wealth in benefactions amounting to $350,000,000.

A report on **yellow fever** read by the Yellow Fever Commission to the Pan-American Medical Congress at Havana, Cuba, described experiments proving for the first time that the disease was transmitted by a mosquito *(Stegomyia calopus)*. Such a theory had been held for 20 years by Dr. Carlos Finlay of Havana, but he had been unable to offer proof and had been ridiculed by the medical profession. The Yellow Fever Commission, sent by the U.S. government to Cuba after the Spanish-American War, included Walter Reed, Aristides Agramonte, Jesse W. Lazear, and James Carroll. Doctors Lazear and Carroll both died from the effects of yellow fever contracted during the experiments.

An early **panoramic film,** *New York in a Blizzard,* was described in the Edison Catalogue of 1901–1902. "Our

Men who were to become legends of baseball were coming to the fore in the early years of the century. Among them was Connie Mack (Cornelius Alexander McGillicuddy), who began as a catcher for Washington (NL) in 1886, then played for Buffalo in the Players League in 1890 before joining Pittsburgh, where he ended his career as player-manager (1894–1896) with a .247 career batting average. In 1901 he was named manager of the Philadelphia Athletics (AL) and eventually became owner of the team. Under his long management the Athletics won nine league championships and five World Series. Mack was elected to the Baseball Hall of Fame in 1937. He did not fully retire until 1954, when the team was sold and moved to Kansas City, Mo.

This year's **national college football championship** was won by Michigan, with a record of 11 wins, no losses, no ties.

The **U.S. Lawn Tennis Association singles championships** were won by Elizabeth Moore in the women's division and William A. Larned in the men's division.

Apr. 19 The fifth **Boston Marathon** was won by James J. Caffrey of Hamilton, Ontario, Canada, with a time of 2 hrs., 29 min., 23.6 sec.

Apr. 29 The 27th annual **Kentucky Derby** was won by His Eminence, with a time of 2:07¾. The jockey was Jimmy Winkfield.

May 23 The 35th annual **Belmont Stakes** was won by Commando, with a time of 2:21. The jockey was H. Spencer.

the amendment established a quasi-protectorate over Cuba. The amendment was abrogated May 29, 1934.

Mar. 4   Pres. **William McKinley was inaugurated** for his second term. Theodore Roosevelt was sworn in as vice president.

Mar. 23   **Emilio Aguinaldo,** leader of the Filipino insurgents, was captured by a U.S. patrol under Brigadier Gen. Frederick Funston in the province of Isabela, Luzon.

Apr. 19   The **rebellion in the Philippines was ended** by proclamation. It had been the most unpopular war ever fought by the U.S., mainly because many Americans believed that the Philippines should have been given its independence.

May 3   A **fire** in Jacksonville, Fla., destroyed 1700 buildings, caused $11,000,000 worth of damage, and left 10,000 homeless.

May 27   A Supreme Court decision bearing on the so-called **Insular Cases,** dealing with the status of such former Spanish possessions as Puerto Rico and the Philippines, was handed down. It stated that territories acquired as a result of the Spanish-American War were neither foreign countries nor part of the U.S. This point was important in establishing a tariff policy toward the possessions.

Nov. 18   The **Hay-Pauncefote Treaty** was signed, abrogating the Clayton-Bulwer Treaty of 1850. By its terms the British consented to U.S. control of an isthmian canal linking the Atlantic and Pacific oceans. The Senate ratified the treaty on Dec. 16.

This year Prendergast was awarded a medal at the Pan-American Exhibition in Buffalo, N.Y.

The works in sculptural portraiture of **Herbert Adams** were exhibited at the Pan-American Exhibition in Buffalo, N.Y., and received high praise. *Portrait of a Young Lady, Rabbi's Daughter,* and *Julia Marlowe* were included.

Mar.   The song "**High Society**" was composed by Porter Steele. It later was adopted by jazz musicians of New Orleans as a standard tune.

Mar. 21   The play *Uncle Tom's Cabin,* reported *Life* magazine, was "today the greatest money-maker of any attraction on the stage of New York City." It was true as well of every other city in the U.S.

Oct. 7   *Monsieur Beaucaire,* a play by Booth Tarkington based on his 1900 novel of the same title, opened in Philadelphia. Tarkington's first play, it reflected the spirit of romanticism evident in many of his later works. The play dealt with the adventures of the French Duke of Orleans, disguised as a barber, in England.

1902

Interest in conservation of natural resources was growing, and the nation found a strong advocate in Pres. Theodore Roosevelt. During his term of office Roosevelt added almost 150,000,000 acres of land to the government reserve. On July 17, 1902, Congress passed the Newlands Reclamation Act, named for its sponsor, Francis G. Newlands, Democratic congressman from Nevada. By its terms the government would build irrigation dams in 16 western states and use the proceeds from the sale of public lands for further projects. The law also set up the U.S. Bureau of Reclamation in the Department of the Interior.

The traditional blue **U.S. Army uniform** was discarded in favor of olive drab despite the protests of sentimentalists who remembered "the boys in blue." The Spanish-American War had taught that blue was too good a target.

Jan. 24   A treaty with Denmark for the purchase of the **Virgin Islands** (Danish West Indies) was signed. The U.S. Senate approved the treaty, but the Danish Rigsdag rejected it. In 1917, after a Danish plebiscite

Plays dealing with strong characters, both virtuous and otherwise, were successful at this time. Foremost among American playwrights was Clyde Fitch, author of more than 30 popular plays. His play *The Stubbornness of Geraldine,* a study of fidelity, opened in New York City on Nov. 3, 1902. He also produced this year *The Girl With the Green Eyes.* The play dealt with the psychological aspects of jealousy; it was his best work. *The Climbers* (1901) and *The City* (1909) dealt seriously with New York City's financial and political life. Fitch also wrote such popular farces as *Captain Jinks of the Horse Marines* (1901).

Among **books published** this year was *The Virginian* by Owen Wister, a story of life in Wyoming that became one of the most celebrated western novels of all time. Wister dedicated the book to his friend Pres. Theodore Roosevelt. *The Virginian* was reprinted 14 times in eight months, and in two years had sold some 300,000 copies. Other books published this year included *The*

camera is revolved from right to left and takes in Madison Square, Madison Square Garden, looks up Broadway from South to North, passes the Fifth Avenue Hotel, and ends looking down 23rd Street West." Panoramic films were made practicable by a new device on motion picture cameras that made it possible to rotate, or pan, the camera. The age of practical cinematography had come a step closer to realization.

Wilbur and Orville Wright built their second full-scale glider and tested it at Kitty Hawk, N.C. They based their design on lift tables by Otto Lilienthal, the German scientist who had worked out a ratio of wing area to forward motion. Unhappily, this second glider crashed. The Wrights, much discouraged, returned to Dayton, Ohio. They later worked out new tables.

Jan. 10 The first great **oil strike in Texas** launched a fabulous era in the Southwest. The Spindletop claim near Beaumont, Tex., owned by Anthony F. Lucas, blew in on this date to open the door for the international petroleum industry.

Mar. 12 The first extensive **New York City public library system** was made possible by a gift from Andrew Carnegie of $5,200,000. It provided for 39 branch libraries.

May 28 The 26th annual **Preakness Stakes** was won by The Parader, with a time of 1:47$\frac{1}{5}$. The jockey was Fred Landry.

June 15 The **U.S. Open golf tournament** was won by Willie Anderson.

Fall The **National League baseball championship** was won by Pittsburgh, with a season record of 90 victories and 49 defeats.

Fall The **first American League baseball championship** was won by Chicago, with a season record of 83 victories and 53 defeats.

Sept. 2 "Speak softly and carry a big stick" was credited to Theodore Roosevelt a few weeks after becoming president. The saying, emphasizing the need for a strong foreign policy, caught the fancy of the entire nation and "the big stick" proved a favorite prop of political cartoonists.

Sept. 28-Oct. 4 The **America's Cup** was successfully defended by the U.S. yacht *Columbia*, which won three straight races from the British challenger *Shamrock II*.

Oct. 16 The prevalence of **racism** in the U.S. was evidenced when an uproar followed Pres. Roosevelt's dining on this date with the noted black educator Booker T. Washington. There was widespread resentment in the South.

1902

As American business enterprises grew, debate increased as to whether large and powerful corporations were good for the nation. Experience so far indicated that industrial giants cared little for anything except profit and that only government regulation could restrain their actions. Into this argument came the International Harvester Company, incorporated in New Jersey on Aug. 12, 1902, with a capital of $120,000,000. The combination of interests represented by the concern produced 85% of all farm machinery in the U.S. However, Harvester conducted its business in such a moderate manner that there was little complaint. Both capitalists and consumers were beginning to recognize that, given the extent of the nation and its economy, bigness was here to stay.

Feb. Discovery of the **hookworm** was announced by Dr. Charles Wardell Stiles. He declared that the so-called poor whites in the South were neither lazy nor innately slovenly, but were suffering on a wide scale from the debilitating effects of the parasite. An anti-hookworm campaign began throughout the South,

The early years of twentieth-century professional baseball saw the founding of the American League in 1900 out of the Western Association, the new league's first season in 1901, and the start of an annual championship series with the National League in 1903. This expansion created more heroes of the diamond. One of the most admired and successful managers of this period was John J. McGraw, nicknamed "Little Napoleon," who left as manager for Baltimore (AL) midway through the 1902 season to become manager of the New York Giants (NL). McGraw held that position for 31 years, during which the Giants won ten National League championships, four in succession, and three World Series. McGraw was elected to the Baseball Hall of Fame in 1937.

This year's **national college football championship** was won by Michigan, with a record of 11 wins, no losses, no ties.

(Dec. 14, 1916) favored the sale, the islands of St. Croix, St. Thomas, and St. John were finally purchased for $25,000,000.

Apr. 29 The **Chinese Exclusion Act** was extended to prohibit immigration of Chinese laborers from the Philippine Islands.

May 20 **Cuban independence** was achieved, four years after the end of the Spanish-American War. The U.S. flag was lowered from government buildings in Cuba and replaced with the new Cuban flag.

June 28 The **Isthmian Canal Act** was passed by Congress. It authorized financing and building of a canal across the Isthmus of Panama, and also authorized an alternative route across Nicaragua in the event the president could not obtain a concession from the Panama Canal Company of France (which he eventually did for $40,000,000) and negotiate a proper treaty with Colombia. Treaty difficulties were obviated by the successful rebellion and separation of Panama from Colombia in Nov. 1903. The new republic immediately granted a ten-mile-wide strip of land for the canal.

July 1 The **Philippine Government Act** was passed by Congress. It declared the Philippine Islands an unorganized territory and all inhabitants territorial citizens. It authorized a commission, appointed by the president, to govern the territory. On July 4 Pres. Theodore Roosevelt issued an order establishing civil government and granting amnesty to all political prisoners.

Nov. 4 In **congressional elections** both major parties made gains in the Senate from minor party or vacant seats, but the Republicans maintained their majority over the Democrats, 57–33. In the House of Representatives the total number of seats rose from 357 to 386, and the Republicans kept their majority over the Democrats, 208–178.

Captain of the Gray-Horse Troop by Hamlin Garland, a novel chronicling the exploitation of the Sioux by white men; *The Mississippi Bubble* by Emerson Hough, a historical novel; *The Wings of the Dove* by Henry James, a novel; *The Story of My Life,* the autobiography of Helen Keller; *A Daughter of the Snows* by Jack London, the author's first novel, and *The Cruise of the Dazzler,* for children, also by London; *Brewster's Millions* by George Barr McCutcheon, a novel that sold in the millions and was the basis for at least six motion pictures; *Dorothy Vernon of Haddon Hall,* a novel by Charles Major; and *The Blazed Trail* by Stewart Edward White, a novel.

Floradora, a phenomenally successful musical, closed in New York City after 547 performances. The musical's most popular feature was its famous sextet of beautiful girls and their escorts, who sang "Tell Me, Pretty Maiden."

One of the most popular **songs** of the year was Hughie Cannon's "Bill Bailey, Won't You Please Come Home," which was later taken up by jazz musicians in the South.

The report of the **McMillan Commission** for reconstruction of Washington, D.C., was released. In general it followed the eighteenth-century designs of the city's original planner, Pierre Charles L'Enfant. The report called for creation of a mall from the White House to the Lincoln Memorial; this would require removal of the Pennsylvania Railroad tracks and buildings of Union Station.

1903

By 1903 it became clear that legislation on the books could not keep railroads from engaging in business practices that gave certain shippers a decided advantage. As a result, on Feb. 19 the Elkins Act, named for Sen. Stephen B. Elkins, Republican of West Virginia, was passed by Congress. This law made it illegal for railroads to give rebates on their published freight rates. Finding that this did not solve the problem, Congress on June 29, 1906, passed the Hepburn Act, named for William P. Hepburn, Republican congressman from Ohio. That law empowered the Interstate Commerce Commission to regulate the rates charged by railroads, pipelines, and terminals.

Realism was becoming an influence in adult American fiction, but it was not noticeable in children's literature. Sentimentalism and a happy ending were what sold, as witnessed by the popular books of Kate Douglas Wiggin. *The Birds' Christmas Carol* (1887) was the story of the life and death of an ethereal child. Wiggin's most successful book, *Rebecca of Sunnybrook Farm,* was published this year and sold more than 1,000,000 copies. This children's classic was about a girl's experiences on her widowed mother's farm. Another Wiggin classic was *Mother Carey's Chickens* (1911), about a warm-hearted widow who had a great many children.

Business and Industry; Science; Education; Philosophy and Religion III		IV Sports; Social Issues and Crime; Folkways; Fashion; Holidays

supported by the Rockefeller Foundation.

Mar. 10 Pres. **Theodore Roosevelt,** in his first decisive action since succeeding to the presidency, announced that the federal government would prosecute the Northern Securities Company, a J. P. Morgan interest, under the Sherman Antitrust Act. Pres. William McKinley, who died on Sept. 14, 1901, had let the law lie dormant despite the rapid growth of holding companies under his administration.

May 12 A **coal miners' strike,** which idled 140,000 anthracite coal miners, began in Pennsylvania after United Mine Workers president John Mitchell's suggestion of arbitration had been refused by mine operators. The miners had asked for a 20% increase in wages and an eight-hour day.

June 15 The **New York Central Railroad** reduced the time of its New York to Chicago run to 20 hours.

July 30 A **coal miners' riot** at Shenandoah, Pa., was broken up by the militia.

Sept. The third glider built by **Orville and Wilbur Wright,** designed by the brothers according to new calculations of pressure, drift, and resistance, was flown successfully at Kitty Hawk, N.C. During September and October they made nearly 1000 flights, several of more than 600 feet.

Oct. 16 A commission was named by Pres. Roosevelt to settle the anthracite **coal miners' strike.** Judge George Gray was appointed head of the commission. On Oct. 21 John Mitchell, president of the United Mine Workers, declared the strike at an end after workers accepted the commission's arbitration at a convention in Wilkes-Barre, Pa. The refusal of coal operators to accept arbitration at the beginning of the strike had aroused much popular opinion against big trusts. Consequently, Pres. Roosevelt's announced policy of enforcing antitrust laws was given considerable popular support.

The **U.S. Lawn Tennis Association singles championships** were won by Marion Jones in the women's division and William A. Larned in the men's division.

Jan. 1 The **first Tournament of Roses Association football game,** and the first post-season football game, was held at Pasadena, Calif. Michigan defeated Stanford 49–0. The event came to be known as the Rose Bowl game in 1923.

Apr. 19 The sixth **Boston Marathon** was won by Samuel A. Mellor of Yonkers, N.Y., with a time of 2 hrs., 43 min., 12 sec.

May 3 The 28th annual **Kentucky Derby** was won by Alan-a-Dale, with a time of 2:08¾. The jockey was Jimmy Winkfield, scoring his second straight Derby win.

May 22 The 36th annual **Belmont Stakes** was won by Masterman, with a time of 2:22½. The jockey was John Bullman.

May 27 The 27th annual **Preakness Stakes** was won by Old England, with a time of 1:45⁴/₅. The jockey was L. Jackson.

Aug. 8 The **Davis Cup** international tennis challenge round was won by the U.S. team, defeating the British team three matches to two.

Fall The **National League baseball championship** was won by Pittsburgh, with a season record of 103 victories and 36 defeats.

Fall The **American League baseball championship** was won by Philadelphia, with a season record of 83 victories and 53 defeats.

Oct. 11 The **U.S. Open golf tournament** was won by Lawrence Auchterlonie.

1903

A historic moment in technology and transportation arrived on Dec. 17, when Orville Wright made the first powered flight in a heavier-than-air machine. As early as 1898 Orville and Wilbur Wright, owners of a bicycle repair shop and factory in Dayton, Ohio, had been working on the problem of flight. Years of experimentation had led to their development of a working glider. Meanwhile, refinements of internal combustion engines gave them the power plant they needed to keep the glider aloft. On Dec. 17, 1903, on the beach at Kitty Hawk, N.C., Orville Wright flew the 750-lb. craft, which was powered by a 12-hp gasoline engine, for 12 seconds, traveling about 120 feet. Four flights were made that

This year was born an American sports institution, the World Series. For the first time, the champions of the National and American leagues met for a post-season playoff, which ran from Oct. 1 to Oct. 13; it was a best-of-nine series. The Pittsburgh Pirates, the National League champs, took three of the first four games from the Boston Red Sox, originally called the Red Stockings. On Oct. 7 the American League champs rebounded with an 11–2 romp over the Pirates, then won the next three games to take the series five games to three and prove to the world that the American League had arrived. Boston's win no doubt ruffled a few feathers in the National camp. In 1904, when Boston again took the

Exploration and Settlement; Wars; Government; Civil Rights; Statistics   **I**

II   **Publishing; Arts and Music; Popular Entertainment; Architecture; Theater**

Jan. 22 The **Hay-Herrán Treaty,** granting a 99-year lease and U.S. sovereignty over a canal zone in Panama, was signed with Colombia. The U.S. Senate ratified it on Mar. 17, but on Aug. 12 the Colombian Senate rejected it.

Feb. 14 A bill creating the **Department of Commerce and Labor,** the ninth Cabinet office, was signed by Pres. Theodore Roosevelt. In 1913 the department was divided in two.

Feb. 23 The first declaration of **federal police power** superior to that of the states was handed down by the Supreme Court in the case of *Champion v. Ames.* The Court ruled that Congress had the right to prohibit transmission through the mails of lottery tickets from one state to another. The ruling was the basis for eventual federal regulation of food, drugs, narcotics, and other substances.

May 1 Ending 48 years of total **prohibition,** New Hampshire enacted a system of licenses for liquor sales.

May 31 A **flood** of the Kansas, Missouri, and Des Moines rivers killed more than 200 persons, left some 8000 homeless, and caused about $4,000,000 in damage.

Nov. 3 A **revolt in Panama** against Colombian rule broke out one day after Pres. Roosevelt ordered U.S. naval forces to the area. The U.S. presence kept Colombian forces from halting the rebellion, which was engineered in part by officers of the Panama Canal Company and by Panamanian groups, all with the tacit approval of the Roosevelt administration. On Nov. 6 the U.S. recognized the Republic of Panama, three days after it had been proclaimed.

Nov. 18 The **Hay-Bunau-Varilla Treaty** was negotiated. It gave the U.S. full control of a ten-mile-wide canal zone in Panama in return for $10,000,000 in gold plus a yearly payment of $250,000.

Dec. 30 A **theater fire** at the Iroquois Theater in Chicago, during a performance by Eddie Foy, killed 588 persons. Public reaction led to new theater codes in many U.S. cities: more fire walls, better and more exits, unobstructed alleyways, fireproof scenery, and the like.

Among **books published** this year was *The Ambassadors* by Henry James, a novel about Americans in Paris that showed the author at the peak of his literary powers. Other books published this year included *The Land of Little Rain* by Mary Austin, a collection of sketches; *The Bar Sinister* by Richard Harding Davis, a novel; *The Little Shepherd of Kingdom Come* by John Fox, Jr., a novel; *The Call of the Wild* by Jack London, a study of the forces of nature and civilization in the framework of a classic dog story, and *The People of the Abyss,* also by London, a study of the slums of London's East End; *Canterbury Pilgrims* by Percy MacKaye, a drama in blank verse that set Chaucer's characters in poetic adventures; *The Pit* by Frank Norris, the second volume of the author's *Epic of the Wheat* trilogy; and *The Testimony of the Suns* by George Sterling, a book of poetry.

The Passion Play, one of the longest motion pictures to be presented in the U.S. to date, was first shown. Its running time of about 36 minutes contrasted sharply with the average film time of three or four minutes. It reflected the popularity of religious themes in early films.

The **first male motion picture star** made his debut in *The Great Train Robbery,* a landmark film considered the first motion picture with a plot. The actor, Max Aaronson, also used the names Max Anderson, G. M. Anderson, and Bronco Billy.

Joseph Pulitzer announced his intention of establishing a Graduate School of Journalism at Columbia University. He left $2,000,000 for the school in his will.

One of the earliest buildings of **Frank Lloyd Wright,** the Larkin Administration Building, was built at Buffalo, N.Y.

The **Williamsburg Bridge,** the second important suspension bridge across the East R. (the first was the Brooklyn Bridge, opened in 1883), was opened in New York City.

June 17 *Babes in Toyland* by Victor Herbert was given its first performance in Chicago. It became one of the best-known operettas in the U.S.

1904

By 1904 Pres. Theodore Roosevelt had achieved great popularity as well as control of the Republican Party. His nomination for a term in his own right was certain and his conservative Democratic opponent, Alton B. Parker, conducted a dull campaign. Roosevelt, although

This was the era of the muckrakers, journalists and authors who investigated and wrote about corruption in government and business. One of the leading muckrakers was Lincoln Steffens, a magazine editor who collected his articles on corruption in municipal

Business and Industry; Science; Education; Philosophy and Religion III	IV Sports; Social Issues and Crime; Folkways; Fashion; Holidays

day, with Wilbur setting the record of 59 seconds in the air traveling 852 feet. The aviation age had arrived.

The **first film exchange** in the U.S. was established by Harry J. Miles and his brother Herbert. The film exchange became the economic foundation of the motion picture industry: it enabled producers to sell their products to one buyer who could pay high prices. More than 100 film exchanges had been established by 1907 in 35 cities throughout the U.S. This led to the opening of thousands of new motion picture theaters. Daily changes of program became customary.

The **first federal wildlife refuge,** Pelican Island near the east coast of Florida, was designated by Pres. Theodore Roosevelt.

The **Ford Motor Company** was organized by Henry Ford, who became its first president.

A **heavier-than-air flying machine,** built by Samuel P. Langley, was tested from a houseboat on the Potomac R. On takeoff, its wing hit a houseboat stanchion and the machine crashed. Langley was subjected to much public ridicule for his efforts. In 1914 the machine was reconditioned and flown. It was a 14-ft. model and flew without a pilot. There are those who maintain that Langley achieved powered flight before the Wright brothers.

Mar. 21   In a **victory for organized labor,** the report of the Anthracite Coal Strike Commission, appointed by Pres. Roosevelt to investigate conditions in the mining industry, established that "no person shall be refused employment, or in any way discriminated against, on account of membership or non-membership in any labor organization."

July 4   The **first Pacific communications cable** was opened. Pres. Roosevelt sent a message around the world and back to him in 12 minutes.

July 26   What was probably the **first transcontinental automobile trip** ended when a 20-hp Winton driven by H. Nelson Jackson and Sewell K. Crocker arrived in New York City. Jackson's success raised charges that his car had not made the trip entirely on its own power, but no evidence of fraud was uncovered. Jackson had started out from San Francisco on May 23. On Aug. 21 a 12-hp Packard model F driven by Tommy Fetch and M. C. Karrup arrived in New York. It had started out on June 20 and had made the trip in 51 days' running time.

American League pennant, John J. McGraw, manager of the champion New York Giants, already involved in a running feud with Ban Johnson, president of the American League, refused to allow a post-season playoff. The bitterness between the two leagues was only temporary. In 1905 the World Series resumed and has been played every year since.

This year's **national college football championship** was won by Princeton, with a record of 11 wins, no losses, no ties.

The **U.S. Lawn Tennis Association singles championships** were won by Elizabeth Moore in the women's division and Hugh L. Doherty in the men's division.

Apr. 20   The seventh **Boston Marathon** was won by John C. Lorden of Cambridge, Mass., with a time of 2 hrs., 41 min., 29.8 sec.

Apr. 27   The opening of **Jamaica Race Track** in Long Island, N.Y., was attended by many notable figures from the world of entertainment and gambling, including Lillian Russell, a reigning glamour queen of the time, James Buchanan "Diamond Jim" Brady, and John Warne "Bet-a-million" Gates. On Memorial Day in 1945 the track drew the largest crowd in the history of New York racing, 64,670.

May 2   The 29th annual **Kentucky Derby** was won by Judge Himes, with a time of 2:09. The jockey was Hal Booker.

May 27   The 37th annual **Belmont Stakes** was won by Africander, with a time of 2:23$\frac{1}{5}$. The jockey was John Bullman.

May 30   The 28th annual **Preakness Stakes** was won by Flocarline, with a time of 1:44$\frac{4}{5}$. The jockey was W. Gannon.

June 27   The **U.S. Open golf tournament** was won by Willie Anderson.

Aug. 8   The U.S. lost the **Davis Cup** international tennis challenge round to Great Britain, four matches to one.

Aug. 22–Sept. 2   The **America's Cup** was successfully defended by the U.S. yacht *Reliance,* which won three straight races from the British challenger *Shamrock III.*

1904

The first section of the New York City subway system, which was to become the largest in the country, was opened on Oct. 27, 1904. Work on the line had begun in 1900. It ran from the Brooklyn Bridge north to 145th St. and Broadway in Manhattan. Construction of this

As soon as automobiles were invented and manufactured, men began racing them against time and against one another. Automobile racing as an organized sport began on Oct. 8, 1904, with the Vanderbilt Cup race, sponsored by William K. Vanderbilt. Vanderbilt was an

Exploration and Settlement; Wars; Government; Civil Rights; Statistics	I		II	Publishing; Arts and Music; Popular Entertainment; Architecture; Theater

representing the conservative party in American politics, was the hero of the progressives. The progressives of this period inherited some of the goals of the populists of a few years earlier, but the populists represented chiefly southern and western farm interests. The progressives were urban-oriented, and concerned primarily with problems of industrial monopoly, corruption in government, assimilation of new immigrants, and the relief of poverty.

Jan. 4 In a ruling on the **status of territorial citizens,** the Supreme Court ruled that citizens of Puerto Rico were not aliens and could not be refused admission to the continental limits of the U.S. However, they were not classified as U.S. citizens.

Feb. 7–8 A tremendous **fire** in Baltimore, Md., destroyed 2600 buildings in an 80-block area of the business district. The fire burned for about 30 hours, making it the biggest fire since the great Chicago fire of 1871. Property loss was estimated at $80,000,000.

Feb. 29 The **Panama Canal Commission** was appointed by Pres. Theodore Roosevelt. The seven-man board was charged with overseeing construction of the waterway. On Apr. 22, 1904, the Panama Canal property was transferred to the U.S. by an agreement signed in Paris. John Findley Wallace was named chief engineer of the project on May 10, 1904.

May 5 The **Socialist National Convention nominated Eugene V. Debs** of Indiana for the presidency and Benjamin Hanford of New York for the vice presidency.

June 16 A steamship **fire** that swept through the *General Slocum* in New York harbor killed some 900 persons.

June 21–23 The **Republican National Convention nominated Pres. Roosevelt** for the presidency and Charles W. Fairbanks of Indiana for the vice presidency.

July 29–30 The **Prohibition Party National Convention** nominated Dr. Silas C. Swallow of Pennsylvania for the presidency and George W. Carroll of Texas for the vice presidency.

July 4–5 The **People's Party (Populist) National Convention** nominated Thomas E. Watson of Georgia for the presidency and Thomas H. Tibbles of Nebraska for the vice presidency.

July 6–9 The **Democratic National Convention** nominated Alton B. Parker of New York for the presidency and Henry G. Davis of West Virginia for the vice presidency.

Nov. 8 **Theodore Roosevelt was reelected president** of the United States. Charles W. Fairbanks was elected vice president. The electoral vote was Roosevelt, 336; Alton B. Parker, Democratic candidate, 140. The popular vote was Roosevelt, 7,628,834; Parker, 5,884,401; Eugene V. Debs, Socialist candidate, 402,460; Dr.

government in *The Shame of the Cities* (1904). Steffens held that such corruption stemmed from alliances between businessmen and politicians who were able to enrich each other at the expense of the taxpayer.

Among **books published** this year was *The Golden Bowl* by Henry James. Other books published this year included *The Crossing* by Winston Churchill, a novel set in Kentucky during the American Revolution; *The Deliverance* by Ellen Glasgow, a novel; *Cabbages and Kings* by O. Henry, the author's first collection of short stories; *The Sea Wolf* by Jack London, a study of human nature and the concept of the superman as embodied in the character of a brutal ship's captain; *Freckles* by Gene Stratton-Porter, a novel; and *The History of the Standard Oil Company* by Ida M. Tarbell, a muckraking classic.

The first building designed entirely for **poured concrete construction,** Unity Temple in Chicago, was built from plans by Frank Lloyd Wright.

Arthur Farwell undertook a nationwide lecture tour to stimulate interest in American music and to bring new Russian and French influences to bear on American audiences. Farwell often played his own compositions based on Indian themes. He also gathered a notable collection of folk music from the Southwest.

This year's production of Richard Wagner's *Parsifal* by the Metropolitan Opera Company was much criticized. One critic said the audience was more interested in a scene that included a 45-second kiss than in the depiction of the Lord's Supper. Another called the performance "profanity, sacrilege, blasphemy, and a gigantic outrage."

Instruction Book No. 1 for Rag-Time by Axel Christensen was published. Admitting that only accomplished pianists could play ragtime properly, Christensen nevertheless undertook to teach the rudiments in 20 lessons. The book became widely popular.

The sculptor **Gutzon Borglum** completed *Mares of Diomedes,* a tour de force depicting six stampeding wild ponies gaunt from hunger. In later life Borglum interested himself in jumboism, the art of carving figures out of mountains.

The **American Academy of Arts and Letters** was founded by the National Institute of Arts and Letters. Membership was limited to 50, to be chosen from among the members of the institute.

Sept. 3 *Mrs. Wiggs of the Cabbage Patch* by Anne Crawford Flexner, a dramatization of the 1901 novel

first part of the subway system was supervised by Alexander Ector Orr. Some of the present system runs on elevated tracks, but there are 134 miles of tunnels, some driven through rock. The first tunnel under the East R. was driven between 1903 and 1906 and put into service in 1908.

A study of ways to eliminate **yellow fever** in the Panama Canal area was begun by William C. Gorgas. Eradication of the disease enabled construction of the canal.

The **National Tuberculosis Association** was organized.

The **National Child Labor Committee** was formed to promote child labor laws.

The **diesel engine** was shown for the first time in the U.S. at the St. Louis Exposition. The engine was based on the plans of the German inventor Rudolf Diesel.

Cigarette coupons first came into use as sales gimmicks of new chain tobacco stores.

The **first speed law** was passed in New York State. It mandated a maximum speed of 10 mph in populated districts, 15 mph in villages, and 20 mph in open country.

Mar. 11 Workers on the **Morton Street Tunnel,** working west from New York City and east from New Jersey, linked their tunnel sections beneath the North R., an estuary of the Hudson R. A few minutes later William G. McAdoo, president of the New York and New Jersey Railroad, stepped through, becoming the first man to cross the river on dry land.

Mar. 14 The **Northern Securities Company** was ordered dissolved by the Supreme Court in a landmark case reflecting the federal government's relation to big business. Theodore Roosevelt's reputation as a trust-buster rested largely on the prosecution of this case and the angry comments he drew from J. P. Morgan, who controlled the railroad holding company.

Apr. 15 A **hero fund,** amounting to $5,000,000, was established by Andrew Carnegie for those who endangered their lives to rescue others, and for the survivors of those who lost their lives while attempting rescues.

May 23 A cut in steamship **steerage rates** to $10 a passenger was announced by German, French, Belgian, and Dutch steamship companies. This was to compete with British lines carrying immigrants to the U.S.

July 25 A **textile strike** was begun involving 25,000 workers in Fall River, Mass. It ended when the mills accepted the workers' wage demands on Jan. 8, 1905.

Sept. 9 **Mounted police** were used for the first time in New York City.

early auto fancier. It was said he had garages that would hold 100 cars and that he hired 20 mechanics to service them. The race, on Long Island, was as much a social as a sporting event, with about 25,000 spectators on hand. The winner was George Heath, driving a 90-hp French Panhard. He defeated 17 other starters by completing ten laps around a 28.4-mi. course in 5 hrs., 26 min., 45 sec.

This year's **national college football championship** was won by Pennsylvania, with a record of 12 wins, no losses, no ties.

The vogue for **jujitsu** was started by Pres. Theodore Roosevelt, who had a Japanese instructor call regularly at the White House.

The **U.S. Lawn Tennis Association** singles championships were won by May Sutton in the women's division and Holcombe Ward in the men's division.

The **World Series** was called off this year by John McGraw, manager of the New York Giants, the National League champions. Incensed by the abuse Ban Johnson, president of the American League, had heaped on him when he switched from the Baltimore Americans in 1903, McGraw got even by refusing to let the Giants meet Boston, the American League leaders, for the postseason series. It took the persuasion of owners, managers, players and fans to smooth the incident over. By that time it was too late for the games to be played.

Apr. 19 The eighth **Boston Marathon** was won by Michael Spring of New York City, N.Y., with a time of 2 hrs., 38 min., 4.4 sec.

May 2 The 30th annual **Kentucky Derby** was won by Elwood, with a time of 2:08½. The jockey was Frankie Prior.

May 5 The **first perfect baseball game,** in which the pitcher did not allow any opposing player to reach first base, was pitched by Denton T. "Cy" Young of the Boston Americans (AL), who led his team to a 3–0 victory over Philadelphia.

May 14 The first **Olympic Games** to be held in the U.S. opened as part of the St. Louis Exposition in St. Louis, Mo. The U.S. won 21 events and the unofficial team championship in the third Olympiad of the modern era.

May 25 The 38th annual **Belmont Stakes** was won by Delhi, with a time of 2:06³/₅. The jockey was George Odom.

May 28 The 29th annual **Preakness Stakes** was won by Bryn Mawr, with a time of 1:44¹/₅. The jockey was Eugene Hildebrand.

Silas C. Swallow, Prohibition Party, 259,257; Thomas E. Watson, People's Party, 114,753. The Republicans carried Missouri for the first time since the Civil War in what was the biggest election victory since 1872. They maintained a 57–33 majority over the Democrats in the Senate and picked up 43 seats in the House for a 250–136 majority.

by Alice Hegan Rice, opened in New York City at the Savoy Theatre.

Nov. 15 The highly popular play *Sunday*, starring **Ethel Barrymore**, opened at the Hudson Theatre in New York City. In this play Miss Barrymore improvised the line, "That's all there is, there isn't any more."

1905

Pres. Theodore Roosevelt gained international prominence by arranging a peace conference between Russia and Japan; the nations had been at war since Feb. 10, 1904. Although Japan had fared better in the military and naval engagements of the Russo-Japanese War, neither side was in a position to go on fighting much longer. In a note to the two powers on June 8, Roosevelt urged an end to hostilities and suggested a conference. The peace conference met at Portsmouth, N.H., on Aug. 9, and the belligerents signed the Treaty of Portsmouth on Sept. 5. The U.S. sought to keep a balance of power in the Far East between the two nations and also to preserve the Open Door Policy in China. However, by the terms of the treaty, Japan came out ahead and was on its way to becoming a world power. Japan's paramount interest in Korea was recognized and it was given the South Manchurian Railway and the Southern Liaotung Peninsula. Roosevelt was able to keep Japan from securing more than half of Sakhalin Island. For his efforts Roosevelt was awarded the Nobel Peace Prize in 1906.

Jan. 21 A protocol with the Dominican Republic was signed, giving the U.S. complete charge of its customs and international debt, with the purpose of satisfying European creditors of Santo Domingo. The U.S. was also to guarantee the territorial integrity of the republic. Though the U.S. Senate refused to ratify the protocol, Pres. Theodore Roosevelt made a temporary arrangement with the republic, incorporating the key elements of the protocol. The action was a reflection of the so-called Roosevelt Corollary to the Monroe Doctrine, which Roosevelt stated on Dec. 6, 1904. Roosevelt held that "in flagrant cases of wrongdoing or impotence" of nations in the Western Hemisphere, the U.S. might be obliged to undertake "the exercise of an international police power."

Feb. 20 A mine disaster in Virginia City, Ala., southwest of Birmingham, killed some 116 miners.

Mar. 4 Pres. **Roosevelt was inaugurated** for his first full term. Charles W. Fairbanks was sworn in as vice president.

Higher education joined hands with theater this year when George Pierce Baker established his 47 Workshop at Harvard. He taught playwriting techniques and provided a laboratory for experimental stage productions. Among those whom Baker taught were Eugene O'Neill, Philip Barry, Sidney Howard, and S. N. Behrman. Baker taught at Harvard until 1925, when he went to Yale to continue his work there.

Among **books published** this year was *The House of Mirth* by Edith Wharton, a novel analyzing with great subtlety a group of wealthy, artificial, and oversophisticated people, and their tragic influence over the life of a young woman. Other books published this year included *Isidro* by Mary Austin, the author's first novel; *The Clansman* by Thomas Dixon, Jr., a novel about the Ku Klux Klan that was the basis for D. W. Griffith's landmark motion picture *The Birth of a Nation; The Game* by Jack London, a novel about prizefighting; *The House of a Thousand Candles* by Meredith Nicholson, a novel; and *Sandy* by Alice Hegan Rice, a novel.

A **popular song** of the year was "Everybody Works but Father." It was only partly a comic reference to father's laziness. Women were beginning to work on a large scale, often driving men out of their jobs in offices and factories.

Oct. 3 *The Girl of the Golden West* by David Belasco, the playwright and theatrical producer, opened in Pittsburgh and ran for three years. The final scene, in which the wounded outlaw hero's blood drips down on the sheriff from the attic where the hero is hidden, was taken from an actual event. Giacomo Puccini used the play as the basis for his opera *La Fanciulla del West*, which opened on Dec. 10, 1910, at the Metropolitan Opera, New York City, Enrico Caruso sang the role of Dick Johnson, the hero. Puccini's opera was the first based on an American theme.

Oct. 23 *The Squaw Man* by Edwin Milton Royle opened at Wallack's Theatre in New York City. The play told the story of a British nobleman living in Wyoming and his love for an Indian squaw.

Business and Industry; Science; Education; Philosophy and Religion III		IV Sports; Social Issues and Crime; Folkways; Fashion; Holidays

Oct. 19 The **American Tobacco Company** was formed by a merger of its two subsidiaries, the Consolidated and the American & Continental tobacco companies.

Nov. 2 **Evangeline Booth** was appointed commander of the Salvation Army of the U.S.

Dec. 10 The **Bethlehem Steel Corporation** was founded in New Jersey.

July 9 The **U.S. Open golf tournament** was won by Willie Anderson.

Sept. 28 A **woman was arrested for smoking** a cigarette while riding in an open automobile in New York City. "You can't do that on Fifth Avenue," said the arresting policeman.

1905

Life insurance had joined the ranks of big business, the three largest firms having combined assets of $1,250,000,000 by 1904. The major firms also had arrangements with certain banks by which the insurance company purchased large blocks of securities placed on the market by the banks. The funds for these lucrative transactions came from the thousands who paid insurance premiums. Reports of a scandal surfaced and an investigating commission was appointed by New York State in 1905. Headed by Charles Evans Hughes, it held 57 public hearings from Sept. 6 to Dec. 30 and uncovered numerous excesses. The probe disclosed, for example, that Charles Hazen Hyde, son of the founder of the Equitable Life Assurance Society, earned $100,000 a year, although still in his twenties. Hyde once charged to company expenses a $12,000 dinner for the French ambassador. The investigation resulted in reform legislation. It also brought Hughes into public life. He went on to become governor of New York, Republican candidate for president, and in 1930 chief justice of the U.S. Supreme Court.

The **population density** in New York City's slums had reached 1000 persons an acre in some sections, exceeding the population density of Bombay.

The **first cigarette testimonials** by stars of the entertainment world employed the comedians Fatty Arbuckle and Harry Bulger and the dramatic actor John Mason in advertisements praising the qualities of Murad cigarettes.

The number of **automobiles** registered in the U.S. rose to 77,988, compared with 300 a decade earlier, but the automobile was still considered a useless toy by most people.

Feb. 20 **State compulsory vaccination laws** were ruled constitutional by the U.S. Supreme Court in the case of *Jacobson v. Massachusetts.*

Apr. 17 **State laws limiting working hours** were ruled unconstitutional by the U.S. Supreme Court.

June 7 The highest recorded **retail price for real estate** to date was paid for No. 1 Wall Street in New York City. The 1250-sq.-ft. plot sold for $700,000.

Greyhounds had been chasing hares for several thousand years, but it was not until 1905 that an American developed the idea of racing the dogs around a circular track in pursuit of an artificial hare. Owen Patrick Smith of Hot Springs, S.Dak., decided to promote tourism through such races. There had been public opposition to the slaughter of live hares, so Smith substituted a stuffed rabbit skin attached to a motorcycle, thus launching the greyhound racing industry.

This year's **national college football championship** was won by Chicago, with a record of 11 wins, no losses, no ties.

The **first Rotary Club** was founded by Paul Percy Harris, a Chicago lawyer. The name derived from the early practice of meeting at each member's home in rotation. Clubs soon spread to other cities and a National Association of Rotary Clubs was established in 1910. Overseas branches were established and in 1922 the organization's name was changed to Rotary International. Each club has representatives from all businesses and professions in its locality.

The **world heavyweight boxing championship** was won by Marvin Hart, who knocked out Jack Root in 12 rounds in the final bout of an elimination tourney. He filled the title vacated by James J. Jeffries' retirement this year.

The **U.S. Lawn Tennis Association singles championships** were won by Elizabeth Moore, for the fourth time, in the women's division and Beals C. Wright in the men's division.

At the **Wimbledon** tennis championships in England, May G. Sutton won the women's singles championship, becoming the first foreigner to win the women's singles and the first U.S. player to win any Wimbledon singles title.

Apr. 19 The ninth **Boston Marathon** was won by Frederick Lorz of Yonkers, N.Y., with a time of 2 hrs., 38 min., 25 sec.

May 10 The 31st annual **Kentucky Derby** was won by Agile, with a time of 2:10¾. The jockey was Jack Martin. For the second time in Derby history, only three horses ran in the race.

May 11 A tornado struck Snyder, Okla., killing about 100 persons.

July 22 A severe yellow fever epidemic began in New Orleans. It lasted into October and was finally brought under control by a federal antimosquito campaign, which began in August. There were 3000 cases and about 400 deaths.

Oct. 31 *Mrs. Warren's Profession* by George Bernard Shaw opened and was ordered closed after one performance (Oct. 28) at the Garrick Theater in New York City. Anthony Comstock, self-appointed protector of public morals in New York, had complained and called the play "reekings." Shaw retaliated by coining the word "Comstockery." Comstock took the case against *Mrs. Warren's Profession* to court, but the play was held to be not actionable.

1906

The worst natural disaster in U.S. history occurred on the morning of Apr. 18, 1906, when a devastating earthquake struck San Francisco, Calif. Most of the damage came not from the shock but from the fire that followed. Flames swept the city for three days. By the time the fire was brought under control, 490 blocks had been leveled, 25,000 buildings had been destroyed, 225,000 people had been made homeless, and 452 had been killed. Damage was estimated to be at least $350,000,000. The nation rallied to the aid of the stricken city, whose residents began at once to rebuild. Banks offered to lend money and stores reordered stock.

The **first American Nobel Prize winner** was Pres. Theodore Roosevelt, who was awarded the Nobel Peace Prize this year for his role in mediating an end to the Russo-Japanese War (1904–1905).

Mar. 1 **Woodrow Wilson,** speaking before the North Carolina Association, said: "Nothing has spread socialistic feeling in this country more than the use of the automobile." This was before Henry Ford's mass-produced cars became available to the average wage earner.

June 29 The **Railroad Rate Act,** giving the federal government authority to set rates for interstate shipments, was passed by Congress. Passage of the bill was preceded by 60 days of debate, much of it acrimonious. The bill's opponents feared federal encroachment on states' rights and rising authority over private property ownership.

June 30 The **Pure Food and Drug Act** was passed. It prohibited the sale of adulterated foods and drugs and demanded an honest statement of contents on labels. Dr. Harvey W. Wiley was mainly responsible for pointing up the necessity for this act. On the same day a Meat Inspection Act was passed by Congress. It was the result of the Reynolds and Neill report of June 4, which revealed shockingly unclean conditions in meat-packing plants. The Meat Inspection Act required sanitary conditions and federal inspection

The reading public's fascination with an American West more imaginary than real seemed insatiable. One man who did his best to feed this craving was Zane Grey, whose more than 60 books sold over 13,000,000 copies before he died in 1939. His first western novel, published in 1906, was *The Spirit of the Border.* His most popular novel was *Riders of the Purple Sage* (1912). Grey was quite authentic as to geography and topography, but his plots and characters were melodramatic and sometimes simplistic. Strong and brave heroes, nasty villains, and pretty, innocent heroines were his stock in trade. Many of his novels were made into movies.

Among **books published** this year was *The Jungle* by Upton Sinclair, a novel exposing the sordid aspects of the Chicago meat-packing industry, particularly the hardships imposed on its workers and the practice of selling questionable or tainted meat. The book came to the attention of Pres. Theodore Roosevelt, who summoned Sinclair for further information. Roosevelt then pushed for passage of the Pure Food and Drug Act of 1906. Other books published this year included *The Spoilers* by Rex Beach, a novel of Alaska based on actual events and the author's experiences in the territory; *Coniston* by Winston Churchill, a novel about boss rule in a state legislature; *The Awakening of Helena Ritchie* by Margaret Deland, a novel; *The Wheel of Life* by Ellen Glasgow, a novel; *The Four Million* by O. Henry, his second collection of stories; *White Fang* by Jack London, a sequel to *The Call of the Wild,* and *Before Adam,* a novel also by London; and *What Is Man?* by Mark Twain, a bitter essay in the form of a Platonic dialogue, published privately.

Ruth St. Denis captivated New York City audiences with her modern dances, including several so-called Hindoo dances.

Alla Nazimova, a famous Russian actress, made her English-speaking debut in New York City with a

Business and Industry; Science; Education; Philosophy and Religion III		IV Sports; Social Issues and Crime; Folkways; Fashion; Holidays

June 11 The Pennsylvania Railroad inaugurated an **18-hour train** between New York and Chicago, the "fastest long-distance train in the world." On June 18 the New York Central Railroad also inaugurated 18-hour service with the Twentieth Century Limited. Both trains suffered wrecks within a week, and 19 lives were lost.

July 7 The **Industrial Workers of the World** (IWW) was established in Chicago as a reaction against the more conservative American Federation of Labor. Its members came to be known as Wobblies.

May 24 The 39th annual **Belmont Stakes** was won by Tanya, with a time of 2:08. The jockey was Eugene Hildebrand.

May 27 the 30th annual **Preakness Stakes** was won by Cairgorn, with a time of 1:45⁴⁄₅. The jockey was W. Davis.

Sept. 22 The **U.S. Open golf tournament** was won by Willie Anderson.

Oct. 9–14 The second annual **World Series** was won by the New York Giants (NL), defeating the Philadelphia Athletics (AL) four games to one.

1906

An event rare in U.S. religious history occurred this year when the Rev. Algernon Sidney Crapsey, rector of St. Andrew's Protestant Episcopal Church in Rochester, N.Y., was tried for heresy before an ecclesiastical court. His church was known for its social work, but it was charged that under the influence of the writings of Karl Marx and Ernest Renan, Crapsey had made heretical remarks about the divinity of Christ. The trial began on Apr. 18 at Batavia, N.Y., with detachments of lawyers, secular and clerical, representing both sides. The trial was fully reported by newspapers throughout the U.S. and England. Crapsey was convicted on Dec. 5 and expelled from the ministry.

Mar. 12 In a decision on **testimony in antitrust proceedings,** the Supreme Court, in the case of *Hale v. Henkel,* ruled that witnesses could be compelled to give testimony against their corporations and to produce papers and documents that might prove pertinent to the case.

Apr. 7 Announcement was made of a successful **transatlantic wireless transmission** from a 40,000-watt transmitter at Manhattan Beach, New York City, to Lee De Forest at a receiving station in Ireland. This year De Forest invented the triode tube, the cornerstone for the development of modern wireless communication.

Apr. 28 A complete legislative program to reform the **life insurance business** was passed by the New York State legislature. The program was the result of investigations in the previous year by Charles Evans Hughes. The laws provided for establishing mutual life insurance companies, prohibited speculative investment of insurance company funds, and forbade companies to hold stock in banks or trust companies.

The most talked about murder of the first decade of the twentieth century was the killing of Stanford White, the prominent architect. On the evening of June 25, 1906, White was at the roof garden of New York City's Madison Square Garden, which he had designed, when he was shot and killed by Harry K. Thaw. The wealthy playboy claimed that White had been having an affair with his wife, Evelyn Nesbit Thaw, a former chorus girl. Thaw's trial fascinated the country. After one hung jury, Thaw was found "not guilty because insane" in 1908. In 1913 Thaw escaped from the mental hospital where he was being held but was found in Canada and brought back. In 1915, at still another trial, he was declared sane and released.

This year's **national college football championship** was won by Princeton, with a record of nine wins, no losses, one tie.

The **U.S. Lawn Tennis Association singles championships** were won by Helen Homans in the women's division and William J. Clothier in the men's division.

Feb. 23 The **world heavyweight boxing championship** was won by Tommy Burns, who defeated Marvin Hart in 20 rounds at Los Angeles, Calif. James J. Jeffries, who retired in 1905 because he could find no worthy adversary, refereed the fight.

Mar. 17 The term *muckraker,* taken from a passage in John Bunyan's *Pilgrim's Progress,* was first used in its modern meaning by Pres. Theodore Roosevelt in an address to the Gridiron Club, Washington, D.C. Muckrakers were authors of "literature of exposure," who in the early 1900s helped stimulate reform by exposing unpleasant sides of American life. The best-known muckrakers included Lincoln Steffens, Ida M. Tarbell, Ray Stannard Baker, and David Graham Phillips. A prime example of the influence of muckraking literature can be seen in Upton Sinclair's *The Jungle,* which helped passage of the Meat Packing Act of 1906.

Apr. 19 The tenth **Boston Marathon** was won by

for all plants in interstate commerce.

Aug. 23 A request for U.S. intervention in Cuba was issued by Tomás Estrada Palma, the first president of Cuba, to quell a revolt arising from election disputes. Pres. Roosevelt held off but finally sent troops, who took over the Cuban government for 13 days in October.

Sept. 22 Race riots in Atlanta, Ga., left 21 persons dead, including 18 blacks, and many more injured in one of the worst race riots in U.S. history. The city was placed under martial law.

Sept. 29 The Platt Amendment, authorizing U.S. intervention in Cuba, was invoked and the U.S. assumed military control of the country. Sec. of War William Howard Taft was provisional governor.

Nov. 6 In congressional elections the Republicans gained four Senate seats for a 61–31 majority. In the House the Republicans lost 28 seats but maintained a 222–164 majority.

Nov. 6 Charles Evans Hughes was elected governor of New York, largely on the strength of his investigation of life insurance scandals. He became a vigorous reformer in many fields.

Nov. 9 The first foreign trip by a U.S. president was made by Pres. Roosevelt, who sailed on the battleship *Louisiana* to visit the Isthmus of Panama and inspect the canal. He returned on Nov. 26.

Dec. 12 Oscar S. Straus of New York City was appointed secretary of commerce and labor by Pres. Roosevelt. Straus was the first Jew to receive a Cabinet appointment.

company of Russian actors. Her English version of Ibsen's *Hedda Gabler* (1890) was especially well received by the critics.

George M. Cohan produced *Forty-Five Minutes from Broadway,* one of his most successful musicals.

This season the plays of **George Bernard Shaw** reached their height of popularity in New York City. Six of his plays were on the New York stage during the season: *Caesar and Cleopatra; Arms and the Man; Man and Superman; John Bull's Other Island; Mrs. Warren's Profession,* which had been shut down for alleged obscenity after its opening in Oct. 1905; and *Major Barbara.*

Ferdinand "Jelly Roll" Morton, the celebrated New Orleans ragtime piano player, wrote "The King Porter Stomp." Morton gave the St. Louis ragtime style of Scott Joplin a heavy beat. Among his many other ragtime compositions were "The Pearls," "Kansas City Stomps," "Chicago Breakdown," "Black Bottom Stomp," "Buddy Carter's Rag," and "The Perfect Rag."

Geraldine Farrar made her U.S. opera debut after having played with great success in the Berlin opera.

Oscar Hammerstein opened his second Manhattan Opera Company in New York City (he had opened an earlier company with the same name in 1892) in competition with the Metropolitan Opera Company. His purpose was to produce a preponderance of French and Italian works, in contrast to the Met's emphasis on German opera. The Manhattan Opera Company lasted until 1910, when Hammerstein sold out to the Metropolitan, agreeing not to produce opera for ten years.

1907

Pres. Theodore Roosevelt was especially interested in the preparedness and political value of the U.S. Navy. Now that a powerful Navy existed, he proposed to show it to the world, partly to deter Japan from further adventurism in the Pacific. On Dec. 16, 1907, a squadron of 16 battleships, known as the Great White Fleet because of the ships' appearance, steamed out of Hampton Roads, Va., under Rear Adm. Robley D. Evans. Instead of causing alarm as some had feared, the fleet was enthusiastically received in many ports of call, including those in Japan, Australia, New Zealand, and Gibraltar. The fleet arrived back at Hampton Roads on Feb. 22, 1909, having convinced the world that the U.S. was a major naval power.

Jan. 26 A law prohibiting corporate campaign contributions to candidates for national office was passed by Congress.

The Broadway theater always offered a variety of productions, some dramatic, some humorous, and some appealing as much to the eye as to the ear or the mind. One of the most successful producers of visually lavish entertainment was Florenz Ziegfeld, who offered his first *Ziegfeld Follies* this year. Ziegfeld put on this annual revue for 24 years, featuring "the most beautiful girls in the world" together with comedians and singers. Among the stars he presented were Anna Held, Fanny Brice, Eddie Cantor, and W. C. Fields. Ziegfeld also staged such hits as *Rio Rita* and *Show Boat.*

Among **books published** this year was *Three Weeks,* a romantic novel by the English author Elinor Glyn that was suppressed in Boston because of its description of an illicit affair. It sold 50,000 copies in three weeks and eventually sold in the hundreds of thousands. Other books published this year included *The Trimmed Lamp*

Business and Industry; Science;		**Sports; Social Issues and Crime;**
Education; Philosophy and Religion III	IV	**Folkways; Fashion; Holidays**

June 21 A partial list of **food additives** was read by Rep. James R. Mann, Republican of Illinois, in Congress. The list included the following: "Coffee. Colored with Scheele's green, iron oxide, yellow ochre, chrome yellow, burnt umber, Venetian red, turmeric, Prussian blue, indigo; adulterated with roasted peas, beans, wheat, rye, oats, chicory, brown bread, charcoal, red slate, bark, date stones." Mann had introduced the Pure Food and Drug Act in the House of Representatives, which passed on June 30.

Aug. **Government ownership of railroads** was proposed by William Jennings Bryan, returning from Europe, to the Democrats who assembled to greet him at Madison Square Garden, New York City. Cheers turned to a chilling silence as the audience heard the idea.

Aug. 13 An announcement that only **steel railroad coaches** would be purchased in the future was made by the Pennsylvania Railroad. Wooden coaches, which were fire hazards and tended to disintegrate or telescope into one another in accidents, would be abandoned.

Dec. 24 The first known **radio broadcast of voice and music** was made by Reginald A. Fessenden, a private radio experimenter, at Branch Rock, Mass. Fessenden had demonstrated his system at Branch Rock on Dec. 11. Also this year he established two-way wireless communication with Scotland.

Timothy Ford of Cambridge, Mass., with a time of 2 hrs., 45 min., 45 sec.

Apr. 22–May 2 **Olympic Games** were held in Athens, Greece, but they were not accepted as official by the International Olympic Committee. The U.S. won 12 gold medals, behind France with 15.

May 2 The 32nd annual **Kentucky Derby** was won by Sir Huon, with a time of 2:08⅘. The jockey was Roscoe Troxler.

May 22 The 31st annual **Preakness Stakes** was won by Whimsical, with a time of 1:45. The jockey was Walter Miller.

May 30 The 40th annual **Belmont Stakes** was won by Burgomaster, with a time of 2:20. The jockey was L. Lyne.

June 29 The **U.S. Open golf tournament** was won by Alex Smith.

Oct. 9–14 The third annual **World Series** was won by the Chicago White Sox (AL), who defeated the Chicago Cubs (NL) four games to two.

Nov. 28 **"Philadelphia Jack" O'Brien,** a light heavyweight, fought heavyweight champion Tommy Burns to a 20-round draw in Los Angeles, Calif.

Dec. 29 The first annual convention of the **Intercollegiate Athletic Association** was held. Formed as an educational organization to establish sound requirements for intercollegiate athletics, it changed its name in 1910 to the National Collegiate Athletic Association. In 1931 it set "Standards for the Conduct of Intercollegiate Athletics," with which all members were required to comply as a condition of membership. It strengthened its enforcement powers in 1951 and is now the rule-making body for all intercollegiate athletics.

1907

Once more overspeculation and a flawed and unregulated banking and credit structure caused a financial panic that turned into a brief depression. A large drop in the stock market on Mar. 13 presaged trouble. On Oct. 21 a run on the Knickerbocker Trust Company in New York City caused panic elsewhere. The bank was forced to close its doors. The government called on J. Pierpont Morgan, the nation's leading financier, for help. By the force of his personality, Morgan secured the cooperation of his fellow bankers, who combined their resources to import $100,000,000 in gold from Europe to restore confidence and end what came to be known as the panic of 1907. One result of the panic was passage of the Aldrich-Vreeland Act on May 30, 1908. It levied a tax of up to 10% on notes based on securities other than federal bonds. It also established a commission to investigate the currency and banking system.

One of the best-remembered infield combinations in the game of baseball is the trio of Joe Tinker, Johnny Evers, and Frank Chance, who played shortstop, second base, and first base, respectively, for the Chicago Cubs (NL). These three turned the double play into an art form. Chance had become manager of the Cubs in 1905. In 1907 the team finished first and went on to dominate the Detroit Tigers in the World Series. Evers and Tinker made six errors in the series, but the trio combined to steal eight bases and kept Detroit from scoring effectively. Franklin Pierce Adams later recalled them in a piece called "Baseball's Sad Lexicon":

> Ruthlessly pricking our gonfalon bubble,
> Making a Giant hit into a double,
> Words that are weighty with nothing but trouble:
> "Tinker to Evers to Chance."

Feb. 8 A treaty with the Dominican Republic was signed. It provided for collection of customs by a U.S. agent with the purpose of satisfying foreign and domestic creditors. The Senate ratified the treaty on Feb. 25. This was essentially the same treaty the Senate refused to accept in 1905.

Feb. 12 The steamer *Larchmont* foundered in Long Island Sound, causing 131 deaths.

Feb. 20 The **Immigration Act of 1907** was signed by Pres. Theodore Roosevelt. It included a provision empowering the president to restrict immigration by Japanese laborers.

Feb. 26 The **General Appropriations Act** was passed. It increased the salaries of Cabinet members, the Speaker of the House, and the vice president to $12,-000, and raised the salaries of senators and congressmen to $7500.

Mar. 14 Japanese laborers were excluded from immigrating to the continental U.S. by presidential order.

Mar. 14 The **Inland Waterways Commission** was appointed by Pres. Theodore Roosevelt. It was to study the related problems of forest preservation and commercial waterways. Theodore E. Burton was designated chairman.

Mar. 21 U.S. Marines landed in **Honduras** to protect life and property during a period of political disturbance.

June 15-Oct. 15 The **Second International Peace Conference,** called by Czar Nicholas II of Russia, was held at The Hague, The Netherlands. The conference had originally been proposed by Pres. Roosevelt in 1904, but the Russo-Japanese War interfered. Establishment of a World Court was advocated by the U.S. but was not adopted. The conference adopted a resolution proposed by Luis M. Drago of Argentina, which stipulated that armed force must not be used against American nations for the collection of debts to foreign creditors.

Sept. 17 Oklahoma adopted a new constitution, which included an article providing for prohibition.

Nov. 16 Oklahoma was admitted to the Union, the 46th state.

Dec. 6 A **coal mine explosion** in Monongah, W.Va., one of the worst mine disasters in U.S. history, killed 361 persons.

Dec. 19 A **coal mine explosion** in Jacobs Creek, Pa., killed 239 persons.

and *Heart of the West,* two more collections by O. Henry; *Songs of a Sourdough* by Robert W. Service, which included the celebrated ballad "The Shooting of Dan McGrew" and which was reissued as *The Spell of the Yukon; Christian Science* by Mark Twain; and *The Fruit of the Tree* by Edith Wharton, a novel.

The Education of Henry Adams, a masterpiece of autobiography by the noted historian and author, was privately printed and distributed to Adams's friends. Adams revealed that his education had not prepared him for modern living and expressed skepticism and loss of faith. The work was published posthumously in 1918 and was awarded the Nobel Prize for Biography in 1919.

The Merry Widow by Franz Lehár was given its first U.S. performance this year. The operetta, which included the popular "Merry Widow Waltz," was performed frequently for many years.

The **Plaza Hotel** in New York City was built from designs by Henry Hardenbergh. Its design exemplified early twentieth-century luxury.

The first public showing of a **color motion picture with sound** was held in Cleveland, Ohio. The Chromophone process was used in the film, which consisted of footage of grand opera, a bull-fight with naturalistic sound effects, and a political speech accompanied by derisive sounds.

Florence Lawrence, probably the first motion picture actress to be treated as a star, began her screen career at the Vitagraph Company. She soon joined the Biograph Company when D. W. Griffith became director, and came to be known as the "Biograph girl."

The **first AIA Gold Medal** for architecture, given by the American Institute of Architects, was awarded to Sir Aston Webb of England.

The **Robey House,** one of Frank Lloyd Wright's earliest designs, was built in Chicago. The structure showed the broad low roofs and horizontal lines that were the hallmark of Wright's prairie houses.

Jan. 22 The opera *Salomé* by Richard Strauss, based on the drama by Oscar Wilde, was given its first U.S. performance at the Metropolitan Opera House in New York City. Mary Garden appeared in the title role. Critics violently disputed the merits of the music, but citizens were shocked by the sensational plot. The Metropolitan canceled further performances. Boston, urged on by the New England Watch and Ward Society, prevented Garden from singing the role there.

| Business and Industry; Science;
Education; Philosophy and Religion | III | | IV | Sports; Social Issues and Crime;
Folkways; Fashion; Holidays |

William D. "Big Bill" Haywood, president of the Western Miners Union, was acquitted of the murder of former governor Frank Steunenberg of Idaho. The trial had Clarence Darrow for the defense and William E. Borah as prosecuting attorney.

The **Nobel Prize in Physics** was awarded to Prof. Albert Abraham Michelson, head of the Physics Department at the University of Chicago. Michelson was honored particularly for his studies of the speed of light, carried out with apparatus designed and built by himself.

The **University of Hawaii** was established as the College of Agriculture and Mechanic Arts in Honolulu, Hawaii. Its first classes met in 1908. Its name was changed to the College of Hawaii in 1911, and to the University of Hawaii in 1920.

The **Brush Motor Car Company** was formed in Detroit, Mich., by Frank Briscoe to manufacture the Brush, a two-seater runabout featuring coil springs and a single-cylinder, 12-hp engine. Designed by Alanson P. Brush, the car was advertised as "Everyman's Car." Despite the auto's low price and innovative features, the Brush Company was absorbed into United States Motors in 1910 and production ceased in 1913.

Mar. 9 John Alexander Dowie died. A Scot who came to the U.S. by way of Australia, Dowie in 1896 established the Christian Catholic Church, a sect that grew to more than 100,000 members; its headquarters were at Zion, Ill. Dowie founded the city of Zion (1901), the tabernacle, and industries worth more than $10,000,000. He later became unbalanced and was deposed as leader of the church.

May The first fleet of **taximeter cabs,** imported from Paris, arrived in New York City.

June 6 **Dropsie College for Hebrew and Cognate Learning,** a postgraduate college for rabbinical and biblical studies, was chartered in Philadelphia, Pa.

Sept. 12 The *Lusitania,* the largest steamship in the world, arrived in New York harbor on its maiden voyage. The liner set a new speed record of 5 days, 54 min. between Queenstown (now Cobh), Ireland, and New York.

This year's **national college football championship** was won by Yale, with a record of nine wins, no losses, one tie.

At the **Wimbledon** tennis championships, May G. Sutton won the women's singles title.

The **U.S. Lawn Tennis Association singles championships** were won by Evelyn Sears in the women's division and William A. Larned in the men's division.

Apr. 19 The 11th **Boston Marathon** was won by Thomas Longboat of Hamilton, Ontario, Canada, with a time of 2 hrs., 24 min., 24 sec.

May An early **Mother's Day** observance was held in Grafton, W.Va., through the efforts of Miss Anna M. Jarvis, who arranged a special church service marking the second anniversary of her mother's death in 1905. She requested that those attending the service wear white carnations, which she supplied. The first formal observances of Mother's Day were held in Grafton and in Philadelphia, Pa., on May 10, 1908. The custom spread rapidly until, by 1911, every state in the Union was participating in Mother's Day exercises held on the second Sunday in May.

May 6 The 33rd annual **Kentucky Derby** was won by Pink Star, with a time of 2:12³/₅. The jockey was Andy Minder.

May 21 The 32nd annual **Preakness Stakes** was won by Don Enrique, with a time of 1:45²/₅. The jockey was G. Mountain.

May 30 The 41st **Belmont Stakes** was won by Peter Pan, with a time of 2:15³/₅. The jockey was G. Mountain.

June 21 The **U.S. Open** golf tournament was won by Alex Ross.

Oct. 8–12 The fourth annual **World Series** was won by the Chicago Cubs (NL), who swept the Detroit Tigers (AL) in four games after the first game ended in a tie.

Dec. 2 The **world heavyweight boxing championship** was successfully defended by Tommy Burns, who knocked out Gunner Moir in ten rounds at London, England.

1908

There was little doubt that Pres. Theodore Roosevelt, if he chose to run again in 1908, would be reelected. However, he had said in 1904 he would not seek a third term, although he had been elected in his own right only once. Instead he handpicked the Republican nominee, William Howard Taft, who had been a lawyer, judge, U.S. solicitor general (1890–1892), governor of the Philippines (1901–1904), and secretary of war (1904–1908). The campaign was a dull one, the Democratic candidate, William Jennings Bryan, having lost most of the glamor he showed when first nominated for the presidency 12 years before.

Feb. 18   An agreement on the **restriction of Japanese immigration** was reached through a note sent to the American ambassador to Japan acknowledging Pres. Theodore Roosevelt's order of Mar. 14, 1907. The Japanese government agreed not to issue any more passports to Japanese laborers for immigration to the U.S.

Mar. 4   A **school fire** at the Collinwood School in Cleveland, Ohio, killed 176 persons.

Apr. 2–3   The **People's Party (Populist) National Convention** nominated Thomas E. Watson of Georgia for the presidency and Samuel W. Williams of Indiana for the vice presidency.

Apr. 12   A **fire** destroyed Chelsea, Mass., leaving more than 10,000 people homeless and destroying some $10,000,000 in property.

Apr. 30   Local **prohibition** was approved by voters in Worcester, Mass., which became the largest dry city in the country (population 130,000). Seventy-six saloons were closed and 2000 men were thrown out of work. On the same day 17 cities and 249 towns also went dry in Massachusetts.

May 10–17   The **Socialist Party National Convention** nominated Eugene V. Debs of Indiana for the presidency and Benjamin Hanford of New York for the vice presidency.

June 16–20   The **Republican National Convention nominated William Howard Taft** of Ohio for the presidency and James S. Sherman of New York for the vice presidency. When Chairman Henry Cabot Lodge spoke in praise of Pres. Theodore Roosevelt, who had chosen not to seek renomination, the delegates began a demonstration that lasted 45 minutes, breaking all previous records for both major parties.

July 4   The **Socialist Labor Party National Convention** nominated Martin R. Preston of Nevada, then serving a jail sentence in the Nevada Penitentiary for murder, for the presidency, and Donald L. Munro of Virginia

A new generation of American painters was arriving on the art scene. The work of these painters was realistic and showed concern with the contemporary world. In 1908 they became known as The Eight when they organized an exhibition of their work in February at the Macbeth Gallery in New York City. The eight artists were Arthur B. Davies, Maurice Prendergast, Ernest Lawson, Robert Henri, George Luks, William J. Glackens, John Sloan, and Everett Shinn. Henri was their leader. Their painting represented a turning away from the pretty but insipid pictures of the older, academic school of painting. Some of their works, depicting the seamier side of modern, urban life, won them the title of the Ash Can school from their detractors. Frank Jewett Mather of *The Nation* wrote that there "was more green, yellow and red sickness about their position than positive talent." Nevertheless, they brought to art a new vitality and proved that everyday scenes showing ordinary people could be worthwhile subjects for the painter, even when the subject was a city backyard, a crowded business street, or lonely city people at night.

Among **books published** this year was *The Trail of the Lonesome Pine* by John Fox, Jr., a novel set in the Cumberland Mts. of Kentucky. The author used his own experiences and knowledge of the region and its people in the novel, which became a best seller. Other books published this year included *The Barrier* by Rex Beach, a novel of adventure; *Mr. Crewe's Career* by Winston Churchill, a novel dealing with control of a state government by a railroad; *Friendship Village* by Zona Gale, stories of midwestern life; *The Iron Heel* by Jack London, a novel that predicted the rise of fascism; *The Circular Staircase* by Mary Roberts Rinehart, the mystery novel that launched her career; and *The Metropolis* by Upton Sinclair, a novel.

Censorship of the 1907 novel *Three Weeks* by Elinor Glyn was accomplished in Boston by the Watch and Ward Society's successful prosecution of a book salesman.

Mme. **Luisa Tetrazzini** made her first appearance in New York City with the Manhattan Opera Company. She had appeared in San Francisco in 1904.

There were between 8000 and 10,000 **nickelodeons,** or movie theaters, in the U.S., drawing an estimated 200,000 customers a day. The first such theater had been launched in 1905 in Pittsburgh, Pa., by John P. Harris and Harry Davis.

| Business and Industry; Science; Education; Philosophy and Religion **III** | **IV** Sports; Social Issues and Crime; Folkways; Fashion; Holidays |

1908

The age of the skyscraper was dawning. In Chicago architects and engineers had pioneered in new technology and materials, especially the steel skeleton that made such structures possible. But it was in New York City that the first real skyscrapers were erected. The first New York City skyscraper was the Flatiron Building, constructed between 1902 and 1904. Its name came from the triangular plot on which it was built, at the intersection of Fifth Ave. and Broadway. Its 22 stories rose 180 ft. high. In 1908 the Singer Building set a new record, its 47 stories rising to a height of 612 ft. It held the title of the world's tallest building for less than a year, however, being eclipsed by the Metropolitan Life tower of 50 stories and 700 ft. The Woolworth Building, completed in 1913, set still another record with its 55 stories and height of 760 ft. Although exceeded in height many times since, this distinguished Gothic-ornamented tower remains the proudest symbol of the age of early skyscrapers.

A **Nurse Corps** was established by the U.S. Navy. Esther Voorhees Hasson was appointed its first superintendent. In 1947 the corps became a staff corps, and its nurses were made commissioned officers.

Unemployment resulting from the panic of 1907 continued. The Bowery Mission in New York City reported that 2000 more men than usual applied daily for free breakfasts. Newspapers were full of advertisements stating workers' willingness to accept wages well below the prevailing standard.

The **transatlantic steerage rate** from Genoa, Italy, to New York City was $12.

An announcement that **poison gas** could be used as an effective weapon was made by Carl M. Wheaton of Newtonville, Mass., who offered the Army his formula, the result of nine years of experimentation.

Sky advertising was introduced in the U.S. when a plane flew over Broadway in New York City towing a box kite rigged with a dummy on a trapeze and a banner advertising a theatrical attraction.

Feb. 3 In an **antitrust decision** in the case of *Loewe v. Lawlor,* the so-called Danbury hatters case, the Supreme Court ruled that the antitrust law applied to labor combinations as well as to capital combinations and declared union boycotting illegal.

May 13–15 A **conservation conference** held at the White House in Washington, D.C., was attended by the governors of 44 states and territories to discuss conservation of natural resources.

May 28 A **child labor law** for the District of Columbia was passed by Congress. Its supporters hoped the law would be a model for the rest of the country.

June 8 The **National Commission for the Conservation of Natural Resources** was named by

The sporting event of the year turned out to be an around-the-world auto race, from New York City to Paris, France, by way of Alaska and Siberia. It was sponsored by *The New York Times* and *Le Matin.* The race began on Feb. 12, when six autos and their crews, French, German, Italian, and U.S., left New York City at 11 A.M. and traveled north toward Albany, N.Y. The cars drove west, across the U.S., Russia, and eastern Europe, experiencing breakdowns and encountering muddy roads, snow, ice, timber wolves, and gasoline shortages. The two lead cars were the huge German Protos driven by Lt. Hans Koeppen and the U.S. Thomas Flyer with George Schuster at the wheel. The German team was penalized 30 days for shipping their car by rail to Seattle, Wash., so, despite the fact the Germans arrived in Paris on July 26 and the Americans on July 30, the U.S. team was declared the winner. The only other entrant to finish, the Italian Zust, arrived two weeks later. When the U.S. team returned, New York City turned out in great numbers to greet them. Pres. Theodore Roosevelt received them at the White House on Aug. 20.

This year's **national college football championship** was won by Pennsylvania, with a record of 11 wins, no losses, one tie.

A new item in **women's fashions,** the Directoire, or sheath, gown was imported from Paris. Police had to rescue the first women to wear the gowns in Chicago. This year narrow skirts without petticoats became the style, along with enormous Merry Widow hats, huge dotted veils, boned collars, and net stockings.

The **U.S. Lawn Tennis Association singles championships** were won by Maud Barger-Wallach in the women's division and William A. Larned, for the fourth time, in the men's division.

Jan. 21 **Smoking for women** in public places was made illegal in New York City by passage of the Sullivan Ordinance.

Apr. 13 A **ban on dancing,** card playing, and theatergoing was lifted by the New England Methodist Episcopal Conference.

Apr. 20 The 12th **Boston Marathon** was won by Thomas P. Morrissey of Yonkers, N.Y., with a time of 2 hrs., 25 min., 43.2 sec.

Apr. 27–Oct. 31 At the **Summer Olympics** in London, England, the U.S. won the unofficial team championship by taking 15 of 28 events, with 23 gold medals. The team was honored in New York City on Aug. 29 on its return from the games.

May 5 The 34th annual **Kentucky Derby** was won by Stone Street, with a time of 2:15¹/₅. The jockey was Arthur Pickens.

for the vice presidency. Because Preston was under the constitutional age and serving a prison term, he was ineligible, and August Gillhaus of New York was nominated in his place.

July 7–10   The **Democratic National Convention nominated William J. Bryan** of Nebraska for the presidency and John W. Kern of Indiana for the vice presidency.

July 15–16   The **Prohibition Party National Convention** nominated Eugene W. Chafin of Illinois for the presidency and Aaron S. Watkins of Ohio for the vice presidency.

July 27   The **Independence Party National Convention** nominated Thomas L. Hisgen of Massachusetts for the presidency and John Temple Graves of Georgia for the vice presidency. William Randolph Hearst acted as temporary chairman during the convention.

Oct. 1   A **two-cent postage rate** went into effect between the U.S. and Great Britain.

Nov. 3   **William Howard Taft was elected president** of the United States. James S. Sherman was elected vice president. The electoral vote was Taft, 321; William Jennings Bryan, Democrat of Nebraska, 162. The popular vote was Taft, 7,679,006; Bryan, 6,409,106; Eugene V. Debs, Socialist candidate, 420,820; Eugene W. Chafin, Prohibition candidate, 252,683; Thomas L. Hisgen, Independence Party, 83,562; Thomas E. Watson, Populist, 28,131; August Gillhaus, Socialist Labor Party, 13,825. In congressional elections the Republicans held a 61–32 majority, the Democrats gaining one seat. In the House, which added five new seats, the Republicans lost three seats but maintained a majority, 219–172.

Nov. 28   An **explosion and cave-in** at the Marianna Mine in Monongahela, Pa., entombed more than 100 miners.

Isadora Duncan danced a series of scenes from Christoph Willibald Gluck's *Iphigénie en Aulide* (1774), recreating the postures of Greek dancers shown on ancient statues and pottery. The years of struggle during which she studied Greek art in the British Museum, and the financial collapse of her temple of dancing near Athens and her school of the dance near Berlin, were now being rewarded with riches and fame. On this second American tour, Duncan was high on the rising crest of her career.

Julia Ward Howe, author of the poem "The Battle Hymn of the Republic," became the first woman member of the American Academy of Arts and Letters. This year William Dean Howells was made president of the academy.

Oct.   **Mischa Elman,** the Russian-born violinist, made his first American appearance at Carnegie Hall in New York City.

Nov. 17   The career of the playwright **Edward Sheldon** began with the opening, at the Hackett Theatre in New York City, of *Salvation Nell,* in which the heroine rose out of the depths of moral degradation to a new life. The play ran for 71 performances. Sheldon's play *The Nigger* (1909) depicted the education of a southern gentleman in racial tolerance through his own degradation; *The Boss* (1911) and *The High Road* (1912) concerned politics and the reformation of character.

Dec. 24   Early **film censorship** was spearheaded in New York City by the Society for the Prevention of Crime, which persuaded Mayor George B. McClellan to revoke the licenses of the city's 550 movie houses. Managers were permitted to reapply for licenses only after they signed an agreement not to give Sunday performances or show immoral films.

1909

The tariff remained a controversial issue. The new president, William Howard Taft, had said he would call a special session of Congress to lower rates. When Congress finished with the matter, however, the Payne-Aldrich Tariff Act, signed by Taft on Aug. 5, included some reductions but on the whole made few changes. Sen. Nelson Aldrich, Republican of Rhode Island, advocated a high tariff and led the fight to keep rates high. In September, Taft defended the bill in a speech at Winona, Minn., thus alienating liberals and progressives

The blues as a recognized musical form had been around for some time, but 1909 was a landmark year in the history of the blues. This year W. C. Handy, the composer and bandleader, wrote "Mr. Crump" as a campaign song for Edward H. Crump, the Democratic boss of Memphis, Tenn. In 1912 it was published as "Memphis Blues" and became a hit, the first composition ever to be published as a blues song.

Among **books published** this year was *Martin Eden* by Jack London. It was an autobiographical novel about a

| Business and Industry; Science; Education; Philosophy and Religion | III | | IV | Sports; Social Issues and Crime; Folkways; Fashion; Holidays |

Pres. Theodore Roosevelt. Its 57 members were to be headed by Gifford Pinchot.

Sept. 16   Incorporation papers for the **General Motors Company** were filed in Hudson County, N.J., by representatives of William C. Durant, director of Buick. Soon after, General Motors bought Buick and then Olds. In 1909 Oakland and Cadillac joined the corporation. Chevrolet was added in 1918.

Sept. 17   Orville Wright crashed in his airplane at Fort Myer, Va., when a propeller blade broke and the plane fell 150 ft. to the ground, injuring Wright seriously and killing his passenger, Lt. Thomas W. Selfridge of the U.S. Signal Corps. Selfridge was the first person killed in an airplane accident. Orville and Wilbur Wright, still using their original machine, though with improvements, had made thousands of flights, had remained in the air as long as 38 min., and had flown distances up to 24 mi., but their work was still unknown in the U.S. to all but a few hundred observers. This year Wilbur Wright went to Europe to make tests for the French. Vast crowds watched his flights. On Sept. 21 he set a new flight endurance record over Le Mans, France—1 hr., 31 min., 25 sec. in a flight of 61 miles.

Oct. 1   The celebrated **Model T Ford** was introduced. It originally cost $850 but by 1926 the price, because of efficient manufacturing, had dropped to $310 for a machine that included a self-starter and other improvements.

Dec.   The first Red Cross **Christmas seals** for the campaign against tuberculosis were sold. The sale raised $135,000.

Dec. 2   The **Federal Council of the Churches of Christ in America** was established in Philadelphia. Thirty Protestant denominations were represented.

Dec. 21   At **tariff hearings** before the House Ways and Means Committee, Andrew Carnegie said, "Take back your protection; we are now men, and we can beat the world at the manufacture of steel."

May 30   The 42nd annual **Belmont Stakes** was won by Colin. There was no official time recorded. The jockey was Joe Notter.

June 2   The 33rd annual **Preakness Stakes** was won by Royal Tourist, with a time of 1:46²/₅. The jockey was Eddie Dugan.

Aug. 28   The **U.S. Open golf tournament** was won by Fred McLeod.

Sept. 23   Perhaps the **greatest dispute in baseball** was a call made in what was supposed to be the decisive game, at the Polo Grounds, N.Y., of the Chicago Cubs-New York Giants National League pennant race. In the bottom of the ninth inning with two men out and the score tied at 1–1, New York was at bat with two men on. The batter hit safely to center field, scoring the winning run. The Chicago players claimed, however, that when Fred Merkle, the man on first, saw the winning run score, he started to walk toward the clubhouse without advancing to second base, invalidating the play. Johnny Evers, the Chicago second baseman, tried to get the ball and tag Merkle out, but the fans streamed onto the field and bedlam reigned. Days later Harry C. Pulliam, head of the National Commission of Organized Baseball, decided to call the game a tie. The teams were forced to play a post-season playoff game, which the Cubs took 4–2. Fans invented the terms "boner" and "bonehead" to apply to Merkle's play.

Oct. 10–14   The fifth annual **World Series** was won by the Chicago Cubs (NL), who beat the Detroit Tigers (AL) four games to one.

Oct. 30   Mrs. **William Waldorf Astor,** wife of the British financier and publisher, died at 78. Her death marked the virtual end of old-style society in New York City. She had ruled society with an iron hand, and attendance at "Mrs. Astor's ball" had been the test of social position.

Dec. 26   The **world heavyweight boxing championship** was won by Jack Johnson, who defeated Tommy Burns in 14 rounds at Sydney, Australia.

1909

Although commercial production of celluloid, the first important synthetic plastic, had been achieved in 1872 by John W. Hyatt, it was in the early twentieth century that development of synthetics progressed significantly. In 1902 Arthur D. Little patented rayon (cellulose ester). In 1909 Leo H. Baekeland, Belgian-born inventor, announced his development of Bakelite, a synthetic thermosetting resin. It had many uses, and soon a large number of commercial products were being made in whole or in part of Bakelite. Because of its extremely high electrical resistance, it was used to make insulators

Former Pres. Theodore Roosevelt left for a hunting trip in Africa on Mar. 23, 1909, partly to let Pres. William Howard Taft have the limelight and partly because of his restless, energetic nature. Roosevelt received $50,000 from *Scribner's Magazine* for his account of the trip. When he returned in Feb. 1910 he brought back numerous animal trophies, which were given to the American Museum of Natural History in New York City. On June 18, 1910, he was off again on a trip to Europe. He reviewed troops with Kaiser Wilhelm of Germany

who had thought he would follow in the footsteps of their hero, Theodore Roosevelt.

The **National Association for the Advancement of Colored People** was founded, principally by liberal whites under the leadership of Oswald Garrison Villard, grandson of William Lloyd Garrison, to promote the rights and welfare of black Americans.

Jan. 28 The second **military occupation of Cuba** by U.S. troops, begun in Sept. 1906, ended, and the last troops left the island on Mar. 31.

Feb. 21 The **Great White Fleet,** consisting of 16 battleships and four destroyers painted white, arrived at Hampton Roads, Va., completing a round-the-world cruise begun in 1907. On the next day, the fleet was reviewed by Pres. Theodore Roosevelt.

Mar. 4 William Howard Taft was inaugurated president of the United States, the 27th. A Republican, he served one term.

Apr. 6 Robert Edwin Peary reached the North Pole. With his servant Matt Henson, who was black, and four Eskimos, Peary made a final dash from an advance base and reached latitude 90 degrees north for the first time in recorded history.

July 12 A resolution for a **Sixteenth Amendment** to the U.S. Constitution was passed by the Senate and submitted to the states for ratification. The amendment authorized Congress to impose income taxes.

Sept. 1 Dr. **Frederick Cook,** of Brooklyn, N.Y., claimed to have reached the North Pole on Apr. 21, 1908, beating Robert E. Peary in the feat by nearly a year. The claim sparked a bitter debate, which continued even after Congress and the scientific community at large recognized Peary's claim.

Nov. 13 An **explosion** at the St. Paul mine at Cherry, Ill., killed 259 miners.

Nov. 18 Two **U.S. warships were ordered to Nicaragua** after it was reported that 500 revolutionists, with two Americans among them, had been executed by the Nicaraguan dictator José Santos Zelaya. In the weeks following, the U.S. sent more warships and transports carrying Marines to the area. U.S. support of a rebel-imposed blockade, and the unstated possibility of U.S. intervention in the conflict, forced Zelaya to retire on Dec. 16.

strong and intelligent laborer and seaman who educates himself, strives for wealth and fame as a writer and, once he succeeds, finds life devoid of meaning and commits suicide on a voyage to the South Seas. Other books published this year included *The Silver Horde* by Rex Beach, a novel; *Roads of Destiny* and *Options,* two collections of stories by O. Henry; *54–40 or Fight!* by Emerson Hough, a historical novel about the conflict over the border between Canada and the Oregon Territory; *A Girl of the Limberlost* by Gene Stratton-Porter, a novel; *Three Lives* by Gertrude Stein, stories; and *A Certain Rich Man* by William Allen White, a novel.

Mary Louise Cecilia "Texas" Guinan, an as yet unknown young actress, played one-night stands in the West in a musical called *The Gay Musician.*

Paul Manship, the sculptor, went to Rome, Italy, to study at the American Academy.

The first notable **animated motion picture** shown in the U.S., *Gertie the Dinosaur,* utilized 10,000 drawings by Winsor McCay, a cartoonist for the New York *American.*

The **AIA Gold Medal** for architecture was awarded to Charles F. McKim of New York City.

"Buddy" Bolden, chief among New Orleans jazz musicians, was committed to an insane asylum. His place was taken by Freddie Keppard, a cornet player and leader of the Olympia Band. The band included such musicians as Louis "Big Eye" Nelson, Sidney Bechet, Willy Santiago, Zue Robertson, and Joe "King" Oliver.

John McCormack, the famous Irish tenor, first came to the U.S. He popularized "Mother Machree" (1910) and "When Irish Eyes Are Smiling" (1912).

Mar. 15 *The Faith Healer* by William Vaughn Moody opened in St. Louis. The play told the story of Ulrich Michaelis, a religious healer, who wanders into a midwestern community and performs miracles but loses his power when he succumbs to love.

Sept. 4 *The Fortune Hunter,* a play by the well-known dramatic caricaturist Winchell Smith, opened in New York City.

| Business and Industry; Science; Education; Philosophy and Religion   III | IV   Sports; Social Issues and Crime; Folkways; Fashion; Holidays |

and other components for the electrical, and later the radio, industry. Another feature of Bakelite was that it could be molded to any shape. It offered virtually limitless opportunities for manufacturers.

Henry Ford produced 19,051 **Model T Fords.** He led the auto industry in production and sales by building only one model, the "universal" car, which "customers could have in any color as long as it was black."

The **first wireless message** from New York City to Chicago was sent.

Mar. The **Glenn H. Curtiss** motor works at Hammondsport, N.Y., was taken over by the Herring-Curtiss Company. The company's first airplane, probably the first commercially manufactured airplane in the U.S., was sold to the New York Aeronautical Society for $5000.

Mar. 30 The **Queensboro Bridge** over the East R. was opened for traffic in New York City.

July 27 Orville Wright made a new **flight duration record,** remaining in the air 1 hr., 1 min., 40 sec. and carrying a passenger in addition to Wright.

Aug. 2 The **Lincoln penny,** designed by Victor D. Brenner, was issued by the Philadelphia Mint. It replaced the Indian head penny, which had been in circulation for 50 years. A controversy arose over the presence of Brenner's initials on the reverse side of the coin. The supply of coins bearing his initials sold out, and by mid-August new coins without initials were being issued.

Aug. 26 The first convention of the **National Conservation Congress,** with 37 states represented, met at Seattle, Wash. Charles W. Eliot presided.

Sept. 27 In a **conservation move,** some 3,000,000 acres of public lands in the West were withdrawn from public sale by Pres. William Howard Taft.

Dec. 31 The **Manhattan Bridge,** the fourth span across the East R. in New York City, was opened to traffic.

and lectured at the Sorbonne in Paris and at Oxford University in England.

This year's **national college football championship** was won by Yale, with a record of ten wins, no losses, no ties.

New standards of **fashion and beauty** were adopted as the automobile gained importance in American life. The suntanned, even red-faced Outdoor Girl replaced the soft, pale Gibson Girl when women took up automobile driving. "Automobile wrinkles" were soothed by application of freshly cut cucumbers. A new field was opened for fashion designers: special clothes for motoring, including a long veil to keep a lady's hat in place.

Feb. 12 The 100th anniversary of **Abraham Lincoln's birth** attracted an estimated 1,000,000 New Yorkers to exercises held in that city. Among the speakers were Booker T. Washington, Mayor George B. McClellan, son of the Civil War general, and Lyman Abbott, pastor of Plymouth Church in Brooklyn.

Mar. 7 **Arbor Day** was made a state holiday by the California legislature in honor of Luther Burbank, the horticulturist. Burbank's birth date was officially designated, although the holiday had been observed on that date informally since 1886 by the planting of trees. An Arbor Day had been first observed in Nebraska on Apr. 10, 1872.

Apr. 19 The 13th **Boston Marathon** was won by Henri Renaud of Nashua, N.H., with a time of 2 hrs., 53 min., 36.8 sec.

May 3 The 35th annual **Kentucky Derby** was won by Wintergreen, with a time of 2:08$^1/_5$. The jockey was Vincent Powers.

May 12 The 34th annual **Preakness Stakes** was won by Effendi, with a time of 1:39$^4/_5$. The jockey was Willie Doyle.

June 2 The 43rd annual **Belmont Stakes** was won by Joe Madden, with a time of 2:21$^3/_5$. The jockey was Eddie Dugan.

June 25 The **U.S. Open golf tournament** was won by George Sargent.

June 27 The **U.S. Lawn Tennis Association singles championships** were won by Hazel Hotchkiss in the women's division and William A. Larned in the men's division (Aug. 27).

Oct. 8–16 The sixth annual **World Series** was won by the Pittsburgh Pirates (NL), who defeated the Detroit Tigers (AL) four games to three.

1910

The Mann-Elkins Act was passed by Congress on June 18. Named for Sen. Stephen B. Elkins, Republican of West Virginia, and Rep. James R. Mann, Republican of Illinois, the law increased the authority of the Interstate Commerce Commission in enforcing its rulings on rates. The new law also extended the ICC's jurisdiction to cover telegraph, telephone, and cable companies and authorized the commission to suspend railroad rate increases pending investigation and court decisions. A Commerce Court was set up to hear appeals of the commission's rulings.

The U.S. **Census** recorded a population of 91,972,266. The center of population was at Bloomington, Ind.

Prohibition had been adopted by the following states: Maine (1858), Kansas (1880), North Dakota (1889), Georgia (1907), Oklahoma (1907), Mississippi (1908), North Carolina (1908), Tennessee (1909).

The last five years had seen the worst period for **mine disasters** in U.S. history. From 1906 through 1910 there were 84 coal mine disasters that killed 2494 miners. Most of the accidents were explosions. The worst year was 1907 with a total of 919 fatalities; Dec. 1907 alone saw 702 fatalities.

Mar. 17 A bill to have the **House Committee on Rules** elected by the members of the House of Representatives rather than appointed by the Speaker of the House was introduced by George W. Norris, Republican of Nebraska. The bill was passed Mar. 19 by a combination of Democrats and insurgent Republicans. The new ruling made the structure of the House much freer and in effect reduced the power of the Speaker of the House, Joseph G. Cannon, Republican of Illinois.

Mar. 26 An amendment to the **Immigration Act of 1907** was passed. It forbade entrance to the U.S. of criminals, paupers, anarchists, and persons carrying disease.

June 25 The **Mann Act,** popularly called the "white slave traffic act," was passed by Congress. The act prohibited interstate or international transport of women for "immoral purposes." It grew out of public agitation over "white slavery," particularly the importation of European girls to work in American brothels.

Aug. 31 The famous **New Nationalism speech** was delivered by Theodore Roosevelt at Osawatomie, Kans. In it he stated his Square Deal policy, which

Songs about unrequited love remained popular with Americans. A songwriter who made a fortune from such songs was Carrie Jacobs Bond, a self-taught musician who wrote both the words and music for some 175 songs. In 1910 she brought out one of her most popular, "A Perfect Day." Other hits included "Just a-Wearyin' for You" and "I Love You Truly"; the latter has been sung at innumerable weddings since its composition.

Among **books published** this year was *The Spirit of Romance* by Ezra Pound, the first book of essays by the leading figure in the new imagist movement in American poetry. Pound's subjects included the barrenness of American culture and the need for absolute criteria in evaluating art. Other books published this year included *Molly Make-Believe* by Eleanor Abbott, a book for children; *The Rosary* by Florence Barclay, a novel that sold some 500,000 copies in three years; *A Modern Chronicle* by Winston Churchill, a novel; *Whirligigs* and *Strictly Business,* collections of stories by O. Henry, who died this year; *My Mark Twain: Reminiscences and Criticisms* by William Dean Howells; *The Finer Grain* by Henry James, stories; *Burning Daylight* by Jack London, a novel, and *Lost Face,* also by London, a collection of stories including "To Build a Fire"; *The Town Down the River* by Edwin Arlington Robinson, a collection of poems including the classic "Miniver Cheevy"; and *The Bungalow Book* by Henry L. Wilson, which went through five editions and was immensely popular.

Pennsylvania Station in New York City opened. It was built from plans based on the Tepidarium of the Baths of Caracalla in Rome. The vast and impressive structure was substantially modified in 1966.

The first place of entertainment catering exclusively to a **black audience** was established at the New Palace Theater in New York City.

The first exhibition of the **Younger American Artists** took place with the opening of Alfred Stieglitz's "291." This show, at the Stieglitz Photo-Secession Gallery at 291 Fifth Ave. in New York City, offered works by Max Weber, John Marin, Abraham Walkowitz, William Zorach, Gaston Lachaise, Bernard Karfiol, Joseph Stella, and others.

July 20 A campaign for **movie censorship** was begun by the Christian Endeavor Society of Missouri, which sought to ban all motion pictures depicting kissing between people who were not related.

| Business and Industry; Science; Education; Philosophy and Religion | III | | IV | Sports; Social Issues and Crime; Folkways; Fashion; Holidays |

1910

This year thousands of people became convinced that the end of the world was at hand. The cause of this prognosis was the passage of Halley's Comet, named for the English astronomer Edmund Halley, who had observed the comet's passage in 1682 and determined that it was the subject of similar observations made in 1531 and 1607. Enough people were frightened by stories of impending catastrophe that comet pills, supposed to protect from the comet's dire effects, went on sale. Miners refused to work on May 18, when the earth was due to pass through the fiery tail of the comet; they did not want to die underground. Many workers stayed home to spend their last day with their families. Farm families hid in cyclone cellars. Others took shelter in caves. In Milwaukee, Wis., two men were said to have committed suicide. Mark Twain, who said he had come in with Halley's Comet and expected to go out with it, was not disappointed. He died on Apr. 21, at 74. Halley's Comet returned in 1985–1986, but did not make much of a show, since its path was much farther from the earth. In 1910, by contrast, the comet's tail could be seen across much of the night sky.

The **farm population** continued its steady decline. There were 32,077,000 farm inhabitants this year, 30,529,000 in 1930, and 25,058,000 in 1950.

Illiteracy in the U.S. reached a new low of 7.7% of the population, a decline of 3% from 1900 and 12.3% from 1870.

Andrew Carnegie established the **Carnegie Endowment for International Peace** with a fund of $10,000,000 following his donation of funds for the Temple of Peace at The Hague, the Netherlands. Both projects collapsed in 1914.

The modern **fundamentalist movement** in American religious history was inspired by publication of a booklet entitled *The Fundamentals: A Testimony to the Truth.* The booklet declared that there were five basic truths of Christianity: the accuracy of the Scriptures, the Virgin birth, the physical resurrection of Christ, the vicarious atonement, and the physical second coming of Christ.

Taylorization became a byword of American industrialism and a synonym for scientific management of labor and machinery in factories. Frederick W. Taylor championed industrial efficiency in such pamphlets as *A Piece Rate System* and *Shop Management.*

A **grade-school education** had been acquired by less than half the population over 25 years of age. Only about 4% of the population held college degrees.

The **first American aviation meet** was held at Los Angeles, Calif. Audiences ranging each day from 20,000 to 50,000 watched air pioneers Louis Paulhan of France and Glenn H. Curtiss, an American, break most air

The most successful and popular organization for American boys was chartered on Feb. 6, 1910. It was the Boy Scouts of America. The incorporator was William D. Boyce, a Chicago publisher who took the idea from the English Boy Scout movement, founded in 1908 by Sir Robert Baden-Powell. Daniel Carter Beard, the illustrator and naturalist, had earlier founded the Sons of Daniel Boone, and Ernest Thompson Seton, author and artist, had organized the Woodcraft Indians. Both organizations had much the same purpose as the Boy Scouts.

This year's **national college football championship** was won by Harvard, with a record of eight wins, no losses, one tie.

A new **fishing record** was set when F. R. Steel caught an 83-lb. Chinook salmon in the Umpqua R. in Oregon. Until 1949 this was the largest freshwater fish ever snared by rod and reel. On May 22, 1949, however, Roy A. Groves snared a blue catfish in the James R., S.Dak., weighing 94 lbs., 8 oz., and on Dec. 2, 1951, G. Valverde caught an alligator gar in the Rio Grande R., Tex., weighing 279 lbs.

Mar. 16 A new **land speed record** of 133 mph was set by Barney Oldfield, who ran a timed mile in a Benz auto at Daytona Beach, Fla.

Apr. 19 The 14th **Boston Marathon** was won by Fred L. Cameron of Amherst, Nova Scotia, Canada, with a time of 2 hrs., 28 min., 52.6 sec.

May 7 The 35th annual **Preakness Stakes** was won by Layminster, with a time of 1:40³/₅. The jockey was R. Estep.

May 10 The 36th annual **Kentucky Derby** was won by Donau, with a time of 2:06²/₅. The jockey was Fred Herbert.

May 30 The 44th annual **Belmont Stakes** was won by Sweep, with a time of 2:22. The jockey was Jimmy Butwell.

June 18 The **U.S. Open** golf tournament was won by Alex Smith.

supported a graduated income tax, control of trusts, labor protection, conservation, and an adequate army and navy.

Sept. 7 The long-standing U.S.-British dispute over the **Newfoundland fisheries** was settled by the International Court of Arbitration at The Hague. The U.S. retained the right to buy water and bait in Newfoundland. A commission was established to settle disputes over fishing regulations.

Nov. 8 In **congressional elections** the Democrats took control of Congress for the first time since 1894. In the Senate the Republicans held a 51–41 majority, but combination with insurgent Republicans opposed to the policies of the Taft administration gave the Democrats control. In the House the Democrats took a 228–162 majority. The only minor party representative in the House was Victor L. Berger of Milwaukee, Wis., the first Socialist ever sent to Congress. In state elections, Franklin Delano Roosevelt was elected to the New York legislature. Oregon adopted a presidential preferential primary, and Washington State adopted woman suffrage.

Sept. 10 **George M. Cohan** presented his *Get-Rich-Quick Wallingford* on the New York stage. It was a highly successful satire on the American drive to succeed.

Oct. 3 The British comedian **Charles Chaplin** headed the bill at the opening of *The Wow-Wows,* a vaudeville sketch by the Fred Karno comedy troupe at the Colonial Theatre in New York City. The sketch was weak but Chaplin was warmly received. The group performed in and near New York for six weeks, then went on the road. Chaplin's roommate on tour was another budding comedian, Stan Laurel.

Oct. 24 *Naughty Marietta* by Victor Herbert was given its first performance in Syracuse, N.Y. It was first performed on Broadway in New York City on Nov. 7.

Dec. 10 *The Girl of the Golden West* by Giacomo Puccini was staged in New York City by the Metropolitan Opera Company. It became the most talked about production of the opera season.

1911

A tragic industrial disaster occurred on Mar. 25, 1911, when the Triangle Waist Company, a sweatshop in New York City, caught fire. About 850 employees were trapped in the building, which was full of inflammable materials used in making shirtwaists. The fire began only minutes before the Saturday workday was to end and lasted but half an hour. The building was considered fireproof but had only one fire escape, and its exit doors were blocked. Some 146 persons were killed, most of them young women. The proprietors were tried but acquitted. However, the fire led to revision of the local building code and labor laws. The tragedy also added impetus to the organizational work of the International Ladies Garment Workers Union, which had been formed in 1900.

Jan. 21 The **National Progressive Republican League** was formed in Washington, D.C., by Sen. Robert M. La Follette of Wisconsin. Sen. Jonathan Bourne of Oregon was elected president. The organization's chief aims were enactment of progressive legislation and promotion of popular government. It called for direct primaries, direct election of delegates to national conventions, and amendments to state constitutions providing for initiative, referendum, and recall.

Mar. 7 Continued fighting in the **Mexican Revolution** (1910–1917) prompted the dispatch of 20,000 U.S.

The American appetite for fiction about the West, with rugged heroes and pure heroines, seemed insatiable. An author who catered to this appetite successfully was Harold Bell Wright, whose most popular novel, *The Winning of Barbara Worth,* was published this year; it eventually sold some 1,500,000 copies. Wright's stories were set in the Southwest. They were a careful mix of love story, adventure story, and moral instruction. Wright knew his craft and his readers. He turned out enormously popular novels for nearly 40 years. Other successful Wright books included *The Shepherd of the Hills* (1907), *The Calling of Dan Matthews* (1909), and *When a Man's a Man* (1916).

Among **books published** this year was the novel *Jennie Gerhardt* by Theodore Dreiser, which sold well enough to warrant republication in 1912 of Dreiser's first novel, *Sister Carrie* (1900). Other books published this year included *The Devil's Dictionary* by Ambrose Bierce, which originally appeared as *The Cynic's Word Book* (1906); *The Iron Woman* by Margaret Deland, a sequel to her novel *The Awakening of Barbara Richie* (1906); *Dawn O'Hara* by Edna Ferber, the author's first novel; *The Miller of Old Church* by Ellen Glasgow, a novel; *Sixes and Sevens* by O. Henry, a posthumous collection; *The Outcry* by Henry James, a novel; *South Sea*

speed records. In spite of the popularity of the show and a great desire among many to fly, in three years only five airplanes had been sold to private persons.

Jan. The **United States Motor Company** was organized by Benjamin Briscoe in a move to compete against General Motors. Ironically, GM suffered a reorganization this year because of poor management and a business decline. United States Motors went into receivership in Sept. 1912. After 1913 its main product was the Maxwell automobile.

Apr. 23 An intense **cold spell** in the Midwest destroyed about $30,000,000 in crops and property.

May 16 The **U.S. Bureau of Mines** was established as part of the Department of Interior, with Dr. Joseph Austin Holmes as its first director.

June 24 An act requiring installation of **radio equipment** on all American passenger ships operating from U.S. ports was passed by Congress.

June 25 A **Postal Savings Bank** system was established by Congress.

Nov. 14 The **first naval aircraft launching** from the deck of a U.S. warship was accomplished by Eugene Ely, who took off from the cruiser *Birmingham* at Hampton Roads, Va.

June 19 **Father's Day** was celebrated for the first time in Spokane, Wash. Initiated by Mrs. John B. Dodd, it was backed by the Ministerial Association and the YMCA. Today it is celebrated on the third Sunday of June.

June 26 The **U.S. Lawn Tennis Association singles championships** were won by Hazel Hotchkiss in the women's division and William A. Larned in the men's division (Aug. 25).

July 4 The **world heavyweight boxing championship** was successfully defended by Jack Johnson, who outclassed former champ Jim Jeffries in 15 rounds. After the match, Johnson's mother is reported to have said, "He said he'd *bring home the bacon*, and the honey boy has gone and done it." No earlier citation is known for this expression.

Oct. 17–23 The seventh annual **World Series** was won by the Philadelphia Athletics (AL), who defeated the Chicago Cubs (NL) four games to one.

1911

Before he left office, Pres. Theodore Roosevelt had ordered the Justice Department to act against the Standard Oil Company of New Jersey under the Sherman Antitrust Act of 1890, but it took more than four years for the case to reach the Supreme Court. Standard Oil controlled about 85% of the domestic oil industry at this time. On May 15, 1911, the Court ordered Standard Oil dissolved because it violated the antitrust law. In so doing, it added to the law by ruling that trusts were unlawful if they engaged in "unreasonable" restraint of trade.

The **Roosevelt Dam** on the Salt R., Ariz., was completed at a cost of $3,890,000. It was one of the important conservation projects begun by the federal government under Pres. Theodore Roosevelt's direction.

Feb. The first electric **automotive self-starter** was demonstrated by Henry Leland, head of the Cadillac division of General Motors. The device had been invented in 1899 by Clyde J. Coleman and perfected by Charles Franklin Kettering. The self-starter made the automobile much easier to use. Drivers no longer had to employ the sometimes treacherous hand crank to start the engine.

Baseball continued to produce heroes for American sports fans. The best all-around player of the era was Tyrus Raymond "Ty" Cobb, who joined the Detroit Tigers in 1905 and played for 24 years in the American League. In his first year in the majors he batted .240. After that his batting average was never below .320. When he retired he held an incredible list of records, including a career batting average of .367, a record 2244 runs, 892 stolen bases, and 12 league batting championships. He was perhaps the most spectacular player the game has ever produced. In 1936 he became the first player elected to the Baseball Hall of Fame. His career total of 4191 hits stood as a record until 1985, when Pete Rose surpassed him.

The **Belmont Stakes** was not run in 1911 or 1912.

This year's **national college football championship** was won by Princeton, with a record of eight wins, no losses, two ties.

Apr. 19 The 15th **Boston Marathon** was won by Clarence H. DeMar of Melrose, Mass., with a time of 2 hrs., 21 min., 39.6 sec.

May 13 The 37th annual **Kentucky Derby** was won by Meridian, with a time of 2:05. The jockey was George Archibald.

troops to the Mexican border. The fighting in Mexico sometimes occurred so close to the border that crowds of U.S. citizens gathered to watch. The troops were recalled on June 24, a month after the revolutionaries had succeeded in overthrowing Pres. Porfirio Díaz.

Aug. 22 **Arizona statehood** was vetoed by Pres. William Howard Taft on the grounds that its constitution permitted the recall of judges, which Taft considered a threat to the independence of the judiciary. After removing this provision, Arizona was admitted to the Union in 1912, after which it reinstated the provision.

Oct. 16 The **National Conference of Progressive Republicans** was held in Chicago. Sen. Robert M. La Follette of Wisconsin was nominated for the presidency.

Dec. 18 Pres. Taft informed Russia that the 1832 **treaty with Russia** would be abrogated because of Russia's refusal to recognize U.S. passports held by Jews, clergymen of certain evangelical denominations, and others. On Dec. 21 a joint resolution abrogating the treaty was ratified by Congress.

Tales by Jack London; and *Mother* by Kathleen Norris, the author's first novel, a best seller.

"**Alexander's Ragtime Band**" was composed by Irving Berlin. Although not strictly a ragtime tune, it was the first song to popularize ragtime outside the limited area of the Mississippi Delta.

Apr. 19 The opening of *Kismet* by Edward Knoblock at the Knickerbocker Theatre in New York City brought the romantic atmosphere of the Arabian Nights to the modern stage. Otis Skinner played the part of Hajj, the beggar, who is caught up in the intrigues of Baghdad.

Sept. 26 *Bought and Paid For* by George Broadhurst opened at the Playhouse in New York City. The play illustrated the author's tendency to build the climax around one scene—here the breaking down of a door by a husband to get to his young wife, who rejects his advances because of his drinking. The heightened melodrama of the prewar American theater was best seen in Broadhurst's plays, which included *The Man of the Hour* (1906) and *The Price* (1911).

1912

The 1912 presidential election began as a three-way race but soon became a contest between former Pres. Theodore Roosevelt, the Progressive Party candidate, and Woodrow Wilson, the Democrat. Pres. William Howard Taft, the Republican candidate, fell far behind. The mood of the country called for reform, and Roosevelt and Wilson differed only on the best way to achieve it. Roosevelt talked of the Square Deal and the New Nationalism; Wilson spoke of the New Freedom. Roosevelt would deal with industrial monopoly by regulating it; Wilson called for breaking up big business to restore competition. When Wilson won in November, he was only the second Democrat to be elected to the presidency since the Civil War.

Jan. 6 **New Mexico** was admitted to the Union, the 47th state.

Jan. 22 U.S. troops began **occupation of Tientsin** for the protection of American interests in the Chinese Revolution, which had begun in Oct. 1911.

Feb. 14 **Arizona** was admitted to the Union, the 48th state.

Apr. 14–15 The British liner *Titanic* struck an iceberg off the coast of Newfoundland and sank on its maiden voyage, killing about 1500 persons, including many U.S. and British notables. An investigation showed that the ship had insufficient lifeboats and that safety procedures had not been followed. The company was blamed for poor equipment and for ordering the ship

The writing, or at least the publishing, of poetry in a modern style seemed to lag behind fiction. However, poetry received a decided stimulus in 1912 with the founding of *Poetry: A Magazine of Verse* in Chicago. The founder was Harriet Monroe, a poet. The magazine had a lasting influence on American poetry under her editorship, which continued until her death in 1936. *Poetry* published the work of such poets as Carl Sandburg, Amy Lowell, Ezra Pound, Hilda Doolittle, T. S. Eliot, Vachel Lindsay, and Hart Crane. Many new poets first came to public attention in its pages.

Among **books published** this year was *The Financier* by Theodore Dreiser, the first novel of a trilogy about Frank Cowperwood, a predatory businessman modeled after Charles T. Yerkes, the financier and transportation magnate. Dreiser continued the Cowperwood trilogy with *The Titan* (1914) and the posthumous volume *The Stoic* (1947). Other books published this year included *A Woman of Genius* by Mary Austin, a novel; *The Squirrel Cage* by Dorothy Canfield, a novel of domestic life; *Alexander's Bridge* by Willa Cather, the author's first novel; *Riders of the Purple Sage* by Zane Grey, the author's most popular novel; *The Autobiography of an Ex-Colored Man* by James Weldon Johnson, a novel; *Smoke Bellew* by Jack London, a novel; and the three-volume *Mark Twain, A Biography* by Albert Bigelow Paine.

| Business and Industry; Science; Education; Philosophy and Religion **III** | **IV** Sports; Social Issues and Crime; Folkways; Fashion; Holidays |

May 29 Dissolution of the **American Tobacco Company** was ordered by the Supreme Court on the grounds that it was a monopoly and violated the Sherman Antitrust Act.

Sept. 17–Nov. 5 The **first cross-country flight** was made by Calbraith P. Rodgers, who flew a Burgess-Wright biplane from Sheepshead Bay, N.Y., to Pasadena, Calif., in 82 hrs., 4 min. of flying time.

Nov. 10 **The Carnegie Corporation** of New York was established by Andrew Carnegie with an initial endowment of $125,000,000. It was the first of the great foundations for scholarly and charitable endeavors. Other funds Carnegie established included the Carnegie Institute of Pittsburgh (1896), $24,000,000; the Carnegie Institute of Washington (1902), $22,000,000; the Carnegie Foundation for the Advancement of Teaching (1905), $15,000,000; and the Carnegie Endowment for International Peace (1910), $10,000,000.

May 17 The 36th annual **Preakness Stakes** was won by Watervale, with a time of 1:51. The jockey was Eddie Dugan.

May 30 The **first annual Indianapolis 500** auto race was won by Ray Harroun, completing the 500-mile course in 6 hrs., 42 min., 8 sec., with an average speed of 74.59 mph.

June 17 The **U.S. Lawn Tennis Association singles championships** were won by Hazel Hotchkiss, for the third straight time, in the women's division and William A. Larned, for the fifth straight time, in the men's division (Sept. 3).

June 24 The **U.S. Open golf tournament** was won by John J. McDermott in a playoff round.

Oct. 14–26 The eighth annual **World Series** was won by the Philadelphia Athletics (AL), who beat the New York Giants (NL) four games to two.

1912

A strike of textile workers at Lawrence, Mass., in 1912 brought prominence in the East to the Industrial Workers of the World (IWW), a radical labor union that had hitherto been active chiefly in the West among miners, migratory farm workers, and lumbermen. The strike began on Jan. 12 over a reduction in wages. It lasted two months and there was considerable violence. The workers ultimately prevailed, and the strike established the IWW as a force to be reckoned with in the textile industry. The IWW's best-known leader was William D. "Big Bill" Haywood, an advocate of mass action, and violence if necessary, to achieve better conditions for workers.

Vitamin discoveries in the U.S. were begun by Prof. Elmer V. McCollum of Yale. While studying dietary deficiencies, McCollum discovered the curative values of two food chemicals designated vitamins A and B.

Jan. **Glenn Curtiss** demonstrated a new flying boat, or amphibious airplane, in San Diego bay. Built in Hammondsport, N.Y., the aircraft had two propellers driven by a 60-hp motor and was designed to carry a passenger as well as the pilot. Other new features included an automatic starter and a bilge pump for the floating bulkhead. The airplane was distinctly superior to the earlier Curtiss hydroplane then being tested by the U.S. Navy.

Americans had a new athletic hero to cheer in 1912, James Francis "Jim" Thorpe, perhaps the best all-around athlete in history. An American Indian, Thorpe attended Carlisle Indian School in Pennsylvania. There he participated in several sports and, under the tutelage of Glenn "Pop" Warner, led the small school to football triumphs over such powers as Harvard. At the Olympic Games in Stockholm in 1912, he won both the pentathlon and the decathlon, but his medals were taken from him the next year when it was discovered that he had played semiprofessional baseball in 1909. On Jan. 18, 1983, 30 years after his death, his medals were restored to his daughter. In 1950 Thorpe had been voted by sportswriters "the greatest football player and male athlete of the first half of the twentieth century."

This year's **national college football championship** was won by Harvard, with a record of nine wins, no losses, no ties.

The spreading fad for **ragtime music** led at about this time to a series of so-called animal dances. The dances were execrated in press and pulpit. Among them were the fox trot, horse trot, crab step, kangaroo dip, camel walk, fish walk, chicken scratch, lame duck, snake, grizzly bear, turkey trot, and bunny hug.

Life magazine listed the **slang phrases of the year** as *Flossy, Beat it!, Peeved, Sure!, Classy, It's a cinch, What*

| **Exploration and Settlement; Wars; Government; Civil Rights; Statistics** | **I** | **II** | **Publishing; Arts and Music; Popular Entertainment; Architecture; Theater** |

to speed through dangerous waters.

May 17   The **Socialist National Convention nominated Eugene V. Debs** of Indiana for the presidency and Emil Seidel of Wisconsin for the vice presidency.

June 5   U.S. **Marines landed in Cuba** to protect American interests there.

June 18–22   The **Republican National Convention nominated Pres. William Howard Taft** for a second term, but only after bitter political maneuvering against the progressive elements favoring Theodore Roosevelt. James S. Sherman was renominated for the vice presidency. Taft forces won parliamentary control of the convention through the election of their candidate for convention chairman, Elihu Root, and through the seating of their delegates in disputed delegations. After Taft's nomination on June 22, Roosevelt announced the formation of the Progressive Party, under his own leadership.

June 25–July 2   The **Democratic National Convention nominated Woodrow Wilson** of New Jersey for the presidency and Thomas R. Marshall of Indiana for the vice presidency.

July 10–12   The **Prohibition Party National Convention** nominated Eugene W. Chafin of Arizona for the presidency and Aaron S. Watkins of Ohio for the vice presidency.

Aug. 5   The **Progressive (Bull Moose) Party nominated Theodore Roosevelt** for the presidency and Hiram Johnson of California for the vice presidency. The party platform called for women's suffrage, direct primaries, and other progressive measures.

Aug. 24   The **parcel post system** was authorized. It was put into service on Jan. 1, 1913.

Nov. 5   **Woodrow Wilson was elected president** of the United States in a landslide Democratic victory. Thomas R. Marshall was elected vice president. The electoral vote was Wilson, 435; Theodore Roosevelt, Progressive Party, 88; William Howard Taft, Republican, 8. The popular vote was Wilson, 6,293,454; Roosevelt, 4,119,538; Taft, 3,484,980; Eugene V. Debs, Socialist candidate, 900,672; Eugene W. Chafin, Prohibition candidate, 206,275. In congressional elections the Democrats took a 51–44 majority in the Senate, with one minor party seat, and a 291–127 majority in the House, with 17 seats going to minor parties.

The Playboy of the Western World (1907) by the Irish playwright John Millington Synge was presented in Boston, Philadelphia, and New York City. In each city its performance occasioned public disorders by those who resented Synge's humorous satire of the Irish.

The popular song of the year was "**Waiting for the Robert E. Lee,**" chosen by a group of composers and musicians 40 years later as the best song of the first half of the twentieth century.

Feb. 5   *He and She* by Rachel Crothers opened. It was a play dealing with a woman's struggle to maintain a home and enjoy a career at the same time. Women's role in modern society was explored in a number of Crothers' plays. *A Man's World* (1909) concerned the double standard; *Young Wisdom* (1914) discussed trial marriages; *Ourselves* (1913) dealt with the new woman; *Nice People* (1920) centered around youthful immorality; *As Husbands Go* (1931) compared American and European husbands. Her best-known play was *Susan and God* (1937), which poked light fun at the Oxford religious movement.

Mar. 14   The opera *Mona* by Brian Hooker, with music by Horatio Parker, opened at the Metropolitan Opera House in New York City. Set in first-century Britain, the work had won a $10,000 prize offered by the Metropolitan Opera Company. In 1915 Hooker's libretto for the opera *Fairyland* won a prize given by the American Opera Association. In 1915 *Morven and the Grail* appeared. Hooker's best-known work was his 1923 translation for the stage of Edmond Rostand's *Cyrano de Bergerac.*

July 12   The French-made film *Queen Elizabeth* starring Sarah Bernhardt was first shown in the U.S. This film, more than any other to date, gave motion pictures the prestige accorded an art form.

Nov. 4   *The Yellow Jacket* by George C. Hazelton and J. Harry Benrimo opened at the Fulton Theatre in New York City. The play was a highly successful attempt to adapt conventions of the Chinese theater for American audiences. The Property Man, a character who drifted in and out of the action, and the Chorus, an actor who explained in song the coming scenes and introduced the characters, caught the fancy of American audiences.

1913

For many years tariff revenue had been the largest single source of government income. The adoption on Feb. 25, 1913, of the Sixteenth Amendment to the Constitution, permitting the levying of income tax on individuals and businesses without apportionment on the

The single most important event to date in the American art world was held at the 69th Regiment Armory at Lexington Ave. and 26th St. in New York City, beginning Feb. 17. It was the International Exhibition of Modern Art, known to this day as the Armory Show.

Business and Industry; Science; Education; Philosophy and Religion III	IV Sports; Social Issues and Crime; Folkways; Fashion; Holidays

Jan. 22 The **Florida East Coast Railroad** between Key West and the mainland opened for passenger traffic. Passenger and freight service to New York City was also initiated this year. The line was not very successful, partly because of storms. After bad hurricane damage in 1935, the line was abandoned. In 1938 the roadbed was paved for automobile traffic.

Mar. 14 Action against a **railroad merger** of the Southern Pacific and Union Pacific railroads was begun by the Justice Department. The Union Pacific had acquired 46% of the stock of the Southern Pacific. The subsequent court decision held that the merger could not go through because the new corporation would be able to stifle competition.

Apr. 6 The term *airplane* was suggested by Capt. Washington I. Chambers as a replacement for the term *aeroplane*, it was reported by *The New York Times*. Chambers, head of the U.S. Navy's aviation experiments, also offered the term *landing gear* for what previously had been called the *chassis*. Chambers' suggestion to replace the term *fuselage* with the word *body* did not catch on.

May 1 A new **ship safety regulation** was issued by federal inspectors following the sinking of the *Titanic* in April. Steamships were ordered to carry enough lifeboats to hold all passengers.

June 19 A new **labor law** was passed by Congress. It extended the eight-hour working day to all workers under federal contract.

Aug. 24 The **Panama Canal Act,** authorizing rebates of canal tolls to American coastal ships, was signed by Pres. William Howard Taft. The act caused indignation in England and Europe, and the U.S. was accused of violating the Hay-Pauncefote Treaty of 1901. The law was repealed in 1914.

Oct. 1 A **state labor law** establishing a 54-hour work week was passed in New York State.

do you know about that?, Fussed, Speedy, Peachy, Nutty, and *Getting your goat.*

The **National Hockey League (NHL) Stanley Cup** was won by the Quebec Bulldogs, who beat Moncton two games straight in a best-of-three series.

Mar. 12 The first patrol of **Girl Guides,** forerunners of the Girl Scouts, was formed by Daisy Gordon and ten other girls in an unused stable owned by Miss Gordon's aunt, Mrs. Juliet Low of Savannah, Ga.

Apr. 19 The 16th **Boston Marathon** was won by Michael J. Ryan of New York City with a time of 2 hrs., 21 min., 18.2 sec.

May 5–July 22 At the **Olympic Games** in Stockholm, Sweden, the U.S. won 23 gold medals and took first place in the unofficial team championships.

May 11 The 38th annual **Kentucky Derby** was won by Worth, with a time of 2:09²/₅. The jockey was Carol Shilling.

May 15 The 37th annual **Preakness Stakes** was won by Colonel Holloway, with a time of 1:56²/₅. The jockey was Clarence Turner.

May 30 The second **Indianapolis 500** auto race was won by Joe Dawson. He completed the course in 6 hrs., 21 min., 6 sec., with an average speed of 78.72 mph.

June 15 The **U.S. Lawn Tennis Association singles championships** were won by Mary K. Browne in the women's division and Maurice E. McLoughlin in the men's division (Aug. 26).

Aug. 2 The **U.S. Open golf tournament** was won by John J. McDermott.

Oct. 8–16 The ninth annual **World Series** was won by the Boston Red Sox (AL), who beat the New York Giants (NL) four games to three in an eight-game series. The second game, played at Boston on Oct. 9, was a tie; it had been called in the 11th inning on account of darkness.

1913

For many years the nation had needed a central banking system to bring stability to currency and credit markets. Bankers wanted a system they could control. Agrarian interests and others wanted a system controlled by the federal government that would provide

This period is often looked back on as the golden age of professional baseball. The sport was truly national, with no competition as yet from professional football or basketball. Fans were as enthusiastic about their favorite teams. Millions of people attended National and

basis of the population of states, was soon to affect the importance of tariff revenues. The change did not come at once, however, for the first income tax law specified graduated rates of 1 to 6% of income.

Mar. 1 The **Webb-Kenyon Interstate Liquor Act** was passed over Pres. Taft's veto. It stated that no liquor could be shipped into states where its sale was illegal. This was the first nationwide victory of the Anti-Saloon league.

Mar. 4 **Woodrow Wilson was inaugurated president** of the United States. The 28th president and a Democrat, he served two terms.

Mar. 21–26 What was called the **Dayton flood** raged in the Miami River Valley of Ohio, killing more than 400 people. Property damage was estimated at $100,-000,000. An additional 200 or more persons were killed by floods along the Indiana R. and elsewhere in the West and South. In 1925 five dams were completed across the upper Miami R. and its tributaries at a cost of $32,000,000. These dams provided significantly increased protection against floods.

Apr. 8 Pres. **Wilson appeared before Congress** to deliver his message on tariff revision. He was the first president to address Congress personally since John Adams in 1800.

May 2 Official recognition of the new **Republic of China** was extended by Pres. Wilson.

May 19 The **Webb Alien Land-Holding Bill** was signed by Gov. Hiram W. Johnson of California in the face of objections by Pres. Wilson and Japan. It excluded Japanese from ownership of land in California.

May 31 The **Seventeenth Amendment** to the U.S. Constitution went into effect. It provided for popular election of U.S. senators. Previously, senators had been chosen by their state legislatures. Thus, the amendment reduced the power and status of state governments and increased popular control of the federal legislature.

Aug. 27 In the continuing civil disorder in **Mexico,** Pres. Wilson announced a policy of "watchful waiting." Gen. Victoriano Huerta had seized power following the assassination of Pres. Francisco I. Madero by Huerta's agents on Feb. 22. Despite pressure brought on them by American business interests, neither presidents Taft nor Wilson would recognize Huerta, whose government did not enjoy popular support. Pres. Madero's government had seized

Organized originally to show works of younger U.S. artists, it came to include European artists as well. There were about 1600 paintings and sculptures in all. The show drew large crowds and horrified conservative critics. Ridicule was showered on Marcel Duchamp's cubist painting *Nude Descending a Staircase,* which one commentator called an "explosion in a shingle factory." In reviewing the show, Theodore Roosevelt was sympathetic but wrote that there was "apt to be a lunatic fringe among the votaries of any forward movement." The exhibition did much to change the direction of American painting.

Among **books published** this year was *O Pioneers!* by Willa Cather, the author's second novel and her first set in the Nebraska of her youth. The story dealt with Alexandra Bergsen, a second-generation Swedish-American who, through courage, diligence, and sacrifice, triumphed over the barren land. Other books published this year included *The Inside of the Cup* by Winston Churchill, a novel that became a best seller; *The Enjoyment of Poetry* by Max Eastman, which went through six editions by 1920; *Virginia* by Ellen Glasgow, a study of the life and values of a southern woman; *Rolling Stones* by O. Henry; *A Small Boy and Others* by Henry James, autobiographical writings; *General William Booth Enters into Heaven and Other Poems* by Vachel Lindsay; *The Valley of the Moon* by Jack London, a novel, and *John Barleycorn,* also by London, an autobiographical account of his struggles against alcohol; and *Pollyanna* by Eleanor Hodgman Porter, a juvenile novel that eventually sold more than 1,000,000 copies and inspired the term *Pollyanna,* meaning an irrepressibly optimistic person.

The first exhibition of sculpture by **Paul Manship** was held in New York City. His works were smooth, almost archaic in style. All irregular outlines were done away with. Young sculptors were greatly influenced by the new technique.

The **Woolworth Building,** tallest in the world, was built in New York City. It measured 792 feet and was considered a wonder by New Yorkers when it was first built.

Vernon and Irene Castle, the celebrated dancing couple, made their American debut this year in *The Sunshine Girl,* an English musical.

Feb. 2 **Grand Central Terminal** in New York City, one of the most elegant and spacious public buildings in the U.S., was officially opened. The building was in

| Business and Industry; Science; Education; Philosophy and Religion III | | IV Sports; Social Issues and Crime; Folkways; Fashion; Holidays |

easy credit. Pres. Woodrow Wilson pledged to reform the banking system and on Dec. 23, 1913, the Owen-Glass Act became law. It set up the Federal Reserve System. The act established a central Federal Reserve Board and a dozen regional banks. All national banks were required to join the system. State banks could do so if they wished. The system could issue currency and control credit by raising or lowering the discount rate it charged member banks. The general aim was to increase economic stability and make it impossible for speculators to upset the economy of the nation.

Jan. A **garment workers' strike** began in New York City, taking about 150,000 workers off their jobs. In February the strike spread to Boston. It ended in New York City on Mar. 12 and in Boston on Apr. 21 with wage concessions, reduced hours, and union recognition.

Feb. 25 A **silk workers' strike** began in Paterson, N.J. Directed by the IWW, it was vigorously opposed by local authorities. The strike was abandoned after five months.

Mar. 4 The **Department of Commerce and Labor** was divided by Congress into two departments having Cabinet status. At the same time Congress passed an act establishing a U.S. Board of Mediation and Conciliation to arbitrate labor disputes.

May 14 John D. Rockefeller donated $100,000,000 to the **Rockefeller Foundation,** chartered by the New York State legislature. His contribution was thought to be the largest single philanthropic act in history.

Summer Henry Ford set up his **first automobile assembly line** for production of the inexpensive Model T. Ford introduced a revolutionary high wage for his workers of $5 a day. Between 1909 and 1924, the price of the Model T dropped from $950 to $290. Ford engineers had adapted the meat packers' conveyor belt system, and soon 1000 Fords a day were turned out.

July 1 The **Lincoln Highway Association** was formed. Interested in promoting road construction, the association selected the route for a projected highway between New York City and San Francisco. It then constructed sections of ideal highway at various places to stimulate road building. When U.S. route numbers came into use about 1925, the Lincoln Highway Association began to curtail its function. Actually, the route has been changed often, and today there is no officially designated Lincoln Highway between the East and West coasts.

American League games, and minor league teams were gaining in popularity as well. One of the top minor leagues was the United States League. In 1914 it was reorganized into the Federal League. It had good financial backing and started pulling top players from both the National and American leagues. Despite its claim to major league status, it lasted only through 1915.

A new **baseball record** for the most consecutive shutout innings pitched in one season was set by Walter Johnson, of the Washington Senators (AL). This year Johnson pitched 56 consecutive innings without allowing a run to score.

This year's **national college football championship** was won by Harvard, with a record of nine wins, no losses, no ties.

Feb. 27 The term *lunatic fringe* was coined by former Pres. Theodore Roosevelt in a letter to Sen. Henry Cabot Lodge of Massachusetts. Roosevelt observed that groups with whom he associated "have always developed among their members a large lunatic fringe."

Mar. 8–10 The **NHL Stanley Cup** was won by the Quebec Bulldogs in two games over Sydney.

Apr. 19 The 17th **Boston Marathon** was won by Fritz Carlson of Minneapolis, Minn., with a time of 2 hrs., 25 min., 14.8 sec.

May 10 The 39th annual **Kentucky Derby** was won by the 91–1 longshot, Donerail, with a time of 2:04⅘. The jockey was Roscoe Goose.

May 20 The 38th annual **Preakness Stakes** was won by Buskin, with a time of 1:53⅖. The jockey was Jimmy Butwell.

May 30 The third annual **Indianapolis 500** auto race was won by Jules Goux of France, completing the 500-mile course in 5 hrs., 35 min., 5 sec., with an average speed of 75.93 mph.

June 13 The 45th annual **Belmont Stakes** was won by Prince Eugene, with a time of 2:18. The jockey was Roscoe Troxler.

June 14 The **U.S. Lawn Tennis Association singles championships** were won by Mary K. Browne in the women's division and Maurice E. McLoughlin in the men's division (Aug. 26).

June 30 A reunion at Gettysburg, Pa., of thousands of Civil War veterans began. The veterans, both Union and Confederate, gathered to commemorate the Battle of Gettysburg on its 50th anniversary.

July 25–28 The **Davis Cup** international tennis challenge round was won for the first time since 1902 by the U.S., beating the British team three matches to two.

Sept. 19 The **U.S. Open golf tournament** was won in a major upset by 20-year-old Francis Ouimet in a three-way playoff.

American business holdings in Mexico, and the affected parties saw in Huerta a chance to recoup their losses. On Nov. 7 Wilson requested Huerta's abdication. Later in the month Wilson announced a policy of material support for Huerta's opponents.

Oct. **Floods** in southern Texas caused $50,000,000 in damage and 500 deaths.

Dec. 10 The 1912 **Nobel Peace Prize** was awarded to Elihu Root in recognition of his work as president of the Carnegie Endowment for International Peace.

the eclectic Classic style popular after the Columbian Exposition of 1893.

Sept. 12 **Percy MacKaye,** an exponent of community drama and the masque as an art form, presented *Sanctuary, A Bird Masque* at Meriden, N.H., to celebrate the opening of the Meriden Bird Club. MacKaye also wrote *Caliban, by the Yellow Sands* (1916) to celebrate Shakespeare's Tercentenary. Some 2500 persons helped stage it in Lewisohn Stadium, at the College of the City of New York.

1914

In August the fragile peace that had prevailed in Europe was broken. European armies that had been preparing for the conflict for years mobilized, and guns began firing. The U.S. was completely unprepared for war, and Pres. Woodrow Wilson intended to keep the country out of the conflict. He viewed the U.S. as the nation that would bring the warring parties to the conference table and help fashion a lasting peace. The U.S. had only a small standing army, and much of it was tied down by the continuing dispute with Mexico. Its air arm was virtually nonexistent—a curious fact for the nation that had pioneered powered flight. Even the U.S. Navy was no match for either the British or German navies. Stories of German atrocities in Belgium hurt the Central Powers in U.S. public opinion, but the British blockade of Europe and subsequent seizure of neutral shipping hurt public perception of the Allies. Almost all Americans wanted the U.S. to stay out of the war.

Jan. 27 The **Panama Canal Zone** received a permanent civil government by executive order of Pres. Woodrow Wilson. George W. Goethals was named its first governor and received the confirmation of the Senate on Feb. 4.

Apr. 9 In an incident at **Tampico,** Mexico, several U.S. Marines from the ship *Dolphin,* coming ashore for supplies, were arrested and detained for an hour and a half by Mexican authorities. Their release was followed by an apology from the Mexican commander at Tampico and an expression of regret by Pres. Victoriano Huerta, but the U.S. commander, Adm. Henry T. Mayo, demanded a special salute to the U.S. flag by the Mexican troops. On Apr. 11 Pres. Huerta refused the demanded salute and on Apr. 14 Pres. Wilson ordered the U.S. fleet to Tampico Bay.

Apr. 16 A second **Coxey's Army** was organized at Massillon, Ohio, to march on Washington, D.C. Made up of unemployed workers, it was headed by Jacob S. Coxey, who had organized the first march in 1894.

Most poets were content to write their poetry and see it published in magazines or books. One who was just as much interested in reciting his poetry in public as in writing it was Vachel Lindsay, who began his career by going on tours during which he exchanged his verses for food and lodging. It was not until publication this year of *The Congo and Other Poems* that he was recognized as a leading voice of the so-called new poetry movement. Lindsay's work is full of strong rhythms, sometimes pounding in their effect. He emphasized gestures and chant when he appeared in public, as he did regularly. *The Chinese Nightingale and Other Poems* (1917) probably saw his talent at its peak.

Among **books published** this year was *Tarzan of the Apes* by Edgar Rice Burroughs, an action-filled story of a man raised by apes in Africa. Burroughs' tale appealed to millions of readers and made the author famous and wealthy. Other books published this year included *North of Boston* by Robert Frost, a first collection of poems that included the classic "Mending Wall" and "The Death of the Hired Man"; *The Poet* by Meredith Nicholson, a biography in fictional form of Nicholson's fellow Hoosier writer James Whitcomb Riley; *Insurgent Mexico* by John Reed, who had been sent to cover the Mexican Revolution by *Metropolitan Magazine; Penrod* by Booth Tarkington, an enormously popular novel about the adventures of a 12-year-old midwestern youth that led to two sequels, *Penrod and Sam* (1916) and *Penrod Jashber* (1929); and *The Eyes of the World* by Harold Bell Wright, which became a best seller.

T. S. Eliot left the U.S. for Europe this year. He settled in England and did not return to America until 1932. By that time he had established himself as a leading poet of the twentieth century with such works as *Prufrock and Other Observations* (1917), *The Waste Land* (1922), and "The Hollow Men" (1925). Eliot became a British subject in 1927.

| Business and Industry; Science; Education; Philosophy and Religion | III | | IV | Sports; Social Issues and Crime; Folkways; Fashion; Holidays |

Aug. 26 The **Keokuk Dam,** the world's largest hydro-electric dam to date, was opened across the Mississippi R. from Keokuk, Iowa, to Hamilton, Ill.

Oct. 3 The **Underwood-Simmons Tariff Act** reduced duties on 958 articles, increased 86, and left 307 unaltered.

Oct. 10 The **waterway across the Isthmus of Panama** was completed when the Gamboa Dike was blown up. Pres. Woodrow Wilson set off the explosion by pressing an electric button at the White House.

Oct. 7–11 The tenth annual **World Series** was won by the Philadelphia Athletics (AL), who beat the New York Giants (NL) four games to one.

Nov. 1 The **first Army–Notre Dame football game** was a memorable one. The Notre Dame team was almost unknown in Eastern football circles, so its victory over Army, 35 to 13, stunned the losers. While legend tends to focus on the passing combination of Gus Dorais and Knute Rockne, the team from South Bend, Ind., was in fact bigger than Army and was favored to win. Its All-American fullback is said to have torn "the Army line to shreds." Notre Dame demonstrated that forward passes could be devastating.

1914

One of the greatest construction projects of all time, and one of strategic importance to the U.S. in terms of national defense and foreign commerce, was marked by completion and official opening of the Panama Canal on Aug. 15, 1914. To build the canal, about 240,000,000 cubic yards of earth were moved and $366,650,000 spent. The first passage through the whole length of the canal was made on Jan. 7, 1914, by a small boat, *Alexander la Valley.* On Aug. 15 the *Ancon,* carrying a full load of government officials, sailed from the Atlantic to the Pacific Ocean, a distance of just over 40 miles. In its first year of operation, 1108 ships passed through the canal.

The **death rate** in the Panama Canal Zone had dropped to six per 1000 against 14.1 per 1000 in the U.S. When work on the canal began in 1904, the area was dangerous to human health. The fight against yellow fever and malaria had been won by Gen. William Gorgas, whose campaign to eradicate mosquitoes had been pushed through in spite of official opposition.

The 1914 **Nobel Prize in Chemistry** was awarded to Theodore William Richards, the first American to receive the prize in that category. Richards was honored for his work in determining the exact atomic weights of a number of elements, in some cases correcting erroneous measurements. His investigation of the atomic weights of oxygen and hydrogen led ultimately to discovery of deuterium, commonly known as heavy hydrogen, a key component in atomic research.

Jan. 3 A **direct wireless connection** was established between the U.S. and Germany.

American society's restless favorite son, former Pres. Theodore Roosevelt, set off on an exploring expedition in Brazil in Oct. 1913; he returned in May 1914. In the jungle he explored a 400-mile-long river that had been called Rio da Duvida [River of Doubt] and which was renamed Rio Roosevelt in his honor by the Brazilian government. Roosevelt wrote a book about his journey, *Through the Brazilian Wilderness* (1914).

This year's **national college football championship** was won by Army, with a record of nine wins, no losses, no ties.

Propaganda from both sides during the early stages of World War I tried to sway U.S. opinion. Atrocity stories, almost all of them later disproved, were circulated by both sides. Many rumors appeared in the American press, and some were believed. The most persistent rumor was that a large Russian army had left Archangel and, traveling by way of Scotland and England, had joined the Allied forces on the western front. There was never the slightest truth in it, although U.S. newspapers carried many alleged eyewitness accounts of bearded Russian soldiers in Glasgow, London, or Calais.

America's favorite **dances** were changing. The colorful and elaborate cotillion, once the most fashionable dance of society, took second place about this time to the waltz and two-step.

The **first great football stadium,** the Yale Bowl, seating almost 80,000, opened. After World War I crowds increased and many large stadiums were erected throughout the U.S.

The **NHL Stanley Cup** was won by the Toronto Blueshirts over Victoria, 13 goals to 8.

Mar. 21 U.S. **figure skating championships** were won by Norman N. Scott of Montreal, Canada, for the

Exploration and Settlement; Wars; Government; Civil Rights; Statistics		Publishing; Arts and Music; Popular Entertainment; Architecture; Theater

Apr. 19 A request for **authorization to use force** in Mexico "to obtain from General Huerta and his adherents the fullest recognition of the rights and dignity of the United States" was made to Congress by Pres. Wilson. After considerable debate, approval was given by both houses on Apr. 22.

Apr. 21 At **Vera Cruz,** Mexico, U.S. forces seized the customhouse and Marines occupied the city. The detachment was sent to exact an apology from Pres. Huerta for the arrest of several U.S. Marines early this month. U.S. losses were 4 dead, 20 wounded.

Apr. 22 **Diplomatic relations** with the U.S. were severed by Mexico.

Apr. 25 The **ABC Powers**—Argentina, Brazil, and Chile—offered to mediate the dispute between Mexico and the U.S. Pres. Wilson quickly accepted. While the mediation commission was meeting, the crisis ended when Pres. Huerta of Mexico was forced to resign on July 15.

June 28 The event that was to precipitate **World War I,** the assassination of Archduke Francis Ferdinand of Austria, occurred at Sarajevo, Serbia. It led to breakdown of diplomatic relations among the major European nations. Austria ultimately declared war on Serbia (July 28) and Germany declared war on Russia (Aug. 1), France (Aug. 3), and Belgium (Aug. 4). On Aug. 4 England declared war on Germany, and two days later Austria declared war on Russia. Declarations of war continued throughout the conflict (1914–1918). The U.S. declared neutrality on Aug. 4.

Sept. 26 The **Federal Trade Commission** was established to prevent monopolies and preserve competition in commerce. Pres. Wilson said the bill was meant "to make men in a small way of business as free to succeed as men in a big way and to kill monopoly in the seed." The commission was to incorporate and supersede the Bureau of Corporations.

Nov. 3 In **congressional elections** the Democrats gained five Senate seats for a 56–40 majority. In the House they lost 61 seats but kept a 230–196 majority, with nine seats held by minor parties.

Nov. 23 U.S. forces in **Vera Cruz,** Mexico, were withdrawn.

The poem "Trees" by **Joyce Kilmer** was published.

The **Whitney Studio Club** was established in New York City. It led to the formation of the Whitney Museum. The club was a gathering place for artists; at the same time it provided a gallery for showings of their work.

John Alden Carpenter composed his descriptive suite for orchestra, *Adventures in a Perambulator,* a work with modern tendencies.

Feb. 13 **ASCAP,** the American Society of Composers, Authors and Publishers, was organized at a meeting of more than 100 composers and their associates at the Hotel Claridge in New York City. Victor Herbert, one of those responsible for calling the meeting, was made director and vice president.

Apr. Production of the **first six-reel motion picture** was begun by Mack Sennett. It was the comedy *Tillie's Punctured Romance,* starring Marie Dressler and Charlie Chaplin.

May 29 The first poems by **Edgar Lee Masters** were published in *Reedy's Mirror.* The poems published in *Reedy's* were later collected in Masters' enormously successful *Spoon River Anthology* (1915).

Aug. 14 The farce *Twin Beds* by Salisbury Field and Margaret Mayo opened at the Fulton Theatre in New York City and became a great hit. It recounted the story of a young wife caught up in the craze for a new dance and featured the novelties of twin beds and the tango.

Aug. 19 *On Trial* by Elmer Rice, the author's first play, opened in New York City. It introduced the dramatic device of the flashback. Often used in modern motion pictures, this device gave theater another dimension.

Dec. 8 *Watch Your Step* by Irving Berlin, a "syncopated musical show," opened in New York City. It was the first of many musicals by Berlin that were to establish him as one of the giants of the American stage.

1915

A major step in strengthening the country's coastal maritime services, with regard to lifesaving and prevention of smuggling, was taken on Jan. 28, 1915, when Congress established the U.S. Coast Guard. It combined the Revenue Cutter Service, which had been established in 1790, with the more recent Life Saving Service. The Coast Guard was placed under the authority of

Booker T. Washington, the most important black American of the late nineteenth and early twentieth centuries, died Nov. 14, 1915. Washington was born into slavery in 1856, the son of a mulatto mother and a white father. Securing an education by his own efforts, Washington, at age 25, was selected to organize what became Tuskegee Institute, a school he turned into a leading

| Business and Industry; Science; Education; Philosophy and Religion III | Sports; Social Issues and Crime; Folkways; Fashion; Holidays IV |

Jan. 13 Litigation over **airplane patents** was settled by the U.S. Circuit Court of Appeals in favor of the Wright brothers and against Glenn Curtiss.

Jan. 20 A **Wisconsin marriage law** based on eugenic principles was declared unconstitutional by the Circuit Court. The law had been enacted in 1913.

Apr. 10 Successful **heart surgery** on an animal was announced by Dr. Alexis Carrel. He said the operation was performed while he suspended blood circulation for several minutes.

May 8 The **Smith-Lever Act** was passed by Congress. It provided federal funds for state agricultural colleges to establish instructional and advisory programs for farmers.

May 18 The **Panama Canal** was opened to barge service.

May 30 **Lassen Peak** in California, long considered extinct, began to emit steam and ash. On June 8 and June 14 steam rose to a height of 10,000 feet above its crest.

July 29 The **Cape Cod Canal** was opened, connecting Cape Cod Bay and Buzzards Bay. Travel distance between New York City and Boston was reduced by 70 miles.

July 31 News of the **closing of the London Stock Exchange** was cabled to the U.S. The cause was the outbreak of World War I. Every other important stock exchange in the world soon closed down.

men's singles and by Theresa Weld of Boston, Mass., for the women's singles.

Apr. 20 The 18th **Boston Marathon** was won by James Duffy of Hamilton, Ontario, Canada, with a time of 2 hrs., 25 min., 1 sec.

May 7 A resolution establishing **Mother's Day,** to be celebrated on the second Sunday in May, was passed by Congress. On May 9 Pres. Wilson issued a proclamation calling on the public to display the U.S. flag on that day as an expression "of our love and reverence for the mothers of our country."

May 9 The 40th annual **Kentucky Derby** was won by Old Rosebud, with a record time of 2:03³/₅. The jockey was John McCabe.

May 21 The 39th annual **Preakness Stakes** was won by Holiday, with a time of 1:53⁴/₅. The jockey was Andy Schuttinger.

May 30 The fourth annual **Indianapolis 500** auto race was won by Rene Thomas, who completed the 500-mile course in 6 hrs., 3 min., 45 sec. with an average speed of 82.47 mph.

June 13 The **U.S. Lawn Tennis Association singles championships** were won by Mary K. Browne in the women's division and Norris Williams, II, in the men's division (Sept. 1).

June 20 The 46th annual **Belmont Stakes** was won by Luke McLuke, with a time of 2:20. The jockey was M. Buxton.

Aug. 15 In the **Davis Cup** international tennis challenge round the U.S. was defeated by Australia three matches to two.

Aug. 21 The **U.S. Open golf tournament** was won by Walter Hagen.

Oct. 9–13 The 11th annual **World Series** was won by the Boston Braves (NL), who swept the Philadelphia Athletics (AL) in four straight games.

1915

Although Thomas A. Edison had built his first phonograph in 1877, it was not until the early years of the twentieth century that it became a practical machine. In 1903 an American company issued recordings of opera stars singing to piano accompaniment. About ten years later, orchestral recordings were attempted for the first time. The Victor Talking Machine Company

On Aug. 17 Leo M. Frank, 29, was lynched for the Apr. 26, 1913, murder of Mary Phagan, 14, at the National Pencil Company Factory in Atlanta, Ga. Frank had been superintendent of the factory and was charged with the murder after the girl's body was found there. In a sensational trial, Frank was convicted, largely on testimony by Jim Conley, the factory janitor. After futile

the Treasury Department, except in times of war. It absorbed the Lighthouse Service in 1939 and the Bureau of Marine Inspection and Navigation in 1942.

Jan. 2 A bill to require **literacy tests** for all immigrants was passed by the Senate. It was vetoed by Pres. Woodrow Wilson on Jan. 28.

May 7 The British steamship *Lusitania,* queen of the Cunard fleet, was sunk without warning off Ireland by a German submarine. Of 1924 persons aboard, 1198 were drowned, including 63 infants. The number of Americans drowned was 114. American indignation over the sinking contributed to the U.S. entry into World War I against Germany in 1917.

May 13 What came to be called the **first** *Lusitania note* was sent to Germany by the U.S. It protested the German attack on the *Lusitania* and demanded reparations.

May 28 The **German reply** to the U.S. note of protest justified the sinking of the *Lusitania* as self-defense, asserting that the ship was armed and carried a cargo of munitions.

May 31 A declaration that the *Lusitania was not armed* when attacked by the German submarine, nor had it ever been armed, was sent by the British ambassador to Sec. of State William Jennings Bryan.

June 7 **William Jennings Bryan resigned** as secretary of state in a disagreement with Pres. Wilson over the wording of a second note to Germany. Robert Lansing was named acting secretary of state.

June 9 In the **second** *Lusitania note,* the U.S. asked Germany to take steps to avoid future attacks on unarmed passenger and merchant ships. The note also addressed the German attacks on the American steamers *Cushing* and *Gulflight.*

July 8 The **German reply** to Pres. Wilson's note of June 9 declared that properly marked ships of neutral countries could cross the seas unmolested by German submarines.

July 15 Evidence of **German espionage** in the U.S. was uncovered when Secret Service men came into possession of a portfolio belonging to Dr. Heinrich F. Albert. The contents proved Albert to be the head of a German propaganda and espionage ring. The portfolio was examined on July 24 and its contents turned over by Sec. of the Treasury William G. McAdoo to the New York *World* for publication. Several German-Americans, including George Sylvester Viereck, were implicated along with German consuls, members of the German Embassy staff, and officials of the Hamburg-American Steamship Line.

educational institution for blacks. Washington was a controversial figure after 1895 when he made a speech in which he said blacks should not attempt to achieve social and political equality until they had secured economic equality. This pleased many whites and resulted in financial support for Tuskegee, but other black leaders denounced his approach. Washington's autobiography, *Up From Slavery* (1901), is a classic.

Among **books published** this year was *Spoon River Anthology* by Edgar Lee Masters, a Chicago lawyer who had had a number of collections published but without much success. This collection of poems, written as epitaphs for people buried in a midwestern cemetery, made Masters a national literary figure. Other books published this year included *America's Coming-of-Age* by Van Wyck Brooks, nonfiction; *The Rivet in Grandfather's Neck* by James Branch Cabell, a novel; *The Song of the Lark,* a novel by Willa Cather; *Verse,* a posthumous collection by Adelaide Crapsey; *The Genius* by Theodore Dreiser, a novel; *Bib Ballads* by Ring Lardner, the author's first book, a minor collection of verse; *Dreams and Dust* by Don Marquis, poetry; *The Song of Hugh Glass* by John G. Neihardt, a long poem that was the first part of Neihardt's five-part *A Cycle of the West* (1949); and *The Harbor* by Ernest Poole, a proletarian novel centering on New York harbor.

Margaret Sanger was arrested on obscenity charges in connection with her book *Family Limitation,* a pioneer work on birth control. Taken to court by the New York Society for the Suppression of Vice, she was found guilty of circulating a work "contrary not only to the law of the state, but to the law of God." She was subsequently jailed.

John Marin was an early exponent of modernism in American painting. Following French expressionists, who included Henri Matisse and Georges Rouault, Marin distorted color and form to represent the interior nature of things. In his watercolor *Woolworth Building,* the mass of brick is depicted as swaying. Marin defended this by saying, "Are the buildings themselves dead? . . . I see great forces at work, great movements, the large buildings and the small buildings."

Max Weber exhibited his painting *Chinese Restaurant,* which was attacked mercilessly by the conservatives. Closely associated with Matisse, Henri Rousseau, and other European moderns, he added to their technique the influence of Oriental art.

Feb. The **Neighborhood Playhouse** was founded on Grand St., New York City. The new theater devoted itself to fostering American and European experimental drama.

Business and Industry; Science; Education; Philosophy and Religion	III		IV	Sports; Social Issues and Crime; Folkways; Fashion; Holidays

brought out a phonograph in 1915 under the name Victrola; the name soon was applied to all phonographs. By 1919 Americans were spending more on phonographs and recordings than on musical instruments, books and periodicals, or sporting goods.

The **taxicab** made its appearance on the American scene when automobile owners found that many people were willing to pay for a short ride. The price was a nickel, or *jitney*, and the term soon was applied to the cars themselves. Drivers were known as *hackers* or *hackies* in the East, *cabbies* in the Midwest. Intercity bus lines sprang from regular jitney service.

An important discovery in **vitamin research** was made by Joseph Goldberger of the U.S. Public Health Service, who determined that pellagra was caused by vitamin deficiencies.

Emory University was chartered in Atlanta, Ga., under Methodist auspices. An outgrowth of Emory College in Oxford, Ga., which had been chartered in 1836, the university was established by a $1,000,000 endowment from Asa Griggs Candler, owner of the rights to the Coca-Cola formula. The university's first four buildings were completed in 1919, and Emory College was moved to Atlanta the same year.

Jan. 25 The **Supreme Court** ruled unconstitutional a Kansas state law forbidding employers from requiring that their employees be nonunion.

Jan. 25 The **first transcontinental telephone call** was made by the same men who had made the original telephone call in 1876. Alexander Graham Bell, speaking from New York City, said to Dr. Thomas A. Watson in San Francisco, "Mr. Watson, come here, I want you."

Jan. 26 **Rocky Mountain National Park** was established by an act of Congress.

May 24 Invention of the **telescribe** to record telephone conversations was announced by Thomas A. Edison.

June 3 The **United States Steel Corporation** was ruled lawful and not in violation of antitrust laws by the District Court of New Jersey.

July 1 The **telephone rate** was reduced to five cents in New York City.

July 13 New York State's **workmen's compensation law** was ruled valid by the New York Court of Appeals. The law had been signed in May.

appeals by Frank's attorneys, up to the Supreme Court, Gov. John M. Slayton commuted Frank's sentence to life imprisonment. An enraged mob took him from a jail in Marietta, Ga., and hanged him. Outside the South it was widely believed that Frank, a Jew, was a victim of hatred and bigotry. In 1982 Alonzo Mann, who had worked as Frank's office boy, revealed to the newspaper *The Tennessean* that on the day of the murder he had seen Jim Conley carrying the body of Mary Phagan to the factory basement, and that Conley had threatened him to keep quiet about the matter. In 1986 Frank's conviction was overturned; more than 70 years after his death.

This year's **national college football championship** was won by Cornell, with a record of nine wins, no losses, no ties.

The quip "**What this country really needs is a good five-cent cigar**" originated with Indiana-born Thomas R. Marshall, vice president under Pres. Woodrow Wilson. During one of the tedious debates in the Senate he came out with the observation.

A new **record for the mile run** was set in Cambridge, Mass., by Norman Taber, who completed the distance in 4:12.6, nearly two seconds under the old record.

The **NHL Stanley Cup** was won by the Vancouver Millionaires, who swept the Ottawa Senators in three straight games.

Feb. 20 The **Panama-Pacific International Exposition** opened at San Francisco, Calif.

Feb. 23 An **easy divorce** bill, requiring only six months' residence, was signed into law in Nevada.

Apr. 5 The **world heavyweight boxing championship** was won by Jess Willard, who defeated Jack Johnson in a 23-round bout in Havana, Cuba. It was not clear whether a blow by Willard or the blazing sun caused Johnson's descent to the canvas, described as a slow sinking.

Apr. 19 The 19th **Boston Marathon** was won by Edouard Fabre of Montreal, Canada, with a time of 2 hrs., 31 min., 41.2 sec.

May 8 The 41st annual **Kentucky Derby** was won by Regret, the first filly to win the race, with a time of 2:05²/₅. The jockey was Joe Notter.

May 17 The 49th annual **Preakness Stakes** was won by Rhine Maiden, with a time of 1:58. The jockey was D. Hoffman.

May 31 The fifth annual **Indianapolis 500** auto race was won by Ralph De Palma, completing the 500-mile course in 5 hrs., 33 min., 55.51 sec., with an average speed of 89.84 mph.

June 5 The 47th annual **Belmont Stakes** was won by The Finn, with a time of 2:18²/₅. The jockey was G. Byrne.

June 12 The **U.S. Lawn Tennis Association singles championships** were won by Molla Bjurstedt in the

July 21 The third *Lusitania* note was dispatched to Germany by Pres. Wilson, warning that any future violation of U.S. rights would be regarded as "deliberately unfriendly."

July 24 In a dockside **ship disaster,** the excursion steamer *Eastland* capsized at her pier in Chicago, killing 852 persons.

July 29 U.S. Marines landed in Haiti one day after the assassination of Haitian president Vilbrun Guillaume Sam.

Aug. 5 A **Latin-American conference** to debate ways to end the political disorder in Mexico opened in Washington, D.C. It was attended by representatives from Argentina, Brazil, Bolivia, Chile, Guatemala, Uruguay, and the U.S.

Sept. 16 Haiti became a U.S. protectorate under the terms of a ten-year treaty. The Senate approved the treaty on Feb. 28, 1916.

Oct. 19 Gen. **Venustiano Carranza** was recognized as president of Mexico by the U.S. The next day an embargo was placed on the shipment of arms to Mexico, except to territories controlled by Carranza.

Feb. The **Washington Square Players,** a theater company that was to give tremendous impetus to modern drama, was founded one week after the first production of the Neighborhood Playhouse. Operating at the Bandbox Theater on 57th St., New York City, the group continued until the U.S. entered World War I. In 1919 it was organized as the Theater Guild.

Feb. 8 *The Birth of a Nation,* D. W. Griffith's landmark motion picture, opened at Clune's Auditorium in Los Angeles, Calif. The most spectacular film made up to that time, it aroused bitter protests from liberals for its sympathetic treatment of the Ku Klux Klan during Reconstruction. Black leaders objected to its lurid racism. The film was based on the novel *The Clansman* (1905) by Thomas Dixon.

Summer The **Provincetown Players,** one of America's most significant theater groups, was organized in Massachusetts by a group of writers and artists led by George Cram Cook. The company was the first to produce a play by Eugene O'Neill, *Bound East for Cardiff* (1916).

1916

The presidential election campaign of 1916 was carried on in the shadow of World War I, then ravaging Europe and threatening to embroil the U.S. Pres. Woodrow Wilson, the Democratic candidate, made good use of the slogan "He kept us out of war," although he knew it was unlikely the country could remain neutral much longer. The Republican candidate, Charles Evans Hughes, might have won had he not snubbed Gov. Hiram Johnson of California when he visited that state. Johnson lost his enthusiasm for Hughes, and Hughes lost California.

Prohibition was voted in by Michigan, Montana, Nebraska, South Dakota, and Utah, making it law in 24 states. It now affected about 32,500,000 citizens.

Jan. 7 A German note to Washington, D.C., concerning **submarine warfare** declared that a strict adherence to international law would henceforth be followed.

Mar. 9 The Mexican revolutionary and bandit **Francisco "Pancho" Villa** led a band of 1500 guerrillas across the border and attacked Columbus, N. Mex., killing 17 Americans. U.S. troops pursued the Mexicans, killing 50 on U.S. soil and 70 more in Mexico. Brig. Gen. John J. Pershing was ordered to Mexico to capture Villa.

The nation's growing interest in the ballet was indicated by both the number of visiting foreign dancers and the development of American dance groups. Anna Pavlova, the Russian ballerina, had made her American debut in 1910. In 1916 Serge Diaghilev brought the Ballet Russe from Paris to New York City's Metropolitan Opera House for a January-to-May season. The noted Russian dancer Vaslav Nijinsky made his debut in New York on Apr. 12. Among American dancers, Ruth St. Denis and Ted Shawn were becoming well known.

Among **books published** this year was *Chicago Poems* by Carl Sandburg, a volume that heralded the arrival of a major new poetic voice and reflected the rise of the American Midwest as a force in American literature. Sandburg's book included the poems "Chicago" and "I Am the People, the Mob." Other books published this year included *The Certain Hour* by James Branch Cabell, short stories; *The Rising Tide* by Margaret Deland, a novel dealing with women's suffrage; *Life and Gabriella* by Ellen Glasgow, a novel; *A Heap o' Livin'* by Edgar Guest, verse; *The Man Against the Sky* by Edwin Arlington Robinson, poetry; *Seventeen* by Booth Tarkington, a novel; *The Mysterious Stranger,* a posthumous tale by Mark Twain; *Xingu and Other Stories* by

| Business and Industry; Science; Education; Philosophy and Religion | III | | IV | Sports; Social Issues and Crime; Folkways; Fashion; Holidays |

July 16 The first warships to pass through the Panama Canal, the *Missouri, Ohio,* and *Wisconsin,* made their successful passage during U.S. fleet maneuvers.

July 27 The first direct **wireless service with Japan** from the U.S. was established.

Oct. 15 In the **largest loan** to date, American bankers, organized under J. P. Morgan & Company, agreed to lend the British and French governments $500,000,-000.

Oct. 21 The **first transatlantic radiotelephone communication** was made from Arlington, Va., to the Eiffel Tower in Paris. A wireless transmission using telegraphy had been accomplished in 1913.

Oct. 27 A new U.S. **seaplane flight record** was established by Oscar A. Brindley, flying 544 miles along the California coast in ten hours.

Dec. 4 The long dormant **Ku Klux Klan** was revived in Georgia under a new charter granted by the state.

Dec. 10 In a landmark for **Ford auto production,** the millionth Model T rolled off Ford's Detroit, Mich., assembly line.

women's division and William M. Johnston in the men's division (Sept. 8). This year the men's championships were moved to Forest Hills, N.Y. The women's championships were moved there in 1921.

June 18 The **U.S. Open golf tournament** was won by Jerome D. Travers.

Oct. 8–13 The 12th annual **World Series** was won by the Boston Red Sox (AL), who beat the Philadelphia Phillies (NL) four games to one.

Oct. 9 A new **auto speed record** of 102.6 mph was set by Gil Anderson, who won the celebrated Astor Cup at Sheepshead Bay, N.Y.

Nov. 7 A **protest parade** was held in Chicago by some 40,000 men demonstrating against the closing of saloons on Sunday.

Dec. 4 The **Peace Ship,** chartered by Henry Ford to carry a peace expedition to Europe, left the U.S. on a historic but futile mission. Ford's slogan "Out of the trenches and back to their homes by Christmas," became a rallying cry for the American pacifist movement. Ford's attempt to find a diplomatic end to the world conflict soon collapsed.

Dec. 18 Pres. **Woodrow Wilson married Mrs. Edith Bolling Galt** in Washington, D.C.

1916

The automobile was seen everywhere, and the automobile industry was soon to become the largest single manufacturing section of the economy. In 1916 auto and truck production passed the 1,000,000 mark for the first time; the value of this production was nearly $1,-000,000,000. The average price of a new car was just over $600, but Henry Ford's Model T, of which 577,036 were produced this year, was selling for only $360, down from the $850 price of just eight years earlier. It was estimated that there were about 3,500,000 cars on the nation's roads.

The **National Research Council** was organized by the National Academy of Sciences.

The discovery of **heparin,** a temporary anticoagulant of blood, by a Johns Hopkins medical student marked an important advance in the prevention of internal blood clotting. The need for a more lasting method of anticoagulation with less frequent injections led to the discovery of dicumarol.

The theory of **progressive education** was formulated by John Dewey in his *Democracy and Education.* According to Dewey, intelligence should be seen as an

Among the baseball heroes of the early twentieth century was Grover Cleveland Alexander, a right-handed pitcher who between 1911 and 1930 played for the Philadelphia Phillies (NL), Chicago Cubs (NL), and St. Louis Cardinals (NL). In the 1916 season he set an unsurpassed record by pitching 15 shutouts for the Phillies. In all, Alexander recorded 90 shutouts during his career. He is exceeded in this respect only by Walter Johnson, who had 113 shutouts during his years with the Washington Senators (AL), from 1907 to 1927. Johnson also compiled a record 3503 strikeouts in his 27-year career.

This year's **national college football championship** was won by Pittsburgh, with a record of eight wins, no losses, no ties.

The **NHL Stanley Cup** was won by the Montreal Canadiens over Portland, 15 goals to 13.

Mar. 15 A **punitive expedition to Mexico** began the pursuit of Pancho Villa and his brigands. The expedition entered Mexico under command of Brig. Gen. John J. Pershing.

Apr. 18 In a strongly worded **note to Germany,** Pres. Woodrow Wilson stated that unless the series of U-boat attacks that included the 1915 sinking of the *Lusitania* and additional attacks on passenger liners were immediately discontinued, diplomatic relations between the U.S. and Germany would be severed.

May U.S. **Marines landed in Santo Domingo** to settle internal violence. The occupation continued until 1924.

May 4 A German note in reply to the U.S. note of Apr. 18 pledged not to attack any merchant vessel without warning and without giving passengers a chance to escape.

June 3 The **National Defense Act** was passed. It increased the standing Army to 175,000 and the National Guard to 450,000.

June 7–10 The **Republican National Convention nominated Charles Evans Hughes** of New York for the presidency and Charles Warren Fairbanks of Indiana for the vice presidency.

June 14–16 The **Democratic National Convention renominated Pres. Wilson** for the presidency and Vice Pres. Thomas R. Marshall for the vice presidency.

June 16 In the punitive action in **Mexico,** Gen. Pershing was notified by Mexican Gen. Jacinto Trevino, commander of Pres. Venustiano Carranza's Northern Army, that Mexico would view any further movement of U.S. troops into Mexico as a hostile action.

June 17 **U.S. forces crossed into Mexico** and an ultimatum was issued by the Mexican consul at Brownsville, Tex. It asserted that U.S. forces would be attacked unless withdrawn.

June 20 A note to Mexico by Sec. of State Robert Lansing asserted that troops would not be withdrawn from Mexico until order was restored on the border.

June 21 U.S. troops were attacked at Carrizal, Mexico. The Americans lost 17 killed or wounded; 38 Mexicans were killed, including the Mexican commander.

July 22 A **bombing in San Francisco** during a Preparedness Day parade killed 10 persons and wounded 40. In 1917 labor leader Tom Mooney was sentenced to hang and Warren K. Billings was sentenced to life imprisonment for the deed. Pres. Wilson commuted Mooney's sentence to life imprisonment in 1918, but because of confessions of perjured testimony at the trial the case was an international cause célèbre for many years. On Jan. 7, 1939, Mooney was pardoned by Gov. Culbert L. Olson of California. Billings was released later in the year.

July 28 A **Mexican proposal** to submit differences to a commission was accepted by the U.S. in a note to the

Edith Wharton; and *When a Man's a Man* by Harold Bell Wright, a novel.

In yet another case of **censorship,** Theodore Dreiser's 1915 novel *The Genius* was suppressed in New York City.

Edgard Varèse, one of most uncompromising of experimentalist composers, came to the U.S. after having been rejected for military service in the French army.

D. W. Griffith in his new film *Intolerance* bewildered audiences with sequences dealing with ancient Babylon, the Crucifixion, St. Bartholomew's massacre, and the killing of modern strikers. All were connected by a repeated scene suggested by Walt Whitman's line "Out of the cradle endlessly rocking."

The **Dixieland Jass Band** opened at Schiller's Cafe in Chicago. The band included Dominique La Rocca, Eddie Edwards, Henry Ragas, Alcide "Yellow" Nunez, and Tony Sbarbaro. It achieved great popularity and, with somewhat different personnel, went on to New York City in the following year, where it was billed as The Original Dixieland Jass Band.

Among events marking the **tercentenary of William Shakespeare's death,** the Drama Society paid tribute with its Century Theatre production of *The Tempest* in the Elizabethan manner; Beerbohm Tree brought from England a four-hour production of *Henry VIII,* more notable for its pageantry than for fidelity to the original; and James K. Hackett played Macbeth unsuccessfully, but with Thomas A. Wise as Falstaff did a creditable production of *The Merry Wives of Windsor.* The nadir of the celebration was reached late in May with Percy MacKaye's presentation of his new masque, *Caliban by the Yellow Sands,* in Lewisohn Stadium in New York City.

Our Mrs. McChesney by Edna Ferber, a play about a business woman in the petticoat line, became one of the most popular dramas of the season. The title role was played by Ethel Barrymore. Ferber had written several collections of stories about Emma McChesney, including *Personality Plus* (1914) and *Emma McChesney and Co.* (1915).

Easter by August Strindberg was produced by the Stage Society of New York City.

The **New York building code** was revised to allow skyscraper construction to unlimited height, provided

| Business and Industry; Science; Education; Philosophy and Religion III | Sports; Social Issues and Crime; IV Folkways; Fashion; Holidays |

instrument for changing one's environment and should be trained accordingly. He held that subject matter should be adjusted to the child, not child to the subject matter, and that there should be no distinction between cultural and vocational training.

The **submachine gun** was invented by Brig. Gen. John Taliaferro Thompson. The weapon came to be known as the Tommy gun.

Jan. 24 The **federal income tax** was ruled constitutional by the U.S. Supreme Court in the case of *Brushaber v. Union Pacific Railroad Co.*

Jan. 25 **U.S. exports for 1915** surpassed all previous figures, totaling $3,555,000,000 and showing an excess of $1,772,309,538 over imports.

Jan. 28 **Louis D. Brandeis** was appointed to the Supreme Court by Pres. Woodrow Wilson. The appointment was confirmed on June 1. Brandeis was the first Jew to become a justice of the Supreme Court.

Feb. 29 **Child labor legislation** in South Carolina raised the minimum age of children employed in mills, factories, and mines from 12 to 14 years.

Apr. 26 **Military training in public schools** was voted down by the New York City Board of Education.

July 11 The **Shackleford Good Roads Bill** was signed by Pres. Wilson. The bill authorized the federal government to turn over $5,000,000 to the states for road-building programs; only states willing to contribute equal amounts could benefit. The law remained in force for five years, with increases each year in the amount spent.

July 17 The **Federal Farm Loan Act** was signed by Pres. Wilson. It established a land bank system to provide loans to farmers who needed money for maintenance or improvement.

July 18 *The Official Gazette,* London, published the names of 80 **U.S. firms blacklisted** under England's trading-with-the-enemy act. The U.S. charged that Great Britain had repeatedly violated the rights of neutrals; that ships were convoyed to British ports and searched at leisure; that the mails were rifled and trade secrets filched; and that U.S. exporters to

Jan. 1 In the second **Tournament of Roses Association football game** (the first had been played in 1902), and the first annual game, Washington State defeated Brown 14–0. This game marked the beginning of the annual football contest that in 1923 came to be called the Rose Bowl game.

Jan. 17 The **Professional Golfers Association** (PGA) was formed. The first professional tournament under its auspices, held at the Siwanoy Golf Course in Bronxville, N.Y., on Apr. 10, was won by James M. Barnes.

Apr. 19 The 20th **Boston Marathon** was won by Arthur V. Roth of Roxbury, Mass., with a time of 2 hrs., 27 min., 16.4 sec.

May 13 The 42nd annual **Kentucky Derby** was won by George Smith, with a new record time of 2:04. The jockey was Johnny Loftus.

May 16 The 40th annual **Preakness Stakes** was won by Damrosch, with a time of 1:54⁴/₅. The jockey was Linus McAtee.

May 30 The sixth **Indianapolis 500** auto race was won by Dario Resta. This year the course distance was 300 miles. Resta completed the race in 3 hrs., 34 min., 17 sec., with an average speed of 84 mph. The race was not run in 1917 or 1918.

June 10 The 48th annual **Belmont Stakes** was won by Friar Rock, with a time of 2:22. The jockey was E. Haynes.

June 12 The **U.S. Lawn Tennis Association singles championships** were won by Molla Bjurstedt in the

Carranza government from acting Sec. of State Frank L. Polk.

July 30 **German sabotage** was said to be the cause of the detonation of ammunition and destruction of the docks at Toms River Island near Jersey City, N.J. On Jan. 17, 1917, a munitions plant at Kingsland, N.J., was destroyed. In 1922 the U.S. lost a suit to recover damages, but the case was reopened in 1939. Germany was ordered to pay reparations but did not do so.

Aug. 4 A treaty for the purchase of the **Danish West Indies** (Virgin Islands) for $25,000,000 was signed by the U.S. and Denmark. It was ratified on Jan. 17, 1917.

Nov. 7 **Woodrow Wilson was reelected president** of the United States. Thomas R. Marshall was reelected vice president. The election was so close that the outcome was uncertain for three days, when it became clear that Wilson had carried California, but by fewer than 4000 votes. The electoral vote was Wilson, 277; Charles Evans Hughes, Republican candidate, 254. The popular vote was Wilson, 9,128,837; Hughes, 8,536,380. In congressional elections the Democrats lost three seats in the Senate but maintained a 53–42 majority, with one seat going to a minor party. In the House the Democrats again narrowed their majority over the Republicans, 216–210, with six seats held by minor parties.

Dec. 18 In identical **peace notes** to the belligerent nations in Europe, Pres. Wilson asked each nation to state its war aims. He stated the U.S. was as interested in peace as the warring states and that steps should be taken not only to end the war but "to secure the future peace of the world."

that setbacks based on the width of the adjacent streets were incorporated in the design on three-fourths of the ground area.

The **Massachusetts Institute of Technology** moved to its present location, on the banks of the Charles R., Cambridge, Mass. Magnificent new buildings were designed by William Wells Bosworth.

Mar. 2 The *Eighth Symphony* of **Gustav Mahler** was given its American premiere performance by the Philadelphia Symphony Orchestra. The piece required eight soloists, a mixed chorus of 800, a children's choir of 150, and an augmented orchestra of 110. Critics complained the piece lacked sustained inspiration and felt the musical ideas did not justify employment of such enormous technical apparatus.

Mar. 20 The one-act play *Magical City* by Zöe Akins opened at the Bandbox in New York City. The performance marked the beginning of the author's career as a successful playwright. The play recounted the effects of New York City on a young girl.

May 20 A bill authorizing **motion picture censorship** was vetoed by Gov. Charles S. Whitman of New York.

Nov. 13 The first complete U.S. production of *The Pearl Fishers* by Georges Bizet marked the opening of the Metropolitan Opera's season.

1917

Pres. Woodrow Wilson had tried hard to keep the U.S. out of World War I, although his sympathies were with the Allied cause. Through the course of the war public opinion had shifted to the Allies' favor, but many still hoped to avoid U.S. involvement. By early 1917, however, it was clear that the U.S. would be unable to stay on the sidelines much longer. Wilson called a special session of Congress and on Apr. 2 delivered his war message. The Senate voted for war, 82–6, on Apr. 4 and the House followed on Apr. 6, 373–50. Wilson signed the war resolution the same day.

Jan. 22 Pres. Woodrow Wilson outlined his **Ten Points** under which he would urge the U.S. to enter a world federation designed to prevent future wars. This speech, given before the Senate, came to be known as his "Peace Without Victory" speech.

Jan. 28 U.S. forces were recalled from **Mexico** after nearly a year of fruitless searching for Pancho Villa.

Middle West farm life in the last half of the nineteenth century was a subject that interested authors and readers. Hamlin Garland, who knew farm labor first-hand, had for a number of years been producing realistic books on the subject. In 1917 his autobiography, *A Son of the Middle Border,* was published. In *Main-Travelled Roads* (1891) he fictionalized the hardships of farm life. Garland's influence on the development of realism helped prepare the way for a new wave of writers.

Among **books published** this year was *The Cream of the Jest* by James Branch Cabell, a novel about a jaded writer who escapes to a dream world called Storisende, has a number of adventures, and returns to the real world happier for the experience. Other books published this year included *The Innocents* and *The Job: An American Novel* by Sinclair Lewis, both novels; *Jerry of the Islands,* a posthumous novel by Jack London, who died in 1916; *Tendencies in Modern American Poetry* by

| Business and Industry; Science; Education; Philosophy and Religion III | | Sports; Social Issues and Crime; Folkways; Fashion; Holidays IV |

European neutrals had to submit lists of their customers for British approval and that the lists were then passed to British firms.

Aug. 16 A **migratory bird treaty** to protect insect-destroying birds in North America was signed by the U.S. and Canada.

Aug. 25 The **National Park Service** was established as part of the Interior Department.

Sept. 3 The **Adamson Eight-Hour Act** was signed by Pres. Wilson. The act made an eight-hour day standard for most railroad workers. The bill had been hurriedly passed by both houses of Congress to stave off a nationwide railroad strike called for Sept. 4. The strike was averted, but the president was severely critized and accused of wooing labor during an election year.

Oct. 16 The **first birth control clinic** was opened by Margaret Sanger, Fania Mindell, and Ethel Burne at 46 Amboy St., Brooklyn, N.Y.

Dec. 21 Trading volume on the **New York Stock Exchange** reached a 15-year high following Sec. of State Robert Lansing's statement that the U.S. was being drawn into the war in Europe.

women's division and Norris Williams II in the men's division (Sept. 6).

June 15 **Boy Scouts of America** was incorporated by a bill signed by Pres. Woodrow Wilson.

June 30 The **U.S. Open golf tournament** was won by Charles Evans, Jr. The competition was suspended until 1919 because of U.S. entry into World War I in 1917.

Sept. 30 The **longest baseball winning streak** on record was stopped at 26 games when the New York Giants (NL) were beaten 8–3 by the Boston Braves in the second game of a double header.

Oct. 7–12 The 13th annual **World Series** was won by the Boston Red Sox (AL), defeating the Brooklyn Dodgers (NL) four games to one.

1917

On Oct. 13 in New York City Mayor John P. Mitchell dedicated the Catskill Aqueduct at ceremonies in Central Park. The aqueduct, a remarkable work of engineering and construction, pointed up the need of cities for reliable sources of water. It had been under construction for 12 years and had cost $177,000,000. It was 92 miles long and at Storm King Mt. it passed under the Hudson R. at a depth of 1114 feet. Much of the aqueduct had to be cut through solid rock.

Irving Langmuir performed experiments in molecular chemistry, determining molecular measurements with an accuracy and precision that made them models for later researchers.

The **University of Alaska** was founded as Alaska Agricultural College and School of Mines at College,

Most professional baseball players of the era learned the game on sandlots or in school, but few played the game at college before entering the ranks of the pros. One of the game's top players during this period was Edward T. "Eddie" Collins, a Columbia College graduate of 1907. Beginning in 1906, Collins played for 25 years in the American League with the Philadelphia Athletics and the Chicago White Sox, becoming one of the best second basemen the game has known. His lifetime total of 3311 hits placed him eighth on the all-time list. Collins was four times the American League's base-stealing champion, in 1917 stealing 51 bases. In 1910 he stole 81 bases, his career high.

This year's **national college football championship** was won by Georgia Tech, with a record of nine wins, no losses, no ties.

The **NHL Stanley Cup** championship was won by

| Exploration and Settlement; Wars; Government; Civil Rights; Statistics I | | II Publishing; Arts and Music; Popular Entertainment; Architecture; Theater |

Jan. 31 A note announcing the German renewal of **submarine warfare** against neutral and belligerent ships, effective Feb. 1, was delivered to the State Department by Count Johann-Heinrich von Bernstorff, the German ambassador.

Feb. 3 **Diplomatic relations with Germany** were severed. On the same day the U.S. liner *Housatonic* was sunk by a German submarine after a one-hour warning.

Feb. 5 An **Immigration Act** was passed by Congress over Pres. Wilson's veto (Jan. 29). The law required a literacy test for immigrants and barred Asiatic laborers, except for those from countries with special agreements or treaties with the U.S.

Feb. 24 The **Zimmermann note,** a coded message from German foreign minister Alfred Zimmermann to the German ambassador to Mexico, was given to Walter Hines Page, U.S. ambassador to Great Britain, by the British, who had decoded it. The note suggested that in the event of U.S. entry into the war against Germany, Germany would propose an alliance with Mexico. The contents of the note were made public on Mar. 1.

Mar. 2 The **Jones Act** was passed, making Puerto Rico a U.S. territory and its inhabitants U.S. citizens.

Mar. 5 Pres. **Wilson was inaugurated** for his second term. Thomas R. Marshall was sworn in for his second term as vice president.

Mar. 8 The Senate adopted a **cloture rule,** permitting the majority to terminate a floor debate. Each senator would be permitted to speak for an hour after the rule was invoked.

Mar. 9 Pres. Wilson announced that the legality of **arming merchant vessels** by presidential order had been supported by the attorney general. Wilson stated he would issue the order immediately.

Apr. 2 The **first woman in the House of Representatives,** Rep. Jeannette Rankin, Republican of Montana, was seated.

Apr. 24 The **Liberty Loan Act,** a war finance measure, authorized Sec. of the Treasury William G. McAdoo to issue for public subscription $2,000,000,000 worth of 3½% convertible gold bonds.

May 18 The **Selective Service Act** was passed, authorizing federal conscription for the armed forces. The act required registration of all males from 21 to 30 years of age.

June 15 The **Espionage Act** was passed, making it a crime to obstruct recruitment, foster disloyalty in the armed forces, or engage in other disloyal acts.

June 26 The **first U.S. troops in Europe** arrived at St.-Nazaire, France, under command of Maj. Gen. William L. Sibert.

Nov. 3 The **first engagement** involving U.S. forces in Europe occurred near the Rhine-Marne Canal in

Amy Lowell; *Parnassus on Wheels* by Christopher Morley, a novel; *Susan Lenox: Her Fall and Rise,* a posthumous novel by David Graham Phillips, considered his best work; *Merlin* by Edwin Arlington Robinson, the first volume of a poetic trilogy dealing with the Arthurian legends that concluded with *Lancelot* (1920) and *Tristram* (1927); and *King Coal* by Upton Sinclair, a novel about coal mining in Colorado.

The great French actress **Sarah Bernhardt,** 72, began what was to be her last tour of the U.S. Although she was unable to move about without assistance (one leg had been amputated in 1915 following aggravation of an old stage injury), she thrilled audiences with remarkably youthful portrayals, among them Portia in Shakespeare's *The Merchant of Venice.*

Storyville, also known as The District, a section of New Orleans set aside for honky-tonks and sporting houses, was closed on the insistence of the U.S. Navy. The closing tended to drive jazz musicians out of New Orleans.

The **Original Dixieland Jass Band** opened at Reisenweber's Restaurant in New York City. In this year the group made the first jazz recordings, including "Tiger Rag," "Reisenweber Rag," "Barnyard Blues," "At the Jazz Band Ball," "Ostrich Walk," "Bluin' the Blues," and "Clarinet Marmalade."

Hell Gate Bridge, a cantilevered steel arch spanning the Harlem R. in New York City, was opened for railroad service. It was one of the most striking nonsuspension bridges in the world.

Ornithologists noted that the **starling,** which had been introduced successfully in New York at the turn of the century, was spreading all over the U.S. and becoming a pest.

Feb. 5 The **Morosco Theatre** in New York City opened to the public with a production of *Canary Cottage,* a musical by Oliver Morosco, Elmer Harris, and Earl Carroll.

Apr. 14 The **Committee on Public Information,** headed by George Creel, was created by executive order to control the censorship of news and propaganda releases.

June 4 The **first Pulitzer prizes** were awarded in the following categories: biography, *Julia Ward Howe* by Laura E. Richards and Maude H. Elliott assisted by Florence H. Hall; history, *With Americans of Past and Present Days* by Jean Jules Jusserand, the French

| Business and Industry; Science; Education; Philosophy and Religion **III** | **IV** Sports; Social Issues and Crime; Folkways; Fashion; Holidays |

Alaska. Its first classes were held in 1922. The university's present name was adopted in 1935.

Helium was first produced in quantity this year, at three experimental plants in Texas. The plants produced about 200,000 cubic feet of the gas, but not quickly enough for it to be used in military balloons in France. At war's end most of the gas was awaiting shipment from docks in New Orleans.

There were 4,842,139 **motor vehicles** registered in the U.S., 435,000 of them trucks. In all the other nations of the world it was estimated there were only 719,246 motor vehicles. This year alone, 1,795,840 passenger cars and 181,348 commercial vehicles were made in the U.S., and there were 25,500 garages and 13,500 repair shops to service them. The average price of a new car was $720.

Feb. 23 The **Federal Board for Vocational Education** was created by the Smith-Hughes Act. To stimulate the development of trade and agricultural schools, Congress voted to supplement the expenditures of the various states with grants from the federal government equal to the amounts spent by the states.

Mar. 3 Congress approved the **first excess profits tax,** to help pay for increased military spending. It was a progressive tax, ranging from 20% to 60% on all corporate profit in excess of 7% to 9% of capital. The law was superseded on Oct. 3 by the Revenue Act of 1917.

Mar. 19 An **eight-hour day** for railroad workers was accepted by railroad managers in cooperation with the defense program, thus removing the threat of a railroad tie-up. Labor also gained by keeping the same pay scale.

Apr. 4 The **bushel price of wheat** passed $2.00 on the Chicago Board of Trade for the first time in a normal market. On May 11, when the price reached $3.25, trading was discontinued.

Apr. 19 The **price of cotton** reached 21¼ cents a lb. on the New York Exchange, the highest price since the Civil War.

Aug. 18 The **first two-way radiotelephone communication** between a plane and the ground, and two days

the Seattle Metropolitans, who defeated the Montreal Canadiens three games to one.

Jan. An **anti-prostitution drive** in San Francisco attracted huge crowds to public meetings this month. At one meeting attended by 7000 people, 20,000 were turned away for lack of room. In a conference with the Rev. Paul Smith, the most outspoken foe of vice, 300 prostitutes made a plea for toleration, explaining they had been forced into a life of sin by poverty. When Smith asked if they would take honest work at $8 to $10 a week, the ladies laughed derisively. This lost them public sympathy. The police closed about 200 houses shortly thereafter.

Jan. 1 The second annual **Tournament of Roses Association football game** (Rose Bowl), and the third such game ever played, was won by Oregon over Pennsylvania, 14–0.

Apr. 2 The memorable sentence "**The world must be made safe for democracy**" appeared in a speech by Pres. Woodrow Wilson before Congress, requesting a declaration of war against Germany.

Apr. 19 The 21st **Boston Marathon** was won by William K. Kennedy of Port Chester, N.Y., with a time of 2 hrs., 28 min., 37 sec.

May 2 The **first double no-hit nine-inning baseball game** in the major leagues was played in Chicago. Jim Vaughn of the Chicago Cubs (NL) and Fred Toney of Cincinnati both pitched the full game without allowing a hit. The Reds scored in the tenth inning to win 1–0.

May 12 The 42nd annual **Preakness Stakes** was won by Kalitan, with a time of 1:54³/₅. The jockey was E. Haynes.

May 12 The 43rd annual **Kentucky Derby** was won by Omar Khayyam, with a time of 2:04³/₅. The jockey was Charles Borel.

June 16 The 49th annual **Belmont Stakes** was won by Hourless, with a new track record time of 2:17⁴/₅. The jockey was Jimmy Butwell.

June 23 A **perfect baseball game,** no hits and no walks, was pitched by Ernie Shore of the Boston Red Sox (AL) in a 4–0 win over the Washington Senators.

June 23 The **U.S. Lawn Tennis Association singles championships** were won by Molla Bjurstedt in the women's division and R. Lindley Murray in the men's division (Aug. 25).

July 4 The famous phrase "**Lafayette, we are here**" was spoken by Col. Charles E. Stanton, appearing for

France. German forces attacked American infantry-men training in front-line trenches. American losses: three dead, five wounded, twelve captured or missing.

Nov. 6   **Women's suffrage** was made law in New York State by constitutional amendment.

Nov. 30   The U.S. **42nd "Rainbow" Division,** with troops from every state in the Union, arrived in France.

Dec. 18   The **Eighteenth Amendment** to the U.S. Constitution, outlawing manufacture, sale, or transportation of alcoholic liquors, was passed by Congress and submitted to the states for ratification. It was ratified on Jan. 29, 1919.

ambassador to the U.S. The prizes also included awards in journalism.

Oct. 27   The Russian violinist **Jascha Heifetz,** age 16, made his American debut in New York City. Critics without exception proclaimed him the equal of the greatest living masters both in technique and maturity of conception. He became a U.S. citizen in 1925.

Dec. 25   *Why Marry?* by Jesse Lynch Williams opened on Broadway at the Astor Theatre. The comedy became the first play to win a Pulitzer Prize, in 1918.

1918

World War I ended on the 11th hour of the 11th day of November this year. At the designated moment, the entire western front opened up with gunfire as war-worn troops sought to fire the last shot. Then silence fell. In the U.S. and elsewhere enormous crowds poured into the streets for a noisy celebration. In New York City 150 tons of paper and ticker tape had to be cleaned off the streets after the festivities. Although the U.S. did not enter the war until nearly three years after the conflict began, the country had mobilized 4,743,829 men and women. Of these, 2,084,000 reached France. U.S. intervention was the deciding factor after years of heavy casualties brought England, France, and Germany to virtual exhaustion. U.S. casualties were 53,513 battle deaths; 63,195 other deaths, mostly from disease; 204,-002 wounded. The cost was $21,850,000,000, not counting loans to allies.

Jan. 8   Pres. Woodrow Wilson listed his **14 points** for a just and lasting peace in an address to Congress stating the "war aims and peace terms of the United States." It was translated and distributed to German soldiers and civilians throughout middle Europe by the Office of Public Information.

May 16   The **Sedition Act** was passed. It provided heavy penalties for those who hindered the war effort by making false statements, obstructing enlistment, or speaking against production of war materials, the American form of government, the Constitution, the flag, etc. It was signed by Pres. Wilson on May 21.

June 4   At **Château-Thierry,** the U.S. Second Division halted German forces advancing toward Paris.

June 6–25   In the Battle of **Belleau Wood,** in France, the U.S. Second Division and Fourth Marine Brigade halted the Germans and recaptured the area after bitter fighting. American deaths: 285 officers and 7585 enlisted men.

Despite the many new plays being written and produced every year, interest in the works of great playwrights remained high. In fact, a number of actors and actresses spent all or most of their careers acting Shakespearean roles. A leading actor was Walter Hampden, an American who acted in England before making his New York City debut in 1907. In Shakespeare's plays he acted the roles of Caliban, Oberon, Romeo, Macbeth, Othello, Shylock, and Hamlet. His appearance as Hamlet in 1918 was hailed as the best American interpretation of the role since Edwin Booth. In 1925 Hampden took over the Colonial Theater in New York and renamed it for himself.

Among **books published** this year was *The Education of Henry Adams,* a posthumous volume, privately printed in 1907 that Adams had written to complement his *Mont-Saint-Michel and Chartres* (1913). The work decried the multiplicity of modern society, symbolized by the electric dynamo, and the failure of modern education to prepare Adams for a happy and useful life. Other books published this year included *My Antonia* by Willa Cather, a masterly novel of prairie life; *Cornhuskers* by Carl Sandburg, a collection of poetry; and *The Magnificent Ambersons* by Booth Tarkington, a study of three generations of a family in Indianapolis from 1873 to 1916, years in which Indianapolis grew from a town to a city.

Early portions of *Ulysses* by **James Joyce,** published in the *Little Review,* were burned by the Post Office Department. The complete novel, regarded by some as the greatest twentieth-century novel in the English language, was published in Paris in 1922 by the expatriate American publisher and bookseller Sylvia Beach. It was

Business and Industry; Science; Education; Philosophy and Religion III	IV Sports; Social Issues and Crime; Folkways; Fashion; Holidays

later between two airborne planes, was established at Langley Field, Va.

Sept. 5 Federal **raids on IWW headquarters** in 24 cities were prompted by the labor organization's antiwar activities. Federal agents seized documents and books and made ten arrests, including William D. "Big Bill" Haywood, a leader of the organization.

Oct. 1 The **second Liberty Loan drive** was launched to sell $3,000,000,000 in bonds with a 4% return. It was oversubscribed by half by Nov. 15, the end of the drive.

Gen. John J. Pershing at the tomb of the French nobleman.

Aug. 19 The first baseball game played in New York City's **Polo Grounds** resulted in the arrest of managers John McGraw of the New York Giants (NL) and Christy Mathewson of the Cincinnati Reds for violating a law prohibiting Sunday ball playing.

Oct. 6–15 The 14th annual **World Series** was won by the Chicago White Sox (AL), who defeated the New York Giants (NL) four games to two.

Nov. 18 **Electric advertising signs** were ordered shut off on Sundays and Thursdays by the federal fuel administrator. The purpose was to save fuel.

1918

The U.S. war effort required mobilization and control of the nation's economic life. The War Industries Board, established on July 28, 1917, was reorganized on Mar. 4, 1918, with Bernard Baruch, a financier, as its head. Food and fuel were rationed, taxes were increased, and millions of dollars worth of Liberty bonds were sold. The railroads were taken over by the government by a presidential proclamation on Dec. 26, 1917, an arrangement formalized by the Railroad Control Act of Mar. 21, 1918. Industries such as steel had already been stimulated by the war because of large purchases by the Allies. Between 1914 and 1917 the production of steel ingots and castings nearly doubled. During the 19 months the U.S. was at war, 875 seagoing vessels were built.

A **compulsory school attendance law** was passed in Mississippi, the last state to do so.

The **United Lutheran Church** was organized through the agreement of 45 hitherto divided synods.

The **expectations of business** during the last year of World War I were expressed in the slogan "Change from a debtor to a creditor nation." It was assumed the dollar would replace the pound in international trade and that the favorable trade balance given to the U.S. by the production of war goods for the Allies would never be upset.

In 1918 there were 1,000,000 more **women employed** than in 1915. On Sept. 30 Pres. Woodrow Wilson told the Senate that women's suffrage was a "vitally necessary war measure." But the Senate lacked the strength to pass any legislation on the matter.

Apr. 6 The **third Liberty Loan Drive** was begun with a goal of $3,000,000,000 at 4.5% interest.

The war prompted an innovation in time-keeping this year. On Mar. 31 Pres. Woodrow Wilson signed a law providing for Daylight Savings Time, by which clocks were to be set ahead one hour so that more daylight was available. Daylight savings was disliked by some, especially farmers, and the law was repealed in 1919. It was not reestablished nationwide until World War II.

This year's **national college football championship** was won by Pittsburgh, with a record of four wins, one loss, no ties.

A French box car bearing the inscription *Hommes 40–Chevaux 8* [40 men, 8 horses] provided a source of humor for doughboys. After the war, reminiscences of these crowded conveyances led to formation of the Forty and Eight Society, a part of the American Legion that devotes itself to fun and high jinks.

The fourth **Tournament of Roses Association football game** (Rose Bowl) was won by the Mare Island Marines, who defeated the Camp Lewis Army team 19–7.

The **NHL Stanley Cup** championship was won by the Toronto Arenas, who defeated the Vancouver Millionaires three games to two.

For this year's **Boston Marathon,** individual competition was suspended because of the war. A service team race was won by Camp Devens.

July 15 In the Second Battle of the **Marne,** German forces attacked east and west of Reims but made no substantial gains. Some 85,000 U.S. troops fought in the battle.

July 18–Aug. 6 The **Aisne-Marne offensive** was launched by more than 250,000 Americans in conjunction with French units to counter the German attack of July 15. The offensive forced the Germans out of the Soissons-Reims salient and gave the Allies the initiative.

Aug. 8 At Amiens Allied forces began a prolonged offensive against the German salient at the Somme R.

Sept. 12–13 At St. Mihiel, U.S. forces cut off and reduced the German salient, taking about 15,000 prisoners.

Sept. 14 Eugene V. Debs, four-time Socialist candidate for the presidency, was sentenced to ten years' imprisonment for violating the Espionage Act of 1917. Debs had been arrested on June 30 for allegedly seditious statements against recruiting at Canton, Ohio. His sentence was commuted in 1921.

Sept. 26–Nov. 11 The Battle of the **Meuse-Argonne,** involving 1,200,000 U.S. troops, had as its objective the cutting of the German supply line, the Sedan-Mézières railroad. American forces cut the railway in early November. The armistice of Nov. 11 brought the American advance to a halt.

Oct. 5 In a **German peace initiative,** Prince Max of Baden, a moderate who had recently been appointed imperial chancellor of Germany, wrote to Pres. Wilson and asked him to "take a hand in the restoration of peace." The note said Germany was willing to accept the 14 points Wilson had set forth in his message to Congress on Jan. 8. In his reply of Oct. 15, Pres. Wilson said that any armistice must be arranged by military authorities, that the German armies must stop their illegal and inhuman practices, and that arbitrary government must cease in Germany. The German government accepted these conditions on Oct. 20. Wilson had some difficulty convincing the Allies to accept the 14 points as the basis of negotiations. They accepted, with reservations Wilson allowed, in early November, and Wilson forwarded the mesages to Germany.

Nov. 3 An **armistice with Austria-Hungary,** effective Nov. 4, was signed.

Nov. 5 In **congressional elections** the Republicans gained control of both houses, taking a 49–47 lead in the Senate, and a House majority of 240–190, with three seats going to minor parties.

Nov. 7 An **armistice with Germany** was reported in New York City newspapers after an erroneous United Press dispatch from France. The city broke into wild demonstrations. Later in the day, the report was

banned from the U.S. until 1933.

Some of the **war plays** presented on the New York stage during the season were *Where the Poppies Bloom* with Marjorie Rambeau; *Billeted* with Margaret Anglin; *Under Orders* by Berte Thomas, with Effie Shannon and Shelley Hull; and *The Better 'Ole,* a play built around the cartoons of British artist Bruce Bairnsfather.

The Russian actress **Alla Nazimova** played in three Henrik Ibsen revivals, *The Wild Duck, Hedda Gabler,* and *A Doll's House.*

Regional drama was emphasized by the Carolina Playmakers, started at the University of North Carolina under the supervision of Prof. Frederick H. Koch. Its dramas generally dealt with historical or folk themes significant to the South.

Among the **notable buildings** completed this year were the Commodore and Pennsylvania hotels and St. Bartholomew's Church, all in New York City.

Feb. 8 The first issue of *Stars and Stripes,* the Army newspaper, was published.

Feb. 12 All **Broadway theaters were closed** in New York City in an effort to save coal.

Feb. 15 **Vernon Castle** was killed in an air accident at Fort Worth, Tex. He and his wife Irene were the most popular dance team in the world before the war. Castle had served with the Royal Flying Corps in Europe.

Apr. 15 *Dance in Place Congo* by Henry Franklin Gilbert, a symphonic poem scored for ballet, was presented at the Metropolitan Opera House in New York City. Gilbert was one of the chief advocates of American, as opposed to European, music. The work was based on Creole themes from New Orleans, and its performance brought him national recognition.

June 1 **Pulitzer prizes** were awarded for the following: fiction, *His Family* by Ernest Poole; biography, *Benjamin Franklin, Self-Revealed* by William Cabell Bruce; history, *A History of the Civil War 1861–1865* by James Ford Rhodes; poetry, *Love Songs* by Sara Teasdale; drama, *Why Marry?* by Jesse Lynch Williams.

May 13 The **first airmail stamps** were issued by the Post Office Department, in denominations of 6 cents, 16 cents, and 24 cents.

May 15 The **first airmail service** was inaugurated with regular flights between New York City and Washington, D.C.

May 28 The **American Railroad Express Company** was organized under federal supervision by an enforced merger of the Adams, American, Wells-Fargo, and Southern Express companies. The move was sought by the government to improve shipment of war goods.

May 31 Sec. of War Newton D. Baker ordered that **conscientious objectors** be granted leave from military service without pay to work on farms.

June 3 The **Federal Child Labor Law** of 1916 was declared unconstitutional by the Supreme Court on the grounds that it violated rights reserved to the states under the Tenth Amendment. The Court also held that Congress, in blocking interstate shipments of goods made by underage children, had exceeded its power to regulate interstate commerce.

July 4 Nearly **one hundred ships were launched** at ports around the country this Independence Day as a patriotic gesture.

July 26 The **sugar ration** was reduced to two pounds a person a month by edict of the U.S. Food Board.

Aug. 9 **Automobile production** was suspended as auto makers were ordered by the War Industries Board to convert to 100% war work before Jan. 1, 1919.

Aug. 29 A 17% increase in the **cost of living** in New York City from July 1917 to July 1918 was revealed by Labor Department statistics.

Sept. 10 The first Chicago–New York **airmail trip** to be completed in one day showed an overall time for transportation of mail of 12 hrs., 55 min. The flying time was 10 hrs., 5 min.

Oct. A devastating **influenza epidemic** reached its height. The disease had first appeared in early September in Boston, New York, and Philadelphia. By mid-October the death rate in these cities had risen over 700%. Doctors were baffled. The epidemic spread to 46 states and ultimately killed between 400,000 and 500,000 persons, far more than the number of Americans killed in the war. Many war plants shut down, telephone service was cut in half, and the draft was suspended in several cities. Panic spread rapidly. Newspapers were filled with outlandish theories of the epidemic's cause and long lists of the dead. The epidemic disappeared in 1919, but it left many

Jan. 26 To promote **food conservation,** Food Administrator Herbert Hoover called for one meatless day, two wheatless days, and two porkless days each week.

Mar. 7 **U.S. figure skating championships** were won by Mrs. Seton R. Beresford of Great Britain, women's singles; Nathaniel W. Niles of Boston, men's singles; and Theresa Weld of Boston and Nathaniel W. Niles, pairs.

May 11 The 44th annual **Kentucky Derby** was won by Exterminator, one of the great American racehorses, with a time of 2:10⁴/₅. The jockey was Willie Knapp.

May 15 The 43rd annual **Preakness Stakes** was run in two sections this year. The first was won by War Cloud, with a time of 1:53³/₅. The jockey was Johnny Loftus. The second was won by Jack Hare, Jr., with a time of 1:53²/₅. The jockey was C. Peak.

June 15 The 50th annual **Belmont Stakes** was won by Johren, with a time of 2:20²/₅. The jockey was Frankie Robinson.

June 22 The **U.S. Lawn Tennis Association singles championships** were won by Molla Bjurstedt, for the fourth time in a row, in the women's division and R. Lindley Murray in the men's division (Sept. 3).

July 14 **Quentin Roosevelt,** 21, the youngest son of former Pres. Theodore Roosevelt, was shot down and killed during a dogfight with an enemy plane.

Sept. 1 The **baseball season was cut short** by order of Sec. of War Newton D. Baker.

Sept. 5–11 The 15th annual **World Series** was won by the Boston Red Sox (AL), who beat the Chicago Cubs (NL) four games to two. Each player on the winning team received $1102.51, the all-time low payment to World Series winners.

Oct. 21 A new **typewriting speed record** was established by Margaret B. Owen in New York City. She typed 170 words a minute with no errors.

denied by Sec. of War Newton D. Baker.

Nov. 9   **Kaiser Wilhelm II** of Germany abdicated. Two days later the armistice went into effect and the war was ended.

Nov. 18   Pres. Wilson announced he would attend the **peace conference** in person. Many in the U.S. criticized the announcement as a sign of what they viewed as Wilson's egotism.

Nov. 21   The **Wartime Prohibition Act,** effective from June 30, 1919, until demobilization, was signed by Pres. Wilson. It banned manufacture or sale of liquor except for export.

Aug. 26   *Lightnin'* by Winchell Smith and Frank Bacon opened on Broadway at The Gaiety Theatre. It was destined to have one of the longest runs, 1291 performances, in U.S. stage history.

Dec. 14   *Il Trittico* by Giacomo Puccini, a trio of one-act operas comprising *Il Tabarro, Suor Angelica,* and *Gianni Schicchi,* was given its world premiere at the Metropolitan Opera in New York City.

1919

With the war won, the Allies prepared to make the peace official. At the peace conference convened at Versailles, France, the American delegation was headed by Pres. Woodrow Wilson. His idealism contrasted with the attitudes of England and France, who wanted to punish Germany. When the Treaty of Versailles was signed on June 28, the war was officially ended. Germany was forced to admit guilt for the war and was stripped of Alsace-Lorraine, the Saar Basin, and its overseas colonies. Germany was also to pay reparations, later fixed at $56,000,000,000, and was required to disarm. Wilson got his wish to establish a League of Nations.

Jan. 18   The **peace conference** opened in Paris. For Pres. Woodrow Wilson it was the beginning of a fight to preserve the principles of the 14 points on which he believed a lasting peace should be established. He failed to have many of his most important points included because of the demands of other victorious Allies.

Jan. 29   The **Eighteenth Amendment** to the Constitution, prohibiting transportation and sale of alcoholic beverages, was ratified. It was the first amendment to have a time limit on ratification, seven years, and the only one that was subsequently repealed.

Feb. 14   The draft of the **League of Nations covenant** was presented by Pres. Wilson to the Paris Peace Conference. Wilson embarked from Brest on Feb. 15 for the U.S. Later he returned to Europe, remaining at the peace conference until it ended on June 28 and returning to New York City on July 8.

Mar. 15   The **American Legion,** an organization of war veterans, was formed in Paris by delegates representing 1000 units of the American Expeditionary Force.

July 10   The **Treaty of Versailles** and League of Nations covenant were sent by Pres. Wilson to the Senate for ratification. Wilson declared that acceptance of the treaty would ensure future peace.

Aug. 31   The **Communist Labor Party** of America was founded at Chicago, Ill. The party adopted the

A younger generation of composers was now presenting works that differed from the romantic style. Among them was Charles T. Griffes, whose *The White Peacock* (1915–1916), originally a piano piece, was presented in 1919 in a version orchestrated for ballet at the Rivoli Theater in New York City. It was received with considerable enthusiasm. Griffes composed a major work for orchestra, *The Pleasure Dome of Kubla Khan,* in 1920. That year he died at the age of 35.

Among **books published** this year was *Jurgen, A Comedy of Justice* by James Branch Cabell, an excursion through the world of fantasy, allegory, and escape. A reworking of the story of Faust set in the mythical kingdom of Poictesme, the novel was suppressed because of the erotic adventures of its protagonist. The book became extremely popular and made Cabell's reputation. Other books published this year included *Winesburg, Ohio* by Sherwood Anderson, a series of connected stories hailed by critics and readers, and Anderson's most successful book; *Java Head* by Joseph Hergesheimer, a novel of East and West, and *Linda Condon,* also by Hergesheimer and also a novel; *On the Makaloa Mat* by Jack London, a posthumous collection of stories; *The American Language* by H. L. Mencken, the author's major scholarly work, which he subsequently augmented; and *Ten Days That Shook the World* by John Reed, a firsthand account of the Russian Revolution, later issued with an introduction by Lenin.

Apr. 9   *The Jest* by Edward Sheldon, a play set in medieval Florence, opened at the Plymouth Theatre in New York City and soon became the theatrical success of the season. The cast included John and Lionel Barrymore.

June 2   **Pulitzer prizes** were awarded for the following: fiction, *The Magnificent Ambersons* by

afflicted with Bright's disease, cardiac diseases and tuberculosis.

Oct. 19 The **fourth Liberty Loan drive** ended. Treasury officials estimated that 20,000,000 persons, over half of the adult population, had bought bonds.

Nov. 1 A **subway derailment** on the Brighton Beach line at Malbone St. in Brooklyn, N.Y., virtually destroyed the five-car wooden train and killed nearly 100 persons. The motorman, a dispatcher pressed into service during an ongoing strike, said his brakes had failed.

Nov. 9 **Charlie Chaplin** announced that he had married the actress Mildred Harris at Los Angeles, Calif., on Oct. 23.

Dec. 16 **William Harrison "Jack" Dempsey,** less than a year away from winning the world heavyweight boxing title, knocked out Carl Morris in 14 seconds at New Orleans. On July 27, at Harrison, N.J., he had stopped Fred Fulton in 18 seconds.

1919

Charismatic religious leaders continued to attract followers in large numbers. The latest was Father Divine (George Baker), a black evangelist whose nonsectarian and interracial movement got its start in Harlem, in New York City, during this period. In 1919 his establishment at Sayville, Long Island, N.Y., attracted attention. Divine set up "heavens" for his "angels," mostly women, where he preached fundamentalist religion and stressed the value of economic and social equality and cooperation. Many of his followers believed he was God. During the years of the Great Depression, Father Divine's heavens provided food and shelter for many people.

Behaviorism found its most positive expression in America in *Psychology from the Standpoint of a Behaviorist* by Dr. John B. Watson. His theory that human behavior could be determined entirely by environmental factors provoked controversy among psychologists and the public.

The **Institute for International Education** was established through the efforts of Elihu Root, Nicholas Murray Butler, and Stephen P. Duggan. The institute was sponsored by the Carnegie Endowment for International Peace. The original policymakers declared that the function of the institute was to act as a liaison between students interested in opportunities for international education and "the persons who may make these opportunities available."

July 21 In a **flight accident,** the Goodyear Tire and Rubber Company balloon *Wing Foot* crashed into the Illinois Trust and Savings Bank at La Salle and Jackson streets in Chicago, killing 12 persons and injuring 28.

Jack Dempsey, new and popular king of boxing, who was to set records in coming years, won the world heavyweight boxing championship on July 4. He scored a technical knockout against the defending champion, Jess Willard, after the third round of a bout at Toledo, Ohio. Dempsey fought four championship bouts and one non-title fight as champion, each of which grossed over $1,000,000, an enormous sum in those days. Dempsey was known as the Manassa Mauler (he was born in Manassa, Colo.) and earned more money than any previous boxer in history. In his fights he was ever on the attack, punching savagely. The crowds loved him for it.

This year's **national college football championship** was won by Harvard, with a record of nine wins, no losses, one tie.

The **NHL Stanley Cup** championship was halted because of an outbreak of influenza, which incapacitated several players and killed one. The Seattle Metropolitans and Montreal Canadiens were tied at two games each, with one tie game.

Jan. 1 The fifth **Tournament of Roses Association football game** (Rose Bowl) was won by the Great Lakes Naval Training Station team, which beat the Mare Island Marines 17–0.

Apr. 19 The 23rd **Boston Marathon** was won by Carl W. A. Linder of Quincy, Mass., with a time of 2 hrs., 29 min., 13 sec.

May 10 The 45th annual **Kentucky Derby** was won by Sir Barton, ridden by Johnny Loftus, with a time of 2:09⅘. Sir Barton, ridden by Loftus, went on to win the Preakness and Belmont Stakes, thereby becoming the first horse to win racing's Triple Crown.

May 14 The 44th annual **Preakness Stakes** was won by Sir Barton, with a time of 1:53. The jockey was Johnny Loftus.

May 31 The seventh annual **Indianapolis 500** auto race marked the resumption of the racing classic after

platform of the Third International, including a badge featuring the hammer and sickle encircled by strands of wheat. The party motto was "Workers of the world unite!"

Sept. 3 Pres. Wilson began a **campaign to promote the Treaty of Versailles** and the League of Nations with a speech at Columbus, Ohio. Wilson undertook the nationwide tour against the advice of his doctors and associates. He was obviously exhausted, suffering from what then was called brain fog.

Sept. 26 Pres. **Wilson suffered a stroke** while traveling to Wichita, Kans. His national tour was halted and he was taken back to Washington, D.C.

Oct. 28 The **Volstead Act,** or National Prohibition Act, was passed by Congress over Pres. Wilson's veto of the previous day. The act defined as intoxicating liquor any beverage containing at least one-half of 1% alcohol and provided for enforcement of the provisions of the Eighteenth Amendment.

Nov. 19 The **Treaty of Versailles** failed to achieve ratification in the Senate by a vote of 55–39.

Booth Tarkington; biography, *The Education of Henry Adams* by Henry Adams; poetry, *Old Road to Paradise* by Margaret Widdemer and *Cornhuskers* by Carl Sandburg.

Aug. 7 An **actors' strike resulted in the closing** of 12 theaters in New York City and others in Boston, Philadelphia, and Chicago. The actors pressed for recognition of Actors' Equity Association.

Oct. 7 *Apple Blossoms,* a romantic opera by Fritz Kreisler and Victor Jacoby, opened at the Globe Theatre in New York City. It featured the dancing of Fred and Adele Astaire and scored a success.

Dec. 15 *Abraham Lincoln* by John Drinkwater, the British playwright, opened at the Cort Theatre in New York City. With Frank McGlynn in the leading role, the play was praised by critics as the best of the season.

1920

The presidential election of 1920 was in part a referendum on whether the U.S. should join the League of Nations. The Democratic nominee, James M. Cox, pledged to do his best to take America into the league. The Republican platform straddled the issue; candidate Warren G. Harding did not seem to feel strongly either way. Harding's election was an indicator that the American people wanted to forget the war. They rejected Woodrow Wilson's idealism and returned to everyday pursuits. This was the first presidential election in which women could vote, and they apparently voted the same way as the men—overwhelmingly Republican.

The U.S. **Census** recorded a population of 105,710,-620. The center of population was placed at eight miles south-southeast of Spencer, Owen County, Ind. For the first time a decline was recorded in rural population to less than 50% of the total. The number of farm residents had dwindled to less than 30%.

Apr. 15 In what came to be called the **Sacco and Vanzetti** case, Frank Parmenter and Alexander Berardelli, paymaster and guard for a shoe factory in South Braintree, Mass., were shot and killed. The payroll they were carrying was seized by the murderers. Three weeks later Nicola Sacco and Bartolomeo Vanzetti, workmen of Brockton, Mass., were arrested and charged with the crime.

What was to become a new industry and a new system of public entertainment and communication got its start on Nov. 2, 1920, when radio station KDKA in Pittsburgh, Pa., broadcast the results of the presidential election. There were few listeners, but for the first time radio broadcasting had become a service for the general public. By 1922 there were about 500 stations, but conditions were chaotic because all employed the same wavelength. Sec. of Commerce Herbert Hoover called a conference for Feb. 27, 1922; there, a system for allocating wavelengths was agreed on. In 1921 Americans were to spend about $10,000,000 on radio sets and parts.

Among **books published** this year was *Main Street* by Sinclair Lewis, a novel about life in a midwestern town that caused a sensation across the country and established Lewis as a leading literary figure. The novel, a bitter indictment of the drabness, hypocrisy, stupidity, and pride of the residents of Gopher Prairie, Minn., became an American classic. Other books published this year included *The Ordeal of Mark Twain* by Van Wyck Brooks, a controversial study of the great author; *This Side of Paradise* by F. Scott Fitzgerald, the author's first novel and a smashing success; *Miss Lulu Bett* by Zona Gale, a novel of rural life in the Middle West; *A Few Figs from Thistles,* a collection of poetry by Edna St. Vincent Millay; *The Great Impersonation* by E. Phillips

| Business and Industry; Science; Education; Philosophy and Religion   III | IV   Sports; Social Issues and Crime; Folkways; Fashion; Holidays |

July 23 **Hogs** on the hoof brought $23.50 a hundredweight at the Chicago stockyards, the highest price until that time.

Sept. 9 **A police strike in Boston** began when the policemen's union called its members off the job. Some 1117 out of 1544 patrolmen walked off their jobs. Many merchants locked up their shops, but looting occurred on a wide scale. New police were hired and the strike was put down. Gov. Calvin Coolidge told AFL president Samuel Gompers: "There is no right to strike against the public safety by anybody, anywhere, any time," a sentence that became well known.

Nov. 20 The **first municipal airport** in the U.S., in Tucson, Ariz., was inaugurated. The field, south of Tucson, is still in use.

a two-year suspension. Howard Wilcox won, completing the course in 5 hrs., 40 min., 42.87 sec., with an average speed of 88.05 mph.

June 11 The **U.S. Open golf tournament** was won by Walter Hagen.

June 11 The 51st annual **Belmont Stakes** was won by Sir Barton, with a time of 2:17²/₅. The jockey was Johnny Loftus.

June 21 The **U.S. Lawn Tennis Association singles championships** were won by Hazel Hotchkiss in the women's division and William M. Johnston in the men's division (Sept. 4).

Sept. 20 The **PGA golf tournament** was won by Jim Barnes.

Oct. 1–9 The 16th annual **World Series** was won by the Cincinnati Reds (NL), who defeated the Chicago White Sox (AL) five games to three in a best-of-nine series, which the major leagues adopted from 1919 through 1921.

1920

A new era in transportation and communication was opened this year when the first New York to California mail plane left New York City on Sept. 7, arriving in San Francisco on Sept. 11. At first airmail service was difficult and risky. The planes were barely more than canvas and wood held together with wire, and instrumentation was virtually nonexistent. A plane's range was small, which meant the pilots had to hop from field to field to get across the country. Flying in bad weather was extremely dangerous. Nonetheless, many pilots who had learned to fly during World War I found the air service to their liking. Aircraft technology grew steadily through the 1920s and 1930s, and airmail service, like air transportation itself, became a fact of life.

Illiteracy in the U.S. reached a new low of 6% of the population, a decline of 1.7% from 1910 and a decline of 14% from 1870.

The **first graduate school of geography** in the U.S. was organized at Clark University in Worcester, Mass. Wallace Walter Atwood, formerly professor of physiography at Harvard University, had become president of Clark and had organized the school of geography with himself as director.

Whatever might happen in other sports, finance, or politics, American fans found it hard to believe scandal could ever touch baseball. Yet on Sept. 28, 1920, eight members of the Chicago White Sox (AL) were indicted on charges of having taken bribes to throw the World Series with the Cincinnati Reds the previous fall. Sportswriters soon referred to the team as the Black Sox, a name that stuck. On Aug. 2, 1921, after a few hours of deliberation, a jury acquitted the players. While spectators cheered, the jurors carried the players around on their shoulders. There was considerable doubt as to the justice of the verdict, and the players were banned from organized baseball.

The term *smoke-filled room* came into use to describe machine politics after the Republican National Convention in June. When the convention became hopelessly deadlocked over a presidential candidate, Ohio politician Harry M. Daugherty told the press: "The convention will be dead-locked, and after the other candidates have gone their limit, some twelve or fifteen men, worn out and bleary-eyed for lack of sleep, will sit down about two o'clock in the morning around a table in a smoke-filled room in some hotel and decide the nomination. When that time comes, Harding will be selected."

This year's **national college football championship** was won by California, with a record of nine wins, no losses, no ties.

Jan. 1 The sixth **Tournament of Roses Association**

May 5–10   The **Socialist Labor Party National Convention** nominated William Wesley Cox of St. Louis, Mo., for the presidency and August Gillhaus of Brooklyn, N.Y., for the vice presidency.

May 8–14   The **Socialist Party National Convention** nominated Eugene V. Debs of Indiana for the presidency, for the fifth time, and Seymour Stedman of Ohio for the vice presidency. Debs was serving a ten-year prison sentence.

June 8–12   The **Republican National Convention** nominated Warren G. Harding of Ohio for the presidency and Gov. Calvin Coolidge of Massachusetts for the vice presidency. The nomination was decided on the tenth ballot.

June 12   The **Farmer Labor Party** was formed in Chicago from a section of the National Labor Party.

June 28–July 5   The **Democratic National Convention** nominated Gov. James M. Cox of Ohio for the presidency and Franklin D. Roosevelt of New York for the vice presidency. Other chief candidates for the hotly contested presidential nomination had been A. Mitchell Palmer, attorney general in Pres. Woodrow Wilson's Cabinet, and former Sec. of the Treasury William G. McAdoo.

July 13–16   The **Farmer Labor Party National Convention** nominated Parley P. Christensen of Utah for the presidency and Max S. Hayes of Ohio for the vice presidency.

July 21–22   The **Prohibition Party National Convention** nominated Aaron S. Watkins of Ohio for the presidency and David Leigh Colvin of New York for the vice presidency.

Nov. 2   **Warren G. Harding was elected president** of the United States. Calvin Coolidge was elected vice president. The electoral vote was Harding, 404; James M. Cox, Democratic candidate, 127. The popular vote was Harding, 16,152,200; Cox, 9,147,353; Eugene V. Debs, Socialist candidate, 919,799; Aaron S. Watkins, Prohibition candidate, 189,408; W. W. Cox, Socialist Labor candidate, 31,175; Parley P. Christensen, Farmer Labor candidate, 26,541. The Republicans increased their majorities in both houses, leading 59–37 in the Senate and 301–131, with one minor party seat and two vacancies, in the House.

Oppenheim, an adventure story that sold more than 1,000,000 copies; *Smoke and Steel* by Carl Sandburg, poetry; and *The Age of Innocence* by Edith Wharton, a novel of New York City society in the 1870s.

New York City became the theatrical center of the world in the early 1920s, partly because of the influx of theatrical greats to the U.S. after the war. Among the prominent arrivals were Eleanora Duse, the actress; Nikita Baliev, the manager; Max Reinhardt, the manager and director; and the Moscow Art Players.

Some **popular songs** of the year were "Japanese Sandman," "Margie," "Avalon," and "Whispering."

Feb. 2   *Beyond the Horizon* by Eugene O'Neill opened at the Morosco Theatre in New York City.

June 2   **Pulitzer prizes** were awarded for the following: biography, *The Life of John Marshall* by Albert J. Beveridge; history, *The War with Mexico* by Justin H. Smith; drama, *Beyond the Horizon* by Eugene O'Neill.

Nov. 1   *The Emperor Jones* by Eugene O'Neill opened at the Neighborhood Playhouse in New York City. The play cast aside the conventions of theater. In eight scenes the themes of justice, retribution, and reversion to the primitive were explored through the experiences of a black porter who becomes leader of a West Indies nation. The effect of the play was heightened by the use of drums throughout the production.

Dec. 21   *Sally,* a musical extravaganza by Jerome Kern, opened at the New Amsterdam Theatre in New York City. It broke all box office records by grossing $38,985 in one week.

| Business and Industry; Science; Education; Philosophy and Religion III | | IV Sports; Social Issues and Crime; Folkways; Fashion; Holidays |

The average **life expectancy** in the U.S., as determined by the Bureau of Public Health, was 54.09 years; in 1901 it had been 49.24 years.

The pragmatic philosophy of **John Dewey** found militant expression in his *Reconstruction in Philosophy.* Dewey derided metaphysics as the product of an aristocratic class, a philosophy of escapism that could not come to grips with the practical problems of a democratic society.

The **first measurement of a star** was accomplished by Albert A. Michelson, who calculated a stellar diameter with the aid of the interferometer he had invented in 1880. He demonstrated that the diameter of Alpha Orionis was 260,000,000 miles.

Rail mileage in the U.S. reached its all-time peak at 253,000, as contrasted with 31,000 at the close of the Civil War. After 1920, railroad mileage began to decline.

Wheat prices reached a new high of $2.33 a bushel.

The **automobile** had become part of American life. By 1923 about 15,000,000 cars were registered. One out of every four families in the U.S. bought or sold an automobile each year. There were 1,000,000 fewer cars than telephones and only 7,000,000 fewer cars than dwelling places.

Jan. 18 In a move to regulate **teachers' political affiliations,** New York State public school teachers were made subject to dismissal for active membership in the Communist Party by a ruling handed down by Acting New York State Commissioner Frank B. Gilbert.

June 5 The **Merchant Marine Act** was passed by Congress as an incentive to U.S. shipping. The act specified that government-owned ships be sold to U.S. shipping companies. The Merchant Fleet Corporation was empowered to supply loans to U.S. shippers and to operate unsold government vessels.

football game (Rose Bowl) was won by Harvard, which edged out Oregon 7–6.

Mar. 20 U.S. figure skating championships were won by Sherwin C. Badger, men's singles; Theresa Weld, women's singles; and Theresa Weld and Nathaniel W. Niles, pairs (Mar. 21).

Apr. 1 The **NHL Stanley Cup** championship was won by the Ottawa Senators, who took the fifth game of the series to beat the Seattle Metropolitans three games to two.

Apr. 19 The 24th **Boston Marathon** was won by Peter Trivoulidas of Greece with a time of 2 hrs., 29 min., 31 sec.

Apr. 20–Sept. 12 At the **Olympic Games** in Antwerp, Belgium, the U.S. won the unofficial team championship, winning nine gold medals. Finland was the second-place team.

May 8 The 46th annual **Kentucky Derby** was won by Paul Jones, with a time of 2:09. The jockey was Ral Parr.

May 18 The 45th annual **Preakness Stakes** was won by Man o' War, with a time of 1:51⅗. The jockey was Clarence Kummer.

May 31 The eighth **Indianapolis 500** auto race was won by Gaston Chevrolet, completing the 500-mile course in 5 hrs., 38 min., 32 sec. for an average speed of 88.62 mph.

June 12 The 52nd annual **Belmont Stakes** was won by Man o' War, with a time of 2:14⅕. The jockey was Clarence Kummer.

July 3 At the **Wimbledon** tennis championships in England, William T. Tilden won the men's singles title.

July 9–16 The **Davis Cup** international tennis challenge round was won, for the first time since 1913, by the U.S., which swept Australia in five straight matches.

Aug. 13 The **U.S. Open** golf tournament was won by Ted Ray of England.

Aug. 21 The **PGA** golf tournament was won by J. Fowler Hutchison.

Sept. The **Walker Law,** legalizing boxing in New York State and regulating the conduct of boxing matches, was passed. The subsequent success of boxing in New York led to similar legislation in other states.

Sept. 6 The **U.S. Lawn Tennis Association singles championships** were won by William T. Tilden in the men's division and Mrs. Molla Bjurstedt Mallory in the women's division (Sept. 25).

Oct. 5–12 The 17th annual **World Series** was won by the Cleveland Indians (AL), who beat the Brooklyn Dodgers (NL) five games to two.

Oct. 30 The **Ku Klux Klan** paraded in Jacksonville, Fla. The sudden, rapid growth of the Klan in 1920 aroused much attention in the press.

Exploration and Settlement; Wars; Government; Civil Rights; Statistics **I**		**II** Publishing; Arts and Music; Popular Entertainment; Architecture; Theater

Nov. 20 The **Nobel Peace Prize** was awarded to Pres. Woodrow Wilson in recognition of his efforts to promote world peace through the League of Nations.

1921

The 1920s witnessed several attempts to reduce armaments and lessen the danger of another war. The U.S. invited the major naval powers to the Washington Conference for Limitation of Armament, which opened in Washington, D.C., on Nov. 12, 1921. The U.S. proposed scrapping warships already built and limiting future construction. The conferees agreed on a 5-5-3 ratio for capital ships for the U.S., Great Britain, and Japan. In all, nine treaties were signed on Feb. 6, 1922, including one that restricted use of submarines in warfare and outlawed poison gas, and another in which the U.S., Great Britain, France, and Japan agreed to respect each other's rights over Pacific possessions. Eventually the work of this conference was destroyed by the events leading to World War II, but it did slow down the international arms race for a time.

Jan. 13 **A report on urbanization** by the Census Bureau showed that 51% of Americans lived in cities and towns of more than 2500.

Mar. 4 **Warren G. Harding was inaugurated president** of the United States. The 29th president and a Republican, he died after two years in office.

Apr. 25 Congressman **Andrew Volstead,** author of the Volstead Act of 1919, introduced a new bill to prohibit sale of beer to the sick, even with medical prescriptions.

May 19 The **first generally restrictive immigration act** in the U.S. was signed by Pres. Harding. The act, effective June 3, initiated a quota system that restricted immigration in any given year to 3% of the number of each nationality reported in the Census of 1910. The total number of immigrants allowed to enter in any given year was set at 357,000.

June 3 **Flooding** of the Arkansas R. after a cloudburst caused property damage estimated at $25,000,000, about $15,000,000 of which represented losses in Pueblo, Colo., which was largely destroyed by the flood. More than 1500 persons were reported killed or missing.

June 10 The **Bureau of the Budget** and the office of Comptroller General of the U.S. were established by Congress as part of the Treasury Department. The

The 1920s saw the rise to national prominence of one of the great American humorists and political commentators, William Penn Adair "Will" Rogers, an authentic cowboy, with Indian ancestry, from Oklahoma. Rogers got his start on the stage as a rope twirler. Soon he was commenting wryly on public events. His perceptive remarks took him to fame in the movies and on the stage, especially in the *Ziegfeld Follies,* in which he first appeared in 1915. His newspaper column was syndicated nationally. The growth of radio as an entertainment medium in the late 1920s and early 1930s brought him an immense audience. Typical of his remarks were such gems as, "The U.S. has never lost a war or won a conference," "Everything is funny as long as it happens to somebody else," and "I tell you folks, all politics is applesauce."

Among **books published** this year, the runaway best seller was *The Sheik* by Edith W. Hull, the adventures of a beautiful girl carried off into the desert by an Arab chief. The novel inspired a motion picture of the same name, starring Rudolph Valentino, and a host of imitative books, including the parody *The Shriek* by Charles Somerville. Other books published this year included *The Brimming Cup* by Dorothy Canfield, a novel; *Three Soldiers* by John Dos Passos, a novel dealing with the aftermath of World War I; *A Daughter of the Middle Border* by Hamlin Garland, autobiography; *The Old Soak* by Don Marquis, the journalist and poet; *Collected Poems* by Edwin Arlington Robinson; *Alice Adams* by Booth Tarkington, a novel; and *Nets to Catch the Wind* by Elinor Wylie, poetry.

This year's **popular songs** included "Blue Moon," "If You Would Care for Me," "Look for the Silver Lining," "Kitten of the Keys," "I Never Knew," and "Down in Chinatown."

Apr. 22 In a case of **censorship,** a New York physician, Dr. William Jay Robinson, was fined $250 for publishing and distributing *Love in Marriage* by Dr. Marie C. Stopes.

May 29 **Pulitzer prizes** were awarded for the following: fiction, *The Age of Innocence* by Edith Wharton; biography, *The Americanization of Edward Bok;* history, *The Victory at Sea* by William Sowden Sims in collaboration with Burton J. Hendrick; drama, *Miss Lulu Bett* by Zona Gale.

| Business and Industry; Science; Education; Philosophy and Religion | III | | IV | Sports; Social Issues and Crime; Folkways; Fashion; Holidays |

Nov. 8 Judge **Kenesaw Mountain Landis** of Chicago was appointed baseball commissioner by joint decision of both major leagues.

1921

The war period had brought boom times to American industry and American workers. With the wartime demand for all kinds of goods ended, the nation experienced a depression by the middle of 1921. Fortunately, recovery began as early as the spring of 1922. In its initial stages, the depression brought wage reductions, such as a 22.5% pay cut imposed by the New York Central Railroad on 43,000 workers, and a 15% cut suffered by clothing workers. Sec. of Commerce Herbert Hoover called a national conference on unemployment. It opened on Sept. 21 and recommended a cut in prices instead of wages so that demand would be stimulated. It was also proposed that a program of public works be started to provide jobs.

The **death rate** in the U.S. was 1163.9 per 100,000 population. In 1900 it had been 1755.

Jan. 3 In a significant decision for **labor unions,** the Supreme Court ruled that they could be prosecuted for restraining interstate trade.

Apr. 2 **Albert Einstein,** the celebrated physicist, arrived in New York City from Europe. On Apr. 15, during a lecture at Columbia University on his theory of relativity, he described time as the fourth dimension.

Apr. 30 **Ford Motor Company assets** were reported to be $345,140,557. Henry Ford announced that a temporary crisis had ended. Six months previously, Ford had had 175,000 finished surplus automobiles. Ford then closed his plants and forced the surplus on unwilling dealers. An upsurge of buying saved the day.

May 20 **Marie Curie,** codiscoverer of radium, was presented by Pres. Warren G. Harding with a capsule of radium worth $100,000, contributed by American women.

The Volstead Act, the national prohibition law, was a year old on Jan. 16, but prohibition had not become the law of the land. In fact it fostered the rise of crime in the U.S. and thereby greatly changed America's social fabric. By 1921 bootleggers were doing a good business, although some of the liquor they supplied was of poor quality, even dangerous. Some people made their own, called bathtub gin or homebrew, but others depended on liquor smuggled over the Canadian border. Offshore lay ships loaded with alcoholic beverages, which small speedy boats brought ashore in darkness, defying the Coast Guard. Between 1920 and 1930 some 500,000 people were arrested for violating the Volstead Act.

This year's **national college football championship** was won by Cornell, with a record of eight wins, no losses, no ties.

The **NHL Stanley Cup** was won by the Ottawa Senators, who defeated the Vancouver Millionaires three games to two.

Jan. 1 The seventh **Tournament of Roses Association football game** (Rose Bowl) was won by California, who beat Ohio State 28–0.

Feb. 26–27 **U.S. figure skating championships** were won in Philadelphia by Theresa Weld Blanchard, women's singles; Sherwin C. Badger, men's singles; and Theresa Weld Blanchard and Nathaniel Niles, pairs.

Apr. 19 The 25th **Boston Marathon** was won by Frank Zuna of New York City, with a time of 2 hrs., 18 min., 57.6 sec.

May 7 The 47th annual **Kentucky Derby** was won by Behave Yourself, with a time of 2:04¹/₅. The jockey was Charles Thompson.

May 16 The 46th annual **Preakness Stakes** was won by Broomspun, with a time of 1:54¹/₅. The jockey was F. Coltiletti.

May 30 The ninth annual **Indianapolis 500** auto race was won by Tommy Milton, completing the course in 5 hrs., 34 min., 44.65 sec., with an average speed of 89.62 mph.

June 11 The 53rd annual **Belmont Stakes** was won by Grey Lag, with a time of 2:16⁴/₅. The jockey was Earl Sande.

June 29 At the **Wimbledon** tennis championships, Elizabeth Ryan won the women's singles title. William T. Tilden won the men's title on July 2.

first comptroller general was John Raymond McCarl, who took office on July 1.

June 20   The first woman to preside over the House of Representatives was Rep. Alice Robertson of Oklahoma. She occupied the chair for 30 minutes.

July 2   The **state of war** between the U.S. and Germany was declared at an end by a joint resolution of Congress. The resolution also claimed all rights, reparations, or indemnities awarded to the U.S. under the Treaty of Versailles.

Aug.   A reemergence in the South of the **Ku Klux Klan** was marked by lawlessness. Whippings, brandings, tarrings, and destruction of property were directed against blacks and whites, although no direct motive could be found for some of the violence.

Aug. 25   A **peace treaty with Germany** was signed in Berlin. It stipulated that none of the provisions of the joint resolution of Congress of July 2, 1921, or of the Versailles Treaty would be vitiated by this treaty.

Dec. 23   The prison sentences of **Eugene V. Debs** and 23 others convicted under the Espionage Act of 1917 were commuted by Pres. Harding, with the release of prisoners to take effect on Christmas Day. Debs had served two years and eight months of a ten-year sentence for seditious statements allegedly made at Canton, Ohio, in 1918.

Aug. 13   *Dulcy,* the first comedy by the successful team of George S. Kaufman and Marc Connelly, opened at the Frazee Theatre in New York City.

Sept. 12   *The Circle,* a three-act comedy by W. Somerset Maugham, opened at the Selwyn Theatre in New York City. It starred John Drew and Mrs. Leslie Carter.

Oct. 5   The **first radio coverage of the World Series** was carried by a wireless station set up at the Electrical Show at the 71st Regiment Armory in New York City, and by station WJZ in Newark, N.J. Both stations carried play-by-play bulletins. The first actual play-by-play coverage began in 1922.

Oct. 10   *A Bill of Divorcement,* a comedy by Clemence Dane starring Katharine Cornell and Allan Pollock, opened at the George M. Cohan Theatre in New York City.

Nov. 2   *Anna Christie,* a powerful drama of the waterfront by Eugene O'Neill, opened at the Vanderbilt Theatre in New York City and catapulted O'Neill to international fame.

Nov. 7   *The Perfect Fool,* written, staged, and performed by the comedian Ed Wynn, opened at the George M. Cohan Theatre in New York City.

Nov. 11   The **Unknown Soldier** of World War I was buried at Arlington National Cemetery after lying in state at the Capitol rotunda in Washington, D.C.

1922

A vexing problem of international relations in the postwar world was that of war debts. During World War I and after, U.S. loans to its allies and to newly formed nations totaled $10,350,479,074. Great Britain, France, and Italy were the largest borrowers. In turn, such countries as Great Britain and France were creditors of other nations. The European allies expected to pay their debts with the reparations assessed against Germany by the Treaty of Versailles. Britain had proposed canceling out debts but Pres. Woodrow Wilson had refused. On Feb. 9, 1922, Congress established a Foreign Debt Commission to settle the problem. In the final arrangement, debtor nations accepted obligations of about $11,500,000,000, payable to the U.S. over 62 years at an average interest rate of 2.135%. When Germany became unable to pay reparations, debts owed the U.S. were scaled down in 1925 and 1926.

Feb. 6   The **Nine-Power Treaty** was signed by the nations participating in the Washington Conference.

Jazz, a unique American contribution to music, hit a new peak of popularity and respectability in the 1920s. The period came to be known as the *jazz age.* One of the musicians who made jazz so popular was Louis "Satchmo" Armstrong, who in 1922 joined King Oliver's Creole Jazz Band in Chicago as a cornetist. The melodic development of jazz owed a great deal to Armstrong, and he made solo renditions an important part of band performances. Later Armstrong organized several big bands, appeared on Broadway, and made successful foreign tours.

Among **books published** this year was *The Enormous Room* by E. E. Cummings, the poet and artist. Cummings' only novel, it was based on the author's imprisonment by French authorities during World War I for some indiscreet remarks he made in letters home while serving on the front as an ambulance driver. Other books published this year included *One of Ours* by Willa Cather, a novel; *The Waste Land* by the expatriate poet T. S. Eliot, a remarkable poem echoing the

| Business and Industry; Science;
Education; Philosophy and Religion | III | | IV | Sports; Social Issues and Crime;
Folkways; Fashion; Holidays |

June 25 Samuel Gompers was chosen president of the American Federation of Labor for the 40th time. He polled more than twice as many votes (25,022) as John L. Lewis (12,324), his opponent in the election.

July 21 The possibilities of **concentrated bombing** were shown by an Army test directed by Gen. William "Billy" Mitchell in which the former German battleship *Ostfriesland* was sunk by aircraft. The test was held off Hampton Roads, Va. Many believed that the demonstration vindicated Gen. Mitchell's belief in the superiority of air power over sea power.

Aug. 16 An estimate of **unemployment** throughout the U.S. released by the Labor Department placed the number of jobless at 5,735,000, the greatest number of unemployed of the postwar depression.

Nov. 2 The **American Birth Control League** was founded in New York City under the leadership of Margaret Sanger. It was a combination of the National Birth Control League, which she had founded in 1914, and the Voluntary Parenthood League, founded by Mary Ware Dennett in 1919.

July 2 The **world heavyweight boxing championship** was defended by Jack Dempsey, who knocked out Georges Carpentier in the fourth round. This was the first fight with a $1,000,000 gate.

July 22 The **U.S. Open golf tournament** was won by James M. Barnes.

Aug. 3 In the **Black Sox scandal**, Judge Kenesaw Mountain Landis, the baseball commissioner, ruled that the Chicago White Sox players charged with throwing the 1919 World Series would not be allowed to play again despite their acquittal in 1920.

Aug. 20 The **U.S. Lawn Tennis Association singles championships** were won by Mrs. Molla Bjurstedt Mallory in the women's division and William T. Tilden in the men's division (Sept. 19).

Sept. 3 The **Davis Cup** international tennis challenge round was won by the U.S., defeating the Japanese team in five straight matches.

Sept. 8 The **first Miss America** title was won by Margaret Gorman of Washington, D.C., at the end of a two-day pageant and festival at Atlantic City, N.J.

Sept. 28 The **PGA golf tournament** was won by Gene Sarazen.

Oct. 5–13 The 18th annual **World Series** was won by the New York Giants (NL), who beat the New York Yankees (AL) five games to three.

Nov. 5 **Armistice Day,** Nov. 11, was proclaimed a legal holiday by Pres. Warren G. Harding.

Dec. **Knee-length skirts** for women became the standard fashion by the end of the year, causing much comment in the press.

1922

The year was marked by technical and commercial progress in radio broadcasting, an enterprise that was soon to foster a major industry and profoundly influence American society. On Aug. 28 the first commercial was broadcast over WEAF in New York City, which had begun operation on Aug. 16. The sponsor was the Queensborough Corporation, a real estate firm, that bought ten minutes of air time to extol Hawthorne Court, a group of apartment buildings in Jackson Heights, Queens. This year also saw one of the earliest long-distance relays; it used a telephone hookup to broadcast in New York a football game between the University of Chicago and Princeton University. On Oct. 4 the first radio play-by-play coverage of the World Series, reported directly from the Polo Grounds in New York City by Grantland Rice, was carried by radio station WJZ in Newark, N.J. Radio stations WGY in Schenectady, N.Y., and WBZ in Springfield, Mass., also carried World Series coverage.

The 1920s had more than their share of sensational murder cases, or perhaps it seemed that way because of the extravagant manner in which the press reported them. Typical was the Hall-Mills case, which began on Sept. 16 with the discovery, side by side under a crab apple tree in New Brunswick, N.J., of the bodies of the Rev. Edward Wheeler Hall and his choir leader, Mrs. Eleanor R. Mills. No one was indicted until four years later, when agitation by a New York City tabloid got the case reopened. The dead man's widow, two brothers, and a cousin were indicted for the murders. In the first 11 days of the trial, newsmen sent out some 5,000,000 words of copy. Billy Sunday, the evangelist, was also there to help report. In the end, all the defendants were acquitted and the case was never solved.

The **NHL Stanley Cup** was won by the Toronto St. Pats, who defeated the Vancouver Millionaires three games to two.

This year's **national college football championship**

The contracting countries agreed to respect the territorial integrity of China. Essentially, this was endorsement of the Open Door policy.

Feb. 6 A naval limitation treaty was signed by France, Italy, and Japan, establishing a ten-year moratorium on construction of capital ships and setting a ratio of these ships for the countries. The treaty was to remain in force until Dec. 31, 1936.

Feb. 27 The Nineteenth Amendment to the Constitution, providing for women's suffrage, was declared constitutional by a unanimous decision of the Supreme Court.

Apr. 15 In the first formal action of the investigation that uncovered the Teapot Dome scandal, Sen. John B. Kendrick of Wyoming introduced a resolution that called on Sec. of the Interior Albert B. Fall to explain why the Teapot Dome oil lands in Wyoming, which had been set aside by the Senate for use of the Navy, were being leased secretly to the Mammoth Oil Company, controlled by Harry F. Sinclair. Sen. Kendrick's information had come to him from one of his constituents, a small businessman in Wyoming.

May 13 The first German ambassador to the U.S. since World War I, Otto L. Wiedfeldt, arrived in New York City.

May 26 A bill providing for a Federal Narcotics Control Board was signed by Pres. Warren G. Harding.

Sept. 22 The Cable Act, providing independent citizenship status for married women regardless of the status of their spouses, was signed by Pres. Harding. A woman would not lose her citizenship by marrying an alien; nor would an alien gain it by marrying an American.

Oct. 3 The first woman U.S. senator, Mrs. W. H. Felton, 87, of Cartersville, Ga., was appointed by Gov. Thomas W. Hardwick of Georgia to the seat vacated by the death of Sen. Thomas E. Watson. Voters chose a successor to Felton in November.

Nov. 7 In congressional elections, the Republicans suffered substantial losses but maintained majorities in both houses. In the Senate they led the Democrats 51–43, with two seats going to minor parties. In the House the Republicans lost 76 seats but still led 225–205, with five seats going to minor parties.

disillusionment caused by war and modern life; *Tales of the Jazz Age* by F. Scott Fitzgerald, and *The Beautiful and Damned*, also by Fitzgerald, a novel; *The Covered Wagon* by Emerson Hough, a novel; *Babbitt* by Sinclair Lewis, a novel about a stereotypical midwestern businessman; *Vandemark's Folly* by Herbert Quick, a novel set in Iowa in the mid-nineteenth century, the first of a trilogy that included *The Hawkeye* (1923) and *The Invisible Woman* (1924); *Rootabaga Stories* by Carl Sandburg, a collection of stories for children; and *Merton of the Movies* by Harry Leon Wilson, a novel.

Among the popular songs of the year were "Song of Love," "April Showers," "My Man," "Say It with Music," "Hot Lips," and "Rose of the Rio Grande."

Censorship of books continued. U.S. Post Office officials destroyed 500 copies of *Ulysses* by James Joyce.

Jan. 3 The classic film *Orphans of the Storm* by D. W. Griffith, starring Lillian and Dorothy Gish, opened at the Apollo Theatre in New York City.

Mar. 9 The naturalist drama *The Hairy Ape* by Eugene O'Neill opened at the Provincetown Theatre in New York City. The play focused on the powerful figure of Yank, a ship's coal stoker, and his perception of his position in modern society.

May 21 Pulitzer prizes were awarded for the following: fiction, *Alice Adams* by Booth Tarkington; biography, *A Daughter of the Middle Border* by Hamlin Garland; history, *The Founding of New England* by James Truslow Adams; poetry, *Collected Poems* by Edwin Arlington Robinson; drama, *Anna Christie* by Eugene O'Neill.

May 23 *Abie's Irish Rose* by Anne Nichols opened at the Fulton Theatre in New York City, beginning a record run of 2327 performances before it closed on Oct. 22, 1927. The play dealt with the love of a young Jewish man and an Irish woman.

May 30 The Lincoln Memorial was dedicated in Washington, D.C.

Oct. 9 *R.U.R.* (Rossum's Universal Robots), a play by the Czech writer Karel Capek, translated by Paul Selver and Nigel Playfair, opened at the Garrick Theatre in New York City. The play introduced the term *robot*, with the meaning "automaton."

Oct. 30 The play *Seventh Heaven* by Austin Strong opened at the Booth Theatre in New York City. The play concerned the love of two characters, Diane and Chico, during the war years.

Oct. 30 *Six Characters in Search of an Author,* a landmark drama in modern theater by the Italian playwright Luigi Pirandello, translated by Brock Pemberton, opened at the Princess Theatre in New York City.

The **Evangelical Church** was formed by merger of the United Evangelical Church, which had been formed in the 1890s, and the Evangelical Association.

The first significant **radar research** in the U.S. was conducted by Dr. Hoyt A. Taylor and Leo C. Young of the U.S. Naval Research Aircraft Laboratory in Washington, D.C.

The number of **postage stamps** used by Americans this year was 14,261,948,813; in 1900 3,998,544,564 had been used.

The first successful use of the **Technicolor** film process was made by Herbert T. Kalmus. The process was not to become widely used for motion pictures until almost 20 years later.

Feb. 21   The **aerial explosion** of the lighter-than-air ship *Roma,* after hitting high tension wires at Hampton Roads Army Airbase, Va., killed 34 of its 45-man crew. The airship had been purchased from the Italian government.

May 12   A **20-ton meteor** fell near Blackstone, Va., causing a 500-sq. ft. hole in the earth. A loud explosion was heard, and flames could be seen for miles around.

June 14   The **first president to be heard over radio** was Pres. Warren G. Harding, whose dedication of the Francis Scott Key Memorial in Baltimore was broadcast. The first official government message was not broadcast until Dec. 6, 1923.

Sept. 12   In a major change of the **marriage ceremony,** the House of Bishops of the U.S. Protestant Episcopal Church voted 36–27 to delete the word *obey* from the marriage service.

Oct. 14   The **first mechanical switchboard** was installed in the New York City telephone system. The exchange was called "Pennsylvania."

Nov. 15   Dr. **Alexis Carrel** of the Rockefeller Institute announced his discovery of leukocytes, or white corpuscles, agents in the blood that prevent the spread of infection.

was won by Cornell, with a record of eight wins, no losses, no ties.

Jan. 1   The eighth **Tournament of Roses Association football game** (Rose Bowl) was played to a scoreless tie by Washington and Jefferson College and California.

Mar. 7   **U.S. figure skating championships** were won by Theresa Weld Blanchard, women's singles; Sherwin C. Badger, men's singles; and Theresa Weld Blanchard and Nathaniel W. Niles, pairs.

Apr. 19   The 26th **Boston Marathon** was won by Clarence H. DeMar of Melrose, Mass., with a record time of 2 hrs., 18 min., 10 sec., breaking the old record by 47.53 sec.

May 13   The 48th annual **Kentucky Derby** was won by Morvich, with a time of 2:04⅗. The jockey was Albert Johnson.

May 13   The 47th annual **Preakness Stakes** was won by Pillory, with a time of 1:51⅗. The jockey was L. Morris.

May 30   The tenth annual **Indianapolis 500** auto race was won by Jimmy Murphy, completing the 500-mile course in 5 hrs., 17 min., 30.79 sec. for a record average speed of 94.48 mph.

June 10   The 54th annual **Belmont Stakes** was won by Pillory, with a time of 2:18⅘. The jockey was C. H. Miller.

June 14   The **PGA golf tournament** was won by Charles Hoffner.

July 15   The **U.S. Open golf tournament** was won by Gene Sarazen.

Aug. 19   The **U.S. Lawn Tennis Association singles championships** were won by Molla Bjurstedt Mallory in the women's division and William T. Tilden in the men's division (Sept. 6). Both won for the third consecutive time.

Aug. 28   The **oldest American international team golf match,** the Walker Cup, between the U.S. and Great Britain, was established with the opening of play at the National Golf Links of America, Southampton, N.Y. The U.S. team won on the second day, eight matches to four.

Aug. 31–Sept. 5   The **Davis Cup** international tennis challenge round was won for the third straight year by the U.S., defeating Australia four matches to one.

Sept. 8   The **Miss America** title was won by Mary Campbell, 16, from Columbus, Ohio, at the annual pageant in Atlantic City, N.J.

Oct. 4–8   The 19th annual **World Series** was won by the New York Giants (NL), who took four of five games from the New York Yankees (AL). The second game of the series (Oct. 5) had ended in a 3–3 tie after ten innings, when the game was called on account of darkness.

1923

For the first time since Zachary Taylor's death in 1850, a president of the United States died in office of natural causes. Pres. Warren G. Harding was in poor health by early 1923. His reputation was in decline because friends he had appointed to federal office had proven corrupt or incompetent. Scandals were about to break all around him. To get away from the unpleasantness, Harding began a tour on June 20 of the West and Alaska. He took ill on the return journey and died in a San Francisco hotel on Aug. 2, at the age of 58. Harding died of an embolism while recovering from an attack of ptomaine poisoning and pneumonia, but there were rumors of foul play at the time. At 2:43 A.M. on Aug. 3, Vice Pres. Calvin Coolidge was sworn in as president by his father, a notary public, in the family home in Plymouth, Vt. Harding was buried at Marion, Ohio, on Aug. 10.

Jan. 10 U.S. occupation troops stationed in Germany were ordered to return by Pres. Warren G. Harding.

Mar. 5 The country's **first old age pension grants** were enacted in Montana and Nevada. The Montana pension allotted $25 monthly to qualified septuagenarians.

May 4 A bill repealing the **New York State Prohibition enforcement act** was passed by the state assembly. Despite Pres. Harding's warning that federal authorities would have to take over the enforcement of Prohibition in states that did not do the job themselves, Gov. Alfred E. Smith signed the repeal bill. This was thought by many to have been the beginning of the end of Prohibition.

May 9 Prescriptions for whiskey by physicians were not limited under Prohibition law, declared Judge John C. Knox of the U.S. District Court in New York.

Sept. 15 Oklahoma was placed under martial law by Gov. John Calloway Walton because of terrorist activities of the Ku Klux Klan, which had become a powerful force in Midwest politics. This year several newspapers began exposing the Klan and its secret activities.

Oct. 16 A state law requiring a **literacy test** for new

After jazz was brought north to Chicago by black musicians from New Orleans and other southern cities, white performers took up the style in greater numbers and became important contributors to it. Among them was Leon Bismarck "Bix" Beiderbecke, who was first influenced by recordings of the Original Dixieland Band. It did not take him long to win a reputation as a cornetist, and in 1923 he organized the Wolverine Orchestra in Chicago. Beiderbecke was also a pianist and a composer, one of his works being "In a Mist." A lonely, driven man, he died in 1931 at age 28.

Among **books published** this year was a slim volume entitled *Three Stories & Ten Poems* by Ernest Hemingway, a young expatriate living in France, where the book was published. Two of the stories were republished in Hemingway's *In Our Time* (1925). Other books published this year included *A Lost Lady* by Willa Cather, a novel; *Tulips and Chimneys* by E. E. Cummings, the author's first volume of poetry; *Streets of Night* by John Dos Passos, a novel; *New Hampshire: A Poem with Notes and Grace Notes* by Robert Frost; *Collected Poems* by Vachel Lindsay; *Harmonium* by Wallace Stevens, poetry; and *Cane* by Jean Toomer, a collection of poetry, stories, and a play focusing on the black experience in the U.S.

This year's **popular songs** included "Yes, We Have No Bananas," "Barney Google," "Sonny Boy," and "Linger Awhile."

Feb. 10 *Icebound,* a play by Owen Davis about the members of a Maine family, opened at the Harris Theatre in New York City.

Feb. 27 *Humoresque,* a play by Fannie Hurst and starring Laurette Taylor and Luther J. Adler, opened at the Vanderbilt Theatre in New York City.

Mar. 2 *Roger Bloomer,* an expressionistic play by John Howard Lawson satirizing American middle-class values, opened at the Equity Theatre in New York City.

Mar. 19 *The Adding Machine* by Elmer Rice, a play concerning the life, death, and afterlife of a man discharged from his job after 25 years of counting figures, opened at the Garrick Theatre in New York City. Like *Roger Bloomer,* by John Howard Lawson, the play showed the influence of the expressionist movement in theater.

May 13 **Pulitzer prizes** were awarded for the following: fiction, *One of Ours* by Willa Cather; biography, *The Life and Letters of Walter H. Page* by Burton J. Hendrick; history, *The Supreme Court in United States History* by Charles Warren; poetry, *The Ballad of the Harp-Weaver, A Few Figs from Thistles,* and *Eight Sonnets,* all by Edna St. Vincent Millay; drama, *Icebound* by Owen Davis.

Business and Industry; Science; Education; Philosophy and Religion	III		IV	Sports; Social Issues and Crime; Folkways; Fashion; Holidays

1923

Inventors and scientists had been working for years at laying the technical groundwork for radio, talking pictures, and television. Lee De Forest, who came to be called "the father of radio" as early as 1906, had developed the triode vacuum tube, which made long-distance telephone and radio communications a possibility. On Mar. 13, 1923, in New York City, De Forest demonstrated a sound motion picture process called Phonofilm. The film he showed included a performance by an orchestra. De Forest held more than 300 patents, yet his career was not an easy one. Like many other inventors during this period, De Forest struggled to secure capital for research and was at times forced into court to protect his patent and licensing rights.

Auto production continued to climb. More autos were built this year than had been produced in the first 15 years of the twentieth century. About 15,000,000 passenger cars were in use in the U.S. New York, New Jersey, Pennsylvania, and Maryland combined had more autos than all the rest of the world outside the U.S.

The DuPont Corporation began the production of **cellophane** through the purchase of American rights to the Swiss patent of Jacques F. Brandenberger. Swiss factories had been producing cellophane, cellulose film, since 1912.

Jan. William Jennings Bryan stirred up controversy over evolution in addressing a group of ministers in St. Paul, Minn. The theory of evolution, he said, is a "program of infidelity masquerading under the name of science." The debate was taken up by newspapers, which gave the names *fundamentalist* and *modernist* to the two sides.

Apr. 9 A minimum wage law for women and children in the District of Columbia was ruled unconstitutional by the U.S. Supreme Court.

Oct. 6 A new average air speed record of 243.76 mph was set by Lt. Al Williams, flying a Curtiss racer at the Pulitzer Trophy contest in St. Louis, Mo.

Nov. 6 A patent for the first electric shaver was issued to Col. Jacob Schick. Schick received several additional patents and in 1931 established his own company, the Schick Dry Shaver Company, Inc., Stamford, Conn.

Thanks to the rugged personality and heroic achievements of Jack Dempsey as heavyweight boxing champion, the sport was more popular than ever and had attained a degree of respectability. On the night of Sept. 14, Dempsey met challenger Luis Angel Firpo, called the Wild Bull of the Pampas. The fight, held at the Polo Grounds in New York City, was one of the most exciting ever seen. Firpo was knocked out in the second round after 3 min., 57 sec. fighting time, but not before there had been 11 knockdowns, including one on a first-round punch by Firpo that knocked Dempsey out of the ring. Sportswriters into whose laps he fell shoved the champion back into the ring in time to save him from losing his crown.

The political slogan "**It won't be Long now**" made the rounds in the Louisiana gubernatorial elections and brought to public notice a new, boisterous figure, Huey Long. An opponent of the 30-year-old upstart coined the phrase. Long ran third in the election.

This year's **national college football championship** was won by Illinois, with a record of eight wins, no losses, no ties.

The **NHL Stanley Cup** was won by the Ottawa Senators, who beat the Vancouver Millionaires three games to one. They also defeated the Edmonton Eskimos in two straight games.

Jan. 1 The ninth **Tournament of Roses Association football game**, which was officially named the Rose Bowl game this year, was won by Southern California, beating Penn State 14–3.

Feb. 15–16 U.S. figure skating championships were won by Theresa Weld Blanchard, women's singles; Sherwin C. Badger, men's singles; and Theresa Weld Blanchard and Nathaniel W. Niles, pairs.

Apr. 18 Yankee Stadium in New York City was opened. It became the home park of the New York Yankees (AL).

Apr. 19 The 27th **Boston Marathon** was won by Clarence H. DeMar of Melrose, Mass., with a time of 2 hrs., 23 min., 47.35 sec.

May 12 The 48th annual **Preakness Stakes** was won by Vigil, with a time of 1:53³/₅. The jockey was Benny Marinelli.

May 19 The 49th annual **Kentucky Derby** was won by Zev, with a time of 2:05²/₅. The jockey was Earl Sande, who scored his first Kentucky Derby victory.

May 30 The 11th annual **Indianapolis 500** auto race was won by Tommy Milton, completing the 500-mile course in 5 hrs., 29 min., 50.17 sec. with an average speed of 90.95 mph.

June 9 The 55th annual **Belmont Stakes** was won by Zev, with a time of 2:19. The jockey was Earl Sande.

voters was sustained by the New York State Court of Appeals.

Oct. 25 The first meeting of the Senate subcommittee to investigate the **Teapot Dome** oil leases was held, with Sen. Thomas J. Walsh, Democrat of Montana, as chairman. Walsh had used the 18 months since his appointment as chairman to study the case, and during that time public interest in it had died down. It was quickly reawakened by the hearings.

Dec. 6 In his first annual **message to Congress,** Pres. Coolidge announced support for U.S. adherence to the World Court and Prohibition enforcement. Coolidge also stated his belief in government noninterference with business and in lower taxes.

May 23 In a case of theatrical **censorship,** the owner of the play *God of Vengeance* by Sholem Asch and 12 cast members were convicted of immoral behavior for presenting the play at the Apollo Theatre in New York City in March. It was the second time anyone had been convicted under the law. The first instance had been some 30 years earlier, in connection with the burlesque *Orange Blossoms.*

Sept. 3 *Poppy,* a musical comedy by Dorothy Donnelly, Stephen Jones, and Arthur Samuels, starring Madge Kennedy and W. C. Fields, opened at the Apollo Theatre in New York City.

Nov. 28 *Laugh, Clown, Laugh!,* adapted from the Italian playwright Fausto Martini's drama *Ridi, Pagliaccio* by David Belasco and Tom Cushing, opened at the Belasco Theatre in New York City. It starred Lionel Barrymore as the tragic figure Tito Beppi, the clown destroyed by love.

1924

Republican victory in the presidential election was anticipated. The Democrats had torn themselves apart in a struggle for the nomination. Gov. Alfred E. Smith of New York represented the East and the big cities, and William G. McAdoo of Tennessee, the southern and western parts of the country. The eventual nominee was John W. Davis, an able man but almost unknown to the voters. The Republicans, on the other hand, could point with pride to Calvin Coolidge and a record of prosperity. The Democrats tried to make much of the scandals of the Harding administration but failed to stir the electorate. In fact, despite a strong third party in the field, only about half of those eligible to vote did so.

Mar. 18 The **Soldiers' Bonus Bill,** providing for paid-up 20-year annuities for most veterans at a cost of $2,000,000,000, was passed by the House of Representatives. Only veterans entitled to less than $50 adjusted compensation were to be paid in cash. The bill was passed by the Senate on Apr. 23, vetoed by Pres. Calvin Coolidge on May 15, and repassed over the veto on May 17 by the House and May 19 by the Senate.

May 11–13 The **Socialist Labor Party National Convention** nominated Frank T. Johns of Oregon for the presidency and Verne L. Reynolds of Maryland for the vice presidency.

June 5 The **Prohibition Party National Convention** nominated Herman P. Faris of Missouri for the presidency and Marie C. Brehm of California for the vice presidency.

Light operas were a very popular form of theatrical entertainment in the 1920s. They were upbeat and romantic for the most part, and this went well with the generally content American public. No composer of such works was more popular than Rudolf Friml, who was born in Prague in 1881 and settled in New York City in 1906. Friml wrote the music for some 33 light operas, most of which now are long forgotten. One of his most popular works was *Rose Marie,* with libretto by Otto Harbach and Oscar Hammerstein II and music by Friml and Herbert Stothart. It opened at the Imperial Theatre in New York on Sept. 2 and ran for 557 performances. *Rose Marie* contained two of Friml's best remembered songs, "Indian Love Call" and "Rose Marie." Two other well-known Friml operettas were *The Firefly* (1912) and *The Vagabond King* (1925).

Among **books published** this year was *Billy Budd, Foretopman* by Herman Melville, a work of beauty and force that the author completed shortly before his death in 1891. The manuscript was found in a tin box among the Melville family possessions. The novel's publication was an important event in the growing movement to recognize Melville as a literary giant. Other books published this year included *The Marble Faun* by William Faulkner, poetry; *Tamar and Other Poems* by Robinson Jeffers; *How to Write Short Stories* by Ring Lardner, a collection that brought him recognition as a perceptive and accomplished writer; and the *Autobiography* of Mark Twain.

This year's **popular songs** included "Big Butter and Egg Man," "Lady, Be Good," "Indian Love Call," "I'll

| Business and Industry; Science; Education; Philosophy and Religion **III** | | Sports; Social Issues and Crime; Folkways; Fashion; Holidays **IV** |

Nov. 13 The **Nobel Prize in Physics** was awarded to Robert Andrews Millikan of the California Institute of Technology for his "work on the elementary electric charge and on the photoelectric effect" while professor of physics at the University of Chicago from 1906 and 1916.

Dec. 6 The **first broadcast of an official presidential address** was that of Pres. Calvin Coolidge's second annual address to Congress. The transmission was so clear that technicians in St. Louis, Mo., telephoned Washington, D.C., to ask about the occasional rustling noise; they were told it was caused by the president turning the pages of his address. The message was carried by several stations from Rhode Island to Texas.

July 15 The **U.S. Open golf tournament** was won by Robert T. "Bobby" Jones, an amateur who beat Robert Cruickshank by two strokes in a playoff round.

Aug. 18 The **U.S. Lawn Tennis Association singles championships** were won by Helen Wills in the women's division and William T. Tilden in the men's division (Sept. 15).

Aug. 30–Sept. 1 The **Davis Cup** international tennis challenge round was won for the fourth year in a row by the U.S., defeating Australia four matches to one.

Sept. 7 The **Miss America** title was won for the second time by Mary Campbell, 17, from Columbus, Ohio, at the annual pageant in Atlantic City, N.J.

Sept. 29 The **PGA golf tournament** was won by Gene Sarazen, who beat Walter Hagen by one stroke.

Oct. 10–15 The 20th annual **World Series** was won by the New York Yankees (AL), defeating the New York Giants (NL) four games to two.

1924

By early 1923 Germany, in default in reparations payments called for by the Treaty of Versailles, was undergoing extreme monetary inflation. It was clear that economic instability in Europe was a danger to U.S. economic growth. On Dec. 15, 1923, Pres. Calvin Coolidge had appointed Charles G. Dawes, a banker and government official, to head a commission to study the problem. On Apr. 9, 1924, the commission proposed what came to be known as the Dawes Plan, a program to reorganize German debt payments and stabilize its currency. The plan substantially reduced Germany's reparations, which had been set at the enormous sum of 132,000,000,000 marks. Payments would be graduated from 1,000,000,000 gold marks in the first year to 2,500,-000,000 in the fifth. The plan was agreed to at an international conference that began in London on July 16, and that went into effect on Sept. 1. The economic crisis was alleviated for a time.

Ford auto prices hit their lowest point after a series of price cuts: $290 without a self-starter. The price for the Model T had been $950 back in 1909.

A test run for **transcontinental airmail** was made in 27 hours from New York City to San Francisco. The best time in 1848 was three months (by ship to Panama, then overland across the Isthmus and by ship to San Francisco); in 1869 it took seven and a half days by rail.

Americans' general enthusiasm for sports made college football a natural for prime interest, professional football being in its infancy in the early 1920s. Among players of the time, the best known was Harold "Red" Grange of the University of Illinois, dubbed the Galloping Ghost of the Gridiron, who scored 31 touchdowns in his college career. The best-known team was Notre Dame, known as the Fighting Irish even though many of the team's players had no Irish connection. This year Notre Dame won all nine of its games and took the national college football championship. The team's success was due in large part to its coach, Knute Rockne, who did much to revolutionize the game by stressing the use of the forward pass and by drilling his players to near perfection.

This year's **national college football championship** was won by Notre Dame, with a record of ten wins, no losses, no ties.

Jan. 1 The tenth **Rose Bowl** football game was fought to a 14–14 tie by Washington and Navy.

Jan. 25–Feb. 4 The **first Winter Olympics** was held at Chamonix, France. The U.S. finished fourth in the unofficial team standings, behind Norway, Finland, and Great Britain, and won one gold medal.

Feb. 18 **U.S. figure skating championships** were won in Philadelphia by Theresa Weld Blanchard, women's singles; Sherwin W. Badger, men's singles; and Theresa Weld Blanchard and Nathaniel W. Niles, pairs.

Mar. 25 The **NHL Stanley Cup** was won by the Montreal Canadiens, who defeated the Vancouver Million-

June 12 The **Republican National Convention** nominated Pres. **Coolidge** for reelection and Charles G. Dawes of Illinois for the vice presidency.

June 19 The **Farmer-Labor Progressive Party National Convention** nominated Duncan MacDonald of Illinois for the presidency and William Bouck of Washington for the vice presidency. On July 10 the candidates stepped down and William Z. Foster and Benjamin Gitlow became the nominees.

June 30 In the **Teapot Dome** oil leasing scandal, a federal grand jury indicted Albert B. Fall, former secretary of the interior; Harry Sinclair, president of Mammoth Oil Company; Edward L. Doheny, president of Pan-American Oil and Transport Company; and Edward L. Doheny, Jr., on charges of bribery and conspiracy to defraud the United States. Sinclair was accused of bribing Fall to secure a lease for the Teapot Dome reserve in Wyoming. The Dohenys were charged with giving a $100,000 bribe to Fall in return for leases on the Elk Hills naval reserve in California.

July 4 The **Conference for Progressive Political Action** nominated Sen. **Robert M. La Follette,** Republican of Wisconsin, for the presidency and (July 18) Sen. Burton K. Wheeler of Montana for the vice presidency.

July 9 The **Democratic National Convention** nominated **John W. Davis** of West Virginia for the presidency on the 103rd ballot. Charles W. Bryan of Nebraska, brother of William Jennings Bryan, was nominated for the vice presidency.

July 10 The **Workers' Party National Convention** nominated William Z. Foster of Illinois for the presidency and Benjamin Gitlow of New York for the vice presidency.

Nov. 4 **Calvin Coolidge was reelected president** of the United States. Charles G. Dawes was elected vice president. The electoral vote was Coolidge, 382; John W. Davis, Democratic candidate, 136; Robert M. La Follette, Progressive candidate, 13. The popular vote was Coolidge, 15,725,016; Davis, 8,385,503; La Follette, 4,822,856; Herman P. Faris, Prohibition candidate, 57,520; Frank T. Johns, Socialist Labor candidate, 36,429; and William Z. Foster, Farmer-Labor Progressive and Workers' Party candidate, 36,386. In congressional elections the Republicans picked up five seats in the Senate for a 56–39 majority, with one seat going to a minor party. In the House the Republicans picked up 22 seats for a 247–183 majority, with four seats going to minor parties.

See You in My Dreams," "Yes, Sir, That's My Baby," and "Sweet Georgia Brown."

Feb. 12 *Rhapsody in Blue* by George Gershwin was first performed, with Gershwin himself at the piano, at Aeolian Hall in New York City. Gershwin followed a concert by Paul Whiteman and his orchestra, which played, among other things, four *Serenades* written especially for the event by Victor Herbert, who was in the audience.

May 11 **Pulitzer prizes** were awarded for the following: fiction, *The Able McLaughlins* by Margaret Wilson; biography, *From Immigrant to Inventor* by Michael I. Pupin; history, *The American Revolution—A Constitutional Interpretation* by Charles Howard McIlwain; poetry, *New Hampshire: A Poem with Notes and Grace Notes* by Robert Frost; drama, *Hell-Bent fer Heaven* by Hatcher Hughes.

May 15 *All God's Chillun Got Wings* by Eugene O'Neill opened at the Provincetown Playhouse in New York City. It starred Paul Robeson as Jim Harris, a black man who falls in love with and marries a white woman.

Sept. 5 *What Price Glory?* by Maxwell Anderson and Laurence Stallings, an unromantic treatment of war centering on two soldiers in love with the same woman, opened at the Plymouth Theatre in New York City. It starred Louis Wolheim and William Boyd.

Nov. 3 *S.S. Glencairn* by Eugene O'Neill opened at the Provincetown Playhouse in New York City. It comprised four short plays; *The Moon of the Caribbees, Bound East for Cardiff, In the Zone,* and *The Long Voyage Home.*

Nov. 11 *Desire Under the Elms* by Eugene O'Neill, portraying the complicated relations among members of a New England family, opened at the Greenwich Village Theatre. Its cast included Walter Huston, Mary Morris, and Charles Ellis.

Nov. 24 *They Knew What They Wanted* by Sidney Howard, a three-act comedy about a middle-aged California winemaker and his love for a younger woman, opened at the Garrick Theatre in New York City. It starred Pauline Lord, Richard Bennett, and Glenn Anders.

Dec. 2 *The Student Prince,* an operetta by Sigmund Romberg, was presented at the Fifty-Ninth Street Theatre in New York City.

| Business and Industry; Science; Education; Philosophy and Religion **III** | **IV** Sports; Social Issues and Crime; Folkways; Fashion; Holidays |

Jan. 1 The number of **radios** in U.S. homes was over 2,500,000. In 1920 there had been no more than 5000 receivers in the U.S., most of them in the hands of experimenters and technicians.

Mar. 31 An **Oregon public school law** requiring all children of grammar-school age to attend public schools was ruled unconstitutional by the U.S. Supreme Court. The law had been aimed chiefly at Roman Catholic and Lutheran parochial schools.

May 21 The **theory of evolution** was ruled untenable by the General Assembly of the Presbyterian Church at San Antonio, Tex.

May 27 The **Methodist Episcopal General Conference,** meeting at Springfield, Mass., lifted its ban on dancing and theater attendance.

June 2 The struggle against **child labor** took the form of a proposed amendment to the Constitution. But by 1950 only 26 of the necessary 36 states had ratified the amendment.

June 15 The **Ford Motor Company** announced manufacture of its 10,000,000th automobile. Ford had taken seven years to make the first million cars, but only 132 working days to make the tenth million.

Oct. 15 **Dirigible ZR-3,** a German airship, completed the flight from Friedrichshafen, Germany, to Lakehurst, N.J. It was renamed the *Los Angeles* when taken over by the U.S. Navy.

Nov. 30 **Wireless transmission of photographs** from London to New York City was demonstrated by the Radio Corporation of America. It took 20 to 25 minutes for each photograph to be transmitted.

Dec. 13 **Samuel Gompers,** president of the American Federation of Labor from 1886 (except for 1895), died at 74.

aires in two straight games and the Calgary Tigers in two straight games.

Apr. 19 The 28th **Boston Marathon** was won by Clarence H. DeMar of Melrose, Mass., who broke both the Boston Marathon and Olympic Marathon records with a time of 2 hrs., 29 min., 40.15 sec.

May 4–July 27 At the **Summer Olympics** in Paris, France, the U.S. took first place in unofficial team standings for the eighth consecutive time and won 45 gold medals.

May 12 The **PGA golf tournament** was won by Walter Hagen.

May 12 The 49th annual **Preakness Stakes** was won by Nellie Morse, with a time of 1:57^1/$_5$. The jockey was Johnny Merimee.

May 17 The 50th annual **Kentucky Derby** was won by Black Gold, with a time of 2:05^1/$_5$. The jockey was John D. Mooney.

May 30 The 12th annual **Indianapolis 500** auto race was won by Lora L. Corum, completing the 500-mile course in a record 5 hrs., 5 min., 23.51 sec., with an average speed of 98.23 mph.

June 6 The **U.S. Open golf tournament** was won by Cyril Walker, who beat Bobby Jones by three strokes.

June 7 The 56th annual **Belmont Stakes** was won by Mad Play, with a time of 2:18^4/$_5$. The jockey was Earl Sande.

July 21 **Nathan Leopold and Richard Loeb** were sentenced to life imprisonment for the kidnaping and murder of Bobby Franks in one of the strangest and most publicized crime cases of the twentieth century. The two well-educated young men had decided on a random killing, apparently to see what the experience would be like. Loeb was killed by a fellow inmate on Jan. 28, 1936, after 12 years in prison. Leopold was ultimately released on parole on Mar. 13, 1958. He died on Aug. 29, 1971, at age 66.

Aug. 16 The **U.S. Lawn Tennis Association singles championships** were won by Helen Wills in the women's division and William T. Tilden in the men's division (Sept. 2).

Sept. 6 The **Miss America** title was won by Ruth Malcolmson, 18, from Philadelphia, Pa., at the annual pageant in Atlantic City, N.J.

Sept. 11–13 The **Davis Cup** international tennis challenge round was won for the fourth year running by the U.S., defeating Australia in five straight matches.

Oct. 4–10 The 21st annual **World Series** was won by the Washington Senators (AL), defeating the New York Giants (NL) four games to three.

1925

The rapid development of aviation technology and the use of the airplane in World War I combat led to a controversy over the future of military air power. Gen. William "Billy" Mitchell, who had served during the war in the Army's air service, was convinced that air power would dominate future warfare. He set out to prove it and, in tests from 1921 to 1923, had land-based bombers attack and sink obsolete warships off the Virginia coast. In 1923 he predicted that bombers would make battleships useless, an opinion that was resented by Navy admirals. On Sept. 5 and 9, 1925, he charged government officials and military commanders with "incompetency, criminal negligence, and almost treasonable administration of national defense." As a result Mitchell was brought before a court-martial on Oct. 28, charged with "conduct prejudicial to good order and military discipline, insubordination, and utterances contemptuous of the War and Navy departments." On Dec. 17 he was found guilty and suspended without pay from rank, command, and duty for five years. Mitchell resigned from the service on Jan 29, 1926, and died in 1936.

Jan. 5 The **first woman governor** in U.S. history, Mrs. William B. Ross, was inaugurated governor of Wyoming.

Mar. 4 Pres. **Calvin Coolidge was inaugurated** for his first full term as president of the United States.

Mar. 18 The worst **tornado** in U.S. history ripped through eastern Missouri, southern Illinois, and southern Indiana, killing 689 persons and causing great devastation. Hardest hit were the cities of West Frankfort, Murphysboro, and De Soto, Ill., and Princeton, Ind.

Mar. 23 The **Isle of Pines Treaty**, establishing Cuban possession of the Isle of Pines, was ratified by the Senate. The treaty had been pending since 1904.

Aug. 8 The **Ku Klux Klan** held a massive political demonstration in Washington, D.C. Some 40,000 white-robed klansmen and klanswomen marched down Pennsylvania Ave. in a massive parade that reflected the Klan's resurgence in strength during the 1920s. They did not wear their hoods, which were prohibited by a local ordinance against wearing masks. Many of the marchers were seen to raise their arms in a manner much like the fascist salute. It was probably the largest Klan parade on record, although there had been larger gatherings of Klan members.

The early 1920s saw first publication of several magazines that were unlike any published before. They were in keeping with the faster pace of life in the postwar world. *Reader's Digest*, with its condensed articles for quick reading, was founded in 1921. *Time*, a news magazine with a jazzy, know-it-all-style began publication in 1923. And on Feb. 21, 1925, a new type of magazine appeared with the founding of *The New Yorker*, edited by Harold Ross. It was said to be for the "caviar sophisticates" and "not for the old lady in Dubuque." It set new styles in fiction and humor, and featured cartoons that spoke for themselves or carried only one-line captions. Its reviews of books, plays, and films set high standards. The first issue was 32 pages and sold for 15 cents.

Among **books published** this year was *An American Tragedy* by Theodore Dreiser, a novel based on an actual murder in upstate New York in 1906. Dreiser explored the influence of money on human actions as well as the importance of heredity in this story. Other books published included *Manhattan Transfer* by John Dos Passos, a novel that presented in kaleidoscopic fashion a fictional cross-section of New York City; *The Great Gatsby* by F. Scott Fitzgerald, the classic novel of the Jazz Age; *Porgy* by Du Bose Heyward, a novel that was the basis for his successful 1927 play *Porgy and Bess*, written with his wife Dorothy, and George Gershwin's 1935 opera *Porgy and Bess; Roan Stallion, Tamar, and Other Poems* by Robinson Jeffers; *Arrowsmith* by Sinclair Lewis, a novel about an idealistic medical researcher and the forces at work in the world of scientific research; *The Song of the Indian Wars* by John G. Neihardt, the third installment of the poet's *Cycle of the West;* and *A Draft of XVI Cantos* by Ezra Pound, the first part of a continuing work remarkable for its scholarship, poetic versatility and, for most readers, its obscurity.

This year's **popular songs** included "Show Me the Way to Go Home," "Collegiate," "Thanks for the Buggy Ride," and "Don't Bring Lulu."

Jan. 11 *Symphony for Organ and Orchestra* by Aaron Copland was given its premiere performance by the New York Symphony.

Apr. 26 **Pulitzer prizes** were awarded for the following: fiction, *So Big* by Edna Ferber; biography, *Barrett Wendell and His Letters* by M. A. DeWolfe Howe; history, *A History of the American Frontier* by Frederic L. Paxson; poetry, *The Man Who Died Twice* by Edwin Arlington Robinson; drama, *They Knew What They Wanted* by Sidney Howard.

Sept. 16 *No, No, Nanette,* a musical comedy by Otto Harbach, Frank Mandell, Irving Caesar, and Vincent Youmans, had its New York City premiere at the Globe Theatre and soon became the hit musical of the

1925

Labor unions did not benefit from the prosperity of the 1920s. In 1921 the American Federation of Labor had almost 4,000,000 members, but by 1929 it was down to 2,961,096. The recession of 1921–1922 hurt, and employers' associations offered strong opposition to organized labor. In addition, there were unfavorable court decisions, such as the 1923 Supreme Court ruling declaring unconstitutional a minimum wage law in the District of Columbia. The decision challenged the legality of similar laws in several states.

A **survey of businesses** showed that only 89 firms in the whole country had been owned by the same families for 100 years or more.

Of the many **automobile manufacturing companies** that were founded before 1905, only 15 were still in existence: Apperson (1901); Buick (1903); Cadillac (1902); Ford (1903); Franklin (1900); Haynes (1896); Locomobile (1899); Maxwell (1904); Olds (1897); Overland (1902); Packard (1902); Peerless (1900); Pierce-Arrow (1901); Stearns (1900); and Studebaker (1898). More than 1000 had failed.

William Green was elected president of the American Federation of Labor, succeeding Samuel Gompers, who died in 1924.

The **first dry ice** manufactured commercially was made by the Prest-Air Devices Company, Long Island City, N.Y.

An antitoxin for **scarlet fever** was developed by George Frederick and Gladys Henry Dick of Chicago.

Jan. 24 A **total solar eclipse** was seen in New York City for the first time in three centuries.

Apr. 1 In the **largest cash transaction** in U.S. industrial history to date, Dillon, Read & Company, a New York banking house, purchased the Dodge Brothers automobile company for $146,000,000.

May 13 A bill requiring **daily Bible readings** in all public schools was passed by the Florida legislature.

July 10–21 The celebrated **Scopes monkey trial** was held in Dayton, Tenn. John T. Scopes had been arrested on May 5 for teaching the theory of evolution to his students in violation of state law. Scopes was defended by Clarence Darrow and Dudley Field Malone. William Jennings Bryan was one of the prosecuting attorneys. Darrow questioned Bryan on his fundamentalist beliefs during the trial (July 20). The trial was thought to have been too severe a strain on Bryan, who died on July 26. Scopes was convicted and fined $100.

Sept. 3 In an **airship disaster,** the U.S. Army dirigible *Shenandoah* was wrecked in a storm near Ava, Ohio, killing 14 persons. In spite of this and similar disasters,

The tempos of popular dances increased along with the pace of life in the Jazz Age. Sweeping the country in the early 1920s was the Charleston, an energetic dance that called for outward heel kicks and an up and down movement achieved by bending the knees to the syncopated rhythm of jazz. The dance had been performed in Charleston, S.C., as early as 1903, but its performance in the 1923 Broadway musical *Runnin' Wild* made the Charleston a hit elsewhere. The Charleston went well with short skirts and short hair. One writer claimed that in this period some 30,000,000 Americans danced frequently.

The **national college football championship** was won by Alabama, with a record of ten wins, no losses, no ties.

The **NHL Stanley Cup** was won by the Victoria Cougars, who defeated the Montreal Canadiens three games to one.

Jan. 1 The eleventh **Rose Bowl** football game was won by Notre Dame, defeating Stanford 27–10.

Feb. 15 **U.S. figure skating championships were won in Boston by Beatrix Loughran, women's singles; Nathaniel W. Niles, men's singles; Theresa Weld Blanchard and Nathaniel W. Niles, pairs.**

Apr. 20 The 29th **Boston Marathon** was won by Charles L. Mellor of Chicago, Ill., with a time of 2 hrs., 33 min., 0.35 sec.

May 8 The 50th annual **Preakness Stakes** was won by Coventry, with a time of 1:59. The jockey was Clarence Kummer.

May 16 The 51st annual **Kentucky Derby** was won by Flying Ebony, with a time of 2:07³/₅. The jockey was Earl Sande, who was still recovering from a spill he had taken at Saratoga Springs, N.Y., in 1924. It was his first mount in months and his second Kentucky Derby victory.

May 30 The 13th annual **Indianapolis 500** auto race was won by Peter DePaolo, completing the 500-mile course in 4 hrs., 56 min., 39.47 sec. for a record average speed of 101.13 mph.

June 5 The **U.S. Open golf tournament** was won by Willie Macfarlane, who beat Robert T. "Bobby" Jones by one stroke in the second round of a playoff.

June 13 The 57th annual **Belmont Stakes** was won by American Flag, with a time of 2:16⁴/₅. The jockey was Albert Johnson.

Aug. 24 The **U.S. Lawn Tennis Association singles championships** were won by Helen Wills, for the third time running, in the women's division and William T. Tilden, for the sixth time in a row, in the men's division (Sept. 19).

Nov. 3 James J. "Jimmy" Walker was elected mayor of New York City by an overwhelming majority. Walker, a Democrat, had served in the state assembly from 1909 to 1914 and in the state senate from 1914 to 1925. He was reelected mayor in 1929. He was enormously popular, partly because of his liberal politics and partly because of his colorful personality and enjoyment of sports and the high life. He came under fire, however, for maladministration of the city's affairs. Walker resigned on Sept. 1, 1932, before any conclusions could be reached regarding the charges made against him.

season. It included the hit songs: "Tea for Two" and "I Want to Be Happy."

Dec. 6 Establishment of the **John Simon Guggenheim Memorial Foundation** was announced. The foundation's first fellowships, to promote scholarship and the arts, were planned for Apr. 1926.

Dec. 8 *The Coconuts,* a musical comedy by George S. Kaufman and Irving Berlin and starring the irrepressible Marx Brothers—Groucho, Chico, Harpo, and Zeppo—and their favorite foil, Margaret Dumont, opened at the Lyric Theatre in New York City.

1926

The question of whether the U.S. should join the Permanent Court of International Justice, which had been established in 1919 as part of the League of Nations, continued to be controversial. On Jan. 27, 1926, the Senate approved membership by a 76–17 vote, but it attached five reservations. Four were acceptable to the members of the World Court but one, relating to advisory opinions, was not. On Dec. 9, 1929, Pres. Herbert Hoover authorized the signing of a protocol of adherence that contained provisions agreed to by both the court and the U.S., but when this was submitted to the Senate, action on it was blocked. Pres. Franklin D. Roosevelt made another attempt, on Jan. 16, 1935, but the Senate rejected membership by a vote of 52–35.

Feb. 26 The **Revenue Act,** which abolished many nuisance taxes and reduced income taxes, surtaxes, and taxes on passenger cars, was signed by Pres. Calvin Coolidge.

Apr. 29 A **debt funding agreement** was signed by the U.S. and France providing for repayment of France's wartime debt to the U.S. of about $4,000,000,000 over a period of 62 years and canceling 60.3% of the amount owed.

May 10 U.S. **Marines landed in Nicaragua** following an uprising (May 2) led by Gen. Augusto César Sandino against Emiliano Chamorro, who had seized power in Oct. 1925. The force, under Rear Adm. Julian L. Latimer, was withdrawn on June 5.

May 18 A Preparatory Commission for a **Disarmament Conference** opened its first session at Geneva, Switzerland. The U.S. was represented by Hugh S. Gibson.

About the turn of the century traditional music had begun to give way to a wave of highly original and experimental works by such composers as Charles Ives, Igor Stravinski, and Edgard Varèse. One of the exponents of a dissonant, neoclassic style was the composer Virgil Thomson. His *Sonata da chiesa* [Church Sonata] for E flat clarinet, C trumpet, viola, F horn, and trombone, completed this year, was in this vein. Its second movement incorporated a tango, which aroused considerable comment. Later Thomson changed his style. His works included several operas, the ballet *Filling Station* (1937), and music for the film *River* (1937). He also served as music critic of the New York *Herald Tribune* from 1940 to 1954.

Among **books published** this year was *Abraham Lincoln, The Prairie Years* by Carl Sandburg, the first two volumes of the poet's landmark six-volume biography of Lincoln. Other books published this year included *The Mauve Decade* by Thomas Beer, a study of American life in the 1890s; *The Story of Philosophy* by Will Durant; *Soldiers' Pay* by William Faulkner, the author's first novel; *The Sun Also Rises* by Ernest Hemingway, a novel of postwar disillusion that has become an American classic; *The Weary Blues* by Langston Hughes, poetry; and *Topper* by Thorne Smith, a novel about a timid soul, Cosmo Topper, and two zany ghosts who befriend him.

The **Dramatists' Guild** was organized by playwrights this year as part of the Authors' League.

This year's **popular songs** included "Bye Bye Blackbird," "The Desert Song," "Horses," "One Alone," "Blue Room," "Play, Gypsy," "When Day Is Done," "In a Little Spanish Town," and "I Found a Million-Dollar Baby in a Five and Ten Cent Store."

Ferdinand "Jelly Roll" Morton began a series of recordings made with his Red Hot Peppers in Chicago. The records, some of the most important in the history of jazz, included "Black Bottom Stomp," "Smoke House Blues," "Original Jelly Roll Blues," and "Doctor Jazz."

advocates of lighter-than-air machines continued to espouse their craft.

Oct. The **Florida land boom** reached a peak about this time. Speculation in Florida properties was said to surpass any other business stampede in U.S. history.

Oct. 16 **Evolutionary theory** was prohibited by the Texas State Text Book Board in any of its school textbooks.

Dec. 29 The name **Duke University** was adopted by the Board of Trustees of Trinity College in North Carolina to meet the terms of a $40,000,000 trust fund established by James B. Duke, the tobacco millionaire.

Sept. 11 The **Miss America** title was won by Fay Lamphier, 19, of Oakland, Calif., at the annual pageant in Atlantic City, N.J.

Sept. 12 The **Davis Cup** international tennis challenge round was won for the sixth straight time by the U.S., defeating France in five straight matches.

Sept. 26 The **PGA golf tournament** was won by Walter Hagen.

Oct. 7–15 The 22nd annual **World Series** was won by the Pittsburgh Pirates (NL), who beat the Washington Senators (AL) four games to three.

1926

Evangelists offering various approaches to salvation continued to attract followers. A leading figure in the movement was Aimee Semple McPherson, who had founded the International Church of the Foursquare Gospel and in 1923 had opened the Angelus Temple in Los Angeles, Calif. She was successful in attracting a following in California. Then, on May 18, 1926, she disappeared while at the beach. Her followers believed she had drowned. About a month later Sister Aimee, as she liked to be called, turned up in Mexico, claiming she had been kidnaped. Investigation revealed she had run off with a former operator of her radio station. The affair caused a sensation. McPherson was tried for fraud and acquitted, but her days of glory were coming to an end.

The first successful treatment of **pernicious anemia** was applied by two Boston doctors, George R. Minot and William P. Murphy. They prescribed a liver diet for the victims of the previously mysterious and fatal disease. Minot and Murphy, along with Dr. George H. Whipple, received the Nobel Prize in 1934 for their work on the disease.

In the controversy over **religious instruction** and the right of boards of education to release schoolchildren for one hour each week for such study, a test case was heard in New York State. The court granted the recess for White Plains, N.Y., schools.

Sarah Lawrence College, Bronxville, N.Y., was established as Sarah Lawrence College for Women. Its first classes met in 1928. Its present name was adopted in 1947.

Plans were announced for construction of the **George Washington Bridge,** across the Hudson R. to Manhattan. Terminal sites selected were Fort Lee in New Jersey and Fort Washington on Manhattan.

A new kind of heavyweight boxing champion was crowned in 1926. James Joseph "Gene" Tunney, born in New York City, reflected a more refined background than that of most professional fighters. A man of intellect as well as action, he liked the company of college professors. On Sept. 23 Tunney beat the champion, Jack Dempsey, on points in a ten-round bout in Philadelphia. The fight attracted a crowd of 118,736 and generated record receipts of $1,895,723. The next year, on Sept. 22, the two met in a rematch in Chicago and again Tunney won the decision. That fight was controversial because of a so-called long count in the seventh round, when Tunney was knocked down but the referee refused to start the count until Dempsey went to a neutral corner. The rematch attracted an even larger crowd, about 145,000 people, and set another record for gate receipts, $2,658,660. Tunney, a better boxer but far less colorful figure than the dethroned champion, retired undefeated in 1928.

The **NHL Stanley Cup** championship was won by the Montreal Maroons, who defeated the Victoria Cougars three games to one.

This year's **national college football championship** was won by Stanford, with a record of ten wins, no losses, one tie.

Jan. 1 The 11th annual **Rose Bowl** football game was won by Alabama, defeating Washington 20–19.

Feb. **U.S. figure skating championships** were won in Boston by Beatrix Loughran, women's singles; Chris R. Christienson, men's singles; and Theresa Weld Blanchard and Nathaniel W. Niles, pairs.

Apr. 19 The 30th **Boston Marathon** was won by John C. Miles of Nova Scotia in a time of 2 hrs., 25 min., 40.25 sec.

May 10 The 51st annual **Preakness Stakes** was won by

July 2 The **Army Air Corps** was established by Congress.

July 2 The **Distinguished Flying Cross** was commissioned for anyone who "while serving in the armed services, distinguished himself by heroism or extraordinary achievement while participating in aerial flight." Charles A. Lindbergh, in the Air Corps Reserve, was decorated on June 11, 1927, becoming the first person to receive the medal.

July 10 An **ammunition depot explosion** at Lake Denmark, N.J., was triggered by lightning, killing 31 persons. Sporadic explosions continued for days; damage reached $93,000,000.

Sept. 18 A disastrous **hurricane** swept Florida and the Gulf states, killing 372 people and injuring more than 6000. Some 5000 homes were destroyed by the storm, leaving almost 18,000 families homeless. Property damage was estimated at more than $80,000,000.

Oct. 25 In a major decision on **executive authority,** the U.S. Supreme Court ruled that the president has the power to remove executive officers from their positions. The decision nullified the act of 1876, which required consent of the Senate before removals from office could be ordered.

Nov. 2 In **congressional elections** the Democrats made gains in both houses. In the Senate the Republicans led 49–46, with one seat going to a minor party. In the House the Republicans' majority was reduced to 237–195, with three seats going to minor parties.

Dec. 10 The **Nobel Peace Prize** for 1925 was awarded jointly to Vice Pres. Charles G. Dawes, for his work on the Dawes Plan of 1924 for reconstruction of German finances, and to Sir Austen Chamberlain of England, for his years of work to promote peace in Europe.

The band consisted of George Mitchell, Omer Simeon, Kid Ory, Johnny St. Cyr, John Lindsay, and Andrew Hilaire.

Jan. 23 *The Great God Brown* by Eugene O'Neill, starring William Harrigan, opened at the Greenwich Village Theatre in New York City. The play made heavy use of symbolism, employing masks to represent different aspects of the personalities of the characters.

Feb. 19 *Skyscrapers,* a ballet scored by John Alden Carpenter on a commission from the Russian producer Sergei Diaghilev, was produced at the Metropolitan Opera House in New York City. Notable for its use of jazz idioms, it evoked much comment among concertgoers.

Apr. The **Book-of-the-Month Club** was organized, paving the way for a revolution in book selling and publishing. At the end of the first year 40,000 subscribers were enrolled, a number that later increased to hundreds of thousands.

May 3 **Pulitzer prizes** were awarded for the following: fiction, *Arrowsmith* by Sinclair Lewis; biography, *The Life of Sir William Osler* by Harvey Cushing; history, *The History of the United States* by Edward Channing; poetry, *What's O'Clock* by Amy Lowell; drama, *Craig's Wife* by George Kelly.

May 5 **Sinclair Lewis** declined the Pulitzer Prize award for his novel *Arrowsmith,* declaring that prizes tend to make writers "safe, polite, obedient and sterile." Lewis urged all novelists to refuse such awards if they wished to remain free.

Aug. 5 Perhaps the **first talking picture** to be presented to an audience was *Don Juan,* featuring John Barrymore, which was shown at the Warner Threatre in New York City. The film utilized a phonographic sound system, not a sound-on-film system.

Nov. 30 *The Desert Song,* an operetta by Otto Harbach, Oscar Hammerstein II, Sigmund Romberg, and Frank Mandel, opened at the Casino Theatre in New York City. Its title song became one of the year's big hits.

1927

On May 20, 1927, Charles A. Lindbergh, a 25-year-old aviator, took off from Roosevelt Field, Long Island, in the monoplane *Spirit of St. Louis,* and headed for Paris, 3600 miles away. The world held its breath as infrequent reports of his progress were heard. At last, 33½ hours after he took off, Lindbergh landed at Le Bourget, completing the first nonstop solo flight from New York to Paris. He was welcomed by a crowd estimated at 100,-000. Lindbergh, tall, lanky, shy, and soft spoken, was

This year the monument at Mount Rushmore, S.D., was dedicated, a colossal 500-foot sculpture carved on the side of the mountain by Gutzon Borglum. Visible for 60 miles were the busts of George Washington, Thomas Jefferson, Abraham Lincoln, and Theodore Roosevelt. Borglum died in 1941, and his work was completed by his son, Lincoln. In 1916 Borglum had begun a similar work on Stone Mt., Ga., as a Confederate memorial, but he ended his association with the project in the mid-

The **40-hour work week** was introduced by Henry Ford to boost the ailing automobile industry. American industrial leaders were shocked, but the proposition was warmly received by the AFL as a means of checking overproduction and limiting unemployment.

Feb. 9 Teaching of the **theory of evolution** was prohibited in the public schools of Atlanta, Ga., by a decision handed down by the Board of Education.

Mar. 7 The first successful **transatlantic radiotelephone conversation** was held between New York City and London at a demonstration by the American Telephone and Telegraph Company, The Radio Corporation of America, and the British General Post Office.

May 9 The **first successful flight over the North Pole** was made by Rear Adm. Richard E. Byrd and Floyd Bennett.

May 20 The **Civilian Aviation Act** was signed by Pres. Calvin Coolidge. The act provided for a Bureau of Air Commerce, which was given jurisdiction over civil aviation, including the licensing of aircraft and pilots. The federal government had previously had no connection with civil aviation except through appropriations for airmail service.

June 20 The **first international Eucharistic Congress** in the U.S. convened at Chicago. Cardinal John Bonzano was chosen papal legate by Pope Pius XI and presided over the congress.

July 5 A **subway strike** in New York City began. It ended unsuccessfully for the workers on July 29. During the strike some 150,000 privately owned automobiles and several thousand buses carried New Yorkers to and from work.

July 26 The **Sanctuary of Our Lady of Victory,** Lackawanna, N.Y., became the first Roman Catholic Church in the U.S. to be consecrated as a basilica.

Display, with a time of 1:59⅘. The jockey was Johnny Maiben.

May 15 The 52nd annual **Kentucky Derby** was won by Bubbling Over, with a time of 2:03⅘. The jockey was Albert Johnson.

May 31 The 14th annual **Indianapolis 500** auto race was won by Frank Lockhart, with a time of 4 hrs., 10 min., 14.95 sec., for an average speed of 95.90 mph. This year the race distance was 400 miles.

June 12 The 58th annual **Belmont Stakes** was won by Crusader, with a time of 2:32⅕. The jockey was Albert Johnson. Beginning with this year, the distance for the Belmont became one mile and a half.

July 10 The **U.S. Open golf tournament** was won by Robert T. "Bobby" Jones.

Aug. 6 The **first woman to swim the English Channel** was Gertrude Ederle of New York City, 19, who accomplished the feat in 14 hrs., 31 min.

Aug. 23 The **U.S. Lawn Tennis Association singles championships** were won by Molla Bjurstedt Mallory in the women's division and Rene Lacoste of France in the men's division (Sept. 18).

Aug. 30 The **first Hambletonian Stakes,** the premier event in harness racing, was won at Syracuse, N.Y., by Guy McKinney in two straight heats. The driver was Nat Ray.

Sept. 10 The **Miss America** title was won by Norma Smallwood, 18, of Tulsa, Okla., at the annual pageant in Atlantic City, N.J.

Sept. 11 The **Davis Cup** international tennis challenge round was won for the seventh time in a row by the U.S., defeating France four matches to one.

Sept. 25 The **PGA golf tournament** was won by Walter Hagen.

Oct. 2–10 The 23rd annual **World Series** was won by the St. Louis Cardinals (NL), who defeated the New York Yankees (AL) four games to three.

1927

This was a period of tremendous growth for the radio industry. As stations of all types proliferated and available output power climbed, it became clear that a supervisory body was needed. On Feb. 23, 1927, the Radio Control Act was signed by Pres. Calvin Coolidge. It authorized establishment of a five-man Federal Radio Commission, each commissioner to supervise one of the five zones into which the country was divided. The commission was authorized to classify types of stations,

In the 1920s baseball changed from a pitcher's game, characterized by relatively few runs scored and even fewer home runs, to a slugger's game. The leading hitter was George Herman "Babe" Ruth, who had begun his major league career in 1914 as a pitcher for the Boston Red Sox (AL). Ruth joined the New York Yankees (AL) in 1920 and hit 54 home runs that season, a new record. The next year his total was 59; in 1927 he knocked out a record 60, hitting the last one on Sept. 30. The record-

modest about his feat, but the world considered him a hero. Pres. Calvin Coolidge sent a Navy cruiser to bring him home. Lindbergh's ticker-tape parade up Broadway in New York City was watched by an estimated 4,000,000 people.

Feb. 10 Pres. Calvin Coolidge called for a **conference to limit naval armament.** It met in Geneva, Switzerland, on June 20. France and Italy refused to join. Only the U.S., Great Britain, and Japan were represented. Great Britain and the U.S. could not agree on cruiser restrictions, and the conference ended in stalemate on Aug. 4.

Mar. 7 In a **voting rights case,** the U.S. Supreme Court ruled unconstitutional Texas law prohibiting blacks from voting in Democratic primary elections.

Apr. **Floods** in the Mississippi R. Valley inundated 4,000,000 acres, causing property loss of $300,000,-000. Some 600,000 persons were homeless for weeks, and several hundred drowned.

Apr. 6 A treaty to **outlaw war** was proposed by French foreign minister Aristide Briand. On June 11 Sec. of State Frank B. Kellogg acknowledged Briand's proposal. On June 20 Briand submitted a treaty draft, and on Dec. 28 Kellogg suggested that Briand's treaty be extended to include all nations of the world. The result was to be the Kellogg-Briand Pact of 1928.

Aug. 2 Pres. **Calvin Coolidge declined renomination,** announcing "I do not choose to run for president in 1928." It had been generally assumed that he would seek reelection.

Aug. 23 **Nicola Sacco and Bartolomeo Vanzetti** were executed in Massachusetts despite agitation in support of them. Many thought the two were innocent of the 1920 killing of a factory guard and were being railroaded for their radical beliefs.

Sept. 29 A **tornado** lasting only five minutes struck St. Louis, Mo., killing 87 persons and injuring about 1500. More than 1000 homes were destroyed by the storm, and estimates of property damage exceeded $50,000,000.

Oct. 10 The lease of the **Teapot Dome** oil reserve lands in Wyoming to the Mammoth Oil Company by former interior secretary Albert B. Fall was ruled by

1920s because of disagreement with the sponsors.

Among **books published** this year was *The Bridge of San Luis Rey* by Thornton Wilder, a novel exploring the nature of destiny and divine providence in connection with the deaths of five persons in a bridge collapse. Other books published this year included *Blue Voyage* by Conrad Aiken, the author's first novel; *Death Comes for the Archbishop* by Willa Cather, a novel of the Southwest during the age of Spanish exploration and settlement; *Copper Sun* and *The Ballad of the Brown Girl*, both volumes by the poet Countee Cullen; *Elmer Gantry* by Sinclair Lewis, a novel; *archy and mehitabel* by Don Marquis, adventures in free verse of archy the cockroach and his friend mehitabel, a cat; *Giants in the Earth* by Ole Rölvaag, a novel of the Norwegian settlement of Dakota Territory in the nineteenth century; and *Oil!* by Upton Sinclair, a novel based in part on the Teapot Dome oil leasing scandal.

The **Academy of Motion Picture Arts and Sciences** was organized this year to present annual awards, which came to be known as Oscars, for noteworthy achievement in the motion picture industry. The first Academy Awards were presented in 1929.

This year's **popular songs** included "Old Man River," "My Blue Heaven," "Rain," "Let a Smile Be Your Umbrella," "Blue Skies," "Russian Lullaby," "Tree in the Park," "Sometimes I'm Happy," "Hallelujah," and "My Heart Stood Still."

Jan. 28 The premiere performance of *Concerto for Piano and Orchestra* by Aaron Copland was given by the Boston Symphony, with the composer at the piano.

Jan. 31 *The Road to Rome* by Robert E. Sherwood, the author's first play, opened at the Playhouse in New York City. The play, a sometimes humorous, sometimes satirical treatment of Hannibal's march on Rome, starred Philip Merivale and Jane Cowl.

Apr. 10 *Ballet Mécanique,* with music by George Antheil, was presented at Carnegie Hall in New York City. Scored for ten pianos, auto horns, buzz saws, cowbells, and other unconventional instruments, the work made Antheil's reputation overnight.

Apr. 25 *Hit the Deck,* a musical comedy by Herbert Fields, Leo Robin, Clifford Grey, and Vincent Youmans, adapted from the play *Shore Leave* by Hubert Osborne, opened at the Belasco Theatre in New York City. Its songs included "Sometimes I'm Happy" and "Hallelujah."

May 2 **Pulitzer prizes** were awarded for the following: fiction, *Early Autumn* by Louis Bromfield; biography, *Whitman* by Emory Holloway; history, *Pinckney's Treaty* by Samuel Flagg Bemis; poetry, *Fiddler's Farewell* by Leonora Speyer; drama, *In Abraham's Bosom* by Paul Green.

| Business and Industry; Science; Education; Philosophy and Religion   III | | IV   Sports; Social Issues and Crime; Folkways; Fashion; Holidays |

assign frequency bands for each type, and issue rules and regulations to prevent interference between stations. It also was given power to rule on operating changes requested by radio stations. The Federal Radio Commission was temporary. Its authority reverted to the secretary of commerce after one year, after which the commission became an appellate body, ruling on appeals of decisions made by the secretary of commerce. Nonetheless, it brought some order to radio. In 1934 it was superseded by the Federal Communications Commission (FCC).

The **Brookings Institution** was established in Washington, D.C. It was named after Robert S. Brookings, a businessman and philanthropist who was the driving force behind the institution's formation. Its first president was H. G. Moulton.

New York University in New York City set up seven summer schools in European universities, granting college credit for the courses. The classes were taught by American instructors.

A **mechanical cotton picker** was developed by John D. Rust.

Development of the **first national radio beacon** for air transportation was announced. The beacon automatically informed the pilot if his machine was off course. This led ultimately to refinement of an instrument that automatically kept airplanes on course.

Jan. 7 Commercial **transatlantic telephone service** was opened between New York City and London. Walter S. Gifford, president of the American Telephone and Telegraph Company, officially inaugurated the line by saying, "Hello, London."

Spring The **15,000,000th Model T Ford** rolled off the assembly line. Shortly after this the Model T was discontinued and the Model A was introduced. Retooling took six months and cost $200,000,000, not counting losses attributable to nonproduction.

Apr. 7 The first successful demonstration of **television** took place in New York City. Walter S. Gifford, president of the American Telephone and Telegraph Company, in New York City spoke with and saw Sec. of Commerce Herbert Hoover, who was in his office in Washington, D.C.

June 28 The first successful **airplane flight from San Francisco to Honolulu,** Hawaii, was made by Army Air Corps pilots Lt. Lester J. Maitland and Lt. Albert F. Hegenberger.

July 29 An electric respirator, later called the **iron lung,** was installed at Bellevue Hospital, New York City. Devised by two physicians, Philips Drinker and Louis A. Shaw of Harvard University, the new device was useful in overcoming many kinds of respiratory failure.

setting blow came on a pitch by Tom Zachary, of the Washington Senators. Ruth's record stood until 1961 when another Yankee, Roger Maris, hit 61 home runs. (In Ruth's day the season consisted of 154 games; in Maris's time, 162.) When the Babe's career ended in 1935 he had hit 714 homers, a record surpassed only by Hank Aaron, of the Milwaukee (and later Atlanta) Braves (NL), who reached a total of 755 in 1976.

Walter Johnson, pitcher for the Washington Senators (AL), ended the last season of his 20-year career by setting two major league career records. Johnson had pitched a total of 113 shutouts and struck out 3503 batters.

The **first Golden Gloves** amateur boxing matches were held this year, sponsored by the New York *Daily News.*

This year's **national college football championship** was won by Illinois, with a record of seven wins, no losses, one tie.

Jan. 1 The 13th **Rose Bowl** football game was played to a 7–7 tie by Alabama and Stanford.

Feb. 10–11 **U.S. figure skating championships** were won by Beatrix Loughran, women's singles; Nathaniel W. Niles, men's singles; and Theresa Weld Blanchard and Nathaniel W. Niles, pairs.

Apr. 7–13 The **NHL Stanley Cup** was won by the Ottawa Senators, who beat the Boston Bruins in two games and tied them in two games.

Apr. 19 The 31st **Boston Marathon** was won for the fifth time by Clarence H. DeMar of Melrose, Mass., with a time of 2 hrs., 40 min., 22.2 sec.

May 9 The 52nd annual **Preakness Stakes** was won by Bostonian, with a time of 2:01³/₅. The jockey was A. "Whitey" Abel.

May 14 The 53rd annual **Kentucky Derby** was won by Whiskery, with a time of 2:06. The jockey was Linus McAtee.

May 30 The 15th annual **Indianapolis 500** auto race was won by George Soulders, completing the 500-mile course in 5 hrs., 7 min., 33.08 sec., with an average speed of 97.54 mph.

June 11 The 59th annual **Belmont Stakes** was won by Chance Shot, with a time of 2:32²/₅. The jockey was Earl Sande.

June 16 The **U.S. Open golf tournament** was won by Tommy Armour.

July 2 At the **Wimbledon** tennis championships, Helen Wills won the women's singles title. Other titles won by U.S. players were men's doubles, Francis T. Hunter and William T. Tilden (July 4); women's doubles, Helen Wills and Elizabeth Ryan (July 5); mixed doubles, Francis T. Hunter and Elizabeth Ryan (July 5).

Aug. 30 The **U.S. Lawn Tennis Association singles championship** were won by Helen Wills in the

the Supreme Court to have been fraudulently negotiated and therefore invalid.

Dec. 17 In a **submarine disaster,** the entire crew of 40 of the U.S. submarine *S-4* died after the craft, attempting to surface off Provincetown, Mass., collided with the Coast Guard destroyer *Paulding* and sank. Divers said they heard tappings on the inside of the submarine and pleas for food and water for three days but were helpless to free the trapped men. On Jan. 4 the first bodies were removed.

Oct. 6 The first **full-length** talking picture, with both music and dialogue synchronized on disk, *The Jazz Singer,* was released.

Nov. 3 *A Connecticut Yankee,* a musical by Herbert Fields, Richard Rodgers, and Lorenz Hart based on the novel by Mark Twain, opened at the Vanderbilt Theatre in New York City. It was the first outstanding Broadway success by the Rodgers and Hart team.

Dec. 27 *Show Boat,* a musical by Oscar Hammerstein II and Jerome Kern, adapted from Edna Ferber's 1926 novel of the same name, opened at the Ziegfeld Theatre in New York City and became an enormous success.

1928

The presidential election campaign of 1928 was marked by a clash of personalities and positions. The Republican candidate, Herbert Hoover, was known as a manager who got things done. His Democratic opponent, Gov. Alfred E. Smith of New York, was a Catholic who favored repeal of the Eighteenth Amendment. In addition, he was perceived as a big-city politician, although he was a liberal reformer. Radio played an important part in a campaign for the first time, and Smith's harsh voice did not go over well. The attack on his Catholicism was vicious, and the election brought out nearly two-thirds of the registered voters. For the first time since the Civil War, the Republicans carried some of the southern states.

Apr. 13–18 The **Socialist Party National Convention** nominated **Norman Thomas** of New York for the presidency and James H. Maurer of Pennsylvania for the vice presidency.

May 27 The **Workers' Party National Convention** nominated William Z. Foster of Illinois for the presidency and Benjamin Gitlow of New York for the vice presidency.

June 12–15 The **Republican National Convention** nominated **Herbert Hoover** of California for the presidency and Charles Curtis of Kansas for the vice presidency.

June 26–29 The **Democratic National Convention** nominated **Gov. Alfred E. Smith** of New York for the presidency and Sen. Joseph T. Robinson of Arkansas for the vice presidency.

July 11 The **Farmer Labor Party National Convention** nominated Sen. George W. Norris of Nebraska for the presidency and Will Vereen of Georgia for the vice presidency. Norris subsequently declined the

American poets have frequently used U.S. history as material for their works. The most prominent such writer in the 1920s was Stephen Vincent Benét, whose *John Brown's Body* was published this year. It was a long narrative poem about the abolitionist hero, evoking the period of strained North-South relations before the Civil War. Benét introduced an even larger project in poetic history with the publication of *Western Star* in 1943. It was the first part of an epic poem that was to trace the westward migration across the continent. *Western Star* depicted the settling of Jamestown and Plymouth colonies. Benét's death in 1943 put an end to the work.

Among **books published** this year was *Scarlet Sister Mary* by Julia Peterkin, a realistic and sympathetic chronicling of the life of a black woman on a South Carolina plantation. The novel was awarded the Pulitzer Prize in 1929 and was dramatized the following year. Other books published this year were *West-Running Brook* by Robert Frost, a collection of poetry; *The Man Who Knew Coolidge* by Sinclair Lewis, a novel; *Buck in the Snow,* a collection of poems by Edna St. Vincent Millay; *Good Morning, America* by Carl Sandburg, poetry; and *Boston* by Upton Sinclair, a novel.

Walt Disney introduced his most famous animated character, Mickey Mouse, in the cartoon *Plane Crazy,* the first cartoon released by Walt Disney Productions. It was followed by *Galloping Gaucho* and *Steamboat Willie,* the latter introducing sound to animated film.

The award-winning symphony *America* was composed by Ernest Bloch. Bloch characterized his music as an attempt to realize the "complex, glowing, agitated soul" he felt pulsating through the Bible.

George Gershwin composed *An American in Paris* this year.

This year's **popular songs** included "Makin' Whoopee," "Silver Moon," "Am I Blue?" "You're the Cream in My Coffee," and "Button Up Your Overcoat."

Nov. 10 The **Nobel Prize in Physics** was awarded jointly to Arthur Holly Compton of the University of Chicago for his discovery of the Compton effect, observed in collisions of x-rays and gamma rays and their variation in wavelength; and to Charles Thomson Rees Wilson of Scotland for his development of the vapor condensation method for tracking the paths of electrically charged particles.

Nov. 13 The **Holland Tunnel,** the first underwater motor vehicle tunnel in the U.S., was opened to commercial traffic. The tunnel, linking Manhattan with New Jersey, had two tubes, each large enough to accommodate two lanes of traffic.

women's division and Rene Lacoste of France in the men's division (Sept. 17).
Joliet, Ill., at the annual pageant in Atlantic City, N.J.

Sept. 10 The **Davis Cup** international tennis challenge round was won by France, which defeated the defending U.S. team three matches to two. The U.S. would not regain the cup until 1937.

Oct. 5–8 The 24th annual **World Series** was won by the New York Yankees (AL), who swept the Pittsburgh Pirates (NL) in four straight games.

Nov. 5 The **PGA golf tournament** was won by Walter Hagen for an unprecedented fourth time in a row.

1928

Anthropology was advancing, now concerning itself to a greater degree with the implications of its findings for modern life. No one contributed more to this process than Franz Boas, who became Columbia University's first professor of anthropology in 1899 and held the post for 37 years. The most influential American anthropologist of his time, he taught and inspired generations of younger scientists. Boas was concerned with refuting the idea that race and culture could be correlated. He attacked the idea of a master race in works such as *Anthropology and Modern Life* (1928).

May 22 The **Jones-White Act** was passed by Congress. It provided a stimulus for American shipping in the form of production subsidies and favorable mail contracts. Despite this and other laws, American shipping continued to operate at a deficit.

June 3 The **first woman to fly across the Atlantic,** Amelia Earhart, took off from Boston for Trepassey Bay, Newfoundland, accompanied by fellow pilot Wilmer Stultz and mechanic Lou Gordon, aboard the Fokker trimoter aircraft *Friendship.* On June 17 the three flew across the Atlantic Ocean to Burry Port, Wales in 20 hrs., 40 min.

July 30 The **first color motion pictures** in the U.S. were exhibited by George Eastman at Rochester, N.Y. The scenes ran the gamut of colorful subjects, including goldfish, peacocks, scarlet-beaked doves, butterflies, flowers, Fifth Avenue fashion models, and pretty girls in pretty dresses. Maj. Gen. James Harbord, president of RCA, and E. F. A. Alexanderson, a pioneer in television, on the strength of the showing predicted the application of color to television.

No sport expanded more in the 1920s than golf. Some of this growth was related to the social status of the game rather than to its fun or healthful properties. Along with the growth of suburbia came a proliferation of golf courses and country clubs. This made the game expensive, adding club membership fees to the considerable cost of clubs, balls, and baggy plus-fours, but every rising young executive felt it was the thing to do. By the late 1920s there were more than 5000 courses, and golfers were spending about $200,000,000 a year on the sport.

This year's **national college football championship** was won by Georgia Tech, with a record of ten wins, no losses, no ties.

Jan. 1 The 14th **Rose Bowl** football game was won by Stanford, edging out Pittsburgh 7–6.

Feb. 11–19 At the second **Winter Olympics** in St. Moritz, Switzerland, the U.S. finished second in team standings and won two gold medals.

Mar. 27 U.S. **figure skating championships** were won by Maribel Y. Vinson, women's singles; Roger Turner, men's singles; and Maribel Y. Vinson and Thornton Coolidge, pairs.

Apr. 5–14 The **NHL Stanley Cup** was won by the New York Rangers, defeating the Montreal Canadiens three games to two.

Apr. 19 The 32nd **Boston Marathon** was won by Clarence H. DeMar of Melrose, Mass., who gained his sixth marathon win with a time of 2 hrs., 37 min., 7.8 sec.

May 11 The 53rd annual **Preakness Stakes** was won by Victorian, with a time of 2:00⅕. The jockey was Raymond "Sonny" Workman.

May 19 The 54th annual **Kentucky Derby** was won by Reigh Count, with a time of 2:10⅖. The jockey was Charles Lang.

May 30 The 16th annual **Indianapolis 500** auto race was won by Louis Meyer, completing the 500-mile course in 5 hrs., 1 min., 33.75 sec., with an average speed of 99.48 mph.

nomination, stating that he was a Democrat and for Al Smith. Frank E. Webb of California became the party's presidential candidate.

July 12 The **Prohibition Party National Convention** nominated William F. Varney of New York for the presidency and James A. Edgarton of Virginia for the vice presidency.

Aug. 27 The **Kellogg-Briand Peace Pact** was subscribed to by 15 nations at Paris, France. The pact called for outlawing war and settling international controversies by arbitration. The pact was eventually signed by 62 nations.

Nov. 6 **Herbert Hoover was elected president** of the United States in a landslide Republican victory. Charles Curtis was elected vice president. The electoral vote was Hoover, 444; Alfred E. Smith, Democratic candidate, 87. The popular vote was Hoover, 21, 392,190; Smith, 15,016,443; Norman Thomas, Socialist candidate, 267,835; William Z. Foster, Workers' Party candidate, 48,228; Verne L. Reynolds, Socialist Labor candidate, 21,181; William F. Varney, Prohibition candidate, 20,106; Frank E. Webb, Farmer Labor candidate, 6391. In congressional elections the Republicans increased their majorities in both houses, leading in the Senate 56–39, with one seat going to a minor party, and controlling the House 267–167, with one seat held by a minor party.

Jan. 9 *Marco Millions* by Eugene O'Neill, starring Alfred Lunt as an acquisitive Marco Polo unaware of the beauty or culture of the lands he journeyed through, opened at the Guild Theatre in New York City.

May 7 **Pulitzer prizes** were awarded for the following: fiction, *The Bridge of San Luis Rey* by Thornton Wilder; biography, *The American Orchestra and Theodore Thomas* by Charles Edward Russell; history, *Main Currents in American Thought* by Vernon L. Parrington; poetry, *Tristram* by Edwin Arlington Robinson; drama, *Strange Interlude* by Eugene O'Neill.

May 11 The **first program of scheduled television broadcasts** was inaugurated by station WGY in Schenectady, N.Y.

July 6 The **first talking motion picture** more than 6000 feet long, *The Lights of New York*, premiered at the Strand Theatre in New York City at a special midnight gala. Warner Brothers released the film nationally on July 21.

Aug. 14 *The Front Page* by Ben Hecht and Charles MacArthur, a perennial favorite about a hard-boiled newspaperman, opened at the Times Square Theatre in New York City. The role of the reporter was acted by Lee Tracy.

Nov. 26 *Holiday,* a three-act comedy by Philip Barry, opened at the Plymouth Theatre in New York City.

1929

As the 1920s neared an end, many were convinced the prosperous times that had begun in 1922 would go on forever, but beneath the surface there were signs of trouble. Several aspects of the economy had begun to decline in 1927. The appearance of growth was, in fact, being produced by wild speculation in the stock market. On Sept. 3, 1929, stock prices reached their highest levels ever, but a slow decline began. On Oct. 24 an abrupt decline began. Leading bankers tried without success to stem the tide. On Oct. 29, Black Tuesday, a record 16, 410,030 shares were traded as huge blocks of stock were dumped for whatever they would bring. By Dec. 1 stocks on the New York Stock Exchange had dropped in value by $26,000,000,000. The day after the crash, Pres. Herbert Hoover said, "The fundamental business of the country . . . is on a sound and prosperous basis." In actuality the Great Depression of the 1930s had begun.

Jan. 15 The **Kellogg-Briand Peace Pact** was passed

American painters were taking up the abstract style. A painter who adapted the principles of abstract art to her own distinctive style was Georgia O'Keeffe, whose *Black Flowers and Blue Larkspur* was painted in 1929. Her depictions of flowers, of which she did many, used a close-up technique. O'Keeffe lived in New Mexico for many years, until her death in 1986. Her paintings, done in an almost bleak style, captured the vastness and forbidding beauty of the Southwest in brilliant representations of bleached bones, barren hills, and desert blossoms. Her later work was more abstract than that of her early years.

Among **books published** this year was *Sartoris* by William Faulkner, the author's first novel about the fictional Yoknapatawpha County and its people, including the Sartoris, Benbow, and Snopes families. Yoknapatawpha County was modeled after Lafayette County in Mississippi, Faulkner's home. Other books published this year included *Selected Poems* by Conrad Aiken; *Red Harvest* and *The Dain Curse* by Dashiell Hammett, both detective novels; *A Farewell to Arms* by Ernest

Sept. The first of what were called **nite coaches,** buses equipped with sleeping facilities for transcontinental travel, were completed by Pickwick Stages, Inc., bus manufacturers of Los Angeles, Calif.

Nov. 6 The **first animated electric sign** in the U.S. was mounted by *The New York Times* around the top of the Times Building, Times Square, New York City. Used to report the presidential election returns, it was called the zipper because of the way it circled the building.

Dec. 12 The **International Civil Aeronautics Conference,** called by Pres. Calvin Coolidge as part of the 25th anniversary celebration of the first powered flight, opened in Washington, D.C. Some 137 delegates from 31 countries attended. On Dec. 13 Charles A. Lindbergh was awarded the Clifford Harmon Trophy. The same day the House of Representatives passed a bill to award the Distinguished Flying Cross to Orville Wright and his deceased brother, Wilbur Wright. On Dec. 17 the delegates attended ceremonies at Kitty Hawk, N.C., honoring the first powered flight by the Wrights on Dec. 17, 1903.

June 9 The 60th annual **Belmont Stakes** was won by Vito, with a time of 2:33$^1/_5$. The jockey was Clarence Kummer.

June 24 The **U.S. Open golf tournament** was won by Johnny Farrell, who beat Robert T. "Bobby" Jones by one stroke in a 36-hole playoff.

July 7 At the **Wimbledon** tennis championships, Helen Wills won the women's singles title for the second year in a row. The mixed doubles title was won by Elizabeth Ryan teamed with P. D. B. Spence of South Africa.

July 26 The **world heavyweight boxing championship** was successfully defended by Gene Tunney, who scored a 12th-round knockout over Tom Heeney in a bout in New Zealand. Shortly after, Tunney announced his retirement.

July 29–Aug. 12 At the **Summer Olympics** in Amsterdam, Holland, the U.S. took first place in team standings and won 24 gold medals. U.S. athletes set 17 new Olympic records, 7 world records.

Aug. 27 The **U.S. Lawn Tennis Association singles championships** were won by Helen Wills in the women's division and Henri Cochet of France in the men's division (Sept. 17).

Oct. 4–9 The 25th annual **World Series** was won by the New York Yankees (AL), who swept the St. Louis Cardinals (NL) in four straight games.

Oct. 6 The **PGA golf tournament** was won by Leo Diegel.

1929

Sociologists were beginning to apply accepted anthropological principles and methods to their examinations of contemporary communities. A pioneer study in this field, *Middletown: A Study in American Culture* by Robert S. and Helen M. Lynd, sociologists of Columbia University, was published this year. "Middletown" actually was the city of Muncie, Ind. The Lynds' study covered such areas as education, leisure, religion, government, and community affairs. A basic finding was that the people of Middletown learned and accepted "new ways of behaving toward material things more rapidly than new habits addressed to persons and non-material institutions."

Apr. 15 The **Birth Control Clinical Research Center** established in New York City by Margaret Sanger was raided by New York police. They were acting on a complaint by the Daughters of the American Revolution. Three nurses and two doctors were arrested and

Criminal gangs that battled to control the illegal liquor business were widespread in Chicago, where Al "Scarface" Capone was soon to emerge as the top gangster. Between 1920 and 1927, about 250 persons were murdered in gang warfare. The climax to this almost open warfare came on Feb. 14, 1929. Five members of one gang, some of them dressed as policemen, walked into a garage on Chicago's North Side, where seven members of the rival George "Bugs" Moran gang were about to begin the day's illegal activities. They lined the seven up against a wall and mowed them down with submachine guns. The mass murder became known as the St. Valentine's Day Massacre and it was suspected that Capone was behind the killings.

The **world heavyweight boxing championship** was up for grabs this year. Max Schmeling of Germany became a contender after successful fights against Johnny Risko (Feb. 1) and Paulino Uzcudun (June 27). Jack Sharkey defeated William L. "Young" Stribling in a ten-round bout (Feb. 27). Schmeling and Sharkey met each other in a championship fight in 1930.

by the Senate 85–1, Sen. John J. Blaine of Wisconsin casting the only negative vote.

Mar. 4 Herbert Hoover was inaugurated president of the United States. Charles Curtis was inaugurated vice president. Hoover, the 31st president and a Republican, served one term.

May 27 Use of the **pocket veto** by the president to prevent enactment of legislation was upheld by the U.S. Supreme Court.

June 15 The **Agricultural Marketing Act** was signed by Pres. Herbert Hoover. The act authorized establishment of a Federal Farm Board for promoting the sale of agricultural commodities through agricultural cooperatives and stabilization corporations. Provisions were also made for purchase of surplus farm products for storage and sale to foreign countries to maintain price levels. A $500,000,000 revolving fund was set up to provide loans at low interest to the cooperating agencies to facilitate marketing.

Sept. National **income statistics** showed that at about this time, some 60% of U.S. citizens had annual incomes of less than $2000, which was estimated as the bare minimum to supply a family with the basic necessities of life.

Oct. 7 The **first speech before Congress by a British prime minister** was given by J. Ramsay MacDonald, who was in Washington, D.C., to discuss naval disarmament.

Oct. 7 In the continuing **Teapot Dome** oil leasing scandal, the trial of former Secretary of the Interior Albert B. Fall began in the Supreme Court of the District of Columbia. He was accused of accepting a $100,000 bribe from Edward L. Doheny in return for a lease on the Elk Hills, Calif., naval oil reserve. On Oct. 25 the court declared him guilty as charged. Fall was sentenced to one year in prison and fined $100,-000.

Hemingway, a novel combining a love story with a realistic depiction of war; *Dear Judas and Other Poems* by Robinson Jeffers; *Laughing Boy* by Oliver La Farge, a novel depicting Navajo Indian life; *Round Up*, a collection of stories by Ring Lardner; *Dodsworth* by Sinclair Lewis, a novel chronicling the collapse of a midwestern auto manufacturer's marriage during a trip to Europe; *Cup of Gold* by John Steinbeck, the author's first novel; and *Look Homeward, Angel* by Thomas Wolfe, a novel introducing Wolfe's celebrated alter ego, Eugene Gant, a sensitive and gifted young man whose quest for adventure closely mirrored the author's own.

The first experiment in creating a **garden community** was attempted in Radburn, N.J. The planned community sought to avoid the hazards of urban life and at the same time introduce a new aesthetic standard for communities.

May 12 **Pulitzer prizes** were awarded for the following: fiction, *Scarlet Sister Mary* by Julia Peterkin; biography, *Life and Letters of Walter H. Page* by Burton J. Hendrick; history, *The Organization and Administration of the Union Army, 1861–1865* by Fred Albert Shannon; poetry, *John Brown's Body* by Stephen Vincent Benét; drama, *Street Scene* by Elmer L. Rice.

May 16 The **first Academy Awards** were presented by the Academy of Motion Picture Arts and Sciences. Among the winners were best picture of 1927–28, *Wings;* best actor, Emil Jannings; best actress, Janet Gaynor.

July The **Milam Building** in San Antonio, Tex., was completed. The most modern office structure of its time, it was noted especially for the attempt to air-condition the entire building.

Sept. 16 In a curious case of **censorship,** the Pulitzer Prize-winning play *Strange Interlude* by Eugene O'Neill was banned in Boston by order of the mayor. The Theatre Guild then moved the play to the suburb of Quincy. Quincy mayor Thomas J. McGrath organized a panel of 25 citizens to see the play and judge its fitness, but the Sept. 30 opening performance was quickly sold out and they could not get in.

Sept. 22 The construction contract for the **Empire State Building** was awarded. Demolition of the old Waldorf-Astoria Hotel on the site of the new skyscraper began soon after. The building was completed in 1931.

Nov. 27 *Fifty Million Frenchmen* by Herbert Fields and Cole Porter opened at the Lyric Theatre in New York City. Described as a "musical comedy tour of Paris," it became Porter's first hit show.

| Business and Industry; Science; Education; Philosophy and Religion III | | IV Sports; Social Issues and Crime; Folkways; Fashion; Holidays |

thousands of records were confiscated. The case caused an uproar as physicians and private citizens indicated their support of the clinic. In May the case was thrown out of court as an infringement of a physician's right to practice medicine.

Sept. The Standard Statistics index of **common stock prices** reached an average of 216. Its climb was as follows: 100 during 1926; 114 by June 1927; 148 by June 1928; 191 by June 1929. This increase represented the biggest bull market the U.S. had ever known.

Sept. 24 The **first blind airplane flight,** in which the pilot used only instruments to guide the plane, was completed by Lt. James H. Doolittle at Mitchell Field, N.Y. Doolittle had received pilot training during World War I, then studied at the University of California and MIT. During this period, Doolittle was one of the leading figures in the development of flight. In 1930 he resigned from the Army Air Corps and went to work for Shell Oil Company as head of its aviation department.

Nov. A patent for a **coin-operated vending machine** that could not be tampered with was awarded to Sebastiano Lando.

Nov. 29 The **first flight over the South Pole** was completed by Lt. Commander Richard E. Byrd. The flight, from a base at Little America over the Pole and back, with a stop at an advance fueling station, lasted 19 hours. The flight was made with a Ford trimotor airplane. Byrd had started from Little America on Nov. 28 with Bernt Balchen, pilot; Harold June, radio operator; and Capt. Ashley C. McKinley, photographer and aerial surveyor. The flight to the pole and back to Little America took about 18 hours. At one point, to gain enough altitude, Byrd jettisoned a month and a half's worth of food to lighten the plane.

This year's **national college football championship** was won by Notre Dame, with a record of nine wins, no losses, no ties.

Jan. 1 The 15th **Rose Bowl** football game was won by Georgia Tech, which edged out California 8–7.

Feb. 19 **U.S. figure skating championships** were won by Maribel Y. Vinson, women's singles; Roger Turner, men's singles; and Maribel Y. Vinson and Thornton Coolidge, pairs.

Mar. 28–29 The **NHL Stanley Cup** was won by the Boston Bruins, who took two straight games from the New York Rangers.

Apr. 19 The 33rd **Boston Marathon** was won by Johnny Miles of Hamilton, Ontario, with a time of 2 hrs., 33 min., 8.8 sec.

May 10 The 54th annual **Preakness Stakes** was won by Dr. Freeland, with a time of 2:01^{3}/$_{5}$. The jockey was Louis Schaefer.

May 17 Alphonse "Scarface Al" **Capone** was sentenced to one year in prison in Chicago for carrying a concealed weapon. Capone pleaded guilty to the charge.

May 18 The 55th annual **Kentucky Derby** was won by Clyde Van Dusen, with a time of 2:10^{4}/$_{5}$. The jockey was Linus McAtee.

May 30 The 17th annual **Indianapolis 500** auto race was won by Ray Keech of Philadelphia, completing the 500-mile course in 5 hrs., 7 min., 25.42 sec., with an average speed of 97.58 mph.

June 8 The 61st annual **Belmont Stakes** was won by Blue Larkspur, with a time of 2:32^{4}/$_{5}$. The jockey was Mack Garner.

June 30 The **U.S. Open golf tournament** was won by Robert T. "Bobby" Jones, who beat Al Espinosa by 23 strokes in a playoff.

July 5 At the **Wimbledon** tennis championships in England, the women's singles title was won for the third straight year by Helen Wills. On July 6 the men's doubles was won by Wilmer Allison and John Van Ryn, and the mixed doubles was won by Helen Wills and Francis T. Hunter.

Aug. 24 The **U.S. Lawn Tennis Association** singles **championships** were won by Helen Wills, for the sixth time, in the women's division and William T. Tilden, for the seventh time, in the men's division (Sept. 14).

Oct. 8–14 The 26th annual **World Series** was won by the Philadelphia Athletics (AL), who beat the Chicago Cubs (NL) four games to one.

Dec. 7 The **PGA golf tournament** was won for the second year in a row by Leo Diegel.

1930

Early in 1930 Pres. Herbert Hoover called a special session of Congress to take up tariff revision, which he had promised in his presidential campaign the previous fall. Hoover primarily wanted to have tariff rates raised on agricultural products. By the time Congress finished its work, however, it sent Hoover the Smoot-Hawley Act, a bill that included some of the highest rates in history on manufactured products. In all, duties on 890 articles were raised to high levels. Hoover signed the act into law on June 17 despite the fact that on May 4 a petition signed by 1028 economists had been sent to Washington urging defeat of the proposed legislation. Within two years, 25 nations retaliated by raising duties on U.S. goods. The economic nationalism triggered by this legislation has been blamed for deepening the worldwide depression.

The U.S. **Census** recorded a population of 122,775,046. The center of population was located three miles northeast of Linton, Green County, Ind.

Feb. 3 **Charles Evans Hughes** was appointed chief justice of the Supreme Court by Pres. Herbert Hoover to succeed William Howard Taft, who retired this year. The appointment was confirmed Feb. 13.

Feb. 10 A major **bootlegging operation** was shut down in Chicago with the arrest of 158 persons from 31 organizations. It was estimated that these organizations sold more than 7,000,000 gallons of whiskey to speakeasies all over the country. Total value of this business was some $50,000,000.

Mar. 13 In the **Teapot Dome** oil leasing scandal, the trial of Edward L. Doheny, charged with bribing Albert B. Fall to obtain a lease for the Elk Hills naval oil reserve, began at the Supreme Court of the District of Columbia. Doheny was acquitted on Mar. 22.

Apr. 21 A **prison fire** killed 318 prisoners in the Ohio State Penitentiary at Columbus. The penitentiary, which held about 4300 inmates, had been designed to accommodate 1500.

Apr. 22 The **London Naval Treaty** was signed in London by the U.S., Great Britain, and Japan. France objected to letting Italy have equal status with the other powers, and both eventually refused to sign important provisions. The treaty remained in effect until Dec. 31, 1936. The Senate confirmed the treaty on July 21.

July 3 The **Veterans Administration Act** was signed by Pres. Hoover. It established the Veterans Administration, which combined all federal agencies dealing with benefits for former servicemen in a single department.

This year was notable for a number of events that brought serious music to radio listeners. On Mar. 16, in the first opera broadcast directly from a stage in Europe (Dresden, Germany), station WEAF in New York City carried part of a performance of Beethoven's *Fidelio.* The program was relayed to New York via shortwave transmission. On Apr. 17 the National Broadcasting Company produced the premiere of Charles Sanford Skilton's one-act Indian opera, *The Sun Bride.* And on Oct. 5 the Columbia Broadcasting System began live Sunday broadcasts of the New York Philharmonic Symphony Orchestra. Arturo Toscanini was its conductor. Seven years later the NBC Symphony Orchestra was formed with Toscanini as conductor.

Among **books published** this year was *I'll Take My Stand: Humanism and America,* an anthology of the writings of a number of southern authors, including John Crowe Ransom, Allen Tate, and Robert Penn Warren. Other books published this year included *The Bridge,* Hart Crane's most memorable work; *The 42nd Parallel* by John Dos Passos, the first novel in the author's *U.S.A.* trilogy; *As I Lay Dying* by William Faulkner, a novel; *Cimarron* by Edna Ferber, a novel; *Collected Poems* by Robert Frost; *The Maltese Falcon* by Dashiell Hammett, the classic detective novel; and *Arundel* by Kenneth Roberts, a historical novel.

Literary **censorship** continued this year. A copy of *Ulysses* by James Joyce, en route to a prospective American publisher, Random House, was seized by customs officials on the grounds that it was obscene. In Boston the works of Leon Trotsky were banned.

The painting *American Gothic* was completed by Grant Wood. Wood had applied the techniques of Flemish and German primitives in the work, which he intended as a satire. The result came to be one of the best known American paintings.

An early **cooperative housing project,** Hillman Houses, was built in New York City by a labor union.

The **Annual Festival of American Music** was inaugurated by the Eastman School of Music at the University of Rochester. It was begun by Dr. Howard Hanson, director of the school, to promote contemporary music. This year Hanson's own Second Symphony, which he called an "escape from the rather bitter type of modern musical realism," achieved immediate popular success.

Feb. 13 *The Last Mile* by John Wexley, a play that anticipated the spate of social dramas of the 1930s, opened at the Sam H. Harris Theatre in New York City. Its cast included Spencer Tracy, George Leach, and James Bell. The play was an impassioned protest against capital punishment.

| Business and Industry; Science; Education; Philosophy and Religion | III | | IV | Sports; Social Issues and Crime; Folkways; Fashion; Holidays |

1930

The Institute for Advanced Study was chartered this year and opened its doors three years later in Princeton, N.J. Its establishment was made possible by gifts from Louis Bamberger and his sister, Mrs. Felix Fuld. The institute's first director was Abraham Flexner, a prominent educator; among its first members was Albert Einstein. The institute was formed as a center for graduate studies. It has no classes and does not confer degrees. As the institute developed, it became known particularly as a research center in mathematics and the natural sciences.

Student enrollment in federally supported **vocational classes** rose from 981,882 in 1930 to 2,290,741 in 1940, and to 3,364,613 in 1950. In 1930, 188,311 students were enrolled in classes in agriculture; 618,604 in classes of trade and industry; and 174,967 in classes in home economics. In 1940 the distribution was 584,133 in agriculture; 758,409 in trade and industry; and 818,766 in home economics. In 1950 agriculture classes enrolled 764,975; trade and industry classes 804,602; and home economics classes 1,430,366.

Illiteracy in America reached a new low of 4.3% of the population, a decline of 1.7% from 1920 and a decline of 15.7% from 1870.

According to an **automobile survey,** one of every 4.9 Americans owned an automobile.

Mar. 13   Identification of the planet Pluto was made from a photograph taken on Jan. 21 at Lowell Observatory in Flagstaff, Ariz. The discovery boosted the prestige of mathematical astronomers, who had predicted existence of the planet.

Mar. 30   The first transcontinental glider flight was begun by Capt. Frank M. Hawks, who took off from San Diego, Calif. He was towed by a biplane on a 500-foot line. He reached Van Cortlandt Park, New York City, on Apr. 6. Hawks had flown the first seaplane glider in the U.S. two weeks earlier at Port Washington, N.Y.

May 11   Adler Planetarium, the **first planetarium** in the U.S., opened in Chicago.

Aug. 11   The American Lutheran Church was formed at Toledo, Ohio, by the merger of the Lutheran Synod of Buffalo, the Evangelical Lutheran Synod of Iowa, and the Evangelical Lutheran Joint Synod of Ohio. On Oct. 31 the church, at an organizational convention, completed the merger of seven synods in the U.S. and Canada.

Golf's first nationally known figure and perhaps the best golfer who ever played, Robert Tyre "Bobby" Jones, Jr., announced his retirement on Nov. 17, after a year in which he set records never achieved by any other player. On Sept. 27 he became the only player ever to make the grand slam in golf by winning the 1930 U.S. Amateur golf tournament after winning the U.S. Open, the British Open, and the British Amateur tournaments. Jones had played serious golf for only eight years, spending much of his time studying law, literature, and engineering. But of the 27 major championship tournaments he entered, he won 13. In retirement he made instructional films and, with Clifford Roberts, founded the Augusta National Golf Club in Georgia and organized the Masters Tournament, one of the major U.S. golf tournaments.

This year's **national college football championship** was won by Notre Dame, with a record of ten wins, no losses, no ties.

Jan. 1   The 16th **Rose Bowl** football game was won by Southern California, defeating Pittsburgh 47–14.

Mar. 22–23   U.S. figure skating championships were won by Maribel Y. Vinson, women's singles; Roger Turner, men's singles; and Beatrix Loughran and Sherwin C. Badger, pairs.

Apr. 1–3   The **NHL Stanley Cup** was won by the Montreal Canadiens, who swept the Boston Bruins in two straight games.

Apr. 19   The **Boston Marathon** was won for the seventh time by Clarence H. DeMar of Melrose, Mass., with a time of 2 hrs., 34 min., 48.2 sec.

May 9   The 55th annual **Preakness Stakes** was won by Gallant Fox, with a time of 2:00³/₅. The jockey was Earl Sande.

May 17   The 56th annual **Kentucky Derby** was won by Gallant Fox, with a time of 2:07³/₅. The jockey was Earl Sande, who scored his third Derby victory.

May 30   The 18th annual **Indianapolis 500** auto race was won by Billy Arnold, who completed the course in 4 hrs., 58 min., 39.72 sec., with an average speed of 100.44 mph.

June 7   The 62nd annual **Belmont Stakes** was won by Gallant Fox. The jockey was Earl Sande. This was the second time that a horse had won the Triple Crown. The winning time was 2:31³/₅.

June 12   The **world heavyweight boxing championship** was won by Max Schmeling of Germany. Schmeling was awarded the victory over Jack Sharkey, who fouled him in the fourth round of the bout in New York City.

July 4   At the **Wimbledon** tennis championships, the women's singles title was won by Helen Wills, now called Helen Wills Moody, her married name. Other

Nov. 4 In **congressional elections** the Republicans lost eight seats in the Senate for a nominal 48–47 majority, with one seat going to a minor party. In the House the Democrats took a 220–214 lead, with one seat going to a minor party.

Nov. 27 The **Nobel Peace Prize** for 1929 was awarded to Frank B. Kellogg who, as secretary of state (1925–1929) under Pres. Calvin Coolidge, negotiated the Kellogg-Briand Peace Pact of 1928.

Dec. 2 In a move to provide **jobs for the unemployed,** Pres. Hoover asked Congress for money for construction of public works. On Dec. 20 Congress passed the necessary legislation for an appropriation of $116,000,000. The president had announced in October there were 4,500,000 unemployed. At the beginning of the Depression, Hoover had tried to arrange programs to deal with unemployment through state and local governments and organizations.

Apr. 3 **Academy Awards** were presented to *Broadway Melody* as the oustanding motion picture of 1928–1929; Warner Baxter as best actor for *In Old Arizona;* and Mary Pickford as best actress for *Coquette.*

May 12 **Pulitzer prizes** were awarded for the following: fiction, *Laughing Boy* by Oliver La Farge; biography, *The Raven* by Marquis James; history, *The War of Independence* by Claude H. Van Tyne; poetry, *Selected Poems* by Conrad Aiken; drama, *The Green Pastures* by Marc Connelly.

Nov. 5 **Academy Awards** were presented to *All Quiet on the Western Front* as the outstanding motion picture of 1929–1930; George Arliss as best actor for *Disraeli;* and Norma Shearer as best actress for *The Divorce.*

Nov. 5 The **Nobel Prize in Literature** was awarded to Sinclair Lewis, particularly in recognition of his novel *Babbitt.* Lewis was the first American to win the prize in literature.

1931

Breakdown in enforcement of the Prohibition laws appeared to be affecting law enforcement in general. As a result, in May of 1929 Pres. Herbert Hoover had appointed a National Commission on Law Observance and Law Enforcement. He named George W. Wickersham, a former U.S. attorney general, as its head. The body came to be known as the Wickersham Commission. It issued its report on Jan. 19, 1931, noting that enforcement of antiliquor laws was hindered by the great profits to be earned in illegal traffic and by the apathy, even hostility, of the general public. The commission believed enforcement should be left to the federal government. It recommended revisions but not repeal of the Eighteenth Amendment. Pres. Hoover, in submitting the report to Congress on Jan. 20, said he also did not favor repeal. The report did not result in any effective action.

Feb. 24 The **procedure for the adoption of the Eighteenth Amendment** was ruled valid by the U.S. Supreme Court in a unanimous decision that reversed the ruling of federal Judge William Clark of New Jersey.

Mar. 17 Mayor **James J. Walker** of New York City was charged with malfeasance and negligence of official

Widespread disillusionment with politics, prompted in large part by the seeming inability of the federal government to end the Depression, was reflected in this year's hit musical comedy, *Of Thee I Sing,* with music by George Gershwin, lyrics by Ira Gershwin, and book by George S. Kaufman and Morrie Ryskind. It was a sharp but good-natured satire on presidential politics. The show opened at the Music Box Theatre in New York City on Dec. 26 and ran for 441 performances. When the show won the Pulitzer Prize for drama the next year, it was the first musical ever to be so honored. The title song was a hit too. A sequel, *Let 'Em Eat Cake* (1933), was less successful, having only 90 Broadway performances.

Among **books published** this year was *The Good Earth* by Pearl S. Buck, the author's first novel. For two years this best seller was at the top of the sales list in bookstores. Other books published this year included *Shadows on the Rock* by Willa Cather, a beautifully written novel set in seventeenth-century Quebec; *ViVa* by E. E. Cummings, poetry; *Newspaper Days* by Theodore Dreiser, autobiography; *Sanctuary* by William Faulkner, a novel; *American Beauty* by Edna Ferber, a novel; *The Glass Key* by Dashiell Hammett; the *Autobiography* of Lincoln Steffens; *The Forge* by T. S. Stribling, the first novel of a trilogy dealing with the fictional Vaiden family of Alabama; *The Long Christmas Dinner* by Thornton Wilder, a collection of one-act plays; and *Axel's Castle* by Edmund Wilson, a collection of essays on symbolism and symbolist writers.

Sept. 3 An experimental **electric passenger train** was installed by Thomas A. Edison on the Lackawanna Railroad between Hoboken and Montclair, N.J.

Sept. 17 Construction of the **Hoover Dam,** originally called Boulder Dam, was begun at Las Vegas, Nev. Work was completed in 1936.

Oct. 30 The **Nobel Prize in Physiology or Medicine** was awarded to Dr. Karl Landsteiner of the Rockefeller Institute for his discovery of human blood groups. Landsteiner was the first American citizen to win the prize for medicine.

Dec. 11 The **Bank of the United States** in New York City, with 60 local branches and 400,000 depositors, closed. More than 1300 banks throughout the country had been closed down by the deepening economic crisis.

titles taken by Americans were men's singles, William T. Tilden (July 5); women's doubles, Helen Wills Moody and Elizabeth Ryan (July 5); men's doubles, Wilmer Allison and John Van Ryn (July 7).

July 12 The **U.S. Open golf tournament** was won by Robert T. "Bobby" Jones.

Aug. 23 The **U.S. Lawn Tennis Association singles championships** were won by Betty Nuthall of England in the women's division and John H. Doeg in the men's division (Sept. 13).

Sept. 13 The **PGA golf tournament** was won by Tommy Armour.

Sept. 13–17 The **America's Cup** was successfully defended by the yacht *Enterprise,* which defeated the British challenger *Shamrock V* in four straight races.

Oct. 1–8 The 27th annual **World Series** was won by the Philadelphia Athletics (AL), who defeated the St. Louis Cardinals (NL) four games to two.

1931

Research in physics in the U.S. and Europe was leading to discoveries that in a few years would be applied in production of the atomic bomb. A leader in the U.S. was Harold C. Urey, a professor of physics at Columbia University. This year Urey announced that he and his associates had discovered an isotope of hydrogen with an atomic weight of two instead of one. This was heavy hydrogen, or deuterium. Molecules of water containing deuterium atoms instead of hydrogen atoms came to be known as heavy water. This was a key component in atomic fission experiments. Urey later served as director (1942–1945) of the Manhattan Project, which developed the world's first atomic bombs.

Stellar radio emissions from the Milky Way were first detected by J. G. Lansky, a radio engineer for Bell Telephone Laboratories. Although Lansky could not identify the exact source of the hissing, his observations helped establish the science of radio-astronomy.

Declining membership in **trade unions** was reflected in figures for the following years: 1920, over 5,000,000; 1927, fewer than 4,000,000; 1931, about 3,333,000.

Jan. 7 **Unemployment** was estimated at between 4,000,000 and 5,000,000 by Col. Arthur Woods, head of the President's Emergency Committee for Unemployment Relief.

The American gangster was a prominent personality in the 1920s and 1930s. Foremost was Alphonse "Al" Capone, also known as "Scarface." He ruled the Chicago underworld in the 1920s with unprecedented lawlessness and brutality. It was estimated that in 1927 alone he took in $105,000,000. Finally, in 1931, Capone was indicted for income tax evasion. He was convicted on Oct. 17 and sentenced to 11 years in prison. He was released in 1939, mortally ill from syphilis. In the East, Jack "Legs" Diamond attracted the most attention because of the unusual scrapes he got into and the number of times he was wounded, but not killed, by gunfire. On Dec. 18, 1931, he was shot to death in an Albany, N.Y., boardinghouse shortly after being acquitted of kidnaping.

This year's **national college football championship** was won by Southern California, with a record of ten wins, one loss, no ties.

Jan. 1 The 17th **Rose Bowl** football game was won by Alabama, defeating Washington State 24–0.

Mar. 21 **U.S. figure skating championships** were won in Boston by Maribel Y. Vinson, women's singles; Roger F. Turner, men's singles; Beatrix Loughran and Sherwin C. Badger, pairs.

Apr. 3–14 The **NHL Stanley Cup** was won by the Montreal Canadiens, who defeated the Chicago Black Hawks three games to two.

Apr. 20 The 35th **Boston Marathon** was won by James Henigan of Medford, Mass., with a time of 2 hrs., 46 min., 45.8 sec.

Exploration and Settlement; Wars; Government; Civil Rights; Statistics	I		II	Publishing; Arts and Music; Popular Entertainment; Architecture; Theater

duties. His removal from office was urged in a statement of charges presented to Gov. Franklin D. Roosevelt by John Haynes Holmes, pastor of the Community Church, and Rabbi Stephen S. Wise. On Apr. 20 Walker denied the charges in a statement to Roosevelt, and on Apr. 28 the governor dismissed them as tenuous.

June 20 An **international moratorium on war debts and reparations** was proposed by Pres. Hoover. The president's first important act to break the international financial panic, it seemed successful at first; stock markets rallied and bankers and economists were enthusiastic. But soon the panic became worse than ever.

Sept. A **bank panic** spread across the nation. In September 305 banks closed; in October 522 shut down. Fear that the U.S. would go off the gold standard led to hoarding of the metal throughout the country.

Dec. 10 The **Nobel Peace Prize** was awarded jointly to Nicholas Murray Butler, president of Columbia University, and to Jane Addams of Chicago. Butler had been the first major figure to support the Kellogg-Briand Peace Pact of 1928, and Addams had been the first international president of the Women's International League for Peace and Freedom. She was honorary president at the time of the award.

The **New School for Social Research** was built in New York City. The building, designed specifically for adult education, was considered a striking example of modern architecture.

Feb. 27 The **New York** *World* was merged with a Scripps-Howard paper, the New York *Telegram,* to form the New York *World-Telegram.* The *World's* editor, Walter Lippmann, joined the *Herald Tribune* and launched a syndicated column that immediately became popular throughout the country.

Mar. 3 An act making **"The Star-Spangled Banner"** the national anthem was signed by Pres. Herbert Hoover. Francis Scott Key wrote the words in 1814 during the bombardment of Fort McHenry in the War of 1812.

May 4 **Pulitzer prizes** were awarded for the following: fiction, *Years of Grace* by Margaret Ayers Barnes; biography, *Charles W. Eliot* by Henry James; history, *The Coming of the War: 1914* by Bernadotte E. Schmitt; poetry, *Collected Poems* by Robert Frost; drama, *Alison's House* by Susan Glaspell.

Oct. 26 *Mourning Becomes Electra* by Eugene O'Neill, a marathon play six hours long comprising three parts, *Homecoming, The Hunted,* and *The Haunted,* opened at the Guild Theatre in New York City.

Nov. 10 **Academy Awards** were presented to *Cimarron* as the outstanding motion picture of 1931; to Lionel Barrymore as best actor for *A Free Soul;* and to Marie Dressler as best actress for *Min and Bill.*

1932

It was a trying year for the nation. Pres. Herbert Hoover tried desperately to stem the Great Depression by granting generous credit to industry and ordering a stern check on government spending. Not only did he reduce his personal salary by 20%, but he also persuaded Vice Pres. Charles Curtis and nine members of the Cabinet to accept similar cuts. Public works programs were planned to alleviate staggering unemployment. Hoover's plans, however, were never realized, for

This year 15,279 books were published or reprinted in the U.S. Of these, 1996 were novels. The novelists' main preoccupation this year seemed to be with the problems of the South. Despite the publication of several outstanding works, not much of literary value was offered to the public. In fact, a virtual paralysis had settled over the arts. Opera houses in Chicago and Philadelphia gave no performances. A number of new orchestral works were ventured, but none with serious

| Business and Industry; Science; Education; Philosophy and Religion III | | IV Sports; Social Issues and Crime; Folkways; Fashion; Holidays |

May 1 The **Empire State Building,** the world's tallest building, was dedicated and opened to the public in New York City.

June 4 The **first rocket-powered glider** in the U.S. was flown by William G. Swan, a stunt pilot, at Atlantic City, N.J. The glider traveled 1000 ft. and reached a height of 100 ft. The flight was staged as an entertainment for an audience at the Steel Pier.

June 23 A **flight around the world** was begun by Wiley Post and Harold Gatty, who took off from Roosevelt Field, Long Island, N.Y., in their plane *Winnie May.* They landed back at Roosevelt Field 8 days, 15 hrs., 51 min. later.

July 1 The **National Council of Congregational and Christian Churches** was formed in Seattle, Wash., by the union of the National Council of Congregational Churches and the General Convention of Christian Churches.

Oct. 5 The **first nonstop flight across the Pacific** Ocean was completed by Hugh Herndon and Clyde Pangborn, who flew from Sabishiro, Japan, to Wenatchee, Wash., a distance of 4860 mi., in 41 hrs., 13 min.

Oct. 24 The **George Washington Bridge,** linking Manhattan with New Jersey across the Hudson R., was officially opened. Gov. Franklin D. Roosevelt of New York and Gov. Morgan F. Larson of New Jersey took part in the ceremonies. The Port Authority of New York had completed the bridge eight months ahead of schedule and under budget. The bridge, one of the most beautiful and best known in the world, was opened to traffic the next day.

May 9 The 56th annual **Preakness Stakes** was won by Mate, with a time of 1:59. The jockey was George Ellis.

May 13 In the celebrated **false start race** at Jamaica, N.Y., the entire field of horses went completely around the track before they were recalled. Rideaway and Clock Tower came in first and second in the false start. In the official race, Clock Tower came in first, and Rideaway finished second.

May 16 The 57th annual **Kentucky Derby** was won by Twenty Grand, with a new derby record time of 2:01⅘, which held until 1941. The jockey was Charles Kurtsinger.

May 30 The 19th annual **Indianapolis 500** auto race was won by Louis Schneider, completing the 500-mile course in 5 hrs., 10 min., 27.94 sec., with an average speed of 96.63 mph.

June 13 The 63rd annual **Belmont Stakes** was won by Twenty Grand, with a time of 2:29⅗. The jockey was Charles Kurtsinger.

July 3–4 At the **Wimbledon** tennis championships, the men's singles title was won by Sidney B. Wood, Jr., 20, the youngest winner in the history of the event. The men's doubles title was won by George Lott, Jr., and John Van Ryn, and the mixed doubles was won by George Lott, Jr., and Mrs. L. A. Harper.

July 6 The **U.S. Open golf tournament** was won by Billy Burke, who beat George Von Elm by one stroke after two 36-hole playoffs.

Aug. 20 The **U.S. Lawn Tennis Association singles championships** were won by Mrs. Helen Wills Moody in the women's division and H. Ellsworth Vines, Jr., in the men's division (Sept. 12).

Sept. 19 The **PGA golf tournament** was won by Tom Creavy.

Oct. 1–10 The 28th annual **World Series** was won by the St. Louis Cardinals (NL), who beat the Philadelphia Athletics (AL) four games to three.

Dec. 28 The **U.S. figure skating championships** were won by Maribel Y. Vinson, women's singles; Roger F. Turner, men's singles; Beatrix Loughran and Sherwin C. Badger, pairs.

1932

Poor demand for goods, uncertain manufacturing conditions, and a wobbly stock market combined to make this one of the most unfavorable business years in modern history. Labor, however, hailed its most important victory to date—passage of the Federal Anti-Injunction Law, or Norris-LaGuardia Act. The battle for the five-day work week was also being won, as Pres. Herbert Hoover made it standard for most government employees. With unemployment hovering at about 11,-

The movement to repeal Prohibition received a boost when the redoubtable "dry" John D. Rockefeller spoke out for the repeal of the Volstead Act. Both presidential candidates asked for its erasure from the law books. With such powerful forces against it, Prohibition was doomed. In baseball Jimmy Foxx threatened to eclipse Babe Ruth's home run record of 60, falling short by two. Tennis had a dazzling new name—16-year-old Frankie Parker, who mowed down veteran opposition wherever

1932 *PRES.* HERBERT HOOVER

480

| Exploration and Settlement; Wars; Government; Civil Rights; Statistics | I | | II | Publishing; Arts and Music; Popular Entertainment; Architecture; Theater |

the voters insisted on a change of administration, electing Franklin D. Roosevelt to the presidency in a Democratic landslide.

The number of **unemployed** in the U.S. reached 13,-000,000. National wages were 60% less than in 1929, dividends 56.6% less. Total business loss during the year was placed at $5,000,000,000 to $6,000,000,000. Two and a half years after the Oct. 1929 stock market crash, U.S. industry as a whole was operating at less than half its maximum 1929 volume.

Jan. 22 The **Reconstruction Finance Corporation** was established with $2,000,000,000 at its disposal to lend to failing banks, farm mortgage associations, building and loan societies, railroads, and insurance companies.

Mar. 1 In the **Lindbergh kidnaping,** one of the most highly publicized crimes of the twentieth century, Charles A. Lindbergh, Jr., an infant of 20 months, was kidnaped from his parents' home at Hopewell, N.J. The body of the child was found on May 12, after payment of a $50,000 ransom. Outraged public opinion made kidnaping a federal crime carrying the death penalty.

Apr. 30–May 2 The **Socialist Labor Party** nominated Verne L. Reynolds of New York for the presidency. J. W. Aiken of Massachusetts was nominated for the vice presidency.

May 22–24 The **Socialist Party nominated Norman Thomas** of New York for the presidency and James H. Maurer of Pennsylvania for the vice presidency.

May 28 The **Communist Party of America** nominated William Z. Foster of New York for the presidency and James W. Ford of New York for the vice presidency.

May 29 The so-called **Bonus Army,** a group of some 1000 former servicemen seeking cash payments for their veterans' bonus certificates, arrived in Washington, D.C. In June other groups of veterans arrived from every section of the country, swelling the army to about 17,000. Camped in the open or in unused buildings near the Capitol, they vowed to stay until Congress authorized immediate cash in full for their certificates. A bill authorizing payment passed the House on June 15, but was killed in the Senate on June 17. The government provided money for veterans to return to their homes, but about 2000 refused the offer and did not move. Finally, on July 28, federal troops under Gen. Douglas MacArthur drove them out.

June 14–16 The **Republican National Convention renominated Pres. Hoover** for the presidency on the first ballot. Charles Curtis was renominated for the vice presidency.

claim to stature. Painters looking for inspiration found it in the formalized primitivism of the Mexican artist Diego Rivera and his compatriots. Architects, deprived of the opportunity to build, chose to quarrel over the so-called International school of design. The theater enjoyed only one real hit—Philip Barry's *The Animal Kingdom.*

Among **books published** this year was *Tobacco Road* by Erskine Caldwell. This novel, dealing with the family of Jeeter Lester, a poor Georgia sharecropper, was the basis for an enormously successful dramatization in 1933 by Jack Kirkland; it has since become an American classic. Other books published this year included *Beyond Desire* by Sherwood Anderson, a novel set in the South; *1919* by John Dos Passos, the second novel in his trilogy *U.S.A.; Light in August* by William Faulkner; and *The Store* by T. S. Stribling, the second novel of a trilogy set in the South.

The **Grand Canyon Suite** was composed by Ferde Grofé. It became known throughout the world.

E. Y. "Yip" Harburg wrote one of the most popular songs of the year, "Brother, Can You Spare a Dime."

Charles Sheeler painted *River Rouge Plant,* an example of precisionism, or the use of austere line and proportion to convey a feeling of the architectural and mechanical. The painting combined the tradition of American craftsmanship with modern engineering design.

Grant Wood, in his painting *Daughters of the American Revolution,* added a note of satire to the objective realism of the twentieth century. The painting was considered a wry commentary on American life.

Charles Burchfield painted *November Evening.* It depicted the shabbiness and drabness of small-town life in the Midwest, tinged with a sense of the tragic. Isolation of a building against a darkening sky, a solitary figure, and the monotonous earth spoke of grandeur as well as of bleakness.

Jan. The **rhythmicon,** a machine invented by the composer Henry Cowell and the engineer Leon Theremin to reproduce all rhythmical combinations, however complex, was presented in a concert at the New School for Social Research in New York City. The chief work on the concert program was Cowell's composition *Rhythmicana,* for orchestra and rhythmicon.

Mar. 28 The career of **George M. Cohan** continued with *Confidential Service,* a detective play that revealed the culprit's identity to the audience in the first act.

Apr. 25 The opening of *Another Language* by Rose Franken at the Booth Theatre in New York City marked the beginning of Franken's career as a playwright. This drama studied the relation of parent and child against the background of the family, a popular theme of the 1930s.

| Business and Industry; Science; Education; Philosophy and Religion III | IV Sports; Social Issues and Crime; Folkways; Fashion; Holidays |

000,000, labor could make little headway in its demands for compulsory unemployment insurance. In science, progress was made in the study of cosmic rays; in the discovery of the neutron by James Chadwick; in the enunciation of the uncertainty principle; and in laboratory production of gamma rays. In addition, an isotope of hydrogen was produced and vitamin C was isolated and identified. Automation was fast becoming a specialty of its own with the construction of large and versatile computing machines.

The **first Polaroid glass** was devised by Edwin H. Land.

Construction of the **San Francisco–Oakland Bay Bridge** was begun. The total cost of the bridge was estimated at $70,000,000.

Wheat prices dropped to a new low of 32 cents a bushel. This contrasted with peak prices of $2.33 a bushel in 1920.

Mar. 23 The **Norris–La Guardia Anti-Injunction** Act, a significant gain for labor, was signed into law. It prohibited injunctions as a means of maintaining anti-union employment contracts or inhibiting strikes, picketing, and boycotts.

May 20 **Amelia Earhart** became the first woman to cross the Atlantic in a solo flight when she landed near Londonderry, Ireland, 2026½ miles from Harbor Grace, Newfoundland, her starting point. The flight took 13 hrs., 30 min.

Fall The opening of **Bennington College** in Bennington, Vt., began a notable experiment in progressive education on the college level. A school for women, it eschewed orthodox methods of grading, credits, and points. A similar project was seen at Teachers College at Columbia University in New York City, where graduation was to be based on overall knowledge acquired rather than on completion of prescribed courses.

Oct. 13 The cornerstone was laid for a new **Supreme Court Building** in Washington, D.C. Pres. Hoover, Chief Justice Charles Evans Hughes, and Guy A. Thompson, president of the American Bar Association, officiated.

he played. The greatest blot on the nation's conscience was its fantastic crime wave. The citizens of Chicago this year shelled out some $145,000,000 to racketeers.

Bank Night, offering prizes to members of the audience at movie houses, was introduced by Charles Urban Yeager in theaters in Colorado. Later he copyrighted the idea, and it spread rapidly throughout the country.

Jan. 1 The 18th **Rose Bowl** football game was won by Southern California, defeating Tulane 21–12. Southern California, with a record of ten wins, one loss, no ties, won the national college football championship.

Feb. 4–13 At the 1932 **Winter Olympics** in Lake Placid, N.Y., the third such games in history and the first held in the U.S., the U.S. team won ten gold medals and the unofficial team championship.

Apr. 5–9 The **NHL Stanley Cup** was won by the Toronto Maple Leafs, who defeated the N.Y. Rangers in three straight games.

Apr. 19 The 36th **Boston Marathon** was won by Paul DeBruyn of New York with a time of 2 hrs., 33 min., 36.4 sec.

May 7 The 58th annual **Kentucky Derby** was won by Burgoo King, with a time of 2:05⅕. The jockey was Eugene James.

May 14 The 57th annual **Preakness Stakes** was won by Burgoo King, with a time of 1:59⅘. The jockey was Eugene James.

May 30 The 20th **Indianapolis 500** auto race was won by Fred Frame of Los Angeles, completing the 500-mile course in 4 hrs., 48 min., 3.79 sec., with an average speed of 104.14 mph.

June 4 The 64th annual **Belmont Stakes** was won by Faireno, with a time of 2:32⅘. The jockey was Tommy Malley.

June 21 The world **heavyweight boxing championship** was won by Jack Sharkey, who took a 15-round decision over Max Schmeling of Germany in New York City, thus returning the title to the U.S.

June 25 The **U.S. Open golf tournament** was won by Gene Sarazen.

June 27–July 2 The **Democratic National Convention nominated Franklin D. Roosevelt** for the presidency, ending a deadlock produced by opposing factions supporting Roosevelt, John Nance Garner of Texas, and Alfred E. Smith of New York. The deadlock was broken and Roosevelt nominated on July 1, when Garner was persuaded to give his delegates to Roosevelt in return for the vice presidential nomination. Roosevelt broke precedent by flying to Chicago to accept the nomination. In his speech, he called for a "new deal for the American people."

July 5–7 The **Prohibition Party** nominated William D. Upshaw of Georgia for the presidency and Frank S. Regan of Illinois for the vice presidency.

July 10 The **Farmer Labor Party** nominated Jacob S. Coxey, mayor of Massillon, Ohio, for the presidency.

Nov. 8 **Franklin D. Roosevelt was elected president** of the United States in a Democratic landslide. John Nance Garner was elected vice president. Roosevelt carried all but seven states, with 472 electoral votes to 59 for Herbert Hoover. The popular vote was Roosevelt, 22,821,857; Hoover, 15,761,841; Norman Thomas, Socialist, 881,951; William Z. Foster, Communist, 102,785; Verne L. Reynolds, Socialist Labor, 33,276; William D. Upshaw, Prohibition, 81,869; Jacob S. Coxey, Farmer Labor, 7309. In congressional elections the Democrats gained 13 Senate seats for a 60–35 majority, with one seat held by a minor party. In the House the Democrats gained 90 seats for a 310–117 majority, with five seats going to minor parties.

May 2 **Pulitzer prizes** were awarded for the following: fiction, *The Good Earth* by Pearl S. Buck; biography, *Theodore Roosevelt* by Henry F. Pringle; history, *My Experiences in the World War* by John J. Pershing; poetry, *The Flowering Stone* by George Dillon; drama, *Of Thee I Sing* by George S. Kaufman, Morrie Ryskind, and Ira Gershwin. This was the first time a musical received the drama award.

Oct. 6 *When Ladies Meet,* a delightful comedy by Rachel Crothers, opened. The play studied two women, who were wife and mistress of the same man. It concluded with the inevitable discovery on the part of the wife.

Oct. 31 *The Late Christopher Bean* by Sidney Howard, a comedy of a small-town family who had once known a painter and thought him a ne'er-do-well only to find themselves famous because of their acquaintance with him after his death, opened at the Henry Miller Theatre in New York City.

Nov. 18 **Academy Awards** were presented to *Grand Hotel* as the outstanding motion picture of 1931–1932; to Fredric March as best actor for his dual portrayal in *Dr. Jekyll and Mr. Hyde;* and to Helen Hayes as best actress for *The Sin of Madelon Claudet.* An additional award was presented to Wallace Beery for *The Champ.* The first awards for short subjects were presented to Walt Disney for the cartoon *Flowers and Trees;* to Mack Sennett for *A Wrestling Swordfish;* and to Hal Roach for *Laurel and Hardy in the Music Box.* A special award was presented to Walt Disney for his creation of Mickey Mouse.

1933

The change of administration deepened the economic crisis. The low point was reached by inauguration day, with the nation gripped by a bank panic. To meet the situation, the administration demanded and was given unprecedented powers. These led to wide changes in the monetary system and to creation of an array of federal agencies to regulate private industry and find jobs for millions on government-sponsored projects. While this program, known as the New Deal, restored some confidence, its more radical measures came under conservative attack. Its critics, however, failed to win popular support. In world affairs, America's Good Neighbor policy fostered an era of Pan-American political and economic cooperation. The gravity of domestic problems distracted attention from international affairs: the rise of Adolf Hitler in Germany, warfare in the Far East, and disintegration of the League of Nations.

Theater had a lackluster year despite offerings by established playwrights and stars. The most notable exception was Eugene O'Neill's *Ah, Wilderness!* Opera houses and symphonic societies curtailed their seasons. Painters and sculptors were helped by commissions from the Civil Works Administration. At one time, the government employed as many as 2500 artists and 1000 architects, most of whom worked at supplying murals for public buildings. The two most popular films of the year were *Little Women,* starring Katherine Hepburn, and *She Done Him Wrong,* featuring Mae West.

Among **books published** this year was *Anthony Adverse* by Hervey Allen, a long, sprawling novel set in the Napoleonic era. Despite criticism concerning Allen's historical accuracy, readers made the book a best seller. Other books published this year included *Death*

| Business and Industry; Science; Education; Philosophy and Religion   III | | Sports; Social Issues and Crime; Folkways; Fashion; Holidays   IV |

Nov. The first comprehensive **medical study** of the relation between medical practices and needs was completed as a government project. The investigating group, the Committee on the Costs of Medical Care, suggested modified socialization of medicine under state control, to be supported by health insurance payments or special taxation. The report left room for private cases. Immediate objections were raised by the American Medical Association, who called the plan Utopian, cumbersome, bureaucratic, and impersonal.

Nov. 10 The **Nobel Prize in Chemistry** was awarded to Irving Langmuir "for his discoveries and investigations in surface chemistry." Langmuir conducted his prize-winning research on surface actions of glass, water, and metals. His discoveries led to improvements in incandescent lighting, reduction of light glare from glass surfaces, and cloud seeding to induce rainfall.

Dec. The vogue for **technocracy** reached its height. Conceived of by Howard Scott, an amateur economist in New York City, and based in part on the doctrines of Frederick Soddy and Thorstein Veblen, it stressed management of society by technical experts. The seemingly scientific and semimystical qualities of technocracy gave it great popularity for a time.

July 1 At the **Wimbledon** tennis championships, Helen Wills Moody won the women's singles title. H. Ellsworth Vines, Jr., won the men's singles on July 2.

July 2 The term *New Deal* was introduced by Franklin D. Roosevelt in his speech accepting the Democratic nomination for the presidency. Before the assembled delegates in Chicago, Roosevelt said: "I pledge you, I pledge myself, to a new deal for the American people. Let us all here assembled constitute ourselves prophets of a new order of competence and courage. This is more than a political campaign; it is a call to arms."

July 30–Aug. 14 At the 1932 **Summer Olympics** in Los Angeles, Calif., the U.S. won 16 gold medals and the unofficial team championship.

Aug. 21 The **U.S. Lawn Tennis Association singles championships** were won by Helen Hull Jacobs in the women's division and H. Ellsworth Vines, Jr., in the men's division (Sept. 3).

Sept. 4 The **PGA golf tournament** was won by Olin Dutra.

Sept. 28–Oct. 2 The 29th annual **World Series** was won by the New York Yankees (AL), who swept the Chicago Cubs (NL) in four games.

1933

Encouraged by sympathetic legislation, especially creation of the National Labor Relations Board (NLRB), organized labor became more militant in making its demands—particularly its right to organize. The American Federation of Labor boasted 4,000,000 members in 29,669 local bodies, and counted as allies the workers enrolled in the railroad brotherhoods. Scientists, meanwhile, confirmed the discovery in 1932 of the positron (positive electron). Television pioneers were jubilantly hailing a new communication medium and pointed with pride to a cathode-ray screen already on the market. American education presented a more somber picture. Two thousand rural schools failed to open in the fall. More than 1500 commercial schools and colleges were forced to suspend activities. Some 200,000 certified teachers were unemployed, and it was estimated that 2,280,000 children were not attending school.

The Depression damped most professional sporting activities. The exception was horseracing, which boomed as never before. State legislatures, recognizing the revenue produced by betting at tracks, compromised their moral positions by encouraging the sport. Maryland this year earned some $66,000,000 from racing revenues alone. League-leading baseball clubs played before packed parks, but the losing teams could not fill their stands. College football contests enjoyed a 13% rise in attendance over the previous season—a popularity that extended to the professional game as well.

The **first totalizator** used at an American racetrack was installed at Arlington Park, Chicago, Ill. This completely electrical device, invented and built in the U.S. in 1927, printed and issued betting tickets at the rate of 50 a minute. It then sorted, added, and transmitted totals to indicator boards, flashing new information to

Feb. 6 The **Twentieth Amendment** to the U.S. Constitution was adopted. It abolished the so-called lame-duck session of Congress and changed the presidential inauguration date from Mar. 4 to Jan. 20. It also specified that the vice president-elect would succeed to the presidency if the president-elect died before inauguration.

Mar. 1 **Bank holidays** were declared in six states, effectively preventing runs on bank assets by worried depositors. By Mar. 4 bank panics reached their greatest intensity. At 4:30 A.M. that day, Gov. Herbert H. Lehman of New York declared a state bank holiday; Gov. Henry Horner of Illinois immediately followed suit.

Mar. 4 **Franklin D. Roosevelt was inaugurated president** of the United States. In his inaugural address, Pres. Roosevelt included the memorable sentence: "The only thing we have to fear is fear itself." The address outlined an aggressive policy to deal with the economic emergency.

Mar. 4 **Frances Perkins,** the first woman to hold a Cabinet post, was appointed secretary of labor by Pres. Franklin D. Roosevelt.

Mar. 5 A week-long **national bank holiday** was approved today, Sunday, by a special session of Congress convened by Pres. Roosevelt.

Mar. 12 The **first fireside chat,** a radio address to the entire nation, was delivered by Pres. Roosevelt on this Sunday evening. His subject was the reopening of the banks during the following week.

Mar. 13 **Banks began reopening** across the country. Before the end of the month over 75% of all banks were operating again.

Mar. 31 The **Civilian Conservation Corps** (CCC) was initiated by the Reforestation Unemployment Act to create jobs through a national reforestation program.

May 12 The **Agricultural Adjustment Act** (AAA) restricted production of certain crops, to be determined by farmers, and paid them bounties for uncultivated acreage. The bounties were to be paid from the revenue obtained from a processing tax. The Supreme Court ruled the AAA unconstitutional in 1936.

May 12 The **Federal Emergency Relief Act** and an appropriation of $500,000,000 for the Federal Emergency Relief Administration were approved by Congress.

May 18 The **Tennessee Valley Act** was passed, establishing the Tennessee Valley Authority (TVA). Its purpose was to control Tennessee R. floods, institute a reforestation program on marginal lands in the Tennessee R. Valley, and provide rural electrification.

May 27 The **Federal Securities Act** was passed

in the Woods, a collection of stories by Sherwood Anderson; *Winner Take Nothing* by Ernest Hemingway, also a collection of stories; *Give Your Heart to the Hawks, and Other Poems* by Robinson Jeffers; *Principles of Harmonic Analysis* by Walter Piston, one of the most influential textbooks on the methods of modern composition; *Rabble in Arms* by Kenneth Roberts, a historical novel; and *The Autobiography of Alice B. Toklas* by Gertrude Stein, which sold surprisingly well.

A significant **obscenity ruling** was handed down in New York City concerning Erskine Caldwell's novel *God's Little Acre.* City Magistrate Benjamin Greenspan exonerated the book of the charge of obscenity made by the New York Society for the Prevention of Vice. The decision was based on three criteria: consideration of the book as a whole rather than a few isolated sections, the aptness of coarse language when spoken by coarse characters, and reactions of a cross-section of citizens on reading the work.

The **American Newspaper Guild** was founded by Heywood Broun.

Aaron Copland composed his *Short Symphony,* considered the best of his works during this period.

May 4 **Pulitzer prizes** were awarded for the following: fiction, *The Store* by T. S. Stribling; drama, *Both Your Houses* by Maxwell Anderson; history, *The Significance of Sections in American History* by Frederick J. Turner; biography, *Grover Cleveland* by Allan Nevins; poetry, *Conquistador* by Archibald MacLeish.

Sept. 9 *As Thousands Cheer* by Irving Berlin and Moss Hart, a delightful musical comedy of the newspaper world, opened at the Forrest Theatre in Philadelphia.

Sept. 26 *Men in White* by Sidney Kingsley, a drama recounting the conflict between a doctor's duty and his emotions, opened at the Broadhurst Theatre in New York City.

Oct. 2 *Ah, Wilderness!* by Eugene O'Neill, a comedy of family life and the problems of adolescence, opened at the Guild Theatre in New York City. The

Business and Industry; Science; Education; Philosophy and Religion	III		IV	Sports; Social Issues and Crime; Folkways; Fashion; Holidays

Average **life expectancy** was 59 years, a gain of ten years since the turn of the century.

The first report of the **National Survey of School Finance,** authorized by Congress in 1931, was delivered. The report stated that one-third of America's schoolchildren were receiving an inadequate education.

Jan. 5 The **Jones Parity Plan,** a bill to restore price levels for such agricultural commodities as wheat, cotton, and hogs by introducing subsidies or price supports, was passed by the House of Representatives.

Jan. 16 Electrification of the **Pennsylvania Railroad** between New York City and Philadelphia, Pa., was completed.

Feb. 25 The **first U.S. aircraft carrier** specifically designed for the purpose, the U.S.S. *Ranger,* was christened at Newport News, Va., by Mrs. Herbert Hoover. The U.S. had other carriers, but they were ships that had been converted for use as carriers.

Mar. 7 **Credit** was tightened by New York life insurance companies, which refused to grant further loans on insurance policies.

May 1 The *Humanist Manifesto* was issued under the signature of 11 prominent college and university professors. The manifesto sought to erase all distinctions between what was religious and what was human, between what was secular and what was sacred. All human activity was considered significant. The universe was considered self-existing rather than created, and man was considered the product of evolutionary processes rather than of divine creation. Stressing the importance of happiness, well-being, and creativity for human beings, the manifesto took a strong stand against the capitalistic system as the vehicle of human aspirations.

June 21 A **rise in employment** was noted by the American Federation of Labor, which announced that 1,500,000 of its members, thrown out of work because of the Depression, had once more found employment.

racing fans at the track every 90 seconds. These machines came into use at all major tracks run under the parimutuel system. Depending on the size of the track, from 100 to 350 vending machines operated by 400 to 900 men and women were used at each park.

Jan. 1 In **college football bowl games,** the results were Miami 7, Manhattan 0 in the first annual Orange Bowl; and Southern California 35, Pittsburgh 0 in the Rose Bowl. The 1932 national collegiate football championship was won by Southern California, with a record of ten wins, no losses, no ties.

Mar. 18 **U.S. figure skating championships** were won in New Haven, Conn., by Maribel Y. Vinson, women's singles; Roger Turner, men's singles; Maribel Y. Vinson and George E. B. Hill, pairs.

Apr. 4–13 The **NHL Stanley Cup** was won by the New York Rangers, who defeated the Toronto Maple Leafs three games to one.

Apr. 19 The 37th **Boston Marathon** was won by Leslie Pawson of Pawtucket, R.I., with a time of 2 hrs., 31 min., 1.6 sec.

May 6 The 59th annual **Kentucky Derby** was won by Broker's Tip, with a time of 2:06⁴/₅. The jockey was Don Meade. This was the second straight year in which the Derby was won by a horse owned and bred by Col. E. R. Bradley.

May 13 The 57th annual **Preakness Stakes** was won by Head Play, with a time of 2:02. The jockey was Charles Kurtsinger.

May 27–Nov. 2 The **Century of Progress Exposition** was held in Chicago, Ill., in honor of the centennial of the founding of Chicago.

May 30 The 21st **Indianapolis 500** auto race was won by Louis Meyer of Huntington Park, Calif., completing the 500-mile course in 4 hrs., 48 min., 0.75 sec., with an average speed of 104.16 mph.

June 10 The **U.S. Open golf tournament** was won by Johnny Goodman.

June 10 The 65th annual **Belmont Stakes** was won by Hurryoff, with a time of 2:32³/₅. The jockey was Mack Garner.

June 21 The **world heavyweight boxing championship** was won by the Italian giant, Primo Carnera, who knocked out Jack Sharkey at Long Island City Bowl.

July 6 In the **first all-star baseball game,** the American League defeated the National League by a score of 4–2. The game was held at Comiskey Park in Chicago before 49,200 fans.

requiring registration and approval of all issues of stocks and bonds.

June 16   The **National Industrial Recovery Act** (NIRA) was created. It established the National Recovery Administration (NRA) and the Public Works Administration (PWA). Gen. Hugh Johnson was named administrator of the NRA, and Harold L. Ickes was named head of the PWA.

June 16   The **Banking Act of 1933** was passed by Congress, establishing the Federal Bank Deposit Insurance Corporation.

Aug. 5   The **National Labor Board,** authorized by the National Industrial Recovery Act, was established by Pres. Roosevelt, who appointed Sen. Robert F. Wagner of New York as chairman. The board was empowered to adjudicate collective bargaining disputes.

Nov. 7   **Fiorello La Guardia,** heading the Fusion ticket, was elected mayor of New York City, thereby ending 16 years of Tammany control.

Nov. 8   The **Civil Works Administration** was set up with an initial appropriation of $400,000,000. Its first director was Harry L. Hopkins. The plan was intended to provide work for about 4,000,000 unemployed and to put two-thirds of the families then receiving relief on a self-sustaining basis.

Dec. 5   The **Twenty-first Amendment was adopted** when it was ratified by Utah, the 36th state to do so. Prohibition in the U.S. was thereby repealed.

role of Nat Miller, a father who grows to understand his son, was played by George M. Cohan in New York and Will Rogers in San Francisco.

Nov. 18   *Roberta,* with music by Jerome Kern, opened for a long run at the New Amsterdam Theatre in New York City. It included the songs "Smoke Gets in Your Eyes" and "The Touch of Your Hand."

Dec. 4   *Tobacco Road,* a play written by Jack Kirkland from the novel by Erskine Caldwell, opened in New York City. At first it failed to attract an audience, but soon its reputation spread and it became one of the longest-running plays on Broadway.

Dec. 6   In a major ruling on **censorship,** the ban on *Ulysses* by James Joyce was lifted by Federal Judge John M. Woolsey, who wrote in part: "[It is] a sincere and honest book. . . . I do not detect anywhere the leer of a sensualist."

1934

Federal agencies continued to control many phases of American life, but there was no controlling the weather. Plagued by record cold snaps in February and searing heat in July, farmers watched their crops wither in the most destructive drought the Midwest had ever seen. Rising agricultural prices afforded temporary relief for them, but not for city dwellers. Internal affairs were complicated by congressional and local elections. Republican orators had only one real issue—the dubious constitutionality of some of the more radical New Deal provisions. According to opponents of the New Deal, federal boondoggles had reached outrageous proportions and were seriously crippling the nation's financial resources, as witnessed by 33 new government agencies, 24,303 new employees, and an increase in the national debt of nearly 20%. Few voters responded, for conditions were slowly improving; only 58 banks had failed in 1934—901 had been the annual average since 1921.

Jan. 1   Dr. **Francis E. Townsend** of Long Beach, Calif., announced an Old Age Revolving Pensions Plan, popularly called the Townsend Plan, giving all those

Although the Depression was far from over, an upbeat mood in America was evidenced by a revitalization in publishing. Government-sponsored art projects encouraged the talented and were responsible for some 15,000 works of art being produced. Hollywood introduced to America a new child star, Shirley Temple.

Among **books published** this year was *Tender Is the Night* by F. Scott Fitzgerald, a novel exploring the lives of Dick Diver, a psychiatrist, and his schizophrenic wife Nicole. Now considered a masterpiece, the novel was published at a time when Fitzgerald's prestige as a writer was slipping and his own life was beginning to disintegrate. Other books published this year included *Doctor Martino and Other Stories* by William Faulkner; *The Thin Man* by Dashiell Hammett; and *Goodbye, Mr. Chips* by James Hilton.

Merry Mount, an opera by Howard Hanson, was produced by the Metropolitan Opera Company in New York City. It achieved a total of nine performances.

The **Catholic Legion of Decency** began censorship of motion pictures. Though there were some protests from

| Business and Industry; Science; Education; Philosophy and Religion **III** | **IV** Sports; Social Issues and Crime; Folkways; Fashion; Holidays |

June 22 The **Illinois Ship Canal** was formally opened. The waterway completed a link between the Great Lakes and the Gulf of Mexico.

Oct. 2 The **five-day work week** was officially sanctioned by the American Federation of Labor, which also supported a six-hour workday.

Oct. 13 A **boycott** of all German-made products as a protest against Nazi antagonism to organized labor within Germany was voted by the American Federation of Labor.

Oct. 20 The **Nobel Prize in Physiology or Medicine** was awarded to Thomas Hunt Morgan "for his discoveries concerning the function of the chromosome in the transmission of heredity." Morgan performed his most significant experiments as head of the California Institute of Technology in Pasadena, Calif.

July 8 The **Wimbledon** women's singles championship was won by Mrs. Helen Wills Moody.

Aug. 13 The **PGA golf tournament** was won by Gene Sarazen.

Aug. 26 The **U.S. Lawn Tennis Association singles championships** were won by Helen Hull Jacobs in the women's division and Frederick J. Perry of Great Britain in the men's division (Sept. 10).

Sept. 9 The **Miss America** title was won by Marion Bergeron, 16, fom West Haven, Conn., at the annual pageant in Atlantic City, N.J.

Oct. 3–7 The 30th annual **World Series** was won by the New York Giants (NL), defeating the Washington Senators (AL) four games to one.

Dec. 17 In the **first National Football League (NFL) championship playoff,** the Chicago Bears defeated the New York Giants 23–21 to become NFL champions of 1933. This year the NFL was divided into Eastern and Western divisions, the leaders of the divisions meeting in a playoff game to determine the league winner. Previously the league championship went to the team with the highest winning percentage.

1934

There was hope that the Depression was coming to an end. Unemployment had dropped by more than 4,000,000. Organized labor, which had claimed 58.3% of the national income in 1929, now earned 62.5%. Business failures dropped sharply. The purchasing power of industrial workers went up by 25%. The American Federation of Labor claimed 2,000,000 new members. The near-disastrous plight of the nation's schools was eased as capital outlay for education grew more generous. Scientists induced artificial radioactivity for the first time, extended the periodic table, tapped the sun's energy with two experimental solar motors, and predicted that man would soon harness atomic energy.

Jan. 7 The Rev. Dr. William Ashley Sunday, better known as **Billy Sunday,** began an intensive two-week revival campaign in New York City at the Calvary Baptist Church. Dr. Sunday, 70, had not visited New York City for this purpose since 1917. At that time, he had evangelized for ten weeks in Washington Heights. People looked on Billy Sunday as the last of the old-fashioned revivalists.

Although Prohibition had been repealed nationally, the dry forces stubbornly refused to concede defeat, renewing their campaign on the local level. However, they were powerless to stop the revival of the huge liquor industry. Distillers this year produced 35,000,000 barrels of beer and 42,000,000 gallons of hard liquor. For the sports fan, the two most imposing figures in the country were Dizzy and Daffy Dean, brothers who rolled up 45 victories between them in pitching the St. Louis Cardinals into a world championship and the first million-dollar World Series gate.

Jan. 1 In **college football bowl games,** the results were Duquesne 33, Miami, Fla., 7 in the Orange Bowl; and Columbia 7, Stanford 0 in the Rose Bowl. The 1933 national collegiate football championship was won by Michigan, with a record of seven wins, no losses, one tie.

Mar. 10 **U.S. figure skating championships** were won in Phila., Pa., by Suzanne Davis, women's singles; Roger Turner, men's singles; Grace E. Madden and James L. Madden, pairs.

over 60 years of age $200 to spend. Money not spent would be returned to the government.

Jan. 31 The **Farm Mortgage Refinancing Act,** which created the Federal Farm Mortgage Corporation, was signed by Pres. Franklin D. Roosevelt. This institution was authorized to assist farmers in paying their mortgages by providing easier credit terms.

Mar. 24 The **Tydings-McDuffie Act,** granting independence to the Philippines, was passed by Congress. The Philippine legislature approved it on May 1. Complete independence would not be proclaimed until July 4, 1946.

Apr. 28 The **Home Owners Loan Act** was signed by Pres. Roosevelt. The act supplemented the Home Owners Refinancing Act of 1933. Both measures were designed to stimulate home building.

June 6 The **Securities Exchange Act** was signed by Pres. Roosevelt. It provided for creation of the Securities and Exchange Commission. It also provided for licensing stock exchanges and declared certain speculative practices illegal.

June 12 The **Trade Agreements Act** was signed by Pres. Roosevelt. It authorized the president to cut tariffs by as much as 50% of the prevailing rates for countries honoring the U.S. with most-favored-nation status.

June 19 The **Communications Act,** establishing the Federal Communications Commission, was passed by Congress. The new commission regulated all national and international communication by telegraph, cable, or radio.

June 28 The **Federal Farm Bankruptcy Act,** also known as the Frazier-Lemke Act, was signed by Pres. Roosevelt. It established a moratorium on farm mortgage foreclosures.

June 28 The **National Housing Act** was passed by Congress. It established the Federal Housing Administration to help home owners finance repairs and enlargements and to spur private building through federal mortgages.

July The **Southern Tenant Farmers' Union** was organized in Arkansas by a small group of sharecroppers. It grew to 35,000 members, mostly in Arkansas and Oklahoma, by 1937. It then affiliated with the Congress of Industrial Organizations (CIO).

July 22 **John Dillinger,** public enemy number one, was shot in Chicago, Ill., by FBI agents.

Sept. 8 A **ship fire** aboard the *Morro Castle,* near Asbury Park, N.J., killed some 130 persons.

Nov. 6 In **congressional elections** the Democrats gained nine Senate seats for a 69–25 majority, with two seats held by minor parties. In the House the Democrats gained nine seats for a 310–117 majority, with five seats going to minor parties.

intellectual quarters, surprisingly little opposition was raised to the program.

The first pipeless **Hammond organ** was produced by Laurens Hammond, an electric clock manufacturer of Chicago, Ill. It was marketed for the first time the following year. The new instrument produced sound by amplification of electrical modulations.

Reginald Marsh, a painter of city scenes, common people, flophouses, theaters, beaches, and other public places, painted *Negroes on Rockaway Beach.* In this work Marsh depicted a mass of people in action, with the arrangement of the figures designed to emphasize the dramatic quality of the moment.

Jan. 8 *Days Without End* by Eugene O'Neill, a modern miracle play depicting a person with a split personality, opened at Henry Miller's Theatre in New York City. In the play John Loving, the hero, becomes whole only when he returns to the Catholicism of his youth.

Jan. 26 **Roy Harris's** *First Symphony* was performed by the Boston Symphony Orchestra under the direction of Serge Koussevitzky.

Feb. 8 *Four Saints in Three Acts* by Gertrude Stein, music by Virgil Thomson, an opera completely incomprehensible to most people, was presented by the Society of Friends and Enemies of Modern Music at Hartford, Conn.

Feb. 24 *Dodsworth* by Sidney Howard, a play based on the novel by Sinclair Lewis, opened at the Shubert Theatre in New York City. A moving account of an American businessman in Europe, the play starred Walter Huston.

Mar. 16 **Academy Awards** were presented to *Cavalcade* as the outstanding motion picture of 1932–1933; to Charles Laughton as best actor for *Henry VIII;* and to Katharine Hepburn as best actress for *Morning Glory.* Walt Disney received his second consecutive award, for the cartoon *Three Little Pigs.*

May 7 **Pulitzer prizes** were awarded for the following: fiction, *Lamb in His Bosom* by Caroline Miller; biography, *John Hay* by Tyler Bennett; history, *The People's Choice* by Herbert Agar; poetry, *Collected Verse* by Robert Hillyer; drama, *Men in White* by Sidney Kingsley.

Nov. 21 The musical comedy *Anything Goes* opened at the Alvin Theatre in New York City. Written by Guy Bolton and P. G. Wodehouse, revised by Howard Lindsay and Russel Crouse, and featuring music by Cole Porter, the musical became the hit of the season.

| Business and Industry; Science; Education; Philosophy and Religion   III | | IV   Sports; Social Issues and Crime; Folkways; Fashion; Holidays |

Mar. 13 Henry Ford made a confident gesture in the face of the Depression by restoring the $5.00-a-day minimum wage to 47,000 of his 70,000 workers.

May 23 What became known worldwide as **nylon** was first produced by Dr. Wallace H. Carothers, a research chemist in the Du Pont laboratories. Carothers succeeded in spinning a synthetic fiber that met exhaustive tests of durability. He called his invention polymer 66.

June 26 The **Evangelical and Reformed Church** was established in Cleveland, Ohio, by union of the Reformed Church in the United States and the Evangelical Synod of North America. The first service of the new church was held on June 27.

July 16 The **first general strike** in U.S. history took place in San Francisco, Calif., as an expression of support for the striking 12,000 members of the International Longshoremen's Association.

Oct. 1 **Olivet College** in Olivet, Mich., abandoned the use of credits, grades, and other elements of traditional education. Under a new plan students were required only to pass general examinations and to be in residence for at least three years. Mornings were to be devoted to private study, group discussions, and individual conferences; afternoons to athletic activities, in which the faculty participated; and evenings to debates and other intellectual or aesthetic pursuits.

Oct. 25 The **Nobel Prize in Physiology or Medicine** was awarded jointly to George R. Minot, William P. Murphy, and George H. Whipple for their discovery of liver therapy to combat anemia. They were the fourth, fifth, and sixth Americans to receive the Nobel Prize in this field.

Nov. 15 The **Nobel Prize in Chemistry** was awarded to Harold Clayton Urey for his discovery in Dec. 1931 of deuterium, or heavy hydrogen, an isotope of hydrogen. Deuterium and its oxide, commonly known as heavy water, were used in fission experiments to slow neutrons so they would split atomic nuclei on impact, a major advance in atomic physics.

Mar. 25 The **first annual Masters golf tournament**, held in Augusta, Ga., was won by Horton Smith, who defeated Craig Wood by one stroke.

Apr. 3–10 The **NHL Stanley Cup** was won by the Chicago Black Hawks, who defeated the Detroit Red Wings three games to one.

Apr. 19 The 38th **Boston Marathon** was won by Dave Komonen of Ontario, Canada, with a time of 2 hrs., 32 min., 53.8 sec.

May 5 The 60th annual **Kentucky Derby** was won by Cavalcade, with a time of 2:04. The jockey was Mack Garner.

May 12 The 59th annual **Preakness Stakes** was won by High Quest, with a time of 1:58⅕. The jockey was Robert Jones.

May 30 The 22nd **Indianapolis 500** auto race was won by Bill Cummings of Indianapolis, completing the 500-mile course in 4 hrs., 46 min., 5.20 sec., with an average speed of 104.86 mph.

June 9 The 66th annual **Belmont Stakes** was won by Peace Chance, with a time of 2:29⅕. The jockey was Wayne Wright.

June 9 The **U.S. Open golf tournament** was won by Olin Dutra, beating Gene Sarazen by one stroke.

June 14 The **world heavyweight boxing championship** was won by Max Baer, who scored a technical knockout over Primo Carnera in the 11th round of a fight held before a crowd of 48,495 in New York City.

July 10 The second annual **baseball all-star game** was won by the American League, 9–7.

July 29 The **PGA golf tournament** was won by Paul Runyan.

Aug. 19 The **U.S. Lawn Tennis Association singles championships** were won by Helen Hull Jacobs in the women's division and Frederick J. Perry of Great Britain in the men's division (Sept. 12).

Sept. 17–25 The **America's Cup** was successfully defended by the U.S. yacht *Rainbow,* which defeated the British challenger *Endeavour* four races to two.

Oct. 3–9 The 31st annual **World Series** was won by the St. Louis Cardinals (NL), defeating the Detroit Tigers (AL) four games to three.

Dec. 9 The **NFL championship** was won by the New York Giants, defeating the Chicago Bears 30–13.

1935

The economic gains registered in 1934 seemed to produce a heady effect on the nation this year. Labor and capital squared off for a no-holds-barred brawl. The New Deal suffered a stunning setback when the Supreme Court declared the National Industrial Recovery Act unconstitutional. This provided anti-administration forces with effective ammunition to use against the New Deal, accusing it of being un-American, Bolshevistic, communistic, and socialistic. Rebellions minor and major destroyed Democratic unity in Congress and made it difficult for Pres. Franklin D. Roosevelt to maintain control of his own supporters. In short, the nation was feuding.

Jan. 29 U.S. membership in the **World Court** was killed when the Senate refused by a vote of 52–36 to ratify participation in the court. The vote fell seven short of achieving the necessary two-thirds majority.

Apr. 27 The **Soil Conservation Act** was passed, creating the Soil Conservation Service as a bureau of the Department of Agriculture.

May 6 The **Works Progress Administration** (WPA) was instituted under the authority of the Emergency Relief Appropriation Act, which passed on Apr. 8.

May 11 The **Rural Electrification Administration** was established by executive order to build power lines and finance electricity production in areas not served by private distributors.

May 27 The **National Industrial Recovery Act was declared unconstitutional** by the Supreme Court. The decision invalidated the National Recovery Administration (NRA) and implied that any government attempt to legislate prices, wages, working conditions, etc., would be unconstitutional. This followed from the Court's strict interpretation of interstate commerce.

Aug. 14 The **Social Security Act** was signed by Pres. Roosevelt. It established a Social Security Board to

Conflicting social forces at work were reflected in the new, so-called proletarian novel, which found a receptive audience, and in the establishment of a left-wing book club. The trend even extended to the most conservative of all arts, the theater. Clifford Odets electrified audiences with his glorification of the little man. Imaginative artists discovered American primitivism through a surprising interest in African art. The Federal Music Project sponsored thousands of free concerts and employed some 18,000 musicians. Film makers produced a raft of epics, such as *Mutiny on the Bounty* and *A Tale of Two Cities,* as well as one of the finest films of all time, *The Informer.* The death of Will Rogers in an airplane crash with Wiley Post on Aug. 16 near Point Barrow, Alaska, was widely mourned.

Among **books published** this year was *Of Time and the River* by Thomas Wolfe, the author's second novel about Eugene Gant. Here the young southerner comes in contact with the cosmopolitan world of New York City. Other books published this year included *Judgment Day* by James T. Farrell, the second novel of his trilogy about young Studs Lonigan; *The Last Puritan* by George Santayana, the philosopher's only novel; and *Tortilla Flat* by John Steinbeck, a novel lovingly recounting the lives of the *paisanos* of Monterey, Calif., and the first of Steinbeck's books to become a commercial success.

Jan. 7 *The Old Maid,* a play by Zöe Akins based on the novelette by Edith Wharton, opened at the Empire Theatre in New York City. The play concerned the relationship between the natural and adoptive mothers of an illegitimate child.

Jan. 7 *The Petrified Forest* by Robert E. Sherwood, starring Humphrey Bogart, Leslie Howard, and Peggy Conklin, opened at the Broadhurst Theatre in New York City.

Feb. 19 *Awake and Sing* by Clifford Odets, a poignant drama of lower-middle-class life in The Bronx, opened at the Belasco Theatre in New York City. The play's successful run gave the author immediate recognition. In the same year Odets saw his plays *Till the Day I Die, Paradise Lost,* and *Waiting for Lefty* produced on the New York stage.

Mar. 27 **Academy Awards** were presented to *It Happened One Night* as the outstanding motion picture of 1934, and to its stars Claudette Colbert and Clark Gable as best actress and best actor. Walt Disney received his third consecutive award, for the cartoon *Tortoise and the Hare.*

May 6 **Pulitzer prizes** were awarded for the following: fiction, *Now in November* by Josephine Winslow

1935

Organized labor was furious over the Supreme Court's adverse decision on the NRA, and over management's attitude toward what labor considered to be workers' basic rights. However, labor found itself in the midst of a major civil war on the issue of craft unions vs. industrial unions. The chief opponents were John L. Lewis of the newly organized Committee for Industrial Organization and William Green, head of the American Federation of Labor. Crisis level was reached when Lewis resigned from the parent group and took his followers with him. Widespread unrest disturbed members of the Daughters of the American Revolution and the American Legion, who pressed state legislatures to pass laws requiring loyalty oaths for teachers. In all, 19 states put such measures on their books.

The **largest salary** earned in the U.S. in 1935 was that of William Randolph Hearst. The second largest was Mae West's.

The **Public Health Service Hospital** at Leestown Pike, Lexington, Ky., a federal hospital for narcotics addicts, was completed.

An **automatic propeller** that maintained a constant engine speed under all conditions was developed for use in airplanes.

An epidemic of **infantile paralysis,** or poliomyelitis, sparked renewed interest in combatting the disease. The drive was led by Pres. Roosevelt, who had been stricken with the disease, also known as polio, in 1921.

In a reversal of its **birth control** stand, the General Federation of Women's Clubs, meeting in Detroit, Mich., endorsed a federal law allowing birth control literature to be delivered by mail.

Mar. 22 The use of **blood tests** as evidence in court cases was authorized in New York State when Gov. Herbert H. Lehman of New York signed bills authorizing introduction of blood types as evidence in criminal or civil cases.

June 10 **Alcoholics Anonymous** was organized in New York City.

July 5 The **National Labor Relations Act,** also known as the Wagner-Connery Act, was signed by Pres. Roosevelt. It established the National Labor Relations Board, which was empowered to recognize collective

Troubled times drew fresh blood into Prohibition ranks, and soon many counties were dry again. The highly charged emotional level of the people was reflected in an upsurge of lynchings in the South and intense interest in the trial of Bruno Richard Hauptmann, charged with the kidnaping and murder of the infant son of Charles and Anne Morrow Lindbergh.

The first annual **Heisman Trophy,** for outstanding college football player of 1935, was voted to Chicago halfback Jay Berwanger.

Jan. 1 In **college football bowl games,** the results were Bucknell 26, Miami, Fla., 0 in the Orange Bowl; Alabama 29, Stanford 13 in the Rose Bowl; and Tulane 20, Temple 14 in the first annual Sugar Bowl. Two teams were named 1934 national college football championship in votes by two sports organizations: Minnesota, with a record of eight wins, no losses or ties; and Alabama, with ten wins, no losses or ties.

Feb. 9 **U.S. figure skating championships** were won in New Haven, Conn., by Maribel Y. Vinson, women's singles; Robin H. Lee, men's singles; Maribel Y. Vinson and George E. B. Hill, pairs.

Apr. 4–9 The **NHL Stanley Cup** was won by the Montreal Maroons, who defeated the Toronto Maple Leafs in three straight games.

Apr. 8 The second annual **Masters golf tournament** was won by Gene Sarazen, who won in a playoff round against Craig Wood.

Apr. 19 The 39th **Boston Marathon** was won by John Kelley of Arlington, Mass., with a time of 2 hrs., 32 min., 7.4 sec.

May 4 The 61st annual **Kentucky Derby** was won by Omaha, with a time of 2:05. The jockey was Willis Saunders.

May 11 The 60th annual **Preakness Stakes** was won by Omaha, with a time of 1:58²/₅. The jockey was Willis Saunders.

May 24 The **first night baseball game** in the major leagues was played between the Cincinnati Reds (NL) and the Philadelphia Phillies (NL) before more than 20,000 fans at Crosley Field, Cincinnati, Ohio. The Reds beat the Phillies 2–1.

May 30 The 23rd **Indianapolis 500** auto race was won Kelly Petillo of Los Angeles, Calif., completing the 500-mile course in 4 hrs., 42 min., 22.71 sec., with an average speed of 106.24 mph.

June 8 The 67th annual **Belmont Stakes** was won by Omaha, with a time of 2:30³/₅. The jockey was Willis Saunders. This was the third time that a horse had won the Triple Crown.

June 8 The **U.S. Open golf tournament** was won by Sam Parks, Jr.

supervise payment of old-age benefits, such payments to be determined by the amount of money earned by recipients before their 65th birthdays.

Aug. 26 The **Public Utilities Act,** known as the Wheeler-Rayburn Act, was signed by Pres. Roosevelt. It required public utilities to register with the Securities and Exchange Commission and limited utility holding corporations to the first degree, or simplest form, of incorporation, unless the nature of the enterprise required greater complexity.

Sept. 8 **Huey Long was assassinated.** A powerful demagogue in Louisiana and national politics, he was shot to death in the corridor of the state capitol in Baton Rouge, La., by Dr. Carl Austin Weiss, Jr.

Johnson; drama, *The Old Maid* by Zöe Akins; history, *The Colonial Period of American History* by Charles McLean Andres; biography, *R. E. Lee* by Douglas S. Freeman; poetry, *Bright Ambush* by Audrey Wurdemann.

Sept. 25 *Winterset* by Maxwell Anderson, a powerful verse drama inspired by the Sacco-Vanzetti case, opened at the Martin Beck Theatre in New York City. The play related the story of a boy who gives his life to clear his father's name. Its stage set, a dark street under an immense bridge, helped create a brooding atmosphere. In 1928 Anderson had handled the Sacco-Vanzetti case more directly in *Gods of the Lightning.*

Oct. 10 *Porgy and Bess,* an opera by George Gershwin based on the novel *Porgy* by Du Bose and Dorothy Heyward, opened at the Alvin Theatre in New York City after a short trial run in Boston. It ran for 16 weeks, followed by a road tour of three months. The work has been revived numerous times in the U.S. and abroad.

1936

Despite criticism of New Deal policies by its opponents, the administration received a vote of confidence in the national elections. Pres. Franklin D. Roosevelt carried all but two states, in the largest presidential vote cast to date. Democratic ranks closed and party leaders hailed the advent of good times. However, bad times continued for farmers as another scorching drought created a vast dust bowl and sent thousands westward in search of fertile land. Critics of the New Deal stressed the fact that since its election in 1932 the Roosevelt government had swelled the national debt by $12,000,000,-000. Countering these statistics was the fact that at the same time the national income had risen by $30,000,-000,000. In international affairs, Germany reoccupied the Rhineland, which had been taken from it after World War I; Italy annexed Ethiopia, which it had invaded the year before, thus crippling the League of Nations as an international peacekeeper; and civil war broke out in Spain.

Apr. 25–28 The **Socialist Labor Party** nominated John W. Aiken of Massachusetts for the presidency and Emil F. Teichert of New York for the vice presidency.

May 5–7 The **Prohibition Party** nominated Dr. D. Leigh Colvin of New York for the presidency and Alvin C. York of Tennessee for the vice presidency. York was subsequently succeeded by Claude A.

The theater enjoyed one of the most distinguished seasons in years and was heartened by the founding of the Federal Theater Project under the Works Progress Administration (WPA). As the Depression eased, more concerts meant more new works performed and more musicians employed. Over 5000 artists in 44 states were employed by the Federal Art Project of the WPA. They painted between 600 and 700 murals for government buildings and a great number of works in oil and watercolor. The demand so far outstripped the supply that some artists were turning out a finished work each week. Movies enjoyed their most prosperous year since the Depression, even though four out of five films were called financial failures by their producers. The industry turned out some 500 feature films. Technicolor had been developed, but few ventured to use the innovation.

Among **books published** this year was *Gone with the Wind* by Margaret Mitchell, a blockbuster novel of Georgia in the Civil War that won a Pulitzer Prize in 1937 and was the basis for the classic 1939 motion picture. The novel sold 1,000,000 copies in six months. Other books published this year included *A Further Range* by Robert Frost, which included the poem "Two Tramps in Mud Time"; and *The Big Money* by John Dos Passos, the third novel of his *U.S.A.* trilogy, which included *The 42nd Parallel* (1930) and *1919* (1932). The trilogy was collected in 1938.

Business and Industry; Science; Education; Philosophy and Religion	III		IV	Sports; Social Issues and Crime; Folkways; Fashion; Holidays

bargaining units, supervise elections, and investigate charges of illegal labor practices.

Aug. 9 The **Motor Carrier Act** was signed by Pres. Roosevelt. It gave the Interstate Commerce Commission jurisdiction over all interstate truck and bus traffic.

Nov. The annual **auto show** in New York City was held this month rather than in January in an effort to even out employment in the auto industry and to ease the slack winter season. Automobile manufacturers began this year to emphasize style innovations to stimulate sales.

Nov. 9 The **Committee for Industrial Organization** was established by John L. Lewis from a dissenting faction within the American Federation of Labor. In 1938 its leaders were expelled from the older organization and reorganized their group as the Congress of Industrial Organizations.

June 13 The **world heavyweight boxing championship** was won by James J. Braddock over Max Baer on points in 15 rounds.

July 6 At the **Wimbledon** tennis championships the women's singles title was won by Helen Wills Moody. This was her seventh victory.

July 8 The third annual **baseball all-star game** was won by the American League 4–1.

Sept. 7 The **Miss America** title was won by Henrietta Leaver, 19, of McKeesport, Pa., at the annual pageant in Atlantic City, N.J.

Sept. 11 The **U.S. Lawn Tennis Association singles championships** were won by Helen Hull Jacobs, for the fourth consecutive time, in the women's division and Wilmer L. Allison in the men's division (Sept. 12).

Oct. 2–7 The 32nd annual **World Series** was won by the Detroit Tigers (AL), defeating the Chicago Cubs (NL) four games to two.

Oct. 23 The **PGA golf tournament** was won by Johnny Revolta.

Dec. 15 The **NFL championship** was won by the Detroit Lions, defeating the New York Giants 26–7.

1936

The nation's commerce was much improved over the previous year. Farm prices were up, metals were up, and automobile production increased 20%. However, 8,000,000 still were unemployed. Labor warfare continued and unions discovered a new weapon in the sit-down strike. Education looked considerably brighter as fewer schools cried out for federal assistance. Teachers were granted slight increases in salaries; enrollment in lower grades dropped because of the falling birth rate; and 35,000 illiterates were taught to read and write by Civilian Conservation Corps instructors. Educators hailed widespread interest in adult classes.

The **perfusion pump,** called an artificial heart, was demonstrated by Dr. Alexis Carrel and Charles A. Lindbergh, at a scientific convention in Copenhagen, Denmark. Dr. Carrel, helped by Lindbergh, had developed the pump at the Rockefeller Institute in New York City. The first description of the artificial heart had appeared in *Science* magazine in June 1935.

The **revolt against progressive education** in America was led by Pres. Robert Maynard Hutchins of Chicago University in his controversial book *The Higher Learning in America.* Hutchins believed education had been reduced to mere emphasis on facts. His ideas never achieved the wide influence of John Dewey's in educational circles.

The **Baseball Hall of Fame** was established in Cooperstown, N.Y., by a group of baseball leaders. A shrine and museum were planned to honor the game's immortals. The first players elected to membership were Ty Cobb, infielder; Walter Johnson, pitcher; Christy Mathewson, pitcher; Babe Ruth, outfielder; and Honus Wagner, infielder.

Jan. 1 In **college football bowl games,** the results were Catholic University 20, Mississippi 19 in the Orange Bowl; Stanford 7, SMU 0 in the Rose Bowl; Texas Christian University 3, LSU 2 in the Sugar Bowl. The national college football championship for 1935 was conferred on Minnesota, with a record of eight wins, no losses or ties, and SMU, with 12 wins, one loss, no ties.

Feb. 5–16 At the **Winter Olympics** in Germany, the U.S. won two gold medals and placed fifth in the unofficial team scoring after Norway, Germany, Sweden, and Finland.

Feb. 13 **U.S. figure skating championships** were won in Chicago by Maribel Y. Vinson, women's singles; Robin H. Lee, men's singles; Maribel Y. Vinson and George E. B. Hill, pairs; Marjorie Parker and Joseph K. Savage, dance.

Apr. 5–11 The **NHL Stanley Cup** was won by the Detroit Red Wings, who defeated the Toronto Maple Leafs three games to one.

Watson of California as the vice presidential candidate.

May 25 The **Socialist Party nominated Norman Thomas** of New York for the presidency and George O. Nelson of Wisconsin for the vice presidency.

June 9–12 The **Republican National Convention nominated Gov. Alfred M. Landon** of Kansas for the presidency and Col. Frank Knox of Illinois for the vice presidency. The Republicans were supported during their campaign by some conservative Democrats, among them Alfred E. Smith.

June 19 Rep. William Lemke, Republican of North Dakota, announced his **presidential candidacy on the Union Party ticket.** Thomas C. O'Brien of Massachusetts was the vice presidential candidate. Lemke was endorsed by the Rev. Charles E. Coughlin's National Union for Social Justice, which held its first national convention in Cleveland on Aug. 14.

June 23–27 The **Democratic National Convention renominated Pres. Roosevelt** by acclamation for the presidency. It chose John Nance Garner for the vice presidency. In general the platform took its stand on the administration's record. The American Labor Party endorsed Roosevelt's candidacy.

June 24–28 The **Communist Party nominated Earl Browder** of Kansas for the presidency and James W. Ford of New York for the vice presidency.

Nov. 3 **Franklin D. Roosevelt was reelected president** of the United States in a Democratic landslide that carried every state except Maine and Vermont. John Nance Garner was elected vice president. Congress became more than three-quarters Democratic in both houses. The electoral vote was Roosevelt, 523; Gov. Alfred M. Landon of Kansas, 8. The popular vote was Roosevelt, 27,751,612; Landon, 16,687,913; William Lemke, Union Party, 891,858; Norman Thomas, Socialist, 187,342; Earl Browder, Communist, 80,181; Dr. D. Leigh Colvin, Prohibition candidate, 37,609; John W. Aiken, Socialist Labor Party, 12,729. The campaign was bitter. About 80% of the press opposed Roosevelt. In congressional elections the Democrats gained seven Senate seats, for a 76–16 majority, with four seats going to minor parties. In the House their majority was 331–89, with 13 seats going to minor parties.

The **Living Theater,** a project undertaken by the Federal Theater Project of the WPA, was begun. It presented, with a minimum of plot, national and international news. Prominent sequences included *Ethiopia, Triple-A Plowed Under,* and *Injunction Granted.*

Mar. 14 *Bury the Dead* by Irwin Shaw opened at the Forty-Sixth Street Theatre in New York City. The play, a forceful antiwar drama, dealt with six dead soldiers who, refusing to be buried, incite a full-scale mutiny among the ranks of the living.

Mar. 22 *On Your Toes,* a musical comedy by Richard Rodgers and Lorenz Hart, was given its world premiere at the Shubert Theatre in Boston, Mass. It became the hit of the season. The score included the ballet *Slaughter on Tenth Avenue.*

May 4 **Pulitzer prizes** were awarded for the following: fiction, *Honey in the Horn* by Harold L. Davis; drama, *Idiot's Delight* by Robert E. Sherwood; history, *The Constitutional History of the U.S.* by Andrew C. McLaughlin; biography, *The Thought and Character of William James* by Ralph Barton Perry; poetry, *Strange Holiness* by Robert P. Tristram Coffin.

May 5 **Academy Awards** were presented to *Mutiny on the Bounty* as the outstanding film of 1935; to Victor McLaglen as best actor for *The Informer;* to Bette Davis as best actress for *Dangerous;* and to John Ford as best director for *The Informer.* Walt Disney won his fourth consecutive award in the cartoon category.

Oct. 27 *It Can't Happen Here,* a play by Sinclair Lewis and John C. Moffitt based on Lewis's 1935 novel of the same title, opened at the Adelphi Theatre in New York City. The play reflected Americans' concerns with the rise of fascist states in the world and with the threat of fascism in the U.S. The play was presented by the Federal Theater Project.

Nov. 12 The **Nobel Prize for Literature** was awarded to Eugene O'Neill, the foremost American dramatist.

Nov. 19 *Johnny Johnson* by Paul Green opened at the Forty-Fourth Street Theatre in New York City. The play was a bitter denunciation of war.

Nov. 30 *You Can't Take It with You* by George S. Kaufman and Moss Hart, a sparkling comedy of escapism loaded with eccentric characters and situations, opened at the Chestnut Street Opera House in Philadelphia. On Dec. 14 it opened at the Booth Theatre in New York City.

Dec. 30 *High Tor,* a dramatic fantasy in verse by Maxwell Anderson, opened at the Hanna Theatre, Cleveland, Ohio. The play recounted the strange visitations to a mountaintop overlooking the Hudson R. by the ghosts of the sailors of an old Dutch ship. The ghosts become involved with bank robbers, criminal lawyers, and residents of the mountain. The play opened at the Martin Beck Theatre in New York City on Jan. 9, 1937.

Business and Industry; Science;
Education; Philosophy and Religion III

IV **Sports; Social Issues and Crime;**
Folkways; Fashion; Holidays

The age of the **trailer** reached full swing. It was estimated that there were 160,000 trailers on the road. Observers on Jan. 1, 1937, counted an average of 25 trailers an hour crossing the state line into Florida. Some statisticians, like Roger Babson, predicted that soon half the population of the country would be living in trailers.

Lake Mead Reservoir on the Colorado R. between Arizona and Nevada was completed. Boulder Dam, which contained the reservoir, was later renamed Hoover Dam. The reservoir had a capacity of over 10 trillion gallons of water, or 31,142,000 acre feet, and covered an area of 246 sq. mi., making it the largest reservoir in the U.S.

Jan. 11 The first move against a **sit-down strike** of automobile workers at the Fisher Body Plant No. 2 in Flint, Mich., was taken by General Motors. The strike had begun on New Year's Eve of 1936. Management ordered all heat in the plant buildings turned off. Police tried unsuccessfully to prevent union men on the outside from sending in food, and the strikers continued to control the plant.

Feb. 3 The **National Guard** prepared to assault strikers holding the General Motors plant in Flint, Mich. At the last minute, Walter Knudsen, head of General Motors, agreed to recognize the United Automobile Workers and to negotiate for a union contract.

May 9 The first scheduled **transatlantic dirigible flight** was completed when the *Hindenburg* landed at Lakehurst, N.J. Built by the German Zeppelin Transport Company, the craft was 830 ft. long, 135 ft. in diameter, and propelled by four 1050 hp Daimler Benz Diesel engines. It had a range of 8000 mi.

June 1 The *Queen Mary*, the world's largest liner, arrived in New York harbor from England on its maiden voyage.

Nov. 12 The **Nobel Prize in Physics** was awarded jointly to Carl David Anderson of the California Institute of Technology for his discovery in 1932 of the positron, and to Victor Francis Hess of Austria for his discovery of cosmic radiation. The discoveries opened new areas of nuclear physics for scientists to explore. Anderson's research confirmed theories about the structure of matter.

Apr. 6 The **Masters golf tournament** was won by Horton Smith.

Apr. 20 The 40th **Boston Marathon** was won by Ellison Brown of Alton, R.I., with a time of 2 hrs., 33 min., 40.8 sec.

May 2 The 62nd annual **Kentucky Derby** was won by Bold Venture, with a time of 2:03³/₅. The jockey was Ira Hanford.

May 16 The 61st annual **Preakness Stakes** was won by Bold Venture, with a time of 1:59. The jockey was George Woolf.

May 30 The 24th **Indianapolis 500** auto race was won by Louis Meyer of Huntington Park, Calif., completing the 500-mile course in 4 hrs., 35 min., 3.39 sec., with an average speed of 109.06 mph.

June 6 The 68th annual **Belmont Stakes** was won by Granville, with a time of 2:30. The jockey was Johnny Stout.

June 6 The **U.S. Open golf tournament** was won by Tony Manero, who shot a world's record 282 for a 72-hole title tournament.

July 4 At the **Wimbledon** tennis championships in England, the women's singles title was won by Helen Hull Jacobs.

July 7 The fourth annual **baseball All-Star Game** was won by the National League, which beat the American League 4–1. It was the first time the National League had won the event.

Aug. 5–16 At the **Summer Olympics** in Berlin, Germany, the U.S. won 20 gold medals and placed second in the unofficial team scoring behind Germany. The star of the games was the U.S. athlete Jesse Owens, who won four gold medals.

Sept. 12 The **Miss America** title was won by Rose Coyle, 22, from Philadelphia, Pa., at the annual pageant in Atlantic City, N.J.

Sept. 12 The **U.S. Lawn Tennis Association singles championships** were won by Frederick J. Perry of England in the men's division and Alice Marble in the women's division.

Sept. 30–Oct. 6 The 33rd annual **World Series** was won by the New York Yankees (AL), defeating the New York Giants (NL) four games to two.

Nov. 22 The **PGA golf tournament** was won by Denny Shute.

Dec. 13 The **NFL championship** was won by the Green Bay Packers, defeating the Boston Redskins 21–6.

Exploration and Settlement; Wars; Government; Civil Rights; Statistics **I**		**II** Publishing; Arts and Music; Popular Entertainment; Architecture; Theater

1937

The New Deal entered a period of transition in which its measures lost much of their emotional impact. As administration forces tried to press on, voices were increasingly raised against the program. Economic and political disputes rippled across the nation, aggravated to a degree by world events: civil war in Spain, German rearmament, and Japan's undeclared war on China. The worst of the Depression seemed over, but other dangers threatened.

Jan. 20 Pres. Franklin D. Roosevelt was inaugurated for his second term.

Feb. 5 In a move to alter composition of the **Supreme Court,** Pres. Franklin D. Roosevelt, after informing congressional leaders at a special Cabinet meeting in the morning, sent a message to Congress at noon recommending revision of statutes governing the federal judiciary. Although the recommendations were intended ostensibly to provide more efficient and younger judges in all federal courts, Roosevelt was charged with attempting to pack the Supreme Court, which in the past had invalidated important parts of the New Deal legislative program.

Mar. 18 A **school fire,** the worst in U.S. history, killed 294 in New London, Tex.

May 1 The **Neutrality Act,** prohibiting export of arms and ammunition to belligerent nations, was signed by Pres. Roosevelt. The act also prohibited sale of securities of belligerent nations in the U.S. It further prohibited use of American ships for carrying munitions and military equipment into belligerent zones, insisting that all belligerents pay for certain specified nonmilitary goods on purchase and convey their purchases on their own ships. This became known as the "cash and carry" clause.

May 6 The dirigible *Hindenburg* was destroyed by fire as it approached its mooring mast at Lakehurst, N.J. It was thought that a spark caused while mooring set off the hydrogen contained within the giant airship. The *Hindenburg* burst into flames and fell to earth in a few horrifying seconds. The disaster marked the virtual end of lighter-than-air transport.

July 22 The **Supreme Court Bill,** by which Pres. Roosevelt sought to modify the federal judiciary, specifically the Supreme Court, was voted back into committee by Congress, effectively killing the bill. In the meantime, Justice Willis Van Devanter had resigned from the Supreme Court, allowing Pres. Roosevelt to

Uncertainty in the nation's economic and political situation carried over to its creative life, resulting in a general sense of apathy. Federal support of the arts served merely to keep its practitioners alive and working. Architects debated the merits of functional design and drew much of their inspiration from builders abroad.

Among **books published** this year was *The Late George Apley* by John P. Marquand, a novel told in the form of a memoir recounting the stagnation of Boston's aristocracy. The story traced the history of several generations and showed the impact of new immigration on the old, settled society of Boston. Also published this year was the novelette *Of Mice and Men* by John Steinbeck that became a perennial favorite. It was the basis for a successful play and motion picture.

The **Harlem River Houses,** among the first public housing projects in New York City, were built from designs by many architects. They were four- and five-story walkups strung together.

The **Lincoln Tunnel,** crossing the Hudson R. from New Jersey to 38th St. in New York City, was built to relieve crowding in the Holland Tunnel. A second tube was added in 1945, and a third tube was added in 1957.

Arturo Toscanini signed a contract with the National Broadcasting Company, agreeing to be conductor of the NBC Symphony Orchestra created especially for him. The event indicated the rising importance of radio.

Mar. 4 **Academy Awards** were presented to *The Great Ziegfeld* as the outstanding motion picture of 1936; to Paul Muni as best actor for *The Story of Louis Pasteur;* to Luise Rainer as best actress for *The Great Ziegfeld;* to Walter Brennan as best supporting actor for *Come and Get It;* and to Gail Sondergaard as best supporting actress for *Anthony Adverse.* Walt Disney received his fifth consecutive award in the cartoon category, for *Country Cousin.* This was the first year in which awards were presented for best supporting actor and actress.

May 3 **Pulitzer prizes** were awarded for the following: fiction, *Gone With the Wind* by Margaret Mitchell; biography, *Hamilton Fish* by Allan Nevins; history, *The Flowering of New England* by Van Wyck Brooks; poetry, *A Further Range* by Robert Frost; drama, *You*

Business and Industry; Science; **Education; Philosophy and Religion**	**III**	**IV**	**Sports; Social Issues and Crime;** **Folkways; Fashion; Holidays**

1937

Labor placed the administration in the awkward position of having to choose sides between warring factions. However, despite internal difficulties, significant successes were won by unions in their effort to organize companies and industries that never before had recognized them. In medicine, the National Cancer Institute was founded, and Dr. E. C. Rosenow of the Mayo Clinic announced progress in the search for a serum against infantile paralysis, or polio. Experiments were based on the recent discovery that polio was caused by a transformed streptococcus.

A new approach to the causes of **mental illness** was revealed in *The Neurotic Personality of Our Time* by Karen Horney, which stressed cultural factors over hereditary factors.

In a wave of **industrial unrest** during the winter of 1936–1937, more than 500,000 workers quit their jobs. Many engaged in illegal sit-down strikes.

Jan. 11 The first move against a **sit-down strike** of automobile workers at the Fisher Body Plant No. 2 in Flint, Mich., was taken by General Motors. The strike had begun on New Year's Eve of 1936. Management ordered all heat in the plant buildings turned off. Police tried unsuccessfully to prevent union men on the outside from sending in food, and the strikers continued to control the plant.

Feb. 3 The **National Guard** prepared to assault strikers holding the General Motors plant in Flint, Mich. At the last minute, Walter Knudsen, head of General Motors, agreed to recognize the United Automobile Workers and to negotiate for a union contract.

Mar. 1 The **United Mine Workers** union was recognized by United States Steel, in a surprise announcement citing an agreement between John L. Lewis, head of the Committee for Industrial Organization (CIO), and Myron Taylor, chairman of the board of United States Steel.

Mar. 29 A **minimum wage law for women** was upheld by the U.S. Supreme Court in the decision of *West Coast Hotel v. Parrish.* The judgment reversed two previous rulings.

Apr. 12 The **National Labor Relations Act** of 1935 was upheld by the U.S. Supreme Court.

May Government statistics on **sit-down strikes** indicated that nearly half a million workers had engaged in such strikes since Sept. 1936.

May 6 The **first coast-to-coast radio program** was conducted by Herbert Morrison, reporting the *Hindenburg* disaster.

May 12 In the **first worldwide radio broadcast** received in the U.S., listeners heard the coronation of King George VI of England.

An event affecting the American people was the Spanish Civil War. While the U.S. government took no official position in the conflict, a considerable portion of the public offered highly emotional support to the Loyalist, antifascist side. American volunteers by the hundreds went to Spain, where they joined Loyalist armies.

Jan. 1 In **college football bowl games**, the results were Texas Christian University 16, Marquette 6 in the first annual Cotton Bowl; Duquesne 13, Mississippi State 12 in the Orange Bowl; Pittsburgh 21, Washington 0 in the Rose Bowl; and Santa Clara 21, LSU 14 in the Sugar Bowl. This season the Associated Press, in its first poll of football sportswriters, ranked Minnesota the leading national college football team of 1936.

Jan. 20 Announcement was made of the election into the **Baseball Hall of Fame** of Napoleon Lajoie, second baseman; Tristram E. "Tris" Speaker, outfielder; and Denton T. "Cy" Young, pitcher. Also named were two managers, Connie Mack and John McGraw.

Feb. 13 **U.S. figure skating championships** were won in Chicago by Maribel Y. Vinson, women's singles; Robin H. Lee, men's singles; Maribel Y. Vinson and George E. B. Hill, pairs; Nettie C. Prantel and Harold Hartshorne, dance.

Apr. 4 The **Masters golf tournament** was won by Byron Nelson.

Apr. 6–15 The **NHL Stanley Cup** was won by the Detroit Red Wings, who defeated the New York Rangers three games to two.

Apr. 19 The 41st **Boston Marathon** was won by Walter Young of Verdun, Quebec, Canada, with a time of 2 hrs., 33 min., 20 sec.

May 8 The 63rd annual **Kentucky Derby** was won by War Admiral, with a time of 2:03$\frac{1}{5}$. The jockey was Charles Kurtsinger.

May 15 The 62nd annual **Preakness Stakes** was won by War Admiral, with a time of 1:58$\frac{2}{5}$. The jockey was Charles Kurtsinger.

May 30 The **PGA golf tournament** was won by Denny Shute.

May 31 The 27th **Indianapolis 500** auto race was won by Wilbur Shaw of Indianapolis, completing the 500-mile course in 4 hrs., 24 min., 7.8 sec., with an average speed of 113.58 mph.

June 5 The 69th annual **Belmont Stakes** was won by War Admiral, with a time of 2:28$\frac{3}{5}$. The jockey was Charles Kurtsinger. War Admiral thus became the fourth horse to win the Triple Crown.

June 12 The **U.S. Open golf tournament** was won by Ralph Guldahl.

June 22 The **world heavyweight boxing championship** was won by Joe Louis, who knocked out

appoint a liberal justice, Hugo L. Black, on Aug. 12 and swing the Court's balance in favor of the New Deal.

July 22 The **Farm Security Administration** (FSA) was established through passage of the Bankhead-Jones Act. The FSA was empowered to make four-year loans at 3% interest to aid farm tenants, sharecroppers, and laborers.

Aug. 26 The **Judicial Procedure Reform Act** was signed by Pres. Roosevelt. It permitted Supreme Court justices and other federal judges to retire voluntarily and with full pension at age 70.

Sept. 2 The **National Housing Act,** also called the Wagner-Steagall Act, was signed by Pres. Roosevelt. It created the U.S. Housing Authority for the purpose of administering loans to small communities and states for rural and urban construction.

Dec. 12 The U.S. gunboat *Panay* was sunk in Chinese waters by Japanese air force planes, killing two and sparking a crisis in U.S.-Japanese relations. On Dec. 14 the U.S. demanded an apology and reparations. The Japanese complied immediately but continued to wage war in China.

Can't Take It with You by Moss Hart and George S. Kaufman.

Aug. 27 *El Salón Méjico* by **Aaron Copland** was given its premiere performance in Mexico City.

Nov. 2 *I'd Rather Be Right,* a musical comedy satirizing Pres. Roosevelt by George S. Kaufman and Moss Hart, with music by Richard Rodgers and Lorenz Hart, opened at the Alvin Theatre in New York City and quickly became an enormous success. It starred George M. Cohan as the president.

Nov. 4 *Golden Boy* by Clifford Odets opened at the Belasco Theatre in New York City. The play, dealing with a gifted son of Italian immigrants who deserts music for the quicker rewards of the prize ring, illuminated the tragedy of the American drive for success.

Nov. 27 *Pins and Needles,* produced by Labor Stage, Inc., a group of garment workers, opened in New York City. It quickly became successful and broke records for musical comedies. Its catchiest tune was "Sing Me a Song of Social Significance."

1938

A return of economic adversity led to increased government spending. This eased the situation a little, but led to further disillusionment with the New Deal. Congressional elections saw a sudden increase in the number of Republican winners. However, the center of government activity and concern was swinging toward foreign affairs. German occupation and annexation (Apr. 10) of Austria, and the crisis in September sparked by German demands on Czechoslovakia, culminating in the Munich Pact (Sept. 29), showed the democratic nations to be paralyzed in the face of German aggression. For the first time, isolationism vs. limited intervention became an active national issue. There was widespread nervousness about the possibility of war, but few believed it likely.

Feb. 16 The second **Agricultural Adjustment Act** was signed by Pres. Roosevelt. It maintained the soil conservation program; provided acreage allotments, parity payments, marketing quotas, and commodity loans to farmers; and authorized crop insurance corpora-

It was an active year for performing and creative arts, although little of distinction was produced. Authors rediscovered the past and flooded the market with historical novels. The organization of two world fairs, scheduled for the following year at New York City and San Francisco, sent architects to their drawing boards and artists to their easels. Commissions were made subject to competition, so the level of work done was somewhat more imaginative than it had recently been. Movie attendance dropped some 40%. The top money maker of the year was Walt Disney's *Snow White and the Seven Dwarfs,* which made Disney famous around the world and became a film classic.

Among **books published** this year was *Our Town,* a play by Thornton Wilder that was also produced and awarded a Pulitzer Prize in 1938. A thoughtful fantasy set on a bare stage, the play examined the lives and relationships of the residents of a small New England village. A central character was the "stage manager," who served as narrator. Other books published this year included *The King Was in His Counting House* by James Branch Cabell, a novel; *The Unvanquished* by William

| Business and Industry; Science; Education; Philosophy and Religion III | | IV Sports; Social Issues and Crime; Folkways; Fashion; Holidays |

May 24 The **Social Security Act** of 1935 was upheld by the U.S. Supreme Court.

May 27 The **Golden Gate Bridge** in San Francisco, Calif., was dedicated.

May 30 **Violence** broke out among workers striking against the Republic Steel Corporation in South Chicago, Ill. Ten strikers were killed and many more injured.

June 8 The **world's largest flower** bloomed at the New York Botanical Gardens. It was the *Amorphophallus titanum*, or giant calla lily, whose native home is Sumatra. The flower was 8½ ft. high, 4 ft. in diameter, and 2 ft. in circumference.

Aug. The first signs of a **new recession** became apparent in a selling wave on the stock markets. The retreat became sharper after Labor Day, and many stocks fell rapidly. On Oct. 19 the New York market was near demoralization, with total transactions of 7,290,000 shares—the largest since 1933.

Sept. 28 **Bonneville Dam,** on the Columbia R. in Oregon, was officially dedicated by Pres. Roosevelt.

Nov. 11 The **Nobel Prize in Physics** was awarded jointly to Clinton Joseph Davisson of Bell Telephone Laboratories in New York City and Sir George Paget Thomson of Great Britain, for their independent "discovery of the interference phenomenon in crystals irradiated by electrons."

James J. Braddock in the eighth round at Chicago.

July 2 At the **Wimbledon** tennis championship in England, the men's singles championship was won by J. Donald Budge.

July 7 The fifth annual **baseball All-Star Game** was won by the American League, which defeated the National League 8–3 and picked up its fourth victory in the event.

July 27 The **Davis Cup** tennis tournament was won by the U.S., defeating Great Britain four matches to one.

July 31–Aug. 5 The **America's Cup** was successfully defended by the yacht *Ranger,* which won four straight races from the British challenger *Endeavour II.*

Sept. 11 The **Miss America** title was won by Bette Cooper, 17, of Bertrand Island, N.J., at the annual pageant in Atlantic City, N.J.

Sept. 11 The **U.S. Lawn Tennis Association singles championships** were won by J. Donald Budge in the men's division and Anita Lizana of Chile in the women's division.

Oct. 6–10 The 34th annual **World Series** was won by the New York Yankees (AL), defeating the New York Giants (NL) four games to one.

Dec. 12 The **NFL championship** was won by the Washington Redskins, defeating the Chicago Bears 28–21.

1938

Because of government support, business conditions at year's end were healthier than at the start. Labor forces won two rousing victories—passage of the maximum hour and minimum wage bill and a long-sought measure that prohibited child labor in interstate industries. Isolated sit-down strikes still plagued industry, but public opinion seemed to swing against these tactics, so unions stopped them entirely. Technological advances were steady: James Slayter and John H. Thomas of Newark, Ohio, perfected methods to manufacture fiberglass. In addition, scientists made further advances in atomic physics.

Learning theory was advanced by publication of *Logic: The Theory of Inquiry and Experience and Education* by John Dewey.

The **history of physics** was the subject of *The Evolution of Physics,* an outstanding volume by Albert Einstein and Leopold Infeld.

It was a good year for sports. The number of active golfers was up, winter sports showed phenomenal growth in popularity, and both football and baseball were thriving. In football some 1,100,000 fans flocked to see professional games in 1938. Major league baseball drew about 10,000,000 to the stadiums in a year when many longtime records were broken. The New York Yankees (AL) became the first team to win the World Series three times running (in 1939, the first to win the series four times in a row). Yankee star Lou Gehrig set eight new major league records, including most consecutive games (2122), most consecutive years with 150 or more games (12), and most home runs with bases filled (23).

The number of **automobile-related deaths** for the year was put at more than 32,000 by the National Safety Council. About one-third of the fatalities involved pedestrians. Almost 9000 deaths resulted from collisions between motor vehicles.

The **Lambeth Walk** became popular on American musical stages and dance floors. It had been performed

tions and the "ever-normal granary" proposals of Sec. of Agriculture Henry A. Wallace.

Mar. 2 **Floods and landslides** in southern California claimed 144 lives. Thousands of homes were destroyed, nearly $60,000,000 in property lost.

Mar. 31 Former president **Herbert Hoover** advised the U.S. not to enter into alliances with openly antifascist European democracies because this course might lead to war. This was in answer to Pres. Roosevelt's speech of Oct. 5, 1937, urging collective international sanctions against aggressors.

May 17 The **Naval Expansion Act of 1938** was passed. It authorized expenditure of more than $1,000,000,-000 to increase the tonnage of capital ships, cruisers, and carriers over a ten-year period.

May 26 The **House Committee to Investigate Un-American Activities** (HUAC) was formed. It was also known as the Dies Committee after its chairman, Rep. Martin Dies, Democrat of Texas.

June 24 The **Wheeler-Lea Act** was passed. It superseded the Pure Food Act of 1906, introducing more stringent regulation of food, drugs, and cosmetics.

June 25 The **Wage and Hours Act** was signed by Pres. Roosevelt. It raised the minimum wage for workers engaged in interstate commerce from 25 cents to 40 cents an hour. Hours were limited to 44 per week in the first year of the law's enaction, dropping to 40 after the third year. Congress declared that it possessed the power in this act to ban interstate shipment of products made by unlawful exploitation of child labor.

July 17 Douglas G. "Wrong-way" Corrigan, unable to obtain a flight exit permit to Europe, took off from New York and landed in Dublin, Ireland, claiming he had headed for California. Despite his illegal action, he became a national celebrity for a time.

Sept. 21 A **hurricane struck New England,** taking an estimated 460 lives. Property damage was estimated at $150,000,000.

Sept. 26 Pres. Roosevelt sent **private memorandums** to Britain, France, Germany, and Czechoslovakia. He recommended arbitration of the Sudetenland crisis, brought on by German demands in the Sudetenland, then part of Czechoslovakia. This set the stage for the

Faulkner; the *Selected Poems* of John Gould Fletcher; *The Fifth Column* by Ernest Hemingway, a play dealing with the Spanish Civil War whose title came to mean a body of agents working secretly within a country to overthrow it; *The Selected Poetry of Robinson Jeffers; The Prodigal Parents* by Sinclair Lewis; *Land of the Free,* poetry by Archibald MacLeish; *Black Is My True-love's Hair* by Elizabeth Madox Roberts, a novel; and *Uncle Tom's Children* by Richard Wright, a collection of stories that heralded Wright's arrival as a writer.

One Third of a Nation was presented by the Living Theater, a project of the WPA Federal Theater Project. The dramatic presentation of conditions in the U.S. underscored the plight of Americans poorly housed.

Estimates showed that the *Music Appreciation Hour,* a program conducted by Walter Damrosch over a national radio network, was heard by 7,000,000 schoolchildren each week.

Adolph Alexander Weinman completed the doors for the American Academy of Arts and Letters building in New York City. Weinman was a master of sculpture in low relief, and the doors conveyed beautifully a sense of three-dimensionality. Weinman's works included the panels for the Morgan Library and the facade of the Municipal Building in New York City.

Walter Gropius and Marcel Breuer completed their first work in the U.S., the Haggerty House in Cohasset, Mass.

The Cloisters, a branch of the Metropolitan Museum of Art, was built at Fort Tryon Park in upper Manhattan to house works of medieval art. The building incorporated parts of five different French cloisters dating from the twelfth to fifteenth centuries.

Mar. 3 *Amelia Goes to the Ball,* a one-act opera buffa composed by Gian-Carlo Menotti while a student at the Curtis Institute of Music in Philadelphia, was produced by the Metropolitan Opera Company in New York City.

Mar. 10 **Academy Awards** were presented to *The Life of Emile Zola* as the outstanding motion picture of 1937; to Spencer Tracy as best actor for *Captains Courageous;* to Luise Rainer as best actress for *The Good Earth;* to Joseph Schildkraut as best supporting actor for *The Life of Emile Zola;* and to Alice Brady as best supporting actress for *In Old Chicago.* Walt Disney was awarded his sixth consecutive award in the cartoon category, for *The Old Mill.*

Apr. 13 *What a Life* by Clifford Goldsmith opened at the Biltmore Theatre in New York City. The play poked fun at adolescence, exemplified in Henry Aldrich, a character even more popular later on, in radio and film.

May *The Incredible Flutist,* a ballet score by **Walter Piston,** was performed by the Boston Pops Orchestra.

Patents were issued for **nylon,** the pioneer synthetic fabric. Commercial production began immediately. Du Pont manufactured toothbrushes with nylon bristles, the first nylon product to reach the market.

The **self-propelled combine,** a major advance in farm machinery, was introduced. The tractor-driven combine had been in general use in the U.S. since 1935. The next step, elimination of the tractor, improved the farmer's ability to cut, thresh, and clean grain. It proved valuable when World War II created unprecedented demand for grain.

Howard Hughes won the International Harmon Trophy for his flight around the world in the record time of three days, 19 hrs., 14 min.

Mar. The stock market **recession** reached its lowest point. Most of the leading stocks had fallen 50 points or more since the preceding August. The Federal Reserve Board's Adjusted Index of Industrial Production fell to 76.

Apr. 12 The first law to require **medical tests for marriage license applicants** was passed in New York State. The measure, known as the Desmond-Breitbart law, was passed to prevent the spread of syphilis. A similar law, requiring all pregnant women to take a blood test, had been passed on Mar. 13.

May 27 The continuing **recession** prompted passage of the Revenue Bill of 1938 by Congress, on grounds that tax concessions were needed to stimulate business. The bill reduced taxes on corporations and was supported by Republican and Democratic opponents of the New Deal.

June 23 **Civilian air transportation** in the U.S. came under federal control with passage of the Civil Aeronautics Act, which established the Civil Aeronautics Authority as an independent agency of the federal government. The agency regulated the licensing of civil pilots, use of airways, introduction of new equipment, and rules of flight.

Oct. 9 A new **international bridge** between Port Huron, Mich., and Point Edward, Ontario, Canada, over the St. Clair R. was dedicated. Construction had cost about $3,250,000.

Oct. 13 William Green, head of the American Federation of Labor, was reelected president of the

as far back as 1909 by a dancer named Daphne Pollard.

Jan. 1 In **college football bowl games,** the results were Rice 28, Colorado 14 in the Cotton Bowl; Auburn 6, Michigan State 0 in the Orange Bowl; California 13, Alabama 0 in the Rose Bowl; and Santa Clara 6, LSU 0 in the Sugar Bowl. This season the AP poll selected Texas Christian University as the national collegiate champions of 1937.

Jan. 18 Election to the **Baseball Hall of Fame** of Grover Cleveland Alexander, the pitcher, was announced.

Feb. 26 **U.S. figure skating championships** were won in Ardmore, Pa., by Joan Tozzer, women's singles; Robin H. Lee, men's singles; Joan Tozzer and M. Bernard Fox, pairs; Nettie C. Prantel and Harold Hartshorne, dance.

Apr. 4 The **Masters golf tournament** was won by Henry Picard, who defeated Ralph Guldahl and Harry Cooper by two strokes.

Apr. 5–12 The **NHL Stanley Cup** was won by the Chicago Black Hawks, who defeated the Toronto Maple Leafs three games to one.

Apr. 19 The 42nd **Boston Marathon** was won by Leslie Pawson of Pawtucket, R.I., with a time of 2 hrs., 35 min., 34.8 sec.

May 7 The 64th annual **Kentucky Derby** was won by Lawrin, with a time of 2:04⅘. The jockey was Eddie Arcaro.

May 14 The 63rd annual **Preakness Stakes** was won by Dauber, with a time of 1:59⅘. The jockey was Maurice Peters.

May 30 The 25th **Indianapolis 500** auto race was won by Floyd Roberts of Van Nuys, Calif., completing the 500-mile course in 4 hrs., 15 min., 58.40 sec., with an average speed of 117.20 mph.

June 4 The 70th annual **Belmont Stakes** was won by Pasteurized, with a time of 2:29⅖. The jockey was Jimmy Stout.

June 11 The **U.S. Open golf tournament** was won by Ralph Guldahl.

July 1 At the **Wimbledon** tennis championships in England, the men's singles title was won by J. Donald Budge. The next day Helen Wills Moody won the women's singles.

July 6 The sixth annual **baseball All-Star Game** was

Munich Pact (Sept. 29), which in effect surrendered the Sudetenland to Germany along with all Czechoslovakian fortresses on the frontier with Germany. British Prime Minister Neville Chamberlain, key figure in negotiations with Adolf Hitler, returned to England and announced he had secured "peace in our time."

Nov. 8   In **congressional elections** the Democrats lost seven Senate seats but kept a 69–23 majority, with four seats going to minor parties. In the House Democrats lost 70 seats, for a 261–164 majority, with four seats going to minor parties.

Nov. 14–18   Hugh R. Wilson, the **U.S. ambassador to Germany, was summoned** to Washington, D.C., to confer with Pres. Roosevelt on anti-Jewish activities in Nazi Germany. Although not an official recall, the move marked U.S. displeasure with German policies and reflected heightened tension in international relations. Four days after Ambassador Wilson returned to the U.S., Hans Dieckhoff, German ambassador to the U.S., was recalled to Germany.

The performance was a success and the ballet became Piston's best-known work.

May 2   **Pulitzer prizes** were awarded for the following: fiction, *The Late George Apley* by John P. Marquand; biography, *Pedlar's Progress* by Odell Shepard and *Andrew Jackson* by Marquis James; history, *The Road to Reunion, 1865–1900* by Paul Herman Buck; poetry, *Cold Morning Sky* by Marya Zaturenska; drama, *Our Town* by Thornton Wilder.

Oct. 3   *Abe Lincoln in Illinois* by Robert E. Sherwood, a scholarly and realistic dramatization of Lincoln's life up to his election to the presidency, opened in Washington, D.C. The play, awarded a Pulitzer Prize in 1939, presented Lincoln as a man unsure of himself and unhappy.

Oct. 30   **Orson Welles** staged his radio play *War of the Worlds,* based on the novel by H. G. Wells. The program caused widespread panic when listeners took as true the realistically performed news reports of an invasion from Mars. The experience demonstrated the power of the new medium to influence large numbers of people.

Nov. 10   The **Nobel Prize for Literature** was awarded to Pearl S. Buck, author of the novel *The Good Earth.*

1939

Prosperity seemed just around the corner. Unfortunately, this was largely due to the tremendous volume of orders for military supplies that flooded the nation's factories. The administration could now concentrate for the first time on the problems engendered by approaching war in Europe. Germany completed the dismemberment of Czechoslovakia, and Adolf Hitler turned his attention to Poland. The signing in August of a nonaggression pact between Russia and Germany cleared the path to war between Germany and the other European powers. The principal question for the U.S. was how it would be able to stay out of the conflict.

Jan. 12   A two-year **defense program** costing $535,-000,000 was recommended by Pres. Franklin D. Roosevelt in a special message to Congress.

Mar.   **Czechoslovakia** ceased to exist as an independent nation. Bohemia and Moravia became a German protectorate, Slovakia passed under German control, and Carpatho-Ukraine was annexed by Hungary.

U.S. novelists were taking a long, fond look back on America's past. Historical novels had never been so plentiful. The theater mourned the passing of the Federal Theater Project but rejoiced in a sudden rebirth of interest in the legitimate stage. A shortage of New York City playhouses was felt for the first time in many years. Painters seemed to be exploring two areas: depiction of the regional American scene, which stressed people in relation to their land or locale; and the use of art as a vehicle for political statement or social satire. Film producers faced the bleak prospect of the loss of a lucrative European market. Nonetheless, this was the year of *Gone with the Wind,* one of the most expensive and most successful motion pictures of all time.

Among **books published** this year was *The Grapes of Wrath* by John Steinbeck, a powerful novel dealing with an Oklahoma farm family who lose their farm to the bank and are forced to travel to California to seek work as migrant laborers. Described as a proletarian novel, the book examined in moving detail the plight of the Okies, and by extension the plight of all people caught up in tragic circumstances not of their own making. The novel won a Pulitzer Prize in 1940 and was the basis for an outstanding motion picture. Also published this year were *Adventure of a Young Man* by John Dos Passos, the first novel of a trilogy entitled *District of Columbia; The Wild Palms* by William Faulkner, a novel; *Captain*

organization. In his acceptance speech, Green asked the Committee for Industrial Organization, headed by John L. Lewis and other labor leaders who had left or were expelled from the federation, to return to the parent organization.

Nov. An early **radar** system, developed by the U.S. Army Signal Corps in 1936 and demonstrated before the secretary of war in 1937, was subjected to exhaustive tests by the Coast Artillery.

Nov. 14–18 The **Congress of Industrial Organizations** (CIO) was established by the delegates to the annual convention of the Committee for Industrial Organization, held at Pittsburgh, Pa. John L. Lewis was unanimously elected president.

Dec. 13 The number of Americans receiving **federal relief** had dropped to 2,122,960, compared with 3,184,000 the previous year, according to a report issued by the Works Progress Administration.

won by the National League, which defeated the American League 4–1.

July 16 The **PGA golf tournament** was won by Paul Runyan.

Sept. 5 In the **Davis Cup** international tennis matches, the U.S. defeated Australia three matches to two in the challenge round.

Sept. 10 The **Miss America** title was won by Marilyn Meseke, 21, from Marion, Ohio, at the annual pageant in Atlantic City, N.J.

Sept. 17 The **U.S. Lawn Tennis Association singles championships** were won by J. Donald Budge in the men's division and Alice Marble in the women's division.

Oct. 5–9 The 35th annual **World Series** was won by the New York Yankees (AL), defeating the Chicago Cubs (NL) in four straight games.

Dec. 11 The **NFL championship** was won by the New York Giants, defeating the Green Bay Packers 23–17.

1939

Business underwent a gradual decline from 1938 levels, followed by gradual recovery and then a spectacular upsurge in the fall, attributable to the outbreak of war in Europe. The biggest event of the year, however, received scant press attention. Scientists announced that they had succeeded in splitting uranium, thorium, and protactinium atoms by bombarding them with neutrons.

Discovery of the **Rh factor** in human blood by Dr. Philip Levine and Dr. Rufus Stetson of New York led to a clearer understanding of pregnancy and blood transfusion complications. The Rh factor is a component of red blood cells. Those with the factor are classified as Rh+, and those lacking it are Rh-. Transfusion of one type of blood into a person with the other type can cause a serious immune reaction. In pregnancies, women with Rh- blood bearing Rh+ fetuses can develop an immune reaction to the baby's blood, leading to difficulties in subsequent pregnancies.

Frequency modulation, a new method of radio transmission and reception, was developed by Edwin H. Armstrong. Armstrong had devised the regenerative receiver during World War I. The latter type of radio

World fairs in New York City and San Francisco opened, and millions flocked to the expositions to glimpse wonders of the future. Observers noted the unreality of the enthusiasm, in face of the impending war in Europe. However, Americans paid little notice to the prophets of doom, instead lining up to take "death-defying" rides on the roller coaster and the parachute jump.

The **latest fashions** were advertised in the Sears Roebuck catalog, which offered dresses "inspired by Schiapparelli." In the following year, Sears would announce that "the traditional lapse between the acceptance of new fashions . . . in metropolitan centers and on farms apparently no longer exists."

Jan. 1 In **college football bowl games,** the results were St. Mary's 20, Texas Tech 13 in the Cotton Bowl; Tennessee 17, Oklahoma 0 in the Orange Bowl; Southern California 7, Duke 3 in the Rose Bowl; and TCU 15, Carnegie Tech 7 in the Sugar Bowl. This season the AP poll chose Texas A&M the national collegiate champions of 1938.

Jan. 21 **U.S. figure skating championships** were won in St. Paul, Minn., by Robin H. Lee, men's singles; Joan Tozzer, women's singles; Joan Tozzer and M. Bernard Fox, pairs; Sandy Macdonald and Harold Hartshorne, dance.

June 8 King George VI and Queen Elizabeth of Great Britain arrived in Washington, D.C., on their visit to the U.S. (June 7–12). They were the first British sovereigns to visit the U.S.

July 1 The **Federal Works Agency** was established by Pres. Roosevelt as a consolidation of five existing agencies: the Public Building Administration, Public Roads Administration, Public Works Administration, Works Projects Administration, and U.S. Housing Authority.

Aug. 24 News of the **German-Russian nonaggression pact** reached U.S. newspapers. It had been signed on Aug. 23.

Sept. 1 Germany invaded Poland without declaration of war. On Aug. 24 Pres. Roosevelt had cabled Germany, Poland, and Italy, urging arbitration, conciliation, or negotiation to avoid war.

Sept. 3 Great Britain and France declared war on Germany. On the same day Belgium declared its neutrality and Pres. Roosevelt, in a fireside chat, declared the U.S. to be neutral.

Sept. 3 Thirty Americans died when the British passenger ship *Athenia* was sunk by a submarine. The following day, Sec. of State Cordell Hull advised U.S. citizens to travel to Europe only under "imperative necessity."

Sept. 21 A special session of Congress was convened by Pres. Roosevelt, who urged the repeal of the arms embargo provision of the Neutrality Act of 1937.

Oct. 18 All U.S. ports and waters were closed to belligerent submarines by presidential order.

Nov. 4 The **Neutrality Act of 1939** was passed by Congress. It repealed the prohibition of arms exports

Horatio Hornblower by C. S. Forester; *Collected Poems* by Robert Frost; *Pale Horse, Pale Rider* by Katherine Anne Porter, stories; *Abraham Lincoln: The War Years* (four volumes) by Carl Sandburg; and *Collected Poems* by Mark Van Doren.

An important study of **propaganda and censorship,** *Public Opinion* by William Albig, was published.

Perhaps the best known office building by **Frank Lloyd Wright,** the Johnson Wax Company administration building, was constructed at Racine, Wis.

Jan. 20 The *Second Piano Sonata* of **Charles Ives** received its first performance at Town Hall in New York City. The sonata, performed by John Kirkpatrick and composed by Ives between 1904 and 1915, was subtitled *Concord Sonata.* Its movements were entitled "Emerson," "Hawthorne," "The Alcotts," and "Thoreau." It has been called by some the greatest music composed by an American, and also the most difficult composition for piano ever written. It took Kirkpatrick two years to learn it.

Jan. 21 *The American Way* by George S. Kaufman and Moss Hart opened at the Center Theatre in New York City. The play traced in cavalcade fashion the life of a German immigrant couple in America.

Feb. 23 **Academy Awards** were presented to *You Can't Take It With You* as the outstanding motion picture of 1938; to Spencer Tracy as best actor for *Boys Town;* to Bette Davis as best actress for *Jezebel;* to Walter Brennan as best supporting actor for *Kentucky;* and to Fay Bainter as best supporting actress for *Jezebel.* Walt Disney won his seventh consecutive award in the cartoon category, for *Ferdinand the Bull.*

Feb. 24 The *Third Symphony* of **Roy Harris** was given its first performance by the Boston Symphony Orchestra, Serge Koussevitzky conducting. Although Harris had been recognized by critics and musicians before this, the performance was his first popular success.

May 1 **Pulitzer prizes** were awarded for the following: fiction, *The Yearling* by Marjorie Kinnan Rawlings; biography, *Benjamin Franklin* by Carl Van Doren; history, *A History of American Magazines* by Frank Luther Mott; poetry, *Selected Poems* by John Gould Fletcher; drama, *Abe Lincoln in Illinois* by Robert E. Sherwood.

Oct. 25 *The Time of Your Life* by William Saroyan opened at the Booth Theatre in New York City. The play, one of Saroyan's best-known works, dealt with the dreams and aspirations of a group of patrons of Nick's Saloon in San Francisco.

Nov. 8 *Life with Father,* a highly successful comedy by Howard Lindsay and Russel Crouse, opened at the Empire Theatre in New York City. The play,

| Business and Industry; Science; Education; Philosophy and Religion III | IV Sports; Social Issues and Crime; Folkways; Fashion; Holidays |

became the standard for amplitude modulation, or AM, broadcast applications. However, AM broadcasting was susceptible to static, and in the 1930s and 1940s Armstrong worked to perfect FM transmission and reception, which was not affected by static emissions. He received virtually no support from public opinion, the radio industry, or the FCC. On Jan. 31, 1954, Armstrong, suffering from poor health, plagued by lawsuits, and lacking financial resources, committed suicide.

The **Works Progress Administration** (WPA) was renamed the Works Projects Administration.

Feb. 27 The **sit-down strike,** organized labor's most controversial weapon, was declared illegal by the U.S. Supreme Court.

May 5 The **United Mine Workers,** headed by John L. Lewis, forced virtual stoppage of all soft-coal production when the union and coal operators failed to reach agreement. Work was resumed on May 13 when a contract was signed.

May 10 The **Methodist Church was reunited** after 109 years of division. The conflict within the church had been marked by two major crises. In 1830 the Methodist Protestant Church had separated from the Methodist Episcopal Church over the question of episcopal authority and had established a separate branch in which lay members were given a voice in church government. The Methodist Episcopal Church, South, had separated from the Methodist Episcopal Church in 1844, ostensibly over an administrative dispute, but probably over the slavery question. A Declaration of Union issued on this date unified some 8,000,000 American Methodists.

June 28 The first regular **transatlantic passenger air service** began when *Dixie Clipper,* a Pan American Airways airliner, left Port Washington, Long Island, with 22 passengers aboard. The flight reached Lisbon, Portgual, 23 hrs., 52 min. later.

July 17 The proposed **Brooklyn-Battery bridge** over the East R. in New York City was rejected by the War Department on the grounds that it might pose a hazard to naval forces in wartime.

Jan. 24 Election to the **Baseball Hall of Fame** was announced for Edward T. "Eddie" Collins, William H. "Wee Willie" Keeler, and George Sisler. On May 2, during the centennial celebration of baseball, six more baseball immortals were added to the Hall of Fame: Adrian C. Anson, Charles A. Comiskey, William A. Cummings, William Ewing, Charles Radbourne, and Albert G. Spaulding. Also on that day Lou Gehrig, ill with the disease that would kill him two years later, withdrew from the New York Yankees lineup and ended his career, which included a record 2130 consecutive games played. On Dec. 7 the Baseball Writers Association moved to put Gehrig in the Hall of Fame.

Mar. 27 The **NCAA basketball championship** was won by the University of Oregon, which defeated Ohio State 46–33.

Apr. 2 The **Masters golf tournament** was won by Ralph Guldahl.

Apr. 6–16 The **NHL Stanley Cup** was won by the Boston Bruins, who defeated the Toronto Maple Leafs four games to one.

Apr. 19 The 43rd **Boston Marathon** was won by Ellison Brown of Alton, R.I., with a time of 2 hrs., 28 min., 51.8 sec.

May 6 The 65th annual **Kentucky Derby** was won by Johnstown, with a time of 2:03²/₅. The jockey was Jimmy Stout. Johnstown had been trained by "Sunny Jim" Fitzsimmons, who had trained two previous Derby winners, Gallant Fox and Omaha.

May 13 The 64th annual **Preakness Stakes** was won by Challedon, with a time of 1:59⁴/₅. The jockey was George Seabo.

May 30 The 27th annual **Indianapolis 500** auto race was won by Wilbur Shaw of Indianapolis, who completed the 500-mile course in 4 hrs., 20 min., 47.41 sec., with an average speed of 115.035 mph. Floyd Roberts, the 1938 winner, died in a crash during the race.

June 3 The 71st annual **Belmont Stakes** was won by Johnstown, with a time of 2:29³/₅. The jockey was Jimmy Stout.

June 12 The **U.S. Open golf tournament** was won by Byron Nelson.

July 7–8 At the **Wimbledon** tennis championships in England, Robert L. Riggs won the men's singles title and Alice Marble won the women's singles. Riggs and Elwood T. Cooke took the men's doubles, Marble and Sarah Palfrey Fabyan the women's doubles.

July 11 The seventh annual **baseball All-Star Game** was won by the American League, which beat the National League 3–1 at Yankee Stadium in New York City.

July 17 The **PGA golf tournament** was won by Henry Picard.

in the Neutrality Act of 1937 and authorized the "cash and carry" sale of arms to belligerent powers.

Nov. 30 The **Russo-Finnish War** (1939–1940) began when Russian forces invaded Finland. Finnish forces inflicted massive casualties on the Red Army, but the outnumbered Finns were forced to sue for peace in Mar. 1940.

depicting life in a Victorian household, was based on sketches written by Clarence Day, Jr., for *The New Yorker* magazine. Lindsay played the part of Father.

Nov. 27 *Key Largo* by Maxwell Anderson opened at the Ethel Barrymore Theatre in New York City. The play, about an American volunteer serving with Loyalist forces in the Spanish Civil War, probed the ability of modern intellectuals to build an adequate moral and ethical foundation for their actions.

Dec. 6 *Du Barry Was a Lady* by Herbert Fields and B. G. De Sylva, with music by Cole Porter, opened at the Forty-Sixth Street Theatre in New York City and became the hit musical of the Broadway season.

1940

With the outbreak of war in Europe in Sept. 1939, the key political question facing the U.S. became how to stay out of the conflict and still help the forces of democracy. Realizing that America was facing a crisis, Pres. Franklin D. Roosevelt decided to run for an unprecedented third term. His rival was a political newcomer, Wendell L. Willkie, whose plainspoken manner made him a powerful contender. Roosevelt won, largely because people felt it was better not to change administrations in dangerous times. This year Germany would invade Norway, overrun Denmark, Luxembourg, Belgium, and the Netherlands, and defeat France. In August Adolf Hitler launched the Battle of Britain, a brutal air assault intended to destroy the Royal Air Force and enable invasion of England.

The **U.S. population** was 131,669,275, according to Census Bureau figures. The center of population was two miles southeast by east of Carlisle, Sullivan County, Ind.

Apr. 7 The **Socialist Party** nominated Norman Thomas of New York for the fourth time as its candidate for the presidency. Maynard C. Krueger was nominated for the vice presidency.

Apr. 12 The **Reciprocal Trade Agreement Act** was signed by Pres. Roosevelt. It extended the life of the Trade Agreements Act of 1937 for three more years.

Apr. 28 The **Socialist Labor Party** nominated John W. Aiken of Massachusetts for the presidency and Aaron M. Orange of New York for the vice presidency.

May 10 The **Prohibition Party** nominated Roger W. Babson of Massachusetts for the presidency and Edgar V. Moorman of Illinois for the vice presidency.

Book production was up, with 11,328 titles published, and war novels led in popularity. The New York stage labored through an uninspired season, relying principally on foreign imports. On Broadway, the biggest musical hits of the season were *Du Barry Was a Lady* by Cole Porter and *Louisiana Purchase* by Irving Berlin. Musicologists noted a trend away from ultramodernism—the 12-tone system, for instance—which had intrigued composers. The art world showed the influence of European refugee painters, who were forced by war into American exile. Their work centered on the individual rather than on aesthetics. This tendency was seen in architecture as well, where outstanding work was done on buildings designed for shelter, care of the sick, social services, and recreation.

Among **books published** this year was *Native Son* by Richard Wright, a powerful novel considered by many to be Wright's masterpiece. It told the story of Bigger Thomas, a young black drawn into crime and ultimately to execution as a murderer. The novel was adapted for Broadway by Wright and Paul Green in 1941 and had a successful run. Other books published this year included *The Hamlet* by William Faulkner, the first novel of a trilogy about the Snopes family; *For Whom the Bell Tolls* by Ernest Hemingway, set in Spain during that country's civil war; and *You Can't Go Home Again* by Thomas Wolfe, who had died in 1938. Critics found this novel of Wolfe's quieter and better organized than his earlier works.

The year's **popular songs** included "South of the Border," "Oh Johnny," "Scatterbrain," "Careless," "In an Old Dutch Garden," "When You Wish upon a Star," "Woodpecker Song," "Playmates," "I'll Never Smile Again," "Blueberry Hill," and "Only Forever."

| Business and Industry; Science; Education; Philosophy and Religion | III | | IV | Sports; Social Issues and Crime; Folkways; Fashion; Holidays |

Oct. 25 Nylon stockings first went on sale in the U.S.

Nov. 9 The Nobel Prize in Physics was awarded to Ernest Orlando Lawrence of the University of California for his development of the cyclotron and for subsequent discoveries in the field of radioactivity, specifically the study of artificially radioactive elements. Lawrence's invention of the cyclotron provided nuclear scientists with an invaluable instrument with which to produce the subatomic particles required for study of nuclear reactions.

Sept. 10 The Miss America title was won by Patricia Mary Donnelly, 19, from Michigan, at the annual pageant in Atlantic City, N.J.

Sept. 17 The U.S. Lawn Tennis Association singles championships were won by Robert L. Riggs in the men's division and Alice Marble in the women's division. This year Marble swept the U.S. and British singles, doubles, and mixed doubles championships.

Oct. 4–8 The 36th annual World Series was won by the New York Yankees (AL), sweeping the Cincinnati Reds (NL) in four games.

Dec. 10 The NFL championship was won by the Green Bay Packers, defeating the New York Giants 27–0.

1940

Unemployment dropped dramatically because of the military conscription of many industrial workers as well as increased orders, resulting in increased hiring. Labor suffered setbacks in its right to organize and in efforts for better hours and wages. By and large, this was expected and accepted, as the labor force agreed that sacrifice was necessary to maintain America's pledge to support its allies. The next step toward development of the atomic bomb was taken when scientists determined that a chain reaction was possible and would soon become a reality.

The **first antibiotic** developed in the U.S., actinomycin, was produced by Dr. Selman Waksman of Rutgers University, a pioneer in antibiotics. However, it was found too poisonous for humans.

The average **life expectancy** was 64 years. This represented a major increase from 49 years in 1900.

Illiteracy in the U.S. reached a new low of 4.2% of the population, a decline of 0.1% from 1930, and a 15.8% drop from 1870.

Radios could be found in 30,000,000 homes, according to a survey.

A major philosophical work by **George Santayana** was completed with publication of *The Realm of Spirit*, the fourth volume of a series entitled *The Realms of Being*. The earlier volumes of this series were *The Realm of Essence* (1927), *The Realm of Matter* (1930), and *The Realm of Truth* (1937).

Apr. 20 An electron microscope was first publicly tested at the Radio Corporation of America laboratory in Camden, N.J. The instrument, about 10 ft. high and

The coming of war to Europe threatened a complete halt in international sports competition. The 1940 Olympic Games were not held, and Olympic competition would not resume until 1948. Also suspended were the Davis Cup and Wimbledon tennis championships. Joe Louis did, however, defend the world heavyweight boxing championship in two bouts (Feb. 9 and June 20) against Arturo Godoy of Chile. In baseball the New York Yankees ended up in third place in the American League, losing a chance to become the first team to win five consecutive World Series.

Cornelius Warmerdam became the first person to pole-vault 15 ft. Two years later he set a new record when he vaulted 15 ft. 7¾ in. He retired from competition in 1943 after having vaulted 15 ft. or more 43 times.

Racetrack attendance for the year was 8,500,000. Some $408,500,000 was bet in parimutuel pools, and $16,145,182 was gathered by states in revenue. By 1952 these figures would rise to 26,434,903 attendance; $1,915,220,517 bet; and $119,266,959 in revenue earned by states.

Jan. 1 In college football bowl games the results were Clemson 6, Boston College 3 in the Cotton Bowl; Georgia Tech 21, Missouri 7 in the Orange Bowl; Southern California 14, Tennessee 0 in the Rose Bowl; and Texas A&M 14, Tulane 13 in the Sugar Bowl. This season the AP poll selected Minnesota as national collegiate champions of 1939.

Feb. 10 U.S. figure skating championships were won in Cleveland, Ohio, by Eugene Turner, men's singles; Joan Tozzer, women's singles; Joan Tozzer and M. Bernard Fox, pairs; Sandy Macdonald and Harold Hartshorne, dance.

Mar. 30 The NCAA basketball championship was won by Indiana University, defeating the University of Kansas 60–42.

June 2 The **Communist Party** nominated Earl Browder of Kansas for the presidency and James W. Ford for the vice presidency.

June 24–28 The **Republican National Convention nominated Wendell L. Willkie** of Indiana for the presidency and Charles L. McNary of Oregon for the vice presidency.

June 28 The **Alien Registration Act,** also known as the Smith Act, was passed by Congress. It was signed into law on the next day by Pres. Roosevelt. It required registration and fingerprinting of aliens and made it unlawful to belong to any organization advocating overthrow of the U.S. government. Subsequent registration showed approximately 5,000,000 aliens living in the U.S.

July 15–19 The **Democratic National Convention** nominated Franklin D. Roosevelt for the presidency on the first ballot. Henry A. Wallace of Iowa was nominated for the vice presidency.

Sept. 3 The **U.S. gave 50 outdated destroyers** to Great Britain in exchange for 99-year leases on naval and air bases in Newfoundland and the West Indies.

Sept. 16 The **Selective Service Act** was passed by Congress. The law, the first U.S. peacetime draft, provided for 900,000 selectees to be taken each year. All men between the ages of 20 and 36 were required to register. Length of military service was one year, but this was extended to 18 months in Aug. 1941.

Nov. 5 **Franklin D. Roosevelt was reelected president** of the United States. Henry A. Wallace was elected vice president. The electoral vote was Roosevelt, 449, Wendell L. Willkie, Republican of Indiana, 82. The popular vote was Roosevelt, 27,244,160; Willkie, 22,-305,198; Norman Thomas, Socialist candidate, 100,-264; Roger W. Babson, Prohibition candidate, 57,812; Earl Browder, Communist, 48,579; John W. Aiken, Socialist Labor candidate, 14,861. In congressional elections the Democrats lost three Senate seats but kept a 66–28 majority, with two seats going to minor parties. In the House the Democrats gained seven seats for a 268–162 lead, with five seats going to minor parties.

Hunter College, the first large-scale urban college building of modern design, was built in New York City. A single building of 19 stories, it provided faculty offices and classrooms for 5650 students.

Letter to the World, a dance scored by Hunter Johnson, was presented in New York City by Martha Graham and her dance company.

Jan. 9 *The Male Animal* by Elliott Nugent and James Thurber opened at the Cort Theatre in New York City. The play satirized college types but also dealt with freedom of thought and speech on college campuses.

Jan. 16 *Two on an Island* by Elmer Rice, a play set in New York City, opened at the Mansfield Theatre in New York City.

Feb. 29 **Academy Awards** were presented to *Gone with the Wind* as the outstanding motion picture of 1939; to Robert Donat as best actor for *Goodbye, Mr. Chips;* to Vivien Leigh as best actress for *Gone with the Wind;* to Thomas Mitchell as best supporting actor for *Stagecoach;* and to Hattie McDaniel as best supporting actress for *Gone with the Wind.* Walt Disney won his eighth consecutive award in the cartoon category, for *The Ugly Duckling.*

Mar. 29 *There Shall Be No Night* by Robert Sherwood, a powerful play dramatizing the tyranny of a dictatorship over a scientist, opened at the Playhouse in Providence, R.I.

May 6 **Pulitzer prizes** were awarded for the following: fiction, *The Grapes of Wrath* by John Steinbeck; biography, *Woodrow Wilson, Life and Letters, Vols. VII and VIII* by Ray Stannard Baker; history, *Abraham Lincoln: The War Years* by Carl Sandburg; poetry, *Collected Poems* by Mark Van Doren; drama, *The Time of Your Life* by William Saroyan.

Dec. 26 *My Sister Eileen* by Joseph Fields and Jerome Chodorov, a delightful farce based on the 1938 book of the same title by Ruth McKenney, opened at the Biltmore Theatre in New York City.

1941

Two events overshadowed all others this year. On June 22 Germany invaded the U.S.S.R. After several weeks of spectacular German success it seemed that Russia would fall before year's end. On December 7 Japanese forces launched a surprise attack on the U.S. base at Pearl Harbor, Hawaii. Almost instantly the American

Of all the art forms, theater alone seemed concerned with the fact that the U.S. was at war. A number of propaganda plays were written by new as well as established writers. Unfortunately, many playwrights looked on the stage as a soapbox, and quality suffered. There were, however, the surprising flowering of a truly

| **Business and Industry; Science;**
Education; Philosophy and Religion **III** | | **IV** **Sports; Social Issues and Crime;**
Folkways; Fashion; Holidays |

weighing 700 lbs., magnified by as much as 100,000 diameters. It had been developed by Dr. Ladislaus Marton and coworkers under the supervision of Dr. Vladimir Kasma Zworykin.

Apr. 27 Appointment of **Bertrand Russell** to the William James lectureship at Harvard would not be affected by the dispute over his appointment to the faculty of City College of New York, it was announced by the president and fellows of Harvard University.

May 15 The first successful **helicopter flight** in the U.S. was completed by the VS-300, an experimental helicopter manufactured by the Vought-Sikorsky Corporation.

May 24 A **time capsule** known as the Crypt of Civilization was sealed at Oglethorpe University in Atlanta, Ga. The crypt contained such items as a bottle of beer, an encyclopedia, and a movie magazine, along with thousands of other objects. It was not to be opened until the year 8113.

July 2 The **Lake Washington Floating Bridge** opened to traffic at Seattle, Wash. The main portion of the bridge floated on huge concrete pontoons. Built at a cost of $8,294,000, the bridge was the greatest floating structure ever built.

Oct. 24 The **40-hour work week,** part of the Fair Labor Standards Act of 1938, went into effect.

Oct. 25 John L. Lewis continued his feud with the administration by urging workers to vote for a Republican president. He declared he would resign as CIO president if Pres. Roosevelt were reelected.

Nov. 7 A **suspension bridge collapse** over the Narrows at Tacoma, Wash., was caused by wind vibration. The bridge tumbled 190 feet into Puget Sound.

Nov. 21 True to his promise, **John L. Lewis resigned** as head of the CIO following the Democratic victory at the polls. He was succeeded by Philip Murray.

Apr. 2–13 The **NHL Stanley Cup** was won by the New York Rangers, who defeated the Toronto Maple Leafs four games to two.

Apr. 7 The **Masters golf tournament** was won by Jimmy Demaret, who beat Lloyd Mangrum by four strokes.

Apr. 19 The 44th **Boston Marathon** was won by Gerard Cote of St. Hyacinthe, Quebec, Canada, with a record of 2 hrs., 28 min., 28.6 sec.

May 4 The 66th annual **Kentucky Derby** was won by Gallahadion, with a time of 2:05. The jockey was Carroll Bierman.

May 11 The 65th annual **Preakness Stakes** was won by Bimelech, with a time of 1:58³/₅. The jockey was Fred A. Smith.

May 30 The 28th **Indianapolis 500** auto race was won by Wilbur Shaw of Indianapolis, completing the 500-mile course in 4 hrs., 22 min., 31.17 sec., with an average speed of 114.27 mph. It was his third win, his second in a row.

June 8 The 72nd annual **Belmont Stakes** was won by Bimelech, with a time of 2:29³/₅. The jockey was Fred A. Smith.

June 9 The **U.S. Open golf tournament** was won by W. Lawson Little.

July 9 The eighth annual **baseball All-Star Game** was won by the American League, which defeated the National League 1–0.

Sept. 2 The **PGA golf tournament** was won by Byron Nelson.

Sept. 8 The **Miss America** title was won by Frances Marie Burke, 19, from Philadelphia, Pa., at the annual pageant in Atlantic City, N.J.

Sept. 9 The **U.S. Lawn Tennis Association singles championships** were won by W. Donald McNeill in the men's division and Alice Marble in the women's division.

Oct. 2–8 The 37th annual **World Series** was won by the Cincinnati Reds (NL), defeating the Detroit Tigers (AL) four games to three.

Dec. 8 The **NFL championship** was won by the Chicago Bears, who defeated the Washington Redskins by the incredible score of 73–0.

1941

The nation's industry tooled up for full-scale war production. Realizing that wartime is usually a time of inflation, the government prepared to curb prices and limit consumption. Numerous bureaus were established to develop and direct America's vast economic potential. For the most part, the civilian population took controls

Remember Pearl Harbor became the war cry of the man in the street, who used it more as a grim reminder than as an outburst of patriotism. Women's fashions, reflecting the general restraint, kept to subdued colors and inconspicuous lines. Prior to the Pearl Harbor attack, the greatest fashion furor of the year came when

nation attained a unity it had not known since the dark days of 1933. No longer were Americans to debate the fact that the U.S. was a neutral power and yet had spent $13,000,000,000 on lend-lease appropriations—all of it for war materiel earmarked for use against Germany and Italy—and had created some 35 separate agencies and offices that in effect were war bureaus. The U.S. was in the war at last.

Jan. 20 Pres. **Franklin D. Roosevelt was inaugurated** for an unprecedented third term. Henry A. Wallace was inaugurated vice president.

Feb. 3 The **Federal Wage and Hour Law** was upheld unanimously by the U.S. Supreme Court. The law prohibited employment of children under 16 in mining and manufacturing and children under 18 in any dangerous occupation. The main provision of the law, however, was its regulation of minimum wages and maximum hours for industries engaged in interstate commerce.

Mar. 11 The **Lend-Lease Bill** was signed by Pres. Franklin D. Roosevelt. It furnished a system by which the U.S. could lend goods and munitions to democratic countries in return for services and goods.

May 27 An unlimited national emergency was declared by Pres. Roosevelt in a radio broadcast from the White House. The proclamation came after German forces overran Greece and Yugoslavia and invaded Crete.

June 14 German and Italian assets in the U.S. were ordered frozen by Pres. Roosevelt. The order included freezing all assets belonging to invaded and occupied European countries.

June 16 All German consulates and Nazi propaganda organizations in the U.S. were ordered closed by the State Department.

July 25 An embargo on shipments of scrap iron and gasoline to Japan was ordered by Pres. Roosevelt. The order also froze Japanese assets in the U.S.

Aug. 9–12 The **Atlantic Charter** was formulated by Pres. Roosevelt and Prime Minister Winston Churchill at a secret meeting off Newfoundland. It contained eight articles of agreement and defined the aims of the two governments during and after the war.

Aug. 18 A **Selective Service Act Extension** was signed by Pres. Roosevelt. It extended the period of military service to not more than 30 months in time of peace and removed the 900,000-man limit on selectees.

Sept. 11 An order to **attack on sight** was issued by Pres. Roosevelt, to apply to German or Italian vessels found by American ships or planes to be operating in U.S. defensive waters. The order was issued after a

American painting style and a new musical awareness. New York City was no longer the sole arbiter of these arts; symphonic societies, ballet companies, opera houses, and museums mushroomed across the nation, sometimes presenting works of uncertain quality but always of unflagging enthusiasm despite wartime conditions.

Among **books published** this year was *Berlin Diary* by William L. Shirer, a study of Adolf Hitler and Nazi Germany that became a best seller. Other books published this year included *Random Harvest* by James Hilton; *H. M. Pulham, Esq.,* a novel by John P. Marquand; *The White Cliffs of Dover* by Alice Duer Miller, a book of verse celebrating the British people in wartime; and *My Friend Flicka* by Mary O'Hara, the story of a boy in Wyoming and his horse Flicka.

The growing **commercialism** of the New York City stage made it difficult for new playwrights to see their work produced. The Experimental Theater, sponsored by the Dramatists' Guild and Equity, and the New Play Project of the National Theater Conference were started this year to encourage new plays.

Edward Hopper painted *Nighthawks,* which depicted diners in an all-night restaurant. The painting's contrast of light and shadow imparted a feeling of loneliness and the sense of life seen in a flash, a technique often employed by Hopper.

Louis O. Gugliemi completed *Terror in Brooklyn,* a painting of female figures encased in a vacuumlike bell jar on a lonely city street. Commenting on the painting, Gugliemi remarked, "I thoroughly believe that the inner world of subjective life is quite as real as the objective."

Morris Graves, who lived like a hermit on the West Coast, painted *Little-Known Bird of the Inner Eye.* The work reflected a strange mixture of Japanese art and modernism.

The paintings of **Stuart Davis** showed a movement away from realism. Geometry rather than reality became the keynote in his canvases. In *New York Under Gaslight,* Davis eliminated time itself as a reference, the Gay Nineties being juxtaposed with skyscrapers.

Feb. 12 *Claudia* by Rose Franken, a comedy dealing with the problems of growing up faced by a girl who suffers from a mother fixation, opened at the Booth Theatre in New York City. The play proved extremely popular, especially to matinee audiences made up predominantly of women.

Feb. 21 The premiere performance of the *Fourth Symphony* of **Roy Harris,** called the *Folk Song Symphony* for chorus and orchestra, was given by the Boston Symphony Orchestra.

| Business and Industry; Science; Education; Philosophy and Religion III | | IV Sports; Social Issues and Crime; Folkways; Fashion; Holidays |

in their stride, convinced that they were part of the price of winning the war. Anticipating a wage freeze, labor attempted to win boosts before it was too late. There were some 4000 strikes this year, twice as many as in 1940. Scientists turned their attention to increasing the U.S. arsenal of weapons. Federal educators prepared to meet the shortage of adequately trained personnel.

British pioneers in **penicillin** development, Sir Howard Florey and Dr. N. G. Heatley, flew to the U.S. to argue the necessity of large-scale production of the life-saving substance. American drug companies responded to their appeal, and penicillin in time became a household word.

An important philosophical work by **Reinhold Niebuhr,** the first volume of the two-volume *The Nature and Destiny of Man,* was published. In this book the Protestant theologian and philosopher presented evil and tragedy as evidence of man's failure to set his divine self above his natural self. He also presented a strong argument for the supernatural qualities of man. The second volume was issued in 1943.

Jan. 3 A **shipbuilding program** of 200 merchant vessels was called for by the federal government.

Jan. 7 The **Office of Production Management** (OPM) was created by executive order. The new agency to supervise defense production was headed by an industrialist, William S. Knudsen.

Jan. 22 A wave of **defense industry strikes** began with a work stoppage in the Allis Chalmers plants.

Feb. 19 Work began at Gatun, **Panama Canal,** on a third set of locks.

Feb. 24 The **first industry-wide priority schedule** was released by the OPM. It affected aluminum and machine tools.

Feb. 26 A strike at the Bethlehem Steel plants was called by the CIO. The subsequent settlement according to an OPM formula was acclaimed as the union's greatest victory to date.

Mar. 19 The **National Defense Mediation Board** (NDMB) was established to settle all labor disputes in defense industries. Its first chairman was Clarence A. Dykstra.

Mar. 22 **Grand Coulee Dam** in the state of Washington began operations two years ahead of schedule.

Apr. 11 The **Ford Motor Company** signed its first contract with a labor union. It settled a strike that began Apr. 2, when the CIO called out 85,000 workers at Ford's River Rouge plant. Ford closed the plant after rioting had injured 150.

an embargo on Japanese silk was announced. It caused a panic in the hosiery business and sent thousands into shops to snatch up every available silk stocking. In golf the top money winner was Ben Hogan, with $18,358. In boxing, Joe Louis defended the world heavyweight title five times. When war came Louis entered the military, and title competition was suspended. This year Americans mourned the death of Lou Gehrig, longtime first baseman for the New York Yankees (AL), who died in New York on June 2 at age 37.

Jan. 1 In **college football bowl games** the results were Texas A&M 13, Fordham 12 in the Cotton Bowl; Mississippi State 14, Georgetown 7 in the Orange Bowl; Stanford 21, Nebraska 13 in the Rose Bowl; and Boston College 19, Tennessee 13 in the Sugar Bowl. This season the AP poll chose Minnesota the national collegiate champions of 1940.

Jan. 6 The term *Four Freedoms* was introduced by Pres. Franklin D. Roosevelt in his annual speech before Congress. These freedoms, which he envisaged as the cornerstone of a new world, were freedom of speech and expression, freedom of worship, freedom from fear, and freedom from want.

Feb. 1 **U.S. figure skating championships** were won in Boston by Jane Vaughn, women's singles; Eugene Turner, men's singles; Donna Atwood and Eugene Turner, pairs; Sandy Macdonald and Harold Hartshorne, dance.

Mar. 29 The **NCAA basketball championship** was won by Wisconsin, which defeated Washington State 39–34.

Apr. 6 The **Masters golf tournament** was won by Craig Wood, who beat Byron Nelson by three strokes.

Apr. 6–12 The **NHL Stanley Cup** was won by the Boston Bruins, who swept the Detroit Red Wings in four straight games. It was the first Stanley Cup sweep in hockey history.

Apr. 19 The 45th **Boston Marathon** was won by Leslie Pawson of Pawtucket, R.I., with a time of 2 hrs., 30 min., 38 sec.

May 3 The 67th annual **Kentucky Derby** was won by Whirlaway, with a time of 2:01²/₅, a new Derby record. The jockey was Eddie Arcaro, who had won the event in 1938.

May 10 The 66th annual **Preakness Stakes** was won by Whirlaway, with a time of 1:58⁴/₅. The jockey was Eddie Arcaro.

May 20 Pres. Roosevelt announced **Thanksgiving** would be moved forward again, to the last Thursday of November, after a two-year experiment during which the holiday was celebrated on the next-to-last Thursday in November. Roosevelt had originally moved the holiday to stimulate business activity.

May 30 The 29th **Indianapolis 500** auto race was won by Mauri Rose and Floyd Davis, completing the 500-

number of U.S. vessels had been sunk or fired on by submarines.

Sept. 20 The **largest tax bill** to date, authorizing the raising of $3,553,400,000, was signed by Pres. Roosevelt. The tax bill provided for the following division of sources: corporation and excess profits to yield $1,382,100,060; individual income, $1,144,000,000; capital stock tax, $22,300,000; estates and gifts, $157,600,000; and excise and miscellaneous taxes, $846,800.

Oct. 17 The U.S. destroyer *Kearny* was torpedoed and damaged by a German submarine off the coast of Iceland.

Oct. 30 The U.S. destroyer *Reuben James* was torpedoed and sunk off the coast of Iceland by a German submarine during the night of Oct. 30–31. Some 100 lives were lost. It was the first American warship to be sunk in the war.

Dec. 7 The **Japanese attacked Pearl Harbor,** Hawaii. The American battleships *Arizona, California, Oklahoma,* and *Utah* (an old target battleship) were sunk; the battleship *West Virginia* settled in shallow water and the *Nevada* ran aground. Damaged battleships were the *Pennsylvania, Maryland,* and *Tennessee.* Destroyers *Cassin, Downes,* and *Shaw,* and the minelayer *Oglala,* were sunk or badly damaged. In all, about 19 ships were sunk or damaged. About 3000 Americans lost their lives. The Japanese lost 28 planes and three midget submarines. Japanese forces also attacked Guam, Wake Island, the Philippines, and other strategic points in the Pacific at the same time Pearl Harbor was attacked.

Dec. 8 A **declaration of war** against Japan was passed by Congress. The sole dissenting vote was cast by Rep. Jeannette Rankin, Republican of Montana. She had also cast the sole dissenting vote against entering World War I.

Dec. 10 The **Japanese invaded** Luzon in the Philippines, where Gen. Douglas MacArthur commanded the defending U.S. and Philippine forces.

Dec. 11 **Germany and Italy declared war** against the U.S., and Congress adopted a resolution recognizing a state of war.

Dec. 22 **Wake Island fell** to the Japanese after a heroic 15-day stand by 400 U.S. Marines.

Feb. 27 **Academy Awards** were presented to *Rebecca* as the outstanding motion picture of 1940; to James Stewart as best actor for *The Philadelphia Story;* to Ginger Rogers as best actress for *Kitty Foyle;* to Walter Brennan as best supporting actor for *The Westerner;* and to Jane Darwell as best supporting actress for *The Grapes of Wrath.* Brennan became the first actor to win the best supporting actor award three times.

Mar. 8 **Sherwood Anderson,** the writer, died at 64 of peritonitis in Cristobal, Canal Zone. He had achieved fame in 1919 with the publication of *Winesburg, Ohio,* a critically and popularly acclaimed collection of short stories.

Mar. 17 The **National Gallery of Art** opened in Washington, D.C. The marble building, a gift of Andrew W. Mellon, was designed by John Russell Pope. It housed Mellon's art collection as well as collections donated later by Samuel H. Kress, Joseph E. Widener, and Chester Dale.

Mar. 24 *Watch on the Rhine,* an effective war drama by Lillian Hellman, opened at the Ford Theatre in Baltimore, Md. The drama dealt with the plight of a German resistance leader against a background of American complacency. It opened at the Martin Beck Theatre in New York City on Apr. 1.

Apr. 11 **Arnold Schoenberg,** Viennese-born composer and creator of the 12-tone system of composing, became an American citizen. Schoenberg, 66, had come to the U.S. in 1933 to escape persecution of Jews under the Hitler regime.

May 4 At Staunton, Va., the **birthplace of Woodrow Wilson** was dedicated as a national shrine by Pres. Roosevelt.

May 5 **Pulitzer prizes** were awarded for the following: biography, *Jonathan Edwards* by Ola Elizabeth Winslow; history, *The Atlantic Migration, 1607–1860* by Marcus Lee Hansen; poetry, *Sunderland Capture* by Leonard Bacon; drama, *There Shall Be No Night* by Robert E. Sherwood.

June 30 The **Franklin D. Roosevelt Library** at Hyde Park, N.Y., was dedicated by Pres. Roosevelt, who had deeded the building, its contents, and the site to the federal government.

Apr. 11 The **Office of Price Administration and Civilian Supply** (OPACS, but better known as OPA) was established with limited powers to recommend price control measures. Its first head was Leon Henderson.

Apr. 14 **Wage increases** in the steel industry of ten cents per hour were granted in a move to prevent strikes.

Apr. 16 A **steel price freeze** at the levels of the first quarter of the year was announced by the OPA in its first official act. Industry cooperated.

Apr. 17 A **cut in auto production** of 20% beginning Aug. 1 was agreed to by the auto industry.

May 1 **U.S. Defense Savings Bonds and Stamps** went on sale.

May 16 **Wage increases** of ten cents per hour were granted by General Motors to ward off strikes. The CIO, in turn, waived its demands for a closed shop.

June 18 The $200,000,000 **Colorado Aqueduct** began supplying water to Los Angeles and other southern California cities. The aqueduct ran from Parker Dam on the Colorado R. 240 miles across the Mojave Desert and the San Bernardino Mts., generating in its descent power to lift its own water a total of 1617 feet.

July 24 A **no-strike agreement** for the duration of the national emergency was signed by AFL building trade unions and the OPM.

Aug. 3 A **gasoline curfew** was begun at midnight in 17 eastern states. The curfew closed filling stations from 7 P.M. to 7 A.M.

Nov. 1 The 950-foot **Rainbow Bridge** was opened to traffic across the Niagara R., just below the falls. An ice jam had destroyed the old bridge in Jan. 1938.

Dec. 15 A **no-strike policy** in war industries was adopted by the AFL executive council. The council also offered to make peace with the CIO. On Dec. 23 an industry-labor conference pledged that there would be no strikes or lockouts. All disputes were to be settled by peaceful means, and a War Labor Board was to be established to settle differences. The conference could not agree on the question of closed shops.

Dec. 27 **Rubber rationing** was announced by the OPA. The measure decreased civilian consumption by 80%. Tire rationing was the first rationing regulation.

mile course in 4 hrs., 20 min., 36.24 sec., with an average speed of 115.11 mph.

June 7 The **U.S. Open golf tournament** was won by Craig Wood. This was the last time the U.S. Open would be played until 1946.

June 7 The 73rd annual **Belmont Stakes** was won by Whirlaway, with a time of 2:31. The jockey was Eddie Arcaro. Whirlaway thus became the fifth horse to win racing's Triple Crown.

July 8 The ninth annual **baseball All-Star Game** was won by the American League, which defeated the National League 7–5.

July 13 The **PGA golf tournament** was won by Vic Ghezzi.

July 17 Yankee center fielder **Joe DiMaggio's hitting streak** was ended by pitchers Al Smith and Jim Bagby, Jr., of the Cleveland Indians. DiMaggio had hit safely in 56 consecutive games, from May 15 through July 16, a major league record.

Sept. 6 The **Miss America** title was won by Rosemary LaPlanche, 19, of Los Angeles, Calif., at the annual pageant in Atlantic City, N.J.

Sept. 7 The **U.S. Lawn Tennis Association singles championships** were won by Robert L. Riggs in the men's division and by Sarah Palfrey Cooke in the women's division.

Sept. 23 A six-ton **monument marking a time capsule** from the New York World's Fair of 1939–1940 was unveiled in Flushing Meadow, Queens, N.Y., the site of the fair. The capsule contained artifacts and information about twentieth-century culture and was to be opened in the year 6939.

Oct. 1–6 The 38th annual **World Series** was won by the New York Yankees (AL), defeating the Brooklyn Dodgers (NL) four games to one.

Nov. 21 The **first woman executed in California** died in San Quentin's gas chamber. She was Mrs. Ethel Leta Juanita Spinelli, 52, alias the Dutchess, convicted slayer of a member of her own gang.

Dec. 7 The wartime phrase *praise the Lord and pass the ammunition* was uttered by Howell M. Forgy, chaplain on the U.S. cruiser *New Orleans*, under attack at Pearl Harbor, Hawaii. While sweating sailors kept up a continuing antiaircraft barrage, he kept their spirits up with this phrase.

Dec. 21 The **NFL championship** was won by the Chicago Bears, who defeated the New York Giants 37–9.

| Exploration and Settlement; Wars; Government; Civil Rights; Statistics | I | | II | Publishing; Arts and Music; Popular Entertainment; Architecture; Theater |

1942

American military pride was subjected to rude shocks early this year as U.S. forces were forced from island after island in the Pacific. The chief defeat was the fall of the Bataan peninsula on Luzon in the Philippines, followed a month later by the fall of the island fortress of Corregidor in Manila Bay. Only days later, in early May, American fortunes changed when a U.S. fleet defeated the Japanese in the Battle of the Coral Sea, and again in June when U.S. dive bombers routed a second enemy naval task force in the Battle of Midway. At home, thousands of civilians over draft age flocked to Washington, D.C., to man the offices created to handle the mammoth war program.

Jan. 2 In the Philippines, **Manila fell** to the Japanese, forcing U.S. and Philippine forces under Gen. Douglas MacArthur to withdraw to the Bataan peninsula.

Feb. 27–Mar. 1 The **Battle of the Java Sea** was a major U.S. naval defeat. The Japanese inflicted heavy losses on the U.S. fleet commanded by Adm. Thomas C. Hart.

Mar. 17 Gen. **MacArthur left Bataan** by presidential order when defense of the peninsula became hopeless. He withdrew to Australia and soon was named commander in chief of the Southwest Pacific Command.

Apr. 9 **Bataan fell** to the Japanese after a heroic defense by a greatly outnumbered force. Gen. Jonathan M. Wainwright, with about 3500 soldiers and nurses, withdrew to Corregidor.

Apr. 10 The **Bataan Death March** began at dawn. American and Philippine prisoners taken at Bataan were forced to march 85 miles in six days with but one meal of rice during the period. By the end of the march, which was punctuated with atrocities, more than 5200 Americans and many more Filipinos had lost their lives.

Apr. 18 An **air raid on Tokyo** was conducted by carrier-launched bombers under command of Maj. Gen. James H. Doolittle. This was the first American offensive blow in the Pacific and did much to boost American morale. It also caused consternation in Japan.

May 4–8 In the **Battle of the Coral Sea**, U.S. naval air forces inflicted heavy losses on the Japanese fleet. This battle was the first ever fought in which neither fleet came within sight of the other. All the fighting was carried on by planes. The U.S. lost the carrier *Lexington*, the destroyer *Sims*, and a tanker. Seven Japanese warships, including one carrier, were sunk.

May 6 **Corregidor fell** to the Japanese. Gen. Wainwright surrendered the fortress to Japanese troops under Gen. Tomoyuki Yamashita.

May 14 The **Women's Army Auxiliary Corps** was established by Congress. Oveta Culp Hobby was

Far from destroying the performing arts, World War II gave them an impetus they had not enjoyed for years. Producers scrambled for available playhouses, selling tickets at high prices and counting their profits. Entertainment-hungry civilians and servicemen were given escapist fare, in most cases unclad ladies of the chorus dancing to a loud pit orchestra. Hundreds of serious artists and musicians were absorbed into the armed forces. Architects responded to the demand for fast, prefabricated housing. This year Americans also mourned the loss of some artistic greats: John Barrymore, youngest member of the celebrated family of actors, May 29, at 60; Carole Lombard, actress and wife of Clark Gable, in a plane crash while returning home from a War Bond drive, Jan. 16, at 32; and Grant Wood, known best for *American Gothic* (1930), his portrait of a dour farm couple, Feb. 12, at 50.

Among **books published** this year was *The Moon Is Down* by John Steinbeck, a novel about the military occupation of a small town and the effect of that occupation on both conqueror and conquered. The book was published simultaneously with its dramatization on the New York City stage, an experiment that proved successful. Other books published this year included *The Just and the Unjust* by James Gould Cozzens, a novel about American lawyers; *The Robe* by Lloyd C. Douglas; *Go Down, Moses* by William Faulkner, a collection of stories that included Faulkner's novelette "The Bear"; and *See Here, Private Hargrove* by Marion Hargrove, an immensely popular chronicle of the soldier's life.

This year's **popular songs** included "White Christmas," "Be Careful, It's My Heart," "I left My Heart at the Stage Door Canteen," "The White Cliffs of Dover," "Praise the Lord and Pass the Ammunition," "Sleepy Lagoon," and "Blues in the Night."

The **biggest box office draw** this year was the comedy team of Bud Abbott and Lou Costello. Mickey Rooney, the top attraction for the past three years, fell to fourth place, behind Clark Gable and Gary Cooper.

Feb. 26 **Academy Awards** were presented to *How Green Was My Valley* as the outstanding motion picture of 1941; to Gary Cooper as best actor for *Sergeant York;* to Joan Fontaine as best actress for *Suspicion;* to Donald Crisp as best supporting actor for *How Green Was My Valley;* and to Mary Astor as best supporting actress for *The Great Lie.* Walt Disney was presented

| Business and Industry; Science; Education; Philosophy and Religion | III | | IV | Sports; Social Issues and Crime; Folkways; Fashion; Holidays |

1942

Anti-inflation measures, such as rent ceilings and wage and price freezes, were put into effect as the nation settled down to the grim business of war. The AFL and CIO voluntarily agreed not to strike for the duration of the war and to submit all labor disputes to a federal mediation board. The War Manpower Commission held virtually dictatorial power over all essential workers and was empowered, if the emergency warranted, to mobilize every adult in the country. Hard hit were colleges and universities, whose enrollments dropped off sharply. Adult education classes, however, increased in number and helped keep the schoolrooms at least partially filled.

Henry J. Kaiser, the industrialist, headed the Liberty Ship program, which incorporated techniques of prefabrication and mass production to speed ship production. By June of this year his four West Coast shipyards had been assigned one-third of the U.S. shipbuilding program. His yard in Vancouver built and launched a 10,500-ton liberty ship in a record four days.

Jan. 1 Sale of **new cars and trucks** was banned by the Office of Production Management.

Jan. 12 The **War Labor Board** (WLB) was created by executive order. The new board, whose head was William H. Davis, supplanted the National Defense Mediation Board (NDMB), established in Mar. 1941. The function of the WLB was to maintain the flow of war materials by settling labor disputes.

Jan. 12 The **Georgia Contract Labor Act** was overturned by the U.S. Supreme Court on the grounds that it violated the antislavery amendment to the Constitution. The Court stated in its opinion that "one who has received an advance on a contract for services which he is unable to repay is bound by the threat of penal sanction to remain at his employment until the debt has been discharged. Such coerced labor is peonage." This decision had a profound effect on labor relations, particularly in the South.

Jan. 16 The **War Production Board** (WPB) was established by executive order. In charge of the entire war production program, it supplanted the OPM. Its first head was Donald M. Nelson.

Jan. 30 The **Price Control Bill** was signed by Pres. Franklin D. Roosevelt, officially giving the Office of Price Administration the power to set all prices except those for farm products.

American society underwent enormous changes. Millions of young men went off to combat, women took up new posts in war industries and military support units, and rationing was introduced to control consumption and preserve resources for war production. In contrast to these changes, trends in fashion continued to emphasize simplicity and economy of design. Crime rates across the nation jumped; officials claimed that youths were having one last fling before entering the Army. In golf the top money winner again was Ben Hogan with $13,143.

Jan. 1 In **college football bowl games** the results were Alabama 29, Texas A&M 21 in the Cotton Bowl; Georgia 40, TCU 26 in the Orange Bowl; Oregon State 20, Duke 16 in the Rose Bowl; and Fordham 2, Missouri 0 in the Sugar Bowl. This season the AP poll chose Ohio State the national collegiate champions of 1941.

Jan. 8 The memorable laconic statement *sighted sub, sank same* was radioed from the South Pacific by Navy pilot David F. Mason. Noticing a surfaced Japanese submarine, he swooped down, deposited his depth charges, and then observed the strewn wreckage of the submarine on the water. His accomplishment earned him the Silver Star.

Jan. 9 The world **heavyweight boxing championship** was successfully defended, for the 20th time, by Joe Louis, who knocked out Buddy Baer in the first round.

Jan. 20 Elected to the **Baseball Hall of Fame** was Rogers Hornsby, the second baseman and seven-time National League batting champion.

Feb. 21 **U.S. figure skating championships** were won in Chicago by Jane Vaughn Sullivan, women's singles; Bobby Specht, men's singles; Doris Schubach and Walter Noffke, pairs; Edith B. Whetstone and Alfred N. Richards, Jr., dance.

Mar. 28 The **NCAA basketball championship** was won by Stanford, which defeated Dartmouth 53–38.

Apr. 4–18 The **NHL Stanley Cup** was won by the Toronto Maple Leafs, who defeated the Detroit Red Wings four games to three. Toronto was the first team to win the Stanley Cup after losing the first three games.

chosen its first commander. Its name was shortened to Women's Army Corp (WAC) in 1943.

June 4–6 In the **Battle of Midway** the U.S. gained an important victory over the Japanese. Americans repulsed an attempt to seize the island, sinking 17 Japanese ships, including four aircraft carriers. Japan lost 275 planes and 4800 men. The U.S. lost over 300 men and two ships including the carrier *Yorktown.*

June 28 The **first U.S. ground assault** on the Japanese in the South Pacific was executed when a contingent of commandos assaulted Salamaua, New Guinea, at night.

July 30 **WAVES,** Women Appointed for Voluntary Emergency Service, was organized as a unit of the U.S. Naval Reserve.

Aug. 7 U.S. Marines landed on **Guadalcanal,** in the Solomon Islands, opening the first major U.S. amphibious operation in the Pacific. The struggle to force the Japanese off the island involved some of the bloodiest fighting of the war. The fighting continued until Feb. 1943.

Aug. 18 **Carlson's Raiders,** a special guerrilla unit led by Lt. Col. Evans Fordyce Carlson, landed on Makin Island, at the northern end of the Gilbert Islands, with orders to destroy the radio station on the island. In 40 hours every Japanese member of a force of 350 was killed, 1000 gallons of gasoline were set aflame, and the island was rendered militarily useless.

Sept. 15 The U.S. carrier *Wasp* was sunk off Guadalcanal.

Oct. 23 In a major **counterattack on Guadalcanal,** the Japanese assaulted Henderson Field. After three days of fierce fighting, the veteran unit suffered defeat at the hands of a Marine and Army force.

Nov. 3 In **congressional elections** the Democrats lost eight Senate seats but kept a majority of 58–37, with one seat held by a minor party. In the House they lost 50 seats but held a 218–208 majority, with four seats going to minor parties.

Nov. 7 In **North Africa,** U.S. forces began landing with support of British naval and air units. Lt. Gen. Dwight Eisenhower commanded the 50 vessels and 400,000 troops employed in the operations.

Nov. 12–15 In a **naval engagement off Guadalcanal,** the U.S. scored a major victory, inflicting heavy losses on a Japanese task force and preventing Japanese reinforcements from reaching the island.

Nov. 23 **SPARS,** the Semper Paratus Always Ready Service, was organized as a women's branch of the Coast Guard.

Nov. 28 In the **Cocoanut Grove fire,** the worst single fire of modern times in the U.S., the Boston nightclub was virtually destroyed. The disaster caused 487 deaths, mostly from asphyxia and trampling.

with three awards, including one in recognition of his general contribution to the motion picture industry.

Apr. 14 *Social Justice,* a weekly published by Rev. Charles E. Coughlin, was banned from the mails. Attorney General Francis Biddle charged the magazine had violated the Espionage Act of 1917.

Apr. 14 *Solomon and Balkis,* a new opera by **Randall Thompson,** was given a radio premiere from Harvard University, Cambridge, Mass.

May 1 The opera *A Tree on the Plain* by Ernst Bacon was given its first performance at Converse College in Spartanburg, S.C.

May 4 **Pulitzer prizes** were awarded for the following: fiction, *In This Our Life* by Ellen Glasgow; biography, *Crusader in Crinoline* by Forrest Wilson; history, *Reveille in Washington* by Margaret Leech; poetry, *The Dust Which Is God* by William Rose Benét.

Aug. 3 A lawsuit was filed against American Federation of Musicians' president James C. Petrillo by the Justice Department, charging the union's ban on recorded music for radio and jukebox violated antitrust laws. The suit was dismissed in Chicago on Oct. 12.

Oct. 7 *The Eve of St. Mark* by Maxwell Anderson, the first Broadway play to depict American soldiers fighting in World War II, opened at the Cort Theatre in New York City.

Oct. 16 *Rodeo,* a ballet with score by Aaron Copland, was produced in New York City by the Ballet Russe de Monte Carlo, starring Agnes de Mille.

Nov. 18 *The Skin of Our Teeth* by Thornton Wilder, a philosophical fantasy, opened at the Plymouth Theatre in New York City. In the play the symbolic character of Mr. Antrobus, played by Frederic March, traced the history of man, showing his foibles, courage, and persistence.

Dec. 28 **Artur Rodzinski,** conductor of the Cleveland Symphony Orchestra, became musical director and regular conductor of the New York Philharmonic Symphony.

| Business and Industry; Science; Education; Philosophy and Religion **III** | | Sports; Social Issues and Crime; Folkways; Fashion; Holidays **IV** |

Feb. 9 War time became effective throughout the nation. Clocks were set ahead one hour, as in daylight savings time, and were kept one hour ahead of standard time throughout the year.

Mar. 17 A no-strike agreement was announced by William Green of the AFL and Philip Murray of the CIO.

Apr. 18 The War Manpower Commission was established. The nine-man group was put under the direction of Federal Security Administrator Paul V. McNutt.

Apr. 28 Rents were stabilized by the OPA. The ruling affected 86,000,000 people housed in 301 areas.

May 5 Sugar rationing began.

May 15 Gasoline rationing began in 17 eastern states. The limit set was three gallons a week for nonessential driving. On July 22 a coupon system of rationing was initiated.

June 13 The Office of War Information was established by Pres. Roosevelt to control dissemination of official news and propaganda. Elmer Davis, the newspaperman and radio commentator, was named as OWI head.

June 22 The first V-mail was sent overseas, from New York City to London. V-mail involved the transfer of letters written on prescribed forms to microfilm, which was sent overseas. There the letters were printed on photographic paper and delivered.

Oct. 1 The first American jet airplane, the XP-59, was tested at Muroc Army Base, Calif., by Robert Stanley, chief pilot for Bell Aircraft Corporation.

Oct. 7 The United Mine Workers withdrew from the CIO.

Nov. 29 Coffee rationing began.

Dec. 1 Nationwide gasoline rationing went into effect.

Dec. 2 The first sustained nuclear reaction was demonstrated in Chicago, Ill., before scientists at the University of Chicago, in a project known as the Argonne Project.

Dec. 4 The Work Projects Administration was abolished by executive order.

Apr. 12 The Masters golf tournament was won by Byron Nelson.

Apr. 19 The 46th Boston Marathon was won by Joe Smith of Medford, Mass., with a time of 2 hrs., 26 min., 51.2 sec.

May 2 The 68th annual Kentucky Derby was won by Shut Out, with a time of 2:04²/₅. The jockey was Wayne D. Wright.

May 9 The 67th annual Preakness Stakes was won by Alsab, with a time of 1:57. The jockey was Basil James.

May 31 The PGA golf tournament was won by Sam Snead.

June 6 The 74th annual Belmont Stakes was won by Shut Out, with a time of 2:29¹/₅. The jockey was Eddie Arcaro.

July 6 The tenth annual baseball All-Star Game was won by the American League, which scored three runs in the first inning in beating the National League 3–1.

Sept. 6–7 The U.S. Lawn Tennis Association singles championships were won by Frederick R. Schroeder, Jr., in the men's division and Pauline M. Betz in the women's division.

Sept. 12 The Miss America title was won by Jo-Carroll Dennison, 18, from Texas, at the annual pageant in Atlantic City, N.J.

Sept. 30–Oct.5 The 39th annual World Series was won by the St. Louis Cardinals (NL), defeating the New York Yankees (AL) four games to one.

Dec. 13 The NFL championship was won by the Washington Redskins, who defeated the Chicago Bears 14–6.

Dec. 21 Nevada divorces were ruled valid in all states by the U.S. Supreme Court.

| Exploration and Settlement; Wars; Government; Civil Rights; Statistics | I | | II | Publishing; Arts and Music; Popular Entertainment; Architecture; Theater |

1943

An uncertain year dawned for U.S. military forces. The nation was engaged in a seesaw battle in North Africa and an agonizing struggle in the Pacific. U.S. forces advanced against the Japanese in New Guinea, the Solomons, and the Gilbert Islands, and new names were added to the American battle lexicon—Bougainville, Lae, Tarawa. In the European theater, American troops in North Africa swept across the Mediterranean to Sicily, then to the Italian mainland itself. To the north U.S. bombers wrought destruction in Europe and helped blast Nazi invasion ports in France.

A **polio epidemic** struck the U.S., killing 1151 and crippling thousands more.

Jan. 14 The **Casablanca conference** opened in Morocco. It was attended by Pres. Franklin D. Roosevelt and other Allied officials. The Allies planned their military strategy for 1943 and agreed to demand unconditional surrender from the Axis nations.

Feb. 13 The U.S. **Marine Corps** added a women's unit.

Feb. 20 At the **Kasserine Pass,** Tunisia, U.S. forces were driven back by Gen. Irwin Rommel's Afrika Korps using the 62-ton Mark VI tank. On Feb. 25 U.S. forces recaptured the pass.

Mar. 2–4 In the **Battle of the Bismarck Sea,** a major U.S. victory in the Pacific, an entire Japanese convoy of 22 ships was sunk by American bombers. More than 50 Japanese planes were shot down.

May 7 **Bizerte, Tunisia, was captured** by American troops. The British took Tunis.

May 12 The **North African campaign** ended. Gen. Jurgen von Arnim, commander of Axis forces after Rommel's recall to Europe, was captured in the Cape Bon peninsula along with other Axis officers.

May 30 **Attu** in the Aleutian Islands was retaken by U.S. forces after intense fighting.

July 10 **Sicily was invaded** by Allied forces, including Gen. George S. Patton's Seventh Army, British Field Marshal Bernard Law Montgomery's Eighth Army, and French and Canadian troops.

July 19 **Rome was bombed** by some 500 Allied planes. The highly strategic city, containing a network of railroads and freight yards, had been spared for four years by the Allies because of its religious significance.

July 25 **Benito Mussolini resigned** on the insistence of King Victor Emmanuel III of Italy.

Aug. 1 Rumania's **Ploesti** oil fields and refineries were raided by U.S. bombers.

Aug. 11–24 The **Quebec conference** was held in Canada to work out the Pacific campaign. Some Chinese representatives were present during the conference. There was some difficulty in arriving at an accord with the Russians over future European operations and postwar problems. Pres. Roosevelt and British

Roy Harris, Aaron Copland, and William Schuman all produced fresh, inventive works for the concert stage this year. Led by such painters as Thomas Hart Benton, American regionalism was rediscovered once again. Some artists painted with almost exotic lushness, others with defiant realism. Refugee artists, including Piet Mondrian, Marc Chagall, Fernand Léger, and Yves Tanguy, flourished in the U.S., producing such striking works as Chagall's *The Juggler* and Mondrian's *Broadway Boogie-Woogie.* In theater, Richard Rodgers and Oscar Hammerstein II elevated the musical comedy with their remarkable production of *Oklahoma!* The year was good for the motion picture industry as well. Top box office attractions were Betty Grable, Bob Hope, Abbott and Costello, Bing Crosby, and Gary Cooper. Notables who died included Lorenz Hart, the lyricist who collaborated with Richard Rodgers, Nov. 22, at 47; and Sergei Rachmaninoff, the Russian-born composer who had made his home in the U.S. after World War I, Mar. 28, at 70.

Among **books published** this year was *A Tree Grows in Brooklyn* by Betty Smith, a novel about a young girl and her family living in a Brooklyn slum. Also published this year were *The Human Comedy* by William Saroyan; *Thirty Seconds Over Tokyo* by Capt. Ted W. Lawson; *Here Is Your War* by Ernie Pyle; *God Is My Co-Pilot* by Col. Robert L. Scott, Jr.; *Guadalcanal Diary* by Richard Tregaskis; and *One World* by Wendell Willkie, an optimistic work that sold more than a million copies within two months of publication.

Deaths and Entrances, a dance with musical score by Hunter Johnson, was presented by Martha Graham and her company.

Two works by **Aaron Copland,** *A Lincoln Portrait* and *Piano Sonata,* received their first American performances this year.

The year's **hit songs** included "You'll Never Know," "As Time Goes By," "Brazil," "Comin' in on a Wing and a Prayer," "Taking a Chance on Love," "You'd Be So Nice to Come Home To," "That Old Black Magic," "Moonlight Becomes You," "I've Heard That Song Before," "Don't Get Around Much Any More," "All or Nothing at All," and "Pistol Packin' Mama."

Thomas Hart Benton painted *July Hay,* depicting two farmers cutting hay in a swirling field of flowers and trees.

| Business and Industry; Science; Education; Philosophy and Religion | III | | IV | Sports; Social Issues and Crime; Folkways; Fashion; Holidays |

1943

The CIO and AFL generally kept to their no-strike pledges, making this a quiet year on the labor front. The United Mine Workers, however, stood in defiance of the War Labor Board, claiming that working conditions and wages were unacceptable. A 48-hour minimum work week was proclaimed by Pres. Roosevelt for all essential war industries in labor-scarce areas. Colleges and universities were promised relief in a plan to send thousands of men to school to be trained as officers for the Army and Navy. In October the Swedish government announced that for the fourth year Nobel Prizes would not be awarded. However, in 1944 retroactive prizes were awarded for 1943. George Washington Carver, the scientist and educator known best for his studies on uses of the peanut, died on Jan. 5, at age 78.

Large-scale production of **penicillin** in the U.S. was made possible by the discovery of a mold on a cantaloupe in a fruit market in Peoria, Ill. This mold was found to yield ten times as much penicillin as the original mold obtained by Sir Alexander Fleming of England.

In **salvage drives** this year, 255,513 tons of tin cans, 43,919 tons of fat, 6,000,000 tons of wastepaper, and more than 26,000,000 tons of iron and steel scrap were collected for use in essential industries.

Jan. 18 The **American Medical Association** (AMA) was found by the U.S. Supreme Court to have violated antitrust laws by preventing activities of cooperative health groups. The action had been initiated on Dec. 20, 1938.

Feb. 7 **Shoe rationing** began, limiting civilians to three pairs a year.

Feb. 9 A minimum **48-hour work week** in war plants was ordered by Pres. Franklin D. Roosevelt.

Mar. 1 Rationing of canned goods began.

Mar. 25 Chester C. Davis was appointed **U.S. food administrator** to combat widespread shortages.

Mar. 29 Rationing of meat, fat, and cheese began.

Apr. 17 **Essential workers** were frozen, that is, prohibited from leaving their jobs, by order of the

Conversation everywhere concerned war news; emergence of a new form of music called jive, a danceable form of jazz; and a steady stream of baseball players drafted into the military. Their departure made for a duller game, but the fans remained loyal. This year Judge Kenesaw Mountain Landis, baseball's first commissioner, was elected to the Baseball Hall of Fame. As in several years past, the standard male garb of America's hepcats was the zoot suit. It consisted of a long, one-button jacket for men, with broad, padded shoulders and peaked lapels, high-waisted trousers that ballooned at the knees and gripped the ankles, a wide silk tie worn against a colored or striped shirt, a knee-length key chain, and a broad-brimmed hat. The Jitterbug was the most popular dance of the year, and variations on its basic routine, called the Lindy hop, proliferated. In a nine-page article, *Life* magazine hailed the Lindy hop as "the true national folk dance of America."

Women's fashions were emancipated from the Paris tradition when American designers produced clothing of fabrics available despite wartime shortages. Two silhouettes were featured: a slim, straight, clinging line, caught at the waist by a belt; and a more bulky figure created by wool box coats and suits.

A new **pitching record** for the twentieth century was set by the New York Giants relief pitcher Ace Adams, who pitched in 70 games, only one of them a complete game for him.

Jan. 1 In **college football bowl games**, the results were Texas 14, Georgia Tech 7 in the Cotton Bowl; Alabama 37, Boston College 21 in the Orange Bowl; Georgia 9, UCLA 0 in the Rose Bowl; and Tennessee 14, Tulsa 7 in the Sugar Bowl. This season the AP poll chose Ohio State the national collegiate champions of 1942.

Mar. 8 **U.S. figure skating championships** were won in New York City by Gretchen Merrill, women's singles; Arthur R. Vaughn, Jr., men's singles; Doris V. Schubach and Walter Noffke, pairs; Marcella May and James Lochead, Jr., dance.

Mar. 30 The **NCAA basketball championship** was won by the University of Wyoming, which defeated Georgetown 56–43.

Exploration and Settlement; Wars; Government; Civil Rights; Statistics	I		II	Publishing; Arts and Music; Popular Entertainment; Architecture; Theater

Prime Minister Winston Churchill met privately on Aug. 17.

Aug. 15 **Kiska** in the Aleutians was retaken by American and Canadian units. When the troops landed, the Japanese were gone.

Aug. 17 **Sicily was conquered** by Allied forces 37 days after it was invaded. The Axis powers had lost 167,000 men in the campaign, the Allies 25,000.

Aug. 28 **New Georgia** in the Solomon Islands was secured by U.S. forces.

Sept. 3 **Invasion of Italy** was commenced by Allied forces crossing the Strait of Messina.

Sept. 8 **Italy surrendered unconditionally** to the Allied powers. German troops there fought on.

Sept. 9 The **Allies landed at Salerno,** Italy. Upward of 700 American, British, Dutch, French, and Polish ships took part in the operation. The U.S. Fifth Army, under command of Gen. Mark Clark, participated in the landing.

Oct. 19 The **Moscow conference** opened. Representatives of Great Britain, the U.S., the U.S.S.R., and the Chinese agreed to collaborate on surrender terms for the enemy. The powers recognized the need for an international organization to prevent future wars.

Nov. 1 U.S. forces landed on **Bougainville** Island in the Solomons.

Nov. 2 A U.S. **air raid on Rabaul,** New Britain, proved a major defeat for the Japanese. Gen. Douglas MacArthur, suspecting an attack would be launched from Rabaul on Empress Augusta Bay, off the west coast of Bougainville, had ordered the mission. Nearly every ship in Rabaul's harbor was hit or sunk, about 94,000 tons of shipping.

Nov. 20 U.S. forces landed on **Tarawa and Makin** in the Gilbert Islands. On Nov. 22 landings were made on Abemama. Occupation of the Gilbert Islands was completed on Nov. 23.

Nov. 22 At a **conference in Cairo,** Egypt, Pres. Roosevelt, Prime Minster Churchill, and Generalissimo Chiang Kai-shek planned military strategy against Japan and declared that Japan, when defeated, would be stripped of all Pacific territories seized since 1914.

Nov. 28–Dec. 1 At the **Teheran conference** in Iran, Pres. Roosevelt, Prime Minister Churchill, and Premier Joseph Stalin met to map strategy for the coming Allied invasion of western Europe.

Dec. 17 A bill repealing the **Chinese Exclusion Acts** and setting an annual immigration quota of 105 Chinese was signed by Pres. Roosevelt. On the next day, in Chicago, Edward Bing Kan filed an application for citizenship. On Jan. 18, 1944, he became the first Chinese to be naturalized under the new law.

Dec. 24 Gen. **Dwight D. Eisenhower** was named Supreme Commander of Allied forces for the invasion of Europe.

Jackson Pollock, a young painter from Wyoming, had his first one-man show. His work struck critics as exceptionally original.

Mar. 4 **Academy Awards** were presented to *Mrs. Miniver* as the outstanding motion picture of 1942 and to Greer Garson, its star, as best actress; to James Cagney as best actor for *Yankee Doodle Dandy;* to Van Heflin as best supporting actor for *Johnny Eager;* and to Teresa Wright as best supporting actress for *Mrs. Miniver.*

Mar. 31 *Oklahoma!* by Richard Rodgers and Oscar Hammerstein II, an extremely successful musical based on the 1931 play *Green Grow the Lilacs* by Lynn Riggs, opened at the St. James Theatre in New York City. Set in Oklahoma about 1900, it told the story of a girl's love for a cowboy. Its songs, including "Oh, What a Beautiful Morning," "People Will Say We're in Love," and "Poor Jud Is Dead," soon took hold all over America.

May 3 **Pulitzer prizes** were awarded for the following: fiction, *Dragon's Teeth* by Upton Sinclair; biography, *Admiral of the Ocean Sea* by Samuel Eliot Morison; history, *Paul Revere and the World He Lived In* by Esther Forbes; poetry, *A Witness Tree* by Robert Frost; drama, *The Skin of Our Teeth* by Thornton Wilder. *Secular Cantata No. 2, A Free Song* by William Schuman won the first Pulitzer prize for a musical composition.

May 5 The **Library of Congress** would preserve some 5000 films made from 1897 to 1917, according to an announcement made by Howard L. Walls, its film curator. The films included 75 Keystone comedies and all of D. W. Griffith's Biograph films.

May 5 A **postal-zone numbering system** was inaugurated in 178 cities. Postmaster General Frank C. Walker expected the use of numbers to speed up mail deliveries.

June 16 **Charlie Chaplin,** 54, married Oona O'Neill, 18, daughter of the playwright Eugene O'Neill.

Dec. 11 The first season of the **City Center of Music and Drama** in New York City opened with a concert by the New York Philharmonic-Symphony.

| Business and Industry; Science; Education; Philosophy and Religion   III | IV   Sports; Social Issues and Crime; Folkways; Fashion; Holidays |

War Manpower Commission. The order affected some 27,000,000 workers.

May 1 **Coal mines were seized** by the government after 530,000 miners refused to obey a War Labor Board order to return to the pits.

May 5 **Authority to seize coal stocks** for use in war plants and for civilian purposes in case of emergency was given to Fuel Administrator Harold L. Ickes.

May 19 The **United Mine Workers** (UMW) petitioned for membership in the AFL.

May 27 The **Office of War Mobilization** was established. James F. Byrnes, its chief executive, was made responsible for conduct of the war on the home front.

June 10 The **Current Tax Payment Bill** was signed by Pres. Roosevelt. This was the pay-as-you-go income tax law.

June 14 In a challenge of the **compulsory flag salute** brought by Jehovah's Witnesses, the Supreme Court ruled that under the Bill of Rights, schoolchildren could not be compelled to salute the flag if the ceremony conflicted with their religion.

June 20 **Race riots** hit Detroit, Mich. The influx of some 300,000 whites and blacks to war plants in the area contributed to the outbreak of violence. In two days, 35 people were killed, and more than 500, mostly blacks, were wounded. Police arrested 300 whites. Race riots also broke out this summer in Mobile (May 25), Los Angeles (June 4), Beaumont, Tex. (June 19), and Harlem, New York City (Aug. 1).

July 19 The world's longest **oil pipeline** of its day, the Big Inch, was dedicated. Its main line extended 1254 miles from Longview, Tex., to Phoenixville, Pa., crossing 30 rivers and nearly 200 streams.

Oct. 17 The **Young Communist League** declared itself dissolved at a special convention held in New York City. The 400 delegates organized American Youth for Democracy, which offered membership to non-Communists.

Oct. 17 Chicago's first **subway** was formally opened.

Apr. 1–8 The **NHL Stanley Cup** was won by the Detroit Red Wings, who swept the Boston Bruins in four games.

Apr. 18 The 47th **Boston Marathon** was won by Gerard Cote of Valleyfield, Quebec, Canada, with a time of 2 hrs., 28 min., 25.8 sec.

May 1 The 69th annual **Kentucky Derby** was won by Count Fleet, with a time of 2:04. The jockey was Johnny Longden.

May 8 The 68th annual **Preakness Stakes** was won by Count Fleet, with a time of 1:57²/₅. The jockey was Johnny Longden.

June 5 The 75th annual **Belmont Stakes** was won by Count Fleet, with a time of 2:28¹/₅. The jockey was Johnny Longden. Count Fleet thus became the sixth horse to win racing's Triple Crown.

July 13 The 11th annual **baseball All-Star Game** was won by the American League, which beat the National League 5–3.

Sept. 4 The **Miss America** title was won by Jean Bartel, 18, from California, at the annual pageant in Atlantic City, N.J.

Sept. 5 The **U.S. Lawn Tennis Association singles championships** were won by Lt. Joseph R. Hunt in the men's division and Pauline M. Betz in the women's division.

Oct. 5–11 The 40th annual **World Series** was won by the New York Yankees (AL), defeating the St. Louis Cardinals (NL) four games to one.

Dec. 4 A **Utah polygamy case,** the first such case prosecuted by the federal government in many years, ended in the conviction of John Zenz, his wife, and his son on charges of transporting a 15-year-old girl over state lines for "purposes of debauchery." The elder Zenz had married her in a religious ceremony.

Dec. 26 The **NFL championship** was won by the Chicago Bears, who defeated the Washington Redskins 41–21.

1944

In the European theater Russian forces made spectacular but costly progress against the Germans. In May Italy fell and on June 6 Allied forces landed in Normandy. In August American armored units began to move rapidly across France. By year's end Allied forces were poised on Germany's eastern and western borders, preparing for the final assault. Similar successes in the Pacific theater led many to hope for victory within the year despite repeated warnings by responsible leaders that the Axis war potential was still formidable. In mid-June the Germans introduced a new weapon, the V-1 pilotless bomb; they launched it against London and other British cities. In September they followed it with the V-2, a supersonic rocket causing great destruction.

Jan. 22 Allied troops landed at **Anzio,** Italy, in a move to outflank the German defensive positions on the Gustav line across central Italy. British and American troops were unable to advance and the German line held.

Feb. 2 **Roi Island** in the Marshall Islands was taken by the Fourth Marine Division and positions were secured on Namur and Kwajalein. For the first time Allied troops set foot on prewar Japanese territory.

Mar. 6 **Berlin was bombed** by 800 U.S. Flying Fortresses. Some 2000 tons of bombs were dropped on the German capital.

Apr. 22 **Netherlands New Guinea was invaded** by U.S. forces.

May 18 **Cassino,** the key point on the Germans' Gustav line in Italy, was evacuated after two months of bitter resistance.

May 19 The **Gustav line collapsed** under heavy assault by Allied troops.

June 4 **Allied forces entered Rome** on this day, Trinity Sunday. Out of respect for the religious holiday, the American Fifth and British Eighth armies did not occupy the city until the next morning.

June 6 The **Normandy invasion** began on this date, designated D-Day. Code named Operation Overlord, the invasion included landings on five beachheads in Normandy, France. The operation, under command of Gen. Dwight D. Eisenhower, involved more than 4000 ships, some 3000 planes, and Allied troops eventually numbering more than 4,000,000.

June 16 **Bombing of Japan** began with a raid on the island of Kyushu by U.S. Superfortresses.

June 26–28 The **Republican National Convention nominated Thomas E. Dewey,** governor of New York, for the presidency and Gov. John W. Bricker of Ohio for the vice presidency.

July 6 A **circus tent fire** at an afternoon performance in Hartford, Conn., destroyed the main tent of Ringling Brothers and Barnum & Bailey Circus. The

The arts enjoyed a boom year. Paper shortages forced publishers to experiment with soft-cover books, and the success of the experiment was overwhelming. Painters who had not been drafted profited when a plentiful supply of money created new buyers who could not shop in the European market. Broadway producers found eager audiences for practically everything they presented. The sellers' market did not improve the quality of the offerings. Architects were still learning a new trade—that of the efficiency builder, since the criterion for a contract was speed of construction. All their new ideas were confined to paper to await the end of the war. The movies enjoyed their greatest year in box office history, grossing close to $2,000,000,000 as the European market began to open in liberated areas. Such established stars as Bing Crosby and Gary Cooper took advantage of the tax laws by producing their own films. Top box office draws were Crosby, Cooper, Bob Hope, Betty Grable, and Spencer Tracy. The nation mourned the deaths of Charles Dana Gibson, the artist and illustrator who created the Gibson Girl, Dec. 23, at age 77; and Maj. Glenn Miller, director of the U.S. Air Force Band and, before the war, one of the most talented musicians and big band leaders. Miller was reported missing on a flight from Paris to London on Dec. 24.

Among **books published** this year was *Forever Amber* by Kathleen Winsor, a historical novel laced with sex. Set in England during the Restoration, the novel sold more than 1,000,000 copies in a year. Other books published this year included *Yankee from Olympus* by Catherine Drinker Bowen, a biography of Justice Oliver Wendell Holmes; *The World of Washington Irving* by Van Wyck Brooks; *A Bell for Adano,* a novel by John Hersey; *The Major Phase* by F. O. Matthiessen; *Brave Men* by Ernie Pyle; *Strange Fruit* by Lillian Smith, a novel whose central characters, a black woman and a white man, were torn between their love for each other and the strictures of southern society; and *Immortal Wife* by Irving Stone, a fictionalized biography of Jessie Frémont.

Popular songs of the year included "I'll Be Seeing You," "Mairzy Doats," "I'll Walk Alone," "Don't Fence Me In," "Long Ago and Far Away," and "Bésame Mucho."

| Business and Industry; Science; Education; Philosophy and Religion   III | | Sports; Social Issues and Crime; Folkways; Fashion; Holidays   IV |

1944

Industry had done such a remarkable job in producing war materiel that the government was able to relax many of its priority regulations. Manufacturers took advantage of the move by looking forward to a consumer economy. Labor controls remained in full effect, however, as did the many curbs against inflation. Despite these checks, living costs rose by nearly one-third, engendering unrest in union ranks. Institutions of higher education mourned the virtual end of the ASTP (Army Specialized Training Program). Some 110,000 of the 145,000 young men who had been enrolled in the nation's colleges were removed and sent to active service. Notables who died this year included Aimee Semple McPherson, the Canadian-born evangelist, fundamentalist preacher, and faith healer, Sept. 27, at age 54.

Penicillin, medical wonder of the year, was shown to be effective against wounds and a wide variety of infectious diseases. Further uses were also found for the sulfa drugs. In one of the more important medical feats of the war, the armed forces used the insecticide DDT to control and wipe out typhus, transmitted by body lice among troops and civilians.

In **salvage drives** this year, nearly 7,000,000 tons of wastepaper, 84,807 tons of fat, 18,500,000 tons of iron and steel scrap, 185,676 tons of tin cans, and 544,739 tons of rags were collected.

Jan. 19   **Railways were returned to their owners** after final settlement of a wage dispute. The railroads had been seized on Dec. 27, 1943, by presidential order to prevent a nationwide rail strike.

Feb. 29   American **black marketeers** squeezed an estimated $1,200,000,000 from consumers during the past year, according to OPA Director Chester A. Bowles.

Apr. 19   The **lend-lease** program was extended to June 30, 1945, by the House of Representatives.

Apr. 26   The **Montgomery Ward plant was seized** by the Army. Troops entered the Chicago plant after

Fashions swung toward bare midriffs, slim skirts, and large hats. Victories in both military theaters raised civilian morale and led to hopes the war would soon end. In boxing, a dispute over the lightweight championship arose in March when Bob Montgomery outpointed Beau Jack in 15 rounds at Madison Square Garden in New York City. Five days later his title, recognized by the New York State Athletic Commission, came into dispute when Juan Zurita defeated Sammy Angott in Hollywood and the National Boxing Association recognized Zurita as the lightweight champion. In golf the top money winner was Byron Nelson, with $37,967. Notables who died this year included Kenesaw Mountain Landis, commissioner of organized baseball for nearly 24 years, Nov. 25, at age 78.

Cartoonists **Bill Mauldin and George Baker** gave armed services newspapers their most popular features. In "Up Front with Mauldin," a pair of long-suffering GIs, Willie and Joe, endured combat stoically ("Just gimme th' aspirin. I already got a Purple Heart"). Baker created the "Sad Sack," an unlucky, confused, unkempt but well-meaning GI forever in trouble. In postwar years, Baker's "Sad Sack" became a regular feature of comic sections, and Mauldin took naturally to political cartooning.

The contribution of **dogs in combat** situations was recognized by posthumous awards of certificates of outstanding achievement to seven dogs killed in the South Pacific. A German shepherd received the Distinguished Service Medal for charging a machine gun nest in the invasion of Sicily.

Jan. 1   In **college football bowl games** the results were Randolph Field 7, Texas 7 in the Cotton Bowl; LSU 19, Texas A&M 14 in the Orange Bowl; Southern California 29, Washington 0 in the Rose Bowl; and Georgia Tech 20, Tulsa 18 in the Sugar Bowl. This season the AP poll chose Notre Dame the national collegiate champions of 1943.

Feb. 27   **U.S. figure skating championships** were won by Gretchen Merrill, women's singles; Doris

blazing canvas fell on fleeing spectators. In the scramble 167 persons were killed and more than 175 were injured.

July 10 Saipan fell to U.S. forces after 25 days of hard fighting. Upward of 25,000 Japanese soldiers were killed. Some 2359 Americans died and more than 11,000 were wounded.

July 19–21 The **Democratic National Convention** nominated **Pres. Roosevelt** for his fourth term. Sen. Harry S Truman of Missouri was nominated for the vice presidency.

July 25 A breakout at **St. Lô** by the U.S. First Army under Gen. Omar Bradley led to collapse of the German line in northwestern France.

Aug. 8 **Brittany fell** to the rapid Allied advance south from Normandy. U.S. forces launched a powerful drive eastward toward Paris.

Aug. 9 **Guam fell** to U.S. forces after 20 days of bloody fighting. The conquest cost the Americans 1214 dead and nearly 6000 wounded. Some 17,000 Japanese were killed and almost 500 prisoners were taken.

Aug. 15 **Southern France was invaded** by the U.S. Seventh Army under Lt. Gen. Alexander M. Patch.

Aug. 21 The **Dumbarton Oaks conference** opened at Washington, D.C. It was attended by delegates from the U.S., Great Britain, China, and the U.S.S.R. The conference agreed on "proposals for establishment of a general international organization," laying the groundwork for establishment of the United Nations.

Aug. 25 **Paris was liberated.** The German commander Gen. Dietrich von Choltitz surrendered to French Gen. Jacques-Philippe Leclerc.

Sept. 12 In the **first American engagement on German soil,** the U.S. First Army pushed five miles into west central Germany. For the first time the Allies fought where the local population was hostile.

Sept. 14 A major **hurricane** with winds up to 134 mph racked the Atlantic coast from Cape Hatteras to Canada, killing 390 at sea (mostly on military vessels that sank) and about 50 civilians. Damage was estimated at $50,000,000.

Sept. 17–27 An unsuccessful **airborne invasion of Holland,** code named Operation Market-Garden, was staged by combined British and American forces. Airborne units were dropped behind German lines to seize five bridges across the Rhine R., including the key bridge at Arnhem. The units met unexpected resistance and suffered heavy casualties. Relief forces were unable to link up with airborne troops, who were forced to evacuate.

Oct. 20 Americans landed at **Leyte,** Philippine Islands, fulfilling Gen. Douglas MacArthur's promise to return. It was during the Leyte campaign that the kamikaze, or suicide plane, was first used.

Two great **opera singers** performed in New York City and were hailed by audiences and critics. They were Dorothy Kirsten, who sang several lyric and coloratura roles with the City Center Opera Company, and Regina Resnik, who prepared in 24 hours to debut in *Il Trovatore* at the Metropolitan Opera, replacing Zinka Milanov.

Mar. 2 **Academy Awards** were presented to *Casablanca* as the outstanding motion picture of 1943; to Paul Lukas as best actor for *Watch on the Rhine;* to Jennifer Jones as best actress for *The Song of Bernadette;* to Charles Coburn as best supporting actor for *The More the Merrier;* and to Katina Paxinou as best supporting actress for *For Whom the Bell Tolls.*

Mar. 5 The premiere performance of **Walter Piston**'s *Second Symphony* was given in Washington, D.C. The symphony achieved immediate success and brought Piston's name prominently before the public.

Apr. 18 *Fancy Free,* a ballet by Jerome Robbins with music by Leonard Bernstein, was presented at the Metropolitan Opera House in New York City by the Ballet Theatre. The ballet, the first by Robbins, drew large crowds. Bernstein later incorporated part of the score in the musical comedy *On the Town.*

May 1 **Pulitzer prizes** were awarded for the following: fiction, *Journey in the Dark* by Martin Flavin; history, *The Growth of American Thought* by Merle Curti; biography, *The American Leonardo: The Life of Samuel F. B. Morse* by Carlton Mabee; poetry, *Western Star* by Stephen Vincent Benét. A special award was given to *Oklahoma!* by Richard Rodgers and Oscar Hammerstein II.

Oct. 1 The **Declaration of Independence** and other historic documents sent away from Washington, D.C., for safekeeping in Dec. 1941 were put on display again at the Library of Congress.

Business and Industry; Science; Education; Philosophy and Religion III		IV Sports; Social Issues and Crime; Folkways; Fashion; Holidays

company chairman Sewell Avery refused to extend the firm's contract with the CIO as ordered by the WLB. Labor trouble continued, and on Dec. 28 troops again seized the plant and other company properties.

May 3 Development of **synthetic quinine** was announced by two Harvard University chemists, Dr. Robert R. Woodward and Dr. William E. Doering.

May 3 **Meat rationing was ended,** except for steak and choice cuts of beef, by order of the OPA.

May 8 The **first eye bank** was established by New York Hospital, New York City, in conjunction with 19 other New York hospitals. The eye bank was used to store human corneas, which could be used to restore sight in certain kinds of blindness.

May 20 The **Communist Party voted to disband** at a convention held in New York City. Its leaders formed a non-party group, the Communist Political Association.

June 5 A U.S. Supreme Court decision declared **insurance companies** subject to the Sherman Antitrust Act because they engaged in interstate commerce.

June 22 The **Servicemen's Readjustment Act** was signed by Pres. Franklin D. Roosevelt. The measure provided broad benefits to returning veterans, including a generous educational program, which came to be known as the GI Bill of Rights.

Aug. 14 **Production of consumer goods** such as vacuum cleaners, electric ranges, and cooking utensils was resumed under order of the WPB. The order was provisional and could be revoked depending on war needs.

Oct. 26 The **Nobel Prize in Physiology or Medicine** was awarded to Joseph Erlanger of the Washington University Medical School in St. Louis and to Herbert Spencer Glasser of the Rockefeller Institute in New York for their research on the functions of single

Schubach and Walter Noffke, pairs; Marcella May and James Lochead, Jr., dance. There was no men's singles competition this year.

Mar. 28 The **NCAA basketball championship** was won by Utah, which defeated Dartmouth 42–40.

Apr. 4–13 The **NHL Stanley Cup** was won by the Montreal Canadiens, who defeated the Chicago Black Hawks in four straight games.

Apr. 19 The 48th **Boston Marathon** was won by Gerard Cote of Montreal, Canada, with a time of 2 hrs., 31 min., 50.4 sec. It was his second consecutive and third career win in the event.

May 1 Ninety-year-old **Jacob S. Coxey,** standing on the steps of the Capitol in Washington, D.C., delivered the speech he was prevented from making 50 years before when he led Coxey's Army, a body of unemployed workers demanding a program of federal work projects.

May 6 The 70th annual **Kentucky Derby** was won by Pensive, with a time of 2:04¹⁄₅. The jockey was Conn McCreary.

May 13 The 69th annual **Preakness Stakes** was won by Pensive, with a time of 1:59¹⁄₅. The jockey was Conn McCreary.

June 3 The 76th annual **Belmont Stakes** was won by Bounding Home, with a time of 2:32¹⁄₅. The jockey was G. L. Smith.

July 11 The 12th annual **baseball All-Star Game** was won by the National League, which defeated the American League 7–1.

| Exploration and Settlement; Wars; Government; Civil Rights; Statistics | I | | II | Publishing; Arts and Music; Popular Entertainment; Architecture; Theater |

Oct. 23–26 In the **Battle of Leyte Gulf** the Japanese fleet, which had been unable to halt U.S. invasion of the Philippines, suffered heavy losses. It was the largest naval battle of the war.

Nov. 7 **Franklin D. Roosevelt was reelected president** of the United States, the only person ever to win a fourth term. Harry S Truman was elected vice president. The electoral vote was Roosevelt, 432; Gov. Thomas E. Dewey, Republican, 99. The popular vote was Roosevelt, 25,602,504, Dewey 22,006,285. In congressional elections the Democrats lost two Senate seats but held a 56–38 majority. In the House they gained 24 seats for a 242–190 lead, with two seats held by minor parties.

Dec. 15 The new rank **general of the Army** was conferred by Congress on Henry "Hap" Arnold, Dwight D. Eisenhower, Douglas MacArthur, and George C. Marshall. Popularly known as five-star generals, the new appointees wore insignia of rank consisting of five stars joined in a circle.

Dec. 16 The **Battle of the Bulge,** last major German offensive of the war, began as German forces broke through Allied defenses in the Ardennes. Led by Gen. Karl von Runstedt, the drive was intended to seize Antwerp and split the Allies in the west. Bad weather hampered Allied air and supply operations. U.S. forces at Bastogne, a strategic point, were surrounded but did not surrender. American resistance stiffened after the massacre of American prisoners at Malmédy (Dec. 17). On Dec. 23 Allied air operations resumed when bad weather lifted. German armored columns halted for lack of fuel and were destroyed. By Dec. 27 a U.S. relief column reached Bastogne. By mid-January 1945 all ground taken in the offensive had been recaptured.

Oct. 5 *Bloomer Girl,* a musical with music by Harold Arlen and lyrics by E. Y. Harburg, opened at the Shubert Theatre in New York City.

Oct. 19 *I Remember Mama* by John Van Druten, a two-act play based on the stories of Kathryn Forbes about a Norwegian-American family in San Francisco, opened at the Music Box in New York City.

Oct. 30 *Appalachian Spring,* a ballet with music by Aaron Copland, was performed by Martha Graham and her company at the Library of Congress, Washington, D.C. Graham was the choreographer.

Nov. 1 *Harvey* by Mary Coyle Chase, a play about a six-foot rabbit invisible to all but Elwood P. Dowd, a slightly eccentric fellow fond of drink, opened at the Forty-Eighth Street Theatre in New York City.

Nov. 11 An agreement on **record royalties** ended a two-year battle between recording companies and the American Federation of Musicians. Two major recording companies signed a contract agreeing to pay the union a fee on each record manufactured.

1945

It was a monumental year—the end of an era and the beginning of a new one. Germany and Japan were forced to accept unconditional surrender. Atomic bombs were dropped on two Japanese cities—a fact that changed the complexion of future wars and of the world in general. A new instrument of peace—the United Nations—was launched at San Francisco. The presidency of the United States changed hands as Franklin D. Roosevelt died in office. Another notable who died this year was Gen. George S. Patton, of injuries sustained in an auto accident on Dec. 9. Patton died in Heidelberg, Germany, Dec. 21, at age 60.

Jan. 9 A **landing on Luzon** in the Philippines was made by the U.S. Sixth Army. In the operation, a task force of 850 ships sailed into Lingayen Gulf, 100 miles north of Manila.

Book publishing had a boom year, with the paperback trade continuing to create hundreds of thousands of book buyers. Hollywood, hungry for plots, was willing to pay as much as $250,000 for rights to a good story. With such prizes before them, writers tailored their techniques to fit the requirements of the screen. The result, by and large, was undistinguished. By war's end, the Hollywood Victory Committee had arranged for 55,619 personal appearances of movie stars at bond rallies and military camps. The motion picture industry kept up a high level of production, even though the major companies were under fire by government lawyers who charged them with conspiring to form illegal trusts. Americans mourned the passing of Robert Benchley, the humorist, Nov. 21, at age 56; and Ernie Pyle, the cel-

Business and Industry; Science; Education; Philosophy and Religion III		IV Sports; Social Issues and Crime; Folkways; Fashion; Holidays

nerve fibers and their discovery that various types of nerve fibers conducted impulses at various speeds. At the same time the Nobel Prize in Physiology or Medicine for 1943 was awarded jointly to Edward A. Doisy of the St. Louis University School of Medicine and to Henrik Dam, the Danish biochemist. Dam was credited with discovering vitamin K, and Doisy with isolating vitamin K from alfalfa and determining its chemical nature.

Nov. 10 The **Nobel Prize in Physics** was awarded to I. I. Rabi of Columbia University for his studies of the magnetic properties of atomic nuclei. At the same time the Nobel Prize in physics for 1943 was awarded to Otto Stern of Carnegie Institute of Technology in Pittsburgh, Pa. A German-born physicist who came to America in 1933, Stern was honored for his contributions to the development of the molecular beam method for studying the magnetic attributes of atomic nuclei, and for his discovery of the magnetic movement of the proton.

Nov. 18 A report on **living costs** showed a rise of 29–30% over the previous year.

Nov. 22 At the **CIO convention** in Chicago, delegates voted to make the organization's Political Action Committee a permanent political instrument.

Aug. 20 The **PGA golf tournament** was won by Robert Hamilton, a relatively unknown pro from Indiana who beat Byron Nelson by one stroke in an upset victory.

Sept. 2 The **Miss America** title was won by Venus Ramey, 19, from Washington, D.C., at the annual pageant in Atlantic City, N.J.

Sept. 3 The **U.S. Lawn Tennis Association singles championships** were won by Sgt. Frank A. Parker in the men's division and Pauline M. Betz in the women's division.

Oct. 4–9 The 41st **World Series** was won by the St. Louis Cardinals (NL), defeating the St. Louis Browns (AL) four games to two.

Dec. 17 The **NFL championship** was won by the Green Bay Packers, who defeated the New York Giants 14–7.

1945

Aside from the war victory, the biggest news of the year was the use of atomic energy. Scientists questioned the moral and ethical value of their contribution to victory in the war. At first, the public refused to share the alarm of the physicists, believing that the people who had created this new force would soon tell the world how to control it. Unfortunately, this did not come to pass.

Roosevelt College was established as Thomas Jefferson College in Chicago, Ill. Its first classes met this year. Its present name was adopted in 1954.

Vitamin research in the U.S. continued with the discovery of folic acid, a component of the large vitamin B family and a necessary element for cell growth. Folic

It was a year of changes in sports. A new baseball commissioner was selected and both the Yankees and the Dodgers were sold to new owners. The annual baseball All-Star Game was canceled because of wartime transportation restrictions. In boxing a newcomer named Rocky Graziano scored five knockouts at Madison Square Garden. In golf the top money winner was Byron Nelson, with $63,335.66. American fashion designers stressed delicacy and prettiness in their designs. Crime statistics recorded a startling upward swing, which experts interpreted as symptomatic of postwar uncertainty.

The phrase *Kilroy was here* appeared almost overnight throughout the world, at least wherever American GIs set foot. Kilroy represented a kind of abstract conglomerate of all GIs. The phrase was scribbled by U.S.

Exploration and Settlement; Wars; Government; Civil Rights; Statistics **I**		**II** Publishing; Arts and Music; Popular Entertainment; Architecture; Theater

Feb. 4–11 The **Yalta conference,** a top-secret meeting in the Ukraine attended by Roosevelt, Winston Churchill, and Joseph Stalin, dealt with the postwar reorganization of Europe. Its communiqué, issued Feb. 12, called for a United Nations Conference on Apr. 25 to prepare a charter for a new peacekeeping organization.

Feb. 9 **Iwo Jima was invaded** by U.S. Marines, who established beachheads two hours after landing.

Mar. 7 The **Remagen Bridge** over the Rhine R. was crossed by the U.S. First Army. Not since the days of Napoleon had an invading army crossed the Rhine.

Mar. 16 **Iwo Jima fell** to the U.S. Marines after 36 days of bitter and bloody fighting. More than 4000 Marines were killed, 15,000 wounded. The Japanese lost more than 20,000 men.

Apr. 1 **Okinawa was invaded** by U.S. forces.

Apr. 12 Pres. **Franklin D. Roosevelt died** in Warm Springs, Ga., on the 83rd day of his fourth term; he was 63. He was succeeded by Harry S Truman.

Apr. 24 The **United Nations conference** opened at San Francisco with delegates from 50 nations attending. The UN charter was signed June 26.

May 7 **Germany surrendered** unconditionally to the Allies after almost six years of war. The surrender was signed in Gen. Dwight D. Eisenhower's headquarters in Reims, France.

May 8 On this day, known as **V-E Day,** for victory in Europe, the instrument of unconditional surrender was ratified in Berlin, ending the European phase of World War II.

June 21 Japanese forces on **Okinawa** surrendered after two and a half months of deadly struggle. More than 100,000 Japanese soldiers were killed. American deaths ran to almost 13,000, with nearly 40,000 wounded.

July 5 The **Philippine Islands were declared liberated** by Gen. Douglas MacArthur. In ten months of fighting since the first American landings at Leyte, more than 400,000 Japanese soldiers had been killed and upward of 12,000 Americans had lost their lives.

July 16 The **first atomic bomb** was detonated near Alamogordo, N.Mex., at 5:30 A.M.

July 28 In a bizarre **airplane crash,** a B-25 bomber flew into the Empire State Building in New York City. It became lodged between the 78th and 79th floors, killing 13 persons. The accident occurred on a foggy Saturday morning.

July 28 The **United Nations Charter** was ratified by the U.S. Senate by a vote of 89 to 2.

Aug. 6 **Hiroshima,** Japan, was destroyed by the first atomic bomb to be used in war.

ebrated war correspondent, who was killed on Iwo Jima on Apr. 18, at age 44.

Among **books published** this year was *Black Boy* by Richard Wright, the grim story of the author's childhood. Other books published this year included *A Masque of Reason* by Robert Frost; *Cass Timberlane* by Sinclair Lewis; *The Age of Jackson* by Arthur M. Schlesinger, Jr., a fascinating account of the life and times of Andrew Jackson; and *Captain from Castile* by Samuel Shellabarger, a historical novel.

José de Creeft, a sculptor whose work furthered the use of sheet metal in sculpture, completed his head of *Rachmaninoff.* The sculpture received the first Sculpture Prize at the Pennsylvania Academy of Art.

Ernst Krenek, a 12-tone composer, wrote *The Santa Fe Time Table* for mixed chorus a cappella.

Mar. 15 **Academy Awards** were presented to *Going My Way* as the outstanding motion picture of 1944; to Bing Crosby as best actor for *Going My Way;* to Ingrid Bergman as best actress for *Gaslight;* to Barry Fitzgerald as best supporting actor for *Going My Way;* and to Ethel Barrymore as best supporting actress for *None But the Lonely Heart.* A new award for documentary productions was shared by two combat films: *Fighting Lady* and *With the Marines at Tarawa.*

Apr. 19 *Carousel,* a hit musical comedy by Richard Rodgers and Oscar Hammerstein II opened at the Majestic Theatre in New York City.

May 7 **Pulitzer prizes** were awarded for the following: fiction, *A Bell for Adano,* by John Hersey; history, *Unfinished Business* by Stephen Bonsal; biography, *George Bancroft: Brahmin Rebel* by Russel Blaine Nye; poetry, *V-Letter and Other Poems* by Karl Shapiro; drama, *Harvey* by Mary Coyle Chase; music, *Appalachian Spring* by Aaron Copland.

June 2 The **New York Music Critics Circle Award** for best symphonic composition of the year was awarded to Walter Piston's *Second Symphony.*

June 27 **Commercial television** came a step closer to reality as the Federal Communications Commission allocated 13 channels for the new medium. Channel 1 was subsequently reallocated for noncommercial use.

July 9 **Frank Lloyd Wright** displayed his model for the Solomon R. Guggenheim Museum of Non-Objective Painting in New York City. The structure's

| Business and Industry; Science; Education; Philosophy and Religion | III | IV | Sports; Social Issues and Crime; Folkways; Fashion; Holidays |

acid was found effective in the treatment of pernicious anemia, but later analyses revealed adverse affects on the nervous system.

The **gross national product** of U.S. goods and services was valued at $215,000,000,000 for the year, two-thirds more than in 1939.

Jan. 15 A nationwide **dimout** was ordered to conserve diminishing fuel supplies.

Feb. 26 A **midnight curfew** was ordered on all places of amusement.

Apr. 30 **Sugar rations** were cut by 25% as reserves neared rock bottom.

May 6 **European food requirements** for the coming year were placed at 12,000,000 tons, according to the Department of Agriculture.

May 8 The **nationwide dimout** was lifted.

May 9 The **midnight entertainment curfew** was lifted.

May 10 Seventy-three more **consumer items** were authorized for manufacture as War Production Board (WPB) bans were lifted.

May 25 **Military aircraft production** was ordered reduced by 30%.

June 30 The **Office of Price Administration (OPA)** was granted one more year of life by the House of Representatives.

July 1 The **New York State Commission Against Discrimination,** the first such agency in the U.S., was established. The commission was authorized to take steps to prevent "discrimination in employment because of race, creed, color, or national origin."

July 27 The **Communist Party** was reestablished by the Communist Political Association, which voted to disband itself.

Aug. 14 All **manpower controls** were lifted by the War Manpower Commission.

Aug. 18 Moving to **restore the civilian economy,** Pres. Truman ordered full restoration of civilian consumer production and collective bargaining, and a return of free markets.

Aug. 20 Some 210 **consumer production controls** were lifted by the WPB.

Army gagsters on streets, billboards, latrines, walls, and all other available surfaces.

Jan. 1 In **college football bowl games,** the results were Oklahoma A&M 34, TCU 0 in the Cotton Bowl; Tulsa 26, Georgia Tech 12 in the Orange Bowl; Southern California 25, Tennessee 0 in the Rose Bowl; and Duke 29, Alabama 26 in the Sugar Bowl. This season the AP poll chose Army the national collegiate champions of 1944.

Jan. 20 Ten new members were elected to the **Baseball Hall of Fame:** Roger Bresnahan, Dennis Brouthers, Frederick C. Clarke, James J. Collins, Edward J. Delahanty, Hugh Duffy, Hughey A. Jennings, Michael J. Kelly, James H. O'Rourke, and "Uncle" Wilbert Robinson.

Jan. 26 The **New York Yankees** baseball club was sold by Edward G. Barrow and the heirs of the late Jacob Ruppert to a syndicate headed by Lawrence MacPhail and including Daniel Topping and Del Webb for an estimated price of $2,800,000.

Mar. 2–5 **U.S. figure skating championships** were won in New York City by Gretchen Merrill, women's singles; Donna Jeanne Pospisil and Jean Pierre Brunet, pairs; Kathe Mehl Williams and Robert J. Swenning, dance. There was no men's singles competition this year.

Mar. 29 The **NCAA basketball championship** was won by Oklahoma A&M, which defeated DePaul 52–44.

Apr. 6–22 The **NHL Stanley Cup** was won by the Toronto Maple Leafs, who defeated the Detroit Red Wings four games to three.

Apr. 19 The 49th **Boston Marathon** was won by John Kelley of West Acton, Mass., with a time of 2 hrs., 30 min., 40.2 sec.

Apr. 24 Sen. **Albert B. "Happy" Chandler,** Democrat of Kentucky, was named baseball commissioner, filling the post vacated by the death of Kenesaw Mountain Landis in 1944.

June 9 The 71st annual **Kentucky Derby** was won by Hoop Jr., with a time of 2:07. The jockey was Eddie Arcaro, who scored his third Kentucky Derby victory.

June 16 The 70th annual **Preakness Stakes** was won by Polynesian, with a time of 1:58⁴/₅. The jockey was Wayne D. Wright.

June 23 The 77th annual **Belmont Stakes** was won by Pavot, with a time of 2:30¹/₅. The jockey was Eddie Arcaro.

July 15 The **PGA golf tournament** was won by Byron Nelson.

Aug. 10 The **Brooklyn Dodgers** baseball club gained new owners as the controlling interest was acquired by Branch Rickey, Walter O'Malley, and John L. Smith.

Sept. 2 The **U.S. Lawn Tennis Association singles championships** were won by Sgt. Frank A. Parker in

| Exploration and Settlement; Wars; Government; Civil Rights; Statistics | I | | II | Publishing; Arts and Music; Popular Entertainment; Architecture; Theater |

Aug. 9 **Nagasaki,** Japan, was destroyed by the second atomic bomb to be used in war.

Aug. 14 The unconditional **surrender of Japan** was announced by Pres. Truman.

Aug. 15 **V-J Day,** for victory over Japan, marked the end of the Pacific phase of World War II.

Aug. 30 **Occupation of Japan** began when Gen. MacArthur landed there.

Sept. 2 The formal **document of surrender** was signed aboard the U.S.S. *Missouri* in Tokyo Bay.

Nov. 12 The **Nobel Peace Prize** was awarded to former secretary of state Cordell Hull for his contributions to the establishment of the United Nations.

main element was a round, blunt tower capped with a glass dome and tapered toward the base. Within, exhibit areas were situated along a continuous spiral ramp.

Dec. 27 The **National Institute of Arts and Letters** announced selection of 15 new members, among them Franklin P. Adams, columnist; Robert P. T. Coffin, author; Lillian Hellman, playwright; Charles Ives, composer; Reginald Marsh, painter; William Schuman, composer; and James Thurber, writer.

1946

Spiraling inflation, acute shortage of housing, and bitter labor disputes were facing Americans. In addition there were rumblings of what came to be known as the Cold War, and poverty-stricken Europe was looking to the U.S. for aid. It quickly became apparent that the U.S. would not be returning to a state of political isolation. Soviet expansionism became a new threat to world security, although some disagreed that Russia had territorial designs on the West. The administration took the view that complete isolation was a luxury Americans could not afford, primarily because of the existence of the atomic bomb, so the U.S. assumed the role of peacemaker in a world still in disorder.

May 14 The **Selective Service Act** was extended to Sept. 1.

July 1 **Atomic bomb tests** were held at Bikini Atoll in the Pacific. A Nagasaki-type bomb was dropped from 30,000 feet. It destroyed five ships, heavily damaged nine, and did varying amounts of damage to 45 others.

July 4 **Philippine independence** was proclaimed by Pres. Harry S Truman. He was keeping a promise made by the U.S. on acquiring the islands in 1898.

July 30 The U.S. joined **UNESCO,** the United Nations Educational, Scientific and Cultural Organization.

Aug. 1 The McMahan Act, creating the **Atomic Energy Commission,** was signed by Pres. Truman. The commission was to be composed of a five-man

Literary critics looked for a spate of fine books this year, calling up as their precedent the year immediately following World War I. Unfortunately, they were disappointed and had to be content with noting a new development in fictional technique—a modified stream of consciousness in which a highly sensitive story was told by a perceptive observer. Responding to high building costs, architects designed houses with small rooms and compensated by using more glass. U.S. painters exhibited in London and succeeded in shocking rather than boring viewers. Theatergoers were treated to one of the most extensive revival seasons in memory. The quality of motion pictures was up, as foreign producers made a strong bid for American markets, offering colorful spectacles and realistic dramas. Repeal of the federal excess profits tax and higher admission prices produced a record in box office receipts.

Among **books published** this year was *Memoirs of Hecate County* by Edmund Wilson, stories that caused a furor because of the author's treatment of sex. It raised a censorship issue reminiscent of the one inspired by James Branch Cabell's 1919 novel *Jurgen.* Lawsuits against Wilson and his publishers led eventually to withdrawal of the book for a time. Other books published this year included *Do I Wake or Sleep?* by Isobel Bolton, a novel written in the stream-of-consciousness style; *This Side of Innocence,* a novel by Taylor Caldwell; *Mr. Roberts* by Thomas Heggen; *B.F.'s Daughter* by John P. Marquand, a novel; *The Fields* by Conrad Richter, the second novel in a trilogy about a pioneer family that began with *The Trees* (1940); *The Hucksters* by Frederic Wakeman, a bitter novel about the advertising industry; *All the King's Men* by Robert Penn Warren, a novel about a southern political boss with parallels to the life of Huey Long; and *Delta Wedding,* a novel by Eudora Welty.

Business and Industry; Science; Education; Philosophy and Religion III		IV Sports; Social Issues and Crime; Folkways; Fashion; Holidays

Oct. 30 Shoe rationing ended.

Nov. 21 The **United Auto Workers struck** all General Motors plants.

Nov. 23 Meat and butter rationing ended.

Dec. 20 Tire rationing ended.

Dec. 31 The **National War Labor Board** was replaced by the National Wage Stabilization Board.

the men's division and Sarah Palfrey Cooke in the women's division.

Sept. 8 The **Miss America** title was won by Bess Myerson, 21, from New York City, at the annual pageant in Atlantic City, N.J.

Oct. 3–10 The 42nd annual **World Series** was won by the Detroit Tigers (AL), defeating the Chicago Cubs (NL) four games to three.

Dec. 16 The **NFL championship** was won by the Cleveland Rams, who defeated the Washington Redskins 15–14.

1946

It was a year of confusion and warfare between management and labor. Held down by years of wage controls, practically all the powerful labor unions struck for higher pay. Industry insisted that labor's demands were exorbitant, but could not afford walkouts at a time when consumer buying was at an unparalleled high. The country had a supply of ready money, saved from the days when nothing could be bought, and a new carefree desire to spend it. The changeover from war production to consumer goods took time, and tempers grew short when orders were not met immediately. The government, meanwhile, tried to convince people that the emergency was not yet over, that ruinous inflation still threatened, and that the shift to peacetime habits should be made cautiously.

Strikes this year involved some 4,600,000 workers, at a cost of 116,000,000 man-hours.

Jan. 25 The AFL voted to readmit the **United Mine Workers** under John L. Lewis.

Feb. 15 **ENIAC,** the electronic numerical integrator and computer, was dedicated at the Moore School of Electrical Engineering in Philadelphia, Pa. The first electronic digital computer, it had been developed by Dr. John W. Mauchly and J. Presper Eckert, Jr. It contained 18,000 vacuum tubes, occupied a 30 foot by 60 foot room, and weighed some 30 tons. The computer took 150,000 watts of power to run, had more than 500,000 soldered connections, and had taken 200,000 man-hours to build. Despite the fact that continual replacement of defective tubes was required to keep the machine running, ENIAC heralded a new age for science, engineering, industry, and mathematics.

Baseball stars returning from service improved the game and afforded fans a breathtaking pennant race, with a playoff necessary in the National League. In golf the top money winner was Ben Hogan, with $42,556.36. In keeping with peacetime optimism and to retain leadership in the fashion world now that styles again were coming from Paris, U.S. designers showed lighthearted feminine collections. Chief topics of conversation included rising prices, the shortage of housing, the menace of Russian communism, and the atomic bomb.

Jan. 1 In **college football bowl games,** the results were Texas 40, Missouri 27 in the Cotton Bowl; Miami (Florida) 13, Holy Cross 6 in the Orange Bowl; Alabama 34, Southern California 14 in the Rose Bowl; and Oklahoma A&M 33, St. Mary's 13 in the Sugar Bowl. This season the AP poll chose Army the national collegiate champions of 1945.

Mar. 2–3 **U.S. figure skating championships** were won in Chicago by Gretchen Merrill, women's singles; Richard Button, men's singles; Donna Jeanne Pospisil and Jean Pierre Brunet, pairs; Anne Davies and Carleton C. Hoffner, Jr., dance.

Mar. 23 The **NCAA basketball championship** was won by Oklahoma A&M, which defeated California 52–35.

Mar. 30–Apr. 9 The **NHL Stanley Cup** was won by the Montreal Canadiens, who defeated the Boston Bruins four games to one.

Apr. 7 The **Masters golf tournament** was won by Herman Keiser.

Apr. 20 The 50th annual **Boston Marathon** was won by Stylianos Kyriakides of Greece, with a time of 2 hrs., 29 min., 27 sec.

Apr. 23 Eleven new members were elected to the **Baseball Hall of Fame:** Jesse Burkett, Frank Chance, John Chesbro, John J. Evers, Clark Griffith, Ed Walsh, Tom McCarthy, Joseph McGinnity, Eddie Plank, Joseph Tinker, and Edward "Rube" Waddell.

| Exploration and Settlement; Wars; Government; Civil Rights; Statistics | I | | II | Publishing; Arts and Music; Popular Entertainment; Architecture; Theater |

control board without military representation but with military liaison. The act allowed the Army and Navy to manufacture atomic weapons and prohibited the distribution of fissionable materials or information on atomic energy.

Nov. 5 In **congressional elections** the Republicans gained 13 Senate seats to take a 51–45 majority, and picked up 55 House seats for a 245–188 majority, with one seat held by a minor party.

Nov. 14 The **Nobel Peace Prize** was awarded jointly to John Raleigh Mott and Emily Greene Balch. Mott, a Methodist layman and a leader in international church activities, headed the YMCA's relief activities for prisoners of war during World War I. Balch was a founder, in 1915, of the Women's International League for Peace and Freedom at The Hague, Netherlands.

Dec. 7 In the worst **hotel fire** to date, 127 died and nearly 100 were injured at the Winecoff Hotel in Atlanta, Ga. The hotel, which had no outside fire escapes or sprinkler system, became a death trap when the two elevator shafts and the two narrow stairways caught fire. Many leaped to their deaths from the windows of the 15-story building.

Dec. 14 The **UN accepted a gift** of $8,500,000 from John D. Rockefeller, Jr., for purchase of property along New York City's East R. for permanent UN headquarters.

Dec. 31 The **state of hostilities** was officially ended by Pres. Truman, who reminded the nation that a state of war still existed and that the state of emergency proclaimed by Pres. Franklin D. Roosevelt was not yet rescinded.

The first test of a new **Massachusetts obscene literature statute** was applied to Kathleen Winsor's 1945 best seller *Forever Amber.* The book was cleared in Suffolk County Superior Court and the decision upheld in the Massachusetts Supreme Court with the observation of Judge Frank J. Donahue that the book was more of a "soporific . . . than an aphrodisiac."

The **Dymaxion House,** a startling architectural innovation, was designed by Buckminster Fuller. A circular dwelling, it could be mass produced by assembly-line techniques. It was considered by many to be the answer to the critical housing shortage.

The **ranch style house** caught the architectural fancy of the public this year. Soon the countryside mushroomed with low-slung, one-story and split-level homes.

The year's most **popular song** was "The Gypsy." Other hits included "They Say It's Wonderful," "Doin' What Comes Naturally," and "I Got the Sun in the Morning," all from Irving Berlin's score for *Annie Get Your Gun;* "To Each His Own," "Aren't You Glad You're You?" "Ole Buttermilk Sky," and "Shoo-Fly Pie and Apple Pan Dowdy."

Mar. 7 **Academy Awards** were given to *The Lost Weekend* as the outstanding motion picture of 1945; to Ray Milland as best actor for *The Lost Weekend;* to Joan Crawford as best actress for *Mildred Pierce;* to James Dunn as best supporting actor for *A Tree Grows in Brooklyn;* and to Anne Revere as best supporting actress for *National Velvet.*

May 6 **Pulitzer prizes** were awarded for the following: biography, *Son of the Wilderness* by Linnie Marsh Wolfe; history, *The Age of Jackson* by Arthur M. Schlesinger, Jr.; drama, *State of the Union* by Russel Crouse and Howard Lindsay.

Oct. 9 *The Iceman Cometh* by Eugene O'Neill opened at the Martin Beck Theatre in New York City.

Nov. 18 *Joan of Lorraine* by Maxwell Anderson opened at the Alvin Theatre in New York City. The play, starring Ingrid Bergman, was presented by the Playwrights Company.

Nov. 19 *The Fatal Weakness,* a three-act comedy by George Kelly, opened at the Royale Theatre in New York City.

Nov. 20 *Another Part of the Forest* by Lillian Hellman opened at the Fulton Theatre in New York City.

1947

Economic equilibrium was the administration's chief concern. A restless population complained of constantly rising prices of food, clothing, rent, and other necessities of life. Manufacturers blamed rising costs on industry-

Two noticeable trends in American publishing were a reawakening interest in U.S. history and a turn toward philosophic introspection. The latter may have been prompted by increased concern with the fate of the

| Business and Industry; Science; Education; Philosophy and Religion **III** | **IV** Sports; Social Issues and Crime; Folkways; Fashion; Holidays |

July 7 Mother Frances Xavier Cabrini was canonized in ceremonies presided over by Pope Pius XII. She was the first American to be canonized. Mother Cabrini was the founder of the Missionary Sisters of the Sacred Heart of Jesus. Her principal shrine is at Mother Cabrini High School in New York City; her feast day is Dec. 22.

Oct. 15 **Price controls** on meat were lifted.

Oct. 31 The **Nobel Prize in Physiology or Medicine** was awarded to Hermann Joseph Muller of Indiana University for his discovery of the production of mutations by x-ray irradiation. Muller obtained his first evidence of such mutations while at the University of Texas in 1926. His discoveries contributed greatly to genetics and radiology.

Nov. 9 **Wage and price controls** were ended except for rent, sugar, and rice.

Nov. 14 The **Nobel Prize in Physics** was awarded to Percy Williams Bridgman of Harvard University for his contributions to high-pressure physics. Bridgman developed an apparatus for production of very high pressures and made numerous discoveries in the study of high pressures.

Nov. 14 The **Nobel Prize in Chemistry** was awarded jointly to James B. Sumner of Cornell University, for his work in the crystallization of enzymes, and to John Northrop and Wendell M. Stanley of the Rockefeller Institute, for their preparation of enzymes and virus proteins in pure form. They were the fourth, fifth, and sixth Americans to receive the Nobel Prize in Chemistry.

Nov. 16 The **Evangelical United Brethren Church** was organized at Johnstown, Pa., in a union of the Evangelical Church and the Church of the United Brethren in Christ.

May 4 The 72nd annual **Kentucky Derby** was won by Assault, with a time of 2:06³/₅. The jockey was Warren Mehrtens.

May 11 The 71st annual **Preakness Stakes** was won by Assault, with a time of 2:01²/₅. The jockey was Warren Mehrtens.

May 30 The 30th **Indianapolis 500** auto race was won by George Robson of Los Angeles, completing the course in 4 hrs., 21 min., 16.70 sec., with an average speed of 114.820 mph.

June 1 The 78th annual **Belmont Stakes** was won by Assault, with a time of 2:30⁴/₅. The jockey was Warren Mehrtens. Assault became the seventh horse to win racing's Triple Crown.

June 16 The **U.S. Open golf tournament** was won by Lloyd Mangrum, who defeated Byron Nelson and Vic Ghezzi by one stroke.

July 6 At the **Wimbledon** tennis championships in England, Pauline Betz won the women's singles title. Louise Brough and Margaret Osborne won the women's doubles, and Tom Brown and Jack Kramer won the men's doubles.

July 9 The 13th annual **baseball All-Star Game** was won by the American League, which shut out the National League 12–0.

Aug. 25 The **PGA golf tournament** was won by Ben Hogan.

Sept. 1 The **first U.S. Women's Open golf tournament** was won in Spokane, Wash., by Patty Berg.

Sept. 7 The **Miss America** title was won by Marilyn Buferd, 21, from California, at the annual pageant in Atlantic City, N.J.

Sept. 8 The **U.S. Lawn Tennis Association singles championships** were won by Jack Kramer in the men's division and Pauline Betz in the women's division.

Oct. 6–15 The 43rd annual **World Series** was won by the St. Louis Cardinals (NL), defeating the Boston Red Sox (AL) four games to three. On Oct. 3 the Cardinals had won the first National League playoff, beating the Brooklyn Dodgers in two games straight.

Dec. 15 The **NFL championship** was won by the Chicago Bears, who defeated the New York Giants 24–14.

Dec. 26 In the **Davis Cup** international tennis matches, the U.S. defeated Australia 5–0, regaining the trophy lost to Australia in 1939.

1947

Many of labor's hard-won gains were erased this year by passage of the widely debated Taft-Hartley Bill. While many citizens applauded the law's effective curb on alleged union excesses, labor leaders pledged an all-

Baseball took a historic step forward as Jackie Robinson signed with the Brooklyn Dodgers, of the National League, becoming the first black to play in the major leagues. Later in the year other black athletes played in

wide wage boosts. Housing conditions everywhere became so tight that Pres. Harry S Truman called the shortage "the foremost of the many problems facing the nation." The most dramatic successes of the year were scored in foreign policy. The European Recovery program, or Marshall Plan, earned the gratitude of western European nations but the abuse of Iron Curtain countries. The intensity of the Cold War was stepped up as an executive order banned all members or sympathizers of the Communist Party from holding office in the executive branch of the U.S. government.

Apr. 9 A tornado caused the death of 167 persons and the injury of more than 1300 in Texas and Oklahoma. Two-thirds of Woodward, Okla., was destroyed by the storm.

Apr. 16–18 A ship explosion in Texas City, Tex., killed some 500 persons. The city itself was virtually annihilated by the blast. The nitrate-laden French freighter *Grandcamp* had caught fire early on the morning of Apr. 16. Fireman thought they had gotten the blaze under control until the ship exploded. Fire then swept the Monsanto Chemical Co. plant, and further explosions were set off in the ensuing conflagration. Also destroyed were a number of oil storage tanks. On Apr. 17 the freighter *High Flyer* exploded. The blasts and fires left the waterfront section of the city in complete devastation. Eyewitnesses said the scene was worse than anything they had seen in Europe during World War II.

May 22 The **Greek-Turkish Aid Bill** was signed by Pres. Truman. The bill authorized some $400,000,000 in aid to Greece and Turkey on their request. This authorization was subject to withdrawal on the disapproval of the interested countries, the U.N. Security Council or General Assembly, or the president if he deemed the aid to have been either improperly used or unnecessary. When Pres. Truman requested the legislation on Mar. 12 he said: "I believe that it must be the policy of the United States to support free peoples who are resisting attempted subjugation by armed minorities or by outside pressures." This political stance came to be known as the Truman Doctrine.

June 5 The **Marshall Plan** for reconstruction of Europe was proposed at Harvard University by Sec. of State George C. Marshall. He stated that careful study of European needs, on which U.S. aid should be

human race now that it had discovered the power to destroy itself. Exhibitions of paintings featured non-objective and expressionistic works and leaned less on realism and surrealism. Composers took heart as orchestral societies encouraged production of new works. Despite a continuing boom on Broadway, producers found it difficult to find backers for their plays, with production costs twice what they had been five years earlier. Reluctant to risk so much on new scripts, producers resorted to revivals. Architects produced little that was new, since three-fourths of the building in the country was in the hands of large-scale developers. The biggest news in the movie industry was the investigation of alleged communist subversion. Senate committees claimed that ten screenwriters were communists or sympathizers and should not be allowed to work on films. A 20% federal amusement tax helped drive some customers away from movies to the new medium of television.

Among **books published** this year was *Under the Volcano*, a novel by the English-born writer Malcolm Lowry. The novel recounted the last day in the life of Geoffrey Firmin, an alcoholic British ex-consul in Mexico. The novel met with moderate success and critical acclaim, but eventually was recognized as a masterpiece. Other books published this year included *The Times of Melville and Whitman* by Van Wyck Brooks; *Butterfly* by James M. Cain, a novel; *Inside U.S.A.* by John Gunther; *The Big Sky* by A. B. Guthrie, a novel; *Gentleman's Agreement* by Laura Z. Hobson, a novel exploring anti-Semitism that became a best seller and was adapted for motion pictures; *Kingsblood Royal*, a novel by Sinclair Lewis; *Tales of the South Pacific* by James Michener; *The Harder They Fall*, a novel about boxing by Budd Schulberg; *I, the Jury* by Mickey Spillane; *The Wayward Bus* by John Steinbeck; and *Aurora Dawn* by Herman Wouk, the author's first novel.

The first performance of *Symphony No. Two* by **Roger Sessions** was given in San Francisco, Calif. It provoked considerable hostile reaction. Dedicated to the memory of Franklin D. Roosevelt, it incorporated a dissonant contrapuntal texture, harmonic complexity, and a driving rhythm.

Jan. 10 *Finian's Rainbow,* by E. Y. Harburg and Fred Saidy, opened at the Forty-Sixth Street Theatre in New York City. The musical, relating the tale of an old Irishman who stole a crock of gold from a leprechaun, included such songs as "How Are Things in Glocca Morra?", "If This Isn't Love," and "Old Devil Moon."

Jan. 28 A copy of the *Bay Psalm Book* was bought for $151,000 at an auction of the Parke-Bernet Galleries in New York City. This was the highest price paid to date for a book.

out effort to repeal the legislation, particularly the provision outlawing closed-shop contracts. Despite this setback, organized labor grew more powerful as a continuing business boom sent more and more workers into its ranks. American education was concerned with five major areas: improving the economic lot of teachers; meeting the challenge of increased enrollment; taking advantage of federal aid for schools while keeping schools free of government control; settling the growing controversy over the role of religion in education; and implementing a growing interest in international educational cooperation.

Enrollment of veterans in American colleges, spurred by the Servicemen's Readjustment Act of 1944, known as the G.I. Bill of Rights, reached its peak. Over 1,000,000 former servicemen were among some 2,500,000 students attending college classes.

Magazine circulation figures climbed. Thirty-eight magazines reported circulations of more than 1,000,000. In 1900 no U.S. magazine had a circulation of more than 500,000.

June 11 **Sugar rationing** ended.

June 17 The **first globe-circling passenger airline** was inaugurated by Pan American Airways, Inc. A round-the-world fare was $1700. The new service began when the clipper *America,* a Lockheed Constellation, took off from La Guardia Airport en route to Gander, Newfoundland, the first stop on a 22,170-mile trip around the world. The plane was scheduled to return to New York on June 30.

June 23 The controversial **Taft-Hartley Act** was passed over Pres. Harry S Truman's veto. The act reduced or eliminated many labor union advantages provided for in the National Labor Relations Act of 1935, including the unconditional closed shop, the check-off system, which enabled unions to collect dues from all employed members; the unconditional

the American League for the first time. In boxing, Joe Louis resumed his defense of the world heavyweight title, winning (Dec. 5) a split decision over "Jersey Joe" Walcott. In golf, the top money winner was Jimmy Demaret, $27,936.83. In women's fashion, the topic of conversation was the so-called New Look, inspired by the Paris designer Christian Dior, who screened women's legs with a long skirt, pinched in their waists, and flattened their bosoms.

Jan. 1 In **college football bowl games,** the results were Arkansas 0, LSU 0 in the Cotton Bowl; Rice 8, Tennessee 0 in the Orange Bowl; Illinois 45, UCLA 14 in the Rose Bowl; and Georgia 20, North Carolina 10 in the Sugar Bowl. This season the AP poll chose Notre Dame the national collegiate champions of 1946.

Mar. 9 **U.S. figure skating championships** were won in Berkeley, Calif., by Gretchen Merrill, women's singles; Richard T. Button, men's singles; Yvonne Sherman and Robert Swenning, pairs; Lois Waring and Walter H. Bainbridge, Jr., dance.

Mar. 25 The **NCAA basketball championship** was won by Holy Cross, which defeated Oklahoma 58–47.

Apr. 6 The **Masters golf** tournament was won by Jimmy Demaret.

Apr. 8–19 The **NHL Stanley Cup** was won by the Toronto Maple Leafs, who defeated the Montreal Canadiens four games to two.

Apr. 19 The 51st **Boston Marathon** was won by Yun Bok Sun of Seoul, Korea, with a time of 2 hrs., 25 min., 39 sec.

May 3 The 73rd annual **Kentucky Derby** was won by Jet Pilot, with a time of 2:06^4/s. The jockey was Eric Guerin.

May 10 The 72nd annual **Preakness Stakes** was won by Faultless, with a time of 1:59. The jockey was Douglas Dodson.

May 30 The 31st **Indianapolis 500** auto race was won by Mauri Rose of Chicago, Ill., completing the 500-mile course in 4 hrs., 17 min., 52.17 sec., with an average speed of 116.33 mph.

May 31 The 79th annual **Belmont Stakes** was won by Phalanx, with a time of 2:29^2/s. The jockey was Ruperto Donoso.

June 15 The **U.S. Open golf tournament** was won by Lew Worsham, who beat Sam Snead by one stroke on the last green in an 18-hole playoff.

based, was essential before progress could be made in the economic rehabilitation of Europe.

June 14 Peace treaties between the U.S. and Italy, Rumania, Bulgaria, and Hungary were ratified by the U.S. Senate and signed by Pres. Truman.

June 26–28 The **Prohibition Party** nominated Claude A. Watson of California for the presidency.

July 18 The **Presidential Succession Act** was signed by Pres. Truman. The act designated the Speaker of the House and then the president of the Senate pro tempore next in succession after the vice president.

July 25 The **National Security Act** of 1947 was passed by Congress. The act unified the armed forces, including a newly created Air Force, within a national military establishment headed by a new official of Cabinet rank, the secretary of defense. It also established the National Security Council and the Central Intelligence Agency. The act was signed on July 26 by Pres. Truman, who nominated Sec. of the Navy James V. Forrestal as the first secretary of defense. Forrestal was confirmed by Congress on July 27.

Sept. 17–19 A severe **hurricane** swept in from the Gulf of Mexico, causing widespread damage in Florida, Mississippi, and Louisiana and killing at least 100 people. On Sept. 21, as an aftermath of the hurricane, floodwaters near New Orleans destroyed crops and killed about 60 people.

Dec. 27 A record-breaking **snowstorm** struck the Northeast, dumping a record 25.8 in. of snow on New York City and causing nearly 80 deaths in the North Atlantic states. Stalled trains stranded commuters. Marooned suburbanites crowded downtown hotels.

Feb. 18 *The Medium,* a two-act opera by Gian-Carlo Menotti, was produced at the Heckscher Theater in New York City by the Ballet Theater. On May 1, it opened on Broadway at the Ethel Barrymore Theater and achieved a resounding popular success.

Mar. 13 *Brigadoon* by Alan Jay Lerner and Frederick Loewe opened at the Ziegfeld Theatre in New York City. The musical told the story of two American lads in a mythical town in Scotland.

Mar. 13 **Academy Awards** were presented to *The Best Years of Our Lives* as the outstanding motion picture of 1946 and to its star, Fredric March, as best actor; to Olivia de Havilland as best actress for *To Each His Own;* to Harold Russell, an amputee who had never acted before, as best supporting actor for *The Best Years of Our Lives;* and to Anne Baxter as best supporting actress for *The Razor's Edge.*

Apr. 7 The first annual **Antoinette Perry, or Tony, Awards,** for outstanding contributions to the American theater during the 1946–1947 season, were presented. Among those honored were José Ferrer for his performance in *Cyrano de Bergerac;* Fredric March for *Years Ago;* Ingrid Bergman for *Joan of Lorraine;* Helen Hayes for *Happy Birthday;* and Patricia Neal for *Another Part of the Forest.* The awards were named after Antoinette Perry, who died in 1946. She served as director of the wartime board of the American Theater Wing.

Apr. 26 *Symphony in A* by **John Powell** was given its first performance by the Detroit Symphony Orchestra. Commissioned by the National Federation of Music Clubs, the symphony was one of the last major works in the avowedly nationalistic movement among U.S. composers.

May 5 **Pulitzer prizes** were awarded for the following: fiction, *All the King's Men* by Robert Penn Warren; biography, *The Autobiography of William Allen White*; history, *Scientists Against Time* by James Phinney Baxter III; poetry, *Lord Weary's Castle* by Robert Lowell.

Dec. 3 *A Streetcar Named Desire* by Tennessee Williams opened at the Ethel Barrymore Theatre in New York City. Set in New Orleans, the play depicted the disintegration of its central character, Blanche Dubois, in face of the brutality of modern life.

1948

The administration and the lawmakers fought all year. Pres. Harry S Truman called the 80th Congress the "worst in our history." One of the chief areas of disagreement was over the supposed presence of communists in governmental positions. The House Committee on Un-American Activities wrote alarming reports,

World War II was one of the leading subjects of this year's books, and first novels dealing with the war by Norman Mailer and Irwin Shaw were among the year's best. The newest communication medium, television, was cursed in many quarters as the eventual destroyer of American reading, theater, and movies. Actually, TV

Business and Industry; Science; Education; Philosophy and Religion III		IV Sports; Social Issues and Crime; Folkways; Fashion; Holidays

right to strike at any time; and immunity from employer lawsuits over breaches of contract and strike damage. New obligations for labor unions included publication of financial statements and a mandatory affidavit of all union leaders attesting to nonmembership in the Communist Party.

Oct. 14 The **first supersonic aircraft,** the Bell X-1 research airplane, was piloted faster than the speed of sound for the first time by Capt. Charles E. Yeager, USAF, during a test at Muroc Air Force Base, Calif.

Oct. 23 The **Nobel Prize in Physiology or Medicine** was awarded jointly to Carl F. Cori and his wife Gerty T. Cori of Washington University in St. Louis for "the discovery of how glycogen is catalytically converted," and to Dr. Bernardo A. Houssay of Buenos Aires, Argentina, for his studies of the hormone produced by the pituitary gland. The Coris were the third husband and wife team to be awarded a Nobel Prize in the field of scientific research. Born in Czechoslovakia, they came to the U.S. in 1922.

Oct. 29 In an early attempt at producing **artificial weather,** the General Electric Company seeded cumulus clouds with dry ice over a forest fire at Concord, N.H.; rain fell, drenching the area. But because a natural rain followed soon after the experiment, it was impossible to determine how effective the seeding had been. During 1947 the press carried much comment about artificial weather, but most meteorologists thought rain would result only from the seeding of clouds already at shower stage.

June 24 The **PGA golf tournament** was won by Jim Ferrier.

June 29 The **U.S. Women's Open golf tournament** was won by Betty Jameson.

July 4–5 At the **Wimbledon** tennis championships in England, Jack Kramer won the men's singles title and Margaret Osborne won the women's singles. Kramer teamed with Robert Falkenburg to win the men's doubles, Doris Hart and Patricia Canning Todd won the women's doubles, and Louise Brough teamed with John E. Bromwich of Australia to win the mixed doubles.

July 8 The 14th annual **baseball All-Star Game** was won by the American League, defeating the National League 2–1.

July 21 The **Baseball Hall of Fame** inducted Carl Hubbell, Robert M. "Lefty" Grove, Gordon "Mickey" Cochrane, and Frank Frisch, as well as 11 baseball greats elected to the Hall of Fame in 1946.

Sept. 6 The **Miss America** title was won by Barbara Walker, 21, from Memphis, Tenn., at the annual pageant in Atlantic City, N.J.

Sept. 14 The **U.S. Lawn Tennis Association singles championships** were won by Jack Kramer in the men's division and Louise Brough in the women's division.

Sept. 30–Oct. 6 The 44th annual **World Series** was won by the New York Yankees (AL), defeating the Brooklyn Dodgers (NL) four games to three.

Dec. 28 The **NFL championship** was won by the Chicago Cardinals, who defeated the Philadelphia Eagles 28–21.

Dec. 30 In the **Davis Cup** international tennis challenge round, the U.S. defeated Australia four matches to one.

1948

Bolstered by increased defense expenditures and a costly foreign-aid program, American industry enjoyed a peak year. Relations between labor and management were particularly mellow. General Motors granted an automatic cost-of-living increase to some 265,000 hourly workers. Strikes were fewer and less violent. However,

The major leagues provided baseball fans with the first post-season playoff in the history of the American League when the Cleveland Indians ended the year with the same won-and-lost record as the Boston Red Sox. This year the Baseball Hall of Fame elected two new members: Herbert J. Pennock, the pitcher, and

1948   *PRES.* HARRY S TRUMAN   538

Exploration and Settlement; Wars;   Publishing; Arts and Music; Popular
Government; Civil Rights; Statistics   I   II   Entertainment; Architecture; Theater

which the president largely ignored, calling one finding a "red herring." The president maintained that the FBI together with the Justice Department was more than equal to the task of cleaning house. Some 2,000,000 federal employees were investigated; as a direct result, 526 resigned and 98 were dismissed. In foreign affairs, the European Recovery Program continued with military aid to Greece, Turkey, and China. The most dramatic development of the year was the Soviet blockade of Berlin, which the U.S. broke by maintaining an airlift to resupply the beleaguered city.

Jan. 8 The cost of **European relief** for the first 15 months of the Marshall Plan was estimated as $16,800,000,000 by Sec. of State George C. Marshall.

Mar. 30 The **Rent Control Bill,** which extended controls until Mar. 31, 1949, was signed by Pres. Truman. The bill also designated an Emergency Court of Appeals to decide on decontrols or increases recommended by local boards but rejected by the federal housing expediter.

Apr. 3 The **Foreign Assistance Act** of 1948 was signed by Pres. Truman. The act provided $5,300,000,000 for a one-year European Recovery Program, known popularly as the Marshall Plan. The act also provided $275,000,000 for military aid to Greece and Turkey, $463,000,000 for economic and military aid to China, and $60,000,000 for a UN Fund for Children.

May 2 The **Socialist Labor Party** nominated Edward A. Teichert for the presidency.

May 9 The **Socialist Party nominated Norman M. Thomas** for the presidency for the sixth consecutive time.

June 24 The **Republican National Convention** nominated Gov. Thomas E. Dewey of New York for the presidency. The following day, Gov. Earl Warren of California was chosen as the vice presidential candidate.

June 24 The **Selective Service Act** was signed by Pres. Truman. It provided for the registration of all men between 18 and 25 and the draft of enough men to constitute an Army of 837,000, a Navy and Marine Corps of 666,882, and an Air Force of 502,000.

June 25 The **Displaced Persons Bill** was signed by Pres. Truman. It admitted 205,000 European

broadcasts of concerts and operas led to creation of music festivals and commissions for new composers, while movie studios suffered a 25% drop in employment, in part due to stiff European competition.

Among **books published** this year was *Raintree County* by Ross Lockridge, a first novel that achieved both critical and popular success. It was to be the author's only book. He died on March 6 at the age of 33, an apparent suicide. Other books published this year included the best-selling religious novel *The Big Fisherman* by Lloyd C. Douglas; *Crusade in Europe* by Dwight D. Eisenhower; *The Naked and the Dead* by Norman Mailer, the author's first novel and one of the best fictional works about World War II; and *The Young Lions* by Irwin Shaw, another first novel, also about World War II and a critical and popular success.

The first **Supreme Court hearing on a state obscenity law** related to a specific book concerned Edmund Wilson's *Memoirs of Hecate County* and its suppression in New York State. The Court was deadlocked on the question and thus upheld the lower court conviction of the publisher.

Ben Shahn completed his painting *Miners' Wives,* a work reflecting the artist's lifelong concern with social injustice. The work portrayed a woman receiving the news of the death of her husband.

Popular **song hits** of the year included "Buttons and Bows," "Now Is the Hour," "Nature Boy," "You Call Everybody Darling," "On a Slow Boat to China," and "All I Want for Christmas Is My Two Front Teeth."

Notable **musical premieres** included *Piano Concerto No. 1* by Howard Hanson, *String Quartet* for oboe, violin, cello, and piano and the *Seventh String Quartet* by Bohuslav Martinu; and *Survivor from Warsaw,* a cantata by Arnold Schoenberg.

The first major postwar **architectural competition,** for design of the Jefferson National Expansion memorial in St. Louis, Mo., was won by a team headed by Eero Saarinen. The group, which included an architect, a sculptor, a painter, and a landscape architect, won the $40,000 prize with their design for a huge parabolic arch made of stainless steel.

Red Cross headquarters in San Francisco, Calif., was built from designs by Gardner A. Dailey. The ribbed surface texture of its poured concrete walls was particularly notable.

Jan. 15 *Make Mine Manhattan,* a musical revue by Arnold B. Horwitt and Richard Lewine, opened at the Broadhurst Theatre in New York City. Its cast included a relative newcomer, Sid Caesar.

| Business and Industry; Science; Education; Philosophy and Religion III | | IV Sports; Social Issues and Crime; Folkways; Fashion; Holidays |

education had a number of new problems to consider, including sharply rising enrollments; inadequate facilities; the failure of teachers to gain better economic status, mainly because rising prices offset salary increases; a shortage of teachers; a decline in enrollment of veterans at colleges and universities; and an ever-swelling tide of foreign students on exchange scholarships.

Aureomycin was produced by Dr. Benjamin Minge Duggar at Lederle Laboratories, Pearl River, N.Y.

Conquest of **pernicious anemia** was completed with the discovery of vitamin B-12, the substance in liver extracts responsible for earlier cures. Vitamin B-12 was found to have phenomenal efficiency. A daily dosage equivalent to one hundredth of a grain of salt was sufficient to cure a victim of pernicious anemia, and the same quantity taken twice a week maintained the cured person in good health.

Workmen's compensation laws were adopted in Mississippi, the last state in the Union to do so.

The **Polaroid Land Camera,** patented by Edwin H. Land in 1947, went on sale. The first camera to carry its own darkroom, it processed prints in one minute. It was an instant hit with professional photographers, who saw the value in obtaining instant prints of subjects. The Polaroid gave them greater flexibility in experimenting with lighting and settings for their subjects.

Jan. 2 It was announced that **atomic research** for industrial development would be the major concern of a new partnership between the University of Chicago and seven corporations.

Jan. 12 **Legal education facilities for blacks** in Oklahoma equal to those for whites were ordered by a U.S. Supreme Court ruling.

Feb. 2 In **political endorsements by labor,** the AFL executive council decided not to support Henry A. Wallace, candidate on the Progressive ticket. The CIO executive board had previously passed a similar resolution.

Mar. 5 A new **U.S. rocketry record** was set by the Navy. A speed of 3000 mph and an altitude of 78 miles

Harold "Pie" Traynor, longtime third baseman for the Pittsburgh Pirates. Plaques honoring the two were unveiled at Cooperstown, N.Y., in the 1949 annual ceremonies. In golf the top money winners were Ben Hogan, $36,812, and Mildred "Babe" Didrikson Zaharias, $3400. Meanwhile, the nation's crime rate remained steady. Racketeers concentrated on large-scale gambling operations, some of which had the tacit approval of local authorities. In fashion, the so-called New Look, in vogue last year, was rejected. Women now wanted the more natural lines of the body to show. Notables who died included George Herman "Babe" Ruth, the Sultan of Swat, Aug. 16, at 53.

Jan. 1 In **college football bowl games,** the results were Southern Methodist 13, Penn State 13 in the Cotton Bowl; Georgia Tech 20, Kansas 14 in the Orange Bowl; Michigan 49, Southern California 0 in the Rose Bowl; and Texas 27, Alabama 7 in the Sugar Bowl. This season the AP poll chose Notre Dame the national collegiate champions of 1947.

Jan. 30–Feb. 8 At the **Winter Olympics** in St. Moritz, Switzerland, the U.S. won three gold medals and finished third in unofficial team standings, behind Sweden and Switzerland.

Feb. 13 At the **world figure skating championships** in Davos, Switzerland, the men's singles title was won by Richard T. Button, the first U.S. skater to win the men's title.

Mar. 13 The **NCAA basketball tournament** was won by Kentucky, which defeated Indiana State 82–70.

Apr. 3 **U.S. figure skating championships** were won in Colorado Springs, Colo., by Gretchen Merrill, women's singles, her sixth consecutive win; Richard T. Button, men's singles; Karol and Peter Kennedy, pairs; Lois Waring and Walter H. Bainbridge, Jr., dance.

Apr. 7–14 The **NHL Stanley Cup** was won for the second year in a row by the Toronto Maple Leafs, who defeated the Detroit Red Wings in four straight games.

Apr. 11 The **Masters golf tournament** was won by Claude Harmon.

Apr. 19 The 52nd **Boston Marathon** was won by Gerard Cote of St. Hyacinthe, Quebec, Canada, with a time of 2 hrs., 31 min., 2 sec.

May 1 The 74th annual **Kentucky Derby** was won by Citation, with a time of 2:05²/₅. The jockey was Eddie Arcaro.

May 15 The 73rd annual **Preakness Stakes** was won by Citation, with a time of 2:02³/₅. The jockey was Eddie Arcaro.

May 25 The **PGA golf tournament** was won by Ben Hogan.

May 31 The 32nd **Indianapolis 500** auto race was won by Mauri Rose, completing the 500-mile course in 4

displaced persons, including 3000 nonquota orphans.

July 15 The **Democratic National Convention** nominated **Pres. Truman** for reelection, and Sen. Alben W. Barkley of Kentucky for the vice presidency.

July 17 The **States Rights Democrats** nominated Gov. Strom Thurmond of South Carolina for the presidency and Gov. Fielding L. Wright of Mississippi for the vice presidency. The political group, also known as the Dixiecrats, were members of the Democratic Party who had walked out of the national convention in opposition to the party's strong civil rights platform.

July 20 Twelve American **Communist Party leaders were indicted** and charged with advocating overthrow of the U.S. government.

July 23–25 The **Progressive Party** nominated Henry A. Wallace for the presidency and Sen. Glen H. Taylor for the vice presidency.

Aug. 2–6 The **Communist Party Convention** at New York City supported the Progressive Party nomination of Henry A. Wallace for the presidency.

Nov. 2 **Harry S Truman was reelected president** of the United States in a major political upset. Alben W. Barkley was elected vice president. Political analysts and polls had predicted that Truman's Republican opponent, Gov. Thomas E. Dewey of New York, would win. The electoral vote was Truman 304, Dewey 189. The popular vote was Truman 24,104,-836; Dewey 21,969,500; Strom Thurmond, States Rights Democrat, 1,169,312; Henry A. Wallace, Progressive, 1,157,172; Norman M. Thomas, Socialist, 132,138; and Claude A. Watson, Prohibition Party, 103,343. In congressional elections the Democrats gained nine Senate seats for a 54–42 majority. In the House they gained 75 seats for a 263–171 lead, with one seat going to a minor party.

Dec. 15 **Alger Hiss,** a former State Department official, was indicted by a federal grand jury on two counts of perjury. Hiss, who had worked in the State Department in 1937 and 1938, denied giving official documents to Whittaker Chambers, a self-proclaimed courier for a communist spy group. He also denied ever meeting Chambers after Jan. 1, 1937.

Feb. 18 *Mister Roberts,* by Thomas Heggen and Joshua Logan based on Heggen's best-selling novel, opened at the Alvin Theatre in New York City. Henry Fonda played the title role. The play became one of the hits of the season.

Mar. 20 **Academy Awards** were presented to *Gentleman's Agreement* as the outstanding motion picture of 1947; to Ronald Colman as best actor for *A Double Life;* to Loretta Young as best actress for *The Farmer's Daughter;* to Edmund Gwenn as best supporting actor for *Miracle on 34th Street;* and to Celeste Holm as best supporting actress for *Gentleman's Agreement.*

Mar. 28 **Tony Awards** were presented to *Mister Roberts* as outstanding play of the 1947–1948 season; Henry Fonda for his performance in *Mister Roberts;* Paul Kelly for *Command Decision;* Basil Rathbone for *The Heiress;* Judith Anderson for *Medea;* and Jessica Tandy for *A Streetcar Named Desire.*

Apr. 30 *Inside U.S.A.,* a musical revue by Howard Dietz and Arthur Schwartz, opened at the New Century Theatre in New York City. Its cast included Beatrice Lillie and Jack Haley.

May 3 **Pulitzer prizes** were awarded to the following: fiction, *Tales of the South Pacific* by James Michener; biography, *Forgotten First Citizen: John Bigelow* by Margaret Clapp; history, *Across the Wide Missouri* by Bernard De Voto; poetry, *Age of Anxiety* by W. H. Auden; drama, *A Streetcar Named Desire* by Tennessee Williams.

Oct. 6 *Summer and Smoke* by Tennessee Williams, a play likened in tone and poetic intensity to the author's previous successes, opened at the Music Box in New York City. It was quietly received by both critics and audiences.

Nov. 4 The **Nobel Prize for Literature** was awarded to T. S. Eliot. Born in St. Louis in 1888, Eliot moved to England and in 1927 became a British subject. Among his works of poetry were *The Waste Land* (1922), and *Ash Wednesday* (1930).

Dec. 16 *Lend an Ear,* a musical revue by Charles Gaynor, opened at the National Theatre in New York City.

Dec. 30 *Kiss Me, Kate,* a hit musical comedy based on Shakespeare's *Taming of the Shrew* with music and lyrics by Cole Porter and book by Bella and Samuel Spewack, opened at the New Century Theatre in New York City.

were achieved during tests at White Sands, N.Mex.

Mar. 8 **Religious education** in public schools was declared a violation of the First Amendment by the U.S. Supreme Court.

Mar. 15 More than 200,000 **soft-coal miners struck** for a more liberal old-age pension plan. On Apr. 12 the miners were sent back to the pits by John L. Lewis after a compromise was reached on the pension fund.

May 10 A nationwide **railroad strike was averted** when the federal government was granted an injunction. Pres. Harry S Truman had threatened to order the Army to seize the railroads.

May 25 The **first sliding-scale wage contract,** in which wages depended on the cost of living, was signed by General Motors and the United Auto Workers. It granted some 225,000 workers an immediate increase of 11 cents an hour.

June 3 The **world's largest reflector telescope** was dedicated. It was the 200-inch Hale telescope at Palomar Mountain Observatory, maintained by the California Institute of Technology.

July 31 **Idlewild International Airport** in New York City, the largest in the world, was dedicated by Pres. Truman.

Aug. 16 The **Anti-Inflation Act** was passed. The Federal Reserve System instituted curbs on installment buying.

Sept. 25 Information on a **jet plane** that could travel almost 900 mph was released by the U.S. Air Force.

Nov. 15 The first American-built **electric locomotive with a gas turbine** was tested by the General Electric and American Locomotive companies at Erie, Pa.

Nov. 20 A new **balloon altitude record** was claimed by the U.S. Army Signal Corps. It was 140,000 feet (26½ miles).

hrs., 10 min., 23.33 sec., with an average speed of 119.81 mph. It was his second consecutive win.

June 12 The 80th annual **Belmont Stakes** was won by Citation, with a time of 2:28⅕. Citation thus became the eighth horse in history to win the Triple Crown of racing. The jockey was Eddie Arcaro, who chalked up his second Triple Crown victory.

June 12 The **U.S. Open golf tournament** was won by Ben Hogan, with a tournament record-breaking score of 276, five strokes lower than the previous tournament record.

June 25 The **world heavyweight boxing championship** was successfully defended by Joe Louis, who defeated "Jersey Joe" Walcott in an 11-round bout.

July 2 At the **Wimbledon** tennis championships in England, Robert Falkenburg won the men's singles title. The next day Louise Brough won the women's singles, then teamed with Margaret Osborne du Pont to win the women's doubles, and with John Bromwich of Australia to win the mixed doubles.

July 13 The 15th annual **baseball All-Star Game** was won by the American League, which beat the National League 5–2.

July 29–Aug. 14 At the **Summer Olympics** in London, England, the U.S. won 33 gold medals and the unofficial team championship.

Aug. 15 The **U.S. Women's Open golf tournament** was won by Mildred "Babe" Didrikson Zaharias.

Sept. 6 In the **Davis Cup** international tennis challenge round, the U.S. won its fifth straight match from Australia, sweeping the round 5–0 and retaining the trophy.

Sept. 11 The **Miss America** title was won by Beatrice Vella "Bebe" Shopp, 18, from Minnesota, at the annual pageant in Atlantic City, N.J.

Sept. 19 The **U.S. Lawn Tennis Association singles championships** were won by 20-year-old Richard A. "Pancho" Gonzales in the men's division and Margaret Osborne du Pont in the women's division.

Oct. 6–11 The 45th annual **World Series** was won by the Cleveland Indians (AL), defeating the Boston Braves (NL) four games to two. The Indians had won the American League pennant by beating the Boston Red Sox 8–3 in a single-game playoff, the first time a playoff was needed in the league.

Oct. 24 The term *Cold War* to characterize East-West relations after World War II was given national prominence after a speech by Bernard M. Baruch before the Senate War Investigating Committee. "Although the war is over," said Baruch, "we are in the midst of a cold war which is getting warmer."

Dec. 19 The **NFL championship** was won by the Philadelphia Eagles, who defeated the Chicago Cardinals 7–0.

1949

In his message to Congress this year, Pres. Harry S Truman presented a program of domestic legislation that he called the Fair Deal. It included repeal of the Taft-Hartley law, reenactment of the Wagner Act, a law calling for a minimum wage of 75 cents an hour, generous farm price supports, expansion of Social Security, federal aid to local school systems, low-rent public housing, slum clearance, and broad civil rights proposals. In foreign affairs, the Senate ratified the North Atlantic Treaty Alliance and pledged over $1,250,000,000 to finance a military assistance program. Worry over communists at home continued as the U.S.S.R. disclosed that it too had atomic weapons, and eleven Communist Party leaders in New York City were found guilty of advocating overthrow of the government.

Jan. 20 Pres. **Truman was inaugurated** for his second term, his first elective term. In his inaugural address Truman announced his Four Points of a major program to promote world peace. The most famous became known as the Point Four section, a policy of making available to underdeveloped areas of the world American industrial and scientific knowledge. This Point Four program was sent to Congress June 24.

Feb. 7 The **Hoover Commission on Organization of the Executive Branch of the Government** issued the first part of its report, recommending streamlining of the executive branch. On Feb. 17 the commission suggested that the Post Office Department be placed beyond politics and run on a business basis. On Mar. 21 it suggested creation of a new Cabinet post, secretary of a department of national welfare and education. In its final report, on Apr. 1, the commission characterized many government enterprises as corrupt and inefficient.

Apr. 4 The **North Atlantic Treaty Organization** (NATO) was formed when the North Atlantic Treaty was signed in Washington, D.C., by representatives of Belgium, Canada, Denmark, France, Great Britain, Italy, Iceland, Luxembourg, The Netherlands, Norway, Portugal, and the U.S.

May 18 The first U.S. civilian **high commissioner of Germany** was appointed. He was John J. McCloy, president of the International Bank for Reconstruction and Development.

May 31 The perjury trial of **Alger Hiss** opened in New York City. Hiss had been indicted on Dec. 15, 1948, on two counts of perjury relating to his testimony to

The year in publishing was marked by an increasing popularity of books on religion, studies of world affairs, and books that discussed the plight of black Americans. Architects rejoiced in slightly decreased building costs, which enabled them to plan more luxury residences. The trend toward decentralization of cities afforded new opportunities to design factories, laboratories, and offices in rural areas. The League of New York Theaters instituted an investigation into the ills of the theater. Its findings recommended fairer policies toward the public in the matter of ticket distribution, pooling of production techniques, more careful advertising and promotion, and the training of theater staffs. The motion picture industry regained its momentum and enjoyed a healthy financial year.

Among **books published** this year was *The Man With the Golden Arm* by Nelson Algren, the powerful story of Frankie Machine, a Chicago poker dealer whose heroin addiction keeps him from escaping the slums and ultimately leads him to suicide. Other books published this year included *The Brave Bulls* by Tom Lea, the author's first novel; *The Waters of Siloe* by Thomas Merton, a history of the Trappist Order; *A Rage to Live* by John O'Hara, a novel; *The Greatest Story Ever Told* by Fulton Oursler; *A Guide to Confident Living* by Norman Vincent Peale; and *Peace of Soul* by Fulton J. Sheen.

New **musical compositions** this year included *Symphony No. 6* by George Antheil, *Viola Concerto* by Béla Bártok, *Symphony No. 2 for Piano and Orchestra* by Leonard Bernstein, *Concerto for Flute, Oboe, Clarinet, Bassoon, Harp, and Orchestra* by Paul Hindemith, and *Quartets No. 14 and No. 5* by Darius Milhaud.

The year's **popular songs** included "Some Enchanted Evening," "A Wonderful Guy," "Bali Ha'i," "Younger Than Springtime," "Were Thine That Special Face," "So in Love," "Just One Way to Say I Love You," and "Let's Take an Old Fashioned Walk."

Feb. 10 *Death of a Salesman* by Arthur Miller, starring Lee J. Cobb, opened at the Morosco Theatre in New York City. The drama concerned Willy Loman, a go-getter with a great smile who finds himself at the age of 63 a wrecked man with nothing left but his loyal wife. It received many awards, including the New York Drama Critics Award and the Pulitzer Prize. It also won the distinction of being the first play to become a Book-of-the-Month Club selection.

Feb. 19 The **first Bollingen Prize** for poetry was awarded to Ezra Pound for his 1948 collection *The Pisan Cantos*. The award sparked bitter controversy because Pound had been charged with treason for

1949

A record national debt of $250,000,000,000 was offset by rising national income, estimated at $222,000,000,-000. Agricultural productivity was at an all-time high. Economists noted a slight decline during the first half of the year, but pointed out that such a sag was inevitable after the inflation of 1948. Total salaries and wages reached new highs; the automotive industry sent some 6,000,000 cars and trucks off assembly lines—a new record. Unemployment increased by 1,500,000. Labor pressed for the fourth round of wage increases since the end of the war. The most significant development for labor was growing involvement in national politics. Candidates for elective office took great care to draw up platforms designed to attract the labor vote.

Jan. 3 **Closed shops** could be banned by the states, the Supreme Court ruled.

Jan. 8 A **transcontinental flight** was made by an Air Force XB-47 jet bomber in 3 hrs., 46 min., averaging 607.2 mph.

Jan. 14 An **antitrust suit** against the American Telephone and Telegraph Company was filed by the Department of Justice, which sought to separate the company from its manufacturing subsidiary, Western Electric, Inc.

Feb. 13 A **voluntary medical care plan** was supported by the American Medical Association in opposition to a compulsory health insurance plan proposed by Pres. Harry S Truman.

Feb. 25 A **flight altitude record** was set when an American guided missile, the WAC-Corporal, was launched at White Sands, N.Mex., and reached an

The two major league baseball leagues staged breathtaking shows for their fans as both pennants were clinched on the last day of the season. In golf the top money winners were Sam Snead, $31,593.83, and Mildred "Babe" Didrikson Zaharias, $4650. In boxing, Joe Louis officially retired in March. On June 22 Ezzard Charles defeated "Jersey Joe" Walcott in a 15-round decision and became the new world heavyweight champion. For a change, American men cheered Parisian fashion designers as they decreed daring decolletage for evening wear and bikini bathing suits for the beach.

Jan. 1 In **college football bowl games,** the results were Southern Methodist 21, Oregon 13 in the Cotton Bowl; Texas 41, Georgia 28 in the Orange Bowl; Northwestern 20, California 14 in the Rose Bowl; and Oklahoma 14, North Carolina 6 in the Sugar Bowl. This season the AP poll chose Michigan the national collegiate champions of 1948.

Feb. 17 At the **world figure skating championships** in Paris, France, Richard T. Button won the men's singles title.

Mar. 13 **U.S. figure skating championships** were won in Ardmore, Pa., by Yvonne Sherman, women's singles; Richard T. Button, men's singles; Karol and Peter Kennedy, pairs; Lois Waring and Walter H. Bainbridge, Jr., dance.

Mar. 26 The **NCAA basketball championship** was won by Kentucky, which defeated Oklahoma State 46–36.

Apr. 8–16 The **NHL Stanley Cup** was won for the third consecutive year by the Toronto Maple Leafs, defeating the Detroit Red Wings in a four-game sweep.

Apr. 10 The **Masters golf tournament** was won by Sam Snead.

Apr. 19 The 53rd **Boston Marathon** was won by Karl Gosta Leandersson of Sweden, with a time of 2 hrs., 31 min., 50.8 sec.

May 7 The 75th annual **Kentucky Derby** was won by Ponder, with a time of 2:04¹/₅. The jockey was Steve Brooks.

May 14 The 74th annual **Preakness Stakes** was won by Capot, with a time of 1:56. The jockey was Ted Atkinson.

May 30 The 33rd **Indianapolis 500** auto race was won by Bill Holland of Reading, Pa., completing the 500-mile course in a record time of 4 hrs., 7 min., 15.97 sec., with an average speed of 121.327 mph.

May 31 The **PGA golf tournament** was won by Sam Snead.

June 11 The **U.S. Open golf tournament** was won by Cary Middlecoff.

June 11 The 81st **Belmont Stakes** was won by Capot, with a time of 2:30¹/₅. The jockey was Ted Atkinson.

a federal grand jury on alleged espionage activities while a State Department official. Whittaker Chambers, a confessed courier for a communist spy ring, testified that Hiss had passed him official documents. Hiss denied giving Chambers any documents while at the State Department in 1937 and 1938, and denied seeing Chambers after Jan. 1, 1937. On July 8 the jury reported a deadlock and was dismissed. A new trial opened on Nov. 17.

June 29 The last **U.S. forces in Korea** were withdrawn. They had been occupying the southern portion of the peninsula since the end of World War II. Only a military mission remained.

July 21 The **North Atlantic Treaty** was ratified by the U.S. Senate by a vote of 82 to 13.

Aug. 31 The **Grand Army of the Republic,** veterans of the Civil War, held its 83rd and last encampment. It was attended by six of the 16 surviving veterans at Indianapolis, Ind.

Oct. 14 **Eleven American communist leaders were convicted** of conspiring to advocate the overthrow of the government after a long, bitter trial marked by personal attacks on the presiding federal judge, Harold Medina. All were sentenced on Oct. 21 by Judge Medina to fines of $10,000. Ten were sentenced to five years imprisonment, one to three years. Originally, 12 leaders had been indicted but the case against William Z. Foster had been separated from the others because of Foster's ill health.

Oct. 24 The permanent **UN headquarters** in New York City were dedicated.

making pro-fascist broadcasts in Italy during World War II.

Mar. 24 **Academy Awards** were presented to *Hamlet* as the outstanding motion picture of 1948 and to its star, Sir Laurence Olivier, as best actor; to Jane Wyman as best actress for *Johnny Belinda;* to Walter Huston as best supporting actor for *The Treasure of the Sierra Madre;* to his son, John Huston, as best director for *The Treasure of the Sierra Madre;* and to Claire Trevor as best supporting actress for *Key Largo.*

Apr. 7 *South Pacific,* a musical by Richard Rodgers, Oscar Hammerstein, II, and Joshua Logan, opened at the Majestic Theatre in New York City. Its cast included Mary Martin, Ezio Pinza, and Juanita Hall as Bloody Mary. Among its delightful songs were "Some Enchanted Evening" and "There Is Nothing Like a Dame."

Apr. 24 **Tony Awards** for outstanding contributions to the theater in 1948–49 were awarded to *Death of a Salesman,* play; *Kiss Me Kate,* musical; Rex Harrison for his performance in *Anne of the Thousand Days* and Martita Hunt in *The Madwoman of Chaillot.*

May 2 **Pulitzer prizes** were awarded for the following: fiction, *Guard of Honor* by James Gould Cozzens; biography, *Roosevelt and Hopkins* by Robert E. Sherwood; history, *The Disruption of American Democracy* by Roy Franklin Nichols; poetry, *Terror and Decorum* by Peter Viereck; drama, *Death of a Salesman* by Arthur Miller.

Nov. 3 The **Nobel Prize for Literature** would not be awarded in 1949, it was announced, because no candidate for the prize received a majority vote. However, in 1950 William Faulkner was awarded the 1949 prize.

altitude of 250 miles. It was the highest altitude ever achieved by a manmade projectile.

Feb. 25 The first **automotive price cuts** since the end of the war were announced by General Motors. It affected the company's entire line of cars and trucks.

Mar. 2 The first **nonstop round-the-world flight** was completed by the U.S. Air Force Superfortress *Lucky Lady II*, which touched down at Carswell Air Force Base, Tex. The airplane had been refueled in the air four times.

Mar. 11 A two-week **soft-coal miners' walkout** was ordered by John L. Lewis. The United Mine Workers took the action in protest against the appointment of Dr. James Boyd as director of the Bureau of Mines.

Apr. 20 The discovery of **cortisone** was announced. The hormone promised to bring relief to sufferers of rheumatoid arthritis, the most painful type of arthritis.

May 20 A reaffiliation bid by the **United Mine Workers** was refused by the executive council of the American Federation of Labor.

Oct. 1–Nov. 11 A nationwide **steel strike** affected some 500,000 workers. The strike was settled when steel companies agreed to workers' pension demands.

Oct. 26 A **minimum wage bill** was signed by Pres. Truman, raising the minimum wage in certain industries engaged in interstate commerce from 40 cents to 75 cents an hour.

Nov. 3 The **Nobel Prize for Chemistry** was awarded to William Francis Giauque for his work in chemical thermodynamics, specifically his studies of substances at very low temperatures. Giauque, born in Canada, was professor of chemistry at the University of Canada.

June 13 The **Baseball Hall of Fame** inducted five new members: Mordecai P. "Three Finger" Brown, pitcher; Charles I. Gehringer, second baseman; Charles A. "Kid" Nichols, pitcher; Herbert J. Pennock, pitcher; and Harold J. "Pie" Traynor, third baseman.

July 1–2 At the **Wimbledon** tennis championships in England, Ted Schroeder won the men's singles title and Louise Brough won the women's singles. Louise Brough and Margaret Osborne du Pont won the women's doubles, and Frank Parker and Richard Gonzales won the men's doubles.

July 12 The 16th annual **baseball All-Star Game** was won by the American League, which beat the National League 11–7.

Aug. 3 **Flag Day** was designated by Congress as June 14.

Aug. 28 In the **Davis Cup** international tennis challenge round, the U.S. won the final two matches from Australia to take the round 4–1 and retain the trophy.

Sept. 5 The **U.S. Lawn Tennis Association singles championships** were won for the second year in a row by Richard A. "Pancho" Gonzales in the men's division and Margaret Osborne du Pont in the women's division.

Sept. 10 The **Miss America** title was won by Jacque Mercer, 18, from Arizona, at the annual pageant in Atlantic City, N.J.

Sept. 25 The **U.S. Women's Open** golf tournament was won by Louise Suggs, who beat Mildred "Babe" Didrikson Zaharias by 14 strokes.

Oct. 5–9 The 46th annual **World Series** was won by the New York Yankees (AL), defeating the Brooklyn Dodgers (NL) four games to one.

Dec. 18 The **NFL championship** was won by the Philadelphia Eagles, who defeated the Los Angeles Rams 14–0.

1950

The nation was concerned with inflation, the threat of communism, and a foreign policy that never seemed to bring lasting peace. Profound pessimism gripped the country when in June North Korean troops crossed the 38th parallel and invaded South Korea. The action was given over to the United Nations to handle; the organization sent an international police force with orders to end the hostilities. Since no other nation could afford to enter the area in force, the U.S. embarked on a costly, unpopular war. Hatred of communist influences within the country mounted as FBI director J. Edgar Hoover announced that there were 55,000 party members and 500,000 sympathizers active within the U.S. The Senate appointed a special investigating committee to probe charges of communist activity in the State Department that had been leveled by Sen. Joseph McCarthy, Republican of Wisconsin.

The U.S. **Census** reported a population of 150,697,-361. The center of the population was placed at eight miles north-northwest of Olney, Richland County, Ill.

Jan. 2   **Foreign aid** in the form of grants and credits from July 1, 1945, to Sept. 30, 1949, amounted to $24,-802,000,000, according to a report issued by the U.S. Department of Commerce.

Jan. 21   The first chairman of a new **Civilian Mobilization Office** was appointed by Pres. Harry S Truman. He was Paul J. Larsen, whose responsibility was to streamline plans for wartime civilian defense. He began his duties on Mar. 1.

Jan. 21   **Alger Hiss was convicted** on two counts of perjury. The jury at this, his second trial on the perjury indictments, found Hiss guilty of lying to a federal grand jury. The jury was investigating allegations of espionage made by Whittaker Chambers, an avowed courier for a communist spy group. On Jan. 25 Hiss was sentenced to two concurrent five-year prison terms.

Jan. 31   Development of the **hydrogen bomb** was authorized by Pres. Truman.

June 25   The **Korean War** (1950–1953) began when North Korean forces launched an invasion across the 38th parallel into South Korea. The UN ordered an immediate cease-fire and withdrawal of invading forces.

June 27   **U.S. forces were ordered to Korea** by Pres. Truman to help South Korea repel the North Korean invasion. The president received the approval of Congress for his action, and the UN Security Council

The confusion and uncertainty of the times produced some curious results. The book *Dianetics* by L. Ron Hubbard, a science fiction writer, promulgated a new field of mental health. Architects expended their talents on shopping centers, supermarkets, motels, and outdoor movies, in response to a mass movement to suburbia. That chronic invalid, the theater, reported bad times. Production costs were so high that only smash hits could afford to pay their backers. Yet, with characteristic perversity, the Broadway stage produced some of its most interesting work in recent years. Particularly noteworthy was a renaissance of poetic drama, as witnessed by production of plays of T. S. Eliot, Christopher Fry, and Robinson Jeffers, all of which met with public acclaim.

Among **books published** this year was *World Enough and Time* by Robert Penn Warren, a novel based on an 1825 murder case known as the Kentucky tragedy. Other books published this year included *The Wall* by John Hersey, a story of the last days of the Warsaw ghetto under Nazi attack during World War II; *The Cardinal* by Henry Morton Robinson, the story of the rise of a Catholic priest; and *The Disenchanted* by Budd Schulberg, a biting novel of the struggle for success in Hollywood.

Howard Swanson, a 41-year-old black composer, attained national prominence late in the year when the New York Philharmonic Orchestra, conducted by Dmitri Mitropoulos, performed his *Short Symphony.* The work later won the Music Critics' Circle Award.

The year's **popular songs** included "Good Night, Irene," "Music! Music! Music!", "Tzena, Tzena, Tzena," "My Foolish Heart," and "Mona Lisa." Nearly every song on this list had a melody derived from some previous popular song.

The boiler plant at the **Illinois Institute of Technology,** Chicago, was built as part of an overall campus design by Ludwig Mies van der Rohe. The campus style used exposed steel frames and buff-colored brick panels on major elevations.

The **United Nations Secretariat,** designed by an international board of architects under the direction of Wallace K. Harrison, was built in New York City. It was a 39-story building with narrow end walls of white marble and wide elevations of green-tinted glass.

Construction was begun on **Lever House,** one of New York City's most impressive modern business buildings. It was completed in 1952. Designed by Skidmore, Owings, & Merrill, its main structure of glass seemed to float on a slim colonnade.

Jan. 5   *The Member of the Wedding* by Carson McCullers, based on the author's novel, opened at the Empire Theatre in New York City and quickly garnered critical acclaim and popularity among

1950

A continuing upward trend in prices led organized labor to press for higher wages and improved working conditions. The Korean War cut the number of unemployed down to 1,900,000. The average weekly earning in industry was up to $60.53, an all-time high. Having pledged the defeat of Sen. Robert A. Taft of Ohio, labor entered into the state election campaign. But this, labor's first major attempt to function as a political force, ended in dismal failure when Taft was returned to office by an overwhelming majority. Growing financial difficulties faced colleges and universities. Public schools were beset by the charge that communists had filtered into school systems and by the issue of desegregation in classrooms. Religious leaders reported a rise in church membership. The Roman Catholic Church announced a 2% gain, Protestant churches a 2.9% gain.

The phenomenal popularity of **antihistamines** for the treatment of the common cold was reflected in sales amounting to $100,000,000 despite warnings by medical authorities.

Illiteracy in the U.S. reached a new low of 3.2% of the population, a decline of 1% from 1940 and 16.8% from 1870.

Jan. 24 A minimum wage of 75 cents an hour went into effect under an amendment to the Fair Labor Standards Act. From 1950 to 1981 the federal minimum wage was increased 13 times, to $3.35 an hour. In 1967 the first minimum wage for farm workers, $1.00 an hour, went into effect.

Mar. 13 The **largest corporate income** ever reported was announced by General Motors. Net earnings in 1949 were $656,434,232.

In boxing, Ezzard Charles successfully defended the world heavyweight title against Freddie Beshore (Aug. 15), Joe Louis (Sept. 27), and Nick Barone (Dec. 5). In golf the top money winners were Sam Snead, $35,758.83, and Mildred "Babe" Didrikson Zaharias, $14,800. In fashion, designers acted with more modesty as the bikini bathing suit lost its popularity and dresses became more wearable and natural. The biggest single fashion note was the reappearance of stoles for use during the day as well as at night. The younger set wore their hair short and dressed in dungarees and ballet shoes. This latter fad may have been prompted by an outburst of activity in the dance world. American dance companies won over European audiences, and dancers from abroad toured the U.S., enjoying packed houses wherever they played.

Jan. 1 In **college football bowl games,** the results were Rice 27, North Carolina 13 in the Cotton Bowl; Santa Clara 21, Kentucky 12 in the Orange Bowl; Ohio State 17, California 14 in the Rose Bowl; and Oklahoma 35, LSU 0 in the Sugar Bowl. This season the AP poll chose Notre Dame the national collegiate champions of 1949.

Feb. 8 **Man o' War** was named the greatest horse of the first half of the century by an Associated Press poll. Known as a horse that excelled as sprinter and distance runner, he ran as a two-year-old and a three-year-old, winning 20 out of 21 starts and breaking five track records.

Mar. 7 At the **world figure skating championships** in London, England, Richard T. Button won the men's singles title for the third consecutive year.

Mar. 19 The **U.S. Women's Open golf tournament** was won by Mildred "Babe" Didrikson Zaharias.

Mar. 24 **U.S. figure skating championships** were won in Sherburne Pass, Vt., by Yvonne Sherman, women's singles; Richard T. Button, men's singles; Karol and Peter Kennedy, pairs; Lois Waring and Michael McGean, dance.

Mar. 28 The **NCAA basketball championship** was won by CCNY, defeating Bradley University 71–68.

Apr. 8–23 The **first NBA (National Basketball Association) basketball championship** was won by the Minneapolis Lakers, who beat the Syracuse Nationals four games to two.

Apr. 9 The **Masters golf tournament** was won by Jimmy Demaret.

Apr. 11–23 The **NHL Stanley Cup** was won by the Detroit Red Wings, defeating the New York Rangers four games to three.

adopted a U.S. resolution for armed intervention.

June 30 A naval blockade of the Korean coast and the use of U.S. ground forces were authorized by Pres. Truman.

July 1 The **first U.S. ground forces** landed in Korea.

July 8 Gen. **Douglas MacArthur** was named commander of UN forces in Korea.

Aug. 4 The **U.S. Army** called up 62,000 enlisted reservists for 21 months of active duty.

Sept. 8 **Emergency powers** over the entire national economy were granted to Pres. Truman under the Defense Production Act.

Sept. 15 U.S. forces landed at **Inchon,** on the west coast of Korea just south of the 38th parallel, and began a drive inland. The operation was intended to relieve South Korean and UN forces hemmed in at Pusan on the southeastern end of the Korean peninsula, and to recapture Seoul, which had fallen to North Korean forces on June 28.

Sept. 22 The **Nobel Peace Prize** was awarded to Dr. Ralph J. Bunche, director of the UN Trusteeship Division, for his work as UN mediator between Israel and the Arab states from Sept. 1948 to Apr. 1949. Dr. Bunche was the first black to win the award.

Sept. 23 The **International Security Act** of 1950 became law as Congress overrode Pres. Truman's veto by a vote of 291 to 48 in the House of Representatives and 57 to 10 in the Senate.

Sept. 26 **Seoul,** capital of South Korea, was recaptured by U.S. troops.

Sept. 29 **South Korean troops** reached the 38th parallel.

Oct. 7 U.S. forces invaded **North Korea** across the 38th parallel.

Nov. 6 **Chinese Communist troops** were reported in action along with North Korean forces by Gen. Douglas MacArthur.

Nov. 7 In **congressional elections** the Democrats lost five Senate seats but retained a 49–47 majority. In the House they lost 29 seats but kept a majority of 234–199, with one seat going to a minor party.

Nov. 20 U.S. troops reached the **Yalu** R. on the Manchurian border.

Nov. 29 U.S. forces **retreated** under heavy attack from Chinese Communist units.

theatergoers. The author's first play, it was marked by exceptional performances by Julie Harris, Ethel Waters, and young Brandon DeWilde.

Jan. 28 **Emmy Awards** of the Academy of Television Arts and Sciences were presented at the academy's second annual awards dinner: most outstanding kinescope personality, Milton Berle; best kinescope show, *Texaco Star Theatre;* best children's show, *Time for Beanie;* best film made for TV in 1949, *Life of Riley.*

Mar. 1 The premiere performance of *The Consul,* an opera by Gian-Carlo Menotti, was given at the Shubert Theatre in Philadelphia. On Mar. 15 the Broadway run began at the Ethel Barrymore Theater.

Mar. 16 The **first annual National Book Awards** were awarded for the following: fiction, *The Man With the Golden Arm* by Nelson Algren; poetry, William Carlos Williams for his *Paterson* poems; biography, *The Life of Ralph Waldo Emerson* by Dr. Ralph L. Rusk.

Mar. 23 **Academy Awards** were presented to *All the King's Men* as the outstanding motion picture of 1949 and to its star, Broderick Crawford, as best actor; to Olivia de Havilland as best actress for *The Heiress;* to Dean Jagger as best supporting actor for *Twelve O'Clock High;* and to Mercedes McCambridge as best supporting actress for *All the King's Men.*

Mar. 27 The **Bollingen Prize** for poetry was awarded to Wallace Stevens.

Apr. 9 **Tony Awards** for outstanding contributions to the theater during the 1948–1949 season were presented to the following: *The Cocktail Party* by T. S. Eliot; *South Pacific* by Richard Rodgers, Oscar Hammerstein II, and Joshua Logan (it won eight awards in various categories); Sidney Blackmer and Shirley Booth for their performances in *Come Back, Little Sheba.*

May 1 **Pulitzer prizes** were awarded for the following: fiction, *The Way West* by A. B. Guthrie; biography, *John Quincy Adams and the Foundations of American Foreign Policy* by Samuel Flagg Bemis; history, *Art and Life in America* by Oliver W. Larkin; poetry, *Annie Allen* by Gwendolyn Brooks; drama, *South Pacific* by Richard Rodgers, Oscar Hammerstein II and Joshua Logan.

Oct. 11 A license to begin **color television broadcasting** was issued by the FCC to the Columbia Broadcasting System, effective Nov. 20. This touched off an industry-wide controversy. RCA charged that CBS's device was not the best. On Nov. 15 a temporary restraining order was issued by the Chicago Federal District Court.

Nov. 10 The **Nobel Prize in Literature** for 1949 was awarded to William Faulkner at the 1950 awards ceremony in Oslo, Norway. The prize had not been awarded in 1949 because none of the candidates had won a majority of votes.

Mar. 17 Discovery of a **new element, californium,** was announced by the University of California, Berkeley. This element, the heaviest yet known, was discovered in experiments with the cyclotron, which also yielded another element, berkelium. They were numbered 98 and 97 respectively.

Mar. 23 **Wages** were up 130% from 1939 according to a U.S. Labor Department report. However, buying power increased only 35%.

May 11 **Grand Coulee Dam** in Washington was dedicated by Pres. Harry S Truman. The dam, on the Columbia R. northwest of Spokane, Wash., was 550 feet high and 4173 feet long. It contained the waters of Franklin D. Roosevelt Lake, one of the largest reservoirs in the U.S. Construction of the dam had begun in 1932 and the dam had gone into operation in 1942. It provided hydroelectric power, flood control, and irrigation for more than 1,000,000 acres of farmland.

May 25 The **longest vehicular tunnel** in the U.S., the Brooklyn-Battery Tunnel in New York City, was opened to traffic. Still the longest tunnel for automotive use, it has been surpassed in length by the 3.6-mile Bay Area Rapid Transit (BART) tubes under San Francisco Bay.

Aug. 25 The **Army seized the railroads** by order of Pres. Truman to prevent a strike of trainmen and yardmen called for Aug. 28. Truman acted under a 1916 war emergency measure. The strike was called off.

Oct. 26 The **Nobel Prize in Physiology or Medicine** was awarded jointly to Philip Showalter Hench of the Mayo Clinic; Edward Calvin Kendall, head of the Department of Biochemistry, Mayo Foundation, University of Minnesota; and Tadeus Reichstein of the

Apr. 19 The 54th **Boston Marathon** was won by Ham Kee Yong, 19, of Seoul, Korea, with a time of 2 hrs., 32 min., 39 sec. He was the youngest runner ever to win the event.

May 6 The 76th annual **Kentucky Derby** was won by Middleground, with a time of 2:01³/₅, missing the Derby record by a fifth of a second. The jockey was Bill Boland.

May 20 The 75th annual **Preakness Stakes** was won by Hill Prince, with a time of 1:59¹/₅. The jockey was Eddie Arcaro.

May 31 The 34th **Indianapolis 500** auto race was won by Johnny Parsons of Van Nuys, Calif., completing the course (shortened to 345-mi. because of rain) in 2 hrs., 46 min., 55.97 sec., with an average speed of 124 mph.

June 10 The 82nd annual **Belmont Stakes** was won by Middleground, with a time of 2:28³/₅. The jockey was Bill Boland.

June 10 The **U.S. Open golf tournament** ended regular play with a three-way tie among Ben Hogan, Lloyd Mangrum, and George Fazio. On June 11 Hogan, in a spectacular comeback after an auto accident in 1949, won an 18-hole playoff round, beating Mangrum by four strokes and Fazio by six strokes.

June 27 The **PGA golf tournament** was won by Chandler Harper.

July 7 At the **Wimbledon** tennis championships in England, the men's singles title was won by V. Edward "Budge" Patty. The next day Louise Brough won the women's singles. Louise Brough and Margaret Osborne du Pont won the women's doubles and Brough teamed with Eric Sturgess of South Africa to win the mixed doubles.

July 11 The 17th annual **baseball All-Star Game** was won by the National League, defeating the American League 4–3 on homers by Ralph Kiner and Red Schoendienst.

Aug. 26 In the **Davis Cup** international tennis challenge round, the Australian team won its third straight match from the U.S., thereby ensuring victory. The Australians went on to win the round 4–1.

Sept. 5 The **U.S. Lawn Tennis Association singles championships** were won by Arthur Larsen in the men's division and Margaret Osborne du Pont in the women's division.

Sept. 9 The **Miss America** title was won by Yolande Betbeze, 21, from Alabama, at the annual pageant in Atlantic City, N.J. This title was for the coming year, 1951. Previous titles had been for the year during which the award was made. Consequently, there was

Dec. 16 A state of national emergency was declared by Pres. Truman. Charles E. Wilson was appointed director of defense mobilization.

Dec. 19 Gen. **Dwight D. Eisenhower** was appointed supreme commander of the Western European defense forces by the North Atlantic Council.

Nov. 10 *The Country Girl,* a play by Clifford Odets about the struggle of a man trying to make a comeback with the help of his wife, opened at the Lyceum Theatre in New York City.

Nov. 16 *Clarinet Concerto* by **Aaron Copland** was given its first performance by Benny Goodman and the NBC Symphony Orchestra.

1951

The world hovered close to the brink of a third world war. Chinese Communist troops had unofficially entered the Korean campaign, operating from bases above the Yalu R. Gen. Douglas MacArthur advocated attacks on strategic positions within Chinese territory, a move that would be tantamount to declaring war on China, which had a military alliance with the U.S.S.R. American casualties had reached 100,000 and tempers at home were getting short. With this crisis before them, government leaders framed a foreign policy emphasizing preparation for war. A huge increase in taxes was asked, universal military training was urged, and a ring of bases around the U.S.S.R. was suggested. General war was averted when the administration stood with the UN on the decision not to attack Chinese bases.

Jan. 1 **Chinese Communist troops** in Korea broke through the defense perimeter around Seoul and took Inchon and Kimpo airfield. Seoul was abandoned three days later.

Jan. 15 The **federal budget** for fiscal 1952 was estimated as follows: revenues, \$55,138,000,000; expenditures, \$71,594,000,000, of which \$41,421,000,000 was allocated for military purposes.

Feb. 1 **Communist China** was formally accused of aggression in Korea by the UN.

Feb. 26 The **Twenty-second Amendment** to the U.S. Constitution was adopted. It stipulated that no person may be elected to the presidency for more than two terms. A vice president succeeding to the presidency and serving more than half the term of his predecessor would be eligible for only one more term.

Mar. 14 **Seoul** was recaptured by U.S. forces. This was the second time the South Korean capital was recaptured by UN forces. The reoccupation of Seoul marked a strategic and psychological victory over the enemy forces, whose lines had been broken and who

Some 11,000 book titles were published this year. The phenomenal sale of paperback books led many publishers to launch a series of these editions. Architects were forced to concentrate on industrial and defense work, although some work was accomplished in the design of school buildings. Painters continued to work in abstractions, and American regionalism all but vanished from contemporary exhibitions. After a brief season of experimentation, the theater returned to the tried-and-true musical.

Among **books published** this year was *Requiem for a Nun* by William Faulkner, a novel written partly in the form of a play. The novel continued the story of Temple Drake, central character in Faulkner's 1931 novel *Sanctuary.* Other books published this year included *The Morning Watch* by James Agee, the author's first novel; *The Grass Harp* by Truman Capote, a novel; *The Sea Around Us* by Rachel Carson; *Mr. Lincoln's Army* by Bruce Catton; *Barbary Shore* by Norman Mailer, a novel; *Lie Down in Darkness,* a first novel by William Styron; and *The Caine Mutiny* by Herman Wouk, a novel.

A survey showed 659 **symphonic groups** in the U.S., including 32 professional orchestras, 343 community, 231 college, and various amateur organizations. More than 1500 U.S. cities and towns supported concert series during the year.

The rise of the U.S. **record industry** was indicated by the sale of some 190,000,000 records during the year.

Friedman House, designed by **Frank Lloyd Wright,** was built at Pleasantville, N.Y. Based on a circular pattern of rough stone, it was a marked departure from stereotyped ideas of modern architecture.

One of the best buildings by European-born **Marcel Breuer,** the dormitory at Vassar College, was built in Poughkeepsie, N.Y. Its design showed the influence of Breuer's Bauhaus association.

Some 231,000,000 **paperback reprints** were sold this year by U.S. book publishers.

This year's **popular songs** included "Too Young," "Hello Young Lovers," and "Getting to Know You," the last two from the musical *The King and I.*

Business and Industry; Science;	**III**		**Sports; Social Issues and Crime;**
Education; Philosophy and Religion		**IV**	**Folkways; Fashion; Holidays**

University of Basel, Switzerland, for their research into the nature of suprarenal cortex hormones and the use of cortisone.

no Miss America for 1950.

Oct. 4–7 The 47th annual **World Series** was won by the New York Yankees (AL), defeating the Philadelphia Phillies (NL) in four straight games.

Dec. 24 The **NFL championship** was won by the Cleveland Browns, who defeated the Los Angeles Rams 30–28.

1951

Employment of women in American industry reached its highest point in history, even higher than during World War II. Wages were up, but so were prices; total employment figures were robust. Alarmed over the growing inflation, the administration tried to institute a program of production controls. Two hundred thousand consumer items were placed under price controls, but attempts to freeze all prices and wages failed. Sen. Estes Kefauver of Tennessee, chairman of a Senate committee on organized crime in interstate commerce, opened hearings to television cameras. For weeks the nation watched as underworld figures testified—or refused to do so—before the committee. In education, universities and colleges saw a sharp drop in enrollment.

There were more than 12,000 **trade associations** in the U.S.—so many that in Chicago managers gathered to form a trade association of managers of trade associations.

Jan. 15 A 30-day ban on **commercial construction** was ordered by the National Production Authority to conserve materials for the defense mobilization program. The ban was to take effect on Feb. 15.

Jan. 16 The **margin requirement** for stock purchasing was raised from 50% to 75% by the Federal Reserve System Board of Governors.

Feb. 28 **Organized labor** withdrew representatives from all government defense agencies in protest against administration mobilization policies. Subsequently, organized labor gained representation on the National Advisory Board on Mobilization Policy. A new Wage Stabilization Board was established on Apr. 17, with power to settle all labor disputes threatening national defense. On Apr. 30 the boycott of defense agencies was lifted.

Apr. 28 **Beef price ceilings** were set by the Office of Price Stabilization.

The baseball season gave fans the ultimate home run thrill. The Brooklyn Dodgers and New York Giants battled their way to a tie for the National League pennant. Each team had won one of the playoff games. Brooklyn led in the third and deciding contest 4–1, going into the ninth inning. New York managed one run and then two men got on base. Finally, at the last moment, Bobby Thomson, the Giants' third baseman, slammed a home run off a pitch of Ralph Branca that decided the game and the season. In golf the top money winners were Lloyd Mangrum, $26,088.83, and Mildred "Babe" Didrikson Zaharias (for the fourth year in a row), $15,087.

Jan. 1 In **college football bowl games,** the results were Tennessee 20, Texas 14 in the Cotton Bowl; Clemson 15, Miami, Florida, 14 in the Orange Bowl; Michigan 14, California 6 in the Rose Bowl; and Kentucky 13, Oklahoma 7 in the Sugar Bowl. This season a UPI poll of football coaches selected Oklahoma the national collegiate champions of 1950, as did the annual AP poll.

Feb. 2–4 **U.S. figure skating championships** were won in Seattle, Wash., by Richard T. Button, men's singles (his sixth consecutive win); Sonya Klopfer, women's singles; Karol and Peter Kennedy, pairs; Carmel and Edward L. Bodel, dance.

Feb. 3 The **largest purse** to date in horse racing, $144,323, was won by Great Circle in the Santa Anita Maturity at Santa Anita Park, Arcadia, Calif. The jockey was Willie Shoemaker.

Feb. 25–Mar. 9 The **first Pan-American Games** were held in Buenos Aires, Argentina. The U.S. finished second in unofficial team score, behind Argentina.

Feb. 26 At the **world figure skating championships** in Milan, Italy, Richard T. Button won the men's singles title for the fourth consecutive year.

Mar. 27 The **NCAA basketball championship** was won by Kentucky, which defeated Kansas State 68–58.

Apr. 7 The **Masters golf tournament** was won by Ben Hogan, who beat Robert Riegel by two strokes.

were steadily being forced north, back over the 38th parallel and into North Korea.

Mar. 21 U.S. armed forces numbered 2,900,000 according to Defense Sec. George C. Marshall. This was double the strength of U.S. armed forces at the outbreak of the Korean War (1950–1953).

Apr. 4 SHAPE (Supreme Headquarters, Allied Powers in Europe) was established in Paris. Gen. Dwight D. Eisenhower assumed command.

Apr. 11 Gen. **Douglas MacArthur was relieved** of all commands by Pres. Harry S Truman. His posts as supreme commander, Allied powers; commander in chief, UN command; commander in chief, Far East; and commanding general, U.S. Army, Far East were all filled by Lt. Gen. Matthew Ridgway.

Apr. 19 Gen. **Douglas MacArthur** addressed a joint session of Congress, defending his Korean policies and beliefs and declaring his military career to be at its end. Recalling words of a ballad, "Old soldiers never die, they just fade away," MacArthur stated: "I now close my military career and just fade away, an old soldier who tried to do his duty as God gave him the light to see that duty."

June 19 **Selective Service** was extended to July 1, 1955. The bill of authorization also lowered the draft age to 18½, lengthened the time of service to two years, and established universal military training.

June 23 A **cease-fire in Korea** was proposed by Jacob Malik, Soviet delegate to the UN, who called for withdrawal of troops from the 38th parallel. On June 30 Gen. Matthew Ridgway sent North Korea a proposal to negotiate a cease-fire agreement. Kim Il Sung, the North Korean commander, and Gen. Peng Teh-huai, the Chinese commander, agreed the next day to meet UN representatives to discuss cease-fire proposals.

July 10 The **first Korean truce talks** were held between UN and Korean representatives at Kaesong, on the 38th parallel in North Korea.

July 11–25 The costliest **flood** to date in U.S. history occurred when the Missouri R. and its tributaries flooded more than 1,000,000 acres of farmland in Kansas, Oklahoma, Missouri, and Illinois. Kansas City suffered particularly severe damage on July 14. Property loss was estimated at more than $1,000,000,000.

Sept. 8 A **peace treaty with Japan** was signed in San Francisco by delegates of 48 nations. The U.S.S.R.,

Designed by **Ludwig Mies van der Rohe,** the Lake Shore Drive Apartments, two 26-story buildings, were built in Chicago. Both buildings were walled entirely in glass.

Jan. 13 *Darkness at Noon,* a play by Sidney Kingsley based on the novel by Arthur Koestler, opened at the Alvin Theatre in New York City. Its cast included Claude Rains, Alexander Scourby, and Kim Hunter.

Jan. 23 **Emmy Awards** were presented to the following: best actor, Alan Young; best actress, Gertrude Berg; most outstanding personality, Groucho Marx; best dramatic show, *Pulitzer Prize Playhouse;* best variety show, *The Alan Young Show.*

Feb. 3 *The Rose Tattoo* by Tennessee Williams opened at the Martin Beck Theatre in New York City. The cast included Maureen Stapleton and Eli Wallach.

Feb. 10 *Billy Budd,* a play adapted from Herman Melville's novelette by Louis O. Coxe and Robert Chapman, opened at the Biltmore Theatre in New York City.

Mar. 6 **National Book Awards** were awarded for the following: fiction, *The Collected Stories of William Faulkner;* poetry, *The Auroras of Autumn* by Wallace Stevens; biography, *Herman Melville* by Newton Arvin.

Mar. 25 **Tony Awards** for outstanding contributions to the theater during the 1950–1951 season were presented for the following; play, *The Rose Tattoo* by Tennessee Williams; musical, *Guys and Dolls* by Abe Burrows, Frank Loesser, and Jo Swerling (it won nine awards in various categories); Claude Rains for his performance in *Darkness at Noon;* and Uta Hagen for her performance in *The Country Girl.*

Mar. 28 *Giants in the Earth,* an opera by Douglas Moore, was given its premiere performance by the Columbia University Opera Workshop in New York City. Based on the 1927 novel by Ole Rölvaag, the opera told the story of Norwegian settlers in the Dakota Territory.

Mar. 29 *The King and I* opened at the St. James Theatre in New York City. The musical, by Richard Rodgers and Oscar Hammerstein, II, was based on the novel *Anna and the King of Siam* by Margaret Landon. It starred Yul Brynner as the king and Gertrude Lawrence as Anna.

Mar. 29 **Academy Awards** were presented to *All About Eve* as the outstanding motion picture of 1950; to José Ferrer as best actor for *Cyrano de Bergerac;* to Judy Holliday as best actress for *Born Yesterday;* to George Sanders as best supporting actor for *All About Eve;* and to Josephine Hull as best supporting actress for *Harvey.*

| Business and Industry; Science;
Education; Philosophy and Religion | III | | IV | Sports; Social Issues and Crime;
Folkways; Fashion; Holidays |

May 15 The **American Telephone and Telegraph Company** reported that it was the first corporation to have more than 1,000,000 stockholders.

June 14 **UNIVAC,** an electronic digital computer designed by Dr. John W. Mauchly and J. Presper Eckert, Jr., and the first such computer built for commercial purposes, was dedicated and demonstrated in Philadelphia, Pa. Mauchly and Eckert had developed ENIAC, the world's first electronic digital computer, in the 1940s, then set up their own company to develop computers for business and industry. They ran into financial difficulties, and their operation was ultimately taken over by Remington Rand.

June 25 The **first commercial color TV broadcast** was presented by the Columbia Broadcasting System, which had spent $5,000,000 over 11 years to develop the required new technology. The four-hour program was carried by stations in New York City, Baltimore, Boston, Philadelphia, and Washington, D.C. Unfortunately, no color TV sets were owned by the public. CBS itself had only 30 or 40 color receivers, and most of these were used for technical or monitoring purposes. It would be months before the first color sets would become available for purchase.

July 11 Released time for **religious studies** for schoolchildren in New York State was upheld by the New York State Court of Appeals. It was upheld again by the U.S. Supreme Court on Apr. 28, 1952.

Sept. 4 The **first transcontinental television broadcast** reported Pres. Truman's opening address to the delegates of the Japanese Peace Treaty Conference in San Francisco, Calif. The broadcast was carried by 94 stations.

Oct. 18 The **Nobel Prize in Physiology or Medicine** was awarded to Dr. Max Theiler of the International Health Division of the Rockefeller Institute for development of vaccine 17-D to combat yellow fever.

Nov. 5 The first section of the **New Jersey Turnpike,** a 51-mile stretch from Bordentown to Deepwater, N.J., was opened to traffic. On Nov. 30 the still incomplete toll road was dedicated by Gov. Alfred E. Driscoll, who opened a 40-mile section between Woodbridge and Bordentown.

Nov. 10 The first transcontinental **direct dial telephone service** was inaugurated when Englewood, N.J., mayor M. Leslie Denning called Alameda, Calif.,

Apr. 7–21 The **NBA basketball championship** was won by the Rochester Royals, who beat the New York Knickerbockers 79–75.

Apr. 11–21 The **NHL Stanley Cup** was won by the Toronto Maple Leafs, who defeated the Montreal Canadiens four games to one.

Apr. 19 The 55th **Boston Marathon** was won by Shigeki Tanaka, 19, from Japan, with a time of 2 hrs., 27 min., 45 sec.

May 5 The 77th annual **Kentucky Derby** was won by Count Turf, with a time of 2:02³/₅. The jockey was Conn McCreary, who gained his second Derby win.

May 19 The 76th annual **Preakness Stakes** was won by Bold, with a time of 1:56²/₅. The jockey was Eddie Arcaro, who scored his fourth Preakness win.

May 30 The 45th **Indianapolis 500** auto race was won by Lee Wallard of Altamont, N.Y., completing the 500-mile course in a record 3 hrs., 57 min., 38.05 sec., with an average speed of 126.244 mph.

June 16 The **U.S. Open golf tournament** was won for the second year in a row by Ben Hogan.

June 16 The 83rd annual **Belmont Stakes** was won by Counterpoint, with a time of 2:29. The jockey was David Gorman.

July 3 The **PGA golf tournament** was won by Sam Snead. It was his third PGA victory.

July 6–7 At the **Wimbledon** tennis championships in England, Dick Savitt won the men's singles title and Doris Hart won the women's singles. Hart and Shirley Fry won the women's singles.

July 10 The 18th annual **baseball All-Star Game** was won by the National League, who defeated the American League 8–3.

July 18 The **world heavyweight boxing championship** was won by "Jersey Joe" Walcott, who knocked out Ezzard Charles in the seventh round at Pittsburgh, Pa. At 37 Walcott was the oldest person to gain the title.

July 23 The **Baseball Hall of Fame** inducted James E. "Jimmy" Foxx, first baseman, who had a career slugging average of .609, and Melvin T. "Mel" Ott, longtime star outfielder for the New York Giants.

Sept. 4 The **U.S. Lawn Tennis Association singles championships** were won by Frank Sedgman of Australia in the men's division and 16-year-old Maureen Connolly of San Diego, Calif., in the women's division. Sedgman was the first Australian to win the men's title.

Poland, and Czechoslovakia did not sign.

Oct. 10 The **Mutual Security Act of 1951** was signed by Pres. Truman. It authorized $7,483,400,000 in U.S. foreign economic, military, and technical aid, and established a Mutual Security Agency. W. Averell Harriman was named head of the agency on the following day.

Oct. 24 The **state of war with Germany** was declared officially ended by Pres. Truman.

Nov. 13–15 The **Prohibition Party** nominated Stuart Hamblen of California for the presidency and Enoch A. Holtwick of Illinois for the vice presidency.

May 7 **Pulitzer prizes** were awarded for the following: fiction, *The Town* by Conrad Richter; biography, *John C. Calhoun: American Portrait* by Margaret Louise Coit; history, *The Old Northwest, Pioneer Period 1815–1840, Volumes I–II* by R. Carlyle Buley; poetry, *Complete Poems* by Carl Sandburg.

Nov. 28 *I Am a Camera,* a play by John Van Druten based on sketches by Christopher Isherwood collected in *Goodbye to Berlin* (1939), opened at the Empire Theatre in New York City. The cast included Julie Harris.

Dec. 24 *Amahl and the Night Visitors,* an opera by Gian-Carlo Menotti commissioned by the National Broadcasting Company, was broadcast on TV on Christmas Eve. It was suggested by the painting *The Adoration of the Magi* by Hieronymus Bosch.

1952

Early in the year British Prime Minister Winston Churchill visited the U.S. to reestablish close ties between Great Britain and the U.S. and to formulate unified policy on problems facing the West. The leading problem was the spreading danger of communist domination. U.S. policy was to arm western Europe and make it too costly for the U.S.S.R. to start a war. Opponents of this U.S.-British alliance included former Pres. Herbert Hoover, who claimed the U.S. was carrying Europe at disastrous expense. A far better plan, he maintained, was to retire to the Western Hemisphere and build a "bastion of liberty." Although 1952 was an election year, this issue was never a serious part of the campaign since the two major candidates, Adlai E. Stevenson and Dwight D. Eisenhower, supported the NATO alliance. While both Stevenson and Eisenhower enjoyed enormous popularity, the Democrats suffered from charges of corruption in the administration of Pres. Harry S Truman. Eisenhower's eventual victory was interpreted by many as a rebuke to the Truman administration. In spite of truce negotiations in Korea, some ground and air action continued; it intensified in October when truce talks were temporarily postponed.

Jan. 24 **Korean truce talks were deadlocked,** according to a statement issued by UN headquarters in Tokyo.

Mar. 8 Charges of **germ warfare** were formally lodged against the U.S. by Chinese Foreign Minister Chou En-lai. The charges, reported by Radio Peking, were supported by the Soviet representative to the UN, Jacob A. Malik. An offer by the International Red

A building boom spurred architects to design with distinction, using new types of construction, notably employing prestressed concrete. The year saw much travel by musical organizations both in the U.S. and abroad. The Boston Symphony made its first European tour. George Gershwin's *Porgy and Bess* played to enthusiastic houses in Berlin, Vienna, and London. The most noticeable trend was a growing acceptance of so-called modern works. Igor Stravinsky, for instance, was slowly achieving full acceptance as a composer. In painting, a movement away from abstractionism toward representationalism was noted. This year's Broadway offerings were so lackluster that George Jean Nathan refused to issue his annual volume reviewing the season.

Among **books published** this year was *Invisible Man* by Ralph Ellison, a powerful novel about the struggle of a young black to find a sense of personal worth as a human being. The novel followed the young man as he moved from southern town to university to Harlem, from innocence to bitter pessimism. Other books published this year included *The Old Man and the Sea* by Ernest Hemingway, a short novel relating the symbolic tale of an old Caribbean fisherman struggling to catch a giant marlin; *Collected Poems 1917–1952* by Archibald MacLeish; and *East of Eden* by John Steinbeck, the author's longest novel, a panoramic story of a California family from the late nineteenth century through World War I.

The year's **popular songs** included "Cry," "Kiss of Fire," "Wish You Were Here," "I Went to Your Wedding," "Domino," and "Wheel of Fortune."

mayor Frank P. Osborn. The call marked the beginning of a test program involving some 10,000 customers of the New Jersey Bell system.

Nov. 15 The **Nobel Prize in Chemistry** was awarded jointly to Dr. Edwin M. McMillan and Dr. Glenn T. Seaborg of the University of California for their research in transuranic elements. They were the eighth and ninth Americans to win the Nobel Prize in Chemistry.

Dec. 20 The **first atomic-powered generator** began producing electricity at the U.S. Reactor Testing Station in Idaho.

Sept. 8 The **Miss America** title was won by Colleen Kay Hutchins, 25, from Utah, at the annual pageant in Atlantic City, N.J.

Sept. 16 The **U.S. Women's Open** golf tournament was won by Betsy Rawls.

Oct. 4–10 The 48th annual **World Series** was won by the New York Yankees (AL), who defeated the New York Giants (NL) four games to two. The Giants had won the National League pennant by beating the Brooklyn Dodgers two games to one in a spectacular ninth inning recovery in the third game of the league playoff.

Dec. 23 The **NFL championship** was won by the Los Angeles Rams, who defeated the Cleveland Browns 24–17.

1952

Inflation was now a reality. Employment had reached a record high of 62,500,000. Prices continued to zoom. The U.S. Treasury recorded a deficit of $4,000,000,000. A major development on the labor front was the three-way struggle involving the steel industry, the Steelworkers of America (C.I.O.), and the U.S. president. When the union prepared to walk out for wage hikes, Pres. Truman seized the mills on the grounds that steel was vital to U.S. defense. Management retaliated by securing an injunction against the seizure; a federal district court then pronounced the president's action unconstitutional, a ruling upheld by the Supreme Court. This sent steelworkers out on what developed into a 54-day strike. Pres. Truman asked Congress for legislation permitting seizure of vital industries, but the Senate advised him to use the provisions of the Taft-Hartley law. Instead, he called both sides to the White House, where they settled the dispute in a conference.

Mar. 2 Those considered **subversives could be barred from teaching** in public schools, according to a U.S. Supreme Court decision.

Mar. 6 **Foreign military and economic aid** during the fiscal year was estimated at $7,900,000,000 by Pres. Truman.

Apr. 8 The nation's **steel mills were seized** by presidential order to prevent a shutdown by strikers. The next day three major steel companies instituted legal action in federal court, Washington, D.C., to contest

This was a year of flying saucers, panty raids, and prison riots. Unidentified flying objects, frequently described as luminous disks or saucers, were reported flashing across night skies all over the nation. The Air Force even published photographs of the phenomena. There was widespread conjecture that these objects were manned by emissaries from outer space. While the nation watched the night skies, college boys across the country seemed intent on besieging sorority houses and girls' dormitories demanding as ransom articles of feminine underclothing, which were freely bestowed. Disturbances of a more serious nature plagued prison officials. Inmates pressing for more liberal treatment took guards as hostages while they bargained with prison authorities. These riots led to a review of state and federal prison systems.

Jan. 1 In **collegiate football bowl games,** the results were Kentucky 20, TCU 7 in the Cotton Bowl; Georgia Tech 17, Baylor 14 in the Orange Bowl; Illinois 40, Stanford 7 in the Rose Bowl; and Maryland 28, Tennessee 13 in the Sugar Bowl. This season the AP poll chose Tennessee the national collegiate champions of 1951, as did the UPI poll.

Feb. 15–25 At the **Winter Olympics** in Oslo, Norway, the U.S. won four gold medals and finished second in unofficial team standings .

Feb. 29 At the **world figure skating championships** in Paris, France, Richard T. Button won the men's singles title for the fifth consecutive year.

Mar. 26 The **NCAA basketball championship** was won by Kansas, which defeated St. John's 80–63.

Mar. 28 **U.S. figure skating championships** were won in Colorado Springs, Colo., by Richard T. Button, men's singles (his seventh consecutive win); Tenley Albright, women's singles; Karol and Peter Kennedy,

Cross to investigate was rejected by Malik, and on Mar. 28 the UN ruled Malik's charges out of order.

Mar. 20 The **Japanese Peace Treaty** was ratified by the U.S. Senate by a vote of 66–10.

May 30–June 1 The **Socialist Party** nominated Darlington Hoopes of Pennsylvania for the presidency and Samuel H. Friedman of New York for the vice presidency.

June 25 The **McCarran-Walter Bill** to revise and limit immigration was vetoed by Pres. Truman as un-American and discriminatory. The following day the House of Representatives overrode the veto 278–113. The Senate took similar action on June 27 by a vote of 57–26. The law abolished racial restrictions on immigration and retained a quota system based on the national origins count of 1920.

July 4–6 The **Progressive Party** nominated Vincent Hallinan of California for the presidency and Charlotta A. Bass of New York for the vice presidency.

July 11 The **Republican National Convention** nominated Gen. **Dwight D. Eisenhower** for the presidency. Sen. Richard M. Nixon of California was nominated for the vice presidency.

July 16 A **G.I. Bill of Rights** was signed by Pres. Truman. It offered Korean veterans with 90 days of service as of June 27, 1950, rights and benefits similar to those granted to veterans of World War II.

July 26 The **Democratic National Convention** nominated Gov. **Adlai E. Stevenson** of Illinois for the presidency and Sen. John J. Sparkman of Alabama for the vice presidency.

Oct. 24 Gen. **Eisenhower vowed to go to Korea** to seek an early and honorable conclusion to the conflict there if elected to the presidency. Eisenhower spoke in Detroit, Mich., on the last stop of his whistle-stop campaign tour.

Nov. 4 Dwight D. **Eisenhower was elected president** of the United States. Sen. Richard M. Nixon of California was elected vice president. The electoral vote was Eisenhower, 442, Gov. Adlai E. Stevenson, Democrat,

Serious **musical works** that received their premieres this year included *Trouble in Tahiti* by Leonard Bernstein, at Brandeis University in Waltham, Mass.; *Acres of Sky* by Arthur Kreutz, in New York City; and *The Farmer and the Fairy* by Alexandre Tcherepnin, in Aspen, Colo. Other new works heard this year were *Symphonie Concertante* by Gail Kubik, which was awarded the Pulitzer Prize for music; *Symphony No. Four* by Paul Creston; *Piano Concerto* by Axel Haieff; *Symphony No. Seven* by Roy Harris; and *Temptation of St. Anthony,* a dance-symphony by Gardner Read.

The **Alcoa Building,** in Pittsburgh, Pa., was built from plans by the firm of Harrison & Abramovitz. The entire 30-story tower was sheathed with 6x12 ft. prefabricated aluminum panels.

Jan. 15 *The Shrike,* a first play of Joseph Kramm, produced and directed by José Ferrer, opened at the Cort Theatre in New York City.

Jan. 29 The **National Book Awards** were presented for the following: fiction, *From Here to Eternity* by James Jones; nonfiction, *The Sea Around Us* by Rachel Carson; poetry, *Collected Poems* by Marianne Moore.

Feb. 13 *Venus Observed* by Christopher Fry, staged by Sir Laurence Olivier and starring Rex Harrison and Lilli Palmer, opened at the Century Theatre in New York City.

Feb. 18 **Emmy Awards** were presented to *Studio One* as best dramatic show; *Red Skelton* as best comedy show, and Red Skelton as best comedian; *Your Show of Shows* as best variety show; Sid Caesar as best actor; Imogene Coca as best actress.

Mar. 20 **Academy Awards** were presented to *An American in Paris* as the outstanding motion picture of 1951; to Humphrey Bogart as best actor for *The African Queen;* to Vivien Leigh as best actress for *A Streetcar Named Desire;* and to Karl Malden and Kim Hunter as best supporting actor and actress for *A Streetcar Named Desire.*

Mar. 27 *The Grass Harp,* a first play by Truman Capote, based on the author's novel of the same title,

the seizure. They were denied a temporary restraining order.

Apr. 29 The **seizure of steel mills** was declared unconstitutional by U.S. District Judge David A. Pine. Steelworkers immediately went on strike.

May 2 The **steel strike was ended** by the steelworkers' union at presidential request.

May 8 Development of a **75-ton atomic cannon** was announced by Army Sec. Frank C. Pace.

June 2 Presidential **seizure of steel mills** was declared unconstitutional by the U.S. Supreme Court. Pres. Truman ordered the plants returned to their owners, and the steelworkers resumed their strike.

June 14 The keel of the **first atomic submarine**, the *Nautilus*, was dedicated at Groton, Conn.

June 28 **Wage and rent controls** and priority and material allocations were extended by Congress.

June 30 **American stockholders** numbered some 6,500,000. Of these, 76% earned less than $10,000 a year after taxes, according to a report made by the Brookings Institute.

July 7 A new **transatlantic speed record** for ships was set by the S.S. *United States* on its first round trip with an eastward crossing of 3 days, 10 hrs., 40 min. On July 14 it set a westward crossing record of 3 days, 12 hrs., 12 min.

July 14 **Price controls** were removed from most fresh and processed meats and vegetables.

July 24 The **steel strike was settled** when management and labor reached a compromise agreement at a White House conference called by Pres. Truman.

Oct. 23 The **Nobel Prize in Physiology or Medicine** was awarded to Dr. Selman A. Waksman of Rutgers University for his discovery, with others, of streptomycin.

pairs (their fifth consecutive win); Lois Waring and Michael McGean, dance.

Apr. 6 The **Masters golf tournament** was won by Sam Snead.

Apr. 10–15 The **NHL Stanley Cup** was won by the Detroit Red Wings, defeating the Montreal Canadiens in four straight games. The Red Wings had also swept the Toronto Maple Leafs in the semifinals in four straight games.

Apr. 12–15 The **NBA basketball championship** was won by the Minneapolis Lakers, who beat the New York Knickerbockers four games to three.

Apr. 19 The 56th **Boston Marathon** was won by Doroteo Flores of Guatemala, with a time of 2 hrs., 31 min., 53 sec.

May 3 The 78th annual **Kentucky Derby** was won by Hill Gail, with a time of 2:01³/₅, a fifth of a second off the Derby record set in 1941 by Whirlaway. The jockey was Eddie Arcaro, who picked up his fifth Derby victory.

May 7 The 84th annual **Belmont Stakes** was won by One Count, with a time of 2:30¹/₅. The jockey was Eddie Arcaro.

May 17 The 77th annual **Preakness Stakes** was won by Blue Man, with a time of 1:57²/₅. The jockey was Conn McCreary.

May 30 The 46th **Indianapolis 500** auto race was won by Troy Ruttman, 22, from California, the youngest driver to win the 500-mile race. He completed the course in a record 3 hrs., 52 min., 41.88 sec., with an average speed of 128.922 mph.

June 14 The **U.S. Open golf tournament** was won by Julius Boros, who beat Ed Oliver by four strokes and Ben Hogan, the defending champion, by five.

June 25 The **PGA golf tournament** was won by Jim Turnesa.

June 29 The **U.S. Women's Open golf tournament** was won by Louise Suggs, beating Betty Jameson and Marlene Bauer by seven strokes.

July 5 At the **Wimbledon** tennis championships in England, Maureen Connolly won the women's singles title. Doris Hart and Shirley Fry won the women's doubles.

July 8 The 19th annual **baseball All-Star Game** was won by the National League, which beat the American League 3–2. Jackie Robinson and Hank Sauer hit home runs for the winners.

July 19–Aug. 3 At the **Summer Olympics** in Helsinki, Finland, the U.S. won 40 gold medals and finished first in the unofficial team standings.

July 21 The **Baseball Hall of Fame** inducted two outstanding hitters, Harry E. Heilmann and Paul Waner.

Sept. 6 The **Miss America** title was won by Neva Jane Langley, 19, from Georgia, at the annual pageant in Atlantic City, N.J.

89. The popular vote was Eisenhower, 33,938,285; Stevenson, 27,312,217; Vincent Hallinan, Progressive, 140,138; Stuart Hamblen, Prohibition, 72,881; Darlington Hoopes, Socialist, 20,189. In congressional elections the Republicans gained one Senate seat for a 48–47 majority, with one seat going to a minor party. In the House they gained 22 seats, for a 221–211 majority, one seat going to a minor party.

Nov. 29   President-elect **Eisenhower flew to Korea,** fulfilling his campaign promise, and inspected the UN forces there. On a three-day tour, he visited front-line positions. The tour was kept secret until he had returned from the zone of danger.

opened at the Martin Beck Theatre in New York City.

Mar. 30   **Tony Awards** for outstanding contributions to the theater during the 1951–1952 season were awarded for the following: play, *The Fourposter;* musical, *The King and I;* dramatic actor, José Ferrer for his performance in *The Shrike;* dramatic actress, Julie Harris for *I Am a Camera.*

May 5   **Pulitzer prizes** were awarded for the following: fiction, *The Caine Mutiny* by Herman Wouk; biography, *Charles Evans Hughes* by Merlo J. Pusey; history, *The Uprooted* by Oscar Handlin; poetry, *Collected Poems* by Marianne Moore; drama, *The Shrike* by Joseph Kramm.

1953

The nation watched with interest as a Republican administration took over the reins of government for the first time in 24 years. Pres. Dwight D. Eisenhower had uncertain control of Congress, the Republicans ruling there by the grace of conservative southern Democrats. The president made immediate attempts to improve his position with the legislative branch by announcing he favored a close presidential-congressional partnership. The new chief executive had four major areas of foreign policy to deal with: countering Russian expansion all over the globe; bolstering European allies by economic and military aid; fostering European unity; and forcing an equitable armistice in Korea. The most explosive internal problem was Sen. Joseph R. McCarthy, Republican of Wisconsin, charging Soviet espionage activities in the U.S. The administration's most outstanding success was a peace agreement in Korea. Pres. Eisenhower announced the agreement to a relieved country but warned, "We have won an armistice on a single battleground, not peace in the world."

In the **Korean War** (1950–1953), U.S. armed forces casualties totaled 137,051; of this number, 25,604 were killed; 103,492 were wounded; and 7955 were reported missing.

Jan. 2   A report on the actions of Sen. **Joseph R. McCarthy** of Wisconsin issued by a Senate privileges and elections subcommittee stated that some of McCarthy's political activities had been "motivated by self-interest." McCarthy was known for his headline-grabbing charges of communist infiltration in various organizations.

There was a bountiful supply of good books this year, but few really distinguished ones. Of particular interest was the publication of a large number of books, mostly novels, by highly competent black writers. Architects looked forward to boom times with commercial construction up 43.2%. Important music festivals in the U.S. and abroad attracted many composers. American painting reverted to the abstract form, but it also discovered the primitivism of Grandma Moses, who received worldwide recognition. Despite Broadway's usual complaints of rising production costs and shortages of houses and scripts, the season showed a marked improvement. Filmgoers were treated to several innovations, including stereophonic sound; 3-D, intended to give the illusion of three dimensions; and several wide-screen processes. The most popular type of film was the science fiction thriller.

Among **books published** this year was *The Adventures of Augie March* by Saul Bellow, a novel offering a panoramic view of middle-class Chicago in the 1920s and 1930s. Other books published this year included *Go Tell It on the Mountain* by James Baldwin, the author's first novel; *Simple Takes a Wife* by Langston Hughes; *The Bridges at Toko-ri* by James Michener; *The Light in the Forest* by Conrad Richter; *Always The Young Strangers* by Carl Sandburg, an account of the poet's youth; *Battle Cry* by Leon Uris; and *The Outsider* by Richard Wright.

The year's **popular songs** included "I Believe," "Doggie in the Window," "Till I Waltz Again With You," and "I'm Walking Behind You."

Jan. 1   *Suite Hébraïque* for viola and orchestra by Ernest Bloch was given its first performance by the Chicago Symphony.

Business and Industry; Science; Education; Philosophy and Religion **III**	**IV** **Sports; Social Issues and Crime; Folkways; Fashion; Holidays**

Nov. 6 The **Nobel Prize in Physics** was awarded jointly to Dr. Edward Mills Purcell of Harvard University and to Dr. Felix Bloch of Stanford University for their work in the measurement of magnetic fields in atomic nuclei. They were the eighth and ninth Americans to receive the award in this field.

Nov. 25 **George Meany** of New York was appointed president of the AFL to fill the unexpired term of William Green, who died on Nov. 21.

Dec. 4 **Walter P. Reuther,** president of the United Auto Workers, was chosen to head the CIO.

Sept. 7 The **U.S. Lawn Tennis Association singles championships** were won for the second year in a row by Frank Sedgman of Australia in the men's division. Maureen Connolly of San Diego, Calif., won in the women's division.

Sept. 23 The **world heavyweight boxing championship** was won by Rocky Marciano, who knocked out "Jersey Joe" Walcott in the 13th round of a bout in Philadelphia. It was Marciano's 43rd straight win as a professional boxer, with no losses.

Oct. 1–7 The 49th annual **World Series** was won by the New York Yankees (AL), defeating the Brooklyn Dodgers (NL) four games to three.

Dec. 28 The **NFL championship** was won by the Detroit Lions, who defeated the Cleveland Browns 17–7.

1953

Americans numbered nearly 161,000,000. The country continued to enjoy unprecedented prosperity, even though the 1953 dollar was worth about 52 cents compared with its 1935–1939 equivalent. Greatly increased personal income more than made up the difference for much of the population. This year saw the end of wage and salary controls. Labor continued its fight for abolition of the Taft-Hartley law. A broad economic program was announced by the administration. It included revision of the tax laws—including modification or elimination of the excess profits tax to benefit corporations—and double taxation of dividends; shifting of the national debt to long-term bonds; and providing for a sliding scale interest rate based on demand. This last provision was designed as a check to inflationary borrowing.

The Ford Foundation established **The Fund for the Republic** and gave it $15,000,000 "to help fight restriction on freedom of thought, inquiry and expression."

Jan. 9 The **federal estimated budget** for fiscal 1953–1954 called for expenditures of $78,587,000,000 and revenues of $68,665,000,000.

Jan. 16 **Offshore oil deposits** were set aside as a national reserve by Pres. Truman.

Feb. 5 **U.S. steel production** was up to 117,500,000 short tons a year, according to a report issued by the American Iron & Steel Institute.

Feb. 6 All **wage and salary controls** were lifted, as well as controls on many consumer goods.

The year's biggest fashion news was a designers' invasion into the field of men's clothes. Bermuda shorts were promoted for the hot summer months. For the ladies, a mood of sleek elegance was decreed. Skirts were shorter, and so were hair styles. The Italian haircut became the vogue. It called for a carefully casual female crew cut that gave the wearer a gaminlike, windblown look. This year Rocky Marciano defended his world heavyweight title in bouts against "Jersey Joe" Walcott (May 15) and Roland LaStarza (Sept. 24). In golf the top money winners were Lew Worsham, $34,002, and Louise Suggs, $19,816. Fans mourned the death of one of the greatest athletes of all time, Jim Thorpe, Mar. 28, at age 64.

Jan. 1 In **college football bowl games,** the results were Texas 16, Tennessee 0 in the Cotton Bowl; Alabama 61, Syracuse 6 in the Orange Bowl; Southern California 7, Wisconsin 0 in the Rose Bowl; and Georgia Tech 24, Mississippi 7 in the Sugar Bowl. This season the AP poll chose Michigan State the national collegiate champions of 1952, as did the UPI poll.

Feb. 10 At the **world figure skating championships** in Switzerland, Hayes Alan Jenkins won the men's singles title and Tenley Albright won the women's singles.

Mar. 18 The **NCAA basketball championship** was won by Indiana, defeating Kansas 69–68.

Mar. 28 **U.S. figure skating championships** were won in Hershey, Pa., by Tenley Albright, women's singles; Hayes Alan Jenkins, men's singles; and Carole Ann Ormaca and Robin Greiner, pairs; Carol Ann Peters and Daniel C. Ryan, dance.

| Exploration and Settlement; Wars; Government; Civil Rights; Statistics | **I** | | **II** | Publishing; Arts and Music; Popular Entertainment; Architecture; Theater |

Jan. 20 Dwight D. Eisenhower was inaugurated president of the United States. The 34th president, he served two terms.

Jan. 21 Thirteen communist leaders were convicted by a federal jury in New York City of conspiring to advocate overthrow of the U.S. government.

Apr. 1 The **Department of Health, Education and Welfare** (HEW) was created by joint congressional action. On Apr. 11 Mrs. Oveta Culp Hobby of Texas was sworn in as the department's first head.

Apr. 20 The **U.S. Communist Party** was ordered to register with the Justice Department as an organization controlled and directed by the U.S.S.R.

Apr. 24 Record **taxes** of $68,500,000,000 were collected in 1952 according to the U.S. Bureau of Internal Revenue.

Apr. 25 A **record for filibustering** was set in the U.S. Senate by Sen. Wayne Morse, Independent of Oregon, who held the floor for 22 hrs., 26 min. opposing a bill that would return offshore oil reserves to the individual states. His marathon failed to sway the Senate, which passed the measure on May 5 by a vote of 56–35.

May 11 **Tornadoes** hit Waco and San Angelo, Tex., killing 124 people.

June 8 A **tornado** sliced through Ohio and into Flint, Mich., killing 139 persons.

June 9 A **tornado** hit western Massachusetts, killing 86 persons.

June 18 The worst **air accident** to date occurred near Tokyo, Japan, when a U.S. Air Force Globemaster crashed, killing 129 persons.

June 19 **Julius and Ethel Rosenberg** were executed at Sing Sing Prison in Ossining, N.Y. They were the first civilians to be executed in the U.S. for espionage. The couple had been convicted on Apr. 5, 1951, of passing secret information about the atom bomb to the U.S.S.R. Their deaths were the subject of protests around the world.

July 27 A **Korean armistice** was signed at Panmunjom by UN, North Korean, and Chinese delegates.

Aug. 1 A broader **Social Security Act** was proposed by Pres. Eisenhower, who recommended provisions to include another 10,500,000 persons under the law.

Jan. 9 *Volpone,* an opera by George Antheil, was produced in Los Angeles, Calif.

Jan. 27 The **National Book Awards** were presented for the following: fiction, *Invisible Man* by Ralph Ellison; poetry, *Collected Poems, 1917–1952* by Archibald MacLeish; biography, *The Course of Empire* by Bernard De Voto.

Feb. 7 *The Marriage,* an opera by Bohuslav Martinu, was given its premiere performance by the New York Opera Company at the New York City Center.

Feb. 11 **Emmy Awards** were presented to Donald O'Connor as best actor in a series for Colgate *Comedy Hour;* Eve Arden as best actress in a series for *Our Miss Brooks;* Edward R. Murrow as most outstanding personality; and *U.S. Steel Hour* as best dramatic program.

Feb. 19 *Picnic* by William Inge, the author's second play, opened at the Music Box in New York City. Its cast included Ralph Meeker, Janice Rule, and Kim Stanley.

Feb. 25 *Wonderful Town,* a musical comedy based on the play *My Sister Eileen,* in turn based on the stories of Ruth McKenney, opened at the Winter Garden in New York City. It featured music by Leonard Bernstein, lyrics by Betty Comden and Adolph Green, and a sparkling performance by Rosalind Russell.

Mar. 19 **Academy Awards** were presented to *The Greatest Show on Earth* as the outstanding motion picture of 1952; to Gary Cooper as best actor for *High Noon;* to Shirley Booth as best actress for *Come Back, Little Sheba;* to Anthony Quinn as best supporting actor for *Viva Zapata!;* and to Gloria Grahame as best supporting actress for *The Bad and the Beautiful.*

Mar. 19 *Camino Real* by Tennessee Williams opened at the National Theatre in New York City.

Mar. 29 **Tony Awards** for outstanding contributions to theater during the 1952–1953 season were presented for the following: play, *The Crucible;* musical, *Wonderful Town;* dramatic actor, Tom Ewell for *The Seven Year Itch;* dramatic actress, Shirley Booth for *Time of the Cuckoo.*

May 4 The premiere performance of *The Mighty Casey,* a one-act opera by William Schuman based on Ernest Lawrence Thayer's poem "Casey at the Bat," was given by the Julius Hartt Opera Guild in Hartford, Conn.

May 4 **Pulitzer prizes** were awarded for the following: fiction, *The Old Man and the Sea* by Ernest Hemingway; biography, *Edmund Pendleton, 1721–1803* by David J. Mays; history, *The Era of Good Feeling* by George Dangerfield; poetry, *Collected Poems, 1917–1952* by Archibald MacLeish; drama, *Picnic* by William Inge.

| Business and Industry; Science; Education; Philosophy and Religion | III | | IV | Sports; Social Issues and Crime; Folkways; Fashion; Holidays |

Feb. 12 Price ceilings were withdrawn for many items, including tires, gasoline, poultry, and eggs.

Feb. 13 Allotment **controls on steel,** copper, and aluminum were renewed by the Office of Defense Mobilization.

Feb. 20 **Stock margin requirements** were reduced from 75% to 50% effective Feb. 24.

Feb. 22 A voluntary program of **health insurance** to be financed by federal, state, and municipal funds was recommended by the President's Commission on the Health Needs of the Nation.

Feb. 25 **Price controls** were lifted on cigarettes, dry groceries, copper, and aluminum by the Office of Price Stabilization.

Mar. 17 All **price controls were officially ended** by the Office of Price Stabilization.

Mar. 30 **Jet-propelled guided missiles** were under production according to the U.S. Navy.

May 25 The **first atomic artillery shell** was fired at a military testing range in Nevada.

June 12 A **wage agreement** was signed by the U.S. Steelworkers of America (CIO) and the United States Steel Corporation. It granted an eight and one-half cent per hour wage boost plus a half cent per hour in benefits.

Sept. 10 Sec. of Labor **Martin P. Durkin** resigned his post because of the failure of Pres. Dwight D. Eisenhower's administration to propose amendments to the Taft-Hartley labor law.

Sept. 22 The **International Longshoremen's Association** was expelled from the AFL for refusing to get rid of racketeers in its ranks.

Oct. 22 The **Nobel Prize for Physiology or Medicine** was awarded jointly to Dr. Fritz Albert Lipmann of Harvard University Medical School for his discovery of co-enzyme A and its function in metabolic processes; and to Dr. Hans Adolf Krebs of Sheffield University in England for his discovery of the citric acid cycle, known as the Krebs cycle.

Dec. 9 The **General Electric Company** announced that all communist employees would be discharged.

Apr. 4–10 The **NBA basketball championship** was won by the Minneapolis Lakers, who defeated the New York Knickerbockers four games to one.

Apr. 9–16 The **NHL Stanley Cup** was won by the Montreal Canadiens, who defeated the Boston Bruins four games to one.

Apr. 12 The **Masters golf tournament** was won by Ben Hogan.

Apr. 20 The 57th **Boston Marathon** was won by Keizo Yamada of Japan, with a time of 2 hrs., 18 min., 51 sec., the fastest time recorded for a marathon.

May 2 The 79th annual **Kentucky Derby** was won by Dark Star, with a time of 2:02. The jockey was Henry Moreno.

May 23 The 78th annual **Preakness Stakes** was won by Native Dancer, with a time of 1:57^4/5. The jockey was Eric Guerin.

May 30 The 37th **Indianapolis 500** was won by Bill Vukovich of Fresno, Calif., in 3 hrs., 53 min., 0.69 sec., with an average speed of 128.74 mph.

June 13 The 85th annual **Belmont Stakes** was won by Native Dancer, with a time of 2:28^3/5. The jockey was Eric Guerin.

June 13 The **U.S. Open golf tournament** was won by Ben Hogan, who beat Sam Snead by six strokes to become the third person in history to win the tournament four times.

June 28 The **U.S. Women's Open golf tournament** was won by Betsy Rawls, who beat Jacqueline Pung of Hawaii by six strokes in an 18-hole playoff.

July 3 At the **Wimbledon** tennis championships in England, Victor Seixas won the men's singles title. The next day Maureen Connolly won the women's singles. Doris Hart and Shirley Fry won the women's doubles, and Hart and Seixas won the mixed doubles.

July 7 The **PGA golf tournament** was won by Walter Burkemo.

July 14 The 20th annual **baseball All-Star Game** was won by the National League 5–1.

July 27 The **Baseball Hall of Fame** inducted Jay Hanna Dean, also known as Jerome Herman Dean but universally called "Dizzy" Dean, the pitcher, and Aloysius H. "Al" Simmons, the outfielder.

Sept. 7 The **U.S. Lawn Tennis Association singles championships** were won by Tony Trabert in the men's division, and by Maureen Connolly in the women's division.

Sept. 13 The **Miss America** title was won by Evelyn Margaret Ay, 20, from Pennsylvania, at the annual pageant in Atlantic City, N.J.

Sept. 30–Oct. 5 The 50th annual **World Series** was won by the New York Yankees (AL), defeating the Brooklyn Dodgers (NL) four games to two. This was

The proposed legislation was passed on Sept. 1, 1954.

Aug. 7 The **Refugee Relief Act** of 1953 was signed by Pres. Eisenhower. It admitted 214,000 more refugees than permitted under existing immigration quotas.

May 27 **Frank Lloyd Wright** was presented with the Gold Medal for Architecture by the National Institute of Arts and Letters.

Sept. 30 *Tea and Sympathy* by Robert Anderson, starring Deborah Kerr and John Kerr (not related), opened at the National Theatre in New York City.

1954

Pres. Dwight D. Eisenhower declared that his foreign policy would be dedicated to regaining the initiative in the world fight against communism and to winning the confidence of U.S. allies. With regard to defense, the president advocated intensive research on atomic weapons and an integrated transcontinental transportation system for civil as well as military travel. It included development of the St. Lawrence Seaway to open the central states to seagoing traffic via the Great Lakes. He advocated greater discretion in loyalty investigations, but promised decisive action in all cases of espionage or sabotage. He also revealed that some 2200 government employees had been dropped under the administration's new security system. Later in the year, the president asked Congress to enact legislation to enable the Atomic Energy Commission to share certain atomic secrets with U.S. allies and to pave the way for industrial development of the atom. The U.S. took part in the London conference (Sept. 28–Oct. 3) and the Paris conference (Oct. 20–23) in which it was agreed that U.S. and British forces would remain in Europe to help keep the peace. The West German Federal Republic (West Germany) was admitted to NATO on Oct. 23. But the major international event was the French defeat at Dien Bien Phu on May 7, causing withdrawal of French forces from Vietnam and the partition of the country into northern and southern states, with elections for reunification to be held in July 1956.

Mar. 1 **Five congressmen were shot** on the floor of the House of Representatives by Puerto Rican nationalists. All recovered from their wounds.

Mar. 8 U.S. **foreign military aid** between Oct. 1949 and Dec. 31, 1954, came to nearly $8,000,000,000, according to a report by Pres. Eisenhower.

Mar. 8 A **mutual defense agreement** was signed by Japan and the U.S. It provided for gradual and partial rearming of Japan.

Mar. 10 The **first atomic power plant** was planned for the Duquesne Power Co., Pittsburgh, Pa., by the Atomic Energy Commission. Pres. Eisenhower, using a special remote hookup, broke ground for it from Denver, Colo., on Sept. 6.

Mar. 10 A 50% reduction in most **federal luxury taxes** and other excise taxes was voted by the House of Representatives.

Books on the Cold War, U.S. foreign policy, government loyalty programs, subversion, and the A-bomb filled rental libraries and bookstore. Novelists favored an exploration of the psychopathic mentality, but said little new or surprising. A major development for poets was an ever-increasing list of awards and prizes open to them; they responded by writing more and better verse. The building boom of 1953 showed no signs of letup; in fact, July set a record with $3,135,000,000 in new construction. All areas of musical endeavor reported great demand. Established symphonic societies and popular musical festivals continued to give composers commissions. Four works by Igor Stravinsky were introduced this year: *Septet* for violin, cello, viola, clarinet, horn, bassoon, and piano; *Three Songs from William Shakespeare; In Memoriam: Dylan Thomas;* and *Four Russian Peasant Songs.* Filmgoers were treated to a rash of spectacular historical epics and westerns. Some 7448 movie houses had CinemaScope facilities.

Among **books published** this year was *A Fable* by William Faulkner, a retelling of the crucifixion and resurrection of Jesus set against the background of World War I. Other books published this year included *No Time for Sergeants* by Mac Hyman, a delightful tale of an innocent Georgia youth drafted into the Air Force; *The Bird's Nest* by Shirley Jackson, a novel about a girl with four personalities; *The Bad Seed* by William March, a novel depicting a young girl as the incarnation of evil; *Sweet Thursday* by John Steinbeck, a sequel to his novel *Cannery Row* (1945); *The Collected Poems of Wallace Stevens;* and *The Ponder Heart,* a novel by Eudora Welty.

The year's **popular songs** included "Stranger in Paradise," based on a melody by Alexander Borodin, "Hernando's Hideaway" and "Hey, There," both from the Broadway musical *Pajama Game,* "I Love Paris," "Careless Love," and "Young at Heart."

Some 29,000,000 households had **television** sets. This represented about 60% of American households. Television had not been marketed seriously until about 1947.

The symphonic eulogy *Ahavah* Brotherhood by **David Diamond** was the highlight of a concert arranged by the Jewish Tercentenary Committee, honoring the 300th anniversary of the first Jew to land in America.

| Business and Industry; Science; Education; Philosophy and Religion **III** | | Sports; Social Issues and Crime; Folkways; Fashion; Holidays |

Dec. 16 A new **airplane speed record** was achieved by U.S. Air Force Major Charles E. Yeager, who flew a Bell X-1A rocket powered plane more than 1600 mph.

the first time a team had won five consecutive World Series.

Dec. 27 The **NFL championship** was won by the Detroit Lions, who defeated the Cleveland Browns 17–16.

1954

A business recession coupled with rising unemployment worried some Americans, but administration spokesmen told the nation that some fallback from unprecedented economic highs was desirable. The downward trend was reversed about the middle of the year. By September personal income had exceeded the August figure by $2,000,000,000. Unemployment, though, totaled 2,893,000, about twice the figure reported for 1953. The AFL and CIO agreed to merge, and AFL president George Meany predicted that the merger would take place in 1955. Huge crop surpluses resulted in stringent curbs by the Agriculture Department. Sec. of Agriculture Ezra Benson was given authority to barter surplus crops on the world market in exchange for strategic goods. Schools were suffering from overcrowding and, with the Supreme Court decision on May 14 outlawing segregation in public schools, there was confusion in the ranks of school administrators.

Jan. 11 Widespread changes in the **Taft-Hartley labor law** were urged by Pres. Eisenhower in a special message to Congress. He also advocated a return to flexible farm price supports.

Jan. 19 **General Motors** announced a $1,000,000,000 expansion program.

Jan. 20 Construction of the **St. Lawrence Seaway** was approved by the Senate.

Feb. 2 Detonation of the **first hydrogen bomb** was officially reported by Pres. Eisenhower. It had taken place at Eniwetok Atoll in the Pacific in 1952.

Feb. 23 **Antipolio inoculation** of schoolchildren was begun in Pittsburgh, Pa., by Dr. Jonas E. Salk, developer of the serum.

The continuing antics of Sen. Joseph R. McCarthy was a topic of conversation along with rising juvenile crime and delinquency. Families discussed discipline and examined outside influences. Lurid comic books and violence-spattered pulp magazines came under attack from parents' groups and, in some cases, legislators. Fashion designers introduced a softer silhouette that deemphasized the bust and showed a longer torso. In boxing, Rocky Marciano defended his world heavyweight title twice (June 17, Sept. 17) in bouts with Ezzard Charles. In golf, the top money winners were Bob Toski, $65,891.24, and Patty Berg, $16,011. Studies showed that the average American's favorite meal was fruit cup, vegetable soup, steak and potatoes, peas, rolls with butter, and pie à la mode. Some 90% of adult Americans drank three to four cups of coffee a day; 64% drank beer, wine, or liquor; and 45% smoked one pack of cigarettes a day. About 60% of the male population and 30% of the female population smoked.

Jan. 1 In **college football bowl games,** the results were Rice 28, Alabama 6 in the Cotton Bowl; Oklahoma 7, Maryland 0 in the Orange Bowl; Michigan State 28, UCLA 20 in the Rose Bowl; and Georgia Tech 42, West Virginia 19 in the Sugar Bowl. This season the AP poll and the UPI poll chose Maryland the national collegiate champions of 1953.

Feb. 17 At the **world figure skating championships** in Oslo, Norway, Hayes Alan Jenkins won the men's singles title.

Mar. 19 **U.S. figure skating championships** were won in Los Angeles, Calif., by Tenley Albright, women's singles; Hayes Alan Jenkins, men's singles; Carole Ann Ormaca and Robin Greiner, pairs; Carmel and Edward L. Bodel, dance.

Mar. 20 The **NCAA basketball championship** was won by La Salle, defeating Bradley 92–76.

Mar. 31–Apr. 12 The **NBA basketball championship** was won by the Minneapolis Lakers, who defeated the Syracuse Nationals four games to one.

Apr. 4–16 The **NHL Stanley Cup** was won by the

Apr. 1 A **United States Air Force Academy,** similar to the service schools at West Point and Annapolis, was authorized.

Apr. 8 Construction of an **early warning radar net** stretching 3000 miles across the Canadian far north was announced by the U.S. and Canada.

Apr. 23–June 17 The **Army-McCarthy hearings** were conducted by the Senate Permanent Subcommittee on Investigations. The hearings were held to investigate charges by its chairman, Sen. Joseph R. McCarthy, Republican of Wisconsin, that Sec. of the Army Robert T. Stevens and Army counsel John G. Adams were hampering the committee's attempts to uncover communists in the military. Stevens and Adams countercharged that McCarthy and his staff had tried to get preferential treatment for one of its former staff members, Pvt. G. David Schine. The hearings, given broad television and newspaper coverage, did much to end the anticommunist witch hunt led by McCarthy.

May 17 Racial **segregation in public schools** was declared unconstitutional by the U.S. Supreme Court. The Court handed down a single ruling on four state cases, including *Brown v. Board of Education* of Topeka, Kans., and another involving the District of Columbia. The rulings outlawed the practice of "separate but equal" facilities in public school systems.

May 24 **Communist Party membership** was declared to be sufficient grounds for deportation of aliens in a U.S. Supreme Court decision that upheld the constitutionality of the Internal Security Act of 1950.

June 24 The site of the new **Air Force Academy** would be Colorado Springs, Colo., Air Force Sec. Harold E. Talbott announced.

July 30 A **resolution of censure** against Sen. Joseph R. McCarthy for conduct unbecoming a senator was introduced in the Senate by Sen. Ralph E. Flanders, Republican of Vermont. A Senate select committee subsequently voted to censure McCarthy on two counts of the resolution.

Sept. 1 **Hurricane Carol** struck Long Island, N.Y., and New England, killing 68. Property losses were estimated at $500,000,000.

Sept. 3 The **Espionage and Sabotage Act** of 1954 was signed by Pres. Eisenhower. The death penalty was authorized for peacetime sabotage and the statute of limitations for these crimes was removed.

Sept. 30 The **first atomic-powered submarine,** the U.S.S. *Nautilus,* was commissioned at Groton, Conn.

Oct. 15 **Hurricane Hazel,** the most violent hurricane of the year, killed 99 persons in the U.S. and 249 in Canada. Combined U.S. and Canadian property losses were put at $100,000,000.

The concert was held at Constitution Hall in Washington, D.C.

Jan. 20 *The Caine Mutiny Court Martial* by Herman Wouk, based on the author's novel *The Caine Mutiny,* opened at the Plymouth Theatre in New York City. Its cast included Henry Fonda and Lloyd Nolan.

Jan. 26 The **National Book Awards** were presented for the following: fiction, *The Adventures of Augie March* by Saul Bellow; poetry, *Collected Poems* by Conrad Aiken; biography, *A Stillness at Appomattox* by Bruce Catton.

Jan. 30 *Symphonic Fantasy* by Roy Harris was introduced by the Pittsbugh Symphony at Pittsburgh, Pa.

Feb. 11 *The Confidential Clerk* by T. S. Eliot, a verse play starring Ina Claire, Claude Rains, and Joan Greenwood, opened at the Morosco Theatre in New York City.

Feb. 22 *Concerto No. Five* for piano and orchestra by Alan Hovhaness was performed in New York City by the National Orchestral Association.

Mar. 4 *Violoncello Concerto* by Ernst Krenek was given its first public performance, by the Los Angeles Philharmonic in Los Angeles, Calif.

Mar. 7 **Emmy Awards** were presented for the following: best actor in a series, Danny Thomas for *Make Room for Daddy;* best actress in a series, Loretta Young for *The Loretta Young Show;* best dramatic series, *The U.S. Steel Hour.*

Mar. 25 **Academy Awards** were presented to *From Here to Eternity* as the outstanding motion picture of 1953; to William Holden as best actor for *Stalag 17;* to Audrey Hepburn as best actress for *Roman Holiday;* and to Frank Sinatra and Donna Reed as best supporting actor and actress for *From Here to Eternity.*

Mar. 28 **Tony Awards** for outstanding contributions to the theater during the 1953–1954 season were presented for the following: play, *The Teahouse of the August Moon;* musical, *Kismet;* actor, David Wayne for *The Teahouse of the August Moon;* actress, Audrey Hepburn for *Roman Holiday.*

Apr. 1 *The Tender Land* by Aaron Copland, the composer's first full-length opera, with a libretto by Horace Everett, premiered at the City Center in New York City.

May 3 **Pulitzer prizes** were awarded for the following: biography, *The Spirit of St. Louis* by Charles A. Lindbergh; history, *A Stillness at Appomattox* by Bruce Catton; poetry, *The Waking: Poems 1933–1953* by Theodore Roethke; drama, *The Teahouse of the August Moon* by John Patrick.

Sept. 30 *The Boy Friend,* a musical by Sandy Wilson starring John Hewer and Julie Andrews, opened at the Royale Theatre in New York City.

Mar. 24 A **hydrogen bomb** explosion in the Marshall Islands on Mar. 1 exceeded all estimates of its power, according to a statement made by Pres. Eisenhower.

Apr. 2 The longest and costliest **strike** in the history of New York City, which began Mar. 3 over labor jurisdiction, was terminated by the International Longshoremen's Association.

May 13 The **St. Lawrence Seaway Bill,** authorizing construction of a joint U.S. and Canadian artificial waterway connecting the Great Lakes and the Atlantic Ocean, was signed by Pres. Eisenhower. On June 9 he named Sec. of Defense Charles E. Wilson director of the St. Lawrence Seaway Development Corporation.

June 29 A two-year **labor agreement** was signed between the United Steelworkers of America (CIO) and the United States Steel Corporation. The contract called for wage hikes and increased pension and social insurance benfits.

July 12 A four-point **highway modernization program** was proposed by Pres. Eisenhower. The cost would be shared by federal and state governments.

July 13 The **gross national product** for 1953 was put at $365,000,000,000 by the Department of Commerce.

Aug. 15 The second assembly of the **World Council of Churches** convened at Evanston, Ill.

Sept. 24 The **United Steelworkers of America** (CIO) banned communists, fascists, and members of the Ku Klux Klan from their ranks.

Oct. 13 The **first supersonic bomber,** the B-58, was ordered into production by the Air Force.

Oct. 21 The **Nobel Prize for Physiology or Medicine** was awarded to John F. Enders of the Harvard School of Medicine, Thomas H. Weller of the Harvard School of Public Health, and Frederick C. Robins of Western

Detroit Red Wings, defeating the Montreal Canadiens four games to three.

Apr. 12 The **Masters golf tournament** was won by Sam Snead, who beat Ben Hogan in a playoff round.

Apr. 19 The 58th **Boston Marathon** was won by Viekko Karanen of Finland, with a time of 2 hrs., 20 min., 39 sec.

May 1 The 80th **Kentucky Derby** was won by Determine, with a time of 2:03. The jockey was Ray York.

May 22 The 79th annual **Preakness Stakes** was won by Hasty Road, with a time of 1:57²/₅. The jockey was Johnny Adams.

May 31 The 38th **Indianapolis 500** auto race was won by Bill Vukovich, completing the course in a record 3 hrs., 49 min., 17.27 sec., with an average speed of 130.840 mph. It was his second consecutive win.

June 12 The 86th annual **Belmont Stakes** was won by High Gun, with a time of 2:30⁴/₅. The jockey was Eric Guerin.

June 19 The **U.S. Open golf tournament** was won by Ed Furgol.

July 3 The **U.S Women's Open golf tournament** was won by Mildred "Babe" Didrikson Zaharias.

July 3 At the **Wimbledon** tennis championships in England, Maureen Connolly won the women's singles title, Louise Brough and Margaret Osborne du Pont the women's doubles, and Victor Seixas and Doris Hart the mixed doubles.

July 13 The 21st annual **baseball All-Star Game** was won by the American League, defeating the National League 11–9. Fans were treated to six home runs, four by the winners.

July 27 The **PGA golf tournament** was won by Chick Harbert.

Aug. 9 The **Baseball Hall of Fame** inducted nine new members: Edward G. Barrow, baseball executive; Thomas H. Connolly, umpire; Charles A. "Chief" Bender, pitcher; William M. "Bill" Dickey, catcher; William J. "Bill" Klem, umpire; Walter J.V. "Rabbit" Maranville, infielder; William H. "Bill" Terry, manager; Roderick J. "Bobby" Wallace, pitcher; and Harry Wright, center fielder and manager.

Sept. 6 The **U.S. Lawn Tennis Association singles championships** were won by Victor Seixas in the men's division and Doris Hart in the women's division.

Exploration and Settlement; Wars; Government; Civil Rights; Statistics	I		II	Publishing; Arts and Music; Popular Entertainment; Architecture; Theater

Oct. 25 The first public and televised Cabinet meeting was held. The president and the Cabinet met in the White House to hear Sec. of State John Foster Dulles report on the Paris conference (Oct. 23) dealing with Allied military forces in Europe and the admission of West Germany to NATO.

Nov. 2 In **congressional elections** the Democrats gained one Senate seat for a 48–47 majority, with one seat going to a minor party. In the House they gained 21 seats, for a 232–203 majority.

Dec. 2 Sen. **McCarthy was condemned** in a vote of a special session of the U.S. Senate for his conduct in Senate committees.

Dec. 11 The **largest warship** ever built, the 59,650-ton aircraft carrier U.S.S. *Forrestal,* was launched at Newport News, Va.

Oct. 28 The **Nobel Prize for Literature** was awarded to Ernest Hemingway "for his powerful style-forming mastery of the art of modern narration." Among Hemingway's works were *The Sun Also Rises* (1926), *A Farewell to Arms* (1929), and *For Whom the Bell Tolls* (1940).

Nov. 4 *Fanny,* a musical by S. N. Behrman and Joshua Logan with music and lyrics by Harold Rome, opened at the Majestic Theatre in New York City.

Dec. 8 *The Bad Seed,* a drama by Maxwell Anderson based on the novel by William March, opened at the Forty-Sixth Street Theatre in New York City.

Dec. 27 *The Saint of Bleecker Street* by Gian-Carlo Menotti opened at the Broadway Theater in New York City to critical and popular acclaim.

1955

The marked easing of the Cold War brought about by what was called the Geneva spirit was engendered by Pres. Dwight D. Eisenhower's proposal to the U.S.S.R. for exchange of military blueprints and mutual aerial inspection. Nations that had been suspicious of U.S. foreign policy began to trust the U.S. a little more. At home, Americans enjoyed a new prosperity. They remodeled their cities in an unprecedented building boom, bought more expensive cars, planned dream homes, and flocked to buy home appliances, especially color TV sets. The Far East, however, was still a sorely troubled area, particularly in Indochina following the French defeat at Dien Bien Phu in May 1954.

Jan. 1 **Foreign aid** to South Vietnam, Cambodia, and Laos was begun by the U.S. Foreign Operations Administration. About $216,000,000 was spent in 1955.

Jan. 3 Some 3002 persons considered **security risks** had been discharged from federal employment between May 28, 1953, and Sept. 30, 1954, it was announced.

Jan. 14 The U.S. **Senate investigation of communism** was approved for continuation in a Senate vote of 84–0.

Jan. 17 The **estimated federal budget** for the 1955 fiscal year was announced. Expenditures totaled $62,-408,000,000; revenues, $60,000,000,000.

A noteworthy trend in the year's publishing was the number of nonfiction books, especially those on child behavior. Architects hailed the continuing high level of construction, and church building reached its highest rate in history. New materials such as aluminum and plastics were being used in construction. The New York Philharmonic and Philadelphia orchestras embarked on extensive European tours. The Symphony of the Air headed east and played in Japanese concert halls. Highlights of the year in music included premieres of *Symphony No. Six* by Darius Milhaud (Boston, Oct. 7) and *Symphony No. Five* by Walter Piston (Boston, Nov. 25). A showing of contemporary American and European painters at the Museum of Modern Art, New York City, revealed that for the first time U.S. artists were surpassing their European peers in imaginative style and technique. The show featured Willem de Kooning, Jackson Pollock, Robert Motherwell, and Adolph Gottlieb.

Among **books published** this year was *Andersonville* by MacKinlay Kantor, a powerful Civil War novel about the notorious Confederate prison. Other books published this year included *The Day Lincoln Was Shot* by Jim Bishop; *A Good Man Is Hard to Find, and Other Stories* by Flannery O'Connor; *Band of Angels* by Robert Penn Warren, a novel set in the Civil War; *The Man in the Gray Flannel Suit* by Sloan Wilson; and *Marjorie Morningstar* by Herman Wouk, a novel.

The year's top **popular songs** were based on old melodies. "Melody of Love" was a longtime favorite piece of piano students. "The Yellow Rose of Texas" was a Confederate Civil War song. Other song hits were "Let Me

| Business and Industry; Science; Education; Philosophy and Religion III | | IV Sports; Social Issues and Crime; Folkways; Fashion; Holidays |

Reserve Medical School for their work in the cultivation of the polio virus.

Nov. 3 The **Nobel Prize in Chemistry** was awarded to Linus Pauling of the California Institute of Technology for his study of the forces holding together protein and other molecules.

Dec. 31 **New York Stock Exchange prices** were the highest quoted since 1929. The volume of shares traded during 1954 (573,374,622) was the highest since 1933.

Sept. 11 The **Miss America** title was won by Lee Meriwether, 19, from California, at the annual pageant in Atlantic City, N.J.

Sept. 29–Oct. 2 The 51st annual **World Series** was won by the New York Giants (NL), defeating the Cleveland Indians (AL) in four straight games.

Dec. 26 The **NFL championship** was won by the Cleveland Browns, who defeated the Detroit Lions 56–10.

Dec. 28 The **Davis Cup** international tennis challenge round was won by the U.S., which defeated Australia three matches to two.

1955

The economy enjoyed a year of nearly full employment and peak production. Net business income was up 33% over the previous year. Labor stated new objectives, chief of which was attainment of a guaranteed annual wage. The organized labor force in the U.S. totaled 15,000,000 after the AFL and the CIO merged to become the American Federation of Labor and Congress of Industrial Organizations (AFL-CIO). The major concern of labor leaders was the increasing use of automation in industrial plants. Walter P. Reuther, vice president of the newly merged labor group, predicted a second industrial revolution as a result of automation. Farm income was down 5½% from 1954. Educators reported a shortage of 250,000 classrooms and 141,300 teachers.

Jan. 8 **Thorazine and reserpine,** two new drugs, showed some success in the treatment of mental patients, according to the New York State Department of Mental Hygiene.

Jan. 9 Experimental **atomic power plants** were to be operated by private industry, it was announced by the Atomic Energy Commission.

Feb. 9 The **AFL-CIO merger** agreement was made public.

Apr. 12 A successful **antipolio vaccine** was announced by Dr. Jonas E. Salk. Tests carried out in 44 states indicated its effectiveness against poliomyelitis.

May 19 An unprecedented number of **business mergers** was reported—three times the rate of 1949.

Davy Crockett and rock 'n' roll highlighted the year 1955. Originally, the Davy Crockett fad was started by a Technicolor movie produced in Hollywood by Walt Disney. Publicity agents then parlayed the legend of the frontiersman who died at the Alamo into a national fad—millions of Davy Crockett coonskin hats were manufactured and distributed, and fur dealers in New York City enjoyed one of the most prosperous years ever. Equally contagious was the mania for rock 'n' roll music, which many attacked as immoral, allegedly because of its monotonous, primitive beat. It was a gala year in Flatbush. The faithful rejoiced as the Brooklyn Dodgers won their first baseball championship, doubly welcome since they beat the mighty New York Yankees. In boxing, Rocky Marciano successfully defended the world heavyweight title in bouts with Don Cockell of Great Britain (May 16) and Archie Moore (Sept. 21). In golf the top money winners were Julius Boros, $65,121, and Patty Berg, $16,492. Fashion designers combined sophisticated sex appeal with fresh youthfulness, and favored a semifitted sheath of oriental design and color.

More than 1,000,000,000 **comic books** were sold annually, according to a report issued by the University of California, at an estimated cost of $100,000,000, four times the book budget of all U.S. public libraries combined. New York State passed a law banning the sale of lurid crime and horror comic books to persons under 18 years of age. Violations were punishable by a year in prison and/or a $500 fine.

Jan. 1 In **college football bowl games,** the results were Georgia Tech 14, Arkansas 6 in the Cotton Bowl; Duke 34, Nebraska 7 in the Orange Bowl; Ohio State 20, Southern California 7 in the Rose Bowl; and Navy 21, Mississippi 0 in the Sugar Bowl. This season the AP poll chose Ohio State the national collegiate

Jan. 19 The first filmed presidential press conference took place. Both TV and motion picture newsreel photographers covered the event.

Jan. 28 Defense of **Formosa and the Pescadores Islands** was pledged by the Senate by a vote of 85–3. On the following day the Chinese demanded that the U.N. order U.S. withdrawal from the entire Formosan area.

Feb. 26 Some 4000 **atomic bombs** had been stockpiled by the U.S., and 1000 by the U.S.S.R., according to an unofficial estimate of Prof. Cecil F. Powell, the British scientist and winner of a Nobel Prize in Physics.

Mar. 1 **Congressional salaries** and salaries of federal judges were increased by about 50% in a bill passed by the House of Representatives.

Mar. 16 The **use of atomic weapons** in case of war was upheld in a statement made by Pres. Eisenhower.

Apr. 9 A **Civil Defense Coordinating Board,** to be headed by Civil Defense Administrator Val Peterson, was formed by presidential order. The new agency was to coordinate the defense activities of all federal bureaus.

June 16 **Selective Service** was extended to June 30, 1959, by the House of Representatives.

June 21 The **Reciprocal Trade Agreements Act** was extended to June 30, 1958, by the House of Representatives.

June 28 More than 1,000,000 **federal employees** were granted a 7.5% pay boost.

July 7 A **foreign aid bill** appropriating $3,285,800,000 was passed by Congress.

July 11 The U.S. **Air Force Academy** was officially opened at its temporary site, Lowry Air Force Base, Denver, Colo.

July 18 The **Geneva conference,** attended by heads of state of the U.S., Great Britain, U.S.S.R., and France, opened at Geneva, Switzerland.

Go, Lover," "Learnin' the Blues," "Mr. Sandman," "Unchained Melody," and "I Need You Now."

Jan. 11 *Inherit the Wind* by Jerome Lawrence and Robert E. Lee, based on the celebrated Scopes monkey trial, premiered at Theatre '55 in Dallas, Tex. On Apr. 21 it began its New York City run at the National Theatre.

Jan. 25 The **National Book Awards** were presented for the following: fiction, *A Fable* by William Faulkner; nonfiction, *The Measure of Man* by Joseph Wood Krutch; poetry, *The Selected Poems of Wallace Stevens.* A special citation was awarded to E. E. Cummings for his volume, *Poems: 1923–1954.*

Jan. 27 *Plain and Fancy,* a musical comedy by Joseph Stein and Will Glickman with lyrics by Arnold B. Horwitt and music by Albert Hague, opened at the Mark Hellinger Theatre in New York City. The show's setting was an Amish community in Pennsylvania.

Feb. 24 *Silk Stockings,* Cole Porter's version of *Ninotchka,* opened at the Imperial Theatre in New York City.

Mar. 2 *Bus Stop* by William Inge, starring Kim Stanley and Albert Salmi, opened at the Music Box in New York City.

Mar. 7 **Emmy Awards** were presented to Robert Cummings as best actor for *Twelve Angry Men;* Judith Anderson as best actress for *Macbeth;* and Art Carney and Audrey Meadows as best actor and actress in a series for *The Jackie Gleason Show.*

Mar. 27 **Tony Awards** for outstanding contributions to the theater during the 1954–1955 season were presented for the following: play, *The Desperate Hours;* musical, *The Pajama Game;* dramatic actor, Alfred Lunt for *Quadrille;* dramatic actress, Nancy Kelly for *The Bad Seed.*

Mar. 30 **Academy Awards** were presented to *On the Waterfront* as the outstanding motion picture of 1954 and to its star Marlon Brando as best actor; to Grace Kelly as best actress for *The Country Girl;* to Edmond O'Brien as best supporting actor for *The Barefoot Contessa;* and to Eva Marie Saint as best supporting actress for *On the Waterfront.*

| Business and Industry; Science; Education; Philosophy and Religion   III | | IV   Sports; Social Issues and Crime; Folkways; Fashion; Holidays |

The report was issued by the Federal Trade Commission.

May 23 The ordination of **women ministers** was approved by the General Assembly of the Presbyterian Church.

May 31 **Racial segregation** in U.S. public schools was banned by the U.S. Supreme Court.

June 10 U.S. **postal workers** won an 8% salary hike.

July 5 A **General Motors stock split** was announced by the corporation's board of directors. Some 91,960,366 shares of General Motors common stock were to be split three for one.

July 29 Plans for the first artificial **satellites** were announced by the U.S. The satellites were scheduled to be launched in 1957.

Aug. 21 U.S. **private investments abroad** were estimated at $26,600,000,000 by the U.S. Department of Commerce.

Sept. 8 Studies of **Mars** by the National Geographic Society indicated the presence of large blue-green areas. The announcement sparked speculation that the patches were living vegetation.

Sept. 12 A study of **foundations** by the American Foundations Information Service listed 7300 charitable, welfare, and research foundations in the U.S. Over 4000 had assets above $4,700,000.

Sept. 26 The **New York Stock Exchange** recorded its heaviest single day dollar loss in history, $14,000,000,000. In all, 7,720,000 shares were traded, the highest volume since July 21, 1933. This sharp break in prices occurred two days after an announcement that Pres. Eisenhower had suffered a heart attack in Denver, Colo.

Oct. 7 The aircraft carrier U.S.S. *Saratoga,* the world's most powerful warship, was launched at the Brooklyn (N.Y.) Navy Yard.

Oct. 18 The **antiproton,** a new atomic subparticle, was discovered at the University of California.

champions of 1954. The UPI poll selected UCLA.

Jan. 27 **Serge Rubinstein,** a wealthy financier and convicted World War II draft dodger, was strangled in his New York City home.

Feb. 16–17 At the **world figure skating championships** in Vienna, Austria, Hayes Alan Jenkins won the men's singles title and Tenley Albright won the women's singles title.

Mar. 12–26 At the second **Pan-American Games** in Mexico City, Mexico, the U.S. took first place in the unofficial team championships, followed by Argentina and Mexico.

Mar. 19 The **NCAA basketball championship** was won by San Francisco, defeating La Salle 77–63.

Mar. 21–Apr. 10 The **NBA basketball championship** was won by the Syracuse Nationals, who beat the Fort Wayne Pistons four games to three.

Apr. 1–2 **U.S. figure skating championships** were won in Colorado Springs, Colo., by Hayes Alan Jenkins, men's singles; Tenley Albright, women's singles; Robin Greiner and Carole Ann Ormaca, pairs; Carmel and Edward L. Bodel, dance.

Apr. 3–14 The **NHL Stanley Cup** was won by the Detroit Red Wings, who defeated the Montreal Canadiens four games to three.

Apr. 10 The **Masters golf tournament** was won by Cary Middlecoff, beating Ben Hogan by seven strokes.

Apr. 19 The 59th **Boston Marathon** was won by Hideo Hamamura of Japan, with a record time of 2 hrs., 18 min., 22 sec.

May 7 The 81st annual **Kentucky Derby** was won by Swaps, with a time of 2:01⁴/₅. The jockey was Willie Shoemaker.

May 28 The 80th annual **Preakness Stakes** was won by Nashua, with a time of 1:54³/₅. The jockey was Eddie Arcaro.

May 30 The 39th **Indianapolis 500** auto race was won by Bob Sweikert of Indianapolis, completing the course in 3 hrs., 53 min., 59.53 sec., with an average speed of 128.209 mph. Bill Vukovich, seeking his third consecutive win, was killed in a four-car crash.

June 11 The 87th annual **Belmont Stakes** was won by Nashua, with a time of 2:29. The jockey was Eddie Arcaro.

June 19 The **U.S. Open golf tournament** was won by Jack Fleck, who beat Ben Hogan by three strokes in a playoff round.

July 1–2 At the **Wimbledon** tennis championships in England, Tony Trabert won the men's singles title and Louise Brough won the women's singles. Victor Seixas and Doris Hart won the mixed doubles.

July 2 The **U.S. Women's Open golf tournament** was won by Fay Crocker of Uruguay, beating Mary Lena Faulk and Louise Suggs by four strokes.

| Exploration and Settlement; Wars; Government; Civil Rights; Statistics | I | | II | Publishing; Arts and Music; Popular Entertainment; Architecture; Theater |

July 26 The U.S. **military reserve** was authorized to be increased from 800,000 to 2,900,000 by 1960 in a bill passed by Congress.

Aug. 2 Funding for 45,000 new **public housing** units was approved by the House of Representatives, 187–168. The units were to be built by July 31, 1956.

Aug. 20 **Serious floods** caused Pres. Eisenhower to declare the following major disaster areas: Connecticut, Massachusetts, Pennsylvania, South Carolina, and parts of New Jersey and Rhode Island.

Sept. 8 A treaty establishing **SEATO**, the Southeast Asia Treaty Organization, was signed in Manila, the Philippines, by the U.S., Australia, France, Great Britain, New Zealand, Pakistan, the Phillipines, and Thailand. The mutual defense pact, the Southeast Asia Collective Defense Treaty, was ratified by the Senate on Feb. 1, 1955 and went into effect on Feb. 19. SEATO was formally ended on Feb. 20, 1976.

Nov. 25 **Racial segregation** in interstate trains and buses was banned by the Interstate Commerce Commission.

Apr. 2 *The Wish,* an opera by George Antheil, was given its premiere performance in Louisville, Ky.

May 2 **Pulitzer prizes** were awarded to the following: fiction, *A Fable* by William Faulkner; biography, *The Taft Story* by William S. White; history, *Great River, the Rio Grande in North American History* by Paul Horgan; poetry, *The Collected Poems of Wallace Stevens;* drama, *Cat on a Hot Tin Roof* by Tennessee Williams.

May 5 *Damn Yankees,* a musical comedy by George Abbott and Douglass Wallop based on Wallop's 1954 novel *The Year the Yankees Lost the Pennant,* opened at the Forty-Sixth Street Theatre in New York City. Its cast included Gwen Verdon and Ray Walston.

Oct. 3 *Tiger at the Gates,* an adaptation by Christopher Fry of Jean Giraudoux's play *La Guerre de Troie n'aura pas lieu,* opened at the Plymouth Theatre in New York City.

Nov. 6 *Griffelkin,* an opera written by Lukas Foss for the NBC Opera Theater, was broadcast.

1956

Tension with the U.S.S.R. still dominated the American scene. John Foster Dulles summed up the Cold War in his "brink of war" statement: "The ability to get to the verge without getting into the war is the necessary art." At home, there was bitter rivalry between the armed services, heightened in May by Army charges that the Air Force was not doing its job. Americans again found a conflict between the North and South. Southern states either ignored or rebelled against the Supreme Court ruling against segregation in the public schools. In Montgomery, Ala., blacks boycotted buses, and on Nov. 13 the Supreme Court ruled that segregation on buses and streetcars was unconstitutional. Among those who died this year was Albert Woolson, the last surviving veteran of the Union Army, Aug. 2, at age 109.

The year in publishing was marked by a growing market for books from abroad, perhaps a reflection of Americans' growing interest in world affairs. In architecture, the volume of construction, particularly of industrial and commercial buildings, continued to increase. The outspoken elder statesman of architecture, Frank Lloyd Wright, completed work on the Price Tower in Bartlesville, Okla., and began construction of the Guggenheim Museum in New York City. Contemporary American paintings by such artists as Jackson Pollock were characterized by a distinct abstractionism; in fact, abstractionism had become conventional. On Aug. 11 the art world mourned the death of Pollock, age 44, in an automobile accident.

Among **books published** this year was *The Last Hurrah* by Edwin O'Connor, a novel about an Irish-American politician in his final political campaign. Critics noted the similarities between the fictional politician Frank Skeffington and the Boston mayor, James M. Curley. The novel was a best seller. Other books published this year included *Seize the Day* by Saul Bellow, a

Jan. 9 In what was interpreted as a vote for **segregation,** Virginia amended a state prohibition against the use of public funds for private schools. The amendment helped support private education in a state

| Business and Industry; Science; Education; Philosophy and Religion   III | IV   Sports; Social Issues and Crime; Folkways; Fashion; Holidays |

Nov. 2 The **Nobel Prize in Chemistry** was awarded to Dr. Vincent du Vigneaud of Cornell University Medical College for his work on two hormones important in childbirth and in regulation of vital organs.

Nov. 2 The **Nobel Prize in Physics** was awarded jointly to Dr. Willis E. Lamb of Stanford University and to Dr. Polykarp Kusch of Columbia University for their work on atomic measurements.

Nov. 3 Discovery of a promising **common cold vaccine** was announced by the U.S. Public Health Service.

Dec. 5 The **AFL and CIO formally merged.** The new organization, the American Federation of Labor and Congress of Industrial Organizations (AFL-CIO), was headed by George Meany, former president of the AFL.

Dec. 12 A **record educational grant** of $500,000,000 was awarded by the Ford Foundation to 4157 privately supported colleges, universities, and hospitals.

Dec. 27 **Traffic fatalities** over the Christmas weekend numbered 609, a new record.

July 12 The 22nd annual **baseball All-Star Game** was won by the National League, who beat the American League 6–5 in 12 innings.

July 17 The **first LPGA golf tournament** was won by Beverly Hanson.

July 25 The **Baseball Hall of Fame** inducted six new members: John Franklin "Home Run" Baker, third baseman; Joseph P. "Joe" DiMaggio, center fielder and hitting champion; Charles L. "Gabby" Hartnett, catcher; Theodore A. "Ted" Lyons, pitcher and manager; Ray Schalk, catcher; and Arthur C. "Dazzy" Vance, pitcher.

July 26 The **PGA golf tournament** was won by Doug Ford.

Sept. 10 The **Miss America** title was won by Sharon Kay Ritchie, 18, from Colorado, at the annual pageant in Atlantic City, N.J.

Sept. 11 The **U.S. Lawn Tennis Association singles championships** were won by Tony Trabert in the men's division and Doris Hart in the women's division.

Sept. 28–Oct. 4 The 52nd annual **World Series** was won by the Brooklyn Dodgers (NL), who defeated the New York Yankees (AL) four games to three.

Dec. 26 The **NFL championship** was won by the Cleveland Browns, who defeated the Los Angeles Rams 38–14.

1956

About 2,000,000 workers received pay increases during the first half of the year, while rising business investments and earnings were benefiting all of labor. The new federal hourly wage minimum of $1.00 an hour was expected to help approximately 2,000,000 workers. In addition, despite widespread drought and crop restrictions, American farmers produced a new all-time high in food and fiber output. Although there were no great discoveries in physics or astronomy during 1956, scientists were active in planning for the International Geophysical Year, to take place in 1957–1958.

Automobile production for the year was excellent. About 6,000,000 cars and 1,000,000 trucks came off the assembly lines, putting 1956 at about the same level as 1953, the industry's third best production year. About one out of every eight cars was a station wagon.

American society was being changed by political, social, and technological forces of great magnitude. One result of these pressures was a new spirit of youthful rebelliousness, as evidenced by the rise of a Tennessee rock-'n'-roll singer, Elvis Presley, who skyrocketed to fame despite objections from parents all over the U.S. A cult also grew up around the late James Dean, a promising young actor who had been killed in an automobile accident in 1955. Dean epitomized the American loner, daring to oppose a society that would not or could not understand him. In the more conventional world of boxing, Rocky Marciano retired as the undefeated world heavyweight champion. In golf, the year's top money winners were Ted Kroll, $72,835, and Marlene Bauer Hagge, $20,235.

Jan. 1 In **college football bowl games,** the results were Mississippi 14, TCU 13 in the Cotton Bowl; Oklahoma 20, Maryland 6 in the Orange Bowl; Michigan State 17, UCLA 14 in the Rose Bowl; and Georgia Tech 7, Pittsburgh 0 in the Sugar Bowl. This season the AP poll and the UPI poll chose Oklahoma the national collegiate champions of 1955.

1956 *PRES.* DWIGHT D. EISENHOWER   572

| Exploration and Settlement; Wars; Government; Civil Rights; Statistics | I | | II | Publishing; Arts and Music; Popular Entertainment; Architecture; Theater |

where public schools had been shut down because of the 1954 Supreme Court ruling against segregation in public schools.

Feb. 15 To enforce **school desegregation** in New Orleans, La., a federal court banned all Louisiana laws opposing the Supreme Court ruling against segregation in public schools.

Mar. 27 The communist *Daily Worker* was seized by Internal Revenue Service agents for nonpayment of income taxes. The newspaper's New York, Chicago, and Detroit offices were returned on Apr. 3 after *Daily Worker* officers posted $4500 against their tax bill.

Apr. 2–3 **Tornadoes** in Michigan, Wisconsin, Oklahoma, Kansas, Mississippi, Missouri, Arkansas, and Tennessee killed at least 45 people and caused $15,000,000 worth of property damage.

Apr. 8 **Six Marine recruits drowned** while on a disciplinary march at Parris Island, S.C. Platoon Sgt. Matthew C. McKeon was convicted on Aug. 3 of drinking on duty and negligent homicide. He was reduced in rank to private and served a three-month prison sentence.

June 30 In the worst **commercial air disaster** to date, 128 persons were killed when two airliners crashed into the Grand Canyon. The accident involved a Trans-World Airlines Super-Constellation and a United Air Lines DC-7, which were thought to have collided in midair.

July 14–15 A **fire** destroyed the Wanamaker Building on Astor Place in New York City.

collection including the title novella, a play, and several stories; *A Single Pebble* by John Hersey, a novel; *Peyton Place* by Grace Metalious, a racy novel about the residents of a New Hampshire town that became the best seller of the year; and *The Letters of Thomas Wolfe*, edited by Elizabeth Nowell, which revealed how close the author's novels were to his actual life.

Operas became more popular in the U.S this year. Among the favorites were *La Boheme* by Giacomo Puccini, which was staged 162 times during the year; *Cosi fan Tutte* by Wolfgang Amadeus Mozart, a comic opera; and *Boris Godunov*, the dramatic opera by Modest Petrovich Moussorgsky. In addition to these opera classics, American audiences were offered a number of new works, including *The Wife of Martin Guerre* by William Bergsma; *The Trial at Rouen* by Norman Dello Joio; *Images of Youth* by Felix Labunski; *The Unicorn, the Gorgon and the Manticore* by Gian-Carlo Menotti; and *The Ballad of Baby Doe* by Douglas Moore.

The year's **popular songs** included a number of hits by Elvis Presley, who had skyrocketed to stardom. Among them were "Heartbreak Hotel," "Don't Be Cruel," "Hound Dog," and "Love Me Tender." Other hits this year were "True Love," "No, Not Much," "Poor People of Paris," and "Standing on the Corner."

An unconventional sculpture by **Richard Lippold,** *Variation Within a Sphere, No. 10: The Sun,* was acquired by the Metropolitan Museum in New York City. The sculpture was made of almost two miles of gold wire and had more than 14,000 hand-welded joints.

Feb. 7 The **National Book Awards** were presented for the following: fiction, *Ten North Frederick* by John O'Hara; nonfiction, *American in Italy* by Herbert Kubly; poetry, *Shield of Achilles* by W. H. Auden.

Feb. 8 *Middle of the Night* by Paddy Chayefsky, starring Edward G. Robinson and Gena Rowlands, opened at the ANTA Theatre in New York City.

Mar. 15 *My Fair Lady,* the hit musical by Alan Jay Lerner and Frederick Loewe based on *Pygmalion* by George Bernard Shaw, opened at the Mark Hellinger Theatre in New York City. Its cast included Rex Harrison and Julie Andrews.

| Business and Industry; Science; Education; Philosophy and Religion III | | Sports; Social Issues and Crime; Folkways; Fashion; Holidays IV |

Feb. 6 Three days of **campus violence** at the University of Alabama were climaxed by the suspension of Autherine Lucy, the first black student to be enrolled there. On Mar. 1 she was permanently expelled for her accusations against the school in a legal suit handled by the National Association for the Advancement of Colored People.

Mar. 20 A major **strike** at Westinghouse Electric Corporation, the longest walkout in more than 20 years, was settled after 156 days when the union accepted contract terms proposed by the company.

Apr. 5 **Victor Riesel was blinded** when a hoodlum threw acid in the labor columnist's face as he left a New York City restaurant. On May 4 it was announced that Riesel, a crusader against labor racketeering, had lost the sight of both eyes. On Aug. 28 Johnny Dio, a notorious racketeer, was named by the FBI as the instigator of the assault. On Sept. 7 Dio and six others were indicted by a federal grand jury on conspiracy charges.

Apr. 28 The **New York Coliseum,** the world's largest exhibition building, with nine acres of floor space, opened in New York City. Its total cost was $35,000,-000.

May 2 Racial **segregation in Methodist churches** was ordered abolished by the General Conference of the Methodist Church in Minneapolis, Minn.

May 4 **Private atomic energy plants** were authorized by the Atomic Energy Commission. Soon after, the Consolidated Edison Company of New York began construction of a $55,000,000 plant at Indian Point, N.Y., and the Commonwealth Edison Company began work on a $45,000,000 plant in Grundy County, Ill.

June 11 In Chicago, reports on **polio** were presented to the American Medical Association by Dr. Jonas E. Salk and Surgeon Gen. Leonard A. Scheele. They stated that the crippling disease would be eliminated

Jan. 26–Feb. 5 At the **Winter Olympics** in Cortina d'Ampezzo, Italy, the U.S. won two gold medals. Hayes Alan Jenkins and Tenley Albright took top honors in singles figure skating competitions.

Feb. 17 At the **world figure skating championships** in Garmisch-Partenkirchen, Germany, Hayes Alan Jenkins won the men's singles title for the fourth year in a row. The next day Carol Heiss won the women's singles.

Mar. 12 Dr. Jésus de Galindez, a critic of the Rafael Trujillo regime in the Dominican Republic, disappeared on his way to his New York City home. Police found a note in his apartment directing them to look for his political enemies if anything happened to him. Dominican officials denied involvement in the disappearance.

Mar. 16 **U.S. figure skating championships** were won in Philadelphia, Pa., by Hayes Alan Jenkins, men's singles; Tenley Albright, women's singles; Carole Ann Ormaca and Robin Greiner, pairs; Joan Zamboni and Roland Junso, dance.

Mar. 23 The **NCAA basketball championship** was won by San Francisco, defeating Iowa 83–71.

Mar. 31–Apr. 7 The **NBA basketball championship** was won by the Philadelphia Warriors, who defeated the Fort Wayne Pistons four games to one.

Mar. 31–Apr. 10 The **NHL Stanley Cup** was won by the Montreal Canadiens, who defeated the Detroit Red Wings four games to one.

Apr. 8 The **Masters golf tournament** was won by Jack Burke, who came from eight strokes behind to beat Ken Venturi by one stroke.

Apr. 19 Actress **Grace Kelly,** 26, was married in Monte Carlo to Prince Rainier III of Monaco, 32, in one of the most publicized marriages of the decade. Prince Rainier was a member of the Grimaldi dynasty, founded in 1017.

Apr. 19 The 60th **Boston Marathon** was won by Antti Viskari of Finland, with a record time of 2 hrs., 14 min., 14 sec.

May 5 The 82nd annual **Kentucky Derby** was won by Needles, with a time of 2:03²/₅. The jockey was Dave Erb.

May 19 The 81st annual **Preakness Stakes** was won by Fabius, with a time of 1:58²/₅. The jockey was Bill Hartack.

May 30 The 40th **Indianapolis 500** auto race was won by Patrick Francis Flaherty of Chicago, Ill., completing the 500-mile course in 3 hrs., 53 min., 59.13 sec., with an average speed of 128.490 mph.

June 16 The 88th annual **Belmont Stakes** was won by Needles, with a time of 2:29⁴/₅. The jockey was Dave Erb.

June 16 The **U.S. Open golf tournament** was won by

Aug. 13–17 The **Democratic National Convention** nominated **Adlai E. Stevenson** of Illinois for the presidency on the first ballot. Sen. Estes Kefauver of Tennessee was nominated for the vice presidency.

Aug. 20–24 The **Republican National Convention** nominated **Pres. Dwight D. Eisenhower** for a second term. Vice Pres. Richard M. Nixon was renominated as Eisenhower's running mate.

Aug. 24 The **first transcontinental helicopter flight** was completed by an Army H-21 helicopter, which flew nonstop from San Diego, Calif., to Washington, D.C., in 37 hrs. With a crew of five, it flew 2610 miles.

Nov. 6 **Dwight D. Eisenhower was reelected president** of the United States in a landslide. Eisenhower was the first Republican president to win reelection since William McKinley in 1900. Although Eisenhower carried 41 states, the Democrats retained control of both houses of Congress. The electoral vote was Eisenhower, 457; Adlai E. Stevenson, Democrat of Illinois, 74. The popular vote was Eisenhower, 35,387,015; Stevenson, 25,875,408. In congressional elections the Democrats gained one Senate seat for a 49–47 majority. In the House they gained one seat for a 233–200 majority.

Dec. 17 The worst single **automobile accident** to date occurred near Phoenix, Ariz. Twelve of the vehicle's 13 passengers were killed.

Mar. 17 **Emmy Awards** were presented to Lloyd Nolan as best actor for *The Caine Mutiny Court Martial* and Mary Martin as best actress for *Peter Pan.* Edward R. Murrow received an award as best news commentator, and *Lassie* was honored as best children's program.

Mar. 21 **Academy Awards** were presented to *Marty* as the outstanding motion picture of 1955 and to its star, Ernest Borgnine, as best actor; to Anna Magnani as best actress for *Rose Tattoo;* to Jack Lemmon as best supporting actor for *Mr. Roberts;* and to Jo Van Fleet as best supporting actress for *East of Eden.*

Apr. 1 **Tony Awards** for outstanding contribution to the theater during the 1955–1956 season were presented for the following: play, *The Diary of Anne Frank;* musical, *Damn Yankees;* dramatic actor, Paul Muni for *Inherit the Wind;* dramatic actress, Julie Harris for *The Lark.*

May 7 **Pulitzer prizes** were awarded for the following: fiction, *Andersonville* by MacKinlay Kantor; biography, *Benjamin Henry Latrobe* by Talbot F. Hamlin; history, *The Age of Reform* by Richard Hofstadter; poetry, *North and South—A Cold Spring* by Elizabeth Bishop; drama, *The Diary of Anne Frank* by Frances Goodrich and Albert Hackett.

Oct. 25 *Separate Tables,* an English import from the pen of Terence Rattigan, opened at the Music Box in New York City.

Oct. 29 **Maria Callas** made her debut at the Metropolitan Opera in New York City with a fiery performance in the title role of Vincenzo Bellini's *Norma.* The opera, the season opener, established a new box office record for first-night receipts.

Oct. 31 *Auntie Mame,* a smash hit by Jerome Lawrence and Robert E. Lee based on the novel by Patrick Dennis, opened at the Broadhurst Theatre in New York City. Rosalind Russell appeared in the title role.

as a threat within three years through use of the Salk vaccine.

Aug. 1   The **Salk antipolio vaccine** was put on the open market by manufacturers. It was sold through normal distribution channels.

Sept. 24   The world's **first transatlantic telephone cable system** began operating. The twin cables, 2250 miles long, stretched from Clarenville, Newfoundland, to Oban, Scotland. The cable, which cost $42,-000,000, had three times the capacity of radio telephone circuits between Europe and the U.S.

Oct. 19   The **Nobel Prize in Physiology or Medicine** was awarded jointly to Dr. Dickinson W. Richardson and Dr. Andre F. Cournand of Columbia University, and to Dr. Werner Forssmann of West Germany, for their work in cardiology and their contributions to the treatment of heart disease.

Nov. 1   The **Nobel Prize in Physics** was awarded jointly to William Shockley, Walter H. Brattain, and John Bardeen, all of Bell Telephone Laboratories, for their discovery of the transistor effect in semiconductors and the development of the transistor.

Nov. 25   The **first successful Antarctic parachute jump** was made by Sgt. Richard J. Patton, USAF. The 1500-foot test jump was made to determine the cause of parachute malfunction in below-zero weather.

Dec. 22   The **first gorilla born in captivity**, a female weighing four and a half lbs., was born at the Columbus Zoo, Ohio.

Cary Middlecoff, who beat Ben Hogan and Julius Boros by one stroke.

June 24   The **LPGA golf tournament** was won by Marlene Bauer Hagge.

July 7   At the **Wimbledon** tennis championships in England, Shirley Fry won the women's singles title. Althea Gibson teamed with Angela Buxton of Great Britain to win the women's doubles, and Shirley Fry and Victor Seixas won the mixed doubles.

July 10   The 23rd annual **baseball All-Star Game** was won by the National League, who beat the American League 7–3.

July 16   The **Ringling Brothers & Barnum and Bailey Circus** performed its last show under canvas. Rising costs for a tented show had forced the move to performances in permanent structures.

July 23   The **Baseball Hall of Fame** inducted two active major league managers: Joseph E. "Joe" Cronin of the Boston Red Sox and Henry B. "Hank" Greenberg, manager of the Cleveland Indians. Both Cronin and Greenberg also had outstanding careers as players.

July 25   The **PGA golf tournament** was won by Jack Burke.

Sept. 8   The **Miss America** title was won by Marian Ann McKnight, 19, from South Carolina, at the annual pageant in Atlantic City, N.J.

Sept. 9   The **U.S. Lawn Tennis Association singles championships** were won by Ken Rosewall of Australia in the men's division and Shirley Fry of St. Petersburg, Fla., in the women's division.

Oct. 3–10   The 53rd annual **World Series** was won by the New York Yankees (AL), defeating the Brooklyn Dodgers (NL) four games to three. On Oct. 8 Don Larsen, the Yankee right-hander, pitched the first no-hit, no-run game in World Series history, beating Brooklyn 2–0.

Nov. 22–Dec. 8   At the **Summer Olympics** in Melbourne, Australia, the U.S. won 32 gold medals and finished second in unofficial team standings, behind the U.S.S.R.

Nov. 30   The **world heavyweight boxing championship** was won by Floyd Patterson, who knocked out Archie Moore in the fifth round in Chicago to win the title vacated by Rocky Marciano on Apr. 27. Patterson, 21, was the youngest fighter to win the championship.

Dec. 30   The **NFL championship** was won by the New York Giants, who defeated the Chicago Bears 47–7.

1957

On Oct. 4 the Soviet Union launched the first Earth satellite, Sputnik I. Americans were stunned by the Soviets' technological progress, and politicians, scientists, and educators called for a major U.S. initiative to regain superiority in missiles development and space technology. Thus 1957 was another year of world tension. Pres. Dwight D. Eisenhower presented the Eisenhower Doctrine; its aim was to resist communist aggression in the Middle East. Despite the race against the U.S.S.R. in outer space, the president continued to release uranium-235 for peaceful purposes; by the end of the year a total of 100,000 kilograms of U-235 had been made available for research and energy. The Air Force, which celebrated its golden anniversary (dating from the founding of the Army Air Corps—the Air Force was officially established in 1947), became the largest enterprise in the U.S.; its total assets for the year were over $70,000,000,000. Notables who died included Sen. Joseph R. McCarthy, Republican of Wisconsin, whose widely publicized charges of communist subversion in government earned him Senate censure and condemnation, on May 2, at age 48.

Jan. 5 The Eisenhower Doctrine was proposed by Pres. Eisenhower before a joint session of Congress. The plan offered protection to any Middle East nation seeking aid against communist aggression. Eisenhower requested authority to use U.S. forces to oppose communist or communist-backed attempts to overthrow any government in the region. He stated he would send such forces only under three conditions: first, only if requested by a Mideast nation under attack; second, only with hour-by-hour communication with Congress; third, only in accord with U.S. treaty obligations and the UN Charter.

Jan. 20 Pres. Eisenhower was inaugurated for his second term. Vice Pres. Richard M. Nixon was also sworn in for a second term in the three-minute ceremony at the White House. Because this inauguration day fell on a Sunday, the public inaugural ceremonies were held on the following day, Jan. 21.

Feb. 4 An explosion in a coal mine near Bishop, Va., killed 37 miners.

Feb. 8 The European Atomic Energy Community was pledged full U.S. support for establishment of an atomic energy industry in Europe within ten years.

Feb. 9–12 The U.S. Communist Party held a convention in New York City during which its

Architects continued to explore the use of new construction materials. A highlight of the year was the completion of the Seagram Building in New York City, the first such structure to be sheathed in bronze. Also in 1957 extraordinary prices were being paid for painting and sculpture. The Edward G. Robinson collection was sold for well over $3,000,000, and one painting in the Georges Lurcy collection, Renoir's *La Serre*, brought $200,000. Americans mourned the passing of Humphrey Bogart, actor, Jan. 14, at 57; James Francis "Jimmy" Dorsey, bandleader, June 12, at 53; Oliver Hardy, of the team of Laurel and Hardy, Aug. 7, at 55; Frederick Law Olmsted, landscape architect, Dec. 25, at 87; and Laura Ingalls Wilder, author of the popular "Little House" books, Feb. 10, at 90.

Among **books published** this year was *By Love Possessed* by James Gould Cozzens, the major novel of the year. Not all critics praised the book but it stayed on the top of the best-seller list. The novel depicted two days in the life of a middle-aged lawyer. Other books published this year included *A Death in the Family* by James Agee, the author's only full-length novel, dealing with a boy's reaction to his father's death; *The Wapshot Chronicle* by John Cheever, a novel; *The Town* by William Faulkner, part of the author's Yoknapatawpha County saga; *Simple Stakes a Claim* by Langston Hughes; and *On the Road* by Jack Kerouac, a semiautobiographical novel of the Beat generation in which the author explored the use of jazz, sex, and drugs by young people.

The year's top **popular songs** included "Love Letters in the Sand," "Tammy," "Fascination," "Young Love," "Round and Round," and music from *My Fair Lady*.

A comprehensive **Picasso exhibition** was presented by New York's Museum of Modern Art in honor of Pablo Picasso's 75th birthday. Attendance during the exhibit was 238,646.

Feb. 7 *A Visit to a Small Planet,* a play by Gore Vidal that he had originally written for television, opened at the Booth Theatre in New York City.

Feb. 25 In a **censorship ruling,** the Supreme Court ruled unanimously against the conviction of a Detroit, Mich., bookseller for selling John Howard Griffin's book *The Devil Rides Outside*. The ruling voided the section of Michigan penal law banning the sale of books that might corrupt youth. Justice Felix Frankfurter said the law would reduce adults in Michigan to reading only what might be deemed fit for children.

Mar. 12 The **National Book Awards** were presented for the following: fiction, *The Field of Vision* by Wright Morris; poetry, *Things of This World* by

Business and Industry; Science; Education; Philosophy and Religion III		IV Sports; Social Issues and Crime; Folkways; Fashion; Holidays

1957

In September wages for factory workers averaged $2.08 an hour, $82.99 a week. Employment remained high during most of the year, but in autumn began to decline. Farm production exceeded the crop yield record set in 1956, and farm prices continued the advance begun in 1956. In religion, leaders of various faiths played important parts in the fight to implement the Supreme Court's decision to bar racial segregation in public schools. Official bodies of several southern church groups requested peaceful compliance with the decision, and the Vatican approved the move by the archbishop of New Orleans to desegregate church schools. But at the end of the year, desegregation in the schools was still a major issue. Americans mourned the death of Adm. Richard E. Byrd on Mar. 11 at age 68. He had led five expeditions to Antarctica and was the first person to fly over the North and South Poles.

In a **survey** of 60,000 high school juniors and seniors, Dr. Ernest V. Hollis of the U.S. Office of Education discovered that 51% of students with an IQ of 133 or higher would not attend college because of the expense or because of a lack of goals.

Jan. 21 The first **nationally televised videotaped TV broadcast** was carried by the National Broadcasting Co. The program was a recording of the presidential inauguration ceremonies in Washington, D.C. The first use of videotape in TV had occurred on Nov. 30, 1956, when taped broadcasts of *Douglas Edwards and the News* began running in the western U.S. The first national show to be videotaped was *Truth or Consequences,* beginning on Jan. 22, 1957.

Apr. 4 The **National Education Association** celebrated its 100th anniversary in Philadelphia. The NEA, which was started in 1857 with a membership of 43, had grown to almost 1,000,000 teachers and affiliates.

May 2 Teamsters Union president **Dave Beck was indicted** by a federal grand jury in Seattle, Wash., on charges that he had evaded payment of $56,000 in income taxes in 1950. Further investigation revealed that Beck had used union funds for himself and his family.

June 13 The *Mayflower II* landed at Plymouth, Mass., 54 days after setting out from Plymouth,

The sack was the most discussed fashion since the New Look. The sack's silhouette was an unfitted drape, and men were heard to comment: "It looks like a flour sack." The most highly praised man of the year in boxing was Carmen Basilio, who outpointed Sugar Ray Robinson in a savage fight for the middleweight championship. But by 1958 Robinson had defeated Basilio again. Floyd Patterson defended the world heavyweight title against Tommy "Hurricane" Jackson (July 29). In golf the top money winners were Dick Mayer $65,835, and Patty Berg, $16,272. Baseball was marked by the departure of the New York Giants for San Francisco and the Brooklyn Dodgers for Los Angeles, leaving the pennant-winning Yankees with sole dominion over New York baseball.

A new **baseball attendance record** for the National League was set by the Milwaukee Braves, who drew 2,215,404 fans to home games this year.

Jan. 1 In **college football bowl games,** the results were TCU 28, Syracuse 27 in the Cotton Bowl; Colorado 27, Clemson 21 in the Orange Bowl; Iowa 35, Oregon State 19 in the Rose Bowl; and Baylor 13, Tennessee 7 in the Sugar Bowl. This season both the UPI and the AP polls chose Oklahoma the national collegiate champions of 1956.

Feb. 28–Mar. 3 At the **world figure skating championships** in Colorado Springs, Colo., Carol Heiss won the women's singles title and David Jenkins won the men's singles.

Mar. 15–16 **U.S. figure skating championships** were won in Berkeley, Calif, by Carol Heiss, women's singles; David Jenkins, men's singles; Ronald and Nancy Ludington, pairs; Sharon McKenzie and Bert Wright, dance.

Mar. 23 The **NCAA basketball championship** was won by North Carolina, which beat Kansas 54–53 in three overtime periods.

Mar. 30–Apr. 3 The **NBA basketball championship** was won by the Boston Celtics, defeating the St. Louis Hawks four games to three.

Apr. 6–16 The **NHL Stanley Cup** was won by the Montreal Canadiens, who defeated the Boston Bruins four games to one.

Apr. 7 The **Masters golf tournament** was won by Doug Ford, beating Sam Snead by three strokes.

Apr. 20 The 61st **Boston Marathon** was won by John J. Kelley of West Acton, Mass., with a time of 2 hrs., 20 min., 5 sec. He was the first U.S. runner to win the event since 1945.

May 4 The 83rd annual **Kentucky Derby** was won by

members adopted a new party constitution. One of the new rules in the constitution specified that party members could be expelled for subversion of the U.S. government. FBI chief J. Edgar Hoover stated that the new rules were merely an attempt by the party to gain acceptance by U.S. citizens.

Feb. 17   A fire in a home for the aged in Warrenton, Mo., killed 72 persons.

Mar. 30   The United States' second **atomic submarine,** the *Seawolf,* was commissioned. On May 16, *Skate,* the third atomic submarine and the first designed for assembly-line production, was launched at Groton, Conn.

Apr. 30   Five members were elected to a new **Senate Hall of Fame** by a special committee of the U.S. Senate. They were Robert M. Taft, Robert M. La Follette, John C. Calhoun, Daniel Webster, and Henry Clay.

June 27–28   Hurricane Audrey and a subsequent tidal wave hit the Louisiana and Texas coasts, leaving 531 persons dead or missing.

July 16   A new **transcontinental speed record** (Long Beach, Calif., to Brooklyn, N.Y.) was set by Maj. John H. Glenn, Jr., USN, in a Navy F8U-1P jet. The time was 3 hrs., 23 min., 8.4 sec.

Aug. 30   A new **filibuster record** was set by Sen. Strom Thurmond, Democrat of South Carolina, who held the floor arguing against civil rights legislation for 24 hrs., 27 min.

Sept. 19   The **first underground atomic explosion** was set off at proving grounds near Las Vegas, Nev.

Sept. 24   Racial violence in **Little Rock,** Ark., prompted Pres. Eisenhower to send a force of some 1000 U.S. Army paratroopers to enforce the desegregation of Central High School. The president said that violence had caused the removal of nine black students in the newly integrated school. The students entered the guarded school on Sept. 25.

Oct. 8   **Jack Soble,** a confessed Soviet spy, was sentenced in New York to a seven-year imprisonment for espionage. Soble had pleaded guilty to obtaining national defense secrets with the knowledge that they would go to the U.S.S.R. His wife Myra Soble, and another member of the conspiracy, Jacob Albam, previously had been sentenced to seven years in jail, but their sentences were reduced to four and five years,

Richard Wilbur; nonfiction, *Russia Leaves the War* by George F. Kennan.

Mar. 16   **Emmy Awards** were presented to Jack Palance as best actor for *Requiem for a Heavyweight* (which won five awards, including one to Rod Serling for best teleplay); Claire Trevor as best actress for *Dodsworth;* Robert Young as best actor in a dramatic series for *Father Knows Best;* and Loretta Young as best actress in a dramatic series for the *Loretta Young Show.*

Mar. 27   **Academy Awards** were presented to *Around the World in 80 Days* as the outstanding motion picture of 1956; to Yul Brynner as best actor for *The King and I;* to Ingrid Bergman as best actress for *Anastasia;* to Anthony Quinn as best supporting actor for *Lust for Life;* and to Dorothy Malone as best supporting actress for *Written on the Wind.*

Apr. 21   **Tony Awards** for distinguished contributions to the theater during the 1956–1957 season were presented for the following: play, *Long Day's Journey into Night* by Eugene O'Neill; musical, *My Fair Lady* by Alan Jay Lerner and Frederick Loewe; dramatic actor, Fredric March for *Long Day's Journey into Night;* dramatic actress, Margaret Leighton for *Separate Tables.*

May 6   **Pulitzer prizes** were awarded for the following: biography, *Profiles in Courage* by John F. Kennedy; history, *Russia Leaves the War* by George F. Kennan; poetry, *Things of This World* by Richard Wilbur; drama, *Long Day's Journey into Night* by Eugene O'Neill. A special award was made to Kenneth Roberts for his historical novels.

June 17   Igor Stravinsky's **75th birthday** was celebrated in Los Angeles, Calif., with an all-Stravinsky program that included the world premiere of his ballet score *Agon: A Contest.*

Sept. 26   *West Side Story* by Arthur Laurents, Leonard Bernstein, and Stephen Sondheim, opened at the Winter Garden in New York City. Its cast included Carol Lawrence and Chita Rivera.

Oct. 1   *Look Back in Anger* by John Osborne opened at the Lyceum Theatre in New York City.

Oct. 15   *Under Milk Wood* by Dylan Thomas opened at Henry Miller's Theatre in New York City.

Oct. 16   **Leonard Bernstein** was appointed to serve as one of the two principal conductors of the Philharmonic-Symphony Society of New York. On Nov. 19 it was announced that he would become its sole musical director at the close of the season.

Oct. 19   *The Cave Dwellers,* a play by William Saroyan described by Brooks Atkinson of *The New York Times* as "one of the most enchanting stories he has ever told," opened at the Bijou Theatre in New York City.

Nov. 28   *Look Homeward, Angel* a play by Ketti Frings adapted from the Thomas Wolfe novel, opened

| Business and Industry; Science; Education; Philosophy and Religion III | | Sports; Social Issues and Crime; Folkways; Fashion; Holidays IV |

England, to duplicate the voyage of the Pilgrims.

July 1 The **International Geophysical Year** (July 1, 1957–Dec. 31, 1958) launched its first major scientific project, the firing of a rocket on San Nicolas Island, Calif., by the Naval Research Laboratory. The goal was to study the effects of the sun's radiation on communications. Scientists of 67 nations participated in the International Geophysical Year, a coordinated study of Earth, its atmosphere and oceans, and the sun.

July 12 A link between **cigarette smoking and lung cancer** had been established by scientific research, Surgeon General Leroy E. Burney reported. Burney stated that the studies showed a "direct relationship between the incidence of lung cancer and the amount smoked."

Aug. 19–20 A new **balloon ascent record** was set when Maj. David G. Simons, USAF, went up 101,486 feet supported by a plastic balloon. The record also marked man's longest stay on the edge of space.

Sept. 1 **Billy Graham** closed his 16-week evangelical campaign in New York with a giant rally on Times Square. His meetings had drawn an attendance of almost 2,000,000, and 56,767 of his hearers in New York City made "decisions for Christ."

Sept. 18 **James R. Hoffa,** international vice president of the Teamsters Union, was charged by the Ethical Practices Committee of the AFL-CIO with fostering criminals in the Teamsters Union. The AFL-CIO advised the union to expel Hoffa or leave the AFL-CIO. On Dec. 6 the Teamsters Union was expelled.

Oct. 16 The **first American objects launched into space** were two aluminum pellets lofted by the U.S. Air Force.

Oct. 31 The **Nobel Prize in Physics** was awarded jointly to Dr. Tsung Dao Lee of Columbia University and Dr. Chen Ning Yang of the Institute for Advanced Study at Princeton for their studies of the behavior of subatomic particles.

Nov. 1 The **world's longest suspension bridge,** the Mackinac Straits Bridge between Michigan's upper

Iron Liege, with a time of 2:02¹/₅. The jockey was Bill Hartack.

May 18 The 82nd annual **Preakness Stakes** was won by Bold Ruler, with a time of 1:56¹/₅ . The jockey was Willie Shoemaker.

May 30 The 41st **Indianapolis 500** auto race was won by Sam Hanks of Pacific Palisades, Calif., completing the 500-mile course in 3 hrs., 41 min., 14.25 sec., with an average speed of 135.601 mph.

June 10 The **LPGA golf tournament** was won by Louise Suggs.

June 15 The 89th annual **Belmont Stakes** was won by Gallant Man, with a time of 2:26³/₅. The jockey was Willie Shoemaker.

June 15 The **U.S. Open golf tournament** was won by Dick Mayer, who beat defending champion Cary Middlecoff by seven strokes in a playoff round.

June 29 The **U.S. Women's Open golf tournament** was won by Betsy Rawls after the apparent winner, Jacqueline Pung, was disqualified for turning in an incorrect scorecard.

July 6 At the **Wimbledon** tennis championships in England, Althea Gibson won the women's singles title. She then teamed with her opponent, Darlene Hard, to win the women's doubles. Gardnar Mulloy and V. Edward "Budge" Patty won the men's doubles. Hard teamed with Mervyn Rose of Australia to win the mixed doubles.

July 9 The 24th annual **baseball All-Star Game** was won by the American League, defeating the National League 6–5.

July 19 The **first U.S. runner to break the four-minute mile** was Don Bowden, who ran the mile in 3:58.7 at Stockton, Calif.

July 21 The **PGA golf tournament** was won by Lionel Hebert.

July 22 The **Baseball Hall of Fame** inducted Samuel "Wahoo Sam" Crawford, who held the major league record for career triples (312); and Joseph V. "Joe" McCarthy, former manager of the Chicago Cubs and New York Yankees. McCarthy led the Yankees to eight American League pennants and seven World Series victories.

Sept. 7 The **Miss America** title was won by Marilyn Elaine Van Derbur, 20, from Colorado, at the annual pageant in Atlantic City, N.J.

Sept. 8 The **U.S. Lawn Tennis Association singles championships** were won by Malcolm Anderson of Australia in the men's division and Althea Gibson in the women's division. Gibson was the first black to win the title.

respectively. Soble was sentenced to seven years in jail. Other charges against him were dropped, including one that carried the death penalty.

Nov. 25 At the opening of the **Senate Preparedness Subcommittee** hearings, Dr. Edward Teller urged that the U.S. strengthen its heavy bomber bases as a safeguard against Soviet missile attack.

at the Ethel Barrymore Theatre in New York City. Its cast included Alan Bates, Hugh Griffith, and Arthur Hill.

Dec. 5 *The Dark at the Top of the Stairs* by William Inge opened at the Music Box in New York City. Its cast included Pat Hingle, Teresa Wright, and Eileen Heckart.

Dec. 19 *The Music Man* by Meredith Willson, starring Robert Preston and Barbara Cook, opened at the Majestic Theatre in New York City.

1958

The political scene was heated during the congressional election campaign by Republican charges that Democrats were guilty of radicalism. Former Pres. Harry S Truman countered with the claim that Pres. Dwight D. Eisenhower had surrendered in Korea. Informal polls showed that the Republicans were losing ground because of continued world tension, including that engendered by America's rush to beat the U.S.S.R. into space, but they continued the fight until election day. When the smoke cleared, the Democrats had scored the biggest gains in more than 20 years.

Jan. 3 Formation of two **missile squadrons** armed with intermediate range ballistic missiles (IRBM's) was announced by the U.S. Air Force. The squadrons were to be part of the Strategic Air Command.

Feb. 28 A **school bus collided** with a car and plunged into the Big Sandy R. near Prestonburg, Ky. The driver and 27 children drowned.

Feb. 28 A **postal rate increase,** effective Aug. 4, was approved by the Senate. The rate for regular mail rose from three cents to four cents an ounce, domestic airmail from six cents to seven cents.

Mar. 4 The verdict against Brig. Gen. **William "Billy" Mitchell,** the pioneer in military air power charged with bringing discredit to the Army more than 37 years earlier, was upheld by Sec. of the Air Force James H. Douglas. Douglas added that Mitchell's faith in air power had been vindicated.

Apr. 1 The **first antirecession legislation** of 1958, a bill to stimulate housing construction, was signed by Pres. Eisenhower. On Apr. 4 he signed legislation eliminating the required 2% down payment on GI home loans.

Book publishing had another year of growth in number of new titles and total number of books sold. At the beginning of 1958, some 45,592,000 households had television sets. TV was offering strong competition to the film industry, which produced fewer movies and showed a slight decline in attendance. Music experienced a few changes. Under the direction of a young, dynamic Leonard Bernstein, the New York Philharmonic Orchestra began to play more works by contemporary American composers. Painters were still fighting the battle of abstractionism versus representation, but abstractionism was the winner in most American exhibits. Among notables who died was Mike Todd, 49, the film producer, whose private plane crashed near Grants, N.Mex., Mar. 22.

Among **books published** this year was *Home from the Hill* by William Humphrey, a first novel that became a best seller. It told the story of a Texas family, concentrating on a boy who tried to emulate his father, a man obsessed with hunting and women. Other books published this year included *95 Poems* by E. E. Cummings; *The Ginger Man,* a novel by the expatriate American writer J. P. Donleavy; *The Affluent Society* by John Kenneth Galbraith; *J. B.* by Archibald MacLeish, a verse drama based on the biblical story of Job; and *Lolita* by Vladimir Nabokov, a novel about a middle-aged man and his love affair with a twelve-year-old girl. The book caused a sensation among readers and critics alike.

The top **popular songs** during the year were predominantly rock-'n'-roll favorites such as "Purple People-Eater" and "Bird Dog." Among popular ballads were "A Certain Smile" and "Your Precious Love."

Jan. 7 *Garden District,* a production of two short plays, *Something Unspoken* and *Suddenly Last Summer* by Tennessee Williams, opened at the York Playhouse, off Broadway in New York City.

Jan. 13 The Communist newspaper *Daily Worker suspended daily publication* because of declining

| Business and Industry; Science; Education; Philosophy and Religion **III** | | **IV** Sports; Social Issues and Crime; Folkways; Fashion; Holidays |

and lower peninsulas, was opened for traffic. The bridge cost an estimated $100,000,000.

Dec. 12 A new **jet speed record** was set by Maj. Adrian E. Drew, USAF, in his F-101 Voodoo. Drew's speed, over a course above the Mojave Desert, Calif., was 1207.6 mph.

Oct. 2–10 The 54th annual **World Series** was won by the Milwaukee Braves (NL), defeating the New York Yankees (AL) four games to three.

Oct. 25 **Umberto "Albert" Anastasia,** an underworld figure, was slain by two gunmen as he sat in a barbershop. The gangster had been nicknamed "Lord High Executioner" of a crime syndicate known as Murder, Inc.

Dec. 29 The **NFL championship** was won by the Detroit Lions, who defeated the Cleveland Browns 59–14.

1958

A serious recession affected the entire country. In February the jobless represented 7.7% of the total labor force; by March the total number of unemployed had jumped to 5,198,000. After antirecession legislation, the situation began to improve by early fall. School desegregation was still a major issue. State authorities in Little Rock, Ark., closed the public schools and reopened them as private institutions that would not admit blacks. A new cry was heard for better educational standards as critics of American schools claimed that standards were lower than ever before.

The **Van Allen belt,** a zone of radiation around Earth about 600 miles in space, was detected by U.S. satellites and named after James A. Van Allen, who led development of the satellite experiments. Radiation was shown to be 1000 times more intense than expected.

A nationwide study of **American college students** was concluded by a statement by Dr. W. Max Wise. He described the average student as more serious than his predecessors, older, often married, and probably holding a part-time job.

Jan. 20 Pres. Dwight D. Eisenhower stated in a letter to Congress that **unwarranted wage or price increases** could imperil the economic status of the U.S.

Jan. 23 Congressional **legislation against racketeering** in labor unions was urged by Pres. Eisenhower.

Jan. 31 The **first U.S. Earth satellite,** Explorer I, was launched at 10:48 P.M. from Cape Canaveral, Fla. It was bullet-shaped, 80 in. long, 6 in. in diameter with the last stage attached, and weighed 30.8 lbs.

The year in international sports competition was highlighted by U.S. defense of the America's Cup and by American capture of the grand prize of tennis, the Davis Cup, which the U.S. had lost to Australia in 1955. Althea Gibson announced she would quit tennis for a year to launch a career as a popular singer. In boxing, middleweight champion Sugar Ray Robinson disproved the theory that former champions cannot make a comeback when he regained his crown for the fifth time, and heavyweight champion Floyd Patterson defended his title in a bout (Aug. 18) with Roy Harris. In golf the top money winners were Arnold Palmer, $42,407, and Beverly Hanson, $12,629.

Jan. 1 In **college football bowl games,** the results were Navy 20, Rice 7 in the Cotton Bowl; Oklahoma 48, Duke 21 in the Orange Bowl; Ohio State 10, Oregon 7 in the Rose Bowl; and Mississippi 39, Texas 7 in the Sugar Bowl. This season the AP poll chose Auburn the national collegiate champions of 1957. The UPI poll selected Ohio State.

Jan. 15 **Eleanor Roosevelt** was the most admired woman in the U.S., according to an annual Gallup Poll survey.

Feb. 14–15 At the **world figure skating championships** in Paris, France, David Jenkins won the men's singles title. Carol Heiss won the women's singles title for the third consecutive year.

Feb. 20 **Nathan Leopold, Jr.,** in Statesville Prison, Joliet, Ill., since 1924 for the thrill murder of Bobby Franks, was granted parole. He was released on Mar. 13.

Mar. 22 The **NCAA basketball championship** was won by Kentucky, which defeated Seattle 84–72.

Mar. 25 The **world middleweight boxing championship** was regained for an unprecedented fifth time by

Apr. 16 Dr. **Edward Teller** told a Senate subcommittee that the U.S. would risk the lives of millions in a possible atomic war if it ended nuclear tests.

Apr. 18 Treason charges against **Ezra Pound,** accused of making broadcasts for the fascists in Italy during World War II, were dropped in federal court in Washington, D.C. The poet had been confined at St. Elizabeth's Hospital, a mental institution, since 1946. A key figure in securing Pound's release was his fellow poet Robert Frost. On July 1 Pound sailed with his wife for Italy.

Apr. 23 **Five paratroopers were killed** during a practice jump at Fort Campbell, Ky., conducted by units of the 101st Airborne Division. Strong winds caused the deaths and also left 137 injured.

May 1 **Four antinuclear protesters were seized** on their ship, *Golden Rule,* by the Coast Guard when they attempted to leave Honolulu for Eniwetok, the atomic testing area.

May 16 A new **world jet speed record** was set by Capt. Walter Irwin, USAF, who flew a single-jet F-104A Starfighter over Edwards Air Force Base, Calif., for an average speed of 1404.19 mph.

June 17 **Sherman Adams,** assistant to the president, denied before a House investigating committee that he had interceded with federal agencies on behalf of industrialist Bernard Goldfine. The president backed Adams on June 18, saying he was a man of integrity.

June 30 The **Alaska statehood bill,** authorizing admission of the territory as the 49th state, was passed by the Senate with an overwhelming vote of 64–20. When Gov. Mike Stepovich of Alaska heard the news, he said: "I believe that we will show the United States of America that we will be one of the greatest states in the Union within the next 50 years."

July 7 The **Alaska statehood bill** was signed by Pres. Eisenhower, making Alaska the 49th state on ratification by the voters of the territory in August. A formal declaration of statehood was planned for 1959.

Aug. 5 The world's **first undersea crossing of the North Pole** was made by the U.S. atomic submarine *Nautilus.* The ship submerged near Point Barrow, Alaska, Aug. 1 and sailed under the 50-foot-thick ice cap for 96 hours before surfacing.

Aug. 25 The **first presidential pension law** became

revenue. Its final edition before becoming a weekly declared, "We'll Be Back."

Jan. 15 *Vanessa,* the first opera by Samuel Barber, was given its premiere performance at the Metropolitan Opera House in New York City.

Jan. 16 *Two for the Seesaw* by William Gibson, a play about a divorced man who falls in love with a New York girl, opened at the Booth Theatre in New York City. In the cast of two were Henry Fonda and Anne Bancroft.

Jan. 30 *Sunrise at Campobello* by Dore Schary opened at the Cort Theatre in New York City. The play, starring Ralph Bellamy as Franklin D. Roosevelt, concerned Roosevelt's attack of polio in 1921 and his struggle to overcome his paralysis in order to return to politics.

Mar. 11 The **National Book Awards** were presented for the following: fiction, *The Wapshot Chronicle* by John Cheever; poetry, *Promises: Poems 1954–1956* by Robert Penn Warren; nonfiction, *The Lion and the Throne* by Catherine Drinker Bowen.

Mar. 26 **Academy Awards** were presented to *The Bridge on the River Kwai* as the outstanding motion picture of 1957 and to its star Alec Guinness as best actor; to Joanne Woodward as best actress for *The Three Faces of Eve;* and to Red Buttons and Miyoshi Umeki as best supporting actor and actress for *Sayonara.*

Apr. 11 Texas pianist **Van Cliburn,** 23, won the Tchaikovsky International Piano and Violin Festival held in Moscow. His playing of the *Third Piano Concerto* by Sergei Rachmaninoff filled the auditorium of the Tchaikovsky Conservatory with a frenzy of applause.

Apr. 13 **Tony Awards** for outstanding contributions to the theater during the 1957–1958 season were presented for the following: play, *Sunrise at Campobello;* musical, *The Music Man;* dramatic actor, Ralph Bellamy for *Sunrise at Campobello;* dramatic actress, Helen Hayes for *Time Remembered.*

Apr. 14 The **Moiseyev Dance Company,** a highly respected dance troupe from the U.S.S.R., opened a three-week engagement at the Metropolitan Opera House in New York City. Their performances were received enthusiastically by audiences and critics. After performing in Canada, Los Angeles, and Washington, D.C., the company returned on June 20 to give eight more performances at Madison Square Garden in New York City.

Apr. 15 **Emmy Awards** were presented to Peter Ustinov as best actor for *The Life of Samuel Johnson;* Polly Bergen as best actress for *The Helen Morgan Story;* and Robert Young and Jane Wyatt as best actor and actress in a dramatic series for *Father Knows Best.*

Apr. 15 A **fire** in the Museum of Modern Art in New

Mar. 8 **William Faulkner,** the Nobel Prize–winning novelist, said at Princeton University that parents and educators were endangering U.S. education by not facing up to important realities and that schools were turning into "baby-sitting organizations."

Mar. 17 **Vanguard 1,** a 3¼-lb. satellite, the second U.S. space vehicle, was launched after more than three months of highly publicized delays. The 6.4-in. aluminum sphere, the smallest satellite launched so far, went into a wider orbit than any other manmade satellite.

Apr. The **International Automobile Show** was held in New York City. Most cars in the show were European models, but the U.S. was represented by a few special cars, including the Ford Thunderbird and a specially designed Buick.

Apr. 26 The **highest Vatican post held by an American** pro-prefect of the Vatican's Sacred Congregation for the Propagation of the Faith was given to Samuel Cardinal Stritch, archbishop of Chicago. On Apr. 28 a blood clot forced amputation of his right arm; on May 27 he died after a stroke.

Apr. 28 Speaking on the **danger of nuclear fallout,** the Nobel Prize–winning scientist Dr. Linus Pauling said that radioactive carbon-14 already left in the air by detonated atomic bombs would cause 5,000,000 genetically defective births and millions of cancer and leukemia cases in the next 300 generations.

May 2 A report on **unemployment** showed that the number of insured jobless in the U.S. had declined, with California showing the biggest increase in employment.

June 27 A new **transatlantic speed record** from New York to London was set by Col. Harry Burrell, USAF, flying an Air Force KC-135. The new time was 5 hrs., 27 min., 42.8 sec., for an average of 630.2 mph.

Sept. 2–3 In a Senate **investigation of labor racketeering,** Harold J. Gibbons, chief aide to

Sugar Ray Robinson, who outpointed Carmen Basilio in 15 rounds at Chicago.

Mar. 28–29 **U.S. figure skating championships** were won in Minneapolis, Minn., by Carol Heiss, women's singles; David Jenkins, men's singles; Ronald and Nancy Ludington, pairs; Andree Anderson and Donald Jacoby, dance.

Mar. 29–Apr. 12 The **NBA basketball championship** was won by the St. Louis Hawks, who defeated the Boston Celtics four games to two.

Apr. 4 **Johnny Stompanato,** a known hoodlum, was stabbed and killed by Cheryl Crane, 14, daughter of the actress Lana Turner. Crane testified that she heard Stompanato threaten her mother. A coroner's jury on Apr. 11 called the act justifiable homicide.

Apr. 8–20 The **NHL Stanley Cup** was won by the Montreal Canadiens, who defeated the Boston Bruins four games to two.

Apr. 16 The **Masters golf tournament** was won by Arnold Palmer, who beat Doug Ford and Fred Hawkins by one stroke.

Apr. 19 The 62nd **Boston Marathon** was won by Franjo Mihalic of Yugoslavia, with a time of 2 hrs., 25 min., 54 sec.

May 3 The 84th annual **Kentucky Derby** was won by Tim Tam, with a time of 2:05. The jockey was Ismael Valenzuela.

May 17 The 83rd annual **Preakness Stakes** was won by Tim Tam, with a time of 1:57⅕. The jockey was Ismael Valenzuela.

May 30 The 42nd annual **Indianapolis 500** auto race was won by Jimmy Bryan of Phoenix, Ariz., completing the 500-mile course in 3 hrs., 44 min., 13 sec., with an average speed of 133.791 mph.

June 7 The 90th annual **Belmont Stakes** was won by Cavan, with a time of 2:30⅕. The jockey was Pete Anderson.

June 8 The **LPGA golf tournament** was won by Mickey Wright.

June 14 The **U.S. Open golf tournament** was won by Tommy Bolt.

June 28 A new **world swimming record** for the 100-meter butterfly was set by Nancy Ramey of Seattle, Wash., who won the event with a time of 1:09⅗ during a meet in Los Angeles, Calif.

effective, granting pensions to former presidents of the United States.

Sept. 5 In a **train accident** on the Jersey Central Railroad, a commuter train went through an open drawbridge into Newark Bay; an estimated 40 persons were killed. An autopsy performed on the train engineer revealed that he had suffered a heart attack and been unable to respond to stop signals.

Sept. 22 A new **underwater endurance record** was set by the atomic-powered submarine U.S.S. *Skate.* During a transpolar voyage it ran for 31 days under polar ice without surfacing.

Sept. 22 **Sherman Adams,** assistant to the president, resigned under pressure from fellow Republicans who felt he was endangering GOP chances in the coming elections. In a nationwide radio-TV broadcast, Adams insisted he had done no wrong in accepting gifts from Boston industrialist Bernard Goldfine.

Oct. 6 A new **underwater endurance record** was set by the atomic-powered submarine U.S.S. *Seawolf,* which surfaced after 60 days.

Nov. 4 **Congressional elections** marked the greatest Democratic gains since the New Deal. The Democrats gained 13 Senate seats to take a 62–34 majority. In the House they won 47 new seats to take control 282–153. In state elections the Democrats made a net gain of five governorships to control 34 state houses against the Republicans' 14.

Dec. 1 A catastrophic **school fire,** the third worst on record, swept through Our Lady of the Angels Roman Catholic Parochial School in Chicago, killing 87 children and three nuns.

York City killed one workman and caused an estimated $320,000 in damage.

May 1 The European premiere of the motion picture *South Pacific* marked the U.S. entry into international cultural competitions at the Brussels World's Fair. Other American cultural events there included the New York City Center Light Opera Company production of *Carousel* by Richard Rodgers and Oscar Hammerstein II (June 4–8 and June 17–22), and performances by the American Ballet Theatre (Aug. 5–10).

May 5 **Pulitzer prizes** were awarded for the following: fiction, *A Death in the Family* by James Agee; biography, *George Washington* by Douglas Southall Freeman; history, *Banks and Politics in America—from the Revolution to the Civil War* by Bray Hammond; poetry, *Promises: Poems 1954–1956* by Robert Penn Warren; drama, *Look Homeward, Angel* by Ketti Frings.

May 17 The **AIA Gold Medal** for architecture was awarded to John Wellborn Root of Chicago, Ill.

July 3–6 The **Newport Jazz Festival** in Rhode Island featured the work of jazz pioneer Duke Ellington. Ellington played several of his own works, including excerpts from his jazz suite *Black, Brown, and Beige.*

Aug. 20 *Maria Golovin,* a new opera by Gian-Carlo Menotti, was given its premiere performance at the Brussels World's Fair.

Oct. 2 *A Touch of the Poet* by Eugene O'Neill, believed to be O'Neill's last unproduced full-length play, opened at the Helen Hayes Theatre in New York City.

Oct. 23 *Make a Million,* a comedy by Norman Barasch and Carroll Moore, opened at the Playhouse in New York City. Its star, the experienced comedian Sam Levene, made the show a sure hit.

Dec. 1 *Flower Drum Song* by Richard Rodgers and Oscar Hammerstein II, based on the novel by C. Y. Lee, opened at the St. James Theatre in New York City.

1959

The year was highlighted by a visit of Vice Pres. Richard M. Nixon to the U.S.S.R. in July and August, and by a visit of Soviet Premier Nikita S. Khrushchev to the U.S. in September. Nixon's well-publicized tour increased his chances of gaining the Republican presidential nomination in 1960. His major competitor was Gov. Nelson A. Rockfeller of New York. For the Democrats, however, no fewer than eight possible candidates were making their opening moves. Americans mourned the deaths of William J. "Wild Bill" Donovan, director of the Office of Strategic Services in World War II, Feb. 8, at

One of the year's cultural high points was the extensive foreign tour of Leonard Bernstein and the New York Philharmonic Orchestra. Commencing in Athens (Aug. 5) and concluding in London (Oct. 10), the tour included a series of 18 concerts in the U.S.S.R. The Soviet Union was the scene of another notable artistic event when *Welcome Home,* a painting by Jack Levine that had been sharply criticized by Pres. Eisenhower, proved popular with the Russians. Notables who died this year included Ethel Barrymore, the celebrated actress, June 18, at 79; Ernest Bloch, composer, July 15,

Teamsters Union president James R. Hoffa, denied before a Senate investigating committee that he ran the union with the aid of hoodlums. He said he regretted violence in strikes but could not quarrel with a worker's right to protect his job.

Sept. 30   The Supreme Court ruling against **racial segregation** in public schools was defied by Gov. Orval E. Faubus of Arkansas, who closed four high schools in Little Rock. On Sept. 17 the Little Rock Private School Corp. was chartered in a move to reopen the city's schools on a segregated basis as private but state-financed institutions.

Oct. 11   In a **lunar exploration** mission, a Pioneer rocket was launched in an attempt to circle the moon. The mission failed on Oct. 12, but the vehicle obtained a record maximum altitude of 79,193 miles—30 times the altitude of any previous man-made object.

Oct. 12   A **synagogue was bombed** in Atlanta, Ga. No one was in the building. On Oct. 14 a synagogue in Peoria, Ill., was bombed. Pres. Eisenhower said he was outraged at the action; the FBI began investigations.

Oct. 30   The **Nobel Prize in Physiology or Medicine** was awarded jointly to Joshua Lederberg of the University of Wisconsin for his studies of the genetic organization of bacteria; and to George W. Beadle of the California Institute of Technology and Edward L. Tatum of the Rockefeller Institute for their discovery that genes control specific chemical processes.

July 5   At the **Wimbledon** tennis championships in England, Althea Gibson won the women's singles title. She then teamed with Maria Bueno of Brazil to win the women's doubles.

July 8   The 25th annual **baseball All-Star Game** was won by the American League, beating the National League 4–3.

July 13   The **U.S. Women's Open golf tournament** was won by Patty Berg.

July 20   The **PGA golf tournament** was won by Dow Finsterwald.

Sept. 6   The **Miss America** title was won by Mary Ann Mobley, 21, from Mississippi, at the annual pageant in Atlantic City, N.J.

Sept. 7   The **U.S. Lawn Tennis Association singles championships** were won by Ashley Cooper of Australia in the men's division and Althea Gibson, for the second year in a row, in the women's division.

Sept. 20–27   The **America's Cup** was defended by the U.S. 12-meter sloop *Columbia*, which defeated the British challenger *Sceptre* in four straight races.

Oct. 1–9   The 55th annual **World Series** was won by the New York Yankees (AL), defeating the Milwaukee Braves (NL) four games to three. Yogi Berra, the Yankees catcher, marked his tenth World Series, tying records set by Babe Ruth and Joe DiMaggio.

Dec. 28   The **NFL championship** was won by the Baltimore Colts, who defeated the New York Giants 23–17.

Dec. 31   The U.S. regained the **Davis Cup** when Alejandro "Alex" Olmedo defeated an Australian, Ashley Cooper, in singles competition for the third American match victory. The U.S. went on to win the international challenge round three matches to two.

1959

After a two-week delay at the request of Pres. Dwight D. Eisenhower, the United Steelworkers of America began a nationwide walkout on July 15. Negotiations proceeded slowly. On the order of Pres. Eisenhower, an 80-day Taft-Hartley injunction was issued on Oct. 21 and, after a court fight ending in the Supreme Court, was executed on Nov. 7, halting the 116-day steel strike, the longest in U.S. history. The U.S. scored a spectacular success when it launched an Atlas missile designed to function as a satellite. This was the fifth and largest Earth satellite successfully launched by the U.S. Besides

U.S. fans suffered a major blow when Floyd Patterson lost the world's heavyweight boxing title to Ingemar Johansson in the third round of a Yankee Stadium bout. Archie Moore retained the light heavyweight title by knocking out challenger Yvon Durelle of Canada, also in the third round. In baseball, the Los Angeles Dodgers, in their second season on the West Coast, gave California its first championship by winning the 1959 World Series. In golf, the top money winners were Art Wall, $53,142, and Betsy Rawls, $26,774.

76; John Foster Dulles, secretary of state under Pres. Dwight D. Eisenhower, May 24, at 71; William F. "Bull" Halsey, Jr., one of the most colorful naval commanders in the Pacific during World War II, Aug. 16, at 76; and George C. Marshall, secretary of state under Pres. Harry S Truman and originator of the Marshall Plan for reconstruction of Europe after World War II, Oct. 16, at 78.

Jan. 3 **Alaska was proclaimed the 49th state** by Pres. Eisenhower.

Feb. 3 An American Airlines **plane crashed** into New York City's East R., killing 65 of 73 persons aboard.

Feb. 10 A **tornado** struck St. Louis, Mo., killing 22 persons, injuring 350, leaving 5000 homeless, and causing an estimated $12,000,000 in damage.

Mar. 18 The **Hawaii statehood bill** was signed by Pres. Eisenhower. Statehood was conditional on a later vote for statehood by Hawaii's electorate.

Mar. 30 **Double jeopardy was upheld** in two U.S. Supreme Court decisions stating that a person could be tried for the same offense in both federal and state courts.

Apr. 7 **Prohibition in Oklahoma** was repealed after 51 years, leaving Mississippi the only dry state in the Union.

Apr. 15 Sec. of State **John Foster Dulles resigned** because of incapacitating illness. Dulles was suffering from cancer. He died on May 24 and was given a funeral with full military honors.

Apr. 18 **Christian Archibald Herter** was named secretary of state by Pres. Eisenhower. The Senate waived the normal seven-day interval between introduction and confirmation of a presidential appointment, confirming Herter in four and a half hours by a 93–9 vote.

May 20 **John Foster Dulles** was given the Medal of Freedom, the highest U.S. civilian award, by Pres. Eisenhower.

at 78; Raymond Chandler, author, Mar. 26, at 70; Lou Costello, comedian, Mar. 3, at 50; Cecil B. DeMille, motion picture producer, Jan. 21, at 77; Edgar Guest, poet, Aug. 5, at 77; Billie Holiday, one of the greatest jazz vocalists of all time, July 17, at 44; and Frank Lloyd Wright, celebrated architect and pioneer of modern design, Apr. 9, at 89.

Among **books published** this year was *Advise and Consent* by Allen Drury, a novel dealing with a Senate confirmation hearing for a highly controversial nomination for secretary of state. Other books published this year included *Henderson the Rain King* by Saul Bellow, a novel; *Breakfast at Tiffany's* by Truman Capote, a short novel; *The Mansion* by William Faulkner, the author's last Snopes family novel; *The War Lover* by John Hersey, an antiwar novel; *History of the United States Naval Operations in World War II* by Samuel Eliot Morison; *Goodbye, Columbus* by Philip Roth, which included the title novella and five short stories; and *Poorhouse Fair* by John Updike, a collection of associated stories.

Popular music of the year was made slightly more interesting by the inclusion of occasional folk tunes in the ranks of best sellers. Among these were "Tom Dooley," "Stagger Lee," "The Battle of New Orleans," and "He's Got the Whole World in His Hands."

The number of **jazz** festivals was increasing, as were jazz performances in European music festivals. Television also felt the beat as jazz found its way into the score for such programs as *Richard Diamond, Peter Gunn,* and *M Squad.*

Jan. 5 In a case involving **protection of journalists' sources,** Marie Torre of the New York *Herald Tribune* began a ten-day jail sentence for contempt of court for refusing to reveal a source used in one of her columns.

Mar. 3 The **National Book Awards** were presented for the following: fiction, *The Magic Barrel* by Bernard Malamud; poetry, *Words for the Wind* by Theodore Roethke; biography, *Mistress to an Age* by J. Christopher Herold.

Mar. 3 *Symphony No. 13* by the American composer Henry Cowell was given its world premiere in Madras, India. The work was performed by the Little Orchestra of New York, Thomas Scherman director, during its tour of Asian countries.

Mar. 5 *Wozzeck,* a modern operatic masterpiece by Alban Berg, received its first Metropolitan Opera production. The opera had first been performed 34 years previously in Berlin.

Mar. 11 *A Raisin in the Sun* by Lorraine H. Hansberry, starring Sidney Poitier and Claudia McNeil, opened at the Ethel Barrymore Theatre in New York City.

Apr. 6 **Academy Awards** were presented to *Gigi* as the outstanding motion picture of 1958; to David

| Business and Industry; Science; Education; Philosophy and Religion   III | | IV   Sports; Social Issues and Crime; Folkways; Fashion; Holidays |

much information-collecting instrumentation, the missile contained a recording of Pres. Eisenhower's voice, which was automatically broadcast. The message was subsequently received and recorded by U.S. radio stations and distributed throughout the world.

Jan. 19 **Discriminatory school laws in Virginia,** designed to prevent school integration by automatically closing schools receiving final federal court orders to integrate, were ruled invalid by the Virginia Supreme Court. On Feb. 2 schools in Arlington and Norfolk were desegregated with no serious disorders occurring.

Feb. 17 **Vanguard 2,** a 21.5-lb. satellite designed to function as the first weather station in space, achieved orbit after being launched from Cape Canaveral, Fla., by the U.S. Navy.

Feb. 28 **Discoverer 1,** the first satellite in the Discoverer military research satellite program, was launched successfully from Vandenberg Air Force Base, Calif.

Mar. 31 The federal emergency **employment compensation program** was extended when Pres. Eisenhower signed a compromise bill granting a three-month extension.

Apr. 5 The U.S. Naval Research Laboratory reported an increase in **atmospheric radioactivity** of 300% in the eastern United States following nuclear tests by the U.S.S.R. in Sept.–Oct. 1958.

Apr. 7 A **drop in unemployment** was reported by the Commerce and Labor departments. Unemployment fell from 4,749,000 in mid-February to 4,362,000 in mid-March, a drop about two-thirds larger than usual for the season and the largest drop since the same period in 1950.

Apr. 9 The **first seven U.S. astronauts** were picked from the ranks of military test pilots by NASA. After a vigorous training and testing program, one would be selected to ride a Project Mercury space capsule into Earth orbit in 1961.

Apr. 13 **Discoverer 2,** a military research satellite, was successfully launched from Vandenberg Air Force Base, Calif.

May 3 By vote of the **Unitarian and Universalist churches** and fellowships, the American Unitarian Association and the Universalist Church of America merged.

Jan. 1 In **college football bowl games,** the results were TCU 0, Air Force 0 in the Cotton Bowl; Oklahoma 21, Syracuse 6 in the Orange Bowl; Iowa 38, California 12 in the Rose Bowl; and LSU 7, Clemson 0 in the Sugar Bowl. This season both the UPI and AP polls chose Louisiana State the national collegiate champions of 1958.

Jan. 31–Feb. 1 U.S. **figure skating championships** were won in Rochester, N.Y., by Carol Heiss, women's singles; David Jenkins, men's singles; Nancy and Ronald Ludington, pairs; Andree Anderson Jacoby and Donald Jacoby, dance.

Feb. 14–15 A two-day **narcotics sweep** in New York City smashed a major heroin ring. Recovering an estimated 28.5 lbs. of heroin valued at $3,600,000, and $50,000 in cash, agents arrested 27 importers and distributors.

Feb. 26–28 At the **world figure skating championships** in Colorado Springs, Colo., Carol Heiss won the women's singles title for the fourth year in a row. David Jenkins won the men's singles.

Mar. 21 The **NCAA basketball championship** was won by California, defeating West Virginia 71–70.

Apr. 4–9 The **NBA basketball championship** was won by the Boston Celtics, who defeated the Minneapolis Lakers in a four-game sweep.

Apr. 5 The **Masters golf tournament** was won by Art Wall.

Apr. 9–18 The **NHL Stanley Cup** was won for the fourth year in a row by the Montreal Canadiens, who defeated the Toronto Maple Leafs four games to one.

Apr. 20 The 63rd **Boston Marathon** was won by Eino Oksanen of Finland, with a time of 2 hrs., 22 min., 42 sec.

May 22 The first black general in U.S. history, Brig. Gen. Benjamin O. Davis, Jr., USAF, was promoted to the rank of major general.

June 8 Investigations of communist subversion conducted by Congress and by individual states were ruled constitutional by the U.S. Supreme Court in two 5–4 decisions.

June 21 Sec. of State **Christian Herter,** returning from the Geneva conference (May 11–Aug. 5) attended by the U.S., France, Great Britain, and the U.S.S.R., stated that western officials were convinced that the Soviet Union intended to absorb West Berlin and eventually all of Germany into the communist camp.

July 4 At 12:10 A.M. the U.S. **49-star flag** was raised for the first time at the Capitol in Washington, D.C., and at Ft. McHenry, Md.

July 7 An omnibus housing bill was vetoed by Pres. Eisenhower, who termed it excessive, defective, inflationary, and an obstacle to constructive progress toward better housing for Americans.

July 23 Vice Pres. **Richard M. Nixon arrived in Moscow,** beginning a two-week tour of the U.S.S.R. and Poland. The next day he held a highly publicized kitchen debate, a discussion with Soviet Premier Nikita S. Khrushchev while standing before a kitchen exhibit in the U.S. exhibition in Moscow. After the impromptu, so-called kitchen debate, Nixon formally opened the exhibition.

July 29 The **accidental death rate** for 1958 was declared by the National Safety Council to be the lowest since 1954, 52.5 persons in 100,000. Total deaths were 91,000, of which 37,000 were auto accident deaths, raising the all-time U.S. death toll in auto accidents to 1,265,000.

Aug. 1 In a **radio-TV address from Moscow,** Vice Pres. Nixon told the Russian people that they would live in tension and fear if Premier Khrushchev attempted to propagate communism in countries outside the U.S.S.R.

Niven as best actor for *Separate Tables;* to Susan Hayward as best actress for *I Want to Live;* to Burl Ives as best supporting actor for *The Big Country;* and to Wendy Hiller as best supporting actress for *Separate Tables.*

Apr. 12 **Tony Awards** for outstanding contributions to the theater during the 1958–1959 season were presented for the following: play, *J.B.* by Archibald MacLeish; musical, *Redhead* by Herbert and Dorothy Fields, Sidney Sheldon, David Shaw, and Albert Hague; dramatic actor, Jason Robards, Jr., for *The Disenchanted;* dramatic actress, Gertrude Berg for *A Majority of One.* A special award was given to the cast of the revue *La Plume de Ma Tante,* which was written and directed by its star, Robert Dhéry.

Apr. 26 *Six Characters in Search of an Author* by Hugo Weisgall, based on Luigi Pirandello's play of the same name, was produced by the New York City Opera.

May 2 **George Grosz** announced plans to move to West Berlin but retain his U.S. citizenship. The satirical and impressionist painter fled Germany in 1933 to become a U.S. citizen. Grosz died in Berlin on July 6, at age 65.

May 4 **Pulitzer prizes** were awarded for the following: fiction, *The Travels of Jamie McPheeters* by Robert Lewis Taylor; history, *The Republican Era: 1869–1901* by Leonard D. White with Jean Schneider, who shared the prize with White's estate; biography, *Woodrow Wilson* by Arthur Walworth; poetry, *Selected Poems, 1928–1958* by Stanley Kunitz; drama, *J.B.* by Archibald MacLeish.

May 4 The first annual **Grammy Awards** of the National Academy of Recording Arts and Sciences were presented for the following: best album of 1958, *The Music from Peter Gunn* by Henry Mancini; best record, "Nel Blu Dipinto Di Blu (Volare)" by Domenico Modugno; best male vocalist, Perry Como for "Catch a Falling Star"; best female vocalist, Ella Fitzgerald for *The Irving Berlin Song Book;* best group, Louis Prima and Keely Smith for "That Old Black Magic."

May 6 **Emmy Awards** were presented to Fred Astaire as best actor for *An Evening With Fred Astaire;* Julie Harris as best actress for *Little Moon;* Raymond Burr as best actor in a dramatic series for *Perry Mason;* and Loretta Young as best actress in a dramatic series for *The Loretta Young Show.*

May 11 *Once Upon a Mattress,* a musical comedy by Jay Thompson, Marshall Barer, and Dean Fuller, opened at the Phoenix Theatre in New York City. Its cast included Carol Burnett, who was making her musical comedy debut.

May 18 The $10,000 **Guggenheim international art award** was presented by Pres. Eisenhower to the

| Business and Industry; Science; Education; Philosophy and Religion III | | IV Sports; Social Issues and Crime; Folkways; Fashion; Holidays |

May 28 Two monkeys were launched into space by the U.S. Army from Cape Canaveral, Fla. They were recovered unhurt from the Caribbean area after a 300-mile-high space flight.

June 3 By **bouncing radio signals off the moon,** a message recorded by Pres. Eisenhower was transmitted from Westford, Mass., to Canadian Prime Minister John George Diefenbaker in Prince Albert, Saskatchewan.

June 15 It was announced by the New York Stock Exchange that **stock in public U.S. corporations** was owned by 12,490,000 persons as of early 1959.

June 18 The **Arkansas school law** used by Gov. Orval Faubus to close public schools in Little Rock and maintain de facto segregation was ruled unconstitutional by a three-judge federal court.

June 30 A **federal debt bill** raising the temporary debt limit to $295,000,000,000 and the permanent limit to $285,000,000,000 was signed by Pres. Eisenhower.

July 7 The **American Lutheran Church** was established by merger of the Evangelical Lutherans and the United Evangelical Lutherans.

July 7 The General Synod of the **United Church of Christ,** meeting in Oberlin, Ohio, issued its first major pronouncement, stressing the role of the church ameliorating in social, international, and political problems, and urging an end to segregation.

July 14 A rise in **employment** from 66,016,000 in mid-May to 67,342,000 in mid-June was reported by the Labor Department. As 2,000,000 students were graduated or left school to seek summer jobs, unemployment rose proportionally; however, the number of unemployed heads of families dropped 180,000 below May's level.

July 15 A nationwide **steel strike** was begun by the United Steelworkers against 28 steel companies after a breakdown of negotiations.

July 21 The **first U.S. nuclear merchant ship** was christened *Savannah* by Mrs. Dwight D. Eisenhower at Camden, N.J.

Aug. 7 **Explorer 6,** a 142-lb. satellite called the paddle wheel satellite because of its four vanes of solar cells, was placed in orbit from Cape Canaveral, Fla. It was the first satellite to be handled by NASA from initiation to orbit.

May 2 The 85th annual **Kentucky Derby** was won by Tomy Lee, with a time of 2:02^1/$_5$. The jockey was Willie Shoemaker.

May 16 The 84th annual **Preakness Stakes** was won by Royal Orbit, with a time of 1:57. The jockey was Willie Harmatz.

May 20 Some 4978 **Japanese-Americans** who had renounced their U.S. citizenship during World War II and later applied for restitution were restored to citizenship by the Dept. of Justice.

May 25 A Louisiana ban on **boxing matches between blacks and whites** was declared unconstitutional by the U.S. Supreme Court.

May 30 The 43rd **Indianapolis 500** auto race was won by Roger Ward of Indianapolis, Ind., completing the 500-mile course in 3 hrs., 40 min., 49.20 sec., with an average speed of 135.857 mph.

June 13 The 91st annual **Belmont Stakes** was won by Sword Dancer, with a time of 2:28^2/$_5$. The jockey was Willie Shoemaker.

June 13 The **U.S. Open golf tournament** was won by Billy Casper.

June 22 A 1957 congressional statute restricting **defendants' access to pretrial statements** made by witnesses was upheld by the Supreme Court.

July 6 The **LPGA golf tournament** was won by Betsy Rawls.

July 7 Two **baseball All-Star Games** were played this year. The first was won by the National League, beating the American League 5–4. On Aug. 3 the American League won the second game 5–3.

| Exploration and Settlement; Wars; Government; Civil Rights; Statistics | I | | II | Publishing; Arts and Music; Popular Entertainment; Architecture; Theater |

Aug. 7 The **explosion** of a truck loaded with six and a half tons of dynamite and ammonium nitrate, triggered by a warehouse fire, killed at least 11 persons, injured 100, and leveled eight blocks in Roseburg, Ore.

Aug. 21 **Hawaii was admitted to the Union** as the 50th state, by a proclamation signed by Pres. Eisenhower. Hawaiians had voted by an overwhelming majority on June 27 for statehood in a special referendum. The president also issued the order for a new flag of 50 stars arranged in staggered rows: five 6-star rows and four 5-star rows, the flag to become official July 4, 1960.

Aug. 26 The U.S. **ban on nuclear testing** would be extended two months, to Dec. 31, 1959, the State Department announced. The U.S. government hoped that Great Britain and the U.S.S.R. would make similar extensions.

Sept. 7 In a move to ensure **voting rights** for blacks, the U.S. Civil Rights Commission requested Pres. Eisenhower to appoint federal registrars to supervise voting in areas where local officials had prevented blacks from voting.

Sept. 15–27 Soviet Premier **Khrushchev visited the U.S.** Arriving at Andrews Air Force Base, where he was welcomed by Pres. Eisenhower, the premier stated he was visiting the U.S. with "open heart and good intentions." On Sept. 18 he addressed the UN, calling for total nuclear disarmament within four years, and on Sept. 25 he began a series of negotiations with Pres. Eisenhower at Camp David. On Khrushchev's departure for Moscow on Sept. 27, it was revealed that he and Pres. Eisenhower had reached understandings designed to relieve world tensions, including the withdrawal of a proposal Khrushchev had made in Nov. 1958 for major changes in the status of Berlin.

Oct. 12 In New Jersey, **equine encephalitis**, commonly known as sleeping sickness, recently claimed 20 lives, state officials reported.

Nov. 16 A **defense budget request** for 1961, totaling some $41,000,000,000, was presented by Pres. Eisenhower. It was also decided that there would be no

Spanish painter Joan Miró for his mural *Night and Day.*

May 21 *Gypsy* by Arthur Laurents, Jule Stein, and Stephen Sondheim, based on the memoirs of Gypsy Rose Lee and starring Ethel Merman in the title role, opened at the Broadway Theatre in New York City.

June 11 *Lady Chatterley's Lover,* by D. H. Lawrence, was banned from the mails by Postmaster General Arthur E. Summerfield, who said, "Any literary merit the book may have is far outweighed by the pornographic and smutty passages and words, so that the book, taken as a whole, is an obscene and filthy work."

June 15 An **equal time ruling** issued by the FCC earlier in the year was reaffirmed by the commission. It required radio and television stations to give equal time to opposing political candidates in debate and news broadcasts.

Aug. 5–Oct. 10 An **international concert tour** was completed by the New York Philharmonic under the direction of Leonard Bernstein. The orchestra toured 17 countries, giving a total of 50 concerts. Among the American music performed were Bernstein's *The Age of Anxiety* and Charles Ives's *The Unanswered Question.*

Sept. 14 A bill lifting FCC **equal time** requirements for radio and television news broadcasts was signed by Pres. Eisenhower.

Sept. 14 A **customs bill** making certain art objects, including modern works, duty free was signed by Pres. Eisenhower.

Oct. 1 *The Gang's All Here* by Jerome Lawrence and Robert E. Lee, a play based on the history of corruption in the Warren G. Harding administration, opened at the Ambassador Theatre in New York City. Its cast included Melvyn Douglas and E. G. Marshall.

Oct. 18 *The Drunkard* by William H. Smith closed after its 9477th performance at the Theatre Mart in Los Angeles, Calif., marking the longest run to date in U.S. theatrical history. It had opened on July 6, 1933.

Oct. 19 *The Miracle Worker* by William Gibson opened at the Playhouse in New York City with Anne Bancroft playing the leading role of Anne Sullivan Macy, Helen Keller's childhood teacher. The play was an immediate success.

Oct. 21 **Dmitri Shostakovich** arrived in New York City to begin a one-month tour with various U.S. symphony orchestras. With him were several other Russian composers, including Dmitri Kabalevsky, Fikret Amirov, and Konstantin Dankevich.

Oct. 21 The **Solomon R. Guggenheim Museum** was opened. It was the only building in New York City designed by Frank Lloyd Wright.

Nov. 19 The **discovery of paintings** said to be the work of Michelangelo da Caravaggio, Il Tintoretto (Jacopo

| Business and Industry; Science; Education; Philosophy and Religion III | | IV Sports; Social Issues and Crime; Folkways; Fashion; Holidays |

Aug. 12 High schools in Little Rock, Ark., were reopened, integrating two previously all-white schools. About 200 to 250 segregationists demonstrated near Central High School, but policemen held them back with fire hoses and clubs.

Aug. 13 Discoverer 5 was launched successfully into polar orbit from Vandenberg Air Force Base, Calif. This followed unsuccessful launchings of Discoverer 3 (June 3) and Discoverer 4 (June 25).

Aug. 19 Discoverer 6 was launched into polar orbit from Vandenberg Air Force Base, Calif.

Sept. 7 The National Council of Churches announced that **church membership** as of 1958 had increased to 109,557,741. This was a gain of 5% since 1957 and indicated that 64% of the population were church members.

Sept. 11 A bill was passed by Congress authorizing **food stamps** in a program to distribute surplus food to impoverished Americans.

Sept. 18 **Vanguard 3,** the 12th successful U.S. satellite, was launched from Cape Canaveral, Fla.

Sept. 22 The **International Longshoremen's Association** was readmitted on two-year probation to the AFL-CIO. The ILA had been expelled from the labor organization because of corruption and crime, conditions that AFL-CIO president George Meany said were much improved.

Oct. 1 In a **longshoremen's strike,** some 70,000 members of the International Longshoremen's Association walked off the job in Atlantic and Gulf Coast ports. Pres. Eisenhower invoked the Taft-Hartley Act on Oct. 6 by appointing a board of inquiry. An injunction on Oct. 8 halted the strike.

Oct. 1 Some **$2,000,000,000 in U.S. notes** was offered by the U.S. Treasury at a 5% interest rate, the highest for U.S. securities since 1929.

Oct. 10 Initiation of the **first passenger service circling the globe** was announced by Pan American World Airways.

Oct. 15 The **Nobel Prize in Physiology or Medicine** was awarded to Severo Ochoa of NYU College of Medicine and Arthur Kornberg of Stanford University Medical School for their joint work on the chemistry of heredity.

July 20 The **Baseball Hall of Fame** inducted Zachariah "Zack" Wheat, former outfielder for the Brooklyn Dodgers.

Aug. 2 The **PGA golf tournament** was won by Bob Rosburg.

Aug. 27–Sept. 7 At the third **Pan-American Games,** held at Soldier Field, Portage Park, and several other sites in Chicago, Ill., the U.S. won the unofficial team championship. Argentina was second.

Aug. 28–31 In the **Davis Cup** international tennis challenge round, Australia beat the defending U.S. team three matches to two.

Sept. 12 The **Miss America** title was won by Lynda Lee Mead, 20, from Mississippi, at the annual pageant in Atlantic City, N.J.

Sept. 13 The **U.S. Lawn Tennis singles championships** were won by Neale Frazer of Australia in the men's division and Maria Bueno of Brazil in the women's division.

Oct. 18 The 56th annual **World Series** was won by the Los Angeles Dodgers (NL), defeating the Chicago White Sox four games to two. The Dodgers had won the National League pennant by sweeping two games from the Milwaukee Braves in a league playoff.

Nov. 5 The newly formed **American Football League** announced that eight professional teams would begin play in 1965.

Nov. 9 Consumers were warned against buying **cranberries** grown in Washington and Oregon. Arthur S. Flemming, secretary of Health, Education, and Welfare, announced that a weed killer causing cancer in rats had contaminated cranberries grown in Washington and Oregon during the 1958–1959 season.

immediate reduction in U.S. troops overseas.

Dec. 3   Pres. Eisenhower began a **three-week tour** of 11 nations in Asia, Africa, and Europe.

Dec. 7   **Travel restrictions** imposed by the federal government were upheld by the Supreme Court, which refused to consider lower court decisions banning American travel to China.

Dec. 10–14   **Gus Hall** was named general secretary of the American Communist Party. Hall, 48, had formerly been the party's Midwest secretary.

Dec. 16   Sec. of Defense Thomas S. Gates announced at the NATO Council in Paris that the U.S. had **nuclear superiority** over the U.S.S.R. both in weapons and weapons delivery systems.

Robusti), Titian (Tiziano Vecelli) Lorenzo Lotto, Claude Gile, Luca Giordano, Bernardo Cavallino, Artemisia Gentileschi, and Raffaello Santi (Raphael) in the home of a Pasadena, Calif., TV repairman, Alfonso Follo, was announced by an associate of the family. The announcement was later declared premature and the owners sought expert opinion.

Nov. 23   *Fiorello!* by Jerome Weidman, George Abbott, Sheldon Harnick, and Jerry Bock, opened at the Broadhurst Theatre. The production starred Tom Bosley as Fiorello H. La Guardia and depicted La Guardia's career up to his successful bid for the mayoralty of New York City. La Guardia's widow, who attended the opening, later said she had been startled by Bosley's resemblance to the late mayor.

Nov. 29   **Grammy Awards** were presented for the following: best album of 1959, *Come Dance With Me* by Frank Sinatra; best record, "Mack The Knife" by Bobby Darin; best male vocalist, Frank Sinatra for *Come Dance With Me;* best female vocalist, Ella Fitzgerald for "But Not for Me"; best group, the Mormon Tabernacle Choir for "Battle Hymn of the Republic."

1960

Relations with the U.S.S.R., which improved in 1959 after Vice Pres. Richard Nixon's trip to Moscow and Premier Nikita Khrushchev's tour of the U.S., deteriorated sharply after a U.S. U-2 reconnaissance plane was shot down inside the U.S.S.R. on May 1. The incident gave Khrushchev a propaganda advantage and led to cancellation of a planned Paris summit meeting. The U-2 incident and a later one concerning an American RB-47 airplane, together with U.S. involvement in Laos, the Congo, Germany, Cuba, and Japan, caused a sharp increase in the American public's concern with loss of national prestige. This concern may have played a decisive role in John F. Kennedy's successful bid for the presidency in the November elections after one of the most colorful campaigns and one of the closest votes in U.S. political history.

Jan. 2   **U.S. manned space flights,** according to *The New York Times,* were being hampered by cost overruns and budget restrictions.

Jan. 7   In his **State of the Union** message, Pres. Dwight D. Eisenhower said that prospects for improvement in East-West relations were somewhat better in view of "recent Soviet deportment."

The opera year was highlighted by the performance in San Diego of *Die Frau ohne Schatten* by Richard Strauss, a gigantic musical drama replete with strange people and flying fish. The music season was tragically marked by the deaths of renowned musicians: Ernst von Dohnanyi, Feb. 9, at 82; Dimitri Mitropoulos, Nov. 2, at 64; Jussi Bjoerling, Sept. 9, at 49; and Leonard Warren, Mar. 4, at 48. The country also mourned the deaths of Franklin Pierce Adams, newspaper columnist, Mar. 23, at 78; H.L. Davis, winner of a Pulitzer Prize for his 1935 novel *Honey in the Horn,* Oct. 31, at 64; Oscar Hammerstein II, lyricist and theatrical producer, Aug. 23, at 65; John P. Marquand, novelist and short story writer, July 16, at 66; and Richard Wright, who chronicled the black experience in America in *Native Son* (1940) and *Black Boy* (1945), Nov. 28, at 52.

Among **books published** this year was *To Kill a Mockingbird,* Harper Lee's first novel, which won a Pulitzer Prize in 1961. The novel, set in the South, concerned two children whose father, a lawyer, defended a black man charged with the rape of a white woman. Other books published this year included *Grant Moves South* by Bruce Catton, which dealt with the 1861–1863 campaign of Gen. U.S. Grant during the Civil War; *The Liberal House* by John Kenneth Galbraith, essays on the

Business and Industry; Science; Education; Philosophy and Religion **III**		**IV** Sports; Social Issues and Crime Folkways; Fashion; Holidays

Oct. 26 The **Nobel Prize in Physics** was awarded jointly to Emilio Segre and Owen Chamberlain of the University of California at Berkeley for their discovery of the antiproton.

Nov. 7 **Striking steelworkers** were ordered back to work by the U.S. Supreme Court, which upheld a Taft-Hartley injunction against the strike.

Nov. 18 Development of a **nuclear power generator for satellites** was announced by the Atomic Energy Commission.

Nov. 19 Preliminary talks on **U.S.-Soviet cooperation in space** by scientists from the U.S. and U.S.S.R. were revealed by the White House.

Dec. 15 **John L. Lewis** announced he would resign as president of the United Mine Workers early in 1960, the year of his 80th birthday.

Dec. 30 The U.S.S. *George Washington,* the first nuclear submarine capable of carrying and launching missiles, was commissioned at Groton, Conn.

Dec. 8 **Ingemar Johansson** was selected fighter of the year by the Boxing Writers Association.

Dec. 16 **Roger Touhy,** 61, was shot and killed on the steps of his sister's home in Chicago, Ill. Touhy, a former underworld figure, had only recently been released from Stateville, Mich., prison.

Dec. 19 The **last Civil War veteran,** Walter Williams, died in Houston, Tex., at the age of 117.

Dec. 27 The **NFL championship** was won by the Baltimore Colts, defeating the New York Giants 31–16.

1960

The U.S. demonstrated considerable technical progress by launching 17 space satellites and probes. The most spectacular of the objects sent into space were Tiros 1, which took 22,952 pictures of Earth's cloud cover; Discoverer 13, whose capsule was the first orbited object ever returned to Earth; and Discoverer 14, whose capsule was later retrieved in midair. Other aspects of national life, however, were showing less progress. A dangerous outflow of gold prompted the government to curtail spending abroad by military personnel, and there was a high rate of unemployment. The government continued its fight for southern school integration, but some public schools remained closed and were marred by mob violence and vandalism, such as that which erupted in November during attempts to integrate schools in New Orleans.

Jan. 2 The **age of the solar system** was estimated by Dr. John H. Reynolds of the University of California (Berkeley) to be 4,950,000,000 years. His estimate was based on study of a meteorite found 41 years previously near Richardton, N.D.

Jan. 4 The **longest steel strike** in the nation's history was settled when the steel companies and the United Steel Workers agreed on a wage increase. The strike had begun on July 15, 1959.

Floyd Patterson, using an eclectic boxing style, defeated Ingemar Johansson to become the first man in history to regain the heavyweight championship of the world. Another outstanding fighter, 40-year-old Sugar Ray Robinson, lost the world middleweight title to Paul Pender. Boxing was under fire, and a congressional investigation tried to determine the nature and extent of underworld influence in the sport. Congress also investigated the practice of payola in the recording and broadcasting industries.

Jan. 1 In **college football bowl games,** the results were Syracuse 23, Texas 14 in the Cotton Bowl; Georgia 14, Missouri 0 in the Orange Bowl; Washington 44, Wisconsin 8 in the Rose Bowl; and Mississippi 21, Louisiana State University 0 in the Sugar Bowl. This season both the AP and UPI polls chose Syracuse the national collegiate champions of 1959.

Jan. 2 The **U.S. chess championship** was successfully defended by Brooklyn's 16-year-old chess wonder, Bobby Fischer, in a tournament in New York City.

Jan. 12 The **first 15,000-point NBA player,** Dolph Schayes of the Syracuse professional basketball team,

Jan. 11 A **protest to Cuba** about confiscation of U.S. property was delivered by U.S. Ambassador Philip W. Bonsal in Havana. It was rejected by the Cuban government on the same day.

Jan. 18 A controversial **mutual security treaty** was signed by the Japanese and U.S. governments. Among other pledges, the treaty stated that both the U.S. and Japan would "maintain and develop . . . their capacities to resist armed attacks."

Feb. 22 Pres. Eisenhower began a **Latin American tour** in Puerto Rico. The tour was scheduled to include Brazil, Argentina, Chile, and Uruguay.

Feb. 23 Sen. Stuart Symington, Democrat of Missouri, declared in the Senate that the "American people are being misled" about the **missile gap** between the U.S. and the U.S.S.R. Pres. Eisenhower vehemently denied the charge.

Feb. 24 The **U.S. population** had reached 179,245,000 by Jan. 1, 1960, according to a Census Bureau estimate.

Feb. 25 A **plane collision** over Rio de Janeiro took the lives of 35 U.S. Navy men and 26 Brazilians.

Feb. 29 A filibuster against **civil rights legislation** was begun by 18 southern senators.

Mar. 7 Just returned from a **Latin American goodwill tour**, Pres. Eisenhower stated that U.S.-Latin American relations were better than ever. He also mentioned that during the tour, Sec. of State Christian Herter had held useful conferences with various Latin American leaders.

Mar. 17 A **plane explosion** killed 63 persons on a flight from Chicago to Miami. The Lockheed Electra exploded in midair over Tell City, Ind.

Apr. 8 A **civil rights bill** was passed by the Senate 71–18. Though it was the first civil rights legislation to survive a southern filibuster, Sen. Joseph S. Clark, Democrat of Pennsylvania, an advocate of civil rights, said his side had "suffered a crushing defeat," calling the bill "only a pale ghost of our hopes."

May 5 The **downing of a U.S. plane** over the U.S.S.R. on May 1 was announced by Premier Nikita S. Khrushchev, who called the captured pilot, Francis Gary Powers, a spy and vowed he would be put on trial. On May 7 the U.S. admitted that the unarmed U-2 plane had been on a spy mission.

May 9 The U.S. announced discontinuance of **U-2 flights** similar to the one intercepted by the U.S.S.R.

May 16 The **Paris summit conference** was canceled by Soviet Premier Khrushchev, who cited the U-2 incident as his reason. Khrushchev also canceled an

improvement of the U.S. economic situation; *The Child Buyer,* a novel by John Hersey; *Tristessa,* a novel by Jack Kerouac; *No High Ground* by Fletcher Knebel and Charles W. Bailey, an account of the development of the atomic bomb and the consequences of its use at Hiroshima; *Ourselves to Know,* a novel by John O'Hara; *Thrones* by Ezra Pound, the latest installment of his poetic work *Cantos; The Uncertain Trumpet* by Gen. Maxwell D. Taylor, which described U.S. military competence as dangerously diminished; *Apologies to the Iroquois* by Edmund Wilson, which dealt with the history and social spirit of the Iroquois; and *Marilyn Monroe* by Maurice Zolotow, a biographical study.

Jan. 6 The donation of **Billy Rose's modern sculpture collection** to the newly completed National Museum in Jerusalem, Israel, was made public. Among the sculptors represented in the collection were Jacob Epstein, Aristide Maillol, Auguste Rodin, and William Zorach.

Jan. 25 **Payola,** money illegally offered or accepted by disc jockeys for broadcasting phonograph records, would bring a $500 fine and one-year prison term in a law proposed by Donald H. McGannon, chairman of the National Association of Broadcasters' TV code review board. The proposal followed extensive investigations into payola practices in the broadcasting industry.

Feb. 11 Jack Paar, protesting **NBC censorship** of one of his jokes the night before, walked off his late-night television show. Later, at a meeting with network officials, Paar agreed to return to the program Mar. 7.

Feb. 25 *Toys in the Attic,* a new play by Lillian Hellman, opened in New York City at the Hudson Theater. The play received excellent reviews.

Feb. 26 *A Thurber Carnival* opened at the ANTA Theater in New York City. The musical was based on the works of the humorist James Thurber.

Feb. 29 The publishing firm **Holt, Rinehart & Winston, Inc.** was established when stockholders of Henry Holt & Co., Inc. approved a merger with Rinehart & Co., Inc. and the John C. Winston Company.

Mar. 23 The **National Book Awards** were presented for the following: fiction, *Good-bye Columbus* by Philip Roth; nonfiction, *James Joyce* by Richard Ellmann; poetry, *Life Studies* by Robert Lowell.

Mar. 25 *Lady Chatterley's Lover* by D. H. Lawrence was ruled not obscene, and therefore mailable, by the U.S. Circuit Court of Appeals in New York. Chief Judge Charles E. Clark, alluding to Postmaster General Arthur E. Summerfield, asked, "Should a mature and sophisticated reading public be kept in blinders because a government official thinks reading certain

| Business and Industry; Science; Education; Philosophy and Religion | III | | IV | Sports; Social Issues and Crime; Folkways; Fashion; Holidays |

Jan. 7 A new **ocean diving record** was established when Lt. Donald Walsh, USN, and Jacques Piccard descended 24,000 ft. in the bathyscaphe *Trieste.* The world record dive was made in the Pacific Marianas Trench, 60 miles from Guam. The dive was surpassed on Jan. 23 when the *Trieste* made a dive of 35,800 ft. to the bottom of the Marianas Trench.

Jan. 7 A **$200,000,000 budget surplus** was predicted for 1960 by Pres. Dwight D. Eisenhower in his annual State of the Union message to Congress. The president stated that "1960 promises to be the most prosperous year in our history."

Jan. 9 Some methods and instances of **birth control** were approved by the bishops and other leaders of the Protestant Episcopal Church. The approbation was limited to countries in which the population increase threatened the general welfare.

Jan. 23 Dependence on **local school financing** was described as "unbusinesslike" by the National Education Association. Local governments provided 56%, state governments 40%, and the federal government 4% of school funds.

Feb. 8–16 A **recession in 1961** was predicted by the AFL-CIO Executive Council, which placed the blame on the Eisenhower administration's "nineteenth-century budget policy."

Feb. 17 A study of the feasibility of using **unmanned seismic stations** for the detection of underground nuclear tests was ordered by the Defense Department.

Feb. 25 **Clergy infiltrated by communists** throughout the U.S. in general and the National Council of Churches in particular was charged by Sec. of the Air Force Dudley C. Sharp in a statement before the House Un-American Activities Committee.

Feb. 26 **James R. Hoffa** was called completely dishonest with respect to his promise to rid the Teamsters Union of criminal elements. The charge against Hoffa, president of the union, was made by a Senate select committee.

Mar. 11 **Pioneer 5,** the third spacecraft to be orbited around the sun, was launched by the U.S. from Cape Canaveral. The other two were Pioneer 4 (U.S.) and Lunik 1 (U.S.S.R.).

Mar. 30 A prediction of steadily **rising unemployment** because of the constant growth of the population was made by the Special Senate Committee on Unemployment.

Apr. 1 The **first weather satellite,** Tiros 1, was orbited by the U.S. It sent thousands of photographs of cloud cover back to Earth.

Apr. 2 Considerable **economic expansion** was predicted for the U.S. in the 1960s by the Cabinet Committee on Price Stability for Economic Growth.

reached a 15,013-point total for his career. Schayes was famed for his rebounding ability.

Jan. 24 In a **Chicago police scandal,** Richard Morrison, an ex-convict awaiting trial for burglary, named eight Chicago policemen as confederates. In the ensuing investigation, 17 policemen were suspended on suspicion of robbery, bribery, and burglary.

Jan. 30 **U.S. figure skating championships** were won in Seattle by Carol Heiss, women's singles; David Jenkins, men's singles; Ronald and Nancy Ludington, pairs; Margie Ackles and Charles Phillips, Jr., dance.

Feb. 18–28 At the **Winter Olympics** in Squaw Valley, Calif., the unofficial team championship was won by the U.S.S.R. Sweden was second and the U.S. was third.

Feb. 23 Demolition of **Ebbets Field,** home park of the Brooklyn Dodgers (now the Los Angeles Dodgers), was begun. An apartment project was planned for the site.

Mar. 2–5 At the **world figure skating championships** in Vancouver, B.C., Carol Heiss won the women's singles title.

Mar. 7 In **racial violence,** Felton Turner, a black 27-year-old resident of Houston, Tex., was beaten with a tire iron and suspended upside down in an oak tree. The initials KKK were carved on his chest. Turner had been abducted by four masked youths, who said their actions were related to the sit-down strikes of Texas Southern University black students.

Mar. 19 The **NCAA basketball championship** was won by Ohio State, which defeated California 75–55.

Mar. 25 **Wilt Chamberlain** retired from professional basketball. Though he decried the rough tactics by opponents on the court, Chamberlain admitted that racial difficulties he encountered as a black had influenced his decision. Chamberlain relented later in the year and signed another pro basketball contract.

Mar. 27–Apr. 9 The **NBA basketball championship** was won by the Boston Celtics, who beat the St. Louis Hawks four games to three.

Apr. 7–14 The **NHL Stanley Cup** was won by the Montreal Canadiens, who defeated the Toronto Maple Leafs in four straight games to become the first team to win the cup five times in a row.

invitation to Pres. Eisenhower to visit the U.S.S.R.

June 4 The U.S. accused the Cuban government of undertaking a **campaign of slander** against the U.S. The accusation was made in a note delivered to the Cuban Foreign Ministry in Havana.

June 16 Pres. Eisenhower's **Japanese visit** was canceled in view of riots in Japan against the mutual security treaty between Japan and the U.S.

June 26 On return from his **Far East goodwill tour,** Pres. Eisenhower defended his foreign policies and proclaimed his tour a success despite cancellation of a visit to Japan.

July 4 The **50-star U.S. flag,** reflecting the admission of Hawaii to the Union in 1959, became official.

July 11 The U.S.S.R. announced that a **U.S. plane had been shot down** by a Soviet fighter on July 1. The U.S.S.R. alleged that the RB-47 reconnaissance bomber had been in Soviet air space over Arctic waters and accused the U.S. of continuing the espionage program revealed by the downing of a U-2 over Russia earlier in the year.

July 13 The **Democratic National Convention nominated Sen. Kennedy** of Massachusetts for the presidency. Kennedy was the second Roman Catholic in the party's history to be nominated for that office.

July 25 The **Republican National Convention nominated Vice Pres. Nixon** for the presidency. Nixon was virtually unchallenged for the nomination, although Sen. Barry Goldwater of Arizona received ten votes after his name had been put into nomination against his wishes.

Aug. 19 **Francis Gary Powers,** pilot of the U-2 spy plane shot down in the U.S.S.R., was sentenced by the Soviets to ten years of "deprivation of freedom."

Aug. 26 The **AFL-CIO endorsed Sen. Kennedy** for president. Kennedy was described by the labor leaders as "intelligent, articulate, and forceful."

Sept. 9–12 **Hurricane Donna,** the most destructive hurricane in U.S. Weather Bureau history, ravaged the Atlantic coast from Florida to New England, killing 30 persons and causing heavy damage.

Sept. 12 Sen. Kennedy stated that as president his **actions would be dictated solely by the public welfare** rather than by the Roman Catholic hierarchy, in a speech in Houston, Tex. Kennedy stated he would resign "if the time should ever come . . . when my office would require me to either violate my conscience or violate the national interest."

Sept. 26 The first of a series of **television debates**

works of power and literary value is not good for him?"

Mar. 27 The **AIA Gold Medal** for architecture was awarded to Ludwig Mies van der Rohe.

Mar. 31 Gore Vidal's *The Best Man* received rave reviews when it opened at the Morosco Theater in New York City. The play concerned a struggle for the presidential nomination.

Apr. 4 **Academy Awards** were presented to *Ben-Hur* as the outstanding motion picture of 1959; Charlton Heston as best actor for *Ben-Hur;* Simone Signoret as best actress for *Room at the Top;* Shelley Winters as best supporting actress for *The Diary of Anne Frank;* and Hugh Griffith as best supporting actor for *Ben-Hur.*

Apr. 11 The $1000 **Brunner Award** was awarded to architect Louis Kahn of Philadelphia by the National Institute of Arts and Letters.

Apr. 14 *Bye Bye Birdie,* a musical by Charles Strouse and Lee Adams, opened at the Martin Beck Theater in New York City. Its cast included Dick Van Dyke, Kay Medford, and Chita Rivera.

Apr. 24 **Tony Awards** for the 1959–1960 season were given for the following: best play, *The Miracle Worker;* best musical, a tie between *Fiorello!* and *The Sound of Music;* best actor in a drama, Melvyn Douglas for *The Best Man;* best actress in a drama, Anne Bancroft for *The Miracle Worker.*

Apr. 29 In a **payola investigation,** Dick Clark, one of the nation's best paid and most influential disc jockeys, denied involvement in illegal payments. Clark stated before the Special House Subcommittee on Legislative Oversight, "I believe in my heart that I have never taken payola."

May 2 **Pulitzer prizes** were awarded for the following: fiction, *Advise and Consent* by Allen Drury; biography, *John Paul Jones* by Samuel Eliot Morison; history, *In the Days of McKinley* by Margaret Leech; poetry, *Heart's Needle* by W. D. Snodgrass; drama, *Fiorello!* by George Abbott, Jerome Weidman, Sheldon Harnick, and Jerry Bock.

May 3 *The Fantasticks,* a musical by Tom Jones and Harvey Schmidt, opened off Broadway at the Sullivan Street Playhouse in New York City.

May 19 In the **payola scandal,** Alan Freed, radio disc jockey, television personality, and originator of the term "rock 'n' roll," was arrested on charges of commercial bribery. Seven other persons accused of payola were also arrested.

June 20 **Emmy Awards** were presented to Laurence Olivier as best actor for his performance in *The Moon*

Business and Industry; Science; Education; Philosophy and Religion	III		IV	Sports; Social Issues and Crime; Folkways; Fashion; Holidays

Apr. 9 School integration had reached only 6% of southern schools, it was reported by *Southern School News,* in spite of the 1954 Supreme Court decision against segregation.

Apr. 13 An experimental satellite, Transit 1-B, was put into orbit around Earth by a Thor-Able-Star rocket. The satellite, achieving an elliptical orbit 500 miles high, was expected to be valuable for navigation.

Apr. 14 A Polaris missile was fired from under water off San Clemente Island, Calif., for the first time.

Apr. 27 Sit-ins by blacks in the South were again endorsed by the National Council of the Protestant Episcopal Church.

Apr. 28 Marital sex relations without procreative intentions were declared not to be sinful by leaders of the 100th General Assembly of the Southern Presbyterian Church.

May 10 The first undersea voyage around the world was completed by the nuclear submarine U.S.S. *Triton,* the largest known submarine.

May 12 Lockheed Aircraft announced that the Electra crashes in Sept. 1959 and Mar. 1960 were caused by a structural deficiency. The cost of correcting the fault was estimated at $25,000,000.

May 20 The U.S. set a world missile record when an Atlas intercontinental ballistic missile flew 9000 miles, from Cape Canaveral, Fla., to beyond the tip of Africa.

May 20 The election of Roman Catholics to public office was decried in a resolution by the Southern Baptist Convention in Miami Beach. The resolution stated, "When a public official is inescapably bound by the dogma and demands of his church, he cannot consistently separate himself from these."

May 24 Designed to act as an early warning system against surprise missile attacks, Midas 2, a 5000-lb. satellite, was launched from Cape Canaveral, Fla.

May 31 The Joint Commission on Mental Illness and Health reported that mental illness afflicted 25% of all Americans at one time or another in their lives to the extent that they required professional help.

June 2–13 All 22 legitimate Broadway theaters closed after Actors' Equity struck one theater. The strike was the first since 1919.

June 6 For middle-aged men, coronary death rates "were found to be from 50% to 150% higher among heavy cigarette smokers" than among nonsmokers, according to the American Heart Association.

July 3 U.S. sugar import quotas were severely cut in response to Cuban Premier Fidel Castro's anti-U.S. policies.

July 7 Foreign language teachers' qualifications in public school systems were criticized by the Modern Language Association. In a report to the U.S. Office

Apr. 10 The Masters golf tournament was won by Arnold Palmer, who beat Ken Venturi by one stroke.

Apr. 19 The 64th Boston Marathon was won by Paavo Kotila of Finland, with a time of 2 hrs., 20 min., 54 sec.

May 2 Caryl Chessman, convicted of kidnaping, rape, and robbery in Jan. 1948, was executed in the gas chamber at San Quentin Prison, Calif., after a 12-year battle for his life.

May 7 The 86th annual Kentucky Derby was won by Venetian Way, with a time of 2:02^2/$_5$. Bill Hartack was the jockey.

May 21 The 85th annual Preakness Stakes was won by Bally Ache, with a time of 1:57^3/$_5$. The jockey was Bob Ussery.

May 30 The 44th Indianapolis 500 auto race was won by Jim Rathmann of Miami, completing the 500-mile course in 3 hrs., 36 min., 11.36 sec., with an average speed of 138.757 mph.

June 11 The 92nd annual Belmont Stakes was won by Celtic Ash, with a time of 2:29^3/$_5$. The jockey was Bill Hartack.

June 18 The U.S. Open golf tournament was won by Arnold Palmer, who beat Jack Nicklaus by two strokes.

June 20 The world heavyweight boxing championship was won by Floyd Patterson, who defeated Ingemar Johansson in a fifth-round knockout. Patterson thus became the first fighter in boxing history to regain the heavyweight championship.

July 4 The LPGA golf tournament was won by Mickey Wright, who became the first person to win the championship twice.

July 13 The second baseball All-Star Game of this year was won by the National League, thus sweeping the 1960 games. On July 11, the National League team won the first game 5–3.

July 23 The U.S. Women's Open golf tournament was won by Betsy Rawls, who became the first person to win the title four times.

between Vice Pres. Nixon and Sen. Kennedy took place in Chicago, Ill.

Oct. 10–12 Former Pres. **Harry S Truman** was reported to be campaigning vigorously for Sen. Kennedy in the presidential campaign. It was reported that Truman said Vice Pres. Nixon "never told the truth in his life"; told a San Antonio audience that if it voted for Nixon, "You ought to go to hell"; and responded to a demand for an apology for his San Antonio remark by saying, "Tell 'em to go to hell."

Oct. 20 An **embargo on exports to Cuba** was declared by the U.S. State Department. Some medicines and foods were excluded from the embargo.

Oct 29 A **plane crash killed 16 football teammates** from the California State Polytechnic College. The Arctic Pacific Line plane crashed shortly after take off, killing a total of 22.

Nov. 8 **John Fitzgerald Kennedy was elected president** of the United States. Sen. Kennedy, Democrat of Massachusetts, was the second-youngest man ever to win the nation's highest office. Sen. Lyndon Baines Johnson, Democrat, was elected vice president. The electoral vote was Kennedy, 303; Nixon, 219; and Sen. Harry F. Byrd, 15. Kennedy won 49.7% and Nixon 49.6% of the popular vote, making the election one of the closest in U.S. history. In congressional elections the Democrats took a 65–35 majority in the Senate. In the House they lost 20 seats but kept a majority of 263–174.

Nov. 15 A **change in the number of House seats** was indicated by the 1960 Census. The population of the U.S. had undergone a sufficient shift to necessitate changes in House districts in 25 states.

Dec. 12 The appointment of **David Dean Rusk** as secretary of state was announced by President-elect Kennedy.

Dec. 16 The **worst air disaster** to date occurred when a United Air Lines DC-8 jet and a Trans-World Airlines Lockheed Super-Constellation collided in fog over New York harbor. The death toll was 132.

and Sixpence; Ingrid Bergman as best actress for *The Turn of the Screw;* Robert Stack as best actor in a dramatic series for *The Untouchables;* and Jane Wyatt as best actress in a dramatic series for *Father Knows Best.*

Sept. 20 *The Hostage* by Brendan Behan opened at the Cort Theater in New York City to good reviews and a delighted audience, ever aware of the author's presence in New York and of his occasional interruptions of performances of his own plays.

Sept. 28 Agreement on a **publishing merger** of Harcourt, Brace & Company and World Book Company was announced by the firms' directors. The new corporation, to be called Harcourt, Brace & World, would be one of the largest publishers in the country.

Oct. 8 *An Evening with Mike Nichols and Elaine May* opened to rave reviews at the St. James Theater in New York City. The show was written and performed by Nichols and May.

Oct. 17 **Charles Van Doren,** former star contestant on the TV quiz show *21,* and 13 others were arrested on charges of perjury. They had stated before a grand jury that the quiz shows involved in a recent scandal had not provided contestants with questions and answers before the shows were broadcast.

Oct. 31 Karel Appel was selected to receive the 1960 **Guggenheim International Art Award** ($10,000) for his abstract painting *Woman with Ostrich.*

Nov. 10 *Period of Adjustment,* a play by Tennessee Williams starring Barbara Baxley, James Daly, and Robert Webber, opened at the Helen Hayes Theater in New York City.

Nov. 17 **Anti-integration riots** in New Orleans were the worst since initiation of school integration there. Almost 200 people were arrested.

Nov. 30 *All the Way Home,* a play by Tad Mosel based on the 1957 novel *A Death in the Family* by James Agee, opened at the Belasco Theater in New York City. Its cast included Colleen Dewhurst, Lillian Gish, and Arthur Hill.

1961

John F. Kennedy was inaugurated president of the U.S. in a year that provided many explosive and dangerous situations. He was met with civil war in Laos and the Congo and continued Russian threats in Berlin. Rising tensions in Berlin culminated in the sealing off of East Berlin by East German and Soviet guards on Aug. 13, and the construction of a concrete and barbed wire barrier that came to be called the Berlin Wall. In

Tropic of Cancer by Henry Miller, originally published in France in 1934, became available in the U.S. after many years of prohibition on grounds of obscenity. Imported and reprinted by the same company that was responsible for U.S. publication of *Lady Chatterley's Lover, Tropic of Cancer* encountered considerably less legal difficulty than the D. H. Lawrence novel. The U.S. literary scene was saddened by the death of Ernest

Business and Industry; Science; Education; Philosophy and Religion III		IV Sports; Social Issues and Crime; Folkways; Fashion; Holidays

of Education, the association pointed out that Kansas was the only state that required special certification of instructors in the languages they taught.

July 20 The first successful launching of **Polaris missiles** from a submerged craft was accomplished by the nuclear submarine U.S.S. *George Washington.* The missiles flew 1150 miles.

Aug. 3 The first phone conversation in which **voices were bounced off the moon** was accomplished by U.S. scientists.

Aug. 4 A **world air speed record** of 2196 mph was set by the X-15 experimental U.S. rocket plane. The plane was piloted by Joseph A. Walker, a civilian test pilot.

Aug. 11 The **first payload recovered from orbit** was lifted from the Pacific Ocean by a U.S. helicopter. The capsule was placed in orbit by Discoverer 13 on Aug. 10.

Aug. 19 A **spacecraft was snagged in midair** by the U.S. Air Force. The 300-lb. space capsule was ejected from Discoverer 14 at an altitude of 10,000 ft. and retrieved at 8500 ft.

Oct. 15 A **strike** of the Union Carbide Nuclear Company was begun by 2000 members of the AFL-CIO Oil, Chemical, and Atomic Workers International Union. The strike ended on Oct. 31, when a wage settlement was reached.

Oct. 18 Observation of **nongenetic heredity** was reported by Dr. Tracy Sonneborn of Indiana University. An element in the outer layer of paramecia appeared to control inherited cell characteristics.

Nov. 3 The **Nobel Prize in Chemistry** was awarded to Prof. Willard Frank Libby of the University of California for discovering a method of radioactive carbon dating.

Nov. 3 The **Nobel Prize in Physics** was awarded to Prof. Donald A. Glaser of the University of California for his development of the bubble chamber, a device that makes visible the paths of subatomic particles.

Nov. 18 Discontinuance of the **De Soto** automobile was announced by the Chrysler Corporation. The De Soto had been manufactured by the company since 1928.

July 24 The **PGA golf tournament** was won by Jay Hebert, beating Jim Ferrier by one stroke.

Aug. 12 In a case of **racial discrimination**, a Troy, Mich., cemetery rejected the body of Winnebago Indian George V. Nash because he was not white. Nash, a World War I veteran, was buried in Pontiac, Mich., after his family refused to permit burial in Arlington National Cemetery.

Aug. 25–Sept. 11 At the **Summer Olympics** in Rome, Italy, the U.S. won 34 gold medals and took second place in team standings, behind the U.S.S.R.

Sept. 10 The **Miss America** title was won by Nancy Anne Fleming, 18, from Michigan, at the annual pageant in Atlantic City, N.J.

Sept. 17 The **U.S. Lawn Tennis Association singles championships** were won by Neale Fraser of Australia in the men's division and Darlene Hard of California in the women's division.

Oct. 3 In a **narcotics raid,** U.S. agents confiscated $3,500,000 worth of heroin (110 lbs.) and arrested four people, among them the Guatemalan ambassador to Belgium, Mauricio Rosal.

Oct. 5–13 The 57th **World Series** was won by the Pittsburgh Pirates (NL), defeating the New York Yankees (AL) four games to three.

Oct. 18 **Casey Stengel,** manager of the New York Yankee baseball team since 1949, was fired. Although the official announcement stated that Stengel had reached retirement age, he attributed dismissal to a controversy with the club owners.

Dec. 26 The **NFL championship** was won by the Philadelphia Eagles, who defeated the Green Bay Packers 17–13.

1961

This was a year for adventure in space. Two Americans and two Russians invaded a frontier of the future. Though the U.S. was unable to equal the impressive Soviet feat of putting men into orbit, it succeeded in propelling two men to the threshold of space and then recovering them safely. The U.S. also launched an impressive series of Earth satellites and space probes, mostly designed to transmit data back to Earth. Progress

In boxing Floyd Patterson again defeated Ingemar Johansson in a close but quick fight in Miami Beach, Fla. Patterson withstood the power of the Swedish champion's savage right hand and scored a knockout, the second in a row for the American heavyweight. In golf, the top money winners were Gary Player, $64,540, and Mickey Wright, $22,236. In baseball, the National League announced that it would add two new

| Exploration and Settlement; Wars; Government; Civil Rights; Statistics | **I** | | **II** | Publishing; Arts and Music; Popular Entertainment; Architecture; Theater |

September the Soviets resumed atmospheric nuclear testing. In the domestic arena, the president was confronted with several difficult problems. How to eliminate unemployment continued to be a major concern. Congress refused to provide substantial aid to U.S. education and passed an impotent civil rights bill. Notables who died included Whittaker Chambers, accuser of Alger Hiss, July 9, at 60; William Z. Foster, chairman of the American Communist Party from 1945 to 1957, Sept. 1, at 80; Learned Hand, distinguished jurist, Aug. 18, at 89; Sam Rayburn, longtime Speaker of the House, Nov. 16, at 79; Walter Bedell Smith, chief of staff to Gen. Eisenhower during World War II, Aug. 9, at 75; and Sumner Welles, diplomat, Sept. 24, at 68.

Jan. 3 The **U.S. broke diplomatic relations with Cuba** after a series of mutually hostile actions, the last being Cuba's demand that the U.S. reduce its Havana embassy staff to 11 members.

Jan. 6 A **fire at the Thomas Hotel** in San Francisco killed 20 persons.

Jan. 20 **John F. Kennedy was inaugurated president** of the United States. A Democrat and the 35th president, Kennedy was assassinated on Nov. 22, 1963.

Mar. 8 Concern over growth of the **John Birch Society,** an ultraconservative group, was voiced on the floor of the U.S. Senate. The secret society, founded in 1958 by Robert H. W. Welch, had accused numerous Americans, including former presidents, of aiding world communism.

Mar. 13 **Elizabeth Gurley Flynn,** 70, was named to succeed Eugene Dennis as national chairman of the U.S. Communist Party. She was the first woman to fill the office.

Apr. 17 In what came to be called the **Bay of Pigs invasion,** some 1500 anti-Castro Cuban exiles landed at the Bay of Cochinos in Cuba. Organized by the U.S.-based National Revolutionary Council and trained by the CIA, the force enjoyed initial success but collapsed within a few days because of inadequate supplies, lack of air support, and overwhelming opposing forces. On Apr. 24 Pres. Kennedy stated he accepted full responsibility for failure of the invasion.

May 16–17 On a two-day **visit to Canada,** Pres. Kennedy urged Canada to augment its hemispheric role by increasing aid to underdeveloped countries and by strengthening NATO.

May 25 In an **address to a joint session of Congress,** Pres. Kennedy urged the U.S. to "take a clearly

Hemingway; he was said to have shot himself while cleaning a shotgun. Joan Sutherland made an impressive U.S. debut at the Metropolitan Opera. She displayed a capacity for combining agility, color, subtlety, and volume of sound. Equally impressive was a New York City recital series by pianist Arthur Rubinstein, who enchanted U.S. music lovers. Playing ten Carnegie Hall recitals within 40 days, Rubinstein, at 72, announced joyfully that he had decided not to make the series his "final touch." Notables who died this year included Gary Cooper, actor, May 13, at 60; Hilda Doolittle, poet, Sept. 27, at 75; Dashiell Hammett, detective writer, Jan. 10, at 66; Moss Hart, playwright, Dec. 20, at 57; George S. Kaufman, playwright and producer, June 2, at 71; Chico Marx, Oct. 11, at 70; Grandma Moses, painter, Dec. 13, at 101; Eero Saarinen, architect, Sept. 1, at 51; and James Thurber, writer and cartoonist, Nov. 2, at 66.

Among **books published** this year was *Webster's Third New International Dictionary.* The massive new unabridged dictionary received a mixed response. Many linguists objected to its refusal to set standards of English and felt that too much valuable old material had been omitted. Other books published this year included *The Coming Fury* by Bruce Catton, the first volume of a trilogy to be called *Centennial History of the Civil War; Midcentury* by John Dos Passos, a novel; *Kaddish and Other Poems* by Allen Ginsberg; *Catch-22* by Joseph Heller, an antiwar novel that became a best seller; *Spirit Lake* by MacKinlay Kantor, a novel about frontier life in Iowa in the 1850s; *Franny and Zooey* by J. D. Salinger, stories; *Sinclair Lewis: an American Life* by Mark Schorer; *The Winter of Our Discontent* by John Steinbeck, a novel; and *The Agony and the Ecstasy* by Irving Stone, a novel based on the life of Michelangelo.

The year's **popular songs** included "Never on Sunday," from the film of the same name, "Where the Boys Are," "Apache," "Don't Be Cruel," "It's Now or Never."

Jan. 9 *Rhinoceros* by Eugene Ionesco, translated by Derek Prouse, opened at the Longacre Theatre in New York City. The cast included Zero Mostel, Eli Wallach, and Anne Jackson.

Jan. 23 In a **film censorship** ruling, the U.S. Supreme Court upheld a Chicago, Ill., ordinance forbidding the showing of any motion picture without permission of the city censors.

Feb. 1 *The New York Times* was voted the best daily newspaper in the U.S. in a poll of 276 newspapers.

Mar. 8 *Mary, Mary,* a play by Jean Kerr starring Barbara Bel Geddes, opened at the Helen Hayes Theatre in New York City.

Mar. 9 *The Devil's Advocate* by Dore Schary, adapted from Morris West's novel, opened at the Billy Rose Theatre in New York City.

Mar. 14 The **National Book Awards** were presented for the following: fiction, *The Waters of Kronos* by

| Business and Industry; Science; Education; Philosophy and Religion   III | | IV   Sports; Social Issues and Crime; Folkways; Fashion; Holidays |

of a different sort was made in civil rights in educational facilities. Court after court voided—but some upheld—various state laws designed to prevent school integration. Even though some civil rights battles were won, integration was slow and marked by sporadic violence, such as that encountered during the so-called freedom rides. Education as a whole became more of a national concern as it became increasingly evident that educational facilities were inadequate and growing more so and that the quality of instruction was poor in many parts of the country. Among the notables who died this year was Lee De Forest, whose invention of the audion tube in 1906 ushered in the age of radio, June 30, at 87.

Jan. 28 Plans for establishing the **Peace Corps,** a project advocated by Pres. John F. Kennedy, were made public by the U.S. State Department.

Jan. 30 Pres. Kennedy decried the **crisis in U.S. education** in his first State of the Union message, noting that some 2,000,000 children were being instructed by 90,000 teachers "not properly qualified."

Jan. 31 In a **Project Mercury** suborbital test flight, the U.S. shot a 37½-lb. chimpanzee into space and recovered him successfully. The capsule containing the animal traveled 5000 mph to a height of 155 miles.

Feb. 6–7 In a **price-fixing** and bid-rigging case, 29 large manufacturers of electrical equipment were found guilty by U.S. District Judge J. Cullen Ganey. The penalties exacted included 30 jail sentences, 23 of which were suspended, and $1,924,500 in fines.

Feb. 18 **Discoverer 21** was launched into orbit by a Thor-Agena-B rocket. An unusual feature of the shot was a control mechanism that enabled the rocket engine to be restarted while in orbit.

Feb. 22–23 **Birth control** as a means of family limitation was endorsed by the National Council of Churches at a meeting in Syracuse, N.Y.

Feb. 23 The most costly **airline strike** in aviation history ended. The six-day strike had completely shut down Trans World, Eastern, Flying Tiger, American, and National airlines and had hampered operations of several others.

Apr. 27 **Explorer 11,** a 95-lb. research satellite, was launched into orbit by a Juno 2 rocket. Carrying a "lensless telescope," the satellite was intended to determine the nature of interstellar matter.

franchises in 1962, the Houston Astros and the New York Mets. Americans mourned the death of Tyrus Raymond "Ty" Cobb, considered by many the greatest baseball player of all time, July 17, at 74.

Jan. 1 In **college football bowl games,** the results were Duke 7, Arkansas 6 in the Cotton Bowl; Missouri 21, Navy 14 in the Orange Bowl; Washington 17, Minnesota 7 in the Rose Bowl; and Mississippi 14, Rice 6 in the Sugar Bowl. This season both the AP and UPI polls chose Minnesota the national collegiate champions of 1960.

Jan. 2 The **AFL championship** for 1960 was won by the Houston Oilers, who defeated the Los Angeles Chargers 24–16.

Jan. 27–29 **U.S. figure skating championships** were won in Colorado Springs, Colo., by Laurence Owen, women's singles; Bradley Lord, men's singles; Maribel Owen and Dudley Richards, pairs; Diane Sherbloom and Larry Pierce, dance.

Mar. 12 The **LPGA golf tournament** was won by Mickey Wright, her third win in four years.

Mar. 25 The **NCAA basketball championship** was won by Cincinnati, defeating the defending champions, Ohio State, 70–65.

Apr. 2–11 The **NBA basketball championship** was won by the Boston Celtics, who defeated the St. Louis Hawks four games to one.

Apr. 6–16 The **NHL Stanley Cup** was won by the Chicago Black Hawks, who defeated the Detroit Red Wings four games to two.

Apr. 10 The **Masters golf tournament** was won by Gary Player of South Africa. He was the first foreign golfer to win the event.

Apr. 19 The 65th **Boston Marathon** was won by Eino Oksanen of Finland, with a time of 2 hrs., 23 min., 29 sec.

May 6 The 87th annual **Kentucky Derby** was won by Carry Back, with a time of 2:04. The jockey was John Sellers.

May 14 Two groups of **freedom riders,** people who traveled by private car and public transportation to sites in the South to protest racial segregation, were attacked by white citizens of Anniston and Birmingham, Ala., while on a journey from Washington, D.C., to New Orleans.

| Exploration and Settlement; Wars; Government; Civil Rights; Statistics | I | | II | Publishing; Arts and Music; Popular Entertainment; Architecture; Theater |

leading role in space achievements." He asked for $1,-800,000,000 for space and other programs.

May 27 A bill establishing the **Alliance for Progress** was signed by Pres. Kennedy. The bill provided $600,-000,000 in special aid to Latin America.

June 3–4 At the **Vienna summit meeting,** Pres. Kennedy and Premier Nikita S. Khrushchev discussed problems of mutual interest to the U.S. and the U.S.S.R., particularly nuclear disarmament and troubles in Laos and in Berlin.

June 22 Returning from a **South American goodwill tour,** Adlai Stevenson, U.S. ambassador to the UN, stated that popular discontent had grown and governmental stability had diminished since his 1960 South American tour.

July 3 Gen. **Douglas MacArthur** returned to the Philippines on his first visit since 1946. He was welcomed to Manila by some 2,000,000 Filipinos.

July 8 A reappraisal of **U.S. military strength** was ordered by Pres. Kennedy. His action was attributed to the East-West confrontation in Berlin and to increased Soviet military expenditures.

July 14 The third week in July was designated **Captive Nations Week.** The intention was to show support for the eventual liberation of all captive nations but particularly the communist satellite nations of eastern Europe.

July 24 A U.S. **passenger jet was hijacked.** An armed passenger forced the pilot of an Eastern Airlines Electra en route to Tampa from Miami to divert to Havana. Cuba later entrusted the plane to the UN Security Council to discourage what it alleged to be "imminent military aggression" by the U.S.

Aug. 2 **U.S. support for the Republic of China** and its membership in the UN was reaffirmed in a joint communiqué issued following meetings between Pres. Kennedy and Premier Ch'en Ch'eng of the Republic of China. The statement reiterated U.S. opposition to UN membership for the People's Republic of China.

Sept. 1 In the worst single commercial **plane crash** to date in the U.S., 78 persons died when a TWA Constellation crashed in Hinsdale, Ill., four minutes after takeoff from Chicago's Midway Airport.

Sept. 4 The **Foreign Assistance Act** of 1961, which authorized $4,253,500,000 for use in foreign military and economic programs, was signed by Pres. Kennedy.

Conrad Richter; nonfiction, *The Rise and Fall of the Third Reich* by William L. Shirer; poetry, *The Woman at the Washington Zoo* by Randall Jarrell.

Mar. 19 The **Ford Foundation** announced a four-year grant of $244,000 to "stimulate communication among the various branches of the American theater."

Apr. 12 **Grammy Awards** were presented to the following: best album of 1960, *Button Down Mind* by Bob Newhart; best record, "Theme from a Summer Place" by Henry Mancini; best male vocalist, Ray Charles for "Georgia on My Mind"; best female vocalist, Ella Fitzgerald for "Mack the Knife"; best group, Steve Lawrence and Eydie Gorme for "We Got Us."

Apr. 13 *Carnival,* a musical by Michael Stewart and Bob Merrill, opened at the Imperial Theatre in New York City.

Apr. 16 **Tony Awards** for the 1960–1961 season were presented to the following: best play, *Becket;* best musical, *Bye, Bye, Birdie;* best actor in a drama, Zero Mostel for *Rhinoceros;* best actress in a drama, Joan Plowright for *A Taste of Honey.*

Apr. 17 **Academy Awards** were presented to *The Apartment* as the outstanding motion picture of 1960; to Burt Lancaster as best actor for *Elmer Gantry;* to Elizabeth Taylor as best actress for *Butterfield 8;* to Peter Ustinov as best supporting actor for *Spartacus;* and to Shirley Jones as best supporting actress for *Elmer Gantry.*

Apr. 30 The **Guggenheim Memorial Foundation** announced award of $1,350,000 in fellowships to 265 scholars, scientists, and artists.

May 1 **Pulitzer prizes** were awarded for the following: fiction, *To Kill a Mockingbird* by Harper Lee; biography, *Charles Sumner and the Coming of the Civil War* by David Donald; history, *Between War and Peace: The Potsdam Conference* by Herbert Feis; poetry, *Times Three: Selected Verse from Three Decades* by Phyllis McGinley; drama, *All the Way Home* by Tad Mosel.

May 9 Calling **television a "vast wasteland,"** Newton N. Minow, chairman of the FCC, in a vehement criticism of TV programming, said, "It is not enough to cater to the nation's whims—you must also serve the nation's needs."

May 16 **Emmy Awards** were presented to Maurice Evans and Judith Anderson as best actor and actress for their performances in *Macbeth,* which was chosen outstanding drama; Raymond Burr as best actor in a dramatic series for *Perry Mason;* and Barbara Stanwyck as best actress in a dramatic series for *The Barbara Stanwyck Show.*

Oct. Esquire, Inc. announced that *Coronet magazine* would cease publication with its October issue. The

Business and Industry; Science; **III**		**IV** **Sports; Social Issues and Crime;**
Education; Philosophy and Religion		**Folkways; Fashion; Holidays**

May 4 A new **balloon altitude record** was set by two Navy scientists who ascended to 113,500 ft. aboard the balloon *Stratolab High No. 5.* One of the balloonists drowned after he fell from the sling of the helicopter that had picked him up.

May 5 A bill setting the federal **minimum wage** at $1.25 an hour and expanding coverage to include 3,624,000 workers not covered previously was signed by Pres. Kennedy.

May 5 The **first American in space** was Navy Commander Alan Bartlett Shepard, Jr., who made a successful suborbital flight aboard the Project Mercury capsule *Freedom Seven.*

June 6 A system for **detection of heart defects in children** was perfected by the Chicago Heart Association. The process involved recording the heart sounds of children on high-fidelity tapes that could be read by cardiologists.

June 16 **Discoverer 25** was launched. Its capsule was ejected and recovered on June 18. The satellite carried samples of various minerals to determine how they would be affected by space conditions.

June 29 **Three satellites were launched** simultaneously by a Thor-Able-Star rocket. These satellites, Transit 4-A, Greb 3, and Injun, constituted the first triple launching in history.

July 3 An 18-day **maritime strike** was halted when a Taft-Hartley injunction was issued at the request of the U.S. Deptartment of Justice. According to the Justice Deptartment, the strike was "cutting the lifelines to Puerto Rico and Hawaii."

July 7 **James R. Hoffa** was reelected president of the International Brotherhood of Teamsters by an overwhelming vote. The election was held at the Teamsters' convention in Miami Beach, Fla.

July 21 The **second American in space** was Capt. Virgil I. "Gus" Grissom, USAF, who ascended to an altitude of 118 miles in a suborbital flight aboard the Project Mercury capsule *Liberty Bell Seven.*

July 28 Calling **racial equality** the "scientific hoax of the century," Henry F. Garrett, past president of the American Psychological Association, claimed that evidence indicated that racial differences in mental ability were "innate and genetic."

May 20 The 86th annual **Preakness Stakes** was won by Carry Back, with a time of 1:57³/₅. The jockey was John Sellers.

May 30 The 45th **Indianapolis 500** auto race was won by A. J. Foyt, completing the 500-mile course with an average speed of 139.130 mph, a new race record.

June 3 The 93rd annual **Belmont Stakes** was won by Sherluck, with a time of 2:29³/₅. The jockey was Braulio Baeza.

June 9 In a **college basketball bribery** scandal, four former players were indicted in New York City in connection with a point-shaving plot, in which players would deliberately control the score of a game as instructed by gamblers. Two gamblers, Aaron Wagman and Joseph Hacken, were named as co-conspirators. Both had been indicted earlier on related charges in the grand jury probe that began on Apr. 4. As the summer progressed, further revelations and indictments showed the practice of point-shaving to be widespread.

June 17 The **U.S. Open golf tournament** was won by Gene Littler.

July 1 The **U.S. Women's Open golf tournament** was won by Mickey Wright, who beat the defending champion Betsy Rawls by six strokes.

July 8 At the **Wimbledon** tennis championships in England the women's doubles title was won by Karen Hantze and Billie Jean Moffitt.

July 24 The **Baseball Hall of Fame** inducted former outfielders Max G. "Scoops" Carey and William R. "Billy" Hamilton.

July 30 The **PGA golf tournament** was won by Jerry Barber, who beat Don January by one stroke in a play-off round.

July 31 The second **baseball All-Star Game** of the year ended in a 1–1 tie at the end of the ninth inning due to rain. It was the first tie in the history of the event. The first game (July 11) had been won in ten innings by the National League, beating the American League 5–4.

Aug. 27 *Cuba and the American Negro,* a report issued by the Senate Internal Security Subcommittee, stated that a Cuban campaign to gain sympathy and support among American blacks had failed.

Sept. 9 The **Miss America** title was won by Maria

| Exploration and Settlement; Wars; Government; Civil Rights; Statistics | I | | II | Publishing; Arts and Music; Popular Entertainment; Architecture; Theater |

Sept. 5 A **hijacking bill** making air piracy a crime punishable by death or imprisonment was signed by Pres. Kennedy.

Sept. 27 **Richard M. Nixon** announced his candidacy for the governorship of California. In his statement, the former vice president said: "I shall not be a candidate for president in 1964."

Oct. 6 Speaking on **civil defense**, Pres. Kennedy advised families to build or buy a shelter against atomic fallout. He said that the U.S. civil defense program should provide such protection for every American.

Nov. 6–9 A **fire** in the Bel Air–Brentwood suburbs of Los Angeles destroyed 447 homes, including some owned by Hollywood movie people.

Nov. 8 A **plane crash** killed 74 U.S. Army recruits flying in a chartered Imperial Airlines Constellation over an area near Richmond, Va. It was later revealed that the airline had been penalized twice for infractions of CAA regulations.

Dec. 5 **Broad participation in exercise** by Americans was called for by Pres. Kennedy. The president noted that five of seven men called for the Army were rejected and complained that the U.S. was becoming a nation of spectators rather than a nation of athletes.

25-year-old magazine had 2,310,000 subscribers but had steadily lost money for two years.

Oct. 4 *The Caretaker* by Harold Pinter, starring Alan Bates, Robert Shaw, and Donald Pleasance, opened at the Lyceum Theatre in New York City.

Oct. 12 *World,* a national weekly newspaper, went on sale. Published in Washington, D.C., by Willard W. Garvey of Wichita, Kans., it had initial distribution in about 100 cities.

Oct. 14 *How to Succeed in Business Without Really Trying,* a musical comedy by Abe Burrows, Jack Weinstock, Willie Gilbert, and Frank Loesser, adapted from the book by Shepherd Mead, opened at the Forty-Sixth Street Theatre in New York City.

Oct. 17 The **Ford Foundation** announced grants of $1,470,000 for five new visual arts programs.

Oct. 31 The first **Bollingen Prize for Translation,** carrying a $2500 cash prize, was awarded to Robert Fitzgerald for his translation of Homer's *Odyssey.*

Nov. 15 A **record art price** of $2,300,000 was paid by the New York Metropolitan Museum of Art for Rembrandt's *Aristotle Contemplating the Bust of Homer.* The painting was formerly in the collection of the late Alfred W. Erickson and his wife.

Nov. 22 *A Man for All Seasons* by Robert Bolt, a drama about the life and death of Sir Thomas More starring Paul Scofield and Leo McKern, opened at the ANTA Theatre in New York City.

Nov. 30 *All the Way Home* by Tad Mosel, based on James Agee's novel *A Death in the Family* (1957), opened at the Belasco Theatre in New York City.

1962

In international affairs, Pres. John F. Kennedy appeared stronger and more sure. He visited Mexico and the Bahamas in an effort to strengthen alliances. Communist violation of a cease-fire in Laos in May led Kennedy to order U.S. troops into Thailand until guarantees of Laotian sovereignty could be secured. Chinese invasion of India in September prompted increased U.S. aid to India. The key event of the year came in October, when Pres. Kennedy, on national TV, revealed that Soviet nuclear missiles and jet bombers were located in Cuba and ordered a blockade of Cuba until the weapons were removed. The world appeared to stand on the brink of nuclear war until Premier Khrushchev agreed to withdraw the weapons. At home, the president was less successful. Congress continued to defeat or alter proposed legislation. The nation mourned the death of Eleanor Roosevelt, widow of Pres. Franklin D. Roosevelt and a key figure in the early years of the United Nations, Nov. 7, at 78.

In art, the interest of the general public and collectors focused on so-called pop art, the depiction and sometimes the actual display of the most banal objects of American life: canned foods, electric appliances, comic strips, and the like. An international art scandal broke when Canadian authorities questioned the authenticity of many of the paintings from Walter P. Chrysler's famous collection, then on tour in Canada. Formation of Citizens for Decent Literature kept the question of censorship in the news; two particular targets of this watchdog group were *The Carpetbaggers* by Harold Robbins and *The Tropic of Capricorn* by Henry Miller. In architecture, one of the year's most interesting structures was the 600-foot Space Needle, at the Century 21 Exposition in Seattle, Wash. Notables who died this year included Sylvia Beach, proprietor of the celebrated bookstore Shakespeare & Co. in Paris, about Oct. 5, at 75; William Beebe, naturalist, author, and explorer, June 4, at 84; E. E. Cummings, poet, Sept. 3, at 67; William Faulkner,

Business and Industry; Science;				**Sports; Social Issues and Crime;**
Education; Philosophy and Religion	**III**		**IV**	**Folkways; Fashion; Holidays**

Sept. 8 In a report on **smoking and heart disease** in the *Journal of the American Medical Association,* it was held that there was statistical evidence connecting the two.

Sept. 13 An **artificial astronaut** was orbited in a Project Mercury space capsule launched from Cape Canaveral, Fla. NASA officials described the flight as very successful.

Oct. 19 The **Nobel Prize for Physiology or Medicine** was awarded to Dr. Georg von Bekesy of Harvard University for his studies of the inner ear.

Oct. 30 In a **report on reading skills** published by seven specialists, the whole-word method of reading instruction was called vastly inferior to the phonic method. The report stated that the whole-word method had caused reading retardation in 35% of American youths.

Nov. 2 The **Nobel Prize for Chemistry** was awarded to Melvin Calvin of the University of California at Berkeley for determining the sequence of chemical reactions involved when a plant assimilates carbon dioxide.

Nov. 2 The **Nobel Prize in Physics** was awarded jointly to Robert Hofstadter of Stanford University for his work on the atomic nucleus and to Rudolf L. Mössbauer of West Germany for developing a method of using radiation from excited nuclei to measure time.

Beale Fletcher, 19, from North Carolina, at the annual pageant in Atlantic City, N.J.

Sept. 10 The **U.S. Lawn Tennis Association singles championships** were won by Roy Emerson of Australia in the men's division and Darlene Hard of California, for the second year running, in the women's division.

Sept. 22 A bill authorizing $30,000,000 to fight **juvenile delinquency** was signed by Pres. Kennedy.

Oct. 1 Yankee slugger **Roger Maris** hit his 61st homer, setting a new season record. He did it in a season of 162 games. Babe Ruth had hit 60 home runs in a 154-game season.

Oct. 4–9 The 58th annual **World Series** was won by the New York Yankees (AL), beating the Cincinnati Reds (NL) four games to one.

Dec. 4 The **world heavyweight boxing championship** was successfully defended by Floyd Patterson, who knocked out Tom McNeeley in the fourth round of a bout in Toronto, Canada.

Dec. 24 The **AFL championship** was won by the Houston Oilers, who defeated the San Diego Chargers 10–3.

Dec. 31 The **NFL championship** was won by the Green Bay Packers, who defeated the New York Giants 37–0.

1962

This year's space achievements included the launching of Telstar, a communications satellite, and the orbiting of three astronauts on perfect missions. Experimentation with nuclear submarines and with thermonuclear detonations added to U.S. technological development. In the South, segregation in university education was broken, but only after mob violence and several deaths. Official nondenominational prayers in public schools were ruled unconstitutional by the Supreme Court. Congress took no steps to provide funds for the improvement of educational facilities for the nation's youth. In industry, an effort by steel industry management to raise prices was stopped by Pres. John F. Kennedy. The AFL-CIO announced a drive to establish a national 35-hour work week.

Jan. 12 A **railroad merger** of two of the nation's largest systems, the Pennsylvania and the New York Central railroads, was approved by the companies' boards of directors.

In boxing Floyd Patterson lost his heavyweight crown to Sonny Liston in less than three minutes. In November 20-year-old Cassius Clay knocked out Archie Moore and moved closer to a title match against Liston. In baseball two new teams, the Houston Colt .45's and the New York Mets, joined the National League roster. The New York Yankees won their 20th World Series. In golf the leading money winners were Arnold Palmer, $81,448, and Mickey Wright, $21,641. A new dance craze, the twist, was born in a New York City nightclub, The Peppermint Lounge. In women's fashions wigs became popular, and boots became a fashion accessory. The romance between Elizabeth Taylor and Richard Burton on the set for the motion picture *Cleopatra* in Rome was in and out of the headlines all year. Notables who died in 1962 included Edward Britt "Ted" Husing, sports announcer, Aug. 10, at 50; Charles "Lucky" Luciano, gangster, Jan. 26, at 65; Clem McCarthy, sports announcer, June 4, at 79; and Benny "Kid" Paret, a

| Exploration and Settlement; Wars; Government; Civil Rights; Statistics | I | II | Publishing; Arts and Music; Popular Entertainment; Architecture; Theater |

Jan. 12 American **communists were barred from travel abroad** by new regulations issued by the U.S. State Department denying passports to Communist Party members.

Jan. 15 U.S. tanks were withdrawn from the Berlin Wall in an effort to improve relations with the U.S.S.R. Two days later 12 Soviet tanks that had stationed near the wall since Oct. 1961 were removed.

Jan. 29 The **nuclear test ban conference** of the U.S., U.S.S.R., and Great Britain in Geneva adjourned after 353 sessions in three years. The talks were deadlocked over a monitoring system for international control.

Feb. 3 A **trade ban with Cuba,** effective Feb. 7 and including almost all products, was ordered by Pres. Kennedy.

Feb. 8 Creation of the **Military Assistance Command** (MAC), a new U.S. military command in South Vietnam, was announced by the Defense Department.

Feb. 10 U-2 pilot **Francis Gary Powers** was released in Berlin by Soviet authorities in exchange for Soviet spy Rudolf Abel. Frederic L. Pryor, an American student, was released by the Soviets at the same time.

Feb. 26 **Segregation laws in transportation facilities,** both interstate and intrastate, were ruled unconstitutional by the U.S. Supreme Court. The Court ordered a federal court in Mississippi to act against state segregation laws in terminals.

Mar. 1 A **plane crash** killed 95 persons when a jet heading for Los Angeles plunged into Jamaica Bay, N.Y., seconds after takeoff from Idlewild International Airport.

Mar. 19 The **Communist Party was sued** in New York by the Justice Department, which also sued four of its officials—Elizabeth Gurley Flynn, Gus Hall, Benjamin J. Davis, and Philip Bart—in an effort to collect $500,000 in income taxes and interest for 1951.

Apr. 3 Full **racial integration in military reserve units,** exclusive of the National Guard, was ordered by the Defense Department.

winner of the 1949 Nobel Prize for Literature, July 6, at 64; Robinson Jeffers, poet, Jan 20, at 75; Franz Josef Kline, expressionist painter, May 13, at 51; Ernie Kovacs, television writer, performer, and producer, Jan. 13, at 42; Fritz Kreisler, violinist, Jan. 29, at 86; Marilyn Monroe, who died in her Los Angeles home of an apparent overdose of sleeping pills, Aug. 5, at 36; and Bruno Walter, conductor, Feb. 17, at 85.

Among **books published** this year was *Ship of Fools* by Katherine Anne Porter, a long-awaited novel 20 years in the writing. It was an account of a voyage from Mexico to Germany of a German ship in 1931, on the eve of Adolf Hitler's rise to power. Other books published this year included *Another Country* by James Baldwin, a novel; *Fail-Safe* by Eugene Burdick and Harvey Wheeler, a novel about the accidental launching of a nuclear strike against the U.S.S.R.; *Silent Spring* by Rachel Carson, a well-documented indictment of the indiscriminate use of pesticides and other chemicals; *In the Clearing,* a collection of poems by Robert Frost; *The Thin Red Line* by James Jones, a novel dealing with the invasion of Guadalcanal in World War II; *Seven Days in May* by Fletcher Knebel and Charles W. Bailey II, a novel dealing with the military overthrow of the U.S. government; *Six Crises* by Richard M. Nixon; *A Simple Honorable Man* by Conrad Richter, a novel; and *Travels With Charley: In Search of America* by John Steinbeck.

WNYC-TV, the nation's first **municipally owned television station,** began operation in New York City. The city also received its first publicly supported educational television station, WNDT, this year.

Two of the fastest-selling **record albums** in the history of the recording industry were issued this year. In *The First Family,* Vaughn Meader and others mimicked members of the Kennedy clan. *My Son, the Folk Singer* featured Allan Sherman singing parodies of folk songs ("Sarah Jackman, Sarah Jackman, how's by you?" to the tune of "Frère Jacques"; "The Catskill ladies sing this song," to "The Camptown Races").

Feb. 14 A televised **tour of the White House** by Jacqueline Kennedy, accompanied by Charles Collingwood, was broadcast simultaneously by CBS and NBC and was seen by an estimated 46,500,000 persons.

Feb. 19 **Abraham Lincoln's boyhood home** in Lincoln City, Ind., was established as a national monument.

Feb. 24 The **AIA Gold Medal** for architecture was awarded posthumously to Eero Saarinen.

Feb. 26 *Oh Dad, Poor Dad, Mamma's Hung You in the Closet and I'm Feelin' So Sad,* an ingenious but sometimes baffling play by Arthur Kopit, opened off Broadway at the Phoenix Theatre in New York City.

Mar. 13 **National Book Awards** were presented for the following: fiction, *The Moviegoer* by Walker Percy; nonfiction, *The City in History* by Lewis Mumford; poetry, *Poems* by Alan Dugan.

| Business and Industry; Science; Education; Philosophy and Religion | III | | IV | Sports; Social Issues and Crime; Folkways; Fashion; Holidays |

Jan. 16 An agreement on **tariff reductions** was initialed by representatives of the U.S. and the Common Market nations.

Jan. 23 The **merger of American Airlines and Eastern Air Lines** was voted by their directors. Stockholders approved the creation of what would be the world's biggest airline system on Apr. 17.

Jan. 26 **Ranger 3,** a lunar probe designed to transmit close-up television pictures of the moon before landing scientific instruments on its surface, was launched from Cape Canaveral, Fla. Two days later, because of excessive velocity, it passed the moon and went into orbit around the sun.

Feb. 14 Plans for an **underwater telephone cable** costing $84,000,000 and running between Hawaii and Japan, via Midway, Wake, and Guam islands, was announced by the American Telephone & Telegraph Company.

Feb. 20 The **first American to orbit Earth,** Lt. Col. John Glenn, circled the globe three times aboard a Mercury capsule *Friendship 7* before splashdown. It was launched from Cape Canaveral, Fla.

Mar. 1 In the **biggest antitrust case** in U.S. history, E. I. du Pont de Nemours & Company was ordered by a federal district court to divest itself of 63,000,000 shares of General Motors stock.

Mar. 4 The Atomic Energy Commission announced that the **first atomic power plant in Antarctica** was in operation at McMurdo Sound.

Mar. 7 A broad **reduction of U.S. import duties** was announced by Pres. Kennedy in a message to Congress. The reductions were the result of extensive negotiations in Geneva, Switzerland, with the European Economic Community, the United Kingdom, and 24 other nations, which made similar tariff concessions. The agreements were made to promote trade and support further trade negotiations.

Mar. 8 A two-year **cultural agreement** was signed with the U.S.S.R. to expand cultural, scientific, technical, and educational exchanges.

Mar. 16 **Titan 2,** the most powerful U.S. ICBM, on its maiden flight, covered more than 5000 miles from Cape Canaveral, Fla., to a spot near Ascension Island in the south Atlantic.

Mar. 27 **Segregation** in all Roman Catholic schools in the New Orleans, La., diocese was ordered ended by Archbishop Joseph Francis Rummel.

Apr. 10 A **steel price increase** averaging 3.5%, or $6.00 a ton, was announced by United States Steel following signing of a new union contract on Apr. 1. Five other steel companies announced similar price hikes.

welterweight fighter who died of injuries sustained in a bout with Emile Griffith, Apr. 3, at 24.

A **UPI survey** showed that in the 24 states with legalized betting at race tracks, 33,881,860 fans bet a total of $2,679,461,505. Attendance was up 1.28% over 1961, and betting was up 5.57%. Mrs. Richard C. du Pont's Kelso was named horse of the year for the third straight year. Kelso earned $254,585 to boost lifetime earnings of the horse to $1,011,940. Kelso became the fifth horse in racing history to top the $1,000,000 mark.

Jan. The use of **nudity in advertising** became a national controversy after Christina Paolozzi, a 22-year-old model, appeared in the nude in a full-page color ad in *Harper's Bazaar.* The photograph was the work of fashion photographer Richard Avedon.

Jan. 1 In **college football bowl games,** the results were Texas 12, Mississippi 7 in the Cotton Bowl; LSU 25, Colorado 7 in the Orange Bowl; Minnesota 21, UCLA 3 in the Rose Bowl; and Alabama 10, Arkansas 3 in the Sugar Bowl. This season both the AP and UPI polls chose Alabama the national collegiate champions of 1961.

Feb. 2 The **first person to vault 16 feet** was a Marine Corps corporal, John Uelses, at the Millrose Games in Madison Square Garden in New York City. Using a springy fiberglass pole, he cleared 16 ft. ¼ in. On the following night, in Boston, he raised the mark to 16 ft. ¾ in.

Feb. 3–4 **U.S. figure skating championships** were won in Boston by Barbara Roles Pursley, women's singles; Monty Hoyt, men's singles; Dorothyann Nelson and Pieter Kollen, pairs; Yvonne Littlefield and Peter Betts, dance.

Feb. 10 Jim Beatty, the **first American to break the four-minute mile indoors,** was clocked at 3:58.9 in Los Angeles, a new indoor record. On June 8, also in Los Angeles, he set a new world record of 8:29.8 for two miles. Beatty won the James E. Sullivan Memorial Trophy as the outstanding amateur athlete of 1962.

Mar. 2 The **first basketball player to score 100 points** in a game was Wilt Chamberlain, star of the Philadelphia Warriors, who made 36 goals and 28 foul shots in a game against the N.Y. Knicks.

Mar. 24 The **NCAA basketball championship** was won by Cincinnati, which defeated Ohio State 71–59.

| Exploration and Settlement; Wars; Government; Civil Rights; Statistics | I | | II | Publishing; Arts and Music; Popular Entertainment; Architecture; Theater |

Apr. 8 Cuba announced that 1179 **Bay of Pigs prisoners** had been convicted of treason and sentenced to 30 years in prison. Officials offered to free all prisoners on payment of a $62,000,000 ransom. Six days later, 60 sick and wounded prisoners were returned to the U.S. on a promise to pay the ransom.

Apr. 25 The **U.S. resumed nuclear testing** in the atmosphere after a three-year moratorium, with the explosion of a device near Christmas Island. The U.S.S.R. had broken the U.S.-Soviet moratorium the preceding September.

May 12 Some 1800 U.S. **Marines were sent to Thailand** with other naval, air, and land forces for defense against possible attack by communist forces from Laos. By May 29, more than 5000 U.S. military personnel were in Thailand.

May 20 **Cyrus R. Vance** was named secretary of the Army.

June 16 Two U.S. **Army officers were killed** in an ambush by guerrillas north of Saigon, South Vietnam.

July 19 The **U.S. suspended diplomatic relations with Peru** one day after a military coup there. Economic and military aid were stopped.

July 19 The Treasury Department announced that **federal expenditures** for the fiscal year ending June 30, 1962, were $87,667,980,000, against revenue of $81,360,367,000.

July 27 The last **Marines in Thailand** were withdrawn.

Aug. 1 A **military appropriation bill** authorizing $48,-136,247,000 in the fiscal year ending June 30, 1963, was passed by Congress.

Aug. 15 For the first time in history, the **national debt** exceeded $300,000,000,000.

Aug. 17 **Diplomatic relations with Peru** were resumed and economic aid was restored.

Aug. 27 At the **Geneva disarmament conference,** the U.S. and Great Britain proposed adoption of a total nuclear test ban open to international inspection. They also proposed an alternative plan that would reduce nuclear tests without international inspection.

Mar. 20 **Henry Moore** exhibited 29 bronzes at the Knoedler Gallery in New York City. This was the English sculptor's first one-man show in New York in eight years.

Mar. 26 **Robert Frost** celebrated his 88th birthday at the White House in Washington, D.C.; Pres. Kennedy presented him with a special medal voted by Congress. Frost's first book of poetry in 15 years, *In the Clearing,* was officially published later in the day.

Apr. 9 **Academy Awards** were presented to *West Side Story* as the outstanding motion picture of 1961; to Maximilian Schell as best actor for *Judgment at Nuremberg;* to Sophia Loren as best actress for *Two Women;* and to George Chakiris and Rita Moreno as best supporting actor and actress for *West Side Story.*

Apr. 27 **The Grange,** the Home of Alexander Hamilton on Convent Ave. in New York City, was established as a national monument.

Apr. 29 **Tony Awards** for the 1961–1962 season were presented for the following: best play, *A Man for All Seasons;* best musical, *How to Succeed in Business Without Really Trying;* best American play, *The Night of the Iguana;* best actor, Paul Scofield for *A Man for All Seasons;* best actress, Margaret Leighton for *The Night of the Iguana.*

May 7 **Pulitzer prizes** were awarded for the following: fiction, *The Edge of Sadness* by Edwin O'Connor; history, *The Triumphant Empire: Thunder-Clouds Gather in the West* by Lawrence Gibson; nonfiction, *The Making of the President, 1960* by Theodore H. White; poetry, *Poems* by Alan Dugan; drama, *How to Succeed in Business Without Really Trying* by Frank Loesser and Abe Burrows.

May 8 *A Funny Thing Happened on the Way to the Forum,* a musical comedy by Burt Shevelove, Larry Gelbart, and Stephen Sondheim, starring Zero Mostel, opened at the Alvin Theatre in New York City. In an especially weak theater season, this was the outstanding new work. Even so, a great deal of its success was attributed to Mostel's brilliant performance.

May 22 **Emmy Awards** were presented to Peter Falk as best actor for *The Price of Tomatoes,* presented by the *Dick Powell Show;* Julie Harris as best actress for *Victoria Regina,* from the *Hallmark Hall of Fame;* Don Knotts as best actor in a series for *The Andy Griffith Show;* and Shirley Booth as best actress in a series for *Hazel.* E. G. Marshall was chosen best actor in a dramatic series for *The Defenders,* which was voted the best dramatic series.

May 28 The poured-concrete **Trans World Airlines passenger terminal** at Idlewild International Airport (N.Y.C.) was opened. Designed by Eero Saarinen, who died in 1961, it resembled a graceful bird in flight. The TWA building was the most eye-catching

The following day Pres. Kennedy accused the steel companies of "irresponsible defiance" of the public interest in raising steel prices.

Apr. 11 A 27-day **shipping strike** on the West Coast was halted by an injunction issued under the Taft-Hartley Act.

Apr. 13 **Steel price increases** previously announced by major steel companies were rescinded after Inland Steel refused to raise prices.

Apr. 19 **Skybolt,** the first U.S. airborne ballistic missile, was launched from a B-52 bomber at Cape Canaveral, Fla. Its second stage failed to fire and the missile fell short of its target.

Apr. 23 Agreement on a **world weather watch** was announced. It provided for a network linked by meteorological satellites and operated by U.S. and Soviet scientists.

Apr. 26 The **first international satellite,** Ariel, bearing six British experiments and propelled aloft by a U.S. Delta rocket, was launched from Cape Canaveral, Fla. It was intended to study the ionosphere.

Apr. 26 **Ranger 4** crashed into the far side of the moon 64 hours after being launched from Cape Canaveral, Fla. Fifty-five hours into the flight, its radio system went dead.

May 6 In the **first submarine-launched nuclear detonation,** a Polaris missile armed with a nuclear warhead and launched from the nuclear submarine *Ethan Allen* was successfully exploded near Christmas Island. It was also the first U.S. test of a nuclear warhead carried by a long-range missile.

May 24 The **second American in orbit,** astronaut M. Scott Carpenter, circled Earth three times aboard the Mercury capsule *Aurora 7,* which was launched by an Atlas rocket from Cape Canaveral, Fla.

May 28 In the **largest stock loss since Oct. 29, 1919,** shares on the New York exchange lost $20,800,000,000 in value. The stock market quickly recovered.

June 8 The **Office of Science and Technology** was established by Pres. Kennedy, who nominated Jerome Wiesner as its first director.

June 25 A New York State law permitting recitation of an **official prayer** in public schools was ruled unconstitutional by the Supreme Court.

July 9 A **thermonuclear explosion** equivalent to 1,400,000 tons of TNT was set off by the U.S. 250 miles above Johnston Island in the Pacific. The blast caused a substantial radiation increase in the Van Allen belt, disrupting communications and satellite operations.

July 10 **Telstar,** the experimental communications satellite developed and owned by American Telephone & Telegraph and Bell Telephone Laboratories,

Apr. 3 **Eddie Arcaro,** considered by many the greatest American jockey in modern turf history, retired from racing. During his 31-year career he had ridden 4779 winners and had brought home purses totaling $30,039,543.

Apr. 7–18 The **NBA basketball championship** was won by the Boston Celtics, defeating the Los Angeles Lakers four games to three.

Apr. 9 The **Masters golf tournament** was won by Arnold Palmer, who beat Gary Player and Dow Finsterwald in a three-way playoff.

Apr. 10–22 The **NHL Stanley Cup** was won for the first time since 1951 by the Toronto Maple Leafs, who beat the Chicago Black Hawks four games to two.

Apr. 19 The 66th **Boston Marathon** was won for the third time, second time in a row, by Eino Oksanen of Finland, with a time of 2 hrs., 23 min., 48 sec.

Apr. 21 The **Century 21 Exposition,** the world's fair at Seattle, Wash., was opened by remote control from Palm Beach, Fla., by Pres. Kennedy, who activated the carillon in the 600-foot Space Needle tower.

May 5 The 88th annual **Kentucky Derby** was won by Decidedly, with a time of 2:00^2/$_5$. The jockey was Bill Hartack.

May 19 The 87th annual **Preakness Stakes** was won by Green Money, with a time of 1:56^1/$_5$. The jockey was Johnny Rotz.

May 30 The 46th **Indianapolis 500** auto race was won by Roger Ward, who completed the 500-mile course in 3 hrs., 33 min., 50.33 sec. for a new race record of 140.293 mph.

June 9 The 94th annual **Belmont Stakes** was won by Jaipur, with a time of 2:28^4/$_5$. The jockey was Willie Shoemaker.

June 17 The **U.S. Open golf tournament** was won by Jack Nicklaus, who beat Arnold Palmer by three strokes in a playoff.

June 30 The **U.S. Women's Open golf tournament** was won by Murle Lindstrom.

The U.S.S.R. rejected both proposals.

Aug. 27 The **Twenty-fourth Amendment** to the Constitution, barring the poll tax as a requirement for voting in federal elections, was approved by Congress.

Sept. 24 Congress authorized a **military call-up** of 150,000 reservists for one year, and extension of the term of active duty of servicemen even without declaring a state of emergency.

Oct. 2 A bill authorizing a **loan to the UN** of $100,000,000 to help meet its financial crisis was signed by Pres. Kennedy.

Oct. 4 A **foreign trade bill,** giving Pres. Kennedy authority to negotiate tariff reductions and to assist firms and individuals injured by the lowering of tariffs, was passed by Congress.

Oct. 22 The **Cuban missile crisis** was the subject of a television address by Pres. Kennedy. He said that the U.S.S.R., contrary to its assurances, had been building missile and bomber bases in Cuba. Kennedy authorized a blockade of Cuba effective Oct. 24, to halt shipment of offensive weapons to Cuba. The day after Kennedy's address, the Council of the Organization of American States voted unanimously to authorize the use of armed force to prevent shipment of offensive weapons to Cuba.

Oct. 25 **Aerial photos of offensive missile bases in Cuba** were displayed to the UN by Ambassador Adlai Stevenson. The next day the U.S. Navy boarded and searched a Soviet-chartered freighter en route to Havana.

Oct. 27 Premier **Khrushchev offered to remove the Cuban missile bases** under UN supervision, demanding that the U.S. take corresponding action in Turkey. A U-2 reconnaissance plane was shot down over Cuba.

Oct. 28 **Withdrawal of Soviet missiles,** under UN inspection, and a halt to construction of bases in Cuba, was agreed to by Premier Khrushchev. Pres. Kennedy agreed to lift the trade and weapons ban when the UN had acted, and pledged that the U.S. would not invade Cuba.

Oct. 29 The U.S. **blockade of Cuba** was suspended for the duration of a trip by acting UN Secretary-General U Thant for a conference with Cuban Prime Minister

structure at the airport, which was becoming something of an architectural showplace.

May 29 **Grammy Awards** were presented for the following: best album of 1961, *Judy at Carnegie Hall* by Judy Garland; best record, "Moon River" by Henry Mancini; best male vocalist, Jack Jones for "Lollipops and Roses"; best female vocalist, Judy Garland for *Judy at Carnegie Hall;* best group, Lambert, Hendricks, and Ross for "High Flying."

May 31–June 3 The **first International Jazz Festival,** presented in Washington, D.C., by the President's Committee of the People-to-People Program, proved a disappointment. There was unanimous praise for the Duke Ellington orchestra and the old-style jazz of the Eureka Brass Band of New Orleans, but the classical-jazz hybrid composition called "Third Stream," by Ellington, Gunther Schuller, and André Hodeir, was received coolly.

June 14 **Igor Stravinsky** celebrated his 80th birthday. Also on this date Stravinsky's new ballet music, *Noah and the Flood,* was performed on network television. It was the first work the composer had written expressly for TV. Choreography was by George Balanchine, director of the New York City Ballet, which danced the ballet.

July 25 The **Sagamore Hill National Historic Site** was established by Congress to preserve the home of Theodore Roosevelt in Oyster Bay, N.Y., and his birthplace on East 20th St. in New York City.

Sept. 23 Philharmonic Hall, the first building to be completed in New York City's **Lincoln Center for the Performing Arts,** opened with a gala concert. Live television coverage was supplied as Leonard Bernstein conducted the New York Philharmonic before an audience of dignitaries, musicians, and patrons of the arts. The hall's acoustics were to prove disappointing. For a long time afterward, engineers made adjustments in the ceiling baffles and other sound-enhancing devices.

Sept. 29 The musical *My Fair Lady* closed. It was the longest-running Broadway musical in history, with 2717 performances since its opening on Mar. 15, 1956.

Oct. 3 *Stop the World—I Want to Get Off* by Leslie Bricusse and Anthony Newley, and starring Anthony Newley and Anna Quayle, opened at the Shubert Theater in New York City. Its hit song was "What Kind of Fool Am I?"

Oct. 27 *Who's Afraid of Virginia Woolf?* opened on Broadway at the Billy Rose Theater. It was Edward Albee's first full-length play. The cast, George Grizzard, Uta Hagen, Arthur Hill, and Melinda Dillan, helped make the drama a box-office success and the most talked about play of the season.

was placed in orbit from Cape Canaveral, Fla. It later relayed live TV pictures from Andover, Maine, to France and Great Britain.

Aug. 17   Dr. **Frances O. Kelsey** of the Food and Drug Administration was awarded the gold medal for distinguished public service by Pres. Kennedy for her refusal to clear the drug thalidomide for the U.S. market. It had been found to cause birth defects.

Aug. 22   The *Savannah,* the world's first nuclear-powered ship, completed its maiden voyage from Yorktown, Va., to Savannah, Ga.

Aug. 22   Pres. Kennedy announced that a **submarine rendezvous** beneath the North Pole had been effected by two U.S. nuclear submarines.

Aug. 27   A compromise bill creating a **satellite communications corporation** was passed by Congress.

Aug. 27   **Mariner 2** was launched successfully from Cape Canaveral, Fla., on a projected 15-week trajectory toward the planet Venus.

Sept. 15   A **public works bill** was signed by Pres. Kennedy. It authorized $900,000,000 for projects in economically depressed areas of the U.S.

Sept. 20   The application by **James H. Meredith,** a black, for admission to the University of Mississippi was denied by Mississippi Gov. Ross R. Barnett in defiance of a federal court order.

Sept. 21   The Defense Department announced a move to offset **U.S. gold losses** through a series of agreements by the U.S., West Germany, France, and Italy covering sales of U.S. military equipment.

Sept. 27   Pres. Kennedy signed the **Food and Agricultural Act of 1962,** a compromise bill providing for some of the increased crop controls he had requested.

Sept. 28   Gov. **Ross R. Barnett** of Mississippi was found guilty of civil contempt by a U.S. court of appeals. He was ordered to cease interference with desegregation at the University of Mississippi or face arrest and a fine of $10,000 for each day of further interference.

Sept. 30   **James H. Meredith** was escorted onto the University of Mississippi campus by U.S. marshals. Two men were killed in the ensuing mob violence, which was quelled with the aid of 3000 federal soldiers. The next day Meredith was enrolled and began to attend classes amid continuing disruption by protesters.

Oct. 3   The **third American in orbit,** astronaut Walter N. Schirra, completed five and three-quarter orbits aboard the Mercury capsule *Sigma 7* before splashing down near Midway Island in the Pacific within four miles of the recovery carrier U.S.S. *Kearsarge.*

Oct. 18   The **Nobel Prize for Physiology or Medicine** was awarded jointly to Dr. James D. Watson of

July 7   At the **Wimbledon** tennis championships in England, Karen Hantze Susman won the women's singles title. Susman teamed with Billie Jean Moffitt to win the women's doubles, and Margaret Osborne du Pont teamed with Neale Fraser of Australia to win the mixed doubles.

July 10   The first **baseball All-Star Game** of 1962 was won by the National League, which beat the American League 3–1. The second game, on July 30, was won by the American League, 9–4. In late November the leagues decided to return to playing a single all-star game each year.

July 22   The **PGA golf tournament** was won by Gary Player of South Africa, who became the first nonresident of the U.S. to win the championship.

July 23   The **Baseball Hall of Fame** inducted Robert W. "Bob" Feller, who pitched for the Cleveland Indians for 18 years; William B. "Bill" McKechnie, infielder and manager; Jack Roosevelt "Jackie" Robinson, infielder for the Brooklyn Dodgers from 1947 to 1956; and Edd J. Roush, who played outfield for the Cincinnati Reds and New York Giants from 1916 to 1931.

Sept. 8   The **Miss America** title was won by Jacquelyn Jeanne Mayer, 20, from Ohio, at the annual pageant in Atlantic City, N.J.

Sept. 8   The **richest purse in thoroughbred racing history,** $357,250, was offered in the Arlington-Washington Futurity, a race for two-year-olds. The winner's share, $142,250, went to Candy Spots.

Sept. 10   The **U.S. Lawn Tennis Association singles championships** were won by Rod Laver of Australia in the men's division and Margaret Smith of Australia in the women's division. With his win, Laver completed a grand slam of the four top world amateur championships, the Australian, French, British, and U.S. tournaments. It was the first men's grand slam since 1938.

Sept. 15–25   The **America's Cup** was successfully defended by the U.S. 12-meter yacht *Weatherly,* which defeated the Australian challenger *Gretel* four races to one. It was the closest competition in years and the first time since 1934 that the U.S. entry failed to sweep the first four races.

| Exploration and Settlement; Wars; Government; Civil Rights; Statistics   **I** | | **II**   Publishing; Arts and Music; Popular Entertainment; Architecture; Theater |

Fidel Castro. No agreement was reached after UN inspection.

Nov. 2   The missile bases in Cuba were being dismantled, Pres. Kennedy reported to the nation, adding that "progress is now being made toward restoration of peace in the Caribbean."

Nov. 6   In congressional elections the Democrats gained two Senate seats for a 67–33 majority. In the House they lost five seats for a 258–177 majority.

Nov. 20   Lifting of the naval blockade of Cuba was announced by Pres. Kennedy, following assurances by Premier Khrushchev that all Soviet jet bombers in Cuba would be removed within 30 days.

Nov. 20   An executive order prohibiting racial discrimination in housing built or purchased with federal funds was signed by Pres. Kennedy.

Dec. 17   The U.S. Communist Party was convicted by a federal jury in Washington, D.C., of failing to register as an agent of the U.S.S.R. It was fined $10,000 on each of 12 counts.

Dec. 23   The Cuban government began releasing prisoners captured in the Bay of Pigs invasion under an agreement with a U.S. committee of private citizens by which Cuba would get more than $50,000,000 in food and medical supplies.

Oct. 23   A postal error involving a U.S. commemorative stamp issued on this date to honor the late secretary general of the UN, Dag Hammarskjold, was reported in early November by several stamp collectors, who had obtained stamps with one color printed incorrectly. Postmaster General J. Edward Day subsequently caused an uproar when he ordered 10,000,000 of the errors printed to prevent speculation in the rarities. A suit against Day by a New Jersey collector was withdrawn after the Post Office Department authenticated his 50-stamp pane as a "discovery" item.

Oct. 25   The Nobel Prize for Literature was won by John Steinbeck, whose works included *Tortilla Flat* (1935), *Of Mice and Men* (1937), *The Grapes of Wrath* (1939), *The Moon Is Down* (1942), *Cannery Row* (1945), and *East of Eden* (1952). The award cited his "realistic and imaginative writing . . . distinguished by a . . . social perception." He was the sixth American, the seventh American-born, author to win a Nobel Prize for Literature.

Oct. 27   *Beyond the Fringe,* a revue with delightfully satiric sketches written and performed by a quartet of young Englishmen, Alan Bennett, Peter Cook, Dudley Moore, and Jonathan Miller, opened at the John Golden Theater in New York City.

Dec. 8   A newspaper strike in New York City began with a walkout by members of the International Typographical Union. The strike lasted 114 days and was said to have cost about $100,000,000 before it was settled on Mar. 31, 1963. Because of the strike, the New York Film Critics Circle announced it would postpone its selection of annual awards for motion pictures.

1963

The death of Pres. John F. Kennedy on Nov. 22 shocked the nation and the world. The 34th person elected president of the United States, Kennedy was the fourth to die by an assassin's bullet. The respect he had evoked throughout the world was attested to by the presence at his funeral of representatives of 92 nations, among them Charles de Gaulle of France, Anastas I. Mikoyan of the U.S.S.R., and Prince Philip of Great Britain. Although Kennedy did not live to see the passage of his civil rights bill, his program of medical care for the aged, or his tax-reduction bill, Congress did approve his proposal for aid to the mentally retarded. This year also saw a $3,600,000,000 appropriation for foreign aid, a reduction of $300,000,000 from the previous year. The signing of a limited nuclear test-ban treaty in October was counterbalanced by continuing conflict with Cuba and with the U.S.S.R. The U.S. became more heavily

The best plays on Broadway were revivals, such as Eugene O'Neill's *Strange Interlude;* British imports, such as John Osborne's *Luther;* and translations, such as Bertolt Brecht's *Mother Courage and Her Children.* New buildings at Harvard and Yale made most of the architectural news. Le Corbusier, the great Swiss-French master, designed the Visual Arts Center at Harvard, his first building in the U.S. At Yale two new college buildings, the first since the 1930s, were completed. Eero Saarinen and Associates were the designers. Also new at Yale were the Beinecke Rare Book and Manuscript Library and Paul Rudolph's Art and Architecture Building, a six-story structure that incorporated 36 different floor and ceiling levels. The Ford Foundation made history when it allocated $7,700,000 for development of ballet in the U.S. William Schuman, president of Lincoln Center for the Performing

Business and Industry; Science; **III**		**Sports; Social Issues and Crime;** **IV**
Education; Philosophy and Religion		**Folkways; Fashion; Holidays**

Harvard University, Dr. Maurice H. F. Wilkins of King's College in London, and Dr. Francis H. C. Crick of Cambridge, England, for their discovery of the molecular structure of deoxyribonucleic acid (DNA), the physical basis of heredity.

Nov. 1   The **New York** *Daily News* was struck by the New York Newspaper Guild. Although the guild signed a new contract, the demands of other unions resulted by Dec. 8 in suspension of publication of all nine New York daily newspapers.

Dec. 2   A new **source of nuclear fuel** was identified equal in potential to U.S. uranium reserves. Deposits of thorium, a radioactive element, in the White Mountains of New Hampshire were found to be ten times greater than previously estimated.

Dec. 8   The **first black bishop** to serve a predominantly white diocese of the Protestant Episcopal Church in the U.S., the Right Rev. John Melville Burgess, was consecrated as suffragan bishop of Massachusetts.

Dec. 13   **Relay 1,** an intercontinental communications satellite, was put in orbit. Two days later transmission was turned off for an indefinite period because of a power failure.

Dec. 14   **Mariner 2,** on its 109th day of flight, transmitted information about Venus for 42 minutes.

Dec. 21   Mississippi Gov. **Ross R. Barnett** and Lt. Gov. Paul B. Johnson were charged with criminal contempt of court in the U.S. Fifth Circuit Court of Appeals in New Orleans for their actions in September violating court orders for admission of James H. Meredith to the University of Mississippi.

Sept. 25   The **world heavyweight boxing championship** was won by Sonny Liston, who knocked out the defending champion Floyd Patterson in two minutes and six seconds of the first round.

Sept. 27   The **New York Mets,** a new National League baseball team, finished their first season, under former Yankee manager Casey Stengel. The Mets lost 120 of the 160 games they played. However, the fans loved them; nearly 1,000,000 came to the Polo Grounds to witness the heroic ineptitude of the players and the antics of their manager.

Oct. 4–16   The 59th annual **World Series** was won by the New York Yankees (AL), defeating the San Francisco Giants (NL) four games to three. The Giants had won the National League pennant by beating the Los Angeles Dodgers two games to one in a league playoff.

Oct. 7   The **LPGA golf tournament** was won by Judy Kimball.

Dec. 23   The **AFL championship** was won by the Dallas Texans, who defeated the Houston Oilers 20 to 17. The game went to two extra quarters and was decided by a field goal by Tommy Brooker.

Dec. 30   The **NFL championship** was won for the second year running by the Green Bay Packers, who defeated the N.Y. Giants 16–7.

1963

Progress toward civil rights was made when South Carolina and Alabama opened their colleges to blacks. The federal government appropriated nearly $2,000,-000,000 for construction and improvement of U.S. college facilities and for student loans. The building and construction trades union of the AFL-CIO adopted a program to eliminate racial discrimination. In July demonstrations in New York City supporting increased hiring of minority workers at construction sites led to more than 700 arrests. During the year, the nation's unemployment rate rose. George Meany, president of the AFL-CIO, condemned automation as a "curse to society." A threatened national railroad strike resulted in a congressional act requiring arbitration, the first time arbitration was imposed in peacetime. Federal legislation required that women receive pay equal to that of men for similar work. The nation's farmers, in a

The sports world lost two of its most popular competitors in the retirements of baseball slugger Stan Musial and basketball back-court artist Bob Cousy. The strike zone in major-league baseball was enlarged at the beginning of the season. To compensate for the bigger target, perhaps, National League umpires began applying the rule that a pitcher must wait one second between windup and delivery. Rigorous enforcement of the one-second rule evoked such outrage from fans and players that the Rules Committee dropped it within a month. Golf's leading money winners were Arnold Palmer, $128,230, and Mickey Wright, $31,269. Rogers Hornsby, the great slugger whose .424 batting average for 1924 has never been equaled, died on Jan. 5, at 66. Davey Moore, world featherweight boxing champion, fell into a coma shortly after losing his title on Mar. 21

| Exploration and Settlement; Wars; Government; Civil Rights; Statistics I | II Publishing; Arts and Music; Popular Entertainment; Architecture; Theater |

involved in the war in Vietnam. On Nov. 1 the government of Pres. Ngo Dinh Diem of South Vietnam was overthrown by South Vietnamese armed forces, and Diem was assassinated. On Nov. 7 the U.S. recognized the provisional government of Nguyen Ngoc Tho, Diem's vice president. Notables who died this year included W. E. B. Du Bois, a prominent black writer and educator, Aug. 27, at age 95; and Medgar W. Evers, civil rights leader, assassinated on June 12, at age 37.

Jan. 17 The largest **federal budget** to date, totaling $98,800,000,000 with a projected deficit of $11,900,000,000, was sent to Congress by Pres. Kennedy.

Jan. 31 Informal **nuclear test ban talks** were broken off by the U.S.S.R. The talks had opened in New York City on Jan. 14 and were joined by Great Britain on Jan. 23.

Feb. 8 **Underground nuclear testing** was resumed by the U.S. A suspension of tests had been ordered on Jan. 20 during the U.S.-U.S.S.R. test ban talks.

Feb. 14 A **program for youth,** including a domestic Peace Corps and a Youth Conservation Corps, was proposed by Pres. Kennedy.

Feb. 21 A **U.S. fishing boat was attacked** by two Cuban-based jet aircraft. The disabled shrimp boat *Ala* had been adrift in international waters about 60 nautical miles north of Cuba. Cuba formally denied the attack on Feb. 25.

Feb. 21 **Medicare,** a medical-hospital insurance plan financed through Social Security, was submitted to Congress by Pres. Kennedy.

Mar. 13 Two **Soviet reconnaissance planes flew over Alaska.** On Mar. 16 the U.S. protested what was termed the "first clearly established incident of a Soviet overflight of the U.S."

Mar. 18 The Supreme Court held that **free counsel for all indigents** facing serious criminal charges must be supplied by the states.

Mar. 19 The **Declaration of San José,** calling for a Central American common market, was signed by Pres. Kennedy following a conference in Costa Rica with presidents of six Central American countries.

Apr. 9 Sir **Winston Churchill** was proclaimed an honorary U.S. citizen in a White House ceremony televised worldwide.

Arts in New York City, announced that $300,000 would be spent on improving acoustics in the center's Philharmonic Hall. Notables who died this year included Van Wyck Brooks, critic and biographer, May 2, at 77; Robert Frost, poet and four-time winner of the Pulitzer Prize, Jan. 29, at 88; Paul Hindemith, composer, Dec. 28, at 68; Oliver La Farge, author and anthropologist, Aug. 2, at 83; Elsa Maxwell, the celebrated New York City hostess, Nov. 1, at 80; Adolphe Menjou, actor, Oct. 29, at 73; Clifford Odets, playwright, Aug. 14, at 57; Zasu Pitts, film comedienne, June 7, at 63; Theodore Roethke, poet, Aug. 1, at 55; William Carlos Williams, poet and physician, Mar. 4, at 79; and Edgar Mantillon "Monty" Woolley, the actor who gained fame in *The Man Who Came to Dinner,* May 6, at 74.

Among **books published** this year was *Terrible Swift Sword* by Bruce Catton, the second volume in Catton's trilogy *Centennial History of the Civil War.* The book covered the period from just after the first Battle of Bull Run in June 1861 through Lincoln's Emancipation Proclamation. Other books published this year included *Eichmann in Jerusalem: A Report on the Banality of Evil* by Hannah Arendt; *The Civil War: A Narrative, Fredericksburg to Meridian* by Shelby Foote, the second volume of a history of the war; *Idiots First* by Bernard Malamud, stories; *The Group* by Mary McCarthy, a novel; *The Sand Pebbles* by Richard McKenna, a novel; *The American Way of Death* by Jessica Mitford, a scathing study of American funeral customs; *The Two Ocean War* by Samuel Eliot Morison; *Raise High the Roof Beam, Carpenters* and *Seymour: An Introduction* by J. D. Salinger, two stories in one volume; and *Cat's Cradle* by Kurt Vonnegut, Jr., a novel.

The year in **popular music** was dominated by folk singers such as Peter, Paul, and Mary; Joan Baez; and the Kingston Trio. In November a Belgian nun, Sister Luc-Gabrielle, became an overnight sensation with a single record, "Dominique," a song she wrote and sang under the pseudonym Soeur Sourire. Her album *The Singing Nun,* released in December, also became an immediate best seller.

Jan. 8–Mar. 4 The *Mona Lisa* by Leonardo da Vinci was exhibited in New York City and Washington, D.C., on loan from the Louvre. Nearly 1,000,000 people waited on line to see the painting. Another Louvre masterpiece, James McNeill Whistler's *Portrait of My Mother,* was shown in Atlanta, Ga., in February as a memorial tribute to a group of Georgia art lovers killed in a plane crash near Paris in 1962.

Mar.–June The first large-scale exhibition of **pop art** was held at the Guggenheim Museum in New York City. The show moved on to other American cities later in the year, bemusing critics and public alike with its representational paintings of such prosaic subjects as soup cans and comic strips. Prominent in the

Business and Industry; Science; Education; Philosophy and Religion	III		IV	Sports; Social Issues and Crime; Folkways; Fashion; Holidays

referendum called for by the Food and Agriculture Act of 1962, overwhelmingly voted down a government program to decrease wheat production and to support the price of wheat. Traffic deaths reached an all-time high of 40,804.

Jan. 3 Relay 1, a communications satellite launched Dec. 13, 1962, but silent since Dec. 15 owing to malfunction, was reactivated by radio signals from the ground. It began transmission between North and South America and Europe.

Jan. 26 The **longshoremen's strike** was ended. It had tied up shipping at East Coast and Gulf Coast ports since Dec. 23, 1962, and cost more than $800,000,000.

Jan. 28 School desegregation in South Carolina, the last state to end segregation in its schools, was achieved when a student named Harvey B. Gantt was enrolled in Clemson College, Clemson, S.C.

Feb. 14 Syncom 1, an experimental forerunner of a series of communications satellites, was launched from Cape Canaveral, Fla. Although a near synchronous orbit was achieved, radio contact with Earth was lost the same day.

Mar. 17 Elizabeth Ann Seton was beatified by Pope John XXIII. She was the first native-born American to be so honored. She was declared a saint by Pope Paul VI in 1974 and canonized on Sept. 14, 1975.

Mar. 31 The **costliest newspaper strike** to date, the 114-day New York City newspaper strike, was ended. The shutdown, which began on Dec. 8, 1962, cost some $100,000,000 in lost revenues. The longest newspaper strike on record was a shutdown in Cleveland, Ohio, from Nov. 19, 1962, to Apr. 8, 1963, with an estimated loss of $25,000,000.

Apr. 2 In a **price-fixing** investigation, a federal grand jury indicted United States Steel and six other steel manufacturers.

Apr. 5 J. Robert Oppenheimer, the U.S. physicist declared a security risk in 1954, was named winner of the Atomic Energy Commission's 1963 Fermi Award.

Apr. 9 Steel price increases averaging $6.00 a ton were announced by the Wheeling Steel Corporation. Within the next few days, other major steel companies announced price increases.

in a bout with Ultiminio "Sugar" Ramos. Moore died on Mar. 25, at age 29.

Tom Swifties, jokes capitalizing on the overuse of adverbs in the Tom Swift boys' adventure books, amused the public for some time in spring and summer. Example: "Take the prisoner down to the deepest dungeon," he said condescendingly.

Jan. 1 In **college football bowl games,** the results were LSU 13, Texas 0 in the Cotton Bowl; Alabama 17, Oklahoma 0 in the Orange Bowl; Southern California 42, Wisconsin 37 in the Rose Bowl; and Mississippi 17, Arkansas 13 in the Sugar Bowl. This season the AP and UPI polls chose Southern California the national collegiate champions of 1962.

Feb. 9–10 U.S. **figure skating championships** were won in Long Beach, Calif., by Lorraine Hanlon, women's singles; Thomas Litz, men's singles; Judianne and Jerry Fotheringill, pairs; Sally Schantz and Stanley Urban, dance.

Mar. 20 Hope Cooke, a recent graduate of Sarah Lawrence College, married Crown Prince Palden Thondup Namgyal of Sikkim in a Buddhist ceremony in Gangtok. On Dec. 2 the prince succeeded to the throne as maharajah on the death of his father, Sir Tashi Namgyal.

Mar. 23 The **NCAA basketball championship** was won by Loyola, Ill., which defeated the University of Cincinnati 60–58.

Apr. 7 The **Masters golf tournament** was won by Jack Nicklaus, who beat Tony Lema by one stroke.

Apr. 9–18 The **NHL Stanley Cup** was won by the Toronto Maple Leafs, who defeated the Detroit Redwings four games to one.

Apr. 19 The 67th **Boston Marathon** was won by Aurele Vandendriessche of Belgium with a record time of 2 hrs., 18 min., 58 sec., beating the course record set in 1957 by 1 min., 7 sec.

Apr. 20–May 5 At the fourth **Pan-American Games** in São Paulo, Brazil, the U.S. won the unofficial team championship with 108 gold medals. Brazil was second with 14 gold medals.

| Exploration and Settlement; Wars; Government; Civil Rights; Statistics | I | | II | Publishing; Arts and Music; Popular Entertainment; Architecture; Theater |

Apr. 10 The nuclear-powered submarine *Thresher* sank in the Atlantic with 129 men on board during a test dive. A Navy board of inquiry concluded that a system failure probably created progressive flooding and that the interference with electrical circuits caused loss of power.

May 11 Canadian acceptance of U.S. nuclear warheads for missiles installed on Canadian soil was announced. The decision was a step toward fulfillment of defense commitments by the two nations in North America.

June 12 Medgar Evers was assassinated by a sniper, who shot the civil rights leader in the back outside the Evers home in Jackson, Miss. The crime sparked numerous demonstrations, and Pres. Kennedy and many other leaders condemned the killing. After a funeral in Jackson, Evers was buried in Arlington National Cemetery.

June 23 Pres. Kennedy, beginning a ten-day tour of Europe, arrived in West Germany. On June 26, speaking to a crowd of more than 1,000,000 in West Berlin, Kennedy stated he was proud to say "Ich bin ein Berliner" [I am a Berliner].

July 8 Virtually all financial transactions with Cuba were banned by the U.S. in another move toward economic isolation of that country.

July 12 A modified form of martial law was declared in Cambridge, Md., after National Guard troops were sent into the city for the second time in a month to control racial violence.

July 15 A nuclear test-ban conference opened in Moscow. The U.S., Great Britain, and the U.S.S.R. were represented.

July 25 A limited nuclear test-ban treaty, prohibiting testing in the atmosphere, in space, and under water, was initialed in Moscow by the U.S., Great Britain, and the U.S.S.R.

Aug. 28 A Freedom March on Washington, D.C., brought an estimated 200,000 participants, who listened to speeches by ten civil rights leaders, among them Dr. Martin Luther King. Dr. King told the group, "I have a dream," describing a U.S. free of divisiveness, hatred, and injustice.

three-year-old pop-art movement were Andy Warhol, Jasper Johns, Robert Rauschenberg, and Roy Lichtenstein.

Mar. 7 The new Pan Am Building in New York City, designed by Emery Roth and Sons, was dedicated. An octagonal 59-story structure built over a portion of Grand Central Station, it was considered by many critics an architectural blight. Others complained that it added to congestion in an area already crowded with traffic and buildings, and expressed resentment over the destruction of the design of Grand Central. In addition, the prospect of noisy flights from its rooftop heliport made tenants in the area uneasy. Meanwhile, efforts to save New York's Pennsylvania Station failed, and that classic edifice began to fall to the wrecker's ball to make way for a new Madison Square Garden.

Mar. 11 *Strange Interlude* by Eugene O'Neill was staged in a revival at the Actors Studio Theatre in New York City. Directed by José Quintero, who was making a name for himself as an interpreter of O'Neill, the play was staged in the original nine-act version and ran from 6 P.M. to midnight. There was a one-hour intermission for supper.

Mar. 12 National Book Awards were presented for the following: fiction, *Morte d'Urban* by James Farl Powers; nonfiction, *Henry James, Vol. II: The Conquest of London, 1870–1881* and *Henry James, Vol. III, The Middle Years, 1881–1895* by Leon Edel; poetry, *Traveling Through the Dark* by William Stafford.

Apr. The famous Armory Show was recreated in its original setting, the 69th Regiment Armory in New York City. First presented in 1913, the Armory Show gave Americans their first look at the works of Georges Braque, Pablo Picasso, and other European modernists; the show was considered a decisive factor in the development of modern American art. Of the 1300 works on exhibit in the 1913 show, 370 were assembled for the anniversary show. After 50 years Marcel Duchamp's *Nude Descending a Staircase* was still the main attraction.

Apr. 8 Academy Awards were presented to *Lawrence of Arabia* as the outstanding motion picture of 1962; to Gregory Peck as best actor for *To Kill a Mockingbird;* to Anne Bancroft as best actress for *The Miracle Worker;* to Ed Begley as best supporting actor for *Sweet Bird of Youth;* and to Patty Duke as best supporting actress for *The Miracle Worker.*

Apr. 25 Tony Awards for the 1962–1963 season were presented for the following: best play, *Who's Afraid of Virginia Woolf?* by Edward Albee; best musical, *A Funny Thing Happened on the Way to the Forum* by Burt Shevelove, Larry Gelbart, and Stephen Sondheim; best actor in a drama, Arthur Hill for *Who's*

Business and Industry; Science; Education; Philosophy and Religion III		IV Sports; Social Issues and Crime; Folkways; Fashion; Holidays

Apr. 12 The Rev. **Martin Luther King, Jr.,** was **arrested** in Birmingham, Ala., during a desegregation drive that had begun on Apr. 2.

Apr. 18 Successful **human nerve transplants** were reported by Dr. James B. Campbell of the New York University Medical Center.

May 7 **Telstar 2,** the second communications satellite, was launched from Cape Canaveral, Fla. It began relaying color and black-and-white television signals between the U.S. and Europe.

May 9 A secret **military satellite** was launched by the Air Force from Point Arguello, Calif. It released some 400,000,000 tiny copper hairs into a polar orbit, providing a cloud of reflective material for relaying radio signals from coast to coast within the U.S.

May 15–16 The **fourth American in orbit,** Maj. L. Gordon Cooper, Jr., completed 22 orbits around Earth aboard the Mercury capsule *Faith 7,* in the final flight of Project Mercury.

June 3 The **agency shop labor contract,** in which an employee is not required to join a union but must pay it the equivalent of dues and fees, was ruled constitutional by the Supreme Court where permitted by a state. The Court also ruled that a state could bar the agency shop.

June 4 A **Federal Reserve bill** changing the backing of $1.00 and $2.00 bills from silver to gold was signed by Pres. Kennedy.

June 8 A **drive against cigarette smoking** was opened by the American Heart Association, the first voluntary public agency to do so.

June 10 A bill requiring **equal pay for equal work,** regardless of sex, was signed by Pres. Kennedy.

June 11 The **University of Alabama was desegregated.** Gov. George C. Wallace, who had literally stood in the way of desegregation, stepped aside when confronted by federalized National Guard troops. Two black students were enrolled.

July 1 In a move to end **racial discrimination in construction,** the United Brotherhood of Carpenters,

Apr. 24 The Boston Celtics' brilliant guard **Bob Cousy,** 34, retired from competition after leading the team to its fifth straight NBA championship. The Celtics had downed the Los Angeles Lakers four games to two (Apr. 14–24).

May 4 The 89th annual **Kentucky Derby** was won by Chateaugay, with a time of 2:01⁴/₅. The jockey was Braulio Baeza.

May 18 The 88th annual **Preakness Stakes** was won by Candy Spots, with a time of 1:56¹/₅. The jockey was Willie Shoemaker.

May 30 The 47th annual **Indianapolis 500** auto race was won by Parnelli Jones, completing the course in 3 hrs., 29 min., 35.40 sec., with an average speed of 143.137 mph.

June 8 The 95th annual **Belmont Stakes** was won by Chateaugay, with a time of 2:30¹/₅. The jockey was Braulio Baeza.

June 23 The **U.S. Open golf tournament** was won by Julius Boros, who beat Arnold Palmer and Jacky Cupit in a playoff.

July 6 At the **Wimbledon** tennis championships in England, Chuck McKinley won the men's singles championship.

July 9 The **baseball All-Star Game** was won by the National League, which beat the American League 5–3.

July 20 The **U.S. Women's Open golf tournament** was won by Mary Mills.

July 21 The **PGA golf tournament** was won by Jack Nicklaus.

July 22 The **world heavyweight boxing championship** was successfully defended by Sonny Liston, who knocked out Floyd Patterson 2 min., 10 sec. into the first round.

Aug. 5 The **Baseball Hall of Fame** inducted John G. Clarkson, pitcher; Elmer H. Flick, outfielder; Edgar C. "Sam" Rice, longtime outfielder for the Washington Senators; and Eppa Rixey, who pitched for the Philadelphia Phillies and Cincinnati Reds from 1912 to 1933 and who died on Feb. 28, 1963, at 71.

Exploration and Settlement; Wars; Government; Civil Rights; Statistics I		II Publishing; Arts and Music; Popular Entertainment; Architecture; Theater

Aug. 30 The **hot line** went into operation. It was an emergency communications link between Washington, D.C., and Moscow, intended to reduce the risk of accidental war.

Sept. 15 A **church bombing** in Birmingham, Ala., left four young black girls dead. The attack on the 16th Street Baptist Church sparked further violence in the city, leaving two more dead and 19 injured.

Oct. 7 The **limited nuclear test-ban treaty was signed** by Pres. Kennedy. It went into effect Oct. 10.

Oct. 9 A **wheat sale** to the U.S.S.R. of 4,000,000 metric tons, valued at some $250,000,000, was approved by Pres. Kennedy.

Oct. 16 Two **U.S. military satellites** were secretly launched from Cape Canaveral, Fla., for the detection of any violation of the treaty banning nuclear tests in space.

Oct. 31 A **gas explosion** in the Indiana State Fair Grounds during an ice show killed 68 people and injured 340.

Nov. 4 A **U.S. military convoy was blocked** by Soviet troops at the western border of Berlin. The U.S. protested and after 41 hours the convoy was allowed to proceed.

Nov. 12 **Travel restrictions on diplomats** were imposed by the State Department, which barred diplomats of Bulgaria, Czechoslovakia, Hungary, Poland, and Rumania from 355 U.S. counties, about 11% of the continental U.S., for "reasons of national security."

Nov. 22 Pres. **John F. Kennedy was assassinated** while riding in a motorcade in Dallas, Tex. He was pronounced dead at 1 P.M. Gov. John B. Connally of Texas, accompanying Kennedy, was severely wounded. Vice Pres. Lyndon Baines Johnson was sworn in as the 36th president of the United States at 2:39 P.M. at Love Air Field in Dallas. That same afternoon, Lee Harvey Oswald, a suspect in the assassination, was captured by Dallas police.

Nov. 24 **Lee Harvey Oswald was shot** and killed by a man named Jack Ruby while in the custody of Dallas police. The nation saw the murder on television. Ruby was apprehended immediately.

Afraid of Virginia Woolf?; best actress in a drama, Uta Hagen for *Who's Afraid of Virginia Woolf?*

May 6 **Pulitzer prizes** were awarded to the following: fiction, *The Reivers* by William Faulkner; biography, *Henry James, Vol. II: The Conquest of London, 1870–1881* and *Henry James, Vol. III: The Middle Years, 1881–1895* by Leon Edel; history, *Washington, Village and Capital, 1800–1878* by Constance McLaughlin Green; general nonfiction, *The Guns of August* by Barbara Tuchman; poetry, *Pictures from Brueghel* by William Carlos Williams. A furor was caused when it was announced that there would be no drama award. The advisory board for drama had recommended Edward Albee's *Who's Afraid of Virginia Woolf?* When their recommendation was not announced, both John Mason Brown and John Gassner resigned.

May 15 **Grammy Awards** went to the following: best record of 1962, "I Left My Heart in San Francisco" by Tony Bennett; best album, *The First Family* by Vaughn Meader; best male vocalist, Tony Bennett for "I Left My Heart in San Francisco"; best female vocalist, Ella Fitzgerald for *Ella Swings Brightly with Nelson Riddle;* best group, Peter, Paul, and Mary, for "If I Had a Hammer."

May 22 The **National Institute of Arts and Letters** awarded its gold medal for poetry to William Carlos Williams, who died Mar. 4.

May 26 **Emmy Awards** were presented to Trevor Howard as best actor for *The Invincible Mr. Disraeli;* to Kim Stanley as best actress for "A Cardinal Act of Mercy," an episode of *Ben Casey;* to E. G. Marshall as best actor in a series for *The Defenders;* and to Shirley Booth as best actress in a series for *Hazel.*

June 12 *Cleopatra,* the most expensive motion picture to date, opened in New York City and at 69 theaters in the U.S. and Canada. The film cost $37,000,000, but by the end of the year it was clear that Twentieth Century-Fox would recoup its investment. The picture's record advance sales were no doubt boosted by the well-publicized romance of its stars, Richard Burton and Elizabeth Taylor.

Aug. **Larry Rivers,** a painter and graphic artist, created an original billboard poster to advertise the first New York Film Festival. The 10- by 16-ft. painting was placed at Broadway and 65th St. A private collector had bought the work even before it was finished.

Sept. 11 A retrospective show of the work of **Hans Hofmann** opened at the Museum of Modern Art in New York City. Hofmann, who left Germany in the 1930s, influenced the abstract expressionist movement in America during the 1940s and 1950s.

Oct. 16 The **New York** *Mirror* ceased publication. Although the Hearst newspaper's circulation was the second largest among U.S. dailies, the paper fell

Business and Industry; Science; Education; Philosophy and Religion **III**	**IV** Sports; Social Issues and Crime; Folkways; Fashion; Holidays

the largest U.S. building trade union, ordered its locals to end all such discrimination.

July 7   A plan for **modification of railroad work rules** submitted by Sec. of Labor W. Willard Wirtz was rejected by the railroad operating unions. The plan was one of several efforts by the government to resolve a labor-management deadlock in the industry.

July 26   **Syncom 2** was successfully launched and on Aug. 15 placed over Brazil in a geostationary Earth orbit. It transmitted telephone and Teletype messages between the U.S. and Nigeria.

Aug. 28   A nationwide **railroad strike was averted** when Congress passed legislation requiring compulsory arbitration of two key issues in the work-rules dispute and barring a strike for 18 days.

Sept. 7   **Krebiozen,** a so-called miracle drug, was declared by the Food and Drug Administration to be creatine, a common amino acid, and ineffective against tumors.

Sept. 10   Public **school desegration** in Huntsville, Ala., was effected after Pres. Kennedy federalized the Alabama National Guard, forcing Gov. Wallace to end his attempt to block school integration.

Oct. 10   The deferred 1962 **Nobel Peace Prize** was awarded to Dr. Linus C. Pauling of the California Institute of Technology. The award committee did not specify Pauling's achievements, but his efforts to secure a ban on nuclear testing were well known.

Oct. 22   In a **Chicago school boycott,** about 225,000 pupils were absent from public schools in a one-day action protesting de facto school segregation.

Nov. 5   The **Nobel Prize in Physics** was awarded jointly to Eugene P. Wigner of Princeton, Maria G. Mayer of the University of California, and Hans Jensen of the University of Heidelberg, Germany, for their studies of atomic structure.

Nov. 20   **Losses in poultry exports** to Common Market nations, in what came to be called the "chicken war," were placed at $26,000,000 by a special panel of experts. The U.S., in retaliation, increased its tariffs on imports from market members.

Aug. 5   Craig Breedlove set an unofficial **world auto speed record** of 407.45 mph on the Bonneville Salt Flats in Utah, driving a sleek three-ton, three-wheeled, jet-powered auto. The U.S. Auto Club established a new class for its records: "Jet-Powered Vehicles."

Aug. 24   **Don Schollander** of Santa Clara, Calif., became the first person to break the two-minute mark for the 200-meter freestyle swim. At Osaka, Japan, he won the event with the time of 1:58.4.

Aug. 24   John Pennel became the **first person to pole vault 17 feet,** reaching 17 ft. ¾ in. at a meet in Miami, Fla.

Sept. 7   The **Miss America** title was won by Donna Axum, 21, from Arkansas, at the annual pageant in Atlantic City, N.J.

Sept. 8   The **U.S. Lawn Tennis Association singles championships** were won by Rafael Osuna of Mexico in the men's division and Maria Bueno of Brazil in the women's division.

Sept. 29   **Stan "The Man" Musial** played his last game for the St. Louis Cardinals, retiring at 42 to take an executive position with the club. In his 22 years in baseball, all with the Cards, the great hitter set or tied 17 major league and 30 National League records.

Oct. 2–6   The 60th annual **World Series** was won by the Los Angeles Dodgers (NL), who swept the New York Yankees (AL) in four games. Dodgers pitcher Sandy Koufax set a new series record by striking out 15 players in the opening game.

Oct. 13   The **LPGA golf tournament** was won by Mickey Wright.

Nov. 8   A **riot at Roosevelt Raceway** in Westbury, Long Island, N.Y., was sparked when six of eight trotters in the sixth race were involved in a pileup. Fans who had bet on the daily double were outraged when the race was declared official. They rioted and started a $20,000 fire. In the melee, 20 people were injured.

Dec. 8   **Frank Sinatra, Jr.,** son of the singer-actor, and himself an aspiring popular singer, was kidnaped at Lake Tahoe. He was released unhurt in Los Angeles

Nov. 25   John F. Kennedy was buried at Arlington National Cemetery following a mass at St. Matthew's Roman Catholic Cathedral.

Nov. 29   What came to be called the **Warren Commission** was established by Pres. Johnson. The special commission, headed by Chief Justice Earl Warren, was appointed to investigate the assassination of John F. Kennedy and related events.

victim to an economic squeeze, partly the result of the 114-day New York City newspaper strike (from Dec. 8, 1962 to Mar. 31, 1963), and partly the result of decreasing advertising income. The *Mirror's* assets were sold to the rival *Daily News.*

Dec. 12   Contralto **Marian Anderson** announced that after her 1964–1965 tour was completed, she would retire from the concert stage.

1964

Campaigning on the promise of achieving the Great Society, Pres. Lyndon Baines Johnson was elected to the presidency by a record-breaking vote. For the first time since 1920, the conservative wing had dominated the Republican campaign, alienating moderates and liberals. At the same time, the Democratic Party lost five southern states because of Pres. Johnson's success in putting through a civil rights bill in July. He was equally successful with the other primary legislative aim of his administration, the anti-poverty bill. His economy-in-government drive was reflected in his first budget, which contained a $1,100,000,000 cut in defense spending. Johnson asked for $3,400,000,000 for foreign aid, the smallest amount requested in 16 years. In domestic affairs, the year was marked by racial violence in many U.S. cities, including New York, Philadelphia, and St. Augustine, Fla. In the summer a coalition of civil rights groups mounted a voter registration and education drive in Mississippi; this sparked acts of violence. Foreign relations reflected continuing tension with Cuba and in Berlin. Deterioration of the situation in Southeast Asia resulted in greater U.S. military and economic assistance to South Vietnam. In the Congo, a number of American citizens were taken hostage, along with many Europeans. Two Americans were killed after U.S. aircraft dropped Belgian troops into the area, but most of the hostages were freed. The U.S. and U.S.S.R. made efforts to reduce threat of nuclear war by reducing stockpiles of materials for nuclear weapons. Steps were taken toward international cooperation in developing peaceful uses of atomic energy and sharing technological advances. Notables who died this year included Elizabeth Gurley Flynn, the American communist leader, Sept. 5, at 74; Herbert Clark Hoover, 31st president of the United States, Oct. 20, at 90; Douglas MacArthur, Apr. 5, at 84; and Alvin C. York, whose bravery during World War I earned him some 50 medals, including the Medal of Honor, Sept. 2, at 76.

Great interest was aroused by the purchase of the G. & C. Merriam Co. by Encyclopaedia Britannica, Inc. The Warren Commission's report on the assassination of Pres. John F. Kennedy was published by the U.S. Printing Office and by five commercial publishers. Bantam Books, with the help of *The New York Times,* prepared a paperback edition that was available to the public 80 hours after the report was released. In the year that followed Kennedy's death, more than 50 books about him were published, some quick productions to catch the popular market, many moving tributes to the dead president. A new force in the theater world was The Repertory Theater of Lincoln Center, which had its first season in an off-Broadway theater while construction continued on its permanent home, the Vivian Beaumont Theater. The Robert Joffrey Ballet fell on hard times when the Harkness Foundation withdrew its subsidy and then took Joffrey's sets, scores, and ballets for the new Harkness Ballet. In November the Ford Foundation made a grant to keep the Joffrey Ballet going. Notables who died this year included Gracie Allen, the zany comedian, Aug. 27, at 58; Marc Blitzstein, composer, Jan. 22, at 58; Eddie Cantor, singer and comedian, Oct. 10, at 72; Rachel Carson, biologist and author, Apr. 14, at 56; Ben Hecht, playwright, Apr. 18, at 70; Alan Ladd, actor, Jan. 29, at 50; Peter Lorre, actor, Mar. 23, at 59; Arthur "Harpo" Marx, Sept. 28, at 70; Flannery O'Connor, the author, Aug. 3, at 39; and Cole Porter, songwriter, Oct. 15, at 71.

Among **books published** this year was the posthumous volume *A Moveable Feast* by Ernest Hemingway, a collection of sketches about Paris and its artistic colony during the years 1921–1926. Other books published this year included *The Rector of Justin* by Louis Auchincloss, a novel; *Herzog,* by Saul Bellow, the author's sixth novel; *Little Big Man* by Thomas Berger, a novel of the old West; *77 Dream Songs* by John Berryman, poems; *The Wapshot Scandal* by John Cheever, a novel; *Why We Can't Wait* by Rev. Martin Luther King, Jr., a forceful treatment of the civil rights movement; *Candy,* a sex

Business and Industry; Science; Education; Philosophy and Religion	III		IV	Sports; Social Issues and Crime; Folkways; Fashion; Holidays

Nov. 26 In the **railroad work-rules arbitration,** the federal arbitration board ruled that 90% of diesel locomotive firemen's jobs in freight and yard service were unnecessary. Railroads had sought to eliminate all of the 40,000 firemen's jobs.

Dec. 4 In a major change in the **Roman Catholic mass,** the use of English in the U.S. in place of Latin for parts of the mass and for the sacraments was approved by the Roman Catholic Ecumenical Council.

Dec. 11 after his father paid a ransom of $240,000. Most of the money was recovered two days later when the FBI arrested three suspects.

Dec. 26–29 The U.S. regained the **Davis Cup,** which it had lost in 1959, by beating the Australian tennis team three matches to two.

Dec. 31 The **NFL championship** was won by the Chicago Bears, who defeated the New York Giants 14–0.

1964

The first close-up pictures of the moon's surface were obtained by the U.S. At the same time, the U.S. successfully launched a spacecraft designed to fly by and photograph the surface of Mars. The first cooperative U.S.-U.S.S.R. space program—Echo 2, a communications satellite—was established. Also in this year, racial violence in both the North and South marked the nation's continuing efforts to assure equality in education for all. Harlem, Brooklyn, Rochester, northern New Jersey, Jacksonville, Fla., Chicago, and Philadelphia were scenes of violent rioting. Schools were boycotted in New York City, Cleveland, Cincinnati, Cambridge, Md., Boston, and Chicago to protest de facto segregation. Federal aid to universities was increased and extended. Notables who died this year included Leo Szilard, the atomic physicist who with Enrico Fermi produced the first nuclear chain reaction in 1942, May 30, at 66; and Norbert Wiener, the mathematician who was called the "father of automation," Mar. 18, at 69.

Jan. 11 The **surgeon general's report on cigarette smoking** was released. A commission headed by U.S. Surgeon General Luther Terry found that the use of cigarettes "contributes substantially to mortality from certain specific diseases and to the overall death rate."

Jan. 25 **Echo 2,** the first U.S.-U.S.S.R. cooperative space program, was launched from Vandenberg Air Force Base, Calif. It sent messages around the world by reflecting radio signals from one point on Earth to another.

Jan. 29 A new **weight-into-orbit record** was set by the fifth Saturn rocket test in preparation for the manned Apollo program. A 20,000-lb. payload was boosted into orbit by the rocket from Cape Kennedy, Fla.

At the New York World's Fair, the General Motors Futurama proved to be the most popular attraction. Ranking just behind GM in attendance was the Vatican Pavilion, its chief attraction being Michelangelo's *Pietà.* While this was the largest, most lavish, and in many ways the best fair of all time, attendance lagged behind fair president Robert Moses' predictions, and many exhibitors began to feel an economic pinch. Worst hit were the extravagant shows in the Lake Amusement Area that had been so popular at the 1939–1940 fair. Most of these shows closed before the end of the fair's first season. In baseball the St. Louis Cardinals beat the New York Yankees in the World Series; the following day Cardinal manager Johnny Keane resigned. Yankee manager Yogi Berra was moved to another position in the club, then quit to become player-coach of the New York Mets. Meanwhile, Keane was named manager of the Yankees. In boxing Cassius Clay gained the heavyweight title from Sonny Liston and enthralled many with his declarations of his own beauty, ability, and greatness. This year he also declared that he was a Black Muslim and changed his name to Muhammad Ali. In golf the top money winners were Jack Nicklaus, $113,284, and, for the fourth year in a row, Mickey Wright, $29,800.

Popular **rock 'n' roll dances** of the younger set had animal names: the Dog, the Monkey, the Chicken; but the favorites were the Watusi and the Frug. In these dances the partners gyrated, squirmed, jerked, and waved their arms—at a distance from one another, of course. The swinging set crowded into discothèques, where the music was supplied by records. The "in" places were Shepheard's and Trude Heller's in New York City and Whiskey à Go-Go in Los Angeles. Dancers were often abetted by scantily clad go-go girls, who performed in relays on raised platforms or in cages.

Jan. 1 In **college football bowl games,** the results were Texas 28, Navy 6 in the Cotton Bowl; Nebraska 13, Auburn 7 in the Orange Bowl; Illinois 17,

Jan. 9 Diplomatic relations with Panama were severed after riots broke out in the Canal Zone over the flying of U.S. and Panamanian flags.

Jan. 23 The **Twenty-fourth Amendment** to the U.S. Constitution, abolishing the poll tax, was ratified by South Dakota, the 38th state to do so. The amendment was declared part of the Constitution on Feb. 4.

Feb. 6 The **water supply for the U.S. naval station at Guantánamo,** Cuba, was cut off in retaliation for seizure of four Cuban fishing vessels within U.S. territorial waters near Florida on Feb. 2.

Feb. 13 The Treasury Department announced that the U.S. would borrow from the **International Monetary Fund** for the first time.

Feb. 17 In a controversial **ruling on congressional districts,** the Supreme Court ruled that congressional districts within each state must be substantially equal in population.

Mar. 10 A **U.S. reconnaissance plane was shot down** by Soviet air defense forces after it accidentally crossed into East German airspace. It was the second such incident in six weeks. Following U.S. protests, the plane's three crewmen were released.

Mar. 14 **Jack Ruby was convicted** by a Dallas, Tex., jury of the murder of Lee Harvey Oswald, the accused assassin of Pres. John F. Kennedy. Ruby was sentenced to death.

Mar. 27 A major **earthquake in Alaska,** centered in Anchorage, killed 117 people and caused enormous damage. The next day Pres. Johnson declared Alaska a major disaster area.

Apr. 3 Diplomatic relations with Panama were resumed.

May 18 In a ruling on **citizenship rights,** the Supreme Court declared unconstitutional a federal statute depriving naturalized citizens of U.S. citizenship if they return to the land of their birth for three years.

May 19 The State Department announced the **U.S. embassy in Moscow had been bugged.** A network of more than 40 microphones had been found embedded in the embassy's walls.

June 10 **Cloture on the civil rights bill** was voted by the U.S. Senate, ending a 75-day filibuster.

farce by Terry Southern and Mason Hoffenberg; and *Julian* by Gore Vidal, a novel about the Roman emperor Julian the Apostate.

Jan. 16 *Hello, Dolly!* by Michael Stewart and Jerry Herman, the biggest musical comedy hit of the season, opened at the St. James Theater in New York City. The show was based on Thornton Wilder's *The Matchmaker* and starred Carol Channing, who was at the top of her form. The title song from the show became a hit record, with jazz great Louis Armstrong's version selling over 1,000,000 copies.

Jan. 18 *Dylan,* a drama by Sidney Michaels based on incidents in the life of the late Welsh poet Dylan Thomas, opened at the Plymouth Theater in New York City. The title role was performed by Alec Guinness, and Kate Reid portrayed Caitlin Thomas, the poet's wife.

Jan. 23 The newly formed **Repertory Theater of Lincoln Center,** playing in a temporary shed near Washington Square Park in New York City, gave its first performance. The play was Arthur Miller's *After the Fall.* Strongly autobiographical, the play was not well received by most critics.

Feb. 7 The **Beatles** arrived at Kennedy Airport in New York at the start of their first U.S. musical tour. After appearing on the *Ed Sullivan Show* on television, they gave their first concert on Feb. 12 at Carnegie Hall. Their second U.S. tour, a 33-day sweep beginning Aug. 19 in San Francisco, was a phenomenal success. Also successful were the group's album *Meet the Beatles,* which became an overnight best seller, and their movie *A Hard Day's Night,* which was released just before their second tour.

Feb. 26 *The Deputy,* a play by Rolf Hochhuth adapted by Jerome Rothenberg, opened at the Brooks Atkinson Theater in New York City. A sensation even before its first performance, it charged Pope Pius XII with partial responsibility for the death of millions of Jews during World War II by reason of his failure to take a public stand against the Nazis. The play was bitterly attacked by some and righteously defended by others. The opening was picketed by some 150 persons, mostly members of religious groups, but also by about 15 members of the American Nazi Party.

Mar. 9 A **$500,000 libel judgment against *The New York Times*** issued by the Alabama Supreme Court was reversed unanimously by the U.S. Supreme Court. The case arose out of misstatements in a paid political ad criticizing the conduct of state officials. The Supreme Court ruled that the Constitution prohibits public officials from recovering damages for defamatory statements about their conduct in office unless they can prove the statements were made with actual malice—that is, in the knowledge they were

Business and Industry; Science; Education; Philosophy and Religion **III**		**IV** Sports; Social Issues and Crime; Folkways; Fashion; Holidays

Feb. 25 A nine-day **boycott on loading wheat** to be shipped to the U.S.S.R. ended after government officials assured the International Longshoremen's Association that 50% of the wheat under future contracts would be shipped in U.S. vessels.

Feb. 29 Development of an advanced **experimental jet plane,** the A-11, capable of flying at more than 2000 mph and at an altitude of over 70,000 ft., was disclosed by Pres. Johnson.

Mar. 4 **James R. Hoffa,** president of the International Brotherhood of Teamsters, was found guilty of tampering with a federal jury in 1962 by a Chattanooga, Tenn., federal jury. He was sentenced to eight years in prison and fined $10,000.

Apr. 8 An unmanned **Gemini spacecraft was successfully launched** into orbit from Cape Kennedy, Fla.

Apr. 11 The **Agricultural Act of 1964** was signed by Pres. Lyndon B. Johnson. It established land allotment and diversion procedures and price support programs for wheat and cotton farmers. The legislation was designed to control surplus production, divert acreage for soil conservation, and support producers while keeping domestic prices low.

Apr. 16 A major find of **zinc, copper, and silver ore,** estimated at more than 25,000,000 tons, near Timmins, Ontario, Canada, was confirmed by the Texas Gulf Sulphur Company.

Apr. 27 In a move supporting **arbitration** in labor disputes, the Supreme Court refused to hear a suit brought by the railroad operating unions. The suit challenged an arbitration award of the previous year under which thousands of firemen's jobs were to be eliminated. The Court left standing a lower court decision upholding the constitutionality of the congressional act that created the arbitration panel.

May 19 Federal **noninflationary wage guidelines were denounced** in a statement issued by the AFL-CIO Executive Council.

May 21 The Baltimore Lighthouse, on Chesapeake Bay in Maryland, became the world's **first nuclear-**

Washington 7 in the Rose Bowl; and Alabama 12, Mississippi 7 in the Sugar Bowl. This season both the AP and UPI polls chose Texas the national collegiate champions of 1963.

Jan. 5 The 1963 **AFL championship** was won by the San Diego Chargers, who defeated the Boston Patriots 51–10.

Jan. 11–12 **U.S. figure skating championships** were won in Cleveland, Ohio, by Peggy Fleming, women's singles; Scott Allen, men's singles; Judianne and Jerry Fotheringill, pairs; Darlene Streich and Charles D. Fetter, Jr., dance.

Jan. 29–Feb. 9 At the **Winter Olympics** in Innsbruck, Austria, the U.S. finished eighth in the unofficial team standings, taking one gold, two silver, and three bronze medals.

Feb. 25 The **world heavyweight boxing championship** was won by Muhammad Ali, in a bout at Miami Beach, when Sonny Liston could not answer the bell for the seventh round because of an injury to his left arm. Ali announced he would give Liston a rematch, but the World Boxing Association (WBA), claiming it had a rule forbidding return bouts, declared the heavyweight title vacant and made plans for an elimination tournament. When their contender Cleveland Williams was shot by Texas highway police, the WBA postponed its plans until 1965. The Ali-Liston bout, scheduled for Nov. 16 in Boston, was called off 70 hours before the bell, after Ali went to the hospital for a hernia operation.

Mar. 21 The **NCAA basketball championship** was won by UCLA, which defeated Duke University 98–83. The victory climaxed a perfect season for UCLA, which won all 30 of its games, the first major team to have an undefeated season since 1957.

Apr. 11–25 The **NHL Stanley Cup** was won for the third year in a row by the Toronto Maple Leafs, who beat the Detroit Red Wings four games to three.

Apr. 12 The **Masters golf tournament** was won by Arnold Palmer for the fourth time.

Apr. 18–26 The **NBA basketball championship** was won, for the sixth time in a row, by the Boston Celtics, who defeated the San Francisco Warriors four games to one.

June 15 In a ruling on **apportionment of state legislatures,** the Supreme Court held that both houses of state legislatures must be apportioned on the basis of population. Previously, upper houses had geographical bases. Both houses of Congress made efforts to block the Court's decision.

July 2 The **Civil Rights Act of 1964** was signed by Pres. Johnson in a televised ceremony a few hours after the House approved Senate amendments by a vote of 289–126.

July 15 The **Republican National Convention** nominated Sen. **Barry Goldwater** for the presidency. The next day Rep. William E. Miller of New York was nominated for the vice presidency.

July 18 A **race riot** broke out in Harlem, New York City, after an off-duty policeman shot a black youth who allegedly attacked him with a knife.

July 19 Gov. **George C. Wallace** of Alabama withdrew from the presidential race. Wallace had done well in a number of Democratic primaries and had announced his candidacy as an independent challenger.

July 22 The section of the **Civil Rights Act of 1964** barring racial discrimination in public accommodations was upheld by a federal court in Atlanta, Ga. The court ordered a restaurant and motel in Atlanta to admit blacks.

July 24 An international **satellite communications agreement** was initialed by representatives of 18 nations in Washington, D.C. The agreement specified international management and ownership of the global communications satellite system being developed in the U.S.

Aug. 2 In what came to be called the **Gulf of Tonkin incident,** three North Vietnamese PT boats attacked the U.S. destroyer *Maddox* in the Gulf of Tonkin in international waters, but were fought off by fighter planes from the U.S. carrier *Ticonderoga.* Three days later U.S. planes bombed North Vietnamese installations and naval craft.

Aug. 4 Three young **civil rights workers were found murdered** and buried in an earthen dam on a farm outside Philadelphia, Miss. The three, James Chaney, 21, of Meridian, Miss., and Andrew Goodman, 20, and Michael Schwerner, 24, both of New York City, had disappeared on June 21 after being held for six hours by Neshoba County police on charges of speeding.

false, or with reckless disregard as to whether they were false or not.

Mar. 10 **National Book Awards** were presented for the following: fiction, *The Centaur* by John Updike; history and biography, *The Rise of the West* by William H. McNeil; arts and letters, *John Keats: The Making of a Poet* by Aileen Ward; science, philosophy, and religion, *Man-Made America: Chaos or Control?* by Christopher Tunnard and Boris Pushkarev; poetry, *Selected Poems* by John Crowe Ransom. Announcement was made of a new $5000 National Medal for Literature, to be awarded beginning in 1965.

Mar. 16 The **Gallery of Modern Art,** New York City's newest museum, opened in its brand-new building on Columbus Circle. Sponsored by A & P heir Huntington Hartford, the museum had a faintly ironic name since its permanent collection and special exhibition did not include anything even remotely avant-garde. (The first big show, which opened the next month, was a retrospective of the Pre-Raphaelites of the nineteenth century.) The museum building, designed by Edward Durrell Stone, was praised for its beauty and functional efficiency.

Apr. 13 **Academy Awards** were presented to *Tom Jones* as the outstanding motion picture of 1963; to Sidney Poitier as best actor for *Lilies of the Field;* to Patricia Neal as best actress for *Hud;* to Melvyn Douglas as best supporting actor for *Hud;* and to Margaret Rutherford as best supporting actress for *The V.I.P.'s.*

Apr. 19 **Michelangelo's** *Pietà,* on loan from St. Peter's in Rome, was unveiled at the Vatican Pavilion at the New York World's Fair. The marble statue had arrived by ship from Italy six days before. For its transportation, a special waterproof, floatable crate had been constructed, designed to free itself from a sinking ship. Placed in a dramatic setting ·by stage designer Jo Mielziner, the *Pietà* was one of the most popular attractions at the fair.

Apr. 23 The **400th anniversary of the birth of William Shakespeare** was celebrated in many parts of the U.S. and Canada. During the year great attention was given to the poet and his works. Dozens of books were published that related to Shakespearean scholarship. A number of national magazines, including *Life* and *Saturday Review,* devoted entire issues to the anniversary. In festivals and single performances from coast to coast, 30 of Shakespeare's 37 plays were performed. Two of the finest productions of the year were Richard Burton's *Hamlet,* with Hume Cronyn and Alfred Drake, in New York City; and the Royal Shakespeare Company's *King Lear,* starring Paul Scofield, which played in Boston, Philadelphia, Washington, and New York City.

Apr. 24 The **New York City Ballet,** under George Balanchine, opened its first season in its new house,

| Business and Industry; Science; Education; Philosophy and Religion | III | | IV | Sports; Social Issues and Crime; Folkways; Fashion; Holidays |

powered lighthouse when a new atomic power supply went into service.

May 25 The **closing of schools to avoid desegregation** was ruled unconstitutional by the Supreme Court. The Court ruled that the schools of Prince Edward County, Va., which had been closed in 1959, must be reopened and desegregated.

June 14 An **agreement to end racial discrimination** in the steel industry was announced by the United Steelworkers of American and 11 steel companies.

June 24 **Health warnings on cigarette** packages would be required starting in 1965, the Federal Trade Commission announced.

July 9 The **New Orleans Cotton Exchange,** the second largest commodities exchange in the U.S., stopped futures trading after 93 years of operation. It announced that its action was due to government control exercised by the Agricultural Act of 1964.

July 26 **James R. Hoffa,** president of the International Brotherhood of Teamsters, was convicted of fraud and conspiracy in the handling of his union's pension fund by a federal jury in Chicago. He was sentenced to five years in prison and fined $10,000.

July 31 The U.S. lunar probe **Ranger 7** crashed into the moon after sending back to Earth 4316 photographs of the lunar surface taken within a 1300-mile range.

Aug. 5 A bill authorizing a **National Commission on Technology, Automation and Economic Progress** to study the effect of automation on unemployment was passed by Congress.

Aug. 14 **Elementary school desegregation in Mississippi** began without incident at previously white elementary schools in Biloxi, Miss. This marked the first desegregation of schools below the college level in that state.

Aug. 19 **Syncom 3,** a communications satellite, was successfully launched from Cape Kennedy, Fla. In

Apr. 20 The **Boston Marathon** was won for the second time in a row by Aurele Vandendriessche of Belgium, with a time of 2 hrs., 19 min., 59 sec.

Apr. 22 Opening-day ceremonies of the **New York World's Fair** of 1964–1965 were marred by threats of a massive traffic tie-up by members of the Congress of Racial Equality (CORE), who planned to have their cars run out of gas on all major arteries leading to the fair. The so-called stall-in, intended to dramatize CORE's demand for city action against racial discrimination, did not materialize, but it was probably a major factor along with bad weather in cutting attendance from an expected 250,000 to 92,646. Pres. Lyndon B. Johnson's dedication speech was interrupted by demonstrators' chants. When the fair closed its first season on Oct. 18, it was apparent that it was in dire financial straits. Low attendance was blamed on fear of racial violence, high prices, and characterization of the fair as a cultural desert.

May 2 The 90th annual **Kentucky Derby** was won by Northern Dancer, with a time of 2:00. The jockey was Bill Hartack.

May 16 The 89th annual **Preakness Stakes** was won by Northern Dancer, with a time of 1:56⁴/₅. The jockey was Bill Hartack.

May 30 The 48th annual **Indianapolis 500** auto race was won by A. J. Foyt, completing the course in 3 hrs., 23 min., 35.83 sec., for an average speed of 147.350 mph.

May 31 In the **longest baseball game** to date, the San Francisco Giants beat the New York Mets 8–6 after 7 hrs., 23 min. of the second game of a double header. The end came in the 23rd inning, matching the fourth longest game in innings played.

June 6 The 96th annual **Belmont Stakes** was won by Quadrangle, with a time of 2:28²/₅. The jockey was Manuel Ycaza. A new world record for bets placed in a single day was set, as fans poured $5,834,896 into the mutuel machines on nine races at Aqueduct Race Track.

June 20 The **U.S. Open golf tournament** was won by Ken Venturi, who beat Tommy Jacobs by two strokes.

June 21 A **perfect baseball game,** the first in a regular season since 1922, was pitched by Jim Bunning of the Philadelphia Phillies, who led his team to a 6–0 victory

Their burned station wagon was found June 23, prompting Pres. Johnson to order an FBI search for the three men.

Aug. 7 The **Gulf of Tonkin Resolution,** a joint resolution approving U.S. action in Southeast Asia, was passed by Congress. A resolution passed on Aug. 1 had granted authority to the president to use all necessary measures to repel armed attack and to help any SEATO nation asking assistance in defense of its freedom.

Aug. 26 The **Democratic National Convention** nominated Pres. **Johnson** for the presidency. Sen. Hubert M. Humphrey of Minnesota was nominated for the vice presidency.

Aug. 28 A three-day **race riot** broke out in Philadelphia, Pa. On Aug. 29 Mayor James H. J. Tate closed off 125 blocks of the city to quell the rioting. More than 500 people were injured and more than 350 were arrested.

Aug. 30 The **Economic Opportunity Act of 1964** was signed by Pres. Johnson. The bill authorized $947,500,000 for youth programs, community action antipoverty measures in rural areas, small business loans, and job training, including a Job Corps for youth.

Sept. 3 A bill establishing a permanent **national wilderness** system comprising 9,200,000 acres was passed by Congress and signed by Pres. Johnson.

Sept. 17 Development of **two antisatellite rocket systems,** based on Nike-Zeus and Thor rockets, was announced by Pres. Johnson.

Sept. 27 The **Warren Commission report** on the assassination of John F. Kennedy was released with the finding that there was no conspiracy, either domestic or international, in the assassination, and that Lee Harvey Oswald alone was responsible for it. The report found also that Jack Ruby, convicted murderer of Oswald, had had no prior contact with Oswald.

Nov. 3 **Lyndon Baines Johnson was elected president** of the United States. Sen. Hubert Horatio Humphrey was elected vice president. The electoral vote was Johnson, 486; Sen. Barry M. Goldwater, Republican, 52. The popular vote was Johnson, 43,126,506; Goldwater, 27,176,799. In congressional elections the Democrats gained one Senate seat for a 68–32 majority, and 37 House seats for a 295–140 majority.

the New York State Theater at Lincoln Center for the Performing Arts. A new ballet, *A Midsummer Night's Dream,* was performed in celebration of the 400th anniversary of William Shakespeare's birth. This was also the opening night of the new theater, which had been designed by Philip Johnson. In a modern interpretation of traditional theatrical elegance, the interior was red and gold and studded with giant faceted lamps that resembled jewels.

May 4 **Pulitzer prizes** were awarded for the following: biography, *John Keats* by Walter Jackson Bate; history, *Puritan Village: The Formation of a New England Town* by Sumner Chilton Powell; general nonfiction, *Anti-Intellectualism in American Life* by Richard Hofstadter; poetry, *At the End of the Open Road* by Louis Simpson.

May 12 **Grammy Awards** were presented to the following: best song of 1963, "The Days of Wine and Roses" by Henry Mancini; best album, *The Barbra Streisand Album;* best male vocalist, Jack Jones for *Wives and Lovers;* best female vocalist, Barbra Streisand for *The Barbra Streisand Album;* best group, Peter, Paul, and Mary for "Blowin' in the Wind."

May 24 **Tony Awards** for the 1963–1964 season were presented for the following: best play, *Luther* by John Osborne; best musical, *Hello, Dolly!* by Michael Stewart and Jerry Herman; best actor in a drama, Alec Guinness for *Dylan;* best actress in a drama, Sandy Dennis for *Any Wednesday.*

May 25 The **Museum of Modern Art** in New York City opened two new wings and an expanded sculpture garden. The new construction provided enough space for two major special shows to be given at the same time and allowed room for a changing display of new acquisitions. Above the special exhibition galleries, the museum's first permanent photographic gallery was installed.

May 25 **Emmy Awards** were presented to Jack Klugman as best actor for "Blacklist," *The Defenders;* Shelley Winters as best actress for "Two Is the Number," *Chrysler Theater;* and Dick Van Dyke and Mary Tyler Moore as best actor and actress in a series for *The Dick Van Dyke Show,* which also won an award for best comedy series.

Aug. 20 **Campobello Island,** New Brunswick, Canada, the site of Franklin D. Roosevelt's summer home, was dedicated as a memorial park in honor of the former president. The ceremony was attended by Mrs. Lyndon Johnson, representing the U.S., and Mrs. Lester Pearson, wife of the Canadian prime minister. It was at his vacation estate that Roosevelt was stricken with polio and began his recovery. By terms of an agreement signed in January, the New Brunswick island was designated Roosevelt Campobello International

| Business and Industry; Science; Education; Philosophy and Religion **III** | | **IV** Sports; Social Issues and Crime; Folkways; Fashion; Holidays |

October it transmitted live broadcasts of the 1964 Olympic Games from Tokyo to California.

Aug. 28 Nimbus 1, an advanced meteorological satellite, was launched from Vandenberg Air Force Base, Calif. Although it failed to achieve its intended circular orbit, it sent back exceptionally clear close-up pictures of Earth's nighttime cloud cover.

Sept. 9 A three-year **auto workers' contract** was agreed to by Chrysler Corporation and the United Auto Workers 55 minutes before 74,000 workers were scheduled to strike.

Sept. 18 An **auto workers' strike was averted** when Ford Motor Company and the UAW reached agreement on a new union contract less than an hour before deadline. However, plants went out on strike over local grievances on Nov. 6, tying up production until Nov. 23.

Sept. 25 General Motors Corp. was struck by the United Auto Workers after failure to reach a new labor agreement. A new three-year national contract was agreed to on Oct. 5, but local strikes tied up production until Nov. 7.

Oct. 14 The **Nobel Peace Prize** was awarded to the Rev. Martin Luther King., Jr., civil rights leader of Atlanta, Ga. He donated the award, valued at $54,600, to the civil rights movement.

Oct. 15 The **Nobel Prize for Physiology or Medicine** was awarded jointly to Dr. Conrad E. Block of Harvard University and Feodor Lynen, a German professor, for their work on the relationship between heart disease and cholesterol.

Oct. 29 The **Nobel Prize in Physics** was awarded jointly to Charles H. Townes of the Massachusetts Institute of Technology and to Nikolai Basov and Aleksandr Prokhorov of the U.S.S.R. for their work in quantum electronics.

Nov. 21 The **longest newspaper shutdown** to date— 132 days—was ended when pressmen from the *Detroit News* and *Detroit Free Press* accepted a new settlement.

over the New York Mets at Shea Stadium in New York City.

July 7 The **baseball All-Star Game** was won by the National League, which defeated the American League 7–4.

July 12 The **U.S. Women's Open golf tournament** was won, for the fourth time, by Mickey Wright, who beat Ruth Jessen by two strokes in a playoff.

July 19 The **PGA golf tournament** was won by Bobby Nichols, who beat both Arnold Palmer and Jack Nicklaus by three strokes.

July 27 The **Baseball Hall of Fame** inducted seven new members: Lucius "Luke" Appling, Urban "Red" Faber, Burleigh Grimes, Miller Higgins, Tim Keefe, Henry "Heinie" Manush, and John Montgomery Ward.

Sept. 12 The **Miss America** title was won by Vonda Kay Van Dyke, 21, from Arizona, at the annual pageant in Atlantic City, N.J.

Sept. 12 In the **New Hampshire Sweepstakes,** the first legal sweepstakes in U.S. horse racing history, six persons won the first prize of $100,000 at Rockingham Park in Salem, N.H.

Sept. 13 The **U.S. Lawn Tennis Association singles championships** were won by Roy Emerson of Australia in the men's division and Maria Bueno of Brazil in the women's division.

Sept. 15–21 The **America's Cup,** yachting's oldest trophy, was successfully defended by the U.S racer *Constellation,* which easily outdistanced the British challenger *Sovereign* in four races off Newport, R.I.

Oct. 4 The **LPGA golf tournament** was won by Mary Mills, who beat Mickey Wright by two strokes.

Oct. 7–15 The 61st annual **World Series** was won by the St. Louis Cardinals (NL), defeating the New York Yankees (AL) four games to three. Cardinal pitcher Bob Gibson struck out 31 batters in three games, a Series record. Mickey Mantle of the Yankees hit his 16th Series homer, breaking the record held by Babe Ruth.

Oct. 10–24 At the **Summer Olympics** in Tokyo, Japan, the U.S. won the unofficial team championship with 36 gold medals.

Exploration and Settlement; Wars; Government; Civil Rights; Statistics	I		II	Publishing; Arts and Music; Popular Entertainment; Architecture; Theater

Dec. 4 The **FBI arrested 21 Mississippians** on charges of conspiracy to violate the civil rights of the three civil rights workers found murdered on Aug. 4. On Dec. 10 the charges against 19 of the men were dropped in Meridian, Miss. Charges against the other two were dropped at the federal government's request.

Dec. 5 The **Medal of Honor** was presented to Capt. Roger H. C. Donlon, U.S. Army, for heroism in South Vietnam. He was the first person to receive the medal since the Korean War.

Dec. 22 Oregon and four northern California counties were declared **major disaster areas** because of heavy snow, rain, and floods. At least 40 people had died as a result of weather conditions in Oregon, California, Idaho, Washington, and Nevada.

Park. It was to be administered by a commission made up of three members from each country.

Sept. 22 *Fiddler on the Roof,* a musical by Joseph Stein, Jerry Bock, and Sheldon Harnick based on the stories of Sholem Aleichem, opened at the Imperial Theater in New York City. Destined for a long run, the musical starred Zero Mostel.

Oct. 1 An **equal time ruling** was issued by the FCC. It stated that any radio or television station carrying a presidential press conference in full must grant equal time to other presidential candidates.

Oct. 13 The German pianist **Wilhelm Kempff,** age 69 and long familiar to American music lovers through his recordings, made his U.S. debut at Carnegie Hall in New York City.

Oct. 21 In a **copyright infringement** case, the U.S. Supreme Court declined to review a lower court's decision that there had been no copyright infringement on the songs of Irving Berlin, which were parodied in *Mad* magazine.

1965

U.S. participation in the war in Vietnam was protested by many in demonstrations across the nation. Before year's end, U.S. losses in Vietnam since Jan. 1961 exceeded 1300 dead and 6100 wounded. The use of helicopters for medical evacuation helped keep the fatality rate below 2% of those wounded. Pres. Lyndon B. Johnson's administration obtained passage of most of its programs. Total appropriations were a record high for peacetime: $119,300,000,000, of which $46,900,000,000 went for defense. At the same time, Pres. Johnson's request for foreign aid was the smallest in the history of the program—$3,380,000,000, of which $3,200,000,000 was granted. The Medicare program was passed, as were antipoverty and voting rights bills and increased aid to education. Although turned down on his requests for repeal of Section 14-b of the Taft-Hartley Act, state right-to-work laws, and self-government for the District of Columbia, Pres. Johnson was given a $1,100,000,000 appropriation for development in Appalachia. In addition, excise taxes were cut, a new immigration law was passed to replace the 41-year-old national-origins quota system, and a new Cabinet-level Department of Housing and Urban Development was established. The nation's rate of population growth, 1.21%, was the slowest since 1945. Notables who died this year included Frances Perkins, secretary of labor from 1933 to 1945, May 14, at 83; Adlai E. Stevenson, unsuccessful Democratic candidate for the presidency in 1952 and 1956, July 14, at 65; and Henry A. Wallace, vice president of the United States from 1941 to 1945, Nov. 18 at 77.

The most sensational theatrical offering of the year was Peter Weiss's *The Persecution and Assassination of Marat as Performed by the Inmates of the Asylum of Charenton Under the Direction of the Marquis de Sade,* a production of the Royal Shakespeare Company directed by Peter Brook, which opened Dec. 27. The playwright's cynical view of the French Revolution was conveyed by actors manifesting a wide variety of psychoses. The Repertory Theater of Lincoln Center occupied its new home, the Vivian Beaumont Theater. The most significant development in art this year was the appearance of op (optical) art, abstract painting that commanded viewers' attention by the dazzling interaction of colors and/or optical illusion. The most important op art show, "The Responsive Eye," opened at the Museum of Modern Art in New York City; it was seen subsequently in St. Louis, Seattle, Pasadena, and Baltimore. Notables who died this year included Thornton W. Burgess, author of the Peter Rabbit stories, June 5, at 91; Nat "King" Cole, born Nathaniel Adams Coles, singer, Feb. 15, at 45; T. S. Eliot, the poet, Jan. 4, at 76; Lorraine Hansberry, playwright, Jan. 12, at 34; Judy Holliday, actress, June 7, at 42; Shirley Jackson, writer, Aug. 8, at 45; Stan Laurel, born Arthur Stanley Jefferson, comedian, Feb. 23, at 74; David O. Selznick, motion picture producer, June 22, at 63; and Edgard Varèse, the French-born composer regarded as the father of electronic music, Nov. 6, at 90.

Among **books published** this year were two biographies of John F. Kennedy that became the

| Business and Industry; Science; Education; Philosophy and Religion   III | | IV   Sports; Social Issues and Crime; Folkways; Fashion; Holidays |

Nov. 21 The **Verrazano-Narrows Bridge** between Brooklyn and Staten Island, N.Y., was formally opened. At 6690 feet, it was the world's longest suspension bridge.

Nov. 28 **Mariner 4** was launched from Cape Kennedy, Fla., to transmit close-up TV pictures of Mars on its projected flyby within 8600 miles of that planet in July 1965.

Dec. 16 In the **first long-term contract settlement** in the union's 92-year history, agreement was reached on a four-year contract by the International Longshoremen's Association and the New York Shipping Association. Before ratification of the agreement, a series of wildcat strikes broke out in New York and elsewhere.

Oct. 29 In a daring **jewel robbery,** thieves made off with magnificent jewels from the collection of rare stones of the Museum of Natural History in New York City. Among them were the world's largest sapphire, the 565-carat Star of India, and the 100-carat DeLong ruby. A tip led to the arrest of professional swimmers Allan Kuhn and Jack "Murph the Surf" Murphy, and beach boy Roger Clark. Most of the gems were recovered as part of an agreement by which the trio received a lenient sentence (Apr. 6, 1965). The DeLong ruby was finally ransomed on Sept. 2, 1965.

Dec. 26 The **AFL championship** was won by the Buffalo Bills, who defeated the San Diego Chargers 20–7.

Dec. 27 The **NFL championship** was won by the Cleveland Browns, who shut out the Baltimore Colts 27–0.

1965

The first U.S. walk in space and the successful rendezvous of two Gemini capsules 185 miles above Earth assisted NASA in its preparations for a manned trip to the moon. Photographs of the surface of Mars showed no trace of the famous canals and provided evidence that the planet had little atmosphere. Commercial communication using an Earth satellite was realized with the aid of Early Bird. The most spectacular comet since Comet Halley in 1910 was spotted by two Japanese amateur astronomers; it was named Comet Ikeya-Seki. The U.S. gross national product rose from $628,000,000,000 to $672,000,000,000, exceeding by $14,000,000,000 the predictions of the president's economic advisers. In December it was announced that the unemployment rate had fallen to 4.2%, an eight-year low. Notables who died this year included the religious leader Father Divine, real name believed to be George Baker, Sept. 10, at about 83; H. V. Kaltenborn, radio commentator, June 14, at 86; Edward R. Murrow, radio and television journalist, Apr. 27, at 57; and Paul Tillich, theologian, Oct. 22, at 79.

Feb. 3 In a **cheating scandal** at the U.S. Air Force Academy, 105 cadets resigned for cheating on examinations. Four more resigned later, when the cadet wing honor board found they had had knowledge of the cheating but had not reported it.

Feb. 7 A **railroad contract** based on attrition to reduce the labor force was signed by five AFL-CIO

In clothing and hairstyles, the trend was toward sexual ambiguity. Young men sprouted shoulder-length hair, and girls wore bangs and shingles, a style designed by London hairdresser Vidal Sassoon. The Mod look, also emanating from London, put the young of both sexes into tight, bell-bottom trousers. For dress-up, women wore skirts two inches above the knee and blouses ruffled at the throat and wrist. The Courrèges look was the high-fashion sensation. It featured a solid color A-line dress trimmed with contrasting bands, high white boots, and often a helmet-type hat. Art-inspired fashions included the Mondrian dresses of Yves St. Laurent and op art fabrics favored by Capucci. In sports Muhammad Ali defied World Boxing Association (WBA) rules against rematches and met Sonny Liston in a short and sweet, successful title defense. Nonetheless, the WBA stripped Ali of his title and declared the championship vacant. In golf the top money winners were Jack Nicklaus, $142,752, and Kathy Whitworth, $32,937. Deaths of this year included John Leonard "Pepper" Martin, of the St. Louis Cardinals, Mar. 5, at 61; Branch W. Rickey, baseball executive, Dec. 9, at 84; Helena Rubinstein, founder of a cosmetics empire, Apr. 1, at about 89; and Amos Alonzo Stagg, college football coach for more than 60 years, 41 of them at the University of Chicago, Mar. 17, at 102.

Jan. 1 In **college football bowl games,** the results were Arkansas 10, Nebraska 7 in the Cotton Bowl; Texas 21, Alabama 17 in the Orange Bowl; Michigan

Jan. 20 Lyndon B. Johnson was inaugurated president of the United States. The 36th president, he served one full term after completing Pres. John F. Kennedy's term of office.

Jan. 28 Pres. Johnson asked Congress to propose **constitutional amendments** that would cover presidential disability; provide for filling a vice presidential vacancy; and reform the electoral college system so that voters could not be overridden by electors.

Feb. 5 A **Northeast drought** that began in Sept. 1961 reduced the water in New York City's storage reservoirs to an all-time low of 24.5% of capacity.

Feb. 16 A plot to dynamite the Statue of Liberty, the Liberty Bell, and the Washington Monument was foiled. Four persons were arrested, including the self-styled leader of the Black Liberation Front and a woman member of a Quebec separatist party.

Feb. 21 Malcolm X was assassinated by rival Black Muslims while addressing a gathering at the Audubon Ballroom in Washington Heights, New York City. Born Malcolm Little, the 39-year-old leader founded the extremist Black Nationalist movement after breaking with the Black Muslims in 1964. In recent months he had been moving toward a less violently anti-white stance. Two days after his death, Black Muslim headquarters in San Francisco and New York City were burned.

Mar. 4 The **U.S. Information Agency closed in Indonesia** because of harassment. It was the first time it had withdrawn its facilities from any of the 100 nations in which it operated. The Peace Corps was withdrawn the following month.

Mar. 8 Ruling on **conscientious objectors,** the Supreme Court held unanimously that a person holding a sincere belief in a Supreme Being, even though differing from the beliefs held by accepted religions, may be exempted from military combat training and service.

Mar. 8–9 The first U.S. combat forces in Vietnam, more than 3500 Marines, landed in South Vietnam to guard the U.S. Air Force base at Danang. They joined 23,500 other Americans serving as advisers in South Vietnam.

Mar. 11 The Rev. **James Reeb died** from a beating he received in Selma, Ala., on Mar. 9. A Unitarian minister from Boston, Reeb had been working in a civil rights drive. Three whites were subsequently indicted for the murder, but they were found not guilty on Dec. 10.

Mar. 15 Sweeping **voting rights legislation** was requested by Pres. Johnson in a nationally televised address to a joint session of Congress. Later Johnson submitted a voting rights bill to Congress. One provision of the bill would empower the attorney general

nonfiction standouts of 1965. *Kennedy* by Theodore Sorensen was an intimate account of Kennedy's career from 1953. *A Thousand Days* by Arthur M. Schlesinger, Jr., dealt with Kennedy's tenure as president. Other books published this year included *Going to Meet the Man* by James Baldwin, short stories; *Manchild in the Promised Land* by Claude Brown; *Never Call Retreat* by Bruce Catton, the third volume in the Civil War trilogy *Centennial History of the Civil War; Country Without Maps* by Jean Garrigue, a collection of poems; *Up the Down Staircase* by Bel Kaufman; *The Autobiography of Malcolm X; The Oxford History of the American People* by Samuel Eliot Morison; and *Everything That Rises Must Converge* by Flannery O'Connor, stories.

Mar. 1 A Maryland **movie censorship law** was ruled a violation of the First Amendment. The Supreme Court found that pictures may be censored before showing only if provision is made for swift court relief; and that the burden of proving that a film should not be shown must rest with the censor. Citing this decision, the Court on Mar. 15 declared unconstitutional New York's censorship procedures. That case involved the Danish film *A Stranger Knocks.*

Mar. 9 **National Book Awards** were presented for the following: fiction, *Herzog* by Saul Bellow; history and biography, *The Life of Lenin* by Louis Fischer; arts and letters, *The Oysters of Locmariaquer* by Eleanor Clark; poetry, *The Far Field* by Theodore Roethke; science, philosophy, and religion, *God and Golem, Inc.* by Norbert Wiener.

Mar. 19 **Norton Simon,** a U.S. industrialist, created an uproar at an art auction at Christie's in London by claiming an irregularity after bidding closed on Rembrandt's portrait of his son Titus Rembrandt. Bidding was reopened and Simon got the picture for $2,234,000. Simon planned to put it on exhibition in Los Angeles, Calif. It was also reported that Prince Franz Josef II of Liechtenstein had refused Simon's offer of $6,000,000 for Leonardo da Vinci's *Portrait of a Young Woman.*

Mar. 30 The **Los Angeles County Art Museum** was dedicated. It was the largest art museum west of the Mississippi R., and the largest built since the National Gallery was opened in 1941.

Apr. 5 **Academy Awards** were presented to *My Fair Lady* as the outstanding motion picture of 1964; to Rex Harrison as best actor for *My Fair Lady;* to Julie Andrews as best actress for *Mary Poppins;* to Peter Ustinov as best supporting actor for *Topkapi;* and to Lila Kedrova as best supporting actress for *Zorba the Greek.*

| Business and Industry; Science; Education; Philosophy and Religion   III | | IV   Sports; Social Issues and Crime; Folkways; Fashion; Holidays |

nonoperating railroad unions and railroad management.

Feb. 16   Pegasus 1, a micrometeoroid detection station with 96-foot wings as sensors, was put into orbit.

Feb. 17   Ranger 8, a moon probe, was successfully launched. It sent back 7137 photos of the moon's surface before crashing into the Sea of Tranquillity on Feb. 20.

Mar. 21   Ranger 9 was launched. It transmitted 5814 photos of the moon's surface before crashing into Alphonsus crater on Mar. 24. It was the last moon probe of the Ranger series.

Mar. 23   Gemini 3, the first manned Gemini flight, was successfully launched from Cape Kennedy, Fla. The craft, nicknamed "Molly Brown," was put through delicate maneuvers by its pilots, Maj. Virgil Grissom and Lt. Commander John Young, during its three-orbit flight. It was retrieved by the carrier *Intrepid* in the Atlantic Ocean.

Apr. 6   Early Bird, the world's first commercial communications satellite, was launched and placed in orbit 22,300 miles above Earth. Owned by ComSat, Early Bird transmitted phone calls, TV, Teletype, and other communications.

Apr. 16 The **Saturn S-1C rocket,** to be the first stage for the Apollo lunar flight and the largest U.S. booster ever produced, was successfully fired at Cape Kennedy, Fla.

Apr. 26 An interim **steelworkers' agreement** providing for wage increases for 400,000 steelworkers averted a nationwide strike scheduled for May 1. Negotiations for a new contract continued.

Apr. 29 The commissioner of education announced that **complete desegregation** of the nation's 27,000 public school districts would be required by the beginning of the autumn 1967 term.

May 24 A federal law authorizing **postal interception of communist propaganda** was declared unconstitutional by the Supreme Court. The law, empowering the postmaster general to hold foreign mail deemed to be communist propaganda and to make the addressee submit a written request for it, was ruled to violate the First Amendment.

34, Oregon State 7 in the Rose Bowl; and LSU 13, Syracuse 10 in the Sugar Bowl. This season the AP and UPI polls chose Alabama the national college football champions of 1964.

Feb. 13   U.S. figure skating championships were won at Lake Placid, N.Y., by Peggy Fleming, 16, in the women's singles; Gary Visconti, men's singles; Vivian and Ronald Joseph, pairs; Kristin Fortune and Dennis Sveum, dance.

Feb. 19 In Washington, D.C., **Henry Ford II** married Italian-born Maria Cristina Vettore Austin. It was the second marriage for both.

Mar. 20 The **NCAA basketball championship** was won by UCLA, which defeated Michigan 91–80.

Apr. 11 The **Masters golf tournament** was won by Jack Nicklaus by nine strokes, a tournament record.

Apr. 17–May 1 The **NHL Stanley Cup** was won by the Montreal Canadiens, who defeated the Chicago Black Hawks four games to three.

Apr. 18–25 The **NBA basketball championship** was won for the seventh straight year by the Boston Celtics, who defeated the Los Angeles Lakers four games to one.

Apr. 19 The 69th **Boston Marathon** was won by Morio Shigematsu of Japan with a time of 2 hrs., 16 min., 33 sec.

May 1 The 91st annual **Kentucky Derby** was won by Lucky Debonair, with a time of 2:01⅕. The jockey was Willie Shoemaker.

May 15 The 90th annual **Preakness Stakes** was won by Tom Rolfe, with a time of 1:56⅕. The jockey was Ron Turcotte.

May 25 The **world heavyweight boxing championship** was successfully defended by Muhammad Ali, who knocked out Sonny Liston about a minute into the first round of a rematch. Few fans saw the punch that floored Liston. Despite Ali's win, the World Boxing Association maintained that its heavyweight title belonged to Ernie Terrell, who had outpointed Eddie Machen on Mar. 5. Ali retained the National Boxing Association title.

May 31 The 49th annual **Indianapolis 500** auto race was won by Jim Clark of Scotland, completing the

to assign federal registration examiners in the six states requiring literacy or other voter-qualification tests.

Mar. 21 A five-day **civil rights march from Selma to Montgomery,** Ala., was begun by some 3200 marchers led by Dr. Martin Luther King, Jr. At the end of the march, some 25,000 demonstrators gathered in front of the state capitol in Montgomery.

Mar. 25 **Viola Gregg Liuzzo,** a civil rights worker from Detroit, Mich., was shot and killed in Selma, Ala. On Dec. 3 Collie LeRoy Wilkins and two other Ku Klux Klansmen were convicted of conspiracy charges in the murder. They were sentenced to ten years' imprisonment.

Apr. 11 A series of **37 tornadoes** swept through Indiana, Iowa, Illinois, Wisconsin, Michigan, and Ohio, killing 271 people and injuring 5000. It was the nation's worst tornado disaster in 40 years.

Apr. 26 The **cost of the Vietnam War** to the U.S. was estimated by Sec. of Defense Robert S. McNamara at almost $1,500,000,000 annually, with economic aid at $300,000,000, food and agricultural supplies at $70,-000,000, military assistance at $330,000,000, and the cost of U.S. forces at $800,000,000.

Apr. 28 **Marines were sent to the Dominican Republic** to protect U.S. citizens following a military coup on Apr. 24 and the outbreak of civil war. By May 5 the U.S. had 12,439 Army personnel and 6924 Marines in the Dominican Republic.

June 7 An 1879 **Connecticut law banning the use of contraceptives** by anyone, including married couples, was ruled unconstitutional by the U.S. Supreme Court.

June 17 In the **first mass bombing raid** in the Vietnam War, Guam-based B-52s bombed a Vietcong concentration 30 miles north of Saigon. It was the first combat use of the heavy jet bombers since they were placed in operation in 1952.

July 28 Pres. Johnson announced that **U.S. troop levels in South Vietnam** would be increased from 75,000 to 125,000, and the draft would be doubled from 17,-000 to 35,000 a month.

Aug. 11–16 **Riots in Watts,** a black section of Los Angeles, Calif., left 35 dead and hundreds injured. The riots, which caused about $200,000,000 in damage, were sparked when a white policeman stopped a black driver suspected of being drunk.

Aug. 16 Total **U.S. casualties in Vietnam** since Jan. 1, 1961, were 561 killed, 3024 wounded, 44 missing in action, and 269 dead of noncombat causes.

Aug. 17 A **nuclear nonproliferation treaty** proposed by the U.S. to the UN Disarmament Committee in Geneva was dismissed by the U.S.S.R. delegate as a "joke." The committee adjourned two days later.

Apr. 9 The **Houston Astrodome,** noted for its plastic dome enclosing the stadium and protecting both players and spectators from the elements, was opened with an exhibition game between the Houston Astros and the New York Yankees. Pres. Johnson was among the honored guests. The players were troubled by glaring light from the stadium dome, which was later painted over.

Apr. 26 The *Fourth Symphony* of **Charles Ives** was performed for the first time by Leopold Stokowski and the American Symphony Orchestra. The 50-year-old work was reconstructed from a badly organized manuscript, and two assistant conductors were required for its performance.

May 3 **Pulitzer prizes** were awarded for the following: fiction, *The Keepers of the House* by Shirley Ann Grau; biography, *Henry Adams* by Ernest Samuels; history, *The Greenback Era* by Irwin Unger; poetry, *77 Dream Songs* by John Berryman; drama, *The Subject Was Roses* by Frank D. Gilroy.

May 9 The celebrated pianist **Vladimir Horowitz,** 60, returned to the concert stage after an absence of 12 years. A wildly enthusiastic audience at Carnegie Hall in New York City gave him standing ovations before and after his recital. Critics found the virtuoso pianist at the peak of his musical powers.

May 14 A **monument to Pres. John F. Kennedy** was dedicated by Queen Elizabeth of England at Runnymede, where in 1215 King John had signed the Magna Charta. Its inscription read: "This acre of English ground was given to the United States of America by the people of Great Britain in memory of John Fitzgerald Kennedy."

May 27 In a rare stage appearance, **George Balanchine,** the choreographer, danced the title role at the New York City Ballet's premiere performance of his new work, *Don Quixote.*

June 13 **Tony Awards** for the 1964–1965 season were presented for the following: best play, *The Subject Was Roses* by Frank D. Gilroy; best musical, *Fiddler on the Roof* by Joseph Stein, Sheldon Harnick, and Jerry Bock; best actor in a drama, Jack Albertson for *The Subject Was Roses;* best actress in a drama, Irene Worth for *Tiny Alice* by Edward Albee.

Sept. 12 **Emmy Awards** were presented to Alfred Lunt and Lynn Fontanne as best actor and actress for *The Magnificent Yankee;* to Dick Van Dyke for *The Dick Van Dyke Show;* and to Barbra Streisand for *My Name Is Barbra.* The inconsistent categories for awards contributed to the withdrawal of CBS News from participation this year.

| Business and Industry; Science; Education; Philosophy and Religion **III** | | **IV** Sports; Social Issues and Crime; Folkways; Fashion; Holidays |

June 3   Gemini 4, manned by Maj. James McDivitt and Maj. Edward White, was successfully launched from Cape Kennedy, Fla. During the four-day, 62-orbit mission White completed the first U.S. space walk; it lasted some 20 minutes while White, 135 miles above North America, was attached to the craft by a lifeline.

June 10   The slow pace of **Chicago school desegregation** was protested by mass demonstrations. By June 15 some 350 demonstrators had been arrested.

June 12   The **Big Bang theory** of creation of the universe was supported by the announcement of the discovery of new celestial bodies known as blue galaxies.

June 18   A **Titan 3C rocket** was launched into orbit with a total thrust of 2,400,000 lbs., the greatest thrust of any rocket ever to leave Earth's surface. The launching was the first to use large solid fuel rockets.

July 15   **Mariner 4** began transmission of 21 pictures of the surface of Mars taken at a range of between 7000 and 10,500 miles. Continually transmitting data to Earth since its launch on Nov. 28, 1964, the craft flew within 5700 miles of Mars.

Aug. 21   **Gemini 5,** piloted by Lt. Col. Gordon Cooper and Lt. Commander Charles Conrad, was launched on an eight-day, 120-orbit mission. The flight took as long as a round trip to the moon. There was some difficulty with a new fuel cell system.

Aug. 29   A 75-day **shipping strike** by three unions against eight lines, with losses to lines and employees estimated at $1,800,000 daily, was settled. Part of the dispute concerned procedures by which to negotiate manpower levels and automation of new ships.

Sept. 3   A new **three-year steel contract,** including wage increases and other employee benefits, was agreed to by steelworkers and the major companies just before a nationwide strike was to begin.

Sept. 16   A **newspaper strike** against *The New York Times* by the New York Newspaper Guild set off a suspension of publication of most New York City dailies. It lasted for more than three weeks and cost the industry at least $10,000,000.

Oct. 12   The **Sealab 2** U.S. Navy research program, a series of 15-day stays 205 feet below the surface of the Pacific Ocean, was completed. The purpose was to

course in 3 hrs., 19 min., 5.34 sec., with an average speed of 150.686 mph.

June 5   The 97th annual **Belmont Stakes** was won by Hail to All, with a time of 2:28²/₅. The jockey was Johnny Sellers.

June 21   The **U.S. Open** golf tournament was won by Gary Player of South Africa. He became the third man to win golf's four top pro titles; only Gene Sarazen and Ben Hogan had previously taken the U.S. and British Opens, the Masters, and the PGA.

July 4   The **U.S. Women's Open** golf tournament was won by Carol Mann.

July 13   The baseball **All-Star Game** was won by the National League, which beat the American League 6–5.

July 26   The **Baseball Hall of Fame** inducted James F. "Pud" Galvin, who, during his 16-year career as a pitcher, from 1875 to 1892, gained 365 victories.

Aug. 15   The **PGA** golf tournament was won by Dave Marr.

Aug. 30   Mets manager **Casey Stengel announced his retirement** after 55 years in baseball. On July 25, just a few days before his 75th birthday, he had broken his hip in a fall. Coach Wes Westrum became interim manager and at season's end was given the job permanently.

Sept. 9   A **perfect baseball game** was pitched by Sandy Koufax of the Los Angeles Dodgers (NL) against the Chicago Cubs. Koufax fanned 14 batters in the 1–0 victory. It was the fourth no-hit game of his career, a major league record, and only the eighth perfect game in baseball history.

Sept. 11   The **Miss America** title was won by Deborah Bryant, 19, from Kansas, at the annual pageant in Atlantic City, N.J.

Sept. 12   The **U.S. Lawn Tennis Association singles championships** were won by Manuel Santana of Spain in the men's division and Margaret Smith of Australia in the women's division.

Sept. 26   The **LPGA** golf tournament was won by Sandra Haynie, who beat Clifford Ann Creed by one stroke.

Exploration and Settlement; Wars; Government; Civil Rights; Statistics		Publishing; Arts and Music; Popular Entertainment; Architecture; Theater

Sept. 4 The new **provisional government of the Dominican Republic** was recognized by the U.S.

Sept. 24 Agreement in principle on a new **Panama Canal treaty,** to supersede the 1903 pact giving the U.S. sole control over the Panama Canal, was announced by Pres. Johnson. The new treaty would provide for joint administration of the canal.

Oct. 4 **Pope Paul VI visited New York City** to address the UN General Assembly on world peace. During the visit he celebrated a papal mass in Yankee Stadium and attended the New York World's Fair.

Oct. 15–16 **Nationwide antiwar demonstrations** were held, followed by a series of rallies and petitions supporting U.S. policy. Several persons burned their draft cards publicly; one person was arrested three days later under a law effective Aug. 31 that made destruction of a draft card a crime.

Oct. 19 An **investigation of the Ku Klux Klan** was opened by the House Committee on Un-American Activities.

Nov. 9–10 A massive **Northeast power blackout** struck an 80,000-square-mile area comprising New York, most of New England, parts of New Jersey, Pennsylvania, and Ontario and Quebec, Canada. The blackout, lasting as long as 13 hours in some areas, was initiated by the malfunction of an automatic relay device at a generating plant near Niagara Falls.

Nov. 15 **Mandatory federal registration by American communists,** required by the Subversive Activities Control Act of 1950, was declared unconstitutional by the Supreme Court on grounds that such registration could be self-incriminating under the 1940 Smith Act and other criminal statutes.

Nov. 20 **U.S. casualties** in Vietnam after a week-long battle in the Iadrang Valley were placed at 240 dead, 470 wounded, and six missing, exceeding the Korean War weekly average of 209 killed.

Nov. 27 An **anti–Vietnam War demonstration in Washington, D.C.,** was conducted by some 15,000 to 25,000 protesters from 140 groups.

Dec. 2 A two-hour **power blackout** hit a 13,200-square-mile area of the Southwest, affecting 50 cities and four military bases in southwest Texas, southern New Mexico, and Ciudad Juárez, Mexico.

Dec. 4 **Two airliners collided** in midair over Danbury, Conn. Four persons of the 112 passengers aboard the planes were killed.

Sept. 13 **Grammy Awards** were presented for the following: best song of 1964, "The Girl From Ipanema" by Stan Getz and Astrud Gilberto; best album, *Getz/Gilberto* by Stan Getz and João Gilberto; best male vocalist, Louis Armstrong for "Hello, Dolly!"; best female vocalist, Barbra Streisand for "People"; best group, The Beatles for *A Hard Day's Night.*

Sept. 30 The **Federal Aid to the Arts Act,** establishing the **National Foundation on the Arts and the Humanities,** was signed by Pres. Johnson. The act appropriated $63,000,000 to finance the first three years of the program.

Oct. 21 The **Ford Foundation** announced grants totaling $85,000,000 to 50 symphony orchestras throughout the U.S. to enable them to lengthen their seasons and improve the salaries scales of musicians.

Oct. 21 The **Vivian Beaumont Theater** in New York City was opened with an adaptation of Georg Büchner's *Danton's Death.* The playhouse, the third unit of Lincoln Center to be completed, was designed by Eero Saarinen and Jo Mielziner. In January it was announced that Elia Kazan and Robert Whitehead would be replaced as directors of the company by Herbert Blau and Jules Irving of the San Francisco Actors' Workshop. *Danton's Death* and the company's second production, William Wycherley's *The Country Wife,* were harshly criticized as badly acted and ineptly staged.

Oct. 28 Eero Saarinen's steel **Gateway Arch** in St. Louis, Mo., the year's most awesome architectural project, was topped out. The 630-ft. parabolic arch commemorated the Louisiana Purchase and the city's role in westward expansion. It was part of the 40-block Jefferson National Expansion Memorial along the city's riverfront. The Spanish Pavilion from the New York World's Fair was to be reconstructed near the arch.

Nov. 17 The **Ford Foundation** announced a grant of $3,200,000 to the New York City Ballet and the New York City Opera to help finance productions at the New York State Theater in Lincoln Center.

| Business and Industry; Science; Education; Philosophy and Religion | III | | IV | Sports; Social Issues and Crime; Folkways; Fashion; Holidays |

study the effects on humans of living underwater and to conduct equipment tests.

Oct. 21 The **Nobel Prize in Physics** was awarded jointly to Richard P. Feynman of the California Institute of Technology, Julian S. Schwinger of Harvard University, and Shinichero Tomonaga of Tokyo Education University in Japan for their work in quantum electrodynamics.

Oct. 21 The **Nobel Prize in Chemistry** was awarded to Robert Burns Woodward of Harvard University for his work in synthesizing complex organic compounds.

Nov. 10 An **aluminum price increase** of 2% planned by Alcoa, the largest producer in the U.S., and three other companies was rescinded after the government announced it would sell some of its aluminum stockpile.

Dec. 4 **Gemini 7**, piloted by Lt. Col. Frank Borman and Commander James A. Lovell, Jr., was launched from Cape Kennedy on a 14-day, 206-orbit mission and rendezvous in space with Gemini 6.

Dec. 5 The **Federal Reserve Board raised the discount rate**—the amount charged its 6235 commercial bank members for borrowing funds—from 4% to 4½%, the highest rate in 35 years, in an effort to stabilize prices and counter inflation.

Dec. 7 In a major **communications merger**, International Telephone and Telegraph announced it would acquire the American Broadcasting Company, contingent on the approval of stockholders and federal agencies. The new company would have more than $1,800,000,000 in assets and would outrank the Radio Corporation of America and its NBC subsidiary.

Dec. 15 **Gemini 6,** piloted by Capt. Walter Schirra and Maj. Thomas Stafford, was launched. It made the first successful space rendezvous, with Gemini 7, some 185 miles above Earth. During its 14-orbit flight, it came within six feet of Gemini 7 and traveled in close formation with the sister ship.

Oct. 6–14 The 62nd annual **World Series** was won by the Los Angeles Dodgers (NL), defeating the Minnesota Twins (AL) four games to three. In the seventh game, on Oct. 14, Sandy Koufax pitched his second World Series shutout, blanking the Twins 2–0.

Oct. 17 The **New York World's Fair closed** after two years, drawing its largest crowd, 446,953, on the last day. The final days of the fair were marred by vandalism and looting by souvenir hunters. In its two-year run, the fair had the largest total attendance of any international exposition in history, 51,607,037, but not the predicted 70,000,000. Declared an "artistic, cultural, and educational success" by Robert Moses, president of the fair corporation, it was a financial disappointment; backers faced a return of 39 cents on the dollar of the $30,000,000 they had invested.

Nov. 17 **William D. Eckert** was elected baseball commissioner. He succeeded Ford Frick, who retired after having held the post since 1952.

Nov. 22 **Muhammad Ali** stopped ex-champ Floyd Patterson in the 12th round of what had been billed as a fight for the heavyweight championship. Although the bout had been set up by Jim Deskin, new head of the World Boxing Association, that organization afterward classified Ali as merely the top contender for the crown the WBA had given to Ernie Terrell on Mar. 5.

Dec. 24 The engagement of **Luci Baines Johnson,** daughter of Pres. Lyndon B. Johnson, to Patrick John Nugent, an airman in the Air National Guard, was announced.

Dec. 26 The **AFL football championship** was won by the Buffalo Bills, who defeated the San Diego Chargers 23–0.

Dec. 26 In an **NFL Western Conference playoff,** the Green Bay Packers defeated the Baltimore Colts 13–10 in sudden death overtime. The Packers went on to play the Cleveland Browns for the league title on Jan. 2, 1966.

1966

Steadily escalating participation in the Vietnamese war resulted in 5008 U.S. troop deaths and 30,093 wounded in 1966, bringing total casualties since Jan. 1, 1961, to 6664 killed and 37,738 wounded. By the end of the year, the U.S. had almost 400,000 troops in Southeast Asia. Among the antiwar demonstrations were the International Days of Protest (Mar. 25–27), during which parades and rallies were held in seven U.S. and seven foreign cities. The proposed budget for fiscal 1967 set expenditures at $112,800,000,000, with a predicted deficit of $1,800,000,000, the smallest in seven years. Congress turned down the administration's proposed civil rights bill, largely because of its open housing provisions, but it did pass measures giving the government a major role in determining automobile and highway safety standards, in attacking urban decay, and in controlling air and water pollution. Notables who died this year included Christian A. Herter, secretary of state under Pres. Eisenhower from 1959 to 1961, Dec. 30, at 71; and Chester W. Nimitz, commander in chief of the U.S. Pacific fleet during World War II, Feb. 20, at 80.

Jan. 17 Robert C. Weaver was unanimously confirmed as secretary of the newly created Department of Housing and Urban Development. He was the first black to hold a Cabinet position.

Jan. 17 A military aircraft collision involving a U.S. B-52 bomber and a KC-135 jet tanker over Spain's Mediterranean coast killed seven of the 11 men aboard the planes. The B-52 was refueling. Four hydrogen bombs fell from the B-52, three on land. The fourth bomb was recovered from the Mediterranean Sea on Apr. 7.

Jan. 29–31 The worst blizzard in 70 years struck an area stretching from North Carolina to New England, killing 165 people.

Jan. 31 Pres. Johnson announced resumption of bombing raids on North Vietnam. They had been suspended on Dec. 24. The bombing had been halted in hope of furthering negotiations, but no move toward peace had been made by North Vietnam.

Feb. 8 The Declaration of Honolulu, which formulated major U.S. and South Vietnamese political and military policy in South Vietnam and stressed economic and social reform, was issued following a three-day conference in Hawaii between Pres. Johnson and Premier Nguyen Cao Ky of South Vietnam.

Feb. 21 The first air strike against North Vietnam since the Jan. 31 resumption of bombing was made against a training center at the old French military base at Dien Bien Phu.

Feb. 22 Operation White Wing, a month-long search and destroy mission by more than 20,000 U.S., South Vietnamese, and South Korean troops in Quang Ngai

American theater this year offered a number of literate and entertaining productions. The strongest of these appeared to be the musicals, among them *Mame* and *Cabaret*. One of the year's highlights was the Broadway revival of Hal Holbrook's one-man show *Mark Twain Tonight!*. The New York City Opera moved into its new home in the Lincoln Center for the Performing Arts. The Metropolitan Opera announced in December that its two-year-old touring company, the Metropolitan Opera National Company, would be disbanded in 1967 for financial reasons. Among the year's top motion pictures were *Who's Afraid of Virginia Woolf?*; *Dr. Zhivago*; *Torn Curtain*, Alfred Hitchcock's 50th film; and *Thunderball*, the fourth of the James Bond films and a box office smash. By the time the fall television season began, nearly all network shows were being broadcast in color. Nearly half the 11,000,000 TV sets sold this year were color sets. In architecture, the use of steel and glass in conservatively designed structures continued to be the rule. The leader in this trend was Ludwig Mies van der Rohe. Notables who died in 1966 included Russel Crouse, playwright, Apr. 3, at 73; Walt Disney, pioneer in motion picture animation, Dec. 15, at 65; Hans Hofmann, abstract expressionist, Feb. 17, at 85; Buster Keaton, comedian, Feb. 1, at 69; Kathleen Norris, novelist, Jan. 18, at 85; Maxfield Parrish, painter, Mar. 30, at 95; Billy Rose, theatrical producer, Feb. 10, at 66; Mari Sandoz, novelist, Mar. 10, at about 65; Delmore Schwartz, poet, July 11, at 52; Deems Taylor, composer and music critic, July 3, at 80; Sophie Tucker, the Last of the Red Hot Mamas, Jan. 13, at about 79; and Ed Wynn, comedian and actor, June 19, at 79.

Among books published this year was *In Cold Blood* by Truman Capote. Described as nonfiction, the book employed fictional techniques to recreate the 1959 murder of a farm family in Holcomb, Kans. The book became a best seller. Other books published this year included *The Embezzler* by Louis Auchincloss, a novel; *Tai-Pan* by James Clavell, a novel about Japan in the mid-nineteenth century; *Papa Hemingway* by A. E. Hotchner, a biography; *Rush to Judgment* by Mark Lane, one of a spate of books criticizing the investigation of the Kennedy assassination; *The Fixer* by Bernard Malamud, a novel; *Valley of the Dolls* by Jacqueline Susann, a novel that critics hated but readers turned into a runaway best seller; and *Ariel* by Sylvia Plath, a collection of poems that further increased the posthumous recognition of the poet, a suicide in 1963.

Jan. 18 The first federal performing arts grant, an emergency grant of $100,000 from the National Council on the Arts, enabled the American Ballet

Business and Industry; Science;   **III**   **IV**   **Sports; Social Issues and Crime;**
Education; Philosophy and Religion   **Folkways; Fashion; Holidays**

1966

The movement for school integration showed signs of division, as did the entire civil rights movement. Pacifist followers of the Southern Christian Leadership Conference of Martin Luther King, Jr., differed with militants such as Stokely Carmichael of SNCC and Floyd McKissick of CORE. Carmichael and others used the term *black power* which, depending on the context of its use, meant anything from blacks taking control of their own political and economic destinies to the destruction of western capitalism. A corollary catch phrase, *white backlash,* came into use to describe the vocal and sometimes violent reaction to this emerging militancy and to continuing efforts by local and federal governments to end discrimination in education, housing, and jobs. Proposals to end de facto school segregation by redrawing district lines and busing children to and from black neighborhoods provoked bitter controversy. At the same time, the Gemini space program came to a successful conclusion, and NASA began preparations for Apollo, a program to put U.S. astronauts on the moon. Notables who died this year included Gilbert H. Grosvenor, longtime president of the National Geographic Society, Feb. 4, at 90; and Sebastian Spering Kresge, founder of the S. S. Kresge store chain, Oct. 18, at 99.

Jan. 1   The **first New York City transit strike** began the same day John V. Lindsay took office as mayor. Monumental traffic jams developed as people used autos to get to work. Morning and evening crowds on the streets gave New York the air of a city of refugees. The strike ended Jan. 13.

Feb. 9   The **New York Stock Exchange** reached the peak of a three-and-one-half-year bull market as the Dow Jones industrial average hit an all-time high of 995. A downturn in stock prices for most of the rest of the year set market analysts to worrying about a recession. A low of 744 was reached Oct. 7.

Mar. 16   **Gemini 8,** manned by astronauts Neil Armstrong and David Scott, was launched and made the first successful space docking, closing on its target vehicle after a six-and-one-half-hour chase. A yaw thruster rocket on the Gemini malfunctioned, throwing the connected crafts into a frightening tumble and bringing the projected 71-hour flight to an end in less than 11 hours.

Mar. 22   An **apology to Ralph Nader** was made by General Motors president James Roche before the Senate Subcommittee on Traffic Safety for spying into Nader's private life. Nader's 1965 book *Unsafe at Any Speed* had singled out models of GM's Corvair as dangerous.

Southpaw Sandy Koufax made the Los Angeles Dodgers pay $130,000 for the use of his pitching arm for the season. He demonstrated its worth by winning 27 games and the National League pennant for his club, even though he had to take cortisone shots before each game for his arthritic arm. But the Baltimore Orioles swept the World Series in four straight games. After the season Koufax retired. The San Francisco Giants' Willie Mays hit 37 home runs for a career total of 542, second only to Babe Ruth's 714. Muhammad Ali consolidated his world heavyweight boxing championship by beating five contenders, the last being Cleveland Williams at the Houston Astrodome (Nov. 14) before 34,420 spectators, largest indoor crowd in boxing history. In golf the top money winners were Billy Casper, $121,944, and Kathy Whitworth, $33,517. In fashion the year's rage was the miniskirt, which put hemlines four or five—and occasionally a daring seven—inches above the knee. This year also saw a fad for paper throwaway clothes, especially inexpensive one-wearing dresses. The use of drugs became a national phenomenon, with the emphasis on LSD and other hallucinogens. The word *psychedelic,* first used to describe such drugs or their effects in the 1950s, came into popular use. The high priest of LSD was Timothy Leary, a psychologist fired from Harvard in 1963. Notables who died this year included James "Sunny Jim" Fitzsimmons, active in horse racing for 78 years, Mar. 11, at 91; Hedda Hopper, born Elda Furry, the Hollywood gossip columnist, Feb. 1, at 75; Tony Lema, golfer, July 24, at 32; Margaret Sanger, the pioneer in family planning, Sept. 6, at 82; and Abe Saperstein, founder of the Harlem Globetrotters, Mar. 15, at 63.

Jan. 1   In **college football bowl games,** the results were LSU 14, Arkansas 7 in the Cotton Bowl; Alabama 39, Nebraska 28 in the Orange Bowl; UCLA 14, Michigan State 12 in the Rose Bowl; and Missouri 20, Florida 18 in the Sugar Bowl. This season the AP poll chose Alabama the national collegiate champions of 1965; the UPI poll selected Michigan State.

Jan. 2   The 1965 **NFL championship** was won by the Green Bay Packers, who defeated the Cleveland Browns 23–12.

Jan. 29   **U.S. figure skating championships** were won by Peggy Fleming, women's singles; Scott Allen, men's singles; Cynthia and Ronald Kauffman, pairs; Kristin Fortune and Dennis Sveum, dance.

Province in South Vietnam, ended after enemy resistance collapsed. Communist troop deaths were reported at 1130.

Mar. 2 **U.S. troop strength in Vietnam** was reported by Sec. of Defense Robert S. McNamara to have reached 215,000. Another 20,000 U.S. troops were said to be on the way.

Mar. 7 The **Voting Rights Act of 1965** was unanimously upheld by the Supreme Court.

Mar. 10 A **Green Beret camp was overrun** by about 2000 North Vietnamese troops after a 72-hour siege. About 200 U.S. and South Vietnamese troops were killed or captured at the Special Forces base in the Ashau Valley.

Mar. 25 **Poll taxes** were declared unconstitutional by the Supreme Court on grounds that they represented an economic barrier to voting.

Apr. 12 **B-52 strategic bombers** were used for the first time on targets in North Vietnam.

Apr. 23 **North Vietnamese aircraft** for the first time attacked U.S. aircraft flying over North Vietnam.

May 1 The **first intentional shelling of Cambodian targets** occurred when U.S. artillery fired on forces attacking U.S. troops operating along the Caibac R.

May 15 In an **antiwar demonstration in Washington,** **D.C.,** more than 10,000 persons picketed the White House. At a rally at the Washington Monument, 63,000 voters' pledges to vote only for antiwar candidates were displayed.

May 30 In the heaviest **air raids on North Vietnam** to date, more than 300 U.S. planes bombed targets. On May 31 an important North Vietnamese arsenal was virtually destroyed by U.S. bombers.

June 1–2 The **White House Conference on Civil Rights,** attended by 2400 persons, adopted resolutions urging Congress to pass the administration's proposed civil rights bill. The conference also asked for more effective enforcement of existing civil rights laws, more federal support for establishing civilian review boards to hear charges of police brutality, and more protection by the FBI in racially troubled areas. Floyd McKissick, national director of the Congress of Racial Equality (CORE), termed the conference a hoax. Stokely Carmichael, chairman of the Student Nonviolent Coordinating Committee (SNCC), refused to attend.

June 3–13 A major battle was fought in **Kontum province,** in the Central Highlands of South Vietnam. No figures on U.S. casualties were announced.

June 6 **James Meredith was shot** and wounded while on a lone march from Memphis, Tenn., to Jackson, Miss., to encourage black voter registration. On June 26 groups from across the country joined with Meredith to complete the march, which was highlighted by a debate between Martin Luther King, Jr., the leading

Theater to open its season at the New York State Theater at Lincoln Center for the Performing Arts in New York City.

Feb. 2 *Wait Until Dark* by Frederick Knott, a drama about a blind woman terrorized by gangsters in her home, opened at the Ethel Barrymore Theater in New York City.

Feb. 22 The **New York City Opera,** presenting its first performance in its new home, the New York State Theater in Lincoln Center, gave the Argentinian composer Alberto Ginastera's *Don Rodrigo* its North American premiere.

Mar. 15 **National Book Awards** were presented for the following: fiction, *The Collected Stories of Katherine Anne Porter;* history and biography, *A Thousand Days* by Arthur M. Schlesinger, Jr.; arts and sciences, *Paris Journal of 1944–1965* by Janet Flanner; poetry, *Buckdancer's Choice* by James Dickey. A special citation honored Flannery O'Connor, who died in 1964.

Mar. 15 **Grammy Awards** were presented for the following: best album of 1965, *September of My Years* by Frank Sinatra; best record, "A Taste of Honey" by Herb Alpert; best male vocalist, Frank Sinatra for "It Was a Very Good Year"; best female vocalist, Barbra Streisand for *My Name Is Barbra;* best group, the Anita Kerr Singers for *We Dig Mancini.*

Mar. 21 In a major **censorship** ruling, the Supreme Court upheld the obscenity conviction of Ralph Ginzburg, publisher of *Eros* and other erotica, principally because the materials were advertised with the "leer of the sensualist." In past obscenity cases the Court had considered the material itself, rather than the circumstances of its production and promotion. At the same time, the Court reversed a Massachusetts ruling that the eighteenth-century novel *Fanny Hill* was obscene, by granting that it was not without "redeeming social value."

Apr. 16 At the end of the last performance of the **Metropolitan Opera** in its venerable house at Broadway and 39th St. in New York City, performers and audience joined hands and sang "Auld Lang Syne." The fabulous gold curtain later was cut into small patches and packaged with souvenir recordings of the occasion. A committee was formed to preserve the old house but failed to prevent its demolition.

Apr. 18 **Academy Awards** were presented to *The Sound of Music* as the outstanding motion picture of 1965; to Lee Marvin as best actor for *Cat Ballou;* to Julie Christie as best actress for *Darling;* to Martin Balsam as best supporting actor for *A Thousand*

| Business and Industry; Science; Education; Philosophy and Religion III | | IV Sports; Social Issues and Crime; Folkways; Fashion; Holidays |

Apr. 6 Cesar Chavez's **National Farm Workers Union,** which had started a strike against California grape growers Sept. 8, 1965, scored its first victory when it was recognized as the bargaining agent for farm workers of Schenley Industries, a major grower.

Apr. 13 A major **jet aircraft order** was announced by Pan American Airways. The order was for 25 new Boeing 747 jet transports to be delivered in 1969. The huge craft was designed to carry up to 500 passengers. As other lines put in orders for the 747 during the year, concern was voiced about airport congestion, safety factors, and fare wars.

Apr. 24 The **longest newspaper strike** in a major city began. Fearing loss of jobs as a result of a merger of three ailing New York City papers—the *World-Telegram and Sun,* the *Journal-American,* and the *Herald Tribune*—the Newspaper Guild struck the new World-Journal-Tribune Inc. The strike lasted until Sept. 11.

May 13 **Federal funding for education** was denied to 12 school districts in the deep South, the first such action against violators of the desegregation guidelines of the 1964 Civil Rights Act.

May 17 The **Gemini 9** launch was postponed because of the failure of an Atlas booster rocket to launch an Agena target vehicle into orbit.

June 2 **Surveyor 1,** launched May 30, made the first U.S. soft landing on the moon after a flight of 231,483 miles in 63 hrs., 36 min. It immediately began televising pictures of the moon's surface; by July 14, when its batteries went dead, it had sent more than 11,000 back to Earth. Shots of indentations made by the craft's legs showed that the surface was strong enough to support an astronaut.

June 3 **Gemini 9,** manned by astronauts Thomas Stafford and Eugene Cernan, was successfully launched and attempted to rendezvous with a target vehicle orbited several hours earlier. The astronauts found the target vehicle's nose shroud only partially detached, gaping open like the "jaws of an angry alligator" and making docking impossible. On the second day of the flight, Cernan spent a record 2 hrs., 5 min. in a space walk, but found his equipment so troublesome that he terminated his extravehicular activity early. Gemini 9 splashed down on June 6 after 70 hrs., 20 min. aloft.

July 1 The **Medicare** insurance program for the elderly was inaugurated. The new health plan, condemned by some as the first step toward socialized medicine, covered the cost of care in hospitals and, after Jan. 1, 1967, in nursing homes.

Feb. 27 At the **world figure skating championships** in Davos, Switzerland, Peggy Fleming won the women's singles title.

Mar. 12 **Bobby Hull** of the Chicago Black Hawks scored his 51st hockey goal of the season against the New York Rangers in Chicago. Hull thus became the first player to score more than 50 in a season; he later ran the total to 54.

Mar. 12 Jockey **Johnny Longden,** 59, retired after 40 years of racing and after riding his 6,032nd winner—the most ever for a jockey—in the San Juan Capistrano Handicap at Santa Anita.

Mar. 19 The **NCAA basketball championship** was won by Texas Western College, which defeated Kentucky 72–65.

Apr. 11 The **Masters golf tournament** was won for the third time by Jack Nicklaus, who became the first person to win two years in a row.

Apr. 17–28 The **NBA basketball championship** was won by the Boston Celtics, who beat the Los Angeles Lakers four games to three, thus enabling coach Red Auerbach to retire with his eighth successive championship. Auerbach was replaced by Bill Russell, Celtic center, the first black to coach a major U.S. sports team.

Apr. 19 The 70th **Boston Marathon** was won by Kenji Kimihara of Japan with a time of 2 hrs., 17 min., 11 sec.

Apr. 24–May 5 The **NHL Stanley Cup** was won by the Montreal Canadiens, who defeated the Detroit Red Wings four games to two for their second consecutive NHL championship.

May 7 The 92nd annual **Kentucky Derby** was won by Kauai King, with a time of 2:02. The jockey ws Donald Brumfield.

May 21 The 91st annual **Preakness Stakes** was won by Kauai King, with a time of 1:55²/₅. The jockey was Donald Brumfield.

May 30 At the 50th annual **Indianapolis 500** auto race, nearly half of the 33 starters were involved in a first-lap crash, but only one driver was hurt. Graham Hill led the six finishers, completing the course in 3 hrs., 27 min., 52.53 sec., for an average speed of 144.317 mph.

advocate of nonviolence, and Stokely Carmichael and Floyd McKissick, militant advocates of political confrontation.

June 11 U.S. troop strength in Vietnam would be increased by 18,000 within 45 days, Sec. of Defense McNamara reported, bringing total troop strength to 285,000. U.S. dead since Jan. 1 were placed at 2100.

June 13 In the landmark case of *Miranda v. Arizona,* the U.S. Supreme Court ruled that the provision in the Fifth Amendment to the Constitution against self-incrimination applied to police interrogation of a criminal suspect. Among other guidelines, the Court specified that suspects must be told they have the right to have a lawyer present while being questioned and that, if suspects choose to make a confession without a lawyer and are subsequently put on trial, the prosecution must prove that the defendants understood their rights when they confessed.

June 29 Hanoi and Haiphong were bombed for the first time in the Vietnam War. Oil storage and loading installations, highways, railroads, bridges, and ships were attacked. Approximately two-thirds of North Vietnam's oil supply was destroyed within a week.

July 14 Eight student nurses were murdered in Chicago in what was called the crime of the century. A ninth nurse escaped by rolling under a bed. On July 26 Richard Speck, 24, was indicted for the crimes. He was convicted Apr. 15, 1967.

July 30 The demilitarized zone (DMZ) separating North and South Vietnam was bombed by U.S. planes for the first time.

Aug. 1 In what was called the Texas tower massacre, Charles J. Whitman, 25, barricaded himself in a tower at the University of Texas at Austin, Tex., and shot and killed 13 and wounded 31 before police killed him. Earlier he had killed his wife and mother.

Aug. 4 The highest monthly draft call since the Korean War, 46,200 for October, was announced by the Defense Department.

Aug. 6 Demonstrations against the Vietnam War were held across the country on the anniversary of the atomic bombing of Hiroshima in 1945. In Washington, D.C., pickets demonstrated in front of the White House and the church where Pres. Johnson's daughter Luci was being married. In New York City 5000 marched to Times Square. On Aug. 9, the anniversary of the atomic bombing of Nagasaki, 200 demonstrators attempted a sit-in at the New York office of the Dow Chemical Company, a manufacturer of napalm.

Sept. 18–24 U.S. weekly casualties in the Vietnam War hit a record 970: 142 killed, 825 wounded, 3 missing. During the same period South Vietnamese losses were 98 killed, 280 wounded, 71 missing.

Sept. 23 Aerial defoliation of areas immediately south of the Demilitarized Zone (DMZ) between North and

Clowns; and to Shelley Winters as best supporting actress for *A Patch of Blue.*

May 2 Pulitzer prizes were awarded for the following: fiction, *The Collected Stories of Katherine Anne Porter;* biography, *A Thousand Days* by Arthur M. Schlesinger, Jr.; history, *The Life of the Mind in America* by Perry Miller; general nonfiction, *Wandering Through Winter* by Edwin Way Teale; poetry, *Selected Poems* by Richard Eberhart.

May 22 Emmy Awards were presented to Cliff Robertson as best actor for "The Game," presented by *Chrysler Theatre;* Simone Signoret as best actress for "A Small Rebellion," from *Chrysler Theatre;* Bill Cosby as best actor in a dramatic series for *I Spy;* and Barbara Stanwyck as best actress in a dramatic series for *The Big Valley.*

May 24 *Mame,* a musical by Jerome Lawrence, Robert E. Lee, and Jerry Herman based on Lawrence and Lee's play *Auntie Mame,* in turn based on a book by Patrick Dennis, opened at the Winter Garden Theater in New York City. Angela Lansbury starred.

June 16 Tony Awards for the 1965–1966 season were presented for the following: best play, *Marat/Sade* by Peter Weiss; best musical, *Man of La Mancha* by Dale Wasserman, Mitch Leigh, and Joe Darion; best actor in a drama, Hal Holbrook for *Mark Twain Tonight!;* best actress in a drama, Rosemary Harris for *The Lion in Winter.*

Aug. 6 The Actor's Workshop of San Francisco was disbanded. The resident company had generated excitement and controversy for 14 years.

Sept. 16 The Metropolitan Opera inaugurated its 84th season and its new house in Lincoln Center for the Performing Arts with Samuel Barber's *Antony and Cleopatra,* which was commissioned for the occasion. The backstage facilities and acoustics were rated excellent; the new opera and the nondescript architecture and decor were barely praised. Practically everyone, however, loved the murals by Marc Chagall and the elegant crystal chandeliers that graced the foyer.

Sept. 28 The new home of the Whitney Museum of American Art was inaugurated in New York City. The building, designed by Marcel Breuer and Associates, was a five-story granite structure with the shape of an inverted, stepped pyramid at the front. The building featured a sunken sculpture garden, and its exterior featured seven apparently randomly placed trapezoidal windows.

| Business and Industry; Science; Education; Philosophy and Religion | III | | IV | Sports; Social Issues and Crime; Folkways; Fashion; Holidays |

July 10 Martin Luther King, Jr., at a huge rally in Soldiers Field, Chicago, demanded that the city end discrimination in housing, schools, and jobs, and stop police brutalities. The city had a riot-torn summer.

July 18 **Gemini 10,** manned by astronauts John Young and Michael Collins, was successfully launched and docked in space with an Agena target vehicle. Both astronauts suffered eye irritation when lithium hydroxide leaked from their life-support system. Gemini 10 splashed down on July 21 in full view of TV cameras after a 71-hour flight.

Aug. 8 The **first successful artificial heart pump,** a left ventricle bypass, was installed in a patient at Methodist Hospital in Houston, Tex., by a team headed by heart surgeon Michael DeBakey. It was removed ten days later.

Aug. 10 **Lunar Orbiter 1,** designed to photograph possible landing sites on the moon, was launched from Cape Kennedy. It went into lunar orbit on Aug. 14 and televised 215 pictures. On Oct. 29 it was crashed into the moon, lest its radio signals interfere with Lunar Orbiter 2, scheduled for launch on Nov. 6.

Aug. 15 The **New York *Herald Tribune,*** strikebound since Apr. 24, closed permanently. The paper had been formed in 1924 by a merger of the New York *Herald* (founded in 1835 by James Gordon Bennett) and the New York *Tribune* (founded in 1841 by Horace Greeley).

Aug. 22 The **Consumer Price Index** hit a record high in July, making 1966 the most inflationary year since 1957.

Sept. 12 **Gemini 11,** manned by astronauts Charles Conrad and Richard Gordon, was successfully launched and docked with an Agena target vehicle. On Sept. 14 the joined crafts achieved a record altitude of 851 miles. Gemini 11 landed Sept. 15, its descent controlled entirely by on-board instruments—a space first.

Sept. 12 The New York *World Journal Tribune,* formed by a merger of three defunct dailies, published its first edition in New York City, one day after the end of the newspaper strike, which had begun on Apr. 24.

Sept. 22 **Surveyor 2,** launched two days earlier, crashed into the moon as attempts to correct its tumbling flight failed.

Oct. 7 **Stock prices** hit the year's low, with the Dow Jones industrial average down to 744 from a February high of 995. It was the worst decline since the one-day crash of May 28, 1962.

June 4 The 98th annual **Belmont Stakes** was won by Amberoid, with a time of 2:29³/₅. The jockey was Bill Boland.

June 8 A **merger** of the National and American football leagues, effective in 1970, was announced. The move provided for a common draft of college players in 1967, putting an end to costly competition between the leagues. It also set up a Super Bowl game between the league champions of the 1966–1967 season.

June 19 The **LPGA golf tournament** was won by Kathy Whitworth.

June 20 The **U.S. Open golf tournament** was won by Billy Casper, who beat Arnold Palmer in a playoff.

July 2 At the **Wimbledon** tennis championships in England, Billie Jean King beat Maria Bueno of Brazil to win the women's singles championship.

July 2–3 The **world decathlon record** of 8089 points, held by C. K. Yang, was bested twice at Salina, Kans., by Russ Hodge (8130) and Bill Toomey (8234).

July 3 The **U.S. Women's Open golf tournament** was won by Sandra Spuzich.

July 9 **Jack Nicklaus** won the British Open, joining Gene Sarazen, Ben Hogan, and Gary Player as the only men to have won the four major golf championships of the world. (The other events are the PGA, Masters, and U.S. Open.)

July 12 The **baseball All-Star Game** was won by the National League, which defeated the American League 2–1 in the tenth inning.

July 16–17 At a long awaited **five-nation swimming meet** in Moscow, the U.S. won 11 of the 17 events. The U.S.S.R. won the other six.

July 17 A new **record for the mile run,** 3:51.3, was set by Jim Ryun, a 19-year-old college freshman, trimming 2.3 sec. from the world record.

July 24 The **PGA golf tournament** was won by Al Geiberger.

July 25 The **Baseball Hall of Fame** inducted two new members: Charles Dillon "Casey" Stengel, who had managed the New York Yankees to ten American

South Vietnam had begun, the U.S. military command announced, to deprive infiltrating North Vietnamese of protective cover.

Oct. 5 The **conviction of Jack Ruby** for the 1963 murder of Lee Harvey Oswald, alleged assassin of Pres. John F. Kennedy, was reversed by the Texas Court of Appeals on the grounds of improperly submitted evidence.

Oct. 13 The heaviest **air strike on North Vietnam** to date was made by 173 U.S. bombers. The next day 175 bombers renewed the raid. On Oct. 15 it was announced that 403 U.S. planes and three helicopters had been lost over North Vietnam since Feb. 7, 1965.

Oct. 15 A bill creating the **Department of Transportation,** the 12th Cabinet department, was signed by Pres. Johnson.

Oct. 17 Pres. Johnson began a **17-day Far East tour.** The 26,000-mile trip included stops in Samoa, New Zealand, and Australia before the president attended a seven-nation conference in the Philippines on Vietnam. After a stop at Cam Ranh Bay, South Vietnam, he visited Thailand, Malaysia, and South Korea, returning to the U.S. on Nov. 2.

Oct. 18 **Twelve firemen were killed** in New York City and nine more were injured in a fire that destroyed an old commercial building. It was the worst disaster in the fire department's 100-year history.

Oct. 26 A **fire at sea** on the U.S. carrier *Oriskany,* in the Gulf of Tonkin, killed 43 men and injured 16.

Nov. 8 In **congressional elections** the Republicans gained three Senate seats and 47 House seats, but the Democrats still held a 64–36 Senate majority and a 248–187 House majority. One of the new Republican senators was Edward W. Brooke of Massachusetts, the first black elected to the Senate since Reconstruction.

Oct. 2 In Houston, Tex., the handsome **Jesse H. Jones Hall for the Performing Arts** was inaugurated with a week of concerts. The new theater and concert hall were designed to accommodate audiences of from 1800 to 3000. The foyer was graced with a pair of sculptures by Richard Lippold entitled *Gemini II.* It was part of a projected $40,000,000 arts and entertainment complex.

Oct. 12 *The Visitation,* the first opera by the American composer Gunther Schuller, received 50 curtain calls at its world premiere in Germany by the Hamburg State Opera. The work, a blend of jazz and atonal music, dealt with the persecution of a black in the South.

Oct. 30 In a bizarre **art theft,** a phone call led police to Chicago's Grant Park and to a trash can containing an Italian Renaissance painting just stolen from the Chicago Art Institute. It was Correggio's *Madonna, Child, and St. John,* valued at $500,000.

Nov. 2 It was announced that **Leonard Bernstein,** music director of the New York Philharmonic for a decade, would retire from that post in 1969 and become laureate conductor.

Nov. 5 *The Fantasticks* became the longest-running musical in New York theater history. The off-Broadway production surpassed the previous record run of 2717 performances set by *My Fair Lady.*

Nov. 20 *Cabaret,* a musical by Joe Masteroff, John Kander, and Fred Ebb based on the play *I Am a Camera* by John van Druten, which was in turn based on sketches by Christopher Isherwood, opened at the Broadhurst Theater in New York City.

1967

By mid-November this year, more than 17,000 Americans had died in Vietnam since 1961, 2000 more in the first ten months of 1967 than in the period 1961–1966. U.S. and UN efforts to achieve peace were entirely unsuccessful, with UN Secretary General U Thant asserting that the impasse was caused by the U.S. bombing of North Vietnam. In South Vietnam, in the first election since the 1963 coup, Nguyen Van Thieu and Nguyen Cao Ky were elected president and vice president amid charges of election fraud. At home, Pres. Johnson got a $69,900,000,000 defense appropriation for the 1967–1968 fiscal year, the largest single appropriation ever passed by Congress. But he was

The most important art news this year was the effort to save the cultural treasures damaged by a flood that struck Florence, Italy, on Nov. 4, 1966. U.S. art conservationists and concerned nonprofessionals volunteered their services, and many organizations helped raise money for salvage and restoration work. In theater, the 1966–1967 season was marked by scarcity of good new plays. Welcome visitors from abroad were the Old Vic, which began a 17-week tour of the U.S. in January; and the Jewish State Theater of Poland, which began a U.S. tour in October. In popular music a new element, Indian music, as popularized by the sitarist Ravi Shankar, appeared in the work of rock groups, notably the

Business and Industry; Science; Education; Philosophy and Religion III		IV Sports; Social Issues and Crime; Folkways; Fashion; Holidays

Nov. 6 **Lunar Orbiter 2** was launched. On Nov. 17 it went into orbit, photographing possible landing sites along the lunar equator. NASA scientists said that photographs of domelike formations indicated that the moon formerly had volcanic activity.

Nov. 11 **Gemini 12,** manned by astronauts James Lovell and Edwin Aldrin, was successfully launched and rendezvoused with an Agena target vehicle. This was the last mission of the Gemini program. On Nov. 12 the astronauts took pictures of a solar eclipse. Aldrin spent a total of five and a half hours in extravehicular activity, without the fatigue and equipment difficulties that had marked earlier Gemini flights. Gemini 12 landed safely on Nov. 15.

Nov. 11 A **merger vote** approved the joining in 1968 of the Methodist Church, with 10,000,000 members, and the Evangelical United Brethren Church, with 750,000 members, to form the United Methodist Church, the largest U.S. Protestant church. The move was subject to ratification by members of both sects.

Nov. 18 **Abstinence from meat on Fridays** would no longer be required of U.S. Roman Catholics, except during Lent. The change became effective Dec. 2.

Dec. 3 Pres. Johnson visited the **Armistad Dam,** a $78,000,000 joint U.S.-Mexican project located between the two countries. He had a four-hour meeting with Pres. Gustavo Díaz Ordaz of Mexico.

Dec. 10 The **Nobel Prize in Chemistry** was awarded to Robert S. Mulliken of the University of Chicago for his work on the chemical bond of atoms in a molecule.

Dec. 10 The **Nobel Prize in Physiology or Medicine** was awarded jointly to Charles B. Huggins of the University of Chicago and Francis Peyton Rous, a member emeritus of the Rockefeller Institute, in recognition of their pioneer discoveries of the causes of specific types of cancer.

League pennants and seven World Series wins from 1949 to 1960; and Theodore S. "Ted" Williams, former outfielder for the Boston Red Sox and six-time American League batting champion.

Aug. 23 The newly formed **North American Soccer League** elected James P. McGuire as its president. This year the league increased the number of its franchises to 11 teams, and planned its first games for 1968.

Sept. 10 The **Miss America** title was won by Jane Anne Jayroe, 19, from Oklahoma, at the annual pageant in Atlantic City, N.J.

Sept. 11 The **U.S. Lawn Tennis Association singles championships** were won by Fred Stolle of Australia in the men's division and Maria Bueno of Brazil in the women's division.

Sept. 25 The **LPGA golf tournament** was won by Gloria Ehret, who beat Mickey Wright by three strokes.

Oct. 5–9 The 63rd annual **World Series** was won by the Baltimore Orioles (AL), who swept the Los Angeles Dodgers (NL) in four straight games, the last three being shutouts.

Nov. 19 In the **collegiate football game of the year,** the undefeated teams of Michigan State and Notre Dame battled to a 10–10 tie at East Lansing, Mich.

Nov. 28 **Truman Capote,** celebrating the success of his "nonfiction novel" *In Cold Blood,* threw a party at New York's Plaza Hotel. It was the year's social sensation.

1967

The space program suffered a setback when three astronauts were killed in a fire while taking their Apollo vehicle through tests at Cape Kennedy, Fla. Space exploration news was not all bad. The U.S. made three successful soft landings on the moon to obtain data about the lunar surface and possible landing sites for manned flights. Mariner 5 sent back information about the atmosphere of Venus, and the new Saturn 5 rocket, the world's largest launch vehicle, orbited Earth in a test to determine its use for eventual manned flights to the moon. The economy showed signs of vigor despite civil unrest in U.S. cities. School integration progressed, but campus violence continued, a reminder that change is

In baseball the Boston Red Sox outfielder Carl Yastrzemski led the American League in three batting categories. He finished the year with an average of .326, batted in 121 runs, and tied Harmon Killebrew in home runs, 44 for the season. The Kansas City Athletics moved to Oakland for the 1968 season, and the American League decided to expand to 12 teams in 1969 by creating a new Kansas City franchise and awarding a franchise to Seattle. The NFL granted a franchise to the New Orleans Saints, and split the league into two conferences and four divisions: Eastern Conference (Century and Capitol divisions) and Western Conference (Central and Coastal divisions). This year the AFL and

unsuccessful in his request for an income tax surcharge that he said was needed to fight the war, to conduct the Great Society programs, and to fight inflation. Congress passed bills providing for increased Social Security benefits, aid to education, and antipoverty funds. Administration legislation requests included the smallest appropriation for foreign aid in 20 years, a Civil Rights Act that would end discrimination in housing by 1969 and prevent discrimination in selecting juries, and revision of the Selective Service System through substitution of a lottery to select draftees. In what was called the long hot summer, the U.S. suffered the worst race riots in its history, with trouble in no fewer than 100 American cities. Notables who died this year included John Nance Garner, vice president of the United States from 1933 to 1941, Nov. 7, at 98; and Jack Ruby, convicted killer of Lee Harvey Oswald, alleged assassin of Pres. John F. Kennedy. Ruby died in Dallas, Tex., Jan. 3, at 55, while awaiting retrial after his conviction was overturned.

Jan. 10 **Lester Maddox,** the Georgia restaurant owner who made headlines in 1964 by passing out ax handles to white customers to prevent desegregation of his eatery, was sworn in as governor of Georgia.

Jan. 16 The **first black southern sheriff** since Reconstruction, former paratrooper Lucius Amerson, was sworn in at Tuskegee, Ala.

Jan. 27 A 63-nation **space demilitarization treaty** was signed by the U.S. and the U.S.S.R. The treaty prohibited the orbiting of nuclear weapons and forbade territorial claims on celestial bodies. It became effective on Oct. 10.

Feb. 10 The **Twenty-fifth Amendment** to the U.S. Constitution, providing for presidential succession, took effect when Nevada became the 38th state to ratify it.

Feb. 13 The **National Student Association** admitted that it had secretly received more than $3,000,000 from the CIA between 1952 and 1966 for use in its overseas programs.

Mar. 1 Rep. **Adam Clayton Powell,** Democrat of New York, was denied his seat in the 90th Congress by a vote of 307 to 116. This was the third time the House had taken such action against a duly elected member. A committee investigating Powell's activities found that he had "wrongfully and willfully" misused approximately $46,000 of government money for private purposes and had "improperly maintained" his wife on his office payroll.

Mar. 28 UN Secretary General U Thant revealed that a **general truce in Vietnam** proposed by him, and talks preparatory to a reopening of the Geneva conference, had been rebuffed by the North Vietnamese. The U.S. and South Vietnam had accepted his plan with qualifications.

Beatles, whose new album *Sgt. Pepper's Lonely Hearts Club Band* also showed signs of the growing influence of the drug culture. Notables who died this year included John Coltrane, jazz musician and composer, July 17, at 40; Nelson Eddy, singer and movie actor, Mar. 6, at 65; Mischa Elman, violinist, Apr. 5, at 76; Woodrow Wilson "Woody" Guthrie, folk singer, Oct. 3, at 55; Edward Hopper, realist painter, May 15, at 84; Langston Hughes, poet and writer, May 22, at 65; Bert Lahr, comedian and actor, Dec. 4, at 72; Henry R. Luce, founder of *Time* and *Life,* Feb. 28, at 68; Carson McCullers, writer, Sept. 29, at 50; Paul Muni, actor, Aug. 25, at 71; Dorothy Parker, writer, June 7, at 73; Claude Rains, actor, May 30, at 77; Basil Rathbone, actor, July 21, at 75; Carl Sandburg, poet, biographer, and folklorist, July 22, at 89; Alice B. Toklas, longtime companion of Gertrude Stein, Mar. 7, at 89; Spencer Tracy, actor, June 10, at 67; and Paul Whiteman, king of jazz, Dec. 29, at 77.

Among **books published** this year was *The Death of a President* by William Manchester, about the assassination of Pres. Kennedy. The Kennedy family had sought to halt publication on the grounds that they had not given final approval of the manuscript, as had been agreed with the author. The book was published after the Kennedys won the right to delete from it some particularly sensitive material. Other books published this year included *Tales of Manhattan* by Louis Auchincloss, short stories; *The Arrangement* by Elia Kazan, a novel; *Death at an Early Age* by Jonathan Kozol, dealing with conditions in ghetto schools; *Rosemary's Baby* by Ira Levin, a shocker that was the basis for an enormously successful movie; *The Medium Is the Message* by Marshall McLuhan and Quentin Fiore, a study of the impact of technology and communication on society; *Nicholas and Alexandra* by Robert K. Massie, a biography of the last czar and czarina of Russia; *The Complete Poems of Marianne Moore; The Instrument* by John O'Hara, a novel; *The Chosen* by Chaim Potok, a first novel that became a best seller; *The Confessions of Nat Turner* by William Styron, a novel based on an 1831 slave revolt; and *Pulitzer* by W. A. Swanberg, a biography.

Jan. 5 *The Homecoming,* a play by Harold Pinter, opened at the Music Box Theater in New York City.

Jan. 31 In Seattle, famed Metropolitan Opera tenor **Giovanni Martinelli,** 81, agreed to stand in for a performer with laryngitis. He sang the role of the aged emperor Altoum in Giacomo Puccini's *Turandot.*

Feb. 14 A retrospective show of more than 200 works by **Andrew Wyeth** opened at the Whitney Museum of American Art in New York City. There, and at museums in other cities where it was shown, the exhibit

rarely easy. Notables who died this year included Henry Kaiser, industrialist, Aug. 24, at 85; J. Robert Oppenheimer, nuclear physicist known as the father of the atomic bomb, Feb. 18, at 62; and Francis Cardinal Spellman, archbishop of New York, Dec. 2, at 78.

Jan. 15 The Commerce Department announced that the **gross national product** had risen by 5.4% in 1966.

Jan. 27 A **launch pad fire** during Apollo tests at Cape Kennedy, Fla., killed astronauts Virgil I. "Gus" Grissom, Edward H. White II, and Roger B. Chaffee. An investigation concluded that a faulty electrical wire was the probable cause.

Feb. 3 **Walter P. Reuther,** head of the United Auto Workers, resigned from the executive council of the AFL-CIO in a widening split between Reuther and AFL-CIO president George Meany.

Feb. 4 **Lunar Orbiter 3** was launched from Cape Kennedy, Fla., on its 92-hour mission to the moon. The spacecraft relayed pictures of possible landing sites for manned space vehicles.

Mar. 7 **James R. Hoffa,** president of the International Brotherhood of Teamsters, began an eight-year prison sentence for jury tampering after the Supreme Court refused to review his 1964 conviction.

Mar. 10 The **New York Stock Exchange** had the second greatest trading day to date, surpassed only by Oct. 29, 1929.

Mar. 29 **Complete school desegregation** no later than the fall term was ordered for six southern states by the U.S. Court of Appeals for the Fifth Circuit. The states affected were Alabama, Florida, Georgia, Louisiana, Mississippi, and Texas.

Apr. 2 A report on **school desegregation** by the Southern Education Reporting Service stated that 16% of black students in 11 southern states were attending desegregated schools in 1967, an increase of 10% over 1966.

NFL played the first Super Bowl game, the World Series of professional football. In boxing Muhammad Ali continued to support his claim to be the greatest of all time by successfully defending the world heavyweight crown against Ernie Terrell in a 15-round decision (Feb. 6) and Zora Folley in a seventh-round knockout (Mar. 22). When Ali refused to be drafted into the Army on religious grounds, the World Boxing Association again stripped him of his title. In golf the top money winners were Jack Nicklaus, $188,998, and Kathy Whitworth, $32,937. In fashion there was little new, but women began to wear maxis, which were ankle-length coats, over their miniskirts. A British model, named Twiggy caused a sensation with her closely cropped hair and tomboyish appeal. Notables who died this year included James E. "Jimmy" Foxx, a great hitter with a lifetime record of 534 home runs, July 21, at 59; John J. "Johnny" Keane, of the St. Louis Cardinals, Jan. 6, at 55; and Reese "Goose" Tatum, of the Harlem Globetrotters, Jan. 18, at 45.

Jan. 2 In **college football bowl games,** the results were Georgia 24, SMU 9 in the Cotton Bowl (Dec. 31, 1966); Florida 27, Georgia Tech 12 in the Orange Bowl; Purdue 14, Southern California 13 in the Rose Bowl; and Alabama 34, Nebraska 7 in the Sugar Bowl. This year the AP and UPI polls selected Notre Dame the national collegiate champions of 1966.

Jan. 15 The first annual **Super Bowl** was won by the Green Bay Packers (NFL), who defeated the Kansas City Chiefs (AFL) 35–10. The Packers had won the NFL championship Jan. 1 by beating the Dallas Cowboys 34–27. The same day the Chiefs won the AFL championship over the Buffalo Bills, 31–7.

Jan. 18 Albert De Salvo, self-confessed **Boston strangler,** who allegedly murdered 13 women between June 1962 and Jan. 1964, was sentenced to life imprisonment for armed robbery, assault, and sex offenses. For lack of evidence, he was not tried for the murders.

Jan. 18–21 **U.S. figure skating championships** were won in Omaha, Nebr., by Peggy Fleming, women's singles; Gary Visconti, men's singles; Cynthia and Ronald Kauffman, pairs; Lorna Dyer and John Carrell, dance.

Feb. 2 Formation of the **American Basketball Association** (ABA), a second pro basketball league, with former NBA star George Mikan as commissioner, was

Mar. 31 The first **U.S.-U.S.S.R. consular treaty** since the Russian Revolution was signed by Pres. Johnson.

Apr. 4 Military authorities announced that the **500th U.S. plane** had been shot down over North Vietnam since bombing began in 1964.

Apr. 12–14 The 18-nation **Presidents of America Conference** in Punta del Este, Uruguay, was attended by Pres. Johnson and Sec. of State Dean Rusk. The conference issued a declaration calling for a Latin American common market by 1970, improved transportation and communications facilities, increased efforts to boost trade earnings, and elimination of unnecessary military spending.

Apr. 15 In an **antiwar demonstration** in New York City, some 100,000 to 400,000 persons marched from New York's Central Park to UN headquarters. A similar protest in San Francisco drew about 50,000.

Apr. 20 The North Vietnamese port city of **Haiphong was bombed** by U.S. planes, which destroyed two power plants and struck at North Vietnamese Mig airfields for the first time.

Apr. 21 **Svetlana Aliluyeva,** daughter of Joseph Stalin, the late premier of the U.S.S.R., arrived in New York City after receiving political asylum at the U.S. Embassy in New Delhi, India.

Apr. 21 **Tornadoes** in northeastern Illinois killed 55 people and injured 1000.

May 13 A **pro-Vietnam demonstration,** an eight-hour parade in New York City to show support for U.S. troops in Vietnam, drew about 70,000 participants.

May 19 The **first U.S. air strike on central Hanoi,** North Vietnam's capital, was launched by U.S. planes.

June 1 **U.S. casualties in Vietnam** for the week of May 21–27 were reported as 313 killed and 2616 wounded, the greatest weekly casualty toll of the war.

June 5 In a **terrorist attack in Tierra Amarilla,** N.Mex., a band of Mexican-Americans seized the county courthouse, wounded two policemen, took two hostages, and freed 11 prisoners held for unlawful assembly. The rebels were members of the Political Confederation of Free City States, which sought to reclaim some 2500 sq. mi. of northern New Mexico that the Spanish crown had allegedly granted to their forebears. Most of the rebels were later captured.

June 8 The **U.S. communications ship** *Liberty* was attacked by Israeli torpedo boats and planes in international waters 15 miles north of the Sinai Peninsula; 34 seamen were killed and 75 were wounded. Israel apologized for the accidental attack.

June 12 State laws forbidding **interracial marriages** were ruled unconstitutional by the U.S. Supreme Court.

June 23 and 25 Ten hours of **U.S.-Soviet talks at Glassboro,** N.J., were held by Pres. Johnson and Premier Aleksei Kosygin. Kosygin had headed his

attracted record crowds. A few critics found Wyeth's style too objective, but most praised the evocative studies created by the most popular living U.S. painter.

Feb. 15 Formation of the **American National Opera Company,** a new opera touring group, was announced. The company was organized, with the help of a grant from the National Council on the Arts, to fill the gap left by the foundering of the Metropolitan Opera's touring group. In the fall the new company began its first tour with productions of Verdi's *Falstaff,* Puccini's *Tosca,* and Alban Berg's *Lulu.*

Feb. 20 The **National Gallery of Art** announced it had bought Leonardo da Vinci's *Ginevra dei Benci* from the prince of Liechtenstein. The price was said to be between $5,000,000 and $6,000,000.

Feb. 22 *MacBird* by Barbara Garson opened at the Village Gate in New York City. A fierce political satire, it dealt with contemporary figures, particularly Pres. Johnson and his family, in a parody of Shakespeare's *Macbeth.*

Mar. 2 **Grammy Awards** were presented for the following: best record of 1966, "Strangers in the Night" by Frank Sinatra; best male vocalist, Frank Sinatra for "Strangers in the Night"; best female vocalist, Eydie Gorme for "If He Walked into My Life"; best group, the Anita Kerr Singers for "A Man and a Woman."

Mar. 3 **National Book Awards** were presented for the following: fiction, *The Fixer* by Bernard Malamud; poetry, *Nights and Days* by James Merrill; history and biography, *The Enlightenment* by Peter Gay; arts and letters, *Mr. Clemens and Mark Twain* by Justin Kaplan; science, philosophy, and religion, *La Vida* by Oscar Lewis.

Mar. 17 The opera *Mourning Becomes Electra* by Marvin David Levy, adapted from the Eugene O'Neill play, was given its world premiere by the Metropolitan Opera. Critics found its music uninteresting.

Mar. 26 **Tony Awards** for the 1966–1967 season were presented for the following: best play, *The Homecoming* by Harold Pinter; best musical, *Cabaret* by Joe Masteroff, John Kander, and Fred Ebb; best actor in a drama, Paul Rogers for *The Homecoming;* best actress in a drama, Beryl Reid for *The Killing of Sister George.*

Apr. 10 **Academy Awards** were presented to *A Man for All Seasons* as the outstanding motion picture of 1966 and to its star, Paul Scofield, as best actor; to Elizabeth Taylor as best actress for *Who's Afraid of*

| Business and Industry; Science; Education; Philosophy and Religion | III | | IV | Sports; Social Issues and Crime; Folkways; Fashion; Holidays |

Apr. 17 Surveyor 3 was successfully launched from Cape Kennedy, Fla. The second U.S. spacecraft to make a soft landing on the moon, it studied the lunar surface and sent back more than 6300 pictures.

May 5 The New York *World Journal Tribune* ceased publication. The afternoon daily, which started up Sept. 12, 1966, had been piling up deficits at the rate of $700,000 a month.

May 10–11 **Riots at Jackson State College,** a black college in Jackson, Miss., were reported. The trouble began when two black policemen arrested a speeding motorist on campus. One person was killed and two wounded before National Guardsmen restored order.

May 11 Ceremonies marking installation of the **100,000,000th telephone** in the U.S. were attended by Pres. Johnson and representatives of the Bell System and the U.S. Independent Telephone Association. The U.S. had approximately half the telephones in the world.

May 22 The **Confession of 1967** was adopted by the General Assembly of the Presbyterian Church in the U.S., the first major new confession by the Presbyterians since the Westminster Confession of 1647.

May 29 A **California property law** giving owners "absolute discretion" in housing rental or sales was ruled unconstitutional by the U.S. Supreme Court on the grounds that it was discriminatory and violated the Fourteenth Amendment.

June 14 An eight-day **maritime strike** by merchant marine deck officers began, tying up shipping in Atlantic and Gulf Coast ports.

June 14 **Mariner 5** was successfully launched toward Venus.

June 19 De facto **school segregation in Washington, D.C.,** was ordered ended by autumn by U.S. District Judge J. Skelly Wright.

announced. The new league, with 11 teams, failed to lure stars from the NBA.

Feb. 28–Mar. 4 At the **world figure skating championships** in Vienna, Austria, Peggy Fleming fell during her freestyle event but went on to win the women's singles title for the second year in a row.

Mar. 25 The **NCAA basketball championship** was won for the third time in four years by undefeated UCLA, which beat Dayton 79–64. UCLA's center, sophomore Lew Alcindor, had an all-time high season field goal percentage of .667 in this, his first varsity year.

Apr. 9 The **Masters golf tournament** was won by Gay Brewer.

Apr. 14–24 The **NBA basketball championship** was won by the Philadelphia 76ers, who defeated the San Francisco Warriors four games to two.

Apr. 19 The 71st annual **Boston Marathon** was won by Dave McKenzie of New Zealand in a record 2 hrs., 15 min., 45 sec.

Apr. 20–May 2 The **NHL Stanley Cup** was won by the Toronto Maple Leafs, who beat the Montreal Canadiens four games to two.

May 6 The 93rd annual **Kentucky Derby** was won by Proud Clarion, with a time of 2:00⅗. The jockey was Bob Ussery.

May 14 New York Yankee outfielder **Mickey Mantle** hit his 500th career home run at Yankee Stadium, becoming the sixth player to reach that mark.

May 20 The 92nd annual **Preakness Stakes** was won by Damascus, with a time of 1:55⅕. The jockey was Willie Shoemaker.

May 31 The 51st annual **Indianapolis 500** auto race, started on May 30 and postponed by rain after 18 laps, was won by A. J. Foyt, completing the course in 3 hrs., 18 min., 24.22 sec. for an average speed of 151.207 mph. Andy Granatelli's turbine-engine car, driven by Parnelli Jones, allowed in the race over protests by owners of piston cars, led until the final three laps, when its transmission failed.

nation's delegation to the UN during its attempt to have Israel branded the aggressor in the Six Day War (June 5–10) against Egypt, Syria, and Jordan.

June 30 The **General Agreement on Tariffs and Trade** (GATT), the result of four years of negotiations begun during the Kennedy administration, was signed in Geneva by the U.S. and 45 other nations.

July 2–7 U.S. Marines at **Con Thien,** just south of the DMZ in South Vietnam, suffered heavy casualties in fierce fighting with North Vietnamese units.

July 12–17 A **race riot** in Newark, N.J., left 26 dead and more than 1300 injured before police and National Guard troops restored order.

July 19 A **midair collision** near Hendersonville, N.C., of a private plane and a Boeing 727 killed 82 persons.

July 22 It was announced that **U.S. troop strength in Vietnam** was to be increased to 525,000 by the end of 1968.

July 23 **Puerto Rico voted to remain a commonwealth** of the U.S. Some 60.5% of the votes cast rejected statehood or full independence.

July 23 The **worst race riot** in U.S. history erupted in Detroit, Mich., killing 43 people and causing some $200,000,000 in damage in five days of violence.

July 29 An **aircraft carrier fire** aboard the U.S.S. *Forrestal* in the Gulf of Tonkin, caused by a punctured fuel tank, killed 134 people and injured 62.

Aug. 21 The Defense Department announced that **two U.S. Navy jets had been shot down** over the People's Republic of China after straying off course from a bombing mission over North Vietnam.

Aug. 24 The draft of a **nuclear nonproliferation treaty,** sponsored by the U.S. and U.S.S.R., was presented to the 18-member UN Disarmament Committee meeting in Geneva.

Aug. 25 **George Lincoln Rockwell,** 49, leader of the American Nazi Party, was shot to death in Arlington, Va. John C. Patler, his former aide, was arrested for the shooting.

Sept. 1–Oct. 4 A siege of the U.S. Marine base at **Con Thien,** just south of the DMZ in South Vietnam, raged for more than a month before U.S. firepower forced North Vietnamese gunners to withdraw from their artillery positions in the DMZ.

Sept. 28 **Walter Washington** was sworn in as commissioner of the District of Columbia, the first black to head a major city government.

Oct. 2 **Thurgood Marshall** was sworn in as the first black Supreme Court justice in U.S. history.

Oct. 3 A 10% **tax surcharge** requested by Pres. Johnson was shelved by the House Ways and Means Committee.

Oct. 14 North Vietnamese **mistreatment of U.S. prisoners of war,** in violation of the 1949 Geneva Convention, was charged by the U.S.

Virginia Woolf?; to Walter Matthau as best supporting actor for *The Fortune Cookie;* and to Sandy Dennis as best supporting actress for *Who's Afraid of Virginia Woolf?.*

Apr. 15 **Thomas Hoving,** former parks commissioner for New York City, became director of the Metropolitan Museum of Art at age 36. Hoving had also been curator of the museum's medieval collection at the Cloisters.

Apr. 26 A new **art auction record** was set by David Mann, a New York City art dealer, who bought Pablo Picasso's painting *Mother and Child* at Sotheby's in London for $532,000, the highest price ever paid for a work by a living artist.

May 1 **Pulitzer prizes** were awarded for the following: fiction, *The Fixer* by Bernard Malamud; biography, *Mr. Clemens and Mark Twain* by Justin Kaplan; history, *Exploration and Empire* by William H. Goetzmann; general nonfiction, *The Problem of Slavery in Western Culture* by David Brion Davis; poetry, *Live or Die* by Anne Sexton; drama, *A Delicate Balance* by Edward Albee.

May 19 The world premiere of ***Bomarzo,*** the second opera by the Argentinian composer Alberto Ginastera, was presented by the Opera Society of Washington, D.C. The work had been banned in Buenos Aires, the composer's home city, because the mayor found it "obsessed with sex and violence."

June 4 **Emmy Awards** were presented to Peter Ustinov as best actor for *Barefoot in Athens;* Geraldine Page as best actress for *A Christmas Memory;* Bill Cosby as best actor in a dramatic series for *I Spy;* and Barbara Bain as best actress in a dramatic series for *Mission: Impossible,* which was also voted best dramatic series.

June 16 A major **art gift** was made by New York City art dealer Sidney Janis, who gave his $2,000,000 collection of modern art, 100 works by 54 artists, to New York City's Museum of Modern Art.

June 25 The **first global TV broadcast,** *Our World,* originated live from 19 countries on five continents, and was seen in 39 nations via satellite.

July 27 The **Santa Fe** (N.Mex.) **Opera House** was destroyed by fire just after the opening of its summer season. Enough sets, costumes, and scores were saved to enable the company to continue the season in a high school gym.

Aug. 15 A steel **sculpture by Pablo Picasso,** designed as a gift to the city of Chicago, was unveiled in the

July 5   The **American Telephone and Telegraph Company** was ordered by the FCC to decrease its rates for long-distance and overseas telephone service by $120,000,000 a year.

July 17   **Surveyor 4,** launched from Cape Kennedy on July 14 and programed to land in Sinus Medii in the center of the near side of the moon, lost radio contact with Earth moments before it landed.

July 26   A three-month strike by the **United Rubber Workers** ended when the union signed three-year contracts with the nation's largest tire manufacturers. One of the companies, Firestone, announced price increases on July 31.

Aug. 30   A **price increase** of 1.8% for steel bars was announced by Republic Steel Corporation. By Sept. 1, six other steel producers announced price hikes.

Sept. 6   A strike was called by the **United Auto Workers** against the Ford Motor Company, idling 159,816 workers as the UAW-Ford contract expired. Contracts with General Motors and Chrysler expired at the same time but UAW members reported for work. The union sought a 6% wage hike and extensive fringe benefits. The strike ended on Oct. 25, with workers accepting a new three-year contract.

Sept. 8   **Surveyor 5** was launched from Cape Kennedy and made a soft landing on the moon 65 hours later. By Sept. 24 it had transmitted a total of 18,006 pictures to Earth along with other important information.

Sept. 11   A **teacher strike** in New York City public schools began on the opening day of school. The strike ended Sept. 29, after the teachers won more than $135,000,000 in pay hikes over a 26-month period.

Oct. 18   The **Nobel Prize in Physiology or Medicine** was awarded jointly to Dr. Haldan Keffer Hartline of Rockefeller University, Dr. George Wald of Harvard University, and Dr. Ragnar Granit of Sweden for research on the eye and its transmission of sensory information to the brain.

June 3   The 99th annual **Belmont Stakes** was won by Damascus, with a time of 2:28⁴/₅. The jockey was Willie Shoemaker.

June 18   The **U.S. Open golf tournament** was won by Jack Nicklaus with a score of 275, one stroke better than the record set by Ben Hogan in 1948.

June 20   **Muhammad Ali** was given a five-year sentence and fined $10,000 for refusing to be drafted into the Army. Boxing authorities had earlier stripped him of his world title, rejecting his claim to exemption as a minister of the Nation of Islam.

June 23   A new **world record for the mile** was set by Jim Ryun, who shaved two-tenths of a second from his old record with a run of 3:51.1 in the AAU championships at Bakersfield, Calif. At the same meet, Paul Wilson cleared 17 ft. 7¾ in., a new world record for the outdoor pole vault.

July 2   The **U.S. Women's Open golf tournament** was won by amateur Catherine Lacoste.

July 8   At the **Wimbledon** tennis championships in England, Billie Jean King swept the women's singles; the women's doubles, with Rosemary Casals; and the mixed doubles, with Owen Davidson of Australia.

July 9   The **LPGA golf tournament** was won by Kathy Whitworth.

July 11   The **baseball All-Star Game** was won by the National League, which defeated the American League 2–1 in 15 innings, the longest all-star game ever played.

July 14   **Eddie Mathews** of the Houston Astros became the seventh player to hit 500 home runs.

July 23–Aug. 6   At the fifth **Pan-American Games** in Winnepeg, Canada, the U.S. won the unofficial team championship, taking 120 gold medals.

July 24   The **PGA golf tournament** was won by Don January in a playoff with Don Massengale.

| Exploration and Settlement; Wars; Government; Civil Rights; Statistics **I** | **II** Publishing; Arts and Music; Popular Entertainment; Architecture; Theater |

Oct. 20 Seven **Ku Klux Klan members were convicted** of conspiracy in the 1964 murders of three civil rights workers, James Chaney, Andrew Goodman, and Michael Schwerner, in Mississippi. The federal jury acquitted eight others and could reach no verdict on three others.

Oct. 21–22 An **antiwar march in Washington, D.C.,** drew some 50,000 participants. At least 647 were arrested, most after a clash with police and troops at the Pentagon.

Oct. 26 **Cancellation of draft deferments** of college students who violated draft laws or interfered with recruiting was ordered by Lewis Hershey, director of the Selective Service.

Oct. 28 **El Chamizal,** a 437-acre border area separated from Mexico in the 1850s when the Rio Grande changed its course, was officially returned to Mexico during ceremonies in El Paso, Tex., attended by Pres. Johnson and Pres. Gustavo Díaz Ordaz of Mexico.

Oct. 30–Nov. 4 A North Vietnamese assault on **Loc Ninh,** on the Cambodian border about 90 miles north of Saigon, was broken after six days by U.S. artillery and air strikes. The attack on the town and the U.S. Special Forces camp there was unusually determined, possibly because the communists wanted a victory to offset the Oct. 31 inauguration of Nguyen Van Thieu as president of South Vietnam.

Nov. 7 **Carl B. Stokes,** a Democrat, was elected the first black mayor of Cleveland, Ohio, the eighth largest city in the U.S.

Nov. 20 The U.S. **population** reached 200,000,000, despite the lowest yearly birthrate in history, 17.8 per 1000.

Nov. 22 **Hill 875** near Dak To, about 40 miles north of Kontum in west central South Vietnam, was taken by U.S. Army forces after a 19-day battle, one of the bloodiest of the Vietnam War.

Dec. 5 More than 1000 **antiwar protesters** attempted to close down a New York City induction center. Among the 264 arrested were Dr. Benjamin Spock and the poet Allen Ginsberg.

Dec. 15 A **collapse of the Silver Bridge** on the Ohio R. between Point Pleasant, W.Va., and Kanauga, Ohio, killed 46 people. The collapse occurred during rush hour.

Dec. 20 U.S. **troop strength** in Vietnam reached 474, 300.

plaza of Chicago's Civic Center. The untitled work, usually referred to as "Chicago's Picasso," stood 50 feet high, weighed 163 tons, and was said by some to resemble a winged baboon.

Oct. 11 A **Picasso exhibit** of 275 sculptures, assembled and shown in Paris in honor of the artist's 85th birthday in 1966, opened at New York City's Museum of Modern Art.

Oct. 16 *Rosencrantz and Guildenstern Are Dead,* a play by Tom Stoppard starring Brian Murray and John Wood, opened at the Alvin Theater in New York City.

Oct. 18 The **La Scala Opera Company,** in its first appearance in the U.S., sang Verdi's *Requiem* at Carnegie Hall in New York City.

Nov. 7 A law creating the **Corporation for Public Broadcasting,** a nonprofit public corporation to aid noncommercial television, was signed by Pres. Johnson.

Nov. 12 A revival of *Hello, Dolly!* by Michael Stewart and Jerry Herman, featuring an all-black cast headed by Pearl Bailey and Cab Calloway, opened at the St. James Theater in New York City.

Nov. 13 *Hair* by James Rado, Gerome Ragni, and Galt MacDermot, described as "an American tribal love-rock musical," was given its New York premiere by the New York Shakespeare Festival off Broadway at the Public Theater.

Dec. 6 At a seminar on **art forgery** at New York City's Metropolitan Museum of Art, the museum revealed that one of its most prized pieces was a forgery. It was an elegant statue of a horse, estimated to be 2400 years old when it was acquired in 1923 and since then widely reproduced in casts and used as an illustration in many books on Greek art. A gamma-ray shadowgraph confirmed that the forgery had been cast by a technique developed in the fourteenth century but was probably no more than 50 years old.

Dec. 7 The **New York Philharmonic** celebrated the 125th year of its founding. Leonard Bernstein conducted a program that was a repeat of the orchestra's first program on the same date in 1842.

Oct. 18 The **Nobel Prize in Physics** was awarded to Dr. Hans Albrecht Bethe of Cornell University for his study of energy generation in stars.

Oct. 19 **Mariner 5** passed within 2480 miles of the planet Venus and sent back data indicating that the planet had no magnetic field and that its surface was unfit for human habitation.

Nov. 7 **Surveyor 6** was launched. On Nov. 9 it made a soft landing on the moon and began transmitting pictures and soil analysis data. On Nov. 17 it lifted off the moon's surface and landed a few feet away. Surveyor 6 then took pictures of its original landing site. It was the first spacecraft to lift off the moon.

Nov. 9 The unmanned **Apollo 9** space vehicle completed an 8-hr., 37-min. test orbit of Earth. The capsule was recovered in the Pacific Ocean just ten miles from its target area. It had been launched from Cape Kennedy by the Saturn 5 rocket, the world's largest launch vehicle, designed for eventual manned flights to the moon. It was the first time Saturn 5 was used.

Nov. 15 A **Detroit newspaper strike** began when the *News* was struck by the Teamsters Union. On Nov. 18 the *Free Press* shut down. The strike continued until Aug. 9, 1968.

Dec. 8 Maj. **Robert H. Lawrence, Jr.,** the first black astronaut, was killed in the crash of his F-104 jet at Edwards Air Force Base, Calif.

Dec. 14 **Production of synthetic DNA,** the substance that controls heredity, was announced by biochemists at Stanford University.

July 24 The **Baseball Hall of Fame** inducted Branch Rickey, Charles "Red" Ruffing, and Lloyd Waner.

Sept. 9 The **Miss America** title was won by Debra Dene Barnes, 18, from Kansas, at the annual pageant in Atlantic City, N.J.

Sept. 10 The **U.S. Lawn Tennis Association singles championships** were won by John Newcombe of Australia in the men's division and Billie Jean King in the women's division. King became the first woman to sweep the U.S. and British singles, doubles, and mixed doubles championships since Alice Marble's sweep in 1939.

Sept. 12–18 The **America's Cup** was successfully defended by the U.S. yacht *Intrepid,* which swept the Australian challenger *Dame Pattie* in four straight races.

Sept. 24 Pro **football kicking records** were smashed by Jim Bakken of the St. Louis Cardinals, who scored seven field goals in one game.

Oct. 4–12 The 64th annual **World Series** was won by the St. Louis Cardinals (NL), who defeated the Boston Red Sox (AL) four games to three.

Dec. 9 **Lynda Byrd Johnson,** the older daughter of Pres. Lyndon B. Johnson, was married to Marine Capt. Charles Robb in the White House.

Dec. 31 The **NFL championship** was won by the Green Bay Packers, who defeated the Dallas Cowboys 21–17 with a touchdown scored from the one-yard line by Bart Starr with 13 seconds remaining in the game.

Dec. 31 The **AFL championship** was won by the Oakland Raiders, who routed the Houston Oilers 40–7.

1968

Dissent and doubt regarding the war in Vietnam and the economy at home prompted several Democratic leaders to challenge Pres. Johnson in the run for the presidential nomination, and stimulated the third-party candidacy of George C. Wallace of Alabama. In March, in the wake of the enemy offensive in Vietnam that came to be known as the Tet offensive, Pres. Johnson announced he would not seek another term. Later, the country was shocked by the assassinations of Martin Luther King, Jr., and Sen. Robert F. Kennedy, and by violence surrounding the Democratic National Convention in Chicago. The Republican candidate, Richard M. Nixon, pledging to end the war in Vietnam and restore law and order in the U.S., narrowly won the presidency. Although inflation had become critical, Pres. Johnson's budget was a record $186,000,000,000, with the year's expenditure on Vietnam about $25,000,000,000. In August the U.S.S.R. and other Warsaw Pact forces invaded Czechoslovakia and ended that country's movement toward liberalism. Notables who died this year included Husband Edward Kimmel, commander of the U.S. Pacific Fleet at the time of the Japanese attack on Pearl Harbor in 1941, May 14, at 86; Joseph Martin, Jr., Speaker of the House from 1946–1948 and 1952–1954, Mar. 6, at 83; Norman Thomas, head of the U.S. Socialist Party from 1926–1955, Dec. 19, at 84; and Lurleen Burns Wallace, who in 1966 succeeded her husband George C. Wallace as governor of Alabama, May 7, at 41.

Jan. 5 Indictments for conspiracy to aid and abet draft evasion were handed down against Dr. Benjamin Spock, the eminent pediatrician, the Rev. William Sloane Coffin of Yale, and three other antiwar activists. On June 14 Spock, Coffin, and two others were convicted; the fifth defendant was acquitted.

Jan. 17 In his **State of the Union** message, Pres. Johnson called for a 10% income tax surcharge to reduce the budget deficit estimated at $20,000,000,000 for fiscal 1968 and to curb inflation.

Jan. 21 A nuclear-armed **B-52 bomber crashed** near Greenland. Some radiation was released from its four hydrogen bombs, which broke up in the crash.

Jan. 23 The *Pueblo* incident began when the Navy intelligence ship U.S.S. *Pueblo* was seized off the coast of North Korea by North Korean patrol boats. It was claimed that the *Pueblo* had been caught within North Korean waters. Its crew of 83 were subjected to harsh treatment until their release on Dec. 23.

Jan. 30–Feb. 24 The **Tet offensive,** timed to coincide with the Vietnamese New Year, was a massive assault by enemy forces throughout South Vietnam. U.S. forces were surprised by the scope and size of the operation, whose key targets included Saigon, the

This year several new theatrical companies opened, notably the Negro Ensemble Company and Theatre Atlanta. The motion picture industry adopted a new voluntary film rating code to restrict viewing of inappropriate films by the young. The year in architecture was marked by the opening in Chicago of the John Hancock Building, a 100-story structure crisscrossed with diagonal exterior braces and tapered for stability. Among the notables who died this year were Tallulah Bankhead, stage and screen star, Dec. 12, at 65; Edna Ferber, novelist, Feb. 23, at 78; Dorothy Gish, actress, June 4, at 70; Harold Gray, creator of the *Little Orphan Annie* comic strip, May 9, at 74; Fannie Hurst, novelist, Feb. 23, at 78; Howard Lindsay, playwright, Feb. 11, at 78; Thomas Merton, Trappist monk and writer, Dec. 10, at 53; Charles Münch, conductor of the Boston Symphony from 1949 to 1962, Nov. 6, at 77; Edwin O'Connor, novelist, Mar. 23, at 49; Conrad Richter, novelist, Oct. 30, at 78; Ruth St. Denis, choreographer of modern dance, July 21, at about 90; Upton Sinclair, author, Nov. 25, at 90; John Steinbeck, Nobel Prize–winning author, Dec. 20, at 66; and Walter Wanger, Hollywood producer, Nov. 18, at 74.

Among **books published** this year were two nonfiction works by Norman Mailer. His *The Armies of the Night* was a personal account of the antiwar demonstrations in Washington, D.C., in Oct. 1967 that culminated in a march on the Pentagon. *Miami and the Siege of Chicago* was Mailer's equally personal view of the 1968 political conventions. Other books published this year included *Tell Me How Long the Train's Been Gone* by James Baldwin, a novel; *Lost in the Funhouse* by John Barth, a collection of stories; *A Brand New Life* by James T. Farrell, a sequel to his *Studs Lonigan* trilogy; *The Algiers Motel Incident* by John Hersey, dealing with the murder of three blacks by police during riots in Detroit; *A Small Town in Germany* by John Le Carré, a master of the spy novel; *The Salzburg Connection* by Helen MacInnes, another master of the genre; *The Naked Ape* by Desmond Morris, a nonfiction study of human beings; *The First Circle* and *Cancer Ward* by Alexander Solzhenitsyn, the Russian writer's second and third novels; and *Couples* by John Updike, a novel.

Jan. 17 The respected Boston publishing company of **Little, Brown and Co.** was acquired by Time, Inc., at a price of $17,000,000.

| Business and Industry; Science; Education; Philosophy and Religion | III | | IV | Sports; Social Issues and Crime; Folkways; Fashion; Holidays |

1968

The economy was seriously threatened by inflation, while unemployment remained low, averaging 3.6% of the labor force for the year. A record 9% increase brought the GNP to $860,000,000,000. In April and June William McChesney Martin, chairman of the Federal Reserve Board, warned that unless weaknesses in the economy were corrected, particularly inflation and the balance-of-payments deficit, the nation would face a serious crisis. Following passage of the income tax surcharge bill in June and exercise of fiscal restraints, interest rates dropped. By December, however, the prime rate had risen again, to a record 6.75%. Labor made strong gains, but they were offset in part by inflation and increased taxes. In education, major strikes by teachers hit New York City and Florida. On many campuses college students demanded reforms, including separation of universities from government defense research projects, greater student participation in college administration, increased enrollment of black and impoverished students, and introduction of black-studies programs. Students pressed their demands with calls for strikes, in some cases met by police action. In medicine, new progress was made in organ transplants. Dr. Denton Cooley of Texas, the most successful in the field, performed 17 heart transplant operations. This year Americans noted the deaths of Francis Cardinal Brennan of Philadelphia July 2, at 74; Chester F. Carlson, inventor of xerography, Sept. 19, at 62; Donald L. Hall, who designed the *Spirit of St. Louis,* flown across the Atlantic by Charles A. Lindbergh in 1927, May 2, at 69; Helen A. Keller, who although deaf, blind, and mute from childhood learned to read, write, and speak and became a leader in the drive for educational aid for the handicapped, June 1, at 87; Charles W. Mayo, the son and nephew of the founders of the Mayo Clinic and a noted surgeon, July 28, at 70; and Robert Reynolds "Bob" Jones, founder of Bob Jones University, Jan. 16, at 84.

Jan. 9 **Surveyor 7** made a soft landing on the moon and began sending back data, including photographs. This was the last flight of the Surveyor series.

Jan. 22 The unmanned **Apollo 5** spacecraft was successfully launched into Earth orbit. During the flight its Lunar Excursion Module (LEM) was tested.

Feb. 8 Four days of **student disorder in Orangeburg,** S.C., culminated in the deaths of three black students in a clash between police and students at South Carolina State College. The trouble began when students from the college and nearby Claflin College protested the barring of blacks from a local bowling alley.

In fashion, hemlines remained high, and efforts to introduce the so-called midi length (hemline at midcalf) were unsuccessful. Pantsuits for evening wear, with full flowing lines, gained wide acceptance. More and more men favored bold, extravagant fashions, and both men and women were wearing leather garments. For the first time the Gallup Poll reported that crime ranked number one among the issues that concerned the public. Another serious problem was the rising use of heroin by middle-class and upper-class youths along with an increase in drug abuse throughout American society. In sports, the National League added two new baseball franchises, San Diego and Montreal. Both the National and American leagues formed two divisions, Eastern and Western, with league championships to be determined by five-game playoffs beginning in 1969. In football, the NFL Players Association campaigned for better pensions. In golf there was a split between the PGA and the new American Professional Golfers, with both groups struggling for control of the ever more lucrative tournaments. A compromise agreement was reached on Dec. 13. The year's top golf money winners were Billy Casper, $121,944, and Kathy Whitworth, $48,380. In boxing, Jimmy Ellis became the World Boxing Association champion by outpointing Jerry Quarry in a bout on Apr. 27. New York State, Massachusetts, and Illinois recognized Joe Frazier, who had knocked out Buster Mathis in a title bout on Mar. 4. The new American Basketball Association concluded its first season with a $2,500,000 loss. This year tennis tournaments were opened to professionals as well as amateurs for the first time. Among the notables who died this year were Tommy Bridges, Detroit Tigers pitcher, Apr. 19, at 61; Samuel Earl "Wahoo Sam" Crawford, outfielder for the Detroit Tigers and Cincinnati Reds, June 15, at 88; Lawson Little, golfer, Feb. 1, at 57; Earl Sande, one of racing's most successful jockeys, Aug. 20, at 69; and Jess Willard, world heavyweight boxing champion from 1915 to 1919, Dec. 15, at 86.

Jan. 1 In **college football bowl games,** the results were Texas A&M 20, Alabama 16 in the Cotton Bowl; Oklahoma 26, Tennessee 24 in the Orange Bowl; USC 14, Indiana 3 in the Rose Bowl; and LSU 20, Wyoming 13 in the Sugar Bowl. This season the AP and UPI polls chose USC the national collegiate champions of 1967.

Jan. 14 **Super Bowl II** was won by the Green Bay Packers (NFL), who defeated the Oakland Raiders (AFL) 33–14 for their second Super Bowl victory. Shortly thereafter the Packers' coach, Vince Lombardi, retired to an executive post with the team. The Packers had won the NFL title on Dec. 31, 1967, by

Marine base at Khe Sanh, and the provincial capital Hue. Enemy forces suffered a devastating setback, but the offensive increased antiwar sentiment in the U.S.

Feb. 14 In the *Pueblo* incident, talks intended to resolve the issue began at Panmunjom between the U.S. and North Korea.

Feb. 16 Occupational and graduate-student **draft deferments** were cut back sharply.

Feb. 24 **Hue was recaptured** by U.S. forces in Vietnam.

Feb. 29 The **Kerner Commission report** was released by the President's National Advisory Committee on Civil Disorders. The report condemned racism in the U.S. and called for aid to black communities to avert further racial polarization and violence.

Mar. 12 Sen. **Eugene J. McCarthy** of Minnesota won the majority of convention delegates selected in the New Hampshire Democratic presidential primary. Campaigning on an antiwar platform and aided by student volunteers, McCarthy won 42% of the vote. Although Pres. Johnson won 48% of the vote, McCarthy won 20 of the 24 delegates.

Mar. 13 It was announced that **nerve gas testing** by the Army at Dugway Proving Grounds in Utah might have caused the deaths of some 6400 sheep in the area.

Mar. 28 **Violence in Memphis,** Tenn., erupted during a march led by Dr. Martin Luther King in support of a sanitation workers' strike. One black marcher was killed. Dr. King urged calm as National Guard troops were called to restore order. He promised to return in April to attend another march.

Mar. 31 Pres. **Johnson announced he would not seek the presidency again.** Addressing the nation on television, the president also called for a partial halt to the bombing of North Vietnam and the opening of peace negotiations.

Apr. 4 Dr. **Martin Luther King, Jr., was assassinated** at age 39 by a sniper in Memphis, Tenn. The event was followed by a week of rioting in urban black ghettos. New York City remained calm but Washington, D.C., was seriously disrupted. King's funeral in Atlanta, Ga., on Apr. 9 was attended by an estimated 75,000 people.

Apr. 5 The **siege of Khe Sanh,** site of a U.S. Marine base in Vietnam, was lifted.

Apr. 8 **Operation Complete Victory,** involving 100,000 allied troops in Vietnam, was begun. It aimed to drive enemy forces from the provinces around Saigon.

Apr. 11 The **1968 Civil Rights Act** was signed by Pres. Johnson. Discrimination in housing was made illegal for almost all types of dwellings.

Feb. 15 **Henry Lewis** was appointed director of the New Jersey Symphony, thus becoming the first black in the U.S. to head a major orchestra.

Feb. 29 **Grammy Awards** were presented for the following: best record of 1967, "Up, Up and Away" by the Fifth Dimension; best album, *Sgt. Pepper's Lonely Hearts Club Band;* best male vocalist, Glen Campbell for "By the Time I Get to Phoenix"; best female vocalist, Bobby Gentry for "Ode to Billie Joe"; best group, the Fifth Dimension for "Up, Up and Away."

Mar. 6 **National Book Awards** were presented for the following: fiction, *The Eighth Day* by Thornton Wilder; poetry, *The Light Around the Body* by Robert Bly; history and biography, *Memoirs 1925–1950* by George F. Kennan; arts and letters, *Selected Essays* by William Troy; science, philosophy, and religion, *Death at an Early Age* by Jonathan Kozol. At the awards ceremony Bly turned his check over to a draft protester to dramatize his opposition to the Vietnam War.

Apr. 6 San Antonio, Tex., celebrated its 200th anniversary with the **opening of HemisFair 68,** an attractive world's fair that featured many permanent buildings, including the 622-ft.-high Tower of the Americas, the largest construction of its type since the Eiffel Tower. One of the permanent buildings, the Theater for Performing Arts, opened with a performance of Verdi's *Don Carlo.*

Apr. 10 *George M!,* a musical by Michael Stewart and John and Fran Pascal based on the life of George M. Cohan, opened at the Palace Theater in New York City. It was welcomed as pleasant, nostalgic entertainment.

Apr. 10 **Academy Awards** were presented to *In the Heat of the Night* as the outstanding motion picture of 1967 and to its star, Rod Steiger, as best actor; to Katharine Hepburn as best actress for *Guess Who's Coming to Dinner?;* to George Kennedy as best supporting actor for *Cool Hand Luke;* and to Estelle Parsons as best supporting actress for *Bonnie and Clyde.*

Apr. 16 *The Boys in the Band* by Mart Crowley opened off Broadway at Theater Four. It was well received as a witty, mature, and frank treatment of homosexuality.

| Business and Industry; Science; Education; Philosophy and Religion | III | | IV | Sports; Social Issues and Crime; Folkways; Fashion; Holidays |

Feb. 19 The **first statewide teachers' strike** in U.S. history began when more than half of Florida's public school teachers walked off the job. The strike lasted until Mar. 8.

Mar. 8 Bishop **Terence J. Cooke** was appointed archbishop of New York by Pope Paul VI, succeeding the late Francis Cardinal Spellman. He was formally installed at St. Patrick's Cathedral on Apr. 4.

Mar. 17 A two-tiered **gold price system** was negotiated in Washington, D.C. by representatives of the U.S. and six European nation members of the London Gold Pool. All gold transactions between governments would be at the official price of $35 an ounce, but the private market would be allowed to fluctuate. This resolved a critical rush on gold that had threatened to disrupt the international economy.

Apr. 4 **Apollo 6** was launched in an unmanned mission designed to test, for the second and last time, the Saturn 5 rocket prior to manned flight.

Apr. 23 A **sit-in at Columbia University** was begun by students protesting university plans to build a gymnasium on land used by the neighboring community. The sit-in, involving several university buildings, led to the closing of the university on Apr. 26. On the night of Apr. 30, the police cleared all buildings occupied by the students. In the police action, some 150 students and police were injured. The university did not resume normal operations until the opening of the fall semester.

May 4 The subscription list of the *Saturday Evening Post* would be cut from 6,800,000 to 3,000,000 in an economy move, the Curtis Publishing Company announced. Restricting *Post* subscriptions to areas of high-income consumers was expected to increase revenues by attracting advertisers catering to people of high incomes. The move evoked much humorous publicity as names of unwanted subscribers became known, among them Martin Ackerman, new president of Curtis, and Gov. Winthrop Rockefeller of Arkansas. The device did not save the magazine, which failed early in 1969.

May 16 The **United Auto Workers** were suspended by the **AFL-CIO** for nonpayment of dues. The longstanding split between the two groups culminated in a formal separation in July.

beating the Dallas Cowboys 21–17. The same day the Raiders had clinched the AFL title by beating the Houston Oilers 40–7.

Jan. 18 A **White House luncheon** given by Mrs. Lyndon B. Johnson for a group of nationally influential women was disrupted when actress Eartha Kitt stated with great emotion that it was pointless to discuss remedies for the troubles at home as long as the war in Vietnam continued.

Jan. 19–20 **U.S. figure skating championships** were won by Peggy Fleming, women's singles; Tim Wood, men's singles; Cynthia and Ronald Kauffman, pairs; Judy Schwomeyer and James Sladky, dance.

Feb. 6–18 At the 1968 **Winter Olympics** in Grenoble, France, the unofficial team championship was won by Norway. The U.S. won only one gold medal, the one taken by figure skater Peggy Fleming.

Mar. 2 At the **world figure skating championships** in Geneva, Switzerland, the women's singles title was won for the third straight year by Peggy Fleming. The 19-year-old from Colorado Springs, Colo., then announced her retirement from competitive skating.

Mar. 23 The **NCAA basketball championship** was won by UCLA, which defeated North Carolina 78–55. The day before, UCLA had beaten its archrival, the University of Houston, in the NCAA semifinals.

Apr. 14 The **Masters golf tournament** was won by Bob Goalby after the tournament leader, Roberto de Vicenzo of Argentina, was disqualified for having signed an incorrect scorecard.

Apr. 18–May 4 The **first ABA basketball championship** was won by the Pittsburgh Pipers, who beat the New Orleans Buccaneers four games to three.

Apr. 19 The 72nd annual **Boston Marathon** was won by Ambrose Burfoot, with a time of 2 hrs., 22 min., 17 sec. Burfoot was the first U.S. runner to win the race since 1957.

Apr. 21–May 2 The **NBA basketball championship** was won by the Boston Celtics, who defeated the Los Angeles Lakers four games to two.

May 4 The 94th annual **Kentucky Derby** was won by Dancer's Image, with a time of 2:02¹⁄₅. The jockey was Bob Ussery. Three days later Dancer's Image was disqualified when traces of a pain-killing drug were found in tests, and Forward Pass, ridden by Ismael Valenzuela, was declared the winner. This was the first recalled race in Derby history. Peter Fuller, owner of Dancer's Image, challenged the recall.

Apr. 15 A **shoot to kill** order was issued to Chicago police by Mayor Richard J. Daley in cases of arson, looting, or rioting—an order that was credited with provoking subsequent police violence in August.

May 2 The **Poor People's March on Washington,** planned by Dr. Martin Luther King, Jr., before his death, got under way. It was led by the Rev. Ralph Abernathy. Later in the month some 3000 marchers camped on a muddy site, dubbed Resurrection City, near the Washington Monument.

May 3 Agreement to hold **peace talks in Paris** was reached between the U.S. and North Vietnam.

May 5 Another **major enemy offensive** was launched in South Vietnam against allied strongholds. Although Saigon came under attack from mortar and sniper fire, the assault was judged to be not as severe as the Tet offensive.

May 10 **Peace talks opened** in Paris with W. Averell Harriman representing the U.S. and Xan Thuy representing North Vietnam.

May 29 The U.S. nuclear submarine *Scorpion* was reported missing off the Azores with 99 men aboard.

June 5 Sen. **Robert F. Kennedy was shot** in Los Angeles at 12:15 A.M., shortly after delivering a speech acknowledging his victory in the June 4 California Democratic primary. Sirhan B. Sirhan, a Jordanian, was seized for the shooting. Kennedy died June 6 and Sirhan was indicted for murder on June 7.

June 8 Ex-convict **James Earl Ray was arrested** in London for the murder of Martin Luther King, Jr., on Apr. 4.

June 10 Gen. **William C. Westmoreland** turned over command of U.S. forces in Vietnam to Gen. Creighton W. Abrams. Gen. Westmoreland had been appointed chief of staff by Pres. Johnson on Mar. 22 in a move interpreted as reflecting disappointment with the conduct of the war.

June 13 Chief Justice **Earl Warren submitted his resignation** to Pres. Johnson, effective on the approval of a successor.

June 17 A **ruling against discrimination** in the purchase or lease of property was handed down by the Supreme Court.

June 23 The war in Vietnam became the **longest war in U.S. history.**

June 24 **Resurrection City** in Washington, D.C., was cleared by police, who arrested 124 people after expiration of their camping permit.

June 26 Associate Justice **Abe Fortas was nominated** by Pres. Johnson as chief justice of the Supreme Court.

June 28 The **income tax surcharge bill,** which Congress had tied to a $6,000,000,000 decrease in government spending, was signed by Pres. Johnson.

Apr. 21 **Tony Awards** for the 1967–1968 season were presented for the following: best play, *Rosencrantz and Guildenstern Are Dead* by Tom Stoppard; best musical, *Hallelujah, Baby!* by Jule Stein, Betty Comden, and Adolph Green; best actor in a drama, Martin Balsam for *You Know I Can't Hear You When the Water's Running;* best actress in a drama, Zoe Caldwell for *The Prime of Miss Jean Brodie.* This was the first time the awards ceremony was televised nationally.

May 8 **Pulitzer prizes** were awarded for the following: fiction, *The Confessions of Nat Turner* by William Styron; biography, *Memoirs 1925–1950* by George F. Kennan; history, *The Ideological Origins of the American Revolution* by Bernard Bailyn; general nonfiction, *Rousseau and Revolution* by Will and Ariel Durant; poetry, *The Hard Hours* by Anthony Hecht.

May 15 The **Merce Cunningham Dance Company,** an exciting and respected modern dance group, began its first major season in New York City.

May 19 **Emmy Awards** were presented to Melvyn Douglas as best actor for *Do Not Go Gentle into That Good Night;* to Maureen Stapleton as best actress for *Among the Paths to Eden;* to Bill Cosby as best actor in a dramatic series for *I Spy;* and to Barbara Bain as best actress in a dramatic series for *Mission: Impossible,* which was also voted the best dramatic series.

May 21 **Helen Hayes,** honored as the first lady of the U.S. theater, was given a special Drama Desk Award for her performance in *The Show-Off,* a revival of George Kelly's 1924 comedy produced by the APA-Phoenix Repertory Company.

May 25 The **Gateway Arch** in St. Louis, Mo., designed by Eero Saarinen, was formally dedicated.

June 3 Pop artist **Andy Warhol** was shot and seriously wounded by Valerie Solanis, who had appeared briefly in one of Warhol's films. Later she was judged not mentally competent to stand trial.

June 12 The newly built **Garden State Arts Center** in New Jersey opened with a performance by the

June 13 A new **stock trading record** was set on the New York Stock Exchange, with 2,350,000 shares traded. The marked upsurge in business that had begun in April was attributed to general optimism that the war in Vietnam was coming to an end. The volume of paperwork became so great in this period that, starting on June 12, the exchange closed down trading on Wednesdays.

June 17–July 1 The **chief rabbi of Moscow visited the U.S.** Rabbi Yehuda Leib Levin came with the apparent purpose of convincing U.S. Jews that there was no anti-Semitism in the U.S.S.R. Although he spoke to large groups and was respectfully heard, most Jews remained unconvinced.

July 1 The **United Auto Workers formally separated from the AFL-CIO.** The split followed years of conflict during which UAW head Walter Reuther accused AFL-CIO head George Meany of blocking labor reforms and allowing the movement to stagnate. Three weeks later, the UAW joined with the Teamsters to form the Alliance for Labor Action.

July 4 **Explorer 38,** a giant radio astronomy satellite, was launched into Earth orbit. With its antennas extended, the satellite was 1500 feet in diameter.

July 15 The **first direct U.S.-U.S.S.R. commercial flights began** when a Soviet Aeroflot jet landed at Kennedy Airport in New York City. On the same day, a U.S. commercial jet took off for Moscow.

July 30 A **steelworkers' agreement** was reached between 11 major steel producers and the United Steel Workers of America. The settlement produced an average 6% annual increase in a three-year contract. The next day Bethlehem Steel announced a 5% rise in steel prices.

July 31 A statement on **birth control** was issued by the National Council of Catholic Bishops. It supported Pope Paul VI's encyclical of July 25, which reiterated condemnation of artificial methods of birth control. Nevertheless, some Catholic priests and laymen publicly disagreed with the pope's position.

Aug. 9 The 264-day **Detroit newspaper strike,** which had idled the city's major papers since Nov. 1967, was ended.

Sept. 9 A **New York City teachers' strike** began when public school teachers walked out, protesting school decentralization policies. The conflict centered on

Finally, on Dec. 23, the Kentucky Racing Commission ruled that Dancer's Image had won the race but not the purse.

May 5–11 The **NHL Stanley Cup** was won by the Montreal Canadiens, who swept the St. Louis Blues in four straight games.

May 8 A **perfect baseball game** was pitched by Jim "Catfish" Hunter of the Oakland Athletics, in leading his team to a 4–0 victory over the Minnesota Twins. This was the first American League perfect game since 1922.

May 18 The 93rd annual **Preakness Stakes** was won by Forward Pass, with a time of 1:56⁴/₅. The jockey was Ismael Valenzuela.

May 27 **George Halas,** a leading figure in the National Football League since the 1920s and owner of the Chicago Bears, retired as coach of the Bears.

May 30 The 52nd annual **Indianapolis 500** auto race was won by Bobby Unser, who completed the course in 3 hrs., 16 min., 13.76 sec. for a new record average speed of 152.882 mph.

June 1 The 100th annual **Belmont Stakes** was won by Stage Door Johnny, setting a new track record of 2:27¹/₅. The jockey was Heliodoro Gustines.

June 16 The **U.S. Open golf tournament** was won by Lee Trevino, who beat Jack Nicklaus by four strokes and became the first person in the tournament's history to play all four rounds under par.

June 24 The **LPGA golf tournament** was won by Sandy Post of Canada, who beat Kathy Whitworth in a playoff to become the first non-U.S. player and the first rookie on the LPGA tour to win the event.

July 6 At the **Wimbledon** tennis championships in England, Billie Jean King won the women's singles title for the third straight year. King and Rosemary Casals won the women's doubles title for the second year running.

July 7 The **U.S. Women's Open golf tournament** was won by Susie Maxwell Berning.

July 9 The baseball **All-Star Game** was won by the National League, which beat the American League 1–0.

July 21 The **PGA golf tournament** was won by Julius Boros, who beat Arnold Palmer and Bob Charles by one stroke.

Exploration and Settlement; Wars; Government; Civil Rights; Statistics I		II Publishing; Arts and Music; Popular Entertainment; Architecture; Theater

July 1 The 18-nation **Kennedy Round tariff reduction agreement,** begun when Kennedy was president and concluded in Geneva in May 1967, went into effect for all signatories.

July 1 The **nuclear nonproliferation treaty** was signed by the U.S., U.S.S.R., and 59 other nations, concluding four years of negotiations.

July 23 A **sniper attack** on police in Cleveland, Ohio, initiated four days of rioting, during which four civilians and three policemen were killed.

Aug. 7 **Rioting in Miami,** Fla., broke out in the city's black section. Three people were killed and hundreds injured before National Guard troops could restore order.

Aug. 8 The **Republican National Convention** nominated Richard M. Nixon for the presidency over Gov. Ronald Reagan of California and Gov. Nelson A. Rockefeller of New York. Gov. Spiro T. Agnew of Maryland was nominated for the vice presidency on Aug. 9 at the convention in Miami Beach, Fla.

Aug. 28 John Gordon Mein, U.S. ambassador to Guatemala, was killed by terrorists.

Aug. 29 In Chicago the **Democratic National Convention** nominated Vice Pres. Hubert H. Humphrey for the presidency. Sen. Edmund S. Muskie of Maine was named the vice presidential candidate. The convention, which began Aug. 26, was the most violent in U.S. history. Antiwar protestors clashed with police and national guardsmen. Hundreds of people, including bystanders and members of the press, were beaten by police, some in full view of television cameras.

Oct. 2 Justice **Abe Fortas** asked to be withdrawn from consideration for confirmation as chief justice. The Senate had objected to his advisory services to the president while on the Court.

Oct. 3 George Wallace named his running mate in his third-party bid for the presidency, former Air Force chief of staff Gen. Curtis E. LeMay.

Oct. 31 **Bombing of North Vietnam** was ordered stopped by Pres. Johnson.

Nov. 5 Richard M. Nixon was elected president of the United States, defeating his Democratic opponent Vice Pres. Hubert H. Humphrey in a close race. Spiro T. Agnew, Republican of Maryland, was elected vice president. The electoral vote was Nixon, 302; Humphrey, 191; George C. Wallace, third-party candidate, 45. One Nixon elector later cast his vote for Wallace. The popular vote was Nixon, 31,785,480; Humphrey, 31,275,166; Wallace, 9,906,473. The Republicans gained four seats in the House and five in the Senate, but the Democrats still held majorities of 58–42 in the Senate and 243–192 in the House. The Republicans gained five governorships in the election.

Philadelphia Orchestra, with Van Cliburn as soloist and Eugene Ormandy conductor.

July 23 The **Whitney Museum** opened the show *Light: Object and Image,* dedicated entirely to works of art created with light.

Aug. 22 Sixteen **art works** worth approximately $1,-400,000 were stolen from the Edward Hanley Collection in Pennsylvania. Among the missing items was a $500,000 Picasso. The FBI recovered the works on Aug. 29 but would not discuss the case. No arrests were made.

Sept. 26 *The Man in the Glass Booth* by Robert Shaw, starring Donald Pleasance, opened at the Royale Theater in New York City. A serious drama treating the problem of guilt in relation to the Nazi regime, the play was received with respect if not enthusiasm.

Sept. 28 The **Metropolitan Museum** in New York City opened *The Great Age of Fresco,* an exhibit displaying 70 Italian Renaissance frescoes that had for the first time been removed from their settings. The show was widely acclaimed and extremely popular.

Oct. 3 *The Great White Hope,* a play by Howard Sackler based on the career of black heavyweight champion Jack Johnson, opened on Broadway at the Alvin Theater. The performance of James Earl Jones in the lead conveyed the frustration of a black man struggling for greatness in a white society. The supporting performance by Jane Alexander was also outstanding.

Oct. 5 The **report of the Cox Commission** on the disturbances at Columbia University in April was released.

Oct. 9 A record **art auction price** was paid at a Parke-Bernet auction in New York City by Norton Simon, the California industrialist. He bid $1,550,000 for Pierre Auguste Renoir's *Le Pont des Arts,* a record for an impressionist painting.

Oct. 29 The **Atlanta Memorial Arts Center** officially opened. The complex incorporated the High Museum, and also included facilities for the Atlanta Symphony; ballet, opera, and theater companies; a children's theater; and an art school. Costing $13,000,

| Business and Industry; Science; Education; Philosophy and Religion | III | | IV | Sports; Social Issues and Crime; Folkways; Fashion; Holidays |

the actions of the board of the experimental Ocean Hill–Brownsville school district in Brooklyn, which refused to assign classes to teachers it claimed were undermining its authority. The teachers' union and the board members accused each other of racism. The strike was settled on Nov. 18.

Oct. 11 The **first manned Apollo mission,** Apollo 7, manned by Commander Walter M. Schirra, Jr., Donn F. Eisele, and Walter Cunningham, was successfully launched and began an 11-day Earth orbit during which the crew transmitted live television broadcasts from the spaceship. The men successfully performed a docking maneuver with the lunar module.

Oct. 16 The **Nobel Prize in Physiology or Medicine** was awarded jointly to Dr. Robert W. Holley of the Salk Institute, Dr. H. Gobind Khorana of the University of Wisconsin, and Dr. Marshall W. Nirenberg of the National Institutes of Health for their studies of the genetic code.

Oct. 25 Cardinal **Cushing of Boston announced his retirement,** stating he was partly motivated by his receipt of hate mail relating to his defense of Mrs. John F. Kennedy's Oct. 19 marriage to Aristotle Onassis.

Oct. 30 The **Nobel Prize in Chemistry** was awarded to Lars Onsager of Yale University for his work in thermodynamic theory.

Oct. 30 The **Nobel Prize in Physics** was awarded to Luis W. Alvarez of the University of California at Berkeley for his work in the field of subatomic particles, particularly his development of the bubble chamber.

Nov. 6 A **student strike** was begun by dissident students at San Francisco State College. The students called for reforms, especially in the area of black-studies programs. This initiated almost four months of turmoil, during which the president of the school, S. I. Hayakawa, called in police to help end the strike.

Dec. 4 A new **medical definition of death** was formulated by the American Medical Association in an effort to resolve controversy arising from organ-transplant operations. The AMA declared that a death had to be declared irreversible by two independent physicians before an organ could be removed from an apparently dead patient for transplanting. The term *brain death* was introduced by Dr. Henry K. Beecher of Harvard on Dec. 12 to denote irreversible death.

July 22 The **Baseball Hall of Fame** inducted three new members, the former outfielders Hazen "Kiki" Cuyler, Leon "Goose" Goslin, and Joe "Ducky" Medwick.

Sept. 7 The **Miss America** title was won by Judith Anne Ford, 18, from Illinois, at the annual pageant in Atlantic City, N.J. A few blocks down from the pageant site, at 2:45 A.M. Sept. 8, the first Miss Black America pageant was held. Saundra Williams, 19, of Philadelphia won that title.

Sept. 9 The **first U.S. Open tennis championships** were won by Arthur Ashe in the men's singles division and by Virginia Wade of England (Sept. 8) in the women's singles division.

Sept. 28 The **first North American Soccer League (NASL) championship** was won by the Atlanta Chiefs, who beat the San Diego Toros 3–0. The first game of the two-game championship, played on Sept. 21, had ended in a scoreless tie.

Oct. 2–10 The 65th annual **World Series** was won for the first time since 1945 by the Detroit Tigers (AL), who beat the St. Louis Cardinals (NL) four games to three.

Oct. 12–27 At the **Summer Olympics** in Mexico City, the U.S. won 45 gold medals and took first place in the unofficial team standings. Despite the altitude, many records were broken, and spectacular performances were turned in by Bob Beamon, who broke the world broad jump record by 21 in. with a jump of 29 ft., 2½ in., and Dick Fosbury, who won the high jump at 7 ft., 4½ in., going over the bar backward. On Oct. 18 two U.S. track stars, Tommy Smith and John Carlos, were suspended from competition after giving the black power salute, a clenched fist raised high over the head, at an awards ceremony. Smith and Carlos had won the gold and bronze medals for the 200-meter dash.

Oct. 19 Mrs. **John F. Kennedy married Aristotle Onassis,** the Greek shipping magnate, in a private ceremony on his island of Skorpios. The event was both the most glamorous and most controversial social event in many seasons.

Dec. 6 Baseball Commissioner **William D. Eckert was relieved** of his post at a meeting of team owners. The move was considered a further reflection of the owners' desire to reorganize and streamline major league baseball.

Dec. 22 President-elect **Richard Nixon's** younger daughter, Julie, was married in New York City to

Exploration and Settlement; Wars; Government; Civil Rights; Statistics I		II Publishing; Arts and Music; Popular Entertainment; Architecture; Theater

Nov. 20   A **coal mine explosion** and fire killed 78 miners in Farmington, W.Va.

Dec. 1   Condemning as a **police riot** the actions of Chicago police during the Democratic Convention in August, the National Commission on the Causes and Prevention of Violence warned against a national tendency toward violence.

000, it was built in memory of 122 Atlanta citizens killed in an airplane accident in Europe in 1962.

Nov. 2   The **Funk & Wagnalls** publishing company was acquired by the Reader's Digest Association.

1969

Richard Milhous Nixon assumed the presidency, carrying the burden of the most unpopular war in U.S. history. At the Paris peace talks little progress was made to end the Vietnam War. After Pres. Nixon made the first moves toward U.S. troop reductions in June, Sen. Charles Goodell, Republican of New York, demanded a complete pullout by the end of 1970. In October and November mammoth peace demonstrations were held in the nation's capital and other major cities. These rallies sparked prowar marches by what the president called "the great silent majority." As the year progressed, the new administration came under increasing criticism for allegedly pursuing a so-called southern strategy, a plan purportedly devised by Attorney General John Mitchell to frame policies and make appointments that would mollify the South and encourage Republican victories there in coming years. Congress voted a $5,000,000,000 cut in military spending, but failed by one vote to defeat construction of the Safeguard antiballistic missile system. This year skyjackers made off with 65 planes, a number that exceeded the total for all years since the first such seizure in 1952. Notables who died this year included Sen. Everett McKinley Dirksen, Senate Republican leader since 1959, Sept. 7, at 73; Allen W. Dulles, diplomat and director of the CIA from 1953 to 1961, Jan. 29, at 75; Joseph P. Kennedy, father of John F. and Robert Kennedy, Nov. 18, at 81; and Adm. Raymond A. Spruance, USN (ret.), who commanded the U.S. fleet at the Battle of Midway in 1942 during World War II, Dec. 13, at 83.

Jan.–Mar.   Torrential **rains,** the heaviest in 100 years, caused vast mud slides in southern California, killed more than 100, and destroyed nearly 10,000 homes. Damage exceeded $60,000,000. The worst storms hit on Jan. 18–26 and Feb. 23–26.

Jan. 3   The House voted to seat Rep. **Adam Clayton Powell** of New York in the 91st Congress, but fined him $25,000 for improper use of government funds and stripped him of seniority.

Jan. 14   A **ship fire** combined with a series of explosions aboard the aircraft carrier *Enterprise* killed 27 people and injured 82 at Pearl Harbor, Hawaii.

Most of the year's theatrical excitement was generated on off-Broadway stages, where patrons saw an unusual number of works by black playwrights, including Lorraine Hansberry, LeRoi Jones, and Lonne Elder III. *Ché*, a play about Guevara, the Latin American revolutionist, opened in New York on Mar. 22; two days later its cast and production staff were arrested on obscenity charges. *Oh! Calcutta!* by Kenneth Tynan was panned by critics but soon became one of the season's hits. In December seven cast members and the producer of its Los Angeles troupe were arrested for indecent exposure and lewdness. A strike by opera performers and musicians postponed the opening of the Metropolitan Opera's season until Dec. 29. In art, Pres. Lyndon B. Johnson presided over the groundbreaking ceremonies for the Joseph H. Hirshhorn Museum and Sculpture Garden in Washington, D.C., in January. The museum was to house the art collection Hirshhorn donated to the U.S. in 1966. Also in January, the New York Museum of Modern Art announced it had acquired the art collection of Gertrude Stein, valued at more than $6,000,000. In May Gov. Nelson A. Rockefeller of New York announced he had donated his collection of primitive art to the Metropolitan Museum of Art in New York City. In September, the Metropolitan announced that its late chairman, Robert Lehman, who had died on Aug. 9, had bequeathed his collection, valued at more than $100,000,000, to the museum. Other notables who died this year included Max Eastman, poet and author, Mar. 25, at 86; Judy Garland, singer and actress, June 22, at 47; Walter Gropius, founder of the Bauhaus school of design, July 5, at 86; Jack Kerouac, Beat novelist, Oct. 21, at 47; Frank Loesser, songwriter and composer, July 28, at 59; Giovanni Martinelli, tenor for the Metropolitan Opera for 33 years, Feb. 22, at 83; Ludwig Mies van der Rohe, architect, Aug. 17, at 83; Drew Pearson, columnist, Sept. 1, at 71; Ben Shahn, painter, Mar. 14, at 70; and Gladys Swarthout, mezzo-soprano for the Metropolitan Opera from 1929 to 1945, July 7, at 64.

Business and Industry; Science; Education; Philosophy and Religion	III		IV	Sports; Social Issues and Crime; Folkways; Fashion; Holidays

Dec. 21–27 **Apollo 8,** manned by Commander Frank Borman, James Lovell, Jr., and William Anders, was launched from Cape Kennedy, Fla. It completed a pioneering five-day mission that included ten orbits of the moon (Dec. 24–25) and yielded spectacular photographs of Earth and the moon.

Dwight David Eisenhower II, grandson of the former president.

Dec. 26–28 In Australia, the **Davis Cup** international tennis round was won, for the first time since 1963, by the U.S., which beat Australia four matches to one.

1969

The U.S. economy continued to show danger signs. Inflation had not been adequately checked, and a recession threatened. The GNP rose to $932,300,000,000, about a 7.7% increase. Averaged over the year, the Consumer Price Index rose a sharp 7.2%. In an effort to fight inflation, the Federal Reserve Board acted to impose monetary restraint; by June 9 the prime lending rate had reached a record high of 8.5%. In science, the flights of Apollo 11 and Apollo 12 to the moon dwarfed all other achievements. These manned missions, exploring for the first time a heavenly body other than Earth, caused 1969 to be popularly called the year of the moon. The year in education was marked by increased unrest on college campuses as students watched the government's failure to bring the Vietnam War to an end or to address domestic problems. Notables who died this year included John L. Lewis, president of the United Mine Workers from 1920 to 1960, June 11, at 79; Willy Ley, science writer, June 24, at 62; and Bishop James A. Pike, the controversial Episcopal leader who was charged with heresy in 1966 and left the church in Apr. 1969. Pike died, probably on Sept. 3, after his car broke down in the desert in Israel. He was 56.

Jan. 16 The **first synthesized enzyme,** ribonuclease, was announced by Merck Laboratories and Rockefeller University. It was produced by teams of scientists working independently at the two institutions.

Jan. 20 The first optical identification of a **pulsar,** a dense neutron star, was announced by astronomers at the University of Arizona, who located such a body in the Crab Nebula.

Jan. 21 A government study reported that **chronic hunger and malnutrition,** accompanied by diseases related to malnutrition and unhealthy living conditions, were widespread in the U.S.

Jan. 29 The federal deadline for **school desegregation** was extended 60 days for five southern school districts

Major league baseball's 100th anniversary was a year of change and excitement. The National League added two teams, San Diego and Montreal, to its roster, and the American League added Kansas City and Seattle. Each league was split into divisions, and playoffs for league pennants were inaugurated. Players refused to report for spring training until owners increased their pension benefits. The outfields of six ball parks were shortened to make it easier to hit home runs and, in a further attempt to spark offensive play, the strike zone was narrowed and the pitcher's mound lowered. Mickey Mantle and Don Drysdale retired. The New York Mets astounded everyone with their first World Series victory. In soccer, the North American Soccer League continued to suffer organizational and financial growing pains. The league championship was won, on the basis of final team standings, by the Kansas City Spurs. In boxing, Joe Frazier twice defended his world heavyweight title, but Jimmy Ellis, recognized champion of the World Boxing Association, fought no championship bouts. In golf, the top money winners were Frank Beard, $175,223, and Carol Mann, $49,153. In fashion, bell-bottom pants were in vogue for women and men. Unisex fashions also became popular. People in the news who died this year included Vito Genovese, considered the head of U.S. organized crime, Feb. 14, at 71; Walter Hagen, five-time PGA title winner, Oct. 5, at 76; Rocky Marciano, former world heavyweight boxing champion, in a plane crash on Aug. 31, at 46; and Tom Zachary, pitcher for the Washington Senators, Jan. 24, at 72.

Jan. 1 In **college football bowl games,** the results were Texas 36, Tennessee 13 in the Cotton Bowl; Penn State 15, Kansas 14 in the Orange Bowl; Ohio State 27, Southern California 16 in the Rose Bowl; and Arkansas 16, Georgia 2 in the Sugar Bowl. This season the AP and UPI polls chose Ohio State the national collegiate champions of 1968.

Jan. 12 **Super Bowl III** was won by the New York Jets (AFL), who defeated the Baltimore Colts (NFL) 16–7 to gain the first AFL victory. On Dec. 31, 1968, the Jets had won the AFL championship by beating the

| Exploration and Settlement; Wars; Government; Civil Rights; Statistics **I** | **II** Publishing; Arts and Music; Popular Entertainment; Architecture; Theater |

Jan. 16 At the **Paris peace talks,** U.S. and North Vietnamese delegates finally agreed on the shape of the table to be used when the South Vietnamese and the National Liberation Front joined the negotiations. Four-party talks began Jan. 18.

Jan. 20 **Richard M. Nixon was inaugurated president** of the United States. Spiro T. Agnew was inaugurated vice president. The inaugural ceremonies were marked by antiwar demonstrations.

Mar. 4 Regular rail shipments of **nerve gas** were revealed by the Department of Defense, which reported it was spending $350,000,000 a year on chemical and biological weapons.

Mar. 10 James Earl Ray, convicted assassin of Dr. Martin Luther King, Jr., was sentenced to 99 years in prison.

Mar. 14 Funds for an **antiballistic missile (ABM)** system as a safeguard for the U.S. nuclear-missile deterrent were requested from Congress by Pres. Nixon. Heretofore the ABM had been promoted as protection for cities.

Apr. 3 **U.S. combat deaths in Vietnam** since Jan. 1, 1961, reached 33,641, topping the 33,629 killed in the Korean War.

Apr. 15 A **U.S. reconnaissance plane was shot down** by North Korean MiG jets over the Sea of Japan; 31 crewmen were lost.

Apr. 23 **Sirhan Sirhan** was sentenced to death for the murder of Sen. Robert Kennedy.

Apr. 24 In the **heaviest bombing raid** to date in the Vietnam War, U.S. B-52's dropped nearly 3000 tons of bombs on enemy positions near the Cambodian border northwest of Saigon.

May 14 An eight-point **Vietnam peace plan** was proposed by Pres. Nixon. It included pullout of most foreign troops within a year and elections supervised by an international body.

May 15 Supreme Court Justice **Abe Fortas** announced his resignation. He had been criticized for accepting a fee from the family foundation of Louis E. Wolfson, who was jailed for stock manipulation.

May 20 U.S. and South Vietnamese troops captured **Hamburger Hill** after ten days of bloody battle. Sen. Edward M. Kennedy of Massachusetts criticized such assaults as senseless. The hill was abandoned May 27 and later was reoccupied by North Vietnamese troops.

June 6 Court testimony revealed that the **FBI had tapped the phones of Martin Luther King, Jr.,** despite a 1965 order by Pres. Johnson to tap only for purposes of national security. The testimony was taken in a federal court in Houston, Tex.

June 8 A **U.S. troop reduction** of 25,000 from Vietnam by Aug. 31 was announced by Pres. Nixon after

Among **books published** this year was *Naked Came the Stranger* by Penelope Ashe, a randy novel actually written in collaboration by 24 writers of the Long Island, N.Y., newspaper *Newsday.* Deliberately written as trash, it nonetheless made the best-seller list. Other books published this year included *Ernest Hemingway: A Life Story* by Carlos Baker; *Bullet Park* by John Cheever, a novel; *Henry James: The Treacherous Years 1895–1901* by Leon Edel, volume four in Edel's biography of James; *In This House of Brede* by Rumer Godden, a novel of life in an English convent; *An Unfinished Woman* by Lillian Hellman, autobiography; *Ada* by Vladimir Nabokov, a novel; *The Godfather* by Mario Puzo; *Portnoy's Complaint* by Philip Roth, a novel that became the year's publishing sensation; *Slaughterhouse-Five* by Kurt Vonnegut, Jr., a novel dealing with the Allied bombing of Dresden during World War II; and *The Making of the President, 1968* by Theodore White.

Jan. 2 *To Be Young, Gifted and Black,* a compilation from the works of Lorraine Hansberry adapted for the stage by Robert Nemiroff, opened at the Cherry Lane Theater in New York City.

Jan. 9 The world premiere of *Delusion of the Fury,* a mixed media musical drama by Harry Partch, was presented by the UCLA Committee on Fine Arts Production.

Feb. 5 *Ceremonies in Dark Old Men* by Lonne Elder III, a moving play about a Harlem family, was presented by the Negro Ensemble Company at St. Mark's Playhouse in New York City.

Feb. 8 The last issue of the *Saturday Evening Post* was published. The magazine was first published on Aug. 4, 1821, but Cyrus H. K. Curtis, after acquiring it in 1898, claimed it had been "founded in 1728 by B. Franklin." In the 1970s the magazine was resurrected and issued nine times a year. The new publication lacked many of its predecessor's most attractive qualities.

Feb. 10 *Adaptation,* a first play by **Elaine May,** and *Next* by **Terrence McNally,** opened at the Greenwich Mews Theater in New York City. Both were short plays and both were directed by Elaine May.

| Business and Industry; Science; Education; Philosophy and Religion   III | | IV   Sports; Social Issues and Crime; Folkways; Fashion; Holidays |

before federal funds would be cut off. This reprieve was widely interpreted as a sign that the Nixon administration was not committed to enforcing integration.

Feb. 14 The longest **dock strike** to date, a 57-day strike of Port of New York dock workers, which had begun on Dec. 20, 1968, was ended with agreement on a new three-year contract. But 43,000 other members of the International Longshoremen's Association continued to strike, closing ports along the Atlantic and Gulf coasts until Apr. 2.

Feb. 25 Mariner 6 was successfully launched toward Mars. On July 30 it passed within 2120 miles of the Martian surface, sending back 74 photographs.

Feb. 26 In the largest **automobile recall** to date, some 4,900,000 cars and trucks considered possibly defective were recalled by General Motors.

Mar. 3 **Apollo 9,** manned by James A. McDivitt, Russell L. Schweickart, and David R. Scott, was successfully launched into Earth orbit on a ten-day mission to test the Lunar Excursion Module (LEM). Apollo 9 splashed down on Mar. 13.

Mar. 27 Mariner 7 was successfully launched toward Mars. On Aug. 5 it passed over the planet's south pole and sent back 91 photographs.

Apr. 4 The world's **first totally artificial heart**—made of Dacron and plastic—was implanted in a human by Dr. Denton A. Cooley in Houston, Tex. The patient died Apr. 8.

Apr. 9 In a **student protest,** a group of 300 Harvard students took over the university's main administration building and evicted eight deans. The next day 400 state and local police cleared the building.

Apr. 14 Discovery of the **chemical structure of an antibody** was announced by Dr. Gerald Edelman and other scientists at Rockefeller University.

Apr. 20 Following a 36-hour **student sit-in** at the student union building of Cornell University, black students emerged armed with shotguns and other weapons.

Oakland Raiders 27–23. The same day the Colts had won the NFL title from the Cleveland Browns, 34–0.

Feb. 1–2 **U.S. figure skating championships** were won in Seattle, Wash., by Tim Wood, men's singles; Janet Lynn, women's singles; Cynthia and Ronald Kauffman, pairs (their fourth consecutive win); Judy Schwomeyer and James Sladky, dance.

Feb. 7 The **first woman jockey** to race at a U.S. parimutuel track was Diana Crump. At Hialeah, Fla., she rode her first mount to a tenth-place finish in a field of 12.

Feb. 22 The **first winning woman jockey** at a U.S. thoroughbred track was Barbara Jo Rubin, with a victory at Charles Town, W.Va.

Feb. 25 A **boycott of spring training** by baseball players was ended with the signing of a three-year pact. Club owners agreed to increase their pension contributions and to reduce eligibility for a pension to four years.

Mar. 2 At the **world figure skating championships** in Colorado Springs, Colo., Tim Wood won the men's singles title.

Mar. 22 The **NCAA basketball championship** was won by UCLA, sparked by center Lew Alcindor, defeating Purdue 97–92. Alcindor became the first player to win the tourney's Most Valuable Player award three years in a row. Later, the Milwaukee Bucks were reported to have paid $1,200,000 for Alcindor's services during the next five years.

Apr. 13 The **Masters golf tournament** was won by George Archer.

Apr. 21 The 73rd **Boston Marathon** was won by Yoshiaki Unetani of Japan with a record time of 2 hrs., 13 min., 49 sec.

Apr. 23–May 5 The **NBA basketball championship** was won by the Boston Celtics, who beat the Los Angeles Lakers four games to three. Following this, his tenth victory in 11 years, Celtics player-coach Bill Russell announced his retirement.

Apr. 27–May 4 The **NHL Stanley Cup** was won by the Montreal Canadiens, who swept the St. Louis Blues in four straight games.

Apr. 30–May 7 The **ABA basketball championship**

meeting with Pres. Nguyen Van Thieu of South Vietnam on Midway Island.

June 19   It was learned that contracts worth $87,000,000 for 68 **MIRV**'s (Multiple Independently Targetable Reentry Vehicles) had been awarded by the Pentagon without public announcement. The president had spoken of a halt to tests of such weapons.

June 23   Earl **Warren retired** as chief justice of the U.S. after swearing in Warren Burger as his successor.

July 8   The **first U.S. troop reductions** in Vietnam began, as 814 men of the Ninth Infantry Division left for home.

July 11   The convictions of Dr. **Benjamin Spock** and three codefendants for conspiring to counsel draft evasion were overturned by a U.S. court of appeals.

July 18   Sen. **Edward M. Kennedy** was involved in an auto accident when the car he was driving crashed off a bridge into the waters off Chappaquiddick Island, Mass. Kennedy was unable to rescue his passenger, Mary Jo Kopechne, who drowned. He reported the accident to Edgartown, Mass., police on July 19. On July 25 he pleaded guilty to leaving the scene of an accident. That evening, in a television statement, he called his actions in delaying the report of the accident "indefensible." He asked his constituents to help him decide on whether to continue his political career. Supported by a favorable response, he resumed his Senate duties on July 31.

July 26–Aug. 3   Pres. **Nixon visited five Asian capitals and Rumania.** He indicated that the U.S. expected its Asian allies to assume chief responsibility for that area's security and economic development. On Aug. 2 crowds gave him an enthusiastic welcome to Bucharest.

July 31   **Murder charges against Col. Robert Rheault,** Green Beret commander in Vietnam, and seven of his men were brought by the Army in connection with the killing of a Vietnamese said to have been a double agent. The charges were dropped on Sept. 29 after the CIA, which was involved in the affair, refused to cooperate in the prosecution.

Aug. 4   The **income tax surcharge** was extended by Congress through Dec. 31.

Aug. 17   Hurricane **Camille** killed more than 300 people and left 70,000 homeless in Mississippi, Louisiana, and Alabama. On Aug. 23 floods caused by the storm killed 100 in Virginia.

Aug. 24   A decimated U.S. **infantry company refused direct orders to fight.** The unit, suffering exhaustion after ten days of vicious fighting, finally was coaxed back into battle by a seasoned veteran.

Sept. 9   An **air collision** of a passenger jet and a light plane near Indianapolis, Ind., killed 83 people.

Sept. 21   **Operation Intercept,** a U.S. drive to halt drug traffic from Mexico, brought border traffic to a virtual

Mar. 10   The world premiere of *Triple Concerto* by Gian-Carlo Menotti was performed by the American Symphony, conducted by Leopold Stokowski.

Mar. 10   **National Book Awards** were presented for the following: fiction, *Steps* by Jerzy Kosinski; poetry, *His Toy, His Dream, His Rest* by John Berryman; history and biography, *White Over Black: American Attitudes Toward the Negro, 1550–1812* by Winthrop D. Jordan; arts and letters, *The Armies of the Night* by Norman Mailer; science, philosophy, and religion, *Death in Life: Survivors of Hiroshima* by Robert Jay Lifton.

Mar. 12   **Grammy Awards** were presented for the following: best record of 1968, "Mrs. Robinson" by Simon and Garfunkel; best album, *By the Time I Get to Phoenix* by Glen Campbell; best male pop vocalist, José Feliciano for "Light My Fire"; best female pop vocalist, Dionne Warwick for "Do You Know the Way to San José?"; best pop group, Simon and Garfunkel for "Mrs. Robinson."

Mar. 27   The **Black Academy of Arts and Letters** was formally established. The purpose of the organization was to honor and encourage writers, artists, and scholars who made notable contributions to black culture.

Apr. 4   The *Smothers Brothers Comedy Hour,* one of television's most popular shows, was canceled by CBS because the brothers failed to submit a show for viewing prior to broadcast. The brothers, whose show was noted for its political satire, later filed three suits seeking more than $31,000,000 in damages.

Apr. 7   **Obscenity laws** prohibiting the private possession of obscene materials were ruled unconstitutional by the U.S. Supreme Court. Justice Thurgood Marshall wrote: "Our whole constitutional heritage rebels at the thought of giving government the power to control men's minds."

Apr. 14   **Academy Awards** were presented to *Oliver!* as the outstanding motion picture of 1968; to Cliff

Business and Industry; Science; III		IV	**Sports; Social Issues and Crime;**
Education; Philosophy and Religion			**Folkways; Fashion; Holidays**

May 15 In Berkeley, Calif., the makeshift **People's Park** established by students and area residents on property owned by the University of California was attacked by police and National Guardsmen. Shotguns and tear gas were used. Five days later a National Guard helicopter dropped a stinging chemical powder on demonstrators, including faculty members.

May 18 **Apollo 10,** the first manned mission to the moon, was successfully launched. Manned by Thomas P. Stafford, Eugene A. Cernan, and John W. Young, Apollo 10 went into lunar orbit. On May 22 the Lunar Excursion Module (LEM) descended to within ten miles of the moon's surface before returning to the Command Module. Apollo 10 returned to Earth and splashed down on May 26.

July 1 A federal **Truth-in-Lending Law** went into effect, requiring that charges for credit and loans be made clear to debtors.

July 3 It was announced that the Sept. 1969 **school desegregation deadline** would be enforced for all southern school districts except those with "bona fide educational and administrative problems." The next day, the National Education Association voted overwhelmingly to demand restoration of the deadline without modification.

July 16 **Apollo 11,** manned by Neil A. Armstrong, Edwin E. Aldrin, Jr., and Michael Collins, was successfully launched toward the moon. On July 20 Armstrong and Aldrin entered the Lunar Excursion Module *Eagle* and began the descent to a landing site near the Sea of Tranquillity. Touching down at 4:17 P.M. EDT, it became the first manned vehicle to land on the moon. Armstrong radioed "Houston, Tranquillity Base here. The *Eagle* has landed." About six and a half hours later, Armstrong became the first person to set foot on the moon, saying "That's one small step for [a] man, one giant leap for mankind." Aldrin joined Armstrong. The two spoke via telephone link to Pres. Nixon, set up experiments, and gathered samples of moon rocks during a two-hour moon walk. On July 21 *Eagle* lifted off and docked with the Command Module *Columbia.* Apollo 11 splashed down in the Pacific Ocean on July 24 at 12:50 P.M. EDT.

Aug. 8 Pres. Nixon called for a guaranteed **minimum income** for families with children as part of a comprehensive reform of the welfare system.

was won by the Oakland Oaks, who beat the Indiana Pacers four games to one.

May 3 The 95th **Kentucky Derby** was won by Majestic Prince, with a time of 2:01⁴/₅. The jockey was Bill Hartack.

May 10 Plans for the 1970 **pro football merger** of the AFL and NFL were completed. The new National Football League was to have two conferences of 13 teams each. The old NFL was renamed the National Football Conference (NFC), and three of its teams (Baltimore, Cleveland, and Pittsburgh) were shifted to the new American Football Conference.

May 17 The 94th **Preakness Stakes** was won by Majestic Prince, with a time of 1:55³/₅. The jockey was Bill Hartack.

May 30 The 53rd **Indianapolis 500** auto race was won by Mario Andretti, completing the 500-mile course in 3 hrs., 11 min. for a new record average speed of 156.867 mph. It was Andretti's first win in the classic race.

June 7 The 101st **Belmont Stakes** was won by Arts and Letters, with a time of 2:28⁴/₅. The jockey was Braulio Baeza. Majestic Prince lost its chance at the triple crown, finishing five lengths back.

June 8 In ceremonies at Yankee Stadium, star outfielder **Mickey Mantle formally retired** after 18 years with the Yankees.

June 15 The **U.S. Open golf tournament** was won by Orville Moody by a single stroke over Deane Beman, Al Geiberger, and Bob Rosburg.

June 29 The **U.S. Women's Open Golf tournament** was won by Donna Caponi.

July 23 The baseball **All-Star Game** was won for the seventh year in a row by the National League, beating the American League 9–3.

July 27 The **LPGA golf tournament** was won by Betsy Rawls.

July 28 The **Baseball Hall of Fame** inducted Stanley F. "Stan the Man" Musial, former outfielder for the St. Louis Cardinals; Roy Campanella, former catcher for the Dodgers; Waite Hoyt, former pitcher; and Stan Coveleski, former pitcher.

Aug. 9 **Sharon Tate** and four others were found, apparently murder victims, at the Los Angeles home

halt. Travel eased considerably on Oct. 10 after complaints by the Mexican government.

Sept. 24   The trial of the **Chicago Eight** began. Eight radical leaders had been indicted on Mar. 20 on charges of conspiring to incite riots during the 1968 Democratic convention in Chicago. The eight—Rennie Davis, David Dellinger, John Froines, Tom Hayden, Abbie Hoffman, Jerry Rubin, Bobby Seale, and Lee Weiner—claimed they were being tried for their political views. The trial was marked by numerous disruptions by the defendants, and on Oct. 29 Judge Julius J. Hoffman ordered Seale bound and gagged. On Nov. 5 Seale was sentenced to four years in prison on 16 counts of contempt, and his case was severed from that of the others, who then became known as the Chicago Seven. On Oct. 9–11 National Guard troops were called into Chicago to control demonstrators outside the courtroom.

Oct. 5   In an apparent **breach of U.S. air defenses,** a Cuban defector landed a MiG-17 at Homestead AFB near Miami, Fla., where Pres. Nixon's plane was waiting to return the president to Washington, D.C.

Oct. 15   The **first Vietnam Moratorium Day** was observed by millions with prayer vigils, candlelight processions, mass meetings, and black armbands. Pres. Nixon ignored it. Vice Pres. Agnew on Oct. 19 called protest leaders "an effete corps of impudent snobs."

Oct. 28   Charges that an **illegal war in Laos** was being conducted without congressional knowledge or consent were leveled against the administration and the Pentagon by Sen. J. William Fulbright, chairman of the Senate Foreign Relations Committee.

Nov. 3   Pres. Nixon said that **secret U.S. peace proposals had been rejected** by the North Vietnamese. Nixon asked the nation to support his plans to Vietnamize the war, that is, encourage Vietnam to pursue the war on its own, and withdraw U.S. troops.

Nov. 6   A **weapons procurement bill** that included funds to make a start on the Safeguard ABM system was passed by Congress.

Nov. 11   **Pro-America demonstrations** in support of U.S. policy in Vietnam by U.S. citizens whom Pres. Nixon called "the great silent majority" marked this year's Veterans' Day observances.

Nov. 14   The **second Vietnam Moratorium Day** began with a long, single-file "March Against Death" in Washington, D.C. On the next day 250,000 people marched there against the war. A San Francisco protest against U.S. participation in the war drew 100,000 demonstrators.

Nov. 16   News reports charged a U.S. infantry unit with **massacre at My Lai 4,** a village in the Songmy district in South Vietnam, on Mar. 16, 1968. More than 450 villagers, including many women and babies,

Robertson as best actor for *Charly;* to Barbra Streisand for *Funny Girl* and Katharine Hepburn for *The Lion in Winter* in the first tie for best actress award; to Jack Albertson as best supporting actor for *The Subject Was Roses;* and to Ruth Gordon as best supporting actress for *Rosemary's Baby.*

Apr. 20   **Tony Awards** for the 1968–1969 season were presented for the following: best play, *The Great White Hope;* best musical, *1776;* best actor in a drama, James Earl Jones for *The Great White Hope;* best actress in a drama, Julie Harris for *Forty Carats.*

Apr. 29   **Duke Ellington** was awarded the Presidential Medal of Freedom by Pres. Nixon at a White House dinner honoring the composer and band leader's 70th birthday. A stellar group of jazz musicians played Ellington compositions.

May 2   *The Pied Piper of Hameln,* a secular cantata by Peter Mennin, was given its world premiere by the Cincinnati Symphony during the Cincinnati May Festival. Max Rudolf conducted and John V. Lindsay of New York City narrated.

May 5   **Pulitzer prizes** were awarded for the following: fiction, *House Made of Dawn* by N. Scott Momaday; general nonfiction, *So Human an Animal* by René Dubos and *The Armies of the Night* by Norman Mailer; biography, *The Man from New York: John Quinn and His Friends* by B. L. Reid; history, *Origins of the Fifth Amendment* by Leonard W. Levy; poetry, *Of Being Numerous* by George Oppen; drama, *The Great White Hope* by Howard Sackler.

May 17   **Leonard Bernstein** conducted Gustav Mahler's *Third Symphony* in his last concert as music director of the New York Philharmonic. On June 10 Pierre Boulez, the composer and conductor, was named to a three-year term as director beginning in 1971. George Szell was appointed to direct until 1971.

May 17   A copy of the first printing of the **Declaration of Independence,** one of 16 known to exist, was bought by Ira G. Corn of Dallas for $404,000. Corn outbid Hans P. Kraus of New York, who on Apr. 15 had bought a copy of the first printing of the U.S.

Business and Industry; Science; Education; Philosophy and Religion	III		IV	Sports; Social Issues and Crime; Folkways; Fashion; Holidays

Aug. 27 A **government employees' protest** against the Nixon administration's policies on school desegregation was staged by about half of the lawyers in the Justice Department's Civil Rights Division. The protest followed a government request that 33 Mississippi school districts be allowed to delay integration.

Sept. 14 The **first large vessel to navigate the Northwest Passage** was the SS *Manhattan*, an icebreaking tanker that sailed through the Prince of Wales Strait. The ship, the first commercial vessel to make the journey, had left Chester, Pa., on Aug. 24 and arrived at Point Barrow, Alaska, on Sept. 21. The project tested the feasibility of transporting crude oil by sea from northern Alaska. It cost the three sponsoring oil companies $40,000,000.

Sept. 23 The **Philadelphia Plan,** which set guidelines for the hiring of minorities by six skilled-craft unions working in Philadelphia on projects receiving federal funds, was ordered into effect by Sec. of Labor George Shultz.

Oct. 8 A **blacklist of scientists** by the Department of Health, Education, and Welfare was reported. The department had barred hundreds of renowned scientists from its advisory panels for such offenses as antiwar statements.

Oct. 16 The **Nobel Prize for Physiology or Medicine** was awarded jointly to Dr. Max Delbruck of the California Institute of Technology, Dr. Alfred D. Hershey of the Carnegie Institute, Cold Spring Harbor, N.Y., and Dr. Salvador E. Luria of the Massachusetts Institute of Technology for their work on the genetic structure of viruses.

Oct. 18 The use of **cyclamates,** artificial sweeteners, was banned by the Department of Health, Education, and Welfare. The ban was modified on Dec. 20 to permit use of specified amounts, except in soft drinks.

Oct. 27 A **strike** against the General Electric Company began as some 150,000 workers walked out in a contract dispute that was not settled until Jan. 30, 1970.

Oct. 29 The Supreme Court ordered **immediate school desegregation** of the 33 Mississippi school

of the actress. In December, Charles Manson and several members of his nomadic hippie cult were indicted for the murders.

Aug. 13 **Bowie Kuhn,** temporary commissioner of baseball since February, was formally appointed to that post with a seven-year contract.

Aug. 15–18 At the **Woodstock Music and Art Fair,** a weekend folk-rock festival, inadequate planning and bad weather threatened for a time to make a disaster area of the site, Max Yasgur's farm near Bethel. The crowd was estimated at 300,000 to 400,000, and many more failed to reach the fair when traffic jams clogged all roads leading to the Catskill area. Helicopters were pressed into service to supply food, water, and medicine. Rains made a quagmire of the festival grounds. Drugs circulated freely, and a number of people were treated for bad drug reactions. Almost miraculously, there were only three deaths. The police adopted a hands-off posture, and the youths present enjoyed themselves in a general spirit of peace, cooperation, and enthusiasm. While many treated the affair as an idyll, others expressed alarm at the incontrovertible evidence of a mass drug culture.

Aug. 17 The **PGA golf tournament** was won by Ray Floyd. The tournament was marred by the behavior of civil rights demonstrators, who harassed Gary Player of South Africa on Aug. 16.

Sept. 6 The **Miss America** title was won by Pamela Anne Eldred, 21, from Michigan, at the annual pageant in Atlantic City, N.J.

Sept. 7–8 The **U.S. Open tennis singles championships** were won by Margaret Smith Court of Australia (Sept. 7) in the women's division and Rod Laver of Australia (Sept. 8) in the men's division. With his victory, Laver completed the grand slam of tennis by winning the top four international championships—the Australian, French, Wimbledon, and U.S. singles titles. Laver had won the grand slam once before, in 1962.

Sept. 19–21 The **Davis Cup** was successfully defended by the U.S., defeating Rumania in five straight matches.

Sept. 22 San Francisco Giants outfielder **Willie Mays hit his 600th home run,** becoming the only player other than Babe Ruth to reach that mark.

Oct. 7 **Fourteeen blacks were dropped from the University of Wyoming football team** after they

were said to have been slain. Pending an investigation, Lt. William L. Calley, Jr., in charge of the U.S. unit at that time, was kept on active duty beyond his official tour.

Nov. 17 The first round of **Strategic Arms Limitation Talks** (SALT) between the U.S. and U.S.S.R. opened in Helsinki, Finland. The conference ended on Dec. 22 with an agreement to resume talks in Vienna on Apr. 16, 1970.

Nov. 21 Control of **Okinawa** and other Ryukyu Islands would be returned to Japan by 1972, it was announced.

Nov. 21 The nomination of **Clement Haynsworth** to the Supreme Court was rejected by the Senate after three months of consideration.

Nov. 24 The **nuclear nonproliferation treaty** was signed by the U.S. and U.S.S.R., the 23rd and 24th signatories.

Nov. 25 The U.S. would not engage in **biological warfare** nor make first use of lethal or incapacitating chemicals, Pres. Nixon announced. The White House later said that tear gas and defoliants were not included in the ban.

Nov. 26 A bill establishing a **lottery for Selective Service draftees** was signed by Pres. Nixon. The first drawing was held Dec. 1.

Dec. 4 **Fred Hampton,** Illinois chairman of the Black Panther Party, was shot and killed along with another party member in a predawn police raid in Chicago. On the next day the Illinois ACLU demanded an investigation of the Panthers' charge that Hampton had been murdered in his bed.

Dec. 15 **U.S. troop strength in Vietnam** would be cut to 434,000 by Apr. 12, Pres. Nixon announced. This would represent a total reduction of about 110,000 since he took office.

Dec. 22 The most far-reaching **tax reform bill** in U.S. history was passed by Congress. Although it removed 9,000,000 of the very poor from federal tax rolls, it was criticized as a measure that aided the rich. The bill, signed by Pres. Nixon on Dec. 30, reduced the tax surcharge from 10% to 5% and extended it for six months, reduced the oil depletion allowance from 27.5% to 22%, closed numerous tax loopholes, and increased Social Security benefits by 15%.

Constitution for $155,000. The copy of the Declaration was found in late 1968 in a defunct bookstore in Philadelphia.

June 8 **Emmy Awards** of the Academy of Television Arts and Sciences were presented to Paul Scofield as best actor in a single performance for *Male of the Species;* to Geraldine Page as best actress in a single performance for *The Thanksgiving Visitor;* to Carl Betz as best actor in a dramatic series for *Judd for the Defense;* and to Barbara Bain as best actress in a dramatic series for *Mission: Impossible.*

Aug. 1 The world premiere of *Help! Help! The Globolinks!,* a light, satirical attack on electronic music by Gian-Carlo Menotti, was presented by the Santa Fe Opera Company.

Sept. 11 **Alice Tully Hall** in Lincoln Center for the Performing Arts in New York City was inaugurated with a concert by the new Chamber Music Society of Lincoln Center. The official opening of the Juilliard School of Music on Oct. 26 completed plans for Lincoln Center.

Sept. 17 The **Milwaukee County Performing Arts Center** was formally opened. The $12,000,000 complex had been in planning for 25 years.

Nov. 25 The **American Symphony Orchestra League,** sponsor of a meeting in New York City of 77 presidents of major U.S. symphonies, announced it would seek increased appropriations from the federal government. It was reported that the five most important orchestras (Cleveland, Philadelphia, Boston, Chicago, and New York) had deficits totaling $5,700,000 for the 1967–1968 season, up from an aggregate loss of $2,900,000 in 1963–1964.

1970

One of the major problems confronting Pres. Richard M. Nixon and the nation was the faltering economy. Pres. Nixon countered rising inflation and joblessness with fiscal austerity, marked by severe cuts in U.S. aerospace programs. He also proposed a coordinated plan to improve the natural environment. The president was

The Broadway theater season was marked by the openings of a few outstanding serious plays, accompanied by an increased interest by both producers and theatergoers in comedies and musicals. The motion picture industry, suffering a financial pinch, reduced its offerings by 25%, but presented viewers with a number of

Business and Industry; Science; Education; Philosophy and Religion	III		IV	Sports; Social Issues and Crime; Folkways; Fashion; Holidays

districts for which the federal government had asked a delay. It was the first decision handed down by Chief Justice Warren Burger, who had been appointed by Pres. Nixon.

Oct. 30 The **Nobel Prize in Physics** was awarded to Dr. Murray Gell-Mann of the California Institute of Technology for his contribution to the theory of elementary particles.

Nov. 14 **Apollo 12,** manned by Charles Conrad, Jr., Richard F. Gordon, Jr., and Alan L. Bean, was launched on a lunar flight in rainy weather. Some 36.5 sec. after liftoff, it was hit by an electric charge, which briefly knocked out power in the spacecraft but not in the rocket. On Nov. 19 Conrad and Bean became the third and fourth humans to land on the moon when they brought down the *Intrepid,* their Lunar Excursion Module, on the plain of the Ocean of Storms. They made two moon walks, and the next day successfully blasted off to rejoin Gordon in the command ship, the *Yankee Clipper.* Apollo 12 splashed down on Nov. 24, only three miles from the carrier *Hornet.*

Nov. 20 In the first step toward total **ban of DDT** by 1971, the U.S. Department of Agriculture ordered a halt to its use in residential areas.

Nov. 22 **Isolation of a single gene,** the basic unit of heredity, was announced by scientists at Harvard University. Their feat promised to facilitate study of the mechanism of gene control.

Dec. 2 The **Boeing 747,** which cost $21,400,000 to develop, made its first public flight, from Seattle, Wash., to New York City.

Dec. 18 A law establishing stricter **coal mine safety standards,** and providing compensation for victims of black lung disease, was passed by Congress.

defied the coach's ban against protests and wore black armbands in support of a stand by the Black Students' Alliance. The BSA wanted the university to sever sports ties with Brigham Young University, a school run by Mormons, who had barred blacks from church ministry.

Oct. 11–16 The **World Series** was won by the New York Mets (NL), who won four straight games from the Baltimore Orioles (AL) after losing the opener to the Orioles. The Mets had beaten the Atlanta Braves in three straight games to take the National League pennant. The Orioles had swept three games from the Minnesota Twins for the American League pennant.

Oct. 18 A new **football field goal record** was set by Chester Marcol of Hillsdale College in Michigan, who kicked a 62-yard field goal, the longest on record for either amateur or pro football.

Oct. 24 Actor **Richard Burton** bought for his wife, Elizabeth Taylor, a 69.42-carat diamond from Cartier, the New York City jeweler. The price was not revealed, but Cartier had paid $1,050,000 for the gem the previous day and said it made a profit on the sale to Burton.

Dec. 6 A **football controversy** over honors for the top college football team continued when Pres. Nixon presented Texas with a plaque honoring it as the best football team in the nation following its 15–14 defeat of Arkansas. The presentation had been protested to no effect by Gov. Raymond P. Shafer of Pennsylvania, who noted that Penn State had been undefeated through 30 games in three years.

Dec. 11–12 A new **world record decathlon score** of 8417 points was set by Bill Toomey at the Southern Pacific AAU meet at UCLA.

Dec. 17 Singer **Tiny Tim,** born Herbert Buckingham Khaury, and Miss Vicki, born Victoria May Budinger—he in his mid-40s and she 17—were wed in a ceremony on Johnny Carson's TV show, *Tonight.*

1970

The word *recession* crept back into the public vocabulary. The economic policies of Pres. Richard Nixon sought a controlled contraction in the economy, accompanied by reduced industrial output and temporarily higher unemployment to break the inflationary spiral that began some three years earlier. By year's end it was

The year in sports was marked by unrest. Curt Flood, of the St. Louis Cardinals, objected to being traded to the Philadelphia Phillies and brought an antitrust suit against organized baseball over the so-called reserve clause. The sports year was also marked by ever-increasing salaries for top athletes and record cash

disappointed in his second attempt to secure Senate approval of a so-called strict constructionist, and a southerner, to fill a vacant Supreme Court seat. Perhaps the most damaging event for the administration was the U.S. military invasion of Cambodia, which Pres. Nixon announced to the American people on Apr. 30. The incident sparked a nationwide shutdown of colleges and universities, violent demonstrations, and deaths on two college campuses. By late December U.S. troop strength in Vietnam had dropped to 340,000. By year's end, the total death toll of U.S. personnel had passed 44,000. Among notables who died this year were Brig. Gen. Benjamin O. Davis, Sr., the first black to attain the rank of general, Nov. 26, at 93; and Rep. L. Mendel Rivers, Democrat of South Carolina, chairman of the House Armed Services Committee, Dec. 28, at 65.

Jan. 2 A survey on **military desertions** by the Department of Defense revealed that 1403 service personnel had deserted to foreign countries since July 1, 1966.

Jan. 6 A **heroin-control agreement with France** was announced. It was aimed at halting the illegal production of the drug in France. The diplomatic agreement was part of an effort to halt heroin smuggling into the U.S.

Jan. 22 In his first **State of the Union message**, Pres. Nixon emphasized the need for environmental protection.

Feb. 4 An **environmental cleanup program** was proposed by Pres. Nixon, who called for expenditure of $10,000,000,000 for waste treatment plants.

Feb. 14 Pres. Nixon, discussing **chemical warfare**, stated that the U.S. would not be the first to use lethal and incapacitating chemicals. He had previously renounced U.S. use of biological weapons.

Feb. 26 The Army announced it would discontinue **surveillance of civilian demonstrations** and maintenance of files on civilians who might be involved in civil disturbances.

Feb. 28 Charges of **institutional racism** were leveled at Daniel Patrick Moynihan, domestic adviser to Pres. Nixon, after leak to the press of his private memo stating "the time may have come when the issue of race could benefit from a period of benign neglect." Moynihan later said the memo meant that blacks would fare better if advocates at both ends of the political spectrum were less vocal.

Mar. 4 A move to **reduce military expenditures** was announced by Sec. of Defense Melvin R. Laird, who stated that 371 military bases in the U.S. and abroad would be closed or reduced, with projected savings of $914,000,000.

Mar. 5 The **nuclear nonproliferation treaty**, ratified by the U.S., U.S.S.R., and 41 other nations, went into effect.

excellent films, including *Catch-22*, *The Graduate*, *Patton*, and the rock documentaries *Woodstock*, which recounted the 1969 festival in upstate New York, and *Gimme Shelter*, about the ultimately disastrous 1969 U.S. tour of the Rolling Stones. This year the Metropolitan Museum of Art celebrated its centennial, and George Balanchine, director of the New York City Ballet, celebrated his 50th anniversary as a choreographer. The art world saw another year of record art prices. At the Parke-Bernet Galleries in New York City, Vincent van Gogh's *Le Cyprès et l'Arbe en Fleur* fetched $1,300,000, a record for a van Gogh work. On Nov. 27 Wildenstein Gallery of New York City paid $5,544,000, a record price for a single painting, for a Velázquez portrait. On May 12, 1971, the painting was acquired by the Metropolitan Museum of Art in New York City. On Dec. 10 Parke-Bernet sold Thomas Eakins' *Cowboys in the Badlands* for $210,000, a record for a U.S. painting. Notables who died this year included John Dos Passos, the novelist, Sept. 28, at 74; Erle Stanley Gardner, creator of Perry Mason, Mar. 11, at 80; Reuben Lucius "Rube" Goldberg, whose zany drawings of impossibly complex devices gave birth to the phrase *Rube Goldberg contraption*, Dec. 7, at 87; John Gunther, the author, May 29, at 68; James Marshall "Jimi" Hendrix, rock guitarist, Sept. 18, at 27; Richard Hofstadter, historian, Oct. 24, at 54; Janis Joplin, rock singer, Oct. 4, at 27; Gypsy Rose Lee, real name Rose Louise Hovick, celebrated striptease artist and author, Apr. 26, at 56; John O'Hara, author, Apr. 11, at 65; Erich Maria Remarque, German-born novelist, Sept. 25, at 72; Mark Rothko, painter, Feb. 25, at 66; and George Szell, conductor of the Cleveland Orchestra from 1946, July 30, at 73.

Among **books published** this year was *Everything You Always Wanted to Know About Sex* by Dr. David Reuben, just one of a number of books about sex that became best sellers, including *The Sensuous Woman* by "J.," *Sexual Politics* by Kate Millett, a feminist treatment of the battle of the sexes, and *Human Sexual Inadequacy* by the research team of Dr. William H. Masters and Virginia Johnson. Other books published this year included *Mr. Sammler's Planet* by Saul Bellow, a novel; *Ball Four* by Jim Bouton, which took the baseball establishment to task; *Deliverance* by James Dickey, the poet's first novel; *Islands in the Stream*, a posthumous novel by Ernest Hemingway; *You Might as Well Live: The Life and Times of Dorothy Parker* by John Keats; *The Art of His Life* by Jay Martin, a biography of Nathanael West; *Culture and Commitment* by Margaret Mead; *Zelda* by Nancy Milford, a biography of Zelda Fitzgerald; *The Greening of America* by Charles A. Reich; *Hard Times, An Oral History of the Great Depression* by Studs Terkel; *Bech: A Book* by John Updike, a novel; and *QB VII* by Leon Uris, a novel.

apparent that the brakes had been applied too strongly. On Dec. 4 it was announced that unemployment had risen to 5.8%. Officials began to move to reduce interest rates as a means of stimulating the economy. The space program suffered major cuts in the budget squeeze, and some of the best-known astronauts left the program to pursue other careers. NASA was hurt further by the near-disastrous Apollo 13 lunar mission in April. In education, the year was marked by explosive campus unrest. Pres. Nixon established a Commission on Campus Unrest, which reported that student disorders reflected student opposition to U.S. military activities, concern over racial injustice, and general dissatisfaction with American life. The commission urged Pres. Nixon to use his leadership to bring the nation together. Notables who died this year included Richard Cardinal Cushing of Boston, Nov. 2, at 75; Joseph Wood Krutch, naturalist and author, May 22, at 76; Walter Reuther, president of the United Auto Workers, who died with his wife and four others in a plane crash, May 9, at 62; John T. Scopes, Dayton, Tenn., central figure in the so-called Scopes monkey trial in 1925, Oct. 21, at 70; and Blanche Stuart Scott, a pioneer woman aviator, Jan. 12, at 84.

Jan. 2 HEW Sec. Robert H. Finch stated that a **black-list of scientists** maintained by the Department of Health, Education, and Welfare had been dropped. Scientists had been barred from HEW advisory panels for their political views.

Jan. 5 **Joseph Yablonski,** unsuccessful candidate for president of the United Mine Workers, was found murdered in his home along with his wife and daughter.

Jan. 14 A Feb. 1, 1970, **deadline for desegregation** of public schools in Alabama, Florida, Georgia, Louisiana, Mississippi, and Tennessee was issued by the Supreme Court, overruling the Sept. 1970 deadline set by a lower court.

Jan. 18 The head of the **Mormon Church** since 1951, David O. McKay, died at 96. On Jan. 23 he was succeeded as president of the Church of Jesus Christ of Latter-Day Saints by Joseph Fielding Smith, 93, grand-nephew of the church's founder.

Feb. 18 The **Chicago Seven** were acquitted of conspiracy charges in connection with riots during the 1968 Democratic convention in Chicago. Five were found guilty of crossing a state line with intent to incite a riot. On Feb. 20 they were sentenced to five-year prison terms.

purses for major sports events. In golf, the top money winners were Lee Trevino, $157,037, and Kathy Whitworth, $30,235. In boxing, Joe Frazier was recognized as the world heavyweight champion, and Muhammad Ali, who had been stripped of the title in 1967, made a comeback with victories over Jerry Quarry (Oct. 26) and Oscar Bonavena (Dec. 7). In soccer the North American Soccer League (NASL) split into two divisions and added New York City and Toronto franchises for the 1971 season. In football, the American Football League added three franchises and became the American Conference of the National Football League. The old NFL roster was reorganized into the National Conference, each conference organized into three divisions. Winners of division playoffs in each conference would go to the Super Bowl. In fashion, many designers pushed the midi style, which dropped the hemline to mid-calf. Youth's influence in dress styles was reflected in such apparel as tie-dyed garments, granny dresses, and secondhand military attire. Americans mourned the passing of Charles "Sonny" Liston, 38, heavyweight boxing champion from 1962 to 1964, about Dec. 28; Vincent Thomas "Vince" Lombardi, celebrated coach of the Green Bay Packers, Sept. 3, at 57; and John J. "Johnny" Murphy, former pitcher for the New York Yankees, Jan. 14, at 61.

Jan. 1 In **college football bowl games,** the results were Texas 21, Notre Dame 17 in the Cotton Bowl; Penn State 10, Missouri 3 in the Orange Bowl; USC 10, Michigan 3 in the Rose Bowl; and Mississippi 27, Arkansas 22 in the Sugar Bowl. This season the AP and UPI polls chose Texas the national college champions of 1969.

Jan. 11 **Super Bowl IV** was won by the Kansas City Chiefs (AFL), who defeated the Minnesota Vikings (NFL) 23–7. On Jan. 4 the Chiefs had won the AFL championship by beating the Oakland Raiders 17–7. The same day the Vikings took the NFL title by beating the Cleveland Browns 27–7.

Feb. 6–7 **U.S. figure skating championships** were won at Tulsa, Okla., by Tim Wood, men's singles; Janet Lynn, women's singles; Jo Jo Starbuck and Kenneth Shelley, pairs; Judy Schwomeyer and James Sladky, dance.

Feb. 16 The **world heavyweight boxing championship** was awarded to Joe Frazier, who knocked out Jimmy Ellis in the fifth round in New York City.

Mar. 7 At the **world figure skating championships** at Ljubljana, Yugoslavia, Tim Wood won the men's singles title for the second year in a row.

Mar. 21 The **NCAA basketball championship** was won for the fourth straight time by UCLA, which defeated Jacksonville University 80–69.

Apr. 1 The 19th U.S. **Census** recorded a preliminary population count approaching 205,000,000.

Apr. 8 The nomination of **G. Harrold Carswell** to the U.S. Supreme Court was rejected by the Senate after a prolonged debate. In 1969 the Senate had rejected the nomination of Clement F. Haynsworth, Jr., to the same vacant seat.

Apr. 16 The second round of **Strategic Arms Limitation Talks** (SALT) opened in Vienna, Austria. The talks recessed on Aug. 14, both sides agreeing to resume in Helsinki, Finland, on Nov. 2. The third round (Nov. 2–Dec. 8) ended on a less optimistic note than the Vienna round, but a fourth round was scheduled to begin in Vienna on Mar. 15, 1971.

Apr. 20 A **troop level reduction** of 150,000 U.S. personnel from Vietnam by early 1971 was announced by Pres. Nixon.

Apr. 29 A military **invasion of Cambodia,** called an *incursion* by the White House, was launched by some 50,000 U.S. and South Vietnamese troops. The operation, aimed at destroying Vietcong and North Vietnamese sanctuaries, was announced by Pres. Nixon in a televised address on Apr. 30.

May 4 At **Kent State University** in Kent, Ohio, four students were killed when National Guard troops fired at some 600 antiwar demonstrators, some of whom had been throwing rocks at the guardsmen and taunting them.

May 9 An **antiwar rally in Washington,** D.C., drew some 100,000 protesters to the nation's capital. Similar demonstrations were held in many parts of the country.

May 12 The nomination of Judge **Harry A. Blackmun** of Minnesota to the Supreme Court was approved by the Senate.

June 15 The claim of **conscientious objector status** on moral grounds alone was found constitutional by the Supreme Court in the case of *Welsh v. United States.* Previously such status was granted only on the basis of long-standing religious belief and training.

June 22 **Juries of fewer than 12 persons** were ruled constitutional by the Supreme Court in the case of *Williams v. Florida.*

July 4 **Honor America Day** was observed in Washington, D.C., as thousands gathered to show support for the administration's war policies.

Aug. 3–5 **Hurricane Celia** swept across the Gulf Coast, killing 26 people in Texas and Florida.

Aug. 12 The **Postal Reorganization Act,** establishing the U.S. Postal Service as an independent agency within the executive branch, was signed by Pres. Nixon.

Sept. 22 A bill authorizing **congressional representation for the District of Columbia** through a nonvoting delegate to the House of Representatives was

Jan. 22 The world premiere of the opera *Of Mice and Men* by Carlisle Floyd was presented by the Seattle Opera.

Jan. 29 The canticle for orchestra *In Praise of Shahn* by William Schuman, a tribute to the late artist Ben Shahn, was given its world premiere by the New York Philharmonic, directed by Leonard Bernstein.

Feb. 17 *Child's Play* by Robert Marasco, a psychological thriller set in a boys' school starring Fritz Weaver, Pat Hingle, and Ken Howard, opened at the Royale Theater in New York City.

Feb. 19 **Andrew Wyeth** was honored at the opening of a one-man exhibition of his works at the White House in Washington, D.C., an event believed to be the first such recognition of a living artist.

Mar. 2 **National Book Awards** were presented for the following: fiction, *Them* by Joyce Carol Oates; poetry, *The Complete Poems* by Elizabeth Bishop; history and biography, *Huey Long* by T. Harry Williams; arts and letters, *An Unfinished Woman* by Lillian Hellman; philosophy and religion, *Gandhi's Truth: On the Origins of Militant Non-violence* by Erik H. Erikson.

Mar. 3 A landmark revival of the opera *Norma* by Vincenzo Bellini was presented by the Metropolitan Opera, with Joan Sutherland in the title role and Marilyn Horne in her Met debut singing Adalgisa.

Mar. 11 **Grammy Awards** were presented to the following: best record of 1969, "Aquarius/Let the Sunshine In" by the Fifth Dimension; best album, *Blood, Sweat and Tears;* best male pop vocalist, Harry Nilsson for "Everybody's Talkin'"; best female pop vocalist, Peggy Lee for "Is That All There Is"; best pop group, the Fifth Dimension for "Aquarius/Let the Sunshine In."

Mar. 30 *Applause,* a musical by Betty Comden, Adolph Green, Charles Strouse, and Lee Adams based on the film *All About Eve* and a story by Mary Orr, opened at the Palace Theater in New York City. It starred Lauren Bacall.

Apr. 7 **Academy Awards** were presented to *Midnight Cowboy* as best film of 1969; John Wayne as best actor for *True Grit;* Maggie Smith as best actress for *The Prime of Miss Jean Brodie;* Gig Young as best supporting actor for *They Shoot Horses, Don't They?;* and Goldie Hawn as best supporting actress for *Cactus Flower.*

Apr. 19 **Tony awards** for the 1969–1970 season were presented for the following: best play, *Borstal Boy;* best musical, *Applause;* best actor in a drama, Fritz Weaver for *Child's Play;* best actress in a drama, Tammy Grimes for *Private Lives.*

Apr. 26 *Company,* a musical by Stephen Sondheim and George Furth examining the institution of marriage through the eyes of a bachelor and five of his

Business and Industry; Science;   **III**   **IV**   **Sports; Social Issues and Crime;**
Education; Philosophy and Religion   **Folkways; Fashion; Holidays**

Mar. 16 The *New English Bible* was published in its entirety. Translated directly from ancient texts, it was the work of British scholars of the major Protestant churches, who were assisted by a panel of literary experts. It was the subject of debate because its language departed radically from the rich sonorities of the King James Bible.

Mar. 18 The **first major postal workers' strike** in U.S. history began. On Mar. 23 Pres. Nixon ordered the National Guard to help alleviate mail delays. The strike ended on Mar. 25.

Apr. 1 A bill **banning cigarette advertising** on radio and television, effective Jan. 1, 1971, was signed by Pres. Nixon.

Apr. 11 **Apollo 13** was successfully launched, carrying astronauts James A. Lovell, Jr., John L. Swigert, Jr., and Fred W. Haise, Jr., toward a lunar landing. The mission seemed to be going perfectly, but on Apr. 13 a tank of liquid oxygen exploded, damaging the spacecraft. The crippled spacecraft continued to the moon, circled it and returned to Earth on Apr. 17. Months later scientists reported that faulty design had caused the problem.

Apr. 22 **Earth Day** was observed across the country, dramatizing the concern of many Americans about the dangers of environmental pollution.

Apr. 28 The **Dow Jones average** of industrial stocks plummeted to 724.33, the lowest point since Nov. 22, 1963, when Pres. John F. Kennedy was shot.

June 4 Use of the drug **L-dopa** for treatment of Parkinson's disease was approved by the Food and Drug Administration.

June 13 A **Commission on Campus Unrest** was named by Pres. Nixon. The nine-member panel, headed by former Gov. William W. Scranton of Pennsylvania, was charged with determining the causes of campus violence and suggesting solutions.

June 21 The **Penn Central Railroad,** operator of the nation's largest rail system, was granted a petition for reorganization under federal bankruptcy laws.

Apr. 13 The **Masters golf tournament** was won by Billy Casper, who beat Gene Littler by five strokes in a playoff round.

Apr. 20 The 74th annual **Boston Marathon** was won by Ron Hill of Great Britain, with a time of 2 hrs., 10 min., 30 sec., a new U.S. marathon record.

Apr. 24–May 8 The **NBA basketball championship** was won for the first time in 24 years by the New York Knickerbockers, who beat the Los Angeles Lakers four games to three.

May 2 The 96th annual **Kentucky Derby** was won by Dust Commander, with a time of 2:03²/₅. The jockey was Mike Manganello.

May 3–10 The **NHL Stanley Cup** was won for the first time in 29 years by the Boston Bruins, who swept the St. Louis Blues in four straight games.

May 15–25 The **ABA basketball championship** was won by the Indiana Pacers, who beat the Los Angeles Stars four games to two.

May 16 The 95th annual **Preakness Stakes** was won by Personality, with a time of 1:56¹/₅. The jockey was Eddie Belmonte.

May 30 The 54th **Indianapolis 500** auto race was won by Al Unser, completing the course in 3 hrs., 12 min., 37.04 sec., with an average speed of 155.749 mph.

June 6 The 102nd annual **Belmont Stakes** was won by High Echelon, with a time of 2:34. The jockey was John Rotz.

June 15 The **LPGA golf tournament** was won by Shirley Englehorn, who beat Kathy Whitworth by four strokes in an 18-hole playoff.

June 21 The **U.S. Open golf tournament** was won by Tony Jacklin of Great Britain, beating Dave Hill by five strokes to become the first Englishman to win the tournament in 50 years.

July 4 At the **Wimbledon** tennis championships, the women's doubles title was won by Billie Jean King and Rosemary Casals for the third time in four years. Casals teamed with Ilie Nastase of Rumania to win the mixed doubles title.

July 5 The **U.S. Women's Open golf tournament** was won for the second year running by Donna Caponi, who beat Sandra Spuzich and Sandra Haynie by one stroke.

July 14 The **baseball All-Star Game** was won by the National League for the eighth consecutive year, defeating the American League team 5–4 in the 12th inning.

July 27 The **Baseball Hall of Fame** inducted Lou Boudreau, former shortstop for the Cleveland Indians

signed by Pres. Nixon. The district had not been represented in Congress since 1875.

Sept. 22–28 Brush fires swept across southern California. It was the worst such disaster in the state's history.

Sept. 27 Pres. Nixon began a nine-day **tour of Europe,** including visits with the leaders of Italy, Yugoslavia, Spain, Great Britain, and Ireland.

Oct. 7 Pres. Nixon proposed a five-point **peace plan** for Indochina, including immediate cease-fire and release of all prisoners of war. The proposal was rejected by North Vietnam.

Oct. 13 **Angela Davis,** former faculty member at UCLA, black militant, and self-proclaimed communist, was seized in New York City in connection with an Aug. 7 courtroom shootout in San Raphael, Calif., in which a judge and three others were killed. She was wanted on kidnaping, murder, and conspiracy charges.

Oct. 15 The **Organized Crime Control Act** was signed by Pres. Nixon, who pledged "total war against organized crime."

Oct. 21 The **Nobel Peace Prize** was awarded to Dr. Norman E. Borlaug for his work on high-yield grains to help Third World nations boost food production and overcome the cycle of hunger and poverty.

Oct. 26 The **Legislative Reform Act,** the first attempt since 1946 to improve the federal legislative process, was signed by Pres. Nixon. The act retained the seniority system.

Nov. 2 **Strategic Arms Limitation Talks** (SALT) between the U.S. and U.S.S.R. were resumed at Helsinki, Finland.

Nov. 3 In **congressional elections** the Democrats lost four seats in the Senate but maintained a majority of 54–44, with two seats going to independent and Conservative candidates. In the House the Democrats picked up 12 seats for a 255–180 majority.

Nov. 21 U.S. forces raided **Sontay,** North Vietnam, in an attempt to free U.S. prisoners of war. The prison camp was found to be empty.

Nov. 23 A **treaty with Mexico,** settling long-standing border disputes, was signed by the U.S.

Nov. 27 Testimony that an antiwar group called the **East Coast Conspiracy to Save Lives** was planning to kidnap a high government official and blow up the underground heating system for federal buildings in Washington, D.C., was given to a Senate subcommittee by FBI director J. Edgar Hoover. Hoover named Philip and Daniel Berrigan, both priests, as leaders in the plot. The government official was later identified as presidential adviser Henry Kissinger.

Dec. 2 The **Environmental Protection Agency,** established in July by executive order, was activated. William D. Ruckelshaus was confirmed the same day as its director.

married friends, opened at the Alvin Theater in New York City.

May 4 **Pulitzer prizes** were awarded for the following: fiction, *Collected Stories* by Jean Stafford; biography, *Huey Long* by T. Harry Williams; history, *Present at the Creation: My Years in the State Department* by Dean G. Acheson; general nonfiction, *Gandhi's Truth: On the Origins of Militant Non-violence* by Erik H. Erikson; poetry, *Untitled Subjects* by Richard Howard.

June 7 **Emmy Awards** were presented to Peter Ustinov as best actor in a single dramatic performance for *A Storm in Summer;* Patty Duke as best actress in a single dramatic performance for *My Sweet Charlie;* Robert Young as best actor in a dramatic series for *Marcus Welby, M.D.;* and Susan Hampshire as best actress in a dramatic series for *The Forsyte Saga.*

Oct. 11 **Natalia Makarova,** the prima ballerina with the Leningrad Kirov Ballet who defected from the U.S.S.R. in September, joined the American Ballet Theater.

Oct. 12 *Conduct Unbecoming* by Barry England, a portrayal of nineteenth-century military life in British India, opened at the Ethel Barrymore Theater in New York City.

Nov. 3 The first New York performance of *The Makropoulos Affair* by Leoč Janášek was presented by the New York City Opera. Maralin Niska was acclaimed for her performance in the leading role.

Nov. 10 *Two by Two* by Peter Stone, Richard Rodgers, and Martin Charnin, a musical about Noah and the ark based on the play *The Flowering Peach* by Clifford Odets, opened at the Imperial Theater in New York City. It starred Danny Kaye.

Nov. 11 *Home* by the British playwright David Storey opened at the Morosco Theater in New York City. The play, recounting a day in the lives of four mental patients, starred Sir John Gielgud, Sir Ralph Richardson, Dandy Nichols, and Mona Washbourne.

Nov. 12 *Sleuth* by Anthony Shaffer, a thriller starring Anthony Quayle and Keith Baxter, opened at the Music Box in New York City. The play became a huge success.

Nov. 16 An **actors' strike** by Actors Equity Association closed 17 off-Broadway productions. The dispute was submitted to binding arbitration on Dec. 16.

Nov. 30 **Leopold Stokowski** conducted the first concert ever given in St. Patrick's Cathedral in New York City, a charity benefit honoring the late Francis Cardinal Spellman.

Dec. 9 **Goeran Gentele,** head of the Stockholm Opera, was named to succeed Rudolf Bing as general manager of the Metropolitan Opera in New York City, effective in 1972.

Business and Industry; Science; Education; Philosophy and Religion **III**		**IV** Sports; Social Issues and Crime; Folkways; Fashion; Holidays

July 3 No **deaths from polio** were recorded in 1969, the National Communicable Disease Center reported. It was the first year without fatalities since record-keeping began in 1955.

Aug. 11 The Rev. **Daniel J. Berrigan,** a Jesuit priest who was a fugitive for four months, was seized by FBI agents. Berrigan, his brother the Rev. Philip F. Berrigan, and seven others had been convicted of burning draft records at Catonsville, Md., in 1968. They were known collectively as the Catonsville Nine.

Sept. 6 A **TWA airliner was hijacked** to Jordan by Palestinian terrorists. On Sept. 12 it was blown up along with two other western-owned airplanes.

Sept. 15 A **strike against General Motors** was called by the UAW, idling some 400,000 workers. The strike was settled on Nov. 11.

Sept. 30 The *New American Bible* was published in its entirety for the first time. It was the first Roman Catholic–sponsored translation in English created directly from original sources.

Oct. 14 The Dept. of Commerce announced that **personal income,** measured on a seasonally adjusted basis, had passed $800,000,000,000 for the first time.

Oct. 15 The **Nobel Prize in Physiology or Medicine** was awarded jointly to Dr. Julius Axelrod of the National Institute of Mental Health in Bethesda, Md., Sir Bernard Katz of Great Britain, and Ulf von Euler of Sweden for their study of the chemistry of nerves in controlling the vascular system.

Oct. 16 The **Nobel Prize in Economics** was awarded to Paul A. Samuelson of MIT. It was the second such award, and the first won by an American.

Oct. 30 A bill establishing a **National Railroad Passenger Corporation,** a quasi-governmental corporation to run passenger lines between the major cities, was signed by Pres. Nixon.

Nov. 18 **Linus Pauling,** the Nobel Prize–winning scientist, reported that high doses of vitamin C could ward off the common cold and the flu. Other scientists held that such doses given over a long period of time could be harmful.

and later manager; Earl Combs, called the "Kentucky Colonel," who played center field for the New York Yankees; Ford Frick, the sportswriter and broadcaster and commissioner of baseball from 1961–1965; and Jesse Joseph "Pop" Haines, former pitcher for the St. Louis Cardinals.

Aug. 16 The **PGA golf tournament** was won by Dave Stockton, who topped Arnold Palmer and Bob Murphy by two strokes.

Aug. 29–31 The **Davis Cup** international tennis challenge round was won by the U.S., which swept West Germany in five straight matches.

Sept. 2–13 The **U.S. Open tennis singles championships** were won by Ken Rosewall of Australia in the men's division and Margaret Court of Australia in the women's division.

Sept. 6–13 The **North American Soccer League championship** was won by the Rochester Lancers, who bested the Washington Darts four goals to three in a two-game, total goal playoff.

Sept. 7 A new **world record for winning mounts** was set by Willie Shoemaker, who broke Johnny Longden's record by winning his 6033rd race, at Del Mar, Calif.

Sept. 12 The **Miss America** title was won by Phyllis Ann George, 21, from Texas, at the annual pageant in Atlantic City, N.J.

Sept. 13 The **first New York City Marathon** was won by Gary Muhrcke of the Millrose Athletic Association, with a time of 2 hrs., 31 min., 38.2 sec. Of the 126 starters, 55 finished the 26-mile, 385-yard course.

Sept. 15–28 The **America's Cup** was successfully defended by the U.S. yacht *Intrepid,* which beat the Australian challenger *Gretel II* four races to one. In the second race *Gretel II* was disqualified because it collided with *Intrepid* at the beginning of the race, the first such forfeit in the yachting classic's history.

Oct. 2 Fourteen members of the **Wichita State University football team** were killed when their chartered plane crashed in the Rocky Mts.

Oct. 10–15 The 67th **World Series** was won by the Baltimore Orioles (AL), defeating the Cincinnati Reds four games to one. On Oct. 5 the Orioles had clinched the American League pennant by sweeping the Minnesota Twins in three games; the Reds had taken the National League pennant by beating the Pittsburgh Pirates three straight.

Oct. 23 A new **land speed record** of 622.407 mph was set by Gary Gabelich of Long Beach, Calif. He drove a rocket-powered car at the Bonneville Salt Flats in Utah.

Exploration and Settlement; Wars; Government; Civil Rights; Statistics **I**		**II** Publishing; Arts and Music; Popular Entertainment; Architecture; Theater

Dec. 21 Reduction of the **voting age** in national elections to 18 years was ruled constitutional by the Supreme Court.

Dec. 23 Plans for a speedy **phase-out of herbicide operations** in Indochina were announced by the Nixon administration.

Dec. 23 The north tower of the **World Trade Center** in New York City was topped out, making it the tallest building in the world. At 1350 ft., it was 100 ft. taller than the Empire State Building.

Dec. 27 *Hello, Dolly!*, the longest running musical in Broadway history, closed after 2844 performances. The previous record had been set by *My Fair Lady*, with 2717 performances.

1971

Pres. Richard Nixon announced in July that he would visit the People's Republic of China and the U.S.S.R. in 1972. The indication that the U.S. and China would move toward normalizing relations profoundly affected international relations. The U.S. continued to disengage from combat in Vietnam, and by December U.S. troop strength in South Vietnam had dropped to 184,000. Opposition to continued American involvement there made itself felt in Washington, D.C., in March, when a bomb planted by the radical Weather Underground exploded in the Capitol. In May thousands of people protesting the war were arrested by police when they attempted to shut down the government by blocking all traffic in the city. In other war-related events, Lt. William L. Calley, Jr., was convicted for his role in the My Lai massacre of 1968. His superiors were exonerated, prompting some to claim Calley was being used as a scapegoat. Pres. Nixon sought funds for the treatment and rehabilitation of Vietnam era veterans who suffered from drug addiction. As the 1972 presidential election approached, Pres. Nixon was faced with challenges for the Republican nomination from Rep. Paul N. McCloskey, Jr., of California, a liberal who sought more rapid deescalation of the war, and Rep. John M. Ashbrook of Ohio, a conservative campaigning to cut deficit spending and eliminate wage and price controls introduced in August. Eleven Democrats were registered for Democratic primaries. The Senate confirmed the nomination of Lewis F. Powell and William H. Rehnquist to the Supreme Court. Notables who died this year included Dean Acheson, former secretary of state, Oct. 12, at 78; Ralph Bunche, diplomat and winner of the 1950 Nobel Peace Prize, Oct. 11, at 67; Thomas E. Dewey, former governor of New York, Mar. 16, at 68; Adm. Thomas C. Hart, USN (ret.), commander in chief of the U.S. Pacific Fleet when Pearl Harbor was bombed, July 4, at 94; Audie Murphy, the most decorated U.S. soldier of World War II, May 28, at 46; Sen. Richard B. Russell, Democrat of Georgia, Jan. 21, at 73; Arthur B. Springarn, president of the NAACP from 1940–1965, Dec. 1, at 93; and Whitney M. Young, Jr., head of the National Urban League from 1961, Mar. 11, at 49.

The Broadway season offered few new shows, and museums reduced their hours of operation. The big publishing story of the year was the leak to *The New York Times* of a top secret Pentagon study of U.S. involvement in Vietnam. The series of excerpts that came to be known as the Pentagon Papers prompted heated debate over the newspaper's right to publish sensitive documents and the federal government's need to protect the documents. The motion picture industry continued to experience hard times as fewer pictures were produced by the major studios, even though independent productions were filmed on location throughout the country. Film makers reported that sexually explicit films, which had been the rage for a time, were losing their box office appeal. Americans mourned the deaths of Duane Allman, rock guitarist, Oct. 29, at 24; Louis Daniel "Satchmo" Armstrong, the gravel-voiced jazz singer and trumpeter, July 6, at 71; Margaret Bourke-White, internationally renowned photographer, Aug. 27, at 67; Walter Van Tilburg Clark, author of *The Ox-Bow Incident* (1940), Nov. 10, at 62; Rockwell Kent, artist and illustrator, Mar. 13, at 88; Ted Lewis, real name Theodore L. Friedman, band leader and entertainer, Aug. 25, at 80; Harold Lloyd, comic genius of the silent film, Mar. 8, at 77; James Douglas "Jim" Morrison, rock singer, July 3, at 27; Ogden Nash, poet, known best for his humorous verse, May 19, at 68; Elmo Roper, pioneer pollster, Apr. 30, at 70; and Igor Stravinsky, the Russian-born composer, Apr. 6, at 88.

Among **books published** this year was *The Vantage Point* by former Pres. Lyndon Johnson. In these memoirs, Johnson recalled the events of his years in the White House and discussed many of the details that were revealed this year by *The New York Times* in the Pentagon Papers scandal. Other books published this year included *The Exorcist* by William Peter Blatty, a shocker that was the basis for an enormously successful motion picture; *Bury My Heart at Wounded Knee* by Dee Brown, an account of the virtual destruction of American Indian society between 1860 and 1890; *The Book of Daniel* by E. L. Doctorow, a novel based on the Rosenberg spy case; *Eleanor and Franklin: The Story of*

| Business and Industry; Science; Education; Philosophy and Religion | III | | IV | Sports; Social Issues and Crime; Folkways; Fashion; Holidays |

Dec. 1 Twenty-four **underground nuclear tests** had been conducted during the year at a Nevada test site, the Atomic Energy Commission reported.

Dec. 31 The **National Air Quality Control Act** was signed by Pres. Nixon. It tightened air pollution standards and penalties and called for a 90% reduction in pollution from automobile exhausts by 1975.

Nov. 8 A new **football field goal record** of 63 yards was set by Tom Dempsey of the New Orleans Saints in a two-point win over the Detroit Lions.

Nov. 14 Forty-three players and coaches of the **Marshall University football team** died when their chartered plane crashed in Kenova, W.Va.

1971

Projected GNP figures were off, unemployment was up to 6%, and inflation rose above 4% for the year. For the first time in the twentieth century imports exceeded exports. In August Pres. Richard M. Nixon announced a plan to control wages and prices, coupled with devaluation of the dollar to improve the U.S. balance of trade. In education, the National Science Foundation reported federal aid to colleges and universities was the lowest since 1966 and forecast an oversupply of scientists and engineers with Ph.D. degrees by 1980. The National Education Association reported that teacher demand was the lowest in 20 years. Despite serious cuts in NASA's budget, the U.S. completed two more manned lunar landings and launched Mariner 9 on its way to a Mars orbit. Late in the year Mariner sent back the first of many photographs of the surface of the planet. Back on Earth, underwater research produced a practical system for the recovery of manganese nodules from the ocean bottom, and at the California Institute of Technology, scientists reported they had successfully tested Albert Einstein's General Theory of Relativity. Notables who died this year included Philo T. Farnsworth, pioneer in the development of television, Mar. 11, at 64; Reinhold Niebuhr, Protestant theologian, June 1, at 78; James Cash Penney, founder of the J. C. Penney department store chain, Feb. 12, at 95; and David Sarnoff, a pioneer in television broadcasting, Dec. 12, at 80.

Jan. 12 Formation of the **Earth Act Group** was announced by Ralph Nader. Its purpose was to organize student fund-raising to support court actions and scientific efforts to fight rural and urban environmental problems.

Jan. 25 In its first decision on **sex discrimination in hiring** practices, the Supreme Court upheld the equal hiring provisions of the 1964 Civil Rights Act by ruling that businesses could not deny employment to women with preschool children unless they applied the same hiring criteria to men.

Sports and politics found common ground this year when a team of U.S. table tennis players was invited to China in April for an impromptu tournament. They lost to the Chinese players but their presence in China, combined with the relaxation of U.S. foreign policy toward the People's Republic, led many to speak hopefully of an era of Ping-Pong diplomacy. This year Billie Jean King became the first woman athlete in history to win more than $100,000 in a year. In golf the top money winners were Jack Nicklaus, $244,490, and Kathy Whitworth, $41,182. Lee Trevino became the fourth U.S. golfer to win both the U.S. and British Open tournaments in the same year. In fashion, skirt lengths settled at just below the knee for daytime and just above the ankle for evening. Both blue denim and leather were popular, and short-shorts were jazzed up and renamed *hot pants.* A fad for 1940s styles reflected nostalgia for what some thought of as a simpler time. Among those who died this year were Robert T. "Bobby" Jones, great golfer, Dec. 18, at 69; Nathan Leopold, who was convicted with Richard Loeb for the "thrill murder" of Bobby Franks in 1924, Aug. 28, at 66; and Joseph Valachi, the crime figure who testified in Senate hearings in 1963 about the workings of Cosa Nostra, Apr. 3, at 66.

Jan. 1 In **college football bowl games,** the results were Notre Dame 24, Texas 11 in the Cotton Bowl; Nebraska 17, LSU 12 in the Orange Bowl; Stanford 27, Ohio State 17 in the Rose Bowl; and Tennessee 34, Air Force 13 in the Sugar Bowl. This season the AP poll selected Nebraska the national collegiate champions of 1970. The UPI poll chose Texas.

Jan. 17 **Super Bowl V** was won in the last five seconds by the Baltimore Colts (AFC), who beat the Dallas Cowboys (NFC) 16–13 on a field goal by Jim O'Brien. On Jan. 3 the Colts had beaten the Oakland Raiders 27–17 to win the AFC championship and the Cowboys had topped the San Francisco 49ers 17–10 for the NFC championship.

Jan. 25 **Charles Manson** was convicted, along with Susan Atkins, Leslie Van Houten, and Patricia Krenwinkel, of the 1969 murders of actress Sharon Tate and six others. On Apr. 19 they were sentenced to

Jan. 2 The **Omnibus Crime Control Act,** authorizing $3,600,000,000 in federal aid for state and local law enforcement agencies, was signed by Pres. Nixon.

Jan. 12 The Rev. **Philip F. Berrigan** was indicted with five others for conspiring to kidnap presidential adviser Henry Kissinger and to bomb the heating systems of federal buildings in Washington, D.C. Berrigan was serving a sentence for burning draft cards.

Jan. 22 In his **State of the Union** address, Pres. Nixon proposed a $16,000,000,000 revenue-sharing program for state and local governments.

Feb. 9 An **earthquake** in southern California caused more than $500,000,000 in damage and killed 65 people, including 47 at a Veterans Administration hospital in Sylmar, near San Fernando.

Feb. 11 A treaty banning nuclear weapons from the **seabed** beyond the standard 12-mile coastal limit was signed by the U.S. and 62 other nations at ceremonies in Washington, D.C., London, and Moscow. It was to become effective after ratification by 22 nations.

Feb. 21 **Tornadoes** struck Louisiana, Mississippi, and Texas, killing 90 people and injuring more than 500.

Feb. 24 The Supreme Court ruled that **illegally obtained evidence,** generally inadmissible in a criminal trial, could be used to contradict a defendant's voluntary testimony. The decision marked a significant alteration of the Miranda ruling of 1966.

Mar. 1 In Washington, D.C., the **Capitol was bombed** by the radical Weather Underground. The device, planted in a restroom in the Senate wing, caused some $300,000 in damage but no injuries.

Mar. 8 **Draft exemption for conscientious objectors,** the Supreme Court ruled, must be based on opposition to all war, not just to the Vietnam War.

Mar. 15 The fourth round of **Strategic Arms Limitation Talks** (SALT) between the U.S. and U.S.S.R. began in Vienna, Austria. On May 28 the conference ended with an agreement to resume talks on July 8 in Helsinki, Finland.

Mar. 27 A **ship disaster** claimed 31 lives when the tanker *Texaco Oklahoma* split in two off Cape Hatteras, N.C.

Mar. 29 Lt. **William L. Calley, Jr.,** was convicted of the premeditated murder of 22 people during the 1968 massacre of South Vietnamese civilians at My Lai. On Mar. 31 he was sentenced to life imprisonment. Exoneration on Sept. 22 of Calley's superior, Capt. Ernest L. Medina, coupled with the earlier dropping of charges against 11 superior officers, fueled the public outcry that Calley was being used as a scapegoat. On Apr. 1 Pres. Nixon ordered Calley

Their Relationship Based on Eleanor Roosevelt's Private Papers by Joseph P. Lash; *The Tenants* by Bernard Malamud, a novel; *Wonderland,* a novel by Joyce Carol Oates; *Honor Thy Father* by Gay Talese, a firsthand account of the life of an organized crime family; *The Other* by Thomas Tryon, a novel of the supernatural; *Rabbit Redux* by John Updike, a sequel to *Rabbit Run* (1960); *Meet Me in the Green Glen* by Robert Penn Warren, a novel; and *The Winds of War* by Herman Wouk, a massive novel of the early years of World War II.

This year's **AIA Gold Medal** for architecture was awarded to Louis I. Kahn of Philadelphia, Pa.

Jan. 19 A revival of *No, No, Nanette,* a 1925 musical by Otto Harbach, Frank Mandel, Vincent Youmans, and Irving Caesar, opened at the Forty-Sixth Street Theater in New York City. The production was supervised by Busby Berkeley and starred Ruby Keeler.

Feb. 20 A **false nuclear alert** was broadcast by radio and television stations across the country when an operator at the National Emergency Warning Center in Colorado mistakenly ran an emergency alert tape rather than the usual test tape. It took some 40 minutes to cancel the phony alert.

Mar. 4 **National Book Awards** were presented for the following: fiction, *Mr. Sammler's Planet* by Saul Bellow; poetry, *To See, To Take* by Mona Van Duyn; history and biography, *Roosevelt: The Soldier of Freedom* by James McGregor Burns; arts and letters, *Cocteau* by Francis Steegmuller; science, *Science in the British Colonies of America* by Raymond Phineas Stearns.

Mar. 16 **Grammy Awards** were presented for the following: best record, "Bridge Over Troubled Water" by Simon and Garfunkel; best album, *Bridge Over Troubled Water* by Simon and Garfunkel; best male pop vocalist, Ray Stevens for "Everything Is Beautiful"; best female pop vocalist, Dionne Warwick for "I'll Never Fall in Love Again"; best pop group, The Carpenters for "Close to You."

Mar. 18 Bequest of some 1500 works by the painter **Edward Hopper** to the Whitney Museum of Art in New York City was announced. Hopper died in 1967.

Mar. 28 **Tony awards** for the 1970–1971 season were presented for the following: best play, *Sleuth;* best musical, *Company;* best dramatic actor, Brian Bedford for *The School for Wives;* best dramatic actress, Maureen Stapleton for *The Gingerbread Lady.*

Apr. 4 *Follies* by James Goldman and Stephen Sondheim, a musical about two dancers 30 years after they leave Broadway, opened at the Winter Garden in New York City.

| Business and Industry; Science;
Education; Philosophy and Religion | III | | IV | Sports; Social Issues and Crime;
Folkways; Fashion; Holidays |

Jan. 31 **Apollo 14,** manned by Alan B. Shepard, Jr., Edgar D. Mitchell, and Stuart A. Roosa, was successfully launched. After initial problems in docking the lunar and command modules, the mission proceeded to a successful lunar landing (Feb. 5–6). Apollo 14 returned to Earth on Feb. 9, bringing back more than 100 lbs. of rock for study.

Mar. 1 **Licensing of commercial whale hunters** was ordered halted by Sec. of Commerce Maurice Stans.

Mar. 2 **William A. "Tony" Boyle,** president of the United Mine Workers, was indicted on charges of conspiracy, embezzlement, and illegal campaign contributions.

Mar. 29 Development of an apparently effective **serum hepatitis vaccine** for children was announced by the New York University Research Center.

Apr. 14 Pres. Nixon announced the lifting of a **trade embargo** with the People's Republic of China, which had existed for more than 20 years.

Apr. 20 The use of **school busing** to end racial segregation in public school systems was ruled constitutional by the Supreme Court.

May 1 **Amtrak,** also known as the National Railroad Passenger Corporation, began operation. It was to provide service by 182 trains to more than 300 cities.

May 8 **Mariner 8** fell into the Atlantic Ocean after the launch vehicle's second-stage booster failed.

May 25 The U.S. program for a **supersonic transport** (SST) was killed when Pres. Nixon signed a bill providing phase-out funds for the project's prime contractors.

May 30 **Mariner 9** was successfully launched from Cape Kennedy, Fla., toward a Mars orbit on Nov. 12. After achieving orbit, it began to send back spectacular pictures of the Martian surface as well as shots of the two moons of Mars.

June 10 Substantiation of **advertising claims** would be required of major U.S. manufacturers, the Federal Trade Commission announced. The first business sec-

death. On Oct. 21 Charles Watson was also sentenced to death for the murders.

Jan. 28–31 **U.S. figure skating championships** were won by John Misha Petkevich, men's singles; Janet Lynn, women's singles; Jo Jo Starbuck and Kenneth Shelley, pairs; Judy Schwomeyer and James Sladky, dance.

Feb. 28 The **PGA golf tournament** was won by Jack Nicklaus, beating Billy Casper by three strokes.

Mar. 8 The **world heavyweight boxing championship** was defended by Joe Frazier in a unanimous 15-round decision over Muhammad Ali. The fight, one of the richest sports events in history, grossed nearly $20,-000,000, largely through receipts from closed-circuit television.

Mar. 27 The **NCAA basketball championship** was won for the fifth straight year by UCLA, who beat Villanova 68–62.

Apr. 8 The first legal **off-track betting** (OTB) system in the U.S. went into operation in New York City.

Apr. 10–14 A U.S. **table tennis team** visited the People's Republic of China and played several exhibition matches in Peking. The unprecedented invitation by the Chinese also included visas for seven western newsmen, reversing a policy that had been maintained since the new government took power in 1949.

Apr. 11 The **Masters golf tournament** was won by Charles Coody, who beat Jack Nicklaus and Johnny Miller by two strokes.

Apr. 19 The **Boston Marathon** was won by Alvaro Mejia of Colombia, with a time of 2 hrs., 18 min., 45 sec.

Apr. 30 The **NBA basketball championship** was won by the Milwaukee Bucks in a four-game sweep over the Baltimore Bullets.

May 1 The 97th annual **Kentucky Derby** was won by Canonero II, with a time of 2:03⅕. The jockey was Gustavo Avila.

May 4–18 The **NHL Stanley Cup** was won by the Montreal Canadiens, who defeated the Chicago Black Hawks four games to three.

May 15 The 96th annual **Preakness Stakes** was won by Canonero II, with a new track record time of 1:54. The jockey was Gustavo Avila.

May 18 The **ABA basketball championship** was won by the Utah Stars, who beat the Kentucky Colonels four games to three.

May 29 The 55th annual **Indianapolis 500** auto race was won for the second year in a row by Al Unser, who completed the 500-mile course in 3 hrs., 10 min., 11.56 sec., for a new record average speed of 157.735 mph.

June 5 The 103rd annual **Belmont Stakes** was won by Pass Catcher, with a time of 2:30⅖. The jockey was Walter Blum.

released from the stockade and moved to his quarters at Fort Benning, Ga., pending the appeal process. Nixon announced that he would review Calley's case before sentence was carried out. On Aug. 20 Calley's sentence was reduced to 20 years' imprisonment.

Apr. 23 In an **antiwar protest** on the steps of the Capitol in Washington, D.C., scores of Vietnam veterans returned their medals and military decorations. On the following day, antiwar rallies were held in Washington and San Francisco.

May 3 In what was called the **Mayday antiwar protest** in Washington, D.C., the culmination of several weeks of antiwar activities in the nation's capital, thousands of demonstrators were arrested and confined when they tried to stop government activities by blocking traffic in the city. Most charges were dropped.

June 11 A 19-month **Indian occupation of Alcatraz Island** off San Francisco ended when U.S. marshals removed 15 people from the former prison island. The Indians had claimed the island under a treaty provision giving them unused federal lands.

June 23 Claude E. Vealey confessed to the Dec. 1969 murders of dissident United Mine Workers leader **Joseph A. Yablonski** and his wife and daughter. In a Washington, Pa., court hearing, he stated he would testify against four others indicted for the murders, including Aubran W. Martin and Paul E. Gilly. On Nov. 12 Martin was convicted; he was sentenced to death the next day. Gilly was convicted on Mar. 1, 1972, and was sentenced to death the following day.

June 30 The **Twenty-sixth Amendment** to the U.S. Constitution, lowering the voting age for all elections to 18, went into effect when Ohio became the 38th state to ratify it.

July 8 The fifth round of the **Strategic Arms Limitation Talks** (SALT) convened in Helsinki, Finland. The talks recessed on Sept. 23 with unofficial reports that the U.S. and U.S.S.R. were approaching agreement on limitation of antiballistic missile (ABM) systems. The talks resumed in Vienna on Nov. 15. On Sept. 30 the two powers signed agreements on ways to reduce the risk of accidental nuclear war.

July 10–11 The **National Women's Political Caucus** in Washington, D.C., was attended by more than 200 women. The organization sought equal representation for women at all levels of the nation's political system.

July 28 A **military crackdown on narcotics** use was announced by the U.S. Army. Virtually all U.S. personnel in South Vietnam were to be tested for use of heroin.

Apr. 14 **Academy Awards** were presented to *Patton* as outstanding motion picture of 1970 and to its star, George C. Scott, as best actor; Glenda Jackson as best actress for *Women in Love;* John Mills as best supporting actor for *Ryan's Daughter;* and Helen Hayes as best supporting actress for *Airport.*

May 3 **Pulitzer prizes** were awarded for the following: biography, *Robert Frost: The Years of Triumph, 1915–1938* by Lawrence R. Thompson; history, *Roosevelt, The Soldier of Freedom* by James McGregor Burns; general nonfiction, *The Rising Sun* by John Toland; poetry, *The Carriers of Ladders* by W. S. Merwin; drama, *The Effect of Gamma Rays on Man-in-the-Moon Marigolds* by Paul Zindel.

May 9 **Emmy Awards** were presented to George C. Scott as best actor for *The Price;* Lee Grant as best actress for *The Neon Ceiling;* Hal Holbrook as best actor in a dramatic series, for "The Senator," a segment of *The Bold Ones;* and Susan Hampshire as best actress in a dramatic series, for *The First Churchills.*

May 17 *Godspell,* a musical by Stephen Schwartz based on the Gospel According to St. Matthew, opened at the Cherry Lane Theater in New York City.

May 22 The **Lyndon Baines Johnson Library,** an $18,600,000 complex at the University of Texas to house the former president's papers, was dedicated.

May 28 The premiere performance of *The Goldberg Variations,* a ballet by Jerome Robbins set to the music of Johann Sebastian Bach, was presented by the New York City Ballet.

June 13 The first installment of what came to be known as the **Pentagon Papers,** excerpts from the Pentagon study *History of the U.S. Decision-making Process on Vietnam Policy,* was published in *The New York Times.* Publication of the documents was halted in federal court, but the decision was reversed on June 30 by the Supreme Court. On June 28 a former Defense Department official, Dr. Daniel Ellsberg, admitted that he had given the documents to the *Times.* He was subsequently indicted for theft and possession of secret documents.

June 16 An **El Greco** sketch for *The Immaculate Conception,* which had been stolen in Spain in 1936, was recovered in New York City by the FBI.

June 27 The rock concert halls **Fillmore East and Fillmore West,** located in New York City and San Francisco, respectively, were closed down by their founder, Bill Graham, largely for financial reasons.

tor to come under federal scrutiny was to be the auto industry.

June 28 State programs to underwrite **nonreligious instruction in parochial schools** were ruled unconstitutional by the Supreme Court.

July 1 The **U.S. Postal Service,** the semi-independent corporation organized to replace the Post Office Department, was officially inaugurated at the White House in Washington, D.C.

July 2 A **cancer virus** had been isolated from cells taken from a cancer patient, a research team in Texas announced. The discovery was considered a significant new lead in the search for causes of cancer.

July 26 **Apollo 14,** manned by astronauts David R. Scott, James B. Irwin, and Alfred M. Worden, was successfully launched. Scott and Irwin were the fourth team to land on the moon (July 30–Aug. 2). They traveled 17.3 miles on the lunar surface using a four-wheeled lunar rover and collected what appeared to be a fragment of the moon's original crust. Nicknamed Genesis rock, it was later found to be about 4,000,000,000 years old. Apollo 14 splashed down in the Pacific on Aug. 7.

Aug. 2 A **federal bailout of Lockheed** Aircraft Corporation was authorized by Congress, which passed by a narrow margin a $250,000,000 loan guarantee for the aerospace giant's TriStar airbus program. The guarantee was officially approved by the administration on Sept. 9.

Aug. 15 A **new economic policy** was announced by Pres. Nixon, who called for a 90-day wage and price freeze, reductions in federal spending, and a temporary 10% surcharge on imports. The dollar would be allowed to float from its formerly fixed exchange rate of $35 per ounce of gold. On Nov. 15 the second phase of the new program was instituted. A pay board, responsible for setting standards for wage increases, set a 5.5% guideline, and a price commission established a 2.5% guideline for annual price increases.

Aug. 20 Agreements establishing **INTELSAT,** the International Telecommunications Satellite Consortium, were signed by 50 nations in Washington, D.C.

June 13 The **LPGA golf tournament** was won by Kathy Whitworth.

June 21 The **U.S. Open golf tournament** was won by Lee Trevino, who beat Jack Nicklaus by two strokes in a playoff. On July 10 Trevino won the British Open, becoming the fourth U.S. player to win both championships in the same year.

June 27 The **U.S. Women's Open golf tournament** was won by JoAnne Gunderson Carner.

June 28 **Muhammad Ali** won a four-year legal battle when the Supreme Court overturned his 1967 conviction for draft evasion.

July 3 At the **Wimbledon** tennis championships, the women's doubles title was won for the second year in a row by Billie Jean King and Rosemary Casals. King teamed with Owen Davidson of Australia to win the mixed doubles title.

July 13 The **baseball All-Star Game** was won by the American League, beating the National League 6–4 for its first all-star victory since 1962.

July 30–Aug. 12 At the **Pan-American Games** in Cali, Colombia, the U.S. won 105 gold medals and ranked first in team standings, followed by Cuba and Canada.

Aug. 9 The **Baseball Hall of Fame** inducted eight new members: Dave Bancroft, Jake Beckley, Charles "Chick" Hafey, Harry Hooper, Joseph J. "Joe" Kelley, Richard "Rube" Marquard, LeRoy "Satchel" Paige, and George Weiss.

Aug. 21 **George Jackson,** 29, one of three black convicts known as the Soledad Brothers after being charged with the murder of a guard at Soledad prison in California, was killed while attempting to escape from San Quentin. Two convicts and three guards were also killed in the attempted mass breakout. Jackson's prison writings had been collected in *Soledad Brother* (1970).

Aug. 26 It was announced that the **New York Giants** football team would move to New Jersey after completion there of a 75,000-seat stadium in 1975.

Sept. 5–15 The **U.S. Open tennis singles championships** were won by Stan Smith in the men's division and Billie Jean King in the women's division. It was the first time in 16 years both titles were won by U.S. players.

Sept. 9 **Gordie Howe,** one of the all-time greats of the NHL, announced his retirement at age 43 to take a job in the front office of the Detroit Red Wings, his team for 25 seasons.

Sept. 11 The **Miss America** title was won by Laurie Lea Schaefer, 22, of Ohio, at the annual pageant in Atlantic City, N.J.

Sept. 19 The **North American Soccer League championship** was won by the Dallas Tornado, defeating the

Aug. 2 Admission of the **People's Republic of China to the UN** would not be opposed by the U.S., it was announced. The U.S. also stated it would not agree to depriving Nationalist China of its representation. On Oct. 25 the UN General Assembly voted to admit the People's Republic of China and expel Nationalist China.

Sept. 4 In the **worst single airplane crash** to date in the U.S., 111 people were killed when an Alaska Airlines Boeing 727 crashed into a mountain west of Juneau, Alaska.

Sept. 9–13 A **prison riot at Attica** State Correctional Facility, Attica, N.Y., led to the deaths of 43 people. Nine prison guards held hostage and 28 prisoners were killed when some 1500 state police and other law enforcement officers staged an air and ground assault to end the uprising.

Sept. 26 Japanese Emperor **Hirohito** was greeted by Pres. Nixon at Anchorage, Alaska, in the first foreign trip ever undertaken by a Japanese emperor. It was also the first meeting of a U.S. president and a Japanese monarch.

Dec. 6 The nomination of **Lewis F. Powell, Jr.,** to the Supreme Court was approved by the Senate. Powell succeeded Justice Hugo L. Black, who resigned on Sept. 17 and died a week later.

Dec. 10 The nomination of **William H. Rehnquist** to the Supreme Court was approved by the Senate. Rehnquist succeeded Justice John M. Harlan, who had resigned on Sept. 23.

Dec. 26–30 **Massive air bombardment** of military installations in North Vietnam resumed. The heaviest attack since the Nov. 1968 bombing halt was conducted by U.S. Navy and Air Force planes.

July 21 *Fiddler on the Roof* became the longest-running Broadway musical, its 2845 performances surpassing the record set by *Hello, Dolly!*

Sept. 8–9 The gala two-day opening of the **Kennedy Center for the Performing Arts** in Washington, D.C., was highlighted by the premiere performance of Leonard Bernstein's *Mass.*

Oct. 12 *Jesus Christ Superstar,* a rock opera by Tim Rice and Andrew Lloyd Webber starring Jeff Fenholt, Ben Vereen, and Yvonne Elliman, opened at the Mark Hellinger Theater in New York City. The opera had already been performed across the country by two touring companies, and an album recording had already sold some 2,500,000 copies.

Oct. 19 *Look* magazine ceased publication because of continuing losses aggravated by the soft economy and rising postal rates.

Oct. 25 At the United Nations, **Pablo Casals** conducted the premiere performance of his *Hymn to the United Nations,* with words by W. H. Auden. Casals received the UN Peace Medal from Secretary General U Thant. On Dec. 29 Casals celebrated his 95th birthday at his home in Puerto Rico.

Nov. 11 *The Prisoner of Second Avenue* by Neil Simon, a comedy starring Peter Falk and Lee Grant, opened at the Eugene O'Neill Theater in New York City.

Nov. 16 **Norman Cousins resigned** after 31 years as editor of *Saturday Review,* citing disagreement on editorial policy with the magazine's new owners.

1972

Pres. Richard M. Nixon enhanced his already substantial chances for reelection with trips to the People's Republic of China in February and to the U.S.S.R. in May. These successes were capped in October when two key strategic arms (SALT) agreements were signed. The Paris peace talks stalled when U.S. representatives walked out, claiming the North Vietnamese were not working for a settlement. On Mar. 30 North Vietnam moved into South Vietnam through the DMZ and from Cambodia. This was met by heavy air bombardment of North Vietnam. After initial losses, South Vietnamese forces began to turn back the North Vietnamese. On Apr. 27 the Paris talks resumed. Despite stepped-up air support for South Vietnamese military actions, U.S. disengagement continued. The last U.S. ground combat

This year the publishing world was rocked by a hoax. The giant McGraw-Hill Company had paid Clifford Irving $750,000 for *The Autobiography of Howard Hughes,* supposedly based on some 100 talks with the reclusive billionaire. After telephone calls by a person claiming to be Hughes, the scheme began to unravel. Irving and his wife pleaded guilty to the hoax on Mar. 14, two weeks before the planned, but aborted, publication date of the book. In the art world, museum management came under fire for a practice called deaccessioning, the selling or trading of art works. Thomas Hoving of the Metropolitan Museum in New York City defended the practice as a way to improve collections. Critics charged the transactions put into private hands works that artists and donors had intended for public

| Business and Industry; Science; Education; Philosophy and Religion | III | | IV | Sports; Social Issues and Crime; Folkways; Fashion; Holidays |

Sept. 29 The **Orbiting Solar Observatory VII** was launched to study a solar flare through x-ray observations.

Oct. 14 The **Nobel Prize in Physiology or Medicine** was awarded to Dr. Earl W. Sutherland of Vanderbilt University for his work with hormones.

Oct. 15 The **Nobel Prize in Economics** was awarded to Simon Kuznets, formerly a professor at Harvard University, who pioneered the use of the gross national product as a means of measuring economic output.

Oct. 29 The first successful use of **electricity to repair a bone fracture** was reported by surgeons at the University of Pennsylvania.

Nov. 6 An **underground nuclear test** was carried out on the remote Alaskan island of Amchitka despite attempts by environmentalists and others to halt it. The Spartan warhead had a yield equivalent to 5,000,000 tons of TNT.

Dec. 4 In the **largest voluntary safety recall** in auto industry history, General Motors recalled some 6,700,000 vehicles to secure engines against motor mount failure.

Dec. 20 The 10% **import surcharge** instituted on Aug. 15 was removed.

Atlanta Chiefs 2–0 in the final game of a three-game playoff.

Sept. 19 The second annual **New York City Marathon** was won by Norman Higgins of New London, Conn., with a time of 2 hrs., 22 min., 54.2 sec.

Sept. 21 The **Washington Senators,** often fondly described by baseball fans as "first in war, first in peace, and last in the American League," would move to Texas for the 1972 season, it was announced. The team would be renamed the Texas Rangers.

Oct. 8–11 The **Davis Cup** international tennis challenge round was won by the U.S., defeating Rumania three matches to two. This year it was decided to abolish the challenge round. Beginning in 1972, the defending team would be required to play through the entire competition.

Oct. 9–17 The 68th annual **World Series** was won by the underdog Pittsburgh Pirates (NL), who beat the Baltimore Orioles (AL) four games to three. On Oct. 5 Baltimore had completed a three-game sweep over the Oakland Athletics to take the American League championship. On Oct. 6 the Pirates had clinched the National League pennant, beating the San Francisco Giants three games to one.

Oct. 26 **Bobby Fischer** became the first U.S. chess player to make his way through the elimination matches for the world chess championship. Fischer defeated Tigran Petrosian of the U.S.S.R. in Buenos Aires, Argentina, thus qualifying for competition against Boris Spassky, the world champion, in 1972.

Oct. 30 A new **college football rushing record** was set by Ed Marinaro of Cornell University, who scored a three-year career total of 4132 yards.

Nov. 18 A bill outlawing **hunting from airplanes** was signed by Pres. Nixon.

1972

The inflationary spiral appeared to be coming under control. Unemployment was down, as was inflation, and economic growth was up. The economy's record was the best since 1967, and in November the Dow Jones average hit 1000 for the first time in history. The number of government employees had not risen and, for the first time in a decade, the number of agricultural workers had not dropped. Nevertheless, businessmen worried about the federal deficit, and many labor leaders withdrew from the Federal Pay Board, charging that wages were being more carefully monitored than prices. The big economic news was the $750,000,000 wheat sale to the U.S.S.R., prompting charges that grain dealers had known about the impending sale and had bought up grain at low prices, thus making big profits at farmers'

Professional sports were beset this year by organizational feuds. The new World Hockey Association attracted some of the NHL's best players with big contracts. After several months of conflict, the International Lawn Tennis Federation came to terms with Lamar Hunt's World Championship Tennis (WCT) group by dividing control over the scheduling of tournaments. Because the agreement was not approved until July, professionals under contract to the WCT were barred from playing in many major tournaments, including Wimbledon. In basketball, the American Basketball Association filed a $300,000,000 antitrust suit against the National Basketball Association, charging it with seeking to eliminate competition by encouraging ABA players to jump leagues. For the first time in

troops were withdrawn in August. On the eve of the presidential election, Henry Kissinger, security adviser to Pres. Nixon, reported that a Vietnam peace settlement was close. The Democratic Party proved unable to support its candidate, Sen. George S. McGovern of South Dakota, who had vowed to end the U.S. military presence in Vietnam within 90 days of his inauguration. McGovern also supported cuts in defense spending and proposed amnesty for those who had chosen prison or exile over military service in Vietnam. McGovern's charges of corruption in the Nixon administration, including the role of administration officials in the Watergate affair, failed to influence the electorate. Notables who died this year included J. Edgar Hoover, head of the FBI from 1924, May 2, at 77; and the Rev. Adam Clayton Powell, Jr., controversial Baptist minister and congressman from New York (1945–1970), Apr. 4, at 63.

Feb. 4 The sixth round of the **Strategic Arms Limitation Talks** (SALT) in Vienna, Austria, begun on Nov. 15, 1971, ended with indications of progress. The seventh round opened in Helsinki, Finland, on Mar. 28 and led to the strategic arms agreements signed in Moscow on May 26.

Feb. 21–28 A historic **presidential visit to China** was undertaken by Pres. Nixon. In the Shanghai Communiqué (Feb. 27), the two nations agreed to work to lessen the risk of war, to normalize relations, and to increase scientific and cultural ties. The Chinese held that Taiwan was part of China. The U.S. acknowledged that there was one China and stated that its policy was to withdraw U.S. military forces from Taiwan as tensions in the area decreased.

Feb. 26 A **coal-slag dam collapsed** in Buffalo Creek, W.Va., after three days of torrential rain, killing some 118 people.

Mar. 8 New guidelines for the **classification of documents** were announced by Pres. Nixon, who ordered a reduction in the number of agencies and officials empowered to classify documents.

Mar. 22 The **Twenty-seventh, or Equal Rights, Amendment** to the Constitution, prohibiting discrimination on the basis of sex, was passed by the Senate and sent to the states for ratification. Hawaii was the first to ratify. By the end of the year, 22 of the required 38 states had ratified it.

Apr. 7 The **Federal Election Campaign Act** went into effect. The law set limits on advertising budgets and on candidates' financing of their own campaigns. It also required disclosure of contributors of more than $100.

view. This year's theater season was noted for its numerous revivals, among them *A Funny Thing Happened on the Way to the Forum.* The music world also offered revivals, with a reemergence of '50s rock 'n' roll, ragtime music, and the big band sound of Benny Goodman and Duke Ellington. Many of Hollywood's film offerings were noted for their brutality, among them *The French Connection* and *The Godfather.* Notables who died this year included the poet John Berryman, a suicide, Jan. 7, at 57; Rudolf Friml, composer, Nov. 12, at 93; Ferde Grofé, composer of the *Grand Canyon Suite,* Apr. 3, at 80; Gabriel Heatter, the newscaster, Mar. 30, at 81; Mahalia Jackson, gospel singer, Jan. 27, at 60; José Limón, dancer, Dec. 2, at 64; Marianne Moore, poet, Feb. 5, at 84; Kenneth Patchen, poet, Jan. 1, at 60; Ezra Pound, poet, Nov. 1, at 87; Ted Shawn, dancer, Jan. 9, at 80; Helen Traubel, Wagnerian soprano, July 28, at 69; Edmund Wilson, author and critic, June 12, at 77; and Walter Winchell, columnist and broadcaster, Feb. 20, at 74.

Among **books published** this year was *August 1914* by Alexander Solzhenitsyn, a novel of the first weeks of World War I and culminating in the Russian defeat in the Battle of Tannenberg. Other books published included a slim volume by Richard Bach entitled *Jonathan Livingston Seagull,* a phenomenal best seller; *Delusions, Etc.,* poems by John Berryman; *The Late John Marquand* by Stephen Birmingham, a biography; *Captains and the Kings* by Taylor Caldwell, a novel; *The Best and the Brightest* by David Halberstam, an account of the Kennedy administration and the early years of American involvement in the Vietnam War; *The Boys of Summer* by Roger Kahn, a nostalgic look at the old Brooklyn Dodgers; *Eleanor and Franklin* by Joseph P. Lash, a study of the Roosevelts; *The Human Season: Selected Poems, 1926–1972* by Archibald MacLeish; and *The Optimist's Daughter* by Eudora Welty, a novel.

Jan. 5 A **Russian art and artifact collection,** comprising nearly 1500 objects, arrived at the Corcoran Gallery in Washington, D.C., on the first stop of a six-city tour.

Jan. 17 A **report on TV violence** by the surgeon general found little effect on children but found it harmful to people predisposed to aggressive behavior. Critics said the report was slanted in favor of the TV industry.

Jan. 28 *Treemonisha,* a 1911 opera by Scott Joplin, was given its premiere performance in Atlanta, Ga.

Feb. 2 **Seiji Ozawa** was named music director of the Boston Symphony, beginning with the 1973–1974 season.

Feb. 4–5 The U.S. premiere performance of *The*

| Business and Industry; Science;
Education; Philosophy and Religion | III | | IV | Sports; Social Issues and Crime;
Folkways; Fashion; Holidays |

expense. In medicine the leading topic was acupuncture, the Chinese practice of achieving anesthesia by inserting needles at specific points on the body. In transportation, the rise in airline hijackings sparked an international strike by pilots, which prompted U.S. officials to institute stricter airport screening procedures. Notables who died this year included Saul Alinsky, social activist, June 12, at 63; Lillian Gilbreth, a pioneer in time-motion studies, Jan. 2, at 93; Paul Goodman, writer and social critic, Aug. 2, at 60; Howard Johnson, founder of the restaurant chain bearing his name, June 20, at 75; Igor Sikorsky, developer of the helicopter, Oct. 26, at 83; Harlow Shapley, astronomer, Oct. 20, at 86; and Joseph F. Smith, Jr., president of the Church of Jesus Christ of Latter Day Saints, July 2, at 95.

Jan. 5 An order to begin work on a **reusable space shuttle** was issued to NASA by Pres. Richard M. Nixon.

Jan. 14 Plans were announced for the **first breeder reactor,** a nuclear reactor that produces more fuel than it consumes. It was to be built in Tennessee by a consortium of government and private organizations.

Feb. 5 In a move to prevent **airplane hijacking,** screening of passengers and their luggage became mandatory on all domestic and foreign flights by U.S. scheduled airlines.

Feb. 14 The **first nuclear-powered heart pump** kept a calf's heart beating for five hours at Boston City Hospital.

Feb. 21 A 134-day **dock strike,** the longest to date, was ended when West Coast longshoremen went back to work. The strike had begun on July 1, 1971, but was suspended Oct. 6 by an 80-day injunction. An agreement with the International Longshoremen's and Warehousemen's Union reached on Feb. 8 had been ratified on Feb. 19.

Mar. 1 The Supreme Court ruled that the **Federal Trade Commission** could extend its traditional authority in antitrust cases and bar unfair or deceptive marketing practices.

Mar. 1 In the **Yablonski murder case,** Paul Gilly was convicted for the 1970 murders of United Mine Workers (UMW) dissident Joseph Yablonski, his wife, and his daughter. Gilly was sentenced to death the next day. On Apr. 11 Gilly's wife pleaded guilty and implicated several UMW leaders, including its president, William A. "Tony" Boyle. On May 2 Albert Pass, a union official, was arrested; on the following day,

history, major league baseball players struck, returning to play only after team owners agreed to an increase in players' pensions. Americans became interested in chess this year because of Bobby Fischer's antics in Reykjavik, Iceland. Fischer and the defending world chess champion, Boris Spassky of the U.S.S.R., argued for months about details leading up to the showdown. During play, Fischer made demands of match officials that kept him in the headlines for months. In golf the top money winners were Jack Nicklaus, $320,542, and Kathy Whitworth, $65,063. This year Americans mourned the deaths of Charles Atlas, real name Angelo Siciliano, body builder, Dec. 24, at 79; Roberto Clemente, star outfielder of the Pittsburgh Pirates, who was killed in the crash of a cargo plane taking relief supplies to earthquake victims in Managua, Nicaragua, Dec. 31, at 38; Gilbert R. "Gil" Hodges, former Brooklyn Dodgers star, Apr. 2, at 47; Norman Norell, real name Norman Levinson, fashion designer, Oct. 25, at 72; Jackie Robinson, first black to play in the major leagues, Oct. 24, at 53; Harold J. "Pie" Traynor, in 1969 voted greatest third baseman of all time, Mar. 16, at 72; and George Weiss, former baseball executive, Aug. 13, at 78.

Jan. 1 In **college football bowl games,** the results were Penn State 30, Texas 6 in the Cotton Bowl; Nebraska 38, Alabama 6 in the Orange Bowl; Stanford 13, Michigan 12 in the Rose Bowl; and Oklahoma 40, Auburn 22 in the Sugar Bowl. This season the AP and UPI polls picked Nebraska as the national collegiate champions of 1971.

Jan. 8 In a major ruling on **college sports eligibility,** the NCAA announced that starting in the fall freshmen would be permitted to play on varsity football and basketball teams.

Jan. 14–16 **U.S. figure skating championships** were won by Ken Shelley, men's singles; Janet Lynn, women's singles, for the fourth year in a row; Jo Jo Starbuck and Kenneth Shelley, pairs; Judy Schwomeyer and James Sladky, dance, for the fifth consecutive year.

Jan. 16 **Super Bowl VI** was won by the Dallas Cowboys (NFC), who defeated the Miami Dolphins (AFC) 24–3. On Jan. 2 the Cowboys had stopped the San Francisco 49ers 14–3 for the NFC championship, and the Dolphins had defeated the Baltimore Colts 21–0 for the AFC title.

Feb. 3–13 At the **Winter Olympics** at Sapporo, Japan, U.S. athletes won three gold medals. The U.S.S.R. was first, with eight gold medals, followed by East Germany, Switzerland, and the Netherlands, all with four.

Mar. 19 The **Association for Intercollegiate Athletics for Women** (AIAW) held its first women's collegiate basketball championship. Immaculata College defeated West Chester State 52–48.

Apr. 10 A treaty banning **biological warfare** was signed by the U.S. and some 120 other nations.

May 2 A mine fire in the Sunshine Silver Mine in Kellogg, Idaho, killed 91 people.

May 8 The **mining of Haiphong harbor** and other major North Vietnamese ports was ordered by Pres. Nixon.

May 15 Alabama Gov. **George C. Wallace was shot** in Laurel, Md., by Arthur Bremer, 21, while campaigning in Maryland's Democratic presidential primary. Wallace was paralyzed from the waist down; three others were seriously injured.

May 22–30 The **first presidential visit to Moscow** in history was made by Pres. Nixon. U.S. and Soviet officials signed a number of agreements, including one for a joint space flight in 1975. On May 26 Pres. Nixon and secretary Leonid I. Brezhnev signed a treaty on antiballistic missile systems and an interim agreement on limitation of strategic missiles.

June 4 **Angela Davis,** the black militant, was acquitted in San Jose, Calif., of abetting a 1970 courtroom escape attempt that left four people dead.

June 9–10 **Flash floods** struck Rapid City, S.D., killing 239 people and causing more than $100,000,000 in damage.

June 17 In what became known as the **Watergate affair,** police arrested five men involved in a burglary of Democratic Party headquarters in the Watergate apartment complex in Washington, D.C. Among the five was James McCord, a former CIA agent then working for the Republican National Committee and the Committee to Reelect the President. Democratic Party Chairman Larry O'Brien, charging Pres. Nixon's campaign staff with "political espionage," filed a $1,000,000 civil suit on June 20.

June 19–23 **Hurricane Agnes** swept the East Coast, killing 127 and causing more than $1,000,000,000 in damage.

June 29 **State death penalties** were ruled unconstitutional by the Supreme Court, which held that they constituted cruel and unusual punishment.

July 10–14 The **Democratic National Convention** nominated Sen. **George S. McGovern** of South Dakota for president and Sen. Thomas F. Eagleton of Missouri for vice president. On July 25 Eagleton confirmed rumors that he had received psychiatric treatment three times from 1960 to 1966 for nervous exhaustion and fatigue. On July 31 Eagleton withdrew from the campaign. On Aug. 8, R. Sargent Shriver, former head of the Peace Corps, succeeded Eagleton on the ticket.

Trojans, an opera by Hector Berlioz, was presented by the Boston Opera Company.

Feb. 17 **Ralph Ginzburg** began serving a three-year sentence on a 1963 conviction for sending obscene promotional material through the mails. The material was touting his magazine *Eros.* Ginzburg was paroled in October.

Mar. 14 **Grammy Awards** were presented for the following: best album of 1971, *Tapestry* by Carole King; best record, "It's Too Late" by Carole King; best male pop vocalist, James Taylor for "You've Got a Friend"; best female pop vocalist, Carole King for *Tapestry;* best group, The Carpenters for *The Carpenters.*

Mar. 30 The nude ballet *Mutations* by Glen Tetley was given its U.S. premiere by the Netherlands Dance Theater at the Brooklyn Academy of Music in New York City.

Apr. 9 **Academy Awards** were presented to *The French Connection* as the outstanding motion picture of 1971 and to its star, Gene Hackman, as best actor; to Jane Fonda as best actress for *Klute;* and to Ben Johnson and Cloris Leachman as best supporting actor and actress for *The Last Picture Show.*

Apr. 13 **National Book Awards** were presented for the following: fiction, *The Complete Stories* by Flannery O'Connor; biography, *Eleanor and Franklin: The Story of Their Relationship* by Joseph P. Lash; history, the *Ordeal of the Union* series by Allan Nevins; arts and letters, *The Classical Style: Haydn, Mozart, Beethoven* by Charles Rosen; philosophy and religion, *Righteous Empire: The Protestant Experience in America* by Martin E. Marty; science, *The Blue Whale* by George L. Small; poetry, *Collected Poems* by Frank O'Hara and *Selected Poems* by Howard Moss.

Apr. 20 The opera *Lord Byron* by Virgil Thomson was given its premiere performance by the Juilliard American Opera Center in New York City.

Apr. 22 A farewell gala for **Rudolf Bing** was held at the Metropolitan Opera in New York City. Bing was retiring after 22 years as general manager of the Met.

Apr. 23 A double bill by **Tom Stoppard,** the British playwright, opened off Broadway at Theater Four. The two witty one-act plays were *The Real Inspector Hound* and *After Magritte.*

Apr. 23 **Tony awards** for the 1971–1972 season were awarded for the following: best play, *Sticks and Bones;* best musical, *Two Gentlemen of Verona;* best dramatic actor, Cliff Gorman for *Lenny;* best dramatic actress, Sada Thompson for *Twigs.*

May 1 **Pulitzer prizes** were awarded for the following: fiction, *Angle of Repose* by Wallace Stegner;

Tennessee local president Silous Huddleston confessed to his role in the killings. On Aug. 23 a federal grand jury indicted four union officials—Pass, Chester Philpot, William Prater, and Ernest Stults—and named three others as unindicted co-conspirators.

Mar. 2 **Pioneer 10** was successfully launched on a 22-month voyage that would take it past Jupiter.

Mar. 20–21 Charging **political intervention by big business,** newspaper columnist Jack Anderson reported that International Telephone and Telegraph and the CIA had tried to promote economic instability in Chile in order to topple the elected Marxist government of Salvador Allende Gossens.

Apr. 4 A rise in **venereal disease** was reported by federal health officials, who estimated that there were some 2,300,000 new cases of gonorrhea in 1972 and 100,000 of infectious syphilis, the biggest increases since introduction of antibiotics.

Apr. 13 In a landmark ruling concerning **public care of the mentally ill** and retarded, federal Judge Frank M. Johnson ordered the state of Alabama to meet specified guidelines in its institutions.

Apr. 14 The 685-mile **California Water Project,** a system of aqueducts to carry water from northern California to the semiarid central and southern areas, went into operation.

Apr. 16 **Apollo 16,** manned by astronauts John W. Young, Charles M. Duke, and Thomas K. Mattingly, was successfully launched into orbit around the moon. On Apr. 20 Duke and Young descended to the moon's surface, remaining there until Apr. 23 to conduct tests and collect rock samples Apollo 16 splashed down on Apr. 27.

May 1 The 1969 election of **William A. "Tony" Boyle** as president of the United Mine Workers was declared void by a federal judge because union funds and facilities had been used in Boyle's campaign. On Dec. 19 Boyle resigned after Arnold Miller, a reform candidate, won a new election.

June 3 The **first woman rabbi in the U.S.,** Sally J. Priesand, 25, was ordained in Cincinnati, Ohio.

June 12–17 **Expo '72,** a fundamentalist conference organized by the Campus Crusade for Christ International, was attended by some 80,000 youthful delegates at the Cotton Bowl in Dallas, Tex.

Mar. 25 The **NCAA basketball championship** was won by UCLA, defeating Florida State 81–76 and maintaining its 45-game winning streak.

Mar. 27 In the trial of the two remaining **Soledad Brothers,** John Cluchette and Fleeta Drumgo were found innocent by a San Francisco jury of slaying a prison guard at Soledad state prison in 1970. The third convict charged, George Jackson, was killed during a prison break attempt in Aug. 1971.

Apr. 1 The **first major league baseball strike** in history began as players walked out over a pension dispute. The strike was settled on Apr. 13. The season began on Apr. 15 rather than on the scheduled date of Apr. 5.

Apr. 9 The **Masters golf tournament** was won by Jack Nicklaus.

Apr. 17 The 76th annual **Boston Marathon** was won by Olavi Suomalainen of Finland, with a time of 2 hrs., 15 min., 39 sec. The first women's competition was won by Nina Kuscsik of Huntington, Long Island, N.Y., with a time of 3 hrs., 8 min., 58 sec.

Apr. 28 In a settlement of the **1968 Kentucky Derby controversy,** a Kentucky court of appeals awarded the prize money to the second-place winner, Forward Pass. The winner, Dancer's Image, was disqualified from the money, but not the win, because the horse had been given a pain-killing drug before the race.

Apr. 30–May 11 The **NHL Stanley Cup** was won for the second time in three years by the Boston Bruins, who defeated the New York Rangers four games to two.

May 6 The 98th annual **Kentucky Derby** was won by Riva Ridge, with a time of 2:01⁴/₅. The jockey was Ron Turcotte.

May 7 The **NBA basketball championship** was won by the Los Angeles Lakers, who defeated the New York Knicks four games to one.

May 18 Formation of the **Gray Panthers** was announced by Margaret Kuhn, 67, to combat discrimination against the elderly.

May 20 The **ABA basketball championship** was won by the Indiana Pacers, who beat the New York Nets four games to two.

May 20 The 97th annual **Preakness Stakes** was won by Bee Bee Bee, with a time of 1:55³/₅. The jockey was Eldon Nelson.

May 27 The 56th **Indianapolis 500** auto race was won by Mark Donohue, with a time of 3 hrs., 4 min., 5.54 sec., for a new record average speed of 162.962 mph.

June 10 The 104th annual **Belmont Stakes** was won by Riva Ridge, with a time of 2:28. The jockey was Ron Turcotte.

June 11 The **LPGA golf tournament** was won by Kathy Ahern.

July 14 Jean Westwood was chosen head of the Democratic Party's National Committee. She was the first woman to hold the top job in either of the nation's two major parties.

Aug. 3 The **Strategic Arms Limitation Treaty** (SALT I) was passed by the U.S. Senate. The treaty limited the U.S. and U.S.S.R. to two antiballistic missile systems of 100 missiles each, one for defense of each nation's capital, one for defense of a portion of its ICBM system. A five-year interim agreement on limitation of strategic arms was approved by the House on Aug. 18 and by the Senate on Sept. 14. The two accords were signed in ceremonies at the White House on Oct. 3.

Aug. 4 Arthur Bremer was convicted on nine counts in the May 15 shootings of Gov. George C. Wallace of Alabama and three others. He was sentenced to 63 years in prison.

Aug. 12 The **last U.S. ground combat forces** in Vietnam were withdrawn.

Aug. 21–23 The **Republican National Convention** nominated Pres. **Nixon** and Vice Pres. Spiro T. Agnew for reelection.

Aug. 29 Pres. Nixon announced that a **White House investigation** of the Watergate break-in, conducted by White House counsel John Dean, revealed that administration officials were not involved in the burglary.

Sept. 5 In what was known as the **trial of the Harrisburg Seven,** federal prosecutors moved to drop all conspiracy charges against the Rev. Philip F. Berrigan and six others accused of plotting to kidnap Henry Kissinger and blow up heating tunnels in Washington, D.C. The trial against the seven in Harrisburg, Pa., had ended in a hung jury.

Sept. 15 In the **Watergate break-in** case, a federal grand jury indicted the five originally accused of burglary and former White House aides G. Gordon Liddy and E. Howard Hunt.

Oct. 12–13 A racial brawl on the carrier *Kitty Hawk* off the coast of Vietnam left some 46 sailors injured. In November the carrier *Constellation* returned to port after more than 100 seamen protested what they termed racist actions by officers. On Nov. 10 Adm. Elmo R. Zumwalt, chief of naval operations, reprimanded some 90 naval officers and demanded an end to racist behavior in the Navy.

Oct. 17 A **Supplementary Security Income** (SSI) system was approved by Congress to replace federal and

biography, *Eleanor and Franklin: The Story of Their Relationship* by Joseph P. Lash; history, *Neither Black nor White* by Carl N. Degler; general nonfiction, *Stilwell and the American Experience in China* by Barbara W. Tuchman; poetry, *Collected Poems* by James Wright.

May 2 *That Championship Season* by Jason Miller was presented by Joseph Papp's New York Shakespeare Festival. Described by Clive Barnes as "the perfect Broadway play of the season," it finally opened on Broadway on Sept. 14 at the Booth Theater.

May 14 **Emmy Awards** were presented to Keith Michell as best actor for *The Six Wives of Henry VIII;* Glenda Jackson as best actress for *Elizabeth R;* Peter Falk as best actor in a dramatic series for *Columbo;* and Glenda Jackson as best actress in a dramatic series for *Elizabeth R.*

June 17 *Fiddler on the Roof* became the longest-running Broadway show in history when its 3225th performance broke the record set by *Life With Father* in 1947.

June 18–25 The **Stravinsky Festival,** presented by the New York State Theater to mark the 90th anniversary of the composer's birth, was the dance event of the year. The New York City Ballet performed 30 works set to Stravinsky scores, many of them world premieres and many choreographed by George Balanchine, longtime friend of Stravinsky.

June 28 The sale of some 800 paintings by **Mark Rothko** was halted after the artist's daughter filed a suit in New York charging that her father's estate was being defrauded by its executors.

June 29 In a landmark decision bearing on **freedom of the press,** the Supreme Court ruled that journalists have no right to withhold confidential information from grand juries. On Oct. 4 Peter Bridge of the Newark *News* became the first reporter to be jailed under this decision.

July 1 *Ms.* magazine, a monthly edited by the feminist leader Gloria Steinem, was launched. Steinem described it as a "how to" publication for women, "not how to make jelly but how to seize control of your life."

July 1–9 The **Newport Jazz Festival,** which had been shut down by a riot in 1971, was moved from Rhode Island to New York City, where it expanded its program from four to nine days and attracted an audience in excess of 100,000.

July 8–9 The largest **rock festival** since the 1969 Woodstock event drew some 200,000 rock music lov-

| Business and Industry; Science; Education; Philosophy and Religion   III | IV   Sports; Social Issues and Crime; Folkways; Fashion; Holidays |

June 26 All meat import quotas were lifted until 1973, in a move to control rapidly rising meat prices.

July 8 An agreement on a **grain sale to the U.S.S.R.,** valued at a minimum of $750,000,000, was announced by Pres. Nixon. Farmers were later angered when it was learned that large exporters had had prior knowledge of the deal and had bought up wheat cheaply.

July 20 An agreement limiting **railroad featherbedding** settled the longstanding dispute over the use of firemen on railroads. A new contract allowed drastic reductions in the number of jobs, to be achieved by attrition.

July 23 **ERTS-1,** the first Earth Resources Technology Satellite, was successfully launched into Earth orbit. On July 25 it began sending photographic information about Earth's resources back to scientists on the ground.

Aug. 21 **Copernicus,** an orbiting astronomical observatory designed to study the stars and the nature of the universe, was successfully launched into orbit.

Sept. 11 The **Bay Area Rapid Transit System** (BART), linking Oakland and San Francisco, Calif., went into operation. The automated rail service was the nation's first new regional transit system in 50 years.

Oct. 12 The **Nobel Prize in Physiology or Medicine** was awarded jointly to Gerald M. Edelman of Rockefeller University and Rodney R. Porter of Great Britain for their studies of antibodies.

Oct. 18 The **Water Pollution Control Act** was passed by Congress over Pres. Nixon's veto. It required industry to halt discharges by 1985, set industry-wide standards, and provided massive federal funding for building and improving sewage plants.

Oct. 20 The **Nobel Prize in Physics** was awarded jointly to John Bardeen of the University of Illinois, Leon N. Cooper of Brown University, and John R. Schrieffer of the University of Pennsylvania for their development of the theory of superconductivity.

Oct. 20 The **Nobel Prize in Chemistry** was awarded jointly to Christian B. Anfinsen of the National Institutes of Health and Stanford Moore and William H. Stein of the Rockefeller Institute for their work in enzyme chemistry, particularly their studies of ribonuclease.

June 18 The **U.S. Open golf tournament** was won for the third time by Jack Nicklaus, tying Bobby Jones's record of 13 major golf titles.

June 19 In a decision bearing on **baseball's reserve clause,** the Supreme Court ruled major league baseball exempt from antitrust statutes, thus ending Curt Flood's 1970 suit against organized baseball. The Court called the exemption an "anomaly" and called on Congress to correct the situation through legislation.

July 2 The **U.S. Women's Open golf tournament** was won by Susie Maxwell Berning.

July 7 The **first women FBI agents,** Susan Lynn Roley, a former U.S. Marine, and Joanne E. Pierce, a former nun, were sworn in.

July 7 At the **Wimbledon** tennis championships in England, Billie Jean King won the women's singles title. On July 9 Stan Smith won the men's singles title, completing the first U.S. singles sweep since 1955. King teamed with Betty Stove of the Netherlands to win the women's doubles, and Rosemary Casals teamed with Ilie Nastase of Rumania to take the mixed doubles title.

July 11–Sept. 1 The **world chess championship** was won by Bobby Fischer, who triumphed over the defending champion, Boris Spassky of the U.S.S.R., in competition at Reykjavik, Iceland.

June 13 In an unprecedented **football team swap,** Robert Isray made a no-cash trade of his Los Angeles Rams for Carroll Rosenbloom's Baltimore Colts.

July 25 The **baseball All-Star Game** was won by the National League, beating the American League 4–3 in the tenth inning.

Aug. 6 The **PGA golf tournament** was won by Gary Player.

Aug. 7 The **Baseball Hall of Fame** inducted eight new members: Lawrence P. "Yogi" Berra, Joshua "Josh" Gibson, Vernon "Lefty" Gomez, William "Will" Harridge, Sanford "Sandy" Koufax, Walter "Buck" Leonard, Early Wynn, and Ross Youngs.

Aug. 26 The **North American Soccer League championship** was won by the New York Cosmos, who defeated the St. Louis Stars 2–1.

Aug. 26–Sept. 11 At the **Summer Olympics** in Munich, West Germany, the U.S. won 33 gold medals to the Soviet Union's 50. Swimmer Mark Spitz set an Olympic record by winning seven gold medals. Frank Shorter was the first U.S. athlete in 64 years to win the gold medal for the marathon, and the U.S. basketball team lost for the first time since the game was introduced in 1936. On Sept. 5 Arab terrorists entered the Olympic village, killed two Israeli coaches and took nine Israeli athletes hostage. All nine were killed, along with a number of terrorists, in a shootout at a

state aid to the aged, blind, and disabled. It was to go into effect in 1974.

Oct. 20 A revenue-sharing bill was signed by Pres. Nixon, authorizing distribution of $30,200,000,000 in federal revenues to state and local governments to spend as they saw fit.

Nov. 7 Richard M. Nixon was reelected president of the United States in the greatest Republican landslide in history. Spiro T. Agnew was reelected vice president. The electoral vote was Nixon, 521; Sen. George S. McGovern, Democrat, 17. The popular vote was Nixon, 45,767,218; McGovern 28,357,668. The Democrats picked up two Senate seats for a 57–43 majority. The Republicans gained 13 seats in the House, but the Democrats still led 255–179, with one seat going to an independent.

Nov. 8 A sit-in at the Bureau of Indian Affairs by some 500 Indians ended when officials promised to study the protesters' demands for enforcement of treaties and reform of natural resource policies on Indian lands. The demands were rejected in Jan. 1973.

Nov. 22 A 22-year-old ban on travel to China was lifted.

Dec. 18 Full-scale bombing of North Vietnam was resumed after the Paris peace negotiations reached an impasse. The bombing was again halted on Dec. 30. Private talks were to resume on Jan. 8, 1973.

ers to Pocono International Raceway at Long Pond, Pa.

Aug. 11 The controversial **Valley Curtain** environmental sculpture, a six-ton, 400-foot-high orange curtain designed by the artist Christo, was completed across the quarter-mile Rifle Gap in Colorado. It lasted 24 hours before high winds tore it to shreds.

Sept. 23 *Pippin,* a musical by Roger O. Hirson and Stephen Schwartz based loosely on the life of the son of Charlemagne, opened at the Imperial Theater in New York City. Its cast included John Rubinstein, Ben Vereen, Eric Berry, and Irene Ryan.

Oct. 21 **Kansas City International Airport** was dedicated in Missouri. Parking lots located inside its three doughnut-shaped terminals enabled passengers to park within 400 feet of the planes.

Nov. 17 *The Changing Room* by David Storey, a play set in a rugby team's locker room before, during, and after a game, opened to critical acclaim at the Long Wharf Theater in New Haven, Conn.

Dec. 20 *The Sunshine Boys* by Neil Simon, starring Jack Albertson and Sam Levene as aging vaudeville comedians brought together one last time by fate, opened at the Broadhurst Theater in New York City.

Dec. 29 *Life* magazine, a pioneer in photojournalism, suspended publication after 36 years of weekly publication.

1973

The landslide victory of Pres. Richard M. Nixon in Nov. 1972 was interpreted by some as a vote of confidence in the Nixon administration's policies. U.S. involvement in Vietnam seemed to be drawing to a close. As the year progressed, however, the story of the Watergate break-in was uncovered by journalists and by the Senate Select Committee on Presidential Campaign Activities. Pres. Nixon's attempts to use executive privilege or national security as reasons to withhold evidence and limit testimony by administration aides caused further friction between the White House and investigators. The revelation that Pres. Nixon had had his official conversations recorded since 1971 set off a struggle for the tapes of conversations relating to Watergate. Key tapes became unavailable, and a portion of one was mysteriously erased. In August Vice Pres. Spiro T. Agnew revealed he was under investigation in connection with official corruption in Maryland that took place while he served as Baltimore County executive and governor of Maryland. By year's end the Nixon administration was in deep trouble. Nixon came under pressure to resign,

Broadway show revenues dropped to a ten-year low during the 1972–1973 season. To avoid the financial disaster accompanying a closing on opening night, a number of producers made Broadway their last stop on extensive national tours. *Lorelei,* starring Carol Channing, was scheduled to arrive in New York City in 1974 after a long 13-city tour. Joseph Papp, director of the New York Shakespeare Festival, took over the Vivian Beaumont Theater in Lincoln Center. By year's end he controlled productions on some ten stages, a reflection of the importance of resident, noncommercial theater. In motion pictures nostalgia was popular with audiences, as evidenced by the success of such films as *American Graffiti,* about growing up in the early 1960s, *Paper Moon, The Sting,* and *Dillinger.* Nostalgia carried the day with television audiences as well. The surprise hit was *The Waltons,* a warm view of southern family life during the Great Depression. A view of contemporary family life was offered by a documentary called *An American Family,* about the Loud family of California. Notables who died this year included Conrad Aiken,

| Business and Industry; Science; Education; Philosophy and Religion III | | Sports; Social Issues and Crime; Folkways; Fashion; Holidays IV |

Oct. 25 The **Nobel Prize in Economics** was awarded jointly to Kenneth J. Arrow of Harvard University and John R. Hicks of Great Britain.

Oct. 28 A bill establishing the **Consumer Product Safety Commission** was signed by Pres. Nixon.

Nov. 13 An international convention to control **oceanic pollution** was signed by the U.S. and 90 other nations.

Nov. 14 The **Dow Jones Index** of 30 industrial stocks closed above 1000 on the New York Stock Exchange for the first time in history.

Dec. 7 **Apollo 17,** the sixth and last of the Apollo lunar landing missions, was successfully launched. It was crewed by Eugene Cernan, Ronald Evans, and Harrison Schmitt. During their lunar excursion (Dec. 11–14), Cernan and Schmitt found what they described as orange soil, which was taken to be a possible indication of volcanic activity, and collected some 249 lbs. of rock and soil samples. Apollo 17 splashed down in the Pacific Ocean on Dec. 19.

Dec. 31 A near-total **ban on DDT use,** ordered by the Environmental Protection Agency, went into effect.

nearby airport. The Olympic Games were suspended for the first time in modern history. They were resumed on Sept. 6 after a memorial service for the dead athletes.

Sept. 9 The **Miss America** title was won by Terry Anne Meeuwsen, 23, of Wisconsin, at the annual pageant in Atlantic City, N.J.

Sept. 9–10 The **U.S. Open tennis singles championships** were won by Billie Jean King, for the third time, in the women's division and Ilie Nastase of Rumania in the men's division.

Oct. 1 The third annual **New York City Marathon** was won by Sheldon Karlin, with a time of 2 hrs., 27 min., 52.8 sec. A separate women's competition was boycotted by its ten entrants, who were permitted to run in the main race after a ten-minute sit-in. The first woman to finish was Nina Kuscsik, with an official time of 3 hrs., 18 min., 41 sec.

Oct. 13–15 The **Davis Cup tennis championship** was successfully defended by the U.S., defeating Rumania three matches to two in Bucharest.

Oct. 14–22 The **World Series** was won by the Oakland Athletics (AL), defeating the Cincinnati Reds (NL) four games to three. On Oct. 11 the Reds had won the National League pennant by beating the Pittsburgh Pirates three games to two. The next day the Athletics won the American League title over the Detroit Tigers, three games to two.

1973

Record levels of retail sales, factory output, new car sales, employment, and personal incomes balanced against inflation of 8.5% and the second dollar devaluation in 14 months, added up to what a consumer columnist described as joyless prosperity. As food prices climbed, consumer groups organized a meat boycott. Toward the end of the year the situation was aggravated by an oil embargo imposed on the U.S. and other industrialized nations by members of the Organization of Arab Petroleum Exporting Countries (OAPEC). The oil shortage caused long lines at gas stations and shut down factories. The federal government organized an emergency gas rationing system, but it was not implemented. In education, the end of the military draft, skyrocketing tuition costs, and increasing competition among degree holders for jobs and for admittance to graduate and professional schools led students to question the value of a college education. Enrollment was up only 2%, but enrollment at less expensive public institutions was strong. Notables who died this year included Harvey S. Firestone, Jr., an industrialist, June 1, at 75; Harold B.

Salaries increased and attendance declined for football, basketball, and baseball, to the benefit of other sports, notably hockey, soccer, and tennis. In September the ban on local television coverage of football games was lifted for events sold out in advance, and many ticket-holders stayed home to watch the games. In baseball the American League adopted the designated hitter rule—which provided for a tenth player in the lineup to hit for the pitcher without forcing the pitcher to leave the game—in the hope of increasing scoring and boosting attendance. In hockey the NHL drew 9,299,028 fans for the 1972–1973 season, an increase of more than 1,000,000 over the previous year. In golf the top money winners were Jack Nicklaus, $308,362, and Kathy Whitworth, $82,864. As professional sports were changing and growing, so was the national passion for physical fitness. Some 60,000,000 Americans were involved in sports for exercise, including some 18,000,000 cyclists. Another carefully observed trend was the national crime rate. On Mar. 28 a preliminary report showed the 1972 crime rate was down 2%, but an FBI report

and the House began an investigation to determine whether impeachment proceedings were in order. The year was marked also by the deaths of several national figures. Lyndon Baines Johnson, 36th president of the United States, whose efforts to realize the Great Society were overwhelmed by the tragedy of Vietnam, died on Jan. 22, at 64. Other notables who died this year included Earl Browder, head of the U.S. Communist Party from 1930 to 1945, June 27, at 82; Jeannette Rankin, who as Republican congresswoman from Montana (1917–1919 and 1941–43) was the first woman elected to Congress and the only member to vote against U.S. entry into both world wars, May 18, at 92; and Winthrop Rockefeller, philanthropist, governor of Arkansas from 1967–1971, and grandson of John D. Rockefeller, Feb. 22, at 60.

Jan. 20   Pres. **Nixon was inaugurated** for his second term. Spiro T. Agnew was sworn in for his second term as vice president.

Jan. 22   A **Vietnam peace agreement** was signed in Paris by representatives of the U.S., North and South Vietnam, and the Vietcong. Its key provisions included a cease-fire throughout North and South Vietnam; withdrawal of U.S. forces and dismantling of U.S. installations within 60 days; release of North Vietnamese, Vietcong, and U.S. prisoners of war within 60 days; and reunification of the North and South through peaceful means. The South Vietnamese government was to remain until new elections were held. North Vietnamese forces in the South would remain in place, but could not be replaced or reinforced.

Jan. 27   An **end to draft call-ups** was announced by Sec. of Defense Melvin R. Laird.

Jan. 30   In the continuing **Watergate** scandal, James W. McCord and G. Gordon Liddy, former members of the Nixon reelection campaign, were convicted of breaking into and illegally wiretapping Democratic Party headquarters in 1972. Five others involved had earlier pleaded guilty.

Feb. 28   **Wounded Knee**, S.D., was occupied by militant members of the American Indian Movement (AIM) to dramatize the group's demands for free elections of tribal leaders, investigation of the Bureau of Indian Affairs, and review of all U.S.-Indian treaties. The group surrendered on May 8 after officials promised to investigate the complaints.

Mar. 23   A **letter by James W. McCord** was revealed by Watergate Judge John J. Sirica. In it McCord claimed perjury had been committed during the trial, that political pressure had been applied to defendants to

author and poet, Aug. 17, at 84; W. H. Auden, one of the great poets of the twentieth century, Sept. 28, at 66; S. N. Behrman, playwright, Sept. 9, at 80; Pearl S. Buck, Nobel Prize–winning novelist, Mar. 6, at 80; Lon Chaney, Jr., actor, July 12, at 67; Eddie Condon, jazz guitarist, Aug. 14, at 67; John Ford, director, Aug. 31, at 78; Betty Grable, 1940s pinup girl, July 2, at 56; William Inge, playwright, June 10, at 60; Gene Krupa, big band musician known for his drum solos, Oct. 16, at 64; Jacques Lipchitz, pioneer of cubist sculpture, May 26, at 81; Lauritz Melchior, leading Wagnerian tenor of the 1930s and 1940s, Mar. 18, at 80; Edward G. Robinson, actor, Jan. 26, at 79; Robert Ryan, actor, July 11, at 63; Edward Steichen, photographer, Mar. 25, at 93; and Max Yasgur, whose 600-acre Sullivan County, N.Y., farm had been the site of the 1969 Woodstock rock festival, Feb. 9, at 53.

Among **books published** this year was *Gravity's Rainbow* by Thomas Pynchon, a massive novel that explored the themes of sexuality, death, and warfare and their relationship to the development of twentieth-century history. Other books published this year included *Recovery* by John Berryman, an unfinished novel; *The Ascent of Man* by Jacob Bronowski, nonfiction; *The World of Apples* by John Cheever, stories; *Economics and the Public Purpose* by John Kenneth Galbraith; *The Taking of Pelham One Two Three* by John Godey, a novel about the hijacking of a New York City subway train; *Serpico* by Peter Maas, the true story of a policeman's struggle to overcome police corruption; *Marilyn* by Norman Mailer, another nonfiction novel; *Rembrandt's Hat* by Bernard Malamud, stories; *Do With Me What You Will* by Joyce Carol Oates, a novel; *The Implosion Conspiracy* by Louis Nizer, an account of the spy trial of Julius and Ethel Rosenberg; *The Great American Novel* by Philip Roth, a novel about a third baseball league, made up of misfits; *Breakfast of Champions* by Kurt Vonnegut, an example of the comic novel of despair; and *The Onion Field* by Joseph Wambaugh, a police novel based on fact.

Jan. 19   A so-called **antiwar counterconcert** was held in Washington, D.C., on the night of Pres. Richard M. Nixon's inaugural concert. It featured Leonard Bernstein conducting Joseph Haydn's *Mass in Time of War.*

Feb. 7   *The Hot L Baltimore* by Lanford Wilson, a play set in the lobby of a decrepit hotel, opened at the Circle Theater in New York City. Its cast included Judd Hirsch and Trish Hawkins.

Feb. 25   *A Little Night Music* by Hugh Wheeler and Stephen Sondheim, a musical suggested by a motion picture by Ingmar Bergman, opened at the Shubert Theater in New York City. Its cast included Hermione Gingold, Len Cariou, and Glynis Johns.

| Business and Industry; Science; Education; Philosophy and Religion | III | | IV | Sports; Social Issues and Crime; Folkways; Fashion; Holidays |

Lee, president of the Church of Jesus Christ of Latter Day Saints, Dec. 26, at 74; Marjorie Post, a philanthropist whose wealth was estimated at some $200,000,000, Sept. 12, at 86; and Selman A. Waksman, winner of the 1952 Nobel Prize for Medicine for his discovery of streptomycin, Aug. 16, at 85.

Jan. 11 Phase three of Pres. Nixon's **new economic policy** went into effect. All wage and price controls were lifted except on food, health care, and construction. The administration sought voluntary compliance with federal guidelines.

Jan. 17 **Import quotas on crude oil** were lifted by Pres. Nixon to cope with fuel shortages caused partly by a severe winter.

Jan. 18 In a **job discrimination** case, the American Telephone & Telegraph Company agreed to pay $15,000,000 to women and minority employees who had been treated unfairly, and to set up job-training programs and establish hiring quotas.

Jan. 22 In a decision on **abortion,** the Supreme Court struck down state laws restricting abortions during the first six months of pregnancy.

Feb. 12 The **dollar was devalued** by 10%, the second such move in 14 months.

Feb. 15 A five-year **accord on hijacking** was signed by the U.S. and Cuba, who agreed on measures intended to discourage the pirating of airplanes and ships.

Mar. 21 The use of **property taxes to finance public education,** despite funding inequities based on the economic levels of individual districts, was upheld by the Supreme Court.

Mar. 27 Trading in stock of the **Equity Funding Corporation of America** was halted on the New York Stock Exchange following an investigation of inside dealing. The company subsequently was ordered into bankruptcy and several officers were indicted on charges of falsifying documents and creating $120,-000,000 in phony assets.

Mar. 29 A **price freeze** on beef, pork, and lamb was announced by Pres. Nixon. Consumer groups initiated a nationwide one-week meat boycott on Apr. 1 in an effort to bring prices down.

Apr. 2 **Political intervention by big business** was highlighted by the admission by International

released on Dec. 27 showed the rate for the first nine months of 1973 to be up 1%, and violent crime up 3%. Among those who died this year were Frank Costello, a leading underworld figure, Feb. 18, at 82; Walt Kelly, creator of the comic strip *Pogo,* Oct. 18, at 60; Edward V. "Eddie" Rickenbacker, World War I flying ace, July 23, at 82; and Murat B. "Chic" Young, creator of the comic strip *Blondie,* Mar. 14, at 72.

Jan. 1 In **college football bowl games,** the results were Texas 17, Alabama 13 in the Cotton Bowl; Nebraska 40, Notre Dame 6 in the Orange Bowl; Southern California 42, Ohio State 17 in the Rose Bowl; and Oklahoma 14, Penn State 0 in the Sugar Bowl (Dec. 31, 1972). This season the AP and UPI polls chose Southern California the national college football champions of 1972.

Jan. 7 A **sniper attack** at a New Orleans, La., motel ended when police shot the sniper, Mark Essex, who had killed six persons and wounded 15 others.

Jan. 14 **Super Bowl VII** was won by the Miami Dolphins (AFC), defeating the Washington Redskins (NFC) 14–7. On Dec. 31, 1972, the Dolphins had defeated the Pittsburgh Steelers 21–17 for the AFC championship and the Redskins had beaten the Dallas Cowboys 26–3 for the NFC title.

Jan. 22 The **world heavyweight boxing championship** was won by George Foreman, who defeated Joe Frazier in a second-round knockout. On Sept. 1 he defended the title with a one-round knockout of Joe Roman in Tokyo, Japan.

Jan. 24–27 **U.S. figure skating championships** were won in Bloomington, Minn., by Gordon McKellen, Jr., men's singles; Janet Lynn, women's singles; Melissa and Mark Militano, pairs; and Mary Karen Campbell and Johnny Johns, dance.

Feb. 25 **Juan Corona** was sentenced to 25 consecutive life terms after being convicted for the 1971 murders of 25 migrant workers in California. In 1978 his conviction was overturned, on the grounds his lawyer did not defend him competently, and a new trial was ordered. He was convicted again on Sept. 23, 1982.

Mar. 1 **Robyn Smith** became the first woman jockey to win a stakes race when she rode North Sea to victory in the Paumonok Handicap at Aqueduct Raceway.

Mar. 1 The **birthrate** for the last six months of 1972 was reported at 1.98 children per couple, below the 2.1 rate for zero population growth.

Mar. 5 Terms of the **first comprehensive basketball contract** between the NBA and the Players Association were announced. They included the highest minimum salary in professional sports ($20,000), and pension benefits of $720 for each season played.

plead guilty and keep quiet, and that other officials were involved in the Watergate break-in.

Apr. 11 In Mississippi, the **Mississippi R.** reached its highest flood level, 50.3 feet, in 30 years. By May 4 more than 35,000 in nine states had fled their homes, 11 had died, and damages had reached $500,000,000.

Apr. 27 Acting FBI director **L. Patrick Gray resigned** following revelations he had destroyed records involving Watergate given him by White House counsel John Dean.

Apr. 30 In a televised **address on Watergate,** Pres. Nixon announced he had accepted the resignations of his chief of staff H. R. Haldeman, domestic policy assistant John Ehrlichman, counsel John Dean, and Attorney Gen. Richard G. Kleindienst. He denied any involvement in the Watergate break-in or any subsequent cover-up.

May 14 In a major **equal rights decision,** the Supreme Court ruled that women in the armed forces were entitled to the same benefits for their spouses as those accorded male servicemen.

May 14 David K. E. Bruce arrived in **Peking** to head the first U.S. liaison office in the People's Republic of China.

May 17 The **Senate Select Committee on Presidential Campaign Activities,** headed by Sen. Sam J. Ervin, Democrat of North Carolina, opened public hearings to explore the alleged cover-up of administration involvement in the Watergate affair.

May 25 Archibald Cox, a professor at Harvard Law School, was sworn in as special Watergate prosecutor.

June 16–25 U.S.S.R. Party Sec. **Leonid I. Brezhnev** visited the U.S. He signed agreements to reduce the risk of accidental nuclear war, increase air travel, and promote scientific exchanges between the U.S. and U.S.S.R.

June 25–29 John Dean **testified** before the Senate committee investigating Watergate. He implicated himself, H. R. Haldeman, John Ehrlichman, Pres. Nixon, John Mitchell, and others in a cover-up. Dean testified that Nixon had discussed the use of executive privilege as a means of avoiding personal involvement in Watergate, and so-called hush money. Dean also produced what was described as a White House enemies list, naming scores of administration foes.

July 1 A bill barring military operations in Indochina without congressional approval was signed by Pres. Nixon.

Mar. 3 **Grammy Awards** were presented for the following: best album of 1972, *Concert for Bangladesh;* best record, "The First Time Ever I Saw Your Face" by Roberta Flack; best male pop vocalist, Harry Nilsson for "Without You"; best female pop vocalist, Helen Reddy for "I Am Woman"; best pop group, Roberta Flack and Donny Hathaway for "Where Is the Love."

Mar. 6 *The Changing Room* by David Storey, which premiered in New Haven, Conn., in 1972, opened at the Morosco Theater in New York City.

Mar. 25 **Tony Awards** for the 1972–1973 season were presented for the following: best drama, *That Championship Season;* best musical, *Pippin,* which won five Tonys; best actor in a drama, Alan Bates for *Butley;* best actress in a drama, Julie Harris for *The Last of Mrs. Lincoln.*

Mar. 27 **Academy Awards** were presented to *The Godfather* as outstanding motion picture of 1972 and to its star Marlon Brando as best actor; to Liza Minnelli as best actress and Joel Grey as best supporting actor for *Cabaret,* which won eight awards in all; and Eileen Heckart as best supporting actress for *Butterflies Are Free.* Brando declined to accept his award.

Apr. 2 **U.S.-Soviet cultural exchange** was highlighted by the opening at the National Gallery of Art in Washington, D.C., of an exhibit of French impressionist and post-impressionist works from museums in the U.S.S.R.

Apr. 10 **National Book Awards** were presented for the following: fiction, *Chimera* by John Barth and *Augustus* by John Williams; poetry, *Collected Poems: 1951–1971* by A. R. Ammons; biography, *George Washington: Anguish and Farewell* by James Thomas Flexner; arts and letters, *Diderot* by Arthur M. Wilson; philosophy and religion, *A Religious History of the American People* by Stanley E. Ahlstrom.

Apr. 26 The new **Agnes de Mille Heritage Dance Theater** gave its first performance at the North Carolina School of the Arts.

May 1 The **Martha Graham Dance Company** opened its two-week season at the Alvin Theater in New York City with a performance of *Clytemnestra* featuring Mary Hinkson in the lead. It marked the first time the title role was not performed by Martha Graham.

May 3 The 110-story **Sears Tower** in Chicago, Ill., was topped out at 1450 feet, making it the world's tallest building.

May 4 An **Alexander Calder stabile** was dedicated at a federal building in Chicago. The sculpture was the first work commissioned under a federal program to put U.S. art into government buildings.

May 7 **Pulitzer prizes** were awarded for the following: fiction, *The Optimist's Daughter* by Eudora Welty; biography, *Luce and His Empire* by W. A. Swanberg;

Business and Industry; Science; Education; Philosophy and Religion III		IV Sports; Social Issues and Crime; Folkways; Fashion; Holidays

Telephone and Telegraph that it had offered funds to the CIA to oppose the election of Salvador Allende Gossens, a Marxist, to the presidency of Chile in 1970. Allende was elected, but on Sept. 11, 1973, his government was overthrown by a military junta and he was killed.

Apr. 5 **Pioneer 11** was launched toward a December rendezvous with the planet Jupiter.

Apr. 15 The signing of **contracts with California grape growers** by the International Brotherhood of Teamsters was announced. It prompted a strike by César Chávez's United Farm Workers Union, which charged the Teamsters with union busting by taking over contracts held by the UFW.

May 14 **Skylab,** the first U.S. space station, was launched into Earth orbit, but a launch mishap damaged one of its solar-power panels and jammed the other. On May 25, Skylab 2 carried astronauts Charles Conrad, Joseph Kerwin, and Paul Weitz to a rendezvous with the station. The crew deployed the stuck panel, made further repairs, and conducted scientific experiments before splashing down in the Pacific on June 22.

June 13 A 60-day **retail price freeze,** excluding rents, wholesale farm prices, and interest and dividends, was announced by Pres. Nixon.

June 25 Several programs for **state aid to parochial schools** were declared unconstitutional by the Supreme Court.

June 29 Establishment of a **Federal Energy Office** to promote conservation and research into alternative sources of energy was announced by Pres. Nixon. It later assumed responsibility for mandatory fuel allocations and potential gasoline rationing.

June 30 The **largest merchant ship** built in the U.S., the 1094-foot, 230,000-ton supertanker *Brooklyn,* was christened at the Brooklyn, N.Y., Navy Yard.

July 18 Phase four of Pres. Nixon's **new economic policy** began. By Sept. 12 all food price restrictions and health-care cost controls were to be lifted. A system of mandatory price controls allowed price increases only to match cost increases.

July 28 **Skylab 3** carried astronauts Alan Bean, Owen Garriott, and Jack Lousma to a rendezvous with the Skylab orbiting laboratory. They made repairs to the

Mar. 24 The second **AIAW basketball championship** was won by Immaculata College, beating Queens College 59–52 for their second women's college championship.

Mar. 26 The **NCAA basketball championship** was won for the seventh consecutive year by UCLA, defeating Memphis State 87–66.

Apr. 9 The **Masters golf tournament** was won by Tommy Aaron.

Apr. 17 The **Boston Marathon** was won by Jon Anderson of Oregon, with a time of 2 hrs., 16 min., 3 sec. He was the first U.S. winner in four years. The first woman to cross the finish line was Jacqueline Hansen of California, with a time of 3 hrs., 5 min., 59 sec.

Apr. 28–May 12 The **ABA basketball championship** was won by the Indiana Pacers, who defeated the Kentucky Colonels four games to three.

Apr. 29–May 10 The **NHL Stanley Cup** was won by the Montreal Canadiens, who defeated the Chicago Black Hawks four games to two.

May 5 The 99th annual **Kentucky Derby** was won by Secretariat, with a record time of 1:59²/₅. The jockey was Ron Turcotte.

May 6 The **first World Hockey Association championship** was won by the New England Whalers, defeating the Winnipeg Jets four games to one.

May 10 The **NBA basketball championship** was won by the New York Knicks, who beat the Los Angeles Lakers four games to one.

May 19 The 98th annual **Preakness Stakes** was won by Secretariat, with a time of 1:55. The jockey was Ron Turcotte.

May 21 The **first athletic scholarship awarded to a woman** was given to Lynn Genesko, a swimmer from Woodbridge, N.J., by the University of Miami (Fla.).

May 27 A new **track record** for the 880-yd. run was set by Rick Wohlhuter, who ran the distance in 1:44.6 at the AAU meet in Los Angeles, Calif.

May 30 The 57th **Indianapolis 500** auto race was won by Gordon Johncock, who completed the course (332.5 mi.) in 2 hrs., 5 min., 26.59 sec. for an average speed of 159.014 mph.

June 9 The 105th annual **Belmont Stakes** was won by Secretariat, with a record time of 2:24, thus becoming the ninth horse to win racing's Triple Crown. Secretariat won by 31 lengths in a performance often called the best ever by a thoroughbred. The jockey was Ron Turcotte.

June 10 The **LPGA golf tournament** was won by Mary Mills.

| Exploration and Settlement; Wars; Government; Civil Rights; Statistics | I | | II | Publishing; Arts and Music; Popular Entertainment; Architecture; Theater |

July 16 The existence of what were to be called the **Watergate tapes,** recordings of White House conversations, was revealed by former White House aide Alexander P. Butterfield. On July 23 special prosecutor Archibald Cox and the Senate committee subpoenaed the tapes. On July 26 Pres. Nixon refused to release them, appealing the case through the courts until Oct. 19, when he offered a summary of requested tapes in return for no further requests for tapes or papers. This was rejected by Cox.

July 31 A **jetliner crashed** on landing at Logan International Airport in Boston, killing 88 people.

Sept. 4 **John Ehrlichman and G. Gordon Liddy were indicted** along with two White House officials in connection with the burglary of the office of Daniel Ellsberg's psychiatrist in 1971. The action had been instigated by the so-called White House plumbers' unit, created to stop security leaks, following Ellsberg's release of Pentagon documents to the press.

Oct. 10 Vice Pres. **Agnew resigned** and pleaded nolo contendere (no contest) to one charge of income tax evasion in return for the dropping of other charges. Agnew was fined and given three years' probation. He was only the second vice president to resign. John C. Calhoun resigned in 1832 to take a Senate seat.

Oct. 12 Rep. **Gerald R. Ford,** Republican of Michigan, was nominated by Pres. Nixon for the vice presidency.

Oct. 16 The **first black mayor of a major southern city,** Maynard Jackson, was elected to office in Atlanta, Ga.

Oct. 16 The **Nobel Peace Prize** was awarded jointly to Sec. of State Henry A. Kissinger and to Le Duc Tho of North Vietnam for their efforts in ending the Vietnam War. Tho declined the award.

Oct. 20 In what came to be called the **Saturday night massacre,** Attorney General Elliot Richardson resigned after refusing to fire special Watergate prosecutor Archibald Cox. Deputy Attorney General William Ruckelshaus was fired after refusing also. Solicitor General Robert Bork then fired Cox, who had earlier in the day announced he would not accept White House summaries of the Watergate tapes.

Oct. 23 Eight **impeachment resolutions** were introduced in the House, even as Pres. Nixon announced he would turn over the subpoenaed Watergate tapes.

Oct. 31 Two of the nine **Watergate tapes** subpoenaed had never been made, the White House revealed.

Nov. 1 **Leon A. Jaworski** was appointed special Watergate prosecutor by Pres. Nixon, who pledged to

history, *People of Paradox: An Inquiry Concerning the Origin of American Civilization* by Michael Kammen; general nonfiction, *Fire in the Lake: The Vietnamese and the Americans in Vietnam* by Frances Fitzgerald and *Children of Crisis,* volumes two and three, by Robert Coles; drama, *That Championship Season* by Jason Miller.

May 11 In the **Pentagon Papers** trial of Daniel Ellsberg and Anthony Russo, Jr., charges of espionage, theft, and conspiracy in connection with release of sensitive Pentagon documents to the press were dismissed. Federal Judge William Byrne, Jr., cited "improper government conduct," including the burglary of the office of Ellsberg's psychiatrist.

May 20 **Emmy Awards** were presented to Laurence Olivier as best actor for *Long Day's Journey Into Night;* Cloris Leachman as best actress for *A Brand New Life;* Richard Thomas as best actor in a dramatic series for *The Waltons;* Michael Learned as best actress in a dramatic series for *The Waltons.*

May 26 In a major decision on **radio and TV advertising,** the Supreme Court ruled that stations were not obligated to sell equal air time for political or controversial issues.

May 30 *Raisin,* a musical by Robert Nemiroff, Charlotte Zaltzberg, Judd Woldin, and Robert Brittan based on the play *A Raisin in the Sun* (1959) by Lorraine Hansberry, opened at the Arena Stage in Washington, D.C. Mayor Walter E. Washington had declared May 30 Lorraine Hansberry Day. The musical opened on Broadway at the 46th Street Theater on Oct. 18.

June 21 In a series of decisions on **obscenity,** the Supreme Court ruled that juries could establish the prurient appeal of materials on the basis of prevailing attitudes in their own communities.

July 29 A **rock festival** at Watkins Glen, N.Y., drew some 600,000 fans to hear music by such groups as the Allman Brothers Band, the Grateful Dead, and The Band.

Sept. 12 A ten-day **Chinese concert tour** was begun by the Philadelphia Orchestra, which arrived in Peking on the first tour of the People's Republic by a U.S. performing group.

Sept. 20 Audio equipment manufacturer **Avery Fisher** announced an $8,000,000 grant to Philharmonic Hall in New York City. The auditorium was subsequently renamed Avery Fisher Hall.

Sept. 21 A new **record art price** for a painting by a U.S. artist, $2,000,000, was paid by the Australian National Gallery in Canberra for Jackson Pollock's *Blue Poles.*

Oct. 26 Acknowledging past unfairness in dealing with **homosexuality** on television, NBC officials agreed to seek advice from homosexuals in future instances.

Business and Industry; Science; Education; Philosophy and Religion III		IV Sports; Social Issues and Crime; Folkways; Fashion; Holidays

station and performed a number of experiments before returning to Earth on Sept. 25.

Aug. 3 Restrictions on **funding of mass transit** through revenues of the Highway Trust Fund were lifted by Congress.

Sept. 1 The nation's strongest **drug control law** went into effect in New York State. It imposed mandatory life sentences for those convicted of trafficking in hard drugs and for addicts who commit violent crimes.

Sept. 6 Former United Mine Workers president **W. A. "Tony" Boyle was indicted** on charges of ordering the 1969 murders of labor dissident Joseph Yablonski, his wife, and his daughter.

Sept. 11 **Fixed brokers' commission rates** were abolished by the Securities and Exchange Commission.

Sept. 14 An **auto workers' strike** against the Chrysler Corporation was begun by the United Auto Workers Union. On Sept. 23 an agreement was signed allowing workers to reject overtime work under certain conditions and granting full pensions to those with 30 years' service. Similar agreements were later signed with Ford and GM.

Sept. 22 **Dallas–Fort Worth Airport** was dedicated. It was the world's largest (27 sq. mi.) and most expensive ($700,000,000) airport and featured its own 13-mile transit system.

Oct. 17 An **embargo on oil** shipped to the U.S. and other nations supporting Israel was instituted by 11 Middle Eastern oil-exporting states.

Oct. 18 The **Nobel Prize in Economics** was awarded to Wassily Leontief of Harvard University.

Oct. 23 The **Nobel Prize in Physics** was awarded jointly to Ivar Giaver of the General Electric Company in Schenectady, N.Y.; Leo Esaki, a Japanese citizen working for IBM in Yorktown Heights, N.Y.; and Brian D. Josephson of Great Britain for their theoretical work in the field of microelectronics.

Nov. 3 **Mariner 10,** the first U.S. probe of the planet Mercury, was launched. It was to fly by Venus on its way to Mercury.

Nov. 7 A call for **energy self-sufficiency** by 1980 was made by Pres. Nixon. He also asked for extension of

June 17 The **U.S. Open golf tournament** was won by Johnny Miller.

June 19 **Janet Lynn,** five-time U.S. figure skating champion, signed a three-year, $1,455,000 contract with the Ice Follies.

July 7–8 At the **Wimbledon** tennis championships in England, Billie Jean King won the women's singles title for the second straight year. King teamed with Rosemary Casals to win the women's doubles, and with Owen Davidson of Australia to win the mixed doubles. Jimmy Connors teamed with Ilie Nastase of Rumania to take the men's doubles. Many tennis professionals boycotted the championship because of the International Lawn Tennis Federation's suspension of Yugoslavian player Nikki Pilic for refusing to play on the Yugoslavian Davis Cup team.

July 22 The **U.S. Women's Open golf tournament** was won by Sue Berning.

July 24 The **baseball All-Star Game** was won by the National League, beating the American League 7–1.

Aug. 6 The **Baseball Hall of Fame** inducted five new members: Roberto Clemente, William G. "Billy" Evans, Monte Irvin, George Kelly, and Warren Spahn.

Aug. 12 The **PGA golf tournament** was won by Jack Nicklaus.

Aug. 14 In a **serial murder case** in Texas, two Houston teenagers were indicted for the homosexual abuse and killings of 27 persons over a three-year period.

Aug. 25 The **North American Soccer League championship** was won by the Philadelphia Atoms, who defeated the Dallas Tornado 2–0.

Aug. 29–Sept. 9 The **U.S. Open tennis singles championships** were won by John Newcombe of Australia in the men's division and Margaret Smith Court of Australia, for the fifth time, in the women's division.

Sept. 8 The **Miss America** title was won by Rebecca Ann King, 23, of Colorado, at the annual pageant in Atlantic City, N.J.

Sept. 20 In a nationally televised tennis mismatch billed as the **"Battle of the Sexes,"** Billie Jean King beat Bobby Riggs in three straight sets and went home $100,000 richer.

Sept. 25 **Willie Mays** of the New York Mets, retiring at season's end after 22 years in the majors, was honored in a ceremony at Shea Stadium in New York City. In his career Mays hit a total of 660 home runs.

Sept. 30 The fourth annual **New York City Marathon** was won by Tom Fleming of Bloomfield, N.J., with a course record time of 2 hrs., 21 min., 54.2 sec. Of the

| Exploration and Settlement; Wars; Government; Civil Rights; Statistics I | II Publishing; Arts and Music; Popular Entertainment; Architecture; Theater |

seek congressional approval before interfering with his investigation.

Nov. 7 The **War Powers Act,** requiring congressional approval for commitment of U.S. forces in combat abroad longer than 60 days, was passed by Congress over Pres. Nixon's veto.

Nov. 21 An **18-minute gap** in a key Watergate tape was revealed by the White House. The tapes requested were turned over to Judge John J. Sirica. On Nov. 27 Rose Mary Woods, Pres. Nixon's personal secretary, testified she had accidentally caused about five minutes of the erasure. The remaining gap was unexplained.

Dec. 4 In the **Chicago Seven** conspiracy case, David Dellinger, Abbie Hoffmann, Jerry Rubin, and their attorney William Kunstler were convicted of contempt of court, but no sentence was imposed.

Dec. 6 **Gerald R. Ford was sworn in as vice president,** the first to take office under the terms of the Twenty-fifth Amendment.

Nov. 5 *When You Comin' Back, Red Ryder?* by Mark Medoff, a drama set in a New Mexico diner, was given its premiere performance by the Circle Repertory Theater Company in New York City.

Nov. 10 **Book burning** was reported in Drake, N.D., where 36 copies of *Slaughterhouse-Five* (1969) by Kurt Vonnegut were put to the torch as "tools of the devil." The local school board voted not to renew the contract of the teacher who assigned the book.

Nov. 13 A **dancers' strike** hit the New York City Ballet for the first time in its 25-year history. The strikers, demanding guaranteed work or pay for the fall-winter season, ended the strike Dec. 7.

Dec. 11 The **Pierpont Morgan Library** in New York City received the country's largest and best collection of Italian drawings, the gift of Janos Scholz.

Dec. 29 A revival of *A Moon for the Misbegotten* by Eugene O'Neill, starring Jason Robards, Colleen Dewhurst, and Ed Flanders, opened at the Morosco Theater in New York City.

1974

The scandals revealed by the Watergate affair continued to cripple the Nixon presidency. The climax came when the Supreme Court ordered the White House to release transcriptions of recorded presidential conversations; the tapes indicated that Nixon had been involved in the cover-up of the Watergate burglary. The House Judiciary Committee, after several months of hearings, voted three articles of impeachment, and it seemed likely an impeachment trial would take place in the Senate. As Nixon's base of support disappeared, he made a tour of the Middle East (June 10–18) and traveled to the U.S.S.R. (June 25–July 3) to sign a limited accord on nuclear weapons testing. These trips were not enough to restore his popular support and in August, faced with impeachment, Nixon became the first U.S. president to resign. Meanwhile, Sec. of State Henry Kissinger followed a policy of shuttle diplomacy, flying from one capital to another in the Middle East. By year's end he had obtained agreement in principle by all parties to resume peace talks in Geneva. This success contrasted with disclosures that the FBI had carried out counterintelligence operations against civil rights groups in the U.S. and that the CIA had been involved in the destabilization or overthrow of foreign governments, particularly the elected Marxist government of Chile. Notables who died this year included Gen. Creighton W. Abrams, Army chief of staff, Sept. 4, at 59; former Sen. Wayne L. Morse of Oregon, July 22, at 73; Gen. Carl A. Spaats, the

The year in theater was dominated again by British imports, notably works by Tom Stoppard and Alan Ayckbourn. In motion pictures nostalgia maintained its box office appeal. *That's Entertainment,* a pastiche of musicals from the 1930s to the 1950s, grossed $18,000,000, and *Chinatown* was reminiscent of the classic 1940s detective films. Disaster films such as *Towering Inferno* were also popular. In the art world, a study entitled *Museums USA* indicated the gravity of U.S. museums' financial woes. The report showed that 36% of the nation's museums had been forced to cut personnel and services since 1966, 37% had been forced to charge admission, and almost 57% of museum staffs were volunteers. Americans mourned the deaths this year of William A. "Bud" Abbott, straight man of the comedy team Abbott and Costello, Apr. 24, at 78; Jack Benny, the comedian, Dec. 26, at 80; Edward Kennedy "Duke" Ellington, the jazz composer and musician, May 24, at 75; Cassandra "Mama Cass" Elliot, the entertainer, July 29, at 33; Dorothy Fields, composer of such song hits as "I'm in the Mood for Love" and "The Way You Look Tonight," Mar. 28, at 68; Samuel Goldwyn, real name Goldfish, the Hollywood producer, Jan. 31, at 91; Adolph Gottlieb, the artist and pioneer in abstract expressionism, Mar. 4, at 71; Chester R. "Chet" Huntley, who was co-anchorman of NBC's nightly *Huntley-Brinkley Report* from 1956–1970, Mar. 20, at 62; Solomon I. "Sol" Hurok, the impresario, Mar. 5, at 85; Louis

Business and Industry; Science; Education; Philosophy and Religion III		IV Sports; Social Issues and Crime; Folkways; Fashion; Holidays

Daylight Savings Time (passed Dec. 14) and reduction of the highway speed limit to 55 mph (passed Dec. 22); set heating oil allocations for homes, schools, and industries; reduced jet fuel allocations; and ordered lower temperatures in federal buildings. On Nov. 25 he called for a Sunday ban on gasoline sales. On Dec. 27 the Federal Energy Office outlined a standby gasoline rationing program.

Nov. 13   Plans for a **trans-Alaska oil pipeline,** designed to supply 2,000,000 barrels of oil a day, were approved by Congress.

Dec. 11   **Most-favored-nation status** was denied the U.S.S.R. by the House of Representatives, barring such status to all nations with emigration restraints.

Dec. 15   **Homosexuality** was not a mental illness, the American Psychiatric Association announced, overturning its 100-year-old position on the subject.

12 women entrants, the first to finish was Nina Kuscsik of Long Island, N.Y., with a time of 2 hrs., 57 min., 7 sec.

Oct. 13–21   The **World Series** was won for the second year in a row by the Oakland Athletics (AL), defeating the New York Mets (NL) four games to three. The Mets had won the National League pennant on Oct. 10 by beating the Cincinnati Reds three games to two. The Athletics had won the American League title Oct. 11, beating the Baltimore Orioles three games to two.

Nov. 30–Dec. 2   The **Davis Cup** tennis championship was won in Cleveland, Ohio, by Australia, beating the U.S. in five straight matches.

Dec. 1   **Jack Nicklaus** won the Disney World Open, becoming the first professional golfer to hit a career total of $2,000,000.

Dec. 16   A new **NFL rushing record** was set by O. J. Simpson, running back for the Buffalo Bills, who broke Jim Brown's 1963 total of 1863 yds. Simpson later set a new pro record of 2003 yds.

1974

The economy slid into crisis. Inflation hit 10.3%, auto sales were off 20%, and housing starts were down 40%. Unemployment soared to 7.2% by December. Nevertheless, the economic depression feared by many did not occur. Foreign trade did not decline, and the international banking system withstood the impact of a dramatic rise in oil prices. In education, community control surfaced as a burning issue in the fall. In Kanawha County, W.Va., parents protested their schools' use of books reflecting contemporary sexual mores and dissident views about the U.S. In Boston, the busing of students to achieve integration led to violence and to a confrontation between a citizens group and the federal judge who ordered integration of the city's schools. In science, there were questions regarding the safety of modern genetic research and warnings of possible environmental problems, such as depletion of the ozone layer in the atmosphere. In religion, even as membership in major church denominations declined, attendance at fundamentalist churches continued to climb. Notables who died this year included Vannevar Bush, who pioneered the development of electronic analog computers, June 28, at 84; Adelle Davis, the nutritionist, May 31, at 70; Haroldson Lafayette Hunt, one of the world's wealthiest men, Nov. 29, at 75; Charles A. Lindbergh, the pioneer aviator, Aug. 26, at 72; Alexander P. Seversky, an early advocate of strategic air power, Aug. 24, at 80; Stephen Gill Spottswood, bishop of the African

A Harris survey showed that tennis claimed 26% of 1974 sports audiences, compared with a 17.7% share in 1973. A Nielsen poll showed that 33,900,000 Americans played the game in 1974, a jump of 68% over the previous year. In golf the top money winners were Johnny Miller, $353,201, and JoAnne Carner, $87,094. In baseball Frank Robinson became the first black manager in major league baseball, Henry Aaron topped the home-run record set by Babe Ruth, and Lou Brock broke the record for stolen bases set by Maury Wills in 1962. Motorcycle stunt driving became a high-paying occupation this year as Robert Craig "Evel" Knievel managed (Sept. 8) to jump the Snake R. Canyon in Twin Falls, Idaho. The year's top fad was streaking, or running naked through a variety of settings. College students were especially fond of the new, short-lived sport. Among the notables who died this year were Jay Hanna "Dizzy" Dean, the baseball pitcher, July 17, at 63; Anne Klein, the fashion designer, Mar. 19, at 51; Peter Revson, a top U.S. race car driver, Mar. 22, at 35; Daniel R. Topping, New York Yankees baseball executive, May 18, at 61; and Amy Vanderbilt, writer on etiquette, Dec. 27, at 66.

Jan. 1   In **college football bowl games,** the results were Nebraska 19, Texas 3 in the Cotton Bowl; Penn State 16, LSU 9 in the Orange Bowl; Ohio State 42, USC 21 in the Rose Bowl; and (Dec. 31, 1973) Nebraska 13, Florida 10 in the Sugar Bowl. This

first chief of staff of the United States Air Force, in 1947, July 14, at 83; Lewis L. Strauss, head of the Atomic Energy Commission from 1953–1958, Jan. 21, at 78; and Earl Warren, former chief justice of the Supreme Court, July 19, at 83.

Jan. 15   In testimony on the **White House tapes,** an expert stated the 18½-minute gap in a critical tape had been caused by deliberate and repeated erasures.

Feb. 6   An **impeachment inquiry** against Pres. Nixon by the House Judiciary Committee was approved by the House of Representatives.

Feb. 28   The **$6,400,000 lawsuit against the Committee to Reelect the President** for its involvement in the Watergate break-in was settled. The Democratic National Committee accepted $775,000.

Apr. 3   Pres. Nixon announced he would comply with an **IRS tax reassessment** and would pay some $465,000 in back taxes and interest owed from 1969 to 1972.

Apr. 3–4   **Tornadoes** struck from Georgia north to Ontario, Canada, killing about 350 people, injuring 1200, and causing about $1,000,000,000 in damage.

Apr. 28   Former Cabinet officials **Maurice Stans and John Mitchell were acquitted** of blocking a government investigation of the financial affairs of Robert Vesco, a major contributor to Pres. Nixon's reelection campaign.

May 2   Former Vice Pres. **Spiro T. Agnew was disbarred** in Maryland, the only state in which he was licensed to practice law.

May 23   Following revelation of **cheating by Annapolis midshipmen,** some 900 were ordered by the U.S. Naval Academy to retake an examination.

June 7   Former attorney general **Richard Kleindienst** was fined $100 and given a one-month suspended sentence for lying to a Senate committee investigating Pres. Nixon's involvement in quashing a Justice Department antitrust suit against International Telephone and Telegraph, a large campaign contributor.

July 18   An **independent legal services corporation** was established by Congress to provide legal aid for the poor.

July 24   In a decision on the **White House tapes,** the Supreme Court ordered that special prosecutor Leon Jaworski's subpoena of tapes and documents be

I. Kahn, the architect, Mar. 17, at 73; Walter Lippmann, the journalist, Dec. 14, at 85; John Crowe Ransom, the poet, July 3, at 86; Cornelius Ryan, known for his books about World War II, Nov. 23, at 54; Anne Sexton, the poet, Oct. 4, at 45; Edward V. "Ed" Sullivan, newspaper columnist and television host, Oct. 13, at 73; and Jacqueline Susann, the best-selling novelist, Sept. 21, at 53.

Among **books published** this year was *Something Happened* by Joseph Heller, the long-awaited second novel by the author of the 1961 classic *Catch-22.* In this new work Heller presented the perspective of a middle-aged man examining his life and finding it to be a mixture of stifled hopes, disillusionment, minor victories, and a sense of loss. Other books published this year included *Watership Down* by Richard Adams, an allegory of life, death, and continuity in the form of a touching animal story; *If Beale Street Could Talk* by James Baldwin, a novel; *Jaws* by Peter Benchley, a novel; *All the President's Men* by Carl Bernstein and Robert Woodward, a study of the people around Pres. Richard Nixon in the shadow of Watergate; *The Hawkline Monster* by Richard Brautigan, described as a Gothic western; *Fear of Flying* by Erica Jong, a novel; *The CIA and the Cult of Intelligence* by Victor Marchetti and John D. Marks, a study of the U.S. intelligence community; *Centennial* by James Michener, a novel examining the history of Colorado and Wyoming from prehistoric to recent times; *Plain Speaking, An Oral Biography of Harry S Truman* by Merle Miller; and *My Life as a Man* by Philip Roth, a novel.

Jan. 25   The so-called **Vinland map was declared a fake** by Yale University, its owner. The map, discovered in 1957 and first published in 1965, indicated that Leif Ericson had discovered North America centuries before Christopher Columbus sailed to the New World.

Jan. 27   *Lorelei* by Jule Styne, Betty Comden, Adolph Green, Kenny Solms, and Gail Parent, a reworking of the 1949 musical *Gentlemen Prefer Blondes,* opened at the Palace Theater in New York City. It starred Carol Channing reprising her role as Lorelei Lee.

Mar. 2   **Grammy Awards** were presented for the following: best album of 1973, *Innervisions* by Stevie Wonder; best record, "Killing Me Softly with His Song" by Roberta Flack; best male pop vocalist, Stevie Wonder for "You Are the Sunshine of My Life"; best female pop vocalist, Roberta Flack for "Killing Me Softly with His Song"; best pop group, Gladys Knight and the Pips for "Neither One of Us."

Mar. 5   What was said to be the **world's oldest song,** an ode of love to gods and goddesses, was performed before an audience at the University of California at Berkeley. It was accompanied by music from a reproduction of a Sumerian lyre dating to 2000 B.C.

Business and Industry; Science; Education; Philosophy and Religion III	IV Sports; Social Issues and Crime; Folkways; Fashion; Holidays

Methodist Episcopal Zion Church and chairman of the NAACP from 1961, Dec. 1, at 77; Earl W. Sutherland, the Nobel Prize–winning pharmacologist, Mar. 9, at 58; and Arthur K. Watson, a key figure in the phenomenal growth of IBM in the 1950s and 1960s, July 26, at 55.

Jan. 13 A Gallup poll on **religious attendance** showed that fewer Roman Catholics and Protestants were attending weekly services than ten years earlier, but attendance at Jewish services was up.

Jan. 21 **Bilingual education** was bolstered by a Supreme Court ruling that schools must teach English to students for whom it is not a first language.

Mar. 7 The Civil War ironclad *Monitor,* which had sunk in a gale in 1862, was reported found off Hatteras, N.C.

Mar. 18 The **Arab oil embargo** against the U.S. was officially lifted following Sec. of State Henry Kissinger's efforts to mediate between Egypt and Israel.

Apr. 8 A bill extending the **minimum wage** to some 8,000,000 additional workers, and gradually raising it to $2.30 an hour, was signed by Pres. Richard M. Nixon.

Apr. 11 **William A. "Tony" Boyle,** former president of the United Mine Workers, was found guilty by a Media, Pa., jury of ordering the 1969 murders of Joseph Yablonski and Yablonski's wife and daughter.

Apr. 18–May 9 **U.S. oil company profits** were reported to have risen sharply in the first quarter of 1974. The rises ranged from 29% for Standard Oil of Ohio to 748% for Occidental Petroleum.

Apr. 30 Federal **wage and price controls were lifted.** A number of price increases by the steel and copper industries followed.

May 2 Legislation for a **Federal Energy Administration,** to be established by July 1975, was passed by Congress. The new agency would be responsible for gas rationing, emergency planning, conservation measures, curbing exorbitant profits, and shaping foreign trade policies.

May 28 In a decision bearing on **class-action suits,** the Supreme Court ruled that plaintiffs in such cases must pay the costs of notifying those they claim to represent.

season the AP poll chose Notre Dame the national college football champions of 1973. The UPI poll selected Alabama.

Jan. 13 **Super Bowl VIII** was won by the Miami Dolphins, defeating the Minnesota Vikings 24–7 for their second consecutive Super Bowl win. On Dec. 30, 1973, the Dolphins had defeated the Oakland Raiders 27–10 for the NFC championship, and the Vikings had defeated the Dallas Cowboys 27–10 for the AFC championship.

Jan. 14 **Mass strip searches of soldiers** and their property for concealed drugs were declared unconstitutional by a federal court.

Jan. 24 **World Championship Tennis** (WCT), the organization of professional tennis players, severed its ties with the U.S. Lawn Tennis Association, WCT head Lamar Hunt announced.

Feb. 5 **Patricia Hearst,** daughter of publisher Randolph Hearst, was kidnaped from her Berkeley, Calif., apartment by members of a group calling itself the Symbionese Liberation Army. On Feb. 12 a ransom message from her abductors demanded $70 in food for every needy person in California. The Hearst family started a $2,000,000 food giveaway on Feb. 22.

Feb. 6–9 **U.S. figure skating championships** were won in Providence, R.I., by Gordon McKellen, Jr., men's singles; Dorothy Hamill, women's singles; Melissa Militano and Johnny Johns, pairs; Colleen O'Connor and Jim Millns, dance.

Mar. 23 The third annual **AIAW basketball championship** was won by Immaculata College, defeating Mississippi State 68–53 for its third consecutive women's college title.

Mar. 24 The **NCAA basketball championship** was won by North Carolina State University, defeating Marquette University 76–64.

Apr. 3 **Patricia Hearst,** in a tape to authorities sent by her abductors, declared she was joining the Symbionese Liberation Army of her own free will. On Apr. 15 a camera took a picture of her participating in the robbery of a San Francisco bank. On June 6 she was indicted by a federal grand jury for her role in the crime.

Apr. 8 **Henry "Hank" Aaron** of the Atlanta Braves (NL) hit his 715th career home run in Atlanta against the Los Angeles Dodgers, breaking the record set decades earlier by the great Babe Ruth. Aaron finished the year with a career total of 733 homers.

Apr. 14 The **Masters golf tournament** was won by Gary Player, who picked up his second Masters win.

Apr. 15 The 78th annual **Boston Marathon** was won by Neil Cusack of Ireland with a time of 2 hrs., 13

honored by the White House. It ruled that presidential privilege did not apply to evidence required in prosecuting Watergate-related crimes. Pres. Nixon turned over the materials on July 30 and Aug. 5.

July 30 **Three articles of impeachment** were voted against Pres. Nixon by the House Judiciary Committee: for blocking the investigation of the Watergate affair, for abuse of presidential powers, and for hindering the impeachment process by not complying with the committee's subpoena for taped White House conversations.

Aug. 5 Pres. **Nixon released tape transcripts** revealing he had impeded the Watergate investigation. One example of the evidence was an order to H. R. Haldeman on June 23, 1972, to tell the FBI: "Don't go any further in this case, period!"

Aug. 8 Pres. **Nixon announced in a televised address that he would resign.** Nixon told an audience of some 100,000,000 he had made some wrong decisions but that he was resigning because he no longer had enough support in Congress.

Aug. 9 Pres. **Nixon resigned.** Gerald R. Ford was sworn in as the 38th president of the United States.

Aug. 20 Nelson A. Rockefeller, former governor of New York, was nominated for the vice presidency by Pres. Ford.

Sept. 4 **Diplomatic relations with East Germany** were established by the U.S.

Sept. 7 In a revelation of **CIA covert operations**, it was disclosed that in April CIA director William Colby had told a congressional committee that from 1970 to 1973 some $8,000,000 had been budgeted for operations against Chile's Marxist government.

Sept. 8 Pres. **Nixon was pardoned** by Pres. Ford for any crimes he may have committed or may have participated in while in office. On Oct. 17 Ford defended this action before the House Judiciary Committee, saying he wanted to end the national divisions created by the Watergate affair.

Sept. 16 Mary Louise Smith of Iowa became the first woman to head the Republican National Committee.

Sept. 16 A limited **amnesty proclamation** was issued by Pres. Ford, offering clemency to thousands of Vietnam-era draft resisters and military deserters if they

Mar. 11 *Candide,* a musical by Hugh Wheeler and Leonard Bernstein based on the classic satire by Voltaire, opened at the Broadway Theater in New York City. It had premiered at the Chelsea Theater Center of the Brooklyn Academy of Music on Dec. 20, 1973.

Apr. 1 In a decision on **censorship for national security,** a federal court ruled that *The CIA and the Cult of Intelligence* by Victor Marchetti and John D. Marks could be published with only 15 deletions made in the original text. The CIA had asked for 168 cuts.

Apr. 2 **Academy Awards** were presented to *The Sting* as outstanding motion picture of 1973; Jack Lemmon as best actor for *Save the Tiger;* Glenda Jackson as best actress for *A Touch of Class;* John Houseman as best supporting actor for *The Paper Chase;* and Tatum O'Neal as best supporting actress for *Paper Moon.*

Apr. 18 **National Book Awards** were presented for the following: fiction, *Gravity's Rainbow* by Thomas Pynchon and *A Crown of Feathers and Other Stories* by Isaac Bashevis Singer; poetry, *The Fall of America: Poems of These States, 1965–1971* by Allen Ginsberg and *Diving Into the Wreck, 1971–1972* by Adrienne Rich; biography, *Malcolm Lowry* by Douglas Day; history, *Macaulay: The Shaping of the Historian* by John Clive; arts and letters, *Deeper into Movies* by Pauline Kael; philosophy and religion, *Edmund Husserl: Philosopher of Infinite Tasks* by Maurice Natanson; science, *Life: The Unfinished Experiment* by S. E. Luria.

Apr. 21 **Tony awards** for the 1973–1974 season were presented for the following: best play, *The River Niger;* best musical, *Raisin;* best actor in a drama, Michael Moriarty for *Find Your Way Home;* best actress in a drama, Colleen Dewhurst for *A Moon for the Misbegotten.*

May 7 **Pulitzer prizes** were awarded for the following: biography, *O'Neill, Son and Artist* by Louis Sheaffer; history, *The Americans: The Democratic Experience* by Daniel J. Boorstin; general nonfiction, *The Denial of Death* by Ernest Becker; poetry, *The Dolphin* by Robert Lowell.

May 16 The controversial work *Dybbuk,* choreographed by Jerome Robbins to music by Leonard Bernstein, was given its first performance by the New York City Ballet.

May 28 **Emmy Awards** were presented to Hal Holbrook as best actor for *Pueblo;* Cicely Tyson as best actress for *The Autobiography of Miss Jane Pittman;* Telly Savalas as best actor in a dramatic series for *Kojak;* and Michael Learned as best actress in a dramatic series for *The Waltons.*

June 4–6 At the **First American Congress of Theater** in Princeton, N.J., the traditional rift between commercial and subsidized theater was overcome as producers discussed the need to develop new marketing, funding, and advertising techniques.

Business and Industry; Science; Education; Philosophy and Religion III		IV Sports; Social Issues and Crime; Folkways; Fashion; Holidays

July 6 **Heart disease,** chief cause of death in the U.S., had declined 10% since 1963, according to a report by the National Center for Health Statistics.

July 9 Difficult times for the **New York Stock Exchange** were reflected in the fact that the price for a seat on the exchange fell to $70,000, lowest price since Feb. 1958.

July 12 The **National Research Act,** establishing guidelines for scientific research on humans, was signed by Pres. Nixon.

July 25 A **school busing plan** to achieve integration in Detroit public schools was rejected by the Supreme Court.

July 29 The **first women Episcopal priests** were ordained by four bishops in Philadelphia, Pa. The ordination of the 11 women was ruled invalid by the House of Bishops on Aug. 15, but on Oct. 17 the same body approved in principle the ordination of women as priests.

Aug. 31 In an effort to provide **deprogramming from cult influence,** the Citizens Freedom Foundation was organized. The group was led by Ted Patrick, who was experienced in removing young people from cult environments and convincing them to return to their families.

Sept. 2 The **Employee Retirement Income Security Act** was signed by Pres. Gerald R. Ford. It was to bring some 300,000 private pension plans under federal regulation by Jan. 1976, when uniform standards would become enforceable and a federal reinsurance program would go into effect to protect benefits if private plans should fail.

Sept. 3 Protesting **schoolbook content** at the opening of schools in Kanawha County, W.Va., parents declared the contents of some books to be profane, anti-American, and vulgar. The controversy continued throughout the fall.

Sept. 12 Opposition to **court-ordered school busing** in Boston turned into violence on opening day of classes. Subsequent violence prompted mobilization of the National Guard on Oct. 15.

Sept. 29 Controversy over the accepted treatment **of breast cancer** was heightened by a report from the National Cancer Institute indicating that radical mastectomy, the prevailing treatment, was too drastic in many cases. The study pressed for surgery that was

min., 39 sec. The first woman to finish was Michiko "Miki" Gorman of Los Angeles, Calif., with a time of 2 hrs., 47 min., 11 sec.

Apr. 25 **Football rule changes** were announced by the NFL, including a 15-minute sudden death period to avoid tie games and the moving of goal posts ten yards back from the goal lines to make it more difficult to score a field goal.

Apr. 28–May 12 The **NBA basketball championship** was won by the Boston Celtics, who took their 12th title win in 18 years by beating the Milwaukee Bucks four games to three.

Apr. 30–May 10 The **ABA basketball championship** was won by the New York Nets, who beat the Utah Stars four games to one.

May 4 The 100th annual **Kentucky Derby** was won by Cannonade, with a time of 2:04. The jockey was Angel Cordero, Jr..

May 4 **Expo '74** opened in Spokane, Wash. Its focus was environmental issues and solutions. The 100-acre site of the mini-world's fair was designed for future use as a park. Washington State's pavilion was intended to serve after Expo '74 as an opera house and convention center.

May 7–19 The **NHL Stanley Cup** was won by the Philadelphia Flyers, who beat the Boston Bruins four games to two.

May 16 In a serial murder case known as the **Zebra killings,** four Black Muslims were indicted in San Francisco for the murder of three persons and attempted murder of six others. Twelve people, all of them white, had been killed, apparently at random, over a five-month period.

May 17 A shootout with the **Symbionese Liberation Army** in Los Angeles left six of eight known members of the terrorist group dead after police opened fire on their headquarters and the building caught fire. Among the dead were the group's leader, Donald D. DeFreeze, self-styled General Field Marshall Cinque. Patty Hearst and William and Emily Harris, wanted for bank robbery, were not in the building at the time of the attack.

May 18 The 99th annual **Preakness Stakes** was won by Little Current, with a time of 1:54³/₅. The jockey was Miguel Rivera.

May 26 The 58th **Indianapolis 500** auto race was won by Johnny Rutherford, who completed the 500-mile course in 3 hrs., 9 min., 10.06 sec., with an average speed of 158.589 mph.

June 8 The 106th annual **Belmont Stakes** was won by Little Current, with a time of 2:29¹/₅. The jockey was Miguel Rivera.

swore allegiance to the U.S. and performed up to two years of public service work.

Sept. 16   Charges stemming from the 1973 **occupation of Wounded Knee,** S.D., against Russell Means and Dennis Banks, leaders of the American Indian Movement (AIM), were dismissed in federal court. The judge criticized the government's handling of witnesses and evidence.

Oct. 10   Legislation providing for **public funding of presidential primaries and elections** was passed by Congress. It set limits on donations and outlays for congressional and presidential campaigns.

Nov. 5   In **congressional elections** the Democrats gained a 61–37 majority in the Senate, with two seats held by independents. In the House the Democrats gained 43 seats, for a 291–144 majority. The Democrats also won four governorships, for a total of 36. Among the new Democratic governors was Ella Grasso of Connecticut, the first elected woman governor. In this election voters in the District of Columbia chose for the first time a mayor and a 14-member city council, posts previously filled by presidential appointment.

Nov. 8   Charges against eight Ohio National Guardsmen stemming from the 1970 **Kent State** tragedy were dropped in federal court.

Nov. 17   It was reported that **special IRS files** were maintained from 1969 to 1973 on 2873 groups and 8585 people involved in dissident causes.

Nov. 18   It was reported that **FBI counterintelligence operations** had been conducted against civil rights organizations such as the Southern Christian Leadership Organization and the Congress of Racial Equality, as well as such extremist groups as the Ku Klux Klan.

Nov. 21   The **Freedom of Information Act,** providing expanded public access to government files, was passed by Congress over Pres. Ford's veto. The law provided that secrecy classification could be challenged in court and had to be justified by federal authorities.

Nov. 23–24   At a **summit meeting in Vladivostok,** U.S.S.R., Pres. Ford and Secretary Leonid Brezhnev agreed to limits on the numbers of ICBMs, MIRVs, heavy bombers, and submarine-launched missiles.

June 12   The **National Theater of Washington, D.C., disbanded.** It was faced with a $300,000 deficit.

June 13   The **Radio City Music Hall Ballet Company,** New York City's oldest resident dance troupe, disbanded after 42 years. This left the Rockettes as Radio City's only dance company.

June 25   In a **decision on editorial rebuttals,** the Supreme Court ruled unconstitutional a Florida law requiring newspapers to print political candidates' replies to editorials that were critical of them.

July 24   At the **international ballet competition** in Varna, Bulgaria, Fernando Bujones became the first U.S. dancer to win the top prize.

July 27   **Mikhail Baryshnikov,** who had defected while touring in Canada with a Soviet ballet troupe, made his U.S. debut with the American Ballet Theater in a performance of *Giselle* in New York City.

Sept. 12–15   The 100th anniversary of the birth of **Arnold Schoenberg** was celebrated by the University of Southern California with musical performances and the creation of the Arnold Schoenberg Institute.

Sept. 23   A revival of the 1959 musical *Gypsy,* by Arthur Laurents, Jule Styne, and Stephen Sondheim, opened at the Winter Garden Theater in New York City. It starred Angela Lansbury.

Sept. 27   A **record price for an American painting** was set with the sale of Willem de Kooning's *Woman V* to the Australian National Gallery for $850,000. The painting had been sold in 1953 for $30,000.

Sept. 30   **Cynthia Gregory,** a principal dancer in the American Ballet Theater, announced she would perform in Cuba. She was the first important U.S. artist to visit Cuba since 1961, when diplomatic relations between the two countries were severed.

Oct. 4   The **Joseph H. Hirshhorn Museum and Sculpture Garden,** part of the Smithsonian Institution in Washington, D.C., opened. Its collection comprised 6000 contemporary paintings and sculptures.

Oct. 8   *Absurd Person Singular,* a comedy by Alan Ayckbourn starring Larry Blyden, Carole Shelley, Richard Kiley, Geraldine Page, and Sandy Dennis, opened at the Music Box in New York City.

Oct. 17–21   A **Charles Ives festival,** celebrating the 100th anniversary of the composer's birth, was observed in New York City and New Haven, Conn., with a large number of lectures, concerts, and recitals.

Oct. 24   *Equus* by Peter Shaffer, starring Anthony Hopkins and Peter Firth, opened at the Plymouth Theater in New York City. The play concerned the blinding of six horses by a young stable hand, and the attempt by the boy's psychiatrist to learn why he committed the crime.

Nov. 2   **J. D. Salinger,** ending a 21-year public silence, announced he was suing a publisher and several major

less deforming and that reduced the lingering pain, weakness, and other effects associated with radical mastectomy.

Oct. 8 A program to control inflation, called **WIN (Whip Inflation Now),** was proposed by Pres. Ford. It called for voluntary energy conservation measures to help combat spiraling oil prices. Pres. Ford also asked for a 5% tax surcharge on corporate profits and on personal incomes of more than $15,000.

Oct. 8 In the **biggest bank failure in U.S. history** to date, the Franklin National Bank, of New York, was declared insolvent. On Oct. 17 the Securities and Exchange Commission filed fraud charges against the bank's holding company and nine members of the firm.

Oct. 10 An independent **Commodity Futures** Trading **Commission** was established by Congress to oversee stock exchanges, curb manipulation and other abuses, and check imbalances resulting from government activities.

Oct. 10 The **Nobel Prize in Physiology or Medicine** was awarded jointly to Albert Claude, formerly of the Rockefeller Institute and currently director of the Institut Jules Bordet in Belgium, Emil Palade of Yale University Medical School, and Christian de Duve of Belgium, associated with the Rockefeller Institute and the University of Louvain, for their research into the inner workings of cells.

Oct. 15 The **Nobel Prize in Chemistry** was awarded to Paul J. Flory of Stanford University for his research on macromolecules, which led to development of new plastics and other synthetic materials.

Nov. 13 **Blueprint for Project Independence,** a plan to reduce U.S. reliance on oil imports, was released by the Federal Energy Administration. The study called for a federal tax of 15 cents a gallon on gasoline; a mandatory fuel standard of 20 miles a gallon for autos; tax credits for insulating homes and buildings; efficiency criteria for electrical appliances; and national standards for heating, cooling, and lighting.

Nov. 15 The **retail price of sugar** soared to 65 cents a pound following the sixth major price increase by two leading U.S. refiners since Oct. 9. On Jan. 1 the price of a pound of sugar had been about 18 cents.

Nov. 26 A bill providing **federal subsidies** for **mass transit,** involving a six-year expenditure totaling $11,-800,000,000, was signed by Pres. Ford.

June 12 **Little League baseball** announced that its teams would be open to girls.

June 16 The **U.S. Open golf tournament** was won by Hale Irwin, beating Forrest Fezler by two strokes.

June 23 The **LPGA golf tournament** was won by Sandra Haynie.

July 5 At the **Wimbledon** tennis championships in England, Chris Evert won the women's singles title. On July 6 Jimmy Connors won the men's singles title. Peggy Michel teamed with Evonne Goolagong of Australia to win the women's doubles, and Billie Jean King teamed with Owen Davidson of Australia to win the mixed doubles.

July 21 The **U.S. Women's Open golf tournament** was won by Sandra Haynie.

July 23 The **baseball All-Star Game** was won by the National League, beating the American League 7–2 for its 11th win in 12 years.

Aug. 11 The **PGA golf tournament** was won by Lee Trevino, beating Jack Nicklaus by one stroke.

Aug. 12 The **Baseball Hall of Fame** inducted six new members: James "Cool Papa" Bell, James "Sunny Jim" Bottomley, John Bertrand "Jocko" Conlan, Edward Charles "Whitey" Ford, Mickey Mantle, and Samuel Thompson.

Aug. 25 The **North American Soccer League championship** was won by the Los Angeles Aztecs, who defeated the Miami Toros 4–3.

Sept. 8 The **Miss America** title was won by Shirley Cothran, 21, of Fort Worth, Tex., at the annual pageant in Atlantic City, N.J.

Sept. 9 The **U.S. Open tennis singles championships** were won by Jimmy Connors in the men's division and Billie Jean King in the women's division.

Sept. 10 **Lou Brock** of the St. Louis Cardinals (NL) broke the major league record for stolen bases in a season, set by Maury Wills in 1962, when he stole base number 105 in a home game against the Philadelphia Phillies. Brock finished the year with a National League career record of 753 stolen bases.

Sept. 10–17 The **America's Cup** was successfully defended by the U.S. yacht *Courageous,* which won four straight races from the Australian challenger *Southern Cross.*

Sept. 29 The fifth annual **New York City Marathon** was won by Dr. Norbert Sander, Jr., of New York City, with a time of 2 hrs., 26 min., 30 sec. The first woman to complete the race was Kathy Switzer of New York City, with a time of 3 hrs., 7 min., 29 sec.

Dec. 1 A jet airplane bound for Washington, D.C., crashed in the Blue Ridge Mts. of Virginia, killing 92 people.

Dec. 10 Rep. **Wilbur D. Mills,** Democrat of Arkansas, resigned his chairmanship of the Ways and Means Committee. Several well-publicized incidents had linked him with Fanne Fox, a burlesque performer.

Dec. 16 A 1925 **Geneva protocol against chemical and biological weapons** was approved by the Senate.

Dec. 19 Nelson A. Rockefeller was sworn in as vice president of the United States.

Dec. 21 Allegations of **illegal CIA activities** were leveled by *The New York Times*. The newspaper reported that during the Nixon administration, the agency had maintained files on some 10,000 U.S. citizens and had engaged in illegal domestic operations against opponents of U.S. policy in Vietnam as well as other dissidents. On Dec. 26 CIA director William Colby acknowledged the truth of the allegations in a letter to Pres. Ford.

bookstores for unauthorized publication and distribution of short stories he had written early in his career.

Nov. 13 *Sizwe Banzi Is Dead* by Athol Fugard, John Kani, and Winston Ntshona, starring Kani and Ntshona, opened at the Edison Theater in New York City. Directed by Fugard, the play was a moving drama centering on South African racial policy.

Dec. 10 A **royalty accord with the U.S.S.R.** was signed in New York City. It promised royalties for live performances in the U.S.S.R. of U.S. works published after 1972.

Dec. 12 An **art theft** occurred at the Brooklyn Museum in New York City. The museum reported that it lost a painting by Renoir, *Still Life with Blue Cup.*

Dec. 29 *All Over Town,* a comedy by Murray Schisgal directed by Dustin Hoffman, opened at the Booth Theater in New York City. Its cast included Cleavon Little, Barnard Hughes, and Zane Lasky.

Dec. 30 A **boycott of UNESCO-sponsored cultural activities** by some 25 leading dancers and musical artists was announced. The action was taken because of the organization's decision to cut all cultural aid to Israel.

1975

The Vietnam War reached its conclusion this year. In January the North Vietnamese stepped up military actions in South Vietnam. In mid-March the South Vietnamese army began a withdrawal from northern South Vietnam that soon became a full-scale retreat. On Apr. 30 the last U.S. citizens were airlifted out of Saigon. On the same day, Gen. Duong Van Minh, who had been installed as president two days earlier, surrendered to the Vietcong. In March the new government of Thailand announced it would seek complete U.S. withdrawal from that country within a year, conditions permitting. In mid-April Cambodia fell to the Khmer Rouge. The agony of Vietnam would continue for the U.S. The war had divided the nation politically and philosophically for more than a decade, and its end prompted disillusionment and a new spirit of isolationism. Thus, Congress and the nation proved unwilling to commit itself against insurgents in Angola and Ethiopia. At home further revelations in the Watergate scandal, investigations of illegal FBI and CIA activities, and growing concern over the faltering national economy continued to erode Americans' faith in their government and in themselves. Notables who died this year included Hannah Arendt, the political philosopher noted for her writings on totalitarianism, Dec. 5, at 69; Gen. Anthony C. McAuliffe, acting commander of the 101st Airborne Division at Bastogne, Belgium, during the Battle of the

In New York City, hard times notwithstanding, Broadway revenues for the 1974–1975 season hit $57,-400,000, almost 25% more than the preceding year. Inflation and recession, however, did take their toll on museums. As the value of endowments fell, museums attempted to reduce operating deficits. They fired employees, curtailed services, shortened schedules, and instituted or increased admission fees. By contrast, the motion picture industry enjoyed a second straight year of record revenues, some $2,000,000,000. Fewer films were made, but income from such blockbusters as *Jaws* and *The Godfather, Part II,* as well as such slick sex films as *Emmanuelle* and *The Story of O* helped boost the box office take. This year Americans mourned the passing of Julian E. "Cannonball" Adderley, the jazz musician, Aug. 8, at 46; Josephine Baker, the cabaret singer, Apr. 10, at 68; Thomas Hart Benton, the artist, Jan. 19, at 85; Walker Evans, the photographer known best for his stark portraits of Depression-era subjects, Apr. 10, at 71; Susan Hayward, the actress, Mar. 14, at 55; Vincent Lopez, the band leader and pianist, Sept. 20, at 80; Fredric March, the actor, Apr. 14, at 77; Ozzie Nelson, the radio and television performer, June 3, at 68; Rod Serling, the author and screenwriter, June 28, at 50; George Stevens, the film director, Mar. 8, at 70; Rex Stout, the creator of fictional detective Nero Wolfe, Oct. 27, at 88; Richard Tucker, the opera tenor, Jan. 8, at 60; Charles

Nov. 27 The longest surviving heart transplant patient, Louis B. Russell, Jr., died in Richmond, Va., at 49. He had received his new heart in 1968.

Dec. 18 In a massive **auto industry layoff** forced by sharply reduced car sales, some 142,000 workers lost their jobs and another 76,000 were temporarily thrown out of work.

Dec. 20 Legislation tying **improved trade benefits for the U.S.S.R.** to that country's relaxation of emigration policies was passed by Congress.

Dec. 30 The **Boston School Committee was fined** by federal Judge W. Arthur Garrity, and its members were barred from participation in school integration matters unless they backed a new public school desegregation plan by Jan. 7, 1975.

Dec. 31 A 41-year ban on **private possession of gold** was lifted. Early sales of bullion were light.

Oct. 3 **Frank Robinson** became the first black manager in major league baseball when he signed a $175,000-a-year contract as player-manager with the Cleveland Indians (AL).

Oct. 12–17 The **World Series** was won for the third straight year by the Oakland Athletics (AL), who beat the Los Angeles Dodgers four games to one. On Oct. 9 the Athletics had won the American League pennant, beating the Baltimore Orioles three games to one. The same day the Dodgers took the National League pennant from the Pittsburgh Pirates, winning three games to one.

Oct. 29 A bill forbidding **discrimination in credit applications** on the basis of sex or marital status was signed by Pres. Ford.

Oct. 30 The **world heavyweight boxing championship** was regained by Muhammad Ali, who triumphed over George Foreman with an eighth-round knockout in Kinshasa, Zaire.

Nov. 11 Competition in the **Little League World Series** was seriously impaired, as foreign teams were barred from participating. Japan and Taiwan had won seven of the last eight baseball championships.

1975

Soaring prices prompted many to turn to gardening and home canning to trim food expenses, which were at an eight-year high as a percentage of take-home pay. There were as many as 6,000,000 new gardeners, according to estimates by the Department of Agriculture. Recovery from the recession began in spring but was hampered by steep interest rates and record high savings levels. Pres. Ford secured a federal tax cut but was unsuccessful in trimming the federal deficit. The budget for 1976 included a deficit of about $52,000,000,000, about 11.5% more than in 1975. This year a Senate committee and the Securities and Exchange Commission investigated illegal payoffs by U.S. businesses overseas. In medicine the increasing number of malpractice suits and high court awards produced skyrocketing insurance premiums, and in some cases withdrawal of malpractice coverage. In a number of states physicians threatened job actions if legislative remedies were not taken. This year also saw publication of a landmark religious work, *The Torah—A Modern Commentary,* Reform Judaism's first comprehensive and authorized commentary on the first five books of the Old Testament. Notables who died this year included John R. Dunning, the physicist, Aug. 25, at 67; Euell Gibbons, the naturalist and author, Dec. 29, at 64; Elijah Muhammad, leader of the Nation of Islam for 41 years, Feb. 25, at 77; Charles H. Revson, the business executive, Aug.

Declining attendance and failure to secure a profitable television contract led to the demise of the World Football League. The American Basketball Association, reduced from eleven teams to eight by season's end, also faced collapse. Increasing violence in hockey led to the first criminal trial of a player for conduct during a game. New federal guidelines requiring equal access for women in school sports were criticized by officials as burdening schools with oppressive costs. Athletics for females traditionally had been neglected in sports budgets. For example, in 1974–1975 UCLA spent $180,000 of its $3,000,000 sports budget for women's athletics. At the University of Nebraska, women's athletics was allocated $45,000 of a $4,000,000 sports budget. In professional golf the top money winners were Jack Nicklaus, $323,149, and Sandra Palmer, $94,805. This year many Americans found recreation in discothèques, where they could dance to music they enjoyed and be treated to colorful lighting effects. Jewelry for men became popular this year. Among the most fashionable items were pendants, rings, bracelets, and neck chains with shark teeth, a fad sparked by the motion picture *Jaws.* Notables who died this year included Avery Brundage, president of the International Olympic Committee from 1952–1972, May 8, at 87; Ezzard Charles, world heavyweight boxing champion from 1949–1951, May 27, at 53; Leland Stanford "Larry" MacPhail, the

1975 *PRES.* GERALD R. FORD   708

| Exploration and Settlement; Wars; Government; Civil Rights; Statistics | I | | II | Publishing; Arts and Music; Popular Entertainment; Architecture; Theater |

Bulge in 1944, Aug. 11, at 77; and Raymond Moley, a member of Pres. Roosevelt's so-called Brain Trust, Feb. 18, at 88.

Jan. 5 A commission on **CIA domestic activities** was appointed by Pres. Gerald R. Ford to investigate whether the agency had violated its charter by engaging in domestic intelligence operations. Headed by Vice Pres. Nelson A. Rockefeller, the commission reported on June 10 that the CIA had undertaken unlawful surveillance of some 300,000 persons or organizations and had supplied Pres. Nixon with information to use against political foes.

Jan. 16 In a challenge to the **congressional seniority system**, Democrats in the House voted to oust F. Edward Hébert, Democrat of Louisiana, as head of the Armed Services Committee and W. R. Poage, Democrat of Texas, as head of the Agriculture Committee. On Jan. 22 Wright Patman, Democrat of Texas, was unseated as chairman of the Banking and Currency Committee. The chairmen were replaced, respectively, by Melvin Price, Democrat of Illinois, Thomas S. Foley, Democrat of Illinois, and Henry S. Reuss, Democrat of Wisconsin.

Jan. 24 **Fraunces Tavern was bombed** in New York City, killing four persons and injuring 53. A terrorist group seeking Puerto Rican independence claimed responsibility.

Jan. 27 A bipartisan **Senate investigation of FBI and CIA activities,** headed by Sen. Frank Church of Idaho, was begun. On Nov. 20 the committee released its report. It charged both agencies with illegal surveillance of U.S. citizens and the CIA with plotting to assassinate foreign leaders and maintaining a secret stockpile of poisons despite a presidential order to destroy the poisons.

Jan. 31 Pres. Ford's **clemency program** for Vietnam-era military resisters was extended to Mar. 1.

Feb. 21 For their parts in the **Watergate** cover-up, former White House aides H. R. Haldeman and John D. Ehrlichman, and former attorney general John Mitchell were each sentenced to 30 months' imprisonment.

Feb. 24 Actuaries of the **Social Security Advisory Council** warned that the $45,900,000,000 trust fund

Weidman, the modern dancer and choreographer, July 15, at 73; Thornton Wilder, the author, Dec. 7, at 78; and P. G. Wodehouse, the English-born author and humorist, Feb. 14, at 93.

Among **books published** this year was *Ragtime* by E. L. Doctorow, a novel set in the U.S. at the turn of the century. The novel carefully intermingled its fictional characters with such real figures as Henry Ford, Harry Houdini, and Stanford White. Other books published this year included *Humboldt's Gift* by Saul Bellow, a novel; *Thurber* by Burton Bernstein, a biography; *How the Good Guys Finally Won* by Jimmy Breslin, one of several books published this year dealing with the Watergate scandal and the Nixon administration; *Against Our Will: Men, Women and Rape* by Susan Brownmiller; *The Lonely Hunter: A Biography of Carson McCullers* by Virginia Spencer Carr; *Shogun, A Novel of Japan* by James Clavell; *Poems: Selected and New, 1950–1974* by Adrienne Rich; *Looking for Mr. Goodbar* by Judith Rossner, a novel that became one of the year's best sellers; *Passions*, stories by Isaac Bashevis Singer; *Breach of Faith* by Theodore H. White, a study of Richard M. Nixon and the Watergate scandal; *A Time to Die* by Tom Wicker, a study of the 1971 Attica prison riot; and *The Twenties,* a posthumous publication from the notebooks of Edmund Wilson.

Jan. 7 *Shenandoah,* a musical by Gary Geld, Peter Udell, James Lee Barrett, and Philip Rose, opened at the Alvin Theater in New York City. Based on the 1965 movie starring Jimmy Stewart, it related the struggle of a Virginia farmer to keep his family together and safe during the Civil War.

Jan. 20 *The Ritz* by Terrence McNally, a comedy set in a steambath frequented by homosexuals, opened at the Longacre Theater in New York City. Its cast included Jerry Stiller, Jack Weston, and Rita Moreno.

Jan. 23 **Recovery of five paintings** stolen in 1969 and valued at $1,000,000 was announced by the FBI.

Feb. 1 The first issue of *Stolen Paintings and Objets d'Art* was published in an effort to help museums, galleries, and collectors identify stolen works.

Mar. 1 **Grammy Awards** were presented for the following: best album of 1974, *Fullfullingness' First Finale* by Stevie Wonder; best record, "I Honestly Love You" by Olivia Newton-John; best male pop vocalist, Stevie Wonder for *Fullfullingness' First Finale;* best female pop singer, Olivia Newton-John for "I Honestly Love You"; best pop group, Paul McCartney & Wings for "Band on the Run."

Mar. 1 *Esplanade* by Paul Taylor, a vigorous modern dance work set to the music of Johann Sebastian Bach and based on such natural movements as running, walking, and skipping, received its premiere performance in Washington, D.C.

| Business and Industry; Science; Education; Philosophy and Religion III | IV Sports; Social Issues and Crime; Folkways; Fashion; Holidays |

24, at 69; and Henry P. Van Dusen, the Protestant theologian, Feb. 13, at 77.

Jan. 5 Women with advanced degrees suffered **discrimination in employment,** both in pay and promotions, a report by the Educational Testing Service revealed.

Jan. 12 Several insurers announced they would no longer offer **medical malpractice insurance** because of increasingly costly court awards.

Feb. 3 **Auto industry layoffs,** caused by poor sales, climbed to a record 274,380 production workers, or 38.5% of the industry's payroll.

Feb. 26 **Wallace Muhammad** was named head of the Nation of Islam a day after the death of his father, Elijah Muhammad, in Chicago.

Feb. 27 Procedures to reduce the **dangers of genetic research,** including the possibility of creating organisms that cause cancer or are drug-resistant, were agreed to by biologists from 17 countries at a conference in California.

Mar. 11 The **proportion of blacks in predominantly white schools** was higher in the South than in the North, according to a report by the Commission on Civil Rights.

Mar. 17–20 In the first major **doctors' strike** in U.S. history, some 2000 interns and resident physicians successfully struck New York City's 21 metropolitan hospitals. They achieved their goal of securing shorter work shifts.

Mar. 18 For his role in the 1973 **Equity Funding Corporation** insurance and equities fraud, former chairman Stanley Goldblum was sentenced to eight years in jail and fined $20,000. A score of other company officials and employees were later imprisoned, fined, or given probation.

Mar. 28 Authorization for so-called **no-frills airline fares** was given for the first time, to National Airlines, by the Civil Aeronautics Board. The fares were for travelers willing to forego such amenities as free meals and drinks.

baseball executive, Oct. 1, at 85; Perle Mesta, the Washington hostess with the mostest, Mar. 16, at 85; Joan Whitney Payson, owner of the New York Mets, Oct. 4, at 72; and Charles Dillon "Casey" Stengel, who managed the New York Yankees and later the New York Mets and mismanaged the English language to the endless delight of sports fans, Sept. 29, at 85.

Jan. 1 In **college football bowl games,** the results were Penn State 41, Baylor 20 in the Cotton Bowl; Notre Dame 13, Alabama 11 in the Orange Bowl; USC 18, Ohio State 17 in the Rose Bowl; and (Dec. 31, 1974) Nebraska 13, Florida 10 in the Sugar Bowl. This season the AP poll chose Oklahoma the national college football champions, and the UPI poll chose USC.

Jan. 12 **Super Bowl IX** was won by the Pittsburgh Steelers (AFC), who defeated the Minnesota Vikings (NFC) 16–6 for their first Super Bowl win. On Dec. 29, 1974, the Steelers had beaten the Oakland Raiders 24–13 for the AFC championship and the Vikings had defeated the Los Angeles Rams 14–10 for the NFC title.

Jan. 31–Feb. 2 **U.S. figure skating championships** were won in Oakland, Calif., by Gordon McKellen, Jr., men's singles; Dorothy Hamill, women's singles; Melissa Melitano and Johnny Johns, pairs; Colleen O'Connor and Jim Millns, dance.

Feb. 1 Otis Francis Tabler, a computer scientist, became the first declared **homosexual to get security clearance** for work on a Defense Department contracts.

Feb. 16 **Jimmy Connors** won the National Indoor Tennis tournament, becoming the first player to win the event three consecutive times.

Mar. 22 The fourth annual **AIAW basketball championship** was won by Delta State, which defeated the three-time women's national champion Immaculata College 90–81.

Mar. 31 The **NCAA basketball championship** was won for the tenth time in 12 years by UCLA, defeating the University of Kentucky 92–85. On Mar. 29 UCLA coach John Wooden had announced he was retiring, after compiling a 620-147 career record.

Apr. 3 **Bobby Fischer** was stripped of his world chess title after he failed to accept a match with U.S.S.R. challenger Anatoly Karpov. Karpov became champion by default.

1975 *PRES.* GERALD R. FORD   710

Exploration and Settlement; Wars;   I   II   Publishing; Arts and Music; Popular
Government; Civil Rights; Statistics   Entertainment; Architecture; Theater

would be exhausted by 1981 unless new sources of revenue were found.

Mar. 18 A CIA attempt at **recovery of a sunken Soviet submarine** in 1974 was revealed. The attempt, involving the salvage vessel *Glomar Explorer,* cost some $250,000,000. A third of the sub was recovered, but not its missiles or codes.

Apr. 4 A U.S. **C-5A transport plane crashed** shortly after takeoff from Saigon, South Vietnam. Some 200 of the refugees being airlifted to the U.S., most of them children, were killed.

Apr. 9 A private **pledge of aid to South Vietnam** in the event of renewed North Vietnamese aggression had been made by Pres. Richard M. Nixon, the White House revealed.

May 12 The U.S. merchant ship *Mayaguez* was seized by Cambodian forces and its crew charged with spying within Cambodia's territorial waters. The crew of 39 was freed on May 14 in a U.S. military rescue operation. Fifteen U.S. soldiers died and 50 were wounded. The operation received virtually unanimous approval by U.S. citizens.

June 24 One hundred and thirteen people were killed when their **jet crashed while attempting to land** in a thunderstorm at Kennedy International Airport in New York City.

July 14 Allegations of **FBI burglaries and break-ins** were confirmed by agency director Clarence B. Kelley, who stated that such activities occurred in national-security cases. On July 16 the Washington *Post* revealed that some of the incidents involved ordinary criminal cases.

July 29 **U.S. bases in Turkey were seized** by the Turkish government after a U.S. embargo on military aid to Turkey. The embargo had been imposed because of a stalemate in negotiations between Turkey and Greece over Cyprus.

Aug. 1 The charter of the **Conference on Security and Cooperation in Europe** was signed by Pres. Ford and leaders of 34 other nations in Helsinki, Finland. The declaration recognized boundaries formed at the end of World War II, renounced use of force, and pledged

Mar. 5 A revival of *A Doll's House* by Henrik Ibsen, adapted by Christopher Hampton and starring Liv Ullmann and Sam Waterston, opened at the Vivian Beaumont Theater in New York City. The entire engagement was sold out before opening night.

Mar. 9 The first **International Women's Art Festival,** held in New York City, featured a three-hour concert by women composers. The program ranged from American folk music to Latin American revolutionary songs to avant-garde works.

Mar. 13 *Same Time, Next Year,* a comedy by Bernard Slade starring Ellen Burstyn and Charles Grodin as two happily married people who meet on the same date and at the same place each year for an extramarital get-together, opened at the Brooks Atkinson Theater in New York City.

Mar. 17 *The Taking of Miss Janie* by Ed Bullins was presented by the New Federal Theater at the Henry Street Settlement in New York City. The play dealt with the relationship of an innocent young white woman and a militant black in the 1960s, exemplifying the relationship between white and black America.

Mar. 28 **Mstislav Rostropovich,** an acclaimed cellist and pianist who voluntarily exiled himself from the U.S.S.R., was appointed musical director and conductor of the National Symphony Orchestra in Washington, D.C., beginning with the 1977–1978 season.

Mar. 28 A **Chinese music and dance troupe** canceled a tour of the U.S. after the State Department requested elimination of a song dealing with the conquest of Taiwan.

Apr. 7 **Beverly Sills** made a highly praised debut with the Metropolitan Opera. The soprano had performed for 20 years with the New York City Opera.

Apr. 8 **Academy Awards** were presented to *The Godfather, Part II* as outstanding motion picture of 1974; Art Carney as best actor for *Harry and Tonto;* Ellen Burstyn as best actress for *Alice Doesn't Live Here Any More;* Robert De Niro as best supporting actor for *The Godfather, Part II;* and Ingrid Bergman as best supporting actress for *Murder on the Orient Express.*

Apr. 8 The principle of **family viewing time** was adopted by the directors of the National Association of Broadcasters, representing two-thirds of all television stations. For two hours in the early evening, stations were to avoid broadcasting shows with strong themes of violence or sex.

Apr. 16 **National Book Awards** were presented for the following: fiction, *Dog Soldiers* by Robert Stone and *The Hair of Harold Roux* by Thomas Williams; poetry, *Presentation Piece* by Marilyn Hacker; history, *The Ordeal of Thomas Hutchinson* by Bernard Bailyn; biography, *The Life of Emily Dickinson* by Richard B. Sewall; arts and letters, *The Lives of a Cell* by Lewis

May Exxon Corporation was listed as the nation's wealthiest company in the annual *Fortune* magazine listing of 500 top industrial firms. Exxon bumped General Motors, number one in the listing for 40 years. Of the top 20 corporations, ten were oil companies.

May 22 A bill providing broad **securities industry reforms** was passed by Congress. It abolished fixed brokerage fees and ordered the Securities and Exchange Commission to set up a national securities clearance system that would give investors up-to-date information on dealings across the country.

May 27 The number of **abortion-related deaths** had been drastically reduced by liberal abortion laws, a report by the National Academy of Sciences revealed. Compared with 320 deaths in 1961, when illegal abortions were common, there had been only 47 deaths in 1973, including 16 linked to illegal operations.

June 4 Discovery of the **oldest animal fossils** in the U.S., large marine worms dating back some 620,000,000 years, was reported by paleontologists in North Carolina.

June 16 Uniform minimum legal fees were held to be in violation of antitrust laws by the Supreme Court.

June 26 Forced confinement of mental patients was barred by the Supreme Court, provided that the patients could care for themselves and did not endanger others.

June 30 The **discovery of a galaxy** approximately 8,000,000,000 light-years away from Earth, identified as Galaxy 3C123, was announced by astronomers at the University of California. The farthest known galaxy from Earth, 3C123 was estimated to be five to ten times larger than the Milky Way.

July 15 The **Apollo-Soyuz** joint space mission began with the launch of Soyuz 19 from the U.S.S.R. and the launch of Apollo, carrying astronauts Thomas P. Stafford, Donald K. Slayton, and Vance D. Brand, from Kennedy Space Center in Florida. On July 17 the craft docked with one another. During their 44-hour linkup, the crews performed a number of experiments. Soyuz returned to Earth on July 21, and Apollo splashed down on July 24.

Apr. 13 The **Masters golf tournament** was won for the fifth time by Jack Nicklaus.

Apr. 21 The 79th annual **Boston Marathon** was won by Bill Rodgers of Boston, with a time of 2 hrs., 9 min., 55 sec., the fastest time by a U.S. runner. The first woman to finish was Liane Winter of West Germany, with a time of 2 hrs., 42 min., 24 sec.

May 3 The 101st annual **Kentucky Derby** was won by Foolish Pleasure, with a time of 2:02. The jockey was Jacinto Vasquez.

May 13–22 The **ABA basketball championship** was won by the Kentucky Colonels, who defeated the Indiana Pacers four games to one.

May 15–27 The **NHL Stanley Cup** was won for the second straight year by the Philadelphia Flyers, defeating the Buffalo Sabres four games to two.

May 17 The 100th annual **Preakness Stakes** was won by Master Derby, a longshot, with a time of 1:56²/₅. The jockey was Darrel McHargue.

May 18–25 The **NBA basketball championship** was won by the Golden State Warriors, who swept the Washington Bullets in four games.

May 18–28 In their **first track and field meet in China**, U.S. athletes won 91 of 99 events.

May 30 The 59th **Indianapolis 500** auto race, cut short by rain, was won by Bobby Unser, who completed 435 miles in 2 hrs., 54 min., 55.08 sec., with an average speed of 149.213 mph.

June 1 The **LPGA golf tournament** was won by Kathy Whitworth.

June 3 It was reported that **Pelé**, the Brazilian soccer star (born Edson Arantes do Nascimento), would come out of retirement to play for the New York Cosmos. His three-year, $7,000,000 contract made him the highest-paid team athlete in the world.

June 3 Guidelines concerning **women in school sports,** affirming the right of women to equal participation in athletics, were sent by the Department of Health, Education, and Welfare to public schools and colleges receiving federal aid.

reduction of military forces and respect for freedom of thought, conscience, and religion.

Aug. 5 **Alger Hiss** was ordered reinstated to the Massachusetts bar 25 years after he lost his right to practice law because of a conviction for perjury before a grand jury investigating espionage against the U.S.

Aug. 6 **Literacy requirements for voting** were abolished and a number of linguistic minorities were brought under the protection of the Voting Rights Act of 1965. The act itself was extended for seven years.

Sept. 5 An **assassination attempt** against Pres. Ford in Sacramento, Calif., was ended when a Secret Service agent wrested a pistol from Lynette A. "Squeaky" Fromme, a follower of Charles Manson.

Sept. 22 In a second **assassination attempt** against Pres. Ford, this time in San Francisco, Calif., the president was shot at by Sara Jane Moore, a police and FBI informer.

Sept. 28 A bill authorizing **admission of women to the military academies** for the three major services by the fall of 1976 was passed by Congress.

Oct. 22 Air Force Sgt. **Leonard Matlovich,** a much-decorated Vietnam veteran, was given a general discharge after publicly declaring his homosexuality. His intent was to challenge the ban against homosexuals in the military. His discharge was later upgraded to honorable.

Nov. 3 In an **administration shakeup** that came to be known as the Halloween massacre, Sec. of State Henry Kissinger resigned his second post as head of the National Security Council, and Sec. of Defense James R. Schlesinger and CIA director William E. Colby were dismissed by Pres. Ford. The president subsequently nominated Donald Rumsfeld for secretary of defense and George Bush for CIA director.

Nov. 4 State **equal rights amendments** were voted down in New York and New Jersey.

Nov. 12 **William O. Douglas,** 77, suffering from effects of a stroke incurred in 1974, announced his retirement from the Supreme Court after 36 years of service. During his tenure, longest of any Supreme

Thomas and *Marcel Proust* by Roger Shattuck; philosophy and religion, *Anarchy, State and Utopia* by Robert Nozick; sciences, *Interpretation of Schizophrenia* by Silvano Arieti.

Apr. 20 A $6,000,000 **Museum of Our National Heritage** was inaugurated in Lexington, Mass., by the Scottish Rite Masons one day after the bicentennial of the battles of Lexington and Concord.

Apr. 21 **Tony awards** for the 1974–1975 season were presented for the following: best play, *Equus;* best musical, *The Wiz;* best dramatic actor, John Kani and Winston Ntshona for *Sizwe Banzi Is Dead;* best dramatic actress, Ellen Burstyn for *Same Time, Next Year.*

Apr. 24 The **Gotham Book Mart** in New York City, in one of the largest retail sales made by a bookstore, was reported to have sold some 65% of its stock of books to New Mexico State University for $485,000.

May 5 **Pulitzer prizes** were awarded for the following: fiction, *The Killer Angels* by Michael Shaara; biography, *The Power Broker: Robert Moses and the Fall of New York* by Robert Caro; history, *Thomas Jefferson and His Times* by Dumas Malone; general nonfiction, *Pilgrim at Tinker Creek* by Annie Dillard; poetry, *Turtle Island* by Gary Snyder; drama, *Seascape* by Edward Albee.

May 12 Vice Pres. Nelson Rockefeller announced he had bought a **surrealist bed** designed by Max Ernst for $35,000. The bed, called *Apparatus for Dreaming,* was installed in the newly established vice-presidential mansion in Washington. D.C.

May 15–31 A **Maurice Ravel Centennial** was presented by the New York City Ballet, featuring 16 new works, including *Le Tombeau de Couperin* by George Balanchine and *Concerto in G* by Jerome Robbins.

May 19 **Emmy Awards** were presented to Sir Laurence Olivier and Katharine Hepburn as best actor and actress for *Love Among the Ruins;* Robert Blake as best actor in a dramatic series for *Baretta;* and Jean Marsh as best actress in a dramatic series for *Upstairs, Downstairs.*

May 21 *A Chorus Line,* a musical by James Kirkwood, Nicholas Dante, Marvin Hamlisch, and Edward Kleban, opened at the New York Shakespeare Festival's Newman Theater and became an instant smash hit. On July 25 it opened on Broadway at the Shubert Theater.

May 22 **James Levine** was named musical director of the Metropolitan Opera beginning with the 1976–1977 season.

May 27 In a landmark case dealing with **government censorship,** the Supreme Court let stand a lower court ruling requiring former CIA agent Victor Marchetti to submit all writings about the CIA to the agency for prior approval. It was the first such ruling on record.

| Business and Industry; Science; Education; Philosophy and Religion III | | Sports; Social Issues and Crime; Folkways; Fashion; Holidays IV |

July 21   The **Bunge Corporation was indicted** for theft in short-weighing of grain shipments. A New Orleans grand jury charged the company, one of the world's leading grain exporters, with short-weight grain shipments between 1961 and 1973 and then engaging in a cover-up. Similar indictments were brought later against other grain exporters.

July 25   **Electricity rates** had risen a record 30% in 1974, the Environmental Protection Agency reported.

July 31   Former Teamsters president **James R. Hoffa** was reported missing by his family. Hoffa, who had served a prison term for jury tampering and mail fraud, had been trying to regain leadership of the Teamsters. It was speculated that he had been murdered by organized crime figures.

July 31   The **cancer death rate** was placed at 176.3 persons per 100,000 by the National Center for Health Statistics. The rate was 105.9 in 1933 and 169.5 in 1974.

Sept. 4   The first court-ordered **cross-district school busing** in a metropolitan area began in Louisville and adjacent Jefferson County in Kentucky. The National Guard was called in on Sept. 6 because of violence in two working-class suburbs.

Sept. 11   Former United Mine Workers president **William A. "Tony" Boyle** was sentenced to three consecutive life terms in Media, Pa., for ordering the 1969 murders of union opponent Joseph Yablonski and Yablonski's wife and daughter.

Sept. 14   Mother **Elizabeth Ann Bayley Seton** was canonized in Rome by Pope Paul VI. She was the first U.S.-born saint.

Oct. 14   The **Nobel Prize in Economics** was awarded jointly to Tjalling C. Koopmans of Yale University and to Leonid Kantorovich of the U.S.S.R.

Oct. 15   **Bankruptcy petitions** were reported to have climbed to a record 254,484 during fiscal 1975, a 34.3% increase over 1974.

Oct. 16   The **Nobel Prize in Physiology or Medicine** was awarded jointly to David Baltimore of the Center for Cancer Research at MIT, Howard M. Temin of the University of Wisconsin, and Dr. Renato Dulbecco of

June 7   The 107th annual **Belmont Stakes** was won by Avatar, with a time of 2:28⅕. The jockey was Willie Shoemaker.

June 23   The **U.S. Open golf tournament** was won by Lou Graham, who beat John Mahaffey in a playoff.

July 4–5   At the **Wimbledon** tennis championships in England, Billie Jean King won the women's singles title and Arthur Ashe became the first black to win the men's singles title. The men's doubles was won by Vitas Gerulaitis and Sandy Mayer. Ann Kiyomura teamed with Kazuko Sawamatsu of Japan to win the women's doubles, and Marty Riessen teamed with Margaret Court of Australia to win the mixed doubles.

July 15   The **baseball All-Star Game** was won by the National League, defeating the American League 6–3.

July 18   The first pro athlete indicted for a **crime committed during play**, Dave Forbes of the Boston Bruins hockey team, saw his trial for criminal assault end with a hung jury. The prosecution decided not to seek a retrial.

July 20   The **U.S. Women's Open golf tournament** was won by Sandra Palmer.

Aug. 10   **Betty Ford,** wife of Pres. Gerald R. Ford, created an uproar when she said during a television interview that she suspected all four of her children had tried marijauna, that she would not be surprised if her 18-year-old daughter Susan told her she was having an affair, and that the Supreme Court had made a "great, great decision" in legalizing abortion.

Aug. 10   The **PGA golf tournament** was won by Jack Nicklaus, who beat Bruce Crampton and Tom Weiskopf by two strokes.

Aug. 17   Seagram heir **Samuel Bronfman** was freed by New York City police and FBI agents eight days after he was kidnaped in Westchester County, N.Y., two days after a $2,300,000 ransom had been paid for his release. Two men were charged with the kidnaping.

Aug. 18   The **Baseball Hall of Fame** inducted five new members: Howard Earl Averill, Stanley R. "Bucky" Harris, William Jennings Bryan "Billy" Herman, William J. "Rudy" Johnson, and Ralph Kiner.

Court justice in history, he earned a reputation as a civil libertarian.

Nov. 18 Eldridge Cleaver, a former leader of the Black Panther Party, returned to the U.S. after seven years of exile to face criminal charges stemming from a shoot-out with Oakland, Calif., police.

Nov. 24 Maryland governor **Marvin Mandel was indicted** with five associates by a federal grand jury. They were charged with bribery, mail fraud, income tax fraud, and racketeering. The charges grew out of the investigation that led to Vice Pres. Spiro T. Agnew's resignation in 1973.

Nov. 26 Pres. Ford announced support for a **federal loan for New York City,** amounting to some $2,300,000,000 annually, to help the city avoid bankruptcy. The fiscal crisis had begun when securities markets declined to buy New York City notes. Ford's announcement reversed his earlier stand on aid to the city.

Dec. 4 A staff report of the Senate Committee investigating **illegal CIA activities** absolved the agency of direct participation in the 1973 military overthrow and subsequent murder of Chilean president Salvador Allende Gossens. The CIA was reported to have spent some $13,400,000 from 1963 on Chilean operations, mostly for anti-Allende activities.

Dec. 7 Following a **presidential trip to China** (Dec. 1–5), Indonesia, and the Philippines, Pres. Ford in Honolulu, Hawaii, enunciated a new Pacific doctrine, which stressed maintenance of U.S. strength in the region, recognized Japan as a pillar of U.S. strategy, and pledged improved ties with the People's Republic of China.

Dec. 19 U.S. covert aid to factions in Angola was cut by the Senate, despite warnings that U.S. security was at stake in the resolution of the civil war. The war had broken out after Portugal granted independence to Angola.

Dec. 20 The last of some 130,000 **Indochinese refugees** resettling in the U.S. left the processing center at Fort Chaffee, Ark.

Dec. 29 An **airport bombing** in the main passenger terminal at LaGuardia Airport in New York City killed 11 people and injured 70.

June 3 *Chicago,* a musical by Fred Ebb, Bob Fosse, and John Kander, opened at the Forty-Sixth Street Theater in New York City. Its cast included Gwen Verdon, Chita Rivera, and Jerry Orbach.

June 19 At a special performance celebrating the upcoming 50th anniversary of the **Martha Graham Dance Company,** held at the Uris Theater in New York City, Rudolf Nureyev and Margot Fonteyn gave the premiere performance of *Lucifer,* a work choreographed especially for them by Martha Graham.

Aug. 1 A **record for paperback reprint rights,** $1,850,000, was reported to have been advanced by Bantam Books for the novel *Ragtime* by E. L. Doctorow.

Aug. 1 The **New Orleans Superdome,** the world's largest indoor sports and entertainment center, was dedicated. It cost $162,000,000 and seated 97,000 people.

Aug. 23 Purchase of the **Packard collection** of rare Japanese art objects for $5,100,000 was announced by the Metropolitan Museum of Art in New York City. The purchase exhausted the museum's acquisition funds for the next five years.

Aug. 29 An agreement for **U.S.-U.S.S.R. art exchanges** from 1975 to 1980 was signed by Soviet officials and Thomas P. F. Hoving, director of the Metropolitan Museum of Art.

Sept. 18 A **theater strike** by the American Federation of Musicians shut down 12 Broadway musicals. The strike ended on Oct. 11.

Sept. 25 The FCC lifted the **equal time ruling** that required radio and television stations to offer equal broadcast time for all political candidates.

Oct. 2 The 70-story **Peachtree Plaza** in Atlanta, Ga., the tallest building in the South, was completed.

Oct. 9 *Drums, Dreams, and Banjos,* a work choreographed by Gerald Arpino as a contribution to the nation's bicentennial celebration, and featuring the songs of Stephen Foster, was given its premiere performance by the Joffrey Ballet in New York City.

Oct. 30 *Travesties,* a play by Tom Stoppard, opened at the Ethel Barrymore Theater in New York City and ran for 156 performances.

Dec. 14 The **Ford Foundation,** faced with depletion of its investment income, announced it would cut back its grants from $208,000,000 to $100,000,000 over the next four years.

Dec. 18 Executors of the estate of **Mark Rothko** and Marlborough Galleries were fined $9,252,000 by a New York court for conflict of interest and negligence in disposing of the 798 paintings in the artist's estate.

Dec. 30 The **New York Film Critics Awards** were voted to *Nashville* as best film of 1975; Jack Nicholson as best actor for *One Flew Over the Cuckoo's Nest;* and Isabelle Adjani as best actress for *The Story of Adele H.*

Italy for their studies of tumor viruses and the effect of the viruses on genetic material.

Oct. 17 The **Nobel Prize in Physics** was awarded jointly to James Rainwater of Columbia University and to Aage N. Bohr and Ben Mottelson of Copenhagen, Denmark, for their work on the asymmetry of the atomic nucleus.

Oct. 20 In a decision on **corporal punishment,** the Supreme Court ruled that teachers could spank students if the students were told in advance of the behavior that would warrant such punishment.

Nov. 10 The parents of **Karen Anne Quinlan,** a young woman who had been comatose in a hospital for seven months, lost a bid in New Jersey Superior Court to have the respirator believed to be keeping their daughter alive turned off. The court ruled that although her condition was irreversible, she was not dead according to legal or medical criteria. On Mar. 31, 1976, the New Jersey Supreme Court gave its approval for disconnecting the respirator. Quinlan proved able to breathe without assistance.

Nov. 29 Legislation requiring states to provide, within five years, **free education for the handicapped** from age 3 to 21 was signed by Pres. Ford.

Dec. 2 A federal law prohibiting the **mailing** of **firearms** that could be hidden on one's person was upheld by the Supreme Court.

Dec. 6 Creation of the **first artificial animal gene** was reported by a team of four Harvard scientists.

Dec. 9 **South Boston High School** was placed under federal court receivership by Judge W. Arthur Garrity after charging the Boston School Committee with failing to implement a court-ordered busing plan to desegregate the school.

Dec. 11 Legislation for **voluntary conversion to the metric system** within ten years was passed by Congress.

Dec. 18 A bill to discourage **redlining,** the practice of arbitrarily rejecting mortgages for homes in certain neighborhoods, was passed by Congress. Mortgage lenders were required to furnish data on the amounts of their home loans and the locations of homes they mortgaged.

Aug. 24 The **North American Soccer League championship** was won by the Tampa Bay Rowdies, who beat the Portland Timbers 2–0.

Sept. 1 **Tom Seaver,** pitcher for the New York Mets (NL), set a new major league record of eight consecutive years with 200 strikeouts or more in a season.

Sept. 6 The **Miss America** title was won by Tawney Elaine Godin, 18, from Yonkers, N.Y., at the annual pageant in Atlantic City, N.J.

Sept. 6–7 The **U.S. Open** tennis singles championships were won by Chris Evert Lloyd in the women's division and Manuel Orantes of Spain in the men's division.

Sept. 18 **Patricia Hearst was captured** in a San Francisco apartment, ending a 19-month FBI search for the kidnaped newspaper heiress who subsequently joined her abductors, the terrorist Symbionese Liberation Army. Hearst and William and Emily Harris were indicted by a Los Angeles jury on Oct. 2 on charges of assault, robbery, and kidnaping in connection with a 1974 shoplifting incident.

Sept. 28 The sixth annual **New York City Marathon** was won by Tom Fleming of New York City, with a course record time of 2 hrs., 19 min., 27 sec. The first woman to finish was Kim Merritt of Wisconsin, with a time of 2 hrs., 46 min., 14 sec.

Oct. 1 In what he called the **Thriller in Manila,** the Philippines, heavyweight champion Muhammad Ali defeated Joe Frazier in 14 rounds in his fourth title defense of the year.

Oct. 11–22 The **World Series** was won for the first time in 35 years by the Cincinnati Reds (NL), who beat the Boston Red Sox (AL) four games to three. On Oct. 7 the Reds had beaten the Pittsburgh Pirates in three straight games for the National League pennant, and the Red Sox had swept the Oakland Athletics in three straight.

Oct. 16–26 At the seventh **Pan-American Games** in Mexico City, Mexico, the U.S. won 116 gold medals and first place in unofficial team standings, followed by Cuba, Canada, and Mexico.

Oct. 22 The **World Football League was disbanded** 12 weeks into its second season because of declining attendance and lack of a national television contract.

| Exploration and Settlement; Wars; Government; Civil Rights; Statistics | I | | II | Publishing; Arts and Music; Popular Entertainment; Architecture; Theater |

1976

Former governor James Earl "Jimmy" Carter of Georgia pulled off a clear-cut victory in the presidential election by sweeping the South and carrying four of the most populous northern industrial states. Having served only one term as governor, Carter made his neophyte status an asset by appealing to voters' mistrust of politicians, particularly those in Washington, D.C. Voters appeared to believe he would keep his promises. "I'll never tell you a lie," he pledged. In Washington, Rep. Wayne Hays was forced to resign in the wake of a sex scandal, and influential congressmen admitted to receiving illegal donations from Gulf Oil Corporation, although they denied having known the source of the donations. The Justice Department conducted a probe of a scheme by South Korean lobbyists to secure support for the government of Park Chung Hee with lavish gifts and political contributions to congressmen. The scandal almost predictably became known as Koreagate. Notables who died this year included Richard J. Daley, longtime mayor and political boss of Chicago, Dec. 20, at 74; James A. Farley, a leading political figure during the first two terms of Pres. Franklin D. Roosevelt, June 9, at 88; Sen. Philip A. Hart, Democrat of Michigan (1958–1976), Dec. 26, at 64; and Martha Mitchell, wife of former attorney general John Mitchell, who herself made headlines during Watergate by providing information of the scandal to the press, May 31, at 56.

Jan. 30 Ruling on the **Federal Election Campaign Act** of 1974, the Supreme Court upheld the provisions for government financing of presidential campaigns, disclosure of campaign contributions, and a ceiling on contributions. The court struck down limits on campaign expenditures except those placed on funds spent by candidates accepting federal subsidies. It declared unconstitutional the Federal Election Commission as set up, stating that its officers would have to be appointed by the executive branch, not the legislative.

Feb. 10 U.S. officials confirmed that **microwave radiation** had been trained on the U.S. Embassy in Moscow. Soviet officials later contended that the emissions had been intended to incapacitate U.S. listening devices.

Feb. 17 In a move to **restructure the U.S. intelligence community,** Pres. Gerald R. Ford announced creation of an independent board to oversee U.S. foreign intelligence operations. The next day he issued an executive order curtailing domestic surveillance of U.S.

The year in theater was noteworthy for its excellent revivals of *Porgy and Bess, My Fair Lady, Guys and Dolls,* and *Fiddler on the Roof.* In film the year was highlighted by such foreign works as Ingmar Bergman's version of Mozart's *The Magic Flute* and Lina Wertmuller's *Seven Beauties.* But in Hollywood, the biggest success came with *Rocky,* starring Sylvester Stallone as a small-time boxer given an improbable shot at the championship. The movie made Stallone a star and led to several sequels. Television hits included the miniseries *Rich Man, Poor Man,* the lightweight series *Charlie's Angels,* featuring three eye-catching private investigators, and the soap opera spoof *Mary Hartman, Mary Hartman.* Notables who died this year included Busby Berkeley, real name William Berkeley Enos, the Hollywood choreographer, Mar. 14, at 80; Alexander Calder, the sculptor, Nov. 11, at 78; Lee J. Cobb, the actor, Feb. 11, at 64; Paul Gallico, the writer, July 15, at 78; Bobby Hackett, the jazz cornetist, June 7, at 61; Fritz Lang, the motion picture director, Aug. 2, at 85; Lotte Lehmann, the German-born soprano, Aug. 26, at 88; Johnny Mercer, writer of such songs as "Moon River" and "That Old Black Magic," June 25, at 66; Samuel Eliot Morison, the historian, May 15, at 89; Phil Ochs, songwriter and folk singer, Apr. 9, at 35; Walter Piston, the composer, Nov. 12, at 82; Lily Pons, the French-born Metropolitan Opera star for some 25 years, Feb. 13, at 71; Man Ray, the artist and leading exponent of Dada, Nov. 18, at 86; Paul Robeson, the singer and actor, Jan. 23, at 77; Rosalind Russell, the actress, Nov. 28, at 63; Mark Tobey, the abstract painter, Apr. 24, at 85; Dalton Trumbo, the novelist and screenwriter who was blacklisted in the late 1940s, Sept. 10, at 70; and Adolph Zukor, the motion picture executive who founded Paramount Pictures, June 10, at 103.

Among **books published** this year was *Roots* by Alex Haley, a fictionalized account of the author's discovery of his lineage in Africa. The book became a best seller and was the basis for an enormously popular television miniseries. Other books published this year included *The Black Family in Slavery and Freedom* by Herbert Gutman, which attacked the notion that blacks lacked strong family units in the past; *Scoundrel Time* by Lillian Hellman, memoirs; *World of Our Fathers* by Irving Howe, a study of the lives of Jews who emigrated from eastern Europe; *Lyndon Johnson and the American Dream* by Doris Kearns, a sympathetic portrait of the former president; *Agent in Place* by Helen MacInnes, a spy thriller; *The Russians* by Hedrick Smith, nonfiction; *Spandau* by Albert Speer, memoirs; *Adolf Hitler* by John Toland, biography; *Trinity* by Leon Uris, a novel; *Slapstick* by Kurt Vonnegut, a novel; and *The Final*

Business and Industry; Science; Education; Philosophy and Religion	III		IV	Sports; Social Issues and Crime; Folkways; Fashion; Holidays

1976

The state of the economy was probably a major contributor to Jimmy Carter's election to the presidency this year. Voters were wary of inflation, which fluctuated between 5% and 6%, and unemployment, which was about 8%. In this year, business ethics came under scrutiny following revelations of corporate payoffs to win sales abroad. Lockheed and Northrop were two major firms that were strongly criticized. Public indignation was also kindled by reports that a number of multinational corporations were cooperating with an Arab embargo on trade with Israel. Congress sought to discourage such behavior by eliminating tax incentives to participating firms. Census Bureau reports indicated that the number of Americans with high-school diplomas had doubled since 1950, but public concern about the quality of education was reflected in calls for greater emphasis on traditional educational skills. A number of states began to require high-school students to pass a comprehensive test before receiving diplomas. The year in science was highlighted by a clean sweep of Nobel Prizes by Americans. Notables who died this year included Jean Paul Getty, the billionaire oil tycoon, June 6, at 83; Howard R. Hughes, Jr., the reclusive billionaire, Apr. 5, at 72; Gerald L. K. Smith, the anti-Semitic, anti-Catholic founder of the so-called National Christian Crusade, Apr. 15, at 78; and Luther Allan Weigle, the biblical scholar who oversaw compilation of the Revised Standard Version of the Bible, Sept. 2, at 96.

Jan. 12 The **first report on national health** issued by the Department of Health, Education, and Welfare indicated that Americans were generally healthy. Infant mortality rates had dropped from their 1950 level of 29.2 per 1000 births to 16.5. Heart disease among those 55 to 64 years of age had declined by almost 15% since 1970. The role of insurance companies in medical payments expanded. In 1950 they paid one-third of all health bills, but in 1975 they paid two-thirds.

Feb. 5 A 35-day **work slowdown** was ended by physicians in southern California, who protested against steep increases in medical malpractice insurance rates.

Feb. 12 Production of **Red Dye No. 2,** most frequently used in drugs, foods, and cosmetics, was banned by the Food and Drug Administration after studies indicated that the dye was carcinogenic.

Professional athletes in baseball, basketball, and football gained greater freedom as team owners revised reserve and option clauses. The issue centered on the tying of players to clubs until retirement or disposal by the team. Owners' fears that so-called free agents would cripple sports proved groundless. Only 24 football players and 24 baseball players chose free-agent status. In basketball, free trading was slated to start in 1980. In boxing, Muhammad Ali defended his heavyweight title in three bouts and then announced his retirement. In golf the top money winners were Jack Nicklaus, $266, 438, and Judy Rankin, $150,734. This year Americans found new sources of amusement in Citizen Band radios and in electronic games that hooked up to television sets. Among the year's deaths was that of Carlo Gambino, reportedly a leading figure in organized crime, Oct. 15, at 74.

Jan. 1 In **college football bowl games,** the results were Arkansas 31, Georgia 10 in the Cotton Bowl; Oklahoma 14, Michigan 6 in the Orange Bowl; UCLA 23, Ohio State 10 in the Rose Bowl; and Alabama 13, Penn State 6 in the Sugar Bowl (Dec. 31, 1975). This season the AP and UPI polls chose Oklahoma the national college champions of 1975.

Jan. 10–11 **U.S. figure skating championships** were won in Colorado Springs, Colo., by Dorothy Hamill, women's singles; Terry Kubicka, men's singles; Tai Babilonia and Randy Gardner, pairs; Colleen O'Connor and Jim Millns, dance.

Jan. 18 **Super Bowl X** was won by the Pittsburgh Steelers (AFC), who defeated the Dallas Cowboys (NFC) 21–17 to pick up their second straight victory. On Jan. 4 the Steelers had beaten the Oakland Raiders 16–10 for the AFC championship and the Cowboys had beaten the Los Angeles Rams 37–7 for the NFC title.

Feb. 4–15 At the **Winter Olympics** in Innsbruck, Austria, the U.S. won three gold medals and tied with West Germany for third place, behind the U.S.S.R. and East Germany. Dorothy Hamill, who won a gold medal on Feb. 13, emerged from the games as an Olympic star.

Mar. 6 At the **world figure skating championships** in Göteborg, Sweden, Dorothy Hamill won the women's singles title.

Mar. 20 **Patricia Hearst** was convicted by a San Francisco jury of taking part in a 1974 bank robbery.

1976 *PRES.* GERALD R. FORD

718

Exploration and Settlement; Wars;   **I**
Government; Civil Rights; Statistics

II   Publishing; Arts and Music; Popular
Entertainment; Architecture; Theater

citizens and proscribing burglaries, illegal use of federal tax returns, and drug tests of unsuspecting subjects. Political assassination in foreign covert operations was also forbidden.

Feb. 25 Seeking passage of the **Equal Rights Amendment**, ERAmerica, a bipartisan group, began operations in Washington, D.C.

Mar. 26 A new four-year **U.S.-Turkish military pact** was signed, providing for reopening of U.S. military bases in Turkey and for $1,000,000,000 in military and economic aid to Turkey. On Apr. 15 a similar agreement, amounting to $700,000,000, was initialed by the U.S. and Greece.

Apr. 26 and 28 The heavily censored, two-part report of the **Senate Select Committee on Intelligence** was issued. It urged stricter guidelines for intelligence activities, closer congressional oversight, and more stringent safeguards against violation of civil liberties.

May 28 A **nuclear test pact** was signed by the U.S. and U.S.S.R. It limited underground tests to devices of no more than 150 kiloton yields and permitted examination of Soviet test sites by the U.S..

June 5 In Idaho, the **Teton R. Dam collapsed** as it was being filled for the first time, flooding an area of 300 sq. mi. Fourteen people were killed, and estimated damage was $1,000,000,000.

June 16 The **U.S. ambassador to Lebanon was assassinated.** Francis E. Meloy, Jr., and an aide were killed in Beirut by unidentified gunmen. Meloy and his aide were en route to a meeting with president-elect Elias Sarkis.

July 2 **Death penalty laws** in Georgia, Florida, and Texas were upheld by the Supreme Court, but those in North Carolina and Louisiana, which prescribed death sentences for specific crimes, were struck down.

Days by Robert Woodward and Carl Bernstein, an account of the end of the Nixon presidency.

Jan. 8 The **first National Book Critics Circle Awards** were presented for the following: fiction, *Ragtime* by E. L. Doctorow; nonfiction, *Edith Wharton* by R. W. B. Lewis; criticism, *The Great War and Modern Memory* by Paul Fussell; poetry, *Self-Portrait in a Convex Mirror* by John Ashbery.

Jan. 9 Twyla Tharp's **Push Comes to Shove,** an energetic, humorous blend of classical ballet and jazz, was given its premiere performance by the American Ballet Theater in New York City. The ballet starred Mikhail Baryshnikov and Martine van Hamel.

Jan. 13 **Sarah Caldwell** became the first woman to conduct at the Metropolitan Opera House in New York City. Critics praised her interpretation of Verdi's *La Traviata.*

Feb. 9 The **first Avery Fisher Prizes** for promising young instrumentalists were announced. The prizes were noncompetitive and consisted of $1000 grants and performances with the New York Philharmonic and six other U.S. orchestras. The first winners were Ursula Oppens and Paul Shenly, pianists; Ani Kavafian, violinist; and Heidi Lehwalder, harpist.

Feb. 11–18 The New York City weekly *The Village Voice* published major portions of a secret House of Representatives report on intelligence agencies. CBS news reporter Daniel Schorr admitted on Feb. 12 that he had provided the *Voice* with a copy of the report. Schorr was suspended by CBS on Feb. 23, after the House ordered an inquiry to determine how he obtained the document. The inquiry proved unsuccessful and was halted on Sept. 22.

Feb. 28 **Grammy Awards** were presented for the following: best album of 1975, *Still Crazy After All These Years* by Paul Simon, who was voted best male pop vocalist as well; best record, "Love Will Keep Us Together" by The Captain and Tennille; best female pop vocalist, Janis Ian for "At Seventeen"; best pop group, The Eagles for "Lyin' Eyes."

Mar. 2 *Bubblin' Brown Sugar,* a musical revue by Loften Mitchell featuring the music of such greats as Eubie Blake, Cab Calloway, and Duke Ellington, opened at the ANTA Theater in New York City.

Mar. 29 **Academy Awards** were presented to *One Flew Over the Cuckoo's Nest* as the outstanding motion picture of 1975 and to its stars, Jack Nicholson and Louise Fletcher, as best actor and actress; to George Burns as best supporting actor for *The Sunshine Boys;* and to Lee Grant as best supporting actress for *Shampoo.*

Apr. 2 In a **literary suit,** Pulitzer Prize–winning playwright Frank D. Gilroy won a settlement in excess of $1,000,000 in a New York court to recompense him for illegal use of his fictional character detective Amos

| Business and Industry; Science; Education; Philosophy and Religion | III | | IV | Sports; Social Issues and Crime; Folkways; Fashion; Holidays |

Apr. 1 **Conrail,** a federally funded corporation, took over operation of six bankrupt northeastern railroads. Federal subsidies were slated to end after five years.

Apr. 15 Funds for a **swine flu vaccination program,** totaling some $135,000,000, were allocated to combat an influenza epidemic expected to strike the U.S. in late 1976.

Apr. 21 **Production of convertibles** by the U.S. auto industry halted as General Motors rolled the last of its Cadillac Eldorado convertibles off the assembly line. The move was made in response to declining sales.

Apr. 22 Widespread **cheating at West Point** was reported. By September, 700 cadets at the U.S. Military Academy were implicated in violations of the academy's honor code.

May 24 **Concorde supersonic jet service** between the U.S. and Europe was inaugurated when two Anglo-French Concorde jets arrived from Paris and London at Dulles International Airport, near Washington, D.C.

June 8 In what was viewed as a **victory for nuclear power,** voters in California defeated a proposition to curb operation of existing nuclear power plants and ban additional construction.

June 25 **Discrimination** by private nonsectarian schools was ruled unconstitutional by the Supreme Court.

June 28 **Strip mining of coal** in Wyoming, Montana, and North and South Dakota was approved by the Supreme Court, which rejected a request by the Sierra Club to delay the mining practice until a regional environmental study was completed.

July 9 The tranquilizer **Valium and alcohol** were the leading causes of drug-related ailments, according to a report of the National Institute on Drug Abuse. Valium, used by some 65,000,000 Americans, was the most often prescribed drug. The report stated that alcohol surpassed all other drugs in social costs.

She was sentenced to seven years in jail on Sept. 24 and released on bail pending appeal.

Mar. 27 The fifth **AIAW basketball championship** was won by Delta State College, defeating Immaculata College 69–64 to win their second consecutive title.

Mar. 29 The **NCAA basketball championship** was won by Indiana, defeating Michigan 86–68.

Apr. 11 The **Masters golf tournament** was won by Ray Floyd, who beat Ben Crenshaw by eight strokes and tied the tournament record 271 set by Jack Nicklaus in 1965.

Apr. 19 The 80th annual **Boston Marathon** was won by Jack Fultz of Arlington, Va., with a time of 2 hrs., 20 min., 19 sec. The first woman to finish was Kim Merritt of Kenosha, Wis., with a time of 2 hrs., 47 min., 19 sec.

May 1 The 102nd **Kentucky Derby** was won in an upset by Bold Forbes, with a time of 2:01³/₅. The jockey was Angel Cordero, Jr.

May 1–13 The **ABA basketball championship** was won by the New York Nets, who defeated the Denver Nuggets four games to two to take their second championship in three years.

May 9–16 The **NHL Stanley Cup** was won for the 19th time by the Montreal Canadiens, who swept the Philadelphia Flyers in four straight games.

May 15 The 101st **Preakness Stakes** was won by Elocutionist, with a time of 1:55. The jockey was John Lively.

May 23–June 6 The **NBA basketball championship** was won for the 13th time by the Boston Celtics, defeating the Phoenix Suns four games to two.

May 30 The 60th **Indianapolis 500** auto race, shortened to 255 miles because of rain, was won by Johnny Rutherford, with a time of 1 hr., 42 min., 52.46 sec., for an average speed of 148.725 mph.

May 30 The **LPGA golf tournament** was won by Betty Burfeindt, beating Judy Rankin by one stroke.

June 5 The 108th **Belmont Stakes** was won by Bold

July 8 Former president **Richard M. Nixon** was declared ineligible to practice law in New York because of his role in the Watergate affair.

July 14 The **Democratic National Convention nominated Jimmy Carter** for the presidency on the first ballot. The next day Sen. Walter F. Mondale of Minnesota was nominated for the vice presidency.

July 20 The last **U.S. forces in Thailand** were withdrawn at the Thai government's request.

July 27 Some 160 **Americans were evacuated from Beirut,** Lebanon, along with 148 other foreigners, by the U.S. Navy acting in conjunction with the Palestine Liberation Organization and the Lebanese Army.

July 31 In Colorado, a **flash flood** in Big Thompson R. Canyon killed 139 persons.

Aug. 18 Two **U.S. soldiers were killed** by North Korean troops, who attacked a work party setting out to prune a tree that blocked surveillance of the demilitarized zone between North and South Korea. The U.S. protested the slayings. On Aug. 21 North Korea called the incident regrettable but did not accept responsibility.

Aug. 19 The **Republican National Convention nominated Pres. Ford** for reelection in a narrow victory over former governor Ronald Reagan of California. Sen. Robert J. Dole of Kansas was nominated for the vice presidency.

Sept. 1 Rep. **Wayne L. Hays,** Democrat of Ohio, resigned from the House of Representatives after the House Ethics Committee voted to investigate Hays's sexual liaison with a former employee, Elizabeth Ray.

Sept. 10–12 An **airplane was hijacked** at La Guardia Airport in New York City by five Croatian terrorists, who forced the crew of the TWA 727 to fly the airplane to Paris. There the Croatians surrendered on Sept. 12. On the day before, a bomb left in New York by the terrorists exploded, killing a police bomb expert and wounding three others. The five terrorists

Burke by publishers and television stations in the series *Burke's Law.*

Apr. 18 **Tony awards** for the 1975–1976 season were presented for the following: best play, *Travesties* by Tom Stoppard; best musical, *A Chorus Line;* best actor in a drama, John Wood for *Travesties;* best actress in a drama, Irene Worth for *Sweet Bird of Youth.*

Apr. 19 **National Book Awards** were presented for the following: fiction, *J. R.* by William Gaddis; poetry, *Self-Portrait in a Convex Mirror* by John Ashbery; arts and letters, *The Great War and Modern Memory* by Paul Fussell; history and biography, *The Problem of Slavery in the Age of Revolution: 1770–1823* by David Brion Davis; contemporary affairs, *Passage to Ararat* by Michael J. Arlen.

Apr. 22 **Barbara Walters** became the first anchorwoman of a network television news program and the highest-paid journalist in history when she accepted a five-year, $5,000,000 contract with ABC.

Apr. 28 *The Belle of Amherst* by William Luce, a one-character play with Julie Harris as Emily Dickinson, opened at the Longacre Theater in New York City.

Apr. 30 In an **obscenity case,** porno star Harry Reems was among those convicted by a Memphis, Tenn., federal court of conspiracy to ship obscene materials, the film *Deep Throat,* across state lines. It was the first time an actor without artistic control over a film was cited for helping to distribute it.

May 3 **Pulitzer prizes** were awarded for the following: fiction, *Humboldt's Gift* by Saul Bellow; biography, *Edith Wharton: A Biography* by R. W. B. Lewis; history, *Lamy of Santa Fe* by Paul Horgan; general nonfiction, *Why Survive? Being Old in America* by Robert N. Butler; poetry, *Self-Portrait in a Convex Mirror* by John Ashbery; drama, *A Chorus Line* by Michael Bennett, Nicholas Dante, Marvin Hamlisch, James Kirkwood, and Edward Kleban.

May 11 The premiere performance of *Pas de "Duke,"* choreographed by Alvin Ailey in honor of jazz composer Duke Ellington, was presented in New York City. Mikhail Baryshnikov and Judith Jamison were the featured dancers.

May 17 **Emmy Awards** were presented for the following: best actor in a special, Anthony Hopkins for *The Lindbergh Kidnapping Case;* best actress in a special, Susan Clark in *Babe;* best actor in a dramatic series, Ed Asner for *Rich Man, Poor Man;* best actress in a dramatic series, Kathryn Walker for *The Adams Chronicles.*

May 18 What was billed as the **Concert of the Century** was presented at Carnegie Hall in New York City to benefit a $6,500,000 fund drive for the concert hall. Among the musical greats who participated were Leonard Bernstein, Yehudi Menuhin, Mstislav

| Business and Industry; Science; Education; Philosophy and Religion **III** | | **IV** Sports; Social Issues and Crime; Folkways; Fashion; Holidays |

July 18 Discovery of **Lyme arthritis,** a new, infectious strain of arthritis, was reported by researchers at Yale University's School of Medicine. Some 51 cases of the disease, apparently caused by an insect-borne virus, were recorded in and around Lyme, Conn.

July 20 **Viking 1,** launched on Aug. 20, 1975, landed on Mars. It was the first spacecraft to reach the planet. Data collected by Viking 1 and by **Viking 2,** launched on Sept. 9, 1975, and landed on Mars on Sept. 3, 1976, showed Mars to be a barren, rocky planet. Tests to detect the presence of life there were inconclusive.

July 27–Aug. 31 What came to be called **Legionnaires' disease** claimed the lives of 29 people who had attended an American Legion convention in Philadelphia, Pa., on July 21–24. Another 151 were hospitalized for high fever and respiratory problems, symptoms of the disease.

Aug. 28 **Synthesis of a bacterial gene** had been accomplished for the first time, scientists at the Massachusetts Institute of Technology reported. The gene functioned properly when implanted in a living cell.

Aug. 30 **Medicaid waste** from fraud, abuse, and government bungling devoured some 25–50% of the $15,000,000,000 Medicaid budget, a Senate study reported. About half the $3,000,000,000 spent on physicians, dentists, pharmacies, and laboratories went for substandard or unnecessary care provided by Medicaid mills, privately owned clinics usually located in poor urban neighborhoods.

Sept. 16 The **ordination of women** was approved by the 65th triennial General Convention of the Episcopal Church. By year's end, some of those who disapproved of the change were preparing to break with the church.

Sept. 18 The Rev. **Sun Myung Moon,** head of the evangelical Unification Church, presided over a "God Bless America" rally in Washington, D.C., that drew some 50,000 persons. Moon, who advocated U.S. defense of South Korea, was denounced by established church leaders for perverting Christian doctrine. He was also under attack from parents who claimed brainwashing tactics had been used to recruit young people into the church. The converts, who solicited contributions in public places, were frequently referred to as *Moonies.*

Forbes, with a time of 2:29. The jockey was Angel Cordero, Jr.

June 15 **Charles O. Finley,** owner of the Oakland Athletics, sold three of his ace players, Vida Blue, Rollie Fingers, and Joe Rudi, to other clubs for $3,500,000. On June 18 baseball commissioner Bowie Kuhn voided the sale as not being good for baseball.

June 17 In a **basketball merger,** the 18 teams of the NBA merged with four of the six remaining teams of the ABA.

June 20 The **U.S. Open golf tournament** was won in an upset by golf rookie Jerry Pate, who beat Tom Weiskopf and Al Geiberger by two strokes.

July 2–3 At the **Wimbledon** tennis championships in England, Chris Evert Lloyd won the women's singles title. Brian Gottfried teamed with Paul Ramirez of Mexico to win the men's doubles, and Evert Lloyd teamed with Martina Navratilova of Czechoslovakia to win the women's doubles.

July 4 A year of festivities celebrating the **bicentennial of U.S. independence** was capped at 2 P.M. by the ringing of bells nationwide. Among the special events this day were Operation Sail, a parade in New York harbor of more than 50 warships and 16 windjammers from many nations; convergence at Valley Forge, Pa., of six wagon trains that had trekked across the country; sealing of time capsules; and a 76-hour vigil (starting July 2) at the National Archives to honor the signing of the Declaration of Independence.

July 11 The **U.S. Women's Open golf tournament** was won by JoAnne Carner.

July 12 A change in the baseball **reserve clause** was agreed to by major league owners and players. The new rule allowed players to become free agents after five years.

July 13 The baseball **All-Star Game** was won for the fifth straight year by the National League, beating the American League 7–1.

July 15 Three **gunmen kidnaped 26 children** and their school bus driver near Chowchilla, Calif., and imprisoned them in an underground cell 100 miles away. The captives dug their way out, and by July 29 the suspected kidnapers had been arrested.

July 17–Aug. 1 At the **Summer Olympics** in Montreal, Canada, the U.S. won 34 gold medals and finished second in unofficial team standings behind

were returned to the U.S. to face charges of air piracy and murder.

Sept. 17 A special **committee to review the assassinations of John F. Kennedy and Martin Luther King, Jr.,** was created by the House of Representatives. Revelations during the 1975 congressional hearings on abuses in intelligence agencies prompted the move.

Sept. 20 A *Playboy* interview with Jimmy Carter provoked considerable controversy when the November issue was released early. In discussing his Baptist religious beliefs, Carter was reported to have said, "[I have] committed adultery in my heart many times."

Sept. 27 In the **first presidential TV debate** between an incumbent and a challenger, Pres. Ford and Democratic candidate Jimmy Carter discussed domestic issues before a television audience estimated at 90,000,000. Two more debates were held on Oct. 6 and Oct. 22. A fourth debate was held between vice-presidential candidates Walter Mondale and Robert Dole (Oct. 15). It was the first televised debate between candidates for vice president.

Oct. 4 Sec. of Agriculture **Earl Butz resigned** his post in the face of national outrage over a racial slur he was reported to have made.

Oct. 20 A **ship collision** on the Mississippi R., 20 miles above New Orleans, killed 78 people when the ferryboat *George Prince* struck the Norwegian tanker *Frosta.*

Oct. 20 In what came to be called **Koreagate,** the Justice Department reported that a major probe was under way concerning the activities of a South Korean lobby, led by businessman Tongsun Park. The purpose of the lobby was to influence congressmen and other government officials through cash grants and campaign contributions estimated at $500,000 to $1,000,000 annually.

Nov. 2 James Earl "Jimmy" Carter, Jr., **was elected president** of the United States. Walter F. Mondale was elected vice president. The electoral vote was Carter, 297; Pres. Ford, 240. The popular vote was Carter, 40,828,929; Ford, 39,148,940. In congressional elections

Rostropovich, Vladimir Horowitz, and Isaac Stern.

June 1 *For Colored Girls Who Have Considered Suicide/When the Rainbow Is Enuf* by Ntozake Shange, a drama about the lives of black women, opened at the Public/Anspacher Theater in New York City. It opened on Broadway at the Booth Theater on Sept. 15

June 2 A **journalist's car was bombed** in Phoenix, Ariz. Don Bolles, an investigative reporter for the *Arizona Republic,* had been probing the role of leading politicians in land swindles. He died on June 13.

June 30 A **television production of** *Swan Lake,* the first live television broadcast of a full-length ballet, was performed by the American Ballet Theater at Lincoln Center in New York City. The ballet featured Natalia Makarova and Ivan Nagy.

July 4 A 455-mile-long so-called **sculpture garden** was unveiled in Nebraska. It offered works by ten U.S. sculptors that were installed at rest areas along Interstate 80.

July 19–31 The **Martha Graham Dance Company,** celebrating its 50th anniversary, became the first modern dance troupe to perform in the Royal Opera House in London, England.

Sept. 7 Italy's renowned opera company, **La Scala,** of Milan, made its U.S opera debut, opening a week of performances at the Kennedy Center for the Performing Arts in Washington, D.C.

Sept. 8 The **Paris Opera Company** made its U.S. debut at the Metropolitan Opera House in New York City, opening its ten-day stay with Mozart's *Marriage of Figaro.*

Sept. 29 A new **record art price** for a painting by Rembrandt, $3,250,000, was set by the industrialist Armand Hammer, who announced acquisition of Rembrandt's *Juno.*

Sept. 30 In the first major attempt at **copyright reform** since 1909, Congress approved legislation, effective Jan. 1, 1978, extending copyright protection for 50 years after the death of an author, artist, or composer. It also restricted reproduction of copyrighted material and set royalty rates for phonograph records played by broadcasters or used in jukeboxes.

Oct. 6 The last privately owned painting by **Jackson Pollock,** *Lavender Mist,* was reported to have been acquired by the National Gallery of Art in Washington, D.C., for $2,000,000. It had been bought in 1950 for about $1500.

Oct. 7 The **Cooper-Hewitt Museum of Design** opened its new quarters at the former Andrew Carnegie mansion in New York City.

Oct. 19 **Avery Fisher Hall** reopened in New York City after a $6,400,000 construction program to improve acoustics. The project was judged a great success.

Sept. 28 The **Toxic Substances Control Act,** was passed by Congress. It prohibited the marketing of new chemical compounds before testing their impact on human health and the environment. The law also forbade production of polychlorinated biphenyls, or PCBs, after 1979. Studies of PCBs had shown they did not break down in the environment and were linked to cancer.

Sept. 30 An **Arab boycott of Israel** had wide support among businesses, the Commerce Department reported. Of the U.S. companies studied by the department between Sept. 1975 and Mar. 1976, the findings of the report showed that 94% went along with the boycott.

Sept. 30 The first state **right-to-die law** was passed in California. It granted to adult patients the right to authorize a physician to shut off their life-support equipment when death was imminent. The law went into effect on Jan. 1, 1977.

Oct. 14 The **Nobel Prize in Physiology or Medicine** was awarded jointly to Dr. Baruch S. Blumberg of the University of Pennsylvania Medical School and to Dr. D. Carleton Gajdusek of the National Institute for Neurological Diseases for their work on infectious diseases.

Oct. 14 The **Nobel Prize in Economics** was awarded to Milton Friedman of the University of Chicago.

Oct. 18 The **Nobel Prize in Chemistry** was awarded to William N. Lipscomb, Jr., of Harvard University for his studies of the structure and bonding of chemical compounds known as boranes.

Oct. 18 The **Nobel Prize in Physics** was awarded jointly to Burton Richter of Stanford University and to Samuel C. C. Ting of MIT for their discovery of the psi, or J, particle.

Dec. 4 The **Association of Evangelical Lutheran Churches** was formed at a meeting of Lutheran moderates in Chicago, Ill. The new denomination's 75,000 members had broken with the conservative Lutheran Church–Missouri Synod over that body's insistence on a literal interpretation of the Bible.

the U.S.S.R. Among the stars of the games was decathlon champion Bruce Jenner.

Aug. 9 The **Baseball Hall of Fame** inducted six new members; Oscar Charleston, a star of the old Negro Leagues; Roger Connor, batting star; Cal Hubbard, umpire; Bob Lemon, pitcher; Fred Lindstrom, batting star; and Robin Roberts, pitcher.

Aug. 16 The **PGA golf tournament** was won by Dave Stockton for the second time.

Aug. 27 A new type of **sexual discrimination** in sports was highlighted when transsexual Renee Richards, formerly Richard Raskind, an eye surgeon, was barred from competing at the U.S. Open tennis championships at Forest Hills, N.Y., after refusing to submit to a chromosome qualification test.

Aug. 28 The **North American Soccer League championship** was won by the Toronto Metros, who beat the Minnesota Kicks 3–0.

Sept. 11 The **Miss America** title was won by Dorothy Kathleen Benham, 20, from Minnesota, at the annual pageant in Atlantic City, N.J.

Sept. 11–12 The **U.S. Open tennis singles championships** were won by Chris Evert Lloyd in the women's division and Jimmy Connors in the men's division.

Oct. 16–21 The **World Series** was won in a four-game sweep by the Cincinnati Reds (NL) over the New York Yankees (AL). On Oct. 12 the Reds had won the National League pennant over the Philadelphia Phillies in a three-game sweep, and the Yankees had taken the American League pennant from the Kansas City Royals three games to two.

Oct. 24 The seventh **New York City Marathon** was won by Bill Rodgers, with a time of 2 hrs., 10 min., 10 sec. The first woman to finish was Miki Gorman of California, with a time of 2 hrs., 39 min., 11 sec. It was New York's first city-wide marathon. Previous marathons had been run within the confines of Central Park.

Nov. 4 In major league baseball's **first free-agent draft,** 24 players from 13 clubs participated. Reggie Jackson signed the most lucrative contract, calling for $2,900,000 over five years with the New York Yankees (AL).

Dec. 10 In the **Bronfman kidnaping case,** a White Plains, N.Y., jury acquitted Mel Lynch and Dominic Byrne of kidnaping Samuel Bronfman, II, in 1975. The two men were convicted of extorting $2,300,000

the Democrats kept a 2–1 Senate majority, 61–38, with one seat going to an independent, and a House majority of 292–143.

Nov. 12 **Normalization talks** between the U.S. and Vietnam were begun in Paris. On Nov. 15, however, the U.S. vetoed Vietnam's application for membership in the UN.

Oct. 21 The **Nobel Prize in Literature** was awarded to Saul Bellow "for the human understanding and subtle analysis of contemporary culture that are combined in his work."

Dec. 22 *Your Arms Too Short to Box With God*, a musical celebration based on the Book of Matthew and written by Alex Bradford and Micki Grant, opened at the Lyceum Theater in New York City.

1977

In the first months of Pres. Jimmy Carter's administration, most Vietnam-era draft resisters were pardoned, the planned pullout of U.S. forces from South Korea was announced, and administration officials spoke out against human rights violations worldwide. Pres. Carter also established guidelines to prevent conflict of interest among officials, opened communication between the White House and ordinary citizens, ended U.S. opposition to the admission of Vietnam to the UN, and signed two treaties returning control of the Panama Canal to Panama. The new president suffered setbacks when Congress challenged the financial dealings of Bert Lance, director of the Office of Management and Budget, and opposed passage of Carter's energy conservation program. Vernon Jordan of the National Urban League charged the administration with not doing enough to reduce unemployment among blacks. Notables who died this year included Lewis B. Hershey, director of the Selective Service System from 1941 to 1973, May 20, at 83; Sen. John L. McClellan, chairman of the Senate Appropriations Committee, Nov. 27, at 81; and Francis Gary Powers, the pilot shot down over the U.S.S.R. in 1960, Aug. 1, at 48.

Jan. 19 **Tokyo Rose,** real name Iva Toguri D'Aquino, was pardoned by Pres. Gerald R. Ford 27 years after her conviction for treason. She had made propaganda broadcasts from Japan during World War II in an attempt to demoralize U.S. troops.

Jan. 20 **Jimmy Carter was inaugurated** president of the United States. The 39th president, he served one term. Walter F. Mondale was sworn in as vice president.

Jan. 21 A **presidential pardon** for most of the nation's Vietnam draft resisters was issued by Pres. Carter.

Even as the nation's interest in the arts boomed, the top 200 nonprofit performing arts groups were sinking under a $125,000,000 deficit incurred during the 1976–1977 season. The Metropolitan Opera in New York City confronted a $14,000,000 deficit; museums in New York, Chicago, and San Diego cut viewing hours to save costs. The American Shakespeare Festival in Stratford, Conn., failed to open for the season, and the City Center Joffrey Ballet in New York scrapped its spring season. In contrast, motion picture revenues were up to a record $2,300,000,000, largely because of such phenomenally successful films as *Star Wars* and *Close Encounters of the Third Kind.* Television's hit show of the year was the miniseries *Roots,* based on the book by Alex Haley. Americans mourned the passing this year of James M. Cain, the novelist, Oct. 27, at 85; Maria Callas, the opera singer, Sept. 16, at 53; Joan Crawford, the actress, May 10, at 69; Harry Lillis "Bing" Crosby, Oct. 14, at 73; Howard Hawks, the motion picture director, Dec. 26, at 81; James Jones, the novelist, May 9, at 55; Guy Lombardo, the band leader, Nov. 5, at 75; Robert Lowell, the poet, Sept. 12, at 60; Alfred Lunt, who performed with his wife Lynn Fontanne in numerous Broadway plays, Aug. 3, at 83; Julius Henry "Groucho" Marx, Aug. 19, at 86, and his brother, Milton "Gummo" Marx, Apr. 21, at 84; Samuel J. "Zero" Mostel, the actor, Sept. 8, at 62; Vladimir Nabokov, the writer, July 2, at 78; Elvis Presley, the king of rock 'n' roll, Aug. 16, at 42; and Ethel Waters, the blues singer and actress, Sept. 1, at 80.

Among **books published** this year was *A Rumor of War* by Philip Caputo. The book was hailed as one of the year's best of several works dealing with the Vietnam War. Other books published this year included *Falconer* by John Cheever, a novel examining the soul of a convict; *Six Men* by Alistair Cooke, essays on six well-known figures of the twentieth century; *A Book of Common Prayer* by Joan Didion, a novel dealing with the inability of its middle-aged characters to find meaning in their lives; *The Immigrants* by Howard Fast, a novel; *The Age of Uncertainty* by John Kenneth Galbraith; *The Thorn Birds* by Colleen McCullough, a novel that became a

| Business and Industry; Science; Education; Philosophy and Religion III | | IV Sports; Social Issues and Crime; Folkways; Fashion; Holidays |

Dec. 15 A major **oil spill** began when the Liberian-registered tanker *Argo Merchant* ran aground near Nantucket Island, Mass., and its 7,700,000-gallon oil cargo leaked.

Dec. 16 The **swine flu immunization program** was halted after it was reported that 51 people had suffered temporary paralysis after getting the vaccine. Some 35,000,000 had been inoculated.

from Bronfman's father. The defense had contended that the scheme was engineered by the younger Bronfman.

Dec. 21 The highly publicized retrial of **Rubin "Hurricane" Carter and John Artis** for the 1966 murders of three people in a Paterson, N.J., bar ended with conviction of the defendants despite the fact that two of the key witnesses in the original trial recanted their testimony.

1977

The U.S. faced a high trade deficit, primarily because of oil imports and the falling value of the dollar. Uncertainty about Pres. Carter's legislative program for tax reform and concern about new, inflationary social programs slowed investment by the private sector. The Dow Jones average declined more than 165 points during the year, and unemployment remained at 7% of the work force. The retail price of a pound of coffee hit $5.00, mainly because of a killing frost in Brazil in 1975. Many consumers struck back by switching to tea. Tea imports rose by nearly 30%, and tea prices rose as well. In transportation, the year was marked by sharp air fare reductions on domestic and transatlantic routes as airlines began offering no-frills flights. Transportation Sec. Brock Adams ruled that airbags or safety belts would be required automotive equipment beginning in 1984. In education, amendments to the Rehabilitation Act of 1973 required that handicapped children be included in regular school settings. Notables who died this year included Wernher von Braun, the German-born rocket pioneer, June 16, at 65; Loren C. Eiseley, the anthropologist and author, July 9, at 69; and John R. Powers, founder of the Powers modeling agency, July 19, at 80.

Jan. 1 The **first woman Episcopal priest** in the U.S., Jacqueline Means, was ordained.

Jan. 11 **Discriminatory zoning laws,** enabling suburbs to block racially integrated housing for low- and middle-income families, were upheld by the Supreme Court. The Court ruled that the refusal of a suburb to change zoning laws was not inherently unconstitutional.

Feb. 23 The **Environmental Protection Agency** was held by the Supreme Court to have the authority to establish industry-wide standards to control discharge of pollutants into waterways.

With star player Pelé in action with an American professional team, soccer became the fastest growing team sport in the U.S. Growth of soccer (some 350,000 persons under 18 years of age were playing the game) was enhanced further by availability of inexpensive equipment, low injury rate, and accessibility for women players. The price of a professional soccer franchise had risen tenfold since 1971, when the going price was $10,000. Baseball attendance leaped 24% over 1976 levels, and basketball attendance edged the 10,000,000 mark. In horse racing 17-year-old Steve Cauthen drew wide attention for his remarkable achievements as a jockey. In boxing, Muhammad Ali decided not to retire and defended his heavyweight crown twice. In golf the top money winners were Tom Watson, $310,653, and Judy Rankin, $122,890. Also this year, skateboards became a new activity for vast numbers of youngsters. Notables who died this year included Robert Calvin "Cal" Hubbard, the baseball umpire, Oct. 17, at 77; Bernard "Toots" Shor, the celebrated New York City barkeeper, Jan. 23, at 73; and Philip K. Wrigley, owner of the Chicago Cubs baseball team, Apr. 12, at 82.

Jan. 1 In **college football bowl games,** the results were Houston 30, Maryland 21 in the Cotton Bowl; Ohio State 27, Colorado 10 in the Orange Bowl; USC 14, Michigan 6 in the Rose Bowl; and Pittsburgh 27, Georgia 3 in the Sugar Bowl. This season the AP and UPI polls chose Pittsburgh the national college champions of 1976.

Jan. 9 **Super Bowl XI** was won by the Oakland Raiders (AFC), who defeated the Minnesota Vikings (NFC) 32–14. On Dec. 26, 1976, the Raiders had beaten the Pittsburgh Steelers 24–7 for the NFC championship, and the Vikings had beaten the Los Angeles Rams 24–13 for the AFC title.

Jan. 17 Convicted murderer **Gary Gilmore** was executed by a Utah firing squad, ending a ten-year halt on capital punishment in the U.S.

Jan. 28–29 A **blizzard** paralyzed much of the East and Midwest, worsening a severe shortage of natural gas. Among the hardest hit cities was Buffalo, N.Y., which already had a cumulative snowfall of 160 inches.

Feb. 24 Citing **human rights violations** as the reason, Sec. of State Cyrus Vance announced a reduction in U.S. aid to Argentina, Ethiopia, and Uruguay. Vance stated that strategic nations such as South Korea did not face similar treatment.

Mar. 1 In a move interpreted as **U.S. support for Soviet dissidents,** Pres. Carter met with Vladimir K. Bukovsky, a leading Soviet activist.

Mar. 2 A new **House ethics code** was adopted. It limited outside income for members of the House of Representatives, broadened financial disclosure requirements, and restricted gifts by lobbyists. The Senate adopted a similar code on Apr. 1.

Mar. 9 **U.S. ground forces in Korea** would be withdrawn within five years, Pres. Carter announced.

Mar. 18 U.S. **travel restrictions** to Cuba, Vietnam, North Korea, and Cambodia were lifted.

Apr. 7 An indictment for **illegal wiretapping and mail surveillance** was handed down against John J. Kearney, a retired FBI inspector alleged to have committed such acts while pursuing fugitive terrorists.

Apr. 27 A **task force on illegal aliens** reported to Pres. Carter that 6,000,000 to 8,000,000 illegal aliens were living in the U.S. About 876,000 had been caught in 1976, compared with 89,000 in 1961.

Apr. 28 An agreement on **fishing rights** in overlapping zones was announced by the U.S. and Cuba.

Apr. 28 In a major **espionage** case, a U.S. citizen named Christopher J. Boyce was convicted of supplying data on satellites and CIA codes to the U.S.S.R. in complicity with another American, Andrew Lee. On Sept. 12 Boyce was sentenced to 40 years in prison. Lee was convicted on May 14 and sentenced on July 18 to life imprisonment.

runaway best seller; *Coming into the Country* by John McPhee, an excellent book about Alaska and Alaskans; and *Ring* by Jonathan Yardley, a biography of Ring Lardner.

Jan. 1 A **Resale Royalties Act** went into effect in California. It was the first statute guaranteeing artists a royalty when their works were resold at a profit for $1000 or more.

Jan. 6 **National Book Critics Circle Awards** were presented for the following: fiction, *October Light* by John Gardner; poetry, *Geography III* by Elizabeth Bishop; nonfiction, *The Woman Warrior: Memoirs of a Girlhood Among Ghosts* by Maxine Hong Kingston; criticism, *The Uses of Enchantment: The Meaning and Importance of Fairy Tales* by Bruno Bettelheim.

Jan. 31 The prestigious *American Poetry Review* was characterized by some 50 well-known poets as racist, antifeminist, and antiyouth. The group demanded that a third of the publication be devoted to works by women and members of minorities.

Feb. 2 *Otherwise Engaged,* a comedy by Simon Gray starring Tom Courtenay, opened at the Plymouth Theater in New York City.

Feb. 7 Former Secretary of State **Henry Kissinger** sold his memoirs for $2,000,000. On Feb. 17 he was reported to have signed a $1,500,000, five-year contract as a TV consultant on world affairs.

Feb. 8 **Larry Flynt,** publisher of the sexually explicit magazine *Hustler,* was convicted in Cincinnati of promoting obscenity and involvement in organized crime.

Feb. 16 *American Buffalo* by David Mamet, a play about three petty gangsters starring Kenneth McMillan, John Savage, and Robert Duvall, opened at the Ethel Barrymore Theater in New York City.

Feb. 19 **Grammy Awards** were presented for the following: best album of 1976, *Songs in the Key of Life* by Stevie Wonder; best record, "This Masquerade" by George Benson; best male pop vocalist, Stevie Wonder for *Songs in the Key of Life;* best female pop vocalist, Linda Ronstadt for *Hasten Down the Wind;* best pop group, Chicago for "If You Leave Me Now."

Mar. 16 **Alex Haley** sued Doubleday for $5,000,000, claiming the publisher had not promoted his immensely popular book *Roots* and had not secured an adequate paperback contract because it sold the rights to its own subsidiary firm.

Mar. 28 **Academy Awards** were presented to *Rocky* as the outstanding motion picture of 1976; Peter Finch and Faye Dunaway as best actor and actress for *Network;* Jason Robards as best supporting actor for *All the President's Men;* and Beatrice Straight as best supporting actress for *Network.*

Mar. 31 *The Shadow Box* by Michael Cristofer, a play about the effects of terminal illness on other patients,

Business and Industry; Science;   **III**   **Sports; Social Issues and Crime;**   **IV**
Education; Philosophy and Religion   **Folkways; Fashion; Holidays**

Mar. 1 The U.S. extended its **fishing limits** to 200 miles offshore to protect depleted fisheries against the activities of foreign fishing fleets.

Mar. 9 A ban on **saccharin** was proposed by the Food and Drug Administration after tests suggested that the artificial sweetener might be carcinogenic. Consumer resistance and intense lobbying led the FDA to allow saccharin to be sold as an over-the-counter drug. On Nov. 4 Congress postponed the ban for 18 months, pending new tests.

Mar. 10 A five-year **farm workers' accord** was reached in the West between the United Farm Workers and the Teamsters, ending years of competition to organize western agricultural workers.

Apr. 18 An all-out campaign for **energy conservation** was called for by Pres. Carter, who called the effort "the moral equivalent of war." On Apr. 20 he asked Congress for new legislation designed to discourage energy waste and encourage conservation measures.

Apr. 26 The **first instant color motion picture system,** capable of processing film in 90 seconds and projecting it on a screen, was displayed by the Polaroid Corporation.

Apr. 28 Regulations banning **discrimination against the handicapped** by employers, schools, and institutions receiving federal funds were signed by Joseph Califano, secretary of the Department of Health, Education, and Welfare.

Apr. 30 Some 2000 **opponents of nuclear energy** occupied the construction site of a nuclear generating plant at Seabrook, N.H. By May 2 some 1414 protesters had been arrested for trespassing.

May 1 Controversy over **Laetrile,** a purported anticancer compound derived primarily from apricot pits, continued as the state of Indiana passed the first law legalizing its manufacture, sale, and use.

May 30 **Viking 1 and 2** biological experiments on the planet Mars, which had proven inconclusive, were terminated by NASA scientists.

Feb. 1 Television rights to the **1980 Olympics** in Moscow were secured by the National Broadcasting Company, which agreed to pay $35,000,000 for exclusive rights to the games and an additional $50,000,000 for production and equipment costs.

Feb. 3–5 **U.S. figure skating championships** were won in Hartford, Conn., by Charles Tickner, men's singles; Linda Fratianne, women's singles; Tai Babilonia and Randy Gardner, pairs; Judi Genovesi and Kent Weigle, dance.

Mar. 3 At the **world figure skating championships** in Tokyo, Japan, Linda Fratianne won the women's singles title.

Mar. 9–11 A **terrorist raid** was staged in Washington, D.C., by 12 Hanafi Muslim gunmen. The terrorists seized three buildings and demanded custody of five Black Muslims who had been imprisoned for the 1973 murder of seven Hanafis and of three more Black Muslims who had been imprisoned for the 1965 murder of Malcolm X. One person was killed during the raid, and 139 were held prisoner for 39 hours before the terrorists surrendered.

Mar. 26 The **AIAW basketball championship** was won for the third consecutive year by Delta State, defeating Louisiana State 68–55.

Mar. 28 The **NCAA basketball championship** was won by Marquette University, defeating North Carolina 67–59.

Apr. 10 The **Masters golf tournament** was won by Tom Watson, who beat Jack Nicklaus by two strokes.

Apr. 18 The 81st **Boston Marathon** was won by Jerome Drayton of Canada, with a time of 2 hrs., 14 min., 46 sec. The first woman to finish was Miki Gorman of California, with a time of 2 hrs., 48 min., 44 sec.

May 7 The 103rd **Kentucky Derby** was won by Seattle Slew, with a time of 2:02⅕. The jockey was Jean Cruguet.

May 7–14 The **NHL Stanley Cup** was won by the Montreal Canadiens, who swept the Boston Bruins in four games.

May 3 **Normalization talks** between the U.S. and Vietnam began in Paris. On the next day, the U.S. agreed to stop blocking Vietnam's request for admission to the UN.

May 4 **Richard M. Nixon,** in the first of five television interviews with David Frost, for which the former president was paid, acknowledged that he had "let the American people down" through his actions in the Watergate cover-up. In the May 19 interview, Nixon argued that sanctioning burglary and other illegal activities taken against dissidents is not illegal "when the president does it."

May 23 The end of the road in the **Watergate** scandal came for three former U.S. officials, John Ehrlichman, H. R. Haldeman, and John Mitchell, when the Supreme Court refused to hear their appeals. On June 22 Mitchell became the first former attorney general to begin serving a prison sentence.

May 28 A **fire** at the Beverly Hills Supper Club in Southgate, Ky., killed 164 people. It was the worst such accident since 1942.

June 6 Development of a **neutron bomb** by the U.S. was reported by the Washington *Post.* The weapon was designed to kill people but cause minimal destruction of property.

June 7 An ordinance prohibiting **discrimination against homosexuals** in housing and employment was rescinded by voters in Dade County, Fla. Anita Bryant, the entertainer, drew national attention to the statute through her highly publicized efforts to have it revoked.

June 30 A halt in production of the **B-1 bomber** was announced by Pres. Carter.

July 1 **Water rationing** was instituted in Los Angeles, Calif., in the midst of a severe West Coast drought.

July 13–14 A 25-hour **power failure** struck New York City and suburban Westchester County, leading to

friends, and family, opened at the Morosco Theater following critically acclaimed runs at the Mark Taper Forum in Los Angeles and the Long Wharf Theater in New Haven, Conn.

Apr. 10 The **Renaissance Center** in downtown Detroit, Mich., was dedicated. Designed by John C. Portman, it was a $337,000,000 complex consisting of a 73-story hotel amid four 39-story office towers.

Apr. 13 **National Book Awards** were presented for the following: fiction, *The Spectator Bird* by Wallace Stegner; biography, *Norman Thomas: The Last Idealist* by W. A. Swanberg; history, *World of Our Fathers* by Irving Howe; contemporary thought, *The Uses of Enchantment: The Meaning and Importance of Fairy Tales* by Bruno Bettelheim; poetry, *Collected Poems 1930–1976* by Richard Eberhart. A special citation was given to *Roots,* written by Alex Haley.

Apr. 13 An **antipornography rally** at New York City's Times Square was joined by the casts of some 25 Broadway shows.

Apr. 17 *I Love My Wife,* a musical by Michael Stewart and Cy Coleman based on a play by Luis Rego, opened at the Ethel Barrymore Theater in New York City. It dealt with two couples coming to grips with the opposing forces of marital fidelity and the sexual revolution.

Apr. 18 **Pulitzer prizes** were awarded for the following: biography, *A Prince of Our Disorder* by John E. Mack; history, *The Impending Crisis: 1841–1861* by David M. Potter; general nonfiction, *Beautiful Swimmers* by William W. Warner; poetry, *Divine Comedies* by James Merrill; drama, *The Shadow Box* by Michael Cristofer. A special award was given for *Roots,* written by Alex Haley.

Apr. 19 The **Center for British Art,** the last building designed by Louis I. Kahn and the new home of the Paul Mellon collection, was dedicated at Yale University.

Apr. 21 *Annie,* a musical by Thomas Meehan, Charles Strouse, and Martin Charnin, starring Andrea McArdle as the lovable redheaded orphan of comic strip fame, opened at the Alvin Theater in New York City.

Apr. 24 *The Basic Training of Pavlo Hummel,* an antiwar play by David Rabe that formed a Vietnam trilogy with *Sticks and Bones* and *Streamers,* opened at the Longacre Theater in New York City. It starred Al Pacino.

May 14 **Pierre Boulez** retired as director of the New York Philharmonic. Zubin Mehta was chosen to succeed him in the 1978–1979 season, with guest conductors finishing the 1977–1978 season.

May 15 *America Windows* by **Marc Chagall,** a set of three 30-foot-wide by 8-foot-high stained glass panels completed by the artist to honor the American bi-

| Business and Industry; Science; Education; Philosophy and Religion | III | | IV | Sports; Social Issues and Crime; Folkways; Fashion; Holidays |

May 31 The use of a **seniority system** in business was declared by the Supreme Court to be constitutional, provided it was not devised to discriminate against black workers.

June 19 Bishop **John N. Neumann** of Philadelphia, known for his development of the parochial school system, was canonized by the Roman Catholic Church. He became the first American male to achieve sainthood.

June 20 **Medicaid funding for elective abortions** was ruled by the Supreme Court to be not obligatory under the Constitution or federal law.

June 21 A federally funded study reported that a **New York State drug law** passed in 1973 had cost $76,-000,000 to administer and had failed to limit drug use or drug-related crime.

June 27 **Legal advertising** of fees for specific, routine services was upheld by the Supreme Court in a decision with wide-ranging implications for a number of professions.

June 29 **Robert Hall,** the nation's largest retail clothing chain, closed its 366 stores after losing nearly $100,000,000 in the previous three years.

July 28 The 799-mile **trans-Alaska pipeline** went into full operation as the first oil from Alaska's Prudhoe Bay fields arrived at the loading port of Valdez at 11:02 P.M. (4:02 A.M. July 29, EST). Pumping operations had begun on June 20.

Aug. 12 The **space shuttle** *Enterprise,* with astronauts C. Gordon Fullerton and Fred W. Haise, Jr., aboard, made its first free flight at Edwards Air Force Base after being lifted to 25,000 feet on the back of a Boeing 747.

Aug. 23 The 77-pound aircraft *Gossamer Condor,* powered by its pilot, was flown by Bryan Allen over a one-mile, figure-eight course at Shafter, Calif. The craft won for its designer, Paul MacCready, the $86,000 Kremer prize for human-powered aircraft.

Sept. 13 The first **U.S. diesel automobiles** were introduced by General Motors. The cars, Oldsmobile

May 9 **Patricia Hearst,** serving a prison sentence for a 1974 robbery, was released on probation.

May 21 The 102nd **Preakness Stakes** was won by Seattle Slew, with a time of 1:54²/₅. The jockey was Jean Cruguet.

May 22–June 5 The **NBA basketball championship** was won by the Portland Trail Blazers, who beat the Philadelphia 76ers four games to two after losing the first two games of the series.

May 25 A furor over **leniency in rape cases** was unleashed when Wisconsin Judge Archie Simonson gave a light sentence to a rapist, suggesting that seductively clad women provoked assaults. He was removed on Sept. 7 by a recall vote.

May 26 One of the towers of the **World Trade Center was scaled** by George Willig, a toy designer, who climbed the south tower in three and a half hours. He was fined $1.10, one cent for each story of the building.

May 29 The 61st **Indianapolis 500** auto race was won by A. J. Foyt, completing the 500-mile course in 3 hrs., 5 min., 57.7 sec., with an average speed of 161.331 mph. Janet Guthrie became the first woman to compete in the racing classic.

June 11 The 109th annual **Belmont Stakes** was won by Seattle Slew, finishing in 2:29³/₅ to take the race and become the tenth horse to win racing's Triple Crown. The jockey was Jean Cruguet.

June 12 The **LPGA golf tournament** was won by Chako Higuchi of Japan.

June 19 The **U.S. Open golf tournament** was won by Hubert Green, beating Lou Graham by one stroke.

June 29 **Capital punishment** for rape was ruled unconstitutional by the Supreme Court.

July 2 At the **Wimbledon** tennis championships in England, the only U.S. player to win in finals play was Joanne Russell, who teamed with Helen Gourlay Cawley of Australia to win the women's doubles championship.

July 19 The baseball **All-Star Game** was won for the sixth time running by the National League, beating the American League 7–5.

extensive looting and arson in the city. Some 3776 looters were arrested and 100 policemen injured. Property damage was estimated at $135,000,000.

July 19 **Flooding** struck the Johnstown, Pa., area, killing 76 people and causing some $200,000,000 in damage.

July 20 In the so-called **Koreagate** lobbying scandal, former Watergate prosecutor Leon Jaworski agreed to lead a House Ethics Committee probe into alleged congressional influence-buying by South Korean lobbyists. On Dec. 30 the Justice Department announced that South Korean businessman Tongsun Park had agreed to testify in return for immunity from prosecution.

Aug. 4 Legislation creating the **Department of Energy,** the twelfth Cabinet-level department and the first new one since 1966, was signed by Pres. Carter. James R. Schlesinger was nominated and quickly confirmed as the first secretary of energy.

Aug. 26 In the midst of a **New York City financial crisis,** the Securities and Exchange Commission charged Mayor Abraham Beame, Comptroller Harrison Goldin, six banks, and a stock brokerage house with intentionally misleading investors in New York City bonds concerning the city's worsening finances.

Sept. 7 Two **Panama Canal treaties,** transferring control of the canal to Panama by the year 2000, were signed by Pres. Carter and Panama's head of state, Brig. Gen. Omar Torrijos Herrera. The accords, capping 13 years of negotiations, were subject to ratification by each nation's legislature.

Sept. 21 **Bert Lance resigned** as director of the Office of Management and Budget following severe criticism of his past financial practices as a banker in Georgia.

Oct. 28 **Prisoner repatriation legislation,** allowing U.S. citizens in Canadian or Mexican jails to be transferred to U.S. prisons, was signed.

Nov. 18–21 The first **National Women's Conference,** the largest feminist gathering since the Seneca Falls,

centennial, were unveiled in the Marc Chagall gallery in the Art Institute of Chicago.

May 16 **Christie's,** the London art auction house, opened a branch in New York City.

June 5 **Tony awards** for the 1976–1977 season were presented for the following: best play, *The Shadow Box* by Michael Cristofer; best musical, *Annie* by Thomas Meehan, Charles Strouse, and Martin Charnin; best dramatic actor, Al Pacino for *The Basic Training of Pavlo Hummel;* best dramatic actress, Julie Harris for *The Belle of Amherst.*

June 30 The **Newport Jazz Festival,** citing prohibitive costs and acoustical problems, announced it was ending its six-year tenure in New York City and moving in 1978 to Saratoga Springs, N.Y.

Aug. 12 A landmark **victims' rights** bill, granting crime victims first claim on income earned by criminals through sale of their life stories, was signed by Gov. Hugh Carey of New York.

Sept. 11 **Emmy Awards** were presented for the following: best actor in a special, Ed Flanders for *Harry S Truman: Plain Speaking;* best actress in a special, Sally Field for *Sybil;* best actor in a dramatic series, James Garner for *The Rockford Files;* best actress in a dramatic series, Lindsay Wagner for *The Bionic Woman;* best dramatic series, *Upstairs, Downstairs.*

Sept. 11 It was reported that an article on a **CIA-journalist link** was to appear in a forthcoming issue of *Rolling Stone.* Carl Bernstein, its author, claimed that some 400 U.S. journalists had given the agency information and assistance since 1950. On Sept. 12, *The New York Times, Newsweek, Time,* network news departments, and other organizations denied knowledge of a connection between the CIA and news organizations.

Sept. 21 Establishment of the **American Musical Theater Center** was announced by Duke University in North Carolina. The Broadway-style production corporation was created to stage shows in regional theaters across the nation. Four days later the university announced that the American Dance Festival had agreed to move to Durham, N.C., in 1978, after a 30-year tenure in New London, Conn. The company's move followed Duke's pledge to create a $1,000,000 trust fund for the dance company.

Oct. 6 *The Gin Game,* a play by D. L. Coburn about a man and a woman in a home for the aged, opened at the Globe Theater in New York City. It starred Hume Cronyn and Jessica Tandy.

Oct. 29 *The Act,* a musical by George Furth, John Kander, and Fred Ebb starring Liza Minelli as a young woman struggling for success as an actress, opened at the Majestic Theater in New York City. It was received enthusiastically by critics and audiences.

88 and 98 models, were said to have 40% greater fuel efficiency than gasoline-powered cars.

Sept. 26 Freddie Laker, president of Great Britain's Laker Airways, introduced the airline's London to New York Skytrain service, which required no reservations. Fares were less than half of conventional economy fares.

Sept. 27 An Army study of West Point, prompted by the 1976 cadet cheating scandal, proposed more than 150 reforms at the U.S. Military Academy to improve morale and management and reverse a "slackening of the pursuit of excellence."

Oct. 1 A longshoremen's strike was launched by some 500,000 workers against container ships in selected Atlantic and Gulf Coast ports. The strike ended on Nov. 29 after companies agreed to a three-year contract granting a 30.5% pay hike and guarantees of job security.

Oct. 3 Five Japanese steel companies that had been dumping steel plate in the U.S. at below-cost prices were hit with a 32% penalty duty by the Treasury Department.

Oct. 11 The Nobel Prize in Physics was awarded jointly to John H. Van Vleck of Harvard University, Philip W. Anderson of Bell Laboratories and Princeton University, and Nevill F. Mott of Great Britain for their contributions to the field of solid state electronic circuitry.

Oct. 13 The Nobel Prize in Physiology or Medicine was awarded jointly to Rosalyn S. Yalow of the Veterans Administration Hospital, Bronx, N.Y., Roger C. L. Guillemin of the Salk Institute, and Andrew V. Schally of Veterans Administration Hospital, New Orleans, La., and Tulane University for their independent studies of the production of peptide hormones in the brain and the relation of the hypothalamus in controlling the pituitary gland.

Oct. 19 The Concorde SST made its first flight from France to Kennedy Airport in New York two days after the Supreme Court refused to stay a lower court ruling authorizing the flights. Concorde flights to Washington, D.C., had begun in May 1976.

July 24 The U.S. Women's Open golf tournament was won by Hollis Stacy, who beat Nancy Lopez by two strokes.

Aug. 1 A return to bell-bottom trousers, white caps, and jumpers for sailors' uniforms was announced by the Navy after an experiment with coat-and-shirt uniforms.

Aug. 8 The Baseball Hall of Fame inducted six new members: Ernie Banks, infielder; Martin Dihigo, pitcher for the old Negro league; John Henry "Pop" Lloyd, shortstop in the Negro league; Al Lopez, manager; Amos Rustie, pitcher, known as the "Hoosier Thunderbolt"; and Joe Sewell, infielder.

Aug. 10 The so-called Son of Sam serial murder case in New York City culminated in the arrest of David Berkowitz, 24, suspected of murdering six people and wounding seven more over a 13-month period.

Aug. 14 The PGA golf tournament was won by Lanny Wadkins, who beat Gene Littler on the third hole of a sudden-death playoff.

Aug. 15 A new U.S. soccer attendance record of 77,961 was established in a playoff game between the New York Cosmos and the Fort Lauderdale Strikers in East Rutherford, N.J.

Aug. 28 The North American Soccer League championship was won by the New York Cosmos, who beat the Seattle Sounders 2–1.

Sept. 10 The Miss America title was won by Susan Yvonne Perkins, 23, from Ohio, at the annual pageant in Atlantic City, N.J.

Sept. 10–11 The U.S. Open tennis singles championships were won by Chris Evert Lloyd, for the third straight time, in the women's division and Guillermo Vilas of Argentina in the men's division.

Sept. 13–18 The America's Cup was successfully defended by the U.S. yacht *Courageous*, which beat the challenger *Australia* in four straight races.

Oct. 11–18 The World Series was won by the New York Yankees (AL), defeating the Los Angeles Dodgers (NL) four games to two. On Oct. 8 the Dodgers had won the National League pennant over the Philadelphia Phillies, three games to one, and the following day the Yankees had clinched the American

N.Y., convention in 1848, drew 1442 delegates to Houston, Tex., to call for passage of the Equal Rights Amendment and elimination of institutional discrimination. Opponents of ERA and abortion held a so-called pro-family rally five miles away.

Dec. 20 Legislation authorizing a **Social Security tax increase** was signed by Pres. Carter. The tax revision was expected to cost workers and employers $227,-000,000,000 in the next ten years.

Dec. 22 A **grain elevator explosion** in Westwego, La., killed 35 people. On Dec. 27 a similar disaster in Galveston, Tex., killed 18.

Nov. 13 The final installment of *L'il Abner,* the comic strip created by Al Capp in 1934, marked Capp's retirement.

Nov. 18 The **Pierpont Morgan Library** in New York City was given a $10,000,000 collection of books and papers by the Heinemann Foundation.

Nov. 22 What was said to be a **record price for sculpture**—between $3,500,000 and $5,000,000—was reported to have been paid by the J. Paul Getty Museum in California for a fourth-century B.C. bronze.

Nov. 28 The final sculpture of **Jacques Lipchitz,** the five-story, 23-ton *Bellerophon Taming Pegasus,* was dedicated at Columbia University in New York City.

Dec. 31 **Thomas P. F. Hoving** ended his tenure as director of New York City's Metropolitan Museum of Art.

1978

Pres. Jimmy Carter returned on Jan. 6 from a nine-day, seven-nation tour of Europe, the Middle East, and India to a U.S. that was beset by grave domestic problems. The availability of energy was a major concern for the government and for business, and short supplies were reflected in rising inflation. To deal with inflation Carter announced (Apr. 11) that wage increases for federal employees would be held to 5.5% and asked (Oct. 24) for voluntary compliance on guidelines for wage and price increases. In the Koreagate lobbying scandal, Tongsun Park, a South Korean businessman, told the Justice Department he had given some $750,000 to members of Congress and political groups to influence legislation from 1970 to 1975. Americans mourned the passing of Gen. Lucius D. Clay, military governor of the U.S. zone in Berlin after World War II, Apr. 16, at 80; and Hubert Horatio Humphrey, former senator from Minnesota and vice president from 1965 to 1969 under Lyndon B. Johnson, Jan. 13, at 66.

Jan. 6 A precedent-setting **Indian land claim suit** was lost by the Wampanoag Indians of Mashpee, Mass., who had gone to court to recover some 13,700 acres on Cape Cod. The jury decided the Indians did not legally constitute a tribe in 1870, when the land was supposedly taken from them, or in Aug. 1976, when they filed their lawsuit. The decision was expected to affect similar cases pending in the Northeast.

Jan. 6 The **Crown of St. Stephen,** prime symbol of the Hungarian nation, was returned to Hungary by the U.S., which had taken custody of it in July 1945 at the end of World War II.

Jan. 25–26 A **blizzard** struck the Midwest, with temperatures of 50 below zero and winds of 100 mph.

The year in theater was disappointing despite a handful of above average plays. The year's biggest hit was the musical *Ain't Misbehavin'.* In May Mikhail Baryshnikov left the American Ballet and joined the New York City Ballet. Both companies had severe financial problems this year but managed to stay afloat. Art auction prices continued to climb. George Caleb Bingham's *The Jolly Flatboatmen* brought $980,000, the highest price paid to date for an American painting. Notables who died this year included Faith Baldwin, a writer known for her romantic novels, Mar. 18, at 84; Edgar Bergen, ventriloquist, Sept. 30, at 75; Charles Boyer, actor, Aug. 26, at 79; Maybelle "Mother" Carter, grand old lady of the Grand Ole Opry and matriarch of the musical Carter family, Oct. 23, at 69; Bruce Catton, author and historian known for his books on the Civil War, Aug. 28, at 78; James Gould Cozzens, Pulitzer Prize–winning novelist, Aug. 9, at 74; Charles Eames, designer known best for his molded plywood, form-fitting chairs, Aug. 21, at 71; Ruth Etting, Ziegfeld Follies girl and popular singer, Sept. 24, at 80; Phyllis McGinley, Pulitzer Prize-winning poet, Feb. 22, at 72; Jack Oakie, comedian, Jan. 23, at 74; Norman Rockwell, artist known best for his cover illustrations for the *Saturday Evening Post,* Nov. 9, at 84; Edward Durrell Stone, architect, Aug. 6, at 76; and Jack L. Warner, motion picture producer, Sept. 9, at 86.

Among **books published** this year was *The Stories of John Cheever,* a collection that won the Pulitzer Prize. Other books published this year included *The World According to Garp* by John Irving, a novel; *American Caesar* by William Manchester, a biography of Douglas MacArthur; *Chesapeake* by James Michener, a novel; *In Search of History: A Personal Adventure* by Theodore

Business and Industry; Science;
Education; Philosophy and Religion   III

IV   **Sports; Social Issues and Crime;**
Folkways; Fashion; Holidays

Nov. 1 A law raising the **minimum wage** from $2.30 to $3.35 an hour by 1981 was signed by Pres. Carter.

Nov. 2 Identification of **methanogens,** a form of life dating back some 3,500,000,000 years, was reported by scientists at the University of Illinois. Methanogens, which thrive on carbon dioxide, produce methane.

Dec. 1 The Food and Drug Administration recommended that **predigested liquid protein** be sold only in containers bearing warning labels that serious illness or death could ensue from its use. The action followed reports linking 31 deaths to the popular diet food since July 1.

League pennant from the Kansas City Royals, three games to two.

Oct. 23 The eighth annual **New York City Marathon** was won by Bill Rodgers with a time of 2 hrs., 11 min., 28.2 sec. The first woman to finish was Miki Gorman of California, with a time of 2 hrs., 43 min., 10 sec.

Dec. 2 A prominent veterinarian, Mark J. Gerard, was indicted in a **horse-switching scandal.** A purportedly dead four-year-old champion colt, Cinzano, had apparently won a Sept. 23 race at Belmont Park disguised as Lebón, a 57-1 longshot.

Dec. 10 **Steve Cauthen** became the first jockey to win more than $5,000,000 in purse money in one year. Cauthen ended 1977 with 488 wins.

1978

The nation's economic woes continued. Inflation rose to 8%, productivity increased only 0.4%, the smallest rise since 1974, and the annual U.S. trade deficit reached $28,450,000. Pres. Jimmy Carter was not successful in pushing labor law reforms through Congress, nor was he able to get Congress to move toward a national health plan to be phased in during the 1980s. Health costs continued to rise, prompting the Department of Health, Education, and Welfare to ask hospitals to hold to a 9.7% increase in 1979. Congress voted a five-year, $50,000,000,000 extension of the Elementary and Secondary Education Act. This year the Mormon Church ended its 148-year ban on the ordination of black men. Notables who died this year included James Bryant Conant, longtime president of Harvard University, Feb. 11, at 84; John Donald MacArthur, billionaire insurance company tycoon, Jan. 6, at 80; Margaret Mead, anthropologist, Nov. 15, at 76; John D. Rockefeller III, eldest of John D. Rockefeller's five grandsons and a noted philanthropist, Jan. 10, at 72; and Harry Winston, jeweler to the rich and famous, Dec. 28, at 82.

Jan. 3 A system of **trigger prices** for imported steel, effective Feb. 15, was announced by the Treasury Department in a move to halt dumping of foreign steel on the U.S. market. The prices were based on delivery costs for Japanese producers, the most efficient in the industry. Prices falling below these benchmarks were subject to import penalties.

Jan. 13 **Japan** agreed to some opening of its domestic market to U.S. products in order to reduce Japan's export trade surplus. Tariffs on some 300 items were

Professional sports prospered this year. Major league baseball drew a record 40,000,000 fans, and the Los Angeles Dodgers (NL) drew 3,347,776 customers to become the first team to break the 3,000,000 mark. In basketball, David Thompson of the Denver Nuggets negotiated an $800,000 contract for the year, highest to date for any professional athlete. Pro football increased its regular season from 14 to 16 games. In golf the top money winners were Tom Watson, $362,429, and Nancy Lopez, $153,097. The boom in jogging and physical fitness activities was good news for sportswear manufacturers, and even the fashion world began paying attention to Americans' interest in fitness and health. Americans also burned up the calories on the dance floors of discothèques, which became enormously popular in the wake of the hit film *Saturday Night Fever.* Notables who died this year included Ford C. Frick, former president of the National League (1934–1951), Apr. 8, at 83; Joseph V. McCarthy, who managed the New York Yankees to eight American League championships and seven World Series victories between 1931 and 1946, Jan. 13, at 90; and James Joseph "Gene" Tunney, undefeated heavyweight champion of the world from 1926 to 1928, Nov. 17, at 80.

Jan. 2 In **college football bowl games,** the results were Notre Dame 38, Texas 10 in the Cotton Bowl; Arkansas 31, Oklahoma 6 in the Orange Bowl; Washington 27, Michigan 20 in the Rose Bowl; and Alabama 35, Ohio State 6 in the Sugar Bowl. This season the AP and UPI polls chose Notre Dame the national collegiate champions of 1977.

Jan. 9 In a major ruling on **coeducational sports,** a federal judge in Dayton, Ohio, ruled against

About 100 people were killed.

Feb. 5–7 A blizzard in New England killed 60 people.

Feb. 8 Pres. **Anwar el-Sadat** of Egypt began a six-day visit to the U.S. He conferred at length with Pres. Carter, urging the U.S. to exert pressure on Israel to negotiate a Middle East peace settlement.

Feb. 22 Two days after a **train derailment** in Waverly, Tenn., two tank cars containing liquid propane exploded, killing 15 people and leveling two blocks of Waverly's business district.

Mar. 16 A **Panama Canal treaty,** the first of two Canal treaties negotiated in 1977, was ratified by the Senate. The treaty guaranteed neutrality of the canal after Panama assumes control at the end of 1999.

Apr. 6 A **retirement age bill,** giving most workers the option of retiring at age 70 rather than 65, was signed by Pres. Carter.

Apr. 7 Production of the **neutron bomb** was deferred by Pres. Carter pending final decision on its construction and deployment.

Apr. 18 The second **Panama Canal treaty** was ratified by the Senate. The treaty stated conditions for the operation and defense of the canal until 1999, when control of the canal passes to Panama. Ratification of both treaties was a triumph for Pres. Carter over strong opposition.

Apr. 27 A **construction accident** at the site of a nuclear power plant at Willow Island, W.Va., killed 51 workers when a scaffolding collapsed inside a cooling tower. The workers, including 11 members of one family, fell 170 feet and were buried under tons of concrete.

May 11 The **first woman Marine Corps general,** Margaret A. Brewer, 47, was appointed.

May 15 A controversial **sale of jet fighters** to Egypt, Saudi Arabia, and Israel became possible when the Senate voted not to block the proposal. Some claimed the sale would endanger Israel's security, but others stated it would help bolster moderate Arab forces in the Middle East.

June 6 **Proposition 13,** a California constitutional amendment that would reduce property taxes by 57%, was approved by 65% of the Californians who voted on the controversial proposal.

June 28 The concept of **racial quotas** came under fire when the Supreme Court ruled in the case of *Bakke v. the University of California* that the university had to admit Allan P. Bakke to its medical school. Bakke, who was white, claimed his civil rights had been violated when he was refused admission because of racial quotas designed to increase the number of minority students in the medical school.

July 15 What was called the **longest walk** ever taken, a 2700-mile march from Alcatraz Island, Calif., by some 1000 American Indians and a similar number of

H. White; and *War and Remembrance,* a novel by Herman Wouk.

Jan. 11 The **National Book Critics Circle Awards** were presented for the following: fiction, *Song of Solomon* by Toni Morrison; nonfiction, *Samuel Johnson* by Walter Jackson Bate; poetry, *Day by Day* by Robert Lowell; criticism, *On Photography* by Susan Sontag.

Jan. 21 An **art theft** at the St. Louis, Mo., Art Museum netted the robbers four sculptures worth $100,000. On Feb. 20 thieves struck again, taking three bronze statues by the French sculptor Auguste Rodin.

Feb. 23 **Grammy Awards** were presented for the following: best album of 1977, *Rumours* by Fleetwood Mac; best record, "Hotel California" by the Eagles; best male pop vocalist, James Taylor for "Handy Man"; best female pop vocalist, Barbra Streisand for "Evergreen"; best group, the Bee Gees for "How Deep Is Your Love."

Mar. 4 The Chicago *Daily News,* the only afternoon paper in the Windy City, ceased publication. Founded in 1875, it won 15 Pulitzer prizes.

Apr. 3 **Academy Awards** were presented to *Annie Hall* as outstanding motion picture of 1977; Richard Dreyfuss as best actor for *The Goodbye Girl;* Diane Keaton as best actress for *Annie Hall;* and Jason Robards, Jr., and Vanessa Redgrave as best supporting actor and actress for *Julia. Star Wars* won seven awards.

Apr. 7 A **record book auction price** was set in New York City when The Stuttgart Museum bought a Gutenberg Bible for $2,000,000.

Apr. 10 **National Book Awards** were presented for the following: fiction, *Blood Ties* by Mary Lee Settle; history, *The Path Between the Seas* by David McCullough; biography, *Samuel Johnson* by Walter Jackson Bate; poetry, *Collected Poems* by Howard Nemerov; contemporary thought, *Winners and Losers* by Gloria Emerson. A special citation was awarded to the humorist S. J. Perelman.

Apr. 17 **Pulitzer prizes** were awarded for the following: fiction, *Elbow Room* by James A. McPherson; biography, *Samuel Johnson* by Walter Jackson Bate; history, *The Visible Hand* by Alfred D. Chandler, Jr.; poetry, *Collected Poems* by Howard Nemerov; general nonfiction, *The Dragons of Eden* by Carl Sagan; drama, *The Gin Game* by Donald L. Coburn.

Apr. 21 An apparent **literary hoax,** a biography of Greta Garbo by Antoni Gronowitz, was reported by

| Business and Industry; Science; Education; Philosophy and Religion | III | | IV | Sports; Social Issues and Crime; Folkways; Fashion; Holidays |

to be reduced, and quotas on 12 items, 11 of them agricultural, were to be removed.

Jan. 16 Thirty-five new **astronaut candidates** out of 8079 applicants, were chosen by NASA for its space shuttle program. Among those chosen were six women, three blacks, and one Oriental.

Mar. 15 At a **farmers' rally** in Washington, D.C., more than 1000 striking farmers gathered at the Capitol steps, where 73 goats were released. On the next day a small group occupied the Department of Agriculture building. The actions were taken to protest proposed farm legislation.

Mar. 25 A 110-day **coal miners' strike,** longest in the industry's history, ended when miners accepted a new three-year contract and went back to work. The strike had caused fears of power shortages and industrial layoffs, but stockpiling before the strike prevented them.

Apr. 17 A new **stock trading record** was set by the New York Stock Exchange, which saw 63,500,000 shares change hands.

Apr. 19 The **first black woman pilot** for a major U.S. airline, Jill E. Brown, 27, from Baltimore, Md., began working for Texas International Airlines.

May 2 Development of a **core curriculum** to replace the general education program that had been in effect since 1947 was approved by the arts and science faculty at Harvard University. Undergraduates would be required to take at least six courses in the following academic areas: literature and the arts; history, social and philosophical analysis; science and mathematics; and foreign language and culture.

May 5 **Organized medicine** was declared by Pres. Carter to be the major obstacle to better health care. Carter affirmed that doctors care about their patients, but said the American Medical Association was concerned only with doctors' interests.

May 20 **Pioneer Venus 1** was launched toward Venus. On Dec. 4 it went into orbit around Venus and began sending back data on the planet's atmosphere.

June 15 The $100,000,000 **Tellico Dam** project in Tennessee was halted indefinitely when the Supreme Court ruled that the snail darter, a rare species of perch, was protected by the Endangered Species Act of 1973 and that construction of the dam threatened its extinction.

preventing high-school girls from playing on the same sports teams as boys.

Jan. 15 **Super Bowl XII** was won by the Dallas Cowboys (NFC), defeating the Denver Broncos (AFC) 27–10. On Jan. 1 the Cowboys had beaten the Minnesota Vikings 23–6 for the NFC championship and the Broncos had defeated the Oakland Raiders 20–17 to take the AFC title.

Feb. 12 **U.S. figure skating championships** were won in Portland, Oreg., by Charles Tickner, men's singles; Linda Fratianne, women's singles; Tai Babilonia and Randy Gardner, pairs; Stacey Smith and John Summers, dance.

Feb. 15 The **world heavyweight boxing championship** was won by Leon Spinks in a 15-round decision over Muhammad Ali at Las Vegas, Nev.

Mar. 9 At the **world figure skating championships** in Ottawa, Canada, Charles Tickner won the men's singles title.

Mar. 25 The **AIAW basketball championship** was won by UCLA, beating the University of Maryland 90–74.

Mar. 27 The **NCAA basketball championship** was won by the University of Kentucky, beating Duke University 94–88.

Apr. 9 The **Masters golf tournament** was won by Gary Player.

Apr. 17 The 82nd **Boston Marathon** was won by Bill Rodgers, with a time of 2 hrs., 10 min., 13 sec. The first woman to finish was Gayle Barron of Georgia, with a time of 2 hrs., 44 min., 52 sec.

May 6 The 104th **Kentucky Derby** was won by Affirmed, with a time of 2:01⅕. The jockey was Steve Cauthen.

May 13–25 The **NHL Stanley Cup** was won by the Montreal Canadiens, defeating the Boston Bruins four games to two.

May 20 The 103rd **Preakness Stakes** was won by Affirmed, with a time of 1:54⅖. The jockey was Steve Cauthen.

May 21–June 7 The **NBA basketball championship** was won by the Washington Bullets, who beat the Seattle Supersonics four games to three.

May 26 The **first legal casino** in the U.S. outside Nevada was opened in Atlantic City, N.J., by Resorts International Hotel Casino.

May 28 The 62nd **Indianapolis 500** auto race was won by Al Unser, completing the 500-mile course in 3 hrs., 5 min., 54.99 sec., with an average speed of 161.363 mph.

June 9 The World Boxing Council **heavyweight boxing championship** was won by Larry Holmes, in a

supporters, ended at the Capitol steps in Washington, D.C. Only about 20 of the original marchers, organized by the American Indian Movement (AIM), made it all the way. The march was intended to protest legislation that AIM contended would deprive American Indians of their land rights and to gain national attention for Indians' rights.

Aug. 7 The **Love Canal** area of Niagara Falls, N.Y., considered to be environmentally unfit for human habitation, was declared a disaster area by Pres. Carter. Evacuation of the area, which had been used as a toxic waste dump from 1947 to 1952, had begun on Aug. 4.

Sept. 6–17 A **Middle East peace conference** at Camp David, Md., was attended by Pres. Carter, Pres. Anwar el-Sadat of Egypt, and Prime Minister Menachem Begin of Israel. On Sept. 17 Sadat and Begin signed an agreement at the White House to conclude a peace treaty between Egypt and Israel within three months.

Sept. 25 A **midair collision** over San Diego, Calif., of a Southwest Airlines jet and a private plane killed all 137 people aboard the two craft and at least ten more on the ground.

Oct. 6 The deadline for ratification of the **Equal Rights Amendment** was extended to June 30, 1982, by Congress. Since its passage in 1972, all but three of the required 38 states had ratified the measure. This was the first extension granted for ratification of a proposed constitutional amendment since 1917, when Congress set seven years as the limit for the process.

Oct. 15 The **National Energy Act of 1978** was passed by Congress. The bill regulated natural gas prices, encouraged use of coal by utilities, set fuel efficiency standards, and provided tax credits for energy conservation. It was signed by Pres. Carter on Nov. 9.

Nov. 7 In **congressional elections** the Republicans gained three Senate seats, but the Democrats still held a majority of 58–41, with one seat held by an independent. In the House the Republicans gained 12 seats, but the Democrats led 276–159.

Nov. 18 A grizzly **mass suicide in Guyana** was prefaced by the murder of Rep. Leo J. Ryan of California and four others visiting the People's Temple on a fact-finding mission to the country. When Jim Jones, leader of the religious sect, learned of the event he led the group in a mass suicide by poison. The final count was 911 dead, including more than 200 children. Most of Jones's followers, like Jones himself, were American citizens.

Nov. 27 **George Moscone and Harvey Milk,** the mayor and city supervisor of San Francisco, respectively, were shot to death in City Hall by Dan White, a former supervisor.

The New York Times. Gronowitz had sold the manuscript to Simon and Schuster, but Garbo circulated an affidavit saying she had never met the author. Gronowitz claimed he had known Garbo since 1938.

May 1 *Da,* a play by Hugh Leonard starring Barnard Hughes and Brian Murray, opened at the Morosco Theater in New York City.

May 1 **Richard Rodgers,** the noted composer, gave $1,000,000 to the American Academy and Institute of Arts and Letters to endow an annual award for librettists and composers not yet recognized by the professional theater.

May 9 *Ain't Misbehavin',* a celebration of the songs of Fats Waller, conceived and directed by Richard Maltby, Jr., opened at the Longacre Theater in New York City.

June 1 The East Building of the **National Gallery of Art** in Washington, D.C., was opened officially. Designed by I. M. Pei, it cost $94,400,000. To mark the event, *The Splendors of Dresden,* also opened. It was probably the most lavish and expensive exhibit in U.S. history.

June 4 **Tony awards** for the 1977–1978 season were presented for the following: best play, *Da;* best musical, *Ain't Misbehavin';* best dramatic actor, Barnard Hughes for *Da;* best dramatic actress, Jessica Tandy for *The Gin Game.*

July 7 The **censorship** controversy involving former CIA employees continued. On this date, Frank W. Snepp III, who wrote an unauthorized book about the agency, was held by a federal judge to have violated his contract with the CIA. Snepp was ordered to hand over his earnings from the book to the federal government.

Sept. 17 **Emmy Awards** were presented for the following: best actor in a special, Fred Astaire for *A Family Upside Down;* best actress in a special, Joanne Woodward for *See How She Runs;* best dramatic actor in a series, Ed Asner for *Lou Grant;* best actress in a dramatic series, Sada Thompson for *Family.*

Sept. 23 The New York City premiere of *Billy Budd,* an opera by Benjamin Britten, marked the opening of the Metropolitan Opera's season.

Oct. 5 The **Nobel Prize for Literature** was awarded to Isaac Bashevis Singer, the Polish-born author who writes in Yiddish. He was cited for his "impassioned narrative art."

Oct. 17 Congress voted the contralto **Marian Anderson** a special gold medal for her "unselfish

June 22 In studying photos of **Pluto,** James W. Christy of the U.S. Naval Observatory discovered a hitherto unknown small moon of Pluto in orbit around it, only 12,000 miles from the planet.

July 6–10 A **scientific delegation to China** headed by Frank Press, director of the Office of Science and Technology, and including 14 high-level scientists, visited the People's Republic to promote scientific and technological exchanges.

Aug. 8 **Pioneer Venus 2** was successfully launched toward a December rendezvous with Venus. On Dec. 9 it sent four probes to the planet's surface and began relaying data about atmosphere and surface conditions of Venus.

Aug. 9 A **newspaper strike** in New York City shut down *The New York Times,* the New York *Daily News,* and the New York *Post* for 88 days. Pressmen, who struck to prevent work-force reductions, went back to work on Nov. 6.

Aug. 11 The bacterium causing **legionnaires' disease** had been isolated, the Centers for Disease Control in Atlanta, Ga., announced. Previously it could only be studied in the tissue of a victim.

Oct. 6 The **first woman university president** in the U.S., Hannah H. Gray, was inaugurated at the University of Chicago.

Oct. 15 The **Humphrey-Hawkins full employment bill,** named for the late Hubert H. Humphrey of Minnesota and Rep. Augustus F. Hawkins, Democrat of California, was passed by Congress. A watered-down version of the original 1976 bill, it called for a national policy of reducing unemployment to 4% and inflation to 3% by 1983. It was signed by Pres. Carter on Oct. 27.

Oct. 16 The **Nobel Prize in Economics** was awarded to Herbert A. Simon of Carnegie-Mellon University.

Oct. 17 The **Nobel Prize in Physics** was awarded jointly to Arno A. Penzias and Robert W. Wilson of Bell Laboratories for their discovery of weak electromagnetic radiation existing throughout the universe, and to Per Kapitsa of the U.S.S.R. for his studies of liquid helium.

Nov. 1 In a move to **bolster the U.S. dollar,** Pres. Carter announced a "massive intervention" in international currency markets, including steps to quintuple the sale of U.S. gold and a steep increase in the discount rate. The dollar rose immediately, and the Dow

15-round decision over Ken Norton.

June 10 The 110th **Belmont Stakes** was won by Affirmed, with a time of 2:26⁴/₅ to become the 11th horse to win racing's Triple Crown. The jockey, once again, was Steve Cauthen. As in the Kentucky Derby and Preakness, Alydar finished second—the only horse ever to be runner-up in all three events. This was the first time there were Triple Crown winners in consecutive years, Seattle Slew having won in 1977.

June 11 The **LPGA golf tournament** was won by Nancy Lopez with a tournament record 13 under par.

June 18 The **U.S. Open golf tournament** was won by Andy North, beating J. C. Snead and Dave Stockton on the last hole after seeing a substantial lead vanish.

July 11 The **baseball All-Star Game** was won for the seventh consecutive year by the National League, beating the American League 7–3.

July 23 The **U.S. Women's Open golf tournament** was won by Hollis Stacy.

Aug. 6 The **PGA golf tournament** was won by John Mahaffey, beating Tom Watson and Jerry Pate on the second hole of a sudden-death playoff.

Aug. 8 The **Baseball Hall of Fame** inducted three new members: Adrian Joss, pitcher; Larry MacPhail, baseball executive; and Eddie Matthews, third baseman for 17 years with the Braves.

Aug. 11–17 The first successful **transatlantic balloon crossing** was made by Max Anderson, Ben Abruzzo, and Larry Newman, who flew from Presque Isle, Maine, to Paris, France, in 137 hrs., 18 min.

Aug. 27 The **North American Soccer League championship** was won by the New York Cosmos, who beat the Tampa Bay Rowdies 3–1.

Sept. 9 The **Miss America** title was won by Kylene Barker, 22, from Galax, Va., at the annual pageant in Atlantic City, N.J.

Sept. 10 The **U.S. Open tennis singles championships** were won by Chris Evert in the women's division and Jimmy Connors in the men's division.

Sept. 15 The World Boxing Association **heavyweight boxing championship** was won by Muhammad Ali, who beat Leon Spinks in 15 rounds to regain the title for an unprecedented third time.

Oct. 10–17 The **World Series** was won by the New York Yankees (AL), defeating the Los Angeles Dodgers (NL) four games to two. On Oct. 7 the Yankees had won the American League pennant, beating the Kansas City Royals three games to one, and the Dodgers had taken the National League title, downing the Philadelphia Phillies three games to one.

| Exploration and Settlement; Wars; Government; Civil Rights; Statistics **I** | | **II** Publishing; Arts and Music; Popular Entertainment; Architecture; Theater |

Dec. 15 The city of **Cleveland, Ohio, defaulted** on $15,500,000 in short-term notes, thus becoming the first major U.S. city to default on its obligations since the 1930s.

Dec. 15 The **People's Republic of China** and the U.S. announced the two nations would initiate full diplomatic relations on Jan. 1, 1979. The U.S. was to sever diplomatic ties with the Republic of China (Taiwan).

devotion to the promotion of the arts" and her "untiring efforts on behalf of the Brotherhood of Man." In 1939 the black singer had been refused the use of Constitution Hall by the Daughters of the American Revolution. She subsequently performed before 75,-000 at the Lincoln Memorial in Washington, D.C.

1979

The nation's attention was focused this year on events in Iran, where in January a wave of revolutionary unrest toppled the regime of Shah Mohammad Reza Pahlavi and installed a fundamentalist Islamic dictatorship under the Ayatollah Ruhollah Khomeini. In November Islamic revolutionaries seized the U.S. embassy in Tehran, taking many hostages and demanding that the Shah, then in the U.S. for medical reasons, be returned to Iran to stand trial for alleged crimes. Pres. Jimmy Carter refused the terrorists' demands and retaliated by banning the import of Iranian oil, freezing Iranian assets in the U.S., and threatening military action to free the hostages. Thus began a diplomatic nightmare that came to be known as the hostage crisis. Notables who died this year included Nelson A. Rockefeller, four times governor of New York, and vice president of the United States from 1974 to 1977, Jan. 26, at 70.

Jan. 4 The legal battle over the **Kent State** University shootings in Ohio in 1970 ended when an out-of-court settlement was reached. The parents of the four students killed by National Guardsmen and the nine wounded by the guardsmen were awarded a total of $675,000.

Jan. 12 The worst **Midwest blizzard** since 1967 killed at least 100 people.

Feb. 8 Military ties with **Nicaragua** had been severed, Pres. Carter announced, adding that economic aid to the repressive regime of Anastasio Somoza DeBayle would be reduced as well. The moves were intended to force Somoza to negotiate with the revolutionary Sandinista movement threatening to topple the Nicaraguan government.

Feb. 14 The U.S. **ambassador to Afghanistan was kidnaped** in Kabul and then killed when Afghan government forces attempted to free him.

Mar. 5 **Alimony laws** requiring payments by divorced husbands but not by divorced wives were ruled unconstitutional by the Supreme Court, which struck

The Broadway theater prospered this year, with 119 productions generating $40,600,000 in profits, up 10% over the previous season. There were 46 off-Broadway shows. Among the year's hits were The *Elephant Man* and the musical *Sugar Babies.* On Dec. 8 the musical *Grease* gave its 3243rd performance and became the longest-running Broadway musical in history. The music industry faced hard times as oil price hikes translated into higher prices for records. Sales of recordings showed a decided drop after 25 years of steady growth. A new art auction price for an American work was set when *Icebergs,* a painting by Frederick Church that had hung unnoticed in England since 1863, sold for $2,500,-000. Notables who died this year included Elizabeth Bishop, Pulitzer Prize–winning poet, Oct. 6, at 68; Al Capp, cartoonist, Nov. 11, at 70; James T. Farrell, author of the *Studs Lonigan* trilogy, Aug. 22, at 75; Arthur Fiedler, conductor of the Boston Pops Orchestra for 50 years, July 10, at 84; Emmett Kelly, clown, Mar. 28, at 80; Peggy Guggenheim, art collector and patron, Dec. 23, at 81; Roy Harris, composer, Oct. 1, at 81; S. J. Perelman, humorist, Oct. 17, at 75; Mary Pickford, first major star of silent movies, May 29, at 86; Richard Rodgers, composer, Dec. 30, at 77; Jean Stafford, writer, Mar. 26, at 63; and John Wayne, actor, June 11, at 72.

Among **books published** this year, the most talked-about work was Norman Mailer's nonfiction novel *The Executioner's Song,* a treatment of the life and death of Gary Gilmore, who was executed in 1977. The book became a best seller and won a Pulitzer Prize. Other books published this year included *A Streak of Luck* by Robert Conot, a biography of Thomas Edison; *Hanta Yo* by Ruth Beebe Hill, a historical novel that drew fire from some American Indians but became a best seller; *The Poems of Stanley Kunitz,* a collection of the poet's work over 50 years; *The Rise of Theodore Roosevelt* by Edmund Morris; *The Ghost Writer* by Philip Roth, fiction; *Sophie's Choice* by William Styron, a novel; and *Jailbird* by Kurt Vonnegut, a novel panned by critics but kept firmly on the best-seller lists by the public.

Jan. 15 The **National Book Critics Circle Awards** were presented for the following: fiction, *The Stories of John Cheever;* nonfiction, *Facts of Life* by Maureen

Jones industrial stock average rose 35.34 points, a record for a single day.

Nov. 4   The Rev. **M. William Howard, Jr.,** 32, a black, was elected president of the National Council of Churches. He was the youngest person ever elected to the post.

Oct. 22   The ninth **New York City Marathon** was won by Bill Rodgers, with a time of 2 hrs., 12 min., 12 sec. The first woman to finish was Grete Waitz of Norway, with a time of 2 hrs., 32 min., 30 sec.

Dec. 8–10   The **Davis Cup** international tennis challenge round was won by the U.S., defeating Great Britain four matches to one.

1979

The economic news continued bad: interest rates, inflation, and the foreign trade deficit all were higher. The Consumer Price Index was up 13.3%, the largest jump in 33 years. In December United States Steel announced it would close 13 plants, putting 13,000 steelworkers out of work and causing further unemployment in other industries. The Dow Jones Average of industrial stocks closed out the year at 838.4, up 4.2% over 1978. Trading was heavy, and a new record of shares traded was set: 8,155,915,314. Consumption of petroleum products declined 1.8%, the first drop since 1975. In education, costs were up and enrollment was down to 58,400,000, a full 3,000,000 fewer students than in 1975. Several events of religious significance highlighted the year. Reader's Digest announced it would publish a condensed version of the Bible, using the Revised Standard Version and reducing it by 40%. In September the Dalai Lama, religious leader of some 6,000,000 Tibetan Buddhists, came to the U.S. on a month-long visit. In October Pope John Paul II visited the U.S. Notables who died this year included Charles E. Coughlin, conservative, anti-Semitic "radio priest" of the 1930s, Oct. 27, at 88; Cyrus S. Eaton, Canadian-born multimillionaire, May 9, at 95; Conrad Hilton, founder of the Hilton hotel chain, Jan. 3, at 91; James Francis Cardinal McIntyre, Roman Catholic archbishop of Los Angeles, July 16, at 93; Samuel I. Newhouse, founder of the Newhouse publishing and broadcasting conglomerate, Aug. 29, at 84; Talcott Parsons, sociologist, May 8, at 76; A. Philip Randolph, labor and civil rights leader, May 16, at 90; Bishop Fulton J. Sheen, who reached millions through his radio and television broadcasts, Dec. 9, at 84; and Rexford Guy Tugwell, a leading figure in Franklin D. Roosevelt's so-called Brain Trust in the 1930s, July 21, at 88.

Jan. 11   **Cigarette smoking** was labeled the "single most important environmental factor contributing to early death," in a report issued by U.S. Surgeon General Julius B. Richmond.

Feb. 13   A report on **school desegregation** by the U.S. Civil Rights Commission stated that 46% of the nation's minority children were attending segregated

One incident reflecting the changes American society had undergone in the last several decades was the so-called palimony case involving the actor Lee Marvin and his former companion Michelle Triola Marvin. The couple had broken up in 1970, but Miss Marvin sued the actor for half of the $3,600,000 he had earned during their six-year relationship. In April a judge ruled against Michelle Marvin but awarded her $104,000 for purposes of rehabilitation. In sports, Muhammad Ali retired from boxing, leaving the World Boxing Association heavyweight crown up for grabs. John Tate won the heavyweight championship in October. In golf the top money winners were Tom Watson, $462,636, and Nancy Lopez, $215,987.

Jan. 1   In **college football bowl games,** the results were Notre Dame 35, Houston 34 in the Cotton Bowl; Oklahoma 31, Nebraska 24 in the Orange Bowl; Southern California 17, Michigan 10 in the Rose Bowl; and Alabama 14, Penn State 7 in the Sugar Bowl. This season the AP poll chose Alabama national collegiate champions of 1978 and the UPI poll picked Southern California.

Jan. 21   **Super Bowl XIII** was won by the Pittsburgh Steelers (AFC), defeating the Dallas Cowboys (NFC) 35–31. On Jan. 7 the Steelers had beaten the Houston Oilers 34–5 for the AFC championship and the Cowboys had defeated the Los Angeles Rams 28–0 for the NFC title.

Feb. 2–3   **U.S. figure skating championships** were won in Cincinnati, Ohio, by Charles Tickner, men's singles; Linda Fratianne, women's singles; Tai Babilonia and Randy Gardner, pairs; Stacey Smith and John Summers, dance.

Mar. 17   At the **world figure skating championships** in Vienna, Austria, Linda Fratianne won the women's singles title. On Mar. 14 Tai Babilonia and Randy Gardner had won the pairs title, marking the first pairs victory for the U.S. since 1950.

down an Alabama law as violating the Fourteenth Amendment.

Mar. 26 An **Egyptian-Israeli peace treaty** ended the 30-year state of war between the two nations. The treaty was signed by Pres. Anwar el-Sadat of Egypt and Prime Minister Menachem Begin of Israel at the White House.

Apr. 3 **Jane Byrne** was elected the first woman mayor of Chicago by the largest majority in that city since 1901.

Apr. 5 An order for domestic **oil price deregulation,** to be phased in beginning June 1 and completed one year later, was issued by Pres. Carter.

Apr. 10 **Tornadoes** struck "Tornado Alley," along the Texas-Oklahoma border, leaving at least 60 dead and more than 800 injured. Wichita Falls, Tex., was hardest hit.

May 25 An **airline crash** of an American Airlines DC-10 jet shortly after takeoff in Chicago killed all 272 passengers and three people on the ground.

June 13 An **Indian land claim suit** was settled, granting the Sioux nation $17,500,000 for an area of the Black Hills of South Dakota taken from them in 1877. Including interest, the award was estimated to exceed $100,000,000. It was the largest award ever received by an Indian group.

June 18 The **SALT 2** strategic arms limitation treaty was signed in Vienna, Austria, by Pres. Carter and Pres. Leonid Brezhnev of the U.S.S.R.

June 29 A plan to limit **oil imports** through 1985 was adopted by the six major western nations and Japan. By its terms the U.S. maximum import level was set at 8,500,000 barrels a day.

July 2 Attendance at **criminal pretrial proceedings** is not a constitutional right of the public or the press, the Supreme Court ruled. The decision left open the possibility that public access to criminal trials could be limited as well.

July 15 A new **energy conservation program** was proposed by Pres. Carter in a televised address. The plan, to cost $140,000,000,000 over ten years, called for limiting oil imports, reducing oil use by utilities, and shifting to other forms of fuel.

Howard and *Inventing America: Jefferson and the Declaration of Independence* by Garry Wills; poetry, *Hello, Darkness: The Collected Poems of L. E. Sissman;* criticism, *Modern Art: 19th and 20th Centuries, Selected Papers* by Meyer Shapiro.

Feb. 2 **Sid Vicious,** the British punk rocker, died in New York City of an overdose of heroin at a party celebrating his release from prison. He had been charged with the stabbing murder of his girlfriend in 1978.

Feb. 9 The **Peabody Museum** of Harvard University, facing financial difficulties, announced it would sell 106 oil paintings of North American Indians by the artist Henry Inman, but would retain the David I. Bushnell collection of Indian artifacts. Objections to the sale had been raised by scholars who feared the paintings would be sold to private collectors and become unavailable for study.

Feb. 9 The will of **Nelson A. Rockefeller,** who died on Jan. 26, left some $13,500,000 worth of paintings, sculptures, and primitive art to the Museum of Modern Art and the Metropolitan Museum of Art, both in New York City.

Feb. 9 In the first major **art theft** from the Metropolitan Museum of Art in its 110-year history, thieves stole an ancient Greek marble head valued at $250,000.

Feb. 16 **Grammy Awards** were presented for the following: best album of 1978, *Saturday Night Fever* by the Bee Gees; best record, "Just the Way You Are" by Billy Joel; best male pop vocalist, Barry Manilow for "Copacabana"; best female pop vocalist, Anne Murray for "You Needed Me"; best pop group, the Bee Gees for *Saturday Night Fever.*

Feb. 27 **Barbara Tuchman,** the Pulitzer Prize–winning historian, was elected the first woman president of the American Academy and Institute of Arts and Letters.

Mar. 1 *Sweeney Todd,* a musical by Hugh Wheeler and Stephen Sondheim starring Angela Lansbury and Len Cariou, opened at the Uris Theater in New York City.

Apr. 3 **Eugene Ormandy** announced he would retire as musical director of the Philadelphia Orchestra at the end of the season, ending a 44-year association with the orchestra.

Apr. 4 **Academy Awards** were presented to *The Deer Hunter* as outstanding motion picture of 1978; Jon Voight and Jane Fonda as best actor and actress for *Coming Home;* Christopher Walken as best supporting actor for *The Deer Hunter;* and Maggie Smith as best supporting actress for *California Suite.*

Apr. 10 A set of **Gilbert Stuart portraits** of the first five U.S. presidents was acquired by the National Gallery of Art. Known as the Gibbs-Coolidge Collection and owned by the Coolidge family of Boston since 1916,

| Business and Industry; Science; Education; Philosophy and Religion III | | IV Sports; Social Issues and Crime; Folkways; Fashion; Holidays |

schools 25 years after the Supreme Court declared segregation unconstitutional.

Mar. 5 **Voyager 1,** launched in 1977, made its closest approach to Jupiter, coming within 172,000 miles of the planet's turbulent cloud cover.

Mar. 28 A **nuclear near-disaster** occurred at Three Mile Island, near Harrisburg, Pa., when a power plant malfunctioned and its operators were unable to deal with the situation. The plant's containment building was flooded and a disaster of enormous magnitude was averted. However, two days later the governor of Pennsylvania advised pregnant women and preschool children living within five miles of the plant to leave the area.

June 7 A **truckers' strike** was begun by independent truckers to protest rising costs of diesel fuel and scarce supplies. The strike was most effective in the West and Midwest. By June 14 some 60% of the nonfleet truckers were said to be on strike. Violence erupted against nonstriking truckers, and National Guard troops were called out in several states. The action led to increased fuel allocations and payment of a surcharge to help offset fuel costs.

June 25 The **Public Broadcasting Service** announced a major reorganization into three separate networks using satellite transmissions. Member stations would choose their own programing from three fields: entertainment and culture; special interest and regional; and education. A basic program service would for the first time allow a uniform schedule of prime-time programs.

June 27 The Supreme Court ruled that **black employees** could be promoted ahead of whites with greater work experience provided the move was part of an affirmative action program intended to offset racial discrimination.

July 11 **Skylab,** the 77-ton U.S. orbiting laboratory, reentered Earth's atmosphere and broke up, showering debris over the Indian Ocean and Australia. No one was hurt.

Sept. 1 **Pioneer 2,** launched in 1973, flew past Saturn, discovering two new rings and an eleventh moon.

Sept. 9 **Karen Stevenson,** 22, a graduate of the University of North Carolina, became the first black American woman to win a Rhodes scholarship.

Oct. 1–7 **Pope John Paul II** paid a six-day visit to the U.S., stopping at Boston, New York City, Philadelphia, Des Moines, Chicago, and Washington, D.C. On Oct. 6 he became the first pope to meet a U.S. president at the White House.

Oct. 3 Authorization for a major **grain sale** to the U.S.S.R., up to 25,000,000 metric tons of wheat and corn over the next year, was announced by the federal

Mar. 25 The **AIAW basketball championship** was won by Old Dominion, defeating Louisiana Tech 75–65.

Mar. 26 The **NCAA basketball championship** was won by Michigan State, defeating Indiana State 75–64.

Apr. 15 The **Masters golf tournament** was won by Fuzzy Zoeller in a sudden-death playoff. He was the first player to win the Masters in his initial appearance.

Apr. 16 The 83rd **Boston Marathon** was won by Bill Rodgers with a time of 2 hrs., 9 min., 27 sec. The first woman to finish was Joan Benoit, with a time of 2 hrs., 35 min., 15 sec.

May 5 The 105th **Kentucky Derby** was won by Spectacular Bid, with a time of 2:02²/₅. The jockey was Ron Franklin.

May 13–21 The **NHL Stanley Cup** was won by the Montreal Canadiens, who defeated the New York Rangers four games to one.

May 19 The 104th **Preakness Stakes** was won by Spectacular Bid, with a time of 1:54¹/₅. The jockey was Ron Franklin.

May 20–June 1 The **NBA basketball championship** was won by the Seattle Supersonics, who defeated the Washington Bullets four games to one after losing the opening game.

May 27 The 63rd **Indianapolis 500** auto race was won by Rick Mears, completing the 500-mile course in 3 hrs., 8 min., 27.97 sec., with an average speed of 158.899 mph.

June 9 The 111th **Belmont Stakes** was won by Coastal, with a time of 2:28³/₅, foiling Spectacular Bid's attempt at a Triple Crown victory. The jockey was Ruben Hernandez.

June 10 The **LPGA golf tournament** was won by Donna Caponi Young.

June 17 The **U.S. Open golf tournament** was won by Hale Irwin, repeating his 1974 victory.

July 1–15 At the eighth **Pan-American Games** in San

July 19 In a major **Cabinet reorganization,** Pres. Carter dismissed four members, including the secretaries of the treasury and of energy; a fifth resigned. At a meeting of his Cabinet and staff, Carter had bluntly expressed his dissatisfaction, prompting the tendering of resignations by all his Cabinet members and by his senior White House staff.

July 25 **Paul Volcker** was appointed chairman of the Federal Reserve Board by Pres. Carter. He was confirmed on Aug. 2 and sworn in on Aug. 6.

Aug. 15 **Andrew Young** resigned as U.S. ambassador to the UN following controversy over his unauthorized meeting with representatives of the Palestine Liberation Organization in July.

Sept. 12–14 **Hurricane Frederic** struck the Gulf Coast, causing some $1,500,000,000 in damage with winds of up to 130 mph. Only eight people were killed, but some 500,000 were forced to evacuate.

Sept. 23 A **nuclear weapons protest,** the largest to date, drew about 200,000 demonstrators in New York City.

Nov. 3 A **shootout in Greensboro,** N.C., between Ku Klux Klan members and participants in an anti-Klan rally left five demonstrators dead and eight wounded. Fourteen Klansmen were arrested and 12 of them were charged with first-degree murder.

Nov. 4 The **U.S. embassy in Teheran** was seized by Iranian revolutionaries, so-called students, who took some 90 hostages, including about 65 Americans. The revolutionaries released the non-U.S. hostages and 13 U.S. hostages, all women or blacks, but kept about 50. The revolutionaries demanded that the U.S. return the deposed Shah to Iran to stand trial. He was in the U.S. undergoing medical treatment. The U.S. refused to comply.

Nov. 21 The **U.S. embassy in Islamabad,** Pakistan, was besieged for five hours before Pakistani soldiers restored order. One U.S. Marine was killed.

Dec. 2 The **U.S. embassy in Tripoli,** Libya, was attacked by a mob. Two floors were damaged but the 21 people in the building escaped unharmed.

Dec. 4 Pres. **Carter** announced his candidacy for reelection.

the portraits were painted between 1810 and 1815.

Apr. 16 **Pulitzer prizes** were awarded for the following: fiction, *The Stories of John Cheever;* biography, *Days of Sorrow and Pain* by Leonard Baker; history, *The Dred Scott Case* by Don E. Fehrenbacker; general nonfiction, *On Human Nature* by Edward O. Wilson; poetry, *Now and Then Poems* by Robert Penn Warren; drama, *Buried Child* by Sam Shepard.

Apr. 19 *The Elephant Man,* a play by Bernard Pomerance starring Philip Anglim, Carole Shelley, and Kevin Conway, opened at the Booth Theater in New York City.

Apr. 23 **National Book Awards** were presented for the following: fiction, *Going After Cacciato* by Tim O'Brien; poetry, *Mirabell: Books of Numbers* by James Merrill; biography, *Robert Kennedy and His Times* by Arthur M. Schlesinger, Jr.; history, *Intellectual Life in the Colonial South, 1585–1763* by Richard Beale Davis; contemporary thought, *The Snow Leopard* by Peter Matthiesen.

June 3 **Tony awards** for the 1978–1979 season were presented for the following: best play, *The Elephant Man;* best musical, *Sweeney Todd;* best dramatic actor, Tom Conti for *Whose Life Is It, Anyway?;* best dramatic actress, Constance Cummings for *Wings* and Carole Shelley for *The Elephant Man.*

July 16 A holographic manuscript of the *Haffner Symphony* by **Wolfgang Amadeus Mozart** was purchased from the National Orchestral Association by the Pierpont Morgan Library in New York City. It is the only manuscript of a major Mozart symphony in the U.S. available to scholars.

Aug. 23 **Alexander Godunov,** a principal dancer with the Russian Bolshoi Ballet, was given political asylum in the U.S. He was the first member of the Bolshoi to defect.

Sept. 9 **Emmy Awards** were presented for the following: best actor in a limited series, Peter Strauss for *The Jericho Mile;* best actress in a limited series, Bette Davis for *Strangers;* best actor in a dramatic series, Ron Leibman for *Kaz;* best actress in a dramatic series, Mariette Hartley for *The Incredible Hulk.*

Sept. 25 *Evita,* a musical by Andrew Lloyd Webber and Tim Rice about the rise of Evita Perón from poverty to become wife of the Argentine dictator Juan Perón, opened at the Broadway Theater in New York City. It starred Patti Lupone and Bob Gunton.

Dec. 3 A **rock concert disaster** claimed the lives of 11 youths who were trampled to death at Riverfront Coliseum in Cincinnati, Ohio. Fans were scrambling to get seats at a concert by The Who.

| Business and Industry; Science; Education; Philosophy and Religion III | | IV Sports; Social Issues and Crime; Folkways; Fashion; Holidays |

government. This exceeded the record 18,000,000-ton limit permitted in 1972.

Oct. 6 A **financial and stock panic** was sparked when the Federal Reserve Board announced—on a Saturday night—a raise in its discount rate from 11% to 12% and took stiff actions to tighten control of the money supply. In the next few days bond prices plunged, stock prices dropped in the heaviest trading since 1929, and banks raised their prime rates to 14.5%. By Oct. 11 the markets regained their balance and recovered most of their losses.

Oct. 12 The **Nobel Prize in Physiology or Medicine** was awarded jointly to Allan M. Cormack of Tufts University and Geoffrey N. Hounsfield of Great Britain for their development of the CAT scan, an advanced type of x-ray equipment.

Oct. 16 The **Nobel Prize in Chemistry** was awarded jointly to Herbert C. Brown of Purdue University and Georg Wittig of West Germany for their discoveries in the chemistry of boron and phosphorus.

Oct. 16 The **Nobel Prize in Physics** was awarded jointly to Steven Weinberg and Sheldon L. Glashow of Harvard University, and to Abdus Salam of Pakistan for their contributions to the development of a unified field theory.

Oct. 17 The **Nobel Prize in Economics** was awarded jointly to Theodore W. Schultz of the University of Chicago and Arthur Lewis of Princeton University for their work on the economic problems of developing nations.

Oct. 17 A bill creating the **Department of Education,** the 13th Cabinet-level agency, was signed by Pres. Carter. On Oct. 30 the president appointed Shirley Hufstedler, a U.S. Court of Appeals judge in Louisiana, to head the new agency. The Department of Health, Education, and Welfare became the Department of Health and Human Services.

Nov. 8 In what was probably the **largest single donation** in the history of philanthropy, Emory University in Atlanta, Ga., was designated to receive $100,000,000 from Robert W. Woodruff, retired head of the Coca-Cola Company.

Nov. 15 **George Meany** retired as head of the AFL-CIO, a post he had held since the merger of the two unions in 1955. On Nov. 19 Lane Kirkland, secretary-treasurer of the union since 1969, was elected to succeed him.

Dec. 21 A bill authorizing a **federal bailout for Chrysler Corporation** by providing $1,500,000,000 in federal loan guarantees for the ailing automotive company was passed by Congress. It was signed by Pres. Carter on Jan. 7, 1980.

Juan, Puerto Rico, the U.S. took 127 gold medals and finished first in unofficial team standings.

July 15 The **U.S. Women's Open golf tournament** was won by Jerilyn Britz, whose score of 284 was the lowest in the tournament's history.

July 17 The **baseball All-Star Game** was won by the National League, defeating the American League 7–6 for their 16th victory in 17 games.

Aug. 5 The **Baseball Hall of Fame** inducted three new members: Warren G. Giles, Willie Mays, and Lewis "Hack" Wilson.

Aug. 6 The **PGA golf tournament** was won by David Graham of Australia, beating Ben Crenshaw on the third hole of a playoff.

Sept. 8 The **North American Soccer League championship** was won by the Vancouver Whitecaps, who beat the Tampa Bay Rowdies 2–1.

Sept. 8 The **Miss America** title was won by Cheryl Prewitt, 22, of Ackerman, Miss., at the annual pageant in Atlantic City, N.J.

Sept. 9 The **U.S. Open tennis singles championships** were won by John McEnroe in the men's division and Tracy Austin, 16, in the women's division. Austin became the youngest player to win the women's singles title.

Oct. 10–17 The **World Series** was won by the Pittsburgh Pirates (NL), defeating the Baltimore Orioles (AL) four games to three. On Oct. 5 the Pirates completed a three-game sweep of the Cincinnati Reds for the National League pennant. The following day the Orioles had taken the American League championship from the California Angels, three games to one.

Oct. 21 The tenth **New York City Marathon** was won by Bill Rodgers, with a time of 2 hrs., 11 min., 42 sec. The first woman to finish was Grete Waitz of Norway, with a new women's world record of 2 hrs., 27 min., 33 sec.

Oct. 21 The World Boxing Association **heavyweight boxing championship** was won in Pretoria, South Africa, by John Tate, who took a 15-round decision over Gerrie Coetzee.

1980

It was a heartbreaking year for Pres. Jimmy Carter, whose administration seemed unable to achieve significant successes in domestic or foreign affairs. The national economy slumped under skyrocketing inflation and rising unemployment. The Carter administration was unable to bring the Iranian hostage crisis to a conclusion, and the Soviet invasion of Afghanistan in Dec. 1979 chilled U.S.-Soviet relations to the freezing point. Meanwhile, the Republican Party, solidly behind Ronald Reagan, expended great energy and vast resources in the presidential election campaign and swept their candidate into power in a Republican landslide. Another factor in U.S. politics was the 1980 Census, which reported a population of 226,504,825 and indicated a shift of 17 seats in the House of Representatives from the Northeast and Midwest to the South and West. This year Americans mourned the deaths of Helen Gahagan Douglas, former actress and Democratic congresswoman from 1944 to 1950 who lost her House seat to Richard M. Nixon in a bitterly fought campaign, June 28, at 79; and William O. Douglas, who had served on the Supreme Court for 36 years beginning in 1939, longer than any other justice in the Court's history, Jan. 19, at 81.

Jan. 4 In a protest against the **Soviet invasion of Afghanistan** in December, Pres. Carter announced that the 17,000,000 metric tons of grain ordered by the U.S.S.R. would not be delivered. Carter also suspended the sale of high-technology equipment, postponed the opening of new consulates in the two countries, and curtailed Soviet fishing privileges in U.S. waters. Carter also entertained the idea of a U.S. boycott of the 1980 Summer Olympics in Moscow, a move he announced on Jan. 20.

Jan. 8 Joint **U.S.-Egyptian Air Force exercises** had been conducted in Dec. 1979, it was revealed. About 300 U.S. airmen had taken part in the exercises in Egypt.

Jan. 23 In his **State of the Union** message, Pres. Carter said that Persian Gulf oil supply routes would be defended by force if necessary.

Jan. 29 **Six Americans escaped from Iran** with the aid of Canadian embassy personnel, it was revealed. The U.S. citizens, who had posed as Canadians, had not been among those held in the U.S. embassy in Teheran.

Feb. 2 Details of **Abscam,** an FBI sting operation to uncover official corruption, were released. Some 31 public officials were named as targets of the investigation, including Sen. Harrison Williams, Republican of New Jersey, and six members of the House of Representatives. In the operation an FBI agent posed as an

The Broadway theater season was marked by revivals of such former hits as *West Side Story, The Music Man,* and *Brigadoon.* The American Ballet Theater celebrated its 40th anniversary this year, and Mikhail Baryshnikov became its director. Conflicts between the Metropolitan Opera Company and its orchestra led to cancellation of its 1980–1981 season. After a last-minute settlement on Dec. 10, the season was begun two months late. Plans for the long-awaited New York City Exposition and Convention Center were finally approved. The single structure would cover five blocks, have 500,000 sq. ft. of exhibition space, and be the largest structure of its kind. This year viewers crowded New York City's Museum of Modern Art to see more than 1000 works by Pablo Picasso. In May a Picasso painting brought $3,000,000 at auction. This sale soon was eclipsed by a $3,900,000 bid for a painting by Paul Cézanne, and $5,200,000 for a painting by Vincent Van Gogh. In music, digitally recorded LP records were widely marketed for the first time. In publishing, two of the nation's most respected magazines, *Harper's* and *Atlantic,* nearly failed but were saved at the last minute. Americans mourned the deaths this year of Gower Champion, choreographer, who died hours before his last show, *42nd Street,* opened, Aug. 25, at 61; Harold E. Clurman, director, drama critic, and author, Sept. 9, at 78; Jimmy Durante, entertainer, Jan. 29, at 86; Jane Froman, big band singer of the 1930s and 1940s, Apr. 23, at 72; José Iturbi, Spanish-born pianist, June 28, at 84; Andre Kostelanetz, conductor, Jan 13, at 78; Henry Miller, author of *Tropic of Cancer* and other controversial works, June 7, at 88; Katherine Anne Porter, Pulitzer Prize–winning author, Sept. 18, at 90; and Mae West, sex queen of the movies for 60 years, Nov. 22, at 87.

Among **books published** was *A Confederacy of Dunces* by John Kennedy Toole, who committed suicide after being unable to find a publisher for his work. Years later his mother found a publisher for his novel, which went on to win a Pulitzer Prize. Other books published this year included *Creek Mary's Blood* by Dee Brown, a novel; *Loon Lake* by E. L. Doctorow, a novel; *Walt Whitman,* a biography by Justin Kaplan; *The White House Years* by Henry Kissinger, which focused on the Vietnam War and prompted much debate; *The Covenant,* another blockbuster by James Michener; and *The Second Coming* by Walker Percy, the author's fifth novel.

Jan. 7 **National Book Critics Circle Awards** were presented for the following: fiction, *The Year of the French* by Thomas Flanagan; general nonfiction, *Munich: The Price of Peace* by Telford Taylor; poetry, *Ashes* and *Seven Years from Somewhere* by Philip

1980

Inflation reached 12.4% by year's end, marking the second successive year of double-digit inflation. The Federal Reserve raised its discount rate to 13%, and unemployment hit an average of 7.1% for the year. Sales of U.S. automobiles were at a 19-year low, down 20% from 1979 levels, and the Ford Motor Co. reported a third-quarter loss of $595,000,000, the biggest ever for a U.S. corporation. This year the federal government took steps to deregulate the trucking industry and railroads. On July 1 Pres. Jimmy Carter signed a bill giving truckers more freedom to raise or lower rates without having to seek ICC permission. On Oct. 14 Pres. Carter signed a bill giving the railroads greater flexibility in setting rates. New federal assistance for railroads in financial trouble was also provided. A noteworthy development was the decline in computer prices. Sales of personal computers were up, although the expected production boom was hurt by short supply of integrated circuit chips. Notables who died this year included Jacqueline Cochran, first woman to fly faster than the speed of sound, Aug. 8, at 70; George Meany, president of the AFL-CIO from 1955 to 1979, Jan. 10, at 85; and Harland "Colonel" Sanders, founder of the Kentucky Fried Chicken food chain, Dec. 16, at 90.

Jan. 2 Of the 68 operating **nuclear power plants** in the U.S., 38 had failed to meet a Jan. 1 deadline for mandated safety changes in equipment and procedures, the Nuclear Regulatory Commission reported. The NRC then said it would give the utilities more time to comply.

Jan. 3 An 11-week **school strike** in Cleveland, Ohio, ended when public school teachers accepted a contract raising their salaries 20% over a 15-month period.

Jan. 14 A surgeon general's report revealed that **lung cancer in women** was increasing sharply, and that within three years it could overtake breast cancer as the leading cause of cancer deaths in women.

Jan. 16 The successful **synthesis of human interferon,** thought to be effective against viral diseases and possibly against some types of cancer, was announced by a group of scientists in Boston.

On Jan. 20 Pres. Carter announced U.S. withdrawal from the Summer Olympics, to be held in Moscow in July, in response to the Soviet invasion of Afghanistan in 1979. Some 50 nations followed suit, but many athletes who had trained for years for the games felt great bitterness at the move. In February Americans witnessed an athletic miracle as the U.S. Olympic hockey team defeated the favored Finnish and Russian hockey teams to take the gold medal and become national heroes. Another top story this year was Muhammad Ali's attempt to win the world heavyweight boxing title for an unprecedented fourth time. Ali had retired from boxing in 1979 after defeating Michael Spinks. On Oct. 2 he faced off against WBA champion Larry Holmes in Las Vegas, but his dream of victory was not to become reality. Nonetheless, the former champ earned $8,000,000 for his part in what many considered a terrible match. In golf, the year's top money winners were Tom Watson, $530,808, and Beth Daniel, $231,000. The year's fashion rage was the bulky coat, down-filled, quilted, and often reaching almost to the ground. Among those who died in 1980 were Alice Longworth Roosevelt, last surviving child of Theodore Roosevelt, Feb. 20, at 96; Richard "Rube" Marquard, one of baseball's all-time great pitchers, June 1, at 90; and Jesse Owens, track star who won four gold medals at the 1936 Olympics in Germany and shattered the Nazi myth of racial superiority, Mar. 30, at age 66.

Jan. 1 In **college football bowl games,** the results were Houston 17, Nebraska 14 in the Cotton Bowl; Oklahoma 24, Florida State 7 in the Orange Bowl; Southern California 17, Ohio State 16 in the Rose Bowl; and Alabama 24, Arkansas 9 in the Sugar Bowl. This season the AP and UPI polls chose Alabama the national collegiate champions of 1979.

Jan. 18–20 **U.S. figure skating championships** were won in Atlanta, Ga., by Charles Tickner, men's singles; Linda Fratianne, women's singles; Tai Babilonia and Randy Gardner, pairs; Stacey Smith and John Summers, dance.

Jan. 20 **Super Bowl XIV** was won by the Pittsburgh Steelers (AFC), defeating the Los Angeles Rams (NFC) 31–19. On Jan. 6 the Steelers had beaten the Houston Oilers 27–13 for the AFC title and the Rams had defeated the Tampa Bay Buccaneers 9–0 for the NFC championship.

Feb. 12–24 At the **Winter Olympics** in Lake Placid, N.Y., the U.S. won six gold medals and finished third behind the U.S.S.R. and East Germany. The U.S. hockey team scored a major upset over the U.S.S.R. team, which had been favored to win the gold medal. Eric Heiden swept the speed skating events,

Arab sheik and offered bribes for political favors.

Feb. 2–3 A **prison riot** at a Santa Fe, N.Mex., state prison left 33 inmates dead and 89 injured. Some 250 state troopers and National Guardsmen were called out to restore order.

Mar. 15 An **Indian land claim suit** was settled when the Penobscot Indian tribe in Maine accepted an $81,-500,000 settlement for land taken from it in violation of the Indian Non-Intercourse Act of 1790.

Mar. 17 The **Refugee Act of 1980** was signed by Pres. Carter. It broadened the definition of the term *refugee* to include people from any part of the world, and increased the maximum annual number to be admitted to the U.S. from 290,000 to 320,000.

Apr. 7 The U.S. broke **diplomatic relations with Iran** in the wake of the continuing hostage crisis. All exports to Iran were banned and Iranian diplomats in the U.S. were expelled.

Apr. 11 Regulations prohibiting **sexual harassment of women** by their superiors in government or business were issued by the Equal Opportunity Commission.

Apr. 24 A U.S. **hostage rescue mission** in Iran ended in disaster. During the operation, three of the eight helicopters of the airborne operation failed. At the staging area inside Iran, the mission was canceled, but during the withdrawal one of the remaining helicopters collided with one of six C-130 transports, killing eight and injuring five.

Apr. 26 Sec. of State **Cyrus Vance resigned,** stating his opposition to the U.S. military rescue attempt in Iran. He was succeeded by Sen. Edmund Muskie, Democrat of Maine.

May 9 A **marine accident** killed at least 35 people when the freighter *Summit Venture* rammed the Sunshine Skyway Bridge over Tampa Bay, Fla., collapsing one of its twin highway spans. On Jan. 28 a Coast Guard cutter had struck an oil tanker near the bridge, killing 23 sailors.

May 17–19 **Race riots** in Miami, Fla. [Liberty City], left at least 14 dead and more than 300 injured, and caused some $100,000,000 in damage. Nearly 1000 people were arrested in the violence, which erupted after an all-white jury acquitted four former Miami policemen charged with the fatal beating of a black man.

May 18 The eruption of **Mt. St. Helens** in southwestern Washington State blew the top of the mountain into the atmosphere, leveled some 120 sq. mi., and set off a series of fires, mudslides, and floods. About 400 people had been evacuated before the eruption, but a count in July showed 15 others dead and about 40 missing. The volcano had been dormant since 1857.

Levine; criticism, *The Gnostic Gospels* by Elaine Pagels.

Jan. 10 The **Boston Pops** Orchestra named John Williams to succeed the late Arthur Fiedler as conductor. Williams, an Academy Award–winning composer, had been assistant conductor.

Feb. 6 **Sulamith Messerer,** a member of the Russian Bolshoi Ballet since 1926, defected to the U.S. with her son Mikhail by way of the U.S. embassy in Tokyo, Japan.

Feb. 15 **Lillian Hellman sued Mary McCarthy** for defamation of character. Hellman filed the $2,500,000 lawsuit after McCarthy, appearing on a television program on Jan. 25, called her a "dishonest writer."

Feb. 15 **Walter Cronkite,** 63, announced his intention to retire in 1981 as anchorman of the *CBS Evening News* program. Cronkite, who held the post since 1950, was to be succeeded by fellow CBS newsman Dan Rather.

Feb. 27 **Grammy Awards** were presented for the following: best album of 1979, *52nd Street* by Billy Joel; best record, "What a Fool Believes" by the Doobie Brothers; best male pop vocalist, Billy Joel for *52nd Street;* best female pop vocalist, Dionne Warwick for "I'll Never Love This Way Again"; best pop group, the Doobie Brothers for "Minute by Minute."

Mar. 6 **Marguerite Yourcenar** became the first woman to be elected to the French Academy. A naturalized U.S. citizen, the author had resided in Maine for more than 30 years.

Apr. 14 **Pulitzer prizes** were awarded for the following: fiction, *The Executioner's Song* by Norman Mailer; biography, *The Rise of Theodore Roosevelt* by Edmund Morris; history, *Been in the Storm So Long* by Leon F. Litwack; general nonfiction, *Gödel, Escher, Bach* by Douglas R. Hofstadter; poetry, *Selected Poems* by Donald R. Justice; drama, *Talley's Folly* by Lanford Wilson.

Apr. 14 **Academy Awards** were presented to *Kramer vs. Kramer* as the outstanding motion picture of 1979 and to its star Dustin Hoffman as best actor; to Sally Field as best actress for *Norma Rae;* to Melvyn Douglas as best supporting actor for *Being There;* and to Meryl Streep as best supporting actress for *Kramer vs. Kramer.*

May 1 The first **American Book Awards,** formerly known as the National Book Awards, were presented for the following: fiction, *Sophie's Choice* by William Styron; general nonfiction, *The Right Stuff* by Tom Wolfe; biography, *The Rise of Theodore Roosevelt* by Edmund Morris; history, *The White House Years* by Henry Kissinger; poetry, *Ashes* by Philip Levine. The National Medal for Literature was presented to Eudora Welty.

| Business and Industry; Science; Education; Philosophy and Religion **III** | | Sports; Social Issues and Crime; Folkways; Fashion; Holidays **IV** |

Feb. 14 The 1500-lb. **Solar Maximum Observatory,** designed to study solar flares, was successfully launched into orbit.

Mar. 13 In the **first criminal trial of a U.S. corporation** in a product defect case, the Ford Motor Company was found not guilty by a jury in Winimac, Ind., of reckless homicide. The case involved the 1978 deaths of three women killed in a Ford Pinto.

Mar. 27 **Michele Sindona** was convicted on 65 counts of fraud in connection with events leading to the 1974 failure of the Franklin Bank in New York City.

Apr. 2 The **Crude Oil Windfall Profits Tax** bill was signed by Pres. Carter. It was expected to produce $227,000,000,000 in tax revenues from the nation's oil companies by 1990.

Apr. 28 A report on **cancer death rates** issued by the American Cancer Society projected that 8,500,000 Americans would die from cancer in the 1980s, at least 2,000,000 more than had died in the 1970s.

Apr. 29 A **Washington for Jesus rally** brought 200,000 evangelical Christians to the nation's capital. One speaker declared the world to be "aflame in sin."

May 5 The **largest U.S. corporation,** according to the annual report by *Fortune* magazine, was Exxon, with sales of $79,106,471,000 in 1979. Exxon moved from second to first place, dropping General Motors to number two.

May 28 The **first women graduates** from the service academies numbered 61 from West Point, 55 from Annapolis, and 97 from the Air Force Academy.

May 30 The **index of leading economic indicators** dropped 4.8% in April, the largest monthly drop on record, the Commerce Department reported. February and March also had shown declines, indicating trouble ahead for the economy.

June 16 In a landmark ruling on **genetic engineering,** the Supreme Court ruled that organisms created in the laboratory could be patented.

becoming the first athlete to win five gold medals in the Winter Olympics.

Mar. 10 Dr. **Herman Tarnower,** coauthor of a best-selling diet book, was shot and killed by his longtime friend Jean Harris, headmistress of a prestigious girls' school in Virginia.

Mar. 14 Twenty-two members of a **U.S. amateur boxing team died** when the Polish airliner they were traveling on crashed near Warsaw. The crash killed 87.

Mar 23 The **AIAW basketball championship** was won for the second consecutive year by Old Dominion, defeating Tennessee 68–53.

Mar. 24 The **NCAA basketball championship** was won by the University of Louisville, beating UCLA 59–54.

Mar. 31 The World Boxing Association **heavyweight boxing championship** was won by Mike "Hercules" Weaver, who knocked out John Tate in the 15th round at Knoxville, Tenn.

Apr. 13 The **Masters golf tournament** was won by Severiano "Seve" Ballesteros of Spain, 23, the youngest player ever to win the tournament.

Apr. 21 The 84th **Boston Marathon** was won by Bill Rodgers, his third consecutive win, with a time of 2 hrs., 12 min., 11 sec. Rosie Ruiz of New York was declared the first woman to finish, but on Apr. 29 she was disqualified on grounds she had not actually run the distance. Jacqueline Garreau of Canada, who had finished in 2 hrs., 34 min., 26 sec., was declared the women's winner.

May 3 The 106th **Kentucky Derby** was won by Genuine Risk, the second filly to ever win the race, with a time of 2:02. The jockey was Jacinto Vasquez.

May 4–16 The **NBA basketball championship** was won by the Los Angeles Lakers, who defeated the Philadelphia 76ers four games to two.

May 12 The first nonstop **transcontinental balloon flight** was completed by Maxie Anderson and his son Kris, who flew 3100 miles from Fort Baker, Calif., to Matane, Quebec, on the Gaspé Peninsula, in four days aboard the balloon *Kitty Hawk.*

May 13–24 The **NHL Stanley Cup** was won for the first time by the New York Islanders, who beat the Philadelphia Flyers four games to two.

May 17 The 105th **Preakness Stakes** was won by Codex, with a time of 1:54¹/₅. The jockey was Angel Cordero, Jr.

May 25 The 64th **Indianapolis 500** auto race was won by Johnny Rutherford, who clinched his third Indy victory with a time of 3 hrs., 29 min., 59.56 sec., with an average speed of 142.862 mph.

June 7 The 112th **Belmont Stakes** was won by

June 3 A total of 101,476 **Cuban refugees** had fled to the U.S. since mid-April with the tacit approval of Fidel Castro's government, it was reported. At first the refugees had been welcomed by the U.S., but by mid-May steps were taken to slow the tide and screen the refugees. It was feared Castro was using the exodus as a way to empty his prisons of criminals.

June 23–Aug. 15 A summer-long **heat wave and drought** devastated crops and livestock and left 1272 people dead in 20 states. The mid–Mississippi R. Valley, the Southwest, and the South were hardest hit in the worst drought since the Dust Bowl days of the 1930s.

June 27 A law requiring **draft registration** by men 19 to 20 years of age was signed by Pres. Carter. Registration was to begin in July, but no actual draft was contemplated.

July 14–17 The **Republican National Convention** nominated **Ronald W. Reagan** for the presidency by a nearly unanimous vote. George Bush of Texas, former ambassador to the UN and former director of the CIA, was nominated for the vice presidency.

Aug. 11–14 The **Democratic National Convention** nominated **Pres. Carter** and Vice Pres. Walter F. Mondale for reelection. Carter defeated Sen. Edward M. Kennedy of Massachusetts by a margin of nearly two to one.

Sept. 19 A **fuel explosion** at a Titan 2 missile site near Damascus, Ark., killed one Air Force employee and injured 21. The blast left a crater 250-feet wide and forced the evacuation of 1400 people from the area for 12 hours.

Nov. 4 **Ronald W. Reagan was elected president** of the United States, carrying 44 states. The electoral vote was Reagan 489, Pres. Jimmy Carter 49. The popular vote was Reagan, 42,797,153; Carter, 34,434,100; John Anderson, independent candidate, 5,533,927. In congressional elections the Republicans picked up 12 Senate seats for a 53–46 majority, with one independent seat. In the House the Democrats lost 33 seats but kept a majority of 242–192, with one seat going to an independent.

Nov. 21 A **hotel fire** at the MGM Grand Hotel in Las Vegas, Nev., killed 84 pople. It was the second worst hotel fire in U.S. history.

May 29 A **world auction record** for a painting was set when J. M. W. Turner's *Juliet and Her Nurse* was sold in New York City for $6,400,000.

June 8 **Tony awards** for the 1979–1980 season were presented for the following: best play, *Children of a Lesser God* by Mark Medoff; best musical, *Evita* by Andrew Lloyd Webber and Tim Rice; best dramatic actor and actress, John Rubinstein and Phyllis Frelich for *Children of a Lesser God.*

Aug. 25 *42nd Street,* a musical by Harry Warren, Al Dubin, Michael Stewart, and Mark Bramble, opened at the Winter Garden Theater in New York City. Gower Champion, who directed and choreographed the musical, died a few hours before it opened.

Sept. 7 **Emmy Awards** were presented for the following: best actor and actress in a limited series or special, Powers Boothe for *Guyana Tragedy* and Patty Duke Astin for *The Miracle Worker;* best actor in a dramatic series, Ed Asner for *Lou Grant;* best actress in a dramatic series, Barbara Bel Geddes for *Dallas.*

Oct. 9 The **Nobel Prize in Literature** was awarded to Czeslaw Milosz, a self-exiled Pole living and teaching in California.

Oct. 17 The second-highest **art auction price** for an American painting was paid for Winslow Homer's *Signal of Distress.*

Oct. 27 **Beverly Sills** gave her final performance, singing the role of Rosalinda in a New York City Opera production of *Die Fledermaus.*

Nov. 21 The so-called **Who Shot J. R.?** episode of the TV evening soap *Dallas* was seen by more U.S. viewers than any other television program in history. More than half the nation's audience watched to see who had tried to kill J. R. Ewing, a question unanswered at the end of the spring season.

Dec. 8 **John Lennon was shot** and killed outside his apartment building in New York City. Mark David Chapman, 25, a former mental patient, was held for the shooting.

Dec. 12 A notebook of sketches and writings by **Leonardo da Vinci** was bought at auction by Armand Hammer, the industrialist, for $5,280,000. He planned to bequeath the book to the Los Angeles County Museum of Art.

Dec. 17 *Amadeus,* a play by Peter Shaffer starring Tim Curry as Wolfgang Amadeus Mozart and Ian McKellan as Antonio Salieri, opened at the Broadhurst Theater in New York City.

| Business and Industry; Science; Education; Philosophy and Religion | III | IV | Sports; Social Issues and Crime; Folkways; Fashion; Holidays |

July 3 A tire recall of 1,800,000 steel-belted radials was announced by Firestone Tire and Rubber Company. In 1978 Firestone had recalled 10,000,000 tires, the largest such recall ever.

Sept. 22 The risk of **toxic shock syndrome** led to recall of a tampon product manufactured by Procter and Gamble. Federal studies had linked use of the tampon with the deaths of 25 women.

Oct. 10 The **Nobel Prize in Physiology or Medicine** was awarded jointly to Baruj Benacerraf of Harvard University, George Snell of the Jackson Laboratory in Maine, and Jean Dausset of France for their studies of antigens, protein-carbohydrate complexes found in the body.

Oct. 14 The **Nobel Prize in Chemistry** was awarded jointly to Paul Berg of Stanford University for his studies of the manipulation of gene structures, and to Walter Gilbert of Harvard University and Frederick Sanger of England for their work on reading the fine details of the structure of DNA.

Oct. 14 The **Nobel Prize in Physics** was awarded jointly to James Cronin of the University of Chicago and Val L. Fitch of Princeton University for their discoveries concerning the symmetry of subatomic particles.

Oct. 15 The **Nobel Prize in Economics** was awarded to Lawrence R. Klein of the Wharton School of the University of Pennsylvania for his development of models for forecasting economic trends.

Nov. 12 **Voyager 1,** launched in Sept. 1977, flew within 77,000 miles of Saturn and found far more rings around the planet than had been previously identified, some with eccentric orbits. The spacecraft also found three new moons, making 15 known in all.

longshot Temperence Hill, with a time of 2:29⁴/₅. The jockey was Eddie Maple.

June 8 The **LPGA golf tournament** was won by Sally Little. It was her first major win and she was the only player to finish under par.

June 15 The **U.S. Open golf tournament** was won by Jack Nicklaus. It was his fourth U.S. Open win.

July 8 The **baseball All-Star Game** was won for the ninth consecutive year by the National League, defeating the American League 4–2.

July 13 The **U.S. Women's Open golf tournament** was won by Amy Alcott by nine strokes.

Aug. 3 The **Baseball Hall of Fame** inducted four new members: Albert W. "Al" Kaline, longtime Detroit Tigers (AL) outfielder; Charles H. "Chuck" Klein, outfielder for the Philadelphia Phillies (NL) and the Cincinnati Reds (NL); Edwin D. "Duke" Snider, outfielder and slugger; and Tom Yawkey, former owner of the Boston Red Sox.

Aug. 10 The **PGA golf tournament** was won for the fifth time by Jack Nicklaus.

Sept. 6 The **Miss America** title was won by Susan Powell, 21, from Elk City, Okla., at the annual pageant in Atlantic City, N.J.

Sept. 6–7 The **U.S. Open tennis singles championships** were won by John McEnroe in the men's division and Chris Evert Lloyd in the women's division.

Sept. 16–25 The **America's Cup** was successfully defended by the U.S. yacht *Freedom,* which beat the challenger *Australia* four races to one.

Sept. 21 The **North American Soccer League championship** was won by the New York Cosmos, who defeated the Fort Lauderdale Strikers 3–0.

Oct. 14–21 The **World Series** was won by the Philadelphia Phillies (NL), defeating the Kansas City Royals (AL) four games to two. On Oct. 10 the Royals completed a three-game sweep of the New York Yankees to win the American League pennant. On Oct. 12 the Phillies won the National League pennant, beating the Houston Astros three games to two.

Oct. 26 The 11th **New York City Marathon** was won by Alberto Salazar of Wayland, Mass., with a time of 2 hrs., 9 min., 41 sec. The first woman to finish was Grete Waitz of Norway, with a time of 2 hrs., 25 min., 41 sec.

1981

The UN Conference on the Law of the Sea, which had worked for several years on the question of how to apportion underseas resources, met in New York City on Mar. 9 in what was expected to be its final session. However, the fledgling administration of Pres. Ronald Reagan, reversing the position of the previous administration, objected to some of the terms of the proposed treaty, and the U.S. did not sign it. In domestic matters, the Bureau of the Census estimated the nation's population as 230,500,000 at year's end, an increase of 2,200,000 over 1980. Divorces in 1981 hit a record 1,210,000, the government reported. Notables who died this year included Roger Baldwin, a founder of the American Civil Liberties Union, Aug. 26, at 97; Gen. Omar N. Bradley, called the "GI's general" during World War II, Apr. 8, at 88; Emanuel Celler, Democrat of New York, who served 50 years (1923–1973) in the House of Representatives, Jan. 15, at 92; David E. Lilienthal, former chairman of the Tennessee Valley Authority and first chairman of the Atomic Energy Commission, Jan. 15, at 81; Carl Vinson, Democrat of Georgia, who served 50 years (1914–1964) in the House of Representatives, June 1, at 97; and Roy Wilkins, leader of the NAACP from 1931 to 1977, Sept. 8, at 80.

Jan. 14 In his **farewell address,** Pres. Jimmy Carter stressed the "threat of nuclear destruction, our stewardship of the physical resources of our planet, and the preeminence of the basic rights of human beings" as the nation's most pressing problems.

Jan. 20 **Ronald Reagan was inaugurated president** of the United States. A Republican, he was at 69 the oldest person ever to assume the presidency. George Bush was inaugurated vice president.

Jan. 20 The Iranian **hostage crisis** ended when Iran released the 52 U.S. captives seized at the U.S. embassy in Teheran in Nov. 1979. The release was accomplished with the help of Algeria minutes after Ronald Reagan succeeded Jimmy Carter as president. On Jan. 21 Carter flew to Wiesbaden, West Germany, to greet the freed Americans.

Feb. 18 In his first **State of the Union** message, Pres. Reagan called for cuts of $41,000,000,000 in the budget Pres. Carter had submitted. He also proposed a 10% income tax cut in each of the next three years, an increase of about $5,000,000,000 in defense

The worldwide recession weakened the art market, and a strong U.S. dollar discouraged foreign buyers. Nevertheless, in May a Picasso self-portrait sold in New York City for $5,300,000, a new auction record for a twentieth-century painting. The Joffrey Ballet celebrated its 25th anniversary in October. In the same month, theatergoers greeted the opening of a British import, *The Life and Adventures of Nicholas Nickleby,* which coincided with publication of new paperback editions of the Dickens novel. Tickets for the play cost $100. An advertisement for a $5 edition of the novel suggested buying the book and saving $95. Among the year's top motion pictures were *Superman II* and *Raiders of the Lost Ark*. In music, videocassettes became an important part of the marketing strategy for many rock groups, who found that airtime on MTV, a rock music channel carried by 252 cable television stations, translated into big sales in record stores. In architecture, increasing attention was being paid to preserving and restoring old buildings. A restoration of particular interest was that of the elaborate terra cotta facade of the Woolworth Building in New York City. Americans mourned the deaths of Nelson Algren, known best for his 1949 novel *The Man With the Golden Arm,* May 9, at 72; Samuel Barber, Pulitzer Prize–winning composer, Jan. 23, at 70; Hoagy Carmichael, popular composer, Dec. 27, at 82; Ariel and Will Durant, husband and wife authors of the 11-volume *The Story of Civilization,* she on Oct. 25, at 83, and he on Nov. 7, at 96; Howard Hanson, composer and director of the Eastman School of Music for 40 years, Feb. 26, at 84; Joseph H. Hirshhorn, millionaire art collector and founder in 1974 of the Hirshhorn Museum in Washington, D.C., Aug. 31, at 82; George Jessel, comedian, May 24, at 83; Anita Loos, novelist and playwright, Aug. 18, at 88; Rosa Ponselle, first U.S.-trained singer to star at the Metropolitan Opera, May 25, at 84; Robert Montgomery, actor, Sept. 27, at 77; William Saroyan, author and playwright, May 18, at 72; and Dewitt Wallace, founder in 1922 of *Reader's Digest,* Mar. 30, at 91.

Among **books published** this year was Dumas Malone's six-volume life of *Thomas Jefferson,* a work 40 years in the making. Its publication was greeted with unanimous acclaim. Other books published this year included *The Company of Women* by Mary Gordon, her second novel; *The Hotel New Hampshire* by John Irving, a novel that disappointed many who had praised his earlier novel *The World According to Garp; Tar Baby* by Toni Morrison, fiction; *The Collected Poems* of the late Sylvia Plath; and *Rabbit Is Rich* by John Updike, the author's third novel about Harry "Rabbit" Angstrom.

Jan. 5 The **National Book Critics Circle Awards** were presented for the following: fiction, *Transit of Venus*

1981

The economy continued to falter in 1981. Inflation hit an annual rate of 14%. Unemployment hit 7.4% and continued to rise. The Census Bureau reported that average household income before taxes had declined 2.6%. Automobile production was at its lowest level in 20 years, with Detroit producing only 6,200,000 passenger cars. The cost of medical care climbed 12.5% and was the highest since records were begun in 1935. In January, Pres. Ronald Reagan lifted oil price controls. Crude oil and oil product prices shot up at once, but an oversupply of crude soon brought them back down. The U.S. imported 40% less oil than in the peak importing year of 1978. The ten major airlines reported a total operating loss of $577,000,000, more than double their losses in 1980. In July a potentially devastating pest, the Mediterranean fruit fly, was found in California. An area of 550 square miles was quarantined, and Gov. Jerry Brown ordered ground spraying and the stripping of fruit from trees. In September, threatened with a federal quarantine of the state's produce, Gov. Brown ordered aerial spraying in spite of protests from environmentalists. The last outbreak of fruit flies was reported in August. By October it appeared a disaster had been averted. Probably the year's brightest news concerned the introduction of a personal computer by IBM, a development that lent legitimacy to the growing personal computer industry and that was to turn it into a major economic force in a few short years. Among those who died this year were Donald W. Douglas, airplane designer, Feb. 2, at 88; John S. Knight, founder of the Knight newspaper empire, June 16, at 87; Lowell Thomas, broadcast pioneer, Aug. 30, at 89; and Harold C. Urey, winner of the Nobel Prize for his discovery of heavy hydrogen, Jan. 5, at 87.

Jan. 7 A stock market run began when Joe Granville, a popular market forecaster, advised investors to "sell everything." The Dow Jones average of industrial stocks fell 23.8 points, and trading on the New York Stock Exchange set a new daily record of 93,700,000 shares. By Jan. 19 the situation had stabilized and stocks had rebounded.

Jan. 8 An increase in the risk of coronary death was linked to consumption of large amounts of cholesterol, according to a report in the *New England Journal of Medicine.* The report was based on a 20-year study of 1900 men.

A trend toward dullness that had prevailed in fashion gave way to a new freshness, characterized by a simple, sexy look. A touch of opulence also became stylish, perhaps inspired by the dress of Nancy Reagan, wife of the president. This year a maintenance worker won $5,000,000 in the New York State Lottery, the largest lottery payoff to date. State lotteries in the U.S. were estimated to take in $3,600,000,000 annually. Crime continued to be a concern. The Burns Detective Agency estimated that white collar crime in 1981 would amount to between $1,200,000,000 and $1,800,000,000 and that only 15% of such crimes would be detected. Divorces in the U.S. totaled a record 1,200,000 this year, the government reported. In sports, the National Football League set a new attendance record of 13,392,000, an average of about 60,000 fans present at a game. In boxing Larry Holmes successfully defended his World Boxing Association heavyweight title in a three-round bout (June 12) against Leon Spinks. In pro golf the top money winners were Tom Kite, $375,699, and Beth Daniel, $206,977. Notables who died included John Kieran, sportswriter who became a star of the radio show *Information Please* in the 1930s and 1940s, Dec. 10, at 89; and Joe Louis, the "Brown Bomber," who held the heavyweight boxing title from 1937 to 1949, the longest reign ever, Apr. 12, at 66.

Jan. 1 In college football bowl games, the results were Alabama 30, Baylor 2 in the Cotton Bowl; Oklahoma 18, Florida State 17 in the Orange Bowl; Michigan 23, Washington 6 in the Rose Bowl; and Georgia 17, Notre Dame 10 in the Sugar Bowl. This season the AP and UPI polls chose Georgia the national collegiate champions of 1980.

Jan. 25 Super Bowl XV was won by the Oakland Raiders (AFC), defeating the Philadelphia Eagles (NFC) 27–10. On Jan. 11 the Raiders had beaten the San Diego Chargers 34–27 for the AFC championship and the Eagles had defeated the Dallas Cowboys 20–7 for the NFC title.

Feb. 3–8 U.S. figure skating championships were won in San Diego, Calif., by Scott Hamilton, men's singles; Elaine Zayak, women's singles; Kitty and Peter Carruthers, pairs; Judy Blumberg and Michael Seibert, dance.

Mar. 5 At the world figure skating championships in Hartford, Conn., Scott Hamilton won the men's singles title.

spending, and more liberal depreciation rules for business.

Mar. 30 Pres. **Reagan was shot** by John W. Hinckley, Jr., 25, outside a Washington, D.C., hotel. Reagan underwent two hours of surgery for a wound in his left lung. Presidential press secretary James Brady was shot in the head but survived. Also wounded were Secret Service agent Timothy J. McCarthy and Washington police officer Thomas K. Delahanty. Reagan returned to the White House on Apr. 11.

Apr. 4 The **first Mexican-American mayor** of a major U.S. city, Henry Gabriel Cisneros, 33, was elected in San Antonio, Tex.

Apr. 21 A major **Saudi arms sale** was announced. The U.S. agreed to sell $1,000,000,000 worth of military equipment to Saudi Arabia, including five AWACS electronic surveillance aircraft. Israel protested the sale.

Apr. 24 The 15-month **embargo on grain** shipments to the U.S.S.R. would be lifted, Pres. Reagan announced, thus fulfilling a campaign pledge he had made.

Apr. 24 A **new military command** would be given the task of protecting U.S. interests in the Persian Gulf, it was announced. The command would take over responsibilities in the region assigned to the year-old Rapid Deployment Force.

June 8 In a ruling on **wage discrimination,** the Supreme Court ruled women could sue for equal pay even if the work they did was not identical with that of male employees.

June 16 A decision to sell **arms to the People's Republic of China** was announced by Sec. of State Alexander Haig at the end of a visit to China. This decision was a reversal of previous U.S. policy.

June 25 The Supreme Court ruled that **draft registration** and, by extension, a military draft, could exclude women without violating the Constitution.

by Shirley Hazzard; general nonfiction, *Walter Lippmann and the American Century* by Ronald Steel; poetry, *Sunrise* by Frederick Seidel; criticism, *Part of Nature, Part of Us: Modern American Poets* by Helen Vendler.

Jan. 14 **Broadcasting regulations** for radio stations were eased by the FCC, freeing stations to air as many commercials an hour as they pleased and removing any obligation to allocate time for news or public affairs programing.

Feb. 5 *Piaf,* a play by Pam Gems starring Jane Lapotaire as Edith Piaf, opened at the Plymouth Theater in New York City.

Feb. 25 **Grammy Awards** were presented for the following: best album of 1980, *Christopher Cross* by Christopher Cross; best record, "Sailing" by Christopher Cross; best male pop vocalist, Kenny Loggins for "This Is It"; best female pop vocalist, Bette Midler for "The Rose"; best rock group, Bob Seger and the Silver Bullet Band for "Against the Wind."

Mar. 13 The **world's largest diamond,** the 170.45 carat Star of Peace, was sold for $20,000,000, believed to be the highest price ever paid for a gem. The stone had been owned by Thomas Loder of New York City and was reported to have been purchased by an unidentified Arab.

Mar. 31 **Academy Awards** were presented to *Ordinary People* as the outstanding motion picture of 1980; Robert De Niro as best actor for *Raging Bull;* Sissy Spacek as best actress for *Coal Miner's Daughter;* Timothy Hutton as best supporting actor for *Ordinary People;* and Mary Steenburgen as best supporting actress for *Melvin and Howard.*

Apr. 11 **Maksim Shostakovich,** son of the Russian composer Dmitri Shostakovich, defected with his son in West Germany. Five days later the U.S. granted the two political asylum. On May 25 Shostakovich, a conductor and pianist, conducted the National Symphony Orchestra in Washington, D.C.

Apr. 13 **Pulitzer prizes** were awarded for the following: fiction, *A Confederacy of Dunces* by John Kennedy Toole; biography, *Peter the Great* by Robert K. Massie; history, *American Education: The National Experience, 1783–1876* by Lawrence A. Cremin; general nonfiction, *Fin-de-Siècle Vienna: Politics and Culture* by Carl E. Schorske; poetry, *The Morning of the Poem* by James Schuyler; drama, *Crimes of the Heart* by Beth Henley.

Apr. 30 **American Book Awards** were presented for the following: fiction, *Plains Song* by Wright Morris; history, *Christianity, Social Tolerance and Homosexuality* by John Boswell; biography, *Walt Whitman* by Justin Kaplan; general nonfiction, *China Men* by Maxine Hong Kingston; poetry, *The Need to Hold Still* by Lisel Mueller. The National Medal for Literature was

| Business and Industry; Science; Education; Philosophy and Religion **III** | **IV** Sports; Social Issues and Crime; Folkways; Fashion; Holidays |

Feb. 23 Equal **athletic programs** for men and women do not have to be provided by educational institutions receiving federal funds, a federal judge in Detroit ruled. The decision was praised by the NCAA but was termed "disastrous" by proponents of equal funding.

Feb. 23 A major **automobile recall** was announced by General Motors. The company recalled 6,400,000 mid-size autos built between 1978 and 1981 to replace two bolts in the cars' rear suspensions.

Mar. 5 **Teaching evolution** in public schools did not violate the rights of religious fundamentalists, a Superior Court judge ruled in a California case. He said, however, that dogmatic teaching about the origin of life was not to be permitted.

Mar. 12 In a major **industrial merger,** Standard Oil of Ohio (Sohio), 13th largest oil company in the U.S., purchased the Kennecott Corp., the largest U.S. copper producer, for $1,700,000,000.

Apr. 12–14 The **space shuttle** *Columbia,* with Robert L. Crippen and John W. Young aboard, was launched from Cape Canaveral, Fla., on its maiden flight. After a flight of 54 hrs., 20 min., 48 sec., including 36 orbits of Earth, *Columbia* touched down at Edwards Air Force Base, Calif., making the first wheels-down landing by any spacecraft.

June 18 A vaccine produced by **genetic engineering** and effective against hoof and mouth disease was announced. The vaccine was believed to be the first product of gene splicing to provide protection against disease in animals or humans.

July 9 The **herpes simplex virus** had been successfully suppressed by an experimental drug, acyclovir, it was reported in the *New England Journal of Medicine.* Genital herpes, caused by the virus, was identified as the most rapidly spreading sexually transmitted disease in the U.S.

Aug. 3 A nationwide **air traffic controllers' strike** was begun by the 13,000 members of the traffic controllers' union, PATCO. Pres. Reagan announced that the strikers had to return to work by Aug. 5 or face dismissal. Many stayed home and were fired. On Aug. 17 the Federal Aviation Administration began accepting applications for new air controllers. On Oct. 22 the

Mar. 29 The **AIAW basketball championship** was won by Louisiana Tech, defeating Tennessee 79–59.

Mar. 30 The **NCAA basketball championship** was won by Indiana, which defeated North Carolina 63–50.

Apr. 12 The **Masters golf tournament** was won by Tom Watson, who beat Jack Nicklaus by two strokes to take his second Masters championship.

Apr. 20 The 85th **Boston Marathon** was won by Toshihiko Seko of Japan, with a time of 2 hrs., 9 min., 26 sec. The first woman to finish was Allison Roe of New Zealand, with a time of 2 hrs., 26 min., 45 sec., a new course record for women.

May 2 The 107th **Kentucky Derby** was won by Pleasant Colony, with a time of 2:02. The jockey was Jorge Velasquez.

May 5–14 The **NBA basketball championship** was won by the Boston Celtics, who defeated the Houston Rockets four games to two.

May 12–21 The **NHL Stanley Cup** was won by the New York Islanders, who defeated the Minnesota North Stars four games to one.

May 16 The 106th **Preakness Stakes** was won by Pleasant Colony, with a time of 1:54⅗. The jockey was Jorge Velasquez.

May 24 The 65th **Indianapolis 500** auto race ended in controversy. A day after the race, Mario Andretti, who had finished second, was named winner over Bobby Unser because Unser had broken a rule during a slowdown period near the end of the race. On Oct. 8 the U.S. Auto Club (USAC) reversed the decision and gave the victory to Unser, but fined him $40,000 for his infraction. Unser had completed the race in 3 hrs., 35 min., 41.78 sec., with an average speed of 139.085 mph.

June 6 The 113th **Belmont Stakes** was won by Summing, with a time of 2:29, to foil Pleasant Colony's chance at winning the Triple Crown. The jockey was George Martins.

June 12 A **baseball strike,** the first mid-season strike ever, began when players walked out in a controversy over compensation of free agents. An agreement was reached between the players' organization and the owners on July 31, but a third of the season had been lost.

July 7 Sandra Day O'Connor, a judge of the Arizona Court of Appeals, was nominated by Pres. Reagan to become the first woman member of the Supreme Court. She was confirmed by the Senate on Sept. 21 and sworn in on Sept. 25.

July 17 A hotel disaster in Kansas City, Mo., in which two indoor aerial walkways collapsed, killed 111 people and injured 190. About 1500 persons were attending a tea dance when the steel and concrete structures plunged to the floor below.

Aug. 4 Pres. Reagan's **income tax reduction plan** was passed by Congress with only a slight modification. The bill reduced income taxes by 5% (rather than the requested 10%) as of Oct. 1, 10% as of July 1, 1982, and 10% as of July 1, 1983.

Aug. 10 Production of the **neutron bomb** as a warhead for missiles and artillery was authorized by Pres. Reagan. The decision reversed U.S. policy set by Pres. Carter in 1978. The weapons were to be kept in the U.S.

Aug. 19 Two **Libyan jets were shot down** by U.S. Navy fighters about 60 miles from the Libyan coast after the Libyan fighters opened fire on the U.S. jets. Libya claimed control of all of the Gulf of Sidra, where the Navy was holding military exercises. The U.S. maintained that the gulf was an international body of water.

Oct. 8 A ban on **commercial reprocessing of nuclear fuel** was lifted by Pres. Reagan. It had been ordered by Pres. Carter in 1977 as a step to control international manufacture of weapons-grade plutonium.

Nov. 18 A four-point **arms control proposal** was presented by Pres. Reagan in a televised address that was broadcast live in Europe. Reagan stated that the U.S would cancel its plans for deployment of new medium-range Pershing 2 and cruise missiles in Europe if the U.S.S.R. would dismantle comparable missiles it had already deployed against other European nations.

Dec. 4 **Covert domestic intelligence operations** by the CIA and other agencies were authorized for the first time in an executive order issued by Pres. Reagan.

presented to Kenneth Burke.

June 4–14 A **Tchaikovsky Festival** was celebrated by the New York City Ballet. The company presented more than 20 ballets, including several new works. Critics considered the festival the U.S. dance event of the year.

June 6 A nationwide competition to design a **Vietnam War Memorial** for Washington, D.C., was won by Maya Yang Lin, a 21-year-old Yale undergraduate in architecture. The winning design consisted of two long, low granite walls in the form of an open V, on which the names of all the U.S. war dead in the Vietnam War would be inscribed.

June 7 **Tony awards** for the 1980–1981 season were presented for the following: best play, *Amadeus;* best musical, *42nd Street;* best actor in a drama, Ian McKellan for *Amadeus;* best actress in a drama, Jane Lapotaire for *Piaf.*

Aug. 8 The **Washington *Evening Star*** ceased publication after 128 years. Time, Inc., had bought the ailing paper in 1978 and spent $85,000,000 in an unsuccessful attempt to make it profitable. The *Star* had been losing circulation and advertising to the Washington *Post.*

Sept. 10 *Guernica*, Pablo Picasso's celebrated antiwar painting, arrived in Spain after having been at the Museum of Modern Art in New York City since 1939. The 10-by-25-foot painting, done in 1937, was inspired by the bombing of the Basque town of Guernica during the Spanish Civil War. Picasso would not allow it to be seen in Spain until the country was freed from the rule of Francisco Franco.

Sept. 13 **Emmy Awards** were presented for the following: best actor in a dramatic series, Daniel J. Travanti for *Hill Street Blues;* best actress in a dramatic series, Barbara Babcock for *Hill Street Blues;* best dramatic series, *Hill Street Blues;* best limited series, *Shogun;* best actor in a limited series, Anthony Hopkins for *The Bunker;* best actress in a limited series, Vanessa Redgrave for *Playing for Time.*

Sept. 19 The popular group **Simon and Garfunkel** was reunited after 11 years when Paul Simon and Art Garfunkel gave a free concert in Central Park, New York City, attended by some 400,000 fans.

Oct. 4 *The Life and Adventures of Nicholas Nickleby,* an eight-and-one-half-hour, two-part play by David Edgar and Stephen Oliver based on the novel by Charles Dickens, opened at the Winter Garden Theater in New York City.

Nov. 20 *A Soldier's Play* by Charles Fuller, performed by the Negro Ensemble Company, opened at Theater Four in New York City. Its cast included Adolph Caesar and Charles Brown.

Dec. 5 The **AIA Gold Medal** for architecture was

| Business and Industry; Science; Education; Philosophy and Religion **III** | **IV** Sports; Social Issues and Crime; Folkways; Fashion; Holidays |

federal Labor Relations Authority decertified PATCO, removing any possibility of a negotiated settlement with striking air controllers.

Aug. 4 The **largest industrial merger** to date took place when E. I. du Pont de Nemours, the largest chemical company in the U.S., agreed to buy Conoco, the ninth largest oil company, for $7,540,000,000.

Aug. 25 **Voyager 2**, launched in 1977, flew within 63,000 miles of Saturn. Data sent back by the spacecraft showed thousands of rings around the planet, many more than the several hundred previously believed to exist.

Sept. 29 **Scholastic aptitude test scores** of high-school seniors were about the same in 1981 as they had been in 1980, the College Board reported. Thus there appeared to be a leveling off of scores after 18 years of decline.

Oct. 9 The **Nobel Prize in Physiology or Medicine** was awarded jointly to David H. Hubel and Tlosten N. Wiesel of Harvard University for their studies of the way the brain processes visual information; and to Roger W. Sperry of the California Institute of Technology for demonstrating the different functions of the right and left hemispheres of the brain.

Oct. 13 The **Nobel Prize in Economics** was awarded to James Tobin of Yale University for his development of the portfolio selection theory of investment.

Oct. 19 The **Nobel Prize in Chemistry** was awarded jointly to Ronald Hoffman of Cornell University and Kenichi Fukui of Japan for applying theories of quantum mechanics to predict the course of chemical reactions.

Oct. 19 The **Nobel Prize in Physics** was awarded jointly to Nicolaas Bloembergen of Harvard University and Arthur Schawlow of Stanford University for their contribution to the development of laser spectroscopy.

Nov. 14 The **space shuttle** *Columbia* completed its second mission, the second flight ever of a reusable spacecraft. The mission was cut short by the failure of a fuel cell.

June 14 The **LPGA golf tournament** was won by Donna Caponi.

June 21 The **U.S. Open golf tournament** was won by David Graham of Australia, the fifth foreign player to win this title.

July 3–4 At the **Wimbledon** tennis championships in England, John McEnroe won the men's singles title and Chris Evert Lloyd won the women's singles. McEnroe teamed with Peter Fleming to win the men's doubles, and Pam Shriver teamed with Martina Navratilova to win the women's doubles.

Aug. 2 The **Baseball Hall of Fame** inducted three new members: Andrew "Rube" Foster, a pitcher and a founder of the National Negro League; Robert M. "Bob" Gibson, who pitched for the St. Louis Cardinals (NL); and John R. "Johnny" Mize, first baseman and slugger.

Aug. 9 The baseball **All-Star Game** was won for the tenth consecutive time by the National League, defeating the American League 5–4.

Aug. 9 The **PGA golf tournament** was won by Larry Nelson, beating Fuzzy Zoeller by three strokes.

Sept. 9–13 The **U.S. Open Tennis singles championships** were won by John McEnroe in the men's division and Tracy Austin in the women's division.

Sept. 12 The **Miss America** title was won by Elizabeth Ward, 20, of Russellville, Ark., at the annual pageant in Atlantic City, N.J.

Sept. 26 The **North American Soccer League championship** was won by the Chicago Sting, who shut out the New York Cosmos 1–0.

Oct. 20 What came to be called the **Brinks robbery**, a bungled armored-car holdup in Nanuet, N.Y., ended with two policemen and one guard dead and two guards wounded. Four persons were arrested, including three members of the terrorist Weather Underground group.

Oct. 20–28 The **World Series** was won by the Los Angeles Dodgers (NL), defeating the New York Yankees (AL) four games to two. On Oct. 15 the Yankees had won the American League pennant over the Oakland Athletics in a three-game sweep. On Oct. 19 the Dodgers won the National League pennant, defeating the Montreal Expos three games to two.

Dec. 29 Reprisals against the U.S.S.R. for its role in the imposition of martial law in Poland and the outlawing of the Solidarity movement were announced by Pres. Reagan. The measures included a halt on all U.S.-bound flights by the Soviet airline Aeroflot, cessation of sales of equipment that could be used for the Siberian gas pipeline, and stopping of negotiations on a new long-term agreement on grain purchases.

awarded to the Italian-born architect Ronaldo Giurgola.

Dec. 20 *Dreamgirls,* a musical by Tom Eyen and Henry Kreiger, directed by Michael Bennett, opened at the Imperial Theater in New York City. It starred Sheryl Lee Ralph, Jennifer Holliday, and Loretta Devine as an up-and-coming musical group reminiscent of the Supremes.

1982

In January Pres. Ronald Reagan predicted that the recession, which had begun in 1981, would be short and followed by a strong recovery. His prediction proved overly optimistic, but at year's end there were encouraging signs in the economy. In foreign affairs the freeze in U.S.-Soviet relations continued as the U.S.S.R. stepped up its war in Afghanistan. The declaration of martial law in Poland on Dec. 13, 1981, viewed as a response to Soviet pressure, contributed to the broadening in June of a U.S. embargo on goods to the U.S.S.R. The Middle East again became a battleground as Israeli forces advanced into Lebanon in June in response to continued Palestinian attacks on Israel from Lebanon. Attempts by the U.S. to bring peace to the region were complex and generally fruitless, but the president decided to commit U.S. Marines as a peacekeeping force in Beirut, an action that provoked much controversy. Americans mourned the deaths this year of former Supreme Court Justice Abe Fortas, Apr. 5, at 71, and Bess Truman, widow of Pres. Harry S Truman, Oct. 18, at 97.

Jan. 4 **Richard V. Allen** resigned as Pres. Reagan's national security adviser. Allen had been accused of taking $1000 from Japanese journalists to arrange an interview with Nancy Reagan. The Justice Department cleared him of any misconduct. Allen was succeeded by Deputy Sec. of State William P. Clark.

Jan. 9–17 A winter freeze with record low temperatures hit the South, Midwest, and Plains states, causing 261 deaths.

Jan. 13 An Air Florida jet crashed into a bridge over the Potomac R. in Washington, D.C., shortly after taking off from National Airport, killing 78 people, including seven who were on the bridge.

The Broadway season was relatively quiet. Biggest hits of the year were the musicals *Nine* and *Cats.* The cost of Broadway productions continued to climb. Cost of producing a musical approached $5,000,000. Opera companies and orchestras continued to have financial problems. The American Ballet Theater's season was shortened by a two-month lockout of its dancers in the fall. The dancers were finally given large salary increases. The Joffrey Ballet, in a move to gain a wider audience, decided to become a resident company in Los Angeles for part of the year while keeping its New York City season. This year movie theaters grossed $3,449,000,000, up 16% over 1981. The most successful film of the year was *E.T.: The Extraterrestrial,* which captured the hearts of millions. The recession was reflected in a softening of art auction prices, but a Henry Moore sculpture, *Reclining Figure,* brought $1,265,000. The 58-year-old *Saturday Review* suspended publication this year after losing $3,000,000 in the previous two years. Notables who died this year included Stringfellow Barr, educator known for his curriculum based on "100 Great Books," Feb. 2, at 85; Ingrid Bergman, actress, Aug. 29, at 67; John Cheever, writer, June 19, at 70; Frederick Dannay, who with his cousin Manfred B. Lee wrote the popular Ellery Queen mystery stories, Sept. 3, at 76; Babette Deutsch, poet, Nov. 13, at 87; Henry Fonda, actor, Aug. 12, at 77; John Gardner, novelist, Sept. 14, at 49; Melville Bell Grosvenor, president of the National Geographic Society, Apr. 22, at 80; Archibald MacLeish, poet, Apr. 20, at 89; Thelonius Monk, jazz pianist and composer, Feb. 17, at 64; Ayn Rand, novelist and champion of a controversial form of individualism, Mar. 6, at 77; Lee Strasberg, proponent of the method theory of acting, Feb. 17, at 80; King Vidor, pioneer film director, Nov. 1, at 87; and John Hay Whitney, millionaire horse breeder, Feb. 8, at 77.

Among **books published** this year were a number of volumes on the arms race and the threat of nuclear war. Perhaps the best was *The Fate of the Earth* by Jonathan Schell, which caused much discussion and gained a wide readership. Other books published this year included

Business and Industry; Science;
Education; Philosophy and Religion   III

IV   **Sports; Social Issues and Crime;**
Folkways; Fashion; Holidays

Dec. 8 The constitutionality of **religious services in campus buildings** by student organizations at public colleges and universities was upheld by the Supreme Court. Many considered this to be the most significant ruling on the issue of separation of church and state in years.

Oct. 25 The 12th **New York City Marathon** was won by Alberto Salazar, a recent graduate of the University of Oregon, with a time of 2 hrs., 8 min., 13 sec. The first woman to finish was Allison Roe of New Zealand, with a time of 2 hrs., 25 min., 28 sec. Both times were new records for this event.

Dec. 11–13 The **Davis Cup** international tennis competition was won by the U.S., defeating Argentina three matches to one in Cincinnati, Ohio.

1982

The recession that began in the summer of 1981 had run its course by November of this year. In 1982 the rate of inflation dropped to 6% and the Consumer Price Index rose only 3.9% for the year, smallest increase since 1972. The gross national product fell 1.8%, largest decrease since 1946. Unemployment rose to 10.8% by December and averaged 9.7% for the year. Some 4,600,000 people were receiving unemployment compensation by October, the largest number since such payments began in the 1930s. More than 30 banks failed, and high interest rates crippled new housing starts. Yet there were signs that U.S. business was on the rebound. Boeing introduced a new jet, the 767, said to be 35% more fuel efficient than older aircraft. Kodak introduced the disc camera, its most important new product in nearly 20 years. The camera was about the size of a pack of cigarettes. In September IBM introduced its 3084 computer, almost twice as powerful as its predecessor and able to process instructions at the rate of 26,000,000 a second. The largest solar plant yet built, expected to produce 10,000 kilowatts of electricity, was completed in the Mojave Desert. The U.S. Institute of Medicine estimated that of the fatalities caused by the ten leading causes of death, fully 50% could be traced to their victims' styles of living, and that some 320,000 deaths a year were caused by smoking. The spread of genital herpes alarmed the nation. It was estimated that 20,000,000 Americans had the disease, and that 300,000 to 500,000 new cases were occurring every year. In education, there were 520,000 fewer students in all U.S. schools than in the previous school year. The College Board reported that black students on average scored 100 points lower on both verbal and math Scholastic Aptitude Tests than white students. Notables who died this year included William Bernbach, founder in 1939 of the Doyle Dane Bernbach advertising firm, Oct. 2, at 71; John Cardinal Cody, Roman Catholic archbishop of Chicago since 1965 and an outspoken advocate of integration, Apr. 25, at 74; and René Dubos, biologist, environmentalist, and author, Feb. 20, at 81.

This year the NCAA sponsored for the first time a major college basketball championship for women. The Association for Intercollegiate Athletics for Women (AIAW), which had been holding championship games since 1972, held its annual game this year, but it was clearly at the end of its existence and disgruntled at the NCAA takeover after years of lack of interest in women's competition. Major league baseball set an attendance record of 44,500,000. Tom Watson was the outstanding golfer of the year, winning both the British and U.S. Open championships. The top pro golf money winners were Craig Stadler, $446,462, and JoAnne Carner, $320,399. Fashions showed a tendency toward greater elegance. Women's winter styles included ponchos and knickers. Sports fans mourned the passing of Leroy "Satchel" Paige, one of the great pitchers of all time, June 8, at 75; and Walter W. "Red" Smith, Pulitzer Prize-winning sportswriter, Jan. 15, at 76.

Jan. 1 In **college football bowl games,** the results were Texas 14, Alabama 12 in the Cotton Bowl; Clemson 22, Nebraska 15 in the Orange Bowl; Washington 28, Iowa 0 in the Rose Bowl; and Pittsburgh 24, Georgia 20 in the Sugar Bowl. This season the AP and UPI polls picked Clemson the national collegiate champions of 1981.

Jan. 24 **Super Bowl XVI** was won by the San Francisco 49ers (NFC), defeating the Cincinnati Bengals (AFC) 26–21. On Jan. 10 the 49ers had beaten the Dallas Cowboys 28–27 for the NFC title, and Cincinnati had beaten the San Diego Chargers 27–7 for the AFC championship.

Jan. 28–31 **U.S. figure skating championships** were won in Indianapolis, Ind., by Scott Hamilton, men's singles; Rosalynn Sumners, women's singles; Kitty and Peter Carruthers, pairs; and Judy Blumberg and Michael Seibert, dance.

Mar. 11–13 At the **world figure skating championships** in Copenhagen, Denmark, Scott Hamilton won the men's singles title and Elaine Zayak won the women's singles title.

Jan. 26 In his **State of the Union** message Pres. Reagan proposed transfer to the states of many social programs, including the welfare system and the food stamp program. He called such changes a "new federalism."

Feb. 6 Pres. Reagan's **proposed budget** for fiscal 1982 of $757,600,000,000 included a projected deficit of $91,500,000,000. Reagan called for deep cuts in domestic spending but asked for an 18% increase in the defense budget.

Mar. 10 Economic **sanctions against Libya** were announced by the Reagan administration in response to Libya's involvement with international terrorist organizations. The sanctions included an embargo on Libyan oil shipments to the U.S. and a ban on export of high-technology products to Libya.

June 18 Exports to the **U.S.S.R.** of equipment to be used to build or operate the Siberian gas pipeline were banned. The ban also applied to the sale of such equipment produced by foreign subsidiaries or licensees of U.S. corporations. The move was protested four days later by the European Economic Community, but the ban was not lifted until Nov. 13.

June 21 John W. Hinckley, Jr., was found not guilty by reason of insanity in the Mar. 30, 1981, shooting of Pres. Reagan and three others. The verdict caused widespread shock and demands for revision of laws governing insanity pleas.

June 24 In a ruling on **presidential liability**, the Supreme Court ruled that a president could not be sued for damages for actions he took while in office. The decision was made in ruling on a suit brought against former president Richard M. Nixon by a government employee.

June 25 Alexander M. Haig, Jr., resigned as secretary of state following disagreements with Pres. Reagan and some of his advisers. George P. Shultz, a former Cabinet member and a businessman, was appointed to succeed Haig. Shultz was confirmed on July 15 and sworn in the next day.

June 30 The **Equal Rights Amendment** failed to achieve ratification despite an extension granted by Congress in 1978. At that time 35 of the required 38

The Dean's December by Saul Bellow, a novel; *Oh, What a Paradise It Seems* by John Cheever, the author's last novel; *God's Grace* by Bernard Malamud, a novel; and *The Mosquito Coast* by Paul Theroux, the story of a modern, unsuccessful Swiss Family Robinson. This year the Library of America, embarking on a program to issue uniform, quality editions of works of major U.S. authors, issued volumes of the works of Nathaniel Hawthorne, Herman Melville, Harriet Beecher Stowe, and Mark Twain.

Jan. 28 The **National Book Critics Circle Awards** were awarded for the following: fiction, *Rabbit Is Rich* by John Updike; general nonfiction, *The Mismeasure of Man* by Stephen Jay Gould; poetry, *A Coast of Trees* by A. R. Ammons; criticism, *A Virgil Thomson Reader* by Virgil Thomson.

Feb. 24 **Grammy Awards** were presented for the following: best album of 1981, *Double Fantasy* by John Lennon and Yoko Ono; best record, "Bette Davis Eyes" by Kim Carnes; best male pop vocalist, Al Jarreau for *Breaking Away;* best female pop vocalist, Lena Horne for *Lena Horne: The Lady and Her Music;* best pop group, Manhattan Transfer for "Boy From New York City."

Mar. 1 The **J. Paul Getty Museum of Art** in Malibu, Calif., became the wealthiest museum in the U.S., and probably in the world, when it received some $1,100,000,000 from the estate of the oil magnate J. Paul Getty.

Mar. 4 The **Metropolitan Museum of Art** in New York City was given a collection of prints valued at $60,000,000, the gift of Belle Linsky. She and her late husband Jack had spent 40 years putting the collection together.

Mar. 12 **Pulitzer prizes** were awarded for the following: fiction, *Rabbit Is Rich* by John Updike; biography, *Grant, A Biography* by William S. McFeeley; history, *Mary Chestnut's Civil War* by C. Vann Woodward; general nonfiction, *The Soul of a New Machine* by Tracy Kidder; poetry, *The Collected Poems* of Sylvia Plath; drama, *A Soldier's Play* by Charles Fuller.

Mar. 29 **Academy Awards** were presented to *Chariots of Fire* as the outstanding motion picture of 1981; Henry Fonda and Katharine Hepburn as best actor and actress for *On Golden Pond;* John Gielgud as best supporting actor for *Arthur;* and Maureen Stapleton as best supporting actress for *Reds.*

Apr. 27 **American Book Awards** were given for the following: fiction, *Rabbit Is Rich* by John Updike; biography, *Mornings on Horseback* by David McCullough; history, *People of the Sacred Mountain* by Peter John Powell; general nonfiction, *The Soul of a New Machine* by Tracy Kidder; poetry, *Life Supports* by William Bronk. The National Medal for Literature

Jan. 5   An Arkansas law requiring the teaching of **creation science,** a theory of creation based on the Bible, in schools in which the theory of evolution was taught was struck down by a federal judge in Arkansas. The court ruled that the teaching of creation science violated the constitutional requirement of separation of church and state.

Jan. 8   The **American Telephone and Telegraph Company** agreed to divest itself of its 22 Bell Telephone operating systems. The agreement ended an eight-year antitrust suit by the Justice Department that charged AT&T with monopolizing U.S. telephone service.

Feb. 26   Widespread **use of marijuana** in the U.S. "justifies serious national concern," the National Academy of Sciences contended in reporting the results of the most comprehensive study yet of the effects of marijuana smoking.

Mar. 11   The second-largest **merger** in U.S. history occurred when Marathon Oil Company agreed to merge with United States Steel Corporation, in a $6,-000,000,000 deal. Mobil Oil had been unsuccessful in its attempt to acquire Marathon Oil.

May 13   **Braniff International Corporation,** operator of the nation's eighth-largest airline, filed for bankruptcy. Braniff was the first major U.S. airline to go bankrupt.

June 15   **Tuition-free public school education** is the right of children of illegal aliens, the Supreme Court ruled, striking down a Texas law.

June 29   A major **Protestant church merger** brought together the United Presbyterian Church and the Presbyterian Church in the United States. The new church would have 3,000,000 members.

July 5   The **Penn Square Bank** in Oklahoma City, Okla., was closed by federal regulators. The bank had suffered heavy losses through loans to depressed energy-based businesses in the Southwest. Some of the bank's $2,000,000,000 in loans had been bought by other banks, causing tremors throughout the banking industry.

July 16   The Rev. **Sun Myung Moon,** leader of the controversial Unification Church, was sentenced to 18 months in prison and fined $25,000 after being convicted of tax fraud and conspiracy to obstruct justice.

Mar. 28   The **NCAA women's basketball championship** was won by Louisiana Tech, which defeated Cheyney State 76–62.

Mar. 29   The **NCAA men's basketball championship** was won by North Carolina, which defeated Georgetown 63–62.

Apr. 11   The **Masters golf tournament** was won by Craig Stadler, who defeated Dan Pohl in a sudden-death playoff.

Apr. 19   The 86th **Boston Marathon** was won by Alberto Salazar of Eugene, Oreg., with a new record time of 2 hrs., 8 min., 51 sec. The first woman to finish was Charlotte Teske of West Germany, with a time of 2 hrs., 29 min., 33 sec.

May 1   The 108th **Kentucky Derby** was won by Gato del Sol, with a time of 2:02²/₅. The jockey was Eddie Delahoussaye.

May 8–16   The **NHL Stanley Cup** was won by the New York Islanders, who swept the Vancouver Canucks in four straight games.

May 15   The 107th **Preakness Stakes** was won by Aloma's Ruler, with a time of 1:55²/₅. The jockey was Jack Kaenel.

May 27–June 8   The **NBA basketball championship** was won by the Los Angeles Lakers, who defeated the Philadelphia 76ers four games to two.

May 30   The 66th **Indianapolis 500** auto race was won by Gordon Johncock, completing the 500-mile course in 3 hrs., 5 min., 9.33 sec., with an average speed of 162.026 mph.

June 5   The 114th **Belmont Stakes** was won by Conquistador Cielo, with a time of 2:28¹/₅. The jockey was Laffit Pincay, Jr.

June 13   The **LPGA golf tournament** was won by Jan Stephenson of Australia.

June 20   The **U.S. Open golf tournament** was won by Tom Watson, who beat Jack Nicklaus by two strokes.

July 3–4   At the **Wimbledon** tennis championships in England, Jimmy Connors won the men's singles title and Martina Navratilova won the women's singles. Navratilova teamed with Pam Shriver to win the women's doubles, and Anne Smith teamed with Kevin Curran of South Africa to win the mixed doubles.

July 13   The **baseball All-Star Game** was won for the 11th consecutive time by the National League, beating the American League 4–1.

July 25   The **U.S. Women's Open golf tournament** was won by Janet Alex.

Aug. 1   The **Baseball Hall of Fame** inducted Henry Louis "Hank" Aaron, who played for the Milwaukee (and later Atlanta) Braves (NL) for 20 years; A. B. "Happy" Chandler, former commissioner of baseball; Travis C. "Stonewall" Jackson, former shortstop for the New York Giants (NL); and Frank Robinson,

1982 *PRES.* RONALD REAGAN   760

| Exploration and Settlement; Wars; Government; Civil Rights; Statistics | I | | II | Publishing; Arts and Music; Popular Entertainment; Architecture; Theater |

states had ratified, but no others had done so in the intervening years.

July 9 A Pan American jet crashed after takeoff in New Orleans, La., killing 154 people. It was the second worst single-plane disaster in U.S. history.

Aug. 19 Congress passed a bill authorizing a tax increase of $93,800,000,000

Aug. 20 About 800 U.S. Marines landed in Beirut, Lebanon, as part of a multinational force to oversee withdrawal of PLO fighters from the city. The Marines were withdrawn on Sept. 10, but they returned to Beirut on Sept. 29 following massacres of Palestinians in the Sabra and Shattila refugee camps by so-called Christian militiamen (Sept. 16–18) and a Lebanese request (Sept. 20) for assistance. On Sept. 30 one Marine was killed and three others wounded while attempting to defuse a bomb.

Sept. 29–Oct. 1 Cyanide placed in Tylenol capsules caused the deaths of seven persons in the Chicago area. By Oct. 6 a nationwide alert was sounded. Suspicious deaths in other parts of the country were reported but none appeared to be related to the Chicago murders. The makers of Tylenol, a pain reliever, recalled 264,000 bottles of the drug. The killer was never found.

Nov. 2 In congressional elections the Republicans kept their 54–46 Senate majority, but the Democrats picked up 26 House seats for a 269–166 majority.

Nov. 22 Construction of the MX missile was proposed by Pres. Reagan, who called for deployment of 100 of the multiple-warhead missiles in "dense pack mode," a relatively small area thought to be easier to defend against an enemy's first strike. The cost of the proposal was put at $26,000,000,000.

Dec. 2–9 Storms and floods struck the Midwest, particularly Illinois, Arkansas, and Missouri, killing 22 and forcing evacuation of 35,000. Damage was estimated at $600,000,000.

was awarded to John Cheever.

May 2 *Medea,* a revival adapted from Euripides starring Zoe Caldwell and Judith Anderson, opened at the Cort Theater in New York City.

May 9 *Nine,* a musical by Arthur Kopit and Maury Yeston based on Federico Fellini's *8,* opened at the 46th Street Theater in New York City. Its cast included Raul Julia, Karen Akers, and Anita Morris.

May 29 *Little Shop of Horrors,* a musical by Howard Ashman and Alan Menken based on the film by Roger Corman, opened at the WPA Theater in New York City.

June 6 Tony awards for the 1981–1982 season were presented for the following: best play, *The Life and Adventures of Nicholas Nickleby;* best musical, *Nine;* best actor in a drama, Roger Rees for *The Life and Adventures of Nicholas Nickleby;* best actress in a drama, Zoe Caldwell for *Medea.*

June 26 *Torch Song Trilogy,* a play by Harvey Fierstein, opened at the Little Theater in New York City after a successful run off Broadway.

July 10 A painting by Samuel F. B. Morse, *The Gallery of the Louvre,* brought $3,250,000 in a private sale, the most ever paid for an American work of art to date. The painting had been owned since 1884 by Syracuse University.

Sept. 15 *Today,* a new national newspaper produced by the Gannett newspaper group, began publication. It was first distributed in the Baltimore–Washington, D.C., area and was characterized by short articles touching only on highlights of the news and the heavy use of color. National distribution was planned.

Sept. 19 Emmy Awards were presented for the following: best actor in a limited series or special, Mickey Rooney for *Bill;* best actress in a limited series or special, Ingrid Bergman for *A Woman Named Golda;* best actor in a dramatic series, Daniel J. Travanti for *Hill Street Blues;* best actress in a dramatic series, Michael Learned for *Nurse;* best dramatic series, *Hill Street Blues.*

Oct. 7 *Cats,* a musical by Andrew Webber based on *Old Possum's Book of Practical Cats* by T. S. Eliot, opened at the Winter Garden in New York City.

Dec. 2 The AIA Gold Medal for architecture was awarded to Nathaniel Alexander Owings, a founding partner of Skidmore, Owings and Merrill. His firm designed the Air Force Academy in Colorado Springs, Colo.

| Business and Industry; Science; Education; Philosophy and Religion | III | IV | Sports; Social Issues and Crime; Folkways; Fashion; Holidays |

Sept. 8 Agreement on a Lutheran church **merger of three Lutheran denominations** was announced. The American Lutheran Church, the Association of Evangelist Lutheran Churches, and the Lutheran Church in America voted to form a single denomination, which would have 5,500,000 members.

Oct. 15 A new **weekly stock trading record** was set by the New York Stock Exchange, 592,460,000 shares. On Oct. 7 the NYSE had reached a new one-day high of 147,070,000 shares.

Oct. 16 The first sighting of **Halley's Comet,** due to pass near Earth in 1985, was reported by astronomers manning a telescope on Mt. Palomar, Calif. It was about 1,000,000,000 miles from Earth.

Oct. 18 The **Nobel Prize in Physics** was awarded to Kenneth G. Wilson of Cornell University for development of a mathematical system explaining changes in the behavior of matter at critical points of pressure and temperature.

Oct. 20 The **Nobel Prize in Economics** was awarded to George Stigler of the University of Chicago for his study of government regulation and its effect on the economy.

Nov. 11–16 The **first operational space shuttle flight** was completed by the shuttle *Columbia,* which successfully carried two satellites into orbit.

Dec. 2 The first successful **artificial heart transplant** was completed at the University of Utah Medical Center. The recipient was Barney C. Clark, 61, who had been near death at the time of the operation.

Dec. 23 A bill increasing the **federal fuel tax** on gasoline and diesel fuel by five cents a gallon was passed by Congress. The increased revenues, estimated at $5,500,000,000 a year, were to be used to repair roads, bridges, and mass transit systems.

Dec. 27 The **Dow Jones average** of industrial stocks closed at a record high of 1070.55.

former outfielder and batting great.

Aug. 8 The **PGA golf tournament** was won by Raymond Floyd, who posted a record opening round score of 63.

Sept. 11 The **Miss America** title was won by Debra Sue Maffett, 25, from Anaheim, Calif., at the annual pageant in Atlantic City, Calif.

Sept. 11–12 The **U.S. Open tennis singles championships** were won by Jimmy Connors in the men's division and by Chris Evert Lloyd in the women's division.

Sept. 19 The **North American Soccer League championship** was won by the New York Cosmos, who defeated the Seattle Sounders 1–0.

Sept. 21 The first regular season **pro football strike** began when the NFL players' association and the team owners failed to agree on a basic contract. It continued until Nov. 16 and became the costliest strike in sports to date. Half the season's games were canceled and the season was cut to nine games for each team.

Oct. 12–20 The **World Series** was won by the St. Louis Cardinals (NL), defeating the Milwaukee Brewers four games to three. On Oct. 10 the Cardinals had won the National League pennant over the Atlanta Braves in three straight games. The same day the Brewers won the American League pennant over the California Angels, three games to two. The Brewers became the first team to win a playoff after losing the first two games.

Oct. 24 The 13th **New York City Marathon** was won by Alberto Salazar of Eugene, Oreg., with a time of 2 hrs., 19 min., 13 sec. The first woman to finish was Grete Waitz of Norway, with a time of 2 hrs., 27 min., 14 sec.

Nov. 1 The contract of **Bowie Kuhn,** commissioner of baseball, would not be renewed, the owners of the 26 major league teams announced. Kuhn, a controversial figure, was in the final year of his second seven-year term.

Nov. 26–28 The **Davis Cup** international tennis championship was won in Grenoble, France, by the U.S., defeating France four matches to one.

Dec. 10 The **WBA heavyweight boxing championship** was won by Michael Dokes, who knocked out Mike Weaver in the first round of a bout at Las Vegas, Nev.

Dec. 12 The **largest cash robbery** in U.S. history occurred when thieves in New York City made off with $9,800,000 from an armored truck company.

1983

Pres. Ronald Reagan's administration faced a difficult year in foreign relations. In Lebanon the U.S. was unsuccessful in its attempt to secure withdrawal of Syrian and Israeli forces and to aid the Lebanese government in its struggle to assert authority over the many political and religious factions fighting in Beirut. Disaster struck the U.S. peacemaking effort in April when the U.S. embassy in Beirut was bombed. The crushing blow came in October when terrorists blew up U.S. Marine headquarters in Beirut. In Central America the U.S. sent military aid to the government of El Salvador in its long and bloody civil war. Pres. Reagan described the Salvadoran insurgents as terrorists. Meanwhile the U.S. sent aid to the anti-Sandinista, anticommunist "freedom fighters" in Nicaragua. Politicians and private citizens alike called for a consistent foreign policy for both the Middle East and Central America and voiced concern that U.S. policies would eventually involve the country in a war. In October U.S. forces were committed in an invasion of the island of Grenada, ostensibly to protect U.S. citizens there after a coup by Marxist radicals. In domestic affairs, the Census Bureau reported that the number of Americans living in poverty grew from 34,400,000 in 1982 to 35,300,000 in 1983, boosting the poverty rate to its highest level in 18 years. Even the weather was dismal in 1983. Heat, cold, and storms killed some 700 people, nearly twice the 1982 total, and caused an estimated $27,000,000,000 in damage. Among the notables who died this year were Benjamin V. Cohen, who wrote much of the precedent-setting legislation of the New Deal of the early 1930s, Aug. 15, at 88; Gen. Alfred M. Gruenther, a principal aide to Gen. Dwight D. Eisenhower in World War II and NATO commander from 1953 to 1956, May 30, at 84; and Sen. Henry M. "Scoop" Jackson, Democrat of Washington, who had served in Congress for nearly 43 years, Sept. 1, at 71.

Jan. 12 **Eugene Rostow was dismissed** by Pres. Reagan as director of the Arms Control and Disarmament Agency because of policy differences with the Reagan administration. Kenneth Adelman, deputy U.S. representative at the UN, was appointed to succeed Rostow.

Jan. 15 Changes in the **Social Security system** were recommended by the National Commission on Social Security Reform. The changes, calculated to produce $168,700,000,000 by 1989 and make the system solvent, included tax increases, a reduction in the growth rate of benefits, and an eventual raising of the retirement age. A bill incorporating these modifications was passed by Congress on Mar. 25 and signed by Pres. Reagan on Apr. 20.

Feb. 22 Discovery of large amounts of **dioxin,** a carcinogenic chemical, in the soil around Times

Americans all over the country this year celebrated the 100th anniversaries of New York City's Metropolitan Opera and the Brooklyn Bridge. The celebrations at the Brooklyn Bridge on May 24, witnessed by an estimated 2,100,000 persons, were climaxed by a spectacular fireworks display staged by the master pyrotechnicians, the Grucci family. The year's major art exhibitions included *The Vatican Collections: The Papacy and Art,* which was seen in New York City, Chicago, and San Francisco; and a comprehensive exhibit of the works of Grant Wood, which was organized by the Minneapolis Institute of Art. A collection of 16 French impressionist works collected by Mr. and Mrs. H. O. Havemayer sold at auction for $16,800,000. Mark Rothko's *Black, Maroon, and White* sold for $1,815,000 and Willem de Kooning's *Two Women* fetched $1,200,000. Movie theaters had record attendance for the third consecutive year, with revenues of nearly $3,700,000,000. The two most popular films were *The Return of the Jedi,* the third completed film in George Lucas's projected nine-film *Star Wars* series; and *Never Say Never Again,* featuring Sean Connery as the super agent James Bond. Television offered two highly successful miniseries, *The Thorn Birds* and *The Winds of War,* both based on best-selling novels. The number of cable television subscribers reached 25,000,000. This year some 4,100,000 videocassette recorders were sold, auguring a strong new electronics market and promising a fundamental change in TV viewing habits. Sales of rock videos, records, and tapes were all up, but the craze for arcade video games came to a sudden halt in 1983. Rupert Murdoch, the Australian newspaper magnate, made headlines of his own by buying the Chicago *Sun-Times* for $90,000,000. Notables who died this year included George Balanchine, choreographer, Apr. 30, at 79; Eubie Blake, ragtime composer and pianist, Feb. 12, at 100; John Cowles, Sr., head of the Cowles publishing empire, Feb. 25, at 84; George Cukor, a leading film director for over 50 years, Jan. 24, at 83; Lynn Fontanne, who with her late husband Alfred Lunt starred in numerous Broadway plays, July 30, at 95; Ira Gershwin, celebrated lyricist, Aug. 17, at 86; Earl "Fatha" Hines, father of modern jazz piano, Apr. 22, at 77; Harry James, trumpeter and band leader, July 6, at 67; Raymond Massey, Canadian-born actor, July 29, at 86; José Luis Sert, architect, Mar. 15, at 80; Norma Shearer, actress, June 12, at 80; Gloria Swanson, film star, Apr. 4, at 84; and Tennessee Williams, playwright, Feb. 25, at 71.

Among **books published** this year was *Ironweed* by William Kennedy, a novel showing the seamier side of the author's hometown, Albany, N.Y. Kennedy had great difficulty securing publication for his book, but its

1983

The economy showed strong signs of improvement this year. Consumer prices rose only 3.8%, slightly less than in 1982, and personal income was up 6.3%, slightly more than in 1982. Orders for manufactured goods rose 10.6%, the largest increase in four years. Automobile production increased 10.2%, and major appliance production was up 21.3%. The greatest increase of all was in new home construction, which jumped 60% over 1982. The country's top executives did spectacularly well. Forty-six captains of industry had cash compensation of more than $1,000,000, and the leader in total compensation took home $13,229,000. The New York Stock Exchange set a new record of 21,589,000,000 shares traded in 1982, and the Dow Jones industrial average closed the year at 1258.64, about 200 points ahead of the 1982 closing mark. The nation's airlines continued to have problems, however, and the foreign trade deficit hit a record for the year of $60,600,000,000. The worst drought since 1936 devastated the South and Midwest, wiping out crops and raising food prices. Elementary school enrollment was down for the eighth year in a row, but gifts to institutions of higher education were up 6.2% to a record $5,100,000,000. Hospital costs rose 10.7%. At the end of August the administration announced a new schedule of Medicare fees for hospital and medical costs in a move to slow the increase in medical bills. This year the number of persons killed in auto accidents dropped to 43,028, the lowest figure in 20 years, in part because of increased use of safety belts and a growing campaign against drunk driving. Notables who died this year included Terence Cardinal Cooke, Roman Catholic archbishop of New York and vicar of the U.S. armed forces, Oct. 6, at 62; R. Buckminster Fuller, architect and inventor of the geodesic dome, July 3, at 87; Herman Kahn, futurist and nuclear stragetist, July 7, at 71; and Humberto Cardinal Madeiros, Roman Catholic archbishop of Boston since 1973 and a noted conservative, Sept. 17, at 67.

Feb. 2 Bishop **Joseph L. Bernardin,** archbishop of Chicago, was among 18 new cardinals invested by Pope John Paul II.

Feb. 14 In the fourth largest **bank failure** in the U.S. in 50 years, the United American Bank of Knoxville, Tenn., was declared insolvent and closed its doors. The bank had deposits of $760,000,000.

Mar. 23 **Barney Clark,** 62, the first recipient of a permanent artificial heart, died 112 days after receiving the device.

Baseball was the top spectator sport in 1983, drawing 78,051,343 fans and dropping horse racing, with 75,784,430 fans, to second place. In golf the year's top money winners were Hal Sutton, $426,668, and JoAnne Carner, $291,404. In fashion the key words were clean lines and classic shapes. Black was the favorite color, but winter brought a craze for brightly colored leg warmers. This year's top craze, however, was the Cabbage Patch doll, a soft cloth doll made by hand, so no two were exactly alike. The supply was nowhere near the demand, and by Christmas many a parent could not find one for sale at any price. Price was no object for some furniture buyers this year. A Rhode Island Chippendale dining table brought $687,000 at auction in 1983, a new record for American furniture. Notables who died this year included Paul "Bear" Bryant of the University of Alabama, the winningest football coach in history, Jan. 26, at 69; Jack Dempsey, world heavyweight boxing champion from 1919 to 1926, May 31, at 86; George Halas, longtime coach of the Chicago Bears, Oct. 31, at 88; and Meyer Lansky, reputed to have been for 40 years the top boss of organized crime, Jan. 15, at 80.

Jan. 1 In **college football bowl games,** the results were SMU 7, Pittsburgh 3 in the Cotton Bowl; Nebraska 21, Louisiana State 17 in the Orange Bowl; UCLA 24, Michigan 14 in the Rose Bowl; and Penn State 27, Georgia 23 in the Sugar Bowl. This season the AP and UPI polls picked Penn State the national collegiate champions of 1982.

Jan. 30 **Super Bowl XVII** was won by the Washington Redskins (NFC), defeating the Miami Dolphins (AFC) 27–17. On Jan. 22 the Redskins had beaten the Dallas Cowboys 31–17 for the NFC championship and the Dolphins had shut out the New York Jets 14–0 for the AFC title.

Feb. 3–4 **U.S. figure skating championships** were won in Pittsburgh, Pa., by Scott Hamilton, men's singles; Rosalynn Sumners, women's singles; Kitty and Peter Carruthers, pairs; Judy Blumberg and Michael Seibert, dance.

Mar. 6 The new **United States Football League** (USFL) began its first season, with five games nationwide. The new league had 12 teams and was scheduled to play an 18-game spring schedule.

Mar. 10–11 At the **world figure skating championships** in Helsinki, Finland, Scott Hamilton won the men's singles title and Rosalynn Sumners won the women's singles title.

Apr. 2 The **NCAA women's basketball championship**

Beach, Mo., led the federal government to offer to buy any homes or businesses there if the owners wished to move. The money would come from a $1,-600,000,000 cleanup fund established in 1980.

Apr. 11 A presidential panel reviewing the **MX missile** recommended that 100 of the ICBMs be installed in existing missile silos in Wyoming and Nebraska. The panel also recommended development of a smaller, single-warheaded missile, dubbed Midgetman.

Apr. 12 The **first black mayor of Chicago,** Harold Washington, a Democratic congressman, was elected to office by a narrow margin.

Apr. 18 The **U.S. embassy in Beirut,** Lebanon, was almost totally destroyed by a car-bomb explosion that killed 63 people, including 17 Americans. Pro-Iranian terrorists were blamed but the perpetrators were not found.

Apr. 20 **Construction of nuclear power plants** could be barred by states for economic reasons, the Supreme Court ruled. The decision upheld a 1976 California law placing a moratorium on such building.

May 24 **MX missile** research and development funds, totaling $625,000,000, were authorized by Congress. Some Democrats supported Republicans on the measure after Pres. Reagan promised to be more flexible in arms control negotiations.

June 15 In a ruling on **legal abortions** involving five different cases, the Supreme Court curbed the power of state and local governments to limit access to such operations. The decision reaffirmed the 1973 ruling giving women unrestricted rights to abortions during the first three months of pregnancy.

June 23 The so-called **legislative veto,** by which Congress overruled actions of federal agencies, was ruled unconstitutional by the Supreme Court as an invasion of executive authority by the legislative branch.

June 28 A proposed **abortion amendment,** allowing legislation to curb or ban abortions, was rejected by the Senate. The vote was 50–49 in favor, but a two-thirds majority was required.

July 28 **Soviet grain purchases** were increased by at least 50% as a result of a new five-year agreement. The U.S.S.R. was to buy a minimum of 9,000,000 metric tons a year, up from 6,000,000, and could purchase as much as 12,000,000 tons.

Aug. 27 A **march on Washington,** D.C., commemorating the famous 1963 civil rights march led by the Rev. Martin Luther King, Jr., brought some 250,000 persons to the nation's capital.

Sept. 5 **Sanctions against the U.S.S.R.,** in response to the Sept. 1 downing of a South Korean airliner by a Soviet fighter, were announced by Pres. Reagan. The largely token measures included suspension of negotiations for a U.S. consulate in Kiev. The airliner had

release to enthusiastic reviews was accompanied by the reissue of two of Kennedy's earlier books, *Legs* (1975) and *Billy Phelan's Greatest Game* (1978). *Ironweed* went on to win the Pulitzer Prize. Other books published this year included *During the Reign of the Queen of Sheba* by Joan Chase, a novel; *Ancient Evenings* by Norman Mailer, a novel of ancient Egypt that received mixed reviews; *The Cannibal Galaxy* by Cynthia Ozick, a novel; *In Search of Excellence* by Thomas J. Peters and Robert H. Waterman, Jr., a best-selling study of what the authors considered to be the best-run companies in the U.S.; and *The Anatomy Lesson* by Philip Roth, a novel.

Jan. 27 The **National Book Critics Circle Awards** were voted for the following: fiction, *George Mills* by Stanley Elkin; general nonfiction, *The Path to Power: Vol. I: The Years of Lyndon Johnson* by Robert A. Caro; poetry, *Antarctic Traveller* by Katha Pollitt; criticism, *The Second American Revolution and Other Essays, 1976–1982* by Gore Vidal.

Feb. 23 **Grammy Awards** were presented for the following: best album of 1982, *Toto IV* by Toto; best record, "Rosanna" by Toto; best male pop vocalist, Lionel Ritchie for "Truly"; best female pop vocalist, Melissa Manchester for "You Should Hear How She Talks About You"; best pop group, Joe Cocker and Jennifer Warnes for "Up Where We Belong."

Mar. 2 The **final episode of** *M*A*S*H,* a long-running series on U.S. medics in the Korean War, was seen by the largest television audience to date for a nonsports program, 125,000,000 viewers.

Mar. 27 *Brighton Beach Memoirs* by Neil Simon, based on the playwright's own experiences in 1937, opened at the Alvin Theater in New York City.

Apr. 11 **Academy Awards** were presented to *Gandhi* as outstanding motion picture of 1982 and to its star, Ben Kingsley, as best actor; to Meryl Streep as best actress for *Sophie's Choice;* to Louis Gossett, Jr., as best supporting actor for *An Officer and a Gentleman;* and to Jessica Lange as best supporting actress for *Tootsie.*

Apr. 18 **Pulitzer prizes** were awarded for the following: fiction, *The Color Purple* by Alice Walker; biography, *Growing Up* by Russell Baker; history, *The Transformation of Virginia, 1740–1790* by Rhys L. Isaac; general nonfiction, *Is There No Place on Earth for Me?* by Susan Sheehan; poetry, *Selected Poems* by Galway Kinnell; drama, *'Night, Mother* by Marsha Norman.

Business and Industry; Science; Education; Philosophy and Religion **III**		**IV** Sports; Social Issues and Crime; Folkways; Fashion; Holidays

Mar. 30 The first **California condor chick** born in captivity was hatched at the San Diego Zoo. A second one was hatched on Apr. 5.

Apr. 4–9 The **space shuttle** *Challenger,* the second U.S. space shuttle, made its maiden voyage into orbit with astronauts Paul Weitz, Donald Peterson, Karol Bobko, and Story Musgrave aboard.

Apr. 26 The **quality of American education** is so poor that it "threatens our very future as a nation and a people," a federal report announced. It decried what it called a "rising tide of mediocrity," which was reflected in high school test scores that were lower than those of 1957. It calculated that some 23,000,000 Americans were functionally illiterate.

May 3 The nuclear **arms race was condemned** in a pastoral letter issued by the Roman Catholic bishops of the U.S.

May 24 **Tax exemptions** for private schools that practice racial discrimination can be denied by the Internal Revenue Service, the Supreme Court ruled.

June 18–24 **Sally K. Ride** became the first U.S. woman astronaut in space as a member of the crew of the space shuttle *Challenger* in its second flight.

June 25 The **Washington Public Power Supply System** defaulted on debts of $2,250,000,000, becoming the largest governmental unit to fail in U.S. history. Of the five nuclear power plants it set out to build in Washington State, only one was ever completed.

Aug. 9 The first direct evidence supporting the existence of **stellar systems** was reported by the Jet Propulsion Laboratory in Pasadena, Calif. An orbiting satellite had detected solid objects orbiting the star Vega. This was the first time that solid objects of any size had been identified in orbit around a star other than the sun.

Aug. 21 **Computer break-ins** of some 60 computers nationwide were accomplished by a band of Milwaukee youths, ages 17 to 22. Among the computers they gained access to were those at Memorial Sloan Kettering Cancer Center in New York City and the Los

was won by Southern California, which defeated Louisiana Tech 69–67.

Apr. 4 The **NCAA men's basketball championship** was won by North Carolina State, defeating the University of Houston 54–52.

Apr. 11 The **Masters golf tournament** was won by Severiano "Seve" Ballesteros of Spain, beating Tom Kite and Ben Crenshaw by four strokes.

Apr. 18 The 87th **Boston Marathon** was won by Greg Meyer of Wellesley, Mass., with a time of 2 hrs., 9 min. The first woman to finish was Joan Benoit of Boston, with a women's record time of 2 hrs., 22 min., 42 sec.

May 7 The 109th **Kentucky Derby** was won by Sunny's Halo, with a time of 2:02^1/$_5$. The jockey was Eddie Delahoussaye.

May 10–17 The **NHL Stanley Cup** was won by the New York Islanders, who defeated the Edmonton Oilers in four straight games.

May 21 The 108th **Preakness Stakes** was won by Deputed Testamony, with a time of 1:55^2/$_5$. The jockey was Donald Miller.

May 22–31 The **NBA basketball championship** was won by the Philadelphia 76ers, who swept the Los Angeles Lakers in four straight games.

May 29 The 67th **Indianapolis 500** was won by Tom Sneva, in 3 hrs., 5 min., 3.066 sec., with an average speed of 162.117 mph.

June 11 The 115th **Belmont Stakes** was won by Caveat, with a time of 2:27^4/$_5$. The jockey was Laffit Pincay Jr.

June 12 The **LPGA golf tournament** was won by Patty Sheehan, beating Sandra Haynie by two strokes.

June 20 The **U.S. Open golf tournament** was won by Larry Nelson, who beat Tom Watson by one stroke.

July 2–3 At the **Wimbledon** tennis championships in England, John McEnroe won the men's singles title and Martina Navratilova won the women's singles. McEnroe teamed with Peter Fleming to win the men's doubles, and Navratilova teamed with Pam Shriver to win the women's doubles.

July 6 The **baseball All-Star Game** was won by the American League, stampeding the National League 13–3 for its first all-star win since 1971. Fred Lynn of the California Angels hit the first grand slam home run in the 50-year history of the All-Star Game.

July 17 The first **USFL championship** was won by the Michigan Panthers, defeating the Philadelphia Stars 24–22.

been shot down after violating Soviet airspace, killing all 269 people aboard.

Sept. 20 A resolution reaffirming the **War Powers Act of 1973,** the Multinational Force in Lebanon Resolution, was passed by Congress. The measure authorized U.S. Marines to remain in Lebanon for another 18 months as a peacekeeping force.

Oct. 9 Sec. of the Interior **James Watt resigned** under fire after his description of a commission as consisting of "a black, a woman, two Jews, and a cripple." Watt had been under fire from environmentalists for his policies. William P. Clark, the national security adviser, was named to succeed Watt.

Oct. 23 The **U.S. Marine headquarters in Beirut,** Lebanon, was destroyed when an explosive-laden truck evaded security measures and blew up outside the building. The driver of the truck was killed in the blast, which took the lives of 241 Marine and Navy personnel.

Oct. 25 An **invasion of Grenada,** an island nation in the Caribbean, was launched by U.S. forces a week after a bloody coup by pro-Cuban Marxists. The guerrillas murdered Grenada's top leaders. By Nov. 2 the Department of Defense reported the end of hostilities. U.S. casualties were listed as 18 dead, 115 wounded. The action was taken to restore order and protect the 1100 U.S. citizens, mostly students, on the island.

Nov. 8 The **first woman governor of Kentucky,** Martha Layne Collins, was elected. Also this day W. Wilson Goode was elected the first black mayor of Philadelphia, Pa.

Nov. 11 The first U.S. **cruise missiles** arrived in Great Britain. In all, 572 of the intermediate-range missiles were to be deployed in Europe, including 160 in Great Britain.

Nov. 23 The U.S.S.R. withdrew from **arms limitation talks** aimed at reducing the number of intermediate-range missiles in Europe. The action was in response to deployment of such weapons by the U.S.

Dec. 4 Carrier-based **U.S. warplanes attacked Syrian positions** near Beirut, Lebanon, for the first time. Two planes were shot down. One pilot was killed and one captured. Syrian forces had fired on U.S. reconnaissance planes on the previous day, prompting the strike.

Dec. 28 **U.S. withdrawal from UNESCO,** the United Nations Educational, Scientific, and Cultural Organization, as of Dec. 31, 1984, was announced. The reasons for the withdrawal included UNESCO's increasing political bias and financial mismanagement. The U.S. deferred withdrawing pending attempts to achieve improvements in UNESCO operations and management, but on Dec. 19, 1984, the decision to withdraw was reaffirmed.

Apr. 24 **American Book Awards** were presented for the following: fiction, *The Color Purple* by Alice Walker; biography, *Isak Dinesen* by Judith Thurman; history, *Voices of Protest: Huey Long, Father Coughlin and the Great Depression* by Alan Brinkley; general nonfiction, *China: Alive in the Bitter Sea* by Fox Butterfield; poetry, *Selected Poems* by Galway Kinnell and *Country Music* by Charles Wright.

May 4 A work of **environmental art** was begun by Javacheff Christo. Eleven Biscayne Bay, Fla., islets were to be surrounded with a tarpaulin of pink plastic. The work, requiring 6,000,000 feet of material, would cost $3,000,000 and remain in place for two weeks.

June 5 **Tony awards** for the 1982–1983 season were presented for the following: best play, *Torch Song Trilogy* by Harvey Fierstein; best musical, *Cats* by Andrew Lloyd Webber; best actor in a drama, Harvey Fierstein for *Torch Song Trilogy;* best actress in a drama, Jessica Tandy for *Foxfire.*

Aug. 21 *La Cage aux Folles,* a musical by Stephen Sondheim and Jerry Herman based on the play by Jean Poiret, opened at the Palace Theater in New York City.

Sept. 19 **Sotheby Park Bernet,** the celebrated British auction house, was sold to Alfred Taubman, a U.S. art patron and head of the Taubman Company, for $125,000,000 after the British Monopolies and Merger Commission gave its somewhat reluctant approval.

Sept. 20 The **J. Paul Getty Museum** in Malibu, Calif., announced it would spend $100,000,000 to construct a fine arts center. It would include its museum, a center for the history of art, and a conservation institute.

Sept. 25 **Emmy Awards** were presented for the following: best actor in a dramatic series, Ed Flanders for *St. Elsewhere;* best actress in a dramatic series, Tyne Daly for *Cagney and Lacey;* best dramatic series, *Hill Street Blues;* best actor in a limited series or special, Tommy Lee Jones for *The Executioner's Song;* best actress in a limited series or special, Barbara Stanwyck for *The Thorn Birds.*

Sept. 27 *A Chorus Line* became the **longest-running Broadway show,** presenting its 3389th performance to top the record set by *Grease.* The show opened on Oct. 25, 1975.

Nov. 20 *The Day After,* a television drama depicting the effects of a nuclear attack on the U.S., was seen by some 100,000,000 viewers, the second-largest TV audience to date.

| Business and Industry; Science; Education; Philosophy and Religion III | | IV Sports; Social Issues and Crime; Folkways; Fashion; Holidays |

Alamos National Laboratory in New Mexico.

Aug. 30–Sept. 5 The first black astronaut in space, Lt. Col. Guion S. Bluford, USAF, was part of the crew on space shuttle *Challenger*'s third mission. On Sept. 5 *Challenger* made the first nighttime shuttle landing.

Sept. 10 A report on public education by the Carnegie Endowment for the Advancement of Teaching recommended that a core curriculum, representing two-thirds of a student's time, should be given over to study of literature, history, mathematics, science, and foreign languages.

Sept. 23 In the largest employee buyout in U.S. history, workers at the Weirton Steel Works in West Virginia voted to buy the plant from National Steel Corporation after the company announced plans to close the plant.

Oct. 10 The Nobel Prize in Physiology or Medicine was awarded to Barbara McClintock, a botanist at the Cold Spring Harbor Laboratory, Long Island, N.Y., for her studies of gene shifting on plant chromosomes and their effect on hereditary factors.

Oct. 14 A new translation of Bible readings to eliminate references to God as solely male was announced by the National Council of Churches. The three-volume work would incorporate about 40% of the Old Testament and 90% of the New Testament.

Oct. 17 The Nobel Prize in Economics was awarded to Gerard Debreu, a French-born professor at the University of California, Berkeley, for his study of the way prices in a free-market economy work to balance consumer and producer forces.

Oct. 19 The Nobel Prize in Physics was awarded jointly to Subrahmanyan Chandrasekhar of the University of Chicago for his work on the density of stars, and to William Fowler of the California Institute of Technology for his theory of the formation of the elements in the universe.

Dec. 22 A joint U.S.-Japanese auto venture by General Motors and Toyota of Japan was approved by the Federal Trade Commission. The new plant, in Fremont, Calif., was expected to produce from 200,000 to 250,000 autos a year. Ford and Chrysler had both opposed the plan.

July 31 The Baseball Hall of Fame inducted four new members: Walter Alston, former manager of the Brooklyn (and later Los Angeles) Dodgers (NL); George Kell, former third baseman; Juan Marichal, who pitched for the San Francisco Giants from 1960 to 1973; and Brooks Robinson, star third baseman for the Baltimore Orioles (AL) for 19 years.

July 31 The U.S. Women's Open golf tournament was won by Jan Stephenson of Australia, beating JoAnne Carner and Patty Sheehan by one stroke.

Aug. 7 The PGA golf tournament was won by Hal Sutton, beating Jack Nicklaus by one stroke.

Aug. 14–18 At the Pan-American Games in Caracas, Venezuela, the U.S. won 137 gold medals and finished first in unofficial team standings.

Sept. 11 The U.S. Open tennis singles championships were won by Jimmy Connors in the men's division, and by Martina Navratilova in the women's division.

Sept. 14–26 The America's Cup was lost by the U.S. for the first time in the yachting classic's 132-year history. The Australian challenger *Australia II* defeated the U.S. yacht *Liberty* four races to three.

Sept. 17 The Miss America title was won by Vanessa Williams, 20, from Millwood, N.Y., at the annual pageant in Atlantic City, N.J. She was the first black to win the title.

Sept. 23 The World Boxing Association heavyweight boxing championship was won by Gerrie Coatzee of South Africa, who knocked out Michael Dokes in ten rounds at Richfield, Ohio.

Oct. 1 The North American Soccer League championship was won by the Tulsa Roughnecks, defeating the Toronto Blizzard 2–0.

Oct. 11–16 The World Series was won by the Baltimore Orioles (AL), defeating the Philadelphia Phillies (NL) four games to one. On Oct. 8 the Orioles won the American League pennant over the Chicago White Sox, three games to one, and the Phillies won the National League pennant from the Los Angeles Dodgers, three games to one.

Oct. 23 The 14th New York City Marathon was won by Rod Dixon of New Zealand with a time of 2 hrs., 8 min., 59 sec. The first woman to finish was Grete Waitz of Norway, with a time of 2 hrs., 27 min.

Nov. 2 A federal holiday honoring Dr. Martin Luther King, Jr., the slain civil rights leader, was designated for observance on the third Monday of January in a bill signed by Pres. Reagan. King was the first person honored with a federal holiday since George Washington's birthday was so named.

1984

The year's top domestic story was the presidential campaign, a race between former vice president Walter F. Mondale and Pres. Ronald Reagan, a highly popular incumbent and master of the media campaign. The Democrats tried unsuccessfully to challenge Reagan's ability to manage the government, even to comprehend the major issues of the day. The Republicans pointed to the booming national economy and assailed the Democrats for their free-spending ways and lack of political vision. In foreign affairs the U.S. and U.S.S.R. jockeyed for position in the debate over resuming nuclear arms limitation talks, so no progress was made. The U.S. appeared also to have lost the initiative in seeking peace in the Middle East. Congress and Pres. Reagan clashed on aid for El Salvador, where the established government was fighting insurgents, and on aid for the so-called *contras* in Nicaragua. There insurgents were fighting the established government, led by the Marxist-dominated Sandinistas. At home in midyear the Census Bureau estimated the U.S. population at 236,158,000. Almost all the population growth of the previous four years had been in the South and West. Two other items of current demographic information were also remarkable: Seven states had more than 1,000,000 residents aged 65 or older, and 454,136 people were in prison, almost double the total of ten years earlier. This year Los Angeles displaced Chicago as the nation's second largest city. Notables who died this year included George D. Aiken, Republican senator from Vermont from 1941 to 1975, Nov. 19, at 92; Ellsworth Bunker, a diplomat who served under six presidents, Sept. 30, at 90; Sen. Frank Church, Democrat of Ohio from 1957 to 1981, Apr. 7, at 59; Gen. Mark W. Clark, a top U.S. commander during World War II, Apr. 17, at 87; and Glen H. Taylor, former senator from Idaho who was Henry A. Wallace's vice presidential running mate on the Progressive ticket in 1948, Apr. 28, at 80.

Jan. 10 Restoration of full **diplomatic relations with the Vatican** after a period of 117 years was announced in Washington, D.C. The move came at a time when the Vatican apparently was taking much interest in international affairs.

Although at year's end almost half of Broadway's 37 theaters were dark, prospects for the theater were promising. Gross receipts were up, and the 1983–1984 season had produced three sellout musicals, *La Cage aux Folles, Cats,* and *Sunday in the Park With George.* The American Academy of Dramatic Arts celebrated its centennial this year, and the Long Wharf Theater in New Haven, Conn., its 20th year anniversary. Major museum exhibits included the *Van Gogh at Arles* exhibit at the Metropolitan Museum in New York City, a complete sellout; an extensive James McNeill Whistler show at the Freer Gallery in Washington, D.C.; and a showing of works of traditional art of the Maori people of New Zealand at the Metropolitan Museum. In mid-May the Museum of Modern Art in New York City opened its new and greatly enlarged facilities. In the fall the Indianapolis Symphony Orchestra moved to a renovated movie palace, but orchestras in St. Louis, Pittsburgh, and Miami moved into new homes. Of the year's top films, *Indiana Jones and the Temple of Doom* earned $42,267,345 in its first six days of release, and went on to break virtually every box office record. The top recording artist of the year was Michael Jackson, whose album *Thriller* sold more than 20,000,000 copies worldwide in 1983 and 1984. Among those who died this year were Ansel Adams, photographer, Apr. 22, at 82; Brooks Atkinson, the drama critic, Jan. 13, at 89; William "Count" Basie, jazz pianist and band leader, Apr. 26, at 79; Richard Burton, the actor, Aug. 5, at 58; Truman Capote, the author, Aug. 25, at 59; Jackie Coogan, first major child star in U.S. film history, Mar. 1, at 69; Janet Gaynor, winner of the first Academy Award for best actress, Sept. 14, at 77; Lillian Hellman, the playwright, June 30, at 79; Alfred A. Knopf, founder of the publishing house bearing his name, Aug. 11, at 91; Mabel Mercer, a singer whose style greatly influenced popular music, Apr. 20, at 84; Ethel Merman, star of musical comedy, Feb. 15, at 76; Jan Peerce, tenor with the Metropolitan Opera for 27 years, Dec. 15, at 80; Lee Krasner Pollock, abstract expressionist painter, June 19, at 75; William Powell, the movie star, Mar. 5, at 91; Irwin Shaw, the author, May 16, at 71; Fred Waring, the band leader, July 29, at 84; Johnny Weissmuller, Olympic star and movie Tarzan, Jan. 20, at 79; and Meredith Willson, Broadway composer and lyricist, June 15, at 82.

Business and Industry; Science;
Education; Philosophy and Religion   III

III   **IV**

Sports; Social Issues and Crime;
Folkways; Fashion; Holidays

Dec. 8   The contract of **Bowie Kuhn** as commissioner of baseball was extended to Mar. 1, 1984, by the major league team owners. They had voted in 1982 not to renew his contract.

1984

The year was excellent for businesses and consumers. The economy expanded 6.8%, its best performance since 1951. The rise in consumer prices was only 4%, and personal income rose 6.8%. New housing starts hit 1,700,000, the highest number since 1979. Americans bought 14,100,000 cars and light trucks, the largest volume since 1979. This helped put Detroit back on its feet, and the big three automobile makers earned $9,810,000,000, a new record. Not all the news was good, however. The foreign trade deficit hit a record $107,600,000,000, the Dow Jones average finished the year about 60 points below its opening price, and 79 banks failed, the largest number since 1938. Although employment was up, the unemployment rate stood at 7.1% in December, down only 0.3% from a year earlier. Organized labor's membership declined to 18.8% of wage and salary workers, compared with 23% in 1980. For the third year in a row, the value of farmland dropped, with the largest declines registered in Iowa and Nebraska. This was bad news for farmers, many of whom had borrowed heavily on their land and now were faced with bankruptcy. Medical costs continued to rise, contributing to the growth of prepaid medical plans and health maintenance organizations, known as HMOs. In November the Great American Smokeout saw more than 5,000,000 smokers kick the habit, according to the American Cancer Society; another 15,000,000 cut back their smoking. In education, this year's high-school graduates scored an average of four points higher on scholastic aptitude tests than the year before. Black students continued to improve their scores faster than white students but remained below the national averages. A study by the National Council of Churches showed members of the clergy to be among the lowest-paid professionals in the country, and women in the clergy to be the lowest paid. Among notables who died this year were the Rev. Martin Luther King, Sr., father of the slain civil rights leader, Nov. 11, at 84; John Rock, who helped develop the birth control pill, Dec. 4, at 94; and George G. Simpson, a world authority on vertebrate paleontology, Oct. 6, at 82.

Jan. 8   In the **largest corporate merger** to date, Texaco, Inc., the third-largest U.S. oil company, agreed to take over the Getty Oil Company in a deal valued at $10,000,000,000.

This year saw the centennial of the American Kennel Club, on Sept. 17. Another institution celebrating its centennial was the roller coaster, first put in operation at Coney Island, N.Y., on June 16, 1884. A different kind of celebration was held in Chicago, where a 28-year-old printer won $40,000,000 in the Illinois state lottery. It was the largest lottery win by one person in North America. The divorce rate dropped for the third year in a row, down to 4.9% of marriages. After three years of decline, traffic fatalities were up. Safety experts thought the increase was associated with the booming economy, which meant traffic was heavier than in recent years. Sales of home exercise equipment passed the $1,000,000,000 mark in 1984, and the growing U.S. mania for fitness and personal appearance also helped the cosmetics industry. It sold $10,000,000,000 worth of skin care products. The mania for Cabbage Patch dolls and their accessories continued. In fashion, the introduction of oversize men's clothing for women triggered a boom for used clothing stores, where women snapped up men's coats at bargain prices. In sports the NFL reported an increase in attendance at football games, but major league baseball showed a drop in attendance. A Gallup poll showed that swimming, bicycling, and fishing were the most popular activities of adult Americans. This year the memory of track star Jesse Owens, star of the 1936 Olympics in Berlin, was honored in West Berlin with the naming of an avenue after him. In professional golf, the year's top money winners were Tom Watson, $476,200, and Betsy King, $266,771. Americans mourned the deaths this year of Walter Alston, manager of the Los Angeles Dodgers for 23 years, Oct. 1, at 72; Joe Cronin, former star shortstop and later president of the American League, Sept. 7, at 77; Jim Fixx, whose books about running fueled the American passion for jogging, July 20, at 52; Waite Hoyt, former pitching great, Aug. 25, at 84; Oswald Jacoby, one of the great contract bridge players of all time, July 27, at 81; and Al Schacht, a player and coach who entertained fans at baseball games with pantomime antics that won him the title of Clown Prince of Baseball, July 14, at 91.

Jan. 1   In **college football bowl games,** the results were Georgia 10, Texas 9 in the Cotton Bowl; Miami 31, Nebraska 30 in the Orange Bowl; UCLA 45, Illinois 3 in the Rose Bowl; and Auburn 9, Michigan 7 in the Sugar Bowl. This season the AP and UPI polls

Exploration and Settlement; Wars; Government; Civil Rights; Statistics I		II Publishing; Arts and Music; Popular Entertainment; Architecture; Theater

Jan. 25 In his **State of the Union** message, Pres. Reagan noted a "renewed energy and optimism throughout the land." He also asked Republicans and Democrats to join together to reduce the enormous projected budget deficit.

Feb. 5–28 A series of **storms** lashed the nation. Winds of up to 100 mph tore through the Plains states, killing 22 in North Dakota and Minnesota. A blizzard dumped three feet of snow in Colorado and Utah and killed 29 people.

Feb. 7 **Withdrawal of U.S. Marines from Beirut,** Lebanon was announced by Pres. Reagan. The troops were completely redeployed to Navy ships offshore by Feb. 29.

Feb. 28 In the **New Hampshire Democratic primary,** Sen. Gary Hart of Colorado scored an upset over front runner Walter F. Mondale, taking 39% of the vote to Mondale's 29%.

Mar. 5 In a major decision on **separation of church and state,** the Supreme Court ruled that a city may make a Nativity scene part of an official Christmas display without violating the constitutional separation of government and organized religion.

Mar. 20 A constitutional **school prayer amendment,** permitting organized spoken prayer in public schools, was rejected by the U.S. Senate. The 56–44 vote fell 11 short of the required two-thirds majority.

Mar. 29 A series of **tornadoes** killed at least 67 people in the Carolinas. At the same time, a hurricane-force storm of sleet, snow, and hail swept the East Coast as far north as southern New England.

Apr. 26–May 1 A **presidential trip to China** was made by Pres. Reagan. He was party to formal agreements on scientific and cultural exchanges, economic cooperation, and development of nuclear energy.

May 7 Establishment of an **Agent Orange victims' fund** of $180,000,000 was announced. The fund, provided by Dow Chemical Company and six other manufacturers of the herbicide, was intended to provide assistance for Vietnam veterans suffering from exposure to Agent Orange and for the families of victims.

Among **books published** this year was a reissue of George Orwell's 1949 classic novel of totalitarianism, *1984.* Critics noted that Orwell had intended the novel to be a warning of things that might occur, not a prediction of the inevitable. Readers put the book firmly on the best-seller lists. Other books published this year included *Him With His Foot in His Mouth and Other Stories* by Saul Bellow; *Lives of the Poets* by E. L. Doctorow, six stories and a novella; *Iacocca* by Lee Iacocca with William Novak, an autobiography of the man credited with returning Chrysler Corporation to prosperity from virtual bankruptcy; The *Aquitaine Progression* by Robert Ludlum, a spy thriller that topped the hardcover best-seller lists; and *Walt Whitman,* a biography by Paul Zweig.

Jan. 5 *The Real Thing* by Tom Stoppard, starring Jeremy Irons and Glenn Close, opened at the Plymouth Theater in New York City.

Jan. 9 **National Book Critics Circle Awards** were voted for the following: fiction, *Ironweed* by William Kennedy; general nonfiction, *The Price of Power: Kissinger in the Nixon White House* by Seymour M. Hersh; biography, *Minor Characters* by Joyce Johnson; criticism, *Hugging the Shore* by John Updike; poetry, *The Changing Light at Sandover* by James Merrill.

Feb. 14 **Ronald Reagan's presidential library** and museum would be located at Stanford University, Palo Alto, Calif., it was announced. A decision on accepting a Ronald Reagan Public Affairs Institute was postponed by university officials.

Feb. 28 **Grammy Awards** were presented for the following: best album of 1983, *Thriller* by Michael Jackson; best record, "Beat It" by Michael Jackson; best male pop vocalist, Michael Jackson for *Thriller;* best female pop vocalist, Irene Cara for "Flashdance"; best pop group, The Police for "Every Breath You Take."

Mar. 4 A **Television Academy Hall of Fame** was established. Its first inductees were Lucille Ball, Milton Berle, Paddy Chayefsky, Norman Lear, Edward R. Murrow, William S. Paley, and David Sarnoff.

Apr. 9 **Academy Awards** were presented to *Terms of Endearment* as outstanding motion picture of 1983; Robert Duvall as best actor for *Tender Mercies;* Shirley MacLaine as best actress for *Terms of Endearment;* Jack Nicholson as best supporting actor for *Terms of Endearment;* and Linda Hunt as best supporting actress for *The Year of Living Dangerously.*

| Business and Industry; Science;
Education; Philosophy and Religion III | | IV Sports; Social Issues and Crime;
Folkways; Fashion; Holidays |

Jan. 13 A nuclear operating license was withheld from a nearly completed power plant in Illinois. It was the first time the Nuclear Regulatory Commission had refused to license a nuclear power facility that was close to completion.

Feb. 3 In the first case of **surrogate conception,** the birth of a baby conceived in one woman's womb and brought to term by another woman was announced by a team of California physicians.

Feb. 7 The **first human satellites** floated in space, two astronauts powered by jet packs and without lifelines connected to their spacecraft. The astronauts were Bruce McCandless and Robert Stewart, crew members on the fourth orbital flight (Feb. 3–11) of the space shuttle *Challenger.*

Feb. 13 The **first heart and liver transplant** was performed on a six-year-old Texas girl, Stormie Jones.

Apr. 23 Identification of a virus thought to **cause acquired immune deficiency syndrome** (AIDS) was announced by federal researchers. The disease, which destroys the body's natural immune system and is considered to be ultimately fatal, was estimated to have afflicted 4000 Americans to date.

May 9 The **largest black-owned business** was reported to be the Johnson Publishing Company. Johnson moved Motown Industries, the recording and entertainment company, to second place.

May 9 **Ordination of noncelibate homosexuals** was prohibited by the General Conference of the United Methodist Church.

May 23 Kristine Holderied became the **first woman midshipman** to graduate at the top of her class at the U.S. Naval Academy at Annapolis, Md.

May 24 **Beatrice Foods Company** agreed to purchase Esmark, Inc., for $2,800,000,000. The sale made Beatrice the second largest food and consumer products company in the world.

May 30 Scientists reported that an effective **chicken pox vaccine** had been developed. The disease claimed some 100 to 150 lives in the U.S. each year.

June 4 Successful **cloning of DNA** from an extinct animal was reported by scientists at the University of California. The gene fragments, cloned from an

picked Miami as the national collegiate champions of 1983.

Jan. 20–21 **U.S. figure skating championships** were won at Salt Lake City, Utah, by Scott Hamilton, men's singles; Rosalynn Sumners, women's singles; Kitty and Peter Carruthers, pairs; Judy Blumberg and Michael Seibert, dance.

Jan. 22 **Super Bowl XVIII** was won by the Los Angeles Raiders (AFC), defeating the Washington Redskins (NFC) 38–9. On Jan. 8 the Raiders had defeated the Seattle Seahawks 30–14 to win the AFC championship, and the Redskins had beaten the San Francisco 49ers 24–21 for the NFC title.

Feb. 8–19 At the **Winter Olympics** in Sarajevo, Yugoslavia, the U.S. won four gold medals and finished fifth in unofficial team standings.

Mar. 3 **Peter V. Ueberroth,** president of the Los Angeles Olympic Organizing Committee, was elected commissioner of baseball by the major league team owners.

Mar. 9 The World Boxing Council **heavyweight boxing championship** was won by Tim Witherspoon, who outpointed Greg Page in a 12-round bout at Las Vegas, Nev.

Mar. 23 At the **world figure skating championships** in Ottawa, Canada, Scott Hamilton won the men's singles title.

Apr. 1 The **NCAA women's basketball championship** was won by Southern California, defeating Tennessee 72–61.

Apr. 2 The **NCAA men's basketball championship** was won by Georgetown, which defeated Houston 84–75.

Apr. 15 The **Masters golf tournament** was won by Ben Crenshaw, who beat Tom Watson by two strokes.

Apr. 16 The 88th **Boston Marathon** was won by Geoff Smith of Great Britain, with a time of 2 hrs., 10 min., 34 sec. The first woman to finish was Lorraine Moller of New Zealand, with a time of 2 hrs., 29 min., 28 sec.

Apr. 29 The **WBA heavyweight boxing championship** was won by Tony Tubbs in a 15-round decision over Greg Page at Buffalo, N.Y.

May 5 The 110th **Kentucky Derby** was won by Swale, with a time of 2:02²/₅. The jockey was Laffit Pincay, Jr.

May 8 The **U.S.S.R. withdrew from the 1984 Olympics.** The U.S.S.R. Olympic Committee said Soviet athletes could not compete because of "gross flouting" of Olympic ideals by the U.S. The move was seen in some quarters as revenge for the boycott of the 1980 games in Moscow by the U.S. and some other Western nations.

May 10–19 The **NHL Stanley Cup** was won by the Edmonton Oilers, who defeated the New York Islanders four games to one.

Exploration and Settlement; Wars; Government; Civil Rights; Statistics	I		II	Publishing; Arts and Music; Popular Entertainment; Architecture; Theater

May 22 In a decision on **job discrimination,** the Supreme Court ruled that law firms may not discriminate on the basis of sex, race, religion, or national origin in promoting associates to partnership. The decision affirmed that partnerships are covered by federal laws against discrimination, as are other forms of businesses.

June 6 On the **40th anniversary of D-Day,** Pres. Reagan joined with representatives from Great Britain, Canada, and other nations in ceremonies at Normandy, where Allied armies landed first in the invasion of France in 1944.

June 11 In a ruling on **admissibility of evidence,** the Supreme Court declared that illegally obtained evidence may be admitted at a trial provided it could be proved that the evidence would have been discovered inevitably by lawful means. On July 5 the Court ruled that some evidence obtained with defective search warrants could be used in a trial.

July 3 The all-male **Jaycees,** Junior Chamber of Commerce, organization was directed to obey state laws against discrimination and accept women as members. On Aug. 16 the Jaycees passed a resolution allowing full membership to women.

July 16–19 The **Democratic National Convention** nominated **Walter F. Mondale** of Minnesota for the presidency and Rep. Geraldine Ferraro of New York for the vice presidency.

July 17 To promote raising of the **legal drinking age** to 21, Pres. Reagan signed a bill giving states until Oct. 1, 1986, to do so or face a 5% cut in federal highway funds.

July 18 The **Deficit Reduction Act of 1984,** raising taxes by about $50,000,000,000 and cutting spending by $13,000,000,000 through 1987, was signed by Pres. Reagan.

Aug. 20–23 The **Republican National Convention** nominated Pres. Reagan for reelection. George Bush was renominated for the vice presidency.

Sept. 20 The **U.S. Embassy in Beirut was bombed.** A suicide car-bomb exploded outside the Embassy, killing at least 23, including two Americans.

Apr. 16 **Pulitzer prizes** were awarded for the following: fiction, *Ironweed* by William Kennedy; general nonfiction, *Social Transformation of American Medicine* by Paul Starr; biography, *Booker T. Washington* by Louis R. Harlan; poetry, *American Primitive* by Mary Oliver; drama, *Glengarry Glen Ross* by David Mamet.

Apr. 25 In a major **publishing merger,** Macmillan, Inc. took over the Scribner Book Companies, which included the 138-year-old firm Charles Scribner's Sons.

Apr. 29 **André Previn,** music director of the Pittsburgh Symphony Orchestra, was named director of the Los Angeles Philharmonic beginning with the 1986–1987 season.

May 2 *Sunday in the Park With George,* a musical by Stephen Sondheim and James Lapine starring Mandy Patinkin as the artist Georges Seurat, opened at the Booth Theater in New York City.

May 3 The **Mark Rothko Foundation** announced that most of its collection of the works of Mark Rothko, the abstract expressionist painter, would be given to 19 museums in the U.S. and abroad. The core of the nearly 1000-work collection would be given to the National Gallery of Art in Washington, D.C.

May 8 A collection of **illuminated manuscripts,** the William S. Glazier collection of medieval and Renaissance manuscripts, would be given to the Pierpont Morgan Library in New York City, the library announced.

May 9 A sculpture by **Alexander Calder,** a 24-foot-high mobile entitled *Big Crinkly,* sold at auction in New York City for $852,000, a new record for sculpture by an American.

June 3 **Tony awards** for the 1983–1984 season were presented for the following: best play, *The Real Thing* by Tom Stoppard; best musical, *La Cage aux Folles* by Jerry Herman and Harvey Fierstein; best actor in a drama, Jeremy Irons for *The Real Thing;* best actress in a drama, Glenn Close for *The Real Thing.*

June 7 A three-volume **reissue of James Joyce's** *Ulysses* was published, correcting 5000 omissions, transpositions, and other errors in previous editions. Scholars predicted that the new edition would lead to reinterpretation of episodes and characters in the novel.

June 9 **Donald Duck's 50th birthday** was celebrated at Disneyland in California. Donald's career began in

| Business and Industry; Science; Education; Philosophy and Religion III | IV Sports; Social Issues and Crime; Folkways; Fashion; Holidays |

animal related to the zebra and the horse, were the first to be extracted from a vanished animal species.

June 12 In a decision supporting the **last hired, first fired** policy of many businesses, the Supreme Court ruled that courts could not overrule seniority programs to prevent layoffs of employees hired under affirmative action programs. Labor leaders applauded the decision, but civil rights groups and others condemned it.

June 14 A resolution opposing the **ordination of women** was passed by the Southern Baptist Convention. The resolution was nonbinding on local congregations and did not apply to women already ordained for the Baptist ministry.

June 15 In the **largest corporate merger** to date, Gulf Corporation agreed to a takeover by the Standard Oil Company of California (SOCAL) for $13,400,000,000. The deal made SOCAL the third largest U.S. oil concern.

June 21 In the **largest single stock transaction** in the history of the New York Stock Exchange, 10,000,000 shares of Superior Oil stock were sold for $423,800,000.

July 26 In the **largest federal loan guarantee** to a private enterprise, the U.S. government committed itself to $4,500,000,000 in loan guarantees to the Continental Illinois National Bank and Trust Company.

Aug. 3 A new **daily volume record** of 236,600,000 shares was set by the New York Stock Exchange. It was the first time the volume exceeded 200,000,000 shares.

Aug. 9 In a statement on **political action by Roman Catholics,** Catholic bishops of the U.S. urged church members to promote the church's position on public policy issues. The statement also called on the clergy to refrain from supporting political candidates.

Aug. 11 A bill protecting **student meetings** for religious or political purposes outside of normal school hours was signed by Pres. Reagan.

Aug. 30–Sept. 5 The **space shuttle** *Discovery,* the third of four U.S. space shuttles, made its maiden flight. Its crew of six included Judith Resnick, the second U.S. woman astronaut in space.

May 19 The 109th **Preakness Stakes** was won by Gate Dancer, with a time of 1:53³/₅. The jockey was Angel Cordero, Jr.

May 27 The 68th **Indianapolis 500** auto race was won by Rick Mears, completing the 500-mile course in 3 hrs., 3 min., 21 sec., with an average speed of 163.612 mph.

May 27–June 12 The **NBA basketball championship** was won by the Boston Celtics, who beat the Los Angeles Lakers four games to three.

June 3 The **LPGA golf tournament** was won by Patty Sheehan by a record margin of ten strokes.

June 9 The 116th **Belmont Stakes** was won by Swale, with a time of 2:27¹/₅. The jockey was Lafitt Pincay, Jr. Eight days after the race Swale collapsed and died suddenly.

June 18 The **U.S. Open golf tournament** was won by Fuzzy Zoeller in an 18-hole playoff with Greg Norman.

June 27 In a major decision on the **televising of college football games,** the Supreme Court ruled that the NCAA's exclusive control over TV coverage of college football constituted an "unreasonable restraint of trade" and violated the Sherman Antitrust Act.

July 7–8 At the **Wimbledon** tennis championships in England, John McEnroe won the men's singles title and Martina Navratilova won the women's singles. McEnroe teamed with Peter Fleming to win the men's doubles, and Navratilova teamed with Pam Shriver to win the women's doubles.

July 11 The baseball **All-Star Game** was won by the National League, 3–1.

July 15 The **U.S. Women's Open golf tournament** was won by Hollis Stacy, who beat Rosie Jones by one stroke.

July 15 The second **USFL football championship** was won by the Philadelphia Stars, who routed the Arizona Wranglers 23–3.

July 18 A **gunman killed 21 people** in and near a McDonald's restaurant in San Ysidro, Calif. James Humberty, heavily armed, walked into the fast food store and began shooting, then continued killing people on the street before he was shot and killed by police officers.

July 23 **Vanessa Williams** resigned as Miss America after nude photos of her appeared in *Penthouse* magazine. Suzette Charles, first runner-up in the 1983 pageant, was named to complete Williams's reign.

July 28–Aug. 12 At the **Summer Olympics** in Los Angeles, Calif., the U.S. won 83 gold medals and finished first in unofficial team standings. Carl Lewis won four gold medals in track and field events, and Mary Lou Retton won four in gymnastics. Joan Benoit won the first Olympic women's marathon.

Oct. 3 The first **FBI agent charged with espionage,** Richard W. Miller, was arrested. He was accused of passing a classified document to two Soviet émigrés.

Oct. 7 In the first **presidential debate** of the 1984 campaign, Democratic candidate Walter F. Mondale handled himself ably in a discussion of domestic issues with Pres. Reagan, who at times seemed disoriented and unsure of his facts.

Oct. 11 A **vice presidential debate** was held between Vice Pres. Bush and Democratic challenger Geraldine Ferraro. The debate was spirited and at one point Rep. Ferraro accused the vice president of being "patronizing" toward her.

Oct. 14 A bill introducing **major changes in U.S. criminal law** was signed by Pres. Reagan. The new law, permitting detention without bail for the first time in peacetime, was denounced by some as a threat to civil liberty.

Oct. 21 In the second **presidential debate** of 1984, Pres. Reagan appeared to have the upper hand in a discussion of foreign affairs with Democratic challenger Walter Mondale.

Nov. 2 In the first **execution of a woman** in 22 years, Margie Velma Barfield, 52, convicted of murder, was put to death in North Carolina.

Nov. 6 **Ronald Reagan was reelected president** of the United States in the greatest Republican landslide in history. Reagan carried 49 states. Walter F. Mondale carried Minnesota and the District of Columbia. The electoral vote was Reagan, 525; Mondale 13. The popular vote was Reagan, 54,455,075; Mondale, 37,577, 185. In congressional elections the Republicans gained two Senate seats for a 53–47 majority. In the House the Democrats lost 14 seats but kept a majority of 253–182.

Nov. 22 A **preliminary arms-control meeting,** to negotiate an agenda for upcoming talks between the U.S. and U.S.S.R., was scheduled for January in Geneva, Switzerland. Sec. of State George P. Shultz and Soviet foreign minister Andrei Gromyko were announced as the principal participants in the talks.

1934 with a bit part in the animated film *Wise Little Men.*

June 23 An **auction of John Lennon's possessions** and those of his widow, Yoko Ono, including furniture, jewelry, and assorted memorabilia, brought $430,000. One of the former Beatle's guitars sold for $19,000.

June 26 An **auction of 32 Hebrew books and manuscripts** thought to have been destroyed by the Nazis during World War II brought $1,450,000 in New York City. It was later learned that the works had been smuggled out of Germany by an emeritus professor of a rabbinical seminary in Cincinnati, Ohio. The books were sold despite controversy over their ownership.

Aug. 3 Establishment of a **National Dance Hall of Fame,** including a National Museum of Dance at Saratoga, N.Y., was announced.

Sept. 23 **Emmy Awards** were presented for the following: best actor in a dramatic series, Tom Selleck for *Magnum, P.I.;* best actress in a dramatic series, Tyne Daly for *Cagney and Lacey;* best actor in a limited series or special, Sir Laurence Olivier for *Laurence Olivier's King Lear;* best actress in a limited series or special, Jane Fonda for *The Dollmaker;* best dramatic series, *Hill Street Blues.*

Nov. 1 A 1953 painting by **Willem de Kooning,** *Two Women,* sold at auction for $1,980,000, the highest auction price ever paid for a post–World War II artwork.

Nov. 9 The actress **Vanessa Redgrave** was awarded $100,000 in damages from the Boston Symphony Orchestra, which had canceled her scheduled performance as narrator in Igor Stravinsky's *Oedipus Rex.* Redgrave, an outspoken supporter of the Palestine Liberation Organization, had sued for breach of contract and also for violation of her civil rights, but the jury rejected the latter charge.

Nov. 16 **American Book Awards** were presented for the following: fiction, *Victory over Japan* by Ellen Gilchrist; nonfiction, *Andrew Jackson and the Course of American Democracy, 1833–1845, vol. III* by Robert V. Remini; first fiction, *Stones for Ibarra* by Harriet Doerr.

Nov. 20 In what was said to be the **biggest magazine acquisition** in history, CBS, Inc., paid $362,500,000 for 12 publications owned by the Ziff-Davis Publishing Company. The next day Rupert Murdoch, the Australian publisher, bought 12 trade journals from Ziff-Davis for $350,000,000.

| Business and Industry; Science; Education; Philosophy and Religion III | | IV Sports; Social Issues and Crime; Folkways; Fashion; Holidays |

Oct. 11 Dr. Kathryn D. Sullivan became the **first U.S. woman astronaut to walk in space.** She was one of seven crew members on the sixth flight of the space shuttle *Challenger* (Oct. 5–13). Also aboard in addition to the crew was the first Canadian astronaut, Marc Garneau.

Oct. 16 A baboon heart transplant to a human, the first operation of its kind, was performed on a 15-day-old baby girl, identified only as Baby Fae, at Loma Linda University Medical Center in California. Baby Fae lived until Nov. 15.

Oct. 17 The **Nobel Prize in Chemistry** was awarded to Dr. Bruce Merrifield of Rockefeller University for protein research offering promise of development of important new drugs.

Nov. 11 In a **pastoral letter on economic justice,** a committee of Roman Catholic bishops called for sweeping economic changes to aid the poor, stating that the level of inequality between the wealthy and the poor was "morally unacceptable."

Nov. 12 The **first space salvage operation** was performed during the second flight (Nov. 8–16) of the space shuttle *Discovery.* Astronauts Joseph Allen and Dale Gardner retrieved a nonfunctioning satellite and brought it into the shuttle's cargo bay. A second retrieval was accomplished on Nov. 14.

Nov. 25 The **second artificial heart transplant** was performed at Humana Heart Institute International in Louisville, Ky. The recipient was William J. Schroeder, 52, of Jasper, Ind.

Nov. 30 The basis for a **Protestant church merger** by nine major Protestant denominations was reached by the Consultation on Church Union, after 22 years of effort. The nine denominations were: African Methodist Episcopal Church; African Methodist Episcopal Zion Church; Christian Church (Disciples of Christ); Christian Methodist Episcopal Church; Episcopal Church; International Council of Community Churches; Presbyterian Church (U.S.A.); United Methodist Church; and United Church of Christ.

Dec. 11–12 Discovery of **7000-year-old human skulls with brains virtually intact** was reported by archeologists in Florida. The skulls were found buried in peat at the bottom of a lake. They were described as the oldest skulls from which it had thus far been possible to extract and analyze DNA.

Aug. 12 The **Baseball Hall of Fame** inducted Luis Aparicio, former shortstop; Don Drysdale, pitcher for the Los Angeles Dodgers from 1956 to 1969; Richard B. "Rick" Ferrell, center fielder; Harmon Killebrew, who ranked fifth in all-time major league home runs; and Harold H. "Pee Wee" Reese, shortstop for the Dodgers from 1940 to 1958.

Aug. 19 The **PGA golf tournament** was won by Lee Trevino, who shot a 15 under par 273 to finish four strokes ahead of Gary Player and Lanny Wadkins.

Aug. 22 The **USFL** voted to switch to a fall schedule for 1986, abandoning its spring football season. The move would put it in direct competition with the NFL.

Aug. 31 The World Boxing Council **heavyweight boxing championship** was won by Pinklon Thomas, who outpointed Tim Witherspoon in a 12-round bout in Las Vegas, Nev.

Sept. 8–9 The **U.S. Open tennis singles championships** were won by John McEnroe in the men's division and Martina Navratilova in the women's division.

Sept. 14–18 The **first transatlantic solo balloon flight** was completed by Joe W. Kittinger, who flew 3535 miles from Caribou, Maine, to near Savona, Italy. He made the flight in the gondola of his ten-story-tall, helium-lifted craft named *Rosie O'Grady's Balloon of Peace.*

Sept. 15 The **Miss America** title was won by Sharlene Wells, 20, from Salt Lake City, Utah, at the annual pageant in Atlantic City, N.J.

Oct. 3 The **North American Soccer League championship** was won by the Chicago Sting, who beat the Toronto Blizzard 3–2.

Oct. 9–14 The **World Series** was won by the Detroit Tigers (AL), defeating the San Diego Padres (NL) four games to one. On Oct. 5 the Tigers had won the American League pennant over the Kansas City Royals in a three-game sweep, and on Oct. 7 the Padres had taken the National League pennant over the Chicago Cubs, three games to two.

Oct. 21 A new **world marathon record** of 2 hrs., 8 min., 5 sec., was set by Stephen Jones of Great Britain at the America's Marathon-Chicago race in Chicago.

Oct. 28 The 15th **New York City Marathon** was won by Orlando Pizzolato of Italy, with a time of 2 hrs., 14 min., 53 sec. The first woman to finish was Grete Waitz of Norway, with a time of 2 hrs., 29 min., 30 sec.

Nov. 5 In a decision on **football franchise** shifts, the Supreme Court ruled the NFL could not prevent its teams from moving to different cities. The Court refused to hear an appeal of a lower court ruling that the NFL's refusal to allow the Oakland Raiders to move to Los Angeles in 1980 constituted a violation of federal antitrust law.

Nov. 26 The **World Court** declared it had jurisdiction in a case brought by Nicaragua to have the U.S. declared an aggressor nation. On May 10 the court had ruled unanimously that the U.S. should halt any attempts to blockade or mine Nicaraguan ports. The U.S. had stated it would not be bound by the decision of the World Court.

Nov. 30 The first volume of the **first Sumerian dictionary,** a projected 17-volume treatment of the world's first written language, was issued by the University of Pennsylvania.

Dec. 18 The *New York Review of Books* was sold for about $5,000,000 to Rea Hederman, a publisher and cable television executive. Established in 1963 during a 114-day New York newspaper strike, the *Review* had become an influential literary journal.

1985

The nation was stunned by what appeared to be an epidemic of spying. Thirteen Americans were charged with espionage in the course of the year. Of those charged, most were past or present CIA or Navy personnel and one was an FBI agent. Most of those accused were said to have turned to spying not for reasons of ideology but for money. One of the accused had been supplying Israel, an ally, with information, much to the discomfiture of the U.S. and Israel. Late in November *The New York Times* reported that since 1968 U.S. citizens had been attacked by terrorists in 72 countries. In 1985 seventeen Americans were killed in terrorist attacks and 154 had been wounded. The government reported that 90 planned terrorist attacks had been foiled in a 12-month period. The Social Security system celebrated its 50th anniversary on Aug. 14, having paid $1,800,000,000 in benefits and carrying 36,700,000 people on its rolls. Americans mourned the passing of former Sen. Sam J. Ervin, Jr., Democrat of North Carolina, who headed the Senate Watergate investigation that led to Pres. Richard Nixon's resignation, Apr. 23, at 88; Patricia Roberts Harris, who served in two Cabinet posts under Pres. Jimmy Carter, Mar. 23, at 60; Henry Cabot Lodge, former Republican senator from Massachusetts and diplomat, Feb. 27, at 82; former Sen. John J. Sparkman, Democrat of Alabama, who served 42 years in Congress, Nov. 16, at 85; Potter Stewart, who served on the Supreme Court from 1958 to 1981, Dec. 7, at 70; and Robert H. W. Welch, Jr., who in 1958 founded the John Birch Society and headed it until 1983, Jan. 6, at 85.

Jan. 18 The **U.S withdrew from World Court proceedings** in a case brought against it by Nicaragua, stating that the court had overextended its jurisdiction. Nicaragua had charged the U.S. with conducting a secret war by aiding rebel *contra* forces and mining Nicaraguan harbors. On Oct. 7 the U.S. announced it no longer would comply automatically with World Court decisions because its procedures had been

On Broadway, fewer shows were staged than in any other year in the century. After two good seasons, attendance and ticket sales were down. Only musicals seemed to attract patrons. A surprise hit of the season was the musical *Tango Argentino,* which opened in October for a projected five-week run and made it big. The Dance Theater of Harlem celebrated its tenth anniversary this year, and the Metropolitan Opera Guild observed its 50th anniversary. The Boston Pops celebrated its centennial with a performance before a full house of 2000. Sales of compact discs and compact disc players far exceeded supply. Music lovers seemed to hover in record stores and buy up the discs as fast as they were unpacked. Manufacturers and audiophiles predicted that the CD would eventually replace the LP record. Books on cassettes were big sellers as well. Book lovers found they could enjoy literature while doing other things, even while driving to work. In art, Rembrandt Peale's portrait of his younger brother, *Rubens Peale With a Geranium,* sold for $4,070,000, the most ever paid at auction for an American painting. Museums across the country opened or planned new facilities. The Arthur M. Sackler Museum opened at Harvard in October. The Whitney Museum planned an addition, the design of which sparked instant controversy. The Metropolitan Museum proposed a new wing, the Dallas Art Museum opened one, and Ft. Lauderdale was finishing work on its first art museum. A landmark in book publishing was reached this year when Shel Silverstein's 1981 collection of poems and drawings, *A Light in the Attic,* made the best-seller list of *The New York Times* for the 112th week in a row, longer than any other book in the list's 59-year history. The movie industry suffered a 7% drop in ticket sales in 1985. Among the top films of the year were *Back to the Future, Rambo: First Blood Part II,* and *Rocky IV.* Videocassette recorder sales began to skyrocket, producing a new form of competition for movie houses. Notables who died this year included Yul Brynner, known for his almost nonstop

Business and Industry; Science;   III
Education; Philosophy and Religion

IV   **Sports; Social Issues and Crime;**
Folkways; Fashion; Holidays

Dec. 20 Development of the long-awaited **megabit memory chip,** able to store more than 1,000,000 bits of electronic data, was announced by Bell Laboratories. The chip could store four times as much information as the most powerful chip heretofore available. It was stated that mass production could begin in about a year.

Nov. 9 The first world heavyweight boxing match under the auspices of the **International Boxing Federation** (IBF) was won by Larry Holmes, who knocked out James "Bonecrusher" Smith in the 12th round of a bout in Las Vegas, Nev. Holmes had vacated his WBC title when arrangements to fight Greg Page, the top contender, were not completed.

Dec. 1 The **WBA heavyweight boxing championship** was won by Greg Page, who knocked out Gerrie Coetzee of South Africa in the eighth round of a bout in Sun City, Bophuthatswana.

1985

The economy continued to expand, but at the low rate of 2.3%. The unemployment rate at the end of the year was 6.8%, lowest in nearly five years. Consumer prices rose only 3.8% and personal income rose 5.95%. Consumer spending rose by 6.6%. Americans bought a record 15,600,000 automobiles and light trucks. All this good news was balanced by some distressing statistics. The federal deficit hit a record $211,900,000,000 for the fiscal year ending Sept. 30, and the trade deficit for calendar 1985 climbed to a record $148,500,000,000. By mid-September the U.S. for the first time since World War I became a debtor nation, owing more to other countries than was owed to it. To alleviate this imbalance, the U.S., Great Britain, France, West Germany, and Japan agreed on Sept. 22 to take steps to lower the value of the dollar. On the next day the dollar fell in value by 4.29% against other major currencies. In business 1985 was the year of the corporate merger, with about $125,000,000,000 changing hands in buy-out transactions. There were 24 mergers involving $1,000,000,000 or more each. A government report released in October said that at least 6928 accidents involving toxic chemicals had occurred in the past five years, killing more than 135 people. The American Medical Association reported that nearly three times as many medical malpractice suits were being filed compared with ten years earlier. According to a congressional investigation, more than 500,000 persons had obtained false degrees or other credentials in fields ranging from architecture to medicine to zoology. Notables who died this year included Eugene Carson Blake, general secretary of the World Council of Churches from 1966 to 1972, July 31, at 78; Sarah G. Blanding, president of Vassar College from 1946 to 1964, the first woman to hold the position, Mar. 3, at 86; Stuart Chase, the economist and semanticist, Nov. 16, at 97; Archibald M. Crossley, a founder of modern public opinion polling, May 1, at 88; Gardner Cowles, Jr., head of the Cowles publishing and communications empire, July 8, at 82; Milton S. Eisenhower,

The Coca-Cola Company shocked the public on Apr. 23 when it announced it was doing away with its 99-year-old recipe for the famous soft drink and offering a new formula. Faithful Coke drinkers responded so forcefully against the change that on July 10 Coca-Cola was forced to reintroduce the old Coke under a new name, Coca-Cola Classic. In fashion elegance continued to gain favor. Career women were beginning to wear more colorful suits, not just feminized copies of men's traditional wear. Meanwhile, the U.S. Army ruled that its male officers were not allowed to carry umbrellas. The national craze for Cabbage Patch dolls continued, and the classic Barbie doll was given a new French-designed wardrobe as well as a business suit with attaché case. In sports the North American Soccer League went out of business after heavy financial losses. Professional basketball and major league baseball, however, reported record attendance in 1985. This year the major league baseball playoffs were extended to best-of-seven series. Critics of the move said it would detract from the importance of the World Series. In golf the top money winners were Curtis Strange, $542,321, and Nancy Lopez, $416,472. Notables who died this year included James Beard, authority on cooking, Jan. 23, at 81; Rudi Gernreich, avant-garde fashion designer who introduced the topless bathing suit for women in the 1960s, Apr. 21, at 62; Burleigh Grimes, pitcher and member of the Baseball Hall of Fame, Dec. 6, at 92; John B. Kelly, Jr., president of the U.S. Olympic Committee, Mar. 2, at 57; Roger Maris, Yankee batting champ who broke Babe Ruth's single-season home run record in 1961, Dec. 14, at 51; John Scarne, international authority on games and gambling, July 7, at 82; and Joseph "Smoky Joe" Wood, a pitcher who won 34 games for the Boston Red Sox in 1912, July 27, at 95.

Jan. 1 In **college football bowl games,** the results were Boston College 45, Houston 28 in the Cotton Bowl; Washington 28, Oklahoma 17 in the Orange Bowl; USC 20, Ohio State 17 in the Rose Bowl; and

"abused for political ends."

Jan. 20 Pres. **Ronald Reagan was inaugurated** for his second term. Vice Pres. George Bush was also sworn in. Because of bitter cold and snow the inauguration parade scheduled for Jan. 21 was canceled.

Jan. 20–21 A record **cold wave** hit much of the U.S., killing at least 40 people in 15 states. A record temperature of −27° F was reached in Chicago.

Mar. 27 In a decision on the **use of lethal force,** the Supreme Court ruled that police could not shoot fleeing criminal suspects who were unarmed and not considered dangerous. Laws in nearly half the states were invalidated by this decision.

May 5 A ceremony in which Pres. Reagan laid a wreath in a **military cemetery in Bitburg,** West Germany, caused controversy in the U.S. and abroad because among those buried in the cemetery were 49 members of the Nazi Waffen-SS. Earlier in the day Pres. Reagan had placed a wreath at a memorial on the site of the Bergen-Belsen concentration camp.

May 31 **Tornadoes** swept through parts of Pennsylvania, Ohio, New York, and Ontario, Canada, killing 93 people and destroying a number of towns.

June 14 A **TWA jetliner was hijacked in Athens,** Greece, by two Shiite Muslim terrorists, who forced the plane to Beirut, Lebanon, and demanded the release of 766 Shiites held in Israel. Some of the hostages were released, but 39 Americans were removed from the plane and kept hostage. Complicated negotiations led to their release on June 30, after Israel independently began to release the interned Shiites.

July 13 Pres. **Reagan underwent surgery** to remove a cancerous tumor from his colon. For eight hours Vice Pres. George Bush exercised the powers of the presidency.

July 23 A **nuclear energy accord** was signed in Washington, D.C., by Pres. Reagan and Li Xiannian, president of the People's Republic of China. The agreement cleared the way for sale of nonmilitary nuclear technology to China.

Aug. 1 The **federal budget** for the fiscal year beginning Oct. 1 was passed by Congress. It authorized expenditures of $967,600,000,000 and revenues of $795,700,000,000. The resulting deficit was put at $171,900,000,000.

Aug. 2 An **airplane crash** of a Delta Airlines L-1011 at the Dallas–Fort Worth Airport killed 133 people. The plane crashed during an attempted landing in a violent thunderstorm.

Aug. 27 The controversial **Sergeant York** mobile antiaircraft system was scrapped by the Defense Department. Purchases of the weapon were halted. The

acting role in *The King and I,* Oct. 10, at 65; Marc Chagall, the artist, Mar. 28, at 97; Stepin Fetchit, born Lincoln Theodore Perry, the first well-known black Hollywood actor, Nov. 19, at 83; Ruth Gordon, the stage and screen actress, Aug. 28, at 88; Rock Hudson, a movie actor who became the first major public figure known to have died of AIDS, Oct. 2, at 59; Eugene List, the concert pianist, Mar. 1, at 66; Helen MacInnes, master of the spy novel, Sept. 30, at 77; Robert Nathan, the author, May 25, at 91; Eugene Ormandy, musical director of the Philadelphia Orchestra for 44 years, Mar. 12, at 85; Roger Sessions, one of America's foremost composers, Mar. 16, at 88; Eric Sloane, the artist, Mar. 6, at 80; Orson Welles, director and actor, Oct. 10, at 70; E. B. White, author and longtime contributor to *The New Yorker* magazine, Oct. 1, at 86; and Efrem Zimbalist, internationally renowned violinist, Feb. 22, at 94.

Among **books published** this year was *Yeager* by Chuck Yeager with Leo Janos. The autobiography of the celebrated test pilot became a best seller. Other books published this year included *The Kingdom of the Wicked* by Anthony Burgess, a novel; *Chapterhouse: Dune* by Frank Herbert, the sixth novel in the author's science fiction epic; *The Cider House Rules* by John Irving, a novel; *Lake Wobegon Days* by Garrison Keillor, the witty host of the radio show *Prairie Home Companion; Skeleton Crew* by Stephen King, stories in the horror fiction genre; *Masters of Atlantis* by Charles Portis, a novel; *All Fall Down: America's Tragic Encounter with Iran* by Gary Sick; *Family Album* by Danielle Steel, a novel that became a best seller; *Dashiell Hammett* by Julian Symons, a biography of the celebrated mystery writer; *The Old Forest and Other Stories* by Peter Taylor; *Gods of War* by John Toland, the author's first novel; and *Galapagos* by Kurt Vonnegut, a novel.

Jan. 3 **Leontyne Price** gave her farewell performance at the Metropolitan Opera in New York City, 24 years after she first sang there. She was the first black American to become a worldwide star of grand opera.

Jan. 14 **National Book Critics Circle Awards** were voted for the following: fiction, *Love Medicine* by Louise Erdrich; general nonfiction, *Weapons and Hope* by Freeman Dyson; biography, *Dostoevsky: The Years of Ordeal, 1850–59* by Joseph Frank; poetry, *The Dead and the Living* by Sharon Olds; criticism, *Twentieth Century Pleasures* by Robert Hass.

Jan. 21 The **American Book Awards** were presented for the following: fiction, *White Noise* by Don DeLillo; nonfiction, *Common Ground: A Turbulent Decade in the Lives of Three American Families* by J. Anthony Lukas; first fiction, *Easy in the Islands* by Bob Shacochis.

Jan. 24 In a **libel suit against** *Time* magazine, a federal jury decided that the publication had not libeled Ariel Sharon, former Israeli defense minister, in an

diplomat, presidential adviser, and brother of Dwight D. Eisenhower, May 2, at 85; Spencer Kimball, president of the Mormon Church since 1973, Nov. 15, at 90; Simon Kuznets, Nobel Prize–winning economist, July 8, at 84; Charles F. Richter, for whom the Richter scale of earthquake measurement is named, Sept. 30, at 85; and Robert W. Woodruff, who turned the Coca-Cola Company into an international business giant, Mar. 7, at 95.

Jan. 24–27 The **first secret space shuttle flight** was made by the shuttle *Discovery.* Even the launch time had been kept secret for the mission, which was devoted entirely to achieving military objectives.

Feb. 17 A **$120,000,000 libel suit against CBS** was dropped by Gen. William C. Westmoreland, former commander of U.S. forces in Vietnam, after 18 weeks of court testimony. The case involved a 1982 CBS documentary that claimed Westmoreland had withheld important information on enemy troop strength.

Mar. 4 A virtual **ban on leaded gasoline** was ordered by the Environmental Protection Agency, which required removal of 90% of the lead in automobile fuel by the end of the year. The agency contemplated ordering a total ban by 1988.

Mar. 18 The **American Broadcasting Company** was bought by Capital Cities Communications, Inc., for $3,500,000,000. It was the first time one of the three major networks had been sold.

Apr. 8 The **Union Carbide Corporation was sued** by the government of India in connection with a plant disaster at Bhopal, India, on Dec. 3, 1984, that killed some 1700 persons and injured as many as 200,000.

Apr. 24 Two new **U.S. Roman Catholic cardinals** were named by Pope John Paul II. They were Archbishop John J. O'Connor of New York and Archbishop Bernard F. Law of Boston.

May 12 The **first woman Conservative rabbi,** Amy Eilberg, 30, was ordained during graduation ceremonies at Jewish Theological Seminary in New York City.

May 15 It was announced that the skeleton of what was believed to be the **earliest known dinosaur** had been unearthed in the Painted Desert of Arizona. The 225,000,000-year-old skeleton was that of a creature the size of a small ostrich.

May 21 In the **largest multiple birth** on record in the U.S., Patricia Frustaci gave birth to seven children, one stillborn, in California. Three died within a short

Nebraska 28, LSU 10 in the Sugar Bowl. This season the AP and UPI polls chose Brigham Young, which had beaten Michigan 24–17 in the Holiday Bowl, the national collegiate champions of 1984.

Jan. 20 **Super Bowl XIX** was won by the San Francisco 49ers (NFC), defeating the Miami Dolphins (AFC) 38–16. On Jan. 6 the 49ers had shut out the Chicago Bears 23–0 for the NFC championship, and the Dolphins had beaten the Pittsburgh Steelers 45–28 for the AFC title.

Feb. 1–2 **U.S. figure skating championships** were won in Kansas City, Mo., by Brian Boitano, men's singles; Tiffany Chin, women's singles; Jill Watson and Peter Oppegard, pairs; Judy Blumberg and Michael Seibert, dance (fifth consecutive win).

Mar. 3 The **first jockey to win $100,000,000** in career purse money was Willie Shoemaker, who rode Lord at War to victory in the Santa Anita Handicap in Arcadia, Calif.

Mar. 31 The **NCAA women's basketball championship** was won by Old Dominion, defeating Georgia 70–65.

Apr. 1 The **NCAA men's basketball championship** was won by Villanova, which beat Georgetown 66–64.

Apr. 14 The **Masters golf tournament** was won by Bernhard Langer of West Germany, who beat Curtis Strange, Raymond Floyd, and Seve Ballesteros by two strokes.

Apr. 15 The 89th **Boston Marathon** was won by Geoff Smith of Great Britain, who scored his second consecutive win with a time of 2 hrs., 14 min., 5 sec. The first woman to finish was Lisa Larsen Weidenbach of Battle Creek, Mich., with a time of 2 hrs., 34 min., 6 sec.

Apr. 29 The **WBA heavyweight boxing championship** was won by Tony Tubbs in a 15-round decision over Greg Page at Buffalo, N.Y.

May 4 The 111th **Kentucky Derby** was won by Spend a Buck, with a time of 2:00¹/₅. The jockey was Angel Cordero, Jr.

May 18 The 110th **Preakness Stakes** was won by Tank's Prospect, with a time of 1:53²/₅. The jockey was Pat Day.

May 21–30 The **NHL Stanley Cup** was won for the second consecutive year by the Edmonton Oilers, who beat the Philadelphia Flyers four games to one.

May 26 The 69th **Indianapolis 500** auto race was won by Danny Sullivan, completing the 500-mile course in 3 hrs., 16 min., 6.069 sec., with an average speed of 152.982 mph.

May 27–June 9 The **NBA basketball championship** was won by the Los Angeles Lakers, who defeated the Boston Celtics four games to two.

June 2 The **LPGA golf tournament** was won by

Sergeant York, which never performed up to specifications, had cost U.S. taxpayers $1,800,000,000.

Sept. 1 The wreck of the *Titanic,* the luxury liner that sank on its maiden voyage in 1912, was found by a U.S.-French exploratory team. The wreck was found about 500 miles south of Newfoundland, but its exact location was kept secret to discourage salvage attempts.

Sept. 9 Sanctions against South Africa were announced by Pres. Reagan to protest that country's policy of apartheid. Sale of computers was banned, and imports of the Kruggerand were halted. The sanctions, which were relatively mild, were viewed as an effort to head off demands by Congress for sterner measures.

Sept. 18 A U.S. hostage in Lebanon, the Rev. Benjamin Weir, was back in the U.S., Pres. Reagan announced. Weir had been held prisoner in Lebanon for 16 months. Six other Americans, kidnaped between Mar. 1984 and June 1985, were still in the hands of terrorists in Lebanon.

Sept. 26–27 Hurricane Gloria struck off the coast of North Carolina, then moved north to the New York metropolitan region. The storm forced evacuation of some 280,000 coastal residents, but only three people were killed. Winds of up to 130 mph caused massive power line damage. Repairs on Long Island continued for more than a week after the storm.

Oct. 7–10 The Italian liner *Achille Lauro* was hijacked in the Mediterranean by four members of the Palestinian Liberation Front (PLF). En route to Port Said, Egypt, the terrorists shot and killed a wheelchair-bound American, Leon Klinghoffer, 69, and dumped his body overboard. The hijackers surrendered in Egypt on Oct. 9. On the next day an Egyptian airliner flew them out of the country. The jet was intercepted by U.S. fighters and forced to land in Italy, where the four were arrested by Italian authorities. Also with them were Muhammad Abbas, head of the PLF, and another PLF representative, who had joined the others after the hijacking. Abbas was subsequently released and fled to Yugoslavia. The four original hijackers were convicted in Italy on Nov. 19 and imprisoned for possession of guns and explosives.

Oct. 11 The Nobel Peace Prize was awarded to the International Physicians for the Prevention of Nuclear War, a Boston-based group founded by doctors from the U.S. and U.S.S.R. The cofounders were Dr. Bernard Lown of the Harvard School of Public Health and Dr. Yevgeny I. Chazov of the U.S.S.R.

Oct. 27–Nov. 7 Hurricane Juan struck the Gulf Coast, killing seven people and causing some $1,000,000,000

article about the 1982 massacres of Palestinians committed by Lebanese troops in two refugee camps in Lebanon. The jury did find, however, that the article contained a false and defamatory paragraph.

Feb. 26 Grammy Awards were presented for the following: best album of 1984, *Can't Slow Down* by Lionel Richie; best record, "What's Love Got to Do With It" by Tina Turner; best male pop vocalist, Phil Collins for "Against All Odds"; best female pop vocalist, Tina Turner for "What's Love Got to Do With It"; best pop group, the Pointer Sisters for "Jump."

Mar. 8 *The New Yorker* magazine was sold to Samuel I. Newhouse, Jr., for $142,000,000.

Mar. 17 The artist Louise Nevelson announced that more than 25 of her sculptures would be donated to museums in the U.S. and Europe. Among the beneficiaries were the Metropolitan Museum of Art and Cooper Union, both in New York City.

Mar. 25 Academy Awards were presented to *Amadeus* as the outstanding motion picture of 1984; F. Murray Abraham as best actor for *Amadeus;* Sally Field as best actress for *Places in the Heart;* Haing S. Ngor as best supporting actor for *The Killing Fields;* and Peggy Ashcroft as best supporting actress for *A Passage to India.*

Mar. 27 *Joe Egg,* a play by Peter Nichols starring Jim Dale and Stockard Channing, opened at the Longacre Theater in New York City.

Apr. 24 Pulitzer prizes were awarded for the following: fiction, *Foreign Affairs* by Alison Lurie; general nonfiction, *The Good War: An Oral History of World War II* by Studs Terkel; biography, *The Life and Times of Cotton Mather* by Kenneth Silverman; history, *Prophets of Regulation* by Thomas K. McCraw; poetry, *Yin* by Carolyn Kizer; drama, *Sunday in the Park With George* by Stephen Sondheim and James Lapine.

Apr. 25 *Big River* by Roger Miller and William Hauptman, a musical based on Mark Twain's *The Adventures of Huckleberry Finn* starring Daniel H. Jenkins and Ron Richardson, opened at the Eugene O'Neill Theater in New York City.

May 5 *The Art of India: 3000 B.C. to A.D. 1300,* an impressive exhibit including stone and bronze sculptures, opened at the National Gallery of Art in Washington, D.C.

June 2 Tony awards for the 1984–1985 season were presented for the following: best play, *Biloxi Blues;* best musical, *Big River;* best actor in a drama, Derek Jacobi for *Much Ado About Nothing;* best actress in a drama, Stockard Channing for *Joe Egg.*

June 20 The Metropolitan Opera announced that it would abandon its national tour after 1986 because of rising costs and other considerations. The Met had

time. The last of the three survivors did not leave the hospital until Oct. 4. On Dec. 3 the Frustacis filed a $3,200,000 malpractice suit against the physicians and the clinic that had given her fertility drugs.

June 4 In a decision on **school prayers** the Supreme Court struck down an Alabama law permitting one minute of prayer or meditation in public schools. The ruling suggested that other state laws might be found constitutional if they did not have as their sole purpose the fostering of religious activity.

July 1 In a decision on **separation of church and state,** the Supreme Court ruled that public school teachers could not enter parochial school classrooms to provide remedial or enrichment instruction. The ruling applied specifically to programs in New York City and Grand Rapids, Mich.

July 19 **Christa McAuliffe,** 36, a high-school teacher and mother of two from Concord, N.H., was selected from 11,000 applicants to become the first teacher to fly aboard a space shuttle.

Aug. 2 Publication of the **Montgomery Ward & Company catalog** would be discontinued, the retail giant announced, because of increasing costs. The first mail order catalog in the nation, it appeared in 1872 and became an American institution, especially on farms and in small towns.

Aug. 11 In an **industrial accident** reminiscent of the 1984 disaster in Bhopal, India, a cloud of toxic gas was released from a Union Carbide plant in Institute, W.Va. At least 135 people were injured.

Sept. 10 The **Episcopal Church** elected a new leader, Bishop Edmund L. Browning of Hawaii, to a 12-year term as presiding bishop. The election indicated that the church would be under liberal leadership.

Oct. 14 The **Nobel Prize in Physiology or Medicine** was awarded to Michael S. Brown and Joseph L. Goldstein of the University of Texas Health Center in Dallas for their discoveries in the field of cholesterol metabolism and contributions to the treatment of diseases linked to presence of the substance.

Oct. 15 The **Nobel Prize in Economics** was awarded to Franco Modigliani of MIT for his work in analyzing the behavior of household savers and the functioning of financial markets.

Oct. 16 The **Nobel Prize in Chemistry** was awarded jointly to Herbert A. Hauptman of the Medical

Nancy Lopez, who beat Alice Miller by eight strokes with a 15-under-par 273.

June 8 The 117th **Belmont Stakes** was won by Creme Fraiche, with a time of 2:27. The jockey was Eddie Maple. Creme Fraiche was the first gelding ever to win the Belmont, and the trainer Woody Stephens was the first to win the Belmont four successive times.

June 16 The **U.S. Open golf tournament** was won by Andy North, who came from behind to beat Tze-Chung Chen of Taiwan by one stroke.

July 6–7 At the **Wimbledon** tennis championships in England, Martina Navratilova won the women's singles title. Navratilova teamed with Paul McNamee of Australia to win the mixed doubles, and Kathy Jordan teamed with Elizabeth Smylie of Australia to win the women's doubles.

July 11 **Nolan Ryan** of the Houston Astros (NL) became the first pitcher in major league history to strike out 4000 batters when he fanned Danny Heep of the New York Mets on three pitches in the sixth inning at Houston. The Astros won 4–3.

July 14 The **USFL football championship** was won by the Baltimore Stars, who defeated the Oakland Invaders 28–24.

July 14 The **U.S. Women's Open golf tournament** was won by Kathy Baker, who beat Judy Clark by three strokes.

July 16 The **baseball All-Star Game** was won by the National League, 6–1.

July 23 A new **record auction price for a thoroughbred** was set at Lexington, Ky., when a yearling son of Nijinsky II and My Charmer sold for $13,100,000.

July 28 The **Baseball Hall of Fame** inducted Lou Brock, former outfielder; Enos Slaughter, former outfielder; Joseph "Arky" Vaughn, who played shortstop for the Pittsburgh Pirates (1932–1941) and Brooklyn Dodgers (1942–1948); and James "Hoyt" Wilhelm, ace relief pitcher from 1952 to 1972, who compiled major league records in games played, wins, losses, and saves.

Aug. 4 **Tom Seaver** of the Chicago White Sox (AL) became the 17th pitcher in major league history to win 300 games when he led his team to a 4 to 1 win over the New York Yankees at Yankee Stadium. On Oct. 6 the Yankees' Phil Niekro became the 18th 300-game winner, winning 8–0 over the Toronto Blue Jays.

Aug. 11 The **PGA golf tournament** was won by Hubert Green, who beat defending champion Lee Trevino by two strokes.

Aug. 25 **Dwight Gooden,** the 20-year-old pitching phenomenon for the New York Mets (NL), became the youngest major league pitcher to win 20 games in a season. Dr. K, as he was called by his fans, was 20

in damage in Louisiana. Downgraded to a tropical storm, Juan moved north, dumping heavy rains on West Virginia, Virginia, Maryland, and Pennsylvania, causing great damage and killing 42 more people.

Nov. 20–21 A summit meeting in Geneva, Switzerland, was conducted by Pres. Reagan and Mikhail Gorbachev, Communist Party secretary of the U.S.S.R. The meeting was characterized as friendly. No major breakthroughs were reached, but both sides agreed to work toward strategic arms reductions and planned to hold another summit meeting in the U.S. in 1986.

Dec. 11 The so-called **Gramm-Rudman bill** to eliminate the federal deficit by 1991 was passed by Congress. Pres. Reagan signed it the following day. The bill called on the president to impose automatic spending reductions if Congress did not meet each year's deficit ceiling. Social Security, interest on the national debt, and some programs for the poor were exempted from cuts.

Dec. 12 An Arrow Airlines **charter jet crashed** in Gander, Newfoundland, killing all 248 U.S. Army soldiers aboard and the plane's crew of eight. The soldiers, members of the 101st Airborne Division, were on their way to Fort Campbell, Ky., after a tour of duty in the Sinai Peninsula. It was reported that the DC-8 had a history of mechanical problems.

Dec. 30 Nine men and one woman accused of **conspiracy to start a racist revolution** were convicted in Seattle, Wash., on racketeering charges. Members of a white supremacist gang called the Order, they were said to have committed crimes in a coast-to-coast spree to finance their plan to create a homeland free of Jews, blacks, and "white traitors."

gone on tour each year ever since its founding in 1883.

July 16 It was announced that a collection of **rare Hebrew books and manuscripts** sold by Sotheby's in 1984 would be recalled. It had been charged that the scholar who smuggled them out of Nazi Germany and later gave them up for sale did not actually own them. Sotheby's said the works would be given to institutions so that they would be available to scholars and the public.

Aug. 5 Establishment of a **Rock and Roll Hall of Fame** was announced by a group of recording executives. A permanent museum and archive were to be established and the first awards made in Jan. 1986.

Sept. 22 **Emmy Awards** were presented for the following: best actor in a dramatic series, William Daniels for *St. Elsewhere;* best actress in a dramatic series, Tyne Daly for *Cagney and Lacey;* best actor in a limited series or special, Richard Crenna for *The Rape of Richard Beck;* best actress in a limited series or special, Joanne Woodward for *Do You Remember Love?;* best dramatic series, *Cagney and Lacey.*

Oct. 9 *Tango Argentino,* a musical celebration of the tango created by Claudio Segovia and Hector Orezzoli, opened at the Mark Hellinger Theater in New York City.

Nov. 3 *The Treasure Houses of Great Britain,* a lavish exhibit, opened at the National Gallery of Art in Washington, D.C. More than 600 priceless objects were assembled from the stately mansions of Great Britain.

Nov. 26 The rights to **Ronald Reagan's autobiography** were acquired by Random House for $3,000,000. The bid was believed to be the highest ever for a single book. The biography was to be written by Edmund Morris for completion early in 1991.

1986

On New Year's Day Pres. Ronald Reagan appeared on television in the U.S.S.R., and Soviet leader Mikhail S. Gorbachev appeared on U.S. television. Both leaders expressed their hopes for world peace. Despite this apparent warming of U.S.-Soviet relations, the Reagan administration continued its tough policy toward the U.S.S.R. A statement of policy issued Mar. 14 committed the U.S. to "democratic revolution" around the world and implied a lessening of support for dictatorships based simply on the fact they were anticommunist. On Feb. 7 President-for-life Jean-Claude Duvalier of Haiti was forced to flee his country; he was flown to France aboard a U.S. jet. On Feb. 26 Pres. Ferdinand Marcos of the Philippines was forced out of office by a bloodless

For the second year in a row, the Broadway theater set a new record for fewest productions: 26, of which only six were very successful. One of the latter was a revival of an old-fashioned musical, *Me and My Girl.* The movies continued to cater generally to teenagers over other age groups with such films as *Ferris Bueller's Day Off.* Major movies of the year included Woody Allen's amusing *Hannah and Her Sisters; Top Gun,* featuring the exploits of a fighter pilot; and *The Color of Money,* with the ever-popular Paul Newman. In art, the Brooklyn Museum presented *From Courbet to Cezanne: A New 19th Century,* a show exhibiting 130 works from the new Musée D'Orsay in Paris, France. Brooklyn, N.Y., was also the site of the first U.S. performance by

Foundation of Buffalo, N.Y., and Jerome Karle of the Naval Research Laboratory, Washington, D.C., for developing techniques for determining the structures of molecules vital to life.

Nov. 11 The **Mormon Church** elected a new president, Ezra Taft Benson, 80, who had served as secretary of agriculture from 1953 to 1960 under Pres. Dwight D. Eisenhower. Benson succeeded Spencer Kimball, who died on Nov. 15.

Dec. 5 A **libel suit against CBS** and a commentator, Walter Jacobson, by the Brown & Williamson Tobacco Company ended when the jury awarded B&W damages of $5,050,000. Jacobson had charged on the air that the cigarette makers were attempting to lure children into smoking, and called them liars.

Dec. 10 The **highest award for damages** in U.S. history was upheld by a Texas state judge. A jury had ordered Texaco, Inc., to pay $11,100,000,000 to the Pennzoil Company because it had interfered with an agreement for Pennzoil to acquire the Getty Oil Company in 1984. Texaco announced it would appeal the decision.

Dec. 19 The **first woman to receive an artificial heart** was Mary Lund of Kensington, Minn., who was given a small version of the Jarvik-7 pump at Abbot-Northwestern Hospital in Minneapolis, Minn., to keep her alive until a human donor could be found.

Dec. 23 The **costliest farm bill** in history was signed by Pres. Reagan. Estimated to cost $169,000,000,000 over five years, it nonetheless reduced income and price supports to farmers for the first time since 1933.

years, 9 months, and 9 days old when he pitched the Mets to a 9–3 victory over the San Diego Padres.

Sept. 7–8 The **U.S. Open tennis singles championships** were won by Ivan Lendl of Czechoslovakia in the men's division and Hana Mandlikova of Czechoslovakia in the women's division.

Sept. 11 **Pete Rose** of the Cincinnati Reds (NL) set a new major league baseball record of 4192 career hits in a 2–0 win over the San Diego Padres at Cincinnati. The old record of 4191 hits was set by Ty Cobb in 1928.

Sept. 14 The **Miss America** title was won by Susan Akin, 21, from Meridian, Miss., at the annual pageant in Atlantic City, N.J.

Sept. 21 The International Boxing Federation **heavyweight boxing championship** was won by Michael Spinks in a 15-round decision over Larry Holmes in Las Vegas, Nev.

Oct. 5 Eddie Robinson of Grambling State University became the "winningest" college football coach in history when his team picked up its 324th win in his 44-year career. During that time Grambling State had lost 106 games and tied 15.

Oct. 19–27 The **World Series** was won by the Kansas City Royals (AL), defeating the St. Louis Cardinals (NL) four games to three. On Oct. 16 the Royals had won the American League pennant against the Toronto Blue Jays four games to three, and the Cardinals had won the National League pennant against the Los Angeles Dodgers four games to two.

Oct. 27 The 16th **New York City Marathon** was won by Orlando Pizzolato of Italy, gaining his second consecutive win with a time of 2 hrs., 11 min., 34 sec. The first woman finisher was Grete Waitz of Norway, who picked up her seventh win with a time of 2 hrs., 28 min., 34 sec.

1986

The year's top story was the tragic loss of the NASA space shuttle *Challenger* and the deaths of all seven persons aboard. Investigations led to the conclusion that failure of a joint on one of the shuttle's solid-fuel booster rockets had caused the disaster. NASA records showed that agency officials had been warned of problems with the rocket joints. The disaster prompted fresh debate on the U.S. space program, particularly over use of the space shuttle as opposed to unmanned vehicles. For the most part it was a successful year for the national economy. Car and truck sales set a record of 16,000,000, with 28.2% of the vehicles imported. The price of oil fell as low as $12 a barrel in July, lowering the price of gasoline but damaging the domestic oil industry. By late

Drug use by professional athletes became an issue this year following 1985 courtroom revelations by baseball players concerning cocaine use in the major leagues. In February Michael Ray Richardson of the New York Nets basketball team was banned from playing in the NBA after his third drug violation, and John Lucas of the Houston Rockets was released after he failed a drug test. On June 19 Len Bias, a University of Maryland basketball star, died of cocaine poisoning, and on June 27 Don Rogers of the Cleveland Browns football team also died after using cocaine. In football, the major television networks announced they were dropping one-third of the 18 scheduled college bowl game broadcasts for lack of advertising support. This year marked the hundredth

1986 *PRES.* RONALD REAGAN   784

| Exploration and Settlement; Wars; Government; Civil Rights; Statistics | I | | II | Publishing; Arts and Music; Popular Entertainment; Architecture; Theater |

popular uprising. The Reagan administration had urged him to resign following his victory in a rigged election. The Office of Management and Budget announced on Oct. 23 that the federal deficit for the year ended Sept. 30 reached $220,700,000,000, the fourth record figure in five years. Notables who died this year included Rep. Joseph P. Addabbo, Democrat of New York, a powerful figure in the shaping of defense policy, Apr. 10, at 61; Chester Bowles, senator, ambassador, and advertising executive, May 25, at 85; Sen. John P. East, Republican of North Carolina, June 29, at 55; James O. Eastland, Democratic senator from Mississippi for 36 years, Feb. 19, at 81; Charles A. Halleck, Republican of Indiana, who served 16 terms in the House of Representatives and was both minority and majority leader, Mar. 3, at 85; Jacob J. Javits, Republican senator from New York from 1954 to 1981, Mar. 7, at 81; Philip C. Jessup, an authority in the field of international law who served on the International Court of Justice from 1960 to 1969, Jan. 31, at 89; and Adm. Hyman G. Rickover, the "father of the nuclear navy," July 8, at 86.

Jan. 7 Economic sanctions against Libya were ordered by Pres. Reagan in retaliation for alleged Libyan involvement in terrorist attacks on Dec. 27, 1985, at the Rome and Vienna airports. Five U.S. citizens had been among the victims. All Libyan assets in the U.S. were frozen, and all U.S. citizens in Libya were ordered home.

Feb. 19 A United Nations **treaty outlawing genocide** was ratified by the Senate. The treaty had been signed by the U.S. in 1948, but the Senate had never acted on it.

Mar. 24 An **armed clash with Libya** occurred in the Gulf of Sidra after Libyan shore installations launched missiles at a U.S. fleet on maneuvers in the gulf. U.S. missiles damaged the Libyan missile site and destroyed two patrol boats advancing on the fleet.

Mar. 25 Military aid to Honduras amounting to $20,000,000 was approved by Congress following reports of a Nicaraguan military incursion to destroy rebel Contra bases just inside the Honduran border.

the Central Ballet of China. After the company's final appearance at the Brooklyn Academy of Music on Mar. 16, the young dancers from the People's Republic of China began a tour of other U.S. cities. In publishing, the Louisville (Ky.) *Times* and *Courier-Journal* newspapers, owned by the Bingham family for nearly 70 years, were acquired by the Gannett newspaper group on May 19 for $305,000,000. On May 28 the Baltimore *Sun* and *Evening Sun* papers were purchased by the Times Mirror Company of Los Angeles for some $450,000,000. In the newspaper world in general, the trend to abandon the publishing of evening papers continued, with 26 of them shifting to the morning field. In book publishing, the year was marked by the purchase on Sept. 28 of Doubleday & Co. by Bertelsmann AG, a large West German publisher, for $475,000,000. In November Bertelsmann sold the 95% interest Doubleday held in the Mets, New York's NL baseball team, to Nelson Doubleday, Jr., and Fred Wilpon for $95,000,000. Of magazines, one survey showed that the most popular among college students was *Cosmopolitan.*

Notables who died this year included Harold Arlen, composer of such hit songs as "Over the Rainbow," Apr. 23, at 81; Desi Arnaz, prominent television actor, musician, and producer, Dec. 2, at 69; Cass Canfield, a leading book publisher for 40 years, Mar. 27, at 88; Lucia Chase, who helped found the American Ballet Theater in 1940, Jan. 9, at 88; John Ciardi, the poet and translator, Mar. 30, at 69; Broderick Crawford, the actor, Apr. 26, at 74; Benny Goodman, the "King of Swing," June 13, at 77; Cary Grant, suave leading man of the movies for 30 years, Nov. 29, at 82; Frank Herbert, the writer known best for his *Dune* series of science fiction novels, Feb. 11, at 65; L. Ron Hubbard, science fiction writer and founder of Scientology, Jan. 24, at 71; Joseph Kraft, the Washington columnist whose work appeared in some 200 newspapers, Jan. 10, at 61; Alan Jay Lerner, the lyricist and playwright known best for his collaboration with Frederick Loewe on *My Fair Lady* and other hits, June 14, at 67; Raymond Loewy, the father of "streamlining" and industrial design, July 14, at 92; Bernard Malamud, the Pulitzer Prize–winning novelist and short-story writer, Mar. 18, at 71; Una Merkel, one of the few silent film stars able to make the transition to sound films, Jan. 2, at 82; Gordon McRae, the movie actor and singer known best for his performance in *Oklahoma*, Jan. 24, at 64; Ray Milland, the actor, Mar. 10, at 81; Vincente Minnelli, producer of some of Hollywood's best musicals, July 25, at 76; Reuben Nakian, distinguished sculptor, Dec. 4 at 89; Georgia O'Keeffe, the artist, known for her desert paintings and exotic, colorful studies of flowers, Mar. 6, at 98; Otto Preminger, the movie director and producer, Apr. 23, at 80; Kate Smith, one of the most popular singers of the twentieth century, who made "God Bless America" an unofficial

December the price was back up to $16.90 as OPEC threatened to cut production. Hot weather and drought in some mid-Atlantic and southern states did great damage to crops and livestock, so that by the end of July losses were estimated at $2,000,000,000. At the year's end unemployment was down to 6.6%, the lowest figure in six years, while producer prices fell 2.5% for the year, the first decline since 1963. On the other hand the GNP grew only 2.5%, the worst showing in four years, bu the CPI rose only 1.1%, the smallest increase since 1961. The foreign trade deficit, however, rose to $169,780,000,000, a record. The Labor Department reported that in February the number of women professionals in the U.S. topped for the first time the number of men holding professional jobs, by a margin of 29,000. A National Science Board report in March revealed that programs in college-level science, mathematics, and engineering had so declined as to constitute a "grave long-term threat" to the country. The Educational Testing Service of Princeton, N.J., announced it would spend $30,000,000 over 15 years to develop new tests that would focus less on absolute scores and concentrate more on what the test-taker knows and does not know. In June the federal government reported 21,915 cases of the disease AIDS in the U.S. and that 12,008 of these persons had already died. The sale of videocassette recorders continued to boom, with a total of 13,174,000 in 1986. Sales of compact discs reached $930,000,000. Notables who died this year included Herbert W. Armstrong, founder of the Worldwide Church of God, Jan. 15, at 93; Harrison Brown, pioneer in producing plutonium and later a foe of nuclear weapons, Dec. 8, at 93; Arthur F. Burns, Federal Reserve Board chairman and ambassador to West Germany, June 26, at 83; Edwin T. Dahlberg, former president of the National Council of Churches, Sept. 6, at 93; Edward Doisy, St., Nobel Prize winner who isolated vitamin K, Oct. 23, at 92; Dana McLean Greeley, president of the Unitarian Universalist Association, June 13, at 77; Fritz A. Lipman, joint Nobel Prize winner for the discovery of coenzyme, important in the body's metabolism, July 24, at 87; Robert S. Mulliken, Nobel Prize winner for his study of the chemistry of atoms, Oct. 31, at 90; James Rainwater, the Nobel Prize-winning physicist, May 31, at 68; Albert Szent-Györgyi, Nobel Prize winner for isolating vitamin C, Oct. 22, at 93; and Helen Taussig, the founder of pediatric cardiology, May 20, at 87.

Jan. 12–18 The space shuttle *Columbia* completed its seventh orbital mission after liftoff had been postponed a record seven times. Its landing was postponed twice.

anniversary of the tuxedo, first worn by Griswold Lorillard to a ball in Tuxedo Park, N.Y., in the fall of 1886. A rise in tux sales and rentals this year was fueled, no doubt, by the growing popularity of weekend weddings, three-day affairs including dinners, brunches, barbecues, sports activities and, of course, the wedding ceremony itself. The Statue of Liberty also turned 100 this year. Its centennial celebration in New York City in July included a breathtaking parade of tall ships from around the world. Texas celebrated the 150th anniversary of its independence from Mexico with 10,000 different events, including the "World's Largest Rattlesnake Roundup." The Oreo cookie marked its 75th anniversary this year. The ever-popular Popsicle underwent a change, as the manufacturer announced the frozen treat in future would sport only one stick. The company, which began manufacturing Popsicles more than 50 years ago, reported annual sales of 100,000,000 dozen. Vanilla was reported to be the nation's favorite flavor of ice cream. Bloomingdale's, the trendy New York City department store, offered eight rules on how to eat caviar properly (it should be eaten with a fork, and never put lemon on it. The Census Bureau reported there were 2,220,000 unwed couples in the U.S., compared with 523,000 in 1970. In fashion, dress design was more relaxed in comparison with the spare style of 1985. The lean silhouette was in. Notables who died this year included James H. "Jim" Crowley, last surviving member of the so-called Four Horsemen of Notre Dame, the backfield that made football history in the 1920s under coach Knute Rockne, Jan. 15, at 83; Vincent Paul "Vince" DiMaggio, oldest of the three DiMaggio brothers in major league baseball, who played ten seasons in the NL, Oct. 3, at 74; Henry "Hank" Greenberg, slugging first baseman for the Detroit Tigers and member of the Baseball Hall of Fame, Sept. 4, at 75; William "Billy" Haughton, top harness racing driver, after a racing accident, July 15, at 62; Robert L. "Bobby" Layne, star quarterback of the Detroit Lions and member of the Pro Football Hall of Fame, Dec. 1, at 59; Theodore H. "Tedd" Lyons, pitcher for 21 years for the Chicago White Sox and member of the Baseball Hall of Fame, July 25, 85; and William "Bill" Veeck, the maverick baseball team owner known as the "Barnum of Baseball," Jan. 1, at 71.

Jan. 1 In **college football bowl games,** the results were Texas A&M 36, Auburn 16 in the Cotton Bowl; Oklahoma 25, Penn State 10 in the Orange Bowl; UCLA 45, Iowa 28 in the Rose Bowl; and Tennessee 35, Miami 7 in the Sugar Bowl. This season both the AP and UPI polls selected Oklahoma the national collegiate champions of 1985.

Jan. 8 The **Baseball Hall of Fame** elected first baseman and slugger Willie McCovey in his first year

Apr. 2 A terrorist bombing aboard a TWA jet flying from Rome, Italy, to Athens, Greece, killed four American passengers, including one infant. Nine other passengers were injured. An Arab terrorist group claimed responsibility.

Apr. 5 A terrorist bombing in a West Berlin discothèque killed a U.S. soldier and a Turkish woman and wounded 155 other persons, including about 60 Americans. U.S. officials later stated they had firm evidence that Libya was involved in the crime.

Apr. 14 A U.S. air strike against Libya was launched in retaliation for Libya's involvement in the West Berlin bombing of Apr. 5 and other terrorist acts. Sixteen U.S. F-111s flying from Great Britain were joined by U.S. carrier-based planes in attacks on five military bases and terrorist centers near Tripoli and Benghazi.

May 5 The Supreme Court ruled that opponents of capital punishment may be barred from juries in capital cases even if such actions increase the likelihood of conviction. The decision, reversing a lower court ruling, invalidated some pending appeals by death-row inmates.

May 13 A Justice Department commission on pornography concluded that such material was potentially harmful and could lead to violent behavior, particularly against women and children. The commission urged stringent action against the pornography industry. Critics claimed the commission's findings were not supported by available scientific evidence.

May 19 A new gun control law, weakening the 1968 federal gun control law, was signed by Pres. Reagan. Among other provisions, the new law allowed interstate retail sales of rifles. Police organizations had been among the groups that had lobbied against the bill.

May 27 Pres. Reagan announced that U.S. strategic arms policy would no longer be bound by the terms of the unratified SALT II arms agreement. At the

national anthem, June 17, at 79; Blanche Sweet, early film star who appeared in D. W. Griffith movies, Sept. 6, at 90; Rudy Vallee, an enormously popular singer and band leader in the 1920s and 1930s, July 3, at 84; Hal B. Wallis, producer of some 400 movies, including *The Maltese Falcon,* Oct. 5, at 88; Theodore H. White, the Pulitzer Prize–winning writer and acknowledged dean of political journalism, May 15, at 71; and Teddy Wilson, jazz pianist with a 50-year career, July 31, at 73.

Among books published this year was *The Garden of Eden,* a posthumous novel by Ernest Hemingway that received mixed reaction from critics. Another novel, *Gone With the Wind* by Margaret Mitchell, turned 50 on June 30 with publication of a facsimile edition of 50,000. The novel, which sold 25,000,000 copies in its first half century, hit the best-seller list once again. Among novels praised and popular were *Kate Vaiden* by Reynolds Price, *The Beet Queen* by Louise Erdrich, *A Summons to Memphis* by Peter Taylor, and *Roger's Version* by John Updike. Representative of an excellent array of nonfiction titles were *The Man Who Mistook His Wife for a Hat,* the recounting of a number of curious medical cases, by Dr. Oliver Sacks; *Ford: The Men and the Machine* by Robert Lacey; *Crabgrass Frontier: The Suburbanization of America,* winner of two prestigious history prizes, by Kenneth T. Jackson; *Tombee: Portrait of a Cotton Planter* by Theodore Rosengarten; and *The Triumph of Politics: Why the Reagan Revolution Failed* by David A. Stockman, former director of the Office of Management and Budget. None of these matched in sales Bill Cosby's *Fatherhood* or Tom Clancy's thriller *Red Storm Rising.*

Jan. 11 A new record book price was set when William Morrow & Company and Avon Books bid $5,000,000 for North American hardbound and paperback rights to James Clavell's novel *Whirlwind.*

Feb. 17 The National Book Critics Circle Awards were given for the following: fiction, *The Accidental Tourist* by Anne Tyler; general nonfiction, *Common Ground* by J. Anthony Lukas; biography, *Henry James: A Life* by Leon Edel; poetry, *The Triumph of Achilles* by Louise Gluck; criticism, *Habitations of the Word* by William Gass.

Feb. 25 Grammy Awards of the National Academy of Recording Arts and Sciences were given for the following: best record of 1985, "We Are the World" by the all-star rock cast USA for Africa; best album, *No Jacket Required* by Phil Collins; best male pop vocalist, Phil Collins for *No Jacket Required;* best female pop vocalist, Whitney Houston for "Saving All My Love for You"; best pop group, USA for Africa for "We Are the World."

Feb. 26 Robert Penn Warren became the first official poet laureate of the U. S. Daniel Boorstin, the Librarian of Congress, made the appointment.

Jan. 24 The spacecraft *Voyager 2* flew within 50,679 miles of the planet Uranus, discovering new moons and rings and obtaining the first evidence of a magnetic field around the planet.

Jan. 28 The **space shuttle *Challenger*** exploded 74 seconds after liftoff at Cape Canaveral, Fla., killing all seven astronauts aboard, including Christa McAuliffe, 37, a Concord, N.H., schoolteacher, the first private citizen chosen for a space shuttle flight. On June 9 a presidential commission report identified failure of a seal on a solid-fuel booster rocket as the cause of the explosion and criticized NASA for a long history of managerial and engineering mistakes. On July 2 NASA announced it would modify the faulty booster rocket joints to eliminate the danger of further booster failures.

Mar. 10 The only **California condor egg** produced in the wild this season was found destroyed in the Ventura Valley in California, biologists reported. Only five California condors were known to exist in the wild.

Mar. 11 In a controversy over the **teaching of Roman Catholic doctrine,** the Rev. Charles E. Curran, a liberal theologian at the Catholic University of America in Washington, D.C., was ordered by the Vatican to retract his views on birth control and other sexual issues or lose the right to teach Roman Catholic doctrine.

Mar. 15 In a statement on the **treatment of terminal patients,** the American Medical Association said it was ethical for doctors to withhold "all means of life-prolonging medical treatment."

Apr. 3 The **U.S. national debt** exceeded $2,000,000,000,000, having doubled in five years.

Apr. 16 The first **surrogate birth of a test-tube baby,** a girl, was announced by spokesmen at Mount Sinai Hospital in Cleveland, Ohio.

Apr. 17 Computers using the **megabit memory chip,** capable of storing more than 1,000,000 bits of electronic data, were being manufactured for the first time, IBM officials announced.

Apr. 22 The first **genetically altered virus** to be released into the environment was approved by the Department of Agriculture. It was to be used to fight a form of herpes affecting swine, which caused an annual $60,000,000 in damage.

of eligibility. On Mar. 10 second baseman Bobby Doerr and catcher Ernie "Schnozz" Lombardi were also voted into the Hall of Fame.

Jan. 17 The **WBA heavyweight boxing championship** was won by Tim Witherspoon in a 15-round decision over Tony Tubbs in Atlanta, Ga.

Jan. 26 **Super Bowl XX** was won by the Chicago Bears (NFC), who defeated the New England Patriots (AFC) 46–10. The Bears had beaten the Los Angeles Rams 24–0 for the NFC title on Jan. 11. On the next day the Patriots had defeated the Miami Dolphins 31–14 for the AFC title.

Feb. 6–8 **U.S. figure skating championships** were won in Uniondale, N.Y., by Brian Boitano, men's singles; Debi Thomas, women's singles; Gillian Wachsman and Todd Waggoner, pairs; Renee Roca and Donald Adair, dance. Thomas was the first black to win the singles championship.

Mar. 22 The **WBC heavyweight boxing championship** was won by Trevor Berbick in a 12-round decision over Pinklon Thomas in Las Vegas, Nev.

Mar. 30 The **NCAA women's basketball championship** was won by Texas, defeating USC 97–81.

Mar. 31 The **NCAA men's basketball championship** was won by Louisville, defeating Duke 72–69.

Apr. 2 The **three-point field goal** in men's basketball, made from a minimum distance of 16 ft., 9 in. from the basket, was adopted by the NCAA. The association also approved use of instant TV replays to check scoring and timing decisions.

Apr. 11 A new **sailing record** for a solo nonstop circumnavigation of the globe was set by Dodge Morgan, 54, who arrived in St. George, Bermuda, aboard his 60-foot sloop *American Promise.* Morgan, the first American to complete such a voyage, had left Bermuda on Nov. 12, 1985, and had sailed 27,000 miles in 150 days. The previous record had been 292 days.

Apr. 13 The **Masters golf tournament** was won for a record sixth time by Jack Nicklaus, who at 46 also became the oldest golfer to win the Masters.

Apr. 21 The 90th **Boston Marathon** was won by Bob de Castella of Australia, with a time of 2 hrs., 7 min., 51 sec. The winner in the women's division was Ingrid Kristiansen of Norway, with a time of 2 hrs., 24 min., 55 sec.

May 2 An **expedition to the North Pole** was completed by six U.S. and Canadian adventurers, the first expedition since 1909 to reach the pole assisted only by dogs. They made the 500-mile trek from Ward

same time, he announced that two Poseidon submarines would be dismantled to make room for a new Trident submarine and keep the U.S. in step with the treaty's provisions.

June 11 Constitutional protection for the **right to abortion** was narrowly reaffirmed by the Supreme Court. The decision voided a Pennsylvania law because some of its provisions were designed to deter women from having abortions and others would require doctors to risk the health of pregnant women.

June 17 Pres. Reagan announced that **Warren E. Burger** would retire as chief justice of the Supreme Court, effective July 10. The president named Associate Justice William H. Rehnquist as Burger's successor, and also named Antonin Scalia, of the U.S. Court of Appeals for the District of Columbia, to the Court. The changes were interpreted as a gain for conservative judicial philosophy.

June 18 A **midair collision** between a plane and a helicopter over the Grand Canyon killed all 25 persons aboard the two aircraft.

June 19 **Cyanide poisoning** was declared the cause of death of two persons in the Seattle, Wash., area. Both had taken Extra-Strength Excedrin capsules containing the poison. Bristol-Myers, the maker of Excedrin, announced the next day it was withdrawing all its nonprescription capsule drugs from sale.

June 27 A **federal budget** for fiscal 1987, providing for spending of $995,000,000,000 and a deficit of $142,600,000,000, was passed by Congress. The bill cut Pres. Reagan's request for defense spending by $28,000,000,000, but the overall price tag was virtually the same as the president's Feb. 5 budget request.

June 27 **U.S. actions against Nicaragua,** including aid to antigovernment rebels, was ruled a violation of national law by the International Court of Justice. The U.S. was ordered to stop arming and training the insurgents and to pay Nicaragua for damages. U.S.

Mar. 24 **Academy Awards** were presented to *Out of Africa* as the outstanding motion picture of 1985; William Hurt as best actor for *Kiss of the Spider Woman;* Geraldine Page as best actress for *The Trip to Bountiful;* Don Ameche as best supporting actor for *Cocoon;* and Anjelica Huston as best supporting actress for *Prizzi's Honor.*

Apr. 2 Rare **Chinese manuscripts** dating to the twelfth century were discovered by curators at the New Orleans Museum of Art. The curators had been examining a recently donated Buddhist sculpture when they found the manuscripts inside, apparently undisturbed for 800 years.

Apr. 8 **Clint Eastwood,** the actor and director, was elected mayor of Carmel, Calif., by a landslide in a much publicized election.

Apr. 17 **Pulitzer prizes** were awarded for the following: fiction, *Lonesome Dove* by Larry McMurtry; general nonfiction, *Move Your Shadow: South Africa, Black and White* by Joseph Lelyveld and *Common Ground: A Turbulent Decade in the Lives of Three American Families* by J. Anthony Lukas; biography, *Louise Bogan: A Portrait* by Elizabeth Frank; poetry, *The Flying Change* by Henry Taylor. No award was given for drama.

Apr. 27 A **video pirate** interrupted the showing of a cable TV movie by Home Box Office by overriding the broadcast with a message saying he would not pay for his cable service. The FCC and commercial users of satellite transmissions expressed dismay that an unknown person could override the HBO signal.

Apr. 29 Probably the worst **library fire** in U.S. history destroyed or damaged some 800,000 books at the Los Angeles Central Library. On May 5 officials reported that the fire, which caused $22,000,000 in damage, had been deliberately set.

May 6 A new record **auction price for a contemporary sculpture,** $1,300,000, was bid by a New York City art dealer for David Smith's 1963 welded-steel work *Voltri-Bolton XXIII.*

May 23 The 75th anniversary of the opening of the **New York Public Library**'s building on Fifth Ave. was celebrated. Restoration of the landmark structure to its original condition, while adapting it to modern needs, had begun in 1981 and was nearing completion.

June 1 **Television coverage of Senate proceedings** was begun, in a test that was to continue until July 15. The House of Representatives had allowed such coverage since Mar. 19, 1979.

June 1 The **Metropolitan Opera** completed its final national tour with a performance of *La Traviata* at Northrup Auditorium in Minneapolis, Minn.

Apr. 27 Formation of the **largest ad agency** in the world was announced. The new company, formed by the merger of BBDO International, the Doyle Dane Bernbach Group, and Needham Harper Worldwide, would have some $5,000,000,000 a year in advertising billings.

Apr. 29 "Clear and unconditional" **opposition to use of nuclear weapons** was voted unanimously by the Council of Bishops of the United Methodist Church.

May 6 The **first American Indian to become a Roman Catholic bishop,** the Rev. Donald E. Pelotte, 41, was ordained in Gallup, N.Mex.

May 30 The first outdoor test of **genetically engineered plants** was begun when genetically altered tobacco was planted on a Wisconsin farm. The field test opened up the possibility of creating high-yield crops that would reduce farmers' dependence on toxic chemicals to control pests.

June 9 Life-prolonging medical treatment for severely handicapped infants could not be required by federal regulations, the Supreme Court ruled, noting there was no evidence of discrimination against such infants and therefore no basis for federal intervention.

June 10 In what was seen as a **victory for fundamentalism,** the Rev. Adrian Rodgers of Memphis, Tenn., was elected president of the Southern Baptist Convention in Atlanta, Ga. He defeated the Rev. Winfred Moore of Amarillo, Tex., a moderate.

June 12 The number of **deaths from AIDS** (acquired immune deficiency syndrome) would increase more than tenfold in five years, federal health officials predicted. By 1991 the disease would afflict some 270,000, causing 179,000 deaths, at a health cost of up to $16,000,000,000 annually.

June 19 The **third artificial heart recipient,** Murray P. Haydon, died at 59 in a Louisville, Ky., hospital. He had received the heart on Feb. 17, 1985. His death left William J. Schroeder the only surviving artificial heart recipient.

July 1 Barber B. Conable, a highly regarded former Republican congressman from New York, began work as president of the World Bank. The White House had announced his appointment Mar. 13.

Hunt Island, Canada, in 56 days and returned from the pole by airplane.

May 3 The 112th **Kentucky Derby** was won by Ferdinand, with a time of 2:02⁴/₅. The jockey was Willie Shoemaker, 54, who picked up his fourth Derby win and became the oldest jockey to win the annual racing classic.

May 16–24 The **NHL Stanley Cup** championship was won by the Montreal Canadiens, who beat the Calgary Flames four games to one.

May 17 The 111th **Preakness Stakes** was won by Snow Chief, with a time of 1:54⁴/₅. The jockey was Alex Solis.

May 25 In an event called **Hands Across America,** nearly 6,000,000 people linked hands in a chain that stretched 4150 miles from New York City to Long Beach, Calif., broken only along a few desert stretches. Sponsors hoped to raise $50,000,000 to aid the hungry and homeless in the U.S.

May 26–June 8 The **NBA basketball championship** was won by the Boston Celtics, beating the Houston Rockets four games to two for their 16th NBA title.

May 31 The 70th **Indianapolis 500** auto race was won by Bobby Rahal, completing the 500-mile course in 2 hrs., 55 min., 43.48 sec., with an average speed of 170.722 mph. It was the first time the race was run in under three hours. Originally scheduled for May 25, the race had been postponed because of rain, the first postponement since 1915.

June 1 The **LPGA golf tournament** was won by Pat Bradley, who became the first to win all four of the top women's tournaments: the LPGA, the U.S. Women's Open, the du Maurier Classic, and the Nabisco Dinah Shore. On May 18 she had become the first woman to exceed $2,000,000 in career earnings.

June 7 The 118th **Belmont Stakes** was won by Danzig Connection, with a time of 2:29⁴/₅, the slowest time since 1980. The jockey was Chris McCarron. It was trainer Woody Stephens' fifth straight Belmont victory.

June 8 In the **longest nine-inning game** in American League baseball history, the Baltimore Orioles beat the New York Yankees 18–9 at Yankee Stadium in 4 hrs., 16 min.

June 15 The **U.S. Open golf tournament** was won by Raymond Floyd, 43, who beat Chip Beck and Lanny Wadkins by two strokes to become the oldest golfer to win the championship.

July 3–6 **Liberty Weekend,** a gala national celebration, capped a three-year, $70,000,000 restoration of the Statue of Liberty. On July 3 Pres. Reagan

Exploration and Settlement; Wars; Government; Civil Rights; Statistics	I		II	Publishing; Arts and Music; Popular Entertainment; Architecture; Theater

missile defense system, popularly known as "Star Wars."

Oct. 14 The **Nobel Peace Prize** was awarded to Elie Wiesel, author and human rights activist. He was cited as a "spiritual leader" against "violence, repression, and racism."

Oct. 22 A revised **federal income tax law** was signed by Pres. Ronald Reagan. The most complete revision of the tax code in more than 40 years, the new law lowered tax rates for almost everyone while eliminating many previous deductions and other tax preferences. The top rate for individuals was lowered from 50% to 38.5%. Most of the changes were to go into effect on Jan. 1, 1987. The total amount of taxes to be collected was expected to remain about the same.

Nov. 2 One **American hostage in Lebanon,** David P. Jacobsen, director of the American Hospital in Beirut, Lebanon, held by kidnapers for 18 months, was freed. Another kidnap victim of Moslem terrorists, the Rev. Lawrence M. Jenco, had been released on July 26. However, on Apr. 17 another hostage, Peter Kilburn, a librarian at the American University of Beirut, was found dead. The terrorists subsequently seized Frank Reed, an American educator, on Sept. 9; Joseph J. Cicippio, chief accountant at the American University, on Sept. 12; and Edward A. Tracy, an author, on Oct. 21.

Nov. 3 What became known as the **Iran–Contra affair** was revealed when a Lebanese magazine reported that the U.S. had been secretly selling arms to Iran in the hope of securing the release of hostages held in Lebanon. American intelligence sources on Nov. 6 confirmed that the operation had taken place. On Nov. 12 Pres. Reagan admitted that he knew of the arms sale, but on Nov. 25 he said he had not been fully informed of all that went on. That same day it was revealed that some of the money received from the sale of arms to Iran had been secretly diverted to the Nicaraguan rebels, known as Contras. Also on Nov. 25 the two officials who were the major planners and overseers of the scheme left office: Vice Adm. John M. Poindexter, national security adviser, resigned, and his assistant, Marine Lt. Col. Oliver L. North, was dismissed. On Nov. 26 the president appointed a three–member panel, headed by former Sen. John G. Tower, to investigate the actions of the National Security Council staff. Meanwhile, Congress prepared to carry out its own investigation, and on Dec. 19 an independent counsel was named to head another inquiry into what was becoming a national scandal.

Nov. 4 In **congressional elections** the Democrats won control of the Senate, 53–47, with a gain of eight seats. They retained control of the House of Representatives, 253–182, a loss of five seats.

May 6 A new record **auction price for a contemporary sculpture**, $1,300,000, was bid by a New York City art dealer for David Smith's 1963 welded-steel work *Voltri-Bolton XXIII.*

May 23 The 75th anniversary of the opening of the **New York Public Library**'s building on Fifth Ave. was celebrated. Restoration of the landmark structure to its original condition, while adapting it to modern needs, had begun in 1981 and was nearing completion.

June 1 **Television coverage of Senate proceedings** was begun, in a test that was to continue until July 15. The House of Representatives had allowed such coverage since Mar. 19, 1979.

June 1 The **Metropolitan Opera** completed its final national tour with a performance of *La Traviata* at Northrup Auditorium in Minneapolis, Minn.

June 1 The **Antoinette Perry, or Tony, Awards** for the 1985–1986 season were presented for the following: best play, *I'm Not Rappaport* by Herb Gardner; best musical, *The Mystery of Edwin Drood;* best actor in a play, Judd Hirsch for *I'm Not Rappaport;* best actress in a play, Lily Tomlin for *The Search for Signs of Intelligent Life in the Universe.*

June 18 Some 1000 works by **Thomas Eakins,** the nineteenth-century U.S. painter, were acquired by the Pennsylvania Academy of Fine Arts. The collection, held privately since Eakins' death in 1916, was expected to shed new light on the artist's life and work.

Aug. 9 The artist **Andrew Wyeth** revealed the existence of 240 works of art secretly painted by him over 15 years. All but one of them were of a woman known only as Helga but later revealed to be a Wyeth neighbor. The collection was bought for an estimated $10,-000,000 or more by a collector, Leonard E. B. Andrews.

Sept. 21 **Emmy Awards** were presented for the following: best drama series, *Cagney and Lacey;* best comedy series, *The Golden Girls;* best actor in a drama series, William Daniels in *St. Elsewhere;* best actress in a drama series, Sharon Gless in *Cagney and Lacey;* best actor in a comedy series, Michael J. Fox in *Family Ties;* best actress in a comedy series, Betty White in *The Golden Girls.*

Business and Industry; Science; Education; Philosophy and Religion III		IV Sports; Social Issues and Crime; Folkways; Fashion; Holidays

Aug. 6   The **longest-surviving recipient of an artificial heart,** William J. Schroeder, died at age 54. He had suffered a series of strokes. Schroeder received the implant on Nov. 25, 1984, and lived 620 days. He was the second recipient and the last survivor of five persons to have had permanent artificial hearts implanted.

Aug. 29   The **Evangelical Lutheran Church** in America was established by the merging of the Lutheran Church in America, the American Lutheran Church, and the Association of Evangelical Lutheran Churches. The new church, with 5,300,000 members, represented about two-thirds of all Lutherans in the U.S.

Sept. 4   In an unusual action, **the Vatican** ordered an American archbishop to turn over to an auxiliary bishop authority in five areas involving such social issues as birth control and homosexuality. Archbishop Raymond Hunthausen of Seattle, Wash., had previously been criticized for his liberal position on certain issues. The next day 140 Catholic leaders in the diocese protested in a letter to the Vatican. On May 27, 1987, full authority was restored to Archbishop Hunthausen.

Oct. 13   The **Nobel Prize in Physiology or Medicine** was awarded to Rita Levi–Montalcini, holder of dual U.S. and Italian citizenship, of the Institute of Cell Biology in Rome, and Stanley Cohen of Vanderbilt University. They were honored for their discovery of substances that influence cell growth.

Oct. 15   The **Nobel Prize in Chemistry** was awarded to Dudley R. Herschback of Harvard University, Yuan T. Lee of the University of California, and John C. Polanyi of the University of Toronto for their discovery of a method of studying chain reactions molecule by molecule.

Oct. 16   The **Nobel Prize in Economics** was awarded to James M. Buchanan of George Mason University for his studies in applying economic principles to political decision making.

Oct. 20   **Withdrawal from South Africa** was announced by General Motors, the largest American company with business interests there. It said it was selling its operations. On Oct. 21 International Business Machines made a similar announcement, followed by Eastman Kodak on Nov. 19 and Citibank, formerly opposed to such action, on June 16, 1987.

Dec. 23   The **first nonstop flight around the world without refueling** was completed when the experimental airplane *Voyager* landed at Edwards Air Force Base, California, after a journey of 25,012 miles that took 9 days, 3 min., 44 sec. Made of plastic and stiffened paper, the fragile-looking plane carried five

Shriver to win the women's doubles. Ken Flach and Kathy Jordan won the mixed doubles.

July 14   The **U.S. Women's Open golf tournament** was won by Jane Geddes in an 18-hole playoff with Sally Little.

July 15   The **baseball All-Star Game** was won by the American League over the National League, 3–2.

July 27   Greg LeMond became the **first American to win the Tour de France,** the best-known bicycle racing event in the world. LeMond covered the 2500-mile over-the-road route in 119 hrs., 35 min., 19 sec., beating his nearest competitor by 3 min., 10 sec. The race began on July 4.

Aug. 11   The **PGA golf tournament** was won by Bob Tway, who sank a spectacular bunker shot on the final hole to edge out Greg Norman.

Aug. 20   The third worst **mass murder** in U.S. history to date took place in Edmond, Okla. Patrick Henry Sherrill, described as always lonely and who had lost his post-office job for lack of competence, shot and killed 14 of his former co-workers, wounded 6 others, and then killed himself.

Sept. 7   The **U.S. Open tennis singles championships** were won by Martina Navratilova over Helena Sukova of Czechoslovakia in the women's division and by Ivan Lendl of Czechoslovakia over his countryman, Miloslav Mecir, in the men's division.

Sept. 17   The **Miss America** title was won by Kellye Cash, 21, of Memphis, Tenn., at the annual pageant in Atlantic City, N.J.

Sept. 23   Congress voted to make the rose the **official national flower** of the U.S. The subject had been debated off and on for about 100 years.

Oct. 18–27   The **World Series** was won by the New York Mets (NL), who defeated the Boston Red Sox (AL) four games to three. New York lost the first two games at home, and the Sox lost the next two in Boston before winning game five to take a three games to two advantage. The sixth game, played in New York, went to the Mets 6–5 in the tenth.

Nov. 2   The 17th **New York City Marathon** was won in the men's division by Gianni Poli of Italy in a time of 2 hrs., 11 min., 6 sec. The women's division was won for the eighth time by Grete Waitz of Norway with a time of 2 hrs., 28 min., 6 sec.

Nov. 14   In one of the nation's **biggest financial scandals,** Ivan F. Boesky agreed to pay the government $100,000,000 as a penalty for illegal insider trading. The Securities and Exchange Commission announced that Boesky was barred for life from participating in the securities business, but he was allowed to liquidate stocks in order to pay off $1,400,000,000 of debt owed by his firm. On Apr. 23, 1987, he pleaded guilty to one charge of conspiracy to file false documents with the federal government; on Dec. 18 he was sentenced to

Nov. 6 An **immigration act** that established new and drastically changed policies concerning aliens in the U.S. was signed into law by Pres. Reagan. Employers were to be prohibited from employing illegal aliens, but many such persons would be given an opportunity to secure legal status, by showing that they entered the U.S. before Jan. 1, 1982, and had resided here continuously "in an illegal status."

Dec. 31 At least **95 persons died in a fire** in a high-rise hotel in San Juan, Puerto Rico. It was later determined that the fire was caused by a disgruntled employee who probably did not intend to do more than shake up the management.

Nov. 17 The **American Book Awards** were presented as follows: fiction, *World's Fair* by E. L. Doctorow; nonfiction, *Arctic Dreams* by Barry Lopez.

Dec. 15 America's most famous music auditorium, **Carnegie Hall** in New York City, reopened with a gala concert featuring many noted musicians. It had been closed for seven months for a $50,000,000 remodeling.

1987

The nation celebrated the 200th anniversary of its Constitution with two separate ceremonies in Philadelphia, where it was written in 1787. On May 25 delegates from the 13 original states held a ceremony on Independence Mall. On July 16, 200 members of Congress assembled in the Quaker City, ending their visit the next day with a ceremony commemorating the signing of the Constitution and featuring the ringing of a replica of the Liberty Bell. In Washington the *Post* reported that in fiscal 1987 the U.S. gave $660,000,000 in military aid to the Afghans resisting the Soviet invasion. About the same time, in Waukee, Iowa, the plight of some farmers was dramatized when a bank foreclosed the mortgage on the home of Ann Zimmerman, who had been the state's first woman lieutenant governor. Back in Washington, it was revealed that for over 50 years the FBI had been busy keeping a number of America's leading authors under surveillance, including John Steinbeck, Gertrude Stein, Norman Mailer, and William F. Buckley, Jr. Also in Washington, in March, the "Grate American Sleep-Out" took place to publicize the distress of the homeless in the nation's capital. Taking part were actor Martin Sheen, Mayor Marion Barry, Jr., and Congressman Tony Coelho. The Hispanic population in the U.S., the Census Bureau reported, had grown by 30% since 1980 and stood at 18,800,000. In the good old summertime a heat wave in the Midwest and East was blamed for nearly 100 deaths, with some areas suffering temperatures near or above 100° for 17 days. Notable people who died during the year included William J. Casey, director if the CIA and former chairman of the Securities and Exchange Commission, May 6, at 74; Ira C. Eaker, who was commander of U.S. air forces in Europe in World War II and helped establish the Air Force as a separate service, Aug. 6, at 92; Alfred M. Landon, Republican candidate for president in 1936, Oct.

Successful Broadway musicals were bigger, if not better, than ever. *Les Misérables* (from England) had advance ticket sales (some as high as $50) of $11,000,000, and *Starlight Express*, a show whose main features were its setting and gadgetry, cost $8,000,000 to stage, a record. The only successful drama was *Fences* by August Wilson. The movies provided a varied fare, including such comedies as *Three Men and a Baby, Raising Arizona*, and *Moonstruck*. *Full Metal Jacket* and *Good Morning, Vietnam* concerned the Vietnam war. Also popular and worthy were *Broadcast News, The Last Emperor*, and *Empire of the Sun*. An unusual art exhibit opened in March in Leningrad, displaying 116 works by the three Wyeths—N.C., son Andrew, and grandson James. As another sign, perhaps, of more cordial relations between the U.S. and the U.S.S.R., a temporary exchange of masterpieces was arranged with the National Gallery of Art, sending an El Greco to the Hermitage in Leningrad, which in turn sent a Titian to Washington. In Philadelphia, the Museum of Art staged the largest display of Chinese ceramic sculpture ever seen outside China, and in New York the Metropolitan Museum held the most important exhibit ever to come out of Israel, "Treasures of the Holy Land: Ancient art from the Israel Museum." Both these exhibits were to go to Houston and Los Angeles. In North Adams, Mass., 28 vacant factory buildings were slated to house one of the largest collections of contemporary art, on loan from Count Giuseppe Pahza di Biumo. On the West Coast, Norton Simon, the industrialist, and the University of California at Los Angeles reached an agreement calling for the transfer of the large art collections owned by Simon to the school. The gift was said to be worth $750,000,000. At auction, artworks by Americans commanded higher prices than ever: a Georgia O'Keeffe work selling for $1,900,000, a record for the artist; an

| Business and Industry; Science; Education; Philosophy and Religion | III | | IV | Sports; Social Issues and Crime; Folkways; Fashion; Holidays |

times its weight in fuel. The pilot was Richard G. Rutan and the copilot Jeana Yeager.

Dec. 31 The production of alloys that provide **superconductivity** at much higher temperatures than ever before was announced by Bell Laboratories and by University of Houston researchers. The Bell Labs material was reported to achieve full superconductivity at 36 K (0° on the Kelvin scale is equal to −460°, or absolute zero, on the Fahrenheit scale).

Dec. 31 On the **New York Stock Exchange** the Dow Jones average of industrial stocks closed the year at 1895.95. On Dec. 2 it had reached a record high of 1955.57, and on Dec. 19 a record 244,700,000 shares were traded.

three years in prison; and on Mar. 24, 1988, he began to serve his sentence.

Nov. 22 The WBC heavyweight boxing championship was won by Mike Tyson, who knocked out Trevor Berbick in the second round at Las Vegas, Nev. Tyson, 20 years old, became the youngest heavyweight champion in boxing history.

Dec. 12 The WBA heavyweight boxing championship was won by James "Bonecrusher" Smith, who knocked out Tim Witherspoon in the first round of a bout in New York City.

1987

In spite of staging in October the greatest stock market crash in history, the national economy had a more or less successful year. Unemployment was down to 5.7%, the lowest since mid-1979, and the GNP rose 3.8%, increasing for the sixth consecutive year. On the other hand, the CPI was up 4.4%, the highest rate of inflation since 1981, and the trade deficit, at $171,220,000,000, set a record for the fifth year in a row, although the December deficit was the lowest in 11 months. The dollar weakened, ending the year at 121.05 Japanese yen, down 23% compared with the previous year end. Black-owned industrial and service businesses set a record, with $4,100,000,000 of sales. The recorded-music business prospered again. Unit sales of compact discs were up 93% to 102,000,000, with a value of $1,600,000,000. Sales of cassette tapes rose 19% to 410,000,000, worth about $2,900,000,000. However, sales of record albums and LPs declined 15% to 107,000,000, worth $793,000,000. *Forbes* magazine declared that Sam Moore Walton, 69, founder of the Wal-Mart discount stores, was, for the third year in a row, the richest American, worth $8,500,000,000. During the year 30 states, compared with only five in 1983, appropriated money to fight the disease AIDS, and one estimate of what it would cost to battle AIDS nationwide in 1991 was $8,500,000,000. Among notable persons who died were I. W. Abel, a founder of the United Steel Workers of America and its president from 1965 to 1977, Aug. 10, at 78; Walter H. Brattain, cowinner of the 1956 Nobel Prize in Physics for the invention of the transistor, Oct. 13, at 85; Henry Ford II, grandson of the founder of the giant automaking company, whose management brought the concern back from a sharp decline, Sept. 29, at 70; and Walter W. Heller, economic adviser to presidents John F. Kennedy and Lyndon B. Johnson, June 15, at 71.

As in other years, Americans faced new problems, tried new or unusual things, set records, committed crimes. A commercial for condoms, a protection against the disease AIDS, first appeared on TV in a major market on Jan. 16, on KRON in San Francisco. In fashion, the miniskirt was back for the first time since the early 1970s. Many women refused to exhibit their thighs, and this time, more than before, the mini raised the question of appropriate wear at work for women aspiring to the executive suite. Noteworthy people who died included Wayne W. "Woody" Hayes, successful football coach at Ohio State, Mar. 12, at 74; Richard D. "Dick" Howser, baseball player and manager who led the Kansas City Royals to their only World Series victory, in 1985, June 18, at 51; Travis Jackson, shortstop for the New York Giants for 15 years and a member of the Baseball Hall of Fame, July 27, at 83; Thomas G. Lanphier, Jr., who in World War II shot down the plane carrying Adm. Isoroku Yamamoto, commander of the Japanese navy, Nov. 26, at 71; and William M. Masland, who in 1943 commanded the first round-the-world flight by a commercial aircraft, Feb. 20, at 79.

Jan. 1–2 In **college football bowl games,** the results were Ohio State 28, Texas A&M 12 in the Cotton Bowl; Oklahoma 42, Arkansas 8 in the Orange Bowl; Arizona State 22, Michigan 15 in the Rose Bowl; and Nebraska 30, Louisiana State 15 in the Sugar Bowl. Both the AP and UPI polls chose Penn State as national champion for 1986 after Pennsylvania's Nittany Lions, in a battle of previously undefeated teams, triumphed over Miami (Fla.) 14–10 in the Fiesta Bowl on Jan. 2.

Jan. 25 **Super Bowl XXI** was won by the New York Giants (NFC), defeating the Denver Broncos (AFC) 39–20. On Jan. 11, the Giants had won the NFC title by defeating the Washington Redskins 17–0 and

12, at 100; Bayard Rustin, longtime civil rights leader, Aug. 24, at 77; and Maxwell D. Taylor, commander of airborne troops in World War II, Apr. 19, at 85.

Jan. 4 The **crash of a 12-car Amtrak passenger train** with three Conrail freight engines near Chase, Md., killed 15 people and injured more than 175. It was the worst accident in Amtrak's history and occurred when the train and engines were mistakenly merged onto the same track.

Jan. 22 An **East Coast blizzard** raged from Maine to Florida, causing at least 37 deaths. Parts of North Carolina received 20 inches of snow.

Jan. 24 Three **Americans were taken hostage in Lebanon.** All members of the faculty of Beirut University College, they were kidnaped by gunmen in West Beirut. They were Allen Steen, Jesse Turner, and Robert Polhill. On June 17 another American, Charles Glass, a journalist, was kidnaped, but on Aug. 18 he either escaped or was allowed to escape. At this time five other Americans were being held captive by Moslem terrorists.

Feb. 4 Pres. Ronald Reagan's veto of a **Clean Water Act** was overridden by Congress, the Senate acting this day and the House having taken action the previous day. The law authorized the spending of $20,000,000,000 through 1994 for sewer construction and the cleaning up of estuaries and toxic "hot spots" and for other purposes. Reagan said the bill was "loaded with waste and larded with pork."

Feb. 19 **Trade sanctions against Poland** were lifted by Pres. Reagan after the Communist regime freed political prisoners. The action removed the ban on trade credits and restored Poland's "most favored nation" status for export-import purposes.

Feb. 26 The **Tower Commission report** on the Iran-Contra affair was critical of Pres. Reagan for failing to understand or control the secret attempt to trade arms to Iran for the release of American hostages being held in Lebanon and divert profits from the sale to the Nicaraguan Contras. The commission, appointed by the president in Nov. 1986, said Reagan must take responsibility for the policy, which ended in "chaos" and caused the U.S. much embarrassment abroad. Blame was placed also on Donald T. Regan, the White House chief of staff, whom the president replaced with former Senator Howard H. Baker, Jr., on Feb. 27. In a television address on Mar. 4, the president said he took "full responsibility," but he did not

Elie Nadelman sculpture going for $2,000,000; a Willem de Kooning painting bringing $3,600,000; and a George Caleb Bingham oil topping all with a reported price of $6,000,000 in a private sale. The American Ballet Theater sold $6,200,000 worth of tickets for its new production of *Sleeping Beauty,* but the dancers of the Dallas Ballet had to raise $500,000 or else disband. Publishing mergers continued to make news. In March media tycoon Rupert Murdoch, who owned newspapers and book publishing houses in Britain, Australia, and the U.S., acquired Harper & Row for $300,000,000. In June British publishing entrepreneur and corporate raider Robert Maxwell attempted to buy Harcourt Brace Jovanovich for $1,730,000,000, but HBJ fought back with a reorganization plan that saved the company from Maxwell but burdened it with an enormous debt. The circulation of daily newspapers dropped by a slight 0.4% and the number of papers from 1676 to 1657. In July it was estimated that 43,260,000 U.S. households, 49.5% of the total, had cable TV. This was an increase of about 2,000,000 in a year.

Noteworthy persons who died included Fred Astaire, the popular dancer, June 22, at 88; the actress Mary Astor, Sept. 25, at 81; Bill Baird, master puppeteer, Mar. 18, at 82; James Baldwin, whose writings spurred the civil rights movement, Dec. 1, at 63; Michael Bennett, Broadway choreographer and winner of eight Tony Awards, July 2, at 44; Ray Bolger, actor best known as the Scarecrow in the movie *The Wizard of Oz,* Jan. 15, at 83; James Burnham, founding editor of the conservative *National Review,* July 28, at 82; Erskine Caldwell, author of novels about the South, such as *Tobacco Road,* Apr. 11, at 83; Jackie Gleason, comedian whose TV show of the 1950s, *The Honeymooners,* developed a cult following, June 24, at 71; Rita Hayworth, glamorous movie star, May 14, at 68; Jascha Heifetz, violin virtuoso, Dec. 10, at 86; Woody Herman, popular leader of big bands, Oct. 29, at 74; John Huston, noted movie director, Aug. 28, at 81; Danny Kaye, comedian, dancer, and singer, Mar. 3, at 74; Nora Kaye, ballerina who created a new, contemporary look among dancers, Feb. 28, at 67; Sammy Kaye, popular musician noted for the music of his "sweet bands," June 2, at 77; Mervyn LeRoy, who directed 75 films over 40 years, including *Little Caesar,* Sept. 13, at 86; Clare Boothe Luce, sharp-tongued playwright, ambassador, and politician, Oct. 9, at 84; Rouben Mamoulian, stage and film director whose productions included *Porgy and Bess* and *Oklahoma!,* Dec. 4, at 90; Pola Negri, exotic vamp of the movies of the 1920s and 1930s, Aug. 1, at 88; Geraldine Page, stage and screen actress, June 13, at 62; Andrés Segovia, who restored the guitar to top rank in classical music, June 2, at 94; Myron Stout, abstract artist of minimal black and white

| **Business and Industry; Science; Education; Philosophy and Religion** III | | IV **Sports; Social Issues and Crime; Folkways; Fashion; Holidays** |

Mar. 19   The Rev. **Jim Bakker,** a successful TV evangelist, resigned his ministry, admitting that he had had an extramarital sexual encounter with a church secretary seven years earlier. The founder of PTL (Praise the Lord, or People That Love) said he had paid what he called blackmail to the woman involved. His wife, Tammy, had also been active in the ministry and had her own line of cosmetics for sale. PTL operated a $172,000,000, 2300-acre theme park, Heritage USA, in Fort Mill, S.C., and in 1986 Bakker was paid $1,600,000 in salary and bonuses. On May 6 the Assemblies of God dismissed Bakker as a minister. On June 12 the new management of PTL filed for bankruptcy, noting $71,000,000 of debt, and on Feb. 1, 1988, sued Bakker for $52,800,000, charging mismanagement and unjustified compensation. In Oct., 1989, Bakker was convicted on 24 fraud and conspiracy charges and sentenced to 45 years in prison and fined $500,000. On Feb. 12, 1991, an appeals court threw out the sentence as excessive and on Aug. 23, 1991, he was resentenced to 18 years in prison.

Mar. 20   The **first drug to benefit AIDS patients** was approved by the federal government. The drug was azidothymidine, or AZT, and while it would not cure AIDS, tests showed it could help victims of the disease live longer. Because AZT could have severe side effects, its use was to be limited to selected categories of patients, totalling about 15,000. The drug was estimated to cost as much as $10,000 per patient per year. On Aug. 18 the Food and Drug Administration approved the trial use, for the first time on humans, of a possible AIDS vaccine. Similar tests were already being carried out in France. The test vaccine used a protein, CD4, that seemed to attract the AIDS virus, thus preventing it from entering nearby body cells.

Apr. 4   A revised **New Testament** was introduced by the nation's Roman Catholic bishops. It avoids the use of the word "man" when the reference is to both men and women. A passage that read "Not on bread alone is man to live" has been changed to "One does not live by bread alone." Known as the Revised New Testament of the American Bible, it was now the authorized version for America's 50,000,000 Catholics.

Apr. 16   The **patenting of new forms of life** created through gene splicing would be allowed, the federal government announced. The U.S. was the first country to take such a step. The policy allowed the patenting of organisms with new traits created by recently devised reproductive technologies, including genetic engineering. Specifically banned was the patenting of new genetic characteristics in human beings.

Denver had won the AFC championship by defeating the Cleveland Browns 30–23 in overtime.

Jan. 31–Feb. 4   The **America's Cup** was regained by the U.S. when the American challenger *Stars & Stripes,* skippered by Dennis Connor of San Diego, Calif., defeated the Australian yacht *Kookaburra III* in four straight races at Fremantle, Australia.

Feb. 7–8   **U.S. figure skating championships** were won at Tacoma, Wash., by Brian Boitano, men's singles; Jill Trenary, women's singles; Peter Oppegard and Jill Watson, pairs; Suzanne Semanick and Scott Gregory, dance.

Feb. 26   Michael Spinks was stripped of his **IBF heavyweight championship.** The action was taken because he failed to defend his title within nine months of winning the crown from Larry Holmes at Apr. 19, 1986, thus failing to live up to IBF rules.

Mar. 7   The combined **WBA and WBC heavyweight boxing championship** was won by Mike Tyson, who defeated James "Bonecrusher" Smith by a unanimous decision in a 15-round bout at Las Vegas, Nev.

Mar. 29   The **NCAA women's basketball championship,** held in Austin, Tex., was won by Tennessee over Louisiana Tech 67–44.

Mar. 30   The **NCAA men's basketball championship** was won by Indiana, defeating Syracuse 74–73.

Mar. 31   In a major ruling concerning **surrogate motherhood,** custody of a baby born to a surrogate mother was awarded to the father. Baby M, as the girl was known during the trial before a New Jersey judge, was born Mar. 27, 1986, the result of the artificial insemination of Mary Beth Whitehead by William Stern. Stern and his wife, Elizabeth, had agreed to pay Whitehead $10,000 and she in turn would relinquish all rights to the child. Whitehead, however, refused to give up the baby, and a suit brought by the Sterns to enforce the contract began on Jan. 5, 1987. Saying he was creating law, the judge in his decision upheld the legality of such a surrogate agreement and stripped the birth mother of all parental rights. On Feb. 3, 1988, however, the Supreme Court of New Jersey ruled unanimously that commercial surrogate motherhood contracts were illegal. The Baby M dispute went back to a lower court, and on Apr. 6, 1988, Whitehead was granted broad rights to see the child, although the Sterns retained custody.

Apr. 12   The **Masters golf tournament** was won by Larry Mize on the second hole of a three-way playoff.

Apr. 20   The 91st **Boston Marathon** was won by Toshihiko Seko of Japan in the men's division with a time of 2 hrs., 11 min., 50 sec. The winner in the women's division was Rosa Mota of Portugal with a time of 2 hrs., 25 min., 21 sec.

May 2   The 113th **Kentucky Derby** was won by Alysheba, with a time of 2:03²/₅. The jockey was

1987 *PRES.* RONALD REAGAN

796

| Exploration and Settlement; Wars; Government; Civil Rights; Statistics | I | | II | Publishing; Arts and Music; Popular Entertainment; Architecture; Theater |

admit that the plan for dealing with Iran was basically wrong.

Apr. 27 **Kurt Waldheim** will not be allowed to enter the U.S., the Justice Dept. announced. The president of Austria and former secretary general of the United Nations was banned because he had "participated in activities amounting to persecution" of Jews and others while he was serving with the German army in the Balkans from 1942 to 1945. Waldheim was the first head of state ever put on a list of persons excluded from the U.S.

May 17 **A missile attack on a U.S. frigate** in the Persian Gulf killed 37 sailors and badly damaged the U.S.S. *Stark.* An Iraqi warplane fired two missiles by mistake and Iraq apologized for the attack. On July 22 U.S. warships began escorting Kuwaiti tankers reregistered under the American flag through the gulf to protect them from possible Iranian attacks. On Sept. 22 an American helicopter attacked and damaged an Iranian minelayer, and on Oct. 19 U.S. naval forces shelled two offshore installations in retaliation for Iranian attacks on Persian Gulf shipping.

Aug. 16 **A Northwest Airlines jet crashed** on takeoff from the Detroit Metropolitan Airport, killing 156 of the 157 persons on board. The only survivor was a four-year-old girl, who was injured but recovered. On May 10, 1988, a federal investigative report blamed the crash on the failure of the two pilots to follow required checklist procedures before takeoff.

Oct. 1 **A severe earthquake** shook the Los Angeles area, killing at least 8 people and injuring more than 100. It was the strongest quake in the region since 1971 and registered 6.1 on the Richter scale. Glass fell from skyscraper windows and in Whittier 30 buildings collapsed.

Oct. 23 The **Supreme Court nomination of Robert H. Bork** was rejected by the Senate by a vote of 58–42. Bork, a member of the federal Appeals Court in Washington, had been nominated by Pres. Reagan to fill the vacancy caused by the resignation of Justice Lewis F. Powell, Jr., on July 1. Lobbying against Bork by many liberal groups, who accused him of extreme right-wing views on issues of civil rights and individual privacy, was intense. After two weeks of hearings in September, the Senate Judiciary Committee on Oct. 6 voted 9–5 to recommend rejection of the nomination. On Oct. 29 Reagan nominated Douglas H. Ginsburg, also an Appeals Court judge. Ginsburg withdrew on Nov. 7 after charges of a conflict of interest in the past and the admission that he used

compositions, Aug. 2, at 79; Antony Tudor, who introduced psychological motivation in his choreography, Apr. 20, at 78 or 79; Andy Warhol, founder of Pop Art, Feb. 22, at 58; Glenway Wescott, novelist, acclaimed at age 26 for *The Grandmothers,* Feb. 22, at 85; and Marguerite Yourcenar, author, holder of dual French and U.S. citizenship, known particularly for *Memoirs of Hadrian,* an imaginary autobiography, and for being the first woman elected to the Académie Française, Dec. 17, at 84.

Among **books published** this year, most talked about novels were Toni Morrison's *Beloved,* the story of a woman escaped from slavery, and Tom Wolfe's *The Bonfire of the Vanities,* an account of a New York yuppie in big trouble. Other important novels were *Patriot Games* by Tom Clancy; *The Counterlife,* the fourth in Philip Roth's Zuckerman series; *Crossing to Safety,* Wallace Stegner's account of the friendship of two couples; and *Presumed Innocent* by Scott Turow. Among nonfiction works were *The Closing of the American Mind* by Allan Bloom and *Cultural Literacy* by E. D. Hirsch, Jr., two critical views of American education; *Man of the House,* an autobiography by former Speaker Thomas P. O'Neill, Jr.; and *Trump: The Art of the Deal* by the real estate developer Donald Trump.

Feb. 24 **Grammy Awards** were presented for the following: best album of 1986, *Graceland* by Paul Simon; best record and best pop vocalist, Steve Winwood for "Higher Love"; best female pop vocalist, Barbra Streisand for *The Broadway Album;* best male rock vocalist, Robert Palmer for "Addicted to Love"; best female rock vocalist, Tina Turner for "Back Where You Started."

Mar. 30 **Academy Awards** were presented to *Platoon* as the outstanding motion picture of 1986; Paul Newman as best actor for *The Color of Money;* Marlee Matlin as best actress for *Children of a Lesser God;* and Michael Caine and Dianne Wiest as best supporting actor and actress for *Hannah and Her Sisters.*

Mar. 30 Acquisition of the **Arturo Toscanini Archives** was announced by the New York Public Library. The large collection of scores, recordings, letters, and memorabilia of the late conductor, valued at $2,000,000, had been inaccessible since 1970 while negotiations went on.

Apr. 6 The first American to win the **Ritz Paris Hemingway Award,** worth $50,000, was Peter Taylor for his novel *A Summons to Memphis.*

| Business and Industry; Science; Education; Philosophy and Religion | III | | IV | Sports; Social Issues and Crime; Folkways; Fashion; Holidays |

May 12 A three-way heart and lung transplant, believed to be a medical first, was performed in Baltimore, Md. A healthy heart was taken from a living person and transplanted to another. The heart donor then received the heart and lungs of an accident victim who had died in a nearby hospital. On May 14 a spokesman for a British hospital said similar operations had been performed there the last week in April and the first week in May.

June 2 A new chairman of the Federal Reserve Board, economist Alan Greenspan, was named by Pres. Ronald Reagan. He succeeded Paul A. Volcker, who had held the post for eight years and who was noted for the strong measures he had taken to quell the high inflation in the economy when he took office. In financial markets, where it had been expected Volcker would serve a third term, there was a sharp drop in bond prices. Greenspan, who had worked in both business and government, was known for his free-market sympathies and was not expected to change noticeably the policies Volcker had followed.

June 19 Teaching the **creationist theory** of human origin may not be required in public schools alongside the theory of evolution when the intent is to promote religious belief, according to the Supreme Court. Thus, by a 7–2 vote, the Court held unconstitutional a Louisiana law of 1984. The decision was seen as a serious blow to the efforts of fundamentalist Christians to mold public school curriculums to fit their beliefs.

June 30 By adopting the declaration "**Judaism has not been superseded by Christianity,**" the United Church of Christ became the first major U.S. Protestant denomination to so affirm the position of the Jewish religion. The declaration, adopted at the convention of the church in Cleveland, Ohio, also stated "God has not rejected the Jewish people."

Sept. 5–7 Infant **twins joined at the head** were separated in a lengthy and unusual operation at the Johns Hopkins University Hospital in Baltimore, Md. Metal plates were implanted over the skull holes caused by the operation. On Apr. 7, 1988, the hospital announced the twins would be discharged in a few days to return to West Germany, where they were born. They suffered some brain damage and might have vision problems but otherwise seemed likely to lead normal lives.

Oct. 12 The **Nobel Prize in Medicine** was awarded to Susumu Tonegawa, a Japanese scientist working at the Massachusetts Institute of Technology. He had

Chris McCarron. Alysheba went on to become racing's all-time leading money earner with $6,679,242 in purses.

May 4 **Women must be admitted to Rotary Clubs,** hitherto all male, the Supreme Court ruled, 7–0. On July 4 the Lions Club International voted to admit women and on July 7 Kiwanis International followed suit.

May 10–18 The **NHL Stanley Cup** championship was won by the Edmonton Oilers, who beat the Philadelphia Flyers four games to three.

May 16 The 112th **Preakness Stakes** was won by Alysheba, with a time of 1:55⁴/₅. The jockey was Chris McCarron.

May 24 A record **10,000th winning harness race** was won by Hervé Filion, a French-Canadian driver, at Yonkers Raceway, N.Y.

May 24 The 71st **Indianapolis 500** auto race was won by Al Unser, completing the 500-mi. course in 3 hrs., 4 min., 59.147 sec. In winning this race for the fourth time, Unser became the oldest Indy winner, five days short of his 48th birthday.

May 24 The **LPGA golf tournament** was won by Jane Geddes by one stroke.

June 2–14 The **NBA basketball championship** was won by the Los Angeles Lakers over the Boston Celtics four games to two.

June 6 The 119th **Belmont Stakes** was won by Bet Twice by 14 lengths, with a time of 2:28²/₅. The jockey was Craig Perret. In addition, Bet Twice won $1,000,-000 in the first Triple Crown participation bonus. Bet Twice finished second in both the Kentucky Derby and the Preakness Stakes. Alysheba had won those two races but finished fourth in the Belmont. On a 5–3–1 point basis, Bet Twice earned 11 points to Alysheba's 10.

June 15 In a bout promoted as deciding the **heavyweight championship,** Michael Spinks knocked out Gerry Cooney in the fifth round of a scheduled 15-round fight. The WBA and the WBC said they would not recognize the winner as champion, but several state boxing commissions said they would.

June 21 The **U.S. Open golf tournament** was won by Scott Simpson, who defeated Tom Watson by one stroke.

July 4 At the **Wimbledon tennis championships,** London, the women's title was won for the sixth consecutive year by Martina Navratilova.

July 14 In the **baseball All-Star game** the National League defeated the American League, 2–0, in 13 innings.

July 26 The **Baseball Hall of Fame** inducted Billy Williams, outfielder, Jim "Catfish" Hunter, pitcher, and Ray Dandridge, who had played 14 seasons in the Negro League.

marijuana while teaching at Harvard Law School. The president then nominated Anthony Kennedy, a federal judge in California, on Nov. 11. Finally, on Feb. 3, 1988, the Senate unanimously confirmed Kennedy by a vote of 97–0.

Nov. 15 A **Continental Airlines jet crashed** while taking off in a snowstorm at Denver's Stapleton Airport, flipping over and breaking into three pieces. Of the 81 persons aboard, 28 were killed and more than 50 injured.

Nov. 18 The Congressional committees' **report on the Iran-Contra affair** blamed Pres. Reagan for failing in his constitutional duty and said he bore "the ultimate responsibility" for the wrongdoing of his aides. The committees' 690-page report also said "the rule of law was subverted" and that if the president did not know what his national security advisers were up to, he should have. The report provided the most complete accounting to date of what became of the nearly $48,000,000 that was raised by the sale of arms to Iran. The two committees had held joint hearings from May 5 to Aug. 15, during which they heard more than 250 hours of testimony from 28 witnesses. The chief witnesses were John M. Poindexter, national security adviser at the time of the affair, and his assistant, Lt. Col. Oliver L. North. The latter was briefly somewhat of a hero, for his gung-ho defense of his actions.

Nov. 20 A **deficit reduction plan** to cut the federal budget deficit by $30,000,000,000 for the fiscal year that had begun on Oct. 1 and by $46,000,000,000 in the following year was agreed to by Pres. Reagan and congressional leaders. On Dec. 22 Reagan signed budget bills totalling $603,900,000,000, a record that would presumably reduce the deficit by $3,400,000,000 more than previously agreed on.

Nov. 21 A **federal prison riot** at Oakdale, La., by about 1000 Cuban refugees being held for possible deportation began with the seizure of 30 hostages. On Nov. 23 a similar group of 1392 detainees at the federal prison in Atlanta, Ga., also took action, seizing the prison and 75 hostages. The detainees were aroused by reports of a new agreement between the U.S. and Cuba whereby Cuba would take back more than 2000 "undesirables." After negotiations and without violence, the riot ended at Oakdale on Nov. 29 and at Atlanta on Dec. 4. The detainees were assured they would receive individual and full reviews of their status. By late Apr. 1988, 1153 of the detainees had been released, ten times more than in the previous five months.

Apr. 7 The **National Museum of Women in the Arts** opened in Washington, D.C., the first museum devoted entirely to women artists. It already held more than 500 examples of such art from the Renaissance to the 20th century. Some feminists felt it would segregate women's artistic work rather than promoting it.

Apr. 16 **Pulitzer prizes** were awarded for the following: fiction, *A Summons to Memphis* by Peter Taylor; general nonfiction, *Arab and Jew: Wounded Spirits in a Promised Land* by David K. Shipler; biography, *Bearing the Cross: Martin Luther King, Jr., and the Southern Christian Leadership Conference* by David J. Garrow; history, *Voyagers to the West: A Passage in the Peopling of America on the Eve of the Revolution* by Bernard Bailyn; poetry, *Thomas and Beulah* by Rita Dove; drama, *Fences* by August Wilson.

Apr. 17 **Richard Wilbur** was appointed the second poet laureate of the U.S. by the Librarian of Congress, succeeding Robert Penn Warren.

June 7 **Tony awards** for the 1986–87 season were presented for the following: best play, *Fences* by August Wilson; best musical, *Les Misérables;* best actor in a drama, James Earl Jones for *Fences;* best actress in a drama, Linda Lavin for *Broadway Bound;* best actor and actress in a musical, Robert Lindsay and Maryann Plunkett for *Me and My Girl.*

Sept. 14 A new method of **measuring TV audiences** was introduced by the A. C. Nielsen Co., which for 20 years had relied on a system of diaries kept by a sampling of households. The new system featured "people meters," which registered opinion by viewers' pushing buttons. Early results of the new method made the TV networks unhappy, as it seemed to register fewer viewers than the diary system.

Sept. 20 **Emmy Awards** were presented for the following: best drama series, *L.A. Law;* best comedy series, *The Golden Girls;* best actor in a dramatic series, Bruce Willis for *Moonlighting;* best actress in a dramatic series, Sharon Gless for *Cagney and Lacey;* best actor in a comedy series, Michael J. Fox for *Family Ties;* best actress in a comedy series, Rue McClanahan for *The Golden Girls.*

Sept. 28 **Two new museums** opened in Washington, D.C., as part of the Smithsonian Institution. One was the National Museum of African Art, which had existed since 1964 but was now greatly expanded; the

Business and Industry; Science; Education; Philosophy and Religion III		IV **Sports; Social Issues and Crime; Folkways; Fashion; Holidays**

discovered how the human body marshals its immunological defenses against many different diseases it has never met before. Dr. Tonegawa was the first Japanese to win the Nobel Prize in this category.

Oct. 14 The **Nobel Prize in Chemistry** was awarded jointly to Donald J. Cram of the University of California at Los Angeles, Charles J. Pedersen, formerly a research chemist with E. I. du Pont de Nemours & Co., and Jean-Marie Lehn, a French professor of chemistry. The three had carried out varied researches that included the creation of artificial molecules that mimic vital chemical reactions of live processes.

Oct. 16 The **youngest person to undergo a heart transplant,** a baby only three hours old, was given a new heart at the Loma Linda (Calif.) Medical Center after the baby was delivered by Caesarean section. The donor of the heart was an infant who had been declared legally dead a few days earlier.

Oct. 19 The **worst stock crash** in the history of the New York Stock Exchange occurred when the Dow Jones industrial average fell 508 points, closing at 1738.74, a decline of 22.6%, nearly double the decline in 1929 that ushered in the Great Depression. The volume of stocks traded, 604,330,000, was nearly twice the previous record of 338,500,000, set on Oct. 16. Computerized program trading, as well as various factors in the national and international economy, was blamed for the collapse of a market that had exhibited a case of the jitters in recent weeks. On Oct. 20 the Dow Jones rose 102.27 points and trading set another new record for volume with 608,120,000 shares traded. In spite of the gain, largely confined to blue chip issues, many more stocks fell than rose. The Dow gained another 186 points the following day but dropped 77.42 points on Oct. 22. The major markets set temporarily shorter hours in hopes of easing the tension, but on Oct. 26 there was another drop of 156.83 points. After a short period of relative quiet, the Dow fell 50.56 on Nov. 3, ending a five–day rally, and on Nov. 9 the average was down another 58.85 points, closing at 1900.20.

Oct. 21 The **Nobel Prize in Economics** was awarded to Robert M. Solow of the Massachusetts Institute of Technology for his contributions to the theory of economic growth.

Dec. 10 **Teaching about the use of condoms** in the battle against the disease AIDS was given qualified support by the Roman Catholic bishops of the U.S. in spite of the church's opposition to birth control. The

July 28 The **U.S. Women's Open golf tournament** was won by Laura Davies of Great Britain in an 18-hole playoff.

Aug. 1 The unified **heavyweight boxing championship** was won by Mike Tyson, who earned a unanimous 12-round decision over Tony Tucker at Las Vegas, Nev. Tyson held the World Boxing Association and World Boxing Council titles, and Tucker was the champion of the International Boxing Federation. Tyson thus became the first undisputed titleholder since Feb. 1978, when Leon Spinks beat Muhammad Ali.

Aug. 2 In the **fastest race in Indy car history,** Michael Andretti won the Marlboro 500 at Michigan International Speedway in Brooklyn, Mich., with an average speed of 171.490 mph. This bettered the mark of 170.722 mph set by Bobby Rahal when he won the Indianapolis 500 in 1986.

Aug. 8–23 At the tenth **Pan-American Games,** in Indianapolis, Ind., the U.S. won 369 medals, including 168 gold medals. Cuba was second with 75 gold medals and 175 in all, and Canada was third with 30 and 162.

Aug. 9 The **PGA championship** was won by Larry Nelson, who defeated Lanny Wadkins on the first hole of a sudden death playoff.

Aug. 16 The tenth anniversary of the death of **Elvis Presley,** rock-and-roll idol, was marked by the pilgrimage of some 20,000 fans to his home, Graceland, in Memphis, Tenn. Carrying lighted candles, the singer's worshippers gathered at his grave, where a spotlight shone on a statue of Jesus Christ.

Aug. 18 **Donald Harvey,** 35, was found guilty of killing 24 people since 1983 by a jury in Ohio. Of his victims 21 died, most by poison, in a Cincinnati hospital where he was an orderly. Harvey was sentenced to three consecutive life terms.

Aug. 29 **Little League baseball** celebrated the 40th anniversary of its world series. It claims 2,500,000 participants in 16,000 chartered programs. The world championship was won by Hua Lian, the Taiwanese team, beating the Irvine, Calif., team 21–1 at Williamsport, Pa. Teams from the Far East had won 17 Little League championships in the last 21 years.

Sept. 12 The women's division of the **U.S. Open tennis singles championships** was won by Martina Navratilova over Steffi Graf of West Germany. It was Navratilova's fourth victory in five years in this event. After a 24-hour rain delay, Ivan Lendl on Sept. 14 defeated Mats Wilander of Sweden for the men's title.

Sept. 19 The **Miss America** title was won by Kaye Lani Rae Rafko, 24, from Monroe, Mich., at the annual pageant in Atlantic City, N.J.

Sept. 29 A new **major league record for grand slam home runs in a season** was set by Don Mattingly of the

Dec. 8 The first treaty to reduce nuclear arsenals was signed in Washington by Pres. Reagan and General Secretary Mikhail S. Gorbachev of the U.S.S.R. Under the terms of the treaty 2611 U.S. and Soviet medium- and short–range missiles sited in Europe would be destroyed. The pact provided for on-site verification by both countries. The agreement was seen as a first step toward agreement on the reduction of U.S. and soviet long-range missiles.

Dec. 16 Michael K. Deaver was found guilty on three of five counts of perjury stemming from his lobbying activities after he left the position of aide to Pres. Reagan. He had been tried on charges of having lied to a House subcommittee about efforts to arrange a meeting between the president and a South Korean trade representative and also of having lied to a federal grand jury. At the base of Deaver's troubles were accusations that he violated the 1978 Ethics in Government Act, which regulates lobbying by former government officials. White House deputy chief of staff until May 1985, Deaver was the highest-ranking Reagan administration official to be convicted of a crime. On Sept. 23, 1988, he was given a three–year suspended sentence.

Dec. 22 A compromise Contra aid appropriation, authorizing $14,000,000 for nonlethal assistance to the Nicaraguan rebels, was signed by Pres. Reagan.

other was the all-new Arthur M. Sackler Museum for Asian and Near East Art. The museums, 96% underground, were on three levels and cost $73,000,000. They exhibited 6000 objects of African and 2500 of Asian art.

Oct. 22 The Nobel Prize for Literature was awarded to Joseph Brodsky, Soviet-born exile, now a citizen of the U.S. A poet and essayist, in both English and Russian, Brodsky at 47 was the second youngest to win this award.

Nov. 9 National Book Awards, called the American Book Awards from 1980 to 1986, were presented for the following: fiction, *Paco's Story* by Larry Heinemann; nonfiction, *The Making of the Atomic Bomb* by Richard Rhodes.

Nov. 11 The highest price for a painting, $53,900,000, was bid at auction in New York for *Irises* by Vincent Van Gogh. The painting had been owned by John Whitney Payson, a member of a wealthy family. Some of the proceeds were to go to the Payson Foundation and to Westbrook College, Portland, Me. On Mar. 21, 1990, the J. Paul Getty Museum of Malibu, Calif., announced it had acquired the painting from the person who had bought it at auction.

1988

The nation entered another presidential election year with the certainty that it would be selecting a new tenant for the White House, because Ronald Reagan would have served the maximum two terms allowed by the Constitution. More citizens than ever would be eligible to vote. The Census Bureau reported on Apr. 4 that as of July 1, 1987, there were 90,031,000 households. Within those households, the median age of Americans was increasing, exceeding 32 for the first time: 32.1 on July 1, 1987. The many baby boomers born in the early post–World War II years were now producing children in large numbers. The government reported in August that there were 3,829,000 births in 1987, the most in nearly a quarter of a century. Whether baby boomers or not, Americans were deserting their farms. About 240,000 left such rural places in 1987, bringing the nation's farm population to its lowest level since before the Civil War. Notables who died this year included Burnita S. Matthews, the first woman to serve as a federal district court judge, appointed in 1949, Apr. 25, at 93; Franklin D. Roosevelt, Jr., son of the late president,

In box office receipts, the 1987–1988 Broadway theater season was the best ever. Theaters took in $253,000,000, an increase of 21% over the previous year. Musicals—such as *The Phantom of the Opera, Les Misérables, Starlight Express,* and *Me and My Girl*—accounted for most of the ticket sales. Dramas like *Speed-the-Plow, Joe Turner's Come and Gone,* and *Walk in the Woods* were critical successes. The most successful drama was *M. Butterfly* whose plot involved a Chinese transvestite serving the communists in an attempt to worm secrets out of a French diplomat. A pleasant surprise was a revival of *Anything Goes,* originally staged in 1934, which played all season at Lincoln Center in New York. The catastrophe of the season was the musical *Carrie,* on which work began seven years earlier and which closed after 16 previews and 5 regular performances with a loss of $7,000,000. The most talked about movie of the year received most of its attention before the public saw it. This was *The Last Temptation of Christ,* based on the novel by Nikos Kazantzakis and directed by Martin Scorsese. It was vociferously

| Business and Industry; Science; Education; Philosophy and Religion III | | IV Sports; Social Issues and Crime; Folkways; Fashion; Holidays |

bishops' position paper called on all Catholic schools to teach AIDS prevention.

Dec. 11   In a ruling on the **Dalkon Shield** birth control device, a federal judge ordered the A. H. Robins Co., producer of the IUD, to establish a fund of $2,475,000,000 to cover possible claims resulting from its use as part of the company's reorganization plan. Robins had filed for bankruptcy in Aug. 1985 because of the thousands of claims against it by women who said they became infertile or suffered injuries as a result of using the shield. About 9500 women had already received compensation.

Dec. 19   In the **largest cash settlement** in U.S. corporate history, Texaco agreed to pay Pennzoil $3,000,000,000 to settle a bitter lawsuit. In 1985 a Texas court had ordered Texaco to pay $10,100,000,000, plus interest, to Pennzoil for having illegally interfered with the latter's attempt to take over the Getty Oil Co. In its battle to overturn this decision, and in its very unfriendly negotiations to reach a less costly settlement with Pennzoil, Texaco filed for bankruptcy on Apr. 12, 1987. The agreed-upon settlement was paid to Pennzoil on Apr. 7, 1988. That same day Texaco ended 361 days in bankruptcy.

Dec. 31   The **Dow Jones** average of industrial stocks closed the year at 1938.83. Although it was off 29% from its August peak, it was up 2.26% for the year in spite of the shattering crash of Oct. 19.

New York Yankees when he hit his sixth of the year.

Oct. 9   A **world record stamp price** for a single postage stamp was paid when a Japanese bank bought for $1,100,000 a stamp that had sold in Pittsburgh, Pa., in 1852 for two cents. The stamp was from a wedding invitation mailed to a Rev. and Mrs. McGill and is known as the Lady McGill. The previous highest price paid for a stamp was $935,000 in 1980.

Oct. 17–25   The **World Series** was won by the Minnesota Twins (AL), who defeated the St. Louis Cardinals four games to three. On Oct. 12, the Twins had won the American League pennant against the Detroit Tigers four games to one, and two days later the Cardinals won the National League pennant against the San Francisco Giants four games to three.

Nov. 1   The 18th **New York City Marathon** was won by Ibrahim Hussein of Kenya in a time of 2 hrs., 11 min., 1 sec. The winner in the women's division was Priscilla Welch of Great Britain in a time of 2 hrs., 30 min., 17 sec.

Nov. 1   The richest prize in tournament golf history, $384,000, was won by Tom Watson at the $3,000,000 Nabisco Championship at San Antonio, Tex. The first place money brought Watson's total PGA tournament earnings to $4,701,629 in 17 years on the PGA tour. Although Curtis Strange finished last in this tournament, he won the title for highest golf earnings in 1987, a record $925,941.

1988

More than halfway through 1988, the national economy showed strong growth but also an increase in inflation. As a result, the Federal Reserve on Aug. 9 raised its discount rate a half point, to 6.5%. Banks in turn increased their prime rate to 10%, the highest since June 1985. In July the nation's factories, mines, and utilities operated at their highest level in eight years, aiding economic growth but also causing inflationary pressures. The most serious problem facing the economy was the Midwest and Southwest drought, with conditions not seen since the Dust Bowl years of the 1930s. In foreign trade, there was considerable improvement because the decrease in the value of the dollar stimulated exports of American goods. Imports, however, did not decrease as much as expected, so that the foreign trade deficit was not lowered very much. The environment was not in as good shape as the economy. In June a NASA scientist said global warming had begun, the earth having been warmer in the first five months of 1988 than in any comparable period in the past 130 years. The Environmental Protection Agency reported

Statistics reported in April for 1987 showed that baseball was still the national game. It attracted 88,200,000 spectators. Horse racing came in second with attendance at 73,600,000, followed by football with 50,000,000 fans. By opening day of the 1988 baseball season, the game had set a salary record: major league owners were paying their players a total of $300,511,924 for the season. The 100th anniversary of golf in the U.S. was observed on June 20 at the St. Andrews Golf Club in Hastings-on-Hudson, N.Y., near where the first match was played. Curtis Strange became the first professional golfer to win more than $1,000,000 in a year when he garnered $1,147,644. On the crime front, the Justice Department reported that there were 581,609 inmates in state and federal prisons, an increase of 6.7% in a year and more than double the 1970 prison population. Notable persons who died included Alan Ameche, Baltimore Colts running back, Aug. 8, at 55; Henry Armstrong, the only boxer ever to hold three world titles at the same time, Oct. 22, at 75; Gregory "Pappy" Boyington, Marine ace of World War II who shot down 28 Japanese

a U.S. representative, Aug. 17, at 74; and J. Skelly Wright, federal judge who was a pioneer in the desegregation of schools and transportation in New Orleans, Aug. 6, at 77.

Jan. 2 One of the **largest inland oil spills** ever, 20 miles up the Monongahela River from Pittsburgh, Pa., dumped 860,000 gallons into the stream when a 40-year-old tank of the Ashland Oil Co. collapsed. Flowing into the Ohio River, the spill caused extensive damage to water supplies and wildlife before dissipating.

Feb. 5 Gen. **Manuel Antonio Noriega**, the most powerful figure in the government of Panama since he became commander of the armed forces on Aug. 12, 1983, was indicted by a federal grand jury in Miami, Fla., in connection with illegal drug dealings. He was charged with receiving more than $4,600,000 in payoffs for allowing large-scale drug dealers to use airstrips under his protection. The president of Panama, Eric Arturo Delvalle, on Feb. 25 tried to remove him from his post, but the general's armed forces drove the president from office.

Feb. 11 A federal jury convicted **Lyn Nofziger**, former White House political director, on three counts of illegal lobbying under the 1978 Ethics in Government Act. The law forbids lobbying a federal agency for a year after a person has left it. Nofziger was charged with violating this law on behalf of the Wedtech Corp., which sought defense contracts, and two other clients. On Apr. 8 he was sentenced to 90 days in jail and fined $30,000. The guilty verdict was overturned by a Court of Appeals on June 27, 1989, on the grounds the prosecution had failed to prove its case.

Feb. 17 Another **American hostage in Lebanon**, U.S. Marine Lt. Col. William R. Higgins, was kidnaped in southern Lebanon, presumably by Palestinian terrorists. His abduction brought to nine the number of Americans missing in Lebanon. One of them, Terry A. Anderson, a journalist, had been held since March 16, 1985.

Feb. 24 The **right to criticize public figures** was strongly endorsed by the Supreme Court, 8–0, when it overturned a $200,000 award to the Rev. Jerry Falwell, founder of the Moral Majority. The award had been made on the basis of an insulting parody in *Hustler* magazine. The court said such free speech is to be protected even when it is "outrageous." Civil libertarians and press organizations hailed the decision.

Mar. 16 In the **Iran-Contra affair** two key figures were indicted on charges of conspiracy to defraud the U.S. by illegally providing the Nicaraguan rebels with profits from the sale of American weapons to Iran. They were Vice Adm. John M. Poindexter and Marine Lt. Col. Oliver L. North. Indicted with them on 23 counts were two others involved in the scheme. The

condemned by fundamentalist Protestants and some Roman Catholics, who had not yet viewed it, as being blasphemous and sacrilegious. Many viewers found it a well-meant but not overly successful cinematic effort to show how Christ might have been tempted to give up the role of messiah and live an ordinary family life. Hollywood was said to be making more movies to appeal to older audiences, but the year's production did not attest to that except perhaps for such different films as *Broadcast News*, a comedy, and *The Unbearable Lightness of Being*, a love story from the novel by Milan Kundera. On the other hand there was the popular *Who Framed Roger Rabbit?*, which cleverly used both animated and live characters. Other box office successes included *Coming to America*, in which comedian Eddie Murphy played an African prince; *Crocodile Dundee II*, again starring Paul Hogan as a he-man from the outback; and *Bull Durham*, a baseball comedy with sex. The National Gallery of Art in Washington staged a centennial exhibit of the works of Georgia O'Keefe whose large, exotic, and vividly colored paintings of flowers had made her somewhat of a cult figure since her death in 1986. Dance in America took on an international flavor. The School of Paris Opéra Ballet performed at the Metropolitan Opera in New York in June; the New York City Ballet made its first tour of Japan since 1958; the American Ballet Theater performed in Paris; and Fernando Bujones became the first American male dancer to appear with the Bolshoi Ballet. In the field of architecture, Rice University in Houston engaged the Spanish architect Ricardo Bofill to design a new building for the Shepherd School of Music that would cover 10.35 acres. Michael Graves was picked to design a new resort and convention center for the Walt Disney World and Epcot Center in Florida. To cost $375,000,000, it would include two luxury hotels: the Swan Resort was to be topped by two 47-foot-high swans, described as "whimsical"; the Dolphin Hotel and Convention Center was to be topped off with a pair of 55-foot dolphins. Everything would be painted in blue-green and coral.

In television there were both bright and dim spots. With the start of its reruns *The Cosby Show* sold $60,000,000 worth of commercials immediately. But there was a falling off of network viewing by children, costing millions in lost advertising revenue. The continued growth of cable television was also a factor in the loss of revenue, with 47,000,000 American homes now subscribing representing 52.8% of all households having TV. VCR and videocassettes also affected the home viewing market with nearly 50,000,000 homes, representing 56% of all households, owning the recording and viewing device. Cassette sales continued to boom and were expected to reach nearly $7,000,000,000 in

that clean air standards for ozone were violated in 1987 in more areas than before. The Fish and Wildlife Service revealed that the development of oil fields in northern Alaska had done far more environmental damage than the government originally predicted. For education, the report card showed mixed grades. At the college level the demand for admission was so great that some students near the top in high school were not being admitted anywhere. At the public school level, the children of the baby boomers were forcing the reopening of schools closed in the 1970s and early 1980s when the school population dropped. A bright spot was the growing interest young people were showing in the teaching profession. Education schools reported increases of up to 50% in applications. Secretary of Education William J. Bennett stirred controversy when he said in April that the overall performance of American schools was "unacceptably low," an evaluation at once challenged by a number of educators. Charitable donations for religious, educational, and other purposes were a record $93,600,000,000 in 1987, but the rate of increase was the lowest in 12 years. On July 27 the surgeon general of the U.S., in the most comprehensive report on nutrition and health ever issued by the government, said fat was a leading cause of disease and that its overconsumption was a major American health problem. In the business world, a boom in facsimile-transmission machines marked the year. Documents were being sent across the country in 20 seconds. American business was active in the Soviet Union. Pepsico, Inc., producer of Pepsi-Cola, claimed the honor of being the first American company to buy commercial time on Soviet TV, as of May 17. McDonald's in April prepared to open 20 stores in Moscow to sell the Big Mac—*Bolshoi Mak* in Russian. Notable persons who died in 1988 included Luis W. Alvarez, Nobel Prize–winning physicist, Sept. 1, at 77; Kingman Brewster, Jr., former president of Yale and ambassador to Great Britain, Nov. 8, at 69; John Cardinal Dearden, liberal Catholic prelate and archbishop of Detroit, Aug. 1, at 80; Richard F. Feynman, Nobel Prize–winning theoretical physicist, Feb. 15, at 69; Raymond W. Goldsmith, economist, July 12, at 83; James R. Killian, Jr., in 1957 the first presidential assistant for science and technology, and president of MIT, Jan. 29, at 83; Gardiner C. Means, economist, Feb. 15, at 91; Jackie Presser, president of the International Brotherhood of Teamsters, July 9, at 61; Isidor Isaac Rabi, pioneer atomic scientist and Nobel Prize winner, Jan. 11, at 89; Merryle S. Rukeyser, long–time financial columnist, Dec. 21, at 91; Sewall Wright, geneticist who established a mathematical basis for evolution, Mar. 3, at 98.

Jan. 8   The **stock market plunge** of Oct. 19, 1987, was blamed on automatic trading programs of large money management firms, which generated huge sell orders, in a report of the Presidential Task Force on

planes and won the Medal of Honor, Jan. 11, at 75; Glenn Cunningham, world-record holder for the mile, Mar. 10, at 78; Robert Lee "Bobby" Dodd, famed football coach at the Georgia Institute of Technology, June 21, at 79; Carl Hubbell, ace pitcher for the New York Giants, Nov. 21, at 85; Ted Kluszewski, slugging first baseman, Mar. 29, at 63; Peter Press "Pistol Pete" Maravich, college and professional basketball star whose 3667 points in his college career remained a record, Jan. 5, at 40; Arthur Joseph Rooney, Sr., a leading American sportsman and founder of the Pittsburgh Steelers of the NFL, Aug. 25, at 87; Edd Roush, twice batting champion of the National League, 1917 and 1919, Mar. 21, at 94.

Jan. 1   In **college football bowl games,** the results were Texas A&M 35, Notre Dame 10 in the Cotton Bowl; Miami 24, Oklahoma 14 in the Orange Bowl; Michigan State 20, USC 17 in the Rose Bowl; and Syracuse 12, Auburn 12 in the Sugar Bowl. Both the AP and UPI declared Miami the national champions for 1987.

Jan. 8–9   **U.S. figure skating championships** were won by Brian Boitano, men's singles, for the fourth consecutive year; Debi Thomas, women's singles, her second win; Peter Oppegard and Jill Watson, pairs; Suzanne Semanick and Scott Gregory, dance.

Jan. 24   A year-long celebration of **Hawaii's 1000-year-old native culture** ended with a party attended by 41,000 in Aloha Stadium in Honolulu, marking Ho'olokah, or Hawaii Unity Day.

Jan. 31   **Super Bowl XXII** was won by the Washington Redskins (NFC), who defeated the Denver Broncos (AFC) 42–10. On Jan. 17 the Redskins had defeated the Minnesota Vikings 17–10 to win the NFC championship and the Broncos had beaten the Cleveland Browns 38–33 for the AFC title.

Feb. 9   New York City's largest single **art theft** occurred when 18 paintings and 10 drawings valued at $6,000,000 were taken from the Colnaghi Ltd. gallery on the Upper East Side. The most valuable items taken were two paintings by Fra Angelico.

Feb. 13–28   **The XVth Olympic Winter Games,** held in Calgary, Can., saw the U.S. win only six medals: two gold, one silver, and three bronze. The two American gold medalists were Brian Boitano, men's figure skating champion, and Bonnie Blair, winner of the women's 500-meter speed skating event. The Soviet Union took the most medals, 29, including 11 gold. East Germany was second with a total of 25.

Feb. 27   A new **round-the-world speed record** was set by a Gulfstream IV jet when it landed in Houston after a flight of 36 hrs., 8 min. The former record had been set as recently as Jan. 30 by a Boeing 747-SP, which made the flight in 36 hrs., 54 min., 15 sec.

indictments came after a 14-month grand jury investigation conducted by independent prosecutor Lawrence E. Walsh. The indictments said that weapon sales to Iran totaled about $30,000,000 and that the U.S. government received $12,000,000. On June 8 the judge in the case ruled that the four defendants must be tried separately. The ruling permitted each defendant to use the testimony his codefendants gave to Congress.

Mar. 16 **U.S. troops were ordered to Honduras** on the basis of reports that 1500 or more Nicaraguan troops had made an incursion into Honduras to attack Contra bases there. The Nicaraguan government denied this. The American troops, four battalions of about 3200 men, were not involved in any fighting and were returned to the U.S. by Mar. 28.

Mar. 22 The **Civil Rights Restoration Act** became law when both houses of Congress overrode a presidential veto. The new law stemmed from a Supreme Court decision of Feb. 28, 1984, known as the Grove City College case, in which the court held that if civil rights laws were violated in connection with a specific program receiving federal funds, other such programs at the same institution need not suffer. The new law said, in effect, that violations in connection with one program affected all parts of the institution receiving federal money.

Apr. 1 A bill providing $47,900,000 of **humanitarian aid for the Nicaraguan Contras** was signed by Pres. Reagan. The bill included $17,700,000 for children who were victims of the civil war.

Apr. 4 The **governor of Arizona was convicted** of misconduct and removed from office by a vote of 21–9 in the state senate. It was the first impeachment trial of a governor in 60 years. Evan Mecham was found guilty of two charges of misconduct, one of which involved his lending $80,000 of state money to his auto dealership. He was also convicted of obstructing justice by trying to prevent an inquiry into charges that one of his aides had made a death threat against a grand jury witness. On June 16 a state jury found Mecham and his brother Willard not guilty of concealing a $350,000 campaign loan.

Apr. 14 The **withdrawal of Soviet forces from Afghanistan,** which the U.S.S.R. had invaded in Dec. 1979, was provided for in agreements signed by the U.S., the U.S.S.R., Afghanistan, and Pakistan. The U.S. and the Soviet Union agreed not to interfere in Afghan and Pakistani affairs, and Afghanistan and Pakistan would not interfere in each other's internal affairs. The troop withdrawal began on May 15.

Apr. 18 The **U.S. Navy attacked Iranian forces** in the southern half of the Persian Gulf. The Americans destroyed two Iranian oil platforms and crippled or sank six armed Iranian vessels. One American

1988, but there were so many videocassette stores selling and renting cassettes—25,000—that competition was driving profits down. A new recording by the group Run–D.M.C., *Tougher Than Leather,* was said to show that rap music was now in the mainstream of American culture. Rap began among young urban blacks, but now its rhymed chanting to a driving beat and its culture, known as hip-hop, were widely acceptable if not always respectable. The book publishing industry prospered, which perhaps accounted for the number of mergers, takeovers, and offers in the works. The big takeover news was the sale of the Crown Publishing Group to Random House on Aug. 15. No price was announced. One estimate projected the growth of book sales at an annual rate of 3.3% through 1992. Sales of children's books were increasing and might reach more than $800,000,000 in 1988, double their sales of five years earlier. Export sales of American books were also expanding, to $739,000,000 in 1987, an increase in one year of 22%. Only in mass market paperbacks did the situation not seem rosy. Dollar sales were going up, but unit sales were down. Nevertheless, Simon & Schuster signed Mary Higgins Clark, a popular author of mystery fiction, to a five-book contract calling for $10,100,000 or $11,600,000 depending on bonuses, while Houghton Mifflin set a record in the children's book field when it agreed to pay $801,000 for a retelling of *Swan Lake* by novelist Mark Helprin with illustrations by Chris Van Allsburg. Newspaper publishing was not as upbeat as book publishing. Although the number of households increased 41.4% from 1970 to 1987, weekday newspaper circulation rose only 1% and Sunday circulation 22.4%. The number of daily papers published declined from 1,657 to 1,645.

Among notable persons who died were the poet Leonie Adams, June 27, at 88; Charles Addams, cartoonist of macabre humor, Sept. 29, at 76; Romare Bearden, collagist, Mar. 12, at 75; Barry Bingham, Sr., newspaper publisher, Aug. 15, at 82; Milton A. Caniff, comic strip artist, creator of *Terry and the Pirates,* Apr. 3, at 81; singer and actress Hazel Dawn, Aug. 28, at 98; Dennis Day, singer and comic with the Jack Benny radio show, June 22, at 71; Florence Eldridge, stage and movie star, Aug. 1, at 86; Gil Evans, jazz composer and arranger, Mar. 20, at 75; Robert A. Heinlein, science fiction writer, May 8, at 80; John Houseman, actor and producer, Oct. 30, at 86; Robert Joffrey, founder and artistic director of the ballet troupe bearing his name, Mar. 25, at 57; Jim Jordan, star of the radio show *Fibber McGee and Molly,* Apr. 1, at 91; Louis L'Amour, author of best-selling westerns, June 10, at 80; composer Frederick Loewe, Feb. 14, at 86; Joshua L. Logan, Broadway director, July 12, at 79; James McCracken, dramatic tenor,

Market Mechanisms. The task force recommended that the Federal Reserve Board be made responsible for regulating trading. On Feb. 2 a staff report of the Securities and Exchange Commission said the crash was accelerated by trading in stock futures. It recommended that certain computerized trading in such futures be limited and that higher margins be required. The NYSE announced on Feb. 4 that it would curb the use of its electronic trading system when the Dow Jones average of industrial stocks rose or fell more than 50 points in a day.

Jan. 13 The **oldest and most distant objects** ever seen in the universe were detected by astronomers, according to a report made before the American Astronomical Society. The objects appeared to be beyond any observed quasar and, being perhaps 17,000,000,000 years old, their radiations were coming from the creation of some of the universe's first galaxies.

Jan. 28 Controversy over a **nuclear power plant** caused the Public Service Co. of New Hampshire to file for bankruptcy. The Seabrook plant, 15 years in construction, was completed in July 1986 at a cost of $5,200,000,000 but had never been granted an operating license because of disputes over emergency evacuation plans. On May 27, in a similar dispute about emergency evacuation, the Long Island Lighting Co. agreed with New York State to abandon plans to operate its Shoreham nuclear plant, which over 20 years had cost $5,300,000,000 without ever being put to use.

Mar. 14 A **treaty to protect the earth's ozone shield** was ratified by the Senate, 83–0, making the U.S. the first major user and producer of chlorofluorocarbons to approve an international agreement reached in Montreal in Sept. 1987. The agreement first froze and then called for a rollback of the use of such chemicals, which are believed to damage the ozone in the upper atmosphere.

Mar. 15 The **first black Catholic archbishop** in the U.S. was named by Pope John Paul II. Eugene Antonio Marino was installed on May 5 as head of the Archdiocese of Atlanta, Ga.

Apr. 1 The **largest department store takeover** in the U.S. was completed when Federated Department Stores, Inc., accepted a bid of $6,600,000,000 from the Campeau Corp. of Canada. The deal was the fifth largest acquisition in U.S. history. Fifteen months earlier Campeau had purchased another American department store chain, Allied Stores Corp., for $3,600,000,000.

Apr. 8 Television evangelist **Jimmy Swaggart was defrocked** as a minister of the Assemblies of God after he rejected punishment ordered by the church. He had been directed to stop preaching for a year after

Mar. 15 The transfer of the **St. Louis Cardinals' NFL franchise** to Phoenix was approved by the league. The owners also voted to continue the use of the instant replay by officials for another season.

Mar. 31 The U.S. and Italy joined in a **drug case** that brought charges against 233 suspected members of a Sicilian Mafia drug ring. More than 100 suspects were under arrest. The investigation had been underway for more than two years. Italian officials said it showed that all three of Italy's major underworld organizations were involved in the drug trade and that New York's Mafia families had had more contact with them than previously thought.

Apr. 4 The **NCAA men's basketball championship** was won by Kansas, which defeated Oklahoma 83–79.

Apr. 10 The **Masters golf tournament** was won by Sandy Lyle of Great Britain when he birdied the final hole.

Apr. 18 The 92nd **Boston Marathon** was won by Ibrahim Hussein of Kenya in the men's division with a time of 2 hrs., 8 min., 43 sec. The women's division was won by Rosa Mota of Portugal with a time of 2 hrs., 24 min., 30 sec.

Apr. 20 A new **team home-run record** was set by the New York Yankees (AL), who became the first major league team to hit more than 10,000 when Jack Clark hit no. 10,001. It was his first home run of the season.

Apr. 22 For the first time in its 37 years, the **Little 500**, a bicycle race held on the Indiana University campus in Bloomington, included an event for women's teams. Hitherto women had been restricted to a tricycle race and cheering the men. The Willkie Sprint team, representing a dormitory quadrangle, won this first women's event.

Apr. 28 By **losing 21 consecutive games** at the start of the baseball season, the Baltimore Orioles set an American League record. They then won a game, but followed that with two more losses. The previous mark of 20 losses was set by Boston in 1906 and tied in 1916 and 1943 by Philadelphia.

May 3 The **largest cocaine seizure** in U.S. history was made by officials at Tarpon Springs, Fla., when they found 9200 pounds of the drug in hollowed-out lumber that had been shipped from Colombia. The cocaine was estimated to have a street value of more than $2,000,000,000. The largest previous cocaine seizure occurred in Fort Lauderdale, Fla., in Nov. 1987, when 8700 pounds were found.

May 4 **Anthony "Fat Tony" Salerno,** reputed to be the boss of the Genovese crime family, was convicted with eight other men of racketeering. The numerous crimes he was charged with included a multimillion-dollar scheme to rig bids in the construction industry. Those convicted faced up to 20 years in prison on the racketeering charge. Salerno was already serving a

helicopter and its crew of two were lost. The U.S. said this strike was in retaliation for Iranian mining of gulf waters that resulted in damage to a Navy ship. On Apr. 29 the government announced that U.S. forces in the gulf would broaden their mission and protect all neutral ships attacked by Iran.

Apr. 28 An **air disaster** caused by the explosionlike rupture of the fuselage of an Aloha Airlines Boeing 737 jet flying at 24,000 feet between Hilo and Honolulu, Hawaii, resulted in the death of a flight attendant, who was swept to her death, and injuries to 60 of the 94 other persons aboard. The plane made an emergency landing safely. Investigators said the cause of the disaster was apparently structural failure.

May 4 An **explosion** in a chemical plant near Henderson, Nev., injured about 200 people. The shock of the explosion was felt for 15 miles and hundreds of windows were shattered in nearby Las Vegas. The plant, which was leveled by four blasts, made fuel for the NASA space shuttles.

May 14 The fiery **head-on crash** of a pickup truck and a bus carrying 67 people near Carrollton, Ky., took the lives of 27, mostly teenagers, returning from a church youth outing. The driver of the truck, who was traveling the wrong way on an interstate highway, was charged two days later with 27 counts of capital murder. Police said he was drunk at the time of the accident.

May 23 Maryland became the **first state to ban cheap pistols,** effective Jan. 1, 1990. The ban covered the manufacture and sale of pistols that were determined to be easily concealed, inaccurate, unsafe, or poorly made. Provision was made to ban plastic guns also.

May 24 A **trade bill** that Congress had been working on for three years was vetoed by Pres. Reagan. The House overrode the veto the same day, 308–113, but on June 8 the Senate failed to register a two-thirds vote to override, 61–37. The president objected particularly to a provision that would require businesses to give 60 days' notice of plant closings or large–scale layoffs. In general the bill was protectionist, intending to defend the nation's industries against what were considered by its supporters unfair trading practices of other countries.

May 27 The **Intermediate-Range Nuclear Forces Treaty,** which called for the elimination of land-based medium-range and short-range missiles now installed in Europe by the U.S. and the Soviet Union, was ratified by the Senate by a vote of 95–3. It was the first U.S.–Soviet arms accord approved by the Senate since 1972.

May 29–June 1 A fourth **summit meeting** was held in Moscow by Pres. Reagan and General Secretary Mikhail S. Gorbachev of the Soviet Union. The meeting was notable chiefly for the extent to which Reagan

Apr. 30, at 61; Colleen Moore, who in the silent movies was the personification of the 1920s flapper, Jan. 25, at 87; Louise Nevelson, pioneering artist in creating environmental sculpture, Apr. 17, at 88; Isamu Noguchi, sculptor, Dec. 30, at 84; Melvin James "Cy" Oliver, jazz composer and orchestra leader, May 27, at 77; Irene Rich, star of silent movies, Apr. 22 at 96; Adela Rogers St. John, journalist, author, and screenwriter, Aug. 10, at 94; Max Shulman, humorist and creator of the TV character Dobie Gillis, Aug. 28, at 69.

Among **books published** this year were *Chaos: Making a New Science* by James Gleick and *A Brief History of Time* by Stephen W. Hawking. Biographies included *Oscar Wilde* by Richard Ellmann and *Freud: A Life for Our Times* by Peter Gay. Historians offered *Reconstruction: America's Unfinished Revolution* by Eric Foner and *Battle Cry of Freedom* by James M. McPherson, a vivid account of the Civil War. Fiction as usual offered a wide range of titles and subjects and included *Emperor of the Air* by Ethan Canin, a noteworthy first collection of short stories that sold 50,000 copies in its hardbound edition; *The Mysteries of Pittsburgh*, a coming-of-age novel by Michael Chabon; *The Cardinal of the Kremlin,* a thriller by Tom Clancy; *Libra,* a recounting of the Kennedy Assassination by Don DeLillo; *The Tenants of Time,* about 19th-century Ireland, by Thomas Flanagan; *Quinn's Book,* set in 19th–century Albany, N.Y., by William Kennedy; and *Freaky Deaky,* a suspense novel by Elmore Leonard. Among poetry offerings was *New and Collected Poems* by Richard Wilbur.

Mar. 2 **Grammy Awards** were presented for the following: best album of 1987, *Joshua Tree* by U2; best record, "Graceland" by Paul Simon; best male pop vocalist, Sting for "Bring on the Night"; best female pop vocalist, Whitney Houston for "I Wanna Dance with Somebody"; best male rock vocalist, Bruce Springsteen for *Tunnel of Love.* There was no award for best female rock vocalist.

Mar. 26 An exhibition of **art treasures from the Hermitage Museum** in Leningrad opened at the Metropolitan Museum in New York, consisting of 51 Dutch and Flemish paintings from the 17th century, most of which had never been seen in the U.S. The exhibit was to go to the Art Institute of Chicago, which was the joint organizer with the Metropolitan of the exhibit. In exchange, the two American museums arranged a display of 51 19th- and early-20th-century French paintings to be shown at the Hermitage and later in Moscow.

| Business and Industry; Science; Education; Philosophy and Religion | III | | IV | Sports; Social Issues and Crime; Folkways; Fashion; Holidays |

he publicly confessed "moral failure" on Feb. 21 following reports that he had committed lewd acts with a prostitute. He left his pulpit on Feb. 21 but on May 22 Swaggart appeared in the pulpit of his Family Worship Center in Baton Rouge, La., preaching without ministerial credentials.

Apr. 11 Expansion of the **roles of women in the Roman Catholic Church** was recommended by a committee of Catholic bishops. Women's leadership roles would be expanded at almost all levels of the church except the priesthood. The report also condemned the "sin of sexism." Women should be encouraged to preach and to distribute communion, and the possibility of ordaining women as deacons should be studied.

Apr. 12 The **world's first patent for a higher form of life,** a mouse, was issued to Harvard University. The patent for "transgenic nonhuman mammals" was in the names of two scientists, Dr. Philip Leder and Dr. Timothy A. Stewart, who injected a gene that causes cancer in many mammals into fertilized mouse eggs and so developed a new breed of genetically altered mice.

Apr. 13 Christian, Moslem, and Jewish **fundamentalism was rejected** by the Conservative movement of Judaism in the first statement of principles in its 143-year history. Conservative Judaism, the report said, should follow a moderate course, with loyalty to tradition but "without resigning from the 20th century."

Apr. 23 A **ban on smoking** in passenger planes went into effect. The no-smoking rule applied to all flights of two hours or less, except for travel clubs, charter trips, and flights to foreign destinations. Northwest Airlines announced it would ban smoking on all domestic flights regardless of their duration.

May 1 The Reagan administration announced an **increase in arms sales abroad.** Its aim was to sell $15,000,000,000 worth, which would be $3,000,000,000 more than it sold in the previous fiscal year. In that year another $2,000,000,000 worth was sold for export directly by manufacturers.

May 13 A **second genetic code** had been deciphered, according to a report in *Nature* by two scientists at MIT. This code directed one of several steps in the synthesis of proteins inside cells. Solution to the problem had been sought by molecular biologists for 20 years. It was a step in providing scientists a way to make proteins to order.

May 13 The **drug AZT** prolonged the lives of AIDS patients, according to the company that produced it. Of 144 patients who participated in the first human trials of azidothymidine (AZT), 84.5% were alive after one year. So far, however, efforts to develop a vaccine for AIDS were discouraging. With nearly 35,000 Americans reported to have died of AIDS, Congress

100-year sentence for his conviction as a member of the Mafia's ruling "commission."

May 7 The 114th **Kentucky Derby** was won by Winning Colors, only the third filly ever to take this event. The jockey was Gary Stevens and the time 2:02⅕.

May 19 **Carlos Lehder Rivas** was convicted of smuggling tons of cocaine into the U.S. Lehder was the reputed leader of a violent Colombian drug ring and, with a codefendant, was found guilty of conspiring to bring 3.3 tons of cocaine into the U.S. between 1978 and 1980.

May 21 The 113th **Preakness Stakes** was won by Risen Star, with a time of 1:56⅕. Eddie Delahoussaye was the jockey.

May 26 The **NHL Stanley Cup** was won for the fourth time in five years by the Edmonton Oilers who swept the Boston Bruins in four games.

May 29 The 72nd **Indianapolis 500** auto race was won for the third time by Rick Mears with an average speed of 114.809 mph in a race marred by a number of accidents. His time was 3 hrs., 27 min., 10.204 sec.

June 7–21 The **NBA basketball championship** was won by the Los Angeles Lakers, defeating the Detroit Pistons four games to three. It was the first time since 1969 that a team had won the title two years in succession.

June 11 The 120th **Belmont Stakes** was won by Risen Star, with a time of 2:26⅖. Eddie Delahoussaye was the jockey.

June 12 The **Tour of Italy bicycle race** was won by an American for the first time since the race was first held in 1909. The winner was Andy Hampsten, 26, who dropped out of the University of North Dakota to take up bicycling. He defeated 198 other cyclists and finished 1 min., 43 sec. ahead of his nearest challenger.

June 20 A law to force the **admission of women to private clubs** was upheld unanimously by the Supreme Court. At issue was a New York City law requiring women to be admitted to large, private clubs that are said to play important roles in business and professional life. In New York the University Club had already voted to admit women. By the end of August the Union League Club, the Century Association, and the Friars Club in New York agreed to admit women. The Friars Club in California admitted its first female member in 1987. On June 18 the exclusive Cosmos Club in Washington, D.C., unassailably male for 110 years, voted by a large majority to accept women. It too had been threatened with legal action.

June 20 The **U.S. Open golf tournament** was won by Curtis Strange, who defeated Nick Faldo by four strokes in an 18-hole playoff.

pushed Gorbachev on the matter of human rights in the Soviet Union and the irritation publicly expressed in return by the Communist leader. Although some progress was made on a number of issues, there was no movement on arms reductions.

June 29 A federal law providing for **independent prosecutors** to investigate high-ranking government officials suspected of criminal activities was upheld by the Supreme Court, 7–1. The decision was a sharp rebuff for the Reagan administration, which had argued that the law was unconstitutional because it encroached on the executive power of the president. The law, enacted in 1978 as a result of the Watergate scandal, allowed the special prosecutors to be appointed by a three-judge federal appellate court.

July 3 An **Iranian passenger jet was shot down** by a U.S. Navy warship at the southern end of the Persian Gulf when it was mistaken for an Iranian F-14 fighter plane. A missile fired from the cruiser *Vincennes* resulted in the death of all 290 persons aboard the Airbus A300. The cruiser at the time was fighting off attacks by Iranian gunboats. There was confusion over what led the commander of the *Vincennes,* Capt. Will C. Rogers III, to believe that the jetliner was a hostile aircraft. On Aug. 2 it was revealed that the report of an investigation by the military blamed crew error caused by psychological stress on men in combat for the first time.

July 5 Attorney General **Edwin Meese III** under criticism for some time for alleged criminal or ethical wrongdoing, announced he would resign later in the summer. He asserted that the report of an independent prosecutor, who had been investigating Meese for 14 months, "vindicated" him because it recommended that no criminal charges be brought. The report, made public on July 18, said that Meese had willfully filed a false income tax return but had intended to pay. It also said there was insufficient evidence to seek indictments in two other matters. One concerned Meese's ties to the Wedtech Corp. of New York City, which had apparently tried to bribe its way into government defense contracts. The other involved an aborted plan to build a $1,000,000,000 oil pipeline in Iraq, the negotiations for which might have violated the Foreign Corrupt Practices Act.

July 18–21 The **Democratic National Convention** nominated Gov. **Michael S. Dukakis** of Massachusetts for president and Sen. Lloyd M. Bentsen, Jr., of Texas for vice president.

Aug. 10 Interned **Japanese-Americans** who were forced into relocation camps during World War II would receive compensation for their ordeal, according to a bill signed by Pres. Reagan. The 120,000 surviving internees, about half the original number, and their beneficiaries would each receive $20,000 tax-

Mar. 31 **Pulitzer prizes** were awarded for the following: fiction, *Beloved* by Toni Morrison; general nonfiction, *The Making of the Atomic Bomb* by Richard Rhodes; biography, *Look Homeward: A Life of Thomas Wolfe* by David Herbert Donald; history, *The Launching of Modern American Science, 1846–1876* by Robert V. Bruce; poetry, *Partial Accounts: New and Selected Poems* by William Meredith; drama, *Driving Miss Daisy* by Alfred Uhry.

Apr. The **archives of Duke Ellington,** late great jazz musician and composer, were acquired by the Smithsonian Institution in Washington, D.C. The material consisted of some 3,000 items of music, files, TV scripts, photography, and business records.

Apr. 1 The **first nightly news anchorman** in American broadcasting retired. He was Douglas Edwards, who joined the CBS radio network in 1942 and held the anchor position for 20 years.

Apr. 3 **Grolier, Inc.,** an American publisher of educational and reference materials, agreed to a takeover by Hachette S. A., a French book and magazine publisher, for about $450,000,000. On Apr. 13 Hachette became the largest magazine publisher in the world, with 74 publications in ten countries, by acquiring an American company, Diamandis Communications, Inc., for $712,000,000.

Apr. 11 **Academy Awards** were presented to *The Last Emperor* as the outstanding motion picture of 1987; Michael Douglas as best actor for *Wall Street;* Cher as best actress for *Moonstruck;* Sean Connery as best supporting actor for *The Untouchables;* Olympia Dukakis as best supporting actress for *Moonstruck.*

Apr. 25 Publishing rights to a **sequel to *Gone With the Wind*** by Margaret Mitchell, one of the most popular novels of all time, were sold to Warner Books in an auction for $4,940,000. The sequel, which was scheduled for publication in 1990, was to be written by Alexandra Ripley, author of four novels. *Gone With the Wind* was published in 1936 and had sold about 25,000,000 copies.

May 2 A **Jackson Pollock painting,** *Search* (1955), was purchased at auction in New York for $4,800,000, a record for the artist and for any post–World War II work of art. The purchaser was a Tokyo art dealer. On May 3, also at auction, Jasper Johns's *Diver* (1962) sold for $4,200,000, a record for the artist. The buyer was not identified.

Business and Industry; Science;
Education; Philosophy and Religion III

IV **Sports; Social Issues and Crime;**
Folkways; Fashion; Holidays

and Pres. Reagan approved a $1,000,000,000 program for education, treatment, and research.

May 16 Only slight changes in the **operations of stock markets** were recommended by the White House Working Group, the third federal government body to study the stock market crash of Oct. 19, 1987. The principal proposal was that trading be halted for one hour on all U.S. markets if any of them fell or rose the equivalent of 250 points on the Dow Jones industrial average.

May 29 Two new **American cardinals** of the Roman Catholic Church were among 25 prelates named to the high posts by Pope John Paul II. The Americans, who were officially installed on June 28, were James Aloysius Hickey of Washington and Edmund Casimir Szoka of Detroit. The appointments brought to ten the number of U.S. cardinals.

June 13 In a trial linking **cigarettes and cancer,** a cigarette manufacturer was found guilty for the first time in the cancer death of a longtime smoker. A federal jury in New Jersey awarded $400,000 damages to Antonio Cipollone, whose wife, Rose, who died in 1984, had smoked heavily for 40 years. However, the Liggett Group, found liable, and other tobacco companies were found not guilty of the charge that they had fraudulently misrepresented the risks of smoking and had conspired to misrepresent facts. The suit was the first of more than 300 since 1954 in which any tobacco company had lost a case. However, in 1990 an appeals court ordered the case retried and on Nov. 5, 1992, the case was dropped by the plaintiff.

June 14 The **Southern Baptist Convention** for the tenth consecutive year elected a conservative as its president. The victor was the Rev. Jerry Vines of Jacksonville, Fla., but he won by only 692 votes out of 31,274 cast by delegates. One of the most divisive issues was control of teaching at the denomination's seminaries. On June 16 the delegates voted to condemn homosexuality as "a manifestation of a depraved nature" and "a perversion of divine standards."

June 14 The **General Assembly of the Presbyterian Church** (U.S.A.) adopted a statement on Christian responsibilities in the nuclear age that declared nuclear war immoral. The statement said that under some circumstances noncooperation or disobedience to civil authority "has been deemed an appropriate Christian response."

June 15 More than half of all **new mothers remained in the job market** for the first time in the nation's history, the Census Bureau reported. The figure reached 50.8% in 1987. Of new mothers with college degrees, 63% remained in the work force, compared with 38% of those with only a high school education. It was noted that women who had more education and more

June 25 "Axis Sally" died. Mildred E. Gillars received her nickname during World War II, when, although an American citizen, she broadcast Nazi propaganda to U.S. troops fighting in Europe. Gillars was said to have been influenced by her lover, Max O. Koischwitz, a German citizen and foreign-office official, who had at one time taught at Hunter College in New York City. After the war Gillars was arrested and tried for treason. Convicted, she was sentenced to 10 to 30 years in prison and fined $10,000. Gillars was released after 12 years.

June 27 **Surrogate motherhood** was banned by a state for the first time when Gov. James J. Blanchard of Michigan signed a bill that outlawed commercial contracts for women to bear children for others. Other state legislatures were considering similar measures.

June 27 The **world heavyweight boxing championship** was retained by Mike Tyson when he knocked out Michael Spinks in 1 min., 31 sec. of the first round of a bout in Atlantic City, N.J. This was Tyson's third defense of his title in 1988. On Jan. 22 he knocked out Larry Holmes, a former champion, in the fourth round, and on Mar. 21 he knocked out Tony Tubbs in the second round.

July 11 **Unrestricted free agency** for 280 members of the NFL Players Association was denied by a federal judge in Minneapolis. The players had sought an injunction that would free them to negotiate with any team they chose because there was no collective bargaining agreement between the NFL owners and the players at the time the players' contracts expired in February. The decision meant players must sign with their own teams or not at all. The players' association said it would continue to press an antitrust suit against the owners.

July 11 His **4000th career harness-racing victory** was registered by John Campbell at the Meadowlands in New Jersey. He became the 15th driver in harness racing history to record that many wins. Campbell also led in career earnings, with $60,000,000 in purses.

July 12 The **baseball All-Star Game** was won by the American League, 2–1, over the National League.

July 13 The **oldest U.S. veteran** died. He was Samuel Leroy Mendel, 104, of Galva, Ill. At 14 he attempted to enlist in the army to serve in the Spanish–American War of 1898 but was turned down. He served three years after 1901. His death left Nathan E. Cook, 102, of Tempe, Ariz., as the oldest U.S. veteran.

July 16 A new **world record for the women's heptathlon** was set by Jackie Joyner-Kersee, with a total of 7215 points for the seven events. The record she broke was her own. Florence Griffith Joyner, Joyner-Kersee's sister-in-law, set a new world record of 10.49

free and an apology from the U.S. government. However, because Congress did not at that time appropriate any money to pay the detainees, the first $20,000 checks were not distributed until Oct. 9, 1990, when nine of the oldest internees received their payments.

Aug. 15–18 The **Republican National Convention** nominated Vice Pres. **George Bush** of Texas for president and Sen. Dan Quayle of Indiana for vice president.

Aug. 27 A settlement of **Indian land claims,** one of the largest in U.S. history, was confirmed by a vote of the tribe concerned, the Puyallup. The settlement gave the tribe $162,000,000 in cash, land, and jobs, in return for surrendering further claims to land and buildings in Tacoma, Wash., valued at more than $750,000,000. Each adult member received $20,000 in cash at once; younger members would receive this sum when they reached 21.

Aug. 31 So far this year 66,895 **forest fires** had burned 3,400,000 acres in the U.S. It was the worst record since 1919 and approached the record of 1910, when more than 5,000,000 acres were destroyed.

Sept. 6 The **Hispanic population** of the U.S. had increased 34% since the 1980 census, the Census Bureau reported. There were now approximately 19,400,000 people of Hispanic background, and they represented 8.1% of the total population. More than half of them lived in California and Texas.

Sept. 14 The explosion of a **Soviet nuclear device** in Central Asia was witnessed for the first time by American officials. The U.S. government was in the process of deciding whether to agree to proposals that would allow each country to verify the other's underground tests.

Sept. 22 **Forest fires** in Yellowstone National Park had by now burned half the park's 2,200,000 acres in summer-long blazes. Controversy arose because park officials followed a policy of allowing naturally caused fires to burn themselves out.

Sept. 30 **Nuclear accidents** in government-operated reactors at the Savannah River plant in South Carolina had been kept secret for as long as 31 years, Congressional committees reported. On Oct. 10 the Energy Dept. announced that it was shutting down the plutonium-processing plant near Boulder, Colo., because of safety problems. On Oct. 14 it was revealed that officials at a plant near Fernald, Ohio, knew for decades that it was releasing tons of radioactive uranium waste into the air. All the plants produced material for the nation's nuclear weapons.

Oct. 3 **Kidnapers released one hostage** in Lebanon. He was Mithileshwar Singh, an Indian with resident alien status in the U.S. Nine Americans were still being held by terrorists.

May 3 **Andy Warhol's collection** of art and other objects sold for a total of $25,300,000 over a ten-day period of auctions. About 10,000 items were disposed of in the largest auction ever held by Sotheby's in New York. Warhol, who died in 1987, had an enormous collection of cookie jars, which brought $247,830. Other items included paintings, pottery, antiques, folk art, and American Indian art.

May 10 A **record price for sculpture** was paid at auction in New York when *Little Dancer at 14 Years of Age* by Edgar Degas was sold for $10,120,000. An unidentified European was the purchaser. The bronze of Degas's 1881 wax sculpture is 37 inches tall.

May 11 The **100th birthday of Irving Berlin,** America's most prolific and popular song writer, was celebrated with a gala concert at Carnegie Hall in New York City. Among the well-known performers paying tribute were Frank Sinatra, Willie Nelson, Ray Charles, Marilyn Horne, and Leonard Bernstein. Mr. Berlin could not attend but planned to watch the taped telecast.

May 18 **Howard Nemerov** was named the third poet laureate of the U.S., by the Librarian of Congress, succeeding Richard Wilbur.

June 5 The **Tony awards** for the 1987–1988 season were presented for the following: best play, *M. Butterfly* by David Henry Hwang; best musical, *The Phantom of the Opera* by Andrew Lloyd Webber; best actor in a play, Ron Silver for *Speed the Plow;* best actress in a play, Joan Allen for *Burn This;* best actor in a musical, Michael Crawford for *The Phantom of the Opera;* best actress in a musical, Joanna Gleason for *Into the Woods.*

June 7 Papers of **Saul Bellow,** consisting of notebooks, typescripts, and other materials relating to his novel *Mr. Sammler's Planet* (1969), were sold in New York City for $66,000, a record at auction for a work by a living author. It was the first manuscript the author, winner of the Nobel Prize for Literature in 1976, had sold. The items were bought as an anonymous gift to be presented to the Berg Collection of the New York Public Library.

June 15 A new edition of **James Joyce's** *Ulysses* published four years earlier became the center of a lively literary controversy. The edition, prepared by a team

Business and Industry; Science; Education; Philosophy and Religion III		Sports; Social Issues and Crime; Folkways; Fashion; Holidays IV

work experience before having children were better able to afford child care.

June 21 **No cavities** or other tooth decay were reported by half the nation's school children, according to a federal government survey. The increase to 49.9% of those with no decay, compared with 36.6% in a 1979–1980 survey, was attributed to the widespread use of fluoride and the high level of dental care.

July 3 A 19th-century **American woman was canonized** by Pope John Paul II at the Vatican. Sister Rose Philippine Duchesne, who was born in France in 1769 and immigrated to the U.S. in 1818, was the fourth American to attain sainthood in the Roman Catholic Church. Sister Duchesne, who died in 1862, founded dozens of schools and a convent for young women and directed the American branch of her order, the Society of the Sacred Heart.

July 11 The **General Convention of the Episcopal Church** closed in an atmosphere of compromise on several issues. On the subject of sexual morality, the delegates reaffirmed "the biblical and traditional teaching of chastity and fidelity," but also called for "an open dialogue" on human sexuality. Anticipating the likelihood of women becoming bishops, the convention provided for bishops to come in from outside a diocese where churches were at odds with their local bishop over women as clergy.

Aug. 2 A bill requiring **notice of plant closings** became law without Pres. Reagan's signature. He opposed the bill but heeded Republican appeals that vetoing it would hurt the party's election chances in the fall. Under the bill's terms, a company with 100 or more full-time employees must give 60 days' notice of plans to close a plant. The same notice must be given if either 500 or one-third of a plant's workers are to be laid off.

Aug. 17 The first joint American–Soviet **nuclear test verification experiment** took place in Nevada. Teams of U.S. and Soviet scientists used different methods to determine the strength of a nuclear blast of an American device.

Aug. 23 A **foreign trade bill** with protectionist overtones was signed by Pres. Reagan. Covering a large number of areas, the new law was aimed particularly at what was alleged to be unfair trading practices of other nations. A most important provision allowed the president to negotiate international agreements to enlarge the markets for goods and services such as banking and insurance.

Sept. 19 A **free trade agreement** with Canada was approved by the Senate, 83–9, completing U.S. action. The agreement would do away with almost all trade barriers and tariffs by 1999. The Canadian House of Commons had previously approved the agreement.

sec. for the women's 100-meter dash. Both records were made at the Olympic trials in Indianapolis, Ind.

July 24 The **U.S. Women's Open golf tournament** was won by Liselotte Neumann of Sweden by three strokes.

July 31 The **Baseball Hall of Fame** elected Willie Stargell, who played his entire career of 21 years with the Pittsburgh Pirates.

July 31 The **last Playboy Club**, in Lansing, Mich., closed. The first opened in Chicago in 1960, and by 1972 some 1,000,000 men had joined 22 clubs. Daringly risqué for their time, the clubs featured as waitresses pretty young women barely stuffed into costumes that included bunny ears and tails.

Aug. 8 The **first night baseball game at Wrigley Field,** Chicago, was played 53 years after the first major league night baseball game took place in Cincinnati, Ohio. Light for night games had never been installed until now.

Aug. 9 The **largest trade in professional sports** occurred when the Edmonton Oilers of the NHL sent Wayne Gretzky, superstar of ice hockey, to the Los Angeles Kings for $15,000,000. The deal also sent two other Oilers players to the Kings, which in turn sent three of its skaters to Edmonton.

Aug. 14 The **PGA golf tournament** was won by Jeff Sluman by three strokes. It was his first victory after six years on the pro tour.

Aug. 15 "Casey at the Bat," a poetic baseball classic and one of the most often recited poems in the English language, marked the 100th anniversary of its first performance. It is thought that on this date in 1888, at Wallack's Theater in New York City, it was first recited by the popular actor DeWolf Hopper, who went on to repeat his performance about 10,000 times over the years. The saga of the mighty baseball hero who failed in the clutch was written by a 25-year-old Harvard graduate, Ernest L. Thayer. It was first published on June 3, 1888, in the San Francisco *Examiner* and Thayer was paid $5.

Aug. 20 **Jack Nicklaus** became the first professional golfer to win more than $5,000,000 in tournament play. A small prize of $5275 in the International Golf Tournament at Castle Rock, Colo., brought his total to $5,002,825.

Aug. 28 The **LPGA tournament** was won by Rosie Jones by a margin of one stroke.

Aug. 31 **Collusion against free agents** was the finding of an arbitrator against the owners of the major league baseball clubs. These owners, the ruling said, violated baseball's collective bargaining agreement in relation to 79 players who became free agents at the end of the 1986 season. Almost none of the clubs attempted to sign such players from other clubs. Monetary damages

Oct. 6 The **Ku Klux Klan,** the Southern White Knights, and 11 individuals were convicted in a federal court in Atlanta, Ga., on charges of rioting in connection with a civil rights march in Jan. 1987. Each organization was ordered to pay $400,000 to be distributed among the 50 plaintiffs in the case.

Oct. 13 A **welfare reform bill** was signed into law by Pres. Reagan. The most revolutionary change it made was to require single parents on welfare with children over three years old to get regular jobs. If they could not find work, they had to enroll in job training or educational courses.

Oct. 17 **American military bases** in the Philippines would continue to operate through Sept. 1991 by the terms of a modified agreement. The U.S. would provide the Philippines with $481,000,000 a year in military and economic aid in 1990 and 1991. This was an increase over the current $180,000,000 a year. The Subic Bay Naval Station and Clark Air Force Base were the two principal American installations.

Oct. 18 A bill to raise the **Veterans Administration** to Cabinet level was passed by Congress. Pres. Reagan was expected to sign the measure. The Department of Veterans Affairs was to be officially established on Mar. 15, 1989. It would be the fifth addition to the Cabinet since 1953.

Oct. 21 **Ferdinand and Imelda Marcos** were indicted by a federal grand jury in New York City. The former president of the Philippines and his wife, along with eight associates, were accused of racketeering. It was alleged they had embezzled more than $100,000,000 of government money, and also took bribes, then transferred to money in the U.S. The money, along with $165,000,000 in loans obtained fraudulently, was then used to buy office buildings in New York City.

Nov. 8 **George Bush was elected president** of the United States, carrying 40 states. He defeated Governor Michael Dukakis of Massachusetts, the Democratic candidate. The electoral vote was Bush 426, Dukakis 112. The popular vote was Bush, 47,917,341, Dukakis, 41,013,030. In congressional elections the Democrats gained one Senate seat for a 55–45 majority; in the House they gained 3 seats for a 260–175 majority.

Nov. 18 An **Anti-Drug bill** of large scope was signed into law by Pres. Reagan. It called for the death penalty for drug-related murders; a $10,000 fine for the possession of even small amounts of controlled substances; and provided for the expansion of treatment facilities. A cabinet-level office was established for a drug "czar" to oversee the nation's fight on drugs.

Nov. 22 The **B-2 stealth bomber** was shown publicly for the first time to members of Congress and media

of German scholars, was claimed to correct some 5000 omissions, transpositions, and other errors in earlier editions. But John Kidd of the University of Virginia, in an 8000-word article in *The New York Review of Books,* said the edition had more flaws than its predecessors. Other scholars supported Kidd. As a result Random House, publisher of *Ulysses* in the U.S. since 1933, asked a textual scholar, G. Thomas Tanselle of Columbia University, to organize a committee to decide which edition it should publish.

Aug. 7 The sale of **Triangle Publications,** Inc., publisher of *TV Guide,* the *Daily Racing Form,* and *Seventeen* magazine, to Rupert Murdoch, Australian publishing magnate with interests in the U.S., Great Britain, and Australia, was announced. At $3,000,000,000 the deal was the largest takeover ever in publishing.

Aug. 7 A **writers' strike** by the Writers Guild of America, which began Mar. 7, ended with a compromise agreement with movie and television producers concerning residual rights and creative control. The strike delayed the usual mid-September opening of the television season on the networks.

Aug. 28 **Emmy Awards** were presented for the following: best dramatic series, *Thirtysomething;* best comedy series, *The Wonder Years;* best actor in a dramatic series, Richard Kiley for *A Year in the Life;* best actress in a dramatic series, Tyne Daly for *Cagney and Lacey;* best actor in a comedy series, Michael J. Fox for *Family Ties;* best actress in a comedy series, Beatrice Arthur for *The Golden Girls.*

Sept. 17 The **Art Institute of Chicago** opened a large new gallery of 66,640 square feet. Limestone-sheathed, it was designed to blend with the original Beaux-Arts building of the Institute. The new building cost $23,000,000. The Institute observed the opening of the new building with the largest exhibit—250 items—of the work of Paul Gauguin since 1906.

Sept. 17 The **end of the television season** found NBC the winner over the 52-week period for the fourth consecutive year. CBS was second and ABC third.

Sept. 27 **Soviet and American curators** for the first time organized jointly a museum exhibition. It was entitled "Crossroads of Continents: Cultures of Siberia and Alaska" and opened for a six-month stay at the Smithsonian Institution, Washington, D.C. The exhibit contained nearly 600 objects showing the

| Business and Industry; Science; Education; Philosophy and Religion | III | | IV | Sports; Social Issues and Crime; Folkways; Fashion; Holidays |

Sept. 20 The **first Hispanic member** of the president's Cabinet took office as secretary of education. He was Lauro F. Cavazos, since 1980 president of Texas Tech University.

Sept. 24 The **first woman to be elected a bishop** of the Episcopal Church was chosen to be suffragan bishop of the Diocese of Massachusetts. She was the Rev. Barbara C. Harris, a black who had been a priest for eight years.

Sept. 29–Oct. 3 The **first U.S. manned space flight in 32 months** took place with five astronauts aboard the space shuttle *Discovery.* In the course of its journey the *Discovery* successfully launched a $100,000,000 communications satellite. It was the first American manned flight in space since the *Challenger* blew up shortly after blastoff on Jan. 28, 1986.

Oct. 17 The **Nobel Prize in Physiology or Medicine** was awarded jointly to two Americans, Gertrude B. Elion and George H. Hitchings of the Burroughs Wellcome Co., and a Briton, James Black of London. The award was given for discoveries of "important principles for drug treatment." The winners developed drugs for treating such ailments as heart disease, gout, leukemia, and peptic ulcers.

Oct. 19 The **Nobel Prize in Physics** was awarded to three Americans: Leon M. Lederman, of the Fermi National Accelerator Laboratory; Melvin Schwartz, of Digital Pathways Inc.; and Jack Steinberger, of the European Center for Nuclear Research. They received the award for their experiments in the early 1960s that produced the first laboratory-made beam of neutrinos. This work made possible detailed studies of radioactive decay involving the "weak" nuclear force.

Oct. 21 **Ferdinand Marcos,** former president of the Philippines, his wife Imelda, and eight associates were indicted in New York City by a federal grand jury on racketeering charges. It was alleged that they had embezzled more than $100,000,000 of Philippine government money. The funds were then used to buy office buildings in New York as was $165,000,000 in loans obtained fraudulently.

Oct. 30 The **largest consumer products company in the world** was formed when the Philip Morris Companies Inc. took over Kraft Inc. for $13,100,000,000. It was the largest takeover even after the $13,300,000,000 acquisition of the Gulf Oil Corp. by Chevron in 1984.

Nov. 4 **Bill Cosby,** star of television comedy, and his wife Camille gave $20,000,000 to Spelman College, Atlanta, Ga. It was the largest gift ever from individuals to a predominately black institution.

Nov. 10 The **Superconducting Super Collider** (SSC) would be built in Texas, the Department of Energy

if any were to be determined later. A similar finding was made in 1987 with regard to players who became free agents in 1985.

Sept. 8 A **new commissioner of baseball,** A. Bartlett Giamatti, was named to take office on Apr. 1, 1989. He would succeed Peter Ueberroth. Giamatti, then president of the National League, was formerly president of Yale University and a professor there of Renaissance literature.

Sept. 9 The **America's Cup** was retained by the U.S. when the *Stars & Stripes* defeated the *New Zealand* in two straight races. It was the most unorthodox contest for the cup in the 137-year history of the event. The *Stars & Stripes* was a 60-foot-long catamaran, and the *New Zealand* was a 132-foot-long monohull. The losers sued, claiming the use of a two-hulled boat unfair. After several court decisions, the New York State Court of Appeals made a final ruling on Apr. 26, 1990, that the cup should stay with the Americans.

Sept. 10 The **Miss America** title was won by Gretchen Elizabeth Carlson, 22, from Anoka, Minn., at the annual pageant in Atlantic City, N.J.

Sept. 10–11 The **U.S. Open tennis singles championships** were won by Mats Wilander of Sweden in the men's division and by Steffi Graf of West Germany in the women's division.

Sept. 16 The **14th perfect game** in major league baseball history was pitched by Tom Browning of the Cincinnati Reds. He defeated the Los Angeles Dodgers 1–0.

Sept. 17–Oct. 2 At the **Summer Olympics** in Seoul, South Korea, the U.S. finished third in medal winnings, taking 36 gold and 94 in all. The U.S.S.R. was first, with 55 and 132, East Germany second with 37 and 102. Among American winners were Matt Biondi, who won 7 medals, 5 of them gold, in swimming events; Greg Louganis, who became the first man to win the three-meter springboard event in consecutive Olympics; Jackie Joyner-Kersee, Florence Griffith Joyner, who won the 100-meter and 200-meter dashes, setting a world record in the former.

Sept. 23 **José Canseco** of the Oakland Athletics (AL) became the first major league baseball player ever to hit 40 home runs and steal 40 bases in one season.

Oct. 4 A new major league baseball **pitching record** of 67 innings of scoreless pitching ended for Orel Hershiser of the Los Angeles Dodgers when the New York Mets scored on him in the ninth inning of the first game of the 1988 National League playoffs.

Oct. 8 The **longest losing streak** in major college football came to an end when Columbia defeated Princeton, 16–13. The Lions had lost 44 games over five years before winning this one. The next week they lost again.

representatives. Designed to evade radar on long-range bombing missions, it had not yet been flown. The Air Force hoped to acquire 132 of the craft at an estimated cost of $500,000,000 per plane.

Dec. 14 A "substantial dialogue" with the **Palestine Liberation Organization** (PLO) could now take place, the U.S. government said, because the PLO had recently renounced terrorism and accepted the existence of Israel. Hitherto the U.S. had refused to deal with the PLO. The first meeting took place Dec. 16 in Tunisia.

Dec. 21 A **mid-air explosion** aboard a Pan American Airways Boeing 747 enroute from London to New York City killed all 259 persons aboard and 11 on the ground when it fell on the village of Lockerbie, Scotland. After an investigation British officials said on Feb. 16, 1989, that a bomb had been hidden in a radio-cassette player and had probably been put aboard at Frankfurt, West Germany, where the flight originated. On. Nov. 14, 1991, two Libyan intelligence agents were indicted in both the U.S. and Great Britain for the crime.

prehistoric life of peoples in those parts of the world.

Sept. 29 **Union Station** in Washington, D.C., reopened after renovations that cost $160,000,000. The 81-year-old classical-style station was appropriate in its grandeur to a period when railroad travel was at its peak and when the U.S. capital was becoming an imperial city. It had been neglected and had gone to ruin since a failed attempt to renew it in 1976. It now had shops, restaurants, and theaters.

Oct. 8 A large collection of **Italian Renaissance manuscripts** and other documents had been acquired by Yale University, it was announced. The material comprised the 500-year-old archives of the Spinelli banking family of Florence. The approximately 150,000 documents included business records as well as correspondence with a number of popes and such major figures as Lorenzo de Medici.

Nov. 29 **National Book Awards** were presented for the following: fiction, *Paris Trout* by Pete Dexter; nonfiction, *A Bright Shining Lie: John Paul Vann and America in Vietnam* by Neil Sheehan.

1989

For the first time in eight years the nation had a new president, although not a new face on the Washington scene, George Bush having held various high government positions as well as having been vice president since 1981. In June the Supreme Court decided states could legally execute criminals as young as 16 as well as mentally retarded persons, although it said mental age could be taken into account in sentencing. In October the government announced that for the first time the Hispanic population of the U.S. had passed the 20,000,000 mark, constituting 8.2% of the total compared with 6.5% in 1980. It was also announced that the number of babies born each year was nearing the 4,000,000 mark, a figure not reached since 1964. In spite of a much-publicized war on drugs, 14,500,000 Americans used illicit drugs at least once a month. During the year Americans gave $115,000,000,000 to charitable causes, an increase of 173% in real terms over the 1955 figure. Public figures who died in 1989 included August A. Busch, Jr., head of the country's largest brewing company and owner of the St. Louis Cardinals baseball team, Sept. 29, at 90; Michael Harrington, the leading spokesman for socialist ideas and ideals, July 31, at 61; Huey Newton, black activist and a founder of the Black Panther party, murdered in Oakland, Calif., Aug. 22, at 47; and Claude Pepper, long-time congressman and chief

The 1988–1989 Broadway theater season was not noteworthy for either impressive or especially popular drama but it did set a record for box office receipts at $262,000,000, an increase of 3.6% over the previous season. However, attendance dropped by 100,000 from 8,100,000 in 1987–1988, perhaps partly accounted for by the fact that the 30 fewer productions were a new low. *The Heidi Chronicles* by Wendy Wasserstein, peopled by women who went to college together in the 1970s, was favorably received by critics and theatergoers. Musicals did better, including *Grand Hotel,* based on a hit movie of 1932; *Gypsy,* a revival featuring a mother intent on making a star of her daughter; and *Jerome Robbins' Broadway,* a potpourri of music from hit shows directed and choreographed by Robbins. American movie producers had one of their best years. Moviegoers spent more than $5,000,000,000 at the box office, breaking the previous record set in 1988 of $4,450,000,000, and total attendance was 1,120,000,000, the most in five years. *Batman,* which sold more than $251,000,000 worth of tickets, made its sponsors happy. Other box office successes included *Indiana Jones and the Last Crusade,* another wild adventure of its protagonist; and *Ghostbusters II,* not up to the original. *Dead Poets Society* concerned an unconventional teacher and his students; *Do the Right Thing,*

announced. Most of the 50 states had hoped to be selected as the site of this $4,400,000,000, 55-mile circular tunnel intended to accelerate atomic particles to the highest speeds ever.

Nov. 28 The **prime lending rate** was raised by one half of one percent to 10.5% by the nation's leading banks. It was the fourth time the rate had been increased in 1988 and was the highest since May, 1985.

Dec. 21 **Drexel Burnham Lambert, Inc.,** a major investment firm, agreed to plead guilty to six felony charges and pay a fine of $650,000,000. The firm faced indictment on charges of mail, wire, and securities fraud. On Feb. 13, 1990, Drexel filed for bankruptcy after it defaulted on $100,000,000 of loans. Some 5000 employees lost their jobs.

Dec. 31 The **Federal Home Loan Bank Board** (FHLBB) said that during 1988 it had sold or merged 222 failing savings and loan associations ("thrifts") with $100,000,000,000 in accounts. The Federal Savings and Loan Insurance Corp. supplied $38,600,000,000 in assistance.

Oct. 15–20 The **World Series** was won by the Los Angeles Dodgers (NL) who defeated the Oakland Athletics (AL) four games to one. On Oct. 12 the Dodgers had won the National League pennant over the New York Mets, four games to three. On Oct. 9 the Athletics took the American League pennant by defeating the Boston Red Sox, four games to none.

Nov. 1 What was believed to be the **largest lottery prize** in the world was won by one individual and two group winners of 25 and 15 people respectively. The total prize in the California lottery was $60,900,000.

Nov. 6 The 19th **New York City Marathon** was won in the men's division by Steve Jones of Wales with a time of 2 hrs., 8 min., 20 sec. Grete Waitz of Norway won the women's division with a time of 2 hrs., 28 min., 7 sec.

Dec. 1 In a **TV sports bidding war** NBC won the television rights to the 1992 Olympics in Spain for $401,000,000. On Dec. 14 CBS paid $1,100,000,000 for exclusive rights to major league baseball for four years beginning in 1990. It would telecast all post season games and 12 during the regular season.

1989

The American economy did not prosper during the year. Although the unemployment rate at year's end was 5.3%, a decline of 0.2%, and 2,500,000 new jobs had been created, almost all of them were in the service industries rather than manufacturing where higher wages prevailed on the whole. Industrial production was up only 1.7%, while retail sales increased 5.0% and producer prices rose 4.8%. Nevertheless, the U.S. continued to attract foreign investments. There were 343 such transactions, valued at $51,200,000,000, compared with 299 with a value of $50,000,000,000 in 1988. In the field of education, the government reported that 4,200,000 young adults were not high school graduates and that of them 15% were white, 22% black, and 28% Hispanic. On the other hand, two-year community colleges had been growing for a decade and 6,000,000 students were expected to be enrolled in them for the 1989–1990 school year. The Roman Catholic Church continued to be the largest religious denomination with 54,000,000 members, followed by the Southern Baptist Convention at 14,800,000 and the United Methodist Church at 9,100,000. The largest black denomination, the National Baptist Convention, U.S.A., Inc., built its own headquarters for the first time, a $10,000,000 structure in Nashville, Tenn. The Christian Church (Disciples of Christ) sent 50,000 Russian-language Bibles to

In sports, Ty Murray of Odessa, Tex., became at age 20 the youngest person to win the all-around championship of professional cowboys; Georgia Southern University, playing in the NCAA's Division I-AA, became the first school in the 20th century to win 15 football games in a season; Sunday Silence set a thoroughbred horse racing record for earnings in one season with $4,578,454; at the Henley Regatta in England 60 of the 400 competing crews were from the U.S.; Tom Kite set a record for annual winnings on the PGA tour with $1,395,278; and Tom Watson became the second professional golfer to pass the $5,000,000 mark in winnings. The designers of high fashion brought forth clothes with softer and gentler lines, abandoning the mannish silhouette. Deep and bright colors were featured but most young women seemed to prefer to go around in black. In men's fashions the double breasted suit made a comeback. The population of federal prisons reached 48,017 compared with 24,162 in 1980. This left the 70 available facilities 50% over their rated capacity. In spite of the number in jail, one of every 42 registered automobiles was stolen or looted in the course of the year. Prominent people who died included Earl "Red" Blaik, football coach at West Point from 1941 to 1958, May 6, at 92; John "Jocko" Conlan, feisty major league baseball umpire, as well liked by fans as any ump could be, Apr.

legislative spokesman for the elderly, May 30, at 88.

Jan. 4 Two **Libyan fighter planes were shot down** by American warplanes from the carrier *John F. Kennedy.* The U.S. pilots encountered the soviet-built MiG-23 fighters in international waters off the Libyan coast. Libya claimed its planes were unarmed and on routine patrol; the American pilots claimed they had been trailed in a hostile manner, and the U.S. government said on Jan. 5 it had visual evidence that the Libyan planes were armed with missiles.

Jan. 11 **Use of chemical weapons** was condemned by representatives of 140 nations, including the U.S., at a meeting in Paris. They urged greater efforts to complete a treaty that would ban the development, production, and possession of such weapons. The U.S. and France, which had convoked the conference, did so partly because of their alarm at the large-scale use of chemical weapons in the Iraq–Iran War of 1980–1988.

Jan. 20 **George Bush was inaugurated president** of the United States, the nation's 41st president. Dan Quayle was inaugurated vice president.

Jan. 23 A Richmond, Va., law favoring **minority-owned construction companies** was ruled invalid by the Supreme Court, 6–3. The rule provided that 30% of public works funds must go to such businesses. The court said such a law could be enforced only if it reduced "identifiable discrimination."

Jan. 28 At an **unusual gathering in Moscow** of American, Cuban, and Soviet officials who had been involved in the superpower showdown over Russian nuclear weapons in Cuba in Oct., 1962, the Russians revealed that, unknown to the U.S., there were 20 nuclear warheads in Cuba before Pres. John F. Kennedy declared a naval blockade of Cuba on Oct. 23, 1962. The warheads had not been attached to missiles but the Soviets said that could have been done in a matter of hours.

Jan. 31 The **U.S. population,** the Census Bureau projected, would peak at about 302,000,000 in 2038 and would then gradually decline to 292,000,000 by 2080. The bureau estimated that by 2030 there would be 66,000,000 persons 65 years and older, or 22% of the population, compared with 30,000,000 this year.

Mar. 14 A ban on the **importation of semiautomatic rifles** was announced by the Bush administration, which previously had opposed any ban. The new rule, sought by anti-gun groups and law enforcement agencies, applied to about 80% of such weapons. On Apr. 5 another 24 models were added to the list.

Mar. 21 A **federal drug testing program** was upheld by the Supreme Court, 7–2. It applied to those holding jobs involving public health and safety. This case was a test of a Federal Railroad Administration rule.

Mar. 24 The worst **oil spill** in U.S. territory began when the supertanker *Exxon Valdez,* owned by the

with Spike Lee as director and actor, had a rather unusual slant on racial violence. Steven Soderbergh's *sex, lies, and videotape* won the top prize at the Cannes Film Festival. *Parenthood* was the most popular comedy; *Pet Sematary* was another scary Stephen King production; and *Field of Dreams* showed that faith could even bring back long-dead baseball players. Among serious fare were *Driving Miss Daisy,* about an elderly widow and her long-suffering chauffeur; and *Glory,* the story of the first black regiment to fight in the Civil War. As to entertainment in the home, 56.4% of households now had cable TV, up from 52.8% in 1988, while 62% of households had VCRs, up from 56%. The Denver, Detroit, and Cleveland symphony orchestras faced serious financial problems, but the Dallas Symphony moved into a new and impressive home that cost $81,500,000. The JVC Jazz Festival (at one time the Newport and at another the Kool) took place in New York City and marked its 35th anniversary. Among a number of serious book-length studies of jazz, *The Swing Era: The Development of Jazz, 1930–1945* by Gunther Schuller, the second volume by him on the subject, was outstanding. A major art exhibit at the National Gallery in Washington during the winter of 1988–1989 marked the 400th anniversary of the Venetian painter, Paolo Veronese, with 50 paintings and 55 drawings on display. A praiseworthy addition to the New York City skyline was Rockefeller Plaza West, on Seventh Avenue, a 57-story office building that went well with the older, neighboring Rockefeller Center. It was stepped back in design, built of limestone, stainless steel, and glass, and featured a 10-story glass section at its southeast corner. Book sales showed an upward trend, mass market paperbacks increasing at a rate of 6.5% per year from 1982 to 1989 while adult hardbound books did even better, with a 12.4% annual increase. In dollar sales during this period, the growth in hardbounds was from $770,800,000 to $1,700,000,000, and paperbacks went from $703,000,000 to $1,100,000,000. Magazine publishing, however, did not prosper, with advertising revenue falling as the year went on, and with the competition of 500 to 600 new ones each year—of which eight out of ten would fail. Unique among new ones was *UpTime: The Disk Monthly,* which was about computers, was published as a disk, and required a computer to be read. It was offered at $720 a year.

Among notable persons who died were Alvin Ailey, founder of the American Dance Theater, Dec. 1, at 58; Joseph Alsop, Jr., hawkish political columnist and art collector, Aug. 28, at 78; Lucille Ball, comedienne of movies and television, Apr. 26, at 77; Donald Barthelme, author who wrote with wry humor, July 23, at 58; Irving Berlin, America's all-time greatest song writer, Sept. 22, at 101; Mel Blanc, the voice of Bugs Bunny and other

Business and Industry; Science; **III**	**Sports; Social Issues and Crime;** **IV**
Education; Philosophy and Religion	**Folkways; Fashion; Holidays**

Moscow in April and planned on shipping 450,000 more by 1991. The Salvation Army expanded its activities to a 91st country, El Salvador. Noteworthy people who died included Salo Wittmayer Baron, much respected for his life's work devoted to Jewish history, Nov. 25, at 94; George W. Beadle, Nobel Prize winner for his work in genetics, June 9, at 85; William M. Fairbank, physicist who pursued the elusive quark, Sept. 30, at 72; Sidney Hook, political philosopher and enemy of communism, July 12, at 96; Walter Hoving, who revived from its doldrums the jewel of jewelry stores, Tiffany & Co., Nov. 27, at 91; Timothy Cardinal Manning, archbishop of Los Angeles, June 23, at 79; Owen Lattimore, scholar of Far Eastern affairs, May 31, at 88; Charles J. Pedersen, Nobel Prize winner in chemistry, Oct. 26, at 85; Emilio G. Segre, Nobel Prize–winning nuclear physicist, Apr. 22, at 84; J. C. Street, co-discoverer of the muon, Nov. 7, at 83.

Jan. 2 A comprehensive **free trade agreement** between the U.S. and Canada was signed by Pres. Ronald Reagan and Prime Minister Brian Mulroney of Canada. The agreement will eliminate tariffs and reduce other barriers to trade and investment by the end of the century. The legislatures of both countries ratified the agreement before the end of the year.

Jan. 31 Thirteen-year-old **American students rank last** in math and science, according to the Education Testing Service. The comparison was with students from South Korea, Great Britain, Ireland, Spain, and four Canadian provinces. The Korean students ranked first in math and, with British Columbia students, first in science.

Feb. 3 In the **largest business takeover ever** RJR Nabisco agreed to be acquired for $25,000,000,000 by Kohlberg Kravis and Roberts & Co., an investment firm specializing in mergers and buyouts. With the Beatrice Companies, which had been acquired in a leveraged buyout in 1986, the combined concerns accounted for about 13% of all U.S. food manufacturing.

Mar. 23 A claim to having achieved **nuclear fusion at room temperature** was made by two chemists working at the University of Utah. They were B. Stanley Pons and Martin Fleischmann. Fusion, occurring when two or more light nuclei are combined to make one heavier nucleus, ordinarily takes place at temperatures of several hundred million degrees and had not yet become a practical source of energy. Most scientists were skeptical of the Pons-Fleischmann process as to whether it existed at all or, if it did, whether it could produce enough energy to be practical. A federal conference in May, which brought together hundreds of scientists in different fields, delivered a strong negative verdict.

16, at 89; Lily Daché, designer noted for her hats, especially turbans, Dec. 31, at 97; A. Bartlett Giamatti, Renaissance scholar, president of Yale University, and commissioner of Major League Baseball, Sept. 1, at 51; Vernon "Lefty" Gomez, pitcher for 14 years for the New York Yankees, winner of six World Series games without a loss, and member of the Baseball Hall of Fame, Feb. 17, at 80; William "Billy" Martin, bad boy of baseball and manager at five different times of the New York Yankees, Dec. 25, at 61; William "Bill" Terry, New York Giants player and manager with a .341 batting average over 14 seasons, Jan. 9, at 90; Sugar Ray Robinson, five times middleweight boxing champion, Apr. 12, at 67; Valentina Nicholaevna Sanina Schlee, fashion designer known professionally by her first name only, who dressed many stars of the theater, Sept. 14, age uncertain; Glenna Collett Vare, a pioneer of women's golf and a charter member of the Women's Golf Hall of Fame, Feb. 3, at 89; Diana Vreeland, the most influential fashion editor of her time, Aug. 22, at 86.

Jan. 2 In **college football bowl games** the results were UCLA 10, Arkansas 2 in the Cotton Bowl; Miami 23, Nebraska 3 in the Orange Bowl; Michigan 22, USC 14 in the Rose Bowl; and Florida State 13, Auburn 7 in the Sugar Bowl. Both the AP and the UPI polls chose Notre Dame as the 1988 national champion. Notre Dame defeated West Virginia, 34–12, in the Fiesta Bowl.

Jan. 22 **Super Bowl XXIII** was won by the San Francisco 49ers (NFC) who defeated the Cincinnati Bengals (AFC) 20–16. On Jan. 8 San Francisco had won the NFC title by defeating the Chicago Bears 28–3 and Cincinnati had taken the AFC title by defeating the Buffalo Bills 21–10.

Feb. 3 The **National League** of major league baseball elected Bill White as president. A player for 14 years and then a sports broadcaster, he was the first black elected to head a major sports organization.

Feb. 11–12 **U.S. figure skating championships** were won in Baltimore, Md., by Jill Trenary, women's singles; Christopher Bowman, men's singles; Kristi Yamaguchi and Rudi Galindo, pairs; and Susan Wynne and Joseph Druar, dance.

Apr. 2 The **NCAA women's basketball championship** was won by Tennessee which defeated Auburn 76–60.

Apr. 3 The **NCAA men's basketball championship** was won by Michigan which defeated Seton Hall 80–79 in overtime.

Apr. 9 The **Masters golf tournament** was won by Nick Faldo of England on the second hole of a playoff with Scott Hoch.

Apr. 17 The 93rd **Boston Marathon** was won in the men's division by Abebe Mekonnen of Ethiopia in a time of 2 hrs., 9 min., 6 sec. The women's division was

Exxon Corp., ran aground in Prince William Sound in southeastern Alaska, dumping 240,000 barrels of oil into the water. Wind and currents spread the oil more than 50 miles from its source and 730 miles of coastline were affected. It was estimated that as many as 400,000 birds and animals suffered. It was alleged that the captain of the tanker, Joseph J. Hazelwood, had been drinking and an uncertified officer was at the helm. On Mar. 22, 1990, Hazelwood was convicted of misdemeanor negligence, fined $50,000, and ordered to perform 1000 hours of community service. His captain's license was suspended on July 25, 1990. Exxon was also blamed by the National Transportation Safety Board and on Mar. 13, 1991, Exxon agreed with Alaska and the federal government to pay a penalty of $100,000,000 and provide $1,000,000,000 over a period of ten years to continue the cleanup. However, on May 3, 1991, both Alaska and Exxon changed their minds and rejected the agreement. The matter was finally settled on Oct. 8, 1991, when Exxon agreed to pay an extra $25,000,000 penalty. On July 10, 1992, an Alaska court overturned Hazelwood's conviction, citing a federal statute that grants immunity from prosecution to those who report oil spills.

Apr. 17 **Special aid for Poland** was announced by the Bush administration. It included lowering tariffs, guaranteeing loans, steps to expedite relations between Polish and American businesses, and support for loans to Poland by the International Monetary Fund and the World Bank.

Apr. 19 An **explosion at sea** aboard the battleship *Iowa* in one of its 16-inch gun turrets killed 47 sailors. The warship was about 300 miles north of Puerto Rico at the time. An initial Navy investigation asserted that the blast had been caused when a sailor attempted to commit suicide. The outcry against this verdict was such that another Navy investigation took place and the Navy apologized on Oct. 17, 1991, to the family of the accused sailor, saying the cause of the blast could not be determined.

May 1 Once a woman has presented **evidence of sex discrimination** in hiring and promotion, the burden of proving otherwise lies with the employer, the Supreme Court held, 6–3. An employer would have to show that the same decision would have been made even if gender were not taken into account.

May 4 A federal jury convicted **Oliver L. North,** a former official of the National Security Council, on charges stemming from his part in the Iran-Contra affair in which arms were sold secretly to Iran and money from the operation funneled to the Nicaraguan Contra rebels. North was found guilty on three charges concerning the destruction of documents, and aiding and abetting the obstruction of Congress. He was acquitted of nine other charges. On July 20,

such characters, July 10, at 81; Malcolm Cowley, liberal literary and social critic, Mar. 27, at 90; Bette Davis, one of the movies' greats, Oct. 6, at 81; Vladimir Horowitz, world leader as a pianist, Nov. 5, at 85; Mary McCarthy, outspoken critic and novelist, Oct. 25, at 77; Zinka Milanov, dramatic soprano, May 30, at 83; Richard B. Morris, historian of Colonial America, Mar. 3, at 84; Frederic Prokosch, novelist, June 1, at 81; I. F. Stone, liberal and iconoclastic columnist, June 18, at 81; Virgil G. Thomson, composer and critic, Sept. 30, at 92; Barbara W. Tuchman, historian, Feb. 6, at 77; Robert Penn Warren, the first U.S. poet laureate, Sept. 15, at 84.

Among **books published** in 1989 were a number of worthy works of fiction: Two novellas by Saul Bellow, *A Theft* and *The Bellarosa Connection; Billy Bathgate* by E. L. Doctorow, about a young man and his fascination with gangsters; *Oldest Living Confederate Widow Tells All* by Allan Gurganus, which lived up to its title; *The Mambo Kings Play Songs of Love* by Oscar Hijuelos, telling of the somewhat wild way of life of some Cuban-Americans; *A Prayer for Owen Meany* by John Irving, about a misfit and the life he made; *The Russia House* by John le Carré; *Some Can Whistle* by Larry McMurtry, more Texas goings-on; *American Appetites,* Joyce Carol Oates's 19th book; *Polar Star* by Martin Cruz Smith; and *The Joy Luck Club* by Amy Tan, a first novel concerning Chinese-American families. Nonfiction of the year included three substantial books about blacks: *And the Walls Came Tumbling Down,* Ralph David Abernathy's account of his part in the civil rights movement; *Paul Robeson* by Martin Bauml Duberman, a biography of the singer, actor, and radical; and *Jazz Cleopatra: Josephine Baker in Her Time* by Phyllis Rose, the life of Josephine Baker whose career was made mostly in France. Volumes of poetry included *Human Wishes* by Robert Haas and *Time's Power, Poems 1985–1988* by Adrienne Rich. In a category by itself was *The Good Times,* more "aw shucks" recollections by Russell Baker.

Jan. 8 *42nd Street,* the **second longest-running musical** in the history of the New York theater, closed after 3486 performances. Its run was exceeded only by that of *A Chorus Line* which was still being performed. *42nd Street* opened on Aug. 25, 1980, and was based on a 1933 movie. A London production closed Jan. 7 after 1823 performances.

Feb. 22 **Grammy Awards** were presented for the following: best album of 1988, *Faith* by George Michael; best song and best record, "Don't Worry, Be Happy," by Bobby McFerrin; best new artist and best female pop vocalist, Tracy Chapman for "Fast Car"; best male rock vocalist, Robert Palmer for *Simply Irresistible;* best female rock vocalist, Tina Turner for *Tina Live in Europe.*

| Business and Industry; Science; Education; Philosophy and Religion **III** | | Sports; Social Issues and Crime; Folkways; Fashion; Holidays **IV** |

May 4 The unmanned spacecraft **Magellan** was launched by the space shuttle *Atlantis* to begin a voyage to Venus. It reached Venus orbit Aug. 10, 1990, and began sending back new and astounding information. Active volcanoes, fractured landscapes, and a thin plastic crust were revealed, unlike anything hitherto seen in the solar system. Other photographs showed pancake-shaped lava domes about half a mile high and ten miles in diameter.

May 22 The first successful **transfer of cells containing foreign genes** into a human being was performed at the National Institutes of Health, Bethesda, Md. The altered cancer-fighting cells were placed in the blood stream of a cancer patient. Although the patient was not expected to benefit, doctors hoped that tracking the cells would eventually help them develop techniques for transplanting foreign genes in such a way as to cure or control disease.

June Nearly **106,000 cases of AIDS** had been reported to date in the U.S. and of these sufferers 61,000 had died. It was estimated that by the end of 1992 there would be between 179,000 and 208,000 more cases. Departing from the usual practice, federal drug officials announced Sept. 28 that they would allow an experimental drug to be prescribed while it was still being tested. The drug was dideoxyinosine (DDI). Meanwhile first tests of an earlier approved drug, AZT, showed improvement in patients using it.

June 10 The disbanding of **Moral Majority,** the conservative Protestant political action group established in 1979, was announced by its founder, the Rev. Jerry Falwall, a Baptist clergyman. He said its goal of getting fundamentalist Christians into politics had been achieved. At its peak Moral Majority claimed a membership of 6,500,000 and in 1984 raised $11,000,000 for political lobbying. The organization was a strong supporter of Pres. Ronald Reagan.

July 9 The **richest man in the U.S.,** according to *Forbes* magazine, was Sam Moore Walton, founder of the Wal-Mart Stores, said to be worth $8,700,000,000.

July 24 The world's **largest media and entertainment conglomerate** was created by the merger of Warner Communications, Inc., into Time, Inc. As Time Warner, Inc., the new corporation had a stock market value of $15,200,000,000 and annual revenues of $10,000,000,000. Time was chiefly a magazine and book publishing company and Warner was a producer of movies and recordings. Both also had sizable cable television operations.

Aug. 9 A bill to bail out **savings and loan associations** was signed into law by Pres. George Bush. It provided $166,000,000,000, of which 75% would come from

won by Ingrid Kristiansen of Norway in 2 hrs., 24 min., 33 sec.

May 6 The 115th **Kentucky Derby** was won by Sunday Silence with a time of 2:05. The jockey was Pat Valenzuela.

May 20 The 114th **Preakness Stakes** was won by Sunday Silence with a time of 1:53⁴/₅. The jockey was Pat Valenzuela.

May 21 The **LPGA golf tournament** was won by Nancy Lopez by three strokes.

May 25 The **NHL Stanley Cup** was won by the Calgary Flames who defeated the Montreal Canadiens four games to two.

May 26 A new **sailing record** for the New York–San Francisco run was set by a trimaran, *Great American,* when it sailed under the Golden Gate Bridge one hour short of 77 days after a 14,500–mile journey. The previous record had been set Feb. 12 when *Thursday's Child* completed the same voyage in 80 days, 20 hours. Prior to these two voyages the record had been held by a clipper, *Flying Cloud,* which made such a trip in 1854 in 89 days, 8 hours.

May 28 The 73rd **Indianapolis 500** auto race was won by Emerson Fittipaldi of Brazil with an average speed of 167.581 mph.

June 10 The 121st **Belmont Stakes** was won by Easy Goer, with a time of 2:26. The jockey was Pat Day.

June 13 The **NBA basketball championship** was won by the Detroit Pistons who defeated the Los Angeles Lakers four games to none.

June 18 The **U.S. Open golf tournament** was won by Curtis Strange who became the first player since 1950–1951 to win the title two years in succession.

July 11 The baseball **All-Star Game** was won by the American League, which beat the National League 5–3.

July 16 The **U.S. Women's Open golf tournament** was won by Betsy King by a margin of four strokes.

July 23 The **British Open golf tournament** was won by Mark Calcavecchia of the U.S. who defeated Greg Norman and Wayne Grady in a four-hole playoff.

July 23 An American won the **Tour de France** for the second time when Greg Lemond triumphed in the cross-country bicycle race by the smallest victory margin ever, eight seconds. In 1986 Lemond became the first American to win the event.

July 23 The **Baseball Hall of Fame** inducted Johnny Bench, catcher, Carl Yastrzemski, outfielder, Al Barlick, umpire, and Albert F. "Red" Schoendienst, infielder.

Aug. 13 The **PGA golf tournament** was won by Payne Stewart who birdied four of the last five holes.

1990, a federal appeals court suspended North's conviction and overturned one count. Richard V. Secord, a former air force general, who had organized the operation that shipped arms to Iran, pleaded guilty Nov. 8, 1989, to a charge of making false statements to Congress. On Sept. 16, 1991, all charges against North were dropped by a federal judge because the trial testimony used to convict him had been affected by testimony he had given Congress under immunity.

May 31 James C. Wright, Jr., announced his resignation as Speaker of the House of Representatives and retired from the House. The House Ethics Committee had accused him on Apr. 17 of having violated rules concerning the acceptance of gifts and outside income. Wright denied the charges. He was succeeded on June 6 as Speaker by Thomas S. Foley of the state of Washington.

June 12 White workers claiming unfair treatment in affirmative action cases can sue under civil rights laws, the Supreme Court ruled, 5–4. The decision arose from a suit brought by white firemen in Birmingham, Ala., who claimed legislation to increase the number of black firemen discriminated against them.

June 12 Burning the American flag as a political protest is protected by the First Amendment's guarantee of free speech, the Supreme Court ruled, 5–4. On Oct. 12 Pres. Bush said he would let a bill passed by Congress banning such burning become law without his signature. He wanted a constitutional amendment. The Supreme Court, 5–4, declared on June 11, 1990, that the law was unconstitutional.

July 3 A restrictive Missouri law on abortion was upheld by the Supreme Court, 5–4. The law forbade public employees to perform abortions; banned the use of public buildings for abortions; and required doctors treating women 20 weeks or more pregnant to determine whether the fetus could survive if born.

July 19 A United Airlines DC-10 jet crashed short of the runway at Sioux City, Iowa, and 112 of the 296 persons aboard died. The pilot had struggled for 45 minutes to control the plane after an explosion in its tail engine. On Nov. 1, 1990, the National Transportation Safety Board blamed the airline for failure to detect the flaw in the engine that caused it to disintegrate.

Sept. 18–24 Hurricane Hugo, one of the worst storms of the century, struck Puerto Rico, the U.S. Virgin Islands, and the east coast of the mainland where Charleston, S.C., was hardest hit. On St. Croix 97% of the buildings were destroyed; in Charleston many landmark structures were destroyed and thousands of trees felled. Damage in South Carolina was estimated at $3,700,000,000 and in Puerto Rico at

Mar. 29 Academy Awards were presented to *Rain Man* as outstanding motion picture of 1988; Dustin Hoffman as best actor for *Rain Man;* Jodie Foster as best actress for *The Accused;* Kevin Kline as best supporting actor for *A Fish Called Wanda;* and Geena Davis as best supporting actress for *The Accidental Tourist.*

Mar. 30 Pulitzer prizes were awarded for the following: fiction, *Breathing Lessons* by Anne Tyler; general nonfiction, *A Bright Shining Lie: John Paul Vann and America in Vietnam* by Neil Sheehan; biography, *Oscar Wilde* by Richard Ellmann; history, *Parting the Waters: America in the King Years, 1954–1963* by Taylor Branch, and *Battle Cry of Freedom: The Civil War Years* by James M. McPherson; poetry, *New and Collected Poems* by Richard Wilbur; drama *The Heidi Chronicles* by Wendy Wasserstein.

Apr. 18 All three television networks lost viewers during the 1988–1989 season for the sixth year in succession. The networks had 67.2% of all prime time viewers, compared with 70.7% in the 1987–1988 season. Cable television gained. NBC ranked first in viewership with ABC second and CBS third.

June 4 Tony awards for the 1988–1989 theatrical season were presented for the following: best play, *The Heidi Chronicles* by Wendy Wasserstein; best musical, *Jerome Robbins' Broadway;* best actor in a play, Philip Bosco for *Lend Me a Tenor;* best actress, Pauline Collins for *Shirley Valentine;* best actor in a musical, Jason Alexander for *Jerome Robbins' Broadway;* best actress in a musical, Ruth Brown for *Black and Blue.*

June 4 New York City Ballet paid tribute to Patricia McBride on the occasion of her retirement after 30 years of dancing. Of 90 roles in the ballet company's repertoire, 42 had been created for her, 22 of those by George Balanchine. McBride had begun dancing classes at age seven and became a principal dancer with the ballet in 1961.

June 13 In an obscenity controversy, an exhibition of photographs by Robert Mapplethorpe was cancelled by the Corcoran Gallery of Art, Washington, in the face of controversy in Congress and the National Endowment for the Arts because of the homoerotic and sadomasochistic content of the late photographer's work. The Washington Project for the Arts, a private group, took over the exhibit and opened it July 20.

Sept. 17 Emmy Awards were presented for the following: best dramatic series, *L.A. Law;* best comedy series, *Cheers;* best actor in a dramatic series, Carroll O'Connor for *In the Heat of the Night;* best actor in a comedy series, Richard Mulligan for *Empty Nest;* best actress in a dramatic series, Dana Delany for

taxes over a ten-year period. It was expected that the total cost would be some $300,000,000,000. A new government body, the Resolution Trust Corporation, was established to merge or liquidate the institutions in trouble so as to protect depositors. Many of the thrift institutions got in financial trouble through bad loans, investments in junk bonds, bad management, and criminal acts of executives. The Federal Deposit Insurance Corporation (FDIC) had already seized 261 institutions with assets of $104,000,000,000.

Sept. 27   In the **largest Japanese acquisition** to date of an American company, Sony Corp., producer of electronic products, arranged to buy Columbia Pictures Entertainment, Inc., for $3,400,000,000.

Sept. 28   A compromise on the **ordination of women** in the Episcopal Church was the substance of a statement issued by the House of Bishops meeting in Philadelphia. The statement, which seemed likely to remove the danger of a split within the church, noted that opposition to the ordination of women continued to be "a recognized theological position" and that church leaders should be "pastorally sensitive" to those who will not accept women as priests.

Oct. 9   The **Dow Jones industrial average** closed at a new high of 2791.41, breaking the previous record set Aug. 24, 1987. However, on Oct. 13 the index fell 190.58 points, the second largest decline ever, although only the 12th worst in terms of percentage. The Dow Jones closed at 2569.26.

Oct. 9   The **Nobel Prize in Physiology or Medicine** was awarded jointly to J. Michael Bishop and Harold E. Warmus, both of the University of California at San Francisco, for their discovery of how normal cell growth can change so as to cause cancer.

Oct. 12   The **Nobel Prize in Chemistry** was awarded to Sidney Altman of Yale University and Thomas R. Cech of the University of Colorado for their determination that RNA is not only a passive carrier of genetic information but can also process such information, promote chain reactions, and reproduce itself.

Oct. 12   The **Nobel Prize in Physics** was awarded to Norman F. Ramsey of Harvard University for his development of the atomic clock, and to Hans Dehmelt of the University of Washington and Wolfgang Paul of West Germany for their method of isolating atomic and subatomic particles for prolonged study.

Oct. 18   The unmanned spacecraft *Galileo* was launched on a roundabout trip to Jupiter by astronauts aboard the space shuttle *Atlantis*. It was due to reach Jupiter on Dec. 7, 1995, and to collect gravitational acceleration it flew by Venus Feb. 16, 1990. During its passage there it took photographs of

Aug. 19   One of the most **lavish parties** of the century was given by Malcolm S. Forbes, a magazine publisher, who hosted it in his palace in Tangier, Morocco, to celebrate his 70th birthday. Invited were 600 or so glamorous, rich, and famous guests. The evening's entertainment included hundreds of belly dancers, a charge by Berber horsemen, and fireworks. The party was estimated to have cost $2,000,000.

Aug. 22   The **first pitcher to strike out 5000 batters,** Nolan Ryan of the Texas Rangers (AL), reached this mark in a game against the Oakland Athletics (AL).

Aug. 24   **Pete Rose,** one of the game's superstars, was banned from baseball for life by A. Bartlett Giamatti, commissioner of Major League Baseball, for having bet on games, allegedly including those of his own team, the Cincinnati Reds (NL), for whom he played and managed.

Aug. 30   Wealthy hotel owner **Leona Helmsley** was found guilty in federal court in New York City on 33 counts of tax evasion, fraud, and conspiracy. She was acquitted on eight other counts. On Dec. 12 she was sentenced to four years in prison, fined $7,200,000, and ordered to perform 750 hours of community service.

Sept. 9–10   The **U.S. Open tennis singles championships** were won in the men's division by Boris Becker and in the women's by Steffi Graf, both of West Germany.

Sept. 13   Francis F. "Fay" Vincent was named **commissioner of Major League Baseball,** in succession to A. Bartlett Giamatti, who died Sept. 1. Vincent was a lawyer and a friend of Giamatti and had recently been deputy commissioner.

Sept. 17   The **Miss America** title was won by Debbye Turner, 23, of Columbia, Mo., at the annual pageant in Atlantic City, N.J.

Sept. 20   The murderer known as the "Night Stalker" for his method of operation, Richard Ramirez, a drifter from Texas, was found guilty in Los Angeles of 30 murders and 30 other crimes. He had terrorized Southern California in the summer of 1985 with a series of killings.

Sept. 29   Law officers **seized 20 tons of cocaine** in a raid on a warehouse in Los Angeles. They also found $10,000,000 in cash in what was said to be the largest drug seizure in history. Four persons were arrested. The cocaine had a wholesale value of $2,000,000,000 and a street sale value of up to $7,000,000,000. One of the suspects arrested said 60 tons had passed through the warehouse during the year. In Texas, near the Mexican border, and also on a Panamanian ship, agents seized 14 tons of cocaine on Oct. 14. In New York City more than 5 tons of the drug were found Nov. 10 hidden in drums of a toxic chemical.

$1,000,000,000. In spite of the fury of the storm only 24 Americans lost their lives.

Oct. 17 An **earthquake** struck the San Francisco area, registering 6.9 on the Richter scale, with its epicenter near Santa Cruz. The quake killed 66 persons, most of whom died in the collapse of a section of a double-deck freeway in Oakland. Damage was estimated at $10,000,000,000. The tremor struck just as the third game of the 1989 World Series was to get underway in Candlestick Park in San Francisco. The stadium, with more than 60,000 people in it, was only slightly damaged and spectators were evacuated without incident.

Nov. 8 L. Douglas Wilder became **the first black elected governor** of a state when he won the Virginia election, but with only 50.19% of the vote.

Nov. 21 Pres. Bush signed **an anti-drug law** that appropriated $3,180,000,000 for treatment facilities, federal prison expansion, education, and law enforcement.

Dec. 3 The first **summit meeting** of Pres. Bush and Mikhail S. Gorbachev, president of the U.S.S.R., took place on ships of the two nations in the harbor of Valetta, Malta. The sessions were disrupted by a fierce storm that caused the cancellation of some visiting back and forth. In closing statements both presidents said in effect that the Cold War was over. The two leaders also discussed nuclear disarmament and the improvement of trade relations between the two countries.

Dec. 20 American **armed forces invaded Panama** in an attempt to overthrow and capture Manuel Antonio Noriega, the military dictator of the country who had been indicted in the U.S. on drug trafficking charges. The invasion force numbered about 24,000, half of whom had been stationed in Panama. After fairly stiff resistance by Noriega's Panama Defense Forces, he surrendered on Jan. 3, 1990, and was flown to the U.S. to stand trial. American casualties were 23 killed and 323 wounded. Panamaniam forces suffered 314 killed and 124 wounded. In addition some 200 non–combatants died.

China Beach; best actress in a comedy series, Candice Bergen for *Murphy Brown.*

Oct. 10 A **reception for Helen Hayes** in New York City was a tribute to the actress from colleagues and friends on her 89th birthday. Hayes made her debut in 1919 in *Old Dutch,* a comedy. Through the years she played leading roles in a great variety of plays. One of her early successes was *Dear Brutus* (1918). She starred in *Caesar and Cleopatra* (1925), *Victoria Regina* (1935), and *Long Day's Journey into Night* (1971).

Nov. 1 The resignation of **Lincoln Kirstein,** a dance impresario, writer, and businessman, as general director of the New York City Ballet and as president of the School of American Ballet was announced. In 1933 he invited George Balanchine, a noted choreographer and teacher, to emigrate to the U.S. and the next year they founded what became the New York City Ballet and its school. Kirstein had much to do with the flowering of classical ballet in America. He wrote a number of books, among them *Blast at Ballet* (1938) and *Movement and Metaphor* (1971).

Nov. 29 **National Book Awards** were presented for the following: fiction, *Spartina* by John Casey; nonfiction, *From Beirut to Jerusalem* by Thomas L. Friedman.

Nov. 30 With the **art auction** in New York City of Pablo Picasso's *Pierrette's Wedding* for $51,300,000, six of the ten highest prices ever paid for paintings were registered in 1989 and the Picasso sale was the second highest price so far recorded. Also in 1989 *Yo Picasso,* a self-portrait, went for $47,900,000; a third Picasso, *Au Lapin Agile,* for $40,700,000; *Halberdier,* by Jacopo Pontormo, $35,100,000; *Rue Mosnier, Paris, Decorated with Flags on June 30, 1887,* by Edouard Manet, $26,400,000; and *Mirror,* by Picasso, also $26,400,000. In addition, Willem de Kooning's *Interchange* was sold on Nov. 8 for $10,700,000, a record at the time at auction for a living artist, while Jackson Pollock's *No. 8, 1950* was sold on May 2 for $11,000,000, the most so far paid for a work by this artist.

1990

By the second half of the year the nation faced the start of a recession at home and a war abroad, the latter the result of Iraq's invasion of Kuwait Aug. 2. Pres. George Bush's handling of foreign policy, especially his skill in building an international coalition to oppose Iraq's Pres. Saddam Hussein, was widely praised. Bush

The 1989–1990 Broadway theater season set a record for box office receipts for the third year in a row: $283,000,000, up from $262,000,000. Attendance was 8,030,000, up from 7,970,000 and there were 35 new productions compared with 30 the previous year. Generally judged the best new American plays of the year

| Business and Industry; Science; Education; Philosophy and Religion   III | | IV   Sports; Social Issues and Crime; Folkways; Fashion; Holidays |

Venusian cloud and wind patterns. Galileo next headed for a swing around the earth to give it a further gravitational push and it came within 600 miles of its home planet on Dec. 8, 1990. On this part of its long journey it made photographs on Dec. 7, 1990, of areas of the far side of the moon never seen before. On Oct. 29, 1991, Galileo took the first photographs of a rocky asteroid, Gaspra, a body about 12 miles long.

Oct. 30   A controlling interest in **Rockefeller Center** in New York City was sold by the Rockefeller Group to the Mitsubishi Estate Co. of Tokyo, which bought 51% of the skyscraper complex for $864,000,000. The handsome Art Deco buildings included the GE Building, formerly the RCA Building, considered one of the best examples of skyscraper design.

Nov. 17   A new **minimum wage bill** that increased the rate from $3.35 an hour to $3.80 on Apr. 1, 1990, and to $4.25 on Apr. 1, 1991, was signed into law by Pres. Bush. The law also established a "training wage" minimum of $3.35 an hour for 16- to 19-year-olds for the first three months of employment.

Nov. 19   American astronomers announced they had detected a source of **light coming from the edge of the universe** and the beginning of time.

Nov. 21   A law banning **smoking on most domestic flights** was signed by Pres. Bush. The only exceptions were for flights to Alaska and Hawaii that took more than six hours.

Nov. 27   The first U.S. **liver transplant** using a live donor was successfully completed at the University of Chicago Medical Center. Four other such operations had been performed in other countries. In the operation a mother gave a third of her liver to her 21-month-old daughter. A second operation took place successfully at the same medical center on Dec. 8.

Dec. 11   **Robert E. Peary** did reach the North Pole on Apr. 6, 1909, according to a report sponsored by the National Geographic Society. In recent years doubts had been cast on his claim, either on the grounds that he falsified his data or had made an honest mistake.

Dec. 31   The **Dow Jones industrial average** ended the year at 2753.20, up 584.63 for a gain of 27%.

Oct. 14–28   The **World Series** was won by the Oakland Athletics (AL) when they defeated the San Francisco Giants (NL) four games to none. The last two games had been postponed since Oct. 17 when an earthquake shook Candlestick Park in San Francisco just as the third game of the series was about to start. On Oct. 8 the Athletics had won the American League championship by beating the Toronto Blue Jays four games to one and the next day the Giants had won the National League title, beating the Chicago Cubs four games to one.

Oct. 15   Wayne Gretzky became the **highest scorer in NHL history** when, playing for the Los Angeles Kings against the Edmonton Oilers, he registered his 1850th point. The record broken had been set by Gordie Howe over 26 seasons. This was Gretzky's 11th season.

Oct. 26   Paul Tagliabue was named **commissioner of the National Football League,** succeeding Pete Rozelle who had retired after 30 years. Tagliabue as a lawyer was associated with a law firm that was outside counsel to the NFL.

Nov. 5   The 20th **New York City Marathon** was won in the men's division by Juma Ikangaa of Tanzania with a time of 2 hrs., 8 min., 1 sec. The women's division was won by Ingrid Kristiansen of Norway with a time of 2 hrs., 25 min., 30 sec.

Nov. 21   For the **exclusive right to broadcast all NCAA tournaments** for a seven-year period CBS agreed to pay the college sports organization $1,000,000,000. Seventeen sports were included but the chief prize was the annual national basketball championship.

Nov. 22   Kirby Puckett, a centerfielder, became the **first $3,000,000-a-year baseball player** when he signed a three-year contract with the Minnesota Twins of the American League for $9,000,000. This figure was exceeded Dec. 1 when Mark Langston, a left-handed pitcher, agreed to a five-year contract with the California Angels for $16,000,000, or $3,200,000 a year. Mark Davis, a left-handed relief pitcher, signed on Dec. 11 with the Kansas City Royals for $13,000,000 for four years, or $3,250,000 a year.

1990

The national economy was without doubt in a recession by year's end. GNP rose only 0.9% for the year and declined by 2.1% in the last quarter. Unemployment rose to 6.1%, its highest level since mid-1987, but the consumer price index rose 6.1%, the most since 1981. Sales of new homes fell by 17.5% to the lowest level

A poll in early 1990 showed that football continued to be America's favorite sport with a following of 35%. Baseball stayed in second place with a 16% following, but basketball's fans had increased from 10% to 15% in the last decade. Baseball had reason to worry: its most faithful followers were over 50 years of age. Basketball,

showed less interest in domestic affairs and the year was notable chiefly for a protracted, acrimonious debate between the Republican-controlled executive branch and the Democratic-controlled Congress over the federal budget deficit. The result was a plan intended to cut that deficit nearly $500,000,000,000 over five years, although skeptics doubted this would happen. In midterm elections the Democratic party made small gains and with its Republican opponents managed to spend $203,000,000 on congressional and state elections, an increase of 26% over 1986, the last comparable year. On Dec. 27 the Census Bureau reported that the population of the country as of Apr. 1 was 249,632,692, an increase of 23,000,000 over 1980. The largest relative increases occurred in the southern and sun belt states, especially, California, Florida, and Texas. The net result was that for the first time a majority (50.2%) of Americans lived in metropolitan areas. New York continued to be the largest such area but Los Angeles, in second place, showed the largest gain. Also notable in population change was the fact that the number of Asians and Pacific islanders in the U.S. increased from 3,834,000 in 1980 to 6,880,000 in 1990. Among notable persons who died were James M. Gavin, a top combat commander in World War II, Feb. 23, at 82; Arthur J. Goldberg, former Supreme Court justice and holder of other high government positions, Jan. 19, at 81; Curtis E. LeMay, commander of the air forces that bombed Japan in World War II, Oct. 1, at 83; Louella Luhrman, an army nurse in World War I and the oldest living veteran, Jan. 26, at 108; Spark M. Matsunaga, Democratic senator from Hawaii, 1977–1990, Apr. 15, at 73; Edwin O. Reischauer, East Asian scholar and ambassador to Japan, Sept. 1, at 79.

Jan. 2–Sept. 27 **Six oil spills** dumped 670,000 gallons of oil and petroleum products into the Arthur Kill and the Kill van Kull, two narrow waterways between Staten Island, New York, and New Jersey. The New Jersey side of the waterways is lined with refineries and tanks that can hold nearly 2,000,000,000 gallons of oil products. Also, on the west coast, off Huntington Beach in southern California, a tanker that hit an underwater object on Feb. 7 spilled about 400,000 gallons of crude oil into the Pacific Ocean.

Apr. 7 For his part in the **Iran-Contra affair** John M. Poindexter, a former national security adviser, was found guilty of five criminal charges involving conspiracy, obstruction of Congress, and making false statements. He was sentenced June 11 to six months in prison. On Nov. 15, 1991, a federal appeals court reversed his conviction because testimony he had given before a congressional committee under a promise of immunity had been used unfairly against him.

were *Six Degrees of Separation, The Piano Lesson,* and *Prelude to a Kiss.* The movies had box office receipts at nearly $5,000,000,000 for their second best year ever, but movie theater owners were not happy. With the total number of screens now nearly 23,000, not enough movies of lasting popularity were being produced to keep the seats filled. For 1990 the movies with the highest gross sales were *Ghost, Pretty Woman,* and *Home Alone.* Mostly praised but not all hits were *Dances With Wolves, Dick Tracy, Alice, The Godfather, Part III,* and *Goodfellas. Bonfire of the Vanities* was a flop, but *Teenage Mutant Ninja Turtles* did more than well. In the world of dance there was a festival of Jerome Robbins's ballets, and the American Ballet Theater celebrated its 50th anniversary. From the U.S.S.R. the Georgia State Dance Company was warmly welcomed. Among the many musical events of the year, the New York City Opera's production of Arnold Schoenberg's *Moses and Aaron* was a high point, as was the debut of Yevgeny Kissin, a young Russian pianist, with the New York Philharmonic. Although two new television series, *Twin Peaks* and *The Simpsons,* were far from run of the mill and became hits, the most popular series were old ones: *Cheers,* in its ninth year, *60 Minutes,* and *Murder She Wrote.* The outstanding production by far was *The Civil War,* 11 hours in length on PBS. Newspaper circulation in large cities showed a tendency to decline as that of suburban papers increased. In 1950 New Yorkers bought 9,200,000 copies of the Sunday papers; in 1990 the figure was a little under 3,200,000. In the magazine field 3100 were being published, of which 536 began publication this year. Of the latter, the top categories of subject matter were sex, lifestyle, and service. Reversing a trend of recent years, paperback books showed a greater sales increase than hardbound books: about 7.2% compared with 4.4%. There was good news for publishers and booksellers at the end of the Christmas season: 36% of adult Americans received one or more books as gifts, an increase of 17.5% over 1989.

Notable people who died included Eve Arden, comedienne, particularly known as *Our Miss Brooks* on TV, Nov. 12, at 83; Pearl Bailey, a singer with a warm and mischievous style, Aug. 17, at 72; Joan Bennett, star of the movies and the stage, Dec. 7, at 80; Leonard Bernstein, conductor, composer, and pianist, Oct. 14, at 72; Gordon Bunshaft, a leader among International Style architects, Aug. 6, at 81; Aaron Copland, composer noted for his treatment of American themes, Dec. 2, at 90; Norman Cousins, magazine editor and author, Nov. 30, at 75; Sammy Davis, Jr., black singer, dancer, and actor, May 16, at 74; Hedley Donovan, editor-in-chief of Time, Inc., from 1964 to 1979, June 29, at 74; Irene Dunne, actress in both sophisticated and humorous roles, Sept. 4, at 91; Douglas Edwards, the first TV

Business and Industry; Science; Education; Philosophy and Religion	III		IV	Sports; Social Issues and Crime; Folkways; Fashion; Holidays

since 1981 and sales of motor vehicles dropped 5.1% to the lowest figure since 1983. On the financial front merger deals amounted to $412,500,000,000, down from $518,800,000,000 in 1989, while the rating of $510,000,000,000 of corporate debt was downgraded. On the plus side, the recession helped narrow the trade deficit by reducing imports so that the imbalance for the year was $100,000,000,000, the smallest in seven years, and personal income rose 6.08%, almost matching the inflation rate. For the first time in seven years the consumption of petroleum fell, by 2.1% to 16,960,000 barrels a day, but domestic production decreased by 5.1% to 7,200,000 barrels a day. By 1990 the number of fast food outlets had risen since 1980 to 119,000 from 67,290, while the number of book stores had also grown greatly, from 10,200 to 17,620. Also on the rise was the temperature around the U.S. It averaged 53.94° F in 1990, the seventh highest on record. The 96-year average was 52.5° F, the record having been set in 1934 at 54.67° F. Notable people who died in 1990 included Ralph David Abernathy, pioneer in the civil rights movement, successor to Martin Luther King, Jr., Apr. 17, at 74; Bruno Bettelheim, psychoanalyst who specialized in the emotional problems of children, Mar. 13, at 86; Harry Bridges, left-wing labor leader who led a general strike that tied up San Francisco in 1934, Mar. 30, at 88; Harold E. Edgerton, inventor of the electronic flash for photography, Jan. 4, at 86; Malcolm S. Forbes, flamboyant millionaire magazine publisher, Feb. 24, at 70; Armand Hammer, oil executive known for his business relations with the U.S.S.R. in spite of the Cold War, Dec. 10, at 92; Robert Hofstadter, Nobel Prize physicist who explored nuclear particles, Nov. 17, at 75; Samuel Noah Kramer, the leading authority on ancient Sumeria, Nov. 26, at 93; Karl A. Menninger, innovative psychiatrist, one of the founders of the Menninger Clinic, July 18, at 96; Robert N. Noyce, coinventor of the integrated circuit, which revolutionized the electronics industry, June 3, at 62; William S. Paley, founder and builder of the Columbia Broadcasting System, Oct. 26, at 89; Albert Rose, whose research made possible the television picture tube, July 26, at 80; B. F. Skinner, psychologist whose theories of behavior control were alarming to some, Aug. 18, at 86; Nathaniel C. Wyeth, inventor of the plastic soda bottle, July 4, at 80.

Jan. 11 Approval of the **Jarvik-7 artificial heart** was withdrawn by the Food and Drug Administration saying there were manufacturing problems and reports of adverse reactions. In 1982 it was the first artificial heart in the world and by now had been used about 150 times.

Jan. 22 In the growing **savings and loan crisis,** the Justice Department reported that 403 people had been convicted of fraud in the past two years in connection

on the other hand, had a following made up of younger fans and blacks. As to active participation in athletics, 158,000 women now took part in intercollegiate sports, an increase from the 34,000 cited 18 years earlier. On the PGA Seniors tour, Lee Trevino won $1,190,518, topping Greg Norman's $1,165,477 on the regular tour, the first time a Seniors pro was the top PGA money-winner. Meanwhile, on the LPGA tour, Pat Bradley became the first woman golfer to pass the $3,000,000-mark, her winnings in the year's tournaments putting her at $3,059,718. Crime flourished with most of the nation's cities setting new records for homicides, among them Dallas, Memphis, Milwaukee, New York, Phoenix, San Antonio, and Washington. Figures released this year showed that the homicide rate among black men, ages 15 to 24, rose by two thirds from 1985 through 1988. On the downward trend were drinking and smoking. In 1979 76% of those 18 to 25 years of age said they had used alcohol in the past month; now it was 63%; those who smoked cigarettes decreased to 32% compared with a high of 50% in 1976. Deaths of notable persons included George Allen, a successful but somewhat eccentric football coach, Dec. 31, at 72; Spurgeon F. "Spud" Chandler, a winning pitcher for the New York Yankees in the 1940s, Jan. 10, at 82; "Rocky" Graziano (Thomas Rocco Barbella), middleweight boxing champion, popular for his brawling style, May 22, at 71; Halston (Roy Halston Frowick), an influential fashion designer of the 1970s, Mar. 26, at 57; Tom Harmon, Michigan's All-American running back who scored 33 touchdowns in 24 games, Mar. 15, at 70; Charley Keller, hard-hitting outfielder for the New York Yankees in the 1940s and 1950s, May 23, at 73; Lester J. Maitland, who made the first flight from the U.S. mainland to Hawaii in 1927, Mar. 29, at 91; Alice Marble, champion tennis player of the late 1930s who four times won the U.S. title, Dec. 13, at 77; Bronislaw "Bronko" Nagurski, a running back of great power in college and in the pros in the 1920s and 1930s, Jan. 7, at 81; Joe Sewell, member of the Baseball Hall of Fame who batted .312 over a 14-season career, Mar. 6, at 91; George P. Stavropoulos, fashion designer who specialized in the use of chiffon, Dec. 10, at 70; Horace C. Stoneham, owner of the New York Giants baseball team who in 1958 moved them so that they became the San Francisco Giants, Jan. 7, at 86.

Jan. 1 In **college football bowl games** the results were Tennessee 31, Arkansas 27 in the Cotton Bowl; Notre Dame 14, Colorado 0 in the Orange Bowl; USC 17, Michigan 10 in the Rose Bowl; and Miami 33, Alabama 25 in the Sugar Bowl. Both the AP and UPI picked Miami as the national collegiate champions of 1989.

Jan. 28 **Super Bowl XXIV** was won by the San Francisco 49ers, who defeated the Denver Broncos

Apr. 14 **Flash floods** set off by heavy thunderstorms swept through central and eastern Ohio, northern West Virginia, and western Pennsylvania driving hundreds of people from their homes. Shadyside, Ohio, was especially hard hit with 23 dead and ten others missing.

June 1 At a **summit meeting** in Washington, D.C., Pres. Bush and Pres. Mikhail Gorbachev of the U.S.S.R. signed an agreement to make large cuts in nuclear weapons. The U.S. would reduce its arsenal of missiles from about 12,000 to about 9500; the Soviets would reduce theirs from about 11,300 to about 6900. To achieve these totals both sides would scrap missile submarines and bombers as well as missiles. An agreement concerning chemical weapons called for the destruction of at least 50% of stocks by 1999. The arms agreement was the broadest between the two nations in 20 years.

June 4 The **use of high school facilities** by student political and religious groups was upheld by the Supreme Court, 8–1. The decision meant that a federal law requiring high schools to permit such use was constitutional. The case involved a high school in Omaha, Neb.

June 25 In a case concerning the **right to die**, the Supreme Court decided, 8–1, that if a person's wishes are clearly known, he or she has a constitutional right to have life-sustaining procedures ended. However, the justices also upheld, 5–4, a Missouri law allowing the sustaining of life of a woman, comatose for more than seven years, because there was no "clear and convincing evidence" that she wanted treatment stopped.

July 8 The **U.S. and Greece signed a new eight-year agreement** providing for the continuance of American military bases in Greece and for military supplies to be furnished to Greece by the U.S. The previous agreement had expired in Dec. 1988 and negotiations for a new agreement had been underway for some time. Under the terms of the new pact the U.S. would retain its two large installations on the island of Crete, while shutting down three others. Greece was to be supplied with more than $1,000,000,000 of arms along with other credits.

July 20 **William J. Brennan, Jr.,** announced his resignation from the Supreme Court, where he had served for nearly 34 years. He was the acknowledged leader of the liberal bloc on the court. One of the major decisions he wrote was that establishing the principle of "one man, one vote" in the reapportionment of voting districts.

July 26 A landmark act protecting the **rights of disabled persons** was signed by Pres. Bush. Estimated to affect 43,000,000 Americans, the law forbade discrim-

anchorman, Oct. 13, at 73; Charles Farrell, movie star of the 1930s and 1940s, May 6, at 82; Stuart Berg Flexner, a leading lexicographer, Dec. 3, at 62; Greta Garbo, movie actress of magnetic and elusive beauty, Apr. 15, at 84; Ava Gardner, a most seductive screen star, Jan. 25, at 77; Paulette Goddard, film actress in both sultry and comedy roles, Apr. 23, at 78; Dexter Gordon, jazz saxophonist and pioneer of be-bop, Apr. 25, at 67; Jim Henson, creator of the delightful puppets, the Muppets, May 16, at 53; Werner Janssen, conductor and composer who made use of jazz idioms, Sept. 19, at 91; Eric Larrabee, editor and author, best known as a champion of the arts, Dec. 4, at 68; Mary Martin, vivacious star of musical comedy and of *Peter Pan*, Nov. 3, at 78; Lewis Mumford, critic in various fields and a pioneer advocate of city planning, Jan. 26, at 94; Walker Percy, novelist who wrote of the present-day South, May 10, at 73; George Nakashima, a master of woodworking and design, June 15, at 85; Johnny Ray, a popular singer of great emotion, Feb. 24, at 63; Anya Seton, author of popular historical novels and biographies, Nov. 8, at 86; Bella Spewack, writer, with her husband, of the books for many plays and movies, Apr. 27, at 91; Barbara Stanwyck, accomplished in varied roles on the stage and in the movies, Jan. 20, at 82; Eleanor Steber, soprano, noted for her roles in Mozart and Strauss operas, Oct. 3, at 76; Iphigene Ochs Sulzberger, who behind the scenes had great influence on the development of *The New York Times* for three generations, Feb. 26, at 97; Sarah Vaughan, a jazz singer with a rich and impressive voice, Apr. 3, at 76; Irving Wallace, author of 33 books that sold millions of copies, June 29, at 74.

Books published in 1990, both fiction and nonfiction, displayed the usual diversity of subject matter. In fiction there was *The Plains of Passage,* more adventures in prehistoric times by Jean M. Auel; *Buffalo Girls,* Larry McMurtry's view of the Old West; *Friend of My Youth,* short stories by Alice Munro; *Because It Is Bitter, and Because It Is My Heart,* Joyce Carol Oates's account of a young girl coming of age; *The Things They Carried,* short stories by Tim O'Brien, set among soldiers in Vietnam; *Burden of Proof* by Scott Turow, a complicated tale of financial misdoings; *Rabbit at Rest,* John Updike's ending of the life and times of Harry "Rabbit" Angstrom; and *Hollywood* by Gore Vidal, the sixth of his novels chronicling American history. Nonfiction was marked by two books reflecting the Reagan era just ended: *Barbarians at the Gate: The Fall of RJR Nabisco* by Bryan Burrough and John Helyar was an account of the greedy finagling that accompanied the buyout of RJR Nabisco, and *The Politics of Rich and Poor* by Kevin Phillips showed how well the wealthy fared compared with the poor. Other nonfiction offerings included *A Life on the Road* by Charles Kuralt, the wandering

with misdeeds in 506 savings and loan institutions. Losses from the frauds totalled $6,400,000,000 and 79% of those convicted had received prison terms.

Feb. 27 Federal health officials recommended a **reduction in the fat content of diets** whether or not a person had a high cholesterol level. It was the first time specific recommendations had been made, including consumption targets of no saturated fats, 10% polyunsaturated, and the rest monounsaturated.

Mar. 3 A gift of $50,000,000 to the **United Negro College Fund** was announced by Walter H. Annenberg, wealthy publisher and a former ambassador to Great Britain. The Fund represents 41 predominately black institutions and this gift was the largest ever in this field.

Mar. 27 In a report on **weight loss,** a House subcommittee announced that Americans spent more than $30,000,000,000 a year on weight loss programs and products that are dangerous or ineffective.

Apr. Officials of the **Mormon Church** confirmed that changes had been made in some of the sacred rituals of the church. The church dropped a vow in which women pledged obedience to their husbands and also a requirement that they veil their faces at a point in a ceremony. The changes were in an "endowment" ceremony which the church considers necessary to assure Mormons life after death.

Apr. 22 The **20th anniversary of Earth Day** was celebrated around the world and organizers said 200,000,000 people in 140 countries had participated. In the U.S. in cities and towns there were demonstrations, tree plantings, recycling exhibits, workshops on endangered species, and other events.

Apr. 25 Seven years behind schedule, the **Hubble Space Telescope** was launched by the space shuttle *Discovery* into an orbit 381 miles above the earth. The $1,500,000,000 instrument, weighing 12 tons, was expected to enlarge the vision of astronomers tenfold and to bring into view up to 10,000,000,000,000 objects in the universe. However after the instrument was opened to the heavens with some difficulty it was discovered on June 27 that there was a serious flaw in its main light-gathering mirror. It would not be able to carry out the major part of its planned observations until and unless replacement instruments were installed. Nevertheless the Hubble Telescope produced some valuable observations: an unexpected concentration of stars around what had been thought to be an ordinary galaxy; new views of Saturn and Pluto; the first sighting of a faint quasar billions of light years from earth; and an unusually clear picture of a storm around Saturn.

55–10 and whose total points and victory margin set records. On Jan. 14 San Francisco had won the NFC title by defeating the Los Angeles Rams 30–3, and Denver won the AFC by beating the Cleveland Browns 37–21.

Feb. 3 Record-holding jockey **Bill Shoemaker** retired, having ridden to 8833 victories, including four Kentucky Derby triumphs, five in the Belmont Stakes, and two in the Preakness Stakes.

Feb. 10–11 U.S. **figure skating championships** were won at Salt Lake City, Utah, by Jill Trenary, for the third time, in women's singles; Todd Eldredge, men's singles; Kristi Yamaguchi and Rudi Galindo, pairs; and Susan Wynne and Joseph Druar, dance.

Feb. 11 The **world heavyweight boxing championship** was won by James "Buster" Douglas when he knocked out the titleholder Mike Tyson in the tenth round of a bout in Tokyo. However, Douglas lost his title Oct. 25 in Los Angeles when he was knocked out in the third round of a fight with Evander Holyfield.

Mar. 25 In one of the worst **mass murders** in U.S. history, a fire in a crowded illegal social club, the Happy Land Social Club in the Bronx, New York City, took 87 lives after a man who had been ejected from the club for quarreling with a former girlfriend, returned, threw gasoline near the door and set it afire. The flash fire took its toll by asphyxiation and burns within a few minutes. The arsonist, Julio Gonzalez, 36, a Cuban refugee, was convicted of all 87 murders as well as arson and assault on Aug. 19, 1991, and on September 19, 1991, he was sentenced to 25 years to life in prison.

Apr. 1 The **NCAA women's basketball championship** was won by Stanford which defeated Auburn 88–81.

Apr. 2 The **NCAA men's basketball championship** was won by the University of Nevada, Las Vegas, which defeated Duke 103–73. It was the first time more than 100 points had been scored by a team in this championship game.

Apr. 8 The **Masters golf tournament** was won by Nick Faldo of England who defeated Raymond Floyd on the second hole of a playoff. Faldo became only the second player to win this event two years in succession.

Apr. 16 The 94th **Boston Marathon** was won by Gelindo Bordin of Italy in the men's division with a time of 2 hrs., 8 min., 19 sec. The women's division was won by Rosa Mota of Portugal with a time of 2 hrs., 23 min., 24 sec.

May 5 The 116th **Kentucky Derby** was won by Unbridled with a time of 2:02. The jockey was Craig Perret.

May 19 The 115th **Preakness Stakes** was won by Summer Squall with a time of 1:53^3/5. The jockey was Pat Day.

ination in employment, public accommodations, and transportation.

Aug. 2–Dec. 31 **Iraqi armed forces invaded Kuwait** and overran it in a matter of hours. Iraq laid claim to Kuwait's territory, saying it had been stealing from its part of an oil field lying in both countries. The United Nations Security Council demanded Iraq's withdrawal and on Aug. 6 ordered a trade and financial boycott. The U.S., asserting that Saudi Arabia, Kuwait's neighbor to the south, was also threatened, on Aug. 7 ordered troops, armor, and aircraft to the Saudi kingdom. By Aug. 9 a naval blockade was formed and all export of oil from Iraq and Kuwait was cut off. On Aug. 10 at a meeting in Cairo, 12 of the 21 member nations of the Arab League voted to support the UN and U.S. actions. By Nov. 8 some 230,000 American troops were in Saudi Arabia and Pres. Bush announced that 150,000 more would be sent. The UN Security Council on Nov. 29 voted to authorize the U.S. and its allies to use force to expel Iraq from Kuwait if its troops did not leave by Jan. 15, 1991. By the end of 1990 580,000 Iraqi troops were believed to be in Kuwait or southern Iraq. Facing them were 485,000 troops of 17 allied countries.

Oct. 22 Pres Bush vetoed a **civil rights bill** and two days later the Senate upheld the veto. Bush said the act would have imposed racial and other quotas in employment. It would have put on employers the burden of defending themselves when charged with discrimination.

Nov. 1 An agreement to end all **dumping of industrial waste at sea** by 1995 was made by 43 nations, including the U.S. and all the leading industrial countries of the world at a meeting in London. The measure was legally binding on all 64 nations that had signed the 20-year-old treaty known as the London Dumping Convention.

Nov. 5 Pres. Bush signed a **budget law** intended to reduce the federal budget by $492,000,000,000 over the next five years. This act ended a bitter three-month controversy between the Republican president and Congress, controlled by the Democrats. The law included $140,000,000,000 in new taxes over a five-year period in spite of Bush's campaign promise in 1988 that he would never approve more taxes.

Nov. 5 **Meir Kahane,** the founder of the militant anti-Arab Jewish Defense League, was assassinated in New York City. The suspected gunman, El Sayyid A. Nosair, Egyptian-born and said to be a devout Muslim, was wounded and captured. Kahane, a rabbi, advocated expelling all Arabs from Israel. The party he founded there was banned in Oct. 1988, on the grounds that it was racist and undemocratic. On Dec. 21, 1991, a jury acquitted Nosair of murder but found him guilty of lesser charges.

voice of CBS; *Captain Sir Richard Francis Burton* by Edward Rice, the life of the man most remembered for translating the *Arabian Nights* but who did much, much more; *Baseball: The People's Game,* being the third volume of Harold Seymour's erudite history of the pastime; *Father, Son & Co.: My Life at IBM and Beyond* by Thomas J. Watson, Jr., indicating it was no easy task to follow in the footsteps of his father, the founder; and *Men at Work* by George F. Will, the conservative political columnist's tribute to the skill of the men on the baseball diamond. Finally, in a class by itself, was *Millie's Book: As Dictated to Barbara Bush,* in which the First Dog told of life in the White House.

Feb. 21 **Grammy Awards** were presented for the following: best album of 1989, *Nick of Time* by Bonnie Raitt, who also won the awards for best female pop and rock vocalist; best song, "Wind Beneath My Wings" by Bette Midler; best male rock vocalist, Don Henley for *The End of Innocence;* best male pop vocalist, Michael Bolton for "How Am I Supposed to Live Without You."

Mar. 18 In a nighttime **art theft** at the Isabella Stewart Gardner Museum in Boston, thieves made off with 12 works of art, including paintings by Degas, Rembrandt, Renoir, and Vermeer, valued at about $100,000,000.

Mar. 26 **Academy Awards** were presented to *Driving Miss Daisy* as outstanding motion picture of 1989; Daniel Day-Lewis as best actor for *My Left Foot;* Jessica Tandy as best actress for *Driving Miss Daisy;* Denzel Washington as best supporting actor for *Glory;* and Brenda Fricker as best supporting actress for *My Left Foot.*

Mar. 29 The major producing companies agreed to put a **warning label on recordings** that contain lyrics which might offend some people. The stickers were to have uniform wording and design. Some companies had already been attaching warnings about lyrics that were explicit about violence and sex.

Apr. 7 Indictments for **obscenity** were lodged against the Contemporary Art Center, Cincinnati, Ohio, and its director in connection with an exhibit of photographs by the late Robert M. Mapplethorpe, known for his homoerotic themes. Officials seized 175 of the pictures on exhibit. On Oct. 5 a jury acquitted the museum and the director. It was believed to be the first time obscenity charges had been brought against a museum.

Apr. 12 **Pulitzer prizes** were awarded for the following: fiction, *The Mambo Kings Play Song of Love* by Oscar Hijuelos; biography, *Machiavelli in Hell* by Sebastian de Grazia; history, *In Our Image: America's Empire in the Philippines* by Stanley Karnow;

Business and Industry; Science;
Education; Philosophy and Religion III

Sports; Social Issues and Crime;
Folkways; Fashion; Holidays IV

June 5 The Presbyterian Church (U.S.A.) adopted a **new statement of faith.** While reaffirming the basic Christian beliefs of the denomination, the statement declared that everyone was equal "in God's image, male and female, of every race and people, to live as one community."

June 12 **Conservatives retained control of the Southern Baptist Convention** for the 12th year in succession, electing a fundamentalist, Morris Chapman, a clergyman of Wichita Falls, Tex., as president with 58% of the votes of the delegates.

June 25 The Central Conference of American Rabbis voted to **admit active homosexuals to the rabbinate.** The conference represented Reform Judaism, and with 1,500,000 members was the largest branch of American Judaism. The issue had been before reform rabbis for 15 years.

June 30 The **AIDS epidemic** was not leveling off but was spreading to new groups in society, including black and Hispanic women, the National Academy of Science said. Men and women enlisting in the military were equally infected. By now 16,000 persons had died of AIDS in New York City.

July 18 In a controversy over **homosexuals in the clergy,** the Evangelical Lutheran Church in America suspended two congregations for having ordained an openly gay man and two lesbian women. The church had previously accepted the ordination of gay clergy who were silent about their sexual orientation.

July 31 Experiments in **gene therapy** by the insertion of new genes into body cells were approved for the first time by an advisory committee of the National Institutes of Health. One gene therapy procedure would treat children with adenosine deaminase (ADA), an immune disorder in which there is a lack of an enzyme necessary to break down certain dangerous byproducts that can destroy immune cells.

Sept. 30 The **New Revised Standard Version of the Bible,** successor to the Revised Standard Version of 1952, the Bible used officially by the major Protestant denominations, was published. The new edition made several notable changes: although God is still "our Father," elsewhere masculine terms were changed, as "man" to "one"; "dark, but comely" became "black and beautiful"; and archaic "thees" were modernized.

Oct. 6 The unmanned spacecraft **Ulysses** was put into orbit from the space shuttle *Discovery.* It was intended to survey the southern hemisphere of the Sun from May to September, 1994. Its course was to take it 500,000,000 miles to Jupiter before it used that planet's gravity to head toward the solar orbit.

May 24 The **NHL Stanley Cup** was won by the Edmonton Oilers for the fifth time in seven years when they defeated the Boston Bruins four games to one.

May 27 The 74th **Indianapolis 500** auto race was won by Arie Luyendyk of the Netherlands with an average speed of 185.984 mph, a new record.

June 9 The 122nd **Belmont Stakes** was won by Go and Go, an Irish colt, with a time of 2:27²/₅. The jockey was Michael Kinane.

June 14 The **NBA basketball championship** was won for the second consecutive year by the Detroit Pistons who defeated the Portland Trail Blazers four games to one.

June 18 The **U.S. Open golf tournament** was won by Hale Irwin in a 19-hole playoff. It was the third time he had won this event and he was the oldest player ever to do so.

June 27 Becoming the **highest paid player in professional baseball,** José Canseco of the Oakland Athletics signed a contract that would earn him $23,500,000 over a five-year period. By the end of 1990 23 players had signed contracts giving them more than $3,000,000 a year.

July 2 **Imelda Marcos** was acquitted of four charges of racketeering and fraud in a federal court in New York City. The widow of the former president of the Philippines, she had been accused with her husband Ferdinand of stealing more than $200,000,000 from the government they once headed and using it to buy art, jewelry, and real estate in the U.S. Ferdinand Marcos had also been indicted on Apr. 6, 1989, but had been declared too ill to stand trial. He died on Sept. 28, 1989.

July 7 At the **Wimbledon** tennis championships in England, the women's singles tennis title was won by Martina Navratilova for a record ninth time. She won her other eight titles in 1978–1979 and 1982–1987. Navratilova had been tied with Helen Wills Moody who won the last of her eight championships in 1938.

July 10 The **baseball All-Star Game** was won for the third straight year by the American League, which defeated the National League 2–0.

July 15 The **U.S. Women's Open golf tournament** was won by Betsy King for the second consecutive year, by one stroke.

July 30 **George Steinbrenner,** the general partner of the New York Yankees (AL), was banned by Commissioner of Major League Baseball Fay Vincent from any further involvement in the management of the team. Vincent found that Steinbrenner had violated a major league rule by becoming involved with a known gambler for the past three years. He was

Nov. 6 In **congressional elections** the Democrats gained one seat in the Senate to give them a 56–44 majority, and eight seats in the House for a 267–167 majority, with one place going to an independent.

Nov. 15 The **Clean Air Act of 1990,** which updated and tightened air pollution standards for the first time since 1977, was signed into law by Pres. Bush. The aim of the law was to cut acid rain pollutants by half, reduce urban smog, and eliminate industrial emissions of toxic chemicals by the end of the century. The cost was expected to be $25,000,000,000 a year.

Nov. 19 The most extensive **arms control treaty** in history was signed in Paris by 20 European nations, the U.S., and Canada. NATO and the Warsaw Pact would each be limited to 20,000 tanks, 20,000 artillery pieces, 30,000 armored vehicles, 6800 airplanes, and 2000 helicopters. Current levels of these items ranged from about 10% higher to more than double. In addition the U.S. and now-unified Germany agreed to a level of no more than 195,000 American troops in Central Europe and no more than 370,000 personnel in the German armed forces.

Nov. 21 The **Charter of Paris,** a general peace treaty, was signed in Paris by the U.S. along with 32 European nations and Canada. It was intended to mark the end of the Cold War and called for a "steadfast commitment to democracy based on human rights and fundamental freedoms."

Nov. 29 The **Immigration Act of 1990,** the most far-ranging revision in 66 years, was signed into law by Pres. Bush. It set a total of 700,000 persons to be admitted per year. Of these, 465,000 were to be relatives of American citizens or permanently residing aliens. Another 140,000 places were reserved for skilled workers.

Dec. 3 Rules concerning **police interrogation of suspects** were tightened by the Supreme Court, ruling 6–2 that once such a person has requested a lawyer, no questioning could take place until the lawyer was present.

Dec. 7 Negotiations concerning the **General Agreement on Tariffs and Trade** (GATT) broke down after four years of discussion among 107 nations. Failure came to the Brussels, Belgium, session when the European Community refused to cut its farm subsidies as much as the U.S. demanded. The negotiators also failed to reach agreements to protect drug and software companies whose patents were not recognized in the developing world, and American music and movie companies from copyright pirates.

Dec. 11 **Two chain reaction collisions** of a total of 75 vehicles in southeastern Tennessee on Interstate Highway 75 killed 15 people and injured more than 50. Heavy fog was blamed for the disaster which

general nonfiction, *And Their Children After Them* by Dale Maharidge and Michael Williamson; poetry, *The World Doesn't End* by Charles Simic; drama, *The Piano Lesson* by August Wilson.

Apr. 22 **Shakespeare wrote Shakespeare,** two professors at Claremont McKennan College in California announced, after they had used a computer to check such things as word frequency against the writing of other 16th-century authors, including Francis Bacon, Christopher Marlowe, Sir Walter Raleigh, and the Duke of Oxford.

Apr. 28 The **longest running show on Broadway,** A **Chorus Line,** closed after 6237 performances. It opened July 25, 1975, and on Sept. 29, 1983, became the longest-running production when it surpassed *Grease* with its 3389th performance. In the course of its run *A Chorus Line* was seen by about 6,543,000 people and had 510 different members of the cast.

May 15 In New York the **highest art auction price** ever paid, $82,500,000, was brought by Vincent Van Gogh's painting *Portrait of Dr. Gachet.* On May 17 the second highest price ever paid for a painting was registered when *At the Moulin de la Galette* by Pierre Auguste Renoir went for $78,100,000. The purchaser of both paintings was Ryoei Saito, a Japanese industrialist, who had been an art collector for 40 years.

May 25 Mark Strand was named the fourth **poet laureate** of the U.S. Strand was born in Canada.

June 3 **Tony awards** for the 1989–1990 season were presented for the following: best play, *The Grapes of Wrath* adapted by James Galati; best musical, *City of Angels* by Larry Gelbart, Cy Coleman, and David Zippel; best actor in a play, Robert Morse for *Tru;* best actress in a play, Maggie Smith for *Lettice and Lovage;* best actor in a musical, James Naughton for *City of Angels;* best actress in a musical, Tyne Daly for *Gypsy.*

Sept. 16 **Emmy Awards** were presented for the following: best drama series, *L.A. Law;* best comedy series, *Murphy Brown;* best actor in a drama series, Peter Falk for *Columbo;* best actress in a drama series, Patricia Wettig for *Thirtysomething;* best actor in a comedy series, Ted Danson for *Cheers;* best actress in a comedy series, Candice Bergen for *Murphy Brown.*

Sept. 26 The **movie rating system** was revised by the Motion Picture Association of America, replacing its "X" rating with "NC-17," meaning that no person under 17 years of age should be admitted. Film makers had protested that the "X" rating had been used by pornographers and that on the other hand it had been unfairly applied to serious films. It was also announced that the "R" (Restricted) rating would be

Business and Industry; Science; Education; Philosophy and Religion **III**		Sports; Social Issues and Crime; Folkways; Fashion; Holidays

Oct. 8 The **Nobel Prize for Medicine or Physiology** was awarded jointly to Joseph E. Murray of the Brigham and Women's Hospital in Boston, Mass., and to E. Donnall Thomas of the Fred Hutchinson Cancer Center in Seattle, Wash. In the early 1950s they performed, respectively, the first kidney and the first bone-marrow transplants.

Oct. 12 The **largest award in a patent infringement case** resulted from an order in a federal court that the Eastman Kodak Company pay the Polaroid Corporation $909,400,000. Kodak had been found guilty in 1985 of infringing seven of Polaroid's instant photography patents. On Jan. 11, 1991, a judge reduced the award by $36,000,000.

Oct. 16 The **Nobel Prize in Physics** was awarded to Jerome I. Friedman and Henry W. Kendall, both of the Massachusetts Institute of Technology, and to Richard E. Taylor, a Canadian at Stanford University. All three were honored for their research that confirmed the existence of quarks.

Oct. 16 The **Nobel Prize in Chemistry** was awarded to Elias James Corey of Harvard University who developed methods for synthesizing complex substances.

Oct. 16 The **Nobel Prize in Economics** was awarded to Harry M. Markowitz of the City University of New York for his portfolio investment theories; to Merton H. Miller of the University of Chicago for his work on the best ways to evaluate a corporation's value; and to William F. Sharpe of William F. Sharpe Associates for his explanation of how stock markets move in relation to investors' decisions.

Oct. 25 A historic **transplant operation** was performed at the Stanford University Medical School when part of a mother's lung was transferred into that of her 12-year-old daughter who was dying as a result of severe scarring of the lungs. Hitherto such operations had been performed using organs from persons who had recently died.

Nov. 11 The first recipient of a **heart and liver transplant** in the same operation died. Stormie Jones was not quite seven years old when the operation was performed on her in a Pittsburgh hospital Feb. 14, 1984.

Nov. 16 The world's **first superconducting transistors** able to operate at relatively high temperatures have been built at the Sandia National Laboratories in Albuquerque, New Mexico, it was announced. The new devices were said to be useful mostly in assisting further research in the field.

Nov. 21 The creator of the "junk bond," **Michael R. Milken,** was sentenced to ten years in prison for violating federal securities laws and for other crimes. He had pleaded guilty on Apr. 24, 1990, to six criminal

allowed to retain his partial ownership of the club. On Aug. 15 Robert E. Nederlander, of a theatrical management family, was named to run the Yankees.

July 31 **Nolan Ryan** of the Texas Rangers (AL) became the 10th major league pitcher to win 300 games in his career when he pitched his team to an 11–3 victory over the Milwaukee Brewers.

Aug. 6 The **Baseball Hall of Fame** inducted Joe Morgan, a second baseman who had played for five teams, and Jim Palmer, star pitcher of the Baltimore Orioles. Both had been elected in their first year of eligibility.

Aug. 11 The **PGA golf tournament** was won by Wayne Grady of Australia by three strokes.

Sept. 2 A **major league pitching record** of nine no-hit games in a season was set when Dave Stieb of the Toronto Blue Jays (AL) pitched such a game against the Cleveland Indians. Seven of the no-hitters were pitched in the American League and set a record there.

Sept. 8 **Ellis Island,** in New York Harbor, through which 12,000,000 immigrants entered the U.S. between 1892 and 1924, its busiest years, reopened as a museum of immigration. Passage through the island's facilities ended in 1954 and the ten buildings, badly deteriorated, had now been restored at a cost of $156,000,000 through private contributions. The chief feature of the restoration was the 160-foot long, two-story high Registry Room where began the processing that determined whether a would-be immigrant was allowed to enter the U.S.

Sept. 8 The **Miss America** title was won by Marjorie Judith Vincent, 25, a law student from Oak Park, Ill., and the fourth black to win, at the annual pageant in Atlantic City, N.J.

Sept. 8–9 The **U.S. Open tennis singles championships** were won by Gabriela Sabatini in the women's division and by Pete Sampras, only 19 years old, in the men's division.

Oct. 16–20 The **World Series** was won by the Cincinnati Reds (NL) over the Oakland Athletics (AL), four games to none, in an upset. On Oct. 12 the Reds had won the National League Pennant by defeating the Pittsburgh Pirates four games to two, and on Oct. 10 the Athletics had won the American League title over the Boston Red Sox in four straight games.

Dec. 13 **Serial murderer** Arthur J. Shawcross was convicted of killing ten women in the Rochester, N.Y., area between 1988 and 1990. Shawcross was on parole for having strangled two children in 1972. On Feb. 1, 1991, he was sentenced to a minimum of 250 years in prison, the total being accounted for by sentences of 25 years to life for each of ten counts of second degree murder.

1990 – 1991   *PRES.* GEORGE BUSH

832

Exploration and Settlement; Wars;
Government; Civil Rights; Statistics   I

II   Publishing; Arts and Music; Popular
Entertainment; Architecture; Theater

involved cars and trucks on both sides of the highway.

Dec. 12 A federal loan guarantee for **food purchases by the Soviet Union** was announced by Pres. Bush.

Dec. 27 San Francisco became the first city to regulate the use of **video display terminals** in the workplace. The law set standards for equipment and facilities and required that workers be given 15 minutes of alternate work for every two hours at a terminal if there were no regularly scheduled breaks.

clarified and explained on the basis of themes such as sex and violence.

Nov. 27 **National Book Awards** were presented for the following: fiction, *The Middle Passage* by Charles Johnson; nonfiction, *The House of Morgan: An American Banking Dynasty and the Rise of Modern Finance* by Ron Chernow.

1991

The nation began the year with apprehension over imminent war in the Persian Gulf, became euphoric when victory was quickly achieved, but relapsed into apprehension again when an economic recession hung on and seemed to get worse. Demographically, the year saw a continued shift of population to the South and the West with a considerable part of the movement accounted for by blacks leaving the northern cities. The number of persons identifying themselves as American Indians had tripled to 1,800,000 since 1960; the number of Asian Americans had increased by 107.8% and Hispanics by 53.0% since 1980. Other data this year revealed that about 5,500,000 children under 12 were going hungry; that nearly one out of four babies is born out of wedlock; that in the 1980s more than 900 male farmers in the upper Middle West committed suicide, nearly double the average for white men; that while black-white marriages had more than tripled since 1970, such couples still faced considerable social ostracism; and that women held only 31.3% of high-level state and local government positions, while occupying 43.5% of lower-level jobs. Notable persons who died included Virginia Mae Brown, first woman to be chairman of the Interstate Commerce Commission, Feb. 24, at 67; John Sherman Cooper, liberal Republican senator for more than 20 years, Feb. 21, at 89; Hamilton Fish, an isolationist and bitter enemy of Pres. Franklin D. Roosevelt who served in Congress for 24 years, Jan. 18, at 102; Lloyd K. Garrison, a lawyer who championed liberal social causes, Oct. 2, at 93; James Roosevelt, eldest son of Pres. Roosevelt, a combat Marine and congressman, Aug. 13, at 83; John G. Tower, Republican senator from Texas for 24 years, Apr. 5, at 65; and Robert F. Wagner, Mayor of New York City from 1954 to 1965, Feb. 12, at 80.

Jan. 7 Cancellation of the **largest weapons program ever terminated** was announced by the Defense Dept. Involved was the A-12 Avenger, a navy plane of the radar-evading stealth type. The planes were to have cost $57,000,000,000 but the program was already 16

In tune with the general recession, the Broadway theater did not prosper during the 1990–1991 season. There were 28 productions, a decline of two; attendance was 7,360,000, down from 8,030,000; and ticket sales totalled $267,000,000, down from $283,000,000. The most talked about show of the season was the musical *Miss Saigon*, first because of a controversy as to whether or not its stars from the London production would be allowed to take the stage in New York, and then for establishing a new high for a seat at $100. Other hits included *Lost in Yonkers* by Neil Simon, and *The Will Rogers Follies*. The movie industry did not enjoy a good year either. In particular it suffered a summer of letdowns with admissions the lowest in nearly 20 years, dropping from 390,000,000 in 1990 to 329,000,000 this year. High-tech violence did all right in the case of *Terminator 2: Judgment Day*, which at $85,000,000 was the most expensive film ever made. *Hudson Hawk*, even though it starred Bruce Willis, was a flop. On the other hand, *Hook*, somewhat of a sequel to *Peter Pan*, did well, as did the animated version of *Beauty and the Beast*. The field of dance marked the year with both new and old events and attractions: the Guangdong Modern Dance Company of China made its American debut, and a new staging of *The Sleeping Beauty* at a cost of $2,800,000 was deemed worth the price. Television had its high and low spots. Most impressive, and perhaps most mind numbing, was the PBS six-and-a-half-hour production of the Sanskrit epic, *The Mahabharata*. More down to earth was *Sarah, Plain and Tall*, in which Glenn Close portrayed a determined pioneer in the Midwest. The usual number of new comedy series began and quickly ended. An exception was *Brooklyn Bridge*, about family life in the 1950s. Most spectacular on the home screen, though, were real life events, in particular the Persian Gulf War and the Clarence Thomas–Anita Hill controversy in the Senate concerning the former's nomination to the Supreme Court. The recession hit museums, forcing them to close galleries and shorten visiting hours. Among those affected were

charges and agreed to pay $600,000,000 in fines and other penalties.

Dec. 10 The first essentially new contraceptive device in 25 years was approved by the Food and Drug Administration. It is a set of small soft tubes that are implanted under a woman's skin and which then release progestin, a hormone that can prevent conception for five years.

Dec. 31 The **Dow Jones industrial stock average** closed the year at 2633.66, down 4.3%.

Dec. 21 In the case of **collusion against free agents,** major league baseball club owners agreed to pay certain players $280,000,000 to compensate them for what they presumably lost between 1986 and 1990 when the owners in collusion dealt with free agent players in such a way as to reduce their salaries. As part of the agreement, 15 players became "new-look" free agents, and were allowed to negotiate with any club.

1991

Early in the year the recession that began in May, 1990, seemed to be easing, but as the year went on the economy worsened. By the end of the year unemployment was up to 7.1%, a 5.5 year high; industrial production dropped 1.9%; sales of new homes were down 5.6%, the third straight year of declines; auto sales fared even worse, being down 11.2%, the worst year since 1983; orders for durable goods followed suit, being off 4.6%, the worst since 1982; the total of installment credit fell 1.0%, the first time it had shrunk since 1958; employers' health costs rose 12.1%; and ten large industries announced in the course of the second half of the year that they would lay off 161,000 workers, with General Motors accounting for 70,000 and International Business Machines 20,000. The economic news was not all bad: the consumer price index was up only 3.1%, a five-year low; the international trade deficit of $8,620,000,000 was the lowest for a decade; and nonfarm productivity showed a gain of 0.3%, the first in three years. Even the troubled savings and loan institutions did better, the 2096 that had not needed government help showing an overall profit of almost $2,000,000,000, although by now 700 other institutions had been seized by the government. Not everyone was faring badly: the Census Bureau reported that the income of the top 20% of households rose by 14% from 1984 to 1988, but the median for all households in that period dropped from $37,012 to $35,752 per year. Among the affluent, according to *Forbes* magazine were 71 billionaires, an increase of 5 for the year. The number of owners of farm land, 2,950,000 people, was the smallest this century, and 47% of such land was held by only 124,000 owners. In March the 5,000,000th patent was issued, for an up-to-the-minute product, a genetically engineered microbe. A poll showed that 61% of women had met with some form of sexual harassment at work, but only 4.0% reported such incidents. More than 400,000 Americans were dying each year from smoking, according to the Federal Centers for Disease Controls. Late in the year there was a decrease in the number of

Thanks to Title IX of the Educational Amendments Act of 1972, many more young women were participating in sports at all levels. This law prohibited sexual discrimination in programs in schools receiving federal financing. As a result, high schools now reported an increase of participation from 7% to 36%, while in colleges where previously all NCAA activities were male, women now accounted for 33% of participants. In spite of the recession the National Football League recorded its third consecutive year of gains in attendance, to 17,752,139, up about 100,000. Thoroughbred horse racing, however, began the year with decreases in both attendance and betting, attributed to the recession and the Persian Gulf War. Hard times also hit Las Vegas, Nev., heart of the gambling industry, where some of the games were down as much as a third in Oct., the busiest month, and two casinos went bankrupt. Rodeo, on the other hand, was prospering. In four years the number of rodeos increased by 25% to 800, while prize money now totalled $2,600,000 at the National Rodeo Finals, compared with about $150,000 in 1970. In professional golf Corey Pavin was the leading money winner at $979,430. At the beginning of the year there were 695,000 inmates in state prisons and 60,000 in federal penitentiaries, an increase in one year of 80,000, the most ever. After five years of mostly miniskirts, the fashion world began to offer some longer hemlines, to the calf or beyond. Of course many women had ignored fashion's decrees and wore whatever length skirt they thought suited them. Among people of note who died were Luke Appling, Hall of Famer, shortstop for 20 years, Jan. 3, at 83; Laz Berrera, trainer of the Triple Crown winner Affirmed, Apr. 25, at 66; James "Cool Papa" Bell, legendary figure of the Negro Baseball League, Mar. 7, at 87; Paul Brown, innovative pro football coach, Aug. 5, at 82; A. B. "Happy" Chandler, commissioner of baseball from 1945 to 1951, June 15, at 92; Leo Durocher, fiery baseball manager known as "Leo the Lip," Oct. 7, at 86; Charles H. Goren, deviser of the most popular contract bridge bidding system, Apr. 3, at

months behind schedule and more than $2,700,000,000 over budget.

Jan. 15 In a **school desegregation case,** the Supreme Court, 5–2, ruled that districts may be released from court-ordered busing when they have taken all "practicable" steps to eliminate segregation. The case concerned the Oklahoma City, Okla., schools.

Jan. 15 The **first elected Navajo tribal president** was inaugurated at Window Rock, Ariz. He was Peter Zah, a former chairman of the Navajo Nation, which has 219,000 members. The ceremony ended two years of disputes and upheavals among officials of the Navajos.

Jan. 15–Feb. 27 The **Persian Gulf War,** codenamed Operation Desert Storm, authorized by the U.N. and led by the U.S., began with an all-out air war against Iraq. Its objective was to drive Iraqi forces out of Kuwait, which Iraq had occupied since Aug. 2, 1990. Ground action began Feb. 24 and three days later Pres. George Bush halted the fighting with Iraqi forces routed. Iraq agreed to destroy its facilities for making chemical, nuclear, and biological weapons, but stalled the actual carrying out of the relevant UN resolutions. American casualties were 146 dead and 467 wounded.

Jan. 27 The **first female ACLU president** in its 71-year history was elected by the American Civil Liberties Union. She was Nadine Strossen, a professor of constitutional law at the New York Law School.

Feb. 1 The State Department's annual report on **human rights** around the world said Iraq had an "abysmal record" of torture and summary executions, but it also criticized Kuwait, Saudi Arabia, Syria, and Turkey, all U.S. allies in the Persian Gulf War.

Feb. 1 A head-on **airplane crash** at the Los Angeles airport, involving a USAir Boeing 737 about to land and a SkyWest commuter craft about to take off from the same runway, killed 22 of 69 persons aboard the former and all 12 on the latter. The planes were mistakenly cleared to use the same runway.

Feb. 3 A **postal rate increase** for first class postage, from 25 to 29 cents for the first ounce, was announced by the U.S. Postal Service. Other rates were to go up in proportion.

Feb. 6 An **act to benefit Vietnam War veterans** who were exposed to the herbicide Agent Orange, which was used to defoliate jungle cover, was signed by Pres. Bush. The law extended disability benefits to those suffering from two kinds of cancer, Non-Hodgkin's lymphoma and soft-tissue sarcoma.

Mar. 4 The Supreme Court ruled, 7–1, that **juries have broad discretion on damage awards,** including

the Brooklyn Museum and the Detroit Institute of Arts. Two noted artists had retrospective shows: Stuart Davis at the Metropolitan Museum in New York, and Robert Rauschenberg at both the Whitney Museum in New York and the Corcoran Gallery of Art in Washington.

Notable persons who died included Berenice Abbott, a pioneer of modern photography, Dec. 10, at 93; Jean Arthur, a most charming actress in comedy dramas, June 19, at 90; Charlie Barnet, jazz saxophonist of the swing era, Sept. 4, at 77; Ralph Bellamy, a character actor who appeared in more than 100 movies, Nov. 29, at 87; Homer Bigart, war correspondent who won two Pulitzer prizes, Apr. 16, at 83; Niven Busch, novelist and screen writer, best known for *Duel in the Sun,* Aug. 25, at 88; Frank Capra, Academy Award–winning movie director, noted for his films in praise of the common man, Sept. 3, at 94; Oona O'Neill Chaplin, daughter of playwright Eugene O'Neill and wife of the movie actor Charlie Chaplin, Sept. 27, at 66; John Charles Daly, Jr., popular host of the television quiz show *What's My Line,* Feb. 25, at 77; Miles Davis, jazz trumpeter and protagonist of cool jazz, Sept. 28, at 65; George T. Delacorte, publisher and philanthropist who was especially fond of donating fountains, May 4, at 97; Colleen Dewhurst, a foremost star of the American theater, closely identified with the plays of Eugene O'Neill, Aug. 22, at 67; Mildred Dunnock, stage and movie actress, remembered particularly for her role in *Death of a Salesman,* July 5, at 90; Sumner Locke Elliott, novelist and playwright who came to the U.S. from Australia, June 24, at 73; Paul Engle, poet, editor, and teacher, Mar. 22, at 82; Tennessee Ernie Ford, whose homespun manner made him popular as a host and as a country and Western singer, Oct. 17, at 72; Redd Foxx, black comedian whose humor was bawdy and who was at his best in the television series *Sanford and Son,* Oct. 11 at 68; Stan Getz, who had great influence on jazz with his tenor saxophone, June 6 at 64; Martha Graham, one of the greatest dancers and choreographers the world has known, Apr. 1, at 96; A. B. Guthrie, Jr., a leading novelist of the American West, Apr. 26, at 90; Eva Le Gallienne, innovative actress, producer, and director, June 3, at 92; Fred MacMurray, a pleasant and popular movie and television star, Nov. 5, at 83; Jimmy McPartland, cornetist and exponent of Chicago-style jazz, Mar. 13, at 83; Robert Motherwell, a giant of the abstract-expressionist school, July 16, at 76; Howard Nemerov, poet laureate of the U.S. and Pulitzer Prize winner, July 5, at 71; Joseph Papp, one of the most influential theatrical producers of his time, Oct. 31, at 70; Lee Remick, attractive and versatile actress, able to portray an assortment of characters, July 2, at 55; Gene Roddenberry, creator of *Star Trek,* the television and movie success that developed a cult following, Oct. 24, at 70; Rudolph Serkin,

births for the first time in five years and it was blamed on the recession. Another government report said life expectancy for blacks was improving, but that they still died about six years younger than whites. Hispanic Americans suffer more than others from diabetes, high blood pressure, kidney disease, and some cancers. The infant mortality rate dropped in 1990 by the largest amount in nearly ten years, from 9.7 deaths per 1000 live births to 9.1. Liberal Protestant denominations lost membership while the Roman Catholic Church and some conservative Protestant denominations gained. The 32 denominations belonging to the National Council of Churches saw membership drop 100,000 to 41,800,000; Catholic membership grew by 2,000,000 to 57,000,000; and the Southern Baptist Convention gained 100,000 to 14,900,000. Overall, reported a 1990 survey, Protestants made up 60.2% of the American population, Catholics 26.2%; non-Christian faiths 3.7%; and those professing no religion 7.5%. Following a series of scandals, the leading television evangelists lost large numbers of followers. Jimmy Swaggart, for example, now had only 20% of his one-time 2,200,000 viewers. General economic conditions were troubling all churches because, while giving rose, expenses, especially for medical and other insurance, and for work for the poor and the homeless, outstripped contributions. In general, education did not do well this year either. Verbal scores on the Scholastic Aptitude Test fell to an all-time low, while math scores fell for the first time since 1980. The proportion of whites taking the test had declined from 87% to 72% since 1972 while the non-white proportion rose from 13% to 28%. College enrollment was up in spite of the recession, but more students were selecting colleges on the basis of cost as tuition fees continued to rise. The report card for elementary and secondary schools was not encouraging. The percentage of pupils earning high school diplomas was no higher than 15 years earlier.

Notable persons who died in 1991 included Carl D. Anderson, Nobel Prize winner in physics for his discovery of the positron, Jan. 11, at 85; John Bardeen, co-inventor of the transistor, for which he received the Nobel Prize in physics, Jan. 30, at 82; John Sloan Dickey, president of Dartmouth College, 1945 to 1970, Feb. 9, at 83; John K. Fairbank, most influential scholar of his time in China studies, Sept. 14, at 84; Louis Finkelstein, the dominant figure of the 20th century in Conservative Judaism, Nov. 21, at 96; James L. Knight, a builder of the Knight-Ridder newspaper chain, Feb. 5, at 81; Edwin H. Land, inventor of instant photography, Mar. 1, at 81; Salvador E. Luria, Nobel Prize winner in medicine and physiology for his work in genetics, Feb. 6, at 78; William A. Lewis, winner of the Nobel Prize in economics, June 15, at 76; Thomas D. Nicholson, director of the American Museum of Natural History from 1969 to

90; Harold "Red" Grange, star college and pro football running back of the 1920s, Jan. 28, at 87; and Arthur Murray, the best-known teacher of ballroom dancing, Mar. 3, at 95.

Jan. 1 In **college football bowl games** the results were Miami 46, Texas 3 in the Cotton Bowl; Colorado 10, Notre Dame 9 in the Orange Bowl; Washington 46, Iowa 34 in the Rose Bowl; and Tennessee 23, Virginia 22 in the Sugar Bowl. The AP picked Colorado as the 1990 national champion, but the UPI selected Georgia Tech, which defeated Nebraska, 45–21, in the Citrus Bowl.

Jan. 5 A new **basketball record** for individual scoring in a game was set by Kevin Bradshaw of United States International University of San Diego, Calif., when he registered 72 points in an NCAA Division I game. The feat broke a 21-year-old record.

Jan. 8–9 Taking steps to **deemphasize college athletics** the NCAA voted to cut coaching staffs in 33 sports, eliminate athletic dormitories, reduce athletic training tables, reduce scholarships by about 10%, and cut time devoted to practice.

Jan. 21 The **exclusion of women** from Princeton's eating clubs was finally ended when the Supreme Court let stand a rule that the Tiger Inn, the last holdout, must admit women. By Feb. 10, some 27 female students had been taken in. The case began in 1979 when a woman student filed a civil rights complaint.

Jan. 27 **Super Bowl XXV** was won by the New York Giants (NFC) who defeated the Buffalo Bills (AFC) 20–19. On Jan. 20 the Giants had won the NFC championship by defeating the San Francisco 49ers 15–13 and Buffalo won the AFC title by beating the Los Angeles Raiders 51–3.

Feb. 2 The **500th basketball victory** of his career was registered by Lou Carnesecca of St. John's University when his basketball team defeated Seton Hall 81–65. St. John's coach for 23 years, Carnesecca became the 30th major college coach to achieve 500 wins.

Feb. 4 The board of directors of the **Baseball Hall of Fame** voted to exclude any player who had been banned from the game. The move was triggered by the 1989 banning for life of Pete Rose, star player and manager of the Cincinnati Reds, for having bet on games.

Feb. 14 A law allowing the **registration of "domestic partnerships"** by homosexual and unmarried heterosexual couples went into effect in San Francisco. Although the law granted no legal rights, about 200 couples registered the first day.

punitive awards, although it was suggested there should be "reasonable constraints." The decision arose out of an Alabama insurance fraud case.

Mar. 20 In a unanimous decision affecting **women in the workplace,** the Supreme Court ruled that employers may not exclude women from jobs that might expose a fetus to toxic substances. The court said such action would be a violation of the federal Civil Rights Act of 1964 which prohibits sex discrimination in employment. The ruling was hailed by labor unions and women's rights groups.

Mar. 26 In a 5–4 decision on **criminal confessions,** the Supreme Court ruled that a coerced confession does not automatically invalidate a conviction. The use of such a confession in a criminal trial, the court said, can be excused if other evidence is adequate to sustain a guilty verdict. This ruling overturned one of 1967 that held such confessions could never be used.

Apr. 1 The use of **racial criteria in jury selection** is unconstitutional, regardless of the race of the defendant or the jurors excluded, the Supreme Court ruled, 7–2. The decision broadened the right of defendants to object to the use of race by prosecutors in jury selection.

Apr. 16 More than 79 **tornadoes** struck seven states in the Midwest and Southwest, killing 23 people, 14 of them in Andover, Kans., where 290 trailer homes and 110 houses were demolished.

June 3 In another ruling on **racial criteria in jury selection,** the Supreme Court voted, 6–3, that jurors may not be excluded from civil lawsuits because of race. The decision extended a 1986 decision that barred prosecutors in criminal cases from excluding jurors on the basis of race.

June 27 **Thurgood Marshall resigned** as a justice of the Supreme Court. A hero of the civil rights movement and the most liberal voice on the court, he had served since 1967, and was the first black to be a justice.

July 1 A 1990 federal law providing expanded **employment rights for the mentally disabled** went into effect. Employers cannot ask applicants whether they have a history of mental illness, and once hired employees are entitled to special support so long as they can perform the requirements of the job.

July 10 Most **economic sanctions against South Africa** were lifted by order of Pres. Bush. He said the movement to end apartheid was now "irreversible." The sanctions had been imposed by a law passed in 1986.

July 30 The **closing of 44 military installations** received final approval from Congress. Reductions

one of the most admired pianists of the century, May 8, at 88; Theodor Seuss Geisel, who as Dr. Seuss delighted children with his fantastic stories, Sept. 24, at 87; Elie Siegmeister, composer of the contemporary American symphonic school, Mar. 10, at 82; Isaac Bashevis Singer, master of portraying the life of his native Poland, July 24, at 87; Danny Thomas, comedian and philanthropist, best remembered for his television show *Make Room for Daddy,* Feb. 6, at 79; and Frank Yerby, historical novelist whose 32 books sold millions of copies, Nov. 29, at 76.

In spite of the recession, dollar sales of **books published** this year (not including mass market paperbacks) were up by 9.1%. Aiding this increase was *Scarlett* by Alexandra Ripley, a deliberately planned sequel to Margaret Mitchell's eternally-popular *Gone With the Wind.* It became a number-one best seller and occupied the same position on the critics' thumbs-down list. Other works of fiction included Norman Mailer's 1328-page novel *Harlot's Ghost,* about the CIA; *How to Make an American Quilt* by Whitney Otto, a novel concerning a women's quilting circle in California; and *The Kitchen God's Wife* by Amy Tan, in which a Chinese matriarch in San Francisco tells the story of her hard life. Nonfiction titles included *The Journals of John Cheever,* the rather sad account of life and its problems the writer noted down over 35 years; and *Final Exit* by Derek Humphry, a how-to book for would-be suicides. In an unusual situation, Simon & Schuster cancelled publication of *American Psycho* by Bret Easton Ellis, considering the fictional tale of a ruthless, amoral psychopath unfit for its list. Vintage took it over, but the book was damned in print even before publication. Writers of spy novels also had their troubles with the fall of the Soviet Union denying them the usual villains of the KGB. New ones were found in drug dealers, terrorists, and even people who committed crimes via computer. More black authors were being published, especially writers of fiction. In addition two volumes of the writings of Richard Wright, who died in 1960, were issued, including a revised version of *Native Son,* which originally had been heavily censored. The largest prize ever given for a single novel, the Turner Tomorrow Award, presented by Ted Turner, a communications magnate, went to Daniel Quinn for *Ishmael,* consisting of philosophical conversations between a man and an ape. Also in the big money was Gen. H. Norman Schwarzkopf, Jr., the victorious commander in the Persian Gulf War, who accepted $5,000,000 for the rights to his memoirs.

Jan. 9 The **Lincoln Center** for the Performing Arts, in New York City, announced that a jazz department will be added to its eight other constituencies. The department will produce concerts and sponsor other events on a year-round basis.

1989, July 9, at 68; Harold R. Perry, the first black to be consecrated a Roman Catholic Bishop in the 20th century, July 17, at 74; and Sylvia Porter, widely read business and financial news columnist, June 5, at 77.

Jan. 8 **Pan American World Airways,** one of the largest U.S. airlines, filed for bankruptcy but would keep flying pending the sale of its planes and routes to other airlines. On Jan. 18 Eastern Airlines, already in bankruptcy, shut down its operations.

Jan. 14 A warning that **racism is a deepening problem** in the U.S. was issued by the United Church of Christ. The church said racist attitudes "permeate most of our institutions" and underlie the economic and social differences between whites and blacks.

Jan. 25 The **death toll from AIDS** had now reached 100,777 and 161,073 cases had been reported since 1981, federal health officials reported. More than 215,000 persons were expected to die of the disease in the next three years.

Feb. 1 Installed as president of the **Teamsters Union,** long noted for its corruption and mob influence, was Ronald R. Carey, a reformer. The insurgent head of a local in New York City, Carey in a Dec. election received 48.5% of the votes in a contest with two insiders.

Feb. 11 **Carter Hawley Hale Stores, Inc.,** the largest department store chain on the West Coast, filed for bankruptcy. Much of the chain's financial problems stemmed from the $1,600,000,000 debt in junk bonds it issued in 1987 to prevent a hostile takeover by the Limited, Inc., a chain of women's specialty stores.

Feb. 21 A new type of **genetically engineered drug** for fighting infections that often affect cancer patients undergoing chemotherapy was approved by the Food and Drug Administration. It was hoped that the drug, granulocyte colony stimulating factor (G-CSF), would also prove effective as a treatment for other types of infections.

Mar. 13 A new **low-fat hamburger** was announced by McDonald's, the largest fast-food chain. It was to be called the McLean Deluxe and would have half the fat of the regular McDonald's offerings.

Apr. 4 **The ozone layer** over the U.S. is being depleted more than twice as fast as previously thought, the Environmental Protection Agency announced.

Apr. 7 The space shuttle *Atlantis* launched into orbit the **Gamma Ray Observatory,** weighing 17 tons and costing $600,000,000. It was to study gamma ray emissions that result from violent explosions in other space when stars collapse and matter and antimatter collide.

Apr. 26 Discovery of the **first catacombs** known to have been used by American Indians for burial and sacred rites was reported by archaeologists. The catacombs were under a 15-acre settlement in eastern

Feb. 15–17 **U.S. figure skating championships** were won in Minneapolis, Minn., by Tonya Harding, women's singles; Todd Eldredge, for the second consecutive year, men's singles; Natasha Kuchiki and Todd Sand, pairs; Elizabeth Punsalan and Jerod Swallow, dance.

Feb. 20 A half interest in the **New York Giants** football team was bought by Preston Robert Tisch, a billionaire businessman. The purchase was made from a member of the Mara family that had owned all of the team since acquiring the NFL franchise in 1925 for $500. Tisch was reported to have paid more than $60,000,000 for his 50%.

Mar. 16 Three American women set a **figure skating record** when they finished one, two, three in the world championships at Munich, Germany. It was the first time in the 73-year history of the event that skaters from the same country accomplished this. The three, in order, were Kristi Yamaguchi, Tonya Harding, and Nancy Kerrigan.

Mar. 31 The **NCAA women's basketball championship** was won by Tennessee, which defeated Virginia 70–67 in overtime.

Apr. 1 The **NCAA men's basketball championship** was won by Duke, which defeated Kansas 72–65.

Apr. 14 The **Masters golf tournament** was won by Ian Woosnam of Wales by one stroke on the last hole.

Apr. 15 The 95th **Boston Marathon** was won in the men's division by Ibrahim Hussein of Kenya with a time of 2 hrs., 11 min., 6 sec. The winner of the women's division was Wanda Panfil of Poland with a time of 2 hrs., 24 min., 18 sec.

May 4 The 117th **Kentucky Derby** was won by Strike the Gold with a time of 2:03. The jockey was Chris Antley.

May 18 The 116th **Preakness Stakes** was won by Hansel with a time of 1:54. The jockey was Jerry Bailey.

May 25 The **NHL Stanley Cup** was won by the Pittsburgh Penguins who defeated the Minnesota North Stars four games to two. It was the first such victory for the Penguins.

May 26 The **Indianapolis 500** auto race was won by Rick Mears, who became only the third racing driver to win the event four times. His average speed was 176.460 mph, and the time was 2 hrs., 50 min., 0.791 sec.

June 8 The 123rd **Belmont Stakes** was won by Hansel with a time of 2:28. The jockey was Jerry Bailey.

June 9 The first championship of the **World League of American Football** was won by the London

and consolidations were to be made at 48 other sites and in all 80,000 military and 37,000 civilian positions would be eliminated.

July 31 A nuclear arms reduction treaty was signed in Moscow by Pres. Bush and Mikhail S. Gorbachev, president of the U.S.S.R. The treaty called for the Soviet Union to cut its nuclear warheads from 10,841 to 8040 within seven years while the U.S. would reduce its total to 10,395 from 12,081.

Aug. 8–Dec. 4 The last six American hostages in Lebanon, who had been held for varying lengths of time, were released by Islamic terrorists. One, Terry Anderson, had been a prisoner since Mar. 16, 1985.

Aug. 31 A museum honoring Martin Luther King, Jr., the black civil rights leader, was opened in the Lorraine Motel in Memphis, Tenn., where he was assassinated in 1968. The exhibits documented many events of the civil rights movement in the 1950s and 1960s.

Sept. 2 Full diplomatic recognition of the Baltic states, Estonia, Latvia, and Lithuania, was granted by the U.S., signifying their freedom from rule by the U.S.S.R.

Sept. 3 A fire in a chicken processing plant killed 25 people in Hamlet, N.C., and injured 45 others. Exits were either blocked or locked. The fire was believed to have started near large vats filled with grease.

Sept. 13 The supplying of arms to Afghanistan would end by Jan. 1, 1992, the U.S. and the U.S.S.R. agreed. Ever since the Soviets invaded the country in 1979 the U.S. had supplied opposition rebels with weapons.

Sept. 19 A military alliance was signed by the U.S. and Kuwait. It allowed the U.S. to use Kuwaiti ports and other facilities, and to store military equipment over a ten-year period, but there was not to be a permanent American military garrison.

Sept. 27 A large unilateral cut in nuclear weapons was announced by Pres. Bush. All tactical weapons in Europe and Asia and on ships would be eliminated; long range bombers and intercontinental missiles would no longer be on 24-hour alert status. On Oct. 5 Pres. Gorbachev of the U.S.S.R. announced a similar reduction.

Oct. 7 Elliott Abrams pleaded guilty to withholding information from Congress in 1986, while serving as assistant secretary of state, in connection with hearings about secret efforts to aid the Nicaraguan Contras. On Nov. 15 a federal judge sentenced Abrams to two years' probation and 100 hours of community service.

Jan. 21 The John and Mable Ringling Museum of Art reopened in Sarasota, Fla., after a $20,000,000 restoration. Noted for its Italian old masters and for four gigantic tapestry cartoons by Rubens, the museum had become badly run down since the death in 1936 of its founder, John Ringling, the circus impresario.

Jan. 27 Observance of the bicentennial of Wolfgang Amadeus Mozart's death began on the anniversary of his birth in 1756. In the U.S. the occasion was to be marked by the performance at Lincoln Center, New York City, of all 835 of his surviving works.

Feb. 8 "Albert Bierstadt: Art and Enterprise," a retrospective exhibit of the work of the artist noted for his large, flamboyant paintings of his idea of the American West, opened at the Brooklyn Museum, New York City. The more than 70 paintings included one six-by-ten-foot work by the artist.

Feb. 13 The long-lost manuscript of the first half of Mark Twain's *Huckleberry Finn,* which had been discovered some months earlier in an attic in Los Angeles, was authenticated. It had disappeared a century earlier from a library in Buffalo, N.Y. The 665-page manuscript was handwritten by Twain between 1876 and 1883.

Feb. 20 The 33rd Grammy Awards were presented for the following: best album of 1990, *Back on the Block* by Quincy Jones; best record, "Another Day in Paradise" by Phil Collins; best male rock vocalist, Eric Clapton for "Bad Love"; best female rock vocalist, Alannah Myles for "Black Velvet"; best male pop vocalist, Roy Orbison for "Oh Pretty Woman"; best female pop vocalist, Mariah Carey for "Vision of Love."

Mar. 11 One of the largest art donations ever was announced by Walter H. Annenberg, a wealthy publisher and philanthropist, who said he would bequeath his collection, valued at at least $1,000,000,000, to the Metropolitan Museum of Art, New York City. The collection is especially strong in the works of the French impressionists and post-impressionists.

Mar. 17 To celebrate the National Gallery of Art's 50th anniversary, the museum opened an exhibit in Washington, D.C., featuring some of the more than 500 works solicited by it to observe the event. The exhibit included paintings, drawings, sculptures, and photographs, among them works by Titian, Albert Bierstadt, Winslow Homer, and Claes Oldenburg.

| Business and Industry; Science; Education; Philosophy and Religion III | IV Sports; Social Issues and Crime; Folkways; Fashion; Holidays |

Arizona known as Casa Malpais. The natural spaces had been enlarged.

May 6 The question of **who first discovered the AIDS virus** was somewhat cleared up when French and American scientists agreed that laboratory mixups had caused the dispute. The French and U.S. strains were contaminated by a third strain of the genetically variable virus.

May 6 The **NCR Corp.** was acquired by the American Telephone and Telegraph Co. (AT&T) in a deal valued at $7,400,000,000. AT&T hoped the merger would enable it to revive its computer operations by virtue of NCR's position as the fifth largest computer manufacturer in the U.S.

May 25 The **first person to receive a fully portable heart pump**, Larry Heinsohn, died in Houston, Tex. He had received the device May 9. Connected with a battery pack that could be slung over the shoulder, the pump was intended to be used only until a human heart donor was available.

May 29 Two Americans were among 23 **new cardinals** of the Roman Catholic Church appointed by Pope John Paul II. They were Anthony J. Bevilacqua of Philadelphia, Pa., and Roger M. Mahony of Los Angeles, Calif. These appointments brought to ten the number of American cardinals.

May 31 A **new national fee schedule for doctors** was announced by Medicare officials. Family doctors and general practitioners would receive larger fees but payments to surgeons and other specialists would be reduced. However, a lower than expected increase for family doctors caused protests.

June 5 In Washington, D.C., the **ordination of a homosexual woman** living in an openly lesbian relationship caused controversy within the Episcopal Church. The woman, Elizabeth L. Carl, was not the first acknowledged homosexual to be ordained but the candor of church officials as well as the candidate was unusual.

June 6 The **Greek Orthodox Church** suspended its ties with the National Council of Churches, the largest ecumenical organization, saying that it was troubled by the "extreme liberalism" shown by the council in the positions it had taken regarding abortion and homosexuality.

June 11 A policy on **sexual misconduct** was adopted by the Presbyterian Church (U.S.A.). The General Assembly's first statement of detailed policy on the subject, it prohibited sexual contact between a parishioner and a clergyman or church employee regardless of who sought to initiate it. Church bodies were urged to establish "sexual misconduct response teams."

June 16 Advancing the search for a **blood substitute**, a biotechnology company announced it had created three pigs that produced hemoglobin, the oxygen-

Monarchs, who defeated the Barcelona Dragons 21–0. The league began its first season Mar. 23 with ten teams. Three of them represented European cities (Barcelona, Frankfurt, and London), and seven North American localities (Birmingham, Montreal, New York/New Jersey, Orlando, Raleigh-Durham, Sacramento, and San Antonio).

June 12 The **NBA basketball championship** was won by the Chicago Bulls, who defeated the Los Angeles Lakers four games to two. It was the first time the Bulls had won the title.

June 17 The **U.S. Open golf tournament** was won by Payne Stewart by two strokes in an 18-hole playoff. On the first day of the tournament, June 13, lightning killed one spectator and injured five others.

June 21 Federal agents announced the **largest heroin seizure** in U.S. history in San Francisco. Nearly 1080 pounds were found in containers shipped from Southeast Asia. Four people were arrested.

June 30 The **LPGA golf tournament** was won by Meg Mallon by one stroke with a birdie putt on the final hole.

July 5 **National League expansion** beginning in 1993, with two new baseball teams, was announced. Owners of the present clubs approved the addition of a Denver team to be known as the Colorado Rockies and a Miami team to be called the Florida Marlins. The additions brought to 28 the total number of major league teams, with 14 in each league.

July 14 The **U.S. Women's Open golf tournament** was won by Meg Mallon by two strokes. She was the only player to finish with an under par score.

July 21 The **Baseball Hall of Fame** inducted Rod Carew, a batting champion; two pitchers, Gaylord Perry and Ferguson Jenkins; Bill Veeck, owner of three different clubs; and Tony Lazzeri, a New York Yankee second baseman.

July 25 **Jeffrey L. Dahmer** was arrested in Milwaukee, Wis., for the serial murder and dismemberment of as many as 17 people. Dahmer later confessed to sexually-motivated-murder charges and on Feb. 17, 1992, was sentenced to 15 consecutive life terms in prison.

July 28 The 15th **perfect baseball game** in major league history was pitched by Dennis Martinez of the Montreal Expos (NL), who retired all 27 Los Angeles Dodgers batters without any reaching base. The first such game was pitched June 12, 1880.

Aug. 2–18 At the 11th **Pan-American Games** in Havana, Cuba, the U.S. won the most medals, 352 to Cuba's 265, but Cuba took the most gold medals, 140

Oct. 15 **Clarence Thomas,** the second black to be appointed to the Supreme Court, was narrowly confirmed by the Senate, 52–48, after a series of bitter confirmation hearings. Besides being opposed by liberals, Thomas was accused of sexual harassment by Anita F. Hill, a black professor of law, whose testimony was savagely attacked by several senators.

Oct. 20–23 The **worst fire in California's history,** started in brush in a hilly section of Oakland, took 23 lives, destroyed 2777 single-family homes and 433 apartment units, and did damage estimated at $5,000,000,000.

Oct. 30 A **Middle East peace conference,** sponsored by the U.S. and the U.S.S.R., opened in Madrid, Spain, with Israel, its Arab neighbors, and the Palestine Liberation Organization represented. Further discussions in Washington, D.C., ended Dec. 18 with little apparent progress.

Nov. 4 The **Ronald Reagan Presidential Library** was dedicated at Simi Valley, Calif., with all five living presidents on hand. Besides Reagan, present were George Bush, Jimmy Carter, Gerald Ford, and Richard Nixon. The new library contains 47,000,000 documents.

Nov. 14 A law that extended **unemployment benefits** was signed by Pres. Bush. At a cost of $5,000,000,000 the law would pay up to 20 weeks of benefits to those who had used up the standard 26 weeks.

Nov. 21 The **Civil Rights Act of 1991** was signed by Pres. Bush. The new law overturned a Supreme Court decision of 1989 by making it easier for employees to sue employers on grounds of discrimination. The burden of defense was now put on the employer.

Nov. 27 Seeking **extradition of suspected terrorists,** Great Britain and the U.S. demanded that Libya turn over to them two intelligence agents they said were responsible for the bombing Dec. 21, 1988, of Pan Am flight 103 over Scotland with the loss of 270 lives. The U.S. had indicted the pair Nov. 14.

Dec. 3 Pres. Bush's chief of staff **John Sununu resigned** after months of controversy over his dictatorial style and his use of military aircraft for personal and political trips. He was succeeded by Samuel K. Skinner, transportation secretary.

Dec. 18 A transportation bill providing $151,000,000,000 for highways and mass transit was signed by Pres. Bush. The money, to be spent over six years, included $31,500,000,000 for transit systems.

Dec. 27 Amid strained **U.S.-Philippine relations,** the Philippine government ordered the U.S. to close its Subic Bay naval base near Manila by Jan. 12, 1992. An

Mar. 24 The largest exhibit in the U.S. of the work of **Kasimir Malevich,** a Russian artist who in 1915 founded suprematism, the first completely abstract style, closed at the Metropolitan Museum of Art, New York City, having been seen previously in Los Angeles and Washington, D.C.

Mar. 25 **Academy Awards** were presented to *Dances With Wolves* as the outstanding motion picture of 1990; Jeremy Irons as best actor for *Reversal of Fortune;* Kathy Bates as best actress for *Misery;* Joe Pesci as best supporting actor for *Goodfellas;* and Whoopie Goldberg as best supporting actress for *Ghost.*

Apr. 9 **Pulitzer prizes** were awarded for the following: fiction, *Rabbit at Rest* by John Updike; general nonfiction, *The Ants* by Berthold K. Holldobler and Edward O. Wilson; history, *A Midwife's Tale: The Life of Martha Ballard, Based on Her Diary 1785–1812* by Laurel Thatcher Ulrich; biography, *Jackson Pollock: An American Saga* by Steven Naifeh and Gregory White Smith; poetry, *Near Changes* by Mona Van Duyn; drama, *Lost in Yonkers* by Neil Simon.

May 10 **Joseph Brodsky** was appointed the fifth poet laureate of the U.S. A one-time inmate of a Soviet prison camp, he emigrated to America in 1972.

May 28 After 13 years **Zubin Mehta retired** as musical director of the New York Philharmonic Orchestra. His tenure was the longest in modern times.

June 2 **Tony awards** for the 1990–1991 theater season were presented for the following: best play, *Lost in Yonkers* by Neil Simon; best musical, *The Will Rogers Follies* by Cy Coleman, Betty Comden, Adolph Green, and Peter Stone; best actor in a play, Nigel Hawthorne for *Shadowlands;* best actress in a play, Mercedes Ruehl for *Lost in Yonkers;* best actor in a musical, Jonathan Pryce for *Miss Saigon;* best actress in a musical, Lea Salonga for *Miss Saigon.*

June 9 The **100th anniversary of the birth of Cole Porter,** the composer of some of the most tuneful and sophisticated popular music of his time, was marked by a concert featuring 40 stars, at Carnegie Hall, New York City.

Aug. 5 **Emmy Awards** were presented for the following: best drama series, *L.A. Law;* best comedy series, *Cheers;* best actor in a drama series, James Earl Jones for *Gabriel's Fire;* best actress in a drama series, Patricia Wettig for *Thirtysomething;* best actor in a comedy series, Burt Reynolds for *Evening Shade;* best actress in a comedy series, Kirstie Alley for *Cheers.*

Business and Industry; Science; Education; Philosophy and Religion III	IV Sports; Social Issues and Crime; Folkways; Fashion; Holidays

carrying component of human blood. The experiment sought a substitute for blood that could be used in all kinds of transfusions and stored for months. The pigs when one day old had been injected with sets of two genes that produce human hemoglobin.

July 5 The **Bank of Credit and Commerce International (BCCI)**, controlled by the emir of Abu Dhabi, was seized by bank regulators in the U.S., Great Britain, and other countries. The bank, supposedly with assets of $20,000,000,000, was bankrupt as the result of false accounting and fictitious loans. It had secretly acquired control of two American banks. BCCI agreed Dec. 19 to pay the U.S. $550,000,000 in penalties.

July 11 An **eclipse of the sun** that was total in Hawaii and partial across part of the continental U.S. attracted many viewers, including scientists who observed it with instruments on top of 13,700-foot-high Mauna Kea in Hawaii.

July 15–Nov. 20 A wave of **bank mergers** created the second, third, and fourth largest banks in the U.S. The third largest was formed July 15 by the merger of Chemical Bank and Manufacturers Hanover Trust of New York, with assets of $139,000,000,000; the second largest Aug. 15 when BankAmerica Corp. and Security Pacific Corp. of California announced a merger with assets of $190,000,000,000; and the fourth largest by the merger Nov. 20 of a North Carolina and a Georgia bank, NCNB Corp. and C&S/Sovran Corp., with assets of $115,000,000,000.

July 19 A **compromise statement on homosexual relationships** was adopted by the General Convention of the Episcopal Church. It reaffirmed the church teaching that sexual relations should be limited to matrimony, but it admitted that many church members did not agree. The statement avoided a decision on the divisive question of ordaining homosexuals.

Aug. 18 The Treasury Dept. suspended **Salomon Brothers** from bidding at its auctions of government securities. However, it changed its mind the same day and said it would allow Salomon, one of Wall Street's largest investment houses, to bid on federal securities for its own account but not for clients. Salomon had admitted that for more than a year it had been buying more than the maximum share allowed any one firm.

Oct. 15 The **Nobel Prize in Economics** was awarded to Ronald H. Coase, a British-born retired professor of the University of Chicago for his theories of why companies, rather than individual businesses, came into being.

Dec. 3 In the continuing **savings and loan crisis,** Pres. Bush signed a bill appropriating $25,000,000,000 to cover losses in the failure of savings and loan institutions. In March $30,000,000,000 had been voted, and

to 130; Canada was third with 22 gold and 127 overall.

Aug. 11 The **PGA golf championship** was won by John Daly by three strokes. He was only the sixth player whose first tournament victory was a major championship.

Aug. 25 A new **world track record** for the 100-meter dash, 9.86 sec., was set by Carl Lewis at the Tokyo World Championships. He bettered the old mark by .04 sec. On Aug. 30 Mike Powell set a new world record for the long jump of 29 ft., 4.5 in., exceeding the old mark by 2 in.

Sept. 7–8 The **U.S. Open tennis singles championships** were won by Monica Seles in the women's division and by Stefan Edberg in the men's division. Both won in straight sets.

Sept. 14 The **Miss America** title was won by Carolyn Suzanne Sapp, 20, of Hawaii, at the annual pageant in Atlantic City, N.J.

Oct. 16 A bloody **mass killing** occurred at Killeen, Tex., when George Jo Hennard rammed his pickup truck into a restaurant and began firing with a semiautomatic pistol, killing 22 people and wounding 20. He then shot himself. No motive was known.

Oct. 19–27 The **World Series** was won by the Minnesota Twins (AL), defeating the Atlanta Braves (NL) four games to three. The Twins had won the American League pennant on Oct. 13 by beating the Toronto Blue Jays four games to one; the Braves had won the National League pennant on Oct. 17, defeating the Pittsburgh Pirates four games to three.

Oct. 24 The members of **Skull and Bones voted to admit women,** thus ending the all-male tradition of Yale University's exclusive secret society, founded in 1832.

Nov. 3 The 22nd **New York City Marathon** was won in the men's division by Salvador Garcia of Mexico with a time of 2 hrs., 9 min., 28 sec. The women's division was won by Liz McColgan of Scotland with a time of 2 hrs., 27 min., 32 sec.

Nov. 7 **Earvin "Magic" Johnson,** a star of the Los Angeles Lakers basketball team, announced his retirement because he was infected with the HIV virus that causes AIDS. A professional basketball player for 12 seasons, Johnson admitted to having had many unprotected sexual contacts. Johnson changed his mind and signed a one-year, $14,600,000 contract with the Lakers, but retired again on Nov. 2, 1992.

Nov. 30 The **first world championship of women's soccer** was won in Guangzhou, China, by the U.S. which defeated Norway, 2–1.

attempt to negotiate a new treaty ended Sept. 16 when the Philippine Senate rejected a new lease. However, on Nov. 5, 1992, the two nations agreed that U.S. forces would continue to have access to military installations in the Philippines.

Nov. 20 National Book Awards were presented for the following: fiction, *Mating* by Norman Rush; nonfiction, *Freedom* by Orlando Patterson; poetry, *What Work Is,* by Philip Levine.

Dec. 5 The $62,000,000 Seattle Art Museum opened its doors and was now able to display most of its entire collection, strong in the field of artifacts of the Indians of the Northwest. The 155,000-square-foot, five-story building was designed by Robert Venturi.

1992

The national elections, besides ending 12 years of Republican control of the executive branch, had several unusual aspects. An independent candidate, H. Ross Perot, a self-made Texas billionaire who entered the race for president, withdrew, and then reentered, polled 19% of the popular vote, an unusually high rating for a third party candidate. Four women were elected to the Senate, bringing the total to six, the most ever; one of these women was the first black female ever elected to the Senate. Also elected to the Senate was the first American Indian, a male. The total turnout of voters was about 55% of those eligible, an increase of about 5% from 1988. Voters in 14 states approved the application of limits to the number of terms senators and representatives may serve. Winning and losing candidates alike spent a great deal of money. A month before the election the average House incumbent had spent about $293,000, while the average for senators seeking reelection was about $2,350,000. One Senate candidate had raised nearly $9,000,000; the top money raiser among those running for House seats had amassed $4,200,000. Those who won would find in Washington that the federal budget deficit had not eased: for the year ending Sept. 30 it was a record $290,000,000. The 50 state governments had their financial problems also. Though they had a combined estimated surplus of $825,000,000, that was less than 1% of their total spending. The cost of the Medicaid program was alarming governors and state legislators as it presently accounted for 15% of total spending and was expected to rise to 28% by 1995. The nation observed, rather mildly, the 500th anniversary of Christopher Columbus's first voyage to the Western Hemisphere. Native Americans were now vocal in pointing out that their ancestors had "discovered" America and had lived in it for thousands of years before Columbus. As a result, the anniversary witnessed such events as changing the name of Columbus Day to Indigenous People's Day by the city council of Berkeley, Calif., and the canceling of a parade in Denver, Colo., for fear of a clash between paraders and American Indians. In schools not only were textbooks changed to

At the box office the Broadway theater season of 1991–1992 was the best ever, with receipts of $292,000,000. Thirty-seven shows were produced, compared with 28 of the previous season, and more than any in the past five seasons. Attendance was up slightly to 7,352,005. Old and new shows and revivals all contributed to the good times. *Miss Saigon* and *The Phantom of the Opera* continued to be popular, but revivals were most talked about, including *Guys and Dolls,* the musical based on Damon Runyon's tales of New York City's night people, and *Man of La Mancha,* a musical version of *Don Quixote.* A new musical with old music was *Crazy for You,* with a generous collection of George Gershwin's melodies, as was *Jelly's Last Jam,* starring Gregory Hines and remembering "Jelly Roll" Morton of jazz fame. *The Secret Garden* was billed as a "family musical" that children would enjoy. There was a new staging of *A Streetcar Named Desire,* and Judd Hirsch was hailed in *Conversations with My Father.* As usual, Neil Simon's latest play, *Lost in Yonkers,* was a success, and what was billed as the "world's longest running musical," *The Fantasticks,* was in its fourth decade. The first hit of the 1992–1993 season was *The Sisters Rosensweig* by Wendy Wasserstein, a comedy of three women seeking love as well as self-definition. Another new play was David Mamet's *Oleanna,* a drama about sexual politics. The movies, as usual, presented a mixed bag of products. *Batman Returns* was an obvious hit, and vampires were in style, including a new filming of *Bram Stoker's Dracula,* by Francis Ford Coppola. James Fenimore Cooper's *The Last of the Mohicans* was presented with rich historical pageantry and romance. Babe Ruth was the subject of a mythical filmed version of his mythical life, *The Babe. White Men Can't Jump* dealt with racism, but it also pictured two men who didn't want to grow up. Robert Redford's direction of *A River Runs Through It* was an enthralling view of both fly fishing and father-son relationships. If *1492* was supposed to be a tribute to the 500th anniversary of Christopher Columbus's first voyage, it missed the mark with its soap opera style dialogue. Among other failures were *Man*

the total since the fall of 1988 was now $105,000,000,000.

Dec. 31 On the last day of the year the **Dow Jones average** of industrial stocks set a new all-time high mark on the New York Stock Exchange at 3168.83, about 20% above the Jan. 1 figure.

Dec. 2 Bobby Bonilla became the **highest-paid player in professional team sports** when he signed a contract with the New York Mets of the National League that would pay him $29,000,000 over five years. The highest paid pitcher in baseball was Jack Morris of the Toronto Blue Jays, who signed a two-year contract Dec. 18 for $10,850,000. In all, six players were now being paid more than $5,000,000 a year.

1992

The recession that began in the spring of 1990 refused to go away, although the third quarter report for the Gross Domestic product (GDP) showed an encouraging gain of 3.9%. A report on consumer confidence indicated it rose 0.4% in October after having in September reached its lowest point since February. The unemployment picture remained rather bleak although the jobless rate fell to 7.4% in October, from a peak of 7.8% earlier in the year. Payroll jobs increased overall by 27,000 in the month but there was a drop of 55,000 in factory jobs. Fear of bad times was reflected in the report that for seven consecutive months consumers had reduced their debts instead of taking on new obligations. But in October retail sales rose 0.9% and automobile sales in early November were up by 21.6% compared with the previous year. The stock market reflected unease, with the Dow Jones industrial average reaching its low for the year to date at 3136.58 on Oct. 9. Further reflecting a weak economy was a government report that the poverty rate rose for the second year to 14.2%. "Cents-off" coupons were perhaps another indicator, with 4,100,000,000 redeemed in the first six months, an increase over 1991 of 10%. On the health front there was good, bad, and indifferent news. Ordinary people were puzzled by a study which found that 98.6°F is not necessarily a person's normal body temperature; it may vary from 96° to 99.9°. Even more puzzling was a finding that women are more likely to die in the week after their birthdays than any other week of the year, while men tend to die shortly before their birthdays. On the news front, smoking in the U.S. reached its lowest level in 37 years. This good news was countered by a steep rise in cases of tuberculosis, a disease which once had been virtually eradicated. In religion, a poll showed that two-thirds of American Roman Catholics thought women should be allowed to become priests, while 70% believed priests should be allowed to marry. The recession did not stop the cost of a college education from going up. In public colleges the year's increase was 10%; in private colleges, 7%. Average tuition fees at the former were $2253; at the latter,

Women and members of minority groups were not doing well in NCAA Division I athletic departments, according to a report by the federal General Accounting Office. For example, total earnings of a head coach of men's basketball were more than twice that of a head coach of women's basketball. Few blacks were found to hold key positions in athletic departments. In professional sports a survey showed that football is now the favorite sport to watch on TV, with 38% favoring it, compared with 16% for baseball and 12% for basketball. Baseball viewership fell 24% among young men aged 12 to 17, while NBA viewership was up 31% and NFL 16%. This trend was also evident in attendance at major league baseball games in the 1992 season, with a drop of nearly 600,000 in the National League and about 325,000 in the American League. On the other hand, owners of teams in professional sports seemed to be doing all right. The New York Yankees baseball franchise was at the top of the list, being valued at $200,000,000. For the first time the average salary of a major league baseball player passed the $1,000,000 mark. Crime figures were also impressive—or depressing. The U.S. held in prison a higher percentage of its population than any other nation. The 1,100,000 inmates represented an incarceration rate of 455 people per 100,000. In late October the 27th execution in the U.S. this year took place in North Carolina, marking the highest number of executions since 1962, when 47 convicts were put to death. News of weapons was not all in the lethal category. More powerful water guns, able to throw a stream 50 feet, became the rage. All was not peaceful in the field of fashion, either. The New York City consumer affairs commissioner attacked designers and producers of beauty products for not using enough members of minority groups in their advertising. The designers, meanwhile, solved the problem of skirt length by featuring pants for women; but while the women covered up, men bared almost all when they modeled underwear at a fashion show of a leading designer. Notable persons who died during the year included Sandy Amoros, hero of the 1955 World Series

reflect a new attitude, but students reflected it also, as when a jury of seventh graders in Scarsdale, N.Y., at a mock trial voted Columbus a villain. Other anniversaries were less controversial. The Alaska Highway, the 1500-mile road from British Columbia to Fairbanks, Alaska, that was rushed to completion in 1942 during World War II, marked its 50th anniversary. The battleship *Missouri*, on which Japan's surrender in 1945 was received, was decommissioned for the third time. On May 18 an amendment to the Constitution first proposed 203 years ago, prohibiting Congress from voting itself immediate pay raises, was finally ratified. Meanwhile Americans remained much as in days of yore. A survey showed that 80% of us still thought a single-family detached home with a yard was the ideal, but many people were finding it hard to come up with the necessary down payment. Americans were also concerned about the state of race relations, brought only too bloodily to their attention by rioting in Los Angeles in April. A survey showed that the majority believed too little money was being spent on the problems of inner cities and on securing justice and equality for black Americans. Among cities a new study rated Tulsa, Okla., the most typical, with Charleston, W.Va., second, and Midland, Tex., third. In New York City the landmark Pan Am Building, opened in 1963, was renamed the Met Life Building. The insurance company had owned the skyscraper since 1981 and Pan American World Airways, a pioneer in air transportation, had gone into bankruptcy. Whether a result of the recession or not, the nation's well-to-do citizens were not giving as big a share of their incomes to charity, in spite of the riches that accrued to them during the 1980s. The more than 7% of the after-tax income they gave in 1979 had declined to less than 4%. On the other hand the number of millionaires increased so greatly over the decade that the total they gave rose to a record level. Ironically, more than a third of the chief executives of the 100 largest charitable foundations had salaries of $200,000 or more in 1991. The highest was the $624,500 paid to Howard B. Keck, chairman of the Keck Foundation; the lowest was $18,500. One item of good news for most people: the winter that ended in March was the warmest in the 97 years such records have been kept. For the period Dec., 1991, through Feb., 1992, the nationwide average temperature was 4°F above normal. Eastern Montana was 11° above normal, but cities in the Northeast registered only 2° above normal.

Notable persons who died his year included Quentin N. Burdick, Democratic senator from North Dakota for 32 years, Sept. 8, at 84; Millicent H. Fenwick, Republican representative from New Jersey from 1964 to 1982, known for her political independence, Sept. 16, at 82; Philip C. Habib, diplomat for nearly three decades and

Trouble, in which Jack Nicholson, usually a drawing card, played a dog trainer; and *Boomerang,* in which Eddie Murphy played a womanizing advertising executive. The latter did not do nearly as well as Murphy's earlier movies. More popular films included *Unforgiven,* in which Clint Eastwood was a reformed killer facing his past; *Sister Act,* with Whoopi Goldberg as a night club singer who flees to a convent to escape mobsters; and *A League of Their Own,* about a women's baseball team during World War II. Overall, movie attendance was down, being 10,000,000 tickets behind normal by mid-August. Many of America's orchestras were in financial trouble as costs of all kinds continued to increase. In the past five years they had gone up by 42%. On the positive side, orchestras were playing to about 1500 people per performance, an increase of 300 from ten years earlier. The Metropolitan Opera marked the 500th anniversary of the first voyage of Columbus to the Western Hemisphere with a new work commissioned from the composer Philip Glass. Called *The Voyage,* it ran for three and a half hours and cost $2,000,000 to stage. Actually, Columbus figured in only a small part of the work, since it began with a landing of aliens on earth in the Ice Age and concluded with the U.S. finding life on another planet. Another new opera was *McTeague,* based on the 1899 novel by Frank Norris about a greedy San Francisco dentist. The composer was William Bolcom and the work had its world premier at the Lyric Opera, Chicago, Ill. An unusual musical event was the appearance on a North American tour for the first time of the Red Star Red Army Chorus and Dance, 130 members strong.

The fall television season got off to a disappointing start so far as the networks were concerned. Shows seen early on Saturday evening, for example, were drawing only a 56% share of the total audience, compared with 66% a year earlier. Older shows, such as *The Simpsons* and *Doogie Howser, M.D.,* had fewer viewers, and new shows, such as *Angel Street* and *Final Appeal,* were doing poorly compared with their predecessors. On the whole the networks seemed to be less and less interested in older people. Typical of the new shows that were popular were *Love and War,* a sitcom about an oddly matched young couple; and *Mad About You,* involving newlyweds whose personalities were not on the same wavelength. A further indication of changing times was seen in the arrival of a series such as *Middle Ages,* intended to appeal to the "baby boomers" who were now into their forties. It was pointed out that there was now a generation of TV viewers who, via cable and satellite, had a much wider range of choices than their elders. But a study by two economists found that average American workers had less time to enjoy the arts and sports than two decades ago because they worked

Business and Industry; Science; Education; Philosophy and Religion	III		IV	Sports; Social Issues and Crime; Folkways; Fashion; Holidays

$8879. The range was all the way from $321 for a year's education to $24,380. In high schools dropout rates were declining for blacks and whites, but not for Hispanics. Another survey reported that the use of standardized tests may hinder efforts to improve math and science education by leading teachers to emphasize memorization rather than reasoning. Noteworthy persons who died this year included Marguerite Ross Barnett, president of the University of Houston since 1990 and the first black woman to head a major American university, Feb. 26, at 49; Eugene R. Black, president of the World Bank from 1949 to 1962, Feb. 20, at 93; Allan Bloom, conservative critic of American universities whose book *The Closing of the American Mind* (1987) caused controversy, Oct. 7, at 62; S. I. Hayakawa, language scholar, college president, and Republican senator from California, Feb. 27, at 85; Daniel K. Ludwig, self-made ship owner and real estate developer, and one of the richest men in the world, Aug. 27, at 95; Barbara McClintock, a leader in genetic research and a Nobel Prize winner, Sept. 2, at 90; William McGowan, longtime head of MCI Communications Corp., June 8, at 64; Lee Salk, child psychologist and authority on family relationships, May 2, at 65; Marc H. Tanenbaum, popular rabbi who contributed greatly to furthering Christian-Jewish relations, July 3, at 66; Willard L. Thorp, economist who helped draft the Marshall Plan for European recovery after World War II, May 10, at 92; Sam Walton, founder of the Wal-Mart store chain that made his family the richest in the U.S., Apr. 5, at 74; and James E. Webb, head of the National Aeronautics and Space Administration during the period when men first reached the moon, Mar. 27, at 85.

Jan. 6 In a wave of **department store closings,** the Woolworth Corp. announced it would close, sell, or reformat 900 of its 6500 stores because of the recession. On Jan. 27 R. H. Macy & Co., one of the largest department store operators in the country, with 251 stores, filed for bankruptcy, saddled by $3,500,000,000 of debt incurred in a management-led buyout in 1986. On May 20 Macy announced that it would close eight stores in the New York City area, having already shut 64 shops around the country that it operated under other names. On May 15 Alexander's closed all 11 of its stores in the New York area.

Jan. 8 At a **summit meeting** in Tokyo, Pres. George Bush and Prime Minister Kiichi Miyazawa of Japan announced some general plans for battling the current recession by creating momentum for expansion and by fighting inflation. On Jan. 9 Bush announced that Japan had agreed to buy more American cars and

as starter of a spectacular double play, June 27, at 62; Walter "Red" Barber, most popular of sports broadcasters over a 33-year career, Oct. 27, at 84; Danny Biasone, professional basketball team owner who devised the 24-second shot clock to make the game more exciting, May 25, at 83; Easley Blackwood, leading contract bridge expert who invented the Blackwood convention as a bidding device in 1933, Mar. 27, at 89; Anita Colby, called the first "supermodel" and who wrote on beauty, Mar. 27, at 77; Mel Hein, iron man center and linebacker of the pro football Giants in the 1930s and 1940s, Jan. 31, at 82; Billy Herman, second baseman of the Brooklyn Dodgers and a member of the Baseball Hall of Fame, Sept. 5, at 83; Eddie Lopat, star pitcher for the New York Yankees for five championship years, June 15, at 73; Mollie Parnis, designer whose dresses were worn by several First Ladies, July 18, at 90+; Samuel Reshevsky, chess grandmaster, Apr. 4, at 80; Anthony "Fat Tony" Salerno, boss of the Genovese crime family, in prison since 1989, July 27, at 80; Carl Stotz, who founded Little League baseball in 1938, June 4, at 82; and Jean R. Yawkey, majority owner of the Boston Red Sox and a philanthropist, Feb. 26, at 83.

Jan. 1 In **college football bowl games,** the results were Florida State 10, Texas A&M 2 in the Cotton Bowl; Miami 22, Nebraska 0 in the Orange Bowl; Washington 34, Michigan 14 in the Rose Bowl; and Notre Dame 30, Florida 28 in the Sugar Bowl. The AP and *The New York Times* selected Miami as the national collegiate champions of 1991, but the UPI and *USA Today*/CNN polls chose Washington.

Jan. 8 The **NCAA adopted stricter academic standards** for athletes. The changes would require incoming freshman athletes to have a higher grade-point average than before in core subjects in high school, and would strengthen the requirement that athletes show progress toward a degree.

Jan. 9–11 **U.S. figure skating championships** were won in Orlando, Fla., by Christopher Bowman, men's singles; Kristi Yamaguchi, women's singles; Calla Urbanski and Rocky Marval, pairs; April Sargent-Thomas and Russ Witherby, dance.

Jan. 18 **Pat Bradley** became only the 12th member of the LPGA Hall of Fame, having won the required 30 tournament victories during her career. Bradley had also won more prize money—$4,109,165—than any other female golfer.

Jan. 26 **Super Bowl XXVI** was won by the Washington Redskins (NFC) who defeated the Buffalo Bills (AFC) 37–24. On Jan. 12 the Redskins had beaten the Detroit Lions 41–10 for the NFC title and the Bills defeated the Denver Broncos 10–7 for the AFC title.

Feb. 8–23 At the **XVIth Winter Olympic Games,** held in Albertville, France, the U.S. finished sixth in the medal standings, winning five gold medals and 11 in

an accomplished trouble-shooter, May 25, at 72; Wilbur D. Mills, a leading Democrat in the House of Representatives for more than 20 years, May 2, at 82; Joseph L. Rauh, Jr., a foremost civil rights lawyer for nearly 50 years, Sept. 3, at 81; John Joseph Sirica, federal judge whose decisions during the Watergate scandal of the early 1970s did much to end the presidency of Richard M. Nixon, Aug. 14, at 88; James A. Van Fleet, four-decade veteran of the Army, who led major campaigns in both World War II and the Korean War, Sept. 23, at 100; and Ted Weiss, Democratic congressman since 1976 and one of the most outspoken liberals in Congress, Sept. 14, at 64.

Jan. 16 An agreement on **patents, copyrights, and trade secrets** was reached by the U.S. and China to provide protection for American books, music recordings, pharmaceuticals, and computer software. In effect China agreed to adopt international standards, ending what was estimated to be more than $800,000,000 of income lost annually by American firms.

Jan. 26 Provisions of a **federal law to aid the disabled** went into effect, with other rules due to be implemented in July. The new regulations were expected to be of special assistance to those confined to wheelchairs, but would also benefit the visually impaired. The law also called for enhanced employment opportunities and better transportation facilities.

Jan. 31 The State Department's annual **report on human rights** was especially critical of China, India, Peru, and Syria, even though the last had been an ally in the Persian Gulf War.

Feb. 1 The **end of the Cold War** was proclaimed in Washington by Pres. George Bush and Pres. Boris Yeltsin of Russia. On May 23 the U.S. signed with Russia, Belarus, Kazakhstan, and Ukraine an agreement to abide by the nuclear arms reduction treaty negotiated with the U.S.S.R. before its collapse in late 1991. On June 16 Pres. Bush and Pres. Yeltsin announced an agreement to further control nuclear armaments. Each nation was to reduce its nuclear warheads to between 3000 and 3500 by the year 2003 from the present combined total of about 22,500.

Feb. 26 **Students may sue colleges for damages** for sexual harassment and other forms of sex discrimination, the Supreme Court ruled, 9–0. The federal government had claimed that a 1972 education act did not authorize monetary damages.

Mar. 8 In the continuing **savings and loan scandal,** a large law firm agreed to pay the federal government $41,000,000 to settle charges that it had improperly withheld damaging information about a savings association it had represented. The firm was Kaye,

140 hours more a year. Also, paid days off had dwindled as vacation, sick leave, and personal days fell by about 15% during the 1980s. Americans were spending more time working and less time on leisure pursuits in part because real wages had declined.

Deaths of notable people this year included Peter Allen, concert entertainer and winner of both a Grammy and an Academy Award for his songwriting, June 18, at 48; Judith Anderson, Australian-born stage, screen and television actress, Jan. 3, at 93; Isaac Asimov, prolific author of nearly 500 books, Apr. 6, at 72; Freddie Bartholomew, child movie star of the 1930s, best known in *Little Lord Fauntleroy,* Jan. 23, at 69/70; Shirley Booth, star of stage and screen, radio and TV, noted for her role in *Come Back, Little Sheba,* Oct. 16, at 94; Morris Carnovsky, character actor known especially for his Shakespearean roles, Sept. 1, at 94; Mae Clarke, movie actress, remembered forever for the scene in which James Cagney shoved a grapefruit in her face, Apr. 29, at 81; John Cage, minimalist composer who also influenced choreography, Aug. 12, at 79; Sandy Dennis, actress who won two Tony Awards as well as an Academy Award, Mar. 2, at 54; Helen Deutsch, screenwriter of the hit movie *Lili* and co-author of *National Velvet,* Mar. 15, at 85; Pietro di Donato, author remembered for *Christ in Concrete* (1938), Jan. 19, at 80; Marlene Dietrich, perhaps the most glamorous star and singer the movies have known, May 6, at 90; Alfred Drake, baritone who was a sensational hit in the lead role in *Oklahoma!* (1943), and other Broadway shows, July 25, at 77; José Ferrer, writer, actor, and director, famous for his role as Cyrano de Bergerac, Jan. 26, at 80; M. F. K. Fisher, short story writer and author of cookbooks that set a new style for the genre, June 22, at 83; Alex Haley, author of the best-selling novel *Roots* (1976), Feb. 10, at 70; Paul Henreid, actor and director of many TV dramas, remembered most of all for his role in the movie *Casablanca,* Mar. 29, at 84; Hanya Holm, choreographer, Nov. 3, at 99; Lou Jacobs, leading clown of the Ringling Brothers and Barnum & Bailey Circus for some 60 years, Sept. 13, at 89; Allan Jones, romantic tenor who sang in many films, most notably in *Show Boat* (1936), June 27, at 84; Oscar Lewis, historian, July 11, at 99; Pare Lorentz, writer and director of socially conscious documentary films such as *The River,* Mar. 4, at 86; Max Lerner, educator and journalist with strong liberal views, June 5, at 89; Cleavon Little, Tony Award–winning actor of the stage, screen, and TV, Oct. 22, at 53; Joan Mitchell, important among the second generation of American abstract expressionists, Oct. 30, at 66; Bert Parks, television host who emceed the Miss America pageant for 25 years, Feb. 2, at 77; Anthony Perkins, versatile actor known best for his role as a psychopath in *Psycho* (1960), Sept. 12, at 60; Molly Picon,

| Business and Industry; Science; Education; Philosophy and Religion **III** | | **IV** Sports; Social Issues and Crime; Folkways; Fashion; Holidays |

$10,000,000,000 more in auto parts by 1995. The heads of the three major American auto manufacturers, who participated in the meetings, denounced the agreement as inadequate.

Feb. 24 The **closing of 21 auto plants** in the U.S. and Canada over the next several years was announced by General Motors. Twelve plants, affecting 16,300 workers, were to be shut down within three years. At the same time the nation's largest auto manufacturer reported a loss in 1991 of $4,445,000,000, the largest in American corporate history.

Mar. 4 In an **artificial insemination scandal,** an infertility specialist was convicted in Virginia on 52 counts of fraud and perjury for artificially inseminating patients with his own sperm. DNA tests indicated that the doctor, Cecil B. Jacobson, had fathered 15 children in this manner, while the prosecution alleged he had fathered as many as 75.

Mar. 9 The resignation of the chairman of the **Christian Science Church** was announced amid a controversy within the church concerning its direction and its finances. The outgoing chairman, Harvey W. Wood, had been the leader in the establishment of the Monitor Channel, a TV outlet that had lost millions of dollars and had borrowed $41,500,000 from the church's pension fund.

Mar. 12 A **warning about a dangerous heart valve** that had been implanted in more than 20,000 Americans was issued by the Food and Drug Administration. It said there was such a high rate of sudden fatal failure that recipients of this particular type of valve should consider having it replaced. The company that produced the valves admitted that worldwide about 500 had failed, killing two-thirds or more of the patients.

Mar. 24 Donna Redel was elected the **first woman chairperson of the New York Commodity Exchange.** The 39-year-old Redel was an executive vice president of the Redel Trading Co.

Apr. 1 A **Russian aid plan,** to provide $24,000,000,000 to further democratization and a free market economy in Russia, was announced by Pres. Bush and Chancellor Helmut Kohl of Germany. The seven leading industrial nations were to take part and the U.S. share was to be nearly $4,500,000,000.

total. All the gold medals were won by women: Bonnie Blair, two in speed skating; Kristi Yamaguchi, figure skating; Cathy Turner, 500-meter race; and Donna Weinbrecht, mogul skiing.

Feb. 10 Former heavyweight boxing champion **Mike Tyson was convicted of rape** in Indianapolis, Ind., and on Mar. 26 was sentenced to six years in prison. He had been charged with raping an 18-year-old beauty pageant contestant on July 19, 1991.

Feb. 17 **Martina Navratilova** won her 158th tennis title, more than any other player, male or female. She took her first championship in Czechoslovakia in 1973.

Mar. 2 Ryne Sandberg became the **highest paid player in professional baseball** when he signed a contract with the Chicago Cubs (NL) worth $28,400,000 over four years. On Aug. 24 Cal Ripken, Jr., of the Baltimore Orioles (AL) became the second-highest paid player when he signed a five-year contract worth $30,500,000.

Mar. 18 The **NFL abandoned the instant replay** for the 1992 season. In effect for five seasons, the system allowed officials with TV monitors to review a play and confirm or overturn the on-field officials' decisions. The instant replay was criticized for slowing the pace of the game.

Apr. 5 The **NCAA women's basketball championship** was won by Stanford, which defeated Western Kentucky 78–62.

Apr. 6 The **NCAA men's basketball championship** was won by Duke, which defeated Michigan 71–51.

Apr. 8 **Arthur Ashe,** the black tennis champion and rights activist, revealed that he had contracted AIDS, apparently from a blood transfusion. In 1968 Ashe had become the first and only black man to win the U.S. tennis championship, and in 1975, the British title.

Apr. 9 **Manuel Antonio Noriega,** the former dictator of Panama, was convicted in a federal court on eight counts of cocaine trafficking, racketeering, and money laundering. He had surrendered to U.S. forces Jan. 3, 1990, during an invasion of Panama by American troops. On July 10 he was sentenced to 40 years in prison.

Apr. 10 The key figure in a major **savings and loan scandal,** Charles H. Keating, Jr., was sentenced to ten years in prison for having duped about 23,000 depositors of the Lincoln Savings and Loan Association, which he headed, into buying high-risk junk bonds. On July 10 a federal jury ordered Keating to pay $3,300,000,000 in damage claims. On Mar. 30 an accounting firm and a law firm, involved in the financial scandal, had agreed to pay $87,000,000 in damages.

Apr. 10 The **first professional hockey strike** in the history of the NHL, a ten-day walkout, ended with an

Scholer, Fierman, Hays, and Handler of New York City, and its client was the Lincoln Savings and Loan Association of Irvine, Calif.

Mar. 31 A Supreme Court decision, 8–0, concerning **school desegregation** would make it easier for educational institutions to take back local control from federal judges. The justices said this could come about as different aspects of school operations were desegregated, rather than having to wait until all was accomplished.

Apr. 5 A **march to support abortion rights** drew an estimated 500,000 people to Washington, D.C. Thought to be the largest ever protest march in the nation's capital, it came as the Supreme Court was about to consider a Pennsylvania law that limited access to abortion.

Apr. 13 A **flood in Chicago,** caused by water surging through tunnnels beneath buildings in the Loop, the main business section, shut down stores, courts, and commodity exchanges for a week. The flood was caused by 250,000,000 gallons of water that flowed from a leak in the Chicago River into a series of tunnels once used to transport freight and coal. Electricity was shut off in a 12-block area.

Apr. 16 In a **congressional banking scandal,** a list of U.S. representatives who overdrew their checking accounts in the House bank was released, showing that 252 current and 51 former members of Congress had done so. Former Rep. Tommy Robinson of Arkansas was reported to have made the most overdrafts, 996, but he denied that he had made so many.

May 4 **State prison inmates' appeals** to federal courts were made more difficult by a Supreme Court decision, 5–4, which overturned a precedent. Federal courts would no longer be obliged to grant a hearing because a prisoner showed that his lawyer had not properly presented his case.

June 1 In a ruling on the use of **frozen embryos,** Tennessee's highest court said that a divorced man could deny his former wife the use of such an embryo that had been fertilized with his sperm. The court held in effect that a man cannot be forced to become a father against his will.

June 12 Speaking at the **Earth Summit** in Rio de Janeiro, Brazil, Pres. Bush said the U.S. would not sign a treaty agreed to by most of the 172 nations present, which was designed to protect rare and endangered animals and plants. He claimed it would "retard technology and undermine the protection of ideas." The U.S. did sign a treaty aimed at preventing further global warming.

comedienne who starred in the Yiddish theater, Apr. 6, at 94; William Schuman, composer and president of the Juilliard School of Music, Feb. 15, at 81; Eric Sevareid, outstanding radio and television reporter and commentator, July 9, at 79; William A. Swanberg, author who specialized in biographies, Sept. 17, at 84; Nancy Walker, actress who portrayed wild and brassy characters on stage and in the movies, Mar. 25, at 69; and Lawrence Welk, folksy bandleader, May 17 at 89.

Affected by the number of **books published** in relation to the public's ability to buy them, and also by the recession, a number of publishers announced they were cutting back on the size of their lists. Yet a number of very lucrative contracts were signed. Barbara Taylor Bradford was to get about $24,000,000 for three novels in the romance genre; Magic Johnson, the basketball star with AIDS, about $5,000,000 for three books; and Kitty Kelley $4,000,000 for a book about the British royal family. This being a presidential election year, books about politics, politicians, and government in general, were numerous. In the last category the leader was *United We Stand* by H. Ross Perot, outlining the nation's core problems and detailing what he would do to solve them if elected to the presidency. Close on his heels was *Putting People First* by Bill Clinton and Al Gore, the Democratic party candidates for president and vice president. Senator Gore also had a best-selling book on the environment, *Earth in the Balance.* Among the year's fiction offerings were *Vox* by Nicholson Baker, consisting entirely of an erotic telephone conversation between a man and a woman; *Rising Sun* by Michael Crichton, as much an attack on Japan as a murder mystery; *"I" Is for Innocent* by Sue Grafton, continuing alphabetically the adventures of Kinsey Milhone, private detective; *Fatherland* by Robert Harris, a believable account of events after Hitler won World War II; *Gerald's Game* by Stephen King, the tale of a woman handcuffed to a bed for more than a day; *Jazz* by Toni Morrison, with Harlem of the 1920s as background; *Black Water* by Joyce Carol Oates, a retelling of the tragedy of Sen. Edward Kennedy at Chappaquiddick; *The Tale of the Body Thief* by Anne Rice, extending her chronicles of vampires; *Red Square* by Martin Cruz Smith, again featuring Moscow detective Arkady Renko; and *The Volcano Lover* by Susan Sontag, which took an unusual approach to the story of Admiral Horatio Nelson and Lady Hamilton. Nonfiction titles included *America: What Went Wrong?* by Donald L. Bartlett and James B. Steel; *The End of History and the Last Man* by Francis Fukuyama, in which the author claimed that achieving liberal democracy would mean the end of history; *The Government Racket* by Martin L. Gross; *Woodrow Wilson,* a biography by August Heckscher; *Kissinger: A Biography* by Walter Isaacson;

Apr. 16 Sharp restrictions on the use of **silicone gel breast implants** were ordered by the Food and Drug Administration. A panel of experts had concluded that there was not enough evidence to show that the implants were safe or effective. The Dow Corning Corp., the largest maker of the implants, first denied any danger, then admitted it had some evidence to the contrary, and announced it was stopping their production.

May 12 **Homosexual behavior conflicts with Christian teaching,** the General Conference of the United Methodist Church declared. On June 10 the Southern Baptist Convention voted to banish two of its churches for accepting homosexuals and began a process to change its by-laws to exclude any church that accepted homosexuals. On July 1 the Roman Catholic Church urged its bishops in the U.S. to oppose any laws that promote public acceptance of homosexual conduct.

May 12 In a move to strengthen the **bank insurance** system, the Federal Deposit Insurance Corporation raised the premiums that banks and savings associations must pay to insurance funds. They would now pay an average of 28 cents for every $100 of deposits instead of 23 cents. The increase was held necessary because of numerous bank failures in recent years.

May 13 Two "firsts" in **space activity** were registered by American astronauts. Three astronauts from the shuttle *Endeavor* walked in space at the same time, and they used only their gloved hands to wrestle a damaged satellite inside the shuttle for repairs. They were some 230 miles above the earth when they captured the 17-foot, 4.5-ton satellite.

May 26 In an announcement concerning **foods produced through genetic engineering,** the federal government said that new and varied products should result and that no more regulation was required than for ordinary foodstuffs. Although some critics had argued that there could be safety risks in such foods, the government held that except in special cases no extraordinary testing was needed.

June 1 The **Dow Jones average** of industrial stocks passed the 3400 mark for the first time ever, ending the day at 3413.21.

agreement between the owners and the Players Association effective through the 1992–1993 season. Among the terms of the new agreement were the establishment of a minimum salary of $100,000, up from $25,000, and an increase in regular season games from 80 to 84.

Apr. 12 The **Masters golf tournament** was won by Fred Couples by two strokes. It was his first major title in his 12-year career.

Apr. 20 The 96th **Boston Marathon** was won in the men's division by Ibrahim Hussein of Kenya, with a time of 2 hrs., 8 min., 14 sec. Olga Markova of Russia won the women's division with a time of 2 hrs., 23 min., 43 sec. Both times were the second fastest ever run on the course.

Apr. 22 In a major **sexual abuse case,** the operator of a day care center in Edenton, N.C., was convicted on 99 charges of sexually abusing children. The trial of Robert F. Kelly, Jr., operator of the Little Rascals Day Care Center, lasted eight months, the longest and costliest ever in North Carolina.

Apr. 29 A bloody and destructive **riot** in south central Los Angeles broke out after four policemen were acquitted of beating a black man while making an arrest, even though the incident had been videotaped by a bystander. In all, 51 persons died, 30 of them homicide victims. Nearly 1800 people were injured, and 6345 were arrested. In the three days of disorder 3767 buildings were burned.

May 1 The 118th **Kentucky Derby** was won by Lil E. Tee with a time of 2:03. The jockey was Pat Day.

May 9–16 The **America's Cup** was successfully defended by *America 3,* which defeated the Italian yacht *Moro di Venezia* four races to one, off San Diego, Calif.

May 16 The 117th **Preakness Stakes** was won by Pine Bluff, with a time of 1:55³/₅. The jockey was Chris McCarron.

May 17 The **LPGA golf tournament** was won by Betsy King, whose four round total of 267 was the lowest ever for this event.

May 24 The 76th **Indianapolis 500 auto race** was won by Al Unser, Jr., completing the 500-mile course in 3 hrs., 43 min., 4.991 sec., with an average speed of 134.479 mph. Unser won by only .043 sec., a record margin, and his was the eighth victory by a member of his family.

June 1 The **NHL Stanley Cup** was won for the second consecutive year by the Pittsburgh Penguins, who defeated the Chicago Blackhawks in four straight games.

June 6 The 124th **Belmont Stakes** was won by A. P. Indy, with a time of 2:26. The jockey was Eddie Delahoussaye.

June 18 In a decision on **racism in jury selection,** the Supreme Court ruled, 7–2, that criminal defendants cannot exclude jurors on the basis of race. Basing its decision on constitutional guarantees of equal protection under the law, the court extended a rule it had laid down six years earlier concerning prosecutors and broadened in a case last year.

June 22 A **law to aid inner cities** was signed by Pres. Bush. Spurred in part by the recent rioting in Los Angeles (see Apr. 29, IV), the law provided $1,300,-000,000 for relief of that disaster in the form of grants and loans for housing and business, plus a summer employment program for 75 cities.

June 22 Laws criminalizing "hate speech" or "bias crimes" were unconstitutional, the Supreme Court ruled. The decision was based on a St. Paul, Minn., ordinance that the court found violated the First Amendment. Although the decision formally came on a 5–4 vote, all the justices found the law unconstitutional on some grounds.

June 28 The most powerful **earthquake** to strike California in 40 years registered 7.4 on the Richter scale. The quake was centered in the Yucca Valley, east of Los Angeles, and was felt as far north as Idaho and Washington. Considerable damage was done to stores and houses but there was only one fatality. Aftershocks continued for some time.

June 29 The constitutional **right to abortion** was reaffirmed by the Supreme Court, 5–4. At the same time the court permitted states to impose some restrictions. The case involved a Pennsylvania law and the court upheld its provisions for a 24-hour waiting period, and the consent of one parent of a teenager or of a judge, among other points.

July 3 A **bill to aid the jobless** was signed into law by Pres. Bush. It provided for 26 weeks of coverage for the unemployed beyond the basic 26 weeks of benefits.

July 15–16 The **Democratic National Convention** nominated Gov. Bill Clinton of Arkansas for the presidency and Sen. Albert Gore of Tennessee for the vice presidency.

Aug. **Forest fires** destroyed hundreds of thousands of acres of woodland in many parts of California, Colorado, Idaho, Nevada, and Oregon, and Washington. At least 9000 fire-fighters, including National Guardsmen, fought the blazes, most of which were caused by lightning striking trees suffering from severe drought. Many homes were destroyed.

Aug. 5 New rules on **radio station ownership** were issued by the Federal Communications Commission. They raised the number of stations a single company

Truman by David McCullough; *The Making of Middlebrow Culture* by Joan Shelley Rubin, explaining how publishers and others have tried to sell culture to almost everyone; *It Doesn't Take a Hero,* a highly successful autobiography by Gen. H. Norman Schwarzkopf, Jr., the commanding general in the Persian Gulf War; *The Silent Passage* by Gail Sheehy, on the significance of menopause for modern women; *The Diversity of Life* by Edward O. Wilson, which argued that human beings were their own worst enemies by their disregard for other species; and *The Radicalism of the American Revolution* by Gordon S. Wood, which argued that the war for independence was indeed much more radical than is usually thought. Finally, in a class by itself, was *Sex,* a sensational collection of photographs of the superstar Madonna.

Jan. 23 In observance of the **100th birthday of Hal Roach** (on Jan. 14), the the the Smithsonian Institution awarded the movie producer and director its highest honor, the James Smithson Medal. Starting as an actor in 1912, Roach by 1919 was beginning to produce some of the most popular comedy films ever made, with stars such as Laurel and Hardy, and Harold Lloyd, along with more than 200 of the "Our Gang" movies. Roach died on Nov. 2.

Feb. 2 The **William S. Paley Collection,** consisting of nearly 80 paintings, drawings, and sculptures, went on exhibit at the Museum of Modern Art, New York City. Featuring works of the modern French masters, the collection of the late founder of the Columbia Broadcasting System was the most significant gift the museum had received in recent years.

Feb. 26 **Grammy Awards** were presented for the following: best album of 1991, *Unforgettable* by Natalie Cole; best record, "Unforgettable" by Natalie Cole; best male pop vocalist, Michael Bolton for "When a Man Loves a Woman"; best female pop and rock vocalist, Bonnie Raitt for "Something to Talk About" and "Luck of the Draw."

Feb. 28 In a tribute to the *Star Trek* television series of the 1960s, the National Air and Space Museum, Washington, D.C., placed on exhibit more than 80 costumes, props, and models from the show. Included were Capt. Kirk's uniform, Mr. Spock's Vulcan ears, and models of the starship *Enterprise.*

Mar. 31 **Academy Awards** were presented to *The Silence of the Lambs* as the outstanding motion picture of 1991; Anthony Hopkins as best actor for *The Silence of the Lambs;* Jodie Foster as best actress for *The Silence of the Lambs;* Jack Palance as best supporting actor for *City Slickers;* and Mercedes Ruehl as best supporting actress for *The Fisher King.*

June 8 A somewhat modified **stand on abortion** was adopted by the General Assembly of the Presbyterian Church (U.S.A.). Nine years earlier it had taken a strong stand in favor of abortion rights, but while still endorsing a woman's right to abortion, it adopted a statement that discouraged women from exercising the right.

June 24 **Damage suits by cigarette smokers** were made possible by a Supreme Court decision, 7–2. In effect the court ruled that the federal law requiring warning labels on cigarette packs did not protect the manufacturers from lawsuits.

June 24 Affirming its previous ruling on state sponsored **prayer in public schools,** the Supreme Court, 5–4, again held that such practices are unconstitutional and violate the First Amendment.

June 26 The Supreme Court ruled, 8–1, that **Mississippi had failed to end racial segregation** in its state university system as required to meet constitutional standards. Although the state's eight public universities were nominally open to all, five remained largely white and three mostly black.

June 28 A baboon's **liver was transplanted into a human** for the first time. The 11.5-hour operation was performed at a Pittsburgh, Pa., hospital on a 35-year-old man who was dying of hepatitis B.

July 6 The **largest educational gift** ever made to a public university or college by an individual was announced by Henry M. Rowan, a wealthy founder of a manufacturing company. The recipient of the $100,000,000 donation was Glassboro State College, Glassboro, N.J., which then changed its name to Rowan College of New Jersey.

July 9 Ending the **longest space shuttle flight** to date, the *Columbia* landed at Cape Canaveral, Fla., after two weeks in orbit. The craft traveled 5,760,000 miles and circled the earth 221 times.

Sept. The **oldest DNA** ever recovered from fossils was reported to have been found in gene fragments extracted from insects preserved in amber for up to 40,000,000 years. Scientists said that this showed DNA could survive far longer than had been believed possible.

June 6 The second **World League of American Football championship** was won by the Sacramento Surge, defeating the Orlando Thunder 21–17.

June 11 The first **foreign ownership of a major league baseball team** by non–North Americans came about when the Seattle Mariners (AL) were sold for $125,000,000 to a seven-member group that included the president of the Nintendo Co. of Japan.

June 14 The **NBA basketball championship** was won for the second consecutive year by the Chicago Bulls, who defeated the Portland Trail Blazers four games to two.

June 21 The **U.S. Open golf tournament** was won by Tom Kite by two strokes.

June 23 **John Gotti,** head of the Gambino crime family, was sentenced to life imprisonment in federal court in Brooklyn, N.Y. He had been convicted on Apr. 2 on 13 counts, including murder, conspiracy, tax fraud, and obstruction of justice.

July 5 At the **Wimbledon** tennis championships in England, Andre Agassi won the title in five sets over Goran Ivaniasevic of Croatia. Agassi was the first American to win this title since 1984.

July 11 **Tracy Austin,** 29, became the youngest inductee of the International Tennis Hall of Fame in a ceremony at Newport, R.I. Austin, at age 16, had in 1979 become the youngest U.S. Open champion. However, an injury suffered in an auto accident halted her career in 1989.

July 14 The **baseball All-Star Game** was won by the American League over the National League, 13–6.

July 23 **Judit Polgar,** the youngest person ever to earn the rank of chess grandmaster, celebrated her 16th birthday. She had achieved this ranking the previous Dec. There were only 401 active grandmasters in the world.

July 24 **George Steinbrenner** was returned to control of the New York Yankee baseball club as of Mar. 1, 1993. The principal owner of the team, he had been banned from major league baseball on July 30, 1990, by Fay Vincent, commissioner of Major League Baseball, for having paid a known gambler to try to secure discrediting information about a Yankee player, Dave Winfield. Settlement of a number of legal and other matters led Vincent to rescind the ban.

July 25–Aug. 9 At the **25th Summer Olympic Games** in Barcelona, Spain, the U.S. finished second in medal winnings with 37 gold and 108 in all. The Unified Team, representing 12 of the former U.S.S.R. republics, was first with 45 gold and 112 in all. Among American winners were: Gail Devers, who won the gold medal in the 100-meter dash 18 months after she came near having her feet amputated as a result of radiation treatment for Graves' disease; Jackie Joyner-Kersee, who for the second time won the gold in the

1992 *PRES.* GEORGE BUSH   852

| Exploration and Settlement; Wars; Government; Civil Rights; Statistics | I | | II | Publishing; Arts and Music; Popular Entertainment; Architecture; Theater |

may control to 18 AM and 18 FM stations from the previous limit of 12 each.

Aug. 19–20 The **Republican National Convention,** meeting in Houston, Tex., nominated Pres. George Bush and Vice Pres. Dan Quayle for reelection.

Aug. 23 **James A. Baker III** resigned as secretary of state and was appointed chief of staff to Pres. Bush. In his new post Baker was to take over command of Bush's reelection campaign, which was seen as floundering.

Aug. 24 **Hurricane Andrew,** the most powerful hurricane ever to strike the continental U.S., ravaged southern Florida with winds of up to 150 mph. Although only 38 persons were killed, either directly or in the storm's aftermath, 85,000 homes were damaged or destroyed, and 250,000 persons were made homeless. Damage was estimated as high as $30,000,000,000, including the destruction of Homestead Air Force Base. Andrew struck southern Louisiana on Aug. 26, leaving at least 25,000 people homeless. More than 20,000 federal troops and National Guardsmen were called in to assist in relief efforts.

Aug. 25 In a new **sanction against Iraq,** the U.S. and its allies ordered Iraq to stop all military flights over the southern part of the country below the 32nd parallel, to prevent armed repression of large numbers of dissident Shiite Muslims. With support from France and Great Britain, allied warplanes flew their first missions over the area Aug. 28 without meeting any resistance.

Aug. 28 **Typhoon Omar** struck the U.S. territory of Guam in the Pacific with winds of 150 mph. Military installations were damaged and about 4300 of the island's 32,000 homes were destroyed or damaged. Total damage was estimated at $250,000,000.

Sept. 11 **Hurricane Iniki,** the most powerful storm to strike Hawaii in the 20th century, blasted the island of Kauai. With gusts up to 160 mph, Iniki killed two persons and injured 98, also destroying or damaging 10,000 homes on the island, which has a population of 55,000.

Sept. 24 An inquiry into the **Tailhook sexual assault scandal** at a naval aviators' convention reported that high-ranking officers had deliberately covered up the affair to avoid unfavorable publicity for the U.S. Navy. As a result, two admirals who supervised the inquiry were forced to retire and a third was reassigned. The affair took place in 1991 at a convention, in Las Vegas, Nev., of the Tailhook Association, an organization of past and present naval aviators, at which 26 women naval personnel were harassed and had clothing torn off.

Apr. 7 **Pulitzer Prizes** were awarded for the following: fiction, *A Thousand Acres* by Jane Smiley; general nonfiction, *The Prize: The Epic Quest for Oil, Money and Power* by Daniel Yergin; biography, *Fortunate Son: The Healing of a Vietnam Vet* by Lewis B. Puller, Jr.; history, *The Fate of Liberty: Abraham Lincoln and Civil Liberties* by Mark E. Neely, Jr.; poetry, *Selected Poems* by James Tate; drama, *The Kentucky Cycle* by Robert Schenkkan.

Apr. 30 *The Cosby Show,* the most popular situation comedy ever to appear on TV, presented its last weekly episode. The comedy series had begun on Sept. 20, 1984. Starring the comedian Bill Cosby as a physician with a large and active family, including a wife who was a lawyer, the program held first place in the ratings for 69 consecutive weeks.

June 1 **Tony Awards** for the 1991–1992 theater season were presented for the following: best play, *Dancing at Lughnasa* by Brian Friel; best musical, *Crazy for You* by George Gershwin, Ira Gershwin, and Ken Ludwig; best actor in a play, Judd Hirsch for *Conversations With My Father;* best actress in a play, Glenn Close for *Death and the Maiden;* best actor in a musical, Gregory Hines for *Jelly's Last Jam;* best actress in a musical, Faith Prince for *Guys and Dolls.*

June 14 **Mona Van Duyn** was appointed the **sixth poet laureate** of the U.S. She was the first woman so named.

June 28 The **Guggenheim Museum** in New York City opened a new ten-story addition and its renovated Frank Lloyd Wright original landmark building. The changes nearly tripled, to 80,000 sq. ft., the amount of exhibit space.

July 7 The **National Gallery of Art** announced that more than 2444 works of art had been promised to it in 1991 when it celebrated its 50th anniversary. The largest and most important gift to the Washington institution was the collection of Herbert and Dorothy Vogel, consisting of more than 2000 works of minimalist, conceptual, and post-1960 art.

Aug. 20 **Leonard Bernstein's personal music library** will be given to the New York Philharmonic Orchestra. The late musician, who was musical director of the orchestra from 1958 to 1969, had assembled more than 3300 scores, many of them annotated by Bernstein or other noted conductors.

Aug. 30 **Emmy Awards** were presented for the following: best drama series, *Northern Exposure;* best comedy series, *Murphy Brown;* best actor in a drama series, Christopher Lloyd for *Avonlea;* best actress in a drama series, Dana Delany for *China Beach;* best actor in a comedy series, Craig T. Nelson for *Coach;*

Business and Industry; Science; Education; Philosophy and Religion **III**	**IV** Sports; Social Issues and Crime; Folkways; Fashion; Holidays

Sept. 20 The **first space flight devoted to Japanese research** ended when the space shuttle *Endeavor* landed after an eight-day mission. Thirty-four experiments had been carried out on behalf of Japanese scientists. The flight also carried the first married couple, first black woman, and first Japanese astronaut into space.

Sept. 21 A nine-member commission to investigate future charges of **sexual abuse by Catholic priests** was appointed by Joseph Cardinal Bernadin, archbishop of the large Chicago diocese. An earlier study of 2252 priests who had served in the diocese since 1963 concluded that complaints of sexual abuse of minors against 39 priests were well-founded.

Sept. 21 The American branch of the ancient **Ethiopian Orthodox Church** declared itself independent of the mother church in Addis Ababa. Church leaders claimed that the recently appointed Patriarch Abuna Paulos was named illegally.

Sept. 25 The 5,700-pound **Mars Observer** was launched on an 11-month voyage to Mars. The first U.S. spacecraft to head for Mars in 17 years, it was intended to map the planet and explore its geological and climatological history after its arrival on Aug. 24, 1993.

Oct. 7 **Heart disease** may be promoted by oils used in the manufacture of margarine, the Department of Agriculture reported. Some vegetable oils found in margarine and other products can in the manufacturing process create, at room temperature, trans-fatty acids which act like saturated fats.

Oct. 9 A major **U.S.-Chinese trade agreement** was signed. By its terms, China would reduce barriers that hinder the importation of such U.S. produced goods as computers, cameras, and chemicals. In Aug. the U.S. had threatened to impose restrictive tariffs on many Chinese goods if such an agreement were not reached.

Oct. 9 The spacecraft *Pioneer 12* ceased operation after 14 years of service. Launched on May 30, 1978, it originally had been expected to send back data

heptathlon; Mike Conley, who set an Olympic record of 57 ft., 10.5 in. in the triple jump; and Carl Lewis, who won his eighth gold medal in three Olympics as part of the 400-meter relay team. The Americans who attracted the most attention were the members of the basketball "Dream Team," composed for the first time almost entirely of professionals from the NBA. They defeated all their opponents by an average of almost 44 points a game. They were also considered arrogant and selfish, enjoying such luxuries as chartered planes and lavish hotel rooms.

July 27 The **U.S. Women's Open golf tournament** was won by Betsy Sheehan, who defeated Juli Inkster by two strokes in an 18-hole playoff.

Aug. 2 The **Baseball Hall of Fame** inducted pitcher Tom Seaver; Rollie Fingers, pitcher; Hal Newhouser, pitcher; and Bill McGowan, umpire. Seaver, in his first year of eligibility, received the highest percentage (98.8%) of the votes ever cast for a player.

Aug. 11 Abandoning its neutral **position on abortion,** the American Bar Association voted to oppose laws that restrict women's rights in this matter. The vote in the House of Delegates was 276–168.

Aug. 16 The **PGA championship** was won by Nick Price of Zimbabwe by three strokes. It was his first major title.

Sept. 5 A **world record in the decathlon** of 8891 points was set by Dan O'Brien at a meet in Talence, France. He bettered the previous 1984 record by 44 points.

Sept. 7 **Baseball commissioner Fay Vincent resigned,** bowing to the demands of the club owners. On Sept. 3 the owners had voted, 18–9 with one abstention, to ask him to leave office. On Sept. 9 Bud Selig of the Milwaukee Brewers (AL) was chosen by the owners to be chairman of the executive council, in effect taking over from Vincent temporarily. The owners felt Vincent had been too independent and would not be firm enough in upcoming labor negotiations with the players.

Sept. 9 **Robin Yount** of the Milwaukee Brewers (AL) made his 3000th career hit, becoming the 17th player in the history of major league baseball to achieve this feat. On Oct. 1 George Brett of the Kansas City Royals (AL) joined this exclusive group.

Sept. 10 The **NFL free-agent system** was ruled illegal by a federal court jury. Under the so-called Plan B, the teams were able to prevent their best players from joining other teams for more money. Damages totalling $1,629,000 were awarded to four of the plaintiffs under the antitrust laws. The outlawed rule had meant that the best players never achieved free agency during the peaks of their careers.

Sept. 12–13 The **U.S. Open tennis championships** were won by Monica Seles in the women's division

Sept. 25 In a landmark **children's rights** case, a court in Orlando, Fla., permitted a 12-year-old boy to "divorce" his parents, ending the rights of his natural mother and permitting him to be adopted by his foster parents as he wished. It was believed to be the first time family rights were ended on the basis of a legal action brought by a child.

Oct. 5 In the first **veto override** since 1989, Congress voted to overturn Pres. Bush's veto of a bill to regulate cable TV companies. Congress had failed to override any of Bush's 35 earlier presidential vetoes. Under the new law, the Federal Communications Commission was to write guidelines by which local governments would set "reasonable" prices for cable service, an action intended to encourage competition. It would also allow over-the-air stations to seek royalties from cable companies for carrying their programs.

Oct. 14 **Alger Hiss** never spied for the Soviet Union, according to the chairman of the Russian government's military intelligence archives. He based his finding on a review of newly accessible files. Hiss, a former State Department employee, had been convicted of perjury in 1951 in connection with testimony before a federal grand jury considering spy charges leveled against him.

Oct. 24 Pres. Bush signed a new **energy bill** that promoted competition between utilities in generating power, made it easier to license nuclear power plants, and took steps to promote gasoline substitutes. However, a provision in the original bill to allow oil drilling in the Arctic National Wildlife Refuge was removed before final passage of the bill by Congress.

Oct. 30 An **Omnibus Water Bill,** authorizing diversion of some water formerly reserved for farmers in California to environmentally endangered areas, was signed by Pres. Bush. The new law would also allow farmers to sell some of the water from irrigation projects to California cities.

Nov. 2 A bill prohibiting **fishing with drift nets** was signed by Pres. Bush. The law would impose trade sanctions on any country using drift nets, as of 1993, in the North Pacific Ocean. The penalties would also apply to the North Atlantic in 1994. Japan, South Korea, and Taiwan were the chief users of the nets, which extend as much as 30 miles and which critics say kill all marine life in their path.

Nov. 3 **William Jefferson Clinton was elected president** of the United States. Sen. Al Gore, Jr., was elected vice president. Bill Clinton defeated the Republican candidate, Pres. George Bush, by 370 to 168 electoral votes. Independent candidate H. Ross

best actress in a comedy series, Candice Bergen for *Murphy Brown.*

Sept. 4 The **death of Superman,** hero of comic books and movies, was foretold by the editor of the publication in which he has appeared for many years. It was said he would fight to his death in November as he tried to save Metropolis from doomsday. However, it was hinted that Superman, as a native of the planet Krypton, might not die for good.

Sept. 5 The pop artist **Prince,** it was announced, had signed a $100,000,000 recording contract with Warner Brothers, making him the highest-paid performer in his field.

Sept. 12 A retrospective exhibit of the art of **René Magritte** opened at the Metropolitan Museum of Art, New York City. The show included about 150 works of the Belgian artist who was a leader of the surrealist movement.

Sept. 16 **The New York Philharmonic Orchestra,** founded in 1842 and the oldest orchestra in the U.S., began the observance of its 150th year with a gala benefit concert at Avery Fisher Hall, New York City. The orchestra made its debut on Dec. 7, 1842.

Sept. 24 The largest exhibit of the art of **Henri Matisse** opened at the Museum of Modern Art, New York City. It included 300 paintings, as well as drawings and sculptures, and was assembled from public collections in Russia and France and also private collectors from around the world. It was the most expensive show the museum had ever mounted, and the art shown was valued at about $1,000,000,000.

Oct. The largest exhibit of the **art of the Plains Indians** opened at the Minneapolis (Minn.) Institute of Arts. It surveyed the period from A.D. 1200 to the present, and included tepees erected on the museum's grounds. Also seen in the exhibition were painted buffalo robes, beaded and quilted mocassins, and amulets made to hold the umbilical cords of newborn children. The exhibit was to be on view later in St. Louis, Mo., and Omaha, Nebr.

Oct. 2 The **musical collection of Irving Berlin,** the late composer, will be donated by his heirs to the Library of Congress in Washington, D.C. Amounting to 750,000 items, the collection included original scores, manuscripts, scrapbooks, and other materials recording the 60-year career of Berlin.

Oct. 8 A new **postage stamp series** honoring rock-and-roll and country musicians would be issued in 1993, the U.S. Postal Service announced. Foremost among those included would be Elvis Presley. Among others would be Patsy Cline, Buddy Holly, Dinah Washington, and Hank Williams.

| Business and Industry; Science; Education; Philosophy and Religion   III | | Sports; Social Issues and Crime; Folkways; Fashion; Holidays   IV |

about Venus over a one-year period only. It had by now sent 400,000,000,000 bits of data.

Oct. 12 The **Nobel Prize in Physiology or Medicine** was shared by two scientists at the University of Washington, Edmond H. Fischer and Edwin G. Krebs. They were honored for their discovery of the way proteins are altered or switched to perform functions within cells.

Oct. 12 The most concentrated **search for life on other worlds** began when programs directed to the world's largest radio telescope in Puerto Rico and another in California were activated. The ten-year, $100,000,000 project was to search more than 10,000,000 different frequency channels for possible signals from extraterrestrials.

Oct. 13 The **Nobel Prize in Economics** was awarded to Gary S. Becker of the University of Chicago for his studies of the economic bases of decisions people make in such areas as education, family size, and crime. This was the third successive year in which a University of Chicago economist won this prize.

Oct. 14 The **Nobel Prize in Chemistry** was awarded to Rudolph A. Marcus, a Canadian-born scientist at the California Institute of Technology, for providing a mathematical explanation for puzzling chemical interactions involving the transfer of electrons between molecules.

Oct. 15 **Fuller disclosure of executives' salaries** was ordered by the Securities and Exchange Commission. Companies would have to explain how they determined the value of such pay and bonuses, and publish charts comparing the pay rates with the performance of the company's stock. The new rules followed many complaints of excessive salaries and unclear and confusing explanations.

Oct. 29 An **injectable contraceptive** that prevents pregnancy for three months was approved by the FDA. The drug contains synthetic progesterone, which inhibits ovulation. Controversy over the drug's use had gone on in the U.S. for two decades, although the drug has been available in more than 90 other countries.

and by Stefan Edberg in the men's division. Both repeated their 1991 victories.

Sept. 17 **Little League Baseball** stripped a Philippine team of the title it had won in the league's World Series on Aug. 29. The Zamboanga team was forced to forfeit its championship because in the series it had used players from other teams. Such a decision, never before made, gave the title to the team from Long Branch, Calif., which represented the U.S. and had lost the final game to Zamboanga, 15–4.

Sept. 17 Operation of the **World League of American football** was suspended by the NFL for one year after two years of play. Expansion of the NFL by two teams was also delayed until at least 1994. Both decisions were based on labor unrest, with owners and players at odds on several issues. When and if the World League resumed play it was expected that more European and fewer American teams would be involved.

Sept. 19 The **Miss America** title was won by Leanza Cornett, 21, of Jacksonville, Fla., at the annual pageant in Atlantic City, N.J.

Sept. 20 **Ray Floyd** became the first golfer to win tournaments in the same year on both the regular and the Senior PGA tour when he was the victor in a Senior tournament played in Indianapolis, Ind. He had won the Doral–Ryder tournament on the regular tour on Mar. 8.

Sept. 20 The first **unassisted triple play** in the National League in 65 years was made by Mickey Morandini, second baseman of the Philadelphia Phillies, in a game against the Pirates at Pittsburgh.

Sept. 23 In an advance for **women in professional sports,** Manon Rheaume became the first woman to play in one of the four major professional sports (baseball, football, basketball, ice hockey) when she appeared as goaltender for the Tampa Bay Lightning in an exhibition ice hockey game. She played one period, faced nine shots, and allowed two goals.

Oct. 11 LeRoy Walker became the **first black president of the U.S. Olympic Committee.** Walker had been treasurer of the U.S.O.C., head coach of the men's track and field team for the 1976 Olympics, and chancellor of North Carolina Central University.

Oct. 17–24 The **World Series** was won by the Toronto Blue Jays (AL), who defeated the Atlanta Braves (NL) four games to two. On Oct. 14 the Blue Jays had won the American League pennant, beating the Oakland Athletics four games to two, and the Braves had won the National League championship, defeating the Pittsburgh Pirates four games to three. For the first time a team located outside the U.S. won the series, although no player on the Blue Jays was a Canadian.

Nov. 1 The 23rd **New York City Marathon** was won in the men's division by Willi Mtolo of South Africa, with a time of 2 hrs., 9 min., 29 sec. The women's division

Perot received no electoral votes. The popular vote was Clinton, 43,728,375; Bush, 38,167,416; and Perot, 18,237,247. The Democrats held their 57–43 majority in the Senate. In the House the Democrats lost nine seats but retained a majority of 259–175, with one independent.

Nov. 1 An exhibition of the art of **Ellsworth Kelly,** an abstract artist of the post–World War II period, entitled "Ellsworth Kelly: The Years in France, 1948–1954," opened at the National Gallery of Art, Washington, D.C. As Kelly developed his style, he produced large paintings with much color, as seen in some of the 120 or so of his works in this exhibit.

Business and Industry; Science; Education; Philosophy and Religion	III		IV	Sports; Social Issues and Crime; Folkways; Fashion; Holidays

Oct. 30 Women need not submit to abusive husbands, a statement by the nation's Roman Catholic bishops declared. There is nothing in the Bible requiring such submission, they said, and added: "Violence in any form—physical, sexual, psychological, or verbal—is sinful."

was won by Lisa Ondieki of Australia, with a time of 2 hrs., 24 min., 40 sec., a new course record for women.

How to Use the Index

Each index entry includes a date and column number. When a subject appears more than once in the book the index supplies a date and column number for each instance.

When a text entry is dated by month and day, this information appears in the index. The citation

Abrams, Elliott, 1991 Oct. 7, I

directs the reader to the time period 1991 and the entry dated October 7 in column I.

Introductory paragraphs, which appear at the beginning of each column for every time period, are identified in the index solely by year and column number. For example,

Alaska Highway, 1992, I

means that information on Alaska Highway is to be found in the column I introductory paragraph of the time period 1992.

Undated text entries appear directly *after* the introductory paragraphs and are identified in the index by consecutive numbers in parentheses. Thus,

Actinomycin, 1940(1), III

directs the reader to the first undated entry *after* the introductory paragraph in column III of the time period 1940. Similarly, parenthetical numbers are used to identify multiple entries having the same date. The index entry

Albee, Edward, 1963 Apr. 25(1), II

directs the reader to the time period 1963 and the first entry dated April 25 in column II.

The early time periods—from the beginning through 1799—are organized in multiple-year blocks. Therefore, for the index entry

Abingdon Press, 1789(4), II

the reader, realizing there is no discrete time period for the year 1789, turns to the time period 1785-1789, then locates the fourth entry dated 1789 in column II.

INDEX

A & P *see* Great Atlantic and Pacific Tea Co.

Aaron, Hank, 1927, IV; 1974, IV; 1974 Apr. 8, IV

Aaron, Tommy, 1973 Apr. 9, IV

Aaronson, Max, 1903(3), II

Abbas, Muhammad, 1985 Oct. 7–10, I

Abbott, Berenice, 1991, II

Abbott, Bud, 1942(3), II; 1943, II; 1974, II

Abbott, George, 1955 May 5, II; 1959 Nov. 23, II; 1960 May 2, II

ABC *see* American Broadcasting Co.

Abel, I. W., 1987, III

Abel, Rudolf, 1962 Feb. 10, I

Abelman v. *Booth*, 1859, I

Abernathy, Ralph, 1968 May 2, I; 1989(1), II; 1990, III

Abilene (Kans.), 1867(10), III

Abingdon Press, 1789(4), II

Abolitionist, The (Channing), 1836(8), II

Abolition movement (*see also* Personal Liberty Laws):
  American Anti-Slavery Society formed, 1833, I
  American Slavery As It Is (Weld), 1839(1), I
  Anti-Slavery Society, 1835(2), I
  Brown activities, 1855 Sept. 5, I
  Brown's raid on Harpers Ferry, 1859 Oct. 16, I
  Channing's role, 1836(8), II
  Conn., 1784, I
  Douglass's role, 1855, IV
  Emancipator published, 1820(6), III
  first society, 1775 Apr. 14, I
  first state (Vt.), 1777 July, I
  Genius of Universal Emancipation, The (Lundy), 1821(4), II
  Lawrence (Kan.) founded, 1854 Apr. 26, I
  Liberator, The, 1831(1), I; 1831 Jan. 1, II; 1831 Jan. 1, IV
  Liberty Party, 1839 Nov. 13, I
  Lovejoy's martyrdom, 1837 Nov. 7, I
  Mass., 1783, I
  N.J., 1786(1), I
  newspaper published, 1817 Aug. 29, II
  N.Y., 1785, I
  Pa. legal action, 1780 Mar. 1, I
  petitions to Congress, 1836 May 25, I
  Philanthropist issued, 1836 Jan., II
  Phillips's "Eternal vigilance", 1852 Jan. 28, IV
  Phillips's first speech (Boston, Mass.), 1837 Dec. 8, I
  presidential election candidates, 1843 Aug. 31, I
  Quaker leadership, 1743, I
  R.I., 1784, I
  riots (Phila., Pa.), 1834 Oct., I
  Slavery tract, 1835(1), II
  Underground Railroad, 1838, I
  Whittier's writings, 1838(1), II

Abolition movement (*cont.*)
  women refused admission to London convention, 1840(3), IV

Abortion:
  ABA opposed restrictions, 1992 Aug. 11, IV
  early advertisement, 1850(1), IV
  B. Ford's views on, 1975 Aug. 10(1), IV
  legalized nationally, 1973 Jan. 22, III
  Medicaid funding not obligatory, 1977 June 20, III
  Presbyterian Church modified endorsement, 1992 June 8, III
  reduced deaths from, 1975 May 27, III
  right reaffirmed, 1986 June 11, I; 1992 June 29, I
  rights march (Wash., D.C.), 1992 Apr. 5, I
  Senate rejected amendment to curb, 1983 June 28, I
  state laws restricting, 1989 July 3, I
  state restrictions struck down, 1983 June 15, I

Abraham, F. Murray, 1985 Mar. 25, II

Abrams, Creighton W., 1968 June 10, I; 1974, I

Abrams, Elliott, 1991 Oct. 7, I

Abscam operation, 1980 Feb. 2, I

Academy Awards *see* Oscar awards

Acadians, 1755 Nov. 30, I; 1847(3), II

Accidents and disasters (*see also* specific kinds; under subject headings):
  Ashfield dam collapsed (Mass.), 1874 May 16, I
  Carnegie's hero fund, 1904 Apr. 15, III
  death rate, 1959 July 29, I
  lightning killed U.S. Open spectator, 1991 June 17, IV
  movie reportage, 1900(5), II
  nuclear weapons' plants, 1988 Sept. 30, I
  Patch's diving accident, 1829 Nov. 13, IV
  Va. Supreme Ct. building collapsed, 1870 Apr. 27, I
  worst to date, 1906, I

Acheson, Dean G., 1970 May 4, II; 1971, I

Achille Lauro hijacking, 1985 Oct. 7–10, I

ACLU *see* American Civil Liberties Union

Actinomycin, 1940(1), III

Actor's Workshop of San Francisco, 1966 Aug. 6, II

Acupuncture, 1972, III

Adair, William Penn *see* Rogers, Will

Adams, Ace, 1943(2), IV

Adams, Ansel, 1984, II

Adams, Brock, 1977, III

Adams, Charles Francis:
  presidential candidacy, 1848 Aug. 9, I

Adams, Franklin P., 1907, IV; 1945 Dec. 27, II; 1960, II

Adams, Henry, 1889(1), II; 1907(2), II; 1918(1), II; 1919 June 2, II

Adams, Herbert, 1901(3), II

Adams, John:
  born, 1735 Oct. 30, I
  Declaration of Independence, 1775–1779, I
  died, 1826 July 4, I
  elected president, 1796 Dec. 7, I
  holiday menus, 1795–1799, IV
  inaugurated, 1797 Mar. 4, I
  "Independence now ... " quote, 1826 June 30, IV
  minister to Britain, 1785 Feb. 24, I
  "Sink or swim" quote, 1826 Aug. 2, IV
  vice president, 1792 Dec. 5, I
  XYZ, 1795–1799, I

Adams, John G., 1954 Apr. 23–June 17, I

Adams, John Quincy:
  attended Boston (Mass.) swimming school, 1827 July 23, IV
  born, 1767 July 11, I
  died, 1848 Feb. 23, I
  doughface term, 1820 Apr. 12, IV
  elected president by House, 1824 Dec. 1, I; 1825 Feb. 9, I
  Florida Purchase Treaty, 1819 Feb. 22, I
  foreign relations policy, 1823 Dec. 2, I
  House gag rule lifted, 1844 Dec. 3, I
  inaugurated president, 1825 Mar. 4, I
  political views, 1828(2), I
  returned to Congress, 1831 Mar. 4, I
  slave ship mutiny, 1839, I
  Tariff of Abominations, 1828, I

Adams, Lee, 1960 Apr. 14, II; 1970 Mar. 30, II

Adams, Leonie, 1988, II

Adams, Richard, 1974(1), II

Adams, Sherman, 1958 June 17, I; 1958 Sept. 22(2), I

Adams mansion (Quincy, Mass.), 1732(3), II

Adamson Eight-Hour Act, 1916 Sept. 3, III

Addabbo, Joseph P., 1986, I

Addams, Charles, 1988, II

Addams, Jane, 1889(1), III; 1931 Dec. 10, I

Adderley, Cannonball (Julian E.), 1975, II

Adelman, Kenneth, 1983 Jan. 12, I

Adjani, Isabelle, 1975 Dec. 30, II

Adler, Dankmar, 1898(4), II

Adler, Felix, 1876(4), III

Adler Planetarium (Chicago, Ill.), 1930 May 11, III

Adolphe, Mme., 1819 June 1, IV

Adultery:
  Carter "in heart" remark, 1976 Sept. 20, I
  colonial divorce grounds, 1660(1), IV
  colonial punishments, 1639(3), IV
  scarlet letter discontinued, 1782(2), IV

Adventist movement *see* Seventh Day Adventists
Advertising:
    on book matches, 1896(5), III
    cigarette on radio-TV banned, 1970 Apr. 1, III
    claim substantiation required, 1971 June 10, III
    electric signs shut off, 1917 Nov. 18, IV
    equal political time overruled, 1973 May 26, II
    first agencies, 1864(2), III
    first exhibition (Phila., Pa.), 1728 Aug.1–8, II
    largest agency in world formed, 1986 Apr. 27, III
    of legal fees upheld, 1977 June 27, III
    missing persons, 1809 Oct. 31, IV
    nudity used, 1962 Jan., IV
    sky introduced, 1908(5), III
AEC *see* Atomic Energy Commission
Affirmative action *see* Equal employment opportunity; Reverse discrimination
Afghanistan:
    Soviet invasion, 1980, I; 1980, IV; 1980 Jan. 4, I; 1982, I
    Soviet troop withdrawal, 1988 Apr. 14, I
    U.S. ambassador kidnaped, 1979 Feb. 14, I
    U.S. arms aid ended, 1991 Sept. 13, I
    U.S. military aid, 1987, I
AFL-CIO *see* American Federation of Labor—Congress of Industrial Organizations
African Methodist Episcopal Church, 1816, III
Agassi, Andre, 1992 July 5, IV
Agassiz, Louis:
    Brazil expedition, 1865(8), III
    rejected Darwinism, 1860(2), III
Aged *see* Gray Panthers; Medicare; Nursing homes; Older people; Pensions
Agee, James, 1951(1), II; 1957(1), II; 1958 May 5, II; 1960 Nov. 30, II; 1961 Nov. 30, II
Agent Orange, 1984 May 7, I; 1991 Feb. 6, I
Age of Reason, The (Paine), 1794(6), II
Agnew, Spiro T.:
    corruption scandal, 1973, I
    disbarred, 1974 May 2, I
    "effete snobs" statement, 1969 Oct. 15, I
    elected vice president, 1968 Nov. 5, I
    inaugurated vice president, 1969 Jan. 20(1), I; 1973 Jan. 20, I
    reelected vice president, 1972 Nov. 7, I
    resigned vice presidency, 1973 Oct. 10, I
    vice presidential candidacy, 1968 Aug. 8, I; 1972 Aug. 21–23, I
Agramonte, Aristides, 1901(1), III
Agrarian Justice (Paine), 1797(1), II
Agricultural Acts, 1933 May 12(1), I; 1938 Feb. 16, I; 1964 Apr. 11, III; 1964 July 9, III

Agricultural Marketing Act, 1929 June 15, I
Agriculture, Department of:
    Butz resigned, 1976 Oct. 4, I
    Cabinet status, 1889 Feb. 11, I
    established, 1862(5), III
Agriculture and agricultural products (*see also* Bimetalism; Diet and nutrition; Drought; Livestock; Pests and pesticides; crop names; farm and farmer headings; types of farm machinery):
    cold spell crop destruction, 1910 Apr. 23, III
    costliest bill to date, 1985 Dec. 23, III
    county fairs, 1810 Oct. 1, IV
    crop controls bill, 1962 Sept. 27, III
    crop diversification, 1880(5), III
    crop yield highest to date, 1956, III
    early scientific approach to, 1748, II
    exports, 1891, III
    Farmer's Alliance, 1873(1), I
    Farmer's Almanac first published (Mass.), 1792, IV
    farmers' rally (Wash., D.C.), 1978 Mar. 15, III
    farmland value dropped, 1984, III
    Farm Mortgage Refinancing Act, 1934 Jan. 31, I
    Farm Security Administration established, 1937 July 22(2), I
    Federal Farm Bankruptcy Act, 1934 June 28(1), I
    Federal Farm Board powers, 1929 June 15, I
    financial plight, 1987, I
    first binder, 1850(3), III
    first fair (Wash., D.C.), 1804(2), IV
    first genetically altered plant tested, 1986 May 30, III
    first Grange, 1867, III
    first magazine, 1810 July, III
    first plow patent, 1797 June 26, III
    first successful journal, 1819 Apr. 2, III
    labor-saving devices, 1831, III
    land-bank system established, 1916 July 17, III
    land-grant college experiment stations, 1887 Mar. 2, II
    National Farmers' Alliance, 1880 Apr., I
    New-Old World exchange, 1550–1600, III
    plow patents, 1813, III
    popular colonial book on, 1710, II
    Populist Party, 1891 May 19, I
    price support, 1933 Jan. 5, III
    record crop yield, 1957, III
    Rochester (N.Y.) fair, 1868 Oct. 1(1), IV
    self-propelled combine introduced, 1938(5), III
    Soil Conservation Act, 1935 Apr. 27, I
    Southern Tenant Farmers' Union, 1934 July 1, I
    surplus, 1954, III
    tying device to bind grain sheaves, 1859(4), III
    western farm workers' accord, 1977 Mar. 10, III

Aguinaldo, Emilio, 1899 Feb. 4, I; 1899 Mar. 30, I; 1901 Mar. 23, I
Ahern, Kathy, 1972 June 11, IV
Ahlstrom, Stanley E., 1973 Apr. 10, II
AIDS (acquired immune deficiency syndrome):
    Ashe infected, 1992 Apr. 8, IV
    beneficial drug, 1988 May 13, III; 1989 June, III
    cases, 1986, III; 1989 June, III
    condom protection, 1987 Dec. 10, III
    death rate, 1986 June 12, III; 1988 May 13, III; 1991 Jan. 25, III
    discoverer of virus dispute, 1991 May 6(1), II
    epidemic spreading, 1990 June 30, III
    first beneficial drug, 1987 Mar. 20, III
    fund appropriations, 1987, III; 1988 May 13, III
    Magic Johnson infected, 1991 Nov. 7, IV
    virus identified, 1984 Apr. 23, III
Aid to the Arts Act, 1965 Sept. 30, II
Aiken, Conrad, 1927(1), II; 1929(1), II; 1930 May 12, II; 1954 Jan. 26, II; 1973, II
Aiken, George D., 1984, I
Aiken, George L., 1852, II
Aiken, John W., 1932 Apr. 30-May 2, I; 1936 Apr. 25–28, I; 1936 Nov. 3, I; 1940 Apr. 28, I; 1940 Nov. 5, I
Ailey, Alvin, 1976 May 11, II; 1989, II
Ainsworth, Henry, 1620(1), II
Air conditioning:
    early attempt (Tex.), 1929 July, II
    first theater, 1848 June 27, III
Air Corps *see* Armed forces
Air Force Academy, U.S. *see* United States Air Force Academy
Airplanes and airlines *see* Aviation; Aviation accidents; specific airline names
Airports:
    Dallas-Fort Worth (Tex.), 1973 Sept. 22, III
    first municipal (Tucson, Ariz.), 1919 Nov. 20, III
    Idlewild International (N.Y.C.) dedicated, 1948 July 31, III
    Kansas City (Mo.) dedicated, 1972 Oct. 21, III
    LaGuardia bombing (N.Y.C.), 1975 Dec. 29, I
    Trans World Airlines terminal (Idlewild, N.Y.) opened, 1962 May 28, II
Air Quality Control Act, 1970 Dec. 31, III
Airships:
    Dirigible ZR-3 flight, 1924 Oct. 15, III
    Hindenburg disaster (N.J.), 1937 May 6, I
    Hindenburg landed (N.J.), 1936 May 9, III
Aisne-Marne offensive, 1918 July 18-Aug. 6, I
Aix-la-Chapelle, Treaty of, 1745–1749, I
Akin, Susan, 1985 Sept. 14, IV
Akins, Zöe, 1916 Mar. 20, II; 1935 Jan. 7(1), II; 1935 May 6, II

Alabama:
    civil rights movement, 1965 Mar. 21,
        I; 1965 Mar. 25, I
    congressional representation
        regranted, 1868 June 25(2), I
    first black sheriff since
        Reconstruction, 1967 Jan. 16, I
    German settlers, 1722 June 4, I
    National Guard federalized, 1963
        Sept. 10, III
    seceded, 1861 Jan. 11, I
    statehood, 1819 Dec. 14, I
    Territory formed, 1817 Mar. 3(1), I
Alabama, University of:
    campus violence in wake of first black
        student, 1956 Feb. 6, III
    desegregated, 1963 June 11, III
Alabama letters (Clay), 1844 July 1–27, I
Alabama (ship), 1864 June 19, I; 1871 May
    8, I
Alamo, The (Tex.):
    built, 1722(2), II
    captured, 1836 Mar. 6, I
    slogan, 1836(3), IV
Alaska:
    earthquake, 1964 Mar. 27, I
    first major gold strike, 1880(6), III
    first settlement, 1811, IV
    Nome founded, 1898(2), III
    oil pipeline plans approved, 1973 Nov.
        13, II
    oil spill, 1989 Mar. 24, I
    purchased, 1867, I
    Russian Orthodox Church influence
        ended, 1872(1), III
    Russian Orthodox Church mission,
        1792(1), III
    "Seward's folly" phrase, 1867(1), IV
    statehood, 1958 June 30, I; 1958 July
        7, I; 1959 Jan. 3, I
    trans-pipeline into operation, 1977
        July 28, III
Alaska, University of, 1917(2), III
Alaska Highway, 1992, I
Albam, Jacob, 1957 Oct. 8, I
Albany Congress, 1750–1754, I
Albany (N.Y.):
    British takeover, 1664 Sept. 7, I
Albee, Edward, 1962 Oct. 13, II; 1963
    Apr. 25(1), II; 1965 June 13, II; 1967
    May 1, II; 1975 May 5, II
Albee, Harriet Ryan, 1857 May, III
Albee, William, 1963 May 6, II
Albert, Heinrich F., 1915 July 15, I
Albert Medal (G.B.), 1884 June, III
Albertson, Jack, 1969 Apr. 14, II
Albig, William, 1939(2), II
Albright, Jacob, 1803(2), III
Albright, Tenley, 1952 Mar. 28, IV; 1954
    Mar. 19, IV; 1955 Feb. 16–17, IV; 1955
    Apr. 1–2, IV; 1956 Jan. 26–Feb. 5, IV;
    1956 Mar. 16, IV
Alcatraz Island (San Francisco), 1971 June
    11, I
Alcindor, Lew, 1967 Mar. 25, IV; 1969
    Mar. 22, IV
Alcoa Building (Pittsburgh, Pa.), 1952(4), II

Alcohol and alcoholism (*see also* Bars,
    saloons, and taverns; Beer; Prohibition
    and temperance movement; Prohibition
    Party; Rum; Whiskey Rebellion; Wine):
    colonial abuse, 1728(4), IV; 1741(2), IV
    colonial favorites, 1710–1714, IV
    colonial prohibitions (Mass.),
        1630–1639, IV; 1633, IV
    early reform societies, 1840, IV
    first cocktail (N.Y.C.), 1776(1), IV
    first excise tax (Pa.), 1684, III
    leading abused drug, 1976 July 9, III
    legal drinking age raised, 1984 July
        17, I
    Mass. state excise, 1782(1), IV
    percentage of drinkers, 1954, IV
    percentage of drinkers declined, 1990,
        IV
    Rush's studies, 1780–1784, III
    Whiskey Ring scandal, 1875, I
    Whiskey Trust, 1886(4), III; 1887, III
Alcoholics Anonymous, 1935 June 10, III
Alcott, Amy, 1980 July 13, IV
Alcott, Louisa May:
    Little Women, 1868, II
Alcott, William A., 1832(2), IV; 1836(5), IV;
    1856(5), IV
Alden, John, 1620–1629, II
Aldrich, Henry (fictional character), 1938
    Apr. 13, II
Aldrich, Nelson, 1909, I
Aldrich, Thomas Bailey, 1870(1), II;
    1873(1), II
Aldrich-Vreeland Act, 1907, III
Aldrin, Edwin E., Jr., 1966 Nov. 11(1), III;
    1969 July 16, III
Aleutian Islands, 1943 May 30, I; 1943
    Aug. 15, I
Alex, Janet, 1982 July 25, IV
Alexander, Grover Cleveland, 1916, IV;
    1938 Jan. 18, IV
Alexander, Jane, 1968 Oct. 3, II
Alexander, Jason, 1989 June 4(1), II
Alexander, Leslie, 1986 Aug. 2, III
Alexander's (dept. store), 1992 Jan. 6, III
Alger, Horatio, Jr., 1867, II; 1889 Feb. 2, II
Algeria:
    U.S. war against, 1815 Mar. 3, I; 1815
        June 17, I; 1815 June 30, I
Algren, Nelson, 1949(1), II; 1950 Mar. 16,
    II; 1981, II
Ali, Muhammad (Cassius Clay):
    attempt to regain title, 1980, IV
    barred from competition, 1968, IV
    boxing championship, 1966, IV
    defended title, 1977, IV
    draft avoidance, 1967, IV; 1967 June
        20, IV
    draft evasion conviction overturned,
        1971 June 28, IV
    regained world heavyweight
        championship, 1974 Oct. 30, IV
    retired, 1979, IV
    third title regain, 1978 Sept. 15, IV
    thriller in Manila, 1975 Oct. 1, IV
    title bouts, 1962, IV; 1964, IV; 1964
        Feb. 25, IV; 1965, IV; 1965 May 25,
        IV; 1965 Nov. 22, IV; 1970, IV;
        1971 Mar. 8, IV; 1976, IV

Alien and Sedition Acts, 1798 June 18, I;
    1798 June 25, I; 1798 July 6, I; 1798 July
    14, I
Alien Registration Act, 1940 June 28, I
Aliens *see* Citizenship; Immigration
Aliluyeva, Svetlana, 1967 Apr. 21(1), I
Alimony *see* Divorce; Palimony
Alinsky, Saul, 1972, III
Allegheny College (Pa.), 1815(5), III
Allemagne, De l' (Staël, de), 1814(3), III
Allen, Ethan, 1775 May 10(1), I; 1775
    Sept. 25, I; 1876 Feb. 28, II
Allen, George, 1990, IV
Allen, Gracie, 1964, II
Allen, Hervey, 1933(1), II
Allen, Joan, 1988 June 5, II
Allen, Joseph, 1984 Nov. 12, III
Allen, Peter, 1992, II
Allen, Richard V., 1982 Jan. 4, I
Allen, Scott, 1964 Jan. 11–12, IV; 1966 Jan.
    29, IV
Allen, Tom, 1869, IV; 1873 Sept. 23, IV
Allende Gossens, Salvador, 1972 Mar.
    20–21, III; 1973 Apr. 2, III; 1975 Dec. 4,
    I
Alley, Kirstie, 1991 Aug. 5, II
Alliance for Progress, 1961 May 27, I
Allison, Michael, 1800(3), IV
Allison, Wilmer, 1929 July 5, IV; 1930 July
    4, IV; 1935 Sept. 11, IV
Allman, Duane, 1971, II
Allston, Washington, 1804, II; 1813(2), II;
    1819(2), II
Almanacs:
    Ame's *Astronomical Diary*, 1725(1), II
    Farmer's first published (Mass.), 1792,
        IV
    first, 1638(3), II
    Poor Richard's (Franklin), 1732 Dec.
        19, II
    popularity, 1690–1699, II
    World Almanac, The, 1868(2), II
Aloha Airlines, 1988 Apr. 28, I
Alpert, Herb, 1966 Mar. 15(2), II
Alphadelphia Phalanx (Mich.), 1844(1), III
Alsop, George, 1666, II
Alsop, Joseph, Jr., 1989, II
Alston, Walter, 1984, IV
Altgeld, John Peter, 1886, I; 1894 July 3,
    III
Altman, Benjamin, 1865(10), III
Altman, Sidney, 1989 Oct. 12(1), III
Aluminum:
    cheap method to extract, 1886(1), III
    price increase, 1965 Nov. 10, III
Alvarez, Luis W., 1968 Oct. 30(2), III;
    1988, III
Amateur Athletes, of America, Assn. of
    Intercollegiate (ICAAAA), 1876(6), IV
Amateur Athletic Union (AAU), 1888 Jan.
    21, IV
Amchitka (Ala.):
    nuclear tests, 1971 Nov. 6, III
Ameche, Alan, 1988, IV
Ameche, Don, 1986 Mar. 24, II
American Academy and Institute of Arts
    and Letters:
    Rogers endowment, 1978 May 1(2), II
    Tuchman first woman president, 1979
        Feb. 27, II

American Academy of Arts, 1802(1), II
American Academy of Arts and Letters, 1904(7), II; 1908(6), II; 1938(4), II
American Academy of Arts and Sciences, 1780–1784, II
   first woman inducted, 1847 Oct., IV
American Academy of Political and Social Science, 1889 Dec. 14, III
American Airlines:
   merged, 1962 Jan. 23, III
American Antiquarian Society, 1812(4), IV
American Art Union, 1848(1), II
American Association for the Advancement of Science, 1848 Sept., III
American Ballet Theater, 1980, II; 1987, II
   dancers' lockout, 1982, II
   50th anniversary, 1990, II
American Bar Association (ABA):
   formed, 1878, III
   opposed restrictive abortion laws, 1992 Aug. 11, IV
American Book Awards, 1980 May 1, II; 1981 Apr. 30, II; 1982 Apr. 27, II; 1983 Apr. 24, II; 1984 Nov. 16, II; 1985 Jan 21, II; 1986 Nov. 17, II
American Broadcasting Co. (ABC):
   bought, 1985 Mar. 18, III
   ITT merger, 1965 Dec. 7, III
American Chemical Society, 1876(1), III
American Civil Liberties Union, 1991 Jan. 27, I
American Dance Festival (N.C.), 1977 Sept. 21, II
American Dialect Society, 1889 Dec. 14, III
American Dictionary of the English Language (Webster), 1828(2), II
American Economic Association, 1885(1), III
American Federation of Labor:
   five-day week, six-hour day sanctioned, 1933 Oct. 2, III
   formed, 1886, III
   German-made products boycotted, 1933 Oct. 13, III
   Gompers died, 1924 Dec. 13, III
   Gompers elected president, 1921 June 25, III
   Green bid for CIO return, 1938 Oct. 13, III
   Green elected president, 1925(3), III
   growth, 1894 Aug. 3, III
   Longshoremen expelled, 1953 Sept. 22, III
   Meany appointed president, 1952 Nov. 25, III
   membership, 1933, III
   membership decline, 1925, III
   Mine Workers petitioned to join, 1943 May 19, III
   no-strike agreement, 1941 July 24, III; 1941 Dec. 15, III; 1942 Mar. 17, III
   UMW readmittance, 1946 Jan. 25, III
   UMW reaffiliation bid refused, 1949 May 20, III
   Wallace presidential candidacy, 1948 Feb. 2, III
American Federation of Labor-Congress of Industrial Organizations (AFL-CIO):
   against socialism, 1894(2), III

American Federation of Labor-Congress of Industrial Organizations (AFL-CIO) (*cont.*)
      denounced noninflationary wage guidelines, 1964 May 19, III
      endorsed Kennedy presidential candidacy, 1960 Aug. 26, I
      Longshoremen readmitted, 1959 Sept. 22, III
      Meany retired, 1979 Nov. 15, III
      merged, 1955, III; 1955 Feb. 9, III; 1955 Dec. 5, III
      predicted recession, 1960 Feb. 8–16, III
      Reuther resigned, 1967 Feb. 3, III
      Teamsters expelled, 1957 Sept. 18, III
      UAW formally separated, 1968 July 1, III
      UAW suspended, 1968 May 16, III
American Fine Arts Society, 1892(4), II
American Folklore Society, 1888(1), III
American Forestry Association, 1882(5), III
American Historical Association, 1884, III
American Home Missionary Society, 1826(2), III
American Horologe Company, 1849(1), III
American Humane Association, 1877 Oct., III
American Indian Movement (AIM), 1978 July 15, I
American Institute of Electrical Engineers, 1884(2), III
American Labor Party:
   endorsed Democratic ticket, 1936 June 23–27, I
American Law Journal, 1808(1), III
American Legion (*see also* Legionnaire's disease):
   formed, 1919 Mar. 15, I
American Library Association, 1876 Oct. 6, III
American Magazine, The, 1757 Oct., II
American Mathematical Society, 1888(1), III
American Medical Association (AMA):
   antitrust violation, 1943 Jan. 18, III
   organized, 1847 May 7, III
   scored by Carter, 1978 May 5, III
   terminal patients' treatment policy, 1986 Mar. 15, III
American National Opera Co., 1967 Feb. 15, II
American Newspaper Guild, 1933(3), II
American Osteopathic Association, 1897(3), III
American Party *see* Know-Nothing Party
American Peace Society:
   on Civil War, 1860 May 28, III
American Philosophical Society, 1725–1729, IV; 1740–1744, III
American Physical Assn., 1889 Dec. 14, III
American Poetry Review (publication), 1977 Jan. 31, II
American Protective Association, 1887 Mar. 3, I
American Psychiatric Association, 1844(2), III
American Psychological Association, 1892(7), III
American Quarterly Review, 1827(2), II

American Railway Union, 1894 June 26, III; 1894 July 2, III; 1894 July 3, III; 1894 July 10, III; 1894 Aug. 3, III
American Republican Party *see* Know-Nothing Party
American Revolution *see* Revolutionary War
American Revolution, Daughters of the (DAR):
   founded, 1881, IV
American Revolution, Sons of the, 1881, IV; 1889(4), IV
American School of Classical Studies (Athens, Greece), 1882(3), III
American Shooter's Manual (publication), 1827(2), IV
American Society of Civil Engineers, 1852 Nov. 5, III
American Society of Composers, Authors and Publishers *see* ASCAP
American Speller, The (Webster), 1783, II
American States, International Conference of, 1889 Oct. 2, I
American Sugar Refining Co., 1891(1), III
American Symphony Orchestra League, 1969 Nov. 25, II
American Telephone and Telegraph Co. (AT&T):
   acquired NCR Corp., 1991 May 6(2), III
   affirmative action program, 1973 Jan. 18, III
   antitrust suit, 1949 Jan. 14, III
   divestiture, 1982 Jan. 8, III
   first corporation with over 1,000,000 stockholders, 1951 May 15, III
   rate decrease order, 1967 July 5, III
American Tobacco Co., 1890(8), III; 1904 Oct. 19, III; 1911 May 29, III
American Tract Society, 1817, III
American Trotting Association, 1887 Mar. 2, IV
America's Cup, 1851, IV; 1857(6), IV; 1870, IV; 1876 Aug. 11–12, IV; 1881 Nov. 9–10, IV; 1885 Sept. 14–16, IV; 1886 Sept. 9–11, IV; 1887 Sept. 17–30, IV; 1893 Oct. 7–13, IV; 1895 Sept. 7–12, IV; 1899 Oct. 16–20, IV; 1901 Sept. 28-Oct. 4, IV; 1903 Aug. 22-Sept. 3, IV; 1930 Sept. 13–17, IV; 1934 Sept. 17–25, IV; 1937 July 31-Aug. 5, IV; 1958, IV; 1958 Sept. 20–27, IV; 1962 Sept. 15–25, IV; 1964 Sept. 15–21, IV; 1967 Sept. 12–18, IV; 1970 Sept. 15–28, IV; 1974 Sept. 10–17, IV; 1977 Sept. 13–18, IV; 1980 Sept. 16–25, IV; 1983 Sept. 14–26, IV; 1987 Jan. 31–Feb. 4, IV; 1988 Sept. 9, IV; 1992 May 9–16, IV
"America" (song), 1831, II
America (term), 1507, IV
Ames, Nathaniel, 1725(1), II
Ames, Oakes, 1867(1), III; 1867(2), I; 1872(1), I
Amherst College (Mass.):
   chartered, 1825 Feb. 21, III
   hazing condemned, 1868(6), IV
Ammons, A. R., 1973 Apr. 10, II; 1982 Jan. 28, II
Amoros, Sandy, 1992, IV

Amtrak (National Railroad Passenger Corporation), 1971 May 1, III
    worst accident to date, 1987 Jan. 4, I
Amusement parks:
    Coney Island (N.Y.), 1881(3), IV
    first Ferris wheel, 1892(3), IV
    Palisades (N.J.), 1898, IV
    roller coaster centennial, 1984, IV
Anarchism:
    "equity" store (Warren), 1827 May, III
    Haymarket Riot (Chicago, Ill.), 1886, I
Anastasia, Umberto, 1957 Oct. 25, IV
Anders, William, 1968 Dec. 21–27, III
Andersen, Hans Christian, 1848(9), II
Anderson, Carl David, 1936 Nov. 12, III; 1991, III
Anderson, Jack, 1972 Mar. 20–21, III
Anderson, John:
    lost presidential bid, 1980 Nov. 4, I
Anderson, Jon, 1973 Apr. 17, IV
Anderson, Joshua R., 1831 Oct. 13, II
Anderson, Judith, 1948 Mar. 28, II; 1955 Mar. 7, II; 1961 May 16, II; 1992, II
Anderson, Malcolm, 1957 Sept. 8, IV
Anderson, Marian, 1963 Dec. 12, II; 1978 Oct. 17, II
Anderson, Maxwell, 1924 Sept. 5, II; 1933 May 4, II; 1935 Sept. 25, II; 1936 Dec. 30, II; 1939 Nov. 27, II; 1942 Oct. 7, II; 1946 Nov. 18, II; 1954 Dec. 8, II
Anderson, Philip W., 1977 Oct. 11, III
Anderson, Robert, 1953 Sept. 30, II
Anderson, Robert (Major), 1861 Apr. 11, I
Anderson, Sherwood, 1919(1), II; 1932(1), II; 1933(1), II; 1941 Mar. 8, II
Anderson, Terry A., 1988 Feb. 17, I; 1991 Aug. 8–Dec. 4, I
Anderson, Willie, 1903 June 27, IV; 1904 July 9, IV; 1905 Sept. 22, IV
Andover Controversy, 1886(2), III
André, John, 1780 Oct. 2, I
Andretti, Mario, 1981 May 24, IV
Andretti, Michael, 1987 Aug. 2, IV
Andrews, Julie, 1965 Apr. 5, II
Andrews, Leonard E. B., 1986 Aug. 9, II
Androboros (play), 1714, II; 1725–1729, II
Andros, Edmund (Sir), 1687, I; 1687 Mar.22, III; 1689(2), I
Anemia, 1926(1), III; 1948(2), III
Anesthesia:
    chloroform, 1831(2), III
    development in U.S., 1842, III
    first public demonstration, 1846 Oct. 16, III
Anfinsen, Christian B., 1972 Oct. 20(2), III
Anglican Church (*see also* Episcopal Church):
    foothold in colonies, 1700–1704, III
    founded in Mass., 1686 May 15, III; 1687 Mar.22, III
    King's Chapel organ (Boston, Mass.), 1713, II
    Md., 1692(2), I; 1702, I
    New England, 1722 Oct. 23, III
    N.C., 1701(1), I; 1705(1), I; 1715, I; 1765, I
    Trinity Church (Boston, Mass.) established, 1729(1), III
    Va., 1620–1629, III

Angola:
    U.S. covert aid cut, 1975 Dec. 19, I
    U.S. support of Savimbi, 1986, I
Animal Industry, Bureau of (U.S.), 1884 May 29, III
Animals (*see also* Endangered and extinct species; Hunting and trapping; Wildlife; Zoos; specific types):
    American Humane Association formed, 1877 Oct., III
    baboon heart transplant, 1984 Oct. 16, III
    welfare promoted, 1866, III
Annapolis (Md.) (*see also* Naval Academy, U.S.):, 1781, IV
Annenberg, Walter, 1990 Mar. 3, III; 1991 Mar. 11, II
Annuals, 1826(3), II
Antarctica *see* Arctic and Antarctica
Antheil, George, 1927 Apr. 10, II; 1949(2), II; 1953 Jan. 9, II; 1955 Apr. 2, II
Anthony, Susan B.:
    failed voting attempt, 1872(2), I
    founded newspaper, 1868(2), I
    National Woman Suffrage Association, 1869 May 15, I
    Seneca Falls (N.Y.) convention, 1848 July 19–20, I
Anthropology:
    Boas's contribution, 1928, III
Antiballistic missile (ABM):
    appropriations, 1969 Nov. 6, I
    funds requested, 1969 Mar. 14, I
Antibiotics *see* Drugs and drug products; specific names
Antibodies, 1972 Oct. 12, III
Antietam, Battle of (Md.), 1862 Sept. 17, I
Antigens, 1980 Oct. 10, III
Antihistamines, 1950(1), III
Anti-Inflation Act, 1948 Aug. 16, III
Anti-Masonic Party, 1826(1), I; 1830 Sept., I; 1831 Sept. 26, I; 1834, I; 1835 Dec. 16, I
Anti-Monopoly Party, 1884 May 14, I
Antioch College (Ohio), 1853 Sept., III
Antiproton, 1959 Oct. 26, III
Antirent War (N.Y.S.), 1839(2), I
Anti-Saloon Republicans, 1886 Sept. 16, I
Antitrust *see* Trusts and antitrust
Apache Indians, 1886 Sept. 4, I
Apollo Project:
    Apollo 6, 1968 Apr. 4, III
    Apollo 8 launched, 1968 Dec. 21–27, III
    Earth orbit, 1967 Nov. 9, III; 1968 Jan. 22, III
    first manned landing, 1969 July 16, III
    first manned mission, 1968 Oct. 11, III
    first manned mission to moon, 1969 May 18, III
    first stage test, 1965 Apr. 16, III
    fourteen launched, 1971 Jan. 31, III; 1971 July 26, III
    joint Soyuz mission, 1975 July 15, III
    launch pad fire, 1967, III; 1967 Jan. 27, III
    lunar module test, 1969 Mar. 3, III
    manned moon flights, 1969, III
    near-disaster, 1970 Apr. 11, III

Apollo Project (*cont.*)
    seventeen landing, 1972 Dec. 7, III
    sixteen moon landing, 1972 Apr. 16, III
    twelve, power loss, 1969 Nov. 14, III
Apparel *see* Clothing and fashion
Appel, Karel, 1960 Oct. 31, II
Appleby, John Francis, 1859(4), III
Appleseed, Johnny, 1800, IV
Appling, Luke, 1991, IV
AP poll *see* under Football
Aquariums, 1896(1), III
Aqueducts *see* Water supply
Arab League:
    Gulf War, 1990 Aug. 2–Dec. 31, I
Arabs *see* Israeli-Arab conflict
Arbor Day, 1872 Apr. 10, IV; 1909 Mar. 7, IV
Arcaro, Eddie, 1962 Apr. 3, IV
Archeology (*see also* Fossils):
    human skulls with brains intact (Fla.), 1984 Dec. 11–12, III
    methanogens life form identified, 1977 Nov. 2, III
    Native American catacombs found (Ariz.), 1991 Apr. 26, III
    painting of first complete skeleton of American mastodon, 1806(3), II
Archer, George, 1969 Apr. 13, IV
Archery, 1828(3), IV
Architecture (*see also* Brunner Award; Building materials; Buildings; Housing; Mansions and manor homes; Religion and churches; Skyscrapers; names of specific architects and edifices):
    Adam style, 1796(5), II
    AIA Gold Medal, 1907(7), II; 1909(6), II; 1958 May 17, II; 1960 Mar. 27, II; 1962 Feb. 24, II; 1971(2), II; 1981 Dec. 5, II; 1982 Dec. 2, II
    Bayard Building (N.Y.C.), 1898(4), II
    Boston Custom House, 1857(4), II
    Breuer's works, 1951(5), II; 1966 Sept. 28, II
    cast-iron buildings (N.Y.C.), 1848, II
    Chicago Art Institute addition, 1988 Sept. 17(1), II
    Classic Revival, 1794(2), II; 1805, II; 1812(3), II
    Crystal Palace, 1853(2), II
    Damon's style, 1824(2), II
    deaths, 1990, II
    Dutch gambrel roof, 1704, II
    early building materials, 1600–1609, II
    example of Federal (Waltham, Mass.), 1805(4), II
    first Classic Revival style (Va.), 1789(3), II
    first course in, 1866(3), II
    first cruciform church (Va.), 1710, II
    first Gropius and Breuer work in U.S., 1938(5), II
    first hipped roof (Md.), 1680, II
    first independent Wright commission, 1893(7), II
    first postwar design competition, 1948(6), II
    French-inspired (Vassar College), 1865(12), II

Architecture (*cont.*)

Gateway Arch (St. Louis, Mo.), 1965 Oct. 28, II

Georgian, 1720–1724, II; 1730(3), II

Gothic Revival, 1835(7), II; 1839, II; 1839(5), II; 1846(4), II; 1848(10), II

Greek Revival, 1799(4), II; 1802(2), II; 1819(1), II; 1819(4), II; 1830(7), II; 1831 Dec. 26, II; 1834(3), II; 1835(8), II; 1836(4), II; 1841(6), II; 1844(6), II

industrial (Mass.), 1846(3), II

innovations, 1952, II

Italian Gothic Revival, 1869(2), II

jerkin-head roof, 1693, II

John Hancock Building (Chicago, Ill.), 1968, II

Latrobe's contribution, 1805, II

McKim's works, 1888(4), II

Mies's designs, 1950(4), II; 1951(8), II

National Institute of Arts and Letters Gold Medal, 1953 May 27, II

new buildings, 1988, II

notable buildings, 1918(6), II

Octagon style, 1848(7), II

Pan Am Building controversy (N.Y.C.), 1963 Mar. 7, II

people-oriented, 1940, II

pre-Greek Revival (N.Y.C.), 1820(2), II

preservation and restoration, 1981, II

Rationalism style, 1812(5), II

Richardson's influence on commercial, 1885(2), II

Richardson's work, 1881(2), II

Rockefeller Plaza West (N.Y.C.), 1989, II

Romanesque Revival, 1891(3), II

school buildings, 1951, II

Seagram Building (N.Y.C.), 1957, II

shingled houses, 1880(3), II

steel and glass use, 1966, II

Sullivan's works, 1890(4), II

trends, postwar, 1946, II

Union Station (Wash., D.C.) renovation, 1988 Sept. 29, II

UN Secretariat design, 1950(5), II

Victorian Gothic, 1872(5), II

White's murder, 1906, IV

Wright's house, 1951(4), II

Wright's works, 1892(7), II; 1893(7), II; 1903(5), II; 1904(2), II; 1907(8), II; 1956, II; 1959 Oct. 21(2), II

Arctic and Antarctica:

Cook-Peary dispute on reaching N. Pole first, 1909 Sept. 1, I

first atomic power plant, 1962 Mar. 4, III

first discovery, 1820(3), I

first flight over S. Pole, 1929 Nov. 29, III

first successful flight over N. Pole, 1926 May 9, III

first successful parachute jump, 1956 Nov. 25, III

first underwater crossing of N. Pole, 1958 Aug. 5, I

Grinnell expedition to rescue Franklin, 1850 May 22, I

North Pole expedition, 1986 May 2, IV

Arctic and Antarctica (*cont.*)

Peary reached N. Pole, 1909 Apr. 6, I; 1989 Dec. 11, III

second Arctic expedition, 1853 May 31, I

Wickes's exploration, 1838 May 18, I

Wilkes's expedition, 1840 Jan 19., I

Arden, Eve, 1953 Feb. 11, II; 1990, II

Arendt, Hannah, 1963(1), II; 1975, I

Argall, Samuel, 1613, I; 1618, IV

Argentina:

Mexican-U.S. dispute, 1914 Apr. 25, I

Argonne Project, 1942 Dec. 2, III

Arieti, Silvano, 1975 Apr. 16, II

Ariss, John, 1758, II

Aristocracy *see* Society

Arizona:

governor impeached, 1988 Apr. 4, I

statehood, 1911 Aug. 22, I; 1912 Feb. 14, I

territory acquired, 1853 Dec. 30, I

Territory formed, 1863 Feb. 24, I

Arizona, University of, 1885(5), III

Arkansas:

seceded, 1861 May 6, I

statehood, 1836 June 15, I

Arkansas, University of, 1871 Mar. 27, III

Arkansas River:

flood, 1921 June 3, I

Arlen, Harold, 1986, II

Arlen, Michael J., 1976 Apr. 19, II

Arlington House (Va.), 1802(2), II

Arliss, George, 1930 Nov. 5(1), II

Armed forces (*see also* Court martials; Draft; Veterans; war names):

aircraft production reduced, 1945 May 25, III

Air Force golden anniversary, 1957, I

air power possibilities, 1921 July 21, III

appraisal and review of forces ordered, 1961 July 8, I

appropriation bill, 1962 Aug. 1, I

appropriations, 1964, I

appropriations cut, 1969, I

Army Air Corps established, 1926 July 2(1), I

Army Dental Corps formed, 1901 Feb. 2(1), I

Army Nurse Corps formed, 1901 Feb. 2(2), I

A-12 Avenger canceled, 1991 Jan. 7, I

base in Philippines, 1988 Oct. 17, I

base in Philippines closed, 1991 Dec. 27, I

bases in Greece extended, 1990 July 8, I

B-2 stealth bomber, 1988 Nov. 22, I

Chileans attacked sailors (Valparaiso), 1891 Oct. 16, I

Continental Marines established, 1775 Nov. 10, I

Continental Navy established, 1775 Oct. 13, I

defense program, 1939 Jan. 12, I

doubled, 1951 Mar. 21, I

early revolutionary force (Phila., Pa.), 1774 Nov. 17, I

expenditures reduced, 1970 Mar. 4, I

Armed forces (*cont.*)

federal budget allocations, 1951 Jan. 15, I

first black general, 1959 May 22, I

first issue of Army newspaper *Stars and Stripes*, 1918 Feb. 8, II

first naval aircraft launching, 1910 Nov. 14, III

first soldier executed by military court order, 1776 June 27, I

five paratroopers killed (Ky.), 1958 Apr. 23, I

flogging outlawed, 1850 Sept. 28(2), I

full racial integration ordered, 1962 Apr. 3, I

general of Army rank conferred, 1944 Dec. 15, I

Great White Fleet, 1907, I; 1909 Feb. 21, I

homosexual ban challenged, 1975 Oct. 22, I

Iowa (battleship) explosion, 1989 Apr. 19, I

Marine Corps women's unit, 1943 Feb. 13, I

Marines drowned (Parris Island, S.C.), 1956 Apr. 8, I

military call-up granted, 1962 Sept. 24, I

military installations closed, 1991 July 30, I

Mitchell court-martial, 1925, I

Mitchell verdict upheld, 1958 Mar. 4, I

National Defense Act passed, 1916 June 3, I

Naval Expansion Act passed, 1938 May 17, I

Navy Nurse Corps established, 1908(1), III

Navy rebuilding, 1883 Mar. 3(2), I

Navy reinstated bell-bottom trousers, 1977 Aug. 1, IV

Navy Tailhook scandal, 1992 Sept. 24, I

personnel statistics, 1850 June 1, III

presidential power to call out militia, 1827 Feb. 2, I

recruits killed in air crash, 1961 Nov. 8, I

reduced in Europe, 1990 Nov. 19, I

reserve increased, 1955 July 26, I

rivalry between services, 1956, I

Semper Paratus Always Ready Service (SPARS), 1942 Nov. 23, I

Sergeant York antiaircraft system scrapped, 1985 Aug. 27, I

unification, 1947 July 25, I

uniform color changed, 1902(1), I

weapons procurement bill, 1969 Nov. 6, I

woman Marine Corps general appointed, 1978 May 11, I

Women Appointed for Voluntary Emergency Service (WAVES), 1942 July 30, I

Women's Army Corps (WAC), 1942 May 14, I

women's spouses ruled equal benefits, 1973 May 14(1), I

Arminian Magazine, 1789 Jan.(1), II
Armistad Dam, 1966 Dec. 3, III
Armistice Day, 1921 Nov. 5, IV
Armour, Tommy, 1927 June 16, IV; 1930 Sept. 13, IV
Armour and Co., H. O., 1868(3), III
Arms control and disarmament:
    Canadian treaty, 1817, I
    Carnegie Peace Endowment (Hague), 1910(3), III
    chemical weapons condemned, 1989 Jan. 11, I
    chemical weapons reduction agreement, 1990 June 1, I
    Eisenhower proposals, 1955, I
    European Security and Cooperation charter signed, 1975 Aug. 1, I
    first Hague conference, 1899, I
    first joint nuclear test verification, 1988 Aug. 17, III
    Geneva Disarmament Conference, 1926 May 18, I
    intermediate-range missile removal pact, 1987 Dec. 8, I; 1988 May 27, I
    Kellogg-Briand Peace Pact, 1928 Aug. 27, I; 1929 Jan. 15, I
    limited nuclear test-ban treaty initialed (Moscow), 1963 July 25, I
    limited nuclear test-ban treaty signed, 1963 Oct. 7, I
    London Naval Treaty signed, 1930 Apr. 22, I
    Methodist opposition to nuclear arms, 1986 Apr. 29, III
    missile agreements, 1972 May 22–30, I
    most extensive treaty to date signed, 1990 Nov. 19, I
    naval limitation conference, 1927 Feb. 10, I
    naval limitation treaty, 1922 Feb. 6(2), I
    Nine-Power Treaty, 1922 Feb. 6(1), I
    nuclear arsenals reduced, 1990 June 1, I
    nuclear nonproliferation treaty, 1970 Mar. 5, I
    nuclear nonproliferation treaty draft, 1967 Aug. 24, I
    nuclear nonproliferation treaty proposal rejected, 1965 Aug. 17, I
    nuclear nonproliferation treaty signed, 1968 July 1(2), I; 1969 Nov. 24, I
    nuclear reduction treaty, 1991 July 31, I
    nuclear stockpiles reduced, 1964, I
    nuclear test-ban conference opened (Moscow), 1963 July 15, I
    nuclear weapons unilateral cuts, 1991 Sept. 27, I; 1992 Feb. 1, I
    preliminary meeting, 1984 Nov. 22, I
    Reagan proposal, 1981 Nov. 18, I
    Rostow dismissed as agency director, 1983 Jan. 12, I
    SALT accords signed, 1972, I; 1972 Feb. 4, I; 1972 Aug. 3, I
    SALT fifth round opened, 1971 July 8, I
    SALT fourth round opened, 1971 Mar. 15, I
    SALT opened, 1969 Nov. 17, I

Arms control and disarmament (*cont.*)
    SALT second and third rounds, 1970 Apr. 16, I
    SALT seventh round opened, 1972 Feb. 4, I
    SALT sixth round ended, 1972 Feb. 4, I
    SALT third round opened, 1970 Nov. 2, I
    SALT 2 treaty signed, 1979 June 18, I
    SALT 2 unratified, 1986 May 27, I
    satellites launched to detect test-ban treaty violations, 1963 Oct. 16, I
    seabed treaty, 1971 Feb. 11, I
    second International Peace Conference, 1907 June 15-Oct. 15, I
    Soviets withdrew from missile talks, 1983 Nov. 23, I
    Soviet-U.S. summit conference (Geneva), 1985 Nov. 20–21, I
    Soviet-U.S. summit (Reykjavik), 1986 Oct. 11–12, I
    space treaty, 1967 Jan. 27, I
    Teller's testimony, 1957 Nov. 25, I
    test ban conference (Geneva), 1962 Jan. 29, I
    test ban talks halted, 1963 Jan. 31, I
    total nuclear test ban proposed, 1962 Aug. 27(1), I
    treaty outlawing war proposed, 1927 Apr. 6, I
    underground nuclear test pact signed, 1976 May 28, I
    underground test verification, 1988 Sept. 14, I
    U.S. strategic arms policy, 1986 May 27, I
    Vladivostok summit meeting, 1974 Nov. 23–24, I
    Washington Conference for Limitation of Armament, 1921, I
Arms sales, 1988 May 1, III
    Iran-Contra affair, 1986 Nov. 3, I; 1987 Feb. 26, I; 1987 Nov. 18, I; 1988 Mar. 16, I; 1989 May 4, I; 1990 Apr. 7, I; 1991 Oct. 7, I
Armstrong, Edwin H., 1939(2), III
Armstrong, Henry, 1988, IV
Armstrong, Herbert W., 1986, III
Armstrong, Louis, 1922, II; 1964 Jan. 16, II; 1965 Sept. 13, II; 1971, II
Armstrong, Neil A., 1966 Mar. 16, III; 1969 July 16, III
Army, Department of:
    Vance named secretary, 1962 May 20, I
Army-McCarthy hearings *see* McCarthy, Joseph R.
Arnaz, Desi, 1986, II
Arnold, Benedict, 1777 Oct. 7, I; 1780 Oct. 2, I; 1781 Sept. 8, I
Arnold, Henry ("Hap"), 1944 Dec. 15, I
Aroostock War, 1839 Feb. 12, I
Arpino, Gerald, 1975 Oct. 9, II
Arrow, Kenneth J., 1972 Oct. 25, III
Arson *see* Fires
Art and artists (*see also* Cartoons; Murals; Sculpture; names of artists and galleries):
    abstract, 1929, II; 1951, II; 1956, II; 1958, II

Art and artists (*cont.*)
    Allston's and Vanderlyn's European studies, 1804, II
    Allston's romantic style, 1813(2), II; 1819(2), II
    American Art Union formed, 1839(1), II
    American girl glorification, 1880(5), II
    American Gothic (Wood), 1930(3), II
    American objection to nude, 1877(2), II
    American regionalism, 1943, II
    American Union membership, 1848(1), II
    American Water Color Society founded, 1867(3), II
    Annenberg donation, 1991 Mar. 11, II
    Armory Show (N.Y.), 1913, II
    Armory Show recreated, 1963 Apr., II
    Ash Can school, 1908, II
    auction prices softened, 1982, II
    auction record, 1961 Nov. 15, II; 1967 Apr. 26, II; 1968 Oct. 9, II; 1968 Oct. 9, II; 1970, II; 1973 Sept. 21, II; 1974 Sept. 27, II; 1976 Sept. 29, II; 1978, II; 1979, II; 1980 May 29, II; 1980 Oct. 17, II; 1987, II; 1987 Nov. 11, II; 1988 May 2, II; 1989 Nov. 30, II; 1990 May 15, II
    Badger's portraiture, 1765–1769, II
    Benton's *July Hay*, 1943(5), II
    best-known by an American, 1871(2), II
    Bierstadt retrospective, 1991 Feb. 8, II
    Bierstadt's landscapes, 1861(5), II
    Bryan Gallery of Christian Art (N.Y.C.), 1853(4), II
    Cassatt's works, 1881(3), II; 1894, II
    Center for British Art (Conn.) dedicated, 1977 Apr. 19, II
    Chagall's *America Windows* unveiled (Chicago), 1977 May 15, II
    Chicago Art Institute addition opening, 1988 Sept. 17(1), II
    Christie's opened N.Y.C. branch, 1977 May 16, II
    Civil War-inspired, 1865(9), II
    Cloisters (N.Y.C.), 1938(6), II
    Cole's landscapes, 1836(1), II
    Copley portraiture, c1760, II; 1765(2), II; 1770–1774, II; 1785(1), II
    Corcoran Art Gallery (Wash., D.C.), 1870(4), II
    Currier & Ives, 1833(4), II
    customs bill, 1959 Sept. 14(2), II
    Davis's move from realism, 1941(6), II
    deaccessioning, 1972, II
    de Kooning painting auction price, 1983, II; 1984 Nov. 1, II
    Eakins's *Gross Clinic*, 1875(3), II
    Eakins's *Turning Stake Boat*, 1873(3), II
    Eakins's *William Rush Carving the Allegorical Figure of the Schuylkill River, 1877(2)*, II
    Eakins' works acquired (Pa.), 1986 June 18, II
    earliest painting of N.Y.C., 1647(2), II
    Earl's landscapes, 1800(1), II

Art and artists (cont.)

early drawings of Indians, 1564, IV; 1585, IV
early expressionist portrait, 1721(1), II
Eight, The, 1908, II
El Greco stolen work recovered (N.Y.C.), 1971 June 16, II
environmental (Biscayne Bay, Fla.), 1983 May 4, II
European refugees' influence, 1940, II
Exhibition of Great Paintings (N.Y.C.), 1860(10), IV
Federal Art Project, 1936, II
Feke portraiture, 1745–1749, II
first American painter to study in Paris, 1812(2), II
first hunting scene engraving, 1774(3), IV
first joint Soviet-U.S. exhibition, 1988 Sept. 27, II
first lithograph, 1818(2), II
first public commission, 1721(4), II
first romanticism, 1775(2), II
first Younger American Artists exhibition, 1910(4), II
five stolen paintings recovered, 1975 Jan. 23, II
Florence (Italy) flood destruction, 1967, II
French impressionist sale, 1983, II
Gallery of Modern Art (N.Y.C.) opened, 1964 Mar. 16, II
Gauguin exhibit, 1988 Sept. 17(1), II
Gibson died, 1944, II
Gibson Girl, 1895, IV
golden day of American, 1860(9), II
Grandma Moses, 1953, II
Graves's Little-Known Bird of the Inner Eye, 1941(5), II
Great Age of Fresco exhibit (N.Y.C.), 1968 Sept. 28, II
Great Depression, 1935, II
Grosz died, 1959 May 2, II
Guggenheim addition opened, 1992 June 28, II
Guggenheim international award, 1959 May 18, II; 1960 Oct. 31, II
Guggenheim Museum (N.Y.C.), 1945 July 9, II; 1959 Oct. 21(2), II
Gugliemi's Terror in Brooklyn, 1941(4), II
high-priced collections sold, 1957, II
high-priced sales, 1980, II; 1982 July 10, II
Hirshhorn Museum and Sculpture Garden (Wash., D.C.), 1969, II; 1974 Oct. 4, II
History of the Rise and Progress of the Arts of Design in the U.S., 1834(2), II
Hofmann retrospective, 1963 Sept. 11, II
Homer's works, 1876(8), II; 1884(2), II; 1980 Oct. 17, II
Hopper's works, 1941(3), II; 1971 Mar. 18, II
Hudson River school, 1823(1), II; 1830, II; 1837(6), II
Icebergs (Church), 1979, II
impressionism, 1861(3), II

Art and artists (cont.)

India exhibit (Wash., D.C.), 1985 May 5, II
Indian art exhibit (Minneapolis, Minn.), 1992 Oct., II
Indian collection sale (Peabody Museum, Mass.), 1979 Feb. 9(1), II
Inness's landscapes, 1865(8), II; 1873(2), II
international scandal, 1962, II
Janis modern art gift, 1967 June 16, II
Japanese influence, 1864(5), II
Johnson's portraits, 1881(5), II
Karel's Woman with Ostrich, 1960 Oct. 31, II
Kelly exhibit, 1992 Nov. 1, II
lack of appreciation in U.S., 1838(3), II
Lehman collection, 1969, II
Leonardo da Vinci, 1963 Jan. 8–Mar. 4, II
Leonardo da Vinci, notebook bought, 1980 Dec. 12, II
Linsky collection (N.Y.C.), 1982 Mar. 4, II
Los Angeles County Museum (Calif.), 1965 Mar. 30, II
Louvre loan exhibitions, 1963 Jan. 8–Mar. 4, II
Malevich exhibition, 1991 Mar. 24, II
Maori exhibit (N.Y.C.), 1984, II
Marin's modernism, 1915(3), II
Marsh's depiction of cities, 1934(5), II
Metropolitan Museum (N.Y.C.), 1880, II
Metropolitan Museum forgery (N.Y.C.), 1967 Dec. 6, II
Miró's work, 1959 May 18, II
Mona Lisa (da Vinci) exhibited (N.Y.C. and Wash., D.C.), 1963 Jan. 8–Mar. 4, II
Morgan Library Italian drawings gift (N.Y.C.), 1973 Dec. 11, II
Morse painting sold at highest price to date, 1982 July 10, II
Mount's works, 1850(6), II
Museum of Modern Art (N.Y.C.), 1964 May 25(1), II; 1984, II
museums' financial plight, 1974, II
National Academy of Design, 1825 Nov. 8, II
National Gallery acquired new works, 1992 July 7, II
National Gallery (Mellon) (Wash., D.C.) opened, 1941 Mar. 17, II
National Gallery (Wash., D.C.) purchased da Vinci work, 1967 Feb. 20, II
National Gallery (Wash., D.C.) 50th anniversary, 1991 Mar. 17, II
November Evening, 1932(6), II
Nude Descending a Staircase (Duchamps), 1963 Apr., II
N.Y. Picture Gallery opened, 1819(1), IV
O'Keeffe centennial exhibit, 1988, II
O'Keeffe's style, 1929, II
Old Art Museum (Boston, Mass.), 1872(5), II
oldest extant institution (Pa.), 1805(1), II

Art and artists (cont.)

op art show, 1965, II
Packard collection purchased, 1975 Aug. 23, II
painting on velvet, 1811(2), IV
Paley collection exhibited, 1992 Feb. 2, II
panoramic, 1840(1), II
Paris mecca for U.S. painters, 1870(5), II
Peale's painting of mastodon, 1806(3), II
Peale's portrait auction sale, 1985, II
Peale's scientific influence, 1809(2), II
Pelham portraiture, 1751 Dec., II
Picasso exhibition (N.Y.C.), 1957(3), II
Picasso record price (N.Y.C.), 1981, II
Picasso's Guernica returned to Spain, 1981 Sept. 10, II
Picasso show and auction, 1980, II
Pietà (Michelangelo) displayed at N.Y. World's Fair, 1964 Apr. 19, II
Pine's portraiture, 1784(1), II
Pollock's one-man show, 1943(6), II
Pollock's works, 1956, II; 1973 Sept. 21, II; 1976 Oct. 6, II
pop, 1962, II
pop exhibit, 1963 Mar.-June, II
popular mid-nineteenth century, 1853(4), II
portrait, 1670(1), II; 1670(3), II; 1670(4), II
portrait of Columbus, 1519, II
Pratt, Matthew, 1805(3), II
Prendergast's works, 1901(2), II
primitivism, 1830(1), II; 1830(2), II
recession weakened market, 1981, II
refugee artists, 1943, II
regional American, 1939, II
Renoir theft (Brooklyn, N.Y.), 1974 Dec. 12, II
River Rouge Plant (Sheeler) precisionism, 1932(4), II
Rivers billboard, 1963 Aug., II
N. Rockefeller legacies, 1979 Feb. 9(2), II
Rockefeller primitive collection, 1969, II
Roger Sherman portrait, c1775, II
Rossiter's romanticism, 1856(4), II
Rothko died, 1970, II
Rothko estate fined, 1975 Dec. 18, II
Rothko Foundation collection, 1984 May 3, II
Rothko sale, 1983, II
Rothko sale halted, 1972 June 28, II
Ruskin's criticism of American, 1856(7), II
Ruskin-Whistler libel suit, 1877(3), II
Russian collection six-city tour, 1972 Jan. 5, II
Ryder's works, 1900, II
Sargent's portraits, 1881(6), II; 1884(4), II
Seattle Museum (Wash.) opened, 1991 Dec. 5, II
Shahn's Miners' Wives, 1948(3), II
Simon's bid for Rembrandt work, 1965 Mar. 19, II
Smibert's portraiture, 1751 Apr. 2, II

Art and artists (*cont.*)
Society of American Artists founded, 1877 June 1, II
Society of Artists of U.S. founded, 1810(2), II
Sotheby Park Bernet auction house sold, 1983 Sept. 19, II
Soviet French impressionists loan, 1973 Apr. 2, II
Soviet-U.S. exchanges, 1975 Aug. 29, II; 1987, II; 1988 Mar. 26, II
Soviet-U.S. joint exhibits, 1988 Sept. 27, II
Stein collection, 1969, II
Stolen Paintings and Objects d'Art published, 1975 Feb. 1, II
Stuart portrait of G. Washington, 1796(2), II
Stuart's portraiture, 1782(2), II; 1979 Apr. 10, II
Studio Building (N.Y.C.), 1857(5), II
Sully's portraits, 1812, II
symbolic, 1947, II
theft (Chicago, Ill.), 1966 Oct. 30, II
theft (Gardner Museum, Boston), 1990 Mar. 18, II
theft (Metropolitan Museum, N.Y.C.), 1979 Feb. 9(3), II
theft (N.Y.C.), 1988 Feb. 9, IV
theft (Pa.), 1968 Aug. 22, II
theft (St. Louis, Mo.), 1978 Jan. 21, II
Treasure Houses of Great Britain exhibit (Wash., D.C.), 1985 Nov. 3, II
trompe l'oeil, 1885(4), II
Trumbull's contribution, 1817, II
Turner's works, 1980 May 29, II
U.S. surpassing European, 1955, II
Vanderlyn's contribution, 1812(2), II
Van Gogh at Arles exhibit (N.Y.C.), 1984, II
Vatican exhibition, 1983, II
Vedder's illustrations, 1884(5), II
Veronese exhibit, 1989, II
vogue for romantic and emotional, 1856(4), II
Warhol collection sold, 1988 May 3, II
Washington Crossing the Delaware (Leutze), 1850(7), II
Washington portraits, 1772, II; 1796(2), II
Weber's *Chinese Restaurant,* 1915(4), II
West's historical paintings, 1792(5), II; 1802, II
Wetherby's portraits, 1852(4), II
Whistler and Royal Society of British artists, 1886(3), II
Whistler exhibit (Wash., D.C.), 1984, II
Whistler's *Mother,* 1871(2), II
Whistler's *Mother* exhibited (Atlanta, Ga.), 1963 Jan. 8–Mar. 4, II
Whistler's paintings, 1863(1), II; 1963 Jan. 8–Mar. 4, II
Whitney Museum (N.Y.C.), 1914(4), II; 1966 Sept. 28, II
Whitney Museum (N.Y.C.) light show, 1968 July 23, II

Art and artists (*cont.*)
women artists' museum opened (Wash., D.C.), 1987 Apr. 7, II
Wood died, 1942, II
Wood exhibition (Minneapolis, Minn.), 1983, II
works found in Calif. home, 1959 Nov. 19, II
Wyeth retrospective, 1967 Feb. 14, II
Wyeth secret Helga collection sold, 1986 Aug. 9, II
Wyeths' three-generational exhibit, 1987, II
Wyeth's White House show, 1970 Feb. 19, II
Arthritis, 1949 Apr. 20, III; 1976 July 18, III
Arthur, Beatrice, 1988 Aug. 28, II
Arthur, Chester A.:
born, 1830 Oct. 5, I
elected vice president, 1880 Nov. 2, I
inaugurated president, 1881 Sept. 20, I
succeeded to presidency, 1881, I
vice presidential nomination, 1880 June 2–8, I
Arthur, Jean, 1991, II
Arthur, Timothy S., 1854(4), II
Articles of Confederation, 1777 Nov. 15, I; 1781 Mar. 1, I
Artificial heart *see* Heart
Artificial insemination *see* Pregnancy and birth
Art Institute of Chicago (Ill.):
Hermitage exchange, 1988 Mar. 26, II
new gallery opened, 1988 Sept. 17(1), II
Artis, John, 1976 Dec. 21, IV
Arts and culture (*see* also specific forms, e.g., Music)
activity in, 1938, II
American Academy founded, 1802(1), II
American Academy of Arts and Letters founded, 1904(7), II
American Fine Arts Society formed, 1892(4), II
apathetic climate, 1937, II
Black Academy of Arts and Letters established, 1969 Mar. 27, II
British derision of American, 1820 Jan., II; 1827 Dec., II
Brooklyn Museum shows French exhibit, 1986, II
Chinese tour canceled, 1975 Mar. 28(2), II
current scene, 1939, II; 1940, II; 1945, II; 1947, II
deficit, 1977, II
first federal performing arts grant, 1966 Jan. 18, II
first International Women's Festival (N.Y.C.), 1975 Mar. 9, II
first U.S. performance of Central Ballet of China, 1986, II
first woman elected to French Academy, 1980 Mar. 6, II
Ford Foundation grants, 1961 Oct. 17, II
German, 1800–1819, III; 1814(3), III

Arts and culture (*cont.*)
Great Depression impact, 1932, II; 1933, II
Guggenheim Foundation established, 1925 Dec. 6, II
Guggenheim grants, 1961 Apr. 30, II
Ingersoll's defense of U.S., 1810(3), II; 1823(2), III
Jones Hall opened (Houston, Tex.), 1966 Oct. 2, II
Milwaukee Center opened (Wis.), 1969 Sept. 17, II
National Institute of Arts and Letters established, 1898(2), II
N.Y. Academy founded, 1808(1), II
record for fewest Broadway productions, 1986, II
revitalization, 1934, II
Soviet exchange, 1962 Mar. 8, III
U.S. in international competitions, 1958 May 1, II
U.S.-Soviet exchanges, 1973 Apr. 2, II
wartime boom, 1944, II
World War II impact on, 1941, II; 1942, II
Asbestos:
curtains in theaters, 1885(3), II
Asbury, Francis, 1784 Dec. 24, III
ASCAP (American Society of Composers, Authors and Publishers), 1914 Feb. 13, II
Asch, Sholem, 1923 May 23, II
Ashbery, John, 1976 Jan. 8, II; 1976 Apr. 19, II; 1976 May 3, II
Ashbrook, John M., 1971, I
Ashcroft, Peggy, 1985 Mar. 25, II
Ashe, Arthur, 1968 Sept. 9, IV; 1975 July 4–5, IV; 1992 Apr. 8, IV
Ashley, William, 1822, IV
Ashman, Howard, 1982 May 29, II
Ashmun, Jehudi, 1821, IV
Asia *see* Far East; country and region names
Asian-Americans:
population increase, 1990, I; 1991, I
Asimov, Isaac, 1992, II
Asner, Ed, 1976 May 17, II; 1978 Sept. 17, II; 1980 Sept. 7, II
Assassinations and assassination attempts:
attempt on congressmen by Puerto Rican nationalists, 1954 Mar. 1, I
books on, 1964, II
civil rights leader Evers (Miss.), 1963 June 12, I
Ford threatened (Calif.), 1975 Sept. 5, I; 1975 Sept. 22, I
Francis Ferdinand (Archduke of Austria), 1914 June 28, I
Garfield, James A., 1881 July 2, I
Garfield's assassin tried, 1881 Nov. 14, I
Jackson, Andrew, 1835 Jan. 30, I
Kahane shot (N.Y.C.), 1990 Nov. 5, I
J. Kennedy (Tex.), 1963, I; 1963 Nov. 22, I
J. Kennedy reviewed, 1976 Sept. 17, I
R. Kennedy (Los Angeles, Calif.), 1968 June 5, I
King reviewed, 1976 Sept. 17, I

Assassinations and assassination attempts
(*cont.*)

King's alleged killer held, 1968 June 8, I

King's assassin convicted, 1969 Mar. 10, I

King shot (Memphis, Tenn.), 1968 Apr. 4, I

Lennon killed (N.Y.C.), 1980 Dec. 8, II

Lincoln, Abraham, 1865, I; 1865 Apr. 14, I

Long, Huey, 1935 Sept. 8, I

McKinley, William, 1901, I

Malcolm X, 1965 Feb. 21, I

Manchester's book on J. Kennedy, 1967(1), II

Reagan assailant found insane, 1982 June 21, I

Reagan shot (Wash., D.C.), 1981 Mar. 30, I

Ruby convicted of Oswald's murder, 1964 Mar. 14, I

Ruby conviction for Oswald's murder reversed, 1966 Oct. 5, I

Sirhan sentenced for R. Kennedy murder, 1969 Apr. 23, I

U.S. ambassador to Lebanon, 1976 June 16, I

U.S. overseas political curtailed, 1976 Feb. 17, I

Wallace, George C. (Md.), 1972 May 15, I

Wallace's assailant convicted, 1972 Aug. 4, I

Warhol shot, 1968 June 3, II

Warren Commission, 1963 Nov. 29, I; 1964, II; 1964 Sept. 27, I

Assemblies of God, 1988 Apr. 8, III

Associated Press (AP):

founded, 1848(1), III

Associations and clubs (*see also* specific names):

colonial, 1725–1729, IV

early trade (Boston, Mass.), 1785(6), III

first chamber of commerce (N.Y.C.), 1768 Apr. 5, III

first historical (Mass.), 1791(1), III

first legal society, 1747(2), III

first scientific, 1740–1744, III

Jaycees membership for women, 1984 July 3, I

last Playboy Club closed, 1988 July 31, IV

N.Y.C. social clubs, 1733, IV

oldest gentlemen's club (Phila., Pa.), 1834(5), IV

patriotic and other types, 1881, IV

Robert's Rules of Order, 1876, II

Rotary Clubs founded, 1905(2), IV

scientific, encouraged (Mass.), 1780(1), III

specialized scholarship, 1884, III; 1888(1), III; 1889 Dec. 14, III

trade associations, 1951(1), III

Union Club founded (N.Y.C.), 1836(4), IV

Vauxhall opened (N.Y.C.), 1811 Dec. 12, IV

Associations and clubs (*cont.*)

women admitted to all-male, 1987 May 4, IV

women admitted to Princeton eating clubs, 1991 Jan. 21, IV

women admitted to Yale Skull and Bones, 1991 Oct. 24, IV

women's admission upheld, 1988 June 20, IV

women's clubs, 1889(1), IV

Astaire, Adele, 1919 Oct. 7, II

Astaire, Fred, 1919 Oct. 7, II; 1959 May 6, II; 1978 Sept. 17, II; 1987, II

Astin, Patty Duke (*see also* Duke, Patty): 1980 Sept. 7, II

Astor, John Jacob, 1808, III; 1811(6), III; 1811 Apr. 12, I; 1822(1), III; 1836 May 31, IV; 1854, III

Astor, Mary, 1942 Feb. 26, II; 1987, II

Astor, William Waldorf (Mrs.), 1908 Oct. 30, IV

Astor Library (N.Y.C.), 1854, III

Astronauts and astronautics *see* Space program

Astronomy (*see also* Solar eclipse; Solar system; Telescope):

Big Bang theory, 1965 June 12, III

Comet Ikeya-Seki, 1965, III

comet orbit, 1680(2), III

Copernican, 1714(2), III

Copernican views accepted by Harvard, 1656, III

Copernicus (orbiting observatory) launched, 1972 Aug. 21, III

early observatory (Mass.), 1840(2), III

Explorer 38 satellite, 1968 July 4, III

first book on Copernican (Mass.), 1659(2), II

first field expedition, 1786 Oct. 20, III

first measurement of a star, 1920(5), III

first photograph of solar spectrum, 1876(2), III

first planetarium, 1767, III

first planetarium (Chicago, Ill.), 1930 May 11, III

first pulsar identification, 1969 Jan. 20, III

first woman professor of, 1847 Oct., IV

galaxy discovered, 1975 June 30, III

Halley's Comet first sighting for 1985 orbit, 1982 Oct. 16, III

Hall's detection of two Mars satellites, 1877(3), III

Harvard Observatory telescope, 1843(4), III

Hubble Space Telescope launched, 1990 Apr. 25, III

Jupiter satellite detected, 1892(11), III

largest telescope to date, 1895, III

Lick Observatory (Calif.), 1888(4), III

life on other worlds search, 1992 Oct. 12(2), III

light from universe edge detected, 1989 Nov. 19, III

Mars study, 1955 Sept. 8, III

Mitchell's comet discovery, 1847 Oct., IV

M. Mitchell's contribution, 1865, III

Astronomy (*cont.*)

observatories, 1895, III; 1897(1), III

oldest, most distant objects yet seen in universe, 1988 Jan. 13, III

photography, 1892(11), III

Pluto identified, 1930 Mar. 13, III

Pluto moon discovered, 1978 June 22, III

solar system age estimated, 1960 Jan. 2, III

stellar radio emissions, 1931(1), III

stellar systems evidence, 1983 Aug. 9, III

Venus observation, 1761(1), III

Asylum for Friendless Boys, The (N.Y.C.), 1851(1), IV

AT&T *see* American Telephone and Telegraph Co.

Atheism, 1697 Oct., III

Atherton, Charles G., 1838 Dec. 11, I

Atkins, Susan, 1971 Jan. 25, IV

Atkinson, Brooks, 1984, II

Atkinson, Juliette P., 1895(3), IV; 1897(3), IV; 1898(3), IV

Atlanta Constitution (publication), 1876(6), II

Atlanta (Ga.):

first black mayor, 1973 Oct. 16(1), I

Peachtree Plaza, 1975 Oct. 2, II

race riots, 1906 Sept. 22, I

Union troops occupied, 1864 Sept. 1, I

Atlanta Memorial Arts Center (Ga.), 1968 Oct. 29, II

Atlantic Charter, 1941 Aug. 9–12, I

Atlantic City (N.J.), 1870(5), IV; 1978 May 26, IV

Atlantic crossings:

air speed record over, 1958 June 27, III

balloon hoax, 1844(6), IV

cable communication chartered, 1854 May 6, III

cable completed, 1866 July 27, III

cable laid, 1857 Mar. 3, III

first cable message, 1857 Mar. 3, III; 1858 Aug. 16, III

first yacht race across, 1866(5), IV

regular U.S.-Britain shipping schedule, 1850 Apr. 27, III

ship speed record, 1850 Aug. 21, III; 1952 July 7, III

Atlantic (magazine), 1980, II

Atlantic Monthly (publication):

founded, 1857(1), II

Atlas, Charles, 1972, IV

Atomic Energy Commission:

created, 1946 Aug. 1, I

Atoms (*see also* Nuclear energy; Nuclear weapons):

antiproton discovered, 1955 Oct. 18, III

bubble chamber developed, 1960 Nov. 3, III

chain reaction possible, 1940, III

chemical bonding, 1966 Dec. 10(1), III

cyclotron developed, 1939 Nov. 9, III

first split, 1939, III

first sustained nuclear reaction, 1942 Dec. 2, III

Atoms (*cont.*)

fusion at room temperature, 1989 Mar. 23, III

magnetic fields, 1952 Nov. 6, III

measurement, 1955 Nov. 2(2), III

molecular chemistry experiments, 1917(1), III

nucleus, 1961 Nov. 2(2), III; 1975 Oct. 17, III

oxygen and hydrogen weights, 1914(2), III

research for industry, 1948 Jan. 2, III

splitting, 1934 Nov. 15, III

structure studies, 1963 Nov. 5, III

subparticles, 1957 Oct. 31, III; 1968 Oct. 30(2), III; 1980 Oct. 14(2), III

Superconducting Super Collider (SSC), 1988 Nov. 10, III

Attica State Correctional Facility (Attica, N.Y.), 1971 Sept. 9–13, I

Attorney General:

first, 1789 Sept. 26(3), I

Meese resigned, 1988 July 5, I

Attorneys *see* Legal profession; personal names

Atwood, Charles B., 1895(5), II

Auchincloss, Louis, 1964(1), II; 1966(1), II; 1967(1), II

Auchterlonie, Lawrence, 1902 Oct. 11, IV

Auden, W. H., 1948 May 3, II; 1956 Feb. 7, II; 1971 Oct. 25, II; 1973, II

Audubon, John J., 1803 Apr., III; 1827, II; 1827 July 23, IV

Auel, Jean M., 1990(1), II

Auerbach, Red, 1966 Apr. 17–28, IV

Augusta (Ga.), 1735, I

Aureomycin, 1948(1), III

Austin, Stephen, 1821 Dec., I; 1823, I; 1825 Mar. 24, I

Austin, Tracy, 1979 Sept. 9, IV; 1981 Sept. 9–13, IV; 1992 July 11, IV

Austin College (Tex.), 1849 Nov. 22, III

Austria:

Waldheim barred from U.S., 1987 Apr. 27, I

Automation, 1932, III; 1955, III; 1963, III; 1964, III; 1964 Aug. 5, III; 1965 Aug. 29, III

Automobiles (*see also* Tires; Traffic accidents; Traffic regulations):

all production suspended, 1918 Aug. 9, III

annual show (N.Y.C.), 1935 Nov., III

Brush two-seater, 1907(4), III

Chrysler bailout, 1979 Dec. 21, III

Chrysler Corp. workers' contract, 1964 Sept. 9, III

Chrysler strike, 1973 Sept. 14, III

De Soto discontinued, 1960 Nov. 18, III

Dodge Bros. purchased, 1925 Apr. 1, III

electric, 1888 July 27, III; 1892 Sept.(2), III

emission controls, 1970 Dec. 31, III

fifteen millionth Model T, 1927 Spring, III

first assembly line, 1913 Summer, III

first diesel, 1977 Sept. 13, III

first electric self-starter, 1911 Feb., III

Automobiles (*cont.*)

first Ford assembled, 1896 June 4, III

first gasoline-driven patent, 1895 June 11, III

first (Phila., Pa.), 1804(2), III

first president to ride in, 1899 Summer, IV

first quantity-production factory (Detroit, Mich.), 1900(8), III

first successful gas-powered, 1892 Sept.(1), III

first transcontinental trip, 1903 July 26, III

Ford assets, 1921 Apr. 30, III

Ford Co. formed, 1903(3), III

Ford Pinto defect case, 1980 Mar. 13, III

Ford prices low, 1924(1), III

Ford reached ten millionth mark, 1924 June 15, III

Ford restored minimum wage, 1934 Mar. 13, III

Ford's early models, 1893 Dec. 24, III

Ford workers' contract, 1964 Sept. 18, III

Ford workers' strike, 1967 Sept. 6, III

40-hour work week, 1926(5), III

gasoline rationing, 1942 May 15, III; 1942 Dec. 1, III

GM expansion program, 1954 Jan. 19, III

GM incorporated, 1908 Sept. 16, III

GM plant closings, 1992 Feb. 24, III

GM strike, 1964 Sept. 25, III; 1970 Sept. 15, III

GM-Toyota joint venture (Calif.), 1983 Dec. 22, III

GM wage increases, 1941 May 16, III

horseless carriage failure predicted, 1899 Oct. 14, III

increased production and use, 1900, III

International Show (N.Y.C.), 1958 Apr., III

Japanese-U.S. agreement, 1992 Jan. 8, III

landmark Model T production, 1915 Dec. 10, III

largest recall to date, 1969 Feb. 26, III

manufacturing companies in existence, 1925(2), III

massive workers' layoff, 1974 Dec. 18, III

Model A introduced, 1927 Spring, III

Model T, 1908 Oct. 1, III; 1909(1), III; 1913 Summer, III; 1916, III

Nader's safety charges, 1966 Mar. 22, III

new sales banned, 1942 Jan. 1, III

number registered, 1905(3), III; 1916, III; 1917(4), III; 1920(8), III

overtime and pension agreements, 1973 Sept. 14, III

ownership, 1930(3), III

price cuts, 1949 Feb. 25(2), III

prices, 1916, III; 1917(4), III

production, 1916, III; 1923(1), III; 1956(1), III

production by Duryea brothers, 1896(4), III

Automobiles (*cont.*)

production cut, 1941 Apr. 17, III

production increased, 1983, III

production low, 1981, III

production of convertibles halted, 1976 Apr. 21, III

record layoffs, 1975 Feb. 3, III

record sales, 1985, III

safety belt requirements, 1977, III

safety recalls, 1971 Dec. 4, III; 1981 Feb. 23(2), III

sales and earnings, 1984, III

sales down, 1980, III; 1990, III; 1991, III

Selden patent suit, 1895 Nov. 5, III

Selden's patent, 1879 May 8, III

station wagons, 1956(1), III

stolen, 1989, IV

U.S. Motor Co. organized, 1910 Jan., III

Wilson's production for mass use, 1906 Mar. 1, I

women drivers, 1909(2), IV

Auto Racing:

around-the-world (N.Y.C.-Paris), 1908, IV

Astor Cup, 1915 Oct. 9, IV

Duryea's impact, 1896(4), III

early (N.Y.), 1900 Apr. 15, IV

fastest race in Indy history to date, 1987 Aug. 2, IV

first gasoline-powered (Ill.), 1895 Nov. 28, IV

first Indianapolis 500, 1911 May 30, IV

first self-propelled vehicle, 1895 Nov. 2, III

Indianapolis 500, 1912 May 30, IV; 1913 May 30, IV; 1914 May 30, IV; 1915 May 31, IV; 1916 May 30, IV; 1919 May 31, IV; 1920 May 31, IV; 1921 May 30, IV; 1922 May 30, IV; 1923 May 30, IV; 1924 May 30, IV; 1925 May 30, IV; 1926 May 31, IV; 1927 May 30, IV; 1928 May 30, IV; 1929 May 30, IV; 1930 May 30, IV; 1931 May 30, IV; 1932 May 30, IV; 1933 May 30, IV; 1934 May 30, IV; 1935 May 30, IV; 1936 May 30, IV; 1937 May 31, IV; 1938 May 30, IV; 1939 May 30, IV; 1940 May 30, IV; 1941 May 30, IV; 1946 May 30, IV; 1947 May 30, IV; 1948 May 31, IV; 1949 May 30, IV; 1950 May 31, IV; 1951 May 30, IV; 1952 May 30, IV; 1953 May 30, IV; 1954 May 31, IV; 1955 May 30, IV; 1956 May 30, IV; 1957 May 30, IV; 1958 May 30, IV; 1959 May 30, IV; 1960 May 30, IV; 1961 May 30, IV; 1962 May 30, IV; 1963 May 30, IV; 1964 May 30, IV; 1965 May 31, IV; 1966 May 30, IV; 1967 May 31, IV; 1968 May 30, IV; 1969 May 30, IV; 1970 May 30, IV; 1971 May 29, IV; 1972 May 27, IV; 1973 May 30, IV; 1974 May 26, IV; 1975 May 30, IV; 1976 May 30(1), IV; 1977 May 29, IV; 1978 May 28, IV; 1979 May 27, IV; 1980 May 25, IV; 1981 May 24, IV; 1982 May 30,

Auto Racing (*cont.*)
   IV; 1983 May 29, IV; 1984 May 27,
      IV; 1985 May 26, IV; 1986 May 31,
      IV; 1987 May 24, IV; 1988 May 29,
      IV; 1989 May 28, IV; 1990 May 27,
      IV; 1991 May 26, IV; 1992 May 24,
      IV
   Indianapolis 500 controversy, 1981
      May 24, IV
   land speed record, 1910 Mar. 16, IV;
      1970 Oct. 23, IV
   Marlboro 500, 1987 Aug. 2, IV
   oldest Indy winner, 1987 May 24, IV
   organized as sport, 1904, IV
   speed records, 1915 Oct. 9, IV
   Vanderbilt Cup, 1904, IV
   world speed record, 1963 Aug. 5(2),
      IV
Avedon, Richard, 1962 Jan., IV
Aviation (*see also* Airports; Airships;
   Aviation Accidents; Helicopters;
   Hijacking; SST (super-sonic transport)):
   airline operating losses, 1981, III
   airlines' problems, 1983, III
   airplane term suggested, 1912 Apr. 6,
      III
   air speed record, 1923 Oct. 6, III
   air traffic controllers' strike, 1981
      Aug. 3, III
   American-Eastern merger, 1962 Jan.
      23, III
   amphibious, 1912 Jan., III
   Army Air Corps established, 1926 July
      2(1), I
   around-the-world flight, 1931 June 23,
      III
   automatic propeller developed,
      1935(3), III
   A-12 Avenger navy plane canceled,
      1991 Jan. 7, I
   Boeing 747 jets, 1966 Apr. 13, III
   Boeing 767 introduced, 1982, III
   Braniff bankruptcy, 1982 May 13, III
   B-1 bomber halted, 1977 June 30, I
   B-2 stealth bomber, 1988 Nov. 22, I
   Civilian Aviation Act, 1926 May 20,
      III
   experimental jet capability, 1964 Feb.
      29, III
   federal control of civilian, 1938 June
      23, III
   first black woman pilot, 1978 Apr. 19,
      III
   first blind flight, 1929 Sept. 24, III
   first cross-country flight, 1911 Sept.
      17-Nov. 5, III
   first direct U.S.-U.S.S.R. commercial
      flights, 1968 July 15, III
   first flight over N. Pole, 1926 May 9,
      III
   first globe-circling passenger airline,
      1947 June 17, III
   first globe-circling passenger service,
      1959 Oct. 10, III
   first jet tested, 1942 Oct. 1, III
   first naval aircraft launching, 1910
      Nov. 14, III
   first nonstop flight across Pacific
      Ocean, 1931 Oct. 5, III

Aviation (*cont.*)
   first nonstop round-the-world flight,
      1949 Mar. 2, III
   first nonstop round-the-world flight
      without refueling, 1986 Dec. 23, III
   first N.Y.-Calif. mail plane, 1920, III
   first plane commercially made in U.S.,
      1909 Mar., III
   first postal service (N.Y.C.-Wash.,
      D.C.), 1918 May 15, III
   first powered flight (Kitty Hawk,
      N.C.), 1903, III
   first regular transatlantic passenger
      service (N.Y.-Portugal), 1939 June
      28, III
   first rocket-powered glider, 1931 June
      4, III
   first successful Antarctic parachute
      jump, 1956 Nov. 25, III
   first successful San Francisco-Honolulu
      flight, 1927 June 28, III
   first transcontinental glider flight,
      1930 Mar. 30, III
   first two-way air-ground
      communication, 1917 Aug. 18, III
   first woman solo across Atlantic, 1932
      May 20, III
   first woman to cross Atlantic, 1928
      June 3, III
   first 747 flight, 1969 Dec. 2, III
   Gossamer Condor human-powered,
      1977 Aug. 23, III
   Hughes' around-the-world flight,
      1938(6), III
   International Civil Aeronautics
      Conference, 1928 Dec. 12, III
   jet possibilities revealed, 1948 Sept.
      25, III
   jet transcontinental flight, 1949 Jan. 8,
      III
   Laker economy service, 1977 Sept.
      26, III
   Langley's machine tested, 1903(4), III
   Lindbergh's flight (N.Y.-Paris), 1927, I
   military production reduced, 1945
      May 25, III
   model plane flight, 1896(6), III
   most costly strike to date, 1961 Feb.
      23, III
   national radio beacon, 1927(4), III
   new flight altitude record, 1949 Feb.
      25(1), III
   new jet speed record, 1957 Dec. 12,
      III; 1988 Feb. 27, IV
   no-frills fares, 1975 Mar. 28, III
   Pan Am bankruptcy, 1991 Jan. 8, III
   passenger smoking ban, 1988 Apr. 23,
      III; 1989 Nov. 21, III
   patent litigation settled, 1914 Jan. 13,
      III
   seaplane flight record, 1915 Oct. 27,
      III
   sharp fare reductions, 1977, III
   sky advertising, 1908(5), III
   speed record, 1953 Dec. 16, III
   terminology changes, 1912 Apr. 6, III
   transatlantic speed record, 1958 June
      27, III
   transcontinental airmail test run,
      1924(3), III

Aviation (*cont.*)
   transcontinental jet speed record,
      1957 July 16, I
   U.S. meet (Los Angeles, Calif.),
      1910(7), III
   world jet speed record, 1958 May 16,
      I
   world speed record, 1960 Aug. 4, III
   Wright brothers' first glider (Kitty
      Hawk, N.C.), 1900(7), III
   Wright brothers' glider tested (Kitty
      Hawk, N.C.), 1901(3), III; 1902
      Sept., I
   Wright flight duration record, 1909
      July 27, III
   Wright tests in France, 1908 Sept. 17,
      III
Aviation accidents:
   Air Florida jet crashed (Wash., D.C.),
      1982 Jan. 13, I
   airship *Roma* aerial explosion, 1922
      Feb. 21, III
   airship *Shenandoah* (Ohio), 1925 Sept.
      3, III
   American Airlines crash (Chicago, Ill.),
      1979 May 25, I
   Army recruits killed (Va.), 1961 Nov.
      8, I
   Arrow Airlines charter jet
      (Newfoundland), 1985 Dec. 12, I
   causes of Electra crashes, 1960 May
      12, III
   collision (Danbury, Conn.), 1965 Dec.
      4, I
   collision (Ind.), 1969 Sept. 9, I
   collision over N.Y. harbor, 1960 Dec.
      16, I
   collision (Rio de Janeiro, Brazil), 1960
      Feb. 25, I
   Continental Airlines crash (Denver,
      Colo.), 1987 Nov. 15, I
   C-5A transport plane (S. Vietnam),
      1975 Apr. 4, I
   Delta (Dallas-Ft. Worth, Tex.), 1985
      Aug. 2, I
   East R. crash (N.Y.C.), 1959 Feb. 3, I
   Empire State Building hit (N.Y.C),
      1945 July 28(1), I
   first person killed, 1908 Sept. 17, III
   football players killed (Calif.), 1960
      Oct. 29, I
   head-on runway crash (Los Angeles),
      1991 Feb. 1(2), I
   Hindenburg fire (N.J.), 1937 May 6, I;
      1937 May 6, III
   Iowa crash, 1989 July 19, I
   Iranian jetliner downed, 1988 July 3, I
   jetliner plunged into Jamaica Bay
      (N.Y.C.), 1962 Mar. 1, I
   Kennedy Airport (N.Y.C.) jet crash,
      1975 June 24, I
   Lockheed Electra explosion, 1960
      Mar. 17, I
   Logan Airport crash (Boston, Mass.),
      1973 July 31, I
   Marshall Univ. football team, 1970
      Nov. 14, IV
   midair collision (Grand Canyon), 1986
      June 18, I

Aviation accidents (*cont.*)
  midair collision (Los Angeles, Calif.),
    1986 Aug. 13, I
  midair collision (N.C.), 1967 July 19, I
  midair collision (San Diego, Calif.),
    1978 Sept. 25, I
  midair explosion (Hawaii), 1988 Apr.
    28, I
  midair explosion (Lockerbie,
    Scotland), 1988 Dec. 21, I; 1991
    Nov. 27, I
  Northwest Airlines crash (Detroit,
    Mich.), 1987 Aug. 16, I
  nuclear-armed B-52 bomber
    (Greenland), 1968 Jan. 21, I
  Pan American jet crashed (New
    Orleans, La.), 1982 July 9, I
  second worst single-plane disaster to
    date, 1982 July 9, I
  TWA jet bombing (Rome-Athens),
    1986 Apr. 2, I
  U.S. amateur boxing team death
    (Poland), 1980 Mar. 14, IV
  U.S. military aircraft collision (Spain),
    1966 Jan. 17(2), I
  Wash., D.C.-bound jet (Va.), 1974 Dec.
    1, I
  Wichita State Univ. football team,
    1970 Oct. 2, IV
  worst commercial single plane to
    date, 1961 Sept. 1, I
  worst commercial to date (Grand
    Canyon), 1956 June 30, I
  worst single plane crash to date
    (Alaska), 1971 Sept. 4, I
  worst to date (Japan), 1953 June 18, I
  worst to date (N.Y. harbor), 1960 Dec.
    16, I
Avocado, 1833(1), IV
Avon Books, 1986 Jan. 11, II
Awards and honors *see* specific fields and
  award names
Axelrod, Julius, 1970 Oct. 15, III
Axis Sally (Mildred E. Gillars), 1988 June
  25, IV
Axum, Donna, 1963 Sept. 7, IV
Ay, Evelyn Margaret, 1953 Sept. 13, IV
Ayckbourn, Alan, 1974 Oct. 8, II
Ayer & Son, N.W., 1864(2), III
AZT (AIDS drug), 1987 Mar. 20, III; 1988
  May 13, III; 1989 June, III

Bártok, Béla, 1949(2), II
Büchner, Georg, 1965 Oct. 21(2), II
Babbitt, Benjamin T., 1843(3), III
Babcock, Barbara, 1981 Sept. 13, II
Babcock, Orville E., 1870, I; 1875, I
Babilonia, Tai, 1979 Mar. 17, IV
Babson, Roger W., 1940 May 10, I; 1940
  Nov. 5, I
Baby Fae, 1984 Oct. 16, III
Baby M case, 1987 Mar. 31, IV
Bacall, Lauren, 1970 Mar. 30, II
Bach, Richard, 1972(1), II
Bacon, Ernst, 1942 May 1, II
Bacon, Francis, 1688, II
Bacon's Rebellion (Va.), 1676 Sept. 19, I
Bacteriology, 1892(3), III
Badger, Joseph, 1765–1769, II
Baekeland, Leo H., 1893(2), III; 1909, III

Baer, Max, 1934 June 14, IV; 1935 June
  13, IV
Baffin, William, 1600–1609, I
Bagby, Jim, Jr., 1941 July 17, IV
Bailey, Charles W., 1960(1), II; 1962(1), II
Bailey, James A., 1875, IV
Bailey, Pearl, 1990, II
Baily, Francis, 1796(2), IV
Bailyn, Bernard, 1968 May 8, II; 1975 Apr.
  16, II; 1987 Apr. 16, II
Bain, Barbara, 1967 June 4, II; 1968 May
  19, II; 1969 June 8, II
Bainter, Fay, 1939 Feb. 23, II
Baird, Bill, 1987, II
Baird, Stephen F., 1887(2), III
Bakelite, 1909, III
Baker, Carlos, 1969(1), II
Baker, George, 1944(1), IV
Baker, George Pierce, 1905, II
Baker, Howard H., Jr., 1987 Feb. 26, I
Baker, James, 1765(1), III
Baker, James A., III, 1992 Aug. 23, I
Baker, Josephine, 1975, II
Baker, Kathy, 1985 July 14(2), IV
Baker, Leonard, 1979 Apr. 16, II
Baker, Nicholson, 1992(1), II
Baker, Russell, 1983 Apr. 18, II; 1989(1), II
Bakers:
  Dutch laws, 1656(3), IV
Bakke, Allan P., 1978 June 28, I
Bakken, Jim, 1967 Sept. 24, IV
Bakker, Jim, 1987 Mar. 19, III
Bakker, Tammy, 1987 Mar. 19, III
Bakke v. *University of California*, 1978
  June 28, I
Balance of payments, 1891, III; 1971, III
  U.S. debtor nation, 1985, III
Balanchine, George, 1962 June 14, II;
  1964 Apr. 24, II; 1965 May 27, II; 1970,
  II; 1972 June 18–25, II; 1975 May 15–31,
  II; 1983, II; 1989 Nov. 1, II
Balch, Emily Greene, 1946 Nov. 14, I
Baldwin, Faith, 1978, II
Baldwin, James, 1953(1), II; 1962(1), II;
  1965(1), II; 1974(1), II; 1987, II
Baldwin, Joseph Glover, 1853, II
Baldwin, Roger, 1981, I
Ball, Lucille, 1984 Mar. 4, II; 1989, II
Ball, Thomas, 1864(6), II; 1876(9), II
Ballesteros, Seve (Severiano), 1980 Apr.
  13, IV; 1983 Apr. 11, IV
Ballet *see* Dances and dancing
Balloons:
  first nonstop transcontinental flight,
    1980 May 12, IV
  first successful transatlantic crossing,
    1978 Aug. 11–17, IV
  first transatlantic solo flight, 1984
    Sept. 14–18, IV
  Goodyear disaster, 1919 July 21, III
  new altitude record, 1948 Nov. 20, III;
    1961 May 4, III
  new ascent record, 1957 Aug. 19–20,
    III
  Poe's hoax, 1844(6), IV
  record voyage (Ohio-S.C.), 1861 Apr.
    20, III
  for Union aerial reconnaissance,
    1862(3), II
Ballou, Hosea, 1775–1779, III; 1805, III

Balls and dances *see* Dances and dancing
Balsam, Martin, 1966 Apr. 18, II; 1968
  Apr. 21, II
Baltic States *see* Estonia; Latvia; Lithuania
Baltimore, David, 1975 Oct. 16, III
Baltimore and Ohio Railroad, 1828, III
Baltimore (Lord), 1632 June 20, I; 1634
  Mar. 25, III; 1649 Apr. 21, III; 1655
  Mar. 25, I
Baltimore (Md.):
  fire, 1904 Feb. 7–8, I
  settled, 1730(2), I
Bamberger, Louis, 1930, III
Bancroft, Aaron, 1807(1), IV
Bancroft, Anne, 1960 Apr. 24, II; 1963
  Apr. 8, II
Bancroft, George, 1834, II
Banister, John, 1680(1), III
Bankhead, Charles, 1847 June 6, I
Bankhead, Tallulah, 1968, II
Banking (*see also* Credit; Federal Reserve
  System; Savings and loan associations;
  bank names):
  Aldrich-Vreeland Act passed, 1907, III
  Bank of North America charter
    revoked (Pa.), 1785(5), III
  Bank of North America established,
    1781 Dec. 31, III
  Bank of Pennsylvania, 1799(4), II
  Bank of the U.S., 1791 Dec. 12, III;
    1832 July 10, I; 1833 Sept. 23, I;
    1833 Oct. 1, I; 1833 Dec. 26, I; 1834
    Mar. 28, I; 1930 Dec. 11, III
  BCCI scandal, 1991 July 5, III
  congressional scandal, 1992 Apr. 16, I
  credit expansion, 1837(3), III
  failures, 1890 May 1, III; 1934, I; 1974
    Oct. 8(2), III; 1982, III; 1983 Feb.
    14, III; 1984, III
  Federal Bank Deposit Insurance
    Corp. established, 1933 June 16(2), I
  first savings bank (Boston, Mass.), 1816
    Dec. 13, III
  Fiscal Bank of the U.S. bill vetoed,
    1841 June 12, I; 1841 Sept. 11, I
  Franklin failure (N.Y.C.), 1980 Mar.
    27, III
  Great Depression closures, 1930 Dec.
    11, III; 1931 Sept., I
  holidays declared, 1933 Mar. 1, I;
    1933 Mar. 5, I
  insurance premiums raised, 1992 May
    12(2), III
  largest federal loan guarantee, 1984
    July 26, III
  Latrobe's design for Second Bank of
    U.S., 1819(1), II
  mergers, 1991 July 15–Nov. 20, III
  national banks created, 1863 Feb. 25,
    I
  panics, 1819(1), I; 1837, I; 1893, III;
    1907, III; 1933, I; 1979 Oct. 6, III
  Penn Square failure (Okla. City), 1982
    July 5, III
  Postal Savings established, 1910 June
    25, III
  reopenings, 1933 Mar. 13, I
  second Bank of the U.S., 1823, III
  second national bank established,
    1816 Apr. 10, III

Banking (cont.)
  second U.S. Bank opened (Phila., Pa.),
    1817 Jan.7, I
  stimulated by War of 1812, 1812(2),
    III
  United American Bank failed
    (Knoxville, Tenn.), 1983 Feb. 14, III
Banking Act of 1933, 1933 June 16(2), I
Bank of America:
  failed (Phila., Pa.), 1890 May 1, III
Bank of Credit and Commerce see BCCI
Bank robberies:
  Hearst convicted, 1976 Mar. 20, IV
  Hearst implicated (San Francisco),
    1974 Apr. 3, IV
  Leslie's Manhattan Savings $3,000,000
    heist, 1878 Oct. 27, IV
Bankruptcy, 1992 Jan. 6, III
  BCCI, 1991 July 5, III
  Carter Hawley Hale Stores, 1991 Feb.
    11, III
  Dalkon Shield claims, 1987 Dec. 11,
    III
  Drexel Burnham Lambert, 1988 Dec.
    21, III
  federal law enacted, 1841 Aug. 19, I
  Macy, R. H., & Co., 1992 Jan. 6, II
  Ohio Life Insurance Co., 1857 Aug.
    24, III
  Pan Am Airways, 1991 Jan. 8, III
  petitions increased, 1975 Oct. 15, III
  Seabrook (N.H.) nuclear power plant,
    1988 Jan. 28, III
  Texaco, Inc., 1987 Dec. 19, III
Banks, Dennis, 1974 Sept. 16(3), I
Banneker, Benjamin, 1754, III
Bannister, Nathaniel, 1847, II
Banvard, John, 1840(1), II
Baptist Church:
  condemnation of homosexuality, 1992
    May 12(1), III
  first (R.I.), 1638, III
  First Baptist Church (Boston, Mass.)
    built, 1872(4), II
  first exiles from Mass., 1668 May 27,
    III
  first separate black (Va.), 1725(1), III
  first Seventh Day (R.I.), 1671, III
  first social union, 1864(3), III
  fundamentalist elected president,
    1986 June 10, III; 1990 June 12, III
  membership, 1900(2), III; 1989, III;
    1991, III
  ordination of women resolution
    opposing, 1984 June 14, III
  persecuted in Mass., 1651, III
  scorned Catholics in public office,
    1960 May 20(2), III
Barasch, Norman, 1958 Oct. 23, II
Barbed wire see Wire
Barbee, William Randolph, 1859(4), II
Barber, Jerry, 1961 July 30, IV
Barber, Red (Walter), 1992, IV
Barber, Samuel, 1958 Jan. 15, II; 1966
  Sept. 16, II; 1981, II
Barbers and beauticians see Beards and
  mustaches; Hair and wigs; Shaving
Bard, Samuel, 1807, III
Bard College (N.Y.), 1860 Mar. 20, III

Bardeen, John, 1956 Nov. 1, III; 1972 Oct.
  20(1), III; 1991, III
Barfield, Margie Velma, 1984 Nov. 2, I
Barger-Wallach, Maud, 1908(3), IV
Barker, James N., 1824 May 12, II;
  1836(10), II
Barker, Kylene, 1978 Sept. 9, IV
Barker, Wharton, 1900 May 10, I
Barkley, Alben:
  elected vice president, 1948 Nov. 2, I
  vice presidential candidacy, 1948 July
    15, I
Barlick, Al, 1989 July 23(3), IV
Barlow, Joel, 1784(2), II; 1790 Mar., I;
  1796(3), II
Barnard, Edward Emerson, 1892(11), III
Barnard, George Grey, 1894(2), II
Barnard, Henry, 1855(1), III
Barnard, John, 1846(3), IV
Barnard College (N.Y.C.):
  established, 1889(2), III
Barnes, Debra Dene, 1967 Sept. 9, IV
Barnes, James M., 1916 Jan. 17, IV; 1919
  Sept. 20, IV; 1921 July 22, IV
Barnet, Charles, 1991, II
Barnett, Marguerite Ross, 1992, III
Barnett, Ross, 1962 Sept. 20, III; 1962
  Sept. 28, III; 1962 Dec. 21, III
Barnum, Phineas T.:
  freak shows, 1837, IV
  Lind tour, 1850, II
  three-ring circus, 1875, IV
Barr, Stringfellow, 1982, II
Barré, Isaac, 1765(1), IV
Barrett, James Lee, 1975 Jan. 7(1), II
Barron, James, 1807, I
Barry, Philip, 1928 Nov. 26, II
Barrymore, Ethel, 1904 Nov. 15, II;
  1916(7), II; 1945 Mar. 15, II; 1959, II
Barrymore, John, 1942, II
Barrymore, Lionel, 1931 Nov. 10, II
Bars, saloons, and taverns:
  colonial, 1630–1639, IV
  colonial prohibitions, 1638(1), IV
  paintings in, 1885(4), II
  Wayside Inn (Mass.), 1690(1), II
  widows' livelihood, 1647(4), IV
Barsimson, Jacob, 1654 July 8, III
Bart, Philip, 1962 Mar. 19, I
Bartel, Jean, 1943 Sept. 4, IV
Barth, John, 1973 Apr. 10, II
Barthelme, Donald, 1989, II
Bartholdi, Frédéric Auguste, 1884 Aug. 5,
  I
Bartholomew, Freddie, 1992, II
Bartlett's Familiar Quotations, 1855(2), II
Barton, Clara, 1865(1), IV; 1881, III; 1882
  Mar. 16, I
Bartram, William, 1790–1794, II
Baruch, Bernard, 1918, III; 1948 Oct. 24,
  IV
Baryshnikov, Mikhail, 1974 July 27, II;
  1978, II; 1980, II

Baseball (see also Little League):
  all-star game, 1934 July 10, IV; 1935
    July 8, IV; 1936 July 7, IV; 1937 July
    7, IV; 1938 July 6, IV; 1939 July 11,
    IV; 1940 July 9, IV; 1941 July 8, IV;
    1942 July 6, IV; 1943 July 13, IV;
    1944 July 11, IV; 1945, IV; 1946
    July 9, IV; 1947 July 8, IV; 1948 July
    13, IV; 1949 July 12, IV; 1950 July
    11, IV; 1951 July 10, IV; 1952 July
    8, IV; 1953 July 14, IV; 1954 July
    13, IV; 1955 July 12, IV; 1956 July
    10, IV; 1957 July 9, IV; 1958 July 8,
    IV; 1959 July 7, IV; 1960 July 13,
    IV; 1961 July 31, IV; 1962 July 10,
    IV; 1963, IV; 1963 July 9, IV; 1964
    July 7, IV; 1965 July 13, IV; 1966
    July 12, IV; 1967 July 11, IV; 1968
    July 9, IV; 1969 July 23, IV; 1970
    July 14, IV; 1971 July 13, IV; 1972
    July 25, IV; 1973 July 24, IV; 1974
    July 23, IV; 1975 July 15, IV; 1976
    July 13, IV; 1977 July 19, IV; 1978
    July 11, IV; 1979 July 17, IV; 1980
    July 8, IV; 1981 Aug. 9(1), IV; 1982
    July 13, IV; 1983 July 6, IV; 1984
    July 11, IV; 1985 July 16, IV; 1986
    July 15, IV; 1987 July 14, IV; 1988
    July 12, IV; 1989 July 11, IV; 1990
    July 10, IV; 1992 July 14, IV
  American Assn. disbanded, 1891 Fall,
    IV
  American Assn. formed, 1882(1), IV
  American League expanded, 1967, IV
  American League formed, 1900 Jan.
    29, IV
  American League pennant, 1901
    Fall(2), IV; 1902 Fall(2), IV
  antitrust case, 1970, IV
  antitrust exemption ruled, 1972 June
    19, IV
  attendance, 1988, IV
  attendance drop, 1984, IV
  attendance record, 1957(1), IV; 1978,
    IV; 1982, IV
  attendance up, 1977, IV
  ball park changes, 1969, IV
  Baltimore chop, 1890(4), IV
  Black Sox (Chicago White Sox
    scandal), 1920, IV; 1921 Aug. 3, IV
  books on, 1990(1), II
  Bouton on, 1970(1), II
  called balls and strikes, 1863(2), IV
  Cartwright's rule and standards,
    1845(3), IV
  catcher's mask invented, 1876(3), IV
  Chandler named commissioner, 1945
    Apr. 24, IV
  Clemente killed in plane crash, 1972,
    IV
  clubs established, 1854(8), IV
  Collins's career, 1917, IV
  commissioner Giamatti died, 1989
    Sept. 13, IV
  commissioner Giamatti named, 1988
    Sept. 8, IV
  commissioner Landis died, 1944, IV
  commissioner Vincent resigned, 1992
    Sept. 7, IV
  Dean brothers, 1934, IV

Baseball (*cont.*)

designated hitter allowed, 1973, IV

DiMaggio's hitting streak ended, 1941 July 17, IV

divisions formed, 1968, IV

Dodgers sold, 1945 Aug. 10, IV

Dodgers to Los Angeles, 1957, IV

early form of, 1833(2), IV

early indication of popularity, 1856(1), IV

Ebbets Field demolished (Brooklyn, N.Y.), 1960 Feb. 23, IV

Eckert dismissed, 1968 Dec. 6, IV

Eckert elected commissioner, 1965 Nov. 17, IV

expansion, 1902, IV

first admission charge, 1858 July 20, IV

first all-star game, 1933 July 6, IV

first all-star tie, 1961 July 31, IV

first American League pennant, 1901 Fall(2), IV

first association formed, 1857(3), IV

first base-stealing, 1863(3), IV

first black in major league, 1947, IV

first Calif. baseball championship, 1959, IV

first deliberate bunt, 1866(4), IV

first double header, 1882 Sept. 25, IV

first double no-hit nine-inning game, 1917 May 2, IV

first electrically lit game, 1883 June 2, IV

first enclosed field (Brooklyn, N.Y.), 1862(2), IV

first free-agent draft, 1976 Nov. 4, IV

first game in Polo Grounds (N.Y.C.), 1917 Aug. 19, IV

first intercollegiate game, 1859 July 1, IV

first Ladies' Day, 1883 June 16, IV

first major league black player, 1884(6), IV

first mid-season strike, 1981 June 12, IV

first newspaper story, 1853(7), IV

first night baseball game played at Wrigley Field (Chicago), 1988 Aug. 8, IV

first night game, 1935 May 24, IV

first no-hit, no-run Series game, 1956 Oct. 3–10, IV

first no-hitter in National League history, 1876 May 23, IV

first non-North American team ownership, 1992 June 11, IV

first official National League game, 1876 Apr. 2, IV

first organized, 1845(3), IV

first organized in San Francisco (Calif.), 1860(6), IV

first organized team, 1839, IV

first paid players, 1864, IV

first perfect game, 1904 May 5, IV

first pitched curve ball, 1864(5), IV

first players' strike, 1972, IV; 1972 Apr. 1, IV

first post-season playoff, 1948, IV

first professional association, 1871 Mar. 17, IV

Baseball (*cont.*)

first professional team (Cincinnati), 1869 Mar. 15, IV

first radio coverage of World Series, 1921 Oct. 5, II

first recorded game (N.J.), 1846 June 19, IV

first rule stipulating ball weight and size, 1854(7), IV

first trophy, 1861(3), IV

first uniforms, 1851 June 3, IV

first World Series, 1903, IV

franchise value, 1992, IV

Gehrig died, 1941, IV

Giants to San Francisco, 1957, IV

glove introduced, 1875(2), IV

golden age of professional, 1913, IV

greatest dispute in, 1908 Sept. 23, IV

Hall of Fame, 1901, IV; 1902, IV; 1911, IV; 1937 Jan. 20, IV; 1938 Jan. 18, IV; 1939 Jan. 24, IV; 1942 Jan. 20, IV; 1943, IV; 1945 Jan. 20, IV; 1946 Apr. 23, IV; 1947 July 21, IV; 1948, IV; 1949 June 13, IV; 1951 July 23, IV; 1952 July 21, IV; 1953 July 27, IV; 1954 Aug. 9, IV; 1955 July 25, IV; 1956 July 23, IV; 1957 July 22, IV; 1959 July 20, IV; 1961 July 24, IV; 1962 July 23, IV; 1963 Aug. 5(1), IV; 1964 July 27, IV; 1965 July 26, IV; 1966 July 25, IV; 1967 July 24(2), IV; 1968 July 22, IV; 1969 July 28, IV; 1970 July 27, IV; 1971 Aug. 9, IV; 1972 Aug. 7, IV; 1973 Aug. 6, IV; 1974 Aug. 12, IV; 1975 Aug. 18, IV; 1976 Aug. 9, IV; 1977 Aug. 8, IV; 1978 Aug. 8, IV; 1979 Aug. 5, IV; 1980 Aug. 3, IV; 1981 Aug. 2, IV; 1982 Aug. 1, IV; 1983 July 31(1), IV; 1984 Aug. 12, IV; 1985 July 28, IV; 1986 Jan. 8, IV; 1987 July 26, IV; 1988 July 31, IV; 1989 July 23(3), IV; 1990 Aug. 6, IV; 1991 July 21, IV; 1992 Aug. 2, IV

Hall of Fame established (Cooperstown, N.Y.), 1936(2), IV

Hall of Fame exclusions, 1991 Feb. 4, IV

Hall of Fame founded (N.Y.C.), 1900 Mar. 5, III

heroes, 1911, IV; 1916, IV

highest batting average, 1894(2), IV

highest paid players, 1991 Dec. 2, IV; 1992 Mar. 2, IV

hitting records, 1985 Sept. 11, IV; 1992 Sept. 9, IV

home run records, 1927, IV; 1932, IV; 1961 Oct. 1, IV; 1964 Oct. 7–15, IV; 1966, IV; 1967, IV; 1967 May 14, IV; 1967 July 14, IV; 1969 Sept. 22, IV; 1973 Sept. 25, IV; 1974, IV; 1974 Apr. 8, IV; 1983 July 6, IV; 1987 Sept. 29, IV; 1988 Apr. 20, IV; 1988 Sept. 23, IV

hot corner term, 1880(6), IV

Houston Astrodome (Tex.) opened, 1965 Apr. 9, II

Houston Astros franchise, 1961, IV

Baseball (*cont.*)

Houston Colt .45's joined National League, 1962, IV

hundredth anniversary, 1969, IV

Koufax's pitching and retirement, 1966, IV

Kuhn contract ended, 1982 Nov. 1, IV

Kuhn contract extended, 1983 Dec. 8, IV

Kuhn named commissioner, 1969 Aug. 13, IV

Landis named commissioner, 1920 Nov. 8, IV

league split into divisions, 1969, IV

longest consecutive losses, 1988 Apr. 28, IV

longest game to date, 1964 May 31, IV

longest nine-inning game, 1986 June 8, IV

longest winning streak, 1916 Sept. 30, IV

McGraw's career, 1902, IV

Mack's career, 1901, IV

Mantle retired, 1969 June 8, IV

Mays retired, 1973 Sept. 25, IV

minor leagues, 1913, IV

Musial retired, 1963 Sept. 29, IV

National Assn. of Baseball Players, 1858(2), IV

National League expansion, 1991 July 5, IV

National League formed, 1876 Feb. 2, IV

National League pennant, 1878(3), IV; 1879 Fall, IV; 1880 Fall, IV; 1881 Fall, IV; 1882 Fall, IV; 1883 Fall, IV; 1884 Fall, IV; 1885 Fall, IV; 1886 Fall, IV; 1887 Fall, IV; 1888 Fall, IV; 1889 Fall, IV; 1890 Fall, IV; 1891 Fall, IV; 1892 Fall, IV; 1893 Fall, IV; 1894 Fall, IV; 1895 Fall, IV; 1896 Fall, IV; 1897 Fall, IV; 1898 Fall, IV; 1899 Fall, IV; 1900 Fall, IV; 1901 Fall(1), IV; 1902 Fall(1), IV

new American League franchises, 1968, IV

new franchises, 1961, IV

nine-inning rule, 1857(4), IV

N.Y.-Brooklyn rivalry began, 1853(6), IV

N.Y. Mets first season, 1962 Sept. 27, IV

N.Y. Mets first World Series victory, 1969, IV

N.Y. Mets franchise, 1961, IV

N.Y. Mets joined National League, 1962, IV

origins, 1839, IV

pennant race, 1946, IV; 1988 Oct. 15–20, IV

perfect game, 1917 June 23(1), IV; 1964 June 21, IV; 1965 Sept. 9, IV; 1968 May 8, IV; 1988 Sept. 16, IV; 1991 July 28, IV

pitched curve ball, 1870 Aug. 16, IV

pitching, 1888(3), IV; 1904 May 5, IV; 1913(1), IV; 1916, IV; 1917 June 23(1), IV; 1927(1), IV; 1934, IV;

Baseball (*cont.*)

1943(2), IV; 1963 Oct. 2–6, IV; 1964 Oct. 7–15, IV; 1965 Sept. 9, IV; 1968 May 8, IV; 1975 Sept. 1, IV; 1985 July 11, IV; 1985 Aug. 4, IV; 1985 Aug. 25, IV; 1988 Oct. 4, IV; 1989 Aug. 22, IV; 1990 July 31, IV; 1990 Sept. 2, IV; 1991 July 28, IV

players' boycott of spring training, 1969 Feb. 25, IV

players' free-agency collusion damages, 1990 Dec. 21, IV

players' free-agency ruled illegal, 1992 Sept. 10, IV

players' free-agent status, 1976, IV; 1988 Aug. 31, IV

players' free-agent status restricted, 1988 July 11(1), IV

players' salaries, 1988, IV; 1991 Dec. 2, IV; 1992 Mar. 2, IV

players' salary records, 1992, IV

players signed for three million annually, 1989 Nov. 22, IV; 1990 June 27, IV

playoffs extended, 1985, IV

popularity, 1933, IV; 1988, IV

popularity decline, 1992, IV

record attendance, 1985, IV

records, 1911, IV; 1913(1), IV; 1916, IV; 1938, IV; 1963 Sept. 29, IV

reserve clause, 1972 June 19, IV; 1976 July 12, IV

F. Robinson first black manager, 1974, IV; 1974 Oct. 3, IV

Rose banned for gambling, 1989 Aug. 24, IV

rules, 1834(6), IV; 1848(1), IV; 1872(3), IV; 1877(2), IV; 1879(1), IV; 1880(7), IV; 1881(1), IV; 1884(5), IV; 1891(1), IV; 1893(8), IV; 1894(1), IV; 1899(1), IV; 1900(3), IV; 1963, IV; 1973, IV

Ruth died, 1948, IV

sale of Oakland players voided, 1976 June 15, IV

season cut, 1918 Sept. 1, IV

second Koufax shutout, 1965 Oct. 6–14, IV

seventh-inning stretch, 1860(4), IV

squeeze play, 1894 June 16, IV

Steinbrenner banned from N.Y. Yankee management, 1990 July 30, IV

Steinbrenner ban rescinded, 1992 July 24, IV

Stengel fired, 1960 Oct. 18, IV

Stengel retirement, 1965 Aug. 30, IV

stolen-base records, 1974, IV; 1974 Sept. 10, IV; 1988 Sept. 23, IV

term *battery* first used, 1869(1), IV

Texas leaguer origins, 1889(3), IV

Thomson's home run, 1951, IV

"Tinker to Evers to Chance", 1907, IV

top spectator sport, 1983, IV; 1988, IV

TV rights, 1988 Dec. 1, IV

Ueberroth elected commissioner, 1984 Mar. 3, IV

umpire expelled for dishonesty, 1882 June 24, IV

Baseball (*cont.*)

unassisted triple play, 1992 Sept. 20(2), IV

unofficial championship won by Brooklyn, 1866(3), IV

upsurge of teams, 1865(2), IV

Vincent named commissioner, 1989 Sept. 13, IV

Washington Senators moved to Tex., 1971 Sept. 21, IV

White elected National League president, 1989 Feb. 3, IV

World Series, 1905 Oct. 9–14, IV; 1906 Oct. 9–14, IV; 1907 Oct. 8–12, IV; 1908 Oct. 10–14, IV; 1909 Oct. 8–16, IV; 1910 Oct. 17–23, IV; 1911 Oct. 14–26, IV; 1912 Oct. 8–16, IV; 1913 Oct. 7–11, IV; 1914 Oct. 9–13, IV; 1915 Oct. 8–13, IV; 1916 Oct. 7–12, IV; 1917 Oct. 6–15, IV; 1918 Sept. 5–11, IV; 1919 Oct. 1–9, IV; 1920 Oct. 5–12, IV; 1921 Oct. 5–13, IV; 1922 Oct. 4–8, IV; 1923 Oct. 10–15, IV; 1924 Oct. 4–10, IV; 1925 Oct. 7–15, IV; 1926 Oct. 2–10, IV; 1927 Oct. 5–8, IV; 1928 Oct. 4–9, IV; 1929 Oct. 8–14, IV; 1930 Oct. 1–8, IV; 1931 Oct. 1–10, IV; 1932 Sept. 28-Oct. 2, IV; 1933 Oct. 3–7, IV; 1934 Oct. 3–9, IV; 1935 Oct. 2–7, IV; 1936 Sept. 30-Oct. 6, IV; 1937 Oct. 6–10, IV; 1938 Oct. 5–9, IV; 1939 Oct. 4–8, IV; 1940, IV; 1940 Oct. 2–8, IV; 1941 Oct. 1–6, IV; 1942 Sept. 30–Oct. 5, IV; 1943 Oct. 5–11, IV; 1944 Oct. 4–9, IV; 1945 Oct. 3–10, IV; 1946 Oct. 6–15, IV; 1947 Sept. 30–Oct. 6, IV; 1948 Oct. 6–11, IV; 1949 Oct. 5–9, IV; 1950 Oct. 4–7, IV; 1951 Oct. 4–10, IV; 1952 Oct. 1–7, IV; 1953 Sept. 30–Oct. 5, IV; 1954 Sept. 29–Oct. 2, IV; 1955 Sept. 28–Oct. 4, IV; 1956 Oct. 3–10, IV; 1957 Oct. 2–10, IV; 1958 Oct. 1–9, IV; 1959 Oct. 18, IV; 1960 Oct. 5–13, IV; 1961 Oct. 4–9, IV; 1962 Oct. 4–16, IV; 1963 Oct. 2–6, IV; 1964, IV; 1964 Oct. 7–15, IV; 1965 Oct. 6–14, IV; 1966, IV; 1966 Oct. 5–9, IV; 1967 Oct. 4–12, IV; 1968 Oct. 2–10, IV; 1969 Oct. 11–16, IV; 1970 Oct. 10–15, IV; 1971 Oct. 9–17, IV; 1972 Oct. 14–22, IV; 1973 Oct. 13–21, IV; 1974 Oct. 12–17, IV; 1975 Oct. 11–22, IV; 1976 Oct. 16–21, IV; 1977 Oct. 11–18, IV; 1978 Oct. 10–17, IV; 1979 Oct. 10–17, IV; 1980 Oct. 14–21, IV; 1981 Oct. 20–28, IV; 1982 Oct. 12–20, IV; 1983 Oct. 11–16, IV; 1984 Oct. 9–14, IV; 1985 Oct. 19–27, IV; 1986 Oct. 18–27, IV; 1987 Oct. 17–25, IV; 1988 Oct. 15–20, IV; 1989 Oct. 14–28, IV; 1989 Oct. 17, I; 1990 Oct. 16–20, IV; 1991 Oct. 19–27, IV; 1992 Oct. 17–24, IV

World Series canceled, 1904(4), IV

World Series forerunner, 1882 Fall, IV

World Series records, 1938, IV

Baseball (*cont.*)

Yankees and Dodgers sold, 1945, IV

Yankees' fifth consecutive World Series, 1953 Sept. 30–Oct. 5, IV

Yankees sold, 1945 Jan. 26, IV

Yankee Stadium (N.Y.C.) opened, 1923 Apr. 18, IV

Basie, Count, 1984, II

Basilio, Carmen, 1957, IV; 1958 Mar. 25, IV

Basketball, 1989 June 13, IV

ABA championship, 1969 Apr. 30–May 7, IV; 1970 May 15–25, IV; 1971 May 18, IV; 1972 May 20(1), IV; 1973 Apr. 28–May 12, IV; 1974 Apr. 30–May 10, IV; 1975 May 13–22, IV; 1976 May 1–13, IV

ABA first season financial loss, 1968, IV

ABA reduced, 1975, IV

ABA second pro league formed, 1967 Feb. 2, IV

AIAW championship, 1973 Mar. 24, IV; 1974 Mar. 23, IV; 1975 Mar. 22, IV; 1976 Mar. 27, IV; 1977 Mar. 26, IV; 1978 Mar. 25, IV; 1979 Mar. 25, IV; 1980 Mar. 23, IV; 1981 Mar. 29, IV

Alcindor's firsts, 1969 Mar. 22, IV

antitrust suit, 1972, IV

attendance up, 1977, IV

Auerbach retired, 1966 Apr. 17–28, IV

bribery scandal, 1961 June 9, IV

Carnesecca 500th coaching victory, 1991 Feb. 2, IV

CBS rights to broadcast NCAA tournaments, 1989 Nov. 21, IV

Chamberlain retired, 1960 Mar. 25, IV

drug use, 1986, IV

first ABA championship, 1968 Apr. 18–May 4, IV

first AIAW women's collegiate championship, 1972 Mar. 19, IV

first black coach, 1966 Apr. 17–28, IV

first comprehensive NBA contract, 1973 Mar. 5, IV

first NBA championship, 1950 Apr. 8–23, IV

first player to score 100 points, 1962 Mar. 2, IV

first 15,000-point NBA player, 1960 Jan. 12, IV

invented, 1891, IV

Johnson retirement, 1991 Nov. 7, IV

NBA-ABA merger, 1976 June 17, IV

NBA championship, 1951 Apr. 7–21, IV; 1952 Apr. 12–15, IV; 1953 Apr. 4–10, IV; 1954 Mar. 31–Apr. 12, IV; 1955 Mar. 21–Apr. 10, IV; 1956 Mar. 31–Apr. 7, IV; 1957 Mar. 30–Apr. 3, IV; 1958 Mar. 29–Apr. 12, IV; 1959 Apr. 4–9, IV; 1960 Mar. 27–Apr. 9, IV; 1961 Apr. 2–11, IV; 1962 Apr. 7–18, IV; 1963 Apr. 24, IV; 1964 Apr. 18–26, IV; 1965 Apr. 18–25, IV; 1966 Apr. 17–28, IV; 1967 Apr. 14–24, IV; 1968 Apr. 21–May 2, IV; 1969 Apr. 23–May 5, IV; 1970 Apr. 24–May 8, IV; 1971

Basketball (*cont.*)
Apr. 30, IV; 1972 May 7, IV; 1973 May 10, IV; 1974 Apr. 28–May 12, IV; 1975 May 18–25, IV; 1976 May 23–June 6, IV; 1977 May 22–June 5, IV; 1978 May 21–June 7, IV; 1979 May 20–June 1, IV; 1980 May 4–16, IV; 1981 May 5–14, IV; 1982 May 27–June 8, IV; 1983 May 22–31, IV; 1984 May 27–June 12, IV; 1985 May 27–June 9, IV; 1986 May 26–June 8, IV; 1987 June 2–14, IV; 1988 June 7–21, IV; 1989 June 13, IV; 1990 June 14, IV; 1991 June 12, IV; 1992 June 14, IV

NCAA championship, 1939 Mar. 27, IV; 1940 Mar. 30, IV; 1941 Mar. 29, IV; 1942 Mar. 28, IV; 1943 Mar .30, IV; 1944 Mar. 28, IV; 1945 Mar. 29, IV; 1946 Mar. 23, IV; 1947 Mar. 25, IV; 1948 Mar. 13, IV; 1949 Mar. 26, IV; 1950 Mar. 28, IV; 1951 Mar. 27, IV; 1952 Mar. 26, IV; 1953 Mar. 18(1), IV; 1954 Mar. 20, IV; 1955 Mar. 19, IV; 1956 Mar. 23, IV; 1957 Mar. 23, IV; 1958 Mar. 22, IV; 1959 Mar. 21, IV; 1960 Mar. 19, IV; 1961 Mar. 25, IV; 1962 Mar. 24, IV; 1963 Mar. 23, IV; 1964 Mar. 21, IV; 1965 Mar. 20, IV; 1966 Mar. 19, IV; 1967 Mar. 25, IV; 1968 Mar. 23, IV; 1969 Mar. 22, IV; 1970 Mar. 21, IV; 1971 Mar. 27, IV; 1972 Mar. 25, IV; 1973 Mar. 26, IV; 1974 Mar. 24, IV; 1975 Mar. 31, IV; 1976 Mar. 29, IV; 1977 Mar. 28, IV; 1978 Mar. 27, IV; 1979 Mar. 26, IV; 1980 Mar. 24, IV; 1981 Mar. 30, IV

NCAA men's championship, 1982 Mar. 29, IV; 1983 Apr. 4, IV; 1984 Apr. 2, IV; 1985 Apr. 1, IV; 1986 Mar. 31, IV; 1987 Mar. 30, IV; 1988 Apr. 4, IV; 1989 Apr. 3, IV; 1990 Apr. 2, IV; 1991 Apr. 1, IV; 1992 Apr. 6, IV

NCAA women's championship, 1982, IV; 1982 Mar. 28, IV; 1983 Apr. 2, IV; 1984 Apr. 1, IV; 1985 Mar. 31, IV; 1986 Mar. 30, IV; 1987 Mar. 29, IV; 1989 Apr. 2, IV; 1990 Apr. 1, IV; 1991 Mar. 31, IV; 1992 Apr. 5, IV

Olympic "Dream Team," 1992 July 25–Aug. 9, IV

players' free-agent status, 1976, IV

popularity increased, 1990, IV

record attendance, 1985, IV

scoring record, 1991 Jan. 5, IV

Thompson's record salary, 1978, IV

three-point field goal adopted, 1986 Apr. 2, IV

UCLA coach Wooden retired, 1975 Mar. 31, IV

Basov, Nikolai, 1964 Oct. 29, III
Bass, Charlotta A., 1952 July 4–6, I
Bastille Day, 1790 July 14, IV
Bate, Walter Jackson, 1978 Jan. 11, II; 1978 Apr. 10, II; 1978 Apr. 17, II
Bates, Alan, 1973 Mar. 25, II
Bates, Katherine Lee, 1895 July 4, II

Bates, Kathy, 1991 Mar. 25, II
Bathrooms *see* Plumbing
Batterson, James G., 1863(2), III
Battles *see* place names, e.g., Lexington, Battle of
Baum, L. Frank, 1900(1), II
Baxter, Anne, 1947 Mar. 13(2), II
Baxter, Keith, 1970 Nov. 12, II
Baxter, Richard, 1664(3), II
Baxter, Warner, 1930 Apr. 3, II
Bayard, Thomas F., 1893 Apr. 3, I
Bay Area Rapid Transit System (BART) (Calif.), 1972 Sept. 11, III
Baylor University (Tex.), 1845 Feb. 1, III; 1861 Dec. 24, III
Bay of Pigs invasion (Cuba), 1961 Apr. 17, I; 1962 Apr. 8, I; 1962 Dec. 23, I
Bayonne Decree, 1808 Apr. 17, I
BCCI (Bank of Credit and Commerce International), 1991 July 5, III
Beach, Moses Yale, 1844(3), IV; 1844(6), IV; 1848(1), III
Beach, Sylvia, 1962, II
Beaches:
first boardwalk (N.J.), 1870(5), IV
N.Y.C., 1881(3), IV
Beacon, The (publication), 1840(8), III
Beadle, Erastus, 1860(1), II
Beadle, George W., 1958 Oct. 30, III
Beame, Abraham, 1977 Aug. 26, I
Beamon, Bob, 1968 Oct. 12–27, IV
Bean, Alan L., 1969 Nov. 14, III; 1973 July 28, III
Beard, Daniel Carter, 1910, IV
Beard, Frank, 1969, IV
Beard, James, 1985, IV
Bearden, Romare, 1988, II
Beards and mustaches:
Civil War-era popularity, 1865, IV
Hawthorne on, 1837(5), IV
Bear Flag Revolt (Calif.), 1845 Spring, I; 1846 June 14, I
Beat generation, 1957(1), II
Beatles (group), 1964 Feb. 7, II; 1965 Sept. 13, II; 1967, II
Beatrice Foods Co., 1984 May 24, III
Beatty, Jim, 1962 Feb. 10, IV
Beauregard, Pierre G.T., 1861 Apr. 12, I; 1862 Apr. 6–7, I
Beauty and cosmetics:
Carolinian women, 1753 May 10, IV
sales of products, 1984, IV
Beck, Dave, 1957 May 2, III
Becker, Boris, 1989 Sept. 9–10, IV
Becker, Ernest, 1974 May 7, II
Becker, Gary S., 1992 Oct. 13, III
Beckley, John, 1802 Jan. 29, I
Bedford, Brian, 1971 Mar. 28, II
Beebe, William, 1962, II
Beecher, Henry K., 1968 Dec. 4, III
Beecher, Henry Ward:
adultery trial, 1874 Aug. 21, IV
"Beecher's Bibles" in Kans., 1854(2), IV
English lecture tour, 1863(1), I
Plymouth Church (Brooklyn, N.Y.), 1847(5), II
sermons' popularity, 1868(5), IV
Beecher, Lyman, 1810(1), IV

Bee Gees (group), 1978 Feb. 23, II; 1979 Feb. 16, II
Beer:
first brewery in Baltimore (Md.), 1744, III
first brewery in Ga., 1740(2), III
Begin, Menachem, 1978 Sept. 6–17, I; 1979 Mar. 26, I
Begley, Ed, 1963 Apr. 8, II
Behan, Brendan, 1960 Sept. 20, II
Behrman, S. N., 1954 Nov. 4, II; 1973, II
Beiderbecke, Bix, 1923, II
Beissel, J. Conrad, 1747(2), II
Belasco, David, 1865(10), II; 1889(3), II; 1905 Oct. 3, II
Belcher, Supply, 1794(4), II
Bel Geddes, Barbara, 1980 Sept. 7, II
Bell, Alexander Graham, 1876 Mar. 7, III; 1915 Jan. 25(2), III
Bell, Cool Papa (James), 1991, IV
Bell, John, 1860 May 9, I
Bellaman House (Mass.), 1880(3), II
Bellamy, Edward, 1888(1), II
Bellamy, Ralph, 1958 Apr. 13, II; 1991, II
Belleau Wood, Battle of, 1918 June 6–25, I
Bellini, Vincenzo, 1970 Mar. 3, II
Bellow, Saul, 1953(1), II; 1954 Jan. 26, II; 1956(1), II; 1959(1), II; 1964(1), II; 1965 Mar. 9, II; 1970(1), II; 1971 Mar. 4, II; 1975(1), II; 1976 May 3, II; 1976 Oct. 21, II; 1982(1), II; 1984(1), II; 1989(1), II
auction of papers, 1988 June 7, II
Bells, 1831(1), III
Belmont Stakes (N.Y.), 1986 June 7, IV
Bemis, Samuel Flagg, 1950 May 1, II
Bemis Heights, Battles of (N.Y.), 1777 Sept. 19(1), I; 1777 Oct. 7, I
Benét, Stephen Vincent, 1928, II; 1929 May 12, II; 1944 May 1, II
Benét, William Rose, 1942 May 4, II
Benacerraf, Baruj, 1980 Oct. 10, III
Bench, Johnny, 1989 July 23(3), IV
Benchley, Peter, 1974(1), II
Benchley, Robert, 1945, II
Benham, Dorothy Kathleen, 1976 Sept. 11, IV
Benjamin, Asher, 1806(1), II
Bennett, Alan, 1962 Oct. 27, II
Bennett, Floyd, 1926 May 9, III
Bennett, Joan, 1990, II
Bennett, Michael, 1976 May 3, II; 1987, II
Bennett, Tony, 1963 May 15, II
Bennett, William J., 1988, III
Bennington College (Vt.), 1932 Fall, III
Benny, Jack, 1974, II
Benoit, Joan, 1983 Apr. 18, IV; 1984 July 28–Aug. 12, IV
Benson, Ezra Taft, 1985 Nov. 11, III
Benson, George, 1977 Feb. 19, II
Benton, Thomas Hart, 1943, II; 1943(5), II; 1975, II
Benton, Thomas Hart (Mo. Sen.):
states' rights, 1830 Jan. 19–27, I
Bent's cold water crackers, 1801(1), IV
Bentsen, Lloyd M., Jr., 1988 July 18–21, I
Benz, Karl, 1895 June 11, III
Berg, Alban, 1959 Mar. 5, II
Berg, Gertrude, 1951 Jan. 23, II; 1959 Apr. 12, II
Berg, Joseph F. (Rev.), 1856(5), III

Berg, Patty, 1946 Sept. 1, IV; 1954, IV; 1955, IV; 1957, IV; 1958 July 13, IV
Berg, Paul, 1980 Oct. 14(1), III
Bergen, Candice, 1989 Sept. 17, II; 1990 Sept. 16, II; 1992 Aug. 30, II
Bergen, Edgar, 1978, II
Bergen, Polly, 1958 Apr. 15(1), II
Berger, Thomas, 1964(1), II
Berger, Victor L., 1910 Nov. 8, I
Bergeron, Marion, 1933 Sept. 9, IV
Bergh, Henry, 1875(3), III
Bergman, Ingrid, 1945 Mar. 15, II; 1946 Nov. 18, II; 1947 Apr. 7, II; 1957 Mar. 27, II; 1960 June 20, II; 1975 Apr. 8(1), II; 1982, II; 1982 Sept. 19, II
Berkeley, Busby, 1971 Jan. 19, II; 1976, II
Berkeley, John (Lord), 1664 June 24, I
Berkeley, William, 1640–1649, II; 1647(2), IV; 1676 Sept. 19, I
Berkenhead, John L., c1794, II
Berkowitz, David, 1977 Aug. 10, IV
Berkshire Cattle Show (Mass.), 1810 Oct. 1, IV
Berle, Milton, 1950 Jan. 28, II; 1984 Mar. 4, II
Berlin, Irving, 1911(2), II; 1914 Dec. 8, II; 1925 Dec. 8, II; 1933 Sept. 9, II; 1989, II
    musical collection donated to Library of Congress, 1992 Oct. 2, II
    100th birthday celebration, 1988 May 11, II
Berlin (Germany):
    bombed by Allies, 1944 Mar. 6, I
    discothèque bombing, 1986 Apr. 5, I
    J. Kennedy visit, 1963 June 23, I
    Soviet blockade, 1948, I
    Soviet intentions, 1959 June 21, I
    U.S. military convoy blocked, 1963 Nov. 4, I
    U.S. tanks withdrawn from wall, 1962 Jan. 15, I
    wall built, 1961, I
Bernadin, Joseph Cardinal, 1983 Feb. 2, III; 1992 Sept. 21(1), III
Bernbach, William, 1982, III
Bernhardt, Sarah, 1880 Nov. 8, II; 1912 July 12, II; 1917(2), II
Berning, Susie Maxwell, 1968 July 7, IV; 1972 July 2(2), IV; 1973 July 22, IV
Bernstein, Burton, 1975(1), II
Bernstein, Carl, 1974(1), II; 1976(1), II; 1977 Sept. 11(2), II
Bernstein, Leonard, 1990, II
    antiwar counterconcert (Wash., D.C.), 1973 Jan. 19, II
    appointed N.Y. Philharmonic conductor, 1957 Oct. 16, II
    Candide, 1974 Mar. 11, II
    compositions, 1944 Apr. 18, II; 1949(2), II; 1952(3), II; 1953 Feb. 25, II; 1957 Sept. 26, II; 1959 Aug. 5–Oct. 10, II; 1971 Sept. 8–9, II; 1974 May 16, II
    conducted at Philharmonic Hall (N.Y.C.) opening, 1962 Sept. 23, II
    international tour, 1959, II; 1959 Aug. 5–Oct. 10, II
    last Philharmonic concert, 1969 May 17(1), II

Bernstein, Leonard (cont.)
    music library donated to N.Y. Philharmonic, 1992 Aug. 20, II
    N.Y. Philharmonic anniversary concert, 1967 Dec. 7, II
    premiered In Praise of Shahn (Schuman), 1970 Jan. 29, II
    retirement from N.Y. Philharmonic announced, 1966 Nov. 2, II
Berra, Yogi, 1958 Oct. 1–9, IV; 1964, IV
Berrera, Laz, 1991, IV
Berrigan, Daniel J., 1970 Aug. 11, III; 1970 Nov. 27, I
Berrigan, Philip F., 1970 Aug. 11, III; 1970 Nov. 27, I; 1971 Jan. 12, I; 1972 Sept. 5, I
Berryman, John, 1964(1), II; 1965 May 3, II; 1969 Mar. 10(2), II; 1972, II; 1972(1), II; 1973(1), II
Berwanger, Jay, 1935(1), IV
Bessemer, Henry, 1857, III
Betbeze, Yolande, 1950 Sept. 9, IV
Bethany College (W. Va.), 1840 Mar. 2, III
Bethe, Hans Albrecht, 1967 Oct. 18(2), III
Bethel (communal settlement, Mo.), 1845(3), III
Bethlehem Steel Corp., 1904 Dec. 10, III; 1941 Feb. 26, III
Bettelheim, Bruno, 1977 Jan. 6, II; 1977 Apr. 13(1), II; 1990, III
Betz, Carol, 1969 June 8, II
Betz, Pauline, 1942 Sept. 6–7, IV; 1943 Sept. 5, IV; 1944 Sept. 3, IV; 1946 July 6, IV; 1946 Sept. 8, IV
Beverages (see also types):
    cider's popularity (N.Y.), 1749(1), IV
    drinking habits, 1954, IV
    new Coca-Cola, 1985, IV
    popular colonial, 1710–1714, IV
    root beer marketed, 1877(2), III
Beverley, Robert, 1705, II; 1705(2), IV
Bevilacqua, Anthony J., 1991 May 29, III
Bias, Len, 1986, IV
Biasone, Danny, 1992, IV
Bible (see also Fundamentalism):
    American Society founded, 1816(2), III
    Berg's argument that U.S. is Promised Land, 1856(5), III
    creation science theory, 1982 Jan. 5, III
    critical works and interpretations, 1891(5), III; 1891(6), III
    first American edition, 1777(3), II
    first Catholic, 1790(4), III
    first complete English, 1782(1), II
    first Greek New Testament printed, 1800(3), II
    first printed in colonies, 1653(2), II; 1661, II
    Gideon, 1899, III
    Gutenberg auctioned at record price (N.Y.C.), 1978 Apr. 7, II
    modernist views of, 1892(4), III
    New American published, 1970 Sept. 30, III
    New English published, 1970 Mar. 16, III
    New Revised Standard, 1990 Sept. 30, III

Bible (cont.)
    new translation eliminating male references to God, 1983 Oct. 14, III
    Reader's Digest condensed, 1979, III
    Reform Judaism commentary, The Torah, 1975, III
    revised New Testament, 1987 Apr. 4, III
    society formed, 1808 Dec. 12, III
    Webster's bowdlerized version, 1833(3), II
Bicentennial:
    ballet Drums, Dreams, and Banjos (N.Y.C.), 1975 Oct. 9, II
    battles of Lexington and Concord (Mass.), 1975 Apr. 20, II
    Chagall's America Windows unveiled (Chicago), 1977 May 15, II
    Constitution, 1987, I
    festivities, 1976 July 4, IV
    Mozart death, 1991 Jan. 27, II
Bicycling:
    "Daisy Bell" song, 1892(2), II
    failure as transportation mode, 1872 Nov. 1, III
    first American Tour de France winner, 1986 July 27, IV
    first American to win Tour of Italy race, 1988 June 12, IV
    first inclusion of women in Little 500 (Ind.), 1988 Apr. 22, IV
    first international six-day race (N.Y.C.), 1891 Oct. 18, IV
    first recorded race, 1883(2), IV
    popularity, 1878, IV; 1889(2), IV; 1892(2), II; 1893(2), IV
    safety bicycle, 1889(2), IV
    Tour de France, 1989 July 23(2), IV
    velocipeding, 1868(2), IV
    women's skirts shortened for, 1895(1), IV
Biddle, Nicholas, 1823, III; 1834(5), II
Bidwell, John, 1892 Nov. 8, I
Bienville, Sieur de, Le Moyne, Jean Baptiste, 1749 May 19, I
Bierce, Ambrose, 1891(1), II; 1893(1), II; 1911(1), II
Bierstadt, Albert, 1991 Feb. 8, II
Bierstadt, Frederick, 1861(5), II
Bigart, Homer, 1991, II
Big Bang theory, 1965 June 12, III
Bigelow, Erastus B., 1846(2), III; 1848(2), III
Billiards:
    colonial, 1722 Apr. 30, IV; 1796(2), IV
    composition ball patented, 1865(3), IV
    first championship, 1858 Apr. 12, IV
    first intercollegiate, 1860(7), IV
    first national champion, 1859(3), IV
Billings, Warren, 1916 July 22, I
Billings, William, 1770(1), II
Bill of Rights:
    adopted, 1790–1794, I
Biltmore Forest School (N.C.), 1898(1), III
Bimetallism:
    backing of bills, 1963 June 4, III
    Bryan's "cross of gold" speech, 1896 July 7, IV; 1896 July 11, I
    Coinage Act, 1792 Apr. 2, I

Bimetallism (*cont.*)
  Democratic Silver Convention (Neb.),
    1894 June 21, I
  free silverites, 1891 May 19, I;
    1894(1), II; 1894 June 21, I; 1895
    Mar. 5, I; 1900 Mar. 14, I
  gold hoarding, 1931 Sept., I
  gold standard, 1900 Mar. 14, I
  gold standard endorsed, 1897 Jan. 12,
    I
  gold standard supporters, 1895 Feb. 8,
    I
  National League formed, 1893 Aug. 1,
    III
  National Monetary Conference (Ind.),
    1897 Jan. 12, I
  political issue, 1890(7), III
  presidential campaign issue, 1896, I;
    1896 July 11, I; 1896 July 22–24, I
  Sherman Silver Purchase Act, 1890
    July 14, I; 1893, I
  silver coinage bill vetoed, 1894 Mar.
    30, I
  silver content in coins reduced, 1853
    Feb. 21, I
  sixteen-one ratio, 1834 June 28, I
  suspension of compulsory coinage of
    silver dollars recommended, 1885
    Dec., I
  three-dollar gold pieces, 1853 Feb. 21,
    I
Bing, Rudolf, 1970 Dec. 9, II; 1972 Apr.
  22, II
Bingham, Barry, Sr., 1988, II
Bingham, George Caleb, 1978, II; 1987, II
Bingham, William, 1796–1799, IV
Biological warfare *see* Chemical and
  biological warfare
Biondi, Matt, 1988 Sept. 17–Oct. 2, IV
Birch Society, John, 1961 Mar. 8, I
Bird, Robert Montgomery, 1831 Sept. 26,
  II; 1837(3), II
Birds:
  American Ornithology published,
    1808(2), III
  Audubon's paintings, 1827, II
  first banded by Audubon, 1803 Apr.,
    III
  migratory treaty (U.S.-Canada), 1916
    Aug. 16, III
  sparrow imported, 1850(9), III
  starlings becoming pests, 1917(6), II
Birds of America, The (Audubon), 1827, II
Birmingham, Stephen, 1972(1), II
Birmingham (Ala.):
  church bombing, 1963 Sept. 15, I
  King arrested, 1963 Apr. 12, III
Birney, James G., 1836 Jan., II; 1839 Nov.
  13, I; 1843 Aug. 31, I; 1844, I; 1844 Dec.
  4, I
Birth control (*see also* Abortion):
  American Birth Control League
    founding, 1921 Nov. 2, III
  Catholic bishops condemned, 1968
    July 31, III
  Catholic doctrinal controversy, 1986
    Mar. 11, III
  Conn. ban unconstitutional, 1965 June
    7(1), I

Birth control (*cont.*)
  Dalkon Shield damage claims, 1987
    Dec. 11, III
  endorsed by Church Council, 1961
    Feb. 22–23, III
  Episcopal Church stance, 1960 Jan. 9,
    III
  first clinic (N.Y.), 1916 Oct. 16, III
  first U.S. book on, 1830 Dec., III
  General Federation of Women's Clubs
    endorsed, 1935(5), III
  injectable contraceptive, 1992 Oct.
    29, III
  new hormone-releasing contraceptive,
    1990 Dec. 10, III
  Sanger arrested, 1915(2), II
  Sanger Clinical Research Center
    (N.Y.C.) raided, 1929 Apr. 15, III
  Wright's *Unwelcomed Child*, 1858(1),
    IV
Births (*see also* Illegitimacy; Pregnancy
  and birth):
  first English, 1587 Aug. 18, IV
  first in New Amsterdam, 1625, IV
  first white (Vinland), 1007, IV
  lowest yearly rate to date, 1967 Nov.
    20, I
  rate down, 1965, I; 1991, III
  rate up, 1988, I; 1989, I
Bishop, Elizabeth, 1956 May 7, II; 1970
  Mar. 2, II; 1977 Jan. 6, II; 1979, II
Bishop, Jim, 1955(1), II
Bishop, J. Michael, 1989 Oct. 9, III
Bismarck Sea, Battle of the (Pacific), 1943
  Mar. 2–4, I
Bison, 1873, IV
Bitburg (W. Ger.), 1985 May 5, I
Bizet, Georges, 1916 Nov. 13, II
Bjoerling, Jussi, 1960, II
Bjurstedt, Molla, 1915 June 12, IV; 1916
  June 12, IV; 1917 June 23(2), IV; 1918
  June 22, IV; 1920 Sept. 6, IV; 1921 Aug.
  20, IV; 1922 Aug. 19, IV; 1926 Aug. 23,
  IV
Black, Eugene R., 1992, III
Black, Hugo L., 1937 July 22(1), I
Black, James, 1988 Oct. 17, III
Black Academy of Arts and Letters, 1969
  Mar. 27, II
Blackbeard (Edward Teach), 1715–1719,
  IV
Black Hawk (Indian chief), 1831 June 27,
  I; 1832 Apr. 6, I; 1832 Aug. 2, I; 1832
  Aug. 27, I
Black Liberation Front, 1965 Feb. 16, I
Blacklisting *see* Subversion and loyalty
  issue
Black market:
  U.S. World War II, 1944 Feb. 29, III
Blackmer, Sidney, 1950 Apr. 9, II
Blackmun, Harry A., 1970 May 12, I
Black Muslims:
  Malcolm X assassinated, 1965 Feb. 21,
    I
  subject of terrorist raid (Wash., D.C.),
    1977 Mar. 9–11, IV
  zebra killings, 1974 May 16, IV
Blackouts and dimouts:
  first (Md.), 1813 Aug. 9, IV
  massive Northeast, 1965 Nov. 9–10, I

Blackouts and dimouts (*cont.*)
  nationwide, 1945 Jan. 15, III
  nationwide dimout lifted, 1945 May 8,
    III
  N.Y.C. area, 1977 July 13–14, I
  Southwest, 1965 Dec. 2, I
Black Panthers:
  Cleaver returned to U.S., 1975 Nov.
    18, I
  Hampton shot, 1969 Dec. 4, I
Black power (*see also* names of specific
  organizations and leaders):
  Davis acquitted, 1972 June 4, I
  Davis capture and trial, 1970 Oct. 13,
    I
  goals, 1966, III
  salute given at Summer Olympics
    (Mexico City), 1968 Oct. 12–27, IV
  Univ. of Wyoming black football
    players' protest, 1969 Oct. 7, IV
Blacks (*see also* Abolition movement;
  Black power; Civil rights; Equal
  Employment Opportunity; Minstrel
  shows; Reconstruction; Reverse
  discrimination; Riots and mob violence;
  subject areas):
  Baptist Convention built headquarter,
    1989, III
  books by, 1991(1), II
  books on, 1976(1), II; 1989(1), II
  brutality against (Tex.), 1960 Mar. 7,
    IV
  business-ownership record, 1987, III
  citizenship, 1868 July 28, I
  Colored Episcopal Methodist Church
    founded, 1870 Dec. 16, III
  conspiracy to start racist revolution
    against, 1985 Dec. 30, I
  Cosbys' philanthropy, 1988 Nov. 4, III
  Cubans sought support from, 1961
    Aug. 27, IV
  Douglass's achievements, 1855, IV
  education, 1758(2), III; 1785(2), III;
    1881 July 4, III; 1882 Apr. 28, III
  education fund gift, 1990 Mar. 3, III
  emigration to Liberia, 1895 Mar. 18, I
  first American-born depicted on stage,
    1795 May 22, II
  first astronaut, 1967 Dec. 8, III; 1983
    Aug. 30–Sept. 5, III
  first Catholic archbishop, 1988 Mar.
    15, III
  first Chicago mayor, 1983 Apr. 12, I
  first comprehensive college (Wash.,
    D.C.), 1867(3), III
  first conductor of major orchestra,
    1968 Feb. 15, II
  first Episcopal bishop in white
    diocese, 1962 Dec. 8, III
  first in Cabinet, 1966 Jan. 17(1), I
  first in Congress, 1870 Feb. 25, I
  first independent Methodist Church
    (Phila., Pa.), 1794(3), III
  first major league baseball manager,
    1974, IV; 1974 Oct. 3, IV
  first major league baseball players,
    1884(6), IV; 1947, IV
  first major political party chairman,
    1880 June 2–8, I

Blacks (*cont.*)
first major sports team coach, 1966 Apr. 17–28, IV
first Miss America, 1983 Sept. 17, IV
first national labor group, 1869 Dec. 6, III
first Nobel winner, 1950 Sept. 22, I
first participation in national political convention, 1872 June 5–6, I
first Phila. mayor, 1983 Nov. 8, I
first senator since Reconstruction, 1966 Nov. 8(1), I
first separate Baptist church (Va.), 1725(1), III
first southern city mayor (Atlanta, Ga.), 1973 Oct. 16(1), I
first southern sheriff since Reconstruction (Ala.), 1967 Jan. 16, I
first state governor elected (Va.), 1989 Nov. 8, I
first Supreme Court justice, 1967 Oct. 2, I
first to head major city government, 1967 Sept. 28, I
first to head U.S. Olympic Committee, 1992 Oct. 11, IV
first troops, 1862 July, I
first U.S. general, 1959 May 22, I
first U.S. Military Academy graduate, 1877 June 15, I
first woman Episcopal bishop, 1988 Sept. 24, III
first woman pilot, 1978 Apr. 19, III
first woman to win Rhodes scholarship, 1979 Sept. 9, III
first worldwide grand opera star, 1985 Jan. 3, II
free tradition (Mass.), 1763(1), I
intermarriage opposition (Phila., Pa.), 1723, IV
intermarriage prohibitions (Mass.), 1705(1), IV
Jefferson's attitude toward, 1809 Feb. 25, III
"Jim Crow" originated, 1828, IV
juries, 1875 Mar. 1, I; 1880 Mar. 1, I
Kerner Commission report, 1968 Feb. 29, I
largest business owned by, 1984 May 9(1), III
life expectancy, 1991, III
literature, 1952(1), II; 1965(1), II
male homicide rate, 1990, IV
Mass. colonial population, 1763(1), I
mayors, 1967 Nov. 7, I
Miss. voting rights restricted, 1890 Nov. 1, I
Mormon ordination ban ended, 1978, III
Moynihan's "benign neglect" statement, 1970 Feb. 28, I
music, 1833(5), II
NAACP founded, 1909(1), I
New Palace Theater (N.Y.C.), 1910(3), II
plays about, 1976 June 1, II
population, 1810(1), I; 1860(1), I
population shift, 1991, I
portrayed on stage, 1823, II
prevalent racism, 1901 Oct. 16, IV

Blacks (*cont.*)
psychologist charged racial equality a hoax, 1961 July 28, III
racism deepening, 1991 Jan. 14, III
racism in Navy charged, 1972 Oct. 12–13, I
religion, 1816, III; 1989, III
SAT scores, 1982, III
school for (Phila., Pa.), 1758(2), III
sports, 1937 June 22, IV; 1957 Sept. 8, IV
status in N.Y.C., 1853 Aug. 15, II
suffrage (Wash., D.C.), 1867 Jan. 8, I
voting rights, 1927 Mar. 7, I
voting rights rejected (Va.), 1867 Mar. 5, I
B. T. Washington on equality, 1915, II
Wilson first novelist, 1859 Sept. 5, II
writers, 1938(1), II; 1940(1), II; 1953, II
Black Sox scandal *see* Baseball
Blackwell, Elizabeth, 1849(3), III
Blackwood, Easley, 1992, IV
Blaine, James G.:
Latin American relations, 1881 Nov. 29, I; 1889 Oct. 2, I
mugwump term, 1872(1), IV
presidential candidacy, 1884, I; 1884 June 3–6, I; 1884 June 6, I
Blaine, John J., 1929 Jan. 15, I
Blair, Bonnie, 1988 Feb. 13–28, IV; 1992 Feb. 8–23, IV
Blair, Francis P., Jr., 1868 July 4–9, I
Blair, Henry W., 1890 Mar. 10, III
Blair Education Bill, 1890 Mar. 10, III
Blake, Eubie, 1983, II
Blake, Eugene Carson, 1985, III
Blake, Robert, 1975 May 19, II
Blanc, Mel, 1989, II
Blanchard, James J., 1988 June 27(1), IV
Blanchard, Joshua, 1729(1), II
Blanchard, Thomas, 1820(5), III
Bland, Richard P., 1895 Mar. 5, I
Bland-Allison Act, 1885 Dec., I
Bland Bill, 1894 Mar. 30, I
Blanding, Sarah G., 1985, III
Blatty, William Peter, 1971(1), II
Blau, Herbert, 1965 Oct. 21(2), II
"Bleeding Kansas" (term), 1856 Aug. 1, I
Blind *see* Handicapped
Blitzstein, Marc, 1964, II
Blizzards *see* Snow storms
Bloch, Ernest, 1928(3), II; 1953 Jan. 1, II; 1959, II
Bloch, Felix, 1952 Nov. 6, III
Block, Conrad E., 1964 Oct. 15, III
Bloembergen, Nicolaas, 1981 Oct. 19(2), III
Blondin, Charles, 1859 June 30, IV
Blood:
anemia therapy, 1934 Oct. 25, III
anticoagulants, 1916(2), III
leukocytes discovered, 1922 Nov. 15, III
Rh factor discovered, 1939(1), III
substitute created, 1991 June 16, III
tests as evidence in courts endorsed, 1935 Mar. 22, III
Bloody Marsh, Battle of (Ga.), 1742 June 9, I

Bloom, Allan, 1987(1), II; 1992, III
Bloomer, Amelia, 1849 Jan., IV; 1850, IV; 1850 Apr., IV; 1853(5), IV
Blount, James Henderson, 1893 Feb. 15, I; 1893 Apr. 13, I; 1893 July 17, I
Blue, Vida, 1976 June 15, IV
Blue laws:
against baseball, 1917 Aug. 19, IV
Conn. travel, 1721 May, IV
New Amsterdam, 1656(2), IV
Va., 1618, IV
Bluford, Guion S., 1983 Aug. 30–Sept. 5, III
Blumberg, Baruch S., 1976 Oct. 14(1), III
Bly, Nellie, 1889, IV; 1890 Jan. 23, III
Bly, Robert, 1968 Mar. 6, II
Boardwalks *see* Beaches
Boas, Franz, 1928, III
Boating (*see also* America's Cup; Rowing; Sculling):
first ice yacht club (N.Y.), 1869(2), IV
first intercollegiate regatta, 1859 July 26, IV
first transoceanic yacht race, 1866(5), IV
N.Y.-San Francisco record, 1989 May 26, IV
N.Y. Yacht Club founded, 1844 July 29, IV
popularity and social prestige, 1843, IV
racing, 1824(1), IV
sailing circumnavigation record, 1986 Apr. 11, IV
U.S. Henley Regatta participants, 1989, IV
Bobko, Karol, 1983 Apr. 4–9, III
Bock, Jerry, 1959 Nov. 23, II; 1960 May 2, II; 1964 Sept. 22, II; 1965 June 13, II
Body of Liberties (Mass. code), 1641 Dec., I
Boehm, John Philip, 1725(2), III
Boeing 747 airplane, 1969 Dec. 2, III
Boesky, Ivan F., 1986 Nov. 14, IV
Bofill, Ricardo, 1988, II
Bogan, Louise, 1986 Apr. 17, II
Bogardus, James, 1848, II
Bogart, Humphrey, 1952 Mar. 20, II; 1957, II
Bohr, Aage N., 1975 Oct. 17, III
Boitano, Brian, 1985 Feb. 1–2, IV; 1986 Feb. 6–8, IV; 1987 Feb. 7–8, IV; 1988 Jan. 8–9, IV; 1988 Feb. 13–28, IV
Bok, Edward W., 1883(4), II; 1889, II; 1921 May 29, II
Boker, George Henry, 1864(1), II
Bolcom, William, 1992, II
Bolden, Charles (Buddy), 1890(5), II; 1909(7), II
Bolger, Ray, 1987, II
Bolles, Don, 1976 June 2, II
Bollingen Prize, 1949 Feb. 19, II; 1950 Mar. 27, II
first for translation, 1961 Oct. 31, II
Boll weevil, 1892(6), III
Bolshoi Ballet:
Godunov defected, 1979 Aug. 23, II
Messerer defected, 1980 Feb. 6, II
Bolt, Robert, 1961 Nov. 22, II
Bolt, Tommy, 1958 June 14, IV

Bolton, Isobel, 1946(1), II
Bolton, Michael, 1990 Feb. 21, II; 1992 Feb. 26, II
Bombs and bombings (*see also* Explosions; Nuclear weapons; Terrorism; country and war names):
    Capitol (Wash., D.C.), 1971, I; 1971 Mar. 1, I
    concentrated air possibilities tested, 1921 July 21, III
    Croatian terrorists (N.Y.C.), 1976 Sept. 10–12, I
    Fraunces Tavern (N.Y.C.), 1975 Jan. 24, I
    journalist's car (Ariz.), 1976 June 2, II
    LaGuardia Airport (N.Y.C.), 1975 Dec. 29, I
    Mitchell's tests, 1925, I
    Mooney-Billings case (San Francisco, Calif.), 1916 July 22, I
    V-1 and V-2 bombs, 1944, I
Bonavena, Oscar, 1970, IV
Bond, Carrie Jacobs, 1910, II
Bonds *see* Government bonds; Stocks and bonds
Bonilla, Bobby, 1991 Dec. 2, IV
Bonneville Dam (Oreg.), 1937 Sept. 28, III
Bonnin and Morris porcelain, 1769(2), III
Bonsal, Philip W., 1960 Jan. 11, I
Bonus Bill, 1817 Mar. 3(2), I
Bonzano, John (Cardinal), 1926 June 20, III
Book-of-the-Month Club, 1926 Apr., II
Books and literature (*see also* Almanacs; American Book Awards; Bible; Censorship; Cookbooks; Copyright laws; Dictionaries; Education and schools (for textbooks); Humor; Illiteracy; National Book Awards; National Medal for Literature; Poetry; Pornography; Publishing; Pulitzer prizes; Royalties; Satire; subjects of books):,
    1961, II
    account of Indian life, 1682(2), II
    Adventures of Augie March, The (Bellow), 1953(1), II
    Adventures of Tom Sawyer, The (Twain), 1876(1), II
    Advise and Consent (Drury), 1959(1), II
    Age of Fable, The (Bullfinch), 1855(6), II
    Agrarian Justice (Paine), 1797(1), II
    Algren's works, 1949(1), II
    Alice's Adventures in Wonderland (Carroll) first published in U.S., 1866(2), II
    All the President's Men (Woodward and Bernstein), 1974(1), II
    American Company of Booksellers organized, 1801(2), II
    American Quarterly Review, 1827(2), II
    Anderson's works, 1933(1), II
    Andersonville (Kantor), 1955(1), II
    Anthony Adverse (Allen), 1933(1), II
    Antiquities of the Jews (Josephus), 1721(3), II
    Aquitaine Progression, The (Ludlum), 1984(1), II

Books and literature (*cont.*)
    arms-race-related, 1982(1), II
    Around the World in Eighty Days (Verne), 1873(1), II
    Auchincloss's works, 1964(1), II; 1966(1), II; 1967(1), II
    August 1914 (Solzhenitsyn), 1972(1), II
    Autocrat of the Breakfast Table, The (Holmes), 1858(3), II
    Bacon's *Essays*, 1688, II
    Bad Seed, The (March), 1954(1), II
    Baldwin's *Flush Times of Alabama and Mississippi*, 1853, II
    Baldwin's works, 1953(1), II; 1962(1), II; 1965(1), II; 1974(1), II
    Beet Queen(Erdrich), 1986, II
    Bellow papers sold, 1988 June 7, II
    Bellow's works, 1953(1), II; 1956(1), II; 1959(1), II; 1964(1), II; 1970(1), II; 1975(1), II; 1982(1), II; 1984(1), II; 1989(1), II
    Ben-Hur (Wallace), 1880(1), II
    Berlin Diary (Shirer), 1941(1), II
    best-selling women writers, 1853(1), II
    Bierce's works, 1891(1), II; 1893(1), II
    Big Bear of Arkansas, The (Bangs), 1841(3), II
    Bird's Nest, The (Jackson), 1954(1), II
    Black Beauty (Sewell), 1890(1), II
    Black Boy (Wright), 1945(1), II
    black themes, 1976(1), II
    bookselling, 1710–1714, II
    boom year, 1945, II
    Brainard's *Literary Remains*, 1832(7), II
    Bridge of San Luis Rey, The (Wilder), 1927(1), II
    British novels pirated, 1818(2), II
    Bury My Heart at Wounded Knee (Brown), 1971(1), II
    By Love Possessed (Cozzens), 1957(1), II
    Capote's works, 1951(1), II; 1959(1), II
    cassettes, 1985, II
    Catch-22 (Heller), 1961(1), II
    Cather's works, 1912(1), II; 1913(1), II; 1915(1), II; 1918(1), II; 1922(1), II; 1923(1), II; 1927(1), II; 1931(1), II
    Century Illustrated Monthly's influence, 1881, II
    Century of Dishonor, A (Jackson), 1881(1), II
    Champions of Freedom (Woodworth), 1816(1), II
    Channing's address, 1830(6), II
    Charlotte Temple's (Rowson) popularity, 1794(5), II
    Cheever's works, 1957(1), II; 1964(1), II; 1969(1), II; 1973(1), II; 1977(1), II; 1978(1), II; 1982(1), II; 1991(1), II
    on child behavior, 1955, II
    children's, c1645, II; 1719(1), II; 1868, II; 1903, II
    Chinese manuscripts found (New Orleans, La.), 1986 Apr. 2, II
    Chosen, The (Potok), 1967(1), II
    Christmas Carol's (Dickens) popularity, 1844(5), II
    on Civil War, 1965(1), II
    Civil War-inspired, 1863, II

Books and literature (*cont.*)
    classic travel, 1704 Oct., II
    Cloister and the Hearth, The (Reade) published in U.S., 1861(4), II
    colonial, c1645, II
    colonial best sellers, 1679, II; 1681(2), II; 1699(1), II
    colonial satire, 1676, II
    Confederacy of Dunces, A (Toole), 1980(1), II
    Confessions of Nat Turner, The (Styron), 1967(1), II
    Conquest of Mexico, The (Prescott), 1843(1), II
    Cooper's Leatherstocking Tales, 1841(2), II
    Cooper's popularity, 1826(1), II
    Cooper's sea novels, 1842(2), II
    Cooper's themes, 1827(3), II
    Cooper's works, 1840(3), II
    Cooper's writing incentive, 1811(3), II
    Cozzen's works, 1942(1), II; 1957(1), II
    Crabgrass Frontier: The Suburbanization of America (Jackson), 1986, II
    Crane's works, 1893(1), II; 1895(1), II; 1898(1), II; 1900(1), II; 1930(1), II
    Cream of the Jest (Cabell), 1917(1), II
    current publications, 1867(1), II; 1868(1), II; 1869(1), II; 1870(1), II; 1871(1), II; 1872(1), II; 1873(1), II; 1874(1), II; 1875(1), II; 1876(1), II; 1877(1), II; 1878(1), II; 1879(1), II; 1880(1), II; 1881(1), II; 1882(1), II; 1883(1), II; 1884(1), II; 1885(1), II; 1886(1), II; 1887(1), II; 1888(1), II; 1889(1), II; 1890(1), II; 1891(1), II; 1892(1), II; 1893(1), II; 1894(1), II; 1895(1), II; 1896(1), II; 1897(1), II; 1898(1), II; 1899(1), II; 1900(1), II; 1901(1), II; 1902(1), II; 1903(1), II; 1904(1), II; 1905(1), II; 1906(1), II; 1907(1), II; 1908(1), II; 1909(1), II; 1910(1), II; 1911(1), II; 1912(1), II; 1913(1), II; 1914(1), II; 1915(1), II; 1916(1), II; 1917(1), II; 1918(1), II; 1919(1), II; 1920(1), II; 1921(1), II; 1922(1), II; 1923(1), II; 1924(1), II; 1925(1), II; 1926(1), II; 1927(1), II; 1928(1), II; 1929(1), II; 1930(1), II; 1931(1), II; 1932(1), II; 1933(1), II; 1934(1), II; 1935(1), II; 1936(1), II; 1937(1), II; 1938(1), II; 1939(1), II; 1940(1), II; 1941(1), II; 1942(1), II; 1943(1), II; 1944(1), II; 1945(1), II; 1946(1), II; 1947(1), II; 1948(1), II; 1949(1), II; 1950(1), II; 1951(1), II; 1952(1), II; 1953(1), II; 1954(1), II; 1955(1), II; 1956(1), II; 1957(1), II; 1958(1), II; 1959(1), II; 1960(1), II; 1961(1), II; 1962(1), II; 1963(1), II; 1964(1), II; 1965(1), II; 1966(1), II; 1967(1), II; 1968(1), II; 1969(1), II; 1970(1), II; 1971(1), II; 1972(1), II; 1973(1), II; 1974(1), II; 1975(1), II; 1976(1), II; 1977(1), II; 1978(1), II; 1979(1), II; 1980(1), II; 1981(1), II; 1982(1), II; 1983(1), II; 1984(1), II;

Books and literature (*cont.*)
1985(1), II; 1986(1), II; 1987(1), II; 1988(1), II; 1989(1), II; 1990(1), II; 1991(1), II; 1992(1), II
David Harum (Westcott), 1898(1), II
Death in the Family, A (Agee), 1957(1), II
Death of a President, The (Manchester), 1967(1), II
Deliverance (Dickey), 1970(1), II
Dianetics (Hubbard), 1950, II
Dickens's popularity, 1867 Dec. 2, II
Didion's works, 1977(1), II
dime novels, 1860(1), II
Doctorow's works, 1971(1), II; 1980(1), II; 1984(1), II; 1989(1), II
Dos Passos's works, 1923(1), II; 1925(1), II; 1930(1), II; 1932(1), II; 1936(1), II; 1939(1), II; 1961(1), II
Douglas's works, 1942(1), II; 1948(1), II
Dreiser's works, 1900(1), II; 1911(1), II; 1912(1), II; 1915(1), II; 1925(1), II; 1931(1), II
Dumas's popularity, 1844(4), II
Dutch language (N.Y.C.), 1794(3), II
early catalog (Boston, Mass.), 1804(3), II
early children's, c1645, II
on early Md., 1666, II
early western, *John Brent* (Winthrop), 1862(2), II
East Lynne (Wood), 1861, II
Education of Henry Adams, The (Adams), 1907(2), II; 1918(1), II
Emerson's works, 1841(1), II; 1844(7), II; 1850(5), II
English Grammar (Murray), 1795(1), II
Enormous Room, The (Cummings), 1922(1), II
Essays (Emerson), 1841(1), II; 1844(7), II
Everything You Always Wanted to Know About Sex (Reuben), 1970(1), II
Executioner's Song, The (Mailer), 1979(1), II
Exorcist, The (Blatty), 1971(1), II
on exploration, 1609(1), II; 1610–1619, II; 1612, II; 1624, II
extolling nature, 1790–1794, II
Fable, A (Faulkner), 1954(1), II
Fail-Safe (Burdick and Wheeler), 1962(1), II
Fate of the Earth, The (Schell), 1982(1), II
Fatherhood (Cosby), 1986, II
Faulkner's works, 1924(1), II; 1926(1), II; 1929(1), II; 1930(1), II; 1931(1), II; 1934(1), II; 1939(1), II; 1940(1), II; 1942(1), II; 1951(1), II; 1954(1), II; 1957(1), II; 1959(1), II
FBI surveillance of authors, 1987, I
Fear of Flying (Jong), 1974(1), II
Ferber's works, 1930(1), II; 1931(1), II
first, 1608, II
first American novel, 1789(2), II
first best seller, 1664(3), II
first history of American, 1829(2), II

Books and literature (*cont.*)
first in Indian language, 1653(2), II
first Latin grammar, 1706(2), II
first music (Mass.), 1620(1), II
first novel by a black (Wilson), 1859 Sept. 5, II
first sheet music, 1698(2), II
first U.S. publication of H. C. Andersen, 1848(9), II
Fitzgerald's works, 1920(1), II; 1925(1), II; 1934(1), II
Fitzhugh's *Cannibals All!* defending slavery, 1857, II
Five Little Peppers and How They Grew (Sidney), 1880(2), II
Ford: The Men and the Machine (Lacey), 1986, II
foreign, 1956, II
Forester's works, 1939(1), II
Forever Amber (Winsor), 1944(1), II
Forge, The (Stribling), 1931(1), II
Fuller's criticism, 1846(2), II
Garbo biography hoax (Gronowitz), 1978 Apr. 21, II
Garden of Eden, The (Hemingway, posthumous), 1986, II
Garland's realism, 1917, II
Georgia Scenes (Longstreet), 1835(5), II
Gilroy legal suit, 1976 Apr. 2, II
Glasgow's works, 1906(1), II; 1911(1), II; 1913(1), II; 1916(1), II
Godfather, The (Puzo), 1969(1), II
Goethe's popularity, 1774(2), II
gold discovery, impact on writers, 1848 Jan. 24, IV
Gone With the Wind (Mitchell), 1936(1), II; 1937 May 3, II
Gone With the Wind (Mitchell, facsimile edition), 1986, II
Gone With the Wind (Mitchell) sequel, 1988 Apr. 25, II; 1991(1), II
Good Earth, The (Buck), 1931(1), II
Good Old Way, The (Mather), 1706(3), II
Gordon's works, 1981(1), II
Gotham Book Mart sold (N.Y.C.), 1975 Apr. 24, II
Grapes of Wrath, The (Steinbeck), 1939(1), II
Gravity's Rainbow (Pynchon), 1973(1), II
Greening of America, The (Reich), 1970(1), II
Green Mountain Boys, The (Thompson), 1839(4), II
Grey's works, 1906, II
Group, The (McCarthy), 1963(1), II
Hammett's works, 1930(1), II; 1931(1), II; 1934(1), II
Hans Brinker (Dodge), 1865(1), II
Harris's works, 1881(1), II; 1893(1), II
Hawthorne's works, 1828(1), II; 1837(4), II; 1846(5), II; 1851(2), II; 1860(3), II
Heidenmauer, The (Cooper), 1832(8), II
Heller's works, 1974(1), II
Hellman-McCarthy character defamation suit, 1980 Feb. 15(1), II

Books and literature (*cont.*)
Hemingway's works, 1923(1), II; 1926(1), II; 1929(1), II; 1933(1), II; 1940(1), II; 1952(1), II; 1964(1), II; 1970(1), II
Henry's works, 1904(1), II; 1906(1), II; 1907(1), II; 1909(1), II; 1910(1), II; 1911(1), II; 1913(1), II
Hersey's works, 1959(1), II
Hidden Hand, The (Southworth), 1859(1), II
highest price paid for, 1947 Jan. 28, II
Hill, Ruth Beebe, 1979(1), II
historical novels, 1837, II; 1899(1), II; 1939, II
History and Present State of Virginia, The (Beverley), 1705, II; 1705(2), IV
Holmes's works and popularity, 1854(3), II; 1856(9), II; 1861(6), II; 1872(1), II
Home From the Hill (Humphrey), 1958(1), II
Horatio Alger series, 1867, II
Howells's works, 1882(1), II; 1885(1), II; 1886(1), II; 1889(1), II; 1890(1), II; 1892(1), II; 1894(1), II; 1900(1), II; 1910(1), II
Huckleberry Finn lost manuscript authenticated, 1991 Feb. 13, II
Hughes biography hoax (Irving), 1972, II
Human Comedy, The (Saroyan), 1943(1), II
Human Sexual Inadequacy (Masters and Johnson), 1970(1), II
Iacocca autobiography, 1984(1), II
idealist fiction, 1872(2), II
I'll Take My Stand: Humanism and America (anthology), 1930(1), II
Impending Crisis of the South (Helper), 1857, II
In Cold Blood (Capote), 1966(1), II; 1966 Nov. 28, IV
on Indian captivity, 1705–1709, II
informal essay style, 1807 Jan.24, II
Innocents Abroad (Twain), 1869(1), II
Invisible Man (Ellison), 1952(1), II
Ironweed (Kennedy), 1983(1), II
Irving, J.'s works, 1978(1), II; 1981(1), II; 1985(1), II; 1989(1), II
Irving, W.'s works, 1828(3), II
James's works, 1875(1), II; 1877(1), II; 1878(1), II; 1879(1), II; 1881(1), II; 1886(1), II; 1897(1), II; 1902(1), II; 1903(1), II; 1904(1), II; 1910(1), II; 1911(1), II; 1913(1), II
Jane Eyre's (Brontë) popularity, 1848(8), II
Jaws (Benchley), 1974(1), II
on jazz, 1989, II
Jewett's works, 1896(1), II
on J. Kennedy, 1964, II; 1965(1), II; 1966(1), II; 1967(1), II
John Godfrey's Fortunes (Taylor), 1864(7), II
John Halifax, Gentleman's (Craik) popularity, 1856(2), II
Jonathan Livingston Seagull (Bach), 1972(1), II
Jones's works, 1962(1), II

Books and literature (*cont.*)

Jungle Book, The (Kipling), 1894(5), II
Jurgen (Cabell), 1919(1), II
King's works, 1985(1), II
Kipling in Vt., 1894(5), II
Kipling's works, 1894(1), II; 1895(1), II; 1897(1), II
Knickerbocker Group, 1820, II
"Lady or the Tiger?, The" (Stockton), 1882(2), II
Lake Wobegon Days (Keillor), 1985(1), II
Lardner's works, 1924(1), II; 1929(1), II
largest printed to date, 1726, II
Last Days of Pompeii, The (Bulwer-Lytton), 1834(4), II
Last Hurrah, The (O'Connor), 1956(1), II
Late George Apley, The (Marquand), 1937(1), II; 1938 May 2, II
Lectures on American Literature (Knapp), 1829(2), II
Lena Rivers (M. J. Holmes), 1856(9), II
Letters from an American Farmer (Crèvecoeur), 1782(5), II; 1793(4), II
Lewis's works, 1917(1), II; 1922(1), II; 1925(1), II; 1927(1), II; 1928(1), II; 1929(1), II; 1938(1), II; 1945(1), II; 1947(1), II
Library of America uniform volumes issued, 1982(1), II
Light in the Attic, A (Silverstein), 1985, II
Linwoods, The (Sedgwick), 1835(3), II
literary sites, 1835(7), II
Little Big Man (Berger), 1964(1), II
Little Lord Fauntleroy (Burnett), 1886(1), II
Little Women (Alcott), 1868, II
Lolita (Nabokov), 1958(1), II
London's works, 1900(1), II; 1902(1), II; 1903(1), II; 1904(1), II; 1905(1), II; 1906(1), II; 1908(1), II; 1909(1), II; 1910(1), II; 1911(1), II; 1912(1), II; 1913(1), II; 1917(1), II; 1919(1), II
Look Homeward, Angel (Wolfe), 1929(1), II
Looking Backward (Bellamy), 1888(1), II
Looking for Mr. Goodbar (Rossner), 1975(1), II
Lovell's Library (cheap books), 1882(4), II
Luck of Roaring Camp and Other Sketches, The (Harte), 1870(1), II
lucrative contracts, 1992(1), II
McCarthy's works, 1963(1), II
Mailer's works, 1948, II; 1948(1), II; 1951(1), II; 1973(1), II; 1979(1), II; 1983(1), II; 1991(1), II
Main Street (Lewis), 1920(1), II
Malamud's works, 1963(1), II; 1966(1), II; 1971(1), II; 1973(1), II; 1982(1), II
Man Who Mistook His Wife for a Hat, The (Sachs), 1986, II
Man Without a Country, The (Hale), 1863, II
Man With the Golden Arm, The (Algren), 1949(1), II

Books and literature (*cont.*)

Marquand's works, 1941(1), II; 1946(1), II
Medium Is the Massage, The (McLuhan), 1967(1), II
Melville's works, 1847(2), II; 1850(4), II; 1855(1), II; 1876(1), II; 1924(1), II
Memoirs of Hecate County (Wilson), 1946(1), II
Michener's works, 1953(1), II; 1974(1), II; 1978(1), II; 1980(1), II
Mitchell novel plagiarized, 1811, II
Moby-Dick (Melville), 1846, II
Moon Is Down, The (Steinbeck), 1942(1), II
Moonstone, The (Collins), 1868(3), II
Morrison's works, 1981(1), II; 1987(1), II; 1988 Mar. 31, II; 1992(1), II
Motley on Netherlands, 1856, II
Moveable Feast, A (Hemingway), 1964(1), II
muckraking, 1906 Mar. 17, IV
Myles Standish courtship, 1620–1629, II
Naked and the Dead, The (Mailer), 1948(1), II
Naked Came the Stranger (Ashe), 1969(1), II
Napoleon and His Marshals (Headley), 1846(1), II
Native Son (Wright), 1940(1), II
Nicholas Nickleby (Dickens), 1981, II
Nick of the Woods (Bird), 1837(3), II
1984 (Orwell) reissued, 1984(1), II
nonfiction emphasis, 1955, II
Norris's works, 1901, II; 1903(1), II
North American Review, 1815(2), II
No Time for Sergeants (Hyman), 1954(1), II
Oates's works, 1971(1), II; 1973(1), II; 1989(1), II; 1990(1), II; 1992(1), II
Of Mice and Men (Steinbeck), 1937(1), II
Of Time and the River (Wolfe), 1935(1), II
O'Hara's works, 1949(1), II; 1960(1), II; 1967(1), II
One World (Willkie), 1943(1), II
On the Road (Kerouac), 1957(1), II
Ozick's works, 1983(1), II
Pamela printed in America, 1744(2), II
Papa Hemingway (Hotchner), 1966(1), II
paperbacks, 1944, II; 1951, II
paperback sales, 1951(6), II
Parson Brownlow's Book (Brownlow), 1862(3), II
Paulding's works, 1835(2), II; 1836(5), II
by Penn, William, 1681(1), II; 1687, II
Percy's works, 1980(1), II
Peyton Place (Metalious), 1956(1), II
Pickwick Papers, The (Dickens), 1837(5), II
Pilot, The (Cooper), 1822(1), II
about Pocahontas, 1808, II
Poe introduced detective story, 1841, II
Poe's works, 1840(5), II; 1845 June, II; 1848(2), II

Books and literature (*cont.*)

political biographies, 1992(1), II
popular farming, 1710, II
popularity of historical novels, 1939, II
Porter's works, 1939(1), II
Portnoy's Complaint (Roth), 1969(1), II
post-Civil War, 1866(1), II
Practice of Piety popularity, 1665, II
production up, 1940, II
proletarian novel, 1935, II
Public Burning, The (Coover), 1977(1), II
on Puritans, 1659(1), II
Quo Vadis? (Sienkiewicz), 1896(1), II
Ragtime (Doctorow), 1975(1), II; 1975 Aug. 1(1), II
Raintree County (Lockridge), 1948(1), II
rare Hebrew sale recalled, 1985 July 16, II
realistic pioneering accounts, 1845, II
Rebecca of Sunnybrook Farm (Wiggin), 1903, II
record auction price (N.Y.C.), 1978 Apr. 7, II
Red Badge of Courage, The (Crane), 1895(1), II
Red Storm Rising (Clancy), 1986, II
Requiem for a Nun (Faulkner), 1951(1), II
Ritz Paris Hemingway Award, 1987 Apr. 6, II
Roberts's works, 1930(1), II
Roger's Version (Updike), 1986, II
romanticism, 1814(2), II
romanticism of Indians, 1820(1), II
Roots (Haley), 1976(1), II; 1977 Mar. 16, II; 1977 Apr. 13(1), II; 1977 Apr. 18, II
Rosemary's Baby (Levin), 1967(1), II
Roth's works, 1959(1), II; 1973(1), II; 1974(1), II; 1979(1), II; 1983(1), II; 1987(1), II
Rowson's popularity, 1813, II
Rumor of War, A (Caputo), 1977(1), II
Rutledge (M.C. Harris), 1860(2), II
St. Nicholas magazine for children, 1873, II
sales up, 1958, II; 1988, II; 1989, II; 1991(1), II
Salinger lawsuit, 1974 Nov. 2, II
Salinger's works, 1961(1), II; 1963(1), II
Salmagundi (Irving and Paulding), 1807 Jan.24, II
Sartoris (Faulkner), 1929(1), II
satire against tolerance, 1647(1), II
Scarlet Letter, The (Hawthorne), 1850(3), II
Scarlet Sister Mary (Peterkin), 1928(1), II
Scottish Chiefs' popularity, 1810(4), II
Scott's influence, 1811(1), II; 1813(4), II; 1814(2), II
Scott's popularity, 1820(4), II; 1821(1), II
See Here, Private Hargrove (Hargrove), 1942(1), II

Books and literature (*cont.*)

Sensuous Woman, The ("J"), 1970(1), II

Seven Days in May (Knebel and Bailey), 1962(1), II

Sexual Politics (Millett), 1970(1), II

Shaw's works, 1948, II; 1948(1), II

She (Haggard), 1887(1), II

Sheik, The (Hull), 1921(1), II

Ship of Fools (Porter), 1962(1), II

Shogun (Clavell), 1975(1), II

Shoshone Valley, The (Flint), 1830(3), II

Silent Spring (Carson), 1962(1), II

Sinclair's works, 1901(1), II; 1906(1), II; 1908(1), II; 1917(1), II; 1927(1), II; 1928(1), II

Singer's works, 1975(1), II

Six Crises (Nixon), 1962(1), II

Sketch Book (Irving), 1819(3), II

Smart Set, The literary monthly, 1900 Mar., II

by Smith, John, 1608, II

Soldiers of Fortune (Davis), 1897(1), II

Something Happened (Heller), 1974(1), II

southern writers' themes, 1838, II; 1866, II; 1930(1), II; 1932, II

Spirit of Romance (Pound), 1910(1), II

Spy, The (Cooper), 1821(2), II

Steffens's works, 1931(1), II

Steinbeck's works, 1929(1), II; 1935(1), II; 1937(1), II; 1942(1), II; 1947(1), II; 1952(1), II; 1954(1), II; 1961(1), II; 1962(1), II

Stevenson's works, 1893(1), II

Stone's works, 1961(1), II

Story of a Bad Boy, The (Aldrich), 1870(1), II

Stowe's *Dred*, 1856(3), II

Stowe's *Minister's Wooing, The*, 1859(6), II

Stowe's works, 1852, II; 1869(1), II

Strange Fruit (Smith), 1944(1), II

stream-of-consciousness technique, 1946, II

Study in Scarlet, A (Doyle), 1890 Feb., II

Styron's works, 1979(1), II

Summons to Memphis, A (Taylor), 1986, II

Swiss Family Robinson (Wyss), 1832(4), II

symbolism, 1931(1), II

Taking of Pelham One Two Three (Godey), 1973(1), II

Tales of a Wayside Inn (Longfellow), 1863(4), II

Tarkington's works, 1899(1), II; 1916(1), II; 1918(1), II; 1921(1), II

Tarzan of the Apes (Burroughs), 1914(1), II

temperance story vogue, 1837(1), IV

Temperance Tales (Sargent), 1848(4), II

Tender Is the Night (Fitzgerald), 1934(1), II

Ten Nights in a Barroom (Arthur), 1854(4), II

Terkel's works, 1970(1), II

Books and literature (*cont.*)

Terrible Swift Sword (Catton), 1963(1), II

Theroux's works, 1982(1), II

Thomas Jefferson, 1981(1), II

Thorn Birds, The (McCullough), 1977(1), II

Three Musketeers, The (Dumas) published, 1844(4), II

Three Weeks (Glyn), 1907(1), II

Tiger-Lilies (Lanier), 1867(1), II

Tobacco Road (Caldwell), 1932(1), II

Token for Children, A (Janeway), 1700(3), II

To Kill a Mockingbird (Lee), 1960(1), II

Tombee: Portrait of a Cotton Planter (Rosengarten), 1986, II

Trail of the Lonesome Pine, The (Fox), 1908(1), II

Tree Grows in Brooklyn, A (Smith), 1943(1), II

Triumph of Politics: Why the Reagan Revolution Failed, The (Stockman), 1986, II

Twain's works, 1872(1), II; 1882(1), II; 1883(1), II; 1884(1), II; 1889(1), II; 1894(1), II; 1896(1), II; 1906(1), II; 1907(1), II; 1916(1), II; 1924(1), II

Twenty Thousand Leagues Under the Sea (Verne), 1873(1), II

Two Years Before the Mast (Dana), 1840(2), II

Ulysses (Joyce), 1922(3), II

Ulysses new edition controversy, 1988 June 15, II

Ulysses reissued, 1984 June 7, II

"Uncle Remus" stories (Harris), 1876(6), II

Uncle Tom's Cabin (Stowe), 1852, II

Under the Volcano (Lowry), 1947(1), II

Updike's works, 1959(1), II; 1970(1), II; 1971(1), II; 1981(1), II; 1990(1), II

Up the Down Staircase (Kaufman), 1965(1), II

Uris's works, 1970(1), II

U.S.A. trilogy (Dos Passos), 1936(1), II

Valley of the Dolls (Susann), 1966(1), II

Vantage Point (Johnson), 1971(1), II

Vidal's works, 1964(1), II

on Vietnam War, 1980(1), II

Virginian, The (Wister), 1902(1), II

Vonnegut's works, 1963(1), II; 1969(1), II; 1973(1), II; 1976(1), II; 1979(1), II; 1985(1), II

Walden (Thoreau), 1854(2), II

Wall, The (Hersey), 1950(1), II

Wambaugh's works, 1973(1), II

Warren's works, 1971(1), II

on Watergate, 1975(1), II; 1976(1), II

Watership Down (Adams), 1974(1), II

Weems's biographies, 1800, II

Welty's works, 1954(1), II; 1972(1), II

western fiction's popularity, 1844, II; 1906, II; 1911, II

Wharton's works, 1905(1), II; 1907(1), II; 1920(1), II

Whirlwind (Clavell), 1986 Jan. 11, II

Books and literature (*cont.*)

Wieland (Brockden) published, 1798(2), II

Wilder's works, 1931(1), II

Willis, Nathaniel Parker, 1840(4), II

Wilson's works, 1960(1), II; 1975(1), II

Winesburg, Ohio (Anderson), 1919(1), II

Wolfe's works, 1929(1), II; 1935(1), II; 1940(1), II

Woman in the Nineteenth Century (Fuller), 1845, II

women's equality, 1797(1), IV

Wonderful Wizard of Oz, The (Baum), 1900(1), II

World Enough and Time (Warren), 1950(1), II

World War II themes, 1943(1), II; 1948, II

Wouk's works, 1951(1), II; 1971(1), II; 1978(1), II

Wright's works, 1938(1), II; 1945(1), II; 1953(1), II

Wuthering Heights, 1848(6), II

Yeager (Yeager), 1985(1), II

Zelda (Milford), 1970(1), II

Boone, Daniel:
folk hero, 1765–1769, IV
in La., 1798(2), I
territory land grant, 1798(2), I
Wilderness Road, 1775 Mar. 10, III

Boone and Crockett Club, 1887(5), III

Boorstin, Daniel J., 1974 May 7, II

Booth, Edwin, 1850 Sept. 27, II; 1891, II

Booth, Evangeline, 1880, III; 1904 Nov. 2, III

Booth, John Wilkes, 1850 Sept. 27, II; 1865, I; 1865 Apr. 14, I; 1865 Apr. 26(2), I

Booth, Sherman M., 1859, I

Booth, Shirley, 1950 Apr. 9, II; 1953 Mar. 19(1), II; 1953 Mar. 29, II; 1962 May 22, II; 1963 May 26, II; 1992, II

Boothe, Powers, 1980 Sept. 7, II

Boots *see* Shoes and footwear

Borah, William E., 1907(1), III

Borax, 1856 Jan. 8, III

Borden, Gail, 1853 May, III; 1856(6), III

Borden, Lizzie (Lisbeth A.), 1892, IV

Bordin, Gelindo, 1990 Apr. 16, IV

Borglum, Gutzon, 1904(6), II; 1927, II

Borgnine, Ernest, 1956 Mar. 21, II

Bork, Robert, 1973 Oct. 20, I; 1987 Oct. 23, I

Borlaug, Norman E., 1970 Oct. 21, I

Borman, Frank, 1965 Dec. 4, III; 1968 Dec. 21–27, III

Boron, 1979 Oct. 16(1), III

Boros, Julius, 1952 June 14, IV; 1955, IV; 1956 June 16(2), IV; 1963 June 23, IV; 1968 July 21, IV

Bosco, Philip, 1989 June 4(1), II

Bosley, Tom, 1959 Nov. 23, II

Bosom bottles, 1756 July 26, IV

Boston Academy of Music, 1833(6), II

Boston Athenaeum, 1807(1), III

Boston Crown Glass Co., 1809(4), III

Boston Custom House, 1857(4), II

Boston Daily Advertiser (newspaper), 1813(1), II

Boston Latin School (Mass.), 1630–1639, III

Boston Marathon, 1897 Apr. 19, IV; 1898 Apr. 19, IV; 1899 Apr. 19, IV; 1900 Apr. 19, IV; 1901 Apr. 19, IV; 1902 Apr. 19, IV; 1903 Apr. 20, IV; 1904 Apr. 19, IV; 1905 Apr. 19, IV; 1906 Apr. 19, IV; 1907 Apr. 19, IV; 1908 Apr. 20, IV; 1909 Apr. 19, IV; 1910 Apr. 19, IV; 1911 Apr. 19, IV; 1912 Apr. 19, IV; 1913 Apr. 19, IV; 1914 Apr. 20, IV; 1915 Apr. 19, IV; 1916 Apr. 19, IV; 1917 Apr. 19, IV; 1918(5), IV; 1919 Apr. 19, IV; 1920 Apr. 19, IV; 1921 Apr. 19, IV; 1922 Apr. 19, IV; 1923 Apr. 19, IV; 1924 Apr. 19, IV; 1925 Apr. 20, IV; 1926 Apr. 19, IV; 1927 Apr. 19, IV; 1928 Apr. 19, IV; 1929 Apr. 19, IV; 1930 Apr. 19, IV; 1931 Apr. 20, IV; 1932 Apr. 19, IV; 1933 Apr. 19, IV; 1934 Apr. 19, IV; 1935 Apr. 19, IV; 1936 Apr. 20, IV; 1937 Apr. 19, IV; 1938 Apr. 19, IV; 1939 Apr. 19, IV; 1940 Apr. 19, IV; 1941 Apr. 19, IV; 1942 Apr. 19, IV; 1943 Apr. 18, IV; 1944 Apr. 19, IV; 1945 Apr. 19, IV; 1946 Apr. 20, IV; 1947 Apr. 19, IV; 1948 Apr. 19, IV; 1949 Apr. 19, IV; 1950 Apr. 19, IV; 1951 Apr. 19, IV; 1952 Apr. 19, IV; 1953 Apr. 20, IV; 1954 Apr. 19, IV; 1955 Apr. 19, IV; 1956 Apr. 19(2), IV; 1957 Apr. 20, IV; 1958 Apr. 19, IV; 1959 Apr. 20, IV; 1960 Apr. 19, IV; 1961 Apr. 19, IV; 1962 Apr. 19, IV; 1963 Apr. 19, IV; 1964 Apr. 20, IV; 1965 Apr. 19, IV; 1966 Apr. 19, IV; 1967 Apr. 19, IV; 1968 Apr. 19, IV; 1969 Apr. 21, IV; 1970 Apr. 20, IV; 1971 Apr.19, IV; 1974 Apr. 15, IV; 1975 Apr. 21, IV; 1976 Apr. 19, IV; 1977 Apr. 18, IV; 1978 Apr. 17, IV; 1979 Apr. 16, IV; 1984 Apr. 16, IV; 1985 Apr. 15, IV; 1986 Apr. 21, IV; 1987 Apr. 20, IV; 1988 Apr. 18, IV; 1989 Apr. 17, IV; 1990 Apr. 16, IV; 1991 Apr. 15, IV; 1992 Apr. 20, IV

    Benoit set women's record, 1983 Apr. 18, IV

    first woman to finish, 1973 Apr. 17, IV; 1974 Apr. 15, IV

    first women's competition, 1972 Apr. 17, IV

    new record time, 1982 Apr. 19, IV

    new women's record, 1981 Apr. 20, IV

    Rodgers's third consecutive win, 1980 Apr. 21, IV

    Ruiz disqualified, 1980 Apr. 21, IV

Boston (Mass.):

    British troops landed, 1768 Oct. 1, I

    censorship, 1898(3), II

    colonial bookselling center, 1710–1714, II

    Common enclosed, 1728(1), IV

    Common established, 1640, I

    English High School opened, 1821 May, III

    fire destroyed 65 acres, 1872 Nov. 9, I

    first tavern, 1630–1639, IV

    great fire, 1679, I

    importance as seaport, 1749(2), III

    Marquand on, 1937(1), II

    musical life, 1810, II

    police strike, 1919 Sept. 9, III

Boston (Mass.) (cont.)

    Quincy Market, 1826(5), II

    school busing controversy, 1974 Sept. 12, III; 1975 Dec. 9, III

    School Committee fined, 1974 Dec. 30, III

    Symphony Hall opened, 1900 Oct. 15, II

    Tremont St. subway, 1897, III

Boston Massacre, 1770 Mar. 5, I

Boston Pops, 1980 Jan. 10, II; 1985, II

Boston Post Road, 1673 Jan. 1, III

Boston Public Library, 1854(2), III; 1855 Sept. 17, III; 1888(4), II

Boston Society for the Moral and Religious Instruction of the Poor, 1815(2), IV

Boston Symphony Orchestra, 1972 Feb. 2, II; 1984 Nov. 9, II

Boston Tea Party, 1773 Dec. 16, I; 1774 Mar. 31, I

Boswell, John, 1981 Apr. 30, II

Botany:

    first professor, 1768(2), III

Boucher, Jonathan, 1763(2), I

Boucicault, Dion, 1857 Dec. 8, II; 1860 Mar. 29, II

Bouck, William, 1924 June 19, I

Boulder, University of (Colo.), 1861(2), III

Boulder Dam see Hoover Dam

Boulez, Pierre, 1977 May 14, II

Bourke-White, Margaret, 1971, II

Bourne, Jonathan, 1911 Jan. 21, I

Bouton, Jim, 1970(1), II

Bowden, Don, 1957 July 19, IV

Bowditch, Nathaniel, 1802, III; 1847(1), II

Bowdoin, James, 1780–1784, II; 1785(2), III

Bowdoin College (Me.), 1794 June 24, III; 1828(1), II

Bowen, Catherine Drinker, 1944(1), II; 1958 Mar. 11, II

Bowery, The (N.Y.C.), 1700–1704, IV

Bowie, James, 1835(4), III; 1836(2), IV

Bowling:

    American Congress formed, 1895 Sept. 9, IV

    popularity, 1818, IV

Bowling Green (N.Y.C.), 1732(1), IV

Bowman, Christopher, 1989 Feb. 11–12, IV; 1992 Jan. 9–11, IV

Boxer Rebellion, 1900, I

Boxing:

    Ali attempt to regain title, 1980, IV

    Ali defended title, 1977, IV

    Ali retirement, 1976, IV; 1979, IV

    Ali's third title regain, 1978 Sept. 15, IV

    Ali stripped of title, 1965 May 25, IV; 1967 June 20, IV

    Allen-McCoole match, 1869, IV

    bare knuckle world heavyweight championship, 1876 Sept. 7, IV; 1880(4), IV; 1882 Feb. 7, IV

    black-white ban declared unconstitutional (La.), 1959 May 25, IV

    brutality and popularity, 1849, IV

    Burns-O'Brien fight, 1906 Nov. 28, IV

    Coburn heavyweight champion, 1863 May 5, IV

Boxing (cont.)

    Corbett defeated Choynski, 1889 June 5, IV

    current scene, 1963, IV; 1965, IV; 1965 Nov. 22, IV

    Dempsey-Firpo bout, 1923, IV

    Dempsey knocked out Morris and Fulton, 1918 Dec. 16, IV

    Dempsey's career, 1919, IV; 1926, IV

    first champion, 1816(4), IV

    first IBF heavyweight championship, 1984 Nov. 9, IV

    first unofficial heavyweight champion, 1810 Dec. 10, IV

    Golden Gloves, 1927(2), IV

    Graziano knockouts, 1945, IV

    Heenan-Sayers match, 1859, IV

    Hyer championship, 1841(2), IV

    Hyer-Sullivan bout, 1849 Feb. 7, IV

    IBF heavyweight championship, 1985 Sept. 21, IV

    investigation of underworld influence, 1960, IV

    Johansson named fighter of year, 1959 Dec. 8, IV

    last bare knuckle bout, 1889 July 8, IV

    light heavyweight championship, 1959, IV

    lightweight championship dispute, 1944, IV

    Louis retired, 1949, IV

    Mace's world heavyweight title, 1870 May 10, IV

    Morrissey heavyweight champion, 1853 Oct. 12, IV

    Patterson first to regain heavyweight championship, 1960, IV; 1960 June 20, IV

    Spinks stripped of IBF heavyweight championship, 1987 Feb. 26, IV

    thriller in Manila, 1975 Oct. 1, IV

    Tunney-Dempsey bouts, 1926, IV

    Tyson youngest heavyweight champion, 1986 Nov. 22, IV

    U.S. amateur team death in Polish air crash, 1980 Mar. 14, IV

    Walker Law legalizing (N.Y.S.), 1920 Sept., IV

    WBA heavyweight championship, 1983 Sept. 23, IV; 1986 Jan. 17, IV

    WBC heavyweight championship, 1986 Mar. 22, IV

    Willard, Jess, 1915 Apr. 5, IV

    world heavyweight championship, 1873 Sept. 23, IV; 1892 Sept. 7, IV; 1897 Mar. 17, IV; 1899 June 9, IV; 1905(3), IV; 1906 Feb. 23, IV; 1907 Dec. 2, IV; 1908 Dec. 26, IV; 1910 July 4, IV; 1915 Apr. 5, IV; 1921 July 2, IV; 1928 July 26, IV; 1929(1), IV; 1930 June 12, IV; 1932 June 21, IV; 1933 June 21, IV; 1934 June 14, IV; 1935 June 13, IV; 1937 June 22, IV; 1940, IV; 1941, IV; 1942 Jan. 9, IV; 1947, IV; 1948 June 25, IV; 1949, IV; 1950, IV; 1951 July 18, IV; 1952 Sept. 23, IV; 1953, IV; 1954, IV; 1955, IV; 1956, IV; 1956 Nov. 30, IV; 1957, IV; 1958, IV; 1959, IV; 1961, IV; 1961 Dec. 4, IV; 1962, IV;

Boxing (*cont.*)
  1962 Sept. 25, IV; 1963 July 22, IV;
    1964, IV; 1964 Feb. 25, IV; 1965
    May 25, IV; 1966, IV; 1967, IV;
    1969, IV; 1970, IV; 1970 Feb. 16,
    IV; 1971 Mar. 8, IV; 1973 Jan. 22,
    IV; 1974 Oct. 30, IV; 1976, IV; 1978
    Feb. 15, IV; 1978 June 9, IV; 1978
    Sept. 15, IV; 1979, IV; 1979 Oct.
    21(2), IV; 1980, IV; 1980 Mar. 31,
    IV; 1981, IV; 1982 Dec. 10, IV;
    1984 Mar. 9, IV; 1984 Apr. 29, IV;
    1984 Aug. 31, IV; 1984 Dec. 1, IV;
    1985 Apr. 29, IV; 1986 Nov. 22, IV;
    1986 Dec. 12, IV; 1987 Mar. 7, IV;
    1987 June 15, IV; 1987 Aug. 1, IV;
    1988 June 27(2), IV; 1990 Feb. 11,
    IV
  world middleweight championship,
    1957, IV; 1958, IV; 1958 Mar. 25, IV
Boyce, Christopher J., 1977 Apr. 28(2), I
Boyce, William D., 1910, IV
Boyd, James, 1949 Mar. 11, III
Boyer, Charles, 1978, II
Boyington, Gregory (Pappy), 1988, IV
Boyle, John T., 1888(2), II
Boyle, Robert, 1723(1), III
Boyle, Tony (William A.), 1971 Mar. 2, III;
    1972 Mar. 1(2), III; 1972 May 1, III;
    1973 Sept. 6, III
  found guilty of Yablonski murder,
    1974 Apr. 11, III
  sentenced for Yablonski murder, 1975
    Sept. 11, III
Boylston, Zabdiel, 1706, III; 1720–1724, III
Boy Scouts of America:
  chartered, 1910, IV
  incorporated, 1916 June 15, IV
Brackenridge, Hugh Henry, 1792(4), II;
    1805, IV
Braddock, Edward, 1755 July 9, I
Braddock, James J., 1935 June 13, IV
Bradford, Alex, 1976 Dec. 22, II
Bradford, Andrew, 1740–1744, II
Bradford, Barbara Taylor, 1992(1), II
Bradford, William, 1620(1), III; 1622, II;
    1623(1), IV; 1628 May 1, IV; 1630, II;
    1725–1729, II
Bradford, William (printer), 1690–1699, II
Bradley, Omar, 1944 July 25, I; 1981, I
Bradley, Pat, 1986 June 1, IV; 1990, IV;
    1992 Jan. 18, IV
Bradshaw, Kevin, 1991 Jan. 5, IV
Bradstreet, Anne, 1650, II; 1678, II
Brady, Alice, 1938 Mar. 10, II
Brady, James, 1981 Mar. 30, I
Brain:
  research, 1981 Oct. 9, III
Brainard, John Gardiner, 1832(7), II
Brallier, John, 1895 Aug. 31, IV
Bramble, Mark, 1980 Aug. 25, II
Branch, Taylor, 1989 Mar. 30, II
Brand, Vance D., 1975 July 15, III
Brandeis, Louis D., 1916 Jan. 28, III
Brando, Marlon, 1955 Mar. 30, II; 1973
    Mar. 27, II
Brandywine, Battle of (Pa.), 1777 Sept. 11,
    I
Braniff International Corp., 1982 May 13,
    III

Brass:
  bowl patent, 1851 Dec. 16, III
  first mill (Conn.), 1802(2), III
Brattain, Walter H., 1956 Nov. 1, III;
    1987, III
Brattle, Thomas, 1680(2), III
Brattle, William, 1720–1724, I
Brautigan, Richard, 1974(1), II
Bray, Thomas (Rev.), 1700–1704, III; 1702,
    I
Brazil:
  Mexican-U.S. dispute, 1914 Apr. 25, I
Breasts:
  silicone gel implants restricted, 1992
    Apr. 16, III
Breckinridge, John C., 1856 June 2–5, I;
    1856 Nov. 4, I; 1860 June 28, I
Breda, Peace of, 1667 July 21, I
Breedlove, Craig, 1963 Aug. 5(2), IV
Breed's Hill (Boston, Mass.), 1775 June 16,
    I; 1775 June 17, I
Brehm, Marie C., 1924 June 5, I
Bremer, Arthur, 1972 May 15, I; 1972
    Aug. 4, I
Brennan, Francis Cardinal, 1968, III
Brennan, Walter, 1939 Feb. 23, II; 1941
    Feb. 27, II
Brennan, William J., Jr., 1990 July 20, I
Brenner, Victor D., 1909 Aug. 2, III
Brent, Margaret, 1639(1), I; c1640, I;
    1869(1), I
Breslin, Jimmy, 1975(1), II
Brett, George, 1992 Sept. 9, IV
Breuer, Marcel, 1938(5), II; 1951(5), II;
    1966 Sept. 28, II
Breweries *see* Beer
Brewer, Gay, 1967 Apr. 9, IV
Brewer, Lucy, 1812 Aug. 19, IV
Brewer, Margaret A., 1978 May 11, I
Brewster, Kingman, Jr., 1988, III
Brewster, William, 1620(1), III
Brezhnev, Leonid I., 1972 May 22–30, I;
    1973 June 16–25, I; 1974 Nov. 23–24, I;
    1979 June 18, I
Briand, Aristide, 1927 Apr. 6, I
Bribery:
  Abscam operation, 1980 Feb. 2, I
  basketball scandal, 1961 June 9, IV
Bricker, John W., 1944 June 26–28, I
Bricusse, Leslie, 1962 Oct. 3, II
Bridge, Peter, 1972 June 29, II
Bridges, Harry, 1990, III
Bridges, Tommy, 1968, IV
Bridges and tunnels:
  Brooklyn-Battery Tunnel (N.Y.C.),
    1950 May 25, III
  Brooklyn Bridge (N.Y.C.) completed,
    1883, II
  Brooklyn Bridge (N.Y.C.) construction
    begun, 1870 Jan. 2, III
  Brooklyn Bridge (N.Y.C.) hundredth
    anniversary, 1983, II
  Cayuga (N.Y.) completed, 1800 Sept.,
    III
  collapsed (Ohio R.), 1967 Dec. 15, I
  Eads's projects, 1884 June, III
  first across East R. (N.Y.C.), 1883, II
  first important railroad tunnel (Mass.),
    1873, III

Bridges and tunnels (*cont.*)
  first important suspension bridge (Pa.),
    1796(2), III
  first (Mass.), 1634(1), III
  first railroad over Miss. R., 1856 Apr.
    21, III
  first steel arch spanning Miss. R.,
    1874(3), III
  first toll (Mass.), 1654(3), III
  first underwater motor vehicle tunnel
    (N.Y.-N.J.), 1927 Nov. 13, III
  first wooden truss (Vt.), 1792(3), III
  floating (Lake Washington, Wash.),
    1940 July 2, III
  George Washington Bridge (N.Y.-N.J.)
    opened, 1931 Oct. 24, III
  George Washington Bridge (N.Y.-N.J.)
    planned, 1926(4), III
  Golden Gate Bridge dedicated (San
    Francisco, Calif.), 1937 May 27, III
  Hell Gate Bridge (N.Y.C.) opened,
    1917(5), II
  Holland Tunnel (N.Y.-N.J.), 1927 Nov.
    13, III
  Lincoln Tunnel built (N.Y.-N.J.),
    1937(3), II
  longest cantilever (Cincinnati, Ohio),
    1876(7), III
  longest pontoon in war (James R.,
    Va.), 1864 June 14, I
  longest vehicular tunnel (N.Y.C.), 1950
    May 25, III
  Manhattan Bridge (N.Y.C.) opened,
    1909 Dec. 31, III
  Mich.-Canada dedicated, 1938 Oct. 9,
    III
  Morton St. Tunnel (N.Y.-N.J.), 1904
    Mar. 11, III
  most famous nineteenth century
    suspension (Mass.), 1810(1), III
  Newburyport (Mass.), 1810(1), III
  pneumatic foundation caissons first
    used, 1874(3), II
  proposed Brooklyn-Battery (N.Y.C.)
    bridge rejected, 1939 July 17, III
  Queensboro Bridge (N.Y.C.) opened,
    1909 Mar. 30, III
  Rainbow Bridge opened (Niagara R.),
    1941 Nov. 1, III
  San Francisco-Oakland Bay Bridge
    (Calif.), 1932(2), III
  second across East R. (N.Y.), 1903(6),
    II
  suspension, 1855, III
  suspension bridge collapsed (Wash.),
    1940 Nov. 7, III
  Town's designs, 1821, III
  Verrazano-Narrows (N.Y.C.), 1964
    Nov. 21(2), III
  world's longest suspension (Mich.),
    1957 Nov. 1, III
  world's longest suspension (N.Y.C.),
    1964 Nov. 21(2), III
Bridgman, Percy Williams, 1946 Nov.
    14(1), III
Briggs, Benjamin S., 1872 Nov. 7, IV
Briggs, Charles A., 1892(4), III
Brillat-Savarin, Anthelme, 1793(1), IV
Brinkley, Alan, 1983 Apr. 24, II

Brinks Co.:
   holdup (Nanuet, N.Y.), 1981 Oct. 20,
      IV
Brisbane, Albert, 1834(1), III; 1844(1), III;
   1850(10), IV
Briscoe, Benjamin, 1910 Jan., III
Briscoe, Frank, 1907(4), III
Bristow, George F., 1855, II; 1856 Mar. 1,
   II; 1859 Mar. 26, II
British Art, Center for, 1977 Apr. 19, II
Brittan, Robert, 1973 May 30, II
Britten, Benjamin, 1978 Sept. 23, II
Britz, Jerilyn, 1979 July 15, IV
Broadcasting (see also Television):
   ABC-ITT merger, 1965 Dec. 7, III
   CBS awarded NCAA rights, 1989 Nov.
      21, IV
   cigarette ads banned, 1970 Apr. 1, III
   Citizen Band radios, 1976, IV
   Communications Act, 1934 June 19, I
   Damrosch's Music Appreciation Hour,
      1938(3), II
   direct wireless connection
      (U.S.-Germany), 1914 Jan. 3, III
   equal political time overruled, 1973
      May 26, II
   equal political time ruling, 1959 June
      15, II
   equal political time ruling lifted, 1959
      Sept. 14(1), II; 1964 Oct. 1, II; 1975
      Sept. 25, II
   FCC regulations eased, 1981 Jan. 14,
      II
   first coast-to-coast radio program,
      1937 May 6, III
   first coverage of World Series, 1921
      Oct. 5, II
   first major network to change hands,
      1985 Mar. 18, III
   first nightly news anchorman retired,
      1988 Apr. 1, II
   first of official presidential address,
      1923 Dec. 6, III
   first of voice and music, 1906 Dec. 24,
      III
   first president on radio, 1922 June 14,
      III
   first transatlantic radiotelephone
      communication (U.S.-France), 1915
      Oct. 21, III
   first wireless message
      (N.Y.C.-Chicago), 1909(2), III
   first wireless U.S.-Japan service, 1915
      July 27, III
   first worldwide radio, 1937 May 12,
      III
   frequency modulation (fm) developed,
      1939(2), III
   musical programs, 1930, II; 1942 Apr.
      14(2), II
   NBC Symphony Orchestra, 1937(4), II
   number of radios, 1924 Jan. 1, III
   payola, 1960 Jan. 25, II; 1960 Apr. 29,
      II; 1960 May 19, II
   PBS reorganized, 1979 June 25, III
   Petrillo ban on recorded music, 1942
      Aug. 3, II
   Radio Control Act, 1927, III
   radio firsts, 1922, III
   radio set statistics, 1940(4), III

Broadcasting (cont.)
   radio's growth, 1920, II
   radio signals bounced off moon, 1959
      June 3, III
   radio station ownership rules change,
      1992 Aug. 5, I
   ship radio equipment required, 1910
      June 24, III
   stellar radio emissions, 1931(1), III
   Time Warner merger, 1989 July 24,
      III
   transatlantic wireless transmission,
      1906 Apr. 7, III
   Welles's radio play "War of the
      Worlds", 1938 Oct. 30, II
   wireless photography transmission
      (London-N.Y.), 1924 Nov. 30, III
   wireless telegraphy, 1891 Dec. 29, III
Broadhead, James O., 1878, III
Broadhurst, George, 1911 Sept. 26, II
Brock, Isaac, 1812 Aug. 16, I; 1812 Oct.
   13, I
Brock, Lou, 1974, IV; 1974 Sept. 10, IV
Brodie, Steve, 1886, IV
Brodsky, Joseph, 1987 Oct. 22, II; 1991
   May 10, II
Bromwich, John E., 1947 July 4–5, IV;
   1948 July 2, IV
Bronfman, Samuel, 1975 Aug. 17, IV; 1976
   Dec. 10, IV
Bronk, William, 1982 Apr. 27, II
Bronowski, Jacob, 1973(1), II
Brontë, Charlotte, 1848(8), II
Brontë, Emily, 1848(6), II
Bronze:
   first equestrian casting, 1853 Jan. 8, II
   first structure sheathed in, 1957, II
Brooke, Edward W., 1966 Nov. 8(1), I
Brook Farm (Mass.), 1841(3), III
Brookings, Robert S., 1927(1), III
Brookings Institution, 1927(1), III
Brooklyn-Battery Tunnel (N.Y.C.), 1950
   May 25, III
Brooklyn Bridge (N.Y.C.):
   Brodie's jump from, 1886, IV
   completed, 1883, II
   contruction begun, 1870 Jan. 2, III
   hundredth anniversary, 1983, II
Brooklyn Museum (N.Y.C.):
   Bierstadt retrospective, 1991 Feb. 8,
      II
   Renoir stolen, 1974 Dec. 12, II
Brooks, James, 1872(1), I
Brooks, John A., 1888 May 31, I
Brooks, Preston S., 1856 May 22, I
Brooks, Van Wyck, 1920(1), II; 1937 May
   3, II; 1944(1), II; 1947(1), II; 1963, II
Brough, Louise, 1946 July 6, IV; 1947 July
   4–5, IV; 1947 Sept. 14, IV; 1948 July 2,
   IV; 1949 July 1–2, IV; 1950 July 7, IV;
   1954 July 3(2), IV; 1955 July 1–2, IV
Broun, Heywood, 1933(3), II
Browder, Earl, 1936 June 24–28, I; 1936
   Nov. 3, I; 1940 June 2, I; 1940 Nov. 5, I;
   1973, I
Brown, Benjamin Gratz, 1872 May 1, I;
   1872 July 9, I
Brown, Charles Brockden, 1795–1799, II;
   1797(1), IV; 1798(2), II
Brown, Claude, 1965(1), II

Brown, Dee, 1971(1), II; 1980(1), II
Brown, Ebenezer, 1819(2), III
Brown, Edmund G., Jr. (Jerry):
   fruit fly spraying, 1981, III
Brown, Harrison, 1986, III
Brown, Henry Kirke, 1856 July 4, II
Brown, Herbert C., 1979 Oct. 16(1), III
Brown, Jill E., 1978 Apr. 19, III
Brown, Jim, 1973 Dec. 16, IV
Brown, John (abolitionist):
   Benét's poem on, 1928, II; 1929 May
      12, II
   Harpers Ferry (W. Va.) raid, 1859 Oct.
      16, I
   Kans. agitation, 1855 Sept. 5, I; 1856
      May 21, I
Brown, John Mason, 1963 May 6, II
Brown, Michael S., 1985 Oct. 14, III
Brown, Olympia, 1860(1), IV
Brown, Paul, 1991, IV
Brown, Ruth, 1989 June 4(1), II
Brown, Tom, 1946 July 6, IV
Brown, Virginia Mae, 1991, I
Brown, William Hill, 1789(2), II
Browne, Charles Farrar see Ward,
   Artemus
Browne, Mary K., 1912 June 15, IV; 1913
   June 14, IV; 1914 June 13, IV
Brownie Box Camera, 1900(5), IV
Browning, Edmund L., 1985 Sept. 10, III
Brownlow, William G., 1862(3), II
Brownmiller, Susan, 1975(1), II
Brown v. Board of Education, 1954 May
   17, I
Brown & Williamson Tobacco Co., 1985
   Dec. 5, III
Bruce, Blanche Kelso, 1880 June 2–8, I
Bruce, David K. E., 1973 May 14(2), I
Bruce, Robert V., 1988 Mar. 31, II
Brundage, Avery, 1975, IV
Brunner Award, 1960 Apr. 11, II
Brushaber v. Union Pacific Railroad Co.,
   1916 Jan. 24, III
Brush Motor Car Co., 1907(4), III
Bryan, Charles W., 1924 July 9, I
Bryan, Jimmy, 1958 May 30, IV
Bryan, Thomas Jefferson, 1853(4), II
Bryan, William Jennings:
   bimetallism, 1890(7), III
   "cross of gold" speech, 1896 July 7,
      IV; 1896 July 11, I
   Democratic Silver Convention, 1894
      June 21, I
   evolution controversy, 1923 Jan., III
   free silver, 1895 Mar. 5, I
   lost presidential bid, 1896 Nov. 3, I
   Omaha World-Herald editor, 1894
      Nov. 6, I
   presidential candidacy, 1896, I; 1896
      July 11, I; 1896 July 22–24, I; 1896
      July 25, I; 1900 July 5, I; 1908, I;
      1908 July 7–10, I; 1908 Nov. 3, I
   proposed federal ownership of
      railroads, 1906 Aug., III
   resigned over Lusitania note, 1915
      June 7, I
   Scopes trial, 1925 July 10–21, III
   Senate-bid defeat, 1894 Nov. 6, I
Bryant, Anita, 1977 June 7, I
Bryant, Bear (Paul), 1983, IV

Bryant, Deborah, 1965 Sept. 11, IV
Bryant, William Cullen, 1817 Sept., II
    collected poems, 1832(6), II
    "Lifetime" and "Flood of Years",
      1876(3), II
    N.Y. *Post* editorship, 1801(2), II;
      1826(2), II
    Thirty Poems, 1864(1), II
Bryn Mawr College (Pa.), 1880(4), III
Brynner, Yul, 1957 Mar. 27, II; 1985, II
Buchanan, James:
    born, 1791 Apr. 23, I
    elected president, 1856 Nov. 4, I
    inaugurated, 1857 Mar. 4, I
    presidential nomination, 1856 June
      2–5, I
Buchanan, James M.:
    Nobel Prize in Economics, 1986 Oct.
      16, III
Buck, Pearl S., 1931(1), II; 1932 May 2, II;
    1938 Nov. 10, II; 1973, II
Buckingham, James, 1841, IV
Bucknell University (Pa.), 1846 Feb. 5, III
Buckner, Simon P., 1896 Sept. 2–3, I
Budge, Don, 1937 July 2, IV; 1937 Sept.
    11(2), IV; 1938 July 1, IV; 1938 Sept. 17,
    IV; 1969 Sept. 7–8, IV
Budget, Bureau of:
    established, 1921 June 10, I
Budget, U.S. (*see also* Debt, U.S.):
    balancing act found partially
      unconstitutional, 1986 July 7, I
    defense, 1959 Nov. 16, I; 1964, I;
      1965, I
    deficit, 1975, III; 1992, I
    deficit-cutting plans, 1990, I
    Deficit Reduction Act, 1984 July 18, I
    deficit reduction plan, 1987 Nov. 20, I
    estimated, 1951 Jan. 15, I; 1953 Jan. 9,
      III; 1955 Jan. 17, I
    expenditures and deficit, 1962 July
      19(2), I; 1985 Aug. 1, I
    largest to date, 1963 Jan. 17, I; 1966, I
    projected smallest in seven years,
      1966, I
    Reagan cuts, 1981 Feb. 18, I
    Reagan proposals, 1982 Feb. 6, I
    Reagan's passed, 1986 June 27(1), I
    record, 1968, I
    reduction legislation signed, 1990
      Nov. 5, I
    surplus predicted, 1960 Jan. 7(2), III
    Treasury surpluses, 1883 Mar. 3(1), I
Buena Vista, Battle of, 1847 Feb. 22–23, I
Bueno, Maria, 1958 July 5, IV; 1959 Sept.
    13, IV; 1963 Sept. 8, IV; 1964 Sept. 13,
    IV; 1966 July 2, IV; 1966 Sept. 11, IV
Buferd, Marilyn, 1946 Sept. 7, IV
Buffalo (*see also* Bison):
    early hunting description, 1693(3), IV
Buffalo Bill, 1883, IV
"Buffalo Gals" (song), 1844(2), II
Buffalo (N.Y.):
    blizzard, 1977 Jan. 28–29, I
Building materials:
    first imitation, 1750(1), II
    first poured concrete construction
      (Chicago, Ill.), 1904(2), II
    first Quincy granite (Boston, Mass.),
      1749, II

Buildings (*see also* Architecture;
    Carpentry; Elevators; Housing; Mansions
    and Manor homes; Office buildings;
    Religion and churches; Skyscrapers;
    edifice names):
      boom in, 1952, II; 1954, II
      commercial construction banned,
        1951 Jan. 15, III
      tallest to date (Chicago, Ill.), 1883(2),
        II; 1891(3), II
      Transportation (Chicago, Ill.), 1893(8),
        II
      unions ordered to end racial
        discrimination, 1963 July 1, III
      world's largest exhibition, 1956 Apr.
        28, III
Bujones, Fernando, 1974 July 24, II; 1988,
    II
Bukovsky, Vladimir K., 1977 Mar. 1, I
Bulfinch, Charles, 1795(2), II; 1804(2), II
Bulge, Battle of the, 1944 Dec. 16, I
Bull, Dixy, 1632, IV
Bull, Ole Broneman, 1852, IV
Bull baiting, 1774(1), IV
Bullfinch, Charles, 1794(2), II
Bullfinch, Thomas, 1855(6), II
Bullins, Ed, 1975 Mar. 17, II
Bull Moose Party *see* Progressive Party
Bullock, William, 1863 Apr. 14, III
Bull Run, Battles of (Va.), 1861 July 21, I;
    1862 Aug. 29–30, I
Bulwer-Lytton, Edward, 1834(4), II
Bunche, Ralph J., 1950 Sept. 22, I; 1971, I
Bundling, 1785–1789, IV
Bunge Corp., 1975 July 21, III
Bunker, Ellsworth, 1984, I
Bunker Hill, Battle of (Mass.), 1775 June
    17, I; 1775 June 17, IV; 1776 Jan. 8, II
Bunning, Jim, 1964 June 21, IV
Bunshaft, Gordon, 1990, II
Bunyan, John, 1681(2), II
Burbank, Luther, 1872(7), III; 1875(2), III;
    1909 Mar. 7, IV
Burchard, Samuel D., 1884, I
Burchfield, Charles, 1932(6), II
Burdick, Eugene, 1962(1), II
Burdick, Quentin N., 1992, I
Burfeindt, Betty, 1976 May 30(2), IV
Burger, Warren, 1969 June 23, I; 1969
    Oct. 29, III; 1986 June 17, I
Burgess, Anthony, 1985(1), II
Burgess, Gelett, 1895(3), II
Burgess, John Melville, 1962 Dec. 8, III
Burgess, John W., 1890(4), III
Burgess, Thornton W., 1965, II
Burgesses, House of (Va.), 1619 July 30, I
Burgoyne, John, 1774(1), II; 1775 May 25,
    I; 1776 Jan. 8, II; 1777 Sept. 14, I; 1777
    Oct. 8, I; 1777 Oct. 17, I
Burk, John Daly, 1798 Apr., II
Burke, Billy, 1931 July 6, IV
Burke, Frances Marie, 1940 Sept. 8, IV
Burke, Jack, 1956 Apr. 8, IV; 1956 July 25,
    IV
Burke, Kenneth, 1981 Apr. 30, II
Burkemo, Walter, 1953 July 7, IV
Burlesque:
    early shows, 1866, IV
    musical satire and living model shows,
      1847, IV

Burling, Thomas, 1773(2), IV
Burnett, Carol, 1959 May 11, II
Burnett, Frances Hodgson, 1886(1), II
Burney, Leroy E., 1957 July 12, III
Burnham, Daniel H., 1891(3), II; 1895(5),
    II
Burnham, James, 1987, II
Burns, Arthur F., 1986, III
Burns, George, 1976 Mar. 29, II
Burns, James McGregor, 1971 Mar. 4, II;
    1971 May 3, II
Burns, Tommy, 1906 Feb. 23, IV; 1906
    Nov. 28, IV; 1907 Dec. 2, IV; 1908 Dec.
    26, IV
Burnside, Ambrose E., 1862 Nov. 5, I;
    1863 June 1, II
Burr, Aaron:
    acquitted of treason, 1807 Sept. 1, I
    charged with treason, 1806, I
    Hamilton duel, 1804 July 11, I
    presidential election tie, 1800, I; 1801,
      I
Burr, Aaron (father), 1745–1749, III
Burr, Raymond, 1959 May 6, II; 1961 May
    16, II
Burrell, Harry, 1958 June 27, III
Burrough, Bryan, 1990(1), II
Burroughs, Edgar Rice, 1914(1), II
Burroughs, John, 1871, II
Burrows, Abe, 1951 Mar. 25, II; 1961 Oct.
    14, II; 1962 May 7, II
Burstyn, Ellen, 1975 Apr. 8(1), II; 1975
    Apr. 21, II
Burton, Richard, 1962, IV; 1963 June 12,
    II; 1969 Oct. 24, IV; 1984, II
Burton, Theodore E., 1907 Mar. 14(2), I
Busch, August A., Jr., 1989, I
Busch, Niven, 1991, II
Buses (*see also* School busing):
    accidents, 1988 May 14, I
    first nite coaches, 1928 Sept., III
    freedom riders, 1961 May 14, IV
    interstate racial segregation banned,
      1955 Nov. 25, I
    Montgomery (Ala.) boycott, 1956, I
Bush, Barbara, 1990(1), II
Bush, George:
    arms control, 1991 July 31, I; 1991
      Sept. 27, I; 1992 Feb. 1, I
    budget deficit, 1990, I; 1990 Nov. 5, I
    Cold War end, 1992 Feb. 1, I
    Earth Summit, 1992 June 12, I
    elected president, 1988 Nov. 8, I
    flag burning issue, 1989 June 12(2), I
    Gulf War, 1990, I; 1990 Aug. 2–Dec.
      31, I; 1991 Jan. 15–Feb. 27, I
    inaugurated as president, 1989 Jan.
      20, I
    Japanese summit, 1992 Jan. 8, III
    legislation signed, 1989 Aug. 9, III;
      1989 Nov. 17, III; 1989 Nov. 21, I;
      1989 Nov. 21, III; 1990 July 26, I;
      1990 Nov. 5, I; 1990 Nov. 15, I;
      1990 Nov. 29, I; 1991 Feb. 6, I;
      1991 Nov. 14, I; 1991 Nov. 21, I;
      1991 Dec. 3, III; 1991 Dec. 18, I;
      1992 June 22(1), I; 1992 July 3, I;
      1992 Oct. 24, I; 1992 Oct. 30, I;
      1992 Nov. 2, I

Bush, George (*cont.*)
lifted S. African sanctions, 1991 July 10, I
named CIA head, 1975 Nov. 3, I
presidency, 1989, I
presidential defeat, 1992 Nov. 3, I
presidential nomination, 1988 Aug. 15–18, I
presidential reelection campaign, 1992 Aug. 19–20, I; 1992 Aug. 23, I
Soviet food purchases, 1990 Dec. 12, I
summit meeting (Malta), 1989 Dec. 3, I
summit meeting (Wash., D.C.), 1990 June 1, I
Sununu resigned, 1991 Dec. 3, I
temporary presidential power, 1985 July 13, I
vetoed civil rights bill, 1990 Oct. 22, I
veto override, 1992 Oct. 5, I
vice presidency, 1980 July 14–17, I; 1984 Aug. 20–23, I; 1984 Oct. 11, I; 1984 Nov. 6, I; 1985 Jan. 20, I
Bush, Vannevar, 1974, III
Bushnell, David I., 1979 Feb. 9(1), II
Bushnell, Horace, 1847, III
Bushy Run, Battle of, 1763 Aug. 5, I
Business (*see also* Corporations; Economics and economy; Great Depression; Manufacturing; Multinational corporations; Prices and price fixing; Stocks and bonds; Trusts and antitrust; names of specific companies and industries):
alleged political intervention, 1972 Mar. 20–21, III
Arab boycott of Israel compliance, 1976, III; 1976 Sept. 30(1), III
Beatrice Foods' purchase of Esmark, 1984 May 24, III
boom in production, 1898, III
car and truck sales record, 1986, III
CPI smallest increase since 1961, 1986, III
ethics criticized, 1976, III
ethos defended in *Wealth and Worth* (Hunt), 1856(4), IV
family-held, 1925(1), III
fax machine boom, 1988, III
first time greater number of women professionals than men, 1986, III
foreign trade deficit record, 1986, III
GNP worst showing in four years, 1986, III
illegal overseas payoffs, 1975, III
importance in U.S., 1790(2), IV
largest black-owned, 1984 May 9(1), III
largest cash transaction, 1925 Apr. 1, III
mergers, 1955 May 19, III
muckrakers on, 1904, II
Norris's novels condemning, 1901, II
overview, 1988, III; 1989, III
panic of 1873, 1873, I; 1874, I
peak year, 1948, III
political intervention in Chile, 1973 Apr. 2, III
priority regulations relaxed, 1944, III

Business (*cont.*)
producer prices first decline since 1963, 1986, III
record black-owned, 1987, III
seniority system upheld, 1977 May 31, III
Taylorization, 1910(5), III
unfavorable, 1932, III
upsurge, 1939, III
U.S. companies in Soviet Union, 1988, III
War Production Board (WPB), 1942 Jan. 16, III
Wharton School founded, 1881(3), III
World War II priority schedule, 1941 Feb. 24, III
World War II production, 1941 Jan. 7, III
Busing *see* School busing
Butler, Benjamin F., 1884 May 14, I; 1884 May 28, I
Butler, Nicholas Murray, 1919(2), III; 1931 Dec. 10, I
Butler, Robert N., 1976 May 3, II
Butler, William O., 1848 May 22–26, I
Butter:
rationing ended, 1945 Nov. 23, III
Butterfield, Alexander P., 1973 July 16, I
Butterfield, Fox, 1983 Apr. 24, II
Butterick, Ebenezer, 1863(3), III
Button, Richard, 1948 Feb. 13, IV; 1948 Apr. 3, IV; 1949 Feb. 17, IV; 1949 Mar. 13, IV; 1950 Mar. 7, IV; 1950 Mar. 24, IV; 1952 Mar. 28, IV
Buttons, Red, 1958 Mar. 26, II
Butz, Earl J., 1976 Oct. 4, I
Buxton, Angela, 1956 July 7, IV
Buying power *see* Consumers
Byrd, Harry F., 1960 Nov. 8, I
Byrd, Richard E., 1926 May 9, III; 1957, III
first flight over South Pole, 1929 Nov. 29, III
Byrne, Dominic, 1976 Dec. 10, IV
Byrne, Jane, 1979 Apr. 3, I
Byrne, William J., Jr., 1973 May 11, II
Byrnes, James F., 1943 May 27, III
Byron, George Gordon (Lord), 1808(3), II

Cézanne, Paul, 1980, II
Cabell, James Branch, 1917(1), II; 1919(1), II; 1938(1), II
Cabinetmakers *see* Furniture and home furnishings
Cabinets *see* federal department names; personal names
Cable Act, 1922 Sept. 22, I
Cables *see* Telegraph; Telephone
Cabot, John, 986–1599, III
Cabrillo, Juan Rodriquez, 1542, I
Cabrini, Mother Frances Xavier, 1946 July 7, III
Cadillac, Antoine de la Mothe, 1701 July 24, I
Caesar, Sid, 1948 Jan. 15, II; 1952 Feb. 18, II
Cage, John, 1992, II
Cagney, James, 1943 Mar. 4, II
Cahill, Mabel E., 1891(4), IV; 1892(5), IV
Cain, James M., 1947(1), II; 1977, II

Caine, Michael, 1987 Mar. 30, II
Calcavecchia, Mark, 1989 July 23(1), IV
Calder, Alexander, 1973 May 4, II; 1976, II; 1984 May 9, II
Caldwell, Charles, 1821(3), IV
Caldwell, Erskine, 1932(1), II; 1933(2), II; 1933 Dec. 4, II; 1987, II
Caldwell, Sarah, 1976 Jan. 13, II
Caldwell, Taylor, 1946(1), II; 1972(1), II
Caldwell, Zoe, 1968 Apr. 21, II; 1982 June 6, II
Calhoun, John C., 1817 Mar. 3(2), I; 1957 Apr. 30, I; 1973 Oct. 10, I
on economic panic, 1820(3), IV
elected vice president, 1824 Dec. 1, I
final speech, 1850 Mar. 4, III
identification with southern interests, 1828, I; 1828 Dec. 19, I
opposed Panama Conference, 1826 June, I
reelected vice president, 1828 Dec. 3, I
California (*see also* Chinese-Americans; city names):
Bear Flag Revolt, 1845 Spring, I; 1846 June 14, I
Bel Air-Brentwood fire, 1961 Nov. 6–9, I
disaster area, 1964 Dec. 22, I
earthquake, 1971 Feb. 9, I; 1992 June 28, I
Eastwood elected Carmel mayor, 1986 Apr. 8, II
first book about (Forbes), 1839(2), II
first covered wagon train to, 1841 May, I
first mission, 1769, I
first secular community, 1777 Nov., I
floods and landslides, 1938 Mar. 2, I
Frémont expedition, 1845 Spring, I
fruit fly spraying, 1981, III
gold discovered, 1848 Jan. 24, IV; 1849, I
Japanese excluded from land ownership, 1913 May 19, I
lottery prize, 1988 Nov. 1, IV
mud slides, 1969 Jan.-Mar., I
Nixon gubernatorial candidacy, 1961 Sept. 27, I
oil spill, 1990 Jan. 2–Sept. 27, I
oldest building, 1777(2), II
property law unconstitutional, 1967 May 29, I
Proposition 13, 1978 June 6, I
state government and constitution, 1849 Sept. 1, I
statehood, 1850 Sept. 9(1), I
water project, 1972 Apr. 14, III; 1992 Oct. 30, I
worst brush fires to date, 1970 Sept. 22–28, I
worst fire to date, 1991 Oct. 20–23, I
California, College of, 1855 Apr. 30, III
California, University of:
Bakke case, 1978 June 28, I
chartered in Berkeley, 1868 Mar. 23, III
Los Angeles art collection, 1987, II
People's Park established, 1969 May 15, III

California Institute of Technology, 1891(3), III

California State Polytechnic Institute, 1960 Oct. 29, I

Californium, 1950 Mar. 17, III

Calisthenics, 1832(4), IV

Callas, Maria, 1956 Oct. 29, II; 1977, II

Callender, John, 1739, II

Callendines, George V., 1847(3), IV

Calley, William L., Jr., 1969 Nov. 16, I; 1971, I; 1971 Mar. 29, I

Calvert, Cecilius see Baltimore (Lord)

Calvin, Melvin, 1961 Nov. 2(1), III

Calvinism (see also Congregational Church; Great Awakening; Mather, Cotton; Presbyterian Church):, 1763(2), III

Cambodia:
    foreign aid, 1955 Jan. 1, I
    Khmer Rouge takeover, 1975, I
    Mayaguez incident, 1975 May 12, I
    U.S invasion, 1970, I; 1970 Apr. 29, I
    U.S. travel restrictions lifted, 1977 Mar. 18, I

Camden, Battle of (S.C), 1780 Aug. 16, I

Cameo portraiture, 1849(2), II

Cameras see Photography

Camp, Walter, 1889(5), IV

Campaign financing:
    congressional elections, 1992, I
    corporate contributions banned, 1907 Jan. 26, I
    curbs, 1972 Apr. 7, I

Campbell, Alexander, 1830(4), III

Campbell, Alexander and Thomas, 1810(4), III

Campbell, George W., 1808(1), IV

Campbell, Glen, 1968 Feb. 29, II; 1969 Mar. 12, II

Campbell, John, 1988 July 11(2), IV

Campbell, Mary, 1922 Sept. 8, IV; 1923 Sept. 7, IV

Campbell, Oliver S., 1890(6), IV; 1891(4), IV; 1892(5), IV

Campbell, Thomas, 1809, II

Camp David (Md.):
    Middle East peace conference, 1978 Sept. 6–17, I

Campeau Corp., 1988 Apr. 1, III

Campobello Island (Canada), 1964 Aug. 20, II

Camps and camping:
    first summer camp for boys (Conn.), 1861 Aug., IV
    first summer camp for children, 1881(1), III

Campus Crusade for Christ International, 1972 June 12–17, III

Campus Unrest, Commission on, 1970, III; 1970 June 13, III

Canada (see also Fifty-four forty issue):
    agreement to curtail illegal immigration, 1893 Sept. 7, I
    allowed U.S. nuclear warheads installed, 1963 May 11, I
    Aroostock War, 1839 Feb. 12, I
    Caroline Affair, 1837 Dec. 29, I
    fishing rights reciprocity with U.S., 1877 Nov. 23, I

Canada (cont.)
    free trade agreement, 1988 Sept. 19, III; 1989 Jan. 2, III
    ice hockey, 1893(1), IV
    Kennedy visit, 1961 May 16–17, I
    migratory bird treaty, 1916 Aug. 16, III
    mutual disarmament treaty, 1817, I
    ore findings, 1964 Apr. 16, III
    U.S. neutrality, 1838 Jan. 5, I
    U.S. prisoner repatriation, 1977 Oct. 28, I
    U.S. territorial waters, 1892 Feb. 29, I
    Webster-Ashburton Treaty, 1842, I
    Winter Olympics (Calgary), 1988 Feb. 13–28, IV

Canadian Reciprocity Treaty, 1854 June 5, I

Canals (see also Panama and Panama Canal):
    Cape Cod (Mass.), 1914 July 29, III
    Chesapeake and Delaware, 1829 Oct. 17, III
    early (Conn. R.), 1794(5), III
    Erie (N.Y.), 1817 July 4, III; 1825, III
    Illinois Ship, 1933 June 22, III
    Isthmian Commission, 1899 Mar., III
    mileage, 1830(1), III
    Mohawk (N.Y.), 1800, III
    Ohio and Erie, 1832(2), III
    Santee (S.C.), 1800, III

Cancer:
    breast treatment controversy, 1974 Sept. 29, III
    cigarette manufacturer held liable, 1988 June 13, III
    death rate up, 1975 July 31(2), III
    dioxin carcinogenic discovered (Times Beach, Mo.), 1983 Feb. 22, I
    first breast x-ray treatment, 1896 Jan. 29, III
    genetic engineering, 1989 May 22, III; 1991 Feb. 21, III
    home for destitute victims of, 1896 Sept., III
    interferon synthesis, 1980 Jan. 16, III
    Laetrile controversy, 1977 May 1, III
    lung in women increasing, 1980 Jan. 14, III
    Memorial Hospital (N.Y.) first for treatment of, 1884(1), III
    mortality rate, 1980 Apr. 28, III
    PCBs causing, 1976 Sept. 28, III
    Red Dye No. 2 banned, 1976 Feb. 12, III
    research, 1966 Dec. 10(2), III
    smoking linked with lung, 1957 July 12, III
    virus causing, 1975 Oct. 16, III
    virus isolated, 1971 July 2, III

Cancer, National Institute, 1937, III

Candler, Asa Griggs, 1915(3), III

Canfield, Cass, 1986, II

Canfield, Dorothy, 1921(1), II

Caniff, Milton A., 1988, II

Canin, Ethan, 1988(1), II

Cannibalism, 1847, I

Cannon, Hughie, 1902(3), II

Cannon, Joseph G., 1910 Mar. 17, I

Canova, Antonio, 1821(3), II

Cans see Containers

Canseco, José, 1988 Sept. 23, IV; 1990 June 27, IV

Cantor, Eddie, 1964, II

Cape Cod Canal (Mass.), 1914 July 29, III

Capek, Karel, 1922 Oct. 9, II

Capital punishment:
    Chessman executed (Calif.), 1960 May 2, IV
    decrease in use (Pa.), 1794(3), IV
    electrocution (N.Y.), 1888 June 4, I; 1890 Aug. 6, IV
    eliminated (partially) in Pa., 1794 Apr. 22, I
    first for espionage, 1953 June 19, I
    first for witchcraft (Mass.), 1648(1), III
    first in colonies, 1630 Sept. 30, I
    first state to abolish (Mich.), 1846 May 4, I
    first woman in Calif., 1941 Nov. 21, IV
    first woman in 22 years (N.C.), 1984 Nov. 2, I
    Gilmore case (Utah), 1977 Jan. 17, IV; 1979(1), II
    increased executions, 1992, IV
    last Quaker (Mass.), 1661 Mar. 24, III
    opponents barred from juries, 1986 May 5, I
    for rape ruled unconstitutional, 1977 June 29, IV
    Sacco and Vanzetti (Mass.), 1927 Aug. 23, I
    state laws unconstitutional, 1972 June 29, I
    Supreme Court rulings on, 1976 July 2, I; 1989, I
    Va. trend away from, 1796(1), IV

Capitol (Wash., D.C.), 1792(1), II
    bombed, 1971, I; 1971 Mar. 1, I
    burned, 1814 Aug. 24, I
    enlargement, 1851 July 4, II
    rebuilding, 1805, II

Capone, Al ("Scarface"), 1929, IV; 1929 May 17, IV; 1931, IV

Caponi, Donna, 1969 June 29, IV; 1970 July 5, IV; 1981 June 14, IV

Capote, Truman, 1951(1), II; 1952 Mar. 27, II; 1959(1), II; 1966(1), II; 1966 Nov. 28, IV; 1984, II

Capp, Al, 1977 Nov. 13, II; 1979, II

Capra, Frank, 1991, II

Captain and Tennille, The (group), 1976 Feb. 28, II

Captive Nations Week, 1961 July 14, I

Caputo, Philip, 1977(1), II

Cara, Irene, 1984 Feb. 28, II

Carbon dating, 1960 Nov. 3, III

Carbon dioxide, 1961 Nov. 2(1), III

Carew, Rod, 1991 July 21, IV

Carey, Henry Charles, 1806, II; 1837, III

Carey, Mariah, 1991 Feb. 20, II

Carey, Mathew, 1806, II; 1822, III

Carey, Ronald R., 1991 Feb. 1, III

Carillons, 1745 Summer, II

Carlisle Indian School (Pa.), 1879(3), III

Carlos, John, 1968 Oct. 12–27, IV

Carlson, Chester F., 1968, III

Carlson, Evans Fordyce, 1942 Aug. 18, I

Carlson, Gretchen Elizabeth, 1988 Sept. 10, IV
Carmel (Calif.), 1986 Apr. 8, II
Carmichael, Hoagy, 1981, II
Carmichael, Stokely, 1966, III; 1966 June 1–2, I; 1966 June 6, I
Carnegie, Andrew, 1976 Oct. 7, II
  against protective tariffs, 1908 Dec. 21, III
  Endowment for International Peace (Hague), 1910(3), III
  hero fund, 1904 Apr. 15, III
  libraries, 1901 Mar. 12, III
  mansion (N.Y.C.), 1884, IV
  philanthropy, 1901, III; 1911 Nov. 10, III
  philanthropy theory, 1889 June, III
  Philippine independence, 1898, I
  steel co., 1901, III
Carnegie Corp., 1911 Nov. 10, III
Carnegie Endowment for International Peace, 1913 Dec. 10, I; 1919(2), III
Carnegie Endowment for the Advancement of Teaching, 1983 Sept. 10, III
Carnegie Hall (N.Y.C.), 1891 May 5, II; 1976 May 18, II
  gala concert reopening, 1986 Dec. 15, II
Carnegie Institute of Technology (Pa.), 1900 Nov. 15, III
Carnegie Steel Co., 1900 Mar. 24, III
Carner, JoAnne Gunderson, 1971 June 27, IV; 1974, IV; 1976 July 11, IV; 1982, IV; 1983, IV
Carnera, Primo, 1933 June 21, IV
Carnes, Kim, 1982 Feb. 24, II
Carnesecca, Lou, 1991 Feb. 2, IV
Carney, Art, 1955 Mar. 7, II; 1975 Apr. 8(1), II
Carnovsky, Morris, 1992, II
Caro, Robert, 1975 May 5, II; 1983 Jan. 27, II
Carolina Playmakers (N.C.), 1918(5), II
Carolina territory see North Carolina; South Carolina
Caroline Affair, The, 1837 Dec. 29, I
Carpenter, John Alden, 1914(5), II; 1926 Feb. 19, II
Carpenter, M. Scott, 1962 May 24, III
Carpenters, The (group), 1971 Mar. 16, II; 1972 Mar. 14, II
Carpenters' Hall (Phila., Pa.), 1742(2), II
Carpentry (see also Building materials):
  Carpenters' Company established (Pa.), 1742(2), II
Carpetbaggers see Reconstruction
Carpets see Furniture and home furnishings
Carr, Benjamin, 1800(4), II
Carr, Virginia Spencer, 1975(1), II
Carranza, Venustiano, 1915 Oct. 19, I
Carrel, Alexis, 1914 Apr. 10, III; 1922 Nov. 15, III; 1936(1), III
Carriages:
  owned in Phila., 1772, IV
Carroll, Charles, 1832, IV
Carroll, George W., 1904 June 29–30, I
Carroll, James, 1901(1), III
Carroll, Lewis, 1866(2), II

Carson, Rachel, 1951(1), II; 1952 Jan. 29, II; 1962(1), II; 1964, II
Carswell, G. Harrold, 1970 Apr. 8, I
Carter, Jimmy (James Earl):
  administration's early accomplishments, 1977, I
  administration's problems, 1980, I
  Cabinet reorganization, 1979 July 19, I
  Camp David Middle East Peace Conference (Md.), 1978 Sept. 6–17, I
  conservation program, 1979 July 15, I
  deferred neutron bomb production, 1978 Apr. 7, I
  deregulation, 1980, III
  economic measures, 1978, I
  elected president, 1976 Nov. 2, I
  energy conservation campaign, 1977 Apr. 18, III
  farewell speech, 1981 Jan. 14, I
  greeted freed hostages, 1981 Jan. 20(2), I
  inaugurated president, 1977 Jan. 20, I
  Iranian crisis, 1979, I
  S. Korean policy, 1977 Mar. 9, I
  Lance case, 1977, I; 1977 Sept. 21, I
  legislation signed, 1977 Aug. 4, I; 1977 Nov. 1, III; 1977 Dec. 20, I; 1978 Apr. 6, I; 1978 Oct. 15, I; 1978 Oct. 15, III; 1979 Oct. 17(2), III; 1979 Dec. 21, III; 1980, III; 1980 Mar. 17, I; 1980 Apr. 2, III; 1980 June 27, I
  lost presidency, 1980 Nov. 4, I
  monetary policy, 1978 Nov. 1, III
  Nicaraguan policy, 1979 Feb. 8, I
  oil price deregulation, 1978 Apr. 5, I
  Panama Canal treaties ratified, 1978 Apr. 18, I
  Panama Canal treaty, 1977 Sept. 7, I
  pardoned Vietnam draft resisters, 1977 Jan. 21, I
  Persian Gulf oil routes, 1980 Jan. 23, I
  Playboy interview, 1976 Sept. 20, I
  presidential candidacy, 1976, I; 1976 July 14, I; 1976 Sept. 27, I; 1979 Dec. 4, I
  protest moves against Soviet invasion of Afghanistan, 1980, IV; 1980 Jan. 4, I
  renominated for presidency, 1980 Aug.11–14, I
  Sadat conference, 1978 Feb. 8, I
  SALT 2 treaty signed, 1979 June 18, I
  scored AMA, 1978 May 5, III
  Soviet dissident support, 1977 Mar. 1, I
  State of the Union message, 1980 Jan. 23, I
Carter, Maybelle ("Mother"), 1978, II
Carter, Rubin ("Hurricane"), 1976 Dec. 21, IV
Carteret, George (Sir), 1664 June 24, I
Carter Hawley Hale Stores, Inc., 1991 Feb. 11, III
Cartoons (see also Comic books; Comic strips):
  Disney's Mickey Mouse, 1928(2), II
  Donald Duck's 50th birthday, 1984 June 9, II

Cartoons (cont.)
  first Democratic donkey, 1870 Jan. 15, I
  first motion picture, 1909(5), II
  first political (Pa.), 1754, II
  first Republican elephant, 1874 Nov. 7, I
  first showing Uncle Sam with beard, 1869 Feb. 6, I
  "Sad Sack" (Baker), 1944(1), IV
  "Up Front" (Mauldin), 1944(1), IV
Cartwright, Alexander J., 1845(3), IV
Carver, George Washington:
  died, 1943, III
Casals, Pablo, 1971 Oct. 25, II
Casals, Rosemary, 1967 July 8, IV; 1968 July 6, IV; 1970 July 4, IV; 1971 July 3, IV; 1972 July 7(2), IV; 1973 July 7–8, IV
Casey, John, 1989 Nov. 29, II
Casey, William J., 1987, I
Cash, Kellye, 1986 Sept. 17, IV
Casket girls, 1728(3), IV
Casper, Billy, 1959 June 13(2), IV; 1966, IV; 1966 June 20, IV; 1968, IV; 1970 Apr. 13, IV
Cass, Lewis, 1848 May 22–26, I; 1854(1), IV
Cassatt, Mary, 1881(3), II; 1894, II
Castle, Vernon and Irene, 1913(4), II; 1918 Feb. 15, II
Castro, Fidel, 1980 June 3, I
Catalogs:
  Montgomery Ward discontinued, 1985 Aug. 2, III
Cather, Willa, 1912(1), II; 1913(1), II; 1915(1), II; 1918(1), II; 1922(1), II; 1923(1), II; 1923 May 13, II; 1927(1), II; 1931(1), II
Catholic Church see Roman Catholic Church
Catholic Legion of Decency, 1934(3), II
Catholic University (Wash., D.C.), 1887 Apr. 19, III
Catonsville Nine, 1970 Aug. 11, III
CAT scan, 1979 Oct. 12, III
Catskill Aqueduct (N.Y.C.), 1917, III
Cattle see Livestock; Meat
Catton, Bruce, 1951(1), II; 1954 Jan. 26, II; 1954 May 3, II; 1960(1), II; 1961(1), II; 1963(1), II; 1965(1), II; 1978, II
Cauthen, Steve, 1977, IV; 1977 Dec. 10, IV
Cavazos, Lauro F., 1988 Sept. 20, III
Cavelier, Robert see La Salle, Sieur de
Caves:
  as settlers' dwellings, 1685(2), IV
Cawley, Helen Gourlay, 1977 July 2, IV
CBS see Columbia Broadcasting System
C.C.N.Y. see New York, College of the City of
Cech, Thomas R., 1989 Oct. 12(1), III
Cedar Creek, Battle of (Va.), 1864 Oct. 19(2), I
Cedar Mountain, Battle of (Va.), 1862 Aug. 9, I
Celler, Emanuel, 1981, I
Cellophane, 1923(2), III
Cells:
  research, 1974 Oct. 10(2), III
Celluloid, 1870 July 12, III

Cemeteries:
    Arlington National (Va.), 1802(2), II
    Native American catacombs found
        (Ariz.), 1991 Apr. 26, III
    racial discrimination, 1960 Aug. 12, IV
Censorship (see also Freedom of
    information; Pornography):,
    1922(3), II
    book burning (N.D.), 1973 Nov. 10, II
    Catholic Legion of Decency, 1934(3),
        II
    Christian Endeavor Society (Mo.)
        campaign for movie, 1910 July 20,
        II
    CIA controversy, 1978 July 7, II
    Citizens for Decent Literature, 1962,
        II
    Coughlin's Social Justice banned, 1942
        Apr. 14(1), II
    Devil Rides Outside, The (Griffin),
        1957 Feb. 25, II
    Fanny Hill ruling reversed, 1966 Mar.
        21, II
    film (N.Y.C.), 1908 Dec. 24, II
    Genius, The (Dreiser), 1916(2), II
    Kreutzer Sonata (Tolstoy), 1890(3), II
    Lady Chatterley's Lover (Lawrence),
        1959 June 11, II
    Love in Marriage (Stopes), 1921 Apr.
        22, II
    Memoirs of Hecate County (Wilson),
        1946(1), II
    motion picture bill vetoed (N.Y.S.),
        1916 May 20, II
    movie laws unconstitutional (Md.,
        N.Y.), 1965 Mar. 1, II
    movie upheld (Chicago, Ill.), 1961 Jan.
        23, II
    for national security decision, 1974
        Apr. 1, II
    opera Salomé (Strauss) (Boston, Mass.),
        1907 Jan. 22, II
    play God of Vengeance (Asch), 1923
        May 23, II
    play Mrs. Warren's Profession (Shaw)
        closed (N.Y.C.), 1905 Oct. 31, II
    play Strange Interlude (O'Neill), 1929
        Sept. 16, II
    Public Opinion (Albig) study on,
        1939(2), II
    Puritan, 1662, II
    schoolbook content protested (W.Va.),
        1974 Sept. 3, III
    Supreme Ct. ruling on government,
        1975 May 27, II
    textbook, 1925 Oct. 16, III
    Three Weeks (Glyn) (Boston, Mass.),
        1907(1), II; 1908(2), II
    Triumph of Death (Boston, Mass.),
        1898(3), II
    Trotsky's works banned (Boston,
        Mass.), 1930(2), II
    TV protested, 1960 Feb. 11, II
    Ulysses ban lifted, 1933 Dec. 6, II
    Ulysses (Joyce), 1918(2), II; 1930(2), II
    World War I, 1917 Apr. 14, II
Census (see also Population):
    first U.S., 1790 Mar. 1, I
Centennial:
    "Casey at the Bat", 1988 Aug. 15, IV

Centennial (cont.)
    golf in U.S., 1988, IV
    Porter birthday concert, 1991 June 9,
        II
Centennial of 1876 (Phila., Pa.), 1876, IV;
    1876(11), III
Central America see Latin America
Central College (Iowa), 1853 June 3, III
Central Intelligence Agency (CIA):
    absolved of direct role in Chile, 1975
        Dec. 4, I
    alleged intervention in Chile, 1972
        Mar. 20–21, III; 1973 Apr. 2, III;
        1974, I; 1974 Sept. 7, I
    alleged link with journalists, 1977
        Sept. 11(2), II
    attempt to recover sunken Soviet
        submarine, 1975 Mar. 18, I
    Bush named director, 1975 Nov. 3, I
    Casey died, 1987, I
    censorship controversy, 1978 July 7, II
    Colby dismissed, 1975 Nov. 3, I
    commission on domestic activities
        named, 1975 Jan. 5, I
    covert domestic operations
        authorized, 1981 Dec. 4, I
    covert operations, 1974 Sept. 7, I
    created, 1947 July 25, I
    funded National Student Assn., 1967
        Feb. 13, I
    illegal domestic operations, 1974 Dec.
        21, I
    Marchetti-Marks book on, 1974(1), II;
        1974 Apr. 1, II; 1975 May 27, II
    Senate investigation of, 1975 Jan. 27,
        I; 1975 Dec. 4, I
Central Park (N.Y.C.), 1857, IV; 1876(5),
    III
Century Illustrated Monthly, The
    (publication), 1881, II
Century 21 Exposition (Seattle, Wash.),
    1962 Apr. 21, IV
Cernan, Eugene, 1966 June 3, III; 1969
    May 18, III; 1972 Dec. 7, III
Chávez, César, 1966 Apr. 6, III; 1973 Apr.
    15, III
Château-Thierry (France), 1918 June 4, I
Chabon, Michael, 1988(1), II
Chadwick, French Ensor, 1882(1), I
Chadwick, George W., 1895(4), II
Chadwick, James, 1932, III
Chaffee, Roger B., 1967 Jan. 27, III
Chafin, Eugene W., 1908 July 15–16, I;
    1908 Nov. 3, I; 1912 July 10–12, I; 1912
    Nov. 5, I
Chagall, Marc, 1966 Sept. 16, II; 1977 May
    15, II; 1985, II
Chain stores see Retail stores
Chakiris, George, 1962 Apr. 9, II
Challenger (space shuttle), 1983 Apr. 4–9,
    III; 1983 June 18–24, III; 1983 Aug.
    30–Sept. 5, III; 1984 Feb. 7, III; 1984
    Oct. 11, III; 1986 Jan. 28, III;
    mid-air disaster, 1986, III;
Chamberlain, Austen (Sir), 1926 Dec. 10, I
Chamberlain, Wilt, 1960 Mar. 25, IV; 1962
    Mar. 2, IV
Chamberland, Owen, 1959 Oct. 26, III
Chambers, B. J., 1878 Feb. 22, I

Chambers, Whittaker, 1948 Dec. 15, I;
    1949 May 31, I; 1950 Jan. 21(2), I; 1961,
    I
Champion, Gower, 1980, II; 1980 Aug. 25,
    II
Champion v. Ames, 1903 Feb. 23, I
Champlain, Samuel de, 1603, III
Chance, Frank, 1907, IV
Chancellorsville, Battle of (Va.), 1863 May
    1–4, I
Chandler, Alfred D., Jr., 1978 Apr. 17, II
Chandler, Happy (Albert B.), 1945 Apr.
    24, IV; 1991, IV
Chandler, Raymond, 1959, II
Chandler, Spurgeon F. (Spud), 1990, IV
Chandrasekhar, Subrahmanyan, 1983 Oct.
    19, III
Chaney, James, 1964 Aug. 4, I; 1964 Dec.
    4, I; 1967 Oct. 20, I
Chaney, Lon, Jr., 1973, II
Channing, Carol, 1964 Jan. 16, II
Channing, Stockard, 1985 June 2, II
Channing, William Ellery, 1812 July 23,
    III; 1813(1), III; 1816(5), IV; 1819(4), III;
    1830(6), II; 1835(1), II; 1836(8), II
Chaplin, Charlie:
    married, 1918 Nov. 9, IV; 1943 June
        16, II
    vaudeville sketch (N.Y.C.), 1910 Oct.
        3, II
Chapman, John (Johnny Appleseed), 1800,
    IV
Chapman, Mark David, 1980 Dec. 8, II
Chapman, Morris, 1990 June 12, III
Chapman, Tracy, 1989 Feb. 22, II
Chappaquiddick accident (Mass.), 1969
    July 18, I
Character of the Province of Maryland, A
    (Alsop), 1666, II
Charles, Ezzard, 1949, IV; 1950, IV; 1954,
    IV; 1975, IV
Charles, Ray, 1961 Apr. 12, II
Charles, Suzette, 1984 July 23, IV
Charles I (King of Great Britain), 1662(2),
    IV
Charles II (King of Great Britain), 1661(2),
    III; 1661 Sept., III; 1662(2), IV; 1664
    Mar. 12, I; 1681 Mar. 4, I; 1684 June 21,
    I; 1686 May 15, III
Charleston, College of (S.C.), 1770(2), III
Charleston (S.C.):
    chief colonial cultural center,
        1760–1764, III
    City Hall built, 1801(1), II
    cyclone, 1893 Aug. 24, I
    epidemic, 1697(1), I
    founded, 1670 Apr., I
    Hurricane Hugo damage, 1989 Sept.
        18–24, I
    independent government, 1776 Mar.,
        I
Charnin, Martin, 1970 Nov. 10, II; 1977
    Apr. 21, II; 1977 June 5, II
Charnley House (Chicago, Ill.), 1892(7), II
Charter Oak, 1687, I
Charters:
    colonial, 1606, I
Chase, Joan, 1983(1), II
Chase, Lucia, 1986, II
Chase, Mary Coyle, 1944 Nov. 1, II

Chase, Salmon P., 1863 Feb. 25, I; 1864 Dec., I
Chase, Stuart, 1985, III
Chattanooga, Battle of (Tenn.), 1863 Nov. 23–25, I
Chauncy, Charles, 1730–1734, III
Chautauqua movement, 1874(1), III
Chauvin, Pierre, 1603, III
Chayefsky, Paddy, 1956 Feb. 8, II; 1984 Mar. 4, II
Cheever, John, 1957(1), II; 1958 Mar. 11, II; 1964(1), II; 1973(1), II; 1977(1), II; 1978(1), II; 1979 Jan. 15, II; 1979 Apr. 16, II; 1982, II; 1982(1), II; 1982 Apr. 27, II; 1991(1), II
Chelsea (Mass.):
    fire, 1908 Apr. 12, I
Chemical and biological warfare:
    Agent Orange victims' fund, 1984 May 7, I
    chemical weapons' stock reduced, 1990 June 1, I
    Chinese-Soviet charges against U.S., 1952 Mar. 8, I
    Defense Dept. shipments, 1969 Mar. 4, I
    Geneva protocol banning, 1974 Dec. 16, I
    nerve gas testing (Utah), 1968 Mar. 13, I
    Nixon ban, 1970 Feb. 14, I
    poison gas developed, 1908(4), III
    use of chemical weapons condemned, 1989 Jan. 11, I
    use of some types banned, 1969 Nov. 25, I
    Vietnam herbicide phase-out, 1970 Dec. 23, I
Chemistry and chemicals (see also Nobel Prizes):
    American Chemical Society formed, 1876(1), III
    first experiment instruction book, 1797(1), III
    first textbook and professorship, 1770(1), III
    five-dollar set, 1860(8), IV
    Gibbs's thermodynamics theory, 1876, III
    Langmuir's research, 1932 Nov. 10, III
    molecular experiments, 1917(1), III
    new elements, 1950 Mar, 17, III
    Phila. (Pa.) society, 1792(2), III
    plant explosion (Nev.), 1988 May 4, I
    transuranic elements, 1951 Nov. 15, III
Cher, 1988 Apr. 11, II
Chernow, Ron, 1990 Nov. 27, II
Cherokee Indians, 1824(3), IV; 1835 Dec., I; 1838(1), IV; 1838 Dec., I
Cherokee Strip (Kans.-Okla.), 1893 Sept. 16, I
Chesapeake and Delaware Canal, 1829 Oct. 17, III
Chesapeake-Leopard affair, 1807, I
Chess:
    American Assn., 1857 Oct. 6, IV

Chess (cont.)
    champions, 1971 Oct. 26, IV; 1972, IV; 1972 July 11–Sept. 1, IV; 1975 Apr. 3, IV
    Fischer defended U.S. championship, 1960 Jan. 2, IV
    youngest grandmaster, 1992 July 23, IV
Chessman, Caryl, 1960 May 2, IV
Cheves, Langdon, 1823, III
Chewing gum:
    first commercially sold, 1848(3), IV
Chiang Kai-shek:
    Cairo conference, 1943 Nov. 22, I
Chicago, University of (Ill.):
    atomic research, 1948 Jan. 2, III
    created, 1891(2), III
    economists won Nobel Prizes for three straight years, 1992 Oct. 13, III
    first woman president, 1978 Oct. 6, III
    summer session integration, 1892(8), III
    Yerkes Observatory, 1897(1), III
Chicago Art Institute (Ill.), 1966 Oct. 30, II
Chicago Daily News (newspaper), 1978 Mar. 4, II
Chicago Eight:
    trial begun, 1969 Sept. 24, I
Chicago (group), 1977 Feb. 19, II
Chicago (Ill.):
    black riots, 1968 Apr. 15, I
    centennial exposition, 1933 May 27-Nov. 2, IV
    civil rights rally, 1966 July 10, III
    displaced as largest U.S. city, 1984, I
    fire, 1871, I; 1894 Aug. 1, I
    fire at World's Columbian Exposition, 1894 Jan. 8, I
    first black mayor, 1983 Apr. 12, I
    first subway, 1943 Oct. 17(2), III
    first woman mayor, 1979 Apr. 3, I
    flood, 1992 Apr. 13, I
    Haymarket Riot, 1886, I
    integration demonstrations, 1965 June 10, III
    library system, 1868(4), III
    Picasso steel sculpture, 1967 Aug. 15, II
    police riot condemned, 1968 Dec. 1, I
    police scandal, 1960 Jan. 24, IV
    priests' sexual abuse of minors charged, 1992 Sept. 21(1), III
    school boycott, 1963 Oct. 22, III
    stockyards, 1865(9), III
    World's Columbian Exposition, 1890 Feb. 24, I; 1892 Oct. 20–23, IV; 1893, IV; 1893(3), II; 1893(4), II; 1893(5), II; 1893(6), IV; 1893(8), II
Chicago Seven, 1970 Feb. 18, III; 1973 Dec. 4, I
Chicago Sun-Times (newspaper), 1983, II
Chicago Times (newspaper):
    anti-Lincoln, 1863 June 1, II
Chickamauga, Battle of (Tenn.), 1863 Sept. 19–20, I
Chicken pox, 1984 May 30, III
"Chicken war" see Poultry
Child, Lydia Maria, 1835(4), II

Children (see also Births; Dolls and toys; Education and schools; Juvenile delinquency; Orphans; Youth culture):
    alcohol abuse, 1741(2), IV
    books for, 1719(1), II; 1868, II; 1873, II; 1880(2), II; 1903, II
    dental hygiene, 1988 June 21, III
    first magazine for (Conn.), 1789 Jan.(2), II
    first summer camp, 1881(1), III
    kidnaped for Va. colony, 1627, IV
    labor, 1790 Dec. 21, III; 1890(1), III; 1904(3), III; 1908 May 28, III; 1916 Feb. 29, III; 1918 June 3, III; 1923 Apr. 9, III; 1924 June 2, III; 1941 Feb. 3, I
    rearing precepts, 1693(1), IV
    taught Latin at early age, 1799(2), IV
    temperance crusade enlisting, 1836(7), IV
    youngest heart transplant recipient to date, 1987 Oct. 16, III
Children's Day, 1856(2), IV
Child welfare:
    Children's Aid Society (N.Y.C.), 1854(6), IV
    day care sexual abuse, 1992 Apr. 22, IV
    divorce from unfit parent allowed, 1992 Sept. 25, I
    first free medical clinics, 1860(3), III
    first legal protection, 1851(1), IV
    heart defect detection, 1961 June 6, III
    labor, protective legislation, 1842 Mar. 3, III
    orthopedic hospital (N.Y.C.), 1863 May 1, III
    sexual abuse by Catholic priests investigated, 1992 Sept. 21(1), III
    Society for the Prevention of Cruelty to Children, 1875(3), III
Chile:
    CIA involvement, 1974, I; 1974 Sept. 7, I; 1975 Dec. 4, I
    human rights abuses criticized, 1986, I
    Mexican-U.S. dispute, 1914 Apr. 25, I
    mob attacked U.S. sailors, 1891 Oct. 16, I
    U.S. alleged involvement in Allende coup, 1972 Mar. 20–21, III
    U.S. political intervention, 1973 Apr. 2, III
Chimpanzee:
    in space, 1961 Jan. 31, III
Chin, Tiffany, 1985 Feb. 1–2, IV
China:
    Boxer Rebellion, 1900, I
    N.Y.C. museum, 1849(1), IV
    Open Door policy, 1922 Feb. 6(1), I
    Republic recognized by U.S., 1913 May 2, I
    U.S. aid, 1948 Apr. 3, I
    U.S. commercial treaty, 1844 July 3, I
    U.S. occupation of Tientsin, 1912 Jan. 22, I
    U.S. support, 1961 Aug. 2, I
China, People's Republic of (Communist):
    Bruce named first U.S. liaison officer, 1973 May 14(2), I

China, People's Republic of (Communist) (*cont.*)

first U.S. track and field meet, 1975 May 18–28, IV

Ford trip, 1975 Dec. 7, I

human rights abuses, 1992 Jan. 31, I

music and dance troupe U.S. tour canceled, 1975 Mar. 28(2), II

Nixon visit, 1972 Feb. 21–28, I

Nixon visit announced, 1971, I

nuclear energy accord with U.S., 1985 July 23, I

patents and copyrights agreement, 1992 Jan. 16, I

Philadelphia Orchestra tour, 1973 Sept. 12, II

Reagan's visit and U.S. cooperative agreements, 1984 Apr. 26–May 1, I

U.N. admission, 1971 Aug. 2, I

U.S. arms sale, 1981 June 16, I

U.S. embargo lifted, 1971 Apr. 14, III

U.S. Ping-Pong team visit, 1971, IV; 1971 Apr. 10–14, IV

U.S. relations eased, 1971, IV; 1971 Apr. 10–14, IV

U.S. scientific delegation visited, 1978 July 6–10, III

U.S. to enter full diplomatic relations, 1978 Dec. 15(2), I

U.S. trade agreement, 1992 Oct. 9(1), III

U.S. travel ban lifted, 1972 Nov. 22, I

U.S. travel restrictions, 1959 Dec. 7, I

Chinaware *see* Pottery

Chinese-Americans:

Calif. restrictions, 1879, I

Calif. riots against, 1877(1), I

citizenship rights, 1898 May 28, I

limited immigration, 1880 Nov. 17, I

Chinese exclusion acts, 1882 May 6, I; 1892 May 5, I; 1893 May 15, I; 1894 Mar. 17, I; 1902 Apr. 29, I; 1943 Dec. 17, I

Chinese Exclusion Treaty, 1880 Nov. 17, I

Chisholm Trail, 1867(10), III

Chocolate:

colonial popularity, 1710–1714, IV

first manufactured (Mass.), 1765(1), III

Chodorov, Jerome, 1940 Dec. 26, II

Cholera epidemics, 1832(1), I; 1832 July 9, IV; 1849 May 17, I; 1850(1), III; 1866(1), I; 1873(3), III

Cholesterol, 1981 Jan. 8, III; 1985 Oct. 14, III

Chou En-lai:

U.S. germ warfare charges, 1952 Mar. 8, I

Choynski, Joe, 1889 June 5, IV

Christ Church (Alexandria, Va.), 1773 Feb. 27, III

Christensen, Axel, 1904(5), II

Christensen, Parley P., 1920 July 13–16, I; 1920 Nov. 2, I

Christian Churches, General Convention of, 1931 July 1, III

Christian Commonwealth, The (Eliot), 1659(1), II

Christian Disciple (magazine), 1813(1), III

Christian Observer (newspaper), 1813 Sept. 4, II

Christian Science:

church membership, 1900(2), III

Church of Christ, Scientist organized, 1879(5), III

controversial chairman resigned, 1992 Mar. 9, III

First Church of Christ, Scientist founded (Boston, Mass.), 1892(5), III

Science and Health published, 1875(4), III

Christie, Julie, 1966 Apr. 18, II

Christie's (N.Y.C.), 1977 May 16, II

Christmas:

first Red Cross seals, 1908 Dec., III

Mass. ban, 1660 May, IV

Nativity display upheld, 1984 Mar. 5, I

traffic fatalities, 1955 Dec. 27, III

Christo, Javacheff, 1972 Aug. 11, II; 1983 May 4, II

Christy, Edwin P., 1842(4), IV

Christy, James W., 1978 June 22, III

Christy Minstrels, 1846 Apr. 27, II

Chrysler, Walter P., 1962, II

Chrysler Corp.:

De Soto discontinued, 1960 Nov. 18, III

federal bailout, 1979 Dec. 21, III

three-year contract, 1964 Sept. 9, III

Church, Benjamin, 1775 July 25, III

Church, Frank, 1975 Jan. 27, I; 1984, I

Church, Frederick, 1979, II

Churches *see* Religion and churches

Churches, National Council of, 1961 Feb. 22–23, III; 1978 Nov. 4, III

Greek Orthodox Church suspended ties, 1991 June 6, III

Churches of Christ:

Federal Council of the, 1908 Dec. 2, III

Churchill, Winston:

Atlantic Charter, 1941 Aug. 9–12, I

Cairo conference, 1943 Nov. 22, I

honorary U.S. citizenship, 1963 Apr. 9, I

Quebec conference, 1943 Aug. 11–24, I

Teheran conference, 1943 Nov. 28–Dec. 1, I

U.S. visit, 1952, I

Yalta conference, 1945 Feb. 4–11, I

Church of Christ, United:

social reform measures, 1959 July 7(2), III

Church of England *see* Anglican Church

Church-state separation:

colonial, 1647 May 29–31, I

compulsory flag salute challenged, 1943 June 14, III

creation science teaching law struck down (Ark.), 1982 Jan. 5, III

creation science teaching law struck down (La.), 1987 June 19, III

first guarantee (Quaker), 1677(1), III

Mass. disestablishment, 1833(1), III

National Fast Day issue, 1832 July 9, IV

Nativity display upheld, 1984 Mar. 5, I

public school teachers banned from parochial schools, 1985 July 1, III

Church-state separation (*cont.*)

religious services in public universities upheld, 1981 Dec. 8, III

school prayer banned (N.Y.S.), 1962 June 25, III

school prayer decision (Ariz.), 1985 June 4, III

school prayer reinstatement amendment rejected, 1984 Mar. 20, I

school prayer struck down, 1992 June 24(2), III

school prayer unconstitutional, 1962, III

student political/religious use of high school facilities upheld, 1990 June 4, I

Supreme Court religion in public schools decision, 1948 Mar. 8, III

CIA *see* Central Intelligence Agency

Ciardi, John, 1986, II

Cicippio, Joseph J., 1986 Nov. 2, I

Cigars and cigarettes *see* Smoking; Tobacco

Cincinnati, Society of, 1783 May 13, IV

Cinema *see* Motion pictures

CIO *see* American Federation of Labor-Committee of Industrial Organization; Committee of Industrial Organization

Cipollone, Antonio and Rose, 1988 June 13, III

Circuses and entertainment (*see also* Burlesque; Freaks; Minstrel shows; Sports; Theater; Vaudeville; other specific types):

Barnum's enterprises, 1875, IV

curfew lifted, 1945 May 9, III

Hippodrome Theater (N.Y.C.) opened, 1853, IV

last tented show, 1956 July 16, IV

midnight curfew, 1945 Feb. 26, III

mime G.W.L. Fox, 1850(8), II

Ricketts', 1793(4), IV

tent fire disaster (Hartford, Conn.), 1944 July 6, I

tightrope performer, Mme. Adolphe, 1819 June 1, IV

traveling shows, 1836, IV

Virginia City (Nev.), 1867, IV

wild West shows, 1878(2), IV

Cisneros, Henry Gabriel, 1981 Apr. 4, I

Citibank, 1986 Oct. 20, III

Cities and urban areas (*see also* specific names):

aid for inner, 1992 June 22(1), I

Cleveland (Ohio) defaulted, 1978 Dec. 15(1), I

colonial population, 1720, I

first community named Washington, 1776(2), IV

first directory (Phila., Pa.), 1785 Oct. 1, III

first garden community (N.J.), 1929(2), II

Los Angeles largest, 1984, I

most typical, 1992, I

population increase, 1990, I

problems in wake of population increases, 1835, IV

Cities and urban areas (*cont.*)
   Riis's exposure of slums, 1890, IV
   slum density (N.Y.C.), 1905(1), III
   urbanization growth, 1921 Jan. 13, I
Citizenship:
   Cable Act, 1922 Sept. 22, I
   children born abroad of U.S. parents,
     1855 Feb. 10, I
   Churchill received honorary, 1963
     Apr. 9, I
   first Chinese citizen under new law,
     1943 Dec. 17, I
   for former slaves, 1868 July 28, I
   Puerto Rican, 1904 Jan. 4, I; 1917
     Mar. 2, I
   returned to Japanese-Americans, 1959
     May 20, IV
   rights rulings, 1964 May 18, I
Citric acid, 1953 Oct. 22, III
City Center of Music and Drama (N.Y.C.),
   1943 Dec. 11, II
Civil Aeronautics Act, 1938 June 23, III
Civil defense:
   J. Kennedy urged fallout shelters,
     1961 Oct. 6, I
Civil Defense Coordinating Board, 1955
   Apr. 9, I
Civil disobedience:
   Army surveillance of civilians
     discontinued, 1970 Feb. 26, I
   CIA surveillance, 1975 Jan. 5, I
   FBI surveillant indicted, 1977 Apr. 7,
     I
   flag burning right upheld, 1989 June
     12(2), I
   illegal CIA domestic operations, 1974
     Dec. 21, I
   Presbyterian advocacy, 1988 June
     14(2), III
   special IRS files on dissenters
     revealed, 1974 Nov. 17, I
   Thoreau's advocacy, 1849, II
Civilian Aviation Act, 1926 May 20, III
Civilian Conservation Corps (CCC), 1933
   Mar. 31, I; 1936, III
Civilian Mobilization Office, 1950 Jan.
   21(1), I
Civil rights (*see also* Black power; Blacks;
   Human rights; School desegregation;
   Voting rights; names of leaders):
   advocates debate, 1966 June 6, I
   bill passed by Senate, 1960 Apr. 8, I
   bill rejected, 1966, I
   bus boycott (Montgomery, Ala.), 1956,
     I
   Bush vetoed bill, 1990 Oct. 22, I
   Chicago (Ill.) rally, 1966 July 10, III
   children's, 1992 Sept. 25, I
   commemorative march (Wash., D.C.),
     1983 Aug. 27, I
   demonstrators' harassment at PGA
     golf tournament, 1969 Aug. 17, IV
   disabled protected, 1990 July 26, I;
     1991 July 1, I; 1992 Jan. 26, I
   equal legal education decision (Okla.),
     1948 Jan. 12, III
   Evers assassinated, 1963 June 12, I
   FBI surveillance, 1974, I; 1974 Nov.
     18, I

Civil rights (*cont.*)
   filibuster against legislation, 1957 Aug.
     30, I; 1960 Feb. 29, I
   filibuster cloture, 1964 June 10, I
   first antidiscrimination agency
     (N.Y.S.), 1945 July 1, III
   first bill to survive filibuster, 1960
     Apr. 8, I
   Freedom March (Wash., D.C.), 1963
     Aug. 28, I
   freedom riders, 1961 May 14, IV
   interstate train and bus segregation
     banned, 1955 Nov. 25, I
   King arrested (Birmingham, Ala.),
     1963 Apr. 12, I
   King museum opened (Memphis,
     Tenn.), 1991 Aug. 31, I
   Ku Klux Klan members convicted of
     rioting, 1988 Oct. 6, I
   Ku Klux Klan members convicted of
     conspiracy, 1967 Oct. 20, I
   Liuzzo killed (Selma, Ala.), 1965 Mar.
     25, I
   Memphis (Tenn.) violence, 1968 Mar.
     28, I
   Meredith shot, 1966 June 6, I
   Methodist abolishment of segregation,
     1956 May 2, III
   militant-pacifist division, 1966, III
   military integrated, 1962 Apr. 3, I
   Poor People's March (Wash., D.C.),
     1968 May 2, I; 1968 June 24, I
   private discrimination upheld, 1883
     Oct. 15, I
   progress, 1963, III
   protests at N.Y. World's Fair, 1964
     Apr. 22, IV
   reverse discrimination applicability
     ruling, 1989 June 12(1), I
   Rev. Reeb died from beatings, 1965
     Mar. 11, I
   Selma-Montgomery (Ala.) march, 1965
     Mar. 21, I
   sit-ins endorsed by Episcopal Church,
     1960 Apr. 27, III
   Supreme Court "separate but equal"
     doctrine, 1896 May 18, I
   three white workers murdered (Miss.),
     1964 Aug. 4, I; 1964 Dec. 4, I
   transportation segregation laws
     banned, 1962 Feb. 26, I
   white backlash, 1966, III
   White House Conference, 1966 June
     1–2, I
Civil Rights Acts, 1866 Apr. 9, I; 1875
   Mar. 1, I; 1883 Oct. 15, I; 1964 July 2, I;
   1964 July 22, I; 1968 Apr. 11, I; 1971
   Jan. 25, III; 1988 Mar. 22, I; 1990 July
   26, I; 1991 Nov. 21, I; 1992 Jan. 26, I
Civil Service Commission *see* Government
   employees
Civil War (*see also* Confederate States of
   America; Secession; Slaves and slavery):
   Alabama sunk, 1864 June 19, I
   American Peace Society opposed,
     1860 May 28, III
   Antietam battle (Md.) halted
     Confederate troops, 1862 Sept. 17, I
   Appomattox (Va.) surrender, 1865
     Apr. 9, I

Civil War (*cont.*)
   art and statues, 1864, II; 1865(9), II;
     1867(2), II
   Atlanta (Ga.) evacuated and occupied
     by Union forces, 1864 Sept. 1, I
   Ball's Bluff (Va.) Union defeat, 1861
     Oct. 21, I
   began with attack on Ft. Sumter
     (S.C.), 1861, I; 1861 Apr. 12, I
   black troops, 1862 July, I; 1864 Apr.
     12, I
   blockade of Confederate ports, 1861
     Apr. 19(2), I; 1861 Nov. 7, I
   books inspired by, 1863, II
   books on, 1936(1), II; 1951(1), II;
     1955(1), II; 1960(1), II; 1961 May 1,
     II; 1963(1), II; 1964(1), II; 1965(1), II
   Bull Run, first battle of (Va.), 1861
     July 21, I
   Bull Run, second battle (Va.), 1862
     Aug. 29–30, I
   Burnside named Union Army of
     Potomac commander, 1862 Nov. 5,
     I
   casualties, 1861 Oct. 21, I; 1862 July
     1(3), I; 1862 Aug. 9, I; 1862 Aug.
     29–30, I; 1862 Dec. 13, I; 1863 May
     1–4, I; 1863 July 1–3, I; 1863 July 4,
     I; 1864 Feb. 20, I; 1864 June 3, I
   Catton's history of, 1961(1), II
   Cedar Creek battle (Va.), 1864 Oct.
     19(2), I
   Cedar Mt. (Va.) battle, 1862 Aug. 9, I
   Chancellorsville battle (Va.), 1863 May
     1–4, I
   Chattanooga battle (Tenn.), 1863 Nov.
     23–25, I
   Chickamauga battle (Tenn.), 1863
     Sept. 19–20, I
   Cold Harbor, Battle of, 1864 June 3, I
   Columbia (S.C.) set afire, 1865 Feb.
     17, I
   Confederate ship *Virginia*, 1862 Mar.
     8, I
   "Copperhead" term, 1862, IV
   Crittenden Compromise proposal,
     1860 Dec. 18, I
   "Damn the torpedoes . . . " expression,
     1864 Aug. 5, IV
   dramas about events of, 1861 Aug. 15,
     II
   Early's tactics, 1864 July 11, I
   eyewitness reports by W. Whitman,
     1863(5), IV
   first casualties (Md.), 1861 Apr. 19(1), I
   first conscription act, 1863 Mar. 3(2), I
   first naval battle (Fla.), 1861 Sept. 13,
     I
   Five Forks battle (Va.), 1865 Apr. 1, I
   Ft. Fisher (N.C.) surrendered, 1865
     Jan. 15, I
   Ft. Pillow massacre (Tenn.), 1864 Apr.
     12, I
   Ft. Sumter relief expedition, 1861
     Apr. 6, I
   Ft. Sumter surrender demanded, 1861
     Apr. 11, I
   Ft. Sumter surrendered, 1861 Apr. 12,
     I

Civil War (cont.)
  Fredericksburg (Va.) battle, 1862 Dec. 13, I
  Gettysburg battle (Pa.), 1863 July 1–3, I
  Gettysburg veterans' reunion, 1913 June 30, IV
  Grant named Union general in chief, 1864 Mar. 10, I
  Halleck named Union Army commander, 1862 July 11, I
  Hampton Roads Peace Conference (Va.), 1865 Feb. 3, I
  Harpers Ferry (W. Va.) captured by Confederates and abandoned, 1862 Sept. 15, I
  Jackson mortally wounded, 1863 May 2, I
  James R. Bridge built (Va.), 1864 June 14, I
  Johnston surrendered (N.C.), 1865 Apr. 26(1), I
  last veteran died, 1959 Dec. 19, IV
  last veterans' encampment, 1949 Aug. 31, I
  Lee named Confederate army commander, 1862 June 1, I
  Lee's conference proposal, 1865 Mar. 2, I
  Lincoln's call for volunteer troops, 1861 Apr. 15, I
  Lincoln's Gettysburg Address, 1863 Nov. 19, II
  McClellan named Army head, 1861 Nov. 1, I
  March to the Sea, 1864 Nov. 16, I
  medical services, 1881, III
  Mobile Bay battle (Ala.), 1864 Aug. 5–23, I
  Monitor construction, 1861 Oct. 4, III
  New Orleans (La.) captured by Union, 1862 May 1, I
  N.Y.C. arson attempt, 1864 Nov. 25, I
  Norfolk Navy Yard (Va.) evacuated by Union forces, 1861 Apr. 19–20, I
  Olustee battle (Fla.), 1864 Feb. 20, I
  peace bid, 1864 July 5, I
  Pea Ridge battle, 1862 Mar. 6–7, I
  Petersburg battle (Va.), 1864 June 15–18, I
  Petersburg (Va.) occupied, 1865 Apr. 3, I
  Petersburg (Va.) siege, 1865 Mar. 25, I
  plays about, 1886, II; 1889 Sept. 9, II
  poetry, 1860, II; 1864(1), II; 1864 Oct. 19(2), I; 1865, II
  Port Hudson battle (Miss.), 1863 July 8, I
  Port Royal Island (S.C.) captured by Union, 1861 Nov. 7, I
  prisoners of war, 1864 Apr. 17, I; 1864 Apr. 20, I
  regional differences leading to, 1852, I
  Richmond (Va.) evacuated, 1865 Apr. 2, I
  Roanoke Island (N.C.) captured by Union, 1862 Feb. 8, I
  St. Albans (Vt.) raid, 1864 Oct. 19(1), I
  Seven Days Campaign, 1862 July 1(3), I

Civil War (cont.)
  Seven Pines and Fair Oaks battles (Va.), 1862 May 31–June 1, I
  Shiloh battle and losses (Tenn.), 1862 Apr. 6–7, I
  slavery issue, 1851 Feb. 15, I
  slogans, 1862 July 16, IV
  songs, 1861(2), II; 1862 July 16, IV
  Spotsylvania campaign (Va.), 1864 May 7–20, I; 1864 May 11, IV; 1864 May 12, I
  Star of the West fired on (S.C.), 1861 Jan. 9(1), I
  submarines, 1864 Feb. 17, III
  termed "insurrection", 1861 Apr. 15, I
  theater closures, 1861(1), II
  TV series on, 1990, II
  Union aerial reconnaissance, 1862(3), III
  Union financing, 1861 Aug. 5, III
  veterans, 1881, IV
  Vicksburg (Miss.) battle, 1863 July 4, I
  Virginia destroyed by its crew, 1862 May 11, I
  Virginia (Merrimack)-Monitor sea battle, 1862 Mar. 9, I
  volunteer army sanctioned by Congress, 1861 July 25, I
  Wilderness battle (Va.), 1864 May 5–6, I
  Wilson's Creek battle won by Confederacy (Mo.), 1861 Aug. 10, I
  women nurses, 1861 June 10, IV; 1881, III
Civil Works Administration: established, 1933 Nov. 8, I
Clairborne, Harry E., 1986 Oct. 9, I
Clancy, Tom, 1987(1), II; 1988(1), II
Clapton, Eric, 1991 Feb. 20, II
Clark, Barney C., 1982 Dec. 2, III; 1983 Mar. 23, III
Clark, Charles E., 1960 Mar. 25, II
Clark, Eleanor, 1965 Mar. 9, II
Clark, Jack, 1988 Apr. 20, IV
Clark, Joseph S., 1960 Apr. 8, I
Clark, Mae, 1992, II
Clark, Mark W., 1984, I
Clark, Mary Higgins, 1988, II
Clark, Susan, 1976 May 17, II
Clark, Walter Van Tilburg, 1971, II
Clark, William, 1804, I; 1814(1), II
Clark, William P., 1982 Jan. 4, I; 1983 Oct. 9, I
Clarke, James Freeman, 1871, III
Clark University (Mass.), 1887(4), III; 1920(2), III
Classical studies, 1882(3), III
Classification of information see Freedom of information
Claude, Albert, 1974 Oct. 10(2), III
Clavell, James, 1966(1), II; 1975(1), II; 1986 Jan. 11, II
Clay, Cassius see Ali, Muhammad
Clay, Henry:
  Anti-Masonic Party, 1831 Sept. 26, I
  Bank of the U.S., 1833 Dec. 26 I
  lost presidential bid, 1832 Dec. 5, I; 1844 Dec. 4, I
  National Fast Day, 1832 July 9, IV

Clay, Henry (cont.)
  opposed Texas annexation, 1844 Apr. 27, I
  political policies, 1828(2), I
  presidential election of 1824, 1825 Feb. 9, I
  presidential nomination, 1831 Dec. 12, I; 1844, I; 1844 May 1, I
  protective tariff advocate, 1828(2), IV
  "rather be right than be president" quote, 1850(4), IV
  Senate censure of Jackson, 1834 Mar. 28, I
  Senate Hall of Fame, 1957 Apr. 30, I
  slavery resolutions, 1850, I
  tariff, 1833 Mar. 2, I
  views on Texas annexation, 1844 July 1–27, I
  Whig Party, 1834, I
Clay, Lucius D., 1978, I
Clayton-Bulwer Treaty, 1850 Apr. 19, I; 1901 Nov. 18, I
Clean Air Act, 1990 Nov. 15, I
Clean Water Act, 1987 Feb. 4, I
Cleaver, Eldridge, 1975 Nov. 18, I
Clemens, Samuel see Twain, Mark
Clemente, Roberto, 1972, IV
Clemson College (S.C.), 1963 Jan. 28, III
Clermont (steamboat), 1803 May, III; 1807 Aug. 11, III
Cleveland, Grover:
  bimetallism, 1885 Dec., I
  born, 1837 Mar. 18, I
  British-Venezuelan boundary dispute, 1895, I
  elected president, 1884 Nov. 4, I; 1892 Nov. 8, I
  gold standard, 1893, I
  Hawaii policy, 1893 Feb. 15, I
  illegitimate child, 1884(2), IV
  inaugurated president, 1885 Mar. 4, I; 1893 Mar. 4, I
  lost presidency, 1888 Nov. 6, I
  mustache, 1865, IV
  presidential candidacy, 1884, I; 1884 July 8–11, I; 1884 July 30, I; 1888, I; 1888 June 5, I
  presidential nomination, 1892 June 21–23, I
  Pullman strike injunction enforcement, 1894 July 3, III
  vetoed immigration literacy requirement bill, 1897 Mar. 2, I
  vetoed silver coinage bill, 1894 Mar. 30, I
Cleveland (Ohio):
  defaulted, 1978 Dec. 15(1), I
  first black mayor, 1967 Nov. 7, I
  race riots, 1968 July 23, I
  school fire, 1908 Mar. 4, I
  teachers' strike, 1980 Jan. 3, III
Clevenger, Shobal Vail, 1836(2), II
Cliburn, Van, 1958 Apr. 11, II; 1968 June 12, II
Clinton, Bill (William Jefferson):
  book by, 1992(1), II
  elected president, 1992 Nov. 3, I
  presidential nomination, 1992 July 15–16, I

Clinton, De Witt, 1812 Dec. 2, I; 1816
    June 22, IV; 1817 July 4, III; 1825, III
Clinton, George, 1804 Dec. 5, I; 1808 Dec.
    7, I
Clinton, Henry (Sir), 1775 May 25, I
Cliosophic Society, 1765(1), II
Clipper ships *see* Ships and shipping
Clive, John, 1974 Apr. 18, II
Clocks and watches (*see also* Time):
    first banjo clock, 1802(1), IV
    first clock made in America, 1754, III
    first eight-day watch, 1850(2), III
    first lasting watch business, 1849(1),
        III
    first patent, 1797(3), III
    first town clock (N.Y.C.), 1780(2), III
    standardized brass clock works,
        1838(2), III
Cloisters, The (N.Y.C.), 1938(6), II
Close, Glenn, 1984 June 3, II; 1992 June 1,
    II
Clothier, William J., 1906(2), IV
Clothing and fashion (*see also* Sewing;
    Sewing machines; Shoes and footwear):
    American designs, 1943(1), IV
    art-inspired, 1965, IV
    banyan (nightgown) forbidden,
        1754(2), IV
    bell-bottom pants, 1969, IV; 1977
        Aug. 1, IV
    bikini bathing suits, 1949, IV
    bloomers' inception, 1850, IV
    bosom bottles, 1756 July 26, IV
    career women's styles, 1985, IV
    caste law (Conn.), 1676(1), IV
    classic shapes, 1983, IV
    colonial codes, 1670–1679, IV; 1675(2),
        IV; 1675(3), IV
    colonial restrictions (Mass.), 1634, IV;
        1639(1), IV
    colonial restrictive laws (Va.), 1660(3),
        IV
    colonial women's (N.Y.), 1704(1), IV
    colonial workmanship, 1775(1), IV
    corsets (stays), 1773(1), IV
    Courrèges look, 1965, IV
    current women's, 1885(1), IV
    detachable collared shirts, 1819(2), III
    Dior, Christian, 1947, IV
    Directoire (sheath gown), 1908(2), IV
    down-filled quilted coat, 1980, IV
    early 19th-century changes, 1817, IV
    elegance emphasis, 1982, IV; 1985, IV
    extravagant colonial, c1710, IV
    fashions in Sears Roebuck catalog,
        1939(1), IV
    feminine, 1945, IV; 1946, IV
    first nylon stockings, 1939 Oct. 25, III
    first tuxedo, 1886 Oct., IV
    galluses (suspenders) patents, 1804(3),
        III
    garment workers' strike (N.Y.C.), 1913
        Jan., III
    hemline dropped, 1970, IV
    high hemlines, 1968, IV
    hot pants, 1971, IV
    knee-length skirts, 1921 Dec., IV
    labor conditions, 1900(4), III
    ladies' tight sleeves vogue, 1841(5), IV
    leg warmers, 1983, IV

Clothing and fashion (*cont.*)
    "lingerie" term popular, 1852(4), IV
    long straight coat introduced,
        c1680(2), IV
    maxicoats, 1967, IV
    men's Bermuda shorts, 1953, IV
    men's styles, c1785, IV; 1865, IV;
        1989, IV
    men's underwear, 1992, IV
    miniskirt, 1966, IV; 1987, IV
    mink muffs advertised, 1860(9), IV
    Mod look, 1965, IV
    New Look, 1947, IV; 1948, IV
    olive drab Army uniform, 1902(1), I
    oversized men's for women, 1984, IV
    pants features, 1992, IV
    pantsuits, 1968, IV
    paper collar invented, 1854(1), III
    paper dresses, 1966, IV
    Paris influence on women's, 1854, IV
    post-1850s fashions, 1854, IV
    Reagan, Nancy, influence, 1981, IV
    sack silhouette, 1957, IV
    sheaths, 1955, IV
    silk stocking sales, 1900(2), IV
    skirt lengths, 1971, IV
    skirt lengths dropped, 1991, IV
    skirts shortened, 1895(1), IV
    social differences, 1887, IV
    softer look, 1989, IV
    softer silhouette, 1954, IV
    Stetson hat originated, 1865(4), IV
    stoles, 1950, IV
    tailors criticized, 1847(3), IV
    tailors' strike (N.Y.C.), 1894 Sept. 4, III
    thin muslin dresses, 1818(1), IV
    tuxedo 100 years old, 1986, IV
    unisex, 1965, IV; 1969, IV
    white stocking craze, c1730, IV
    women's pelerines and cardinals,
        1842(3), IV
    women's return to fancier, 1850(11),
        IV
    World War II fashions, 1941, IV; 1942,
        IV; 1943(1), IV; 1944, IV
    youth influence, 1970, IV
    zoot suit, 1943, IV
Clubs *see* Associations and clubs; specific
    names
Cluchette, John, 1972 Mar. 27, IV
Clurman, Harold E., 1980, II
Clymer, George, 1816(2), II
Coaches, four-in-hand (*see also* Stage
    coaches):, 1879, IV
Coal:
    anthracite first burned in open grate
        (Pa.), 1808 Feb. 11, III
    anthracite first used (Pa.), 1769(5), III
    black lung disease compensation, 1969
        Dec. 18, III
    conservation efforts, 1918 Feb. 12, II
    longest miners' strike to date ended,
        1978 Mar. 25, III
    mine disaster (Avondale, Pa.), 1869
        Sept. 6, I
    mine explosions, 1907 Dec. 6, I; 1907
        Dec. 19, I; 1957 Feb. 4, I; 1968
        Nov. 20, I

Coal (*cont.*)
    miners' strikes, 1894 Apr. 20, III; 1897
        July 2, III; 1900 Sept. 17, III; 1902
        May 12, III; 1902 July 30, III; 1902
        Oct. 16, III
    mine safety standards, 1969 Dec. 18,
        III
    mines seized, 1943 May 1, III
    price rise, 1900 Sept. 17, III
    production stopped by Mine Workers,
        1939 May 5, III
    stock seizure authority given, 1943
        May 5, III
    strike, 1948 Mar. 15, III
    strip mining upheld, 1976 June 28, III
    walkout, 1949 Mar. 11, III
Coase, Ronald, 1991 Oct. 15, III
Coast Guard, U.S.:
    established, 1915, I
Coatzee, Gerrie, 1983 Sept. 23, IV
Cobb, Lee J., 1976, II
Cobb, Lyman, 1847(4), IV
Cobb, Ty, 1911, IV; 1961, IV; 1985 Sept.
    11, IV
Coburn, Charles, 1944 Mar. 2, II
Coburn, Donald L., 1977 Oct. 6, II; 1978
    Apr. 17, II
Coca, Imogene, 1952 Feb. 18, II
Coca-Cola Co., 1985, IV
Cocaine, 1988 May 3, IV; 1988 May 19,
    IV; 1989 Sept. 29, IV
Cochet, Henri, 1928 Aug. 27, IV
Cochran, Jacqueline, 1980, III
Cocker, Joe, 1983 Feb. 23, II
Cock fighting, 1830 Feb. 11, IV
Cocoanut Grove fire (Boston, Mass.), 1942
    Nov. 28, I
Coddington, William, 1640–1649, II
Cody, John Cardinal, 1982, III
Cody, William F., 1883, IV
Coetzee, Gerrie, 1984 Dec. 1, IV
Coffee:
    campaign against, 1821(1), IV
    cups drunk, 1954, IV
    high prices, 1977, III
    introduced into North America,
        1710–1714, IV
    rationing, 1942 Nov. 29, III
Coffee houses, 1670(2), IV; 1745–1749, IV
Coffin, Levi, 1838, I
Coffin, Robert P. T., 1945 Dec. 27, II
Coffin, William Sloane, 1968 Jan. 5, I
Cohan, George M., 1891(4), II; 1906(2), II;
    1910 Sept. 10, II; 1932 Mar. 28, II; 1933
    Oct. 2, II
Cohen, Benjamin V., 1983, I
Coin Act ("Crime of '73"), 1873 Feb. 12, I
Coinage Act, 1834 June 28, I; 1853 Feb.
    21, I
Coins *see* Bimetallism; Currency; metal
    name
Coit, Margaret Louise, 1951 May 7, II
Coke, Thomas, 1765–1769, III
Cokesbury College (Md.), 1787 Dec., III
Colbert, Claudette, 1935 Mar. 27, II
Colby, Anita, 1992, IV
Colby, William, 1974 Sept. 7, I; 1974 Dec.
    21, I; 1975 Nov. 3, I
Cold fusion, 1989 Mar. 23, III
Cold Harbor, Battle of, 1864 June 3, I

Colds, 1955 Nov. 3, III; 1970 Nov. 18, III
Cold War (*see also* Arms control and disarmament; Subversion and loyalty issue):
    Brezhnev U.S. visit, 1973 June 16–25, I
    Captive Nations Week designated, 1961 July 14, I
    Dulles on, 1956, I
    easing of, 1955, I
    Eisenhower Doctrine, 1957, I; 1957 Jan. 5, I
    end marked by Charter of Paris, 1990 Nov. 21, I
    end proclaimed, 1992 Feb. 1, I
    end seen at Malta summit, 1989 Dec. 3, I
    hot line (Wash., D.C.-Moscow), 1963 Aug. 30, I
    increasing, 1960, I
    Khrushchev's visit to U.S., 1959 Sept. 15–27, I
    Nixon kitchen debate, 1959 July 23, I
    Nixon Moscow speech, 1959 Aug. 1, I
    rumblings of, 1946, I
    Soviets invaded Czechoslovakia, 1968, I
    Summit conference (Paris), canceled, 1960 May 16, I
    term coined, 1948 Oct. 24, IV
    U.S. policy differences, 1952, I
    U.S.S.R.-U.S. exchange visits, 1959, I
    U.S. travel restrictions on diplomats, 1963 Nov. 12, I
    Vienna summit meeting, 1961 June 3–4, I
Cole, Natalie, 1992 Feb. 26, II
Cole, Nat "King", 1965, II
Cole, Thomas, 1836(1), II; 1837(6), II; 1838(3), II
Coleman, Cy, 1977 Apr. 17, II; 1991 June 2, II
Coles, Robert, 1973 May 7, II
Colfax, Schuyler, 1868 May 20–21, I; 1868 Nov. 3, I
Colgate University (N.Y.), 1846 Mar. 26, III
Colleges and universities (*see also* Fraternities and sororities; Riots and mob violence; Scholarships; School desegregation; names of specific institutions; subject areas for professional schools):,
    1991, III
    ASTP ended, 1944, III
    black institutions gift, 1990 Mar. 3, III
    Campus Unrest Commission established, 1970, III; 1970 June 13, III
    colonial student life, 1760–1764, IV
    Cornell student sit-in, 1969 Apr. 20, III
    costs up, 1992, III
    Cox Commission report on student protests, 1968 Oct. 5, II
    for deaf (Wash., D.C.), 1864, III
    deaths, 1992, III
    degree holders, 1910(6), III
    early football rules, 1873 Oct. 19, IV
    early Midwest, 1721, III

Colleges and universities (*cont.*)
    educational value questioned, 1973, III
    Eliot's influence, 1869, III
    false degrees and credentials, 1985, III
    federal aid, 1964, III
    federal aid down, 1971, III
    federal aid for state agricultural, 1914 May 8, III
    first arts and letters society (Princeton), 1765(1), II
    first botany professor, 1768(2), III
    first Catholic in deep South, 1836 Jan. 9, III
    first Catholic (Wash., D.C.), 1789 Jan. 23, III
    first Catholic west of Alleghenies, 1832 Dec. 28, III
    first coeducational, 1833(5), III
    first comprehensive black, 1867(3), III
    first fine arts department (Yale), 1865(1), III
    first graduate program in all-women's college, 1880(4), III
    first graduate programs, 1870(1), III
    first graduate school in geography, 1920(2), III
    first in Calif. to match leading eastern, 1855 Apr. 30, III
    first in middle colonies (Pa.), 1726, III
    first Intercollegiate Athletic Assn. convention, 1906 Dec. 29, IV
    first intercollegiate football (N.J.), 1869 Nov. 6, IV
    first intercollegiate rowing race, 1852 Aug. 3, IV
    first large-scale urban building (N.Y.C.), 1940(3), II
    first lectures on electricity, 1746(1), III
    first Lutheran, 1832 Apr. 7, III
    first magazine, 1806 Nov. 15, II
    first mathematics and philosophy professorship, 1717, III
    first Methodist, 1787 Dec., III
    first municipal (Charleston, S.C.), 1770(2), III
    first music chair, 1875, II
    first noncleric to be appointed president, 1787(2), III
    first nonsectarian (Pa.), 1755 June 16, III
    first Ph.D. degree (Yale Univ.), 1861(1), III
    first private military, 1819(1), III
    first Quaker, 1833(4), III
    first rabbinical, 1867 Oct. 25, III
    first state-supported women's (Miss.), 1884 Mar. 12, III
    first summer course (Harvard Univ.), 1869(5), III
    first undergraduate daily newspaper (Ill.), 1871(2), III
    first undergraduate humor magazine (Harvard Univ.), 1876(6), III
    first woman dean, 1880(4), III
    first woman's athletic scholarship, 1973 May 21, IV
    first woman university president (Chicago, Univ. of), 1978 Oct. 6, III
    gifts up, 1983, III

Colleges and universities (*cont.*)
    greater emphasis on science, 1871(1), III
    Harvard student protest (Mass.), 1969 Apr. 9, III
    hazing condemned at Amherst, 1868(6), IV
    Humanist Manifesto, 1933 May 1, III
    Idaho, 1834 June 15, I
    Intercollegiate Association of Amateur Athletes of America (ICAAAA) formed, 1876(6), IV
    intercollegiate football, 1870(6), IV
    land grant, 1862, III
    largest gift to public institution to date, 1992 July 6, III
    lower black SAT scores, 1982, III
    number of graduates, 1820(4), III
    oldest state (Ga.), 1785 Jan. 27, III
    Olivet (Mich.) nontraditional, 1934 Oct. 1, III
    Orangeburg (S.C.) student disorder, 1968 Feb. 8, III
    panty raids, 1952, IV
    progressive education institutions, 1932 Fall, III
    religious services in campus buildings upheld, 1981 Dec. 8, III
    second coeducational (Wis.), 1847(1), III
    seven established before Revolution, 1745–1749, III
    seven new established, 1810(3), III
    Smith book on ideal, 1753, II
    soccer introduced, 1820(1), IV
    sports deemphasis, 1991 Jan. 8–9, IV
    sports discrimination, 1992, IV
    sports eligibility ruling, 1972 Jan. 8, IV
    stricter academic standards for athletes, 1992 Jan. 8, IV
    student as type first satirized, 1807(1), II
    student protests and riots, 1967 May 10–11, III; 1969, III
    student right to sue for damages, 1992 Feb. 26, I
    student strike (San Francisco, Calif.), 1968 Nov. 6, III
    study of American student, 1958(2), III
    survey on attendance, 1957(1), III
    two-year community, 1989, III
    veterans' enrollment, 1947(1), III
    women admitted to all-male clubs, 1991 Jan. 21, IV; 1991 Oct. 24, IV
    World War II impact, 1942, III
Collegiate Reformed Dutch Church *see* Reformed Protestant Dutch Church
Collegiate School (N.Y.C.), 1633, III
Collins, Eddie, 1917, IV; 1939 Jan. 24, IV
Collins, Martha Layne, 1983 Nov. 8, I
Collins, Michael, 1966 July 18, III; 1969 July 16, III
Collins, Pauline, 1989 June 4(1), II
Collins, Phil, 1985 Feb. 26, II; 1986 Feb. 25, II; 1991 Feb. 20, II
Collins, Wilkie, 1868(3), II
Collins Line, 1850 Apr. 27, III; 1850 Aug. 21, III
Colman, Norman J., 1889 Feb. 11, I

Colman, Ronald, 1948 Mar. 20, II
Colnaghi Ltd., 1988 Feb. 9, IV
Colombia:
    drug traffic, 1988 May 3, IV; 1988
        May 19, IV
    Panamanian revolt against, 1903 Nov.
        3, I
    U.S. Panama Canal zone treaty, 1903
        Jan. 22, I; 1903 Nov. 18, I
Colonial Dames of America, 1881, IV
Colonial governors:
    Andros ouster (N.E.), 1689(2), I
    Carolinas separated, 1712 May 9, I
    Charter Oak incident, 1687, I
    first native-born (Mass.), 1673, I
    Glorious Revolution impact,
        1680–1689, I
    Leisler insurrection (N.Y.), 1689(1), I
    N.J., 1738, I
    New Netherland, 1624 May, I
    N.Y.C., 1652(2), I
    political attack on Oglethorpe, 1740, I
    Va., 1610–1619, I
Colonies and settlements (see also
    Immigration; Land grants; Westward
    expansion; specific colony, state, or
    subject headings):
    Board of Trade jurisdiction, 1696(3), I
    British land grants, 1664 Mar. 12, I
    Carolina divided, 1729 June, I
    Cherokee Strip (Kans.-Okla.), 1893
        Sept. 16, I
    Discourse Concerning Western
        Planting, A (Hakluyt), 1584, II
    Dutch patroon system, 1620–1629, I;
        1630(2), I
    English charters, 1606, I
    first attempt to unite, 1750–1754, I
    first Calif. permanent, 1769, I
    first democratic theory, 1644, II
    first Dutch, 1623, I
    first English west of Allegheny Divide,
        1748, I
    first European, 1526 Summer, I
    first federation (N.E.), 1640–1649, I
    first French, 1562 Apr. 30, I
    first German (Pa.), 1683 Oct. 6, I
    first important Dutch (N.Y.), 1614, I
    first in Mich., 1701 July 24, I
    first in northern Ore. Territory, 1836
        Sept. 1, I
    first Moravian (Ga.), 1735(1), III
    first northern French, 1604, I
    first permanent English (Va.), 1607
        May 13, I
    first permanent Pacific Northwest,
        1811 Apr. 12, I
    first permanent white, 1565 Sept. 8, I
    first Russian (Alaska), 1811, IV
    first Swedish, 1624 Dec. 21, I; 1638
        Mar., I
    first termed United States, 1776 Sept.
        9, I
    first Texas, 1821 Dec., I
    first to grant complete religious
        tolerance (R.I.), 1636 June, I
    first to propose independence (N.C.),
        1776 Apr. 12, I
    first Vt., 1720–1724, I

Colonies and settlements (cont.)
    first Welsh settlers (Pa.), 1682 Aug. 13,
        I
    Folger satire, 1676, II
    French Jesuits expelled by British
        from Appalachia, 1763(3), III
    garrison aid appeals, 1689 June 30, IV
    Ga. founding, 1730–1734, I
    Good Speed to Virginia (Gray),
        1609(2), II
    Gray's promotion of Va., 1609(2), II
    Great Migration (Mass.), 1630(1), I
    Hakluyt's promotion of English, 1584,
        II
    Huguenots, 1680–1689, IV
    Idaho's first permanent, 1860 Apr. 14,
        III
    Md. charter, 1632 June 20, I
    Otis opposition to English rule, 1761
        Feb. 24, I
    political and economic theory,
        1705–1709, I
    promotional books, 1584, II; 1609(2),
        II; 1624, II
    religious freedom, 1620–1629, III
    slavery acts, 1664, I
    Swiss and German (Carolinas), 1709
        Sept. 3, I; 1710–1714, I
    Texas, 1823, I
    Treaty of Utrecht provisions, 1713
        Apr. 11, I
    types, 1600–1609, IV
Colorado:
    blizzard, 1984 Feb. 5–28, I
    flash flood, 1976 July 31, I
    nuclear plant accidents, 1988 Sept. 30,
        I
    statehood, 1876 Aug. 1, I
    women's suffrage granted, 1893 Nov.
        7, I
Colorado, University of, 1861(2), III
Colorado Aqueduct, 1941 June 18, III
Colorado River, 1869(2), I; 1878(3), III
Colt, Samuel, 1833, III; 1842(1), III
Coltrane, John, 1967, II
Columbia Broadcasting System (CBS):
    baseball telecast rights, 1988 Dec. 1,
        IV
    Brown & Williamson libel suit, 1985
        Dec. 5, III
    color TV, 1950 Oct. 11, II; 1951 June
        25, III
    Cronkite retirement, 1980 Feb. 15(2),
        II
    NCAA broadcasting rights, 1989 Nov.
        21, IV
    Schorr suspended, 1976 Feb. 11–18, II
    Westmoreland libel suit, 1985 Feb. 17,
        III
    Ziff-Davis magazines acquisition, 1984
        Nov. 20, III
Columbia Pictures Entertainment, Inc.,
    1989 Sept. 27, III
Columbia (S.C.), 1865 Feb. 17, I
Columbia (space shuttle), 1981 Apr. 12–14,
    III; 1981 Nov. 14, III; 1982 Nov. 11–16,
    III; 1986 Jan. 12–18, III; 1992 July 9, III

Columbia University (N.Y.C.) (see also
    Barnard College):
    Cox Commission report on student
        protests, 1968 Oct. 5, II
    founded as King's College, 1754 Oct.
        31, III
    Graduate School of Journalism,
        1903(4), II
    Johnson presidency, 1787(2), III
    Lipchitz collection dedicated, 1977
        Nov. 28, II
    Low's presidency, 1889 Oct. 7, III
    MacDowell appointed head of music
        department, 1896(2), II
    student sit-in, 1968 Apr. 23, III
    Teachers College, 1932 Fall, III
Columbus, Christopher, 1492 Oct. 12, I;
    1519, II; 1792 Oct. 12, II; 1893, IV
    500th anniversary of first voyage,
        1992, I; 1992, II
Columbus Day, 1790–1794, IV; 1792 Oct.
    12, IV
Colvin, David L., 1920 July 21–22, I; 1936
    May 5–7, I; 1936 Nov. 3, I
Combe, George, 1838(4), IV
Comden, Betty, 1953 Feb. 25, II; 1968
    Apr. 21, II; 1970 Mar. 30, II; 1974 Jan.
    27(1), II; 1991 June 2, II
Comic books, 1955(1), IV
Comic strips:
    death of Superman, 1992 Sept. 4, II
    first, 1896, II
    L'il Abner final installment, 1977
        Nov. 13, II
Commentaries on American Law (Kent),
    1826, III
Commerce see Business; Interstate
    commerce; Trade; names of
    commodities
Commerce, Department of, 1913 Mar. 4,
    III
Commerce and Labor, Department of:
    divided, 1913 Mar. 4, III
    founded, 1903 Feb. 14, I
    Straus named sec., 1906 Dec. 12, I
Commercial Review of the South and
    Southwest (publication), 1846 Jan., III
Committee for Industrial Organization
    (CIO):
    established, 1935 Nov. 9, III
Committee of Secret Correspondence,
    1775 Nov. 29(1), I
Commodity Futures Trading Commission,
    1974 Oct. 10(1), III
Commodore Hotel (N.Y.C.), 1918(6), II
Common Sense (Paine), 1776 Jan. 10, II
Communications Act, 1934 June 19, I
Communications satellites see Satellites
Communist Labor Party:
    founded, 1919 Aug. 31, I
Communist Party (see also Subversion and
    loyalty issue; Young Communist
    League):
    convicted for failing to register as
        U.S.S.R. agent, 1962 Dec. 17, I
    Daily Worker seized, 1956 Mar. 27, I
    Daily Worker suspended, 1958 Jan.
        13, II
    eleven leaders convicted, 1949, I;
        1949 Oct. 14, I

Communist Party (*cont.*)
Flynn named chairman, 1961 Mar. 13, I

Hall named secretary, 1959 Dec. 10–14, I

mail interception banned, 1965 May 24, III

mandatory registration of members unconstitutional, 1965 Nov. 15, I

members banned from Steelworkers, 1954 Sept. 24, III

membership subject to deportation, 1954 May 24, I

new constitution, 1957 Feb. 9–12, I

N.Y.S. teachers banned from, 1920 Jan. 18, III

ordered to register with Justice Dept., 1953 Apr. 20, I

presidential ticket, 1932 May 28, I; 1936 June 24–28, I; 1940 June 2, I

reestablished, 1945 July 27, III

sued for back taxes, 1962 Mar. 19, I

supported Wallace presidential candidacy, 1948 Aug. 2–6, I

travel abroad restrictions, 1962 Jan. 12, I

twelve leaders indicted, 1948 July 20, I

voted to disband, 1944 May 20, III

Como, Perry, 1959 May 4(2), II

compact discs, 1986, III

Compromise of 1850 (*see also* Kansas-Nebraska Act)::
1850, I; 1850 Mar. 7, I; 1850 Sept. 9(1), I; 1850 Sept. 9(2), I; 1850 Sept. 18, I; 1850 Sept. 20, I; 1852 June 1–6, I; 1852 June 16–21, I; 1860 Dec. 18, I

Compton, Arthur Holly, 1927 Nov. 10, III

Comptroller General office, 1921 June 10, I

Computers:
break-ins nationwide, 1983 Aug. 21, III

ENIAC, first electronic digital, 1946 Feb. 15, III

IBM 3084, 1982, III

megabit memory chip, 1984 Dec. 20, III; 1986 Apr. 17, III

personal, 1980, III; 1981, III

price decline, 1980, III

stock trading system curbs, 1988 Jan. 8, III

trade magazine on disk, 1989, II

UNIVAC, electronic digital, 1951 June 14, III

workplace video display terminal use regulated, 1990 Dec. 27, I

Comstock, Anthony, 1873 Mar. 3, I; 1905 Oct. 31, II

Comstock Lode (Nev.), 1859(1), I

Conable, Barber B., 1986 July 1, III

Conant, James Bryant, 1978, III

Concord, Battle of (Mass.), 1975 Apr. 20, II

Concorde *see* SST (supersonic transport)

Concrete:
first building utilizing (Chicago, Ill.), 1904(2), II

Condoms:
AIDS prevention, 1987 Dec. 10, III

Condoms (*cont.*)
TV advertising, 1987, IV

Condon, Eddie, 1973, II

Condor, California, 1986 Mar. 10, III

Cone, Orello, 1891(5), III

Conestoga wagon *see* Covered wagons

Coney Island (N.Y.), 1881(3), IV; 1984, IV

Confederate States of America (*see also* Civil War):
capital, 1861 Feb. 18, I; 1861 May 21, I

churches protected by Lincoln order, 1863 Jan., III

coinage bill, 1861 Mar. 9, I

constitution, 1861 Mar. 11, I

Davis captured, 1865 May 10, I

Davis inaugurated as president, 1861 Feb. 18, I

Davis treason trial, 1868 Dec. 3, I

formed (Ala.), 1861 Feb. 4, I

insurrection declared over, 1866 Apr. 2, I

Johnson's amnesty proclamation, 1865 May 29, I

Lee named army commander, 1865 Feb. 6, I

Lincoln amnesty and reconstruction bid, 1863 Dec. 8, I

Memorial Day, 1865 Apr. 26, IV

presidential amnesty proclamation, 1868 Dec. 25, I

provisional congress action, 1861 Feb. 9, I

Richmond (Va.) evacuated, 1865 Apr. 2, I

"Stars and Bars" flag, 1861 Mar. 4(1), I

United Confederate Veterans organized, 1889 June 10, I

Congo, Belgian:
U.S. hostages, 1964, I

Congregational Church:
Andover Controversy, 1886(2), III

Cambridge Synod (Mass.), 1646 Sept. 1, III

Dwight's ministry, 1822, II

first in Boston, 1630 Summer, III

first ministers (Mass.), 1624, III; 1629, III

founded by Separatists (Mass.), 1620(1), III

hostility to Quakers, 1677(2), III

popular book on, 1665, II

Puritan beliefs outlined, 1659(1), II

schism (N.E.), 1662 Mar., III

united with Natl. Convention of Christian Churches, 1931 July 1, III

Wise's pamphlets (Mass.), 1710–1717, II

Congress, U.S. (*see also* Continental Congress; Elections; names of acts; subjects of legislation):
arms accord ratified, 1988 May 27, I

Baltimore American verbatim reports of, 1799(1), II

budget deficit, 1990, I

censures, 1834 Mar. 28, I; 1834 Apr. 15, I; 1872(1), I; 1954 July 30, I

civil rights filibuster, 1960 Feb. 29, I

Congress, U.S. (*cont.*)
Contra aid investigation, 1986 Nov. 3, I; 1987 Feb. 26, I; 1989 May 4, I; 1991 Oct. 7, I

Contra aid report, 1987 Nov. 18, I

Contra aid supplied, 1986 Aug. 13, I; 1987 Dec. 22, I; 1988 Apr. 1, I

corruption uncovered by FBI, 1980 Feb. 2, I

deaths, 1990, I; 1991, I; 1992, I

districts be equally populated, 1964 Feb. 17, I

80th called "worst in history", 1948, I

ethics code, 1977 Mar. 2, I

filibuster cloture on civil rights bill, 1964 June 10, I

filibuster record, 1953 Apr. 25, I; 1957 Aug. 30, I

first American Indian elected to Senate, 1992, I

first black members, 1870 Feb. 25, I

first black senator since Reconstruction, 1966 Nov. 8(1), I

first black woman elected to Senate, 1992, I

first British prime minister to speak before, 1929 Oct. 7(1), I

first duel by members, 1808(1), IV

first former president to serve, 1831 Mar. 4, I

first legislation enacted, 1789 June 1, I

first Senate impeachment trial since 1936, 1986 Oct. 9, I

first session, 1789 Mar. 4, I

first Socialist Party representative, 1910 Nov. 8, I

first special session, 1797 May 15, I

first woman representative, 1917 Apr. 2, I

first woman senator, 1922 Oct. 3, I

first woman to preside over House, 1921 June 20, I

five representatives shot, 1954 Mar. 1, I

gag rule lifted, 1844 Dec. 3, I

gag rule on slavery petitions, 1840 Jan. 8, I

Gallatin barred from Senate, 1794 Feb. 28, I

Gulf Oil Corp. illegal donations, 1976, I

Hays sex scandal, 1976, I; 1976 Sept. 1, I

House Atherton Gag, 1838 Dec. 11, I

House committee to review assassinations, 1976 Sept. 17, I

House gag rules, 1836 May 25, I

House membership shift, 1980, I

House Rules Committee members elected by House, 1910 Mar. 17, I

House seat changes indicated, 1960 Nov. 15, I

House Un-American Committee Activities formed, 1938 May 26, I

intelligence activities report leaked, 1976 Feb. 11–18, II

Korean lobbying, 1977 July 20, I; 1978, I

Korean lobbyist scandals, 1976, I; 1976 Oct. 20(2), I

Congress, U.S. (*cont.*)
  McCarthy censured, 1954 July 30, I
  McCarthy condemned, 1954 Dec. 2, I
  medal to singer Anderson, 1978 Oct.
    17, II
  Mills scandal, 1974 Dec. 10, I
  pay raise restrictions, 1992, I
  popular election of senators, 1913
    May 31, I
  Powell denied House seat, 1967 Mar.
    1, I
  Powell seated, 1969 Jan. 3, I
  refusal to seat Kans. delegates, 1856
    Aug. 1, I
  Rep. Brooks's physical attack on Sen.
    Sumner, 1856 May 22, I
  representation granted to states
    formerly seceded, 1868 June 25(2), I
  representatives' overdrawn bank
    accounts, 1992 Apr. 16, I
  salaries increased, 1955 Mar. 1, I
  Senate censured Jackson, 1834 Mar.
    28, I
  Senate chooses vice president, 1836
    Dec. 7, I
  Senate cloture rule, 1917 Mar. 8, I
  Senate Hall of Fame, 1957 Apr. 30, I
  Senate Select Committee on
    Intelligence report, 1976 Apr. 26
    and 28, I
  seniority system challenged, 1975 Jan.
    16, I
  seniority system retained, 1970 Oct.
    26, I
  special session on Neutrality Act, 1939
    Sept. 21, I
  Thomas confirmation hearings, 1991
    Oct. 15, I
  TV coverage of Senate, 1986 June
    1(1), II
  upheld Bush veto, 1990 Oct. 22, I
  veto on federal agencies overturned,
    1983 June 23, I
  Washington (D.C.) representation,
    1970 Sept. 22, I
  women senators, 1992, I
  Wright resigned as speaker, 1989 May
    31, I
Congress of Industrial Organizations (CIO)
  (*see also* American Federation of
  Labor-Congress of Industrial
  Organizations (AFL-CIO)):
  Bethlehem Steel settlement, 1941
    Feb. 26, III
  established, 1938 Nov. 14–18, III
  Lewis resigned, 1940 Nov. 21, III
  Mine Workers withdrew, 1942 Oct. 7,
    III
  no-strike agreement, 1942 Mar. 17, III
  Political Action Committee, 1944 Nov.
    22, III
  Reuther named head, 1952 Dec. 4, III
  on Wallace presidential candidacy,
    1948 Feb. 2, III
Conkling, Roscoe, 1880 June 5, IV
Conley, Jim, 1915, IV
Conley, Mike, 1992 July 25–Aug. 9, IV
Connally, John B.:
  shot in Tex., 1963 Nov. 22, I

Connecticut:
  charter, 1662 May 3, I
  Constitution, 1639 Jan. 14, I
  contraceptive law unconstitutional,
    1965 June 7(1), I
  elected first woman governor in U.S.,
    1974 Nov. 5, I
  fifth state to ratify U.S. Constitution,
    1788 Jan. 9, I
  outlawed slavery, 1784, I
Connecticut, University of, 1881(4), III
Connecticut Wits *see* Hartford Wits
Connelly, Marc, 1921 Aug. 13, II
  Pulitzer Prize, 1930 May 12, II
Connery, Sean, 1988 Apr. 11, II
Connolly, Maureen, 1951 Sept. 4, IV; 1952
  July 5, IV; 1952 Sept. 7, IV; 1953 July 3,
  IV; 1953 Sept. 7, IV; 1954 July 3(2), IV
Connor, Dennis, 1987 Jan. 31–Feb. 4, IV
Connors, Jimmy, 1973 July 7–8, IV; 1974
  July 5, IV; 1974 Sept. 9, IV; 1975 Feb.
  16, IV; 1976 Sept. 11–12, IV; 1978 Sept.
  10, IV; 1982 July 3–4, IV; 1982 Sept.
  11–12, IV; 1983 Sept. 11, IV
Conoco Corp., 1981 Aug. 4, III
Conot, Robert, 1979(1), II
Conrad, Charles, Jr., 1965 Aug. 21, III;
  1966 Sept. 12(1), III; 1969 Nov. 14, III;
  1973 May 14, III
Conrail, 1976 Apr. 1, III
Conscientious objectors:
  moral grounds ruled constitutional,
    1970 June 15, I
  not confined to Vietnam War, 1971
    Mar. 8(1), I
  Supreme Ct. ruling, 1965 Mar. 8, I
  World War I, 1918 May 31, III
Conscription *see* Draft
Conservation *see* Environmental
  protection
Consolidated Edison Co.:
  Indian Point (N.Y.) plant, 1956 May 4,
    III
Constitution (*see also* Bill of Rights; States'
  rights; Supreme Court):
  bicentennial celebrations, 1987, I
  convention, 1785–1789, I
  Eighteenth Amendment, 1917 Dec.
    18, I; 1919 Jan. 29, I; 1931 Feb. 24,
    I
  Eleventh Amendment, 1798 Jan. 8, I
  Fifteenth Amendment, 1869 Apr. 10,
    I; 1870 Mar. 30(2), I
  Fifth Amendment, 1966 June 13, I
  First Amendment, 1965 May 24, III
  first colonial (Conn.), 1639 Jan. 14, I
  Fourteenth Amendment, 1868 July
    28, I; 1886 May 10, I
  Fourteenth Amendment guarantees,
    1872(2), I
  Montesquieu influence, 1745, II
  Nineteenth Amendment, 1922 Feb.
    27, I
  prohibition amendment first
    introduced, 1876 Dec. 12, I
  proposed amendments on presidential
    issues, 1965 Jan. 28, I
  proposed child labor amendments,
    1924 June 2, III

Constitution (*cont.*)
  proposed school prayer amendment
    rejected, 1984 Mar. 20, I
  ratification, 1787 Dec. 7, I; 1787 Dec.
    12, I; 1787 Dec. 18, I; 1788 Jan. 2, I;
    1788 Jan. 9, I; 1788 Feb. 6, I; 1788
    Apr. 28, I; 1788 May 23, I; 1788
    June 21, I; 1788 June 25, I; 1788
    July 26, I; 1789 Nov. 21, I; 1790
    May 29, I; 1791 Mar. 4, I
  Seventeenth Amendment, 1913 May
    31, I
  Sixteenth Amendment, 1909 July 12,
    I; 1913, I
  Thirteenth Amendment, 1865 Dec. 2,
    I
  Twelfth Amendment, 1800, I; 1804
    Sept. 25, I
  Twentieth Amendment, 1933 Feb. 6,
    I
  Twenty-fifth Amendment, 1886 Jan.
    19, I; 1967 Feb. 10, I
  Twenty-first Amendment, 1933 Dec.
    5, I
  Twenty-fourth Amendment, 1962
    Aug. 27(2), I; 1964 Jan. 23, I
  Twenty-second Amendment, 1951
    Feb. 26, I
  Twenty-seventh Amendment, 1972
    Mar. 22, I
  Twenty-seventh Amendment ratified,
    1992, I
  Twenty-sixth Amendment ratified,
    1971 June 30, I
Constitutional Union Party, 1860 May 9, I
Constitution (ship), 1812 Aug. 19, I; 1812
  Aug. 19, IV; 1812 Dec. 29, I; 1830 Sept.
  16, II
Construction *see* Building materials;
  Buildings
Consumer Product Safety Commission,
  1972 Oct. 28, III
Consumers (*see also* Cost of Living;
  Manufacturing):
  buying power, 1950 Mar. 23, III
  confidence, 1992, III
  ineffective weight-loss spending, 1990
    Mar. 27, III
  meat boycott, 1973, III
  Product Safety Commission
    established, 1972 Oct. 28, III
  prosperity, 1955, I
  Truth-in-Lending Law, 1969 July 1,
    III
Containers:
  canned goods rationing, 1943 Mar. 1,
    III
  commercial canned food, 1831, IV
  first food canning business (N.Y.),
    1819(3), III
  first salmon canneries, 1864(5), III
  Heinz packing, 1869(4), III
  tin can introduced, 1818(2), III
Contemporary Art Center (Cincinnati,
  Ohio), 1990 Apr. 7, II
Conti, Tom, 1979 June 3, II
Continental Congress:
  first meeting, 1770–1774, I
  fled Phila. (Pa.), 1777 Sept. 19(2), I
  formation, 1774 May 17, I

Continental Congress (*cont.*)
  second convened (Phila., Pa.), 1775
    May 10(2), I
  Suffolk Resolves, 1774 Sept. 17, I
Contra aid (*see also* Iran-Contra affair):
  arms-for-hostages link revealed, 1986
    Nov. 3, I
  congressional appropriation, 1986
    Aug. 13, I; 1987 Dec. 22, I; 1988
    Apr. 1, I
Contraceptives *see* Birth control
Contract Labor Law, 1885, I
Contrast, The (Tyler), 1787 Apr. 16, II
Conway, Thomas, 1777 Sept. 25–Dec. 23, I
Coodies (term), 1812(1), IV
Coody, Charles, 1971 Apr. 11, IV
Coogan, Jackie, 1984, II
Cook, Frederick, 1909 Sept. 1, I
Cook, Nathan E., 1988 July 13, IV
Cook, Peter, 1962 Oct. 27, II
Cookbooks, 1761(2), III
Cooke, Alistair, 1977(1), II
Cooke, Elwood T., 1939 July 7–8, IV
Cooke, George Frederick, 1810(6), II
Cooke, Hope, 1963 Mar. 20, IV
Cooke, John Esten, 1866, II; 1866(1), II
Cooke, Sarah Palfrey, 1941 Sept. 7, IV;
  1945 Sept. 2, IV
Cooke, Terence J., 1968 Mar. 8, III; 1983,
  III
Cooke & Co., Jay, 1873, I
Cooley, Denton A., 1969 Apr. 4, III
Coolidge, Calvin:
  Boston (Mass.) police strike, 1919 Sept.
    9, III
  declined renomination, 1927 Aug. 2, I
  elected president, 1924 Nov. 4, I
  elected vice president, 1920 Nov. 2, I
  first broadcast of official presidential
    address, 1923 Dec. 6, III
  first message to Congress, 1923 Dec.
    6, I
  inaugurated, 1925 Mar. 4, I
  presidential candidacy, 1924, I; 1924
    June 12, I
  succeeded to presidency, 1923, I
  vice presidential candidacy, 1920 June
    8–12, I
Cooling systems *see* Air conditioning;
  Fans, electric
Cooney, Gerry, 1987 June 15, IV
Cooper, Anthony Ashley, 1710–1714, III
Cooper, Ashley, 1958 Sept. 7, IV; 1958
  Dec. 31, IV
Cooper, Bette, 1937 Sept. 11(1), IV
Cooper, Elias Samuel, 1859(2), III
Cooper, Gary, 1942(3), II; 1942 Feb. 26, II;
  1943, II; 1944, II; 1953 Mar. 19(1), II;
  1961, II
Cooper, George C., 1894(1), III
Cooper, Gordon, 1965 Aug. 21, III
Cooper, James Fenimore:
  American Democrat, The, 1838(2), II
  career beginnings, 1811(3), II
  Deerslayer, The, 1841(2), II
  estimated college graduates, 1820(4),
    III
  European settings, 1832(8), II
  Last of the Mohicans, The, 1826(1), II
  on N.Y.C.'s growth, 1828(4), IV

Cooper, James Fenimore (*cont.*)
  Pathfinder, The, 1840(3), II
  Pilot, The,, 1822(1), II
  Prairie, The, 1827(3), II
  sea novels, 1842(2), II
  Spy, The, 1821(2), II
Cooper, John Sherman, 1991, I
Cooper, Leon N., 1972 Oct. 20(1), III
Cooper, L. Gordon, Jr., 1963 May 15–16,
  III
Cooper, Peter, 1874, I; 1876 May 18, I
Cooper-Hewitt Museum of Design
  (N.Y.C.), 1976 Oct. 7, II
Cooper Union (N.Y.C.), 1858(1), III
Copland, Aaron, 1925 Jan. 11, II; 1933(5),
  II; 1937 Aug. 27, II; 1942 Oct. 16, II;
  1943(3), II; 1944 Oct. 30, II; 1945 May 7,
  II; 1950 Nov. 16, II; 1954 Apr. 1, II;
  1990, II
Copley, John Singleton, c1760, II; 1765(2),
  II; 1770–1774, II; 1775(2), II; 1782 Dec.
  5, II; 1785(1), II
Copper:
  Canadian findings, 1964 Apr. 16, III
  first sheet (Boston, Mass.), 1802 Nov.
    18, III
Copyright laws:
  Boucicault's efforts for theater, 1857
    Dec. 8, II
  Chinese agreement to honor, 1992
    Jan. 16, I
  Dickens's advocacy, 1842(1), II
  dramatists' problems, 1869(3), II
  first, 1790 May 31, I
  first major reforms, 1976 Sept. 30, II
  infringement case, 1964 Oct. 21, II
  international, 1890(2), II; 1891 Mar. 4,
    I
  pirating, 1818(2), II
  play authorship and performance
    rights, 1856 Aug. 18, II
Coral Sea, Battle of the, 1942 May 4–8, I
Corbett, James J. ("Gentleman Jim"), 1889
  June 5, IV; 1892 Sept. 7, IV; 1897 Mar.
  17, IV
Corcoran Art Gallery (Wash., D.C.):
  incorporated, 1870(4), II
  Mapplethorpe exhibit controversy,
    1989 June 13, II
  Rauschenberg retrospective, 1991, II
Corey, Elias James, 1990 Oct. 16(2), III
Cori, Carl F. and Gerty T., 1947 Oct. 23,
  III
Cormack, Allan M., 1979 Oct. 12, III
Corn:
  Jamestown colony (Va.), 1608, IV
  Plymouth colony (Mass.), 1623(1), IV
Cornell, Ezra, 1856, III; 1865(3), III
Cornell College (Iowa), 1854 Feb., III
Cornell University (N.Y.):
  founded, 1865(3), III
  student sit-in, 1969 Apr. 20, III
Cornett, Leanza, 1992 Sept. 19, IV
Cornwallis, Charles (Sir), 1781 Oct. 19, I
Corona, Juan, 1973 Feb. 25, IV
Coronado, Francisco, 1540, IV
Coronet (magazine), 1961 Oct., II

Corporal punishment:
  flogging outlawed in Navy and
    Merchant Marine, 1850 Sept. 28(2),
    I
  Supreme Ct. upheld, 1975 Oct. 20, III
  use in schools attacked, 1847(4), IV
Corporation for Public Broadcasting:
  created, 1967 Nov. 7, II
Corporations (*see also* Business;
  Multinational corporations; Stocks and
  bonds; Trusts and antitrust; names):
  "as persons," Supreme Court ruling,
    1886 May 10, III
  biggest loss, 1980, III
  election campaign contributions
    banned, 1907 Jan. 26, I
  ethics, 1872(5), III
  excess profits tax, 1917 Mar. 3, III
  executives' salaries fuller disclosure
    ordered, 1992 Oct. 15, III
  Exxon wealthiest, 1975 May, III
  first business (N.Y.), 1675, III
  first commercial (Conn.), 1723(2), III
  first criminal trial of, 1980 Mar. 13, III
  first mercantile, 1872(6), III
  first million-dollar formed, 1901, III
  first to have over 1,000,000
    stockholders, 1951 May 15, III
  government regulation of, 1902, III
  holding companies (N.J.), 1889(1), I
  Japanese takeovers of U.S., 1989 Sept.
    27, III
  largest cash settlement to date, 1987
    Dec. 19, III
  largest to date, 1980 May 5, III; 1984
    June 15, III
  largest income ever reported, 1950
    Mar. 13, III
  largest media/entertainment to date,
    1989 July 24, III
  largest merger to date, 1981 Aug. 4,
    III; 1984 Jan. 8, III; 1988 Oct. 30,
    III; 1989 Feb. 3, III
  mergers, 1985, III; 1990, III; 1991
    May 6(2), III
  second largest merger to date, 1982
    Mar. 11, III
  Standard Oil-Kennecott merger, 1981
    Mar. 12, III
  stock publicly owned, 1959 June 15,
    III
Corrigan, Douglas G. ("Wrong-way"), 1938
  July 17, I
Cortisone, 1949 Apr. 20, III
Cosby, Bill, 1966 May 22, II; 1967 June 4,
  II; 1968 May 19, II; 1992 Apr. 30, II
  Spelman College gift, 1988 Nov. 4, III
Cosby, William, 1734 Oct., IV
Cosmetics *see* Beauty and cosmetics
Cosmopolitan (publication), 1886(2), II
Cosmos Club (Wash., D.C.), 1988 June 20,
  IV
Costello, Frank, 1973, IV
Costello, Lou, 1942(3), II; 1943, II; 1959, II
Cost of living:
  Consumer Price Index, 1969, III
  Consumer Price Index high, 1966
    Aug. 22, III; 1990, III
  eighteenth-century middle class,
    1728(2), IV

Cost of living (*cont.*)
  first wage contract tied to, 1948 May 25, III
  rise, 1918 Aug. 29, III; 1944 Nov. 18, III
Cothran, Shirley, 1974 Sept. 8, IV
Cotton:
  boll weevil damage, 1892(6), III
  federal programs, 1964 Apr. 11, III
  first factory in New England, 1787(3), III
  first mill (R.I.), 1790(3), III
  first power machinery manufacturing plant (Mass.), 1814(2), III
  first seed oil, 1768(1), III
  gin, 1793 Oct. 28, III
  mechanical picker, 1927(3), III
  New Orleans (La.) futures trading stopped, 1964 July 9, III
  phrase "cotton is king", 1855(2), IV
  price rise, 1917 Apr. 19, III
  Slater operation (R.I.), 1790 Dec. 21, III
  textile production, 1898, III
Cotton, John, c1645, II
Coughlin, Charles E., 1942 Apr. 14(1), II; 1979, III
Counterculture *see* Youth culture
Counterfeiting *see* under Currency; Frauds
Couples, Fred, 1992 Apr. 12, IV
Cournand, Andre F., 1956 Oct. 19, III
Court, Margaret, 1969 Sept. 7–8, IV; 1970 Sept 2–13, IV; 1973 Aug. 29–Sept. 9, IV; 1975 July 4–5, IV
Courts (*see also* Impeachment; Juries; Legal profession; Prisons and prisoners; Punishment; Supreme Court):
  America's Cup retained by U.S. ruling, 1988 Sept. 9, IV
  Appeal, Circuit, created, 1891 Mar. 3, I
  blood tests endorsed as evidence, 1935 Mar. 22, III
  cigarette manufacturer found liable for smoker's cancer death, 1988 June 13, III
  class-action suits costs, 1974 May 28, III
  criminal confessions ruling, 1991 Mar. 20(2), I
  criminal pretrial proceedings closed, 1979 July 2, I
  Dalkon Shield injury claims, 1987 Dec. 11, III
  damage awards, 1991 Mar. 4, I
  day-care sexual abuse conviction, 1992 Apr. 22, IV
  Deaver convicted of perjury, 1987 Dec. 16, I
  defendants' access to pretrial statements, 1959 June 22, IV
  defendants' rights, 1966 June 13, I; 1971 Feb. 24, I; 1984 Oct. 14, I; 1990 Dec. 3, I
  double jeopardy upheld, 1959 Mar. 30, I
  evidence admissibility ruling, 1984 June 11, I
  Exxon Valdez case, 1989 Mar. 24, I

Courts (*cont.*)
  first U.S. Claims, 1855 Feb. 24, I
  frozen embryos ruling, 1992 June 1, I
  Helmsley convicted, 1989 Aug. 30, IV
  highest corporate cash settlement to date, 1987 Dec. 19, III
  highest damages awarded to date, 1985 Dec. 10, III
  independent prosecutors upheld, 1988 June 29, I
  Iran-Contra conviction, reversed, 1990 Apr. 7, I
  Iran-Contra conviction, suspended, 1989 May 4, I
  Iran-Contra indictments, 1988 Mar. 16, I
  Iran-Contra sentence, 1991 Oct. 7, I
  Ku Klux Klan convictions, 1988 Oct. 6, I
  Mapplethorpe obscenity indictments, 1990 Apr. 7, II
  Milken sentenced, 1990 Nov. 21, III
  Miranda decision, 1966 June 13, I
  newsmen denied right to withhold information, 1972 June 29, II
  Nofziger convicted for illegal lobbying, 1988 Feb. 11, I
  Noriega convicted, 1992 Apr. 9, IV
  savings and loan fraud convictions, 1990 Jan. 22, III; 1992 Apr. 10(1), IV
  smokers' damage suits upheld, 1992 June 24(1), III
  surrogate mother ruling, 1987 Mar. 31, IV
Courtship and dating:
  bundling, 1785–1789, IV
  separation of couples (Md.), 1704 Sept. 28, IV
Cousins, Norman, 1971 Nov. 16, II; 1990, II
Cousy, Bob, 1963, IV; 1963 Apr. 24, IV; 1963 Apr. 24, IV
Covered wagons:
  Conestoga, 1760–1764, III
  first train to Calif., 1841 May, I
  westward pioneers' use, 1815(3), III
Cowboys, 1871, IV; 1989, IV
  rodeos, 1991, IV
Cowell, Henry, 1932 Jan., II; 1959 Mar. 3(2), II
Cowles, Gardner, Jr., 1985, III
Cowles, John, Sr., 1983, II
Cowley, Malcolm, 1989, II
Cowpens, Battle of (S.C.), 1781 Jan. 17, I
Cox, Archibald, 1973 May 25, I; 1973 July 16, I; 1973 Oct. 20, I
Cox, James M.:
  presidential candidacy, 1920, I; 1920 June 28–July 5, I; 1920 Nov. 2, I
Cox, William W., 1920 May 5–10, I; 1920 Nov. 2, I
Coxe, Daniel, 1722(1), II; 1730(2), IV
Coxey, Jacob S., 1894, I; 1932 July 10, I; 1932 Nov. 8, I; 1944 May 1, IV
Coxey's Army, 1894, I; 1914 Apr. 16, I
Coyle, Rose, 1936 Sept. 12(1), IV
Cozzens, James Gould, 1942(1), II; 1949 May 2, II; 1957(1), II; 1978, II

Crédit Mobilier of America, 1867(1), III; 1867(2), I; 1872(1), I
Crèvecoeur, J. Hector St. John de, 1782(5), II; 1793(4), II
Crabtree, Lotta, 1856(7), IV
Craik, Dinah Maria Mulock, 1856(2), II
Cram, Donald J., 1987 Oct. 14, III
Cranberries, 1959 Nov. 9, IV
Crane, Cheryl, 1958 Apr. 4, IV
Crane, Hart, 1930(1), II
Crane, Stephen, 1893(1), II; 1895(1), II; 1898(1), II; 1900(1), II
Cranfill, James B., 1892 June 29–July 1, I
Crapsey, Algernon Sidney, 1906, III
Craps (game), 1813, IV
Crawford, Broderick, 1950 Mar. 23, II; 1986, II
Crawford, Joan, 1946 Mar. 7, II; 1977, II
Crawford, Michael, 1988 June 5, II
Crawford, Samuel ("Wahoo Sam"), 1968, IV
Crawford, Thomas, 1857 Oct. 10, II
Creavy, Tom, 1931 Sept. 19, IV
Credit (*see also* Balance of payments; Banking):
  consumer buying curbs, 1948 Aug. 16, III
  Dawes Plan, 1924, III
  discrimination against women barred, 1974 Oct. 29, IV
  Federal Reserve discount rate raised, 1965 Dec. 5, III
  first borrowing from IMF, 1964 Feb. 13, I
  France's war debt funding agreement, 1926 Apr. 29, I
  insurance loans tightened, 1933 Mar. 7, III
  international moratorium on war debts and reparations proposed, 1931 June 20, I
  largest federal loan guarantee, 1984 July 26, III
  largest loan to date, 1915 Oct. 15, III
  mortgage redlining discouraged, 1975 Dec. 18, III
  prime rate at record high, 1969, III
  prime rate raised, 1988, III; 1988 Nov. 28, III
  Truth-in-Lending Law, 1969 July 1, III
  U.S. change from debtor to creditor nation, 1918(3), III
  U.S. notes offered at 5%, 1959 Oct. 1(2), III
  World War I debts and reparations, 1922, I
Creeden, Timothy J., 1894 Dec. 14, I
Creeft, José de, 1945(2), II
Creek Indians, 1813, I; 1814 Mar. 29, I; 1825 Feb. 12, I; 1826 Jan. 24, I; 1827 Nov. 15, I; 1832(2), II
CREEP (Committee to Reelect the President) *see* Watergate Affair
Creighton, Jim, 1864, IV
Cremin, Lawrence A., 1981 Apr. 13, II
Crenna, Richard, 1985 Sept. 22, II
Crenshaw, Ben, 1984 Apr. 15, IV
Creole incident, 1841 Oct. 27, I
Creston, Paul, 1952(3), II

Crew *see* Rowing

Crichton, Michael, 1992(1), II

Crick, Francis H. C., 1962 Oct. 18, III

Cricket, 1810, IV; 1840(5), IV; 1859 Oct. 3, IV; 1870(3), IV

Crime (*see also* Courts; Juvenile delinquency; Organized crime; Prisons and prisoners; types, e.g., Murders):
  dead line for arrests (N.Y.C.), 1880 Mar. 12, IV
  Dillinger shot, 1934 July 22, I
  first indictment of sports pro, 1975 July 18, IV
  increase in colonies, 1720–1724, IV
  James brothers legend, 1882, IV
  lethal force against suspects overruled, 1985 Mar. 27, I
  major issue, 1968, IV
  major law changes, 1984 Oct. 14, I
  national rate trend, 1973, IV
  Negro Conspiracy of 1741 (N.Y.C.), 1740–1744, IV
  Omnibus Crime Control Act, 1971 Jan. 2, I
  penalties for hate speech/bias crime struck down, 1992 June 22(2), I
  rate jump, 1942, IV
  upswing, 1945, IV
  victims' rights bill (N.Y.S.), 1977 Aug. 12, II
  white collar, 1981, IV

Crippen, Robert L., 1981 Apr. 12–14, III

Crisis, The (Paine), 1776 Dec. 19, I

Crisp, Donald, 1942 Feb. 26, II

Cristofer, Michael, 1977 Mar. 31, II; 1977 Apr. 18, II; 1977 June 5, II

Crittenden Compromise, 1860 Dec. 18, I

Crocker, Fay, 1955 July 2, IV

Crockett, Davy, 1786 Aug. 17, IV; 1831 Apr. 25, IV; 1833, IV; 1834(2), IV; 1836(2), IV
  fad, 1955, IV

Cronin, James, 1980 Oct. 14(2), III

Cronin, Joe, 1984, IV

Cronkite, Walter, 1980 Feb. 15(2), II

Croquet, 1860, IV; 1864(4), IV; 1882(2), IV

Crosby, Bing, 1943, II; 1944, II; 1945 Mar. 15, II; 1977, II

Cross, Christopher, 1981 Feb. 25, II

Crossley, Archibald M., 1985, IV

Crothers, Rachel, 1912 Feb. 5, II; 1932 Oct. 6, II

Crouse, Russel, 1939 Nov. 8, II; 1946 May 6, II; 1966, II

Crow Indians, 1892 Oct. 15, I

Crowley, Jim (James H.), 1986, IV

Crowley, Mart, 1968 Apr. 16, II

Crown Publishing Group, 1988, II

Crude Oil Windfall Profits Tax Act, 1980 Apr. 2, III

Cruelty to Children, Society for the Prevention of, 1875(3), III

Cruger, John, 1768 Apr. 5, IV

Cruikshank, James, 1867(7), III

Crump, Diana, 1969 Feb. 7, IV

Crump, Edward H., 1909, II

Crystal Palace (N.Y.C.), 1853(2), II; 1853(4), IV

Cuba (*see also* Spanish-American War):
  appropriation for relief of Americans in, 1897 May 24, I
  Bay of Pigs, 1961 Apr. 17, I
  Bay of Pigs prisoners convicted of treason, 1962 Apr. 8, I
  Bay of Pigs prisoners released, 1962 Dec. 23, I
  campaign for U.S. blacks' support, 1961 Aug. 27, IV
  confiscation of U.S. property protested, 1960 Jan. 11, I
  first major U.S. artist to visit since 1961, 1974 Sept. 30, II
  fishing rights agreement, 1977 Apr. 28(1), I
  Guantánamo water supply cut off, 1964 Feb. 6, I
  hijacking accord, 1973 Feb. 15, III
  hijackings, 1961 July 24, I
  independence, 1898, I; 1898 Aug. 12, I; 1902 May 20, I
  Isle of Pines Treaty, 1925 Mar. 23, I
  McKinley's intervention request, 1898 Apr. 11, I
  Maine exploded, 1898(1), IV; 1898 Feb. 15, I
  Maine in Havana harbor, 1898 Jan. 25, I
  missile crisis, 1962, I; 1962 Oct. 22, I; 1962 Oct. 25, I; 1962 Oct. 27, I; 1962 Oct. 28, I; 1962 Oct. 29, I; 1962 Nov. 2, I; 1989 Jan. 28, I
  Platt Amendment, 1901 Mar. 2, I
  rebellion against Spain, 1895 Feb. 24, I; 1897 May 24, I
  refugees in U.S. riot, 1987 Nov. 21, I
  refugees to U.S., 1980 June 3, I
  slander campaign against U.S. charged, 1960 June 4, I
  Spain relinquished, 1899 Feb. 10, I
  trade ban (U.S.), 1962 Feb. 3, I
  U.S. banned financial dealings with, 1963 July 8, I
  U.S. bid to Spain for, 1854 Oct. 18, I
  U.S. blockade ordered, 1898 Apr. 22(1), I
  U.S. broke diplomatic relations, 1961 Jan. 3, I
  U.S. congressional joint resolution on, 1898 Apr. 19, I
  U.S. cut sugar quotas, 1960 July 3, III
  U.S. embargo, 1960 Oct. 20, I
  U.S. fishing boat attacked, 1963 Feb. 21(1), I
  U.S. intervention, 1906 Aug. 23, I; 1906 Sept. 29, I
  U.S. Marines landed, 1912 June 5, I
  U.S. Marines landed at Guantanamo, 1898 June 11, I
  U.S. naval blockade lifted, 1962 Nov. 20(1), I
  U.S. travel restrictions lifted, 1977 Mar. 18, I
  U.S. troop occupation ended, 1909 Jan. 28, I
  U.S. ultimatum to Spain on, 1898 Apr. 20, I

Cukor, George, 1983, II

Cults:
  deprogramming, 1974 Aug. 31, III
  Guyana mass suicide, 1978 Nov. 18, I
  Moon convicted, 1982 July 16, III
  Moon rally (Wash., D.C.), 1976 Sept. 18, III

Culture *see* Arts and culture; specific forms, e.g., Music

Cumberland University (Tenn.), 1843 Dec. 30, III

Cummings, Constance, 1979 June 3, II

Cummings, E. E., 1922(1), II; 1923(1), II; 1931(1), II; 1955 Jan. 25, II; 1958(1), II; 1962, II

Cummings, Robert, 1955 Mar. 7, II

Cummings, William A. ("Candy"), 1864(5), IV

Cunningham, Glen, 1988, IV

Cunningham, Walter, 1968 Oct. 11, III

Curfews:
  midnight, lifted, 1945 May 9, III
  midnight, on amusement places, 1945 Feb. 26, III

Curie, Marie, 1921 May 20, III

Curran, Charles E., 1986 Mar. 11, III

Curran, Kevin, 1982 July 3–4, IV

Currency (*see also* Bimetallism):
  Carter's moves to bolster dollar, 1978 Nov. 1, III
  Confederate, 1861 Mar. 9, I
  continental, 1790(3), IV
  Continental Congress paper, 1775 June 22, I
  counterfeit, 1705–1709, IV
  counterfeiter, Stuart best known, 1854(3), IV
  dollar devalued, 1973 Feb. 12, III; 1985, III
  dollars in circulation, 1865(5), III
  dollar weakened, 1987, III
  first coins made by steam power, 1836 Mar. 23, III
  first mint (Mass.), 1652 June 10, I
  first paper (Mass.), 1690 Feb. 3, I
  foreign coins barred, 1857 Feb. 21, I
  free coinage of silver, 1876 July 25, I
  Greenback Party, 1874, I
  greenbacks, 1864 Dec., I
  greenbacks reached par value, 1878 Dec. 17, I
  "In God We Trust" on coins, 1864(1), IV; 1864 Dec., I
  Jefferson coinage system, 1785 July 6, I
  Know Ye Men (R.I. term), 1783(1), IV
  Lincoln penny issued, 1909 Aug. 2, III
  nickel issued, 1866 May 16, I
  silver omitted, 1873 Feb. 12, I
  specie payment resumed, 1879 Jan. 1, I
  Specie Resumption Act, 1875 Jan. 14, I
  three-cent pieces coined, 1851 Mar. 3, I

Current Tax Payment Act, 1943 June 10, III

Currier, Nathaniel, 1833(4), II

Curtis, Charles, 1928 June 12–15, I; 1928 Nov. 6, I; 1929 Mar. 4, I; 1932 June 14–16, I

Curtis, Cyrus H. K., 1883(4), II; 1969 Feb. 8, II
Curtis, George William, 1856(6), II; 1857(3), II
Curtis, John B., 1848(3), IV
Curtis, Samuel Ryan, 1862 Mar. 6–7, I
Curtis Publishing Co., 1968 May 4, III
Curtiss, Glenn H., 1909 Mar., III; 1912 Jan., III; 1914 Jan. 13, III
Cushing, Caleb, 1844 July 3, I
Cushing, Richard Cardinal, 1968 Oct. 25, III; 1970, III
Custer, George A., 1876 June 25, I
Custis, George Washington Parke, 1802(2), II
Custis-Lee mansion (Arlington, Va.), 1802(2), II
Customs and duties *see* Trade; Travel and tourism
Cuthbert, Eddie, 1863(3), IV
Cutlery:
 four-tined forks, 1800(1), IV
Cutter, Charles, 1876 Oct. 6, III
Cyclamates, 1969 Oct. 18, III
Cyclones:
 Ga. and S.C., 1893 Aug. 24, I
 La. Gulf Coast, 1893 Oct. 2, I
 Mt. Vernon (Ill.), 1888 Feb. 19, I
Cyclotron, 1939 Nov. 9, III
Czechoslovakia (*see also* Munich Pact):
 Germans invade, 1939 Mar., I
 USSR invasion, 1968, I
Czolgosz, Leon, 1901, I

Díaz Ordaz, Gustavo, 1966 Dec. 3, III
Daguerreotypes, 1839(1), III
Dahlberg, Edwin T., 1986, III
Dahmer, Jeffrey L., 1991 July 25, IV
Daily News (N.Y.C. newspaper), 1855(3), II; 1962 Nov. 1, III
Daily Worker (newspaper), 1958 Jan. 13, II
Dairy products (*see also* Milk):
 rationing, 1943 Mar. 29, III; 1945 Nov. 23, III
Dakota territory (*see also* North Dakota; South Dakota):
 established, 1861 Mar. 2, I
Dalai Lama, 1979, III
Dale, Thomas (Sir), 1610–1619, I
Daley, Richard J., 1968 Apr. 15, I; 1976, I
Dall, Caroline H., 1853 Feb., II
Dallas, George M., 1844 May 27–29, I
Dallas Art Museum (Tex.), 1985, II
Dallas-Fort Worth Airport (Tex.), 1973 Sept. 22, III
Dalton gang, 1892 Oct. 5, IV
Daly, Augustin, 1862 Dec. 8, II; 1864(4), II; 1867 Aug. 12, II; 1886 Aug. 19, II
Daly, John Charles, Jr., 1991, II
Daly, John (golfer), 1991 Aug. 11, IV
Daly, Tyne, 1983 Sept. 25, II; 1984 Sept. 23, II; 1985 Sept. 22, II; 1988 Aug. 28, II; 1990 June 3, II
Dam, Henrik, 1944 Oct. 26, III
Damage suits *see* Courts
Damon, Isaac, 1824(2), II
Damrosch, Walter, 1938(3), II

Dams:
 Bonneville (Oreg.) dedicated, 1937 Sept. 28, III
 coal-slag collapsed (W. Va.), 1972 Feb. 26, I
 Grand Coulee dedicated (Wash. state), 1950 May 11, III
 Grand Coulee opened (Wash.), 1941 Mar. 22, III
 Hoover (Nev.), 1930 Sept. 17, III; 1936(4), III
 Keokuk (Miss. R.), 1913 Aug. 26, III
 Miami R. (Ohio) flood protection, 1913 Mar. 21–26, I
 Roosevelt (Ariz.), 1911(1), III
 Tellico (Tenn.) halted, 1978 June 15, III
 Teton R. collapsed (Ida.), 1976 June 5, I
 U.S.-Mexican Armistad, 1966 Dec. 3, III
 world's largest hydroelectric to date, 1913 Aug. 26, III
Dana, Charles A., 1868(5), II; 1884(1), IV
Dana, Richard Henry, Jr., 1840(2), II
Dances and dancing, 1991, II
 activity, 1950, IV
 Agnes de Mille Heritage Theater (N.C.), 1973 Apr. 26, II
 American Ballet Theater anniversary, 1980, II
 American Ballet Theater grant recipient, 1966 Jan. 18, II
 American Ballet Theater lockout, 1982, II
 American Ballet Theater 50th anniversary, 1990, II
 American Dance Festival moved to N.C., 1977 Sept. 21, II
 animal craze, 1912(2), IV
 Appalachian Spring, 1944 Oct. 30, II
 Balanchine stage appearance, 1965 May 27, II
 ballet companies, 1987, II; 1988, II
 ballet debuts and groups, 1916, II
 ballet introduced, 1827 Feb. 7, II
 Ballet Mécanique (Antheil), 1927 Apr. 10, II
 Baryshnikov joined N.Y.C. Ballet, 1978, II
 Baryshnikov's debut, 1974 July 27, II
 belly dance, 1893(3), IV
 Boston prohibitions, 1681, IV
 Boz Ball honoring Dickens (N.Y.C.), 1842 Feb. 14, II
 Castles' debut, 1913(4), II
 charity balls (N.Y.C.), 1857(1), IV
 Charleston, 1925, IV
 cotillion, 1914(3), IV
 Dance in Place Congo (Gilbert), 1918 Apr. 15, II
 Dance Theater of Harlem 10th anniversary, 1985, II
 Deaths and Entrances (Graham), 1943(2), II
 discothèques, 1975, IV
 Drums, Dreams, and Banjos (Arpino), 1975 Oct. 9, II
 Duncan, Isadora, 1908(5), II
 Dybbuk (Robbins), 1974 May 16, II

Dances and dancing (*cont.*)
 Esplanade (Taylor), 1975 Mar. 1(2), II
 Fancy Free (Robbins), 1944 Apr. 18, II
 first fancy dress ball (N.Y.C.), 1829(1), IV
 first live TV ballet, *Swan Lake*, 1976 June 30, II
 Ford Foundation grants, 1963, II; 1965 Nov. 17, II
 Godunov defected, 1979 Aug. 23, II
 Goldberg Variations (Robbins), 1971 May 28, II
 Gregory to dance in Cuba, 1974 Sept. 30, II
 Hall of Fame (Saratoga, N.Y.), 1984 Aug. 3, II
 Harkness Ballet, 1964, II
 Incredible Flutist (Piston), 1938 May, II
 international ballet competition (Bulgaria), 1974 July 24, II
 jitterbug, 1943, IV
 Joffrey Ballet, 1964, II
 Joffrey's Los Angeles season, 1982, II
 Kirstein resignation as New York Ballet director, 1989 Nov. 1, II
 Lambeth Walk, 1938(2), IV
 lavish ball in Waldorf-Astoria, 1897, IV
 Lindy hop, 1943, IV
 Lucifer (Graham) premiered, 1975 June 19, II
 McBride retirement, 1989 June 4(2), II
 Makarova joined American Ballet Theater, 1970 Oct. 11, II
 Martha Graham Dance Co. British performance, 1976 July 19–31, II
 Martha Graham Dance Co. (N.Y.C.), 1973 May 1, II
 Martha Graham Dance Co. 50th anniversary, 1975 June 19, II
 Merce Cunningham Co., 1968 May 15, II
 Messerer defected to U.S., 1980 Feb. 6, II
 Methodist ban lifted (New England), 1908 Apr. 13, IV
 Moiseyev Co. performed, 1958 Apr. 14, II
 Montez's notoriety, 1856(7), IV
 Mutations (Tetley), 1972 Mar. 30, II
 N.Y.C. Ballet, 1964 Apr. 24, II
 N.Y.C. Ballet strike, 1973 Nov. 13, II
 N.Y.C. Ballet Tchaikovsky festival, 1981 June 4–14, II
 N.Y.C. public balls, c1735, IV; 1866(6), IV
 Nureyev, Rudolf, 1975 June 19, II
 Pas de "Duke" (Ailey), 1976 May 11, II
 Phila. Assembly, 1749(2), IV
 popular rock 'n' roll, 1964(1), IV
 public ball vogue (N.Y.), c1735, IV
 Push Comes to Shove (Tharp), 1976 Jan. 9, II
 Radio City Music Hall Ballet Co. disbanded, 1973 June 13, II
 Ravel centennial, 1975 May 15–31, II
 Robbins' festival, 1990, II

Dances and dancing (*cont.*)
  Rodeo (Copland), 1942 Oct. 16, II
  St. Denis's modern, 1906(2), II
  Skyscrapers (Carpenter) ballet, 1926
    Feb. 19, II
  Stravinsky ballet written for TV, 1962
    June 14, II
  Stravinsky Festival (N.Y.C.), 1972 June
    18–25, II
  twist craze, 1962, IV
  two-step vogue, 1890(3), IV
Dandridge, Ray, 1987 July 26, IV
Daniel, Beth, 1980, IV; 1981, IV
Daniel, William, 1884 July 23, I
Daniels, William, 1985 Sept. 22, II; 1986
  Sept. 21, II
Dannay, Frederick, 1982, II
D'Annunzio, Gabriele, 1898(3), II
Danson, Ted, 1990 Sept. 16, II
Dante, Nicholas, 1975 May 21, II; 1976
  May 3, II
DAR *see* American Revolution, Daughters
  of the
Dare, Virginia, 1587 Aug. 18, IV
Darin, Bobby, 1959 Nov. 29, II
Darion, Joe, 1966 June 16, II
Darrow, Clarence:
  defense of Debs, 1894 Dec. 14, III
  Haywood defense, 1907(1), III
  Scopes trial, 1925 July 10–21, III
Dartmouth College (N.H.):
  Supreme Court Case, 1819, III
Darwell, Jane, 1941 Feb. 27, II
Darwin, Charles (*see also* Evolution):
  Origin of Species, 1860(2), III
Dashaway, Dick (fictional character),
  1807(1), II
Dating *see* Courtship and dating
Dausset, Jean, 1980 Oct. 10, III
Davidge, William, 1850 Aug. 19, II
Davidson, Owen, 1967 July 8, IV
Davies, Laura, 1987 July 28, IV
Davies, Samuel, 1730–1734, III
Davis, Adelle, 1974, III
Davis, Angela, 1970 Oct. 13, I; 1972 June
  4, I
Davis, Benjamin J., 1962 Mar. 19, I
Davis, Benjamin O., 1959 May 22, I; 1970,
  I
Davis, Bette, 1936 May 5, II; 1939 Feb.
  23, II; 1979 Sept. 9, II; 1989, II
Davis, Chester C., 1943 Mar. 25, III
Davis, David Brion, 1976 Apr. 19, II
Davis, Dwight F., 1900, IV
Davis, Elmer, 1942 June 13, III
Davis, Geena, 1989 Mar. 29, II
Davis, Henry G., 1904 July 6–9, I
Davis, H.L., 1960, II
Davis, Jefferson:
  birthday made legal holiday, 1892
    June 3, IV
  captured, 1865 May 10, I
  elected president of Confederacy,
    1861 Feb. 4, I
  evacuated from Richmond (Va.), 1865
    Apr. 2, I
  inaugurated president of Confederacy,
    1861 Feb. 18, I
  treason trial, 1868 Dec. 3, I

Davis, John W., 1924, I; 1924 July 9, I;
  1924 Nov. 4, I
Davis, Mark, 1989 Nov. 22, IV
Davis, Miles, 1991, II
Davis, Owen, 1923 Feb. 10, II
  Pulitzer Prize, 1923 May 13, II
Davis, Paulina Wright, 1853 Feb., II
Davis, Richard Beale, 1979 Apr. 23, II
Davis, Richard Harding, 1895, IV; 1897(1),
  II
Davis, Sammy, Jr., 1990, II
Davis, Samuel (Rev.), 1755(2), II
Davis, Stuart, 1941(6), II; 1991, II
Davisson, Clinton Joseph, 1937 Nov. 11,
  III
Dawes, Charles G., 1924, III; 1924 June
  12, I; 1924 Nov. 4, I; 1926 Dec. 10, I
Dawes Severalty Act, 1887 Feb. 8, I
Dawn, Hazel, 1988, II
Day, Benjamin H., 1833, II
Day, Clarence, Jr., 1939 Nov. 8, II
Day, Dennis, 1988, II
Day, Douglas, 1974 Apr. 18, II
Day, J. Edward, 1962 Oct. 23, II
Day, Pat, 1990 May 19, IV
Daye, Stephen, 1630–1639, II; 1638(3), II
Day-Lewis, Daniel, 1990 Mar. 26, II
Day of Doom, The (Wigglesworth),
  1660–1669, II
Dayton, William L., 1856 June 17–19, I
Dazey, Charles T., 1893 Oct. 23, II
D-Day, 1944 June 6, I
DDI (AIDS drug), 1989 June, III
DDT:
  banned, 1969 Nov. 20, III; 1972 Dec.
    31, III
  for typhus, 1944(1), III
Deafness *see* Handicapped
Dean, Daffy, 1934, IV
Dean, Dizzy (Jay Hanna), 1934, IV; 1974,
  IV
Dean, James, 1956, IV
Dean, John, 1972 Aug. 29, I; 1973 Apr. 27,
  I; 1973 Apr. 30, I; 1973 June 25–29, I
Dearborn, Henry A. S., 1847 Sept., I
Dearden, John Cardinal, 1988, III
Death (*see also* Cemeteries; Funerals; Life
  expectancy; Mortality rate; personal
  names):
  AMA on terminal patient treatment,
    1986 Mar. 15, III
  gender differences in dates of, 1992,
    III
  life-prolonging treatment for infants
    ruling, 1986 June 9, III
  medical definition, 1968 Dec. 4, III;
    1975 Nov. 10, III
  right-to-die law (Calif.), 1976 Sept.
    30(2), III
  right-to-die rulings, 1990 June 25, I
  suicide handbook, 1991(1), II
Death penalty *see* Capital punishment
Deaver, Michael K., 1987 Dec. 16, I
DeBakey, Michael, 1966 Aug. 8, III
Debates:
  Lincoln-Douglas, 1858, I
  Webster-Hayne, 1830 Jan. 19–27, I;
    1830 Jan. 27, IV
De Bow's Review (publication), 1846 Jan.,
  III

Debreu, Gerard, 1983 Oct. 17, III
Debs, Eugene V.:
  imprisoned for Espionage Act
    violation, 1918 Sept. 14, I
  presidential candidacy, 1904 May 5, I;
    1904 Nov. 8, I; 1908 May 10–17, I;
    1908 Nov. 3, I; 1912 May 17, I; 1912
    Nov. 5, I; 1920 May 8–14, I; 1920
    Nov. 2, I
  presidential nomination, 1900 Mar.
    6–9, I
  prison sentence commuted, 1921 Dec.
    23, I
  railroad strike, 1894 June 26, III; 1894
    July 10, III
  railroad strike injunction violation,
    1894 Dec. 14, III
  Socialist Party formed, 1901(1), I
Debt, U.S. (*see also* Budget, U.S.):
  $15 per person, 1816 Jan. 1, I
  $250 billion, 1949, III
  exceeded $2,000,000,000,000, 1986
    Apr. 3, III
  exceeded $500 million, 1862 July 1(1),
    I
  executive branch-congressional
    debate, 1990, I; 1990 Nov. 5, I
  first to exceed $300 billion, 1962 Aug.
    15, I
  Gramm-Rudman bill, 1985 Dec. 11, I;
    1986 July 7, I
  limit raised, 1959 June 30, III
  record, 1992, I
  record low, 1985, III
  reduction plan, 1987 Nov. 20, I
Decatur, Daniel *see* Emmett, Dan
Decatur, Stephen, 1804 Feb. 16, I; 1807, I;
  1815 June 17, I; 1815 June 30, I;
  1816(3), IV
Declaration of Independence:
  Adams and Jefferson deaths, 1826 July
    4, I
  Adams's quote, 1826 Aug. 2, IV
  early copy sold, 1969 May 17(2), II
  in Library of Congress, 1944 Oct. 1, II
  last surviving signer's death (Carroll),
    1832, IV
  written and signed, 1775–1779, I;
    1776 July 6, II; 1776 July 8, I; 1776
    Aug. 2, I
Declaration of Rights and Grievances,
  1765 Oct. 7–25, I
Declaratory Act, 1766 Mar. 18, I
Decoration Day (*see also* Memorial Day):,
  1868 May 30, IV
Deere, John, 1837(1), III
Defense, Department of:
  created, 1947 July 25, I
  Rumsfeld named director, 1975 Nov.
    3, I
  Schlesinger dismissed, 1975 Nov. 3, I
Defense bonds *see* Government bonds
Defense budget *see* Budget, U.S.
Defense Mediation Board, National
  (NDMB), 1941 Mar. 19, III
Defense Production Act, 1950 Sept. 8, I
Deficit, U.S. *see* Budget, U.S.; Debt, U.S.
Deficit Reduction Act, 1984 July 18, I
De Forest, Lee, 1906 Apr. 7, III; 1923, III;
  1961, III

DeFreeze, Donald D., 1974 May 17, IV
de Galindez, Jesus, 1956 Mar. 12, IV
Degas, Edgar, 1988 May 10, II
Degler, Carl N., 1972 May 1, II
de Grazia, Sebastian, 1990 Apr. 12, II
de Havilland, Olivia, 1947 Mar. 13(2), II;
   1950 Mar. 23, II
Dehmelt, Hans, 1989 Oct. 12(2), III
Deism, 1710–1714, III
de Kooning, Willem, 1974 Sept. 27, II;
   1983, II; 1984 Nov. 1, II; 1987, II; 1989
   Nov. 30, II
De Koven, Reginald, 1890, II
De Lôme, Enrique, 1898 Feb. 9, I
Delacorte, George T., 1991, II
Delahanty, Thomas K., 1981 Mar. 30, I
Delany, Dana, 1989 Sept. 17, II; 1992 Aug.
   30, II
Delaware:
   awarded to Penn, 1682 Aug. 24, I
   first state to ratify U.S. Constitution,
      1787 Dec. 7, I
Delaware, University of, 1833 Feb. 5, III
Delaware Indians, 1737, I
De La Warr, Thomas West, 1609–10, I;
   1610–1619, I
Delbruck, Max, 1969 Oct. 16, III
DeLillo, Don, 1985 Jan 21, II; 1988(1), II
Dellinger, David, 1973 Dec. 4, I
Delvalle, Eric Arturo, 1988 Feb. 5, I
Demaret, Jimmy, 1940 Apr. 7, IV; 1947,
   IV; 1947 Apr. 6, IV; 1950 Apr. 9, IV
de Mille, Agnes, 1942 Oct. 16, II; 1973
   Apr. 26, II
DeMille, Cecil B., 1959, II
De Mille, Henry, 1889(3), II
Democracy see Government and politics
Democratic Party (see also Presidential
   elections; Republican Party
   (anti-Federalist); States Rights
   Democrats; Watergate):
   adopted name formally, 1832 May 21,
      I
   control of Congress, 1878(1), I; 1986
      Nov. 4, I
   convention adjourned without
      nominating presidential candidate,
      1860 Apr. 23, I
   donkey as symbol, 1870 Jan. 15, I
   first woman to head National
      Committee, 1972 July 14, I
   formed, 1828(1), I
   presidential nominations, 1856 June
      2–5, I
   "Rum, Romanism, and Rebellion",
      1884, I
   sound money branch, 1896 Sept. 2–3,
      I
Demonstrations see Civil rights; Riots and
   mob violence; Vietnam War
   demonstrations
Dempsey, Jack (William Harrison), 1918
   Dec. 16, IV; 1919, IV; 1923, IV; 1926,
   IV; 1983, IV
Dempsey, Tom, 1970 Nov. 8, IV
DeNiro, Robert, 1975 Apr. 8(1), II; 1981
   Mar. 31, II
Denison University (Ohio), 1832 Feb. 2, III
Denmark:
   treaty with U.S., 1916 Aug. 4, I

Dennie, Joseph, 1801, II
Dennis, Sandy, 1964 May 24, II; 1967 Apr.
   10, II; 1992, II
Dennison, Aaron Lufkin, 1850(2), III
Dennison, Jo-Carroll, 1942 Sept. 12, IV
Dentistry:
   declining cavity rate, 1988 June 21,
      III
   first national association, 1840(7), III
   first school in world (Baltimore, Md.),
      1840, III
   U.S. Army Corps formed, 1901 Feb.
      2(1), I
Denton, Daniel, 1670(2), II
Denver (Colo.):
   airport crash, 1987 Nov. 15, I
Department stores see Retail stores
De Salvo, Albert, 1967 Jan. 18, IV
Design, National Academy of, 1825 Nov.
   8, II
De Soto, Fernando, 1539 May 30, I; 1541
   May 8, I; 1609(1), II
Detergents see Soap and detergents
Detroit Free Press (newspaper), 1964 Nov.
   21(1), III
Detroit (Mich.):
   airport crash, 1987 Aug. 16, I
   busing plan rejected, 1974 July 25, III
   founded, 1701 July 24, I
   newspaper strike, 1967 Nov. 15, III
   newspaper strike ended, 1968 Aug. 9,
      III
   race riots, 1943 June 20, III
   Renaissance Center dedicated, 1977
      Apr. 10, II
   surrendered by French, 1760 Nov. 29,
      I
   worst U.S. race riot to date, 1967 July
      23(2), I
Detroit News (newspaper), 1964 Nov.
   21(1), III
Deuterium, 1934 Nov. 15, III
Deutsch, Babette, 1982, II
Deutsch, Helen, 1992, II
Devers, Gail, 1992 July 25–Aug. 9, IV
De Voto, Bernard, 1953 Jan. 27, II
Dewey, George, 1898 May 1, I; 1898 July
   8, I
Dewey, John, 1899(1), II; 1916(3), III;
   1920(4), III; 1938(1), III
Dewey, Melvil (Dewey Decimal System),
   1876(8), III; 1876 Oct. 6, III
Dewey, Thomas E.:
   died, 1971, I
   presidential candidacy, 1944 June
      26–28, I; 1944 Nov. 7, I; 1948 June
      24(1), I; 1948 Nov. 2, I
Dewhurst, Colleen, 1974 Apr. 21, II; 1991,
   II
DeWilde, Brandon, 1950 Jan. 5, II
Dexter, Pete, 1988 Nov. 29, II
DeYoung, Charles, 1865(7), II
DeYoung, Michael, 1865(7), II
Dhéry, Robert, 1959 Apr. 12, II
Diaghilev, Serge, 1916, II
Dial, The (publication), 1836(1), III; 1840,
   II; 1844(8), II
Diamandis Communications, Inc., 1988
   Apr. 3, II
Diamond, David, 1954(4), II

Diamond, Jack ("Legs"), 1931, IV
Diamond Match Co., 1896(5), III
Diamonds:
   Burton's purchase, 1969 Oct. 24, IV
   world's largest sold (N.Y.C.), 1981
      Mar. 13, II
Dickens, Charles:
   Christmas Carol, A, 1844(5), II
   first book published in U.S., 1837(5), II
   first N.Y.C. reading, 1867 Dec. 2, II
   food preferences, 1827, IV
   Nicholas Nickleby dramatized, 1981,
      II; 1981 Oct. 4, II
   popularity, 1820(4), II; 1867 Dec. 2, II
   U.S. tour, 1842(1), II; 1842 Feb. 14, II
Dickey, James, 1966 Mar. 15(1), II;
   1970(1), II
Dickey, John Sloan, 1991, III
Dickinson, Charles, 1806, IV
Dickinson, Emily, 1890(1), II; 1891(1), II;
   1896(1), II; 1976 Apr. 28, II
Dickinson, Jonathan, 1699(1), II;
   1745–1749, III
Dictionaries:
   first American edition of The Royal
      Standard English Dictionary,
      1788(2), II
   first Indian, 1643(1), II
   Sumerian dictionary, first volume
      issued, 1984 Nov. 30, II
   Webster's, 1806(2), II; 1806(3), IV
   Webster's American, 1828(2), II
   Webster's Third International
      Dictionary, 1961(1), II
Dicumarol, 1916(2), III
Didion, Joan, 1977(1), II
di Donato, Pietro, 1992, II
Didrikson, Babe see Zaharias, Babe
   Didrikson
Diegel, Leo, 1928 Oct. 6, IV; 1929 Dec. 7,
   IV
Diem, Ngo Dinh, 1963, I
Dien Bien Phu, 1954, I; 1966 Feb. 21, I
Dies, Martin (see also Un-American
   Activities, House Committee on): 1938
   May 26, I
Diesel engine, 1904(4), III
Diet and nutrition (see also Cookbooks;
   Food stamps; Hunger; Vitamins):
   Americans' favorite meal, 1954, IV
   Borden's condensed products, 1856(6),
      III
   British commentary on American,
      1827, IV
   cold water crackers, 1801(1), IV
   Dutch habits (N.Y.), 1749(3), IV
   early nineteenth-century, 1807, IV
   European food needs, 1945 May 6, III
   explorers' shipboard provisions, 1577,
      IV
   fat overconsumption warnings, 1988,
      III
   food administrator appointed, 1943
      Mar. 25, III
   Graham's crackers and theories, 1830,
      IV
   holiday, 1795–1799, IV
   low-fat McDonald's hamburger, 1991
      Mar. 13, III

Diet and nutrition (*cont.*)
  margarine-heart disease link found, 1992 Oct. 7, III
  Oreo cookie, 1986, IV
  Popsicles changed, 1986, IV
  reduced fat recommended, 1990 Feb. 27, III
  soaring food prices, 1975, III
  weight-loss scams, 1990 Mar. 27, III
Dietrich, Marlene, 1992, II
Dillard, Annie, 1975 May 5, II
Dillinger, John, 1934 July 22, I
DiMaggio, Joe:
  hitting streak, 1941 July 17, IV
Dime novels *see* Books and literature
Dimouts *see* Blackouts and dimouts
Dingley, Nelson, 1897, I
Dinwiddie, Robert, 1753 Oct. 31, I
Dio, Johnny, 1956 Apr. 5, III
Dioxin, 1983 Feb. 22, I
Diplomacy (*see also* country names):
  ambassadorial rank created, 1893 Mar. 1, I
  first ambassador to Court of St. James, 1893 Apr. 3, I
  first foreign diplomat to U.S. (France), 1778 July, I
  first minister to Britain, 1792 Jan. 12, I
  first U.S. consul, 1786(2), I
  first U.S. naval attaché, 1882(1), I
  knee breeches or medals banned, 1853(1), IV
Diplomatic Appropriation Act, 1893 Mar. 1, I
Dirigibles *see* Airships
Dirksen, Everett, 1969, I
Disabled *see* Handicapped
Disarmament *see* Arms control and disarmament
Disasters *see* Accidents and disasters; specific types, e.g., Aviation accidents
Disciples of Christ, 1830(4), III; 1989, III
Discothèques, 1964(1), IV; 1975, IV; 1978, IV
Discoverer (spacecraft), 1959 Feb. 28, III; 1959 Apr. 13, III; 1959 Aug. 13, III; 1959 Aug. 19, III; 1960, III; 1960 Aug. 11, III; 1960 Aug. 19, III; 1961 Feb. 18, III; 1961 June 16, III
Discovery (space shuttle), 1984 Aug. 30–Sept. 5, III; 1984 Nov. 12, III; 1985 Jan. 24–27, III; 1988 Sept. 29–Oct. 3, III
Discrimination *see* Civil rights; Equal employment opportunity; Reverse discrimination; Women's rights; groups and areas of discrimination
Disney, Walt (*see also* Walt Disney World and Epcot Center): 1928(2), II; 1932 Nov. 18, II; 1934 Mar. 16, II; 1936 May 5, II; 1938, II; 1938 Mar. 10, II; 1939 Feb. 23, II; 1942 Feb. 26, II; 1964, IV; 1966, II; 1984 June 9, II
Displaced Persons Bill, 1948 June 25, I
Distribution Bill, 1837 Jan. 1, I
District of Columbia *see* Washington (D.C.)
Divorce:
  alimony laws, 1979 Mar. 5, I

Divorce (*cont.*)
  child's right to end natural parent relationship affirmed, 1992 Sept. 25, I
  colonial, 1660(1), IV
  easy (Nev.), 1915 Feb. 23, IV
  frozen embryos custody, 1992 June 1, I
  rate dropped, 1984, IV
  record number, 1981, I; 1981, IV
  single parents, 1988 Oct. 13, I
  valid in Nev., 1942 Dec. 21, IV
Dix, Dorothea, 1841(3), IV; 1843 Jan., IV; 1861 June 10, IV
Dix, Dorothy (Elizabeth Meriwether Gilmer), 1896, IV
Dixie Clipper (airplane), 1939 June 28, III
Dixiecrats *see* States Rights Democrats
Dixieland *see* Jazz
"Dixie" (song), 1859(2), II
Dixon, Thomas, 1905(1), II
DNA (deoxyribonucleic acid), 1962 Oct. 18, III; 1967 Dec. 14, III; 1984 June 4, III; 1984 Dec. 11–12, III
  oldest recovered from fossils, 1992 Sept., III
Doctorow, E. L., 1971(1), II; 1975(1), II; 1975 Aug. 1(1), II; 1976 Jan. 8, II; 1980(1), II; 1984(1), II; 1986 Nov. 17, II; 1989(1), II
Doctors *see* Medicine
Dodd, Robert Lee (Bobby), 1988, IV
Dodge, Henry, 1848 June 22, I
Dodge, Mary Mapes, 1865(1), II; 1873, II
Doeg, John H., 1930 Aug. 23, IV
Doerr, Harriet, 1984 Nov. 16, II
Dogs:
  Animal Kennel Club 100th anniversary, 1984, IV
  greyhound racing, 1884(7), IV; 1905, IV
  in World War II combat, 1944(2), IV
  Westminster Kennel Club show, 1877(1), IV
Doheny, Edward L., 1924 June 30, I; 1930 Mar. 13, I
Doherty, Hugh L., 1903(2), IV
Dohnanyi, Ernst von, 1960, II
Doisy, Edward A., 1944 Oct. 26, III; 1986, III
Dokes, Michael, 1982 Dec. 10, IV
Dole, Robert J., 1976 Aug. 19, I; 1976 Sept. 27, I
Dole, Sanford B., 1900 Apr. 30, I
Dolls and toys:
  Barbie, 1985, IV
  Cabbage Patch, 1983, IV; 1984, IV; 1985, IV
  first model train, 1798(2), IV
  five-dollar chemistry set, 1860(8), IV
  miniature electric train, 1847 July 26, IV
  sale in Puritan colonies, 1651, IV
Domestic partnership laws, 1991 Feb. 14, IV
Dominican Republic:
  de Galindez disappearance, 1956 Mar. 12, IV
  Pres. Grant land speculation, 1870, I

Dominican Republic (*cont.*)
  protocol signed with U.S., 1905 Jan. 21, I
  U.S. Marines sent in wake of coup, 1965 Apr. 28, I
  U.S recognized new government, 1965 Sept. 4, I
  U.S. trade treaty, 1907 Feb. 8, I
Donald, David, 1961 May 1, II; 1988 Mar. 31, II
Donald Duck (cartoon character), 1984 June 9, II
Donat, Robert, 1940 Feb. 29, II
Donelson, Andrew J., 1856 Feb. 22(2), I; 1856 Sept. 17, I
Donleavy, J. P., 1958(1), II
Donlon, Roger H. C., 1964 Dec. 5, I
Donnelly, Ignatius, 1900 May 10, I
Donnelly, Patricia Mary, 1939 Sept. 10, IV
Donner, George, 1847, I
Donner, Jacob, 1847, I
Donoghue, John, 1885(5), II
Donovan, Hedley, 1990, II
Donovan, William J. ("Wild Bill"), 1959, I
Doobie Brothers, 1980 Feb. 27, II
Doolittle, Hilda, 1961, II
Doolittle, James, 1929 Sept. 24, III; 1942 Apr. 18, I
Doors *see* Windows and doors
Dorais, Gus, 1913 Nov. 1, IV
Dorr, Thomas W., 1842(2), I
Dorr's Rebellion, 1842(2), I
Dorsey, Jimmy, 1957, II
Dos Passos, John, 1921(1), II; 1923(1), II; 1925(1), II; 1930(1), II; 1932(1), II; 1936(1), II; 1939(1), II; 1961(1), II; 1970, II
Doubleday, Abner, 1839, IV
Dougherty, William, 1875 Dec. 25, II
Doughface (term), 1820 Apr. 12, IV
Douglas, Donald W., 1981, III
Douglas, Helen Gahagan, 1980, I
Douglas, James (Buster), 1990 Feb. 11, IV
Douglas, James H., 1958 Mar. 4, I
Douglas, Lloyd C., 1942(1), II; 1948(1), II
Douglas, Melvyn, 1960 Apr. 24, II; 1964 Apr. 13, II; 1968 May 19, II; 1980 Apr. 14(2), II
Douglas, Michael, 1988 Apr. 11, II
Douglas, Stephen A.:
  debates with Lincoln, 1858, I
  held Senate seat, 1858–1859, I
  Illinois RR land grant, 1856(4), III
  Kansas-Nebraska Act, 1854, I; 1854(1), IV
  presidential nomination, 1860 June 18–23, I
Douglas, William O.:
  died, 1980, I
  retired from Supreme Ct., 1975 Nov. 12, I
Douglass, Frederick, 1855, IV
Dove, Rita, 1987 Apr. 16, II
Dow, Neal, 1840, IV; 1880 June 17, I
Dow Chemical Co., 1984 May 7, I
Dow Corning Corp., 1992 Apr. 16, III
Dowie, John Alexander, 1907 Mar. 9, III
Dow Jones & Co., 1889 July 8, II
Dow Jones industrial average *see* Stocks and bonds

Downing, Andrew Jackson, 1839, II; 1841(5), II; 1851(7), II
Doyle, Arthur Conan, 1890 Feb., II; 1892(1), II; 1899(3), II
Draft (see also Conscientious objectors):
 act extension signed, 1941 Aug. 18, I
 Ali evasion conviction overturned, 1971 June 28, IV
 card burnings, 1965 Oct. 15–16, I
 Catonsville (Md.) records burned, 1970 Aug. 11, III
 deferments canceled for violators, 1967 Oct. 26, I
 deferments cut, 1968 Feb. 16, I
 doubled, 1965 July 28, I
 end to call-ups, 1973 Jan. 27(2), I
 extended, 1946 May 14, I; 1951 June 19, I; 1955 June 16, I
 first, Civil War, 1863 Mar. 3(2), I
 first national conscription act, 1792 May 8, I
 first peacetime, 1940 Sept. 16, I
 highest call since Korean War, 1966 Aug. 4, I
 lottery, 1967, I; 1969 Nov. 26, I
 post World War II, 1948 June 24(2), I
 registration of 19- to 20-year-olds, 1980 June 27, I
 resisters' clemency program extended, 1975 Jan. 31, I
 riots against (N.Y.C.), 1863 July 13–16, I
 Spock conviction overturned, 1969 July 11, I
 universal military training established, 1951 June 19, I
 Vietnam resisters pardoned, 1977 Jan. 21, I
 women's exclusion upheld, 1981 June 25, I
 World War I, 1917 May 18, I
Drake, Alfred, 1992, II
Drake, Edwin L., 1859, III
Drake, Francis (Sir), 1579, III; 1579 June 17, I
Drake, Joseph Rodman, 1816 Aug., II; 1819, II
Drama see Theater; Theatrical productions
Draper, John William, 1840(6), III; 1876(2), III
Drapers Meadows (Va.), 1748, I
Dred Scott v. Sandford, 1857, I
Dreiser, Theodore (see also Dresser, Paul):
 American Tragedy, An, 1925(1), II
 book censored, 1916(2), II
 Cowperwood trilogy, 1912(1), II
 Genius, The, 1915(1), II
 Jennie Gerhardt, 1911(1), II
 Newspaper Days, 1931(1), II
 Sister Carrie, 1900(1), II
Dresser, Paul, 1897, II
Dressler, Marie, 1931 Nov. 10, II
Drew, Adrian E., 1957 Dec. 12, III
Drew, George F., 1877 Jan. 2, I
Drexel Burnham Lambert, Inc., 1988 Dec. 21, III
Dreyfuss, Richard, 1978 Apr. 3, II
Drift net fishing:
 prohibited, 1992 Nov. 2, I

Drinking see Alcohol and alcoholism; Bars, Taverns and saloons; types of beverages
Dropsie College for Hebrew and Cognate Learning (Pa.), 1907 June 6, III
Drought:
 Dust Bowl, 1934, I; 1936, I
 N.E., 1965 Feb. 5, I
 Northwest, 1992 Aug., I
 worst since Dust Bowl, 1980 June 23–Aug. 15, I; 1983, III; 1988, III
Drug addiction see Narcotics
Drugs and drug products (see also Food and drug laws; Psychedelic drugs; Narcotics):
 AIDS therapy, 1987 Mar. 20, III; 1988 May 13, III; 1989 June, III
 antihistamines, 1950(1), III
 cyanide in Excedrin (Seattle, Wash.), 1986 June 19, I
 cyanide in Tylenol capsules (Chicago, Ill.), 1982 Sept. 29–Oct. 1, I
 fertility malpractice suit, 1985 May 21, III
 first antibiotic, 1940(1), III
 first pharmacopoeia published, 1778(1), III
 genetically engineered, 1991 Feb. 21, III
 Kiersted Ointment, 1638(3), IV
 large-scale penicillin production, 1941(1), III
Drumgo, Fleeta, 1972 Mar. 27, IV
Drury, Allen, 1959(1), II; 1960 May 2, II
Drysdale, Don, 1969, IV
Duane, William J., 1833 Sept. 23, I
Duberman, Martin Bauml, 1989(1), II
Dubin, Al, 1980 Aug. 25, II
Du Bois, W. E. B., 1963, I
Dubos, René, 1969 May 5, II; 1982, III
Duché, Andrew, 1741(3), III
Duchamps, Marcel, 1963 Apr., II
Duchesne, Rose Philippine, 1988 July 3, III
Dudley, Paul, 1724, III
Dueling:
 Decatur-Barron, 1807, I
 first recorded between two congressmen, 1808(1), IV
 Hamilton-Burr, 1804 July 11, I
 Jackson-Dickinson, 1806, IV
Duffy, Hugh, 1894(2), IV
Dugan, Alan, 1962 Mar. 13, II; 1962 May 7, II
Duggan, Stephen P., 1919(2), III
Duggar, Benjamin Minge, 1948(1), III
Dukakis, Michael S.:
 presidential candidacy, 1988 July 18–21, I
 presidential defeat, 1988 Nov. 8, I
Dukakis, Olympia, 1988 Apr. 11, II
Duke, Charles M., 1972 Apr. 16, III
Duke, James Buchanan, 1890(8), III
Duke, Patty (see also Astin, Patty Duke): 1963 Apr. 8, II; 1970 June 7, II
Duke's laws (N.Y.S.), 1665 Feb. 28, I
Duke University (N.C.), 1852 Nov. 21, III; 1890(8), III; 1925 Dec. 29, III; 1977 Sept. 21, II
Dulbecco, Renato, 1975 Oct. 16, III
Dulles, Allen W., 1969, I

Dulles, John Foster:
 "brink of war" statement, 1956, I
 died, 1959, I; 1959 Apr. 15, I
 Medal of Freedom, 1959 May 20, I
Dumas, Alexandre, 1844(4), II
Dumbarton Oaks Conference (Wash., D.C.) (see also United Nations): 1944 Aug. 21, I
Dummer, William, 1720–1724, I
Dunaway, Faye, 1977 Mar. 28, II
Duncan, Isadora, 1908(5), II
Dunkard church (Pa.), 1723(3), III
Dunlap, William, 1803 Feb. 4, II; 1805 Feb. 22, II; 1834(2), II
Dunmore, John Murray, 1776 Jan. 1, I
Dunn, James, 1946 Mar. 7, II
Dunne, Finley Peter, 1896(3), II
Dunne, Irene, 1990, II
Dunning, John R., 1975, III
Dunnock, Mildred, 1991, II
Dunster, Henry (Rev.), 1636 Oct. 28, III
Duplicating machines:
 mimeograph invented, 1876(3), III
du Pont, Margaret Osborne, 1948 July 2, IV; 1948 Sept. 19, IV; 1949 July 1–2, IV; 1949 Sept. 5, IV; 1950 July 7, IV; 1950 Sept. 5, IV; 1954 July 3(2), IV; 1962 July 7, IV
Du Pont, Samuel F., 1861 Nov. 7, I
du Pont de Nemours, E. I., 1962 Mar. 1, III; 1981 Aug. 4, III
Durand, Peter, 1818(2), III
Durant, Will, 1926(1), II; 1968 May 8, II; 1981, II
Durant, Ariel, 1968 May 8, II; 1981, II
Durante, Jimmy, 1980, II
Durkin, Martin P., 1953 Sept. 10, III
Durocher, Leo, 1991, IV
Duryea, Charles E. and J. Frank, 1892 Sept.(1), III; 1895 June 11, III; 1895 Nov. 28, IV; 1896(4), III
Dutch Reformed Church see Reformed Protestant Dutch Church
Dutra, Olin, 1932 Sept. 4, IV; 1934 June 9(2), IV
Duvalier, Jean-Claude, 1986, I
Duvall, Robert, 1984 Apr. 9, II
Duve, Christian de, 1974 Oct. 10(2), III
du Vigneaud, Vincent, 1955 Nov. 2(1), III
Dvořák, Antonín, 1892(5), II; 1893(2), II
Dwight, Timothy, 1822, II
Dykstra, Clarence, 1941 Mar. 19, III
Dymaxion House, 1946(3), II
Dyott, Thomas, 1833(2), III
Dyson, Freeman, 1985 Jan. 14, II

Eads, James Buchanan, 1874(3), III; 1884 June, III
Eagles, The (group), 1976 Feb. 28, II; 1978 Feb. 23, II
Eagleton, Thomas F., 1972 July 10–14, I
Eaker, Ira C., 1987, I
Eakins, Thomas, 1873(3), II; 1875(3), II; 1877(2), II; 1986 June 18, II
Eames, Charles, 1978, II
Ear:
 inner, research, 1961 Oct. 19, III
Earhart, Amelia, 1928 June 3, III; 1932 May 20, III
Earl, Ralph, 1800(1), II

Early, Jubal A., 1864 July 11, I
Early Bird (communications satellite), 1965 Apr. 6, III
Earth:
  first American to orbit, 1962 Feb. 20, III
Earth Act Group, 1971 Jan. 12, III
Earth Day, 1970 Apr. 22, III; 1990 Apr. 22, III
Earthquakes, 1987 Oct. 1, I
  Alaska, 1964 Mar. 27, I
  California, 1992 June 28, I
  one of greatest (Mo.), 1811 Dec. 16, I
  San Francisco (Calif.), 1906, I; 1989 Oct. 17, I
  southern Calif., 1971 Feb. 9, I
  Winthrop study of, 1735–1739, III
Earth Summit (Rio de Janeiro, Brazil), 1992 June 12, I
East, John P., 1986, I
East Coast Conspiracy to Save Lives, 1970 Nov. 27, I; 1971 Jan. 12, I
Eastern Air Lines:
  merged, 1962 Jan. 23, III
Eastern Exchange Hotel (Boston, Mass.), 1846(1), III
Eastland, James O., 1986, I
Eastman, George, 1870 July 12, III; 1880(9), III; 1888(5), III; 1889(6), III; 1928 July 30, III
Eastman, Max, 1969, II
Eastman Kodak Co., 1893(2), III; 1982, III; 1986 Oct. 20, III; 1990 Oct. 12, III
Eastman School of Music (N.Y.), 1930(5), II
Easton, Treaty of, 1758 Oct., I
East River (N.Y.C.), 1867 Jan. 23, IV
Eastwood, Clint, 1986 Apr. 8, II
Eating see Cutlery; Diet and nutrition; Pottery
Eaton, Cyrus S., 1979, III
Ebb, Fred, 1966 Nov. 20, II; 1967 Mar. 26, II; 1975 June 3, II; 1977 Oct. 29, II
Ebbets Field (Brooklyn, N.Y.), 1960 Feb. 23, IV
Eberhart, Richard, 1966 May 2, II; 1977 Apr. 13(1), II
Echo 2 (satellite), 1964, III; 1964 Jan. 25, III
Eckert, J. Presper, Jr., 1946 Feb. 15, III; 1951 June 14, III
Eckert, William D., 1965 Nov. 17, IV; 1968 Dec. 6, IV
Economic Opportunity Act, 1964 Aug. 30, I
Economics and economy (see also Bankruptcy; Cost of Living; Debt, U.S.; Great Depression; Income and wealth; Nobel Prizes; Prices and price fixing; Unemployment):
  American Assn. organized, 1885(1), III
  Anti-inflation Act, 1948 Aug. 16, III
  antirecession legislation, 1958 Apr. 1, I
  booming recovery and expansion, 1984, III
  Carey's economic nationalism, 1837, III
  Carter's measures, 1978, I
  civilian restored, 1945 Aug. 18, III

Economics and economy (cont.)
  depressions, 1784(1), III; 1893, III; 1907, III
  Eisenhower program, 1953, III
  expansion, 1985, III
  expansion predicted, 1960 Apr. 2, III
  financial panic, 1819(1), I
  forecasting, 1980 Oct. 15, III
  Franklin theory, 1751, II
  Galbraith on, 1960(1), II
  gross national product (GNP), 1945(3), III; 1954 July 13, III; 1965, III; 1967 Jan. 15, III; 1968, III; 1969, III; 1971 Oct. 15, III; 1982, III; 1987, III
  improvement, 1983, III
  inflation, 1952, III; 1968, III; 1971, III; 1973, III; 1978, III; 1980, III; 1981, III; 1987, III; 1988, III
  international panic, 1931 June 20, I
  Jefferson on agrarian, 1804 Feb. 1, IV
  leading indicators index dropped, 1980 May 30, III
  meat price controls lifted, 1946 Oct. 15, III
  national income rise, 1936, I
  Nixon policies, 1970, I; 1970, III; 1971 Aug. 15, III; 1972, III; 1973 Jan. 11, III; 1973 June 13, III; 1973 July 18, III
  overview, 1987, III; 1988, III; 1989, III; 1990, III; 1991, III; 1992, III
  panics, 1820(3), IV; 1836 July 11, I; 1837, I; 1841 Aug. 19, I; 1857 Aug. 24, III; 1869 Sept. 24, III; 1873, I; 1874, I; 1893, III
  peak, 1955, III
  postwar, 1947, I
  post-World War I depression, 1921, III
  recession, 1937 Aug., III; 1938 May 27, III; 1958, III; 1990, I; 1990, III
  recession continued, 1992, III
  recession lessened, 1982, III
  recession predicted, 1960 Feb. 8–16, III
  recession worsened, 1991, III
  revolt against determinist theory, 1885(1), III
  technocracy vogue, 1932 Dec., III
  Theory of the Leisure Class (Veblen), 1899(1), II
  Truman granted emergency powers, 1950 Sept. 8, I
  unemployed march on Wash. (D.C.), 1894, I
  unstable, 1960, III; 1977, III
  upswing, 1938, III
  wage and price controls, 1946 Nov. 9, III; 1971 Aug. 15, III; 1972, III; 1973 Jan. 11, III
  wage and rent controls extended, 1952 June 28, III
  wartime anti-inflation measures, 1942, III
  western wheat crop failure, 1835(1), III
  WIN (Whip Inflation Now) program, 1974 Oct. 8(1), III
  world recession, 1970, III
  worst crisis since Great Depression, 1974, III

Edberg, Stefan, 1991 Sept. 7–8, IV; 1992 Sept. 12–13, IV
Eddy, Mary Baker, 1875(4), III; 1879(5), III; 1892(5), III
Eddy, Nelson, 1967, II
Edel, Leon, 1963 Mar. 12, II; 1963 May 6, II; 1969(1), II; 1986 Feb. 17, II
Edelman, Gerald M., 1969 Apr. 14, III; 1972 Oct. 12, III
Ederle, Gertrude, 1926 Aug. 6, IV
Edgarton, James A., 1928 July 12, I
Edgerton, Harold E., 1990, III
Edison, Thomas A.:
  books on, 1979(1), II
  electric passenger train, 1930 Sept. 3, III
  electric voting machine, 1869(3), III
  first central electric power plant, 1881(2), III
  first movie film, 1889(6), III
  incandescent electric lamp, 1879 Oct. 21, III; 1880 Jan. 27, III
  mimeograph invention, 1876(3), III
  movie camera patent, 1891 Aug. 24, III
  phonograph, 1877 Dec. 6, III
  telephone inventions, 1915 May 24, III
  wireless telegraphy patent, 1891 Dec. 29, III
Edmunds Act, 1862 July 1(2), I; 1882 Mar. 22, I
Edmunds-Tucker Act, 1887(1), III
Education, Department of:
  Cavazos made secretary, 1988 Sept. 20, III
  created, 1979 Oct. 17(2), III
Education and schools (see also Church-state separation; Classical studies; Colleges and universities; Parochial schools; Physical education; School busing; School desegregation):
  adult, 1858(1), III; 1936, III
  American Journal, first national teachers' publication, 1855(1), III
  attendance law (Mass.), 1852(2), III
  Bible reading required (Fla.), 1925 May 13, III
  bilingual ruling, 1974 Jan. 21, III
  Bowdoin speech on importance of, 1785(2), III
  Carlisle Indian School (Pa.), 1879(3), III
  coeducational sports upheld, 1978 Jan. 9, IV
  colonial, 1630–1639, III
  colonial textbook, 1690(2), II
  colonial women, 1765(4), IV
  community control issue, 1974, III
  core curriculum recommended, 1983 Sept. 10, III
  corporal punishment attacked, 1847(4), IV
  corporal punishment upheld, 1975 Oct. 20, III
  correspondence schools, 1892(8), III
  costs up, 1979, III
  cultural literacy, 1987(1), II
  current concerns, 1947, III

Education and schools (*cont.*)
Death at an Early Age (Kozol), 1967(1), II
Dewey's learning theory, 1899(1), II; 1938(1), III
dropout rate, 1992, III
early grammar and reader, 1783, II
Education Testing Service to spend $30,000,000, 1986, III
Elementary and Secondary Act extended, 1978, III
elementary enrollment down, 1983, III
Elementary Instruction in Europe (Stowe), 1837(2), III
enrollment down, 1979, III; 1982, III
facility use by student political/religious groups upheld, 1990 June 4, I
Faulkner on quality of, 1958 Mar. 8, III
fewer college-level science, math, and engineering students, 1986, III
first arithmetic textbook by American, 1729(3), II
first classical elementary school (N.Y.C.), 1659, III
first compulsory law (Mass.), 1647 Nov. 11, III
first correspondence school, 1891 Oct. 16, III
first federal land grant (Ohio), 1785 May 20, I
first for Indians (Va.), 1723(1), III
first free kindergarten (N.Y.C.), 1876(4), III
first free publicly supported high school (Boston, Mass.), 1821 May, III
first inclusion of science in curriculum (Pa.), 1689, III
first kindergarten (English-language) (Boston, Mass.), 1860, III
first kindergarten (German-language) (Wis.), 1856(1), III
first music instruction in public schools (Boston, Mass.), 1838(4), II
first Natl. Survey of School Finance, 1933(2), III
first N.Y. secondary school charter, 1787(2), II
first public land allotment (R.I.), 1640 Aug. 6, III
first public law (Mass.), 1647, III
first schoolmaster (N.Y.C.), 1630–1639, III; 1633, III
first state board (Mass.), 1837 Apr. 20, III
first state high school law (Mass.), 1827(1), III
first state-supported teachers' training school established (Mass.), 1839, III
first statewide teachers' strike (Fla.), 1968 Feb. 19, III
first tax-financed (Mass.), 1639 May 20, III
first U.S. commissioner, 1855(1), III
first vocational (Va.), 1646, III
first written exams (Boston, Mass.), 1845(1), III

Education and schools (*cont.*)
free right of illegal aliens, 1982 June 15, III
Great Depression impact on, 1933, III
for handicapped, 1817(1), III; 1829 Mar. 2, III; 1975 Nov. 29, III; 1977, III
high school diploma-holders doubled, 1976, III
high schools numbered 321, 1860(1), III
inadequate facilities and teaching, 1961, III
Jefferson proposal for public (Va.), 1779(2), III
J. Kennedy on crisis in, 1961 Jan. 30, III
Lancaster system introduced (N.Y.C.), 1806(2), III
language teachers' qualifications criticized, 1960 July 7, III
last state to pass compulsory school attendance (Miss.), 1918(1), III
Latin schools (Mass.), 1765(2), III
level reached, 1910(6), III
local financing of, 1960 Jan. 23, III
McGuffey's *Eclectic Readers*, 1836, III
math and science low rankings, 1989 Jan. 31, III
military, 1968, III
military training vetoed (N.Y.C.), 1916 Apr. 26, III
NEA 100th anniversary, 1957 Apr. 4, III
non-high school graduates, 1989, III
N.Y. teachers banned from Communist Party membership, 1920 Jan. 18, III
oldest U.S. association founded (Boston, Mass.), 1830(5), III
Parent-Teacher Assns., 1897 Feb. 17, III
Pestalozzi's theories introduced, 1809, III
Phila. school for blacks, 1758(2), III
Pierpont's *Readers*, 1825(2), II
poor quality, 1983 Apr. 26, III
Primary Geography text, 1867(7), III
private, 1710, III
progressive, revolt against, 1936(2), III
progressive theory, 1916(3), III
property taxes to finance upheld, 1973 Mar. 21, III
public school attendance law declared unconstitutional (Oreg.), 1924 Mar. 31, III
quality issue, 1976, III
record grant by Ford Foundation, 1955 Dec. 12, III
released time for religious studies upheld (N.Y.S.), 1951 July 11, III
released time for religious study (N.Y.S.), 1926(2), III
religious teachings banned, 1948 Mar. 8, III
SAT scores leveling off, 1981 Sept. 29, III
SAT scores up, 1984, III
school prayer banned (N.Y.S.), 1962 June 25, III

Education and schools (*cont.*)
school prayer ruled unconstitutional, 1962, III
school reopenings, 1988, III
southern colonial curriculum, 1765(2), IV
student religious or political meetings protected, 1984 Aug. 11, III
subversives barred from teaching, 1952 Mar. 2, III
teacher demand down, 1971, III
teacher shortage, 1948, III
teachers' loyalty oaths, 1935, III
teachers' strike ended (Cleveland, Ohio), 1980 Jan. 3, III
teachers' strike (N.Y.C.), 1967 Sept. 11, III; 1968 Sept. 9, III
teaching profession interest, 1988, III
third worst school fire to date (Chicago, Ill.), 1958 Dec. 1, I
Webster's *Spelling Book* reissued, 1855(7), II
women's, 1787(1), III; 1814, III; 1821(1), III
women teachers, 1852(2), IV
worst school fire to date (Tex.), 1937 Mar. 18, I
Edwards, Douglas, 1988 Apr. 1, II; 1990, II
Edwards, Jonathan:
books by, 1737, II; 1742(1), II
Great Awakening, 1730–1734, III
Great Awakening sermon, 1741(2), III
Northampton (Mass.) ministry, 1727, III
"Personal Narrative", 1740(1), III
resignation ended Great Awakening, 1750(2), III
Eggleston, Edward, 1871(1), II; 1873(1), II
Egypt (*see also* Israeli-Arab conflict):
joint U.S. Air Force exercises, 1980 Jan. 8, I
Ehret, Gloria, 1966 Sept. 25, IV
Ehrlichman, John, 1973 Apr. 30, I; 1973 June 25–29, I; 1973 Sept. 4, I; 1975 Feb. 21, I; 1977 May 23, I
Eilberg, Amy, 1985 May 12, III
Einstein, Albert, 1921 Apr. 2, III; 1930, III; 1938(2), III; 1971, III
Eisele, Donn F., 1968 Oct. 11, III
Eiseley, Loren C., 1977, III
Eisenhower, Dwight David:
Adams resigned, 1958 Sept. 22(2), I
against wage and price increases, 1958 Jan. 20, III
atomic weapon use, 1955 Mar. 16, I
backed Adams in Goldfine case, 1958 June 17, I
Crusade in Europe, 1948(1), II
Doctrine, 1957, I; 1957 Jan. 5, I
domestic policies, 1954, I
elected president, 1952, I; 1952 Nov. 4, I
Far East tour, 1960 June 26, I
flew to Korea, 1952 Nov. 29, I
foreign policy, 1954, I
general of Army rank, 1944 Dec. 15, I
heart attack, 1955 Sept. 26, III
highway program proposed, 1954 July 12, III

Eisenhower, Dwight David (*cont.*)
 inaugurated for second term, 1957
  Jan. 20, I
 inaugurated president, 1953 Jan. 20, I
 Japanese tour canceled, 1960 June 16,
  I
 Latin American tour, 1960 Feb. 22, I;
  1960 Mar. 7, I
 legislation signed, 1954 May 13, III;
  1954 Sept. 3, I; 1958 Apr. 1, I; 1958
  July 7, I; 1959 Mar. 31, III; 1959
  June 30, III; 1959 Sept. 14(2), II
 meeting with Khrushchev, 1959 Sept.
  15–27, I
 named Supreme Allied commander,
  1943 Dec. 24, I
 NATO command, 1950 Dec. 19, I
 nominated for second term, 1956
  Aug. 20–24, I
 Normandy invasion, 1944 June 6, I
 North African invasion, 1942 Nov. 7, I
 nuclear policy, 1954, I
 predicted budget surplus, 1960 Jan.
  7(2), III
 presidential candidacy, 1952 July 11, I
 problems of presidency, 1953, I
 proposed military information
  exchanges with Soviets, 1955, I
 reelected president, 1956 Nov. 6, I
 sent troops to Little Rock (Ark.), 1957
  Sept. 24, I
 SHAPE command, 1951 Apr. 4, I
 signed German surrender, 1945 May
  7, I
 Social Security proposals, 1953 Aug. 1,
  I
 on Soviet relations, 1960 Jan. 7, I
 State of the Union message, 1960 Jan.
  7, I; 1960 Jan. 7(2), III
 steel strike, 1959, III
 on subversion, 1954, I
 on synagogue bombings, 1958 Oct. 12,
  III
 on Taft-Hartley Act changes, 1954
  Jan. 11, III
 three-week tour abroad, 1959 Dec. 3,
  I
 urged antiracketeering legislation,
  1958 Jan. 23, III
 vetoed housing bill, 1959 July 7, I
 vowed to go to Korea, 1952 Oct. 24, I
Eisenhower, Milton S., 1985, III
Elder, Lonne, III, 1969 Feb. 5, II
Elderly *see* Gray Panthers; Medicare;
 Nursing homes; Older people
Eldred, Pamela Anne, 1969 Sept. 6, IV
Eldredge, Todd, 1990 Feb. 10–11, IV;
 1991 Feb. 15–17, IV
Eldridge, Florence, 1988, II
Election Campaign Act, 1972 Apr. 7, I;
 1976 Jan. 30, I
Elections (*see also* Campaign financing;
 Electoral college and vote count;
 Presidential elections; Voting rights):
 campaign spending, 1990, I
 congressional, 1800–1801, I;
  1802–1803, I; 1804–1805, I;
  1806–1807, I; 1808–1809, I;
  1810–1811, I; 1812–1813, I;
  1814–1815, I; 1816–1817, I;

Elections (*cont.*)
  1818–1819, I; 1820–1821, I;
  1822–1823, I; 1824–1825, I;
  1826–1827, I; 1828–1829, I;
  1830–1831, I; 1832–1833, I;
  1834–1835, I; 1836–1837, I;
  1838–1839, I; 1840–1841, I;
  1842–1843, I; 1844–1845, I; 1844
  Dec. 4, I; 1846–1847, I; 1848–1849,
  I; 1850–1851, I; 1852–1853, I;
  1854–1855, I; 1856–1857, I;
  1858–1859, I; 1860–1861, I;
  1862–1863, I; 1864–1865, I;
  1866–1867, I; 1868–1869, I;
  1870–1871, I; 1872–1873, I;
  1874–1875, I; 1876–1877, I; 1878(1),
  I; 1880 Nov. 2, I; 1882 Nov. 7, I;
  1884 Nov. 4, I; 1886 Nov. 2, I; 1888
  Nov. 6, I; 1890 Nov. 4, I; 1894 Nov.
  6, I; 1896 Nov. 3, I; 1898 Nov. 8, I;
  1900 Nov. 6, I; 1902 Nov. 4, I; 1904
  Nov. 8, I; 1906 Nov. 6(1), I; 1908
  Nov. 3, I; 1910 Nov. 8, I; 1912 Nov.
  5, I; 1914 Nov. 3, I; 1916 Nov. 7, I;
  1918 Nov. 5, I; 1920 Nov. 2, I; 1922
  Nov. 7, I; 1924 Nov. 4, I; 1926 Nov.
  2, I; 1928 Nov. 6, I; 1930 Nov. 4, I;
  1932 Nov. 8, I; 1934 Nov. 6, I; 1936
  Nov. 3, I; 1938 Nov. 8, I; 1940 Nov.
  5, I; 1942 Nov. 3, I; 1944 Nov. 7, I;
  1946 Nov. 5, I; 1948 Nov. 2, I; 1950
  Nov. 7, I; 1952 Nov. 4, I; 1954 Nov.
  2, I; 1956 Nov. 6, I; 1958 Nov. 4, I;
  1960 Nov. 8, I; 1962 Nov. 6, I; 1964
  Nov. 3, I; 1966 Nov. 8(1), I; 1968
  Nov. 5, I; 1970 Nov. 3, I; 1972 Nov.
  7, I; 1974 Nov. 5, I; 1976 Nov. 2, I;
  1978 Nov. 7, I; 1980 Nov. 4, I; 1982
  Nov. 2, I; 1984 Nov. 6, I; 1986 Nov.
  4, I; 1988 Nov. 8, I; 1990, I; 1990
  Nov. 6, I; 1992, I; 1992 Nov. 3, I
 Crump campaign song (Tenn.), 1909,
  II
 Democratic congressional sweep,
  1958, I; 1958 Nov. 4, I
 direct, of senators, 1913 May 31, I
 electric voting machine, 1869(3), III
 federal supervision of city, 1871 Feb.
  28, I
 first direct primary (Minn.), 1900
  Sept. 18, I
 first Kansas, 1855 Mar. 30, I
 first nominating convention (Utica,
  N.Y.), 1824 Aug., I
 first state to adopt primary (Wis.),
  1900 Sept. 18, I
 gerrymandering originated, 1810(2), I
 reapportionment act, 1842 June 25, I
 voter turnout increased, 1992, I
Electoral college and vote count, 1792
 Dec. 5, I; 1796 Dec. 7, I; 1800, I; 1804
 Dec. 5, I; 1808 Dec. 7, I; 1812 Dec. 2, I;
 1816 Dec. 4, I; 1820 Dec. 6, I; 1824
 Dec. 1, I; 1828 Dec. 3, I; 1832 Dec. 5, I;
 1836 Dec. 7, I; 1840 Dec. 2, I; 1844
 Dec. 4, I; 1848 Nov. 7, I; 1852 Nov. 2, I;
 1856 Nov. 4, I; 1860 Nov. 6, I; 1864
 Nov. 8, I; 1868 Nov. 3, I; 1872 Nov. 5, I;
 1876 Nov. 7, I; 1880 Nov. 2, I; 1884
 Nov. 4, I; 1888 Nov. 6, I; 1892 Nov. 8, I;

Electoral college and vote count (*cont.*)
 1896 Nov. 3, I; 1900 Nov. 6, I; 1904
  Nov. 8, I; 1908 Nov. 3, I; 1912 Nov. 5, I;
  1916 Nov. 7, I; 1920 Nov. 2, I; 1924
  Nov. 4, I; 1928 Nov. 6, I; 1932 Nov. 8, I;
  1936 Nov. 3, I; 1940 Nov. 5, I; 1944
  Nov. 7, I; 1948 Nov. 2, I; 1952 Nov. 4, I;
  1956 Nov. 6, I; 1960 Nov. 8, I; 1964
  Nov. 3, I; 1968 Nov. 5, I; 1972 Nov. 7, I;
  1976 Nov. 2, I; 1980 Nov. 4, I; 1984
  Nov. 6, I; 1988 Nov. 8, I
 proposed reforms, 1965 Jan. 28, I
 separate ballots for president and vice
  president, 1804 Sept. 25, I
 Tilden-Hayes dispute, 1877, I
Electra plane, 1960 Mar. 17, I; 1960 May
 12, III
Electricity (*see also* Blackouts and
 dimouts; Hydroelectric power; Lighting;
 Public utilities):
  auto, 1892 Sept.(2), III
  bell, 1831(1), III
  experimental passenger train (N.J.),
   1930 Sept. 3, III
  first alternating current motor,
   1892(10), III
  first appliances, 1882(4), III; 1882(6),
   III
  first central power plant, 1881(2), III
  first fan, 1882(6), III
  first fire alarm system (Boston, Mass.),
   1847 July 26, IV; 1851(1), III
  first sewing machine, 1889(7), III
  first university lecture on, 1746(1), III
  first used for bone fracture repair,
   1971 Oct. 29, III
  Franklin kite experiment, 1752 June,
   III
  GE formed, 1892(1), III
  miniature train, 1847 July 26, IV
  motors, 1834(2), III
  rate rise, 1975 July 25, III
  Rural Electrification Administration
   established, 1935 May 11, I
  Tesla's inventions, 1888, III
Electronics, 1964 Oct. 29, III; 1973 Oct.
 23, III; 1977 Oct. 11, III
Electron microscope, 1940 Apr. 20, III
Elegy on the Reverend Thomas Shepard
 (Oakes), 1677(2), II
Elementary and Secondary Education Act,
 1978, III
Elevators:
 first in hotel (N.Y.C.), 1859(3), III
 first in office building (N.Y.C.),
  1868(7), III
 first (N.Y.C.), 1852, III
Elion, Gertrude B., 1988 Oct. 17, III
Eliot, Charles W., 1869, III
Eliot, Jared (Rev.), 1735–1739, III; 1748, II
Eliot, John (Rev.), 1631 Nov. 3, III; 1646
 Oct. 28, III; 1653(2), II; 1659(1), II; 1660,
 III; 1661, II
Eliot, T. S., 1914(2), II; 1922(1), II; 1948
 Nov. 4, II; 1950 Apr. 9, II; 1954 Feb. 11,
 II; 1965, II
Elizabeth I (Queen of England), 1584, II
Elkin, Stanley, 1983 Jan. 27, II
Elkins, Stephen B., 1903, I; 1910, I
Elkins Act, 1903, I

Elks, Benevolent Protective Order of, 1868(3), IV
Ellington, Duke, 1958 July 3–6, II; 1962 May 31–June 3, II; 1969 Apr. 29, II; 1974, II; 1976 May 11, II
    archives, 1988 Apr., II
Elliot, Mama Cass (Cassandra), 1974, II
Elliott, Sumner Locke, 1991, II
Ellis, Bret Easton, 1991(1), II
Ellis, Jimmy, 1968, IV; 1969, IV; 1970 Feb. 16, IV
Ellis Island (N.Y.), 1892 Jan. 1, I
    restoration, 1990 Sept. 8, IV
Ellison, Ralph, 1952(1), II; 1953 Jan. 27, II
Ellmann, Richard, 1960 Mar. 23, II; 1988(1), II; 1989 Mar. 30, II
Ellsberg, Daniel, 1971 June 13, II; 1973 May 11, II; 1973 Sept. 4, I
Elman, Mischa, 1908 Oct., II; 1967, II
El Salvador:
    commercial treaty with U.S., 1850 Jan. 2, III
    Reagan-congressional policy clash, 1984, I
    Salvation Army in, 1989, III
    U.S. support of anti-Sandinistas, 1983, I
Elsberg, Louis, 1862(2), III
Ely, Richard T., 1889, III
Emancipation Day, 1865 June 19, IV
Emancipation Proclamation, 1862 July 22, I; 1862 Sept. 22, I; 1863, I; 1871, I
Emancipator (publication), 1820(6), III
Embargo Act, 1807 Dec. 22, I; 1808, I; 1809, I; 1809 Mar. 1(1), I
Embree, Elihu, 1820(6), III
Emerson, Gloria, 1978 Apr. 10, II
Emerson, Ralph Waldo:
    American Scholar speech, 1837 Aug. 31, II
    Conduct of Life, The, 1860(6), II
    English Traits published, 1856(8), II
    Essays, 1841(1), II
    Essays (second series) published, 1844(7), II
    French's bust of, 1879(2), II
    on Mass. intellectual lull, 1807(1), IV
    Nature, 1836, II
    Representative Men, 1850(5), II
Emerson, Roy, 1961 Sept. 10, IV; 1964 Sept. 13, IV
Emmett, Dan, 1843(2), II
Emmy Awards, 1950 Jan. 28, II; 1951 Jan. 23, II; 1952 Feb. 18, II; 1953 Feb. 11, II; 1954 Mar. 7, II; 1955 Mar. 7, II; 1956 Mar. 17, II; 1957 Mar. 16, II; 1958 Apr. 15(1), II; 1959 May 6, II; 1960 June 20, II; 1961 May 16, II; 1962 May 22, II; 1963 May 26, II; 1964 May 25(2), II; 1965 Sept. 12, II; 1966 May 22, II; 1967 June 4, II; 1968 May 19, II; 1969 June 8, II; 1970 June 7, II; 1971 May 9, II; 1972 May 14, II; 1973 May 20, II; 1974 May 28, II; 1975 May 19, II; 1976 May 17, II; 1977 Sept. 11(1), II; 1978 Sept. 17, II; 1979 Sept. 9, II; 1980 Sept. 7, II; 1981 Sept. 13, II; 1982 Sept. 19, II; 1983 Sept. 25, II; 1984 Sept. 23, II; 1985 Sept. 22,

Emmy Awards (*cont.*)
    II; 1987 Sept. 20, II; 1988 Aug. 28, II; 1989 Sept. 17, II; 1990 Sept. 16, II; 1991 Aug. 5, II; 1992 Aug. 30, II
Emory University (Ga.), 1836 Dec. 10, III; 1915(3), III; 1979 Nov. 8, III
Empire State Building (N.Y.C.), 1929 Sept. 22, II; 1931 May 1, III; 1945 July 28(1), I
Employee Retirement Income Security Act, 1974 Sept. 2, III
Employment *see* Labor
Enabling Act, 1802 Apr. 30, I
Encyclopaedia Britannica:
    Dobson's edition, 1790(1), II
Encyclopedia Americana, 1827(3), III; 1829, III
Endangered and extinct species:
    bison, 1873, IV
    Calif. condor egg destroyed, 1986 Mar. 10, III
    DNA cloning from extinct animal, 1984 June 4, III
    seal hunting ban, 1892 Feb. 29, I
    snail darter (perch), 1978 June 15, III
    whale-hunting licenses, 1971 Mar. 1, III
Endeavor (space shuttle), 1992 Sept. 20, III
Enders, John F., 1954 Oct. 21, III
Endicott, John, 1630–1639, I; 1661 Sept., III
End of world predictions (*see also* Seventh Day Adventists):, 1910, III
Energy, Department of:
    created, 1977 Aug. 4, I
Energy Act, 1978 Oct. 15, I
Energy Administration, Federal:
    established, 1974 May 2, III
Energy and power (*see also* specific sources and types):
    Carter conservation program, 1979 July 15, I
    conservation campaign, 1977 Apr. 18, III
    conservation measures, 1945 Jan. 15, III
    development bill signed, 1992 Oct. 24, I
    Nixon conservation measures, 1973 Nov. 7, III
    shortage, 1978, I
Energy Office, Federal:
    formed, 1973 June 29, III
Engineering:
    American Institute of Electrical Engineers, 1884(2), III
    American Society of Civil Engineers, 1852 Nov. 5, III
    American Society of Mechanical Engineers, 1880(1), III
    Eads' awards, 1884 June, III
Engines (*see also* Steam engine):
    caloric, 1856(3), III
    diesel, 1904(4), III
    early gas, 1844 May 25, III
    electric, 1834(3), II
    first alternating current driven, 1892(10), III

Engines (*cont.*)
    internal combustion design, 1826 Apr. 1, III
England *see* Great Britain
England, Church of *see* Anglican Church
England, Barry, 1970 Oct. 12, II
Engle, Paul, 1991, II
Englehorn, Shirley, 1970 June 15, IV
English, William H., 1858 May 4, I; 1880 June 22–24, I
English Channel, 1926 Aug. 6, IV
Engraving *see* Art and artists
Engraving and Printing, Bureau of:
    established, 1862 Aug. 28, III
"Entangling alliances" phrase, 1801 Mar. 4, IV
Enterprise (space shuttle), 1977 Aug. 12, III
Entertainment *see* Circuses and entertainment; types
Environmental protection (*see also* Endangered and extinct species; Pollution; Wildlife):
    drift netting banned, 1992 Nov. 2, I
    Earth Day, 1970 Apr. 22, III
    Earth Day 20th anniversary, 1990 Apr. 22, III
    Earth Summit, 1992 June 12, I
    Expo '74 focus (Spokane, Wash.), 1974 May 4(2), IV
    first convention of National Conservation Congress, 1909 Aug. 26, II
    global warming, 1988, III
    Gore book, 1992(1), II
    leaded gasoline ban, 1985 Mar. 4, III
    Nader's Earth Act Group, 1971 Jan. 12, II
    national commission named, 1908 June 8, III
    Nixon proposals, 1970 Jan. 22, I; 1970 Feb. 4, I
    ozone, 1988, III
    ozone layer depletion, 1991 Apr. 4, III
    ozone layer international protection treaty ratified, 1988 Mar. 14, III
    permanent national wilderness system, 1964 Sept. 3, I
    public lands, 1909 Sept. 27, III
    T. Roosevelt's advocacy, 1902, I
    White House conference, 1908 May 13–15, III
Environmental Protection Agency (EPA):
    established, 1970 Dec. 2, I
    water pollution standards, 1977 Feb. 23, III
Enzymes, 1946 Nov. 14(2), III; 1953 Oct. 22, III; 1969 Jan. 16, III; 1972 Oct. 20(2), III
Epidemics *see* Medicine; disease name
Episcopal Church:
    birth control stance, 1960 Jan. 9, III
    Browning presiding bishop, 1985 Sept. 10, III
    Cathedral of St. John the Divine (N.Y.C.), 1892, II
    Crapsey tried for heresy, 1906, III
    endorsed black sit-ins, 1960 Apr. 27, III

Episcopal Church (*cont.*)
   first bishop, 1783, III; 1784 Nov. 18, III
   first black bishop in white diocese, 1962 Dec. 8, III
   first woman bishop, 1988 Sept. 24, III
   first woman priest, 1977 Jan. 1, III
   first women priests ordained (irregularly) (Phila., Pa.), 1974 July 29, III
   General Convention compromises, 1988 July 11, III
   oldest N.J. building, 1703 Mar. 28, III
   ordination of homosexuals, 1991 June 5, III; 1991 July 19, III
   women's ordination approved, 1976 Sept. 16, III
   women's ordination compromise, 1989 Sept. 28, III
   word "obey" deleted from marriage ceremony, 1922 Sept. 12, III
Equal employment opportunity:
   affirmative action upheld, 1986 July 2, III
   antihomosexual discrimination ordinance defeated, 1977 June 7, I
   AT&T affirmative action program, 1973 Jan. 18, III
   black affirmative action upheld, 1979 June 27, III
   disabled, 1990 July 26, I; 1992 Jan. 26, I
   discrimination against women holding advanced degrees, 1975 Jan. 5, III
   first Supreme Ct. decision on sex discrimination, 1971 Jan. 25, III
   last hired, first fired policy upheld, 1984 June 12, III
   law firm promotion policy ruling, 1984 May 22, I
   legislation imposing quotas vetoed, 1990 Oct. 22, I
   mentally disabled law, 1991 July 1, I
   NCAA athletic departments, 1992, IV
   new civil rights act, 1991 Nov. 21, I
   non-exclusion of women from jobs potentially exposing fetus to toxic substance, 1991 Mar. 20(1), I
   ruling, 1991 Mar. 20(1), I
   sex discrimination ruling, 1989 May 1, I
   Supreme Court rulings, 1989 Jan. 23, I
   women's wage discrimination ruling, 1981 June 8, I
Equal rights *see* Civil rights; Equal Employment Opportunity; Voting rights; Women's rights; specific subject areas
Equal Rights Amendment (ERA):
   ERAmerica pro-group formed, 1976 Feb. 25, I
   failed ratification, 1982 June 30, I
   passed by Senate, 1972 Mar. 22, I
   ratification deadline extended, 1978 Oct. 6, I
   voted down (N.Y. and N.J.), 1975 Nov. 4, I
Equal Rights Party, 1884(1), I
Equine encephalitis, 1959 Oct. 12, I

Equitable Life Assurance Society, 1868(7), III
Equity Funding Corporation of America, 1973 Mar. 27, III; 1975 Mar. 18, III
Erasmus Hall High School (N.Y.), 1787(2), II
Erdman, Jacob, 1898 June 1, III
Erdrich, Louise, 1985 Jan. 14, II
Ericson, Leif, 1974 Jan. 25, II
Ericsson, John, 1856(3), III
Erie Canal (N.Y.), 1817 July 4, III; 1825, III
Erie Railroad, 1851 May 15, III
Erikson, Erik H., 1970 Mar. 2, II; 1970 May 4, II
Erlanger, Joseph, 1944 Oct. 26, III
Ernst, Max, 1975 May 12, II
Ernst, Oswald H., 1898 Aug. 9, I
ERTS-1 (Earth Resources Technology Satellite), 1972 July 23, III
Ervin, Sam J., Jr., 1973 May 17, I; 1985, I
Esaki, Leo, 1973 Oct. 23, III
Esmark, Inc., 1984 May 24, III
Espionage (*see also* Subversion and loyalty issue; Treason):
   Boyce and Lee convicted, 1977 Apr. 28(2), I
   CIA's covert domestic authorized, 1981 Dec. 4, I
   congressional report leaked, 1976 Feb. 11–18, II
   first execution for, 1953 June 19, I
   first FBI agent charged with, 1984 Oct. 3, I
   German in U.S., 1915 July 15, I
   Powers released by Soviets, 1962 Feb. 10, I
   Pueblo incident, 1968 Jan. 23, I; 1968 Feb. 14, I
   RB-47 incident, 1960 July 11, I
   Senate committee report on U.S. intelligence, 1976 Apr. 26 and 28, I
   Soble imprisoned, 1957 Oct. 8, I
   thirteen charged with, 1985, I
   U.S. intelligence activities restructured, 1976 Feb. 17, I
   U.S. plane shot down by Soviets, 1964 Mar. 10, I
   U-2 flights discontinued, 1960 May 9, I
   U-2 incident, 1960, I; 1960 May 5, I; 1960 May 16, I; 1960 Aug. 19, I
Espionage Act, 1917 June 15, I; 1942 Apr. 14(1), II
Espionage and Sabotage Act, 1954 Sept. 3, I
Essay on Field Husbandry, An (Eliot), 1748, II
Essays (Bacon), 1688, II
Essays (Emerson), 1841(1), II; 1844(7), II
Essex, Mark, 1973 Jan. 7, IV
Establishment Act, 1765, I
   Md., 1702, I
Esterbrook, Richard, 1858(2), III
Estonia, 1991 Sept. 2, I
Ethical Culture, New York Society for, 1876(4), III
Ethiopia:
   annexed by Italy, 1936, I

Ethiopian Orthodox Church:
   American branch severed ties, 1992 Sept. 21(2), III
Ethnic groups (*see also* specific kinds, e.g., Chinese-Americans):
   N.Y.C. melting pot, 1890(2), I
Etiquette:
   books reflecting rising interest in, 1878(1), IV
   Manual of Politeness for Both Sexes, A, 1837(2), IV
   popular women's, 1847(5), IV
   proper dinner conversation, 1838 Mar. 3, IV
   Va. code, 1774 May, IV
   Young Man's Guide, The (Alcott), 1832(2), IV
Etting, Ruth, 1978, II
Eureka College (Ill.), 1855 Feb. 6, III
Europe (*see also* country names):
   food needs, 1945 May 6, III
Europe, Conference on Security and Cooperation in, 1975 Aug. 1, I
European Atomic Energy Community, 1957 Feb. 8, I
European Recovery Program *see* Marshall Plan
Eutaw Springs, Battle of (S.C), 1781 Sept. 9, I
Euthanasia *see* Death
Evangelical and Reformed Church, 1934 June 26, III
Evangelical Association, 1803(2), III
Evangelical Church, 1922(1), III
Evangelical Lutheran Church, 1986 Aug. 29, III
Evangelical United Brethren Church, 1946 Nov. 16, III; 1966 Nov. 11(2), III
Evangelism *see* Religion and churches; specific movements
Evans, Charles, Jr., 1916 June 30, IV
Evans, George Henry, 1845, III
Evans, Gil, 1988, II
Evans, Maurice, 1961 May 16, II
Evans, Oliver, 1773(2), III; 1804(2), III
Evans, Ronald, 1972 Dec. 7, III
Evans, Walker, 1975, II
Everett, Edward, 1855 Sept. 17, III; 1860 May 9, I
Evers, Johnny, 1907, IV; 1908 Sept. 23, IV
Evers, Medgar, 1963, I; 1963 June 12, I
Evert, Chris (*see also* Lloyd, Chris Evert): 1974 July 5, IV
Evolution:
   Bryan on controversy, 1923 Jan., III
   Darwin published, 1860(2), III
   differing views (Ward and Sumner), 1883, III
   Fiske's works, 1884(1), II
   rejected by Agassiz, 1860(2), III
   rejected by Presbyterians (Tex.), 1924 May 21, III
   school curriculum inclusion issues, 1987 June 19, III
   Scopes monkey trial, 1925 July 10–21, III
   Scopes trial play, 1955 Jan. 11, II
   teaching prohibited (Ga.), 1926 Feb. 9, III

Evolution (*cont.*)
    teaching upheld (Calif.), 1981 Mar. 5,
       III
    textbook ban (Tex.), 1925 Oct. 16, III
Ewell, Tom, 1953 Mar. 29, II
Executions *see* Capital punishment
Exercise (*see also* Gynasiums and
    gymnastics; Physical education; Sports;
    specific types):
    home equipment sales up, 1984, IV
    increased enthusiasm for, 1973, IV
    J. Kennedy urging participation in,
      1961 Dec. 5, I
Explorers and exploration (*see also*
    personal names; regions and territories
    explored):
    Antarctica, 1820(3), I; 1840 Jan 19., I
    Columbus for Spain, 1492 Oct. 12, I
    Columbus 500th anniversary, 1992, I;
      1992, II
    Drake for England, 1579 June 17, I
    early books about, 1609(1), II
    English, 1600–1609, I
    expedition to rescue Franklin, 1850
      May 22, I
    French claims, 1670–1679, I
    French reach Lake Ontario, 1678, I
    Lewis and Clark, 1814(1), II
    Long's expeditions, 1820(2), III; 1820
      June 6, I
    Norsemen, 986–1599, I
    Pike's expeditions, 1806 July 15, I
    Powell's Colorado R. exploration,
      1878(3), III
    Sacajawea female Indian guide,
      1805(1), IV
    shipboard provisions, 1577, IV
    Spanish, 1513 Apr. 2, I
    Vinland map called fraud, 1974 Jan.
      25, II
    West, 1826, I
    Wickes's South Seas, 1838 May 18, I
    Wilkes's Antarctica, 1840 Jan 19., I
    written reports, 986–1599, II
Explorer (satellite), 1958 Jan. 31, III
Explorer 11 (satellite), 1961 Apr. 27, III
Explorer 38 (satellite), 1968 July 4, III
Explosions:
    airplane (Hawaii), 1988 Apr. 28, I
    airplane (Lockerbie, Scotland), 1988
      Dec. 21, I
    ammunition depot (N.J.), 1926 July 10,
      I
    chemical plant (Nev.), 1988 May 4, I
    coal mine (Pa.), 1907 Dec. 19, I
    coal mine (W. Va.), 1907 Dec. 6, I;
      1968 Nov. 20, I
    Detroit (Mich.), 1895 Nov. 6, I
    Electra plane, 1960 Mar. 17, I
    fuel (Ark.), 1980 Sept. 19, I
    gas, 1963 Oct. 31, I
    grain elevator (La., Tex.), 1977 Dec.
      22, I
    mine (Ill.), 1909 Nov. 13, I
    mine (Pa.), 1908 Nov. 28, I
    mining, 1910(3), I
    ship *Iowa*, 1989 Apr. 19, I
    ship (Tex.), 1947 Apr. 16–18, I
    truck (Ore.), 1959 Aug. 7, I
    Utah mine, 1900 May 1, I

Exports *see* Trade
Expositions *see* Fairs
Extraterrestrial life, 1992 Oct. 12(2), III
Exxon Corp.:
    largest corporation, 1975 May, III;
      1980 May 5, III
    oil spill damages, 1989 Mar. 24, I
Exxon Valdez oil spill, 1989 Mar. 24, I
Eyeglasses:
    bifocals invented, c1760, III
Eyen, Tom, 1981 Dec. 20, II
Eyes:
    first cornea bank (N.Y.C.), 1944 May
      8, II
    research, 1967 Oct. 18(1), III

Fabyan, Sarah Palfrey, 1939 July 7–8, IV
Fads:
    bicycling, 1878, IV
    Cabbage Patch dolls, 1983, IV; 1984,
      IV; 1985, IV
    Citizen Band radios, 1976, IV
    Davy Crockett, 1955, IV
    electronic games, 1976, IV
    jujitsu, 1904(2), IV
    panty raids, 1952, IV
    skateboards, 1977, IV
    streaking, 1974, IV
    Tom Swifties (jokes), 1963(1), IV
    twist (dance), 1962, IV
    water guns, 1992, IV
Fairbank, John K., 1991, III
Fairbanks, Charles W., 1904 June 21–23, I;
    1904 Nov. 8, I; 1905 Mar. 4, I; 1916
    June 7–10, I
Fairbanks, Richard, 1639(2), I
Fair Labor Standards Act, 1940 Oct. 24,
    III; 1950 Jan. 24, III
Fair Oaks, Battle of (Va.), 1862 May
    31–June 1, I
Fairs:
    Centennial of 1876 (Phila., Pa.), 1876,
      IV
    Century of Progress Exposition
      (Chicago, Ill.), 1933 May 27-Nov. 2,
      IV
    Century 21 Exposition (Seattle,
      Wash.), 1962 Apr. 21, IV
    Chicago World's Columbian
      Exposition, 1890 Feb. 24, I; 1892
      Oct. 20–23, IV; 1893, IV; 1893(3), II;
      1893(4), II; 1893(5), II; 1893(6), IV;
      1893(8), II; 1894 Jan. 8, I
    county, 1810 Oct. 1, IV
    Crystal Palace Exhibition (N.Y.C.),
      1853(4), IV
    Expo '72 (Dallas, Tex.), 1972 June
      12–17, III
    Expo '74 (Spokane, Wash.), 1974 May
      4(2), IV
    HemisFair 68 (San Antonio, Tex.),
      1968 Apr. 6, II
    Ind. State Fair Grounds explosion,
      1963 Oct. 31, I
    New Orleans Exposition, 1885, IV
    N.Y.C. Exposition and Convention
      Center, 1980, II
    N.Y. World's, 1939, IV; 1941 Sept. 23,
      IV; 1964, IV; 1964 Apr. 19, II; 1964
      Apr. 22, IV; 1965 Oct. 17, IV

Fairs (*cont.*)
    Panama-Pacific International
      Exposition, 1915 Feb. 20, IV
    Rochester (N.Y.) agricultural, 1868
      Oct. 1(1), IV
    San Francisco World's opened, 1939,
      IV
Faldo, Nick, 1988 June 20, IV; 1989 Apr.
    9, IV; 1990 Apr. 8, IV
Falk, Peter, 1962 May 22, II; 1972 May 14,
    II; 1990 Sept. 16, II
Falkenburg, Robert, 1947 July 4–5, IV;
    1948 July 2, IV
Fall, Albert B., 1922 Apr. 15, I; 1924 June
    30, I; 1927 Oct. 10, I; 1929 Oct. 7(2), I;
    1930 Mar. 13, I
Falwell, Jerry, 1988 Feb. 24, I; 1989 June
    10, III
Famine *see* Hunger
Faneuil Hall (Boston, Mass.), 1742 Sept.
    24, II
Fans, electric, 1882(6), III
Far East (*see also* country names):
    Eisenhower tour, 1960 June 26, I
    Johnson, L., tour, 1966 Oct. 17, I
    SEATO mutual defense pact, 1955
      Sept. 8, I
Faris, Herman P., 1924 June 5, I; 1924
    Nov. 4, I
Farley, James A., 1976, I
Farm Bankruptcy Act, 1934 June 28(1), I
Farm equipment *see* Agriculture and
    agricultural products
Farmer, Moses Gerrish, 1847 July 26, IV
Farmer Labor Party:
    formed, 1920 June 12, I
    presidential ticket, 1920 July 13–16, I;
      1928 July 11, I; 1932 July 10, I
Farmer-Labor Progressive Party:
    presidential ticket, 1924 June 19, I
Farmer's Alliance, 1873(1), I
Farmers' Alliance, National, 1880 Apr., I
Farming *see* Agriculture and agricultural
    products
Farm Loan Act, 1916 July 17, III
Farm Mortgage Refinancing Act, 1934
    Jan. 31, I
Farm Security Administration (FSA), 1937
    July 22(2), I
Farm Workers Union, National:
    recognized as bargaining agent, 1966
      Apr. 6, III
Farnsworth, Philo T., 1971, III
Farragut, David G.:
    captured New Orleans (La.), 1862
      May 1, I
    "Damn the torpedoes . . . ", 1864 Aug.
      5, IV
    Mobile Bay battle (Ala.), 1864 Aug.
      5–23, I
Farrar, Geraldine, 1906(7), II
Farrell, Charles, 1990, II
Farrell, James T., 1935(1), II; 1979, II
Farrell, Johnny, 1928 June 24, IV
Farwell, Arthur, 1904(3), II
Fascism:
    Steelworkers' ban, 1954 Sept. 24, III
Fashion *see* Clothing and fashion
Fast, Howard, 1977(1), II

Fat (dietary) *see* Diet and nutrition; Oils and fats
Father Divine (George Baker), 1919, III; 1965, III
Fatherhood, 1992 June 1, I
Father's Day, 1910 June 19, IV
Faubus, Orval E., 1958 Sept. 30, III; 1959 June 18, III
Faulk, Mary Lena, 1955 July 2, IV
Faulkner, William, 1924(1), II; 1926(1), II; 1929(1), II; 1930(1), II; 1931(1), II; 1932(1), II; 1934(1), II; 1939(1), II; 1940(1), II; 1942(1), II; 1950 Nov. 10(1), II; 1951(1), II; 1951 Mar. 6, II; 1954(1), II; 1955 Jan. 25, II; 1955 May 2, II; 1957(1), II; 1959(1), II; 1962, II; 1963 May 6, II
    on educational quality, 1958 Mar. 8, III
    Nobel Prize, 1949 Nov. 3, II
Fax (facsimile-transmission machines), 1988, III
Fazio, George, 1950 June 10(2), IV
FBI *see* Federal Bureau of Investigation
Feats:
    actress Menken (Virginia City, Nev.), 1863(1), IV
    around-the-world records, 1889, IV; 1890 May 24, I
    Blondin's high-wire, 1859 June 30, IV
    Brodie's Brooklyn Bridge (N.Y.) jump, 1886, IV
    first transcontinental auto trip, 1903 July 26, III
    Knievel's motorcycle stunts, 1974, IV
    Niagara Falls crossed by tightrope walker, 1859 June 30, IV
    thousand-mile walk, 1830(3), IV
    weightlifting, 1885 Dec. 20, IV
    Weston's walking, 1861(1), IV
    World Trade Center scaled (N.Y.C.), 1977 May 26, IV
Federal aid *see* Revenue sharing; subject headings receiving aid, e.g., Education
Federal Bank Deposit Insurance Corporation, 1933 June 16(2), I
Federal Bureau of Investigation (FBI):
    Abscam operation, 1980 Feb. 2, I
    burglaries and break-ins confirmed, 1975 July 14, I
    counterintelligence operations, 1974 Nov. 18, I
    first agent charged with espionage, 1984 Oct. 3, I
    first women agents, 1972 July 7(1), IV
    Gray resigned, 1973 Apr. 27, I
    illegal surveillance indictment, 1977 Apr. 7, I
    Senate investigation of, 1975 Jan. 27, I
    surveillance of authors, 1987, I
    surveillance of civil rights group, 1974, I
Federal Communications Commission (FCC), 1927, III
Federal Deposit Insurance Corp., 1989 Aug. 9, III
Federal Emergency Relief Act (FERA), 1933 May 12(2), I
Federal Home Loan Bank Board, 1988 Dec. 31, III

Federal Housing Administration (FHA), 1934 June 28(2), I
Federalist, The (political essays), 1785–1789, II
Federalist Party:
    Alien and Sedition Acts, 1798 July 14, I
    Dennie's journal, 1801, II
    end of influence, 1814 Dec. 15–Jan. 4, 1815, I
    founding, 1789(1), I
Federal Reserve bill, 1963 June 4, III
Federal Reserve System and Board:
    discount rate raised, 1965 Dec. 5, III; 1988, III
    established, 1913, III
    Greenspan named chairman, 1987 June 2, III
    rediscount rate raised, 1980, III
    Volcker named head, 1979 July 25, I
Federal Securities Act, 1933 May 27, I
Federal Trade Commission (FTC):
    established, 1914 Sept. 26, I
    unfair marketing practices, 1972 Mar. 1(1), III
Federal Wage and Hour Law, 1941 Feb. 3, I
Federal Works Agency, 1939 July 1, I
Federated Department Stores, Inc., 1988 Apr. 1, III
Fehrenbacker, Don E., 1979 Apr. 16, II
Feis, Herbert, 1961 May 1, II
Feke, Robert, 1710–1714, III; 1745–1749, II
Feliciano, José, 1969 Mar. 12, II
Feminism *see* Women's rights
Fencing:
    Boston school, 1673(2), IV
Fenwick, Millicent H., 1992, I
Ferber, Edna, 1911(1), II; 1916(7), II; 1925 Apr. 26, II; 1930(1), II; 1931(1), II; 1968, II
Fermi Award, 1963 Apr. 5, III
Fern, Fanny *see* Willis, Sara Payson
Ferraro, Geraldine, 1984 July 16–19, I; 1984 Oct. 11, I
Ferrer, José, 1947 Apr. 7, II; 1951 Mar. 29(2), II; 1952 Jan. 15, II; 1952 Mar. 30, II; 1992, II
Ferrier, Jim, 1947 June 24, IV; 1960 July 24, IV
Ferries:
    first route (Mass.), 1630 Nov. 9, III
Ferris, George W. G., 1892(3), IV
Fessenden, Reginald A., 1906 Dec. 24, III
Fessenden, Thomas G., 1803(1), II
Fetchit, Stepin, 1985, II
Fewkes, J. Walker, 1889(3), III
Feynman, Richard P., 1965 Oct. 21(1), III; 1988, III
Fiberglass, 1938, III
Fiedler, Arthur, 1979, II
Field, Cyrus W., 1854 May 6, III; 1866 July 27, III; 1881(6), III
Field, James G., 1892 July 4–5, I
Field, Sally, 1977 Sept. 11(1), II; 1980 Apr. 14(2), II; 1985 Mar. 25, II
Field, Stephen, 1874(4), III
Fields, Dorothy, 1974, II

Fields, Herbert and Dorothy, 1959 Apr. 12, II
Fields, Joseph, 1940 Dec. 26, II
Fierstein, Harvey, 1982 June 26, II; 1983 June 5, II; 1984 June 3, II
Fifth Dimension (group), 1968 Feb. 29, II; 1970 Mar. 11, II
Fifty-four forty issue, 1844(1), IV; 1846 Apr. 27, I; 1846 June 15, I
Fifty-four forty treaty, 1824, I
Fillmore, Millard:
    born, 1800 Jan. 7, I
    elected vice president, 1848 Nov. 7, I
    Know-Nothing presidential nominee, 1856 Feb. 22(2), I
    sworn in as president, 1850 July 9, I
    vice presidential nomination, 1848 June 7–9, I
    Whig presidential candidate, 1856 Sept. 17, I
Film industry *see* Motion pictures
Financial scandals:
    Boesky insider trading, 1986 Nov. 14, IV
Finch, Peter, 1977 Mar. 28, II
Finch, Robert H., 1970 Jan. 2, III
Fingers, Rollie, 1976 June 15, IV; 1992 Aug. 2, IV
Fink, Mike, 1829, IV
Finkelstein, Louis, 1991, III
Finlay, Carlos, 1901(1), III
Finley, Charles O., 1976 June 15, IV
Finsterwald, Dow, 1958 July 20, IV; 1962 Apr. 9, IV
Firearms (*see also* Gunpowder):
    "Beecher's Bibles" (Sharps rifles), 1854(2), IV
    Colt revolver, 1833, III
    first popular repeating rifle, 1860(4), III
    first state to ban cheap pistols, 1988 May 23, I
    Gatling gun, 1862 Nov. 4, III
    gun control law signed, 1986 May 19, I
    mailing ban upheld, 1975 Dec. 2, III
    Maxim machine gun, 1884(4), III
    National Rifle Assn. formed, 1871(1), IV
    rifle shooting matches, 1873(4), IV
    semiautomatic rifles import ban, 1989 Mar. 14, I
    submachine gun invented (Tommy gun), 1916(4), III
Fires (*see also* Forest and brush fires; Insurance):
    aircraft carrier (Gulf of Tonkin), 1967 July 29, I
    asbestos curtains precaution in theaters, 1885(3), II
    Baltimore, Md., 1904 Feb. 7–8, I
    Bel Air-Brentwood (Calif.), 1961 Nov. 6–9, I
    Beverly Hills Supper Club (Ky.), 1977 May 28, I
    Boston (Mass.), 1679, I; 1872 Nov. 9, I
    Bronx (N.Y.) social club arson, 1990 Mar. 25, IV
    Chelsea (Mass.), 1908 Apr. 12, I
    Chicago (Ill.), 1871, I; 1894 Aug. 1, I

Fires (*cont.*)

chicken processing plant (N.C.), 1991 Sept. 3, I

circus tent (Hartford, Conn.), 1944 July 6, I

Cleveland (Ohio) school, 1908 Mar. 4, I

Cocoanut Grove (Boston, Mass.), 1942 Nov. 28, I

Columbia (S.C.), 1865 Feb. 17, I

early precautions and firemen, 1640–1649, IV

first efficient engine (Phila., Pa.), 1731(2), III

first electric alarm system (Boston, Mass.), 1847 July 26, IV; 1851(1), III

first fire engine (Mass.), 1654(2), III

first fireproof building (N.Y.C.), 1854(7), II

first paid firemen (N.Y.C.), 1697(2), I

first professional fire department (N.Y.C.), 1865 May 2, III

French Catholic Church (Holyoke, Mass.), 1875 May 27, I

Harper & Brothers (N.Y.C.), 1853(3), II

Harrisburg (Pa.), 1897 Feb. 2, I

Hinckley (Minn.), 1894 Sept. 1, I

Iroquois Theater (Chicago, Ill.), 1903 Dec. 30, I

Jacksonville (Fla.), 1901 May 3, I

Library of Congress (Wash., D.C.), 1851 Dec. 24, I

Metropolitan Opera House (N.Y.C.), 1892 Aug. 27, II

MGM Grand Hotel (Las Vegas, Nev.), 1980 Nov. 21, I

Milwaukee (Wis.), 1892 Oct. 28, I

Minneapolis (Minn.), 1893 Aug. 13, I

Miss. steamboat, 1888 Dec. 24, I

Morro Castle (ship) (N.J.), 1934 Sept. 8, I

Museum of Modern Art (N.Y.C.), 1958 Apr. 15(2), II

Newhall House (Wis.), 1883 Jan. 10, I

New Orleans (La.), 1788 Mar. 21, I

N.Y.C., 1776 Sept. 21, I

nursing home (Mo.), 1957 Feb. 17, I

Ocean Monarch (ship), 1848 Aug. 24, I

Ohio State Penitentiary, 1930 Apr. 21, I

Oriskany (U.S. carrier), 1966 Oct. 26, I

Peshtigo (Wis.), 1871 Oct. 8, I

pier and steamship (Hoboken, N.J.), 1900 June 30, I

Portland (Me.), 1866 July 4, I

St. Louis (Mo.), 1849 May 17, I

San Francisco (Calif.), 1850 May 4, I; 1851 May 3, I; 1906, I

San Juan (Puerto Rico), 1986 Dec. 31, I

Santa Fe (N. Mex.) house, 1967 July 27, II

school (Chicago, Ill.), 1958 Dec. 1, I

ship *Enterprise* (Hawaii), 1969 Jan. 14, I

ship *Phoenix* (Lake Michigan), 1847 Nov. 22, I

Silver Lake (Ore.), 1894 Dec. 29, I

Fires (*cont.*)

silver mine (Ida.), 1972 May 2, I

steamboat *Erie*, 1841 Aug. 9, I

steamboat *Stonewall*, 1869 Oct. 27, I

steam fire engine introduced (Cincinnati, Ohio), 1852(1), III

steamship *General Slocum* (N.Y.), 1904 June 16, I

steamship *Griffith* (Lake Erie), 1850 June 17, I

theaters' propensity to, 1878(2), II

Thomas Hotel (San Francisco, Calif.), 1961 Jan. 6, I

Triangle Waist Co. (N.Y.C.), 1911, I

twelve firemen killed (N.Y.C.), 1966 Oct. 18, I

Wanamaker Building (N.Y.C.), 1956 July 14–15, I

Washington, G., statue destroyed (N.C.), 1831 June 21, II

World's Columbian Exposition (Chicago, Ill.), 1894 Jan. 8, I

worst hotel, to date, 1946 Dec. 7, I

worst in Calif. history, 1991 Oct. 20–23, I

worst library, 1986 Apr. 29, II

worst school, to date (Tex.), 1937 Mar. 18, I

worst theater (Brooklyn, N.Y.), 1876 Dec. 5, I

Firestone, Harvey, Jr., 1973, III

Firestone Tire and Rubber Co., 1980 July 3, III

Firpo, Luis Angel, 1923, IV

First Church of Christ, Scientist *see* Christian Science

"First in war, first in peace" (eulogy), 1799 Dec. 26, IV

Fischer, Bobby, 1960 Jan. 2, IV; 1971 Oct. 26, IV; 1972, IV; 1972 July 11–Sept. 1, IV; 1975 Apr. 3, IV

Fischer, Edmond H., 1992 Oct. 12(1), III

Fischer, Louis, 1965 Mar. 9, II

Fish, Hamilton, 1937 May 3, II; 1991, I

Fish and fishing (*see also* Aquariums; Whaling):

Canadian Reciprocity Treaty, 1854 June 5, I; 1877 Nov. 23, I

Cuban-U.S. rights agreement, 1977 Apr. 28(1), I

dietary importance (Mass.), 1623(2), IV

diplomatic convention with Britain, 1818 Oct. 20, I

drift netting banned, 1992 Nov. 2, I

European fishermen, 986–1599, III

first business corporation (N.Y.), 1675, III

first club (Phila., Pa.), 1732(2), IV

first large-scale expedition, 1614, III

first natl. fly casting tournament, 1893(6), IV

growing colonial, 1715–1719, III

growth in N.E. 1741, 1741(1), III

N.E. colonial ventures, 1670–1679, III

Newfoundland Fisheries dispute settled, 1910 Sept. 7, I

offshore limits extended, 1977 Mar. 1, III

record catches, 1910(2), IV

salmon cannery, 1864(5), III

Fish and fishing (*cont.*)

Soviet privileges halted, 1980 Jan. 4, I

U.S. boat attacked, 1963 Feb. 21(1), I

Fisher, Avery, 1973 Sept. 20, II; 1976 Feb. 9, II

Fisher, Harry C. ("Bud"), 1896, II

Fisher, M. F. K., 1992, II

Fish House Club (Phila., Pa.), 1732(2), IV

Fisk, Clinton B., 1888 May 31, I

Fisk, James, 1869 Sept. 24, III

Fiske, John, 1884(1), II; 1891(1), II

Fitch, Clyde, 1890 May 19, II; 1902, II

Fitch, John, 1786(1), III; 1796–1797, III; 1798(2), IV

Fitch, Val L., 1980 Oct. 14(2), III

Fitzgerald, Barry, 1945 Mar. 15, II

Fitzgerald, Ella, 1959 May 4(2), II; 1959 Nov. 29, II; 1961 Apr. 12, II; 1963 May 15, II

Fitzgerald, Frances, 1973 May 7, II

Fitzgerald, F. Scott, 1920(1), II; 1925(1), II; 1934(1), II

Fitzgerald, Robert, 1961 Oct. 31, II

Fitzgerald, Zelda, 1970(1), II

Fitzhugh, George, 1856(6), IV

Fitzsimmons, Bob, 1897 Mar. 17, IV; 1899 June 9, IV

Fitzsimmons, James ("Sunny Jim"), 1966, IV

Five Forks, Battle of (Va.), 1865 Apr. 1, I

Fixx, Jim, 1984, IV

Flach, Ken, 1986 July 5–6, IV

Flack, Roberta, 1973 Mar. 3, II; 1974 Mar. 2, II

Flag Day, 1777 June 14, IV; 1877, IV; 1893 June 14, IV; 1949 Aug. 3, IV

Flagg, Josiah, 1764(1), II

Flags:

burning American as protest upheld, 1989 June 12(2), I

compulsory salute to challenged, 1943 June 14, III

Confederate, 1861 Mar. 4(1), I

designed by Franklin, 1747, I

early American, 1775–1779, IV; 1775 Sept. 15, IV

fifty-star, 1960 July 4, I

first depiction of American in England, 1782 Dec. 5, I

first representation of striped, 1647(2), II

first salute to a U.S., 1776 Nov. 16, IV

first salute to Stars and Stripes, 1778 Feb. 14, IV

forty-nine-star first raised, 1959 July 4, I

Old Glory, first use of, 1831 Aug. 10, IV

raising first official, 1775 Dec. 3, IV

Stars and Stripes, 1775–1779, IV; 1777 June 14, IV

thirteen stripes, 1818 Apr. 4, IV

Flanagan, Thomas, 1980 Jan. 7, II; 1988(1), II

Flanders, Ed, 1977 Sept. 11(1), II; 1983 Sept. 25, II

Flanders, Ralph E., 1954 July 30, I

Flanner, Janet, 1966 Mar. 15(1), II

Flatiron Building (N.Y.C.), 1895(5), II; 1908, III

Fleck, Jack, 1955 June 19, IV

Fleetwood Mac (group), 1978 Feb. 23, II

Fleischmann, Martin, 1989 Mar. 23, III

Fleming, Nancy Anne, 1960 Sept. 10, IV

Fleming, Peggy, 1964 Jan. 11–12, IV; 1965
  Feb. 13, IV; 1966 Jan. 29, IV; 1966 Feb.
  27, IV; 1967 Jan. 18–21, IV; 1967 Feb.
  28–Mar. 4, IV; 1968 Jan. 19–20, IV; 1968
  Feb. 6–18, IV; 1968 Mar. 2, IV

Fleming, Peter, 1981 July 3–4, IV; 1983
  July 2–3, IV; 1984 July 7–8, IV

Fletcher, John Gould, 1939 May 1, II

Fletcher, Louise, 1976 Mar. 29, II

Fletcher, Maria Beale, 1961 Sept. 9, IV

Flexner, Abraham, 1930, III

Flexner, James T., 1973 Apr. 10, II

Flexner, Stuart Berg, 1990, II

Flint, Timothy, 1830(3), II

Flogging see Corporal punishment

Flood, Curt, 1970, IV

Flood, James C., 1884, IV

Floods:
  Arkansas R., 1921 June 3, I
  Chicago (Ill.), 1992 Apr. 13, I
  Colo. R., 1976 July 31, I
  costliest to date, 1951 July 11–25, I
  Dayton (Ohio), 1913 Mar. 21–26, I
  disaster areas, 1955 Aug. 20, I
  Florence (Italy) art works destroyed,
    1967, II
  Johnstown (Pa.), 1889 May 31, I; 1977
    July 19, I
  Kans., Mo., and Des Moines rivers,
    1903 May 31, I
  Midwest, 1982 Dec. 2–9, I
  Mississippi R., 1882 Mar., I; 1927 Apr.,
    I; 1973 Apr. 11, I
  New Orleans (La.), 1947 Sept. 17–19, I
  Rapid City (S.D.), 1972 June 9–10, I
  Shadyside (Ohio), 1990 Apr. 14, I
  southern Calif., 1938 Mar. 2, I
  Teton R. Dam collapse (Ida.), 1976
    June 5, I
  Tex., 1913 Oct., I
  Tex. Gulf Coast, 1886 Oct. 12, I

Florida (see also names of cities):
  capital punishment laws, 1976 July 2,
    I
  carpetbag government ended, 1877
    Jan. 2, I
  congressional representation
    regranted, 1868 June 25(2), I
  East Fla. annexed, 1818, I
  hurricane, 1970 Aug. 3–5, I
  Hurricane Andrew, 1992 Aug. 24, I
  invaded by Oglethorpe (Ga.), 1740
    Jan., I
  Jacksonville fire, 1901 May 3, I
  Jefferson Davis's birthday made legal
    holiday, 1892 June 3, IV
  land boom, 1925 Oct., III
  Purchase Treaty, 1819 Feb. 22, I
  seceded, 1861 Jan. 10, I
  Spanish claims, 1513 Apr. 2, I; 1539
    May 30, I
  statehood, 1845 Mar. 3, I
  Union bid for reallegiance, 1864 Feb.
    7, I
  West Fla. annexed, 1810, I; 1812 May
    14, I

Florida East Coast Railroad, 1912 Jan. 22,
  III

Flory, Paul J., 1974 Oct. 15, III

Flowers see Horticulture

Floyd, Carlisle, 1970 Jan. 22, II

Floyd, Ray, 1969 Aug. 17, IV; 1976 Apr.
  11, IV; 1982 Aug. 8, IV; 1986 June 15,
  IV; 1992 Sept. 20(1), IV

Flu see Influenza

Flying saucers, 1952, IV

Flynn, Elizabeth Gurley, 1961 Mar. 13, I;
  1962 Mar. 19, I; 1964, I

Flynt, Larry, 1977 Feb. 8, II

FM radio see Broadcasting

Foley, Thomas S., 1975 Jan. 16, I; 1989
  May 31, I

Folger, Peter, 1676, II

Follo, Alfonso, 1959 Nov. 19, II

Fonda, Henry, 1948 Mar. 28, II; 1982, II;
  1982 Mar. 29, II

Fonda, Jane, 1972 Apr. 9, II; 1979 Apr. 4,
  II; 1984 Sept. 23, II

Foner, Eric, 1988(1), II

Fontaine, Joan, 1942 Feb. 26, II

Fontanne, Lynn, 1965 Sept. 12, II; 1983,
  II

Fonteyn, Margot, 1975 June 19, II

Food see Containers; Cookbooks; Diet and
  nutrition; Food and drug laws; Food
  stamps; Fruits and vegetables; Grocery
  stores and supermarkets; Hunger; Meat;
  Milk; Refrigeration; other types

Food administrator, U.S., 1943 Mar. 25, III

Food and Agricultural Act, 1962 Sept. 27,
  III; 1963, III

Food and drug laws:
  additives, 1906 June 21, III
  antithalidomide campaign, 1962 Aug.
    17, III
  cyclamates ban, 1969 Oct. 18, III
  genetically engineered foods, 1992
    May 26, III
  Krebiozen discredited, 1963 Sept. 7,
    III
  L-dopa approved, 1970 June 4, III
  predigested liquid protein, 1977 Dec.
    1, III
  Pure Food and Drug Act, 1906(1), II;
    1906 June 30, I
  Red Dye No. 2 banned, 1976 Feb. 12,
    III
  saccharin ban proposed, 1977 Mar. 9,
    III
  Wheeler-Lea Act, 1938 June 24, I

Food manufacturing, 1989 Feb. 3, III

Food stamps:
  authorization, 1959 Sept. 11, III

Football:
  AFL championship, 1961 Jan. 2, IV;
    1961 Dec. 24, IV; 1962 Dec. 23, IV;
    1964 Jan. 5, IV; 1964 Dec. 26, IV;
    1965 Dec. 26(1), IV; 1967 Dec.
    31(2), IV
  All-American team, 1889(5), IV
  American League, 1959 Nov. 5, IV
  AP poll, 1937 Jan. 1, IV; 1938 Jan. 1,
    IV; 1939 Jan. 1, IV; 1940 Jan. 1, IV;
    1941 Jan. 1, IV; 1942 Jan. 1, IV;
    1943 Jan. 1, IV; 1944 Jan. 1, IV;
    1945 Jan. 1, IV; 1946 Jan. 1, IV;

Football (cont.)
  1947 Jan. 1, IV; 1948 Jan. 1, IV;
  1949 Jan. 1, IV; 1950 Jan. 1, IV;
  1951 Jan. 1, IV; 1952 Jan. 1, IV;
  1953 Jan. 1, IV; 1954 Jan. 1, IV;
  1955 Jan. 1, IV; 1956 Jan. 1, IV;
  1957 Jan. 1, IV; 1958 Jan. 1, IV;
  1959 Jan. 1, IV; 1960 Jan. 1, IV;
  1961 Jan. 1, IV; 1962 Jan. 1, IV;
  1963 Jan. 1, IV; 1964 Jan. 1, IV;
  1965 Jan. 1, IV; 1966 Jan. 1, IV;
  1967 Jan. 2, IV; 1968 Jan. 1, IV;
  1969 Jan. 1, IV; 1970 Jan. 1, IV;
  1971 Jan. 1, IV; 1972 Jan. 1, IV;
  1973 Jan. 1, IV; 1974 Jan. 1, IV;
  1975 Jan. 1, IV; 1976 Jan. 1, IV;
  1977 Jan. 1, IV; 1978 Jan. 2, IV;
  1979 Jan. 1, IV; 1980 Jan. 1, IV;
  1981 Jan. 1, IV; 1982 Jan. 1, IV;
  1983 Jan. 1, IV; 1984 Jan. 1, IV;
  1985 Jan. 1, IV; 1986 Jan. 1, IV;
  1987 Jan. 1–2, IV; 1988 Jan. 1, IV;
  1989 Jan. 2, IV; 1990 Jan. 1, IV;
  1991 Jan. 1, IV; 1992 Jan. 1, IV
  Army-Navy game, 1890 Nov. 29, IV
  attendance, 1988, IV; 1991, IV
  attendance up, 1984, IV
  blacks dropped from Univ. of
    Wyoming team, 1969 Oct. 7, IV
  bowl games, 1933 Jan. 1, IV; 1934 Jan.
    1, IV; 1935 Jan. 1, IV; 1936 Jan. 1,
    IV; 1937 Jan. 1, IV; 1938 Jan. 1, IV;
    1939 Jan. 1, IV; 1940 Jan. 1, IV;
    1941 Jan. 1, IV; 1942 Jan. 1, IV;
    1943 Jan. 1, IV; 1944 Jan. 1, IV;
    1945 Jan. 1, IV; 1946 Jan. 1, IV;
    1947 Jan. 1, IV; 1948 Jan. 1, IV;
    1949 Jan. 1, IV; 1950 Jan. 1, IV;
    1951 Jan. 1, IV; 1952 Jan. 1, IV;
    1953 Jan. 1, IV; 1954 Jan. 1, IV;
    1955 Jan. 1, IV; 1956 Jan. 1, IV;
    1957 Jan. 1, IV; 1958 Jan. 1, IV;
    1959 Jan. 1, IV; 1960 Jan. 1, IV;
    1961 Jan. 1, IV; 1962 Jan. 1, IV;
    1963 Jan. 1, IV; 1964 Jan. 1, IV;
    1965 Jan. 1, IV; 1966 Jan. 1, IV;
    1967 Jan. 2, IV; 1968 Jan. 1, IV;
    1969 Jan. 1, IV; 1970 Jan. 1, IV;
    1971 Jan. 1, IV; 1972 Jan. 1, IV;
    1973 Jan. 1, IV; 1974 Jan. 1, IV;
    1975 Jan. 1, IV; 1976 Jan. 1, IV;
    1977 Jan. 1, IV; 1978 Jan. 2, IV;
    1979 Jan. 1, IV; 1980 Jan. 1, IV;
    1981 Jan. 1, IV; 1982 Jan. 1, IV;
    1983 Jan. 1, IV; 1984 Jan. 1, IV;
    1985 Jan. 1, IV; 1986 Jan. 1, IV;
    1987 Jan. 1–2, IV; 1988 Jan. 1, IV;
    1989 Jan. 2, IV; 1990 Jan. 1, IV;
    1991 Jan. 1, IV; 1992 Jan. 1, IV
  bowl game TV coverage dropped,
    1986, IV
  Calif. State players killed in plane
    crash, 1960 Oct. 29, I
  college rushing record, 1971 Oct. 30,
    IV
  controversy over top college honors,
    1969 Dec. 6, IV
  drug use, 1986, IV
  early collegiate matches, 1870(6), IV

Football (*cont.*)
early collegiate rules drafted, 1873 Oct. 19, IV
favorite sport, 1990, IV
field goal record, 1969 Oct. 18, IV; 1970 Nov. 8, IV
first Army-Notre Dame game, 1913 Nov. 1, IV
first depicted, 1806(2), IV
first intercollegiate game (N.J.), 1869 Nov. 6, IV
first national college championship, 1883(1), IV
first NCAA 15-game wins in 20th century, 1989, IV
first NFL playoffs, 1933 Dec. 17, IV
first professional game (Pa.), 1895 Aug. 31, IV
first Rose Bowl game, 1902 Jan. 1, IV
first Super Bowl, 1967, IV; 1967 Jan. 15, IV
first uniforms, 1875(1), IV
first USFL championship, 1983 July 17, IV
first WLAF championship, 1991 June 9, IV
franchise shifts decision, 1984 Nov. 5, IV
Halas retired as Bears coach, 1968 May 27, IV
Heisman Trophy, 1935(1), IV
instant replay abandoned, 1992 Mar. 18, IV
league merger, 1966 June 8, IV
league reorganization, 1970, IV
Lombardi retired, 1968 Jan. 14, IV
longest college losing streak, 1988 Oct. 8, IV
Marshall Univ. team killed, 1970 Nov. 14, IV
Mich. State-Notre Dame tie, 1966 Nov. 19, IV
national collegiate championship, 1884(4), IV; 1885(3), IV; 1886(1), IV; 1887(1), IV; 1888(1), IV; 1889(7), IV; 1890(5), IV; 1891(3), IV; 1892(4), IV; 1893(4), IV; 1894(3), IV; 1895(2), IV; 1896(1), IV; 1897(2), IV; 1898(2), IV; 1899(2), IV; 1900(1), IV; 1901(1), IV; 1902(1), IV; 1903(1), IV; 1904(1), IV; 1905(1), IV; 1906(1), IV; 1907(1), IV; 1908(1), IV; 1909(1), IV; 1910(1), IV; 1911(2), IV; 1912(1), IV; 1913(2), IV; 1914(1), IV; 1915(1), IV; 1916(1), IV; 1917(1), IV; 1918(1), IV; 1919(1), IV; 1920(2), IV; 1921(1), IV; 1922(2), IV; 1923(2), IV; 1924, IV; 1925(1), IV; 1926(2), IV; 1927(3), IV; 1928(1), IV; 1929(2), IV; 1930(1), IV; 1931(1), IV; 1935 Jan. 1, IV
NFL attendance record, 1981, IV
NFL championship, 1934 Dec. 9, IV; 1935 Dec. 15, IV; 1936 Dec. 13, IV; 1937 Dec. 12, IV; 1938 Dec. 11, IV; 1939 Dec. 10, IV; 1940 Dec. 8, IV; 1941 Dec. 21, IV; 1942 Dec. 13, IV; 1943 Dec. 26, IV; 1944 Dec. 17, IV; 1945 Dec. 16, IV; 1946 Dec. 15, IV; 1947 Dec. 28, IV; 1948 Dec. 19, IV; 1949 Dec. 18, IV; 1950 Dec. 24, IV;

Football (*cont.*)
1951 Dec. 23, IV; 1952 Dec. 28, IV; 1953 Dec. 27, IV; 1954 Dec. 26, IV; 1955 Dec. 26, IV; 1956 Dec. 30, IV; 1957 Dec. 29, IV; 1958 Dec. 28, IV; 1959 Dec. 27, IV; 1960 Dec. 26, IV; 1961 Dec. 31, IV; 1962 Dec. 30, IV; 1963 Dec. 31, IV; 1964 Dec. 27, IV; 1966 Jan. 2, IV; 1967 Dec. 31(1), IV
NFL conference and divisions split, 1967, IV
NFL rushing record, 1973 Dec. 16, IV
NFL Western Conference playoff, 1965 Dec. 26(2), IV
Notre Dame popularity, 1924, IV
N.Y. Giants half interest bought, 1991 Feb. 20, IV
N.Y. Giants move to N.J., 1971 Aug. 26, IV
pensions, 1968, IV
players' free-agent status, 1976, IV
popularity, 1933, IV
popularity of collegiate, 1924, IV
pro AFL-NFL merger, 1969 May 10, IV
prohibited at Yale, 1822(1), IV
pro kicking record, 1967 Sept. 24, IV
prospective rules discussed, 1876 Nov. 23, IV
pro strike, 1982 Sept. 21, IV
Rams-Colts team swap, 1972 July 13, IV
Rose Bowl, 1916 Jan. 1, IV; 1917 Jan. 1, IV; 1918(3), IV; 1919 Jan. 1, IV; 1920 Jan. 1, IV; 1921 Jan. 1, IV; 1922 Jan. 1, IV; 1923 Jan. 1, IV; 1924 Jan. 1, IV; 1925 Jan. 1, IV; 1926 Jan. 1, IV; 1927 Jan. 1, IV; 1928 Jan. 1, IV; 1929 Jan. 1, IV; 1930 Jan. 1, IV; 1931 Jan. 1, IV; 1932 Jan. 1, IV; 1933 Jan. 1, IV; 1934 Jan. 1, IV; 1935 Jan. 1, IV; 1936 Jan. 1, IV; 1937 Jan. 1, IV; 1938 Jan. 1, IV; 1939 Jan. 1, IV; 1940 Jan. 1, IV; 1941 Jan. 1, IV; 1942 Jan. 1, IV; 1943 Jan. 1, IV; 1944 Jan. 1, IV; 1945 Jan. 1, IV; 1946 Jan. 1, IV; 1947 Jan. 1, IV; 1948 Jan. 1, IV; 1949 Jan. 1, IV; 1950 Jan. 1, IV; 1951 Jan. 1, IV; 1952 Jan. 1, IV; 1953 Jan. 1, IV; 1954 Jan. 1, IV; 1955 Jan. 1, IV; 1956 Jan. 1, IV; 1957 Jan. 1, IV; 1958 Jan. 1, IV; 1959 Jan. 1, IV; 1960 Jan. 1, IV; 1961 Jan. 1, IV; 1962 Jan. 1, IV; 1963 Jan. 1, IV; 1964 Jan. 1, IV; 1965 Jan. 1, IV; 1966 Jan. 1, IV; 1967 Jan. 2, IV; 1968 Jan. 1, IV; 1969 Jan. 1, IV; 1970 Jan. 1, IV; 1971 Jan. 1, IV; 1972 Jan. 1, IV; 1973 Jan. 1, IV; 1974 Jan. 1, IV; 1975 Jan. 1, IV; 1976 Jan. 1, IV; 1977 Jan. 1, IV; 1978 Jan. 2, IV; 1979 Jan. 1, IV; 1980 Jan. 1, IV; 1981 Jan. 1, IV; 1982 Jan. 1, IV; 1983 Jan. 1, IV; 1984 Jan. 1, IV; 1985 Jan. 1, IV; 1986 Jan. 1, IV; 1987 Jan. 1-2, IV;

Football (*cont.*)
1988 Jan. 1, IV; 1989 Jan. 2, IV; 1990 Jan. 1, IV; 1991 Jan. 1, IV; 1992 Jan. 1, IV
rule changes, 1974 Apr. 25, IV
St. Louis Cardinals to Phoenix, 1988 Mar. 15, IV
Super Bowl, 1966 June 8, IV; 1967 Jan. 15, IV; 1968 Jan. 14, IV; 1969 Jan. 12, IV; 1970 Jan. 11, IV; 1971 Jan. 17, IV; 1972 Jan. 16, IV; 1973 Jan. 14, IV; 1974 Jan. 13, IV; 1975 Jan. 12, IV; 1976 Jan. 18, IV; 1977 Jan. 9, IV; 1978 Jan. 15, IV; 1979 Jan. 21, IV; 1980 Jan. 20, IV; 1981 Jan. 25, IV; 1982 Jan. 24, IV; 1983 Jan. 30, IV; 1984 Jan. 22, IV; 1985 Jan. 20, IV; 1986 Jan. 26, IV; 1987 Jan. 25, IV; 1988 Jan. 31, IV; 1989 Jan. 22, IV; 1990 Jan. 28, IV; 1991 Jan. 27, IV; 1992 Jan. 26, IV
Super Bowl II, 1968 Jan. 14, IV
Tagliabue named NFL commissioner, 1989 Oct. 26, IV
televising college games ruling, 1984 June 27, IV
Thorpe's triumphs, 1912, IV
TV coverage ban lifted, 1973, IV
TV viewers, 1992, IV
UPI poll, 1953 Jan. 1, IV; 1954 Jan. 1, IV; 1955 Jan. 1, IV; 1956 Jan. 1, IV; 1957 Jan. 1, IV; 1958 Jan. 1, IV; 1959 Jan. 1, IV; 1960 Jan. 1, IV; 1961 Jan. 1, IV; 1962 Jan. 1, IV; 1963 Jan. 1, IV; 1964 Jan. 1, IV; 1965 Jan. 1, IV; 1966 Jan. 1, IV; 1967 Jan. 2, IV; 1968 Jan. 1, IV; 1969 Jan. 1, IV; 1970 Jan. 1, IV; 1971 Jan. 1, IV; 1972 Jan. 1, IV; 1973 Jan. 1, IV; 1974 Jan. 1, IV; 1975 Jan. 1, IV; 1976 Jan. 1, IV; 1977 Jan. 1, IV; 1978 Jan. 2, IV; 1979 Jan. 1, IV; 1980 Jan. 1, IV; 1981 Jan. 1, IV; 1982 Jan. 1, IV; 1983 Jan. 1, IV; 1984 Jan. 1, IV; 1985 Jan. 1, IV; 1986 Jan. 1, IV
USFL, 1983 Mar. 6, IV; 1984 July 15(2), IV; 1984 Aug. 22, IV; 1985 July 14(1), IV
WFL disbanded, 1975, IV; 1975 Oct. 22, IV
Wichita State team killed, 1970 Oct. 2, IV
"winningest" college coach, 1985 Oct. 5, IV
WLAF championship, 1991 June 9, IV; 1992 June 6(2), IV
WLAF suspended, 1992 Sept. 17(2), IV
Yale Bowl first great stadium (Conn.), 1914(4), IV
Foote, Arthur William, 1888, II
Foote, Shelby, 1963(1), II
Foot racing, 1844, IV
Foran Act *see* Contract Labor Law
Forbes, Alexander, 1839(2), II
Forbes, Dave, 1975 July 18, IV
Forbes, Esther, 1943 May 3, II
Forbes, Malcolm S., 1989 Aug. 19, IV; 1990, III

Force Act of 1833, 1833 Mar. 2, I; 1833
   Mar. 15, I
Ford, Betty, 1975 Aug. 10(1), IV
Ford, Doug, 1955 July 26, IV; 1957 Apr. 7,
   IV
Ford, Gerald R.:
   administration shakeup, 1975 Nov. 3, I
   assassination attempt (Calif.), 1975
      Sept. 5, I; 1975 Sept. 22, I
   Chinese trip, 1975 Dec. 7, I
   intelligence operations restructured,
      1976 Feb. 17, I
   legislation signed, 1974 Sept. 2, III;
      1974 Oct. 29, IV; 1974 Nov. 26, III;
      1975 Nov. 29, III
   legislation vetoed, 1974 Nov. 21, I
   lost presidency, 1976 Nov. 2, I
   N.Y.C. loan, 1975 Nov. 26, I
   Pacific doctrine, 1975 Dec. 7, I
   pardoned Nixon, 1974 Sept. 8, I
   pardoned Tokyo Rose, 1977 Jan. 19, I
   presidential candidacy, 1976 Aug. 19,
      I; 1976 Sept. 27, I
   sworn in as president, 1974 Aug. 9, I
   vice presidency, 1973 Oct. 12, I; 1973
      Dec. 6, I
   Vietnam amnesty proclamation, 1974
      Sept. 16(2), I
   Vladivostok summit meeting, 1974
      Nov. 23–24, I
   wife's personal views, 1975 Aug. 10(1),
      IV
   WIN (Whip Inflation Now) program,
      1974 Oct. 8(1), III
Ford, Henry:
   auto co. formed, 1903(3), III
   first auto assembled, 1896 June 4, III
   first successful gasoline engine, 1893
      Dec. 24, III
   minimum wage restored, 1934 Mar.
      13, III
   Peace Ship, 1915 Dec. 4, IV
Ford, Henry, II, 1965 Feb. 19, IV; 1987,
   III
Ford, James W., 1932 May 28, I; 1936 June
   24–28, I; 1940 June 2, I
Ford, John, 1936 May 5, II; 1973, II
Ford, Judith Anne, 1968 Sept. 7, IV
Ford, Susan, 1975 Aug. 10(1), IV
Ford, Tennessee Ernie, 1991, II
Ford Foundation:
   educational grant, 1955 Dec. 12, III
   fund for the Republic, 1953(1), III
   grants cutback, 1975 Dec. 14, II
   grant to ballet, 1963, II
   N.Y.C. ballet and opera grants, 1965
      Nov. 17, II
   symphony orchestra grants, 1965 Oct.
      21(1), II
   theater grant, 1961 Mar. 19, II
   visual arts grants, 1961 Oct. 17, II
Fordham University (N.Y.), 1846 Apr. 10,
   III
Ford Motor Co.:
   assets, 1921 Apr. 30, III
   first labor contract, 1941 Apr. 11(1),
      III
   formed, 1903(3), III
   forty-hour work week, 1926(5), III

Ford Motor Co. (cont.)
   landmark Model T production, 1915
      Dec. 10, III
   loss, 1980, III
   Model A, 1927 Spring, III
   Model T, 1908 Oct. 1, III; 1909(1), III;
      1913 Summer, III
   Pinto defect case, 1980 Mar. 13, III
   price low, 1924(1), III
   ten millionth car, 1924 June 15, III
   union contract, 1964 Sept. 18, III
   workers' strike, 1967 Sept. 6, III
Foreign aid (see also Marshall Plan):
   Afghanistan, 1987, I; 1991 Sept. 13, I
   appropriations, 1955 July 7, I; 1961
      Sept. 4, I
   at $7.9 billion, 1952 Mar. 6, III
   at $8 billion, 1954 Mar. 8(1), I
   China, 1948 Apr. 3, I
   Contra appropriations, 1986 Aug. 13,
      I, 1988 Apr. 1, I
   first act passed, 1812 Mar. 3, I
   grants and credits, 1950 Jan. 2, I
   Greece and Turkey, 1948 Apr. 3, I
   human rights violations linked to,
      1977 Feb. 24, I
   Indochina, 1955 Jan. 1, I
   Mutual Security Act fund
      authorization, 1951 Oct. 10, I
   Philippines, 1988 Oct. 17, I
   Poland, 1989 Apr. 17, I
   Russia, 1992 Apr. 1, III
   smallest appropriations requested to
      date, 1965, I
   Soviet food purchases guarantee, 1990
      Dec. 12, I
   Truman Doctrine, 1947 May 22, I
Foreign Assistance Act, 1948 Apr. 3, I;
   1961 Sept. 4, I
Foreign investments:
   in U.S., 1989, III; 1989 Sept. 27, III;
      1989 Oct. 30, III
   private U.S. abroad, 1955 Aug. 21, III
   U.S. corporate withdrawal from South
      Africa, 1986 Oct. 20, III
Foreign Missions, American Board of
   Commissioners for, 1810(2), III
Foreign relations (see also Diplomacy;
   Treaties; war and country names):
   criticism of Reagan's policy, 1983, I
   during Great Depression, 1933, I
   Eisenhower policies, 1954, I
   Eisenhower's problems, 1953, I
   impact of Vietnam War, 1975, I
   Jefferson on "entangling alliances",
      1801 Mar. 4, IV
   Johnson administration, 1964, I
   Kennedy's policies, 1962, I
   Kissinger's shuttle diplomacy, 1974, I
   manifest destiny doctrine, 1845, IV;
      1898, I
   Monroe Doctrine, 1823 Dec. 2, I
   Neutrality Act, 1937 May 1, I
   neutrality proclamation, 1793 Apr. 22,
      I
   Point Four program, 1949 Jan. 20, I
   Reagan policies, 1986, I
   U.S. deteriorating world position,
      1960, I

Foreign relations (cont.)
   Waldheim first head of state barred
      from U.S., 1987 Apr. 27, I
   Washington's views, 1796 Sept. 17, I
Foreman, George, 1973 Jan. 22, IV; 1974
   Oct. 30, IV
Forest and brush fires:
   California, 1970 Sept. 22–28, I; 1992
      Aug., I
   Northwest, 1992 Aug., I
   worst record in 69 years, 1988 Aug.
      31, I
   Yellowstone National Park, 1988 Sept.
      22, I
Forester, C. S., 1939(1), II
Forests and trees (see also Arbor Day):
   American Forestry Association
      founded, 1882(5), III
   first school (N.C.), 1898(1), III
   U.S. Forestry Division, 1886 June 30, I
Formosa and Pescadores Islands:
   U.S. defense pledged, 1955 Jan. 28, I
Forrest, Edwin, 1820 Nov. 27, II; 1823, II;
   1826, II
Forrest, Nathan B., 1864 Apr. 12, I
Forrestal, James V., 1947 July 25, I
Forssmann, Werner, 1956 Oct. 19, III
Fortas, Abe, 1968 June 26, I; 1968 Oct. 2,
   I; 1969 May 15, I; 1982, I
Fort Caroline (Fla.), 1565 Sept. 20, I
Fort Dearborn (Ill.), 1812 Aug. 15, I
Fort Duquesne (Pa.), 1754 Apr. 17, I; 1758
   Nov. 25, I
Fort Fisher (N.C.), 1865 Jan. 15, I
Fort Frontenac (Ontario), 1758 Aug.27, I
Ft. Lauderdale (Fla.):
   new museum, 1985, II
Fort Leavenworth (Kan.), 1827 (1), I
Fort Louisbourg (Nova Scotia), 1745 June
   16, I
Fort Nassau (N.Y.), 1614, I
Fort Necessity (Pa.), 1754 May 28, I
Fort Okfuskee (Ga.), 1735, I
Fort Orange (N.Y.), 1614, I
Fort Oswego (N.Y.), 1756 Aug. 14, I
Forts:
   Castillo de San Marcos (Fla.), 1672
      Oct. 2, II
   early, 1600–1609, II
   first substantial (Mass.), 1622 Summer,
      II
   French, 1725–1729, I
   French Mississippi Valley, c1720, I
Fort Sumter (S.C.), 1861, I; 1861 Apr. 6, I;
   1861 Apr. 11, I
Fort Ticonderoga (N.Y.), 1758 July 8, I;
   1775 May 10(1), I; 1777 July 6, I
Fort Ticonderoga (Pa.), 1759 July 26, I
Fort Washington (N.Y.), 1776 Nov. 16, I
Fort William Henry (N.Y.), 1757 Aug. 9, I
Fortune magazine survey see Corporations
Fosbury, Dick, 1968 Oct. 12–27, IV
Foss, Lukas, 1955 Nov. 6, II
Fosse, Bob, 1975 June 3, II
Fossils:
   earliest known dinosaur unearthed
      (Ariz.), 1985 May 15, III
   oldest animal (N.C.), 1975 June 4, III
   oldest DNA found, 1992 Sept., III

Foster, Jodie, 1989 Mar. 29, II; 1992 Mar. 31, II

Foster, John, 1670(1), II

Foster, Stephen:
Arpino ballet, 1975 Oct. 9, II
died, 1860(4), II
dropped black dialect in songs, 1852(3), II
first published song, 1844(3), II
"Old Black Joe", 1860(4), II
"Old Folks at Home", 1851(5), II
"Susanna" first performed, 1847 Sept. 11, II

Foster, William Z., 1924 June 19, I; 1924 July 10, I; 1924 Nov. 4, I; 1928 May 27, I; 1928 Nov. 6, I; 1932 May 28, I; 1932 Nov. 8, I
died, 1961, I

Foulis, James, 1896 July 18, IV

Foundations (see also individual names):
study of, 1955 Sept. 12, III

Four Freedoms, 1941 Jan. 6, IV

Fourier, Charles, 1834(1), III; 1850(10), IV

Fowler, Orson Squire, 1834, III; 1846(3), IV; 1848(7), II

Fowler, William, 1983 Oct. 19, III

Fox, George Washington Lafayette, 1850(8), II

Fox, John, Jr., 1908(1), II

Fox, Margaret, 1849, III

Fox, Michael J., 1986 Sept. 21, II; 1987 Sept. 20, II; 1988 Aug. 28, II

Foxbury Golf Club (Pa.), 1887(3), IV

Foxe, Fanne, 1974 Dec. 10, I

Fox hunting see under Hunting

Fox Indians, 1830 July 15, I

Foxx, Jimmy, 1932, IV; 1967, IV

Foxx, Redd, 1991, II

France (see also Colonies and settlements; French and Indian War; French Revolution; Huguenots; XYZ Affair):
debt funding agreement with U.S., 1926 Apr. 29, I
first salute to Stars and Stripes, 1778 Feb. 14, IV
treaties abrogated, 1798 July 7, I
U.S. alliance treaty, 1778 Feb. 6, I; 1778 May 4, I
war declared, 1939 Sept. 3(1), I

Francis Ferdinand (Archduke of Austria), 1914 June 28, I

Frank, Elizabeth, 1986 Apr. 17, II

Frank, Joseph, 1985 Jan. 14, II

Frank, Leo M., 1915, IV

Franken, Rose, 1932 Apr. 25, II; 1941 Feb. 12, II

Frankfurter, Felix, 1957 Feb. 25, II

Franklin, Benjamin:
Autobiography, 1771, II; 1815(1), II
birth celebrations, 1826 Jan. 17, IV; 1885 Jan. 17, IV
born, 1706 Jan. 17, I
bought Pennsylvania Gazette, 1729 Oct., II
colonial unification plan, 1750–1754, I
Declaration of Independence, 1775–1779, I
died, 1790 Apr. 17, I
economic theory, 1751, II
electricity experiment, 1752 June, III

Franklin, Benjamin (cont.)
first abolition society, 1775 Apr. 14, I
flag designs, 1747, I
founded first foreign-language newspaper, 1732 May, II
founded first library, 1731(1), III
French dealings, 1776 Sept., I
glassychord invention, 1761(2), II
invented bifocal lenses, c1760, III
invented stove, 1742(3), III
Junto formed, 1725–1729, IV
magazines published, 1740–1744, II
Northwest Passage, 1753, I
Poor Richard's Almanack, 1690–1699, II; 1732 Dec. 19, II; 1734(1), IV; 1739, IV; 1747, IV; 1758, IV; 1838 Dec. 15, IV
postmaster general, 1775 July 26, I
published first political cartoon, 1754, II
religious views, 1728, III
Royal Society medal (G.B.), 1753(1), III
settled in Phila. (Pa.), 1723, I
street lighting, 1757(2), IV
University of Pennsylvania, 1749 Nov. 13, III; 1755 June 16, III

Franklin, John (Sir), 1850 May 22, I; 1853 May 31, I

Franklin and Marshall College (Pa.), 1787 Mar. 10, III

Franklin College (Ind.), 1836 Jan 30, III

Franklin National Bank (N.Y.C.), 1974 Oct. 8(2), III; 1980 Mar. 27, III

Franks, Bobby, 1924 July 21, IV; 1958 Feb. 20, IV

Fraser, Neale, 1960 Sept. 17, IV

Fraternal organizations (see also individual names):
Elks formed (N.Y.C.), 1868(3), IV
first Freemason, 1682(1), IV
Knights of Labor formed, 1869(6), III
Knights of Pythias founded (Wash., D.C.), 1864 Feb. 19, IV
Temple of Honor, 1845(1), IV

Fraternities and sororities:
first fraternity house (Williams College, Mass.), 1876(2), IV

Fratianne, Linda, 1977 Feb. 3–5, IV; 1977 Mar. 3, IV; 1978 Feb. 12, IV; 1979 Feb. 2–3, IV; 1979 Mar. 17, IV; 1980 Jan. 18–20, IV

Frauds (see also Medicine (for quack cures)):
artificial insemination donor, 1992 Mar. 4, III
balloon, 1844(6), IV
Drexel securities, 1988 Dec. 21, III
Edwards heirs, 1880(3), IV
Equity Funding Corp. insurance, 1975 Mar. 18, III
Franklin Bank (N.Y.C.) case, 1980 Mar. 27, III
Garbo biography (Gronowitz), 1978 Apr. 21, II
gold brick swindle, 1880(2), IV
Hughes biography (Irving), 1972, II
Marcos charges, 1990 July 2, IV
Marcos indictments, 1988 Oct. 21, III
Medicaid, 1976 Aug. 30, III

Frauds (cont.)
savings and loan, 1990 Jan. 22, III; 1991 Dec. 3, III; 1992 Apr. 10(1), IV
TV evangelist, 1987 Mar. 19, III
Vinland map, 1974 Jan. 25, II
Yazoo land (Ga.), 1795(1), I

Fraunces Tavern (N.Y.C.), 1719(3), II; 1975 Jan. 24, I

Frazer, Neale, 1959 Sept. 13, IV

Frazier, Joe, 1968, IV; 1969, IV; 1970, IV; 1970 Feb. 16, IV; 1971 Mar. 8, IV; 1973 Jan. 22, IV; 1975 Oct. 1, IV

Frazier-Lemke Act, 1934 June 28(1), I

Freaks:
albino, 1818(3), IV
Barnum's, 1837, IV

Fredericksburg, Battle of (Va.), 1862 Dec. 13, I

Freed, Alan, 1960 May 19, II

Freedmen's Bureau, 1865 Mar. 3, I; 1866 Feb. 19, I

Freedom March (Wash., D.C.), 1963 Aug. 28, I

Freedom of information:
Act passed, 1974 Nov. 21, I
new document classification guidelines, 1972 Mar. 8, I
Pentagon Papers, 1971, II; 1971 June 13, II
Village Voice published House report on intelligence activities, 1976 Feb. 11–18, II

Freedom of the press see Censorship; Newspapers

Freedom riders, 1961 May 14, IV

Freeman, Douglas Southall, 1958 May 5, II

Freeman, Mary Wilkins, 1891(1), II

Freemasons (see also Anti-Masonic Party):
first grand master, 1730(2), IV
first military lodge, 1738, IV
first settler, 1682(1), IV
Morgan kidnaping, 1826(1), I

Freer Gallery (Wash., D.C.), 1984, II

Free-Soil Party, 1847 Nov., I; 1848 Aug. 9, I; 1852 Aug. 11, I

Free trade see Trade

Frelich, Phyllis, 1980 June 8, II

Frelinghuysen, Theodore, 1844 May 1, I

Frémont, Jesse, 1944(1), II

Frémont, John C.:
first expedition, 1842(1), I
presidential nomination, 1856 June 2, I
Republican presidential candidate, 1856 June 17–19, I
second expedition, 1843 May 29, I
third expedition, 1845 Spring, I

French, Daniel Chester, 1879(2), II; 1893(4), II

French and Indian War (see also King William's War; Paris, Treaty of; Queen Anne's War; Seven Years' War):
Braddock mortally wounded, 1755 July 9, I
Detroit surrendered by French, 1760 Nov. 29, I
first refugees, 1755 Nov. 30, I
first skirmish, 1754 May 28, I
Ft. Duquesne captured, 1758 Nov. 25, I

French and Indian War (*cont.*)
Ft. Frontenac (Ontario) captured, 1758 Aug.27, I
Ft. Loudon surrendered, 1760 Aug. 7, I
Ft. Necessity surrendered, 1754 July 4, I
Ft. Oswego (N.Y.) captured, 1756 Aug. 14, I
Ft. Ticonderoga, 1758 July 8, I; 1759 July 26, I
Ft. William Henry (N.Y.) captured, 1757 Aug. 9, I
French surrendered Louisbourg (Nova Scotia), 1758 July 26, I
French Revolution, 1790 July 14, IV; 1793(5), II; 1794(5), IV
Freneau, Philip, 1775–1779, II; 1788(1), II; 1793(5), II; 1815, II
Frick, Ford C., 1978, IV
Fricker, Brenda, 1990 Mar. 26, II
Friedman, Jerome I., 1990 Oct. 16(1), III
Friedman, Milton, 1976 Oct. 14(2), III
Friedman, Samuel H., 1952 May 30–June 1, I
Friedman, Thomas L., 1989 Nov. 29, II
Friedman House (Pleasantville, N.Y.), 1951(4), II
Friel, Brian, 1992 June 1, II
Friendly Sons of St. Patrick, Society of, 1784(1), IV
Friends, Society of *see* Quakers
Friml, Rudolf, 1924, II; 1972, II
Frings, Ketti, 1957 Nov. 28, II; 1958 May 5, II
Frobisher, Martin (Sir), 1577, IV; 1600–1609, I
Froebel, Friedrich, 1860, III
Froman, Jane, 1980, II
Fromme, Lynette (Squeaky), 1975 Sept. 5, I
Frontier (*see also* Cowboys; Forts; Homestead Act; Westward expansion):
Colt revolver, 1833, III
early meaning, 1690(2), I
folk heroes, 1833, IV
frontiersman as comedic type, 1831 Apr. 25, IV
Mass.-Conn., 1692(1), I
Mills's report on, 1812(2), IV
plays about, 1870 Feb. 14, II
rough sports, 1819, IV
tall stories (*Mince Pie for the Million*), 1846(1), IV
tough image, 1820, IV
Turner on, 1893(1), III
Frontier Day (Wyo.), 1897(1), IV
Frost, David, 1977 May 4, I
Frost, Robert, 1914(1), II; 1923(1), II; 1928(1), II; 1930(1), II; 1936(1), II; 1939(1), II; 1945(1), II; 1962(1), II
aided Pound, 1958 Apr. 18, I
died, 1963, II
Pulitzer Prize, 1924 May 11, II; 1931 May 4, II; 1937 May 3, II; 1943 May 3, II
White House birthday celebration, 1962 Mar. 26, II

Fruits and vegetables (*see also* specific types):
citrus, 1832(1), IV
first banana shipment to U.S., 1804(3), IV
loganberry developed, 1881(5), III
price controls lifted, 1952 July 14, III
Frustaci, Patricia, 1985 May 21, III
Fry, Christopher, 1952 Feb. 13, II; 1955 Oct. 3, II
Fry, Shirley, 1951 July 6–7, IV; 1952 July 5, IV; 1953 July 3, IV; 1956 July 7, IV; 1956 Sept. 9, IV
Fry, William Henry, 1845 June 4, II; 1855, II
Fry, Christopher, 1952 Feb. 13, II
Fry, Shirley, 1956 July 7, IV
Fuel *see* Energy and power; Heating; types
Fugard, Athol, 1974 Nov. 13, II
Fugitive Slave laws, 1802, IV; 1826(2), I; 1850 Sept. 18, I; 1851, I; 1851 Feb. 15, I; 1859, I
Fukui, Kenichi, 1981 Oct. 19(1), III
Fukuyama, Francis, 1992(1), II
Fulbright, J. William:
on U.S. involvement in Laos, 1969 Oct. 28, I
Fuller, Charles, 1981 Nov. 20, II; 1982 Mar. 12, II
Fuller, Margaret, 1840, II; 1845, II; 1846(2), II
Fuller, R. Buckminster, 1946(3), II; 1983, III
Fuller, Samuel, 1620 Dec. 21, III
Fullerton, C. Gordon, 1977 Aug. 12, III
Fulton, Fred, 1918 Dec. 16, IV
Fulton, Robert, 1803 May, III; 1807 Aug. 11, III; 1811(5), III; 1814 Oct. 29, III
Fundamental Constitutions (Locke), 1660–1669, III
Fundamentalism (*see also* Evolution):
early brush with science, 1878(1), III
Expo '72 conference (Tex.), 1972 June 12–17, III
growth, 1974, III
inspiration for modern, 1910(4), III
modernist controversy with, 1892(4), III
Moral Majority disbanded, 1989 June 10, III
rejected by Conservative Judaism, 1988 Apr. 13, III
Southern Baptist Convention, 1990 June 12, III
Sunday's advocacy, 1896, III
victory for, 1986 June 10, III
Fund for the Republic, 1953(1), III
Funerals:
colonial customs, 1735–1739, IV
Dutch customs, 1691(1), IV
Funk & Wagnalls Co., 1968 Nov. 2, II
Funston, Frederick, 1901 Mar. 23, I
Furgol, Ed, 1954 June 19, IV
Furniture and home furnishings:
Allison cabinets, 1800(3), IV
banister-back chair, c1680(1), IV
begun in Phila (Pa.), 1791(2), III
Bigelow's power carpet loom, 1848(2), III

Furniture and home furnishings (*cont.*)
Burling cabinetmaking, 1773(2), IV
chief colonial designers, 1780–1784, IV
Chippendale influence, 1754(1), IV
colonial manufacturers, 1650–1659, IV
colonial wallpaper, 1730(2), III
Empire style, 1804, IV
fancy chair manufacturing, 1830(5), II
Hepplewhite, 1788, IV
high-backed settle, 1640, IV
highboy, c1690, IV
Hitchcock chair, 1820(2), IV
Pa. walnut stretcher table, c1685, IV
Queen Anne style, 1725, IV
record auction prices, 1983, IV
settle table, c1650, IV
Sheraton and Directoire styles, 1800(2), IV
Sheraton's designs, 1791(1), II
slat-back chair, c1700, IV
Furth, George, 1970 Apr. 26, II; 1977 Oct. 29, II
Fur trading:
Ashley's expedition, 1822, IV
Astor's enterprises, 1808, III; 1811(6), III; 1811 Apr. 12, I; 1822(1), III
black market crackdown (N.Y.), 1725–1729, I
Monts's monopoly, 1603, III
U.S.-British competition (Ore.), 1827, I
westward advance, 1700, III
Fussell, Paul, 1976 Jan. 8, II; 1976 Apr. 19, II
Futures trading, 1964 July 9, III

Gable, Clark, 1935 Mar. 27, II; 1942(3), II
Gaddis, William, 1976 Apr. 19, II
Gadsden Purchase, 1853 Dec. 30, I
Gajdusek, D. Carleton, 1976 Oct. 14(1), III
Galbraith, John Kenneth, 1958(1), II; 1960(1), II; 1973(1), II; 1977(1), II
Galileo (spacecraft), 1989 Oct. 18, III
Gallatin, Abraham, 1794 Feb. 28, I
Gallaudet, Thomas, 1817(1), III
Gallaudet College (Wash., D.C.), 1864, III
Gallery of Modern Art, The (N.Y.C.), 1964 Mar. 16, II
Gallico, Paul, 1976, II
Gallup poll *see* Public opinion
Galt, Edith Bolling, 1915 Dec. 18, IV
Gambino, Carlo, 1976, IV
Gambling (*see also* Horse racing; Lotteries):
baseball, 1990 July 30, IV; 1992 July 24, IV
colonial, 1699 June, IV
decreased, 1991, IV
first bookmakers, 1873(2), IV
first legal casino (outside Nev.) opened (N.J.), 1978 May 26, IV
first legalized horse racing (N.H.), 1964 Sept. 12(2), IV
riverboat, 1856, IV
Rose banned from baseball, 1989 Aug. 24, IV
track betting legalized (N.Y.), 1887 May 26, IV

Games and recreation (*see also* Sports; specific games and sports):
arcade video craze, 1983, II
banned during Revolutionary crisis, 1774(2), IV
card playing suppressed (Mass.), 1699 June, IV
coaching and fox-hunting, 1879, IV
colonial, 1610–1619, IV; 1660–1669, IV
craps, 1813, IV
electronic, 1976, IV
Methodist card playing ban lifted (N.E.), 1908 Apr. 13, IV
mid-eighteenth century, 1750–1754, IV
most popular activities, 1984, IV
pioneer farmers, 1801, IV
Plymouth strictures, 1621 Dec. 25, IV
popular N.Y.C. colonial, 1766(2), IV
town ball, 1830(2), IV
Gamma Ray Observatory, 1991 Apr. 7, III
Gangsters *see* Organized crime
Gantt, Harvey B., 1963 Jan. 28, III
Garbage *see* Waste disposal
Garbo, Greta, 1978 Apr. 21, II; 1990, II
García, Manuel del Pópolo Vincente, 1826(6), II
Garden, Mary, 1907 Jan. 22, II
Gardenier, Barent, 1808(1), IV
Gardens *see* Horticulture
Garden State Arts Center (N.J.), 1968 June 12, II
Gardner, Ava, 1990, II
Gardner, Dale, 1984 Nov. 12, III
Gardner, Erle Stanley, 1970, II
Gardner, Herb, 1986 June 1(3), II
Gardner, Isabella Stuart, Museum (Boston, Mass.), 1990 Mar. 18, II
Gardner, John, 1977 Jan. 6, II; 1982, II
Gardner, Randy, 1979 Mar. 17, IV
Garfield, James A.:
assassinated, 1881, I; 1881 July 2, I
assassin tried, 1881 Nov. 14, I
born, 1831 Nov. 19, I
elected president, 1880 Nov. 2, I
inaugurated, 1881 Mar. 4, I
presidential campaign, 1880, I; 1880 June 2–8, I
Garfunkel, Art, 1969 Mar. 12, II; 1971 Mar. 16, II; 1981 Sept. 19, II
Garland, Hamlin, 1891(1), II; 1902(1), II; 1917, II; 1921(1), II; 1922 May. 21, II
Garland, Judy, 1962 May 29, II; 1969, II
Garner, James, 1977 Sept. 11(1), II
Garner, John Nance, 1932 June 27-July 2, I; 1932 Nov. 8, I; 1936 June 23–27, I; 1936 Nov. 3, I; 1967, I
Garrett, Henry F., 1961 July 28, III
Garrigue, Jean, 1965(1), II
Garriott, Owen, 1973 July 28, III; 1973 July 28, III
Garrison, Lloyd K., 1991, I
Garrison, Wendell Phillips, 1865(11), II
Garrison, William Lloyd, 1831(1), I; 1831 Jan. 1, I; 1831 Jan. 1, IV; 1833, I; 1835 Oct. 21, I; 1857 Jan. 15, I
Garritse, William, 1645 June, IV
Garrity, W. Arthur, 1974 Dec. 30, III; 1975 Dec. 9, III

Garrow, David J., 1987 Apr. 16, II
Garson, Barbara, 1967 Feb. 22, II
Garson, Greer, 1943 Mar. 4, II
Gas, natural:
first sold (N.Y.S.), 1865(6), III
first well (N.Y.), 1821(2), III
Gas lights *see* Lighting
Gasoline *see* Automobiles; Oil and oil products
Gaspra (asteroid), 1989 Oct. 18, III
Gass, William, 1986 Feb. 17, II
Gassner, John, 1963 May 6, II
Gates, Horatio, 1777 Sept. 25–Dec. 23, I; 1777 Oct. 17, I
Gates, Thomas (Sir), 1609–10, I
Gateway Arch (St. Louis, Mo.), 1965 Oct. 28, II; 1968 May 25, II
Gatling, Richard Jordan, 1862 Nov. 4, III
Gatty, Harold, 1931 June 23, III
Gauguin, Paul, 1988 Sept. 17(1), II
Gavin, James M., 1990, I
Gay, Peter, 1967 Mar. 8, II; 1988(1), II
Gaynor, Charles, 1948 Dec. 16, II
Gaynor, Janet, 1929 May 16, II; 1984, II
Gay rights *see* Homosexuality
Gazette of the United States (newspaper), 1789 Apr. 11, II
Geary Chinese Exclusion Act, 1892 May 5, I; 1893 May 15, I
Geddes, Jane, 1986 July 14, IV; 1987 May 24, IV
Gehrig, Lou, 1938, IV; 1939 Jan. 24, IV; 1941, IV
Geiberger, Al, 1966 July 24, IV
Geisel, Theodor Seuss, 1991, II
Gelbart, Larry, 1962 May 8, II; 1963 Apr. 25(1), II
Geld, Gary, 1975 Jan. 7(1), II
Gell-Mann, Murray, 1969 Oct. 30, III
Gemini Project:
11 docking, 1966 Sept. 12(1), III
first manned flight, 1965 Mar. 23, III
first space docking, 1966 Mar. 16, III
first U.S. space walk, 1965 June 3, III
5 launched, 1965 Aug. 21, III
last mission, 1966 Nov. 11(1), III
launching postponed, 1966 May 17, III
9 launched and attempted rendezvous, 1966 June 3, III
rendezvous in space, 1965 Dec. 4, III; 1965 Dec. 15, III
success, 1966, III
10 docking, 1966 July 18, III
unmanned spacecraft launched, 1964 Apr. 8, III
Gems, Pam, 1981 Feb. 5, II
General Agreement on Tariffs and Trade (GATT), 1967 June 30, I; 1990 Dec. 7, I
General Appropriations Act, 1907 Feb. 26, I
General Electric Co. (GE):
communist employee ban, 1953 Dec. 9, III
formed, 1892(1), III
strike, 1969 Oct. 27, III
General Motors Corp. (GM):
all plants struck, 1945 Nov. 21, III
anti-sit-down strike measures (Mich.), 1936 Jan. 11, III; 1936 Feb. 3, III

General Motors Corp. (GM) (*cont.*)
antitrust case, 1962 Mar. 1, III
automatic cost-of-living increase, 1948, III; 1948 May 25, III
auto recalls, 1969 Feb. 26, III; 1971 Dec. 4, III; 1981 Feb. 23(2), III
earnings, 1950 Mar. 13, III
expansion program, 1954 Jan. 19, III
Futurama exhibit (N.Y.), 1964, IV
incorporated, 1908 Sept. 16, III
layoffs, 1991, III
Nader case, 1966 Mar. 22, III
plant closings, 1992 Feb. 24, III
second largest corporation, 1980 May 5, III
South African interests terminated, 1986 Oct. 20, III
stock split, 1955 July 5, III
strike, 1964 Sept. 25, III; 1970 Sept. 15, III
Toyota joint venture, 1983 Dec. 22, III
wage increases, 1941 May 16, III
Genesko, Lynn, 1973 May 21, IV
Genetics:
bacterial gene synthesis, 1976 Aug. 28, III
chromosome function, 1933 Oct. 20, III
code studies, 1968 Oct. 16, III
DNA cloning, 1984 June 4, III
DNA discovery, 1962 Oct. 18, III
DNA extracted from ancient skull (Fla.), 1984 Dec. 11–12, III
DNA recovered from oldest fossils, 1992 Sept., III
DNA research, 1980 Oct. 14(1), III
engineered infection-fighting drug, 1991 Feb. 21, III
engineering, 1981 June 18, III
engineering ruling, 1980 June 16, III
first artificial gene created, 1975 Dec. 6, III
first cell transfer of foreign genes, 1989 May 22, III
first engineered virus released, 1986 Apr. 22, III
first plants engineered by, 1986 May 30, III
food engineering, 1992 May 26, III
gene shifting, 1983 Oct. 10, III
gene splicing to produce vaccine, 1981 June 18, III
gene therapy experiments, 1990 July 31, III
heredity, 1959 Oct. 15, III
isolation of single gene, 1969 Nov. 22, III
marriage eugenic law unconstitutional, 1914 Jan. 20, III
Nobel Prizes, 1958 Oct. 30, III
nongenetic heredity, 1960 Oct. 18, III
patented new life forms, 1987 Apr. 16, III; 1988 Apr. 12, III
racial equality dispute, 1961 July 28, III
research safety questioned, 1974, III; 1975 Feb. 27, III
second code deciphered, 1988 May 13, III

Genetics (*cont.*)
    structure of viruses, 1969 Oct. 16, III
    synthetic DNA produced, 1967 Dec. 14, III
Geneva conference:
    opened, 1955 July 18, I
Geneva Convention, 1882 Mar. 16, I
Genocide, 1986 Feb. 19, I
Genovese, Vito, 1969, IV
Gentele, Goeran, 1970 Dec. 9, II
Gentry, Bobby, 1968 Feb. 29, II
Geography:
    Cruikshank's published, 1867(7), III
    early gazette, 1793, III
    first graduate school in, 1920(2), III
Geological Society of America, 1888(1), III
Geological Survey, U.S., 1879 Mar. 3, I
Geology:
    first U.S. map, 1809, III
Geophysical Year, International, 1957 July 1, III
George, Henry, 1888(1), I
George, Phyllis Ann, 1970 Sept. 12, IV
Georgetown University (Wash., D.C.), 1789 Jan. 23, III; 1815(4), III
George VI (King of Great Britain), 1937 May 12, III; 1939 June 8, I
George Washington Bridge (N.Y.-N.J.), 1926(4), III; 1931 Oct. 24, III
George Washington (submarine), 1959 Dec. 30, III
George Washington University (Wash., D.C.), 1821 Feb. 6, III
Georgia:
    Augusta established, 1735, I
    capital punishment laws, 1976 July 2, I
    congressional representation regranted, 1868 June 25(2), I
    founding, 1730–1734, I
    fourth state to ratify U.S. Constitution, 1788 Jan. 2, I
    Maddox elected governor, 1967 Jan. 10, I
    Methodist Church, 1736 Feb. 5, III
    readmitted to Union, 1869 Apr. 10, I; 1870 July 15, I
    seceded, 1861 Jan. 19, I
Georgia, University of, 1785 Jan. 27, III
Georgia Contract Labor Act, 1942 Jan. 12(2), III
Gerard, Conrad Alexandre, 1778 July, I
Gerard, Mark J., 1977 Dec. 2, IV
Gerard, William W., 1837(4), III
German culture, 1800–1819, III; 1814(3), III
Germany:
    attacked Soviet Union, 1941, I
    boycott of products, 1933 Oct. 13, III
    Dawes Plan, 1924, III
    first post-World War I ambassador to U.S., 1922 May 13, I
    first U.S. civilian commissioner, 1949 May 18, I
    Kaiser Wilhelm abdicated, 1918 Nov. 9, I
    nonaggression pact with Soviets, 1939 Aug. 24, I
    Rhineland reoccupied, 1936, I
    Samoan controversy, 1889, I

Germany (*cont.*)
    Samoan treaty, 1890 Feb. 4, I
    Turnverein societies, 1850(6), IV
    U.S. on Nazi anti-Jewish programs, 1938 Nov. 14–18, I
    U.S. sabotage (N.J.), 1916 July 30, I
Germany, East:
    U.S. established diplomatic relations, 1974 Sept. 4, I
Germany, West:
    NATO admittance, 1954, I
Germ warfare *see* Chemical and biological warfare
Gernreich, Rudi, 1985, IV
Geronimo (Apache Indian), 1886 Sept. 4, I
Gerry, Elbridge, 1810(2), I; 1812(3), IV; 1812 Dec. 2, I; 1813 Mar. 4, I; 1875(3), III
Gerrymandering, 1812(3), IV
Gershwin, George, 1924 Feb. 12, II; 1928(4), II; 1931, II; 1935 Oct. 10, II; 1992 June 1, II
Gershwin, Ira, 1983, II; 1992 June 1, II
Gerulaitis, Vitas, 1975 July 4–5, IV
Getty, J. Paul, 1976, III
Getty, J. Paul, Museum of Art (Malibu, Calif.), 1977 Nov. 22, II; 1982 Mar. 1, II; 1983 Sept. 20, II; 1987 Nov. 11, II
Getty Oil Co., 1984 Jan. 8, III; 1987 Dec. 19, III
Gettysburg, Battle of (Pa.), 1863 July 1–3, I; 1913 June 30, IV
Gettysburg Address (Lincoln), 1863 Nov. 19, II
Gettysburg College (Pa.), 1832 Apr. 7, III
Getz, Stan, 1965 Sept. 13, II; 1991, II
Ghent, Treaty of, 1814, I; 1815 Feb. 11, I
Ghezzi, Vic, 1941 July 13, IV
Giamatti, A. Bartlett, 1988 Sept. 8, IV; 1989 Aug. 24, IV; 1989 Sept. 13, IV
Giauque, William F., 1949 Nov. 3, III
Giaver, Ivar, 1973 Oct. 23, III
Gibbons, Euell, 1975, III
Gibbons, Harold J., 1958 Sept. 2–3, III
Gibbons v. Ogden, 1824 Mar. 2, I
Gibbs, James Ethan Allen, 1857 June 2, III
Gibbs, Josiah Willard, 1876, III
GI Bill *see* Servicemen's Readjustment Act
Gibson, Althea, 1956 July 7, IV; 1957 July 6, IV; 1957 Sept. 8, IV; 1958, IV; 1958 July 5, IV; 1958 Sept. 7, IV
Gibson, Charles Dana, 1895, IV; 1944, II
Gibson, William, 1958 Jan. 16, II; 1959 Oct. 19, II
Giddings, Joshua, R., 1841 Oct. 27, I
Gideons International, 1899, III
Gielgud, John, 1982 Mar. 29, II
Gilbert, Humphrey (Sir), 1583, III
Gilbert, Walter, 1980 Oct. 14(1), III
Gilbert, William S., 1879 June 16, II
Gilbert, Willie, 1961 Oct. 14, II
Gilberto, Astrud, 1965 Sept. 13, II
Gilberto, João, 1965 Sept. 13, II
Gilbreth, Lillian, 1972, III
Gilchrist, Ellen, 1984 Nov. 16, II
Gilded Age, 1872, IV; 1880, II; 1884, IV; 1897, IV
Gilder, Richard Watson, 1881, II
Giles, Charles, 1835(4), IV

Gillette, William, 1881 June 1, II; 1886, II; 1899(3), II
Gillhaus, August, 1908 July 4, I; 1908 Nov. 3, I; 1920 May 5–10, I
Gilly, Paul E., 1971 June 23, I; 1972 Mar. 1(2), III
Gilmore, Gary, 1977 Jan. 17, IV; 1979(1), II
Gilroy, Frank D., 1965 May 3, II; 1965 June 13, II; 1976 Apr. 2, II
Ginsberg, Allen, 1961(1), II; 1967 Dec. 5, I; 1974 Apr. 18, II
Ginsburg, Douglas H., 1987 Oct. 23, I
Ginzburg, Ralph, 1966 Mar. 21, II; 1972 Feb. 17, II
Girard, Stephen, 1823, III; 1831 Dec. 26, II
Girard College (Phila., Pa.), 1848 Jan. 3, III
Giraudoux, Jean, 1955 Oct. 3, II
Girl Guides:
    formed, 1912 Mar. 12, IV
Gish, Dorothy, 1968, II
Gist, Christopher, 1750, I; 1753 Oct. 31, I
Gitlow, Benjamin, 1924 June 19, I; 1924 July 10, I; 1928 May 27, I
Giurgola, Ronaldo, 1981 Dec. 5, II
Gladden, Washington, 1889, III; 1891(6), III
Glaser, Donald A., 1960 Nov. 3, III
Glasgow, Ellen, 1904(1), II; 1906(1), II; 1911(1), II; 1913(1), II; 1916(1), II; 1942 May 4, II
Glashow, Sheldon L., 1979 Oct. 16(2), III
Glass:
    Boston Crown Glass Co. incorporated, 1809(4), III
    first cheap, standardized sets, 1825(4), IV
    first midwest works (Pittsburgh, Pa.), 1797(2), III
    first plate, 1850(4), III
    first Polaroid, 1932(1), III
    house (Mass.), 1850(4), III
    Jamestown colony (Va.), 1607, III
    La Farge's stained windows, 1870, II
    mechanical pressing of, 1825(2), III
    New Amsterdam, 1654(1), III
    Ohio, 1815(1), IV
    Stiegel (Pa.), 1769(1), III
    Wistar's South Jersey, 1739, III
Glass, Charles, 1987 Jan. 24, I
Glass, Henry, 1898 June 21, I
Glass, Philip, 1992, II
Glassboro State College (N.J.), 1992 July 6, III
Glasser, Herbert, 1944 Oct. 26, III
Glazier, William S., 1984 May 8, II
Gleason, Jackie, 1987, II
Gleason, Joanna, 1988 June 5, II
Gleick, James, 1988(1), II
Glenn, John H., Jr.:
    Earth orbit, 1962 Feb. 20, III
    transcontinental speed record, 1957 July 16, I
Gless, Sharon, 1986 Sept. 21, II; 1987 Sept. 20, II
Glickman, Will, 1955 Jan. 27, II
Glidden, Carlos, 1867(9), III; 1868 June 23, III
Glidden, Joseph F., 1874, III

Gliders, 1883(3), III
Global warming, 1988, III
    international treaty, 1992 June 12, I
Glomar Explorer, 1975 Mar. 18, I
Glorious Revolution, 1680–1689, I;
    1689(2), I
Gluck, Louise, 1986 Feb. 17, II
Glyn, Elinor, 1908(2), II
Goalby, Bob, 1968 Apr. 14, IV
Goddard, John, 1780–1784, IV
Goddard, Paulette, 1990, II
Godden, Rumer, 1969(1), II
Godey, John, 1973(1), II
Godey's Lady's Book (publication), 1828,
    II; 1852(1), IV
Godin, Tawney Elaine, 1975 Sept. 6, IV
Godkin, Edwin Lawrence, 1865(11), II
God's Protecting Providence (Dickinson),
    1699(1), II
Godunov, Alexander, 1979 Aug. 23, II
Goethals, George W., 1914 Jan. 27, I
Goethe, Johann Wolfgang von, 1774(2), II
Gold and gold rush (*see also* Bimetallism):
    Black Friday panic, 1869 Sept. 24, III
    counterfeit brick swindle, 1880(2), IV
    cyanide extraction process, 1890(6), III
    discovered in Calif., 1848 Jan. 24, I;
    1848 Jan. 24, IV
    federal purchase of, 1895 Feb. 8, I
    first major Alaska strike, 1880(6), III
    Klondike, 1897 July 14, I
    measures to offset U.S. losses, 1962
    Sept. 21, III
    Ore. discovery, 1850 July 25, IV
    overland statistics, 1850 July 8, I
    Pike's Peak (Colo.), 1858, IV
    price system, 1968 Mar. 17, III
    private possession ban lifted, 1974
    Dec. 31, III
    production doubled, 1890(6), III
    reserve, 1894 Jan. 17, I
    sailors deserted ships for, 1850 July,
    IV
    scope of rush, 1849, I
    second rush (Klondike R.), 1896 Aug.
    12, III
    total value mined to date, 1828(1), III
Goldberg, Arthur, 1990, I
Goldberg, Rube (Reuben Lucius), 1970, II
Goldberg, Whoopie, 1991 Mar. 25, II
Goldberger, Joseph, 1915(2), III
Goldblum, Stanley, 1975 Mar. 18, III
Golden Gate Bridge (San Francisco, Calif.),
    1937 May 27, III
Goldfine, Bernard, 1958 June 17, I; 1958
    Sept. 22(2), I
Goldin, Harrison, 1977 Aug. 26, I
Goldman, James, 1971 Apr. 4, II
Goldsmith, Clifford, 1938 Apr. 13, II
Goldsmith, Fred, 1870 Aug. 16, IV
Goldsmith, Raymond W., 1988, III
Goldstein, Joseph L., 1985 Oct. 14, III
Goldwater, Barry:
    presidential candidacy, 1964 July 15,
    I; 1964 Nov. 3, I
    presidential nomination votes, 1960
    July 25, I
Goldwyn, Samuel, 1974, II
Golf:
    Bradley firsts, 1986 June 1, IV

Golf (*cont.*)
    British Open, 1989 July 23(1), IV
    centennial in U.S., 1988, IV
    Disney World Open, 1973 Dec. 1, IV
    early miniature (N.Y.C.), 1652, IV
    first LPGA Tournament, 1955 July 17,
    IV
    first pro to win $2,000,000, 1973 Dec.
    1, IV
    first reference (N.Y.S.), 1657(1), IV
    first Senior pro top money winner,
    1990, IV
    first simultaneous winner on PGA
    regular and Senior tour, 1992 Sept.
    20(1), IV
    first true club (Pa.), 1887(3), IV
    first U.S. Open (Newport, R.I.), 1895
    Oct. 4, IV
    first Women's Open, 1946 Sept. 1, IV
    Jones's retirement, 1930, IV
    leading money winners, 1962, IV;
    1988 Aug. 20, IV; 1990, IV
    leading women money winners, 1990,
    IV
    Lema plane crash, 1966, IV
    LPGA Hall of Fame, 1992 Jan. 18, IV
    LPGA Tournament, 1956 June 24, IV;
    1957 June 10, IV; 1958 June 8, IV;
    1959 July 6, IV; 1960 July 4, IV;
    1961 Mar. 12, IV; 1962 Oct. 7, IV;
    1963 Oct. 13, IV; 1964 Oct. 4, IV;
    1965 Sept. 26, IV; 1966 Sept. 25, IV;
    1967 July 9, IV; 1968 June 24, IV;
    1969 July 27, IV; 1970 June 15, IV;
    1971 June 13, IV; 1972 June 11, IV;
    1973 June 10, IV; 1974 June 23, IV;
    1975 June 1, IV; 1976 May 30(2),
    IV; 1977 June 12, IV; 1978 June 11,
    IV; 1979 June 10, IV; 1980 June 8,
    IV; 1981 June 14, IV; 1982 June 13,
    IV; 1983 June 12, IV; 1984 June 3,
    IV; 1985 June 2, IV; 1986 June 1,
    IV; 1987 May 24, IV; 1988 Aug. 28,
    IV; 1989 May 21, IV; 1991 June 30,
    IV; 1992 May 17, IV
    Masters Tournament, 1930, IV; 1934
    Mar. 25, IV; 1935 Apr. 8, IV; 1936
    Apr. 6, IV; 1937 Apr. 4, IV; 1938
    Apr. 4, IV; 1939 Apr. 2, IV; 1940
    Apr. 7, IV; 1941 Apr. 6, IV; 1942
    Apr. 12, IV; 1946 Apr. 7, IV; 1947
    Apr. 6, IV; 1948 Apr. 11, IV; 1949
    Apr. 10, IV; 1950 Apr. 9, IV; 1951
    Apr. 7, IV; 1952 Apr. 6, IV; 1953
    Apr. 12, IV; 1954 Apr. 12, IV; 1955
    Apr. 10, IV; 1956 Apr. 8, IV; 1957
    Apr. 7, IV; 1958 Apr. 16, IV; 1959
    Apr. 5, IV; 1960 Apr. 10, IV; 1961
    Apr. 10, IV; 1962 Apr. 9, IV; 1963
    Apr. 7, IV; 1964 Apr. 12, IV; 1965
    Apr. 11, IV; 1966 Apr. 11, IV; 1967
    Apr. 9, IV; 1968 Apr. 14, IV; 1969
    Apr. 13, IV; 1970 Apr. 13, IV; 1971
    Apr. 11, IV; 1972 Apr. 9, IV; 1973
    Apr. 9, IV; 1974 Apr. 14, IV; 1975
    Apr. 13, IV; 1976 Apr. 11, IV; 1977
    Apr. 10, IV; 1978 Apr. 9, IV; 1979
    Apr. 15, IV; 1980 Apr. 13, IV; 1981
    Apr. 12, IV; 1982 Apr. 11, IV; 1983
    Apr. 11, IV; 1984 Apr. 15, IV; 1985

Golf (*cont.*)
    Apr. 14, IV; 1986 Apr. 13, IV; 1987
    Apr. 12, IV; 1988 Apr. 10, IV; 1989
    Apr. 9, IV; 1990 Apr. 8, IV; 1991
    Apr. 14, IV; 1992 Apr. 12, IV
    Nicklaus won four major
    championships, 1966 July 9, IV
    oldest Masters winner, 1986 Apr. 13,
    IV
    oldest U.S. Open winner, 1986 June
    15, IV
    PGA and American Professional
    Golfers split, 1968, IV
    PGA formed, 1916 Jan. 17, IV
    PGA tournament, 1919 Sept. 20, IV;
    1920 Aug. 21, IV; 1921 Sept. 28, IV;
    1922 June 14, IV; 1923 Sept. 29, IV;
    1924 May 12(1), IV; 1925 Sept. 26,
    IV; 1926 Sept. 25, IV; 1927 Nov. 5,
    IV; 1928 Oct. 6, IV; 1929 Dec. 7,
    IV; 1930 Sept. 13, IV; 1931 Sept. 19,
    IV; 1932 Sept. 4, IV; 1933 Aug. 13,
    IV; 1934 July 29, IV; 1935 Oct. 23,
    IV; 1936 Nov. 22, IV; 1937 May 30,
    IV; 1938 July 16, IV; 1939 July 17,
    IV; 1940 Sept. 2, IV; 1941 July 13,
    IV; 1942 May 31, IV; 1944 Aug. 20,
    IV; 1945 July 15, IV; 1946 Aug. 25,
    IV; 1947 June 24, IV; 1948 May 25,
    IV; 1949 May 31, IV; 1950 June 27,
    IV; 1951 July 3, IV; 1952 June 25,
    IV; 1953 July 7, IV; 1954 July 27,
    IV; 1955 July 26, IV; 1956 July 25,
    IV; 1957 July 21, IV; 1958 July 20,
    IV; 1959 Aug. 2, IV; 1960 July 24,
    IV; 1961 July 30, IV; 1962 July 22,
    IV; 1963 July 21, IV; 1964 July 19,
    IV; 1965 Aug. 15, IV; 1966 July 24,
    IV; 1967 July 24(1), IV; 1968 July
    21, IV; 1969 Aug. 17, IV; 1970 Aug.
    16, IV; 1971 Feb. 28, IV; 1972 Aug.
    6, IV; 1973 Aug. 12, IV; 1974 Aug.
    11, IV; 1975 Aug. 10(2), IV; 1976
    Aug. 16, IV; 1977 Aug. 14, IV; 1978
    Aug. 6, IV; 1979 Aug. 6, IV; 1980
    Aug. 10, IV; 1981 Aug. 9(2), IV;
    1982 Aug. 8, IV; 1983 Aug. 7, IV;
    1984 Aug. 19, IV; 1985 Aug. 11, IV;
    1986 Aug. 11, IV; 1987 Aug. 9, IV;
    1988 Aug. 14, IV; 1989 Aug. 13, IV;
    1990 Aug. 11, IV; 1991 Aug. 11, IV;
    1992 Aug. 16, IV
    popularity and social status, 1888, IV;
    1928, IV
    records, 1967 June 18, IV; 1972 June
    18, IV; 1976 Apr. 11, IV
    richest tournament prize to date,
    1987 Nov. 1, IV
    Rosburg, Bob, 1959 Aug. 2, IV
    top money winners, 1941, IV; 1942,
    IV; 1944, IV; 1945, IV; 1946, IV;
    1947, IV; 1948, IV; 1949, IV; 1950,
    IV; 1951, IV; 1953, IV; 1954, IV;
    1955, IV; 1956, IV; 1957, IV; 1958,
    IV; 1959, IV; 1961, IV; 1962, IV;
    1963, IV; 1964, IV; 1965, IV; 1966,
    IV; 1967, IV; 1968, IV; 1969, IV;
    1970, IV; 1971, IV; 1972, IV; 1973,
    IV; 1974, IV; 1975, IV; 1976, IV;
    1977, IV; 1978, IV; 1979, IV; 1980,

Golf (*cont.*)
IV; 1981, IV; 1982, IV; 1983, IV; 1984, IV; 1985, IV; 1986, IV; 1987 Nov. 1, IV; 1989, IV; 1990, IV; 1991, IV; 1992 Jan. 18, IV

U.S. Golf Assn. formed, 1894, IV

U.S. Open, 1896 July 18, IV; 1897 Sept. 17, IV; 1898 June 18, IV; 1899 Sept. 15, IV; 1900 Oct. 5, IV; 1901 June 15, IV; 1902 Oct. 11, IV; 1903 June 27, IV; 1904 July 9, IV; 1905 Sept. 22, IV; 1906 June 29, IV; 1907 June 21, IV; 1908 Aug. 28, IV; 1909 June 25, IV; 1910 June 18, IV; 1911 June 24, IV; 1912 Aug. 2, IV; 1913 Sept. 19, IV; 1914 Aug. 21, IV; 1915 June 18, IV; 1916 June 30, IV; 1919 June 11(1), IV; 1920 Aug. 13, IV; 1921 July 22, IV; 1922 July 15, IV; 1923 July 15, IV; 1924 June 6, IV; 1925 June 5, IV; 1926 July 10, IV; 1927 June 16, IV; 1928 June 24, IV; 1929 June 30, IV; 1930 July 12, IV; 1931 July 6, IV; 1932 June 25, IV; 1933 June 10(1), IV; 1934 June 9(2), IV; 1935 June 8(2), IV; 1936 June 6(2), IV; 1937 June 12, IV; 1938 June 11, IV; 1939 June 12, IV; 1940 June 9, IV; 1941 June 7(1), IV; 1946 June 16, IV; 1947 June 15, IV; 1948 June 12(2), IV; 1949 June 11(1), IV; 1950 June 10(2), IV; 1951 June 16(1), IV; 1952 June 14, IV; 1953 June 13(2), IV; 1954 June 19, IV; 1955 June 19, IV; 1956 June 16(2), IV; 1957 June 15(2), IV; 1958 June 14, IV; 1959 June 13(2), IV; 1960 June 18, IV; 1961 June 17, IV; 1962 June 17, IV; 1963 June 23, IV; 1964 June 20, IV; 1965 June 21, IV; 1966 June 20, IV; 1967 June 18, IV; 1968 June 16, IV; 1969 June 15, IV; 1970 June 21, IV; 1971 June 21, IV; 1972 June 18, IV; 1973 June 17, IV; 1974 June 16, IV; 1975 June 23, IV; 1976 June 20, IV; 1977 June 19, IV; 1978 June 18, IV; 1979 June 17, IV; 1980 June 15, IV; 1981 June 21, IV; 1982 June 20, IV; 1983 June 20, IV; 1984 June 18, IV; 1985 June 16, IV; 1986 June 15, IV; 1987 June 21, IV; 1988 June 20, IV; 1989 June 18, IV; 1990 July 15, IV; 1991 June 17, IV; 1992 June 21, IV

U.S. Women's Open, 1947 June 29, IV; 1948 Aug. 15, IV; 1949 Sept. 25, IV; 1950 Mar. 19, IV; 1951 Sept. 16, IV; 1952 June 29, IV; 1953 June 28, IV; 1954 July 3(1), IV; 1955 July 2, IV; 1957 June 29, IV; 1958 July 13, IV; 1960 July 23, IV; 1961 July 1, IV; 1962 June 30, IV; 1963 July 20, IV; 1964 July 12, IV; 1965 July 4, IV; 1966 July 3, IV; 1967 July 2, IV; 1968 July 7, IV; 1969 June 29, IV; 1970 July 5, IV; 1971 June 27, IV; 1972 July 2(2), IV; 1973 July 22, IV; 1974 July 21, IV; 1975 July 20, IV; 1976 July 11, IV; 1977 July 24, IV; 1978 July 23, IV; 1979 July 15, IV;

Golf (*cont.*)
1980 July 13, IV; 1982 July 25, IV; 1983 July 31(2), IV; 1984 July 15(1), IV; 1985 July 14(2), IV; 1986 June 1, IV; 1986 July 14, IV; 1987 July 28, IV; 1988 July 24, IV; 1989 July 16, IV; 1990 July 15, IV; 1991 July 14, IV; 1992 July 27, IV

Walker Cup, 1922 Aug. 28, IV

Watson's championships, 1982, IV

Gompers, Samuel, 1886, III; 1894(2), III; 1921 June 25, III; 1924 Dec. 13, III

Gone With the Wind (book and film), 1936(1), II; 1939, II
sequel, 1988 Apr. 25, II; 1991(1), II

Gonzales, Pancho, 1948 Sept. 19, IV; 1949 Sept. 5, IV

Gonzales, Richard, 1949 July 1–2, IV

Gonzalez, Julio, 1990 Mar. 25, IV

Goodale, Samuel D., 1863 Dec. 1, III

Goode, W. Wilson, 1983 Nov. 8, I

Goodell, Charles, 1969, I

Gooden, Dwight, 1985 Aug. 25, IV

Goodman, Andrew, 1964 Aug. 4, I; 1964 Dec. 4, I; 1967 Oct. 20, I

Goodman, Benny, 1950 Nov. 16, II; 1986, II

Goodman, Johnny, 1933 June 10(1), IV

Goodman, Paul, 1972, III

Goodrich, Frances, 1956 May 7, II

Goodyear, Charles, 1839(2), III; 1844, III

Goodyear Tire and Rubber Co.:
balloon disaster, 1919 July 21, III

Gorbachev, Mikhail S., 1985 Nov. 20–21, I; 1986, I
arms control, 1991 July 31, I; 1991 Sept. 27, I
arms control treaty, 1987 Dec. 8, I
summit conference (Malta), 1989 Dec. 3, I
summit conference (Moscow), 1988 May 29–June 1, I
summit conference (Reykjavik), 1986 Oct. 11–12, I
summit conference (Wash., D.C.), 1990 June 1, I

Gordon, Daisy, 1912 Mar. 12, IV

Gordon, Dexter, 1990, II

Gordon, Mary, 1981(1), II

Gordon, Richard F., Jr., 1966 Sept. 12(1), III; 1969 Nov. 14, III

Gordon, Ruth, 1969 Apr. 14, II; 1985, II

Gore, Al (Albert, Jr.):
books by, 1992(1), II
elected vice president, 1992 Nov. 3, I
vice-presidential nomination, 1992 July 15–16, I

Goren, Charles H., 1991, IV

Gore Place (Waltham, Mass., house), 1805(4), II

Gorgas, William C., 1904(1), III; 1914(1), III

Gorillas, 1956 Dec. 22, III

Gorman, Arthur P., 1865(2), IV

Gorman, Cliff, 1972 Apr. 23(2), II

Gorman, Margaret, 1921 Sept. 8, IV

Gorme, Eydie, 1961 Apr. 12, II; 1967 Mar. 2, II

Gosnold, Bartholomew, 1602 May 15, I

Goss, Joe, 1876 Sept. 7, IV

Gossett, Louis, Jr., 1983 Apr. 11, II

Gostelow, Jonathan, 1780–1784, IV

Gotham Book Mart (N.Y.C.), 1975 Apr. 24, II

Gottfried, Brian, 1976 July 2–3, IV

Gotti, John, 1992 June 23, IV

Gottlieb, Adolph, 1974, II

Gottschalk, Louis Moreau, 1850(1), II; 1851(6), II; 1853 Feb. 11, II

Gough, John Bartholomew, 1845(2), IV; 1846, IV

Gouging, 1800(5), IV

Gould, Hannah, 1832(5), II

Gould, Jay, 1836 May 27, III; 1869 Sept. 24, III

Gould, Stephen Jay, 1982 Jan. 28, II

Gould, Thomas, 1869(4), II

Government agencies *see* specific names, inverted; under subject headings, e.g., World War II

Government and politics (*see also* Colonial governors; Elections; Presidential elections; States' rights; political party names):
Catholics in public office issue, 1960 May 20(2), III
deaths, 1989, I; 1990, I; 1991, I
drug testing upheld, 1989 Mar. 21, I
European interest in U.S. system, 1835, III
Federalist, The, 1785–1789, II
first black Cabinet member, 1966 Jan. 17(1), I
first democratic theory, 1644, II
first Hispanic Cabinet member, 1988 Sept. 20, III
first independent local, 1772, I
first legislative assembly (Va.), 1619 July 30, I
first woman in Cabinet, 1933 Mar. 4(2), I
Hoover Commission on Executive Branch, 1949 Feb. 7, I
independent prosecutors upheld, 1988 June 29, I
internal improvements, 1830, I
legislature apportionment, 1964 June 15, I
Montesquieu influence, 1745, II
muckrakers on, 1904, II
N.Y. machine, 1820(2), I
Paine's views, 1791 Mar.(1), II; 1794(6), II
spoils system, 1829(1), I; 1832 Jan. 21, IV; 1883, I
twelfth Cabinet department created, 1966 Oct. 15, I

Government bonds:
authorized by Congress, 1790 Aug. 4, III
first U.S. war bonds issued, 1812 Mar. 14, I
issued to replenish gold reserve, 1894 Jan. 17, I
Liberty Loan Act, 1917 Apr. 24, I
Liberty Loan drive ended, 1918 Oct. 19, III
Liberty Loan drives, 1917 Oct. 1, III; 1918 Apr. 6, III

Government bonds (*cont.*)
Treasury notes issued, 1812 June 30, III
World War II defense, 1941 May 1, III
Government employees:
Civil Service Commission established, 1883, I
eight-hour day, 1868 June 25(1), I
first civil service commission, 1871 Mar. 4, I
first homosexual security clearance, 1975 Feb. 1, IV
House Un-American Activities Committee investigation of, 1948, I
pay raise, 1955 June 28, I
protested Nixon school desegregation policies, 1969 Aug. 27, III
salaries increased, 1907 Feb. 26, I
security risks discharged, 1955 Jan. 3, I
Government Printing Office, 1860 June 23, III
Government spending *see* Budget, U.S.; Debt, U.S.; areas of spending
Governors (*see also* Colonial governors; state names):
first black elected (Va.), 1989 Nov. 8, I
first woman, 1925 Jan. 5, I
first woman elected (Conn.), 1974 Nov. 5, I
first woman elected (Ky.), 1983 Nov. 8, I
Mecham impeached (Ariz.), 1988 Apr. 4, I
Republican gains, 1968 Nov. 5, I
Governor's Palace (Williamsburg, Va.), 1706(1), II; 1720, IV
Grégoire, Henri, 1809 Feb. 25, III
Grable, Betty, 1943, II; 1944, II; 1973, II
Grace Church (N.Y.C.), 1846(4), II
Gracie Mansion (N.Y.C.), 1799(2), II
Grady, Wayne, 1990 Aug. 11, IV
Graf, Steffi, 1987 Sept. 12, IV; 1988 Sept. 10–11, IV; 1989 Sept. 9–10, IV
Grafton, Sue, 1992(1), II
Graham, Billy, 1957 Sept. 1, III
Graham, David, 1979 Aug. 6, IV; 1981 June 21, IV
Graham, Lou, 1975 June 23, IV
Graham, Martha, 1940(4), II; 1943(2), II; 1944 Oct. 30, II; 1973 May 1, II; 1975 June 19, II; 1976 July 19–31, II; 1991, II
Graham, Sylvester, 1830, IV
Graham, William A., 1852 June 16–21, I
Grahame, Gloria, 1953 Mar. 19(1), II
Grain:
crop failure, 1835(1), III
elevator explosions (La., Tex.), 1977 Dec. 22, I
federal programs, 1964 Apr. 11, III
government production and price control, 1963, III
short-weighing shipments, 1975 July 21, III
Soviet embargo lifted, 1981 Apr. 24(1), I
Soviet purchases increased, 1983 July 28, I
Soviet sale halted, 1980 Jan. 4, I

Grain (*cont.*)
Soviet wheat deal, 1963 Oct. 9, I; 1972, III; 1972 July 8, III; 1979 Oct. 3, III
wheat loading boycott ended, 1964 Feb. 25, III
wheat price high, 1920(7), III
wheat price rise, 1917 Apr. 4, III
wheat prices at new low, 1932(3), III
wheat's importance as cash crop, 1839(3), III
Grambling State University, 1985 Oct. 5, IV
Gramercy Park (N.Y.C.), 1831(1), II
Gramm-Rudman Act, 1986 July 7, I
Grammy Awards, 1959 May 4(2), II; 1959 Nov. 29, II; 1961 Apr. 12, II; 1962 May 29, II; 1963 May 15, II; 1964 May 12, II; 1965 Sept. 13, II; 1966 Mar. 15(2), II; 1967 Mar. 2, II; 1968 Feb. 29, II; 1969 Mar. 12, II; 1970 Mar. 11, II; 1971 Mar. 16, II; 1972 Mar. 14, II; 1973 Mar. 3, II; 1974 Mar. 2, II; 1975 Mar. 1(1), II; 1976 Feb. 28, II; 1977 Feb. 19, II; 1978 Feb. 23, II; 1979 Feb. 16, II; 1980 Feb. 27, II; 1981 Feb. 25, II; 1982 Feb. 24, II; 1983 Feb. 23, II; 1984 Feb. 28, II; 1985 Feb. 26, II; 1986 Feb. 25, II; 1987 Feb. 24, II; 1988 Mar. 2, II; 1989 Feb. 22, II; 1990 Feb. 21, II; 1991 Feb. 20, II; 1992 Feb. 26, II
Grandcamp (ship), 1947 Apr. 16–18, I
Grand Canyon:
airliner collision over, 1956 June 30, I
airplane-helicopter collision over, 1986 June 18, I
Grand Central Station (N.Y.C.), 1871(5), II; 1913 Feb. 2, II
Grand Coulee Dam (Wash.), 1941 Mar. 22, III; 1950 May 11, III
Grandma Moses (A. M. Robertson), 1953, II; 1961, II
Grange, Red, 1924, IV; 1991, IV
Grange movement, 1867, III
Granger, Francis, 1835 Dec. 16, I
Granite, 1749, II; 1846(3), II
Grant, Cary, 1986, II
Grant, Lee, 1971 May 9, II; 1976 Mar. 29, II
Grant, Micki, 1976 Dec. 22, II
Grant, Ulysses S.:
born, 1822 Apr. 27, I
died, 1885 July 23, I
Dominican Republic land speculation, 1870, I
elected president, 1868 Nov. 3, I
funeral, 1885 July 23, I
inaugurated president, 1869 Mar. 4, I; 1873 Mar. 4, I
Personal Memoirs, 1885(1), II
Petersburg (Va.) siege, 1864 June 15–18, I
presidency, 1869, I
prisoners of war, 1864 Apr. 17, I
reelected president, 1872 Nov. 5, I
renominated for presidency, 1872 June 5–6, I
Republican presidential nomination, 1868 May 20–21, I
Shiloh battle (Tenn.), 1862 Apr. 6–7, I

Grant, Ulysses S. (*cont.*)
Spotsylvania campaign (Va.), 1864 May 7–20, I; 1864 May 11, IV
Supreme C. packing, 1871 May 1, III
third-term bid, 1875 Dec. 15, I; 1876, I; 1880 June 5, IV
Union general in chief, 1864 Mar. 10, I
Vicksburg (Miss.) surrendered to, 1863 July 4, I
Whiskey Ring scandal, 1875, I
Wilderness battle (Va.), 1864 May 5–6, I
Workingmen's Party presidential nomination, 1872 May 23, I
Granville, Joe, 1981 Jan. 7, III
Grapes:
Teamsters' contract with growers (Calif.), 1973 Apr. 15, III
workers' strike (Calif.), 1973 Apr. 15, III
workers' unionization, 1966 Apr. 6, III
Grasso, Ella, 1974 Nov. 5, I
Grau, Shirley Ann, 1965 May 3, II
Graupner, Gottlieb, 1810, II
Graves, John T., 1908 July 27, I
Graves, Michael, 1988, II
Graves, Morris, 1941(5), II
Gray, Asa, 1860(2), III
Gray, Hannah H., 1978 Oct. 6, III
Gray, Harold, 1968, II
Gray, L. Patrick, 1973 Apr. 27, I
Gray, Robert, 1609(2), II
Gray, Simon, 1977 Feb. 2, II
Gray Panthers, 1972 May 18, IV
Grayson, William, 1854(5), II
Graziano, Rocky, 1945, IV; 1990, IV
Great Atlantic and Pacific Tea Co., 1870(2), III
Great Awakening, 1730–1734, III; 1737, II; 1741(2), III; 1742(1), II; 1745–1749, III; 1750(2), III
Great Britain (*see also* Colonies and settlements; Explorers and exploration; Trade; war names):
backed Cleveland, 1888, I
blockade of European coast, 1806 May 16, I
boundary dispute with Venezuela, 1895, I
Buckingham's tour and impressions of U.S., 1841, IV
Emerson's admiration of, 1856(8), II
first prime minister to speak before U.S. Congress, 1929 Oct. 7(1), I
first sovereigns to visit U.S., 1939 June 8, I
first U.S. ambassador to, 1893 Apr. 3, I
Jay Treaty, 1794 Nov. 19, I
jetliner bombing (Lockerbie, Scotland), 1991 Nov. 27, I
London Stock Exchange closed, 1914 July 31, III
Martineau on America, 1837(2), II
neutrality treaty with U.S., 1850 Apr. 19, I
Newfoundland Fisheries dispute settled, 1910 Sept. 7, I
Panama Canal treaty with U.S., 1901 Nov. 18, I

Great Britain (*cont.*)
    Prince of Wales in U.S., 1860 Oct. 4,
        IV
    Samoan controversy, 1889, I
    Samoan treaty, 1890 Feb. 4, I
    tension with U.S., 1895, I
    Treaty of Washington, 1871 May 8, I;
        1877 Nov. 23, I
    war declared, 1939 Sept. 3(1), I
    Webster-Ashburton Treaty, 1842, I
Great Depression (*see also* Banking; Stocks
    and bonds; Unemployment):
    Black Tuesday, 1929, I
    breaks in, 1934, III
    Hard Times: Oral History (Terkel),
        1970(1), II
    Hoover programs, 1932, I
    impact on education, 1933, III
    impact on sports, 1933, IV
    impact on the arts, 1932, II; 1933, II;
        1934, II
    low point, 1933, I
    Reconstruction Finance Corporation
        formed, 1932 Jan. 22, I
    recovery, 1936, III
    songs, 1932(3), II
    statistics, 1932(1), I
    U.S. economic nationalism, 1930, I
Great Seal of the United States, 1782 June
    20, I
Great White Fleet, 1907, I; 1909 Feb. 21,
    I
Greece:
    U.S. aid, 1948 Apr. 3, I
    U.S. military bases agreement, 1990
        July 8, I
Greek Orthodox Church, 1991 June 6, III
Greek-Turkish Aid Act, 1947 May 22, I
Greeley, Dana McLean, 1986, III
Greeley, Horace:
    on advertising, 1851(2), IV
    Civil War peace bid, 1864 July 5, I
    defeated for presidency, 1872 Nov. 5,
        I
    diet, 1830, IV
    founded N.Y. *Tribune*, 1841(4), IV;
        1841 Apr. 10, II
    "Go West, young man . . . ", 1851(4),
        IV
    presidential candidacy, 1872, I; 1872
        May 1, I; 1872 July 9, I
Green, Adolph, 1953 Feb. 25, II; 1968
    Apr. 21, II; 1970 Mar. 30, II; 1974 Jan.
    27(1), II; 1991 June 2, II
Green, Hubert, 1977 June 19, IV; 1985
    Aug. 11, IV
Green, Paul, 1936 Nov. 19, II
Green, William, 1925(3), III; 1935, III;
    1938 Oct. 13, III; 1952 Nov. 25, III
Greenback-Labor Party, 1878 Feb. 22, I;
    1880 June 9, I
Greenback Party, 1874, I; 1876 May 18, I;
    1884 May 28, I
Greenbacks *see* Currency
Greene, Francis V., 1898 July 31, I
Greenhouse effect *see* Global warming
Green Mountain Boys:
    Thompson's novel about, 1839(4), II
Greenough, Horatio, 1829, II; 1833(1), II

Greensboro College (N.C.), 1838 Dec. 28,
    III
Greensboro (N.C.):
    Ku Klux Klan shootout, 1979 Nov. 3, I
Greenspan, Alan, 1987 June 2, III
Greenwood, Isaac, 1735–1739, III
Gregory, Cynthia, 1974 Sept. 30, II
Gregory, Samuel, 1848 Nov. 1, III
Grenada, 1983, I; 1983 Oct. 25, I
Gretzky, Wayne, 1988 Aug. 9, IV; 1989
    Oct. 15, IV
Grey, Joel, 1973 Mar. 27, II
Grey, Zane, 1906, II; 1912(1), II
Greyhound racing *see* Dogs
Gridley, Jeremy, 1740–1744, II
Gridley, Richard, 1775 June 16, I
Griffes, Charles T., 1919, II
Griffin, John Howard, 1957 Feb. 25, II
Griffith, Clark, 1894 June 16, IV
Griffith, D. W., 1915 Feb. 8, II; 1916(4), II;
    1922 Jan. 3, II
Griffith, Hugh, 1960 Apr. 4, II
Grimes, Burleigh, 1985, IV
Grimes, Tammy, 1970 Apr. 19, II
Grimké, Angelina, 1839(1), I
Grinnell, Henry, 1850 May 22, I; 1853
    May 31, I
Grinnell College (Iowa), 1846 June 17, III
Grissom, Virgil I., 1961 July 21, III; 1965
    Mar. 23, III; 1967 Jan. 27, III
Griswold, Rufus Wilmot, 1842(4), II
Grocery stores and supermarkets:
    A&P founded, 1870(2), III
Grofé, Ferde, 1932(2), II; 1972, II
Grolier, Inc., 1988 Apr. 3, II
Gromyko, Andrei, 1984 Nov. 22, I
Gronowitz, Antoni, 1978 Apr. 21, II
Gropius, Walter, 1938(5), II; 1969, II
Gross National Product *see* Economics and
    economy
Grosvenor, Gilbert H., 1966, III
Grosvenor, Melville Bell, 1982, II
Grosz, George, 1959 May 2, II
Grove Street houses (N.Y.C.), 1820(2), II
Grucci family, 1983, II
Gruenther, Alfred M., 1983, I
Guadalupe Hidalgo, Treaty of, 1848, I
Guam:
    surrendered to U.S., 1898 June 21, I
    typhoon, 1992 Aug. 28, I
    U.S. acquisition, 1898, I; 1898 Aug. 12,
        I; 1899 Feb. 10, I
Guast, Pierre du, 1603, III; 1604, I
Guatemala:
    U.S. ambassador killed, 1968 Aug. 28,
        I
Guerrière (ship), 1811, I; 1812 Aug. 19, I;
    1812 Aug. 19, IV
Guest, Edgar, 1959, II
Guggenheim, Peggy, 1979, II
Guggenheim International Art Award,
    1960 Oct. 31, II
Guggenheim Memorial Foundation, 1925
    Dec. 6, II; 1961 Apr. 30, II
Guggenheim Museum (N.Y.C.), 1945 July
    9, II; 1959 Oct. 21(2), II; 1963 Mar.-June,
    II
    ten-story addition, 1992 June 28, II
Gugliemi, Louis O., 1941(4), II

Guilford Court House, Battle of (N.C.),
    1781 Mar. 15, I
Guillemin, Roger C. L., 1977 Oct. 13, III
Guinan, "Texas" (Mary Louise Cecilia),
    1909(3), II
Guinness, Alec, 1958 Mar. 26, II; 1964
    May 24, II
Guiteau, Charles J., 1881 July 2, I; 1881
    Nov. 14, I
Guldahl, Ralph, 1937 June 12, IV; 1938
    June 11, IV; 1939 Apr. 2, IV
Gulf of Tonkin incident *see* Tonkin, Gulf
    of
Gulf Oil Corp., 1976, I; 1984 June 15, III
Gulf War, 1991, I; 1991, II; 1991(1), II;
    1991 Jan. 15–Feb. 27, I
    coalition forces, 1990 Aug. 2–Dec. 31,
        I
Gunn, Frederick William, 1861 Aug., IV
Gunpowder:
    first mill (Mass.), 1639 June 6, III
Guns *see* Firearms; Gunpowder
Gunther, John, 1947(1), II; 1970, II
Gurganus, Allan, 1989(1), II
Guthrie, A. B., 1947(1), II; 1950 May 1, II;
    1991, II
Guthrie, Woody, 1967, II
Gutman, Herbert, 1976(1), II
Guyana mass suicide, 1978 Nov. 18, I
Guy Fawkes Day, 1665, IV
Gwenn, Edmund, 1948 Mar. 20, II
Gymnasiums and gymnastics, 1825(3), IV;
    1826(1), IV; 1850(6), IV

Hébert, F. Edward, 1975 Jan. 16, I
Haas, Robert, 1989(1), II
Habib, Philip C., 1992, I
Hachette S.A., 1988 Apr. 3, II
Hacker, Marilyn, 1975 Apr. 16, II
Hackett, Albert, 1956 May 7, II
Hackett, Bobby, 1976, II
Hackman, Gene, 1972 Apr. 9, II
Hagen, Uta, 1951 Mar. 25, II; 1963 Apr.
    25(1), II
Hagen, Walter, 1914 Aug. 21, IV; 1919
    June 11(1), IV; 1923 Sept. 29, IV; 1924
    May 12(1), IV; 1925 Sept. 26, IV; 1926
    Sept. 25, IV; 1927 Nov. 5, IV; 1969, IV
Haggard, Henry Rider, 1887(1), II
Hagge, Marlene Bauer, 1956, IV; 1956
    June 24, IV
Haggerty House (Cohasset, Mass.), 1938(5),
    II
Hague (Neth.) conferences, 1899, I;
    1910(3), III
Haieff, Axel, 1952(3), II
Haig, Alexander M., Jr.:
    Chinese arms sale, 1981 June 16, I
    resigned as state secretary, 1982 June
        25, I
Hair and wigs (*see also* Beards and
    mustaches):
    barber-hairdresser's wages (Phila.,
        Pa.), 1794(4), IV
    barbers' prices, 1860(2), IV
    Italian style for women, 1953, IV
    long-haired men arrested (Conn.),
        1675(2), IV
    men's long, 1965, IV
    periwigs opposed in N.E., 1660(3), IV

Hair and wigs (*cont.*)
  powdering unfashionable, 1794(2), IV
  Sassoon's styles, 1965, IV
  style influence, 1782(3), IV
  tower style, c1770, IV
  women's wigs popular, 1962, IV
Haise, Fred W., Jr., 1970 Apr. 11, III; 1977 Aug. 12, III
Haiti:
  Reagan policies, 1986, I
  U.S. Marines landed, 1915 July 29, I
  U.S. protectorate, 1915 Sept. 16, I
Hakluyt, Richard, 986–1599, II; 986–1599, III; 1584, II; 1609(1), II
Halas, George, 1968 May 27, IV; 1983, IV
Halberstam, David, 1972(1), II
Haldeman, H. R., 1973 Apr. 30, I; 1973 June 25–29, I; 1974 Aug. 5, I; 1975 Feb. 21, I; 1977 May 23, I
Hale, Edward Everett, 1863, II
Hale, George E., 1891(4), III
Hale, John P., 1847 Nov., I; 1852 Aug. 11, I; 1852 Nov. 2, I
Hale, Nathan, 1776 Sept. 22, I; 1813(1), II
Hale, Sarah Josepha, 1828, II; 1855(1), IV
Hale v. Henkel, 1906 Mar. 12, III
Haley, Alex, 1976(1), II; 1977, II; 1977 Mar. 16, II; 1977 Apr. 13(1), II; 1977 Apr. 18, II; 1992, II
Haley, Jack, 1948 Apr. 30, II
Half-Way Covenant (N.E.), 1662 Mar., III
Hall, Asaph, 1877(3), III
Hall, Donald L., 1968, III
Hall, Granville Stanley, 1882(1), III
Hall, Gus, 1959 Dec. 10–14, I; 1962 Mar. 19, I
Hall, John Elihu, 1808(1), III
Hallam, Lewis, 1750–1754, II
Halleck, Charles A., 1986, I
Halleck, Fitz-Greene, 1820, II
Halleck, Henry W.:
  Union Army commander, 1862 July 11, I
Halley's Comet, 1835(5), IV; 1910, III; 1982 Oct. 16, III
Hallinan, Vincent, 1952 July 4–6, I; 1952 Nov. 4, I
Hall of Fame (N.Y.C.), 1900 Mar. 5, III
Halsey, William F., Jr. ("Bull"), 1959, I
Halston, 1990, IV
Hamblen, Stuart, 1951 Nov. 13–15, I; 1952 Nov. 4, I
Hamill, Dorothy, 1974 Feb. 6–9, IV; 1975 Jan. 31–Feb. 2, IV; 1976 Jan. 10–11, IV; 1976 Feb. 4–15, IV; 1976 Mar. 6, IV
Hamilton, Alexander:
  Burr-Jefferson presidential election tie, 1801, I
  Federalist, 1785–1789, II
  Federalist Party, 1789(1), I
  home, The Grange, national monument (N.Y.C.), 1962 Apr. 27, II
  killed in duel, 1804 July 11, I
  manufacturing and tariff views, 1790–1794, III
  secretary of the treasury, 1789 Sept. 2, I
Hamilton, Andrew, 1730(3), II; 1734 Oct., II

Hamilton, Robert, 1944 Aug. 20, IV
Hamilton, Scott, 1981 Feb. 3–8, IV; 1981 Mar. 5, IV; 1982 Jan. 28–31, IV; 1982 Mar. 11–13, IV; 1983 Feb. 3–4, IV; 1983 Mar. 10–11, IV; 1984 Jan. 20–21, IV; 1984 Mar. 23, IV
Hamilton College (N.Y.), 1812 May 26, III
Hamlin, Hannibal, 1860 May 16–18, I; 1860 Nov. 6, I; 1861 Mar. 4(2), I
Hamlin, Talbot F., 1956 May 7, II
Hamlisch, Marvin, 1975 May 21, II; 1976 May 3, II
Hammarskjold, Dag, 1962 Oct. 23, II
Hammer, Armand, 1976 Sept. 29, II; 1980 Dec. 12, II; 1990, III
Hammerstein, Oscar, 1883 Feb. 27, III; 1906(8), II
Hammerstein, Oscar, II, 1927 Dec. 27(1), II; 1943, II; 1943 Mar. 31, II; 1944 May 1, II; 1945 Apr. 19, II; 1949 Apr. 7, II; 1950 Apr. 9, II; 1950 May 1, II; 1951 Mar. 29(1), II; 1958 Dec. 1, II; 1960, II
Hammett, Dashiell, 1929(1), II; 1930(1), II; 1931(1), II; 1934(1), II; 1961, II
Hammond, Bray, 1958 May 5, II
Hammond, George Henry, 1870(8), III
Hammond, Laurens, 1934(4), II
Hampden, Walter, 1918, II
Hampshire, Susan, 1970 June 7, II; 1971 May 9, II
Hampsten, Andy, 1988 June 12, IV
Hampton, Fred, 1969 Dec. 4, I
Hancock, Winfield Scott, 1864 May 12, I; 1880, I; 1880 June 22–24, I
Hand, Learned, 1961, I
Handel and Haydn Society (Boston, Mass.), 1821, II
Handicapped:
  capital punishment upheld for mentally retarded, 1989, I
  civil rights law, 1990 July 26, I; 1992 Jan. 26, I
  deaf-mutes: Gallaudet College (Wash., D.C.) founded, 1864, III
  discrimination ban, 1977 Apr. 28, III
  education requirements, 1977, III
  first free school for deaf, 1817(1), III
  first school for the blind (Boston, Mass.), 1829 Mar. 2, III
  free education for, 1975 Nov. 29, III
  infant life-prolonging treatment, 1986 June 9, III
  Supplementary Security Income (SSI), 1972 Oct. 17, I
Handlin, Oscar, 1952 May 5, II
Hands Across America (event), 1986 May 25, IV
Handy, W.C., 1909, II
Hanford, Benjamin, 1904 May 5, I; 1908 May 10–17, I
Hangings see Capital punishment; Riots and mob violence
Hanlon, Lorraine, 1963 Feb. 9–10, IV
Hanover College (Ind.), 1828 Dec. 30, III
Hansberry, Lorraine H., 1959 Mar. 11, II; 1965, II; 1969 Jan. 2, II; 1973 May 30, II
Hansell, Ellen, 1887(4), IV
Hansen, Jacqueline, 1973 Apr. 17, IV
Hanson, Beverly, 1955 July 17, IV; 1958, IV

Hanson, Howard, 1930(5), II; 1934(2), II; 1948(5), II; 1981, II
Hantze, Karen, 1961 July 8, IV
Harbert, Chick, 1954 July 27, IV
Harcourt, Brace & World, 1960 Sept. 28, II
Harcourt Brace Jovanovich, 1987, II
Hard, Darlene, 1957 July 6, IV; 1960 Sept. 17, IV; 1961 Sept. 10, IV
Hardenbergh, Henry Janeway, 1897 Jan. 30, II
Harding, Tonya, 1991 Feb. 15–17, IV; 1991 Mar. 16, IV
Harding, Warren G. (*see also* Teapot Dome scandal):
  died, 1923, I
  elected president, 1920 Nov. 2, I
  first president heard on radio, 1922 June 14, III
  inaugurated president, 1921 Mar. 4, I
  presidential candidacy, 1920, I; 1920 June 8–12, I
Hardy, Oliver, 1957, II
Hardy, Samuel, 1679, II
Hargrove, Marion, 1942(1), II
Hariot, Thomas, 986–1599, II
Harkness Foundation, 1964, II
Harlan, Louis R., 1984 Apr. 16, II
Harlem River Houses (N.Y.C.), 1937(2), II
Harmon, Claude, 1948 Apr. 11, IV
Harmon, Tom, 1990, IV
Harmony Society, 1803, III
Harness racing, 1987 May 24, IV
  4000th victory, 1988 July 11(2), IV
Harnett, William Michael, 1885(4), II
Harnick, Sheldon, 1959 Nov. 23, II; 1960 May 2, II; 1964 Sept. 22, II; 1965 June 13, II
Harper, Chandler, 1950 June 27, IV
Harper, Robert Goodloe, 1798 June 18, IV
Harper, William Rainey, 1891(2), III; 1892(8), III
Harper & Brothers:
  fire, 1853(3), II
  fireproof building constructed, 1854(7), II
Harper & Row, 1987, II
Harpers Ferry (W. Va.):
  abandoned by Confederates, 1862 Sept. 15, I
  captured by Stonewall Jackson, 1862 Sept. 15, I
  John Brown's raid, 1859 Oct. 16, I
Harper's (magazine), 1980, II
Harper's Monthly Magazine, 1850(2), II
Harper's Weekly (publication):
  founded, 1857(3), II
Harrigan, Edward, 1870(2), II
Harriman, Job, 1900 Mar. 6–9, I
Harriman, W. Averell:
  Mutual Security Agency head, 1951 Oct. 10, I
  Paris peace talks, 1968 May 10, I
Harrington, Michael, 1989, I
Harris, Barbara C., 1988 Sept. 24, III
Harris, Chapin Aaron, 1840, III
Harris, Charles K., 1892(6), II
Harris, Jean, 1980 Mar. 10, IV
Harris, Joel Chandler, 1876(6), II; 1893(1), II

Harris, Julie, 1950 Jan. 5, II; 1952 Mar. 30, II; 1956 Apr. 1, II; 1959 May 6, II; 1962 May 22, II; 1969 Apr. 20, II; 1973 Mar. 25, II; 1976 Apr. 28, II; 1977 June 5, II

Harris, Miriam Coles, 1860(2), II

Harris, Patricia Roberts, 1985, I

Harris, Robert, 1992(1), II

Harris, Rosemary, 1966 June 16, II

Harris, Roy, 1934 Jan. 26, II; 1939 Feb. 24, II; 1941 Feb. 21, II; 1952(3), II; 1954 Jan. 30, II; 1979, II

Harris, Townsend:
    Japanese trade, 1858, III

Harris, William and Emily, 1974 May 17, IV; 1975 Sept. 18, IV

Harrisburg (Pa.):
    fire, 1897 Feb. 2, I

Harrisburg Seven, 1972 Sept. 5, I

Harrison, Benjamin:
    antistrike policy, 1892(2), III
    born, 1833 Aug. 20, I
    defeated for reelection, 1892 Nov. 8, I
    elected president, 1888 Nov. 6, I
    inaugurated, 1889 Mar. 4, I
    nominated for second term, 1892 June 7–11, I
    presidential candidacy, 1888, I; 1888 June 25, I

Harrison, Peter, 1720–1724, II; 1749, II

Harrison, Rex, 1949 Apr. 24, II; 1965 Apr. 5, II

Harrison, Wallace K., 1950(5), II

Harrison, William Henry:
    born, 1773 Feb. 9, I
    died, 1841, I; 1841 Mar. 4, I
    elected president, 1840 Dec. 2, I
    inaugurated president, 1841 Mar. 4, I
    Indian wars, 1811 Nov. 7, I; 1813 Oct. 5, I
    nominated for presidency, 1839 Dec. 4–7, I
    political slogan, 1836(1), IV
    presidential candidacy, 1836, I; 1836 Dec. 7, I
    presidential nomination, 1835 Dec. 16, I; 1840, I
    War of 1812, 1813 Sept. 10, I

Harrison & Abramovitz, 1952(4), II

Harrison Gray Otis House (Boston, Mass.), 1796(5), II

Harroun, Ray, 1911 May 30, IV

Hart, Doris, 1947 July 4–5, IV; 1951 July 6–7, IV; 1952 July 5, IV; 1953 July 3, IV; 1954 July 3(2), IV; 1954 Sept. 6, IV; 1955 July 1–2, IV; 1955 Sept. 11, IV

Hart, Gary, 1984 Feb. 28, I

Hart, Lorenz, 1927 Nov. 3, II; 1936 Mar. 22, II; 1937 Nov. 2, II; 1943, II

Hart, Marvin, 1905(3), IV

Hart, Moss, 1933 Sept. 9, II; 1936 Nov. 30, II; 1937 May 3, II; 1937 Nov. 2, II; 1939 Jan. 21, II; 1961, II

Hart, Philip A., 1976, I

Hart, Thomas C., 1942 Feb. 27-Mar. 1, I; 1971, I

Hart, Tom, 1870(2), II

Harte, Bret:
    Chronicle contributor, 1865(7), II
    first poems, 1867(1), II

Harte, Bret (*cont.*)
    "Luck of Roaring Camp, The", 1868(2), II
    Mrs. Skaggs's Husbands and Other Stories, 1873(1), II
    Overland Monthly, The, edited, 1868 July, II

Hartford, Huntington, 1964 Mar. 16, II

Hartford (Conn.):
    first church, 1636, III

Hartford Convention, 1814 Dec. 15–Jan. 4, 1815, I

Hartford Courant (newspaper), 1764(2), II

Hartford Wits, 1793(1), II; 1807, II

Hartley, Mariette, 1979 Sept. 9, II

Hartline, Haldan Keffer, 1967 Oct. 18(1), III

Harvard University (Mass.) (*see also* Radcliffe College):
    Astronomical Observatory, 1843(4), III
    astronomy, 1761(1), III
    banyan (nightgown) forbidden, 1754(2), IV
    Battle Window, 1870, II
    clubs, 1814(1), IV
    Copernican system accepted, 1656, III
    core curriculum adopted, 1978 May 2, III
    cost of education, 1814(1), IV
    crew racing, 1870(7), IV
    drama workshop, 1905, II
    early entrance requirements, 1636 Oct. 28, III
    early observatory, 1840(2), III
    Eliot's innovations, 1869, III
    first astronomical field expedition, 1786 Oct. 20, III
    first building, 1638(1), II
    first divinity degree, 1692(2), III
    first divinity professor, 1722 Jan. 24, III
    first graduate programs, 1870(1), III
    first honorary LL.D, 1773(3), III
    first lecture on electricity, 1746(1), III
    first summer course, 1869(5), III
    founded, 1636 Oct. 28, III
    Lampoon started, 1876(6), III
    Mather's connection with, 1674, III
    medical school opened, 1782(1), III
    music chair, 1875, II
    new buildings, 1963, II
    Peabody Museum Indian collection sale, 1979 Feb. 9(1), II
    ranking students socially discontinued, 1773(3), IV
    Russell appointed to faculty, 1940 Apr. 27, III
    student protest, 1969 Apr. 9, III

Harvey, Donald, 1987 Aug. 18, IV

Harvey, William Hope, 1894(1), II

Hass, Robert, 1985 Jan. 14, II

Hatch Act, 1887 Mar. 2, I

Hathaway, Donny, 1973 Mar. 3, II

Hauptman, Herbert A., 1985 Oct. 16, III

Hauptman, William, 1985 Apr. 25, II

Hauptmann, Bruno, 1935, IV

Havemeyer, Henry O., 1891(1), III

Haverford College (Pa.), 1833(4), III

Hawaii:
    Hurricane Iniki, 1992 Sept. 11, I

Hawaii (*cont.*)
    midair jet explosion, 1988 Apr. 28, I
    native culture celebration, 1988 Jan. 24, IV
    Pearl Harbor attacked, 1941, I; 1941, IV; 1941 Dec. 7, I
    Pearl Harbor leased from, 1887 Jan. 20, I
    provisional government recognized, 1893 Feb. 1, I
    rebellion, 1893 Jan. 17, I; 1893 July 17, I
    Reciprocity Treaty, 1875 Jan. 30, I
    republic recognized by U.S., 1894 Aug. 8, I
    statehood, 1959 Mar. 18, I; 1959 Aug. 21, I
    Territory established, 1900 Apr. 30, I
    total eclipse of sun, 1991 July 11, III
    U.S. annexation, 1893 Feb. 15, I; 1893 July 17, I; 1898 June 15, I
    U.S. protectorate ended, 1893 Apr. 13, I
    U.S. recognition of independence and trade treaty, 1843, I

Hawaii, University of, 1907(3), III

Hawking, Stephen W., 1988(1), II

Hawkins, John, 1565, IV

Hawkins, John H.W., 1833(3), IV

Hawks, Frank M., 1930 Mar. 30, III

Hawks, Howard, 1977, II

Hawn, Goldie, 1970 Apr. 7(1), II

Hawthorne, Nathaniel:
    daughter, 1896 Sept., III
    Fanshawe (first novel), 1828(1), II
    House of Seven Gables, The, 1670–1679, II; 1851(2), II
    Library of America issues works, 1982(1), II
    Marble Faun, The (Hawthorne), 1860(3), II
    and Margaret Fuller, 1846(2), II
    "Maypole of Merry-Mount, The", 1637(2), II
    Scarlet Letter, The, 1850(3), II
    short stories, 1846(5), II
    Twice-Told Tales, 1837(4), II

Hawthorne, Nigel, 1991 June 2, II

Hayakawa, S. I., 1968 Nov. 6, III; 1992, III

Hay-Bunau-Varilla Treaty, 1903 Nov. 18, I

Hayden, Horace A., 1840(7), III

Haydon, Murray P., 1986 June 19, III

Hayes, Helen, 1932 Nov. 18, II; 1947 Apr. 7, II; 1958 Apr. 13, II; 1968 May 21, II; 1971 Apr. 14, II
    tribute to, 1989 Oct. 10, II

Hayes, Max S., 1920 July 13–16, I

Hayes, Rutherford B.:
    born, 1822 Oct. 4, I
    disputed election, 1876 Nov. 7, I; 1877, I
    inaugurated president, 1877 Mar. 5, I
    refused second term, 1880, I
    Republican presidential nomination, 1876 June 14–16, I

Hayes, Wayne W. (Woody), 1987, IV

Hay-Herrán Treaty, 1903 Jan. 22, I

Haymarket Riot (Chicago, Ill.), 1886, I

Hayne, Paul Hamilton, 1857(2), II; 1860(8), II

Hayne, Robert Y.:
   Webster debate, 1830 Jan. 19–27, I
Haynie, Sandra, 1965 Sept. 26, IV; 1974
   June 23, IV; 1974 July 21, IV
Haynsworth, Clement, 1969 Nov. 21(2), I;
   1970 Apr. 8, I
Hay-Pauncefote Treaty, 1901 Nov. 18, I;
   1912 Aug. 24, III
Hays, Wayne, 1976, I; 1976 Sept. 1, I
Hayward, Susan, 1959 Apr. 6, II; 1975, II
Haywood, William D. ("Big Bill"), 1907(1),
   III; 1912, III
Hayworth, Rita, 1987, II
Hazelwood, Joseph J., 1989 Mar. 24, I
Hazzard, Shirley, 1981 Jan. 5, II
Headley, Joel T., 1846(1), II
Health, Education and Welfare,
   Department of (HEW):
      created, 1953 Apr. 1, I
      Finch dropped scientists' blacklist,
         1970 Jan. 2, III
      first head, 1953 Apr. 1, I
      renamed, 1979 Oct. 17(2), III
Health insurance (see also Medicaid;
   Medicare):
      expanded, 1976 Jan. 12, III
      prepaid plans and HMOs, 1984, III
      voluntary program recommended,
         1953 Feb. 22, III
Hearst, Patricia:
      absent from SLA shootout, 1974 May
         17, IV
      captured, 1975 Sept. 18, IV
      convicted for bank robbery, 1976
         Mar. 20, IV
      joined SLA abductors, 1974 Apr. 3, IV
      kidnaped, 1974 Feb. 5, IV
      released from prison, 1977 May 9, IV
Hearst, William Randolph:
      Boston Daily Advertiser, 1813(1), II
      circulation war with Pulitzer, 1883
         May 9, II
      Independence Party chairmanship,
         1908 July 27, I
      largest salary earned, 1935(1), III
      published de Lôme letter, 1898 Feb.
         9, I
      San Francisco Examiner, 1865(6), II
Heart:
      antismoking drive, 1963 June 8, III
      baboon transplant, 1984 Oct. 16, III
      cholesterol effect, 1964 Oct. 15, III;
         1981 Jan. 8, III
      Cooley, Denton, 1968, III
      defective artificial implanted valve
         recalled, 1992 Mar. 12, III
      defects in children, detection, 1961
         June 6, III
      disease decline, 1974 July 6, III; 1976
         Jan. 12, III
      first artificial heart recipient died,
         1983 Mar. 23, III
      first artificial pump, 1966 Aug. 8, III
      first artificial transplant, 1982 Dec. 2,
         III
      first nuclear-powered pump, 1972
         Feb. 14, III
      first portable pump recipient died,
         1991 May 25, III

Heart (cont.)
      first three-way transplant, 1987 May
         12, III
      first totally artificial, 1969 Apr. 4, III
      first transplant with liver, 1984 Feb.
         13, III
      first transplant with live recipient
         died, 1990 Nov. 11, III
      first woman to receive artificial, 1985
         Dec. 19, III
      Jarvik-7 artificial withdrawn, 1990 Jan.
         11, III
      longest-surviving artificial recipient
         died, 1986 Aug. 6, III
      longest surviving transplant patient
         died, 1974 Nov. 27, III
      margarine found disease promoting,
         1992 Oct. 7, III
      perfusion pump, 1936(1), III
      research, 1956 Oct. 19, III
      second artificial transplant, 1984 Nov.
         25, III
      smokers' death rate, 1960 June 6, III
      smoking linked to disease, 1961 Sept.
         8, III
      successful animal surgery, 1914 Apr.
         10, III
      third recipient of artificial died, 1986
         June 19, III
      transplants, 1968, III
      youngest transplant recipient to date,
         1987 Oct. 16, III
Heating (see also Stoves):
      first steam-heated public building
         (Boston, Mass.), 1846(1), III
      fuel shortages, 1973 Jan. 17, III
Heatter, Gabriel, 1972, II
Heat waves, 1980 June 23–Aug. 15, I;
   1987, I
Hebert, Jay, 1960 July 24, IV
Hebert, Lionel, 1957 July 21, IV
Hebrew Congregations, Union of
   American, 1873(1), III
Hebrew Union College (Ohio), 1875(1), III
Hecht, Anthony E., 1968 May 8, II
Hecht, Ben, 1928 Aug. 14, II; 1964, II
Heckart, Eileen, 1973 Mar. 27, II
Heckscher, August, 1992(1), II
Heenan, John C., 1859, IV
Heep, Danny, 1985 July 11, IV
Heflin, Van, 1943 Mar. 4, II
Heidelberg College (Ohio), 1851 Feb.
   13(2), III
Heiden, Eric, 1980 Feb. 12–24, IV
Heifetz, Jascha, 1917 Oct. 27, II; 1987, II
Hein, Mel, 1992, IV
Heinemann, Larry, 1987 Nov. 9, II
Heinemann Foundation, 1977 Nov. 18, II
Heinlein, Robert A., 1988, II
Heinrich, Anton Philip, 1820(3), II
Heinz, Henry J., 1869(4), III
Heiss, Carol, 1956 Feb. 17, IV; 1957 Feb.
   28–Mar. 3, IV; 1957 Mar. 15–16, IV;
   1958 Feb. 14–15, IV; 1958 Mar. 28–29,
   IV; 1959 Jan. 31–Feb. 1, IV; 1959 Feb.
   26–28, IV; 1960 Jan. 30, IV; 1960 Mar.
   2–5, IV
Helderberg War see Antirent War
Helicopters:
      first successful, 1940 May 15, III

Helicopters (cont.)
      first transcontinental flight, 1956 Aug.
         24, I
      use in Vietnam, 1965, I
Helium, 1917(3), III; 1978 Oct. 17, III
Heller, Joseph, 1961(1), II; 1974(1), II
Heller, Walter W., 1987, III
Hell Gate Bridge (N.Y.C.), 1917(5), II
Hellman, Lillian, 1941 Mar. 24, II; 1945
   Dec. 27, II; 1946 Nov. 20, II; 1960 Feb.
   25, II; 1969(1), II; 1970 Mar. 2, II;
   1976(1), II; 1980 Feb. 15(1), II; 1984, II
Hellwig, Helen, 1894(4), IV
Helmsley, Leona, 1989 Aug. 30, IV
Helmuth, Justus Christian Henry, 1769(3),
   III
Helper, Hinton Rowan, 1857, II
Helprin, Mark, 1988, II
Helyar, John, 1990(1), II
Hemenway, Mary, 1889(3), III
Hemingway, Ernest:
      books on, 1966(1), II; 1969(1), II
      died, 1961, II
      Farewell To Arms, A, 1929(1), II
      Fifth Column, The, 1938(1), II
      first publications, 1923(1), II
      For Whom the Bell Tolls, 1940(1), II
      Moveable Feast, A, 1964(1), II
      Nobel Prize, 1954 Oct. 28, II
      Old Man and the Sea, The, 1952(1), II
      posthumous work, 1970(1), II
      Pulitzer Prize, 1953 May 4(2), II
      Sun Also Rises, The, 1926(1), II
      Winner Take Nothing, 1933(1), II
Hench, Philip Showalter, 1950 Oct. 26, III
Hendricks, Thomas A., 1876 June 27–28, I;
   1884 July 8–11, I; 1884 July 30, I; 1884
   Nov. 4, I; 1885 Nov. 25, I
Hendrie, G. M., 1883(2), IV
Hendrix, Jimi (James Marshall), 1970, II
Henley, Beth, 1981 Apr. 13, II
Henley, Don, 1990 Feb. 21, II
Henley Regatta, 1989, IV
Hennard, George Jo, 1991 Oct. 16, IV
Hennepin, Louis (Fr.), 1670–1679, I
Henreid, Paul, 1992, II
Henri, Robert, 1908, II
Henry, George W., 1859(2), IV
Henry, Joseph, 1831(1), III
Henry, O., 1894 Mar., II
      first story collection, 1904(1), II
      Four Million, The, 1906(1), II
      Options, 1909(1), II
      Roads of Destiny, 1909(1), II
      Rolling Stones, 1913(1), II
      Sixes and Sevens, 1911(1), II
      Strictly Business, 1910(1), II
      Trimmed Lamp and Heart of the
         West, 1907(1), II
      Whirligigs, 1910(1), II
Henry, Patrick:
      attacked Stamp Act, 1765 May 29, I
      "Give me liberty" speech, 1775 Mar.
         23, I
      Wirt's book on, 1803, II
Henson, Jim, 1990, II
Henson, Matt, 1909 Apr. 6, I
Heparin, 1916(2), III
Hepatitis, 1971 Mar. 29, III

Hepburn, Audrey, 1954 Mar. 25, II; 1954 Mar. 28, II

Hepburn, Katharine, 1934 Mar. 16, II; 1968 Apr. 10(2), II; 1969 Apr. 14, II; 1975 May 19, II; 1982 Mar. 29, II

Hepburn, William P., 1903, I

Hepburn Act, 1903, I

Herbert, Frank, 1985(1), II; 1986, II

Herbert, Victor, 1890, II; 1894(3), II; 1903 June 17, II; 1910 Oct. 24, II; 1914 Feb. 13, II

Herbicides see Chemical and biological warfare

Herd, Fred, 1898 June 18, IV

Heredity see Genetics

Heresy see Religion and churches; Witchcraft

Hering, Constantine, 1836(2), III

Herjulfson, Bjarni, 986–1599, I

Herman, Billy, 1992, IV

Herman, Jerry, 1964 Jan. 16, II; 1964 May 24, II; 1966 May 24, II; 1967 Nov. 12, II; 1983 Aug. 21, II; 1984 June 3, II

Herman, Woody, 1987, II

Hermitage, (Jackson's home), 1804(1), II

Hermitage (Leningrad museum), 1987, II; 1988 Mar. 26, II

Hermits, 1832 Apr. 1, IV

Herndon, Hugh, 1931 Oct. 5, III

Herne, James A., 1893, II

Heroin see Narcotics

Herold, J. Christopher, 1959 Mar. 3(1), II

Herpes, 1981 July 9, III; 1982, III

Herschback, Dudley R., 1986 Oct. 15, III

Hersey, John, 1945 May 7, II; 1950(1), II; 1956(1), II; 1959(1), II; 1960(1), II

Hersh, Seymour M., 1984 Jan. 9, II

Hershey, Alfred D., 1969 Oct. 16, III

Hershey, Lewis B., 1967 Oct. 26, I; 1977, I

Hershiser, Orel, 1988 Oct. 4, IV

Herter, Christian Archibald:
    died, 1966, I
    named secretary of state, 1959 Apr. 18, I
    on Soviet role in Germany, 1959 June 21, I

Hess, Victor Francis, 1936 Nov. 12, III

Heston, Charlton, 1960 Apr. 4, II

Hewitt, Abram S., 1868(2), III

Heyward, Du Bose, 1925(1), II

Hibernian Hall (Charleston, S.C.), 1841(6), II

Hickey, James Aloysius, 1988 May 29, III

Hickok, "Wild Bill", 1867(3), IV

Hicks, John R., 1972 Oct. 25, III

Higgins, William R., 1988 Feb. 17, I

Higham, Richard, 1882 June 24, IV

Highways see Roads and highways

Highway Trust Fund, 1973 Aug. 3, III

Higsen, Thomas L., 1908 Nov. 3, I

Hijacking:
    Achille Lauro Italian liner, 1985 Oct. 7–10, I
    Croatian terrorists (N.Y.C.), 1976 Sept. 10–12, I
    Cuban-U.S. accord, 1973 Feb. 15, III
    Eastern Airlines jet (Fla.-Cuba), 1961 July 24, I
    highest annual total since first, 1969, I

Hijacking (cont.)
    international pilots' strike protesting, 1972, III
    law against signed, 1961 Sept. 5, I
    mandatory passenger screening, 1972 Feb. 5, III
    Palestinian terrorists, 1970 Sept. 6, III
    TWA jetliner (Athens), 1985 June 14, I

Hijuelos, Oscar, 1989(1), II; 1990 Apr. 12, II

Hill, Anita F., 1991 Oct. 15, I

Hill, Arthur, 1963 Apr. 25(1), II

Hill, Dave, 1970 June 21, IV

Hill, Ruth Beebe, 1979(1), II

Hiller, Wendy, 1959 Apr. 6, II

Hillquit, Morris, 1901(1), I

Hilton, Conrad, 1979, III

Hilton, James, 1934(1), II; 1941(1), II

Hinckley, John W., Jr., 1981 Mar. 30, I; 1982 June 21, I

Hindemith, Paul, 1949(2), II; 1963, II

Hindenburg (airship), 1936 May 9, III; 1937 May 6, I; 1937 May 6, III

Hines, Earl ("Fatha"), 1983, II

Hines, Gregory, 1992 June 1, II

Hip-hop culture, 1988, II

Hires, Charles Elmer, 1877(2), III

Hirohito (Emperor of Japan), 1971 Sept. 26, I

Hiroshima (Japan):
    atomic bomb dropped on, 1945 Aug. 6, I

Hirsch, E. D., Jr., 1987(1), II

Hirsch, Judd, 1986 June 1(3), II; 1992, II; 1992 June 1, II

Hirshhorn, Joseph H., 1981, II

Hirshhorn Museum and Sculpture Garden, Joseph (Wash., D.C.), 1969, II; 1974 Oct. 4, II

Hirson, Roger O., 1972 Sept. 23, II

Hiscox, Thomas (Rev.), 1745–1749, II

Hisgen, Thomas L., 1908 July 27, I

Hispanic-Americans:
    dropout rate, 1992, III
    educational level, 1989, III
    first Cabinet member, 1988 Sept. 20, III
    health problems, 1991, III
    population, 1987, I; 1988 Sept. 6, I; 1989, I; 1991, I

Hiss, Alger, 1948 Dec. 15, I; 1949 May 31, I; 1950 Jan. 21(2), I; 1975 Aug. 5, I
    exonerated by Russian official, 1992 Oct. 14, I

Historia Plantarum (Ray), 1680(1), III

Historical Discourse, An (Callender), 1739, II

History and historians:
    account of N.E. Indians, 1677(1), II
    Adams' History of the U.S., 1889(1), II
    American Historical Assn., 1884, III
    Antiquarian Society founded (Mass.), 1812(4), IV
    Bancroft's nationalistic approach, 1834, II
    changing critical standards, 1858, II
    colonial primary source, 1630 May 29, II
    current publications, 1888(1), II
    "father of American", 1630, II

History and historians (cont.)
    first association, 1791(1), III
    first comic, of U.S., 1812(1), II
    first comprehensive (N.E.), 1669, II
    Fiske's works, 1891(1), II
    Palfrey's History of New England, 1858, II
    Parkman's works, 1851(4), II; 1865(5), II; 1874(1), II
    Pioneers of France in the New World (Parkman), 1865(5), II
    Prescott's Spanish histories, 1859 Jan. 28, II
    Prescott's works, 1837(1), II; 1859 Jan. 28, II
    societies founded, 1804(1), III
    Sparks's works, 1835, II
    Turner's contribution, 1893(1), III

Hitchings, George H., 1988 Oct. 17, III

Hoaxes see Frauds

Hobart, Garret A., 1896 June 18, I; 1896 Nov. 3, I

Hobart College (N.Y.), 1822 Apr. 10, III

Hobby, Oveta Culp, 1942 May 14, I; 1953 Apr. 1, I

Hoboken, N.J.:
    fire, 1900 June 30, I

Hobson, Henry, 1891(3), II

Hobson, Laura Z., 1947(1), II

Hochhuth, Rolf, 1964 Feb. 26, II

Hockey, Ice:
    attendance increased, 1973, IV
    first NHL strike to date ended, 1992 Apr. 10(2), IV
    first U.S. league, 1896 Nov., IV
    first woman pro player, 1992 Sept. 23, IV
    first World Hockey Assn. championship, 1973 May 6, IV
    Forbes's criminal indictment, 1975 July 18, IV
    Gretzky traded, 1988 Aug. 9, IV
    highest scorer in NHL history, 1989 Oct. 15, IV
    Howe retired, 1971 Sept. 9, IV
    Hull's 51st goal scored, 1966 Mar. 12(1), IV
    introduced in U.S., 1893(1), IV
    Stanley Cup, 1912(4), IV; 1913 Mar. 8–10, IV; 1914(5), IV; 1915(4), IV; 1916(2), IV; 1917(2), IV; 1918(4), IV; 1919(2), IV; 1920 Apr. 1, IV; 1921(2), IV; 1922(1), IV; 1923(3), IV; 1924 Mar. 25, IV; 1925(2), IV; 1926(1), IV; 1927 Apr. 7–13, IV; 1928 Apr. 5–14, IV; 1929 Mar. 28–29, IV; 1930 Apr. 1–3, IV; 1931 Apr. 3–14, IV; 1932 Apr. 5–9, IV; 1933 Apr. 4–13, IV; 1934 Apr. 3–10, IV; 1935 Apr. 4–9, IV; 1936 Apr. 5–11, IV; 1937 Apr. 6–15, IV; 1938 Apr. 5–12, IV; 1939 Apr. 6–16, IV; 1940 Apr. 2–13, IV; 1941 Apr. 6–12, IV; 1942 Apr. 4–18, IV; 1943 Apr. 1–8, IV; 1944 Apr. 4–13, IV; 1945 Apr. 6–22, IV; 1946 Mar. 30–Apr. 9, IV; 1947 Apr. 8–19, IV; 1948 Apr. 7–14, IV; 1949 Apr. 8–16, IV; 1950 Apr. 11–23, IV; 1951 Apr. 11–21, IV; 1952 Apr. 10–15, IV; 1953 Apr.

Hockey, Ice (cont.)
  9–16, IV; 1954 Apr. 4–16, IV; 1955
    Apr. 3–14, IV; 1956 Mar. 31–Apr.
    10, IV; 1957 Apr. 6–16, IV; 1958
    Apr. 8–20, IV; 1959 Apr. 9–18, IV;
    1960 Apr. 7–14, IV; 1961 Apr. 6–16,
    IV; 1962 Apr. 10–22, IV; 1963 Apr.
    9–18, IV; 1964 Apr. 11–25, IV; 1965
    Apr. 17–May 1, IV; 1966 Apr.
    24-May 5, IV; 1967 Apr. 20–May 2,
    IV; 1968 May 5–11, IV; 1969 Apr.
    27–May 4, IV; 1970 May 3–10, IV;
    1971 May 4–18, IV; 1972 Apr.
    30–May 11, IV; 1973 Apr. 29–May
    10, IV; 1974 May 7–19, IV; 1975
    May 15–27, IV; 1976 May 9–16, IV;
    1977 May 7–14, IV; 1978 May
    13–25, IV; 1979 May 13–21, IV;
    1980 May 13–24, IV; 1981 May
    12–21, IV; 1982 May 8–16, IV; 1983
    May 10–17, IV; 1984 May 10–19, IV;
    1985 May 21–30, IV; 1986 May
    16–24, IV; 1987 May 10–18, IV;
    1988 May 26, IV; 1989 May 25, IV;
    1990 May 24, IV; 1991 May 25, IV;
    1992 June 1, IV
  World Hockey Assn., 1972, IV
Hodges, Gil, 1972, IV
Hodges-Field House (Mass.), 1836(4), II
Hoffa, James R.:
  began prison term, 1967 Mar. 7, III
  convicted of fraud and conspiracy,
    1964 July 26, III
  corruption charges, 1957 Sept. 18, III
  jury-tampering conviction, 1964 Mar.
    4, III
  racketeering charges, 1960 Feb. 26,
    III
  reelected Teamsters president, 1961
    July 7, III
  reported missing, 1975 July 31(1), III
Hoffenberg, Mason, 1964(1), II
Hoffman, Dustin, 1974 Dec. 29, II; 1980
  Apr. 14(2), II; 1989 Mar. 29, II
Hoffman, Julius J., 1969 Sept. 24, I
Hoffman, Ronald, 1981 Oct. 19(1), III
Hoffmann, Abbie, 1973 Dec. 4, I
Hoffner, Charles, 1922 June 14, IV
Hofmann, Hans, 1963 Sept. 11, II; 1966, II
Hofstadter, Douglas R., 1980 Apr. 14(1), II
Hofstadter, Richard, 1964 May 4, II; 1970,
  II
Hofstadter, Robert, 1961 Nov. 2(2), III;
  1990, III
Hogan, Ben, 1941, IV; 1942, IV; 1946, IV;
  1946 Aug. 25, IV; 1948 May 25, IV;
  1948 June 12(2), IV; 1950 June 10(2), IV;
  1951 Apr. 7, IV; 1951 June 16(1), IV;
  1953 Apr. 12, IV; 1953 June 13(2), IV;
  1955 Apr. 10, IV; 1955 June 19, IV;
  1956 June 16(2), IV; 1965 June 21, IV;
  1966 July 9, IV
Holbrook, Hal, 1966, II; 1966 June 16, II;
  1971 May 9, II; 1974 May 28, II
Holden, William, 1954 Mar. 25, II
Holder, Charles Frederick, 1886 Jan. 1, IV
Holderied, Kristine, 1984 May 23, III
Holding companies see Corporations
Holiday, Billie, 1959, II
Holidays see specific names

Holland Tunnel (N.Y.-N.J.), 1927 Nov. 13,
  III
Holldobler, Berthold K., 1991 Apr. 9, II
Holley, Robert W., 1968 Oct. 16, III
Holliday, Judy, 1951 Mar. 29(2), II; 1965,
  II
Holm, Celeste, 1948 Mar. 20, II
Holm, Hanya, 1992, II
Holme, Thomas, 1681 July 11, III
Holmes, John Haynes, 1931 Mar. 17, I
Holmes, Larry, 1978 June 9, IV; 1980, IV;
  1981, IV; 1984 Nov. 9, IV; 1985 Sept.
  21, IV; 1988 June 27(2), IV
Holmes, Mary Jane, 1854(3), II; 1856(9), II
Holmes, Oliver Wendell (physician):
  Autocrat of the Breakfast Table,
    1857(1), II; 1858(3), II
  early poems, 1836(6), II
  Elsie Venner, 1861(6), II
  "Old Ironsides" poem, 1830 Sept. 16,
    II
  Poet of the Breakfast Table, The,
    1872(1), II
  puerperal fever treatise, 1843(2), III
Holmes, Oliver Wendell (jurist):
  books on, 1944(1), II
  Mass. Supreme Court dissent on
    picketing, 1896(3), III
Holmes, Sherlock (fictional character),
  1886, II; 1890 Feb., II; 1892(1), II;
  1899(3), II
Holt, Rinehart & Winston, Inc., 1960 Feb.
  29, II
Holtwick, Enoch A., 1951 Nov. 13–15, I
Homans, Helen, 1906(2), IV
Homeless:
  "Grate American Sleep-Out", 1987, I
  N.Y.C., 1850(5), IV
Home Owners Loan Act, 1934 Apr. 28, I
Homer, Winslow, 1865(9), II; 1876(8), II;
  1884(2), II; 1980 Oct. 17, II
Homestead Act, 1862, I
"Home Sweet Home" (song), 1823 May 8,
  II
Homosexuality (see also AIDS):
  antidiscrimination measure defeated
    (Fla.), 1977 June 7, I
  church condemnation, 1992 May
    12(1), III
  domestic partnership law, 1991 Feb.
    14, IV
  Episcopal Church ordination, 1991
    June 5, III; 1991 July 19, III
  first security clearance, 1975 Feb. 1,
    IV
  Lutheran suspension of openly gay
    clergy, 1990 July 18, III
  Mapplethorpe photography exhibit,
    1989 June 13, II; 1990 Apr. 7, II
  Matlovich challenged military ban,
    1975 Oct. 22, I
  mental illness classification reversed,
    1973 Dec. 15, III
  Methodist ordination of noncelibate
    homosexuals banned, 1984 May 9(2),
    III
  NBC acknowledged unfair treatment,
    1973 Oct. 26, II
  Reform Judaism to admit to rabbinate,
    1990 June 25, III

Homosexuality (cont.)
  serial murder victims case (Tex.), 1973
    Aug. 14, IV
  Supreme Court ruling, 1986 June 30, I
Honduras:
  U.S. Marines landed in, 1907 Mar. 21,
    I
  U.S. military aid approved, 1986 Mar.
    25, I
  U.S. troops ordered to, 1988 Mar. 16, I
Honolulu, Declaration of, 1966 Feb. 8, I
Honor America Day, 1970 July 4, I
Hoochy-koochy (dance), 1893(3), IV
Hood, John B., 1864 Sept. 1, I
Hoof and mouth disease, 1981 June 18, III
Hook, Sidney, 1989, III
Hooker, Brian, 1912 Mar. 14, II
Hooker, Thomas, 1636, III
Hookworm, 1902 Feb., III
Hoopes, Darlington, 1952 May 30–June 1,
  I; 1952 Nov. 4, I
Hoosac Tunnel (Mass.), 1873, III
Hoover, Herbert:
  Cold War views, 1952, I
  Depression programs, 1932, I
  died, 1964, I
  elected president, 1928 Nov. 6, I
  Great Depression, 1929, I
  high tariffs, 1930, I
  inaugurated, 1929 Mar. 4, I
  lost presidency, 1932 Nov. 8, I
  presidential candidacy, 1928, I; 1928
    June 12–15, I; 1932 June 14–16, I
  Prohibition enforcement commission,
    1931, I
  proposed war debt moratorium, 1931
    June 20, I
  unemployment measures, 1930 Dec.
    2, I
  urged against alliances with antifascist
    countries, 1938 Mar. 31, I
Hoover, J. Edgar:
  Berrigan plot, 1970 Nov. 27, I
  on communist subversion, 1950, I
  died, 1972, I
Hoover Commission on Organization of
  the Executive Branch, 1949 Feb. 7, I
Hoover Dam (Nev.), 1930 Sept. 17, III;
  1936(4), III
Hope, Anthony, 1894(1), II
Hope, Bob, 1943, II
Hopkins, Anthony, 1976 May 17, II; 1981
  Sept. 13, II; 1992 Mar. 31, II
Hopkins, Esek, 1775 Dec. 22, I
Hopkins, Harry L., 1933 Nov. 8, I
Hopkinson, Francis, 1755–1759, II;
  1775–1779, II; 1775–1779, IV
Hopkinson, Joseph, 1784(1), II; 1798(1), II
Hopper, DeWolf, 1988 Aug. 15, IV
Hopper, Edward, 1941(3), II; 1967, II;
  1971 Mar. 18, II
Hopper, Hedda, 1966, IV
Horgan, Paul, 1955 May 2, II; 1976 May 3,
  II
Horlick, William, 1882(4), IV
Hormones, 1955 Nov. 2(1), III; 1971 Oct.
  14, III; 1977 Oct. 13, III
Horne, Lena, 1982 Feb. 24, II
Horne, Marilyn, 1970 Mar. 3, II
Horney, Karen, 1937(1), III

Hornsby, Rogers, 1942 Jan. 20, IV; 1963, IV

Horowitz, Vladimir, 1965 May 9, II; 1989, II

Horseback riding *see* Horses

Horse racing:

American Childers' win (Long Island), 1757(1), IV

American Trotting Assn. formed, 1887 Mar. 2, IV

Arcaro, jockey, retired, 1962 Apr. 3, IV

attendance, 1988, IV

Belmont horse-switching scandal, 1977 Dec. 2, IV

Belmont Stakes (N.Y.), 1867 June 19, IV; 1868 June 10, IV; 1869 June 5, IV; 1870 June 4, IV; 1871 June 10, IV; 1872 June 1, IV; 1873 June 7, IV; 1874 June 13, IV; 1875 June 12, IV; 1876 June 10, IV; 1877 June 9, IV; 1878 June 8, IV; 1879 June 5, IV; 1880 June 14, IV; 1881 June 7, IV; 1882 June 8, IV; 1883 June 9, IV; 1884 June 4, IV; 1885 June 6, IV; 1886 June 5, IV; 1887 June 9, IV; 1888 June 9, IV; 1889 June 13, IV; 1890 June 10(2), IV; 1891 June 10, IV; 1892 June 9, IV; 1893 June 10, IV; 1894 June 19, IV; 1895 Nov. 2, IV; 1896 June 2, IV; 1897 May 29, IV; 1898 May 26, IV; 1899 May 25, IV; 1900 May 24, IV; 1901 May 23, IV; 1902 May 22, IV; 1903 May 27, IV; 1904 May 25, IV; 1905 May 24, IV; 1906 May 30, IV; 1907 May 30, IV; 1908 May 30, IV; 1909 June 2, IV; 1910 May 30, IV; 1911(1), IV; 1913 June 13, IV; 1914 June 20, IV; 1915 June 5, IV; 1916 June 10, IV; 1917 June 16, IV; 1918 June 15, IV; 1919 June 11(2), IV; 1920 June 12, IV; 1921 June 11, IV; 1922 June 10, IV; 1923 June 9, IV; 1924 June 7, IV; 1925 June 13, IV; 1926 June 12, IV; 1927 June 11, IV; 1928 June 9, IV; 1929 June 8, IV; 1930 June 7, IV; 1931 June 13, IV; 1932 June 4, IV; 1933 June 10(2), IV; 1934 June 9(1), IV; 1935 June 8(1), IV; 1936 June 6(1), IV; 1937 June 5, IV; 1938 June 4, IV; 1939 June 3, IV; 1940 June 8, IV; 1941 June 7(2), IV; 1942 June 6, IV; 1943 June 5, IV; 1944 June 3, IV; 1945 June 23, IV; 1946 June 1, IV; 1947 May 31, IV; 1948 June 12(1), IV; 1949 June 11(2), IV; 1950 June 10(1), IV; 1951 June 16(2), IV; 1952 May 7, IV; 1953 June 13(1), IV; 1954 June 12, IV; 1955 June 11, IV; 1956 June 16(1), IV; 1957 June 15(1), IV; 1958 June 7, IV; 1959 June 13(1), IV; 1960 June 11, IV; 1961 June 3, IV; 1962 June 9, IV; 1963 June 8, IV; 1964 June 6, IV; 1965 June 5, IV; 1966 June 4, IV; 1967 June 3, IV; 1968 June 1, IV; 1969 June 7, IV; 1970 June 6, IV; 1971 June 5, IV; 1972 June 10, IV; 1973 June 9, IV; 1974

Horse racing (*cont.*)

June 8, IV; 1975 June 7, IV; 1976 June 5, IV; 1977 June 11, IV; 1978 June 10, IV; 1979 June 9, IV; 1980 June 7, IV; 1981 June 6, IV; 1982 June 5, IV; 1983 June 11, IV; 1984 June 9, IV; 1985 June 8, IV; 1986 June 7, IV; 1987 June 6, IV; 1988 June 11, IV; 1989 June 10, IV; 1990 June 9, IV; 1991 June 8, IV; 1992 June 6(1), IV

betting legalized (N.Y.), 1887 May 26, IV

colonial Md., 1765–1775, IV

colonial N.Y., 1664(2), IV; 1668, IV; 1669, IV

decreased attendance and betting, 1991, IV

Fair Grounds (La.), 1873(3), IV

first bookmakers, 1873(2), IV

first jockey club (S.C.), 1734(2), IV

first jockey to win $100,000,000, 1985 Mar. 3, IV

first jockey to win over $5,000,000, 1977 Dec. 10, IV

first legal off-track betting (N.Y.C.), 1971 Apr. 8, IV

first major (N.Y.), 1823 May, IV

first organized (N.Y.), 1660–1669, IV

first recalled Kentucky Derby race, 1968 May 4, IV

first totalizator, 1933(1), IV

first winning woman jockey, 1969 Feb. 22, IV

first woman jockey, 1969 Feb. 7, IV

first woman jockey stakes winner, 1973 Mar. 1(1), IV

forbidden in New Amsterdam, 1657(2), IV

Hambletonian Stakes (N.Y.), 1926 Aug. 30, IV

Hempstead Plains (N.Y.), 1780 Nov., IV

hurdles introduced, 1834(4), IV

Jamaica Race Track (N.Y.) false start race, 1931 May 13, IV

Jamaica Race Track (N.Y.) opened, 1903 Apr. 27, IV

jockey Cauthen's achievements, 1977, IV; 1977 Dec. 10, IV

Jockey Club formed, 1894 Feb., IV

jockey Longden retired, 1966 Mar. 12(2), IV

jockeys, 1892 Mar. 18, IV

jockey Shoemaker retired, 1990 Feb. 3, IV

Kentucky Derby, 1875 May 17, IV; 1876 May 15, IV; 1877 May 22, IV; 1878 May 21, IV; 1879 May 20, IV; 1880 May 18, IV; 1881 May 17, IV; 1882 May 16, IV; 1883 May 23, IV; 1884 May 16, IV; 1885 May 14, IV; 1886 May 14, IV; 1887 May 11, IV; 1888 May 14, IV; 1889 May 9, IV; 1890 May 14, IV; 1891 May 13, IV; 1892 May 11, IV; 1893 May 10, IV; 1894 May 15, IV; 1895 May 6, IV; 1896 May 6, IV; 1897 May 4, IV; 1898 May 4, IV; 1899 May 4, IV; 1900 May 3, IV; 1901 Apr. 29, IV;

Horse racing (*cont.*)

1902 May 3, IV; 1903 May 2, IV; 1904 May 2, IV; 1905 May 10, IV; 1906 May 2, IV; 1907 May 6, IV; 1908 May 5, IV; 1909 May 3, IV; 1910 May 10, IV; 1911 May 13, IV; 1912 May 11, IV; 1913 May 10, IV; 1914 May 9, IV; 1915 May 8, IV; 1916 May 13, IV; 1917 May 12(2), IV; 1918 May 11, IV; 1919 May 10, IV; 1920 May 8, IV; 1921 May 7, IV; 1922 May 13(1), IV; 1923 May 19, IV; 1924 May 17, IV; 1925 May 16, IV; 1926 May 15, IV; 1927 May 14, IV; 1928 May 19, IV; 1929 May 18, IV; 1930 May 17, IV; 1931 May 16, IV; 1932 May 7, IV; 1933 May 6, IV; 1934 May 5, IV; 1935 May 4, IV; 1936 May 2, IV; 1937 May 8, IV; 1938 May 7, IV; 1939 May 6, IV; 1940 May 4, IV; 1941 May 3, IV; 1942 May 2, IV; 1943 May 1, IV; 1944 May 6, IV; 1945 June 9, IV; 1946 May 4, IV; 1947 May 3, IV; 1948 May 1, IV; 1949 May 7, IV; 1950 May 6, IV; 1951 May 5, IV; 1952 May 3, IV; 1953 May 2, IV; 1954 May 1, IV; 1955 May 7, IV; 1956 May 5, IV; 1957 May 4, IV; 1958 May 3, IV; 1959 May 2, IV; 1960 May 7, IV; 1961 May 6, IV; 1962 May 5, IV; 1963 May 4(1), IV; 1964 May 2, IV; 1965 May 1, IV; 1966 May 7, IV; 1967 May 6, IV; 1968 May 4, IV; 1969 May 3, IV; 1970 May 2, IV; 1971 May 1, IV; 1972 May 6, IV; 1973 May 5, IV; 1974 May 4(1), IV; 1975 May 3, IV; 1976 May 1, IV; 1977 May 7, IV; 1978 May 6, IV; 1979 May 5, IV; 1980 May 3, IV; 1981 May 2, IV; 1982 May 1, IV; 1983 May 7, IV; 1984 May 5, IV; 1985 May 4, IV; 1986 May 3, IV; 1987 May 2, IV; 1988 May 7, IV; 1989 May 6, IV; 1990 May 5, IV; 1991 May 4, IV; 1992 May 1, IV

Kentucky Derby controversy, 1972 Apr. 28, IV

largest purse to date, 1951 Feb. 3, IV

laws relaxed (N.Y.S.), 1821(2), IV

legalized betting survey, 1962(1), IV

N.H. Sweepstakes, 1964 Sept. 12(2), IV

Newmarket (Long Island) popularity, 1750(1), IV

new mile record, 1816(1), IV

North-South races, 1842, IV

N.Y. Trotting Club, 1825(2), IV

oldest Kentucky Derby jockey winner, 1986 May 3, IV

outlawed on public roads (Ky.), 1793(2), IV

Pimlico track built (Baltimore, Md.), 1870(4), IV

Plymouth colony ban, 1674, IV

popularity, 1842, IV; 1933, IV

popular weekly sheet, 1831 Dec. 10, IV

Horse racing (cont.)
Preakness Stakes, 1873 May 27, IV;
1874 May 26, IV; 1875 May 28, IV;
1876 May 25, IV; 1877 May 24, IV;
1878 May 27, IV; 1879 May 24, IV;
1880 May 28, IV; 1881 May 27, IV;
1882 May 27, IV; 1883 May 26, IV;
1884 May 23, IV; 1885 May 22, IV;
1886 May 21, IV; 1887 May 13, IV;
1888 May 11, IV; 1889 May 10, IV;
1890 June 10(1), IV; 1891(5), IV;
1894 May 17, IV; 1895 May 25, IV;
1896 June 6, IV; 1897 June 8, IV;
1898 June 11, IV; 1899 May 30, IV;
1900 May 29, IV; 1901 May 28, IV;
1902 May 27, IV; 1903 May 30, IV;
1904 May 28, IV; 1905 May 27, IV;
1906 May 22, IV; 1907 May 21, IV;
1908 June 2, IV; 1909 May 12, IV;
1910 May 7, IV; 1911 May 17, IV;
1912 May 15, IV; 1913 May 20, IV;
1914 May 21, IV; 1915 May 17, IV;
1916 May 16, IV; 1917 May 12(1),
IV; 1918 May 15, IV; 1919 May 14,
IV; 1920 May 18, IV; 1921 May 16,
IV; 1922 May 13(2), IV; 1923 May
12, IV; 1924 May 12(2), IV; 1925
May 8, IV; 1926 May 10, IV; 1927
May 9, IV; 1928 May 11, IV; 1929
May 10, IV; 1930 May 9, IV; 1931
May 9, IV; 1932 May 14, IV; 1933
May 13, IV; 1934 May 12, IV; 1935
May 11, IV; 1936 May 16, IV; 1937
May 15, IV; 1938 May 14, IV; 1939
May 13, IV; 1940 May 11, IV; 1941
May 10, IV; 1942 May 9, IV; 1943
May 8, IV; 1944 May 13, IV; 1945
June 16, IV; 1946 May 11, IV; 1947
May 10, IV; 1948 May 15, IV; 1949
May 14, IV; 1950 May 20, IV; 1951
May 19, IV; 1952 May 17, IV; 1953
May 23, IV; 1954 May 22, IV; 1955
May 28, IV; 1956 May 19, IV; 1957
May 18, IV; 1958 May 17, IV; 1959
May 16, IV; 1960 May 21, IV; 1961
May 20, IV; 1962 May 19, IV; 1963
May 18, IV; 1964 May 16, IV; 1965
May 15, IV; 1966 May 21, IV; 1967
May 20, IV; 1968 May 18, IV; 1969
May 17, IV; 1970 May 16, IV; 1971
May 15, IV; 1972 May 20(2), IV;
1973 May 19, IV; 1974 May 18, IV;
1975 May 17, IV; 1976 May 15, IV;
1977 May 21, IV; 1978 May 20, IV;
1979 May 19, IV; 1980 May 17, IV;
1981 May 16, IV; 1982 May 15, IV;
1983 May 21, IV; 1984 May 19, IV;
1985 May 18, IV; 1986 May 17, IV;
1987 May 16, IV; 1988 May 21, IV;
1989 May 20, IV; 1990 May 19, IV;
1991 May 18, IV; 1992 May 16, IV
public forbidden (N.Y.S.), 1802(3), IV
richest purse, 1962 Sept. 8(2), IV
Roosevelt Raceway (N.Y.) riot, 1963
Nov. 8, IV
Saratoga (N.Y.) track built, 1864(3), IV
Selima and offsprings' success (Md.),
1752(1), IV
South vs. North race, 1836(3), IV
sprint (Va.), 1779, IV

Horse racing (cont.)
track attendance and bets, 1940(2), IV
trotting racing popularity, 1862(1), IV
trotting record, 1806 June 5, IV
Va. aristocrats, 1673(1), IV
wagers in single day record, 1964
June 6, IV
world record for winning mounts,
1970 Sept. 7, IV
Horses:
breeding, 1750(2), IV; c1790, IV;
1798(1), IV
Dancer's Image disqualified, 1968
May 4, IV
Expectation, 1802(4), IV
first annual N.Y. Horse Show, 1883
Oct. 22, IV
first female thief, 1839(1), IV
introduced in U.S., 1540, IV
Kelso horse of year, 1962(1), IV
Man o' War named greatest, 1950
Feb. 8, IV
Messenger breeding line, 1788 May,
IV
Morgan breed, 1808, IV
Peacemaking record, 1803(2), IV
Prioress first U.S. horse to race in
Europe, 1857(7), IV
race with steam locomotive, 1830
Sept. 18, IV
record auction price, 1985 July 23, IV
record earnings, 1989, IV
Secretariat ninth to win Triple
Crown, 1973 June 9, IV
trotter mile running record, 1854(5),
IV
women cautioned against riding,
1837(6), IV
women's riding vogue, 1855(3), IV
Horseshoes, 1835 Nov. 23, III
Horticulture (see also Botany):
Burbank's nursery (Calif.), 1875(2), III
Burbank's potato, 1872(7), III
Downing's treatise on landscape
gardening, 1841(5), II
Downing's Wash., D.C., landscaping,
1851(7), II
early Dutch gardens, 1653(1), II
first horticulturist, 1724, III
first seed business, 1784(3), III
gardening upswing, 1975, III
landscape gardening, 1839, II
Perrine's contribution, 1833(1), IV
poinsettia, 1825 Mar. 7, I
rose declared official U.S. flower, 1986
Sept. 23, IV
Va. plants, 1680(1), III
world's largest flower, 1937 June 8, III
Hosmer, Harriet G., 1860(5), II
Hospitals see Medicine; Mental Illness and
health; names
Hostages see Iran; Lebanon
Hotchkiss, Hazel, 1909 June 27, IV; 1910
June 26, IV; 1911 June 17, IV; 1919
June 21, IV
Hotchner, A.E., 1966(1), II
Hotels and inns:
Astor Hotel opened (N.Y.C.), 1836
May 31, IV

Hotels and inns (cont.)
Astoria opened (N.Y.C.), 1897 Jan. 30,
II
Commodore (N.Y.C.), 1918(6), II
disaster (Kansas City, Mo.), 1981 July
17, I
fire (San Francisco, Calif.), 1961 Jan. 6,
I
fire (San Juan, Puerto Rico), 1986 Dec.
31, I
first bridal suite (N.Y.C.), 1844(2), IV
first hotel (N.Y.), 1802(2), IV
first luxury hotel (Boston, Mass.), 1829
Oct. 16, IV
first passenger elevator (N.Y.C.),
1859(3), III
first private bath (N.Y.C.), 1844(2), IV
first steam-heated (Boston, Mass.),
1846(1), III
gas lighting, 1835(3), III
Helmsley convicted, 1989 Aug. 30, IV
Pennsylvania (N.Y.C.), 1918(6), II
Plaza (N.Y.C.), 1907(4), II
racial discrimination barred, 1964 July
22, I
second worst fire to date (Las Vegas,
Nev.), 1980 Nov. 21, I
worst fire to date, 1883 Jan. 10, I;
1946 Dec. 7, I
Hot line (Wash., D.C.-Moscow), 1963 Aug.
30, I
Hounsfield, Geoffrey N., 1979 Oct. 12, III
"House divided" theme, 1856(6), IV; 1858
June 16, IV
Houseman, John, 1974 Apr. 2, II; 1988, II
House of the Seven Gables, The
(Hawthorne), 1670–1679, II
House Un-American Activities Committee
see Un-American Activities, House
Committee on
Housing (see also Heating; Lighting;
Mansions and manor homes; Mobile
homes; Plumbing; Real estate; Windows
and doors; names of specific historic
homes):
American ideal, 1992, I
antihomosexual discrimination law
defeated (Fla.), 1977 June 7, I
best extant N.E. style, 1683, II
Calif. law ruled unconstitutional, 1967
May 29, III
caves, 1685(2), IV
cooperative (Hillman Houses, N.Y.C.),
1930(4), II
discriminatory zoning laws upheld,
1977 Jan. 11, III
Dymaxion House (Fuller), 1946(3), II
earliest remaining in Manhattan,
1719(3), II
early names (Md.), c1650, I
early public (N.Y.C.), 1937(2), II
emerging styles, 1640–1649, II
Federal, fine example, of (Mass.),
1805(4), II
first tenement law (N.Y.C.), 1867(1), I
first Wright design (Chicago, Ill.),
1892(7), II
GI loans, 1958 Apr. 1, I
Home Owners Loan Act, 1934 Apr.
28, I

Housing (*cont.*)
  log cabin introduced (Del.), 1638(2), II; 1638 Mar., I
  Mies's Lake Shore Drive (Chicago) apartments, 1951(8), II
  National Housing Act, 1934 June 28(2), I; 1937 Sept. 2, I
  new construction rate jumped, 1983, III
  new home sales down, 1991, III
  new public units approved, 1955 Aug. 2, I
  numbering (Phila., Pa.), 1793(3), IV
  oldest extant in Midwest (Ill.), c1737, II
  oldest extant (Va.), 1636, II
  oldest frame (Mass.), 1637(1), II
  Old Merchant's House (N.Y.), 1832(1), II
  omnibus bill vetoed, 1959 July 7, I
  racial discrimination prohibited, 1962 Nov. 20(2), I
  ranch style, 1946(4), II
  redlining, 1975 Dec. 18, III
  Renaissance style (N.Y.C.), 1664(4), II
  rent controls, 1948 Mar. 30, I; 1952 June 28, III
  rent stabilization, 1942 Apr. 28, III
  Richard Jackson House (N.H.), 1664(1), II
  Robey House (Chicago, Ill.), 1907(8), II
  servants' staircase, c1720, IV
  shingled, 1880(3), II
  shortage, 1946(3), II; 1947, I
  starts, 1984, III
  Turner House (Salem, Mass.), 1670–1679, II
  Wright's designs, 1892(7), II; 1893(7), II
Housing and Urban Development, Department of:
  Weaver first secretary, 1966 Jan. 17(1), I
Houssay, Bernardo, 1947 Oct. 23, III
Houston, Sam:
  defeated Santa Anna, 1836 Apr. 21, I
  first president of Tex. Republic, 1836 Oct. 22, I
Houston, Whitney, 1986 Feb. 25, II; 1988 Mar. 2, II
Houston Astrodome (Tex.), 1965 Apr. 9, II
Hovey, Fred H., 1895(3), IV
Hovhaness, Alan, 1954 Feb. 22, II
Hoving, Thomas, 1967 Apr. 15, II; 1972, II; 1975 Aug. 29, II; 1977 Dec. 31, II
Hoving, Walter, 1989, III
Howard, Bronson, 1870(6), II; 1889 Sept. 9, II
Howard, Maureen, 1979 Jan. 15, II
Howard, M. William, Jr., 1978 Nov. 4, III
Howard, Oliver O., 1865 Mar. 3, I; 1867(3), II
Howard, Richard, 1970 May 4, II
Howard, Sidney, 1924 Nov. 24, II; 1925 Apr. 26, II; 1932 Oct. 31, II; 1934 Feb. 24, II
Howard, Trevor, 1963 May 26, II
Howard University (Wash., D.C.), 1867(3), III

Howe, Elias, 1846 Sept. 10, III; 1851 Aug. 12, III
Howe, Gordie, 1971 Sept. 9, IV
Howe, Irving, 1976(1), II; 1977 Apr. 13(1), II
Howe, John Ireland, 1832(3), III
Howe, Julia Ward, 1868(1), I; 1908(6), II
Howe, William (Sir), 1775 May 25, I; 1775 June 17, I
Howells, William Dean:
  Annie Kilburn, 1889(1), II
  Hazard of New Fortunes, A, 1890(1), II
  Indian Summer, 1886(1), II
  Modern Instance, A, 1882(1), II
  My Mark Twain, 1910(1), II
  posthumous work, 1900(1), II
  president of American Academy of Arts and Letters, 1908(6), II
  Rise of Silas Lapham, The, 1885(1), II
  Traveler from Ultruia, A, 1894(1), II
  Venetian Life, 1866(1), II
Howser, Richard D. (Dick), 1987, IV
Hoyt, Charles H., 1891 Nov. 9, II
Hoyt, Monty, 1962 Feb. 3–4, IV
Hoyt, Waite, 1984, IV
Hubbard, Cal (Robert), 1977, IV
Hubbard, Elbert, 1895, II; 1899 Feb. 22, II
Hubbard, L. Ron, 1950, II; 1986, II
Hubbard, William, 1677(1), II
Hubbell, Carl, 1988, IV
Hubble Space Telescope, 1990 Apr. 25, III
Hubel, David H., 1981 Oct. 9, III
Huddleston, Silous, 1972 Mar. 1(2), III
Hudson, Henry, 1600–1609, I
Hudson, Rock, 1985, II
Hudson River and Valley:
  artists' depictions, 1823(1), II; 1830, II; 1837(6), II
  Dutch colonists, 1623, I; 1630(2), I
Huerta, Victoriano, 1913 Aug. 27, I; 1914 Apr. 9, I; 1914 Apr. 25, I
Hufstedler, Shirley, 1979 Oct. 17(2), III
Huggins, Charles B., 1966 Dec. 10(2), III
Hughes, Barnard, 1978 June 4, II
Hughes, Charles Evans:
  chief justice appointment, 1930 Feb. 3, I
  elected N.Y. governor, 1906 Nov. 6(2), I
  life insurance scandal probe, 1905, III
  presidential candidacy, 1916, I; 1916 June 7–10, I
Hughes, Howard, 1938(6), III; 1972, II; 1976, III
Hughes, John Joseph, 1841, III
Hughes, Langston, 1926(1), II; 1953(1), II; 1957(1), II; 1967, II
Hughes, Robert Ball, 1847(1), II
Huguenots:
  S.C., 1562 Apr. 30, I; 1680–1689, IV; 1693(2), IV
Hull, Bobby, 1966 Mar. 12(1), IV
Hull, Cordell, 1945 Nov. 12, I
Hull, Edith M., 1921(1), II
Hull, John, 1652 June 10, I
Hull, Josephine, 1951 Mar. 29(2), II
Hull, William, 1812 Aug. 16, I
Hull House (Chicago, Ill.), 1889(1), III
Hulls, Jonathan, 1778(2), III

Humanism, 1933 May 1, III
Human rights:
  annual report, 1991 Feb. 1(1), I; 1992 Jan. 31, I
  U.S. foreign policy stance, 1977 Feb. 24, I
Humberty, James, 1984 July 18, IV
Humor (*see also* Satire):
  Artemus Ward, His Book, 1862, II
  first undergraduate magazine (Harvard Univ.), 1876(6), III
  folksy, 1843, II
  A History of New York (Irving), 1809(1), II
  Josh Billings, His Sayings (Shaw), 1865(2), II
  Life magazine, 1883(3), II
  Will Rogers's rise, 1921, II
Humphrey, Hubert H.:
  died, 1978, I
  elected vice president, 1964 Nov. 3, I
  lost presidential bid, 1968 Nov. 5, I
  presidential candidacy, 1968 Aug. 29, I
  vice presidential candidacy, 1964 Aug. 26, I
Humphrey, William, 1958(1), II
Humphrey-Hawkins Act, 1978 Oct. 15, III
Humphry, Derek, 1991(1), II
Hungary:
  Crown of St. Stephen returned by U.S., 1978 Jan. 6(2), I
Hunger:
  Borlaug's efforts against, 1970 Oct. 21, I
  widespread U.S., 1969 Jan. 21, III
Hunt, E. Howard, 1972 Sept. 15, I
Hunt, Freeman, 1856(4), IV
Hunt, H. L., 1974, III
Hunt, Joseph R., 1943 Sept. 5, IV
Hunt, Lamar, 1974 Jan. 24, IV
Hunt, Linda, 1984 Apr. 9, II
Hunt, Martita, 1949 Apr. 24, II
Hunt, Richard Morris, 1871(3), II
Hunt, Robert Morris, 1857(5), II
Hunt, Thomas P., 1836(7), IV
Hunt, Walter, 1854(1), III
Hunt, William, 1812 Feb. 15, I
Hunt, William H., 1883 Mar. 3(2), I
Hunter, "Catfish" (Jim), 1968 May 8, IV
Hunter, Francis T., 1927 July 2, IV; 1929 July 5, IV
Hunter, Kim, 1952 Mar. 20, II
Hunter, Robert, 1714, II; 1725–1729, II
Hunter College (N.Y.C.), 1940(3), II
Hunthausen, Raymond, 1986 Sept. 4, III
Hunting and trapping (*see also* Fur trading):
  from airplanes outlawed, 1971 Nov. 18, IV
  American Shooter's Manual, 1827(2), IV
  buffalo, 1693(3), IV
  colonial tall tale (Mass.), 1767 Dec. 21, IV
  deer closed season (N.Y.), 1706, IV
  early drawings, 1564, IV
  first engraving of, 1774(3), IV
  first organized fox-hunting group (Phila., Pa.), 1766(1), IV

Hunting and trapping *(cont.)*
    fowl closed season (N.Y.), 1708, IV
    fox, 1879, IV
    foxes imported (Md.), 1730(1), IV
    fur seal ban, 1892 Feb. 29, I
    game available (N.Y.), 1670(1), IV
    game protection law, 1796 May 19, I
    nocturnal deer (Carolina), 1784(2), IV
    Va. methods described, 1705(2), IV
Huntley, Chet, 1974, II
Hurok, Sol, 1974, II
Hurricanes:
    Agnes (Atlantic Coast), 1972 June
      19–23, I
    Andrew (Fla., La.), 1992 Aug. 24, I
    Atlantic coast, 1944 Sept. 14, I
    Audrey (La. and Tex.), 1957 June
      27–28, I
    Camille (South), 1969 Aug. 17, I
    Carol (L.I. and N.E.), 1954 Sept. 1, I
    Celia (Tex. and Fla.), 1970 Aug. 3–5, I
    Donna (Atlantic Coast), 1960 Sept.
      9–12, I
    Fla. and Gulf states, 1926 Sept. 18, I
    Frederic (Gulf Coast), 1979 Sept.
      12–14, I
    Galveston, Tex., 1900 Sept. 8, I
    Gloria, 1985 Sept. 26–27, I
    Gulf states, 1947 Sept. 17–19, I
    Hazel, 1954 Oct. 15, I
    Hugo (Puerto Rico, Virgin Islands,
      South Carolina), 1989 Sept. 18–24, I
    Iniki, 1992 Sept. 11, I
    Juan (Gulf Coast), 1985 Oct. 27–Nov.
      7, I
    Last Island (La.) casualties, 1856 Aug.
      10, I
    most destructive to date, 1960 Sept.
      9–12, I
    N.E., 1938 Sept. 21, I
Hurst, Fannie, 1923 Feb. 27, II; 1968, II
Hurt, William, 1986 Mar. 24, II
Husing, Ted (Edward Britt), 1962, IV
Hussein, Ibrahim, 1987 Nov. 1, IV; 1988
    Apr. 18, IV; 1991 Apr. 15, IV; 1992 Apr.
    20, IV
Hussein, Saddam, 1990, I
Hussey, Obed, 1831, III
Huston, Anjelica, 1986 Mar. 24, II
Huston, John, 1949 Mar. 24, II; 1987, II
Huston, Walter, 1949 Mar. 24, II
Hutchins, Colleen Kay, 1951 Sept. 8, IV
Hutchins, Robert M., 1936(2), III
Hutchinson, Anne, 1637 Nov. 7, III
Hutchinson, Thomas, 1750–1754, I
Hutchison, J. Fowler, 1920 Aug. 21, IV
Hutton, Timothy, 1981 Mar. 31, II
Hwang, David Henry, 1988 June 5, II
Hyatt, John Wesley, 1865(3), IV
Hyde, Charles Hazen, 1905, III
Hyde Park Library (N.Y.), 1941 June 30, II
Hydroelectric power:
    first plant (Wis.), 1882(7), III
    Westinghouse generators (N.Y.),
      1895(1), III
    world's largest dam to date (Miss. R.),
      1913 Aug. 26, III
Hydrofluoric acid, 1823(1), III
Hydrogen bomb *see* Nuclear weapons
Hydrotherapy, 1840(4), IV

Hyer, Jacob, 1816(4), IV; 1841(2), IV
Hyer, Tom, 1841(2), IV; 1849 Feb. 7, IV
Hymns *see* Music

Iacocca, Lee, 1984(1), II
Ian, Janis, 1976 Feb. 28, II
IBM (International Business Machines):
    layoffs, 1991, III
    South African interests terminated,
      1986 Oct. 20, III
Ibsen, Henrik, 1918(4), II; 1975 Mar. 5, II
Ice *see* Refrigeration
Ice hockey *see* Hockey, Ice
Ice skating *see* Skating, Ice
Ickes, Harold L., 1933 June 16(1), I; 1943
    May 5, III
Iconoclast (publication), 1894 Mar., II
Idaho:
    first permanent settlement, 1860 Apr.
      14, III
    Fort Hall first settlement, 1834 June
      15, I
    statehood, 1890 July 3, I
    Territory created, 1863 Mar. 3(1), I
Idaho, University of, 1889 Jan. 30, III;
    1892 Oct. 3, III
Idlewild International Airport (N.Y.C.),
    1948 July 31, III; 1962 May 28, II
Ikangaa, Juma, 1989 Nov. 5, IV
ILGWU *see* Ladies' Garment Workers
    Union, International
Illegitimacy (*see also* single parents):
    Cleveland's child, 1884(2), IV
    Randolph's child, 1803(3), IV
    statistics, 1991, I
Illinois:
    Emancipation Day, 1824 Aug. 2, IV
    important road development in,
      1811(4), III
    opened by railroad, 1856(4), III
    statehood, 1818 Dec. 3, I
    tornado, 1925 Mar. 18, I
Illinois, University of, 1867(6), III; 1871(2),
    III
Illinois Central Railroad, 1856(4), III
Illinois Institute of Technology:
    Mies design of campus buildings,
      1950(4), II
Illinois Ship Canal, 1933 June 22, III
Illinois Wesleyan University, 1853 Feb. 12,
    III
Illiteracy:
    Blair Education Bill, 1890 Mar. 10, III
    CCC instruction, 1936, III
    colonial newspapers countering, 1745,
      III
    colonial women, 1655, III
    decrease in, 1880(2), III; 1890(2), III;
      1900(3), III; 1930(2), III
    immigration literacy requirement,
      1915 Jan. 2, I
    immigration literacy requirement act
      passed, 1917 Feb. 5, I
    immigration literacy requirement
      vetoed, 1897 Mar. 2, I
    literacy widespread, 1817(2), II
    Mass. literacy voting requirement,
      1857 May 1, I
    new low, 1910(2), III; 1920(1), III;
      1950(2), III

Illiteracy *(cont.)*
    statistics, 1940(3), III; 1983 Apr. 26, III
    voting requirement tests, 1923 Oct.
      16, I
Immigration (*see also* Citizenship; Ethnic
    groups; Refugees):
    Alien and Sedition Acts, 1798 June 18,
      I; 1798 June 25, I; 1798 July 6, I;
      1798 July 14, I
    "alien is person" ruling, 1886 May 10,
      I
    Alien Registration Act, 1940 June 28,
      I
    Asian laborers banned, 1917 Feb. 5, I
    British and German, 1815, IV;
      1834(1), I
    Calif. efforts to restrict Chinese, 1879,
      I
    Chinese, 1848(1), I
    Chinese citizenship rights, 1898 May
      28, I
    Chinese Exclusion Act declared
      unconstitutional, 1893 May 15, I
    Chinese Exclusion Acts, 1882 May 6,
      I; 1902 Apr. 29, I; 1943 Dec. 17, I
    Chinese Exclusion Treaty, 1880 Nov.
      17, I
    Chinese further restricted, 1892 May
      5, I
    Chinese workers' restrictions, 1888(6),
      III
    Contract Labor Law, 1885, I
    cut by British Passenger Act, 1803, IV
    deportation of communist aliens, 1954
      May 24, I
    disease carriers banned, 1910 Mar. 26,
      I
    eastern and southern Europe, 1891, I
    eleven Sicilians lynched (New
      Orleans, La.), 1891 Mar. 14, I; 1892
      Apr. 12, I
    Ellis Island (N.Y.C.), 1892 Jan. 1, I
    Ellis Island (N.Y.C.) restoration, 1990
      Sept. 8, IV
    encouraged to South and Northwest,
      1883(1), I
    fares and steerage conditions, 1850(6),
      III
    federal naturalization act, 1790 Mar.
      26, I
    first federal restrictions, 1882, I
    first generally restrictive act, 1921
      May 19, I
    first law enacted, 1819 Mar. 2, I
    illegal aliens' right to free education,
      1982 June 15, III
    illegal alien status revision act signed,
      1986 Nov. 6, I
    illegal alien task force, 1977 Apr. 27, I
    illegal surveillance, 1893 Sept. 7, I
    increased, 1855, I
    influx, 1891, I
    Irish in wake of potato famine,
      1846(4), IV
    Japanese restrictions, 1907 Feb. 20, I;
      1907 Mar. 14(1), I; 1908 Feb. 18, I
    Know-Nothing Party against, 1853(2),
      I

Immigration (*cont.*)
  legislative revisions, 1990 Nov. 29, I
  literacy requirement act, 1917 Feb. 5,
    I
  literacy requirement bill vetoed, 1897
    Mar. 2, I
  literacy requirements, 1915 Jan. 2, I
  McCarran-Walter Bill, 1952 June 25, I
  Middle Eastern, 1891, I
  Native American Party founded
    against, 1843 June, I
  Naturalization Act passed, 1795 Jan.
    29, I
  New Era shipwreck, 1854 Nov. 13, I
  N.Y.C. Tammany Hall influence,
    1850(8), IV
  N.Y.S. law requiring reports on, 1837
    Feb., I
  quota system, 1921 May 19, I
  R.I. discrimination, 1729, IV
  Scandinavian, 1838(5), II
  spurred by contract labor act, 1864
    July 4, III
  statistics, 1850(2), I; 1882, I
  steerage rate reduced, 1904 May 23,
    III; 1908(3), III
  superintendent position created, 1891,
    I
  U.S. bureau created, 1894 Aug. 18, I
  World War II displaced persons, 1948
    June 25, I
Immigration Act, 1907 Feb. 20, I; 1910
  Mar. 26, I; 1990 Nov. 29, I
Immunization *see* Vaccination; disease
  names
Impeachment:
  first president (Johnson), 1868, I
  first Senate trial in 50 years, 1986 Oct.
    9, I
  governor (Ariz.), 1988 Apr. 4, I
  Nixon articles voted, 1974 July 30, I
  Nixon inquiry, 1974, I; 1974 Feb. 6, I
  resolutions against Nixon, 1973 Oct.
    23, I
Imports *see* Trade
Inchiquin, The Jesuit's Letters (Ingersoll),
  1810(3), II
Income and wealth, personal, 1991, III
  $100,000 annual, 1866 Sept. 15, IV
  conspicuous consumption, 1897, IV
  control of, 1896(2), III
  corporate heads, 1983, III
  declined, 1981, III
  first roster (N.Y.C.), 1844(3), IV
  largest salary earned, 1935(1), III
  mansions, 1884, IV
  millionaires' support of art, 1880, II
  "millionaire" term popularized,
    1843(1), IV
  N.Y.C. society, 1872, IV
  number of millionaires increased,
    1992, I
  passed $800 billion, 1970 Oct. 14, III
  prosperity and increased, 1953, III
  richest American, 1987, III
  richest man worldwide, 1989 July 9,
    III
  rise in, 1954, III; 1990, III
  statistics, 1929 Sept., I
Income tax *see* Taxation

Indentured servants, 1620–1629, IV;
  1680–1689, III
Independence, War of *see* Revolutionary
  War
Independence Day (*see also* Bicentennial):
  Liberty Weekend, 1986 July 3–6, IV
  100 ships launched to celebrate, 1918
    July 4, III
Independence Hall (Phila., Pa.), 1730(3), II
Independence Party, 1908 July 27, I
India:
  sued Union Carbide Corp., 1985 Apr.
    8, III
Indiana:
  capital, 1816 Dec. 11, I
  statehood, 1816 Dec. 11, I
  tornado, 1925 Mar. 18, I
Indiana University, 1828 Jan. 24, III
  Little 500 bicycle race, 1988 Apr. 22,
    IV
Indian Removal Act, 1830(2), I
Indians (*see also* Indian wars; Massacres;
  specific tribes):
  Alcatraz Island occupation (San
    Francisco), 1971 June 11, I
  Appropriation Act, 1871 Mar. 3, I
  art exhibit, 1992 Oct., II
  baptism, 1540, III; 1613, III
  books on, 1979(1), II
  books on captives of, 1705–1709, II;
    1824, II
  books romanticizing, 1820(1), II
  Carlisle School (Pa.), 1879(3), III
  catacombs found (Ariz.), 1991 Apr. 26,
    III
  characterized as vicious (Bird),
    1837(3), II
  Cherokee land (Kans.-Okla.), 1893
    Sept. 16, I
  Cherokee Phoenix (newspaper), 1828
    Feb. 21, II
  colonial encroachment on lands, 1760
    Dec. 2, I
  colonial relations, 1650–1659, I
  Columbus anniversary protests, 1992,
    I
  Crow reservation opened (Mont.),
    1892 Oct. 15, I
  early drawings of, 1564, IV; 1585, IV
  early federal act, 1786 Aug. 7, III
  early population, 1600, IV
  factory system established, 1795(2), I
  federal department established, 1834
    June 30, I
  federal policy, 1850(9), IV
  first book in own language, 1653(2), II;
    1661, II
  first Catholic bishop, 1986 May 6, III
  first church (Mass.), 1660, III
  first drawings of, 1564, IV
  first language dictionary, 1643(1), II
  first permanent school for (Va.),
    1723(1), III
  first play about, 1766(2), II
  first Protestant convert (Va.), 1587, III
  first Protestant service, 1646 Oct. 28,
    III
  first reservation (N.J.), 1758 Aug., I
  first U.S. senator, 1992, I

Indians (*cont.*)
  first written language (Cherokee),
    1824(3), IV
  game protection law, 1796 May 19, I
  Hubbard account of N.E., 1677(1), II
  Iroquois treaty with settlers, 1722, I
  Jamestown, Va., uprising, 1644 Mar.
    18, I
  lacrosse, 1775(2), IV
  land claim suit (Mass.), 1978 Jan. 6(1),
    I
  land claim suit settled (Me.), 1980
    Mar. 15, I
  land claim suit settled (S.D.), 1979
    June 13, I
  land claim suit settled (Wash.), 1988
    Aug. 27, I
  land deals, 1830 July 15, I
  land opened for settlement (Okla.),
    1891 Sept. 22, I
  lands, 1809, IV
  lands act, 1887 Feb. 8, I
  lands ceded to U.S., 1890 Feb. 10, I
  longest walk to promote rights, 1978
    July 15, I
  Mass. church founded, 1670 Aug. 22,
    III
  Mass. settlers' protective measures,
    1703 Fall, IV
  Meurin dialect dictionary, 1746(2), III
  Moravian hymns in language of, 1763,
    II
  "Only good Indian is a dead Indian"
    quote, 1869 Jan., IV
  Peabody Museum painting and
    artifacts sale, 1979 Feb. 9(1), II
  Pa. land deed, 1737, I
  plays about, 1830(4), II
  pre-colonization, 986–1599, IV
  refused burial in Mich. cemetery,
    1960 Aug. 12, IV
  resettlement, 1834 Oct. 28, I; 1835
    Dec., I; 1838(1), IV; 1838 Dec., I;
    1840(2), I
  rise in, 1991, I
  Rowlandson book about, 1682(2), II
  Sacajawea on Lewis and Clark
    expedition, 1805(1), IV
  Schoolcraft's research on culture and
    history, 1820, III
  sculpture of, 1888(2), II; 1900(2), II
  Seattle Museum of artifacts, 1991 Dec.
    5, II
  Seminole treaty and resistance, 1835,
    I
  settlers' impact, 986–1599, IV; 1600,
    IV
  sit-in to demand land reforms, 1972
    Nov. 8, I
  Sitting Bull killed, 1890 Dec. 15, I
  smallpox epidemics, 1616, III
  speech and music first recorded,
    1889(3), III
  Tecumseh's leadership, 1809, IV
  in theater, 1832(2), II
  Treaty of Easton (Pa.), 1758 Oct., I
  treaty with Pilgrims, 1621, I
  Wounded Knee (S.D.) occupation,
    1973 Feb. 28, I

Indians (cont.)
    Wounded Knee (S.D.) occupation
       charges dismissed, 1974 Sept. 16(3),
       I
Indian wars:
    Black Hawk, 1832 Apr. 6, I; 1832 Aug.
       27, I
    Creek, 1813, I; 1814 Mar. 29, I
    early, 1675–1676, I; 1675 June 24, I;
       1675 Aug. 2, I; 1675 Sept. 1, I; 1676
       Feb. 10, I; 1676 Aug. 12, I
    first U.S. Medal of Honor, 1861 Feb.
       13, I
    Geronimo captured, 1886 Sept. 4, I
    Little Big Horn battle, 1876 June 25, I
    Nez Percé Indians, 1877 June–Oct., I
    Northwest Territory, 1794 Aug. 20, I
    Pequot, 1630–1639, I
    Pontiac's Rebellion, 1763 May 7, I;
       1763 Aug. 5, I
    Seminole, 1817 Nov. 20, I; 1818, I;
       1832 May 9, I; 1835, I
    Sioux uprising (Minn.), 1862 Aug. 18, I
    Tecumseh confederacy, 1811 Nov. 7, I
    Tuscarora, 1711 Sept. 22, I; 1713 Mar.
       23, I
Indochina (see also Vietnam War; country
    names):
    U.S. bill barring military operations,
       1973 July 1, I
Industrial Congress of the United States,
    1845(2), III
Industrial Workers of the World (IWW):
    established, 1905 July 7, III
    federal raids on headquarters, 1917
       Sept. 5, III
    silk workers' strike (N.J.), 1913 Feb.
       25, III
    textile strike (Lawrence, Mass.), 1912,
       III
Industry see Business; Manufacturing
Infantile paralysis:
    epidemic, 1935(4), III; 1943(1), I
    first year of no deaths from, 1970 July
       3, III
    Salk vaccine, 1954 Feb. 23, III; 1955
       Apr. 12, III; 1956 June 11, III; 1956
       Aug. 1, III
    serum progress, 1937, III
    virus research, 1954 Oct. 21, III
Infant mortality, 1976 Jan. 12, III; 1991,
    III
Infeld, Leopold, 1938(2), III
Influenza:
    epidemic and deaths, 1918 Oct., III
    first serious epidemic, 1733, I
    swine flu vaccination program, 1976
       Apr. 15, III; 1976 Dec. 16, III
    vitamin C prevention, 1970 Nov. 18,
       III
Information, classified see Freedom of
    information
Information Agency, U.S., 1965 Mar. 4, I
Inge, William, 1953 Feb. 19, II; 1953 May
    4(2), II; 1955 Mar. 2, II; 1973, II
Ingersoll, Charles, 1810(3), II; 1823(2), III
Inheritance see Wills, estates, and trusts
Inkster, Juli, 1992 July 27, IV
Inman, Henry, 1979 Feb. 9(1), II

Inness, George, 1861(3), II; 1865(8), II;
    1873(2), II
Insanity see Mental illness and health
Insects see Pests and pesticides; specific
    types
Institute of Electrical and Electronic
    Engineers, 1884(2), III
Insular Cases, 1901 May 27, I
Insurance (see also Health Insurance):
    banking premiums raised, 1992 May
       12(2), III
    Equity Funding Corp. fraud, 1975
       Mar. 18, III
    first company to focus on life (Pa.),
       1812(3), III
    first fire (Charleston, S.C.), 1735(2), III
    first life co. (Pa.), 1759, III
    first marine and fire (Phila., Pa.), 1721
       May 25, III
    first mutual life co. chartered, 1842
       Apr. 12, III
    first travelers' accident, 1863(2), III
    "Hand-in-hand" fire motto (Phila.,
       Pa.), 1752 May 11, IV
    life cos. reforms, 1906 Apr. 28, III
    life cos. scandal, 1905, III
    loan policies tightened, 1933 Mar. 7,
       III
    mutual life, 1906 Apr. 28, III
    subject to antitrust laws, 1944 June 5,
       III
Intelligence activities see Central
    Intelligence Agency; Espionage; Federal
    Bureau of Investigation; Wiretapping
INTELSAT (International
    Telecommunications Satellite
    consortium), 1971 Aug. 20, III
Interferon, 1980 Jan. 16, III
Interior, Department of:
    created, 1849 Mar. 3(1), I
    Watt resigned, 1983 Oct. 9, I
Intermediate range ballistic missiles
    (IRBM) see Missiles
Intermediate-Range Nuclear Forces
    Treaty, 1987 Dec. 8, I; 1988 May 27, I
Internal revenue see Taxation
Internal Revenue Act, 1864 June 30, III
Internal Security Act, 1950 Sept. 23, I;
    1954 May 24, I
International Business Machines see IBM
International Education, Institute for,
    1919(2), III
International Harvester Co., 1902, III
International Justice, Permanent Court of
    see World Court
International Longshoremen's Assn see
    Longshoremen's Assn., International
International Monetary Fund (IMF):
    first U.S. borrowing, 1964 Feb. 13, I
International relations see Foreign
    relations
International Telephone and Telegraph
    Co. (ITT):
    ABC merger, 1965 Dec. 7, III
    Chilean political intervention, 1972
       Mar. 20–21, III; 1973 Apr. 2, III
    Nixon reelection campaign finances,
       1974 June 7, I

Interstate commerce:
    federal control established, 1824 Mar.
       2, I
    federal regulatory commission, 1887,
       I; 1906 June 29, I; 1910, I
    ICC's authority increased, 1910, I
    Motor Carrier Act, 1935 Aug. 9, III
    unions subject to prosecution for
       restraining, 1921 Jan. 3, III
    Wage and Hours Act, 1938 June 25, I
Interstate Commerce Act, 1887, I
Interstate Commerce Commission:
    increased jurisdiction, 1910, I
Intolerable Acts, 1774 Mar. 31, I; 1774
    June 22, I; 1774 Sept. 17, I
Inventions see Patents; subject headings
Ionesco, Eugene, 1961 Jan. 9, II
Iowa:
    flood, 1903 May 31, I
    jet crash, 1989 July 19, I
    new territory formed, 1838 June 12, I
    statehood, 1846 Dec. 28, I
Iowa, University of, 1847 Feb. 25, III
Iowa Wesleyan College, 1855 Jan. 25, III
Iran:
    hostage crisis ended, 1981 Jan. 20(2), I
    hostage rescue mission aborted, 1980
       Apr. 24, I
    six Americans escaped, 1980 Jan. 29, I
    U.S. broke relations with, 1980 Apr. 7,
       I
    U.S. hostage crisis, 1979, I; 1979 Nov.
       4, I
    U.S. naval attacks, 1988 Apr. 18, I
    U.S. ship downed jetliner, 1988 July 3,
       I
Iran-Contra affair (see also Contra aid):
    Abrams guilty plea, 1991 Oct. 7, I
    congressional report, 1987 Nov. 18, I
    indictments, 1988 Mar. 16, I
    North convicted, later suspended,
       1989 May 4, I
    Poindexter convicted, later reversed,
       1990 Apr. 7, I
    revealed, 1986 Nov. 3, I
    Tower Commission report, 1987 Feb.
       26, I
Iran-Iraq war:
    Persian Gulf shipping, 1987 May 17, I
Iraq:
    Gulf War, 1991 Jan. 15–Feb. 27, I
    human rights abuse, 1991 Feb. 1(1), I
    invaded Kuwait, 1990, I; 1990 Aug.
       2–Dec. 31, I
    missile attacked U.S. tanker, 1987 May
       17, I
    new sanctions imposed, 1992 Aug. 25,
       I
IRBMs see Missiles
Ireland:
    emigration to U.S. halted by British,
       1803, IV
    potato famine, 1846(4), IV
Ireson, Benjamin, 1808 Oct. 30, IV
Irish-Americans:
    N.Y.C. riots, 1871 July 12, I
Irish National Convention, 1895 Sept. 27, I
Iron see Steel and iron
Irons, Jeremy, 1984 June 3, II; 1991 Mar.
    25, II

Irons and ironing:
  first electric flatiron, 1882(4), III
Iroquois Indians, 1650–1659, I; 1722, I;
  1744, I
Irving, Clifford, 1972, II
Irving, John, 1978(1), II; 1981(1), II;
  1985(1), II; 1989(1), II
Irving, Jules, 1965 Oct. 21(2), II
Irving, Washington:
  "almighty dollar" phrase, 1836 Nov.
    12, IV
  Bracebridge Hall, 1822(2), II
  on frontier, 1820, IV
  A History of New York, 1809(1), II
  Knickerbocker Group, 1820, II
  "Rip Van Winkle", 1818, IV; 1828(5),
    II
  Salmagundi, 1807 Jan.24, II
  Sketch Book, 1819(3), II
  Spanish romances, 1828(3), II
  Sunnyside (N.Y.), 1835(7), II
  Tales of a Traveler, 1824(1), II
Irwin, Bernard John Dowling, 1861 Feb.
  13, I
Irwin, Hale, 1974 June 16, IV; 1979 June
  17, IV; 1990 June 18, IV
Irwin, James B., 1971 July 26, III
Isaac, Rhys L., 1983 Apr. 18, II
Isaacson, Walter, 1992(1), II
Isherwood, Christopher, 1951 Nov. 28, II;
  1966 Nov. 20, II
Islam, Nation of, 1975 Feb. 26, III
Isle of Pines Treaty, 1925 Mar. 23, I
Israel:
  attacked U.S. ship *Liberty*, 1967 June
    8, I
  U.S. informer, 1985, I
Israeli-Arab conflict:
  economic boycott of Israel, 1976, III;
    1976 Sept. 30(1), III
  Lebanese conflict, 1982, I
  oil embargo lifted, 1974 Mar. 18, III
  oil shortage, 1973, III; 1973 Oct. 17,
    III
  Olympic Games terrorist attack (W.
    Ger.), 1972 Aug. 26–Sept. 11, IV
  peace conference (Camp David, Md.),
    1978 Sept. 6–17, I
  peace conference (Madrid, Sp.), 1991
    Oct. 30, I
  peace treaty, 1979 Mar. 26, I
  Sadat visited U.S., 1978 Feb. 8, I
  Time libel suit, 1985 Jan. 24, II
  TWA hijacking (Jordan), 1970 Sept. 6,
    III
  UNESCO cultural aid to Israel cut,
    1974 Dec. 30, II
  U.S. arms sale to Saudi Arabia, 1981
    Apr. 21, I
  U.S. jet fighter sale, 1978 May 15, I
  U.S.-PLO dialogue opened, 1988 Dec.
    14, I
  Young's unauthorized PLO meeting,
    1979 Aug. 15, I
Isray, Robert, 1972 July 13, IV
Isthmian Canal Act, 1902 June 28, I
Italy:
  Ethiopia annexed, 1936, I
  Mafia drug case, 1988 Mar. 31, IV

Italy (*cont.*)
  Renaissance manuscripts, 1988 Oct. 8,
    II
  repercussions of immigrants' lynching
    (New Orleans, La.), 1891 Mar. 14, I;
    1892 Apr. 12, I
Iturbi, José, 1980, II
Ives, Burl, 1959 Apr. 6, II
Ives, Charles, 1939 Jan. 20, II; 1945 Dec.
  27, II; 1965 Apr. 26, II; 1974 Oct. 17–21,
  II
Ives, James Merritt, 1833(4), II

Jack, Beau, 1944, IV
Jacklin, Tony, 1970 June 21, IV
Jackson, Andrew:
  assassination attempt, 1835 Jan. 30, I
  Bank of the U.S., 1833 Sept. 23, I;
    1833 Dec. 26, I
  Battle of New Orleans, 1815, I
  books on, 1945(1), II; 1946 May 6, II
  born, 1767 Mar. 15, I
  church-state separation, 1832 July 9,
    IV
  Creek War, 1814 Mar. 29, I
  died, 1845 June 8, I
  duels, 1806, IV
  elected president, 1828 Dec. 3, I
  equestrian bronze casting of, 1853
    Jan. 8, II
  financial policies, 1837, I
  first Democratic Party presidential
    nominee, 1828(1), I
  Hermitage, The, 1804(1), II
  inaugurated, 1829 Mar. 4, I
  inaugurated for second term, 1833
    Mar. 4, I
  internal improvements issue, 1830, I
  kitchen cabinet, 1829(2), I
  nullification controversy, 1833 Mar. 2,
    I
  opponents, 1828(2), I; 1834, I
  policies as 1836 campaign factor,
    1836, I
  recognized Tex. Republic, 1837 Mar.
    3(2), I
  reelected president, 1832 Dec. 5, I
  second term nomination, 1832 May
    21, I
  Seminole Wars, 1818, I
  Senate censured, 1834 Apr. 15, I
  song about, 1822(2), IV
  S.C. secession threat, 1832, I
  species circular, 1836 July 11, I
  spoils system, 1829(1), I
  symbolic of new era, 1829, I
  tariff policy, 1828, I
  Tex. purchase offer, 1829 Aug. 25, I
  vetoed banking bill, 1832 July 10, I
Jackson, George, 1971 Aug. 21, IV; 1972
  Mar. 27, IV
Jackson, Glenda, 1971 Apr. 14, II; 1972
  May 14, II; 1974 Apr. 2, II
Jackson, Helen Hunt, 1881(1), II; 1884(1),
  II
Jackson, Henry M., 1983, I
Jackson, James, 1795(1), I
Jackson, Mahalia, 1972, II
Jackson, Maynard, 1973 Oct. 16(1), I
Jackson, Michael, 1984, II; 1984 Feb. 28, II

Jackson, Reggie, 1976 Nov. 4, IV
Jackson, Shirley, 1954(1), II; 1965, II
Jackson, Thomas J. ("Stonewall"):
  Bull Run, second battle (Va.), 1862
    Aug. 29–30, I
  captured Harpers Ferry (W. Va.),
    1862 Sept. 15, I
  Cedar Mt. battle (Va.), 1862 Aug. 9, I
  mortally wounded, 1863 May 2, I
  nicknamed "Stonewall", 1861 July 21,
    I
Jackson, Tommy ("Hurricane"), 1957, IV
Jackson, Travis, 1987, IV
Jackson State College (Miss.):
  riots, 1967 May 10–11, III
Jacobi, Abraham, 1860(3), III
Jacobi, Derek, 1985 June 2, II
Jacobs, Helen Hull, 1932 Aug. 21, IV; 1933
  Aug. 26, IV; 1934 Aug. 19, IV; 1935
  Sept. 11, IV; 1936 July 4, IV
Jacobs, Lou, 1992, II
Jacobsen, David P., 1986 Nov. 2, I
Jacobson, Cecil B., 1992 Mar. 4, III
Jacobson, Walter, 1985 Dec. 5, III
Jacoby, Oswald, 1984, IV
Jagger, Dean, 1950 Mar. 23, II
James, Harry, 1983, II
James, Henry:
  Ambassadors, The, 1903(1), II
  American, The, 1877(1), II
  books on, 1944(1), II; 1969(1), II; 1986
    Feb. 17, II
  Daisy Miller, 1879(1), II
  Europeans, The, 1878(1), II
  Finer Grain, The, 1910(1), II
  Golden Bowl, The, 1904(1), II
  Niagara Falls description, 1871(2), IV
  Outcry, The, 1911(1), II
  Passionate Pilgrim, A, 1875(1), II
  Princess Casamassima, 1886(1), II
  Pulitzer Prize, 1931 May 4, II
  Small Boy and Others, 1913(1), II
  Spoils of Poynton, 1897(1), II
  What Maisie Knew, 1897(1), II
  Wings of the Dove, The, 1902(1), II
James, Jesse and Frank, 1882, IV
James, William, 1882(1), III; 1890, III
James II (King of Great Britain),
  1680–1689, I; 1687, I; 1687 June 28, IV
Jameson, Betty, 1947 June 29, IV
James R. Bridge (Va.), 1864 June 14, I
Jamestown colony (Va.):
  burned, 1676 Sept. 19, I
  founded, 1607 May 13, I
  Indian uprising, 1644 Mar. 18, I
  social stratum, 1607, IV
  starvation, 1608, IV; 1609–10, I
Janáček, Leoč, 1970 Nov. 3, II
Janeway, James, 1700(3), II
Janis, Sidney, 1967 June 16, II
Jannings, Emil, 1929 May 16, II
Janssen, Werner, 1990, II
January, Don, 1961 July 30, IV; 1967 July
  24(1), IV
Japan:
  art influence in U.S., 1864(5), II
  atomic bombs dropped on Hiroshima
    and Nagasaki, 1945, I; 1945 Aug. 6,
    I; 1945 Aug. 9, I
  Bush meetings, 1992 Jan. 8, III

Japan (*cont.*)
  business acquisitions in U.S., 1989 Sept. 27, III; 1989 Oct. 30, III
  domestic market opened to U.S. products, 1978 Jan. 13, III
  Eisenhower visit canceled, 1960 June 16, I
  first embassy in U.S., 1860 Mar. 9, I
  Hirohito visit to U.S., 1971 Sept. 26, I
  immigration restricted, 1907 Feb. 20, I; 1907 Mar. 14(1), I; 1908 Feb. 18, I
  joint auto venture with U.S., 1983 Dec. 22, III
  major league U.S. baseball team ownership, 1992 June 11, IV
  more ports opened to U.S., 1858, III
  mutual defense agreement with U.S., 1954 Mar. 8(2), I
  opened to U.S. trade, 1854 Mar. 31, I
  peace treaty ratified, 1952 Mar. 20, I
  Pearl Harbor attack, 1941, I; 1941 Dec. 7, I
  Perry trade treaty, 1853, I
  sank U.S. gunboat *Panay*, 1937 Dec. 12, I
  space research, 1992 Sept. 20, III
  steel dumping in U.S., 1978 Jan. 3, III
  steel-dumping penalty, 1977 Oct. 3, III
  Treaty of Portsmouth provisions, 1905, I
  U.S. mutual security treaty, 1960 Jan. 18, I
  U.S. occupation, 1945 Aug. 30, I
  World War II peace treaty signed, 1951 Sept. 8, I
Japanese-Americans:
  citizenship returned, 1959 May 20, IV
  excluded from land ownership (Calif.), 1913 May 19, I
  recompensed for internment, 1988 Aug. 10, I
Jarreau, Al, 1982 Feb. 24, II
Jarrell, Randall, 1961 Mar. 14, II
Java Sea, Battle of, 1942 Feb. 27-Mar. 1, I
Javits, Jacob J., 1986, I
Jaworski, Leon A., 1973 Nov. 1, I; 1974 July 24, I; 1977 July 20, I
Jay, John, 1789 Sept. 26(1), I
Jaycees:
  women's membership, 1984 July 3, I
Jayroe, Jane Anne, 1966 Sept. 10, IV
Jay Treaty, 1794 Nov. 19, I
Jazz:
  age, 1922, II; 1925, IV
  Armstrong's popularization of, 1922, II
  Beiderbecke in Chicago, Ill., 1923, II
  "Bill Bailey", 1902(3), II
  Bolden insane, 1909(7), II
  books on, 1989, II
  Dixieland Band opened (Chicago, Ill.), 1916(5), II
  Ellington archives, 1988 Apr., II
  first International Festival (Wash., D.C.), 1962 May 31–June 3, II
  first recordings, 1917(4), II
  first white Dixieland band, 1892(3), II
  growing influence, 1959(3), II

Jazz (*cont.*)
  "High Society" song adopted, 1901 Mar., II
  "Jelly Roll" Morton, 1926(4), II
  JVC Jazz Festival (N.Y.C.), 1989, II
  Lincoln Center (N.Y.C.) department, 1991 Jan. 9, II
  Newport Festival moved to N.Y.C., 1972 July 1–9, II
  Newport Festival moved to Saratoga Springs (N.Y.), 1977 June 30, II
  Newport Festival (R.I.), 1958 July 3–6, II
  Original Dixieland Jass Band opened (N.Y.C.), 1917(4), II
  revived, 1982, II
  Storyville (New Orleans) closed, 1917(3), II
  "You've Been a Good Old Wagon but You've Done Broke Down" (song) (Harney), 1895(2), II
Jeanneret, Charles-Eduard *see* Le Corbusier
Jeffers, Robinson, 1924(1), II; 1925(1), II; 1929(1), II; 1933(1), II; 1938(1), II; 1962, II
Jefferson, Joseph, 1796(1), II
Jefferson, Thomas:
  agrarian society vision, 1804 Feb. 1, IV
  architectural views, 1812(3), II
  book collection to Library of Congress, 1815(1), III
  books on, 1981(1), II
  born, 1743 Apr. 13, I
  coinage system, 1785 July 6, I
  coined "entangling alliances" phrase, 1801 Mar. 4, IV
  college experiences, 1760–1764, IV
  Declaration of Independence, 1775–1779, I
  died, 1826 July 4, I
  elected vice president, 1796 Dec. 7, I
  Enabling Act, 1802 Apr. 30, I
  encouraged R. Fulton, 1807 Aug. 11, III
  first president inaugurated in Wash., D.C., 1801 Mar. 4, I
  on freedom of speech, press, and religion, 1800 Sept. 23, IV
  inaugurated for second term, 1805 Mar. 4, I
  Lewis and Clark Expedition, 1804, I
  Louisiana Purchase, 1802, I; 1803 Jan. 11, I
  minister to France, 1785 Mar. 10, I
  Monticello, 1770(2), II
  plow studies, 1797 June 26, III
  presidential election tie, 1800, I; 1801, I
  primogeniture abolishment, 1785(4), IV
  public education proposal (Va.), 1779(2), III
  reelected president, 1804 Dec. 5, I
  religious views, 1822, III
  retirement, 1809 Mar. 4(2), I
  secretary of state, 1789 July 27, I
  slave emancipation bill, 1782, I
  states' rights, 1815 Dec. 5, I

Jefferson, Thomas (*cont.*)
  tax views, 1805 Mar. 4, IV
  trade policy, 1807 Dec. 22, I
  University of Virginia, 1819(5), III
  views on blacks, 1809 Feb. 25, III
  Virginia Capitol, 1789(3), II
  William and Mary, College of, 1779(1), III
Jefferson National Expansion memorial (St. Louis, Mo.), 1948(6), II
Jeffries, James J., 1899 June 9, IV
Jehovah's Witnesses:
  flag salute challenged, 1943 June 14, III
  organized, 1872(2), III
Jemison, Mary, 1824, II
Jencks, Joseph, 1640–1649, III
Jenco, Lawrence M., 1986 Nov. 2, I
Jenkins, David, 1957 Feb. 28–Mar. 3, IV; 1957 Mar. 15–16, IV; 1958 Feb. 14–15, IV; 1958 Mar. 28–29, IV; 1959 Jan. 31–Feb. 1, IV; 1959 Feb. 26–28, IV; 1960 Jan. 30, IV
Jenkins, Ferguson, 1991 July 21, IV
Jenkins, Hayes Alan, 1954 Feb. 17, IV; 1954 Mar. 19, IV; 1955 Feb. 16–17, IV; 1955 Apr. 1–2, IV; 1956 Jan. 26–Feb. 5, IV; 1956 Feb. 17, IV; 1956 Mar. 16, IV
Jenkins, Robert, 1735–1739, I
Jensen, Hans, 1963 Nov. 5, III
Jersey Central Railroad, 1958 Sept. 5, I
Jessel, George, 1981, II
Jessup, Philip C., 1986, I
Jet planes *see* Aviation
Jewelry (*see also* Diamonds):
  men's, 1975, II
Jewett, Sarah Orne, 1877(1), II; 1884(1), II; 1896(1), II
Jewish Defense League, 1990 Nov. 5, I
Jews (*see also* Israeli-Arab conflict):
  book, *Antiquities of the Jews* (Josephus), 1721(3), II
  books on, 1976(1), II; 1977 Apr. 13(1), II
  Conservatives rejected all forms of fundamentalism, 1988 Apr. 13, III
  Dropsie College founded (Pa.), 1907 June 6, III
  first appointed to Cabinet, 1906 Dec. 12, I
  first hospital (N.Y.C.), 1852 Jan. 15, III
  first in North America (N.Y.C.), 1654 July 8, I
  first rabbinical college, 1867 Oct. 25, III
  first rabbis' conference (Ohio), 1855 Oct. 17, III
  first Supreme Ct. justice, 1916 Jan. 28, III
  first to die in American Revolution, 1775 Jan. 11, I
  first to hold elective post, 1775 Jan. 11, I
  first woman Conservative rabbi, 1985 May 12, III
  first woman rabbi, 1972 June 3, III
  founded congregation (N.Y.C.), 1654 July 8, III
  Hebrew papers and books auction price (N.Y.C.), 1984 June 26, II

Jews (*cont.*)
 Hebrew Union College founded
  (Ohio), 1875(1), III
 homosexuals admitted to Reform
  rabbinate, 1990 June 25, III
 impact in colonies, 1725–1729, III
 Kahane assassinated, 1990 Nov. 5, I
 land for first settlement purchased
  (S.C.), 1755 Nov. 27, I
 landmark work, *The Torah*, published,
  1975, III
 Moscow chief rabbi visited U.S., 1968
  June 17–July 1, III
 Protestant affirmation, 1987 June 30,
  III
 rare Hebrew books and manuscript
  sale recalled, 1985 July 16, II
 religious attendance up, 1974 Jan. 13,
  III
 settled in Ga., 1733 July, I
 synagogue bombed (Ga.), 1958 Oct.
  12, III
 three hundredth anniversary of first
  in U.S., 1954(4), II
 Union of American Hebrew
  Congregations, 1873(1), III
 U.S. reaction to Nazi programs, 1938
  Nov. 14–18, I
 women rabbis, 1986 Aug. 2, III
 Young Men's Hebrew Association,
  1874 Mar. 22, III
"Jim Crow" (term), 1828, IV
Job discrimination *see* Equal employment
 opportunity; specific industries
Jockey Club, 1894 Feb., IV
Joel, Billy, 1979 Feb. 16, II; 1980 Feb. 27,
 II
Joffrey, Robert, 1988, II
Joffrey Ballet Co., 1975 Oct. 9, II; 1982, II
Jogging, 1968, IV
Johansson, Ingemar, 1959, IV; 1959 Dec.
 8, IV; 1960, IV; 1960 June 20, IV
John Paul II (Pope), 1979, III; 1979 Oct.
 1–7, III; 1984 Jan. 10, I
Johns, Frank T., 1924 May 11–13, I; 1924
 Nov. 4, I
Johns, Jasper, 1988 May 2, II
Johns Hopkins University, The (Md.):
 chartered, 1867(5), III
 psychology laboratory, 1882(1), III
Johnson, Andrew:
 amnesty proclamation, 1865 May 29, I
 born, 1808 Dec. 29, I
 elected vice president, 1864 Nov. 8, I
 impeachment, 1868, I
 Reconstruction views, 1866, I
 sworn in as president, 1865 Apr. 15, I
 vetoed black suffrage bill, 1867 Jan. 8,
  I
 vetoed Civil Rights Act, 1866 Apr. 9, I
 vetoed Freedmen's Bureau bill, 1866
  Feb. 19, I
 vetoed Reconstruction acts, 1867 Mar.
  2(1), I; 1867 Mar. 23, I; 1867 July
  19, I
 vetoed southern state congressional
  representation bill, 1868 June 25(2),
  I
 vice presidency, 1865 Mar. 4, I

Johnson, Andrew (*cont.*)
 vice presidential nomination, 1864
  June 7, I
Johnson, Ben, 1972 Apr. 9, II
Johnson, Charles, 1990 Nov. 27, II
Johnson, Eastman, 1881(5), II
Johnson, Edward, 1650–1659, II
Johnson, Hale, 1896 May 27–28, I
Johnson, Herschel V., 1860 June 18–23, I
Johnson, Hiram, 1912 Aug. 5, I
Johnson, Howard, 1972, III
Johnson, Hugh, 1933 June 16(1), I
Johnson, Jack, 1908 Dec. 26, IV; 1910 July
 4, IV
Johnson, Joyce, 1984 Jan. 9, II
Johnson, Lady Bird:
 White House luncheon disrupted,
  1968 Jan. 18, IV
Johnson, Luci Baines, 1965 Dec. 24, IV
Johnson, Lynda Byrd, 1967 Dec. 9, IV
Johnson, Lyndon B.:
 appropriations requests, 1967, I
 books on, 1976(1), II
 constitutional amendments proposed,
  1965 Jan. 28, I
 daughter Luci engaged, 1965 Dec. 24,
  IV
 daughter Lynda married, 1967 Dec. 9,
  IV
 Declaration of Honolulu, 1966 Feb. 8,
  I
 declined to seek presidential
  renomination, 1968 Mar. 31, I
 died, 1973, I
 elected president, 1964 Nov. 3, I
 elected vice president, 1960 Nov. 8, I
 Far East tour, 1966 Oct. 17, I
 Glassboro (N.J.) talks, 1967 June 23
  and 25, I
 Great Society programs, 1964, I
 inaugurated president, 1965 Jan. 20, I
 income tax surcharge proposed, 1967
  Oct. 3, I
 legislation signed, 1964 Apr. 11, III;
  1964 July 2, I; 1964 Sept. 3, I; 1965
  Sept. 30, II; 1966 Oct. 15, I; 1967
  Nov. 7, II; 1968 Apr. 11, I; 1968
  June 28, I
 Library (University of Tex.) dedicated,
  1971 May 22, II
 MacBird (Garson) satirization of, 1967
  Feb. 22, II
 memoirs published, 1971(1), II
 Mexican visit, 1966 Dec. 3, III; 1967
  Oct. 28, I
 ordered N. Vietnam bombing halt,
  1968 Oct. 31, I
 presidential candidacy, 1964, I; 1964
  Aug. 26, I
 presidential reelection challenge,
  1968, I
 programs passed, 1965, I
 State of the Union message, 1968 Jan.
  17, I
 sworn in as president, 1963 Nov. 22, I
 voting rights legislation, 1965 Mar. 15,
  I
 wilderness legislation, 1964 Sept. 3, I
Johnson, Magic (Earvin), 1991 Nov. 7, IV;
 1992(1), II

Johnson, Paul B., 1962 Dec. 21, III
Johnson, Philip, 1964 Apr. 24, II
Johnson, Richard M., 1835 May 20, I; 1836
 Dec. 7, I
Johnson, Virginia, 1970(1), II
Johnson, Walter, 1913(1), IV; 1916, IV;
 1927(1), IV
Johnson, William Samuel, 1787(2), III
Johnson Publishing Co., 1984 May 9(1), III
Johnson Wax Co., 1939(3), II
Johnston, Albert S., 1862 Apr. 6–7, I
Johnston, Joseph E., 1862 May 31–June 1,
 I; 1865 Apr. 26(1), I
Johnston, W. F., 1856 June 2, I
Johnston, William M., 1915 June 12, IV;
 1919 June 21, IV
Johnstown (Pa.), 1977 July 19, I
Joliet, Louis, 1670–1679, I
Jones, Allan, 1992, II
Jones, Bobby, 1926 July 10, IV; 1928 June
 24, IV; 1929 June 30, IV; 1930, IV; 1930
 July 12, IV; 1971, IV; 1972 June 18, IV
Jones, Bob (Robert Reynolds), 1968, III
Jones, "Casey" (John Luther), 1900 Apr.
 30, IV
Jones, Jack, 1962 May 29, II; 1964 May 12,
 II
Jones, James, 1952 Jan. 29, II; 1962(1), II;
 1977, II
Jones, James Earl, 1968 Oct. 3, II; 1969
 Apr. 20, II; 1987 June 7, II; 1991 Aug. 5,
 II
Jones, Jennifer, 1944 Mar. 2, II
Jones, Jim, 1978 Nov. 18, I
Jones, John Paul, 1779 Sept. 23, I; 1822(1),
 II
Jones, Joseph Stevens, 1832 June 17, II
Jones, Margaret, 1648(1), II
Jones, Marion, 1899(3), IV; 1902(2), IV
Jones, Quincy, 1991 Feb. 20, II
Jones, Robert T., 1923 July 15, IV
Jones, Rosie, 1988 Aug. 28, IV
Jones, Shirley, 1961 Apr. 17, II
Jones, Stephen, 1984 Oct. 21, IV
Jones, Steve, 1988 Nov. 6, IV
Jones, Tom, 1960 May 3, II
Jones, Tommy Lee, 1983 Sept. 25, II
Jones Act, 1917 Mar. 2, I
Jones Hall (Houston, Tex.), 1966 Oct. 2, II
Jones Parity Plan, 1933 Jan. 5, III
Jones-White Act, 1928 May 22, III
Jong, Erica, 1974(1), II
Joplin, Janis, 1970, II
Joplin, Scott, 1885, II; 1899(2), II; 1972
 Jan. 28, II
Jordan, Jim, 1988, II
Jordan, Kathy, 1985 July 6–7, IV; 1986 July
 5–6, IV
Jordan, Vernon, 1977, I
Jordan, Winthrop D., 1969 Mar. 10(2), II
Josephson, Brian D., 1973 Oct. 23, III
Josselyn, John, 1674(1), II
Journalism *see* Newspapers and
 publications; Television
Journeymen Cordwainers trial, 1810 July
 12, III
Joyce, James, 1918(2), II; 1922(3), II;
 1930(2), II; 1933 Dec. 6, II; 1984 June 7,
 II; 1988 June 15, II

Joyner, Florence Griffith, 1988 July 16, IV; 1988 Sept. 17–Oct. 2, IV
Joyner-Kersee, Jackie, 1988 July 16, IV; 1988 Sept. 17–Oct. 2, IV; 1992 July 25–Aug. 9, IV
Judaism *see* Jews
Judicial Procedure Reform Act, 1937 Aug. 26, I
Judson, Adoniram, 1810(2), III; 1812, III
Judson, E.Z.C., 1849 May 10, II
Juilliard School of Music (N.Y.C.), 1969 Sept. 11, II
Jujitsu, 1904(2), IV
Julian, George W., 1852 Aug. 11, I
Junk bonds, 1990 Nov. 21, III
Jupiter (planet):
    fifth satellite detected, 1892(11), III
    Pioneer 10 launched, 1972 Mar. 2, III
    Pioneer 11 launched, 1973 Apr. 5, III
    Voyager 1 closest approach, 1979 Mar. 5, III
Juries:
    blacks on, 1875 Mar. 1, I; 1880 Mar. 1, I
    broad discretion on damage awards ruling, 1991 Mar. 4, I
    capital punishment opponents barred from, 1986 May 5, I
    fewer than 12 ruled constitutional, 1970 June 22, I
    first all-woman (Md.), 1656 Sept. 22, I
    racial criteria rulings, 1991 Apr. 1, I; 1991 June 3, I; 1992 June 18, I
    women, 1701(3), I
Justice, Department of:
    created, 1870 June 22, I
    Meese resigned, 1988 July 5, I
Justice, Donald R., 1980 Apr. 14(1), II
Juvenile delinquency:
    capital punishment, 1989, I
    legislation to fight, 1961 Sept. 22, IV
    rising rate, 1954, IV

Kael, Pauline, 1974 Apr. 18, II
Kahane, Meir, 1990 Nov. 5, I
Kahn, Herman, 1983, III
Kahn, Louis I., 1960 Apr. 11, II; 1971(2), II; 1974, II; 1977 Apr. 19, II
Kahn, Roger, 1972(1), II
Kaiser, Henry J., 1942(1), III; 1967, III
Kalamazoo College (Mich.), 1855 Feb. 10, III
Kalb, Johann de (Baron), 1780 Aug. 16, I
Kalmus, Herbert T., 1922(4), III
Kaltenborn, H.V., 1965, III
Kammen, Michael, 1973 May 7, II
Kanagawa, Treaty of, 1854 Mar. 31, I
Kander, John, 1966 Nov. 20, II; 1967 Mar. 26, II; 1975 June 3, II; 1977 Oct. 29, II
Kane, Elisha Kent, 1853 May 31, I
"Kangaroo voting", 1888(1), I
Kani, John, 1974 Nov. 13, II; 1975 Apr. 21, II
Kansas:
    antislavery constitution ratified, 1859 July 5, I
    antislavery settlers, 1854(2), IV; 1854 Apr. 26, I
    "bleeding", 1856 Aug. 1, I
    English bill, 1858 May 4, I

Kansas (*cont.*)
    first territorial election, 1855 Mar. 30, I
    flood, 1903 May 31, I
    Free State forces, 1855 Sept. 5, I; 1855 Oct. 23, I; 1855 Nov. 26, I
    Free State legislature elected, 1857 Oct. 5, I
    Lecompton Constitution, 1858 Mar. 23, I; 1858 Aug. 2, I
    Lecompton Constitutional Convention (slavery issue), 1857 Oct. 19, I
    massacre of slavery supporters, 1856 May 21, I
    statehood, 1861 Jan. 29, I
    temperance movement violence, 1900(1), I
    Topeka Constitution, 1855 Oct. 23, I
    Wakarusa War, 1855 Nov. 26, I
    White's editorial on, 1896 Aug. 15, II
Kansas, University of, 1864(1), III
Kansas Agricultural College, 1897(2), III
Kansas City International Airport (Mo.), 1972 Oct. 21, II
Kansas City (Mo.):
    hotel disaster, 1981 July 17, I
Kansas-Nebraska Act, 1854, I; 1854(1), IV; 1857, I
Kantor, MacKinlay, 1955(1), II; 1956 May 7, II; 1961(1), II
Kantorovich, Leonid, 1975 Oct. 14, III
Kapitsa, Per, 1978 Oct. 17, III
Kaplan, Justin, 1967 Mar. 8, II; 1967 May 1, II; 1980(1), II; 1981 Apr. 30, II
Karle, Jerome, 1985 Oct. 16, III
Karlsefni, Thorfinn, 986–1599, I; 1007, IV
Karnow, Stanley, 1990 Apr. 12, II
Karpov, Anatoly, 1975 Apr. 3, IV
Katz, Bernard, 1970 Oct. 15, III
Kaufman, Bel, 1965(1), II
Kaufman, George S., 1921 Aug. 13, II; 1925 Dec. 8, II; 1932 May 2, II; 1936 Nov. 30, II; 1937 May 3, II; 1937 Nov. 2, II; 1939 Jan. 21, II; 1961, II
Kavafian, Ani, 1976 Feb. 9, II
Kaye, Danny, 1987, II
Kaye, Nora, 1987, II
Kaye, Sammy, 1987, II
Kazan, Elia, 1967(1), II
Keane, Johnny, 1964, IV; 1967, IV
Kearney, John J., 1977 Apr. 7, I
Kearns, Doris, 1976(1), II
Keating, Charles H., 1992 Apr. 10(1), IV
Keaton, Buster, 1966, II
Keaton, Diane, 1978 Apr. 3, II
Keats, John (U.S. writer), 1970(1), II
Keck, Howard B., 1992, I
Kedrova, Lila, 1965 Apr. 5, II
Keefe, Tim, 1888(3), IV
Keeler, Ruby, 1971 Jan. 19, II
Keeler, "Wee Willie", 1939 Jan. 24, IV
Kefauver, Estes:
    organized crime hearings, 1951, III
    vice presidential candidacy, 1956 Aug. 13–17, I
Keil, William, 1845(3), III
Keillor, Garrison, 1985(1), II
Keiser, Herman, 1946 Apr. 7, IV
Keith, Benjamin Franklin, 1883(5), II
Keith, George, 1697(1), III

Keller, Charley, 1990, IV
Keller, Helen, 1902(1), II; 1959 Oct. 19, II; 1968, III
Kelley, Clarence B., 1975 July 14, I
Kelley, Kitty, 1992(1), II
Kelley, Oliver H., 1867, III
Kellogg, Frank B., 1927 Apr. 6, I; 1930 Nov. 27, I
Kellogg-Briand Peace Pact, 1927 Apr. 6, I; 1928 Aug. 27, I; 1929 Jan. 15, I
Kelly, Ellsworth, 1992 Nov. 1, II
Kelly, Emmett, 1979, II
Kelly, George, 1926 May 3, II; 1946 Nov. 19, II
Kelly, Grace, 1955 Mar. 30, II; 1956 Apr. 19(1), IV
Kelly, John B., Jr., 1985, IV
Kelly, Nancy, 1955 Mar. 27, II
Kelly, Paul, 1948 Mar. 28, II
Kelly, Robert F., Jr., 1992 Apr. 22, IV
Kelly, Walt, 1973, IV
Kelly, William, 1857, III
Kelsey, Frances O., 1962 Aug. 17, III
Kemble, Fanny, 1832, II
Kemeys, Edward, 1878(4), II
Kempff, Wilhelm, 1964 Oct. 13, II
Kendall, Edward Calvin, 1950 Oct. 26, III
Kendall, Henry W., 1990 Oct. 16(1), III
Kendrick, John B., 1922 Apr. 15, I
Kenilworth (Scott), 1821(1), II
Kennan, George F., 1957 Mar. 12, II; 1957 May 6, II; 1968 Mar. 6, II; 1968 May 8, II
Kennecott Corp.:
    merger, 1981 Mar. 12, III
Kennedy, Anthony, 1987 Oct. 23, I
Kennedy, Edward M.:
    Chappaquiddick (Mass.), 1969 July 18, I
    lost presidential nomination, 1980 Aug. 11–14, I
    on Vietnam War, 1969 May 20, I
Kennedy, George, 1968 Apr. 10(2), II
Kennedy, Jacqueline Bouvier:
    married Onassis, 1968 Oct. 19, IV; 1968 Oct. 25, III
    White House tour, 1962 Feb. 14, II
Kennedy, John F.:
    assassinated (Tex.), 1963, I; 1963 Nov. 22, I
    assassination investigated, 1963 Nov. 29, I
    assassination reviewed, 1976 Sept. 17, I
    Bay of Pigs invasion, 1961 Apr. 17, I
    books on, 1965(1), II; 1966(1), II; 1967(1), II
    Canadian visit, 1961 May 16–17, I
    Catholic issue, 1960 Sept. 12, I
    Cuban missile crisis, 1962 Oct. 22, I; 1962 Oct. 28, I; 1962 Nov. 2, I
    on education crisis, 1961 Jan. 30, III
    elected president, 1960 Nov. 8, I
    election debates, 1960 Sept. 26, I
    European tour, 1963 June 23, I
    on exercise, 1961 Dec. 5, I
    federalized Ala. National Guard, 1963 Sept. 10, III
    foreign policies, 1962, I
    funeral, 1963, I; 1963 Nov. 25, I

Kennedy, John F. (*cont.*)
honored poet Frost, 1962 Mar. 26, II
"Ich bin ein Berliner" statement, 1963 June 23, II
inaugurated as president, 1961 Jan. 20, I
legislation signed, 1961 May 5(1), III; 1961 May 27, I; 1961 Sept. 4, I; 1961 Sept. 5, I; 1961 Sept. 22, IV; 1962 Sept. 15, III; 1962 Sept. 27, III; 1962 Oct. 2, I; 1963 Mar. 19, I; 1963 June 4, III; 1963 June 10, III
Medicare, 1963 Feb. 21(2), I
military call-up, 1962 Sept. 24, I
ordered military appraisal, 1961 July 8, I
Peace Corps, 1961 Jan. 28, III
presidential accomplishments, 1963, I
presidential candidacy, 1960, I; 1960 July 13, I
presidential candidacy endorsed by AFL-CIO, 1960 Aug. 26, I
problems facing, 1961, I
Pulitzer Prize, 1957 May 6, II
Ruby conviction reversed, 1966 Oct. 5, I
Runnymede monument (Eng.), 1965 May 14, II
Science and Technology Office created, 1962 June 8, III
scored steel price hike, 1962 Apr. 10, III
space program priority, 1961 May 25, I
tariff reductions, 1962 Mar. 7, III
Vienna summit, 1961 June 3–4, I
Warren Commission report, 1964 Sept. 27, I
youth programs, 1963 Feb. 14, I
Kennedy, John Pendleton, 1838, II
Kennedy, Joseph P., 1969, I
Kennedy, Robert F.:
books on, 1979 Apr. 23, II
shot (Los Angeles, Calif.), 1968 June 5, I
Sirhan sentenced for murder of, 1969 Apr. 23, I
Kennedy, William, 1983(1), II; 1984 Jan. 9, II; 1984 Apr. 16, II; 1988(1), II
Kennedy Center for the Performing Arts (Wash., D.C.):
La Scala U.S. debut, 1976 Sept. 7, II
opening, 1971 Sept. 8–9, II
Kennedy family:
First Family record album satire, 1962(3), II; 1963 May 15, II
Kennedy Round tariff reduction, 1968 July 1(1), I
Kent, James, 1826, III
Kent, Rockwell, 1971, II
Kent State University (Ohio):
charges against National Guardsmen dropped, 1974 Nov. 8, I
shooting out-of-court settlement, 1979 Jan. 4, I
shootings, 1970 May 4, I
Kentucky:
Boone's exploits, 1765–1769, IV
bus-truck crash, 1988 May 14, I
first woman governor, 1983 Nov. 8, I

Kentucky (*cont.*)
statehood, 1792 June 1, I
Statehood Day, 1792 June 1, IV
Kentucky, University of, 1865(4), III
Kentucky Derby *see* Horse racing
Kenyon College (Ohio), 1824 Jan. 24, III
Keokuk Dam (Miss. R.), 1913 Aug. 26, III
Kern, Jerome, 1920 Dec. 21, II; 1927 Dec. 27(1), II; 1933 Nov. 18, II
Kern, John W., 1908 July 7–10, I
Kerner Commission, 1968 Feb. 29, I
Kerouac, Jack, 1957(1), II; 1960(1), II; 1969, II
Kerr, Jean, 1961 Mar. 8, II
Kerrigan, Nancy, 1991 Mar. 16, IV
Kerr Singers, Anita (group), 1966 Mar. 15(2), II; 1967 Mar. 2, II
Kerwin, Joseph, 1973 May 14, III
Key, Francis Scott, 1814, II; 1931 Mar. 3, II
Khorana, H. Gobind, 1968 Oct. 16, III
Khrushchev, Nikita S.:
Cuban missile crisis, 1962 Oct. 27, I; 1962 Oct. 28, I; 1962 Nov. 20(1), I
debate with Nixon, 1959 July 23, I
U.S. visit, 1959, I; 1959 Sept. 15–27, I
U-2 incident, 1960 May 5, I; 1960 May 16, I
Vienna summit, 1961 June 3–4, I
Kidd, John, 1988 June 15, II
Kidd, William (Capt.), 1699 Spring, IV
Kidder, Tracy, 1982 Mar. 12, II; 1982 Apr. 27, II
Kidnaping (*see also* Terrorism):
Bronfman case (N.Y.), 1975 Aug. 17, IV; 1976 Dec. 10, IV
children for Va. colony, 1627, IV
Hearst case, 1974 Feb. 5, IV; 1974 Apr. 3, IV; 1974 May 17, IV; 1975 Sept. 18, IV; 1976 Mar. 20, IV
Lindbergh baby, 1932 Mar. 1, I; 1935, IV
school bus (Calif.), 1976 July 15, IV
Sinatra son, 1963 Dec. 8, IV
U.S. ambassador to Afghanistan, 1979 Feb. 14, I
Kieft, Willem, 1630–1639, IV
Kier, Samuel M., 1841(1), III
Kieran, John, 1981, IV
Kiersted, Hans, 1638(3), IV
Kilburn, Peter, 1986 Nov. 2, I
Kiley, Richard, 1988 Aug. 28, II
Killebrew, Harmon, 1967, IV
Killian, James R., Jr., 1988, III
Kilmer, Joyce, 1914(3), II
Kilrain, Jake, 1889 July 8, IV
"Kilroy was here" (phrase), 1945(1), IV
Kimball, Judy, 1962 Oct. 7, IV
Kimball, Spencer, 1985, III; 1985 Nov. 11, III
Kimmel, Husband E., 1968, I
Kinane, Michael, 1990 June 9, IV
King, Betsy, 1984, IV; 1989 July 16, IV; 1990 July 15, IV; 1992 May 17, IV
King, Billie Jean (*see also* Moffitt, Billie Jean), 1966 July 2, IV; 1967 July 8, IV; 1967 Sept. 10, IV; 1968 July 6, IV; 1970 July 4, IV; 1971, IV; 1971 July 3, IV; 1971 Sept. 5–15, IV; 1972 July 7(2), IV;

King, Billie Jean (*cont.*)
1972 Sept. 9–10, IV; 1973 July 7–8, IV; 1973 Sept. 20, IV; 1974 July 5, IV; 1974 Sept. 9, IV; 1975 July 4–5, IV
King, Carole, 1972 Mar. 14, II
King, Clarence, 1879 Mar. 3, I
King, Martin Luther, Jr.:
arrested (Birmingham, Ala.), 1963 Apr. 12, III
assassinated, 1968 Apr. 4, I
assassination reviewed, 1976 Sept. 17, I
assassin Ray convicted, 1969 Mar. 10, I
Chicago (Ill.) rally, 1966 July 10, III
debate with Carmichael, 1966 June 6, I
federal holiday honoring, 1983 Nov. 2, IV
"I have a dream" speech, 1963 Aug. 28, I
Memphis (Tenn.) violence, 1968 Mar. 28, I
museum honoring (Memphis, Tenn.), 1991 Aug. 31, I
Nobel Peace Prize, 1964 Oct. 14, III
phones tapped by FBI, 1969 June 6, I
Ray held for assassination, 1968 June 8, I
Why We Can't Wait, 1964(1), II
King, Martin Luther, Sr., 1984, III
King, Rebecca Ann, 1973 Sept. 8, IV
King, Rufus, 1816, I; 1816 Dec. 4, I
King, Stephen, 1985(1), II; 1992(1), II
King, William R., 1852 June 1–6, I; 1852 Nov. 2, I
King George's War, 1740–1744, I; 1745–1749, I; 1745, I
King Philip's War (Mass.), 1675–1676, I; 1675 June 24, I; 1675 Aug. 2, I; 1675 Sept. 1, I; 1676 Feb. 10, I; 1676 Aug. 12, I
King's Chapel (Boston, Mass.), 1749, II
Kingsley, Ben, 1983 Apr. 11, II
Kingsley, Sidney, 1933 Sept. 26, II; 1951 Jan. 13, II
King's Mountain, Battle of (S.C.), 1780 Oct. 7, I
Kingston, Maxine Hong, 1977 Jan. 6, II; 1981 Apr. 30, II
King William's War, 1690–1699, I; 1690 Feb. 8, I; 1690 Oct. 7, I; 1697 Sept. 30, I
Kinnell, Galway, 1983 Apr. 18, II; 1983 Apr. 24, II
Kipling, Rudyard, 1890(2), II; 1894(1), II; 1894(5), II; 1895(1), II; 1897(1), II
Kirkland, Caroline, 1845, II
Kirkland, Jack, 1933 Dec. 4, II
Kirkland, John Thornton, 1814(1), IV
Kirkland, Lane, 1979 Nov. 15, III
Kirkpatrick, John, 1939 Jan. 20, II
Kirkwood, James, 1975 May 21, II; 1976 May 3, II
Kirstein, Lincoln, 1989 Nov. 1, II
Kirsten, Dorothy, 1944(3), II
Kissin, Yevgeny, 1990, II
Kissinger, Henry:
American Book Award, 1980 May 1, II
Berrigan kidnaping plot, 1970 Nov. 27, I; 1971 Jan. 12, I; 1972 Sept. 5, I

Kissinger, Henry (*cont.*)
  biography, 1992(1), II
  memoirs and TV contracts, 1977 Feb. 7, II
  Middle East mediation, 1974 Mar. 18, III
  Nobel Peace Prize, 1973 Oct. 16(2), I
  resigned National Security Council post, 1975 Nov. 3, I
  shuttle diplomacy, 1974, I
  White House Years, The, 1980(1), II
Kite, Tom, 1981, IV; 1989, IV; 1992 June 21, IV
Kitt, Eartha, 1968 Jan. 18, IV
Kittinger, Joe W., 1984 Sept. 14–18, IV
Kitty Hawk (carrier), 1972 Oct. 12–13, I
Kizer, Carolyn, 1985 Apr. 24, II
Kleban, Edward, 1975 May 21, II; 1976 May 3, II
Klein, Anne, 1974, IV
Klein, Lawrence R., 1980 Oct. 15, III
Kleindienst, Richard G., 1973 Apr. 30, I; 1974 June 7, I
Klemm, Johann Gottlob, 1741 Aug., II
Kline, Franz Josef, 1962, II
Kline, Kevin, 1989 Mar. 29, II
Klinghoffer, Leon, 1985 Oct. 7–10, I
Klondike R., 1896 Aug. 12, III; 1897 July 14, I
Klugman, Jack, 1964 May 25(2), II
Kluszewski, Ted, 1988, IV
Knapp, Samuel, 1829(2), II
Knebel, Fletcher, 1960(1), II; 1962(1), II
Knickerbocker Group, 1820, II
Knievel, Evel (Robert), 1974, IV
Knight, Gladys, 1974 Mar. 2, II
Knight, James L., 1991, III
Knight, John S., 1981, III
Knight, Sarah Kemble, 1700–1704, IV; 1704 Oct., I
Knights of Columbus, 1882 Feb. 2, III
Knights of Labor, Noble Order of the, 1869(6), III; 1873(1), I; 1878 Jan. 1, III; 1885, I
Knights of Pythias, 1864 Feb. 19, IV
Knights of St. Crispin, Order of the, 1867 Mar. 7, III
Knights Templar, Grand Encampment of, 1816 June 22, IV
Knitting:
  power machine, 1831 Apr., III
Knives:
  Bowie, 1835(4), III
Knopf, Alfred A., 1984, II
Knott, Frederick, 1966 Feb. 2, II
Knotts, Don, 1962 May 22, II
Know-Nothing Party:
  antislavery faction's presidential nomination, 1856 June 2, I
  Fillmore-Donelson ticket, 1856 Feb. 22(2), I
  formed, 1853(2), I
  proslavery forces, 1855 June 5, I
  proslavery presidential candidates endorsed by Whigs, 1856 Sept. 17, I
  slavery stance, 1856, I
Knox, Frank, 1936 June 9–12, I
Knox, Henry, 1789 Aug. 7, I
Knudsen, William S., 1941 Jan. 7, III
Koch, Frederick H., 1918(5), II

Kodak Co. *see* Eastman Kodak Co. Photography
Kohlberg Kravis and Roberts & Co., 1989 Feb. 3, III
Koopmans, Tjalling C., 1975 Oct. 14, III
Kopechne, Mary Jo, 1969 July 18, I
Kopit, Arthur, 1962 Feb. 26, II; 1982 May 9, II
Korea:
  U.S. forces withdrawn, 1949 June 29, I
  U.S. recognized independence, 1882 May 22, I
Korea, North:
  Pueblo incident, 1968 Jan. 23, I; 1968 Feb. 14, I
  two U.S. soldiers killed, 1976 Aug. 18, I
  U.S. reconnaissance plane downed, 1969 Apr. 15, I
  U.S. travel restrictions lifted, 1977 Mar. 18, I
Korea, South:
  Moon support, 1976 Sept. 18, III
  Park lobbyist activities, 1976, I; 1976 Oct. 20(2), I; 1977 July 20, I
  Park's testimony on U.S. lobby, 1978, I
  Soviets shot down airliner, 1983 Sept. 5, I
  Summer Olympics, 1988 Sept. 17–Oct. 2, IV
  U.S. ground forces' withdrawal, 1977 Mar. 9, I
Koreagate (scandal), 1976, I; 1976 Oct. 20(2), I; 1977 July 20, I; 1978, I
Korean War:
  armed forces doubled, 1951 Mar. 21, I
  armistice signed, 1953 July 27, I
  began, 1950 June 25, I
  casualties, 1953(1), I
  cease-fire proposed, 1951 June 23, I
  Chinese Communist aggression charged, 1951 Feb. 1, I
  Chinese Communist troop involvement, 1950 Nov. 6, I
  Eisenhower's vow to visit, 1952 Oct. 24, I
  Eisenhower visited, 1952 Nov. 29, I
  first truce talks, 1951 July 10, I
  implications for third world war, 1951, I
  MacArthur named UN commander, 1950 July 8, I
  MacArthur policy defense before Congress, 1951 Apr. 19, I
  MacArthur recalled, 1951 Apr. 11, I
  national emergency declared, 1950 Dec. 16, I
  peace agreement, 1953, I; 1953 July 27, I
  Seoul recaptured by U.S., 1951 Mar. 14, I
  Seoul taken by Chinese, 1951 Jan. 15, I
  Seoul taken by U.S., 1950 Sept. 26, I
  38th parallel crossed by U.S., 1950 Oct. 7, I
  38th parallel reached by S. Koreans, 1950 Sept. 29, I
  truce talks deadlocked, 1952 Jan. 24, I

Korean War (*cont.*)
  Truman granted emergency economic powers, 1950 Sept. 8, I
  U.S. Army reservists called up, 1950 Aug. 4, I
  U.S. forces ordered into, 1950, I; 1950 June 27, I
  U.S. forces retreated, 1950 Nov. 29, I
  U.S. germ warfare charged, 1952 Mar. 8, I
  U.S. ground forces landed, 1950 July 1, I
  U.S. landed at Inchon, 1950 Sept. 15, I
  U.S. naval blockade, 1950 June 30, I
  Yalu R. reached by U.S., 1950 Nov. 20, I
Kornberg, Arthur, 1959 Oct. 15, III
Kosinski, Jerzy, 1969 Mar. 10(2), II
Kostelanetz, Andre, 1980, II
Kosygin, Aleksei, 1967 June 23 and 25, I
Kotzebue, August von, 1798 Dec. 10, II
Koufax, Sandy, 1963 Oct. 2–6, IV; 1965 Sept. 9, IV; 1965 Oct. 6–14, IV; 1966, IV
Kovacs, Ernie, 1962, II
Kozol, Jonathan, 1967(1), II; 1968 Mar. 6, II
Kraft, Joseph, 1986, II
Kraft Inc., 1988 Oct. 30, III
Kramer, Jack, 1946 July 6, IV; 1946 Sept. 8, IV; 1947 July 4–5, IV; 1947 Sept. 14, IV
Kramer, Samuel Noah, 1990, III
Kramm, Joseph, 1952 Jan. 15, II; 1952 May 5, II
Krebiozen, 1963 Sept. 7, III
Krebs, Edwin G., 1992 Oct. 12(1), III
Krebs, Hans Adolf, 1953 Oct. 22, III
Kreiger, Henry, 1981 Dec. 20, II
Kreisler, Fritz, 1962, II
Krenek, Ernst, 1945(3), II; 1954 Mar. 4, II
Krenwinkel, Patricia, 1971 Jan. 25, IV
Kresge, Sebastian S., 1966, III
Kreutz, Arthur, 1952(3), II
Kristiansen, Ingrid, 1989 Apr. 17, IV; 1989 Nov. 5, IV
Kroll, Ted, 1956, IV
Krupa, Gene, 1973, II
Krutch, Joseph Wood, 1955 Jan. 25, II; 1970, III
Kubicka, Terry, 1976 Jan. 10–11, IV
Kubik, Gail, 1952(3), II
Kubly, Herbert, 1956 Feb. 7, II
Kuhn, Allan, 1964 Oct. 29, IV
Kuhn, Bowie, 1969 Aug. 13, IV; 1976 June 15, IV; 1982 Nov. 1, IV; 1983 Dec. 8, IV
Kuhn, Margaret, 1972 May 18, IV
Ku Klux Klan:
  banned from Steelworkers, 1954 Sept. 24, III
  congressional investigations, 1965 Oct. 19, I
  convictions for rioting, 1988 Oct. 6, I
  Dixon's novel on, 1905(1), II
  formed (Tenn.), 1865 Dec. 24, IV
  Liuzzo murder, 1965 Mar. 25, I
  massive demonstration (Wash., D.C.), 1925 Aug. 8, I
  members convicted of conspiracy, 1967 Oct. 20, I

Ku Klux Klan (*cont.*)

Okla. under martial law, 1923 Sept. 15, I

paraded (Jacksonville, Fla.), 1920 Oct. 30, IV

reemergence in South, 1921 Aug., I

revised constitution, 1868(3), I

revived in Ga., 1915 Dec. 4, III

shootout (N.C.), 1979 Nov. 3, I

Turner abduction (Tex.), 1960 Mar. 7, IV

Kunitz, Stanley, 1979(1), II

Kunstler, William, 1973 Dec. 4, I

Kuralt, Charles, 1990(1), II

Kusch, Polykarp, 1955 Nov. 2(2), III

Kuscsik, Nina, 1973 Sept. 30, IV

Kuwait:

Gulf War, 1991 Jan. 15–Feb. 27, I

invaded by Iraq, 1990, I; 1990 Aug. 2–Dec. 31, I

U.S. military alliance signed, 1991 Sept. 19, I

Kuznets, Simon, 1971 Oct. 15, III; 1985, III

Ky, Nguyen Cao, 1966 Feb. 8, I

Labels and labeling:

cigarette health hazard, 1964 June 24, III

Pure Food and Drug Act, 1906 June 30, I

recordings' explicit lyrics, 1990 Mar. 29, II

Labor (*see also* Equal employment opportunity; Indentured servants; Migrant workers; Slaves and slavery; Strikes; Work day and week; union names; industry names):

actors' unions, 1900(4), II

AFL formed, 1886, III

agency shop labor contract constitutional, 1963 June 3, III

all manpower controls lifted, 1945 Aug. 14, III

antidiscrimination moves, 1963 July 1, III; 1964 June 14, III

anti-injunction Law, 1932, III; 1932 Mar. 23, III

antitrust laws, subject to, 1908 Feb. 3, III

apprentices, 1819(2), IV

arbitration supported by Supreme Ct., 1964 Apr. 27, III

Asian immigrants banned, 1917 Feb. 5, I

automation, 1955, III; 1963, III

child, 1890(1), III; 1941 Feb. 3, I

Child Labor Law (1916) unconstitutional, 1918 June 3, III

child laws, 1842 Mar. 3, III; 1923 Apr. 9, III

child law (Wash., D.C.), 1908 May 28, III

Chinese exclusion, 1894 Mar. 17, I

Chinese workers' restrictions, 1879, I; 1888(6), III

closed shop curbs, 1949 Jan. 3, III

closed shop issue, 1915 Jan. 25(1), III

Coxey's Army, 1894, I; 1944 May 1, IV

Labor (*cont.*)

crafts vs. industrial unions, 1935, III

decline in leisure time, 1992, II

declining trade union membership, 1931(2), III

early organizations, 1845(2), III

Eisenhower on wage increases, 1958 Jan. 20, III

employment compensation program, 1959 Mar. 31, III

employment rise, 1933 June 21, III; 1959 July 14, III

equal pay for equal work, 1963, III; 1963 June 10, III

Erdman Arbitration Act, 1898 June 1, III

federal arbitration began, 1888 Oct. 1, III

federal minimum wage, 1956, III

first apprenticeship (Va.), 1646, III

first cost-of-living wage contract, 1948 May 25, III

first national black group, 1869 Dec. 6, III

first national congress (Baltimore, Md.), 1866 Aug. 20, III

first organization (Mass.), 1648 Oct. 18, III

first state bureau (Mass.), 1869 Jan. 23, III

first use of term "scab", 1799(1), IV

gains, 1938, III; 1950, III

Gompers' views, 1894(2), III

Haywood murder trial, 1907(1), III

Holmes on picketing, 1896(3), III

ILGWU formed, 1900(4), III

immigration restrictions, 1885, I

increased union formation, 1863, III; 1864(6), III

influential newspaper of Civil War period, 1863(2), II

injunctions, 1894 July 2, III; 1894 Aug. 3, III

injunction use upheld, 1895 May 27, III

IWW established, 1905 July 7, III

IWW headquarters raided, 1917 Sept. 5, III

Japanese banned, 1907 Feb. 20, I; 1907 Mar. 14(1), I

jobs of essential workers frozen, 1943 Apr. 17, III

Knights of Labor established, 1878 Jan. 1, III

Knights of St. Crispin, 1867 Mar. 7, III

largest employment buyout, 1983 Sept. 23, III

Mediation and Conciliation Board established, 1913 Mar. 4, III

minimum age (S.C.), 1916 Feb. 29, III

minimum wage, 1923 Apr. 9, III; 1934 Mar. 13, III; 1950 Jan. 24, III; 1961 May 5(1), III

minimum wage extension, 1974 Apr. 8, III

minimum wage law for women, 1937 Mar. 29, III

minimum wage raised, 1949 Oct. 26, III; 1977 Nov. 1, III; 1989 Nov. 17, III

Labor (*cont.*)

mining unions, 1903 Mar. 21, III

minority-hiring policies, 1969 Sept. 23, III

National Child Labor Committee formed, 1904(3), III

National Labor Board, 1933 Aug. 5, I

National Labor Relations Act signed, 1935 July 5, III

National Labor Relations Act upheld, 1937 Apr. 12, III

National Union, 1872(3), I

new mothers remaining in job market, 1988 June 15, III

noninflationary wage guidelines supported, 1964 May 19, III

organization, 1933, III

organized membership decline, 1984, III

paternalism, 1833(2), III

political action, 1950, III

political influence, 1949, III

political organization, 1868(6), III

postwar problems, 1946, III

proposed constitutional amendment against child, 1924 June 2, III

Pullman strike impact on, 1894 Aug. 3, III

railroad brotherhoods, 1868(5), III

railroad brotherhoods rise, 1873(2), III

reform efforts, 1845, III

sit-down strikes, 1936, III; 1936 Jan. 11, III; 1939 Feb. 27, III

spur to immigration, 1864 July 4, III

Taft-Hartley Act, 1947, III; 1947 June 23, III

Teamsters named Carey president, 1991 Feb. 1, III

training wage minimum, 1989 Nov. 17, III

Triangle fire (N.Y.C.), 1911, I

union boycott of defense agencies, 1951 Feb. 28, III

union corruption, 1957 May 2, III; 1957 Sept. 18, III

union growth, 1937, III

union influence decline, 1877(1), III

union legality established (Mass.), 1842(2), III

union membership, 1870(9), III

union racketeering, 1953 Sept. 22, III; 1956 Apr. 5, III; 1958 Jan. 23, III; 1958 Sept. 2–3, III

unions' decline, 1925, III

unions subject to interstate trade prosecution, 1921 Jan. 3, III

unrest, 1886(5), III; 1937(2), III

video display terminal use regulated, 1990 Dec. 27, I

Wage and Hours Act, 1938 June 25, I

Wage and Hours Act upheld, 1941 Feb. 3, I

wage and price controls lifted, 1974 Apr. 30, III

wage and salary controls lifted, 1953 Feb. 6, III

wages, 1957, III

Labor (*cont.*)
  Wage Stabilization Board established, 1945 Dec. 31, III
  wages up, 1950 Mar. 23, III
  War Labor Board created, 1942 Jan. 12(1), III
  wartime scene, 1943, III
  women's employment at highest point, 1951, III
  women's laws, 1923(1), III; 1923 Apr. 9, III; 1937 Mar. 29, III
  working hours limitation ruled unconstitutional, 1905 Apr. 17, III
  workmen's compensation laws adopted (Miss.), 1948(3), III
  workmen's compensation valid, 1915 July 13, III
Labor, Department of (*see also* Commerce and Labor, Department of):
  Cabinet status, 1913 Mar. 4, III
  Durkin resigned, 1953 Sept. 10, III
  established, 1888 June 13, III
  Perkins appointed sec., 1933 Mar. 4(2), I
  U.S. Bureau formed as forerunner, 1884 June 27, I
Labor Day:
  first Monday in Sept. set, 1884(3), IV
  first parade (N.Y.C.), 1882 Sept. 5, IV
  legal holiday, 1894 June 28, IV
  legal holiday (N.Y.), 1887 Sept. 5, IV
Labor Party:
  presidential ticket, 1884 July 30, I
Lacoste, Catherine, 1967 July 2, IV
Lacoste, Rene, 1926 Aug. 23, IV; 1927 Aug. 30, IV
Lacrosse, 1775(2), IV
  first intercollegiate association, 1882(5), IV
Ladd, Alan, 1964, II
Ladd, William, 1828(1), IV
Ladies' Garment Workers Union, International (ILGWU), 1900(4), III
Ladies' Home Journal (publication), 1883(4), II; 1889, II
Laetrile, 1977 May 1, III
La Farge, John, 1870, II; 1876(7), II; 1888(3), II
La Farge, Oliver, 1929(1), II; 1930 May 12, II; 1963, II
Lafayette, Marquis de, 1824, IV
Lafayette College (Pa.), 1826 Mar. 9, III
Lafitte, Jean, 1815(3), IV
La Follette, Robert M.:
  formed Progressive Republican League, 1911 Jan. 21, I
  presidential candidacy, 1924 July 4, I; 1924 Nov. 4, I
  presidential nomination, 1911 Oct. 16, I
  Senate Hall of Fame, 1957 Apr. 30, I
La Guardia, Fiorello H., 1959 Nov. 23, II
  elected mayor, 1933 Nov. 7, I
La Guardia Airport (N.Y.C.):
  bombing, 1975 Dec. 29, I
Lahr, Bert, 1967, II
Laine, Jack ("Papa"), 1892(3), II
Laird, Melvin R., 1970 Mar. 4, I
Lake Champlain, Battle of, 1814 Sept. 11, I

Lake Erie, Battle of, 1813 Sept. 10, I
Laker, Freddie, 1977 Sept. 26, III
Lakes *see* name inverted
Lake Washington Floating Bridge (Wash.), 1940 July 2, III
Lamb, Willis E., 1955 Nov. 2(2), III
Lambert, Hendricks, and Ross (group), 1962 May 29, II
L'Amour, Louis, 1988, II
Lamphier, Fay, 1925 Sept. 11, IV
Lancaster, Burt, 1961 Apr. 17, II
Lancaster, Joseph, 1806(2), III
Lance, Bert, 1977, I; 1977 Sept. 21, I
Land, public *see* Public land
Land, Edwin H., 1948(4), III; 1991, III
Landis, Kenesaw Mountain, 1920 Nov. 8, IV; 1921 Aug. 3, IV; 1943, IV
Land mines, 1840(4), I
Landon, Alfred M., 1936 June 9–12, I; 1936 Nov. 3, I; 1987, I
Landscape gardening *see* Horticulture
Landslides, 1938 Mar. 2, I
Landsteiner, Karl, 1930 Oct. 30, III
Lane, Harriet, 1860 Oct. 4, IV
Lane, Joseph, 1860 June 28, I
Lane, Mark, 1966(1), II
Lang, Fritz, 1976, II
Lange, Jessica, 1983 Apr. 11, II
Langer, Bernhard, 1985 Apr. 14, IV
Langley, Neva Jane, 1952 Sept. 6, IV
Langley, Samuel P., 1896(6), III; 1903(4), III
Langmuir, Irving, 1917(1), III; 1932 Nov. 10, III
Langston, Mark, 1989 Nov. 22, IV
Langtry, Lillie, 1882, II
Language:
  admonitions, 1838 Dec. 15, IV
  airplane replaced *aeroplane,* 1912 Apr. 6, III
  bilingual education fostered, 1974 Jan. 21, III
  campaign slogans, 1884, I; 1884(2), IV; 1888(2), IV; 1910 July 4, IV; 1923(1), III
  Civil War epithet, 1862, IV
  English used in Catholic mass, 1963 Dec. 4, III
  expressions coined, 1812(1), IV; 1820 Apr. 12, IV; 1828, IV; 1831 Aug. 10, IV; 1832 Jan. 21, IV; 1836 Nov. 12, IV; 1841(1), IV; 1843(1), IV; 1855(2), IV; 1858 Oct. 25, IV; 1864(2), IV; 1866(2), IV; 1867(1), IV; 1869 Jan., IV; 1872(1), IV; 1882(3), IV; 1884(1), IV; 1888(2), IV; 1889(3), IV; 1892(2), IV; 1893(3), IV; 1904 Nov. 15, II; 1906 Mar. 17, IV; 1910 July 4, IV; 1913(1), II; 1913 Feb. 27, IV; 1920(1), IV; 1922 Oct. 9, II; 1923(1), IV; 1941 Jan. 6, IV; 1948 Oct. 24, IV
  famous quotes, 1775 June 17, IV; 1800 Sept. 23, IV; 1813 June 1, I; 1813 Sept. 10, I; 1816(3), IV; 1826 June 30, IV; 1826 Aug. 2, IV; 1830 Jan. 27, IV; 1850(4), IV; 1851(4), IV; 1852 Jan. 28, IV; 1864 Aug. 5, IV; 1884 June 5, IV; 1890(1), IV; 1915(2), IV; 1917 Apr. 2, IV; 1917 July 4, IV

Language (*cont.*)
  first formal study of American, 1816, II; 1816(1), III
  first Latin grammar, 1706(2), II
  first use of term "scab", 1799(1), IV
  first written American Indian, 1824(3), IV
  foreign, teaching qualifications, 1960 July 7, III
  gender-specific eliminations, 1987 Apr. 4, III
  hate speech laws unconstitutional, 1992 June 22(2), I
  infants taught Latin, 1799(2), IV
  Know Ye Men term (R.I.), 1783(1), IV
  Modern Language Assn. founded, 1883(2), III
  national language developed, 1789(1), II
  New Testament revision, 1987 Apr. 4, III
  O.K. origins, 1840(1), IV
  origin of *Uncle Sam,* 1812, IV
  phrase origination, 1805 Apr. 27, I
  popular phrases, 1785(1), IV; 1790(3), IV; 1798 June 18, IV; 1838(2), IV; 1844(1), IV; 1845, IV; 1850(2), IV; 1867(2), IV; 1901 Sept. 2, IV; 1941 Dec. 7, IV; 1942 Jan. 8, IV; 1945(1), IV
  revised Bible, 1990 Sept. 30, III
  slang phrases, 1912(3), IV
  southern conservatism, 1817(2), IV
  standard English grammar, 1795(1), II
  ten-gallon hat origin, 1865(4), IV
  term *lingerie,* 1852(4), IV
  Tom Swifties, 1963(1), IV
  Webster's dictionary, 1828(2), II
  Webster's *Dissertations,* 1789(1), II
  Webster's standards, 1806(2), II; 1806(3), IV
  Webster's Third International Dictionary, 1961(1), II
Lanier, James, F. D., 1844(6), II
Lanier, Sidney:
  centennial ode, 1876(2), II
  flute compositions, 1873(4), II
  "Marshes of Glynn, The", 1878(5), II
  only novel, 1867(1), II
  Poems, 1877(1), II
Lanphier, Thomas G., Jr., 1987, IV
Lansing, Robert, 1915 June 7, I
Lansky, J. G., 1931(1), III
Lansky, Meyer, 1983, IV
Laos:
  foreign aid, 1955 Jan. 1, I
  illegal war charges, 1969 Oct. 28, I
Lapine, James, 1984 May 2, II; 1985 Apr. 24, II
LaPlanche, Rosemary, 1941 Sept. 6, IV
Lapotaire, Jane, 1981 June 7, II
Lardner, Ring, 1915(1), II; 1924(1), II; 1929(1), II; 1977(1), II
Larned, William A., 1901(2), IV; 1902(2), IV; 1907(3), IV; 1908(3), IV; 1909 June 27, IV; 1910 June 26, IV; 1911 June 17, IV
Larrabee, Eric, 1990, II
Larsen, Arthur, 1950 Sept. 5, IV
Larsen, Don, 1956 Oct. 3–10, IV

Larsen, Paul J., 1950 Jan. 21(1), I
La Salle, Sieur de (Robert Cavelier), 1670–1679, I; 1678, I; 1685 Jan., I
La Scala Opera Co., 1967 Oct. 18, II; 1976 Sept. 7, II
Las Guasimas, Battle of, 1898 June 24, I
Lash, Joseph P., 1971(1), II; 1972(1), II; 1972 Apr. 13, II; 1972 May 1, II
LaStarza, Roland, 1953, IV
Last of the Mohicans, The (Cooper), 1826(1), II
Las Vegas (Nev.):
    decrease in gambling, 1991, IV
    hotel fire, 1980 Nov. 21, I
Lathrop, Rose Hawthorne, 1896 Sept., III
Latin America (*see also* country names):
    Alliance for Progress, 1961 May 27, I
    Blaine's invitation to conference, 1881 Nov. 29, I
    Central American common market, 1963 Mar. 19, I
    cultural ties promoted, 1811(2), II
    Declaration of San José, 1963 Mar. 19, I
    Eisenhower tour, 1960 Feb. 22, I; 1960 Mar. 7, I
    first Pan-American conference, 1889 Oct. 2, I; 1890 Apr. 14, I
    Good Neighbor policy, 1933, I
    Panama Conference, 1826 June, I
    Presidents of America Conference (Uruguay), 1967 Apr. 12–14, I
    recognition of republics, 1822 Mar. 8, I
    Stevenson goodwill tour, 1961 June 22, I
Latrobe, Benjamin H., 1803 May, III; 1805, II; 1819(1), II
Latta, Alexander Bonner, 1852(1), III
Latter-Day Saints, Church of Jesus Christ of *see* Mormon Church
Lattimore, Owen, 1989, III
Latvia, 1991 Sept. 2, I
Laudonnière, René Goulaine de, 1564, IV
Laughton, Charles, 1934 Mar. 16, II
Laurel, Stan, 1910 Oct. 3, II; 1965, II
Laurents, Arthur, 1957 Sept. 26, II; 1959 May 21, II; 1974 Sept. 23, II
Laver, Rod, 1962 Sept. 10, IV; 1969 Sept. 7–8, IV
Lavin, Linda, 1987 June 7, II
Law, Andrew, 1767(1), II
Law, Bernard F. (Archbishop), 1985 Apr. 24, III
Law, John, 1720 Oct., I; 1732 Jan., I
Law and legislation (*see also* Blue laws; Courts; Crime and criminals; Legal profession; names of acts; under subjects of legislation;):
    American scholarship, 1826, III
    federal bankruptcy, 1841 Aug. 19, I
Lawler, Charles, 1894(4), II
Lawn tennis *see* Tennis
Law of the sea *see* Sea, Law of the
Lawrence, Amos Adams, 1837(3), IV; 1847(1), III; 1854 Apr. 26, I
Lawrence, D. H., 1960 Mar. 25, II
Lawrence, Ernest Orlando, 1939 Nov. 9, III
Lawrence, Florence, 1907(6), II

Lawrence, James, 1813 June 1, I
Lawrence, Jerome, 1959 Oct. 1, II; 1966 May 24, II
Lawrence, Robert H., Jr., 1967 Dec. 8, III
Lawrence, Steve, 1961 Apr. 12, II
Lawrence College (Wis.), 1847(1), III
Lawrence (Kan.), 1854 Apr. 26, I
Lawrence (ship), 1813 Sept. 10, I
Lawson, John Howard, 1923 Mar. 2, II
Lawson, Ted W., 1943(1), II
Lawson, Victor F., 1875 Dec. 25, II
Lawyers *see* Legal profession; personal names
Lazarus, Emma, 1876(5), II
Lazear, Jesse W., 1901(1), III
Lazzeri, Tony, 1991 July 21, IV
L-dopa (drug), 1970 June 4, III
Lea, Tom, 1949(1), II
Leachman, Cloris, 1972 Apr. 9, II; 1973 May 20, II
Lead poisoning:
    first account of, 1735(4), III
League of Nations:
    covenant, 1919 Feb. 14, I
    covenant sent to Senate, 1919 July 10, I
    presidential campaign issue, 1920, I
    Wilson's Ten Points, 1917 Jan. 22, I
League of Six Nations, The, 1722, I
Lear, Norman, 1984 Mar. 4, II
Learned, Michael, 1973 May 20, II; 1974 May 28, II; 1982 Sept. 19, II
Leary, Timothy, 1966, IV
Leather:
    patent first manufactured, 1818 Sept. 20, III
Leaver, Henrietta, 1935 Sept. 7, IV
Lebanon:
    Americans evacuated, 1976 July 27, I
    hostages taken/released, 1986 Nov. 2, I; 1987 Jan. 24, I; 1988 Feb. 17, I; 1988 Oct. 3, I; 1991 Aug. 8–Dec. 4, I
    Shiite Muslim hijacking (Athens), 1985 June 14, I
    U.S. ambassador killed, 1976 June 16, I
    U.S. embassy and Marine headquarters bombed, 1983, I; 1983 Apr. 18, I; 1983 Oct. 23, I
    U.S. Embassy bombed, 1984 Sept. 20, I
    U.S. hostage returned, 1985 Sept. 18, I
    U.S. Marines authorized to remain, 1983 Sept. 20, I
    U.S. Marines in Beirut, 1982, I; 1982 Aug. 20, I
    U.S. Marine withdrawal, 1984 Feb. 7, I
    U.S. warplanes attacked Syrian positions, 1983 Dec. 4, I
Le Carré, John, 1989(1), II
Le Corbusier, 1963, II
Lecture circuit:
    central booking office, 1867(4), II
    Farwell on American music, 1904(3), II
    Gough's temperance speeches, 1845(2), IV; 1846, IV
Leder, Philip, 1988 Apr. 12, III

Lederberg, Joshua, 1958 Oct. 30, III
Lederle Laboratories (Pearl River, N.Y.), 1948(1), III
Lederman, Leon M., 1988 Oct. 19, III
Lee, Andrew, 1977 Apr. 28(2), I
Lee, Ann, 1770–1774, III
Lee, Gypsy Rose (Rose Louise Hovick), 1959 May 21, II; 1970, II
Lee, Harold B., 1972, III; 1973, III
Lee, Harper, 1960(1), II; 1961 May 1, II
Lee, Henry (Light-horse Harry), 1799 Dec. 26, IV
Lee, John D., 1857 Sept. 11, I
Lee, Peggy, 1970 Mar. 11, II
Lee, Richard Henry, 1775–1779, I
Lee, Robert E.:
    Chancellorsville (Va.) victory, 1863 May 1–4, I
    Confederate army commander, 1862 June 1, I
    conference sought with Grant, 1865 Mar. 2, I
    died, 1870 Oct. 12, I
    given command of Confederate armies, 1865 Feb. 6, I
    last victory, 1864 June 3, I
    mansion (Arlington, Va.), 1802(2), II
    Petersburg (Va.) defense, 1864 June 15–18, I
    retreat across Potomac R., 1863 July 1–3, I
    succeeded Gen. J.E. Johnston, 1862 May 31–June 1, I
    surrendered at Appomattox (Va.), 1865 Apr. 9, I
Lee, Robert E. (playwright), 1959 Oct. 1, II; 1966 May 24, II
Lee, Tsung Dao, 1957 Oct. 31, III
Lee, Yuan T., 1986 Oct. 15, III
Leech, Margaret, 1942 May 4, II; 1960 May 2, II
Lefferts, Peter, 1777(5), II
Le Gallienne, Eva, 1991, II
Legal profession:
    abortion restrictions opposed, 1992 Aug. 11, IV
    American Bar Association formed, 1878, III
    deaths, 1988, I
    equal educational facilities ordered (Okla.), 1948 Jan. 12, III
    fee advertising upheld, 1977 June 27, III
    first journal, 1808(1), III
    first society (N.Y.), 1747(2), III
    first woman lawyer in U.S., 1869(1), I
    first woman lawyer (Md.), c1640, I
    free aid for indigents, 1963 Mar. 18, I
    legal aid for poor corp. established, 1974 July 18, I
    partnership antidiscrimination ruling, 1984 May 22, I
    uniform minimum fees unlawful, 1975 June 16, III
    women won right to argue before Supreme Court, 1879 Feb. 15, I
Legal Tender Act, 1864 Dec., I; 1871 May 1, III
Legends:
    Captain Kidd, 1699 Spring, IV

Legends (*cont.*)
    Captain Paddock, 1690, IV
    "Casey" Jones, 1900 Apr. 30, IV
    Davy Crockett, 1834(2), IV
    frontier tall stories, 1846(1), IV
    hunting tall tale (Mass.), 1767 Dec. 21,
        IV
    Ireson abandoning his schooner, 1808
        Oct. 30, IV
    James brothers, 1882, IV
    Johnny Appleseed, 1800, IV
    Mike Fink, 1829, IV
    N.E. caterpillar invasion, 1768, IV
    Nix Mate's Island (Mass.), 1689
        Summer, IV
    Orange Blossom's (Mulholland) stories,
        1880(5), IV
    Tom Cook, the Leveler, 1741(1), IV
    "Wild Bill" Hickok, 1867(3), IV
    Windham Frogs (Conn.), 1758 July, IV
Legionnaires' disease, 1976 July 27–Aug.
    31, III; 1978 Aug. 11, III
Legislative Reform Act, 1970 Oct. 26, I
Legislatures (*see also* Congress, U.S.):
    apportionment ruling, 1964 June 15, I
Lehár, Franz, 1907(3), II
Lehder Rivas, Carlos, 1988 May 19, IV
Lehman, Robert, 1969, II
Lehmann, Lotte, 1976, II
Lehn, Jean-Marie, 1987 Oct. 14, III
Lehwalder, Heidi, 1976 Feb. 9, II
Leibman, Ron, 1979 Sept. 9, II
Leigh, Mitch, 1966 June 16, II
Leigh, Vivien, 1940 Feb. 29, II; 1952 Mar.
    20, II
Leighton, Margaret, 1957 Apr. 21, II; 1962
    Apr. 29, II
Leisler, Jacob, 1689(1), I
Leland, Henry, 1911 Feb., III
Lelyveld, Joseph, 1986 Apr. 17, II
Lema, Tony, 1966, IV
LeMay, Curtis E., 1968 Oct. 3, I; 1990, I
Lemke, William, 1936 June 19, I; 1936
    Nov. 3, I
Lemmon, Jack, 1956 Mar. 21, II; 1974
    Apr. 2, II
Lemond, Greg, 1986 July 27, IV; 1989 July
    23(2), IV
Lemons, 1832(1), IV
Le Moyne, Jacques de Morgues, 1564, IV
Lendl, Ivan, 1985 Sept. 7–8, IV; 1986
    Sept. 7, IV; 1987 Sept. 12, IV
Lend-Lease Act, 1941 Mar. 11, I
L'Enfant, Pierre Charles, 1800 June, I;
    1902(4), II
Lennon, John, 1980 Dec. 8, II; 1982 Feb.
    24, II; 1984 June 23, II
Leonard, Elmore, 1988(1), II
Leonard, Hugh, 1978 May 1(1), II
Leonardo da Vinci, 1967 Feb. 20, II; 1980
    Dec. 12, II
Leontief, Wassily, 1973 Oct. 18, III
Leopold, Nathan, 1924 July 21, IV; 1958
    Feb. 20, IV; 1971, IV
Lerner, Alan Jay, 1947 Mar. 13(1), II; 1956
    Mar. 15, II; 1957 Apr. 21, II; 1986, II
Lerner, Max, 1992, II
LeRoy, Mervyn, 1987, II
Leslie, George L., 1878 Oct. 27, IV

Letters from an American Farmer
    (Crèvecoeur), 1793(4), II
Letters of a British Spy (Wirt), 1803, II
Leutze, Emanuel, 1850(7), II
Lever House (N.Y.C.), 1950(6), II
Levering, Joshua, 1896 May 27–28, I; 1896
    Nov. 3, I
Levin, Ira, 1967(1), II
Levin, Yehuda Leib, 1968 June 17–July 1,
    III
Levine, James, 1975 May 22, II
Levine, Philip, 1980 Jan. 7, II; 1980 May
    1, II; 1991 Nov. 20, II
Levy, Marvin David, 1967 Mar. 17, II
Lewis, Arthur, 1979 Oct. 17(1), III
Lewis, Carl, 1991 Aug. 25, IV; 1992 July
    25–Aug. 9, IV
Lewis, Henry, 1968 Feb. 15, II
Lewis, John L.:
    CIO forerunner, 1935, III; 1935 Nov.
        9, III
    coal strike ended, 1948 Mar. 15, III
    coal walkout, 1949 Mar. 11, III
    died, 1969, III
    feud with Roosevelt, 1940 Oct. 25, III
    first CIO president, 1938 Nov. 14–18,
        III
    lost AFL presidency bid, 1921 June
        25, III
    resigned as CIO head, 1940 Nov. 21,
        III
    stopped coal production, 1939 May 5,
        III
    UMW presidency resignation, 1959
        Dec. 15, III
    UMW recognized, 1937 Mar. 1, III
Lewis, Meriwether, 1804, I; 1805(1), IV;
    1814(1), II
Lewis, Oscar, 1967 Mar. 8, II; 1992, II
Lewis, R. W. B., 1976 Jan. 8, II; 1976 May
    3, II
Lewis, Sinclair:
    biography of, 1961(1), II
    books published, 1917(1), II; 1920(1),
        II; 1922(1), II; 1925(1), II; 1927(1),
        II; 1928(1), II; 1929(1), II; 1934 Feb.
        24, II; 1936 Oct. 27, II; 1938(1), II;
        1945(1), II; 1947(1), II
    Nobel Prize, 1930 Nov. 5(2), II
    Pulitzer Prize, 1926 May 3, II; 1926
        May 5, II
Lewis, Ted, 1971, II
Lewis, William A., 1991, III
Lewis and Clark Expedition, 1804, I;
    1805(1), IV; 1814(1), II
Lexington, Battle of (Mass.), 1775 Apr. 19,
    I; 1975 Apr. 20, II
Ley, Willy, 1969, III
Leyte Gulf, Battle of, 1944 Oct. 23–26, I
Libby, Willard Frank, 1960 Nov. 3, III
Libel and slander:
    Brown & Williamson Co. suit against
        CBS, 1985 Dec. 5, III
    Hellman-McCarthy suit, 1980 Feb.
        15(1), II
    judgment against *N.Y. Times* reversed,
        1964 Mar. 9, II
    right to criticize public figures, 1988
        Feb. 24, I

Libel and slander (*cont.*)
    suit against *Time* magazine, 1985 Jan.
        24, II
    Westmoreland suit against CBS, 1985
        Feb. 17, III
    Whistler-Ruskin suit, 1877(3), II
    Zenger case, 1734 Oct., II
Liberator, The (publication), 1831(1), I;
    1831 Jan. 1, II; 1831 Jan. 1, IV
Liberia, 1821, IV; 1895 Mar. 18, I
Liberty Bell (Phila., Pa.), 1752(2), IV; 1835
    July 8, I; 1965 Feb. 16, I
Liberty Loan Act, 1917 Apr. 24, I
Liberty Party, 1839 Nov. 13, I; 1843 Aug.
    31, I; 1844, I; 1844 Dec. 4, I; 1847 Nov.,
    I
Liberty (ship), 1967 June 8, I
Liberty Weekend (event), 1986 July 3–6,
    IV
Libraries:
    American Library Assn. established,
        1876 Oct. 6, III
    associations, 1820(1), III
    Astor Library opening (N.Y.C.), 1854,
        III
    Boston Public (Mass.) architecture,
        1888(4), II
    Boston Public (Mass.) opened, 1854(2),
        III
    Coonskin (Ohio), 1804(1), IV
    Dewey Decimal System, 1876(8), III
    first circulating (Phila., Pa.), 1731(1),
        III
    first extensive N.Y.C. system, 1901
        Mar. 12, III
    first national librarians' convention,
        1853 Sept. 15, III
    first public (Va.), 1620(2), II
    first state-supported (N.Y., N.H.),
        1820(3), III
    first tax-supported (Conn.), 1803(1), III
    first tax-supported in Mass., 1855 Sept.
        17, III
    Ky.'s first, 1795(1), III
    largest west of the Alleghenies,
        1830(2), III
    Lenox (N.Y.C.), 1871(3), II
    Miller endowment (Chicago, Ill.),
        1868(4), III
    number and collections, 1800(5), II
    number of public, 1731(1), III
    N.Y. Public, 1897(2), II
    N.Y. Public 75th anniversary, 1986
        May 23, III
    oldest public (N.H.), 1833(3), III
    Pittsburgh (Pa.) network, 1814(1), III
    Reagan's presidential (Calif.), 1984
        Feb. 14, II; 1991 Nov. 4, II
    worst fire, 1986 Apr. 29, II
Library of Congress:
    acquired Jefferson's book collection,
        1815(1), II
    Irving Berlin personal music
        collection donated, 1992 Oct. 2, II
    established, 1800(1), II
    film collection, 1943 May 5(1), II
    fire, 1851 Dec. 24, II
    first book catalog, 1802 Apr., II
    first librarian, 1802 Jan. 29, I

Library of Congress (*cont.*)
  historic documents returned to, 1944
    Oct. 1, II
Libya:
  terrorism, 1991 Nov. 27, I
  U.S. air strike, 1986 Apr. 14, I
  U.S. armed clash with, 1986 Mar. 24, I
  U.S. economic sanctions, 1982 Mar.
    10, I; 1986 Jan. 7, I
  U.S. embassy attacked, 1979 Dec. 2, I
  U.S. shot down fighter planes, 1989
    Jan. 4, I
  U.S. shot down jets, 1981 Aug. 19, I
Lick, James, 1888(4), III; 1895, III
Lick Observatory (Calif.), 1888(4), III
Liddy, G. Gordon, 1972 Sept. 15, I; 1973
  Jan. 30, I; 1973 Sept. 4, I
Lieber, Francis, 1827(3), III; 1829, III
Life expectancy, 1920(3), III; 1933(1), III;
  1940(2), III; 1991, III
Life insurance *see* Insurance
Life of George Washington (Marshall),
  1804(4), II
Life of Washington (Bancroft), 1807(1), IV
Life (publication), 1883(3), II; 1972 Dec.
  29, II
Lifton, Robert Jay, 1969 Mar. 10(2), II
Light:
  source from edge of universe
    detected, 1989 Nov. 19, III
  velocity measurement, 1878(2), III
Lighthouses:
  first nuclear-powered (Md.), 1964 May
    21, III
  first Pacific coast (Calif.), 1855(2), III
  oldest still operating, 1790(1), III
Lighting:
  electric in home, 1859 July, III
  first baseball game played under
    electric, 1883 June 2, IV
  first electrical city street system
    (Cleveland, Ohio), 1879(1), III
  first gas experiments, 1796(1), III
  first municipal electric (Conn.),
    1880(8), III
  first street (Boston, Mass.), 1719, IV
  gas for hotel use, 1835(3), III
  gas street, 1806(1), IV; 1816 June, III
  incandescent electric, 1879 Oct. 21,
    III
  incandescent lamp, 1880 Jan. 27, III
  incandescent stage, 1882 Dec. 11, III
  street, 1770–1774, IV
  street (Phila., Pa.), 1757(2), IV
Lilienthal, David E., 1981, I
Liliuokalani, Queen (Hawaii), 1893 Jan. 17,
  I
Lillie, Beatrice, 1948 Apr. 30, II
Lily (publication), 1849 Jan., IV; 1853(3),
  IV
Limón, José, 1972, II
Lime:
  first produced (R.I.), 1662 Jan., III
Lin, Maya Yang, 1981 June 6, II
Lincoln, Abraham (*see also* Civil War):
  amnesty bid to southerners, 1863 Dec.
    8, I
  assassinated, 1865, I; 1865 Apr. 14, I;
    1865 Apr. 15, II

Lincoln, Abraham (*cont.*)
  books on, 1890(1), II; 1926(1), II;
    1939(1), II; 1940 May 6, II
  born, 1809 Feb. 12, I
  boyhood home named national
    monument (Ind.), 1962 Feb. 19, II
  Cooper Union speech (N.Y.C.), 1860
    Feb. 27, I
  debates with Douglas, 1858, I
  defeated for Senate seat, 1858–1859, I
  elected president, 1860, I; 1860 Nov.
    6, I
  Emancipation Proclamation, 1862 July
    22, I; 1862 Sept. 22, I; 1863, I
  first formal birthday observance
    (Wash., D.C.), 1866 Feb. 12, IV
  first inaugural address, 1861 Mar. 4,
    IV
  Gettysburg Address, 1863 Nov. 19, II
  Hampton Roads Peace Conference
    (Va.), 1865 Feb. 3, I
  "house divided" statement, 1856(6),
    IV; 1858 June 16, IV
  inaugurated, 1861 Mar. 4(2), I
  one hundredth birthday celebrated,
    1909 Feb. 12(1), IV
  plays on, 1938 Oct. 3, II
  presidential nomination, 1860 May
    16–18, I
  press freedom, 1863 June 1, II
  protected Confederate churches, 1863
    Jan., III
  reelected, 1864 Nov. 8, I
  reelection bid, 1864, I; 1864(2), IV;
    1864 June 7, I
  second inaugural address, 1865 Mar.
    4, IV
  second inauguration, 1865 Mar. 4, I
  statues of, 1866(4), II; 1887(2), II
  "swap horses" political expression,
    1864(2), IV
  Thanksgiving Day national holiday
    proclamation, 1863 Oct. 3, IV
Lincoln Center for the Performing Arts
  (N.Y.C.):
  Alice Tully Hall opened, 1969 Sept.
    11, II
  Avery Fisher Hall improvement, 1976
    Oct. 19, II
  Avery Fisher Hall renamed, 1973
    Sept. 20, II
  jazz department added, 1991 Jan. 9, II
  Juilliard School of Music, 1969 Sept.
    11, II
  Metropolitan Opera's new house,
    1966 Sept. 16, II
  Mozart bicentennial, 1991 Jan. 27, II
  N.Y.C. Opera, 1966, II
  N.Y. State Theater, 1966 Feb. 22, II
  N.Y. State Theater opening, 1964 Apr.
    24, II
  Philharmonic Hall acoustics
    adjustment, 1963, II
  Philharmonic Hall first building
    completed, 1962 Sept. 23, II
  Philharmonic Hall grant, 1973 Sept.
    20, II
  Repertory Theater, 1964, II; 1964 Jan.
    23, II

Lincoln Center for the Performing Arts
  (N.Y.C.) (*cont.*)
  Vivian Beaumont Theater, 1964, II;
    1965, II; 1965 Oct. 21(2), II; 1973, II
Lincoln Highway Assn., 1913 July 1, III
Lincoln Memorial (Wash., D.C.), 1922 May
  30, II
Lincoln Savings and Loan Association,
  1992 Apr. 10(1), IV
Lincoln Tunnel (N.Y.-N.J.), 1937(3), II
Lind, Jenny, 1850, II
Lindbergh, Charles A.:
  Clifford Harmon Trophy, 1928 Dec.
    12, III
  died, 1974, III
  Distinguished Flying Cross, 1926 July
    2(2), I
  heart perfusion pump development,
    1936(1), III
  Pulitzer Prize, 1954 May 3, II
  solo flight (N.Y.-Paris), 1927, I
  son kidnaped, 1932 Mar. 1, I; 1935, IV
Lindsay, Howard, 1939 Nov. 8, II; 1946
  May 6, II; 1968, II
Lindsay, John V.:
  N.Y.C. transit strike, 1966 Jan. 1, III
Lindsay, Robert, 1987 June 7, II
Lindsay, Vachel, 1914, II; 1923(1), II
Lindstrom, Murle, 1962 June 30, IV
Linguistics *see* Language
Linsky, Belle and Jack, 1982 Mar. 4, II
Lipchitz, Jacques, 1973, II; 1977 Nov. 28,
  II
Lipmann, Fritz, 1953 Oct. 22, III; 1986,
  III
Lippmann, Walter, 1974, II; 1981 Jan. 5, II
Lippold, Richard, 1956(5), II; 1966 Oct. 2,
  II
Lipscomb, William N., Jr., 1976 Oct. 18(1),
  III
Liquor *see* Alcohol and alcoholism; Bars,
  saloons, and taverns; Prohibition and
  temperance movement; types
List, Eugene, 1985, II
List, Friedrich, 1827, III
Liston, Sonny, 1962, IV; 1962 Sept. 25, IV;
  1963 July 22, IV; 1964 Feb. 25, IV;
  1965, IV; 1965 May 25, IV; 1970, IV
Literacy *see* Illiteracy
Literature *see* Books and literature
Literature, National Medal for, 1981 Apr.
  30, II; 1982 Apr. 27, II
Lithography *see* Art
Lithuania, 1991 Sept. 2, I
Little, Brown and Co., 1968 Jan. 17, II
Little, Cleavon, 1992, II
Little, Sally, 1980 June 8, IV
Little, W. Lawson, 1940 June 9, IV; 1968,
  IV
Little Big Horn, Battle of, 1876 June 25, I
Little Egypt (Catherine Devine), 1893(3),
  IV
Little League:
  foreign teams barred from World
    Series, 1974 Nov. 11, IV
  opened to girls, 1974 June 12, IV
  Philippine team stripped of title, 1992
    Sept. 17(1), IV
  world series 40th anniversary, 1987
    Aug. 29, IV

Littler, Gene, 1961 June 17, IV
Little Rock (Ark.):
 racial violence, 1957 Sept. 24, I
 school desegregation, 1958 Sept. 30,
   III; 1959 June 18, III; 1959 Aug. 12,
   III
Little, Sally, 1986 July 14, IV
Litwack, Leon F., 1980 Apr. 14(1), II
Litz, Thomas, 1963 Feb. 9–10, IV
Liuzzo, Viola Gregg, 1965 Mar. 25, I
Liver:
 baboon's transplanted into a human,
   1992 June 28, III
 first live donor transplant, 1989 Nov.
   27, III
 first transplant, 1984 Feb. 13, III
 first transplant recipient died, 1990
   Nov. 11, III
Livestock (see also Meat; Milk):
 Abilene (Kans.) cattle terminal,
   1867(10), III
 American Humane Assn., 1877 Oct.,
   III
 barbed wire impact on ranching,
   1874, III
 cattle epidemic (South), 1695, III
 hogs highest price to date, 1919 July
   23, III
 introduced by Europeans, 1565, III
 sheep breeding, 1802(1), III
Livingston, Robert R., 1803 Jan. 11, I;
   1808(1), II; 1813 Feb. 26, III
Lizana, Anita, 1937 Sept. 11(2), IV
Lloyd, Chris Evert (see also Evert, Chris),
   1975 Sept. 6–7, IV; 1976 July 2–3, IV;
   1976 Sept. 11–12, IV; 1977 Sept. 10–11,
   IV; 1978 Sept. 10, IV; 1980 Sept. 6–7,
   IV; 1981 July 3–4, IV; 1982 Sept. 11–12,
   IV
Lloyd, Christopher, 1992 Aug. 30, II
Lloyd, Harold, 1971, II
Lloyd, Joe, 1897 Sept. 17, IV
Lloyd Webber, Andrew, 1971 Oct. 12, II;
   1979 Sept. 25, II; 1980 June 8, II; 1982
   Oct. 7, II; 1983 June 5, II; 1988 June 5,
   II
Lobbying:
 Deaver perjury conviction, 1987 Dec.
   16, I
 Nofziger convicted for illegal, 1988
   Feb. 11, I
Locke, David Ross (Petroleum Vesuvius
   Nasby), 1864(8), II; 1865(3), II
Locke, John, 1660–1669, III; 1693(1), IV
Lockheed Aircraft Corp.:
 Electra crashes, 1960 Mar. 17, I; 1960
   May 12, III
 federal bailout, 1971 Aug. 2, III
Lockridge, Ross, 1948(1), II
Lockwood, Belva A., 1884(1), I
Locomotive Engineers, Brotherhood of,
   1863, II
Lodge, Henry Cabot:
 died, 1985, I
 speech praising T. Roosevelt, 1908
   June 16–20, I
Loeb, Richard, 1924 July 21, IV
Loesser, Frank, 1951 Mar. 25, II; 1961
   Oct. 14, II; 1962 May 7, II; 1969, II

Loewe, Frederick, 1947 Mar. 13(1), II;
   1956 Mar. 15, II; 1957 Apr. 21, II; 1988,
   II
Loewy, Raymond, 1986, II
Logan, George, 1798 June, III
Logan, John A., 1884 June 3–6, I
Logan, Joshua, 1950 Apr. 9, II; 1950 May
   1, II; 1954 Nov. 4, II; 1988, II
Logan International Airport (Boston,
   Mass.), 1973 July 31, I
Log cabin, 1638(2), II; 1638 Mar., I
Loggins, Kenny, 1981 Feb. 25, II
Lombard, Carole, 1942, II
Lombardi, Vince, 1968 Jan. 14, IV; 1970,
   IV
Lombardo, Guy, 1977, II
London, Jack:
 books published, 1900(1), II; 1902(1),
   II; 1903(1), II
 Burning Daylight, 1910(1), II
 Game, The, 1905(1), II
 Iron Heel, The, 1908(1), II
 Martin Eden, 1909(1), II
 posthumous works, 1917(1), II;
   1919(1), II
 Sea Wolf, The, 1904(1), II
 Smoke Bellew, 1912(1), II
 South Sea Tales, 1911(1), II
 Valley of the Moon, 1913(1), II
 White Fang, 1906(1), II
London conference, 1954, I
London Naval Treaty, 1930 Apr. 22, I
Long, Huey, 1923(1), IV; 1935 Sept. 8, I;
   1970 Mar. 2, II; 1970 May 4, II
Long, Stephen, 1820(2), III; 1820 June 6, I
Longden, Johnny, 1966 Mar. 12(2), IV
Longfellow, Henry Wadsworth:
 Ballads and Other Poems, 1841(4), II
 biography, 1825, II
 born, 1807(1), IV; 1807 Feb. 27, IV
 bust in Westminster Abbey, 1882(3), II
 "Courtship of Miles Standish, The",
   1620–1629, II; 1858(4), II
 Evangeline, 1755 Nov. 30, I; 1839(3),
   II; 1847(3), II
 first verse collection, 1839(3), II
 Hyperion, 1839(3), II
 New England Tragedies, 1630 May 29,
   II; 1868(1), II
 Paul Revere's Ride, 1775–1779, II
 Song of Hiawatha, The, 1820, III;
   1855(5), II
 Tales of a Wayside Inn, 1863(4), II
 Tales of a Wayside Inn 1690 The
   famous
 Wayside Inn of Henry, 1690(1), II
Long Island, Battle of (N.Y.), 1776 Aug. 27,
   I
Longshoremen's Assn., International:
 first long-term contract to date, 1964
   Dec. 16, III
 N.Y.C. strike ended, 1954 Apr. 2, III
 racketeering, 1953 Sept. 22, III
 readmitted to AFL-CIO, 1959 Sept.
   22, III
 strike, 1959 Oct. 1(1), III
 strike ended (East and Gulf coasts),
   1963 Jan. 26, III
Longstreet, Augustus B., 1835(5), II
Look (magazine), 1971 Oct. 19, II

Loos, Anita, 1981, II
Lopat, Eddie, 1992, IV
Lopez, Barry, 1986 Nov. 17, II
Lopez, Nancy, 1978, IV; 1979, IV; 1985,
   IV; 1985 June 2, IV; 1989 May 21, IV
Lopez, Vincent, 1975, II
López expedition, 1851 Aug. 24, I
Lord, Bradley, 1961 Jan. 27–29, IV
Loren, Sophia, 1962 Apr. 9, II
Lorentz, Pare, 1992, II
Lorillard, Griswold, 1986, IV
Lorre, Peter, 1964, II
Los Angeles (Calif.):
 earthquake, 1987 Oct. 1, I; 1992 June
   28, I
 largest city in U.S., 1984, I
 library fire, 1986 Apr. 29, II
 riots, 1992, I; 1992 Apr. 29, IV; 1992
   June 22(1), I
Los Angeles County Art Museum (Calif.),
   1965 Mar. 30, II
Los Angeles Philharmonic, 1984 Apr. 29,
   II
Lost Colony see Roanoke Island colony
Lott, George, Jr., 1931 July 3–4, IV
Lotteries:
 largest N.Y.C. payoff, 1981, IV
 largest prize in world, 1988 Nov. 1, IV
 largest single win (Ill.), 1984, IV
 state proceeds, 1981, IV
 Union College (N.Y.), 1810(2), IV
Loud family, 1973, IV
Loudon, Fort (Tenn.), 1760 Aug. 7, I
Louganis, Greg, 1988 Sept. 17–Oct. 2, IV
Louis, Joe, 1937 June 22, IV; 1940, IV;
   1941, IV; 1942 Jan. 9, IV; 1947, IV; 1948
   June 25, IV; 1949, IV; 1950, IV; 1981, IV
Louisiana:
 capital punishment laws, 1976 July 2,
   I
 carpetbag government ended, 1877
   Apr. 24, I
 casket girls, 1728(3), IV
 concession surrendered to French
   crown, 1732 Jan., I
 congressional representation
   regranted, 1868 June 25(2), I
 French claims, 1670–1679, I
 Hurricane Andrew, 1992 Aug. 24, I
 Law's speculative failure, 1720 Oct., I
 Long assassinated, 1935 Sept. 8, I
 Long's political slogan, 1923(1), IV
 seceded, 1861 Jan. 26, I
 statehood, 1812 Apr. 30, I
 Territory ceded to France by Spain,
   1800 Oct. 1, I
 tornado, 1971 Feb. 21, I
Louisiana, University of, 1847 Feb. 16, III
Louisiana Purchase:
 Madison as envoy, 1803 Jan. 11, I
 negotiations begun, 1802, I
 states included, 1803 Apr. 30, I
Louisiana State University, 1853 Mar. 31,
   III
Louisiana Territory Act, 1804 Mar. 26, I
Louis Philippe, 1796–1799, IV
Louis XIV (King of France), 1670–1679, I
Lousma, Jack, 1973 July 28, III
Lovejoy, Elijah P., 1837 Nov. 7, I

Lovell, James A., Jr., 1965 Dec. 4, III; 1966 Nov. 11(1), III; 1968 Dec. 21–27, III; 1970 Apr. 11, III
Lovell, John W., 1882(4), II
Low, Juliet, 1912 Mar. 12, IV
Low, Seth, 1889 Oct. 7, III
Lowe, Thaddeus Sobieski Coulincourt, 1861 Apr. 20, III; 1862(3), III
Lowell, Amy, 1917(1), II; 1926 May 3, II
Lowell, Francis Cabot, 1814(2), III
Lowell, James Russell:
    Atlantic Monthly editorship, 1857(1), II
    Civil War-inspired works, 1865, II
    "Ode for the Fourth of July", 1876(4), II
    three major works published, 1848(5), II
Lowell, Percival, 1895, III
Lowell, Robert, 1947 May 5, II; 1960 Mar. 23, II; 1974 May 7, II; 1977, II; 1978 Jan. 11, II
Lowry, Malcolm, 1947(1), II
Loyalists *see* Tories
Loyalty and loyalty oaths *see* Subversion and loyalty issue
Loyola College (Md.), 1853 Apr. 13, III
Loyola University (Ill.), 1870(7), III
LSD *see* Psychedelic drugs
Lucas, John, 1986, IV
Luce, Clare Booth, 1987, II
Luce, Henry R., 1967, II
Luce, William, 1976 Apr. 28, II
Luciano, Lucky (Charles), 1962, IV
Lucy, Autherine, 1956 Feb. 6, III
Ludlow, Roger, 1639 Jan. 14, I
Ludlum, Robert, 1984(1), II
Ludwig, Daniel, 1992, III
Ludwig, Ken, 1992 June 1, II
Luhrman, Luella, 1990, I
Lukas, J. Anthony, 1985 Jan 21, II; 1986 Feb. 17, II; 1986 Apr. 17, II
Lukas, Paul, 1944 Mar. 2, II
Lunar Orbiter 1 (satellite), 1966 Aug. 10, III
Lunar Orbiter 2 (satellite), 1966 Nov. 6, III
Lunar Orbiter 3 (satellite), 1967 Feb. 4, III
Lund, Mary, 1985 Dec. 19, III
Lung:
    black lung disease compensation, 1969 Dec. 18, III
    cancer in women increasing, 1980 Jan. 14, III
    cancer-smoking link, 1957 July 12, III
    first three-way transplant, 1987 May 12, III
    iron devised, 1927 July 29, III
    living organ transplant, 1990 Oct. 25, III
Lunt, Alfred, 1955 Mar. 27, II; 1965 Sept. 12, II; 1977, II
Lurcy, Georges, 1957, II
Luria, Salvador E., 1969 Oct. 16, III; 1974 Apr. 18, II; 1991, III
Lurie, Alison, 1985 Apr. 24, II
Lusitania (ship), 1907 Sept. 12, III; 1915 May 7, I; 1915 May 13, I; 1915 May 28, I; 1915 May 31, I; 1915 June 7, I; 1915 June 9, I; 1915 July 21, I

Lutheran Church:
    American Lutheran Church formed (Ohio), 1930 Aug. 11, III
    Evangelical Assn. formed, 1976 Dec. 4, III
    first congregation (Del.), 1638 Mar., I
    membership, 1900(2), III
    merger, 1959 July 7(1), III; 1986 Aug. 29, III
    merger within, 1982 Sept. 8, III
    openly gay clergy condemned, 1990 July 18, III
    ties with Germany, 1769(3), III
    United organized, 1918(2), III
Luyendyk, Arie, 1990 May 27, IV
Lyceums, 1826, IV
Lyle, Sandy, 1988 Apr. 10, IV
Lynch, Mel, 1976 Dec. 10, IV
Lynching *see* Riots and mob violence
Lynd, Robert and Helen, 1929, III
Lynen, Feodor, 1964 Oct. 15, III
Lynn, Fred, 1983 July 6, IV
Lynn, Janet, 1969 Feb. 1–2, IV; 1970 Feb. 6–7, IV; 1971 Jan. 28–31, IV; 1972 Jan. 14–16, IV; 1973 Jan. 24–27, IV; 1973 June 19, IV
Lyon, James, 1761(1), II
Lyon, Mary, 1837 Nov. 8, III

Maas, Peter, 1973(1), II
McAdoo, William G.:
    first to use Morton St. Tunnel (N.Y.-N.J.), 1904 Mar. 11, III
McAllister, Ward, 1872, IV; 1892(1), IV
MacArthur, Arthur, 1899 Mar. 30, I; 1900 June 21, I
MacArthur, Charles, 1928 Aug. 14, II
MacArthur, Douglas:
    Bonus Army, 1932 May 29, I
    book on, 1978(1), II
    died, 1964, I
    general of Army rank, 1944 Dec. 15, I
    Korean War command, 1950 July 8, I
    left Bataan (Philippines), 1942 Mar. 17, I
    occupation of Japan, 1945 Aug. 30, I
    "Old soldiers" speech before Congress, 1951 Apr. 19, I
    Philippine command, 1941 Dec. 10, I
    Philippines invaded, 1944 Oct. 20, I
    Philippines liberated, 1945 July 5, I
    Rabaul air raid, 1943 Nov. 2, I
    relieved of Korean War commands, 1951 Apr. 11, I
    returned to Philippines, 1961 July 3, I
MacArthur, John Donald, 1978, III
McAteer, Myrtle:
    Whitman, Malcolm D., 1900(4), IV
McAuliffe, Anthony C., 1975, I
McAuliffe, Christa, 1985 July 19, III; 1986 Jan. 28, III
McBride, Patricia, 1989 June 4(2), II
McCambridge, Mercedes, 1950 Mar. 23, II
McCandless, Bruce, 1984 Feb. 7, III
McCarl, John Raymond, 1921 June 10, I
McCarran-Walter Bill, 1952 June 25, I
McCarthy, Clem, 1962, IV
McCarthy, Eugene:
    won N.H. presidential primary, 1968 Mar. 12, I

McCarthy, Joseph R.:
    Army subversion charges, 1954 Apr. 23–June 17, I
    censure resolution against, 1954 July 30, I
    communist subversion charges, 1953, I
    condemned by Senate, 1954 Dec. 2, I
    died, 1957, I
    public reaction against, 1954, IV
    Senate committee charges against, 1953 Jan. 2, I
    State Dept. subversion charges, 1950, I
McCarthy, Joseph V., 1978, IV
McCarthy, Mary, 1963(1), II; 1980 Feb. 15(1), II; 1989, II
McCarthy, Timothy J., 1981 Mar. 30, I
McCartney, Paul, 1975 Mar. 1(1), II
McClanahan, Rue, 1987 Sept. 20, II
McClellan, George B.:
    Antietam (Md.), 1862 Sept. 17, I
    commander in chief, 1861 Nov. 1, I
    Peninsular Campaign failure, 1862 July 1(3), I
    presidential candidacy, 1864, I; 1864 Aug. 29, I
McClellan, John L., 1977, I
McClintock, Barbara, 1983 Oct. 10, III; 1992, III
McCloskey, John (Rev.), 1875 Mar. 15, III
McCloskey, Paul N., Jr., 1971, I
McCloy, John J., 1949 May 18, I
McClure, Samuel Sidney, 1884, II
McCollum, Elmer V., 1912(1), III
McComb, H. K., 1867(2), I
McCoole, Mike, 1869, IV
McCord, James W., 1972 June 17, I; 1973 Jan. 30, I; 1973 Mar. 23, I
McCormack, Frank, 1909(8), II
McCormick, Cyrus H., 1831, III; 1834(3), III
McCoy, J. G., 1867(10), III
McCracken, James, 1988, II
McCraw, Thomas K., 1985 Apr. 24, II
MacCready, Paul, 1977 Aug. 23, III
McCullers, Carson, 1950 Jan. 5, II; 1967, II; 1975(1), II
McCullock v. Maryland, 1819, I
McCullough, Colleen, 1977(1), II
McCullough, David, 1978 Apr. 10, II; 1982 Apr. 27, II; 1992(1), II
McDaniel, Hattie, 1940 Feb. 29, II
McDermott, John J., 1897 Apr. 19, IV; 1911 June 24, IV; 1912 Aug. 2, IV
McDivitt, James A., 1965 June 3, III; 1969 Mar. 3, III
MacDonald, Duncan, 1924 June 19, I
MacDonald, J. Ramsay, 1929 Oct. 7(1), I
McDonald, Ronald J., 1898 Apr. 19, IV
McDonald's (fast food chain):
    low-fat hamburger, 1991 Mar. 13, III
    mass shootings (Calif.), 1984 July 18, IV
    Soviet openings, 1988, III
MacDowell, Edward, 1888(5), II; 1889(2), II; 1896(2), II
McDowell, Ephraim, 1807, III
McDowell, Irvin, 1861 July 21, I

MacDowell Colony (Peterborough, N.H.), 1896(2), II
Mace, Jem, 1870 May 10, IV
McEnroe, John, 1979 Sept. 9, IV; 1980 Sept. 6–7, IV; 1981 July 3–4, IV; 1981 Sept. 9–13, IV; 1983 July 2–3, IV; 1984 July 7–8, IV; 1984 Sept. 8–9, IV
Macfarlane, Willie, 1925 June 5, IV
McFeeley, William S., 1982 Mar. 12, II
McFerrin, Bobby, 1989 Feb. 22, II
McGinley, Phyllis, 1961 May 1, II; 1978, II
McGovern, George S.:
    presidential candidacy, 1972, I; 1972 July 10–14, I; 1972 Nov. 7, I
McGowan, Bill, 1992 Aug. 2, IV
McGowan, William, 1992, III
McGraw, John J., 1902, IV; 1903, IV; 1904(4), IV
McGready, James, 1801, III
McGuffey, William H., 1836, III
Machine guns see Firearms
Machinery:
    first practical paper-folding, 1856 Oct. 7, III
    first screw-cutting, 1809(1), III
    interchangeable parts, 1820(5), III
MacInnes, Helen, 1976(1), II; 1985, II
McIntyre, James Francis Cardinal, 1979, III
Mack, Connie, 1901, IV
Mack, John E., 1977 Apr. 18, II
McKay, David O., 1970 Jan. 18, III
McKay, Donald, 1832, III
MacKaye, Percy, 1913 Sept. 12, II
MacKaye, Steele, 1880(6), II
McKellan, Ian, 1981 June 7, II
McKellen, Gordon, Jr., 1973 Jan. 24–27, IV; 1974 Feb. 6–9, IV; 1975 Jan. 31–Feb. 2, IV
McKenna, Richard, 1963(1), II
McKenney, Ruth, 1940 Dec. 26, II
MacKenzie, William Lyon, 1837 Dec. 29, I
McKim, Charles, 1854(2), III
McKim, Charles Follen, 1888(4), II; 1909(6), II
McKim, James Miller, 1865(11), II
Mackinac Straits Bridge (Mich.), 1957 Nov. 1, III
McKinley, Chuck, 1963 July 6, IV
McKinley, William:
    assassinated, 1901, I
    auto ride, 1899 Summer, IV
    born, 1843 Jan. 29, I
    Cuban port blockade, 1898 Apr. 22(1), I
    de Lôme letter on, 1898 Feb. 9, I
    elected president, 1896 Nov. 3, I
    inaugurated president, 1897 Mar. 4, I; 1901 Mar. 4, I
    presidential campaign, 1896, I; 1896 June 18, I; 1896 Aug. 15, II; 1900 June 19–21, I
    protective tariffs, 1897, I
    reelected president, 1900 Nov. 6, I
    requested U.S. intervention in Cuba, 1898 Apr. 11, I
    Spanish-American War peace treaty, 1899 Feb. 10, I

McKinley, William (cont.)
    volunteer call for Spanish-American War, 1898 Apr. 23, I; 1898 May 25(1), I
McKinley Tariff Act, 1890 Oct. 1(1), I
McKissick, Floyd, 1966 June 1–2, I
McKnight, Marian Ann, 1956 Sept. 8, IV
McLaglen, Victor, 1936 May 5, II
MacLaine, Shirley, 1984 Apr. 9, II
MacLeish, Archibald, 1933 May 4, II; 1938(1), II; 1952(1), II; 1953 Jan. 27, II; 1953 May 4(2), II; 1959 Apr. 12, II; 1959 May 4(1), II; 1972(1), II; 1982, II
McLeod, Fred, 1908 Aug. 28, IV
McLoughlin, Maurice E., 1912 June 15, IV; 1913 June 14, IV
McLuhan, Marshall, 1967(1), II
Maclure, William, 1809, III
McMahan Act, 1946 Aug. 1, I
McMillan, Edwin M., 1951 Nov. 15, III
Macmillan, Inc., 1984 Apr. 25, II
MacMonnies, Frederick W., 1893(3), II
MacMurray, Fred, 1991, II
McMurtry, Larry, 1986 Apr. 17, II; 1989(1), II; 1990(1), II
McNally, Terrence, 1969 Feb. 10, II; 1975 Jan. 20, II
McNamee, Paul, 1985 July 6–7, IV
McNary, Charles L., 1940 June 24–28, I
MacNeil, Hermon Atkins, 1900(2), II
McNeil, William H., 1964 Mar. 10, II
McNeill, W. Donald, 1940 Sept. 9, IV
McNutt, Paul V., 1942 Apr. 18, III
Macon's Bill No. Two, 1810 May 1, I
McPartland, Jimmy, 1991, II
MacPhail, Larry, 1975, IV
McPhee, John, 1977(1), II
McPherson, Aimee Semple, 1926, III; 1944, III
McPherson, James A., 1978 Apr. 17, II
McPherson, James M., 1988(1), II; 1989 Mar. 30, II
McRae, Gordon, 1986, II
Macready, William Charles, 1826, II; 1849 May 10, II
Macy, Anne Sullivan, 1959 Oct. 19, II
Macy, R.H., & Co., 1992 Jan. 6, III; 1992 Jan. 6, III
Maddox, Lester, 1967 Jan. 10, I
Madeiros, Humberto Cardinal, 1983, III
Madison, James:
    born, 1751 Mar. 16, I
    died, 1836 June 28, I
    elected president, 1808 Dec. 7, I
    federal improvement policies, 1815 Dec. 5, I
    Federalist, 1785–1789, II
    inaugurated, 1809 Mar. 4(1), I; 1813 Mar. 4, I
    Marbury v. Madison, 1803, I
    reelected president, 1812 Dec. 2, I
    trade policies, 1809, I; 1810 Aug. 5, I; 1811 Feb. 11, I
    vetoed Bonus Bill, 1817 Mar. 3(2), I
Madison Square Garden (N.Y.C.):
    first opened, 1879, II
Madonna, 1992(1), II
Madrid peace conference (Spain), 1991 Oct. 30, I
Maelzel, John Nepomuk, 1830(1), IV

Maffett, Debra Sue, 1982 Sept. 11, IV
Mafia see Organized crime
Magazines see Newspapers and publications
Magellan (spacecraft), 1989 May 4, III
Magnani, Anna, 1956 Mar. 21, II
Magrieritte, René, 1992 Sept. 12, II
Maguire, Matthew, 1896 July 4–9, I
Mahaffey, John, 1978 Aug. 6, IV
Maharidge, Dale, 1990 Apr. 12, II
Mahler, Gustav, 1916 Mar. 2, II
Mahony, Roger M., 1991 May 29, III
Mailer, Norman, 1948, II; 1948(1), II; 1951(1), II; 1969 Mar. 10(2), II; 1969 May 5, II; 1973(1), II; 1979(1), II; 1980 Apr. 14(1), II; 1983(1), II; 1991(1), II
Maimonides College (Pa.), 1867 Oct. 25, III
Maine:
    annexed to Massachusetts Bay Colony, 1652 May 31, I
    elections as national barometer, 1888(2), IV
    first northern French colony, 1604, I
    French settlement, 1613, I
    Indian land claim suit settled, 1980 Mar. 15, I
    provincial grant, 1622 Aug. 10, I
    statehood, 1820 Mar. 15, I
Maine, University of, 1862(4), III
Maine (battleship), 1898(1), IV; 1898 Jan. 25, I; 1898 Feb. 15, I
Maitland, Lester J., 1990, IV
Makarova, Natalia, 1970 Oct. 11, II
Malamud, Bernard, 1959 Mar. 3(1), II; 1963(1), II; 1966(1), II; 1967 Mar. 8, II; 1967 May 1, II; 1971(1), II; 1973(1), II; 1982(1), II; 1986, II
Malcolmson, Ruth, 1924 Sept. 6, IV
Malcolm X, 1965(1), II; 1965 Feb. 21, I; 1977 Mar. 9–11, IV
Malden, Karl, 1952 Mar. 20, II
Malevich, Kasimir, 1991 Mar. 24, II
Malik, Jacob, 1951 June 23, I; 1952 Mar. 8, I
Mallon, Meg, 1991 June 30, IV; 1991 July 14, IV
Malone, Dorothy, 1957 Mar. 27, II
Malone, Dudley Field, 1925 July 10–21, III
Malone, Dumas, 1975 May 5, II; 1981(1), II
Malta summit meeting, 1989 Dec. 3, I
Malvern Hill, Battle of (Va.), 1862 July 1(3), I
Mamet, David, 1977 Feb. 16, II; 1984 Apr. 16, II; 1992, II
Mamoulian, Rouben, 1987, II
Manchester, Melissa, 1983 Feb. 23, II
Manchester, William, 1967(1), II; 1978(1), II
Mancini, Henry, 1959 May 4(2), II; 1961 Apr. 12, II; 1962 May 29, II; 1964 May 12, II
Mandel, Marvin, 1975 Nov. 24, I
Mandlikova, Hana, 1985 Sept. 7–8, IV; 1986 July 5–6, IV
Manero, Tony, 1936 June 6(2), IV
Manet, Edouard, 1989 Nov. 30, II
Mangin, Joseph F., 1812(5), II
Mangrum, Lloyd, 1946 June 16, IV; 1950 June 10(2), IV; 1951, IV

Manhattan Bridge (N.Y.C.), 1909 Dec. 31, III

Manhattan Opera Co. (N.Y.C.), 1906(8), II; 1908(3), II

Manhattan Project, 1931, III

Manhattan Transfer (group), 1982 Feb. 24, II

Manifest destiny (doctrine), 1845, IV; 1898, I

Manila Bay, Battle of, 1898 May 1, I

Manilow, Barry, 1979 Feb. 16, II

Mann, Carol, 1965 July 4, IV; 1969, IV

Mann, David, 1967 Apr. 26, II

Mann, Horace:
    Antioch College presidency, 1853 Sept., III
    educational reforms, 1839, III
    sec. of Mass. state education board, 1837 Apr. 20, III

Mann, James R., 1906 June 21, III; 1910, I

Mann, William D'Alton, 1900 Mar., II

Mann Act, 1910 June 25, I

Mann-Elkins Act, 1910, I

Manners see Etiquette

Manning, Timothy Cardinal, 1989, III

Mansfield, Arabella, 1869(1), I

Manship, Paul, 1909(4), II; 1913(2), II

Mansions and manor homes (see also names of presidential homes):
    Adams (Quincy, Mass.), 1732(3), II
    Arlington House (Va.), 1802(2), II
    Georg Muller House (Pa.), 1752, II
    Gilded Age examples, 1884, IV
    Governor's Palace (Va.), 1706(1), II
    Gracie Mansion (N.Y.C.), 1799(2), II
    Hudson Valley (N.Y.), 1671(1), I; 1693(4), IV
    Lefferts Homestead (N.Y.), 1777(5), II
    Mount Airy (Va.), 1758, II
    Parlange (La.), 1750(2), II
    Vanderbilt (N.Y.C.), 1881(4), IV
    Whitehall (Md.), 1769(1), II

Manson, Charles, 1969 Aug. 9, IV; 1971 Jan. 25, IV; 1975 Sept. 5, I

Manteo (Indian), 1587, III

Mantle, Mickey, 1964 Oct. 7–15, IV; 1967 May 14, IV; 1969, IV; 1969 June 8, IV

Manual training see Vocational training

Manufacturing:
    consumer goods, 1787, IV; 1945 May 10, III
    consumer goods production resumed, 1944 Aug. 14, III
    consumer production controls lifted, 1945 Aug. 20, III
    early enterprises, 1640–1649, III
    early trade associations, 1785(6), III
    Essex Co. mills (Mass.), 1846(3), II
    exports, 1891, III
    federal production controls, 1951, III
    Hamilton's advocacy, 1790–1794, III
    List's economic arguments for, 1827, III
    National Assn.'s first meeting, 1895 Jan. 22, III
    N.E.'s economic shift to, 1828(2), III
    notice of plant closing, 1988 Aug. 2, III
    screw threading machine patent, 1798 Dec. 14, III

Manufacturing (cont.)
    societies to encourage, 1787(4), III
    toxic gas accident (W. Va.), 1985 Aug. 11, III
    Whitney's concept of interchangeable parts, 1798(2), III

Mapmaking:
    first road, 1789, III
    Melish's for U.S., 1812(4), II
    New World, 986–1599, II
    Vinland map called fake, 1974 Jan. 25, II

Mapplethorpe, Robert M., 1989 June 13, II; 1990 Apr. 7, II

Marasco, Robert, 1970 Feb. 17, II

Marathon Oil Co., 1982 Mar. 11, III

Marathons see Boston Marathon; New York City Marathon; Olympic Games; Track and field

Maravich, Peter Press (Pistol Pete), 1988, IV

Marble, Alice, 1936 Sept. 12(2), IV; 1938 Sept. 17, IV; 1939 July 7–8, IV; 1939 Sept. 17, IV; 1940 Sept. 9, IV; 1990, IV

Marbury v. Madison, 1803, I

March, Fredric, 1932 Nov. 18, II; 1947 Mar. 13(2), II; 1957 Apr. 21, II; 1975, II

March, William, 1954(1), II

Marchetti, Victor, 1974(1), II; 1974 Apr. 1, II; 1975 May 27, II

Marciano, Rocky, 1952 Sept. 23, IV; 1953, IV; 1954, IV; 1955, IV; 1956, IV; 1969, IV

Marcol, Chester, 1969 Oct. 18, IV

Marcos, Ferdinand, 1986, I
    indicted, 1988 Oct. 21, I, III; 1990 July 2, IV

Marcos, Imelda:
    acquitted, 1990 July 2, IV
    indicted, 1988 Oct. 21, I, III

Marcus, Rudolph A., 1992 Oct. 14, III

Marcy, William Learned, 1832 Jan. 21, IV

Mardi Gras, 1827(1), IV; 1857(5), IV

Mare Mount (Mass.), 1628 May 1, IV; 1637(2), II

Marietta College (Ohio), 1835 Feb. 14, III

Marijuana see Narcotics

Marin, John, 1915(3), II

Marinaro, Ed, 1971 Oct. 30, IV

Marine Biological Laboratory (Woods Hole, Mass.), 1887(2), III

Marine Corps, U.S.:
    official song, 1805 Apr. 27, I

Mariner Project:
    failed launching, 1971 May 8, III

Mariner 10, first Mercury probe, 1973 Nov. 3, III

Mariner 2, 1962 Aug. 27(2), III; 1962 Dec. 14, III

Mariner 4, 1964 Nov. 28, III; 1965 July 15, III

Mariner 5, 1967 June 14(2), III; 1967 Oct. 19, III

Mariner 6, 1969 Feb. 25, III

Mariner 7, 1969 Mar. 27, III

Mariner 9, 1971, III; 1971 May 30, III

Marino, Eugene Antonio, 1988 Mar. 15, III

Maris, Roger, 1927, IV; 1961 Oct. 1, IV; 1985, IV

Market-Garden, Operation, 1944 Sept. 17–27, I

Marketing:
    FTC authority extended to unfair practices, 1972 Mar. 1(1), III

Markham, Edward, 1899 Jan. 15, II

Markova, Olga, 1992 Apr. 20, IV

Markowitz, Harry M., 1990 Oct. 16(3), III

Marks, John D., 1974(1), II; 1974 Apr. 1, II

Marne, Battle of, 1918 July 15, I

Marquand, John P., 1937(1), II; 1938 May 2, II; 1941(1), II; 1946(1), II; 1960, II

Marquard, Rube (Richard), 1980, IV

Marquette, Jacques, 1670–1679, I; 1701 July 24, I

Marquis, Don, 1921(1), II; 1927(1), II

Marr, Dave, 1965 Aug. 15, IV

Marriages (see also Adultery; Divorce; Polygamy; Spinsterhood):
    advertisement for wives in N.Y.Times, 1856(3), IV
    agency to arrange, 1852(3), IV
    W. A. Alcott's traditional views on, 1836(5), IV
    Boston regulations, 1685(1), IV
    Chaplin-O'Neill, 1943 June 16, II
    civil legal (N.Y.), 1664(1), IV
    colonial customs, 1765(3), IV
    colonial separation law (Conn.), 1660(2), IV
    colonial women's prospects, 1658, IV
    common law, 1647(5), IV
    Cooke-Sikkim Crown Prince, 1963 Mar. 20, IV
    domestic partnership law, 1991 Feb. 14, IV
    dowry nonpayment, 1679, IV
    eugenic-based law unconstitutional (Wis.), 1914 Jan. 20, III
    first hotel bridal suite, 1844(2), IV
    first in colonies (Va.), 1609, IV
    first in Pa., 1682(2), IV
    first medical test law (N.Y.), 1938 Apr. 12, III
    first roster of credit standings and possibilities (N.Y.C.), 1844(3), IV
    Ford-Austin, 1965 Feb. 19, IV
    Franklin epigram, 1734(1), IV
    Gouverneur Morris-Anne Randolph, 1809(1), IV
    independent citizenship for women, 1922 Sept. 22, I
    as inducement for women colonizers (S.C.), 1666, IV
    interracial bans ruled unconstitutional, 1967 June 12, I
    interracial illegal (Mass.), 1705(1), IV
    interracial increase, 1991, I
    interrracial opposed (Phila., Pa.), 1723, IV
    Johnson-Robb, 1967 Dec. 9, IV
    G. Kelly-Rainier (Monaco), 1956 Apr. 19(1), IV
    Kennedy-Onassis, 1968 Oct. 19, IV
    N.J. minor's statute, 1719 Mar., IV
    Nixon-Eisenhower, 1968 Dec. 22, IV
    "obey" deleted from ceremony, 1922 Sept. 12, III
    older women-younger men, 1771 Mar. 15, IV

Marriages (cont.)
    phrenological and physiological
        approach to, 1846(3), IV
    religious ceremony allowed (Mass.,
        Conn.), 1692(1), III
    runaway wives, c1735, IV
    sex relations, 1960 Apr. 28, III
    shortage of women, 1736, IV
    three-day celebrations, 1986, IV
    Tiny Tim-Miss Vicki, 1969 Dec. 17, IV
    wife abuse condemned by Catholic
        bishops, 1992 Oct. 30, III
    women's property rights, 1836(1), I
Marsh, Jean, 1975 May 19, II
Marsh, Reginald, 1934(5), II; 1945 Dec. 27,
    II
Marshall, E. G., 1962 May 22, II; 1963
    May 26, II
Marshall, George C.:
    died, 1959, I
    general of Army rank, 1944 Dec. 15, I
Marshall, John:
    appointed chief justice, 1801 Jan. 20, I
    banquet honoring, 1798 June 18, IV
    biography of Washington, 1804(4), II
    died, 1835 July 8, I
    judicial opinions, 1819, I; 1819, III
Marshall, Thomas R., 1912 June 25-July 2,
    I; 1912 Nov. 5, I; 1915(2), IV; 1916 June
    14-16, I; 1916 Nov. 7, I; 1917 Mar. 5, I
Marshall, Thurgood, 1967 Oct. 2, I; 1969
    Apr. 7, II; 1991 June 27, I
Marshall Field Building (Chicago, Ill.),
    1885(2), II
Marshall Plan:
    Greece, China, and Turkey aid, 1948,
        I
    minimum cost, 1948 Jan. 8, I
    proposed, 1947 June 5, I
    signed, 1948 Apr. 3, I
    success, 1947, I
Marshall University (W. Va.), 1970 Nov.
    14, IV
Mars (planet):
    Mariner 6, 1969 Feb. 25, III
    Mariner 7, 1969 Mar. 27, III
    Observer launched, 1992 Sept. 25, III
    orbits, 1971, III; 1971 May 30, III
    photographs, 1964, III; 1964 Nov. 28,
        III; 1965, III; 1965 July 15, III; 1969
        Feb. 25, III; 1969 Mar. 27, III
    satellites detected, 1877(3), III
    vegetation possibility, 1955 Sept. 8, III
    Viking findings, 1976 July 20, III
    Viking 1 and 2 experiments ended,
        1977 May 30, III
Martin, Aubran W., 1971 June 23, I
Martin, Bradley, 1897, IV
Martin, Jay, 1970(1), II
Martin, Joseph, Jr., 1968, I
Martin, Mary, 1956 Mar. 17, II; 1990, II
Martin, Pepper, 1965, IV
Martineau, Harriet, 1827, IV; 1837(2), II
Martinelli, Giovanni, 1967 Jan. 31, II;
    1969, II
Martinez, Dennis, 1991 July 28, IV
Martinu, Bohuslav, 1948(5), II; 1953 Feb.
    7, II
Martin v. Hunter's Lessee, 1816 Mar. 20(1),
    I

Marty, Martin E., 1972 Apr. 13, II
Marvin, Lee, 1966 Apr. 18, II; 1979, IV
Marvin, Michelle Triola, 1979, IV
Marx, Chico, 1961, II
Marx, Groucho, 1951 Jan. 23, II; 1977, II
Marx, Gummo, 1977, II
Marx, Harpo, 1964, II
Marx, Karl, 1851(8), II
Marx Brothers, 1925 Dec. 8, II
Mary Celeste (ship), 1872 Nov. 7, IV
Maryland:
    Anglican Church, 1702, I
    Baltimore charter, 1632 June 20, I
    banned slave trade, 1783, I
    book on early, 1666, II
    Catholic-Puritan civil war ended, 1655
        Mar. 25, I
    first state to ban cheap pistols, 1988
        May 23, I
    Mandel indicted, 1975 Nov. 24, I
    Protestant rebellion, 1689 Aug. 1, I
    Roman Catholic Church, 1634 Mar.
        25, III
    seventh state to ratify U.S.
        Constitution, 1788 Apr. 28, I
Maryland, University of, 1812 Dec. 29, III
Maryland Day, 1634 Mar. 25, IV
Maryland plantation, c1650, I
Masland, William M., 1987, IV
Mason, Lowell, 1821, II; 1833(6), II;
    1838(4), II; 1858(1), II
Masonic orders see Freemasons
Masonic Temple (Chicago, Ill.), 1891(3), II
Masonry see Buildings
Massachusetts (see also Boston;
    Massachusetts Bay Colony; New
    England):
    anti-Catholicism, 1700 June 17, III
    constitution drafted, 1775 May 16, I
    early independence move, 1641 Dec.,
        I
    first Englishman to land, 1602 May
        15, I
    Gerrymandering, 1812(3), IV
    Indian land-claim suit (Cape Cod),
        1978 Jan. 6(1), I
    Mather dynasty rule, 1635 Aug. 17, I
    Mather ecclesiastical history, 1702(1),
        II
    outlawed slavery, 1783, I
    prohibition in, 1908 Apr. 30, I
    Puritan ban on priests, 1647 May 26,
        III
    separated from N.H., 1680 Sept., I
    sixth state to ratify U.S. Constitution,
        1788 Feb. 6, I
    State House, 1795(2), II
    tornadoes, 1953 June 9, I
Massachusetts, University of:
    founded, 1863(1), III
Massachusetts Bay Colony:
    charter revoked, 1684 June 21, I
    first settlers, 1629 June 27, I
    Me. annexed, 1652 May 31, I
    population growth, 1643(2), I
    united with Plymouth, 1691(1), I
Massachusetts Emigrant Aid Society, 1854
    Apr. 26, I
Massachusetts Historical Society, 1791(1),
    III

Massachusetts Institute of Technology
    (MIT):
    first architecture course, 1866(3), II
    founded, 1859(1), III
    moved to present site, 1916(10), II
Massacres:
    Alamo (Tex.), 1836(2), IV; 1836 Mar.
        6, I
    Boston (Mass.), 1770 Mar. 5, I
    first Indian (Va.), 1622 Mar. 22, I
    Ft. Caroline (Fla.), 1565 Sept. 20, I
    Ft. Dearborn (Mich.), 1812 Aug. 15, I
    Ft. Michilimackinak (Mich.), 1763
        June 2, I
    Ft. Pillow (Tenn.), 1864 Apr. 12, I
    Haverhill (Mass.), 1708 Aug. 30, I
    of Kans. slavery supporters, 1856 May
        21, I
    Malmédy prison (France), 1944 Dec.
        16, I
    Mountain Meadows (Utah), 1857 Sept.
        11, I
    My Lai Songmy, 1969 Nov. 16, I;
        1971, I; 1971 Mar. 29, I
    Queen Anne's War (Deerfield, Mass.),
        1704 Feb. 29, I
    St. Valentine's Day (Chicago, Ill.),
        1929, IV
    Sauk by Ill. militia, 1832 Aug. 2, I
    Texas tower, 1966 Aug. 1, I
    Tuscarora war (N.C.), 1711 Sept. 22, I
    Wyoming Valley (Pa.), 1778 July 3-4,
        I; 1809, II
    Yamassee Indian (S.C.), 1715-1719, I
Massey, Raymond, 1983, II
Massie, Robert K., 1967(1), II; 1981 Apr.
    13, II
Mass transit see Transit systems
Masteroff, Joe, 1966 Nov. 20, II; 1967 Mar.
    26, II
Masters, Edgar Lee, 1914 May 29, II;
    1915(1), II
Masters, William H., 1970(1), II
Matches, 1896(5), III
Matchett, Charles H., 1892 Aug. 28, I;
    1896 July 4-9, I; 1896 Nov. 3, I
Mathematics:
    first algebra book, 1730(2), II
    first professorship, 1717, III
    first textbook by American, 1729(3), II
    U.S. student deficiency in, 1989 Jan.
        31, III
Mather, Cotton, 1661, II; 1688, IV
    accomplishments, 1690-1699, III
    books by, 1702(1), II; 1706(3), II
    colonial grievances manifesto, 1689(2),
        I
    deism, 1710-1714, III
    on first Bible printed in colonies,
        1661, II
    Harvard studies, 1674, III
    personal conduct surveillance, 1702,
        IV
    praised Bradstreet's poetry, 1650, II
    on supernatural events, 1688, IV
    supported Copernican theory, 1714(2),
        III
    urged smallpox inoculations,
        1720-1724, III

Mather, Cotton (*cont.*)
  witchcraft views, 1690–1699, III; 1692 Oct., III
Mather, Increase, 1674, III; 1681, IV; 1692(2), III
Mather, Richard, 1635 Aug. 17, I; 1670(3), II
Mathews, Eddie, 1967 July 14, IV
Matisse, Henri, 1992 Sept. 24, II
Matlin, Marlee, 1987 Mar. 30, II
Matlovich, Leonard, 1975 Oct. 22, I
Matsunaga, Spark M., 1990, I
Matthau, Walter, 1967 Apr. 10, II
Matthews, Burnita S., 1988, I
Matthiesen, Peter, 1979 Apr. 23, II
Matthiessen, F. O., 1944(1), II
Mattingly, Don, 1987 Sept. 29, IV
Mattingly, Thomas K., 1972 Apr. 16, III
Mauchly, John W., 1946 Feb. 15, III; 1951 June 14, III
Maugham, W. Somerset, 1921 Sept. 12, II
Mauldin, Bill, 1944(1), IV
Maurer, James H., 1928 Apr. 13–18, I; 1932 May 22–24, I
Maxim, Hiram Percy, 1884(4), III
Maxwell, Elsa, 1963, II
Maxwell, Robert, 1987, II
May, Elaine, 1960 Oct. 8, II; 1969 Feb. 10, II
Mayaguez (ship), 1975 May 12, I
May Day:
  Mare Mount, 1628 May 1, IV
  Mayday war protest (Wash., D.C.), 1971 May 3, I
Mayer, Dick, 1957, IV; 1957 June 15(2), IV
Mayer, Jacquelyn Jeanne, 1962 Sept. 8(1), IV
Mayer, Maria G., 1963 Nov. 5, III
Mayer, Sandy, 1975 July 4–5, IV
Mayflower Compact:
  first social contract, 1620 Nov. 21, I
Mayflower II (ship), 1957 June 13, III
Mayflower (ship), 1620 Dec. 26, I; 1630, II
Mayhew, Jonathan, 1747(1), III; 1763(2), III
Mayo, Charles W., 1968, III
Mayors:
  first black of Chicago (Ill.), 1983 Apr. 12, I
  first black of Cleveland (Ohio), 1967 Nov. 7, I
  first black of Phila. (Pa.), 1983 Nov. 8, I
  first Mexican-American, 1981 Apr. 4, I
  first southern black (Atlanta, Ga.), 1973 Oct. 16(1), I
  first woman of Chicago (Ill.), 1979 Apr. 3, I
  N.Y.C., 1925 Nov. 3, I; 1933 Nov. 7, I
Maypole, 1645 June, IV
Mays, Willie, 1966, IV; 1969 Sept. 22, IV; 1973 Sept. 25, IV
Mead, Larkin G., 1866(4), II
Mead, Lynda Lee, 1959 Sept. 12, IV
Mead, Margaret, 1970(1), II; 1978, III
Meade, George G.:
  Gettysburg battle (Pa.), 1863 July 1–3, I
Meader, Vaughn, 1963 May 15, II
Meadows, Audrey, 1955 Mar. 7, II

Means, Gardiner C., 1988, III
Means, Jacqueline, 1977 Jan. 1, III
Means, Russell, 1974 Sept. 16(3), I
Meany, George:
  AFL-CIO head, 1955 Dec. 5, III
  AFL presidency, 1952 Nov. 25, III
  automation, 1963, III
  died, 1980, III
  retired, 1979 Nov. 15, III
Mears, Rick, 1988 May 29, IV; 1991 May 26, IV
Meat:
  Armour pork-packing plant, 1868(3), III
  beef price ceilings, 1951 Apr. 28, III
  Catholics' abstinence on Friday lifted, 1966 Nov. 18, III
  consumer boycott, 1973, III; 1973 Mar. 29, III
  import quotas lifted, 1972 June 26, III
  Inspection Act passed, 1906(1), II; 1906 June 30, I
  low-fat McDonald's hamburger, 1991 Mar. 13, III
  packing plants, 1898, III
  price controls, 1946 Oct. 15, III
  price controls lifted, 1952 July 14, III
  price freeze, 1973 Mar. 29, III
  rationing, 1943 Mar. 29, III
  rationing ended, 1944 May 3(2), III; 1945 Nov. 23, III
  Union stockyards (Chicago, Ill.), 1865(9), III
  World War I meatless days, 1918 Jan. 26, IV
Mecham, Evan, 1988 Apr. 4, I
Mecham, Willard, 1988 Apr. 4, I
Mechanical Engineers, American Society of, 1880(1), III
Mecir, Miloslav, 1986 Sept. 7, IV
Mecklenburg Declaration of Independence (N.C.), 1775 May 20, I
Medals and decorations:
  Distinguished Flying Cross, 1926 July 2(2), I
  Ellington received Medal of Freedom, 1969 Apr. 29, II
  first congressional, to foreigner, 1779 July 26, I
  first Medal of Honor, 1861 Feb. 13, I
  Medal of Honor, 1862 July 12, I
  Medal of Honor for heroism in S. Vietnam, 1964 Dec. 5, I
  Purple Heart, 1782 Aug. 7, I
  singer Anderson received congressional, 1978 Oct. 17, II
Medicaid:
  abortion-funding ruling, 1977 June 20, III
  fraud, 1976 Aug. 30, III
  rising costs, 1992, I
Medicare:
  new doctors' fee schedule, 1991 May 31, III
  plan submitted, 1963 Feb. 21(2), I
  started, 1966 July 1, III

Medicine (*see also* Anesthesia; Drugs and drug products; Health insurance; Medicaid; Medicare; Mental illness and health; Nobel Prizes; Nursing profession; Pregnancy and birth; Public health; Smoking; Vaccination; names of diseases, body organs, and parts):
  advances in, 1937, III
  American Medical Assn. antitrust violation, 1943 Jan. 18, III
  antibody chemical structure discovered, 1969 Apr. 14, III
  bacteriology as science, 1892(3), III
  blood substitute created, 1991 June 16, III
  Caldwell's contribution, 1821(3), IV
  Carter scored AMA, 1978 May 5, III
  Channing Home, hospital for indigent women (Boston, Mass.), 1857 May, III
  children's diseases, first professor of, 1860(3), III
  colonial care, 1750–1754, III
  contemporary remedies, 1810(3), IV
  costs highest to date, 1981, III
  death defined, 1968 Dec. 4, III; 1975 Nov. 10, III
  disease-carrying immigrants banned, 1910 Mar. 26, I
  doctors' slowdown (Calif.), 1976 Feb. 5, III
  education, 1780–1784, III; 1782(1), III
  electricity used for bone fracture repair, 1971 Oct. 29, III
  first college clinic (N.Y.C.), 1840(5), III
  first comprehensive service-needs study, 1932 Nov., III
  first cowpox vaccination, 1800(5), III
  first cystotomy, 1840(5), III
  first dispensary (Phila., Pa.), 1785(1), III
  first doctors' strike (N.Y.C.), 1975 Mar. 17–20, III
  first doctor (Va.), 1610, III
  first essay on human dissection, 1750(1), III
  first eye bank established, 1944 May 8, III
  first heart and liver transplant, 1984 Feb. 13, III
  first hospital in N.Y.C., 1658, III
  first hospital in Phila. (Pa.), 1750–1754, III
  first Jewish hospital (N.Y.C.), 1852 Jan. 15, III
  first lithotomy, 1706, III
  first live donor liver transplant, 1989 Nov. 27, III
  first mannequin showing female physiology, 1844(4), IV
  first orthopedic hospital (N.Y.C.), 1863 May 1, III
  first osteopathic college (Mo.), 1892(9), III
  first Pilgrim doctor, 1620 Dec. 21, III
  first public clinic for throat disease, 1862(2), III
  first school entirely for women (Pa.), 1850 Mar. 11, III

Medicine (*cont.*)

first school for women (Boston, Mass.), 1848 Nov. 1, III

first school on Pacific coast, 1859(2), III

first school (Pa.), 1765 May 3, III

first smallpox inoculations (Boston, Mass.), 1720–1724, III

first three-way heart/lung transplant, 1987 May 12, III

first West Coast college, 1859(2), III

first woman doctor, 1849(3), III

first women's hospital, 1849(3), III

gene therapy, 1990 July 31, III

Gerard's contribution, 1837(4), III

Holmes publication, 1843(2), III

home health book by W. A. Alcott, 1856(5), IV

homeopathy, 1836(2), III

homeopathy introduced, 1825(4), III

hospital costs rose, 1983, III

interferon synthesis, 1980 Jan. 16, III

Kier's Rock Oil patent cure-all, 1841(1), III

malpractice suits, 1975, III; 1975 Jan. 12, III; 1976 Feb. 5, III

malpractice suits increased, 1985, III

national convention and association founding, 1847 May 7, III

national health report, 1976 Jan. 12, III

National Research Act, 1974 July 12, III

nerve transplants, 1963 Apr. 18, III

N.Y.C. regulated practice of, 1753(2), III

normal temperature variation, 1992, III

organ transplants, 1968, III; 1968 Dec. 4, II

Osteopathic Assn. formed, 1897(3), III

osteopathy developed, 1874(2), III

pernicious anemia treatment, 1926(1), III

personal nature of practice, 1803(1), IV

phrenology, 1821(3), IV

quack, 1809(3), III; 1838(3), IV

rising costs, 1978, III

Rush's contribution, 1780–1784, III

significant contributions, 1807, III

twins joined at head separated, 1987 Sept. 5–7, III

voluntary care plan, 1949 Feb. 13, III

whiskey prescriptions allowed under Prohibition, 1923 May 9, I

Medill, Joseph, 1852(2), II

Medina, Ernest L., 1971 Mar. 29, I

Medina, Harold:

convicted Communist Party leaders, 1949 Oct. 14, I

Medoff, Mark, 1973 Nov. 5, II; 1980 June 8, II

Meehan, Thomas, 1977 Apr. 21, II; 1977 June 5, II

Meese, Edwin, 1988 July 5, I

Meeting House (Deerfield, Mass.), 1824(2), II

Meeuwsen, Terry Anne, 1972 Sept. 9, IV

Meggy, Percy, 1875 Dec. 25, II

Mehta, Zubin, 1977 May 14, II; 1991 May 28, II

Mein, John Gordon, 1968 Aug. 28, I

Mekonnen, Abebe, 1989 Apr. 17, IV

Melchior, Lauritz, 1973, II

Melish, John, 1812(4), II

Mellon, Andrew W., 1941 Mar. 17, II

Mellon, Paul, 1977 Apr. 19, II

Meloy, Francis E., Jr., 1976 June 16, I

Melville, Herman:

Billy Budd, 1924(1), II

career, 1846, II

Clarel: A Poem and Pilgrimage in the Holy Land, 1876(1), II

Israel Potter, 1855(1), II

Library of Congress reissued works, 1982(1), II

Moby-Dick (Melville) published, 1851(3), II

Omoo, 1847(2), II

White-Jacket published, 1850(4), II

Memorial Day (*see also* Decoration Day):

Confederate, 1865 Apr. 26, IV

N.Y. first to recognize, 1873(1), IV

Memorial Hospital for the Treatment of Cancer (N.Y.C.), 1884(1), III

Memphis (Tenn.):

race riots, 1968 Mar. 28, I

Menéndez de Avilés, Pedro, 1565 Sept. 8, I; 1565 Sept. 20, I

Mencken, H. L., 1900 Mar., II; 1919(1), II

Mendel, Samuel Leroy, 1988 July 13, IV

Menjou, Adolphe, 1963, II

Menken, Adah Isaacs, 1863(1), IV; 1867, IV

Menken, Alan, 1982 May 29, II

Mennin, Peter, 1969 May 2, II

Menninger, Karl A., 1990, III

Mennonites, 1800(4), III

Menotti, Gian-Carlo, 1938 Mar. 3, II; 1947 Feb. 18, II; 1950 Mar. 1, II; 1951 Dec. 24, II; 1954 Dec. 27, II; 1958 Aug. 20, II; 1969 Mar. 10(1), II; 1969 Aug. 1, II

Mental illness and health:

afflicting 25% of all Americans, 1960 May 31, III

American Psychiatric Assn. precursor, 1844(2), III

Dix's crusade for better treatment of insane, 1841(3), IV; 1843 Jan., IV

drug therapy, 1955 Jan. 8, III

employment rights, 1991 July 1, I

first American treatise published, 1812(1), III

first hospital (Va.), 1770(3), III

first insane asylum (Pa.), 1817(2), III

first treatment facility (Phila., Pa.), 1709(2), III

forced confinement of patients barred, 1975 June 26, III

homosexuality exempted, 1973 Dec. 15, III

Horney's theories, 1937(1), III

Rush's studies, 1780–1784, III

state institution guidelines ordered (Ala.), 1972 Apr. 13, III

Mercer, Jacque, 1949 Sept. 10, IV

Mercer, Johnny, 1976, II

Mercer, Mabel, 1984, II

Merchant Marine Act, 1920 June 5, III

Mercury (planet):

first U.S. probe, 1973 Nov. 3, III

Mercury Project, 1961 Jan. 31, III; 1961 May 5(2), III; 1961 July 21, III; 1961 Sept. 13, III; 1963 May 15–16, III

Meredith, James H., 1962 Sept. 20, III; 1962 Sept. 30, III; 1962 Dec. 21, III; 1966 June 6, I

Meredith, William, 1988 Mar. 31, II

Mergenthaler, Ottmar, 1884(5), III

Mergers *see* Corporations; Trusts and antitrust; company and industry names

Meriwether, Lee, 1954 Sept. 11, IV

Merkel, Una, 1986, II

Merkle, Fred, 1908 Sept. 23, IV

Merman, Ethel, 1984, II

Merrifield, Bruce, 1984 Oct. 17, III

Merrill, Bob, 1961 Apr. 13, II

Merrill, James, 1967 Mar. 8, II; 1977 Apr. 18, II; 1979 Apr. 23, II; 1984 Jan. 9, II

Merrimack (ship) *see Virginia* (ship)

Merriwell, Frank (fictional character), 1896(1), II

Merry Mount:

Hanson opera on, 1934(2), II

Hawthorne on, 1637(2), II

Merton, Thomas, 1949(1), II; 1968, II

Merwin, W. S., 1971 May 3, II

Meseke, Marilyn, 1938 Sept. 10, IV

Messerer, Sulamith, 1980 Feb. 6, II

Mesta, Perle, 1975, IV

Metalious, Grace, 1956(1), II

Metcalf, Henry B., 1900 June 27–28, I

Meteorological satellites *see* Weather satellites

Meteors, 1922 May 12, III

Methodist Book Concern (N.Y.C.), 1789(4), II

Methodist Church:

Colored Episcopal founded, 1870 Dec. 16, III

condemnation of homosexuality, 1992 May 12(1), III

established, 1765–1769, III

first annual conference, 1773 July 14, III

first black independent (Phila., Pa.), 1794(3), III

first building (N.Y.C.), 1768 Oct. 30, III

first college (Md.), 1787 Dec., III

first recorded camp meeting (Ky.), 1800 July, III

membership, 1900(2), III; 1989, III

merged with Evangelical United Brethren Church, 1966 Nov. 11(2), III

noncelibate homosexual ordination banned, 1984 May 9(2), III

nuclear weapon use opposed, 1986 Apr. 29, III

organized in America, 1784 Dec. 24, III

personal conduct bans lifted (N.E.), 1908 Apr. 13, IV

promoted by Whitefield tour, 1739 Aug., III

racial segregation abolished, 1956 May 2, III

reunited, 1939 May 10, III

Methodist Church (cont.)
    revoked dancing-theater ban, 1924 May 27, III
    Wesley in Ga., 1736 Feb. 5, III
Metric system, 1975 Dec. 11, III
Metropolitan Museum of Art (N.Y.C.) (see also Cloisters):
    Altman's gifts, 1865(10), III
    Annenberg donation, 1991 Mar. 11, II
    art forgery, 1967 Dec. 6, II
    centennial, 1970, II
    Davis retrospective, 1991, II
    founded, 1880, II
    Great Age of Fresco, 1968 Sept. 28, II
    Greek marble head stolen, 1979 Feb. 9(3), II
    Hermitage exchange, 1988 Mar. 26, II
    Hoving named director, 1967 Apr. 15, II
    Hoving resigned as director, 1977 Dec. 31, II
    Israeli ancient art exhibit, 1987, II
    Lehman collection, 1969, II
    Linsky print collection, 1982 Mar. 4, II
    Magritte retrospective, 1992 Sept. 12, II
    Malevich exhibition, 1991 Mar. 24, II
    Maori exhibit, 1984, II
    proposed new wing, 1985, II
    purchased Packard collection, 1975 Aug. 23, II
    Rembrandt's Aristotle acquired, 1961 Nov. 15, II
    Rockefeller legacy, 1979 Feb. 9(2), II
    Rockefeller primitive art collection, 1969, II
    Soviet art exchanges, 1975 Aug. 29, II
    van Gogh at Arles exhibit, 1984, II
Metropolitan Opera (N.Y.C.):
    Amelia Goes to the Ball (Menotti) produced, 1938 Mar. 3, II
    Billy Budd (Britten), 1978 Sept. 23, II
    Bing farewell gala, 1972 Apr. 22, II
    Caldwell first woman conductor, 1976 Jan. 13, II
    Callas debut, 1956 Oct. 29, II
    deficit, 1977, II
    destroyed by fire, 1892 Aug. 27, II
    Diamond Horseshoe, 1892(2), IV
    final national tour, 1986 June 1(2), II
    first performance in Lincoln Center, 1966 Sept. 16, II
    Gentele named general manager, 1970 Dec. 9, II
    Girl of the Golden West, The (Puccini), 1905 Oct. 3, II; 1910 Dec. 10, II
    Hammerstein's competition, 1906(8), II
    Horne debut, 1970 Mar. 3, II
    hundredth anniversary, 1983, II
    Il Trittico (Puccini) premiered, 1918 Dec. 14, II
    last performance in old house, 1966 Apr. 16, II
    Levine named musical director, 1975 May 22, II
    Melba and Calve's debuts, 1893(5), II
    Merry Mount (Hanson), 1934(2), II

Metropolitan Opera (N.Y.C.) (cont.)
    Mona (Hooker) opened, 1912 Mar. 14, II
    Mourning Becomes Electra (Levy) premiered, 1967 Mar. 17, II
    national tour halted, 1985 June 20, II
    Norma revived, 1970 Mar. 3, II
    opening night production, 1916 Nov. 13, II
    Paris Opera Co. U.S. debut, 1976 Sept. 8, II
    Parsifal (Wagner) production, 1904(4), II
    Price farewell performance, 1985 Jan. 3, II
    Salomé (Strauss) canceled, 1907 Jan. 22, II
    season's beginning postponed, 1980, II
    Sills debut, 1975 Apr. 7, II
    strike, 1969, II
    Sutherland debut, 1961, II
    touring co. disbanded, 1966, II
    Vanessa (Barber), 1958 Jan. 15, II
    Voyage (Glass) premiered, 1992, II
    Wozzeck (Berg), 1959 Mar. 5, II
Meurin, Sébastien Louis (Fr.), 1746(2), III
Meuse-Argonne, Battle of, 1918 Sept. 26-Nov. 11, I
Mexican-Americans:
    first U.S. mayor, 1981 Apr. 4, I
    terrorist attack (N. Mex), 1967 June 5, I
Mexican Revolution:
    U.S. troops sent, 1911 Mar. 7, I
Mexican War:
    Battle of Buena Vista, 1847 Feb. 22-23, I
    Battle of Cerro Gordo, 1847 Apr. 18, I
    Battle of Molino del Rey, 1847 Sept. 8, I
    Battle of Palo Alto, 1846 May 8, I
    Battle of Resaca de la Palma, 1846 May 9, I
    casualties and cost, 1848, I
    Chapultepec taken, 1847 Sept. 13, I
    declared formally, 1846 May 13, I
    Mexicans defeated at Churubusco, 1847 Aug. 20, I
    Mexico City taken, 1847 Sept. 14, I
    Monterrey captured by U.S., 1846 Sept. 25, I
    peace negotiations, 1847 Apr. 15, I; 1847 June 6, I
    Polk declared, 1846, I
    Polk's troop order, 1846 Jan., I
    Thoreau against, 1849, II
    treaty provisions, 1848, I
    U.S. forces crossed Rio Grande, 1846 May 18, I
    U.S. siege of Vera Cruz, 1847 Mar. 9, I
Mexico (see also Texas):
    border treaty with U.S., 1970 Nov. 23(1), I
    Carranza presidency recognized by U.S., 1915 Oct. 19, I
    diplomatic relations severed by U.S., 1914 Apr. 22, I
    El Chamizal border area returned by U.S., 1967 Oct. 28, I

Mexico (cont.)
    first U.S. minister, 1825 Mar. 7, I
    Gadsden Purchase, 1853 Dec. 30, I
    L. Johnson visited, 1966 Dec. 3, III
    Latin-American conference on, 1915 Aug. 5, I
    negotiation with U.S. proposed, 1916 July 28, I
    Tampico incident, 1914 Apr. 9, I
    U.S. diplomatic relations severed, 1845 Mar. 28, I
    U.S. dispute mediated, 1914 Apr. 25, I
    U.S. forces recalled from, 1917 Jan. 28, I
    U.S. forces withdrawn from Vera Cruz, 1914 Nov. 23, I
    U.S. prisoner repatriation, 1977 Oct. 28, I
    U.S. punitive action, 1916 Mar. 15(2), I; 1916 June 16, I; 1916 June 17, I; 1916 June 20, I
    U.S. troops attacked, 1916 June 21, I
    Vera Cruz customhouse seizure, 1914 Apr. 21, I
    Villa forays into U.S., 1916 Mar. 9, I
    Wilmot Proviso, 1846 Aug., I
    Wilson intervention request, 1914 Apr. 19, I
    Wilson's policy, 1913 Aug. 27, I
    Zimmermann note, 1917 Feb. 24, I
Mey, Cornelis J., 1624 May, I
M'Fingal (Trumbull), 1782(4), II
Miami (Fla.):
    race riots, 1968 Aug. 7, I; 1980 May 17-19, I
Miami University (Ohio), 1809 Feb. 17, III
Michael, George, 1989 Feb. 22, II
Michaels, Sidney, 1964 Jan. 18(1), II
Michel, Peggy, 1974 July 5, IV
Michelangelo, 1964 Apr. 19, II
Michelson, Albert A., 1878(2), III; 1907(2), III; 1920(5), III
Michener, James, 1947(1), II; 1948 May 3, II; 1953(1), II; 1974(1), II; 1978(1), II; 1980(1), II
Michigan:
    first colony, 1701 July 24, I
    first state to abolish capital punishment, 1846 May 4, I
    statehood, 1837 Jan. 26, I
    surrogate motherhood banned, 1988 June 27(1), IV
    tornado, 1953 June 8, I
Michigan, University of:
    chartered, 1837 Mar. 18, III
Microelectronics, 1973 Oct. 23, III
Microfilm, 1942 June 22, III
Microscope, electron, 1940 Apr. 20, III
Midas 2 (satellite), 1960 May 24, III
Middlebury College (Vt.):
    chartered, 1800 Nov. 1, III
Middlecoff, Cary, 1949 June 11(1), IV; 1955 Apr. 10, IV; 1956 June 16(2), IV
Middle East (see also Israeli-Arab conflict; country names):
    Eisenhower Doctrine, 1957, I; 1957 Jan. 5, I
Midler, Bette, 1981 Feb. 25, II; 1990 Feb. 21, II
Midway, Battle of, 1942 June 4-6, I

Mielziner, Jo, 1965 Oct. 21(2), II
Mies van der Rohe, Ludwig, 1950(4), II; 1951(8), II; 1960 Mar. 27, II; 1966, II; 1969, II
Migrant workers:
  murderer convicted (Calif.), 1973 Feb. 25, IV
Mikan, George, 1967 Feb. 2, IV
Milanov, Zinka, 1989, II
Miles, Nelson D., 1898 July 25, I; 1898 July 28, I
Milford, Nancy, 1970(1), II
Milhaud, Darius, 1949(2), II; 1955, II
Military see Armed forces; war names
Milk:
  condensing process, 1856(6), III
  evaporated process patented, 1853 May, III
  first malted, 1882(4), IV
Milk, Harvey, 1978 Nov. 27, I
Milken, Michael R., 1990 Nov. 21, III
Milland, Ray, 1946 Mar. 7, II; 1986, II
Millay, Edna St. Vincent, 1920(1), II; 1923 May 13, II; 1928(1), II
Miller, Alice Duer, 1941(1), II
Miller, Arnold, 1972 May 1, III
Miller, Arthur, 1949 Feb. 10, II; 1949 May 2, II; 1964 Jan. 23, II
Miller, Glenn, 1944, II
Miller, Henry, 1961, II; 1962, II; 1980, II
Miller, Jason, 1972 May 2, II; 1973 May 7, II
Miller, Johnny, 1971 Apr. 11, IV; 1973 June 17, IV; 1974, IV
Miller, Jonathan, 1962 Oct. 27, II
Miller, Merle, 1974(1), II
Miller, Merton H., 1990 Oct. 16(3), III
Miller, Perry, 1966 May 2, II
Miller, Richard W., 1984 Oct. 3, I
Miller, Roger, 1985 Apr. 25, II
Miller, William (Adventist leader), 1831 Aug., III; 1844 Mar. 21, III
Miller, William E., 1964 July 15, I
Millett, Kate, 1970(1), II
Millie (White House dog), 1990(1), II
Millikan, Robert Andrews, 1923 Nov. 13, III
Millionaires see Gilded Age; Income and wealth, personal; names of individuals
Mills, Clark, 1853 Jan. 8, II
Mills, John, 1971 Apr. 14, II
Mills, Mary, 1963 July 20, IV; 1964 Oct. 4, IV; 1973 June 10, IV
Mills, Robert, 1815 July 4, II
Mills, Samuel J., 1812(2), IV
Mills, Wilbur, 1974 Dec. 10, I; 1992, I
Mills and milling:
  oldest tide mill (Mass.), 1643(2), II
Milmore, Martin, 1874(2), II
Milosz, Czeslaw, 1980 Oct. 9, II
Milwaukee County Performing Arts Center (Wis.), 1969 Sept. 17, II
Milwaukee (Wis.):
  fire, 1892 Oct. 28, I
  serial sexually-motivated murders, 1991 July 25, IV
Mimeograph see Duplicating machines
Mimes, 1850(8), II
Minerals:
  space research on, 1961 June 16, III

Mines, Bureau of, 1910 May 16, III
Mining (see also product names):
  cave-in (Pa.), 1894 Feb. 13, I
  disaster (Ala.), 1905 Feb. 20, I
  disaster (Franklin, Wash.), 1894 Apr. 24, I
  explosion (Ill.), 1909 Nov. 13, I
  explosion (Pa.), 1908 Nov. 28, I
  explosion (Utah), 1900 May 1, I
  first charter (Conn.), 1709(1), III
  strike violence (Ida.), 1899 Apr. 29, III
  unions recognized, 1903 Mar. 21, III
  worst disaster to date, 1907 Dec. 6, I; 1910(3), I
Minneapolis (Minn.):
  fire, 1893 Aug. 13, I
Minnelli, Liza, 1973 Mar. 27, II
Minnelli, Vincente, 1986, II
Minnesota:
  Hinckley fire, 1894 Sept. 1, I
  statehood, 1858 May 11, I
  territory established, 1849 Mar. 3(2), I
  tornado, 1899 June 12, I
Minnesota, University of:
  founded, 1851 Feb. 13(1), III; 1868(1), III
Minot, George R., 1926(1), III
Minow, Newton N., 1961 May 9, II
Minstrel shows:
  cakewalk, 1877(4), II
  Christy's Minstrels, 1842(4), IV; 1846 Apr. 27, II
  first N.Y. troupe, 1843(2), II
  Rice singing "Jim Crow", 1828, IV
  song "Zip Coon", 1834(1), II
  Virginia Minstrels, 1843(4), II
Mint, U.S. (see also Bimetallism; Currency), 1792 Apr. 2, I
Minuit, Peter, 1625 Spring, I; 1626, I
Miranda v. Arizona, 1966 June 13, I; 1971 Feb. 24, I
Miró, Joan, 1959 May 18, II
MIRV (Multiple Independently-targetable Reentry Vehicle):
  contracts secretly awarded, 1969 June 19, I
Miss America, 1921 Sept. 8, IV; 1922 Sept. 8, IV; 1923 Sept. 7, IV; 1924 Sept. 6, IV; 1925 Sept. 11, IV; 1926 Sept. 10, IV; 1927 Sept. 9, IV; 1933 Sept. 9, IV; 1935 Sept. 7, IV; 1936 Sept. 12(1), IV; 1937 Sept. 11(1), IV; 1938 Sept. 10, IV; 1939 Sept. 10, IV; 1940 Sept. 8, IV; 1941 Sept. 6, IV; 1942 Sept. 12, IV; 1943 Sept. 4, IV; 1944 Sept. 2, IV; 1945 Sept. 8, IV; 1946 Sept. 7, IV; 1947 Sept. 6, IV; 1948 Sept. 11, IV; 1949 Sept. 10, IV; 1950 Sept. 9, IV; 1951 Sept. 8, IV; 1952 Sept. 6, IV; 1953 Sept. 13, IV; 1954 Sept. 11, IV; 1955 Sept. 10, IV; 1956 Sept. 8, IV; 1957 Sept. 7, IV; 1958 Sept. 6, IV; 1959 Sept. 12, IV; 1960 Sept. 10, IV; 1961 Sept. 9, IV; 1962 Sept. 8(1), IV; 1963 Sept. 7, IV; 1964 Sept. 12(1), IV; 1965 Sept. 11, IV; 1966 Sept. 10, IV; 1967 Sept. 9, IV; 1968 Sept. 7, IV; 1969 Sept. 6, IV; 1970 Sept. 12, IV; 1971 Sept. 11, IV; 1972 Sept. 9, IV; 1973 Sept. 8, IV; 1974 Sept. 8, IV; 1975 Sept. 6, IV; 1976 Sept. 11, IV; 1977 Sept. 10,

Miss America (cont.)
  IV; 1978 Sept. 9, IV; 1979 Sept. 8(2), IV; 1980 Sept. 6, IV; 1981 Sept. 12, IV; 1982 Sept. 11, IV; 1983 Sept. 17, IV; 1984 Sept. 15, IV; 1985 Sept. 14, IV; 1986 Sept. 17, IV; 1987 Sept. 19, IV; 1988 Sept. 10, IV; 1989 Sept. 17, IV; 1990 Sept. 8, IV; 1991 Sept. 14, IV; 1992 Sept. 19, IV
  Williams resigned, 1984 July 23, IV
Miss Black America, 1968 Sept. 7, IV
Missiles (see also Antiballistic missile; Arms control and disarmament; MIRV; Rockets):
  first airborne ballistic launched, 1962 Apr. 19, III
  first nuclear submarine to carry, 1959 Dec. 30, III
  first Polaris fired underwater, 1960 July 20, III
  first U.S. cruise in Great Britain, 1983 Nov. 11, I
  first U.S. test of nuclear warhead carried by, 1962 May 6, III
  gap with Soviets, 1960 Feb. 23, I
  IRBM squadrons, 1958 Jan. 3, I
  jet-propelled guided, 1953 Mar. 30, III
  MX development funds approved, 1983 May 24, I
  MX proposed, 1982 Nov. 22, I
  MX recommendations, 1983 Apr. 11, I
  Persian Gulf shipping attack, 1987 May 17, I
  Polaris fired (Calif.), 1960 Apr. 14, III
  "Star Wars" defense system, 1986 Oct. 11–12, I
  Titan 2 maiden flight, 1962 Mar. 16, III
  Titan 2 site explosion (Ark.), 1980 Sept. 19, I
  U.S.-U.S.S.R. agreements, 1972 May 22–30, I
  world record, 1960 May 20(1), III
Missing persons:
  de Galindez, 1956 Mar. 12, IV
  Hoffa, 1975 July 31(1), III
  Mary Celeste crew, 1872 Nov. 7, IV
  reward for apprentice blacksmith, 1819(2), IV
  reward for black women, 1809 Oct. 31, IV
Missions:
  American Home Society, 1826(2), III
  Brown's in La., 1819(2), III
  Calif. oldest building, 1777(2), II
  Catholic choir book, 1813(3), II
  first Calif., 1769, I
  first society founded, 1810(2), III
  Oregon Territory, 1836 July 4, IV
  San Juan Capistrano (Calif.), 1797(2), II
  single surviving Franciscan church (Ariz.), 1784(3), II
  Tex., 1690(1), I
  U.S. abroad, 1812, III
Mississippi:
  abolished slavery, 1865 Aug. 14, I
  civil rights workers murdered, 1964 Aug. 4, I

Mississippi *(cont.)*
compulsory school attendance law
(Miss.), 1918(1), III
elementary school desegregation
began, 1964 Aug. 14, III
FBI arrests in civil rights murders,
1964 Dec. 4, I
last state to adopt workmen's
compensation laws, 1948(3), III
overturned secession ordinance, 1865
Aug. 14, III
readmitted to Congress, 1870 Feb. 23,
I
readmitted to Union, 1869 Apr. 10, I
seceded, 1861 Jan. 9(2), I
statehood, 1817 Dec. 10, I
Territory divided, 1817 Mar. 3(1), I
tornado, 1971 Feb. 21, I
university system ruled still
segregated, 1992 June 26, III
Mississippi, University of:
Barnett and Johnson contempt
charge, 1962 Dec. 21, III
black admission denied, 1962 Sept. 20,
III
established, 1844 Feb. 23, III
Gov. Barnett civil contempt charge,
1962 Sept. 28, III
Meredith enrolled, 1962 Sept. 30, III
Mississippi Bubble, 1720 Oct., I
**Mississippi Industrial Institute and
College,** 1884 Mar. 12, III
Mississippi River and Valley:
ferry-tanker collision, 1976 Oct. 20(1),
I
first Europeans, 1541 May 8, I
first railroad bridge, 1856 Apr. 21, III
first steel arch bridge spanning,
1874(3), III
floods, 1882 Mar., I; 1927 Apr., I; 1973
Apr. 11, I
French exploration, 1670–1679, I
French inroads, c1720, I
surface affected by earthquake, 1811
Dec. 16, I
Mississippi University for Women, 1884
Mar. 12, III
Missouri:
abortion restrictions, 1989 July 3, I
flood, 1903 May 31, I
slavery issue, 1819 Feb. 13, I; 1849
Mar. 10, I
statehood, 1821 Aug. 10, I
tornado, 1899 Apr. 27, I
Missouri, University of, 1839 Feb. 11, III
Missouri Compromise *(see also*
Compromise of 1850):,
1820, I
Missouri River:
flood, 1951 July 11–25, I
Missouri (ship), 1945 Sept. 2, I; 1992, I
Miss Vicki (Victoria May Budinger), 1969
Dec. 17, IV
Mitchell, Billy, 1921 July 21, III; 1925, I;
1958 Mar. 4, I
Mitchell, Edgar D., 1971 Jan. 31, III
Mitchell, Isaac, 1811, II
Mitchell, Joan, 1992, II

Mitchell, John:
acquitted in Vesco dealings, 1974 Apr.
28, I
appeal rejected, 1977 May 23, I
implicated in Watergate, 1973 June
25–29, I
sentenced for Watergate cover-up,
1975 Feb. 21, I
Mitchell, Keith, 1972 May 14, II
Mitchell, Loften, 1976 Mar. 2, II
Mitchell, Margaret, 1936(1), II; 1937 May
3, II; 1988 Apr. 25, II
Mitchell, Maria, 1847 Oct., IV; 1865, III
Mitchell, Martha, 1976, I
Mitchell, Thomas, 1940 Feb. 29, II
Mitchell, William, 1839(3), IV
Mitchill, Samuel Latham, 1795–1799, III
Mitford, Jessica, 1963(1), II
Mitropoulos, Dimitri, 1960, II
Miyazawa, Kiichi, 1992 Jan. 8, III
Mize, Larry, 1987 Apr. 12, IV
Mobile Bay, Battle of (Ala.), 1864 Aug.
5–23, I
Mobile homes:
upsurge, 1936(3), III
Mobley, Mary Ann, 1958 Sept. 6, IV
Mob violence *see* Riots and mob violence
Modern Chivalry (Brackenridge), 1792(4),
II; 1805, IV
Modern Language Association, 1883(2), III
Modigliani, Franco, 1985 Oct. 15, III
Modjeska, Helena, 1877, II
Modugno, Domenico, 1959 May 4(2), II
Moffitt, Billie Jean (*see also* King, Billie
Jean), 1961 July 8, IV; 1962 July 7, IV
Moffitt, John C., 1936 Oct. 27, II
Moiseyev Dance Co., 1958 Apr. 14, II
Molasses, 1715–1719, III
Act, 1733 May 17, I
Moley, Raymond, 1975, I
Molino del Rey, Battle of, 1847 Sept. 8, I
Momaday, N. Scott, 1969 May 5, II
Monaco:
royal wedding, 1956 Apr. 19(1), IV
Monadnock Building (Chicago, Ill.),
1883(2), II
Mondale, Walter F.:
Dole TV debate, 1976 Sept. 27, I
lost presidential bid, 1984 Nov. 6, I
N.H. primary loss, 1984 Feb. 28, I
presidential candidacy, 1984, I; 1984
July 16–19, I; 1984 Oct. 7, I; 1984
Oct. 21, I
vice presidency, 1976 July 14, I; 1976
Sept. 27, I; 1976 Nov. 2, I; 1977 Jan.
20, I; 1980 Aug.11–14, I
Money *see* Bimetallism; Coin Act; Coinage
Acts; Currency
Mongrel Tariff Act, 1883 Mar. 3(1), I
Monitor (ship):
Civil War action, 1861 Oct. 4, III;
1862 Mar. 9, I; 1862 Dec. 31, I
designed, 1856(3), III
found (N.C.), 1974 Mar. 7, III
Monk, Thelonius, 1982, II
Monkeys:
in space, 1959 May 28, III
Monmouth, Battle of (N.J.), 1778 June 28, I
Monongahela River, 1988 Jan. 2, I
Monopolies *see* Trusts and antitrust

Monroe, Harriet, 1912, II
Monroe, James:
born, 1758 Apr. 28, I
died, 1831 July 4, I
elected president, 1816 Dec. 4, I
foreign aid views, 1812 Mar. 3, I
inaugurated, 1817 Mar. 4, I; 1821
Mar. 5, I
Latin American relations, 1822 Mar.
8, I
Louisiana Purchase, 1803 Jan. 11, I
presidential candidacy, 1816, I
reelected president, 1820 Dec. 6, I
vetoed transportation bill, 1822 May
4, I
Monroe, Marilyn:
died, 1962, II
Mailer biography, 1973(1), II
Monroe Doctrine, 1823 Dec. 2, I; 1905
Jan. 21, I
Montana:
statehood, 1889 Nov. 8, I
Territory formed, 1864 May 26, I
Montana, University of, 1893 Feb. 17, III
Montcalm, Joseph de, 1756 Aug. 14, I
Montesquieu, Baron de la Brède et de,
1745, II
Montez, Lola, 1856(7), IV
Montgomery, Bernard, 1943 July 10, I
Montgomery, Bob (boxer), 1944, IV
Montgomery, John J., 1883(3), III
Montgomery, Robert, 1981, II
Montgomery (Ala.):
civil rights march, 1965 Mar. 21, I
Montgomery Ward & Co.:
catalog discontinued, 1985 Aug. 2, III
founded, 1872, III
plant seized by U.S. Army (Chicago,
Ill.), 1944 Apr. 26, III
Monticello (Va.), 1770(2), II
Monumental Church (Va.), 1812(3), II
Monuments, National:
Grange, Hamilton home (N.Y.C.),
1962 Apr. 27, II
Lincoln home (Ind.), 1962 Feb. 19, II
Mt. Rushmore (S.D.), 1927, II
Vietnam War memorial, 1981 June 6,
II
Wilson's birthplace (Va.), 1941 May 4,
II
Moody, Dwight L., 1875, III; 1899 Dec.
22, III
Moody, Orville, 1969 June 15, IV
Moody, William Vaughn, 1909 Mar. 15, II
Moon:
Apollo 13 near-disaster, 1970 Apr. 11,
III
first manned landing, 1969 July 16, III
first manned mission to, 1969 May 18,
III
first photographs, 1840(6), III; 1876(2),
III; 1964, III; 1964 July 31, III
first spacecraft to lift off of, 1967 Nov.
7, III
first U.S. soft landing, 1966 June 2, III
Galileo photographs, 1989 Oct. 18, III
Lunar Orbiter 1, 1966 Aug. 10, III
manned flights, 1969, III
Orbiter launchings, 1966 Aug. 10, III;
1967 Feb. 4, III

Moon (cont.)
   photographs, 1966 June 2, III; 1966
     Aug. 10, III; 1966 Nov. 6, III; 1967
     Feb. 4, III; 1967 Apr. 17, III; 1967
     Sept. 8, III; 1968 Jan. 9, III
   Ranger 3 probe, 1962 Jan. 26, III
   Ranger 4 crashed on side, 1962 Apr.
     26(2), III
   Ranger 7 probe, 1964 July 31, III
   Ranger 8 probe, 1965 Feb. 17, III
   Ranger 9 probe, 1965 Mar. 21, III
   rock samples, 1971 Jan. 31, III; 1971
     July 26, III; 1972 Apr. 16, III; 1972
     Dec. 7, III
   second soft landing on, 1967 Apr. 17,
     III
   soft landings, 1967 Nov. 7, III; 1968
     Jan. 9, III
   Surveyor 2 crashed into, 1966 Sept.
     22, III
   Surveyor 4 radio contact lost, 1967
     July 17, III
   Surveyor 5 soft landing, 1967 Sept. 8,
     III
   third and fourth humans to land on,
     1969 Nov. 14, III
   voices bounced off, 1960 Aug. 3, III
Moon, Sun Myung, 1976 Sept. 18, III;
   1982 July 16, III
Mooney, Tom, 1916 July 22, I
Moore, Archie, 1959, IV
Moore, Carroll, 1958 Oct. 23, II
Moore, Colleen, 1988, II
Moore, Davey, 1963, IV
Moore, Douglas, 1951 Mar. 28, II
Moore, Dudley, 1962 Oct. 27, II
Moore, Elizabeth H., 1896(2), IV; 1901(2),
   IV; 1903(2), IV; 1905(4), IV
Moore, Henry, 1962 Mar. 20, II; 1982, II
Moore, J. Hamilton, 1802, III
Moore, Marianne, 1952 Jan. 29, II; 1952
   May 5, II; 1967(1), II; 1972, II
Moore, Mary Tyler, 1964 May 25(2), II
Moore, Sara Jane, 1975 Sept. 22, I
Moore, Stanford, 1972 Oct. 20(2), III
Moore, Thomas, 1817(2), II
Moore, Zephaniah S., 1825 Feb. 21, III
Moorman, Edgar V., 1940 May 10, I
Morality see Blue laws; Personal conduct;
   specific areas
Moral Majority, 1988 Feb. 24, I; 1989 June
   10, III
Moral Reform Society, American, 1837(4),
   IV
Morandini, Mickey, 1992 Sept. 20(2), IV
Moravian College (Pa.), 1742(2), III
Moravians:
   first community (Ga.), 1735(1), III
   moved from Ga. to Pa., 1741, I
   musical activities, 1741, II; 1744(3), II;
     1745 Sept. 4, II
   published Indian language hymns,
     1763, II
Moreno, Rita, 1962 Apr. 9, II
Morgan, Dodge, 1986 Apr. 11, IV
Morgan, Joe, 1990 Aug. 6, IV
Morgan, J. Pierpont:
   panic of 1907, 1907, III
   railroad organization, 1894(3), III
   U.S. Steel formed, 1901, III

Morgan, Thomas Hunt, 1933 Oct. 20, III
Morgan, William, 1826(1), I
Morgan & Co., J. P.:
   international loan, 1915 Oct. 15, III
Moriarity, Michael, 1974 Apr. 21, II
Morison, Samuel Eliot, 1943 May 3, II;
   1959(1), II; 1960 May 2, II; 1963(1), II;
   1965(1), II; 1976, II
Mormon Church:
   antipolygamy measures, 1882 Mar. 22,
     I
   Benson elected president, 1985 Nov.
     11, III
   black ordination ban ended, 1978, III
   dissolved as corporation by Congress,
     1887(1), III
   first Utah settlement, 1847 July 24, I
   followers' problems, 1838, III
   founded, 1830, III
   on gold discovery, 1848 Jan. 24, IV
   Ida. settlement, 1860 Apr. 14, III
   Lee named president, 1972, III
   McKay died, 1970 Jan. 18, III
   membership, 1900(2), III
   Mich. colony, 1850 July 8, III
   Mountain Meadows Massacre (Utah),
     1857 Sept. 11, I
   polygamy abolished, 1887(1), III; 1890
     Oct. 6, III
   polygamy advocated, 1843 July 12, IV
   ritual changes, 1990 Apr., III
   settled in Utah, 1847 July 24, III
   Smith named head, 1970 Jan. 18, III
   Smiths murdered, 1844 June 27, III
   temple dedicated (Salt Lake City,
     Utah), 1893(4), III
   westward migration, 1846(2), IV; 1846
     Feb. 10, I
Morphy, Paul C., 1857 Oct. 6, IV
Morrell, William, 1625, II
Morrill, Justin Smith, 1862, III
Morrill Act (land-grant colleges), 1862, III;
   1862 July 1(2), I
Morrill Tariff Act, 1860 May 10, III
Morris, Carl, 1918 Dec. 16, IV
Morris, Edmund, 1979(1), II; 1980 Apr.
   14(1), II; 1980 May 1, II
Morris, Gouverneur, 1809(1), IV
Morris, Jack, 1991 Dec. 2, IV
Morris, Lewis, 1738, I
Morris, Richard B., 1989, II
Morris, Thomas, 1843 Aug. 31, I
Morris, William, 1895, II
Morris, Wright, 1957 Mar. 12, II; 1981
   Apr. 30, II
Morrison, Herbert, 1937 May 6, III
Morrison, Jim, 1971, II
Morrison, Toni, 1978 Jan. 11, II; 1981(1),
   II; 1987(1), II; 1992(1), II
   Pulitzer Prize, 1988 Mar. 31, II
Morrissey, John C., 1853 Oct. 12, IV;
   1864(3), IV
Morro Castle (ship), 1934 Sept. 8, I
Morrow & Company, William, 1986 Jan.
   11, II
Morse, Jedidiah, 1793, III
Morse, Robert, 1990 June 3, II
Morse, Samuel F. B.:
   first photographic equipment, 1839(1),
     III

Morse, Samuel F. B. (cont.)
   first telegraph company, 1847 Apr.
     16, III
   National Academy of Design, 1825
     Nov. 8, II
   painting brought highest price to
     date, 1982 July 10, II
   telegraph invention, 1835(2), III; 1844
     May 24, III
   telegraph patent, 1837 Sept., III
Morse, Wayne, 1953 Apr. 25, I; 1974, I
Mortality rate (see also Life expectancy):
   auto accident drop, 1983, III
   cancer, 1975 July 31(2), III
   cancer up, 1980 Apr. 28, III
   cigarette-caused, 1964 Jan. 11, III;
     1982, III
   by cities, 1842(2), IV
   coronary, 1981 Jan. 8, III
   coronary from smoking, 1960 June 6,
     III
   down, 1921(1), III
   infant, 1991, III
   infant dropped, 1976 Jan. 12, III
Morton, "Jelly Roll" (Ferdinand), 1906(6),
   II; 1926(4), II
Morton, Levi P., 1888 June 25, I; 1888
   Nov. 6, I
Morton, Thomas, 1637(2), II
Morton, William T. G., 1846 Oct. 16, III
Moscone, George, 1978 Nov. 27, I
Moscow summit conference, 1988 May
   29–June 1, I
Mosel, Tad, 1960 Nov. 30, II; 1961 May 1,
   II; 1961 Nov. 30, II
Mosquito (see also Yellow fever):,
   1901(1), III; 1914(1), III
Moss, Howard, 1972 Apr. 13, II
Mössbauer, Rudolf L., 1961 Nov. 2(2), III
Mostel, Zero, 1961 Apr. 16, II; 1962 May
   8, II; 1977, II
Mota, Rosa, 1987 Apr. 20, IV; 1988 Apr.
   18, IV; 1990 Apr. 16, IV
Motels see Hotels and inns
Mothers:
   percentage in work force, 1988 June
     15, III
   single parent welfare reform, 1988
     Oct. 3, I
   surrogate legal issues, 1987 Mar. 31,
     IV; 1988 June 27(1), IV
Mothers, National Congress of, 1897 Feb.
   17, III
Mother's Day, 1907 May, IV; 1914 May 7,
   IV
Motherwell, Robert, 1991, II
Motion pictures (see also New York Film
   Critics Awards; Oscar awards):
   Abbott and Costello's box office draw,
     1942(3), II
   amusement tax, 1947, II
   Bank Night, 1932(1), IV
   Bernhardt in Queen Elizabeth, 1912
     July 12, II
   Birth of a Nation, 1905(1), II; 1915
     Feb. 8, II
   blacklisting, 1947, II
   Black Maria pioneer film studio (N.J.),
     1893 Feb. 1, III
   box office record, 1989, II

Motion pictures (*cont.*)
box office sales drop, 1985, II; 1991, II
box office second best year to date, 1990, II
brutality themes, 1972, II
CinemaScope, 1954, II
Cleopatra most expensive film to date, 1963 June 12, II
controversial films, 1988, II
disaster films, 1974, II
disaster reportage, 1900(5), II
early experiments, 1872(3), III
early panoramic film, 1901(2), III
financial pinch, 1970, II
first animated, 1909(5), II
first boxing match filmed, 1897 Mar. 17, IV
first camera patent, 1891 Aug. 24, III
first color, 1928 July 30, III
first color with sound (Ohio), 1907(5), II
first female star, 1907(6), II
first film exchange, 1903(1), III
first film with plot, 1903(3), II
first instant color system, 1977 Apr. 26, III
first lengthy talking, 1928 July 6, II
first male star, 1903(3), II
first movie film developed by Edison, 1889(6), III
first presidential press conference, 1955 Jan. 19, I
first shown on public screen (N.Y.C.), 1896 Apr. 23, II
first six-reel, 1914 Apr., II
first talking, 1926 Aug. 5, II; 1927 Oct. 6, II
first Technicolor process, 1922(4), III
foreign films, 1946, II; 1976, II
Gone with the Wind, 1939, II
greatest box office year to date, 1944, II; 1946, II; 1975, II
Great Train Robbery, The, 1903(3), II
growth of industry, 1900(4), II
independent productions, 1971, II
Indiana Jones broke box office record, 1984, II
Informer, The, 1935, II
innovations, 1953, II
Intolerance (Griffith), 1916(4), II
Japanese acquisition of Columbia Pictures, 1989 Sept. 27, III
Jaws, 1975, II
Jazz Singer, The (Jolson), 1927 Oct. 6, II
Library of Congress collection, 1943 May 5(1), II
Lombard died, 1942, II
nickelodeons, 1908(4), II
nostalgia films, 1973, II; 1974, II
Orphans of the Storm (Griffith), 1922 Jan. 3, II
panorama popularity, 1846(3), IV
Passion Play, The, 1903(2), II
popular films 1933, II; 1933(1), II; 1983, II; 1987, II; 1988, II; 1989, II; 1990, II; 1991, II; 1992, II
production, 1945, II
prosperity, 1936, II
rating code, 1968, II

Motion pictures (*cont.*)
rating code revised, 1990 Sept. 26, II
revenues up, 1977, II
Roach awarded Smithsonian medal, 1992 Jan. 23, II
Rocky, 1976, II
Snow White and the Seven Dwarfs, 1938, II
sound process demonstrated, 1923, III
South Pacific in international competitions, 1958 May 1, II
suffered worst year, 1938, II
teen films, 1986, II
Time Warner merger, 1989 July 24, III
Todd died, 1958, II
top box office stars, 1943, II; 1944, II
top films, 1966, II; 1985, II
U.S. studios' decline, 1948, II
war effort, 1945, II
writers' strike, 1988 Aug. 7(2), II
Motor Carrier Act, 1935 Aug. 9, III
Motorcycle stunt driving, 1974, IV
Motors *see* Engines
Mott, Frank Luther, 1939 May 1, II
Mott, John Raleigh, 1946 Nov. 14, I
Mott, Lucretia, 1840(3), IV; 1848, IV; 1848 July 19–20, I
Mott, Nevill F., 1977 Oct. 11, III
Mottelson, Ben, 1975 Oct. 17, III
Mount, William Sidney, 1850(6), II
Mountain climbing:
Mt. Whitney scaled, 1873 Aug. 18, IV
Mourt's Relation (Bradford and Winslow), 1622, II
Mowatt, Anna Cora, 1845 Mar. 24, II
Moynihan, Daniel P., 1970 Feb. 28, I
Mozart, Wolfgang Amadeus, 1979 July 16, II
bicentennial of death, 1991 Jan. 27, II
Mr. Dooley (fictional character), 1896(3), II
Ms. (magazine), 1972 July 1, II
Mt. Holyoke College (Mass.), 1837 Nov. 8, III
Mtolo, Willi, 1992 Nov. 1, IV
Mt. St. Helens (Wash.), 1980 May 18, I
Mt. Sinai Hospital (N.Y.C.), 1852 Jan. 15, III
Mt. Vernon (Va.), 1757, II
Ladies' Association organized to purchase, 1853(2), IV
national monument dedicated, 1859(1), IV
Mt. Washington Cog Railroad (N.H.), 1866 Aug. 29, III
Muckraking, 1904, II; 1906 Mar. 17, IV
Mudd, Samuel A., 1865, I
Mud slides, 1969 Jan.-Mar., I
Mueller, Lisel, 1981 Apr. 30, II
Mugwumps, 1884(1), IV; 1884 June 6, I
Mugwump (term), 1872(1), IV
Muhammad, Elijah, 1975, III; 1975 Feb. 26, III
Muhammad, Wallace, 1975 Feb. 26, III
Muhammad Ali *see* Ali, Muhammad
Mulberry trees, 1623, III
Muldoon, William, 1880, IV
Mulholland, Joseph M. (Orange Blossom), 1880(5), IV
Mullens, Priscilla, 1620–1629, II

Muller, Hermann, 1946 Oct. 31, III
Mulligan, Richard, 1989 Sept. 17, II
Mulliken, Robert S., 1966 Dec. 10(1), III; 1986, III
Mulloy, Gardnar, 1957 July 6, IV
Mulroney, Brian, 1989 Jan. 2, III
Mumford, Lewis, 1962 Mar. 13, II; 1990, II
Mumford, Stephen, 1671, III
Münch, Charles, 1968, II
Muni, Paul, 1937 Mar. 4, II; 1956 Apr. 1, II; 1967, II
Munich Pact, 1938, I; 1938 Sept. 26, I
Munro, Alice, 1990(1), II
Munro, Donald L., 1908 July 4, I
Munsey, Frank A., 1889 Feb. 2, II
Munsey's Weekly (publication), 1889 Feb. 2, II
Murals:
Boston Public Library (Mass.), 1888(4), II
first major assignment (Boston, Mass.), 1876(7), II
government buildings, 1936, II
La Farge's church (N.Y.), 1888(3), II
Murders (*see also* Assassinations and assassination attempts):
American Nazi Party leader, 1967 Aug. 25, I
Black Panthers chmn. Hampton, 1969 Dec. 4, I
Borden case (Fall River, Mass.), 1892, IV
Boston Strangler sentenced, 1967 Jan. 18, IV
Carter and Artis convicted (N.J.), 1976 Dec. 21, IV
civil rights workers, 1964 Aug. 4, I; 1964 Dec. 4, I; 1967 Oct. 20, I
Corona convicted (Calif.), 1973 Feb. 25, IV
Dahmer serial (Wis.), 1991 July 25, IV
eight student nurses (Chicago, Ill.), 1966 July 14, I
Frank case (Ga.), 1915, IV
Hall-Mills case, 1922, IV
Happy Land Social Club (Bronx, N.Y.), 1990 Mar. 25, IV
Haywood-Steunenberg case, 1907(1), III
homosexual abuse serial case (Tex.), 1973 Aug. 14, IV
hospital patients (Ohio), 1987 Aug. 18, IV
Leopold-Loeb case, 1924 July 21, IV; 1958 Feb. 20, IV
McDonald's restaurant mass killing (Calif.), 1984 July 18, IV
Manson family (Calif.), 1969 Aug. 9, IV; 1971 Jan. 25, IV
mass (Killeen, Tex.), 1991 Oct. 16, IV
mass (Okla.), 1986 Aug. 20, IV
Moscone-Milk case (San Francisco, Calif.), 1978 Nov. 27, I
"Night Stalker" (Los Angeles) convicted, 1989 Sept. 20, IV
Rubinstein strangled (N.Y.C.), 1955 Jan. 27, IV
Ruby conviction reversed, 1966 Oct. 5, I

Murders (*cont.*)
  Sacco and Vanzetti case, 1920 Apr. 15, I
  serial (N.Y.S.) convicted, 1990 Dec. 13, IV
  sniper attack (New Orleans, La.), 1973 Jan. 7, IV
  Son of Sam serial (N.Y.C.), 1977 Aug. 10, IV
  Stompanato-Crane, 1958 Apr. 4, IV
  Tarnower-Harris (N.Y.), 1980 Mar. 10, IV
  Touhy (Chicago, Ill.), 1959 Dec. 16, IV
  urban records set, 1990, IV
  White-Thaw case, 1906, IV
  Yablonski family (Pa.), 1970 Jan. 5, III; 1971 June 23, I; 1972 Mar. 1(2), III; 1973 Sept. 6, III; 1974 Apr. 11, III; 1975 Sept. 11, III
  Zebra serial (San Francisco, Calif.), 1974 May 16, IV
Murdoch, James E., 1836(9), II
Murdoch, Rupert, 1983, II; 1984 Nov. 20, II; 1987, II; 1988 Aug. 7(1), II
Murphy, Audie, 1971, I
Murphy, Jack ("Murph the Surf"), 1964 Oct. 29, IV
Murphy, Johnny (John J.), 1970, IV
Murphy, William P., 1926(1), III
Murray, Anne, 1979 Feb. 16, II
Murray, Arthur, 1991, IV
Murray, John, 1775–1779, III
Murray, Joseph E., 1990 Oct. 8, III
Murray, Lindley, 1795(1), II
Murray, Philip, 1940 Nov. 21, III
Murray, R. Lindley, 1917 June 23(2), IV; 1918 June 22, IV
Murray, Ty, 1989, IV
Murrow, Edward R., 1953 Feb. 11, II; 1956 Mar. 17, II; 1965, III; 1984 Mar. 4, II
Muscat (Oman), 1833 Sept. 21, I
Museum of Art (Phila., Pa.), 1987, II
Museum of Modern Art (N.Y.C.):
  enlarged, 1984, II
  fire damage, 1958 Apr. 15(2), II
  Guernica returned to Spain, 1981 Sept. 10, II
  Janis gift, 1967 June 16, II
  Matisse exhibit, 1992 Sept. 24, II
  new facilities opened, 1964 May 25(1), II
  op art show, 1965, II
  Paley collection exhibited, 1992 Feb. 2, II
  Picasso exhibits, 1967 Oct. 11, II; 1980, II
  Rockefeller legacy, 1979 Feb. 9(2), II
  Stein collection, 1969, II
Museum of Natural History (N.Y.C.):
  jewel robbery, 1964 Oct. 29, IV
Museum of Our National Heritage (Mass.), 1975 Apr. 20, II
Museums (*see also* specific museum names):
  American Museum opened (N.Y.C.), 1811(2), III
  economic pinch, 1991, II
  economic problems, 1975, II

Museums (*cont.*)
  Ellis Island (N.Y.C.) restoration, 1990 Sept. 8, IV
  first (Charleston, S.C.), 1773 Jan. 12, III
  first private natural history (Phila., Pa.), 1809(2), II
  Getty fine arts center (Malibu, Calif.), 1983 Sept. 20, II
  Getty wealthiest (Malibu, Calif.), 1982 Mar. 1, II
  Great Chinese (N.Y.C.), 1849(1), IV
  Guggenheim addition opened, 1992 June 28, II
  King civil rights exhibits (Memphis, Tenn.), 1991 Aug. 31, I
  new facilities, 1985, II
  obscenity indictments, 1990 Apr. 7, II
  Peale's (Phila., Pa.), 1794(1), III
Musgrave, Story, 1983 Apr. 4–9, III
Musial, Stan, 1963, IV; 1963 Sept. 29, IV
Music (*see also* Dances and dancing; Grammy Awards; Jazz; Opera; Recording equipment; Rock music; names of concert halls, groups, orchestras, and performers):
  Adventures in a Perambulator (Carpenter), 1914(5), II
  "After the Ball Is Over" (song), 1892(6), II
  "All Quiet Along the Potomac Tonight" hit song of Civil War, 1861(2), II
  amateur musicians in professional orchestras, 1769 Nov. 30, IV
  "America" (song), 1831, II
  American Symphony Orchestra, 1969 Nov. 25, II
  An American in Paris (Gershwin), 1928(4), II
  Antheil's works, 1949(2), II
  ASCAP founded, 1914 Feb. 13, II
  Barlow's version of hymns, 1784(2), II
  Bay Psalm Book sold at auction (N.Y.C.), 1947 Jan. 28, II
  Belcher songs, 1794(4), II
  Berkenhead's popularity (Boston, Mass.), c1794, II
  Berlin's songs, 1911(2), II
  Berlin 100th birthday celebration, 1988 May 11, II
  Bernstein retirement from N.Y. Philharmonic, 1966 Nov. 2, II
  Bernstein's antiwar counterconcert (Wash., D.C.), 1973 Jan. 19, II
  Bernstein scores donated to N.Y. Philharmonic, 1992 Aug. 20, II
  Bernstein's last Philharmonic concert, 1969 May 17(1), II
  Bernstein's *Mass*, 1971 Sept. 8–9, II
  Bernstein's works, 1949(2), II
  big band sound revived, 1972, II
  "Bill Bailey Won't You Please Come Home" (Cannon), 1902(3), II
  Billings psalms, 1770(1), II
  blackface songs, 1833(5), II
  Bloch's *Suite Hébraïque*, 1953 Jan. 1, II
  Bloch's *Symphony America*, 1928(3), II

Music (*cont.*)
  Boston Pops centennial, 1985, II
  Boston Pops named Williams conductor, 1980 Jan. 10, II
  Boulez retired, 1977 May 14, II
  Bristow's *Second Symphony* performed, 1856 Mar. 1, II
  Bristow's *Third Symphony*, 1859 Mar. 26, II
  "Brother, Can You Spare a Dime" (Harburg) song, 1932(3), II
  campaign songs, 1909, II
  Carnegie Hall opened, 1891 May 5, II
  Carnegie Hall post-renovation reopening, 1986 Dec. 15, II
  Casals UN concert, 1971 Oct. 25, II
  choir book for Catholic missions, 1813(3), II
  Civil War songs, 1862 July 16, IV
  "Clare de Kitchen" (song), 1832(3), II
  Cliburn won Tchaikovsky piano competition, 1958 Apr. 11, II
  Collegium Musicum established (Pa.), 1744(3), II
  colonial concerts and societies, 1760–1764, II
  colonial hymnals, 1735–1739, II
  composer Varèse in U.S., 1916(3), II
  Concert of the Century (N.Y.C.), 1976 May 18, II
  contralto Anderson retirement, 1963 Dec. 12, II
  Copland's *Clarinet Concerto*, 1950 Nov. 16, II
  Copland's *Concerto* premiered, 1927 Jan. 28, II
  Copland's *El Salón Méjico* premiered, 1937 Aug. 27, II
  Copland's *Lincoln Portrait* and *Piano Sonata*, 1943(2), II
  Copland's *Short Symphony*, 1933(5), II
  Copland's *Symphony for Organ and Orchestra*, 1925 Jan. 11, II
  country and rock musician postage stamp issues, 1992 Oct. 8, II
  Cowell's *Symphony No. 13*, 1959 Mar. 3(2), II
  "Daisy Bell" song, 1892(2), II
  Diamond's *Ahavah*, 1954(4), II
  "Dixie" (song), 1859(2), II
  "Dominique" hit song, 1963(5), II
  Dresser's songs, 1897, II
  Dvořák in U.S., 1893(2), II
  Dvořák's N.Y.C. visit, 1892(5), II
  early collection of secular, 1787(1), II
  early hymn collection (Beissel), 1730(1), II
  education, 1821, II; 1833(6), II
  eighteenth-century American, 1715–1719, II
  Ellington archives, 1988 Apr., II
  European recognition of American, 1889 July 12, II
  "Everybody Works but Father" (song), 1905(3), II
  Farwell's promotion of American, 1904(3), II
  Federal Project, 1935, II
  Festival of American (Rochester, N.Y.), 1930(5), II

Music (*cont.*)

first American patriotic song, 1768
July 18, II

first Avery Fisher Prizes, 1976 Feb. 9,
II

first black conductor of major
orchestra (N.J.), 1968 Feb. 15, II

first book with barred notes, 1721(2),
II

first City Center (N.Y.C.) season, 1943
Dec. 11, II

first criticism (Phila., Pa.), 1715–1719,
II

first Hammond organ, 1934(4), II

first important chamber group
(Boston, Mass.), 1842, II

first inclusion in public school
curriculum (Boston, Mass.), 1838(4),
II

first instruction manual, 1715–1719, II

first known mention of instrument,
1664(2), II

first organ built in colonies (N.Y.C.),
1741 Aug., II

first original blues song, 1909, II

first original hymn book (Pa.), 1747(2),
II

first periodical, 1786 May, II

first pianoforte, 1775(4), II

first piano pieces composed in
America, c1790, II

first pipe organs (Pa.), 1700(2), II

first printed orchestral score, 1791
Mar.(2), II

first psalm book (Mass.), 1620(1), II

first public concert (Boston, Mass.),
1715–1719, II

first Pulitzer Prize, 1943 May 3, II

first regular orchestra formed (Boston,
Mass.), 1810, II

first sheet music, 1698(2), II

first spinet, 1769 Sept. 18, II

first store (Phila.,Pa.), 1759 Dec. 13, II

first symphony orchestra (Pa.), 1741,
II

Flagg hymns published, 1764(1), II

folk singers' popularity, 1963(5), II

Ford Foundation grants, 1965 Nov.
17, II

Ford Foundation symphony orchestra
grants, 1965 Oct. 21(1), II

Foster's songs, 1844(3), II; 1851(5), II;
1852(3), II; 1860(4), II

Garden State Arts Center (N.J.)
opened, 1968 June 12, II

glassychord, 1761(2), II

"Good-Bye, Dolly Gray" (song),
1900(3), II

Gottschalk's European tour, 1850(1),
II

Gottschalk's formal debut (N.Y.C.),
1853 Feb. 11, II

Gottschalk's popularity, 1851(6), II

Grand Canyon Suite (Grofé), 1932(2),
II

Griffes's works, 1919, II

Hanson's *Piano Concerto No. 1*,
1948(5), II

Hanson's *Second Symphony*, 1930(5),
II

Music (*cont.*)

Harris's *First Symphony* performed,
1934 Jan. 26, II

Harris's *Fourth Symphony*, 1941 Feb.
21, II

Harris's *Symphonic Fantasy*, 1954 Jan.
30, II

Harris's *Third Symphony*, 1939 Feb.
24, II

Heinrich's compositions, 1820(3), II

Herbert's operettas, 1894(3), II

"High Society" (Steele song), 1901
Mar., II

Hindemith's works, 1949(2), II

"Home Sweet Home" (Payne), 1823
May 8, II

Hopkinson's contribution, 1755–1759,
II

Horowitz's return recital, 1965 May 9,
II

Hovhaness's *Concerto No. Five*, 1954
Feb. 22, II

"Hunters of Kentucky, The" (song),
1822(2), IV

hymnals, 1821, II

immigrant colonial contribution,
1730–1734, II

Indian-language hymns, 1763, II

In Praise of Shahn (Schuman), 1970
Jan. 29, II

"In the Good Old Summer Time"
(song), 1900(3), II

Ives festivals (N.Y.C., New Haven,
Conn.), 1974 Oct. 17–21, II

Ives's *Fourth Symphony*, 1965 Apr.
26, II

Ives's *Second Piano Sonata* (Concord),
1939 Jan. 20, II

jazz, 1890(5), II

jive, 1943, IV

Joplin's works, 1885, II; 1899(2), II

King's Chapel organ (Mass.), 1713, II

Krenek's *Violoncello Concerto*, 1954
Mar. 4, II

Krenek's 12-tone works, 1945(3), II

Lanier's flute compositions, 1873(4), II

Law's contribution, 1767(1), II

lawsuit against Petrillo, 1942 Aug. 3,
II

Lind tour, 1850, II

"Lubly Fan" (song) popularity,
1844(2), II

Lyon hymn book, 1761(1), II

MacDowell's works, 1888(5), II;
1889(2), II; 1896(2), II

Mahler's *Eighth Symphony*
premiered, 1916 Mar. 2, II

Martinu's *String Quartet*, 1948(5), II

Mason's *Carmina Sacra*'s popularity,
1858(1), II

Mehta named N.Y. Philharmonic
director, 1977 May 14, II

Mehta retired from N.Y.
Philharmonic, 1991 May 28, II

Melodies, Duets, Songs, and Ballads
(Woodworth), 1826(4), II

Menotti's *Triple Concerto*, 1969 Mar.
10(1), II

Merry Widow operetta (Lehár),
1907(3), II

Music (*cont.*)

Milhaud's *Symphony No. Six*, 1955, II

Milhaud's works, 1949(2), II

modern works accepted, 1952, II

Morton's rags, 1906(6), II

Mozart bicentennial, 1991 Jan. 27, II

Mozart manuscript (N.Y.C.), 1979 July
16, II

multilanguage Moravian hymn
concert (Pa.), 1745 Sept. 4, II

national anthem designated, 1931
Mar. 3, II

new compositions, 1952(3), II

New England Academicians, 1888, II

N.Y. Philharmonic anniversary
concert, 1967 Dec. 7, II

N.Y. Philharmonic's international tour,
1959, II; 1959 Aug. 5–Oct. 10, II

N.Y. Philharmonic Society founded,
1842, II

Oklahoma! musical, 1944 May 1, II

Olcott's songs, 1899, II

Ormandy retired from Philadelphia
Orchestra, 1979 Apr. 3, II

Ozawa named Boston Symphony
director, 1972 Feb. 2, II

Pachelbel, Carl Theodorus,
1730–1734, II

Paine appointed Harvard Univ.
professor, 1875, II

Paine's *Second Symphony* performed
(Boston, Mass.), 1880(4), II

Patent Analytic Grammatical System
(music teaching), 1819 Feb., IV

patriotic, 1814, II

Philadelphia Orchestra Chinese tour,
1973 Sept. 12, II

Philharmonic Hall (N.Y.C.) acoustics,
1963, II

pianist Kempff debut, 1964 Oct. 13, II

pianist Kissin debut, 1990, II

pianist Rubinstein recitals, 1961, II

Pied Piper of Hamelin cantata
(Mennin) premiered, 1969 May 2, II

Piston's composition textbook, 1933(1),
II

Piston's *Incredible Flutist*, 1938 May,
II

Piston's *Second Symphony*, 1945 June
2, II

Piston's *Second Symphony* premiered,
1944 Mar. 5, II

Piston's *Symphony No. Five*, 1955, II

popular hymnals, 1786(2), II

popular lyric, 1810(4), IV

popular songs, 1823, IV; 1892(2), II;
1892(6), II; 1896(4), II; 1897, II;
1899, II; 1900(3), II; 1902(3), II;
1905(3), II; 1912(3), II; 1920(3), II;
1921(2), II; 1922(2), II; 1923(2), II;
1924(2), II; 1925(2), II; 1926(3), II;
1927(3), II; 1928(5), II; 1932(3), II;
1940(2), II; 1942(2), II; 1943(4), II;
1944(2), II; 1946(5), II; 1948(4), II;
1949(3), II; 1950(3), II; 1951(7), II;
1952(2), II; 1953(2), II; 1954(2), II;
1955(3), II; 1956(3), II; 1957(2), II;
1958(2), II; 1959(2), II; 1961(2), II

Porter birth centennial concert, 1991
June 9, II

Music (*cont.*)

Powell *Symphony in A*, 1947 Apr. 26, II

Presley 10th anniversary of death marked, 1987 Aug. 16, IV

Previn named Los Angeles Philharmonic director, 1984 Apr. 29, II

psalm books, 1640, II

Rachmaninoff died, 1943, II

radio broadcasts, 1930, II; 1937(4), II; 1938(3), II

ragtime, 1885, II; 1899(2), II; 1911(2), II; 1912(2), II

ragtime instruction book (Christensen), 1904(5), II

ragtime revived, 1972, II

rap, 1988, II

V. Redgrave damage suit, 1984 Nov. 9, II

Red Star Red Army Chorus and Dance tour, 1992, II

Rhapsody in Blue (Gershwin) first performed, 1924 Feb. 12, II

rhythmicon invented by Cowell, 1932 Jan., II

Rodgers' endowment grant, 1978 May 1(2), II

Rodzinski named N.Y. Philharmonic conductor, 1942 Dec. 28, II

"Rosary, The" (Nevin song) popularity, 1898, II

Rostropovich named National Symphony director (Wash., D.C.), 1975 Mar. 28(1), II

St. Patrick's Spellman concert (N.Y.C.), 1970 Nov. 30, II

Schoenberg became U.S. citizen, 1941 Apr. 11, II

Schoenberg's 100th birthday celebrated (UCLA), 1974 Sept. 12–15, II

Schoenberg's *Survivor from Warsaw* cantata, 1948(5), II

sentimental songs, 1898, II; 1910, II

Sessions' *Second Symphony*, 1947(2), II

Shankar's Indian influence, 1967, II

M. Shostakovich defected to U.S., 1981 Apr. 11, II

Shostakovich tour, 1959 Oct. 21(1), II

"Sidewalks of New York, The" (song), 1894(4), II

Simon and Garfunkel concert (N.Y.C.), 1981 Sept. 19, II

Singing Nun album, 1963(5), II

Singsters Repository of Ballads Collected from New Yorkers, 1811(3), III

Sousa's marches, 1899, II

steam calliope, 1855 Oct. 9, II

Stravinsky celebration (Calif.), 1957 June 17, II

Stravinsky's popularity, 1954, II

"Susanna" (Foster song), 1847 Sept. 11, II

Swanson's *Short Symphony*, 1950(2), II

Symmes's essay on secular singing, 1720, II

Music (*cont.*)

symphonic groups, 1951(2), II; 1989, II; 1992, II

Symphonic Sketches (Chadwick), 1895(4), II

symphonic tours, 1955, II

Symphony Hall (Boston, Mass.), 1900 Oct. 15, II

R. Taylor's contribution, 1792(3), II

tenor McCormack in U.S., 1909(8), II

Theodore Thomas's tours, 1869, II

"There'll Be a Hot Time in the Old Town To-Night" (song), 1896(4), II

Thomson's style, 1926, II

Toscanini archives, 1987 Mar. 30, II

trend from ultramodernism, 1940, II

TV's promotion of, 1948, II

videocassettes, 1981, II

violinist Bull's Norwegian colony in Pa., 1852, IV

violinist Elman's N.Y. debut, 1908 Oct., II

violinist Heifetz's debut, 1917 Oct. 27, II

vocal recitals, 1818(2), IV

Von Tilzer's songs, 1897, II; 1899, II

"Waiting for the Robert E. Lee" (song), 1912(3), II

war-year compositions, 1943, II

World's Columbian Exposition popularizing, 1893(5), II

world's oldest song performed (Calif.), 1974 Mar. 5, II

"Yankee Doodle" (song), 1755(1), II

"Zip Coon" ("Turkey in the Straw"), 1834(1), II

Musical Journal, 1800(4), II

Muskie, Edmund:

named secretary of state, 1980 Apr. 26, I

vice presidential candidacy, 1968 Aug. 29, I

Mussolini, Benito, 1943 July 25, I

Mustaches *see* Beards and mustaches

Mutinies *see* Court martials; Ships and shipping; Slaves and slavery

Mutual Security Act, 1951 Oct. 10, I

Muybridge, Eadweard, 1872(3), III

Myerson, Bess, 1945 Sept. 8, IV

My Lai massacre *see* Massacres

Myles, Alannah, 1991 Feb. 20, II

Mythology:

Bullfinch's *Age of Fable*, 1855(6), II

Nabokov, Vladimir, 1958(1), II; 1969(1), II; 1977, II

Nadelman, Elie, 1987, II

Nader, Ralph, 1966 Mar. 22, III; 1971 Jan. 12, III

Nagasaki:

atomic bomb dropped on, 1945 Aug. 9, I

Nagurski, Bronislaw (Bronko), 1990, IV

Naifeh, Steven, 1991 Apr. 9, II

Nails, 1777(1), III

Naismith, Jim, 1891, IV

Nakashima, George, 1990, II

Nakian, Reuben, 1986, II

Nantucket (Mass.):

sperm whaling, 1712, III

Napoleon Bonaparte, 1806 May 16, I; 1808 Apr. 17, I; 1810 Mar. 23, I; 1810 Aug. 5, I

Narcotics:

anti-drug bill, 1988 Nov. 18, I

cocaine seized, 1989 Sept. 29, IV

cocaine smuggling conviction, 1988 May 19, IV

Federal Control Board established, 1922 May 26, I

federal hospital completed (Lexington, Ky.), 1935(2), III

federal legislation, 1989 Nov. 21, I

federal testing upheld, 1989 Mar. 21, I

B. Ford's remarks on marijuana, 1975 Aug. 10(1), IV

hallucinogenic, 1966, IV

heroin, use of, 1968, IV

heroin-control agreement with France, 1970 Jan. 6, I

heroin raid, 1960 Oct. 3, IV

heroin ring uncovered (N.Y.C.), 1959 Feb. 14–15, IV

largest cocaine seizure to date, 1988 May 3, IV

largest heroin seizure to date, 1991 June 21, IV

marijuana widespread use, 1982 Feb. 26, III

Noriega convicted, 1992 Apr. 9, IV

Noriega indicted, 1988 Feb. 5, I

Noriega surrendered to U.S., 1989 Dec. 20, I

Operation Intercept (Mex.), 1969 Sept. 21, I

pro athletes' use, 1986, IV

Sicilian-U.S. Mafia arrests, 1988 Mar. 31, IV

strip searches of soldiers unconstitutional, 1974 Jan. 14, IV

strongest control law (N.Y.S.), 1973 Sept. 1, III; 1977 June 21, III

use statistics, 1989, I

U.S. military in Vietnam use of, 1971, I; 1971 July 28, I

Valium and alcohol most abused, 1976 July 9, III

Nasby, Petroleum Vesuvius *see* Locke, David Ross

Nash, George V., 1960 Aug. 12, IV

Nash, Ogden, 1971, II

Nast, Thomas, 1874 Nov. 7, I

Nastase, Ilie, 1970 July 4, IV; 1972 July 7(2), IV; 1972 Sept. 9–10, IV

Natanson, Maurice, 1974 Apr. 18, II

Natchez Trace, 1806, III

Nathan, George Jean, 1900 Mar., II

Nathan, Robert, 1985, II; 1985, II

Nation, Carry, 1900(1), I

Nation, The (publication), 1865(11), II

National. *Note:* for organizations not found here, see under key word inverted

National Academy of Sciences (Wash., D.C.):

founded, 1863 Mar. 3, III

Research Council, 1916(1), III

National Air and Space Museum (Wash., D.C.):

Star Trek exhibit, 1992 Feb. 28, II

National Assn. of Manufacturers, 1895 Jan. 22, III
National Association for the Advancement of Colored People (NAACP): founded, 1909(1), I
National Book Awards (see also American Book Awards):, 1950 Mar. 16, II; 1951 Mar. 6, II; 1952 Jan. 29, II; 1953 Jan. 27, II; 1954 Jan. 26, II; 1955 Jan. 25, II; 1956 Feb. 7, II; 1957 Mar. 12, II; 1958 Mar. 11, II; 1959 Mar. 3(1), II; 1960 Mar. 23, II; 1961 Mar. 14, II; 1962 Mar. 13, II; 1963 Mar. 12, II; 1964 Mar. 10, II; 1965 Mar. 9, II; 1966 Mar. 15(1), II; 1967 Mar. 8, II; 1968 Mar. 6, II; 1969 Mar. 10(2), II; 1970 Mar. 2, II; 1971 Mar. 4, II; 1972 Apr. 13, II; 1973 Apr. 10, II; 1974 Apr. 18, II; 1975 Apr. 16, II; 1976 Apr. 19, II; 1977 Apr. 13(1), II; 1978 Apr. 10, II; 1979 Apr. 23, II; 1987 Nov. 9, II; 1988 Nov. 29, II; 1989 Nov. 29, II; 1990 Nov. 27, II; 1991 Nov. 20, II
National Book Critics Circle Awards, 1976 Jan. 8, II; 1977 Jan. 6, II; 1978 Jan. 11, II; 1979 Jan. 15, II; 1980 Jan. 7, II; 1981 Jan. 5, II; 1982 Jan. 28, II; 1983 Jan. 27, II; 1984 Jan. 9, II; 1985 Jan. 14, II; 1986 Feb. 17, II
National Broadcasting Co. (NBC): first in viewership, 1989 Apr. 18, II first videotaped broadcasts, 1957 Jan. 21, III homosexuality issue, 1973 Oct. 26, II Olympic telecast rights, 1988 Dec. 1, IV ratings win, 1988 Sept. 17(2), II Symphony Orchestra, 1930, II Toscanini contract, 1937(4), II
National Defense Act, 1916 June 3, I
National Education Assn., 1957 Apr. 4, III; 1960 Jan. 23, III
National Endowment for the Arts, 1989 June 13, II
National Foundation on the Arts and the Humanities, 1965 Sept. 30, II
National Gallery of Art (Wash., D.C.): Art of India exhibit, 1985 May 5, II East Building opened, 1978 June 1, II 50th anniversary celebration, 1991 Mar. 17, II French impressionist exhibit, 1973 Apr. 2, II Hermitage exchange, 1987, II Kelly exhibit, 1992 Nov. 1, II Leonardo da Vinci purchase, 1967 Feb. 20, II new art works acquired, 1992 July 7, II O'Keeffe exhibit, 1988, II opened, 1941 Mar. 17, II Pollock work acquired, 1976 Oct. 6, II Rothko collection, 1984 May 3, II Stuart's portraits acquired, 1979 Apr. 10, II Treasure Houses of Great Britain exhibit, 1985 Nov. 3, II Veronese exhibit, 1989, II

National Industrial Recovery Act (NIRA), 1933 June 16(1), I unconstitutional, 1935 May 27, I
National Institute of Arts and Letters, 1898(2), II; 1945 Dec. 27, II; 1963 May 22, II
National Labor Board, 1933 Aug. 5, I
National Labor Reform Party, 1872(3), I
National Labor Relations Act, 1935 July 5, III; 1937 Apr. 12, III
National Medal for Literature, 1964 Mar. 10, II
National Monuments see Monuments, National; specific names
National Museum of African Art (Wash., D.C.), 1987 Sept. 28, II
National Museum of Women in the Arts (Wash., D.C.), 1987 Apr. 7, II
National Party see Greenback-Labor Party
National Railroad Passenger Corporation see Amtrak
National Recovery Act, 1935, I
National Recovery Administration (NRA): established, 1933 June 16(1), I
National Republican Party, 1828(2), I; 1831 Dec. 12, I
National Rifle Association: formed, 1871(1), IV
National Security Act, 1947 July 25, I
National Security Council: created, 1947 July 25, I Iran-Contra affair, 1986 Nov. 3, I Kissinger resigned, 1975 Nov. 3, I
National Statistical Assn., 1888(1), III
National Student Assn.: CIA funding, 1967 Feb. 13, I
National Symphony Orchestra (Wash., D.C.), 1975 Mar. 28(1), II
Native American Party (see also Know-Nothing Party):, 1843 June, I; 1847 Sept., I
Native Americans see Indians
Nativism (anti-Catholic movement), 1841, III
Natural gas see Gas, Natural
Natural Research Act, 1974 July 12, III
Natural resources see Environmental protection; types
Natural Sciences of Philadelphia, Academy of, 1812(5), III
Nature (see also Horticulture; Wildlife): Agassiz's Brazilian studies, 1865(8), III Burroughs's writings on, 1871, II early study, 1674(1), II travel books extolling, 1790–1794, II
Nature (Emerson), 1836, II
Naughton, James, 1990 June 3, II
Nautilus (submarine), 1952 June 14, III; 1954 Sept. 30, I; 1958 Aug. 5, I
Naval Academy, U.S. (Annapolis, Md.): cheating scandal, 1974 May 23, I first woman graduating at top of class, 1984 May 23, III opened, 1845 Oct. 10, III women admitted, 1975 Sept. 28, I women graduates, 1980 May 28, III
Naval Expansion Act, 1938 May 17, I
Navigation Acts (British), 1660–1669, I; 1660 Dec. 1, I

Navratilova, Martina, 1976 July 2–3, IV; 1981 July 3–4, IV; 1982 July 3–4, IV; 1983 July 2–3, IV; 1983 Sept. 11, IV; 1984 July 7–8, IV; 1984 Sept. 8–9, IV; 1985 July 6–7, IV; 1986 July 5–6, IV; 1986 Sept. 7, IV; 1987 July 4, IV; 1987 Sept. 12, IV; 1990 July 7, IV 158th tennis title, 1992 Feb. 17, IV
Navy, U.S. see Armed forces; war names
Navy Department, U.S.: first secretary, 1798(3), I
Nazimova, Alla, 1906(3), II; 1918(4), II
NBA championship see Basketball
NBC see National Broadcasting Co.
NCR Corp., 1991 May 6(2), III
Neal, Patricia, 1964 Apr. 13, II
Nebraska (see also Kansas-Nebraska Act): Omaha as site of first legislature, 1855(2), I statehood, 1867 Mar. 1, I
Nebraska, University of, 1869(1), III; 1869 Feb. 15, III
Nederlander, Robert E., 1990 July 30, IV
Neely, Mark E., Jr., 1992 Apr. 7, II
Negri, Pola, 1987, II
Negro Conspiracy of 1741 (N.Y.C.), 1740–1744, IV
Negroes see Blacks; Slaves and slavery
Neighborhood Guild (N.Y.C.), 1886(3), III
Nelson, Byron, 1937 Apr. 4, IV; 1939 June 12, IV; 1940 Sept. 2, IV; 1942 Apr. 12, IV; 1944, IV; 1945, IV; 1945 July 15, IV
Nelson, Craig T., 1992 Aug. 30, II
Nelson, Donald M., 1942 Jan. 16, III
Nelson, George O., 1936 May 25, I
Nelson, Larry, 1981 Aug. 9(2), IV; 1983 June 20, IV; 1987 Aug. 9, IV
Nelson, Ozzie, 1975, II
Nemerov, Howard, 1978 Apr. 10, II; 1978 Apr. 17, II; 1988 May 18, II; 1991, II
Nemiroff, Robert, 1973 May 30, II
Neptune's Theater, 1606 Nov. 14, II
Nerves, 1970 Oct. 15, III
Nerve transplants, 1963 Apr. 18, III
Nesbit, Evelyn (Thaw), 1906, IV
Netherlands: Motley's Rise of the Dutch Republic, 1856, II
Neumann, John N., 1977 June 19, III
Neumann, Liselotte, 1988 July 24, IV
Neutrality Act, 1937 May 1, I; 1939 Sept. 21, I; 1939 Nov. 4, I
Nevada: chemical plant explosion, 1988 May 4, I divorces ruled valid, 1942 Dec. 21, IV statehood, 1864 Oct. 31, I Territory established, 1861 Mar. 2, I
Nevelson, Louise, 1985 Mar. 17, II; 1988, II
Nevin, Ethelbert, 1898, II
Nevins, Allan, 1933 May 4, II; 1972 Apr. 13, II
New Amsterdam see New York City
Newark College (Del.), 1833 Feb. 5, III
Newark (N.J.): race riot, 1967 July 12–17, I
Newberry College (S.C.), 1856 Dec. 20, III
Newberry Library (Chicago, Ill.), 1868(4), III

Newbold, Charles, 1797 June 26, III
Newcombe, John, 1967 Sept. 10, IV; 1973 Aug. 29–Sept. 9, IV
New Deal *see* Roosevelt, Franklin Delano
New Echota, Treaty of, 1835 Dec., I
New England (*see also* individual colony and state names):
    Anglican Church, 1722 Oct. 23, III; 1729(1), III
    colonial population, 1730–1734(1), I
    colonies' federation, 1640–1649, I
    commerical to industrial transition, 1828(2), III
    confederation dissolved, 1684 June 21, I
    first comprehensive history, 1669, II
    French and English claims, 1720–1724, I
    hurricane, 1938 Sept. 21, I
    Palfrey's history, 1858, II
    Puritans defended, 1650–1659, II
    slave trade, 1696(1), I
    social and intellectual lull, 1807(1), IV
    social snobbery, 1653, IV
New England Primer, 1690(2), II
New England Woman's Club, 1868(1), I
New English Canaan (Morton), 1637(2), II
Newfoundland, 1583, III
New Granada, Treaty of, 1848 June 3, I
New Guinea:
    U.S. ground assault, 1942 June 28, I
New Hampshire:
    first church, 1657, II
    ninth state to ratify U.S. Constitution, 1788 June 21, I
    oldest house, 1664(1), II
    separated from Mass., 1680 Sept., I
New Hampshire, University of, 1866(1), III
New Hampshire Gazette (newspaper), 1756, II
New Hampshire Sweepstakes, 1964 Sept. 12(2), IV
Newhart, Bob, 1961 Apr. 12, II
Newhouse, Samuel I., 1979, III; 1985 Mar. 8, II
Newhouser, Hal, 1992 Aug. 2, IV
New Jersey:
    British proprietorship, 1664 June 24, I
    first colonial governor, 1738, I
    holding companies permitted, 1889(1), I
    oil spills, 1990 Jan. 2–Sept. 27, I
    outlawed slavery, 1786(1), I
    third state to ratify U.S. Constitution, 1787 Dec. 18, I
New Jersey Symphony, 1968 Feb. 15, II
New Jersey Turnpike, 1951 Nov. 5, III
Newley, Anthony, 1962 Oct. 3, II
Newman, Paul, 1987 Mar. 30, II
New Mexico:
    statehood, 1912 Jan. 6, I
    Territory acquired, 1853 Dec. 30, I
    territory boundaries and slavery option established, 1850 Sept. 9(2), I
    terrorism, 1967 June 5, I
New Mexico, University of, 1889(4), III
New Netherland (*see also* New Jersey; New York State):
    British takeover, 1667 July 21, I

New Netherland (*cont.*)
    Dutch surrendered to British, 1664 Sept. 7, I; 1667 July 21, I
    founded, 1624 May, I
    manors, 1671(1), I
    N.Y.C., 1667 July 21, I
New Orleans, Battle of, 1815, I; 1815(3), IV; 1822(2), IV
New Orleans (La.):
    captured by Union, 1862 May 1, I
    Exposition, 1885, IV
    fires destroyed French Quarter, 1788 Mar. 21, I
    founded by French, 1718, I
    Mardi Gras, 1827(1), IV; 1857(5), IV
    opera center, 1791(2), II; 1808(2), II
    school desegregation riots, 1960 Nov. 17, II
    sniper attack, 1973 Jan. 7, IV
    Storyville closed, 1917(3), II
    Superdome, 1975 Aug. 1(2), II
    Yellow fever epidemic, 1853(1), I; 1905 July 22, I
Newport Jazz Festival (N.Y.C.), 1972 July 1–9, II
    moved to Saratoga Springs (N.Y.), 1977 June 30, II
Newport Parish Church (Va.), 1682(3), II
Newport (R.I.):
    Casino, 1881(4), II
    as important port, 1730–1734, IV
    jazz festival, 1958 July 3–6, II
    as popular resort, 1730–1734, IV
    U.S. Lawn Tennis Association, 1881(2), IV
New School for Social Research (N.Y.C.), 1931(2), II
Newspapers and publications (*see also* Censorship; Freedom of information; Publishing; Pulitzer Prizes; publication names):
    American Guild founded, 1933(3), II
    American Museum magazine, 1787 Jan., II
    Associated Press founded, 1848(1), III
    Atlanta Constitution (Ga.) started, 1868(6), II
    Atlantic magazine rescued, 1980, II
    Baltimore American verbatim reports of Congress, 1799(1), II
    Baltimore Sun and *Evening Sun* purchased by Times Mirror, 1986, II
    biggest magazine acquisition to date, 1984 Nov. 20, II
    Boston Daily Advertiser, 1813(1), II
    Boston Gazette, 1719(2), II
    Bryan's editorship, 1894 Nov. 6, I
    Bryant, William Cullen, 1826(2), II
    Chicago *Daily News* founded, 1875 Dec. 25, II
    Chicago *Daily News* halted, 1978 Mar. 4, II
    circulation, 1987, II; 1990, II
    Cleveland Leader established, 1852(2), II
    colonial magazines, 1740–1744, II
    Columbia Graduate School of Journalism, 1903(4), II
    Columbian Magazine, 1786 Sept., II
    comic strips, 1896, II

Newspapers and publications (*cont.*)
    Coronet magazine ceased, 1961 Oct., II
    Cosmopolitan founded, 1886(2), II
    costliest strike to date (N.Y.C.), 1963 Mar. 31, III
    Courier-Journal (Ky.) acquired by Gannett, 1986, II
    criminal pretrial proceedings closed to, 1979 July 2, I
    criticism of public figures upheld, 1988 Feb. 24, I
    criticized, 1838 Jan., IV
    Daily News (N.Y.C.) founded, 1855(3), II
    Daily Worker seized, 1956 Mar. 27, I
    Daily Worker suspended, 1958 Jan. 13, II
    Dana editor of N.Y. *Sun*, 1868(5), II
    decline in circulation and dailies, 1988, II
    Detroit (Mich.) strike, 1967 Nov. 15, III; 1968 Aug. 9, III
    disrupted by Revolution, 1772, III
    distribution, 1850(5), III
    early literary magazine, 1757 Oct., II
    early newspapers, 1700–1704, II
    far western publications, 1850(9), II
    Federalist weekly, 1789 Apr. 11, II
    first Catholic (Boston, Mass.), 1789 Apr. 23, II
    first daily (Phila., Pa.), 1783 May 30, II
    first foreign language (Phila., Pa.), 1732 May, II
    first illustrated magazine, 1774 Jan., II
    first in Colo., 1859 Apr. 23, II
    first Indian, 1828 Feb. 21, II
    first in Ida., 1862(1), II
    first in Kans., 1854 Sept. 15, II
    first in Mont., 1864(3), II
    first in N.D., 1864(2), II
    first in Nebraska Territory, 1854(1), II
    first in N.Y., 1725–1729, II
    first in S.D., 1859(3), II
    first in Wyoming, 1863(3), II
    first juvenile magazine (Conn.), 1789 Jan.(2), II
    first (Mass.), 1690 Sept. 25, II
    first musical periodical, 1786 May, II
    first professional journalist (Freneau), 1815, II
    first religious weekly (Phila., Pa.), 1813 Sept. 4, II
    first sectarian magazine, 1789 Jan.(1), II
    first serial (Pa.), 1729(2), II
    first sports editor, 1832(3), IV
    first *Stars and Stripes*, 1918 Feb. 8, II
    first successful newspaper (Boston, Mass.), 1700–1704, II
    first successful Sunday edition (Phila., Pa.), 1878(3), II
    first syndicate, 1884, II
    first typesetting foundry, 1772, III
    first undergraduate daily, 1871(2), III
    first women-focused magazine (Boston, Mass.), 1784 May, II
    freedom of press landmark decision, 1734 Oct., II; 1972 June 29, II

Newspapers and publications (*cont.*)
Greeley founded N.Y. *Tribune,*
1841(4), IV; 1841 Apr. 10, II
Hachette largest magazine publisher
in world, 1988 Apr. 3, II
Harper's magazine inception, 1850(2),
II
Harper's magazine rescued, 1980, II
O. Henry's publications, 1894 Mar., II
human interest, 1896, IV
important magazines, 1872, II
influential Civil War era labor,
1863(2), II
Jefferson on freedom of, 1800 Sept.
23, IV
journalist's car bombed (Ariz.), 1976
June 2, II
Journal of Commerce, 1827(2), III
Kans. *Gazette,* 1895 June 1, II
Ladies Home Journal magazine
founded, 1883(4), II; 1889, II
largest takeover, 1988 Aug. 7(1), II
Life humor magazine, 1883(3), II
Life magazine discontinued, 1972
Dec. 29, II
Lincoln on press freedom, 1863 June
1, II
link with CIA alleged, 1977 Sept.
11(2), II
Lippmann column launched, 1931
Feb. 27, II
longest major city strike began
(N.Y.C.), 1966 Apr. 24, III
longest strike to date (Cleveland,
Ohio), 1963 Mar. 31, III
longest strike to date (Detroit, Mich.),
1964 Nov. 21(1), III
Look magazine ceased, 1971 Oct. 19,
II
Louisville (Ky.) *Courier-Journal*
founding and outlook, 1868(7), II
lovelorn columns, 1896, IV
McClure's Magazine, 1884, II
magazine ad revenue down, 1989, II
magazine circulation climbed, 1947(2),
III
Missouri Democrat established,
1852(1), II
Mr. Dooley creation, 1896(3), II
Ms. magazine started, 1972 July 1, II
muckrakers, 1904, II
Munsey's Weekly (later monthly),
1889 Feb. 2, II
Murdoch's acquisitions, 1983, II; 1984
Nov. 20, II; 1988 Aug. 7(1), II
Nation founded, 1865(11), II
new magazines, 1925, II
N.Y.C. strike, 1962 Nov. 1, III; 1962
Dec. 8, II; 1965 Sept. 16, III; 1978
Aug. 9, III
N.Y.C. strike ended, 1966 Sept. 12(2),
III
New Yorker, The (magazine) sold,
1985 Mar. 8, II
N.Y.C.'s first daily, 1793(2), II
N.Y. *Herald* founded, 1835(6), II
N.Y. *Herald Tribune* ceased, 1966
Aug. 15, III
N.Y. *Mirror* ceased, 1963 Oct. 16, II
N.Y. *Morning Journal,* 1882(5), II

Newspapers and publications (*cont.*)
N.Y. Review of Books sold, 1984 Dec.
18, II
N.Y. Times founded, 1851(1), II
N.Y. Times libel case, 1964 Mar. 9, II
N.Y. Times voted best daily, 1961 Feb.
1, II
N.Y. *World* purchased by Pulitzer,
1883 May 9, II
N.Y. *World-Telegram* merger, 1931
Feb. 27, II
oldest continuing (N.H.), 1756, II
oldest continuously published paper
(Conn.), 1764(2), II
Overland Monthly, The, 1868 July, II
Pennsylvania Gazette's popularity,
1729 Oct., II
Pentagon Papers, 1973 May 11, II
political, 1801, II; 1813(1), II
political editorial rebuttals decision,
1974 June 25, II
post-Revolutionary War periodicals,
1795–1799, II
protection of journalists' sources, 1959
Jan. 5, II
Pulitzer-Hearst N.Y. circulation war,
1883 May 9, II
Pulitzer's influence, 1878, II
religious, 1813(1), III
St. Louis *Post-Dispatch,* 1878, II
San Francisco *Chronicle* founded,
1865(7), II
San Francisco *Examiner* started,
1865(6), II
Saturday Evening Post (magazine)
economy move, 1968 May 4, III
Saturday Evening Post (magazine) last
issue, 1969 Feb. 8, II
Saturday Review suspended, 1982, II
Scribner's Monthly, 1870(3), II
second U.S. daily (N.Y.C.), 1793(2), II
sensationalism, 1833, II; 1882(5), II
Smart Set, The literary monthly, 1900
Mar., II
social responsibility, 1841(4), IV
Spanish-American War, 1898 Feb. 9, I
specialized magazines, 1840, II
spurring literacy, 1745, III
strike (Detroit, Mich.), 1967 Nov. 15,
III
Today begun, 1982 Sept. 15, II
Wall Street Journal, 1889 July 8, II
Walters highest-paid journalist to date,
1976 Apr. 22, II
Washington *Evening Star* ceased,
1981 Aug. 8, II
White's career, 1895 June 1, II; 1896
Aug. 15, II
women's interest, 1828, II
World began publication, 1961 Oct.
12, II
World Journal Tribune (N.Y.C.)
ceased, 1967 May 5, III
World Journal Tribune (N.Y.C.)
formed, 1966 Sept. 12(2), III
yellow journalism, 1895 Feb. 24, I
New Sweden (Del.), 1655, I
Newton, Huey, 1989, I
Newton, Isaac (Sir), 1680(2), III
Newton-John, Olivia, 1975 Mar. 1(1), II

New Year's Day:
colonial festivities, 1773 Mar., IV
first Tournament of Roses (Calif.),
1886 Jan. 1, IV
presidential receptions, 1791 Jan. 1,
IV
New York, College of the City of
(C.C.N.Y.):
founded, 1853(3), III
New York Academy of Fine Arts, 1808(1),
II
New York Athletic Club, 1868 Nov. 11, IV
New York Bar Association, 1747(2), III
New York Central Railroad:
inaugurated 18-hour train
(N.Y.C.-Chicago), 1905 June 11, III
largest, 1900(9), III
merged, 1962 Jan. 12, III
N.Y.C.-Chicago run time, 1902 June
15, III
New York City (*see also* Hudson River and
Valley; Tweed, William M.; buildings;
sections; institutions):
anti-Vietnam War demonstration,
1967 Apr. 15, I
black segregation, 1853 Aug. 15, II
British takeover, 1664 Sept. 7, I
Central Park proposal, 1850(7), III
colonial self-government, 1652(2), I
Confederate arson attempt, 1864 Nov.
25, I
Continental Army evacuated, 1776
Sept. 15, I
Cooper on growth and change in,
1828(4), IV
cosmopolitan population, 1643(1), I;
1675(1), IV
Dutch churches, 1628, III
Dutch colonial buildings destroyed by
fire, 1776 Sept. 21, I
Dutch influence, 1794(3), II
Dutch laws, 1656(2), IV; 1656(3), IV
Dutch repossess, 1673 Aug. 8, I
Dutch settlement, 1612, I
earliest painting of, 1647(2), II
Ellis Island restoration, 1990 Sept. 8,
IV
enlarged, 1897 May 5, I
ethnic groups, 1890(2), I
extensive library system, 1901 Mar.
12, III
federal loan guarantee, 1975 Nov. 26,
I
financial crisis, 1977 Aug. 26, I
first Brooklyn church, 1666(2), III
first chamber of commerce, 1768 Apr.
5, III
first mounted police, 1904 Sept. 9, III
first police, 1658 Aug. 12, I
first printed account, 1670(2), II
first transit strike, 1966 Jan. 1, III
Grand Panorama exhibition, 1809
Nov. 1, IV
Harlem River Houses, 1937(2), II
Irish riot, 1871 July 12, I
Jewish settlers, 1654 July 8, III
LaGuardia elected mayor, 1933 Nov.
7, I
largest single art theft, 1988 Feb. 9,
IV

New York City (cont.)
　longest and costliest strike, 1954 Apr.
　　2, III
　Manhattan Island sold (Dutch), 1626, I
　mayors, 1889 Oct. 7, III
　New Amsterdam settlement, 1625
　　Spring, I
　newspaper strike, 1962 Nov. 1, III;
　　1962 Dec. 8, II; 1966 Apr. 24, III
　newspaper strike ended, 1963 Mar.
　　31, III; 1966 Sept. 12(2), III
　oil spills, 1990 Jan. 2–Sept. 27, I
　Paulding's tales of New Amsterdam,
　　1836(5), II
　police corruption, 1894 Jan. 30, I;
　　1894 Dec. 14, I
　pro-Vietnam War parade, 1967 May
　　13, I
　slum population density, 1905(1), III
　Stamp Act riot, 1765 Nov. 1, I
　state capital, 1790(1), IV
　subway, 1864(4), III
　Swedish colony (Del.) annexed, 1655, I
　Tammany Hall investigation, 1871
　　Sept. 4, I
　teachers' strike, 1967 Sept. 11, III;
　　1968 Sept. 9, III
　tenderloin section, 1876(5), IV
　transit strike, 1889 Jan. 28, I
　Tweed convicted, 1873 Nov. 19, I
　Walker elected mayor, 1925 Nov. 3, I
　Walker malfeasance charges, 1931
　　Mar. 17, I
　Washington Square North, 1830(7), II
　wealth-based society, 1872, IV
　women admitted to private clubs,
　　1988 June 20, IV
　World's Fair opened, 1939, IV
　world theatrical center, 1920(2), II
　worst fire dept. disaster, 1966 Oct. 18,
　　I
New York City Ballet:
　Baryshnikov joined, 1978, II
　dancer's strike, 1973 Nov. 13, II
　Ford Foundation grant, 1965 Nov. 17,
　　II
　Kirstein resigned as director, 1989
　　Nov. 1, II
　Lincoln Center first season, 1964 Apr.
　　24, II
　McBride retirement, 1989 June 4(2),
　　II
　Tchaikovsky festival, 1981 June 4–14,
　　II
New York City Exposition and Convention
　Center, 1980, II
New York City Hall, 1803(2), II; 1812(5), II
New York City Marathon, 1970 Sept. 13,
　IV; 1971 Sept. 19(2), IV; 1972 Oct. 1, IV;
　1975 Sept. 28, IV; 1977 Oct. 23, IV;
　1978 Oct. 22, IV; 1980 Oct. 26, IV; 1982
　Oct. 24, IV; 1983 Oct. 23, IV; 1984 Oct.
　28, IV; 1985 Oct. 27, IV; 1986 Nov. 2,
　IV; 1987 Nov. 1, IV; 1988 Nov. 6, IV;
　1989 Nov. 5, IV; 1991 Nov. 3, IV; 1992
　Nov. 1, IV
　first city-wide, 1976 Oct. 24, IV
　first woman finisher, 1973 Sept. 30,
　　IV; 1974 Sept. 29, IV

New York City Marathon (cont.)
　new women's world record, 1979 Oct.
　　21(1), IV
　records, 1981 Oct. 25, IV
　women's boycotted, 1972 Oct. 1, IV
New York City Opera:
　first Lincoln Center performance,
　　1966 Feb. 22, II
　Ford Foundation Grant, 1965 Nov. 17,
　　II
　Makropoulos Affair, The (Janáŝek),
　　1970 Nov. 3, II
　Moses and Aaron (Schoenberg), 1990,
　　II
　moved to Lincoln Center, 1966, II
　Sills final performance, 1980 Oct. 27,
　　II
　Six Characters in Search of an Author
　　(Weisgall), 1959 Apr. 26, II
New York Coliseum, 1956 Apr. 28, III
New York Commodity Exchange, 1992
　Mar. 24, III
New York Daily News (newspaper):
　struck, 1978 Aug. 9, III
New Yorker, The (magazine), 1925, II;
　1985 Mar. 8, II
New York Evening Post (newspaper),
　1801(2), II
New York Film Critics Circle Awards,
　1962 Dec. 8, II; 1975 Dec. 30, II
New York Herald Tribune (newspaper),
　1835(6), II; 1966 Aug. 15, II
New-York Historical Society, 1804(1), III
New York Horse Show, 1883 Oct. 22, IV
New York Hospital for Ruptured and
　Crippled Children (N.Y.C.), 1863 May 1,
　III
New York Hospital (N.Y.C.):
　first eye bank established, 1944 May
　　8, III
New York Mirror (newspaper), 1840(4), II;
　1963 Oct. 16, II
New York Music Critics Circle Award,
　1945 June 2, II
New York Philharmonic:
　anniversary concert, 1967 Dec. 7, II
　Bernstein retirement, 1966 Nov. 2, II
　Bernstein's last concert as director,
　　1969 May 17(1), II
　Bernstein's scores donated, 1992 Aug.
　　20, II
　Boulez retired, 1977 May 14, II
　Carnegie Hall, 1891 May 5, II
　Mehta named conductor, 1977 May
　　14, II
　Mehta retired, 1991 May 28, II
　150th anniversary, 1992 Sept. 16, II
　radio broadcasts begun, 1930, II
　Rodzinski named conductor, 1945
　　June 2, II
New York Philharmonic Society, 1856
　Mar. 1, II
New York Post (newspaper):
　struck, 1978 Aug. 9, III
New York Public Library (N.Y.C.):
　Bellow papers, 1988 June 7, II
　Toscanini Archives acquired, 1987
　　Mar. 30, II
New York Review of Books (publication),
　1984 Dec. 18, II

New York State (see also Hudson River
　and Valley; city names):
　Albany Regency, 1825, I
　civil disturbance during power failure,
　　1977 July 13–14, I
　constitution, 1839(2), I
　eleventh state to ratify U.S.
　　Constitution, 1788 July 26, I
　Erie Canal impact, 1825, III
　fifty-four-hour work week, 1912 Oct.
　　1, III
　first antidiscrimination agency, 1945
　　July 1, III
　first Dutch colony, 1614, I
　Guy Fawkes Day observed, 1665, IV
　Hughes elected governor, 1906 Nov.
　　6(2), I
　Leisler insurrection, 1689(1), I
　manors, 1693(4), IV
　T. Roosevelt elected governor, 1898
　　Nov. 8, I
New York Stock Exchange (see also Stocks
　and bonds):
　closed, 1873 Sept. 20, I
　electronic trading system curbs, 1988
　　Jan. 8, III
　organized, 1792 May 17, III
　seat price drop, 1974 July 9, III
　second greatest trading day to date,
　　1967 Mar. 10, III
　worst crash in history, 1987 Oct. 19,
　　III; 1988 Jan. 8, III
New York Sun (newspaper), 1833, II;
　1868(5), II
New York Times, The (newspaper):
　first animated electric sign, 1928 Nov.
　　6, III
　founding, 1851(1), II
　increased pages, 1868 Oct. 1(2), IV
　libel judgment reversed, 1964 Mar. 9,
　　II
　Pentagon Papers, 1971, II; 1971(1), II;
　　1971 June 13, II
　political stance, 1851(1), II
　struck, 1965 Sept. 16, III; 1978 Aug. 9,
　　III
　on velocipede's limitation, 1872 Nov.
　　1, III
　voted best daily, 1961 Feb. 1, II
New York Tribune (newspaper):
　began publication, 1841 Apr. 10, II
　Karl Marx columns, 1851(8), II
　social responsibility, 1841(4), IV
New York Trotting Club, 1825(2), IV
New York University (N.Y.C.):
　chartered, 1831 Apr. 18, III
　Hall of Fame, 1900 Mar. 5, III
　summer schools in Europe, 1900 Mar.
　　5, III
New York v. Miln, 1837 Feb., I
New York World Journal Tribune
　(newspaper), 1967 May 5, III
New York World (newspaper), 1889, IV;
　1896, II
New York World-Telegram (newspaper),
　1931 Feb. 27, II
New York Yacht Club, 1844 July 29, IV
Nez Percé Indians, 1877 June–Oct., I
Ngor, Haing S., 1985 Mar. 25, II

Niagara Falls (N.Y.):
H. James's description of, 1871(2), IV
Love Canal disaster area, 1978 Aug. 7, I

Nicaragua (*see also* Iran-Contra affair):
U.S. aid to insurgents barred, 1986 June 27(2), I
U.S. Contra aid appropriated, 1986 Aug. 13, I; 1987 Dec. 22, I; 1988 Apr. 1, I
U.S. intervention in revolution, 1909 Nov. 18, I
U.S. Marines landed, 1926 May 10, I
U.S. ties severed, 1979 Feb. 8, I
Walker's seizure and rule, 1855(1), I
World Court case against U.S., 1984 Nov. 26, I; 1985 Jan. 18, I

Nicholas II (Czar of Russia), 1907 June 15-Oct. 15, I
Nichols, Anne, 1922 May 23, II
Nichols, Bobby, 1964 July 19, IV
Nichols, George Ward, 1867(3), IV
Nichols, Mike, 1960 Oct. 8, II
Nichols, Peter, 1985 Mar. 27, II
Nicholson, Jack, 1975 Dec. 30, II; 1976 Mar. 29, II; 1984 Apr. 9, II
Nicholson, Thomas D., 1991, III
Nicklaus, Jack, 1960 June 18, IV; 1962 June 17, IV; 1963 Apr. 7, IV; 1963 July 21, IV; 1964, IV; 1965, IV; 1965 Apr. 11, IV; 1966 Apr. 11, IV; 1966 July 9, IV; 1967, IV; 1967 June 18, IV; 1971, IV; 1971 Feb. 28, IV; 1971 Apr. 11, IV; 1972, IV; 1972 Apr. 9, IV; 1972 June 18, IV; 1973, IV; 1973 Aug. 12, IV; 1973 Dec. 1, IV; 1975, IV; 1975 Apr. 13, IV; 1975 Aug. 10(2), IV; 1976, IV; 1980 June 15, IV; 1983 Aug. 7, IV; 1986 Apr. 13, IV; 1988 Aug. 20, IV
Nicolls, Richard, 1664(2), IV; 1664 Mar. 12, I; 1664 Sept. 7, I
Niebuhr, Reinhold, 1941(2), III; 1971, III
Niekro, Phil, 1985 Aug. 4, IV
Nielson, A. C., Co., 1987 Sept. 14, II
Nijinsky, Vaslav, 1916, II
Nilsson, Harry, 1970 Mar. 11, II; 1973 Mar. 3, II
Nimbus 1 (satellite), 1964 Aug. 28, III
Nimitz, Chester W., 1966, I
Nirenberg, Marshall W., 1968 Oct. 16, III
Niska, Maralin, 1970 Nov. 3, II
Niven, David, 1959 Apr. 6, II
Nix Mate's Island legend (Mass.), 1689 Summer, IV
Nixon, John, 1776 July 8, I
Nixon, Julie:
married David Eisenhower, 1968 Dec. 22, IV

Nixon, Richard M. (*see also* Watergate):
ABM policy, 1969 Mar. 14, I
Asian visit, 1969 July 26–Aug. 3, I
bills vetoed, 1972 Oct. 18, III; 1973 Nov. 7, I
books on, 1976(1), II
Calif. gubernatorial candidacy, 1961 Sept. 27, I
Calley case, 1971 Mar. 29, I
Cambodian incursion, 1970, I; 1970 Apr. 29, I
Campus Unrest Commission, 1970, III

Nixon, Richard M. (*cont.*)
chemical warfare ban, 1970 Feb. 14, I
China visit, 1972 Feb. 21–28, I
complied with tax reassessment, 1974 Apr. 3, I
Cuban defector's plane landed (Fla.), 1969 Oct. 5, I
daughter Julie married David Eisenhower, 1968 Dec. 22, IV
denied Watergate involvement, 1973 Apr. 30, I
document classification relaxation, 1972 Mar. 8, I
domestic policies, 1970, I
economic measures, 1971, III; 1973 Jan. 11, III; 1973 July 18, III
elected president, 1968 Nov. 5, I
elected vice president, 1952 Nov. 4, I
election debates, 1960 Sept. 26, I
enemies' list, 1973 June 25–29, I
energy self-sufficiency program, 1973 Nov. 7, III
environmental protection, 1970 Jan. 22, I
European tour, 1970 Sept. 27, I
Hirohito meeting (Alaska), 1971 Sept. 26, I
illegal use of CIA, 1975 Jan. 5, I
impeachment attempts, 1973 Oct. 23, I; 1974, I; 1974 Feb. 6, I; 1974 July 30, I
inaugurated president, 1969 Jan. 20(1), I; 1973 Jan. 20, I
international successes, 1972, I
ITT antitrust suit, 1974 June 7, I
legal practice in N.Y. barred, 1976 July 8, I
legislation signed, 1969 Nov. 26, I; 1969 Dec. 22, I; 1970 Apr. 1, III; 1970 Aug. 12, I; 1970 Sept. 22, I; 1970 Oct. 15, I; 1970 Oct. 26, I; 1970 Oct. 30, III; 1970 Dec. 31, III; 1971 Jan. 2, I; 1971 May 25, III; 1971 Nov. 18, IV; 1972 Oct. 20, I; 1972 Oct. 28, III; 1973 July 1, I; 1974 Apr. 8, III; 1974 July 12, III
loss of support, 1974, I
lost presidency, 1960 Nov. 8, I
Medal of Freedom awarded, 1969 Apr. 29, II
Middle East trip, 1974, I
nominated Ford for vice presidency, 1973 Oct. 12, I
ordered Haiphong harbor mined, 1972 May 8, I
and organized crime, 1970 Oct. 15, I
pardoned, 1974 Sept. 8, I
presidential candidacy, 1960 July 25, I; 1968, I; 1968 Aug. 8, I; 1972 Aug. 21–23, I
presidential liability suit against, 1982 June 24, I
presidential renomination challengers, 1971, I
presidential tapes, 1973 July 16, I
private pledge to S. Vietnam, 1975 Apr. 9, I
reelected president, 1972 Nov. 7, I
reelection campaign financing, 1974 Apr. 28, I; 1974 June 7, I

Nixon, Richard M. (*cont.*)
resignation, 1974 Aug. 8, I; 1974 Aug. 9, I
resignation and impeachment issues, 1973, I
retail price freeze, 1973 June 13, III
revenue-sharing program, 1971 Jan. 22, I
Rumanian visit, 1969 July 26–Aug. 3, I
school desegregation policies protested, 1969 Aug. 27, III
"silent majority" statement, 1969 Nov. 11, I
Six Crises published, 1962(1), II
southern strategy, 1969, I
Soviet visits, 1959, I; 1959 July 23, I; 1959 Aug. 1, I; 1972 May 22–30, I; 1974, I
Soviet wheat deal, 1972 July 8, III
space shuttle, 1972 Jan. 5, III
State of the Union message, 1970 Jan. 22, I; 1971 Jan. 22, I
Supreme Ct. nominees, 1970, I; 1970 Apr. 8, I; 1970 May 12, I
Supreme Ct. nominees approved, 1971, I; 1971 Dec. 6, I; 1971 Dec. 10, I
sworn in as vice president, 1957 Jan. 20, I
Thieu meeting, 1969 June 8, I
Truman lambasts, 1960 Oct. 10–12, I
TV interview on Watergate, 1977 May 4, I
vice presidential candidacy, 1952 July 11, I; 1956 Aug. 20–24, I
Vietnamization policy, 1969 Nov. 3, I
Vietnam peace plan, 1969 May 14, I; 1970 Oct. 7, I
Vietnam War policy, 1969, I
welfare reforms, 1969 Aug. 8, III
White House tapes, 1973 Nov. 21, I
White House tapes transcripts released, 1974 July 24, I; 1974 Aug. 5, I
Nizer, Louis, 1973(1), II
Nobel Prizes:
Americans won all, 1976, III
Chemistry, 1914(2), III; 1932 Nov. 10, III; 1934 Nov. 15, III; 1946 Nov. 14(2), III; 1949 Nov. 3, III; 1951 Nov. 15, III; 1954 Nov. 3, III; 1955 Nov. 2(1), III; 1960 Nov. 3, III; 1961 Nov. 2(1), III; 1965 Oct. 21(2), III; 1966 Dec. 10(1), III; 1968 Oct. 30(1), III; 1972 Oct. 20(2), III; 1974 Oct. 15, III; 1976 Oct. 18(1), III; 1979 Oct. 16(1), III; 1980 Oct. 14(1), III; 1981 Oct. 19(1), III; 1984 Oct. 17, III; 1985 Oct. 16, III; 1986 Oct. 15, III; 1987 Oct. 14, III; 1989 Oct. 12(1), III; 1990 Oct. 16(2), III; 1992 Oct. 14, III
Economics, 1970 Oct. 16, III; 1971 Oct. 15, III; 1972 Oct. 25, III; 1973 Oct. 18, III; 1975 Oct. 14, III; 1976 Oct. 14(2), III; 1978 Oct. 16, III; 1979 Oct. 17(1), III; 1980 Oct. 15, III; 1981 Oct. 13, III; 1982 Oct. 20, III; 1983 Oct. 17, III; 1985 Oct. 15,

Nobel Prizes (*cont.*)
  III; 1986 Oct. 16, III; 1987 Oct. 21,
  III; 1990 Oct. 16(3), III; 1991 Oct.
  15, III; 1992 Oct. 13, III
  Literature, 1930 Nov. 5(2), II; 1936
    Nov. 12, II; 1938 Nov. 10, II; 1948
    Nov. 4, II; 1949 Nov. 3, II; 1950
    Nov. 10(1), II; 1954 Oct. 28, II; 1962
    Oct. 25, II; 1976 Oct. 21, II; 1978
    Oct. 5, II; 1980 Oct. 9, II; 1987 Oct.
    22, II
  not awarded for past four years, 1943,
    III
  Peace, 1905, I; 1906(1), I; 1913 Dec.
    10, I; 1920 Nov. 20, I; 1926 Dec. 10,
    I; 1930 Nov. 27, I; 1931 Dec. 10, I;
    1945 Nov. 12, I; 1946 Nov. 14, I;
    1950 Sept. 22, I; 1963 Oct. 10, III;
    1964 Oct. 14, III; 1970 Oct. 21, I;
    1973 Oct. 16(2), I; 1985 Oct. 11, I;
    1986 Oct. 14, I
  Physics, 1907(2), III; 1923 Nov. 13, III;
    1927 Nov. 10, III; 1936 Nov. 12, III;
    1937 Nov. 11, III; 1939 Nov. 9, III;
    1944 Nov. 10, III; 1946 Nov. 14(1),
    III; 1952 Nov. 6, III; 1955 Nov. 2(2),
    III; 1956 Nov. 1, III; 1957 Oct. 31,
    III; 1959 Oct. 26, III; 1960 Nov. 3,
    III; 1961 Nov. 2(2), III; 1963 Nov. 5,
    III; 1964 Oct. 29, III; 1965 Oct.
    21(1), III; 1967 Oct. 18(2), III; 1968
    Oct. 30(2), III; 1969 Oct. 30, III;
    1972 Oct. 20(1), III; 1973 Oct. 23,
    III; 1975 Oct. 17, III; 1976 Oct.
    18(2), III; 1977 Oct. 11, III; 1978
    Oct. 17, III; 1979 Oct. 16(2), III;
    1980 Oct. 14(2), III; 1981 Oct. 19(2),
    III; 1982 Oct. 13, III; 1983 Oct. 19,
    III; 1988 Oct. 19, III; 1989 Oct.
    12(2), III; 1990 Oct. 16(1), III
  Physiology or Medicine, 1930 Oct. 30,
    III; 1933 Oct. 20, III; 1933 Oct. 20,
    III; 1934 Oct. 25, III; 1944 Oct. 26,
    III; 1946 Oct. 31, III; 1947 Oct. 23,
    III; 1950 Oct. 26, III; 1951 Oct. 18,
    III; 1952 Oct. 23, III; 1953 Oct. 22,
    III; 1954 Oct. 21, III; 1956 Oct. 19,
    III; 1958 Oct. 30, III; 1959 Oct. 15,
    III; 1961 Oct. 19, III; 1962 Oct. 18,
    III; 1964 Oct. 15, III; 1966 Dec.
    10(2), III; 1967 Oct. 18(1), III; 1968
    Oct. 16, III; 1969 Oct. 16, III; 1970
    Oct. 15, III; 1971 Oct. 14, III; 1972
    Oct. 12, III; 1974 Oct. 10(2), III;
    1975 Oct. 16, III; 1976 Oct. 14(1),
    III; 1977 Oct. 13, III; 1979 Oct. 12,
    III; 1980 Oct. 10, III; 1981 Oct. 9,
    III; 1983 Oct. 10, III; 1985 Oct. 14,
    III; 1987 Oct. 12, III; 1988 Oct. 17,
    III; 1989 Oct. 9, III; 1990 Oct. 8, III;
    1992 Oct. 12(1), III
Nofziger, Lyn, 1988 Feb. 11, I
Noguchi, Isamu, 1988, II
Nolan, Lloyd, 1956 Mar. 17, II
Non-Intercourse Act, 1809, I; 1809
  Mar.1(2), I
Norell, Norman, 1972, IV
Norfolk Navy Yard (Va.), 1861 Apr. 19–20,
  I

Norfolk (Va.):
  burned by British, 1776 Jan. 1, I
Noriega, Manuel Antonio:
  convicted, 1992 Apr. 9, IV
  indicted, 1988 Feb. 5, I
  surrendered to U.S., 1989 Dec. 20, I
Norman, Greg, 1984 June 18, IV; 1986
  Aug. 11, IV; 1989 July 23(1), IV; 1990,
  IV
Norman, Marsha, 1983 Apr. 18, II
Norris, Frank, 1901, II; 1903(1), II; 1992, II
Norris, George W., 1910 Mar. 17, I; 1928
  July 11, I
Norris, Kathleen, 1911(1), II; 1966, II
Norris-LaGuardia Anti-Injunction Act,
  1932, III; 1932 Mar. 23, III
North, Andy, 1978 June 18, IV; 1985 June
  16, IV
North, Frederick (Lord), 1770 Apr. 12, I
North, Oliver L.:
  convicted, later suspended, 1989 May
    4, I
  dismissed from office, 1986 Nov. 3, I
  indicted, 1988 Mar. 16, I
  testified on Iran-Contra, 1987 Nov.
    18, I
North Adams (Mass.):
  contemporary art exhibit, 1987, II
North American Phalanx (N.J.
  community), 1843, III
North American Review (publication),
  1815(2), II
North Atlantic Treaty Organization
  (NATO):
  Eisenhower appointed supreme
    commander, 1950 Dec. 19, I
  formed, 1949 Apr. 4, I
  ratified, 1949, I; 1949 July 21, I
  U.S. troops reduced, 1990 Nov. 19, I
  West German Federal Republic
    admitted, 1954, I
North Carolina:
  abolished slavery, 1865 Nov. 9, I
  Anglican Church, 1701(1), I; 1705(1),
    I; 1715, I; 1765, I
  blizzard, 1987 Jan. 22, I
  capital punishment laws, 1976 July 2,
    I
  congressional representation
    regranted, 1868 June 25(2), I
  first colony to propose independence,
    1776 Apr. 12, I
  Mecklenburg Declaration of
    Independence, 1775 May 20, I
  named, 1691(2), I
  overturned secession ordinance, 1865
    Nov. 9, I
  seceded, 1861 May 20, I
  separate colonial governor, 1712 May
    9, I
  separate royal province, 1729 June, I
  twelfth state to ratify U.S.
    Constitution, 1789 Nov. 21, I
  Va. colonists' settlements, 1653, I
North Carolina, University of, 1789 Dec.
  11, III
North Dakota:
  statehood, 1889 Nov. 2, I
North Dakota, University of, 1883 Feb. 23,
  III

Northern Securities Co., 1902 Mar. 10, III;
  1904 Mar. 14, III
North Pole *see* Arctic and Antarctic
Northrop, John, 1946 Nov. 14(2), III
Northwestern University (Ill.), 1851 Jan.
  28, III
Northwest Passage:
  Argo expedition, 1753, I
  early explorations, 1600–1609, I
  first large ship to navigate, 1969 Sept.
    14, III
Northwest Territory:
  divided, 1800 May 7, I
  ordinance provisions, 1787 July 13, I
  Russian claims, 1824, I
Norton, Ken, 1976, IV; 1978 June 9, IV
Norway:
  Rynning book encouraging U.S.
    immigration, 1838(5), II
Norwich University (Vt.), 1819(1), III
Nosair, El Sayyid A., 1990 Nov. 5, I
Notre Dame, University of (Ind.):
  football team's fame, 1924, IV
  founded, 1844 Jan. 15, III
  last of Four Horsemen died, 1986, IV
Nott, Eliphalet, 1838(5), IV
Nova Anglia (Morrell), 1625, II
Noyce, Robert N., 1990, III
Noyes, John Humphrey, 1848, III
Nozick, Robert, 1975 Apr. 16, II
Ntshona, Winston, 1974 Nov. 13, II; 1975
  Apr. 21, II
Nuclear energy (*see also* Atomic Energy
  Commission; Atoms):
  bankruptcy (Seabrook, N.H.), 1988
    Jan. 28, III
  Chinese-U.S. accord, 1985 July 23, I
  construction accident (W. Va.), 1978
    Apr. 27, I
  emergency evacuation disputes, 1988
    Jan. 28, III
  EURATOM support, 1957 Feb. 8, I
  failure to meet safety mandates, 1980
    Jan. 2, III
  Fermi Award, 1963 Apr. 5, III
  first Antarctica plant, 1962 Mar. 4, III
  first atomic-powered generator, 1951
    Dec. 20, III
  first atomic power plant (Pittsburgh,
    Pa.), 1954 Mar. 10(1), I
  first breeder reactor, 1972 Jan. 14, III
  first heart pump, 1972 Feb. 14, III
  first lighthouse (Md.), 1964 May 21, III
  fuel, commercial reprocessing ban
    lifted, 1981 Oct. 8, I
  fusion at room temperature, 1989
    Mar. 23, III
  international cooperation, 1964, I
  operating license refused (Ill.), 1984
    Jan. 13, III
  opponents' protest (Seabrook, N.H.),
    1977 Apr. 30, III
  private industry experimental plants,
    1955 Jan. 9, III
  private plants authorized, 1956 May 4,
    III
  satellite generator, 1959 Nov. 18, III
  state plant construction bans upheld,
    1983 Apr. 20, I

Nuclear energy (*cont.*)
  thorium as new source, 1962 Dec. 2,
    III
  Three Mile Island (Pa.) near-disaster,
    1979 Mar. 28, III
  uranium-235, 1957, I
  vote to curb defeated (Calif.), 1976
    June 8, III
  Washington (State) Public Power
    Supply System defaulted, 1983 June
    25, III
Nuclear weapons (*see also* Arms control
  and disarmament; Missiles):
  atomic bomb dropped, 1945, I
  atomic bomb dropped on Nagasaki,
    1945 Aug. 9, I
  atomic bombs stockpiled, 1955 Feb.
    26, I
  atomic cannon, 1952 May 8, III
  Bikini Atoll tests, 1946 July 1, I
  Catholic bishops condemned arms
    race, 1983 May 3, III
  Eisenhower defense of use, 1955 Mar.
    16, I
  fallout detected, 1959 Apr. 5, III
  false alert, 1971 Feb. 20, II
  first atomic artillery shell fired (Nev.),
    1953 May 25, III
  first atomic bomb detonated (N.M.),
    1945 July 16, I
  first atomic bomb dropped
    (Hiroshima), 1945 Aug. 6, I
  first atomic submarine, 1952 June 14,
    III
  first atomic submarine commissioned,
    1954 Sept. 30, I
  first hydrogen bomb detonated, 1954
    Feb. 2, III
  first submarine launched, 1962 May 6,
    III
  first underground explosion (Nev.),
    1957 Sept. 19, I
  four test protesters seized (Hawaii),
    1958 May 1, I
  hydrogen bomb development
    authorized, 1950 Jan. 31, I
  hydrogen bomb fell into
    Mediterranean, 1966 Jan. 17(2), I
  hydrogen bombs shattered in crash
    (Greenland), 1968 Jan. 21, I
  hydrogen bomb tested (Marshall
    Islands), 1954 Mar. 24, III
  neutron bomb, 1977 June 6, I
  neutron bomb authorized, 1981 Aug.
    10, I
  neutron bomb deferred, 1978 Apr. 7,
    I
  Pauling on fallout danger, 1958 Apr.
    28, III
  physicists' moral questions, 1945, III
  plant accidents concealed, 1988 Sept.
    30, I
  Presbyterian Church condemned use
    of, 1988 June 14(2), III
  protest (N.Y.C.), 1979 Sept. 23, I
  second and third atomic submarines,
    1957 Mar. 30, I
  Soviet device exploded, 1988 Sept. 14,
    I

Nuclear weapons (*cont.*)
  Teller's defense of tests, 1958 Apr. 16,
    I
  test of missile-carried, 1962 May 6, III
  thermonuclear explosion causing
    radiation increase, 1962 July 9, III
  underground tests (Amchitka, Ala.),
    1971 Nov. 6, III
  underground tests (Nev.), 1970 Dec.
    1, III
  underground tests resumed (U.S.),
    1963 Feb. 8, I
  unmanned seismic stations for test
    detection, 1960 Feb. 17, III
  Urey's development of, 1931, III
  U.S. resumed testing in atmosphere,
    1962 Apr. 25, I
  U.S. superiority, 1959 Dec. 16, I
  U.S. test ban extended, 1959 Aug. 26,
    I
  U.S. warheads allowed in Canada,
    1963 May 11, I
  warheads in Cuba, 1989 Jan. 28, I
Nudity:
  ballet *Mutations* (Tetley), 1972 Mar.
    30, II
  in advertising, 1962 Jan., IV
Nugent, Elliott, 1940 Jan. 9, II
Nugent, Patrick John, 1965 Dec. 24, IV
Nullification controversy, 1833 Mar. 2, I;
  1833 Mar. 15, I
Nursing homes:
  fire (Mo.), 1957 Feb. 17, I
Nursing profession:
  Army Corps formed, 1901 Feb. 2(2), I
  Dix headed Union Army, 1861 June
    10, IV
  first major education institution
    (N.Y.C.), 1873(5), III
  first professional instruction, 1798(1),
    III
  Navy Corps established, 1908(1), III
Nuthall, Betty, 1930 Aug. 23, IV
Nutrition *see* Diet and nutrition
Nylon:
  first produced, 1934 May 23, III
  first product marketed, 1938(4), III
  first stockings, 1939 Oct. 25, III

Oakes, Urian, 1677(2), II
Oakie, Jack, 1978, II
Oates, Joyce Carol, 1970 Mar. 2, II;
  1971(1), II; 1973(1), II; 1989(1), II;
  1990(1), II; 1992(1), II
Oberlin College (Ohio), 1833(5), III
O'Brien, Dan, 1992 Sept. 5, IV
O'Brien, Edmond, 1955 Mar. 30, II
O'Brien, Fitz-James, 1862 Apr. 6, II
O'Brien, Larry, 1972 June 17, I
O'Brien, "Philadelphia Jack", 1906 Nov.
  28, IV
O'Brien, Thomas C., 1936 June 19, I
O'Brien, Tim, 1979 Apr. 23, II; 1990(1), II
Obscenity *see* Pornography
Ocean Hill-Brownsville school district
  (Brooklyn, N.Y.), 1968 Sept. 9, III
Oceanography:
  diving record, 1960 Jan 7(1), III
  manganese nodule recovery, 1971, III
  Sealab 2 program, 1965 Oct. 12, III

Oceans *see* Oceanography; Seabed treaty;
  Sea, Law of the; specific names
Oceans:
  first undersea around the world
    voyage, 1960 May 10, III
  international pollution control
    agreement, 1972 Nov. 13, III; 1990
    Nov. 1, I
Ochoa, Severo, 1959 Oct. 15, III
Ochs, Phil, 1976, II
O'Connor, Carroll, 1989 Sept. 17, II
O'Connor, Donald, 1953 Feb. 11, II
O'Connor, Edwin, 1956(1), II; 1962 May 7,
  II; 1968, II
O'Connor, Flannery, 1955(1), II; 1964, II;
  1965(1), II; 1966 Mar. 15(1), II; 1972
  Apr. 13, II
O'Connor, John J. (Archbishop), 1985 Apr.
  24, III
O'Connor, Sandra Day, 1981 July 7, I
Odd Fellows, Independent Order of, 1819
  Apr. 26, IV
Odets, Clifford, 1935, II; 1935 Feb. 19, II;
  1937 Nov. 4, II; 1950 Nov. 10(2), II;
  1963, II; 1970 Nov. 10, II
Office buildings (*see also* Skyscrapers):
  Alcoa (Pittsburgh, Pa.), 1952(4), II
  first elevator, 1868(7), III
  Larkin (Buffalo, N.Y.), 1903(5), II
  Lever House (N.Y.C.), 1950(6), II
  Marshall Field (Chicago, Ill.), 1885(2),
    II
  Milam (San Antonio, Tex.), 1929 July,
    II
  Monadnock (Chicago, Ill.), 1883(2), II
  Pan Am Building (N.Y.C.), 1963 Mar.
    7, II
  Seagram (N.Y.C.), 1957, II
  Tower (N.Y.C.), 1889(8), III
  Wainwright (St. Louis, Mo.), 1890(4),
    II
  Wright's designs, 1939(3), II
Office of Price Administration (OPA):
  extended, 1945 June 30, III
Off-track betting (OTB) *see* Horse racing
Oglethorpe, James Edward, 1730–1734, I;
  1735–1739, I; 1735, I; 1735–1739, I;
  1736 Feb. 5, III; 1740, I; 1740 Jan., I
Oglethorpe University (Ga.), 1835 Dec. 21,
  III
O'Hara, Frank, 1972 Apr. 13, II
O'Hara, John, 1949(1), II; 1956 Feb. 7, II;
  1960(1), II; 1967(1), II; 1970, II
O'Hara, Mary, 1941(1), II
Ohio:
  Dayton flood, 1913 Mar. 21–26, I
  floods, 1990 Apr. 14, I
  French colony, 1790 Mar., I
  nuclear plant accidents, 1988 Sept. 30,
    I
  statehood, 1803 Feb. 19, I
  tornado, 1953 June 8, I
Ohio and Erie Canal, 1832(2), III
Ohio Life Insurance Co., 1857 Aug. 24, III
Ohio River and Valley:
  French claims, 1749 May 19, I; 1754
    Apr. 17, I; 1754 July 4, I
  French-English claims competition,
    1725–1729, I

Ohio River and Valley (cont.)
    George II chartered Ohio Co., 1749
        May 19, I
    Gist charts, 1750, I
    Iroquois ceded to English, 1744, I
    oil spill, 1988 Jan. 2, I
    G. Washington survey, 1753 Oct. 31, I
Ohio State University, 1870(6), III
Ohio Wesleyan University, 1802 Jan. 9, III;
    1842 Mar. 7, III; 1853 Apr. 1, III
Oil, Chemical, and Atomic Workers
    International Union, 1960 Oct. 15, III
Oil and oil products (see also Teapot
    Dome scandal):
    Alaskan pipeline opened, 1977 July
        28, III
    Alaskan pipeline plans approved, 1973
        Nov. 13, III
    Arab embargo, 1973, III; 1973 Oct.
        17, III
    Arab embargo lifted, 1974 Mar. 18, III
    Carter on Persian Gulf routes, 1980
        Jan. 23, I
    consumption declined, 1990, III
    co. profits' sharp rise, 1974 Apr.
        18–May 9, III
    earliest commercial use, 1841(1), III
    economic impact of first well, 1859,
        III
    Energy Office allocations, 1973 June
        29, III
    environmental impact, 1988, III
    federal fuel tax passed, 1982 Dec. 23,
        III
    first gas-powered auto, 1892 Sept.(1),
        III
    first Tex. strike, 1901 Jan. 10, III
    first U.S. corp., 1854 Dec. 30, III
    gas curfew, 1941 Aug. 3, III
    gas rationing, 1942 May 15, III
    gas rationing standby program and
        Sunday sales ban, 1973 Nov. 7, III
    Gulf War, 1990 Aug. 2–Dec. 31, I
    import quotas lifted on crude, 1973
        Jan. 17, III
    imports limitation, 1979 June 29, I
    leaded gasoline ban, 1985 Mar. 4, III
    longest pipeline (Big Inch), 1943 July
        19, III
    offshore reserves, 1953 Jan. 16, III
    plan to reduce U.S. reliance on
        foreign, 1974 Nov. 13, III
    price controls lifted, 1981, III
    price deregulation, 1978 Apr. 5, I
    Rockefeller interests, 1862(1), III;
        1870, III
    shortage, 1973, III
    six spills (N.Y.-N.J.), 1990 Jan. 2–Sept.
        27, I
    spill (Alaska), 1989 Mar. 24, I
    spill (Calif.), 1990 Jan. 2–Sept. 27, I
    spill (Mass.), 1976 Dec. 15, III
    spill (Pa.-Ohio), 1988 Jan. 2, I
    Standard Oil Co. dividends, 1900
        Apr., III
    U.S. interests in Persian Gulf
        protected, 1981 Apr. 24(2), I
    windfall profits bill signed, 1980 Apr.
        2, III

Oils and fats:
    first cottonseed, 1768(1), III
    margarine-heart disease link found,
        1992 Oct. 7, III
O'Keeffe, Georgia, 1929, II; 1986, II; 1987,
    II; 1988, II
Okinawa, 1969 Nov. 21(1), I
Oklahoma:
    land rush, 1889 Apr. 22, I
    martial law in, 1923 Sept. 15, I
    prohibition enacted, 1907 Sept. 17, I
    prohibition repealed, 1959 Apr. 7, I
    statehood, 1907 Nov. 16, I
    territory created, 1890 May 2, I
    tornado, 1905 May 11, I; 1979 Apr.
        10, I
Oklahoma, University of, 1892 Dec. 19, III
Olcott, Chauncey, 1899, II
Older people (see also Pensions):
    population increase, 1989 Jan. 31, I
Oldfield, Barney, 1910 Mar. 16, IV
"Old Glory" (flag), 1831 Aug. 10, IV
Oldham, John, 1630–1639, I
Old Ironsides see Constitution (ship)
"Old Oaken Bucket, The" (song), 1826(4),
    II
Olds, Sharon, 1985 Jan. 14, II
Olds Co. (Detroit, Mich.), 1900(8), III
Old Ship Meeting House (Hingham,
    Mass.), 1681(3), II
Old South Meeting House (Boston, Mass.),
    1729(1), II
Old Swedes Church (Del.), 1698(1), II
Old West Church (Boston, Mass.), 1806(1),
    II
Oleana (Pa. commune), 1852, IV
Oliver, Mary, 1984 Apr. 16, II
Oliver, Melvin James (Cy), 1988, II
Olivet College (Mich.), 1934 Oct. 1, III
Olivier, Laurence, 1949 Mar. 24, II; 1960
    June 20, II; 1973 May 20, II; 1975 May
    19, II; 1984 Sept. 23, II
Olmedo, Alex, 1958 Dec. 31, IV
Olmsted, Frederick Law, 1857, IV;
    1876(5), III; 1957, II
Olustee, Battle of (Fla.), 1864 Feb. 20, I
Olympic Games:
    Athens, Greece, 1906 Apr. 22-May 2,
        IV
    first, 1896 Apr. 6, IV
    first black to head U.S. Committee,
        1992 Oct. 11, IV
    first five gold medals winner, 1980
        Feb. 12–24, IV
    first in U.S. (St. Louis, Mo.), 1904 May
        14, IV
    first U.S. basketball loss, 1972 Aug.
        26–Sept. 11, IV
    first U.S. gold medal marathon
        winner, 1972 Aug. 26–Sept. 11, IV
    first Winter (France), 1924 Jan.
        25-Feb. 4, IV
    first women's marathon, 1984 July
        28–Aug. 12, IV
    gold medal winners, 1900 May
        20-Oct. 28, IV; 1920 Apr. 20-Sept.
        12, IV
    NBC granted TV rights (Moscow),
        1977 Feb. 1, IV
    Owens honored (W. Berlin), 1984, IV

Olympic Games (cont.)
    Soviets withdrew, 1984 May 8, IV
    Stockholm, Sweden, 1912 May 5-July
        22, IV
    Summer (Amsterdam), 1928 July
        29-Aug. 12, IV
    Summer (Barcelona, Spain), 1992 July
        25–Aug. 9, IV
    Summer (Berlin Ger.), 1936 Aug.
        5–16, IV
    Summer (France), 1924 May 4-July 27,
        IV
    Summer (Helsinki, Finland), 1952 July
        19–Aug. 3, IV
    Summer (London, Eng.), 1908 Apr.
        27-Oct. 31, IV; 1948 July 28–Aug.
        14, IV
    Summer (Los Angeles, Calif.), 1932
        July 30-Aug. 14, IV; 1984 July
        28–Aug. 12, IV
    Summer (Melbourne, Australia), 1956
        Nov. 22–Dec. 8, IV
    Summer (Mexico City, Mex.), 1968
        Oct. 12–27, IV
    Summer (Montreal, Canada), 1976
        July 17–Aug. 1, IV
    Summer (Moscow), 1980, IV
    Summer (Munich, W. Ger.), 1972 Aug.
        26–Sept. 11, IV
    Summer (Rome, Italy), 1960 Aug.
        25–Sept. 11, IV
    Summer (Seoul, S. Korea), 1988 Sept.
        17–Oct. 2, IV
    Summer (Tokyo, Japan), 1964 Oct.
        10–24, IV
    suspended, 1940, IV
    terrorist attack, 1972 Aug. 26–Sept.
        11, IV
    TV rights, 1988 Dec. 1, IV
    U.S. hockey team upset win, 1980, IV;
        1980 Feb. 12–24, IV
    U.S. withdrawal from Summer
        (Moscow), 1980, IV
    Winter (Albertville, France), 1992
        Feb. 8–23, IV
    Winter (Calgary, Can.), 1988 Feb.
        13–28, IV
    Winter (Cortina d'Ampezzo, Italy),
        1956 Jan. 26–Feb. 5, IV
    Winter (Germany), 1936 Feb. 5–16, IV
    Winter (Grenoble, France), 1968 Feb.
        6–18, IV
    Winter (Innsbruck, Austria), 1964 Jan.
        29–Feb. 9, IV; 1976 Feb. 4–15, IV
    Winter (Japan), 1972 Feb. 3–13, IV
    Winter (Lake Placid, N.Y.), 1932 Feb.
        4–13, IV; 1980 Feb. 12–24, IV
    Winter (Oslo, Norway), 1952 Feb.
        15–25, IV
    Winter (St. Moritz, Switz.), 1928 Feb.
        11–19, IV; 1948 Jan. 30–Feb. 8, IV
    Winter (Sarajevo, Yugoslavia), 1984
        Feb. 8–19, IV
    Winter (Squaw Valley, Calif.), 1960
        Feb. 18–28, IV
Onassis, Aristotle, 1968 Oct. 19, IV
Onassis, Jacqueline see Kennedy,
    Jacqueline Bouvier
Ondieki, Lisa, 1992 Nov. 1, IV
O'Neal, Tatum, 1974 Apr. 2, II

Oneida Community (N.Y.), 1848, III
O'Neill, Eugene:
   Ah, Wilderness!, 1933, II; 1933 Oct. 2, II
   All God's Chillun Got Wings, 1924 May 15, II
   Anna Christie, 1921 Nov. 2, II
   Beyond the Horizon, 1920 Feb. 2, II
   Days Without End, 1934 Jan. 8, II
   Desire Under the Elms, 1924 Nov. 11, II
   Emperor Jones, The, 1920 Nov. 1, II
   Great God Brown, The, 1926 Jan. 23, II
   Hairy Ape, The, 1922 Mar. 9, II
   Iceman Cometh, The, 1946 Oct. 9, II
   Marco Millions, 1928 Jan. 9, II
   Mourning Becomes Electra, 1930 Oct. 26, II
   Nobel Prize, 1936 Nov. 12, II
   Provincetown Players, 1915 Summer, II
   Pulitzer Prize, 1920 June 2, II; 1922 May. 21, II; 1928 May 7, II; 1957 May 6, II
   S.S. Glencairn, 1924 Nov. 3, II
   Strange Interlude, 1929 Sept. 16, II; 1963 Mar. 11, II
   Tony awards, 1957 Apr. 21, II
   Touch of the Poet, A, 1958 Oct. 2, II
O'Neill, Oona, 1943 June 16, II; 1991, II
O'Neill, Thomas P., Jr., 1987(1), II
Ono, Yoko, 1982 Feb. 24, II; 1984 June 23, II
Onsager, Lars, 1968 Oct. 30(1), III
Ontario, Lake:
   first vessel, 1678, I
Opechancanough (Indian), 1644 Mar. 18, I
Opera (*see also* Metropolitan Opera; New York City Opera):
   Academy of Music opening (N.Y.C.), 1854, II
   Amahl and the Night Visitors (Menotti), 1951 Dec. 24, II
   Amelia Goes to the Ball (Menotti), 1938 Mar. 3, II
   American composers, 1855, II
   American National Opera Co. formed, 1967 Feb. 15, II
   Antony and Cleopatra (Barber), 1966 Sept. 16, II
   Apple Blossoms (Kreisler and Jacoby), 1919 Oct. 7, II
   Astor Place Opera House (N.Y.C.), 1847(1), IV
   Bomarzo (Ginastera) premiered, 1967 May 19, II
   Consul, The (Menotti), 1950 Mar. 1, II
   Die Frau ohne Schatten (Strauss), 1960, II
   early American, 1796(6), II
   first American grand (Phila., Pa.), 1845 June 4, II
   first broadcast, 1930, II
   first house (New Orleans, La.), 1791(2), II
   first libretto, 1767(2), II
   first on American theme, 1905 Oct. 3, II

Opera (*cont.*)
   first produced and performed (Charleston, S.C.), 1735 Feb. 8, II
   first prominent American-trained singer, 1859, II
   first Schuller, *Visitation*, premiered, 1966 Oct. 12, II
   Ford Foundation grants, 1965 Nov. 17, II
   Four Saints in Three Acts (Thomson), 1934 Feb. 8, II
   Friml's light, 1924, II
   Giants in the Earth (Moore), 1951 Mar. 28, II
   Girl of the Golden West, The (Puccini), 1905 Oct. 3, II; 1910 Dec. 10, II
   grand Italian introduced in N.Y., 1825 Nov. 29, II
   Griffelkin (Foss), 1955 Nov. 6, II
   Hammerstein's Manhattan Co. (N.Y.C.), 1906(8), II
   Help! Help! The Globolinks! (Menotti), 1969 Aug. 1, II
   Hooker's works, 1912 Mar. 14, II
   Il Trittico (Puccini) premiered, 1918 Dec. 14, II
   Italian, 1826(6), II
   Italian Opera House opened, 1833 Nov. 16, II
   Jesus Christ Superstar (Rice and Webber), 1971 Oct. 12, II
   Kirsten hailed (N.Y.C.), 1944(3), II
   La Scala U.S. appearances, 1967 Oct. 18, II; 1976 Sept. 7, II
   light, 1890, II
   Little Tycoon (Spenser), 1886 Jan. 4, II
   Lord Byron (Thomson) premiered, 1972 Apr. 20, II
   McTeague (Bolcom) premiered, 1992, II
   Makropoulos Affair, The (Janáček), 1970 Nov. 3, II
   Maria Golovin (Menotti), 1958 Aug. 20, II
   Marriage, The (Martinu), 1953 Feb. 7, II
   Medium, The (Menotti), 1947 Feb. 18, II
   Merry Mount (Hanson), 1934(2), II
   Metropolitan fire (N.Y.C.), 1892 Aug. 27, II
   Metropolitan's Diamond Horseshoe, 1892(2), IV
   Mighty Casey, The (Schuman), 1953 May 4(1), II
   Moses and Aaron (Schoenberg), 1990, II
   New Orleans as U.S. capital, 1791(2), II; 1808(2), II
   new works, 1956(2), II
   Norma revived (Bellini), 1970 Mar. 3, II
   Of Mice and Men (Floyd), 1970 Jan. 22, II
   Opera House (N.Y.C.) opened, 1833(6), IV
   Paris Opera Co. U.S. debut (N.Y.C.), 1976 Sept. 8, II

Opera (*cont.*)
   Parsifal (Wagner) production criticized, 1904(4), II
   Pearl Fishers (Bizet), 1916 Nov. 13, II
   popular classics, 1956(2), II
   Porgy and Bess (Gershwin), 1935 Oct. 10, II
   Resnik debut (N.Y.C.), 1944(3), II
   Salomé (Strauss) first U.S. performance, 1907 Jan. 22, II
   Santa Fe (N. Mex.) house destroyed by fire, 1967 July 27, II
   Schumann-Heink's U.S. debut, 1898 Nov. 7, II
   Sills's final performance, 1980 Oct. 27, II
   Sills's Met debut, 1975 Apr. 7, II
   singer Farrar's debut, 1906(7), II
   Solomon and Balkis (Thompson) radio premiere, 1942 Apr. 14(2), II
   sopranos Melba and Calve's debuts, 1893(5), II
   Tender Land, The (Copland) premiered, 1954 Apr. 1, II
   tenor Martinelli stand-in performance, 1967 Jan. 31, II
   Tetrazzini's N.Y. debut, 1908(3), II
   Treemonisha (Joplin) premiered, 1972 Jan. 28, II
   Tree on the Plain (Bacon), 1942 May 1, II
   Trojans, The (Berlioz) U.S. premiere, 1972 Feb. 4–5, II
   Volpone (Antheil), 1953 Jan. 9, II
   Wish, The (Antheil), 1955 Apr. 2, II
Oppen, George, 1969 May 5, II
Operation Desert Storm *see* Gulf War
Oppenheimer, J. Robert, 1963 Apr. 5, III; 1967, III
Oppens, Ursula, 1976 Feb. 9, II
Opper, Frederick Burr, 1896, II
Orange, Aaron M., 1940 Apr. 28, I
Orange Blossom *see* Mulholland, Joseph
Oranges, 1832(1), IV
Orantes, Manuel, 1975 Sept. 6–7, IV
Orbison, Roy, 1991 Feb. 20, II
Orbiting Solar Observatory VII, 1971 Sept. 29, III
Oregon:
   American Society for Encouraging the Settlement of, 1829(3), I
   arrival of 1000 settlers, 1843 May 22, I
   boundary, 1844(1), IV
   congressional resolution to terminate boundary agreement with British, 1846 Apr. 27, I
   disaster area, 1964 Dec. 22, I
   first settlement in northern territory, 1836 Sept. 1, I
   first white women in territory, 1836 July 4, IV
   gold discovered, 1850 July 25, IV
   local government formed, 1843 May 2, I
   Silver Lake fire, 1894 Dec. 29, I
   statehood, 1859 Feb. 14, II
   territory claims, 1827, I
   treaty establishing boundary signed, 1846 June 15, I
Oregon, University of, 1872(4), III

Oregon Trail, 1812 Feb. 15, I; 1834 June 15, I
Organization of Arab Petroleum Exporting Countries (OAPEC), 1973, III
Organizations *see* Associations and clubs; specific names
Organized crime:
  Anastasia slain, 1957 Oct. 25, IV
  Capone's career, 1931, IV
  Capone sentenced, 1929 May 17, IV
  Chicago (Ill.) wave, 1932, IV
  Diamond's career, 1931, IV
  Gotti convicted, 1992 June 23, IV
  Honor Thy Father (Talese), 1971(1), II
  Kefauver hearings, 1951, III
  Nixon's countermeasures, 1970 Oct. 15, I
  St. Valentine's Day Massacre (Chicago, Ill.), 1929, IV
  Salerno convicted, 1988 May 4, IV
  Sicilian-U.S. Mafia drug ring, 1988 Mar. 31, IV
  Touhy murdered (Chicago, Ill.), 1959 Dec. 16, IV
Organized Crime Control Act, 1970 Oct. 15, I
Ormandy, Eugene, 1979 Apr. 3, II; 1985, II
Ornithology *see* Birds
Orphans:
  Bethesda Orphanage (Ga.), 1740 Mar. 25, IV
  Girard College (Phila., Pa.), 1831 Dec. 26, II; 1848 Jan. 3, III
Orr, Alexander E., 1904, III
Orthodox churches *see* Greek Orthodox Church; Russian Orthodox Church
Orwell, George, 1984(1), II
Osborn, Charles, 1817 Aug. 29, II
Osborne, John, 1957 Oct. 1, II; 1964 May 24, II
Osborne, Margaret, 1946 July 6, IV; 1947 July 4–5, IV
Oscar awards, 1927(2), II; 1929 May 16, II; 1930 Apr. 3, II; 1930 Nov. 5(1), II; 1931 Nov. 10, II; 1932 Nov. 18, II; 1934 Mar. 16, II; 1935 Mar. 27, II; 1936 May 5, II; 1937 Mar. 4, II; 1938 Mar. 10, II; 1939 Feb. 23, II; 1940 Feb. 29, II; 1941 Feb. 27, II; 1942 Feb. 26, II; 1943 Mar. 4, II; 1944 Mar. 2, II; 1945 Mar. 15, II; 1946 Mar. 7, II; 1947 Mar. 13(2), II; 1948 Mar. 20, II; 1949 Mar. 24, II; 1950 Mar. 23, II; 1951 Mar. 29(2), II; 1952 Mar. 20, II; 1953 Mar. 19(1), II; 1954 Mar. 25, II; 1955 Mar. 30, II; 1956 Mar. 21, II; 1957 Mar. 27, II; 1958 Mar. 26, II; 1959 Apr. 6, II; 1960 Apr. 4, II; 1961 Apr. 17, II; 1962 Apr. 9, II; 1963 Apr. 8, II; 1964 Apr. 13, II; 1965 Apr. 5, II; 1966 Apr. 18, II; 1967 Apr. 10, II; 1968 Apr. 10(2), II; 1969 Apr. 14, II; 1970 Apr. 7(1), II; 1971 Apr. 14, II; 1972 Apr. 9, II; 1973 Mar. 27, II; 1974 Apr. 2, II; 1975 Apr. 8(1), II; 1976 Mar. 29, II; 1977 Mar. 28, II; 1978 Apr. 3, II; 1979 Apr. 4, II; 1980 Apr. 14(2), II; 1981 Mar. 31, II; 1982 Mar. 29, II; 1983 Apr. 11, II; 1984 Apr. 9, II; 1985 Mar. 25, II; 1986 Mar. 24, II;

Oscar awards (*cont.*)
  1987 Mar. 30, II; 1988 Apr. 11, II; 1989 Mar. 29, II; 1990 Mar. 26, II; 1991 Mar. 25, II; 1992 Mar. 31, II
Osceola (Indian chief), 1835, I
Osgood, Samuel, 1789 Sept. 26(2), I
Ostend Manifesto, 1854 Oct. 18, I
Osteopathy, 1892(9), III
Osuna, Rafael, 1963 Sept. 8, IV
Oswald, Lee Harvey:
  captured, 1963 Nov. 22, I
  found responsible for Kennedy assassination, 1964 Sept. 27, I
  killed, 1963 Nov. 24, I
  Ruby convicted for murder of, 1964 Mar. 14, I
  Ruby conviction reversed, 1966 Oct. 5, I
Otis, Elisha Graves, 1852, III
Otis, Elwell Stephens, 1899 Apr. 28, I; 1899 Nov. 24, I
Otis, James, 1761 Feb. 24, I
Otterbein College (Ohio), 1849 Feb. 13, III
Otto, Whitney, 1991(1), II
Ouimet, Francis, 1913 Sept. 19, IV
Oursler, Fulton, 1949(1), II
Outcault, Richard F., 1896, II
Outlines of American Political Economy (List), 1827, III
Overland Monthly, The (publication), 1868 July, II
Owen, Laurence, 1961 Jan. 27–29, IV
Owen, Robert, 1803, III; 1825, I; 1830 Dec., III
Owen-Glass Act, 1913, III
Owens, Jesse, 1936 Aug. 5–16, IV; 1980, IV; 1984, IV
Owings, Nathaniel Alexander, 1982 Dec. 2, II
Ozawa, Seiji, 1972 Feb. 2, II
Ozick, Cynthia, 1983(1), II
Ozone layer, 1988, III
  depletion, 1991 Apr. 4, III
  protection treaty ratified, 1988 Mar. 14, III

Paar, Jack, 1960 Feb. 11, II
Pachelbel, Carl Theodorus, 1730–1734, II
Pacific, College of the (Calif.), 1851 July 10, III
Pacific Ocean and Coast:
  first cable communication, 1903 July 4, III
  first Europeans, 1542, I
  first permanent Northwest colony, 1811 Apr. 12, I
  illegal immigration surveillance, 1893 Sept. 7, I
  Wickes's expedition, 1838 May 18, I
Pacific University (Ore.), 1854 Jan. 13, III
Pacifism (*see also* Conscientious objectors; Nobel Prizes—Peace; Vietnam War demonstrations):
  American Peace Society, 1837(1), I
  American Peace Society established, 1828(1), IV
  Civil War, 1860 May 28, III
  Erikson on, 1970 Mar. 2, II; 1970 May 4, II

Pacifism (*cont.*)
  Logan's efforts, 1798 June, III
  Mass. Peace Society, 1816(5), IV
  stance against World War, 1915 Dec. 4, IV
Pacino, Al, 1977 June 5, II
Page, Geraldine, 1967 June 4, II; 1969 June 8, II; 1986 Mar. 24, II; 1987, II
Page, Greg, 1984 Nov. 9, IV; 1984 Dec. 1, IV; 1985 Apr. 29, IV
Pagels, Elaine, 1980 Jan. 7, II
Pahlavi, Mohammad Reza (Shah of Iran), 1979 Nov. 4, I
Pahza di Biumo, Count Giuseppe, 1987, II
Paige, Satchel (Leroy), 1982, IV
Paine, Albert Bigelow, 1912(1), II
Paine, John Knowles, 1875, II; 1880(4), II
Paine, Robert, 1870 Dec. 16, II
Paine, Thomas:
  Age of Reason, 1794(6), II
  Agrarian Justice, 1797(1), II
  Common Sense, 1776 Jan. 10, II
  Crisis, The, 1776 Dec. 19, I
  Rights of Man, 1791 Mar.(1), II
  steamboat subsidy proposal, 1778(2), III
Paint:
  first standard formula for house, 1880(11), III
Painters *see* Art and artists
Pakenham, Edward (Sir), 1815, I
Pakistan:
  U.S. embassy seized, 1979 Nov. 21, I
Palade, Emil, 1974 Oct. 10(2), III
Palance, Jack, 1957 Mar. 16, II; 1992 Mar. 31, II
Palden Thondup Namgyal (Prince of Sikkim), 1963 Mar. 20, IV
Paleontology *see* Fossils
Palestine Liberation Organization (PLO), 1988 Dec. 14, I
Palestinian Liberation Front (PLF), 1985 Oct. 7–10, I
Paley, William S., 1984 Mar. 4, II; 1990, III
  art collection exhibited at Museum of Modern Art (N.Y.C.), 1992 Feb. 2, II
Palfrey, John Gorham, 1858, II
Palimony, 1979, IV
Palmer, Arnold, 1958, IV; 1958 Apr. 16, IV; 1960 June 18, IV; 1962, IV; 1962 Apr. 9, IV; 1963, IV; 1963 June 23, IV; 1964 Apr. 12, IV
Palmer, Erastus D., 1876(10), II
Palmer, Jim, 1990 Aug. 6, IV
Palmer, John M., 1896 Sept. 2–3, I; 1896 Nov. 3, I
Palmer, Nathaniel Brown, 1820(3), I
Palmer, Potter, 1884, IV
Palmer, Robert, 1987 Feb. 24, II; 1989 Feb. 22, II
Palmer, Sandra, 1975, IV; 1975 July 20, IV
Palo Alto, Battle of, 1846 May 8, I
Panama and Panama Canal:
  Act signed, 1912 Aug. 24, III
  act to build passed, 1902 June 28, I
  British-U.S. neutrality agreement on projected canal, 1850 Apr. 19, I
  canal survey, 1867 Feb. 25, I
  civil government in zone, 1914 Jan. 27, I

Panama and Panama Canal (*cont.*)
  Commission appointed, 1904 Feb. 29, I
  Delvalle ousted, 1988 Feb. 5, I
  disease rate decline, 1914(1), III
  first warships to pass through, 1915 July 16, III
  Hay-Pauncefote Treaty, 1901 Nov. 18, I
  inspected by T. Roosevelt, 1906 Nov. 9, I
  need for canal, 1898(3), III
  new treaty agreement, 1965 Sept. 24, I
  Noriega convicted in U.S., 1992 Apr. 9, IV
  Noriega indicted, 1988 Feb. 5, I
  Noriega surrendered to U.S., 1989 Dec. 20, I
  officially opened, 1914, III
  opened to barge service, 1914 May 18, III
  railroad across isthmus, 1855(3), III
  resumed U.S. diplomatic relations, 1964 Apr. 3, I
  revolt, 1903 Nov. 3, I
  severed U.S. relations, 1964 Jan. 9, I
  third locks begun, 1941 Feb. 19, III
  treaties transferring U.S. control signed, 1977 Sept. 7, I
  treaty ratified, 1978 Mar. 16, I; 1978 Apr. 18, I
  U.S. invasion, 1989 Dec. 20, I
  U.S. right of way across Isthmus, 1848 June 3, I
  U.S. sovereignty, 1903 Jan. 22, I; 1903 Nov. 18, I
  waterway across Isthmus completed, 1913 Oct. 10, III
  yellow fever eradication, 1904(1), III
Pan Am Building (N.Y.C.), 1963 Mar. 7, II
  renamed, 1992, I
Pan America *see* Latin America
Pan American Airways, Inc., 1947 June 17, III; 1966 Apr. 13, III; 1991 Jan. 8, III
  midair explosion (Lockerbie, Scotland), 1988 Dec. 21, I
Pan-American Games, 1951 Feb. 25–Mar. 9, IV; 1955 Mar. 12–26, IV; 1959 Aug. 27–Sept. 7, IV; 1963 Apr. 20–May 5, IV; 1967 July 23–Aug. 6, IV; 1971 July 30–Aug. 12, IV; 1975 Oct. 16–26, IV; 1979 July 1–15, IV; 1983 Aug. 14–18, IV; 1987 Aug. 8–23, IV; 1991 Aug. 2–18, IV
Pan-American Union, 1890 Apr. 14, I
Panay (gunboat), 1937 Dec. 12, I
Panfil, Wanda, 1991 Apr. 15, IV
Pangborn, Clyde, 1931 Oct. 5, III
Panics *see under* Banking; Economics and economy; Stocks and bonds
Panoplist, The (newspaper), 1813(1), III
Panoramas, 1846(3), IV
Paolozzi, Christina, 1962 Jan., IV
Paper:
  first mill and watermark (Pa.), 1690(2), III
  machine-made, 1817(3), III
  manila, 1838(1), III
Papp, Joseph, 1973, II; 1991, II
Parent, Gail, 1974 Jan. 27(1), II

Parents and Teachers, National Congress of, 1897 Feb. 17, III
Paret, Kid (Benny), 1962, IV
Paris, Charter of, 1990 Nov. 21, I
Paris, Treaty of, 1760–1764, I; 1783 Sept. 3, I
Paris conference, 1954, I; 1954 Oct. 25, I
Paris (France):
  liberated, 1944 Aug. 25, I
Paris peace talks *see* Vietnam War
Park, Tongsun, 1976 Oct. 20(2), I; 1977 July 20, I; 1978, I
Park Chung Hee, 1976, I
Parker, Alton B., 1904 July 6–9, I
Parker, Dorothy, 1967, II; 1970(1), II
Parker, Frank A., 1944 Sept. 3, IV; 1945 Sept. 2, IV; 1949 July 1–2, IV
Parker, Frankie, 1932, IV
Parker, John, 1775 Apr. 19, I
Parker, Theodore (Rev.), 1841(2), III
Parker, Willard, 1840(5), III
Parkinson's disease, 1970 June 4, III
Parkman, Francis, 1851(4), II; 1865(5), II; 1874(1), II; 1884(1), II
Parks, Bert, 1992, II
Parks, Sam, 1935 June 8(2), IV
Parks and recreation areas (*see also* Amusement Parks; Resorts):
  Boston Common, 1640, I
  Central Park (N.Y.C.), 1850(7), III; 1876(5), III
  city, 1899, IV
  Gramercy (N.Y.C.), 1831(1), II
  National Park Service established, 1916 Aug. 25, III
  Olmsted's designs, 1857, IV
  Rocky Mountain National established, 1915 Jan. 26, III
  Sequoia National, 1890(5), III
  Yellowstone National, 1872(2), IV
  Yosemite National, 1890(5), III
Park Street Church (Boston, Mass.), 1810(1), II
Parnis, Mollie, 1992, IV
Parochial schools:
  nativism movement against state-supported, 1841, III
  public school teachers banned from, 1985 July 1, III
  state-aid programs unconstitutional, 1973 June 25, III
  state programs ruled unconstitutional, 1971 June 28, III
Parrish, Maxfield, 1966, II
Parson Capen House (Topsfield, Mass.), 1683, II
Parsons, Estelle, 1968 Apr. 10(2), II
Parsons, Talcott, 1979, III
Partch, Harry, 1969 Jan. 9, II
Partnerships, 1984 May 22, I
Pascal, John and Fran, 1968 Apr. 10(1), II
Pass, Albert, 1972 Mar. 1(2), III
Pastor, Antonio (Tony), 1861, IV
Pastorius, Francis Daniel, 1683 Oct. 6, I; 1690(1), III; 1697(1), III
Patch, Sam, 1829 Nov. 13, IV
Patchen, Kenneth, 1972, II
Pate, Jerry, 1976 June 20, IV
Patent medicines *see* Medicine

Patents:
  aviation litigation settled, 1914 Jan. 13, III
  barbed wire, 1873 Oct. 27, III
  billiard ball, 1865(3), IV
  brass bowls, 1851 Dec. 16, III
  celluloid, 1870 July 12, III
  Chinese agreement to honor, 1992 Jan. 16, I
  cigar-rolling machine, 1883 Feb. 27, III
  coin-operated vending machine, 1929 Nov., III
  Colt revolver, 1833, III
  condensed milk, 1856(6), III
  continuous-roll printing press, 1863 Apr. 14, III
  De Forest's, 1923, III
  electric flatiron, 1882(4), III
  evaporated milk, 1853 May, III
  first colonial (Mass.), 1641 Oct., III
  first electric shaver, 1923 Nov. 6, III
  first for higher form of life, 1988 Apr. 12, II
  first gasoline-driven auto, 1895 June 11, III
  first issued, 1790 July 31, III
  first law passed, 1790 Apr. 10(1), I
  first laws, 1809(2), III
  first machinery, 1640–1649, III
  first movie camera, 1891 Aug. 24, III
  first practical paper-folding machine, 1856 Oct. 7, III
  first sewing machine with eye-pointed needle, 1846 Sept. 10, III
  5,000,000th issued, 1991, III
  gas engine, 1844 May 25, III
  gasoline-driven auto, 1879 May 8, III; 1895 Nov. 5, III
  genetically engineered organisms allowed, 1987 Apr. 16, III
  genetically engineered organisms upheld, 1980 June 16, III
  hollow tile design, 1871(4), II
  horseshoe manufacturing machine, 1835 Nov. 23, III
  ice-maker, 1851 May 6, III
  largest infringement award to date, 1990 Oct. 12, III
  Linotype automatic typesetting machine, 1884(5), III
  manila paper, 1838(1), III
  nylon, 1938(4), III
  plows, 1813, III
  pneumatic hammer, 1890(3), III
  Polaroid camera, 1948(4), III
  postmarking and stamp-canceling machine, 1857(1), III
  reapers, 1834(3), III
  refrigerated car, 1868 Jan. 16, III
  safety pin, 1849(2), III
  Selden (auto), 1895 Nov. 5, III
  sewing machine, 1857 June 2, III
  sewing machine (Singer), 1851 Aug. 12, III
  steam calliope, 1855 Oct. 9, II
  steel processing, 1857, III
  stereoscope, 1863 Dec. 1, III
  telegraph, 1835(2), III; 1837 Sept., III
  telephone, 1876 Mar. 7, III

Patents (*cont.*)
  thresher fanning mill, 1837 Dec. 29, III
  typewriter, 1829 July 23, III; 1867(9), III; 1868 June 23, III
  U.S. Office opened, 1790 July 31, III
  vacuum cleaner, 1869 June 8, III
  Velox papers, 1893(2), III
  vulcanization of rubber, 1844, III
  wireless telegraphy, 1891 Dec. 29, III
  zipper, 1893(3), III
Patman, Wright, 1975 Jan. 16, I
Patrick, John, 1954 May 3, II
Patrick, Ted, 1974 Aug. 31, III
Patriotism, 1831, II
Patterson, Floyd, 1956 Nov. 30, IV; 1957, IV; 1958, IV; 1959, IV; 1960, IV; 1960 June 20, IV; 1961, IV; 1961 Dec. 4, IV; 1962 Sept. 25, IV; 1963 July 22, IV; 1965 Nov. 22, IV
Patterson, Orlando, 1991 Nov. 20, II
Patti, Adelina, 1859, II
Patton, George S., 1943 July 10, I; 1945, I
Patty, Budge, 1950 July 7, IV; 1957 July 6, IV
Paul, Wolfgang, 1989 Oct. 12(2), III
Paulding, James Kirke, 1807 Jan.24, II; 1813(4), II; 1817(2), IV; 1835(2), II; 1836(5), II
Pauling, Linus, 1954 Nov. 3, III; 1958 Apr. 28, III; 1963 Oct. 10, III; 1970 Nov. 18, III
Paul VI, Pope, 1965 Oct. 4, I
Pavin, Corey, 1991, IV
Pavlova, Anna, 1916, II
Paxinou, Katina, 1944 Mar. 2, II
Payne, John Howard, 1818, II; 1823 May 8, II; 1824 May 27, II
Payne-Aldrich Tariff Act, 1909, I
Payne's Landing, Treaty of, 1832 May 9, I
Payola, 1960 Jan. 25, II; 1960 Apr. 29, II; 1960 May 19, II
Payson, Joan Whitney, 1975, IV
Payson, John Whitney, 1987 Nov. 11, II
PCBs (polychlorinated biphenyls), 1976 Sept. 28, III
Peabody, Elizabeth Palmer, 1860, III
Peabody Museum (Cambridge, Mass.), 1979 Feb. 9(1), II
Peace *see* Arms control and disarmament; Nobel Prizes—Peace; Pacifism
Peace Corps:
  plans revealed, 1961 Jan. 28, III
  withdrawn from Indonesia, 1965 Mar. 4, I
Peachtree Plaza (Atlanta, Ga.), 1975 Oct. 2, II
Peale, Charles Willson, 1772, II; 1794(1), III; 1805(1), II; 1806(3), II; 1809(2), II
Peale, Norman Vincent, 1949(1), II
Peale, Rembrandt, 1985, II
Pea Ridge, Battle of (Ark.), 1862 Mar. 6–7, I
Pearl Harbor (Hawaii):
  Japanese attack, 1941, I; 1941, IV; 1941 Dec. 7, I
  leased by U.S., 1887 Jan. 20, I
Pearson, Drew, 1969, II
Peary, Robert E., 1909 Apr. 6, I; 1909 Sept. 1, I; 1989 Dec. 11, III

Peck, Gregory, 1963 Apr. 8, II
Pedersen, Charles J., 1987 Oct. 14, III; 1989, III
Peerce, Jan, 1984, II
Pegasus 1 (weather satellite), 1965 Feb. 16, III
Pei, I. M., 1978 June 1, II
Peirce, Charles Sanders, 1876(9), III; 1890, III
Pelé (Arantes do Nascimento, Edson), 1975 June 3(1), IV; 1977, IV
Pelham, Peter, 1751 Dec., II
Pellagra, 1915(2), III
Pelotte, Donald E., 1986 May 6, III
Penal code *see* Prisons and prisoners
Pencils *see* Pens and pencils
Pender, Paul, 1960, IV
Pendleton, George H., 1864 Aug. 29, I
Pendleton Act, 1883, I
Penicillin:
  large-scale production, 1941(1), III; 1943(1), III
  uses, 1944(1), III
Penmanship, 1864 May 16, IV
Penn, Thomas, 1737, I
Penn, William:
  awarded Del., 1682 Aug. 24, I
  Charles II charter grant, 1681 Mar. 4, I
  church-state separation, 1677(1), III
  frame of Government, 1682 May 5, I
  liquor excise tax, 1684, III
  Phila. laid out, 1681 July 11, III; 1682(2), I
  real estate transaction regulation, 1681 July 11, III
  writings, 1680–1689, III; 1681(1), II; 1687, II
Penn Central Railroad:
  bankruptcy, 1970 June 21, III
Pennel, John, 1963 Aug. 24(2), IV
Penney, J. C., 1971, III
Penn Square Bank (Okla. City), 1982 July 5, III
Pennsylvania:
  abortion law upheld, 1992 June 29, I
  charter, 1681 Mar. 4, I
  Delaware Indians' relations, 1737, I
  first German settlers, 1683 Oct. 6, I
  first state to abolish slavery, 1780 Mar. 1, I
  first Welsh settlers, 1682 Aug. 13, I
  floods, 1990 Apr. 14, I
  Frame of Government (William Penn), 1682 May 5, I
  Lancaster capital, 1790 Dec. 6, IV
  promotional account, 1681(1), II
  second state to ratify U.S. Constitution, 1787 Dec. 12, I
  Swedish and Finnish colonists, 1655, I
Pennsylvania, University of:
  chartered, 1755 June 16, III
  founded, 1749 Nov. 13, III
  medical school founded, 1765 May 3, III
  Wharton School founded, 1881(3), III
Pennsylvania Academy of Fine Arts, 1805(1), II; 1986 June 18, II
Pennsylvania Hotel (N.Y.C.), 1918(6), II

Pennsylvania Railroad:
  chartered, 1846 Apr. 13, III
  electrification (N.Y.C.-Phila., Pa.), 1933 Jan. 16, III
  inaugurated 18-hour train (N.Y.C.-Chicago), 1905 June 11, III
  merged, 1962 Jan. 12, III
  steel coaches, 1906 Aug. 13, III
Pennsylvania Rock Oil Co., 1854 Dec. 30, III
Pennsylvania State College, 1854(3), III
Pennsylvania Station (N.Y.C.):
  demolished, 1963 Mar. 7, II
  opened, 1910(2), II
Pennzoil Co., 1985 Dec. 10, III; 1987 Dec. 19, III
Penrod (Tarkington), 1914(1), II
Pens and pencils:
  first lead pencils, 1812(4), III
  fountain pen developed, 1883(1), III
  steel pens, 1858(2), III
Pensions (*see also* Social Security):
  first military (Mass.), 1636, I
  first old age (Mont. and Nev.), 1923 Mar. 5, I
  first presidential, 1958 Aug. 25, I
  for presidents' widows, 1882 Mar. 31, I
  private brought under federal regulation, 1974 Sept. 2, III
  retirement age raised, 1978 Apr. 6, I
  Townsend Plan, 1934 Jan. 1, I
Pentagon Papers, 1971, II; 1971(1), II; 1971 June 13, II; 1973 May 11, II; 1973 Sept. 4, I
Penthouse (magazine), 1984 July 23, IV
Penzias, Arno A., 1978 Oct. 17, III
People's Park (Berkeley, Calif.), 1969 May 15, II
People's Party *see* Farmers' Alliance; Populist Party
People's Temple, 1978 Nov. 18, I
Pepper, Claude, 1989, I
Pepsico, Inc., 1988, III
Perón, Evita, 1979 Sept. 25, II
Percy, Walker, 1962 Mar. 13, II; 1980(1), II; 1990, II
Perelman, S. J., 1978 Apr. 10, II; 1979, II
Perkins, Anthony, 1992, II
Perkins, Frances, 1933 Mar. 4(2), I; 1965, I
Perkins, Josephine Amelia, 1839(1), IV
Perkins, Susan Yvonne, 1977 Sept. 10, IV
Perot, H. Ross, 1992, I; 1992(1), II; 1992 Nov. 3, I
Perret, Craig, 1990 May 5, IV
Perrine, Henry, 1833(1), IV
Perry, Antoinette *see* Tony awards
Perry, Frederick J., 1933 Aug. 26, IV; 1934 Aug. 19, IV; 1936 Sept. 12(2), IV
Perry, Gaylord, 1991 July 21, IV
Perry, Harold R., 1991, III
Perry, Matthew C.:
  Japanese relations, 1853, I
  Treaty of Kanagawa, 1854 Mar. 31, I
Perry, Oliver, 1813 Sept. 10, I
Perry, Stuart, 1844 May 25, III
Pershing, John J.:
  Mexico, 1916 Mar. 9, I; 1916 Mar. 15(2), I; 1916 June 16, I; 1932 May 2, II

Persian Gulf (*see also* Gulf War):
  Iranian jetliner downed, 1988 July 3, I
  Iraqi missile attacked U.S. tanker, 1987 May 17, I
  new U.S. military command in, 1981 Apr. 24(2), I
  U.S. naval attack on Iranian forces, 1988 Apr. 18, I
Personal conduct:
  American Moral Reform Society convention, 1837(4), IV
  Conn. Moral Society, 1810(1), IV
  distinctive U.S. habits, 1850(7), IV
  Mass. codes, 1702, IV
  Methodist ban on dancing and theatergoing lifted, 1924 May 27, III
  Methodist bans lifted (N.E.), 1908 Apr. 13, IV
  moral hygiene model set by A. Lawrence, 1837(3), IV
  Plymouth codes, 1621 Dec. 25, IV
  Puritan codes, 1610–1619, IV
  smoking, 1890(2), IV
  Va. codes, 1618, IV; 1619, IV
  women smoking bans, 1904 Sept. 28, IV; 1908 Jan. 21, IV
Personal income *see* Income and wealth, personal
Personal liberty laws, 1851 Feb. 15, I
Peru:
  U.S. diplomatic relations resumed, 1962 Aug. 17, I
  U.S. suspended diplomatic relations, 1962 July 19(1), I
Pesci, Joe, 1991 Mar. 25, II
Pests and pesticides:
  boll weevil first seen (Tex.), 1892(6), III
  cranberry contamination, 1959 Nov. 9, IV
  DDT ban, 1969 Nov. 20, III; 1972 Dec. 31, III
  DDT used for typhus, 1944(1), III
  fruit fly (Calif.), 1981, III
  N.E. caterpillar invasion legend, 1768, IV
  potato bug, 1874(2), IV
  Silent Spring (Carson), 1962(1), II
Peter, Paul, and Mary (group), 1963 May 15, II; 1964 May 12, II
Peterkin, Julia, 1928(1), II; 1929 May 12, II
Peters, Thomas J., 1983(1), II
Petersburg, Battle of (Va.), 1864 June 15–18, I
Petersburg (Va.), 1865 Mar. 25, I; 1865 Apr. 2, I; 1865 Apr. 3, I
Peterson, Donald, 1983 Apr. 4–9, III
Peterson, Val, 1955 Apr. 9, I
Petkevich, John Misha, 1971 Jan. 28–31, IV
Petrillo, James C., 1942 Aug. 3, II
Petroleum *see* Oil and oil products
Petrosian, Tigran, 1971 Oct. 26, IV
Phagan, Mary, 1915, IV
Pharmacy *see* Drugs and drug products
Phi Beta Kappa:
  founded, 1776 Dec. 5, III
Philadelphia Club, 1834(5), IV

Philadelphia Orchestra, 1973 Sept. 12, II; 1979 Apr. 3, II
Philadelphia (Pa.):
  anti-Catholic riots, 1844, I
  capital of new U.S., 1790 Dec. 6, IV
  Centennial of 1876, 1876, IV
  Constitution bicentennial ceremonies, 1987, I
  evacuated by British, 1778 June 18, I
  first black mayor, 1983 Nov. 8, I
  Market Street, 1790(2), IV
  Merchant's Exchange, 1834(3), II
  Mummers' parade, 1876 Jan. 1, IV
  occupied by British, 1777 Sept. 26, I
  planning and site, 1682(2), I
  poor people's riot, 1726, I
  race riot, 1964 Aug. 28, I
  St. David's Day celebration, 1729 Mar. 1, IV
  St. George's Day celebration, 1729 Apr. 23, IV
  survey, 1681 July 11, III
Philadelphia Plan, 1969 Sept. 23, III
Philadelphia Times (publication), 1878(3), II
Philadelphia Troop of Light Horse, 1774 Nov. 17, I
Philanthropist (publication), 1836 Jan., II
Philanthropy:
  Altman's contributions, 1865(10), III
  black education fund, 1882 Apr. 28, III; 1990 Mar. 3, III
  Carnegie Corp., 1911 Nov. 10, III
  Carnegie's hero fund, 1904 Apr. 15, III
  Cosby gift to Spelman College, 1988 Nov. 4, III
  donation record, 1988, III
  donations increased, 1989, I
  first systematic theory of, 1889 June, III
  Foundation executives' salaries, 1992, I
  largest gift made to public college to date, 1992 July 6, III
  largest single donation, 1979 Nov. 8, III
  Lathrop's efforts, 1896 Sept., III
  Rockefeller projects, 1913 May 14, III
  total contributions rose, 1992, I
Philately *see* Stamp collecting
Philip Morris Companies Inc., 1988 Oct. 30, III
Philippine Government Act, 1902 July 1, I
Philippines:
  amnesty granted to insurgents, 1900 June 21, I
  Bataan fell, 1942 Apr. 9, I
  Chinese Exclusion Act, 1902 Apr. 29, I
  Corregidor fell, 1942 May 6, I
  Death March, 1942 Apr. 10, I
  first U.S. troops sent, 1898 May 25(2), I
  Government Act passed, 1902 July 1, I
  independence, 1934 Mar. 24, I; 1946 July 4, I
  insurgent Aguinaldo captured, 1901 Mar. 23, I

Philippines (*cont.*)
  Isla Grande occupied by U.S., 1898 July 8, I
  Japanese victories, 1942, I
  Japan invaded, 1941 Dec. 10, I
  liberated, 1945 July 5, I
  MacArthur left Bataan, 1942 Mar. 17, I
  MacArthur returned, 1944 Oct. 20, I
  Malate assaulted by Spain, 1898 July 31, I
  Malolos occupied by U.S., 1899 Mar. 30, I
  Manila Bay battle, 1898 May 1, I
  Manila occupied, 1942 Jan. 2, I
  Marcos charges, 1990 July 2, IV
  Marcos forced out, 1986, I
  Marcos indictments, 1988 Oct. 21, I; 1988 Oct. 21, III
  rebellion against U.S., 1899 Feb. 4, I; 1899 Apr. 28, I; 1899 Nov. 24, I
  rebellion ended, 1901 Apr. 19, I
  U.S. acquisition, 1898, I; 1899 Feb. 10, I
  U.S. base closed, 1991 Dec. 27, I
  U.S. landed on Luzon, 1945 Jan. 9, I
  U.S. military bases, 1988 Oct. 17, I
  U.S.-Spanish agreement, 1898 Aug. 12, I
Philipsborough (N.Y.), 1693(4), IV
Phillips, Eleazar, 1710, II
Phillips, Kevin, 1990(1), II
Phillips, Wendell, 1837 Dec. 8, I; 1851(3), IV; 1852 Jan. 28, IV
Phillips, Willard, 1828(2), III
Philosophy:
  Dewey's pragmatism, 1920(4), III
  first professorship, 1717, III
  Niebuhr's *Nature and Destiny of Man*, 1941(2), III
  pragmatism, 1876(9), III
  rationalism, 1756, III; 1782(2); 1797(1), II
  Santayana's works, 1896(1), II; 1940(5), III
Phipps, William, 1687 June 28, IV
Phonographs *see* Recording equipment
Phosphorus, 1979 Oct. 16(1), III
Photography (*see also* Daguerrotypes; Motion pictures):
  Brownie Box Camera, 1900(5), IV
  celestial, 1892(11), III
  celluloid patented, 1870 July 12, III
  deaths, 1991, II; 1991, III
  disc camera, 1982, III
  first aerial reconnaissance, 1862(3), III
  first equipment in U.S., 1839(1), III
  first of moon, 1840(6), III; 1876(2), III
  first of solar spectrum, 1876(2), III
  first of sun, 1891(4), III
  first pocket Kodak, 1880(9), III
  first successful roll film, 1880(9), III
  Kodak camera introduced, 1888(5), III
  Kodak patent infringement of Polaroid, 1990 Oct. 12, III
  Mapplethorpe obscenity allegations, 1989 June 13, II; 1990 Apr. 7, II
  as pastime, 1900(5), IV
  Polaroid Land Camera, 1948(4), III

Photography (*cont.*)
  wireless transmission (London-N.Y.),
    1924 Nov. 30, III
Phrases, popular *see* Languages
Phrenology, 1832(1), III; 1834, III; 1838(4),
  IV; 1846(3), IV
Phyfe, Duncan, 1780–1784, IV
Physical education, 1826(1), IV; 1829, III
Physical fitness *see* Exercise
Physicians for Prevention of Nuclear War,
  1985 Oct. 11, I
Physick, Philip Syng, 1807, III
Physics (*see also* Atoms; Nobel Prizes):
  atomic, 1932, III
  Einstein's theory tested, 1971, III
  high-pressure discoveries, 1946 Nov.
    14(1), III
  history of Einstein and Infeld, 1938(2),
    III
  light velocity measurement, 1878(2),
    III
  nuclear, 1936 Nov. 12, III
  relativity theory, 1921 Apr. 2, III
  superconductive higher-temperature
    alloys produced, 1986 Dec. 31(1), III
  superconductivity theory, 1972 Oct.
    20(1), III
Physiology *see* Nobel Prizes
Picard, Henry, 1938 Apr. 4, IV; 1939 July
  17, IV
Picasso, Pablo, 1957(3), II; 1967 Apr. 26,
  II; 1967 Aug. 15, II; 1967 Oct. 11, II;
  1980, II; 1981, II; 1981 Sept. 10, II
  record auction prices, 1989 Nov. 30, II
Piccard, Jacques, 1960 Jan 7(1), III
Pickering, John, 1816, II; 1816(1), III
Pickering, Timothy, 1809, I
Pickett, George E., 1863 July 1–3, I; 1865
  Apr. 1, I
Pickford, Mary, 1930 Apr. 3, II; 1979, II
Picon, Molly, 1992, II
Pierce, Dickey, 1866(4), IV
Pierce, Franklin:
  died, 1869 Oct. 8, I
  elected president, 1852 Nov. 2, I
  inaugurated as president, 1853 Mar. 4,
    I
  presidential nomination, 1852 June
    1–6, I
Pierce, Joanne E., 1972 July 7(1), IV
Pierce, William, 1638(3), II
Pierpont, John, 1825(2), II
Pierpont Morgan Library (N.Y.C.), 1973
  Dec. 11, II; 1977 Nov. 18, II; 1979 July
  16, II; 1984 May 8, II
Pike, James A., 1969, III
Pike, Zebulon, 1806 July 15, I; 1813 Apr.
  27, I
Pike's Peak (Colo.), 1806 July 15, I; 1858,
  IV
Pilgrims *see* Congregational Church;
  Massachusetts Bay Colony; New
  England; Plymouth Colony
Pilgrim's Progress, The (Bunyan), 1681(2),
  II
Pinckney, Charles Cotesworth, 1795–1799,
  I; 1798 June 18, IV
Pinckney, Thomas, 1792 Jan. 12, I
Pine, David A., 1952 Apr. 29, III
Pine, Robert Edge, 1784(1), II

Ping-Pong, 1971, IV; 1971 Apr. 10–14, IV
Pins, 1832(3), III; 1849(2), III
Pintard, John, 1804(1), III
Pinter, Harold, 1961 Oct. 4, II; 1967 Jan.
  5, II; 1967 Mar. 26, II
Pioneer Project, 1958 Oct. 11, III; 1960
  Mar. 11, III; 1972 Mar. 2, III; 1973 Apr.
  5, III; 1978 May 20, III; 1978 Aug. 8, III;
  1979 Sept. 1, III; 1992 Oct. 9(2), III
Pioneers *see* Colonies and settlements;
  Covered wagons; Frontier; Westward
  expansion; state names
Pipes *see* Smoking
Pirandello, Luigi, 1922 Oct. 30(2), II
Pirates and privateering (*see also*
  Tripolitan War; War of 1812):
  Algerian, 1815 June 30, I
  Captain Kidd, 1699 Spring, IV
  first reports (Me.), 1632, IV
  Lafitte, 1815(3), IV
  steps to end, 1715–1719, IV
Piston, Walter, 1933(1), II; 1938 May, II;
  1944 Mar. 5, II; 1945 June 2, II; 1955, II;
  1976, II
Pitcher, Moll ("witch"), 1813(1), IV
Pitts, Zasu, 1963, II
Plains Indians:
  art exhibit, 1992 Oct., II
Planetariums *see* Astronomy; names
Planets *see* Astronomy; names
Plantations:
  early names (Md.), c1650, I
Plantation system:
  beginning, 1749 Oct. 26, I
Plants *see* Horticulture
Plastics:
  Baekeland's development of, 1893(2),
    III
  macromolecular research, 1974 Oct.
    15, III
Plath, Sylvia, 1966(1), II; 1981(1), II; 1982
  Mar. 12, II
Platt, Orville H., 1901 Mar. 2, I
Platt Amendment, 1906 Sept. 29, I
Playboy Club, 1988 July 31, IV
Playboy (magazine), 1976 Sept. 20, I
Player, Gary, 1961, IV; 1961 Apr. 10, IV;
  1962 Apr. 9, IV; 1962 July 22, IV; 1965
  June 21, IV; 1966 July 9, IV; 1969 Aug.
  17, IV; 1972 Aug. 6, IV; 1974 Apr. 14,
  IV; 1978 Apr. 9, IV
Plays *see* Theater; Theatrical productions
Plaza Hotel (N.Y.C.), 1907(4), II
Plessy v. Ferguson, 1896 May 18, I
Plimpton, James L., 1863, IV
Plowright, Joan, 1961 Apr. 16, II
Plows, 1813, III; 1837(1), III
Plumbing:
  colonial interior water closet (Md.),
    1769(1), II
  first house with running water (R.I.),
    1723(2), II
  first private bath in hotel (N.Y.C.),
    1844(2), IV
  major improvements in home
    facilities, 1880(7), III
Plunkett, Maryann, 1987 June 7, II
Plutonium, 1981 Oct. 8, I
Pluto (planet), 1930 Mar. 13, III; 1978
  June 22, III

Plymouth Church of the Pilgrims
  (Brooklyn, N.Y.), 1847(5), II
Plymouth colony (Mass.):
  earliest harvest festival, 1621 Dec., IV
  first exports, 1623 Sept. 10, III
  first history begun, 1630, II
  first ministers, 1624, III; 1629, III
  first Sunday school, 1669, III
  founded, 1620 Dec. 26, I
  Indian treaty, 1621, I
  journal of founding, 1622, II
  united with Massachusetts Bay
    Colony, 1691(1), II
Poage, W. R., 1975 Jan. 16, I
Pocahontas, 1607 Dec.(1), I; 1608, II; 1611,
  III; 1613, III; 1808, II
Poe, Edgar Allan:
  balloon hoax, 1844(6), IV
  "Bells" and *Eureka* published, 1848(2),
    II
  financial problems, 1845 June, II
  first book of poems, 1827(1), II
  first collection published, 1840(5), II
  introduced detective story, 1841, II
  problems and despair, 1847 Jan. 30, II
  Southern Literary Messenger, 1833(2),
    II
  Tales published, 1845 June, II
Poetry (*see also* Bollingen Prize; National
  Book Awards; Pulitzer Prizes):,
  1988(1), II; 1989(1), II
  Aiken's works, 1929(1), II
  Airs of Palestine (Pierpont), 1816(3), II
  Allston's works, 1813(2), II
  American Poetry Review charged with
    discrimination, 1977 Jan. 31, II
  "America the Beautiful" (Bates), 1895
    July 4, II
  Ariel (Plath), 1966(1), II
  Arlington's works, 1916(1), II
  awards, 1954, II
  Bailey's rural frolic description, 1755,
    IV
  "Bells, The" (Poe) published, 1848(2),
    II
  Benét's works, 1928, II
  Berryman's works, 1964(1), II; 1972(1),
    II
  Bradstreet's works, 1650, II; 1678, II
  Brodsky fifth U.S. laureate, 1991 May
    10, II
  Bryant's collected poems, 1832(6), II
  Bryant's poems, 1876(3), II
  Byron's popularity in U.S., 1808(3), II
  "Casey at the Bat" (Thayer), 1888
    May, II; 1988 Aug. 15, IV
  Chicago Poems (Sandburg), 1916(1), II
  Civil War-inspired, 1860, II; 1864(1),
    II; 1864 Oct. 19(2), I; 1865, II
  *Collection of Poems by Several Hands,
    A*, 1744(1), II
  "Culprit Fay, The" (Drake), 1816
    Aug., II
  Cummings's works, 1923(1), II;
    1931(1), II; 1958(1), II
  describing early N.E., 1625, II
  Dickinson's works, 1890(1), II; 1891(1),
    II; 1896(1), II
  Drake's satirical, 1819, II
  Eliot in England, 1914(2), II

Poetry (cont.)
Eliot's works, 1948 Nov. 4, II
Evangeline (Longfellow), 1847(3), II
famous anthology (Hartford Wits),
1793(1), II
"Father Abbey's Will" (Seccomb),
1730(4), II
Fern Leaves from Fanny's Portfolio,
1853(1), II
first collection by a woman (Mass.),
1678, II
Freneau's works, 1788(1), II; 1815, II
Frost received medal, 1962 Mar. 26,
II
Frost's works, 1914(1), II; 1923(1), II;
1928(1), II; 1930(1), II; 1936(1), II;
1939(1), II; 1945(1), II; 1962(1), II
Ginsberg's works, 1961(1), II
Gould's popularity, 1832(5), II
Greenfield Hill (Dwight), 1822, II
Griswold anthology of American,
1842(4), II
on G. Washington's death, 1800(2), II
Hasty Pudding, The (Barlow)
published, 1796(3), II
Hayne's southern, 1860(8), II
Hireling, The (Grayson), 1854(5), II
Holmes's contribution, 1836(6), II
Hughes's works, 1926(1), II
Jeffers's works, 1924(1), II; 1925(1), II;
1929(1), II; 1933(1), II; 1938(1), II
Kunitz's works, 1979(1), II
Lalla Rookh (Moore) popularity,
1817(2), II
Lanier's works, 1878(5), II
Leaves of Grass (Whitman), 1855(4), II
Lindsay's new poetry movement,
1914, II
Lindsay's works, 1923(1), II
Longfellow first American honored in
Westminster Abbey (G.B.), 1882(3),
II
Longfellow's popularity, 1858(4), II
Longfellow's works, 1825, II; 1839(3),
II; 1841(4), II; 1855(5), II
J. R. Lowell's works, 1848(5), II;
1917(1), II
MacLeish's works, 1938(1), II; 1952(1),
II; 1972(1), II
"Man with the Hoe, The" (Markham),
1899 Jan. 15, II
M'Fingal (Trumbull), 1782(4), II
Millay's works, 1920(1), II; 1928(1), II
Moore's works, 1967(1), II
Mouse-Trap printed (Md.), 1728(1), II
Nemerov third U.S. laureate, 1988
May 18, II
Night Thoughts (Young), 1777(1), II
Oakes's Elegy, 1677(2), II
"Ode for the Fourth of July" (Lowell),
1876(4), II
"Old Ironsides" (Holmes), 1830 Sept.
16, II
patriotic, 1798(1), II
Paulding's parody of Scott, 1813(4), II
Plath's works, 1981(1), II
Poe's works, 1827(1), II; 1847 Jan. 30,
II
Poetry magazine founded, 1912, II

Poetry (cont.)
Pope's Essay on Man popularity,
1747(1), II
popular satiric, 1708, II
Pound's works, 1925(1), II; 1960(1), II
Puritan, 1660–1669, II
"Purple Cow" (Burgess), 1895(3), II
Revolutionary War-inspired,
1775–1779, II
Rich's works, 1975(1), II
Riley, James Whitcomb, 1883(1), II
Robinson's works, 1896(1), II; 1897(1),
II; 1910(1), II; 1917(1), II; 1921(1), II
Sandburg's works, 1918(1), II; 1920(1),
II
Seasons, The (Thomson), 1777(4), II
"Sheridan's Ride" (Read), 1864 Oct.
19(2), I
Snow-Bound (Whittier), 1866(1), II
"Spagnoletto" (Lazarus), 1876(5), II
Spoon River Anthology (Masters),
1914 May 29, II; 1915(1), II
Stevens's works, 1923(1), II; 1954(1), II
Strand named fourth U.S. laureate,
1990 May 25, II
Tennyson's Poems, 1842(3), II
"Trees" (Kilmer), 1914(3), II
Van Doren's works, 1939(1), II
Van Duyn sixth U.S. laureate, 1992
June 14, II
Warren first U.S. laureate, 1986 Feb.
26, II
Waste Land, The (Eliot), 1922(1), II
White Cliffs of Dover (Miller),
1941(1), II
Whitman's works, 1859(5), II; 1865(4),
II; 1871(1), II; 1891(1), II; 1892(1), II
Whittier's New England-inspired,
1843(3), II
Whittier's works, 1849(1), II; 1856(1),
II; 1860(7), II
Wilbur second U.S. laureate, 1987
Apr. 17, II
Wylie's works, 1921(1), II
Wyoming Valley (Pa.) massacre:
Campbell on, 1809, II
Pohl, Dan, 1982 Apr. 11, IV
Poindexter, John M.:
convicted, later reversed, 1990 Apr. 7,
I
dismissed from office, 1986 Nov. 3, I
indicted, 1988 Mar. 16, I
testified on Iran-Contra, 1987 Nov.
18, I
Poinsett, Joel R., 1825 Mar. 7, I
Pointer Sisters (group), 1985 Feb. 26, II
Poison gas see Chemical and biological
warfare
Poisons:
cyanide in Excedrin (Seattle, Wash.),
1986 June 19, I
cyanide in Tylenol capsule (Chicaco,
Ill.), 1982 Sept. 29–Oct. 1, I
lead, 1735(4), III
Poitier, Sidney, 1964 Apr. 13, II
Poland:
invaded by Germany, 1939 Sept. 1, I
Soviet intervention, 1981 Dec. 29, I;
1982, I
U.S. special aid, 1989 Apr. 17, I

Poland (cont.)
U.S. trade sanctions lifted, 1987 Feb.
19, I
Polanyi, John C., 1986 Oct. 15, III
Polaris missile, 1962 May 6, III
Polaroid Corporation, 1977 Apr. 26, III;
1990 Oct. 12, III
Polaroid glass, 1932(1), III
Polaroid Land Camera, 1948(4), III
Polgar, Judit, 1992 July 23, IV
Polhill, Robert, 1987 Jan. 24, I
Poli, Gianni, 1986 Nov. 2, IV
Police:
action in Chicago (Ill.) condemned,
1968 Dec. 1, I
Chicago (Ill.) scandal, 1960 Jan. 24, IV
first mounted (N.Y.C.), 1904 Sept. 9,
III
first (N.Y.C.), 1658 Aug. 12, I
interrogation of suspects rules
tightened, 1990 Dec. 3, I
Los Angeles (Calif.) riots, 1992 Apr.
29, IV
N.Y.C. corruption, 1894 Jan. 30, I;
1894 Dec. 14, I
strike (Boston, Mass.), 1919 Sept. 9, III
Police, The (group), 1984 Feb. 28, II
Poliomyelitis see Infantile paralysis
Political parties see names of parties
Political scandals see Scandals; personal
names
Political science:
Burgess and Willoughby's views,
1890(4), III
Politics see Elections; Government and
politics; Presidential elections
Polk, Frank L., 1916 July 28, I
Polk, James K.:
born, 1795 Nov. 2, I
dark horse presidential nomination,
1844 May 27–29, I
elected president, 1844 Dec. 4, I
fifty-four forty campaign issue,
1844(1), IV
inaugurated, 1845 Mar. 4, I
Mexican War, 1846, I; 1846 Jan., I;
1846 Sept. 25, I; 1847 Apr. 15, I
Pollard, Ann, 1721(1), II
Pollitt, Katha, 1983 Jan. 27, II
Pollock, Jackson, 1943(6), II; 1956, II; 1973
Sept. 21, II; 1976 Oct. 6, II; 1988 May 2,
II; 1989 Nov. 30, II
Pollock, Lee Krasner, 1984, II
Polls see Public opinion
Poll tax see Voting rights
Pollution:
air quality controls, 1970 Dec. 31, III
Clean Air Act signed, 1990 Nov. 15, I
Clean Water Act, 1987 Feb. 4, I
EPA's standards for water upheld,
1977 Feb. 23, III
Love Canal disaster area (N.Y.), 1978
Aug. 7, I
oceanic control international
agreement, 1972 Nov. 13, III; 1990
Nov. 1, I
oil spill (Alaska), 1989 Mar. 24, I
oil spill (Calif.), 1990 Jan. 2–Sept. 27, I
oil spill (Mass.), 1976 Dec. 15, III
oil spill (Pa.-Ohio), 1988 Jan. 2, I

Pollution (*cont.*)
    oil spills (N.Y.-N.J.), 1990 Jan. 2–Sept. 27, I
    ozone, 1988, III
    sea dumping banned, 1990 Nov. 1, I
    Toxic Substances Control Act, 1976 Sept. 28, III
    Water Control Act, 1972 Oct. 18, III
Pollyanna (book and term), 1913(1), II
Polo, 1876(1), IV; 1886(2), IV
Polygamy:
    Edmunds Act suppressing, 1882 Mar. 22, I
    federal legislation against, 1862 July 1(2), I
    Mormons abolished, 1887(1), III; 1890 Oct. 6, III
    Oneida (N.Y.) colony, 1848, III
    sanctioned by Smith, 1843 July 12, IV
    Utah case, 1943 Dec. 4, IV
Pomerance, Bernard, 1979 Apr. 19, II
Ponce de León, Juan, 1513 Apr. 2, I
Pons, B. Stanley, 1989 Mar. 23, III
Pons, Lily, 1976, II
Ponselle, Rosa, 1981, II
Pontiac's Rebellion, 1763 May 7, I; 1763 June 2, I; 1763 Aug. 5, I
Pontormo, Jacopo, 1989 Nov. 30, II
Pony Express, 1860 Apr. 3, III; 1861, III
Poole, F. W., 1876 Oct. 6, III
Poor *see* Poverty
Poor People's March (Wash., D.C.), 1968 May 2, I; 1968 June 24, I
Poor relief *see* Welfare
Poor Richard's Almanack (Franklin), 1690–1699, II; 1732 Dec. 19, II; 1734(1), IV; 1739, IV; 1747, IV; 1758, IV
Pope, Alexander, 1747(1), II
Popsicles, 1986, IV
Popular Science Monthly (publication), 1872, II
"Popular sovereignty" (*see also* Kansas-Nebraska Act):, 1854, I; 1854(1), IV
Population:
    Asian-American, 1991, I
    birth rate below zero growth, 1973 Mar. 1(2), IV
    black, 1810(1), I; 1860(1), I
    center, 1820(1), I; 1830(1), I; 1840(1), I; 1850(1), I; 1860(1), I; 1870(1), I; 1880(1), I; 1890(1), I; 1900(2), I; 1910(1), I; 1920(1), I; 1930(1), I; 1940(1), I; 1950(1), I
    colonial, 1610–1619(1), I; 1620–1629(1), I; 1630–1639(1), I; 1640–1649(1), I; 1650–1659(1), I; 1660–1669(1), I; 1670–1679(1), I; 1680–1689(1), I; 1690–1699(1), I; c1700, I; 1710–1714(1), I; 1720, I; 1730–1734(1), I; 1740–1744(1), I; 1750–1754(1), I; 1760–1764(1), I; 1770–1774(1), I; 1780, I
    colonial slave, 1725, I
    farm, 1910(1), III
    fourth Census, 1820(1), I
    growth rate slowed, 1965, I
    Hispanic-American, 1987, I; 1988 Sept. 6, I; 1989, I; 1991, I
    Massachusetts Bay Colony, 1643(2), I

Population (*cont.*)
    Mass. black, 1763(1), I
    N.E., 1730(1), I
    N.Y.C., 1790(1), IV
    N.Y.C. slum density, 1905(1), III
    161,000,000, 1953, III
    recorded, 1800(1), I; 1810(1), I
    rural, 1920(1), I
    shift, 1800(1), I; 1810(1), I; 1960 Nov. 15, I; 1980, I; 1984, I; 1991, I
    slave, 1800(1), I
    statistics, 1830(1), I; 1840(1), I; 1860(1), I; 1870(1), I; 1880(1), I; 1890(1), I; 1900(2), I; 1910(1), I; 1920(1), I; 1930(1), I; 1940(1), I; 1950(1), I; 1960 Feb. 24, I; 1967 Nov. 20, I; 1970 Apr. 1, I; 1981, I; 1984, I; 1988, I; 1989 Jan. 31, I; 1990, I; 1991, I
    for 31 states, 1850(1), I
    urban growth, 1835, IV
Populist Party:
    middle-of-the-road presidential ticket, 1900 May 10, I
    presidential campaign issues, 1892, I
    presidential ticket, 1892 July 4–5, I; 1896 July 25, I; 1904 July 4–5, I; 1908 Apr. 2–3, I
    started, 1891 May 19, I
Porcelain *see* Pottery
Pornography (*see also* Nudity):
    community attitudes ruling, 1973 June 21, II
    Deep Throat (film) conviction, 1976 Apr. 30, II
    Flynt convicted, 1977 Feb. 8, II
    Forever Amber (Winsor) test case (Mass.), 1946(2), II
    Ginzburg conviction, 1972 Feb. 17, II
    Ginzburg conviction upheld, 1966 Mar. 21, II
    God's Little Acre (Caldwell) ruling, 1933(2), II
    Justice Dept. commission findings, 1986 May 13, I
    Lady Chatterley's Lover (Lawrence) ruled not obscene, 1960 Mar. 25, II
    mailing prohibited, 1873 Mar. 3, I
    Mapplethorpe exhibit controversy, 1989 June 13, II; 1990 Apr. 7, II
    Memoirs of Hecate County (Wilson), Supreme Court hearing, 1948(2), II
    prohibition of private material unconstitutional, 1969 Apr. 7, II
    rally against (N.Y.C.), 1977 Apr. 13(2), II
    "redeeming social value" ruling, 1966 Mar. 21, II
    Tropic of Cancer (Miller) made available, 1961, II
Porter, Cole, 1929 Nov. 27, II; 1934 Nov. 21, II; 1939 Dec. 6, II; 1948 Dec. 30, II; 1955 Feb. 24, II; 1964, II
    birth centennial anniversary, 1991 June 9, II
Porter, Eleanor Hodgman, 1913(1), II
Porter, Jane, 1810(4), II
Porter, Katherine Anne, 1939(1), II; 1962(1), II; 1966 Mar. 15(1), II; 1966 May 2, II; 1980, II

Porter, Rodney R., 1972 Oct. 12, III
Porter, Sylvia, 1991, III
Porter, William Trotter, 1832(3), IV
Porteus, James, 1720–1724, II
Port Hudson, Battle of (Miss.), 1863 July 8, I
Portis, Charles, 1985(1), II
Portland (Me.):
    fire, 1866 July 4, I
Portman, John C., 1977 Apr. 10, II
Portraiture *see* Art and artists; Cameo portraiture; Daguerrotype; Photography
Ports:
    Boston (Mass.) importance, 1749(2), III
    closed to World War II belligerents, 1939 Oct. 18, I
    longest strike to date ended (N.Y.C.), 1969 Feb. 14, III
    longest strike to date ended (West Coast), 1972 Feb. 21, III
    Longshoremen's strike, 1959 Oct. 1(1), III; 1977 Oct. 1, III
    merchant marine strike (Atlantic and Gulf Coast), 1967 June 14(1), III
    strike ended (East and Gulf coasts), 1963 Jan. 26, III
Portsmouth, Treaty of, 1905, I
Post, Marjorie, 1973, III
Post, Sandy, 1968 June 24, IV
Post, Wiley, 1931 June 23, III
Postal Reorganization Act, 1970 Aug. 12, I
Postal Savings Bank system, 1910 June 25, III
Postal Service (*see also* Stamp collecting):
    airmail time (Chicago-N.Y.C.), 1918 Sept. 10, III
    censorship, 1959 June 11, II
    congressional act on delivery, 1836 July 2, I
    Continental Congress established, 1775 July 26, I
    early airmail service, 1920, III
    English patent to found, 1692 Apr., I
    error in commemorative stamp, 1962 Oct. 23, II
    firearm ban upheld, 1975 Dec. 2, III
    first airmail (N.Y.C.-Wash., D.C.), 1918 May 15, III
    first airmail stamps issued, 1918 May 13, III
    first major strike, 1970 Mar. 18, III
    first (Mass.), 1639(2), I
    first official stamps, 1847 July 1, III
    first overland delivery west of Missouri R., 1850 July 1, I
    first penny postcards, 1873 May 1, III
    first postmaster general, 1789 Sept. 26(2), I
    first regular mounted (N.Y.C.-Boston), 1673 Jan. 1, III
    first transcontinental overland mail service, 1858 Oct. 9, III
    first V-mail, 1942 June 22, III
    franking privileges, 1800 Apr. 3, IV
    free delivery, 1865(7), III; 1887(1), III
    free delivery in cities, 1863(2), I; 1873(6), III
    Indian mail carriers (N.Y.C.), 1672, IV

Postal Service (*cont.*)
interception of communist propaganda banned, 1965 May 24, III
Lady Chatterley's Lover (Lawrence) ruled mailable, 1960 Mar. 25, II
motorized mail collection (Ohio), 1899(1), III
number of stamps used, 1922(3), III
obscene literature mailing prohibited, 1873 Mar. 3, I
parcel post authorized, 1912 Aug. 24, I
Pony Express, 1860 Apr. 3, III
postmarking and stamp-canceling machine, 1857(1), III
railroads legalized as carriers, 1838(4), III
rate increase, 1958 Feb. 28(2), I; 1991 Feb. 3, I
rates lowered, 1883 Mar. 3(1), I; 1885 July 1, I
rural free delivery, 1900(1), III
rural free delivery established, 1896 Oct. 1, I
semi-independent corp. inaugurated, 1971 July 1, III
special delivery service started, 1885 Mar. 3, I
stamp series honoring rock and country musicians, 1992 Oct. 8, II
three-cent rates, 1851 Mar. 3, I
transcontinental air test, 1924(3), III
two-cent rate (G.B.-U.S.), 1908 Oct. 1, I
U.S. Postal Service as independent agency, 1970 Aug. 12, I
workers' salary increase, 1955 June 10, III
zone numbering system, 1943 May 5(2), II
Potatoes, 1719, III; 1846(4), IV
Burbank originated, 1872(7), III
Potok, Chaim, 1967(1), II
Potter, David M., 1977 Apr. 18, II
Pottery:
Canton ware, 1785(2), IV
cup plates popularity, 1817(1), IV
first kiln (N.Y.C.), 1730(1), III
first porcelain manufacturers (Phila., Pa.), 1769(2), III
first significant production of chinaware, 1828(3), III
first true porcelain manufactured (Ga.), 1741(3), III
Pennsylvania Dutch kilns, c1733, III
Poultry:
export losses, 1963 Nov. 20, III
Pound, Ezra, 1910(1), II; 1925(1), II; 1949 Feb. 19, II; 1958 Apr. 18, I; 1960(1), II; 1972, II
Poverty (*see also* Welfare):
apprenticeships (Va.), 1646, III
Association for Improving the Condition of the Poor of N.Y.C., 1843(2), IV
Boston (Mass.) steps against, 1835(1), IV

Poverty (*cont.*)
Channing Home, hospital for indigent women, opened (Boston, Mass.), 1857 May, III
Economic Opportunity Act, 1964 Aug. 30, I
growing in N.Y.C., 1840(2), IV
growing rate, 1983, I
Hands Across America, 1986 May 25, IV
homeless class (N.Y.C.), 1850(5), IV
increase in rate, 1992, III
lifestyle, 1887, IV
Phila. (Pa.) riot, 1726, I
public relief (N.Y.C.), 1695(1), IV
public works bill, 1962 Sept. 15, III
Quaker public almshouse (Phila., Pa.), 1732(1), III
right to free legal aid, 1963 Mar. 18, I
Roman Catholic stance on economic justice, 1984 Nov. 11, III
Powell, Adam Clayton, Jr., 1967 Mar. 1, I; 1969 Jan. 3, I; 1972, I
Powell, John, 1947 Apr. 26, II
Powell, John Wesley, 1869(2), I; 1878(3), III
Powell, Lewis F., Jr., 1971, I; 1971 Dec. 6, I; 1987 Oct. 23, I
Powell, Mike, 1991 Aug. 25, IV
Powell, Peter John, 1982 Apr. 27, II
Powell, Susan, 1980 Sept. 6, IV
Powell, William, 1984, II
Powers, Francis Gary, 1960 May 5, I; 1960 Aug. 19, I; 1962 Feb. 10, I; 1977, I
Powers, Hiram, 1851, II; 1868(4), II
Powers, James Farl, 1963 Mar. 12, II
Powers, John R., 1977, III
Practical Navigator, The (Moore), 1802, III
Practice of Piety, The (Bayly), 1665, II
Pragmatism, 1890, III
Pratt, Matthew, 1805(3), II
Pratt, Philip W., 1888 July 27, III
Preakness Stakes, 1992 May 16, IV
Preble, Edward, 1803 May 23, I
Pregnancy and birth (*see also* Abortion; Birth control; Illegitimacy):
artificial insemination scandal, 1992 Mar. 4, III
birthrate below zero population growth, 1973 Mar. 1(2), IV
employment rulings, 1991 Mar. 20(1), I
first surrogate conception, 1984 Feb. 3, III
first test-tube surrogate birth (Ohio), 1986 Apr. 16, III
frozen embryos ruling, 1992 June 1, I
handicapped infant life-prolonging treatment ruling, 1986 June 9, III
Holmes on puerperal fever, 1843(2), III
largest multiple birth, 1985 May 21, III
Rh factor discovered, 1939(1), III
surrogate mother case, 1987 Mar. 31, IV
surrogate motherhood banned (Mich.), 1988 June 27(1), IV
Preminger, Otto, 1986, II
Prendergast, Maurice, 1901(2), II

Presbyterian Church:
Briggs's heresy trial, 1892(4), III
Confession of 1967 adopted, 1967 May 22, III
declared nuclear war immoral, 1988 June 14(2), III
doctrine standardized, 1729(2), III
endorsed nonprocreative marital sex relations, 1960 Apr. 28, III
evolution theory rejected (Tex.), 1924 May 21, III
first congregation, 1611, III
first constructed (N.J.), 1666(1), III
membership, 1900(2), III
merger within, 1982 June 29, III
modified pro-abortion stance, 1992 June 8, III
new statement of faith, 1990 June 5, III
sexual misconduct policy adopted, 1991 June 11, III
women ordained, 1955 May 23, III
Prescott, William Hickling, 1775 June 17, I; 1775 June 17, IV; 1837(1), II; 1843(1), II; 1859 Jan. 28, II
Presidential elections (*see also* Electoral college and vote count; Watergate; personal names):
abolitionist candidates, 1843 Aug. 31, I; 1844, I; 1847 Nov., I
abolitionist party's strong showing, 1844 Dec. 4, I
Adams-Calhoun winners, 1824 Dec. 1, I
AFL-CIO endorsed Kennedy, 1960 Aug. 26, I
Anti-Masonic showing, 1831 Sept. 26, I
Anti-Monopoly Party ticket, 1884 May 14, I
Baker control of Bush campaign, 1992 Aug. 23, I
Barnburners, 1848 June 22, I
Bidwell, John, 1892 June 29–July 1, I
Blaine-Logan ticket, 1884 June 3–6, I
books by candidates, 1992(1), II
Breckinridge-Lane ticket, 1860 June 28, I
Bryan-Kern ticket, 1908 July 7–10, I
Bryan-Sewall ticket, 1896 July 11, I
Bryan-Stevenson ticket, 1900 July 5, I
Buchanan-Breckinridge winners, 1856 Nov. 4, I
Burr-Jefferson tie, 1800, I; 1801, I
Bush-Quayle ticket, 1988 Aug. 15–18, I; 1992 Aug. 19–20, I
Bush-Quayle winners, 1988 Nov. 8, I
campaign and nominees, 1840, I; 1844, I
candidates, 1836, I
Carter campaign, 1976, I; 1979 Dec. 4, I
Carter-Ford TV debate, 1976 Sept. 27, I
Carter-Mondale ticket, 1976 July 14, I; 1980 Aug.11–14, I
Carter-Mondale winners, 1976 Nov. 2, I
Cass-Butler candidacies, 1848 May 22–26, I

Presidential elections (*cont.*)

Chicago Seven acquitted, 1970 Feb. 18, III

Chicago Seven case, 1973 Dec. 4, I

Civil War issue, 1864, I; 1864 Aug. 29, I

Clay nominated, 1844 May 1, I

Cleveland-Hendricks ticket, 1884 July 8–11, I

Cleveland-Hendricks winners, 1884 Nov. 4, I

Cleveland-Stevenson ticket, 1892 June 21–23, I

Cleveland-Stevenson winners, 1892 Nov. 8, I

Cleveland-Thurman ticket, 1888 June 5, I

Clinton-Gore ticket, 1992 July 15–16, I

Clinton-Gore winners, 1992, I; 1992 Nov. 3, I

Communist Party ticket, 1932 May 28, I; 1936 June 24–28, I; 1940 June 2, I

communist support for Wallace, 1948 Aug. 2–6, I

Constitutional Union Party nominees, 1860 May 9, I

Coolidge-Dawes ticket, 1924 June 12, I

Coolidge-Dawes winners, 1924 Nov. 4, I

Cox-F. D. Roosevelt ticket, 1920 June 28-July 5, I

Davis-Bryan ticket, 1924 July 9, I

debates, Mondale-Reagan, 1984 Oct. 7, I; 1984 Oct. 21, I

debates, Nixon-Kennedy, 1960 Sept. 26, I

Democratic Convention violence (Chicago, Ill.), 1968 Aug. 29, I

Democratic N.H. primary upset, 1984 Feb. 28, I

Democratic ticket, 1852 June 1–6, I; 1856 June 2–5, I; 1860 June 18–23, I

Dewey-Bricker ticket, 1944 June 26–28, I

Dewey-Warren ticket, 1948 June 24(1), I

Dixiecrats' ticket, 1948 July 17, I

Douglas-Johnson ticket, 1860 June 18–23, I

Dukakis-Bentsen ticket, 1988 July 18–21, I

easy Republican victory, 1924, I

Eisenhower-Nixon ticket, 1952 July 11, I; 1956 Aug. 20–24, I

Eisenhower-Nixon winners, 1952 Nov. 4, I; 1956 Nov. 6, I

equal broadcasting time ruling, 1964 Oct. 1, II

Farmer Labor Party ticket, 1920 July 13–16, I; 1928 July 11, I; 1932 July 10, I

Farmer-Labor Progressive Party, 1924 June 19, I

Federalist Party's decline, 1816, I

first black delegate participation in major convention, 1872 June 5–6, I

Presidential elections (*cont.*)

first nominating convention, 1831 Dec. 12, I

first reported by telegraph, 1844 May 27–29, I

first third party, 1830 Sept., I

first TV debate between incumbent and challenger, 1976 Sept. 27, I

first woman candidate, 1884(1), I

Ford-Dole ticket, 1976 Aug. 19, I

Foster-Gitlow ticket, 1924 July 10, I

free silverites, 1891 May 19, I; 1896, I

Free-Soil ticket, 1848 Aug. 9, I; 1852 Aug. 11, I

Frémont-Dayton ticket, 1856 June 17–19, I

Garfield-Arthur ticket, 1880 June 2–8, I

Garfield-Arthur winners, 1880 Nov. 2, I

Garfield campaign against Hancock, 1880, I

Goldwater-Miller ticket, 1964 July 15, I

Grant administration scandals, 1876, I

Grant-Colfax ticket, 1868 May 20–21, I

Grant-Colfax winners, 1868 Nov. 3, I

Grant reelected, 1872 Nov. 5, I

Grant's third-term nomination, 1880 June 5, IV

Grant-Wilson ticket, 1872 June 5–6, I

greatest Republican landslide to date, 1972 Nov. 7, I; 1984 Nov. 6, I

Greeley-Brown ticket, 1872 May 1, I; 1872 July 9, I

Greeley's candidacy, 1872, I

Greenback-Labor Party candidates, 1878 Feb. 22, I

Greenback-Labor Party ticket, 1880 June 9, I

Greenback Party candidates, 1874, I

Greenback Party ticket, 1876 May 18, I; 1884 May 28, I

Hancock-English ticket, 1880 June 22–24, I

Harding-Coolidge ticket, 1920 June 8–12, I

Harding-Coolidge winners, 1920 Nov. 2, I

Harrison-Morton ticket, 1888 June 25, I

Harrison-Morton winners, 1888 Nov. 6, I

W. H. Harrison nominated, 1835 Dec. 16, I

Harrison-Reid ticket, 1892 June 7–11, I

Harrison-Tyler winners, 1840 Dec. 2, I

Hayes-Tilden dispute, 1876 Nov. 7, I

Hayes-Wheeler ticket, 1876 June 14–16, I

Hoopes-Friedman ticket, 1952 May 30–June 1, I

Hoover-Curtis ticket, 1928 June 12–15, I; 1932 June 14–16, I

Hoover-Curtis winners, 1928 Nov. 6, I

House decision, 1824 Dec. 1, I; 1825 Feb. 9, I

Presidential elections (*cont.*)

Hughes-Fairbanks ticket, 1916 June 7–10, I

Humphrey-Muskie ticket, 1968 Aug. 29, I

Independence Party ticket, 1908 July 27, I

issues, 1916, I; 1928, I; 1952, I; 1960, I; 1964, I; 1984, I

Jackson-Calhoun winners, 1828 Dec. 3, I

Jackson-Van Buren winners, 1832 Dec. 5, I

Jefferson and Clinton elected, 1804 Dec. 5, I

L. Johnson-Humphrey ticket, 1964 Aug. 26, I

L. Johnson-Humphrey winners, 1964 Nov. 3, I

L. Johnson's landslide, 1964, I

L. Johnson withdrew, 1968 Mar. 31, I

J. Kennedy-Johnson winners, 1960 Nov. 8, I

J. Kennedy nominated, 1960 July 13, I

J. Kennedy's Catholicism, 1960 Sept. 12, I

Know-Nothing antislavery faction ticket, 1856 June 2, I

Know-Nothing ticket, 1856 Feb. 22(2), I

Labor Party ticket, 1884 July 30, I

Landon-Knox ticket, 1936 June 9–12, I

League of Nations issue, 1920, I

Liberal Republican Party ticket, 1872 May 1, I

Liberty Party nominees, 1839 Nov. 13, I

Lincoln carried all free states, 1860, I

Lincoln-Hamlin ticket, 1860 May 16–18, I

Lincoln-Hamlin winners, 1860 Nov. 6, I

Lincoln-Johnson ticket, 1864 June 7, I

Lincoln-Johnson winners, 1864 Nov. 8, I

McCarthy's candidacy, 1968 Mar. 12, I

McClellan-Pendleton ticket, 1864 Aug. 29, I

McGovern-Shriver ticket, 1972 July 10–14, I

McKinley-Hobart ticket, 1896 June 18, I

McKinley-Hobart winners, 1896 Nov. 3, I

McKinley-Roosevelt ticket, 1900 June 19–21, I

McKinley-Roosevelt winners, 1900 Nov. 6, I

Madison-Clinton winners, 1808 Dec. 7, I

Madison-Gerry winners, 1812 Dec. 2, I

major upset, 1948 Nov. 2, I

Me. vote as barometer, 1888(2), IV

Mondale-Ferraro ticket, 1984 July 16–19, I

Monroe-Tompkins winners, 1816 Dec. 4, I; 1820 Dec. 6, I

Mugwump revolt, 1884 June 6, I

Presidential elections (*cont.*)
National Democratic Party (Sound Money) ticket, 1896 Sept. 2–3, I
National Labor Reform Party candidate, 1872(3), I
National Silver Republican ticket, 1896 July 22–24, I
Native American Party candidates, 1847 Sept., I
Nixon-Agnew ticket, 1968 Aug. 8, I; 1972 Aug. 21–23, I
Nixon-Agnew winners, 1968 Nov. 5, I; 1972 Nov. 7, I
Nixon candidacy, 1972, I
Nixon-Goldwater ticket, 1960 July 25, I
Nixon reelection campaign dealings, 1974 Apr. 28, I
Nixon renomination challengers, 1971, I
nomination race, 1959, I
Parker-Davis ticket, 1904 July 6–9, I
parties split on slavery, 1856, I
Pierce-King ticket, 1852 June 1–6, I
Pierce-King winners, 1852 Nov. 2, I
Polk elected, 1844 Dec. 4, I
Polk nominated, 1844 May 27–29, I
Populist Party issues and showing, 1892, I
Populist Party ticket, 1892 July 4–5, I; 1896 July 25, I; 1900 May 10, I; 1904 July 4–5, I; 1908 Apr. 2–3, I
Progressive Party ticket, 1911 Oct. 16, I; 1912 Aug. 5, I; 1924 July 4, I; 1948 Feb. 2, III; 1948 July 23–25, I; 1952 July 4–6, I
Prohibition Party ticket, 1872 Feb. 22, I; 1876 May 17, I; 1880 June 17, I; 1884 July 23, I; 1888 May 31, I; 1892 June 29–July 1, I; 1896 May 27–28, I; 1900 June 27–28, I; 1904 June 29–30, I; 1908 July 15–16, I; 1912 July 10–12, I; 1920 July 21–22, I; 1924 June 5, I; 1928 July 12, I; 1932 July 5–7, I; 1936 May 5–7, I; 1940 May 10, I; 1947 June 26–28, I; 1951 Nov. 13–15, I
public funding, 1974 Oct. 10, I
Reagan-Bush ticket, 1980 July 14–17, I; 1984 Aug. 20–23, I
Reagan-Bush winners, 1980 Nov. 4, I; 1984 Nov. 6, I
Reagan's landslide, 1980, I
reform issues, 1912, I
Republican landslide, 1980, I
Republican Party split, 1912 June 18–22, I
Republican ticket, 1856 June 17–19, I; 1860 May 16–18, I
T. Roosevelt-Fairbanks ticket, 1904 June 21–23, I
T. Roosevelt-Fairbanks winners, 1904 Nov. 8, I
F. D. Roosevelt-Garner ticket, 1932 June 27-July 2, I; 1936 June 23–27, I
F. D. Roosevelt-Garner winners, 1932 Nov. 8, I
F. D. Roosevelt landslide, 1936, I; 1936 Nov. 3, I

Presidential elections (*cont.*)
F. D. Roosevelt third-term bid, 1940, I; 1940 July 15–19, I
F. D. Roosevelt-Truman ticket, 1944 July 19–21, I
F. D. Roosevelt-Wallace ticket, 1940 July 15–19, I
F. D. Roosevelt-Wallace winners, 1940 Nov. 5, I
scandals as issue, 1884, I; 1884(2), IV
second Catholic nominee, 1960 July 13, I
second-youngest to win, 1960 Nov. 8, I
Seymour-Blair ticket, 1868 July 4–9, I
Sherman declined candidacy, 1884 June 5, IV
slavery issue, 1860, I
slogans, 1836(1), IV; 1884, I; 1884(2), IV; 1888(2), IV; 1924, IV
Smith-Robinson ticket, 1928 June 26–29, I
Smith's campaign, 1894(4), II
"smoke-filled room" expression, 1920(1), IV
Social Democrat ticket, 1900 Mar. 6–9, I
Socialist Labor Party ticket, 1892 Aug. 28, I; 1896 July 4–9, I; 1908 July 4, I; 1920 May 5–10, I; 1924 May 11–13, I; 1932 Apr. 30-May 2, I; 1936 Apr. 25–28, I; 1940 Apr. 28, I; 1948 May 2, I
Socialist Party ticket, 1904 May 5, I; 1908 May 10–17, I; 1912 May 17, I; 1920 May 8–14, I; 1928 Apr. 13–18, I; 1932 May 22–24, I; 1936 May 25, I; 1940 Apr. 7, I; 1948 May 9, I
southern Democratic ticket, 1860 June 28, I
Stevenson-Kefauver ticket, 1956 Aug. 13–17, I
Stevenson-Sparkman ticket, 1952 July 26, I
Supreme Ct. rulings on Campaign Act, 1976 Jan. 30, I
Taft candidacy, 1908, I
Taft-Sherman ticket, 1908 June 16–20, I; 1912 June 18–22, I
Taft-Sherman winners, 1908 Nov. 3, I
tariff issue, 1888, I
Taylor-Fillmore ticket, 1848 June 7–9, I
Taylor-Fillmore winners, 1848 Nov. 7, I
Tilden-Hayes dispute, 1877, I
Tilden-Hendricks ticket, 1876 June 27–28, I
"Tippecanoe and Tyler too", 1836(1), IV
Truman-Barkley ticket, 1948 July 15, I
Truman-Barkley winners, 1948 Nov. 2, I
Truman lambasted Nixon, 1960 Oct. 10–12, I
TV debates, 1960 Sept. 26, I; 1976 Sept. 27, I; 1984 Oct. 7, I; 1984 Oct. 21, I
Tyler nominated, 1844 May 27, I

Presidential elections (*cont.*)
uniform day set by Congress, 1845 Jan. 23, I
Union Party ticket, 1936 June 19, I
Van Buren-Adams candidacy, 1848 Aug. 9, I
Van Buren-Dodge candidacy, 1848 June 22, I
Van Buren-R. Johnson winners, 1836 Dec. 7, I
vice presidential debate, Bush-Ferraro, 1984 Oct. 11, I
Vietnam War issue, 1968, I
Wallace-LeMay ticket, 1968 Oct. 3, I
Wallace withdrew candidacy, 1964 July 19, I
Webster's Whig candidacy, 1835 Jan.(1), I
Whig candidates, 1839 Dec. 4–7, I; 1856 Sept. 17, I
Whig ticket, 1852 June 16–21, I
White's candidacy, 1835 Jan.(2), I
Willkie-McNary ticket, 1940 June 24–28, I
Wilson-Marshall ticket, 1912 June 25-July 2, I; 1916 June 14–16, I
Wilson-Marshall winners, 1912 Nov. 5, I; 1916 Nov. 7, I
Workers' Party ticket, 1928 May 27, I
Workingmen's Party nomination, 1872 May 23, I
Presidential Succession Act, 1947 July 18, I
Presidents and presidency (*see also* Electoral college and vote count; personal names):
anti-third-term resolution, 1875 Dec. 15, I
beards and mustaches, 1865, IV
executive authority ruling, 1926 Oct. 25, I
first broadcast of official presidential address, 1923 Dec. 6, III
first filmed press conference, 1955 Jan. 19, I
first foreign trip, 1906 Nov. 9, I
first heard on radio, 1922 June 14, III
first inaugural ball, 1789 May 7, IV
first meeting with Japanese monarch, 1971 Sept. 26, I
first pension law, 1958 Aug. 25, I
first Pope to meet in White House, 1979 Oct. 1–7, III
first to marry in office, 1844 June 26, IV
first to ride in auto, 1899 Summer, IV
first to visit Moscow, 1972 May 22–30, I
first U.S. citizen by birth, 1782 Dec. 5, I
first vice president to succeed to, 1841, I; 1841 Mar. 4, I
Jacksonian era as turning point in, 1829, I
lame duck amendment, 1933 Feb. 6, I
liability ruling, 1982 June 24, I
New Year's Day reception, 1791 Jan. 1, IV
oldest to date, 1981 Jan. 20(1), I
only third term, 1941 Jan. 20, I
pocket veto upheld, 1929 May 27, I

Presidents and presidency (*cont.*)
    proposed constitutional amendments
        on disability, 1965 Jan. 28, I
    style of address debated, 1789 Apr.
        23, IV
    succession, 1933 Feb. 6, I; 1967 Feb.
        10, I
    succession act, 1886 Jan. 19, I
    succession changed, 1947 July 18, I
    Tenure of Office Act, 1867 Mar. 2(2),
        I; 1868, I
    two-term restriction, 1951 Feb. 26, I
    widows' pensions, 1882 Mar. 31, I
Presley, Elvis, 1956, IV; 1977, II; 1987
    Aug. 16, IV
Press *see* Newspapers and publications
Presser, Jackie, 1988, III
Preston, Martin R., 1908 July 4, I
Prevention of Cruelty to Animals,
    American Society for the, 1866, III
Previn, André, 1984 Apr. 29, II
Prewitt, Cheryl, 1979 Sept. 8(2), IV
Price, Leontyne, 1985 Jan. 3, II
Price, Melvin, 1975 Jan. 16, I
Price, Nick, 1992 Aug. 16, IV
Price, William, 1720–1724, II
Price Administration, Office of (OPA),
    1941 Apr. 11(2), III; 1942 Jan. 30, III
Prices and price fixing (*see also* Economics
    and economy; commodity names):
    aluminum, 1965 Nov. 10, III
    ceilings lifted, 1953 Feb. 12, III
    Consumer Price Index up, 1979, III
    controls lifted, 1953 Feb. 25, III
    controls officially ended, 1953 Mar.
        17, III
    domestic oil deregulation, 1978 Apr.
        5, I
    early colonial, 1695(2), IV
    Eisenhower on increases, 1958 Jan.
        20, III
    electrical equipment manufacturers
        guilty of fixing, 1961 Feb. 6–7, III
    food controls removed from, 1952 July
        14, III
    meat price freeze, 1973 Mar. 29, III
    Nixon controls, 1973 July 18, III
    oil controls lifted, 1981, III
    OPA established, 1941 Apr. 11(2), III
    Price Control Bill signed, 1942 Jan.
        30, III
    retail freeze, 1973 June 13, III
    Salem (Mass.), 1633, IV
    shoe (Mass.), 1676, III
    steel, 1941 Apr. 16, III; 1963 Apr. 2,
        III
    steel raise, 1962 Apr. 10, III; 1963
        Apr. 9, III; 1967 Aug. 30, III; 1968
        July 30, III
    steel raise rescinded, 1962 Apr. 13, III
    U.S. Steel and others indicted, 1963
        Apr. 2, III
Priesand, Sally J., 1972 June 3, III
Priestley, Joseph, 1804, III
Prima, Louis, 1959 May 4(2), II
Primaries *see* Elections; Presidential
    elections
Prince, Faith, 1992 June 1, II
Prince (musician), 1992 Sept. 5, II
Princeton, Battle of (N.J.), 1777 Jan. 3, I

Princeton University (N.J.):
    first arts and letters society, 1765(1), II
    founding, 1745–1749, III
    Institute for Advanced Study, 1930,
        III
    invited discussion of football rules,
        1876 Nov. 23, IV
    women admitted to eating clubs, 1991
        Jan. 21, IV
Printing *see* Publishing
Prior, William, 1830(1), II
Prisons and prisoners (*see also* Capital
    punishment; Punishment):
    appeals restricted, 1992 May 4, I
    Attica riot (N.Y.), 1971 Sept. 9–13, I
    Auburn system, 1790(5), IV
    convict importation prohibited,
        1670(2), I
    Cuban detainees' riots, 1987 Nov. 21,
        I
    fire (Ohio State Penitentiary), 1930
        Apr. 21, I
    number of inmates doubled, 1984, I;
        1988, IV
    N.Y. Assn. established, 1844(5), IV
    Pa. reforms, 1790(4), IV; 1790(5), IV;
        1794(3), IV
    population up, 1989, IV; 1991, IV;
        1992, IV
    repatriation of Canadian and Mexican,
        1977 Oct. 28, I
    riots, 1952, IV
    riot (Santa Fe, N. Mex.), 1980 Feb.
        2–3, I
    Soledad (Calif.) escape attempt, 1971
        Aug. 21, IV
    Soledad case (Calif.), 1972 Mar. 27, IV
    three federal penitentiaries
        constructed, 1891(2), IV
Privateering *see* Pirates and privateering
Private schools *see* Education and schools;
    Parochial schools; School desegregation
Prizefighting *see* Boxing
Production Management, Office of (OPM),
    1941 Jan. 7, III
Progressive Party:
    founded, 1911 Jan. 21, I
    issues, 1904, I
    La Follette presidential nomination,
        1911 Oct. 16, I
    platform, 1912 Aug. 5, I
    presidential ticket, 1912 June 18–22, I;
        1912 Aug. 5, I; 1924 July 4, I; 1948
        July 23–25, I; 1952 July 4–6, I
Progressive Republican League *see*
    Progressive Party
Prohibition and temperance movement:
    amendment ratified, 1919 Jan. 29, I
    Anti-Saloon League organized (Ohio),
        1893(7), IV
    beer sale restriction proposed, 1921
        Apr. 25, I
    Bloomer report on drinking contest,
        1850 Apr., IV
    bootlegging, 1921, IV
    bootlegging operation closed
        (Chicago, Ill.), 1930 Feb. 10, I
    burgeoning societies, 1840, IV
    campaign against coffee, 1821(1), IV
    cold water societies, 1836(7), IV

Prohibition and temperance movement
    (*cont.*)
    commentary on dangers of drink,
        1838(5), IV
    Congressional Temperance Society
        founded, 1833(3), IV
    constitutional amendment first
        introduced, 1876 Dec. 12, I
    Eighteenth Amendment passed, 1917
        Dec. 18, I
    first organization, 1826 Feb. 13, IV
    first organized group (Conn.), 1789(2),
        I
    first U.S. law (Tenn.), 1838 Jan. 26, I
    gangsters, 1929, IV
    Giles on alcohol abuse, 1835(4), IV
    Gough's lectures, 1845(2), IV; 1846, IV
    in Okla., 1907 Sept. 17, I
    Me. law, 1851 June 2, I
    Miss. strictures, 1839(2), IV
    N.H. ends total, 1903 May 1, I
    N.Y.S. bill repealing, 1923 May 4, I
    political party organized, 1869 Sept. 1,
        I
    protest against Sunday saloon closing
        (Chicago, Ill.), 1915 Nov. 7, IV
    Protestant ministers' total abstinence
        pledge, 1836(6), IV
    repeal, 1932, IV; 1933 Dec. 5, I; 1934,
        IV
    repealed in Okla., 1959 Apr. 7, I
    Sargent's stories, 1835(2), IV
    selective law enforcement (N.Y.C.),
        1855(5), IV
    Sons of Temperance founded, 1842(1),
        IV
    states adopting, 1910(2), I; 1916(1), I
    Supreme Ct. decisions, 1931 Feb. 24, I
    temperance story vogue, 1837(1), IV
    Temperance Tales (Sargent), 1848(4),
        II
    Temple of Honor, 1845(1), IV
    Ten Nights in a Barroom (Arthur),
        1854(4), II
    upsurge of, 1935, IV
    violence (Kans.), 1900(1), I
    Volstead Act passed, 1919 Oct. 28, I
    Wartime Act, 1918 Nov. 21, I
    Webb-Kenyon Interstate Liquor Act
        passed, 1913 Mar. 1, I
    whiskey medical prescriptions
        allowed, 1923 May 9, I
    Wickersham Commission on, 1931, I
    Woman's Christian Temperance
        Union founded, 1874(1), I
    Worcester (Mass.) enforced, 1908 Apr.
        30, I
Prohibition Party (*see also* Anti-Saloon
    Republicans):
    first convention, 1872 Feb. 22, I
    presidential ticket, 1876 May 17, I;
        1880 June 17, I; 1884 July 23, I;
        1888 May 31, I; 1892 June 29–July
        1, I; 1896 May 27–28, I; 1900 June
        27–28, I; 1904 June 29–30, I; 1908
        July 15–16, I; 1912 July 10–12, I;
        1920 July 21–22, I; 1924 June 5, I;
        1928 July 12, I; 1932 July 5–7, I;

Prohibition Party (*cont.*)
  1936 May 5–7, I; 1940 May 10, I;
    1947 June 26–28, I; 1951 Nov.
    13–15, I
Prokhorov, Aleksandr, 1964 Oct. 29, III
Prokosch, Frederic, 1989, II
Prompter, The (Webster), 1791(3), II
Propaganda:
  interception of communist mail
    banned, 1965 May 24, III
  OWI established, 1942 June 13, III
  Public Opinion (Albig), study of,
    1939(2), II
  World War II plays, 1941, II
Proposition 13 (Calif.), 1978 June 6, I
Prostitution:
  Boston rampage against, 1737 Mar. 9,
    IV
  French in La., 1721, IV
  Mann Act, 1910 June 25, I
  San Francisco drive against, 1917 Jan.,
    IV
Proteins, 1984 Oct. 17, III
Protestant churches (*see also* sect names):
  alcohol abstinence pledges, 1836(6),
    IV
  attendance down, 1974 Jan. 13, III
  black groups, 1816, III
  colonial diversification, 1705–1709, III
  Federal Council of the Churches of
    Christ established, 1908 Dec. 2, III
  first English-language service, 1579,
    III
  first important minister (Mass.), 1631
    Nov. 3, III
  first Indian convert (Va.), 1587, III
  first Indian service, 1646 Oct. 28, III
  first U.S. to affirm, 1987 June 30, III
  liberal-conservative conflict, 1813(1),
    III
  liberalization, 1847, III
  major merger, 1982 June 29, III
  Md. rebellion, 1689 Aug. 1, I
  membership, 1991, III
  New English Bible, 1970 Mar. 16, III
  nine-denomination merger, 1984 Nov.
    30, III
  oldest in continuous use (Del.),
    1698(1), II
  sect membership, 1900(2), III
  social gospel movement, 1885(3), III;
    1889, III
Protests *see* Civil rights; Rebellions; Riots
  and mob violence; Vietnam War
  demonstrations; subject areas
Pryce, Jonathan, 1991 June 2, II
Psychedelic drugs, 1966, IV
Psychology:
  American Assn. formed, 1892(7), III
  behaviorism, 1919(1), III
  Hall's work, 1882(1), III
  James's work, 1882(1), III; 1890, III
PTL (Praise the Lord, or People That
  Love), 1987 Mar. 19, III
Public Broadcasting Service (PBS):
  reorganized, 1979 June 25, III
Public debt *see* Debt, U.S.
Public health:
  first state board (Mass.), 1869(2), III

Public Health Service Hospital (Lexington,
  Ky.), 1935(2), III
Public houses *see* Bars, saloons, and
  taverns
Public lands:
  conservation move, 1909 Sept. 27, III
  fencing of western prohibited, 1885
    Feb. 25, I
  railroad subsidies, 1894, III
  Sioux territory, 1890 Feb. 10, I
  species circular, 1836 July 11, I
Public opinion:
  most admired woman, 1958 Jan. 15,
    IV
Public utilities:
  first electric light company (N.Y.C.),
    1878 Oct. 15, III
  first gas company (Baltimore, Md.),
    1816 June, III
  first municipal electric lighting plant
    (Conn.), 1880(8), III
Public Utilities Act, 1935 Aug. 26, I
Public works:
  appropriations, 1962 Sept. 15, III
  artists and architects, 1933, II
  Federal Works Agency established,
    1939 July 1, I
  minority-owned business preferences
    ruled invalid, 1989 Jan. 23, I
Public Works Administration (PWA), 1933
  June 16(1), I
Publishers' Weekly (publication), 1872, II
Publishing (*see also* Books and literature;
  Censorship; Newspapers and
  publications):,
    1991(1), II
  annuals' vogue, 1826(3), II
  Book-of-the-Month Club begun, 1926
    Apr., I
  Bradford's contribution, 1725–1729, II
  continuous-roll printing press, 1863
    Apr. 14, III
  decline after Revolution, 1782(3), II
  Doubleday purchased by
    Bertelsmann, 1986, II
  emerging book firms, 1806, II
  first book printed (Mass.), 1640, II
  first cheap paperback novels, 1842(5),
    II
  first copyright law (Mass.), 1672 May
    15, I
  first Linotype machine, 1884(5), III
  first paper-folding machine, 1856 Oct.
    7, III
  first presses, 1690–1699, II
  first printing press (Mass.), 1630–1639,
    II
  first printing press (Pa.), 1685, II
  first printing press (Va.), 1682(1), II
  first rotary printing press (Phila., Pa.),
    1846(3), III
  first U.S. edition of Shakespeare's
    Plays, 1796(4), II
  Funk & Wagnalls bought by Reader's
    Digest, 1968 Nov. 2, II
  Government Printing Office
    established, 1860 June 23, III
  Haley sued Doubleday, 1977 Mar. 16,
    II
  hand-press improvements, 1816(2), II

Publishing (*cont.*)
  Harcourt–World Book merger, 1960
    Sept. 28, II
  Holt, Rinehart & Winston established,
    1960 Feb. 29, II
  Hubbard's ventures, 1895, II
  Little, Brown acquired by Time, Inc.,
    1968 Jan. 17, II
  Macmillan-Scribner merger, 1984
    Apr. 25, II
  mergers, 1987, II; 1988, II; 1988 Apr.
    3, II; 1988 Aug. 7(1), II
  Merriam Co. purchased, 1964, II
  oldest continuous operation (N.Y.C.),
    1789(4), II
  paperback sales, 1990, II
  Printers Assn. celebration of
    Franklin's birthday, 1885 Jan. 17, IV
  Random House, 1985 Nov. 26, II
  Reagan autobiography rights highest
    bid to date, 1985 Nov. 26, II
  record book price bid, 1986 Jan. 11, II
  record paperback reprint rights, 1975
    Aug. 1(1), II
  sequel rights sold to *Gone With the
    Wind*, 1988 Apr. 25, II
  I. Thomas's ventures, 1800(3), II
  Time Warner merger, 1989 July 24,
    III
Puccini, Giacomo, 1905 Oct. 3, II; 1910
  Dec. 10, II; 1918 Dec. 14, II
Puckett, Kirby, 1989 Nov. 22, IV
Pueblo incident, 1968 Jan. 23, I; 1968 Feb.
  14, I
Puerto Ricans:
  citizenship status, 1904 Jan. 4, I
Puerto Rico:
  hotel fire disaster, 1986 Dec. 31, I
  Hurricane Hugo damage, 1989 Sept.
    18–24, I
  invaded by U.S., 1898 July 25, I
  made U.S. territory, 1917 Mar. 2, I
  nationalists shot congressmen, 1954
    Mar. 1, I
  Ponce surrendered, 1898 July 28, I
  rejected statehood or independence,
    1967 July 23(1), I
  terrorist independence activities, 1975
    Jan. 24, I
  U.S. acquisition, 1898, I; 1898 Aug. 12,
    I; 1899 Jan. 15, II; 1899 Feb. 10, I
  U.S. victory at Coamo, 1898 Aug. 9, I
Pulaski, Casimir, 1779 Sept. 3–Oct. 28, I
Pulitzer, Joseph, 1868(2), II; 1878, II; 1883
  May 9, II; 1903(4), II
Pulitzer Prizes, 1917 June 4, II; 1918 June
  1, II; 1919 June 2, II; 1920 June 2, II;
  1921 May 29, II; 1922 May. 21, II; 1923
  May 13, II; 1924 May 11, II; 1925 Apr.
  26, II; 1926 May 3, II; 1926 May 5, II;
  1927 May 2, II; 1928 May 7, II; 1929
  May 12, II; 1930 May 12, II; 1931 May
  4, II; 1932 May 2, II; 1933 May 4, II;
  1934 May 7, II; 1935 May 6, II; 1936
  May 4, II; 1937 May 3, II; 1938 May 2,
  II; 1939 May 1, II; 1940 May 6, II; 1941
  May 5, II; 1942 May 4, II; 1943 May 3,
  II; 1944 May 1, II; 1945 May 7, II; 1946
  May 6, II; 1947 May 5, II; 1948 May 3,
  II; 1949 May 2, II; 1950 May 1, II; 1951

Pulitzer Prizes (cont.)
  May 7, II; 1952 May 5, II; 1953 May
    4(2), II; 1954 May 3, II; 1955 May 2, II;
    1956 May 7, II; 1957 May 6, II; 1958
    May 5, II; 1959 May 4(1), II; 1960 May
    2, II; 1961 May 1, II; 1962 May 7, II;
    1963 May 6, II; 1964 May 4, II; 1965
    May 3, II; 1966 May 2, II; 1967 May 1,
    II; 1968 May 8, II; 1969 May 5, II; 1970
    May 4, II; 1971 May 3, II; 1972 May 1,
    II; 1973 May 7, II; 1974 May 7, II; 1975
    May 5, II; 1976 May 3, II; 1977 Apr. 18,
    II; 1978 Apr. 17, II; 1979 Apr. 16, II;
    1980 Apr. 14(1), II; 1981 Apr. 13, II;
    1982 Mar. 12, II; 1983 Apr. 18, II; 1984
    Apr. 16, II; 1985 Apr. 24, II; 1986 Apr.
    17, II; 1987 Apr. 7, II; 1987 Apr. 16, II;
    1988 Mar. 31, II; 1989 Apr. 30, II; 1990
    Apr. 12, II; 1991 Apr. 9, II; 1992 Apr. 7,
    II
Puller, Lewis B., Jr., 1992 Apr. 7, II
Pullman, George M., 1859 Sept. 1, III;
    1867(11), III
Pung, Jacqueline, 1953 June 28, IV
Punishment (see also Capital punishment):
    adulterous woman's (Mass.), 1639(3),
      IV
    adultery, 1782(2), IV
    ducking stool, 1691(2), IV
    early Dutch, 1638(2), IV
    severe colonial (N.Y.C.), 1659 Jan., IV
    for sexual misconduct (Mass.), 1656(1),
      IV
    social differences (Va.), 1623(3), IV
Purcell, Edward Mills, 1952 Nov. 6, III
Purchas, Samuel:
    Purchas His Pilgrimes, 1613, II
Purdue University (Ind.), 1865(2), III
Pure Food and Drug Act, 1906 June 30, I
Puritans see Congregational Church;
    Massachusetts Bay Colony; New
    England; Plymouth Colony
Pursley, Barbara Roles, 1962 Feb. 3–4, IV
Pusey, Merlo J., 1952 May 5, II
Putnam, Gideon, 1802(2), IV
Putnam, Israel, 1775 June 17, IV
Puyallup Indians, 1988 Aug. 27, I
Puzo, Mario, 1969(1), II
Pyle, Ernie, 1943(1), II; 1944(1), II; 1945,
    II
Pynchon, Thomas, 1973(1), II; 1974 Apr.
    18, II

Quack cures see Medicine
Quakers (see also Abolition movement):
    antislavery, 1754, I
    church-state separation, 1677(1), III
    dissenting faction, 1697(1), III
    first annual meeting (R.I.), 1661(1), III
    first significant settlement (N.J.), 1677
      Aug., I
    Flushing, N.Y., meeting house,
      1694(2), II
    humanitarianism, 1732(1), III
    last executed (Mass.), 1661 Mar. 24, III
    Mass. persecution halted, 1661 Sept.,
      III
    Penn charter, 1681 Mar. 4, I
    Pa. colonies, 1620–1629, III
    persecuted in colonies, 1650–1659, III

Quakers (cont.)
    Puritan hostility, 1677(2), III
    slave importation banned, 1696(2), I
Quarry, Jerry, 1969, IV; 1970, IV
Quartering Act, 1765 Mar. 24, I; 1774
    June 2, I
Quayle, Anthony, 1970 Nov. 12, II
Quayle, Dan:
    inaugurated as vice president, 1989
      Jan. 20, I
    nominated as vice-president, 1988
      Aug. 15–18, I
    renominated as vice president, 1992
      Aug. 19–20, I
Quebec:
    French repulsed English, 1690 Oct. 7,
      I
Quebec Act, 1774 June 22, I
Queen Anne's War, 1700–1704, I; 1704
    Feb. 29, I; 1713 Apr. 11, I
Queen Mary (ship), 1936 June 1, III
Queensboro Bridge (N.Y.C.), 1909 Mar. 30,
    III
Quincy Market (Boston, Mass.), 1826(5), II
Quinine, 1944 May 3(1), III
Quinlan, Karen Anne, 1975 Nov. 10, III
Quinn, Anthony, 1953 Mar. 19(1), II; 1957
    Mar. 27, II
Quinn, Daniel, 1991(1), II

Rabe, David, 1977 Apr. 24, II
Rabi, Isidor Isaac, 1944 Nov. 10, III; 1988,
    III
Race riots see Riots and mob violence
Rachmaninoff, Sergei, 1943, II
Racial quotas see Equal employment
    opportunity; Reverse discrimination
Racism, 1991 Jan. 14, III
    criminalizing hate speech/bias crimes
      unconstitutional, 1992 June 22(2), I
    jury selection criteria, 1991 Apr. 1, I;
      1992 June 18, I
Racquet ball, 1863(4), IV
Radar:
    early system, 1938 Nov., III
    early warning system, 1954 Apr. 8, I
    first significant research, 1922(2), III
Radburn (N.J.), 1929(2), II
Radcliffe College (Mass.):
    forerunner established, 1879(4), III
Radiation effects:
    Muller's work on, 1946 Oct. 31, III
    research, 1978 Oct. 17, III
Radio see Broadcasting
Radioactivity:
    following USSR nuclear tests, 1959
      Apr. 5, III
    nuclear fallout danger, 1958 Apr. 28,
      III
Radio-astronomy, 1931(1), III
Radio City Music Hall (N.Y.C.):
    ballet co. disbanded, 1973 June 13, II
Radio Control Act, 1927, III
Radium, 1921 May 20, III
Rafko, Kaye Lani Rae, 1987 Sept. 19, IV
Ragtime see Jazz; Music
Rahal, Bobby, 1986 May 31, IV
Railroad disasters:
    Amtrak (Md.), 1987 Jan. 4, I

Railroad disasters (cont.)
    Cannon Ball express, 1900 Apr. 30,
      IV
    Chatsworth (Ill.), 1887 Aug. 10, I
    derailment, 1978 Feb. 22, I
    Pacific Express (Ohio), 1876 Dec. 29, I
    sixty-six children killed (Pa.), 1856 July
      17, I
Railroad Express Co., American, 1918 May
    28, III
Railroad Rate Act, 1906 June 29, I
Railroads (see also Railroad disasters; Train
    robberies; Transit systems (for
    interurban and commuter)):
    affluence, 1894, III
    air brake invented, 1868, III
    Amtrak started, 1971 May 1, III
    antimerger action, 1912 Mar. 14, III
    Army seizure, 1950 Aug. 25, III
    bankruptcies, 1893, III
    brotherhoods rise of, 1868(5), III
    "Casey" Jones legend, 1900 Apr. 30,
      IV
    Conrail begun, 1976 Apr. 1, III
    contract based on attrition, 1965 Feb.
      7, III
    Crédit Mobilier scandal, 1867(2), I;
      1872(1), I
    deregulation, 1980, III
    eastern system and services, 1855(4),
      IV
    eight-hour act signed, 1916 Sept. 3, III
    eight-hour day, 1917 Mar. 19, III
    Erie, longest line to date in world,
      1851 May 15, III
    experimental electric passenger (N.J.),
      1930 Sept. 3, III
    featherbedding limited, 1972 July 20,
      III
    federal land grant, 1850(11), III
    federal mediation beginnings, 1888
      Oct. 1, III
    federal ownership proposed, 1906
      Aug., III
    federal troops, 1894 July 3, III; 1894
      July 20, III
    financial deals, 1840(4), III
    firemen organized, 1873(2), III
    firemen's jobs ruled unnecessary, 1963
      Nov. 26, III
    first bridge over Miss. R., 1856 Apr.
      21, III
    first charter (N.J.), 1816 Feb. 6, III
    first electric locomotive with gas
      turbine, 1948 Nov. 15, III
    first important tunnel (Hoosac, Mass.),
      1873, III
    first in Calif., 1856(2), III
    first mountain-climbing (N.H.), 1866
      Aug. 29, III
    first printed suggestion for
      transcontinental, 1832 Feb. 6, III
    first refrigerated car, 1868 Jan. 16, III
    first sleeping car, 1859 Sept. 1, III
    first steam locomotive, 1826(1), III
    first transcontinental, 1869 May 10,
      III
    Florida East Coast, 1912 Jan. 22, III
    Gould system strike, 1886(5), III

Railroads (*cont.*)

Grand Central Terminal (N.Y.C.) opened, 1913 Feb. 2, II

growth and largest line, 1900(9), III

Illinois Central opened up Ill., 1856(4), III

initiation of era of, 1828, III

interstate racial segregation banned, 1955 Nov. 25, I

interstate rates, 1906 June 29, I

interstate regulation, 1887, I

labor unions organized, 1863, III

legalized as mail carriers, 1838(4), III

line networks, 1853, III

longest cantilever bridge (Cincinnati, Ohio), 1876(7), III

Morgan's empire, 1894(3), III

National Convention (St. Louis, Mo.), 1875 Nov. 23, IV

National Passenger Corp. established, 1970 Oct. 30, III

nationwide strikes, 1877, III

N.Y.C.-Chicago run time, 1902 June 15, III

N.Y. Central and Hudson River strike, 1890 Aug. 8, III

Panama, 1855(3), III

Penn Central bankruptcy, 1970 June 21, III

Pennsylvania chartered, 1846 Apr. 13, III

Pennsylvania electrification (N.Y.C.-Phila., Pa.), 1933 Jan. 16, III

Pennsylvania-N.Y. Central merger, 1962 Jan. 12, III

Pennsylvania Station (N.Y.C.) opened, 1910(2), II

Pullman cars, 1867(11), III

Pullman strike (Chicago, Ill.), 1894 May 11, III; 1894 June 26, III; 1894 July 6, III; 1894 July 20, III; 1894 Aug. 3, III

Pullman strike injunction (Chicago, Ill.), 1894 July 2, III; 1894 July 3, III; 1894 July 10, III; 1894 Dec. 14, III

rates regulation, 1903, I

refrigerated cars, 1870(8), III

returned to owners, 1944 Jan. 19, III

secret rebates contract, 1872(5), III

segregation, 1878 Jan. 14, I

speed record, 1890 Jan. 23, III

standard time established, 1883 Nov. 18, I

station architecture, 1881(2), II

stations, 1871(5), II

steel coaches, 1906 Aug. 13, III

strike averted, 1948 May 10, III

strike averted by compulsory arbitration rule, 1963 Aug. 28, III

telegraph essential to, 1856, III

Tom Thumb locomotive race with horse, 1830 Sept. 18, IV

track mileage, 1840(1), III; 1880(3), III; 1894, III; 1920(6), III

track width gauge set, 1863 Mar. 2, III

T-rail invented, 1830(3), III

transcontinental, 1862 July 1, III

transcontinental survey authorized, 1853 Mar. 3, I

Railroads (*cont.*)

Twentieth Century Limited, 1905 June 11, III

Union Station (Wash., D.C.) renovation, 1988 Sept. 29, II

Vanderbilt's "public be damned" statement, 1882(3), IV

work-rules arbitration, 1963 Nov. 26, III

work rules modification plan rejected, 1963 July 7, III

Rain (*see also* Floods):

torrential causing mud slides (Calif.), 1969 Jan.-Mar., I

Rainbow Bridge (Niagara R.), 1941 Nov. 1, III

Rainer, Luise, 1937 Mar. 4, II; 1938 Mar. 10, II

Rainey, Joseph H., 1870 Feb. 25, I

Rainier (Prince of Monaco), 1956 Apr. 19(1), IV

Rains, Claude, 1951 Mar. 25, II; 1967, II

Rains, Gabriel J., 1840(4), I

Rainwater, James, 1975 Oct. 17, III; 1986, III

Raitt, Bonnie, 1990 Feb. 21, II; 1992 Feb. 26, II

Raleigh, Walter (Sir), 1584, II; 1585 Aug., I; 1587, III

Rambouillet Decree, 1810 Mar. 23, I

Ramey, Nancy, 1958 June 28, IV

Ramey, Venus, 1944 Sept. 2, IV

Ramirez, Paul, 1976 July 2–3, IV

Ramirez, Richard, 1989 Sept. 20, IV

Ramsey, Norman F., 1989 Oct. 12(2), III

Rand, Ayn, 1982, II

Randolph, Anne Cary, 1809(1), IV

Randolph, A. Philip, 1979, III

Randolph, Edmund J., 1789 Sept. 26(3), I

Randolph, John, 1803(3), IV; 1820 Apr. 12, IV

Random House, 1985 Nov. 26, II; 1988, II; 1988 June 15, II

Ranger (lunar probe), 1962 Jan. 26, III; 1962 Apr. 26(2), III; 1964 July 31, III; 1965 Feb. 17, III; 1965 Mar. 21, III

Rankin, Jeannette, 1917 Apr. 2, I; 1941 Dec. 8, I; 1973, I

Rankin, Judy, 1976, IV; 1977, IV

Ransom, John Crowe, 1964 Mar. 10, II; 1974, II

Rape:

capital punishment unconstitutional, 1977 June 29, IV

judicial leniency in sentencing, 1977 May 25, IV

Tyson convicted, 1992 Feb. 10, IV

Rap music, 1988, II

Rapp, George, 1803, III

Rasle, Sébastien, 1720–1724, I

Ratcliffe, Robert (Rev.), 1686 May 15, III

Rathbone, Basil, 1948 Mar. 28, II; 1967, II

Rather, Dan, 1980 Feb. 15(2), II

Rationalism, 1756, III; 1782(2), III; 1797(1), II

Rationing:

canned goods, 1943 Mar. 1, III

coffee, 1942 Nov. 29, III

food, 1943 Mar. 29, III

Rationing (*cont.*)

gasoline, 1942 May 15, III; 1942 Dec. 1, III

meat and butter ended, 1945 Nov. 23, III

meat ended, 1944 May 3(2), III

rubber, 1941 Dec. 27, III

shoes, 1943 Feb. 7, III

shoes ended, 1945 Oct. 30, III

standby gasoline program, 1973 Nov. 7, III

sugar, 1918 July 26, III; 1942 May 5, III; 1945 Apr. 30, III

sugar ended, 1947 June 11, III

tires ended, 1945 Dec. 20, III

water (Los Angeles, Calif.), 1977 July 1, I

Rattigan, Terence, 1956 Oct. 25, II

Rauh, Joseph L., 1992, I

Rauschenberg, Robert, 1991, II

Rauschenbusch, Walter, 1889, III

Rauson, Edmund, 1639 June 6, III

Ravel, Maurice, 1975 May 15–31, II

Rawlings, Marjorie Kinnan, 1939 May 1, II

Rawlins, Horace, 1895 Oct. 4, IV

Rawls, Betsy, 1951 Sept. 16, IV; 1953 June 28, IV; 1957 June 29, IV; 1959, IV; 1959 July 6, IV; 1960 July 23, IV; 1961 July 1, IV; 1969 July 27, IV

Ray, Elizabeth, 1976 Sept. 1, I

Ray, James Earl, 1968 June 8, I; 1969 Mar. 10, I

Ray, Johnny, 1990, II

Ray, Man, 1976, II

Ray, Ted, 1920 Aug. 13, IV

Rayburn, Sam, 1961, I

Razors *see* Shaving

RB-47 incident, 1960 July 11, I

Reach, Albert J. ("Al"), 1864, IV

Read, Gardner, 1952(3), II

Reade, Charles, 1861(4), II

Reader's Digest (magazine), 1925, II

Reading (*see also* Illiteracy):

whole word teaching method scored, 1961 Oct. 30, III

Reading clubs (Phila., Pa.), 1803(4), IV

Reagan, Nancy, 1981, IV; 1982 Jan. 4, I

Reagan, Ronald:

air traffic controllers' strike, 1981 Aug. 3, III

arms control proposal, 1981 Nov. 18, I

arms control treaty, 1987 Dec. 8, I

assassin Hinckley ruled insane, 1982 June 21, I

autobiography rights sold, 1985 Nov. 26, II

budget approved, 1986 June 27(1), I

budget cuts, 1981 Feb. 18, I

cancer surgery, 1985 July 13, I

Chinese nuclear energy accord, 1985 July 23, I

Chinese trip, 1984 Apr. 26–May 1, I

CIA covert domestic intelligence operations authorized, 1981 Dec. 4, I

Contra aid-arms sale diversion revealed, 1986 Nov. 3, I

Contra aid-arms sale diversion role, 1987 Feb. 26, I

Reagan, Ronald (*cont.*)
    Contra aid bill signed, 1987 Dec. 22,
      I; 1988 Apr. 1, I
    Contra aid request honored, 1986
      Aug. 13, I
    D-Day anniversary celebration, 1984
      June 6, I
    Deaver perjury conviction, 1987 Dec.
      16, I
    deficit reduction, 1987 Nov. 20, I
    "democratic revolution" commitment,
      1986, I
    dismissed Rostow, 1983 Jan. 12, I
    elected president, 1980 Nov. 4, I
    Federal Reserve appointment, 1987
      June 2, III
    free trade agreement, 1989 Jan. 2, III
    German cemetery wreath-laying
      controversy, 1985 May 5, I
    Gramm-Rudman bill signed, 1985
      Dec. 11, I
    Haig resignation, 1982 June 25, I
    inaugurated for second term, 1985
      Jan. 20, I
    inaugurated president, 1981 Jan.
      20(1), I
    landslide presidential victory, 1980, I
    Law of the Sea treaty rejected, 1981, I
    legislation signed, 1983 Nov. 2, IV;
      1984 July 17, I; 1984 Aug. 11, III;
      1984 Oct. 14, I; 1985 Dec. 23, III;
      1986 May 19, I; 1986 Oct. 22, I;
      1986 Nov. 6, I; 1987 Nov. 20, I;
      1987 Dec. 22, I; 1988 Apr. 1, I;
      1988 Aug. 10, I; 1988 Aug. 23, III;
      1988 Oct. 13, I; 1988 Nov. 18, I
    Libyan sanctions, 1986 Jan. 7, I
    lifted nuclear fuel commercial
      reprocessing ban, 1981 Oct. 8, I
    lifted oil price controls, 1981, III
    lifted Polish trade sanctions, 1987
      Feb. 19, I
    lost presidential nomination, 1976
      Aug. 19, I
    Marine withdrawal from Beirut, 1984
      Feb. 7, I
    Moral Majority support, 1989 June 10,
      III
    MX missile proposed, 1982 Nov. 22, I
    national security adviser Allen
      resigned, 1982 Jan. 4, I
    neutron bomb authorized, 1981 Aug.
      10, I
    "new federalism", 1982 Jan. 26, I
    Nofziger lobbying conviction, 1988
      Feb. 11, I
    notice of plant closing law, 1988 Aug.
      2, III
    official biography, 1985 Nov. 26, II
    political criticism of, 1984, I
    presidential candidacy, 1980 July
      14–17, I
    presidential library (Calif.), 1984 Feb.
      14, II; 1991 Nov. 4, I
    presidential reelection campaign,
      1984, I; 1984 Aug. 20–23, I; 1984
      Oct. 7, I; 1984 Oct. 21, I
    proposed budget, 1982 Feb. 6, I
    reelected president, 1984 Nov. 6, I

Reagan, Ronald (*cont.*)
    reprisals against Soviets, 1981 Dec. 29,
      I
    Salvador policy, 1984, I
    shot (Wash., D.C.), 1981 Mar. 30, I
    Soviet grain embargo lifted, 1981 Apr.
      24(1), I
    Soviet relations, 1986, I
    Soviet sanctions, 1983 Sept. 5, I
    State of the Union message, 1981 Feb.
      18, I; 1982 Jan. 26, I; 1984 Jan. 25, I
    strategic arms policy, 1986 May 27, I
    summit conference (Geneva), 1985
      Nov. 20–21, I
    summit conference (Moscow), 1988
      May 29–June 1, I
    summit conference (Reykjavik), 1986
      Oct. 11–12, I
    Supreme Court appointments, 1986
      June 17, I; 1987 Oct. 23, I
    vetoed trade bill, 1988 May 24, I
    veto of Clean Water Act overridden,
      1987 Feb. 4, I
    veto of South African sanctions bill
      overriden, 1986 Aug. 13, I
Real estate (*see also* Housing):
    early transaction regulation, 1681 July
      11, III
    highest price to date (N.Y.C.), 1905
      June 7, III
    ruling against discrimination, 1968
      June 17, I
    women's rights, 1847(2), IV; 1848(2),
      IV
Reapers, 1831, III; 1834(3), III
Reapportionment Act, 1842 June 25, I
Rebellions (*see also* Revolutionary War):
    Bear Flag Revolt (Calif.), 1845 Spring,
      I; 1846 June 14, I
    conspiracy to start racist, 1985 Dec.
      30, I
    Dorr's (R.I.), 1842(2), I
    Shays', 1787 Jan. 25, I
    Whiskey (Pa.), 1794 July-Nov., I
Reciprocal Trade Agreement Act, 1940
    Apr. 12, I; 1955 June 21, I
Reconnaissance plane flights *see*
    Espionage; RB-47 incident; U-2 incident
Reconstruction:
    ended, 1877, I
    ended in Fla., 1877 Jan. 2, I
    ended in La., 1877 Apr. 24, I
    ended in S.C., 1877 Apr. 10, I
    first act passed, 1867 Mar. 2(1), I
    "forty acres and a mule", 1866(2), IV
    fourth act passed, 1868 Mar. 11, I
    Joint Committee established, 1865
      Dec. 4, I
    opposing political views of, 1866, I
    second act passed, 1867 Mar. 23, I
    Southern Homestead Act repealed,
      1876(1), I
    third act passed, 1867 July 19, I
Reconstruction Finance Corporation, 1932
    Jan. 22, I
Recording equipment (*see also* Grammy
    Awards):
    books on cassettes, 1985, II
    compact disc players and discs, 1985,
      II

Recording equipment (*cont.*)
    compact disc sales up, 1987, III
    digital LP records, 1980, II
    drop in record sales, 1979, II
    fastest-selling albums to date, 1962(3),
      II
    first jazz records, 1917(4), II
    Jackson's album sales, 1984, II
    payola, 1960 Jan. 25, II; 1960 Apr. 29,
      II; 1960 May 19, II
    phonograph patent application, 1877
      Dec. 6, III
    phonograph record sales, 1951(3), II
    phonograph's popularity, 1915, III
    record royalties agreement, 1944 Nov.
      11, II
    warning labels on recordings, 1990
      Mar. 29, II
Recreation *see* Games and recreation;
    Parks and recreation areas; Resorts;
    types
Red Cross, American, 1881, III; 1948(7), II
Red Cross, International, 1945 Nov. 12, I
Reddy, Helen, 1973 Mar. 3, II
Red Eagle *see* Weatherford, William
Redel, Donna, 1992 Mar. 24, III
Redgrave, Vanessa, 1978 Apr. 3, II; 1981
    Sept. 13, II; 1984 Nov. 9, II
Redpath, James, 1867(4), II
Reeb, James (Rev.), 1965 Mar. 11, I
Reed, Donna, 1954 Mar. 25, II
Reed, Frank, 1986 Nov. 2, I
Reed, John, 1919(1), II
Reed, Walter, 1901(1), III
Reems, Harry, 1976 Apr. 30, II
Rees, Roger, 1982 June 6, II
Reformed Church, 1725(2), III
Reformed Protestant Dutch Church:
    British toleration (N.Y.C.), 1665 Feb.
      28, I
    education, 1633, III
    established (N.Y.C.), 1628, III
    first minister to preach in English,
      1764, IV
Refrigeration:
    first commercial dry ice, 1925(4), III
    first ice-making machine patent, 1851
      May 6, III
    first important ice shipment from
      N.E., 1805(1), III
    railroad cars, 1868 Jan. 16, III;
      1870(8), III
Refugee Act of 1980, 1980 Mar. 17, I
Refugee Relief Act, 1953 Aug. 7, I
Refugees:
    Cuban, 1980 June 3, I
    Cuban riots, 1987 Nov. 21, I
    last Vietnamese settled in U.S., 1975
      Dec. 20, I
    term *refugee* broadened, 1980 Mar.
      17, I
    World War II, 1948 June 25, I
Refuse *see* Waste Disposal
Regan, Donald T., 1987 Feb. 26, I
Regan, Frank S., 1932 July 5–7, I
Rego, Luis, 1977 Apr. 17, II
Regulatory commissions:
    federal power superseding state, 1903
      Feb. 23, I

Regulatory commissions (*cont.*)
  increased interstate commerce
    control, 1910, I
  interstate commerce, 1887, I; 1906
    June 29, I
Rehabilitation Act, 1977, III
Rehan, Ada, 1874, II; 1887, II
Rehnquist, William H., 1971, I; 1971 Dec.
  10, I; 1986 June 17, I
Reich, Charles A., 1970(1), II
Reichstein, Tadeus, 1950 Oct. 26, III
Reid, Beryl, 1967 Mar. 26, II
Reid, B. L., 1969 May 5, II
Reid, Whitelaw, 1892 June 7–11, I
Reinagle, Alexander, c1790, II
Reischauer, Edwin O., 1990, I
Relay 1 (satellite), 1962 Dec. 13, III; 1963
  Jan. 3, III
Reliance Building (Chicago, Ill.), 1895(5),
  II
Relief *see* Poverty; Welfare
Religion and churches (*see also* Bible;
  Church-state separation; Evolution;
  Fundamentalism; Great Awakening;
  Missions; Music; Parochial schools; sect
  and denomination names):
  Albrights, 1803(2), III
  attendance survey, 1974 Jan. 13, III
  baptism edict (Va.), 1662(1), IV
  Beacon, The (publication), 1840(8), III
  Buddhist leader's U.S. visit, 1979, III
  Calvinist theology book, 1641, II
  Campbellites, 1810(4), III
  Christian Catholic Church founded,
    1907 Mar. 9, III
  church building peak, 1955, II
  church membership, 1959 Sept. 7, III
  church membership rise, 1950, III
  clergy lowest-paid professionals, 1984,
    III
  colonial, 1620–1629, III
  colonial Pentecost celebration, c1660,
    IV
  colonial sects, 1700–1704, III
  communist infiltration charges, 1960
    Feb. 25, III
  compulsory education (Va.), 1631, III
  condemnation of homosexuality, 1992
    May 12(1), III
  Confederate churches protected, 1863
    Jan., III
  denomination memberships, 1989, III
  dominance over science, 1769(4), III
  Duke's laws (N.Y.S.), 1665 Feb. 28, I
  early Gothic Revival church, 1846(4),
    II
  early toleration document (Carolinas),
    1660–1669, III
  Evangelical and Reformed Church
    established, 1934 June 26, III
  Evangelical United Brethren Church
    organized, 1946 Nov. 16, III
  evangelism, 1896, III
  evangelism rampant, 1858(4), III
  evangelist Graham, 1957 Sept. 1, III
  evangelist McPherson, 1926, III; 1944,
    III
  evangelist Moody, 1875, III; 1899
    Dec. 22, III
  Father Divine, 1919, III

Religion and churches (*cont.*)
  finest extant example of late colonial
    meeting house (Mass.), 1785(2), II
  first baptism, 1540, III
  first bishop, 1112, III
  first brick meeting house (Mass.),
    1694(1), II
  first Brooklyn church (N.Y.), 1666(2),
    III
  First Church (Quincy, Mass.), 1828(4),
    II
  first church-state separation
    guarantee, 1677(1), III
  first cruciform church (Va.), 1710, II
  first divinity degree, 1692(2), III
  first divinity professor, 1722 Jan. 24,
    III
  first Hartford (Conn.) church, 1636,
    III
  first Indian church, 1660, III
  first N.E. minister to challenge Trinity
    doctrine, 1747(1), III
  first N.H. church, 1657, II
  first published weekly (Phila., Pa.),
    1813 Sept. 4, II
  first Sunday school (Mass.), 1669, III
  first woman ordained, 1860(1), IV
  frontier revivalism, 1801, III
  Georgian-style structures, 1720–1724,
    II
  Gothic Revival First Congregational
    Church (Haverhill, Mass.), 1848(10),
    II
  Henry the Holy Shouter, 1859(2), IV
  heresy laws (Mass.), 1697 Oct., III
  heresy (Mass.), 1637 Nov. 7, III
  Indian church founded (Mass.), 1670
    Aug. 22, III
  Jefferson on freedom of, 1800 Sept.
    23, IV
  late meeting house style (Brooklyn,
    N.Y.), 1847(5), II
  liberal social positions questioned,
    1991 June 6, III
  literature distributed, 1817, III
  mandatory church attendance (Va.),
    1618, IV; 1624, IV
  Mass. colonies' charter, 1691(1), I
  Mass. strictures, 1675 May 3, IV;
    1676(2), IV
  Methodist merger, 1966 Nov. 11(2),
    III
  National Council of Churches head,
    1978 Nov. 4, III
  Newport Parish Church (Va.), 1682(3),
    II
  oldest surviving Manhattan church,
    1766(1), II
  Old Ship Meeting House erected
    (Mass.), 1681(3), II
  Old West Church (Boston, Mass.),
    1806(1), II
  Park Street Church (Boston, Mass.)
    built, 1810(1), II
  Pastorius treatise, 1690(1), III; 1697(1),
    III
  Plan of Union, 1801(1), III
  Pope John Paul's U.S. visit, 1979, III;
    1979 Oct. 1–7, III

Religion and churches (*cont.*)
  public school released time upheld
    (N.Y.S.), 1951 July 11, III
  racism deplored, 1991 Jan. 14, III
  released time in schools to study,
    1926(2), III
  R.I. tolerance, 1636 June, I
  St. Bartholomew's Church (N.Y.C.)
    built, 1918(6), II
  school Bible reading required (Fla.),
    1925 May 13, III
  slave conversion law repealed (Va.),
    1682(1), I
  slave conversions, 1667, I; 1670(1), I;
    1671(2), I
  Sunday schools, 1824, III; 1874(1), III
  Sunday's preaching, 1896, III; 1934
    Jan. 7, III
  Ten Great Religions (Clarke), 1871, III
  Toleration Act (Md.), 1649 Apr. 21, III
  Trinity Church (Del.), 1698 May 29, II
  TV evangelist scandals, 1987 Mar. 19,
    III; 1988 Apr. 8, III
  Va. clergy salaries, 1758(1), III
  Washington for Jesus rally (Wash.,
    D.C.), 1980 Apr. 29, III
  women ministers ordained, 1955 May
    23, III
  World Council of Churches convened,
    1954 Aug. 15, III
Remarque, Erich Maria, 1970, II
Rembrandt van Rijn, 1976 Sept. 29, II
Remick, Lee, 1991, II
Remington Co., 1868 June 23, III
Remini, Robert V., 1984 Nov. 16, II
Renoir, Pierre Auguste, 1968 Oct. 9, II;
  1990 May 15, II
Rensselaer Polytechnic Institute (N.Y.),
  1824 Oct. 3, III
Rensselaerswyck (Dutch patroonship),
  1630(2), I
Rent Control Bill, 1948 Mar. 30, I
Renwick, James, 1839, II; 1858(2), II;
  1865(12), II
Republican Party (*see also* Presidential
  elections):
  adopted National Republican Party
    name, 1868 May 20–21, I
  Anti-Saloon, 1886 Sept. 16, I
  first black chairman, 1880 June 2–8, I
  first national meeting, 1856 Feb.
    22(1), I
  first presidential campaign, 1856, I;
    1856 June 17–19, I
  first use of elephant symbol, 1874
    Nov. 7, I
  first woman to head Natl. Committee,
    1974 Sept. 16(1), I
  formed (Mich.), 1854 July 6, I
  Medill role in, 1852(2), II
  Mugwumps, 1884(1), IV; 1884 June 6,
    I
  National Silver convention, 1896 July
    22–24, I
  presidential election split, 1872, I
  Progressive faction, 1911 Jan. 21, I;
    1911 Oct. 16, I
  strong congressional election showing,
    1858–1859, I

Resaca de la Palma, Battle of, 1846 May 9, I

Reserpine, 1955 Jan. 8, III

Reservoirs *see* Dams; Water supply

Reshevsky, Samuel, 1992, IV

Resnick, Judith, 1984 Aug. 30–Sept. 5, III

Resnik, Regina, 1944(3), II

Resolution Trust Corporation, 1989 Aug. 9, III

Resorts:
    mineral springs (Va.), 1740, IV
    Newport (R.I.), 1730–1734, IV; 1881(4), II

Restaurants (*see also* Bars, saloons, and taverns; Coffee houses):
    first licensed (Mass.), 1643, IV
    racial discrimination barred, 1964 July 22, I
    variety performances, 1857(2), IV
    variety programs banned (N.Y.C.), 1862 Apr., II
    waitresses, 1853(5), IV
    waitresses serving liquor banned (N.Y.C.), 1862 Apr., II

Resurrection City (Wash., D.C.), 1968 May 2, I; 1968 June 24, I

Retail stores (*see also* Grocery stores and supermarkets):
    B. Altman (N.Y.C.), 1865(10), III
    Carter Hawley Hale bankruptcy, 1991 Feb. 11, III
    country stores, 1814, IV
    department store closings, 1992 Jan. 6, III
    development of chains, 1879, III
    first female clerks (Phila., Pa.), 1850(3), III
    five-and-ten cent stores, 1879, III
    largest department store takeover, 1988 Apr. 1, III
    largest store in world (N.Y.C.), 1862(3), IV
    Montgomery Ward & Co., 1872, III
    overview, 1990, III
    Robert Hall clothing chain closed, 1977 June 29, III

Retardation *see* Handicapped

Retirement *see* Pensions

Reuben, David, 1970(1), II

Reuss, Henry S., 1975 Jan. 16, I

Reuther, Walter P.:
    AFL-CIO resignation, 1967 Feb. 3, III
    on automation, 1955, III
    CIO head, 1952 Dec. 4, III
    died, 1970, III

Revels, Hiram R., 1870 Feb. 25, I

Revenue Act, 1926 Feb. 26, I

Revenue sharing:
    bill signed, 1972 Oct. 20, I
    Nixon proposal, 1971 Jan. 22, I

Revere, Anne, 1946 Mar. 7, II

Revere, Paul:
    commemorative bowl, 1768, II
    engravings for magazine, 1774 Jan., II

Reverse discrimination:
    Bakke case (Calif.), 1978 June 28, I
    civil rights laws applicability ruling, 1989 June 12(1), I

Revivalism *see* Great Awakening; Religion and churches; specific movements

Revolta, Johnny, 1935 Oct. 23, IV

Revolution, The (publication), 1868(2), I

Revolutionary War:
    account by contemporary, 1805(2), II
    André–Arnold plot, 1780 Oct. 2, I
    appeal for army coats, 1775(1), IV
    Battle of Brandywine, 1777 Sept. 11, I
    Battle of Bunker Hill, 1775 June 17, I; 1775 June 17, IV
    Battle of Camden (S.C.), 1780 Aug. 16, I
    Battle of Cowpens (S.C.), 1781 Jan. 17, I
    Battle of Eutaw Springs, 1781 Sept. 9, I
    Battle of Guilford Court House (N.C.), 1781 Mar. 15, I
    Battle of King's Mountain (S.C.), 1780 Oct. 7, I
    Battle of Lexington, 1775 Apr. 19, I
    Battle of Long Island, 1776 Aug. 27, I
    Battle of Monmouth, 1778 June 28, I
    Battle of Princeton, 1777 Jan. 3, I
    Bemis Heights battles, 1777 Sept. 19(1), I; 1777 Oct. 7, I
    British defeated at Bennington (Vt.), 1777 Aug. 16, I
    British evacuated Boston, 1776 Mar. 17, I
    British evacuated Phila., 1778 June 18, I
    British occupied Savannah (Ga.), 1778 Dec. 29, I
    British reinforcements, 1775 May 25, I
    British troops in Boston, 1768 Oct. 1, I
    British victory at Briar Creek (Ga.), 1779 Mar. 3, I
    Burgoyne crossed the Hudson to encamp at Saratoga (N.Y.), 1777 Sept. 14, I
    Burgoyne's retreat to Saratoga (N.Y.), 1777 Oct. 8, I
    Burgoyne's surrender at Saratoga (N.Y.), 1777 Oct. 17, I
    causes, 1660–1669, I
    Charleston (S.C.) defended, 1776 Mar., I
    Chesapeake Bay naval battle, 1781 Sept. 5, I
    Common Sense (Paine) published, 1776 Jan. 10, II
    Continental forces withdrawn from R.I., 1778 Aug. 30, I
    Continental naval victory, 1775 Nov. 29(2), I
    Conway Cabal, 1777 Sept. 25–Dec. 23, I
    Crisis (Paine) written, 1776 Dec. 19, I
    dramas about, 1844(1), II
    ending, 1780–1784, I; 1781 Oct. 19, I; 1783 Sept. 3, I
    Ethan Allen captured, 1775 Sept. 25, I
    events leading to, 1765–1769, I; 1765 Mar. 24, I; 1767 June 29, I
    first clashes, 1770–1774, I
    first Continental Navy commander, 1775 Dec. 22, I
    first military encounter (N.H.), 1774 Dec. 14, I
    first submarine attack, 1776 Sept. 6, I

Revolutionary War (*cont.*)
    first surgeon general, 1775 July 25, III
    Ft. Ticonderoga abandoned, 1777 July 6, I
    Ft. Ticonderoga taken, 1775 May 10(1), I
    Ft. Washington (N.Y.C.) captured by British, 1776 Nov. 16, I
    Germantown (Pa.) attack, 1777 Oct. 4, I
    Hale executed, 1776 Sept. 22, I
    Hessian troops captured (Trenton, N.J.), 1776 Dec. 26, I
    Hickey hanged as traitor, 1776 June 27, I
    Jones naval role, 1779 Sept. 23, I
    Marine battalions established, 1775 Nov. 10, I
    mine attack against British shipping, 1778 Jan. 5, I
    navy established, 1775 Oct. 13, I
    New London (Conn.) looted, 1781 Sept. 8, I
    N.Y.C. evacuated, 1776 Sept. 15, I
    Norfolk (Va.) burned, 1776 Jan. 1, I
    paintings depicting, 1817, II
    Phila. occuped by British, 1777 Sept. 26, I
    poems about, 1775–1779, II
    retreat to Valley Forge (Pa.), 1777 Dec. 17, I
    satire on, 1776, II; 1779, II
    Savannah (Ga.) siege, 1779 Sept. 3–Oct. 28, I
    Stony Point (N.Y.) captured, 1779 July 15, I; 1779 July 26, I
    theater suspended, 1774 Oct. 20, II
    veterans, 1881, IV; 1889(4), IV
    veteran's organization, 1783 May 13, IV; 1784(1), IV
    Washington, George, 1777 Sept. 25–Dec. 23, I
    Yorktown (Va.) occupied by British, 1781 Aug. 1, I
    Yorktown (Va.) shelled, 1781 Oct. 9, I
    Yorktown (Va.) surrender, 1781 Oct. 19, I

Revson, Charles H., 1975, III

Revson, Peter, 1974, IV

Reykjavik summit conference, 1986 Oct. 11–12, I

Reynolds, Burt, 1991 Aug. 5, II

Reynolds, John H., 1960 Jan. 2, III

Reynolds, Verne L., 1924 May 11–13, I; 1928 Nov. 6, I; 1932 Apr. 30-May 2, I; 1932 Nov. 8, I

Rheault, Robert, 1969 July 31, I

Rheaume, Manon, 1992 Sept. 23, IV

Rhine River:
    Remagen Bridge crossed by U.S., 1945 Mar. 7, I

Rhode Island:
    Callender history published, 1739, II
    charter, 1643 Mar., I
    Constitution, 1647 May 29–31, I
    Dorr's Rebellion, 1842(2), I
    founded, 1636 June, I
    outlawed slavery, 1784, I
    religious tolerance, 1636 June, I

Rhode Island (*cont.*)
thirteenth state to ratify U.S. Constitution, 1790 May 29, I
Rhodes, Richard, 1987 Nov. 9, II; 1988 Mar. 31, II
Rhodes scholarship, 1979 Sept. 9, III
Ribaut, Jean, 1562 Apr. 30, I
Rice:
first planting (Va.), 1647(2), IV
Rice, Anne, 1992(1), II
Rice, Edward, 1990(1), II
Rice, Elmer, 1914 Aug. 19, II; 1923 Mar. 19, II; 1929 May 12, II; 1940 Jan. 16, II
Rice, Grantland, 1922, III
Rice, Thomas Darmouth, 1828, IV
Rice, Tim, 1971 Oct. 12, II; 1979 Sept. 25, II; 1980 June 8, II
Rice University (Tex.), 1891 May 19, III; 1988, II
Rich, Adrienne, 1974 Apr. 18, II; 1975(1), II; 1989(1), II
Rich, Irene, 1988, II
Rich, Richard, 1609(2), II
Richards, Renee (Richard Raskind), 1976 Aug. 27, IV
Richards, Theodore William, 1914(2), III
Richardson, Dickinson W., 1956 Oct. 19, III
Richardson, Elliot:
resigned, 1973 Oct. 20, I
Richardson, Henry Hobson, 1872(4), II; 1880(3), II; 1881(2), II; 1885(2), II
Richardson, Michael Ray, 1986, IV
Richardson, Samuel, 1744(2), II
Richie, Lionel, 1983 Feb. 23, II; 1985 Feb. 26, II
Richmond, James N., 1850(4), III
Richmond, University of (Va.), 1840 Mar. 4, III
Richmond (Va.):
Confederacy capital, 1861 May 21, I; 1865 Apr. 2, I
Richter, Burton, 1976 Oct. 18(2), III
Richter, Charles F., 1985, III
Richter, Conrad, 1946(1), II; 1951 May 7, II; 1953(1), II; 1961 Mar. 14, II; 1962(1), II; 1968, II
Rickenbacker, Eddie (Edward V.), 1973, IV
Ricketts Circus, 1793(4), IV
Rickey, Branch, 1965, IV
Rickover, Hyman G., 1986, I
Ride, Sally K., 1983 June 18–24, III
Ridgway, Matthew, 1951 Apr. 11, I; 1951 June 23, I
Riesel, Victor, 1956 Apr. 5, III
Riessen, Marty, 1975 July 4–5, IV
Rifles *see* Firearms
Riggs, Bobby, 1939 July 7–8, IV; 1939 Sept. 17, IV; 1941 Sept. 7, IV; 1973 Sept. 20, IV
Rights of Man, The (Paine), 1791 Mar.(1), II
Right to die *see* Death
Riis, Jacob A., 1890, IV; 1900(4), III
Riley, James Whitcomb, 1883(1), II
Rinehart, William H.:
Clytie (sculpture), 1872(3), II
Ringling, John and Mable, Museum of Art (Sarasota, Fla.), 1991 Jan. 21, II

Ringling Brothers and Barnum and Bailey Circus, 1956 July 16, IV
Riots and mob violence (*see also* Rebellions; Terrorism; Vietnam War demonstrations):
anti-Chinese-Americans (Calif.), 1877(1), I
anti-integration (New Orleans, La.), 1960 Nov. 17, II
Atlanta (Ga.) race, 1906 Sept. 22, I
Attica Prison (N.Y.), 1971 Sept. 9–13, I
Berkeley (Calif.) People's Park confrontation, 1969 May 15, III
blacks (Vicksburg, Miss.), 1874 Dec. 7, I
Boston (Mass.) school busing, 1974 Sept. 12, III
Catholic (Phila., Pa.), 1844, I
Chicago Seven (Ill.), 1970 Feb. 18, III
Chileans attacked U.S. sailors (Valparaiso), 1891 Oct. 16, I
church bombing (Birmingham, Ala.), 1963 Sept. 15, I
civil rights march (Memphis, Tenn.), 1968 Mar. 28, I
coal miners (Pa.), 1902 July 30, III
Columbia University (N.Y.) sit-in, 1968 Apr. 23, III
Cuban detainees, 1987 Nov. 21, I
Democratic National Convention (Chicago, Ill.), 1968 Aug. 29, I; 1968 Dec. 1, I
Detroit (Mich.) race, 1943 June 20, III
Frank lynching (Ga.), 1915, IV
Harlem (N.Y.C.) race, 1964 July 18, I
Haymarket (Chicago, Ill.), 1886, I
Jackson State College (Miss.), 1967 May 10–11, III
Ku Klux Klan shootout (N.C.), 1979 Nov. 3, I
Little Rock (Ark.) racial violence, 1957 Sept. 24, I
Los Angeles (Calif.), 1992, I; 1992 Apr. 29, IV; 1992 June 22(1), I
Louisville (Ky.) school busing, 1975 Sept. 4, III
lynchings in South, 1935, IV
martial law (Cambridge, Md.), 1963 July 12, I
Miami (Fla.) race, 1968 Aug. 7, I
national violence condemned, 1968 Dec. 1, I
N.Y.C. Irish Protestants-Catholics, 1871 July 12, I
Orangeburg (S.C.) student disorder, 1968 Feb. 8, III
prison (Santa Fe, N. Mex.), 1980 Feb. 2–3, I
race (Atlanta, Ga.), 1906 Sept. 22, I
race (Cambridge, Md.), 1963 July 12, I
race (Miami, Fla.), 1980 May 17–19, I
race (Newark, N.J.), 1967 July 12–17, I
race (Phila., Pa.), 1964 Aug. 28, I
racial, 1964, I; 1964, III
Roosevelt Raceway (N.Y.), 1963 Nov. 8, IV
Sicilian immigrants lynched (New Orleans, La.), 1891 Mar. 14, I; 1892 Apr. 12, I

Riots and mob violence (*cont.*)
sniper attack provoking (Cleveland, Ohio), 1968 July 23, I
strikers (Ill.), 1898 Oct. 12, III
striking Pa. miners, 1894 Apr. 5, I
truck strike, 1979 June 7, III
University of Ala., 1956 Feb. 6, III
University of Mississippi desegregation, 1962 Sept. 30, III
urban race, 1968 Apr. 4, I; 1968 Apr. 15, I
Vicksburg (Miss.), 1874 Dec. 7, I
Watts (Los Angeles, Calif.), 1965 Aug. 11–16, I
worst race riot to date (Detroit, Mich.), 1967, I; 1967 July 23(2), I
Ripken, Cal, Jr., 1992 Mar. 2, IV
Ripley, Alexandra, 1988 Apr. 25, II; 1991(1), II
Ripley, George, 1841(3), III
Ripon College (Wis.), 1851 Jan. 29, III
Rip Van Winkle (fictional character), 1828(5), II
Ritchie, Sharon Kay, 1955 Sept. 10, IV
Rittenhouse, David, 1767, III; 1792 Apr. 2, I
Ritz Paris Hemingway Award, 1987 Apr. 6, II
Rivers, Larry, 1963 Aug., II
Rivers, L. Mendel, 1970, I
Rivers and Harbors Act, 1882 Aug. 2, I
Rivers and waterways (*see also* names of specific rivers):
colonial transportation importance, 1686, III
Inland Commission appointed, 1907 Mar. 14(2), I
St. Lawrence Seaway, 1954 Jan. 20, III; 1954 May 13, III
RJR Nabisco, 1989 Feb. 3, III; 1990(1), II
Roach, Hal, 1932 Nov. 18, II; 1992 Jan. 23, II
Roads and highways (*see also* Streets; Traffic regulations):
Alaska highway anniversary, 1992, I
Boston Post Road, 1673 Jan. 1, III
colonial, 1755–1759, III
federal improvements, 1830, I
federal legislation, 1991 Dec. 18, I
federal programs, 1916 July 11, III
first large-scale construction (National Road), 1811, III
first major turnpike (Pa.), 1794(4), III
first published maps, 1789, III
first speeding fines (Phila., Pa.), 1712, IV
first turnpike (Va.), 1785(4), III
highway modernization program, 1954 July 12, III
important Ill., 1811(4), III
Lincoln Highway Assn. to promote, 1913 July 1, III
Monroe vetoed transportation bill, 1822 May 4, I
Natchez Trace, 1806, III
N.J. Turnpike, 1951 Nov. 5, III
sculpture garden (Neb.), 1976 July 4, II
turnpikes (Pa.), 1794(4), III; 1838(3), III

Roads and highways (*cont.*)
    Wilderness Road, 1775 Mar. 10, III;
        1790(2), III
Roanoke Island colony (N.C.), 986–1599,
    II; 1585 Aug., I
Roanoke Island (N.C.):
    captured by Union forces, 1862 Feb.
        8, I
Robards, Jason, Jr., 1959 Apr. 12, II; 1977
    Mar. 28, II; 1978 Apr. 3, II
Robb, Charles, 1967 Dec. 9, IV
Robberies (*see also* Bank robberies; Train
    robberies):
    art theft (Brooklyn Museum), 1974
        Dec. 12, II
    art theft (Gardner Museum, Boston),
        1990 Mar. 18, II
    art theft (Hanley collection, Pa.), 1968
        Aug. 22, II
    auto, 1989, IV
    Brinks' armored-car holdup (Nanuet,
        N.Y.), 1981 Oct. 20, IV
    Chicago Art Institute, 1966 Oct. 30, II
    Conn. Mutual Life Insurance Co.,
        1889 Jan. 24, IV
    Dalton gang, 1892 Oct. 5, IV
    jewels (N.Y.C.), 1964 Oct. 29, IV
    largest cash to date (N.Y.C.), 1982
        Dec. 12, IV
    theft (N.Y.C.), 1988 Feb. 9, IV
Robbins, Harold, 1962, II
Robbins, Jerome, 1944 Apr. 18, II; 1971
    May 28, II; 1974 May 16, II; 1975 May
    15–31, II; 1989, II; 1989 June 4(1), II;
    1990, II
Roberts, Kenneth, 1930(1), II; 1933(1), II;
    1957 May 6, II
Robertson, Agnes, 1854(6), II
Robertson, Alice, 1921 June 20, I
Robertson, Cliff, 1966 May 22, II; 1969
    Apr. 14, II
Robert's Rules of Order, 1876, II
Robeson, Paul, 1924 May 15, II; 1976, II
Robey House (Chicago, Ill.), 1907(8), II
Robins, A. H., Co., 1987 Dec. 11, III
Robins, Frederick C., 1954 Oct. 21, III
Robinson, Eddie, 1985 Oct. 5, IV
Robinson, Edward G., 1957, II; 1973, II
Robinson, Edwin Arlington, 1896(1), II;
    1897(1), II; 1910(1), II; 1916(1), II;
    1917(1), II; 1921(1), II; 1922 May. 21, II;
    1925 Apr. 26, II; 1928 May 7, II
Robinson, Frank, 1974, IV; 1974 Oct. 3, IV
Robinson, Henry Morton, 1950(1), II
Robinson, Jackie, 1947, IV; 1952 July 8,
    IV; 1972, IV
Robinson, Joseph T., 1928 June 26–29, I
Robinson, Sugar Ray, 1957, IV; 1958, IV;
    1958 Mar. 25, IV; 1960, IV
Robinson, Tommy, 1992 Apr. 16, I
Robots *see* Automation
Roche, James, 1966 Mar. 22, III
Rock, John, 1984, III
Rockefeller, John D.:
    monopolies, 1882, III
    oil interests, 1862(1), III; 1870, III
    philanthropy, 1913 May 14, III
    for Prohibition repeal, 1932, IV
Rockefeller, John D., Jr.:
    UN bequest, 1946 Dec. 14, I

Rockefeller, John D. III, 1978, III
Rockefeller, Nelson:
    art legacies, 1979 Feb. 9(2), II
    bought surrealist bed, 1975 May 12, II
    died, 1979, I
    donated art collection, 1969, II
    headed commission to investigate
        CIA, 1975 Jan. 5, I
    nominated for vice presidency, 1974
        Aug. 20, I
    vice presidency, 1974 Dec. 19, I
Rockefeller, Winthrop, 1973, I
Rockefeller Center (N.Y.C.):
    Japanese controlling interest, 1989
        Oct. 30, III
Rockefeller Foundation, 1902 Feb., III;
    1913 May 14, III
Rockefeller Plaza West (N.Y.C.), 1989, II
Rockets (*see also* Missiles):
    first glider, 1931 June 4, III
    new record, 1948 Mar. 5, III
    Saturn, 1967 Nov. 9, III
    Saturn S-1C, 1965 Apr. 16, III
    Thor-Agena-B launched Discoverer
        21, 1961 Feb. 18, III
    Titan 3C launched, 1965 June 18, III
    two antisatellite systems, 1964 Sept.
        17, I
    weight-into-orbit record, 1964 Jan. 29,
        III
Rock music:
    Beatles' U.S. tour, 1964 Feb. 7, II
    cable MTV popularity, 1981, II
    commemorative stamps, 1992 Oct. 8,
        II
    concert disaster, 1979 Dec. 3, II
    Fillmore East and West closed, 1971
        June 27, II
    Gimme Shelter (film), 1970, II
    Hair opened off-Broadway, 1967 Nov.
        13, II
    Hall of Fame, 1985 Aug. 5, II
    Jesus Christ Superstar (opera) (Rice
        and Webber), 1971 Oct. 12, II
    largest festival since Woodstock (Pa.),
        1972 July 8–9, II
    Prince recording contract, 1992 Sept.
        5, II
    punk star Sid Vicious died from drug
        overdose, 1979 Feb. 2, II
    rock 'n roll, 1955, IV
    rock 'n' roll revived, 1972, II
    Watkins Glen (N.Y.) festival, 1973 July
        29, II
    Woodstock (film), 1970, II
    Woodstock (N.Y.), 1969 Aug. 15–18,
        IV
Rockne, Knute, 1913 Nov. 1, IV; 1924, IV
Rockwell, George Lincoln, 1967 Aug. 25, I
Rockwell, Norman, 1978, II
Rocky Hill Meeting House (Mass.), 1785(2),
    II
Rocky Mountain National Park, 1915 Jan.
    26, III
Rocky Mountains:
    South Pass gateway, 1824(1), I
Roddenberry, Gene, 1991, II
Rodeos, 1991, IV
Rodgers, Adrian, 1986 June 10, III

Rodgers, Bill, 1975 Apr. 21, IV; 1980 Apr.
    21, IV
Rodgers, Calbraith, 1911 Sept. 17-Nov. 5,
    III
Rodgers, Richard, 1927 Nov. 3, II; 1936
    Mar. 22, II; 1937 Nov. 2, II; 1943, II;
    1943 Mar. 31, II; 1944 May 1, II; 1945
    Apr. 19, II; 1949 Apr. 7, II; 1950 Apr. 9,
    II; 1950 May 1, II; 1951 Mar. 29(1), II;
    1958 Dec. 1, II; 1970 Nov. 10, II; 1978
    May 1(2), II; 1979, II
Rodin, Auguste, 1978 Jan. 21, II
Rodzinski, Artur, 1942 Dec. 28, II
Roe, Allison, 1981 Apr. 20, IV; 1981 Oct.
    25, IV
Roe, Edward Payson, 1872(1), II
Roebling, John A., 1855, III; 1883, II
Roelantsen, Adam, 1630–1639, III; 1633,
    III
Roethke, Theodore, 1954 May 3, II; 1959
    Mar. 3(1), II; 1963, II; 1965 Mar. 9, II
Rogers, Don, 1986, IV
Rogers, Ginger, 1941 Feb. 27, II
Rogers, John, 1867(2), II; 1875(2), II
Rogers, Paul, 1967 Mar. 26, II
Rogers, Will, 1921, II; 1933 Oct. 2, II;
    1935, II
Rogers, Will C., 3d, 1988 July 3, I
Roley, Susan Lynn, 1972 July 7(1), IV
Rolfe, John, 1610–1619, III; 1613, III
Roller skating:
    figure, 1870(1), IV
    introduced, 1863, IV
Rolling Stone, The (O. Henry publication),
    1894 Mar., II
Rolling Stone (publication), 1977 Sept.
    11(2), II
Rolling Stones (group), 1970, II
Rölvaag, Ole, 1927(1), II
Roman Catholic Church (*see also* Parochial
    schools):
    AIDS prevention, 1987 Dec. 10, III
    American Protective Assn. against,
        1887 Mar. 3, I
    antichurch movements, 1841, III
    antichurch organizations, 1850(10), III
    anti-family violence statement, 1992
        Oct. 30, III
    attendance down, 1974 Jan. 13, III
    Bernardin made cardinal, 1983 Feb.
        2, III
    Cardinal Cushing retirement (Boston,
        Mass.), 1968 Oct. 25, III
    condemnation of homosexuality, 1992
        May 12(1), III
    Cooke appointed archbishop (N.Y.),
        1968 Mar. 8, III
    deaths, 1988, III; 1989, III
    doctrine-teaching controversy, 1986
        Mar. 11, III
    Duchesne canonized, 1988 July 3, III
    election to public office decried, 1960
        May 20(2), III
    English used in mass, 1963 Dec. 4, III
    expansion of role of women
        recommended, 1988 Apr. 11, III
    first American-born nun, 1752 Jan. 31,
        III
    first American canonized, 1946 July 7,
        III

Roman Catholic Church (*cont.*)
first American cardinal, 1875 Mar. 15, III
first basilica (N.Y.C.), 1926 July 26, III
first Bible, 1790(4), III
first Bible in English, 1970 Sept. 30, III
first bishop (Baltimore, Md.), 1790 Aug. 15, III
first black archbishop in U.S., 1988 Mar. 15, III
first cathedral (Baltimore, Md.), 1821 May 31, III
first church built in Boston (Mass.), 1803 Sept. 29, III
first church built (St. Marys, Md.), 1634, II
first college (Wash., D.C.), 1789 Jan. 23, III; 1815(4), III
first council (Baltimore, Md.), 1852 May 9, III
first Indian bishop, 1986 May 6, III
first international Eucharistic Congress (Chicago, Ill.), 1926 June 20, III
first Jesuit missionaries, 1566, III
first laity Congress (Baltimore, Md.), 1889 Nov. 11, III
first male U.S. saint, 1977 June 19, III
first mass in only colonial built and maintained church (Phila., Pa.), 1732 Feb. 26, III
first men's fraternal organization, 1882 Feb. 2, III
first newspaper (Boston, Mass.), 1789 Apr. 23, III
first nun (La.), 1729 Mar. 15, III
first parish (Fla.), 1565 Sept. 8, III
first priest ordained in U.S., 1793 May 25, III
first U.S.-born saint, 1975 Sept. 14, III
French aid, 1850(8), III
French Jesuit missionaries expelled from Appalachian region, 1763(3), III
Friday meat ban lifted, 1966 Nov. 18, III
highest Vatican post held by American, 1958 Apr. 26, III
Kennedy candidacy issue, 1960 Sept. 12, I
largest denomination in U.S., 1989, III
liberal archbishop's authority challenged, 1986 Sept. 4, III
Md., 1620–1629, III; 1634 Mar. 25, III; 1649 Apr. 21, III; 1655 Mar. 25, I
Mass. priest ban, 1700 June 17, III
membership, 1991, III
movie censorship, 1934(3), II
New American Bible, 1970 Sept. 30, III
nuclear arms race condemned, 1983 May 3, III
opposed birth control, 1968 July 31, III
ordination of women survey, 1992, III
pastoral letter on economic justice, 1984 Nov. 11, III
Phila. (Pa.) riots, 1844, I

Roman Catholic Church (*cont.*)
political action statement, 1984 Aug. 9, III
Pope John Paul's U.S. visit, 1979, III; 1979 Oct. 1–7, III
Pope Paul's U.S. visit, 1965 Oct. 4, I
priests prohibited (Mass.), 1647 May 26, III
priests' sexual abuse of minors charged, 1992 Sept. 21(1), III
revised New Testament, 1987 Apr. 4, III
school segregation ordered ended (La.), 1962 Mar. 27, III
second presidential nominee, 1960 July 13, I
Seton beatified, 1963 Mar. 17, III
Seton canonized, 1975 Sept. 14, III
two new American cardinals named, 1991 May 29, III
two new cardinals named, 1985 Apr. 24, III
two new U.S. cardinals, 1988 May 29, III
Romberg, Sigmund, 1924 Dec. 2, II
Rome (Italy):
occupied by Allies, 1944 June 4, I
Rommel, Irwin, 1943 Feb. 20, I
Ronstadt, Linda, 1977 Feb. 19, II
Rooney, Arthur Joseph, Sr., 1988, IV
Rooney, Mickey, 1942(3), II; 1982 Sept. 19, II
Roosa, Stuart A., 1971 Jan. 31, III
Roosevelt, Alice Longworth, 1980, IV
Roosevelt, Eleanor:
died, 1962, I
Lash's biography of, 1971(1), II; 1972(1), II
most admired woman, 1958 Jan. 15, IV
Roosevelt, Ellen C., 1890(6), IV
Roosevelt, Franklin D.:
appointed Perkins to Labor Dept., 1933 Mar. 4(2), I
Atlantic Charter, 1941 Aug. 9–12, I
attack-on-sight order, 1941 Sept. 11, I
Cairo conference, 1943 Nov. 22, I
Campobello Island home (Canada) dedicated, 1964 Aug. 20, II
Casablanca conference, 1943 Jan. 14, I
defense program recommendation, 1939 Jan. 12, I
died, 1945, I; 1945 Apr. 12, I
dismissed charges against N.Y.C. Mayor Walker, 1931 Mar. 17, I
drive against polio, 1935(4), III
elected president, 1932 Nov. 8, I
elected state legislator (N.Y.), 1910 Nov. 8, I
fireside chats, 1939 Sept. 3(1), I
first fireside chat, 1933 Mar. 12, I
Four Freedoms, 1941 Jan. 6, I
German and Italian assets in U.S. freeze, 1941 June 14, I
inaugurated, 1933 Mar. 4(1), I
inaugurated for second term, 1937 Jan. 20, I
inaugurated for third term, 1941 Jan. 20, I
on invasion of Poland, 1939 Sept. 1, I

Roosevelt, Franklin D. (*cont.*)
Japanese embargo ordered, 1941 July 25, I
legislation signed, 1934 Jan. 31, I; 1934 Apr. 28, I; 1934 June 6, I; 1934 June 12, I; 1935 July 5, III; 1935 Aug. 9, III; 1935 Aug. 14, I; 1935 Aug. 26, I; 1937 May 1, I; 1937 Aug. 26, I; 1937 Sept. 2, I; 1938 Feb. 16, I; 1938 June 25, I; 1940 Apr. 12, I; 1940 June 28, I; 1941 Mar. 11, I; 1941 Aug. 18, I; 1941 Sept. 20, I; 1942 Jan. 30, III; 1943 June 10, III; 1943 Dec. 17, I; 1944 June 22, III
Library dedicated (Hyde Park, N.Y.), 1941 June 30, II
national emergency proclaimed, 1941 May 27, I
New Deal opposition, 1938 May 27, III
New Deal policies, 1933, I
New Deal speech, 1932 June 27-July 2, I; 1932 July 2, IV
New Deal transition, 1937, I
nominated for fourth term, 1944 July 19–21, I
nominated for third term, 1940 July 15–19, I
opponents, 1934, I; 1935, I; 1935 May 27, I; 1940 Oct. 25, III
presidential candidacy, 1932 June 27-July 2, I; 1936 June 23–27, I
press opposition, 1936 Nov. 3, I
Quebec conference, 1943 Aug. 11–24, I
reelected for fourth term, 1944 Nov. 7, I
reelected president, 1936 Nov. 3, I; 1940 Nov. 5, I
satire on, 1937 Nov. 2, II
on Sudetenland crisis, 1938 Sept. 26, I
Supreme Court packing move, 1937 Feb. 5, I; 1937 July 22(1), I
Teheran conference, 1943 Nov. 28–Dec. 1, I
Thanksgiving Day date, 1941 May 20, IV
third-term presidential bid, 1940, I
U.S. neutrality, 1939 Sept. 3(1), I
vice presidential candidacy, 1920 June 28-July 5, I
Yalta conference, 1945 Feb. 4–11, I
Roosevelt, Franklin D., Jr., 1988, I
Roosevelt, James, 1991, I
Roosevelt, Quentin, 1918 July 14, IV
Roosevelt, Theodore:
African hunting trip, 1909, IV
antitrust actions, 1902 Mar. 10, III; 1902 Oct. 16, III; 1904 Mar. 14, III; 1911, III
appointed Straus to cabinet, 1906 Dec. 12, I
on Armory Show (N.Y.), 1913, II
books on, 1979(1), II
born, 1858 Oct. 27, I
Brazil expedition, 1914, IV
coal miners' strike (Pa.), 1902 Oct. 16, III
Commerce and Labor Dept. created, 1903 Feb. 14, I

Roosevelt, Theodore (*cont.*)
  conservation measures, 1902, I;
    1903(2), III; 1908 June 8, III;
    1911(1), III
  Cuban intervention, 1906 Aug. 23, I
  daughter Alice died, 1980, IV
  declined presidential third term,
    1908, I
  dined with Booker T. Washington,
    1901 Oct. 16, IV
  elected N.Y. governor, 1898 Nov. 8, I
  elected vice president, 1900 Nov. 6, I
  Great White Fleet, 1907, I; 1909 Feb.
    21, I
  inaugurated for first full term, 1905
    Mar. 4, I
  Inland Waterways Commission, 1907
    Mar. 14(2), I
  Japanese immigration restrictions,
    1908 Feb. 18, I
  jujitsu instruction, 1904(2), IV
  Lodge speech praising, 1908 June
    16–20, I
  lost presidential bid, 1912 Nov. 5, I
  "lunatic fringe" expression, 1913 Feb.
    27, IV
  Monroe Doctrine application, 1905
    Jan. 21, I
  muckrakers, 1904, II; 1906 Mar. 17,
    IV
  New Nationalism speech, 1910 Aug.
    31, I
  Nobel Peace Prize, 1905, I; 1906(1), I
  Panama Canal Commission, 1904 Feb.
    29, I
  Panama Canal inspection tour, 1906
    Nov. 9, I
  Panamanian revolt, 1903 Nov. 3, I
  political stance, 1904, I
  presidential third-term bid, 1912, I
  Progressive Party presidential
    candidacy, 1912 June 18–22, I; 1912
    Aug. 5, I
  Pure Food and Drug Act, 1906(1), II
  reelected president, 1904 Nov. 8, I
  Republican presidential nomination,
    1904 June 21–23, I
  Rough Riders, 1896(4), II; 1898 Apr.
    22(3), I; 1898 June 24, I; 1898 July
    1–2, I; 1898 Aug. 7, I
  Russo-Japanese War peace conference,
    1905, I
  Sagamore Hill home named historic
    site, 1962 July 25, II
  slum reform, 1890, IV
  son killed in World War I, 1918 July
    14, IV
  "Speak softly and carry a big stick",
    1901 Sept. 2, IV
  Square Deal, 1910 Aug. 31, I
  succeeded to presidency, 1901, I
  on Tolstoy, 1890(3), II
  vice presidency, 1901 Mar. 4, I
  vice presidential campaign, 1900 June
    19–21, I
  wildlife protection, 1887(5), III
  Winning of the West, The, 1889(1), II;
    1896(1), II
Roosevelt College (Ill.), 1945(1), III
Roosevelt Dam (Ariz.), 1911(1), III

Roosevelt Raceway (N.Y.), 1963 Nov. 8, IV
Root, Elihu, 1912 June 18–22, I; 1913 Dec.
  10, I; 1919(2), III
Root, John Wellborn, 1891(3), II; 1895(5),
  II; 1958 May 17, II
Roper, Elmo, 1971, II
Rose:
  declared official national flower, 1986
    Sept. 23, IV
Rose, Albert, 1990, III
Rose, Billy, 1960 Jan. 6, II; 1966, II
Rose, Ernestine L., 1836(1), I
Rose, Mauri, 1948 May 31, IV
Rose, Mervyn, 1957 July 6, IV
Rose, Pete, 1911, IV; 1985 Sept. 11, IV;
  1989 Aug. 24, IV
Rose, Philip, 1975 Jan. 7(1), II
Rose, Phyllis, 1989(1), II
Rosen, Charles, 1972 Apr. 13, II
Rosenberg, Julius and Ethel, 1953 June 19,
  I; 1973(1), II
Rosenbloom, Carroll, 1972 July 13, IV
Rosewall, Ken, 1956 Sept. 9, IV; 1970 Sept
  2–13, IV
Ross, Alex, 1907 June 21, IV
Ross, Betsy, 1775–1779, IV
Ross, William B. (Mrs.), 1925 Jan. 5, I
Rossiter, Thomas P., 1856(4), II
Rossner, Judith, 1975(1), II
Rosters:
  first commercial, 1773(1), III
Rostow, Eugene, 1983 Jan. 12, I
Rostropovich, Mstislav, 1975 Mar. 28(1), II
Rotary Clubs, 1905(2), IV
  women admitted, 1987 May 4, IV
Roth, Philip, 1959(1), II; 1960 Mar. 23, II;
  1969(1), II; 1973(1), II; 1974(1), II;
  1979(1), II; 1983(1), II; 1987(1), II
Roth and Sons, Emery, 1963 Mar. 7, II
Rothko, Mark, 1970, II; 1972 June 28, II;
  1975 Dec. 18, II; 1983, II; 1984 May 3,
  II
Rough Riders *see* Roosevelt, Theodore
Rous, Francis Peyton, 1966 Dec. 10(2), III
Roush, Edd, 1988, IV
Rowan, Henry M., 1992 July 6, III
Rowell, George Presbury, 1864(2), III
Rowing (*see also* Sculling):
  first Childs Cup, 1879 June 24, IV
  first intercollegiate rowing race, 1852
    Aug. 3, IV
  first significant race, 1811(1), IV
  Harvard-Yale crew match, 1870(7), IV
  intercollegiate rowing contests
    institutionalized, 1860(3), IV
  oarsmen as sport idols, 1873(4), IV
Rowlandson, Mary, 1682(2), II; 1705–1709,
  II
Rowson, Susanna, 1794(5), II; 1813, II
Royal American Magazine, 1774 Jan., II
Royalties:
  accord with U.S.S.R., 1974 Dec. 10, II
  recordings, 1944 Nov. 11, II
  Resale Act (Calif.), 1977 Jan. 1, II
Royle, Edwin Milton, 1905 Oct. 23, II
Rubber:
  Goodyear vulcanizing patent, 1839(2),
    III; 1844, III
  rationing, 1941 Dec. 27, III
  strike ended, 1967 July 26, III

Rubin, Barbara Jo, 1969 Feb. 22, IV
Rubin, Jerry, 1973 Dec. 4, I
Rubin, Joan Shelley, 1992(1), II
Rubinstein, Arthur, 1961, II
Rubinstein, Helena, 1965, IV
Rubinstein, John, 1980 June 8, II
Rubinstein, Serge, 1955 Jan. 27, IV
Ruby, Jack, 1963 Nov. 24, I; 1964 Mar. 14,
  I; 1964 Sept. 27, I; 1966 Oct. 5, I; 1967,
  I
Ruckelshaus, William D., 1970 Dec. 2, I;
  1973 Oct. 20, I
Rudi, Joe, 1976 June 15, IV
Ruehl, Mercedes, 1991 June 2, II; 1992
  Mar. 31, II
Rugs *see* Furniture and home furnishings
Ruiz, Rosie, 1980 Apr. 21, IV
Rukeyser, Merryle S., 1988, III
Rum:
  colonial importation, 1728(4), IV
  importation permitted (Ga.), 1749
    Oct. 26, I
  Molasses Act, 1733 May 17, I
Rummel, Joseph Francis (Archbishop),
  1962 Mar. 27, III
Rumsfeld, Donald, 1975 Nov. 3, I
Running (*see also* Boston Marathon; Foot
  racing; Jogging; New York City
  Marathon; Track and field):
  Deerfoot's sensation in England,
    1861(2), IV
  ten-mile foot race, 1835(3), IV
Runstedt, Karl von, 1944 Dec. 16, I
Runyan, Paul, 1934 July 29, IV; 1938 July
  16, IV
Rural areas:
  free mail delivery, 1896 Oct. 1, I;
    1900(1), III
  Garland's realistic fiction on, 1917, II
  population, 1920(1), I
  population decline, 1910(1), III; 1988,
    I
Rural electrification, 1933 May 18, I
Rural Electrification Administration
  (REA), 1935 May 11, I
Rush, Benjamin, 1770(1), III; 1775 Apr. 14,
  I; 1787(1), III; 1800 Sept. 23, IV; 1812(1),
  III
Rush, Norman, 1991 Nov. 20, II
Rush, William, 1814(3), II; 1833 Jan. 17, II
Rusk, Dean, 1960 Dec. 12, I
Rusk, Ralph L., 1950 Mar. 16, II
Ruskin, John, 1856(7), II; 1872(5), II;
  1877(3), II
Russell, Bertrand, 1940 Apr. 27, III
Russell, Bill, 1966 Apr. 17–28, IV; 1969
  Apr. 23–May 5, IV
Russell, Charles E., 1928 May 7, II
Russell, Harold, 1947 Mar. 13(2), II
Russell, Joanne, 1977 July 2, IV
Russell, John Henry, 1861 Sept. 13, I
Russell, Louis B., Jr., 1974 Nov. 27, III
Russell, Richard B., 1971, I
Russell, Rosalind, 1976, II
Russell's Magazine, 1857(2), II
Russia (*see also* Cold War; Soviet Union):
  aid plan to promote free market, 1992
    Apr. 1, III
  Alaska settlement, 1811, IV
  fifty-four forty treaty, 1824, I

Russia (cont.)
 U.S. abrogated 1832 treaty, 1911 Dec. 18, I
Russian Orthodox Church, 1792(1), III; 1872(1), III
Russian Revolution, 1919(1), II
Russo, Anthony, Jr., 1973 May 11, II
Russo-Finnish War, 1939 Nov. 30, I
Russo-Japanese War, 1905, I
Rustin, Bayard, 1987, I
Rutgers University (N.J.):
 founded, 1766 Nov. 10, III
Ruth, Babe (George Herman), 1927, IV; 1948, IV; 1961 Oct. 1, IV; 1964 Oct. 7–15, IV; 1966, IV; 1969 Sept. 22, IV; 1974, IV; 1974 Apr. 8, IV; 1992, II
Rutherford, Margaret, 1964 Apr. 13, II
Rutledge, John, 1776 Mar., I
Ryan, Cornelius, 1974, II
Ryan, Elizabeth, 1921 June 29, IV; 1927 July 2, IV; 1928 July 7, IV; 1930 July 4, IV
Ryan, Leo J., 1978 Nov. 18, I
Ryan, Nolan, 1985 July 11, IV; 1989 Aug. 22, IV; 1990 July 31, IV
Ryan, Robert, 1973, II
Ryder, Albert Pinkham, 1900, II
Rynning, Ole, 1838(5), II
Ryswick, Treaty of, 1697 Sept. 30, I
Ryukyu Islands, 1969 Nov. 21(1), I
Ryun, Jim, 1966 July 17, IV; 1967 June 23, IV

Saarinen, Eero, 1948(6), II; 1961, II; 1962 Feb. 24, II; 1962 May 28, II; 1963, II; 1965 Oct. 21(2), II; 1965 Oct. 28, II; 1968 May 25, II
Sabatini, Gabriela, 1990 Sept. 8–9, IV
Sabotage, 1916 July 30, I
 peacetime penalties, 1954 Sept. 3, I
Sacajawea, 1805(1), IV
Saccharin, 1977 Mar. 9, III
Sacco-Vanzetti case, 1920 Apr. 15, I; 1927 Aug. 23, I
 Anderson's plays on, 1935 Sept. 25, II
Sackler, Howard, 1968 Oct. 3, II; 1969 May 5, II
Sackler Museum, Arthur M. (Cambridge, Mass.), 1985, II
Sackler Museum, Arthur M. (Wash., D.C.), 1987 Sept. 28, II
Sadat, Anwar el-, 1978 Feb. 8, I; 1978 Sept. 6–17, I; 1979 Mar. 26, I
Safety pin, 1849(2), III
Sagamore Hill (Oyster Bay, N.Y.), 1962 July 25, II
Sagan, Carl, 1978 Apr. 17, II
Sailing see America's Cup; Boating
Saint, Eva Marie, 1955 Mar. 30, II
St. Albans (Vt.) raid, 1864 Oct. 19(1), I
St. Andrews Club (Yonkers, N.Y.), 1888, IV
St. Anne's Church (Brooklyn, N.Y.), 1869(2), II
St. Augustine (Fla.), 1565 Sept. 8, I; 1565 Sept. 8, III
St. Bartholomew's Church (N.Y.C.), 1918(6), II
St. David's Day, 1729 Mar. 1, IV
St. Denis, Ruth, 1906(2), II; 1916, II; 1968, II

Saint-Gaudens, Augustus, 1887(2), II; 1891(2), II
St. George's Day, 1729 Apr. 23, IV
St. John, Adela Rogers, 1988, II
St. John, John P., 1884 July 23, I
St. John's College (Md.), 1784 Nov., III
St. John's University (N.Y.C.), 1991 Feb. 2, IV
St. Lawrence Seaway, 1954, I; 1954 Jan. 20, III; 1954 May 13, III
St. Lawrence University (N.Y.), 1856 Apr. 3, III
St. Louis (Mo.):
 cholera epidemic, 1866(1), I
 fire and cholera epidemic, 1849 May 17, I
 Gateway Arch, 1965 Oct. 28, II; 1968 May 25, II
 tornado, 1896 May 27, I; 1927 Sept. 29, I; 1959 Feb. 10, I
St. Louis University (Mo.), 1832 Dec. 28, III
St. Lusson, Daumont de, 1670–1679, I
St. Mark's in-the-Bouwerie (N.Y.C.), 1799(3), II
St. Nicholas magazine, 1873, II
St. Patrick's Cathedral (N.Y.C.), 1839, II; 1858(2), II; 1970 Nov. 30, II
St. Patrick's Day:
 first celebrations, 1737 Mar. 17, IV
St. Paul's Chapel (N.Y.C.), 1766(1), II
St. Paul's Episcopal Church (Augusta, Ga.), 1819(4), II
St. Philip's Church (S.C.), 1835(8), II
St. Stephen's Catholic Church (Boston, Mass.) only extant Bulfinch-designed, 1804(2), II
St. Stephen's College (N.Y.), 1860 Mar. 20, III
St. Tammany Society, 1792 Oct. 12, IV
Saito, Ryoei, 1990 May 15, II
Salam, Abdus, 1979 Oct. 16(2), III
Salazar, Alberto, 1981 Oct. 25, IV; 1982 Apr. 19, IV
Salerno, "Fat Tony" (Anthony), 1988 May 4, IV; 1992, IV
Salinger, J. D., 1961(1), II; 1963(1), II; 1974 Nov. 2, II
Salk, Jonas E., 1954 Feb. 23, III; 1955 Apr. 12, III; 1956 June 11, III
Salk, Lee, 1992, III
Salmagundi (Irving and Paulding), 1807 Jan.24, II
Salomon Brothers, 1991 Aug. 18, III
Salonga, Lea, 1991 June 2, II
Saloons see Bars, saloons, and taverns
Salt:
 first patent, 1641 Oct., III
Salt Lake City (Utah):
 Mormons established, 1847 July 24, III
SALT (Strategic Arms Limitation Talks) see under Arms Control and disarmament
Salvador, Francis, 1775 Jan. 11, I
Salvation Army, 1880, III; 1904 Nov. 2, III; 1989, III
Samoa, 1878 Jan. 17, I; 1889, I; 1890 Feb. 4, I
 partition treaty, 1899 Dec. 2, I
Sampras, Pete, 1990 Sept. 8–9, IV

Sampson, William T., 1898 Apr. 22(1), I
Samuels, Ernest, 1965 May 3, II
Samuelson, Paul A., 1970 Oct. 16, III
San Antonio (Tex.):
 HemisFair 68, 1968 Apr. 6, II
Sandberg, Ryne, 1992 Mar. 2, IV
Sandburg, Carl, 1916(1), II; 1918(1), II; 1919 June 2, II; 1920(1), II; 1922(1), II; 1926(1), II; 1939(1), II; 1940 May 6, II; 1951 May 7, II; 1953(1), II; 1967, II
Sande, Earl, 1968, IV
Sanders, George, 1951 Mar. 29(2), II
Sanders, Harland ("Colonel"), 1980, III
Sandoz, Mari, 1966, II
Sandwich glass, 1825(2), III; 1825(4), IV
San Francisco (Calif.):
 anti-Vietnam War demonstration, 1967 Apr. 15, I; 1971 Apr. 23, I
 bomb thrown, 1916 July 22, I
 domestic partnership law, 1991 Feb. 14, IV
 early fires, 1850 May 4, I; 1851 May 3, I
 earthquake, 1989 Oct. 17, I
 earthquake and fire, 1906, I
 heroin seized, 1991 June 21, IV
 mayor and city supervisor murdered, 1978 Nov. 27, I
 video display terminal workplace regulations, 1990 Dec. 27, I
 World Fair opened, 1939, IV
San Francisco-Oakland Bay Bridge (Calif.), 1932(2), III
San Francisco State College (Calif.), 1968 Nov. 6, III
Sanger, Frederick, 1980 Oct. 14(1), III
Sanger, Margaret, 1915(2), II; 1916 Oct. 16, III; 1929 Apr. 15, III; 1966, IV
 American Birth Control League founding, 1921 Nov. 2, III
San Jacinto, Battle of, 1836(2), IV; 1836 Apr. 21, I; 1836 Apr. 21, IV
San José, Declaration of, 1963 Mar. 19, I
San José (Calif.), 1777 Nov., I
San Juan Capistrano (Calif.), 1777(2), II
Santa Anna, Antonio López de, 1836(2), IV; 1836 Mar. 6, I; 1836 Apr. 21, I
Santa Clara, University of (Calif.), 1855 Apr. 28, III
Santa Fe Opera House, 1967 July 27, II
Santa Fe Trail, 1821, I
 Fort Leavenworth (Kan.), 1827(1), I
Santana, Manuel, 1965 Sept. 12, IV
Santayana, George, 1896(1), II; 1935(1), II; 1940(5), III
Santo Domingo:
 U.S. Marines landed, 1916 May, I
San Xavier del Bac (Ariz.), 1784(3), II
Saperstein, Abe, 1966, IV
Sapp, Carolyn Suzanne, 1991 Sept. 14, IV
Sarah Lawrence College (N.Y.), 1926(3), III
Saranac Lake (N.Y.), 1885, III
Saratoga (N.Y.):
 attacked and burned, 1745 Nov. 28–29, I
Saratoga (warship), 1955 Oct. 7, III
Sarazen, Gene, 1921 Sept. 28, IV; 1922 July 15, IV; 1923 Sept. 29, IV; 1932 June 25, IV; 1933 Aug. 13, IV; 1935 Apr. 8, IV; 1965 June 21, IV; 1966 July 9, IV

Sargent, George, 1909 June 25, IV
Sargent, John Singer, 1881(6), II; 1884(4), II
Sargent, Lucius Manlius, 1835(2), IV; 1848(4), II
Sarnoff, David, 1971, III; 1984 Mar. 4, II
Saroyan, William, 1939 Oct. 25, II; 1940 May 6, II; 1943(1), II; 1957 Oct. 19, II; 1981, II
Sassacus (Indian chief), 1630–1639, I
Satellites (see also Weather satellites):
    astronomy, Explorer 38, 1968 July 4, III
    Atlas missile, 1959, III
    bill creating communications corporation, 1962 Aug. 27(1), III
    communications, first commercial, 1965 Apr. 6, III
    communications, international agreement, 1964 July 24, I
    communications (Echo 2), 1964, III; 1964 Jan. 25, III
    communications (Relay 1), 1963 Jan. 3, III
    communications (Syncom 1), 1963 Feb. 14, III
    communications (Syncom 2), 1963 July 26, III
    communications (Syncom 3), 1964 Aug. 19, III
    communications (Telstar 2), 1963 May 7, III
    Discoverer 1, 1959 Feb. 28, III
    Discoverer 2, 1959 Apr. 13, III
    Discoverer 21, 1961 Feb. 18, III
    Discoverer 25, 1961 June 16, III
    Discoverer 5, 1959 Aug. 13, III
    Discoverer 6, 1959 Aug. 19, III
    early warning system, 1960 May 24, III
    experimental Earth orbit, 1960 Apr. 13, III
    Explorer 11, 1961 Apr. 27, III
    Explorer 6, 1959 Aug. 7, III
    first announced, 1955 July 29, III
    first ERTS-1 launched, 1972 July 23, III
    first human, 1984 Feb. 7, III
    first international, 1962 Apr. 26(1), III
    first U.S. Earth launched (Fla.), 1958 Jan. 31, III
    INTELSAT agreement, 1971 Aug. 20, III
    launched to monitor nuclear test-ban treaty violations, 1963 Oct. 16, I
    Lunar Orbiter 1, 1966 Aug. 10, III
    Lunar Orbiter 2, 1966 Nov. 6, III
    nuclear generator, 1959 Nov. 18, III
    Relay 1 intercontinental communications, 1962 Dec. 13, III
    secret military launched, 1963 May 9, III
    Surveyor 2, 1966 Sept. 22, III
    Telstar communications, 1962, III; 1962 July 10, III
    three launched simultaneously, 1961 June 29, III
    Van Allen belt discovered, 1958(1), III
    Vanguard 1, 1958 Mar. 17, III
    Vanguard 2, 1959 Feb. 17, III

Satellites (cont.)
    Vanguard 3, 1959 Sept. 18, III
Satire (see also Humor):
    on American Revolution, 1776, II; 1779, II
    on colonies, 1775(3), II
    Contrast, The (play), 1790(2), II
    Drake's poetry, 1819, II
    Fanny (Halleck), 1820, II
    Fashion (Mowatt) theatrical comedy, 1845 Mar. 24, II
    Fessenden's works, 1803(1), II
    first of college student, 1807(1), II
    Hartford Wits, 1807, II
    Hoyt's plays, 1891 Nov. 9, II
    of Kennedy family, 1962(3), II
    MacBird (Garson) on Johnson administration, 1967 Feb. 22, II
    M'Fingal (on Tories), 1775(1), II; 1782(4), II
    Modern Chivalry (Brackenridge), 1792(4), II; 1805, IV
    Nasby's works (Locke), 1864(8), II; 1865(3), II
    on New World settlements, 1613, II
    on Plymouth Pilgrims, 1637(2), II
    poem on Md., 1708, II
    Prue and I (Curtis), 1856(6), II
    on tolerance, 1647(1), II
Saturday Evening Post, The (magazine), 1729 Oct., II; 1968 May 4, III; 1969 Feb. 8, II
Saturday Review of Literature (magazine), 1971 Nov. 16, II; 1982, II
Saturn (planet):
    moon and rings discovered, 1979 Sept. 1, III
    more moons and rings discovered, 1980 Nov. 12, III
    Voyager 2 data, 1981 Aug. 25, III
Saudi Arabia:
    Gulf War, 1990 Aug. 2–Dec. 31, I
    U.S. arms sale, 1981 Apr. 21, I
Sauer, Hank, 1952 July 8, IV
Sauk Indians, 1830 July 15, I; 1831 June 27, I; 1832 Apr. 6, I; 1832 Aug. 2, I
Savalas, Telly, 1974 May 28, II
Savannah (Ga.):
    British occupied, 1778 Dec. 29, I
    cyclone, 1893 Aug. 24, I
    siege, 1779 Sept. 3–Oct. 28, I
Savannah (ship), 1959 July 21, III; 1962 Aug. 22(1), III
Savery, William, 1780–1784, IV
Savimbi, Jonas, 1986, I
Savings and loan associations:
    bail-out bill, 1989 Aug. 9, III
    failures, 1988 Dec. 31, III
    federal bail out, 1991 Dec. 3, III
    fraud convictions, 1990 Jan. 22, III
    improved, 1991, III
    insurance premiums raised, 1992 May 12(2), III
    Keating sentenced, 1992 Apr. 10(1), IV
    law firm settlement agreement, 1992 Mar. 8, I
Savings bonds see Government bonds
Savitt, Dick, 1951 July 6–7, IV
Say, Jean Baptiste, 1804 Feb. 1, IV

Scalia, Antonin, 1986 June 17, I
Scandals (see also Watergate):
    Annapolis midshipmen cheating, 1974 May 23, I
    artificial insemination fraud, 1992 Mar. 4, III
    BCCI, 1991 July 5, III
    Black Sox (Chicago White Sox), 1920, IV; 1921 Aug. 3, IV
    Boesky insider trading, 1986 Nov. 14, IV
    congressional sex, 1976, I; 1976 Sept. 1, I
    Crédit Mobilier, 1867(1), III; 1867(2), I; 1872(1), I
    Grant administration, 1875, I; 1876, I
    horse-switching, 1977 Dec. 2, IV
    House banking, 1992 Apr. 16, I
    illegal corporate donations to congressmen, 1976, I
    independent prosecutors upheld, 1988 June 29, I
    Iran-Contra, 1986 Nov. 3, I; 1987 Feb. 26, I; 1987 Nov. 18, I; 1988 Mar. 16, I; 1989 May 4, I; 1990 Apr. 7, I; 1991 Oct. 7, I
    Korean lobbyist (Koreagate), 1976, I; 1976 Oct. 20(2), I; 1978, I
    life insurance (N.Y.), 1905, III
    Mills linked with burlesque performer, 1974 Dec. 10, I
    Navy Tailhook sexual harassment, 1992 Sept. 24, I
    payola, 1960 Jan. 25, II; 1960 Apr. 29, II; 1960 May 19, II
    police (Chicago, Ill.), 1960 Jan. 24, IV
    savings and loan crisis, 1989 Aug. 9, III; 1990 Jan. 22, III; 1991 Dec. 3, III; 1992 Mar. 8, I; 1992 Apr. 10(1), IV
    securities, 1990 Nov. 21, III; 1991 Aug. 18, III
    Teapot Dome, 1922 Apr. 15, I; 1923 Oct. 25, I; 1924 June 30, I; 1927 Oct. 10, I; 1929 Oct. 7(2), I; 1930 Mar. 13, I
    TV evangelists, 1987 Mar. 19, III; 1988 Apr. 8, III
    TV quiz show, 1960 Oct. 17, II
    U.S. Air Force Academy cheating, 1965 Feb. 3, III
    West Point widespread cheating, 1976 Apr. 22, III; 1977 Sept. 27, III
Scarlet fever, 1736, III; 1925(5), III
Scarne, John, 1985, IV
Schacht, Al, 1984, IV
Schaefer, Laurie Lea, 1971 Sept. 11, IV
Schally, Andrew V., 1977 Oct. 13, III
Schary, Dore, 1958 Jan. 30, II; 1961 Mar. 9, II
Schawlow, Arthur, 1981 Oct. 19(2), III
Schayes, Dolph, 1960 Jan. 12, IV
Schell, Jonathan, 1982(1), II
Schell, Maximilian, 1962 Apr. 9, II
Schenkkan, Robert, 1992 Apr. 7, II
Schick, Jacob, 1923 Nov. 6, III
Schiff, Jacob, 1893(5), III
Schildkraut, Joseph, 1938 Mar. 10, II
Schine, G. David, 1954 Apr. 23–June 17, I

Schirra, Walter M., Jr., 1962 Oct. 3, III; 1965 Dec. 15, III; 1968 Oct. 11, III
Schisgal, Murray, 1974 Dec. 29, II
Schlesinger, Arthur M., Jr.:
    historical works, 1945(1), II
    National Book Awards, 1966 Mar. 15(1), II; 1979 Apr. 23, II
    Pulitzer Prize, 1946 May 6, II; 1966 May 2, II
    Thousand Days, A, 1965(1), II
Schlesinger, James R., 1975 Nov. 3, I
    named energy secretary, 1977 Aug. 4, I
Schmeling, Max, 1929(1), IV; 1930 June 12, IV
Schmidt, Harvey, 1960 May 3, II
Schmitt, Harrison, 1972 Dec. 7, III
Schoenberg, Arnold, 1941 Apr. 11, II; 1948(5), II; 1974 Sept. 12–15, II; 1990, II
Schoendienst, Albert F. (Red), 1989 July 23(3), IV
Scholarships:
    first black woman to win Rhodes, 1979 Sept. 9, III
Scholastic aptitude tests (SATS), 1981 Sept. 29, III; 1991, III
Schollander, Don, 1963 Aug. 24(1), IV
Scholz, Janos, 1973 Dec. 11, II
School busing:
    Boston (Mass.) issue, 1975 Dec. 9, III
    Boston School Committee fined, 1974 Dec. 30, III
    collision and drowning (Ky.), 1958 Feb. 28(1), I
    first cross-district busing (Ky.), 1975 Sept. 4, III
    plan rejected (Detroit, Mich.), 1974 July 25, III
    Supreme Ct. modification, 1991 Jan. 15(1), I
    upheld, 1971 Apr. 20, III
    violence (Boston, Mass.), 1974, III; 1974 Sept. 12, III
Schoolcraft, Henry Rowe, 1820, III
School desegregation:
    Ala. National Guard federalized, 1963 Sept. 10, III
    anti-integration riots (New Orleans, La.), 1960 Nov. 17, II
    Ark. law closing schools ruled against, 1959 June 18, III
    backlash to, 1966, III
    Chicago (Ill.) boycott against segregation, 1963 Oct. 22, III
    Chicago (Ill.) slow-paced protested, 1965 June 10, III
    closings to avoid desegregation unconstitutional, 1964 May 25, III
    college, 1962, III
    colleges opened to blacks (S.C. and Ala.), 1963, III
    complete compliance ordered, 1967 Mar. 29, III
    complete public, 1967 deadline announced, 1965 Apr. 29, III
    continued noncompliance, 1979 Feb. 13, III
    deadline enforcement modifications, 1969 July 3, III
    de facto boycotts, 1964, III

School desegregation (*cont.*)
    elementary school (Miss.), 1964 Aug. 14, III
    federal deadline extended, 1969 Jan. 29, III
    federal funding denied to southern violators, 1966 May 13, III
    federal lawyers protested Nixon policies, 1969 Aug. 27, III
    immediate of Miss. districts ordered, 1969 Oct. 29, III
    in Catholic schools (New Orleans, La.), 1962 Mar. 27, III
    increased southern compliance, 1967 Apr. 2, III
    in S.C., 1963 Jan. 28, III
    Little Rock (Ark.) defiance, 1958 Sept. 30, III
    Little Rock (Ark.) high schools reopened, 1959 Aug. 12, III
    Little Rock (Ark.) racial violence, 1957 Sept. 24, I
    local control returned ruling, 1992 Mar. 31, I
    La. segregation laws banned, 1956 Feb. 15, I
    Miss. university system ruled noncomplying, 1992 June 26, III
    only 6% in South in six years, 1960 Apr. 9, III
    private nonsectarian ordered, 1976 June 25, III
    private schools' tax exemptions denied, 1983 May 24, III
    religious leaders' support, 1957, III
    southern states' reaction, 1956, I
    South higher than North, 1975 Mar. 11, III
    state-supported private schools (Va.), 1956 Jan. 9, I
    Supreme Ct. deadline, 1970 Jan. 14, III
    Supreme Ct. declared against, 1954 May 17, I
    Supreme Ct. ordered, 1955 May 31, III; 1991 Jan. 15(1), I
    token, 1960, III
    University of Alabama desegregated, 1963 June 11, III
    University of Mississippi, 1962 Sept. 20, III; 1962 Sept. 28, III; 1962 Sept. 30, III; 1962 Dec. 21, III
    Va. discriminatory laws ruled invalid, 1959 Jan. 19, III
    Wash., D.C., ordered to end, 1967 June 19, III
School prayer *see* Church-state separation
School taxes *see* Education and schools
Schorer, Mark, 1961(1), II
Schorr, Daniel, 1976 Feb. 11–18, II
Schorske, Carl E., 1981 Apr. 13, II
Schrieffer, John R., 1972 Oct. 20(1), III
Schroeder, Frederick R., Jr., 1942 Sept. 6–7, IV
Schroeder, Ted, 1949 July 1–2, IV
Schroeder, William J., 1984 Nov. 25, III; 1986 June 19, III; 1986 Aug. 6, III
Schulberg, Budd, 1947(1), II; 1950(1), II
Schuller, Gunther, 1966 Oct. 12, II; 1989, II

Schultz, Theodore W., 1979 Oct. 17(1), III
Schuman, William, 1943 May 3, II; 1945 Dec. 27, II; 1953 May 4(1), II; 1963, II; 1970 Jan. 29, II; 1992, II
Schumann-Heink, Ernestine, 1898 Nov. 7, II
Schurz, Carl (Mrs.), 1856(1), III
Schuyler, James, 1981 Apr. 13, II
Schwartz, Delmore, 1966, II
Schwartz, Melvin, 1988 Oct. 19, III
Schwartz, Stephen, 1971 May 17, II; 1972 Sept. 23, II
Schwarzkopf, H. Norman, Jr., 1991(1), II; 1992(1), II
Schweickart, Russell L., 1969 Mar. 3, III
Schwerner, Michael, 1964 Aug. 4, I; 1964 Dec. 4, I; 1967 Oct. 20, I
Schwinger, Julian S., 1965 Oct. 21(1), III
Schwomeyer, Judy, 1970 Feb. 6–7, IV
Science (*see also* Evolution; specific disciplines):
    American Assn. for the Advancement of founded, 1848 Sept., III
    associations encouraged (Mass.), 1780(1), III
    blacklists, 1969 Oct. 8, III
    colonial developments, 1735–1739, III
    deaths, 1988, III; 1989, III; 1990, III; 1991, III
    early brush with fundamentalism, 1878(1), III
    first association, 1740–1744, III
    Gibbs's contribution, 1876, III
    greater educational emphasis on, 1871(1), III
    Maclure's contribution, 1809, III
    Mitchill's contributions, 1795–1799, III
    National Academy founded (Wash., D.C.), 1863 Mar. 3, III
    Phila. (Pa.) Academy founded, 1812(5), III
    popularization, 1806(3), III
    practical approach to, 1802, III
    Priestley's studies, 1804, III
    religious dominance over, 1769(4), III
    Silliman's contribution, 1818, III
    Smithsonian Institution (Wash., D.C.), 1846, III
    U.S. delegation visited China, 1978 July 6–10, III
    U.S. student deficiency in, 1989 Jan. 31, II
Science and Technology, Office of, 1962 June 8, III
Scioto Company, 1790 Mar., I
Scofield, Paul, 1962 Apr. 29, II; 1967 Apr. 10, II; 1969 June 8, II
Scopes, John T., 1925 July 10–21, III; 1970, III
Scott, Blanche Stuart, 1970, III
Scott, David R., 1966 Mar. 16, III; 1969 Mar. 3, III; 1971 July 26, III
Scott, Dred, 1857, I
Scott, George C., 1971 Apr. 14, II; 1971 May 9, III
Scott, Norman N., 1914 Mar. 21, IV
Scott, Robert L., Jr., 1943(1), II
Scott, Walter (Sir), 1811(1), II; 1812 Apr. 13, II; 1813(4), II; 1814(2), II; 1820(4), II; 1821(1), II

Scott, Winfield:
    Aroostock War, 1839 Feb. 12, I
    entered Mexico City, 1847 Sept. 14, I
    Mexican War, 1847 Mar. 9, I; 1847
        Apr. 18, I; 1847 Aug. 20, I; 1847
        Sept. 8, I; 1847 Sept. 13, I
    "Old Fuss and Feathers" coined,
        1841(1), IV
    retired as Army head, 1861 Oct. 31, I
    Trail of Tears term, 1838(1), IV
    Whig presidential candidacy, 1852
        June 16–21, I; 1852 Nov. 2, I
Scranton, William W.:
    Campus Unrest Commission, 1970
        June 13, III
Scribner's Monthly (publication), 1870(3),
    II
Scribner's Sons, Charles, 1984 Apr. 25, II
Scrimshaw, 1829(1), II
Sculling, 1851(5), IV
Sculpture:
    Adams's works, 1901(3), II
    Barbee's works, 1859(4), II
    Borglum's *Mares of Diomedes*,
        1904(6), II
    Calder record auction price, 1984
        May 9, II
    Calder stabile (Chicago, Ill.), 1973
        May 4, II
    Canova statue of Washington, 1821(3),
        II
    Centennial of 1876 influence on
        American, 1876(11), II
    Chicago's Picasso steel, 1967 Aug. 15,
        II
    Chinese ceramic exhibit (Phila., Pa.),
        1987, II
    Clevenger's contribution, 1836(2), II
    Crawford's works, 1857 Oct. 10, II
    Creeft's *Rachmaninoff*, 1945(2), II
    Donoghue's work, 1885(5), II
    early equestrian statue of G.
        Washington, 1856 July 4, II
    equestrian (Boston Public Gardens),
        1864(6), II
    Ethan Allen statue, 1876 Feb. 28, II
    first American-born sculptor, 1814(3),
        II
    first equestrian bronze casting, 1853
        Jan. 8, II
    first known American, 1769(2), II
    first life-sized bronze statue, 1847(1),
        II
    French's for Columbian Exposition,
        1893(4), II
    French's works, 1879(2), II
    garden (Neb.), 1976 July 4, II
    Gaudens' *Grief* (Wash., D.C.), 1891(2),
        II
    Gould's *West Wind*, 1869(4), II
    Greenough's contribution, 1829, II
    Hosmer's *Puck*, 1860(5), II
    Indian subjects and themes, 1888(2),
        II
    Kemeys' animals, 1878(4), II
    Lincoln statues, 1866(4), II; 1887(2), II
    Lipchitz final collection dedicated
        (N.Y.C.), 1977 Nov. 28, II
    MacMonnies' Columbian fountain,
        1893(3), II

Sculpture (*cont.*)
    MacNeil's works, 1900(2), II
    Manship in Rome, 1909(4), II
    Manship's works, 1913(2), II
    Moore bronzes (N.Y.C.), 1962 Mar. 20,
        II
    Nevelson museum donation, 1985
        Mar. 17, II
    Palmer's *Chancellor Robert R.
        Livingston*, 1876(10), II
    Picasso exhibit (N.Y.C.), 1967 Oct. 11,
        II
    Powers's *Clytie*, 1868(4), II
    Powers's *Greek Slave* statue, 1851, II
    Reclining Figure (Moore) price, 1982,
        II
    record auction price, 1986 May 6, II;
        1988 May 10, II
    record price paid (Calif.), 1977 Nov.
        22, II
    Rinehart's *Clytie*, 1872(3), II
    Rogers's Civil War scenes, 1867(2), II
    Rose donation, 1960 Jan. 6, II
    Rush's work, 1833 Jan. 17, II
    small plaster groups vogue, 1875(2), II
    Soldiers' and Sailors' Monument
        (Boston, Mass.), 1874(2), II
    Struggle of the Two Natures in Man
        (Barnard), 1894(2), II
    Tilden's sports, 1885(6), II
    Valley Curtain (Christo), 1972 Aug.
        11, II
    *Variation Within a Sphere, No. 10:
        The Sun* (Lippold), 1956(5), II
    J. Q. A. Ward's statues, 1864, II
    G. Washington statue destroyed by
        fire (N.C.), 1831 June 21, II
    Washington statues, 1833(1), II
    D. Webster statue (N.Y.C.), 1876(9), II
    Weinman's works, 1938(4), II
Sea, Law of the, 1981, I
Seabed treaty:
    signed, 1971 Feb. 11, I
Seaberg, Glenn T., 1951 Nov. 15, III
Seabury, Samuel (Rev.), 1783, III; 1784
    Nov. 18, III
Seafood *see* Fish and fishing
Seagram Building (N.Y.C.), 1957, II
Sealab program:
    Pacific Ocean research, 1965 Oct. 12,
        III
Seale, Bobby, 1969 Sept. 24, I
Seals, 1892 Feb. 29, I
Seaman, Elizabeth Cochrane *see* Bly,
    Nellie
Sears, Evelyn, 1907(3), IV
Sears, Richard D., 1881(2), IV; 1882(6), IV;
    1883(3), IV; 1884(8), IV; 1885(2), IV;
    1886(3), IV; 1887(4), IV
Sears, Roebuck & Co.:
    latest fashions in catalog, 1939(1), IV
Sears Tower (Chicago, Ill.), 1973 May 3, II
Seattle Art Museum (Wash.), 1991 Dec. 5,
    II
Seattle Mariners:
    Japanese ownership, 1992 June 11, IV
Seaver, Tom, 1975 Sept. 1, IV; 1985 Aug.
    4, IV; 1992 Aug. 2, IV
Seawolf (submarine), 1958 Oct. 6, I
Sebastiano del Piombo, 1519, II

Seccomb, John, 1730(4), II
Secession (*see also* Civil War; Confederate
    States of America):
    Ala., 1861 Jan. 11, I
    Ark., 1861 May 6, I
    bid for Fla.'s return to Union, 1864
        Feb. 7, I
    Fla., 1861 Jan. 10, I
    Ga., 1861 Jan. 19, I
    La., 1861 Jan. 26, I
    Miss., 1861 Jan. 9(2), I
    N.C., 1861 May 20, I
    S.C., 1860 Dec. 20, I
    State Disunion Convention (Mass.),
        1857 Jan. 15, I
    states readmitted, 1870 Jan. 26, I;
        1870 Feb. 23, I; 1870 Mar. 30(1), I;
        1870 July 15, I
    Tenn., 1861 June 8, I
    Tex., 1861 Feb. 23, I
    Va., 1861 Apr. 17, I
Second Coinage Act, 1834 June 28, I
Secord, Richard V., 1989 May 4, I
Secret Service:
    organized, 1778 June, I
Securities Exchange Act, 1934 June 6, I
Sedgman, Frank, 1951 Sept. 4, IV; 1952
    Sept. 7, IV
Sedgwick, Catherine Maria, 1835(3), II
Sedition Act (*see also* Alien and Sedition
    Acts):,
        1918 May 16, I
Seely, Henry W., 1882(4), III
Seger, Bob, and the Silver Bullet Band
    (group), 1981 Feb. 25, II
Segovia, Andrés, 1987, II
Segre, Emilio, 1959 Oct. 26, III; 1989, III
Seidel, Emil, 1912 May 17, I
Seidel, Frederick, 1981 Jan. 5, II
Seixas, Victor, 1953 July 3, IV; 1954 July
    3(2), IV; 1954 Sept. 6, IV; 1955 July 1–2,
    IV; 1956 July 7, IV
Seko, Toshihiko, 1987 Apr. 20, IV
Selden, George B., 1879 May 8, III; 1895
    Nov. 5, III
Selective Service *see* Draft
Selective Service Act:
    World War I, 1917 May 18, I
    World War II, 1940 Sept. 16, I; 1946
        May 14, I; 1948 June 24(2), I
Selective Service Act Extension, 1941 Aug.
    18, I
Seles, Monica, 1991 Sept. 7–8, IV; 1992
    Sept. 12–13, IV
Selfridge, Thomas W., 1908 Sept. 17, III
Selleck, Tom, 1984 Sept. 23, II
Selma (Ala.):
    civil rights march, 1965 Mar. 21, I
    Liuzzo killed, 1965 Mar. 25, I
Selznick, David O., 1965, II
Seminole Indians, 1817 Nov. 20, I; 1818, I;
    1821 Sept., I; 1832 May 9, I; 1834 Oct.
    28, I; 1835, I
Senf, Christian, 1800, III
Sennett, Mack, 1914 Apr., II; 1932 Nov.
    18, II
Sequoia National Park, 1890(5), III
Sequoyah, 1824(3), IV
Serkin, Rudolph, 1991, II
Serling, Rod, 1975, II

Sert, José Luis, 1983, II
Service, Robert W., 1907(1), II
Servicemen's Readjustment Act, 1944
    June 22, III; 1947(1), III; 1952 July 16, I
Sessions, Roger, 1947(2), II; 1985, II
Seton, Anya, 1990, II
Seton, Elizabeth Ann, 1963 Mar. 17, III;
    1975 Sept. 14, III
Seton, Ernest Thompson, 1910, IV
Settle, Mary Lee, 1978 Apr. 10, II
Settlement houses:
    first Neighborhood Guild (N.Y.C.),
        1886(3), III
    Henry Street (N.Y.C.), 1893(5), III
    Hull House (Chicago, Ill.), 1889(1), III
    Livingston Street (N.Y.C.), 1893(5), III
Seuss, Dr. (Theodor Seuss Geisel), 1991, II
Sevareid, Eric, 1992, II
Seven Pines, Battle of (Va.), 1862 May
    31–June 1, I
Seventh Day Adventists, 1831 Aug., III;
    1844 Mar. 21, III
Seven Years' War (see also Paris, Treaty
    of):,
    1755–1759, I
Seversky, Alexander P., 1974, III
Sevier, John, 1806, IV
Sewall, Arthur, 1896 July 11, I; 1896 July
    22–24, I
Sewall, Richard B., 1975 Apr. 16, II
Sewall, Samuel, 1674(2), II; 1677(2), III;
    1697(2), III; 1699 June, IV; 1700(1), II;
    1702(2), II; 1714(2), III; 1714 May 12, IV
Seward, William Henry, 1858 Oct. 25, IV;
    1867, I; 1867(1), IV
Sewell, Joe, 1990, IV
Sewers see Waste disposal
Sewing:
    first paper clothes patterns, 1863(3),
        III
Sewing machines:
    first electric, 1889(7), III
    first with eye-pointed needle, 1846
        Sept. 10, III
    Gibbs's patent, 1857 June 2, III
    Singer-Howe royalty suit, 1851 Aug.
        12, III
Sex (see also Homosexuality):
    books on, 1970(1), II
    Love in Marriage (Stopes) censored,
        1921 Apr. 22, II
    marital relations, 1960 Apr. 28, III
    Presbyterian Church's misconduct
        code adopted, 1991 June 11, III
    Puritan codes, 1649–1660, IV; 1656(1),
        IV
    record warning labels for explicit
        language, 1990 Mar. 29, II
    Richards sports discrimination case,
        1976 Aug. 27, IV
Sexton, Anne, 1967 May 1, II; 1974, II
Sexual abuse (see also Rape):
    Catholic priests investigated, 1992
        Sept. 21(1), III
    day care center (N.C.), 1992 Apr. 22,
        IV
Sexual harassment, 1980 Apr. 11, I
    Navy Tailhook scandal, 1992 Sept. 24,
        I
    statistics, 1991, III

Sexual harassment (cont.)
    students' rights for damages, 1992
        Feb. 26, I
    Thomas-Hill hearings, 1991, II; 1991
        Oct. 15, I
Seymour, Harold, 1990(1), II
Seymour, Horatio, 1868 July 4–9, I
Shaara, Michael, 1975 May 5, II
Shackleford Good Roads Act, 1916 July 11,
    III
Shacochis, Bob, 1985 Jan 21, II
Shafer, Raymond P., 1969 Dec. 6, IV
Shaffer, Anthony, 1970 Nov. 12, II
Shaffer, Peter, 1974 Oct. 24, II; 1980 Dec.
    17, II
Shafter, William R., 1898 June 12–14, I;
    1898 July 17, I
Shahn, Ben, 1948(3), II; 1969, II; 1970 Jan.
    29, II
Shakers:
    founding and decline, 1770–1774, III
    furniture, c1700, IV
Shakespeare, William, 1796(4), II; 1916(6),
    II; 1918, II; 1964 Apr. 23, II; 1990 Apr.
    22, II
Shange, Ntozake, 1976 June 1, II
Shankar, Ravi, 1967, II
SHAPE (Supreme Headquarters, Allied
    Powers in Europe):
    established, 1951 Apr. 4, I
Shapiro, Karl, 1945 May 7, II
Shapiro, Meyer, 1979 Jan. 15, II
Shapley, Harlow, 1972, III
Sharkey, Jack, 1929(1), IV; 1930 June 12,
    IV
Sharon, Ariel, 1985 Jan. 24, II
Sharp, Dudley C., 1960 Feb. 25, III
Sharpe, William F., 1990 Oct. 16(3), III
Shattuck, Roger, 1975 Apr. 16, II
Shaving:
    first electric shaver, 1923 Nov. 6, III
    safety razor devised, 1880(10), III
Shaw, George Bernard, 1905 Oct. 31, II;
    1906(5), II
Shaw, Henry Wheeler, 1865(2), II
Shaw, Irwin, 1936 Mar. 14, II; 1948, II;
    1948(1), II; 1984, II
Shaw, Samuel, 1786(2), I
Shawcross, Arthur J., 1990 Dec. 13, IV
Shawn, Ted, 1916, II; 1972, II
Shays' Rebellion, 1784(1), III; 1787 Jan. 25,
    I
Sheaffer, Louis, 1974 May 7, II
Shearer, Norma, 1930 Nov. 5(1), II; 1983,
    II
Sheehan, Betsy, 1992 July 27, IV
Sheehan, Neil, 1988 Nov. 29, II; 1989 Mar.
    30, II
Sheehan, Patty, 1983 June 12, IV; 1984
    June 3, IV
Sheehan, Susan, 1983 Apr. 18, II
Sheehy, Gail, 1992(1), II
Sheeler, Charles, 1932(4), II
Sheen, Fulton J., 1949(1), II; 1979, III
Sheep see Livestock
Sheldon, Charles M., 1896(1), II
Sheldon, Edward, 1908 Nov. 17, II; 1919
    Apr. 9, II
Shellabarger, Samuel, 1945(1), II
Shelley, Carole, 1979 June 3, II

Shelley, Ken, 1972 Jan. 14–16, IV
Shenly, Paul, 1976 Feb. 9, II
Shepard, Alan B., Jr., 1961 May 5(2), III;
    1971 Jan. 31, III
Shepard, Sam, 1979 Apr. 16, II
Shepard, Thomas, 1641, IV
Sheridan, Philip H., 1864 Oct. 19(2), I;
    1865 Apr. 1, I; 1869 Jan., IV
Sheridan, Richard Brinsley, 1832(2), II
Sherlock Holmes (fictional character) see
    Holmes, Sherlock
Sherman, Allan, 1962(3), II
Sherman, James S., 1908 June 16–20, I;
    1908 Nov. 3, I; 1912 June 18–22, I
Sherman, Roger, c1775, II
Sherman, William Tecumseh:
    Columbia (S.C.) fire, 1865 Feb. 17, I
    declined Republican presidential
        nomination, 1884 June 5, IV
    Johnston's surrender, 1865 Apr. 26(1),
        I
    March to the Sea, 1864 Nov. 16, I
    occupied Atlanta (Ga.), 1864 Sept. 1, I
Sherman Antitrust Act, 1890, I; 1890 July
    14, I; 1894 Aug. 3, III
Sherman Silver Purchase Act, 1893, I;
    1893 Aug. 1, III
Sherrill, Patrick Henry, 1986 Aug. 20, IV
Sherwood, Robert E., 1927 Jan. 31, II;
    1935 Jan. 7(2), II; 1938 Oct. 3, II; 1939
    May 1, II; 1940 Mar. 29, II; 1941 May 5,
    II; 1949 May 2, II
Shevelove, Burt, 1962 May 8, II; 1963 Apr.
    25(1), II
Shiloh, Battle of (Tenn.), 1862 Apr. 6–7, I
Ship disasters:
    Athenia sunk, 1939 Sept. 3(2), I
    carrier fire (Gulf of Tonkin), 1967 July
        29, I
    carrier Oriskany fire (Gulf of Tonkin),
        1966 Oct. 26, I
    Collins Line, 1850 Apr. 27, III
    collision (Miss. R.), 1976 Oct. 20(1), I
    collision (Tampa Bay, Fla.), 1980 May
        9, I
    Eastland capsized (Chicago, Ill.), 1915
        July 24, I
    Enterprise fire (Hawaii), 1969 Jan. 14,
        I
    Erie fire, 1841 Aug. 9, I
    Evening Star, 1866 Oct. 3, I
    explosion (Tex.), 1947 Apr. 16–18, I
    General Slocum fire (N.Y.C.), 1904
        June 16, I
    Griffith fire (Lake Erie), 1850 June
        17, I
    Hoboken (N.J.) fire, 1900 June 30, I
    Housatonic sunk, 1917 Feb. 3, I
    Lady Elgin-Augusta collision (Lake
        Michigan), 1860 Sept. 7–8, I
    Larchmont (L.I. Sound), 1907 Feb. 12,
        I
    Lusitania sunk, 1915 May 7, I
    Miss. steamboat fires, 1888 Dec. 24, I
    Morro Castle fire (N.J.), 1934 Sept. 8, I
    New Era shipwreck, 1854 Nov. 13, I
    Ocean Monarch fire, 1848 Aug. 24, I
    Ohio R. collision, 1847 Nov. 19, I
    Pacific sinking, 1875 Nov. 4, I

Ship disasters (*cont.*)
   Pennsylvania explosion (Miss. R.),
      1858 June 13, I
   Phoenix fire (Lake Michigan), 1847
      Nov. 22, I
   safety requirements after *Titanic*,
      1912 May 1, III
   St. Louis (Mo.) fire, 1849 May 17, I
   San Francisco sinking, 1853 Dec. 24, I
   Schiller ran aground, 1875 May 7, I
   Scorpion missing, 1968 May 29, I
   steamboat *Lexington* fire, 1840 Jan.
      13, I
   steamboat *Stonewall* fire (Ohio R.),
      1869 Oct. 27, I
   steamer *Moselle* exploded, 1838 Apr.
      25, I
   steamer *Pulaski* exploded, 1838 June
      14, I
   S-4 disaster, 1927 Dec. 17, I
   Texaco Oklahoma tanker (N.C.), 1971
      Mar. 27, I
   Thresher sank, 1963 Apr. 10, I
   Titanic sunk, 1912 Apr. 14–15, I
   Titanic wreck found, 1985 Sept. 1, I
   worst to date, 1865 Apr. 27, I
Shipler, David K., 1987 Apr. 16, II
Ships and shipping (*see also* Barges;
   Canals; Ferries; Pirates and
   privateering; Ports; Ship disasters;
   Steamboats; submarines; names of
   specific ships):
   clipper, 1832, III
   Collins Line regular transatlantic
      crossing, 1850 Apr. 27, III
   colonial growth, 1715–1719, III
   federal call for 200, 1941 Jan. 3, III
   first American-built to cross Atlantic,
      1564 Spring, III
   first battle cruiser (Conn.), 1646, I
   first built in Boston, 1644, III
   first built on Lake Ontario, 1798(3),
      III
   first English-made on Lake Ontario,
      1755 June 28, III
   first global circumnavigation, 1790
      Apr. 10(2), I
   first large to navigate Northwest
      Passage, 1969 Sept. 14, III
   first navigating quadrant, 1730(3), III
   first nuclear merchant, 1959 July 21,
      III
   first nuclear-powered cargo, 1962
      Aug. 22(1), III
   first schooner, 1713, III
   first specially designed aircraft carrier,
      1933 Feb. 25, III
   flatboat invented, 1750(3), III
   French seizure of U.S., 1808 Apr. 17, I
   Great White Fleet, 1907, I; 1909 Feb.
      21, I
   Jones-White Act, 1928 May 22, III
   Kaiser's Liberty Ship program,
      1942(1), III
   largest U.S.-built merchant christened
      (Brooklyn, N.Y.), 1973 June 30, III
   largest warship to date, 1954 Dec. 11,
      I
   lifeboat requirements, 1912 May 1, III

Ships and shipping (*cont.*)
   Longshoremen's contract, 1964 Dec.
      16, III
   Lusitania maiden voyage speed
      record, 1907 Sept. 12, III
   Mary Celeste crew disappearance,
      1872 Nov. 7, IV
   Merchant Marine Act, 1920 June 5, III
   Monitor design, 1861 Oct. 4, III
   one hundred launched, 1918 July 4,
      III
   Pacific transatlantic speed record,
      1850 Aug. 21, III
   Persian Gulf incidents, 1987 May 17,
      I; 1988 Apr. 18, I
   Queen Mary maiden voyage, 1936
      June 1, III
   radio installation required, 1910 June
      24, III
   Rambouillet Decree, 1810 Mar. 23, I
   Revolutionary War construction, 1776
      July 3, III
   speed record for clipper, 1850(12), III
   steerage rates cut, 1904 May 23, III;
      1908(3), III
   strike ended, 1965 Aug. 29, III
   strike halted by injunction, 1961 July
      3, III; 1962 Apr. 11, III
   sunken *Monitor* found (N.C.), 1974
      Mar. 7, III
   transatlantic crossings initiated, 1818
      Jan., III
   transatlantic speed record, 1952 July
      7, III
   U.S.S. Saratoga launched, 1955 Oct. 7,
      III
Shirer, William L., 1941(1), II; 1961 Mar.
   14, II
Shockley, William, 1956 Nov. 1, III
Shoemaker, Willie, 1970 Sept. 7, IV; 1985
   Mar. 3, IV; 1986 May 3, IV; 1990 Feb. 3,
   IV
Shoes and footwear:
   first distinctively right/left, 1800(3),
      III
   first organized union (Mass.), 1648
      Oct. 18, III
   high heels unfashionable, 1790(6), IV
   industry unemployment, 1867 Mar. 7,
      III
   Lynn (Mass.) strike, 1860(5), IV; 1860
      Feb. 22, III
   price regulations (Mass.), 1676, III
   rationing, 1943 Feb. 7, III
   rationing ended, 1945 Oct. 30, III
   women's boots fashionable, 1828(5),
      IV; 1962, IV
Sholes, Christopher Latham, 1867(9), III;
   1868 June 23, III
Shopp, Bebe (Beatrice Vella), 1948 Sept.
   11, IV
Shor, Toots, 1977, IV
Shore, Ernie, 1917 June 23(1), IV
Shorter, Frank, 1972 Aug. 26–Sept. 11, IV
Shostakovich, Dmitri, 1959 Oct. 21(1), II
Shostakovich, Maksim, 1981 Apr. 11, II
Showboats, 1836, IV
Shriver, Pam, 1981 July 3–4, IV; 1982 July
   3–4, IV; 1983 July 2–3, IV; 1984 July
   7–8, IV; 1986 July 5–6, IV

Shriver, R. Sargent, 1972 July 10–14, I
Shulman, Max, 1988, II
Shultz, George P., 1982 June 25, I; 1984
   Nov. 22, I
Shute, Denny, 1936 Nov. 22, IV; 1937
   May 30, IV
Siam, 1833 Mar. 20, I
Siamese twins, 1987 Sept. 5–7, III
Siberian gas pipeline, 1982 June 18, I
Sick, Gary, 1985(1), II
Sidney, Margaret, 1880(2), II
Siegmeister, Elie, 1991, II
Sienkiewicz, Henryk, 1896(1), II
Sieur de Monts colony, 1604, I
Signoret, Simone, 1960 Apr. 4, II; 1966
   May 22, II
Signs:
   first animated electric, 1928 Nov. 6,
      III
Sikkim:
   Cooke-Crown Prince marriage, 1963
      Mar. 20, IV
Sikorsky, Igor, 1972, III
Silk:
   colonial production (Va.), 1623, III
   embargo on Japanese, 1941, IV
   Nassau popularity (Boston, Mass.),
      1734 Mar., IV
   Va. cultivation, 1661(2), III
   workers' strike, 1913 Feb. 25, III
Silliman, Benjamin, 1818, III
Sills, Beverly, 1975 Apr. 7, II; 1980 Oct.
   27, II
Silver (*see also* Bimetallism):
   Canadian findings, 1964 Apr. 16, III
   Comstock Lode (Nev.), 1859(1), I
   first U.S. mining co. (N.C.), 1839 Jan.
      7, III
   inflation, 1890(7), III
   mine fire (Ida.), 1972 May 2, I
   Revere bowl, 1768, II
Silver, Ron, 1988 June 5, II
Silverman, Kenneth, 1985 Apr. 24, II
Silverstein, Shel, 1985, II
Simic, Charles, 1990 Apr. 12, II
Simon, Herbert A., 1978 Oct. 16, III
Simon, Neil, 1971 Nov. 11, II; 1972 Dec.
   20, II; 1983 Mar. 27, II; 1991 Apr. 9, II;
   1991 June 2, II; 1992, II
Simon, Norton, 1965 Mar. 19, II; 1968
   Oct. 9, II; 1987, II
Simon, Paul, 1969 Mar. 12, II; 1971 Mar.
   16, II; 1976 Feb. 28, II; 1981 Sept. 19,
   II; 1987 Feb. 24, II; 1988 Mar. 2, II
Simon and Garfunkel, 1981 Sept. 19, II
Simpson, George G., 1984, III
Simpson, Louis, 1964 May 4, II
Simpson, O. J., 1973 Dec. 16, IV
Simpson, Scott, 1987 June 21, IV
Sinatra, Frank, 1954 Mar. 25, II; 1959
   Nov. 29, II; 1966 Mar. 15(2), II; 1967
   Mar. 2, II
Sinatra, Frank, Jr., 1963 Dec. 8, IV
Sincere Convert, The (Shepard), 1641, II
Sinclair, Harry, 1924 June 30, I
Sinclair, Upton, 1901(1), II; 1906(1), II;
   1908(1), II; 1917(1), II; 1927(1), II;
   1928(1), II; 1943 May 3, II; 1968, II
Sindona, Michele, 1980 Mar. 27, III
Singer, Isaac, 1851 Aug. 12, III

Singer, Isaac Bashevis, 1974 Apr. 18, II; 1975(1), II; 1978 Oct. 5, II; 1991, II
Singer Manufacturing Co., 1889(7), III
Singh, Mithileshwar, 1988 Oct. 3, I
Single parents:
 welfare reform, 1988 Oct. 13, I
Sioux Indians, 1862 Aug. 18, I; 1876 June 25, I; 1890 Feb. 10, I; 1979 June 13, I
Sirhan, Sirhan B., 1968 June 5, I; 1969 Apr. 23, I
Sirica, John J., 1973 Mar. 23, I; 1973 Nov. 21, I; 1992, I
Sisler, George, 1939 Jan. 24, IV
Sissman, L. E., 1979 Jan. 15, II
Sitting Bull (Indian chief), 1876 June 25, I; 1890 Dec. 15, I
Skateboards, 1977, IV
Skate (submarine), 1958 Sept. 22(1), I
Skating *see* Hockey, Ice; Roller skating
Skating, Ice:
 American figure championship record, 1991 Mar. 16, IV
 Fleming retirement, 1968 Mar. 2, IV
 Lynn signed with Ice Follies, 1973 June 19, IV
 popularity, 1868, IV
 U.S. figure championships, 1914 Mar. 21, IV; 1918 Mar. 7, IV; 1920 Mar. 20, IV; 1921 Feb. 26–27, IV; 1922 Mar. 7, IV; 1923 Feb. 15–16, IV; 1924 Feb. 18, IV; 1925 Feb. 15, IV; 1926 Feb., IV; 1927 Feb. 10–11, IV; 1928 Mar. 27, IV; 1929 Feb. 19, IV; 1930 Mar. 22–23, IV; 1931 Mar. 21, IV; 1931 Dec. 28, IV; 1933 Mar. 18, IV; 1934 Mar. 10, IV; 1935 Feb. 9, IV; 1936 Feb. 13, IV; 1937 Feb. 13, IV; 1938 Feb. 26, IV; 1939 Jan. 21, IV; 1940 Feb. 10, IV; 1941 Feb. 1, IV; 1942 Feb. 21, IV; 1943 Mar. 8, IV; 1944 Feb. 27, IV; 1945 Mar. 2–5, IV; 1946 Mar. 2–3, IV; 1947 Mar. 9, IV; 1948 Apr. 3, IV; 1949 Mar. 13, IV; 1950 Mar. 24, IV; 1951 Feb. 2–4, IV; 1952 Mar. 28, IV; 1953 Mar. 28, IV; 1954 Mar. 19, IV; 1955 Apr. 1–2, IV; 1956 Mar. 16, IV; 1957 Mar. 15–16, IV; 1958 Mar. 28–29, IV; 1959 Jan. 31–Feb. 1, IV; 1960 Jan. 30, IV; 1961 Jan. 27–29, IV; 1962 Feb. 3–4, IV; 1963 Feb. 9–10, IV; 1964 Jan. 11–12, IV; 1965 Feb. 13, IV; 1966 Jan. 29, IV; 1967 Jan. 18–21, IV; 1968 Jan. 19–20, IV; 1969 Feb. 1–2, IV; 1970 Feb. 6–7, IV; 1971 Jan. 28–31, IV; 1972 Jan. 14–16, IV; 1973 Jan. 24–27, IV; 1974 Feb. 6–9, IV; 1975 Jan. 31–Feb. 2, IV; 1976 Jan. 10–11, IV; 1977 Feb. 3–5, IV; 1978 Feb. 12, IV; 1979 Feb. 2–3, IV; 1980 Jan. 18–20, IV; 1981 Feb. 3–8, IV; 1981 Mar. 5, IV; 1982 Jan. 28–31, IV; 1983 Feb. 3–4, IV; 1984 Jan. 20–21, IV; 1985 Feb. 1–2, IV; 1986 Feb. 6–8, IV; 1987 Feb. 7–8, IV; 1988 Jan. 8–9, IV; 1989 Feb. 11–12, IV; 1990 Feb. 10–11, IV; 1991 Feb. 15–17, IV; 1992 Jan. 9–11, IV
 Winter Olympics, 1988 Feb. 13–28, IV

Skating, Ice (*cont.*)
 world figure championships, 1948 Feb. 13, IV; 1949 Feb. 17, IV; 1950 Mar. 7, IV; 1951 Feb. 26, IV; 1952 Feb. 29, IV; 1953 Feb. 10, IV; 1954 Feb. 17, IV; 1955 Feb. 16–17, IV; 1956 Feb. 17, IV; 1957 Feb. 28–Mar. 3, IV; 1958 Feb. 14–15, IV; 1959 Feb. 26–28, IV; 1960 Mar. 2–5, IV; 1966 Feb. 27, IV; 1967 Feb. 28–Mar. 4, IV; 1968 Mar. 2, IV; 1969 Mar. 2, IV; 1970 Mar. 7, IV; 1976 Mar. 6, IV; 1977 Mar. 3, IV; 1978 Mar 9, IV; 1979 Mar 17, IV; 1982 Mar. 11–13, IV; 1983 Mar. 10–11, IV; 1984 Mar. 23, IV
Skelton, Red, 1952 Feb. 18, II
Skidmore, Owings & Merrill, 1950(6), II
Skinner, B. F., 1990, III
Skinner, Otis, 1877, II; 1911 Apr. 19, II
Skinner, Samuel K., 1991 Dec. 3, I
Skybolt (missile), 1962 Apr. 19, III
Skylab:
 mishap, 1973 May 14, III
 reentered Earth's atmosphere, 1979 July 11, III
 three rendezvous, 1973 July 28, III
Skyscrapers (*see also* Office buildings):
 Bessemer steel I beams, 1889(5), III
 early steel frame (Chicago, Ill.), 1895(5), II
 Empire State Building (N.Y.C.) contract awarded, 1929 Sept. 22, II
 Empire State Building (N.Y.C.) dedicated, 1931 May 1, III
 first steel skeleton construction (Chicago Ill.), 1884(3), II
 highest to date (Chicago, Ill.), 1973 May 3, II
 Manhattan Life Insurance Building (N.Y.C.), 1893(6), II
 N.Y.C., 1908, III
 N.Y.C. building code revised, 1916(9), II
 Sullivan's, 1890(4), II
 tallest building in South (Ga.), 1975 Oct. 2, II
 tallest to date (N.Y.C.), 1913(3), II
 World Trade Center world's tallest (N.Y.C.), 1970 Dec. 23, II
Slade, Bernard, 1975 Mar. 13, II
Sladky, James, 1970 Feb. 6–7, IV
Slander *see* Libel and slander
Slang *see* Language
Slater, John Fox, 1882 Apr. 28, III
Slater, Samuel, 1790 Dec. 21, III
Slaves and slavery (*see also* Abolition movement; Compromise of 1850; Emancipation Proclamation, Fugitive Slave laws; Kansas-Nebraska Act; Reconstruction):
 abolished in Ill., 1824 Aug. 2, IV
 abolished in Miss., 1865 Aug. 14, I
 abolished in N.C., 1865 Nov. 9, I
 acts passed by colonies, 1664, I
 African resettlement, 1816, IV; 1820 Feb. 6, I; 1821, IV; 1821(4), II
 African resettlement resolutions (Va.), 1800(2), I

Slaves and slavery (*cont.*)
 African trade prohibited, 1807 Mar. 2, I
 banned in Tex., 1830 Apr. 6, I
 barred in Northwest Territory, 1787 July 13, I
 books defending and scoring, 1857, II
 colonial population, 1725, I
 congressional gag rule on petitions, 1840 Jan. 8, I
 congressional gag rule on petitions lifted, 1844 Dec. 3, I
 Creole mutiny, 1841 Oct. 27, I
 crime charges against (N.Y.C.), 1740–1744, IV
 Curtis's address against, 1856(6), II
 Dred Scott decision, 1857, I
 Dutch colonial importation, 1652(1), I
 emancipation bill (Va.), 1782, I
 Emancipation Day, 1865 June 19, IV
 first denunciation of, 1700(1), II
 first in French La., 1716 June 6, III
 first new state to outlaw (Ohio), 1803 Feb. 19, I
 first shipment (Va.), 1619 Aug., I
 Fitzhugh's defense of, 1856(6), IV; 1857, II
 Freedmen's Bureau created, 1865 Mar. 3, I
 Fugitive Slave Act nullified (Pa.), 1826(2), I
 Ga. Contract Labor Act overturned, 1942 Jan. 12(2), III
 "house divided" statement and theme, 1856(6), IV; 1858 June 16, IV
 House resolution denies petition rights, 1837 Feb. 6, I
 indentured servants and,, 1680–1689, III
 in Kans. issue, 1855 Mar. 30, I; 1855 Sept. 5, I
 in newly acquired territory issue, 1846 Aug., I; 1848 Aug. 9, I
 insurrection (La.), 1811 Jan., IV
 insurrections, 1822, I
 "irrepressible conflict" statement, 1858 Oct. 25, IV
 Lincoln-Douglas debates, 1858, I
 Missouri Compromise, 1820, I
 Mo. legislature stance, 1849 Mar. 10, I
 Mo.'s status, 1819 Feb. 13, I
 North-South division, 1802, IV
 N.Y. tension, 1735 Jan., IV
 Pentecost celebration (N.Y.S.), c1660, I
 population, 1800(1), I; 1860(1), I
 presidential campaign issue, 1856, I; 1860, I
 Quaker ban, 1696(2), I
 religious conversion laws, 1670(1), I; 1671(2), I
 religious conversion laws repealed (Va.), 1682(1), I
 religious conversions, 1667, I; 1671(2), I
 religious protest against, 1690(1), III
 sanctioned in Ga., 1749 Oct. 26, I
 shipboard mutiny, 1839, I

Slaves and slavery (cont.)
 "sold down the river" phrase, 1850(2), IV
 S.C. uprisings, 1739, I
 Stowe's *Dred* on economic and moral evils of, 1856(3), II
 subject to Confederate military duty, 1865 Mar. 13, I
 Thirteenth Amendment prohibiting, 1865 Dec. 2, I
 trade, 1680–1689, III; 1696(1), I
 trade abolished (Md.), 1783, I
 trade abolished (Wash., D.C.), 1850 Sept. 20, I
 trade urged reopened by Vicksburg convention, 1859 May 12, I
 Turner insurrection (Va.), 1831, I
 Uncle Tom's Cabin rebutted, 1854(5), II
 Uncle Tom's Cabin's depiction of, 1852, II
 Va. act limiting to blacks, 1705(2), I
 Va. laws, 1667, I
 Wilmot Proviso, 1846 Aug., I
 Woolman against, 1754, I
Slayton, Donald K., 1975 July 15, III
Sleeping sickness *see* Equine encephalitis
Slidell, John, 1846, I
Sloane, Eric, 1985, II
Slocum, Henry W., 1888(4), IV; 1889(6), IV
Sloughter, Henry, 1689(1), I
Slums *see* Cities and urban areas
Small, George L., 1972 Apr. 13, II
Smallpox:
 epidemics, 1697(1), I; 1720–1724, III; 1873(3), III
 first inoculation (Boston, Mass.), 1720–1724, III
 Indian epidemics, 1616, III
Smallwood, Norma, 1926 Sept. 10, IV
Smart Set, The (publication), 1900 Mar., II
Smede, Jan, 1654(1), III
Smibert, John, 1742 Sept. 24, II; 1751 Apr. 2, II
Smiley, Jane, 1992 Apr. 7, II
Smith, Alex, 1906 June 29, IV; 1910 June 18, IV
Smith, Alfred E., 1936 June 9–12, I
 presidential candidacy, 1928, I; 1928 June 26–29, I; 1928 Nov. 6, I
 "Sidewalks of New York, The" (song), 1894(4), II
Smith, Al (pitcher), 1941 July 17, IV
Smith, Anne, 1982 July 3–4, IV
Smith, Betty, 1943(1), II
Smith, Charles S., 1876(7), III
Smith, David, 1986 May 6, II
Smith, Francis Hopkinson, 1891(1), II
Smith, Gerald L. K., 1976, III
Smith, Green Clay, 1876 May 17, I
Smith, Gregory White, 1991 Apr. 9, II
Smith, Hedrick, 1976(1), II
Smith, James (Bonecrusher), 1986 Dec. 12, IV; 1987 Mar. 7, IV
Smith, Jedediah Strong, 1824(1), I; 1826, I; 1830 Apr. 10–July 16, I
Smith, John, 1607 Dec.(1), I; 1608, II; 1608, IV; 1610–1619, II; 1612, II; 1613, III; 1614, III; 1624, II

Smith, Joseph, 1830, III
 advocated polygamy, 1843 July 12, IV
 murdered, 1844 June 27, III; 1847 July 24, III
 Nauvoo (Ill.), 1838, III
Smith, Joseph Fielding, 1970 Jan. 18, III; 1972, III
Smith, Kate, 1986, II
Smith, Keely, 1959 May 4(2), II
Smith, Lillian, 1944(1), II
Smith, Maggie, 1970 Apr. 7(1), II; 1979 Apr. 4, II; 1990 June 3, II
Smith, Margaret, 1962 Sept. 10, IV; 1965 Sept. 12, IV
Smith, Martin Cruz, 1989(1), II; 1992(1), II
Smith, Mary Louise, 1974 Sept. 16(1), I
Smith, Nathan, 1807, III
Smith, Red (Walter), 1982, IV
Smith, Richard Penn, 1829 Mar. 26, II
Smith, Robyn, 1973 Mar. 1(1), IV
Smith, Samuel Francis, 1831, II
Smith, Seba, 1843, II
Smith, Stan, 1971 Sept. 5–15, IV; 1972 July 7(2), IV
Smith, Sydney, 1820 Jan., II
Smith, Thorne, 1926(1), II
Smith, Tommy, 1968 Oct. 12–27, IV
Smith, Walter Bedell, 1961, I
Smith, William (writer), 1753, II
Smith, Willie, 1899 Sept. 15, IV
Smith, Winchell, 1909 Sept. 4, II
Smith Act *see* Alien Registration Act
Smith College (Mass.), 1871(3), III
Smith-Lever Act, 1914 May 8, III
Smithsonian Institution (Wash., D.C.):
 Ellington archives, 1988 Apr., II
 established, 1846, III; 1847 May 1, III
 Smithsonian Medal awarded, 1992 Jan. 23, II
 Soviet-U.S. joint exhibit, 1988 Sept. 27, II
 two new museums opened, 1987 Sept. 28, II
Smoking (*see also* Tobacco):
 banned on passenger planes, 1988 Apr. 23, III; 1989 Nov. 21, III
 cigarette appearance in U.S., 1867(8), III
 cigarette health hazard, 1979 Jan. 11, III
 cigarette manufacturer found guilty in cancer death, 1988 June 13, III
 cigarette package labeling, 1964 June 24, III
 cigarette percentages, 1954, IV
 cigarette production, 1900(6), III
 cigarette radio-TV ads banned, 1970 Apr. 1, III
 cigarette testimonials, 1905(2), III
 cigar prohibitions, 1789(1), IV
 coronary death rate from, 1960 June 6, II
 damage suits upheld, 1992 June 24(1), III
 declined to lowest level to date, 1992, III
 decreased, 1990, IV
 drive against, 1963 June 8, III
 Dutch (N.Y.), 1678, IV
 first cigarette coupons, 1904(5), III

Smoking (cont.)
 first cigar-rolling machine, 1883 Feb. 27, III
 Great American Smokeout, 1984, III
 illegal for women (N.Y.C.), 1908 Jan. 21, IV
 introduced to England, 1565, IV
 laws, 1646, IV; 1647(1), IV
 leading cause of death, 1982, III
 libel suit against CBS, 1985 Dec. 5, III
 linked to heart disease, 1961 Sept. 8, III
 lung cancer link, 1957 July 12, III
 smokers' damage suits upheld, 1992 June 24(1), III
 socially acceptable for men, 1890(2), IV
 surgeon general's report, 1964 Jan. 11, III
 woman arrested for public (N.Y.C.), 1904 Sept. 28, IV
Smoot-Hawley Act, 1930, I
Smothers Brothers, 1969 Apr. 4, II
Smylie, Elizabeth, 1985 July 6–7, IV
Snead, Sam, 1942 May 31, IV; 1949, IV; 1949 Apr. 10, IV; 1949 May 31, IV; 1950, IV; 1951 July 3, IV; 1952 Apr. 6, IV; 1953 June 13(2), IV; 1954 Apr. 12, IV
Snell, George, 1980 Oct. 10, III
Snepp, Frank W., III; 1978 July 7, II
Snodgrass, W. D., 1960 May 2, II
Snorro (first N. American white birth), 1007, IV
Snowstorms:
 blizzard (Midwest), 1978 Jan. 25–26, I; 1979 Jan. 12, I
 blizzard (N.E.), 1978 Feb. 5–7, I; 1987 Jan. 22, I
 blizzard (N.Y.C.), 1888 Mar. 12, I; 1901(2), III
 blizzard paralyzed East and Midwest, 1977 Jan. 28–29, I
 Colo. and Utah, 1984 Feb. 5–28, I
 East R. (N.Y.C.) frozen, 1867 Jan. 23, IV
 hurricane-force (East Coast), 1984 Mar. 29, I
 record-breaking (N.Y.C.), 1947 Dec. 27, I
 worst blizzard in 70 years, 1966 Jan. 29–31, I
Snyder, Gary, 1975 May 5, II
Soap and detergents:
 soap powder introduced, 1843(3), III
Soble, Jack, 1957 Oct. 8, I
Soble, Myra, 1957 Oct. 8, I
Soccer:
 attendance record, 1977 Aug. 15, IV
 fastest-growing team sport, 1977, IV
 first introduced, 1820(1), IV
 first NASL championship, 1968 Sept. 28, IV
 first women's world championship, 1991 Nov. 30, IV
 NASL split, 1970, IV
 North American Soccer League championships, 1968 Sept. 28, IV; 1969, IV; 1970 Sept. 6–13, IV; 1971 Sept. 19(1), IV; 1972 Aug. 26, IV;

Soccer (*cont.*)
    1973 Aug. 25, IV; 1974 Aug. 25, IV;
        1975 Aug. 24, IV; 1976 Aug. 28, IV;
        1977 Aug. 28, IV; 1978 Aug. 27, IV;
        1979 Sept. 8(1), IV; 1980 Sept. 21,
        IV; 1981 Sept. 26, IV; 1982 Sept. 19,
        IV; 1983 Oct. 1, IV; 1984 Oct. 3, IV
    North American Soccer League
        defunct, 1985, IV
    North American Soccer League
        formed, 1966 Aug. 23, IV
    Pelé returned from retirement, 1975
        June 3(1), IV
Social customs *see* Personal conduct;
    Society
Social Democrat Party, 1900 Mar. 6–9, I
Socialism:
    AFL against, 1894(2), III
Socialist Labor Party, 1896 July 4–9, I
    presidential ticket, 1892 Aug. 28, I;
        1908 July 4, I; 1920 May 5–10, I;
        1924 May 11–13, I; 1932 Apr.
        30-May 2, I; 1936 Apr. 25–28, I;
        1940 Apr. 28, I; 1948 May 2, I
Socialist Party:
    first congressional representative,
        1910 Nov. 8, I
    formed, 1901(1), I
    presidential ticket, 1904 May 5, I;
        1908 May 10–17, I; 1912 May 17, I;
        1920 May 8–14, I; 1928 Apr. 13–18,
        I; 1932 May 22–24, I; 1936 May 25,
        I; 1940 Apr. 7, I; 1948 May 9, I;
        1952 May 30–June 1, I
Social reform (*see also* specific
    movements, e.g., Abolition movement):
    Bloomer's publication, 1849 Jan., IV
    burgeoning of societies for, 1840, IV
    decades before Civil War, 1834, IV
    Frances Wright's tour, 1824(2), IV
    Phillips's speech on, 1851(3), IV
    Protestant social gospel movement,
        1885(3), III
    religious involvement in, 1889, III
    Roman Catholic stance on economic
        justice, 1984 Nov. 11, III
    Woolman essay, 1793(3), II
    Wright's tour, 1825, IV
Social Security (*see also* Medicare):
    Act signed, 1935 Aug. 14, I
    Act upheld, 1937 May 24, III
    Advisory Council warned of fund
        exhaustion, 1975 Feb. 24, I
    broader act proposed, 1953 Aug. 1, I
    fiftieth anniversary, 1985, I
    modification legislation, 1983 Jan. 15,
        I
    tax increase, 1977 Dec. 20, I
Social stratification and snobbery *see*
    Society
Society (*see also* Etiquette; Gilded Age;
    Income and wealth, personal):
    Buckingham's characterization of
        N.Y., 1841(6), IV
    Capote's party (N.Y.C.), 1966 Nov. 28,
        IV
    caste clothing law (Conn.), 1676(1), IV
    changes from World War II, 1942, IV
    customs mid-eighteenth century,
        1750–1754, IV

Society (*cont.*)
    Forbes's lavish birthday party, 1989
        Aug. 19, IV
    the 400, 1892(1), IV
    golf's association with, 1928, IV
    Governor's Palace (Williamsburg, Va.)
        as center of fashion, 1720, IV
    grand opera house construction
        (N.Y.C.), 1847(1), IV
    Harvard students' position listed,
        1773(3), IV
    Jamestown stratum, 1607, IV
    lavish balls, 1897, IV
    lifestyle, 1887, IV
    Martineau's impressions of America,
        1837(2), II
    Morris-Randolph wedding, 1809(1), IV
    Mrs. Astor as arbiter of, 1908 Oct. 30,
        IV
    N.E. snobbery, 1653, IV
    N.Y.C. charity balls, 1857(1), IV
    N.Y.C. clubs, 1733, IV
    Phila. carriage ownership, 1772, IV
    primogeniture abolished (Va.),
        1785(4), IV
    rigid Va. code, 1774 May, IV
    rowing and sailing popularity, 1843,
        IV
    southern aristocracy, 1670–1690, IV
    at Symphony Hall (Boston, Mass.),
        1900 Oct. 15, II
    titles of rank opposed, 1776 July 13,
        IV
    upper class culture domination,
        1802(1), II
    Va. penal code, 1623(3), IV
    wealth-based N.Y.C., 1872, IV
Society of American Artists, 1877 June 1,
    II
Sociology:
    Middletown (Lynd), 1929, III
    Ward and Sumner's views, 1883, III
Soeur Sourire (Luc-Gabrielle), 1963(5), II
Soil Conservation Act, 1935 Apr. 27, I
Solanis, Valerie, 1968 June 3, II
Solar eclipse, 1925 Jan. 24, III; 1991 July
    11, III
Solar Maximum Observatory, 1980 Feb.
    14, III
Solar power, 1982, III
Solar system (*see also* Astronomy; specific
    planets or components)
    age, 1960 Jan. 2, III
Soledad Brothers, 1971 Aug. 21, IV; 1972
    Mar. 27, IV
Solis, Alex, 1986 May 17, IV
Solms, Kenny, 1974 Jan. 27(1), II
Solow, Robert M., 1987 Oct. 21, III
Solzhenitsyn, Alexander, 1972(1), II
Somoza DeBayle, Anastasio, 1979 Feb. 8, I
Sondheim, Stephen, 1957 Sept. 26, II;
    1959 May 21, II; 1962 May 8, II; 1963
    Apr. 25(1), II; 1970 Apr. 26, II; 1971
    Apr. 4, II; 1973 Feb. 25, II; 1974 Sept.
    23, II; 1979 Mar. 1, II; 1983 Aug. 21, II;
    1984 May 2, II; 1985 Apr. 24, II
Songmy *see* Vietnam War
Songs *see* Music
Sonneborn, Tracy, 1960 Oct. 18, III

Sons of Liberty (*see also* Tammany
    Society):,
        1765(1), IV
Sons of the American Revolution, 1889(4),
    IV
Sontag, Susan, 1978 Jan. 11, II; 1992(1), II
Sony Corp., 1989 Sept. 27, III
Sorensen, Theodore, 1965(1), II
Sotheby Park Bernet, 1983 Sept. 19, II;
    1985 July 16, II
    largest auction to date, 1988 May 3, II
Sothern, Edward Hugh, 1887, II
Soulé, Pierre, 1854 Oct. 18, I
Soulé, Samuel W., 1867(9), III; 1868 June
    23, III
Soule, John B. L., 1851(4), IV
Sousa, John Philip, 1899, II
South, University of the (Tenn.), 1858 Jan.
    6, III
South, U.S. (*see also* Civil War;
    Confederate States of America;
    Plantations; Secession; Slaves and
    slavery; state names):
    Baldwin's tales of, 1853, II
    De Bow's Review reflecting society
        and economy, 1846 Jan., III
South Africa:
    U.S. corporate withdrawal, 1986 Oct.
        20, III
    U.S. sanctions, 1986 Aug. 13, I
    U.S. sanctions against, 1985 Sept. 9, I
    U.S. sanctions lifted, 1991 July 10, I
South America *see* Latin America
South Boston High School (Mass.), 1975
    Dec. 9, III
South Carolina:
    carpetbag government ended, 1877
        Apr. 10, I
    congressional representation
        regranted, 1868 June 25(2), I
    eighth state to ratify U.S. Constitution,
        1788 May 23, I
    first colony, 1526 Summer, I
    Huguenots, 1562 Apr. 30, I;
        1680–1689, IV; 1693(2), IV
    Hurricane Hugo damage, 1989 Sept.
        18–24, I
    nullification ordinance revoked, 1833
        Mar. 15, I
    rejected Tariff of Abominations, 1828
        Dec. 19, I
    royal control restored, 1729, I
    Savannah River plant nuclear
        accidents, 1988 Sept. 30, I
    seceded, 1860 Dec. 20, I
    secession threat, 1832, I
    seized public lands, 1860 Dec. 22, I
    separate colonial governor, 1712 May
        9, I
    separate royal province, 1729 June, I
South Carolina, University of:
    chartered, 1801(3), III
South Dakota:
    Rapid City flash floods, 1972 June
        9–10, I
    statehood, 1889 Nov. 2, I
South Dakota, University of, 1882(2), III
Southeast Asia Treaty Organization
    (SEATO), 1955 Sept. 8, I
Southern, Terry, 1964(1), II

Southern Baptist Convention, 1986 June 10, III; 1989, III; 1990 June 12, III; 1991, III; 1992 May 12(1), III

Southern California, University of, 1880 Oct. 4, III

Southern Education Fund, 1882 Apr. 28, III

Southern Homestead Act, 1876(1), I

Southern Immigration Association, 1883(1), I

Southern Pacific Railroad, 1912 Mar. 14, III

Southern Railroad Co., 1894(3), III

Southern Tenant Farmers' Union, 1934 July, I

South Pole see Arctic and Antarctica

Southworth, E.D.E.N. (Mrs.), 1859(1), II

Soviet Union (see also Arms control and disarmament; Cold War; Espionage; Russia):
 Afghanistan invasion, 1980, I; 1980, IV; 1980 Jan. 4, I; 1982, I
 Afghanistan withdrawal, 1988 Apr. 14, I
 attacked by Germany, 1941, I
 Baltic states declared independent, 1991 Sept. 2, I
 Boyce-Lee espionage case, 1977 Apr. 28(2), I
 Brezhnev visited U.S., 1973 June 16–25, I
 CIA attempt to recover sunken submarine, 1975 Mar. 18, I
 Cuban missile crisis revelation, 1989 Jan. 28, I
 cultural exchange with U.S., 1962 Mar. 8, III
 defectors, 1970 Oct. 11, II; 1974 July 27, II; 1979 Aug. 23, II; 1980 Feb. 6, II; 1981 Apr. 11, II
 denied most-favored-nation status, 1973 Dec. 11, III
 files showed Hiss did not spy, 1992 Oct. 14, I
 first consular treaty with U.S., 1967 Mar. 31, I
 first direct commercial flight to U.S., 1968 July 15, III
 Glassboro (N.J.) talks, 1967 June 23 and 25, I
 microwave radiation of U.S. embassy, 1976 Feb. 10, I
 Nixon visit, 1972 May 22–30, I
 nonaggression pact with Germany, 1939 Aug. 24, I
 Polish intervention, 1982, I
 Reagan administration policy, 1986, I
 reconnaissance flights over Alaska, 1963 Mar. 13, I
 religion, 1989, III
 royalty accord with U.S., 1974 Dec. 10, II
 space achievements, 1961, III
 space cooperation, 1959 Nov. 19, III
 Stalin's daughter requested political asylum, 1967 Apr. 21(1), I
 summit conference (Geneva), 1985 Nov. 20–21, I
 summit conference (Malta), 1989 Dec. 3, I

Soviet Union (cont.)
 summit conference (Moscow), 1988 May 29–June 1, I
 summit conference (Reykjavik), 1986 Oct. 11–12, I
 summit conference (Wash., D.C.), 1990 June 1, I
 U.S. art exchanges, 1975 Aug. 29, II; 1987, II; 1988 Mar. 26, II
 U.S. Art joint exhibit, 1988 Sept. 27, II
 U.S. businesses in, 1988, III
 U.S. cultural exchanges, 1959, II; 1973 Apr. 2, II
 U.S. embargo, 1982, I
 U.S. embassy bugged, 1964 May 19, I
 U.S. exports of Siberian pipeline equipment, 1982 June 18, I
 U.S. federal loan guaranteed food purchases, 1990 Dec. 12, I
 U.S. grain deal, 1963 Oct. 9, I; 1964 Feb. 25, III; 1972, III; 1972 July 8, III; 1979 Oct. 3, III
 U.S. grain embargo lifted, 1981 Apr. 24(1), I
 U.S. grain purchases increased, 1983 July 28, I
 U.S. grain sale halted, 1980 Jan. 4, I
 U.S. plane shot down, 1964 Mar. 10, I
 U.S. reprisals for Polish policy, 1981 Dec. 29, I
 U.S. sanctions, 1983 Sept. 5, I
 U.S. support of dissidents, 1977 Mar. 1, I
 U.S. trade benefits linked to emigration policies, 1974 Dec. 20, III
 U.S. witnessed nuclear test explosion, 1988 Sept. 14, I
 weather watch with U.S., 1962 Apr. 23, III
 withdrew from Olympics, 1984 May 8, IV

Spaats, Carl A., 1974, I

Spacek, Sissy, 1981 Mar. 31, II

Space Needle (Seattle, Wash.), 1962, II

Space program (see also Missiles; Moon, Rockets; Satellites; names of planets and specific spacecraft):
 Apollo launch pad fire, 1967 Jan. 27, III
 Apollo-Soyuz joint mission, 1975 July 15, III
 Apollo 4 Earth orbit, 1967 Nov. 9, III
 Apollo 5, 1968 Jan. 22, III
 Apollo 6 launched, 1968 Apr. 4, III
 Apollo 7, 1968 Oct. 11, III
 Apollo 8 manned mission, 1968 Dec. 21–27, III
 Apollo 9, 1969 Mar. 3, III
 artificial astronaut orbited, 1961 Sept. 13, III
 Apollo 13 mishap, 1970, III; 1970 Apr. 11, III
 Apollo 14, 1971 Jan. 31, III
 Bluford first black astronaut, 1983 Aug. 30–Sept. 5, III
 Challenger disaster, 1986 Jan. 28, III
 Challenger space shuttle, 1984 Oct. 11, III

Space program (cont.)
 Challenger space shuttle maiden voyage, 1983 Apr. 4–9, III
 chimpanzee in, 1961 Jan. 31, III
 Columbia completed first space shuttle flight, 1982 Nov. 11–16, III
 Columbia completed second mission, 1981 Nov. 14, III
 Columbia seventh orbit, 1986 Jan. 12–18, III
 Columbia space shuttle launched, 1981 Apr. 12–14, III
 Discovery space shuttle, 1984 Aug. 30–Sept. 5, III; 1984 Nov. 12, III; 1988 Sept. 29–Oct. 3, III
 Enterprise first free flight, 1977 Aug. 12, III
 financial cuts, 1970, I; 1970, III
 first American in space, 1961 May 5(2), III
 first American to orbit Earth, 1962 Feb. 20, III
 first black astronaut killed, 1967 Dec. 8, III
 first flight devoted to Japanese research, 1992 Sept. 20, III
 first manned Apollo mission, 1968 Oct. 11, III
 first manned Gemini flight, 1965 Mar. 23, III
 first manned moon landing, 1969 July 16, III
 first manned moon mission, 1969 May 18, III
 first Mercury probe, 1973 Nov. 3, III
 first on-board instrument-controlled descent, 1966 Sept. 12(1), III
 first payload recovered from orbit, 1960 Aug. 11, III
 first salvage operation, 1984 Nov. 12, III
 first secret shuttle flight, 1985 Jan. 24–27, III
 first seven astronauts, 1959 Apr. 9, III
 first space docking, 1966 Mar. 16, III
 first space station launched (Skylab), 1973 May 14, III
 first teacher selected to fly in space shuttle, 1985 July 19, III
 first U.S. objects launched, 1957 Oct. 16, III
 first U.S. space walk, 1965, III; 1965 June 3, III
 first U.S.-U.S.S.R. cooperative venture, 1964, III; 1964 Jan. 25, III
 first woman astronaut, 1983 June 18–24, III
 first woman to walk in space, 1984 Oct. 11, III
 fourth American in orbit, 1963 May 15–16, III
 Galileo launched, 1989 Oct. 18, III
 Gamma Ray Observatory launched, 1991 Apr. 7, III
 Gemini rendezvous, 1965, III; 1965 Dec. 4, III; 1965 Dec. 15, III
 Gemini 4 launched, 1965 June 3, III
 Gemini 5, 1965 Aug. 21, III
 Gemini 9 attempted docking, 1966 June 3, III

Space program (*cont.*)

Gemini 9 launching postponed, 1966 May 17, III

Gemini 10 docking, 1966 July 18, III

Gemini 11 docking, 1966 Sept. 12(1), III

Gemini 12 last mission, 1966 Nov. 11(1), III

Hubble Telescope launched, 1990 Apr. 25, III

international demilitarization treaty, 1967 Jan. 27, I

Jupiter orbits, 1979 Mar. 5, III

Kennedy's call for, 1961 May 25, I

Lockheed bailout, 1971 Aug. 2, III

longest space shuttle flight to date, 1992 July 9, III

Magellan launched, 1989 May 4, III

manned flights hampered by finances, 1960 Jan. 2, I

Mariner 2 Venus probe, 1962 Aug. 27(2), III; 1962 Dec. 14, III

Mariner 8 failed, 1971 May 8, III

Mars experiments ended, 1977 May 30, III

Mars exploration, 1971, III; 1971 May 30, III

Mars photographs, 1964 Nov. 28, III; 1965 July 15, III

Mars probes, 1969 Feb. 25, III; 1969 Mar. 27, III; 1992 Sept. 25, III

Mercury Project, 1961 Jan. 31, III

monkeys launched, 1959 May 28, III

moon exploration, 1958 Oct. 11, III

moon landings, 1966 June 2, III; 1967 Apr. 17, III; 1967 Sept. 8, III; 1967 Nov. 7, III; 1968 Jan. 9, III; 1971 July 26, III; 1972 Apr. 16, III; 1972 Dec. 7, III

moon orbits, 1966 Sept. 22, III; 1966 Nov. 6, III; 1967 Feb. 4, III; 1967 July 17, III

moon probes, 1962 Jan. 26, III; 1965 Feb. 17, III; 1965 Mar. 21, III

new astronaut candidates, 1978 Jan. 16, III

orbiting astronauts, 1962, III

Orbiting Solar Observatory VII, 1971 Sept. 29, III

photographer, 1964, III

Pioneer 10, 1972 Mar. 2, III

Pioneer 11 launched, 1973 Apr. 5, III

Pioneer 12 ceased operations, 1992 Oct. 9(2), III

Ranger 4 spacecraft crashed, 1962 Apr. 26(2), III

reusable shuttle, 1972 Jan. 5, III

Saturn data, 1981 Aug. 25, III

Saturn moon and rings, 1979 Sept. 1, III; 1980 Nov. 12, III

second American in orbit, 1962 May 24, III

second American in space, 1961 July 21, III

second lunar landing, 1969 Nov. 14, III

second woman in space, 1984 Aug. 30–Sept. 5, III

seventeen launches, 1960, III

Skylab rendezvous, 1973 July 28, III

Space program (*cont.*)

Skylab's reentry, 1979 July 11, III

Solar Maximum Observatory launched, 1980 Feb. 14, III

Soviet achievements, 1961, III

Soviet-U.S. cooperation, 1959 Nov. 19, III; 1975 July 15, III

spacecraft snagged in midair, 1960 Aug. 19, III

Sputnik, 1957, I

sun orbits, 1960 Mar. 11, III

Telstar, 1962, III

third American in orbit, 1962 Oct. 3, III

three simultaneous space walks, 1992 May 13, III

Ulysses launched, 1990 Oct. 6, III

unmanned Gemini spacecraft launched, 1964 Apr. 8, III

U.S. achievements, 1961, III

U.S.-Soviet race, 1957, I

Van Allen belt discovered, 1958(1), III

Venus findings, 1967 Oct. 19, III; 1989 May 4, III; 1989 Oct. 18, III

Venus orbits and probes, 1967 June 14(2), III; 1978 May 20, III; 1978 Aug. 8, III

Viking Mars findings, 1976 July 20, III

worst accident to date, 1967, III

Spain:

civil war, 1936, I; 1937, IV

Cuban independence, 1898, I

Cuban rebellion, 1895 Feb. 24, I; 1897 May 24, I; 1898 Feb. 15, I; 1898 Apr. 11, I

diplomatic relations severed with U.S. over Cuba, 1898 Apr. 19, I

U.S. ultimatum on Cuba, 1898 Apr. 20, I

Spalding, Eliza Hart, 1836 July 4, IV

Spalding, H. H., 1836 Sept. 1, I

Spanish-American War (*see also* Cuba):

Battle of Las Guasimas, 1898 June 24, I

Battle of Manila Bay, 1898 May 1, I

Buena Ventura captured by U.S., 1898 Apr. 22(2), I

Coamo, Puerto Rico, U.S. victory, 1898 Aug. 9, I

declared, 1898 Apr. 24, I

de Lôme letter, 1898 Feb. 9, I

disease-caused casualties, 1898 Aug. 1, I

El Caney taken, 1898 July 1–2, I

first troops to Manila, 1898 May 25(2), I

hostilities halted, 1898 Aug. 12, I

Isla Grande occupied, 1898 July 8, I

McKinley call for volunteers, 1898 Apr. 23, I; 1898 May 25(1), I

Malate assaulted by Spain, 1898 July 31, I

"Message to Garcia" (Hubbard), 1895, II; 1899 Feb. 22, II

peace treaty signed, 1898 Dec. 10, I; 1899 Feb. 10, I

Ponce, Puerto Rico, surrendered, 1898 July 28, I

"Remember the Maine" slogan, 1898(1), IV

Spanish-American War (*cont.*)

Revenue Act passed, 1898 June 10, I

Rough Riders, 1896(4), II; 1898 Apr. 22(3), I; 1898 June 24, I; 1898 July 1–2, I; 1898 Aug. 7, I

San Juan Heights taken, 1898 July 1–2, I

Santiago de Cuba surrendered, 1898 July 17, I

songs, 1896(4), II

Spanish fleet destroyed, 1898 July 3, I

U.S. acquisitions from, 1898, I; 1898 June 21, I; 1898 Aug. 12, I; 1901 May 27, I

U.S. forces embark from Key West (Fla.) to Cuba, 1898 June 12–14, I

U.S. Marines landed (Guantanamo, Cuba), 1898 June 11, I

U.S. peace commissioners appointed, 1898 Sept. 9, I

Volunteer Army Act, 1898 Apr. 22(3), I

Spanish civil war, 1936, I; 1937, IV

Sparkman, John J., 1952 July 26, I; 1985, I

Sparks, Jared, 1835, II

Spassky, Boris, 1972, IV; 1972 July 11–Sept. 1, IV

Specie Resumption Act, 1875 Jan. 14, I

Species circular, 1836 July 11, I

Speck, Richard, 1966 July 14, I

Speculation:

land (Fla.), 1925 Oct., III

Speer, Albert, 1976(1), II

Spelling:

American Speller, The (Webster), 1783, III

Spellman, Francis Cardinal, 1967, III; 1970 Nov. 30, II

Spelman College (Ga.), 1988 Nov. 4, III

Spence, P. D. B., 1928 July 7, IV

Spencer, Platt Rogers, 1864 May 16, IV

Spenser, Willard, 1886 Jan. 4, II

Sperry, Roger W., 1981 Oct. 9, III

Spewack, Bella, 1990, II

Spillane, Mickey, 1947(1), II

Spinks, Leon, 1978 Feb. 15, IV; 1981, IV

Spinks, Michael, 1980, IV; 1985 Sept. 21, IV; 1987 Feb. 26, IV; 1987 June 15, IV; 1988 June 27(2), IV

Spinning and weaving *see* Textile industry

Spinsterhood:

colonial penalties, 1637, IV

Spiritualism *see* Supernatural

Spitz, Mark, 1972 Aug. 26–Sept. 11, IV

Spock, Benjamin:

arrested, 1967 Dec. 5, I

conviction overturned, 1969 July 11, I

indicted for draft conspiracy, 1968 Jan. 5, I

Sports (*see also* Games and recreation; specific sports):

AAU founded, 1888 Jan. 21, IV

CBS awarded NCAA broadcasting rights, 1989 Nov. 21, IV

collegiate deemphasis, 1991 Jan. 8–9, IV

collegiate eligibility, 1972 Jan. 8, IV

equal male-female program federal funding, 1981 Feb. 23(1), III

favorite idols, 1873(4), IV

Sports (*cont.*)
first black coach, 1966 Apr. 17–28, IV
first criminal indictment during play, 1975 July 18, IV
first intercollegiate, 1843, IV
first organized (N.Y.C.), 1664(2), IV
first trophy, 1668, IV
first woman's athletic scholarship, 1973 May 21, IV
frontier, 1819, IV
gouging's popularity, 1800(5), IV
Great Depression impact on, 1933, IV
highest paid on pro team, 1991 Dec. 2, IV
highest pro salary, 1978, IV
high school coeducational upheld, 1978 Jan. 9, IV
increased participation by women, 1990, IV; 1991, IV
Intercollegiate Assn. of Amateur Athletes of America (ICAAAA) formed, 1876(6), IV
Intercollegiate Athletic Assn.'s first convention, 1906 Dec. 29, IV
largest trade to date, 1988 Aug. 9, IV
narcotics, 1986, IV
NCAA adopted stricter academic standards for athletes, 1992 Jan. 8, IV
New Orleans Superdome (La.), 1975 Aug. 1(2), II
oldest organization (Phila., Pa.), 1732(2), IV
poll of favorite, 1990, IV
popularity statistics, 1988, IV
Preakness Stakes, 1991 May 18, IV
sexual discrimination, 1976 Aug. 27, IV
Thorpe died, 1953, IV
Thorpe's performance, 1912, IV
Tilden's sculptures of, 1885(6), II
TV bidding war, 1988 Dec. 1, IV
women's increased participation in, 1880(1), IV
women students' equal participation ruling, 1975, IV; 1975 June 3(2), IV
Spotsylvania, Battle of (Va.), 1864 May 7–20, I; 1864 May 12, I
Spotsylvania campaign (Va.), 1864 May 11, IV
Spottswood, Stephen Gill, 1974, III
Springarn, Arthur B., 1971, I
Springer v. United States, 1881 Jan. 24, I
Spring Hill College (Ala.), 1836 Jan. 9, III
Springsteen, Bruce, 1988 Mar. 2, II
Spruance, Raymond A., 1969, I
Spuzich, Sandra, 1966 July 3, IV
"Squatter sovereignty" *see* "Popular sovereignty"
SST (supersonic transport):
Concorde service started to Dulles Airport, 1976 May 24, III
first flight to Kennedy Airport (N.Y.C.), 1977 Oct. 19, III
first supersonic aircraft, 1947 Oct. 14, III
first supersonic bomber, 1954 Oct. 13, III
Supreme Ct. refused to ban, 1977 Oct. 19, III

SST (supersonic transport) (*cont.*)
U.S. program halted, 1971 May 25, III
Stack, Robert, 1960 June 20, II
Stacy, Hollis, 1977 July 24, IV; 1978 July 23, IV; 1984 July 15(1), IV
Stadler, Craig, 1982, IV; 1982 Apr. 11, IV
Stafford, Jean, 1970 May 4, II; 1979, II
Stafford, Thomas P., 1965 Dec. 15, III; 1966 June 3, III; 1969 May 18, III; 1975 July 15, III
Stafford, William, 1963 Mar. 12, II
Stage coaches:
first line, 1732(2), III
N.Y.–Phila. line, 1766, III
routes, 1755–1759, III; 1785(3), III
Stagg, Amos Alonzo, 1965, IV
Stained glass *see* Glass
Stalin, Joseph:
daughter's political asylum request, 1967 Apr. 21(1), I
Teheran conference, 1943 Nov. 28–Dec. 1, I
Yalta conference, 1945 Feb. 4–11, I
Stamp Act, 1765–1769, I; 1765 May 29, I; 1765 Oct. 7–25, I; 1765 Nov. 1, I; 1766 Mar. 17, I
Stamp collecting:
world record price paid, 1987 Oct. 9, IV
Standard Oil Co.:
antitrust actions against, 1911, III
dividends, 1900 Apr., III
forerunner, 1862(1), III
founded, 1870, III
trust, 1882, III
Standard Oil Co. of California, 1984 June 15, III
Standard Oil of Ohio, 1981 Mar. 12, III
Standish, Myles, 1620–1629, II; 1858(4), II
Stanford University (Calif.), 1885(4), III
Reagan library, 1984 Feb. 14, II
Stanley, Kim, 1963 May 26, II
Stanley, Wendell M., 1946 Nov. 14(2), III
Stanley Cup, 1947 Apr. 8–19, IV
Stans, Maurice H.:
acquitted in Vesco dealings, 1974 Apr. 28, I
whale-hunting licenses ordered, 1971 Mar. 1, III
Stanton, Charles E., 1917 July 4, IV
Stanton, Edwin M., 1868, I
Stanton, Elizabeth Cady, 1848, IV; 1848 July 19–20, I; 1869 May 15, I
Stanwyck, Barbara, 1961 May 16, II; 1966 May 22, II; 1983 Sept. 25, II; 1990, II
Stapleton, Maureen, 1968 May 19, II; 1971 Mar. 28, II; 1982 Mar. 29, II
Stargell, Willie, 1988 July 31, IV
Starr, Paul, 1984 Apr. 16, II
Stars and stripes *see* Flags
"Star Spangled Banner, The" (song), 1814, II; 1931 Mar. 3, II
"Star Wars" (Strategic Defense Initiative), 1986 Oct. 11–12, I
State, Department of:
Dulles died, 1959 Apr. 15, I
established, 1789 July 27, I
Haig resigned as secretary, 1982 June 25, I

State, Department of (*cont.*)
Herter named secretary, 1959 Apr. 18, I
human rights report, 1991 Feb. 1(1), I; 1992 Jan. 31, I
McCarthy's charges against, 1950, I
Muskie named secretary, 1980 Apr. 26, I
Randolph succeeded Jefferson, 1789 Sept. 26(3), I
Rusk named secretary, 1960 Dec. 12, I
Shultz appointed secretary, 1982 June 25, I
Vance resigned as secretary, 1980 Apr. 26, I
State of the Union messages *see* names of presidents (*see also* specific states):
States, U.S.:
provisions for statehood, 1802 Apr. 30, I
slavery issue, 1820, I
States' rights (*see also* Secession):
federal power, 1819, I; 1819, III
Hartford Convention, 1814 Dec. 15–Jan. 4, 1815, I
Madison's vs. Jefferson's views, 1815 Dec. 5, I
S.C. secession threat, 1832, I
Supreme Ct. on (Wis.), 1859, I
Webster-Hayne debate, 1830 Jan. 19–27, I; 1830 Jan. 27, IV
States Rights Democrats, 1948 July 17, I
Statue of Liberty (N.Y.C.) (*see also* Ellis Island):
centennial, 1986, IV; 1986 July 3–6, IV
cornerstone laid, 1884 Aug. 5, I
dedicated, 1886 Oct. 28, I
dynamite plot, 1965 Feb. 16, I
Statues *see* Sculpture
Stavropoulos, George P., 1990, IV
Stealth technology:
B-2 bomber, 1988 Nov. 22, I
Steamboats (*see also* Ship disasters):
Clermont, 1803 May, III; 1807 Aug. 11, III
federal building subsidy proposed, 1778(2), III
first American to cross Atlantic, 1819 May 26, III
first built in America, 1763(1), III
first built in U.S., 1786(1), III
first down Miss. R., 1811(1), III
first ferry (N.Y.–N.J.), 1811(5), III
first normal transatlantic, 1840(3), III
first steam-powered, 1787 Dec.3, III
first successful sea voyage, 1809(2), III
first transatlantic, 1838 Apr. 23, III
first warship, 1814 Oct. 29, III
Fitch's efforts to develop, 1796–1797, III
Lexington fire, 1840 Jan. 13, I
Livingston's monopoly, 1813 Feb. 26, III
Moselle exploded, 1838 Apr. 25, I
Pulaski exploded, 1838 June 14, I
Steam engine:
for fire fighting, 1852(1), III

Steam engine (*cont.*)
  first locomotive, 1826(1), III
  first (N.J.), 1753(3), III
  first successful propulsion
    experiments, 1773(2), III
  Latrobe on future of, 1803 May, III
  locomotive race with horse, 1830
    Sept. 18, IV
  miniatures, 1798(2), IV
Steamheat *see* Heating
Stearns, Raymond Phineas, 1971 Mar. 4, II
Steber, Eleanor, 1990, II
Stedman, Seymour, 1920 May 8–14, I
Steegmuller, Francis, 1971 Mar. 4, II
Steel, Ronald, 1981 Jan. 5, II
Steel and iron:
  allotment controls renewed, 1953
    Feb. 13, III
  antitrust rulings, 1915 June 3, III
  Bethlehem Steel formed, 1904 Dec.
    10, III
  Carnegie Co. incorporated (N.J.), 1900
    Mar. 24, III; 1901, III
  Carnegie on tariffs, 1908 Dec. 21, III
  cast-iron buildings (N.Y.C.), 1848, II
  contract, 1954 June 29, III
  end to racial discrimination
    agreement, 1964 June 14, III
  first Bessemer I beams, 1889(5), III
  first building skeleton (Chicago, Ill.),
    1884(3), II
  first building skeleton (N.Y.C.),
    1889(8), III
  first railroad coaches, 1906 Aug. 13,
    III
  first successful ironworks (Mass.),
    1640–1649, III
  first works (Va.), 1620(2), III
  frame skyscraper, 1895(5), II
  freeze on prices, 1941 Apr. 16, III
  furnaces (Va.), 1714(1), III
  government mill seizure, 1952, III;
    1952 Apr. 8, III; 1952 Apr. 29, III;
    1952 June 2, III
  Homestead Strike (Pa.), 1892, III
  Japanese dumping, 1977 Oct. 3, III
  Kelly and Bessemer's processing,
    1857, III
  labor agreement, 1968 July 30, III
  labor violence (Chicago, Ill.), 1937
    May 30, III
  longest strike to date settled, 1960
    Jan. 4, III
  Marquette range discovered (Mich.),
    1844 Sept. 19, III
  nail manufacture, 1777(1), III
  nationwide strike settled, 1949 Oct.
    1–Nov. 11, III
  new three-year contract, 1965 Sept. 3,
    III
  open-hearth process, 1868(2), III
  price-fixing, 1941 Apr. 16, III; 1963
    Apr. 2, III
  price hike, 1962 Apr. 10, III; 1963
    Apr. 9, III; 1967 Aug. 30, III; 1968
    July 30, III
  price hike rescinded, 1962 Apr. 13, III
  production up, 1953 Feb. 5, III
  rolled iron produced (Pa.), 1817(4), III
  strike begun, 1959 July 15, III

Steel and iron (*cont.*)
  strike canceled, 1952 May 2, III
  strike longest to date ended, 1959, III
  strikers ordered back, 1959 Nov. 7, III
  strike settled, 1952 July 24, III; 1960
    Jan. 4, III
  trigger prices to halt dumping, 1978
    Jan. 3, III
  United Mine Workers recognized,
    1937 Mar. 1, III
  U.S. Steel Corp. formed, 1901, III
  wage agreement, 1953 June 12, III
  wage increases, 1941 Apr. 14, III
  Weirton Steel Works buyout (W.Va.),
    1983 Sept. 23, III
  West Point Foundry (N.Y.), 1818(1),
    III
  workers' interim agreement, 1965
    Apr. 26, III
  workers' unemployment, 1979, III
Steele, Danielle, 1985(1), II
Steele, Porter, 1901 Mar., II
Steen, Allen, 1987 Jan. 24, I
Steenburgen, Mary, 1981 Mar. 31, II
Steffens, Lincoln, 1904, II; 1931(1), II
Stegner, Wallace, 1972 May 1, II; 1977
    Apr. 13(1), II; 1987(1), II
Steichen, Edward, 1973, II
Steiger, Rod, 1968 Apr. 10(2), II
Stein, Gertrude, 1933(1), II; 1934 Feb. 8,
    II; 1969, II
Stein, Joseph, 1955 Jan. 27, II; 1964 Sept.
    22, II; 1965 June 13, II
Stein, William H., 1972 Oct. 20(2), III
Steinbeck, John, 1929(1), II; 1935(1), II;
    1937(1), II; 1939(1), II; 1940 May 6, II;
    1942(1), II; 1947(1), II; 1952(1), II;
    1954(1), II; 1961(1), II; 1962(1), II; 1962
    Oct. 25, II; 1968, II
Steinberger, Jack, 1988 Oct. 19, III
Steinbrenner, George, 1990 July 30, IV;
    1992 July 24, IV
Steinem, Gloria, 1972 July 1, II
Stengel, Casey, 1960 Oct. 18, IV; 1962
    Sept. 27, IV; 1965 Aug. 30, IV; 1966 July
    25, IV; 1975, IV
Stephens, Woody, 1985 June 8, IV
Stephenson, Jan, 1982 June 13, IV; 1983
    July 31(2), IV
Stepovitch, Mike, 1958 June 30, I
Stereoscope, 1863 Dec. 1, III
Stern, Otto, 1944 Nov. 10, III
Stern, William and Elizabeth, 1987 Mar.
    31, IV
Sternberg, George Miller, 1892(3), III
Stetson, John Batterson, 1865(4), IV
Steunenberg, Frank, 1907(1), III
Stevens, George, 1975, II
Stevens, John, 1809(2), III; 1811(5), III
Stevens, John L., 1893 Jan. 17, I; 1893
    Feb. 1, I; 1893 July 17, I
Stevens, Ray, 1971 Mar. 16, II
Stevens, Robert L., 1830(3), III
Stevens, Robert T., 1954 Apr. 23–June 17,
    I
Stevens, Thaddeus, 1865 Dec. 4, I
Stevens, Wallace, 1923(1), II; 1950 Mar.
    27, II; 1951 Mar. 6, II; 1954(1), II; 1955
    Jan. 25, II; 1955 May 2, II

Stevens Institute of Technology (N.J.),
    1870(3), III
Stevenson, Adlai:
  vice presidential candidacy, 1892 June
    21–23, I; 1892 Nov. 8, I; 1893 Mar.
    4, I; 1900 July 5, I
Stevenson, Adlai E.:
  Cuban missile crisis, 1962 Oct. 25, I
  died, 1965, I
  presidential candidacy, 1952 July 26,
    I; 1956 Aug. 13–17, I; 1956 Nov. 6, I
  presidential defeat, 1952 Nov. 4, I
  South American goodwill tour, 1961
    June 22, I
Stevenson, Karen, 1979 Sept. 9, III
Stevenson, Robert Louis, 1893(1), II
Stewart, Alexander T., 1862(3), IV
Stewart, Gideon T., 1876 May 17, I
Stewart, James, 1941 Feb. 27, II
Stewart, Michael, 1961 Apr. 13, II; 1964
    Jan. 16, II; 1964 May 24, II; 1967 Nov.
    12, II; 1968 Apr. 10(1), II; 1977 Apr. 17,
    II; 1980 Aug. 25, II
Stewart, Payne, 1989 Aug. 13, IV; 1991
    June 17, IV
Stewart, Potter, 1985, I
Stewart, Robert, 1984 Feb. 7, III
Stewart, Timothy A., 1988 Apr. 12, III
Stieb, Dave, 1990 Sept. 2, IV
Stiegel, Henry William, 1769(1), III
Stieglitz, Alfred, 1910(4), II
Stigler, George, 1982 Oct. 20, III
Stiles, Ezra, 1735–1739, III
Stocks and bonds (*see also* Government
    bonds; New York Stock Exchange):
  Black Friday panic, 1869 Sept. 24, III
  Commodity Futures Trading
    Commission established, 1974 Oct.
    10(1), III
  crash, 1987 Oct. 19, III
  crash (Black Tuesday), 1929, I
  crash blamed on automatic trading
    programs, 1988 Jan. 8, III
  daily volume record set, 1984 Aug. 3,
    III
  different voting rights, 1986 July 3, III
  Dow Jones all-time high, 1966 Feb. 9,
    III
  Dow Jones average, 1983, III; 1987
    Dec. 31, III
  Dow Jones average down, 1984, III;
    1990 Dec. 31, III
  Dow Jones average low, 1970 Apr. 28,
    III; 1992, III
  Dow Jones average passed 3400 mark,
    1992 June 1, III
  Dow Jones average record drop, 1987
    Oct. 19, III
  Dow Jones average record high, 1982
    Dec. 27, III; 1989 Oct. 9, III; 1991
    Dec. 31, III
  Dow Jones average record
    high/shares traded, 1986 Dec. 31(2),
    III
  Dow Jones average second largest
    decline, 1989 Oct. 9, III
  Dow Jones average up, 1989 Dec. 31,
    III
  Dow Jones decline, 1977, III

Stocks and bonds (*cont.*)
  Dow Jones record single-day rise, 1978 Nov. 1, III
  Drexel felony charges, 1988 Dec. 21, III
  electronic trading systems curbs, 1988 Jan. 8, III
  Equity Funding Corp. inside dealings, 1973 Mar. 27, III
  federal registration required, 1933 May 27, I
  first Dow Jones 1000 closing, 1972, III; 1972 Nov. 14, III
  fixed brokers' commission rates abolished, 1973 Sept. 11, III
  GM split, 1955 July 5, III
  heaviest single day loss, 1955 Sept. 26, III
  insider trading, 1986 Nov. 14, IV
  largest dividend to date, 1900 Apr., III
  largest loss since 1929, 1962 May 28, III
  largest single transaction to date, 1984 June 21, III
  London Stock Exchange closed, 1914 July 31, III
  margin requirements, 1951 Jan. 16, III
  margin requirements reduced, 1953 Feb. 20, III
  market operations reforms proposed, 1988 May 16, III
  market run, 1981 Jan. 7, III
  Milken sentenced, 1990 Nov. 21, III
  new trading record, 1978 Apr. 17, III
  number of holders, 1952 June 30, III
  N.Y. Stock Exchange closed, 1873 Sept. 20, I
  ownership, 1959 June 15, III
  panic, 1979 Oct. 6, III
  price climb, 1929 Sept., III
  price downturn, 1966 Feb. 9, III
  prices at year's low, 1966 Oct. 7, III
  prices highest since 1929, 1954 Dec. 31, III
  railroad, 1894, III
  recession at lowest, 1938 Mar., III
  record shares traded, 1979, III
  Salomon Brothers suspended from auctions, 1991 Aug. 18, III
  second greatest trading day to date (N.Y.S.E.), 1967 Mar. 10, III
  Securities Exchange Act, 1934 June 6, I
  securities reforms, 1975 May 22, III
  selling rate signaled new recession, 1937 Aug., III
  shares traded, 1983, III
  trading high, 1916 Dec. 21, III
  trading record, 1968 June 13, III; 1981 Jan. 7, III
  volume highest since 1933, 1954 Dec. 31, III
  weekly trading record, 1982 Oct. 15, III
  worst crash in history, 1987 Oct. 19, III; 1988 Jan. 8, III
Stockton, Dave, 1970 Aug. 16, IV; 1976 Aug. 16, IV
Stockton, Frank R., 1882(2), II

Stockton, Robert F., 1846 June 14, I
Stoddard, Joshua C., 1855 Oct. 9, II
Stoddard, Solomon (Rev.), 1703 Fall, IV
Stoddert, Benjamin, 1798(3), I
Stokes, Carl B., 1967 Nov. 7, I
Stokowski, Leopold, 1965 Apr. 26, II; 1970 Nov. 30, II
Stolle, Fred, 1966 Sept. 11, IV
Stompanato, Johnny, 1958 Apr. 4, IV
Stone, Edward Durrell, 1964 Mar. 16, II; 1978, II
Stone, I. F., 1989, II
Stone, Irving, 1944(1), II; 1961(1), II
Stone, Lucy, 1870(2), I
Stone, Melville E., 1875 Dec. 25, II
Stone, Peter, 1970 Nov. 10, II; 1991 June 2, II
Stone, Robert, 1975 Apr. 16, II
Stoneham, Horace C., 1990, IV
Stony Point, Battle of (N.Y.), 1779 July 15, I; 1779 July 26, I
Stopes, Marie C., 1921 Apr. 22, II
Stoppard, Tom, 1967 Oct. 16, II; 1968 Apr. 21, II; 1972 Apr. 23(1), II; 1975 Oct. 30, II; 1976 Apr. 18, II; 1984 Jan. 5, II; 1984 June 3, II
Stores *see* Grocery stores and supermarkets; Retail stores
Storey, David, 1970 Nov. 11, II; 1972 Nov. 17, II; 1973 Mar. 6, II
Storms *see* types, e.g., Rain; Snowstorms
Stotz, Carl, 1992, IV
Stoughton, Israel, 1634(1), III
Stout, Myron, 1987, II
Stout, Rex, 1975, II
Stove, Betty, 1972 July 7(2), IV
Stoves:
  first mentioned, 1702(2), II
  Franklin, 1742(3), III
Stowe, Calvin, 1837(2), III
Stowe, Harriet Beecher:
  Dred, A Tale of the Great Dismal Swamp, 1856(3), II
  Library of America edition of works, 1982(1), II
  Minister's Wooing, The, 1859(6), II
  Oldtown Folks, 1869(1), II
  Uncle Tom's Cabin, 1839(1), I; 1852, II
Strachey, William, 1610, II
Straight, Beatrice, 1977 Mar. 28, II
Strang, James Jesse, 1850 July 8, III
Strange, Curtis, 1985, IV; 1987 Nov. 1, IV; 1988, IV; 1988 June 20, IV; 1989 June 18, IV
Strasberg, Lee, 1982, II
Strategic Arms Limitation Talks (SALT) *see* Arms control and disarmament
Straus, Oscar S., 1906 Dec. 12, I
Strauss, Lewis L., 1974, I
Strauss, Peter, 1979 Sept. 9, II
Strauss, Richard, 1907 Jan. 22, II
Stravinsky, Igor, 1954, II; 1957 June 17, II; 1962 June 14, II; 1971, II; 1972 June 18–25, II
Streep, Meryl, 1980 Apr. 14(2), II; 1983 Apr. 11, II
Street, J. C., 1989, III
Streetcars:
  cable (San Francisco, Calif.), 1873(4), III

Streetcars (*cont.*)
  first electric (Wis.), 1882(7), III
  first in world (N.Y.C.), 1832 Nov. 26, III
  first successful electric, (Richmond, Va.), 1887(3), III
  inventions leading to cable, 1871(4), III
Streets:
  cleaning, 1690–1699, IV
  first electric lights for entire city (Cleveland, Ohio), 1879(1), III
  first lights (Boston, Mass.), 1719, IV
  first naming plan (R.I.), 1679 Sept., IV
  gas lighting introduced (R.I.), 1806(1), IV
  gas lights, 1816 June, III
  lighting, 1770–1774, IV
  lighting (Phila., Pa.), 1757(2), IV
  naming, 1701, IV; 1790(2), IV
  paving, 1755–1759, IV
Streisand, Barbra, 1964 May 12, II; 1965 Sept. 12, II; 1965 Sept. 13, II; 1966 Mar. 15(2), II; 1969 Apr. 14, II; 1978 Feb. 23, II; 1987 Feb. 24, II
Streptomycin, 1952 Oct. 23, III
Stribling, T. S., 1931(1), II; 1933 May 4, II
Strikes:
  actors, 1919 Aug. 7, II
  actors' off-Broadway, 1970 Nov. 16, II
  AFL no-strike agreement, 1941 July 24, III; 1941 Dec. 15, III
  air traffic controllers, 1981 Aug. 3, III
  auto workers, 1967 Sept. 6, III; 1973 Sept. 14, III
  auto workers' averted, 1964 Sept. 9, III; 1964 Sept. 18, III
  baseball, 1972, IV; 1972 Apr. 1, IV
  baseball, first mid-season, 1981 June 12, IV
  Bethlehem Steel, 1941 Feb. 26, III
  Broadway musicians, 1975 Sept. 18, II
  Broadway theaters closed, 1960 June 2–13, III
  carpenters (Boston, Mass.), 1825(1), III
  coal, 1943 May 1, III
  coal miners, 1900 Sept. 17, III
  coal miners (Ohio), 1894 Apr. 20, III
  coal miners (Pa.), 1902 May 12, III; 1902 July 30, III; 1902 Oct. 16, III
  coal miners (Pa., Ohio, W. Va.), 1897 July 2, III
  costliest in sports to date, 1982 Sept. 21, IV
  defense industry, 1941 Jan. 22, III
  early union (Phila., Pa.), 1794(2), III
  federal troops, 1894 July 3, III; 1894 July 20, III
  first court appeal by employer, 1805(2), III
  first doctors' (N.Y.C.), 1975 Mar. 17–20, III
  first general to date, 1934 July 16, III
  first industry-wide (N.Y.C.), 1806(1), III
  first involving women (R.I.), 1824, III
  first major postal workers', 1970 Mar. 18, III
  first move against sit-down (Mich.), 1936 Jan. 11, III

Strikes (*cont.*)

first recorded factory workers' (N.J.), 1828(4), III

first recorded (Phila., Pa.), 1786(2), III

first statewide teachers' (Fla.), 1968 Feb. 19, III

Ford Motor Co., 1941 Apr. 11(1), III

garment workers (N.Y.C.), 1894 Sept. 4, III; 1913 Jan., III

GE workers, 1969 Oct. 27, III

GM, 1964 Sept. 25, III; 1970 Sept. 15, III

GM Flint (Mich.) plant, 1936 Jan. 11, III; 1936 Feb. 3, III

GM plants, 1945 Nov. 21, III

grape workers (Calif.), 1966 Apr. 6, III; 1973 Apr. 15, III

hockey, 1992 Apr. 10(2), IV

Homestead (Pa.), 1892, III

injunction first used, 1894 July 2, III

injunction use upheld, 1895 May 27, III

international pilots, 1972, III

longest and costliest N.Y.C., 1954 Apr. 2, III

longest coal to date ended, 1978 Mar. 25, III

longest newspaper began (N.Y.C.), 1966 Apr. 24, III

longest newspaper to date (Detroit, Mich.), 1964 Nov. 21(1), III

longest port to date ended (West Coast), 1972 Feb. 21, III

longest steel to date settled, 1960 Jan. 4, III

Longshoremen, 1959 Oct. 1(1), III

Longshoremen's (East and Gulf Coasts), 1977 Oct. 1, III

Longshoremen's ended (East and Gulf Coasts), 1963 Jan. 26, III

Lynn (Mass.) shoemakers', 1860(5), IV; 1860 Feb. 22, III

maritime, halted by injunction, 1961 July 3, III

Metropolitan Opera (N.Y.C.), 1969, II

most costly aviation to date, 1961 Feb. 23, III

National Guard involvement (Mich.), 1936 Feb. 3, III

nationwide railroad, 1877, III

newspaper (Cleveland, Ohio), 1963 Mar. 31, III

newspaper (Detroit, Mich.), 1967 Nov. 15, III

newspaper ended (Detroit, Mich.), 1968 Aug. 9, III

newspaper ended (N.Y.C.), 1963 Mar. 31, III; 1966 Sept. 12(2), III

newspaper (N.Y.C.), 1962 Nov. 1, III; 1962 Dec. 8, II; 1965 Sept. 16, III; 1978 Aug. 9, III

N.Y.C. ballet, 1973 Nov. 13, II

N.Y.C. sailors', 1800(2), III

N.Y.C. transit workers, 1889 Jan. 28, I

nuclear workers, 1960 Oct. 15, III

N.Y. Central and Hudson River RR, 1890 Aug. 8, III

Pa. miners' riot, 1894 Apr. 5, I

police (Boston, Mass.), 1919 Sept. 9, III

port ended (N.Y.), 1969 Feb. 14, III

Strikes (*cont.*)

pro football, 1982 Sept. 21, IV

Pullman (Chicago, Ill.), 1894 May 11, III; 1894 June 26, III; 1894 July 2, III; 1894 July 3, III; 1894 July 6, III; 1894 July 10, III; 1894 Aug. 3, III

Pullman injunction (Chicago, Ill.), 1894 July 20, III; 1894 Dec. 14, III

railroad averted by compulsory arbitration, 1963 Aug. 28, III

railroad injunction, 1948 May 10, III

railroads seized by Army, 1950 Aug. 25, III

riot and casualties (Ill.), 1898 Oct. 12, III

rubber ended, 1967 July 26, III

shipping halted by injunction, 1962 Apr. 11, III

shipping settled, 1965 Aug. 29, III

silk workers, 1913 Feb. 25, III

sit-down, 1937(2), III; 1937 May, III

sit-down found illegal, 1939 Feb. 27, III

soft coal, 1948 Mar. 15, III

steel, 1952, III; 1952 Apr. 8, III; 1952 Apr. 29, III; 1952 June 2, III; 1959, III; 1959 July 15, III; 1959 Nov. 7, III

steel canceled, 1952 May 2, III

steel settled, 1949 Oct. 1–Nov. 11, III; 1952 July 24, III

subway (N.Y.C.), 1926 July 5, III

teachers' ended (Cleveland, Ohio), 1980 Jan. 3, III

teachers' (N.Y.C.), 1967 Sept. 11, III; 1968 Sept. 9, III

textile (Fall River, Mass.), 1904 July 25, III

textile (Lawrence, Mass.), 1912, III

transit (N.Y.C.), 1966 Jan. 1, III

truckers', 1979 June 7, III

TV and film writers, 1988 Aug. 7(2), II

union conspiracy issue tried, 1810 July 12, III

uprising in, 1941, III

violence in miners' (Idaho), 1899 Apr. 29, III

violence in steel strike (Chicago, Ill.), 1937 May 30, III

wartime ban on, 1942, III

Westinghouse, 1956 Mar. 20, III

widespread, 1892(2), III; 1946(1), III

Strindberg, August, 1916(8), II

Strip mining *see* Coal

Stritch, Samuel (Cardinal), 1958 Apr. 26, III

Strong, Austin, 1922 Oct. 30(1), II

Strong, Josiah, 1885(3), III

Strossen, Nadine, 1991 Jan. 27, I

Strouse, Charles, 1960 Apr. 14, II; 1970 Mar. 30, II; 1977 Apr. 21, II; 1977 June 5, II

Strugess, Eric, 1950 July 7, IV

Stuart, Gilbert, 1782(2), II; 1796(2), II; 1979 Apr. 10, II

Stuart, James Ewell Brown ("Jeb"), 1864 May 11, I

Stuart, William (counterfeiter), 1854(3), IV

Student protests and sit-ins *see* Colleges and universities; Vietnam War demonstrations; names of specific colleges

Stuyvesant, Peter, 1640–1649, IV; 1652(2), I; 1654 July 8, III; 1655, I; 1657(2), IV; 1659 Sept. 30, IV; 1664 Sept. 7, I

Styne, Jule, 1959 May 21, II; 1968 Apr. 21, II; 1974 Jan. 27(1), II; 1974 Sept. 23, II

Styron, William, 1951(1), II; 1967(1), II; 1968 May 8, II; 1979(1), II; 1980 May 1, II

Submarines:

CIA attempt to recover sunken Soviet, 1975 Mar. 18, I

first atomic commissioned, 1954 Sept. 30, I

first atomic keel dedicated, 1952 June 14, I

first launch of nuclear warhead, 1962 May 6, III

first missile-capable nuclear, 1959 Dec. 30, III

first Polaris missile launch, 1960 July 20, III

first successful attack, 1864 Feb. 17, III

first undersea voyage around world, 1960 May 10, III

Nautilus crossed N. Pole, 1958 Aug. 5, I

nuclear *Scorpion* missing (Azores), 1968 May 29, I

nuclear *Thresher* sank, 1963 Apr. 10, I

Poseidon dismantled, 1986 May 27, I

rendezvous beneath N. Pole, 1962 Aug. 22(2), III

second and third atomic, 1957 Mar. 30, I

S-4 disaster, 1927 Dec. 17, I

Trident, 1986 May 27, I

underwater endurance record, 1958 Sept. 22(1), I; 1958 Oct. 6, I

underwater mine detonation, 1842(1), III

use in World War I, 1916 Jan. 7, I; 1916 Apr. 18, I; 1917 Jan. 31, I

Subversion and loyalty issue (*see also* Espionage; Treason):

Alien Registration Act, 1940 June 28, I

Army-McCarthy hearings, 1954 Apr. 23–June 17, I

clergy infiltrated by communists charged, 1960 Feb. 25, III

communists in government charges, 1948, I

Coughlin's *Social Justice*, 1942 Apr. 14(1), II

J. Edgar Hoover on, 1950, I

federal government employee restrictions, 1947, I

GE communist employee ban, 1953 Dec. 9, III

Hiss case, 1948 Dec. 15, I; 1949 May 31, I

Hiss convicted, 1950 Jan. 21(2), I

Hiss exonerated by Russians, 1992 Oct. 14, I

Subversion and loyalty issue (*cont.*)
  International Security Act, 1950 Sept. 23, I
  investigations ruled constitutional, 1959 June 8, I
  John Birch Society's activities, 1961 Mar. 8, I
  Ku Klux Klan investigated, 1965 Oct. 19, I
  McCarthyism attacked, 1954, IV
  McCarthy's charges, 1953, I; 1953 Jan. 2, I
  Rosenbergs executed, 1953 June 19, I
  scientists' blacklist dropped, 1970 Jan. 2, III
  scientists blacklisted, 1969 Oct. 8, III
  screenwriters' blacklisting, 1947, II
  security-risk personnel discharged, 1955 Jan. 3, I
  Senate investigation of communism, 1955 Jan. 14, I
  teachers' restrictions, 1952 Mar. 2, III
  thirteen communist leaders convicted, 1953 Jan. 21, I
Subways:
  Chicago's first, 1943 Oct. 17(2), III
  derailment (Brooklyn, N.Y.), 1918 Nov. 1, III
  first in U.S. planned (N.Y.C.), 1864(4), III
  first practical (Boston, Mass.), 1897, III
  N.Y.C. strike, 1926 July 5, III
  N.Y.C. system opened, 1904, III
Suffolk Resolves, 1774 Sept. 17, I
Suffrage *see* Voting rights; Women's suffrage
Sugar:
  American Sugar's control of market, 1891(1), III
  first cane grown (La.), 1751, III
  price soars, 1974 Nov. 15, III
  rationed, 1918 July 26, III; 1942 May 5, III
  rationing ended, 1947 June 11, III
  rations cut, 1945 Apr. 30, III
  trust, 1887, III
  U.S. import quotas from Cuba cut, 1960 July 3, III
Suggs, Louise, 1949 Sept. 25, IV; 1952 June 29, IV; 1953, IV; 1955 July 2, IV; 1957 June 10, IV
Suits and claims *see* Courts
Sukova, Helena, 1986 Sept. 7, IV
Sullivan, Arthur (Sir), 1879 June 16, II
Sullivan, Ed, 1974, II
Sullivan, John L., 1882 Feb. 7, IV; 1889 July 8, IV
Sullivan, Kathryn D., 1984 Oct. 11, III
Sullivan, Louis H., 1890(4), II; 1893(8), II; 1898(4), II
Sully, Thomas, 1812, II
Sultana (ship), 1865 Apr. 27, I
Sulzberger, Iphigene Ochs, 1990, II
Summerfield, Arthur E., 1959 June 11, II; 1960 Mar. 25, II
Sumner, Charles:
  caned and severely injured, 1856 May 22, I
  Reconstruction views, 1865 Dec. 4, I
Sumner, James B., 1946 Nov. 14(2), III

Sumner, William Graham, 1883, III
Sumners, Rosalynn, 1982 Jan. 28–31, IV; 1983 Feb. 3–4, IV; 1983 Mar. 10–11, IV; 1984 Jan. 20–21, IV
Sun (*see also* Solar):
  first photographs, 1891(4), III
  orbits around, 1960 Mar. 11, III
Sunday, Billy, 1896, III; 1934 Jan. 7, III
Sunday School Magazine, 1824, III
Sunnyside (Tarrytown, N.Y.), 1835(7), II
Sununu, John, 1991 Dec. 3, I
Superconducting Super Collider (SSC), 1988 Nov. 10, III
Superconductivity, 1986 Dec. 31, III
  first transistors, 1990 Nov. 16, III
Superdome (New Orleans, La.), 1975 Aug. 1(2), II
Supermarkets *see* Grocery stores and supermarkets
Supernatural:
  Mather's reports, 1688, IV
  séance cult, 1849, III
  satanic visitation (Conn.), 1789 Oct. 7, IV
Supersonic transport *see* SST
Supreme Court, U.S.:
  abortion legalized, 1973 Jan. 22, III
  abortion restrictions upheld, 1989 July 3, I
  abortion ruling reaffirmed, 1983 June 15, I; 1986 June 11, I; 1992 June 29, I
  affirmative action upheld, 1986 July 2, III
  agency shop labor contract upheld, 1963 June 3, III
  Ali draft evasion conviction overturned, 1971 June 28, IV
  "alien is person" ruling, 1886 May 10, I
  alimony laws, 1979 Mar. 5, I
  antiparochial school law voided (Oreg.), 1924 Mar. 31, III
  antitrust decisions, 1904 Mar. 14, III; 1906 Mar. 12, III; 1908 Feb. 3, III; 1911, III; 1911 May 29, III; 1943 Jan. 18, III; 1944 June 5, III
  arbitration upheld, 1964 Apr. 27, III
  baseball exempted from antitrust, 1972 June 19, IV
  bilingual education ruling, 1974 Jan. 21, III
  black affirmative action upheld, 1979 June 27, III
  Blackmun approved, 1970 May 12, I
  blacks on juries, 1880 Mar. 1, I
  black-white boxing ban unconstitutional, 1959 May 25, IV
  Bork nomination rejected, 1987 Oct. 23, I
  Brandeis appointed, 1916 Jan. 28, III
  Brennan resigned, 1990 July 20, I
  budget balancing act found partially unconstitutional, 1986 July 7, I
  Burger retired, 1986 June 17, I
  Burger sworn in, 1969 June 23, I
  business seniority system upheld, 1977 May 31, III
  capital punishment, 1976 July 2, I; 1989, I

Supreme Court, U.S. (*cont.*)
  capital punishment advocates barred from juries, 1986 May 5, I
  capital punishment for rape unconstitutional, 1977 June 29, IV
  censorship, 1957 Feb. 25, II
  Chase as chief justice, 1864 Dec., I
  child labor law unconstitutional, 1918 June 3, III
  Chinese exclusion unconstitutional, 1893 May 15, I
  church-state separation decision, 1985 July 1, III
  citizenship rights, 1898 May 28, I; 1964 May 18, I
  civil rights decisions, 1878 Jan. 14, I; 1883 Oct. 15, I; 1968 June 17, I
  class-action suits ruling, 1974 May 28, III
  closed criminal pretrial proceedings upheld, 1979 July 2, I
  closed shops, 1949 Jan. 3, III
  coerced confessions ruling, 1991 Mar. 20(2), I
  Communist Party membership, 1965 Nov. 15, I
  Communist Party membership deportation upheld, 1954 May 24, I
  communist subversion investigations upheld, 1959 June 8, I
  compulsory flag salute ruling, 1943 June 14, III
  compulsory vaccination laws, 1905 Feb. 20, III
  Concorde ban upheld, 1977 Oct. 19, III
  congressional districts equally populated, 1964 Feb. 17, I
  conscientious objectors' status rulings, 1965 Mar. 8, I; 1970 June 15, I; 1971 Mar. 8(1), I
  contraceptive ban unconstitutional (Conn.), 1965 June 7(1), I
  Contract Labor Act (Ga.) overturned, 1942 Jan. 12(2), III
  copyright infringement case, 1964 Oct. 21, II
  corporal punishment upheld, 1975 Oct. 20, III
  "corporations as persons" ruling, 1886 May 10, III
  creationist theory in school curriculum struck down, 1987 June 19, III
  death penalty laws, 1972 June 29, I
  defendants' rights, 1959 June 22, IV; 1966 June 13, I; 1971 Feb. 24, I; 1990 Dec. 3, I; 1991 Mar. 20(2), I
  double jeopardy upheld, 1959 Mar. 30, I
  Douglas retired, 1975 Nov. 12, I
  editorial rebuttals decision, 1974 June 25, II
  eighteen-year-old vote constitutional, 1970 Dec. 21, I
  EPA pollution-control authority upheld, 1977 Feb. 23, III
  equal legal educational facilities (Okla.), 1948 Jan. 12, III

Supreme Court, U.S. (*cont.*)

equal political advertising air time overruled, 1973 May 26, II

equal rights decisions, 1973 May 14(1), I

evidence admissibility ruling, 1984 June 11, I

executive authority, 1926 Oct. 25, I

federal drug testing upheld, 1989 Mar. 21, I

Federal Election Campaign Act, 1976 Jan. 30, I

federal vs. state power, 1819, I; 1819, III; 1903 Feb. 23, I

firearm mailing ban upheld, 1975 Dec. 2, III

first black justice, 1967 Oct. 2, I

first black justice resigned, 1991 June 27, I

first chief justice, 1789 Sept. 26(1), I

first state obscenity law hearing (N.Y.S.), 1948(2), II

first woman member, 1981 July 7, I

flag burning rulings, 1989 June 12(2), I

football franchise shifts upheld, 1984 Nov. 5, IV

Fortas chief justice nomination withdrawn, 1968 Oct. 2, I

Fortas nominated as chief justice, 1968 June 26, I

Fortas resigned, 1969 May 15, I

Fourteenth Amendment rulings, 1886 May 10, I; 1886 May 10, III

free counsel for indigents, 1963 Mar. 18, I

freedom of press decision, 1972 June 29, II

freedom to criticize public figures upheld, 1988 Feb. 24, I

free education for illegal aliens upheld, 1982 June 15, III

genetic engineering ruling, 1980 June 16, III

government censorship ruling, 1975 May 27, II

Grant appointments, 1871 May 1, III

hate speech/bias crime laws denied, 1992 June 22(2), I

Haynsworth nomination rejected, 1969 Nov. 21(2), I

homosexual relations ruling, 1986 June 30, I

housing discrimination, 1967 May 29, III

Hughes appointed chief justice, 1930 Feb. 3, I

illegal evidence ruling, 1971 Feb. 24, I

immigration, 1837 Feb., I; 1882, I

income tax constitutional, 1881 Jan. 24, I; 1916 Jan. 24, III

independent prosecutors upheld, 1988 June 29, I

interception of communist propaganda banned, 1965 May 24, III

interracial marriages upheld, 1967 June 12, I

Supreme Court, U.S. (*cont.*)

interstate commerce, 1824 Mar. 2, I; 1895 May 27, III; 1898 June 1, III

job discrimination ruling, 1984 May 22, I

judicial review doctrine, 1803, I

jury rulings, 1970 June 22, I; 1991 Mar. 4, I; 1991 Apr. 1, I; 1991 June 3, I; 1992 June 18, I

justice retirement act, 1937 Aug. 26, I

labor unions subject to interstate trade regulations, 1921 Jan. 3, III

last hired, first fired policy upheld, 1984 June 12, III

legal fee advertising upheld, 1977 June 27, III

Legal Tender Act, 1871 May 1, III

legislative veto struck down, 1983 June 23, I

lethal force against criminal suspects barred, 1985 Mar. 27, I

life-prolonging treatment ruling, 1986 June 9, III

longest justice's tenure, 1980, I

malice aforethought judgment, 1964 Mar. 9, II

Marshall resigned, 1991 June 27, I

Marshall's contribution, 1801 Jan. 20, I

Medicaid-funded abortion not mandatory, 1977 June 20, III

membership increased, 1837 Mar. 3(1), I

mental institutions guidelines, 1972 Apr. 13, III

mental patients' forced confinement barred, 1975 June 26, III

minimum wage law, 1923 Apr. 9, III

minority-owned construction company preference law invalid, 1989 Jan. 23, I

Mississippi university system ruled still segregated, 1992 June 26, III

Miss. school desegregation ordered, 1969 Oct. 29, III

movie censorship, 1961 Jan. 23, II; 1965 Mar. 1, II

National Labor Relations Act upheld, 1937 Apr. 12, III

Nativity display upheld, 1984 Mar. 5, I

Nev. divorces, 1942 Dec. 21, IV

new building cornerstone laid, 1932 Oct. 13, III

New Deal measures, 1933 May 12(1), I; 1935, I; 1935 May 27, I

Nixon nominees, 1970 May 12, I

Nixon nominees approved, 1971, I; 1971 Dec. 6, I; 1971 Dec. 10, I

Nixon nominees rejected, 1970, I; 1970 Apr. 8, I

nuclear plant construction bans upheld, 1983 Apr. 20, I

obscenity rulings, 1966 Mar. 21, II; 1973 June 21, II

parochial school aid barred, 1973 June 25, III

parochial school aid rulings, 1971 June 28, III

pocket veto upheld, 1929 May 27, I

poll taxes unconstitutional, 1966 Mar. 25, I

Supreme Court, U.S. (*cont.*)

Powell approved, 1971, I; 1971 Dec. 6, I

power consolidation, 1816 Mar. 20(1), I

presidential liability ruling, 1982 June 24, I

presidential powers, 1827 Feb. 2, I

prisoners' appeals restricted, 1992 May 4, I

private nonsectarian school discrimination banned, 1976 June 25, III

private possession of obscene material allowed, 1969 Apr. 7, II

Prohibition decisions, 1931 Feb. 24, I

property tax financing of public education upheld, 1973 Mar. 21, III

public school religious education barred, 1948 Mar. 8, III

Puerto Rican citizenship, 1904 Jan. 4, I

Rehnquist approved, 1971, I; 1971 Dec. 10, I

religious services in public universities upheld, 1981 Dec. 8, III

reverse discrimination ruling, 1989 June 12(1), I

right-to-die rulings, 1990 June 25, I

F. D. Roosevelt's move to pack, 1937 Feb. 5, I; 1937 July 22(1), I

school busing plan rejected (Detroit, Mich.), 1974 July 25, III

school busing to desegregate ruling, 1971 Apr. 20, III

school desegregation issues, 1955 May 31, III; 1964 May 25, III; 1991 Jan. 15(1), I; 1992 Mar. 31, I

school desegregation unconstitutional, 1954 May 17, I

school facilities' use by student political/religious groups upheld, 1990 June 4, I

school prayer banned (N.Y.), 1962 June 25, III

school prayer law struck down, 1985 June 4, III

school prayer law struck down again, 1992 June 24(2), III

segregation in transportation banned, 1962 Feb. 26, I

separate but equal doctrine, 1896 May 18, I

sex hiring discrimination ruling, 1971 Jan. 25, III; 1989 May 1, I

sit-down strike illegal, 1939 Feb. 27, III

slavery, 1826(2), I; 1857, I; 1859, I

smokers' damage suits upheld, 1992 June 24(1), III

Social Security Act, 1937 May 24, III

southern school desegregation deadline, 1970 Jan. 14, III

state legislature apportionment, 1964 June 15, I

steel mill seizure, 1952, III; 1952 June 2, III

steel strike, 1959 Nov. 7, III

strip coal mining upheld, 1976 June 28, III

Supreme Court, U.S. (*cont.*)
strip searches of soldiers banned, 1974 Jan. 14, IV
student rights to sue colleges ruling, 1992 Feb. 26, I
subversion decisions, 1952 Mar. 2, III
Taney as chief justice, 1834 June 24, I
Tariff Act income tax clauses voided, 1895 May 20, III
tax exemptions for private schools that discriminate ruled against, 1983 May 24, III
Teapot Dome ruling, 1927 Oct. 10, I
televising college football games ruling, 1984 June 27, IV
Tellico Dam (Tenn.) halted, 1978 June 15, III
Thomas confirmed, 1991 Oct. 15, I
travel restrictions upheld, 1959 Dec. 7, I
unfair marketing practices, 1972 Mar. 1(1), III
uniform minimum legal fees barred, 1975 June 16, III
union membership, 1915 Jan. 25(1), III
U.S. territorial possessions, 1901 May 27, I
Voting Rights Act upheld, 1966 Mar. 7, I
voting rights decisions, 1927 Mar. 7, I
wage and hour law upheld, 1941 Feb. 3, I
Warren resigned, 1968 June 13, I
Warren retired, 1969 June 23, I
Watergate appeals rejected, 1977 May 23, I
White House tapes subpoenaed, 1974, I; 1974 July 24, I
women admitted to all-male clubs, 1987 May 4, IV
women in workplace ruling, 1991 Mar. 20(1), I
women lawyers permitted to argue cases, 1879 Feb. 15, I
women's admission to private clubs upheld, 1988 June 20, IV
women's exclusion from draft upheld, 1981 June 25, I
women's minimum wage law upheld, 1937 Mar. 29, III
women's suffrage, 1922 Feb. 27, I
women's wage discrimination ruling, 1981 June 8, I
working hours limitations, 1905 Apr. 17, III
zoning laws upheld, 1977 Jan. 11, III
Surrogate motherhood, 1987 Mar. 31, IV; 1988 June 27(1), IV
Surveyor 1, 1966 June 2, III
Surveyor 2, 1966 Sept. 22, III
Surveyor 3, 1967 Apr. 17, III
Surveyor 4, 1967 July 17, III
Surveyor 5, 1967 Sept. 8, III
Surveyor 6, 1967 Nov. 7, III
Surveyor 7, 1968 Jan. 9, III
Susann, Jacqueline, 1966(1), II; 1974, II
Susman, Karen Hantze, 1962 July 7, IV
Sutherland, Earl W., 1971 Oct. 14, III; 1974, III

Sutherland, Joan, 1961, II; 1970 Mar. 3, II
Sutter, John, 1848 Jan. 24, IV
Sutton, Hal, 1983, IV; 1983 Aug. 7, IV
Sutton, May G., 1904(3), IV; 1905(5), IV; 1907(2), IV
Swaggart, Jimmy, 1988 Apr. 8, III
Swallow, Silas C., 1904 June 29–30, I; 1904 Nov. 8, I
Swan, William G., 1931 June 4, III
Swanberg, W. A., 1967(1), II; 1973 May 7, II; 1977 Apr. 13(1), II
Swanberg, William A., 1992, II
Swanson, Gloria, 1983, II
Swanson, Howard, 1950(2), II
Swarthout, Gladys, 1969, II
Swedenborg, Emanuel, 1800, IV
Sweet, Blanche, 1986, II
Swerling, Jo, 1951 Mar. 25, II
Swift, Gustavus Franklin, 1870(8), III
Swigert, John L., Jr., 1970 Apr. 11, III
Swimming:
first school (Boston, Mass.), 1827 July 23, IV
first woman across English Channel, 1926 Aug. 6, IV
five-nation meet (Moscow), 1966 July 16–17, IV
two-minute mark freestyle record, 1963 Aug. 24(1), IV
world record, 1958 June 28, IV
Swindles see Frauds
Symbionese Liberation Army (SLA):
Hearst captured and indicted, 1975 Sept. 18, IV
Hearst joined, 1974 Apr. 3, IV
ransom for P. Hearst kidnaping, 1974 Feb. 5, IV
shootout (Los Angeles, Calif.), 1974 May 17, IV
Symington, Stuart:
missile gap charges, 1960 Feb. 23, I
Symmes, Thomas (Rev.), 1720, II
Symons, Julian, 1985(1), II
Symphony Hall (Boston, Mass.), 1900 Oct. 15, II
Syncom 1 (satellite), 1963 Feb. 14, III
Syncom 2 (satellite), 1963 July 26, III
Syncom 3 (satellite), 1964 Aug. 19, III
Synge, John Millington, 1912(2), II
Synthetics (*see also* types):
early 20th century, 1909, III
quinine developed, 1944 May 3(1), III
Syracuse University (N.Y.), 1870(4), III
Szell, George, 1970, II
Szent-Györgyi, Albert, 1986, III
Szilard, Leo, 1964, III
Szoka, Edmund Casimir, 1988 May 29, III

Taber, Norman, 1915(3), IV
Tabler, Otis Francis, 1975 Feb. 1, IV
Table tennis see Ping-Pong
Taft, Robert M., 1957 Apr. 30, I
Taft, William Howard:
Bastille Day celebration arranged, 1790 July 14, IV
born, 1857 Sept. 15, I
conservation move, 1909 Sept. 27, III
Cuban governorship, 1906 Sept. 29, I
defended high tariffs, 1909, I
elected president, 1908 Nov. 3, I

Taft, William Howard (*cont.*)
inaugurated president, 1909 Mar. 4, I
lost presidential bid, 1912 Nov. 5, I
presidential candidacy, 1908 June 16–20, I
retired from Supreme Ct., 1930 Feb. 3, I
Russian treaty abrogated, 1911 Dec. 18, I
second term presidential nomination, 1912 June 18–22, I
selected for presidency by T. Roosevelt, 1908, I
vetoed Ariz. statehood, 1911 Aug. 22, I
Taft-Hartley Act:
amendments, 1953 Sept. 10, III
Eisenhower urged changes, 1954 Jan. 11, III
passed, 1947, III; 1947 June 23, III
Tagliabue, Paul, 1989 Oct. 26, IV
Tailhook scandal, 1992 Sept. 24, I
Takeovers see Corporations
Talese, Gay, 1971(1), II
Talleyrand, Charles Maurice de, 1795–1799, I
Tallmadge, James, 1819 Feb. 13, I
Tall tales see Legends
Tammany societies:
citizens' investigation of corruption (N.Y.C.), 1871 Sept. 4, I
Daily News support, 1855(3), II
first Columbus Day celebration, 1792 Oct. 12, IV
first meeting, 1789 May 12, IV
inception and growth, 1790–1794, IV
influence on immigrants, 1850(8), IV
Sons of Liberty precursor, 1734 Oct., II
Tampons, 1980 Sept. 22, III
Tan, Amy, 1989(1), II; 1991(1), II; 1991(1), II
Tandy, Jessica, 1948 Mar. 28, II; 1978 June 4, II; 1983 June 5, II; 1990 Mar. 26, II
Tanenbaum, Marc H., 1992, II
Taney, Roger Brooke, 1833 Sept. 23, I; 1834 June 24, I
Tanselle, G. Thomas, 1988 June 15, II
Tappan, Arthur, 1827(2), III; 1833, I
Tarawa and Makin landings:
Gilbert Islands occupied by U.S., 1943 Nov. 20, I
Tarbell, Ida M., 1904(1), II
Tariff Act, 1842 Aug. 30, I
Hamilton's advocacy, 1790–1794, III
Tariff acts:
income tax clauses voided, 1895 May 20, III
Tariff of Abominations, 1828, I; 1828(2), IV; 1828 Dec. 19, I; 1832, I
Tariffs see Trade
Tarkington, Booth, 1899(1), II; 1901 Oct. 7, II; 1914(1), II; 1916(1), II; 1918(1), II; 1919 June 2, II; 1921(1), II; 1922 May. 21, II
Tarnower, Herman (Dr.), 1980 Mar. 10, IV
Tate, James, 1992 Apr. 7, II
Tate, John, 1979, IV; 1979 Oct. 21(2), IV; 1980 Mar. 31, IV

Tate, Sharon, 1969 Aug. 9, IV; 1971 Jan. 25, IV

Tatum, Edward L., 1958 Oct. 30, III

Tatum, Goose (Reese), 1967, IV

Taubman, Alfred, 1983 Sept. 19, II

Taunton (Mass.):
  founded, 1637, IV

Taussig, Helen, 1986, III

Taverns see Bars, saloons, and taverns

Taxation (see also Stamp Act):
  Bush pledge, 1990 Nov. 5, I
  Civil War income, 1861 Aug. 5, III
  corporate concessions, 1938 May 27, III
  cut, 1975, III
  excess profits, 1917 Mar. 3, III
  federal income, authorized, 1909 July 12, I
  federal income, constitutional, 1916 Jan. 24, III
  federal law (1862) constitutional, 1881 Jan. 24, I
  first federal law, 1791 Mar. 3, I
  first graduated income, 1894 Aug. 27, I
  first income rates, 1913, I
  income, 1864 June 30, III
  income, reduction plan, 1981 Aug. 4, I
  income clauses in Tariff Act, 1895 May 20, III
  income revision enacted, 1986 Oct. 22, I
  income surcharge, 1968 Jan. 17, I
  income surcharge bill, 1968 June 28, I
  income surcharge extended, 1969 Aug. 4, I
  income surtax, 1967 Oct. 3, I
  increase authorized, 1982 Aug. 19, I
  IRS files on dissenters revealed, 1974 Nov. 17, I
  Jefferson's view, 1805 Mar. 4, IV
  largest bill to date, 1941 Sept. 20, I
  most extensive reform bill to date, 1969 Dec. 22, I
  pay-as-you-go, 1943 June 10, III
  property, reduction (Calif.), 1978 June 6, I
  property financing public education upheld, 1973 Mar. 21, III
  raised, 1984 July 18, I
  record amount collected, 1953 Apr. 24, I
  reduced by 50%, 1954 Mar. 10(2), I
  Revenue Act reductions, 1926 Feb. 26, I
  single, promoted, 1890 Sept. 3, I

Taxicabs:
  first fleet of meter (N.Y.C.), 1907 May, III
  first use, 1915(1), III

Taylor, Bayard, 1864(7), II

Taylor, Deems, 1966, II

Taylor, Elizabeth, 1961 Apr. 17, II; 1962, IV; 1967 Apr. 10, II
  diamond from Burton, 1969 Oct. 24, IV
  romance with Burton, 1963 June 12, II

Taylor, Frederick W., 1910(5), III

Taylor, Glen H., 1948 July 23-25, I; 1984, I

Taylor, Henry, 1986 Apr. 17, II

Taylor, James, 1972 Mar. 14, II; 1978 Feb. 23, II

Taylor, Maxwell D., 1960(1), II; 1987, I

Taylor, Myron, 1937 Mar. 1, III

Taylor, Paul, 1975 Mar. 1(2), II

Taylor, Peter, 1985(1), II; 1987 Apr. 6, II; 1987 Apr. 16, II

Taylor, Raynor, 1792(3), II

Taylor, Richard E., 1990 Oct. 16(1), III

Taylor, Telford, 1980 Jan. 7, II

Taylor, Zachary:
  born, 1784 Nov. 24, I
  died, 1850 July 9, I
  elected president, 1848 Nov. 7, I
  inaugurated president, 1849 Mar. 5, I
  Mexican War, 1846 Jan., I; 1846 May 18, I; 1846 Sept. 25, I
  presidential nomination, 1847 Sept., I; 1848 June 7-9, I

Taylor University (Ind.), 1847 Jan. 18, III

Tchaikovsky, Peter Ilyich, 1981 June 4-14, II

Tcherepnin, Alexandre, 1952(3), II

Tea:
  colonial popularity, 1710-1714, IV
  colonial resentments, 1706, I
  high prices, 1977, III

Tea Act, 1773 Apr. 27, I; 1773 Dec. 16, I

Teach, Edward see Blackbeard

Teale, Edwin Way, 1966 May 2, II

Teamsters Union:
  Beck indicted, 1957 May 2, III
  Carey elected president, 1991 Feb. 1, III
  farm workers' accord, 1977 Mar. 10, III
  Gibbons denied racketeering charges, 1958 Sept. 2-3, III
  grape workers' contract (Calif.), 1973 Apr. 15, III
  Hoffa began prison term, 1967 Mar. 7, III
  Hoffa reelected president, 1961 July 7, III
  Hoffa reported missing, 1975 July 31(1), III
  Hoffa's conviction, 1964 Mar. 4, III; 1964 July 26, III
  Hoffa's ethics, 1957 Sept. 18, III
  joined with UAW, 1968 July 1, III
  racketeering, 1960 Feb. 26, III

Teapot Dome scandal, 1922 Apr. 15, I; 1923 Oct. 25, I; 1924 June 30, I; 1927 Oct. 10, I; 1929 Oct. 7(2), I; 1930 Mar. 13, I

Tear gas see Chemical and biological warfare

Technocracy, 1932 Dec., III

Tecumseh, 1809, IV; 1811 Nov. 7, I; 1813, I; 1813 Oct. 5, I

Teenagers see Juvenile delinquency; Youth; Youth culture

Teheran conference, 1943 Nov. 28-Dec. 1, I

Teichert, Edward A., 1948 May 2, I

Teichert, Emil F., 1936 Apr. 25-28, I

Telegraph:
  Atlantic cable completed, 1866 July 27, III
  early wireless, 1891 Dec. 29, III
  essential to railroads, 1856, III
  first company, 1847 Apr. 16, III
  first direct Brazil-U.S., 1883 Sept. 21, III
  first message, 1844 May 24, III
  first transatlantic message, 1857 Mar. 3, III; 1858 Aug. 16, III
  first transcontinental message, 1861, III
  first transpacific, 1903 July 4, III
  first U.S. subsidy of overseas cable, 1857 Mar. 3, III
  invented, 1835(2), III
  national system, 1856, III
  patent, 1837 Sept., III
  term telegram first used, 1852 Apr. 6, IV
  transatlantic cable charter granted, 1854 May 6, III
  Western Union monopoly, 1866 Apr. 1, III

Telephone:
  antitrust suit, 1949 Jan. 14, III
  AT&T divestiture, 1982 Jan. 8, III
  direct dial, 1951 Nov. 10, III
  first Boston-N.Y.C., 1884(3), III
  first commercial exchange, 1878 Jan. 28, III
  first conversation bounced off moon, 1960 Aug. 3, III
  first intercity system, 1879(2), III
  first mechanical switchboard, 1922 Oct. 14, III
  first N.Y.C.-Chicago service, 1883 Mar. 24, III
  first patent, 1876 Mar. 7, III
  first successful transatlantic radiotelephone conversation, 1926 Mar. 7, III
  first switchboard line interconnection, 1877(4), III
  first transatlantic cable system (Newfoundland-Scotland), 1956 Sept. 24, III
  first transcontinental call, 1915 Jan. 25(2), III
  installation of 100 millionth marked, 1967 May 11, III
  long-distance rates decreased, 1967 July 5, III
  N.Y.C. expansion, 1884(3), III
  number in use, 1900(5), III
  rate reduced (N.Y.C.), 1915 July 1, III
  telescribe to record invented, 1915 May 24, III
  transatlantic opened (N.Y.C.-London), 1927 Jan. 7, III
  underwater cable plans (Hawaii-Japan), 1962 Feb. 14, III

Telescope, 1825(3), III; 1843(4), III; 1948 June 3, III
  extraterrestrial signals search, 1992 Oct. 12(2), III
  Hubble launched in space, 1990 Apr. 25, III

Television (*see also* Emmy Awards):
   American Family, An documentary, 1973, II
   audience measurement, 1987 Sept. 14, II
   Burke's Law suit, 1976 Apr. 2, II
   cable regulation bill veto overridden, 1992 Oct. 5, I
   cable subscribers, 1983, II; 1987, II; 1988, II; 1989, II; 1989 Apr. 18, II
   cable video pirate, 1986 Apr. 27, II
   CBS awarded NCAA broadcasting rights, 1989 Nov. 21, IV
   CBS Evening News anchor Cronkite retirement, 1980 Feb. 15(2), II
   cigarette ads banned, 1970 Apr. 1, III
   Civil War, PBS series, 1990, II
   college football ruling, 1984 June 27, IV
   color licenses, 1950 Oct. 11, II
   color sets, 1951 June 25, III
   color sets and shows, 1966, II
   condom ads, 1987, IV
   Corp. for Public Broadcasting created, 1967 Nov. 7, II
   Cosby Show final episode, 1992 Apr. 30, II
   Day After, The largest audience, 1983 Nov. 20, II
   equal political air time overruled, 1973 May 26, II
   equal political time ruling, 1959 June 15, II; 1964 Oct. 1, II
   equal political time ruling lifted, 1959 Sept. 14(1), II; 1975 Sept. 25, II
   evangelist scandals, 1987 Mar. 19, III; 1988 Apr. 8, III
   family viewing time, 1975 Apr. 8(2), II
   first demonstrated, 1927 Apr. 7, III
   first global broadcast, 1967 June 25, II
   first live ballet, *Swan Lake*, 1976 June 30, II
   first municipally owned station (WNYC-TV), 1962(2), II
   first news anchorwoman, 1976 Apr. 22, II
   first presidential press conference, 1955 Jan. 19, I
   first public Cabinet meeting shown, 1954 Oct. 25, I
   first scheduled program, 1928 May 11, II
   first transcontinental broadcast, 1951 Sept. 4, III
   first videotaped broadcasts, 1957 Jan. 21, III
   football coverage ban lifted, 1973, IV
   football favorite viewer sport, 1992, IV
   homosexuality issue, 1973 Oct. 26, II
   Kennedy White House tour, 1962 Feb. 14, II
   largest audience to date, 1980 Nov. 21, II
   *M*A*S*H* final episode, 1983 Mar. 2, II
   music promotion, 1948, II
   NBC granted Olympics coverage (Moscow), 1977 Feb. 1, IV

Television (*cont.*)
   NBC season's ratings winner, 1988 Sept. 17(2), II
   network viewership down, 1989 Apr. 18, II
   new shows, 1992, II
   nine-inch screen, 1933, III
   Nixon interview on Watergate, 1977 May 4, II
   nostalgia, 1973, II
   opera *Amahl and the Night Visitors* (Menotti), 1951 Dec. 24, II
   organized crime hearings, 1951, III
   Paar walked off show, 1960 Feb. 11, II
   popular series, 1990, II
   popular shows, 1976, II
   presidential debates, 1960 Sept. 26, I; 1976 Sept. 27, I
   quiz show scandal, 1960 Oct. 17, II
   revenue losses, 1988, II
   Roots hit show, 1977, II
   season overview, 1991, II
   Senate proceedings coverage, 1986 June 1(1), II
   sets, 1954(3), II; 1958, II
   sex and violence themes, 1975 Apr. 8(2), II
   Smothers Brothers show canceled, 1969 Apr. 4, II
   Soviet commercials, 1988, III
   sports bidding war, 1988 Dec. 1, IV
   Star Trek exhibit, 1992 Feb. 28, II
   Stravinsky ballet written for, 1962 June 14, II
   thirteen channels allocated, 1945 June 27, II
   Time Warner merger, 1989 July 24, III
   "vast wasteland" designation, 1961 May 9, II
   videocassette recorders (VCRs), 1981, II; 1983, II; 1985, II; 1988, II; 1989, II
   violence report, 1972 Jan. 17, II
   Walters highest paid journalist to date, 1976 Apr. 22, II
   Waltons popularity, 1973, II
   "Who Shot J. R.?" *Dallas* episode, 1980 Nov. 21, II
   writers' strike, 1988 Aug. 7(2), II
Television Academy Hall of Fame, 1984 Mar. 4, II
Teller, Edward, 1957 Nov. 25, I; 1958 Apr. 16, I
Teller, Henry M., 1896 July 22–24, I
Tellico Dam (Tenn.), 1978 June 15, III
Telstar (communications satellite), 1962, III; 1962 July 10, III; 1963 May 7, III
Temin, Howard M., 1975 Oct. 16, III
Temperance movement *see* Prohibition and temperance movement
Temple, Shirley, 1934, II
Templeman, John, 1810(1), III
Temple of Honor, 1845(1), IV
Tennent, William, 1730–1734, III
Tennessee:
   seceded, 1861 June 8, I
   statehood, 1796 June 1, I
Tennessee, University of, 1794 Sept. 10, III

Tennessee Valley Authority (TVA), 1933 May 18, I
Tennis:
   Ashe revealed AIDS infection, 1992 Apr. 8, IV
   banned in New Amsterdam, 1659 Sept. 30, IV
   "Battle of the Sexes" (King-Riggs), 1973 Sept. 20, IV
   Connors first third consecutive winner of Natl. Indoor title, 1975 Feb. 16, IV
   Davis Cup, 1902 Aug. 8, IV; 1903 Aug. 8, IV; 1913 July 25–28, IV; 1914 Aug. 15, IV; 1920 July 9–16, IV; 1921 Sept. 3, IV; 1922 Aug. 31–Sept. 5, IV; 1923 Aug. 30–Sept. 1, IV; 1924 Sept. 11–13, IV; 1925 Sept. 12, IV; 1926 Sept. 11, IV; 1927 Sept. 10, IV; 1937 July 27, IV; 1938 Sept. 5, IV; 1946 Dec. 26, IV; 1947 Dec. 30, IV; 1948 Sept. 6, IV; 1949 Aug. 28, IV; 1950 Aug. 26, IV; 1954 Dec. 28, IV; 1958, IV; 1958 Dec. 31, IV; 1959 Aug. 28–31, IV; 1963 Dec. 26–29, IV; 1968 Dec. 26–28, IV; 1969 Sept. 19–21, IV; 1970 Aug. 29–31, IV; 1971 Oct. 8–11, IV; 1972 Oct. 13–15, IV; 1973 Nov. 30–Dec. 2, IV; 1978 Dec. 8–10, IV; 1981 Dec. 11–13, IV; 1982 Nov. 26–28, IV
   Davis Cup founded, 1900, IV
   Davis Cup suspended, 1940, IV
   first men's singles championship, 1881(2), IV
   first U.S. Open, 1968 Sept. 9, IV
   first U.S. Wimbledon winner, 1905(5), IV
   first women's singles championship, 1887(4), IV
   grand slam, 1969 Sept. 7–8, IV
   King's winnings, 1971, IV
   lawn tennis introduced, 1874, IV
   Navratilova top title winner, 1992 Feb. 17, IV
   Parkers's fame, 1932, IV
   Richards barred from U.S. Open, 1976 Aug. 27, IV
   tournaments open to pros, 1968, IV
   U.S. Lawn Tennis Assn., 1881(2), IV
   USLTA singles championships, 1881(2), IV; 1882(6), IV; 1883(3), IV; 1884(8), IV; 1885(2), IV; 1886(3), IV; 1887(4), IV; 1888(4), IV; 1889(6), IV; 1890(6), IV; 1891(4), IV; 1892(5), IV; 1893(5), IV; 1894(4), IV; 1895(3), IV; 1896(2), IV; 1897(3), IV; 1898(3), IV; 1899(3), IV; 1900(4), IV; 1901(2), IV; 1902(2), IV; 1903(2), IV; 1904(3), IV; 1905(4), IV; 1906(2), IV; 1907(3), IV; 1908(3), IV; 1909 June 27, IV; 1910 June 26, IV; 1911 June 17, IV; 1912 June 15, IV; 1913 June 14, IV; 1914 June 13, IV; 1915 June 12, IV; 1916 June 12, IV; 1917 June 23(2), IV; 1918 June 22, IV; 1919 June 21, IV; 1920 Sept. 6, IV; 1921 Aug. 20, IV; 1922 Aug. 19, IV; 1923 Aug. 18, IV; 1924 Aug. 16, IV; 1925 Aug. 24, IV;

Tennis (*cont.*)
1926 Aug. 23, IV; 1927 Aug. 30, IV; 1928 Aug. 27, IV; 1929 Aug. 24, IV; 1930 Aug. 23, IV; 1931 Aug. 20, IV; 1932 Aug. 21, IV; 1933 Aug. 26, IV; 1934 Aug. 19, IV; 1935 Sept. 11, IV; 1936 Sept. 12(2), IV; 1937 Sept. 11(2), IV; 1938 Sept. 17, IV; 1939 Sept. 17, IV; 1940 Sept. 9, IV; 1941 Sept. 7, IV; 1942 Sept. 6–7, IV; 1943 Sept. 5, IV; 1944 Sept. 3, IV; 1945 Sept. 2, IV; 1946 Sept. 8, IV; 1947 Sept. 14, IV; 1948 Sept. 19, IV; 1949 Sept. 5, IV; 1950 Sept. 5, IV; 1951 Sept. 4, IV; 1952 Sept. 7, IV; 1953 Sept. 7, IV; 1954 Sept. 6, IV; 1955 Sept. 11, IV; 1956 Sept. 9, IV; 1957 Sept. 8, IV; 1958 Sept. 7, IV; 1959 Sept. 13, IV; 1960 Sept. 17, IV; 1961 Sept. 10, IV; 1962 Sept. 10, IV; 1963 Sept. 8, IV; 1964 Sept. 13, IV; 1965 Sept. 12, IV; 1966 Sept. 11, IV; 1967 Sept. 10, IV; 1968 Sept. 9, IV; 1969 Sept. 7–8, IV
U.S. Open, 1970 Sept 2–13, IV; 1971 Sept. 5–15, IV; 1972 Sept. 9–10, IV; 1973 Aug. 29–Sept. 9, IV; 1974 Sept. 9, IV; 1975 Sept. 6–7, IV; 1976 Sept. 11–12, IV; 1977 Sept. 10–11, IV; 1978 Sept. 10, IV; 1979 Sept. 9, IV; 1980 Sept. 6–7, IV; 1981 Sept. 9–13, IV; 1982 Sept. 11–12, IV; 1983 Sept. 11, IV; 1984 Sept. 8–9, IV; 1985 Sept. 7–8, IV; 1986 Sept. 7, IV; 1987 Sept. 12, IV; 1988 Sept. 10–11, IV; 1989 Sept. 9–10, IV; 1990 Sept. 8–9, IV; 1991 Sept. 7–8, IV; 1992 Sept. 12–13, IV
WCT severed ties with USLTA, 1974 Jan. 24, IV
Wimbledon, 1905(5), IV; 1907(2), IV; 1920 July 3, IV; 1921 June 29, IV; 1927 July 2, IV; 1928 July 7, IV; 1929 July 5, IV; 1930 July 4, IV; 1931 July 3–4, IV; 1932 July 1, IV; 1933 July 8, IV; 1935 July 6, IV; 1936 July 4, IV; 1937 July 2, IV; 1938 July 1, IV; 1939 July 7–8, IV; 1946 July 6, IV; 1947 July 4–5, IV; 1948 July 2, IV; 1949 July 1–2, IV; 1950 July 7, IV; 1951 July 6–7, IV; 1952 July 5, IV; 1953 July 3, IV; 1954 July 3(2), IV; 1955 July 1–2, IV; 1956 July 7, IV; 1957 July 6, IV; 1958 July 5, IV; 1961 July 8, IV; 1962 July 7, IV; 1963 July 6, IV; 1966 July 2, IV; 1967 July 8, IV; 1968 July 6, IV; 1970 July 4, IV; 1971 July 3, IV; 1972 July 7(2), IV; 1973 July 7–8, IV; 1974 July 5, IV; 1975 July 4–5, IV; 1976 July 2–3, IV; 1977 July 2, IV; 1981 July 3–4, IV; 1982 July 3–4, IV; 1983 July 2–3, IV; 1984 July 7–8, IV; 1985 July 6–7, IV; 1986 July 5–6, IV; 1987 July 4, IV; 1990 July 7, IV; 1992 July 5, IV
Wimbledon boycotted, 1973 July 7–8, IV
Wimbledon suspended, 1940, IV

Tennis (*cont.*)
women's singles title record, 1990 July 7, IV
World Championship Tennis (WCT) tournament scheduling conflict, 1972, IV
youngest International Hall of Fame inductee, 1992 July 11, IV
youngest women's singles winner, 1979 Sept. 9, IV
Tennyson, Alfred Lord:
Poems published in U.S., 1842(3), II
Tenure of Office Act, 1867 Mar. 2(2), I; 1868, I
Terkel, Studs, 1970(1), II; 1985 Apr. 24, II
Terra cotta, 1853(1), III
Terrell, Ernie, 1965 May 25, IV; 1965 Nov. 22, IV
Terrorism (*see also* Bombs and bombing; Hijacking; Massacres):
Brinks robbery (Nanuet, N.Y.), 1981 Oct. 20, IV
Hanafi Muslim raid (Wash., D.C.), 1977 Mar. 9–11, IV
jetliner bombing (Lockerbie, Scotland), 1991 Nov. 27, I
Lebanese, 1985 Sept. 18, I
Lebanon, arms-for-hostages deal, 1986 Nov. 3, I
Lebanon, hostages, 1986 Nov. 2, I; 1987 Jan. 24, I; 1988 Feb. 17, I; 1988 Oct. 3, I; 1991 Aug. 8–Dec. 4, I
Mexican-Americans (Tierra Amarilla, N. Mex.), 1967 June 5, I
Olympic Games (W. Ger.), 1972 Aug. 26–Sept. 11, IV
Pan Am flight explosion, 1988 Dec. 21, I
PLO reported renouncing, 1988 Dec. 14, I
Rome and Vienna airports, 1986 Jan. 7, I
Statue of Liberty dynamite plot, 1965 Feb. 16, I
TWA jet bombing (Rome-Athens), 1986 Apr. 2, I
U.S. ambassador to Guatemala killed, 1968 Aug. 28, I
U.S. citizens victims abroad, 1985, I
U.S. economic sanctions to protest Libyan, 1982 Mar. 10, I
U.S. retaliation for Libyan, 1986 Apr. 14, I
W. Berlin discothèque bombing, 1986 Apr. 5, I
Terry, Aline, 1893(5), IV
Terry, Luther, 1964 Jan. 11, III
Tesla, Nikola, 1888, III; 1892(10), III
Test bans *see* Arms Control and disarmament
Tetley, Glen, 1972 Mar. 30, II
Teton River Dam (Ida.), 1976 June 5, I
Tetrazzini, Luisa, 1908(3), II
Texaco, Inc., 1984 Jan. 8, III; 1985 Dec. 10, III; 1987 Dec. 19, III
Texas (*see also* Mexican War):
Alamo, 1836(2), IV
Alamo captured, 1836 Mar. 6, I

Texas (*cont.*)
American settlements, 1823, I; 1825 Mar. 24, I
annexation and U.S. protection assurance, 1845 June 15, I
annexation opponents, 1844 Apr. 27, I
annexation request withdrawn, 1838 Oct. 12, I
Annexation Treaty voted down by Senate, 1844 June 8, I
Annexation Treaty with U.S., 1844 Apr. 12, I
annexed by congressional joint resolution, 1845, I
capital punishment laws, 1976 July 2, I
Clay's Alabama letters on annexation, 1844 July 1–27, I
Emancipation Day, 1865 June 19, IV
first American settlement, 1821 Dec., I
first European settlement, 1682(3), I
floods, 1913 Oct., I
Franciscans' history of, 1745–1763, III
French expedition, 1685 Jan., I
Galveston hurricane, 1900 Sept. 8, I
holidays, 1836 Mar. 2, IV; 1836 Apr. 21, IV
hurricane, 1970 Aug. 3–5, I
independence, 1836 Mar. 2, I; 1836 Mar. 2, IV; 1836 Apr. 21, I; 1836 Oct. 22, I
Jackson's offer to purchase, 1829 Aug. 25, I
mass murder (Killeen), 1991 Oct. 16, IV
Mexico banned further U.S. colonization, 1830 Apr. 6, I
Rangers (mounted police) authorized, 1835 Nov. 24, I
readmitted to Union, 1869 Apr. 10, I; 1870 Mar. 30(1), I
republic recognized, 1837 Mar. 3(2), I
seceded, 1861 Feb. 23, I
Spindletop oil strike, 1901 Jan. 10, III
statehood, 1845 Dec. 29, I
Superconducting Super Collider (SSC), 1988 Nov. 10, III
tornadoes, 1953 May 11, I; 1971 Feb. 21, I; 1979 Apr. 10, I
Texas, University of:
classes began, 1883 Sept. 15, III
Johnson, L. B., Library dedicated, 1971 May 22, II
tower massacre, 1966 Aug. 1, I
Texas and New Mexico Act, 1850 Sept. 9(2), I
Texas Gulf Sulphur Co., 1964 Apr. 16, III
Textbooks *see* under Education and schools
Textile industry (*see also* Clothing and fashion; types of material):
first factory (Mass.), 1640–1649, III
first gingham factory (Mass.), 1846(2), III
first joint stock manufacturing company, 1775 Feb. 22, III
Lawrence (Mass.) strike, 1912, III
N.E. dominance, 1850, III

Textile industry (*cont.*)
power knitting machine, 1831 Apr.,
III
silk workers strike (N.J.), 1913 Feb. 25,
III
spinning and carding invention, 1764,
III
strike (Fall River, Mass.), 1904 July 25,
III
weaver apprentices (Va.), 1777(2), III
woolen mills, 1802(1), III
Théâtre d'Orleans (La.), 1808(2), II
Thailand:
last Marines withdrawn, 1962 July 27,
I
sought complete U.S. withdrawal,
1975, I
U.S. forces withdrawn, 1976 July 20, I
U.S. Marines sent, 1962 May 12, I
Thalidomide, 1962 Aug. 17, III
Thames, Battle of, 1813 Oct. 5, I
"Thanatopsis" (Bryant) acclaimed, 1817
Sept., II
Thanksgiving:
day changed, 1863 Oct. 3, IV
earliest celebration (Mass.), 1621 Dec.,
IV
first celebrated as national holiday,
1789 Nov. 26, IV
first in New Amsterdam, 1644, IV
first public celebration (Mass.), 1631
Feb. 22, IV
moved to last Thursday, 1941 May 20,
IV
proclaimed national holiday, 1863
Oct. 3, IV
Thant, U, 1967 Mar. 28, I
Tharp, Twyla, 1976 Jan. 9, II
Thaw, Harry K., 1906, IV
Thayer, Eli, 1854 Apr. 26, I
Thayer, Ernest L., 1988 Aug. 15, IV
Theater (*see also* Burlesque; Censorship;
Copyright laws; Lincoln Center for the
Performing Arts; Minstrel shows; New
York Drama Critics Circle Awards;
Theaters; Theatrical productions;):
Acadia, 1606 Nov. 14, II
actor's payment, 1800(4), IV
actors' strike, 1919 Aug. 7, II
actors' strike off-Broadway, 1970 Nov.
16, II
Actor's Workshop of San Francisco
disbanded, 1966 Aug. 6, II
American Musical Theater Center
(N.C.), 1977 Sept. 21, II
antipornography rally, 1977 Apr.
13(2), II
asbestos curtains, 1885(3), II
Astor Place riot, 1849 May 10, II
Baker's Harvard Univ. 47 Workshop,
1905, II
Bannister's plays, 1847, II
Barker's plays, 1836(10), II
Barrymore, John, 1919 Apr. 9, II;
1942, II
Barrymore, Lionel, 1919 Apr. 9, II;
1923 Nov. 28, II
Belasco's career as playwright,
1865(10), II

Theater (*cont.*)
benefit performance (N.Y.C.), 1809
May 31, IV
Berlin's musicals, 1914 Dec. 8, II
Bernhardt's debut, 1880 Nov. 8, II
Bernhardt's last tour, 1917(2), II
black experience themes, 1976, II
black playwrights, 1969, II
blacks, portrayal of, 1823, II
Booth in *Hamlet*, 1891, II
Booth's career, 1891, II
Booth's N.Y.C. debut, 1850 Sept. 27,
II
Boston (Mass.) ban, 1792 Dec. 5, II
Boston (Mass.) reopened, 1794(1), II
Boucicault's plays, 1857 Dec. 8, II;
1860 Mar. 29, II
box office record, 1992, II
British imports, 1974, II
British-American actors' competition,
1826, II
Broadway musicians' strike, 1975
Sept. 18, II
Broadway revenues down, 1973, II
Broadway revenues up, 1975, II; 1990,
II
Broadway slump, 1985, II
Carolina Playmakers, 1918(5), II
"Casey at the Bat" recitation, 1888
May, II
Civil War events dramatized, 1861
Aug. 15, II
Civil War-inspired plays, 1886, II;
1889 Sept. 9, II
Cohan's first appearance, 1891(4), II
Cohan's plays, 1906(4), II
colonial opposition, 1665 Aug. 27, II;
1749 Aug. 22, II
colonial quality, 1762 May 3, IV
comedian Davidge debut, 1850 Aug.
19, II
comedienne Ada Rehan, 1874, II
comedies and musicals, 1970, II
Cooke's popularity and decline,
1810(6), II
current N.Y.C. plays, 1887, II
Daly French adaptations, 1864(4), II
double-feature performances, 1819
Feb. 5, IV
Dramatic Arts Academy 100th
anniversary, 1984, II
dramatic treatment of modern
women, 1912 Feb. 5, II
Dramatists' Guild organized, 1926(2),
II
early farce, 1792 Apr. 24, II
Experimental Theater (N.Y.C.),
1941(2), II
Federal Theater Project, 1936, II;
1936(2), II; 1936 Oct. 27, II
first American-born black depicted,
1795 May 22, II
first American comedy, 1787 Apr. 16,
II
first American Congress (N.J.), on,
1974 June 4–6, II
first comedy performed in public,
1790(2), II
first English-speaking company
touring Europe, 1886 Aug. 19, II

Theater (*cont.*)
first extended engagement (N.Y.C.),
1786(1), II
first melodrama, 1803 Feb. 4, II
first performance in Va., 1665 Aug.
27, II
first permanent (Phila., Pa.), 1766
Oct., II
first play composed and written in
U.S., 1714, II
first professional actors (S.C.), 1703, II
first professionally performed
American play, 1767 Apr. 24, II
first summer (N.Y.C.), 1800 July 9, II
first U.S. performance of *Hamlet*,
1786(1), II
Fitch's plays, 1902, II
Ford Foundation grant, 1961 Mar. 19,
II
foreign companies, 1967, II
foreign plays adapted, 1836(11), II
Forrest's debut, 1820 Nov. 27, II
frontier drama, 1870 Feb. 14, II
frontiersman as comedic type, 1831
Apr. 25, IV
Gilbert and Sullivan first performed in
N.Y., 1879 June 16, II
Gillette's plays, 1881 June 1, II; 1886,
II
Gillette's *Sherlock Holmes*, 1886, II;
1899(3), II
Hallam troupe, 1750–1754, II
Hampden's Shakespearean roles,
1918, II
Hayes received Drama Desk Award,
1968 May 21, II
Indian extras, 1832(2), II
J. Jefferson's first appearance, 1796(1),
II
Kemble's popularity, 1832, II
Kotzebue adaptations, 1798 Dec. 10,
II
lackluster season, 1952, II
Langtry's popularity, 1882, II
laws prohibiting repealed (Pa.), 1789
Mar. 2, II
league investigation of ills, 1949, II
Lincoln Center Repertory, 1964, II
Living Theater, 1936(2), II; 1938(2), II
longest consecutive-running play to
date, 1891 Nov. 9, II
longest-running musical closed, 1970
Dec. 27, II
longest-running musical to date, 1962
Sept. 29, II; 1971 July 21, II
longest run to date, 1959 Oct. 18, II;
1972 June 17, II; 1983 Sept. 27, II
long-running play *Abaellino, The
Great Bandit*, 1801 Feb. 11, II
long-running plays, 1918 Aug. 26, II;
1933 Dec. 4, II
MacKaye's masques, 1913 Sept. 12, II
melodrama, 1829 Mar. 26, II
melodrama *East Lynne*'s popularity,
1861, II
melodrama *Hazel Kirke* (MacKaye),
1880(6), II
Menken's feats, 1863(1), IV
Methodist ban lifted (New England),
1908 Apr. 13, IV

Theater (*cont.*)
H. Modjeska debut, 1877, II
Mulligan Guard plays, 1879 Jan. 13, II
Murdoch's debut, 1836(9), II
Murray-Kean Company of Comedians, 1750 Mar. 5, II
musical revivals, 1976, II
musicals' rising costs, 1982, II
National Theater of Washington (D.C.) disbanded, 1974 June 12, II
Nazimova in Ibsen revivals, 1918(4), II
Nazimova N.Y. debut, 1906(3), II
Negro Ensemble Co., 1968, II
Neighborhood Playhouse (N.Y.C.) founded, 1915 Feb.(1), II
new American plays, 1854(6), II
New Play Project (N.Y.C.), 1941(2), II
New Theatre (Phila., Pa.) opened, 1794 Feb. 17, II
N.Y.C. problems, 1827(3), IV
N.Y.C. riot against British actor, 1831 Oct. 13, II
N.Y.C. world center, 1920(2), II
Odets' works, 1935, II; 1935 Feb. 19, II
off-Broadway, 1969, II
pantomime *Planche*, 1856(5), II
Papp's productions, 1973, II
Payne's comedies, 1818, II; 1824 May 27, II
Pa. law forbidding, 1759 May 31, II
Peters the Antipodean, 1829 Sept. 14, II
plays about Indians, 1766(2), II; 1830(4), II
plays about Pocahontas, 1808, II
poetic drama, 1950, II
pre-Broadway tours, 1973, II
prosperous, 1979, II
Provincetown Players organized (Mass.), 1915 Summer, II
Puritan influence, 1761 June 10, IV
record-running plays, 1922 May 23, II
regional drama, 1918(5), II
revivals, 1946, II; 1947, II; 1963, II; 1972, II; 1980, II
Revolutionary War theme, 1844(1), II
rich-poor contrast theme, 1850 July 22, II
Rip Van Winkle dramatizations, 1828(5), II
road companies started (Ky.), 1810(5), II
Robertson's debut, 1854(6), II
sexually explicit plays, 1969, II
Shakespeare death tercentenary, 1916(6), II
Shakespeare's 400th anniversary celebrated, 1964 Apr. 23, II; 1964 Apr. 24, II
Shaw's popularity, 1906(5), II
Sheldon's plays, 1908 Nov. 17, II
Skinner debut, 1877, II
southern mountaineers as dramatic types introduced, 1846 Feb. 9, II
Stoppard double bill off-Broadway, 1972 Apr. 23(1), II
suspended during Revolution, 1774 Oct. 20, II
"Texas" Guinan, 1909(3), II

Theater (*cont.*)
Thomas's plays, 1894 July 26, II
Tory dramas, 1774(1), II
tribute to H. Hayes, 1989 Oct. 10, II
Washington's patronage (N.Y.C.), 1789(2), IV
Washington Square Players (N.Y.C.) founded, 1915 Feb.(2), II
women actors (N.Y.C.), 1779 Jan. 9, II
World War I plays, 1918(3), II
World War II propaganda plays, 1941, II
Yankee as stock character, 1825(1), II; 1832 June 17, II
Ziegfeld's shows, 1907, II
Theaters:
Bowery Theater opened (N.Y.C.), 1826 Oct.23, II
Brougham's Lyceum (N.Y.C.) opened, 1850 Dec. 3, II
closed to conserve coal, 1918 Feb. 12, II
closures in wake of Civil War, 1861(1), II
commemoration of first in U.S., 1852 Sept. 6, II
early air conditioning, 1848 June 27, III
eight operating in N.Y.C., 1837(7), II
fire (Chicago, Ill.), 1903 Dec. 30, I
fire hazards, 1878(2), II
first building (Williamsburg, Va.), 1716, II
first house exclusively for blacks, 1910(3), II
first incandescent lighting (Boston, Mass.), 1882 Dec. 11, III
Hippodrome Theater (N.Y.C.) opened, 1853, IV
Morosco Theatre (N.Y.C.) opened, 1917 Feb. 15, II
N.Y.C. closure for Lincoln's death, 1865 Apr. 15, II
Olympic Theater (N.Y.C.) reopened, 1839(3), IV
Park Theater's elegant decor, 1834(1), IV
Park Theatre (N.Y.C.) closed by bankruptcy, 1805 Feb. 22, II
reopened in Phila., Pa., 1784 Apr. 1, II
second building opened (N.Y.C.), 1732(2), II
strike closed Broadway theaters (N.Y.C.), 1960 June 2–13, III
third in colonies (Charleston, S.C.), 1735 Feb. 12, II
Wharf Theater (Conn.) 20th anniversary, 1984, II
worst fire to date (Brooklyn, N.Y.), 1876 Dec. 5, I
Theatrical productions, 1987, II; 1988, II; 1989, II; 1990, II; 1991, II; 1992, II
Abe Lincoln in Illinois (Sherwood) opened, 1938 Oct. 3, II
Abie's Irish Rose (Nichols), 1922 May 23, II
Abraham Lincoln, 1919 Dec. 15, II
Absurd Person Singular (Ayckbourn), 1974 Oct. 8, II

Theatrical productions (*cont.*)
Act, The musical, 1977 Oct. 29, II
Adaptation (May), 1969 Feb. 10, II
Adding Machine, The (Rice) expressionism, 1923 Mar. 19, II
After the Fall (Miller), 1964 Jan. 23, II
A Funny Thing Happened . . . musical, 1962 May 8, II; 1972, II
Ah, Wilderness! (O'Neill), 1933, II; 1933 Oct. 2, II
Ain't Misbehavin' musical, 1978, II; 1978 May 9, II
All God's Chillun Got Wings (O'Neill), 1924 May 15, II
All Over Town (Schisgal), 1974 Dec. 29, II
All the Way Home (Mosel), 1960 Nov. 30, II; 1961 Nov. 30, II
Amadeus (Shaffer), 1980 Dec. 17, II
American Buffalo (Mamet), 1977 Feb. 16, II
American Way (Kaufman and Hart) opened, 1939 Jan. 21, II
Anna Christie (O'Neill), 1921 Nov. 2, II
Annie musical, 1977 Apr. 21, II
Another Language (Franken), 1932 Apr. 25, II
Another Part of the Forest (Hellman), 1946 Nov. 20, II
Anything Goes musical, 1934 Nov. 21, II
Applause musical, 1970 Mar. 30, II
As Thousands Cheer (Berlin and Hart), 1933 Sept. 9, II
Auntie Mame (Lawrence and Lee), 1956 Oct. 31, II
Awake and Sing (Odets), 1935 Feb. 19, II
Babes in Toyland (Herbert), 1903 June 17, II
Bad Seed, The (Anderson), 1954 Dec. 8, II
Basic Training of Pavlo Hummel, The (Rabe), 1977 Apr. 24, II
Beau Brummell (Fitch), 1890 May 19, II
Belle of Amherst, The (Luce), 1976 Apr. 28, II
Best Man, The (Vidal), 1960 Mar. 31, II
Beyond the Fringe revue, 1962 Oct. 27, II
Big River musical, 1985 Apr. 25, II
Bill of Divorcement, A (Dane), 1921 Oct. 10, II
Billy Budd (Coxe and Chapman) opened, 1951 Feb. 10, II
Bloomer Girl musical comedy opened, 1944 Oct. 5, II
Bought and Paid For (Broadhurst) opened, 1911 Sept. 26, II
Boy Friend, The musical (Wilson), 1954 Sept. 30, II
Boys in the Band, The (Crowley), 1968 Apr. 16, II
Brigadoon musical, 1947 Mar. 13(1), II
Brighton Beach Memoirs (Simon), 1983 Mar. 27, II

Theatrical productions (*cont.*)

Bubblin' Brown Sugar musical, 1976 Mar. 2, II

Bunker Hill (Burk), 1797 Feb. 17, II

Bury the Dead (Shaw) opened, 1936 Mar. 14, II

Bus Stop (Inge), 1955 Mar. 2, II

Bye Bye Birdie musical, 1960 Apr. 14, II

Cabaret musical, 1966, II; 1966 Nov. 20, II

Cage aux Folles, La musical, 1983 Aug. 21, II; 1984, II

Caine Mutiny Court Martial, The (Wouk), 1954 Jan. 20, II

Camino Real (Williams), 1953 Mar. 19(2), II

Candide (Bernstein), 1974 Mar. 11, II

Caretaker, The (Pinter), 1961 Oct. 4, II

Carnival musical, 1961 Apr. 13, II

Carousel musical, 1945 Apr. 19, II

Cats musical, 1982 Oct. 7, II; 1984, II

Cave Dwellers, The (Saroyan), 1957 Oct. 19, II

Ceremonies in Dark Old Men (Elder), 1969 Feb. 5, II

Changing Room, The (Storey), 1972 Nov. 17, II; 1973 Mar. 6, II

Charity Ball, The (Belasco and De Mille), 1889(3), II

Chicago musical, 1975 June 3, II

Child's Play (Marasco), 1970 Feb. 17, II

Chorus Line, A longest-running musical, 1989 Jan. 8, II

Chorus Line, A musical, 1975 May 21, II; 1983 Sept. 27, II

Chorus Line, A, musical and longest-running show to date, closed, 1990 Apr. 28, II

Circle, The (Maugham), 1921 Sept. 12, II

Claudia (Franken), 1941 Feb. 12, II

Coconuts musical, 1925 Dec. 8, II

Company musical, 1970 Apr. 26, II

Conduct Unbecoming (England), 1970 Oct. 12, II

Confidential Clerk, The (Eliot), 1954 Feb. 11, II

Confidential Service (Cohan), 1932 Mar. 28, II

Connecticut Yankee, A musical, 1927 Nov. 3, II

Country Girl, The (Odets), 1950 Nov. 10(2), II

Da (Leonard), 1978 May 1(1), II

Damn Yankees musical, 1955 May 5, II

Danton's Death (Büchner), 1965 Oct. 21(2), II

Dark at the Top of the Stairs, The (Inge), 1957 Dec. 5, II

Darkness at Noon (Kingsley), 1951 Jan. 13, II

Days Without End (O'Neill), 1934 Jan. 8, II

Death of a Salesman (Miller), 1949 Feb. 10, II

Delusion of the Fury musical, 1969 Jan. 9, II

Theatrical productions (*cont.*)

Deputy, The (Hochhuth), 1964 Feb. 26, II

Desert Song, The operetta, 1926 Nov. 30, II

Desire Under the Elms (O'Neill), 1924 Nov. 11, II

Devil's Advocate (Schary), 1961 Mar. 9, II

Dodsworth (Howard), 1934 Feb. 24, II

Doll's House, A (Ibsen), 1975 Mar. 5, II

Dreamgirls musical, 1981 Dec. 20, II

Drunkard, The (Smith), 1959 Oct. 18, II

Du Barry Was a Lady musical, 1939 Dec. 6, II; 1940, II

Dulcy (Kaufman-Connelly), 1921 Aug. 13, II

Dylan (Michaels), 1964 Jan. 18(1), II

Easter (Strindberg) produced, 1916(8), II

Elephant Man, The (Pomerance), 1979 Apr. 19, II

Emperor Jones (O'Neill), 1920 Nov. 1, II

Equus (Shaffer), 1974 Oct. 24, II

Evening with Mike Nichols and Elaine May, An revue, 1960 Oct. 8, II

Eve of St. Mark, The (Anderson), 1942 Oct. 7, II

Evita musical, 1979 Sept. 25, II

Faith Healer, The (Moody) opened (St. Louis, Mo.), 1909 Mar. 15, II

Fanny musical (Behrman and Logan), 1954 Nov. 4, II

Fantasticks longest-running musical to date, 1966 Nov. 5, II

Fantasticks musical, 1960 May 3, II

Fashion (Mowatt) social satire, 1845 Mar. 24, II

Fatal Weakness, The (Kelly), 1946 Nov. 19, II

Female Patriotism, or the Death of Joan d'Arc (Burk), 1798 Apr., II

Fiddler on the Roof longest-running Broadway show to date, 1972 June 17, II

Fiddler on the Roof musical, 1964 Sept. 22, II; 1971 July 21, II

Fifth Column (Hemingway), 1938(1), II

Fifty Million Frenchmen musical, 1929 Nov. 27, II

Finian's Rainbow musical, 1947 Jan. 10, II

Fiorello! musical, 1959 Nov. 23, II

Floradora musical, 1902(2), II

Flower Drum Song musical, 1958 Dec. 1, II

Flowering Peach, The (Odets), 1970 Nov. 10, II

Follies musical, 1971 Apr. 4, II

For Colored Girls Who Have Considered Suicide... (Shange), 1976 June 1, II

Fortune Hunter, The (Smith), 1909 Sept. 4, II

42nd Street musical, 1980 Aug. 25, II

Theatrical productions (*cont.*)

42nd Street second longest-running musical, 1989 Jan. 8, II

Front Page, The (Hecht and MacArthur), 1928 Aug. 14, II

Gang's All Here, The (Lawrence and Lee), 1959 Oct. 1, II

Garden District (Williams), 1958 Jan. 7, II

George M! musical, 1968 Apr. 10(1), II

Get-Rich-Quick Wallingford musical, 1910 Sept. 10, II

Gin Game, The (Coburn), 1977 Oct. 6, II

Girl of the Golden West (Belasco), 1905 Oct. 3, II

Gladiator, The (Bird), 1831 Sept. 26, II

Glance at New York, A (Bacon), 1848(11), II

Godspell musical, 1971 May 17, II

Golden Boy (Odets), 1937 Nov. 4, II

Grass Harp, The (Capote) opened, 1952 Mar. 27, II

Grease longest-running musical to date, 1979, II

Great God Brown, The (O'Neill), 1926 Jan. 23, II

Great White Hope, The (Sackler), 1968 Oct. 3, II

Gypsy musical, 1959 May 21, II; 1974 Sept. 23, II

Hair musical, 1967 Nov. 13, II

Hairy Ape, The (O'Neill), 1922 Mar. 9, II

Harvey (Chase) opened, 1944 Nov. 1, II

He and She (Crothers) opened, 1912 Feb. 5, II

Hello, Dolly! musical, 1964 Jan. 16, II; 1967 Nov. 12, II; 1970 Dec. 27, II

High Tor (Anderson) opened, 1936 Dec. 30, II

Hit the Deck musical, 1927 Apr. 25, II

Holiday (Barry) opened, 1928 Nov. 26, II

Homecoming, The (Pinter) opened, 1967 Jan. 5, II

Home (Storey), 1970 Nov. 11, II

Hostage, The (Behan), 1960 Sept. 20, II

Hot L Baltimore, The (Wilson), 1973 Feb. 7, II

How to Succeed in Business Without Really Trying musical, 1961 Oct. 14, II

Humoresque (Hurst), 1923 Feb. 27, II

I Am a Camera (Van Druten), 1951 Nov. 28, II

Icebound (Davis), 1923 Feb. 10, II

Iceman Cometh, The (O'Neill), 1946 Oct. 9, II

I'd Rather Be Right musical, opened, 1937 Nov. 2, II

I Love My Wife musical, 1977 Apr. 17, II

Inherit the Wind (Lawrence and Lee), 1955 Jan. 11, II

In Old Kentucky (Dazey), 1893 Oct. 23, II

Theatrical productions (*cont.*)

Inside U.S.A. musical revue, 1948 Apr. 30, II

I Remember Mama (Van Druten), 1944 Oct. 19, II

It Can't Happen Here (Lewis and Moffitt), 1936 Oct. 27, II

Jest, The (Sheldon), 1919 Apr. 9, II

Jesus Christ Superstar musical, 1971 Oct. 12, II

Joan of Lorraine (Anderson), 1946 Nov. 18, II

Joe Egg (Nichols), 1985 Mar. 27, II

Johnny Johnson (Green), 1936 Nov. 19, II

Key Largo (Anderson), 1939 Nov. 27, II

King and I, The musical opened, 1951 Mar. 29(1), II

Kismet musical, 1911 Apr. 19, II

Kiss Me, Kate musical, 1948 Dec. 30, II

Last Mile, The (Wexley), 1930 Feb. 13, II

Late Christopher Bean, The (Howard), 1932 Oct. 31, II

Laugh, Clown, Laugh! (Martini), 1923 Nov. 28, II

Leah the Forsaken (Daly), 1862 Dec. 8, II

Lend an Ear (Gaynor) musical, 1948 Dec. 16, II

Life with Father (Lindsay and Crouse), 1939 Nov. 8, II

Lightnin' (Smith and Bacon), 1918 Aug. 26, II

Little Katy comment on American life, 1854(4), IV

Little Night Music, A musical, 1973 Feb. 25, II

Little Shop of Horrors musical, 1982 May 29, II

Look Back in Anger (Osborne), 1957 Oct. 1, II

Look Homeward, Angel (Frings), 1957 Nov. 28, II

Lorelei musical, 1974 Jan. 27(1), II

Louisiana Purchase (Berlin), 1940, II

MacBird (Garson), 1967 Feb. 22, II

Magical City (Akins), 1916 Mar. 20, II

Make a Million (Barasch and Moore), 1958 Oct. 23, II

Make Mine Manhattan revue, 1948 Jan. 15, II

Male Animal, The (Nugent and Thurber), 1940 Jan. 9, II

Mame musical, 1966, II; 1966 May 24, II

Man for All Seasons, A (Bolt), 1961 Nov. 22, II

Man in the Glass Booth, The (Shaw), 1968 Sept. 26, II

Marat Sade (Weiss), 1965, II

Marco Millions (O'Neill) opened, 1928 Jan. 9, II

Mark Twain Tonight! one-man show, 1966, II

Marmion (Barker) opened (N.Y.C.), 1812 Apr. 13, II

Mary, Mary (Kerr), 1961 Mar. 8, II

Theatrical productions (*cont.*)

Medea revived, 1982 May 2, II

Member of the Wedding, The (McCullers), 1950 Jan. 5, II

Men in White (Kingsley), 1933 Sept. 26, II

Middle of the Night (Chayefsky), 1956 Feb. 8, II

Miracle Worker, The (Gibson), 1959 Oct. 19, II

Miss Saigon, 1991, II

Mister Roberts (Heggen and Logan), 1948 Feb. 18, II

Monsieur Beaucaire (Tarkington), 1901 Oct. 7, II

Moon for the Misbegotten, A (O'Neill), 1973 Dec. 29, II

Mourning Becomes Electra (O'Neill) opened, 1930 Oct. 26, II

Mrs. Warren's Profession (Shaw), 1905 Oct. 31, II

Mrs. Wiggs of the Cabbage Patch (Flexner), 1904 Sept. 3, II

Music Man, The musical, 1957 Dec. 19, II

My Fair Lady closed, 1962 Sept. 29, II

My Fair Lady musical, 1956 Mar. 15, II

My Sister Eileen (Field and Chodorov), 1940 Dec. 26, II

Naughty Marietta operetta (Herbert), 1910 Oct. 24, II

New Blood (Thomas), 1894 July 26, II

New York Fireman and Bond Street Heiress (Johnson), 1850 July 22, II

Next (McNally), 1969 Feb. 10, II

Nicholas Nickleby (Dickens), 1981, II; 1981 Oct. 4, II

Nine musical, 1982 May 9, II

No, No, Nanette musical, 1925 Sept. 16, II; 1971 Jan. 19, II

Oath of Office, The (Cannon), 1850 Mar. 18, II

Of Thee I Sing musical, 1931, II

Oh! Calcutta!, 1969, II

Oh Dad, Poor Dad . . . , 1962 Feb. 26, II

Oklahoma! musical, 1943, II; 1943 Mar. 31, II; 1944 May 1, II

Old Maid, The (Akins), 1935 Jan. 7(1), II; 1935 May 6, II

Once Upon a Mattress musical, 1959 May 11, II

One Third of a Nation WPA production, 1938(2), II

On Trial (Rice), 1914 Aug. 19, II

On Your Toes musical, 1936 Mar. 22, II

Othello performed (N.Y.C.), 1866 Dec. 29, II

Otherwise Engaged (Gray), 1977 Feb. 2, II

Our Mrs. McChesney (Ferber), 1916(7), II

Our Town (Wilder), 1938(1), II; 1938 May 2, II

Perfect Fool, The (Wynn), 1921 Nov. 7, II

Period of Adjustment (Williams), 1960 Nov. 10, II

Theatrical productions (*cont.*)

Petrified Forest, The (Sherwood), 1935 Jan. 7(2), II

Piaf (Gems), 1981 Feb. 5, II

Picnic (Inge), 1953 Feb. 19, II

Pins and Needles revue, 1937 Nov. 27, II

Pippin musical, 1972 Sept. 23, II

Plain and Fancy musical, 1955 Jan. 27, II

Playboy of the Western World, The (Synge), 1912(2), II

Ponteach, first play about Indians, 1766(2), II

Poppy (Donnelly, Jones, Samuels), 1923 Sept. 3, II

Porgy and Bess (Heyward), 1925(1), II

Prisoner of Second Avenue, The (Simon), 1971 Nov. 11, II

Prophet of St. Paul's, The (Brown), 1837 Mar. 20, II

Raisin in the Sun, A (Hansberry), 1959 Mar. 11, II

Raisin musical, 1973 May 30, II

Real Thing, The (Stoppard), 1984 Jan. 5, II

revivals, 1992, II

Rhinoceros (Ionesco), 1961 Jan. 9, II

Ritz, The (McNally), 1975 Jan. 20, II

Road to Rome, The (Sherwood), 1927 Jan. 31, II

Roberta (Kern) musical, 1933 Nov. 18, II

Roger Bloomer (Lawson), 1923 Mar. 2, II

Rosencrantz and Guildenstern Are Dead (Stoppard), 1967 Oct. 16, II

Rose Tattoo, The (Williams), 1951 Feb. 3, II

R.U.R. (Capek), 1922 Oct. 9, II

Saint of Bleecker Street, The (Menotti), 1954 Dec. 27, II

Sally (Kern) musical, 1920 Dec. 21, II

Same Time, Next Year (Bernard), 1975 Mar. 13, II

Saratoga (Howard), 1870(6), II

Separate Tables (Rattigan), 1956 Oct. 25, II

Seventh Heaven (Strong), 1922 Oct. 30(1), II

Shadow Box, The (Cristofer), 1977 Mar. 31, II

Shenandoah (Howard), 1889 Sept. 9, II

Shenandoah musical, 1975 Jan. 7(1), II

Sherlock Holmes, 1886, II

Shore Acres (Herne), 1893, II

Show Boat musical, 1927 Dec. 27(1), II

Shrike, The (Kramm), 1952 Jan. 15, II

Silk Stockings musical, 1955 Feb. 24, II

Six Characters in Search of an Author (Pirandello), 1922 Oct. 30(2), II

Sizwe Banzi Is Dead (Fugard), 1974 Nov. 13, II

Skin of Our Teeth, The (Wilder), 1942 Nov. 18, II

Sleuth (Shaffer), 1970 Nov. 12, II

Soldier's Play, A (Fuller), 1981 Nov. 20, II

Theatrical productions (*cont.*)

South Pacific musical, 1949 Apr. 7, II

Squaw Man, The (Royle), 1905 Oct. 23, II

S.S. Glencairn (O'Neill), 1924 Nov. 3, II

Stop the World . . . musical, 1962 Oct. 3, II

Strange Interlude (O'Neill) revived, 1963 Mar. 11, II

Streetcar Named Desire, A (Williams), 1947 Dec. 3, II

Student Prince, The (Romberg) operetta, 1924 Dec. 2, II

Summer and Smoke (Williams), 1948 Oct. 6, II

Sunday, 1904 Nov. 15, II

Sunday in the Park with George musical, 1984, II; 1984 May 2, II

Sunrise at Campobello (Schary), 1958 Jan. 30, II

Sunshine Boys, The (Simon), 1972 Dec. 20, II

Superstition (Barker), 1824 May 12, II

Sweeney Todd musical, 1979 Mar. 1, II

Taking of Miss Janie, The (Bullins), 1975 Mar. 17, II

Tango Argentino musical, 1985, II; 1985 Oct. 9, II

Tea and Sympathy (Anderson), 1953 Sept. 30, II

That Championship Season (Miller), 1972 May 2, II

There Shall Be No Night (Sherwood), 1940 Mar. 29, II

They Knew What They Wanted (Howard), 1924 Nov. 24, II

Thurber Carnival, 1960 Feb. 26, II

Tiger at the Gates (Fry), 1955 Oct. 3, II

Time of Your Life, The (Saroyan), 1939 Oct. 25, II

Tobacco Road (Kirkland), 1933 Dec. 4, II

To Be Young, Gifted and Black (Hansberry), 1969 Jan. 2, II

Torch Song Trilogy (Fierstein), 1982 June 26, II

Touch of the Poet, A (O'Neill), 1958 Oct. 2, II

Toys in the Attic (Hellman), 1960 Feb. 25, II

Travesties (Stoppard), 1975 Oct. 30, II

Twin Beds (Field and Mayo) farce, 1914 Aug. 14, II

Two by Two musical, 1970 Nov. 10, II

Two for the Seesaw (Gibson), 1958 Jan. 16, II

Two on an Island (Rice), 1940 Jan. 16, II

Uncle Tom's Cabin, 1852, II

Uncle Tom's Cabin popularity as a play, 1901 Mar. 21, II

Under Milk Wood (Thomas), 1957 Oct. 15, II

Under the Gaslight (Daly), 1867 Aug. 12, II

Venus Observed (Fry), 1952 Feb. 13, II

Theatrical productions (*cont.*)

Visit to a Small Planet, A (Vidal), 1957 Feb. 7, II

Wait Until Dark (Knott), 1966 Feb. 2, II

Watch on the Rhine (Hellman), 1941 Mar. 24, II

West Side Story musical, 1957 Sept. 26, II

What a Life (Goldsmith), 1938 Apr. 13, II

What Price Glory? (Anderson), 1924 Sept. 5, II

When Ladies Meet (Crothers), 1932 Oct. 6, II

When You Comin' Back, Red Ryder? (Medoff), 1973 Nov. 5, II

Who's Afraid of Virginia Woolf? (Albee), 1962 Oct. 13, II; 1963 May 6, II

Why Marry? (Williams), 1917 Dec. 25, II

Winterset (Anderson), 1935 Sept. 25, II

Wonderful Town musical, 1953 Feb. 25, II

Yellow Jacket (Hazelton and Benrimo) opened, 1912 Nov. 4, II

You Can't Take It with You (Kaufman and Hart), 1936 Nov. 30, II

Your Arms Too Short to Box with God musical, 1976 Dec. 22, II

Theiler, Max, 1951 Oct. 18, III

Theosophical Society of America (N.Y.C.), 1875 Nov. 17, III

Theroux, Paul, 1982(1), II

Thieu, Nguyen Van, 1969 June 8, I

Tho, Le Duc, 1973 Oct. 16(2), I

Tho, Nguyen Ngoc, 1963, I

Thomas, Augustus, 1894 July 26, II

Thomas, Charence, 1991 Oct. 15, I

Thomas, Danny, 1954 Mar. 7, II; 1991, II

Thomas, Debi, 1986 Feb. 6–8, IV; 1988 Jan. 8–9, IV

Thomas, Dylan, 1957 Oct. 15, II; 1964 Jan. 18(1), II

Thomas, E. Donnall, 1990 Oct. 8, III

Thomas, Isaiah, 1800(3), II; 1806, II; 1812(4), IV

Thomas, Lewis, 1975 Apr. 16, II

Thomas, Lowell, 1981, III

Thomas, Martha Carey, 1880(4), III

Thomas, Norman:

presidential candidacy, 1928 Apr. 13–18, I; 1928 Nov. 6, I; 1932 May 22–24, I; 1932 Nov. 8, I; 1936 May 25, I; 1936 Nov. 3, I; 1940 Apr. 7, I; 1940 Nov. 5, I; 1948 May 9, I; 1948 Nov. 2, I; 1968, I

Thomas, Pinklon, 1984 Aug. 31, IV

Thomas, Richard, 1973 May 20, II

Thomas, Robert Bailey, 1792, IV

Thomas, Theodore, 1869, II

Thompson, Daniel Pierce, 1839(4), II

Thompson, David, 1978, IV

Thompson, John Taliaferro, 1916(4), III

Thompson, Lawrence R., 1971 May 3, II

Thompson, Martin, 1830(7), II

Thompson, Randall, 1942 Apr. 14(2), II

Thompson, Sada, 1972 Apr. 23(2), II; 1978 Sept. 17, II

Thompson, William Tappan, 1843, II

Thomson, Bobby, 1951, IV

Thomson, George Paget (Sir), 1937 Nov. 11, III

Thomson, Virgil, 1926, II; 1934 Feb. 8, II; 1972 Apr. 20, II; 1982 Jan. 28, II died, 1989, II

Thorazine, 1955 Jan. 8, III

Thoreau, Henry David:

"Civil Disobedience", 1849, II

Walden, 1854(2), II

Thorium, 1962 Dec. 2, III

Thorp, Willard L., 1992, III

Thorpe, Jim, 1912, IV; 1953, IV

Thorpe, Thomas Bangs, 1841(3), II

Three Mile Island (Pa.), 1979 Mar. 28, III

Thresher (nuclear submarine), 1963 Apr. 10, I

Threshers, 1837 Dec. 29, III

Thrift institutions *see* Savings and loan associations

Thumb, Tom (dwarf), 1837, IV

Thurber, James, 1940 Jan. 9, II; 1945 Dec. 27, II; 1960 Feb. 26, II; 1961, II

Thurman, Allen G., 1888 June 5, I

Thurman, Judith, 1983 Apr. 24, II

Thurmond, Strom, 1948 July 17, I; 1948 Nov. 2, I; 1957 Aug. 30, I

Thuy, Xan, 1968 May 10, I

Tibbles, Thomas H., 1904 July 4–5, I

Tickner, Charles, 1977 Feb. 3–5, IV; 1978 Feb. 12, IV; 1978 Mar 9, IV; 1979 Feb. 2–3, IV; 1980 Jan. 18–20, IV

Ticknor, George, 1855 Sept. 17, III

Tilden, Douglas, 1885(6), II

Tilden, Samuel J.:

Democratic nomination for presidency, 1876 June 27–28, I

disputed election, 1876 Nov. 7, I; 1877, I

Tilden, William T., 1920 July 3, IV; 1920 Sept. 6, IV; 1921 June 29, IV; 1921 Aug. 20, IV; 1922 Aug. 19, IV; 1923 Aug. 18, IV; 1924 Aug. 16, IV; 1925 Aug. 24, IV; 1927 July 2, IV; 1929 Aug. 24, IV; 1930 July 4, IV

Tiles, 1871(4), II

Tillich, Paul, 1965, III

Time (*see also* Clocks and watches):

Daylight Savings Time, 1918, IV

standard adopted throughout U.S., 1883 Nov. 18, I

war time effective, 1942 Feb. 9, III

Time capsules:

Crypt of Civilization, 1940 May 24, III

N.Y. World's Fair, 1941 Sept. 23, IV

Time (magazine), 1925, II

Time Warner, Inc.:

formation, 1989 July 24, III

Timrod, Henry, 1860, II

Ting, Samuel C. C., 1976 Oct. 18(2), III

Tinker, Joe, 1907, IV

Tiny Tim (singer), 1969 Dec. 17, IV

Tippecanoe, Battle of, 1809, IV

"Tippecanoe and Tyler too" slogan, 1836(1), IV; 1840, I

Tires:

rationing ended, 1945 Dec. 20, III

Tires (*cont.*)
  recall, 1980 July 3, III
Tiros 1 (satellite), 1960, III; 1960 Apr. 1,
  III
Tisch, Preston Robert, 1991 Feb. 20, IV
Titanic (ship), 1912 Apr. 14–15, I; 1985
  Sept. 1, I
Titan 2 (ICBM), 1962 Mar. 16, III
Titan 3C (rocket), 1965 June 18, III
Tobacco (*see also* Smoking):
  American Tobacco Co. formed, 1904
    Oct. 19, III
  chewing and spitting, 1850(7), IV
  colonial economic asset (Va.),
    1610–1619, III
  genetically altered planted (Wis.),
    1986 May 30, III
  trade with England, 1620 June 29, I
Tobey, Mark, 1976, II
Tobin, James, 1981 Oct. 13, III
Tocqueville, Alexis de, 1835, III
Today (newspaper), 1982 Sept. 15, II
Todd, Mike, 1958, II
Todd, Patricia Canning, 1947 July 4–5, IV
Toklas, Alice B., 1967, II
Tokyo Rose (Iva Toguri D'Aquino), 1977
  Jan. 19, I
Toland, John, 1971 May 3, II; 1976(1), II;
  1985(1), II
Toleration Act (Md.), 1649 Apr. 21, III;
  1655 Mar. 25, I
Tolstoy, Leo, 1890(3), II
Tomatoes, 1834(3), IV
Tomkins, Daniel, 1816 Dec. 4, I
Tomlin, Lily, 1986 June 1(3), II
Tomonaga, Shinichero, 1965 Oct. 21(1), III
Tompkins, Daniel, 1820 Dec. 6, I
Tonegawa, Susumu, 1987 Oct. 12, III
Tonkin, Gulf of:
  Oriskany U.S. carrier fire, 1966 Oct.
    26, I
  resolution granting president
    authority to repel attack, 1964 Aug.
    7, I
  N. Vietnamese attacked U.S.
    destroyer, 1964 Aug. 2, I
Tony awards, 1947 Apr. 7, II; 1948 Mar.
  28, II; 1949 Apr. 24, II; 1950 Apr. 9, II;
  1951 Mar. 25, II; 1952 Mar. 30, II; 1953
  Mar. 29, II; 1954 Mar. 28, II; 1955 Mar.
  27, II; 1956 Apr. 1, II; 1957 Apr. 21, II;
  1958 Apr. 13, II; 1959 Apr. 12, II; 1960
  Apr. 24, II; 1961 Apr. 16, II; 1962 Apr.
  29, II; 1963 Apr. 25(1), II; 1964 May 24,
  II; 1965 June 13, II; 1966 June 16, II;
  1967 Mar. 26, II; 1968 Apr. 21, II; 1969
  Apr. 20, II; 1970 Apr. 19, II; 1971 Mar.
  28, II; 1972 Apr. 23(2), II; 1973 Mar. 25,
  II; 1974 Apr. 21, II; 1975 Apr. 21, II;
  1976 Apr. 18, II; 1977 June 5, II; 1978
  June 4, II; 1979 June 3, II; 1980 June 8,
  II; 1981 June 7, II; 1982 June 6, II; 1983
  June 5, II; 1984 June 3, II; 1985 June 2,
  II; 1986 June 1(3), II; 1987 June 7, II;
  1988 June 5, II; 1989 June 4(1), II; 1990
  June 3, II; 1991 June 2, II; 1992 June 1,
  II
Toole, John Kennedy, 1980(1), II; 1981
  Apr. 13, II

Tools:
  pneumatic hammer, 1890(3), III
Toomey, Bill, 1969 Dec. 11–12, IV
Topeka Constitution, 1855 Oct. 23, I
Topping, Daniel, 1974, IV
Tories:
  Boucher's views, 1763(2), I
  plays supporting, 1774(1), II
  post-Revolution treatment of, 1783(4),
    IV; 1784(3), IV
  satire on, 1775(1), II
Tornadoes:
  Carolinas, 1984 Mar. 29, I
  from Ga. to Canada, 1974 Apr. 3–4, I
  Ill., 1967 Apr. 21(2), I
  La., Miss., Tex., 1971 Feb. 21, I
  Lake Pepin (Minn.), 1890 July 13, I
  Mass., 1953 June 9, I
  Mich., 1953 June 8, I
  Midwest, 1991 Apr. 16, I
  Minn., 1899 June 12, I
  Mo., 1899 Apr. 27, I
  Ohio, 1953 June 8, I
  Ohio, Pa., N.Y., Ontario, 1985 May 31,
    I
  property damage, 1956 Apr. 2–3, I
  St. Louis (Mo.), 1896 May 27, I; 1927
    Sept. 29, I; 1959 Feb. 10, I
  Snyder, Okla., 1905 May 11, I
  southern states, 1884 Feb. 9, I
  Tex., 1953 May 11, I
  Tex. and Okla., 1947 Apr. 9, I
  Tex.-Okla., 1979 Apr. 10, I
  Wisc., 1899 June 12, I
  worst in 40 years (Middle West), 1965
    Apr. 11, I
  worst to date, 1925 Mar. 18, I
Torre, Marie, 1959 Jan. 5, II
Torrijos Herrera, Omar, 1977 Sept. 7, I
Toscanini, Arturo, 1930, II; 1937(4), II
  archives, 1987 Mar. 30, II
Toski, Bob, 1954, IV
Touhy, Roger, 1959 Dec. 16, IV
Tourism *see* Travel and tourism
Tournament of Roses (Calif.), 1886 Jan. 1,
  IV; 1902 Jan. 1, IV; 1916 Jan. 1, IV;
  1917 Jan. 1, IV; 1918(3), IV; 1919 Jan. 1,
  IV; 1920 Jan. 1, IV; 1921 Jan. 1, IV;
  1922 Jan. 1, IV; 1923 Jan. 1, IV
Tower, John G.:
  died, 1991, I
  Iran-Contra investigation commission,
    1986 Nov. 3, I
Tower Building (N.Y.C.), 1889(8), III
Tower Commission, 1986 Nov. 3, I; 1987
  Feb. 26, I
Town, Ithiel, 1821, III
Townes, Charles H., 1964 Oct. 29, III
Townsend, Bertha L., 1888(4), IV; 1889(6),
  IV
Townsend, Francis E., 1934 Jan. 1, I
Townshend Acts, 1767 June 29, I; 1770
  Apr. 12, I
Toxic chemicals, 1985, III
Toxic shock syndrome, 1980 Sept. 22, III
Toxic Substances Control Act, 1976 Sept.
  28, III
Toxic waste *see* Pollution
Toyota Co., 1983 Dec. 22, III

Toys *see* Dolls and Toys
Trabert, Tony, 1953 Sept. 7, IV; 1955 July
  1–2, IV; 1955 Sept. 11, IV
Track and field (*see also* Boston Marathon;
  New York City Marathon):
  decathlon world record, 1992 Sept. 5,
    IV
  first indoor amateur (N.Y.C.), 1868
    Nov. 11, IV
  first U.S. meet in China, 1975 May
    18–28, IV
  first 100-yard race, 1876(4), IV
  first 16-ft. pole vault, 1962 Feb. 2, IV
  first 17-ft. pole vault, 1963 Aug. 24(2),
    IV
  four-minute mile broken, 1957 July
    19, IV
  four-minute mile indoor record
    broken, 1962 Feb. 10, IV
  mile run records, 1915(3), IV; 1966
    July 17, IV; 1967 June 23, IV
  pole vault records, 1940(1), IV; 1967
    June 23, IV
  records, 1973 May 27, IV
  restrictions on communist diplomats,
    1963 Nov. 12, I
  women's heptathlon record, 1988 July
    16, IV
  world decathlon record, 1966 July
    2–3, IV; 1969 Dec. 11–12, IV
  world marathon record (Chicago),
    1984 Oct. 21, IV
  world records, 1991 Aug. 25, IV
  world 100-meter dash record, 1988
    Sept. 17–Oct. 2, IV
Tracy, Edward A., 1986 Nov. 2, I
Tracy, Spencer, 1938 Mar. 10, II; 1939
  Feb. 23, II; 1944, II; 1967, II
Trade (*see also* Interstate commerce;
  Stamp Act; Townshend Acts;
  commodities traded):
  S. African sanctions lifted, 1991 July
    10, I
  anti-unfair trading practices bill, 1988
    Aug. 23, III
  balance of, 1891, III; 1971, III; 1985,
    III
  banned with Cuba, 1962 Feb. 3, I
  bill passed allowing president to
    reduce tariffs, 1962 Oct. 4, I
  Boston (Mass.) center for, 1715–1719,
    III
  British blacklist of U.S. firms, 1916
    July 18, III
  British prohibited, 1811 Feb. 11, I
  Canadian free trade agreement, 1988
    Sept. 19, III; 1989 Jan. 2, III
  Cape Horn to China route, 1784(2),
    III
  China treaty, 1844 July 3, I
  Chinese agreement, 1992 Oct. 9(1), III
  Chinese embargo lifted, 1971 Apr. 14,
    III
  colonial unfair profit charge, 1639(2),
    IV
  colonies with England, 1705–1709, I
  deficit, 1988, III
  deficit down, 1990, III; 1991, III
  deficit record, 1983, III; 1984, III;
    1985, III; 1987, III

Trade (*cont.*)
deficit rise, 1978, III
Embargo Act, 1808, I
Embargo Act repealed, 1809, I; 1809
Mar. 1(1), I
Embargo Act signed, 1807 Dec. 22, I
exports exceeded imports, 1916 Jan.
25, III
Federal Trade Commission (FTC)
established, 1914 Sept. 26, I
first exports, 1600–1609, III
first exports (Mass.), 1623 Sept. 10, III
first tariff bill, 1789 July 4, III
first treaty with El Salvador, 1850 Jan.
2, III
Force Act, 1833 Mar. 2, I
GATT negotiations fail, 1990 Dec. 7, I
GATT signed, 1967 June 30, I
growing colonial, 1715–1719, III
growth (Mass.), 1735(3), III
Hamilton's tariff advocacy,
1790–1794, III
highest tariff to date, 1890 Oct. 1(1), I
import duties lowered, 1857 Mar. 3, I
imports exceeded exports, 1971, III
import surcharge recalled, 1971 Dec.
20, III
Iraqi embargo/blockade, 1990 Aug.
2–Dec. 31, I
Japan eased domestic market for U.S.,
1978 Jan. 13, III
Japanese Kanagawa Treaty, 1854 Mar.
31, I
Japanese steel-dumping penalty, 1977
Oct. 3, III
Japanese treaties, 1853, I; 1858, III
Kennedy Round tariff reduction, 1968
July 1(1), I
McKinley Tariff Act, 1890 Oct. 1(1), I
Macon's Bill No. Two, 1810 May 1, I
Mongrel Tariff Act, 1883 Mar. 3(1), I
Morrill Tariff Bill passed, 1860 May
10, III
Muscat (Oman) treaty, 1833 Sept. 21,
I
Navigation Acts (British), 1660–1669,
I; 1660 Dec. 1, I
new Iraqi sanctions, 1992 Aug. 25, I
Non-Intercourse Act, 1809, I; 1809
Mar.1(2), I; 1810 Aug. 5, I
Perry Japanese treaty, 1853, I
Polish sanctions lifted, 1987 Feb. 19, I
protectionist bill vetoed, 1988 May 24,
I
protective tariffs, 1816 Mar. 20(2), I;
1822, III; 1828(2), III; 1842 Aug. 30,
I; 1897, I; 1908 Dec. 21, III; 1909, I;
1930, I
Reciprocal Act extended, 1955 June
21, I
Reciprocal Agreement Act, 1940 Apr.
12, I
routes, 1600–1609, I
Samoan treaty, 1878 Jan. 17, I
Siam treaty, 1833 Mar. 20, I
Smoot-Hawley Act, 1930, I
South African sanctions, Aug. 13, I
South's objection to high tariffs, 1832,
I

Trade (*cont.*)
Soviet benefits linked to emigration
policies, 1974 Dec. 20, III
Soviets denied most-favored-nation
status, 1973 Dec. 11, III
strictures on British imports, 1806
Apr. 18, I
tariff cuts, 1934 June 12, I; 1962 Jan.
16, III; 1962 Mar. 7, III
Tariff of Abominations, 1828, I;
1828(2), IV; 1828 Dec. 19, I
Tariff of 1833, 1833 Mar. 2, I
Underwood-Simmons Tariff Act, 1913
Oct. 3, III
wool tariffs, 1827 Feb. 28, I
Yorktown (Va.) customhouse, 1706, I
Trade Agreements Act, 1934 June 12, I
Traffic accidents:
automobile-related statistics, 1938(1),
IV
chain reaction collisions (Tenn.), 1990
Dec. 11, I
Christmas weekend fatalities, 1955
Dec. 27, III
death rate, 1959 July 29, I
deaths at all-time high, 1963, III
fatalities dropped, 1983, III
fatalities up, 1984, IV
truck-bus crash (Ky.), 1988 May 14, I
worst single to date (Ariz.), 1956 Dec.
17, I
Traffic regulations:
first speed law (N.Y.), 1904(6), III
Trailers *see* Mobile homes
Trail of Tears (Cherokee resettlement),
1838(1), IV; 1838 Dec., I
Train, George Francis, 1890 May 24, I
Train accidents *see* Railroad disasters
Train robberies:
first (Ohio), 1865 May 5, IV
Transcendental Club, 1836(1), III
Transcendentalism:
Brook Farm (Mass.), 1841(3), III
Conduct of Life, The (Emerson),
1860(6), II
Dial suspended publication, 1844(8),
II
Dial voice of, 1840, II
Emerson's *Essays*, 1841(1), II
Emerson's *Nature*, 1836, II
Transistors, 1956 Nov. 1, III
first superconducting, 1990 Nov. 16,
III
Transit systems (*see also* Buses; Subways):
Bay Area Rapid Transit System
(BART), 1972 Sept. 11, III
bill signed, 1991 Dec. 18, I
cable car invented, 1873(4), III
commuter train accident (N.J.), 1958
Sept. 5, I
elevated railroad (N.Y.C.), 1867(12),
III
federal subsidies, 1974 Nov. 26, III
first electric streetcar (Wis.), 1882(7),
III
first elevated railroad (N.Y.C.),
1881(6), III
first N.Y.C. strike, 1966 Jan. 1, III
first street trains (Mass.), 1856 Mar.
26, III

Transit systems (*cont.*)
first successful electric trolley system
(Richmond, Va.), 1887(3), III
funding from Highway Trust
restricted, 1973 Aug. 3, III
inventions leading to cable car,
1871(4), III
N.Y.C. strike, 1889 Jan. 28, I
Phila.'s first horsecar, 1858(3), III
third rail invented, 1874(4), III
Transportation (*see also* types):
colonial importance of water, 1686, III
segregation laws banned, 1962 Feb.
26, I
slow pace, 1783(3), IV
Vanderbilt's promotion, 1810, III
velocipede's failure, 1872 Nov. 1, III
Transportation, Department of:
created, 1966 Oct. 15, I
Trans World Airlines (TWA):
airliner hijacked, 1970 Sept. 6, III
passenger terminal (N.Y.C.), 1962 May
28, II
Transylvania College (Ky.), 1821(3), IV
Transylvania University library, 1830(2),
III
Trapping *see* Hunting and trapping
Traubel, Helen, 1972, II
Travanti, Daniel J., 1981 Sept. 13, II; 1982
Sept. 19, II
Travel and tourism (*see also* Resorts):
Bly's around-the-world record, 1889,
IV
Buckingham's U.S. tour and
impressions, 1841, IV
Chinese ban lifted, 1972 Nov. 22, I
classic book, 1704 Oct., II
customs regulations scored, 1868(4),
IV
Dickens's impressions of U.S., 1842(1),
II
early challenges and dangers, 1796(3),
IV
English impressions of U.S. habits,
1850(7), IV
federal restrictions, 1959 Dec. 7, I
first guidebook, 1732(1), II
guidebooks, 1825(1), IV
passport denials, 1962 Jan. 12, I
popularity at mid-century, 1855(4), IV
restrictions lifted, 1977 Mar. 18, I
Train's around-the-world trip record,
1890 May 24, I
Travels in the United States (Melish),
1812(4), II
Travelers Insurance Co., 1863(2), III
Travers, Jerome D., 1915 June 18, IV
Traynor, Pie (Harold J.), 1972, IV
Treason:
B. Arnold, 1780 Oct. 2, I
J. Davis trial, 1868 Dec. 3, I
Pound charges dropped, 1958 Apr. 18,
I
Tokyo Rose pardoned, 1977 Jan. 19, I
Treasury Bonds *see* Government Bonds
Treasury Department:
Duane replaced as secretary, 1833
Sept. 23, I
established, 1789 Sept. 2, I

Treasury Department (*cont.*)
  Senate rejection of Taney as secretary, 1834 June 24, I
  suspended Salomon Brothers from auctions, 1991 Aug. 18, III
Treaties (*see also* names, inverted):
  abrogation of French (1778), 1798 July 7, I
  banning biological warfare, 1972 Apr. 10, I
  banning genocide, 1986 Feb. 19, I
  Chinese exclusion, 1894 Mar. 17, I
  Dominican Republic trade, 1907 Feb. 8, I
  first foreign alliance (France), 1778 Feb. 6, I
  limited nuclear test ban, 1963 Oct. 7, I
  Mexican border, 1970 Nov. 23(1), I
  migratory birds (Canada), 1916 Aug. 16, III
  nuclear nonproliferation signed, 1968 July 1(2), I
  Panama Canal, 1977 Sept. 7, I
  Panama Canal ratified, 1978 Mar. 16, I; 1978 Apr. 18, I
  Russian (1832) abrogated, 1911 Dec. 18, I
  SALT 2, 1979 June 18, I
  SEATO, 1955 Sept. 8, I
  space demilitarization, 1967 Jan. 27, I
  Virgin Island purchase, 1916 Aug. 4, I
Trees *see* Arbor Day; Forests and trees
Tregaskis, Richard, 1943(1), II
Tremont Temple (Boston, Mass.), 1864(3), III
Trenary, Jill, 1987 Feb. 7–8, IV; 1989 Feb. 11–12, IV; 1990 Feb. 10–11, IV
Trenton, Battle of (N.J.), 1776 Dec. 26, I
Trevino, Jacinto, 1916 June 16, I
Trevino, Lee, 1968 June 16, IV; 1970, IV; 1971, IV; 1971 June 21, IV; 1974 Aug. 11, IV; 1984 Aug. 19, IV; 1990, IV
Trevor, Claire, 1949 Mar. 24, II; 1957 Mar. 16, II
Trial (ship), 1644, III
Triangle Publications, Inc., 1988 Aug. 7(1), II
Triangle trade *see* Slavery
Triangle Waist Co., 1911, I
Trichinosis, 1885(2), III
Trinity Church (Boston, Mass.), 1729(1), III
Trinity Church (Del.), 1698 May 29, II
Trinity Church (N.Y.C.), 1741 Aug., II; 1766(1), II; 1790(5), III; 1839(5), II
Trinity School (N.Y.C.), 1710, III
Tripolitan War, 1801 May 14, I; 1802 Feb. 6, I; 1803 May 23, I; 1804 Feb. 16, I; 1805, I; 1805 Apr. 27, I
Trist, Nicholas P., 1847 Apr. 15, I
Trollope, Frances, 1827, IV; 1827 Dec., II
Trotsky, Leon, 1930(2), II
Trucks:
  deregulation, 1980, III
  new sales banned, 1942 Jan. 1, III
  strike, 1979 June 7, III
Trudeau, Edward Livingston, 1885, III; 1894(1), III
Truman, Bess, 1982, I

Truman, Harry S:
  anti-Nixon remarks, 1960 Oct. 10–12, I
  biography, 1992(1), II
  communists in government, 1948, I
  declared national emergency, 1950 Dec. 16, I
  elected vice president, 1944 Nov. 7, I
  emergency powers, 1950 Sept. 8, I
  ended World War II state of hostilities, 1946 Dec. 31, I
  Fair Deal, 1949, I
  hydrogen bomb authorization, 1950 Jan. 31, I
  inaugurated for second term, 1949 Jan. 20, I
  International Security Act veto overridden, 1950 Sept. 23, I
  Korean War, 1950 June 27, I; 1950 June 30, I
  legislation signed, 1946 Aug. 1, I; 1947 May 22, I; 1947 July 18, I; 1948 Mar. 30, I; 1948 Apr. 3, I; 1948 June 24(2), I; 1948 June 25, I; 1949 Oct. 26, III; 1951 Oct. 10, I; 1952 July 16, I
  oral biography of (Miller), 1974(1), II
  Point Four program, 1949 Jan. 20, I
  presidential candidacy, 1948 July 15, I
  railroads seizure, 1950 Aug. 25, III
  railroad strike injunction, 1948 May 10, III
  recalled MacArthur, 1951 Apr. 11, I
  reelected president, 1948 Nov. 2, I
  steel mill seizure, 1952, III; 1952 Apr. 8, III; 1952 May 2, III; 1952 June 2, III
  steel settlement, 1952 July 24, III
  succeeded to presidency, 1945 Apr. 12, I
  vetoed McCarran-Walter Bill, 1952 June 25, I
  vetoed Taft-Hartley Act, 1947 June 23, III
  vice presidential candidacy, 1944 July 19–21, I
Truman Doctrine, 1947 May 22, I
Trumbo, Dalton, 1976, II
Trumbull, John, 1775(1), II; 1782(4), II; 1817, II
Trump, Donald, 1987(1), II
Trusts and antitrust:
  American Medical Assn. violation, 1943 Jan. 18, III
  American Tobacco Co. dissolved, 1911 May 29, III
  antitrust applied to labor, 1894 Aug. 3, III
  AT&T divestiture, 1982 Jan. 8, III
  AT&T suit, 1949 Jan. 14, III
  baseball antitrust case, 1970, IV
  baseball exempted, 1972 June 19, IV
  basketball suit, 1972, IV
  biggest case to date, 1962 Mar. 1, III
  first antitrust laws, 1889 Mar. 2, I
  football franchise shifts ruling, 1984 Nov. 5, IV
  insurance cos. subject to antitrust, 1944 June 5, III
  labor application, 1908 Feb. 3, III

Trusts and antitrust (*cont.*)
  legal fees decision, 1975 June 16, III
  Northern Securities Co. dissolved, 1904 Mar. 14, III
  organization and growth of trusts, 1882, III
  prosecution of Northern Securities Co., 1902 Mar. 10, III
  T. Roosevelt's antitrust enforcement, 1902 Oct. 16, III
  rush to form trusts, 1887, III; 1888(3), III
  Sherman Antitrust Act passed, 1890, I
  Standard Oil Co. case, 1911, III
  tobacco, 1890(8), III
  TV college football ruling, 1984 June 27, IV
  U.S. Steel ruled lawful, 1915 June 3, III
  Whiskey Trust, 1886(4), III
  witnesses compelled to testify in court proceedings, 1906 Mar. 12, III
Tryon, Thomas, 1971(1), II
Tubbs, Tony, 1984 Apr. 29, IV; 1985 Apr. 29, IV; 1986 Jan. 17, IV; 1988 June 27(2), IV
Tuberculosis:
  case upsurge, 1992, III
  first Red Cross Christmas seals, 1908 Dec., III
  National Assn. organized, 1904(2), III
  sanatoriums, 1885, III; 1894(1), III
Tubman, Harriet, 1838, I
Tuchman, Barbara, 1963 May 6, II; 1972 May 1, II; 1979 Feb. 27, II; 1989, II
Tucker, Richard, 1975, II
Tucker, Sophie, 1966, II
Tucker, Tony, 1987 Aug. 1, IV
Tuckerman, Joseph, 1835(1), IV
Tudor, Antony, 1987, II
Tudor, Frederick, 1805(1), III
Tugwell, Rexford Guy, 1979, III
Tulane University (La.), 1847 Feb. 16, III; 1884(6), III
Tulsa (Okla.):
  rated most typical U.S. city, 1992, I
Tunnels *see* Bridges and tunnels; specific names
Tunney, Gene, 1926, IV; 1928 July 26, IV; 1978, IV
Turkey:
  U.S. aid, 1948 Apr. 3, I
  U.S. bases seized, 1975 July 29, I
  U.S. military pact, 1976 Mar. 26, I
"Turkey in the Straw" (song), 1834(1), II
Turner, Cathy, 1992 Feb. 8–23, IV
Turner, Debbye, 1989 Sept. 17, IV
Turner, Felton, 1960 Mar. 7, IV
Turner, Frederick J., 1893(1), III; 1933 May 4, II
Turner, Jesse, 1987 Jan. 24, I
Turner, J. M. W., 1980 May 29, II
Turner, Lana, 1958 Apr. 4, IV
Turner, Nat, 1831, I
Turner, Ted, 1991(1), II
Turner, Tina, 1985 Feb. 26, II; 1987 Feb. 24, II; 1989 Feb. 22, II
Turnesa, Jim, 1952 June 25, IV
Turnverein societies, 1850(6), IV
Turow, Scott, 1987(1), II; 1990(1), II

Turtel Taube (hymn book), 1747(2), II
Tuskegee Institute (Ala.), 1881 July 4, III
Tuxedo Club (N.Y.), 1886 Oct., IV
Tuxedo Park (N.Y.), 1986, IV
TV *see* Television
TVA *see* Tennessee Valley Authority
Twain, Mark:
  adopted pseudonym, 1862, II
  Adventures of Tom Sawyer, The,
    1876(1), II
  Autobiography, 1924(1), II
  biography of, 1920(1), II
  books on, 1967 Mar. 8, II; 1967 May 1,
    II
  born, 1835(5), IV
  "Celebrated Jumping Frog of
    Calaveras County, The", 1865 Nov.
    18, II
  Christian Science, 1907(1), II
  Connecticut Yankee in King Arthur's
    Court, A, 1889(1), II
  died, 1910, III
  on frontier, 1820, IV
  Gilded Age, The, 1874(1), II
  Halley's Comet, 1835(5), IV; 1910, III
  Holbrook's one-man show revived,
    1966, II
  Huckleberry Finn, 1884(1), II
  Huckleberry Finn lost manuscript
    authenticated, 1991 Feb. 13, II
  Innocents Abroad, 1869(1), II
  Joan of Arc, 1896(1), II
  Library of America edition of works,
    1982(1), II
  Life on the Mississippi, 1883(1), II
  Mysterious Stranger, The, 1916(1), II
  Paine biography of, 1912(1), II
  Prince and the Pauper, The, 1882(1),
    II
  Pudd'nhead Wilson, 1894(1), II
  Roughing It, 1872(1), II
  San Francisco *Chronicle,* 1865(7), II
  weather quote, 1890(1), IV
  What Is Man?, 1906(1), II
Tway, Bob, 1986 Aug. 11, IV
Tweed, William Marcy ("Boss"):
  convicted of fraud, 1873 Nov. 19, I
  corruption investigation, 1871 Sept. 4,
    I
  escaped from prison, 1875 Dec. 4, I
  returned to N.Y. prison, 1876 Nov. 23,
    I
Twiggy (model), 1967, IV
Two Penny Act (Va.), 1758(1), III
Tydings-McDuffie Act, 1934 Mar. 24, I
Tylenol, 1982 Sept. 29–Oct. 1, I
Tyler, Anne, 1986 Feb. 17, II; 1989 Mar.
  30, II
Tyler, John:
  born, 1790 Mar. 29, I
  Cabinet resigned, 1841 Sept. 11, I
  elected vice president, 1840 Dec. 2, I
  married, 1844 June 26, IV
  nominated for president, 1844 May
    27, I
  succeeded to presidency, 1841, I;
    1841 Mar. 4, I
  vetoed banking bill, 1841 June 12, I
  vice presidential candidacy, 1836(1),
    IV

Tyler, John (*cont.*)
  vice presidential nomination, 1839
    Dec. 4–7, I; 1840, I
  withdrew from second-term attempt,
    1844, I; 1844 May 27, I
Tyler, Royall, 1787 Apr. 16, II; 1790(2), II
Typewriter:
  early, 1843(1), III
  first patent, 1829 July 23, III
  first successful, 1867(9), III
  "now is the time . . . " test phrase
    created, 1867(2), IV
  two patents granted, 1868 June 23, III
  typing speed record, 1918 Oct. 21, IV
Typhoid and typhus, 1837(4), III; 1944(1),
  III
Typhoons:
  Omar, 1992 Aug. 28, I
Tyson, Cicely, 1974 May 28, II
Tyson, Mike, 1986 Nov. 22, IV; 1987 Mar.
  7, IV; 1987 Aug. 1, IV; 1988 June 27(2),
  IV; 1990 Feb. 11, IV
  rape conviction, 1992 Feb. 10, IV

Udell, Peter, 1975 Jan. 7(1), II
Ueberroth, Peter V., 1984 Mar. 3, IV;
  1988 Sept. 8, IV
Uelses, John, 1962 Feb. 2, IV
Uhry, Alfred, 1988 Mar. 31, II
Ulrich, Laurel Thatcher, 1991 Apr. 9, II
Ulysses (spacecraft), 1990 Oct. 6, III
Umbrellas, 1771, IV; 1985, IV
Umeki, Miyoshi, 1958 Mar. 26, II
Un-American Activities, House Committee
  on:
    communists in government charges,
      1948, I
    formed, 1938 May 26, I
    Ku Klux Klan investigation, 1965 Oct.
      19, I
Una (publication), 1853 Feb., II
Uncle Sam, term, 1812, IV; 1869 Feb. 6, I
Uncle Tom's Cabin (Stowe), 1839(1), I;
  1852, II; 1854(5), II; 1901 Mar. 21, II
Underground Railroad, 1838, I
Underwood-Simmons Tariff Act, 1913 Oct.
  3, III
Unemployment:
  automation-effect study, 1964 Aug. 5,
    III
  benefits extended, 1991 Nov. 14, I;
    1992 July 3, I
  bleak outlook, 1992, III
  Civil Works Administration, 1933
    Nov. 8, I
  Coxey's Army (second), 1914 Apr. 16,
    I
  decline, 1934, III; 1958 May 2, III;
    1959 Apr. 7, III; 1987, III
  doubled, 1954, III
  dropped drastically, 1940, III
  GM plant closings, 1992 Feb. 24, III
  Great Depression, 1931 Jan. 7, III
  higher, 1970, III
  Hoover's measures, 1930 Dec. 2, I
  Humphrey-Hawkins bill, 1978 Oct.
    15, III
  large industry layoffs, 1991, III
  level, 1936, III
  low, 1968, III

Unemployment (*cont.*)
  notice of plant closing law, 1988 Aug.
    2, III
  from panic of 1907, 1908(2), III
  peak number of compensation
    recipients, 1982, III
  post-World War I depression, 1921
    Aug. 16, III
  public works program, 1930 Dec. 2, I
  rate, 1981, III; 1989, III
  rate fall, 1965, III
  rate lowest in five years, 1985, III
  rate rose, 1990, III
  record auto industry layoffs, 1975 Feb.
    3, III
  rise, 1958, III; 1959 July 14, III; 1980,
    III
  rising predicted, 1960 Mar. 30, III
  statistics, 1932(1), I; 1949, III
  steelworkers, 1979, III
UNESCO *see* United Nations
Unger, Irwin, 1965 May 3, II
UNICEF *see* United Nations
Unification Church, 1976 Sept. 18, III;
  1982 July 16, III
Union Carbide Corp., 1985 Apr. 8, III;
  1985 Aug. 11, III
Union Carbide Nuclear Co., 1960 Oct. 15,
  III
Union Club (N.Y.C.), 1836(4), IV
Union College (N.Y.), 1795 Feb. 25, III
Union Oyster House, The (Boston, Mass.),
  1725(2), II
Union Pacific Railroad, 1862 July 1, III;
  1912 Mar. 14, III
Union Party, 1936 June 19, I
Unions *see* Labor; Strikes; names
Union Station (Wash., D.C.), 1988 Sept. 29,
  II
Unitarian Church (Lexington, Mass.),
  1847(4), II
Unitarianism:
  beliefs and growth, 1785–1789, III
  Channing's sermon, 1819(4), III
  Chauncy founding, 1730–1734, III
  Emlyn's work, 1756, III
  merged with Universalists, 1959 May
    3, III
  Parker's unorthodox views, 1841(2),
    III
United American Bank (Knoxville, Tenn.),
  1983 Feb. 14, III
United Auto Workers (UAW):
  Chrysler contract, 1964 Sept. 9, III
  Ford contract, 1964 Sept. 18, III
  GM strike, 1964 Sept. 25, III; 1970
    Sept. 15, III
  joined with Teamsters, 1968 July 1, III
  separated from AFL-CIO, 1968 July 1,
    III
  struck GM, 1945 Nov. 21, III
  suspended by AFL-CIO, 1968 May 16,
    III
United Brethren in Christ, Church of the,
  1800(4), III
United Church of Christ, 1987 June 30,
  III; 1991 Jan. 14, III
United Farm Workers, 1973 Apr. 15, III;
  1977 Mar. 10, III

United Mine Workers (UMW):
   AFL readmittance, 1946 Jan. 25, III
   AFL refused reaffiliation, 1949 May
      20, III
   Boyle found guilty of Yablonski
      murder, 1974 Apr. 11, III
   Boyle indicted, 1971 Mar. 2, III; 1973
      Sept. 6, III
   Boyle's election voided, 1972 May 1,
      III
   forced coal production stoppage, 1939
      May 5, III
   Lewis resigned presidency, 1959 Dec.
      15, III
   petitioned to join AFL, 1943 May 19,
      III
   recognized by U.S. Steel, 1937 Mar. 1,
      III
   riot and violence (Ill.), 1898 Oct. 12,
      III
   wartime defiance, 1943, III
   withdrew from CIO, 1942 Oct. 7, III
   Yablonski family murder, 1970 Jan. 5,
      III; 1972 Mar. 1(2), III
United Nations (UN) (see also Korean
War):
   Casals received Peace Medal, 1971
      Oct. 25, II
   Charter ratified by Senate, 1945 July
      28(2), I
   Communist China admission, 1971
      Aug. 2, I
   established, 1945, I
   Fund for Children, 1948 Apr. 3, I
   genocide banned, 1986 Feb. 19, I
   Gulf War, 1991 Jan. 15–Feb. 27, I
   Iraq invasion of Kuwait, 1990 Aug.
      2–Dec. 31, I
   permanent headquarters dedicated
      (N.Y.), 1949 Oct. 24, I
   Rockefeller gift for headquarters'
      property (N.Y.C.), 1946 Dec. 14, I
   San Francisco conference opened,
      1945 Apr. 24, I
   Secretariat design, 1950(5), II
   two-China issue, 1961 Aug. 2, I
   UNESCO joined by U.S., 1946 July 30,
      I
   UNESCO-sponsored cultural events
      boycotted, 1974 Dec. 30, II
   U.S. financial loan to, 1962 Oct. 2, I
   U.S. withdrew from UNESCO, 1983
      Dec. 28, I
   Vietnam's admission vetoed, 1976
      Nov. 12, I
   Young resigned, 1979 Aug. 15, I
United Negro College Fund, 1990 Mar. 3,
III
United Press International (UPI):
   football poll, 1951 Jan. 1, IV; 1952 Jan.
      1, IV; 1953 Jan. 1, IV; 1954 Jan. 1,
      IV; 1955 Jan. 1, IV; 1956 Jan. 1, IV;
      1957 Jan. 1, IV; 1958 Jan. 1, IV;
      1959 Jan. 1, IV; 1960 Jan. 1, IV;
      1961 Jan. 1, IV; 1962 Jan. 1, IV;
      1963 Jan. 1, IV; 1964 Jan. 1, IV;
      1965 Jan. 1, IV; 1966 Jan. 1, IV;
      1967 Jan. 2, IV; 1968 Jan. 1, IV;
      1969 Jan. 1, IV; 1970 Jan. 1, IV;
      1971 Jan. 1, IV; 1972 Jan. 1, IV;

United Press International (UPI) (cont.)
   1973 Jan. 1, IV; 1974 Jan. 1, IV;
   1975 Jan. 1, IV; 1976 Jan. 1, IV;
   1977 Jan. 1, IV; 1978 Jan. 2, IV;
   1979 Jan. 1, IV; 1980 Jan. 1, IV;
   1981 Jan. 1, IV; 1982 Jan. 1, IV;
   1983 Jan. 1, IV; 1984 Jan. 1, IV;
   1985 Jan. 1, IV; 1986 Jan. 1, IV;
   1987 Jan. 1–2, IV; 1988 Jan. 1, IV;
   1989 Jan. 2, IV; 1990 Jan. 1, IV;
   1991 Jan. 1, IV; 1992 Jan. 1, IV
United Rubber Workers:
   strike, 1967 July 26, III
United States Air Force Academy (Colo.):
   authorized, 1954 Apr. 1, I
   cheating scandal, 1965 Feb. 3, III
   opened, 1955 July 11, I
   site announced, 1954 June 24, I
   women admitted, 1975 Sept. 28, I
   women graduates, 1980 May 28, III
United States Military Academy (West
Point, N.Y.):
   cheating widespread, 1976 Apr. 22, III
   first black graduate, 1877 June 15, I
   founded, 1802 Mar. 16, I
   reforms in wake of cheating scandal,
      1977 Sept. 27, III
   women admitted, 1975 Sept. 28, I
   women graduates, 1980 May 28, III
United States Motor Co., 1910 Jan., III
United States Naval Academy see Naval
Academy
United States (ship), 1952 July 7, III
United States Steel Corp.:
   contract with Steelworkers, 1954 June
      29, III
   formed, 1901, III
   merger, 1982 Mar. 11, III
   price-fixing indictment, 1963 Apr. 2,
      III
   recognized Mine Workers, 1937 Mar.
      1, III
   ruled lawful, 1915 June 3, III
United States (term), 1776 Sept. 9, I
United Steelworkers of America:
   banned communists, fascists, Ku Klux
      Klan members, 1954 Sept. 24, III
   canceled strike, 1952 May 2, III
   injunction against mill seizure, 1952,
      III
   U.S. Steel contract, 1954 June 29, III
   wage agreement signed, 1953 June
      12, III
Universalism:
   doctrinal change (Ballou), 1805, III
   dogma, 1790(6), III
   founding and spread of, 1730–1734,
      III; 1775–1779, III
   merged with Unitarians, 1959 May 3,
      III
Universities see Colleges; specific names
Unknown Soldier, 1921 Nov. 11, II
Unser, Al, 1987 May 24, IV
Unser, Al, Jr., 1992 May 24, IV
Unser, Bobby, 1981 May 24, IV
Updike, John, 1959(1), II; 1964 Mar. 10, II;
   1970(1), II; 1971(1), II; 1981(1), II; 1982
   Jan. 28, II; 1982 Mar. 12, II; 1982 Apr.
   27, II; 1984 Jan. 9, II; 1990(1), II; 1991
   Apr. 9, II

Upjohn, Richard, 1839, II; 1839(5), II
Upshaw, William D., 1932 July 5–7, I;
   1932 Nov. 8, I
Uranium-235, 1957, I
Uranus (planet), 1986 Jan. 24, III
Urban areas see Cities
Urey, Harold C., 1934 Nov. 15, III; 1981,
   III
Uris, Leon, 1953(1), II; 1970(1), II; 1976(1),
   II
USA for Africa (group), 1986 Feb. 25, II
Ustinov, Peter, 1958 Apr. 15(1), II; 1961
   Apr. 17, II; 1965 Apr. 5, II; 1967 June 4,
   II; 1970 June 7, II
Utah (see also Mormon Church):
   blizzard, 1984 Feb. 5–28, I
   boundaries and slavery status
      established, 1850 Sept. 9(3), I
   statehood, 1896 Jan. 4, I
   women's suffrage, 1895 Nov. 5, I
   Young first territory governor, 1850
      Sept. 28(1), I
Utah Act, 1850 Sept. 9(3), I
Utilities see Public utilities; types
Utopianism:
   Alphadelphia Phalanx (Mich.), 1844(1),
      III
   Bethel (Mo.), 1845(3), III
   Brisbane's advocacy of Fourierian,
      1834(1), III
   Brook Farm (Mass.), 1841(3), III
   Fourier and Brisbane-inspired
      communes, 1850(10), IV
   Harmony communities, 1803, III
   N. American Phalanx (N.J.), 1843, III
   Oneida Community (N.Y.), 1848, III
   Owen's New Harmony (Ind.), 1825, I
   Rappites, 1803, III
   Volney's influence, 1795(2), III
Utrecht, Treaty of, 1713 Apr. 11, I;
   1735–1739, I
U-2 incident, 1960, I; 1960 May 5, I; 1960
   May 9, I; 1960 May 16, I; 1960 Aug. 19,
   I; 1962 Feb. 10, I

Vaccination:
   chicken pox, 1984 May 30, III
   common cold, 1955 Nov. 3, III
   compulsory, 1905 Feb. 20, III
   hepatitis, 1971 Mar. 29, III
   hoof and mouth disease, 1981 June 18,
      III
   swine flu program, 1976 Apr. 15, III;
      1976 Dec. 16, III
Vacuum cleaners:
   first patent, 1869 June 8, III
Valachi, Joseph M., 1971, IV
Valentine's Day, 1754(3), IV
Valium (tranquilizer), 1976 July 9, III
Vallandigham, Clement L., 1863, II
Vallee, Rudi, 1986, II
Valley Forge (Pa.), 1777 Dec. 17, I
Van Allen, James A., 1958(1), III
Van Allen belt, 1962 July 9, III
Van Buren, Martin:
   Albany Regency, 1825, I
   born, 1782 Dec. 5, I
   died, 1862 July 24, I
   elected president, 1836 Dec. 7, I
   elected vice president, 1832 Dec. 5, I

Van Buren, Martin (*cont.*)
  Free Soil Party presidential
    candidacy, 1848 Aug. 9, I
  inaugurated, 1837 Mar. 4, I
  influence on 1828 presidential
    election, 1828 Dec. 3, I
  link to O.K. expression, 1840(1), IV
  neutrality proclamation, 1838 Jan. 5, I
  nominated for presidency, 1835 May
    20, I
  nominated for vice presidency, 1832
    May 21, I
  opposed Panama Conference, 1826
    June, I
  opposed Texas annexation, 1844 Apr.
    27, I
  presidential candidacy, 1836, I; 1847
    Nov., I; 1848 June 22, I
  renominated for presidency, 1840, I;
    1840 May 5, I
  vice presidency, 1833 Mar. 4, I
Vance, Cyrus, 1962 May 20, I; 1977 Feb.
  24, I; 1980 Apr. 26, I
Vanderbilt, Amy, 1974, IV
Vanderbilt, Cornelius, 1810, III; 1855(1), I
Vanderbilt, George W., 1892(4), II
Vanderbilt, William H., 1882(3), IV
Vanderbilt, William Kissam, 1881(4), IV;
  1904, IV
Vanderbilt University (Tenn.), 1878(1), III
Van Derbur, Marilyn, 1957 Sept. 7, IV
Vanderlyn, John, 1804, II; 1812(2), II
Van der Stucken, Frank, 1889 July 12, II
Van Doren, Carl, 1939 May 1, II
Van Doren, Charles, 1960 Oct. 17, II
Van Doren, Mark, 1939(1), II; 1940 May 6,
  II
Van Dorn, Earl, 1862 Mar. 6–7, I
Van Druten, John, 1944 Oct. 19, II; 1951
  Nov. 28, II; 1966 Nov. 20, II
Van Dusen, Henry P., 1975, III
Van Duyn, Mona, 1971 Mar. 4, II; 1991
  Apr. 9, II; 1992 June 14, II
Van Dyke, Dick, 1964 May 25(2), II; 1965
  Sept. 12, II
Van Dyke, Henry, 1896(1), II
Van Dyke, Vonda Kay, 1964 Sept. 12(1),
  IV
Van Fleet, James A., 1992, I
Van Fleet, Jo, 1956 Mar. 21, II
Van Gogh, Vincent, 1980, II; 1987 Nov.
  11, II; 1990 May 15, II
Vanguard 1, 1958 Mar. 17, III
Vanguard 3, 1959 Sept. 18, III
Van Houten, Leslie, 1971 Jan. 25, IV
Van Rensselaer, Stephen, 1812 Oct. 13, I
Van Ryn, John, 1929 July 5, IV; 1930 July
  4, IV; 1931 July 3–4, IV
Van Vleck, John H., 1977 Oct. 11, III
Vanzetti, Bartolomeo *see* Sacco-Vanzetti
  case
Varèse, Edgard, 1916(3), II; 1965, II
Vardon, Harry, 1900 Oct. 5, IV
Varney, William F., 1928 July 12, I; 1928
  Nov. 6, I
Vassar College (N.Y.):
  architecture, 1865(12), II
  Breuer-designed dormitory, 1951(5), II
  first woman astronomy professor,
    1865, III

Vassar College (N.Y.) (*cont.*)
  founded, 1861 Jan. 18, III
Vatican:
  clashed with American archbishop's
    authority, 1986 Sept. 4, III
  full U.S. diplomatic relations restored,
    1984 Jan. 10, I
Vaudeville:
  Harrigan and Hart, 1870(2), II
  Keith circuit, 1883(5), II
  Pastor originated, 1861, IV
  White Rats union, 1900(4), II
  Wow-Wows, The, 1910 Oct. 3, II
Vaughan, Sarah, 1990, II
Vaux, Calvert, 1857, IV; 1876(5), III
Vauxhall (N.Y.C.), 1811 Dec. 12, IV
Vealey, Claude E., 1971 June 23, I
Veblen, Thorstein, 1899(1), II
V-E Day, 1945 May 8, I
Vedder, Elihu, 1884(5), II
Veeck, Bill (William), 1986, IV; 1991 July
  21, IV
Vegetables *see* Fruits and vegetables;
  types
Velocipeding *see* Bicycling
Velvet, 1811(2), IV
Vending machines, 1929 Nov., III
Vendler, Helen, 1981 Jan. 5, II
Venereal disease:
  herpes simplex virus, 1981 July 9, III
  herpes spread, 1982, III
  increase, 1972 Apr. 4, III
  law to prevent spread of (N.Y.), 1938
    Apr. 12, III
Venezuela:
  boundary dispute with Great Britain,
    1895, I
Venturi, Ken, 1964 June 20, IV
Venus de Medici (statue), 1784(1), II
Venus (planet):
  Magellan probe, 1989 May 4, III
  Mariner 2 probe, 1962 Aug. 27(2), III;
    1962 Dec. 14, III
  Mariner 5 probe, 1967 June 14(2), III;
    1967 Oct. 19, III
  Pioneer 1 launched, 1978 May 20, III
  Pioneer 2 launched for rendezvous,
    1978 Aug. 8, III
Vereen, Will, 1928 July 11, I
Vermont:
  christened, 1763 Oct., IV
  constitution provision, 1777 July, I
  first permanent settlement,
    1720–1724, I
  fourteenth state to ratify U.S.
    Constitution, 1791 Mar. 4, I
  Kipling home, 1894(5), II
  slavery abolished, 1777 July, I
  universal male suffrage, 1777 July, I
  women's legal status improved,
    1847(2), IV
Vermont, University of, 1791 Nov. 3, III
Verne, Jules, 1873(1), II
Veronese, Paolo, 1989, II
Verrazano-Narrows Bridge (N.Y.C.), 1964
  Nov. 21(2), III
Versailles, Treaty of, 1919, I; 1919 July 10,
  I; 1919 Sept. 3, I; 1919 Nov. 19, I
Vesco, Robert, 1974 Apr. 28, I
Vesey, Denmark, 1822, I

Vespucci, Amerigo, 1507, II
Vestry Act, 1701(1), I; 1705(1), I; 1715, I
Veterans (*see also* Pensions; specific
  organizations):
  Administration Act signed, 1930 July
    3, I
  Administration raised to Cabinet
    level, 1988 Oct. 18, I
  Agent Orange disability benefits
    increased, 1991 Feb. 6, I
  American Revolution, 1783 May 13,
    IV; 1784(1), IV; 1881, IV; 1889(4),
    IV
  anti-Vietnam War protests, 1971 Apr.
    23, I
  Bonus Army, 1932 May 29, I
  Civil War, 1913 June 30, IV
  Civil War, last survivor died, 1959
    Dec. 19, IV
  Civil War, last Union Army survivor
    died, 1956, I
  first national encampment of Grand
    Army of the Republic, 1866 Nov.
    20, IV
  Forty and Eight Society, 1918(2), IV
  GI Bill, 1944 June 22, III; 1947(1), III
  GI bill signed, 1952 July 16, I
  Grand Army of the Republic, 1881, IV
  last Grand Army of the Republic
    encampment, 1949 Aug. 31, I
  narcotics addiction, 1971, I
  oldest to date died, 1988 July 13, IV;
    1990, I
  Soldiers' Bonus Bill, 1924 Mar. 18(1), I
  United Confederate organized, 1889
    June 10, I
Veterans Affairs, Department of:
  created, 1988 Oct. 18, I
Veterans' Day:
  pro-Vietnam War demonstrations,
    1969 Nov. 11, I
Vice presidency (*see also* Presidential
  elections; specific names):
  resignations, 1973 Oct. 10, I
  third to succeed to presidency, 1881, I
Vicious, Sid, 1979 Feb. 2, II
Vicksburg, Battle of (Miss.), 1863 July 4, I
Vicksburg convention, 1859 May 12, I
Vidal, Gore, 1957 Feb. 7, II; 1960 Mar. 31,
  II; 1964(1), II; 1983 Jan. 27, II; 1990(1),
  II
Videocassette recorders, 1986, III
  sales, 1988, II
Video games, 1983, II
Videotape, 1957 Jan. 21, III
Vidor, King, 1982, II
Vienna summit meeting, 1961 June 3–4, I
Viereck, Peter, 1949 May 2, II
Vietnam:
  Diem overthrown, 1963, I
  foreign aid, 1955 Jan. 1, I
  French defeat at Dien Bien Phu,
    1954, I
  Military Assistance Command (MAC)
    created, 1962 Feb. 8, I
  partition, 1954, I
  S. Vietnamese elections, 1967, I
  U.S. aid, 1964, I

Vietnam (*cont.*)
U.S. airlift plane crashed, 1975 Apr. 4, I
U.S. normalization talks, 1976 Nov. 12, I
U.S. normalization talks begun, 1977 May 3, I
U.S. officers killed, 1962 June 16, I
U.S. travel restrictions lifted, 1977 Mar. 18, I
Vietnam War (*see also* Cambodia; Conscientious objectors; Draft; Indochina; Laos; Pentagon Papers; Tonkin, Gulf of; Veterans; Vietnam War demonstrations:
Abrams relieved Westmoreland, 1968 June 10, I
Agent Orange victims compensated, 1991 Feb. 6, I
Agent Orange victims' fund, 1984 May 7, I
bombing of N. Vietnam halted, 1968 Oct. 31, I
bombing of N. Vietnam resumed, 1966 Jan. 31, I; 1966 Feb. 21, I; 1971 Dec. 26–30, I; 1972 Dec. 18, I
books on, 1972(1), II; 1977(1), II; 1980(1), II
Calley convicted, 1971, I; 1971 Mar. 29, I
clemency program for resisters extended, 1975 Jan. 31, I
concluded, 1975, I
Con Thien heavy casualties, 1967 July 2–7, I
Con Thien siege, 1967 Sept. 1–Oct. 4, I
cost to U.S., 1965 Apr. 26, I
Declaration of Honolulu, 1966 Feb. 8, I
defoliation, 1966 Sept. 23, I
demilitarized zone bombed, 1966 July 30, I
deserters and evaders offered amnesty, 1974 Sept. 16(2), I
draft resisters pardoned, 1977 Jan. 21, I
eight-point peace plan, 1969 May 14, I
enemy offensive, 1968 May 5, I
first B-52 bombers used on N. Vietnam, 1966 Apr. 12, I
first intentional shelling of Cambodian targets, 1966 May 1, I
first mass bombing raid, 1965 June 17, I
first Medal of Honor, 1964 Dec. 5, I
first U.S. air strike on central Hanoi, 1967 May 19, I
first U.S. combat forces, 1965 Mar. 8–9, I
five hundredth U.S. plane shot down over N. Vietnam, 1967 Apr. 4, I
Green Beret camp overrun, 1966 Mar. 10, I
Green Beret murder charges, 1969 July 31, I
Haiphong bombed, 1967 Apr. 20, I
Hamburger Hill captured, 1969 May 20, I

Vietnam War (*cont.*)
Hanoi and Haiphong bombed, 1966 June 29, I
heaviest bombing of N. Vietnam to date, 1966 May 30, I; 1966 Oct. 13, I; 1969 Apr. 24, I
herbicide phase-out, 1970 Dec. 23, I
Hill 875 taken by U.S., 1967 Nov. 22, I
Hue recaptured, 1968 Feb. 24, I
Khe Sanh siege lifted, 1968 Apr. 5, I
Kontum major battle, 1966 June 3–13, I
last refugees settled in U.S., 1975 Dec. 20, I
last U.S. ground combat forces withdrawn, 1972, I; 1972 Aug. 12, I
Loc Ninh attacked, 1967 Oct. 30–Nov. 4, I
longest U.S. war to date, 1968 June 23, I
memorial-design competition, 1981 June 6, II
military desertions, 1970 Jan. 2, I
mining of Haiphong harbor, 1972 May 8, I
mistreatment of U.S. POWs charged, 1967 Oct. 14, I
My Lai (Songmy) massacre, 1969 Nov. 16, I; 1971, I; 1971 Mar. 29, I
narcotics use, 1971, I; 1971 July 28, I
Navy jets shot down over China, 1967 Aug. 21, I
Nixon peace plan, 1970 Oct. 7, I
Nixon private pledge to S. Vietnam, 1975 Apr. 9, I
Nobel Peace Prize awards, 1973 Oct. 16(2), I
Operation Complete Victory, 1968 Apr. 8, I
Operation White Wing, 1966 Feb. 22, I
Paris peace talks, 1968 May 3, I; 1968 May 10, I; 1969 Jan. 16, I
Paris peace talks stalled, 1972, I
peace agreement signed, 1973 Jan. 27(1), I
plays on, 1977 Apr. 24, II
racial brawl, 1972 Oct. 12–13, I
secret peace proposals rejected, 1969 Nov. 3, I
Sontay raided, 1970 Nov. 21, I
Tet offensive, 1968 Jan. 30–Feb. 24, I
truce rebuffed, 1967 Mar. 28, I
U.S. casualties, 1965, I; 1965 Aug. 16, I; 1965 Nov. 20, I; 1966, I; 1966 Sept. 18–24, I; 1967, I; 1967 June 1, I; 1969 Apr. 3, I; 1970, I
U.S. expenditures, 1968, I
U.S. infantry co. refused orders to fight, 1969 Aug. 24, I
U.S. troop levels, 1965 July 28, I; 1966, I; 1966 Mar. 2, I; 1966 June 11, I; 1967 July 22, I; 1967 Dec. 20, I; 1970, I
U.S. troop reductions, 1969, I; 1969 June 8, I; 1969 July 8, I; 1969 Dec. 15, I; 1970 Apr. 20, I; 1971, I
N. Vietnamese air attacks on U.S. aircraft, 1966 Apr. 23, I

Vietnam War (*cont.*)
N. Vietnamese offensive, 1968 Jan. 30–Feb. 24, I; 1972, I
Vietnam Moratorium Day, 1969 Oct. 15, I; 1969 Nov. 14, I
Westmoreland libel suit, 1985 Feb. 17, III
Vietnam War demonstrations:
against increased U.S. involvement, 1965, I
against U.S. invasion of Cambodia, 1970, I
anti and prowar, 1969, I
antiwar rally (Wash., D.C.), 1970 May 9, I
antiwar scientists blacklisted, 1969 Oct. 8, III
attempted shutdown of N.Y.C. induction center, 1967 Dec. 5, I
Bernstein's counterconcert (Wash., D.C.), 1973 Jan. 19, II
Berrigan plot, 1970 Nov. 27, I; 1971 Jan. 12, I
D. Berrigan seized, 1970 Aug. 11, III
bomb exploded in Capitol (Wash., D.C.), 1971, I; 1971 Mar. 1, I
Chicago Eight trial, 1969 Sept. 24, I
Chicago Seven, 1973 Dec. 4, I
Democratic National Convention (Chicago, Ill.), 1968 Aug. 29, I; 1968 Dec. 1, I
Harrisburg Seven case dropped, 1972 Sept. 5, I
on Hiroshima-Nagasaki bombing anniversaries, 1966 Aug. 6, I
Honor America Day prorally (Wash., D.C.), 1970 July 4, I
International Days of Protest, 1966, I
Kent State shootings, 1970 May 4, I; 1974 Nov. 8, I
Kent State shooting settlement, 1979 Jan. 4, I
Mayday protest (Wash., D.C.), 1971 May 3, I
nationwide, 1965 Oct. 15–16, I
N.Y.C., 1967 Apr. 15, I
at Nixon's inauguration, 1969 Jan. 20(1), I
Pentagon clash (Wash., D.C.), 1967 Oct. 21–22, I
pro-America demonstrations, 1969 Nov. 11, I
protesters arrested (Wash., D.C.), 1971, I
prowar parade (N.Y.C.), 1967 May 13, I
San Francisco (Calif.), 1967 Apr. 15, I
Spock and Coffin indicted, 1968 Jan. 5, I
veterans' antiwar protests (Wash., D.C., and San Francisco, Calif.), 1971 Apr. 23, I
Wash., D.C., 1965 Nov. 27, I
Wash., D.C., demonstrations, 1966 May 15, I
Viking Project:
reached Mars, 1976 July 20, III
terminated, 1977 May 30, III
Vilas, Guillermo, 1977 Sept. 10–11, IV

Villa, Pancho (Francisco), 1916 Mar. 9, I; 1916 Mar. 15(2), I; 1917 Jan. 28, I

Village Voice, The (newspaper), 1976 Feb. 11–18, II

Villanova University (Pa.), 1848 Mar. 10, III

Villard, Oswald Garrison, 1909(1), I

Vincennes (ship), 1988 July 3, I

Vincent, Francis F. (Fay), 1989 Sept. 13, IV; 1990 July 30, IV; 1992 July 24, IV; 1992 Sept. 7, IV

Vincent, Marjorie Judith, 1990 Sept. 8, IV

Vines, H. Ellsworth, Jr., 1931 Aug. 20, IV; 1932 July 1, IV; 1932 Aug. 21, IV

Vinland, 986–1599, I
 map called fake, 1974 Jan. 25, II

Vinson, Carl, 1981, I

Violence *see* Bombs and bombings; Crime; Riots and mob violence; Terrorism;

Virginia (*see also* Jamestown colony):
 Assembly Acts printed, 1682(1), II
 British royal family ties, 1662(2), IV
 Capitol, 1789(3), II
 colonists settle N.C., 1653, I
 early accounts, 1610, II; 1612, II
 early history book, 1705, II
 first black governor, 1989 Nov. 8, I
 readmitted to Union, 1869 Apr. 10, I; 1870 Jan. 26, I
 seceded, 1861 Apr. 17, I
 social stratification, 1670–1690, IV
 tenth state to ratify U.S. Constitution, 1788 June 25, I

Virginia, University of:
 founded, 1819(5), III

Virginia City (Nev.), 1867, IV

Virginia (ship), 1861 Apr. 19–20, I; 1862 Mar. 8, I; 1862 Mar. 9, I; 1862 May 11, I

Virginia "tea party", 1706, I

Virgin Islands:
 negotiations to purchase, 1900 Dec. 29, I
 purchased, 1916 Aug. 4, I
 U.S. acquired, 1902 Jan. 24, I

Viruses:
 AIDS identified, 1984 Apr. 23, III
 cancer-causing, 1971 July 2, III; 1975 Oct. 16, III
 discoverer of AIDS, 1991 May 6(1), III
 first genetically altered to be released, 1986 Apr. 22, III
 herpes simplex, 1981 July 9, III
 interferon synthesis, 1980 Jan. 16, III
 legionnaires' disease-causing isolated, 1978 Aug. 11, III

Visconti, Gary, 1965 Feb. 13, IV; 1967 Jan. 18–21, IV

Vitamins:
 A and B discovered, 1912(1), III
 B-12 for pernicious anemia, 1948(2), III
 C high dosage against colds, 1970 Nov. 18, III
 C isolated, 1932, III
 folic acid discovered, 1945(2), III
 pellagra caused by deficiency of, 1915(2), III

V-J Day, 1945 Aug. 15, I

Vocabulary of Words and Phrases Peculiar to the United States:
 (Pickering), 1816, II; 1816(1), III

Vocational training:
 enrollment in federally supported classes, 1930(1), III
 federal board created, 1917 Feb. 23, III
 first free (Md.), 1750(4), III

Vogel, Herbert and Dorothy, 1992 July 7, II

Voight, Jon, 1979 Apr. 4, II

Volcanoes:
 Lassen Peak (Calif.), 1914 May 30, III
 Mt. St. Helens erupted (Wash. State), 1980 May 18, I

Volcker, Paul A., 1979 July 25, I; 1987 June 2, III

Volney, Comte de, 1795(2), III

Volstead, Andrew, 1921 Apr. 25, I

Volstead Act, 1919 Oct. 28, I; 1921, IV; 1932, V

von Bekesy, Georg, 1961 Oct. 19, III

von Braun, Wernher, 1977, III

von Euler, Ulf, 1970 Oct. 15, III

Vonnegut, Kurt, Jr., 1963(1), II; 1969(1), II; 1973(1), II; 1973 Nov. 10, II; 1976(1), II; 1979(1), II; 1985(1), II

Von Tilzer, Harry, 1897, II; 1899, II

Voting rights (*see also* Women's suffrage):
 Act upheld, 1966 Mar. 7, I
 blacks granted (Wash., D.C.), 1867 Jan. 8, I
 blacks prohibited from primaries ruled unconstitutional (Tex.), 1927 Mar. 7, I
 blacks rejected (Va.), 1867 Mar. 5, I
 eighteen-year-old in effect, 1971 June 30, I
 eighteen-year-old ruled constitutional, 1970 Dec. 21, I
 federal registrars to help blacks, 1959 Sept. 7, I
 Fifteenth Amendment guarantees, 1869 Apr. 10, I; 1870 Mar. 30(2), I
 first state to restrict black (Miss.), 1890 Nov. 1, I
 first universal male suffrage (Vt.), 1777 July, I
 L. Johnson legislative proposals, 1965 Mar. 15, I
 laws extending, 1818(1), I
 literacy requirement (Mass.), 1857 May 1, I
 literacy tests, 1923 Oct. 16, I
 literary requirements abolished, 1975 Aug. 6, I
 machines authorized, 1899 Feb. 14, III
 poll tax abolished, 1962 Aug. 27(2), I; 1964 Jan. 23, I
 poll taxes unconstitutional, 1966 Mar. 25, I
 restrictive colonial (Mass.), 1631 May 18, I
 secret ballot first used (Ky.), 1888(1), I
 Twenty-Fourth Amendment barring poll tax passed, 1962 Aug. 27(2), I
 Twenty-Fourth Amendment ratified, 1964 Jan. 23, I

Voting rights (*cont.*)
 Washington (D.C.) residents denied, 1878 June 11, I

Voting Rights Act, 1966 Mar. 7, I
 extended, 1975 Aug. 6, I

Voyager Project:
 closest approach to Jupiter, 1979 Mar. 5, III
 found Saturn rings and moons, 1980 Nov. 12, III
 Saturn data, 1981 Aug. 25, III
 Uranus data, 1986 Jan. 24, III

Wabash College (Ind.), 1834(4), III

Waco University (Tex.), 1861 Dec. 24, III

Waddell, Reed, 1880(2), IV

Wade, Virginia, 1968 Sept. 9, IV

Wadkins, Lanny, 1977 Aug. 14, IV; 1987 Aug. 9, IV

Wage and Hours Act, 1938 June 25, I

Wage Stabilization Board:
 established, 1945 Dec. 31, III

Wagner, Lindsay, 1977 Sept. 11(1), II

Wagner, Richard, 1904(4), II

Wagner, Robert F., 1933 Aug. 5, I; 1991, I

Wagner-Connery Act *see* National Labor Relations Act

Wagner-Steagall Act, 1937 Sept. 2, I

Wainwright, Jonathan, 1942 Apr. 9, I; 1942 May 6, I

Wainwright Building (St. Louis, Mo.), 1890(4), II

Waitz, Grete, 1979 Oct. 21(1), IV; 1986 Nov. 2, IV; 1988 Nov. 6, IV

Wakarusa War, 1855 Nov. 26, I

Wake Forest College (N.C.), 1838 Dec. 26, III

Wake Island, 1941 Dec. 22, I

Wakeman, Frederic, 1946(1), II

Waksman, Selman A., 1952 Oct. 23, III; 1973, III

Walcott, "Jersey Joe", 1947, IV; 1948 June 25, IV; 1949, IV; 1951 July 18, IV; 1952 Sept. 23, IV; 1953, IV

Wald, George, 1967 Oct. 18(1), III

Wald, Lillian D., 1893(5), III

Waldheim, Kurt, 1987 Apr. 27, I

Waldseemüller, Martin, 1507, II

Walken, Christopher, 1979 Apr. 4, II

Walker, Alice, 1983 Apr. 18, II; 1983 Apr. 24, II

Walker, Anne, 1638(1), IV

Walker, Barbara, 1947 Sept. 6, IV

Walker, Cyril, 1924 June 6, IV

Walker, James J., 1925 Nov. 3, I; 1931 Mar. 17, I

Walker, Kathryn, 1976 May 17, II

Walker, LeRoy, 1992 Oct. 11, IV

Walker, Moses Fleetwood, 1884(6), IV

Walker, Nancy, 1992, II

Walker, William, 1855(1), I

Walking:
 long-distance record, 1867(4), IV
 popular spectator sport, 1870(2), IV
 Weston's feats, 1861(1), IV

Wall, Art, 1959, IV; 1959 Apr. 5, IV

Wallace, Dewitt, 1981, II

Wallace, George C.:
 antischool desegregation actions, 1963 Sept. 10, III

Wallace, George C. (*cont.*)
assailant convicted, 1972 Aug. 4, I
presidential candidacy, 1968, I; 1968 Oct. 3, I; 1968 Nov. 5, I
shot (Md.), 1972 May 15, I
University of Ala. desegregated, 1963 June 11, III
withdrew presidential candidacy, 1964 July 19, I
Wallace, Henry A.:
communist support, 1948 Aug. 2–6, I
died, 1965, I
elected vice president, 1940 Nov. 5, I
labor declined support, 1948 Feb. 2, III
presidential candidacy, 1948 July 23–25, I; 1948 Nov. 2, I
vice presidency, 1941 Jan. 20, I
vice presidential candidacy, 1940 July 15–19, I
Wallace, Irving, 1990, II
Wallace, John Findley, 1904 Feb. 29, I
Wallace, Lew, 1880(1), II
Waller, Fats, 1978 May 9, II
Wallis, Hal B., 1986, II
Wallop, Douglass, 1955 May 5, II
Wall Street Journal (newspaper), 1889 July 8, II
Walsh, Donald, 1960 Jan 7(1), III
Walsh, Lawrence E., 1988 Mar. 16, I
Walsh, Thomas J., 1923 Oct. 25, I
Walt Disney World and Epcot Center (Fla.), 1988, II
Walter, Bruno, 1962, II
Walters, Barbara, 1976 Apr. 22, II
Walton, Sam Moore, 1987, III; 1989 July 9, III; 1992, III
Wambaugh, Joseph, 1973(1), II
Wanamaker, John, 1862(3), IV
Wanamaker Building (N.Y.C.), 1956 July 14–15, I
Wanger, Walter, 1968, II
War (*see also* Pacifism; specific war names):
Geneva Convention ratified, 1882 Mar. 16, I
longest U.S. to date, 1968 June 23, I
War bonds *see* Government bonds
Ward, Aaron Montgomery, 1872, III
Ward, Artemus (Charles Farrar Browne), 1862, II; 1865(2), II
Ward, Elizabeth, 1981 Sept. 12, IV
Ward, Holcombe, 1904(3), IV
Ward, John Quincy Adams, 1864, II
Ward, Lester Frank, 1883, III
Ward, Nathaniel, 1647(1), II
War Department, U.S.:
established, 1789 Aug. 7, I
Ware, William, 1837, II
Warhol, Andy, 1968 June 3, II; 1987, II; 1988 May 3, II
War Industries Board, 1918, III
War Information, Office of (OWI), 1942 June 13, III
Waring, Fred, 1984, II
War Labor Board (WLB), 1942 Jan. 12(1), III; 1945 Dec. 31, III
War Manpower Commission, 1942, III; 1942 Apr. 18, III; 1945 Aug. 14, III

War Mobilization, Office of, 1943 May 27, III
Warmus, Harold E., 1989 Oct. 9, III
Warner, Charles Dudley, 1874(1), II; 1890(1), IV
Warner, Jack L., 1978, II
Warner, Olin Levi, 1888(2), II
Warner, William W., 1977 Apr. 18, II
Warner Books, 1988 Apr. 25, II
Warner Communications, Inc., 1989 July 24, III
Warnes, Jennifer, 1983 Feb. 23, II
War of Jenkins' Ear, 1735–1739, I; 1740 Jan., I; 1742 June 9, I
War of the Austrian Succession, 1740–1744, I; 1745–1749, I
War of 1812:
Battle of Lake Champlain, 1814 Sept. 11, I
Battle of Lake Erie, 1813 Sept. 10, I
Battle of New Orleans, 1815, I; 1815(3), IV
Battle of Thames (Canada), 1813 Oct. 5, I
British naval victory, 1813 Aug. 14, I
British surrendered York, Canada, 1813 Apr. 27, I
Channing on, 1812 July 23, III
Chesapeake-Leopard affair, 1807, I
declared, 1812, I
derisive term *Coodies*, 1812(1), IV
"Don't give up the ship", 1813 June 1, I
events leading to, 1811, I
financing, 1812 Mar. 14, I; 1812 June 30, III
Fort McHenry (Md), 1814, II
Hartford Convention, 1814 Dec. 15–Jan. 4, 1815, I
Hornet captured *Peacock*, 1813 Feb. 24, I
Hull surrendered Detroit, 1812 Aug. 16, I
Lake Erie naval engagement, 1812 Oct. 9, I
Old Ironsides (*Constitution*), 1812 Aug. 19, I; 1812 Aug. 19, IV; 1812 Dec. 29, I
stimulated banking expansion, 1812(2), III
term *Uncle Sam* first used, 1812, IV
Treaty of Ghent, 1814, I; 1815 Feb. 11, I
Van Rensselaer defeated at Queenstown Heights, 1812 Oct. 13, I
Washington (D.C.) captured, 1814 Aug. 24, I
women's participation, 1812 Aug. 19, IV
War Powers Act, 1973 Nov. 7, I; 1983 Sept. 20, I
War Production Board (WPB), 1942 Jan. 16, III; 1945 May 10, III; 1945 Aug. 20, III
Warren, Earl:
died, 1974, I
Kennedy assassination investigation, 1963 Nov. 29, I

Warren, Earl (*cont.*)
resigned from Supreme Ct., 1968 June 13, I
retired as chief justice, 1969 June 23, I
separate but equal doctrine, 1896 May 18, I
vice presidential candidacy, 1948 June 24(1), I
Warren, Harry, 1980 Aug. 25, II
Warren, Josiah, 1827 May, III
Warren, Leonard, 1960, II
Warren, Mercy Otis, 1775(3), II; 1779, II; 1805(2), II
Warren, Robert Penn, 1946(1), II; 1947 May 5, II; 1950(1), II; 1955(1), II; 1958 Mar. 11, II; 1958 May 5, II; 1971(1), II; 1979 Apr. 16, II; 1986 Feb. 26, II; 1987 Apr. 17, II; 1989, II
Warren Commission, 1963 Nov. 29, I; 1964 Sept. 27, I
War Revenue Act, 1898 June 10, I
Wartime Prohibition Act, 1918 Nov. 21, I
Warwick, Dionne, 1969 Mar. 12, II; 1971 Mar. 16, II; 1980 Feb. 27, II
Washington, Booker T., 1881 July 4, III; 1901 Oct. 16, IV; 1915, II
Washington, Denzel, 1990 Mar. 26, II
Washington, George (*see also* Mount Vernon):
biographies, 1800, II; 1804(4), II; 1807(1), IV; 1835, II
born, 1732 Feb. 22, I
Cambridge (Mass.) troop command, 1775 July 3, I
Christ Church (Alexandria, Va.), 1773 Feb. 27, III
Continental Army commander, 1775 June 15, I
Conway Cabal, 1777 Sept. 25–Dec. 23, I
Crossing the Delaware painting, 1850(7), II
death commemorations, 1800(2), II
died, 1799 Dec. 14, I
equestrian statue of, 1856 July 4, II
Farewell Address, 1719(3), II; 1796 Sept. 17, I
first inaugural ball, 1789 May 7, IV
first town named for (N.C.), 1776(2), IV
French and Indian War, 1754 May 28, I; 1754 July 4, I; 1755 July 9, I
Germantown (Pa.) attack, 1777 Oct. 4, I
holiday menus, 1795–1799, IV
monuments, 1815 July 4, II
Mount Vernon, 1757, II
neutrality proclamation, 1793 Apr. 22, I
New Year's Day reception, 1791 Jan. 1, IV
Ohio territory survey, 1753 Oct. 31, I
portraits, 1772, II
presidential inauguration, 1789 Apr. 30, I
reelected president, 1792 Dec. 5, I
resigned military command, 1783 Dec. 24, I
retired from hunting, 1785(3), IV
Samuel Davis on, 1755(2), II

Washington, George (*cont.*)
  second inauguration, 1793 Mar. 4, I
  statues of, 1821(3), II; 1833(1), II;
    1864(6), II
  Stuart portrait of, 1796(2), II
  theater going, 1789(2), IV
  Trinity Church (N.Y.C.), 1790(5), III
  Valley Forge (Pa.), 1777 Dec. 17, I
  Webster on, 1838, IV
Washington, Harold, 1983 Apr. 12, I
Washington, Martha, 1800 Apr. 3, IV
Washington, Treaty of, 1826 Jan. 24, I;
  1871 May 8, I; 1877 Nov. 23, I
Washington, University of, 1861(3), III
Washington, Walter E., 1967 Sept. 28, I;
  1973 May 30, II
Washington and Jefferson College (Pa.),
  1802 Jan. 15, III
Washington and Lee University (Va.), 1782
  Oct., III
Washington College (Md.), 1782 Apr., III
Washington (D.C.):
  abortion rights march, 1992 Apr. 5, I
  anti-Vietnam War protests, 1965 Nov.
    27, I; 1966 May 15, I; 1967 Oct.
    21–22, I; 1970 May 9, I; 1971, I;
    1971 May 3, I
  became U.S. capital, 1800 June, I
  captured by British, 1814 Aug. 24, I
  civil rights march, 1983 Aug. 27, I
  commission government, 1878 June
    11, I
  congressional representation granted,
    1970 Sept. 22, I
  design, 1800 June, I
  farmers' rally, 1978 Mar. 15, III
  first black commissioner, 1967 Sept.
    28, I
  first mayor and city council elected,
    1974 Nov. 5, I
  Freedom March, 1963 Aug. 28, I
  Honor America Day rally, 1970 July 4,
    I
  Ku Klux Klan mass rally, 1925 Aug. 8,
    I
  McMillan Commission report for
    reconstruction of, 1902(4), II
  Mayday anti-Vietnam War protest,
    1971 May 3, I
  National Theater disbanded, 1974
    June 12, II
  Poor People's March, 1968 May 2, I;
    1968 June 24, I
  public ground landscaping, 1851(7), II
  segregation ordered ended, 1967 June
    19, III
  territorial government, 1871 Feb. 21,
    I
  territorial government abolished, 1874
    June 20, I
  Union Station renovation, 1988 Sept.
    29, II
  Vietnam Moratorium Day, 1969 Nov.
    14, I
  Vietnam veterans' antiwar protest,
    1971 Apr. 23, I
  women admitted to private clubs,
    1988 June 20, IV
Washington (D.C.) summit meeting, 1990
  June 1, I

Washington *Evening Star* (newspaper),
  1981 Aug. 8, II
Washington Memorial Arch (N.Y.C.), 1890
  May 30, II
Washington Monument (Wash., D.C.),
  1836(3), II; 1885 Feb. 21, II
  dynamite plot, 1965 Feb. 16, I
Washington Opera Co., 1967 May 19, II
Washington (State):
  Franklin mine disaster, 1894 Apr. 24,
    I
  Indian land claims settled, 1988 Aug.
    27, I
  Mt. St. Helens erupted, 1980 May 18,
    I
  statehood, 1889 Nov. 11, I
  territory formed, 1853 Mar. 2, I
  women's suffrage adopted, 1910 Nov.
    8, I
Washington University (Mo.), 1853 Feb.
  22, III
Wasp (ship), 1942 Sept. 15, I
Wasserman, Dale, 1966 June 16, II
Wasserstein, Wendy, 1989, II; 1989 Mar.
  30, II; 1989 June 4(1), II; 1992, II
Waste disposal (*see also* Pollution):
  early, 1690–1699, IV
  first underground sewer, 1704(2), IV
  furnaces, 1885(2), III
  salvage drives, 1944(2), III
  sea dumping banned, 1990 Nov. 1, I
  treatment programs, 1970 Feb. 4, I
  World War II drives, 1943(2), III
Watauga Association, 1772, I
Watch and Ward Society (Boston, Mass.),
  1898(3), II
Watches *see* Clocks and watches
Watergate (*see also* Pentagon Papers):
  administration involvement
    uncovered, 1973, I
  administration resignations, 1973 Apr.
    27, I; 1973 Apr. 30, I
  All the President's Men (Woodward
    and Bernstein), 1974(1), II
  books on, 1975(1), II; 1976(1), II
  convicted officials' appeals rejected,
    1977 May 23, I
  Cox named special prosecutor, 1973
    May 25, I
  Dean testimony before Senate
    committee, 1973 June 25–29, I
  Democratic Party headquarters
    burglarized (Wash., D.C.), 1972
    June 17, I
  FBI destruction of records, 1973 Apr.
    27, I
  Haldeman, Ehrlichman, Mitchell
    sentenced, 1975 Feb. 21, I
  impeachment inquiry, 1974 Feb. 6, I;
    1974 July 30, I
  indictments, 1972 Sept. 15, I
  Jaworski named special prosecutor,
    1973 Nov. 1, I
  lawsuit against CREEP settled, 1974
    Feb. 28, I
  Liddy and McCord convicted, 1973
    Jan. 30, I
  McCord letter implicating
    administration, 1973 Mar. 23, I

Watergate (*cont.*)
  Nixon impeachment resolutions, 1973
    Oct. 23, I
  Nixon impeded investigation, 1974
    Aug. 5, I
  Nixon pardoned, 1974 Sept. 8, I
  Nixon resignation, 1974 Aug. 8, I;
    1974 Aug. 9, I
  Nixon TV address denying
    involvement, 1973 Apr. 30, I
  Nixon TV interview on, 1977 May 4, I
  Saturday night massacre, 1973 Oct.
    20, I
  Senate Select Committee opened
    hearings, 1973 May 17, I
  White House investigation of, 1972
    Aug. 29, I
  White House tapes issue, 1973 Oct.
    23, I; 1973 Oct. 31, I; 1974, I
  White House tapes revealed, 1973
    July 16, I
  White House tapes subpoenaed, 1974
    July 24, I
  White House tapes' transcripts
    released, 1974 Aug. 5, I
  White House tapes' 18½-minute gap,
    1973 Nov. 21, I; 1974 Jan. 15, I
Waterman, Lewis E., 1883(1), III
Waterman, Robert H., Jr., 1983(1), II
Water Pollution Control Act, 1972 Oct.
  18, III
Waters, Ethel, 1950 Jan. 5, II; 1977, II
Water supply (*see also* Plumbing):
  Calif. Project, 1972 Apr. 14, III
  Catskill Aqueduct (N.Y.C.), 1917, III
  Clean Water Act, 1987 Feb. 4, I
  Colorado Aqueduct opened, 1941
    June 18, III
  early Phila. (Pa.), 1797(2), IV
  first Phila. aqueduct, 1801 Oct. 19, III
  Guantánamo (Cuba) cut off, 1964 Feb.
    6, I
  Lake Mead Reservoir, 1936(4), III
  N.Y.C. storage at all-time low, 1965
    Feb. 5, I
  omnibus bill signed, 1992 Oct. 30, I
  rationing (Los Angeles, Calif.), 1977
    July 1, I
  sluicing process improvement,
    1853(2), III
Waterways *see* Canals; Rivers and
  waterways; specific names
Watkins, Aaron S., 1908 July 15–16, I;
  1912 July 10–12, I; 1920 July 21–22, I;
  1920 Nov. 2, I
Watkins Glen (N.Y.), 1973 July 29, II
Watson, Arthur K., 1974, III
Watson, Charles, 1971 Jan. 25, IV
Watson, Claude A., 1936 May 5–7, I; 1947
  June 26–28, I; 1948 Nov. 2, I
Watson, Elkanah, 1810 Oct. 1, IV
Watson, James D., 1962 Oct. 18, III
Watson, John B., 1919(1), III
Watson, Thomas A., 1915 Jan. 25(2), III
Watson, Thomas E., 1896 July 25, I; 1904
  July 4–5, I; 1904 Nov. 8, I; 1908 Apr.
  2–3, I; 1908 Nov. 3, I
Watson, Thomas J., Jr., 1990(1), II

Watson, Tom, 1977, IV; 1977 Apr. 10, IV; 1978, IV; 1979, IV; 1980, IV; 1981 Apr. 12, IV; 1982, IV; 1982 June 20, IV; 1984, IV; 1987 June 21, IV; 1987 Nov. 1, IV; 1989, IV

Watt, James, 1983 Oct. 9, I

Watts, Isaac, 1719(1), II; 1735–1739, II; 1784(2), II

Watts riots (Los Angeles, Calif.), 1965 Aug. 11–16, I

Waverley (Scott), 1814(2), II

Waverly (Tenn.), 1978 Feb. 22, I

Wayland, Francis, 1855 Sept. 17, III

Wayne, Anthony, 1779 July 15, I; 1794 Aug. 20, I

Wayne, David, 1954 Mar. 28, II

Wayne, John, 1970 Apr. 7(1), II; 1979, II

Wayside Inn (Sudbury, Mass.), 1690(1), II

WCTU *see* Women's Christian Temperance Union

Wealth *see* Income and wealth, personal

Weapons sales *see* Arms sales

Weather (*see also* specific conditions, e.g., Rain; Snowstorms):
  artificial, 1947 Oct. 29, III
  average temperature rise, 1990, III
  cold spell destruction (Midwest), 1910 Apr. 23, III
  damage and casualties, 1983, I
  "Everybody talks about the" quote, 1890(1), IV
  freak New England summer, 1816(2), IV
  Ore. and Calif. disaster areas, 1964 Dec. 22, I
  record cold wave, 1985 Jan. 20–21, I
  U.S. Bureau established, 1870 Feb. 9, III
  warmest winter to date, 1992, I
  Weather Bureau created, 1890 Oct. 1(2), I
  winter deep freeze, 1982 Jan. 9–17, I

Weatherford, William (Red Eagle), 1813, I

Weather satellites:
  first, Tiros 1, orbited, 1960 Apr. 1, III
  first station in space launched, 1959 Feb. 17, III
  Nimbus 1, 1964 Aug. 28, III
  Pegasus 1 launched, 1965 Feb. 16, III
  world watch network (U.S.-Soviet), 1962 Apr. 23, III

Weather Underground, 1971, I; 1971 Mar. 1, I; 1981 Oct. 20, IV

Weaver, Fritz, 1970 Apr. 19, II

Weaver, James B., 1878 Feb. 22, I; 1880 June 9, I; 1892 July 4–5, I; 1892 Nov. 8, I

Weaver, Mike ("Hercules"), 1980 Mar. 31, IV; 1982 Dec. 10, IV

Weaver, Robert C., 1966 Jan. 17(1), I

Weaving *see* Textile industry

Webb, Aston (Sir), 1907(7), II

Webb, Frank E., 1928 Nov. 6, I

Webb, James E., 1992, III

Webb Alien Land-Holding Bill (Calif.), 1913 May 19, I

Webber, Andrew Lloyd *see* Lloyd Webber, Andrew

Webber, Charles W., 1844, II

Webb-Kenyon Interstate Liquor Act, 1913 Mar. 1, I

Weber, Max, 1915(4), II

Webster, Daniel:
  Dartmouth College case, 1819, III
  Hayne debate, 1830 Jan. 19–27, I
  oratory, 1825 June 17, II
  presidential candidacy, 1836, I; 1836 Dec. 7, I
  presidential nomination, 1835 Jan.(1), I
  protective tariff advocate, 1828(2), III
  Senate Hall of Fame, 1957 Apr. 30, I
  statue of, 1876(9), II
  supported Clay compromise, 1850 Mar. 7, I
  views on slavery, 1841 Oct. 27, I
  on G. Washington, 1838, IV

Webster, Noah, 1783, II; 1789(1), II; 1790 May 31, I; 1791(3), II; 1793(2), II; 1806(2), II; 1806(3), IV; 1828(2), II
  bowdlerized Bible, 1833(3), II
  Spelling Book reissued, 1855(7), II

Webster-Ashburton Treaty, 1839 Feb. 12, I; 1842, I

Wedtech Corp., 1988 Feb. 11, I; 1988 July 5, I

Weems, Mason L. (Parson), 1800, II; 1815(1), II

Weidman, Charles, 1975, II

Weidman, Jerome, 1959 Nov. 23, II; 1960 May 2, II

Weightlifting, 1885 Dec. 20, IV

Weigle, Luther, 1976, III

Weinberg, Steven, 1979 Oct. 16(2), III

Weinbrecht, Donna, 1992 Feb. 8–23, IV

Weinman, Adolph Alexander, 1938(4), II

Weinstock, Jack, 1961 Oct. 14, II

Weir, Benjamin (Rev.), 1985 Sept. 18, I

Weir, John F., 1865(1), III

Weisgall, Hugo, 1959 Apr. 26, II

Weiss, George, 1972, IV

Weiss, Peter, 1965, II; 1966 June 16, II

Weiss, Ted, 1992, I

Weissmuller, Johnny, 1984, II

Weitz, Paul, 1973 May 14, III; 1983 Apr. 4–9, III

Welch, Priscilla, 1987 Nov. 1, IV

Welch, Robert H. W., Jr., 1961 Mar. 8, I; 1985, I

Weld, Theodore Dwight, 1835(2), I; 1839(1), I

Weld, Theresa, 1914 Mar. 21, IV

Welfare (*see also* Child welfare; Poverty; Settlement houses):
  guaranteed minimum income request, 1969 Aug. 8, III
  reform bill, 1988 Oct. 13, I
  relief recipients, drop in, 1938 Dec. 13, III

Welk, Lawrence, 1992, II

Weller, Charles, 1867(2), IV

Weller, Thomas H., 1954 Oct. 21, III

Welles, Orson, 1938 Oct. 30, II; 1985, II

Welles, Sumner, 1961, I

Wellesley College (Mass.), 1870(5), III

Wells, Sharlene, 1984 Sept. 15, IV

Welsh v. United States, 1970 June 15, I

Welty, Eudora, 1946(1), II; 1954(1), II; 1972(1), II; 1973 May 7, II; 1980 May 1, II

Wertherism, 1774(2), II

Wescott, Glenway, 1987, II

Wesley, Charles, 1735–1739, II

Wesley, John, 1735–1739, II; 1736 Feb. 5, III

Wesleyan University (Conn.), 1831 May 26, III

West, Alanson M., 1884 May 28, I

West, Benjamin, 1792(5), II; 1802, II; 1805(3), II

West, Mae, 1935(1), III; 1980, II

West, Nathaniel, 1970(1), II

West Coast Hotel v. Parrish, 1937 Mar. 29, III

Westcott, Edward Noyes, 1898(1), II

Western Reserve University (Ohio), 1826 Feb. 7, III

Western Union Telegraph Co., 1856, III

Westinghouse, George, 1868, III; 1895(1), III

Westinghouse Electric Corp.:
  strike, 1956 Mar. 20, III

Westminster Abbey (G.B.), 1882(3), II

Westminster College (Mo.), 1851 Feb. 18, III

Westminster Kennel Club *see under* Dogs

Westmoreland, William C., 1968 June 10, I; 1985 Feb. 17, III

Weston, Edward P., 1861(1), IV; 1867(4), IV

West Point *see* United States Military Academy

West Point Foundry (N.Y.), 1818(1), III

West Virginia:
  floods, 1990 Apr. 14, I
  statehood, 1863 June 20, I

West Virginia University, 1867(4), III

Westward expansion (*see also* Covered wagons; Cowboys; Frontier; Public land; names of states):
  books on frontier life, 1845, II
  Boone's exploits, 1765–1769, IV
  "Buffalo Bill's" Wild West Show, 1883, IV
  Donner party ordeal, 1847, I
  early account of lands, 1722(1), II
  fiction about, 1911, II
  fiction's popularity, 1844, II
  Frémont expeditions, 1842(1), I; 1843 May 29, I; 1845 Spring, I
  French-English competition, 1725–1729, I
  Grey's books on, 1906, II
  Homestead Act, 1862, I
  Hunt's arrival in Ore., 1812 Feb. 15, I
  Lewis and Clark Expedition, 1804, I
  Mountain Meadows Massacre (Utah), 1857 Sept. 11, I
  Plan of Union, 1801(1), III
  Powell's exploration of Colorado R., 1869(2), I
  Smith's expeditions, 1826, I; 1830 Apr. 10–July 16, I
  Southwest, 1821, I
  Wilderness Road, 1775 Mar. 10, III; 1790(2), III

Westwood, Jean, 1972 July 14, I

Wetherby, Isaac Augustus, 1852(4), II

Wettig, Patricia, 1990 Sept. 16, II; 1991 Aug. 5, II

Wexley, John, 1930 Feb. 13, II

Whaling:
    Captain Paddock legend, 1690, IV
    first sperm whale captured, 1712, III
    hunting licenses, 1971 Mar. 1, III
    Nantucket (Mass.), 1690(3), III
    oil and tallow, 1815(2), III
    rise and decline, 1815, III
    scrimshaw, 1829(1), II

Wharton, Edith:
    Age of Innocence, The, 1920(1), II
    Fruit of the Tree, The, 1907(1), II
    House of Mirth, The, 1905(1), II
    play based on novelette, 1935 Jan. 7(1), II
    Pulitzer Prize, 1921 May 29, II

Wharton School of Finance and Economy (Pa.), 1881(3), III

Wheat *see* Grain

Wheaton College (Ill.), 1860 Feb. 15, III

Wheeler, Burton K., 1924 July 4, I

Wheeler, Harvey, 1962(1), II

Wheeler, Hugh, 1973 Feb. 25, II; 1974 Mar. 11, II; 1979 Mar. 1, II

Wheeler, Joseph, 1898 June 24, I

Wheeler, William A., 1876 June 14–16, I

Wheeler-Lea Act, 1938 June 24, I

Wheeling Steel Corp., 1963 Apr. 9, III

Whig Party:
    discord during Tyler administration, 1841, I; 1841 June 12, I; 1841 Sept. 11, I
    emergence, 1828(2), I
    endorsed Know-Nothing presidential candidates, 1856 Sept. 17, I
    first president, 1841 Mar. 4, I
    formed, 1834, I
    N.Y. *Tribune*, 1841 Apr. 10, II
    presidential election of 1836, 1836, I
    Scott-Graham ticket, 1852 June 16–21, I

Whipple, George H., 1926(1), III

Whiskey Rebellion (Pa.), 1794 July–Nov., I

Whiskey Ring scandal, 1875, I

Whiskey Trust, 1886(4), III; 1887, III

Whist, c1745, IV

Whistler, James McNeill:
    born, 1834 July 10, II
    caused furor in art world, 1863(1), II
    elected Royal Society of British Artists presidents, 1886(3), II
    Freer Gallery show (Wash., D.C.), 1984, II
    Japanese influence, 1864(5), II
    libel suit against Ruskin, 1877(3), II

Whistler's Mother, 1871(2), II

Whitaker, Alexander (Rev.), 1611, III; 1613, III

White, Andrew Dickson, 1865(3), III

White, Betty, 1986 Sept. 21, II

White, Dan, 1978 Nov. 27, I

White, E. B., 1985, II

White, Edward H., II, 1965 June 3, III; 1967 Jan. 27, III

White, Hugh L., 1835 Jan.(2), I; 1836, I; 1836 Dec. 7, I

White, John, 1585, IV; 1585 Aug., I; 1587 Aug. 18, IV

White, Stanford:
    killed by Thaw, 1906, IV
    Newport (R.I.) Casino, 1881(4), II
    Washington Memorial Arch (N.Y.C.), 1890 May 30, II

White, Theodore H., 1962 May 7, II; 1969(1), II; 1975(1), II; 1978(1), II; 1986, II

White, William Allen, 1895 June 1, II; 1896 Aug. 15, II

White, William (Bill), 1989 Feb. 3, IV

White, William S., 1955 May 2, II

Whitefield, George, 1730–1734, III; 1739 Aug., III; 1740 Mar. 25, IV

Whitehead, Mary Beth, 1987 Mar. 31, IV

White House (Wash., D.C.):
    burned, 1814 Aug. 24, I
    restored, 1818 Jan.1, IV
    televised tour, 1962 Feb. 14, II
    work begun, 1792(2), II
    Wyeth's one-man show, 1970 Feb. 19, II

Whiteman, Paul, 1967, II

White Slave Act *see* Mann Act

White Wing Operation, 1966 Feb. 22, I

Whitman, Charles J., 1966 Aug. 1, I

Whitman, Malcolm D., 1898(3), IV; 1899(3), IV

Whitman, Marcus, 1836 Sept. 1, I

Whitman, Narcissa Prentiss, 1836 July 4, IV

Whitman, Walt:
    books on, 1980(1), II; 1984(1), II
    Drum-Taps, 1865(4), II
    eyewitness Civil War reports by, 1863(5), IV
    final collection, 1891(1), II
    Leaves of Grass, 1855(4), II; 1892(1), II
    "Out of the Cradle Endlessly Rocking", 1859(5), II
    Passage to India (poems), 1871(1), II
    on visiting brother in Union Army, 1862 Dec. 29, IV

Whitney, Caspar, 1889(5), IV

Whitney, Eli, 1793 Oct. 28, III; 1798(2), III

Whitney, John Hay, 1982, II

Whitney Museum (N.Y.C.), 1914(4), II; 1966 Sept. 28, II; 1968 July 23, II; 1971 Mar. 18, II
    addition, 1985, II
    Rauschenberg retrospective, 1991, II

Whittier, John Greenleaf:
    abolition pieces, 1838(1), II
    "Barefoot Boy", 1856(1), II
    born, 1807(1), IV
    edited Brainard's writings, 1832(7), II
    Home Ballads, Poems and Lyrics, 1860(7), II
    In War Time, 1864(1), II
    Moll Pitcher, 1813(1), IV
    N.E. poetry, 1843(3), II
    Poems second edition published, 1849(1), II
    "Skipper Ireson's Ride", 1808 Oct. 30, IV
    Snow-Bound, 1866(1), II

Whitworth, Kathy, 1965, IV; 1966, IV; 1967, IV; 1967 July 9, IV; 1968, IV; 1968 June 24, IV; 1970, IV; 1971, IV; 1971 June 13, IV; 1972, IV; 1973, IV; 1975 June 1, IV

Who Wrote the Bible? (Gladden), 1891(6), III

Wichita State University, 1970 Oct. 2, IV

Wicker, Tom, 1975(1), II

Wickersham, George W., 1931, I

Wickes, Charles, 1838 May 18, I

Wiedfeldt, Otto L., 1922 May 13, I

Wiener, Norbert, 1964, III; 1965 Mar. 9, II

Wiesel, Elie, 1986 Oct. 14, I

Wiesel, Tlosten, 1981 Oct. 9, III

Wiesner, Jerome, 1962 June 8, III

Wiest, Dianne, 1987 Mar. 30, II

Wiggin, Kate Douglas, 1903, II

Wigglesworth, Edward, 1722 Jan. 24, III

Wigglesworth, Michael, 1660–1669, II

Wigner, Eugene P., 1963 Nov. 5, III

Wigs *see* Hair and wigs

Wilander, Mats, 1987 Sept. 12, IV; 1988 Sept. 10–11, IV

Wilbur, Richard, 1957 Mar. 12, II; 1957 May 6, II; 1987 Apr. 17, II; 1988(1), II; 1988 May 18, II; 1989 Mar. 30, II

Wilder, Laura Ingalls, 1957, II

Wilder, L. Douglas, 1989 Nov. 8, I

Wilder, Thornton, 1927(1), II; 1931(1), II; 1938(1), II; 1938 May 2, II; 1942 Nov. 18, II; 1943 May 3, II; 1968 Mar. 6, II; 1975, II
    Pulitzer Prize, 1928 May 7, II

Wilderness, Battle of the (Va.), 1864 May 5–6, I

Wildlife (*see also* Endangered and extinct species; Environmental protection; Nature):
    first federal refuge (Fla.), 1903(2), III
    T. Roosevelt's interest in, 1887(5), III

Wild West shows, 1878(2), IV

Wiley, Harvey W., 1906 June 30, I

Wilhelm II (Kaiser of Germany), 1918 Nov. 9, I

Wilkes, Charles, 1840 Jan 19., I

Wilkins, Maurice H. F., 1962 Oct. 18, III

Wilkins, Roy, 1981, I

Wilkinson, James, 1806, I

Will, George F., 1990(1), II

Willamette University (Ore.), 1853 Jan. 12, III

Willard, Emma, 1814, III; 1821(1), III

Willard, Jess, 1968, IV

Willard, Samuel (Rev.), 1726, II

Willard, Simon, 1802(1), IV

Willcox, James, 1857 June 2, III

William and Ellen (Smith), 1811(1), II

William and Mary, the College of (Va.):
    charter, 1693 Feb. 8, III
    cornerstone laid, 1695, II
    first professorship in mathematics and philosophy, 1717, III
    Jefferson's experiences at, 1760–1764, IV
    Phi Beta Kappa founded, 1776 Dec. 5, III
    school for Indians, 1723(1), III
    university status, 1779(1), III

William III (King of Great Britain), 1696(3), I

William Jewell College (Mo.), 1849 Feb. 27, III

Williams, Billy, 1987 July 26, IV

Williams, Harrison, 1980 Feb. 2, I

Williams, Henry, 1763(1), III

Williams, John, 1973 Apr. 10, II; 1980 Jan. 10, II

Williams, John (writer), 1705–1709, II

Williams, Norris (II), 1914 June 13, IV; 1916 June 12, IV

Williams, Roger, 1631 Feb. 5, III; 1636 June, I; 1638, III; 1643(1), II; 1643 Mar., I; 1644, II

Williams, Samuel W., 1908 Apr. 2–3, I

Williams, Saundra, 1968 Sept. 7, IV

Williams, Ted, 1966 July 25, IV

Williams, Tennessee, 1947 Dec. 3, II; 1948 May 3, II; 1948 Oct. 6, II; 1951 Feb. 3, II; 1951 Mar. 25, II; 1953 Mar. 19(2), II; 1955 May 2, II; 1958 Jan. 7, II; 1960 Nov. 10, II; 1983, II

Williams, T. Harry, 1970 Mar. 2, II; 1970 May 4, II

Williams, Thomas, 1975 Apr. 16, II

Williams, Vanessa, 1983 Sept. 17, IV; 1984 July 23, IV

Williams, Walter, 1959 Dec. 19, IV

Williams, William Carlos, 1950 Mar. 16, II; 1963, II; 1963 May 6, II; 1963 May 22, II

Williamsburg Bridge (N.Y.C.), 1903(6), II

Williams College (Mass.), 1793 Feb. 22, III
    first fraternity house in U.S., 1876(2), IV

Williamson, Michael, 1990 Apr. 12, II

Williams v. Florida, 1970 June 22, I

Willig, George, 1977 May 26, IV

Willis, Bruce, 1987 Sept. 20, II

Willis, Nathaniel Parker, 1840(4), II

Willis, Sara Payson (Fanny Fern), 1853(1), II

Willkie, Wendell L.:
    One World, 1943(1), II
    presidential candidacy, 1940, I; 1940 June 24–28, I; 1940 Nov. 5, I

Willoughby, W. W., 1890(4), III

Wills, estates, and trusts:
    Edwards heirs fraud, 1880(3), IV

Wills, Garry, 1979 Jan. 15, II

Wills, Helen, 1923 Aug. 18, IV; 1924 Aug. 16, IV; 1925 Aug. 24, IV; 1927 July 2, IV; 1927 Aug. 30, IV; 1928 July 7, IV; 1928 Aug. 27, IV; 1929 July 5, IV; 1929 Aug. 24, IV; 1930 July 4, IV; 1931 Aug. 20, IV; 1932 July 1, IV; 1933 July 8, IV; 1935 July 6, IV; 1938 July 1, IV

Wills, Maury, 1974 Sept. 10, IV

Willson, Meredith, 1957 Dec. 19, II; 1984, II

Wilmot Proviso, 1846 Aug., I

Wilson, Alexander, 1808(2), III

Wilson, Arthur M., 1973 Apr. 10, II

Wilson, August, 1987 Apr. 16, II; 1987 June 7, II; 1990 Apr. 12, II

Wilson, Charles E., 1950 Dec. 16, I; 1954 May 13, III

Wilson, Charles Thomson Rees, 1927 Nov. 10, III

Wilson, Edmund, 1931(1), II; 1946(1), II; 1948(2), II; 1960(1), II; 1972, II; 1975(1), II

Wilson, Edward O., 1979 Apr. 16, II; 1991 Apr. 9, II; 1992(1), II

Wilson, Harriet E., 1859 Sept. 5, II

Wilson, Henry, 1872 May 23, I; 1872 June 5–6, I; 1873 Mar. 4, I

Wilson, Hugh R., 1938 Nov. 14–18, I

Wilson, Kenneth G., 1982 Oct. 13, III

Wilson, Lanford, 1973 Feb. 7, II; 1980 Apr. 14(1), II

Wilson, Robert W. (physicist), 1978 Oct. 17, III

Wilson, Sloan, 1955(1), II

Wilson, Teddy, 1986, II

Wilson, Woodrow:
    appointed Brandeis to Supreme Court, 1916 Jan. 28, III
    on automobile, 1906 Mar. 1, I
    biography, 1992(1), II
    birthplace made national shrine (Va.), 1941 May 4, II
    books on, 1940 May 6, II
    born, 1856 Dec. 28, I
    elected president, 1912 Nov. 5, I
    established Federal Reserve System, 1913, III
    Fourteen Points, 1918 Jan. 8, I; 1919 Jan. 18, I
    German war debts, 1922, I
    inaugurated president, 1913 Mar. 4, I; 1917 Mar. 5, I
    married, 1915 Dec. 18, IV
    merchant vessels armed, 1917 Mar. 9, I
    Mexican civil disorder, 1913 Aug. 27, I
    Mexican intervention, 1914 Apr. 19, I
    Nobel Peace Prize, 1920 Nov. 20, I
    peace conference, 1918 Nov. 18, I; 1919, I; 1919 Jan. 18, I; 1919 Feb. 14, I
    peace notes, 1916 Dec. 18, I
    presidential candidacy, 1912, I; 1912 June 25–July 2, I; 1916, I; 1916 June 14–16, I
    recognized Chinese Republic, 1913 May 2, I
    reelected president, 1916 Nov. 7, I
    stroke, 1919 Sept. 26, I
    Tampico (Mex.) incident, 1914 Apr. 9, I
    tariff message delivered before Congress, 1913 Apr. 8, I
    Ten Points, 1917 Jan. 22, I
    U-boat note to Germany, 1916 Apr. 18, I
    Versailles Treaty campaign, 1919 Sept. 3, I
    vetoed immigrants' literacy requirement bill, 1915 Jan. 2, I
    women's suffrage advocacy, 1918(4), III
    "world safe for democracy" speech, 1917 Apr. 2, IV
    World War I entry, 1917, I; 1917 Apr. 2, IV
    World War I neutrality, 1914, I

Wilson's Creek, Battle of (Mo.), 1861 Aug. 10, I

Winchell, Alexander, 1878(1), III

Winchell, Walter, 1972, II

Winchester, Oliver F., 1860(4), III

Windmills see Mills and milling

Windows and doors:
    first sliding sash-windows (Va.), 1699(2), II

Windstorms (Plains states), 1984 Feb. 5–28, I

Wine:
    colonial favorites, 1710–1714, IV
    first commercial, 1647(3), IV

Wing, Simon, 1892 Aug. 28, I; 1892 Nov. 8, I

Wings (group), 1975 Mar. 1(1), II

Winslow, Edward, 1620(1), III; 1622, II

Winslow, Josiah, 1673, I

Winslow, Samuel, 1641 Oct., III

Winsor, Kathleen, 1946(2), II

Winston, Harry, 1978, II

Winston Co., John C., 1960 Feb. 29, II

Winters, Shelley, 1960 Apr. 4, II; 1964 May 25(2), II; 1966 Apr. 18, II

Winthrop, John, 1629 June 27, I; 1630 May 29, II; 1640–1649, I; 1640–1649, III; 1648(1), III; 1761(1), III; 1773(3), III

Winthrop, John IV, 1735–1739, III; 1746(1), III

Winthrop, John, Jr., 1662 May 3, I

Winthrop, Theodore, 1862(2), II

Winwood, Steve, 1987 Feb. 24, II

Wire, barbed, 1873 Oct. 27, III; 1874, III

Wireless see Broadcasting

Wiretapping (see also Watergate):
    FBI illegal, indictment for, 1977 Apr. 7, I
    of M. L. King's phones, 1969 June 6, I
    of U.S. embassy in Moscow, 1964 May 19, I

Wirt, William, 1803, II; 1831 Sept. 26, I

Wisconsin:
    first to adopt primary election system, 1900 Sept. 18, I
    Peshtigo destroyed by fire, 1871 Oct. 8, I
    statehood, 1848 May 29, I
    states' rights case, 1859, I
    tornado, 1899 June 12, I

Wisconsin, University of:
    chartered, 1848 July 26, III

Wise, Isaac Mayer, 1875(1), III

Wise, John, 1710–1717, II

Wise, Stephen S., 1931 Mar. 17, I

Wise, W. Max, 1958(2), III

Wistar, Caspar, 1739, III

Wister, Owen, 1902(1), II

Witchcraft:
    first execution (Mass.), 1648(1), III
    Mather role, 1690–1699, III; 1692 Oct., III
    Moll Pitcher, 1813(1), IV
    Salem trials, 1674(2), II; 1692 Mar., III; 1697(2), III

Witherspoon, Tim, 1984 Mar. 9, IV

Wittenmyer, Annie, 1874(1), I

Wittig, Georg, 1979 Oct. 16(1), III

WNYC-TV (N.Y.C.), 1962(2), II

Wodehouse, P. G., 1975, II

Wohlhuter, Rick, 1973 May 27, IV

Woldin, Judd, 1973 May 30, II

Wolfe, Thomas, 1929(1), II; 1935(1), II; 1940(1), II; 1956(1), II; 1957 Nov. 28, II
Wolfe, Tom, 1980 May 1, II; 1987(1), II
Wollstonecraft, Mary, 1794(1), IV
Woman's Christian Temperance Union, 1874(1), I
Woman's Journal (publication), 1870(2), I
Woman's Medical College of Pennsylvania, 1850 Mar. 11, III
Women (*see also* Abortion; Mothers; Pregnancy and birth; Prostitution; Sexual harassment; Spinsterhood; Witchcraft; Women's rights; Women's suffrage):
    AIDS case, 1990 June 30, III
    in armed forces, 1942 May 14, I; 1942 July 30, I; 1942 Nov. 23, I; 1943 Feb. 13, I
    artistic glorification of, 1880(5), II
    artists and sculptors, 1860(5), II; 1881(3), II; 1894, II
    art museum opened (Wash., D.C.), 1987 Apr. 7, II
    astronomy, 1847 Oct., IV
    beauty of Carolinian, 1753 May 10, IV
    changing status, c1735, IV
    Civil War service, 1861 June 10, IV
    clubs, 1889(1), IV
    colonial illiteracy, 1655, III
    colonizers, 1617, IV; 1620, IV; 1658, IV; 1666, IV; 1728(3), IV
    in Congress, 1917 Apr. 2, I; 1992, I
    dramatizations of modern, 1912 Feb. 5, II
    early editorial employment, 1852(1), IV
    education, 1742(2), III; 1765(4), IV; 1787(1), III; 1814, III; 1821(1), III; 1833(5), II; 1837 Nov. 8, III; 1838 Dec. 28, III; 1870(5), III; 1871(3), III; 1879(4), III; 1880(4), III; 1884 Mar. 12, III; 1889(2), III
    employment, 1905(3), II; 1918(4), III; 1923 Apr. 9, III; 1951, III
    employment of new mothers, 1988 June 15, III
    Episcopal ordination approved, 1976 Sept. 16, III
    Episcopal ordination compromise, 1989 Sept. 28, III
    equality espoused in Alcuin (Brockden), 1797(1), IV
    etiquette manual, 1847(5), IV
    exercise, 1837(6), IV
    first ACLU president, 1991 Jan. 27, I
    first AIAW collegiate basketball championship, 1972 Mar. 19, IV
    first all-woman jury (Md.), 1656 Sept. 22, I
    first artificial heart recipient, 1985 Dec. 19, III
    first Arts and Letters Institute president, 1979 Feb. 27, II
    first athlete to win over $100,000 in year, 1971, IV
    first athletic scholarship, 1973 May 21, IV
    first black pilot, 1978 Apr. 19, III
    first black senator, 1992, I

Women (*cont.*)
    first black to win Rhodes scholarship, 1979 Sept. 9, III
    first Boston Marathon competitor, 1972 Apr. 17, IV
    first Cabinet member, 1933 Mar. 4(2), I
    first Conservative rabbi, 1985 May 12, III
    first doctor, 1849(3), III
    first elected state governor (Conn.), 1974 Nov. 5, I
    first elected to French Academy, 1980 Mar. 6, II
    first Episcopal bishop, 1988 Sept. 24, III
    first Episcopal priest, 1977 Jan. 1, III
    first Episcopal priests irregularly ordained, 1974 July 29, III
    first executed in Calif., 1941 Nov. 21, IV
    first executed in 22 years (N.C.), 1984 Nov. 2, I
    first FBI agents, 1972 July 7(1), IV
    first governor, 1925 Jan. 5, I
    first governor of Ky., 1983 Nov. 8, I
    first hockey pro player, 1992 Sept. 23, IV
    first horse thief, 1839(1), IV
    first hospital solely for, 1849(3), III
    first inclusion in Little 500 bicycle race, 1988 Apr. 22, IV
    first International Arts Festival, 1975 Mar. 9, II
    first jockey, 1969 Feb. 7, IV
    first jockey stakes winner, 1973 Mar. 1(1), IV
    first lawyer in colonies (Md.), c1640, I
    first lawyers in U.S., 1869(1), I
    first magazine for (Boston, Mass.), 1784 May, II
    first mannequin, 1844(4), IV
    first mayor of Chicago (Ill.), 1979 Apr. 3, I
    first on Supreme Ct., 1981 July 7, I
    first ordained minister, 1860(1), IV
    first poet (Mass.), 1678, II
    first presidential candidate, 1884(1), I
    first rabbi, 1972 June 3, III
    first retail clerks, 1850(3), IV
    first strike involving (R.I.), 1824, III
    first to conduct at Metropolitan Opera (N.Y.C.), 1976 Jan. 13, II
    first to finish N.Y.C. Marathon, 1973 Sept. 30, IV
    first to fly across Atlantic, 1928 June 3, III
    first to graduate at top of Naval Academy class, 1984 May 23, III
    first to head Republican National Committee, 1974 Sept. 16(1), I
    first to preside over House of Representatives, 1921 June 20, I
    first to solo fly over Atlantic, 1932 May 20, III
    first to swim English Channel, 1926 Aug. 6, IV
    first TV anchorwoman, 1976 Apr. 22, II

Women (*cont.*)
    first university president, 1978 Oct. 6, III
    first U.S. astronaut, 1983 June 18–24, III
    first U.S. poet laureate, 1992 June 14, II
    first U.S. senator, 1922 Oct. 3, I
    first vice presidential candidate, 1984 July 16–19, I
    first white in Ore. Territory, 1836 July 4, IV
    first winning jockey, 1969 Feb. 22, IV
    Gibson Girl as ideal, 1895, IV
    Godey's Lady's Book, editorial employment of, 1852(1), IV
    golf firsts, 1986 June 1, IV
    History of the Condition of Women in Various Ages and Nations (Child), 1835(4), II
    home opened for released convicts, 1844(5), IV
    horseback riding, 1855(3), IV
    in journalism, 1828, II
    Jewish rabbis, 1986 Aug. 2, III
    labor conditions, 1900(4), III
    lawyers, 1879 Feb. 15, I
    legal process, 1701(3), I
    Little League baseball opened to girls, 1974 June 12, IV
    lung cancer increasing, 1980 Jan. 14, III
    Marine Corps general, 1978 May 11, I
    medical education, 1848 Nov. 1, III; 1850(1), IV; 1850 Mar. 11, III
    military service, 1812 Aug. 19, IV
    minimum wage law upheld, 1937 Mar. 29, III
    most admired, 1958 Jan. 15, IV
    N.Y.C. Marathon boycotted, 1972 Oct. 1, IV
    nursing, 1865(1), IV
    ordination, 1955 May 23, III; 1992, III
    Outdoor Girl ideal, 1909(2), IV
    publications for, 1883(4), II; 1889, II
    refused admission to antislavery convention (London), 1840(3), IV
    rising status, 1701(3), I
    scientists, 1865, III; 1921 May 20, III
    second in space, 1984 Aug. 30–Sept. 5, III
    service academy graduates, 1980 May 28, III
    smoking, 1890(2), IV; 1904 Sept. 28, IV; 1908 Jan. 21, IV
    sports, 1880(1), IV
    sports participation increase, 1990, IV; 1991, IV
    teaching profession, 1852(2), IV
    waitresses, 1853(5), IV
    F. Wright's lectures, 1825, IV
    writers, 1813, II; 1853(1), II
Women's Clubs, Greater Federation of, 1889(1), IV
Women's Conference, National (Houston, Tex.), 1977 Nov. 18–21, I
Women's Political Caucus, National, 1971 July 10–11, I

Women's rights (*see also* Equal
Employment Opportunity; Equal Rights
Amendment; Women's suffrage):
  admitted to military academies, 1975
    Sept. 28, I
  admitted to Princeton's eating clubs,
    1991 Jan. 21, IV
  admitted to Rotary Club, 1987 May 4,
    IV
  admitted to Yale Skull and Bones,
    1991 Oct. 24, IV
  antisexual harassment rules, 1980 Apr.
    11, I
  Bloomer's style of dress, 1850, IV
  coeducational high school sports
    upheld, 1978 Jan. 9, IV
  credit application discrimination
    barred, 1974 Oct. 29, IV
  draft exclusion upheld, 1981 June 25,
    I
  equal athletic program federal
    funding decision, 1981 Feb. 23(1),
    III
  equal participation in school sports
    ruling, 1975, IV; 1975 June 3(2), IV
  equal pay for equal work, 1963, III;
    1963 June 10, III
  equal property (N.Y.) (Miss.) (Me.),
    1848(2), IV
  expansion of role in Catholic Church,
    1988 Apr. 11, III
  failed voting attempt, 1872(2), I
  first national convention (Worcester,
    Mass.), 1850 Oct. 23–24, I
  Fuller's advocacy, 1845, II; 1846(2), II
  improved in Vt., 1847(2), IV
  Jaycees full membership, 1984 July 3,
    I
  largest gathering since 1848, 1977
    Nov. 18–21, I
  Lily magazine, 1853(3), IV
  Ms. magazine started, 1972 July 1, II
  New England Woman's Club
    organized, 1868(1), I
  N.Y. petition, 1836(1), I
  objection to designation as "female",
    1855(1), IV
  private club admissions upheld, 1988
    June 20, IV
  property rights, 1836(1), I; 1847(2), IV
  Seneca Falls (N.Y.) convention, 1848,
    IV; 1848 July 19–20, I
  sex discrimination ruling, 1989 May 1,
    I
  Sexual Politics (Millett), 1970(1), II
  Southern Baptist resolution opposing
    ordination of women, 1984 June 14,
    III
  spouse benefits ruling, 1973 May
    14(1), I
  *Vindication of The Rights of Women,
    A*, (Wollstonecraft), 1794(1), IV
  Woman's Journal, 1870(2), I
Women's suffrage:
  first colony to grant women suffrage
    (N.J.), 1776 July 2, I
  first state to grant suffrage (Wyo.),
    1890 July 10, I
  first suffrage (Wyoming Territory),
    1869 Dec. 10, I

Women's suffrage (*cont.*)
  first women's suffrage magazine, 1853
    Feb., II
  National Woman Suffrage Association,
    1869 May 15, I
  Revolution, The, suffrage newspaper,
    1868(2), I
  suffrage association, 1869 May 15, I
  suffrage newspaper *The Revolution*,
    1868(2), I
  Wash. (state) adopted women's
    suffrage, 1910 Nov. 8, I
  Wilson's advocacy of women's,
    1918(4), III
  women granted (Colo.), 1893 Nov. 7, I
  women granted (N.Y.S.), 1917 Nov. 6,
    I
  women's attempt to test Fourteenth
    Amendment, 1872(2), I
  women's suffrage constitutional, 1922
    Feb. 27, I
  women's suffrage initiated, 1639(1), I
  Wyoming Territory grants first
    women's, 1869 Dec. 10, I
Wonder, Stevie, 1974 Mar. 2, II; 1975 Mar.
  1(1), II; 1977 Feb. 19, II
*Wonder-Working Providence of Sions
  Saviour*, 1650–1659, II
Wood, Craig, 1941 Apr. 6, IV; 1941 June
  7(1), IV
Wood, Gordon S., 1992(1), II
Wood, Grant, 1930(3), II; 1932(5), II; 1942,
  II; 1983, II
Wood, Harvey W., 1992 Mar. 9, III
Wood, Jethro, 1813, III
Wood, John, 1976 Apr. 18, II
Wood, Joseph ("Smoky Joe"), 1985, IV
Wood, Leonard:
  Rough Riders, 1898 Apr. 22(3), I; 1898
    June 24, I
Wood, Sidney B., 1931 July 3–4, IV
Wood, Tim, 1968 Jan. 19–20, IV; 1969
  Feb. 1–2, IV; 1969 Mar. 2, IV; 1970 Feb.
  6–7, IV; 1970 Mar. 7, IV
Wooden, John, 1975 Mar. 31, IV
Woodford, Stewart L., 1898 Apr. 20, I
Woodruff, Robert W., 1979 Nov. 8, III;
  1985, III
Woodruff, Wilford, 1887(1), III
Woods, Rose Mary, 1973 Nov. 21, I
Woodstock Music and Art Fair (N.Y.), 1969
  Aug. 15–18, IV
  film, 1970, II
Woodward, C. Vann, 1982 Mar. 12, II
Woodward, Joanne, 1958 Mar. 26, II; 1978
  Sept. 17, II; 1985 Sept. 22, II
Woodward, Robert, 1974(1), II; 1976(1), II
Woodward, Robert Burns, 1965 Oct. 21(2),
  III
Woodworth, Samuel, 1826(4), II
Wool:
  protective tariffs, 1827 Feb. 28, I;
    1897, I
Woolley, John G., 1900 June 27–28, I
Woolley, Monty, 1963, II
Woolman, John, 1743, I; 1754, I; 1793(3),
  II
Woolson, Albert, 1956, I
Woolworth, Frank W., 1879, III

Woolworth Building (N.Y.C.), 1908, III;
  1913(3), II; 1981, II
Woolworth Corp., 1992 Jan. 6, III
Worden, Alfred M., 1971 July 26, III
Work day and week:
  5-day, 1932, III; 1933 Oct. 2, III
  8-hour day, 1867(2), III; 1868 June
    25(1), I; 1912 June 19, III; 1916
    Sept. 3, III
  10-hour day, 1840 Mar. 31, III
  35-hour work week, 1962, III
  40-hour week, 1926(5), III; 1940 Oct.
    24, III
  48-hour week, 1943 Feb. 9, III
  54-hour week (N.Y.S.), 1912 Oct. 1, III
Workers' Party:
  presidential ticket, 1924 July 10, I;
    1928 May 27, I
Workingmen's National Party, 1872 May
  23, I
Workmen's compensation law, 1915 July
  13, III
Works Progress Administration (WPA),
  1935 May 6, I; 1936, II; 1936(2), II
  abolished, 1942 Dec. 4, III
  renamed, 1939(3), III
World Bank, 1986 July 1, III
World Book Co., 1960 Sept. 28, II
World Council of Churches, 1954 Aug. 15,
  III
World Court:
  Senate killed U.S. participation in,
    1935 Jan. 29, I
  U.S.-Nicaragua dispute, 1984 Nov. 26,
    I
  U.S. rejected membership, 1926, I
  U.S. withdrew from Nicaragua case,
    1985 Jan. 18, I
World fairs see Fairs
World Journal Tribune (newspaper), 1966
  Sept. 12(2), III
World (newspaper), 1961 Oct. 12, II
World Trade Center (N.Y.C.), 1970 Dec.
  23, II; 1977 May 26, IV
World War I:
  Aisne-Marne offensive, 1918 July
    18-Aug. 6, I
  Amiens offensive, 1918 Aug. 8, I
  armistice, 1918, I
  Austria-Hungary armistice, 1918 Nov.
    3, I
  Austrian archduke assassinated, 1914
    June 28, I
  Battle of Belleau Wood, 1918 June
    6–25, I
  British trade blacklist, 1916 July 18,
    III
  casualties, 1918, I; 1918 June 6–25, I
  Château-Thierry battle, 1918 June 4, I
  conservation efforts, 1918 Jan. 26, IV
  cost, 1918, I
  covenant, 1919 Feb. 14, I
  debts and reparations, 1922, I; 1924,
    III; 1926 Apr. 29, I
  energy conservation, 1917 Nov. 18, IV
  Espionage Act, 1917 June 15, I
  false armistice, 1918 Nov. 7, I
  first U.S. military engagement, 1917
    Nov. 3, I

World War I (*cont.*)

first U.S. troops in Europe, 1917 June 26, I

Ford's Peace Ship, 1915 Dec. 4, IV

Fourteen Points, 1918 Jan. 8, I; 1919 Jan. 18, I

German note on submarine warfare, 1916 Jan. 7, I

German note pledging merchant vessel safety, 1916 May 4, I

German peace initiative, 1918 Oct. 5, I

German spy ring uncovered in U.S., 1915 July 15, I

German submarine warfare renewed, 1917 Jan. 31, I

Hommes 40-Chevaux 8, 1918(2), IV

Housatonic sunk, 1917 Feb. 3, I

"Lafayette, we are here," quote, 1917 July 4, IV

Liberty Loan Act, 1917 Apr. 24, I; 1917 Oct. 1, III; 1918 Apr. 6, III; 1918 Oct. 19, III

Lusitania declared unarmed when attacked, 1915 May 31, I

Lusitania sinking, U.S.-German note exchanges, 1915 May 13, I; 1915 May 28, I; 1915 June 7, I; 1915 June 9, I; 1915 July 8, I; 1915 July 21, I

Lusitania sunk, 1915 May 7, I

Meuse-Argonne battle, 1918 Sept. 26-Nov. 11, I

peace treaty, 1921 Aug. 25, I

plays about, 1918(3), II

propaganda, 1914(2), IV

Public Information Committee created, 1917 Apr. 14, II

St. Mihiel action, 1918 Sept. 12–13, I

Second Battle of Marne, 1918 July 15, I

Sedition Act, 1918 May 16, I

Selective Service Act passed, 1917 May 18, I

ship launching, 1918 July 4, III

stock exchanges closed, 1914 July 31, III

Treaty of Versailles, 1919, I; 1919 July 10, I; 1919 Sept. 3, I; 1919 Nov. 19, I

Unknown Soldier buried (Arlington, Va.), 1921 Nov. 11, II

U.S. arming of merchant vessels, 1917 Mar. 9, I

U.S. economic mobilization, 1918, III; 1918 Aug. 9, III

U.S. entry, 1917, I; 1917 Apr. 2, IV

U.S. German occupation troops returned, 1923 Jan. 10, I

U.S.-German relations severed, 1917 Feb. 3, I

U.S.-Germany state of war ended, 1921 July 2, I

U.S. losses, 1917 Nov. 3, I

U.S. neutrality, 1914, I

U.S. protested German U-boats, 1916 Apr. 18, I

U.S. "Rainbow" Division (42nd) in France, 1917 Nov. 30, I

World War I (*cont.*)

Wilson at peace conference, 1918 Nov. 18, I; 1919, I; 1919 Jan. 18, I; 1919 Feb. 14, I

Wilson peace notes, 1916 Dec. 18, I

"world safe for democracy" speech, 1917 Apr. 2, IV

Zimmermann note, 1917 Feb. 24, I

World War II:

airborne invasion of Holland unsuccessful, 1944 Sept. 17–27, I

Aleutians taken by U.S., 1943 May 30, I

Allied advances, 1944, I

Anzio landing, 1944 Jan. 22, I

Athenia sunk, 1939 Sept. 3(2), I

Atlantic Charter, 1941 Aug. 9–12, I

atomic bomb dropped on Nagasaki, 1945 Aug. 9, I

"Axis Sally" died, 1988 June 25, IV

Bataan fell, 1942 Apr. 9, I

Battle of Java Sea, 1942 Feb. 27-Mar. 1, I

Battle of Leyte Gulf, 1944 Oct. 23–26, I

Battle of Midway, 1942 June 4–6, I

Battle of the Bismarck Sea (Pacific), 1943 Mar. 2–4, I

Battle of the Bulge, 1944 Dec. 16, I

Battle of the Coral Sea, 1942 May 4–8, I

Berlin bombed, 1944 Mar. 6, I

Bizerte (Tunisia) captured by U.S., 1943 May 7, I

books on, 1943(1), II; 1948, II; 1948(1), II

Bougainville Island (Solomons) invaded by U.S., 1943 Nov. 1, I

Brittany fell to Allies, 1944 Aug. 8, I

Cairo conference, 1943 Nov. 22, I

Carlson's Raiders, 1942 Aug. 18, I

cartoons, 1944(1), IV

Casablanca conference, 1943 Jan. 14, I

Cassino evacuated, 1944 May 18, I

civilian impact, 1942, IV

civilian measures, 1942, III

coal mines seized, 1943 May 1, III

congressional sessions on, 1939 Sept. 21, I

Corregidor fell, 1942 May 6, I

D-Day 40th anniversary celebrated, 1984 June 6, I

dogs in combat, 1944(2), IV

Dumbarton Oaks conference (Wash., D.C.), 1944 Aug. 21, I

Eisenhower named Supreme Allied Commander, 1943 Dec. 24, I

ended, 1945, I

first atom bomb dropped (Hiroshima), 1945 Aug. 6, I

first U.S. engagement on German soil, 1944 Sept. 12, I

first U.S. ground assault on Japanese (New Guinea), 1942 June 28, I

first U.S. warship sunk, 1941 Oct. 30, I

German advances, 1940, I

German and Italian assets frozen in U.S., 1941 June 14, I

German consulates in U.S. closed, 1941 June 16, I

World War II (*cont.*)

German V-1 and V-2 bombs, 1944, I

Germany and Italy declared war against U.S., 1941 Dec. 11, I

Germany attacked Russia, 1941, I

Germany surrendered, 1945 May 7, I

Great Britain and France war declaration, 1939 Sept. 3(1), I

Guadalcanal fighting, 1942 Aug. 7, I; 1942 Oct. 23, I; 1942 Nov. 12–15, I

Guam fell to U.S., 1944 Aug. 9, I

Gustav line collapsed, 1944 May 19, I

impact on arts, 1942, II

invasion of Czechoslovakia, 1939 Mar., I

Italy invaded, 1943 Sept. 3, I

Italy surrendered, 1943 Sept. 8, I

Iwo Jima fell to U.S., 1945 Mar. 16, I

Iwo Jima invaded by U.S., 1945 Feb. 9, I

Japan bombed, 1944 June 16, I

Japanese assets frozen by U.S., 1941 July 25, I

Japanese peace treaty ratified, 1952 Mar. 20, I

Japanese peace treaty signed, 1951 Sept. 8, I

Japan invaded Philippines, 1941 Dec. 10, I

Japan surrendered, 1945 Aug. 14, I

job freeze, 1943 Apr. 17, III

Kasserine Pass (Tunisia) action, 1943 Feb. 20, I

Kiska (Aleutians) retaken by U.S., 1943 Aug. 15, I

last major German offensive, 1944 Dec. 16, I

lend-lease, 1940 Sept. 3, I; 1941, I; 1941 Mar. 11, I

lend-lease extended, 1944 Apr. 19, III

Leyte (Philippines) occupied by U.S., 1944 Oct. 20, I

Luzon landing, 1945 Jan. 9, I

MacArthur left Bataan, 1942 Mar. 17, I

Malmédy massacre, 1944 Dec. 16, I

Marine ace died, 1988, IV

Moscow conference opened, 1943 Oct. 19, I

Mussolini resigned, 1943 July 25, I

Netherlands New Guinea invaded by U.S., 1944 Apr. 22, I

New Georgia (Solomon Islands) taken by U.S., 1943 Aug. 28, I

Normandy invasion, 1944 June 6, I

North African advances, 1943, I

North African campaign ended, 1943 May 12, I

North African invasion, 1942 Nov. 7, I

Okinawa invaded by U.S., 1945 Apr. 1, I

Okinawa surrendered by Japan, 1945 June 21, I

Pacific area advances, 1943, I

Paris liberated, 1944 Aug. 25, I

peace treaties, 1947 June 14, I

Pearl Harbor attacked, 1941, I; 1941 Dec. 7, I

Philippines Death March, 1942 Apr. 10, I

World War II (*cont.*)
Philippines liberated, 1945 July 5, I
plays on, 1942 Oct. 7, II
Ploesti oil fields (Rumania) bombed by U.S., 1943 Aug. 1, I
Poland invaded, 1939 Sept. 1, I
"praise the Lord . . ." phrase coined, 1941 Dec. 7, IV
Quebec conference (Canada), 1943 Aug. 11–24, I
Rhine R. crossed by U.S., 1945 Mar. 7, I
Roi Island (Marshalls) taken by U.S., 1944 Feb. 2, I
Rome bombed, 1943 July 19, I
Rome occupied by Allies, 1944 June 4, I
St. Lô breakout by U.S., 1944 July 25, I
Saipan fell to U.S., 1944 July 10, I
Salerno (Italy) invaded by Allies, 1943 Sept. 9, I
salvage drives, 1943(2), III; 1944(2), III
second Neutrality Act passed, 1939 Nov. 4, I
Sicily invaded, 1943 July 10, I
Sicily taken by Allies, 1943 Aug. 17, I
"sighted sub . . ." phrase coined, 1942 Jan. 8, IV
southern France invaded by U.S., 1944 Aug. 15, I
sporting events suspended in wake of, 1940, IV
state of hostilities ended, 1946 Dec. 31, I
state of war with Germany officially ended, 1951 Oct. 24, I
Sudetenland crisis, 1938 Sept. 26, I
surrender document signed, 1945 Sept. 2, I
Tarawa and Makin landing, 1943 Nov. 20, I
Teheran Conference, 1943 Nov. 28–Dec. 1, I
U.S. agencies created, 1942 Jan. 12(1), III; 1942 Jan. 16, III; 1942 Apr. 18, III; 1942 June 13, III; 1943 Mar. 25, III; 1943 May 27, III
U.S. air raid on Rabaul, 1943 Nov. 2, I
U.S. air raid on Tokyo, 1942 Apr. 18, I
U.S. arms sales authorized, 1939 Nov. 4, I
U.S. attack on sight order, 1941 Sept. 11, I
U.S. black market, 1944 Feb. 29, III
U.S. civilian preparation for, 1941, III
U.S. coal stocks seizure authority, 1943 May 5, III
U.S. consumer goods production resumed, 1944 Aug. 14, III
U.S. defeats in Pacific, 1942, I; 1942 Feb. 27-Mar. 1, I; 1942 Apr. 9, I
U.S. defense agencies, 1941 Jan. 7, III; 1941 Apr. 11(2), III
U.S. defense industry strikes, 1941 Jan. 22, III
U.S. Defense Mediation Board established, 1941 Mar. 19, III
U.S. embargo against Japan, 1941 July 25, I

World War II (*cont.*)
U.S. entered war, 1941, I; 1941 Dec. 8, I
U.S. industry priority schedule, 1941 Feb. 24, III
U.S. isolationism vs. intervention, 1938, I; 1938 Mar. 31, I; 1939, I
U.S. *Kearny* torpedoed, 1941 Oct. 17, I
U.S. national emergency proclaimed, 1941 May 27, I
U.S. neutrality, 1939 Sept. 3(1), I; 1939 Sept. 21, I
U.S. ports and waters closed, 1939 Oct. 18, I
U.S. *Reuben James* torpedoed and sunk, 1941 Oct. 30, I
V-E Day, 1945 May 8, I
V-J Day, 1945 Aug. 15, I
Wake Island fell to Japan, 1941 Dec. 22, I
Wasp, U.S. carrier, sunk, 1942 Sept. 15, I
Yalta conference, 1945 Feb. 4–11, I
Worsham, Lew, 1947 June 15, IV; 1953, IV
Worth, Irene, 1965 June 13, II; 1976 Apr. 18, II
Wouk, Herman, 1947(1), II; 1951(1), II; 1952 May 5, II; 1954 Jan. 20, II; 1955(1), II; 1971(1), II; 1978(1), II
Wounded Knee (S.D.), 1973 Feb. 28, I; 1974 Sept. 16(3), I
Wrenn, Robert D., 1893(5), IV; 1894(4), IV; 1896(2), IV; 1897(3), IV
Wrestling:
Muldoon's accomplishment, 1880, IV
Wright, Beals C., 1905(4), IV
Wright, Charles, 1983 Apr. 24, II
Wright, Fielding L., 1948 July 17, I
Wright, Frances, 1824(2), IV; 1825, IV
Wright, Frank Lloyd:
died, 1959, II
first home design, 1892(7), II
first independent commission, 1893(7), II
Friedman House (Pleasantville, N.Y.), 1951(4), II
Gold Medal, 1953 May 27, II
Guggenheim Museum (N.Y.C.), 1945 July 9, II; 1959 Oct. 21(2), II
Johnson Wax Co. office building (Wis.), 1939(3), II
Larkin Building (Buffalo, N.Y.), 1903(5), II
Price Tower (Okla.), 1956, II
Robey House (Chicago, Ill.), 1907(8), II
Unity Temple (Chicago, Ill.), 1904(2), II
Wright, Harold Bell, 1911, II
Wright, H. C., 1858(1), IV
Wright, James, 1972 May 1, II
Wright, James C., Jr., 1989 May 31, I
Wright, J. Skelly, 1988, I
Wright, Mickey, 1958 June 8, IV; 1960 July 4, IV; 1961, IV; 1961 Mar. 12, IV; 1961 July 1, IV; 1962, IV; 1963, IV; 1963 Oct. 13, IV; 1964, IV; 1964 July 12, IV; 1966 Sept. 25, IV

Wright, Orville:
built first glider, 1900(7), III
crashed in plane (Va.), 1908 Sept. 17, III
Distinguished Flying Cross, 1928 Dec. 12, III
first powered flight (Kitty Hawk, N.C.), 1903, III
flight duration record, 1909 July 27, III
glider tested, 1902 Sept., III
patent claim settled, 1914 Jan. 13, III
second glider, 1901(3), III
Wright, Patricia Lovelly, 1769(2), II
Wright, Richard, 1938(1), II; 1940(1), II; 1945(1), II; 1953(1), II; 1960, II; 1991(1), II
Wright, Sewall, 1988, III
Wright, Teresa, 1943 Mar. 4, II
Wright, Wilbur:
air tests in France, 1908 Sept. 17, III
built first glider, 1900(7), III
Distinguished Flying Cross, 1928 Dec. 12, III
first powered flight, 1903, III
glider tested, 1902 Sept., III
patent claim settled, 1914 Jan. 13, III
second glider, 1901(3), III
Wrigley, Philip K., 1977, IV
Writers Guild of America, 1988 Aug. 7(2), II
Wyatt, Jane, 1958 Apr. 15(1), II; 1960 June 20, II
Wyeth, Andrew, 1967 Feb. 14, II; 1970 Feb. 19, II
Helga paintings revealed, 1986 Aug. 9, II
three-generational exhibit, 1987, II
Wyeth, Andrew, Jr., 1987, II
Wyeth, James, 1987, II
Wyeth, Nathaniel C., 1990, III
Wyeth, Nathaniel Jarvis, 1834 June 15, I
Wylie, Elinor, 1921(1), II
Wyman, Jane, 1949 Mar. 24, II
Wynn, Ed, 1921 Nov. 7, II; 1966, II
Wyoming:
first woman governor, 1925 Jan. 5, I
statehood, 1890 July 10, I
Wyoming, University of, 1886 Mar. 4, III; 1969 Oct. 7, IV
Wyoming Valley massacre (Pa.), 1778 July 3–4, I; 1809, II

X-Ray:
CAT scan, 1979 Oct. 12, III
XYZ Affair, 1795–1799, I; 1798 June 18, IV

Yablonski, Joseph A., 1970 Jan. 5, III; 1971 June 23, I; 1972 Mar. 1(2), III; 1973 Sept. 6, III
Boyle found guilty of murder, 1974 Apr. 11, III
Boyle sentenced for murder, 1975 Sept. 11, III
Yachting *see* America's Cup; Boating
Yale University (Conn.):
center for British Art, 1977 Apr. 19, II
colonial enrollment, 1783(2), IV
crew racing, 1870(7), IV

Yale University (Conn.) (cont.)
   Dwight's presidency, 1822, II
   first college magazine, 1806 Nov. 15,
      II
   first fine arts department, 1865(1), III
   first graduate programs, 1870(1), III
   first great football stadium, 1914(4),
      IV
   football game depicted, 1806(2), IV
   football prohibited, 1822(1), IV
   founded, 1701 Oct. 16, III
   granted first Ph.D. degree in U.S.,
      1861(1), III
   Italian Renaissance manuscripts
      acquired, 1988 Oct. 8, II
   liberalized curriculum, 1735–1739, III
   medical school, 1818, III
   new buildings, 1963, II
   science courses, 1871(1), III
   women admitted to Skull and Bones,
      1991 Oct. 24, IV
Yalow, Rosalyn S., 1977 Oct. 13, III
Yalta conference, 1945 Feb. 4–11, I
Yamaguchi, Kristi, 1991 Mar. 16, IV; 1992
   Jan. 9–11, IV; 1992 Feb. 8–23, IV
Yang, Chen Ning, 1957 Oct. 31, III
Yardley, Jonathan, 1977(1), II
Yasgur, Max, 1969 Aug. 15–18, IV; 1973, II
Yastrzemski, Carl, 1967, IV; 1989 July
   23(3), IV
Yawkey, Jean R., 1992, IV
Yazoo land fraud (Ga.), 1795(1), I
Yeager, Charles E., 1953 Dec. 16, III
Yeager, Charles Urban, 1932(1), IV
Yellow fever:
   cause found, 1901(1), III
   death rate decline, 1914(1), III
   epidemic (Fla.), 1888 July 29, I
   epidemic (La. and Miss.), 1853(1), I
   epidemic (New Orleans, La.), 1905
      July 22, I
   epidemic (N.Y.), 1798(1), I
   epidemics, 1873(3), III
   Panama Canal zone, 1904(1), III
   southern toll, 1878, I
   Spanish-American War casualties,
      1898 Aug. 1, I
   vaccine, 1951 Oct. 18, III
Yellowstone National Park, 1872(2), IV
   forest fires, 1988 Sept. 22, I
Yeltsin, Boris, 1992 Feb. 1, I

Yerby, Frank, 1991, II
Yergin, Daniel, 1992 Apr. 7, II
Yerkes, Charles Tyson, 1895, III; 1897(1),
   III
Yeston, Maury, 1982 May 9, II
Yick Wo v. Hopkins, 1886 May 10, I
Yom Kippur War, 1973, III
York, Alvin C., 1936 May 5–7, I; 1964, I
Yorktown (Va.):
   British occupied, 1781 Aug. 1, I
   Cornwallis surrendered, 1781 Oct. 19,
      I
   shelled, 1781 Oct. 9, I
Yosemite National Park, 1890(5), III
Young, Alan, 1951 Jan. 23, II
Young, Andrew, 1979 Aug. 15, I
Young, Bennett H., 1864 Oct. 19(1), I
Young, Brigham:
   first Utah territory governor, 1850
      Sept. 28(1), I
   led Mormons to Utah, 1847 July 24,
      III
   Mormon Temple site, 1893(4), III
   Mormon westward migration, 1846
      Feb. 10, I
Young, Chic (Murat B.), 1973, IV
Young, Cy (Denton T.), 1904 May 5, IV
Young, Donna Caponi, 1979 June 10, IV
Young, Edward (Rev.), 1777(1), II
Young, Gig, 1970 Apr. 7(1), II
Young, John W., 1965 Mar. 23, III; 1966
   July 18, III; 1969 May 18, III; 1972 Apr.
   16, III; 1981 Apr. 12–14, III
Young, Loretta, 1948 Mar. 20, II; 1954
   Mar. 7, II; 1957 Mar. 16, II; 1959 May 6,
   II
Young, Robert, 1957 Mar. 16, II; 1958
   Apr. 15(1), II; 1970 June 7, II
Young, Whitney M., Jr., 1971, I
Young Communist League:
   dissolved, 1943 Oct. 17(1), III
Young Men's Christian Association
   (Y.M.C.A.), 1851, III
Young Men's Hebrew Association
   (Y.M.H.A.), 1874 Mar. 22, III
Young Women's Christian Association
   (Y.W.C.A.), 1866(1), IV
Yount, Robin, 1992 Sept. 9, IV
Yourcenar, Marguerite, 1980 Mar. 6, II;
   1987, II

Youth (see also Children; Education and
   schools; Juvenile delinquency; Youth
   culture):
   Economic Opportunity Act, 1964 Aug.
      30, I
   J. Kennedy programs, 1963 Feb. 14, I
Youth culture:
   Beat generation, 1957(1), II
   fashions, 1970, IV
   Greening of America, The (Reich),
      1970(1), II
   Presley and Dean cults, 1956, IV
   Woodstock (N.Y.), 1969 Aug. 15–18,
      IV

Zachary, Tom, 1969, IV
Zaharias, Mildred "Babe" Didrikson, 1948
   Aug. 15, IV; 1949, IV; 1949 Sept. 25, IV;
   1950, IV; 1950 Mar. 19, IV; 1951, IV;
   1954 July 3(1), IV
Zaltzberg, Charlotte, 1973 May 30, II
Zayak, Elaine, 1981 Feb. 3–8, IV; 1982
   Mar. 11–13, IV
Zelaya, José Santos, 1909 Nov. 18, I
Zenger, John Peter, 1734 Oct., II
Ziegfeld, Florenz, 1907, II
Ziff-Davis Publishing Co., 1984 Nov. 20, II
Zimbalist, Efrem, 1985, II
Zimmerman, Ann, 1987, I
Zimmermann note, 1917 Feb. 24, I
Zinc, 1964 Apr. 16, III
Zindel, Paul, 1971 May 3, II
Zipper, 1893(3), III
Zoeller, Fuzzy, 1979 Apr. 15, IV; 1984
   June 18, IV
Zolotow, Maurice, 1960(1), II
Zoning, 1977 Jan. 11, III
Zoos:
   Arabian camels exhibited, 1790 June
      30–July 7, IV
   first condor chick born in captivity
      (San Diego, Calif.), 1983 Mar. 30, III
   first public (Phila. Pa.), 1874(1), IV
   first wild animal exhibited, 1714 May
      12, IV
Zukor, Adolph, 1976, II
Zumwalt, Elmo R., 1972 Oct. 12–13, I
Zurita, Juan, 1944, IV
Zweig, Paul, 1984(1), II